Roget's

INTERNATIONAL

THESAURUS®

Roget's

INTERNATIONAL

THESAURUS®

7

SEVENTH EDITION

Edited by Barbara Ann Kipfer, Ph.D.

COLLINS REFERENCE

An Imprint of HarperCollins Publishers
www.harpercollins.com

Lithograph of Peter Mark Roget:
Edward Mansfield Burbank, *Sketches of the Lives & Works of the Honorary Medical Staff of the Manchester Infirmary, from 1752 to 1830*, Volume 1, 1904. Courtesy of the New York Public Library.

Designed by C. Linda Dingler

Library of Congress Cataloging-in-Publication Data has been applied for.

ISBN
978-0-06-171522-8 (plain)
978-0-06-171523-5 (thumb-indexed)

15   QGT   10   9   8   7   6   5

Contents

P. M. Roget.

Peter Mark Roget

1779–1869

The author of the "Treasury of Words" could hardly have thought that his name would become forever associated with a particular book, even though he hoped that he was suggesting a unique way of utilizing the richness and flexibility of the English language. But for more than 150 years Roget's work has been the constant companion of all those who aspire to use the language most effectively.

The career of Peter Mark Roget prior to the publication of his *Thesaurus* in 1852, when he was seventy-three years old, while largely devoted to science and to medicine, required of him a facility with words in the delivery of ideas and concepts. A lifetime of secretaryships for several learned societies had thoroughly familiarized him with the need for clarity and forcefulness of expression. That he was justified in his concept is made obvious by the universal acceptance of his thesaurus as an indispensable tool for all those who wish to write and speak with eloquence.

Born in London the son of a Protestant pastor who died at an early age, Roget was raised by his mother. He studied at the University of Edinburgh from 1793 to 1798 and received an M.D. after his successful defense of his Latin thesis dealing with the laws of chemical affinity. He was, however, too late to share in that institution's happy days as a stunning example of the Scottish Enlightenment. He was not to know William Cullen, the great nosologist, nor Alexander Monro primus, who brought Hermann Boerhaave's ethos of a medical school from Leyden; but he did learn anatomy from Monro secundus and medicine from John Gregory. The bright stars of David Hume, denied professorship at the university for his radical thinking, and of Adam Smith had long since blazed across the Scottish intellectual world. Moreover, Roget was too early for Sir James Young Simpson and chloroform, or for the dexterous Syme, who was mentor and father-in-law to the great Lord Lister. While Roget was in Edinburgh, the soil was being prepared for the phenomenon of Paris Medicine, the next wave of medical advance, which would be built on the ruins of the French Revolution.

After his graduation, the young physician looked about for the connections he would need to launch a medical career. In this he was fortunate in having the concerned attention of his uncle, Sir Samuel Romilly, whose own promising political potential, shortened by his suicide, provided an entrée to certain segments of English scientific and intellectual life. Through his uncle, Roget was introduced to Lord Lansdowne, for whom he served briefly as personal physician, and to Jeremy Bentham. On his own initiative, Roget spent some time in Bristol in Thomas Beddoes's Pneumatic Institute, devoted to the treatment of human illness using various gases. There he may have met illustrious figures Humphry Davy, James Watt, Samuel Taylor Coleridge, William Wordsworth, and Robert Southey.

In the midst of his desultory round of attendance at lectures and dispensary duties, Roget learned that his uncle had maneuvered for him an opportunity to tutor two scions of a wealthy Manchester manufacturer on a grand tour of Europe. The Peace of Amiens had been signed in 1802, and Continental travel was once again open to English families anxious to provide their children with the advantages of foreign scenes.

Roget was twenty-three when he shepherded his charges across the English Channel and on to Paris, where they entered into the round of parties and dinners opened to them through letters from Sir Samuel and from the boys' family. But there was more than that. Roget hired a French tutor and supervised his charges' studies in mathematics, chemistry, and geology. He also saw to it that there were the obligatory trips to museums as well as to the theater and that the boys wrote their impressions and comments after each visit.

The little party pushed on to Geneva, not without encountering obstructions, delays, and disappointments injected by the French bureaucracy. In Geneva, although the city had recently been annexed by Napoleon, the group felt secure enough to settle down to a life of studies, parties, and local sight-seeing. The respite was short-lived, however. The Peace of Amiens was abrogated by Napoleon in 1803, and the position of any Englishman in French territory was in doubt. Warned by Madame de Staël that he faced internment, Roget undertook to establish for himself Genevan citizenship on the basis of his father's birth in that city. Through prodigious effort and resourcefulness remarkable in so young a man, Roget sneaked the party, dressed as peasants, into Germany. He was successful in making his way to Denmark and thence to England, delivering his charges back to their family.

Manchester now offered the best opportunity to establish a medical practice, since Roget could count on the support of the wealthy Philips family, whose sons had shared his French experience. He quickly became associated with the local infirmary and with the Manchester Literary and Philosophical Society, before which body he gave a series of lectures on physiology that historians credit as forming the basis of what became the School of Medicine in that city. As D. L. Emblen points out in his biography of Roget, "[he] showed that his chief interest in the new science of physiology lay in the organization and order of several aspects of that subject and in the relationship of the subject to such kindred fields as anatomy" (D. L. Emblen, *Peter Mark Roget: The Word and the Man*, New York: Thomas Crowell, 1970, p. 96). It was Roget's meticulous, precise way of looking at order, at plan, and at interdependence in animal economy that would eventually find expression in his unique and practical lexicographic experiment.

But the great metropolis beckoned, and the young physician finally decided on a London career. Roget was never outstandingly successful as a medical practitioner. He had, however, become associated with the establishment of the Northern Dispensary, the quintessential Victorian expression of medical charity, to which he devoted a lifetime of practice. Roget's métier was teaching and institutional activities. He lectured in the Theory and Practice of Physic at the Great Windmill Street School, which served as the school of anatomy of Middlesex Hospital before that institution was eclipsed by the new University College on Gower Street. The Medical and Chirurgical Society, founded to bridge the gap between medicine and surgery, commanded much of Roget's attention during his London days. He served as the society's secretary for twelve years and contributed to its journal, *Transactions*. In 1814 he became a fellow in the Royal Society on the basis of a paper he wrote describing a forerunner of the slide rule. He contributed many articles to the *Encyclopaedia Britannica* that were carried through several editions. In those pages he crossed swords with George Combe, the ardent promoter of phrenology, a discipline which Roget could not support. While serving as secretary of the Royal Society he wrote the Bridgewater Treatise of Physiology, which demonstrated anew Roget's ability to organize and classify the essentials of a rapidly developing science.

Although extremely occupied during these years, as a list of his extensive memberships in scientific and cultural organizations shows, Roget seems never to have captured the attention of his peers to the extent that many of his contemporaries enjoyed. There is a hint that he was always just below the top rank, never in the front. It was, after all, an age of giants, and to be even in the midst of all that ferment was remarkable enough. His active public life came to an end when he was eased out of the secretaryship of the Royal Society after a conflict over the operation of the library, and was literally forced into retirement.

An inactive retirement was not compatible with Roget's lifestyle. Since childhood, putting ideas and concepts in writing had been second nature to him. He dwelt in a world of language, and his orderly, systematic mind lent itself to classification. More than a list of synonyms, more than a dictionary, the thesaurus Roget devised and constantly improved upon during this time was a unique ordering of the English language to be used by those desiring to impart an exacting and felicitous tone to written or spoken material. Grouped by ideas rather than by a mere alphabetical listing, the thesaurus enabled the user to find the exact word or phrase needed for a specific purpose. Roget had been keeping such a word list for many years. He now proposed to enlarge it and present it to the world of users of the English language.

The success of this venture was never in doubt. Roget supervised some twenty-five editions and printings of the thesaurus and was actively at work on his masterpiece when he died in 1869 at the age of ninety. *Roget's International Thesaurus*® continues to be issued. For all those who deal with words and with ideas as expressed in words it has become indispensable. It remains a monument of scholarship and a tribute to the industry and breadth of knowledge of one of the lesser-known Victorian greats.

DONALD F. KENT, M.D.

How to Use this Book

Like other great reference books, *Roget's International Thesaurus*® is the product of continuous improvement and long-term investment by its editors. The process began almost two centuries ago, in 1805, when Dr. Peter Mark Roget began compiling a list of useful words for his own convenience.

The revolutionary achievement of Dr. Roget was his development of a brand new principle: *the grouping of words according to ideas*. If the user cannot find something in a reference book, it is often because of the restriction of searching alphabetically by "known" headwords. Dr. Roget's thesaurus reversed the access to allow the user to find a word from another word, or a concept or idea. When in 1852 Roget published the first book ever to realize this concept with thoroughness and precision, he called it a "thesaurus" (from the Greek and Latin, meaning "treasury" or "storehouse"). And *thesaurus* it has remained to this day.

So successful was Roget's *Thesaurus of English Words and Phrases, Classified and Arranged so as to Facilitate the Expression of Ideas and Assist in Literary Composition* that a second edition followed one year later in 1853. By Dr. Roget's death in 1869 there had been no less than twenty-eight editions and printings.

Each subsequent edition introduced more efficient and useful features, all of which have contributed to the quality of the present edition. Over the years, tens of thousands of new words and phrases were added, the coverage of foreign expressions increased, and the scope of the book expanded to include slang and useful quotations: a recent innovation was the numbering of the paragraphs for the user's convenience. By 1992, when the fifth edition was published by HarperCollins, *Roget's International Thesaurus*® had become a greatly expanded and improved book, yet one which still retained Roget's brilliant organization.

The seventh edition of *Roget's International Thesaurus*®, prepared by Barbara Ann Kipfer, Ph.D, has a text of about 464,000 words and phrases, arranged in categories by their meanings, and a comprehensive index.

The search for a word that you need is a simple, two-step process that begins in the index. Suppose that you want a word to describe something that first occurred in the past:

Step 1. In the index, look up the word *first* and pick the subentry closest to the meaning you want, which would likely be "previous."

Step 2. Follow its number (834.4) into the text of the thesaurus and you will find a whole paragraph of adjectives starting with **previous, prior, early.**

firmament 1072.2
first
  n baseball 745.1
  first ever 818.3
  adj leading 165.3
  front 216.10
  chief 249.14
  preceding 814.4
  beginning 818.15
  foremost 818.17
  previous 834.4
  novel 841.11
  adv before 216.12
  preferably 371.28
  firstly 818.18
first aid 91.14
first base 745.1
first-born
  n senior 304.5
  adj older 842.19
first-class
  superlative 249.13
  first-rate 999.17

834 PREVIOUSNESS
NOUNS **1 previousness,** earliness 845, antecedence *or* antecedency, priority, **anteriority, precedence** *or* precedency 814, precession; *status quo ante* <L>, previous *or* prior state, earlier state; preexistence; **anticipation,** predating, antedating; antedate; **past time** 837.1
  2 antecedent, precedent, premise; forerunner, **precursor** 816, ancestor
VERBS **3 be prior,** be before *or* early *or* earlier, come on the scene *or* appear earlier, **precede, antecede, forerun,** come *or* go before, set a precedent; **herald,** usher in, proclaim, announce; **anticipate,** antedate, predate; **preexist**

ADJS **4 previous, prior, early** 845.7, **earlier,** *ci-devant or ci-dessus* <Fr>, **former,** fore, prime, first, **preceding** 165.3, foregoing, above, anterior, **anticipatory,** antecedent; **preexistent;** older, elder, senior

Tracking down words in this way is the most obvious and direct use of the thesaurus. However, there are other ways in which the unique features of *Roget's International Thesaurus*® will help you solve word problems.

The thesaurus is a device for finding specific words or phrases for general ideas. A dictionary will tell you many things about a word—spelling, pronunciation, meaning, and origins. You use a thesaurus when you have an idea but do not know, or cannot remember, the word or phrase that expresses it best or when you want a more accurate or effective way of saying what you mean. A thesaurus gives you possibilities and you choose the one that you think is best within your particular context. The range of possibilities includes not only meaning as we usually think of it, but the special sense and force given by nonformal words and phrases (slang and informal), of which many are included and labeled.

Roget's International Thesaurus® is an efficient word-finder because it has a structure especially designed to stimulate thought and help you organize your ideas. The backbone of this structure is the ingenious overall arrangement of the main categories. The plan is outlined in the "Synopsis of Categories," which begins on page xix. To make good use of the thesaurus's structure all you need to remember is that it contains many sequences of closely related categories. Beginning at 48, for example, you will see **HEARING, DEAFNESS, SOUND, SILENCE, FAINTNESS OF SOUND, LOUDNESS**, etc., a procession of similar, contrasting and opposing concepts, all dealing with the perception and quality of sounds. So, when you are not quite satisfied with what you find in one place, glance at nearby categories too; it may be that your original intention was not the best. If you are having trouble framing a thought in a positive way, you may find that it can be more effectively expressed negatively. Seeing related terms, and antonyms, often opens up lines of thought and chains of association that had not occurred to you.

You will have already noticed that the large categories of ideas are numbered in sequence; there are 1075 of them in this edition of *Roget's International Thesaurus*®. Within each category the terms are presented in short paragraphs by basic meaning, and these are also numbered. References from the index to the text are made with two-part numbers such as 247.4, the first part being the number of the main category, the second the number of the paragraph within that category. This system, unique to this book, makes for quick and easy pinpointing of the place where you will find the words you need.

The terms within a category are organized also by part of speech, in this order: nouns, verbs, adjectives, adverbs, prepositions, conjunctions, and interjections. When you are casting about for a way of saying something, rather than looking for a specific word, do not limit your search to the narrow area of the category suggested by the index reference, but examine the offerings in all parts of speech.

There is a further refinement of word arrangement. The sequence of terms within a paragraph, far from being random, is determined by close, semantic relationships. The words closest in meaning are offered in clusters that are set off with semicolons; the semicolon signals a slight change in sense or application. A close examination of the clusters will make you aware of the fine distinctions between synonyms, and you will soon recognize that few words are exactly interchangeable. As an aid in focusing on the *right* word, terms with special uses are identified by labels in angle brackets—such as the label <nf> for nonformal terms, <Fr> for French terms, or <technical> for technical terms. A full list of the abbreviations often used within brackets can be found on page xxvii.

The connector "and" is used to group things so as to avoid using a label (say, <nf>) for each individual item. The connector "or" is used similarly to avoid needless repetition of a term that can be used with several modifiers.

Cross references are also an important feature of the text. They suggest additional meanings of the words you are examining. Notice also that the paragraphs of text are highlighted with terms in boldface type. The boldfaced words are those most commonly used for the idea at hand.

"Word elements" such as prefixes, suffixes, and combining forms, are listed when helpful after the final text paragraph of the category, and before any word lists.

The use of an appropriate quotation often enlivens one's prose. Here, again, *Roget's International Thesaurus*® can help you, for it contains thousands of such quotes on scores of subjects. Another useful feature of the thesaurus is its word lists. These contain the names of specific things—animals, plants, measurements, and many other entities—few of which have synonyms. The lists can save you many excursions to specialized reference books.

Thus, *Roget's International Thesaurus*® can help you in countless ways to improve your writing and speech and to enrich your active vocabulary. But you should remember the caution that very few words are true synonyms: Use the thesaurus in conjunction with a good dictionary whenever a selected word or phrase is unfamiliar to you.

Peter Roget's Preface to the First Edition

(1852)

It is now nearly fifty years since I first projected a system of verbal classification similar to that on which the present work is founded. Conceiving that such a compilation might help to supply my own deficiencies, I had, in the year 1805, completed a classed catalog of words on a small scale, but on the same principle, and nearly in the same form, as the Thesaurus now published. I had often during that long interval found this little collection, scanty and imperfect as it was, of much use to me in literary composition, and often contemplated its extension and improvement; but a sense of the magnitude of the task, amidst a multitude of other avocations, deterred me from the attempt. Since my retirement from the duties of Secretary of the Royal Society, however, finding myself possessed of more leisure, and believing that a repertory of which I had myself experienced the advantage might, when amplified, prove useful to others, I resolved to embark in an undertaking which, for the last three or four years, has given me incessant occupation, and has, indeed, imposed upon me an amount of labor very much greater than I had anticipated. Notwithstanding all the pains I have bestowed on its execution, I am fully aware of its numerous deficiencies and imperfections, and of its falling far short of the degree of excellence that might be attained. But, in a work of this nature, where perfection is placed at so great a distance, I have thought it best to limit my ambition to that moderate share of merit which it may claim in its present form; trusting to the indulgence of those for whose benefit it is intended, and to the candor of critics who, while they find it easy to detect faults, can at the same time duly appreciate difficulties.

P. M. ROGET

April 29, 1852

Foreword

by Barbara Ann Kipfer, Ph.D.

In developing this new edition, I chose to focus on the modernity and scope of the language coverage in the sixth edition of *Roget's International Thesaurus*®. We live in the Internet Age, making the *International Thesaurus* ever more valuable. It can now be used in the wording of queries for search engines accessing the World Wide Web. To this end, I have included as many new words and phrases as possible from general vocabulary to scientific and technological terms.

The lists have been revised to add new terms, delete obsolete ones, and expand treatment. Quotations were retained if they could conceivably be valuable in a user's writings. Otherwise, unuseful quotations and outdated terms were set aside to make room for new synonyms, additional synonyms, and new lists.

I wish to acknowledge the help, support, and guidance of Dr. Robert L. Chapman, who passed away in 2002. I am honored to have been his choice of successor.

I also thank Stephanie Meyers of HarperCollins and Susan Baker of Westchester Book Group who have helped and supported this edition's publication.

No one is luckier than I to have the time and the environment I need to complete such a massive undertaking. To that I owe gratitude to my husband and frequent collaborator, Paul Magoulas. To him and to my sons, Kyle and Keir, I would like to repay their love and encouragement.

BARBARA ANN KIPFER, PH.D.

October 2009

Synopsis of Categories

Abbreviations Used in This Book

ADJS	adjectives
ADVS	adverbs
Anon	anonymous
Arab	Arabic
Austral	Australia, Australian
Brazil Pg	Brazilian Portuguese
Brit	British
Can	Canada, Canadian
Can Fr	Canadian French
Chin	China, Chinese
CONJ	conjunction
Cz	Czechoslovakian
Dan	Danish
E	East, Eastern
Eng	England, English
etc	et cetera
fem	feminine
Fr	France, French
Ger	Germany, German
Gk	Greece, Greek
gram	grammar
Heb	Hebrew
Hindu	Hinduism
Hung	Hungary, Hungarian
INTERJS	interjections
Ir	Ireland, Irish
Ital	Italy, Italian
L	Latin
masc	masculine
N	North, Northern
nf	nonformal usage
Norw	Norway, Norwegian
old	older usage
Pg	Portugal, Portuguese
PHRS	phrases
pl	plural
Pol	Poland, Polish
PREP	preposition
Russ	Russia, Russian
S	South, Southern
Scot	Scotland, Scottish
sing	singular
Skt	Sanskrit
Sp	Spanish
Sp Amer	Spanish American
Swah	Swahili
Swed	Sweden, Swedish
Turk	Turkey, Turkish
UN	United Nations
US	United States
W	West, Western

1 BIRTH

NOUNS **1 birth,** genesis, **nativity,** nascency, **childbirth, childbearing, having a baby, giving birth, birthing,** parturition, biogenesis, the stork <nf>, patter of tiny feet; **confinement,** lying-in, being brought to bed, **childbed,** accouchement <Fr>; **labor,** travail, birth throes or pangs; **delivery,** blessed event <nf>; the Nativity; multiparity; **hatching;** littering, whelping, farrowing; active birth, alternative birth; obstetrics

VERBS **2 be born,** have birth, come forth, issue forth, see the light of day, come into the world; **hatch;** be illegitimate or born out of wedlock, have the bar sinister, be born on the wrong side of the blanket, come in through a side door <nf>

3 give birth, bear, bear or have young, **have; have a baby,** bear a child, have children; drop, cast, throw, pup, whelp, kitten, foal, calve, fawn, lamb, cub, yean, farrow, litter, spawn, lay eggs; lie in, be confined, labor, travail

ADJS **4 born,** given birth, post-natal; **hatched;** bred, begotten, cast, dropped, whelped, foaled, calved, etc; "cast naked upon the naked earth"—Pliny the Elder; née; newborn; stillborn; **bearing,** giving birth, natal

2 THE BODY

NOUNS **1 body,** the person, carcass, anatomy, frame, bodily or corporal or corporeal entity, physical self, physical or bodily structure, physique, soma, somatotype, bod <nf>; torso, trunk; organism, organic complex, flesh and blood <nf>; the material or physical part

2 the skeleton, the bones <see list>, one's bones, framework, frame, form, structure, shell, bony framework, endoskeleton, bag of bones; axial skeleton, appendicular skeleton, visceral skeleton; rib cage; skeletology; **bone <see list>;** cartilage

3 the muscles, myon, voluntary muscle, involuntary muscle; **musculature,** physique; **connective tissue,** connectivum; thew, sinew, tendon, ligament, cartilage

4 the skin, skin, dermis, integument, **epidermis,** scarfskin, ecderon; hypodermis, hypoderma; dermis, derma, derm, corium, true skin, cutis, cuticle; epithelium, pavement epithelium; endothelium; mesoderm; endoderm, entoderm, blastoderm; ectoderm, epiblast, ectoblast; enderon; connective tissue; age spot, liver spot

5 <castoff skin> slough, cast, desquamation, exuviae, molt

6 membrane, membrana, pellicle, chorion; basement membrane, membrana propria; allantoic membrane; amnion, amniotic sac, arachnoid membrane; serous membrane, serosa, membrana serosa; **eardrum,** tympanic membrane, tympanum, membrana tympana; **mucous membrane; velum; peritoneum;** periosteum; pleura; pericardium; meninx, **meninges;** perineurium, neurilemma; conjunctiva; **hymen** or maidenhead

7 member, appendage, external organ; head, noggin and noodle <nf>; **arm;** forearm; wrist; elbow; upper arm, biceps; **leg,** limb, shank, gam and pin <nf>, legs, wheels <nf>; shin, cnemis; ankle, tarsus; calf; knee; thigh, ham; popliteal space; **hand,** paw <nf>, finger; **foot,** dog and puppy <nf>, toe

8 teeth, dentition, ivories and choppers <nf>, pearly whites; periodontal tissue, alveolar ridge, alveolus; **tooth,** fang, tusk; snag, snaggletooth, peg; bucktooth, gagtooth or gang tooth <nf>; pivot tooth; cuspid, bicuspid; canine tooth, canine, dogtooth, eyetooth, carnassial, tush <nf>; molar, grinder, gnasher; premolar; incisor, cutter, fore-tooth; wisdom tooth; milk tooth, baby tooth, deciduous tooth; permanent tooth; crown, cusp, dentine, enamel

9 eye, visual organ, organ of vision, oculus, optic, **orb,** peeper <nf>; clear eyes, bright eyes, starry orbs; saucer eyes, banjo eyes <nf>, popeyes, goggle eyes; naked eye, unassisted or unaided eye; corner of the eye; epicanthus, epicanthic fold; eyeball; retina; lens; cornea; sclera; optic nerve; iris; pupil; eyelid, lid, nictitating membrane; choroid coat, aqueous humor, vitreous humor

10 ear, auditory apparatus, hearing organ, lug <Scot>; external ear, **outer ear;** auricle, pinna; tragus; cauliflower ear; concha, conch, shell; ear lobe, lobe, lobule; auditory canal, acoustic or auditory meatus; helix; **middle ear,** tympanic cavity, tympanum; eardrum, drumhead, tympanic membrane; auditory ossicles; malleus, hammer, incus, anvil; stapes, stirrup; mastoid process; eustachian or auditory tube; **inner ear;** round window, secondary eardrum; oval window; bony labyrinth, membraneous labyrinth, utricle; perilymph, endolymph; vestibule; semicircular canals; cochlea; basilar membrane, organ of Corti; auditory or acoustic nerve

11 nose, nasal organ, snout, smeller, proboscis, beak, schnoz <nf>, snout, muzzle; nostril, naris, nasal cavity, olfactory nerve

12 mouth, oral cavity; lips, tongue, taste buds; mandible, jaw; maw; gums, periodontal tissue; uvula; teeth

13 genitals, genitalia, sex organs, reproductive organs, pudenda, private parts, privy parts, private parts; privates *or* meat *or* naughty bits <nf>; **crotch,** groin, pubic region, perineum, pelvis; **male organs; penis, phallus,** *lingam* <Skt>, glans penis; gonads; **testes, testicles,** balls *and* nuts *and* rocks *and* ballocks *and* nads *and* family jewels <nf>, cullions <old>; spermary; scrotum, bag *and* basket <nf>, cod <old>; vas deferens; **female organs; vulva,** *yoni* <Skt>, cunt <nf>; **vagina;** clitoris, glans clitoridis; pudenda; labia, labia majora, labia minora, lips, nymphae; cervix; ovary; uterus, womb, fallopian tubes; secondary sex characteristic, mons pubis, mons veneris, pubic hair, beard, breasts

14 **nervous system, nerves,** central nervous system, peripheral nervous system; autonomic nervous system; sympathetic *or* thoracolumbar nervous system, parasympathetic *or* craniosacral nervous system; **nerve; neuron;** nerve cell, sensory *or* afferent neuron, sensory cell; motor *or* afferent neuron; association *or* internuncial neuron; nerve fiber, axon, dendrite, myelin *or* medullary sheath; **synapse;** effector organ; nerve trunk; **ganglion;** plexus, solar plexus; **spinal cord**

15 **brain,** encephalon; cerebrum, cerebellum, cerebral matter

16 **viscera, vitals, internal organs, insides, innards** <nf>, entrails, inwards, internals, thoracic viscera, abdominal viscera; inner mechanism, works <nf>; peritoneum, peritoneal cavity; **guts** *and* kishkes *and* giblets <nf>; **heart,** ticker *and* pump <nf>, endocardium, atria, ventricles, aorta; **lung, lungs; liver;** gallbladder; spleen; pancreas; **kidney, kidneys;** urethra

17 **digestion,** ingestion, assimilation, absorption; primary digestion, secondary digestion, peristalsis; predigestion; salivary digestion, gastric *or* peptic digestion, pancreatic digestion, intestinal digestion; digestive system, alimentary canal, gastrointestinal tract; salivary glands, gastric glands, liver, pancreas; digestive secretions, saliva, gastric juice, pancreatic juice, intestinal juice, bile

18 <digestive system> mouth, maw, salivary glands; gullet, crop, craw, **throat,** pharynx; esophagus, gorge, weasand <old>, wizen <Brit nf>; fauces, isthmus of the fauces; **abdomen; stomach, belly** <nf>, **midriff,** diaphragm; swollen *or* distended *or* protruding *or* prominent belly, beer belly, *embonpoint* <Fr>, **paunch,** ventripotence; underbelly; pylorus; **intestine, intestines,** entrails, **bowels;** small intestine, villus, odenum, jejunum, ileum; blind gut, cecum; foregut, hindgut, midgut, mesogaster; **appendix,** vermiform appendix *or* process; large intestine, colon, sigmoid flexure, rectum; anus

19 <nf terms> goozle, guzzle; tum, tummy, tum-tum, breadbasket, **gut,** bulge, fallen chest, corporation, spare tire, bay window, **pot,** potbelly, potgut, beerbelly, German *or* Milwaukee goiter, pusgut, swagbelly; **guts,** tripes, stuffings

20 **metabolism,** metabolic process; basal metabolism, acid-base metabolism, energy metabolism; **anabolism,** substance metabolism, constructive metabolism, assimilation; **catabolism,** destructive metabolism, disassimilation; endogenous metabolism, exogenous metabolism; pharmacokinetic metabolism; uricotelic metabolism; metabolic rate

21 **breathing, respiration,** aspiration, **inspiration, inhalation; expiration, exhalation;** insufflation, exsufflation; **breath,** wind, breath of air; three-part breath; pant, puff; wheeze, asthmatic wheeze; broken wind; gasp, gulp; snoring, snore, stertor; sniff, sniffle, snuff, snuffle; sigh, suspiration; sneeze, sternutation; cough, hack; hiccup; **artificial respiration,** kiss of life, mouth-to-mouth resuscitation; anaerobic respiration

22 <respiratory system> **lungs,** bellows <nf>, lights <old>; diaphragm; **windpipe, trachea,** weasand <old>, wizen <Brit nf>; bronchus, bronchi <pl>, bronchial tube; epiglottis

23 **duct, vessel,** canal, passage; gland; vasculature, vascularity, vascularization; vas, meatus; thoracic duct, lymphatic; emunctory <old>; pore; urethra, urete; vagina; oviduct, fallopian tube; salpinx; eustachian tube; ostium; fistula; **blood vessel; artery,** aorta, pulmonary artery, carotid; **vein,** jugular vein, vena cava, pulmonary vein; portal vein, varicose vein; venation; **capillary;** arteriole, veinlet, veinule, venule

24 <body fluids> humor, **lymph,** chyle, choler, yellow bile, black bile; rheum; serous fluid, serum; plasma; **pus, matter,** purulence, peccant humor <old>; suppuration; ichor, sanies; discharge; gleet, leukorrhea, the whites; mucus; **phlegm,** snot <nf>; **saliva, spit** <nf>; **urine, piss** <nf>; **perspiration, sweat** <nf>; **tear,** teardrop, lachryma; **milk,** mother's milk, colostrum, lactation; **semen;** cerumen, earwax

25 **blood** <see list>, whole blood, lifeblood, vital fluid, venous blood, arterial blood, **gore;** ichor, humor; grume; **serum,** blood serum; blood substitute; **plasma,** synthetic plasma, plasma substitute, dextran, clinical dextran; **blood cell** *or* **corpuscle,** hemocyte; **red corpuscle** *or* **blood cell,** erythrocyte; **white corpuscle** *or* **blood cell,** leukocyte, blood platelet; **hemoglobin;** blood pressure; circulation; **blood group** *or* **type,** type O *or* A *or* B *or* AB; Rh-type, Rh-positive, Rh-negative; **Rh factor** *or* Rhesus factor; antigen,

antibody, isoantibody, globulin; opsonin; blood grouping; blood count; hematoscope, hematoscopy, hemometer; bloodstream

ADJS **26 skeleton, skeletal; bone,** osteal, **bony,** osseous, ossiferous; ossicular; ossified; **spinal,** myelic; **muscle, muscular,** myoid; cartilage, cartilaginous

27 cutaneous, cuticular; skinlike, skinny; skin-deep; **epidermal,** epidermic, ecderonic; hypodermic, hypodermal, subcutaneous; dermal, dermic; ectodermal, ectodermic; endermic, endermatic; cortical; epicarpal; testaceous; membranous

28 eye, optic, ophthalmic, optical; visual; **ear,** otic; aural

29 genital; phallic, penile, penial; testicular; scrotal; spermatic, seminal; vulvar, vulval; vaginal; clitoral; cervical; ovarian; uterine; reproductive, generative, hormonal, sexual

30 nerve, neural, neurological; **brain, cerebral,** cerebellar, nervous, synaptic

31 digestive; stomachal, stomachic, abdominal; ventral, celiac, **gastric,** ventricular; big-bellied 257.18; **metabolic,** basal metabolic, anabolic, catabolic; assimilative, dissimilative

32 respiratory, breathing; inspiratory, expiratory; nasal, rhinal; bronchial, tracheal; **lung,** pulmonary, pulmonic, pneumonic; puffing, huffing, snorting, wheezing, wheezy, asthmatic, stertorous, snoring, panting, heaving; sniffy, sniffly, sniffling, snuffy, snuffly, snuffling; sneezy, sternutative, sternutatory, errhine

33 circulatory, vascular, vascularized, circulating; vasiform; venous, veinal, venose; capillary; arterial, aortic; **blood,** hematal, hematic; bloody, gory, sanguinary; lymphatic, rheumy, humoral, phlegmy, ichorous, serous, sanious; chylific, chylifactive, chylifactory; **puslike,** purulent, suppurated or suppurating, suppurative; teary, tearing, tearlike, **lachrymal,** lacrimal, lacrimatory; mucous; sweaty, perspiring; urinary

34 blood types

A–	B+
A+	O–
AB–	O+
AB+	Rh-negative
B–	Rh-positive

35 bones

acetabelum
aitchbone
alveolar bone
anklebone
anvil
astragalus or anklebone
backbone or spine or spinal column or myel
basilar or basioccipital bone
breastbone or sternum
calcaneus
calf bone or fibula
cannon bone
carpal or carpus

cheekbone
chin
clavicle
coccyx
collarbone
costa
cranial bones
cranium
cuboid
edgebone
ethmoid bone
femur
fibula
floating rib
frontal bone
funny or crazy bone
gladiolus
hallux
hammer
haunch bone
heel bone
hipbone
humerus
hyoid or lingual bone
ilium
incus
inferior maxillary
innominate bone
intermaxillary or premaxillary or incisive bone
interparietal or incarial bone
ischium
kneecap or patella or whirl bone
lacrimal bone
lenticular bone or os orbiculare
lentiform or pisiform or postular bone
malar or zygomatic bone
malleus
mandible and maxilla or jawbones
mastoid
maxillary
metacarpal or metacarpus
metatarsal or metatarsus

multangular bone large or trapezium
multangular bone small or trapezoid
nasal bone
occipital bone
palate bone
parietal bone
patella
pelvis
periotic bone or otocrane
petrosal or petrous bone
phalanx or phalanges <pl>
pterygoid bone
pubis
pyramidal bone or os triquetrum
rachidial
rachis or vertebral column
radius
rib
sacrum or resurrection bone
scaphoid bone
scapula
semilunar bone
sesamoid bones
shinbone
shoulder blade
skull
sphenoid bone
stapes
sternum
stirrup
sutural or wormian bone
talus
tarsal or tarsus
temporal bone
thighbone or femur
tibia
ulna
vertebra
vomer
wristbone
zygomatic

36 muscles

abdominal or abs
anterior tibial
biceps brachii
biceps femoris
crural ligaments soleus
deltoid
erector
external oblique
extensor

fascia lata
flexor
gastrocnemius
gluteus maximus
gracilis
hamstring
latissimus dorsi
pectoralis major
pectoralis minor

quadriceps
rectus abdominis
rectus femoris
rotator cuff
sartorius

sternomastoid
tendon of Achilles
trapezius
triceps brachii *or*
   triceps

3 HAIR

NOUNS **1 hairiness, shagginess,** hirsuteness, pilosity, fuzziness, frizziness, **furriness,** downiness, fluffiness, woolliness, fleeciness, bristliness, stubbliness, burrheadedness, mopheadedness, shockheadedness; crinosity, hispidity, villosity; hypertrichosis, pilosis, pilosism, pilosity

2 hair, pile, **fur** 4.2, coat, pelt, **fleece,** fuzz, wool, camel's hair, horsehair, hide; **mane;** shag, tousled *or* matted hair, **mat of hair;** pubescence, pubes, pubic hair; hairlet, villus, capillament, cilium, ciliolum 271.1; seta, setula; bristle 288.3

3 gray hair, grizzle, silver *or* silvery hair, white hair, salt and pepper hair *or* beard, graying temples, "hoary hair"—Thomas Gray, "the silver livery of advised age"—Shakespeare

4 head of hair, head, crine; **crop,** crop of hair, mat, elflock, **thatch,** mop, **shock,** shag, fleece, **mane; locks, tresses,** crowning glory, helmet of hair

5 lock, tress; flowing locks, flowing tresses; **curl, ringlet,** wisp; earlock, *payess* <Yiddish>; lovelock; frizz, frizzle; crimp; ponytail

6 tuft, flock, fleck; forelock, widow's peak, crest, quiff <Brit>, fetlock, cowlick; **bang, bangs,** fringe

7 braid, plait, twist; **pigtail,** rat's-tail *or* rat-tail, tail; **queue,** cue; coil, knot; topknot, scalplock, pigtail, bunches; bun, chignon; widow's peak; dreadlock, cornrow

8 beard, whiskers, facial hair; beaver <nf>; full beard, chin whiskers, side whiskers; **sideburns,** burnsides, **muttonchops; goatee,** tuft; imperial, **Vandyke,** spade beard; adolescent beard, pappus, down, peach fuzz, "the soft down of manhood"—Callimachus; **stubble,** bristles, five o'clock shadow, designer stubble

9 <plant beard> awn, brush, arista, pile, pappus, nettle

10 <animal and insect whiskers> tactile process, tactile hair, **feeler, antenna,** vibrissa; barb, barbel, barbule, tentacle, palpus; cat whisker

11 mustache, mustachio, soup-strainer <nf>, mustachios, toothbrush, handle bars *or* handlebar mustache, Fu Manchu mustache, Zapata mustache, walrus mustache, tash <nf>

12 eyelashes, lashes, cilia; **eyebrows,** brows

13 false hair, hair extensions, switch, fall, chignon, rat <nf>; false eyelashes

14 wig, peruke, toupee, hairpiece, rug *and* divot *and* doormat <nf>, hair weave, merkin <old>, periwig <old>; hair extensions

15 hairdo, hairstyle, haircut, do <nf>, **coiffure,** coif, headdress; wave; marcel, marcel wave; **permanent,** permanent wave; home permanent; cold wave; blow-drying, finger-drying

16 feather, plume, pinion; **quill;** pinfeather; contour feather, penna, down feather, plume feather, plumule, tail feather; filoplume; hackle; scapular; **crest,** tuft, topknot; panache

17 <parts of feathers> quill, calamus, barrel; barb, shaft, barbule, barbicel, cilium, filament, filamentule, plumule

18 plumage, feathers, feather, feathering; contour feathers; breast feathers, mail <of a hawk>; hackle; flight feathers; remiges, primaries, secondaries, tertiaries; covert, tectrices; speculum, wing bay

19 down, fluff, flue, floss, **fuzz, fur,** pile, fleece, fine hair; eiderdown, eider; swansdown; thistledown; lint

VERBS **20** grow *or* sprout hair; whisker, **bewhisker**

21 feather, fledge, feather out; sprout wings

22 cut *or* dress the hair, trim, **barber, coiffure,** coif, style *or* shape the hair; pompadour, wave, marcel; process, conk; **bob, shingle**

ADJS **23 hairlike,** trichoid, capillary; filamentous, filamentary, filiform; bristlelike 288.10

24 hairy, hirsute, barbigerous, crinose, crinite, pubescent; pilose, pilous, pileous; **furry,** furred; bushy; villous; villose; ciliate, cirrose; hispid, hispidulous, setal; **woolly, fleecy,** lanate, lanated, flocky, flocculent, floccose; woolly-headed, woolly-haired, ulotrichous; bushy, tufty, **shaggy,** shagged; matted, tomentose; mopheaded, burrheaded, shockheaded, unshorn; **bristly** 288.9; fuzzy

25 bearded, whiskered, whiskery, **bewhiskered,** barbate, barbigerous; mustached *or* mustachioed; awned, awny, pappose; goateed; unshaved, **unshaven;** stubbled, stubbly, bristly

26 wigged, periwigged, peruked, toupeed

27 feathery, plumy; hirsute; featherlike, plumelike, pinnate, pennate; **downy,** fluffy, nappy, velvety, peachy, fuzzy, flossy, furry

28 feathered, plumaged, flighted, **pinioned, plumed,** pennate, plumate, plumose

29 tufted, crested, topknotted

4 CLOTHING MATERIALS

NOUNS **1 material, fabric, cloth, textile,** textile fabric, texture, tissue, stuff, weave, weft, woof, web, **goods,** drapery, *étoffe or tissu* <Fr>; thread, yarn, rope; napery, table linen, felt; silk; lace; cotton; wool; polyester; nylon; rag, rags

2 fur, pelt, hide, coat, fell, fleece, vair <heraldry>; imitation fur, fake fur, synthetic fur; furring; peltry, skin(s); **leather** <see list>, rawhide; imitation leather, leather paper, leatherette

3 leather

alligator
buckskin
buff
cabretta
calf leather
capeskin
chamois *or* chammy
chamois skin
chevrette
Cordovan
cowhide
deerskin
doeskin
goatskin
grain leather
horsehide
kid
lambskin
levant morocco
mocha

morocco
nappa
nubuck
oxhide
patent leather
pebble leather
pigskin
pig suede
rawhide
Russian leather
saddle leather
shagreen
sheepskin
snakeskin
sole-leather *or* shoe-leather
stirrup leather
suède
tawed leather
whitleather *or* white leather

4 fabrics, fibers

acetate
acrylic
alpaca
angora
astrakhan
baize
balbriggan
baldachin
barathea
batik
batiste
bayadere
bengaline
bombazine
bombazine
boucle
brilliantine
broadcloth
brocade
brocatel or brocatelle
buckram
bunting
burlap
byssus
calico
cambric
camel hair or camel's hair
candlewick
Canton crepe
canvas

cashmere
castor
challis
chambray
charmeuse
cheesecloth
chenille
cheviot
chiffon
chinchilla
chino
chintz
cire
cloque
cloth
combing wool
cord
corduroy
cotton
Courtelle
crash
crepe de Chine
cretonne
Crimplene
crinoline
Dacron
damask
denim
dimity
doeskin

Donegal tweed
drill
drugget
duck
duffel or duffle
dungaree
duetyn or duvetyne
ecru
faille
felt
flannel
flannelette
fleece
foulard
frieze
fustian
gabardine
galatea
gauze
Georgette
gingham
gossamer
grenadine
grogram
grosgrain
gunny
haircloth
Harris tweed
herringbone
homespun
honan
hopsack
horsehair
houndstooth
huckaback
jaconet
jacquard
jardiniere
jean
jersey
jute
Kendal green
kersey
khaki
lace
lame
lawn
leatherette
leno
linen
linsey-woolsey
lisle
lisse
loden
Lurex
mackintosh
mackinaw
mackintosh or macintosh
madras

maline
marocain
marquisette
Marseille or Marseilles
mat
melton
merino
mesh
messaline
mohair
moire
moleskin
monk's cloth
moquette
mousseline
muslin
nainsook
nankeen
net or netting
ninon
nylon
oilcloth
oilskin
organdy
organza
organzine
paisley
panne
paramatta
percale
percaline
petersham
Pima
pique
plaid
plush
polar fleece
polyester
pongee
poplin
prunella
quilting
ragg
ratine
rayon
rep
ruched
russet
sackcloth
sacking
sailcloth
samite
sarcenet
sateen
satin
scrim
seersucker
serge

shalloon
shantung
sharkskin
Shetland wool
sheer
shoddy
shot silk
silk
spandex
stockinette
suede
supima
surah
swansdown
swanskin
tabaret
tabby
taffeta
tapestry
terry cloth

ticking
tiffany
toile
toweling
tricot
tricotine
tulle
tussah
tweed
twill
velour
velvet
velveteen
Venetian cloth
vicuna
voile
webbing
whipcord
wool
worsted

5 CLOTHING

NOUNS **1 clothing, clothes, apparel, wear, wearing apparel, daywear, dress,** dressing, **raiment,** garmenture, **garb, attire, array,** habit, habiliment, fashion, style 578.1, guise, **costume,** costumery, gear, toilette, trim, bedizenment; **vestment,** vesture, investment, investiture, canonicals, liturgical garment; **garments,** robes, robing, rags <nf>, drapery, finery, feathers; toggery or togs or **duds** or threads <nf>, sportswear; work clothes, fatigues; linen; menswear, men's clothing, womenswear, women's clothing; unisex clothing; latest fashion

2 wardrobe, furnishings, things, accouterments, trappings, gear; **outfit,** livery, harness, caparison; turnout and getup and rig and rig-out <nf>; wedding clothes, bridal outfit, trousseau; maternity clothes

3 garment, vestment, vesture, robe, frock, gown, rag <nf>

4 ready-mades, ready-to-wear, off-the-rack clothes, off-the-peg clothes, store or store-bought clothes, wash-and-wear, dry goods

5 rags, tatters, secondhand clothes, seconds, old clothes, castoff clothes, preowned clothing, consignment clothes, Goodwill clothes; worn clothes, **hand-me-downs** and reach-me-downs <nf>, castoffs; slops

6 suit <see list>, suit of clothes, set of clothes, ensemble; **frock,** dress, rig <nf>, **costume, habit,** bib and tucker <nf>

7 uniform <see list>, **livery,** monkey suit <nf>; nurse's uniform, police officer's uniform, etc; athletic team uniform, baseball uniform, etc

8 mufti, civilian dress or clothes, **civvies** and cits <nf>, plain clothes

9 costume, costumery, character dress; outfit and getup and rig <nf>; masquerade, disguise, mask; tights, leotards; ballet skirt, tutu, bodysuit; motley, cap and bells; silks; buskin

10 finery, frippery, fancy dress, fine or full feather <nf>, investiture, regalia, caparison, fig or full fig <Brit nf>; **best clothes,** best bib and tucker <nf>; **Sunday best** and Sunday clothes and Sunday-go-to-meeting clothes and Sunday-go-to-meetings <nf>, **glad rags** <nf>, ostrich feathers <nf>, party dress, dress-up clothes, dressy clothes; power dressing

11 formal dress, formals, **evening dress,** evening wear, **full dress,** dress clothes, evening wear, white tie and tails, **soup-and-fish** <nf>; dinner clothes; dress suit, full-dress suit, tail coat, tails <nf>; tuxedo, tux <nf>, dinner jacket; **regalia,** court dress; dress uniform, full-dress uniform, special full-dress uniform, social full-dress uniform; whites <nf>, dress whites, white tie; evening gown or dress, dinner dress or gown; prom dress, ball dress; morning dress, morning coat; semiformal dress; black tie, bow tie, cummerbund

12 cloak, overgarment <see list>

13 outerwear; coat, jacket <see list>; **overcoat** <see list>, great-coat, **topcoat,** surcoat; **rainwear;** rain gear, raincoat, slicker, rainsuit, foul weather gear

14 waistcoat, weskit <nf>, **vest;** down vest

15 shirt <see list>, waist, **shirtwaist,** linen, sark and shift <nf>; **blouse,** bodice; pullover, shell, T-shirt; dickey; sweater <see list>

16 dress <see list>, **gown, frock;** skirt

17 apron, tablier <Fr>; pinafore, bib, tucker; smock

18 pants, trousers, pair of trousers or pants, **breeches,** britches <nf>, **pantaloons;** jeans, designer jeans, blue jeans, dungarees; **slacks;** khakis, chinos; corduroys or cords, flannels, ducks, pinstripes, bell-bottoms, hiphuggers, Capri pants or Capris, pegged pants, pedal pushers, leggings, overalls, knickers, breeches, jodhpurs, sweatpants, cargo pants, carpenter pants; shorts, short pants, Bermuda shorts, hot pants, Jamaica shorts, surfer shorts, board shorts, short shorts, cycling shorts, gym shorts

19 waistband, belt 280.3; **sash,** cummerbund; **loincloth,** breechcloth or breechclout, waistcloth, **G-string,** loinguard, dhoti, moocha; **diaper,** dydee <nf>, napkins <Brit>, nappies <Brit nf>

20 dishabille, déshabillé <Fr>, **undress,** something more comfortable; **negligee,** négligé <Fr>; **wrap,** wrapper; sport clothes, playwear, activewear, sportswear, casual wear, leisurewear, **casual clothes** or **dress,** fling-on clothes, loungewear, plain clothes, dress-down clothes, knock-around clothes, grubbies <nf>; business casual; dress-down day, casual day

21 nightwear, night clothes, sleepwear; **nightdress, nightgown, nightie** *and* shortie nightie <nf>, negligee, nightshirt; **pajamas,** pyjamas <Brit>, pj's <nf>, baby doll pajamas; sleepers; robe, bathrobe, dressing gown, housecoat, caftan, bed jacket

22 underclothes, underclothing, undergarments <see list>, underthings, bodywear, **underwear, undies** <nf>, skivvies, BVD, body clothes, smallclothes, unmentionables <nf>, tighty whities <nf>, intimate apparel, **lingerie, linen,** underlinen; flannels, woolens, long johns

23 corset, stays, foundation garment, corselet; **girdle,** undergirdle, panty girdle; garter belt

24 brassiere, bra <nf>, sports bra, bandeau, crop top, underbodice, push-up bra; padded bras, falsies <nf>

25 headdress, headgear, headwear, headclothes; **millinery;** headpiece, **chapeau, cap, hat,** helmet; bonnet, stocking cap, cowboy hat, visor, baseball cap; lid <nf>; headcloth, **kerchief,** bandanna, coverchief; **handkerchief**

26 veil, veiling, veiler, net; *yashmak* <Turk>, *chador* <Iran>; mantilla

27 footwear, footgear, *chaussure* <Fr>; **shoes, boots,** overshoes; clodhoppers *and* gunboats *and* waffle-stompers *and* shitkickers <nf>, work shoes; oxfords, saddle shoes, pumps, slides, flats, slingbacks, espadrilles, high heels, platform shoes, penny loafers *or* loafers; sandals, flip-flops, zoris, jellies; athletic shoes, tennis shoes, sneakers; wooden shoes, clogs; slippers, moccasins

28 hosiery <see list>, legwear, pantyhose, **hose, stockings,** nylons; **socks**

29 swimwear; bathing suit, swimsuit, swimming suit, tank suit, tank top, *maillot* or *maillot de bain* <Fr>, one-piece suit, two-piece suit; **trunks;** bikini, string bikini *or* string, thong; swimming trunks, surfer shorts; wet suit; coverup

30 children's wear; rompers, jumpers; creepers; layette, baby clothes, infantwear, infants' wear, baby linen; swaddling clothes, swaddle

31 <clothing accessory> scarf, belt, glove, mitten, handkerchief, sunglasses, jewelry; neckwear, tie, necktie; collar, dickey

32 garment making, **tailoring; dressmaking, the rag trade** <nf>, fashion design, haute couture, **Seventh Avenue, the garment industry,** Garment District; **millinery,** hatmaking, hatting; hosiery; **shoemaking,** bootmaking, **cobbling;** habilimentation

33 clothier, haberdasher, draper <Brit>, outfitter; costumier, costumer; glover; hosier; furrier; dry goods dealer, mercer <Brit>

34 garmentmaker, garmentworker, needleworker; cutter, stitcher, finisher

35 tailor, tailoress, *tailleur* <Fr>, sartor; fitter; busheler, bushelman; furrier, cloakmaker, outfitter

36 dressmaker, modiste, *couturière* or *couturier* <Fr>; fashion designer; seamstress 741.2

37 hatter, hatmaker, **milliner**

38 shoemaker, bootmaker, booter, **cobbler**

VERBS **39 clothe,** enclothe, **dress, garb, attire,** tire, array, **apparel,** raiment, garment, habilitate, **tog** *and* tog out <nf>, dud <nf>, robe, enrobe, invest, endue, **deck,** bedeck, dight, rag out *or* up <nf>; drape, bedrape; wrap, enwrap, lap, envelop, sheathe, shroud, enshroud, invest; wrap *or* bundle *or* muffle up; swathe, swaddle

40 cloak, mantle; coat, jacket; gown, frock; breech; shirt; **hat,** coif, bonnet, cap, hood; boot, shoe; stocking, sock

41 outfit; equip, **accouter,** uniform, caparison, rig, rig out *or* up, fit, **fit out,** turn out, **costume,** habit, suit; design; **tailor,** tailor-make, custom-make, make to order

42 dress up, get up, doll *or* **spruce up** <nf>, **primp** *and* prink *and* prank <nf>, gussy up <nf>, spiff *or* fancy *or* slick up <nf>, pretty up <nf>, deck out *or* up, trick out *or* up, tog out *or* up <nf>, rag out *or* up <nf>, fig out *or* up <nf>; dress to kill, titivate, bedeck, dizen, bedizen; overdress; put on the dog *or* style <nf>; **dress down,** underdress

43 don, put on, slip on *or* into, get on *or* into, try on, assume, dress in, adorn, dight <old>; change; suit up

44 wear, have on, dress in, be dressed in, put on, slip on, affect, sport <nf>; change into; try on

ADJS **45 clothing; dress,** vestiary, sartorial; **clothed, clad, dressed, attired, togged** <nf>, tired, arrayed, **garbed,** garmented, habited, habilimented, decked, bedecked, decked-out, turned-out, tricked-out, rigged-out, vested, vestmented, robed, gowned, raimented, **appareled,** invested, endued, liveried, uniformed; **costumed,** in costume, cloaked, mantled, disguised; breeched, trousered, pantalooned; coifed, capped, bonneted, hatted, hooded; **shod,** shoed, booted, *chaussé* <Fr>

46 dressed up, dolled *or* **spruced up** <nf>; spiffed *or* fancied *or* slicked up <nf>, gussied up <nf>; spruce, dressed to advantage, dressed to the nines, dressed *or* fit to kill <nf>; in Sunday best, *endimanché* <Fr>, in one's best bib and tucker <nf>, in fine *or* high feather; *en grande tenue* <Fr>, *en grande toilette* <Fr>, in full dress, in full feather, in white tie and tails, in tails; **well-dressed, chic,** *soigné* <Fr>, stylish, modish, well-turned, well turned-out, très chic; retro-chic; **dressy; overdressed**

47 in dishabille, en déshabillé <Fr>, **in negligee; casual,** nonformal, dress-down, sporty, in one's shirtsleeves; baggy, sloppy; skintight, décolleté, low-necked, low-cut; underdressed, half-dressed

48 tailored, custom-made, tailor-made, made-to-order, bespoke <Brit>; ready-made, store-bought and off-the-rack <nf>, ready-to-wear; vestmental; sartorial

49 suits

bodysuit
boiler suit
business suit
camouflage suit or camo
casual suit
cat suit
coordinates
coveralls
double-breasted suit
dress suit
ensemble
flight suit
jogging suit or track suit
jumpsuit
leisure suit
livery
lounge suit
monkey suit
one-piece suit
pants suit or pantsuit
pinstripe suit
playsuit
rain suit
riding habit
romper suit or rompers
sack suit
separates
single-breasted suit
ski suit
slack suit
snowsuit
space suit
sports suit
summer suit
sun suit
sweat suit
swimsuit
tailored suit
tank suit
three-piece suit
town-and-country suit
track suit
tropical suit
trouser suit
tuxedo
two-piece suit
wet suit
zoot suit

50 uniforms

battle dress
blues
continentals
dress blues
dress whites
fatigues
full dress
khaki
livery
nauticals
olive-drab or OD
regimentals
sailor suit
school uniform
soldier suit
stripes <prison uniform>
undress
whites

51 cloaks, overgarments

academic gown
academic hood
academic robe
Afghan coat
bachelor's gown
burnoose
caftan
cap and
   gown
cape
capelet
capote
capuchin
cardinal
cashmere or cashmere
   shawl
cassock
chlamys
cowl
doctor's gown
domino
duster
frock
gaberdine
haik
houppelande
Inverness cape
judge's robe or gown
kaftan
kimono
kirtle
manta
manteau
mantelet
mantelletta
mantellone
mantilla
mantle
mantua
master's gown
military cloak
monk's robe
opera cloak or
   cape
pallium
pelerine
pelisse
peplos
peplum
plaid
poncho
robe
roquelaure
sagum
serape
shador
shawl
shoulderette
slop
smock
soutane
stole
tabard
talma
tippet
toga
toga virilis
tunic
wrap-around
wrapover
wrapper
wrap-up

52 coats, jackets, overcoats

anorak
balmacaan
benjamin
blanket coat
blazer
blouse
body-coat
bolero
bomber jacket
box coat
Burberry <trademark>
bush jacket
camelhair coat
capote
capuchin
car coat
chaqueta <Sp>
chesterfield
claw-hammer coat or claw
   hammer
cloth coat
coach coat
coatee
coolie jacket or coat
cutaway coat or cutaway
denim jacket or jean jacket
dinner coat or jacket
dolman
double-breasted jacket
doublet
down jacket
dreadnought
dress coat
dressing jacket
duffle coat
duster
Eton jacket
fearnought
fingertip coat
fitted coat
flack jacket
fleece jacket
frock coat or frock
fur coat
fur-lined coat
fur-trimmed coat
greatcoat
hacking jacket
happi coat
Inverness
jerkin
jumper
leather coat
loden coat
London Fog <trademark>
long coat
lounging jacket
mackinaw or mackinaw
   coat
mackintosh or mac
macfarlane
Mao jacket
maxicoat
mess jacket
midicoat
monkey jacket
morning coat
Nehru jacket
Newmarket or Newmarket
   coat
Norfolk jacket
oilskins

paletot
parka
peacoat *or* pea jacket
pilot jacket
Prince Albert *or* Prince
    Albert coat
raglan
raincoat
redingote
reefer *or* reefer jacket
sack *or* sack coat
safari jacket
sanbenito
shawl
shell jacket
shirtjac *or* shirt jacket
shooting jacket
single-breasted jacket
ski jacket
sleeve waistcoat
slicker
slip-on
smoking jacket
sou'wester
spencer

spiketail
sport coat *or* jacket
sports jacket
suit coat
surtout
swagger coat
swallow-tailed coat *or*
    swallowtail
sweater coat
swing coat
tabard
tail coat *or* tails
topcoat
topper
trench coat
tuxedo coat *or* jacket
ulster
watch coat
waterproof
Windbreaker
    <trademark>
winter coat
woolly
wrap-around *or* wrap
wraprascal

matador *or* toreador pants
moleskins
overalls
painter's pants
pantaloons
parachute pants
pedal pushers
pegleg trousers
plus fours
riding breeches

shorts
short shorts
ski pants
slacks
stirrup pants
stretch pants
sweat pants *or*
    sweatpants
trunk hose
waders

55 shirts

aloha *or* Hawaiian shirt
bandeau
basque
blouse
blouson
body shirt
body suit
bush shirt
bustier
button down
camp shirt
chambray shirt
coat shirt
crop top
denim shirt
benjamin
crop top
dickey
doublet
dress shirt
evening shirt
flannel shirt
garibaldi shirt
golf shirt
habit shirt
hair shirt
halter, halter top
hoodie

jersey
lawn shirt
long-sleeved shirt
middy blouse
muscle shirt
olive-drab *or* OD shirt
overblouse
Oxford shirt
polo shirt
pourpoint
pullover
rugby shirt
sark
shell
shirt-jacket *or* shirt-jac
shirtwaist
short-sleeved shirt
sleeveless shirt
sport shirt
sweatshirt
tank top
tee-shirt *or* T-shirt
three-quarter sleeve shirt
top
tube top
tunic
turtleneck
workshirt

53 sweaters

bolero
boucle
bulky
cable-knit sweater
cardigan *or* cardigan
    jacket
cashmere sweater
coat sweater
crewneck sweater
Fair Isle sweater
fisherman's sweater
Guernsey
hand-knit
jersey
mock turtleneck
mohair sweater
polo sweater

poor boy sweater
pull-on sweater
pullover
rollneck sweater
shell
shoulderette
ski sweater
slip-on
slipover
sloppy Joe
sweat shirt
sweater vest
turtleneck sweater
twin sweater set *or*
    twin set
V-neck sweater
woolly

54 trousers and pants

baggies
bell-bottoms
Bermuda shorts
bloomers
blue jeans
boot-cut pants
breeches
buckskins
Capri pants
cargo pants
carpenter pants
chaps
chinos
clamdiggers
corduroys *or* cords

cutoffs
ducks
dungarees
gaiters
harem pants
high-waters
hiphuggers
hot pants
jeans
jodhpurs
knee breeches
knickers *or* knickerbockers
lederhosen
Levi's <trademark>
loincloth

56 dresses, skirts

A-line skirt
ballet skirt
backwrap
ball gown
body dress
bridal gown
cheongsam
chiton
coat dress
cocktail dress
crinoline
culottes *or* divided skirt
dinner dress *or* gown
dirndl
divided skirt
evening dress
evening gown
farthingale
formal

full skirt
gown *or* evening gown
granny dress
grass skirt
harem skirt
hobble skirt
hoop skirt
housedress
hula skirt
jumper
kilt *or* filibeg *or* tartan
kimono
kirtle
little black dress
mantua
maternity dress
maxiskirt
microskirt *or* micromini-
    skirt

midiskirt
miniskirt
Mother Hubbard
muu-muu
overdress
overskirt
pannier
pantdress
pantskirt
peplum
petticoat
pinafore
pleated skirt
poodle skirt
princess dress
prom dress
sack
sari

sarong
sheath
shift
shirtdress *or* shirtwaist
    dress
skort
slit skirt
sundress
sweater dress
tank dress
T-dress
tea gown
tent dress
tube dress
tunic dress
tutu
wrap dress
wrap skirt *or* wraparound

57 nightclothes

baby doll pajamas
bathrobe
bed gown
bed jacket
dishabille
dressing gown
dressing jacket
housecoat
jammies *or* p.j.'s <nf>
lounging pajamas
morning dress

negligee
nightgown
nightie <nf>
nightshirt
pajamas
peignoir
robe
robe de chambre
romper
sleeper
smoking jacket

58 undergarments

all-in-one
athletic supporter *or*
    jockstrap
Balmoral
bandeau
bloomers
bikini
bodice
body stocking
body suit
boxer shorts
brassiere *or* bra
breechclout *or* loin-cloth
briefs
bustle
BVD's <trademark>
cami-knickers
camisole
chemise
corselet
corset
crinoline
diapers
drawers
foundation garment
full slip
garter
garter belt

girdle
G-string
half-slip
Jockey <trademark> shorts
knickers <Brit>
leotard
lingerie
long underwear *or* long
    johns
napkins *or* nappies <Brit>
pannier
panties
pants
panty girdle
peekaboo
petticoat
push-up bra
scanties
shift
shorts
singlet <Brit>
skivvies
slip
smock
soakers
sport bra *or* sports bra
step-ins
strapless bra

support garment
tap pants
teddy
tee-shirt *or* T-shirt
thermal underwear *or*
    thermals
thong
tournure <Fr>
underdrawers
underpants

undershirt
undershorts
underskirt
undervest
underwire bra
undies
union suit
unitard
unmentionables
woolens

59 hosiery

anklets *or* ankle socks
argyles
athletic socks
bobbysocks
boothose
boot socks
crew socks
dress sheers
fishnet stockings
footlets
full-fashioned
    stockings
garter stockings
hose
body stocking
knee-highs
knee-socks
leggings
leg-warmers
lisle hose

nylons
pantyhose
Peds <trademark>
rayon stockings
seamless stockings
sheer stockings *or*
    sheers
silk stockings
slouch socks
socks
stocking hose
stockings
stretch stockings
support hose
sweat socks
tights
tube socks
varsity socks
wigglers *or* toe socks
work socks

6 UNCLOTHING

NOUNS **1 unclothing,** divestment, divestiture,
divesture; **removal; stripping,** denudement,
denudation; baring, stripping *or* laying bare,
uncovering, **exposure,** exposing; indecent
exposure, exhibitionism, flashing <nf>;
decortication, excoriation; desquamation,
exfoliation; exuviation, ecdysis

2 disrobing, undressing, undress, disrobement,
unclothing; uncasing, discasing; shedding,
molting, peeling; striptease, stripping;
skinny-dipping <nf>, mooning <nf>,
flashing <nf>

3 nudity, nakedness, bareness; **the nude, the
altogether** *and* **the buff** <nf>, **the raw** <nf>; state
of nature, state of undress, full frontal, **birthday
suit** <nf>; not a stitch, not a stitch to one's name,
not a stitch on one's back; full-frontal nudity;
décolleté, décolletage, toplessness; nudism,
naturism, gymnosophy; nudist, naturist,
gymnosophist, exhibitionist; stripper, stripteaser,
ecdysiast, topless dancer, lap dancer

4 hairlessness, baldness, acomia, alopecia; calvities;
hair loss; beardlessness, bald-headedness *or*

-patedness; baldhead, baldpate, baldy <nf>, skinhead; pattern baldness; shaving, tonsure, depilation; hair remover, depilatory

VERBS **5** **divest, strip, strip away, remove; uncover,** uncloak, unveil, **expose,** lay open, bare, lay *or* strip bare, strip naked, **denude,** denudate; fleece, shear; pluck; strip-search

6 **take off, remove, doff,** off with, put off, slip *or* step out of, slip off, slough off, cast off, throw off, drop; unwrap, undo

7 **undress, unclothe,** undrape, ungarment, unapparel, unarray, disarray; **disrobe;** unsheathe, discase, uncase; **strip,** strip to the buff <nf>, do a strip-tease; skinny-dip, flash <nf>, moon <nf>

8 **peel, pare, skin, strip,** flay, excoriate, decorticate, bark; scalp; depilate, shave

9 **husk, hull,** pod, **shell,** shuck

10 **shed, cast,** throw off, **slough, molt,** slough off, exuviate

11 **scale, flake,** scale *or* flake off, desquamate, exfoliate

ADJS **12** **divested, stripped, bared,** denuded, denudated, **exposed, uncovered,** stripped *or* laid bare, unveiled, showing; unsheathed, discased, uncased

13 **unclad, undressed, unclothed, unattired, disrobed,** ungarmented, undraped, ungarbed, unrobed, unapparreled, uncased; **clothesless,** garbless, garmentless, raimentless; half-clothed, underclothed, *en déshabillé* <Fr>, in dishabille, nudish; low-necked, low-cut, décolleté, strapless, topless; **seminude,** scantily clad

14 **naked, nude; bare,** peeled, raw <nf>, **in the raw** <nf>, *in puris naturalibus* <L>, in a state of nature, in nature's garb; in one's birthday suit, **in the buff** *and* in native buff *and* stripped to the buff *and* **in the altogether** <nf>, with nothing on, without a stitch, without a stitch to one's name *or* on one's back; **stark-naked,** bare-ass <nf>, buck naked, bare as the back of one's hand, naked as the day one was born, naked as a jaybird <nf>, starkers <Brit nf>; topless, bare-breasted, bottomless, bare-bottomed, "naked as a worm"—Chaucer; nudist, naturistic, gymnosophical

15 **barefoot,** barefooted, unshod; discalced, discalceate

16 bare-ankled, bare-armed, bare-backed, bare-breasted, topless, bare-chested, bare-faced, bare-handed, bare-headed, bare-kneed, bare-legged, bare-necked, bare-throated

17 **hairless,** depilous; **bald,** acomous; bald as a coot, bald as an egg; **bald-headed,** bald-pated, tonsured; **beardless,** whiskerless, shaven, clean-shaven, smooth-shaven, smooth-faced; smooth, glabrous

18 exuvial, sloughy; desquamative, exfoliatory; denudant *or* denudatory; peeling, shedding

ADVS **19** nakedly, barely, baldly
WORD ELEMENTS **20** de-, dis-, un-

7 NUTRITION

NOUNS **1** **nutrition, nourishment,** nourishing, feeding, nurture; alimentation, sustenance; **food** *or* **nutritive value, food intake;** food chain *or* cycle; food pyramid, recommended daily vitamins and minerals

2 **nutritiousness,** nutritiveness, **digestibility,** assimilability; healthfulness

3 **nutrient,** nutritive, **nutriment** 10.3, food; nutrilite, growth factor, growth regulator; **natural food,** health food <see list>; roughage, fiber, dietary fiber

4 **vitamin** <see list>, vitamin complex; provitamin, provitamin A *or* carotene; food additive, vitamin supplement

5 **carbohydrate,** carbo *or* carbs <nf>, simple carbohydrate, complex carbohydrate; hydroxy aldehyde, hydroxy ketone, glycogen, cellulose, ketone, saccharide, monosaccharide, disaccharide, trisaccharide, polysaccharide *or* polysaccharose; **sugar;** artificial sweetener; **starch**

6 **protein** *or* proteid, simple protein, conjugated protein, protein structure; **amino acid,** essential amino acid; peptide, dipeptide, polypeptide, etc; globulin, collagen, gluten, immunoglobulin, hemoglobin

7 **fat,** glyceride, **lipid,** lipoid; lecithin; fatty acid; steroid, sterol; **cholesterol,** glycerol-cholesterol, cephalin-cholesterol; triglyceride; **lipoprotein,** high-density lipoprotein *or* HDL, low-density lipoprotein *or* LDL; polyunsaturated fat; saturated fat; unsaturated fat

8 **digestion,** ingestion, assimilation, absorption; primary digestion, secondary digestion; predigestion; salivary digestion, gastric *or* peptic digestion, pancreatic digestion, intestinal digestion; digestive system, alimentary canal, gastrointestinal tract; salivary glands, gastric glands, liver, pancreas; digestive secretions, saliva, gastric juice, pancreatic juice, intestinal juice, bile

9 **digestant,** digester, digestive; pepsin; **enzyme,** proteolytic enzyme

10 **enzyme,** apoenzyme, coenzyme, isoenzyme; transferase, hydrolase, lyase, isomerase, polymerase, amylase, diastase; pepsin, rennin; proenzyme, trypsin, zymogen

11 **essential element,** macronutrient; carbon, hydrogen, oxygen, nitrogen, calcium, phosphorus, potassium, sodium, chlorine, sulfur, magnesium; trace element, micronutrient; iron, manganese, zinc, copper, iodine, cobalt, selenium, molybdenum, chromium, silicon

12 metabolism, basal metabolism, metabolic process, acid-base metabolism, energy metabolism; **anabolism,** assimilation; **catabolism,** disassimilation

13 diet, dieting, dietary; dietetics; **regimen,** regime; bland diet; soft diet, pap, spoon food *or* meat, spoon victuals <nf>; balanced diet; diabetic diet, allergy diet, reducing diet, weight-loss diet, obesity diet; high-calorie diet, low-calorie diet, watching one's weight *or* calories, calorie-counting; liquid diet; high-protein diet, low-carbohydrate diet; low-salt diet, low-sodium diet, salt-free diet; low-fat diet, fat-free diet; low-cholesterol diet; sugar-free diet; vegetarianism, lactovegetarianism, vegan diet; macrobiotic diet; crash diet, fad diet; portion control; eating disorder, anorexia, anorexia nervosa, bulimia; diet book, calorie counter

14 vitaminization, **fortification, enrichment,** restoration

15 nutritionist, dietitian, vitaminologist, enzymologist

16 <science of nutrition> **dietetics,** dietotherapeutics, dietotherapy; vitaminology; threpsology; enzymology

VERBS **17 nourish,** feed, sustain, aliment, nutrify <old>, nurture, provide for, fatten up; **sustain,** strengthen; cook for, wine and dine, regale, chef; force-feed

18 digest, assimilate, absorb; metabolize; predigest

19 diet, go on a diet; watch one's weight *or* calories, count calories

20 vitaminize, **fortify, enrich,** restore

ADJS **21 nutritious,** nutritive, nutrient, **nourishing;** good for, healthful; alimentary, alimental; organic; digestible, assimilable

22 digestive, assimilative; peptic, eupeptic

23 dietary, dietetic, dietic <old>; regiminal

24 foods, bland

broth	milk
cake	pasta
cooked cereals	pie
cookie	plain rice
crackers	potatoes
decaffeinated coffee	pudding
eggs	refined breads
fruit juice	refined
Jell-O ™	cereals
lean meat	rice pudding
marshmallows	soft banana
mild-flavored vegetable	tofu
juice	yogurt

25 foods, soft

applesauce	canned fruit
breakfast drink	cooked cereal
cooked fruit	muffin
cooked vegetables	pasta
cottage cheese	pastry
couscous	pudding
custard	smooth peanut butter
eggs	soft bread
ice cream	soft cheese
Jell-O ™	soft fruit
macaroni and cheese	soft vegetables
mashed potatoes	sorbet
meat loaf	soup
milkshake	yogurt

26 vitamins

vitamin A	*or* cyanocobalamin *or*
vitamin A1 *or* antiophthal-	extrinsic factor *or*
mic factor *or* axeroph-	pentothenic acid *or*
thol, retinol	lipoid acid
vitamin A2	biotin *or* vitamin H
biotin	choline
carotene	folic acid *or* pteroylglu-
choline	tamic acid *or* para-ami-
cryptoxanthin	nobenzoic acid *or* PABA
vitamin B	inositol
vitamin B complex	niacin *or* nicotinic acid
vitamin B1 *or* thiamine *or*	vitamin C *or* ascorbic acid
aneurin *or* anti-beriberi	vitamin D2 *or* calciferol
factor	ergocalciferol
vitamin B2 *or* vitamin G *or*	cholecalciferol *or* vitamin
riboflavin *or* lactoflavin	D3
or ovoflavin *or* hepatofla-	vitamin E *or* tocopherol
vin	vitamin K *or* naphthoqui-
vitamin M *or* vitamin Bc	none
vitamin B6 *or* pyridoxine	menadione
or adermin	vitamin P *or* bioflavinoid
vitamin B12 *or* cobalamin	

8 EATING

NOUNS **1 eating, feeding, dining,** messing; the nosebag <nf>; ingestion, consumption, consuming, deglutition; **tasting,** relishing, savoring; **gourmet eating** *or* **dining,** fine dining, gourmandise, gastronomy; nibbling, pecking, licking, **munching;** snacking; **devouring,** gobbling, wolfing, downing, gulping; **gorging, overeating,** gluttony, overconsumption; **chewing,** mastication, manducation, rumination; **feasting, regaling,** regalement; **appetite, hunger** 100.7; nutrition 7; **dieting** 7.13; gluttony 672.1; carnivorism, carnivorousness, carnivority; herbivorism, herbivority, herbivorousness, grazing, browsing, cropping, pasturing, pasture; vegetarianism, phytophagy; omnivorism, omnivorousness, pantophagy; cannibalism, anthropophagy; omophagia *or* omophagy

2 bite, morsel, taste, swallow; mouthful, gob <nf>, piece, slice, scrap, tidbit; nibble, munchies; cud, quid; bolus, gobbet; **chew,** chaw <nf>; nip, niblet; munch; gnash; champ, chomp <nf>; appetizer, hors d'oeuvre, amuse-bouche

3 **drinking,** imbibing, imbibition, potation; lapping, sipping, tasting, nipping, tippling; quaffing, gulping, swigging <nf>, swilling *and* guzzling <nf>, pulling <nf>; winebibbing; compotation, symposium; barhopping; drunkenness 88.1,3

4 **drink,** potation, beverage <see list>, potion, libation, oblation, thirst-quencher; draft, dram, drench, **swig** <nf>, swill *and* guzzle <nf>, quaff, tipple, **sip,** sup, suck, tot, bumper, snort *and* slug <nf>, pull <nf>, lap, gulp, slurp <nf>; nip, peg; toast, health; mixed drink, cocktail; nightcap <nf>

5 **meal, repast,** feed *and* sit-down <nf>, mess, spread <nf>, menu, table, board, meat, *repas* <Fr>; **refreshment,** refection, regalement, collation, entertainment, treat; frozen meal

6 <meals> **breakfast,** *petit déjeuner* <Fr>, continental breakfast, English breakfast, American breakfast, meat breakfast, *déjeuner à la fourchette* <Fr>, banquet, smorgasbord; power breakfast *or* lunch *or* dinner; **brunch** <nf>, Sunday brunch, elevenses <Brit nf>; **lunch, luncheon,** tiffin, hot lunch, light lunch, box lunch, brown-bag lunch, packed lunch <Brit>; blue-plate special; tapas; **tea,** teatime, high tea, afternoon tea, cream tea; **dinner,** *diner* <Fr>, evening meal, dinner party; **supper,** *souper* <Fr>; buffet supper *or* lunch; fast food, takeout, drive-through meal; precooked frozen meal, TV dinner; **picnic, cookout,** alfresco meal, fête champêtre, tailgate picnic, **barbecue,** fish fry, clambake, wiener roast *or* wienie roast; pot luck; midnight supper *or* snack; progressive dinner; dashboard *or* cupholder meal

7 **light meal, refreshments,** light repast, light lunch, spot of lunch <nf>, collation, **snack** *and* nosh <nf>, **bite** <nf>, bite to eat <nf>, *casse-croûte* <Fr>; informal meal; coffee break, tea break

8 **hearty meal, full meal,** healthy meal, large *or* substantial meal, heavy meal, nosh-up, **square meal,** man-sized meal, large order; three squares; formal meal, sit-down meal

9 **feast, banquet,** regale, buffet, smorgasbord, festal board, groaning board, spread; finger buffet; Lucullan banquet, bacchanalia; Passover; blow *or* blowout <nf>, feeding frenzy <nf>; dinner party; bean feast

10 **serving,** service; **portion, helping,** serving suggestion; second helping, seconds; **course;** dish, plate; *plat du jour* <Fr>; antepast <old>; first course, starter, soup, entree, *entrée* <Fr>, main course, entremets, side dish, tapas; dessert

11 <manner of service> service, table service, counter service, self-service, curb service,

take-out service, drive-through; table d'hôte, ordinary; à la carte; cover, *couvert* <Fr>; cover charge; American plan, European plan

12 **tableware,** dining utensils; **silverware,** silver, silver plate, stainless-steel ware; **flatware,** flat silver; hollow ware; **cutlery,** knives, fish knife, carving knife, fruit knife, steak knife, butter knife; forks, fish fork, salad fork, fondue fork; spoons, tablespoon, teaspoon, soup spoon, dessert spoon, coffee spoon, serving spoon; chopsticks; **dishware, china, dishes,** plates, cups, saucers, bowls, fingerbowls; glasses, **glassware**, tumbler, goblet, wineglass, crystal, flute; **dish,** salad dish, fruit dish, dessert dish; **bowl,** cereal bowl, fruit bowl, punchbowl; **tea service, tea set,** tea things, tea strainer, tea-caddy, tea-cozy

13 **table linen, napery,** tablecloth, table cover, table-mat, table pad, place mat, setting; **napkin, table napkin,** serviette <Brit>

14 **menu, bill of fare,** carte, a la carte, menuboard

15 **gastronomy,** gastronomics, gastrology, **epicurism,** epicureanism

16 **eater,** feeder, consumer, devourer, partaker; **diner,** luncher; picnicker; mouth, hungry mouth, big eater; diner-out, eater-out; boarder, board-and-roomer; **gourmet,** gastronome, epicure, gourmand, connoisseur of food *or* wine, bon vivant, Lucullus, foodie, chowhound; overeater, pig *and* wolf <nf>, trencherman, big eater, **glutton** 672.3; light eater, nibbler, picky eater, fussy eater; omnivore, pantophagist; **flesh-eater, meat-eater, carnivore,** omophagist, predacean; **man-eater, cannibal; vegetarian,** lactovegetarian, vegan, fruitarian, plant-eater, **herbivore,** phytophagan, phytophage; grass-eater, graminivore; grain-eater, granivore

17 **restaurant,** eating place, eating house, dining room; eatery *and* beanery *and* hashery *and* hash house *and* greasy spoon <nf>, chain restaurant, theme restaurant; **fast-food restaurant,** takeout, hamburger joint <nf>; *trattoria* <Ital>; **lunchroom,** luncheonette; **café,** *caffè* <Ital>, roadside cafe; **tearoom,** *bistro* <Fr>; **coffeehouse,** coffeeroom, **coffee shop,** coffee bar; **tea shop,** tea-garden, teahouse; pub, tavern, brew pub, gastropub <Brit>; chop-house; **grill,** grillroom, steakhouse, carvery; brasserie; pancake house, waffle house; cookshop; buffet, smorgasbord, self-service restaurant; **lunch counter,** quick-lunch counter; salad bar; hot-dog stand, hamburger stand, drive-in restaurant, drive-in; **snack bar,** sandwich bar, *buvette* <Fr>, *cantina* <Sp>; milk bar; sushi bar; juice bar; raw bar; pizzeria; **cafeteria,** automat; mess hall, dining hall, refectory; canteen; cookhouse, cookshack, lunch wagon,

chuck wagon; **diner,** dog wagon <nf>; delicatessen, deli; ice-cream parlor, soda fountain; dining car; vending machine; **kitchen** 11.4, breakfast nook, dining room, dinette

VERBS **18 feed, dine,** wine and dine, mess; nibble, snack, graze <nf>; satisfy, gratify; regale; bread, meat; board, sustain; pasture, put out to pasture, graze, browse; forage, fodder; provision 385.9

19 nourish, nurture, nutrify, aliment, foster; **nurse, suckle,** lactate, breast-feed, wet-nurse, dry-nurse; fatten, fatten up, stuff, force-feed

20 eat, feed, fare, take, partake, partake of, *mange* <Fr>, take nourishment, subsist, break bread, break one's fast, feast on; refresh *or* entertain the inner man, feed one's face *and* put on the feed bag <nf>, fall to, pitch in <nf>; **taste,** relish, savor; hunger 100.19; get *or* have the munchies, **diet,** go on a diet, watch one's weight, count calories

21 dine, dinner; **sup,** breakfast; lunch; have dinner, have lunch, have breakfast; picnic, cook out; **eat out, dine out;** board; mess with, break bread with; brown-bag

22 devour, swallow, ingest, **consume,** take in, tuck in *or* away *and* tuck into *and* chow down <nf>, down, get down, scarf down, put away <nf>, snarf <nf>; **eat up;** dispatch *or* dispose of <nf>

23 gobble, gulp, bolt, wolf, gobble *or* gulp *or* bolt *or* wolf down

24 feast, banquet, regale; eat heartily, have a good appetite, eat up, lick the platter *or* plate, do oneself proud <nf>, do one's duty, do justice to, clean one's plate, polish the platter, put it away <nf>

25 stuff, gorge 672.4, pig out <nf>, oink out <nf>, engorge, glut, guttle, binge, cram, eat one's fill, stuff *or* gorge oneself, gluttonize, eat everything in sight

26 pick, peck <nf>, **nibble; snack** <nf>, nosh <nf>; pick at, peck at <nf>, eat like a bird, show no appetite

27 chew, chew up, chaw <nf>, bite into; **masticate,** manducate; ruminate, chew the cud; **bite,** grind, champ, chomp <nf>; **munch,** crunch; gnash; **gnaw;** mouth, mumble; gum

28 feed on *or* **upon, feast on** *or* **upon,** batten upon, fatten on *or* upon; prey on *or* upon, live on *or* upon, pasture on, browse, graze, crop

29 drink, drink in, **imbibe,** wet one's whistle <nf>; **quaff, sip, sup,** bib, swig *and* swill *and* guzzle *and* pull *and* gulp <nf>; **suck,** suckle, suck in *or* up; drink off *or* up, toss off *or* down, knock back, drain the cup; wash down; **toast,** drink to, pledge; tipple, **booze** 88.23

30 lap up, sponge *or* soak up, lick, lap, slurp <nf>

ADJS **31 eating, feeding, gastronomical, dining,** mensal, commensal, prandial, postprandial, preprandial; **nourishing, nutritious** 7.21; empty-calorie; **dietetic; omnivorous,** pantophagous, **gluttonous** 672.6; **flesh-eating, meat-eating, carnivorous,** omophagic, omophagous, predacious; **man-eating, cannibal,** cannibalistic; insect-eating, insectivorous; vegetable-eating, **vegetarian,** lactovegetarian, vegan, fruitarian; plant-eating, **herbivorous,** phytivorous, phytophagous; grass-eating, graminivorous; grain-eating, granivorous; organic

32 chewing, masticatory, masticating, manducatory; ruminant, ruminating, cud-chewing; tasting, nibbling

33 edible, eatable, comestible, consumable, safe to eat, esculent, digestible, gustable, esculent; kosher; **palatable,** succulent, mouth-watering, **delicious,** dainty, savory, good to eat, finger-licking; **fine, fancy, gourmet;** calorific, fattening, rich

34 drinkable, potable, quaffable

INTERJS **35** chow down!, soup's on!, grub's on!, come and get it!; *bon appétit!* <Fr>, eat hearty!, eat up!

WORD ELEMENTS **36** phag-, phago-, -phagia, -phagy; -phage, -vore, -vora

9 REFRESHMENT

NOUNS **1 refreshment,** refection, refreshing, freshening up, **bracing, exhilaration, stimulation,** enlivenment, vivification, **invigoration,** reinvigoration, reanimation, rejuvenation, revival, revivification, revivescence *or* revivescency, renewal, recreation, rest and recreation, R and R; regalement, regale; **tonic,** bracer, breath of fresh air, pick-me-up *and* a shot in the arm *and* an upper <nf>; cordial

VERBS **2 refresh, freshen,** freshen up, fresh up <nf>; **revive,** revivify, **reinvigorate,** reanimate; **exhilarate, stimulate, invigorate,** fortify, enliven, liven up, restore, animate, vivify, quicken, brisk, brisken; brace, **brace up,** buck up *and* pick up <nf>, perk up *and* chirk up <nf>, set up, set on one's legs *or* feet <nf>; renew one's strength, put *or* breathe new life into, give a breath of fresh air, blow out the cobwebs, give a shot in the arm <nf>; renew, recreate, charge *or* recharge one's batteries <nf>, give a break, give a breather; **regale, cheer,** refresh the inner man

ADJS **3 refreshing,** refreshful, **fresh,** brisk, crisp, crispy, fortifying, zesty, zestful, **bracing, tonic,** cordial; analeptic; **exhilarating, stimulating, stimulative, stimulatory, invigorating,** rousing, energizing; regaling, cheering; rejuvenating; recreative, recreational

4 refreshed, restored, invigorated, exhilarated, freshened up, enlivened, stimulated, energized, recharged, animated, reanimated, **revived,** renewed, recreated, ready for more, ready for another round

5 unwearied, untired, unfatigued, unexhausted

10 FOOD

NOUNS **1 food,** foodstuff, food and drink, sustenance, kitchen stuff, victualage, **comestibles, edibles,** eatables, viands, **cuisine,** tucker <Austral>, ingesta <pl>; soul food; fast food, junk food; **fare,** cheer, creature comfort; provision, provender; meat <old>, bread, daily bread, bread and butter, staff of life; health food; board, table, feast 8.9, spread <nf>; nouvelle cuisine, designer food; processed food

2 <nf terms> **grub,** grubbery, **eats, chow,** chuck, grits, groceries, nosh, the nosebag, scarf *or* scoff, nibbles, tuck <Brit>, victuals *or* vittles; fast food; Frankenfood

3 nutriment, nourishment, nurture; pabulum, pap; aliment, alimentation, fare; **refreshment,** refection; **sustenance,** support, keep

4 feed, fodder, provender, animal food; forage, pasture, eatage, pasturage; grain; corn, oats, barley, wheat, cereal grain; meal, bran, chop; **hay,** timothy, clover, straw; ensilage, silage; chicken feed, scratch, scratch feed, mash; slops, swill; pet food, dog food, cat food; bird seed

5 provisions, groceries, provender, supplies, stores, larder, food supply, food and drink, victuals; fresh foods, canned foods, frozen foods, dehydrated foods, precooked foods, convenience foods; commissariat, commissary, grocery

6 rations, board, meals, commons <chiefly Brit>, mess, allowance, allotment, food allotment, tucker <Austral>; short commons <chiefly Brit>; emergency rations; K ration, C ration, garrison *or* field rations

7 dish, culinary preparation *or* concoction; cover, **course** 8.10; casserole; grill, broil, boil, roast, fry; **main dish, entree,** main course, *pièce de résistance* <Fr>, culinary masterpiece, dish fit for a king; hors d'oeuvre, starter, appetizer; side dish, side, salad, vegetables; dessert; dish of the day, soup of the day, specialty

8 delicacy, dainty, goody <nf>, treat, kickshaw, **tidbit,** titbit; gourmet food; **morsel,** choice morsel, *bonne bouche* or *amuse-gueule* <Fr>; savory; dessert; ambrosia, nectar, cate, manna

9 appetizer, whet, *apéritif* <Fr>; foretaste, antepast <old>, *antipasto* <Ital>, *Vorspeise* <Ger>; **hors d'oeuvre;** *crostato* <Ital>, starter, nibbles, tidbits; smorgasbord; crackers and cheese, crudites, **dip,** guacamole, salsa, pâté, cheese dip, nachos,

potato skins, hummus; falafcl; rumaki; **pickle,** dill pickle

10 soup, *potage* <Fr>, *zuppa* or *minestra* <Ital>, cream soup, clear soup, consomme, stock, bouillon, broth, potage, bisque, borscht, gumbo, chowder, bouillabaisse, alphabet soup, avgolemono

11 stew, olla, olio, *olla podrida* <Sp>; hot pot; meat stew, *étuvée* <Fr>; Irish stew, mulligan stew *or* mulligan <nf>, burgoo; goulash, Hungarian goulash; ragout; salmi; *bouillabaisse* <Fr>, *paella* <Catalan>, oyster stew; fricassee; curry

12 sauce; tomato sauce, ketchup *or* catsup; brown sauce, Worcestershire sauce, soy sauce, Bordelaise; Tabasco sauce <trademark>, barbecue sauce; tartar sauce, horseradish; condiment, dip, dressing, salsa, guacamole, pesto; applesauce; mayonnaise, salad dressing, vinaigrette; white sauce, veloute, Alfredo, Bearnaise, hollandaise, bechamel

13 meat, flesh, red meat, *viande* <Fr>, white meat; butcher's meat, *viande de boucherie* <Fr>; **cut of meat;** game, *menue viande* <Fr>; venison; **roast,** joint, *rôti* <Fr>; pot roast; chop, cutlet, grill; barbecue, boiled meat, *bouilli* <Fr>; forcemeat; mincemeat, mince; hash, *hachis* <Fr>; *civet* <Fr>; pemmican, jerky; sausage meat, scrapple; aspic; meat substitute, tofu, bean curd

14 beef, *bœuf* <Fr>; roast beef, *rosbif* <Fr>; chuck, rib roast, tenderloin, sirloin, steak, round, filet *or* fillet, beefsteak, boneless rump, shank, brisket; hamburger, ground beef; corned beef; dried beef; chipped beef; jerky, charqui; pastrami; beef extract, bouillon; suet

15 veal, *vitello* <Ital>, *veau* <Fr>; veal cutlet, *côtelette de veau* <Fr>; shoulder, rib roast, chops, loin, rump, shank, leg, cutlet, escallop, breast, neck; *poitrine de veau* <Fr>; fricandeau; calf's head, *tête de veau* <Fr>; calf's liver, *foie de veau* <Fr>; sweetbread, *ris de veau* <Fr>; calf's brains

16 mutton, *mouton* <Fr>; muttonchop; **lamb,** *agneau* <Fr>; breast of lamb, rack of lamb, crown roast, *poitrine d'agneau* <Fr>; leg of lamb, leg of mutton, *gigot* <Fr>, *jambe de mouton* <Fr>; saddle of mutton

17 pork, *porc* <Fr>, pig, pigmeat <nf>, spareribs, ribs

18 steak, *tranche* <Fr>, **beefsteak,** *bifteck* <Fr>, *tranche de bœuf* <Fr>, *bistecca* <Ital>, minute steak, filet, tournedo

19 chop, cutlet, *côtelette* <Fr>; pork chop, *côtelette de porc frais* <Fr>; mutton chop, *côtelette de mouton* <Fr>; scallop, papillote, Saratoga chop; veal cutlet, veal chop, *côtelette de veau* <Fr>, *Wiener Schnitzel* <Ger>

20 <variety meats> kidneys; heart; brains; liver; gizzard; tongue; sweetbread <thymus>; beef bread <pancreas>; tripe <stomach>; marrow;

cockscomb; chitterlings *or* chitlins <intestines>; prairie *or* mountain oyster <testis>; haslet, giblets, *abattis* <Fr>, offal

21 **sausage,** *saucisse* <Fr>, *saucisson* <Fr>, *salsiccia* <Ital>, *Wurst* <Ger>, banger, hot dog; **pâté**

22 **poultry, fowl,** bird, edible bird, chicken, turkey, *volaille* <Fr>

23 <parts of poultry> leg, drumstick, thigh, wing, wishbone, breast; white meat, dark meat, giblets, pope's *or* parson's nose <nf>

24 **fish,** *poisson* <Fr>; seafood; fruits de mer; fried fish, broiled fish, boiled fish, poached fish, smoked fish, fish cake *or* fish ball, fish stick, fish pie; fish and chips; food fish; finnan haddie; kipper, kippered salmon *or* herring, gravlax; smoked salmon, lox; smoked herring, red herring; eel, *anguille* <Fr>; fish eggs, roe, caviar; ceviche, sushi; squid, calamari; flatfish, sole, lemon sole, Dover sole, flounder, fluke, dab, sanddab

25 **shellfish,** *coquillage* <Fr>; **mollusc,** mollusk, snail, *escargot* <Fr>

26 **eggs,** *œufs* <Fr>; fried eggs, *œufs sur le plat* <Fr>; hard- and soft-boiled eggs, *œufs à la coque* <Fr>, coddled eggs; poached eggs, over-easy, sunny-side up, *œufs pochés* <Fr>; scrambled eggs, buttered eggs, *œufs brouillés* <Fr>; dropped eggs, shirred eggs, stuffed eggs, deviled eggs; omelet *or* omelette; soufflé; Scotch egg, eggs Benedict; egg salad

27 **stuffing, dressing,** forcemeat *or* farce

28 **bread,** *pain* <Fr>, *pane* <Ital>, the staff of life; French bread, Italian bread, sourdough bread, ciabatta; loaf of bread; crust, breadcrust, crust of bread; breadstuff; **leaven,** leavening, ferment

29 **corn bread;** pone, ash pone, corn pone, corn tash, ash cake, hoecake, johnnycake; dodger, corn dodger, corn dab, hush puppy; cracklin' bread <nf>; *tortilla* <Sp>

30 **biscuit,** sinker <nf>; hardtack, sea biscuit, ship biscuit, pilot biscuit *or* bread; shortcake; **cracker,** soda cracker *or* saltine, graham cracker, *biscotto or biscotti* <Ital>, cream cracker, potato chip, potato crisp <Brit>, sultana, water biscuit, butter cracker, oyster cracker, pilot biscuit; wafer; rusk, zwieback, melba toast, Brussels biscuit; pretzel

31 **roll, bun, muffin;** bagel, bialy *or* bialystoker; brioche, croissant; English muffin; popover; scone; hard roll, kaiser roll, dinner roll, Parker House roll, Portuguese roll

32 **sandwich,** *canapé* <Fr>, *smörgasbord* <Swed>; club sandwich, Dagwood; hamburger, burger; submarine *or* sub *or* hero *or* grinder *or* hoagy *or* poorboy; wedge; gyro; veggieburger *or* vegeburger *or* gardenburger

33 **noodles,** pasta, Italian paste, paste; **spaghetti,** spaghettini, ziti, penne, fettuccine, linguine,

fusilli, radiattore, vermicelli, rigatoni, tortellini, ravioli, gnocchi, **macaroni,** lasagne; *kreplach* <Yiddish pl>, won ton; **dumpling;** spaetzle, dim sum; matzo balls, *knaydlach* <Yiddish>

34 **cereal,** breakfast food, dry cereal, hot cereal; **flour,** meal

35 **vegetables,** produce, *légumes* <Fr>, veg *and* veggies <nf>; **greens;** potherbs; **beans,** *frijoles* <Sp>, *haricots* <Fr>; leafy vegetable, stem vegetable, root vegetable, tuber, flower vegetable, seed vegetable, pulse; **potato,** spud <nf>, tater <nf>, *pomme de terre* <Fr>, Irish potato, pratie <nf>, white potato; **tomato,** love apple; mushroom; eggplant, *aubergine* <Fr>, mad apple; rhubarb, pieplant; cabbage, *Kraut* <Ger>; ratatouille, mixed vegetables

36 **rice,** white rice, long-grain rice, brown rice, wild rice, pilaf, orzo, couscous, risotto, Arborio rice

37 **salad,** *salade* <Fr>; **greens,** *crudités* <Fr>, tossed salad, chef's salad, Caesar salad; fruit salad, pasta salad, potato salad, coleslaw, Cobb salad, composed salad

38 **fruit;** produce; stone fruit, drupe, berry, pome, pepo, sorosis, syconium, hesperidium; simple fruit, true fruit, composite fruit, aggregate fruit, multiple fruit, false fruit, succulent fruit; citrus fruit; tropical fruit; dry fruit, dehiscent fruit, indehiscent fruit, fruiting body; fruit compote, fruit soup, fruit cup, fruit cocktail, fruit salad, stewed fruit

39 **nut,** *noix* <Fr>, *noisette* <Fr>; kernel, meat

40 **sweets,** sweet stuff, **confectionery; sweet, sweetmeat; confection; candy;** bonbon, comfit, confiture; **jelly, jam;** preserve, conserve; marmalade; toffee, butterscotch, caramel, dulce de leche, chocolate, fudge; gelatin, Jell-O <trademark>; compote; pudding, custard, mousse; tutti-frutti; maraschino cherries; honey; icing, frosting, glaze; meringue; whipped cream

41 **pastry,** *patisserie* <Fr>; French pastry, Danish pastry; **tart,** tarlet; turnover; timbale; **pie,** *tarte* <Fr>, fruit pie, tart, single-crust pie, double-crust pie, deep-dish pie, fruit pie, custard pie, meringue pie; *quiche or quiche Lorraine* <Fr>; cobbler, crisp; bread pudding; patty, patty cake; patty shell, *vol-au-vent* <Fr>; rosette; dowdy, pandowdy; phyllo *or* filo, strudel, baklava; puff pastry, flake pastry; puff, cream puff, croquembouche, profiterole; cannoli, cream horn; éclair; tiramisu; croissant, scone, shortbread, brioche

42 **cake,** *gâteau* <Fr>, *torte* <Ger>; *petit-four* <Fr>; layer cake, Bundt cake, pound cake, sponge cake, upside-down cake, fruitcake, gingerbread, cheesecake, shortcake, cupcake, tiramisu, brownie; petit four, madeleine; doughnut, doughnut hole

43 cookie, biscuit <Brit>, fortune cookie, biscotti, bar cookie, drop cookie, refrigerator *or* icebox cookie, sandwich cookie; cereal bar, energy bar

44 doughnut, donut, friedcake, sinker <nf>, olykoek <nf>; French doughnut, raised doughnut; glazed doughnut; doughnut hole; fastnacht; **cruller,** twister; jelly doughnut, bismarck; fritter, *beignet* <Fr>; apple fritter

45 pancake, griddlecake, **hot cake,** battercake, flapcake, **flapjack,** flannel cake; buckwheat cake; chapatty <India>; **waffle;** blintz, cheese blintz, *crêpe* and *crêpe suzette* <Fr>, *Pfannkuchen* <Ger>, Swedish pancake, latke

46 pudding, custard, mousse, flan, tapioca

47 ice, *glace* <Fr>, frozen dessert; **ice cream,** ice milk; **sherbet,** water ice <Brit>, Italian ice, sorbet, bombe; gelato; tortoni; parfait; sundae, ice-cream sundae, banana split; ice-cream soda; ice-cream float, frappé; ice-cream cone; frozen pudding; frozen custard, soft ice cream; frozen yogurt; ice cream sandwich

48 dairy products, milk products, butter, cream, yogurt; **cheese,** *fromage* <Fr>; **tofu,** bean curd

49 beverage <see list>, drink, thirst quencher, potation, potable, drinkable <nf>, **liquor,** liquid, hard liquor, alcoholic drink, libation, liqueur, mixed drink, cocktail, **beer** <see list>, brew, brewski <nf>, alcopop; **wine** <see list>; **soft drink,** nonalcoholic beverage; cooler, spritzer; cold drink; carbonated water, soda water, sparkling water, tap water, spring water, mineral water, seltzer water; **soda,** pop, soda pop, tonic; milk shake *or* milkshake, shake *and* frosted <nf>; malted milk, malt <nf>, hot chocolate, cocoa; smoothie; **milk,** pasteurized milk, homogenized milk, skim milk, condensed milk, evaporated milk, low-fat milk, chocolate milk; **coffee,** cappuccino, espresso, decaffeinated coffee *or* decaf, café latté *or* latté, café au lait, java *and* joe <nf>; **tea,** iced tea; **fruit juice,** lemonade, vegetable juice, tomato juice; juice box

50 <food packaging terms> use-by date, best-before date, sell-by date

51 breads

andama	flatbread
bagel	foccaccia
baguette	French bread
breadstick	Irish soda bread
brown bread	lavash
challah	matzo
corn bread	Melba toast
croissant	nut bread
dinner roll	oatmeal bread
egg bread	pita
English muffin	plain white roll

poppy-seed roll	scone
potato bread	sourdough bread
pumpernickel bread	tortilla
raisin bread	Vienna bread
roll	white bread
rye bread	whole-wheat bread

52 cheeses

American	Lancashire
Banon	Leicester
Bel paese	Liederkranz
bleu cheese	Limburger
Bleu de Bresse	Liptauer
blue cheese	Longhorn
Blue Cheshire	Maroilles
Boursin	Mimolette
brick	Monterey Jack
Brie	mozzarella
Caciocavallo	Muenster
Caerphilly	Neufchâtel
Camembert	Parmesan
Cheddar	Parmigiano
Cheshire	Reggiano
chevre	pecorino
Colby	Port Salut
cottage cheese *or* curds	pot cheese
and whey	process cheese
cream cheese	provolone
Danish blue	ricotta
Dunlop	Romano
Edam	Roquefort
Emmenthaler	Samsoe
Epoisses	sapsago
Feta	Scamorze
Fontina	smoked cheese
fromage	St. Marcellin
Gjetost	St. Nectaire
Gloucester	Stilton
goat cheese	string cheese
Gorgonzola	Swiss
Gouda	Teleme
Gruyere	Tillamook
Havarti	Trappist
hoop cheese	cheese
Jaalsberg *or* Jarlsberg	Vacherin
jack cheese	White Wensleydale

53 desserts

angel food cake	brandy snap
apple brown betty	bread pudding
apple crisp	brownie
apple pie	cake
baked Alaska	cannoli
baklava	carrot cake
banana split	charlotte
bananas Foster	charlotte russe
Bavarian cream	cheesecake
blancmange	chocolate chip cookie
blondie	clafouti
bombe	cobbler
Boston cream pie	coffeecake

compote
cookie
coupe
cream puff
crème brûlée
crème caramel
crepe suzette
crisp
cruller
cupcake
custard
Danish
deep dish pie
devil's food cake
doughnut
eclair
egg cream
Eskimo pie
fig bar
flan
floating island
flummery
frappe
frozen custard
frozen yogurt
fruitcake
fruit cup
fruit pie
frumenty
galatoboureko
gateau
gelatin
gelato
gingerbread
gingersnap
granita
halvah
ice cream
ice cream bar
ice cream cake
ice cream float
ice cream sandwich
ice cream soda
Indian pudding
Italian ice
Jell-O <trademark>
jelly roll
junket
key lime pie
kuchen
lady finger
layer cake
lemon meringue pie
macaroon

marble cake
marshmallow
mela stregata
milkshake
mousse
mud pie
napoleon
Nesselrode
pandowdy
panettone
parfait
pastry
peach Melba
pie
pound cake
profiteroles
pudding
rice pudding
sacher torte
scone
sheet cake
sherbet
shortbread
shortcake
s'mores
snow cone
snow pudding
sorbet
souffle
spice cake
sponge cake
strawberry
   shortcake
streusel
strudel
sugar cookie
sundae
sweet potato pie
sweet roll
tapioca
tart
tartlet
tiramisu
Toll House cookie
torte
tres leches cake
trifle
turnover
upside-down cake
vacherin
wafer
wedding cake
zabaglione
zuppa inglese

54 meat cuts and joints

back rib
belly slice
blade
brain

breast
brisket
butt
center loin chop

chop
chuck
collar
cubes
cutlet
escalope
filet mignon
fillet *or* tenderloin
flank
fore rib
hock
joint
knuckle
leg
loin
loin chop
medallion
middle neck
neck fillet
noisette

55 beers

abbey ale
ale
amber ale
barley wine
bitter
bitter stout
bittersweet
bock beer
brown ale
bruised beer
caramel malt
cask-conditioned ale
chicha
copper ale
craft-brewed beer
cream ale
crystal malt
dark beer
diat pils
doppelbock
draft beer *or* draught beer
dry beer
dunkel beer
dunkel weissbier
eisbock
faro
festbier
fire-brewed beer
fruit beer
golden ale
home brew
ice beer
India pale ale
kellerbier
kolsch
krausen
kriek
kristall weizen

rack
rib
ribeye
riblet
round
rump
saddle
shank
shin
shoulder
shoulder chop
side
sirloin
skirt
spare rib
steak
T-bone
tenderloin
tournedos
undercut

kruidenbier
Kulmbacher beer
kumiss
kvass
lager
lambic beer
light beer
loster bier
maibock
malt liquor
marzen
mead
melomel
Munchener
near beer
nonalcoholic
   beer
nut brown ale
oatmeal stout
obergarig
old ale
oscura
pale ale
pilsener
poker beer
pony beer
porter
saison
Scotch ale
schwarzbier
specialty malt
spruce beer
starkbier
steam beer
stout
summer ale
Trappist
tripel beer

ur-bock
Vienna beer
weiss
weizenbier
wheat beer
white beer
winter beer
zwickelbier

56 beverage types

ade
alcoholic beverage
ambrosia
apple juice
beef tea
beer
birch beer
black tea
brew
buttermilk
café au lait
café filtre
café noir
café latte
cappuccino
chicory
chocolate milk
cider
club soda
cocktail
cocoa
coconut milk
coffee
cola
cordial
cranberry juice
cream soda
dairy drink
Darjeeling tea
Earl Grey tea
egg cream
eggnog
espresso
float
frappé
fruit juice
ginger ale
ginger beer
ginseng tea
grape juice
grapefruit juice
green tea
herb tea
hot chocolate
ice cream soda
ice water
iced coffee
iced tea

infusion
juice
kava
kefir
koumiss
lemonade
limeade
liquor
malted *or* malted milk
milk
milk shake *or* milkshake
mineral water
mixed drink
mixer
mocha
mulled cider
nectar
orange juice
orange pekoe tea
orangeade
pearl milk tea
phosphate
pineapple juice
punch
root beer
root beer float
sarsaparilla
seltzer
shrub
soda *or* soda
    pop
soda water
soft drink
soybean milk
spice tea
spirits
sports drink
syllabub
tea
tisane
tomato juice
tonic water
Turkish coffee
vegetable juice
water
whiskey
wine
wine cooler

57 cocktails, mixed drinks

Adam and Eve
after-dinner cocktail
Alabama slammer
Alaska cocktail
alexander
Allegheny
Americana
Bacardi cocktail

B & B
Bahama mama
banshee
Basin street
bay breeze
beachcomber
bee stinger
Bellini
Bermuda Rose
Betsy Ross
B-52
bijou cocktail
black Maria
Black Russian
black velvet
bloody Caesar
Bloody Mary
blue Hawaiian
blue lagoon
blue whale
bocce ball
Bombay cocktail
Boston cocktail
bourbon on the rocks
brandy alexander
brandy fizz
brandy smash
Bronx cocktail
buck's fizz
bull and bear
bull's eye
bull's milk
bullshot
buttered rum
Cape Codder
champagne cocktail
champagne cooler
cherry blossom
chi-chi
clamato cocktail
coffee grasshopper
cooler
Cosmopolitan *or* Cosmo
daiquiri
dirty banana
dixie julep
dream cocktail
dry martini
eggnog
English highball
Fifth Avenue
firefly
fizz
flip
foxy lady
frappe
French connection
frozen daiquiri
frozen Margarita

fuzzy navel
gentleman's cocktail
Georgia mint julep
Georgia peach
Gibson
gimlet
gin and bitters
gin and sin
gin and tonic
gin fizz
gin highball
gin rickey
gin sling
gin sour
gluhwein
golden Cadillac
grasshopper
greyhound
grog
Harvard cocktail
Harvard cooler
Harvey Wallbanger
highball
hole-in-one
Hollywood
Honolulu cocktail
hot buttered rum
hot toddy
hurricane
Indian Summer
Irish coffee
Jack Rose
kamikaze
Kentucky blizzard
Kentucky cocktail
kiddie cocktail *or* Shirley
    Temple *or* mocktail
King Alphonse
Kir
Kir royale
Long Island iced tea
Louisville lady
lover's kiss
madras
mai-tai
Manhattan
Margarita
martini
melon ball
merry widow
Mexican coffee
mimosa
mint julep
Mojito
muddled drink
mudslide
Narragansett
New York cocktail
nutcracker

nutty professor
old-fashioned
orange blossom
orgeat
peach sangaree
peppermint pattie
Peter Pan cocktail
Pimm's cup
pina colada
pink lady
pink squirrel
planter's punch
posset
pousse café
prairie oyster
presbyterian
punch
rickey
Rob Roy
rum and coke
rum cooler
rusty nail
salty dog
sangria
San Juan cooler
Scarlett O'Hara
Scotch and soda
scotch on the rocks
screwdriver
seabreeze
Seven and Seven
shandy
shrub
sidecar cocktail

Singapore sling
slam dunk
sloe gin fizz
smash
snake bite
snowball
sombrero
soother cocktail
southern lady
southern peach
spritzer
stinger
syllabub
tequila sunrise
thoroughbred
    cooler
toasted almond
toddy
Tom and Jerry
Tom Collins
velvet hammer
virgin Mary
vodka and tonic
vodka gimlet
vodka martini
Wassail
whiskey sour
white lady
White Russian
white satin
white spider
wine cooler
wu-wu
zombie

58 milk varieties

breast milk *or* mother's
    milk
buttermilk
chocolate milk
coconut milk
condensed milk
cow's milk
dried milk
evaporated milk
filtered milk
fortified milk
goat's milk *or*
    goats' milk
homogenized milk
ice milk
lactose-reduced milk
low-fat milk
malted milk
nonfat milk
one-percent milk

organic milk
pasteurized milk
powdered milk
raw milk
rice milk
skim milk *or* skimmed
    milk
soy milk
sterilized milk
strawberry milk
sweetened condensed
    milk
two-percent milk
UHT milk *or* ultra-heat
    treatment milk *or*
    long-life milk
ultra-high temperature
    milk
untreated milk
whole milk

59 wines

Alsace
amontillado

amoroso
apple wine

Asti spumante
Aveleda
Barbera
Bardolino
Barolo
Beaujolais
Bergerac
blanc de noir
blush
Bordeaux
Bordeaux Blanc
Burgundy
Cabernet Sauvignon
cabinet wine
California wine
Chablis
Champagne
Chardonnay
Chateauneuf-du-Pape
Chenin blanc
Chianti
Christi
claret
cold duck
Condrieu
Cote Rotie
Cotes de Nuit
Cotes du Rhone
dandelion wine
Dao
dessert wine
Dolcetto
Douro
dry wine
Entre-deux-Mers
fortified wine
Frascati
Fume Blanc
German wine
Gewurztraminer
Graves
Grenache
Hermitage
hock
Johannisberg
    Riesling
jug wine
Lacrima
Lambrusco
Liebfraumilch
Macon
Madeira
Malaga
Marsala
Mateus Rose
Medoc
Merlot
Montepulciano
Moselle

Muscadet
Muscat
Muscatel
Napa Valley
    wine
Navarra
Nierstein
noble wine
Oporto
Orvieto
Pauillac
Pinot Blanc
Pinot Grigio
Pinot Gris
Pinot Noir
Pomerol
Pommard
port
Pouilly-Fuissé
Pouilly-Fume
red wine
retsina
Rhine
Rhone
Riesling
Rioja
rose
ruby port
sake
Sancerre
Sangiovese
Sauternes
Sauvignon
    Blanc
Sekt
sherry
Shiraz
Soave
sparkling
    wine
St. Estephe
St. Julien
sweet wine
Sylvaner
Syrah
table wine
tawny port
Tokay-Pinot
    Gris
Valdepenas
Valpolicella
vermouth
vinho verde
vintage wine
Vouvray
white cabernet
white wine
white zinfandel
zinfandel

11 COOKING

NOUNS **1 cooking, cookery, cuisine, culinary art;** food preparation, food processing; home economics, domestic science, home management, culinary science; haute cuisine, *nouvelle cuisine* <Fr>; gastronomy; catering; nutrition 7

2 <cooking technique> manner of preparation, style of recipe; baking, toasting, roasting, oven-roasting, frying, deep-frying, pan-frying, stir-frying, searing, flash-frying, blackening, smoking, curing, sautéing, boiling, parboiling, simmering, steaming, stewing, basting, braising, poaching, shirring, blanching, steaming, barbecuing, steeping, brewing, grilling, broiling, pan-broiling, charbroiling, microwaving, pressure-cooking; canning, pickling, preserving

3 cook, chef, *cuisinier* or *cuisinière* <Fr>, kitchener, culinarian, culinary artist; **chief cook, head chef,** *chef de cuisine* <Fr>, cordon bleu cook; sous chef, apprentice chef, fry cook or grease-burner <nf>, short-order cook, food preparer, prep cook; **baker,** *boulanger* <Fr>, pastry cook, pastry chef, *patissier* <Fr>, saucier; caterer

4 kitchen, cookroom, cookery, **scullery,** cuisine; back of the house; kitchenette, cooking area; **galley;** cookhouse; **bakery,** bakehouse; barbecue; **cookware, kitchen ware,** cooker <see list>; pots and pans; refrigerator, fridge <nf>, freezer; cookbook, recipe, receipt

VERBS **5 cook,** prepare food, prepare, prepare a meal, do, cook up, fry up, boil up, rustle up <nf>; precook; boil, heat, heat up, stew, simmer, parboil, blanch; brew; poach, coddle; bake, fire, ovenbake; **microwave,** micro-cook, nuke <nf>; scallop; shirr; roast; toast; fry, deep-fry or deep-fat fry, griddle, pan, pan-fry; sauté, stir-fry; frizz, frizzle; sear, blacken, braise, brown; broil, grill, pan-broil; barbecue; fricassee; steam, blanch; devil; curry; baste; **do to a turn,** do to perfection, whip something up and throw something together <nf>

ADJS **6 cooking, culinary,** kitchen, gastronomic, epicurean; mealtime, mensal; preprandial, postprandial, after-dinner; au naturel, a la mode, a la carte, table d'hôte

7 cooked, heated, stewed, fried, barbecued, curried, fricasseed, deviled, sautéed, shirred, toasted; roasted, roast; fired, pan-fried, deep-fried or deep-fat fried, stir-fried; broiled, grilled, pan-broiled; seared, blackened, braised, browned; boiled, simmered, parboiled; steamed; blanched; poached, coddled; baked, fired, oven-baked; scalloped

8 done, well-done, well-cooked; *bien cuit* <Fr>, done to a turn or to perfection; overcooked, **overdone,** burned; medium, medium-rare; doneness

9 underdone, undercooked, not done, **rare,** red, raw, *saignant* <Fr>; al dente; sodden, fallen

10 cookers

baker	galley stove
barbecue	griddle
boiler	grill
brazier	hibachi
broiler	hot plate
camp stove	infrared broiler
chafer	infrared cooker
chafing dish or pan	microwave oven
coffee maker	oven
convection oven	percolator
cook stove	pots and pans
cooktop	pressure cooker or
corn popper	autoclave
Crockpot	range
<trademark>	roaster
deep fat fryer	rotisserie
double boiler	samovar
Dutch oven	slow cooker
electric cooker	smoker
electric frying pan	steamer
electric roaster	stove
electric toaster	toaster
field range	toaster oven
fireless cooker	waffle iron
fry-cooker	waterless cooker

12 EXCRETION
<bodily discharge>

NOUNS **1 excretion,** egestion, extrusion, **elimination, discharge,** expulsion, call of nature <nf>; **emission;** eccrisis; **exudation,** transudation; extravasation, effusion, flux, flow; ejaculation, ejection 909; **secretion** 13

2 defecation, dejection, **evacuation,** voidance; movement, **bowel movement** or BM, number two <nf>, **stool,** shit and crap <nf>; **diarrhea,** loose bowels, flux; trots and runs and shits and GI's and GI shits <nf>; turistas or tourista and Montezuma's revenge and Aztec two-step <nf>; lientery; **dysentery,** bloody flux; catharsis, purgation, purge

3 excrement, dejection, dejecta, dejecture, **discharge,** ejection; matter; **waste,** waste matter; **excreta,** egesta, ejecta, ejectamenta; exudation; exudate; transudation; extravasation; effluent; sewage, sewerage

4 feces, feculence; defecation, movement, bowel movement or **BM; stool, shit** <nf>, **ordure,** night soil, jakes <Brit nf>, crap and ca-ca and doo-doo and number two and poo-poo and poop <nf>; turd <nf>; dingleberry <nf>; **manure, dung, droppings;** cow pats, cow flops <nf>; cow chips, buffalo chips; guano; coprolite, coprolith; sewage, sewerage

5 urine, water, **piss** <nf>, number one, *pish* <Yiddish>, pee *and* pee-pee *and* wee-wee *and* whizz <nf>, piddle, leak, stale; **urination,** micturition, emiction, a piss *and* a pee *and* a whizz <nf>; golden shower <nf>; urea, uric acid

6 pus; matter, purulence, peccant humor <old>, discharge, ichor, sanies; pussiness; **suppuration, festering,** rankling, mattering, running, weeping; gleet, leukorrhea

7 sweat, perspiration, perspiring, sweating, water, moisture, dampness, wetness; exudation, exudate; diaphoresis, sudor, sudation, sudoresis; honest sweat, the sweat of one's brow; beads of sweat, beaded brow; cold sweat; **lather,** swelter, streams of sweat; sudoresis; body odor *or* **BO,** perspiration odor

8 hemorrhage, hemorrhea, **bleeding;** nosebleed; ecchymosis, petechia

9 menstruation, menstrual discharge *or* flow *or* flux, catamenia, catamenial discharge, flowers <old>, **the curse** <nf>, the curse of Eve; flow <nf>; **menses, monthlies,** courses, period, one's friend, time of the month, that time

10 latrine, convenience, **toilet,** toilet room, water closet *or* WC <nf>; **john** *and* johnny *and* **can** *and* crapper *and* head <nf>; loo <Brit nf>; **lavatory,** washroom; **bathroom,** basement; **rest room,** comfort station *or* room, commode; ladies' *or* women's *or* girls' *or* little girls' *or* powder room <nf>; men's *or* boys' *or* little boys' room <nf>, the ladies', the gents'; head; privy, outhouse, backhouse, shithouse <nf>, johnny house <nf>, earth closet <Brit>, jakes, closet *and* necessary <nf>; bog <Brit>; urinal

11 toilet, stool, **water closet; john** *and* johnny *and* **can** *and* crapper *and* thunderbox <nf>; latrine; commode, closetstool, potty-chair <nf>; **chamber pot,** chamber, pisspot <nf>, potty <nf>, jerry <Brit nf>, jordan <Brit nf>, thunder mug <nf>; throne <nf>; chemical toilet, chemical closet; urinal; bedpan

VERBS **12 excrete,** egest, **eliminate, discharge,** emit, give off, pass, expel; ease *or* relieve oneself, go to the bathroom *or* toilet <nf>; **exude,** exudate, transude; weep; effuse, extravasate; answer the call of nature, pay a call, make a pit stop, make a comfort stop; **secrete** 13.5

13 defecate, shit *and* crap <nf>, **evacuate,** void, **stool,** dung, have a bowel movement *or* BM, move one's bowels, soil, take a shit *or* crap <nf>, ca-ca *or* number two <nf>; have the runs *or* trots *or* shits <nf>

14 urinate, pass *or* **make water, wet,** stale, **piss** <nf>, piddle, pee, tinkle; pee-pee *and* wee-wee *and* whizz *and* take a whizz *and* take a leak <nf>, spend a penny, pump bilge, do number one

15 fester, suppurate, matter, rankle, run, weep; ripen, come *or* draw to a head

16 sweat, perspire, exude; break out in a sweat, **get all in a lather** <nf>; sweat like a trooper *or* horse *or* pig, swelter, wilt, steam

17 bleed, hemorrhage, lose blood, **shed blood,** spill blood; bloody; ecchymose, extravasate

18 menstruate, come sick, bleed, come around, have one's period, have the curse, have one's friend, be on the rag <nf>, flow

ADJS **19 excretory,** excretive, excretionary; eliminative, eliminant, egestive; exudative, transudative; **secretory** 13.7

20 excremental, excrementary; **fecal,** feculent, shitty *and* crappy <nf>, scatologic *or* scatological, stercoral, stercorous, stercoraceous, dungy; **urinary,** urinative

21 festering, suppurative, rankling, mattering; pussy, purulent

22 sweaty, perspiry <nf>; sweating, perspiring; wet with sweat, beaded with sweat, **sticky** <nf>, **clammy;** bathed in sweat, drenched with sweat, wilted; in a sweat; sudatory, sudoric, sudorific, diaphoretic

23 bleeding, bloody, hemorrhaging; ecchymosed; blood-borne

24 menstrual, catamenial, menstruating; on the rag <nf>

13 SECRETION

NOUNS **1 secretion,** secreta, secernment; **excretion** 12; external secretion, internal secretion; exudation, transudation; lactation; weeping, lacrimation; ooze

 2 digestive secretion *or* juice, salivary secretion, gastric juice, digestive juice, pancreatic juice, intestinal juice; bile, gall; endocrine; prostatic fluid, seminal fluid, semen, sperm; thyroxin; autacoid, **hormone,** chalone; mucus; tears; rheum; sebum, musk, pheromone; milk, colostrum; gland

 3 saliva, spittle, sputum, spit, expectoration, spitting; phlegm, sputum; salivation, ptyalism, sialorrhea, sialagogue, **slobber,** slabber, slaver, **drivel,** dribble, **drool;** froth, foam; mouth-watering

 4 endocrinology, eccrinology, hormonology

VERBS **5 secrete,** produce, give out *or* off, exude, transude, release, emit, discharge, eject; **excrete** 12.12; water; lactate; weep, tear, cry, lacrimate; sweat, perspire; ooze

 6 salivate, ptyalize; **slobber,** slabber, slaver, **drool, drivel,** dribble; **expectorate, spit,** spit up; spew; hawk, clear the throat

ADJS **7 secretory,** secretive, secretional, secretionary, secreting; **excretory** 12.19; exudative, transudatory, emanative, emanatory, emanational; lymphatic, serous; seminal, spermatic; watery, watering; lactational; lacteal, lacteous, lactating; lachrymal, lacrimatory, lachrymose; rheumy; salivary, salivant, salivous, salivating, sialoid, sialagogic; sebaceous, sebiferous; sweating, sweaty, sudatory; oozing

8 **glandular,** glandulous; **endocrine,** humoral, exocrine, eccrine, apocrine, holocrine, merocrine; **hormonal** *or* hormonic; adrenal, pancreatic, gonadal; ovarian; luteal; prostatic; splenetic; thymic; thyroidal

14 BODILY DEVELOPMENT

NOUNS 1 **bodily** *or* **physical development,** growth, development 861.1, maturation, maturing, maturescence, coming of age, growing up, reaching one's full growth, upgrowth; growing like a weed <nf>; plant growth, vegetation 310.32, germination, pullulation; sexual maturity, pubescence, puberty; nubility, marriageability, marriageableness; adulthood, manhood, womanhood; reproduction, procreation 78, burgeoning, sprouting; budding, gemmation; outgrowth, excrescence; overgrowth 257.5

VERBS 2 **grow, develop,** wax, **increase** 251; gather, brew; **grow up,** mature, maturate, spring up, ripen, come of age, **shoot up,** sprout up, upshoot, upspring, upsprout, upspear, overtop, tower, get bigger, get taller; grow like a weed <nf>; burgeon, **sprout** 310.34, blossom 310.35, reproduce 78.7, procreate 78.8, grow out of, germinate, pullulate; vegetate 310.34; **flourish, thrive;** mushroom, balloon; outgrow; overgrow, hypertrophy, overdevelop, grow uncontrollably

ADJS 3 **grown, full-grown, grown-up,** developed, well-developed, fully developed, **mature, adult, full-fledged,** fully fledged; **growing,** adolescent, maturescent, pubescent; nubile, marriageable; **sprouting,** crescent, budding, in full bloom, flowering 310.38, florescent, **flourishing,** blossoming, blooming, burgeoning, fast-growing, thriving; overgrown, hypertrophied, overdeveloped

15 STRENGTH
<inherent power>

NOUNS 1 **strength, might,** mightiness, powerfulness, stamina; **force, potency, power** 18; **energy** 17; **vigor, vitality,** vigorousness, heartiness, lustiness, lustihood; **stoutness, sturdiness,** stalwartness, robustness, hardiness, ruggedness; **guts** *and* gutsiness <nf>, fortitude, intestinal fortitude <nf>, **toughness** 1049, **endurance, stamina,** staying *or*

sticking power, stick-to-it-iveness <nf>; **strength of will,** decisiveness, obstinacy 361

2 **muscularity,** brawniness; beefiness *and* huskiness *and* heftiness *and* burliness <nf>, thewiness, sinewiness; **brawn,** beef <nf>; **muscle,** brawn, sinew, sinews, thew, thews; musculature, build, physique; tone, elasticity 1048; brute strength

3 **firmness, soundness,** staunchness, stoutness, **sturdiness, stability,** solidity, **hardness** 1046, temper

4 **impregnability,** impenetrability, **invulnerability,** inexpugnability, inviolability; **unassailability,** unattackableness; resistlessness, **irresistibility; invincibility,** indomitability, insuperability, unconquerableness, unbeatableness; invincibility

5 **strengthening, invigoration,** fortification; **hardening,** toughening, firming; case hardening, tempering; **restrengthening,** reinforcement; **reinvigoration,** refreshment, revivification; fortifying

6 **strong man, stalwart, tower of strength,** muscle man, piledriver, bulldozer, hunk <nf>, hardbody; **giant,** Samson, Goliath; Charles Atlas, Mr Universe; superhero, Hercules, Atlas, Antaeus, Cyclops, Briareus, colossus, Polyphemus, Titan, Brobdingnagian, Tarzan, Superman; the strong, the mighty; bouncer; he-man

7 <nf terms> **hulk, powerhouse, muscle man,** man mountain, big bruiser, bruiser, strapper, strong-arm man, bully, bullyboy, ape, tough, toughie, tough guy, bozo, **goon** 671.10, gorilla, meat-eater

8 <comparisons> horse, ox, lion; pig-shit <nf>; oak, heart of oak; rock, Gibraltar; iron, steel, nails; lumberjack

VERBS 9 **be strong,** overpower, overwhelm; have what it takes, pack a punch

10 **not weaken,** not flag; **bear up, hold up,** keep up, stand up; **hold out,** stay *or* see it out, not give up, **never say die,** not let it get one down, gird up one's loins

11 <nf terms> **tough it out, hang tough, hang in,** stick *or* take it, take it on the chin, sweat it out, go *or* stay the distance

12 **exert strength,** put beef *or* one's back into it <nf>; use force, get tough <nf>, muscle *and* manhandle *and* strong-arm <nf>; push around

13 **strengthen, invigorate, fortify,** beef up <nf>, brace, batten, buttress, prop, shore up, support, undergird, brace up; gird, gird up one's loins; steel, harden, case harden, anneal, stiffen, **toughen,** temper, nerve; confirm, sustain; **restrengthen, reinforce; reinvigorate,** refresh, revive, recruit one's strength; tone; soup up, beef up

14 **proof,** insulate, weatherproof, soundproof, muffle, quietize, fireproof, waterproof, goofproof <nf>, etc

ADJS **15 strong, forceful,** forcible, **mighty, powerful,** puissant <nf>, **potent** 18.12; **stout, sturdy, stalwart, rugged,** hale; hunky *and* husky *and* hefty *and* beefy <nf>, strapping, durable, doughty <nf>, **hardy,** hard, hard as nails, cast-iron, iron-hard, steely; **robust,** robustious, gutty *and* gutsy <nf>; strong-willed, obstinate 361.8; **vigorous, hearty,** nervy, **lusty,** bouncing, full- *or* red-blooded; bionic, sturdy as an ox, strong as a lion *or* an ox *or* a horse, strong as brandy, strong as pig-shit <nf>, strong as strong; full-strength, double-strength, industrial-strength <nf>

16 able-bodied, well-built, well-set, well-set-up <nf>, well-knit, of good *or* powerful physique, broad-shouldered, barrel-chested, **athletic; muscular,** well-muscled, heavily muscled, thickset, burly, **brawny;** buff; thewy, sinewy, **wiry;** muscle-bound, all muscle; strapping

17 herculean, Briarean, Antaean, Cyclopean, Atlantean, gigantic, gigantesque, Brobdingnagian, huge 257.20; Amazonian

18 firm, sound, stout, sturdy, tough, hard-boiled <nf>, **staunch, stable,** solid; sound as a dollar, solid as a rock, firm as Gibraltar, made of iron; buffed; rigid, unbreakable, infrangible; braced, buttressed

19 impregnable, impenetrable, **invulnerable,** inviolable, inexpugnable; **unassailable,** unattackable, insuperable, unsurmountable; resistless, **irresistible; invincible,** indomitable, **unconquerable,** unsubduable, unyielding 361.9, incontestable, unbeatable, more than a match for; overpowering, overwhelming, avalanchine

20 resistant, proof, tight; impervious; foolproof; shatterproof; weatherproof, dampproof, watertight, hermetically sealed, vacuum-packed, leakproof; hermetic, airtight; soundproof, noiseproof; puncture proof, holeproof; bulletproof, ballproof, shellproof, bombproof; rustproof, corrosionproof; fireproof, flameproof, fire-resisting; burglarproof

21 unweakened, undiminished, unallayed, unbated, unabated, unfaded, unwithered, unshaken, unworn, unexhausted; **unweakening, unflagging, unbowed;** in full force *or* swing, **going strong** <nf>; in the plenitude of power

22 <of sounds and odors> **intense, penetrating,** piercing; **loud,** deafening, thundering 56.12; **pungent,** five-alarm, three-alarm, **reeking** 69.10

ADVS **23 strongly, stoutly, sturdily,** stalwartly, robustly, ruggedly; **mightily, powerfully, forcefully,** forcibly; **vigorously, heartily,** lustily; **soundly, firmly,** staunchly; impregnably, invulnerably, **invincibly, irresistibly,** unyieldingly; resistantly, imperviously; **intensely; loudly,** at the top of one's lungs, clamorously, deafeningly; **pungently**

WORD ELEMENTS **24** muscul-, musculo-, my-, myo-; -eus

16 WEAKNESS

NOUNS **1 weakness,** weakliness, **feebleness,** enfeeblement, strengthlessness; **flabbiness, flaccidity,** softness; **impotence** or impotency 19; **debility,** debilitation, prostration, invalidism, collapse; **faintness,** faintishness, dizziness, lightheadedness, shakiness, gone *or* blah feeling <nf>; **fatigue** 21, exhaustion, weariness, dullness, sluggishness, languor, lassitude, **listlessness,** tiredness, languishment, atony, burn-out *or* burnout; anemia, bloodlessness, etiolation, asthenia, adynamia, cachexia *or* cachexy

2 frailty, slightness, **delicacy, daintiness,** lightness; **flimsiness, unsubstantiality,** wispiness, sleaziness, shoddiness; **fragility,** frangibility *or* frangibleness, brittleness, breakableness, destructibility; disintegration 806; **human frailty,** fatal flaw; gutlessness <nf>, cowardice 491; moral weakness, irresolution, **indecisiveness,** infirmity of will, velleity, changeableness 854; inherent vice

3 infirmity, unsoundness, incapacity, unfirmness, unsturdiness, **instability, unsubstantiality;** decrepitude; **unsteadiness, shakiness,** ricketiness, wobbliness, wonkiness <Brit nf>, weediness <nf>; caducity, senility, invalidism; wishy-washiness, insipidity, vapidity, wateriness

4 weak point, weakness, weak place, **weak side,** weak link, vulnerable point, chink in one's armor, Achilles' heel *or* heel of Achilles, soft underbelly; fatal flaw; feet of clay

5 weakening, enfeeblement, debilitation, exhaustion, inanition, attrition; languishment; **devitalization,** enervation, evisceration; fatigue; attenuation, extenuation; softening, mitigation, damping, abatement, slackening, relaxing, relaxation, blunting, deadening, dulling; **dilution,** watering, watering-down, attenuation, thinning, reduction

6 weakling, weak *or* meek soul, weak sister <nf>, hothouse plant, softy <nf>, softling, **jellyfish,** invertebrate, gutless wonder <nf>, **baby,** big baby, crybaby, chicken <nf>, scaredy-cat, coward, wimp, wussy, Milquetoast, sop, **milksop, namby-pamby, mollycoddle,** mama's boy, mother's boy, mother's darling, teacher's pet; sissy *and* pansy *and* pantywaist <nf>, pushover <nf>, softie, lightweight; **wimp,** poor *or* weak *or* dull tool <nf>; **nonentity,** hollow man, doormat *and* empty suit *and* nebbish *and* sad sack <nf>

7 <comparisons> kitten, reed, thread, matchwood, rope of sand; house of cards, eggshell, glass, house built on sand, sand castle, cobweb; water, milk and water, gruel, dishwater, cambric tea

VERBS 8 <be weak> **shake,** tremble, quiver, quaver, cringe, cower 491.9, totter, teeter, dodder; halt, limp; be on one's last leg, have one foot in the grave

9 <become weak> **weaken,** grow weak *or* weaker, go soft <nf>; **languish, wilt,** faint, **droop,** drop, dwindle, **sink, decline, flag, pine, fade, tail away** *or* off, fail, fall *or* drop by the wayside, ebb, wane; crumble, go to pieces, disintegrate 806.3; go downhill, hit the skids <nf>; give way, break, collapse, cave in <nf>, surrender, cry uncle <nf>; give out, have no staying power, run out of gas <nf>, conk *or* peter *or* poop *or* peg *or* fizzle out <nf>; come apart, come apart at the seams, come unstuck *or* unglued <nf>; yield; die on the vine <nf>; wear thin *or* away

10 <make weak> **weaken, enfeeble, debilitate,** unstrengthen, unsinew, undermine, soften up <nf>, unbrace, unman, unnerve, rattle, shake up <nf>, impair, **devitalize, enervate,** eviscerate; **sap,** sap the strength of, exhaust, gruel, take it out of <nf>; shake, unstring; reduce, lay low; attenuate, extenuate, mitigate, abate; blunt, deaden, dull, damp *or* dampen, take the edge off; draw the teeth, defang; cramp, cripple

11 **dilute, cut** <nf>, **reduce, thin,** thin out, attenuate, rarefy; **water,** water down, adulterate, irrigate *and* baptize <nf>; soften, muffle, mute; negate

ADJS 12 **weak,** weakly, **feeble,** debilitated, imbecile; **strengthless,** sapless, marrowless, pithless, sinewless, listless, out of gas <nf>, nerveless, lustless; **impotent, powerless** 19.13; spineless, lily-livered, whitelivered, wimpy *and* wimpish *and* chicken *and* gutless *and* wussy <nf>, cowardly 491.10; unnerved, shookup <nf>, unstrung, faint, faintish, lightheaded, dizzy, gone; dull, slack; **soft, flabby,** flaccid, unhardened; **limp,** limber, limp *or* limber as a dishrag, floppy, rubbery; **languorous,** languid, **drooping,** droopy, pooped <nf>; asthenic, anemic, bloodless, effete, etiolated; not what one used to be

13 "weak as water"—Bible, weak as milk and water, weak as a drink of water, weak as a child *or* baby, weak as a chicken, weak as a kitten, weak as a mouse, "weak as a rained-on bee"—F R Torrence

14 **frail, slight, delicate, dainty;** puny; light, lightweight; effeminate; namby-pamby, sissified, pansyish; **fragile,** frangible, **breakable,** destructible, shattery, crumbly, brittle, fragmentable, fracturable; **unsubstantial, flimsy,** sleazy, tacky <nf>, wispy, cobwebby, gossamery,

papery; gimcrack *and* gimcracky *and* cheap-jack *and* ticky-tacky <nf>; jerry-built, jerry; gimpy

15 **unsound, infirm,** unfirm, **unstable, unsubstantial,** unsturdy, unsolid, decrepit, crumbling, fragmented, fragmentary, disintegrating 806.5; poor, poorish; rotten, rotten to the core

16 **unsteady, shaky, rickety,** ricketish, wonky <Brit nf>, spindly, spidery, teetering, teetery, tottery, tottering, doddering, tumbledown, ramshackle, dilapidated, rocky <nf>; groggy, wobbly, staggery

17 **wishy-washy,** tasteless, bland, **insipid,** vapid, neutral, watery, milky, milk-and-water, mushy; halfhearted, infirm of will *or* purpose, **indecisive,** irresolute, changeable 853.7; limp-wristed, gutless

18 **weakened, enfeebled, disabled,** incapacitated, challenged <nf>, debilitated, infirm; **devitalized,** drained, exhausted, sapped, burned-out, maxed-out, used up, played out, spent, *ausgespielt* <Ger>, effete, etiolated; **fatigued, enervated,** eviscerated; **wasted, rundown,** worn, worn-out, worn to a frazzle <nf>; stressed out; on one's last legs

19 **diluted, cut** <nf>, **reduced, thinned,** rarefied, attenuated; adulterated; watered, watered-down

20 **weakening, debilitating, enfeebling; devitalizing,** enervating, sapping, exhausting, fatiguing, grueling, trying, draining, unnerving

21 **languishing, drooping,** sinking, declining, flagging, pining, fading, failing; on the wane

ADVS 22 **weakly, feebly,** strengthlessly, languorously, listlessly; faintly; delicately, effeminately, daintily; infirmly, unsoundly, unstably, unsubstantially, unsturdily, flimsily; shakily, unsteadily, teeteringly, totteringly

17 ENERGY

NOUNS 1 **energy, vigor, force, power, vitality,** strenuousness, **intensity, dynamism,** demonic energy; **potency** 18; **strength** 15; actual *or* kinetic energy; dynamic energy; potential energy; **energy source** 1021.1, electrical energy, hydroelectric energy *or* power, water power, nuclear energy, solar energy, wind energy, alternative energy

2 **vim, verve,** fire, adrenalin, **dash, drive; aggressiveness, enterprise,** initiative, proactiveness, thrust, spunk; **eagerness** 101, zeal, heartiness, keenness, gusto, passion

3 <nf terms> **pep,** bang, biff, get-up-and-go, ginger, gism, jazz, sizzle, kick, moxie, oomph, pepper, piss and vinegar, **pizzazz,** poop, punch, push, snap, spizzerinctum, spark, starch, steam, zing, zip, zizz, sparkle, wallop, balls, oomph, adrenaline rush

4 **animation, vivacity,** liveliness, energy, **ardor,** vitality, glow, warmth, enthusiasm, vibrancy,

lustiness, robustness, mettle, **zest,** zestfulness, **gusto, élan,** éclat, impetus, impetuosity, *joie de vivre* <Fr>, *brio* <Ital>, spiritedness, **briskness,** perkiness, sprightliness, pertness, sensibility, **life, spirit,** life force, vital force *or* principle, *élan vital* <Fr>; activity 330

5 <energetic disapproval or criticism> **acrimony,** acridity, acerbity, acidity, **bitterness,** tartness, **causticity,** mordancy *or* mordacity, **virulence; harshness,** fierceness, **rigor,** roughness, **severity, vehemence,** violence 671, stringency, astringency, stridency 58.1, **sharpness, keenness, poignancy,** trenchancy; edge, point; bite, teeth, grip, sting; animosity; backstabbing

6 **energizer, stimulus,** stimulator, vitalizer, arouser, needle <nf>, restorative; **stimulant, tonic** 86.8; **activator,** motivator, motivating force, motive power; **animator,** spark plug *and* human dynamo *and* ball of fire <nf>; life, life of the party; spinach

7 <units of energy> atomerg, dinamode, dyne, erg, energid, foot-pound, horsepower-hour, horsepower-year, joule, calorie 1019.19, kilogram-meter, kilowatt-hour, photon, quantum

8 **energizing, invigoration, animation, enlivenment,** quickening, **vitalization,** revival, revitalization; **exhilaration, stimulation**

9 **activation,** reactivation; viability

VERBS 10 **energize,** dynamize; **invigorate, animate, enliven, liven, liven up,** vitalize, quicken, goose *or* jazz up <nf>; **exhilarate, stimulate,** hearten, galvanize, enthuse, electrify, fire, build a fire under, inflame, warm, kindle, charge, charge up, psych *or* pump up <nf>, rouse, arouse, act like a tonic, be a shot in the arm <nf>, **pep** *or* snap *or* jazz *or* zip *or* perk up <nf>, put pep *or* zip into it <nf>

11 **have energy,** be energetic, be vigorous, **thrive,** burst *or* overflow with energy, flourish, tingle, feel one's oats, be up and doing, be full of beans *or* pep *or* ginger *or* zip <nf>, be full of piss and vinegar <nf>, champ at the bit <nf>; come on like gangbusters <nf>

12 **activate,** reactivate, recharge, reanimate; step on the gas <nf>

ADJS 13 **energetic, vigorous, strenuous, forceful, forcible, strong, dynamic,** kinetic, intense, acute, keen, incisive, trenchant, vivid, vibrant, passionate; **enterprising, aggressive,** proactive, activist, can-do *and* gung ho *and* take-over *and* take-charge <nf>, go-getting; **active, lively,** living, **animated, spirited,** go-go <nf>, **vivacious,** brisk, bright-eyed and bushy-tailed <nf>, feisty, lusty, **robust,** hearty, enthusiastic, mettlesome, zesty, zestful, impetuous, spanking, smacking; pumped *and* pumped up *and* jazzed-up *and* charged up *and*

switched on <nf>, full-on, snappy *and* zingy *and* zippy *and* peppy <nf>, full of pep *or* pizzazz *or* piss and vinegar <nf>, full of beans <nf>

14 **acrimonious, acrid,** acidulous, acid, acerbic, **bitter,** tart, **caustic,** escharotic <med>, mordant *or* mordacious, **virulent, violent, vehement,** vitriolic; **harsh,** fierce, **rigorous,** severe, rough, stringent, astringent, strident 58.12, **sharp, keen,** sharpish, incisive, trenchant, **cutting,** biting, stinging, **scathing,** stabbing, **piercing, poignant,** penetrating, edged, double-edged

15 **energizing, vitalizing, enlivening,** quickening; tonic, bracing, rousing; **invigorating,** invigorative; **animating,** animative; **exhilarating,** exhilarative; **stimulating,** stimulative, stimulatory, vivifying; activating; viable

ADVS 16 **energetically, vigorously, strenuously, forcefully,** forcibly, intensely, like a house afire *and* like gangbusters <nf>, zestfully, lustily, heartily, keenly, passionately; **actively,** briskly; **animatedly, spiritedly,** vivaciously, with pep <nf>, *con brio* <Ital>

18 POWER, POTENCY
<effective force>

NOUNS 1 **power, potency** *or* potence, prepotency, **force, might,** mightiness, **vigor,** vitality, vim, push, drive, charge, puissance <old>; dint, virtue; moxie *and* oomph *and* pizzazz *and* poop *and* punch *and* bang *and* clout *and* steam <nf>; powerfulness, forcefulness; virulence, vehemence; **strength** 15; **energy** 17; **virility** 76.2; cogence *or* cogency, validity, effect, impact, **effectiveness,** effectivity, effectuality, competence *or* competency; productivity, productiveness; power structure, corridors of power; **influence** 894, pull; **authority** 417, weight; **superiority** 249; power pack, amperage, wattage; main force, *force majeure* <Fr>, main strength, brute force *or* strength, compulsion, duress; muscle power, sinew, might and main, beef <nf>, strong arm; full force, full blast; power struggle; mana; charisma

2 **ability, capability, capacity,** potentiality, faculty, facility, fitness, qualification, talent, flair, genius, caliber, **competence,** competency, adequacy, sufficiency, **efficiency,** efficacy; **proficiency** 413.1; the stuff *and* the goods *and* what it takes <nf>; susceptibility

3 **omnipotence, almightiness, all-powerfulness,** invincibility; omnicompetence

4 manpower; horsepower, brake horsepower *or* bhp, electric power, electropower, hydroelectric power; hydraulic power, water power; steam

power; geothermal power; solar power; atomic power, nuclear power, thermonuclear power; rocket power, jet power; **propulsion, thrust,** impulse

5 force of inertia, *vis inertiae* <L>, torpor; dead force, *vis mortua* <L>; living force, *vis viva* <L>; force of life, *vis vitae* <L>

6 centrifugal force *or* action, centripetal force *or* action, force of gravity

7 <science of forces> dynamics, statics, mechanics

8 **empowerment, enablement;** investment, endowment, enfranchisement

9 **work force,** hands, men, manpower; **fighting force,** troops, units, the big battalions, firepower; **personnel** 577.11, human resources; **forces**

VERBS 10 **empower, enable;** invest, clothe, invest *or* clothe with power, commission, deputize, warrant; enfranchise; endue, endow, **authorize;** arm; strengthen

11 **be able,** be up to, up to, **lie in one's power; can,** may, can do; make it *or* make the grade <nf>; hack it *and* cut it *and* cut the mustard <nf>; charismatize; **wield power,** possess authority 417.13; **take charge** 417.14, get something under one's control *or* under one's thumb, hold all the aces *and* have the say-so <nf>

ADJS 12 **powerful, potent,** prepotent, powerpacked, **mighty,** irresistible, avalanchine, **forceful,** forcible, dynamic; **vigorous,** vital, **energetic,** puissant, ruling, in power; **cogent,** striking, telling, effective, impactful, valid, operative, in force; **strong;** high-powered, high-tension, high-pressure, high-performance, high-potency, bionic; **authoritative;** armipotent, mighty in battle; kick-ass <nf>

13 **omnipotent, almighty, all-powerful;** plenipotentiary, pre-eminent, absolute, unlimited, **sovereign** 417.17; **supreme** 249.13; omnicompetent

14 **able, capable, equal to,** up to, **competent,** adequate, effective, effectual, efficient, efficacious, can-do; productive; **proficient** 413.22

ADVS 15 **powerfully, potently, forcefully,** forcibly, mightily, with might and main, **vigorously, energetically,** dynamically; **cogently,** strikingly, tellingly, impactfully; **effectively,** effectually; productively; with telling effect, to good account, to good purpose, with a vengeance

16 **ably, capably, competently,** adequately, effectively, effectually, **efficiently, well; to the best of one's ability,** as lies in one's power, so far as one can, as best one can; with all one's might, with everything that is in one

17 **by force,** by main *or* brute force, by *force majeure,* with the strong arm, with a high hand, high-

handedly; **forcibly,** amain, with might and main; by force of arms, at the point of the sword, by storm

PREPS 18 by dint of, by virtue of

WORD ELEMENTS 19 dynam-, dynamo-; -dynamia

19 IMPOTENCE

NOUNS 1 **impotence** *or* impotency, **powerlessness,** impuissance <old>, forcelessness, feebleness, softness, flabbiness, wimpiness *or* wimpishness <nf>, **weakness** 16; power vacuum

2 **inability, incapability, incapacity,** incapacitation, **incompetence** *or* incompetency, inadequacy, insufficiency, ineptitude, **inferiority** 250, inefficiency, unfitness, imbecility; disability, disablement, disqualification; legal incapacity, wardship, minority, infancy

3 **ineffectiveness, ineffectualness,** ineffectuality, inefficaciousness, **inefficacy,** counterproductiveness *or* counterproductivity, invalidity, **futility, uselessness,** inutility, bootlessness, failure 410; fatuity, inanity

4 **helplessness, defenselessness,** unprotectedness, vulnerability; **debilitation,** invalidism, effeteness, etiolation, enervation; wimpiness <nf>

5 **emasculation,** demasculinization, defeminization, effeminization, neutering, maiming, castration 255.4

6 **impotent,** weakling 16.6, invalid, incompetent, unable; flash in the pan, blank cartridge, wimp *and* dud <nf>; eunuch, *castrato* <Ital>, gelding; pushover, easy mark <nf>

VERBS 7 be impotent, lack force; be ineffective, avail nothing, not work *or* do not take <nf>; **waste one's effort,** bang one's head against a brick wall, have one's hands tied, spin one's wheels, tilt at windmills, run in circles, get nowhere

8 **cannot, not be able,** be unable, not have it *and* not hack it *and* not cut it *and* not cut the mustard <nf>, not make it *and* not make the grade *and* not make the cut <nf>

9 **disable,** disenable, unfit, **incapacitate,** drain, de-energize; enfeeble, debilitate, **weaken** 16.9,10; cripple, maim, lame, hamstring, knee-cap, defang, pull the teeth of <nf>; wing, clip the wings of; **inactivate,** disarm, unarm, put out of action, put *hors de combat;* **put out of order,** put out of commission <nf>, throw out of gear; bugger *and* bugger up *and* queer *and* queer the works *and* gum up *or* screw up <nf>, throw a wrench *or* monkey wrench in the machinery <nf>, sabotage, wreck; kibosh *and* put the kibosh on <nf>; spike, spike one's guns, put a spoke in one's wheels

10 <put out of action> **paralyze,** prostrate, shoot down in flames <nf>, put *hors de combat,* knock out <nf>, break the neck *or* back of; hamstring; handcuff, tie the hands of, hobble, enchain, manacle, hog-tie <nf>, **tie hand and foot,** truss up; throttle, strangle, get a stranglehold on; muzzle, gag, silence; **take the wind out of one's sails,** deflate, knock the props out from under, undermine, cut the ground from under, not leave a leg to stand on

11 **disqualify; invalidate,** knock the bottom out of <nf>

12 **unman, unnerve, enervate,** exhaust, etiolate, **devitalize; emasculate,** cut the balls off <nf>, demasculinize, effeminize; desex, desexualize; sterilize; castrate 255.11, neuter

ADJS **13** **impotent, powerless, forceless, out of gas** <nf>; feeble, soft, flabby, **weak** 16.12, weak as a kitten, wimpy *or* wimpish <nf>, wussy

14 **unable, incapable, incompetent,** inefficient, ineffective; **unqualified,** inept, unendowed, ungifted, untalented, **unfit,** unfitted; **outmatched,** out of one's depth, in over one's head, outgunned; **inferior** 250.6

15 **ineffective, ineffectual, inefficacious,** counterproductive, feckless, not up to scratch *or* up to snuff <nf>, **inadequate** 250.7; **invalid, inoperative,** of no force; nugatory, nugacious; fatuous, fatuitous; **vain, futile, inutile, useless,** unavailing, bootless, fruitless; all talk and no action, all wind; **empty,** inane; **debilitated,** effete, enervated, etiolated, barren, sterile, washed-out <nf>

16 **disabled, incapacitated; crippled,** hamstrung; disqualified, invalidated; disarmed; paralyzed; hog-tied <nf>; prostrate, **on one's back,** on one's beam-ends; challenged

17 **out of action, out of commission** and out of it <nf>, out of gear; *hors de combat* <Fr>, out of the battle, off the field, out of the running; laid on the shelf, obsolete, life-expired

18 **helpless, defenseless, unprotected;** vulnerable, like a sitting duck <nf>, dead in the water <nf>, aidless, friendless, unfriended; fatherless, motherless; leaderless, guideless; **untenable,** pregnable, vulnerable; disenfranchised

19 **unmanned, unnerved, enervated,** debilitated, **devitalized;** nerveless, sinewless, marrowless, pithless, lustless; **castrated,** emasculate, emasculated, gelded, eunuchized, unsexed, deballed <nf>, demasculinized, effeminized

ADVS **20** **beyond one,** beyond one's power *or* capacity *or* ability, beyond one's depth, out of one's league <nf>, above one's head, too much for

INTERJ **21** no can do!

20 REST, REPOSE

NOUNS **1** **rest, repose, ease, relaxation,** leisure, slippered *or* unbuttoned ease, decompression <nf>; **comfort** 121; comfort zone; restfulness, quiet, tranquility; inactivity 331; sleep 22

2 **respite, recess, rest, pause,** halt, stay, lull, **break,** surcease, suspension, interlude, **intermission,** spell <Austral>, letup <nf>, **time out** <nf>, time to catch one's breath; **breathing spell,** breathing time, breathing place, breathing space, breath; **breather;** coffee break, tea break, cigarette break; cocktail hour, happy hour <nf>; enforced respite, downtime; R and R *or* rest and recreation

3 **vacation,** holiday <Brit>, getaway; **time off;** day off, week off, month off, etc; paid vacation, paid holiday <Brit>; personal day, personal time, personal time off; weekend; **leave, leave of absence, furlough; liberty,** shore leave; day trip, scenic route; **sabbatical,** sabbatical leave *or* year; **weekend; busman's holiday;** package tour *or* holiday; honeymoon; spring break, winter break; Cook's tour

4 **holiday, day off; red-letter day,** gala day, fete day, festival day, day of festivities, field day; national holiday, legal holiday, bank holiday <Brit>; High Holiday, High Holy Day; holy day; feast, feast day, high day, church feast, fixed feast, movable feast; half-holiday; mini-break

5 **day of rest,** *dies non* <L>; **Sabbath,** Sunday, Lord's day, First day

VERBS **6** **rest, repose,** take rest, take one's ease, **take it easy** <nf>, lay down one's tools, rest from one's labors, rest on one's oars, take life easy; go to rest, settle to rest; lie down, have a lie-down, go to bed, snuggle down, curl up, tuck up, bed, bed down, couch, recline, lounge, drape oneself, sprawl, loll; take off one's shoes, unbuckle one's belt, get *or* take a load off one's feet, put one's feet up

7 **relax,** unlax <nf>, unbend, unwind, slack, slacken, **ease; ease up, let up,** slack up, slack off, **ease off,** let down, **slow down,** take it slow, take time to catch one's breath; mellow out, chill, lay back *and* kick back *and* decompress <nf>

8 **take a rest, take a break, break, take time out** and grab some R and R <nf>, pause, lay off, **knock off** <nf>, recess, **take a recess,** take ten *and* take five <nf>; stop for breath, catch one's breath, breathe; stop work, suspend operations, call it a day; go to bed with the chickens, sleep in; take a nap, catch some Zs <nf>; take a moment

9 **vacation, get away from it all,** holiday, take a holiday, make holiday; **take a leave of absence,** take leave, go on leave, go on furlough, take one's sabbatical; weekend; Sunday, Christmas, etc

ADJS **10 vacational, holiday,** ferial <old>, festal; sabbatical; **comfortable** 121.11; **restful,** quiet 173.12

ADVS **11 at rest, at ease,** at one's ease; abed, in bed

12 on vacation, on leave, on furlough; off duty, on one's own time, having a field day

21 FATIGUE

NOUNS **1 fatigue, tiredness, weariness,** wearifulness; **burnout,** end of one's tether, overtiredness, overstrain; faintness, goneness, weakness, enfeeblement, lack of staying power, enervation, debility, debilitation 16.1; jadedness; lassitude, languor; tension fatigue, stance fatigue, stimulation fatigue; fatigue disease, fatigue syndrome or post-viral fatigue syndrome, chronic fatigue syndrome; combat fatigue; mental fatigue, brain fag <nf>; strain, mental strain, heart strain, eyestrain; jet lag sleepiness 22.1

2 exhaustion, exhaustedness, draining, inanition; **collapse, prostration,** breakdown, crack-up <nf>, nervous exhaustion or prostration, burn-out or burnout; blackout

3 breathlessness, shortness of breath, windedness, short-windedness; panting, gasping; dyspnea, labored breathing

VERBS **4 fatigue, tire, weary, exhaust,** wilt, flag, jade, harass; **wear,** wear on or upon, **wear down; tire out, wear out, burn out; use up; do in; wind,** put out of breath; overtire, overweary, overfatigue, overstrain; weaken, enervate, debilitate 16.10; weary or tire to death, take it out of; prostrate; deprive of sleep

5 burn out, get tired, grow weary, tire, weary, fatigue, jade; **flag, droop,** faint, sink, feel dragged out, wilt; **play out,** run out, run down, burn out; gasp, wheeze, pant, puff, blow, puff and blow, puff like a grampus; collapse, break down, crack up <nf>, give out, drop, fall or drop by the wayside, drop in one's tracks, succumb; need a break

6 <nf terms> **beat, poop,** frazzle, fag, tucker; fag out, tucker out, knock out, do in, do up; **poop out,** peter out

ADJS **7 tired, weary, fatigued,** wearied, weariful, jaded, run-down, good and tired; unrefreshed, unrestored, in need of rest, ready to drop; **faint,** fainting, feeling faint, **weak,** rocky <nf>, enfeebled, enervated, debilitated, seedy <nf>, weakened 16.18; drooping, droopy, wilting, flagging, sagging; languid; worn, worn-down, **worn to a frazzle** or shadow, toilworn, weary-worn; wayworn, way-weary; foot-weary, weary-footed, footsore; tired-armed; tired-winged, weary-winged; weary-laden

8 <nf terms> **beat, pooped, bushed,** poohed, paled, frazzled, bagged, fagged, tuckered, plumb tuckered, done, done in, all in, dead, dead beat, dead on one's feet, gone; **pooped out,** knocked out, wiped out, tuckered out, played out, fagged out; run ragged; used up, done up, beat up, washed-up, whacked out

9 tired-looking, weary-looking, tired-eyed, tired-faced, haggard, hollow-eyed, ravaged, drawn, cadaverous, worn, wan, zombiish

10 burnt-out, burned-out, **exhausted,** drained, **spent,** unable to go on, gone; **tired out, worn-out,** beaten; maxed-out; bone-tired, bone-weary; **dog-tired,** dog-weary; **dead-tired, tired to death,** weary unto death, dead-alive or dead-and-alive, more dead than alive, ready to drop, on one's last legs; prostrate

11 overtired, overweary, overwrought, overwearied, overstrained, overdriven, overfatigued, overspent; hackneyed

12 breathless, winded; wheezing, puffing, panting, **out of breath,** short of breath or wind, gasping for breath, agasp; short-winded, short-breathed, dyspneic

13 fatiguing, wearying, wearing, **tiring,** straining, stressful, trying, **exhausting,** draining, **grueling,** punishing, killing, demanding; **tiresome,** fatiguesome, **wearisome,** weariful; toilsome 725.18

ADVS **14 out,** to the point of exhaustion

22 SLEEP

NOUNS **1 sleepiness, drowsiness,** keif, doziness, heaviness, lethargy, oscitation, somnolence or somnolency, yawning, stretching, oscitancy, pandiculation; languor 331.6; sand in the eyes, heavy eyelids; REM sleep or rapid-eye-movement sleep or dreaming sleep; dormition

2 sleep, slumber; repose, silken repose, somnus <L>, the arms of Morpheus; bye-bye or beddy-bye <nf>; doss <Brit nf>, blanket drill and shut eye <nf>; light sleep, fitful sleep, **doze, drowse,** snoozle <nf>; beauty sleep <nf>; sleepwalking, somnambulism; somniloquy; **land of Nod,** slumberland, sleepland, dreamland; hibernation, winter sleep, aestivation; bedtime, sack time <nf>; unconsciousness 25.2

3 nap, snooze <nf>, **catnap,** wink, **forty winks and** some Zs <nf>, zizz <Brit nf>, wink of sleep, spot of sleep; **siesta,** blanket drill and sack or rack time <nf>; power nap

4 sweet sleep, balmy sleep, downy sleep, soft sleep, gentle sleep, smiling sleep, golden slumbers; "the honey-heavy dew of slumber"—Shakespeare; peaceful sleep, sleep of the just; restful sleep, good night's sleep

5 **deep sleep,** profound sleep, heavy sleep, **sound sleep,** cataphor, unbroken sleep, wakeless sleep, drugged sleep, dreamless sleep, the sleep of the dead; paradoxical *or* orthodox *or* dreaming *or* REM sleep, synchronized *or* S *or* NREM sleep; lucid dreaming

6 **stupor,** sopor, **coma, swoon,** lethargy <old>, persistent vegetative state; **trance;** narcosis, narcohypnosis, narcoma, narcotization, narcotic stupor *or* trance; sedation; high <nf>; nod <nf>; narcolepsy; catalepsy; thanatosis, shock; sleeping sickness, encephalitis lethargica

7 **hypnosis,** mesmeric *or* **hypnotic sleep, trance,** somnipathy, hypnotic somnolence; lethargic hypnosis, somnambulistic hypnosis, cataleptic hypnosis, animal hypnosis; narcohypnosis; autohypnosis, self-hypnosis; hypnotherapy

8 **hypnotism, mesmerism;** hypnology; hypnotization, mesmerization; **animal magnetism,** od, odyl, odylic force; hypnotic suggestion, posthypnotic suggestion, autosuggestion

9 **hypnotist, mesmerist,** hypnotizer, mesmerizer; Svengali, Mesmer

10 **sleep-inducer,** sleep-producer, sleep-provoker, sleep-bringer, hypnotic, soporific, somnifacient; poppy, mandrake, mandragora, opium, opiate, morphine, morphia; nightcap; sedative 86.12; anesthetic; lullaby

11 **Morpheus,** Somnus, Hypnos; sandman, dustman <Brit>

12 **sleeper, slumberer;** sleeping beauty; **sleepyhead,** lie-abed, slugabed, sleepwalker, somnambulist; somniloquist, dreamer

VERBS 13 **sleep, slumber,** rest in the arms of Morpheus; **doze, drowse; nap, catnap,** take a nap, catch a wink, sleep soundly, **sleep like a top** *or* **log,** sleep like the dead; *dormir sur les deux oreilles* <Fr>; snore, saw wood *and* saw logs <nf>; have an early night, go to bed betimes; sleep in; oversleep

14 <nf terms> **snooze,** get some shut-eye, get some sack time, flake *or* sack out, crash, catch forty winks *or* some zs, zizz <Brit>; pound the ear, kip *or* doss <Brit>, log zs

15 **hibernate,** aestivate, lie dormant

16 **go to sleep,** settle to sleep, go off to sleep, **fall asleep,** drop asleep, **drop off,** drift off, drift off to sleep; **doze off, drowse off,** nod off, dope off <nf>; close one's eyes

17 **go to bed, retire;** lay me down to sleep; bed, bed down; go night-night *and* go bye-bye *and* go beddy-bye <nf>

18 <nf terms> **hit the hay, hit the sack,** crash, turn in, crawl in, flop, sack out, sack up, kip down *or* doss down <Brit>, lights out

19 **put to bed,** bed; nestle, cradle; **tuck in**

20 **put to sleep; lull to sleep,** rock to sleep; **hypnotize, mesmerize,** magnetize; **entrance,** trance, put in a trance; narcotize, drug, dope <nf>; anesthetize, put under; sedate

ADJS 21 **sleepy, drowsy,** dozy, snoozy <nf>, **slumberous,** slumbery, dreamy, sleepful; **half asleep,** asleep on one's feet; sleepful, sleep-filled; yawny, stretchy <nf>, oscitant, yawning, napping, **nodding,** ready for bed; heavy, **heavy-eyed, heavy with sleep,** sleep-swollen, sleep-drowned, sleep-drunk, drugged with sleep; **somnolent,** soporific; **lethargic,** comatose, narcose *or* narcous, stuporose *or* **stuporous, in a stupor,** out of it <nf>; narcoleptic; cataleptic; narcotized, drugged, doped <nf>; sedated; anesthetized; **languid**

22 **asleep, sleeping, slumbering,** in the arms *or* lap of Morpheus, in the land of Nod; **sound asleep, fast asleep,** dead asleep, deep asleep, in a sound sleep, flaked-out <nf>; **unconscious, oblivious, out,** out like a light, out cold; comatose; dormant; dead, **dead to the world;** unwakened, unawakened

23 **sleep-inducing,** sleep-producing, sleep-bringing, sleep-causing, sleep-compelling, sleep-inviting, sleep-provoking, sleep-tempting; **narcotic,** hypnotic, **soporific, somniferous,** somnifacient; sedative 86.45

24 **hypnotic,** hypnoid, hypnoidal, **mesmeric;** odylic; narcohypnotic; somnambulant, somnambulic

23 WAKEFULNESS

NOUNS 1 **wakefulness,** wake; **sleeplessness,** restlessness, tossing and turning; **insomnia,** insomnolence *or* insomnolency, white night; vigilance, vigil, all-night vigil, lidless vigil, *per vigilium* <L>; insomniac; consciousness, sentience; alertness 339.5

2 **awakening, wakening,** rousing, **arousal;** rude awakening, rousting out <nf>; reveille

VERBS 3 **keep awake,** keep one's eyes open; keep alert, be vigilant 339.8; stay awake, **toss and turn, not sleep a wink,** not shut one's eyes, count sheep; have a white night

4 **awake, awaken, wake, wake up, get up,** rouse, come alive <nf>; open one's eyes, stir <nf>

5 <wake someone up> **awaken, waken, rouse, arouse,** awake, wake, **wake up,** shake up, knock up <Brit>, roust out <nf>

6 **get up,** get out of bed, **arise,** rise, **rise and shine** <nf>, greet the day, **turn out** <nf>; roll out *and* pile out *and* **show a leg** *and* hit the deck <nf>

ADJS 7 **wakeful, sleepless,** slumberless, **unsleeping,** insomniac, insomnious; restless; watchful, vigilant, lidless

8 **awake,** conscious, **up; wide-awake,** broad awake; sentient; alert 339.14

ADVS 9 **sleeplessly, unsleepingly; wakefully,** with one's eyes open; alertly 339.17

24 SENSATION
<physical sensibility>

NOUNS 1 **sensation, sense, feeling;** sense impression, sense-datum *or* -data, percept, perception, sense perception; experience, sensory experience, sense impression; **sensuousness,** sensuosity, sensuality; **consciousness,** awareness, apperception; response, response to stimuli

2 **sensibility,** sensibleness, physical sensibility, sentience *or* sentiency; openness to sensation, readiness of feeling, receptiveness, receptivity; sensation level, threshold of sensation, limen; impressionability, impressibility, affectibility; **susceptibility,** susceptivity, perceptibility; esthesia, aesthesia, esthesis

3 **sensitivity, sensitiveness;** perceptivity, perceptiveness, feelings; responsiveness; **tact, tactfulness, considerateness,** courtesy, politeness; **compassion, sympathy;** empathy, identification; **concern,** solicitousness, solicitude; capability of feeling, passibility; **delicacy, exquisiteness,** tenderness, fineness; **oversensitiveness,** oversensibility, hypersensitivity, **thin skin,** hyperesthesia, hyperpathia, supersensitivity, overtenderness; **irritability,** prickliness, soreness, **touchiness,** tetchiness; ticklishness, nervousness 128; allergy, anaphylaxis; sensitization; photophobia

4 **sore spot,** sore point, soft spot, raw, exposed nerve, raw nerve, nerve ending, tender spot, the quick, where the shoe pinches, where one lives *and* in the gut <nf>; agitation, agita <nf>, hot spot

5 **senses, five senses,** sensorium; touch 74, taste 62, smell 69, sight 27, hearing 48; sixth sense, second sight, extrasensory perception *or* ESP; sense *or* sensory organ, sensillum, receptor; synesthesia, chromesthesia, color hearing; phonism, photism; kinesthesia, muscle sense, sense of motion; sense organ; horse sense

VERBS 6 **sense, feel,** experience, **perceive,** apprehend, be sensible of, be conscious *or* aware of, apperceive; taste 62.7, smell 69.8, see 27.12, hear 48.11,12, touch 73.6; respond, respond to stimuli; be sensitive to, have a thing about <nf>; overreact

7 **sensitize,** make sensitive; sensibilize, sensify; **sharpen, whet, quicken,** stimulate, excite, stir, cultivate, refine

8 **touch a sore spot,** touch a soft spot, touch on the raw, touch a raw spot, touch to the quick, hit *or*
touch a nerve *or* nerve ending, touch where it hurts, hit one where he lives <nf>, strike *or* hit home

ADJS 9 **sensory,** sensorial; **sensitive,** receptive, responsive; **sensuous;** sensorimotor, sensimotor; kinesthetic, somatosensory; feeling, percipient; centripetal

10 **neural, nervous,** nerval; neurologic, neurological

11 sensible, sentient, sensile; **susceptible,** susceptive; **receptive,** impressionable, impressive <old>, impressible; **perceptive; conscious,** cognizant, **aware,** sensitive to, alive to, clued in, sussed <nf>

12 **sensitive,** responsive, sympathetic, compassionate; empathic, empathetic; passible; delicate, tactful, considerate, courteous, solicitous, tender, refined; **oversensitive, thin-skinned;** oversensible, hyperesthetic, hyperpathic, hypersensitive, supersensitive, overtender, overrefined, overwhelmed; **irritable, touchy,** irascible, tetchy <nf>, quick on the draw *or* trigger *or* uptake, itchy, ticklish, prickly; goosey <nf>, skittish; nervous; allergic, anaphylactic

13 *<keenly sensitive>* **exquisite,** poignant, **acute,** sharp, **keen,** biting, vivid, intense, extreme, excruciating

14 sensate, perceptible, audible, visible, tactile, palpable, tangible, noticeable

25 INSENSIBILITY
<physical unfeeling>

NOUNS 1 **insensibility,** insensibleness, **insensitivity,** insensitiveness, insentience, impassibility, lack of feeling; **unperceptiveness,** imperceptiveness, imperception, imperceptivity, impercipience, blindness, lack of concern, obtuseness; inconsiderateness; unsolicitousness; tactlessness; discourtesy, boorishness; philistinism; **unfeeling,** unfeelingness, **apathy,** affectlessness, lack of affect; thick skin *or* hide, callousness 94.3; **numbness,** dullness, hypothymia, **deadness;** pins and needles; hypesthesia; anesthesia, analgesia; narcosis, electronarcosis; narcotization; lack of awareness

2 **unconsciousness, senselessness;** nothingness, oblivion, obliviousness, indifference, heedlessness, unawareness; nirvana; **faint, swoon, blackout,** syncope, athymia, lipothymy *or* lipothymia; **coma;** torpor, **stupor;** trance; catalepsy, catatony *or* catatonia, sleep 22; knockout *or* KO *or* kayo <nf>; semiconsciousness, grayout; suspended animation

3 **anesthetic,** general anesthetic, local anesthetic, analgesic, anodyne, balm, ointment, **pain killer,** pain-reliever, antiodontalgic; tranquilizer, **sedative,** sleeping pill *or* tablet, somnifacient,

knockout drops *and* Mickey Finn *and* Mickey
<nf>; drug, dope <nf>, narcotic, opiate;
acupuncture; desensitization; ether
VERBS **4 deaden, numb,** benumb, blunt, dull,
obtund, **desensitize;** paralyze, palsy; **anesthetize,
put to sleep,** slip one a Mickey *or* Mickey Finn
<nf>, chloroform, etherize; narcotize, drug, dope
<nf>; freeze, **stupefy, stun,** bedaze, besot; knock
unconscious, knock senseless, **knock out, KO** *and*
kayo *and* lay out *and* coldcock *and* knock stiff *and*
brain <nf>; concuss
5 faint, swoon, drop, succumb, keel over <nf>, fall
in a faint, fall senseless, **pass** *or* zonk out <nf>,
black out, dim, go out like a light; gray out
ADJS **6 insensible, unfeeling, insensitive,** insentient,
insensate, impassible; nerveless, senseless,
unemotional; unsympathetic, uncompassionate;
unconcerned, unsolicitous, non-caring, uncaring,
impassive, cold-blooded, apathetic, hardhearted;
tactless, boorish, heavy-handed; **unperceptive,**
imperceptive, impercipient, blind, unmindful;
thick-skinned, hardened, **dull,** obtuse, obdurate;
numb, numbed, benumbed, dead, **deadened,**
asleep, unfelt; **unfeeling, apathetic,** affectless;
stoic; deaf; callous 94.12; anesthetized, narcotized,
hypnotized
7 stupefied, stunned, dazed, bedazed, astonied <old>
8 unconscious, senseless, oblivious, unaware,
comatose, asleep, dead, lifeless, **dead to the world,**
cold, out, **out cold;** heedless, unmindful; nirvanic;
half-conscious, semiconscious; drugged,
narcotized; doped *and* stoned *and* spaced out *and*
strung out *and* zonked *and* zonked out *and* out of
it <nf>; catatonic, cataleptic; stunned, concussed,
knocked out; desensitized; out for the count <nf>
9 deadening, numbing, dulling; **anesthetic,**
analgesic, narcotic; stupefying, stunning,
numbing, mind-boggling *or* -numbing;
anesthetizing, narcotizing

26 PAIN
<physical suffering>

NOUNS **1 pain; suffering, hurt, hurting,** painfulness,
misery <nf>, **distress,** *Schmerz* <Ger>, dolor
<old>; **discomfort,** malaise; aches and pains;
pain threshold
2 pang, pangs, throe, throes; seizure, spasm,
paroxysm; ouch <nf>; **twinge,** twitch, wrench,
jumping pain; crick, kink, hitch, cramp *or* cramps;
nip, thrill, pinch, tweak, bite, prick, pinprick, **stab,**
stitch, sharp *or* piercing *or* stabbing pain, acute
pain, **shooting pain,** darting pain, fulgurant pain,
lancinating pain, shooting; boring *or* terebrant *or*

terebrating pain; gnawing, gnawing *or* grinding
pain; stitch in the side; charley horse <nf>;
phantom limb pain; hunger pang *or* pain;
wandering pain; psychalgia, psychosomatic pain,
soul pain, mind pain
3 smart, smarting, **sting,** stinging, urtication, **tingle,**
tingling; **burn,** burning, burning pain, fire; pins
and needles
4 soreness, irritation, inflammation, tenderness,
sensitiveness; algesia; rankling <old>, festering;
sore; sore spot 24.4
5 ache, aching, throbbing, throbbing ache *or* pain,
throb; **headache,** cephalalgia, misery in the head
<nf>; splitting headache, **sick headache, migraine,**
megrim, hemicrania; **backache; earache,** otalgia;
toothache, odontalgia; **stomachache,** tummyache
<nf>, bellyache *or* gut-ache <nf>; **colic,**
collywobbles, gripes, gripe, gnawing, gnawing of
the bowels, fret <nf>; **heartburn,** acid reflux,
agita, pyrosis; **angina**
6 agony, anguish, torment, torture, ordeal, exquisite
torment *or* torture, the rack, excruciation,
crucifixion, martyrdom, martyrization,
excruciating *or* agonizing *or* atrocious pain, hell
on earth, punishment; pain in the neck
VERBS **7 pain,** give *or* inflict pain, **hurt, wound,
afflict, distress,** injure; **burn;** sting; nip, bite,
tweak, pinch; pierce, prick, stab, cut, lacerate,
thrash; **irritate, inflame,** sear, harshen,
exacerbate, intensify; chafe, gall, fret, rasp, rub,
grate; gnaw, grind; gripe; fester, rankle <old>;
torture, torment, rack, put to torture, put *or* lay on
the rack, **agonize, harrow,** crucify, martyr,
martyrize, traumatize, excruciate, wring, twist,
contorse, convulse; wrench, tear, rend; prolong
the agony, kill by inches
8 suffer, feel pain, feel the pangs, anguish 96.19;
hurt, ache, have a misery <nf>, ail, be afflicted;
smart, tingle; throb, pound; shoot; twinge, thrill,
twitch; **wince,** blanch, shrink, make a wry face,
grimace; **agonize,** writhe
ADJS **9 pained,** in pain, **hurt,** hurting, **suffering,**
afflicted, wounded, distressed, in distress;
tortured, tormented, racked, agonized, harrowed,
lacerated, crucified, martyred, martyrized,
wrung, twisted, convulsed, anguished; on the
rack, under the harrow; traumatized; stressed out,
bothered
10 painful; hurtful, **hurting,** distressing, afflictive,
miserable; **acute, sharp,** piercing, stabbing,
shooting, stinging, biting, gnawing; **poignant,**
pungent, burning, searing, **severe,** cruel, harsh,
grave, hard; griping, cramping, spasmic,
spasmatic, spasmodic, paroxysmal; **agonizing,**

excruciating, exquisite, atrocious, torturous, tormenting, martyrizing, racking, **harrowing,** unbearable, intolerable

11 **sore, raw;** pained; smarting, tingling, **burning; irritated, inflamed, tender,** sensitive, fiery, angry, red; algetic; chafed, galled; **festering,** rankling <old>; black-and-blue

12 **aching,** achy, **throbbing;** headachy, migrainous, backachy, toothachy, stomachachy, colicky, griping

13 **irritating,** irritative, irritant; **chafing, galling,** fretting, bothersome, rasping, boring, grating, grinding, stinging, scratchy

27 VISION

NOUNS 1 **vision, sight, eyesight,** seeing; **sightedness;** visioning; eye, power of sight, sense of sight, visual sense; **perception,** discernment; perspicacity, perspicuity, sharp or acute or keen sight, visual acuity, quick sight, **20/20** vision; farsight, farsightedness; nearsightedness; astigmatism; clear sight, unobstructed vision; rod vision, scotopia; cone vision, photopia; color vision, twilight vision, daylight vision, day vision, night vision; eye-mindedness; **field of vision,** visual field, scope, ken, purview, horizon, sweep, range; line of vision, line of sight, sight-line; peripheral vision, peripheral field; field of view 31.3; sensitivity to light, phototonus

2 **observation,** observance; **looking, watching, viewing, seeing,** witnessing, espial; **notice,** note, respect, **regard;** watch, lookout; spying, espionage

3 **look, sight,** the eye and a look-see and a gander <nf>, glad eye <nf>, dekko <Brit nf>, eye, view, regard; sidelong look; leer, leering look, lustful leer; sly look; look-in; preview; scene, prospect 33.6

4 **glance,** glance or flick of the eye, squiz <Austral>, slant <nf>, rapid glance, cast, side-glance; **glimpse,** flash, quick sight; **peek, peep;** wink, blink, flicker or twinkle of an eye; casual glance, **half an eye;** coup d'œil <Fr>

5 **gaze, stare,** gape, goggle; sharp or piercing or penetrating look; **ogle,** glad eye, come-hither look <nf>, bedroom eyes <nf>; **glare, glower,** glaring or glowering look, black look, dirty look; evil eye, malocchio <Ital>, whammy <nf>; withering look, hostile look, chilly look, the fisheye or stinkeye or hairy eyeball <nf>; rubbernecking

6 **scrutiny,** overview, **survey,** contemplation, surveillance; **examination, inspection** 938.3, scrutiny, the once-over <nf>, visual examination,

a vetting <Brit nf>, ocular inspection, eyeball inspection <nf>

7 **viewpoint, standpoint, point of view,** vantage, vantage point, perspective, point or coign of vantage, where one stands; bird's-eye view, worm's-eye view, fly on the wall; **outlook,** angle, slant, angle or field of vision, optique <Fr>, eyeshot; mental outlook 978.2

8 observation post or point or deck; **observatory; lookout,** outlook, overlook, scenic overlook; planetarium; **watchtower,** tower; Texas tower; beacon, lighthouse, pharos; gazebo, belvedere; bridge, conning tower, crow's nest; peephole, sighthole, spyhole, loophole; **ringside,** ringside seat; **grandstand,** bleachers, stands; **gallery,** top gallery; paradise and peanut gallery <nf>; window

9 **eye,** visual organ, organ of vision, oculus, optic, **orb, peeper** <nf>, baby blues <nf>; clear eyes, bright eyes, starry orbs; saucer eyes, popeyes and goggle eyes and banjo eyes and googly eyes and sparklers <nf>; naked eye, unassisted or unaided eye; corner of the eye; eyeball; iris; pupil; eyelid, lid, nictitating membrane; eyeglasses

10 **sharp eye,** keen eye, piercing or penetrating eye, gimlet eye, X-ray eye; **eagle eye,** hawkeye, peeled eye <nf>, watchful eye; **weather eye**

11 <comparisons> eagle, hawk, cat, lynx, ferret, weasel; Argus

VERBS 12 **see, behold, observe, view, witness, perceive, discern, spy,** espy, **sight,** have in sight, make out, pick out, descry, spot <nf>, twig <Brit nf>, discover, notice, take notice of, have one's eye on, distinguish, recognize, ken <nf>, **catch sight of,** get a load of <nf>, take in, get an eyeful of <nf>, look on or upon, cast the eyes on or upon, **set** or **lay eyes on, clap eyes on** <nf>; **glimpse,** get or catch a glimpse of; see at a glance, see with half an eye; see with one's own eyes

13 **look, peer,** have a look, take a gander and take a look <nf>, direct the eyes, turn or bend the eyes, cast one's eye, lift up the eyes; **look at,** take a look at, eye, **eyeball** <nf>, have a look-see <nf>, have a dekko <Brit nf>, look on or upon, gaze at or upon; **watch, observe, view, regard;** keep one's eyes peeled or skinned, be watchful or observant or vigilant, keep one's eyes open; keep in sight or view, hold in view; look after; **check** and **check out** <nf>, scope <nf>, scope on or out <nf>; keep under observation, spy on, have an eye out, keep an eye out, keep an eye on, keep a weather eye on, follow, tail and shadow <nf>, stake out; **reconnoiter,** scout, get the lay of the land; **peek, peep,** pry, take a peep or peek; play peekaboo

14 scrutinize, survey, eye, contemplate, look over, give the eye *or* the once-over <nf>; **ogle,** ogle at, **leer,** leer at, give one the glad eye; examine, vet <Brit nf>, **inspect** 938.24; **pore,** pore over, peruse; take a close *or* careful look; take a long, hard look; size up <nf>; take stock of; have eyes in the back of one's head

15 gaze, gloat <old>, fix one's gaze, fix *or* fasten *or* rivet one's eyes upon, keep one's eyes upon, feast one's eyes on; **eye, ogle; stare,** stare at, stare hard, stare out, zone out, look, goggle, **gape, gawk** *or* gawp <nf>, gaze open-mouthed; crane, crane the neck, stand on tiptoe, rubberneck <nf>; strain one's eyes; look straight in the eye, look full in the face, hold one's eye *or* gaze, stare down

16 glare, glower, look daggers, look black; give one the evil eye, give one a whammy <nf>; give one the fish eye <nf>, give one a dirty look

17 glance, glimpse, glint, cast a glance, glance at *or* upon, give a *coup d'œil* <Fr>, take a glance at, take a squint at <nf>

18 look askance *or* askant, give a sidelong look; squint, look asquint; cock the eye; **look down one's nose** <nf>

19 look away, look aside, **avert the eyes,** look another way, break one's eyes away, stop looking, turn away from, turn the back upon; drop one's eyes *or* gaze, cast one's eyes down; avoid one's gaze

ADJS **20 visual, ocular,** eye, eyeball <nf>; **sighted,** seeing, having sight *or* vision; **optic, optical;** ophthalmic; retinal; visible 31.6

21 clear-sighted, clear-eyed; twenty-twenty; **farsighted,** farseeing, telescopic; **sharp-sighted,** keen-sighted, sharp-eyed, **eagle-eyed,** hawk-eyed, ferret-eyed, lynx-eyed, cat-eyed, Argus-eyed; eye-minded, perceptive, aware

ADVS **22 at sight,** as seen, visibly, at a glance; by sight, by eyeball <nf>, visually; at first sight, **at the first blush,** *prima facie* <L>; out of the corner of one's eye; from where one stands, from one's viewpoint *or* standpoint

WORD ELEMENTS **23** opto-, -opsia, -opsy, -opsis; -opy, -opia; -scopy; ocul-, oculo-, ophthalm-, ophthalmo-

28 DEFECTIVE VISION

NOUNS **1** faulty eyesight, bad eyesight, visual handicap, defect of vision *or* sight, poor sight, impaired vision, imperfect vision, blurred vision, reduced sight, partial sightedness, partial blindness; legal blindness; **astigmatism,** astigmia; nystagmus; albinism; double vision, double sight, diplopia; tunnel vision; photophobia; **blindness** 30

2 dim-sightedness, dull-sightedness, near-blindness, amblyopia, gravel-blindness, sand-blindness, **purblindness,** dim eyes; blurredness, blearedness, bleariness, lippitude <old>; eyestrain, bloodshot eyes, redness, red eyes

3 nearsightedness, myopia, shortsightedness, short sight

4 farsightedness, hyperopia, longsightedness, long sight; presbyopia

5 strabismus, heterotropia; cast, cast in the eye; **squint,** squinch <nf>; **cross-eye, cross-eyedness;** convergent strabismus, esotropia; upward strabismus, anoöpsia; walleye, exotropia; detached retina; tic

6 <defective eyes> cross-eyes, cockeyes, squint eyes, lazy eye, swivel eyes <nf>, goggle eyes, walleyes, bug-eyes *and* popeyes <nf>, saucer eyes <nf>

7 winking, blinking, fluttering the eyelids, nictitation; winker, blinkard <old>; tic

VERBS **8** see badly *or* poorly, barely see, be half-blind; have a mote in the eye; see double

9 squint, squinch <nf>, squint the eye, look asquint, screw up the eyes, skew, goggle <old>

10 wink, blink, nictitate, bat the eyes <nf>

ADJS **11** poor-sighted; visually impaired, visually handicapped, sight-impaired; legally blind; **blind** 30.9; **astigmatic, astigmatical;** nystagmic; **nearsighted, shortsighted, myopic,** mope-eyed <old>; **farsighted,** longsighted, presbyopic; dayblind, hereralopic; nightblind, nyctalopic; colorblind; sand-blind; **squinting,** squinty, asquint, squint-eyed, squinch-eyed <nf>, strabismal, strabismic; winking, **blinking,** blinky, blink-eyed, nictating; blinkered; photophobic

12 cross-eyed, cockeyed, swivel-eyed <nf>, goggle-eyed, bug-eyed *and* popeyed <nf>, **walleyed,** saucer-eyed, glare-eyed; one-eyed, monocular, cyclopean; moon-eyed

13 dim-sighted, dim, dull-sighted, dim-eyed, weak-eyed, feeble-eyed, mole-eyed; **purblind,** half-blind, gravel-blind, sand-blind; bleary-eyed, blear-eyed; filmy-eyed, film-eyed; snow-blind; sand-blind; bloodshot, red-eyed; dry-eyed

29 OPTICAL INSTRUMENTS

NOUNS **1 optical instrument** <see list>, optical device, viewer; **microscope** <see list>; **spectroscope, spectrometer** <see list>

2 lens, glass; prism, objective prism; eyepiece, objective, condenser; mirror system, catadioptric system, telecentric system; **camera** 714.11

3 spectacles, specs <nf>, **glasses, eyeglasses,** pair of glasses *or* spectacles, barnacles <Brit nf>, cheaters *and* peepers <nf>; reading glasses, readers;

bifocals, divided spectacles, trifocals, pince-nez, nippers <nf>; progressive lenses; lorgnette, *lorgnon* <Fr>; horn-rimmed glasses; harlequin glasses; granny glasses; mini-specs <nf>; colored glasses, sunglasses, sun-specs <nf>, dark glasses, Polaroid <trademark> glasses, shades <nf>; goggles, blinkers; eyeglass, monocle, quizzing glass; thick glasses, thick-lensed glasses, thick lenses, Coke-bottle glasses <nf>; **contacts,** contact lenses, hard lenses, soft lenses, extended-wear lenses; progressive lenses

4 **telescope** <see list>, scope, **spy glass,** terrestrial telescope, glass, **field glass; binoculars,** zoom binoculars, opera glasses, binocs <nf>

5 **sight;** sighthole; finder, viewfinder; panoramic sight; bombsight; peep sight, open sight, leaf sight

6 **mirror,** glass, **looking glass,** seeing glass <Brit nf>, reflector, speculum; hand mirror, window mirror, rear-view mirror, cheval glass, pier glass, shaving mirror; steel mirror; convex mirror, concave mirror, distorting mirror

7 **optics,** optical physics; **optometry;** microscopy, microscopics; telescopy; stereoscopy; spectroscopy, spectrometry; infrared spectroscopy; spectrophotometry; electron optics; fiber optics; **photography** 714

8 **oculist,** ophthalmologist, **optometrist;** microscopist, telescopist; optician

ADJS **9** **optic, optical,** ophthalmic, ophthalmologic, ophthalmological, optometrical; acousto-optic, acousto-optical; ocular, binocular, monocular

10 microscopic, telescopic, etc; stereoscopic, three-dimensional, 3-D

11 **spectacled, bespectacled,** four-eyed <nf>; goggled; monocled

12 **optical instruments and viewers**

abdominoscope	microfilm viewer *or* reader
amblyoscope	ophthalmoscope
blink comparator	optometer
bronchoscope	oscilloscope
camera lucida	periscope
chromatoscope	pharyngoscope
chromoscope	photometer
cystoscope	photomultiplier
diaphanoscope	photoscope
diffractometer	polariscope
endoscope	polemoscope
epidiascope	prism
eriometer	pseudoscope
fiberscope	radarscope
gastroscope	radioscope
goniometer *or*	rangefinder
gonioscope	retinoscope
image orthicon	saccarimeter
kaleidoscope	sniperscope
laser	snooperscope

spectroscope	stroboscope
stereopticon	telestereoscope
stereoscope	thaumatrope

13 **microscopes**

acoustic microscope	phase contrast microscope
binocular microscope	*or* phase microscope
blink microscope	photomicroscope
comparison microscope	pinion focusing microscope
compound microscope	polarizing microscope
conoscope	power microscope
dark-field microscope	projecting microscope
dissecting microscope	scanning electron
electron microscope	microscope
field-emission microscope	scanning microscope
field-ion microscope	scanning tunneling
fluorescence microscope	microscope
gravure microscope	simple *or* single microscope
high-powered microscope	spectromicroscope
interference microscope	stereomicroscope *or*
laboratory microscope	stereoscopic microscope
light microscope	surface microscope
metallograph	transmission electron
metallurgical microscope	microscope
microprojector	ultramicroscope
optical microscope	ultraviolet microscope
oxyhydrogen microscope	X-ray microscope

14 **spectroscopes, spectrometers**

analytical spectrometer	microwave spectroscope
diffraction spectroscope	monochromator
direct-reading spectrometer	ocular spectroscope
direct-reading spectroscope	prism spectroscope
direct-vision spectroscope	reversion spectroscope
mass spectrograph	spectrograph
mass spectroscope	spectrophotometer
microspectrophotometer	spectroradiometer
microspectroscope	star spectroscope

15 **telescopes**

astronomical telescope *or*	mercurial telescope
Kepler telescope	Mills cross
Cassegrain telescope	Multiple Mirror Telescope
collimator	*or* MMT
coudé telescope	Newtonian telescope
Dobsonian telescope	optical telescope
double-image	panoramic telescope
telescope	prism *or* prismatic
elbow telescope	telescope
electron telescope	radio telescope
equatorial telescope	reflecting telescope
finder telescope	refracting telescope
Galilean telescope	Schmidt telescope
Gregorian telescope	spotting scope
guiding telescope	telescopic sight
Hale telescope	terrestrial telescope
heliometer	tower telescope
Hubble Space	twin telescope
Telescope	vernier telescope
inverting telescope	water telescope
Maksutov telescope	zenith telescope *or* tube

30 BLINDNESS

NOUNS **1 blindness, sightlessness,** cecity, ablepsia, unseeingness, sightless eyes, lack of vision, eyelessness; stone-blindness, total blindness; darkness, "total eclipse without all hope of day"—Milton; legal blindness; partial blindness, reduced sight, **blind side; blind spot;** dimsightedness; snow blindness, niphablepsia; amaurosis, *gutta serena* <L>, drop serene; cataract; glaucoma; trachoma; mental *or* psychic blindness, mind-blindness, soul-blindness, benightedness, unenlightenment, spiritual blindness; **blinding,** making blind, depriving of sight, putting out the eyes, excecation <old>; blurring the eyes, blindfolding, hoodwinking, blinkering; tunnel vision

2 day blindness, hemeralopia; **night blindness,** nyctalopia; moon blindness, moon-blind

3 color blindness; dichromatism; monochromatism, achromatopsia; red blindness, protanopia, green blindness, deuteranopia, red-green blindness, Daltonism; yellow blindness, xanthocyanopia; blue-yellow blindness, tritanopia; violet-blindness

4 the blind, the sightless, the unseeing; blind man; bat, mole; "blind leaders of the blind"—Bible

5 blindfold; eye patch; blinkers, blinds, blinders, rogue's badge

6 <aids for the blind> sensory aid, **Braille,** New York point, Gall's serrated type, Boston type, Howe's American type, Moon *or* Moon's type, Alston's Glasgow type, Lucas's type, sight-saver type, Frere's type; line letter, string alphabet, writing stamps; noctograph, writing frame, embosser, high-speed embosser; visagraph; talking book; optophone, Visotoner, Optacon; personal sonar, Pathsounder; ultrasonic spectacles; cane; Seeing Eye dog, guide dog; white stick *or* cane

VERBS **7 blind,** blind the eyes, deprive of sight, **strike blind,** render *or* make blind, excecate <old>; darken, dim, obscure, eclipse; **put one's eyes out,** gouge; **blindfold,** blinker, hoodwink, bandage; throw dust in one's eyes, benight; **dazzle,** bedazzle, daze; glare; snow-blind

8 be blind, not see, walk in darkness, grope in the dark, feel one's way; go blind, lose one's sight *or* vision, black out; be blind to, close *or* shut one's eyes to, wink *or* blink at, look the other way, blind oneself to, wear blinkers *or* have blinders on, avert one's eyes; have a blind spot *or* side

ADJS **9 blind, sightless, unsighted,** ableptical, eyeless, visionless, **unseeing,** undiscerning, unobserving, unperceiving; in darkness, rayless, bereft of light, dark <nf>, "dark, dark, dark, amid the blaze of noon"—Milton; **stone-blind,** stark blind, **blind as a bat,** blind as a mole *or* an owl; amaurotic; dim-sighted 28.13; hemeralopic; nyctalopic; color-blind; glaucomatous; legally blind; mind-blind, soul-blind, mentally *or* psychically *or* spiritually blind, benighted, unenlightened

10 blinded, excecate <old>, darkened, obscured; **blindfolded,** blindfold, hoodwinked, blinkered; **dazzled,** bedazzled, dazed; snow-blind, snow-blinded; sand-blind

11 blinding, obscuring; **dazzling,** bedazzling, stunning

31 VISIBILITY

NOUNS **1 visibility,** visibleness, perceptibility, discernibleness, observability, detectability, visuality, seeableness; exposure; manifestation; outcrop, outcropping; the visible, the seen, what is revealed, what can be seen; revelation, epiphany

2 distinctness, plainness, evidence <old>, evidentness, obviousness, patentness, manifestness, recognizability; **clearness, clarity,** crystal-clearness, lucidity, limpidity; **definiteness,** definition, sharpness, microscopical distinctness; resolution, high resolution, low resolution; **prominence, conspicuousness,** conspicuity; **exposure,** public exposure, high profile, low profile; high *or* low visibility; atmospheric visibility, seeing, ceiling, ceiling unlimited, visibility unlimited, CAVU *or* ceiling and visibility unlimited, severe clear <nf>, visibility zero

3 field of view, field of vision, range *or* scope of vision, visual range, **sight,** limit of vision, eyereach, **eyesight,** eyeshot, ken; **vista, view, horizon, prospect, perspective, outlook,** survey, visible horizon; range, scan, scope; line of sight, sightline, line of vision; naked eye; command, domination, outlook over; **viewpoint, observation point** 27.8

VERBS **4 show,** show up, show through, shine out *or* through, **surface, appear** 33.8, **be visible,** be seen, be revealed, be evident, be noticeable, be obvious, meet the gaze, impinge on the eye, present to the eye, meet *or* catch *or* hit *or* strike the eye; **stand out,** stand forth, loom large, glare, **stare one in the face,** hit one in the eye, **stick out like a sore thumb;** dominate; emerge, come into view, materialize

5 be exposed, be conspicuous, have high visibility, stick out, hang out <nf>, crop out; live in a glass house; have *or* keep a high profile

ADJS **6 visible,** visual, **perceptible,** perceivable, **discernible, seeable,** viewable, witnessable, beholdable, observable, detectable, noticeable, recognizable, to be seen; **in sight,** in view, in plain sight, in full view, present to the eyes, before one's eyes, under one's eyes, open, naked, outcropping, hanging out <nf>, exposed, showing, open *or* exposed to view; **evident,** in evidence, **manifest, apparent;** revealed, disclosed, unhidden, unconcealed, unclouded, undisguised

7 **distinct, plain, clear, obvious, evident, patent,** unmistakable, unmissable, not to be mistaken, much in evidence, plain to be seen, for all to see, showing for all to see, apparent, plain as a pikestaff, plain as the nose on one's face, plain as day, clear as day, plain as plain can be, big as life and twice as ugly; **definite, defined, well-defined,** well-marked, well-resolved, in focus; **clear-cut,** clean-cut; crystal-clear, clear as crystal; **conspicuous,** glaring, staring, **prominent,** pronounced, well-pronounced, in bold *or* strong *or* high relief, high-profile; identifiable, recognizable

ADVS 8 **visibly, perceptibly,** perceivably, discernibly, seeably, recognizably, observably, markedly, noticeably; **manifestly, apparently,** evidently; **distinctly, clearly,** with clarity *or* crystal clarity, **plainly,** obviously, patently, definitely, unmistakably; conspicuously, undisguisedly, unconcealedly, prominently, pronouncedly, glaringly, starkly, staringly

32 INVISIBILITY

NOUNS 1 **invisibility,** imperceptibility, unperceivability, undetectability, indiscernibility, unseeableness, viewlessness; nonappearance; disappearance 34; the invisible, the unseen; more than meets the eye; unsubstantiality 764, immateriality 1053, **secrecy** 345, **concealment** 346; hidden depths, tip of the iceberg; zero visibility

2 **inconspicuousness,** half-visibility, semivisibility, low profile, latency; **indistinctness, unclearness,** unplainness, **faintness,** paleness, feebleness, weakness, **dimness,** bedimming, bleariness, darkness, shadowiness, **vagueness,** vague appearance, indefiniteness, obscurity, uncertainty, indistinguishability; **blurriness,** blur, soft focus, defocus, **fuzziness, haziness,** mistiness, filminess, fogginess; blackout, brownout

VERBS 3 be invisible *or* unseen, escape notice; lie hid 346.8, **blush unseen;** disappear 34.2; white out, black out

4 **blur, dim, pale,** soften, film, mist, fog; defocus, lose resolution *or* sharpness *or* distinctness, go soft at the edges

ADJS 5 **invisible; imperceptible,** unperceivable, **indiscernible,** undiscernible, undetectable,

unseeable, viewless, unbeholdable, unapparent, insensible; **out of sight,** *à perte de vue* <Fr>, out of range; **secret** 345.11,15; **unseen,** sightless, unbeheld, unviewed, unwitnessed, unobserved, unnoticed, unperceived; unsubstantial, transparent; behind the curtain *or* scenes; disguised, camouflaged, hidden, **concealed** 346.11,14; undisclosed, unrevealed, *in petto* <L>; latent, unrealized, submerged

6 **inconspicuous,** half-visible, semivisible, low-profile; **indistinct, unclear,** unplain, **indefinite,** undefined, ill-defined, ill-marked, **faint,** pale, feeble, weak, **dim,** dark, **shadowy, vague, obscure,** indistinguishable, unrecognizable; half-seen, merely glimpsed; low-profile, half-seen, low-definition; uncertain, confused, out of focus, **blurred, blurry,** bleared, bleary, blear, **fuzzy, hazy,** misty, filmy, foggy

33 APPEARANCE

NOUNS 1 **appearance, appearing,** apparition, coming, forthcoming, showing-up, coming forth, coming on the scene, making the scene <nf>, putting in an appearance, arrival; **emergence,** issuing, issuance; **arising,** rise, rising, occurrence; **materialization, materializing,** coming into being; **manifestation,** realization, incarnation, revelation, showing-forth; epiphany, theophany, avatar, ostent <old>; **presentation, disclosure, exposure,** opening, unfolding, unfoldment, showing; rising of the curtain

2 **appearance,** exterior, externals, **mere externals, facade,** outside, **show, outward show, image,** display, front <nf>, outward *or* external appearance, surface appearance, surface show, vain show, apparent character, public image, window dressing, cosmetics; whitewash; whited sepulcher; **glitz** *and* tinsel <nf>, gaudiness, speciousness, meretriciousness, superficies, **superficiality;** PR *and* flack <nf>; pretense

3 aspect, look, view; feature, lineaments; **seeming, semblance, image,** imago, icon, eidolon, likeness, simulacrum; guise, mien; effect, impression, total effect *or* impression; **form, shape,** figure, configuration, gestalt; **manner,** fashion, wise, guise, style; **respect, regard,** reference, light; **phase; facet, side,** angle, viewpoint 27.7, slant *and* twist *and* spin <nf>

4 **looks, features, lineaments,** traits, lines; **countenance,** face, visage, feature, favor, brow, physiognomy; cast of countenance, **cut of one's jib** <nf>, facial appearance *or* expression, cast, turn; **look, air, mien,** demeanor, carriage, bearing, port,

deportment, posture, stance, poise, presence; guise, garb, dress, complexion, color

5 <thing appearing> **apparition, appearance,** phenomenon, semblance; **vision, image, shape, form,** figure, presence; false image, mirage, phasm <old>, specter, **phantom** 988.1

6 **view, scene, sight; prospect, outlook, lookout, vista, perspective; scenery,** scenic view; panorama, sweep; scape, **landscape,** seascape, riverscape, waterscape, airscape, skyscape, cloudscape, cityscape, townscape; bird's-eye view, worm's-eye view; best seat in the house

7 **spectacle, sight;** exhibit, **exhibition,** exposition, **show, stage show** 704.4, **display, presentation,** representation; dog and pony show; tableau, tableau vivant; panorama, diorama, cosmorama, myriorama, cyclorama, georama; *son et lumière* <Fr>, sound-and-light show; phantasmagoria, shifting scene, light show; psychedelic show; **pageant,** pageantry; parade, pomp

VERBS **8** **appear,** become visible; **arrive, make one's appearance,** make *or* put in an appearance, appear on the scene, make the scene *and* weigh in <nf>, appear to one's eyes, meet *or* catch *or* strike the eye, **come in sight** *or* **view, show,** show oneself, show one's face, nip in <nf>, **show up** <nf>, **turn up,** come, **materialize,** pop up, present oneself, present oneself to view, **manifest oneself,** become manifest, **reveal oneself,** discover oneself, uncover oneself, declare oneself, expose *or* betray oneself, flash; **come to light,** see the light, see the light of day; **emerge,** issue, issue forth, stream forth, come forth, come to the fore, present itself, come out, come forward, come to the surface, come one's way, come to hand, come into the picture; enter 189.7, come upon the stage; **rise, arise,** rear its head; look forth, peer *or* peep out; crop out, outcrop; loom, heave in sight, appear on the horizon; crawl out of the woodwork; fade in, wax

9 **burst forth,** break forth, debouch, erupt, irrupt, explode; **pop up, bob up** <nf>, start up, spring up, burst upon the view; flare up, flash, gleam

10 appear to be, seem to be, **appear, seem, look,** feel, sound, look to be, appear to one's eyes, have *or* present the appearance of, give the feeling of, strike one as, come on as <nf>; **appear like, seem like, look like,** have *or* wear the look of, **sound like; have every appearance of,** have all the earmarks of, have all the features of, show signs of, have every sign *or* indication of; assume the guise of, take the shape of, exhibit the form of

ADJS **11** **apparent,** appearing, **seeming, ostensible;** outward, surface, superficial; material, incarnate; **visible** 31.6

ADVS **12** **apparently, seemingly, ostensibly, to** *or* by all appearances, to *or* by all accounts, to all seeming, evidently, as it seems, to the eye; on the face of it, *prima facie* <L>; on the surface, outwardly, superficially; at first sight *or* view, at the first blush

34 DISAPPEARANCE

NOUNS **1** **disappearance,** disappearing, **vanishing,** vanishment; **going, passing, departure, loss;** dissipation, dispersion; dissolution, dissolving, melting, evaporation, evanescence, dematerialization 1053.5; fade, fadeout, fading, fadeaway, blackout; wane, ebb; wipe, wipeout, wipeoff, erasure; eclipse, occultation, blocking; sunset; delitescence; vanishing point; elimination 773.2; extinction 395.6; disappearing act

VERBS **2** **disappear, vanish,** vanish from sight, do a vanishing act <nf>, depart, fly, **flee** 368.10, go, be gone, **go away,** pass, pass out *or* away, pass out of sight, exit, pull up stakes <nf>, leave the scene *or* stage, clear out, pass out of the picture, pass *or* retire from sight, become lost to sight, be seen no more, take a powder; **perish, die,** die off; die out *or* away, dwindle, wane, fade, **fade out** *or* **away,** do a fade-out <nf>; sink, sink away, dissolve, melt, melt away, dematerialize 1053.6, evaporate, evanesce, **vanish** *or* **disappear into thin air,** go up in smoke; disperse, dispel, dissipate; cease, cease to exist, **cease to be;** cease publication, go out of print, go off the air, become obsolete, close down; leave no trace; waste, waste away, erode, be consumed, wear away; undergo *or* suffer an eclipse; **hide** 346.8; blend into the background

ADJS **3** **vanishing, disappearing,** passing, fleeting, fugitive, transient, flying, fading, dissolving, melting, evaporating, evanescent, waning, here today gone tomorrow

4 **gone,** away, gone away, past and gone, extinct, missing, no more, poof <nf>, lost, lost to sight *or* view, long-lost, **out of sight; unaccounted for;** nonexistent; out of the picture

35 COLOR

NOUNS **1** **color, hue; tint,** tinct, tincture, **tinge, shade, tone,** cast; key; **coloring, coloration;** color harmony, color balance, color scheme; decorator color; **complexion,** skin color *or* coloring *or* tone, pigmentation; chromatism, chromaticism, chromism; achromatism 36.1; natural color; undercolor; pallor 36.2; color perception, color vision, color blindness

2 warmth, warmth of color, warm color; **blush, flush, glow,** healthy glow or hue

3 softness, soft color, subtle color, pale color, pastel, pastel color, pastel shade

4 colorfulness, color, bright color, pure color, **brightness, brilliance, vividness,** intensity, saturation; **richness,** gorgeousness, gaiety; riot or splash of color; Technicolor <trademark>; Day-Glo <trademark>; variegation, multicolor, polychrome; color scheme, color coordination

5 garishness, loudness, luridness, glitz <nf>, gaudiness 501.3; loud or screaming color <nf>; shocking pink, jaundiced yellow, chartreuse; clashing colors, color clash

6 color quality; chroma, Munsell chroma, brightness, purity, saturation; **hue,** value, lightness; colorimetric quality, chromaticity, chromaticness; tint, **tone;** chromatic color, achromatic or neutral color; warm color; cool color; tinge, shade

7 color system, chromaticity diagram, color triangle, Maxwell triangle; hue cycle, color disk, color wheel, color circle, chromatic circle, color cycle or gamut, color chart; Munsell scale; color solid; fundamental colors; **primary color,** primary pigment, primary; secondary color, secondary; tertiary color, tertiary; complementary color; chromaticity coordinate; color mixture curve or function; spectral color, spectrum color, pure or full color; metamer; **spectrum,** solar spectrum, color spectrum, chromatic spectrum, color index; rainbow; monochrome; demitint, half tint, halftone, mezzotint, half-light, patina; chromatic aberration

8 <coloring matter> **color, coloring, colorant,** tinction, tincture, **pigment, stain;** chromogen; **dye,** dyestuff, artificial coloring, food coloring, color filter, color gelatin; paint, distemper, tempera, enamel, glaze; coat, coating, **coat of paint; undercoat,** undercoating, **primer,** priming, prime coat, **ground, flat coat,** dead-color; interior paint, exterior paint, floor enamel; wash, wash coat, flat wash, colorwash, whitewash; opaque color, transparent color; medium, vehicle; drier; thinner; turpentine, turps <nf>; additive color, subtractive color; artist's colors, colored pencils, crayons, chalk

9 <persons according to hair color> **brunet; blond,** Goldilocks; bleached blond, peroxide blond; ash blond, platinum blond, strawberry blond, honey blond, dirty blond; **towhead; redhead,** carrottop <nf>; gray

10 <science of colors> chromatology; chromatics, chromatography, chromatoscopy, colorimetry; spectrum analysis, spectroscopy, spectrometry, spectrography; color theory

11 <applying color> **coloring,** coloration; **staining, dyeing; tie-dyeing; tinting,** tinging, tinction; pigmentation; illumination, emblazonry; color printing; lithography

12 painting, paint-work, coating, covering; **enameling,** glossing, glazing; **varnishing,** japanning, lacquering, shellacking; staining; **calcimining, whitewashing;** gilding; stippling; frescoing, fresco; undercoating, priming; watercoloring, gouache, oil-painting, crayoning

13 spectrum, rainbow; red, orange, yellow, green, blue, indigo, violet

VERBS **14 color,** hue, lay on color; **tinge, tint,** tinct, **tincture,** tone, complexion; pigment; bedizen; variegate, colorize; **stain, dye,** dip, tie-dye; imbue; deep-dye, fast-dye, double-dye, dye in the wool, yarn-dye; ingrain, grain; shade, shadow; illuminate, emblazon; **paint,** apply paint, paint up, **coat,** cover, face, watercolor, crayon; dab, **daub,** bedaub, smear, besmear, brush on paint, slap or slop on paint; **enamel,** gloss, glaze; **varnish,** japan, **lacquer, shellac; white out; calcimine, whitewash,** parget; wash; **gild,** begild, engild; stipple; fresco; distemper; undercoat, prime; emblazon; color-code

15 <be inharmonious> **clash,** conflict, collide, fight

ADJS **16 chromatic,** colorational; **coloring,** colorific, colorative, tinctorial, tingent; pigmental, pigmentary; monochrome, monochromic, monochromatic; dichromatic; many-colored, parti-colored, medley or motley <old>, rainbow, **variegated** 47.9, polychromatic, multicolored, kaleidoscopic, Technicolored; prismatic, spectral; matching, toning, harmonious; warm, glowing; cool, cold

17 colored, hued, in color, colorized, in Technicolor <trademark>; **tinged, tinted,** tinctured, tinct, toned; **painted, enameled; stained, dyed;** tie-dyed; imbued; complexioned, complected <nf>; full-colored, full; deep, deep-colored; wash-colored; washed

18 deep-dyed, fast-dyed, double-dyed, **dyed-in-the-wool;** ingrained, ingrain; permanent, colorfast, fast, fadeless, unfading, indelible, constant

19 colorful, colory; **bright, vivid,** intense, **rich,** exotic, **brilliant,** burning, **gorgeous, gay,** bright-hued, bright-colored, rich-colored, gay-colored, high-colored, deep-colored

20 garish, lurid, loud, screaming, shrieking, glaring, flaring, flashy, glitzy <nf>, flaunting, crude, blinding, overbright, raw, gaudy 501.20; Day-Glo <trademark>

21 off-color, off-tone; **inharmonious, discordant,** incongruous, **harsh,** clashing, conflicting, colliding

22 soft-colored, soft-hued, **soft,** softened, **subdued,** understated, muted, delicate, light, creamy, peaches-and-cream, **pastel, pale,** palish, subtle, mellow, delicate, quiet, tender, sweet; pearly, nacreous, mother-of-pearl, iridescent, opalescent; patinaed; somber, simple, sober, sad; flat, eggshell, semigloss, gloss; weathered, heathered

WORD ELEMENTS **23** -chroia, -chromasia, chrom-, chromo-, chromat-, chromato-; -phyll; pigmento-; -chrome, -chromia, -chromy; pallidi-; -chroic, -chroous

36 COLORLESSNESS

NOUNS **1 colorlessness,** lack *or* absence of color, huelessness, tonelessness, achromatism, achromaticity; dullness, lackluster 1027.5; neutral hue *or* tint

2 **paleness, dimness,** weakness, **faintness,** fadedness; lightness, fairness; **pallor,** pallidity, pallidness, prison pallor, **wanness, sallowness,** pastiness, ashiness; wheyface; muddiness, dullness; grayness, griseousness; **anemia,** hypochromic anemia, hypochromia, chloranemia; bloodlessness, exsanguination; **ghastliness, haggardness,** lividness, sickly hue, sickliness, deadly *or* deathly pallor, deathly hue, cadaverousness

3 **decoloration,** decolorizing, decolorization, discoloration, achromatization, lightening; **fading, paling; dimming, bedimming; whitening,** blanching, etiolation, whiteness, albinism, pigment deficiency; bleeding, bleeding white; weathering

4 **bleach,** bleaching, bleaching agent *or* substance; whitener; color remover, decolorant, decolorizer, achromatizer

VERBS **5** decolor, decolorize, discolor, achromatize, etiolate; **fade, wash out; dim, dull, tarnish,** tone down; **pale, whiten,** blanch, drain, drain of color; **bleach,** peroxide; etiolate

6 **lose color, fade,** fade out; **bleach,** bleach out; **pale, turn pale,** grow pale, **change color,** change countenance, turn white, **whiten, blanch,** wan; come out in the wash; discolor

ADJS **7 colorless, hueless,** toneless, uncolored, achromic, achromatic, achromatous, unpigmented; neutral; dull, flat, mat, dead, dingy, muddy, leaden, lusterless, lackluster 1027.17; **faded, washed-out,** dimmed, discolored, decolored, etiolated, weathered; **pale, dim,** weak, **faint; pallid, wan, sallow,** fallow; pale *or* blue *or* green around the gills, drained of color; **white,** white as a sheet; crystal; **pasty,** mealy, waxen; **ashen,** ashy, ashen-hued, cinereous, cineritious, gray, griseous,

mousy, dingy; **anemic,** hypochromic, chloranemic; bloodless, exsanguine, exsanguinated, exsanguineous, bled white; **ghastly,** livid, lurid, **haggard,** cadaverous, unhealthy, sickly, deadly *or* deathly pale; pale as death *or* a ghost *or* a corpse; pale-faced, tallow-faced, wheyfaced, white-skinned

8 **bleached,** decolored, decolorized, achromatized, whitened, blanched, lightened, bleached out, bleached white; drained, drained of color; etiolated

9 **light, fair,** light-colored, light-hued; pastel; whitish 37.8

WORD ELEMENTS **10** achromat-, achromato-, achro-, achroö-

37 WHITENESS

NOUNS **1 whiteness, white, whitishness;** albescence; **lightness, fairness;** paleness 36.2; silveriness; snowiness, frostiness; chalkiness; pearliness; **creaminess,** off-whiteness, chalkiness; blondness; hoariness, grizzliness, canescence; milkiness, lactescence; glaucousness; glaucescence; silver; albinism, achroma, achromasia, achromatosis; albino; leukoderma, vitiligo; wheyface; white race 312.2,3

2 <comparisons> alabaster, bone, chalk, cream, ivory, lily, lime, milk, pearl, sheet, swan, sheep, fleece, flour, foam, paper, phantom, silver, snow, driven snow, tallow, teeth, wax, wool

3 **whitening,** albification, blanching; etiolation; **whitewashing; bleaching** 36.4; silvering, frosting, grizzling

4 whitening agent, whitener, whiting, whitening, **whitewash,** calcimine; pipe clay; correction fluid, Wite-Out <trademark>; bleach

VERBS **5 whiten,** white, etiolate, **blanch; bleach** 36.5; pale, blench; decolorize; fade; silver, grizzle, frost, besnow; chalk

6 **whitewash,** white <old>, calcimine; pipe-clay; clean

ADJS **7 white,** pure white, white as alabaster *or* bone *or* chalk *or* snow, etc 37.2, **snow-white,** snowy, niveous, frosty, frosted; **hoary,** hoar, **grizzled,** grizzly, griseous, canescent; silver, **silvery,** silvered, argent <heraldry>, argentine; platinum; chalky, cretaceous; fleece- *or* fleecy-white; swan-white; foam-white; **milk-white,** milky, lactescent; marble, marmoreal; lily-white, white as a lily; white as a sheet, wheyfaced, ghastly; albescent; whitened, bleached, blanched, achromatic; crystal

8 **whitish,** whity, albescent; **light, fair;** pale 36.7; off-white; eggshell; glaucous, glaucescent; pearl,

pearly, pearly-white, pearl-white; alabaster, alabastrine; cream, **creamy;** ivory, ivory-white; gray-white; dun-white

9 **blond** or blonde; flaxen-haired, fair-haired; artificial blond, bleached-blond, peroxide-blond; ash-blond, platinum-blond, strawberry-blond, honey-blond, blond-headed, blond-haired; **towheaded,** tow-haired; golden-haired 43.5; white-haired

10 **albino,** albinic, albinistic, albinal

WORD ELEMENTS 11 alb-, albo-, leuc-, leuco-, leuk-, leuko-

12 **white color varieties**

alabaster	milk-white
antimony white	nacre
argent	off-white
bismuth white	oyster white
blond	Paris white
bone white	pearl or pearl white
chalk	platinum
Chinese white	pure white
columbine	putty
dove	silver
Dutch white	snow white
eggshell	strontium white
flake white	swan white
gauze	titanium white
ivory	white lead
lily white	zinc white
marble	

38 BLACKNESS

NOUNS 1 **blackness,** nigritude, nigrescence; inkiness; **black, sable, ebony;** melanism; black race 312.2,3; darkness 1027

2 **darkness, darkishness,** darksomeness, blackishness; total darkness, lightlessness; **swarthiness,** swartness, swarth; **duskiness,** duskness; pitchiness; soberness, sobriety, **somberness,** graveness, sadness, funereality; hostility, sullenness, anger, black mood, black looks, black words

3 **dinginess, griminess, smokiness,** sootiness, fuliginousness, fuliginosity, smudginess, smuttiness, blotchiness, dirtiness, **muddiness,** murkiness

4 <comparisons> ebony or ebon <old>, jet, ink, sloe, pitch, tar, coal, charcoal, smoke, soot, smut, raven, obsidian, sable, crow, night, hell, sin, one's hat <Brit>, pitch

5 **blackening, darkening,** nigrification, melanization, melanism, melanosis, denigration; shading; **smudging,** smutching, **smirching;** smudge, smutch, smirch, smut

6 **blacking,** blackening, blackening agent, blackwash; charcoal, burnt cork, black ink; lampblack, carbon black, stove black, gas black, soot; japan; melanin

VERBS 7 **blacken,** black, nigrify, melanize, denigrate; **darken,** bedarken; shade, shadow; blackwash, ink, charcoal, cork; **smudge,** smutch, **smirch,** besmirch, murk, blotch, blot, dinge, dirty; smut, soot; smoke, oversmoke, singe, scorch, char; ebonize; **smear** 661.9/512.10, **blacken one's name** or **reputation,** give one a black eye; japan, niello

ADJS 8 **black,** black as ink or pitch or tar or coal, etc 38.4; **sable** <heraldry>, nigrous, nigrescent; **ebony,** ebon; deep black, of the deepest dye; **pitch-black, pitch-dark,** pitchy, black or dark as pitch, tar-black, tarry; night-black, night-dark, black or dark as night; midnight, black as midnight; **inky,** inky-black, atramentous, achromatic, ink-black, black as ink; **jet-black,** jet, jetty; **coal-black,** coaly, black as coal, coal-black; sloe, sloe-black, sloe-colored; raven, **raven-black,** black as a crow; blue-black, brown-black; **dark** 1027.13–16

9 **dark,** dark-colored, **darkish,** darksome, blackish; nigrescent; **swarthy,** swart; **dusky,** dusk; **somber,** sombrous, **sober, grave,** sad, funereal; hostile, sullen, angry; achromatic

10 **dark-skinned,** black-skinned, **dark-complexioned; black, colored;** swarthy, swart; melanian, melanic, melanotic, melanistic, melanous

11 **dingy, grimy, smoky,** sooty, fuliginous, **smudgy,** smutty, blotchy, dirty, **muddy,** murky, smirched, besmirched, dusky; blackened, singed, charred

12 **livid, black-and-blue**

13 **black-haired, raven-haired,** raven-tressed, black-locked, dark-haired; brunet or brunette

WORD ELEMENTS 14 atro-, mel-, mela-, melo-, melano-, melam-

15 **black color varieties**

aniline black	japan
arsenic black	jet or jet black
black	lampblack
blue-black	night black
Brunswick black	nigrosine
carbon black	pitch-black
charcoal black	Prussian black
chrome black	pure black
coal black	raven black
corbeau	sable
direct black	slate black
drop black	sloe black
ebony	soot black
ink black	subfusc
ivory black	sulfur black

39 GRAYNESS

NOUNS **1 grayness, gray,** grayishness, canescence; glaucousness, glaucescence; silveriness; ashiness; neutral tint; smokiness; mousiness; slatiness; leadenness; lividness, lividity; dullness, drabness, soberness, somberness; grisaille; oyster, taupe, greige; gunmetal, iron, lead, pewter, silver, slate, steel

2 gray-haired *or* **gray-headed person,** gray-hair, graybeard, grisard, salt-and-pepper, hoariness

VERBS **3 gray,** grizzle, silver, frost

ADJS **4 gray, grayish,** gray-colored, gray-hued, gray-toned, grayed, griseous; canescent; iron-gray, steely, steel-gray; Quaker-gray, Quaker-colored; acier, gray-drab; Oxford gray; dove-gray, dove-colored; pearl-gray, pearl, pearly; silver-gray, silver, silvery, silvered; **grizzly,** grizzled, grizzle; ash-gray, ashen, ashy, cinerous, cinereous, cineritious, cinereal; dusty, dust-gray; smoky, smoke-gray; charcoal-gray; slaty, slate-colored; leaden, livid, lead-gray, iron-gray; glaucous, glaucescent; wolf-gray; mousy, mouse-gray, mouse-colored; taupe; dapple-gray, dappled-gray; gray-spotted, gray-speckled, salt-and-pepper; gray-black, gray-brown, etc; taupe, ecru, greige; neutral; **dull, dingy,** dismal, **somber, sober, sad, dreary;** winter-gray, hoar, hoary, frost-gray, rime-gray

5 gray-haired, gray-headed, silver-headed; hoar, hoary, hoary-haired, grizzled; gray-bearded, silver-bearded, salt-and-pepper *or* pepper-and-salt; frosty

6 gray color varieties

ash *or* ash gray	lilac gray
bat	merle
battleship gray	mole gray
blue-gray	moleskin
cadet gray	mouse
charcoal gray	mushroom
cinder	neutral
cloud	nutria
crystal gray	obsidian
dark gray	olive gray
dove	opal gray
field gray	Oxford gray
flint	oyster gray
French gray	pale gray
glaucous gray	pearl *or* pearl gray
granite	pelican
gray *or* grey	plumbago
gray-white	powder gray
greige *or* grege	Quaker gray
gun metal	salt-and-pepper *or*
iron	pepper-and-salt
lead	shell gray
light gray	silver

silver-gray	steel gray
slate gray	taupe
smoke gray	zinc gray

40 BROWNNESS

NOUNS **1 brownness, brownishness, brown,** browning, infuscation; brown race 312.2; ochre, sepia, raw sienna, burnt sienna, raw umber, burnt umber; caramel, pumpernickel, coffee, chocolate, paper bag

VERBS **2 brown,** embrown, infuscate; rust; **tan, bronze,** suntan; sunburn, burn; fry, sauté, scorch, braise; toast; caramelize

ADJS **3 brown, brownish;** cinnamon, hazel; fuscous; **brunet,** brune; tawny, fulvous; dark brown; tan, tan-colored; tan-faced, tan-skinned, tanned, sun-tanned; khaki, khaki-colored; drab, olive-drab; **dun,** dun-brown, dun-drab, dun-olive; beige, grege, buff, biscuit, mushroom; **chocolate,** chocolate-colored, chocolate-brown; cocoa, cocoa-colored, cocoa-brown; coffee, coffee-colored, coffee-brown; toast, toast-brown; nut-brown; oatmeal; walnut, walnut-brown; seal, seal-brown; fawn, fawn-colored; grayish-brown; brownish-gray, fuscous, taupe, mouse-dun, mouse-brown, tweed; snuff-colored, snuff-brown, mummy-brown; umber, umber-colored, umber-brown; olive-brown; **sepia;** sorrel; sable; yellowish-brown, brownish-yellow; lurid <old>; brown as a berry, berry-brown

4 reddish-brown, rufous-brown, brownish-red; roan; henna; terra-cotta; rufous, foxy; livid-brown; **mahogany,** mahogany-brown; auburn, Titian; **russet,** russety; rust, rust-colored, rusty, ferruginous, rubiginous; liver-colored, liver-brown; **bronze,** bronze-brown, bronze-colored, bronzed, brazen; copper, coppery, copperish, cupreous, copper-colored; **chestnut,** chestnut-brown, castaneous; bay, bay-colored; bayard <old>; sunburned, adust <old>

5 brunet *or* **brunette; brown-haired; auburn-haired;** xanthous

6 brown color varieties

acorn	beige
alesan	biscuit
amber	Bismarck brown
antique bronze	bistre
antique brown	bone brown
antique drab	Bordeaux
auburn	brick
autumn leaf	brindle
baize	bronze
bay	brown
beaver	brown madder

brunet *or* brunette
buckthorn brown
buff
burgundy
burnt almond
burnt ocher
burnt sienna
burnt umber
butternut
café au lait
café noir
camel
caramel
Castilian brown
chestnut
chocolate
cinnamon
cocoa
coconut
coffee
Cologne brown
copper
cordovan
dark brown
dead leaf
doeskin
drab
Dresden brown
dun
earth
ecru
fallow
fawn
foliage brown
fox
ginger
Havana brown
hazel
henna
Italian earth
Italian ocher
ivory brown
khaki
leather
light brown
light red-brown
liver brown
madder brown
mahogany
manganese brown

manila
maple sugar
Mars brown
mineral brown
mink
mocha
nougat
nut
nutmeg
nutria
oatmeal
ocher
olive brown
orange-brown
otter brown
oxblood
pale brown
peat brown
peppercorn
putty
raffia
raw sienna
raw umber
reddish-brown
roan
russet
rust
sand
sandalwood
seal brown
sepia
sienna
sorrel
suntan
tan
tanaura
taupe
tawny
terra cotta
terra sienna
terra umbra
Titian
toast
topaz
tortoiseshell
umber
Vandyke brown *or*
  Verona brown
walnut
yellow-brown

7 reddish-brown color varieties

auburn
baize
bay
brick
burgundy
burnt ocher
burnt sienna
caramel

Castilian brown
chestnut
chocolate
cinnamon
cocoa
Columbian red
cordovan
ginger

henna
India red
light red-brown
liver
madder brown
mahogany
nutmeg
ocher
oxblood
piccolopasso red
red robin
roan

russet
rust
sand
sedge
sepia
sienna
sorrel
terra cotta
titian
Venetian red
vermilion *or*
  vermeil

41 REDNESS

NOUNS **1 redness, reddishness,** rufosity, rubricity; **red,** *rouge* <Fr>, gules <heraldry>; rubicundity, **ruddiness,** color, high color, floridness, floridity; rubor, erythema, erythroderma; erythrism; reddish brown; red race 312.3; "any color, so long as it's red"—Eugene Field; carmine, crimson, henna, rouge, vermilion, cerise; cherry, ruby, fire engine

2 pinkness, pinkishness; rosiness; pink, rose

3 reddening, rubefaction, rubification, rubescence, erubescence, rufescence; **coloring,** mantling, crimsoning, **blushing, flushing; blush,** flush, glow, bloom, rosiness; hectic, hectic flush; flush syndrome, alcohol flush syndrome; rubefacient

VERBS **4** <make red> **redden, rouge,** ruddle, rubefy, raddle, rubric; warm, inflame; crimson, encrimson; vermilion, madder, miniate, henna, rust, carmine; incarnadine, pinkify; **blush;** red-ink, red-pencil, lipstick

5 redden, turn *or* grow red, **color,** color up, **mantle, blush, flush, crimson;** flame, glow

ADJS **6 red, reddish,** gules <heraldry>, red-colored, red-hued, red-dyed, red-looking; **ruddy,** ruddied, rubicund; rubric *or* rubrical, rubricate, rubricose; rufescent, rufous, rufulous; warm, hot, glowing; bright-red; fiery, flaming, flame-colored, flame-red, fire-red, red as fire, lurid, red as a hot *or* live coal; reddened, inflamed; **scarlet, vermilion, vermeil; crimson;** rubiate; maroon; damask; puce; stammel; cerise; iron-red; cardinal, cardinal-red; cherry, cherry-colored, cherry-red; carmine, incarmined; **ruby,** ruby-colored, ruby-red; wine, port-wine, wine-colored, wine-red, vinaceous; carnation, carnation-red; brick-red, bricky, tile-red, lateritious; rust, rust-red, rusty, ferruginous, rubiginous; beet-red, red as a beet; lobster-red, red as a lobster; red as a turkey-cock; copper-red, carnelian; russet; Titian, Titian-red; infrared; reddish-amber, reddish-gray, etc; reddish-brown 40.4

7 **sanguine,** sanguineous, **blood-red,** blood-colored, bloody-red, bloody, gory, red as blood

8 **pink, pinkish,** pinky; **rose, rosy,** rose-colored, rose-hued, rose-red, roseate; primrose; flesh-colored, flesh-pink, incarnadine; coral, coral-colored, coral-red, coralline; salmon, salmon-colored, salmon-pink; damask, carnation; fuchsia

9 **red-complexioned,** ruddy-complexioned, warm-complexioned, red-fleshed, red-faced, ruddy-faced, apple-cheeked, **ruddy,** rubicund, **florid,** sanguine, full-blooded; blowzy, blowzed; rosy, **rosy-cheeked;** glowing, blooming; hectic, blushing, rouged, flushed, flush; burnt, sunburned; erythematous

10 **redheaded,** red-haired, red-polled, red-bearded; erythristic; red-crested, red-crowned, red-tufted; ginger-haired, carroty, carrot-topped, chestnut, auburn, Titian, xanthous

11 reddening, blushing, flushing, coloring; rubescent, erubescent; rubificative, rubrific; rubefacient

12 **pink color varieties**

amaranth pink	opera pink
annatto	orange-pink
begonia	orchid pink
blush	orchid rose
burnt rose	pale pink
cameo pink	peach red
carnation	peach blossom pink
casino pink	petal pink
chrome primrose	primrose
coral pink	purplish pink
deep pink	red-pink *or*
fiesta	reddish pink
flamingo	rose
flesh pink	rose pink
geranium pink	rose quartz
hot pink	royal pink
incarnadine	salmon
livid pink	scarlet madder
mallow pink	shell pink
neon pink	shocking pink
nymph	tea rose
ombre	watermelon

13 **red color varieties**

alizarin crimson	brownish red
alpenglow	Burgundy
annatto	burnt carmine
beet red	burnt ocher
blood red	cadmium red
blush	cardinal
bois de rose	carmine
bougainvillea	carnation
Bordeaux	carnelian
brick red	Castillian red
bright red	cerise
bright rose	cherry

Chinese red	old rose
chrome red	orange-red
cinnabar	oxblood
claret	palladium red
cochineal	paprika
coral pink	peach
cordovan	Persian red
cranberry	pinkish red
crimson	ponceau
damask	poppy
dark red	Prussian red
deep red	puce
English red	purple-red
faded rose	red ocher
fire red	rhodamine
fire-engine red	rose madder
flame red	royal red
fuchsia	ruby
garnet	ruddle
geranium	rust
grenadine	safranine
gules	scarlet
hellebore red	solferino
iron red	stammel
lake *or* lac	strawberry
light red	terra rosa
lobster	tile red
madder	Turkey red
magenta	Venetian red
maroon	vermeil
Mars red	vermilion
murrey	wild cherry
old red	wine

42 ORANGENESS

NOUNS 1 **orangeness,** oranginess; **orange;** cadmium orange, carotene

ADJS 2 **orange, orangeish,** orangey, orange-hued, reddish-yellow; ocherous *or* ochery, ochreous, ochroid, ocherish; old gold; saffron; pumpkin, pumpkin-colored; tangerine, tangerine-colored; apricot, peach, cantaloupe, salmon, mango; carroty, carrot-colored; orange-red, orange-yellow, red-orange, reddish-orange, yellow-orange

3 **orange color varieties**

acid orange	chrome orange
apricot	copper
aurora	copper red
brass	dark orange
burnt ocher	Dutch orange
burnt orange	Florida gold
burnt Roman ocher	helianthin
burnt sienna	hyacinth
cadmium orange	madder orange
carnelian	mandarin
carotene	marigold
carrot	Mars orange

melon
methyl orange
Mikado orange
neon orange
ocher
ocher orange
old gold
orange chrome
 yellow
orange lead
orange madder
orange mineral
orange ocher
orange vermilion
orange-red
orange-yellow
orpiment

pale orange
peach
pumpkin
raw sienna
realgar orange
red-orange
Rubens' madder
saffron
Spanish ocher
sunset orange
tangerine
Tangier ocher
terra cotta
titian *or* Titian
yellow carmine
yellow-orange
zinc orange

43 YELLOWNESS

NOUNS **1 yellowness, yellowishness;** goldenness, aureateness; **yellow,** gold, or <heraldry>; gildedness; fallowness; cadmium yellow, cadmium lemon

2 yellow skin, yellow complexion, sallowness; biliousness; xanthochroism; **jaundice,** yellow jaundice, icterus, xanthoderma, xanthism; yellow race 312.2,3

VERBS **3 yellow,** turn yellow; **gild,** begild, engild; aurify; sallow; **jaundice**

ADJS **4 yellow, yellowish,** yellowy; lutescent, luteous, luteolous; xanthic, xanthous; flavescent; **gold, golden,** gold-colored, golden-yellow, gilt, gilded, auric, aureate; sunshine-yellow; **canary,** canary-yellow; citron, citron-yellow, citreous; **lemon,** lemon-colored, lemon-yellow; sulfur-colored, sulfur-yellow; mustard, mustard-yellow; pale-yellow, **sallow,** fallow; cream, creamy, cream-colored; straw, straw-colored, tow-colored; flaxen, flaxen-colored, flax-colored; sandy, sand-colored; ocherous *or* ochery, ochreous, ochroid, ocherish; buff, buff-colored, buff-yellow; honey-colored; saffron, saffron-colored, saffron-yellow; primrose, primrose-colored, primrose-yellow; topaz-yellow; greenish-yellow, chartreuse; banana; maize

5 yellow-haired, golden-haired, tow-headed, tow-haired, auricomous, xanthous; blond 37.9

6 yellow-faced, yellow-complexioned, sallow, yellow-cheeked; **jaundiced,** xanthodermatous, icteric, icterical, bilious

7 yellow color varieties

acid yellow
amber
apricot yellow
arsenic yellow
auramine

aureate
aureolin
azo yellow
barium yellow
blond

brass
brazilin
brownish-yellow
buff
butter
cadmium yellow
calendula
canary
Cassel yellow
chalcedony
chamois
champagne
chartreuse yellow
chrome lemon
chrome yellow
citron
cobalt yellow
corn
cream
crocus
dandelion
ecru
flax
gamboge
gold
golden yellow
goldenrod
green-yellow
honey
jonquil
lemon
linen
madder yellow

maize
marigold yellow
mikado yellow
mustard
Naples yellow
ocher *or* ochre
oil yellow
old gold
orange-yellow
orpiment
pale yellow
palomino
Paris yellow
peach yellow
pear
primrose
purree
quince yellow
reed
saffron
sallow
sand
snapdragon
straw
sulfur
sunflower
sunshine yellow
topaz yellow
yellow madder
yellow ocher
yellowstone
yolk yellow
zinc yellow

44 GREENNESS

NOUNS **1 greenness,** viridity; greenishness, virescence, viridescence; verdantness, verdancy, **verdure,** glaucousness, glaucescence; **green,** greensickness, chlorosis, chloremia, chloranemia; chlorophyll; grass, emerald

2 verdigris, patina, aerugo; patination

VERBS **3 green;** verdigris, patinate, patinize

ADJS **4 green,** virid; **verdant,** verdurous, vert <heraldry>; grassy, leafy, leaved, foliaged; springlike, summerlike, summery, vernal, vernant, aestival; **greenish,** viridescent, virescent; **grass-green,** green as grass, grassy; citrine, citrinous; **olive,** olive-green, olivaceous; pea-green; avocado; jade; loden green; bottle-green; forest-green; sea-green; beryl-green, berylline; leek-green, porraceous <old>; holly, holly-green; ivy, ivy-green; emerald, emerald-green, smaragdine; chartreuse, yellow-green, yellowish-green, greenish-yellow; glaucous, glaucescent, glaucous green; blue-green, bluish-green, green-blue, greenish-blue; greensick, chlorotic, chloremic, chloranemic

5 verdigrisy, verdigrised, patinous, patinaed, patinated *or* patinized, aeruginous

6 green color varieties

absinthe	Kendal green
apple green	leaf green
aqua green	leek green
aquamarine	light green
avocado	lime
bay	Lincoln green
beryl	lizard
bice	loden
blue-green	lotus
bottle green	malachite
Brunswick green	marine
cadmium green	methyl green
celadon	mignonette
chartreuse *or* chartreuse	mint
green	moss
chrome green *or*	myrtle
chromium green	Niagara green
chrome oxide green	Nile green
chrysolite green	olive
citron green	pale green
civette green	Paris green
clair de lune	parrot
cobalt green	patina
corbeau	pea green
cucumber	pistachio green
cypress	Quaker green
dark green	reseda
drake	sage green
duck green	sap green
eau de nil	sea green *or* sea-water
Egyptian green	green
emerald	serpentine
fir green *or* fir	shamrock
flagstone	Spanish green
forest green	spruce
gallein	teal
glauconite	terre-verte
glaucous green	tourmaline
grass green	turquoise
gray-green	verdant green
green ocher	verdet
Guinea green	verdigris
gunpowder	vert
holly green	Vienna green
Irish green	viridian
ivy green	Wedgwood green
jade	willow green
Janus green	yellow-green
jungle green	yew
kelly green	zinc

45 BLUENESS

NOUNS 1 **blueness, bluishness;** azureness; **blue, azure**, cyan, indigo, ultramarine; lividness, lividity; cyanosis

VERBS 2 **blue,** azure

ADJS 3 **blue, bluish,** cerulescent, cerulean, ceruleous; cyanic, cyaneous, cyanean, cyanotic; **azure** <heraldry>, azurine, azurean, azureous, azured, azure-blue, azure-colored, azure-tinted; sky-blue, sky-colored, sky-dyed; ice-blue; light-blue, lightish-blue, pale-blue; dark-blue, deep-blue, midnight-blue, navy-blue; peacock-blue, pavonine, pavonian; beryl-blue, berylline; turquoise, turquoise-blue; aquamarine; cornflower; electric-blue; ultramarine; royal-blue; indigo; sapphire, sapphire-blue, sapphirine; Wedgwood-blue, robin's-egg blue; livid

4 blue color varieties

air force blue	ice blue
aniline blue	indigo
aquamarine	kingfisher blue
azul *or* azulene	lapis lazuli
azure	lavender blue
azurite blue	light blue
baby blue	lucerne
beryl	lupine
bice	madder blue
blue	marine blue
blue turquoise	midnight blue
blueberry	milori blue
bluebonnet	Napoleon blue
blue-gray	navy blue *or*
blue-green	navy
blue-violet	pale blue
bright blue	peacock blue
Brunswick blue	perse
cadet blue	Persian blue
calamine blue	powder blue
cerulean	Prussian blue
Chinese blue	purple-blue
cobalt blue	reddish blue
Copenhagen blue	robin's-egg blue
cornflower	royal blue
cyan	sapphire blue
dark blue	Saxe blue
daylight blue	sea blue
deep blue	sky blue
delft blue	slate blue
denim blue	smalt
Dresden blue	smoke blue
electric blue	steel blue
Empire blue	teal blue
flag blue	turquoise
French blue	ultramarine
gentian blue	Venetian blue
gray-blue	violet-blue
greenish blue	water blue
Havana lake	Wedgwood
Helvetia blue	blue
huckleberry	wisteria blue
hyacinth	woad
hydrangea	zaffer

46 PURPLENESS

NOUNS **1 purpleness, purplishness,** purpliness;
  purple; violet, lavender, lilac, magenta, mauve,
  amethyst**;** lividness, lividity, bruise
VERBS **2 purple,** empurple, purpurate <old>
ADJS **3 purple,** purpure <heraldry>, purpureal,
  purpureous, purpurean, purpurate <old>; royal
  purple; **purplish,** purply, purplescent, empurpled;
  violet, violaceous; plum, plum-colored, plum-
  purple; amethystine; **lavender,** lavender-blue; lilac;
  magenta; mauve; mulberry; orchid; pansy-purple,
  pansy-violet; raisin-colored; fuchsia, puce,
  aubergine, orchid; purple-blue; livid

4 purple color varieties

amaranth	madder violet
amethyst	magenta
aniline purple	maroon
Argyle purple	Mars violet
aubergine	mauve
blue-violet	monsignor
bluish purple	mulberry
Burgundy	orchid
violet	pale purple
campanula	pansy violet
cerise	periwinkle
clematis	phlox
dahlia	plum
damson	prune
dark purple	puce
deep purple	purple-blue
eggplant	purple-red
fuchsia	raisin
grape	raspberry
gridelin	red-violet
heliotrope	reddish purple
hyacinth	royal purple _or_ regal
imperial purple	purple
indigo	rubine
king's purple	solferino
lavender	tulip
light purple	Tyrian purple
lilac	violet
livid purple	wine purple
livid violet	wisteria

47 VARIEGATION
  <diversity of colors>

NOUNS **1 variegation, multicolor;** parti-color;
  medley _or_ mixture of colors, spectrum, rainbow of
  colors, rainbow, riot of color; polychrome,
  polychromatism; dichromatism, trichromatism,
  etc; dichroism, trichroism, etc
2 iridescence, iridization, irisation, **opalescence,**
  nacreousness, pearliness, chatoyancy, **play of
  colors** _or_ **light;** light show; moiré pattern, tabby;
  burelé _or_ burelage

3 spottiness, maculation, freckliness, speckliness,
  mottledness, mottlement, dappleness,
  dappledness, stippledness, spottedness,
  dottedness; **fleck, speck, speckle;** freckle; **spot,**
  dot, polka dot, macula, macule, blotch, splotch,
  patch, splash, bullet point; **mottle, dapple;**
  brindle; **stipple,** stippling, pointillism, pointillage;
  pinpointing; spattering
4 check, checker, checks, checking, checkerboard,
  chessboard; **plaid,** tartan; checker-work, variegated
  pattern, harlequin, colors in patches, crazy-work,
  patchwork; parquet, parquetry, marquetry, mosaic,
  tesserae, tessellation; crazy-paving <Brit>; hound's
  tooth; inlay, damascene; graph
5 stripe, striping, candy-stripe, pinstripe; barber
  pole; **streak, streaking;** striation, striature, stria;
  striola, striga; crack, craze, crackle, reticulation;
  bar, band, belt; list
6 <comparisons> spectrum, rainbow, iris,
  chameleon, leopard, jaguar, cheetah, ocelot,
  zebra, barber pole, candy cane, Dalmatian,
  firedog, peacock, butterfly, mother-of-pearl, nacre,
  tortoise shell, opal, kaleidoscope, stained glass,
  serpentine, calico cat, marble, mackerel sky,
  confetti, crazy quilt, patchwork quilt, shot silk,
  moiré, watered silk, marbled paper, Joseph's coat,
  harlequin, tapestry; bar code, checkerboard,
  graph paper
VERBS **7 variegate,** motley; parti-color; polychrome,
  polychromize; pattern; harlequin; **mottle, dapple,**
  stipple, **fleck,** flake, **speck, speckle,** bespeckle,
  freckle, **spot,** bespot, dot, sprinkle, blot, spangle,
  bespangle, pepper, stud, maculate; blotch, splotch;
  tattoo, stigmatize <old>; **check, checker;**
  tessellate; **stripe, streak,** striate, band, bar, vein,
  craze; marble, marbleize; engrail; tabby
8 opalesce, opalize; iridesce
ADJS **9 variegated, many-colored,** many-hued,
  diverse-colored, **multicolored,** multicolor,
  multicolorous, **varicolored,** varicolorous,
  polychrome, polychromic, polychromatic;
  parti-colored, parti-color; of all manner of colors,
  of all the colors of the rainbow; versicolor,
  versicolored, versicolorate, versicolorous;
  engrailed; motley, medley <old>, harlequin;
  colorful, colory; daedal; crazy; thunder and
  lightning; kaleidoscopic, kaleidoscopical;
  prismatic, prismatical, prismal, spectral; shot,
  shot through; bicolored, bicolor, dichromic,
  dichromatic; tricolored, tricolor, trichromic,
  trichromatic; two color _or_ colored, three color
  _or_ -colored, two-tone _or_ -toned, etc
10 iridescent, iridal, iridial, iridine, iridian, iridiated;
  irised, irisated, **rainbowy,** rainbowlike, rainbowed;
  opalescent, opaline, opaloid; nacreous, nacry,

nacré <Fr>, nacred, **pearly,** pearlish, mother-of-pearl; tortoise-shell; peacock-like, pavonine, pavonian; chatoyant; moiré, burelé; watered

11 **chameleonlike,** chameleonic, changeable

12 **mottled, motley; pied, piebald,** skewbald, pinto; **dappled,** dapple; calico; marbled; clouded; salt-and-pepper

13 **spotted, dotted,** polka-dot, sprinkled, peppered, studded, pocked, pockmarked; **spotty,** dotty, patchy, pocky; **speckled, specked,** speckledy, speckly, specky; **stippled,** pointillé, pointillistic; **flecked,** fleckered; spangled, bespangled; maculate, maculated, macular; punctate, punctated; freckled, frecked, freckly; blotched, blotchy, splotched, splotchy; flea-bitten; tortoiseshell; foxed

14 **checked, checkered,** checkedy, check, **plaid,** plaided; tessellated, tessellate, mosaic

15 **striped,** stripy, candy-stripe, pinstripe; **streaked,** streaky; **striated,** striate, striatal, striolate, strigate *or* strigose; barred, banded, listed; veined; **brindle,** brindled, brinded; marbled, marbleized; reticulate; tabby

48 HEARING

NOUNS 1 **hearing,** audition; sense of hearing, auditory *or* aural sense, auditory sensation; ear; listening, heeding, attention, hushed attention, rapt attention, eager attention, mind; auscultation, aural examination, examination by ear; audibility

2 **audition,** hearing, tryout, call <nf>, **audience, interview,** conference; attention, favorable attention, ear; **listening,** listening in; **eavesdropping,** overhearing, wiretapping, electronic surveillance, bugging <nf>

3 good hearing, refined *or* acute sense of hearing, sensitive ear, nice *or* quick *or* sharp *or* correct ear; **an ear for;** musical ear, ear for music, musicality; ear-mindedness; bad *or* poor ear, no ear, tin ear <nf>

4 **earshot,** earreach, **hearing,** range, auditory range, reach, carrying distance, **sound of one's voice**

5 **listener,** hearer, auditor, audient, hearkener, auditioner, earwitness; **eavesdropper,** overhearer, monitor; little pitcher with big ears, snoop <nf>, listener-in; fly on the wall <nf>

6 **audience,** auditory <old>, **house, congregation;** studio audience, live audience, captive audience, theatregoers, gallery, crowd, grandstand; orchestra, pit; groundling, boo-bird <nf>, spectator 918

7 **ear** 2.10, auditory apparatus, hearing organ; external ear, **outer ear;** cauliflower ear, jug ear, bat ear

8 listening device; **hearing aid,** hard-of-hearing aid; electronic hearing aid, transistor hearing aid; vacuum-tube hearing aid; ear trumpet; amplifier, speaking trumpet, megaphone; stethoscope

9 <science of hearing> otology; otoscopy, auriscopy; audiometry; otoneurology, otopathy, otography, otoplasty, otolaryngology, otorhinolaryngology; ear, nose, and throat *or* ENT; audiology; acoustic phonetics, phonetics 524.13; auriscope, otoscope, auscultator, stethoscope; audiometer

VERBS 10 **listen,** hark, **hearken, heed, hear, attend,** give attention, **give ear,** give *or* lend an ear, bend an ear; list <old>, **listen to,** listen at <nf>, attend to, pay attention, give a hearing to, give audience to, sit in on; **listen in; eavesdrop,** wiretap, tap, intercept, bug <nf>; **keep one's ears open,** be all ears <nf>, listen with both ears, strain one's ears; prick up the ears, cock the ears, keep one's ear to the ground, have long ears; hang on the lips of, hang on every word; hear out; auscultate, examine by ear

11 **hear,** catch, get <nf>, take in, hear from; **overhear; hear of,** hear tell of <nf>, pick up; get an earful <nf>, get wind of, get word; have an ear for, have perfect pitch

12 be heard, **fall on the ear,** sound in the ear, catch *or* reach the ear, carry, sound, resound, echo, reverberate, come within earshot, come to one's ear, register, make an impression, get across <nf>; **have one's ear,** reach, contact, get to; make oneself heard, get through to, gain a hearing, reach the ear of; ring in the ear; caress the ear; assault *or* split *or* assail the ear

ADJS 13 **auditory,** audio, audile, **hearing, aural,** auricular, otic, audial, auditive, auditorial; audio-visual; audible; otological, otoscopic, otopathic, etc; acoustic, acoustical, phonic

14 **listening, attentive,** open-eared, **all ears** <nf>, hearing; wired

15 **eared,** auriculate; big-eared, cauliflower-eared, crop-eared, dog-eared, droop-eared, flap-eared, flop-eared, jug-earned, lop-eared, long-eared, mouse-eared, prick-eared, quick-eared; **sharp-eared;** tin-eared; ear-minded; ear-shaped, earlike, auriform

INTERJS 16 **hark!,** hark ye!, hear ye!, hearken!, hear!, oyez!, hear ye, hear ye!, now hear this!, list!, **listen!,** listen up!, attend!, attention!, hist!, whisht!, psst!, yo!

49 DEAFNESS

NOUNS 1 **deafness, hardness of hearing,** dull hearing, deaf ears; **stone-deafness;** nerve-deafness; mind deafness, word deafness; **tone**

deafness, asonia, unmusicalness; cophosis; impaired hearing, hearing *or* auditory impairment; loss of hearing, **hearing loss; deaf-muteness,** deaf-mutism, surdimutism <old>

2 **the deaf,** the hard-of-hearing; **deaf-mute,** surdo-mute <old>, deaf-and-dumb person; lip reader; silent person

3 deaf-and-dumb alphabet, manual alphabet, finger alphabet, fingerspelling; dactylology, sign language, American Sign Language; lip reading, oral method; hearing aid

VERBS 4 **be deaf;** have no ears, be earless; lose one's hearing, suffer hearing loss *or* impairment, go deaf; shut *or* stop *or* close one's ears, **turn a deaf ear;** fall on deaf ears; lipread, use sign language, sign

5 **deafen, stun,** split the ears *or* eardrums

ADJS 6 **deaf, hard-of-hearing,** hearing-impaired, dull *or* thick of hearing, deaf-eared, dull-eared; surd <old>; deafened, stunned; **stone-deaf,** deaf as a stone, deaf as a door *or* a doorknob *or* doornail, **deaf as a post,** deaf as an adder; **unhearing;** earless; word-deaf; tone-deaf, unmusical; deafish, half-deaf, quasi-deaf; **deaf and dumb,** deaf-mute

50 SOUND

NOUNS 1 **sound,** sonance, acoustic, acoustical *or* acoustic phenomenon; auditory phenomenon *or* stimulus, auditory effect; noise; ultrasound; sound wave, sound propagation; sound intensity, sound intensity level, amplitude, loudness 53; phone, speech sound 524.12; resonance

2 **tone, pitch, frequency,** audio frequency *or* AF; monotone, monotony, tonelessness; overtone, harmonic, partial, partial tone; undertone; fundamental tone, fundamental; intonation 524.6

3 **timbre,** tonality, **tone quality,** tone color, color, coloring, clang color *or* tint, *Klangfarbe* <Ger>, register

4 **sounding,** sonation, sonification

5 **acoustics,** phonics, radioacoustics, acoustic theory, harmonics; acoustical engineer, acoustician; radiophonics

6 **sonics;** subsonics, **supersonics,** ultrasonics; speed of sound 174.2; sound barrier, transonic barrier, sonic barrier *or* wall; sonic boom; ultrasonic frequency, infrasonic frequency

7 <sound unit> **decibel,** db; bel, phon, sone

8 **loudspeaker, speaker,** dynamic speaker; speaker unit, speaker system; crossover network; voice coil; cone, diaphragm; acoustical network; horn <nf>; **headphone, earphone,** stereo headset, headset, ear buds

9 **microphone, mike** <nf>; radiomicrophone; concealed microphone, **bug** <nf>

10 **audio amplifier, amplifier, amp <nf>; preamplifier,** preamp <nf>

11 sound reproduction system, audio sound system; **high-fidelity** system *or* hi-fi <nf>; **record player, phonograph,** gramophone, Victrola; **jukebox,** nickelodeon; radio-phonograph combination; monophonic *or* monaural system, **mono** <nf>, stereophonic *or* binaural system, stereo <nf>; four-channel stereo system, discrete four-channel system, derived four-channel system, quadraphonic sound system; multitrack player *or* recorder *or* sound system; **pickup** *or* cartridge, magnetic pickup *or* cartridge, ceramic pickup *or* cartridge, crystal pickup, photoelectric pickup; stylus, needle; tone arm; turntable, transcription turntable, record changer, changer; **public-address system** *or* PA *or* PA system; sound truck; loud-hailer, bullhorn; intercommunication system, **intercom** <nf>, squawk box <nf>; **tape recorder,** tape deck, cassette *or* audio-cassette player, cassette *or* audio-cassette recorder, recording system; boom box, ghetto blaster; compact disk *or* CD player; media player; iPod <trademark>; hi-fi fan *or* freak <nf>, audiophile

12 **record, phonograph record,** disc, wax, long-playing record *or* LP; transcription, electrical transcription, digital transcription, digital recording; **recording,** wire recording, tape recording; digital stereo; digital disc; tape, tape cassette, cassette; tape cartridge, cartridge; digital audio tape *or* DAT, DVD; compact disk *or* CD; video-cassette recorder *or* VCR

13 **audio distortion, distortion;** interference, static 1034.21; scratching, shredding, hum, 60-cycle hum, rumble, hissing, howling, blurping, blooping, woomping, fluttering, flutter, squeals, whistles, birdies, motorboating; feedback

VERBS 14 **sound,** make a sound *or* noise, give forth *or* emit a sound; noise; speak 524.19; resound, reverberate, echo; **record,** tape, tape-record; prerecord; play back; broadcast, amplify

ADJS 15 **sounding,** sonorous, soniferous; **sounded;** tonal; monotone, monotonic, toneless, droning; voiced

16 **audible,** hearable, heard; **distinct, clear,** plain, definite, articulate; distinctive, contrastive; high-fidelity, hi-fi <nf>, stereophonic; microphonic

17 **acoustic, acoustical,** phonic, sonic; subsonic, supersonic, ultrasonic, hypersonic; transonic *or* transsonic, faster than sound

ADVS 18 **audibly, aloud,** out, **out loud;** distinctly, clearly, plainly

51 SILENCE

NOUNS 1 silence, silentness, soundlessness, noiselessness, **stillness,** "lucid stillness"—T S Eliot, **quietness,** quietude, quiescence 173, **quiet, still,** peace, whisht <Scot & Ir>, **hush,** mum; lull, rest, calm; golden silence; total silence, deathlike *or* tomblike silence, dead silence, perfect silence, solemn *or* awful silence, radio silence, the quiet *or* silence of the grave *or* the tomb; dull roar; hush *or* dead of night, dead; tacitness, taciturnity, reticence, reserve; inaudibility; tranquillity; not a sound *or* peep

2 muteness, mutism, **dumbness,** voicelessness, tonguelessness; speechlessness, wordlessness; inarticulateness; anaudia, aphasia, aphonia; hysterical mutism; deaf-muteness 49.1; standing mute, refusal to speak, stonewalling <nf>, the code of silence *or* omertà <Ital>, keeping one's lip buttoned <nf>; laryngitis

3 mute, dummy; deaf-mute 49.2

4 silencer, muffler, muffle, **mute,** baffle *or* baffler, quietener, cushion; **damper,** damp; dampener; **soft pedal,** sordine, sourdine, *sordino* <Ital>; hushcloth, silence cloth; **gag, muzzle;** antiknock; **soundproofing,** acoustic tile, sound-absorbing material, sound-proofing insulation

VERBS 5 be silent, keep silent *or* silence, **keep still *or* quiet; keep one's mouth shut, hold one's tongue,** keep one's tongue between one's teeth, bite one's tongue, put a bridle on one's tongue, seal one's lips, shut *or* close one's mouth, hold one's breath, muzzle oneself, **not breathe a word,** not speak, forswear speech *or* speaking, **keep mum, hold one's peace,** not let a word escape one, not utter a word, not open one's mouth, not make a sound, not make a peep; make no sign, keep to oneself; not have a word to say, be mute, stand mute; choke up, have one's words stick in one's throat; be taciturn, spare one's words, have little to say, keep one's counsel, hush up

6 <nf terms> **shut up,** keep one's trap *or* yap shut, button up, button one's lip, save one's breath, shut one's bazoo, can it, dummy up, clam up, close up like a clam, knock it off, not let out a peep, say nothing, not say 'boo', play dumb, stonewall

7 fall silent, hush, quiet, quieten, quiesce, **quiet down,** pipe down <nf>, check one's speech, stop talking; lose one's voice, get laryngitis

8 silence, put to silence, hush, hush one up, hush-hush, **shush, quiet,** quieten, **still; soft-pedal,** put on the soft pedal, play down; squash, squelch <nf>, stifle, choke, choke off, throttle, put the kibosh on <nf>, put the lid on *and* shut down on <nf>, put the damper on <nf>, **gag, muzzle,** muffle, stifle, stop one's mouth, cut one short; strike dumb *or* mute, dumbfound; tongue-tie

9 muffle, mute, dull, soften, deaden, quietize, cushion, baffle, damp, **dampen,** deafen; subdue, stop, tone down, **soft-pedal,** put on the soft pedal

ADJS 10 silent, still, stilly, **quiet,** quiescent 173.12, **hushed, soundless,** noiseless; taciturn, uncommunicative, tight-lipped, clammed up <nf>; echoless; **inaudible,** subaudible, below the limen *or* threshold of hearing, unhearable; quiet as a mouse *or* lamb, mousy; silent as a post *or* stone, so quiet that one might hear a feather *or* pin drop; silent as the grave *or* tomb, still as death; **unsounded, unvoiced,** unpronounced

11 tacit, wordless, unspoken, unuttered, unexpressed, unsaid, unarticulated, unvocalized; **implicit** 519.8

12 mute, mum, dumb, voiceless, tongueless, **speechless,** wordless, breathless, at a loss for words, choked up; inarticulate; **tongue-tied,** dumbstruck, dumbstricken, stricken dumb, **dumbfounded;** anaudic, aphasic, aphonic

ADVS 13 silently, in silence, **quietly, soundlessly,** noiselessly; inaudibly

INTERJS 14 silence!, hush!, shush!, sh!, sh-sh!, whist! *or* whish! <Brit nf>, whisht! <Scot & Ir>, peace!, pax!, *tais toi!* <Fr>, **be quiet!,** be silent!, be still!, **keep still!,** keep quiet!, quiet!, quiet please!, soft!, belay that! *or* there!, stow it!; **hold your tongue!,** hold your jaw! *or* lip!, **shut up!** <nf>, **shut your mouth!** <nf>, save your breath!, not another word!, not another peep out of you!, mum!, mum's the word!; hush your mouth!, shut your trap!, shut your face!, button your lip!, pipe down!, clam up!, dry up!, can it!, that's enough!, knock it off!

52 FAINTNESS OF SOUND

NOUNS 1 faintness, lowness, softness, gentleness, subduedness, dimness, feebleness, weakness; indistinctness, unclearness, flatness; subaudibility, inaudibility; decrescendo; distant sound

2 muffled tone, veiled voice, *voce velata* <Ital>, covered tone; **mutedness; dullness, deadness,** flatness; noise abatement, sound reduction, soundproofing

3 thud, dull thud; **thump,** flump, crump, clop, clump, clunk, plunk, tunk, plump, bump; pad, pat; **patter,** pitter-patter, pit-a-pat; **tap,** rap, **click,** tick, flick, pop, peep; tinkle, ting, clink, chink, tingaling

4 murmur, murmuring, murmuration; **mutter,** muttering; **mumble,** mumbling; soft voice, low voice, small *or* little voice; **undertone,** underbreath, bated breath; susurration, susurrus, undercurrent; **whisper,** whispering, stage whisper, breathy voice; breath, sigh, sough, exhalation, aspiration; purl, hum, moan, white noise *or* sound; nonresonance

5 **ripple, splash,** ripple of laughter, ripple of applause; titter, chuckle

6 **rustle,** rustling, froufrou, swoosh, "a little noiseless noise among the leaves"—Keats

7 **hum, humming,** thrumming, low rumbling, booming, bombilation, bombination, **droning, buzzing,** whizzing, whirring, purring

8 **sigh, sighing, moaning,** sobbing, whining, soughing

VERBS **9** **steal** *or* **waft on the ear,** melt in the air, float in the air

10 **murmur, mutter, mumble,** mussitate <old>, maffle <Brit nf>; coo; susurrate; **lower one's voice, speak under one's breath; whisper,** whisper in the ear; breathe, sigh, aspirate

11 **ripple, babble, burble,** bubble, **gurgle,** guggle, **purl, trill;** lap, plash, **splash,** swish, swash, slosh, wash

12 **rustle,** crinkle; **swish,** whish

13 **hum,** thrum, bum <Brit nf>, boom, bombilate, bombinate, **drone, buzz,** whiz, whir, burr, birr <Scot>, purr

14 **sigh, moan, sob, whine,** sough; **whimper**

15 **thud, thump, patter,** clop, clump, clunk, plunk, flump, crump; pad, pat; **tap,** rap, **click,** tick, tick away; pop; tinkle, clink, chink

ADJS **16** **faint, low, soft, gentle, subdued, dim, feeble, weak,** faint-sounding, low-sounding, soft-sounding; soft-voiced, low-voiced, faint-voiced, weak-voiced; murmured, whispered, hushed; half-heard, barely heard, scarcely heard; distant, dying away; indistinct, unclear; barely audible, subaudible, near the limit *or* threshold of hearing; soft-pedaled, piano, pianissimo; decrescendo; unstressed, unaccented

17 **muffled, muted, softened, dampened,** damped, **smothered,** stifled, bated, dulled, deadened, subdued; **dull, dead, flat,** *sordo* <Ital>; nonresonant

18 **murmuring,** murmurous, murmurish, **muttering, mumbling;** susurrous, susurrant; **whispering,** whisper, whispery; whimpering; **rustling**

19 **rippling, babbling, burbling,** bubbling, **gurgling,** guggling, **purling, trilling;** lapping, splashing, plashing, sloshing, swishing

20 **humming,** thrumming, **droning,** booming, bombinating, **buzzing,** whizzing, whirring, purring, burring

ADVS **21** **faintly, softly,** gently, subduedly, hushedly, dimly, feebly, weakly, low; piano, pianissimo; *sordo* and *sordamente* <Ital>, *à la sourdine* <Fr>

22 **in an undertone,** *sotto voce* <Ital>, **under one's breath,** with bated breath, in a whisper, in a stage whisper, between the teeth; aside, in an aside; out of earshot

53 LOUDNESS

NOUNS **1** **loudness,** intensity, volume, amplitude, fullness; sonorousness, sonority; surge of sound, surge, swell, swelling; loudishness, high volume

2 **noisiness,** noisefulness, **uproariousness,** racketiness, tumultuousness, thunderousness, clamorousness, clangorousness, boisterousness, obstreperousness; vociferousness 59.5; stridency, stridor; intensity

3 **noise,** loud noise, **blast** 56.3, tintamarre, **racket, din, clamor;** outcry, **uproar,** hue and cry, noise and shouting; howl; clangor, clang, clatter, clap, jangle, rattle; roar, rumble, thunder, thunderclap 56.5; **crash, boom,** sonic boom; **bang,** percussion; brouhaha, **tumult, hubbub,** bobbery <India>, vociferation, ululation; fracas, **brawl,** commotion, drunken brawl; **pandemonium,** bedlam, hell *or* bedlam let loose; charivari, shivaree <nf>; discord 61; shattered silence; cachinnation, stertor; explosion, bombardment; crescendo, forte, fortissimo, tutti

4 <nf terms> row, flap, hullabaloo, brannigan, shindy, donnybrook, free-for-all, shemozzle, rumble, rhubarb, dustup, rumpus, ruckus, ruction, rowdydow, hell broke loose, foofooraw, hoo-ha, Katy-bar-the-door, tzimmes

5 **blare, blast,** shriek 58.4, peal; **toot,** tootle, **honk,** beep, blat, trumpet, report; bay, bray; **whistle,** tweedle, squeal; trumpet call, trumpet blast *or* blare, sound *or* flourish of trumpets, Gabriel's trumpet *or* horn, **fanfare,** tarantara, tantara, tantarara, clarion call; tattoo; taps; full blast

6 **noisemaker;** ticktack, bull-roarer, catcall, whizzer, whizgig, snapper, cricket, clapper, clack, clacker, cracker; firecracker, cherry bomb; rattle, rattlebox; horn, Klaxon <trademark>; whistle, thunderer, steam whistle, siren; boiler room, boiler factory; loud-hailer, bullhorn <nf>

VERBS **7** **din; boom,** thunder 56.9; **resound,** ring, peal, ring *or* resound in the ears, din in the ear, **blast the ear,** pierce *or* split *or* rend the ears, rend *or* split the eardrums, split one's head; **deafen,** stun; blast 56.8, **bang, crash** 56.6; **rend the air** *or* skies *or* firmament, rock the sky, fill the air, make the welkin ring; shake *or* rattle the windows; awake *or* startle the echoes, set the echoes ringing, awake the dead, shatter the peace; surge, swell, rise, crescendo; **shout** 59.6

8 drown out, outshout, outroar, shout down, overpower, overwhelm; jam

9 be noisy, make a noise *or* **racket,** raise a clamor *or* din *or* hue and cry, noise, racket, **clamor,** roar, clangor; brawl, row, rumpus; **make an uproar,** kick up a dust *or* racket, kick up *or* raise a hullabaloo, raise the roof, raise Cain *or* Ned, howl like all the devils of hell, raise the devil, raise hell, whoop it up, maffick <Brit>; not be able to hear oneself think

10 blare, blast; shriek 58.8; **toot,** tootle, sound, peal, wind, blow, blat; pipe, trumpet, bugle, clarion; bay, bell, bray; **whistle,** tweedle, squeal; **honk,** honk *or* sound *or* blow the horn, beep; sound taps, sound a tattoo; go off

ADJS **11 loud,** loud-sounding, forte, fortissimo, crescendo; loudish; **resounding,** ringing, plangent, pealing; full, sonorous; **deafening,** ear-deafening, **ear-splitting,** head-splitting, ear-rending, ear-piercing, piercing; **thunderous,** thundering, tonitruous, tonitruant; **crashing, booming** 56.12; window-rattling, earthshaking, enough to wake the dead *or* the seven sleepers

12 loud-voiced, loudmouthed, fullmouthed, full-throated, big-voiced, clarion-voiced, trumpet-voiced, trumpet-tongued, brazen-mouthed, **stentorian,** stentorious, stentorophonic, like Stentor, booming

13 noisy, noiseful, rackety, clattery, clangorous, clanging, **clamorous,** clamoursome <Brit nf>, clamant, blatant, blaring, brassy, brazen, blatting; uproarious, **tumultuous,** turbulent, blustering, brawling, **boisterous,** rip-roaring, rowdy, mafficking <Brit>, strepitous, strepitant, obstreperous; vociferous 59.10

ADVS **14 loudly, aloud,** loud, lustily; **boomingly, thunderously, thunderingly; noisily,** uproariously; ringingly, resoundingly; with a loud voice, at the top of one's voice, at the pitch of one's breath, in full cry, with one wild yell, with a whoop and a hurrah; forte, *fortemente* <Ital>, fortissimo

54 RESONANCE

NOUNS **1 resonance, resoundingness,** resonancy, **sonorousness,** sonority, plangency, **vibrancy;** mellowness, richness, fullness; deepness, lowness, bassness; hollowness; **snore,** snoring

2 reverberation, resounding; rumble, rumbling, thunder, thundering, boom, booming, growl, growling, grumble, grumbling, reboation; rebound, resound, **echo,** reecho

3 ringing, tintinnabulation, **pealing, chiming, tinkling,** tingling, **jingling,** dinging, donging; **tolling,** knelling; clangor, clanking, clanging; **ring, peal, chime; toll,** knell; **tinkle,** tingle, **jingle,** dingle, ding, dingdong, ding-a-ling, ting-a-ling; clink, tink, ting, ping, chink; clank, clang; jangle, jingle-jangle; campanology, bell ringing, change ringing, peal ringing; tinnitis, ringing of *or* in the ear

4 bell <see list>, tintinnabulum; **gong,** triangle, **chimes,** door chimes, clock chimes, Westminster chimes; clapper, tongue; carillon, set of bells; ringtone

5 resonator, resounder, reverberator; **sounding board,** soundboard, sound box; resonant chamber *or* cavity; echo chamber; loud pedal, damper pedal, sustaining pedal

VERBS **6 resonate, vibrate,** pulse, throb; snore

7 reverberate, resound, sound, **rumble,** roll, boom, echo, reecho, rebound, bounce back, be reflected, be sent back, echo back, send back, return

8 ring, tintinnabulate, **peal,** sound; **toll,** knell, sound a knell; **chime;** gong; **tinkle,** tingle, **jingle,** ding, dingdong, dong; clink, tink, ting, chink; clank, clang, clangor; jangle, jinglejangle; ring changes *or* peals; ring in the ear

9 <deep voices> bass, basso, basso profundo, baritone, bass-baritone, contralto

ADJS **10 resonant, reverberant, vibrant, sonorous,** plangent, rolling; mellow, rich, full; resonating, reverberating, echoing, reechoing, vibrating, pulsing, throbbing

11 deep, deep-toned, deep-pitched, deep-sounding, deepmouthed, deep-echoing; **hollow, sepulchral; low,** low-pitched, low-toned, grave, heavy; **bass;** baritone; contralto; throaty, gravelly

12 reverberating, reverberant, reverberatory, reboant, **resounding,** rebounding, repercussive, sounding; **rumbling,** thundering, booming, growling; echoing, reechoing, echoic; undamped; persistent, lingering

13 ringing, pealing, tolling, belling, sounding, chiming; **tinkling,** tinkly, tingling, **jingling,** dinging; tintinnabular *or* tintinnabulary *or* tintinnabulous; campanological

14 bells

air bell	dinner bell *or* gong *or*
alarm bell	chimes
anchor bell	doorbell
angelus bell	fire bell
Big Ben	fog bell
bourdon	gong bell
breakfast bell	hand bell
call bell	harness bell
chiming bell	hour bell
church bell	jingle bell
clinkum bell	Liberty Bell
computer bell	minute bell
cowbell	news bell

night bell
pancake bell
passing bell *or* death bell
   or end bell *or*
     mortbell
ringtone
Sanctus bell *or* sacring bell
   or saunce *or* sauncing
     bell
school bell

sheepbell
shop bell
signal bell
sleigh bell
tap bell
telephone bell
tocsin
vesper bell
watch bell
wind-bell

55 REPEATED SOUNDS

NOUNS **1 staccato; drum, thrum, beat, pound, roll;** drumming, tom-tom, beating, pounding, thumping; **throb,** throbbing, pulsation 916.3; **palpitation,** flutter; sputter, spatter, splutter; **patter, pitter-patter,** pit-a-pat; rub-a-dub, rattattoo, rataplan, rat-a-tat, rat-tat, rat-tat-tat, tat-tat, tat-tat-tat; clop-clop; **tattoo,** devil's tattoo, ruff, ruffle, paradiddle; **drumbeat,** drum music; drumfire, barrage; echo, re-echo; ringtone

2 clicking, ticking, tick, ticktock, ticktack, ticktick

3 rattle, rattling, brattle <Scot>, ruckle <Brit nf>, rattletybang; **clatter,** clitter, clunter <Brit nf>, **clitterclatter, chatter,** clack, clacket <nf>; racket 53.3

VERBS **4 drum, thrum, beat, pound, thump, thump out, roll; palpitate,** flutter; sputter, splatter, splutter; patter, pitter-patter, go pit-a-pat *or* pitter-patter; **throb,** pulsate 916.12; beat *or* sound a tattoo, beat a devil's tattoo, ruffle, beat a ruffle

5 tick, ticktock, ticktack, tick away

6 rattle, ruckle <Brit nf>, brattle <Scot>; **clatter,** clitter, **chatter,** clack; rattle around, clatter about

ADJS **7 staccato; drumming, thrumming, beating, pounding, thumping; throbbing;** palpitant, fluttering; sputtering, spattering, spluttering; clicking, ticking

8 rattly, rattling, chattering, **clattery,** clattering

56 EXPLOSIVE NOISE

NOUNS **1 report, crash, crack, clap, bang,** wham, slam, clash, burst; **knock, rap, tap,** smack, whack, thwack, whop, whap, swap <nf>, whomp, splat, crump <Brit nf>, bump, slap, slat <Brit nf>, flap, flop

2 snap, crack; click, clack; **crackle,** snapping, cracking, crackling, crepitation, decrepitation, sizzling, spitting; rale

3 detonation, blast, explosion, fulmination, **discharge, burst, bang, pop, crack,** bark; **shot,** gunshot; backfire; volley, salvo, fusillade; displosion

4 boom, booming, cannonade, **peal, rumble,** grumble, growl, **roll, roar**

5 thunder, thundering, clap *or* crash *or* peal of thunder, **thunderclap,** thunderpeal, thundercrack, thunderstroke; peal; "heaven's artillery"— Shakespeare; thunderstorm 316.3; Thor *or* Donar, Jupiter Tonans, Indra

VERBS **6 crack, clap, crash,** wham, slam, **bang,** clash; **knock, rap, tap,** smack, whack, thwack, whop, whap, swap <nf>, whomp, splat, crump <Brit nf>, bump, slat <Brit nf>, slap, flap

7 snap, crack; click, clack; **crackle,** crepitate, decrepitate; spit

8 blast, detonate, explode, discharge, burst, go off, **bang, pop, crack,** bark, fulminate; burst on the ear

9 boom, thunder, peal, rumble, grumble, growl, **roll, roar;** peal

ADJS **10 snapping, cracking, crackling,** crackly, crepitant

11 banging, crashing, bursting, exploding, explosive, blasting, cracking, popping; knocking, rapping, tapping; slapping, flapping, slatting <Brit nf>

12 thundering, thunderous, thundery, fulminating, tonitruous, tonitruant, thunderlike; **booming,** pealing, rumbling, rolling, roaring; cannonading, volleying; tonant

INTERJS **13** bang!, boom!, wham!, whammo!, blam!, kerboom!, kerblam!

57 SIBILATION

<hissing sounds>

NOUNS **1** sibilation, sibilance *or* sibilancy; **hiss, hissing,** siss, sissing, white noise; hush, hushing, shush, shushing; sizz, sizzle, sizzling; fizz, fizzle, fizzling, effervescing, effervescence; swish, whish, whoosh; whiz, buzz, zip; siffle; wheeze, *râle* <Fr>, rhonchus; whistle, whistling; sneeze, sneezing, sternutation; snort; snore, stertor; **sniff,** sniffle, snuff, snuffle; spit, sputter, splutter; squash, squish, squelch; sigmatism, lisp; assibilation; frication, frictional rustling; interference, static

VERBS **2** sibilate; **hiss,** siss; hush, shush; sizzle, sizz; fizzle, fizz, effervesce; whiz, buzz, zip; swish, whish, whoosh; whistle; wheeze; sneeze; snort; snore; sniff, sniffle, snuff, snuffle; spit, sputter, splutter; squash, squish, squelch; lisp; assibilate

ADJS **3 sibilant; hissing,** hushing, sissing; sizzling, fizzling, effervescent; **sniffing,** sniffling, snuffling; snoring; wheezing, wheezy

58 STRIDENCY

<harsh and shrill sounds>

NOUNS **1 stridency,** stridence, stridor, stridulousness, stridulation; **shrillness,** highness, sharpness, acuteness, arguteness; **screechiness, squeakiness,** creakiness, reediness, pipingness, brassiness

2 raucousness, harshness, raucity; discord, cacophony 61.1; coarseness, rudeness, ugliness, roughness, gruffness; **raspiness,** scratchiness, scrapiness, **hoarseness,** huskiness, dryness; stertorousness; roupiness <Scot>; gutturalness, gutturalism, gutturality, thickness, throatiness; cracked voice

3 rasp, scratch, scrape, grind; crunch, craunch, scranch <old>, scrunch, crump; burr, chirr, buzz; snore, snort, stertor; **jangle, clash, jar;** clank, clang, clangor, twang, twanging; blare, blat, bray; croak, caw, cackle; belch; growl, snarl; grumble, groan

4 screech, shriek, scream, squeal, shrill, keen, squeak, squawk, skirl, screak, skreak <nf>, skriech *or* skreigh <Scot>, creak; bleep; **whistle,** wolf-whistle; pipe; **whine, wail, howl,** ululation, yammer; vibrato; waul, caterwaul

5 <insect sounds> **stridulation,** cricking, creaking, chirking <Scot>; crick, creak, chirk, chirp, chirping, chirrup, scritch

6 <high voices> soprano, mezzo-soprano, treble; tenor, alto; male alto, countertenor; head register, head voice, head tone, falsetto

VERBS **7 stridulate,** crick, creak, chirk, chirp, chirrup, scritch

8 screech, shriek, screak, skreak <nf>, creak, squeak, squawk, **scream, squeal,** shrill, keen; **whistle,** wolf-whistle; pipe, skirl; **whine,** wail, howl, wrawl <Brit nf>, yammer, ululate; waul, caterwaul; raise the roof <nf>

9 <sound harshly> **jangle, clash, jar;** blare, blat, bray; croak, caw, cackle; belch; burr, chirr, buzz; snore; growl, snarl; grumble, groan; clank, clang, clangor; twang

10 grate, rasp, scratch, scrape, grind; crunch, craunch, scranch <old>, scrunch, crump

11 grate on, jar on, grate upon the ear, jar upon the ear, offend the ear, pierce *or* split *or* rend the ears, harrow *or* lacerate the ear, **set the teeth on edge, get on one's nerves,** jangle *or* wrack the nerves, make one's skin crawl

ADJS **12 strident,** stridulant, stridulous; strident-voiced

13 high, high-pitched, high-toned, high-sounding; treble, soprano, mezzo-soprano, tenor, alto, falsetto, countertenor

14 shrill, thin, sharp, acute, argute, keen, keening, peeping, **piercing,** penetrating, ear-piercing, ear-splitting; **screechy,** screeching, shrieky, shrieking, **squeaky,** squeaking, screaky, creaky, creaking; whistling, piping, skirling, reedy; whining, wailing, howling, ululating, ululant; vibrato

15 raucous, raucid, **harsh,** harsh-sounding; coarse, rude, rough, gruff, ragged; **hoarse, husky,** roupy <Scot>, cracked, dry; **guttural,** thick, throaty, croaky, croaking; choked, strangled; squawky, **squawking;** brassy, brazen, tinny, metallic; stertorous

16 grating, jarring, grinding; **jangling,** jangly; **rasping,** raspy; scratching, scratchy; scraping, scrappy; abrasive

59 CRY, CALL

NOUNS **1 cry, call, shout, yell,** hoot; halloo, hollo, yo-ho, hello, hi, yo, hail; **whoop, holler** <nf>; **cheer, hurrah,** huzzah, hooray; **howl,** yowl, yawl <Brit nf>; shout-out; bawl, bellow, roar; **scream, shriek,** screech, squeal, squall, caterwaul; yelp, yap, yammer, yawp, bark; war cry, battle cry, war whoop, rallying cry; jeer, boo, hiss, razz; guffah, cachinnation; raspberry, razzing, heckling; Bronx cheer

2 exclamation, ejaculation, outburst, blurt, ecphonesis; expletive

3 hunting cry; tallyho, yoicks <old>, view halloo

4 outcry, vociferation, clamor; hullabaloo, hubbub, brouhaha, **uproar** 53.3; **hue and cry**

5 vociferousness, vociferance, clamorousness, clamoursomeness <Brit nf>, blatancy; noisiness 53.2

VERBS **6 cry, call, shout, yell, holler** <nf>, hoot; hail, halloo, hollo; **whoop; cheer** 116.6; **howl,** yowl, yammer, yawl <Brit nf>; squawk, yawp; **bawl, bellow,** roar, roar *or* bellow like a bull; cry *or* yell *or* scream bloody murder *or* blue murder; **scream, shriek,** screech, squeal, squall, waul, caterwaul; yelp, yap, bark; heckle

7 exclaim, give an exclamation, ejaculate, burst out, blurt, blurt out, jerk out, spout out; stammer out; shout out

8 vociferate, outcry, **cry out,** call out, bellow out, yell out, holler out <nf>, shout out, sing out; sound off <nf>, pipe up, **clamor,** make *or* raise a clamor; make an outcry, **raise a hue and cry,** make an uproar

9 cry aloud, raise *or* lift up the voice, give voice *or* tongue, shout *or* cry *or* thunder at the top of one's voice, split the throat *or* lungs, strain the voice *or* throat *or* vocal cords, rend the air

ADJS **10 vociferous,** vociferant, vociferating;
clamorous, clamoursome <Brit nf>; **blatant;**
obstreperous, brawling; **noisy;** crying, shouting,
yelling, hollering <nf>, **bawling,** screaming;
yelping, yapping, yappy, yammering; loud-voiced,
loudmouthed, openmouthed, stentorian,
Boanergean; booming
11 exclamatory, ejaculatory, blurting

60 ANIMAL SOUNDS

NOUNS **1** animal noise; **call, cry;** mating call *or* cry;
grunt, howl, bark, howling, waul, caterwaul,
ululation, barking; bird song, birdcall, note,
woodnote, clang; stridulation 58.5; dawn chorus;
warning cry
VERBS **2** cry, call; **howl,** yowl, yawp, yawl <nf>,
ululate; wail, whine, pule; **squeal,** squall, scream,
screech, screak, squeak; troat; **roar; bellow,** blare,
bawl; moo, low; **bleat,** blate, blat; **bray; whinny,
neigh,** whicker, nicker, bray; **bay,** bay at the moon,
bell; **bark,** woof, latrate <old>, give voice *or*
tongue; **yelp, yap,** yip; **mew,** mewl, **meow,** miaow,
waul, caterwaul; weal
3 grunt, gruntle <Brit nf>, oink; **snort**
4 growl, snarl, grumble, gnarl, snap; hiss, spit
5 <birds> **warble, sing,** carol, call; pipe, whistle;
trill, chirr, roll; **twitter,** tweet, twit, chatter,
chitter; **chirp,** chirrup, chirk, **cheep,** peep, pip;
quack, honk, cronk; **croak, caw; squawk,** scold,
screech; **crow,** cock-a-doodle-doo; **cackle,**
gaggle, gabble, guggle, **cluck,** clack, chuck;
gobble; hoot, hoo; **coo; cuckoo;** drum; tu-whit
tu-whoo; whoop
ADJS **6 howling,** yowling, crying, wailing, whining,
puling, bawling, ululant, blatant; barking; lowing,
mugient, snarling, growling; singing, humming

61 DISCORD

<dissonant sounds>

NOUNS **1 discord,** discordance *or* discordancy,
dissonance *or* dissonancy, diaphony, **cacophony;**
stridor, stridency; **inharmoniousness,**
unharmoniousness, disharmony, inharmony;
unmelodiousness, unmusicalness, unmusicality,
untunefulness, tunelessness; atonality, atonalism;
flatness, sharpness, sourness <nf>; dissonant
chord, wolf; false note, sour note *and* clinker *and*
clam <nf>, off note; cipher; dodecaphonism *or*
dodecaphony
2 clash, jangle, jar; noise, mere noise, confusion *or*
conflict *or* jarring *or* jostling of sounds; Babel,
witches' *or* devils' chorus; harshness 58.2; clamor
53.3

VERBS **3** sound *or* strike *or* hit a sour note <nf>, hit
a clinker *or* a clam <nf>; not carry a tune; **clash,
jar, jangle,** conflict, jostle; grate 58.10,11; untune,
unstring; hurt the ears
ADJS **4 dissonant, discordant, cacophonous,**
absonant <old>, disconsonant, diaphonic;
strident, shrill, harsh, raucous, grating 58.16;
inharmonious, unharmonious, disharmonious,
disharmonic, inharmonic; **unmelodious,**
immelodious, nonmelodious; **unmusical,**
musicless, nonmusical, untuneful, tuneless;
untunable, untuned, atonal, toneless; droning,
singsong; cracked, **out of tune,** out of tone, out of
pitch; **off-key, off-tone, off-pitch,** off; flat, sharp,
sour <nf>; "above the pitch, out of tune, and off
the hinges"—Rabelais, "like sweet bells jangled,
out of tune and harsh"—Shakespeare
5 clashing, jarring, jangling, jangly, confused,
conflicting, jostling, warring, ajar; **harsh,** hoarse,
grating 58.16

62 TASTE

<sense of taste>

NOUNS **1 taste,** gust <old>, *goût* <Fr>; sense of taste;
flavor, sapor; **smack, tang; savor, relish,** sapidity,
deliciousness; palate, tongue, tooth, stomach;
taste in the mouth, taste perception; sweetness,
sourness, bitterness, bittersweetness, saltiness;
sharp taste, acid taste, tart taste, salty taste, spicy
taste, sweet taste, sour taste, bitter taste, pungent
taste; aftertaste; tang; savoriness 63
2 sip, sup, lick, bite, try, nip
3 tinge, soupçon, smack hint 248.4
4 sample, specimen, taste, taste test, taster, little
bite, little smack, taste treat; tidbit, sampler;
example 786.2; appetizer, hors d'oeuvre, canape,
aperitif, starter <Brit>, tapas, little plate
5 taste bud *or* bulb *or* goblet, taste *or* gustatory cell,
taste hair; **tongue,** lingua; **palate**
6 tasting, savoring, gustation, nibble, nip, sampling
VERBS **7 taste,** taste of, sample, degust, partake;
savor, savor of, relish; try; sip, sup <nf>, roll on the
tongue, test; lick; smack
ADJS **8 gustatory,** gustative; tastable, gustable <old>
9 flavored, flavorous, flavory, sapid, saporous,
saporific; tasty, savory, flavorful 63.9; sweet, sour,
bitter, bittersweet, salt
10 lingual, glossal; **tonguelike,** linguiform, lingulate

63 SAVORINESS

NOUNS **1 savoriness, palatableness,** palatability,
tastiness, toothsomeness, goodness, good taste,
right taste, **deliciousness,** gustatory

delightfulness, scrumptiousness *and* yumminess <nf>, lusciousness, delectability, **flavorfulness,** flavorsomeness, flavorousness, flavoriness, good flavor, fine flavor, sapidity; full flavor, full-bodied flavor; gourmet quality; succulence, juiciness; sapidity, sapidness

2 savor, relish, zest, gusto, *goût* <Fr>; richness

3 flavoring, flavor, flavorer; **seasoning,** seasoner, **relish, condiment, spice,** condiment; flavor enhancer; artificial flavoring

VERBS **4 taste good,** tickle *or* flatter *or* delight the palate, tempt *or* whet the appetite, make one's mouth water, melt in one's mouth

5 savor, relish, like, love, be fond of, be partial to, enjoy, delight in, have a soft spot for, appreciate; smack the lips; do justice to; taste 62.7

6 savor of, taste of, smack of, have a relish of, have the flavor of, taste like

7 flavor, savor; **season,** salt, pepper, **spice,** sauce

ADJS **8 tasty,** fit to eat *and* finger-lickin' good <nf>, good-tasting, **savory,** savorous, **palatable, toothsome,** gustable <old>, sapid, **good,** good to eat, nice, agreeable, likable, pleasing, mouth-watering, to one's taste, **delicious,** delightful, delectable, exquisite; delicate, dainty; juicy, succulent, **luscious,** lush; for the gods, ambrosial, nectarous, nectareous; fit for a king, gourmet, fit for a gourmet, of gourmet quality, epicurean; scrumptious *and* yummy <nf>

9 flavorful, flavorsome, flavorous, flavory, well-flavored; full-flavored, full-bodied; nutty, fruity; **rich,** rich-flavored; sapid

10 appetizing, mouth-watering, tempting, tantalizing, provocative, piquant

64 UNSAVORINESS

NOUNS **1 unsavoriness, unpalatableness,** unpalatability, **distastefulness,** untastefulness; bad taste, bad taste in the mouth

2 acridness, acridity, tartness, sharpness, causticity, astringence *or* astringency, acerbity, **sourness** 67; pungency 68; **bitterness,** bitter taste; gall, gall and wormwood, wormwood, bitter pill

3 nastiness, foulness, vileness, loathsomeness, repulsiveness, obnoxiousness, odiousness, offensiveness, disgustingness, nauseousness; **rankness,** rancidity, rancidness, overripeness, rottenness, malodorousness, fetor, fetidness; yuckiness <nf>; repugnance 99.2; nauseant, emetic, sickener

VERBS **4 disgust, repel,** turn one's stomach, nauseate; make one's gorge rise; gross one out <nf>

ADJS **5 unsavory, unpalatable, unappetizing,** untasteful, untasty, ill-flavored, foul-tasting, **distasteful,** dislikable, unlikable, uninviting, unpleasant, unpleasing, displeasing, disagreeable

6 bitter, bitter as gall *or* wormwood, amaroidal; **acrid,** sharp, caustic, tart, astringent; hard, harsh, rough, coarse; acerb, acerbic, sour; pungent

7 nasty, offensive 98.18, fulsome, noisome, noxious, rebarbative, mawkish, cloying, brackish, **foul, vile,** bad; gross *and* icky *and* yucky <nf>, **sickening, nauseating,** nauseous, nauseant, vomity *and* barfy <nf>; poisonous, toxic, rank, rancid, maggoty, weevily, spoiled, overripe, high, rotten, stinking, putrid, malodorous, fetid

8 inedible, uneatable, not fit to eat *or* drink, undrinkable, impotable; unfit for human consumption

65 INSIPIDNESS

NOUNS **1 insipidness,** insipidity, **tastelessness, flavorlessness,** blandness, savorlessness, saplessness, unsavoriness, dullness; **weakness, thinness,** mildness, **wishy-washiness,** namby-pambyness; **flatness, staleness,** lifelessness, deadness; vapidity, inanity, jejunity, jejuneness; adulteration, dilution; pablum

ADJS **2 insipid, tasteless, flavorless,** bland, nondescript, unexciting, plain, spiceless, **savorless,** sapless, unsavory, unflavored, unseasoned; pulpy, pappy, gruelly, pasty; **weak, thin,** mild, **wishy-washy,** milktoast, washy, watery, watered, watered-down, diluted, dilute, milk-and-water, dishwater; **flat, stale,** dead, *fade* <Fr>; vapid, inane, jejune; "weary, flat, stale, and unprofitable"—Shakespeare; unappetizing; indifferent, characterless, neither one thing nor the other

66 SWEETNESS

NOUNS **1 sweetness,** sweet, sweetishness, saccharinity, dulcitude <old>; **sugariness,** syrupiness; oversweetness, mawkishness, cloyingness, sickly-sweetness; sweet tooth; confectionery, sweet-shop <Brit>, candy store, bakery

2 sweetening, edulcoration <old>; sweetener; sugar, cane sugar, beet sugar, sugar lump, sugar loaf, caster sugar, granulated sugar, powdered sugar, brown sugar, turbinado sugar; sweetening agent, sugar-substitute, artificial sweetener, saccharin, aspartame, NutraSweet <trademark>, cyclamates, sodium cyclamate, calcium cyclamate; molasses, blackstrap, treacle <Brit>; syrup, maple syrup, cane syrup, corn syrup, sorghum, golden syrup *or* treacle <Brit>; **honey,** honeycomb, honeypot, comb honey, clover honey; honeydew; **nectar, ambrosia;** sugarcoating; sweets, candy, dessert; sugar-making; sugaring off; saccharification

VERBS **3 sweeten,** dulcify, edulcorate *or* dulcorate <old>; **sugar;** honey, nectarize; sugarcoat, glaze, candy; ice, frost, glaze; mull; saccharify; sugar off

ADJS **4 sweet,** sweetish, sweetened; sacchariferous, saccharine; **sugary,** sugared, candied, **honeyed,** syrupy; mellifluous, mellifluent <old>; melliferous, nectarous, nectareous, ambrosial; sugarsweet, honeysweet, sweet as sugar *or* honey, sweet as a nut; sugar-coated; bittersweet; sour-sweet, sweet-sour, sweet and sour, sweet and pungent

5 oversweet, saccharine, rich, **cloying,** mawkish, luscious <old>, sickly-sweet

67 SOURNESS

NOUNS **1 sourness,** sour, sourishness, **tartness,** tartishness, acerbity, astringency, verjuice; acescency; acidity, acidulousness; hyperacidity, subacidity; vinegariness; unsweetness, **dryness; pungency** 68; greenness, unripeness; bitterness, sharpness

2 sour; vinegar, acidulant; **pickle,** sour pickle, dill pickle, bread-and-butter pickle; verjuice; lemon, lime, crab apple, green apple, sour cherry; aloe; sourgrass; sour balls; sourdough; sour cream, sour milk; bitters; wormwood; **acid**

3 souring, acidification, acidulation, acetification, acescence; fermentation; turning

VERBS **4 sour,** turn sour *or* acid, turn, go sour, sharpen, **acidify,** acidulate, acetify; ferment; set one's teeth on edge; curdle, spoil, turn, ferment, go off, go bad, molder

ADJS **5 sour,** soured, sourish; **tart,** tartish; tangy, pungent; crab, **crabbed;** acerb, acerbic, acerbate, acrid; acescent; **vinegarish,** vinegary, sour as vinegar; pickled; lemony; **pungent** 68.6; unsweet, unsweetened, **dry,** sec; green, unripe

6 acid, acidulous, acidulent, acidulated; acetic, acetous, acetose; hyperacid; subacid, subacidulous

68 PUNGENCY

NOUNS **1 pungency, piquancy, poignancy,** spiciness; strong flavor; **sharpness, keenness,** edge, **causticity,** astringency, mordancy, severity, asperity, trenchancy, cuttingness, bitingness, penetratingness, harshness, roughness, **acridity; bitterness** 64.2; acerbity, acidulousness, acidity, **sourness** 67; aroma

2 zest, zestfulness, zestiness, **briskness,** liveliness, raciness; **nippiness, tanginess,** snappiness; **spiciness,** pepperiness, hotness, fieriness; **tang,**

spice, relish; **nip, bite,** kick; sting, punch, snap, zip, ginger, sharpness; **kick,** guts <nf>; heat

3 strength, strongness; high flavor, highness, rankness, gaminess

4 saltiness, salinity, brininess; brackishness; **salt; brine;** pepperiness

VERBS **5 bite, nip,** cut, penetrate, bite the tongue, sting, kick, make the eyes water, go up the nose

ADJS **6 pungent, piquant, poignant; sharp, keen,** piercing, penetrating, nose-tickling, aromatic, stinging, **biting, acrid,** astringent, irritating, harsh, rough, **spicy,** severe, asperous, cutting, trenchant; **caustic,** vitriolic, mordant, escharotic; **bitter** 64.6; acerbic, acid, **sour,** tart, sharp

7 zestful, zesty, **brisk,** lively, racy, zippy, **nippy,** snappy, **tangy,** with a kick, strong; spiced, seasoned, high-seasoned, savory; **spicy,** curried, **peppery,** hot, burning, hot as pepper; mustardy; like horseradish, like Chinese mustard

8 strong, strong-flavored, strong-tasting; **high,** highly flavored, highy seasoned, high-tasted; **rank, gamy,** racy

9 salty, salt, salted, saltish, **saline, briny; brackish;** pickled

69 ODOR

NOUNS **1 odor, smell, scent,** aroma, flavor <old>, savor; **essence,** definite odor, redolence, effluvium, emanation, exhalation, fume, breath, subtle odor, whiff, wafture, trace, detectable odor; trail, spoor; **fragrance** 70; **stink, stench** 71, funk

2 odorousness, smelliness, headiness, pungency 68; aromatherapy

3 smelling, olfaction, nosing, scenting; sniffing, snuffing, snuffling, whiffing, odorizing, odorization

4 sense of smell, smell, smelling, scent, olfaction, olfactory sense

5 olfactory organ; olfactory pit, olfactory cell, olfactory area, **nose; nostrils,** noseholes <nf>, nares, naris, nasal cavity; olfactory nerves; **olfactories;** scent gland, pheromone

VERBS **6** <have an odor> **smell,** be aromatic, smell of, be redolent of; emit *or* emanate *or* give out a smell, reach one's nostrils, yield an odor *or* aroma, breathe, exhale; reek, **stink** 71.4; pong <Brit nf>

7 odorize; scent, aromatize, perfume 70.8

8 smell, scent, nose; **sniff,** snuff, snuffle, inhale, breathe, breathe in; get a noseful of, smell of, catch a smell of, get *or* take a whiff of, whiff, get wind of, follow one's nose

ADJS **9 odorous,** odoriferous, odiferous, odored, odorant, olent, **smelling, smelly,** smellful

<Austral>, smellsome, olent, **redolent, aromatic;** effluvious; **fragrant** 70.9; **stinking, malodorous** 71.5; emanative, pheromonal

10 strong, strong-smelling, strong-scented; **pungent,** penetrating, nose-piercing, sharp, heady; reeking, reeky; funky, foul; suffocating, stifling; noisome, noxious

11 smellable, sniffable, whiffable

12 olfactory, olfactive

13 keen-scented, quick-scented, sharp- or keen-nosed, **with a nose for**

70 FRAGRANCE

NOUNS **1 fragrance,** fragrancy <old>, **perfume, aroma,** scent, redolence, balminess, **incense, bouquet,** nosegay <old>, sweet smell, sweet savor; **odor** 69; spice, spiciness; muskiness; fruitiness; perfume dynamics, aromatherapy

2 perfumery, *parfumerie* <Fr>; **perfume,** *parfum* <Fr>, eau de parfum, **scent, essence,** extract; aromatic, ambrosia; attar, essential or volatile oil; aromatic water; balsam, **balm,** aromatic gum; myrrh; bay oil, myrcia oil; champaca oil; rose oil, attar of roses, lavender oil, heliotrope, jasmine oil, bergamot oil; fixative, musk, civet, ambergris, patchouli, musk

3 toilet water, Florida water; rose water, *eau de rose* <Fr>; lavender water; cologne, cologne water, eau de Cologne; bay rum; **lotion,** after-shave lotion

4 incense; joss stick; pastille; frankincense or olibanum; agalloch or aloeswood, calambac, lignaloes or linaloa, sandalwood, frangipani, resin, myrrh, eucalyptus, attar, ambergris, patchouli

5 perfumer, *parfumeur* <Fr>; thurifer, censer bearer, censer, thurible; **perfuming,** censing, thurification, odorizing

6 <articles> perfumer, *parfumoir* <Fr>, fumigator, scenter, odorator, odorizer; atomizer, purse atomizer, spray; censer, thurible, incensory, incense burner; vinaigrette, scent bottle, smelling bottle, scent box, scent ball; scent strip; scent bag, sachet; pomander, pouncet-box <old>; potpourri; scratch-and-sniff; dryer sheet

VERBS **7 be fragrant,** smell sweet, **smell good,** please the nostrils, smell like a rose

8 perfume, scent, cense, incense, thurify, aromatize, odorize, fumigate, embalm

ADJS **9 fragrant, aromatic,** odoriferous, redolent, perfumy, **perfumed, scented,** odorate or essenced <old>, **sweet, sweet-smelling,** sweet-scented, savory, balmy, ambrosial, incense-breathing; thuriferous; **odorous** 69.9; sweet as a rose, fragrant as new-mown hay; pungent,

heady; flowery; fruity; musky; spicy; aromatherapeutic

71 STENCH

NOUNS **1 stench, stink,** funk, malodor, fetidness, fetidity, fetor, foul or bad odor, offensive odor, unpleasant smell, offense to the nostrils, bad smell, niff and pong <Brit nf>, rotten smell, noxious stench, "the rankest compound of villainous smell that ever offended nostril"— Shakespeare, smell or stench of decay, **reek,** reeking, nidor; fug and frowst <Brit nf>; mephitis, miasma, graveolence <old>, effluvium, osmidrosis; body odor or BO; halitosis, **bad breath,** foul breath

2 fetidness, fetidity, malodourousness, **smelliness,** stinkingness, **odorousness,** noisomeness, **rankness, foulness,** putridness, offensiveness; repulsiveness; **mustiness,** funkiness, must, frowst or frowstiness <Brit nf>, moldiness, mildew, fustiness, frowziness, stuffiness; staleness; **rancidness,** rancidity, reastiness <Brit nf>; rottenness 393.7; putrefaction, putrescence, decay, gaminess

3 stinker, stinkard; skunk or polecat or rotten egg; stink ball, stinkpot, stink bomb; mothball; flatus, fart, cesspool, hydrogen sulfide, sulfur dioxide

VERBS **4 stink,** smell, **smell bad,** niffy and pong <Brit nf>, assail or offend the nostrils, stink in the nostrils, stink to heaven or high heaven, smell of rotten eggs; **reek;** smell up, stink up, stink out

ADJS **5 malodorous, fetid,** olid, **odorous, stinking, reeking,** reeky, nidorous, smelling, bad-smelling, **evil-smelling,** foul-smelling, ill-smelling, heavy-smelling, **smelly,** smellful <Austral>, niffy and pongy <Brit nf>, stenchy; **foul,** vile, putrid, bad, fulsome, noisome, fecal, feculent, excremental, offensive, repulsive, noxious, sulfurous, graveolent <old>; rotten; **rank,** strong, high, gamy; **rancid,** reasty or reasy <Brit nf>, reechy <old>; **musty,** funky, fusty, frowy <nf>, frowzy, frowsty <Brit>, stuffy, moldy, mildewed, mildewy; mephitic, miasmic, miasmal; crappy; asphyxiating

72 ODORLESSNESS

NOUNS **1 odorlessness, inodorousness,** lack of smell, scentlessness, scentlessness, smell-lessness; inoffensiveness; anosmia

2 deodorizing, deodorization, fumigation, ventilation; freshness, fresh air; smoke-free area, no-smoking area

3 deodorant, deodorizer; antiperspirant; fumigant, fumigator; mouthwash, breath freshener; ventilator, air filter, air purifier

VERBS **4 deodorize,** fumigate; ventilate, freshen the air; cleanse

ADJS **5 odorless,** inodorous, nonodorous, smell-less, **scentless,** unscented; fragrance-free; smoke-free, smokeless; fumigated; neutral-smelling; inoffensive; in the fresh air

6 deodorant, deodorizing, freshening

73 TOUCH

NOUNS **1 touch;** sense of touch, tactile sense, tactual sensation, cutaneous sense; taction, **contact** 223.5; **feel,** feeling; hand-mindedness; light touch, lambency, whisper, breath, **kiss,** lip-clap <nf>, **caress,** fondling; loving touch; lick, lap; **brush,** graze, grazing, glance, glancing; stroke, rub; tap, flick; fingertip caress; tentative poke

2 touching, feeling, fingering, palpation, palpating; **handling,** manipulation, manipulating; petting, caressing, stroking, massaging, rubbing, frottage, frication, friction 1044; laying on of hands, fondling; pressure 902.2; feeling up <nf>; osteopathy, chiropractic

3 touchableness, **tangibility, palpability,** tactility, sensitivity, feel

4 feeler, tactile organ, tactor; tactile cell; tactile process, tactile corpuscle, **antenna;** tactile hair, vibrissa; cat whisker; barbel, barbule; palp, palpus; tentaculum

5 finger, digit; forefinger, index finger, index; ring finger, annulary; middle finger, medius, dactylion; little finger, pinkie or pinky <nf>, minimus; thumb, pollex

VERBS **6 touch, feel,** feel of, palpate; **finger,** pass or run the fingers over, feel with the fingertips, thumb; **handle,** palm, paw; **manipulate,** wield, ply; twiddle; poke at, prod, paw; tap, flick; come in contact 223.10

7 touch lightly, touch upon; kiss, **brush,** sweep, graze, brush by, glance, scrape, skim

8 stroke, pet, caress, fondle; **nuzzle,** nose, rub noses; feel up <nf>; rub, rub against, snuggle, massage, knead 1047.6

9 lick, lap, tongue, mouth

ADJS **10 tactile,** tactual; hand-minded

11 touchable, **palpable, tangible,** tactile, tactual; touchy-feely

12 lightly touching, lambent, playing lightly over, barely touching, grazing, skimming, tickling

74 SENSATIONS OF TOUCH

NOUNS **1 tingle,** tingling, thrill, buzz; **prickle,** prickles, prickling, pins and needles; **sting,** stinging, urtication; paresthesia

2 tickle, tickling, **titillation,** pleasant stimulation, **ticklishness,** tickliness

3 itch, itching, itchiness; pruritus; prurigo

4 creeps and **cold creeps** and shivers and **cold shivers** <nf>, creeping of the flesh; gooseflesh, goose bumps, goose pimples; formication

VERBS **5 tingle,** thrill; **itch;** scratch; **prickle,** prick, sting

6 tickle, titillate, thrill

7 feel creepy, feel funny, creep, crawl, **have the creeps** or **cold creeps** or the heebie-jeebies or abdabs <nf>; have gooseflesh or goose bumps; give one the creeps or the willies <nf>

ADJS **8 tingly,** tingling, atingle; **prickly,** prickling

9 ticklish, tickling, tickly, **titillative**

10 itchy, itching; pruriginous

11 creepy, crawly, creepy-crawly, formicative

75 SEX

NOUNS **1 sex,** gender; male, maleness, masculinity 76, female, femaleness, femininity 77; **genitals, genitalia**

2 sexuality, sexual nature, sexualism, sex life, love life; sex education, birds and the bees; **love** 104, sexual activity, lovemaking 562, marriage 563; heterosexuality; homosexuality; bisexuality, ambisexuality; **carnality, sensuality** 663; sexiness, voluptuousness, flesh, fleshiness; **libido,** sex drive, sexual instinct or urge; **potency** 76.2; impotence; frigidity, coldness

3 sex appeal, sexual attraction or attractiveness or magnetism, sexiness, animal magnetism

4 sex object; piece and meat and piece of meat and ass and piece of ass and hot number <nf>; nooky or nookie; sex queen, sex goddess, sex kitten; hottie; skirt <nf>; hunk, sex god; beefcake or stud or stud muffin <nf>, pretty boy

5 sexual desire, sensuous or carnal desire, bodily appetite, **biological urge,** venereal appetite or desire, sexual longing, **lust,** desire, lusts or desires of the flesh, itch, horniness, lech <nf>, chemistry; **erection,** penile erection, hard-on <nf>; **passion,** carnal or sexual passion, fleshly lust, prurience or pruriency, concupiscence, hot blood, aphrodisia, the hots and hot pants and hot rocks and hot nuts <nf>, G-spot; lustfulness, goatishness, libidinousness; lasciviousness 665.5; **eroticism,** erotism; indecency 666; erotomania, eromania, *hysteria libidinosa* <L>; nymphomania, andromania, *furor uterinus* <L>, satyrism, satyriasis, gynecomania; infantile sexuality, polymorphous perversity; **heat,** rut, mating instinct; frenzy or fury of lust; estrus, estrum, estrous cycle, estral cycle

6 aphrodisiac, love potion, philter, love philter; cantharis, blister beetle, Spanish fly

7 copulation, sex act, having sex, having intercourse, *le sport* <Fr>, coupling, mating, pairing, intimacy, coition, **coitus,** pareunia, venery <old>, copula <law>, **sex, intercourse, sexual intercourse,** cohabitation, commerce, sexual commerce, congress, sexual congress, sexual union, sexual relations, relations, marital relations, marriage act, consummation, act of love, making love, sleeping together *or* with, going to bed with, going all the way <nf>; screwing *and* balling *and* nookie *and* diddling *and* making it with <nf>; consenting adult; meat *and* ass <nf>, intimacy, connection, carnal knowledge, aphrodisia; foreplay; **oral sex,** oral-genital stimulation, fellatio, fellation, blow job <nf>; cunnilingus, sixty-nine <nf>; **anal sex,** anal intercourse, sodomy, buggery <nf>; **orgasm,** climax, sexual climax; unlawful sexual intercourse, adultery, hanky-panky, fornication 665.7; coitus interruptus, onanism; tantric sex; group sex, group grope <nf>; serial sex, gang bang <nf>; spouse swapping, wife swapping, husband swapping; casual sex, one-night stand *or* quickie; phone sex; safe sex; sex shop; **lovemaking** 562; **procreation** 78; germ cell, sperm, ovum 305.12

8 masturbation, autoeroticism, self-abuse, onanism, manipulation, playing with oneself, jacking off *and* jerking off *and* pulling off *and* hand job <nf>, wank <nf>; sexual fantasy; wet dream; manustrupration

9 sexlessness, asexuality, neuterness, nonsexualness; **impotence** 19; frigidity; eunuch, *castrato* <Ital>, spado, neuter, gelding; steer

10 sexual preference; sexual orientation; sexual normality, sexual nature; **heterosexuality; homosexuality,** homosexualism, homoeroticism, homophilia, *l'amour bleu* <Fr>, the love that dare not speak its name, sexual inversion, lesbianism, sapphism, tribadism; alternative lifestyle; autoeroticism; transsexuality; **bisexuality,** bisexualism, ambisexuality, ambisextrousness, amphierotism, swinging *or* going both ways <nf>; **lesbianism,** sapphism, tribadism *or* tribady; **sexual prejudice,** sexism, genderism, phallicism, heterosexism, homosexism; coming out of the closet <nf>

11 perversion, sexual deviation, sexual deviance, sexual perversion, sexual abnormality; sexual pathology; psychosexual disorder; sexual psychopathy, *psychopathia sexualis* <L>; paraphilia; zoophilia, zooerastia, bestiality; pedophilia; algolagnia, algolagny, **sadomasochism** *or* s and m; active algolagnia, **sadism;** passive algolagnia, **masochism;** satyrism; fetishism; narcissism; pederasty, pedophilia; exhibitionism; nymphomania; necrophilia; coprophilia; scotophilia, voyeurism; transvestitism, cross-dressing; **incest,** incestuousness, **sex crime,** sexual offense; **sexual abuse,** carnal abuse, molestation; sexual harassment; unlawful sexual intercourse, rape, date rape; cybersex

12 intersexuality, intersexualism, epicenism, epicenity; hermaphroditism, pseudohermaphroditism; androgynism, androgyny, gynandry, gynandrism; transsexuality, transsexualism

13 heterosexual, straight <nf>, breeder <nf>

14 homosexual, gay person, homosexualist, homophile, invert; catamite, *mignon* <Fr>, Ganymede, chicken *and* punk *and* gunsel <nf>; **bisexual,** bi-guy <nf>; **lesbian,** sapphist, tribade, fricatrice <old>; gay pride, gay rights

15 <nf terms for male homosexuals> homo, queer, faggot, fag, fruit , flit, fairy, pansy, nance, auntie, queen, drag queen, closet queen, fruitcake, poof *and* poofter *and* poove <Brit>; <nf terms for female homosexuals> dyke, bull dyke, butchfemme, boondagger, diesel-dyke, lesbo, lez

16 sexual pervert; **pervert,** perve <nf>, **deviant,** deviate, sex pervert, sex fiend, sex criminal, sexual psychopath; sodomist, sodomite, sob <Brit nf>, bugger; pederast; paraphiliac; zoophiliac; pedophiliac; sadist; masochist; sadomasochist, algolagniac; fetishist; transvestite *or* TV, cross-dresser; narcissist; exhibitionist; necrophiliac; coprophiliac; scotophiliac, voyeur; erotomaniac, nymphomaniac, satyr, horndog <nf>; rapist 665.12

17 intersex, sex-intergrade, epicence; hermaphrodite, pseudohermaphrodite; androgyne, gynandroid; transsexual

18 sexology, sex study, sexologist; sexual counselor; sexual surrogate; sexual customs *or* mores *or* practices; sexual morality; new morality, sexual revolution; sexual freedom *or* liberation, free love; trial marriage

VERBS **19** sex, sexualize; genderize

20 lust, **lust after,** itch for, have a lech *and* have hot pants for <nf>, **desire; be in heat** *or* **rut,** rut, come in; get physical <nf>; get an erection, get a hard-on <nf>, tumesce

21 copulate, couple, **mate,** have intercourse, unite in sexual intercourse, **have sexual relations, have sex,** pair, make out <nf>, perform the act of love *or* marriage act, come together, cohabit, cohabitate, shack up <nf>, be intimate; sleep with *or* together, lie with, go to bed with, bonk; fuck *and* screw *and* lay *and* ball *and* frig *and* diddle and do it *and* **make it with** <nf>, go all the way, go to bed with, lie together, get laid <nf>; cover, mount, serve *or* service <of animals>; commit adultery, fornicate 665.19; **make love**

22 **masturbate,** play with *or* abuse oneself, jack off *and* whack off <nf>; fellate, suck *and* suck off <nf>; sodomize, bugger *and* ream <nf>

23 **stimulate,** have foreplay; go down on, give head, suck *or* suck off

24 **climax, come,** achieve satisfaction, achieve *or* reach orgasm; **ejaculate,** get off <nf>

ADJS 25 **sexual,** sex, sexlike, gamic, coital, libidinal; **erotic,** appealing, amorous, magnetic; nuptial; venereal; **carnal, sensual** 663.5, voluptuous, fleshly; desirable, baddable; **sexy;** erogenous, erogenic, erotogenic, ginchy <nf>; sexed, oversexed, hypersexual; procreative 78.15; potent 76.13

26 **aphrodisiac,** aphroditous, **arousing,** stimulating, eroticizing, venereal

27 **lustful, prurient, hot,** steamy, sexy, concupiscent, lickerish, libidinous, **salacious** 666.9, **passionate,** hot-blooded, itching, **horny** *and* hot to trot *and* sexed-up *and* hot and bothered <nf>, excited, aroused, randy, goatish, sexed-up, randy; sex-starved, unsatisfied; lascivious 665.29; **orgasmic,** orgastic, **ejaculatory**

28 **in heat, burning, hot; in rut,** rutting, rutty, ruttish; in must, must, musty; estrous, estral, estrual

29 **unsexual,** unsexed; **sexless,** asexual, esexual, **neuter,** neutral, neutered; castrated, emasculated, eunuchized; **cold, frigid; impotent;** frustrated; undersexed

30 **homosexual,** homoerotic, gay, queer *and* limp-wristed *and* faggoty <nf>; **bisexual,** bisexed, ambisexual, ambisextrous, amphierotic, AC-DC <nf>, autoerotic; lesbian, sapphic, tribadistic; butch *and* dykey <nf>; effeminate 77.14; transvestite; outed; gay-friendly

31 hermaphrodite, hermaphroditic, pseudohermaphrodite, pseudohermaphroditic, epicene, monoclinous; androgynous, androgynal, gynandrous, gynandrian

76 MASCULINITY

NOUNS 1 **masculinity,** masculineness, maleness; **manliness,** manlihood, **manhood,** manfulness, manlikeness; mannishness; gentlemanliness, gentlemanlikeness; boyishness; tomboyishness; a guy thing <nf>

2 **male sex, male sexuality, virility,** virileness, virilism, potence *or* **potency,** sexual power, manly vigor, **machismo;** ultramasculinity; phallicism; male superiority

3 **mankind, man, men, manhood,** menfolk *or* menfolks <nf>, the sword side, patriarchy

4 **male,** male being, masculine; he, him, his, himself; **man,** male person, *homme* <Fr>, *hombre* <Sp>; **gentleman,** gent <nf>

5 <nf terms> **guy,** fellow, feller, lad, blade, chap, chappie, cat, duck, stud, joker, jasper, bugger, bastard, bloke *and* cove *and* johnny *and* bod <Brit nf>, body, dude, gent, Joe, Adam, bud

6 **real man, he-man,** *and* two-fisted man <nf>, hunk *and* jockstrap *and* jock <nf>, man with hair on his chest; caveman *and* bucko <nf>, beefcake

7 <forms of address> **Mister, Mr,** Messrs <pl>, Master; **sir,** my good man, gentleman, my dear sir *or* man; esquire; *monsieur or M* <Fr>, *messieurs or MM* <Fr pl>; *signor and signore and signorino* <Ital>; *señor and Sr and don* <Sp>, *Dom, senhor* <Pg>; *Herr and mein Herr* <Ger>; *mijnheer* <Dutch>, *sahib* <India>, *sri or babu* <Hindu>; *bwana* <Swah>

8 <male animals> cock, rooster, chanticleer; cockerel; drake; gander; peacock; tom turkey, tom, turkey-cock, gobbler, turkey gobbler; dog; boar; stag, hart, buck; stallion, studhorse, stud, top horse <nf>, entire horse, entire, colt; tomcat, tom; he-goat, billy goat, billy; boar, hog; ram, tup <Brit>; wether; bull, bullock, top cow <nf>; steer, stot <Brit nf>; drone

9 <mannish female> **amazon,** virago, androgyne; lesbian, butch *and* dyke <nf>; **tomboy,** hoyden, romp

10 **man of the family,** family man, married man, husband, widower, househusband, patriarch, paterfamilias, father, papa <nf>; son, brother, uncle, nephew, godfather, godson, grandfather, grandson, grandpa

VERBS 11 masculinize, virilize

ADJS 12 **masculine, male,** bull, he-; **manly, manlike, mannish,** manful, andric; uneffeminate; **gentlemanly,** gentlemanlike; yang

13 **virile, potent,** viripotent; ultramasculine, **macho, he-mannish** *and* hunky <nf>, two-fisted <nf>, broad-shouldered, hairy-chested

14 **mannish, mannified; unwomanly, unfeminine,** uneffeminate, viraginous; **tomboyish,** hoyden, rompish

77 FEMININITY

NOUNS 1 **femininity,** feminality, feminacy, feminineness, femaleness, femineity, feminism; **womanliness,** womanlikeness, womanishness, **womanhood,** womanity, muliebrity; girlishness, little-girlishness; maidenhood, maidenliness; **ladylikeness,** gentlewomanliness; **matronliness,** matriarchy, matronage, matronhood, matronship; the eternal feminine; a girl thing <nf>

2 effeminacy, unmanliness, effeminateness, epicenity, epicenism, **womanishness,** muliebrity, **sissiness** <nf>, prissiness <nf>; androgyny, girly man <nf>; feminism

3 womankind, woman, women, femininity, **womanhood,** womenfolk or womenfolks <nf>, the distaff side; **the female sex;** the second sex, **the fair sex,** the gentle sex, the softer sex, **the weaker sex,** the weaker vessel <nf>

4 female, female being; she, her, herself

5 woman, Eve, daughter of Eve, Adam's rib, femme <Fr>, distaff <old>, weaker vessel; frow, Frau <Ger>, vrouw <Dutch>, donna <Ital>, wahine <Hawaii>; **lady,** milady, gentlewoman, domina <L>; feme sole and feme covert <law>; married woman, wife; **matron,** dame, **dowager;** squaw; unmarried woman, bachelor girl <nf>, single woman, spinster, maiden; old maid; lass, lassie, girl 302.6; career woman, businesswoman, working woman, working wife or mother; superwoman; liberated woman, feminist, suffragette, women's libber <nf>

6 <nf terms> **gal, dame,** hen, biddy, skirt, missy, toots, jane, broad, doll, damsel, babe, chick, wench, bird <Brit>, tomato, bitch, minx, momma, mouse, sister, squaw, toots, ball-breaker, dudette

7 woman of the family, married woman, wife, widow, housewife, mother, matriarch, materfamilias; daughter, sister, aunt, niece, godmother, goddaughter, grandmother, granddaughter; soccer mom

8 <forms of address> **Ms;** Miss or miss; Mistress <old>, **Mrs; madam** or ma'am; missus; my good lady, my dear woman or lady, lady; madame or Mme <Fr>; mesdames or Mmes <Fr pl>; Frau and Fraulein <Ger>, vrouw <Dutch>, signora <Ital>, señora <Sp>, senhora <Pg>, mem-sahib <Hindu>; donna <Ital>, doña <Sp>, dona <Pg>, mademoiselle or Mlle <Fr>; Fraülein <Ger>; signorina <Ital>, señorita <Sp>, senhorita <Pg>, Dame and Lady <Brit>

9 <female animals> hen, biddy; guinea hen; peahen; bitch, slut, gyp; sow, gilt; ewe, ewe lamb; she-goat, nanny goat or nanny; doe, hind, roe; jenny; mare, brood mare; filly; cow, bossy; heifer; vixen; tigress; lioness; she-bear, she-lion, queen bee, etc

10 <effeminate male> **mollycoddle,** effeminate; **mother's darling, mother's boy, mama's boy,** Lord Fauntleroy, sissy, Percy, goody-goody, goody two-shoes; **pantywaist,** pansy, nancy or nance, chicken, lily; cream puff, weak sister, milksop, wussy; fag or queen or swish <nf>

11 feminization, womanization, effemination, effeminization, sissification <nf>

VERBS **12** feminize; womanize, demasculinize, effeminize, effeminatize, effeminate, soften, sissify <nf>; emasculate, castrate, geld

ADJS **13 feminine, female;** gynic, gynecic, gynecoid; muliebral, distaff, **womanly, womanish, womanlike,** petticoat; **ladylike,** gentlewomanlike, gentlewomanly; **matronly,** matronal, matronlike; **girlish,** little-girlish, kittenish; maidenly 301.11;

14 effeminate, womanish, fem <nf>, old-womanish, **unmanly,** muliebrous, soft, chicken, prissy, **sissified,** sissy, **sissyish**

78 REPRODUCTION, PROCREATION

NOUNS **1 reproduction, making, re-creation,** remaking, refashioning, reshaping, redoing, re-formation, reworking, rejiggering <nf>; **reconstruction,** rebuilding, redesign, restructuring, perestroika <Russ>; **revision;** reedition, reissue, reprinting; reestablishment, **reorganization,** reinstitution, reconstitution; redevelopment; **rebirth,** renascence, resurrection, revival; regeneration, regenesis, palingenesis; **duplication** 874, **imitation** 336, **copy** 785, **repetition** 849; **restoration** 396, renovation; producing or making or creating anew or over or again or once more; **birth rate,** fertility rate; baby boom or boomlet <nf>

2 procreation, reproduction, generation, begetting, breeding, engenderment, engendering, fathering, siring, spawning; **propagation, multiplication,** proliferation; linebreeding; inbreeding, endogamy; outbreeding, xenogamy; dissogeny; crossbreeding 797.4

3 fertilization, fecundation; impregnation, insemination, begetting, getting with child, knocking up <nf>, mating, servicing; **pollination,** pollinization; germination; cross-fertilization, cross-pollination; self-fertilization, heterogamy, orthogamy; isogamy, artificial insemination; conjugation, zygosis; in vitro fertilization, test-tube baby technique

4 conception, conceiving, inception of pregnancy; superfetation, superimpregnation

5 pregnancy, gestation, incubation, parturiency, gravidness or gravidity, heaviness, greatness, bigness, the family way <nf>; brooding, sitting, covering

6 birth, generation, genesis; development; procreation; abiogenesis, archigenesis, biogenesis, blastogenesis, digenesis, dysmerogenesis, epigenesis, eumerogenesis, heterogenesis, histogenesis, homogenesis, isogenesis, merogenesis, metagenesis, monogenesis, oögenesis, orthogenesis, pangenesis, parthenogenesis, phytogenesis, sporogenesis, xenogenesis; spontaneous generation

VERBS **7 reproduce, remake,** make *or* do over, **re-create,** regenerate, resurrect, revive, re-form, refashion, **reshape,** remold, recast, rework, rejigger <nf>, redo, **reconstruct,** rebuild, redesign, restructure, **revise;** reprint, reissue; reestablish, reinstitute, reconstitute, refound, **reorganize; redevelop; duplicate** 874.3, **copy** 336.5, **repeat** 849.7, **restore** 396.11, **renovate**

8 procreate, generate, breed, beget, get, **engender; propagate, multiply;** proliferate; mother; father; sire; reproduce in kind, reproduce after one's kind, "multiply and replenish the earth"—Bible; breed true; inbreed, breed in and in; outbreed; cross-pollinate, crossbreed; linebreed

9 lay <eggs>, deposit, drop, spawn

10 fertilize, fructify, fecundate, fecundify; **impregnate, inseminate,** spermatize, knock up <nf>, **get with child** *or* **young; pollinate** *or* pollinize, pollen; cross-fertilize, cross-pollinate *or* cross-pollinize

11 conceive, get in the family way <nf>; superfetate

12 be pregnant, be gravid, be great with child, **be with child** *or* **young;** be in the family way *and* have a bun in the oven *and* be expecting *and* anticipate a blessed event <nf>, be infanticipating *and* be knocked up <nf>, be blessed-eventing <nf>; gestate, breed, carry, carry young; **incubate, hatch; brood,** sit, set, cover

13 give birth 1.3

ADJS **14 reproductive, re-creative, reconstructive,** re-formative; renascent, regenerative, resurgent, reappearing; reorganizational; revisional; **restorative** 396.22; Hydraheaded, phoenixlike

15 reproductive, procreative, procreant, **propagative,** life-giving; spermatic, spermatozoic, seminal, germinal, fertilizing, fecundative; multiparous

16 genetic, generative, genial, gametic; genital, genitive; abiogenetic, biogenetic, blastogenetic, digenetic, dysmerogenetic, epigenetic, eumerogenetic, heterogenetic, histogenetic, homogenetic, isogenetic, merogenetic, metagenetic, monogenetic, oögenetic, orthogenetic, pangenetic, parthenogenetic, phytogenetic, sporogenous, xenogenetic

17 bred, impregnated, inseminated; inbred, endogamic, endogamous; outbred, exogamic, exogamous; crossbred; linebred

18 pregnant, enceinte <Fr>, preggers *and* knocked-up <nf>, **with child** *or* **young, in the family way** <nf>, gestating, breeding, teeming, parturient; heavy with child *or* young, great *or* big with child *or* young, wearing her apron high, in a delicate condition, gravid, heavy, great, big-laden;

carrying, carrying a fetus *or* an embryo; **expecting** <nf>, anticipating *and* anticipating a blessed event <nf>, infanticipating <nf>; superfetate, superimpregnated

79 CLEANNESS

NOUNS **1 cleanness, cleanliness; purity,** squeaky-cleanness <nf>, pureness; **immaculateness,** immaculacy; **spotlessness,** unspottedness, stainlessness, whiteness; freshness; fastidiousness, daintiness, cleanly habits, spit and polish; asepsis, sterility, hospital cleanliness; tidiness 807.3

2 cleansing, cleaning, cleaning up, detersion <old>; **purge,** purging, purgation, cleanout, cleaning out, purging, purgation, catharsis, abstersion <old>; **purification,** purifying, lustration; expurgation, bowdlerization; housecleaning, spring-cleaning, cleanup

3 sanitation, hygiene, hygenics; **disinfection, decontamination, sterilization,** sanitization, antisepsis, asepsis; pasteurization; deodorization, fumigation, disinfestation, delousing; chlorination

4 refinement, clarification, purification, depuration; **straining,** colature; elution, elutriation; extraction 192.8; **filtering,** filtration; **percolation,** leaching, edulcoration <old>, lixiviation; **sifting,** separation, **screening,** sieving, bolting, riddling, winnowing; essentialization; sublimation; **distillation,** destructive distillation

5 washing, ablution; lavation, laving, lavage; lavabo; **wash, washup;** soaking, soaping, lathering; dip, dipping; rinse, rinsing; sponge, sponging; shampoo, shampooing; washout, elution, elutriation; irrigation, flush, flushing, flushing out; douche, douching; enema; **scrub,** scrubbing, swabbing, mopping, scouring; **cleaning up** *or* **out,** washing up, scrubbing up *or* out, mopping up *or* down, wiping up *or* down

6 laundering, laundry, tubbing; **wash, washing;** washday

7 bathing, balneation

8 bath, bathe <Brit>, tub <nf>; **shower,** shower bath, needle bath, hot *or* cold shower; douche; sponge bath, sponge; hip bath, sitz bath; footbath; sweat bath, Turkish bath, hummum, Russian bath, Swedish bath, Finnish bath, sauna *or* sauna bath, steam bath, Japanese bath, hot tub, whirlpool bath, Jacuzzi <trademark>, plunge bath

9 dip, bath; acid bath, mercury bath, fixing bath; sheepdip

10 bathing place, bath, baths, public baths, **bathhouse,** bagnio <old>, sauna, Turkish baths; *balneum* and *balneae* and *thermae* <L>; mikvah <Judaism>; watering place, spa; lavatory, washroom, bathroom; steam room, sweat room, sudatorium, sudarium, sudatory, caldarium, tepidarium; rest room

11 washery, laundry; washhouse, washshed; **coin laundry, Laundromat** <trademark>, **launderette,** coin-operated laundry, laundrette <Brit>, washateria; automatic laundry; hand laundry; car wash

12 washbasin, washbowl, washdish, basin; **lavatory, washstand; bathtub,** tub, bath; bidet; basin and pitcher, basin and ewer; **shower,** showers, shower room, shower bath, shower stall, shower head, shower curtain; **sink,** kitchen sink; dishwasher; washing machine, washer; piscina, lavabo, ewer, aquamanile; washtub, washboard, washpot, washing pot, wash boiler, dishpan; finger bowl; wash barrel

13 refinery; refiner, purifier, clarifier; **filter; strainer,** colander; **percolator,** lixiviator; **sifter, sieve, screen,** riddle, cribble; winnow, winnower, winnowing machine, winnowing basket *or* fan; cradle, rocker

14 cleaner, cleaner-up, cleaner-off, cleaner-out; **janitor,** janitress, custodian; cleaning woman *or* lady *or* man, housecleaner, housemaid, maid, daily *or* daily woman *and* charwoman *or* char <Brit>; window cleaner, squeegee <nf>; scrubber, swabber; shoeshiner, bootblack

15 washer, launderer; **laundress,** laundrywoman, **washerwoman,** washwoman; **laundryman,** washerman, washman; dry cleaner; **dishwasher,** pot-walloper *and* pearl-diver <nf>, scullion, scullery maid; dishwiper

16 sweeper; street sweeper, crossing sweeper, whitewing, cleanser *or* scavenger <Brit>; **chimney sweep** *or* sweeper, sweep, flue cleaner; scavenger, beachcomber; garbage collector, trash collector, sanitary engineer

17 cleanser, cleaner; cleaning agent; antiseptic, disinfectant; cold cream, cleansing cream, **soap, detergent,** washing powder, soap flakes, abstergent; dishwashing liquid *or* powder; shampoo; rinse; bubble bath, shower gel; **solvent;** cleaning solvent; water softener; purifier, depurant; mouthwash, gargle; dentifrice, **toothpaste, tooth powder,** whitener; abrasive, pumice, pumice stone, holystone, hearthstone, scouring powder, scouring pad; polish, varnish, wax, whitewah; purge, purgative, cathartic, enema, diuretic, emetic, nauseant, laxative; **cleaning device,** cleaning tool, cleaning cloth

VERBS **18 clean, cleanse, purge,** deterge, depurate; **purify,** lustrate, disinfect; sweeten, **freshen;** whiten, bleach; clean up *or* out, clear out, sweep out, clean up after; houseclean, clean house, spring-clean; spruce, **tidy** 808.12; scavenge; **wipe,** wipe up *or* out, wipe off, mop *or* mop up, swab, scrub, scour; dust, dust off; steam-clean, **dry-clean;** expurgate, bowdlerize

19 wash, bathe, bath <Brit>, shower, lave, have *or* take a bath; **launder,** tub; wash up *or* out *or* away; **rinse,** rinse out, dip, dunk, flush, flush out, irrigate, sluice, sluice out; ritually immerse, baptize, *toivel* <Yiddish>; sponge, sponge down *or* off; **scrub,** scrub up *or* out, **swab, mop,** mop up; **scour;** hose out *or* down; rinse off *or* out; soak out *or* away; soap, lather; shampoo; syringe, douche; gargle

20 groom, dress, fettle <Brit nf>, **brush up; preen,** plume, titivate; manicure

21 comb, curry, card, hackle *or* hatchel, heckle <nf>, rake

22 refine, clarify, clear, purify, rectify, depurate, decrassify; try; **strain;** elute, elutriate; **extract** 192.10; **filter,** filtrate; **percolate,** leach, lixiviate, edulcorate <old>; **sift,** separate, sieve, **screen,** decant, bolt, winnow; sublimate, sublime; **distill,** spiritualize <old>, essentialize

23 sweep, sweep up *or* out, **brush,** brush off, whisk, broom; vacuum <nf>, vacuum-clean

24 sanitize, sanitate, hygienize; **disinfect, decontaminate, sterilize,** antisepticize, radiosterilize; autoclave, boil; pasteurize, flash-pasteurize; disinfest, fumigate, deodorize, delouse; chlorinate

ADJS **25 clean, pure; immaculate, spotless,** stainless, pristine, white, fair, dirt-free, soil-free, fresh; **unsoiled, unsullied,** unmuddied, unsmirched, unbesmirched, unblotted, unsmudged, unstained, untarnished, **unspotted,** unblemished, unmarked, undirtied; smutless, smut-free; bleached, whitened; bright, shiny 1025.34; **unpolluted,** nonpolluted, untainted, unadulterated, **undefiled;** kosher, *tahar* <Heb>, ritually pure *or* clean; **squeaky-clean** *and* clean as a whistle *or* a new penny *or* a hound's tooth <nf>; **sweet, fresh,** fresh as a daisy; **cleanly,** fastidious, dainty, of cleanly habits; well-washed, well-scrubbed, tubbed <nf>

26 cleaned, cleansed, cleaned up, cleaned out, washed, scrubbed; purged, purified; expurgated, bowdlerized; refined, filtered; spruce, spick and span, **tidy** 807.8

27 sanitary, hygienic, prophylactic; sterile, aseptic, antiseptic, **uninfected;** disinfected, decontaminated, sterilized; autoclaved, boiled; pasteurized

28 cleansing, cleaning; detergent, detersive; disinfectant, antibacterial; abstergent, abstersive, depurative; **purifying,** purificatory, lustral;

expurgatory; purgative, purging, cathartic, diuretic, emetic; balneal, ablutionary

ADVS **29 cleanly,** clean; **purely, immaculately, spotlessly**

80 UNCLEANNESS

NOUNS **1 uncleanness,** immundity; **impurity,** unpureness; **dirtiness,** grubbiness, dinginess, griminess, messiness *and* grunginess *and* scuzziness <nf>, scruffiness, slovenliness, sluttishness, untidiness 810.6; miriness, muddiness 1062.4; uncleanliness

2 filthiness, foulness, vileness, scumminess <nf>, feculence, shittiness <nf>, muckiness, ordurousness, nastiness, grossness *and* yuckiness *and* ickiness <nf>; scurfiness, scabbiness; rottenness, putridness 393.7; rankness, fetidness 71.2; odiousness, repulsiveness 98.2; nauseousness, disgustingness 64.3; hoggishness, piggishness, swinishness, beastliness

3 squalor, squalidness, squalidity, **sordidness,** slum, hellhole; slumminess <nf>; insanitation, lack of sanitation; unhealthy conditions

4 defilement, befoulment, dirtying, soiling, besmirchment; **pollution, contamination, infection;** abomination; ritual uncleanness *or* impurity *or* contamination

5 soil, soilure, soilage, smut; **smirch, smudge,** smutch, smear, **spot,** blot, blotch, **stain** 1004.3

6 dirt, grime; dust; soot, smut; **mud** 1062.8

7 filth, muck, slime, mess, sordes, foul matter; ordure, **excrement** 12.3; mucus, snot <nf>; scurf, furfur, dandruff; scuzz *and* mung <nf>; putrid matter, pus, corruption, gangrene, decay, carrion, **rot** 393.7; **obscenity,** smut <nf> 666.4

8 slime, slop, scum, sludge, slush; glop *and* gunk <nf>, **muck, mire,** ooze

9 offal, slough, **offscourings,** scurf, scum, riffraff, scum of the earth; residue; **carrion; garbage, swill,** slop, slops, sullage; dishwater, ditchwater, bilgewater, bilge; **sewage,** sewerage; rubbish, trash, **waste, refuse** 391.4

10 dunghill, manure pile, midden, mixen <Brit nf>, colluvies; compost heap; kitchen midden, refuse heap

11 sty, pigsty, pigpen, hogpen; **stable,** Augean stables; dump *and* hole *and* shithole <nf>, rathole; tenement; warren, **slum,** rookery; the inner city, the ghetto, the slums, asphalt *or* concrete jungle; plague spot, pesthole; hovel

12 <receptacle of filth> sink; sump, **cesspool,** cesspit, septic tank; catchbasin; bilge *or* bilges; **sewer,** drain, *cloaca* and *cloaca maxima* <L>; sewage

farm, purification plant; **dump,** garbage dump, dumpsite, sanitary landfill, landfill; **swamp,** bog, mire, quagmire, marsh

13 pig, swine, hog, slut, sloven, slattern 810.7

VERBS **14** wallow in the mire, live like a pig, roll in the dirt *or* mud

15 dirty, dirty up, dirt <old>, grime, **begrime;** muck, muck up <nf>; **muddy,** bemud <old>; mire, bemire; slime; dust; soot, smoke, besmoke

16 soil, besoil; black, **blacken; smirch,** besmirch, sully, slubber <Brit nf>, smutch *or* smouch, besmutch, smut, **smudge, smear,** besmear, daub, bedaub; **spot, stain** 1004.6; get one's hands dirty, dirty *or* soil one's hands

17 defile, foul, befoul; sully; foul one's own nest, shit where one eats <nf>, nasty *or* benasty <nf>, mess *and* mess up <nf>, make a mess of; **pollute, corrupt, contaminate, infect; taint,** tarnish, poison; profane, desecrate, unhallow

18 spatter, splatter, splash, **bespatter,** dabble, bedabble, spot, splotch

19 draggle, bedraggle, **drabble,** bedrabble, daggle <old>, drabble in the mud

ADJS **20 unclean, unwashed,** unbathed, unscrubbed, unscoured, unswept, unwiped; **impure,** unpure; **polluted, contaminated, infected, corrupted;** ritually unclean *or* impure *or* contaminated, *tref* <Yiddish>, *terefah* <Heb>, nonkosher; not to be handled without gloves; **uncleanly;** septic, unhygienic, contaminated, polluted, toxic

21 soiled, sullied, dirtied, smirched, besmirched, smudged, spotted, **tarnished,** tainted, **stained; defiled,** fouled, **befouled;** draggled, drabbled, bedraggled

22 dirty, dirt-encrusted, **grimy, grubby,** grungy <nf>, scummy <nf>, smirchy, dingy, messy <nf>; scruffy, slovenly, untidy 810.15; miry, **muddy** 1062.14; **dusty;** smutty, smutchy, smudgy; sooty, smoky; snuffy

23 filthy, foul, vile, mucky, **nasty,** icky *and* yecchy *and* yucky *and* gross *and* grungy *and* scuzzy *and* grotty <nf>; malodorous, mephitic, rank, **fetid** 71.5; **putrid, rotten;** pollutive; nauseating, disgusting; **odious, repulsive** 98.18; **slimy;** barfy *and* vomity *and* puky <nf>; sloppy, sludgy; gloppy *and* gunky <nf>, scurfy, scabby; wormy, maggoty, flyblown; feculent, ordurous, crappy *and* shitty <nf>, excremental, excrementitious, fecal 12.20

24 hoggish, piggish, swinish, beastly

25 squalid, sordid, wretched, shabby; slumlike, slummy

ADVS **26 uncleanly, impurely,** unpurely; **dirtily,** grimily; **filthily, foully,** nastily, vilely

81 HEALTHFULNESS

NOUNS **1 healthfulness, healthiness, salubrity,** salubriousness, salutariness, **wholesomeness,** beneficialness, goodness

2 hygiene, hygienics; sanitation 79.3; public health, epidemiology; health physics; **preventive medicine,** prophylaxis, preventive dentistry, prophylactodontia; prophylactic psychology, mental hygiene; **fitness** and **exercise** 84; cleanliness

3 hygienist, hygeist, sanitarian; public health doctor *or* physician, epidemiologist; health physicist; preventive dentist, prophylactodontist; dental hygienist

VERBS **4 make for health,** conduce to health, **be good for,** agree with

ADJS **5 healthful, healthy, salubrious, salutary, wholesome,** health-preserving, health-enhancing, health-giving, life-promoting, **beneficial,** benign, good, **good for;** nutritious, nourishing, roborant; **hygienic, hygienical,** hygeian, sanitary; constitutional, for one's health; conditioning; bracing, refreshing, invigorating, tonic; what the doctor ordered

82 UNHEALTHFULNESS

NOUNS **1 unhealthfulness, unhealthiness, insalubrity,** insalubriousness, unsalutariness, ill health, poor health, **unwholesomeness,** badness; noxiousness, noisomeness, injuriousness, harmfulness 1000.5; pathenogenicity; chronic ill health, valetudinarianism; health hazard, threat *or* danger *or* menace to health; contamination, pollution, environmental pollution, air *or* water *or* noise pollution

2 innutritiousness, indigestibility

3 poisonousness, toxicity, venomousness; virulence *or* virulency, malignancy, noxiousness, destructiveness, deadliness, morbidity; **infectiousness,** infectivity, contagiousness, communicability; poison, venom 1001.3

VERBS **4 disagree with,** not be good for, sicken

ADJS **5 unhealthful, unhealthy, insalubrious, unsalutary, unwholesome,** peccant, bad, **bad for;** noxious, noisome, injurious, baneful, harmful 1000.12; **polluted,** contaminated, tainted, foul, septic, stagnant; unhygienic, unsanitary, insanitary; morbific, pathogenic, pestiferous

6 unnutritious, indigestible, unassimilable

7 poisonous, toxic, toxicant; **venomous,** envenomed, venenate, venenous; veneniferous, toxiferous; pollutive; **virulent, noxious, malignant,** malign, destructive, deadly; pestiferous, pestilential,

pestilent; mephitic, miasmal, miasmic, miasmatic; **infectious,** infective, contagious, communicable, catching, germ-laden; mephitic; lethal, deadly

83 HEALTH

NOUNS **1 health, well-being; fitness,** health and fitness, physical fitness 84; bloom, flush, pink, glow, rosiness; mental health, emotional health; physical condition; Hygeia

2 healthiness, healthfulness, **soundness,** wholesomeness; healthy body, good *or* healthy constitution; **good health,** good state of health; **robust health,** rugged health, rude health, glowing health, picture of health; **fine fettle,** fine whack <nf>, fine *or* high feather <nf>, **good shape,** good trim, fine shape, top shape <nf>, good condition, mint condition; eupepsia, good digestion; clean bill of health

3 haleness, heartiness, robustness, vigorousness, ruggedness, **vitality,** lustiness, hardiness, strength, vigor; longevity

4 immunity, resistance, nonproneness *or* nonsusceptibility to disease; **immunization;** antibody, antigen 86.27

5 health care, health protection, health *or* medical management, **health maintenance, medical care** 91.1; **wellness,** wellness program, disease prevention, preventive medicine; health awareness program; health policy, health-care policy; allied health care; ambulatory care; palliative care; **health plan, health** *or* **medical insurance,** health service, health-care delivery service *or* plan, health maintenance organization *or* HMO, Medicare, Medicaid; National Health Service *or* NHS *or* National Health <Brit>; socialized medicine; health department, health commissioner; health club, health spa

VERBS **6 enjoy good health,** have a clean bill of health, be in the pink; be in the best of health; **feel good,** feel fine, feel fit, feel like a million dollars *or* like a million <nf>, never feel better; feel one's oats, be full of pep; burst with health, bloom, glow, flourish; keep fit, stay in shape; wear well, stay young, be well-preserved

7 get well, recover 396.20, mend, get healthy, be oneself again, feel like a new person, get back on one's feet, bounce back, get over it, perk up, get the color back in one's cheeks; recuperate 396.19

ADJS **8 healthy, healthful,** enjoying health, **fine,** in health, in shape, in condition, **fit,** fit and fine; **in good health,** in the pink of condition, in mint condition, in good case, **in good** *or* **fine shape, in fine fettle,** in A-1 condition, bursting with health, full of life and vigor, feeling one's oats; eupeptic

9 <nf terms> **in the pink,** in fine whack, in fine *or* high feather, chipper, **fit as a fiddle;** alive and kicking, bright-eyed and bushy-tailed; full of beans *or* of piss and vinegar

10 **well, unailing, unsick, unsickly,** unfrail; all right, doing nicely, up and about, sitting up and taking nourishment, alive and well

11 **sound,** whole, wholesome; unimpaired 1002.8; sound of mind and body, sound in wind and limb, sound as a dollar <nf>

12 **hale, hearty,** hale and hearty, **robust,** robustious, robustuous, vital, **vigorous, strong,** strong as a horse *or* an ox, bionic <nf>, stalwart, stout, sturdy, **rugged,** rude, hardy, lusty, bouncing, well-knit, flush <old>; **fit,** in condition *or* shape; of good constitution

13 **fresh,** green, youthful, **blooming;** flush, flushed, **rosy,** rosy-cheeked, apple-cheeked, ruddy, pink, pink-cheeked; fresh-faced, fresh as a daisy *or* rose, fresh as April

14 **immune, resistant,** nonprone *or* nonsusceptible to disease; health-conscious, health-protecting; immune response

84 FITNESS, EXERCISE

NOUNS 1 **fitness, physical fitness, physical conditioning, condition, shape,** trim, tone, fettle, aerobic fitness, anaerobic fitness, cardiovascular fitness, cardiorespiratory fitness, cardio; **gymnasium, gym** <nf>, **fitness center, health club,** health spa, work-out room, weight room, exercise track *or* trail, trim trail <Brit>, *parcourse* or *parcours* <Fr>; **weight, barbell,** dumbbell, exercise machine, Nautilus <trademark>, bench, exercise bike, rowing machine, stair-climbing machine, elliptical trainer, treadmill; whirlpool bath, Jacuzzi <trademark>, hot tub, spa

2 **exercise,** motion, movement, maneuver; **program,** routine, drill, work-out; **exercise systems; warm-up, stretching,** warm-down; **calisthenics,** free exercise, setting-up exercise *or* set-ups, physical jerks <Brit>, daily dozen <nf>, constitutional; **parcourse exercise; gymnastic exercise, gymnastics;** slimnastics; **isometrics,** isometric *or* no-movement exercise; breather, wind sprint; **aerobic exercise, aerobics,** aerobic dancing *or* dance, step aerobics, dancercize *or* dancercizing, fitaerobics, jazz ballet *or* Jazzercise; Callanetics; **bodybuilding,** weightlifting, weight training, pumping iron <nf>, bench press, arm raise, curl, wrist curl; **running, jogging,** roadwork, distance running; obligate running; cross-training, interval training, *fartlek* <Swedish>; **walking,** fitness walking, healthwalking, aerobic walking, powerwalking, powerstriding; **swimming,** swimnastics, water exercise, aquaerobics; yoga, Pilates

3 **physical fitness test;** stress test, treadmill test; cardiovascular text

VERBS 4 **exercise, work out,** warm up, aerobicize, stretch, lift weights, weight-train, pump iron <nf>, jog, run, bicycle, walk, fitness-walk, power-walk; practice

85 DISEASE

NOUNS 1 **disease** <see list>, **illness, sickness, malady, ailment, indisposition, disorder,** complaint, morbidity, *morbus* <L>, **affliction,** affection, distemper <old>, **infirmity; disability,** defect, handicap; deformity 265.3; **birth defect,** congenital defect; abnormality, condition, pathological condition; **signs, symptoms, pathology,** symptomatology, symptomology, syndrome; **sickishness,** malaise, seediness *and* rockiness *and* the pip *and* the crud *and* the creeping crud <nf>; complication, secondary disease *or* condition; plant disease, blight 1001.2

2 **fatal disease,** deadly disease, terminal disease *or* illness, hopeless condition; **death** 307, clinical death, loss of vital signs; apparent death; **brain death,** local death, somatic death; sudden death, unexplained death; liver death; serum death; thymic death *or* mors thymica; cell death, molecular death; cot death *or* crib death *or* sudden infant death syndrome *or* SIDS

3 **unhealthiness,** healthlessness; **ill health,** poor health, delicate *or* shaky *or* frail *or* fragile health; **sickliness,** peakedness <nf>, **feebleness,** delicacy, weakliness, fragility, **frailty** 16.2; **infirmity, unsoundness,** debility, debilitation, enervation, exhaustion, decrepitude; wasting, languishing, languishment <old>, cachexia *or* cachexy; chronic ill health, invalidity, **invalidism;** unwholesomeness, morbidity, morbidness; hypochondria, hypochondriasis, valetudinarianism, history of illness

4 **infection, contagion,** contamination, taint, virus, affliction; **contagiousness, infectiousness, communicability;** pestiferousness, epidemicity, inoculability; carrier, vector; **epidemiology**

5 **epidemic, plague, pestilence,** pest, pandemic, pandemia, scourge, bane; white plague, tuberculosis; pesthole, plague spot

6 **seizure, attack,** access, visitation; arrest; blockage, stoppage, occlusion, thrombosis, thromboembolism; **stroke,** ictus, apoplexy; **spasm, throes, fit, paroxysm, convulsion,** eclampsia, frenzy; **epilepsy,** falling sickness; tonic spasm,

tetany, lockjaw, trismus, tetanus; laryngospasm, laryngismus; clonic spasm, clonus; cramp; vaginismus

7 **fever, feverishness,** febrility, febricity, pyrexia; hyperpyrexia, hyperthermia; **heat, fire, fever heat;** flush, hectic flush; calenture; delirium 926.8, ague; chill, hypothermia, shivers, shakes

8 **collapse, breakdown, crackup** <nf>, **prostration,** exhaustion, burn-out *or* burnout; nervous prostration *or* breakdown *or* exhaustion, neurasthenia; circulatory collapse

9 <disease symptoms> indication, **syndrome;** anemia; ankylosis; asphyxiation, anoxia, cyanosis; ataxia; bleeding, hemorrhage; colic; dizziness, vertigo; ague, chill, chills; hot flash, hot flush; dropsy, hydrops, edema; morning sickness; fainting; fatigue 21; headache, migraine; fever; constipation; diarrhea, flux, dysentery; indigestion, upset stomach, dyspepsia; inflammation 85.10; necrosis; insomnia; malaise; itching, pruritus; jaundice, icterus; backache, lumbago; vomiting, nausea; paralysis; skin eruption, rash; sore, abscess, discharge; hypertension, high blood pressure; hypotension, low blood pressure; tumor, growth; shock; convulsion, seizure, spasm; pain 26; fibrillation, tachycardia; shortness of breath, labored breathing, apnea, dyspnea, asthma; blennorhea; congestion, nasal discharge, rheum, sore throat, coughing, sneezing; wasting, cachexia *or* cachexy, tabes, marasmus, emaciation, atrophy; sclerosis

10 **inflammation,** inflammatory disease, -itis; muscle *or* muscular disease *or* disorder, myopathy; collagen disease, connective-tissue disease

11 **deficiency diseases** <see list>, nutritional disease, vitamin-deficiency disease, acquired immune deficiency syndrome *or* AIDS

12 **genetic disease** <see list>, gene disease, gene-transmitted disease, hereditary *or* congenital disease

13 **infectious disease** <see list>, infection

14 **eye disease,** ophthalmic disease, disease of the eye *or* of vision; cataract; conjunctivitis *or* pink eye; glaucoma; sty; eye *or* visual defect, defective vision 28

15 **ear disease,** otic disease *or* disorder; **deafness; earache,** otalgia; tympanitis; otosclerosis; **vertigo,** dizziness, loss of balance; Ménière's syndrome *or* disease *or* apoplectical deafness

16 **respiratory disease, upper respiratory disease;** lung disease; cold, sinusitis; influenza, flu; bronchitis, pneumonia

17 **tuberculosis** *or* **TB,** white plague, phthisis, consumption

18 **venereal disease** *or* VD, sexually-transmitted disease *or* STD, social disease, Cupid's itch *or* Venus's curse, dose <nf>; chancre, chancroid; gonorrhea *or* clap *or* the clap *or* claps <nf>; syphilis *or* syph *or* the syph *or* the pox <nf>; herpes, crabs; acquired immune deficiency syndrome *or* AIDS

19 **cardiovascular disease;** heart disease, heart condition, heart trouble; vascular disease; hypertension *or* high blood pressure; angina *or* angina pectoris; cardiac *or* myocardial infarction; cardiac arrest; congenital heart disease; congestive heart failure; coronary *or* ischemic heart disease; coronary thrombosis; heart attack, coronary, heart failure; tachycardia; heart surgery, bypass surgery, angioplasty

20 **blood disease,** hemic *or* hematic disease, hematopathology, anemia, leukemia, lymphoma, Hodgkin's disease; blood poisoning, toxemia, septicemia; hemophilia

21 **endocrine disease,** gland *or* glandular disease, endocrinism, endocrinopathy; diabetes; goiter; hyper- *or* hypoglycemia; hyper- *or* hypothyroidism

22 **metabolic disease;** acidosis, alkalosis, ketosis; gout, podagra; galactosemia, lactose intolerance, fructose intolerance; phenylketonuria *or* PKU, maple syrup urine disease, congenital hypophosphatasia

23 **liver disease,** hepatic disease; gallbladder disease; jaundice *or* icterus

24 **kidney disease,** renal disease; nephritis

25 **neural** *or* **nerve disease,** neurological disease, neuropathy; brain disease; amyotrophic lateral sclerosis *or* Lou Gherig's disease; palsy, cerebral palsy, Bell's palsy; chorea *or* St Vitus's dance *or* the jerks <nf>; Huntington's chorea; headache, migraine; multiple sclerosis *or* MS; muscular dystrophy; Parkinson's disease *or* Parkinsonism; Alzheimer's disease; neuralgia; sciatica *or* sciatic neuritis; shingles *or* herpes zoster; spina bifida; meningitis; emotional trauma 92.17

26 **shock, trauma;** traumatism

27 **paralysis,** paralyzation, palsy, impairment of motor function; **stroke,** apoplexy; paresis; motor paralysis, sensory paralysis; hemiplegia, paraplegia, diplegia, quadriplegia; cataplexy, catalepsy; infantile paralysis, poliomyelitis, polio <nf>; atrophy, numbness

28 **heatstroke;** heat prostration *or* exhaustion; sunstroke, *coup de soleil* <Fr>, siriasis, insolation; calenture, thermic fever

29 **gastrointestinal disease,** disease of the digestive tract; stomach condition; colic; colitis; constipation *or* irregularity; diarrhea *or* dysentery *or* looseness of the bowels *or* flux, the trots *or* the shits *or* the runs <nf>, Montezuma's revenge; gastritis; gastroenteritis; indigestion *or* dyspepsia;

stomachache, bellyache; cramps; heartburn, acid reflux, agita; stomach flu; ulcer, peptic ulcer, stomach cancer; food poisoning

30 **nausea,** nauseation, queasiness, squeamishness, qualmishness; qualm, pukes <nf>; motion sickness, travel sickness, **seasickness,** *mal de mer* <Fr>, airsickness, car sickness, motion discomfort; vomiting 909.8

31 **poisoning,** intoxication, venenation; septic poisoning, blood poisoning, sepsis, septicemia, toxemia, pyemia, septicopyemia; autointoxication; food poisoning, ptomaine poisoning, botulism, salmonellosis, listeriosis; milk sickness; ergotism, St Anthony's fire

32 **environmental disease, occupational disease** <see list>, disease of the workplace, environmental *or* occupational hazard, biohazard; tropical disease

33 **vitamin deficiency disease,** avitaminosis; night blindness, xerophthalmia, beriberi, pellagra, pernicious anemia, scurvy, rickets, osteomalacia

34 **allergy,** allergic disorder; allergic rhinitis, **hay fever,** rose cold, pollinosis, spring allergy; **asthma,** bronchial asthma; **hives,** urticaria; eczema; conjunctivitis; cold sore; allergic gastritis; cosmetic dermatitis; Chinese restaurant syndrome *or* Kwok's disease; allergen

35 **skin diseases;** acne, sebaceous gland disorder; dermatitis; eczema; herpes; hives; itch; psoriasis; scabies; athlete's foot; melanoma, skin cancer

36 **skin eruption,** eruption, **rash,** efflorescence, breaking out, acne, pimple; diaper rash; drug rash, vaccine rash; prickly heat, heat rash; hives, urticaria, nettle rash; papular rash; rupia

37 **sore, lesion;** pustule, papule, papula, fester, **pimple,** hickey *and* zit <nf>; pock; ulcer, ulceration; bedsore; tubercle; blister, bleb, bulla, blain; whelk, wheal, welt, wale; **boil,** furuncle, furunculus; carbuncle; canker; canker sore; cold sore, fever blister; sty; abscess, gathering, aposteme <old>; gumboil, parulis; whitlow, felon, paronychia; bubo; chancre; soft chancre, chancroid; hemorrhoids, piles; bunion; chilblain, kibe; polyp; stigma, petechia; scab, eschar; fistula; suppuration, festering; swelling, rising 283.4

38 **trauma, wound, injury,** hurt, lesion; **cut,** incision, scratch, gash; puncture, stab, stab wound; flesh wound; **laceration,** mutilation; abrasion, scuff, scrape, chafe, gall; frazzle, fray; run, **rip,** rent, slash, **tear; burn,** scald, scorch, first- *or* second- *or* third-degree burn; flash burn; **break, fracture,** bone-fracture, comminuted fracture, compound *or* open fracture, greenstick fracture, spiral *or* torsion fracture; rupture; crack, chip, craze, check, crackle; wrench; whiplash injury *or* whiplash; concussion; **bruise, contusion,** ecchymosis, **black-and-blue mark; black eye,** shiner *and* mouse <nf>; **battering;** battered child syndrome; sprain, strain, repetitive strain injury; paper cut

39 **growth,** neoplasm; **tumor,** intumescence; benign tumor, nonmalignant tumor, innocent tumor; malignant tumor, malignant growth, metastatic tumor, **cancer,** sarcoma, carcinoma; morbid growth; excrescence, outgrowth; proud flesh; exostosis; cyst, wen; fungus, fungosity; callus, callosity, **corn,** clavus; **wart,** verruca; **mole,** nevus

40 **gangrene,** mortification, necrosis, sphacelus, sphacelation; noma; moist gangrene, dry gangrene, gas gangrene, hospital gangrene; caries, cariosity, tooth decay; slough; necrotic tissue

41 <animal diseases> anthrax, splenic fever, charbon, milzbrand, malignant pustule; malignant catarrh *or* malignant catarrhal fever; bighead; blackleg, black quarter, quarter evil *or* ill; cattle plague, rinderpest; glanders; foot-and-mouth disease, hoof-and-mouth disease, aphthous fever; distemper; gapes; heaves, broken wind; hog cholera; mad cow disease; loco, loco disease, locoism; mange, scabies; pip; rot, liver rot, sheep rot; staggers, megrims, blind staggers, mad staggers; swine dysentery, bloody flux; stringhalt; Texas fever, blackwater; John's disease, paratuberculosis, pseudotuberculosis; rabies, hydrophobia; myxomatosis

42 **germ,** pathogen, contagium, bug <nf>, disease-causing agent, disease-producing microorganism; **microbe,** microorganism; **virus,** filterable virus, nonfilterable virus, adenovirus, echovirus, reovirus, rhinovirus, enterovirus, picornavirus, retrovirus, virion, bacteriophage, phage; HIV *or* human immunodeficiency virus; rickettsia; bacterium, **bacteria,** germ, coccus, streptococcus, staphylococcus, bacillus, spirillum, vibrio, spirochete, gram-positive bacteria, gram-negative bacteria, aerobe, aerobic bacteria, anaerobe, anaerobic bacteria; protozoon, amoeba, trypanosome; fungus, mold, spore; **carcinogen,** cancer-causing agent

43 **sick person,** ill person, sufferer, victim; valetudinarian, **invalid, shut-in;** incurable, terminal case; **patient, case;** inpatient, outpatient; apoplectic, bleeder, consumptive, dyspeptic, epileptic, rheumatic, arthritic, spastic; addict; **the sick, the infirm;** hypochondriac

44 **carrier,** vector, biological vector, mechanical vector; Typhoid Mary

45 **cripple,** defective, **handicapped person,** disabled person, physically challenged, incapable; amputee; paraplegic, quadriplegic, paralytic; deformity 265.3; the crippled, the handicapped

VERBS **46 ail, suffer,** labor under, be affected with, complain of; **feel ill,** feel under the weather, feel awful *or* feel like hell <nf>, feel something terrible, not feel like anything <nf>, feel like the walking dead; look green about the gills <nf>

47 take sick *or* **ill, sicken; catch, contract, get,** take, sicken for <Brit>, **come down with** <nf>, be stricken *or* seized by, fall a victim to; catch cold; take one's death <nf>; **break out,** break out with, break out in a rash, erupt; run a temperature, fever; be laid by the heels, be struck down, be brought down, be felled; drop in one's tracks, **collapse;** overdose *or* **OD** <nf>; go into shock, be traumatized

48 fail, weaken, sink, decline, run down, lose strength, lose one's grip, dwindle, droop, flag, wilt, wither, wither away, fade, **languish,** waste, waste away, pine, peak

49 go lame, founder

50 afflict, disorder, derange; sicken, indispose; weaken, enfeeble, enervate, reduce, debilitate, devitalize; **invalid,** incapacitate, **disable;** lay up, hospitalize

51 infect, disease, contaminate, taint, pollute; reinfect, superinfect

52 poison, empoison <old>, envenom

ADJS **53 disease-causing, disease-producing, pathogenic;** threatening, life-threatening; unhealthful 82.5

54 unhealthy, healthless, in poor health; **infirm, unsound,** unfit, invalid, valetudinary, valetudinarian, debilitated, cachectic, enervated, exhausted, drained; shut-in, housebound, homebound, wheelchair-bound; **sickly,** peaky *or* peaked <nf>; **weakly, feeble, frail** 16.14; weakened, decrepit, with low resistance, **run-down,** reduced, reduced in health; **dying** 307.32, **terminal,** moribund, languishing, failing 16.21; pale 36.7

55 unwholesome, unhealthy, unsound, morbid, diseased, pathological

56 ill, ailing, sick, unwell, indisposed, taken ill, down, bad, on the sick list; **sickish, seedy** *and* **rocky** <nf>, **under the weather, out of sorts** <nf>, all-overish <nf>, below par <nf>, white as a sheet, off-color, off one's feed <nf>; not quite right, not oneself; faint, faintish, feeling faint; feeling awful *and* feeling something terrible <nf>, feel crummy *and* feel shitty <nf>; sick as a dog <nf>, laid low; in a bad way, critically ill, in danger, on the critical list, on the guarded list, in intensive care; terminal, inoperable, mortally ill, sick unto death, near death; far gone

57 nauseated, nauseous, **queasy, squeamish, qualmish,** qualmy; **sick to one's stomach;** pukish *and* puky *and* barfy <nf>; seasick, carsick, airsick, green around the gills

58 feverish, fevered, feverous, in a fever, febrile, pyretic; **flushed,** inflamed, **hot, burning,** fiery, hectic; hyperpyretic, hyperthermic; delirious 926.31

59 laid up, invalided, hospitalized, in hospital <Brit>; **bedridden, bedfast, sick abed; down,** prostrate, flat on one's back; in childbed, confined

60 diseased, morbid, pathological, bad, **infected, contaminated,** tainted, peccant, **poisoned,** septic; cankerous, cankered, ulcerous, ulcerated, ulcerative, gangrenous, gangrened, mortified, sphacelated; **inflamed;** congested; **swollen,** edematous

61 anemic, chlorotic; bilious; dyspeptic, liverish, colicky; dropsical, edematous, hydropic; gouty, podagric; neuritic, neuralgic; palsied, paralytic; pneumonic, pleuritic, tubercular, tuberculous, phthisic, consumptive; rheumatic, arthritic; rickety, rachitic; syphilitic, pocky, luetic; tabetic, tabid <old>; allergic; allergenic; apoplectic; hypertensive; diabetic; encephalitic; epileptic; laryngitic; leprous; malarial; measly; nephritic; scabietic, scorbutic, scrofulous; variolous, variolar; tumorous; cancerous, malignant; **carcinogenic,** tumorigenic; HIV-positive

62 contagious, infectious, infective, **catching,** taking, spreading, **communicable,** zymotic, inoculable; pathogenic, germ-carrying; pestiferous, pestilent, pestilential, **epidemic,** epidemial, pandemic; epizootic, epiphytotic; endemic; sporadic; septic

63 kinds of disease

acute disease *or* condition	endocrine gland disease
allergy *or* allergic disease	epidemic disease
atrophy	functional disease
autoimmune disease	fungus *or* fungal disease
bacterial disease	gastric *or* stomach
blood disease	disease
bone disease	gastroenterological disease
cancer	gastrointestinal disease
cardiovascular disease	genetic disease
childhood *or* pediatric	geriatric disease
disease	glandular disease
chronic disease *or*	hepatic *or* liver disease
condition	hereditary disease
chronic fatigue syndrome	hypertrophy
circulatory disease	iatrogenic disease
collagen disease	intestinal disease
congenital disease	joint disease
connective-tissue	muscular disease
disease	neurological disease
contagious *or* infectious	nutritional disease
disease	occupational disease
deficiency disease	ophthalmic disease
degenerative disease	organic disease
digestive disease	pandemic disease
endemic disease	parasitic disease
endocrine disease	protozoan disease

psychiatric disease
psychogenic *or* psychoso-
    matic disease
pulmonary disease
radiation disease
renal *or* kidney disease
respiratory disease
skin disease
sexually transmitted
    disease *or* STD *and*
    venereal disease

tropical disease
ulcer
urinogenital *or* urogenital
    disease
venereal *or* sexually-
    transmitted disease
    or STD
virus *or* viral
    disease
wasting disease
worm disease

64 deficiency diseases and disorders

acquired immune
    deficiency syndrome *or*
    AIDS
anemia
anhidrosis
anoxemia
ariboflavinosis
beriberi
cachexia
chlorosis
cretinism
cytopenia
deficiency anemia
dermatitis
goiter
greensickness
hypoadenia
hypochromia
hypothyroidism
immunodeficiency
ischemia
Italian *or* Lombardy
    leprosy

keratomalacia
kwashiorkor
leukopenia *or* leucopenia
lymphopenia
maidism
malnutrition
night blindness
osteomalacia
osteoporosis
pellagra
pernicious anemia
protein deficiency
rickets *or* rachitis
scurvy
severe combined immune
    deficiency
struma
thrombocytopenia
undernutrition
vitamin deficiency
Wernicke-Korsakoff
    syndrome
xerophthalmia

65 genetic diseases and disorders

achromatic vision
adenosine deaminase
    deficiency *or* ADA
    deficiency
albinism
Christmas disease
color blindness
cystic fibrosis
dichromatic vision
Down *or* Down's syndrome
dysautonomia
Hartnup's disease
hemophilia
hip dysplasia
Huntington's chorea
ichthyosis
lipid histiocytosis

maple syrup urine
    disease
Milroy's disease
mongolism *or*
    mongolianism <old>
mucoviscidosis
muscular dystrophy
neurofibromatosis
Niemann-Pick disease
pancreatic fibrosis
sickle-cell anemia *or*
    disease
Tay-Sachs disease
thalassemia
Turner's syndrome
Werdnig-Hoffmann
    disease

66 infectious diseases

acquired immune
    deficiency syndrome *or*
    AIDS
acute articular rheumatism

African lethargy *or*
    encephalitis
    lethargica
ague

AIDS-related complex *or*
    ARC *or* pre-AIDS
alkali disease
amebiasis
amebic dysentery
anthrax *or* pulmonary
    anthrax *or* woolsorter's
    disease
bacillary dysentery
bastard measles
black death
black fever
blackwater fever
breakbone fever
brucellosis
bubonic plague
cachectic fever
cerebral rheumatism
Chagas disease *or*
    American
    trypanosomiasis
Chagres fever
chicken pox *or* varicella
cholera *or* Asiatic cholera
cowpox
dandy fever
dengue *or* dengue fever
diphtheria
dumdum fever
dysentery
elephantiasis
enteric fever
erysipelas
famine fever
five-day fever
frambesia
German measles
glandular fever
grippe
Hansen's disease *or* leprosy
Haverhill fever
hepatitis
herpangina
herpes
histoplasmosis
hookworm
infectious hepatitis
inflammatory rheumatism
influenza *or* flu <nf>
jail fever
jungle rot
kala azar
Kew Gardens spotted fever
legionnaires' disease
lepra
leprosy
leptospirosis
loaiasis *or* loa loa
Lyme disease

lyssa
malaria *or* malarial fever
marsh fever
measles *or* rubeola
meningitis
milzbrand
mononucleosis *or*
    infectious mononucleosis
    or kissing disease *or*
    mono <nf>
mumps
ornithosis
osteomyelitis
paratyphoid fever
parotitis
pneumonia
poliomyelitis *or* infantile
    paralysis *or* polio <nf>
polyarthritis rheumatism
ponos
psittacosis *or* parrot fever
rabies *or* hydrophobia
rat-bite fever
relapsing fever
rheumatic fever
rickettsial pox
ringworm *or* tinea
Rocky Mountain spotted
    fever
rubella
scarlatina
scarlet fever
schistosomiasis
scrub typhus *or*
    tsutsugamushi disease
septic sore throat
shigellosis
sleeping sickness *or* sleepy
    sickness <Brit>
smallpox *or* variola
snail fever
splenic fever
sporotrichosis
spotted fever
St Anthony's fire
strep throat
streptococcus tonsilitis
swamp fever
syphilis
tetanus *or* lockjaw
thrush
tick-borne typhus
tick fever
toxic shock syndrome
tracheitis
trench fever
trench mouth *or* Vincent's
    infection *or* Vincent's
    angina

trypanosomiasis
tuberculosis
tularemia *or* deer fly fever
  or rabbit fever
typhoid fever *or* typhoid
typhus *or* typhus fever
undulant fever
vaccinia

venereal disease *or* VD
viral dysentery
viral pneumonia
whooping cough *or*
  pertussis
yaws
yellow fever *or* yellow jack
zoster *or* shingles *or* zona

67 environmental and occupational diseases and disorders

aeroembolism *or* caisson
  disease *or* decompres-
  sion sickness *or* tunnel
  disease *or* diver's palsy
  or the bends <nf>
altitude sickness
anoxemia
anoxia
anoxic anoxia
anthrax *or* pulmonary
  anthrax *or* woolsorter's
  disease
cadmium poisoning
carpal tunnel syndrome
chilblain
frostbite
housemaid's knee
immersion foot

jet lag
lead poisoning
mercury poisoning
Minamata disease
motion sickness
pneumoconiosis *or*
  black lung <nf>
radiation sickness
radionecrosis
reactive schizophrenia
red-out
repetitive stress injury *or*
  repetitive motion
  disorder
sunstroke
trench foot
writer's cramp *or* palsy *or*
  spasm

86 REMEDY

NOUNS **1 remedy, cure, corrective,** alterative, remedial measure, sovereign remedy; **relief, help, aid, assistance,** succor; balm, balsam; healing agent; restorative, analeptic; healing quality *or* virtue; oil on troubled waters; specific, specific remedy; **prescription,** recipe, receipt; magic bullet

2 nostrum, patent medicine, quack remedy; snake oil

3 panacea, cure-all, universal remedy, theriac, catholicon, philosophers' stone; polychrest, broad-spectrum drug *or* antibiotic; elixir, elixir of life, *elixir vitae* <L>

4 medicine, medicament, medication, medicinal, theraputant, pharmaceutical, **drug, physic,** preparation, mixture; herbs, medicinal herbs, simples, vegetable remedies; wonder drug, miracle drug; balsam, balm; tisane, ptisan; drops; powder; inhalant; electuary, elixir, syrup, lincture, linctus; officinal; specialized drug, orphan drug; **prescription drug,** ethical drug; over-the-counter *or* OTC drug, counter drug, **nonprescription drug;** proprietary medicine *or* drug, proprietary, patent medicine; proprietary name, generic name; materia medica; pharmacognosy; **placebo,** placebo effect

5 drug, narcotic drug, controlled substance, designer drug, illegal drug, dope <nf>

6 dose, dosage, draft, potion, portion, **shot,** injection; broken dose; booster, booster dose, recall dose, booster shot; drops; inhalant

7 pill, bolus, **tablet, capsule,** time-release capsule, lozenge, dragée, troche, pastille

8 tonic, bracer, cordial, restorative, analeptic, roborant, **pick-me-up** <nf>; **shot in the arm** <nf>; stimulant; vitamin shot, herb tea, ginseng, iron

9 stimulant; Adrenalin <trademark> *or* adrenaline <Brit> *or* epinephrine, aloes; amphetamine sulphate, aromatic spirits of ammonia, caffeine, dextroamphetamine sulfate *or* Dexedrine <trademark>, digitalin *or* digitalis, methamphetamine hydrochloride *or* Methedrine <trademark>, smelling salts *or* salts; pep pill

10 palliative, alleviative, alleviatory, lenitive, assuasive, assuager; soothing, abirritant

11 balm, lotion, salve, ointment, unguent, *unguentum* <L>, cream, balm, cerate, unction, balsam, oil, emollient, demulcent; **liniment,** embrocation; vulnerary; collyrium, eyesalve, eyebath, eyewater <old>, eyewash; ear-drops

12 sedative, sedative hypnotic, depressant, amobarbital and secobarbital, amobarbital sodium *or* Amytal <trademark>, atropine, barbital *or* barbitone <Brit>, barbituric acid, belladonna, chloral hydrate *or* chloral, laudanum, meperidine *or* Demerol <trademark>, morphine, pentobarbital *or* Nembutal <trademark>, phenobarbital *or* Luminal <trademark>, Quaalude <trademark>, reserpine, scopolamine, secobarbital *or* Seconal <trademark>; **sleeping pill** *or* tablet *or* potion; **calmative, tranquilizer,** chlorpromazine, Equanil <trademark>, Librium <trademark>, meprobamate, rauwolfia, reserpine, Thorazine <trademark>, Triavil <trademark>, Valium <trademark>; abirritant, soother, soothing syrup, quietener, pacifier; **analgesic,** acetaminophen *or* Tylenol <trademark>, acetanilide, acetophenetidin, aspirin *or* acetylsalicylic acid *or* Bayer <trademark>, buffered aspirin *or* Bufferin <trademark>, headache *or* aspirin powder, ibuprofen *or* Advil <trademark> *or* Motrin <trademark> *or* Nuprin <trademark>, phenacetin, propoxyphene *or* Darvon <trademark>, sodium salicylate; **anodyne,** paregoric <old>; **pain killer** *and* pain pill <nf>; anti-inflammatory drug *or* agent, nonsteroidal anti-inflammatory drug *or* NSAID, muscle relaxant; alcohol, liquor 88.13

13 psychoactive drug, hallucinogen, psychedelic, psychedelic drug

14 antipyretic, febrifuge, fever-reducer, fever pill <nf>

15 anesthetic; local *or* topical *or* general anesthetic; differential anesthetic; chloroform, ether, ethyl chloride, gas, laughing gas, nitrous oxide, novocaine *or* Novocain <trademark>, thiopental sodium *or* Pentothal <trademark> *or* truth serum

16 cough medicine, cough syrup, cough drops; horehound

17 laxative, cathartic, physic, purge, purgative, aperient, carminative, diuretic; stool softener; milk of magnesia, castor oil, Epsom salts; nauseant, emetic; douche, enema

18 emetic, vomitive *or* vomit <old>, nauseant

19 enema, clyster, clysma, lavage, lavement <old>

20 prophylactic, prophylaxis, **preventive,** preventative, protective

21 antiseptic, disinfectant, fumigant, fumigator, **germicide,** bactericide, microbicide; alcohol, carbolic acid, hydrogen peroxide, merbromin *or* Mercurochrome <trademark>, tincture of iodine

22 dentifrice, toothpaste, tooth powder; mouthwash, gargle, fluoride, dental floss

23 contraceptive, birth control device, prophylactic, contraception; condom; **rubber** *and* skin *and* bag <nf>; oral contraceptive, **birth control pill, the pill** <nf>, Brompton *or* Brompton's mixture *or* cocktail, morning-after pill, abortion pill, RU-486; diaphragm, pessary; spermicide, spermicidal jelly, contraceptive foam; intrauterine device *or* IUD, Dalkon shield <trademark>, Lippes loop; abortion issue, anti-choice, pro-choice, pro-life, right-to-life

24 vermifuge, vermicide, worm medicine, anthelminthic

25 antacid, gastric antacid, alkalizer

26 antidote, countermeasure, counterpoison, counteraction, alexipharmic, antitoxin, counterirritant, theriaca *or* theriac

27 antitoxin, antitoxic serum; **antivenin; serum,** antiserum; interferon; **antibody,** antigen-antibody product, anaphylactic antibody, incomplete antibody, inhibiting antibody, sensitizing antibody; gamma globulin, serum gamma globulin, immune globulin, antitoxic globulin; lysin, precipitin, agglutinin, anaphylactin, bactericidin; antiantibody; antigen, Rh antigen, Rh factor; allergen; **immunosuppressive drug**

28 vaccination, inoculation; vaccine

29 antibiotic, ampicillin, bacitracin, erythromycin, gramicidin, neomycin, nystatin, penicillin, polymyxin, streptomycin, tetracycline *or* Terramycin <trademark>; **miracle drug, wonder drug,** magic bullet; bacteriostat; **sulfa drug,** sulfa, sulfanilamide, sulfonamide, sulfathiazole

30 diaphoretic, sudorific

31 vesicant, vesicatory, epispastic

32 miscellaneous drugs, anabolic steroid *or* muscle pill, antihistamine, antispasmodic, beta blocker, counterirritant, decongestant, expectorant, fertility drug *or* pill, hormone, vasoconstrictor, vasodilator, AZT, hormone replacement therapy

33 dressing, application, epithem <old>; plaster, court plaster, mustard plaster, sinapism; **poultice,** cataplasm; formentation; **compress,** pledget; stupe; tent; tampon; **bandage, bandaging,** band <old>, binder, cravat, triangular bandage, roller *or* roller bandage, four-tailed bandage; bandage compress, adhesive compress, adhesive bandage, Band-Aid <trademark>; butterfly dressing; elastic bandage, Ace elastic bandage *and* Ace bandage <trademark>, compression bandage; rubber bandage; plastic bandage *or* strip; **tourniquet;** sling; splint, brace; cast, plaster cast; tape, **adhesive tape;** lint, cotton, gauze, sponge; patch, nicotine patch

34 pharmacology, pharmacy, pharmaceutics; posology; materia medica

35 pharmacist, pharmaceutist, pharmacopolist, **druggist, chemist** <Brit>, **apothecary,** dispenser, gallipot; pharmacologist, pharmaceutical chemist, posologist; pill pusher *or* roller<nf>

36 drugstore, pharmacy, chemist *and* chemist's shop <Brit>, apothecary's shop, dispensary, dispensatory

37 pharmacopoeia, pharmacopedia, dispensatory

VERBS **38** remedy, help, relieve, cure 396.15; medicate; prescribe; treat

ADJS **39 remedial, curative, therapeutic, healing, corrective,** disease-fighting, alterative, restorative, curing, analeptic, sanative, sanatory; salubrious, salutiferous; all-healing, panacean; adjuvant; **medicinal,** medicative, theriac, theriacal, iatric; anticancer; first-aid

40 palliative, lenitive, alleviative, assuasive, soothing, balmy, balsamic, demulcent, emollient, pain-relieving, analgesic, anodyne

41 antidotal, alexipharmic, counteractant; **antitoxic; antibiotic,** synthetic antibiotic, semisynthetic antibiotic, bacteriostatic, antimicrobial; antiluetic, antisyphilitic; antiscorbutic; antiperiodic; antipyretic, febrifugal; vermifugal, anthelmintic; **antacid**

42 prophylactic, preventive, protective

43 antiseptic, disinfectant, germicidal, bactericidal

44 tonic, stimulating, bracing, invigorating, stimulative, reviving, refreshing, restorative, analeptic, strengthening, roborant, corroborant

45 sedative, calmative, calmant, depressant, **soothing, tranquilizing, quietening; narcotic,** opiatic; **analgesic,** anodyne, paregoric <old>; anti-inflammatory; muscle-relaxant; hypnotic, soporific, somniferous, somnifacient, sleep-inducing

46 psychochemical, psychoactive; ataractic; antidepressant, mood drug; hallucinogenic, **psychedelic,** mind-expanding, psychotomimetic

47 anesthetic, deadening, numbing

48 cathartic, laxative, purgative, aperient; carminative; diuretic

49 emetic, vomitive

87 SUBSTANCE ABUSE

NOUNS **1 substance abuse, drug abuse,** narcotics abuse, drug use, glue-sniffing, solvent abuse; **addiction, addictedness, drug addiction,** narcotic addiction, opium addiction *or* habit, opiumism, morphine addiction *or* habit, morphinism, heroin addiction *or* habit, cocaine addiction, cocainism, coke habit <nf>, crack habit, barbiturate addiction, amphetamine addiction; **habit,** drug habit, jones <nf>, drug habituation, drug dependence, physical addiction *or* dependence, psychological addiction *or* dependence, jones *and* monkey on one's back *and* Mighty Joe Young <nf>; **drug experience, drug intoxication,** high *and* buzz *and* rush <nf>; frightening drug experience, bad trip *and* bum trip *and* bummer *and* drag <nf>; **alcoholism** 88.3, alcohol abuse, drinking habit, acute alcoholism, chronic alcoholism, dipsomania, hitting the bottle <nf>, Dutch courage, hard drinking, liquid lunch, barhopping; drunk driving; **smoking,** smoking habit, one- *or* two- *or* three-pack-a-day habit, nicotine addiction 89.10, chain smoking; **tolerance,** acquired tolerance; **withdrawal, withdrawal sickness,** withdrawal syndrome, withdrawal symptoms, bogue *and* coming down *and* crash <nf>, abrupt withdrawal *and* cold turkey <nf>; **detoxification** *or* detox <nf>, drying out, taking the cure; Alcoholics Anonymous, AA; Narcotics Anonymous, NA; drug test; drug czar

2 <drug use> smoking, sniffing, injecting, snorting, freebasing, hitting up, shooting up, skin-popping, mainlining, pill-popping, banging, blowing, cocktailing; buzz, trip, acid trip, bad trip; drug pushing, drug trafficking, holding <nf>

3 drug, narcotic, dope <nf>, dangerous drug, controlled substance, abused substance, illegal drug, addictive drug, **hard drug;** soft drug, gateway drug; lifestyle drug; **opiate; sedative, depressant,** sedative hypnotic, **antipsychotic tranquilizer,** trank <nf>; **hallucinogen,** hallucinogenic drug, psychedelic, psychedelic drug, psychoactive drug, psychoactive chemical *or* psychochemical, psychotropic drug, psychotomimetic drug, mind-altering drug,

mind-expanding drug, mind-blowing drug; designer drug; street drug; recreational drug; **stimulant; antidepressant,** Prozac <trademark>; **inhalant,** volatile inhalant; drug of choice

4 <nf terms for amphetamines> bennies, benz, black mollies, brain ticklers, crank, crystal, dexies, diet pills, dolls, ecstasy, footballs, greenie, hearts, ice, jelly beans, lid poppers, meth, pep pills, purple hearts, speed, uppers, ups, white crosses

5 <nf terms for amyl nitrate> amies, blue angels, blue devils, blue dolls, blue heavens, poppers, snappers; **barbiturates,** barbs, black beauties, candy, dolls, downers, downs, goofballs, gorilla pills, nebbies, nimbies, phennies, phenos, pink ladies, purple hearts, yellow jackets

6 <nf terms for chloral hydrate> joy juice, knockout drops, mickey, Mickey Finn, peter

7 <nf terms for cocaine> basuco, bernice, C, big C, blow, C, charlie, coke, crack, crack cocaine, jumps, dust, flake, girl, gold dust, her, jay, joy powder, lady, lady snow, nose candy, Peruvian marching powder, rock, snow, star dust, toot, white, white girl, white lady, white stuff

8 <nf terms for hashish> black hash, black Russian, hash

9 <nf terms for heroin> big H, boy, brown, caballo, crap, doojee, flea powder, garbage, H, hard stuff, henry, him, his, horse, hombre, jones, junk, mojo, P-funk, scag, schmeck, smack, white stuff

10 <nf terms for LSD> acid, big D, blotter, blue acid, blue cheer, blue heaven, California sunshine, cap, cubes, D, deeda, dots, electric Kool-Aid, haze, L, mellow yellows, orange cubes, pearly gates, pink owsley, strawberry fields, sugar, sunshine, tabs, yellow, yellow sunshine, orange sunshine

11 <nf terms for marijuana> Acapulco gold, aunt mary, bomb, boo, bush, doobie, gage, ganja, grass, grefa, hay, hemp, herb, Indian hay, J, jane, kif, mary, maryjane, mary warner, meserole, mighty mezz, moota, muggles, pod, pot, smoke, snop, tea, Texas tea, weed, yerba

12 <nf terms for marijuana cigarette> joint, joy stick, kick stick, reefer, roach, stick, twist

13 <nf terms for mescaline> beans, big chief, buttons, cactus, mesc

14 <nf terms for morphine> big M, emm, hocus, M, miss emma, miss morph, morph, moocah, white stuff

15 <nf terms for pentobarbital> nebbies, nemmies, nimby, yellow dolls, yellows

16 <nf terms for opium> black pills, brown stuff, hop, O, tar

17 <nf terms for peyote> bad seed, big chief, buttons, cactus, P, topi

18 <nf terms for phencyclidine> angel dust, animal trank, DOA, dust, elephant, hog, PCP, peace, rocket fuel, supergrass, superweed

19 <nf terms for psilocybin> magic mushroom, mushroom, shroom, STP

20 dose, hit *and* fix *and* toke *and* rock <nf>; **shot, injection,** bang *or* bhang <nf>; **portion, packet,** spliff *and* snort *and* blockbuster *and* toke and blast <nf>, shoot-up *and* hype <nf>, bag *and* deck <nf>, dime bag; drug house, shooting gallery *and* needle park <nf>, crack house, opium den, balloon room *and* pot party *and* dope den <nf>

21 addict, drug addict, narcotics addict, user, drug user, drug abuser, junkie *and* head *and* druggy *and* doper *and* toker *and* fiend *and* freak *and* space cadet <nf>; cocaine user, cokie *and* coke head *and* crackhead *and* sniffer *and* snow drifter *and* flaky <nf>; opium user, opium addict, hophead *and* hopdog *and* tar distiller <nf>; heroin user *or* addict, smackhead *and* smack-sack *and* schmecker <nf>; methedrine user *or* methhead <nf>; amphetamine user, pillhead *and* pill popper *and* speed freak <nf>; LSD user, acidhead *and* acid freak *and* tripper *and* cubehead <nf>; marijuana smoker *and* pothead <nf>; **drug seller** *or* dealer, pusher, contact, connection; **alcoholic, alcoholic** 88.11; **smoker,** heavy smoker, chain smoker, nicotine addict

VERBS **22 use, be on,** get on; use occasionally *or* irregularly, have a cotton habit *and* chip *and* chippy *and* joy pop <nf>; **get a rush** *or* flush, go over the hump <nf>; **sniff,** snort, blow, toot, one and one <nf>; **smoke marijuana,** take on a number *and* blow a stick *and* toke *and* blast *and* weed out <nf>; **smoke opium,** blow a fill; freebase; **inject,** mainline, shoot *and* shoot up *and* jab *and* get down *and* get off <nf>, pop *and* skin pop <nf>, **take pills,** pop pills <nf>; **withdraw,** crash *and* come down <nf>, kick *or* go cold turkey *and* go a la canona *and* hang tough *and* water out <nf>, detoxify, disintoxicate, detoxicate, dry out, kick *and* kick the habit <nf>; **trip,** blow one's mind *and* wig out <nf>; **sell drugs,** deal *and* push <nf>; **buy drugs,** score *and* make *and* connect <nf>; **have drugs,** be heeled *and* carry *and* hold *and* sizzle <nf>; **drink** *or* **booze** 88.24–25; **smoke, smoke tobacco,** puff, puff away, drag, chain-smoke, smoke like a chimney

ADJS **23 intoxicated,** under the influence, nodding, narcotized, poppied, far gone

24 <nf terms> **high,** bent, blasted, blind, bombed out, bonged out, buzzed, coked, coked out, flying, fried, geared, geared up, geezed, gonged, gorked, hopped-up, in a zone, junked, luded out, maxed, noddy, ripped, smashed, snowed, spaced, space out, spacey, stoned, strung out, switched on, tanked, totaled, tranqued, tripping, trippy, wankered, wired, wrecked, zoned, zoned out, zonked, zonked out

25 addicted, hooked *and* zunked *and* on the needle <nf>; dependency-prone; **supplied with drugs,** holding *and* heeled *and* carrying *and* anywhere <nf>; using, on, behind acid <nf>

88 INTOXICATION, ALCOHOLIC DRINK

NOUNS **1 intoxication, inebriation, inebriety,** insobriety, besottedness, sottedness, **drunkenness, tipsiness,** befuddlement, fuddle, fuddlement, fuddledness, tipsification *and* tiddliness <nf>; a high, soaking <nf>; Dutch courage, pot-valiance *or* pot-valiancy, pot-valor; hangover, katzenjammer, morning after <nf>

2 bibulousness, bibacity, bibaciousness, bibulosity, sottishness; serious drinking; crapulence, crapulousness; **intemperance** 669; bacchanalianism; Bacchus, Dionysus, fondness for the bottle

3 alcoholism, dipsomania, oenomania, alcoholic psychosis *or* addiction, pathological drunkenness, problem drinking, heavy drinking, habitual drunkenness, ebriosity; delirium tremens 926.9/10; grog blossom *and* bottle nose <nf>; gin drinker's liver, cirrhosis of the liver

4 drinking, imbibing; social drinking; tippling, guzzling, gargling, bibing; winebibbing, winebibbery; toping; hard drinking, serious drinking <nf>; **boozing** *and* swilling <nf>, **hitting the booze** *or* **bottle** *or* **sauce** <nf>; alcoholism, Alcoholics Anonymous

5 spree, drinking bout, bout, **celebration,** potation, compotation, symposium, wassail, **carouse, carousal,** drunken carousal *or* revelry, revel; bacchanal, bacchanalia, bacchanalian; **debauch, orgy**

6 <nf terms> **binge, drunk,** bust, tear, **bender, toot, bat,** pub-crawl <Brit>, jag, booze-up <chiefly Brit>, brannigan, guzzle, randan, rip

7 drink, dram, potation, potion, libation, **nip,** draft, drop, spot, finger or two, sip, sup, suck, drench, guzzle, gargle, jigger; peg, swig, swill, pull; **snort,** jolt, **shot,** snifter, wet; quickie; round, round of drinks

8 bracer, refresher, reviver, pickup *and* **pick-me-up** <nf>, tonic, hair of the dog *or* hair of the dog that bit one <nf>

9 drink, cocktail, highball, long drink, mixed drink; liquor, spirits; **punch; eye-opener** <nf>, **nightcap** <nf>, sundowner <Brit nf>; **chaser** <nf>, *pousse-café* <Fr>, *apéritif* <Fr>; parting cup, stirrup cup, one for the road; hair of the dog; Mickey Finn *or* Mickey *and* knockout drops <nf>; mixer, chaser

10 **toast, pledge,** health

11 **drinker,** imbiber, **social drinker,** tippler, bibber; winebibber, oenophilist; **drunkard, drunk, inebriate, sot,** toper, guzzler, swiller, soaker, lovepot, tosspot, barfly, thirsty soul, **serious drinker,** devotee of Bacchus; swigger; hard drinker, heavy drinker, **alcoholic, dipsomaniac, problem drinker,** chronic alcoholic, chronic drunk, pathological drinker; carouser, reveler, wassailer; bacchanal, bacchanalian; pot companion

12 <nf terms> **drunk, lush,** lusher, **soak,** sponge, hooch hound, **boozer, boozehound,** booze fighter, booze freak, dipso, juicehead, loadie, ginhound, elbow bender *or* crooker, shikker, bottle sucker, swillbelly, swillpot, swillbowl; **souse, stew,** bum, rummy, rumhound, stewbum; wino

13 **spirits, liquor,** intoxicating liquor, adult beverage, **hard liquor,** hard stuff <nf>, **whiskey,** firewater, snake juice, spiritus frumenti, usquebaugh <Scot>, schnapps, ardent spirits, strong waters, **intoxicant,** toxicant, inebriant, **potable,** potation, **beverage, drink, strong drink,** strong liquor, alcoholic drink *or* beverage, **alcohol,** aqua vitae, water of life, brew, **grog,** social lubricant, nectar of the gods; **booze** <nf>; **rum,** the Demon Rum, John Barleycorn; the bottle, the cup, the cup that cheers, "the ruddy cup"—Sir Walter Scott, little brown jug; punch bowl, the flowing bowl

14 <nf terms> **likker, hooch, juice, sauce,** tiger milk, pig *or* tiger sweat, sheepdip, moonshine, white lightning; **medicine,** snake medicine, corpse reviver; **rotgut, poison,** rat poison, formaldehyde, embalming fluid, shellac, **panther piss**

15 **liqueur, cordial;** brandy, flavored brandy

16 **beer,** brew *and* brewskie *and* suds <nf>, swipes <Brit nf>, "barmy beer"—Dryden; small beer; nonalcoholic beer, alcohol-free beer; draft beer, home-brew, microbrew

17 **wine,** *vin* <Fr>, *vino* <Sp & Ital>; vintage wine, nonvintage wine; the grape; red wine, white wine, rosé wine, pink wine, blush wine; dry *or* sweet wine, heavy *or* light wine, full *or* thin wine, rough *or* smooth wine, still wine, sparkling wine; extra sec *or* demi-sec *or* sec *or* brut champagne, bubbly; new wine, must; imported wine, domestic wine; fortified wine; wine of the country, *vin du campagne* <Fr>; jug wine, plonk <Brit>; Beaujolais wine

18 **bootleg liquor, moonshine** <nf>; hooch *and* shine *and* mountain dew <nf>, white lightning *or* mule <nf>; bathtub gin; home brew

19 **liquor dealer,** liquor store owner; **vintner,** wine merchant; winegrower, winemaker, wine expert, oenologist; **bartender,** mixologist, barkeeper, barkeep, barman <Brit>, tapster, publican <Brit>; barmaid, tapstress; **brewer,** brewmaster; **distiller; bootlegger, moonshiner** <nf>

20 **bar,** barroom, *bistro* <Fr>, cocktail lounge; taproom; **tavern, pub,** pothouse, alehouse, rumshop, grogshop, dramshop, groggery, gin mill <nf>, **saloon,** drinking saloon, saloon bar <Brit>; lounge bar, piano bar, sports bar, singles bar, gay bar; waterhole *or* watering hole <nf>; wine bar; public house <Brit>; public *or* local <Brit nf>; beer parlor, beer garden, rathskeller; **nightclub, cabaret;** café, wine shop; barrel house *and* honky-tonk *and* dive <nf>; **speakeasy** *and* blind tiger *and* blind pig *and* after-hours joint <nf>

21 **distillery, still,** distiller; **brewery,** brewhouse; **winery,** wine press; bottling works

VERBS 22 **intoxicate, inebriate, addle, befuddle,** bemuse, besot, go to one's head, make one see double, make one tiddly

23 <nf terms> **plaster,** pickle, swack, crock, stew, souse, stone, pollute, tipsify, booze up, boozify, fuddle, overtake

24 **tipple, drink,** dram <Brit>, nip; grog, **guzzle,** gargle; **imbibe,** have a drink *or* nip *or* dram *or* guzzle *or* gargle, soak, bib, quaff, sip, sup, lap, lap up, take a drop, slake one's thirst, cheer *or* refresh the inner man, drown one's troubles *or* sorrows, commune with the spirits; **down,** toss off *or* down, toss one's drink, knock back, throw one back, drink off *or* up, drain the cup, drink bottoms-up, drink deep; **drink hard,** drink like a fish, drink seriously, **tope;** take to drink *or* drinking, drink one's fill, "follow strong drink"—Bible

25 <nf terms> **booze,** swig, swill, moisten *or* wet one's whistle; **liquor, liquor up,** lush, souse, tank up, **hit the booze** *or* **bottle** *or* **sauce,** exercise *or* bend *or* crook *or* raise the elbow, dip the beak, splice the main brace; chug-a-lug, chug

26 **get drunk,** be stricken drunk, get high, put on a high, take a drop too much; **get plastered** *or* **pickled,** etc <nf>, tie one on *and* get a bun on <nf>

27 **be drunk,** be intoxicated, have a drop too much, have more than one can hold, have a jag on <nf>, see double, be feeling no pain; **stagger, reel; pass out** <nf>

28 **go on a spree; go on a binge** *or* **drunk** *or* **toot** *or* **bat** *or* **bender** <nf>, **carouse, spree, revel,** wassail, debauch, "eat, drink, and be merry"—Bible, paint the town red <nf>, pub-crawl <Brit nf>, club-hop

29 **drink to, toast, pledge,** drink a toast to, drink *or* pledge the health of, give you

30 **distill; brew;** bootleg, moonshine <nf>, moonlight <nf>

ADJS **31 intoxicated, inebriated,** inebriate, inebrious, **drunk, drunken,** *shikker* <Yiddish>, **tipsy,** in liquor, **in one's cups, under the influence,** the worse for liquor, having had one too many; nappy, beery; **tiddly, giddy, dizzy,** muddled, addled, flustered, bemused, reeling, seeing double; **mellow, merry,** jolly, happy, gay, glorious; **full**; **besotted,** sotted, sodden, drenched, far-gone; drunk as a lord, drunk as a fiddler *or* piper, drunk as a skunk, drunk as an owl; staggering drunk, drunk and disorderly; crapulent, crapulous; **maudlin**

32 dead-drunk, blind drunk, overcome, out *and* out cold *and* passed out <nf>, helpless, under the table

33 <nf terms> **fuddled,** muzzy, **boozy,** overtaken; **swacked, plastered,** shnockered, stewed, **pickled,** pissed, **soused,** soaked, boiled, fried, canned, tanked, potted, corned, bombed, ripped, smashed; bent, **crocked,** crocko, shellacked, sloshed, sozzled, zonked, tight, lushy, squiffy, afflicted, jug-bitten, oiled, lubricated, feeling no pain, polluted, raddled, organized, **high,** elevated, high as a kite, lit, **lit up,** lit to the gills, illuminated, **loaded, stinko,** tanked, tanked-up, stinking drunk, pie-eyed, pissy-eyed, shitfaced, cockeyed, cockeyed drunk, roaring *or* rip-roaring drunk, skunk-drunk; half-seas over, three sheets to the wind, well-oiled, **blotto, stiff,** blind, paralyzed, **stoned**

34 full of Dutch courage, pot-valiant, pot-valorous

35 bibulous, bibacious, drunken, sottish, liquorish, given *or* addicted to drink, **liquor-loving,** liquor-drinking, drinking, hard-drinking, swilling <nf>, toping, tippling, winebibbing

36 intoxicating, intoxicative, **inebriating,** inebriative, inebriant, heady

37 alcoholic, spirituous, ardent, strong, hard, with a kick <nf>; winy, vinous

INTERJS **38** <toasts> skoal!, prosit! *or* prost!, *à votre santé!* <Fr>, *¡salud!* <Sp>, *l'chaim!* <Heb>, *sláinte!* <Ir>, *salute!* <Ital>, *na zdorovye!* <Russ>, *salud!* <Sp>, to your health!, long life!, to life!, cheerio!, cheers!, to us!, down the hatch!, bottoms up!, here's how!, here's to you!, here's looking at you!, here's mud in your eye!, here's good luck!, here's to absent friends!, confusion to our enemies!

89 TOBACCO

NOUNS **1 tobacco,** *tabac* <Fr>, nicotine, nicotia *or* nicotian <old>; **the weed** <nf>, fragrant weed, Indian weed *or* drug, filthy weed, sot-weed <old>, "pernicious weed"—Cowper; carcinogenic substance; smoke, tobacco smoke, cigarette smoke, cigar smoke, pipe smoke; secondary smoke, secondhand smoke

2 <tobaccos> flue-cured *or* bright, fire-cured, air-cured; Broadleaf, Burley, Cuban, Havana, Havana seed, Latakia, Turkish, Russian, Maryland, Virginia; plug tobacco, bird's-eye, canaster, leaf, lugs, seconds, shag; pipe tobacco

3 smoking tobacco, smokings <nf>, smoke *and* smokes <nf>

4 cigar, seegar <nf>; rope *and* stinker <nf>; **cheroot, stogie,** corona, belvedere, Havana, panatella, colorado, trichinopoly; cigarillo; box of cigars, cigar box, cigar case, humidor; cigar cutter

5 cigarette; butt *and* cig *and* **fag** *and* coffin nail *and* cancer stick <nf>; filter tip, high tar, low tar, methol; cigarette butt, **butt,** stub; snipe <nf>; pack *or* deck of cigarettes, box *or* carton of cigarettes, cigarette case, cigarette paper

6 pipe, tobacco pipe; corncob, corncob pipe, Missouri meerschaum; briar pipe, briar; clay pipe, clay, churchwarden <Brit>; meerschaum; water pipe, hookah, nargileh, kalian, hubble-bubble; peace pipe, calumet; pipe rack, pipe cleaner, tobacco pouch

7 chewing tobacco, eating tobacco, oral tobacco; navy *or* navy plug, cavendish, twist, pigtail, plug, cut plug; **quid,** cud, fid <Brit nf>, **chew,** chaw; tobacco juice

8 snuff, snoose <nf>; rappee; pinch of snuff; snuff bottle, snuffbox, snuff mill <Scot>

9 nicotine, nicotia <old>

10 smoking, smoking habit, habitual smoking; chain-smoking; smoke, puff, drag <nf>; **chewing;** tobacco *or* nicotine addiction, tobaccoism, tabacosis, tabacism, tabagism, nicotinism; passive smoking

11 tobacco user, smoker, cigarette *or* pipe *or* cigar smoker, chewer, snuffer, snuff dipper

12 tobacconist; snuffman; tobacco store *or* shop, cigar store

13 smoking room, smoking car, **smoker;** smoke-free area, non-smoking section

VERBS **14** <use tobacco> **smoke;** inhale, puff, draw, drag <nf>, pull; smoke like a furnace *or* chimney; chain-smoke; **chew,** chaw <nf>; roll; **take snuff,** dip *or* inhale snuff

ADJS **15 tobacco,** tobaccoy *or* tobaccoey, tobaccolike; **nicotinic;** smoking, chewing; snuffy; smoke-free, non-smoking

90 HEALTH CARE

NOUNS **1 medicine, medical practice,** medical profession, medical care, **health care,** health-care industry, health-care delivery, primary care *or* treatment; **medical specialty** *or* **branch** <see list>; **treatment, therapy** 91; **health insurance** 83.5, Medicare, Medicaid; **care,** nursing care, home care, outpatient care, life care; family practice, general practice

2 **surgery;** operation; cosmetic surgery, plastic surgery, facelift, liposuction, nose job <nf>, tuck <nf>

3 **dentistry** <see list>, dental medicine, dental care

4 **doctor,** doc <nf>, **physician,** Doctor of Medicine *or* **MD** *or* medical doctor, **medical practitioner, medical man, medico** <nf>, leech <old>, croaker *and* sawbones <nf>; **general practitioner** *or* **GP;** family doctor; country doctor; **intern; resident,** house physician, resident physician; fellow; physician in ordinary; medical attendant, attending physician; **specialist,** board-certified physician *or* specialist; **medical examiner,** coroner; oculist, **optometrist,** radiologist, anesthesiologist; health maintenance organization *or* HMO

5 **surgeon,** sawbones <nf>; operator, operative surgeon

6 **dentist,** tooth doctor; **dental surgeon,** oral surgeon, operative dentist; Doctor of Dental Surgery *or* DDS; Doctor of Dental Science *or* DDSc; Doctor of Dental Medicine *or* DMD; orthodondist, perdontist, exodontist, endodontist, prosthodontist

7 **veterinary, veterinarian, vet** <nf>, veterinary surgeon, horse doctor, animal doctor, horse whisperer

8 **health-care professional, health-care provider, physician, nurse, midwife, therapist,** therapeutist, practitioner; physical therapist, physiotherapist, speech therapist, occupational therapist

9 **healer, nonmedical therapist;** theotherapist; Christian *or* spiritual *or* divine healer; **Christian Science practitioner; faith healer,** witch doctor <nf>, shaman, alternative practitioner, **osteopath, chiropractor,** podiatrist, acupuncturist, etc

10 **nurse,** sister *or* nursing sister <Brit>; **probationer,** probationist, probe <nf>; caregiver, hospice caregiver; practical nurse; registered nurse *or* RN, nurse practitioner

11 <hospital staff> paramedic, emergency medical technician *or* EMT; medevac; physician's assistant *or* PA; orderly, attendant, nurse's aide; audiologist; anesthetist; dietician, nutritionist; radiographer, X-ray technician; laboratory technician; radiotherapist; dietitian; hospital administrator; ambulance driver; custodian

12 **Hippocrates,** Galen; Aesculapius, Asclepius

13 **practice of medicine,** medical practice; general practice, restricted *or* limited practice; group practice; professional association *or* PA; family practice, private practice, health maintenance organization *or* HMO; orthodox medicine, conventional medicine, general medicine, preventive medicine, internal medicine, occupational medicine, public-health medicine, community medicine; unorthodox medicine, alternative medicine, acupuncture, faith healing, homeopathy, naturopathy, guided imagery, visualization, Ayurveda, shamanism, color therapy, art therapy, etc.

VERBS 14 **practice medicine,** doctor <nf>; examine, diagnose, screen; treat; prescribe, medicate, administer, inject; make a house call, be on call; intern; practice surgery, perform surgery, operate; practice dentistry; do a procedure

ADJS 15 **medical,** iatric, health, Hippocratic; surgical; chiropodic, pediatric, orthopedic, obstetric, obstetrical, neurological; dental; orthodontic, periodontic, prosthodontic, exodontic; osteopathic, chiropractic, naturopathic, hydropathic, allopathic, homeopathic; gynecological, internal, pathological, forensic; clinical; diagnostic; therapeutic; veterinary

16 **branches of medicine**

adolescence medicine	immunochemistry
anatomy	immunology
anesthesiology	internal medicine
audiology	materia medica
aviation medicine	mental hygiene
bacteriology	midwifery
bariatrics	mycology
cardiography	neonatology
cardiology	nephrology
chemotherapy	neurology
chiropody	neurosurgery
critical care medicine	nosology
dental surgery	nutrition
dentistry	obstetrics
dermatology	oncology
diagnostics	ophthalmology
dolorology	optometry
embryology	orthopedics
endocrinology	orthotics
epidemiology	osteopathy
etiology	otolaryngology
family practice	otology
fetology	parasitology
fluoroscopy	pathology
gastroenterology	pediatrics
general medicine	pharmacology
geriatrics *or* gerontology	physical medicine
gynecology	physiopathology
hematology	physiotherapy
hygiene	plastic surgery

podiatry
psychiatry
psychology
psychoneuroimmunology
pulmonology
radiology
rheumatology
serology
space medicine
surgery
surgical anatomy
symptomatology *or* semeiology
teratology
therapeutics
tocology
toxicology
virology

17 kinds and specialties of dentistry

endodontics *or* endodontia
exodontics *or* exodontia
family dentistry
general dentistry
gerodontics
implantology
operative dentistry
oral surgery *or* surgical dentistry
orthodontics *or* orthodontia
pedodontics *or* pedodontia
periodontics *or* periodontia
prosthetic dentistry *or* prosthodontics *or* prosthodontia
radiodontics *or* radiodontia

18 types of surgery

apicectomy
appendectomy *or* appendicectomy
arterioplasty
autograft *or* autoplasty
cesarean section
cholecystectomy
cholelithotomy
colostomy
cordotomy
craniotomy
cryosurgery
cystectomy
D & C *or* dilatation and curettage
debridement
episiotomy
fenestration
gastrectomy
goniopuncture
hepatectomy
homograft *or* allograft *or* homoplasty
hysterectomy
ileostomy
iridectomy
labioplasty
laparotomy
laryngectomy
lobotomy *or* leukotomy
lithonephrotomy *or* nephrolithotomy
mastectomy
necrotomy
nephrectomy
neurotomy
oophorectomy *or* ovariectomy
orchidectomy *or* orchiectomy *or* testectomy
ostectomy
otoplasty
phlebotomy *or* venesection
pneumonectomy
rhinoplasty
rhizotomy
salpingectomy
thoracotomy
tracheostomy *or* tracheotomy
vasectomy

91 THERAPY, MEDICAL TREATMENT

NOUNS **1 therapy, therapeutics,** therapeusis, **treatment, medical care** *or* **treatment,** medication; noninvasive *or* nonsurgical therapy *or* treatment; disease-fighting, healing; healing arts, physical therapy, psychotherapy 92, medicines 86

2 nonmedical therapy; theotherapy; **healing;** Christian *or* spiritual *or* divine healing; shamanism; **faith healing**

3 hydrotherapy, hydrotherapeutics; hydropathy, water cure; cold-water cure; contrast bath, whirlpool bath

4 heat therapy, thermotherapy; heliotherapy, solar therapy; fangotherapy; hot bath, sweat bath, sunbath

5 diathermy, medical diathermy; electrotherapy, electrotherapeutics; **radiothermy,** high-frequency treatment; shortwave diathermy, ultrashortwave diathermy, microwave diathermy; ultrasonic diathermy; surgical diathermy, radiosurgery, electrosurgery, electrosection, electrocautery, electrocoagulation

6 radiotherapy, radiation therapy, radiotherapeutics; adjuvant therapy

7 radiology, radiography, radioscopy, radiation, fluoroscopy, etc 1037.8; diagnostic radiology, scanning, magnetic resonance imaging *or* MRI

8 <radiotherapeutic substances> radium; cobalt; radioisotope, tracer, labeled *or* tagged element, radioelement; radiocarbon, carbon 14, radiocalcium, radiopotassium, radiosodium, radioiodine; atomic cocktail

9 <diagnostic pictures and graphs> **X ray,** scan, radiograph, radiogram, roentgenogram *or* roentgenograph; photofluorograph; X-ray movie; chest X-ray; pyelogram; orthodiagram; encephalograph, encephalogram; electroencephalograph, electroencephalogram *or* EEG; electrocorticogram; electrocardiogram *or* ECG *or* EKG; electromyogram; computer-assisted tomography *or* CAT, computerized axial tomography *or* computed tomography *or* computer-assisted tomography *or* computerized tomography *or* CAT; CAT scan; magnetic resonance imaging *or* MRI; MRI scan; positron emission tomography *or* PET; PET scan; ultrasound, ultrasonography; sonogram

10 case history, medical history, anamnesis; associative anamnesis; catamnesis, follow-up

11 diagnostics, prognostics; symptomatology, semeiology, semeiotics

12 diagnosis; examination, physical examination; study, test, workup <nf>; medical test, laboratory test, screening, diagnostic procedure; blood test, blood work <nf>, blood count, urinalysis, uroscopy; biopsy; Pap test *or* smear; stress test; electrocardiography, electroencephalography, electromyography; mammography; pregnancy test, amniocentesis *or* amnio, ultrasound

13 prognosis, prognostication, prognostic, **symptom, sign**

14 treatment, medical treatment *or* attention *or* care; **cure,** curative measures; **medication,** medicamentation; **regimen,** regime, protocol; first aid; hospitalization; physical therapy, acupressure, shiatsu

15 immunization; immunization therapy, immunotherapy; vaccine therapy, vaccinotherapy; toxin-antitoxin immunization; serum therapy, serotherapy, serotherapeutics; tuberculin test, scratch test, patch test; **immunology,** immunochemistry; immunity theory, side-chain theory; immunity; immunodeficiency

16 inoculation, vaccination; injection, hypodermic, hypodermic injection, shot *and* bing <nf>, hypospray *or* jet injection; booster, booster shot <nf>; antitoxin, vaccine 86.28

17 <methods of injection> cutaneous, percutaneous, subcutaneous, intradermal, intramuscular, intravenous, intramedullary, intracardiac, intrathecal, intraspinal

18 transfusion, blood transfusion; serum; blood bank, blood donor center, bloodmobile; blood donor

19 surgery, surgical treatment, **operation,** surgical operation, surgical intervention, surgical technique *or* measure, the knife <nf>; **instrument,** device; respirator; unnecessary surgery, *cacoëthes operandi* <L>, tomomania; major surgery, minor surgery, laser surgery, plastic surgery

20 bloodletting, bleeding, venesection, phlebotomy; leeching; cupping

21 hospital, clinic, *hôpital* <Fr>, treatment center; general hospital, teaching hospital, university hospital, health center, base hospital; hospice, infirmary; nursing home, rest home, convalescent home, sanitarium, assisted living; sick bay *or* berth; trauma center; birthing center; wellness center

22 pesthouse, lazar house, lazaretto *or* lazaret <old>

23 health resort, spa, watering place, baths; mineral spring, warm *or* hot spring; pump room, pump house; yoga retreat

VERBS **24 treat, doctor,** minister to, care for, give care to, physic; **diagnose;** nurse; **cure, remedy, heal;** dress the wounds, bandage, poultice, plaster, strap, splint; bathe; massage, rub; operate on; physic, purge, flux <old>; **operate,** perform a procedure; transplant, replant

25 medicate, medicine, drug, dope <nf>, dose; salve, oil, anoint, embrocate

26 irradiate, radiumize, **X-ray,** roentgenize

27 bleed, let blood, leech, phlebotomize; cup; **transfuse,** give a transfusion; perfuse

28 immunize, inoculate, vaccinate, shoot <nf>

29 undergo treatment, take the cure, doctor <nf>, take medicine; go under the knife <nf>

92 PSYCHOLOGY, PSYCHOTHERAPY

NOUNS **1 psychology** <see list>, science of the mind, science of human behavior, mental philosophy; psychologism, pop psychology *and* psychobabble <nf>; mental states, mental processes

2 psychological school, school *or* system of psychology, psychological theory; Adlerian psychology; behaviorism *or* behavior *or* behavioristic psychology *or* stimulus-response psychology; Freudian psychology *or* Freudianism; Gestalt psychology *or* configurationism; Horneyan psychology; Jungian *or* analytical psychology; Pavlovian psychology; Reichian psychology *or* orgone theory; Skinnerian psychology; Sullivanian psychology

3 psychiatry, psychological medicine; neuropsychiatry; social psychiatry; prophylactic psychiatry

4 psychosomatic medicine, psychological medicine, medicopsychology; psychosocial medicine

5 psychotherapy, psychotherapeutics, mind cure, cognitive therapy

6 psychoanalysis, analysis, the couch <nf>, counseling, behavior therapy, behavior modification; psychoanalytic therapy, psychoanalytic method; **depth psychology,** psychology of depths; group analysis *or* psychology, family therapy; play therapy; transactional analysis; psychognosis, psychognosy; dream analysis, interpretation of dreams, dream symbolism; depth interview; hypnotherapy; meditation, transcendental meditation

7 psychodiagnostics, psychodiagnosis, psychological *or* psychiatric evaluation

8 psychometrics, psychometry, psychological measurement; **intelligence testing;** mental test, psychological screening; psychography; psychogram, psychograph, psychological profile; psychometer, IQ meter <nf>; lie detector, polygraph, psychogalvanometer, psychogalvanic skin response

9 psychological test <see list>, mental test; standardized test; developmental test, achievement test

10 psychologist; psychotherapist, therapist, psychotherapeutist; clinical psychologist; licensed psychologist, psychological practitioner; child psychologist; **psychiatrist,** alienist, somatist; neuropsychiatrist; psychopathist, psychopathologist; psychotechnologist, industrial psychologist; hypnotherapist; behavior therapist; psychobiologist, psychochemist, psychophysiologist, psychophysicist;

psychographer; psychiatric social worker; **psychoanalyst, analyst; shrink** *and* headshrinker *and* shrinker <nf>; **counselor,** psychological counselor; counseling service

11 **personality tendency,** complexion <old>, humor; somatotype; **introversion,** introvertedness, ingoingness; inner-directedness; **extroversion,** extrovertedness, outgoingness; other-directedness; syntony, ambiversion; schizothymia, schizothymic *or* schizoid personality; cyclothymia, cyclothymic *or* cycloid personality; mesomorphism, mesomorphy; endomorphism, endomorphy; ectomorphism, ectomorphy

12 <personality type> **introvert, extrovert,** syntone, ambivert; schizothyme, schizoid; cyclothymic, cyclothyme, cycloid; choleric, melancholic, sanguine, phlegmatic; endomorph, mesomorph, ectomorph; Type A; Type B

13 **pathological personality,** psychopathological personality, sick personality, psycho <nf>

14 **mental disorder, emotional disorder,** neurosis; psychonosema, psychopathyfunctional nervous disorder; reaction; emotional instability; **maladjustment,** social maladjustment; nervous *or* mental breakdown, crack-up <nf>; problems in living; brainstorm; **insanity, mental illness** 926.1; **psychosis** 926.3; **schizophrenia; paranoia** 926.4; **manic-depressive psychosis,** bipolar disorder; **depression,** melancholia 926.5; seasonal affective disorder *or* SAD, post-partum depression; melancholia *or* endogenous depression; premenstrual syndrome *or* PMS; **neurosis, psychoneurosis,** neuroticism, neurotic *or* psychoneurotic disorder; brain disease, nervous disorder; cognitive disorder, eating disorder, sleep disorder, somatoform disorder, dissociative disorder, mood disorder, anxiety disorder, sexual disorder, impulse-control disorder, conversion disorder; battle fatigue

15 **personality disorder, character disorder,** moral insanity, sociopathy, **psychopathy; psychopathic personality;** sexual pathology, sexual psychopathy 75.11; compulsion, fixation, complex; obsessive-compulsive disorder; identity crisis, midlife crisis

16 **neurotic reaction,** neurosis, overreaction, disproportionate reaction, depression, mania

17 **psychological stress, stress; frustration,** external frustration, internal frustration; conflict, ambivalence, ambivalence of impulse; **trauma,** psychological *or* emotional trauma, traumatism, mental *or* emotional shock, decompensation; rape trauma syndrome; post-traumatic stress disorder; shell shock

18 **psychosomatic symptom; symptom of emotional disorder,** emotional symptom, psychological

symptom; **thought disturbance,** thought disorder *or* disturbances, dissociative disorder, delirium, delusion, disorientation, hallucination; **speech abnormality**

19 **trance,** daze, stupor; catatonic stupor, catalepsy; cataplexy; dream state, reverie, daydreaming 985.2; somnambulism, sleepwalking; hypnotic trance; fugue, fugue state; **amnesia** 990.2; meditation; brown study

20 **dissociation,** mental *or* emotional dissociation, disconnection, dissociative disorder; dissociation of personality, personality disorganization *or* disintegration; **schizoid personality;** double *or* dual personality; multiple personality, split personality, alternating personality; schizoidism, schizothymia, **schizophrenia** 926.4; depersonalization; **paranoid personality; paranoia** 926.4

21 **fixation,** libido fixation *or* arrest, **arrested development;** infantile fixation, pregenital fixation, father fixation, Freudian fixation, mother fixation, parent fixation; **regression,** retreat to immaturity

22 **complex,** inferiority complex, superiority complex, parent complex, Oedipus complex, mother complex, Electra complex, father complex, Diana complex, persecution complex; castration complex; compulsion complex

23 **defense mechanism,** defense reaction; ego defense, psychotaxis; biological *or* psychological *or* sociological adjustive reactions; resistance; dissociation; **negativism, alienation; escapism,** escape mechanism, avoidance mechanism; escape, flight, **withdrawal; isolation,** emotional insulation; **fantasy,** fantasizing, escape into fantasy, dreamlike thinking, autistic *or* dereistic thinking, idealization, wishful thinking, autism, dereism; wish-fulfillment, wish-fulfillment fantasy; sexual fantasy; **compensation,** overcompensation, decompensation; substitution; **sublimation;** regression, reversion; **projection,** identification, blame-shifting; displacement; intellectualization, **rationalization**

24 **suppression, repression, inhibition,** resistance, restraint, censorship, censor; block, psychological block, blockage, blocking; denial, negation, rejection; reaction formation; rigid control; **suppressed desire**

25 **catharsis,** purgation, abreaction, motor abreaction, psychocatharsis, **emotional release,** relief of tension, outlet; release therapy, acting-out, psychodrama; imaging

26 **conditioning,** classical *or* Pavlovian conditioning; instrumental conditioning; operant conditioning; psychagogy, reeducation, reorientation;

conditioned reflex, conditioned stimulus, conditioned response; reinforcement, positive reinforcement, negative reinforcement; simple reflex, unconditioned reflex, **reflex** 903.1; **behavior** 321; suggestion

27 **adjustment,** adjustive reaction; **readjustment, rehabilitation;** psychosynthesis, integration of personality; fulfillment, self-fulfillment; self-actualization, peak experience; integrated personality, syntonic personality; stress management

28 **psyche,** psychic apparatus, **personality, self,** personhood; **mind** 919.1,3,4, pneuma, soul; preconscious, foreconscious, coconscious; **subconscious, unconscious,** stream of consciousness, subconscious *or* unconscious mind, submerged mind, subliminal, subliminal self; **libido,** psychic *or* libidinal energy, motive force, vital impulse, ego-libido, object libido; **id,** primitive self, pleasure principle, life instinct, death instinct; **ego,** conscious self; **superego,** ethical self, conscience; ego ideal; ego-id conflict; anima, animus, persona; collective unconscious, racial unconscious; hive mind; psychological me; **self**

29 **engram,** memory trace, traumatic trace *or* memory; unconscious memory; archetype, archetypal pattern *or* image *or* symbol; imago, image, father image, etc; race *or* racial memory; cultural memory; **memory** 989

30 **symbol,** universal symbol, father symbol, mother symbol, phallic symbol, fertility symbol, etc; symbolism, symbolization

31 **surrogate,** substitute; father surrogate, father figure, father image; mother surrogate, mother figure, mother image

32 **gestalt,** pattern, figure, configuration, form, sensory pattern; figure-ground

33 **association, association of ideas,** chain of ideas, concatenation, mental linking; controlled association, free association, association by contiguity, association by similarity; association by sound, clang association; stream of consciousness; transference, identification, positive transference, negative transference; synesthesia 24.5

34 **cathexis,** cathection, desire concentration; charge, energy charge, cathectic energy; anticathexis, countercathexis, counterinvestment; hypercathexis, overcharge

35 psychiatric treatment, psychiatric care; psychosurgery, shock treatment, shock therapy, convulsive therapy, electroconvulsive therapy

VERBS **36 psychologize, psychoanalyze,** analyze, counsel; abreact; fixate, obsess on <nf>; neuroticize

ADJS **37 psychological; psychiatric,** neuropsychiatric; psychometric; **psychopathic,** psychopathological; **psychosomatic,** somatopsychic, psychophysical, psychophysiological, psychobiological; psychogenic, psychogenetic, functional; psychodynamic, psychoneurological, psychosexual, psychosocial, psychotechnical; **psychotic**

38 **psychotherapeutic;** psychiatric, psychoanalytic, psychoanalytical; psychodiagnostic; hypnotherapeutic

39 **neurotic, psychoneurotic,** disturbed, disordered; neurasthenic, psychasthenic; hysteric *or* hysterical, hypochondriac, phobic; deluded; dissociated; depressed, poopy <nf>; stressed

40 **introverted,** introvert, introversive, **subjective, ingoing,** inner-directed; withdrawn, isolated; Type B

41 **extroverted,** extrovert, extroversive, **outgoing,** extrospective; other-directed; Type A

42 **subconscious, unconscious;** subliminal, extramarginal; preconscious, foreconscious, coconscious

43 **kinds and branches of psychology**

abnormal psychology	group psychology
academic psychology	haptics
act psychology	hedonics
analytic *or* introspective psychology	holistic psychology
	hormic psychology
animal psychology	individual psychology
applied psychology	industrial psychology
association psychology	introspection
behavioral psychology *or* behaviorism	psychology
	Jungian psychology
biopsychology	mass psychology
child psychology	medical psychology
clinical psychology	morbid psychology
cognitive psychology	neuropsychology
comparative psychology	objective psychology
constitutional psychology	ontogenetic psychology
criminal psychology	parapsychology
depth psychology	phenomenological
developmental psychology	psychology
differential psychology	phylogenetic psychology
dynamic *or* functional	physiologic *or* physiologi-
psychology	cal psychology
ecological psychology	polygenetic psychology
educational psychology	popular psychology
ego psychology	positive psychology
empirical psychology	psychoacoustics
existential psychology	psychoasthenics
experimental psychology	psychobiochemistry
faculty psychology	psychobiology
folk *or* ethnic psychology	psychochemistry
genetic psychology	psychodiagnostics
Gestalt psychology *or*	psychodynamics
configurationism	psychoendocrinology

psychogenetics
psychogeriatrics
psychographics
psychohistory
psycholinguistics
psychological medicine
psychological warfare
psychomathematics
psychometrics *or*
psychometry
psychonomy *or*
psychonomics
psychopathology
psychopharmacology
psychophysics
psychophysiology
psychosociology
psychosomatics
psychotechnics *or*
psychotechnology
psychotherapy *or*
psychotherapeutics
race *or* racial
psychology
rational psychology
reactology
reflexology
reverse psychology
self psychology
social psychology
sports psychology
structural psychology
transpersonal psychology
voluntaristic psychology

44 psychological and mental tests

alpha test
apperception test
aptitude test
association test
Babcock-Levy test
Bernreuter personality
inventory
beta test
Binet *or* Binet-Simon test
Brown personality
inventory
Cattell's infant intelligence
scale
CAVD test
controlled association test
free association test
frustration test
Gesell's development
schedule
Goldstein-Sheerer test
inkblot test
intelligence quotient *or* IQ
intelligence test
interest inventory
IQ test
Kent mental test
Minnesota Multiphasic
Personality Inventory
Minnesota Preschool Scale
Oseretsky test
personality test
Rogers's process
scale
Rorschach test
Rotter incomplete
sentences blank
Stanford revision
Stanford scientific aptitude
test
Stanford-Binet test
Szondi test
thematic apperception test
or TAT
Wechsler Adult
Intelligence Scale
Wechsler-Bellevue
intelligence scale
Wechsler Intelligence
Scale for Children
word association test

93 FEELING

NOUNS **1 feeling, emotion,** affect, **sentiment,**
affection, affections, sympathies, beliefs; affective
faculty, affectivity; emotional charge, cathexis;
feelings, sensitiveness, sensibility, susceptibility,
thin skin; emotional life; the logic of the heart;
sense, deep *or* profound sense, gut sense *or*
sensation <nf>; emotional intelligence; **sensation**
24; **impression,** undercurrent, perception; hunch,
intuition, feeling in one's bones, vibes <nf>,
presentiment 934.3; foreboding; **reaction, response,**
gut reaction <nf>; **instinct** 365.1; emotional
coloring *or* shade *or* nuance, **tone;** drama queen

2 passion, passionateness, strong feeling, powerful
emotion; **fervor, fervency,** fervidness,
impassionedness, **ardor, ardency,** *empressement*
<Fr>, warmth of feeling, **warmth, heat, fire,** verve,
furor, **fury,** vehemence; heartiness, gusto, relish,
savor; spirit, heart, soul; **liveliness** 330.2; **zeal**
101.2; **excitement** 105; **ecstasy**

3 heart, soul, spirit, *esprit* <Fr>, **breast, bosom,**
inmost heart *or* soul, heart of hearts, secret *or*
inner recesses of the heart, secret places, heart's
core, heartstrings, cockles of the heart, bottom of
the heart, being, innermost being, core of one's
being; viscera, pit of one's stomach, **gut** *or* guts
<nf>; bones

4 sensibility, sensitivity, sensitiveness, delicacy,
fineness of feeling, tenderness, affectivity,
susceptibility, impressionability 24.2

5 sympathy, fellow feeling, sympathetic response,
good feeling, responsiveness, relating, warmth,
cordiality, **caring,** concern; response, echo, chord,
sympathetic chord, vibrations, vibes <nf>;
empathy, identification; involvement, sharing;
pathos

6 tenderness, tender feeling, softness, gentleness,
delicacy; **tenderheartedness,** softheartedness,
warmheartedness, tender *or* sensitive *or* warm
heart, soft place *or* spot in one's heart; warmth,
fondness, weakness 100.2

7 bad feeling, hard feelings; immediate dislike,
disaffinity, personality conflict, bad vibes *or*
chemistry *or* juju <nf>, bad blood, **hostility,**
scunner, animosity 589.4; resentment, bitterness,
ill will, intolerance, disappointment;
hard-heartedness 94.3

8 sentimentality, sentiment, sentimentalism,
oversentimentality, oversentimentalism, bathos;
nostalgia, nostomania; romanticism; sweetness
and light, hearts-and-flowers; bleeding heart;
mawkishness, cloyingness, maudlinness, namby-
pamby, namby-pambyness, namby-pambyism;
mushiness *or* sloppiness <nf>; **mush** *and* slush *and*
slop *and* goo *and* schmaltz <nf>; sob story *and*
tearjerker <nf>, soap opera

9 emotionalism, emotionality, lump in one's throat;
emotionalizing, emotionalization; emotiveness,
emotivity; visceralness; nonrationalness,
unreasoningness; demonstrativeness, making
scenes, excitability; **theatrics, theatricality,
histrionics, dramatics,** hamminess *and* chewing
up the scenery <nf>; **sensationalism,
melodrama,** melodramatics, blood and thunder;
yellow journalism; emotional appeal, human
interest, love interest; **overemotionalism,**
hyperthymia, excess of feeling, emotional
instability

VERBS **10 feel,** entertain *or* harbor *or* cherish *or* nurture a feeling; feel deeply, feel in one's viscera *or* bones, feel in one's gut *or* guts <nf>; experience 831.8; have a sensation, get *or* receive an impression, **sense, perceive;** intuit, have a hunch

11 respond, react, be moved, be affected *or* touched, be inspired, echo, catch the flame *or* infection, be in tune; **respond to,** warm up to, take *or* lay to heart, open one's heart to, be turned on to <nf>, nourish in one's bosom, feel in one's breast, cherish at the heart's core, treasure up in the heart; enter into the spirit of, be imbued with the spirit of; care about, feel for, sympathize with, empathize with, identify with, relate to emotionally, dig *and* be turned on by <nf>, be involved, share; color with emotion

12 have deep feelings, be all heart, have a tender heart, take to heart, be a person of heart *or* sentiment; have a soft place *or* spot in one's heart; be a prey to one's feelings; love 104.18–20; hate 103.5

13 emotionalize, emote <nf>, give free play to the emotions, make a scene; be theatrical, theatricalize, ham it up *and* chew up the scenery <nf>; **sentimentalize,** gush *and* slobber over <nf>

14 affect, touch, move, stir; melt, soften, melt the heart, choke one up, give one a lump in the throat; **penetrate,** pierce, go through one, go deep; touch a chord, **touch a sympathetic chord, touch one's heart,** tug at the heart *or* heartstrings, go to one's heart, get under one's skin; come home to; **touch to the quick,** touch on the raw, flick one on the raw, smart, sting

15 impress, affect, strike, hit, smite, rock; **make an impression, get to one** <nf>; make a dent in, make an impact upon, sink in <nf>, strike home, come home to, hit the mark <nf>; tell, have a strong effect, traumatize, strike hard, impress forcibly

16 impress upon, bring home to, make it felt; stamp, stamp on, etch, engrave, engrave on

ADJS **17 emotional, affective,** emotive, affectional, **feeling,** sentient; soulful, of soul, of heart, of feeling, of sentiment; visceral, gut <nf>; glandular; emotiometabolic, emotiomotor, emotiomuscular, emotiovascular; demonstrative, overdemonstrative

18 fervent, fervid, passionate, impassioned, intense, **ardent; hearty, cordial,** enthusiastic, exuberant, unrestrained, vigorous; keen, breathless, **excited** 105.18,20,22; **lively** 330.17; zealous; **warm, burning, heated, hot, volcanic,** red-hot, fiery, flaming, glowing, ablaze, afire, on fire, boiling over, steaming, steamy; delirious, fevered, feverish, febrile, flushed; wired; intoxicated, drunk; obsessed

19 emotionalistic, emotive, overemotional, hysteric, hysterical, sensational, sensationalistic, melodramatic, theatric, theatrical, histrionic, dramatic, overdramatic, hammy <nf>, nonrational, unreasoning; overemotional, hyperthymic

20 sensitive, sensible, emotionable, passible <old>, delicate; responsive, sympathetic, receptive; empathetic, caring; susceptible, impressionable; **tender, soft, tenderhearted, softhearted,** warmhearted

21 sentimental, sentimentalized, soft, **mawkish, maudlin,** cloying; sticky *and* gooey *and* schmaltzy *and* sappy *and* soppy <nf>, oversentimental, oversentimentalized, bathetic; **mushy** *or* sloppy *or* gushing *or* teary *or* beery <nf>, treacly <Brit nf>; tearjerking <nf>; namby-pamby, romantic; nostalgic, nostomanic

22 affecting, touching, moving, emotive, pathetic

23 affected, moved, touched, impressed; impressed with *or* by, penetrated with, seized with, imbued with, devoured by, obsessed, obsessed with *or* by; wrought up by; stricken, wracked, racked, torn, agonized, tortured; worked up, all worked up, wired, **excited** 105.20

24 deep-felt, deepgoing, from the heart, heartfelt, homefelt <old>; **deep, profound;** indelible; pervasive, pervading, absorbing; penetrating, penetrant, piercing; **poignant,** keen, sharp, acute

ADVS **25 feelingly, emotionally,** affectively; affectingly, touchingly, movingly, **with feeling,** poignantly

26 fervently, fervidly, passionately, impassionedly, intensely, **ardently,** zealously; keenly, breathlessly, excitedly; warmly, heatedly, glowingly; heartily, cordially; enthusiastically, exuberantly, vigorously; kindly, heart and soul, with all one's heart, from the heart, from the bottom of one's heart

27 sentimentally, mawkishly, maudlinly, cloyingly; mushily *and* sloppily *and* gushingly <nf>

94 LACK OF FEELING

NOUNS **1 unfeeling,** unfeelingness, affectlessness, lack of affect, lack of feeling *or* feeling tone, emotional deadness *or* numbness *or* paralysis, **anesthesia, emotionlessness,** unemotionalism, unexcitability; **dispassion,** dispassionateness, unpassionateness, **objectivity;** passionlessness, **spiritlessness, heartlessness,** soullessness; **coldness, coolness, frigidity,** chill, chilliness, frostiness, iciness; coldheartedness, cold-bloodedness; cold heart, cold blood; cold fish; **unresponsiveness,** unsympatheticness; lack of touch *or* contact, autism, self-absorption, withdrawal, catatonia; unimpressionableness, unimpressibility; insusceptibility, unsusceptibility; **impassiveness,** impassibility, impassivity; straight face *and* poker face <nf>, deadpan <nf>; immovability, untouchability; **dullness, obtuseness; inexcitability** 106

2 insensibility, insensibleness, **unconsciousness,** unawareness, **obliviousness,** oblivion; anesthesia, narcosis

3 callousness, insensitivity, insensitiveness, philistinism; **coarseness, brutalization, hardness,** hardenedness, **hard-heartedness, hardness of heart,** hard heart, stony-heartedness, heart of stone, stoniness, marbleheartedness, flintheartedness, flintiness; **obduracy,** obdurateness, induration, inuredness; imperviousness, **thick skin,** rhinoceros hide, thick *or* hard-shell, armor, formidable defenses

4 apathy, indifference, unconcern, lack of caring, disinterest; withdrawnness, **aloofness, detachment,** ataraxy *or* ataraxia, **dispassion; passiveness,** passivity, supineness, insouciance, nonchalance; inappetence, lack of appetite; **listlessness, spiritlessness,** burnout, blah *or* blahs <nf>, heartlessness, plucklessness, spunklessness; **lethargy, phlegm,** lethargicalness, phlegmaticalness, phlegmaticness, hebetude, **dullness,** sluggishness, languor, languidness; soporifousness, sopor, coma, comatoseness, torpidness, torpor, torpidity, **stupor,** stupefaction, narcosis; acedia, sloth; **resignation,** resignedness, stoicism; **numbness,** benumbedness; hopelessness 125

VERBS **5** not be affected by, remain unmoved, not turn a hair, not care less <nf>; have a thick skin, have a heart of stone; be cold as ice, be a cold fish, be an icicle; not affect, leave one cold *or* unmoved, unimpress, underwhelm <nf>

6 callous, harden, case harden, **harden one's heart,** ossify, steel, indurate, inure; brutalize

7 dull, blunt, desensitize, obtund, hebetate

8 numb, benumb, paralyze, **deaden,** anesthetize, freeze, **stun, stupefy,** drug, narcotize

ADJS **9 unfeeling, unemotional,** nonemotional, emotionless, affectless, emotionally dead *or* numb *or* paralyzed, anesthetized, drugged, narcotized; **unpassionate, dispassionate,** unimpassioned, **objective;** passionless, **spiritless, heartless,** soulless; lukewarm, Laodicean; **cold, cool, frigid,** frozen, chill, chilly, arctic, frosty, frosted, icy, **coldhearted, cold-blooded,** cold as charity; **unaffectionate,** unloving; **unresponsive,** unresponding, **unsympathetic;** out of touch *or* contact; in one's shell *or* armor, behind one's defenses; autistic, self-absorbed, self-centered, egocentric, catatonic; unimpressionable,

unimpressible, insusceptible, unsusceptible, unperturbed, imperturbable, undisturbed; **impassive,** impassible; immovable, untouchable; dull, obtuse, blunt; **inexcitable** 106.10

10 insensible, unconscious, unaware, **oblivious,** blind to, deaf to, dead to, lost to

11 unaffected, unmoved, untouched, dry-eyed, unimpressed, unshaken, unstruck, **unstirred,** unruffled, unanimated, uninspired

12 callous, calloused, insensitive, Philistine; **thick-skinned,** pachydermatous; **hard, hard-hearted, hardened,** case-hardened, coarsened, brutalized, indurated, stony, stony-hearted, marblehearted, flinthearted, flinty, steely, impervious, inured, armored *or* steeled against, proof against, as hard as nails

13 apathetic, indifferent, unconcerned, uncaring, **disinterested, uninterested; withdrawn, aloof, detached,** Olympian, above it all; **passive,** supine; stoic, stoical; insouciant, nonchalant, blasé, **listless, spiritless,** burned-out, blah <nf>, heartless, pluckless, spunkless; **lethargic, phlegmatic,** hebetudinous, **dull,** desensitized, sluggish, torpid, languid, slack, soporific, comatose, **stupefied,** in a stupor, **numb,** numbed, benumbed; resigned; hopeless 125.12

ADVS **14 unfeelingly, unemotionally,** emotionlessly; with a straight *or* poker face <nf>, deadpan <nf>; **dispassionately,** unpassionately; **spiritlessly, heartlessly,** coldly, coldheartedly, cold-bloodedly, **in cold blood;** with dry eyes

15 apathetically, indifferently, unconcernedly, disinterestedly, uninterestedly, uncaringly, impassively; **listlessly, spiritlessly,** heartlessly, plucklessly, spunklessly; **lethargically, phlegmatically,** dully, numbly

95 PLEASURE

NOUNS **1 pleasure, enjoyment;** quiet pleasure, euphoria, well-being, good feeling, comfort zone, **contentment,** content, **ease, comfort** 121; coziness, warmth; **gratification, satisfaction,** great satisfaction, hearty enjoyment, keen pleasure *or* satisfaction, pleasance; **self-gratification,** self-indulgence; instant gratification; luxury; **relish, zest, gusto,** *joie de vivre* <Fr>; sweetness of life, *douceur de vivre* <Fr>; kicks <nf>, **fun,** entertainment, amusement 743; beer and skittles <Br>; intellectual pleasure, pleasures of the mind; **strokes** *and* stroking *and* ego massage <nf>; physical pleasure, creature comforts, bodily pleasure, sense *or* sensuous pleasure; sexual pleasure, voluptuousness, sensual pleasure, *volupté* <Fr>, animal pleasure, animal comfort, bodily comfort, fleshly *or* carnal delight; forepleasure, titillation, endpleasure, fruition; sensualism

2 **happiness, felicity, gladness, delight,** delectation; **joy, joyfulness,** joyance <old>; **cheer,** cheerfulness, exhilaration, **exuberance, high spirits, glee,** sunshine; gaiety 109.4, overjoyfulness, overhappiness; intoxication; **rapture,** ravishment, bewitchment, **enchantment,** unalloyed happiness; elation, exaltation; **ecstasy,** ecstasies, transport; **bliss,** blissfulness; beatitude, beatification, blessedness; paradise, heaven, seventh heaven, cloud nine; smiley face; eudaimonia; happy camper

3 **treat, regalement,** regale; **feast, banquet** revelment, regale, Lucullan feast; feast *or* banquet of the soul; round of pleasures, mad round; **festivity,** fete, fiesta, festive occasion, celebration, party, merrymaking, revel, revelry, jubilation, joyance; carnival, Mardi Gras; afterparty

4 pleasure-loving, pleasure principle, hedonism, hedonics; epicureanism, Cyrenaicism, eudaemonism, eudemonism; hedonic treadmill

5 <period of pleasure> good time, fun time, happy hour, bread and circuses, *la dolce vita* <Ital>, life of Riley, easy street, bed of roses, Elysium, Elysian fields, land of milk and honey

VERBS 6 **please, pleasure, give pleasure,** afford one pleasure, be to one's liking, sit well with one, meet one's wishes, take *or* strike one's fancy, feel good *or* right, strike one right; do one's heart good, warm the cockles of one's heart, tickle pink <nf>; **suit**

7 <nf terms> **hit the spot,** be just the ticket, be just what the doctor ordered, **make a hit,** go over big, go over with a bang

8 **gratify, satisfy,** sate, satiate; slake, appease, allay, assuage, quench; regale, feed, feast; do one's heart good, warm the cockles of the heart

9 **gladden,** make happy, happify; bless, beatify; cheer 109.7

10 **delight,** delectate, **tickle, titillate, thrill, enrapture, enthrall, enchant,** entrance, fascinate, captivate, bewitch, **charm,** becharm; enravish, ravish, imparadise; ecstasiate, transport, carry away

11 <nf terms> **give one a bang** *or* kick *or* charge *or* rush, knock out, knock off one's feet *or* dead *or* for a loop, knock one's socks off, thrill to death *or* to pieces, tickle to death, tickle pink, **wow,** slay, send, freak out; **stroke,** massage one's ego

12 **be pleased, feel happy,** feel good, sing, purr, smile, laugh, be wreathed in smiles, beam; **delight,** joy, take great satisfaction; look like the cat that swallowed the canary; brim *or* burst with joy, walk *or* tread on air, have stars in one's eyes, be in heaven *or* seventh heaven *or* paradise, be on cloud nine; fall *or* go into raptures; die with delight *or* pleasure

13 **enjoy,** pleasure in, be pleased with, receive *or* derive pleasure from, take delight *or* pleasure in, get a kick *or* boot *or* bang *or* charge *or* lift *or* rush out of <nf>; **like, love,** adore <nf>; **delight in, rejoice in,** indulge in, luxuriate in, revel in, riot in, bask in, wallow in, swim in; groove on *and* get high on <nf>; feast on, gloat over *or* on; **relish, appreciate,** roll under the tongue, do justice to, savor, smack the lips; devour, eat up

14 **enjoy oneself,** have a good time, party, live it up <nf>, have the time of one's life, have a ball *or* blast <nf>; live large

ADJS 15 **pleased, delighted; glad,** gladsome; **charmed,** intrigued <nf>; **thrilled; tickled,** tickled to death *and* tickled pink <nf>, exhilarated; **gratified, satisfied;** pleased with, taken with, favorably impressed with, sold on <nf>, turned-on; pleased as Punch, pleased as a child with a new toy; euphoric, eupeptic; **content, contented,** easy, **comfortable** 121.11, cozy, in clover, snug as a bug in a rug <nf>

16 **happy, glad, joyful, joyous,** flushed with joy, radiant, beaming, glowing, starry-eyed, sparkling, laughing, smiling, smirking, smirky, chirping, purring, singing, dancing, leaping, capering, **cheerful, gay** 109.14; **blissful,** blessed, blessed; beatified, beatific; thrice happy, happy as a lark, happy as a king, happy as the day is long, happy as a clam at high water, happy as a clam, happy as a pig in shit *or* poo <nf>, happy as a sand boy <Brit>

17 **overjoyed,** overjoyful, overhappy, brimming *or* bursting with happiness, on top of the world; **rapturous,** raptured **enraptured, enchanted,** entranced, enravished, ravished, rapt, possessed; sent *and* high *and* freaked-out <nf>, **in raptures,** transported, in a transport of delight, **carried away,** rapt *or* ravished away, beside oneself, beside oneself with joy, all over oneself <nf>; **ecstatic,** in ecstasies, ecstasiating; rhapsodic, rhapsodical; imparadised, **in paradise,** in heaven, in seventh heaven, on cloud nine <nf>; **elated,** elate, exalted, jubilant, exultant, flushed; blessed, blessed-out

18 **pleasure-loving,** pleasure-seeking, fun-loving, hedonic, hedonistic; Lucullan; epicurean, Cyrenaic, eudaemonic; carnivalesque; living large

ADVS 19 **happily, gladly, joyfully, joyously, delightedly,** with pleasure, to one's delight; blissfully, blessedly; **ecstatically,** rhapsodically, **rapturously; elatedly,** jubilantly, exultantly

20 for fun, for kicks, for the hell *or* heck *or* devil of it <nf>

INTERJS **21 goody!,** goody, goody!, goody gumdrops!, good-o! <Brit>; whee!, **wow!,** u-mm!, mmmm!, oooo!, oo-la-la!; oh boy!, boy oh boy!, boy!, man!, hot dog!, hot ziggety!, hot diggety!, whoopee!, wowie zowie!, out of sight! *or* outa sight!, groovy!, keen-o!, keen-o-peachy!, hubba hubba!

96 UNPLEASURE

NOUNS **1 unpleasure, unpleasantness** 98, **lack of pleasure,** joylessness, cheerlessness; unsatisfaction, nonsatisfaction, ungratification, nongratification; grimness; discontent 108; displeasure, dissatisfaction, **discomfort,** uncomfortableness, misease <old>, malaise, **painfulness; disquiet,** inquietude, **uneasiness,** unease, discomposure, vexation of spirit, **anxiety;** angst, anguish, dread, nausea, existential woe, existential vacuum; the blahs <nf>; **dullness,** flatness, staleness, tastelessness, savorlessness; **boredom,** ennui, tedium, tediousness, spleen; emptiness, spiritual void, death of the heart *or* soul; unhappiness 112.2; dislike 99

2 annoyance, vexation, bothersomeness, exasperation, *tracasserie* <Fr>, **aggravation; nuisance, pest, bother,** botheration <nf>, public nuisance, **trouble, problem,** pain <nf>, difficulty, hot potato <nf>; **trial;** bed of nails; **bore,** crashing bore <nf>; **drag** *and* downer <nf>, royal pain; **worry,** worriment <nf>; downside *and* the bad news <nf>; stress, fear, pressure, anxiety, angst; **headache** <nf>; **pain in the neck** *or* **in the ass** <nf>; **harassment,** molestation, persecution, dogging, hounding, harrying; devilment, bedevilment; vexatiousness 98.7; bogey *or* bogy

3 irritation, aggravation, exacerbation, worsening, salt in the wound, twisting the knife in the wound, embitterment, **provocation;** fret, gall, chafe; irritant; pea in the shoe

4 chagrin, distress; embarrassment, abashment, discomfiture, egg on one's face <nf>, disconcertion, disconcertment, discountenance, discomposure, disturbance, confusion; **humiliation, shame,** shamefacedness, mortification, red face

5 pain, distress, grief, stress, stress of life, suffering, passion, dolor; ache, aching; pang, wrench, throes, cramp, spasm, twinge; wound, injury, hurt; **sore,** sore spot, soreness, tender spot, tenderness, lesion; strain, sprain; cut, stroke; shock, blow, hard *or* nasty blow; malady, illness, disease, plague; bane

6 wretchedness, despair, bitterness, infelicity, **misery, anguish, agony, woe,** woefulness, woesomeness <old>, bale, balefulness; **melancholy,** melancholia, **depression, sadness,** disappointment, **grief** 112.10; **heartache,** aching heart, heavy heart, bleeding heart, broken heart, agony of mind *or* spirit; suicidal despair, black night of the soul, **despondency,** gloom and doom, despond, "Slough of Despond"—Bunyan; **desolation,** prostration, crushing; extremity, depth of misery; sloth, acedia

7 torment, torture, cruciation <old>, excruciation, crucifixion, passion, laceration, clawing, lancination, flaying, excoriation; the rack, the iron maiden, thumbscrews; **persecution; martyrdom; purgatory,** living death, hell, hell upon earth; holocaust; nightmare, horror

8 affliction, infliction, **curse, woe,** distress, grievance, **sorrow,** *tsures* <Yiddish>, **trouble,** peck *or* pack of troubles, "sea of troubles"—Shakespeare; **care,** burden of care; **burden,** adversity, **oppression, cross, cross to bear** *or* **be borne, load,** fardel <old>, imposition, encumbrance, weight, albatross around one's neck, millstone around one's neck; thorn, thorn in the side, crown of thorns; white elephant; bitter pill, bitter draft, bitter cup, cup *or* waters of bitterness; gall, gall and wormwood; "the thousand natural shocks that flesh is heir to"—Shakespeare; Pandora's box

9 trial, tribulation, trials and tribulations; **ordeal,** fiery ordeal, the iron entering the soul, perfect storm

10 tormentor, torment; torturer; **nuisance, pest,** pesterer, pain *and* pain in the neck *or* ass <nf>, nag, nudzh <nf>, *nudnik* <Yiddish>, public nuisance; **tease,** teaser; annoyer, harasser, harrier, badgerer, **heckler,** plaguer, persecutor, sadist; molester, **bully**

11 sufferer, victim, prey; **wretch,** poor devil <nf>, object of compassion; martyr

VERBS **12** give no pleasure *or* joy *or* cheer *or* comfort, **disquiet,** discompose, leave unsatisfied; discontent; taste like ashes in the mouth; **bore,** be tedious, cheese off <Brit nf>

13 annoy, irk, vex, nettle, provoke, pique, miff *and* peeve <nf>, distemper, **ruffle, disturb,** discompose, **roil,** rile, **aggravate,** make a nuisance of oneself, **exasperate,** exercise, try one's patience, try the patience of a saint; **put one's back up,** make one bristle; **gripe;** give one a pain <nf>; get, get one down, **get one's goat,** get under one's skin, get in one's hair, tread on one's toes; burn up *and* brown off <nf>; **torment, molest, bother,** pother;

harass, harry, drive up the wall <nf>, hound, dog, nag, nobble <Brit nf>, nudzh <nf>, persecute; heckle, pick or prod at, rub it in and rub one's nose in it <nf>, badger, hector, bait, bullyrag, worry, worry at, nip at the heels of, chivy, hardly give one time to breathe, make one's life miserable, keep on at; bug <nf>, be on the back of and be at and ride <nf>, pester, tease, needle, devil, get after or get on <nf>, bedevil, pick on <nf>, tweak the nose, pluck the beard, give a bad time to <nf>; plague, beset, beleaguer; catch in the crossfire or in the middle; catch one off balance, trip one up; stalk

14 irritate, aggravate, exacerbate, worsen, rub salt in the wound, twist the knife in the wound, step on one's corns, barb the dart; touch a soft spot or tender spot, touch a raw nerve, touch where it hurts; provoke, gall, chafe, fret, grate, grit and gravel <nf>, rasp; get on one's nerves, grate on, set on edge; set one's teeth on edge, go against the grain; rub one or one's fur the wrong way

15 chagrin, embarrass, abash, discomfit, disconcert, discompose, confuse, throw into confusion or a tizzy or a hissy-fit, upset, confound, cast down, mortify, put out, put out of face or countenance, put to the blush

16 distress, afflict, trouble, burden, give one a tough row to hoe, load with care, bother, disturb, perturb, disquiet, discomfort, agitate, upset, put to it; disappoint; worry, give one gray hair

17 pain, grieve, aggrieve, anguish; hurt, wound, bruise, hurt one's feelings; pierce, prick, stab, cut, sting; cut up <nf>, cut to the heart, wound or sting or cut to the quick, hit one where one lives <nf>; be a thorn in one's side

18 torture, torment, agonize, harrow, savage, rack, scarify, crucify, impale, excruciate, lacerate, claw, rip, bloody, lancinate, macerate, convulse, wring; prolong the agony, kill by inches, make life miserable or not worth living; martyr, martyrize; tyrannize, push around <nf>; punish 604.10

19 suffer, hurt, ache, bleed; anguish, suffer anguish; agonize, writhe; go hard with, have a bad time of it, go through hell; quaff the bitter cup, drain the cup of misery to the dregs, be nailed to the cross

ADJS 20 pleasureless, joyless, cheerless, depressed 112.22, grim; sad, unhappy 112.21; unsatisfied, unfulfilled, ungratified; bored, cheesed off <Brit nf>; anguished, anxious, suffering angst or dread or nausea, uneasy, unquiet, prey to malaise; repelled, revolted, disgusted, sickened, nauseated, nauseous

21 annoyed, irritated, bugged <nf>; galled, chafed; bothered, troubled, disturbed, ruffled, roiled, riled; irked, vexed, piqued, nettled, provoked, peeved and miffed <nf>, griped, aggravated, exasperated; burnt-up and browned-off <nf>, cheesed-off <nf>, resentful, angry 152.28

22 distressed, afflicted, put-upon, beset, beleaguered; caught in the middle or in the crossfire; troubled, bothered, disturbed, perturbed, disquieted, discomforted, discomposed, agitated; hung up <nf>; uncomfortable, uneasy, ill at ease; chagrined, embarrassed, abashed, discomfited, disconcerted, upset, confused, mortified, put-out, out of countenance, cast down, chapfallen

23 pained, grieved, aggrieved; wounded, hurt, injured, bruised, mauled; cut, cut to the quick; stung; anguished, aching, bleeding

24 tormented, plagued, harassed, harried, dogged, hounded, persecuted, beset; nipped at, worried, chivied, heckled, badgered, hectored, baited, bullyragged, ragged, pestered, teased, needled, deviled, bedeviled, picked on <nf>, bugged <nf>

25 tortured, harrowed, savaged, agonized, convulsed, wrung, racked, crucified, impaled, lacerated, excoriated, clawed, ripped, bloodied, lancinated; on the rack, under the harrow

26 wretched, miserable; woeful, woebegone, woesome <old>; crushed, stricken, cut up <nf>, heartsick, heart-stricken, heart-struck; deep-troubled; desolate, disconsolate, suicidal

ADVS 27 to one's displeasure, to one's disgust

97 PLEASANTNESS

NOUNS 1 pleasantness, pleasingness, pleasance, pleasure 95, pleasurefulness, pleasurableness, pleasurability, pleasantry <old>, felicitousness, enjoyableness; bliss, blissfulness; felicitousness; sweetness, mellifluousness, douceur <Fr>; mellowness; agreeableness, agreeability, complaisance, rapport, harmoniousness; compatibility; welcomeness; geniality, congeniality, cordiality, Gemütlichkeit <Ger>, affability, amicability, amiability; amenity, graciousness; goodness, goodliness, niceness; fun 743.2/95.1; heaven

2 delightfulness, exquisiteness, loveliness; charm, winsomeness, grace, attractiveness, appeal, appealingness, winningness; sexiness <nf>; glamour; captivation, enchantment, entrancement, bewitchment, witchery, enravishment; charm offensive; fascination 377.1; invitingness, temptingness, tantalizingness; voluptuousness, sensuousness; luxury

3 delectability, delectableness, deliciousness, lusciousness; tastiness, flavorsomeness, savoriness; juiciness; succulence

4 cheerfulness; brightness, sunniness; sunny side, bright side; fair weather

VERBS **5** make pleasant, brighten, sweeten, gild, gild the lily *or* pill; sentimentalize, saccharinize; please, gratify, satisfy; brighten one's day, make one's day <nf>

ADJS **6 pleasant, pleasing, pleasureful, pleasurable;** fair, fair and pleasant, **enjoyable,** pleasure-giving; felicitous, felicific; **likable, desirable,** to one's liking, to one's taste, to *or* after one's fancy, after one's own heart; **agreeable,** complaisant, harmonious, *en rapport* <Fr>, compatible; **blissful;** sweet, mellifluous, honeyed, dulcet; mellow; **gratifying,** satisfying, rewarding, heartwarming, grateful; **welcome,** welcome as the roses in May; genial, congenial, cordial, *gemütlich* <Ger>, affable, amiable, amicable, gracious; good, goodly, nice, fine; cheerful 109.11

7 delightful, exquisite, lovely; thrilling, titillative; good-natured; **charming, attractive, endearing, engaging, appealing,** prepossessing, heartwarming, sexy <nf>, **enchanting,** bewitching, witching, entrancing, enthralling, intriguing, fascinating; **captivating, irresistible, ravishing,** enravishing; **winning,** winsome, taking, fetching, heart-robbing; inviting, tempting, tantalizing; voluptuous, zaftig <nf>, sensuous; luxurious, delicious

8 <nf terms> **fun, kicky,** chewy, dishy, drooly, sexy, toast, yummy

9 blissful, beatific, saintly, divine; sublime; **heavenly,** idyllic, paradisal, paradisiac, paradisiacal, paradisic, paradisical, empyreal *or* empyrean, Elysian; out of sight *or* of this world <nf>

10 delectable, delicious, luscious; tasty, flavorsome, savory; juicy, succulent

11 bright, sunny, fair, mild, balmy; halcyon, Saturnian

ADVS **12 pleasantly, pleasingly, pleasurably,** fair, **enjoyably; blissfully; gratifyingly,** satisfyingly; agreeably, genially, affably, cordially, amiably, amicably, graciously, kindly; cheerfully 109.17

13 delightfully, exquisitely; charmingly, engagingly, appealingly, enchantingly, bewitchingly, entrancingly, intriguingly, fascinatingly; ravishingly, enravishingly; **winningly,** winsomely; invitingly, temptingly, tantalizingly, voluptuously, sensuously; luxuriously

14 delectably, deliciously, lusciously, tastily, succulently, savorously

98 UNPLEASANTNESS

NOUNS **1 unpleasantness,** unpleasingness, displeasingness, displeasure; **disagreeableness,** disagreeability, *désagrément* <Fr>; **abrasiveness,** woundingess, hostility, unfriendliness; **undesirability,** unappealingness, unattractiveness, unengagingness, uninvitingness, unprepossessingness; **distastefulness,** unsavoriness, unpalatability, nastiness, **undelectability; ugliness** 1015; discomfort, pain, annoyance

2 offensiveness, objectionability, objectionableness, unacceptability; repugnance, contrariety, **odiousness, repulsiveness,** repellence *or* repellency, rebarbativeness, disgustingness, offensiveness, nauseousness, grossness *and* yuckiness *and* grunginess *and* scuzziness <nf>; **loathsomeness, hatefulness,** beastliness <nf>; **vileness, foulness,** putridness, putridity, rottenness, noxiousness; **nastiness,** fulsomeness, noisomeness, **obnoxiousness,** abominableness, heinousness; **contemptibleness,** contemptibility, despicability, **despicableness,** baseness, ignobleness, ignobility; unspeakableness; coarseness, grossness, crudeness, rudeness, obscenity

3 dreadfulness, horribleness, horridness, atrociousness, atrocity, hideousness, terribleness, awfulness <nf>; grimness, direness, banefulness

4 harshness, agony, agonizingness, excruciation, excruciatingness, **torture,** torturesomeness, torturousness, **torment,** tormentingness; desolation, desolateness; heartbreak, heartsickness

5 distressfulness, distress, grievousness, grief; painfulness, pain 26; **harshness,** bitterness, sharpness; lamentability, lamentableness, deplorability, deplorableness, pitiableness, pitifulness, pitiability, regrettableness; **woe, sadness, sorrowfulness, mournfulness,** lamentation, woefulness, woesomeness <old>, woebegoneness, pathos, poignancy; comfortlessness, discomfort, misease <old>; dreariness, cheerlessness, joylessness, dismalness, **depression,** bleakness, black *or* dark cloud

6 mortification, humiliation, embarrassment, egg on one's face <nf>; disconcertedness, awkwardness, disappointment

7 vexatiousness, irksomeness, annoyance, annoyingness, aggravation, exasperation, provocation, provokingness, tiresomeness, wearisomeness; **troublesomeness, bothersomeness,** harassment; worrisomeness, plaguesomeness, peskiness *and* pestiferousness <nf>

8 **harshness, oppressiveness, burdensomeness,** onerousness, weightiness, heaviness

9 **intolerability,** intolerableness, unbearableness, insupportableness, insufferableness, **unendurability**

VERBS 10 **be unpleasant; displease,** make unpleasant; be disagreeable *or* undesirable *or* distasteful *or* abrasive

11 **offend,** give offense, **repel,** put off, turn off <nf>, **revolt, disgust,** nauseate, sicken, make one sick, make one sick to *or* in the stomach, make one vomit *or* puke *or* retch, turn the stomach, gross out <nf>; stink in the nostrils; stick in one's throat, stick in one's crop *or* craw *or* gizzard <nf>; **horrify, appall,** shock; make the flesh creep *or* crawl, make one shudder

12 **agonize,** excruciate, **torture, torment,** desolate

13 **mortify,** humiliate, embarrass, disconcert, disturb, chagrin, shame; bitch-slap <nf>

14 **distress, dismay,** grieve, mourn, lament, sorrow; pain, discomfort, misease <old>; get in one's hair, try one's patience, give one a hard time *or* a pain *or* a pain in the neck *or* ass *or* butt <nf>, disturb, put off

15 **vex, irk, annoy, aggravate,** exasperate, provoke, run afoul; **trouble, worry,** give one gray hair, plague, harass, bother, hassle; disappoint

16 **oppress, burden,** weigh upon, weight down, wear one down, be heavy on one, be the bane of one's existence, crush one; **tire, exhaust,** weary, wear out, wear upon one; prey on the mind, prey on *or* upon; **haunt,** haunt the memory, obsess; stalk

ADJS 17 **unpleasant, unpleasing, unenjoyable; displeasing, disagreeable; unlikable,** dislikable; **abrasive,** wounding, hostile, unfriendly; **undesirable,** unattractive, unappealing, unengaging, uninviting, unalluring; tacky *and* low rent *and* low ride <nf>; unwelcome, thankless; **distasteful,** untasteful, **unpalatable,** unsavory, unappetizing, undelicious, **undelectable; ugly** 1015.6; sour, **bitter**

18 **offensive, objectionable,** objectional, **odious, repulsive,** repellent, rebarbative, **repugnant, revolting,** forbidding; **disgusting, sickening, loathsome,** gross *and* yucky *and* grungy *and* scuzzy <nf>, beastly <nf>, **vile, foul, nasty, nauseating** 64.7; grody <nf>; fulsome, mephitic, miasmal, miasmic, malodorous, stinking, fetid, noisome, noxious; coarse, gross, crude, rude, obscene; **obnoxious, abhorrent, hateful, abominable,** heinous, **contemptible, despicable,** detestable, execrable, beneath *or* below contempt, **base,** ignoble, uncouth

19 **horrid, horrible,** horrific, **horrifying,** horrendous, unspeakable, beyond words; **dreadful, atrocious, terrible, rotten,** awful *and* beastly <nf>, **hideous; tragic;** dire, grim, baneful; appalling, shocking, disgusting

20 **distressing,** distressful, dismaying; from hell <nf>; afflicting, afflictive; **painful,** sore, **harsh, bitter,** sharp; **grievous,** dolorous, dolorific, dolorogenic; **lamentable, deplorable,** regrettable, pitiable, piteous, rueful, woeful, woesome <old>, woebegone, **sad,** sorrowful, wretched, mournful, **depressing,** depressive, disappointing; **pathetic,** affecting, touching, moving, saddening, poignant; comfortless, discomforting, uncomfortable; **desolate,** dreary, cheerless, joyless, dismal, bleak

21 **mortifying,** humiliating, **embarrassing,** crushing, disconcerting, awkward, disturbing

22 **annoying, irritating,** galling, **provoking, aggravating** <nf>, **exasperating; vexatious,** vexing, irking, **irksome,** baneful, tiresome, wearisome; **troublesome, bothersome, worrisome,** bothering, troubling, disturbing, plaguing, plaguesome, plaguey <nf>, pestilent, pestilential, **pesky** *and* pesty *and* pestiferous <nf>; tormenting, harassing, worrying; pestering, teasing; importunate, importune; distasteful

23 **agonizing, excruciating, harrowing,** racking, rending, **desolating,** consuming; **tormenting,** torturous; **heartbreaking,** heartrending, **heartsickening,** heartwounding

24 **oppressive, burdensome, crushing,** trying, onerous, heavy, weighty; **harsh,** wearing, wearying, exhausting; overburdensome, tyrannous, grinding

25 **insufferable, intolerable, insupportable, unendurable, unbearable,** past bearing, not to be borne *or* endured, for the birds <nf>, **too much** *or* a bit much <nf>, more than flesh and blood can bear, enough to drive one mad, enough to provoke a saint, enough to make a preacher swear <nf>, enough to try the patience of Job

ADVS 26 **unpleasantly, distastefully** unpleasingly; **displeasingly, offensively, objectionably,** odiously, **repulsively,** repellently, rebarbatively, repugnantly, **revoltingly, disgustingly, sickeningly, loathsomely, vilely,** foully, nastily, fulsomely, mephitically, malodorously, fetidly, noisomely, noxiously, obnoxiously, **abhorrently, hatefully, abominably,** contemptibly, **despicably, detestably,** execrably, nauseatingly

27 **horridly, horribly, dreadfully, terribly,** hideously; **tragically;** grimly, direly, banefully; appallingly, shockingly

28 **distressingly,** distressfully; **painfully,** sorely, **grievously,** lamentably, deplorably, pitiably,

ruefully, woefully, woesomely <old>, sadly, pathetically; **agonizingly, excruciatingly,** harrowingly, heartbreakingly

29 **annoyingly, irritatingly, aggravatingly, provokingly, exasperatingly; vexatiously, irksomely,** tiresomely, wearisomely; **troublesomely, bothersomely,** worrisomely, regrettably

30 **insufferably, intolerably, unbearably, unendurably, insupportably**

INTERJS 31 yuck or eeyuck! or yeeuck! or yeeuch!, phew! or pugh!, ugh!; *feh!* <Yiddish>; alas, alack, bah!, tsk tsk!

99 DISLIKE

NOUNS 1 **dislike, distaste,** disrelish, scunner; disaffection, **disfavor,** disinclination; disaffinity; **displeasure, disapproval,** disapprobation; instant dislike; rejection

2 **hostility,** antagonism, **enmity** 589; **hatred, hate** 103; **aversion, repugnance,** repulsion, **antipathy,** allergy <nf>, grudge, abomination, **abhorrence, horror,** mortal horror; **disgust, loathing;** nausea; shuddering, cold sweat, creeping flesh

VERBS 3 **dislike,** mislike, disfavor, not like, have no liking for, be no love lost between, **have no use for** <nf>, **not care for,** have no time for, have a disaffinity for, have an aversion to, want nothing to do with, not think much of, entertain or conceive or take a dislike to, take a scunner to, not be able to bear or endure or abide, not give the time of day to <nf>, **disapprove of; disrelish,** have no taste for, not stomach, not have the stomach for, not be one's cup of tea; be hostile to, have it in for <nf>; **hate, abhor, detest, loathe** 103.5

4 **feel disgust,** be nauseated, **sicken at,** choke on, have a bellyful of <nf>; **gag, retch,** keck, heave, vomit, puke, chunder and hurl and upchuck and barf <nf>

5 **shudder at,** have one's flesh creep or crawl at the thought of; shrink from, **recoil, revolt at;** grimace, make a face, make a wry face or mouth, turn up one's nose, look down one's nose, look askance, raise one's eyebrows, take a dim view of, show distaste for, disapprove of

6 **repel, disgust** 98.11, gross out <nf>; leave a bad taste in one's mouth, rub the wrong way, antagonize

ADJS 7 **unlikable, distasteful,** mislikable, dislikable, **uncongenial, displeasing,** unpleasant 98.17; **not to one's taste,** not one's sort, not one's cup of tea, counter to one's preferences, offering no delight, against the grain, uninviting; yucky <nf>, unlovable; **abhorrent, odious** 98.18; **intolerable** 98.25

8 **averse, allergic** <nf>, loath, reluctant, undelighted, out of sympathy, disaffected, disenchanted, **disinclined, displeased,** put off <nf>, not charmed, less than pleased; **disapproving, censorious, judgmental,** po-faced <Brit nf>; unamiable, **unfriendly, hostile** 589.10; death on, down on

9 **disliked, uncared-for, unvalued,** unprized, misprized, undervalued; **despised,** detested, lowly, spat-upon, untouchable; **unpopular, out of favor,** gone begging; **unappreciated,** misunderstood; unsung, thankless; unwept, unlamented, unmourned, undeplored, unmissed, unregretted

10 **unloved,** unbeloved, uncherished, loveless; **lovelorn,** forsaken, **rejected,** jilted, thrown over <nf>, spurned, crossed in love

11 **unwanted,** unwished, undesired; **unwelcome,** undesirous, unasked, unbidden, uninvited, uncalled-for, unasked-for

100 DESIRE

NOUNS 1 **desire, wish,** wanting, grasping, **want, need,** desideration; **hope; fancy; will, mind, pleasure,** will and pleasure; heart's desire; **urge,** drive, libido, pleasure principle; concupiscence; horme; wish fulfillment, fantasy; passion, ardor, sexual desire 75.5; **curiosity,** intellectual curiosity, thirst for knowledge, lust for learning; **eagerness** 101

2 **liking, love, fondness;** infatuation, crush; **affection; relish, taste,** gusto, gust <Scot>; **passion, weakness** <nf>

3 **inclination, penchant, partiality, fancy, favor, predilection, preference,** propensity, proclivity, **leaning, bent,** turn, tilt, bias, **affinity,** tendency; mutual affinity or attraction; **sympathy,** fascination

4 **wistfulness,** wishfulness, yearnfulness, **nostalgia;** wishful thinking; sheep's eyes, longing or wistful eye; daydream, daydreaming

5 **yearning, yen** <nf>; **longing,** desiderium, **hankering** <nf>, **pining,** honing <nf>, aching; languishment, languishing; **nostalgia, homesickness,** *Heimweh* <Ger>, *mal du pays* and *maladie du pays* <Fr>; nostomania

6 **craving, coveting, lust; hunger, thirst, appetite,** "appetite, an universal wolf"—Shakespeare, appetition, appetency or appetence; aching void, hungry ghost; **itch, itching,** prurience or pruriency; lech <nf>, **sexual desire** 75.5; *cacoëthes* <L>, **mania** 926.12

7 **appetite,** stomach, relish, taste; **hunger,** hungriness; the munchies <nf>, peckishness <Brit nf>; tapeworm <nf>, eyes bigger than one's

stomach, wolf in one's stomach, canine appetite; empty stomach, emptiness <nf>, hollow hunger; **thirst,** thirstiness, drought <nf>, dryness; polydipsia; torment of Tantalus; sweet tooth <nf>

8 **greed,** greediness, graspingness, **avarice, cupidity, avidity, voracity, rapacity, lust,** avariciousness, *avaritia and cupiditas* <L>; money-grubbing; avidness, esurience, wolfishness; voraciousness, ravenousness, rapaciousness, sordidness, **covetousness,** acquisitiveness; itching palm; grasping; **piggishness, hoggishness,** swinishness; **gluttony** 672, *gula* <L>; inordinate desire, furor, craze, fury *or* frenzy of desire, overgreediness; insatiable desire, insatiability; incontinence, intemperateness 669.1

9 **aspiration,** reaching high, upward looking; high goal *or* aim *or* purpose, dream, ideals, hope; **idealism** 986.7

10 **ambition,** ambitiousness, vaulting ambition; aim, target; climbing, status-seeking, social climbing, careerism; opportunism; power-hunger; "the mind's immodesty"—d'Avenant; noble *or* lofty ambition, magnanimity <old>; American dream

11 <object of desire> **desire,** heart's desire, desideration, *desideratum* <L>; wish; **hope;** catch, quarry, prey, game, plum, prize, trophy, brass ring <nf>; status symbol; collectable; collectible; forbidden fruit, ideal, weakness, temptation; lodestone, magnet; golden vision, mecca, glimmering goal; land of heart's desire 986.11; something to be desired, "a consummation devoutly to be wish'd"—Shakespeare; dearest wish, ambition, the height of one's ambition; a sight for sore eyes, a welcome sight; the light at the end of the tunnel

12 **desirer,** wisher, wanter, hankerer <nf>, yearner, coveter; fancier, collector; addict, freak <nf>, glutton, greedy pig, devotee, votary; **aspirant,** aspirer, solicitant, wannabee *or* wannabe *and* hopeful *and* would-be <nf>, candidate; **lover,** love interest, swain, suitor, toyboy, squeeze <nf>

13 **desirability; agreeability,** acceptability, unobjectionableness; **attractiveness,** attraction, magnetism, **appeal,** seductiveness, provocativeness, pleasingness; likability, lovability 104.6

VERBS 14 **desire,** desiderate, be desirous of, **wish,** lust after, bay after, kill for *and* give one's right arm for <nf>, die for <nf>, **want,** have a mind to, choose <nf>; would fain do *or* have <old>, would be glad of; **like,** have *or* acquire a taste for, fancy, take to, **take a fancy** *or* a shine to, have a fancy for; have an eye to, have one's eye on; lean toward, tilt toward, have a penchant for, have a weakness *or* soft spot in one's heart for; aim at, set one's cap

for, have designs on; wish very much, wish to goodness; **love** 104.18; lust; prefer, favor 371.17

15 **want to, wish to, like to,** love to, dearly love to, choose to; **itch to,** burn to; ache to, long to

16 **wish for, hope for, yearn for,** yen for *and* have a yen for <nf>, **itch for,** lust for, pant for, **long for, pine for,** hone for <nf>, ache for, be hurting for <nf>, weary for, languish for, **be dying for,** thirst for, sigh for, gape for <old>; cry for, clamor for; spoil for <nf>

17 **want with all one's heart, want in the worst way; set one's heart on, have one's heart set on,** give one's kingdom in hell for *or* one's eyeteeth for <nf>

18 **crave, covet, hunger after,** thirst after, crave after, **lust after,** have a lech for <nf>, pant after, run mad after, **hanker for** *or* **after** <nf>; crawl after; aspire after, be consumed with desire; have an itchy *or* itching palm *and* have sticky fingers <nf>

19 **hunger,** hunger for, feel hungry, be peckish <Brit nf>; starve <nf>, be ravenous, raven; **have a good appetite,** be a good trencherman, have a tapeworm <nf>, have a wolf in one's stomach; eye hungrily, lick one's chops <nf>; **thirst,** thirst for; lick one's lips

20 **aspire, be ambitious;** aspire to, try to reach; aim high, keep one's eyes on the stars, raise one's sights, set one's sights, reach for the sky, dream of, "hitch one's wagon to a star"—Emerson

ADJS 21 **desirous,** desiring, desireful <old>, lickerish, **wanting, wishing,** needing, hoping; aspirational; dying to <nf>; tempted; appetitive, desiderative, optative, libidinous, libidinal; orectic; hormic; **eager;** lascivious, **lustful**

22 **desirous of** *or* **to,** keen on, set on <nf>, bent on; fond of, with a liking for, partial to <nf>; fain of *or* to <old>; inclined toward, leaning toward; **itching for** *or* **to,** aching for *or* to, **dying for** *or* **to;** spoiling for <nf>; mad on *or* for, wild to *or* for <nf>, crazy to *or* for <nf>

23 **wistful,** wishful; **longing, yearning,** yearnful, **hankering** <nf>, **languishing, pining,** honing <nf>; **nostalgic, homesick**

24 **craving,** coveting; **hungering,** hungry, thirsting, thirsty, athirst; **itching,** prurient; fervid; **devoured by desire,** in a frenzy *or* fury of desire, mad with lust, consumed with desire

25 **hungry,** hungering, peckish <Brit nf>; empty <nf>, unfilled; ravening, **ravenous,** voracious, sharp-set, **wolfish,** dog-hungry <nf>, hungry as a bear; **starved, famished,** starving, famishing, perishing *or* pinched with hunger; fasting, off food, unfed; keeping Lent, Lenten; underfed; half-starved, half-famished

26 **thirsty,** thirsting, athirst; **dry,** parched, droughty <nf>

27 **greedy, avaricious, avid, voracious, rapacious,** cupidinous, esurient, **ravening, grasping, grabby** <nf>, graspy, acquisitive, mercenary, sordid, overgreedy; ravenous, gobbling, devouring; miserly, money-hungry, money-grubbing, money-mad, venal, **covetous,** coveting; **piggish, hoggish,** swinish, a hog for, greedy as a hog; **gluttonous** 672.6; omnivorous, all-devouring; insatiable, insatiate, unsatisfied, unsated, unappeased, unappeasable, limitless, bottomless, unquenchable, quenchless, unslaked, unslakeable, slakeless; big-eyed <nf>

28 **aspiring, ambitious,** sky-aspiring, upward-looking, high-reaching; high-flying, social-climbing, careerist, careeristic, fast-track, fast-lane, on the make <nf>; power-hungry; would-be, wannabe

29 **desired, wanted,** coveted; **wished-for,** hoped-for, longed-for; sought after, in demand, popular

30 **desirable,** sought-after, much sought-after, to be desired, to die for <nf>, **much to be desired; enviable,** worth having; **likable, pleasing,** after one's own heart; **agreeable,** acceptable, unobjectionable, cromulent; palatable; **attractive,** taking, winning, sexy <nf>, dishy <Brit nf>, **seductive, provocative,** tantalizing, exciting; appetizing, tempting, toothsome, mouth-watering; **lovable,** adorable; buzzworthy

ADVS **31** **desirously, wistfully,** wishfully, **longingly, yearningly,** piningly, languishingly; cravingly, itchingly; hungrily, thirstily; aspiringly, ambitiously

32 **greedily, avariciously,** avidly, ravenously, raveningly, voraciously, rapaciously, **covetously,** graspingly, devouringly; wolfishly, **piggishly, hoggishly,** swinishly

101 EAGERNESS

NOUNS **1** **eagerness, enthusiasm, avidity,** avidness, keenness <chiefly Brit>, forwardness, prothymia, **readiness,** promptness, quickness, **alacrity,** cheerful readiness, *empressement* <Fr>; keen desire, **appetite** 100.7; anxiousness, anxiety; **zest,** zestfulness, gusto, verve, **liveliness,** life, **vitality,** vivacity, élan, spirit, animation; **impatience,** breathless impatience 135.1; keen interest, fascination; **craze** 926.12

2 **zeal, ardor, ardency, fervor, fervency, fervidness, spirit, warmth, fire, heat,** heatedness, **passion,** passionateness, impassionedness, heartiness, intensity, **abandon,** vehemence; intentness, resolution 359; **devotion,** devoutness, devotedness, dedication, commitment, committedness; **earnestness, seriousness,** sincerity; loyalty, faithfulness, faith, fidelity 644.7; discipleship, followership

3 **overzealousness, overeagerness,** overanxiousness, overanxiety; unchecked enthusiasm, **overenthusiasm, infatuation; overambitiousness; frenzy, fury; zealotry,** zealotism; mania, **fanaticism** 926.11

4 **enthusiast, zealot,** infatuate, energumen, rhapsodist; addict; faddist; pursuer; hobbyist, collector; **fanatic,** trainspotter <Brit nf>; stalker; visionary 986.13; **devotee,** votary, aficionada, aficionado, **fancier,** admirer, **follower; disciple,** worshiper, idolizer, idolater; amateur, dilettante

5 <nf terms> **fan, buff, freak,** hound, fiend, demon, nut, bug, head, junkie, groupie, rooter, booster, great one for, sucker for; fan club, fanzine; eager beaver, -aholic

VERBS **6** **jump at,** catch, grab, grab at, go for, snatch, snatch at, fall all over oneself, get excited about, go at hammer and tongs *or* tooth and nail, go hog wild <nf>; go to great lengths, lean *or* bend *or* fall over backwards; **desire** 100.14,18

7 **be enthusiastic, rave, enthuse** *and* be big for <nf>; get stars in one's eyes, **rhapsodize, carry on over** *and* rave on <nf>, make much of, **make a fuss over,** make an ado *or* much ado about, make a to-do over *and* take on over <nf>, be *or* go on over *or* about <nf>, rave about *and* whoop it up about <nf>; go nuts *or* gaga *or* ape over <nf>; gush, gush over; effervesce, bubble over

ADJS **8** **eager, anxious,** agog, all agog; **avid, keen,** forward, prompt, quick, ready, ready and willing, alacritous, bursting to, dying to, raring to, gung ho; **zestful, lively,** full of life, vital, vivacious, vivid, spirited, **animated; impatient** 135.6; breathless, panting, champing at the bit; **desirous** 100.21

9 **zealous, ardent, fervent, fervid,** perfervid, **spirited, intense,** hearty, vehement, abandoned, **passionate,** impassioned, **warm,** heated, hot, hot-blooded, red-hot, fiery, white-hot, flaming, burning, afire, aflame, on fire, like a house afire <nf>; **devout, devoted;** dedicated, committed; **earnest, sincere, serious,** in earnest; loyal, faithful 644.20; intent, intent on, resolute 359.11

10 **enthusiastic,** enthused *and* big <nf>, **gung ho** <nf>, glowing, full of enthusiasm; enthusiastic about, infatuated with

11 <nf terms> **wild about, crazy about, mad about,** ape about *or* over, gone on, all in a dither over, gaga over, starry-eyed over, all hopped up about, hepped up over, hot about *or* for *or* on, steamed up about, **turned-on, switched-on;** hipped on, **cracked on,** bugs on, freaked-out, **nuts on** *or* **over** *or* **about, keen on** *or* **about,** crazy *or* mad about

12 overzealous, ultrazealous, **overeager,** over-
anxious; **overambitious;** overdesirous;
overenthusiastic, infatuated; feverish, perfervid,
febrile, at fever or fevered pitch; hectic, frenetic,
furious, **frenzied,** frantic, **wild,** hysteric,
hysterical, delirious; **insane** 926.26; **fanatical**
926.32

ADVS **13 eagerly, anxiously; impatiently,**
breathlessly; **avidly,** promptly, quickly, keenly,
readily; zestfully, vivaciously, animatedly;
enthusiastically, with enthusiasm; **with alacrity,**
with zest, with gusto, with relish, with open arms,
avidiously

14 zealously, ardently, fervently, fervidly, perfervidly,
heatedly, heartily, vehemently, **passionately,**
impassionedly; intently, intensely; **devoutly,
devotedly;** earnestly, sincerely, seriously

102 INDIFFERENCE

NOUNS **1 indifference,** indifferentness;
indifferentism; halfheartedness, zeallessness,
perfunctoriness, fervorlessness; **coolness,**
coldness, chilliness, chill, iciness, frostiness,
stoicism; tepidness, **lukewarmness,** Laodiceanism;
neutrality, neutralness; insipidity, vapidity;
adiaphorism

**2 unconcern, disinterest, detachment; disregard,
dispassion,** insouciance, **carelessness,**
regardlessness; easygoingness; **heedlessness,**
mindlessness, inattention 984; **unmindfulness,
incuriosity** 982; **insensitivity;** disregardfulness,
recklessness, negligence 340.1; je-m'en-foutisme
or je-m'en-fichisme <Fr>; unsolicitousness,
unanxiousness; pococurantism; **nonchalance,**
inexcitability 106, ataraxy or ataraxia, samadhi;
indiscrimination, casualness 945.1; **listlessness,**
lackadaisicalness, lack of feeling or affect, **apathy**
94.4; sloth, acedia, phlegm, lethargy

3 undesirousness, desirelessness; nirvana;
lovelessness, passionlessness; uneagerness,
unambitiousness; lack of appetite, inappetence

VERBS **4 not care, not mind, not give** or **care a
damn,** not give a hoot or shit or crap <nf>, not
care less or two hoots <nf>, care nothing for or
about, not care a straw about; shrug off, dismiss;
take no interest in, have no desire for, not think
twice about, have no taste or relish for; hold no
brief for; be half-hearted, temper one's zeal; lose
interest

5 not matter to, be all one to, take it or leave it;
make no difference, make no never-mind <nf>; sit
on the fence, remain neutral

ADJS **6 indifferent, halfhearted,** zealless,
perfunctory, fervorless; **cool, cold** 589.9; tepid,

lukewarm, Laodicean; neither hot nor cold,
neither one thing nor the other, "neither fish, nor
flesh, nor good red herring"—John Heywood;
unmoved; blah, **neuter, neutral**

7 unconcerned, uninterested, disinterested,
turned-off, **dispassionate,** insouciant, **careless,**
regardless; easygoing; incurious 982.3; mindless,
unmindful, heedless, inattentive 984.6,
disregardful; **devil-may-care,** reckless, negligent
340.10; unsolicitous, unanxious; pococurante,
nonchalant, inexcitable 106.10; ataractic; **blasé,**
undiscriminating, casual 945.5; **listless,**
lackadaisical, sluggish; bovine; numb, **apathetic**
94.13

8 undesirous, unattracted, desireless; loveless,
passionless; inappetent; nirvanic; **unenthusiastic,**
uneager; **unambitious,** unaspiring

ADVS **9 indifferently, with indifference,** with utter
indifference; coolly, coldly; lukewarmly,
halfheartedly; perfunctorily; for all or aught one
cares

10 unconcernedly, uninterestedly, disinterestedly,
dispassionately, insouciantly, **carelessly,**
regardlessly; mindlessly; **unmindfully, heedlessly,**
recklessly, negligently 340.17; **nonchalantly;**
listlessly, lackadaisically; numbly, **apathetically**
94.15

PHRS **11 who cares?,** I don't care, I couldn't care less
<nf>; who gives a crap?; it's a matter of sublime
indifference; never mind!, **what does it matter?,**
what's the difference?, what's the diff? <nf>, what
are the odds?, what of it?, **so what?,** what the hell
<nf>, it's all one to me, it's all the same to me, it's
no skin off one's nose or ass <nf>; like it or lump it;
forget it!

12 I should worry?, I should fret?, that's your lookout,
that's your problem, I feel for you but I can't reach
you; that's your pigeon <nf>, that's your tough
luck, tough titty and shit <nf>

103 HATE

NOUNS **1 hate, hatred; dislike** 99; **detestation,
abhorrence, aversion, antipathy,** repugnance,
loathing, execration, **abomination,** odium; **spite,**
spitefulness, despite, despitefulness, **malice,
malevolence,** malignity; vials of hate or wrath;
rancor, venom; misanthropy, misanthropism;
misandry, misogyny; misogamy; misopedia;
anti-Semitism; race hatred, racism, racialism;
bigotry; phobia, Anglophobia, Russophobia,
xenophobia, etc; grudge; scorn, despising,
contempt 157; hate crime

2 enmity 589; bitterness, **animosity** 589.4;
hatefulness

3 <hated thing> **anathema, abomination,** detestation, aversion, abhorrence, antipathy, execration, hate; peeve, pet peeve; phobia; bugbear, bête noire, bane, bitter pill; fear; dislike

4 hater, man-hater, woman-hater, misanthropist, misanthrope, misogynist, anti-Semite, racist, racialist, white supremacist, bigot, redneck <nf>; phobic, Anglophobe, xenophobe, etc; detester, loather

VERBS **5 hate, detest, loathe, abhor,** execrate, **abominate,** hold in abomination, take an aversion to, shudder at, utterly detest, be death on, not stand, not stand the sight of, not stomach; scorn, spit on, **despise** 157.3; hate someone's guts <nf>

6 dislike, have it in for <nf>, feel aversion for, disrelish 99.3

ADJS **7 hating, abhorrent,** loathing, despising, venomous, death on; averse 99.8; disgusted 96.20; scornful, **contemptuous** 157.8; antagonistic; execrative

8 hateful, loathesome, accursed, aversive, odious, detestable 98.18; despiteful; unlikable 99.7; **contemptible** 661.12/98.18

WORD ELEMENTS **9** mis-, miso-; -phobia, -phobiac, -phobe

104 LOVE

NOUNS **1 love, affection, attachment, devotion, fondness,** sentiment, warm feeling, soft spot in one's heart, weakness <nf>, like, **liking,** fancy, shine <nf>, amore <Ital>; **partiality, predilection;** intimacy; **passion,** tender feeling or passion, **ardor,** ardency, fervor, heart, flame, the real thing <nf>; physical love, Amor, Eros, bodily love, libido, sexual love, sex 75; desire, yearning 100.5; lasciviousness 665.5; charity, caritas <L>, brotherly love, Christian love, agape, loving concern, fellow feeling, **caring;** sentimental attachment; spiritual love, platonic love; amour-propre; **adoration,** worship, hero worship; **regard,** admiration; idolization, idolism, idolatry; popular regard, popularity; faithful love, truelove; married love, conjugal love, uxoriousness; free love, free-lovism; **lovemaking** 562; self-love, narcissism, autophilia, egotism; patriotism, love of one's country

2 amorousness, amativeness, lovingness, meltingness, **affection, affectionateness,** demonstrativeness; mating instinct, reproductive or procreative drive, libido; carnality, sexiness, goatishness, hot pants and horniness <nf>; romantic love, romanticism, **sentimentality,** susceptibility; lovesickness, lovelornness; ecstasy, rapture; enchantment 95.2

3 infatuation, infatuatedness, passing fancy; **crush** and mash and pash and case <nf>; **puppy love** and young love and calf love <nf>; love at first sight, coup de foudre <Fr>; falling in love

4 parental love, natural affection, mother or maternal love, father or paternal love; filial love; parental instinct; unconditional love

5 love affair, affair, affair of the heart, **amour, romance,** affaire d'amour <Fr>, romantic tie or bond, something between, thing <nf>; relationship, liaison, entanglement, involvement, intrigue, tryst; **dalliance,** amorous play, the love game, flirtation, hanky-panky, lollygagging <nf>; triangle, eternal triangle; illicit or unlawful love, forbidden or unsanctified love, adulterous affair, adultery, unfaithfulness, infidelity, cuckoldry; hookup <nf>; courtship, courting, wooing, pursuit, dating, dallying, betrothal, engagement, going together and going out with <nf>, going steady <nf>

6 loveableness, likeableness, lovability, likability, adoreableness, adorability, sweetness, loveliness, lovesomeness; cuddliness, cuddlesomeness; amiability, attractiveness 97.2, desirability, agreeability, amiability; **charm, appeal,** allurement 377; winsomeness, winning ways

7 Love, Cupid, Amor, Eros, Kama; Venus, Aphrodite, Astarte, Freya

8 <symbols> **cupid,** cupidon, amor, amourette, amoretto, amorino <Ital>; love-knot

9 sweetheart, loved one, love, beloved, darling, dear, dear one, dearly beloved, well-beloved, truelove, beloved object, **object of one's affections,** light of one's eye or life, light of love; sex object, prey, quarry, game; valentine

10 <nf terms> **sweetie, honey,** honeybunch, honey-bunny, honey bun, honeypie, hon, main squeeze, sweetie-pie, sweet patootie, tootsie, tootsie-pie, tootsy-wootsy, dearie, baby, dreamboat, heartthrob, poopsy, poopsy-woopsy, sugar, sugar-bun, sweets, cookie

11 lover, admirer, adorer, amorist; infatuate, paramour, **suitor, wooer,** pursuer, follower; **flirt,** coquette; vampire, vamp; conquest, catch; devotee; escort, companion, date and steady <nf>; significant other, soul mate, bashert <Yiddish>; squeeze <nf>; old flame <nf>, new flame <nf>; love interest; other woman

12 beau, inamorato, swain, suitor, escort, man, gallant, cavalier, squire, esquire, caballero <Sp>; amoroso and cavaliere servente <Ital>; sugar daddy <nf>; gigolo; **boyfriend** and **fellow** and young man and flame <nf>; old man <nf>; love-maker, lover-boy <nf>; **seducer, lady-killer,** ladies' man, sheik, philanderer, cocksman <nf>; Prince

Charming, Lothario, Romeo; Casanova, Don Juan; boy toy <nf>

13 **ladylove, inamorata,** *amorosa* <Ital>, lady, mistress, ladyfriend; lass, lassie, jo <Scot>, gill, jill, Dulcinea

14 <nf terms> **doll, angel,** baby, baby-doll, doll-baby, buttercup, ducks, ducky, pet, snookums, snooky, **girl, girlfriend,** sweetheart, best girl, dream girl; old lady

15 **favorite,** preference; **darling,** idol, jewel, apple of one's eye, fair-haired boy, man after one's own heart; **pet,** fondling, cosset, minion; spoiled child *or* darling, *enfant gâté* <Fr>, lap dog; teacher's pet; matinee idol; tin god, little tin god

16 **fiancé, fiancée,** bride-to-be, affianced, betrothed, future, intended <nf>

17 **loving couple,** soul mates, lovebirds, turtledoves, bill-and-cooers; newlyweds, honeymooners; star-crossed lovers; Romeo and Juliet, Anthony and Cleopatra, Tristan and Isolde, Abélard and Héloïse, Darby and Joan; item <nf>

VERBS 18 **love, be fond of,** be in love with, **care for, like, fancy,** have a fancy for, take an interest in, **dote on** *or* **upon,** be desperately in love, burn with love; be partial to, have a soft spot in one's heart for, have a weakness *or* fondness for; court, woo, romance

19 <nf terms> **go for,** have an eye *or* eyes for, only have eyes for, be sweet on, have a crush *or* mash *or* case on; have it bad, carry a torch *or* the torch for, have designs on

20 **cherish, hold dear,** hold in one's heart *or* affections, think much *or* the world of, prize, treasure; **admire, regard,** esteem, revere; **adore, idolize,** worship, dearly love, think worlds *or* the world of, love to distraction

21 **fall in love, lose one's heart, become enamored,** be smitten; take to, **take a liking** *or* **fancy to,** take a shine to *and* fall for <nf>, become attached to, bestow one's affections on; fall head and ears *or* head over heels in love, be swept off one's feet; cotton to <nf>

22 **enamor, endear;** win one's heart, win the love *or* affections of, take the fancy of, make a hit with <nf>; **charm,** becharm, **infatuate,** hold in thrall, command one's affection, **fascinate,** attract, allure, grow on one, strike *or* tickle one's fancy, **captivate,** bewitch, enrapture, carry away, sweep off one's feet, turn one's head, inflame with love; **seduce,** vamp <nf>, draw on, tempt, tantalize

ADJS 23 **beloved, loved, dear, darling, precious;** pet, favorite; **adored, admired,** esteemed, revered; **cherished,** prized, treasured, held dear; **well-liked,** popular; **well-beloved,** dearly beloved, dear to one's heart, after one's heart *or* own heart, dear as the apple of one's eye

24 **endearing, lovable, likable, adorable,** admirable, **lovely,** lovesome, sweet, winning, winsome; **charming;** angelic, seraphic; caressable, kissable; cuddlesome, cuddly

25 **amorous,** amatory, amative, erotic; **sexual** 75.25; loverly, loverlike; **passionate, ardent,** impassioned; desirous 100.21,22; lascivious 665.29

26 **loving,** lovesome, **fond, adoring, devoted, affectionate,** demonstrative, **romantic, sentimental, tender,** soft <nf>, melting; lovelorn, lovesick, languishing; wifely, husbandly, conjugal, uxorious, faithful; parental, paternal, maternal, filial; charitable, caritative; self-loving, narcissistic

27 **enamored, charmed,** becharmed, **fascinated, captivated,** bewitched, enraptured, enchanted; **infatuated,** infatuate; **smitten,** heartsmitten, heartstruck, lovestruck, besotted with

28 **in love,** head over heels in love, over head and ears in love

29 **fond of, enamored of,** partial to, **in love with,** attached to, wedded to, devoted to, wrapped up in; **taken with,** smitten with, struck with

30 <nf terms> **crazy about,** mad *or* nuts *or* nutty *or* wild about, swacked on, sweet on, stuck on, gone on

ADVS 31 **lovingly, fondly, affectionately, tenderly,** dearly, **adoringly,** devotedly; amorously, ardently, passionately; with love, with affection, with all one's love

WORD ELEMENTS 32 phil-, philo-, -phily; -phile; -philic, -philous

105 EXCITEMENT

NOUNS 1 **excitement,** emotion, excitedness, **arousal, stimulation, exhilaration;** a high <nf>, manic state *or* condition

2 **thrill, sensation,** titillation; **tingle,** tingling; quiver, shiver, shudder, tremor, **tremor of excitement,** rush <nf>; flush, rush of emotion, surge of emotion

3 <nf terms> **kick, charge,** electricity, hullabaloo, boot, bang, belt, blast, flash, hit, jolt, large charge, rush, upper, lift; jollies

4 **agitation, perturbation,** ferment, **turbulence, turmoil,** tumult, embroilment, uproar, **commotion,** disturbance, ado, *brouhaha* <Fr>, to-do <nf>; pell-mell, **flurry,** ruffle, bustle, stir, swirl, swirling, whirl, vortex, eddy, hurry, hurry-scurry, hurly-burly; fermentation, yeastiness, effervescence, ebullience, ebullition; fume; agita <nf>

5 **trepidation,** trepidity; **disquiet,** disquietude, inquietude, **unrest, restlessness,** fidgetiness;

fidgets *or* shakes *and* shivers *and* dithers *and* antsyness <nf>; **quivering, quavering, quaking,** heartquake, **shaking,** trembling; **quiver,** quaver, shiver, shudder, dread, didder <Brit nf>, twitter, **tremor,** tremble, flutter; palpitation, pitapatation <nf>, pit-a-pat, pitter-patter; **throb,** throbbing; panting, heaving

6 **dither, tizzy** <nf>, swivet, foofaraw, **pucker** <nf>, **twitter,** twitteration <nf>, **flutter, fluster,** flusteration *and* flustration <nf>, **fret, fuss,** pother, bother, lather *and* stew *and* snit <nf>, flap; emotional crisis, *crise* <Fr>

7 **fever of excitement, fever pitch,** fever, heat, fever heat, fire; sexual excitement, rut

8 **fury, furor,** furore <Brit>, fire and fury; **ecstasy,** transport, **rapture,** ravishment; intoxication, abandon; **passion, rage,** raging *or* tearing passion, towering rage *or* passion; **frenzy,** orgy, orgasm; madness, craze, **delirium,** hysteria

9 **outburst,** outbreak, **burst, flare-up,** blaze, **explosion,** eruption, irruption, upheaval, convulsion, spasm, seizure, fit, paroxysm; storm, tornado, funnel cloud, whirlwind, cyclone, hurricane, gale, tempest, gust; steroid rage, roid rage <nf>; road rage <nf>

10 **excitability,** excitableness, perturbability, agitability; emotional instability, explosiveness, eruptiveness, inflammability, combustibility, tempestuousness, violence, latent violence; **irascibility** 110.2; irritability, edginess, touchiness, prickliness, **sensitivity** 24.3; skittishness, **nervousness** 128; excessive emotion, hyperthymia, **emotionalism** 93.9

11 **excitation, excitement, arousal,** arousing, **stirring,** stirring up, working up, working into a lather <nf>, lathering up, whipping up, steaming up, **agitation, perturbation; stimulation, stimulus,** **exhilaration,** animation; electrification, galvanization; **provocation, irritation,** aggravation, exasperation, exacerbation, fomentation, inflammation, infuriation, **incitement** 375.4

VERBS 12 **excite, impassion, arouse, rouse,** blow up <old>, **stir, stir up,** set astir, stir the feelings, stir the blood, cause a stir *or* commotion, play on the feelings; **work up,** work into, work up into a lather <nf>, lather up, whip up, **key up,** steam up; **move** 375.12; **foment, incite** 375.17; turn on <nf>; **awaken,** awake, wake, waken, wake up; call up, summon up, call forth; **kindle,** enkindle, light up, light the fuse, **fire, inflame,** heat, warm, set fire to, set on fire, fire *or* warm the blood; fan, fan the fire *or* flame, blow the coals, stir the embers, feed the fire, add fuel to the fire *or* flame, pour oil on the fire; raise to a fever heat *or*

pitch, bring to the boiling point; overexcite; **annoy, incense; enrage, infuriate;** frenzy, madden

13 **stimulate, whet, sharpen,** pique, provoke, quicken, enliven, liven up, pick up, jazz up <nf>, animate, **exhilarate,** invigorate, galvanize, fillip, give a fillip to; infuse life into, give new life to, revive, renew, resuscitate

14 **agitate, perturb, disturb, trouble, disquiet, discompose,** discombobulate <nf>, unsettle, **stir, ruffle, shake, shake up, shock, upset,** make waves, jolt, jar, rock, stagger, electrify, bring *or* pull one up short, give one a turn <nf>; fuss <nf>, flutter, flurry, rattle, disconcert, **fluster**

15 **thrill, tickle,** thrill to death *or* to pieces, give a thrill, **give one a kick** *or* boot *or* charge *or* bang *or* lift <nf>; intoxicate, fascinate, titillate, take one's breath away

16 **be excitable,** excite easily; **get excited, have a fit;** catch the infection; **explode, flare up,** flash up, flame up, fire up, catch fire, take fire; **fly into a passion,** go into hysterics, have a tantrum *or* temper tantrum, come apart; ride off in all directions at once, run around like a chicken with its head cut off; **rage, rave, rant,** rant and rave, rave on, bellow, **storm,** ramp; be angry, smolder, **seethe** 152.15

17 <nf terms> **work oneself up,** work oneself into a sweat, lather, have a short fuse, get hot under the collar, run a temperature, race one's motor, get into a dither *or* tizzy *or* swivet *or* pucker *or* stew; blow up, **blow one's top** *or* stack *or* cool, **flip,** flip out, flip one's lid *or* wig, freak out, pop one's cork, wig out, blow a gasket, fly off the handle, **hit the ceiling,** go ape, go hog wild, go bananas, lose one's cool, go off the deep end

18 <be excited> **thrill,** tingle, **tingle with excitement,** glow; swell, swell with emotion, be full of emotion; thrill to; turn on to *and* get high on *and* freak out on <nf>; heave, pant; **throb,** palpitate, go pit-a-pat; **tremble, shiver, quiver, quaver, quake,** flutter, twitter, **shake,** shake like an aspen leaf, have the shakes <nf>; **fidget,** have the fidgets *and* have ants in one's pants <nf>; toss and turn, toss, tumble, twist and turn, wriggle, wiggle, writhe, squirm; twitch, jerk

19 **change color,** turn color, go all colors; **pale,** whiten, blanch, turn pale; darken, look black; turn blue in the face; **flush, blush,** crimson, glow, mantle, color, redden, turn *or* get red

ADJS 20 **excited,** impassioned; **thrilled,** agog, tingling, tingly, atingle, aquiver, atwitter; **stimulated, exhilarated, high** <nf>; manic; **moved, stirred,** stirred up, **aroused, roused,** switched *or* turned on <nf>, on one's mettle, fired, inflamed, wrought up, **worked up,** all worked up, worked up into a lather <nf>, lathered up, whipped up, steamed up, keyed up, hopped up <nf>; turned-on <nf>; carried away; bursting, ready to burst; effervescent, yeasty, ebullient

21 **in a dither, in a tizzy** <nf>, in a swivet, in a foofaraw, **in a pucker** <nf>, in a quiver, **in a twitter,** in a flutter, all of a twitter *or* flutter, in a fluster, in a flurry, in a pother, in a bother, in a ferment, in a turmoil, in an uproar, in a stew *and* in a sweat <nf>, in a lather <nf>

22 **heated, passionate, warm, hot,** red-hot, flaming, **burning, fiery, glowing, fervent, fervid; feverish,** febrile, on fire, hectic, flushed; sexually excited, in rut 75.28; burning with excitement, het up <nf>, hot under the collar <nf>; seething, boiling, boiling over, steamy, steaming

23 **agitated, perturbed, disturbed, troubled, disquieted, upset,** antsy <nf>, unsettled, **discomposed, flustered,** ruffled, **shaken**

24 **turbulent,** tumultuous, tempestuous, boisterous, clamorous, uproarious

25 **frenzied, frantic; ecstatic,** transported, enraptured, ravished, in a transport *or* ecstasy; intoxicated, abandoned; orgiastic, orgasmic; raging, raving, roaring, bellowing, ramping, storming, howling, ranting, fulminating, frothing *or* foaming at the mouth; freaked out; **wild,** hog-wild <nf>; **violent,** fierce, ferocious, feral, **furious,** ballistic; **mad,** madding, **rabid,** maniac, maniacal, demonic, demoniacal, possessed; carried away, **distracted, delirious, beside oneself,** out of one's wits; uncontrollable, running mad, amok, berserk, hog-wild <nf>; **hysterical,** in hysterics; wild-eyed, wild-looking, haggard; blue in the face

26 **overwrought, overexcited, overstimulated, hyper** <nf>; **overcome,** overwhelmed, overpowered, overmastered; hand-wringing; **upset,** *bouleversé* <Fr>; theatrical

27 **restless,** restive, **uneasy,** unquiet, unsettled, unrestful, tense; **fidgety,** antsy <nf>, fussy, fluttery

28 **excitable, emotional,** highly emotional, overemotional, hyperthymic, perturbable, flappable <nf>, agitable; emotionally unstable; explosive, volcanic, eruptive, inflammable; irascible 110.19; irritable, edgy, touchy, wired <nf>, prickly, **sensitive** 24.13; **skittish,** startlish; **high-strung,** highly strung, on edge, high-spirited, mettlesome, high-mettled; **nervous**

29 **passionate, fiery, vehement,** hotheaded, **impetuous,** violent, volcanic, furious, fierce, **wild;** tempestuous, stormy, tornadic; simmering, volcanic, ready to burst forth *or* explode

30 **exciting, thrilling,** thrilly <nf>, **stirring, moving, breathtaking,** eye-popping <nf>; agitating, agitative, perturbing, disturbing, upsetting, troubling, gut-wrenching, disquieting, unsettling, distracting, jolting, jarring; heart-stirring, heart-thrilling, heart-swelling, heart-expanding, soul-stirring, spirit-stirring, deep-thrilling, mind-blowing <nf>; impressive, striking, telling; **provocative** 375.27, provoking, piquant, tantalizing; **inflammatory** 375.28; **stimulating,** stimulative, stimulatory; exhilarating, heady, intoxicating, maddening, ravishing; **electric,** galvanic, charged, overcharged; **overwhelming,** overpowering, overcoming, overmastering, more than flesh and blood can bear; suspensive, **suspenseful,** cliff-hanging <nf>

31 **penetrating, piercing,** stabbing, cutting, stinging, biting, keen, brisk, sharp, caustic, astringent

32 **sensational, lurid,** yellow, **melodramatic,** Barnumesque; spine-chilling, eye-popping <nf>; blood-and-thunder, cloak-and-dagger; tabloid

ADVS 33 **excitedly, agitatedly,** perturbedly; aflutter; with beating *or* leaping heart, with heart beating high, with heart going pitapat *or* pitter-patter <nf>, thrilling all over, with heart in mouth; with glistening eyes, all agog, all aquiver *or* atwitter *or* atingle; in a sweat *or* stew *or* dither *or* tizzy <nf>

34 **heatedly, passionately,** warmly, hotly, glowingly, fervently, fervidly, **feverishly**

35 **frenziedly, frantically,** wildly, furiously, violently, fiercely, madly, rabidly, distractedly, deliriously, till one is blue in the face <nf>

36 **excitingly, thrillingly,** stirringly, movingly; **provocatively,** provokingly; stimulatingly, exhilaratingly

106 INEXCITABILITY

NOUNS 1 **inexcitability,** inexcitableness, unexcitableness, **imperturbability,** imperturbableness, unflappability <nf>; steadiness, evenness; inirritability, unirritableness; **dispassion,** dispassionateness, unpassionateness, ataraxy *or* ataraxia; quietism; stoicism; **even temper,** steady *or* smooth temper, good *or* easy temper; unnervousness 129; **patience** 134; **impassiveness,** impassivity, stolidity; bovinity, dullness

2 **composure,** countenance; **calm, calmness,** calm disposition, **placidity, serenity,** tranquility, soothingness, peacefulness; mental composure, peace *or* calm of mind; calm *or* quiet mind, easy mind; resignation, resignedness, acceptance, fatalism, stoic calm; philosophicalness, philosophy, philosophic composure; **quiet,** quietness of mind *or* soul, quietude; decompression, imperturbation, indisturbance, unruffledness; **coolness,** coolheadedness, cool <nf>,

sangfroid; icy calm; Oriental calm, Buddha-like composure, Buddha nature; shantih, "the peace that passeth all understanding"—Bible

3 **equanimity,** equilibrium, equability, balance; **levelheadedness,** level head, well-balanced *or* well-regulated mind; **poise,** aplomb, **self-possession, self-control,** self-command, self-restraint, restraint, possession, **presence of mind;** confidence, assurance, **self-confidence, self-assurance,** centered

4 **sedateness, staidness,** soberness, sobriety, sober-mindedness, **seriousness,** gravity, solemnity, sobersidedness; temperance, moderation; sobersides

5 **nonchalance,** casualness, offhandedness; easygoingness, lackadaisicalness; **indifference,** unconcern 102.2

VERBS 6 **be cool** *or* **composed,** not turn a hair, not have a hair out of place, keep one's cool <nf>, look as if butter wouldn't melt in one's mouth; **tranquilize, calm** 670.7; **set one's mind at ease** *or* **rest,** make one easy

7 **compose oneself, control oneself,** restrain oneself, collect oneself, **get hold of oneself,** get a grip on oneself <nf>, get a grip, get organized, master one's feelings, regain one's composure; **calm down, cool off,** cool down, sober down, hold *or* keep one's temper, simmer down *and* cool it <nf>; **relax,** decompress, unwind, take it easy, lay *or* kick back <nf>; **forget it,** get it out of one's mind *or* head, drop it

8 <control one's feelings> **suppress, repress,** keep under, smother, stifle, choke *or* hold back, fight down *or* back, inhibit; sublimate; get it together

9 **keep cool,** keep one's cool <nf>, **keep calm,** keep one's head, keep one's shirt on *and* hang loose <nf>, not turn a hair; take things as they come, roll with the punches <nf>; keep a stiff upper lip

ADJS 10 **inexcitable, imperturbable,** undisturbable, unflappable <nf>; **unirritable,** inirritable; **dispassionate,** unpassionate; **steady;** stoic, stoical; **even-tempered; impassive,** stolid; bovine, dull; unnervous 129.2; **patient;** long-suffering

11 **unexcited, unperturbed,** undisturbed, untroubled, unagitated, **unruffled,** unflustered, unstirred, unimpassioned

12 **calm, placid,** quiet, **tranquil, serene,** peaceful; **cool, coolheaded,** cool as a cucumber <nf>; philosophical

13 **composed, collected,** recollected, **levelheaded; poised,** together <nf>, in equipoise, equanimous, equilibrious, **balanced,** well-balanced; **self-possessed,** self-controlled, controlled, self-restrained; confident, assured, **self-confident, self-assured;** temperate, pacific

14 **sedate, staid,** sober, sober-minded, **serious,** grave, solemn, sobersided; temperate, moderate

15 **nonchalant, blasé, indifferent,** unconcerned 102.7; **casual, offhand, relaxed, laid-back** *and* throwaway <nf>; **easygoing,** easy, free and easy, devil-may-care, lackadaisical, *dégagé* <Fr>

ADVS 16 inexcitably, **imperturbably,** inirritably, **dispassionately;** steadily; stoically; **calmly, placidly,** quietly, **tranquilly, serenely; coolly, composedly,** levelheadedly; impassively, stolidly, stodgily, stuffily

17 **sedately, staidly, soberly, seriously,** sobersidedly

18 **nonchalantly, casually, relaxedly,** offhandedly, easygoingly, lackadaisically

107 CONTENTMENT

NOUNS 1 **contentment, content,** contentedness, satisfiedness; **satisfaction,** entire satisfaction, fulfillment, gratification; ease, peace of mind, eupathy, composure 106.2; comfort 121; **quality of life;** well-being, euphoria; **happiness** 95.2; **acceptance,** resignation, reconcilement, reconciliation; clear *or* clean conscience, dreamless sleep; serenity; satiety; halcyon days

2 **complacency,** complacence; **smugness, self-complacence** *or* self-complacency, self-approval, self-approbation, **self-satisfaction, self-content,** self-contentedness self-contentness; bovinity

3 **satisfactoriness, adequacy, sufficiency** 991; **acceptability,** admissibility, **tolerability,** agreeability, unobjectionability, unexceptionability, tenability, viability; competency

VERBS 4 **content, satisfy;** gratify; put *or* set at ease, set one's mind at ease *or* rest, achieve inner harmony; indulge, satiate

5 **be content, rest satisfied, rest easy,** rest and be thankful, be of good cheer, be reconciled to, take the good the gods provide, accept one's lot, rest on one's laurels, let well enough alone, let sleeping dogs lie, take the bitter with the sweet; come to terms with oneself, learn to live in one's own skin; have no kick coming <nf>, not complain, not worry, have nothing to complain about, not sweat it *and* cool it *and* go with the flow <nf>; content oneself with, settle for; settle for less, take half a loaf, lower one's sights, cut one's losses; **be pleased** 95.12; have one's heart's desire

6 **be satisfactory, do, suffice** 991.4; **suit,** suit one down to the ground, serve, meet the needs of

ADJS 7 **content, contented, satisfied; pleased** 95.12; happy; **easy, at ease,** at one's ease, easygoing; composed 106.13; **comfortable** 121.11, of good comfort; fulfilled, gratified; euphoric, eupeptic;

carefree, without care, *sans souci* <Fr>; accepting, resigned, reconciled; uncomplaining, unrepining

8 **untroubled, unbothered, undisturbed,** unperturbed 106.11, unworried, unvexed, unplagued, untormented, secure

9 **well-content, well-pleased,** well-contented, **well-satisfied,** highly satisfied, satiated, full, full-up

10 **complacent,** bovine; **smug, self-complacent, self-satisfied,** self-content, **self-contented**

11 **satisfactory, satisfying; sufficient** 991.6, sufficing, **adequate, enough,** commensurate, proportionate, proportionable, ample, equal to, competent

12 **acceptable,** admissible, **agreeable,** unobjectionable, unexceptionable, tenable, viable; **OK** *and* okay *and* all right *and* alright <nf>; **passable,** good enough, not bad, so-so; palatable

13 **tolerable, bearable, endurable,** supportable, sufferable

ADVS 14 **contentedly,** to one's heart's content; **satisfiedly,** with satisfaction; **complacently, smugly,** self-complacently, self-satisfiedly, self-contentedly

15 **satisfactorily,** satisfyingly; **acceptably, agreeably,** admissibly; sufficiently, adequately, commensurately, amply, enough; **tolerably, passably**

16 **to one's satisfaction,** to one's delight, to one's great glee; to one's taste, to the king's *or* queen's taste

108 DISCONTENT

NOUNS 1 **discontent,** discontentment, discontentedness; **dissatisfaction,** unsatisfaction, dissatisfiedness, unfulfillment; **resentment, envy** 154; **restlessness, restiveness, uneasiness,** unease; malaise; rebelliousness 327.3; disappointment 132; unpleasure 96; unhappiness 112.2; ill humor 110; **disgruntlement,** sulkiness, sourness, petulance, peevishness, querulousness; vexation of spirit; cold comfort; divine discontent; Faustianism

2 **unsatisfactoriness,** dissatisfactoriness; **inadequacy, insufficiency** 992; **unacceptability,** inadmissibility, unsuitability, undesirability, objectionability, untenability, indefensibility; **intolerability** 98.9

3 **malcontent,** *frondeur* <Fr>; **complainer,** complainant, **faultfinder, grumbler,** growler, smellfungus, griper, grouser, croaker, carper, peevish *or* petulant *or* querulous person, whiner; reactionary, reactionist; rebel 327.5; spoilsport; tough customer, dissatisfied customer, angry young man

4 <nf terms> **grouch, kvetch,** kicker, griper, moaner, moaning Minnie <Brit>, crank, crab, grump, beefer, bellyacher, bitcher, sorehead, picklepuss, sourpuss, churl

VERBS 5 **dissatisfy, discontent, disgruntle, displease,** fail to satisfy, be inadequate, not fill the bill, disappoint, leave much *or* a lot to be desired, dishearten, disillusion, put out <nf>; **be discontented, complain**

6 <nf terms> **beef, bitch, kvetch,** bellyache, boo, hiss, carp, crab, gripe, grouch, grouse, grump, have an attitude, kick, moan, piss, make a stink, squawk

ADJS 7 **discontented, dissatisfied, disgruntled,** unaccepting, unaccommodating, **displeased,** less than pleased, let down, disappointed; **unsatisfied, ungratified,** unfulfilled; resentful, dog-in-the-manger; envious 154.3; restless, restive, uneasy; rebellious 327.11; malcontent, malcontented, **complaining,** complaintful, critical of, pejorative, sour, **faultfinding,** grumbling, growling, murmuring, muttering, griping, croaking, **peevish, petulant,** sulky, brooding, **querulous,** querulant, whiny; unhappy 112.21; out of humor 110.17

8 <nf terms> **grouchy, kvetchy,** cranky, beefing, crabby, crabbing, grousing, griping, bellyaching, bitching

9 **unsatisfactory,** dissatisfactory; **unsatisfying, ungratifying,** unfulfilling; **displeasing** 98.17; disappointing, disheartening, not up to expectation, not good enough, substandard; **inadequate,** incommensurate, **insufficient** 992.9; unpopular, not up to snuff <nf>

10 **unacceptable,** inadmissible, unsuitable, undesirable, **objectionable,** exceptionable, impossible, untenable, indefensible; **intolerable** 98.25; rejected

ADVS 11 **discontentedly, dissatisfiedly**

12 **unsatisfactorily,** dissatisfactorily; **unsatisfyingly, ungratifyingly; inadequately, insufficiently; unacceptably,** nowise, inadmissibly, unsuitably, undesirably, objectionably; intolerably 98.30

109 CHEERFULNESS

NOUNS 1 **cheerfulness,** cheeriness, **good cheer, cheer,** cheery vein *or* mood; blitheness, blithesomeness; **gladness,** felicity, gladsomeness; **happiness** 95.2; **pleasantness,** winsomeness, geniality, conviviality; brightness, radiance, **sunniness;** sanguineness, sanguinity, sanguine humor, euphoric *or* eupeptic mein; optimism, rosy expectation, hopefulness; **irrepressibility,** irrepressibleness

2 good humor, good spirits, good cheer; **high spirits, exhilaration,** rare good humor; *joie de vivre* <Fr>

3 lightheartedness, lightsomeness, lightness, levity; **buoyancy,** buoyance, resilience, resiliency, bounce <nf>, springiness; springy step; **jauntiness,** perkiness, debonairness, carefreeness; **breeziness,** airiness, pertness, chirpiness, light heart

4 gaiety, gayness, *allégresse* <Fr>; **liveliness, vivacity, vitality,** life, **animation, spiritedness, spirit,** esprit, élan, **sprightliness,** high spirits, zestfulness, zest, vim, zip <nf>, vigor, verve, gusto, **exuberance,** heartiness; **spirits,** animal spirits; piss and vinegar <nf>; **friskiness,** skittishness, coltishness, rompishness, rollicksomeness, capersomeness; **sportiveness, playfulness, frolicsomeness,** gamesomeness, kittenishness

5 merriment, merriness; **hilarity,** hilariousness; **joy,** joyfulness, joyousness; **glee,** gleefulness, high glee; **jollity,** jolliness, **joviality,** jocularity, jocundity; frivolity, **levity; mirth,** mirthfulness, amusement 743; **fun,** good time; **laughter** 116.4

VERBS **6** exude cheerfulness, radiate cheer, not have a care in the world, **beam,** burst *or* brim with cheer, glow, radiate, sparkle, sing, lilt, whistle, **chirp,** chirrup, chirp like a cricket; walk on air, dance, skip, caper, frolic, gambol, romp, caracole; **smile, laugh** 116.8; be a Pollyanna

7 cheer, gladden, brighten, put in good humor; **encourage, hearten,** pick up <nf>; **inspire,** inspirit, warm the spirits, **raise the spirits,** elevate one's mood, buoy up, boost, give a lift <nf>, put one on top of the world *and* on cloud nine <nf>; **exhilarate,** animate, invigorate, liven, enliven, vitalize; **rejoice,** rejoice the heart, do the heart good

8 elate, exalt, elevate, lift, uplift, flush

9 cheer up, take heart, drive dull care away; **brighten up,** light up, **perk up; buck up** *and* brace up *and* chirk up <nf>; come out of it, snap out of it <nf>, revive

10 be of good cheer, bear up, **keep one's spirits up,** keep one's chin up <nf>, keep one's pecker up <Brit nf>, keep a stiff upper lip <nf>, grin and bear it

ADJS **11 cheerful, cheery,** of good cheer, in good spirits; in high spirits, exalted, elated, exhilarated, high <nf>; irrepressible; **blithe,** blithesome; **glad, gladsome; happy,** happy as a clam *or* a lark, on top of the world, sitting on top of the world, sitting pretty, on cloud nine, over the moon <nf>; **pleasant, genial,** winsome; **bright, sunny,** bright and sunny, **radiant,** riant, sparkling, beaming, glowing, flushed, perky, rosy, smiling, laughing; sanguine, sanguineous, euphoric, eupeptic,

ebullient, Pollyannaish, exhilarated; optimistic, hopeful; **irrepressible;** up <nf>

12 lighthearted, light, lightsome; **buoyant,** corky <nf>, resilient; **jaunty,** perky, **debonair, carefree,** free and easy; **breezy,** airy

13 pert, chirk <nf>, chirrupy, **chirpy, chipper** <nf>

14 gay, gay as a lark <old>; **spirited,** sprightly, **lively, animated, vivacious,** vital, zestful, zippy <nf>, **exuberant,** hearty; **frisky,** antic, skittish, coltish, rompish, capersome; **full of beans** *and* **feeling one's oats** <nf>, full of piss and vinegar <nf>; **sportive, playful,** playful as a kitten, kittenish, **frolicsome,** gamesome; rollicking, rollicky, rollicksome

15 merry, mirthful, hilarious; joyful, joyous, rejoicing; **gleeful,** gleesome; **jolly,** buxom; **jovial,** jocund, jocular; **frivolous;** laughter-loving, mirth-loving, risible; merry as a cricket *or* grig, "as merry as the day is long"—Shakespeare; tickled to death <nf>, tickled pink <nf>, high as a kite <nf>

16 cheering, gladdening; encouraging, heartening, heartwarming, uplifting; **inspiring,** inspiriting; **exhilarating,** animating, enlivening, invigorating; cheerful, cheery, glad, joyful

ADVS **17 cheerfully,** cheerily, with good cheer, with a cheerful heart; irrepressibly; **lightheartedly,** lightly; jauntily, perkily, airily; **pleasantly,** genially, blithely; **gladly, happily, joyfully,** smilingly; optimistically, hopefully

18 gaily, exuberantly, heartily, spiritedly, animatedly, vivaciously, zestfully, with zest, with vim, with élan, with zip <nf>, with verve, with gusto

19 merrily, gleefully, hilariously; jovially, jocundly, jocularly; frivolously; **mirthfully,** laughingly

PHRS **20** cheer up!, every cloud has a silver lining; don't let it get you down, illegitimati non carborundum <L, don't let the bastards grind you down>; chin up!, buck up!, keep your pecker up! <Brit>; it's always darkest before the dawn, banzai!

110 ILL HUMOR

NOUNS **1 ill humor,** bad humor, **bad temper,** rotten *or* ill *or* evil temper, **ill nature,** filthy *or* rotten *or* evil humor; **sourness,** biliousness, liverishness; choler, bile, gall, spleen; **abrasiveness,** causticity, corrosiveness, asperity 144.8; **anger** 152.5; discontent 108

2 irascibility, irritability, excitability, short *or* quick temper, short fuse <nf>; **crossness,** disagreeableness, disagreeability, gruffness, shortness, peevishness, querulousness, fretfulness, crabbedness, **crankiness, testiness,** crustiness, huffiness, huffishness, churlishness, bearishness, snappishness, waspishness; **perversity,** cross-grainedness, fractiousness

3 <nf terms> **crabbiness, grouchiness,** cantankerousness, crustiness, grumpiness *or* grumpishness, cussedness, huffiness *or* huffishness, **meanness, orneriness,** bitchiness, cussedness, feistiness, ugliness, miffiness, saltiness, scrappiness, shirtiness <Brit>, soreheadedness

4 **hot temper, temper,** quick *or* short temper, irritable temper, warm temper, fiery temper, fierce temper, short fuse <nf>, pepperiness, feistiness *and* spunkiness <nf>, **hotheadedness,** hot blood; sharp tongue

5 **touchiness, tetchiness,** ticklishness, prickliness, quickness to take offense, miffiness <nf>, **sensitiveness,** oversensitiveness, hypersensitiveness, sensitivity, oversensitivity, hypersensitivity, thin skin; temperamentalness, moodiness

6 **petulance** *or* petulancy, **peevishness,** pettishness, **querulousness, fretfulness,** resentfulness; shrewishness, vixenishness

7 **contentiousness, quarrelsomeness** 456.3; **disputatiousness, argumentativeness,** litigiousness; **belligerence,** truculence

8 **sullenness, sulkiness, surliness, moroseness, glumness,** grumness, grimness, mumpishness, dumpishness, dourness, *bouderie* <Fr>; **moodiness,** moodishness; mopishness, mopiness <nf>; dejection, melancholy 112.5

9 **scowl, frown,** lower, **glower, pout,** moue, mow, grimace, wry face; sullen looks, black looks, hangdog look, **long face**

10 **sulks,** sullens, **mopes,** mumps, dumps, grumps <nf>, frumps <Brit nf>, **blues,** blue devils, mulligrubs, **pouts**

11 <ill-humored person> **sorehead, grouch, curmudgeon, grump, crank,** crab, **crosspatch,** feist *or* fice <nf>, wasp, **bear,** grizzly bear, pit bull, junkyard dog <nf>; fury, Tartar, dragon, ugly customer <nf>; **hothead,** hotspur; fire-eater; sulker, churl, bellyacher, neurotic

12 **bitch** <nf>, **shrew, vixen,** virago, termagant, brimstone, fury, witch, beldam, cat, tigress, she-wolf, she-devil, spitfire; fishwife; **scold,** common scold, harpy, nag, Xanthippe; old bag; battle-ax <nf>

VERBS 13 have a temper, have a short fuse <nf>, have a devil in one, be possessed of the devil; be cross, get out on the wrong side of the bed

14 **sulk, mope,** mope around; grizzle <chiefly Brit nf>, grump *and* **grouch** *and* **bitch** <nf>, fret;

get oneself in a sulk; have the blues, be down in the dumps

15 **look sullen,** look black, look black as thunder, gloom, pull *or* make *or* have a long face; **frown, scowl,** knit the brow, lower, **glower, pout,** brood, make a moue *or* mow, grimace, make a wry face, make a lip, hang one's lip, thrust out one's lower lip

16 **sour,** acerbate, exacerbate; **embitter,** bitter, envenom

ADJS 17 **out of humor,** out of temper, out of sorts, **in a bad humor,** in a shocking humor, feeling evil <nf>; **abrasive,** caustic, corrosive, acid; angry; discontented 108.5

18 **ill-humored, bad-tempered,** ill-tempered, evil-humored, evil-tempered, **ill-natured,** ill-affected, ill-disposed

19 **irascible, irritable,** excitable, flappable <nf>; **cross, cranky, testy;** cankered, crabbed, spiteful, spleeny, splenetic, churlish, bearish, snappish, waspish; **gruff,** grumbly, grumbling, growling; **disagreeable; perverse,** fractious, cross-grained

20 <nf terms> **crabby, grouchy,** cantankerous, crusty, grumpy *or* grumpish, cussed, huffy *or* huffish, mean, mean as a junkyard dog, ornery, bitchy, feisty, ugly, miffy, salty, scrappy, shirty <Brit>, soreheaded

21 **touchy, tetchy,** miffy <nf>, ticklish, prickly, quick to take offense, **thin-skinned, sensitive,** oversensitive, hypersensitive, high-strung, highly strung, temperamental, prima-donnaish

22 **peevish, petulant,** pettish, **querulous, fretful,** resentful; catty; shrewish, vixenish, vixenly; nagging, naggy

23 **sour,** soured, **sour-tempered,** vinegarish; prune-faced <nf>; **choleric, dyspeptic, bilious,** liverish, jaundiced; **bitter,** embittered

24 **sullen, sulky, surly, morose,** dour, mumpish, dumpish, **glum,** grum, grim; **moody,** moodish; **mopish,** mopey <nf>, moping; **glowering,** lowering, **scowling, frowning;** dark, black; black-browed, beetle-browed; dejected, melancholy 112.23; somber

25 **hot-tempered, hotheaded, passionate,** hot, fiery, peppery, feisty, spunky <nf>, **quick-tempered, short-tempered;** hasty, quick, explosive, volcanic, combustible, vicious

26 **contentious, quarrelsome** 456.17; **disputatious,** controversial, litigious, polemic, polemical; **argumentative,** argumental; on the warpath, looking for trouble; scrappy <nf>; cat-and-doggish, cat-and-dog; **bellicose, belligerent**

ADVS 27 **ill-humoredly, ill-naturedly; irascibly, irritably, crossly, crankily, testily,** huffily, cantankerously <nf>, crabbedly, sourly, churlishly, crustily, bearishly, snappily; perversely, fractiously, cross-grainedly

28 **peevishly, petulantly,** pettishly, **querulously, fretfully**

29 **grouchily** and **crabbily** and grumpily <nf>, grumblingly

30 **sullenly, sulkily, surlily, morosely,** mumpishly, glumly, grumly, grimly; moodily, mopingly; gloweringly, loweringly, scowlingly, frowningly

111 SOLEMNITY

NOUNS 1 **solemnity, solemness, dignity, soberness, sobriety, gravity,** *gravitas* <L>, weightiness, **somberness, grimness; sedateness, staidness;** demureness, decorousness; **seriousness, earnestness, thoughtfulness, sober-mindedness,** sobersidedness; sobersides, humorlessness; long face, straight face; **formality** 580

VERBS 2 honor the occasion, keep a straight face, look serious, compose one's features, wear an earnest frown; repress a smile, not crack a smile <nf>, wipe the smile off one's face, keep from laughing, make a long face

ADJS 3 **solemn, dignified, sober, grave,** unsmiling, weighty, **somber,** frowning, **grim; sedate, staid;** demure, decorous; **serious, earnest, thoughtful,** pensive; **sober-minded,** sober-sided; in earnest; straight-faced, long-faced, grim-faced, grim-visaged, stone-faced, stony-faced; sober as a judge, grave as an undertaker; **formal** 580.7

ADVS 4 **solemnly, soberly,** gravely, somberly, grimly; **sedately, staidly,** demurely, decorously; with dignity, **seriously, earnestly,** thoughtfully, sober-mindedly, sobersidedly; with a straight face; formally 580.11

112 SADNESS

NOUNS 1 **sadness,** sadheartedness, weight or burden of sorrow; heaviness, **heavyheartedness,** heavy heart, **heaviness of heart;** pathos, bathos

2 **unhappiness,** infelicity; displeasure 96.1; discontent 108; **uncheerfulness,** cheerlessness; **joylessness,** unjoyfulness; mirthlessness, unmirthfulness, humorlessness, infestivity; **grimness; wretchedness, misery**

3 **dejection, depression, oppression,** dejectedness, **downheartedness,** downcastness; **discouragement, disheartenment,** dispiritedness; *Schmerz* and *Weltschmerz* <Ger>; malaise 96.1; lowness, lowness or depression or oppression of spirit, downer and down trip <nf>; chill, chilling effect; **low spirits,** drooping spirits, sinking heart, funk; despondence or **despondency,** spiritlessness,

heartlessness; black or blank despondency, "Slough of Despond"—Bunyan; demotivation, hopelessness 125, **despair** 125.2, pessimism 125.6, gloom and doom, suicidal despair, death wish, self-destructive urge; weariness of life, *taedium vitae* <L>; sloth, acedia, noonday demon

4 **hypochondria,** hypochondriasis, morbid anxiety; neurosis

5 **melancholy, melancholia,** melancholiness, spleen <old>; gentle melancholy, romantic melancholy; **pensiveness, wistfulness,** tristfulness; **nostalgia,** homesickness, nostalgy <old>, *mal du pays* <Fr>

6 **blues** and blue devils and mulligrubs <nf>, mumps, **dumps** <nf>, **doldrums,** dismals, dolefuls <nf>, megrims, blahs and mopes and megrims and sulks and funks<nf>

7 **gloom, gloominess,** darkness, murk, murkiness, **dismalness, bleakness, grimness, somberness, gravity, solemnity; dreariness,** drearisomeness; wearifulness, wearisomeness

8 **glumness,** grumness, **moroseness, sullenness,** sulkiness, **moodiness,** mumpishness, dumpishness; mopishness, mopiness <nf>

9 **heartache, aching heart,** bleeding heart, grieving heart; heartsickness, heartsoreness; **heartbreak, broken heart,** brokenheartedness, heartbrokenness

10 **sorrow,** sorrowing, **grief, care,** carking care, **woe;** heartgrief, heartfelt grief; languishment, pining; **anguish, misery, agony;** prostrating grief, prostration; **lamentation** 115

11 **sorrowfulness, mournfulness,** ruefulness, **woefulness, dolefulness,** woesomeness <old>, dolorousness, **plaintiveness,** plangency, grievousness, aggrievedness, lugubriousness, funerealness; weeping and wailing and gnashing of teeth; *lacrimae rerum* <L>, **tearfulness** 115.2

12 **disconsolateness,** disconsolation, **inconsolability,** inconsolableness, unconsolability, comfortlessness; **desolation,** desolateness; forlornness

13 **sourpuss** and picklepuss and gloomy Gus <nf>, moaning Minnie <Brit nf>; mope, brooder; **melancholic,** melancholiac; depressive; Eeyore

14 **killjoy, spoilsport,** grinch and crepehanger and drag <nf>; damp, damper, **wet blanket,** party pooper; gloomster and doomster <nf>, doomsdayer, apocalypticist, apocalyptician, awfulizer <nf>, crapehanger; fussbudget, worrywart, skeleton at the feast; pessimist 125.7

VERBS 15 hang one's head, pull or make a long face, look blue, sing or get or have the blues <nf>; drag one down; carry the weight or woe of the world on one's shoulders; hang crape <nf>, apocalypticize, catastrophize, awfulize <nf>

16 lose heart, despond, give way, give oneself up *or* over to; despondency; **despair** 125.10, sink into despair, throw up one's hands in despair, be *or* become suicidal, lose the will to live; **droop,** sink, languish, mope; reach *or* plumb the depths, touch *or* hit bottom, hit rock bottom

17 grieve, sorrow; weep, mourn 115.8,10; be dumb with grief; **pine,** pine away *or* over; **brood over, mope, fret,** take on <nf>; **eat one's heart out,** break one's heart over; **agonize,** ache, bleed

18 sadden, darken, cast a pall *or* gloom upon, weigh *or* weigh heavy upon; **deject, depress, oppress, crush,** press down, hit one like a ton of bricks <nf>, **cast down,** lower, lower the spirits, get one down <nf>, take the wind out of one's sails, rains on one's parade, burst one's bubble, **discourage, dishearten,** take the heart out of, **dispirit;** damp, dampen, damp *or* dampen the spirits; dash, knock down, beat down; sink, sink one's soul, plunge one into despair

19 aggrieve, oppress, **grieve, sorrow,** plunge one into sorrow, embitter; draw tears, bring to tears; **anguish, tear up** *and* **cut up** <nf>, wring *or* pierce *or* lacerate *or* rend the heart, pull at the heartstrings; be cut up; afflict 96.16, torment 96.18; **break one's heart, make one's heart bleed;** desolate, leave an aching void; prostrate, break down, crush, bear down, inundate, overwhelm

ADJS 20 sad, saddened; sadhearted, **sad of heart; heavyhearted,** heavy; oppressed, weighed upon, weighed *or* weighted down, bearing the woe *or* weight of the world, burdened *or* laden with sorrow; sad-faced, long-faced; sad-eyed; sad-voiced

21 unhappy, uncheerful, uncheery, **cheerless, joyless, unjoyful,** unsmiling; mirthless, unmirthful, humorless, infestive; funny as a crutch <nf>; **grim; out of humor,** out of sorts, in bad humor *or* spirits; **sorry,** sorryish; discontented 108.5; **wretched, miserable;** pleasureless 96.20

22 dejected, depressed, downhearted, down, downcast, cast down, bowed down, subdued; **discouraged, disheartened, dispirited,** dashed; **low, feeling low,** low-spirited, **in low spirits; down in the mouth** <nf>, **in the doldrums, down in the dumps** *and* **in the dumps** *and* in the doleful dumps <nf>, in the depths; **despondent,** desponding; **despairing** 125.12, weary of life, suicidal, world-weary; pessimistic 125.16; spiritless, heartless, **woebegone; drooping,** droopy, languishing, pining, haggard; hypochondriac *or* hypochondriacal

23 melancholy, melancholic, splenetic <old>, **blue** <nf>, funky <nf>; atrabilious, atrabiliar; **pensive, wistful,** tristful; **nostalgic,** homesick

24 gloomy, dismal, murky, bleak, grim, somber, sombrous, **solemn, grave;** sad, *triste* <Fr>, **funereal,** funebrial, crepehanging <nf>, saturnine; **dark,** black, gray; **dreary,** drear, drearisome; weary, weariful, wearisome

25 glum, grum, **morose, sullen,** sulky, mumpish, dumpish, long-faced, crestfallen, chapfallen; **moody,** moodish, **brooding,** broody; mopish, mopey <nf>, **moping**

26 sorrowful, sorrowing, sorrowed, **mournful, rueful, woeful, woesome** <old>, **doleful, plaintive,** plangent; anguished; dolorous, **grievous, lamentable,** lugubrious; **tearful; care-worn;** grieved, **grief-stricken,** griefful, aggrieved, in grief, bereft, plunged in grief, dumb with grief, prostrated by grief, cut-up *and* torn-up <nf>, **inconsolable**

27 sorrow-stricken, sorrow-wounded, sorrow-struck, sorrow-torn, sorrow-worn, sorrow-wasted, sorrow-beaten, sorrow-blinded, sorrow-clouded, sorrow-shot, sorrow-burdened, sorrow-laden, sorrow-sighing, sorrow-sobbing, sorrow-sick

28 disconsolate, inconsolable, unconsolable, comfortless, prostrate *or* prostrated, **forlorn; desolate,** *désolé* <Fr>; sick, **sick at heart, heartsick,** soul-sick, heartsore

29 overcome, crushed, borne-down, overwhelmed, inundated, spazzed-out, **stricken, cut up** <nf>, **desolated,** prostrate *or* prostrated, broken-down, undone; **heart-stricken,** heart-struck; **brokenhearted,** heartbroken

30 depressing, depressive, depressant, **oppressive; discouraging, disheartening, dispiriting;** morale-sapping, worst-case, downbeat *or* downer <nf>

ADVS 31 sadly, gloomily, dismally, drearily, heavily, bleakly, grimly, somberly, sombrously, solemnly, funereally, gravely, with a long face; **depressingly**

32 unhappily, uncheerfully, cheerlessly, joylessly, unjoyfully

33 dejectedly, downheartedly; discouragedly, disheartenedly, dispiritedly; despondently, despairingly, spiritlessly, heartlessly; **disconsolately,** inconsolably, unconsolably, forlornly

34 melancholily, pensively, wistfully, tristfully; nostalgically

35 glumly, grumly, **morosely, sullenly;** moodily, moodishly, broodingly, broodily; mopishly, mopily <nf>, mopingly

36 sorrowfully, mournfully, ruefully, woefully, woesomely <old>, **dolefully,** dolorously, **plaintively, grievously,** grieffully, lugubriously; with a broken voice; **heartbrokenly,** brokenheartedly; **tearfully,** with tears in one's eyes

113 REGRET

NOUNS **1 regret, regrets,** regretting, regretfulness, rue; **remorse,** remorsefulness, remorse of conscience; buyer's remorse; **shame,** shamefulness, shamefacedness, shamefastness; **sorrow, grief, sorriness,** repining; **contrition,** contriteness, attrition; bitterness; apologies; wistfulness 100.4

2 compunction, qualm, qualms, qualmishness, scruples, scrupulosity, scrupulousness, pang, pangs, **pangs of conscience,** throes, sting *or* pricking *or* twinge *or* twitch of conscience, touch of conscience, **voice of conscience,** pricking of heart, misgiving, better self

3 self-reproach, self-reproachfulness, **self-accusation, self-condemnation,** self-conviction, self-punishment, self-humiliation, self-debasement, **self-hatred,** self-flagellation; hair shirt; self-analysis, soul-searching, examination of conscience

4 penitence, repentance, change of heart; apology, humble *or* heartfelt apology, abject apology; better nature, good angel, guardian angel; reformation 858.2; deathbed repentance; mea culpa; **penance** 658.3; wearing a hairshirt *or* sackcloth *or* sackcloth and ashes, mortification of the flesh

5 penitent, confessor; **prodigal son,** prodigal returned; Magdalen

VERBS **6 regret, deplore, repine, be sorry for; rue,** rue the day; **bemoan, bewail;** curse one's folly, **reproach oneself,** kick oneself <nf>, bite one's tongue, accuse *or* condemn *or* blame *or* convict *or* punish oneself, flagellate oneself, wear a hair shirt, make oneself miserable, humiliate *or* debase oneself, hate oneself for one's actions, hide one's face in shame; examine one's conscience, search one's soul, consult *or* heed one's better self, analyze *or* search one's motives; cry over spilled milk, waste time in regret

7 repent, think better of, change one's mind, have second thoughts; laugh out of the other side of one's mouth; **plead guilty,** own oneself in the wrong, humble oneself, **apologize** 658.5, beg pardon *or* forgiveness, throw oneself on the mercy of the court; **do penance** 658.6; reform

ADJS **8 regretful, remorseful,** full of remorse, **ashamed,** shameful, shamefaced, shamefast, **sorry, rueful, repining,** unhappy about; **conscience-stricken,** conscience-smitten; **self-reproachful,** self-reproaching, self-accusing, self-condemning, self-convicting, self-punishing, self-flagellating, self-humiliating, self-debasing, self-hating; wistful 100.23

9 penitent, repentant; penitential, penitentiary; **contrite,** abject, humble, humbled, **sheepish, apologetic,** touched, softened, melted; atoning

10 regrettable, much to be regretted; **deplorable** 1000.9

ADVS **11 regretfully, remorsefully,** sorrily, ruefully, unhappily

12 penitently, repentantly, penitentially; **contritely,** abjectly, **humbly, sheepishly, apologetically**

114 UNREGRETFULNESS

NOUNS **1 unregretfulness, unremorsefulness, unsorriness,** unruefulness; **remorselessness,** regretlessness, sorrowlessness; **shamelessness,** unashamedness

2 impenitence, impenitentness; nonrepentance, irrepentance, unrepentance; **uncontriteness,** unabjectness; seared conscience, heart of stone, callousness 94.3; **hardness of heart,** hardness, induration, obduracy; **defiance** 454/327.2; **insolence** 142; no regrets, no remorse

VERBS **3 harden one's heart,** steel oneself; **have no regrets,** not look backward, not cry over spilled milk; have no shame, have *or* feel no remorse; feel nothing

ADJS **4 unregretful,** unregretting, **unremorseful, unsorry, unsorrowful,** unrueful; **remorseless,** regretless, sorrowless, griefless; unsorrowing, ungrieving, unrepining; **shameless,** unashamed

5 impenitent, unrepentant, unrepenting, unrecanting; **uncontrite,** unabject; untouched, unsoftened, unmelted, callous 94.12; hard, hardened, obdurate; **defiant** 454.7; **insolent** 142.9

6 unregretted, unrepented, unatoned

ADVS **7 unregretfully, unremorsefully,** unruefully; **remorselessly,** sorrowlessly, impenitently, shamelessly, unashamedly; **without regret,** without looking back, **without remorse,** without compunction, without any qualms *or* scruples

115 LAMENTATION

NOUNS **1 lamentation,** lamenting, **mourning, moaning, grieving, sorrowing, wailing, bewailing, bemoaning,** keening, howling, ululation; **sorrow** 112.10; woe, misery; threnody

2 weeping, sobbing, crying, bawling; blubbering, whimpering, sniveling; **tears,** flood of tears, fit of crying; cry *and* good cry <nf>; **tearfulness, weepiness** <nf>, lachrymosity, melting mood; tearful eyes, swimming *or* brimming *or* overflowing eyes; **tear,** teardrop, lachryma; lacrimatory, tear bottle

3 lament, plaint, *planctus* <L>; **murmur,** mutter; **moan, groan; whine, whimper; wail,** wail of woe; **sob,** *cri du coeur* <Fr>, **cry,** outcry, scream, **howl,** yowl, bawl, yawp, keen, ululation; jeremiad, tirade, dolorous tirade

4 complaint, grievance, peeve, pet peeve, **groan; dissent, protest** 333.2; hard luck story <nf>, sob story, sad story, tale of woe; **complaining,** scolding, groaning, **faultfinding** 510.4, sniping, destructive criticism, **grumbling, murmuring;** whining, petulance, peevishness, querulousness; backstabbing

5 <nf terms> **beef, kick, gripe,** kvetch, grouse, bellyache, howl, holler, **squawk,** bitch; **beefing, grousing, kicking, griping,** kvetching, **bellyaching,** squawking, **bitching,** yapping

6 dirge, funeral or **death song,** coronach, keen, elegy, epicedium, requiem, monody, threnody, threnode, coronach <Ir>, knell, death knell, passing bell, funeral or dead march, muffled drums; eulogy, funeral or graveside oration

7 <mourning garments> **mourning, weeds,** widow's weeds, crape, black; deep mourning; sackcloth, sackcloth and ashes; cypress, cypress lawn, yew; mourning band; mourning ring

8 lamenter, griever, mourner 309.7; moaner, weeper, sniveler; **complainer,** faultfinder, smellfungus, malcontent 108.3

9 <nf terms> **grouch, kvetch,** kicker, griper, moaner, moaning Minnie <Brit>, crank, crab, crybaby, blubberer, grouser, beefer, bellyacher, bitcher, sorehead, picklepuss, sourpuss, bellyacher, grumbler

VERBS **10 lament, mourn, moan, grieve, sorrow,** keen, weep over or for, **bewail, bemoan, deplore, repine, sigh,** rue, give sorrow words; sing the blues <nf>, elegize, dirge, knell, toll the knell; pay one's last respects; wake, hold a wake, go to a funeral, sound the last post

11 wring one's hands, tear one's hair, gnash one's teeth, beat one's breast, sing the blues

12 weep, sob, cry, bawl, boo-hoo; **blubber,** ululate, **whimper, snivel; shed tears,** drop a tear; **burst into tears,** burst out crying, give way to tears, melt or dissolve in tears, break down, break down and cry, turn on the waterworks <nf>; cry one's eyes out, cry oneself blind; cry before one is hurt

13 wail, ululate; **moan, groan; howl,** yowl, yawl <Brit nf>; **cry, squall, bawl,** yawp, **yell, scream,** shriek; cry out, make an outcry; bay at the moon; tirade

14 whine, whimper, yammer <nf>, pule, grizzle <chiefly Brit nf>

15 complain, groan; grumble, murmur, mutter, growl, clamor, croak, grunt, yelp; **fret, fuss, make** a fuss about, fret and fume; air a grievance, lodge or register a complaint; fault, find fault

16 <nf terms> **beef, bitch, kick, kvetch,** bellyache, crab, gripe, grouch, grouse, grump, have an attitude, holler, howl, moan, piss, piss and moan, make a stink, squawk, yap; raise a howl, put up a squawk or howl, take on, cry or yell or scream bloody murder, give one a hard time, piss or kick up a storm or row or fuss, make or raise a stink

17 go into mourning; put on mourning, wear mourning

ADJS **18 lamenting, grieving, mourning, moaning, sorrowing;** wailing, bewailing, bemoaning; **in mourning,** in sackcloth and ashes; depressed, down <nf>

19 plaintive, plangent, **mournful,** moanful, wailful, lamentive, ululant; woebegone, disconsolate; **sorrowful** 112.26; **howling,** Jeremianic; whining, whiny, whimpering, puling; **querulous, fretful,** petulant, peevish; **complaining, faultfinding** 510.23

20 <nf terms> **grouchy, kvetchy,** cranky, beefing, crabby, crabbing, grousing, griping, bellyaching, bitching

21 tearful, teary, **weepy** <nf>; lachrymal, lachrymose, lacrimatory; in the melting mood, on the edge of tears, ready to cry; **weeping,** weepy, **sobbing, crying;** blubbering, whimpering, sniveling; red-eyed; **in tears,** with tears in one's eyes, with tearful or watery eyes, with swimming or brimming or overflowing eyes, with eyes suffused or bathed or dissolved in tears

22 dirgelike, knell-like, elegiac, elegiacal, epicedial, threnodic, plaintive, plangent

ADVS **23 lamentingly, plaintively, mournfully,** moanfully, wailfully; **sorrowfully** 112.36; complainingly, groaningly, querulously, fretfully, petulantly, peevishly

116 REJOICING

NOUNS **1 rejoicing, jubilation,** jubilance, jubilant display, jubilee, show of joy, raucous happiness; **exultation,** elation, triumph; the time of one's life, special day; whoopee and hoopla <nf>, festivity 743.3,4, merriment 109.5; celebration 487

2 cheer, hurrah, huzzah, hurray, hooray, yippee, rah, cowabunga; **cry, shout, yell;** hosanna, hallelujah, alleluia, paean, paean or chorus of cheers, three cheers; **applause** 509.2, fanfare, shout-out; high-five <nf>

3 smile, smiling; bright smile, gleaming or glowing smile, beam; silly smile or grin; **grin,** grinning; broad grin, ear-to-ear grin, toothful grin; stupid grin, idiotic grin; sardonic grin, **smirk, simper**

4 laughter, laughing, hilarity 109.5, risibility; **laugh;** boff *and* boffola *and* yuck <nf>; **titter; giggle; chuckle, chortle;** cackle, crow; **snicker,** snigger, snort; ha-ha, hee-haw, hee-hee, ho-ho, tee-hee, yuk-yuk; guffaw, **horselaugh; hearty laugh, belly laugh** <nf>, Homeric laughter, cachinnation; **shout, shriek,** shout of laughter, burst *or* outburst of laughter, peal *or* roar of laughter, gales of laughter; fit of laughter, convulsion

VERBS **5 rejoice,** jubilate, **exult, glory, joy, delight,** bless *or* thank one's stars *or* lucky stars, congratulate oneself, hug oneself, rub one's hands, clap hands; dance *or* skip *or* jump for joy, dance, skip, frisk, rollick, revel, frolic, caper, gambol, caracole, romp; sing, carol, chirp, chirrup, chirp like a cricket, lilt; make merry

6 cheer, give a cheer, give three cheers, **cry, shout, yell,** cry for joy, yell oneself hoarse; huzzah, hurrah, hurray, hooray; shout hosanna *or* hallelujah, "make a joyful noise unto the Lord"— Bible; **applaud** 509.10; high-five <nf>

7 smile, crack a smile <nf>, break into a smile; **beam,** smile brightly; **grin,** grin like a Cheshire cat *or* chessy-cat <nf>; **smirk, simper**

8 laugh, burst out laughing, burst into laughter, burst out, laugh outright; laugh it up <nf>; **titter; giggle; chuckle, chortle;** cackle, crow; **snicker,** snigger, snort; ha-ha, hee-haw, hee-hee, ho-ho, tee-hee, yuk-yuk; **guffaw,** belly laugh, horselaugh; **shout, shriek,** give a shout *or* shriek of laughter; **roar,** cachinnate, roar with laughter; shake with laughter, shake like jelly; be convulsed with laughter, go into convulsions, fall about <Brit nf>; burst *or* split with laughter, break up *and* crack up <nf>, split <nf>, **split one's sides,** laugh fit to burst *or* bust <nf>, bust a gut *and* pee in *or* wet one's pants laughing <nf>, **be in stitches** <nf>, hold one's sides, roll in the aisles <nf>; laugh oneself sick *or* silly *or* limp, die *or* nearly die laughing; laugh in one's sleeve, laugh up one's sleeve, laugh in one's beard

9 make laugh, kill *and* **slay** <nf>, "set the table on a roar"—Shakespeare, break *or* crack one up <nf>, get a laugh

ADJS **10 rejoicing,** delighting, exulting; **jubilant, exultant, elated,** elate, flushed, euphoric, ecstatic

ADVS **11 rejoicingly,** delightingly, exultingly; **jubilantly, exultantly, elatedly**

117 DULLNESS

<being uninteresting>

NOUNS **1 dullness, dryness,** dustiness, uninterestingness; **stuffiness, stodginess,** woodenness, stiffness; barrenness, sterility, aridity, jejunity; **insipidness,** insipidity, vapidness, vapidity, inanity, hollowness, emptiness, superficiality, **staleness, flatness,** tastelessness; characterlessness, colorlessness, pointlessness; **deadness,** lifelessness, spiritlessness, bloodlessness, paleness, pallor, etiolation, effeteness; **slowness,** pokiness, dragginess <nf>, unliveliness; **tediousness** 118.2; **dreariness,** drearisomeness, dismalness; **heaviness,** leadenness, ponderousness; inexcitability 106; solemnity 111; lowness of spirit 112.3

2 prosaicness, prosiness; prosaism, prosaicism, prose, plainness; **matter-of-factness,** unimaginativeness; matter of fact; **simplicity** 798, **plainness** 499

3 triteness, corniness *and* squareness <nf>, **banality,** banalness, unoriginality, sameness, **hackneyedness, commonplaceness,** commonness, familiarness, platitudinousness; a familiar ring; redundancy, repetition, **staleness,** mustiness, fustiness; cliché 974.3

VERBS **4 fall flat,** fall flat as a pancake; leave one cold *or* unmoved, go over like a lead balloon <nf>, lay an egg *and* bomb <nf>, **wear thin**

5 prose, platitudinize, sing a familiar tune; pedestrianize; warm over; banalize

ADJS **6 dull, dry,** dusty, dry as dust, mind-numbing; **stuffy, stodgy,** wooden, stiff; arid, barren, blank, sterile, jejune; **insipid,** vapid, inane, hollow, empty, superficial; ho-hum *and* blah <nf>, **flat,** tasteless; characterless, colorless, pointless; **dead,** lifeless, spiritless, bloodless, pale, pallid, etiolated, effete; cold; **slow,** poky, draggy <nf>, pedestrian, plodding, unlively; **tedious; dreary,** drearisome, dismal; **heavy,** leaden, ponderous, elephantine; dull as dish water, "weary, stale, flat and unprofitable"—Shakespeare; inexcitable 106.10; solemn 111.3; low-spirited 112.22

7 uninteresting, uneventful, **unexciting; uninspiring; unentertaining,** unenjoyable, **unamusing,** unfunny, unwitty

8 prosaic, prose, prosy, prosing, plain; **matter-of-fact,** unimaginative, unimpassioned

9 trite; corny *and* square *and* square-John *and* Clyde <nf>, hokey, fade, **banal,** unoriginal, platitudinous, **stereotyped,** stock, set, **commonplace, common,** truistic, twice-told, **familiar,** bromidic <nf>, old hat <nf>, back-number, bewhiskered, warmed-over, **cut-and-dried; hackneyed,** hackney; well-known 928.27; **stale,** musty, fusty; **worn,** timeworn, well-worn, moth-eaten, threadbare, **worn thin**

ADVS **10 dully, dryly,** dustily, **uninterestingly;** stuffily, stodgily; aridly, barrenly, jejunely, **insipidly, vapidly,** inanely, hollowly, emptily, superficially, tastelessly, **colorlessly,** pointlessly; lifelessly, spiritlessly, bloodlessly, pallidly, effetely; slowly, draggily <nf>, ploddingly; **tediously;** drearily, drearisomely, dismally; heavily, ponderously

11 **tritely,** cornily <nf>, **banally,** commonplacely, commonly, familiarly, hackneyedly, unoriginally, truistically, stalely

118 TEDIUM

NOUNS 1 **tedium, monotony, humdrum,** irksomeness, irk; **sameness,** sameliness, samesomeness <nf>, wearisome sameness, more of the same, the same old thing *or* story, the same damn thing <nf>; broken record, parrot; platitude, chestnut; undeviation, unvariation, invariability; the round, the daily round *or* grind, the weary round, the treadmill, the squirrel cage, the rat race <nf>, the beaten track *or* path, drag <nf>; time on one's hands, time hanging heavily on one's hands; **protraction, prolongation** 827.2

2 **tediousness, monotonousness, unrelievedness; humdrumness,** humdrumminess; **dullness** 117; **wearisomeness,** wearifulness; **tiresomeness, irksomeness,** drearisomeness; boresomeness, boringness; prolixity, **long-windedness** 538.2; redundancy, repetition, repetitiveness, tick-tock

3 **weariness, tiredness,** wearifulness; jadedness, satiation, satiety; **boredom,** boredness; **ennui,** spleen <old>, melancholy, life-weariness, *taedium vitae* <L>, world-weariness, *Weltschmerz* <Ger>, jadedness; languor, **listlessness** 94.4, **dispiritedness** 112.3

4 **bore,** crashing bore <nf>, frightful bore; **pest, nuisance;** dryasdust; proser, twaddler, **wet blanket;** buttonholer; bromide; egoist

5 <nf terms> drag, drip, pill, flat tire, deadass, deadfanny, dull tool; **headache,** pain, pain in the neck *or* ass; broken record

VERBS 6 **be tedious, drag on,** go on forever; have a certain sameness, be infinitely repetitive, do the same old thing; **weary, tire, irk,** wear, wear on *or* upon, **make one tired,** fatigue, weary *or* tire to death, jade; give one a pain in the ass *and* give one a bellyful *and* make one fed-up <nf>, **pall, satiate, glut**

7 **bore,** leave one cold, set *or* send to sleep; **bore stiff** *or* to tears *or* to death *or* to extinction <nf>, bore to distraction, bore out of one's life, bore out of all patience; buttonhole; wear out one's welcome, stay too long

8 **harp on** *or* **upon, dwell on** *or* **upon,** harp upon one *or* the same string, play *or* sing the same old song *or* tune, play the same broken record

ADJS 9 **tedious, monotonous, humdrum,** singsong, jog-trot, treadmill, unvarying, invariable, uneventful, broken-record, parrotlike, harping, everlasting, too much with us <nf>; blah <nf>, flat, **dreary,** drearisome, dry, dry-as-dust, dusty, **dull** 117.6; protracted, prolonged 827.11; prolix, **long-winded** 538.12; pedestrian, commonplace

10 **wearying,** wearing, **tiring; wearisome,** weariful, fatiguing, **tiresome, irksome; boring, boresome,** stupefyingly boring, stuporific, yawny <nf>

11 **weary,** weariful; **tired,** wearied, irked; good and tired, tired to death, weary unto death; sick, **sick of, tired of, sick and tired of;** jaded, satiated, palled, fed up <nf>, brassed off <Brit nf>; **blasé;** splenetic <old>, melancholy, melancholic, life-weary, world-weary, tired of living, half-dead; **listless** 94.13, **dispirited** 112.22

12 **bored, uninterested;** bored stiff *or* to death *or* to extinction *or* to tears <nf>, stupefied *or* stuporous with boredom; with eyes rolling

ADVS 13 **tediously, monotonously,** harpingly, everlastingly, unvaryingly, endlessly; long-windedly; **boringly,** boresomely; **wearisomely,** fatiguingly, wearyingly, **tiresomely, irksomely,** drearisomely; dully 117.10

14 on a treadmill, in a squirrel cage, on the beaten track, on the same old round; without a change of menu *or* scenery *or* pace

PHRS 15 ho hum!, heigh ho!, what a life!, que sera sera; *plus ça change, plus c'est la même chose* <Fr, the more things change, the more they stay the same>; so what else is new?, go figure; MEGO *or* mine eyes glaze over

119 AGGRAVATION

NOUNS 1 **aggravation, worsening; exacerbation,** embittering, embitterment, souring; deterioration; **intensification, heightening,** stepping-up, sharpening, deepening, **increase,** enhancement, amplification, enlargement, magnification, augmentation, exaggeration; **exasperation, annoyance, irritation** 96.3; hassle <nf>, aggro <chiefly Brit>; deliberate aggravation, provocation; contentiousness

VERBS 2 **aggravate, worsen,** make worse; **exacerbate,** embitter, sour; deteriorate; **intensify, heighten,** step up, sharpen, make acute *or* more acute, bring to a head, deepen, **increase,** enhance, amplify, enlarge, magnify, build up, exaggerate; augment; rub salt in the wound, twist the knife, add insult to injury, inflame, pour oil on the fire, add fuel to the fire *or* flame, heat up *and* hot up <nf>; increase pressure *or* tension, tighten, tighten up, tighten the screws, put the squeeze on <nf>;

bring to a head; **exasperate, annoy, irritate** 96.14; rub it in <nf>; provoke, antagonize, hassle <nf>, be an *agent provocateur*

3 **worsen,** get *or* grow worse, take a turn for the worse, deteriorate, degenerate; go from push to shove, **go from bad to worse; jump out of the frying pan and into the fire,** avoid Scylla and fall into Charybdis

ADJS 4 **aggravated, worsened, worse,** worse and worse, exacerbated, embittered, soured, deteriorated; **intensified, heightened,** stepped-up, **increased,** deepened, enhanced, amplified, magnified, enlarged, augmented, heated *or* hotted up <nf>; **exasperated, irritated, annoyed** 96.21; provoked, deliberately provoked; worse-off, out of the frying pan and into the fire

5 **aggravating,** aggravative; **exasperating,** exasperative; **annoying, irritating** 98.22; provocative; vexing, vexatious; contentious

ADVS 6 from bad to worse; aggravatingly, exasperatingly; annoyingly 98.29

120 RELIEF

NOUNS 1 **relief, easement, easing,** ease; **relaxation,** relaxing, relaxation *or* easing of tension, decompression, slackening, respite, let-up; **reduction,** diminishment, diminution, lessening, abatement, remission; **remedy** 86; **alleviation, mitigation, palliation,** softening, assuagement, allayment, defusing, appeasement, mollification, subduement; soothing, salving, anodyne; lulling; dulling, deadening, numbing, narcotizing, anesthesia, anesthetizing, analgesia; sedating, sedation; doping *or* doping up <nf>; comfort, solace, consolation; charity, benefaction

2 **release, deliverance, freeing,** removal; suspension, intermission, respite, surcease, reprieve; discharge; catharsis, purging, purgation, purge, cleansing, cleansing away, emotional release

3 **lightening, disburdening,** unburdening, unweighting, unloading, disencumbrance, disembarrassment, easing of the load, a load off one's mind, something out of one's system

4 **sense** *or* **feeling of relief,** sigh of relief

VERBS 5 **relieve,** give relief, **ease,** ease matters, **relax,** slacken; **reduce,** diminish, lessen, abate, remit, de-stress; **alleviate, mitigate, palliate,** soften, pad, cushion, assuage, allay, defuse, lay, appease, mollify, subdue, soothe; salve, pour balm into, pour oil on; poultice, foment, stupe; slake; lull; **dull, deaden,** dull *or* deaden the pain, numb, benumb, anesthetize, tranquilize, sedate, narcotize, dope *or* dope up <nf>; temper the wind to the shorn lamb, lay the flattering unction to

one's soul; take the sting out of; comfort, solace, pacify

6 **release, free, deliver,** reprieve, remove, free from, liberate; suspend, intermit, give respite *or* surcease; **relax,** decompress, ease, destress; act as a cathartic, **purge, purge away, cleanse,** cleanse away; give release, cut loose

7 **lighten, disburden,** unburden, unweight, unload, unfreight, disencumber, disembarrass, ease one's load; **set one's mind at ease** *or* **rest,** set at ease, **take a load off one's mind,** smooth the ruffled brow of care; relieve oneself, let one's hair down, pour one's heart out, talk it out, let it all hang out *and* go public <nf>, get it off one's chest

8 **be relieved, feel relief,** feel better about, get something out of one's system, feel *or* be oneself again; get out from under <nf>; **breathe easy** *or* **easier,** breathe more freely, breathe again, rest easier; **heave a sigh of relief,** draw a long *or* deep breath

ADJS 9 **relieving, easing, alleviative,** alleviating, alleviatory, ameliorating, **mitigative,** mitigating, **palliative,** assuaging, lenitive, assuasive, softening, subduing, soothing, demulcent, emollient, balmy, balsamic; **remedial** 86.39; dulling, deadening, numbing, benumbing, anesthetic, analgesic, anodyne, pain killing, sedative, hypnotic; cathartic, purgative, cleansing; **relaxing**

10 **relieved,** breathing easy *or* easier *or* freely, able to breathe again, out from under *and* out of the woods <nf>; alleviated; decompressed; **relaxed;** calmed, restored

121 COMFORT

NOUNS 1 **comfort, ease, well-being;** contentment 107; clover, velvet <nf>, bed of roses; life of ease 1010.1; solid comfort

2 **comfortableness, easiness; restfulness,** reposefulness, peace, peacefulness; softness, cushiness <nf>, cushioniness; **coziness, snugness;** friendliness, warmness; **homelikeness,** homeyness <nf>, homeliness; **commodiousness,** roominess, convenience; luxuriousness 501.5; hospitality 585

3 **creature comforts, comforts, conveniences,** excellent accommodations, amenities, good things of life, cakes and ale, egg in one's beer <nf>, all the comforts of home; all the heart can desire, luxuries, the best

4 **consolation, solace,** solacement, easement, heart's ease; **encouragement,** aid and comfort, **assurance, reassurance,** support, **comfort,** crumb *or* shred of comfort; condolence 147, sympathy; **relief** 120

5 **comforter,** consoler, solacer, encourager; the Holy Spirit *or* Ghost, the Comforter, the Paraclete

VERBS **6 comfort, console, solace,** give *or* bring comfort, bear up; condole with, sympathize with, extend sympathy; ease, **put** *or* **set at ease;** bolster, support; relieve 120.5; **assure, reassure; encourage, hearten,** pat on the back; **cheer** 109.7; wipe away the tears

7 be comforted, take comfort, take heart; take hope, lift up one's heart, pull oneself together, pluck up one's spirits; *sursum corda* <L>

8 be at ease, be *or* feel easy, stand easy <Brit>; **make oneself comfortable,** make oneself at home, feel at home, put one's feet up, take a load off <nf>; **relax,** be relaxed; live a life of ease 1010.10

9 snug, snug down *or* up; tuck in

10 snuggle, nestle, cuddle, cuddle up, curl up; nest; bundle; snuggle up to, snug up *or* together <old>

ADJS **11 comfortable,** comfy <nf>; contented 107.7,9,10; **easy,** easeful; **restful,** reposeful, peaceful, **relaxing;** soft, cushioned, cushy <nf>, cushiony; comfortable as an old shoe; **cozy, snug,** snug as a bug in a rug; friendly, warm; **homelike,** homey *and* down-home <nf>, homely, lived-in; **commodious,** roomy, convenient; low-maintenance, luxurious 501.21

12 at ease, at one's ease, easy, relaxed, laid-back <nf>; at rest, resting easy; **at home,** in one's element; unstressed

13 comforting, consoling, consolatory, of good comfort; condoling, condolent, condolatory, sympathetic; **assuring, reassuring,** supportive; **encouraging, heartening; cheering** 109.16; relieving 120.9; hospitable 585.11; warm-and-fuzzy

ADVS **14 comfortably, easily,** with ease; **restfully,** reposefully, peacefully; **cozily, snugly; commodiously,** roomily, conveniently; luxuriously, voluptuously

15 in comfort, in ease, **in clover, on** *or* **in velvet** <nf>, on *or* in a bed of roses

16 comfortingly, consolingly, assuringly, reassuringly, supportively, encouragingly, hearteningly; hospitably

122 WONDER

NOUNS **1 wonder,** wonderment, sense of wonder, marveling, marvel, **astonishment, amazement,** amaze, **astoundment;** dumbfoundment, stupefaction; **surprise; awe,** breathless wonder *or* awe, sense of mystery, admiration; beguilement, fascination 377.1; bewilderment, puzzlement 971.3

2 marvel, wonder, prodigy, miracle, phenomenon, phenom <nf>; astonishment, amazement, marvelment, wonderment, wonderful thing, nine days' wonder, *annus mirabilis* <L>, amazing *or* astonishing thing, quite a thing, really something, sensation, rocker *and* stunner <nf>; one for the books *and* something to brag about *and* something to shout about *and* something to write home about *and* something else <nf>; **rarity,** nonesuch, nonpareil, exception, one in a thousand, one in a way, oner <Brit nf>; **curiosity, sight, spectacle,** eye-popper <nf>; wonders of the world; masterpiece, chef d-oeuvre, masterstroke

3 wonderfulness, wondrousness, **marvelousness,** miraculousness, phenomenalness, **prodigiousness, stupendousness, remarkableness,** extraordinariness; beguilingness, fascination, enchantingness, enticingness, seductiveness, **glamorousness; awesomeness, mysteriousness,** mystery, numinousness; **transcendence,** transcendentness, surpassingness

4 inexpressibility, ineffability, ineffableness, inenarrability, noncommunicability, noncommunicableness, incommunicability, incommunicableness, indescribability, indefinableness, **unutterability, unspeakability,** unnameableness, innominability, unmentionability

VERBS **5 wonder, marvel,** be astonished *or* amazed *or* astounded, be seized with wonder; **gaze, gape,** drop one's jaw, look *or* stand aghast *or* agog, gawk, **stare,** stare openmouthed, open one's eyes, rub one's eyes, hold one's breath; not know what to say, not know what to make of, not believe one's eyes *or* ears *or* senses

6 astonish, amaze, astound, surprise, startle, stagger, **bewilder, perplex** 971.13, flabbergast <nf>, confound, overwhelm, **boggle, boggle the mind; awe,** strike with wonder *or* awe; **dumbfound** *or* dumbfounder, strike dumb, strike dead; strike all of a heap *and* throw on one's beam ends *and* knock one's socks off *and* bowl down *or* over <nf>, dazzle, bedazzle, daze, bedaze; **stun, stupefy,** petrify, paralyze

7 take one's breath away, turn one's head, make one's head swim, make one's hair stand on end, make one's tongue cleave to the roof of one's mouth, make one stare, make one sit up and take notice, sweep *or* carry off one's feet; blow one's mind

8 beggar *or* baffle description, stagger belief

ADJS **9 wondering,** wrapped *or* rapt in wonder, marveling, **astonished, amazed, surprised, astounded,** flabbergasted <nf>, gobsmacked, **bewildered,** puzzled, confounded, **dumbfounded,** dumbstruck, staggered, overwhelmed, unable to believe one's senses *or* eyes; **aghast,** agape, agog, all agog, gazing, gaping, at gaze staring, gauping, wide-eyed, popeyed, open-eyed, openmouthed, **breathless; thunderstruck,** wonder-struck, wonder-stricken, awestricken, awestruck, struck all of a heap <nf>; **awed, in awe,** in awe of; spellbound, fascinated, captivated, under a charm, beguiled, enthralled, enraptured, enravished, enchanted, entranced, bewitched, hypnotized, mesmerized, stupefied, lost in wonder *or* amazement; transfixed, rooted to the spot

10 **wonderful, wondrous, marvelous,** awesome, **miraculous,** fantastic, fabulous, ace, cool, rad *or* wicked <nf>, phenomenal, brilliant, **prodigious, stupendous,** unheard-of, wicked, unprecedented, extraordinary, exceptional, rare, unique, singular, **remarkable,** striking, **sensational,** bar none; **strange,** passing strange, "wondrous strange"— Shakespeare; **beguiling, fascinating;** incredible, inconceivable, outlandish, unimaginable, incomprehensible; **bewildering, puzzling,** enigmatic; *magnifique* <Fr>; supercalifragilisticexpialidocious *or* supercalifragilistic; must-see

11 **awesome,** awful, awing, awe-inspiring; **transcendent,** transcending, surpassing; **mysterious,** numinous; weird, eerie, uncanny, bizarre, bizarro <nf>; exotic; sweet <nf>

12 **astonishing, amazing, surprising,** startling, **astounding,** confounding, staggering, stunning <nf>, eye-opening, breathtaking, overwhelming, mind-boggling *or* –numbing, mind-blowing, jaw-dropping; **spectacular,** electrifying

13 **indescribable, ineffable,** inenarrable, inexpressible, unutterable, unspeakable, noncommunicable, incommunicable, indefinable, undefinable, unnameable, innominable, unwhisperable, unmentionable

ADVS 14 **wonderfully,** wondrously, **marvelously, miraculously,** fantastically, fabulously, phenomenally, prodigiously, stupendously, extraordinarily, exceptionally, remarkably, strikingly, **sensationally;** strangely, outlandishly, incredibly, inconceivably, unimaginably, incomprehensibly, **bewilderingly, puzzlingly,** enigmatically; **beguilingly,** fascinatingly

15 **awesomely,** awfully, awingly, awe-inspiringly; **mysteriously,** numinously, weirdly, eerily, uncannily, bizarrely; **transcendently,** surpassingly, surpassing, passing *or* passing fair <old>

16 **astonishingly, amazingly, astoundingly,** staggeringly, confoundingly; **surprisingly,** startlingly, to one's surprise *or* great surprise, to one's astonishment *or* amazement, for a wonder, strange to say

17 **indescribably, ineffably,** inexpressibly, unutterably, **unspeakably,** inenarrably, indefinably, unnameably, unmentionably

18 in wonder, in astonishment, in amazement, in bewilderment, in awe, in admiration, with gaping mouth

INTERJS 19 <astonishment or surprise> my word!, I declare!, well I never!, of all things!, as I live and breathe!, what!, indeed!, really!, surely!, how now!, what on earth!, what in the world!, I'll be jiggered!, holy moly!, holy Christmas!, holy cow!, holy mackerel!, holy Moses!, holy guacamole!, holy smoke!, holy shit! <nf>, hush *or* shut my mouth!, blow me down!, strike me dead!, shiver my timbers!, *sacré bleu!* <Fr>

20 oh!, O!, ah!, la!, lo!, lo and behold!, hello!, halloo!, hey!, whew!, phew!, wow!, yipes!, yike!

21 my!, oh, my!, dear!, dear me!, goodness!, gracious!, goodness gracious!, gee!, my goodness!, my stars!, good gracious!, good heavens!, good lack!, lackadaisy!, blimey!, my gosh!, welladay!, hoity-toity!, zounds!, 'sdeath!, gadzooks!, gad so!, bless my heart!, God bless me!, heavens and earth!, for crying out loud! <nf>, jiminy!

22 imagine!, fancy!, fancy that!, just imagine!, only think!, well!, I never!, can you feature that!, can you beat that!, it beats the Dutch!, do tell!, you don't say!, the devil *or* deuce you say!, I'll be!, what do you know!, what do you know about that!, how about that!, who would have thought it!, did you ever!, can it be!, can such things be?, will wonders never cease!, go on!

23 **Seven Wonders of the Ancient World**

The Great Pyramids of Egypt at Giza	The Mausoleum of King Mausolus at Halicarnassus
The Hanging Gardens of Babylon	
The Statue of Zeus at Olympia	The Colossus of Rhodes
The Temple of Artemis (Diana) at Ephesus	The Lighthouse of Alexandria

123 UNASTONISHMENT

NOUNS 1 **unastonishment, unamazement,** unamazedness, nonastonishment, nonamazement, nonamazedness, nonwonder, nonwondering, nonmarveling, unsurprise, unsurprisedness, awelessness, wonderlessness; phlegmaticness, apathy, passivity, nonchalance; **calm,** calmness, coolness, **cool** <nf>, cool *or* calm *or* nodding acceptance, composure, composedness, sangfroid, inexcitability 106, expectation 130, unimpressibleness, refusal to be impressed *or* awed *or* amazed; poker face, straight face; predictability

VERBS 2 **accept, take for granted** *or* as a matter of course *or* in stride *or* as it comes, treat as routine, show no amazement, refuse to be impressed, not blink an eye, not turn a hair, keep one's cool <nf>; see it coming

ADJS **3 unastonished, unsurprised, unamazed,** unmarveling, unwondering, unastounded, undumbfounded, unbewildered; undazzled, undazed; unawed, aweless, wonderless, blasé; **unimpressed,** unmoved; calm, **cool,** cool as a cucumber, composed, nonchalant, inexcitable 106.10; expecting, expected 130.13,14; phlegmatic

124 HOPE

NOUNS **1 hope, hopefulness,** hoping, **hopes,** fond *or* fervent hope, good hope, good cheer; aspiration, **desire** 100; prospect, **expectation** 130; sanguine expectation, happy *or* cheerful expectation; **trust, confidence, faith,** assured faith, **reliance,** dependence; conviction, assurance, security, well-grounded hope; assumption, presumption; auspiciousness; **promise, prospect,** good *or* bright *or* fair prospect, good *or* hopeful prognosis, best case; great expectations, good prospects, high hopes; hoping against hope, prayerful hope; doomed hope *or* hopes; greener pastures; plus side

2 optimism, optimisticalness, Pollyannaism, cheerful *or* bright *or* rosy outlook, rose-colored glasses; **cheerfulness** 109; bright side, silver lining; "the noble temptation to see too much in everything"—Chesterton; wishful thinking; philosophical optimism, Leibnizian *or* Rousseauistic optimism, Pollyanna optimism, utopianism, perfectionism, perfectibilism; millenarianism, chiliasm, millennialism

3 ray of hope, gleam *or* glimmer of hope; faint hope, last hope

4 airy hope, unreal hope, **dream,** false hope, golden dream, pipe dream <nf>, bubble, chimera, fool's paradise, quixotic ideal, utopia 986.11; vision, castles in the air, air castle, cloud-cuckoo-land, lotus land; American dream

5 optimist, hoper, Pollyanna, ray of sunshine <nf>, irrepressible optimist, Dr Pangloss, idealist; Leibnizian optimist, philosophical optimist, utopian, perfectionist, perfectibilist, perfectibilitarian; millenarian, chiliast, millennialist, millennian; aspirer, aspirant, hopeful <nf>, dreamer, visionary

VERBS **6 hope,** be *or* live in hopes, have reason to hope, entertain *or* harbor the hope, cling to the hope, cherish *or* foster *or* nurture the hope; look for, prognosticate, **expect** 130.5; **trust,** confide, presume, feel confident, rest assured; pin one's hope upon, put one's trust in, hope in, rely on, count on, lean upon, bank on, set great store on;

hope for, **aspire to, desire** 100.14; **hope against hope,** hope and pray, hope to God <nf>

7 be hopeful, get one's hopes up, keep one's spirits up, never say die, take heart, cheer up, buck up, be of good hope, be of good cheer, keep hoping, keep hope alive, keep the faith <nf>, keep smiling, cling to hope; **hope for the best,** knock on wood, touch wood <Brit>, cross one's fingers, keep one's fingers crossed, allow oneself to hope; clutch *or* catch at straws; wish

8 be optimistic, look on the bright side; look through *or* **wear rose-colored glasses,** *voir en couleur de rose* <Fr>; call the glass half full, look on the bright side, think positively *or* affirmatively, be upbeat <nf>, think the best of, **make the best of it,** say that all is for the best, put a good *or* bold face upon, put the best face upon; see the light at the end of the tunnel; count one's chickens before they are hatched, count one's bridges before they are crossed

9 give hope, raise hope, yield *or* afford hope, hold out hope, justify hope, inspire hope, **raise one's hopes,** raise expectations, **lead one to expect; cheer** 109.7; inspire, inspirit; **assure, reassure,** support; **promise,** hold out promise, augur well, bid fair *or* well, make fair promise, have good prospects

ADJS **10 hopeful, hoping, in hopes,** full of hope, in good heart, of good hope, of good cheer; **aspiring** 100.28; **expectant** 130.11; **sanguine,** fond; **confident,** assured; undespairing

11 optimistic, upbeat *and* up <nf>, bright, sunny; bullish; **cheerful** 109.11; **rosy,** roseate, rose-colored, *couleur de rose* <Fr>; pollyannaish, Leibnizian, Rousseauistic, Panglossian; utopian 986.23, idealistic, perfectionist, perfectibilitarian, millenarian, chiliastic, millennialistic, visionary

12 promising, of promise, full of promise, bright with promise, pregnant of good, best-case, **favorable,** looking up; aspiring, aspirant; **auspicious, propitious** 133.17; heartening; inspiring, inspiriting, **encouraging,** cheering, reassuring, supportive; on a wing and a prayer

ADVS **13 hopefully,** hopingly; **expectantly** 130.15; **optimistically; cheerfully** 109.17; sanguinely, fondly; confidently

125 HOPELESSNESS

NOUNS **1 hopelessness,** unhopefulness, no hope, not a prayer *and* not a hope in hell <nf>, not the ghost of a chance; small hope, bleak outlook *or* prospect *or* prognosis, worst case, blank future, no future; losing battle; inexpectation 131; futility 391.2; impossibility 967

2 **despair, desperation,** desperateness, loss of hope; no way <nf>, no way out, no exit, despondency 112.3; disconsolateness 112.12; forlornness; letdown; cave of despair, cave of Trophonius; gloom and doom; acedia, sloth; apathy 94.4; downer <nf>

3 **irreclaimability, irretrievability,** irredeemability, irrecoverableness, unsalvageability, unsalvability; incorrigibility, irreformability; irrevocability, **irreversibility; irreparability, incurability,** irremediableness, curelessness, remedilessness, immedicableness; unrelievability, unmitigability

4 **forlorn hope,** vain expectation, doomed *or* foredoomed hope, fond *or* foolish hope, futility; counsel of perfection

5 dashed hopes, blighted hope, hope deferred; disappointment 132

6 **pessimism, cynicism,** malism, nihilism; uncheerfulness 112.2; **gloominess,** dismalness, gloomy outlook; negativism; defeatism; retreatism, Weltschmerz

7 **pessimist, cynic,** malist, nihilist; killjoy 112.14, gloomy Gus *and* calamity howler *and* worrywart <nf>, seek-sorrow, Job's comforter, prophet of doom, Cassandra, Eeyore; negativist; defeatist; retreatist; loser, born loser; drag <nf>

8 lost cause, fool's errand, wild-goose chase; **hopeless case,** hopeless situation; **goner** *and* gone goose *or* gosling *and* dead duck <nf>; terminal case

VERBS **9** **be hopeless,** have not a hope *or* prayer, have no remedy, look bleak *or* dark; **be pessimistic, look on the dark side,** be *or* think downbeat <nf>, think negatively, think *or* make the worst of, put the worst face upon, call *or* see the glass half empty; not hold one's breath

10 **despair,** despair of, **despond** 112.16, falter, lose hope, **lose heart, abandon hope,** give up hope, **give up,** give up all hope *or* expectation, give way *or* over, fall *or* sink into despair, give oneself up *or* yield to despair, throw up one's hands in despair, turn one's face to the wall; curse God and die, write off

11 **shatter one's hopes,** dash *or* crush *or* blight *or* shatter one's hope, burst one's bubble <nf>, bring crashing down around one's head, dash the cup from one's lips, disappoint 132.2, drive to despair *or* desperation

ADJS **12** **hopeless,** unhopeful, without hope, affording no hope, worst-case, bleak, grim, dismal, cheerless, comfortless, down in the mouth; **desperate, despairing, in despair;** despondent 112.22; disconsolate 112.28; forlorn; apathetic 94.13

13 **futile, vain** 391.13; doomed, foredoomed, pointless

14 **impossible,** out of the question, not to be thought of, no-go *and* no-win *and* lose-lose <nf>

15 **past hope, beyond recall,** past praying for, beyond hope, abject; **irretrievable, irrecoverable, irreclaimable,** irredeemable, unsalvageable, unsalvable; incorrigible, irreformable; irrevocable, **irreversible; irremediable, irreparable,** inoperable, **incurable,** cureless, remediless, immedicable, beyond remedy, terminal; unrelievable, unmitigable; **ruined,** undone, kaput <nf>; lost, gone, gone to hell *and* gone to hell in a handbasket <nf>

16 **pessimistic,** pessimist, downbeat <nf>, **cynical,** nihilistic; uncheerful 112.21; **gloomy,** dismal, crepehanging, funereal, lugubrious; negative, negativistic; defeatist; Cassandran *or* Cassandrian, Cassandra-like

ADVS **17** **hopelessly, desperately,** forlornly; impossibly

18 **irreclaimably, irretrievably, irrecoverably,** irredeemably, unsalvageably, unsalvably; irrevocably, **irreversibly; irremediably, incurably, irreparably**

126 ANXIETY
<troubled thought>

NOUNS **1** **anxiety, anxiousness; apprehension, apprehensiveness,** antsyness <nf>, misgiving, foreboding, forebodingness, suspense, strain, tension, stress, nervous strain *or* tension; **dread, fear** 127; **concern,** concernment, anxious concern, **solicitude,** zeal 101.2; **care,** cankerworm of care; **distress,** trouble, vexation, unease; **uneasiness, perturbation, disturbance,** upset, **agitation, disquiet,** disquietude, inquietude, unquietness; **nervousness** 128; malaise, angst 96.1; pucker *and* yips *and* stew *and* all-overs <nf>, pins and needles, tenterhooks, shpilkes <nf>; overanxiety; anxious seat *or* bench; anxiety neurosis *or* hysteria; performance anxiety

2 **worry,** worriment <nf>, worriedness; **worries,** worries and cares, troubles, concerns; worrying, fretting; harassment, torment

3 **worrier, worrywart** *and* nervous Nellie <nf>, fussbudget

VERBS **4** **concern,** give concern, **trouble, bother, distress, disturb, upset,** frazzle, **disquiet, agitate;** rob one of ease *or* sleep *or* rest, keep one on edge *or* on tenterhooks *or* on pins and needles *or* on shpilkes <nf>

5 <make anxious> **worry, upset, vex,** fret, agitate, get to <nf>, **harass,** harry, **torment,** dog, hound, plague, persecute, haunt, beset

6 <feel anxious> **worry,** worry oneself, worry one's head about, worry oneself sick, trouble one's head *or* oneself, be a prey to anxiety, lose sleep; have one's heart in one's mouth, have one's heart miss *or* skip a beat, have one's heart stand still, get butterflies in one's stomach; **fret, fuss, chafe,** stew *and* take on <nf>, fret and fume; tense up, bite one's nails, walk the floor, go up the wall <nf>, be on tenterhooks *or* pins and needles *or* shpilkes <nf>

ADJS **7 anxious, concerned, apprehensive,** foreboding, misgiving, suspenseful, strained, tense, tensed up <nf>, nail-biting, white-knuckle <nf>; **fearful** 127.32; **solicitous,** zealous 101.9; **troubled, bothered; uneasy, perturbed, disturbed, disquieted, agitated; nervous** 128.11; **on pins and needles,** on tenterhooks, on shpilkes <nf>, on the anxious seat *or* bench; all hot and bothered *and* in a pucker *and* in a stew <nf>; over-anxious, overapprehensive; trepidacious

8 worried, vexed, fretted; **harassed,** harried, tormented, dogged, hounded, persecuted, haunted, beset, plagued; worried sick, worried to a frazzle, worried stiff <nf>

9 careworn, heavy-laden, overburdened

10 troublesome, bothersome, **distressing,** distressful, **disturbing, upsetting, disquieting; worrisome,** worrying; fretting, chafing; **harassing,** tormenting, plaguing; **annoying** 98.22

ADVS **11 anxiously, concernedly, apprehensively,** misgivingly, **uneasily;** worriedly; solicitously, zealously 101.14

127 FEAR, FEARFULNESS

NOUNS **1 fear, fright,** affright; **scare, alarm, consternation, dismay; dread,** unholy dread, **awe; terror, horror,** horrification, mortal *or* abject fear; **phobia** <see list>, funk *or* blue funk <nf>; **panic,** panic fear *or* terror, blind panic; stampede; **cowardice** 491

2 fearfulness, frighteningness, frightfulness, awfulness, scariness, fearsomeness, alarmingness, dismayingness, disquietingness, startlingness, disconcertingness, terribleness, **dreadfulness, horror,** horribleness, **hideousness,** appallingness, direness, **ghastliness,** grimness, grisliness, **gruesomeness,** ghoulishness; **creepiness, spookiness,** eeriness, weirdness, uncanniness

3 fearfulness, afraidness; **timidity, timorousness, shyness;** shrinkingness, bashfulness, diffidence, stage fright, mike fright *and* flop sweat <nf>; skittishness, startlishness, jumpiness, goosiness <nf>; shamefacedness

4 apprehension, apprehensiveness, **misgiving, qualm,** qualmishness, funny feeling; **anxiety** 126,

angst; worry; doubt 955.2, mental reservation; foreboding

5 trepidation, trepidity, perturbation, **fear and trembling; quaking, agitation** 105.4; **uneasiness, disquiet,** disquietude, inquietude; **nervousness** 128; palpitation, heartquake; shivers *or* cold shivers <nf>, creeps *or* cold creeps <nf>, heebie-jeebies <nf>, chills of fear *or* terror, icy fingers *or* icy clutch of dread, jimjams <nf>; horripilation, gooseflesh, goose bumps <nf>; sweat, cold sweat; thrill of fear, spasm *or* quiver of terror; sinking stomach; blood running cold, knocking knees, chattering teeth

6 frightening, intimidation, bullying, browbeating, cowing, bulldozing <nf>, hectoring; **demoralization,** psychological warfare, war of nerves

7 terrorization, terrorizing, horrification, scaremongering, panic-mongering, scare tactics; **terrorism,** terror *or* terroristic tactics, *Schrecklichkeit* <Ger>, rule by terror, reign of terror, sword of Damocles, war of nerves; agroterrorism, bioterrorism, cyberterrorism

8 alarmist, scaremonger, panic-monger; **terrorist,** bomber, assassin

9 frightener, scarer, hair-raiser; alarmist; scarebabe, **bogey,** bogeyman, **bugaboo,** bugbear; hobgoblin; **scarecrow; horror, terror,** holy terror; **ogre,** ogress, **monster,** vampire, werewolf, ghoul, bête noire, fee-faw-fum; incubus, succubus, nightmare; witch, goblin; **ghost,** specter, phantom, revenant; Frankenstein, Dracula, Wolf-man; mythical monsters

VERBS **10 fear, be afraid; apprehend,** have qualms, misgive, eye askance; **dread,** stand in dread of, be in mortal dread *or* terror of, stand in awe of, stand aghast; be on pins and needles, sit upon thorns; have one's heart in one's mouth, have one's heart stand still, have one's heart skip *or* miss a beat; quake in one's boots; **sweat,** break out in a cold sweat, sweat bullets <nf>

11 take fright, take alarm, push *or* press *or* hit the panic button <nf>; funk *and* go into a funk <nf>, get the wind up <Brit nf>; lose courage 491.8; pale, grow *or* turn pale, change *or* turn color; look as if one had seen a ghost; freeze, be paralyzed with fear, throw up one's hands in horror, jump out of one's skin; shit in one's pants *and* shit green <nf>

12 start, startle, **jump,** jump out of one's skin, jump a mile, leap like a startled gazelle; **shy,** fight shy, start aside, boggle, jib; **panic,** stampede, skedaddle <nf>

13 flinch, shrink, shy, shy away from, draw back, recoil, funk <nf>, **quail, cringe, wince, blench,**

blink, say *or* cry uncle; put one's tail between one's legs

14 **tremble, shake, quake, shiver, quiver, quaver; tremble** *or* **quake** *or* **shake** in one's boots *or* **shoes,** tremble like an aspen leaf, quiver like a rabbit, shake all over

15 **frighten,** fright, affright, funk <nf>, frighten *or* scare out of one's wits; **scare,** spook <nf>, scare one stiff *or* shitless *or* spitless <nf>, scare the life out of, scare the pants off of *and* scare hell out of *and* scare the shit out of <nf>; scare one to death, scare the daylights *or* the living daylights *or* the wits *or* the shit out of <nf>; give one a fright *or* scare *or* turn; **alarm,** disquiet, raise apprehensions; shake, stagger; **startle** 131.8; **unnerve, unman,** unstring; give one goose-flesh, horripilate, give one the creeps *or* the willies <nf>, make one's flesh creep, chill one's spine, make one's nerves tingle, curl one's hair <nf>, make one's hair stand on end, make one's blood run cold, freeze *or* curdle the blood, make one's teeth chatter, make one tremble, take one's breath away, make one shit one's pants *or* shit green <nf>

16 **put in fear,** put the fear of God into, **throw a scare into** <nf>; **panic,** stampede, send scuttling, throw blind fear into

17 **terrify, awe,** strike terror into; **horrify, appall, shock,** make one's flesh creep; **frighten out of one's wits** *or* **senses;** strike dumb, **stun, stupefy, paralyze, petrify,** freeze

18 **daunt, deter,** shake, stop, stop in one's tracks, set back; **discourage, dishearten;** faze <nf>; **awe, overawe**

19 **dismay, disconcert, appall, astound, confound, abash, discomfit, put out, take aback**

20 **intimidate, cow, browbeat, bulldoze** <nf>, bludgeon, dragoon; **bully, hector, harass,** huff; bluster, bluster out of *or* into; **terrorize,** put in bodily fear, use terror *or* terrorist tactics, pursue a policy of *Schrecklichkeit,* systematically terrorize; threaten 514.2; **demoralize**

21 **frighten off, scare away,** bluff off, put to flight

ADJS 22 **afraid, scared,** scared to death <nf>, spooked <nf>; feared *or* afeared <nf>; fear-stricken, fear-struck; haunted with fear, phobic

23 **fearful,** fearing, fearsome, **in fear; cowardly** 491.10; **timorous, timid, shy,** rabbity *and* mousy <nf>, afraid of one's own shadow; **shrinking,** bashful, diffident; scary; **skittish,** skittery <nf>, startlish, gun-shy, jumpy, goosy <nf>; **tremulous,** trembling, trepidant, shaky, shivery; **nervous;** waiting for the bomb to drop

24 **apprehensive, misgiving,** antsy <nf>, **qualmish,** qualmy; anxious 126.7

25 **frightened,** frightened to death, affrighted, in a fright, frit <Brit nf>, in a funk *or* blue funk <nf>; **alarmed,** disquieted; consternated, **dismayed,** daunted; **startled** 131.13; more frightened than hurt

26 **terrified,** terror-stricken, terror-struck, terror-smitten, terror-shaken, terror-troubled, terror-riven, terror-ridden, terror-driven, terror-crazed, terror-haunted; awestricken, awestruck; **horrified,** horror-stricken, horror-struck; **appalled, astounded, aghast;** frightened out of one's wits *or* mind, **scared to death, scared stiff** *or* **shitless** *or* spitless <nf>; unnerved, unstrung, unmanned, undone, **cowed,** awed, **intimidated; stunned, petrified, stupefied,** paralyzed, frozen; white as a sheet, pale as death *or* a ghost, deadly pale, ashen, blanched, pallid, gray with fear

27 **panicky,** panic-prone, panicked, in a panic, panic-stricken, panic-struck, terror-stricken, out of one's mind with fear, prey to blind fear

28 **frightening, frightful; fearful,** fearsome, fear-inspiring, nightmarish, hellish; **scary,** scaring, chilling; **alarming, startling,** disquieting, dismaying, disconcerting; **unnerving, daunting,** deterring, **deterrent,** discouraging, disheartening, fazing, awing, overawing; stunning, stupefying, mind-boggling *or* –numbing, hair-raising

29 **terrifying,** terrorful, terror-striking, terror-inspiring, terror-bringing, terror-giving, terror-breeding, terror-breathing, terror-bearing, terror-fraught; **bloodcurdling, hair-raising** <nf>; petrifying, paralyzing, stunning, stupefying; **terrorizing, terror, terroristic;** *schrecklich* <Ger>

30 **terrible,** terrific, tremendous; **horrid, horrible, horrifying,** horrific, horrendous; **dreadful, dread,** dreaded; **awful;** awesome, awe-inspiring; **shocking, appalling,** astounding; **dire,** direful, fell; formidable, redoubtable; **hideous, ghastly,** morbid, grim, grisly, gruesome, ghoulish, macabre

31 **creepy, spooky, eerie, weird, uncanny**

ADVS 32 **fearfully, apprehensively, diffidently,** for fear of; **timorously, timidly, shyly,** mousily <nf>, bashfully, shrinkingly; tremulously, tremblingly, quakingly, **with** *or* **in fear and trembling;** with heart in mouth, with bated breath

33 **in fear, in terror,** in awe, in alarm, in consternation; in mortal fear, in fear of one's life

34 **frightfully, fearfully; alarmingly, startlingly,** disquietingly, dismayingly, disconcertingly, **shockingly, appallingly,** astoundingly; **terribly,** terrifically, tremendously; **dreadfully, awfully; horridly, horribly,** horrifyingly, horrifically, horrendously

35 phobias by subject

\<accidents\> dystychiphobia
\<alcohol\> alcoholophobia *or* dipsophobia
\<anemia\> anemophobia
\<animals\> zoophobia
\<ants\> myrmecophobia
\<bacteria\> bacteriophobia
\<baldness\> phalacrophobia
\<beards\> pogonophobia
\<bears\> ursaphobia
\<bees\> apiphobia *or* melissophobia
\<being alone\> autophobia *or* monophobia *or* eremiophobia *or* eremophobia
\<being buried alive\> taphophobia
\<being dirty\> automysophobia
\<being idle\> thaasophobia
\<being in vehicles\> amaxophobia
\<being whipped\> mastigophobia
\<birds\> ornithophobia
\<blood\> hemaphobia *or* hematophobia *or* hemophobia
\<blushing\> erythrophobia
\<body odor\> bromidrophobia *or* bromidrosiphobia
\<books\> bibliophobia
\<bridges\> gephyrophobia
\<bullets\> ballistophobia
\<bulls\> taurophobia
\<cancer\> cancerphobia *or* cancerophobia *or* carcinophobia
\<cats\> ailurophobia *or* aelurophobia *or* galeophobia
\<cemeteries\> coimetrophobia
\<certain places\> topophobia
\<chaos, disorder\> ataxophobia *or* ataxiophobia
\<chickens\> alektorophobia
\<childbirth\> tocophobia *or* maieusiophobia *or* maieuticophobia
\<children\> pedophobia
\<Chinese\> Sinophobia

\<cholera\> cholerophobia
\<church\> ecclesiophobia
\<clouds\> nephelophobia
\<coitus, intercourse\> coitophobia
\<cold\> cheimaphobia *or* cheimatophobia *or* frigophobia
\<color\> chromophobia *or* chromatophobia
\<comets\> cometophobia
\<computers\> cyberphobia
\<constipation\> coprostasophobia
\<corpses\> necrophobia
\<crossing a bridge\> gephyrophobia
\<crossing a street\> agyrophobia
\<crowds\> demophobia
\<crystals\> crystallophobia *or* hyalophobia
\<dampness\> hygrophobia
\<dancing\> chorophobia
\<darkness\> scotophobia *or* achluophobia *or* nyctophobia
\<dawn\> eosophobia
\<daylight, sunlight\> phengophobia
\<death\> thanatophobia
\<decisions\> decidophobia
\<demons\> demonophobia
\<dentists\> dentophobia
\<depth\> bathophobia
\<diabetes\> diabetophobia
\<dirt\> mysophobia
\<disease\> pathophobia
\<doctors, hospitals\> iatrophobia
\<dogs\> cynophobia
\<double vision\> diplopiaphobia
\<draft\> aerophobia
\<dreams\> oneirophobia
\<drink\> potophobia
\<drugs\> pharmacophobia
\<duration, time\> chronophobia
\<dust\> koniophobia *or* coniophobia *or* amathophobia
\<electricity\> electrophobia
\<enclosed places\> claustrophobia
\<English\> Anglophobia
\<everything\> panphobia *or* pantophobia

\<eyes\> ommatophobia
\<failure\> kakorraphiaphobia
\<fatigue\> kopophobia
\<fear\> phobophobia
\<feathers\> pteronophobia
\<feces\> coprophobia *or* scatophobia
\<fever\> febriphobia
\<fire\> pyrophobia
\<fish\> ichthyophobia
\<floods\> antlophobia
\<flowers\> anthophobia
\<flutes\> aulophobia
\<flying\> aviatophobia
\<fog\> homichlophobia
\<food\> cibophobia *or* sitophobia *or* sitiophobia
\<foreigners\> xenophobia
\<forests\> xylophobia
\<freedom\> eleutherophobia
\<French\> Francophobia *or* Gallophobia
\<frogs, reptiles\> batrachophobia
\<fur\> doraphobia
\<gaining weight\> obesophobia *or* pocrescophobia
\<garlic\> alliumphobia
\<Germans\> Germanophobia *or* Teutonophobia
\<germs\> spermophobia *or* spermatophobia
\<ghosts\> phasmophobia
\<God\> theophobia
\<going to bed\> clinophobia
\<gold\> aurophobia
\<gravity\> barophobia
\<growing old\> gerascophobia
\<hair\> chaetophobia *or* trichophobia
\<hair disease\> trichopathophobia
\<Halloween\> samhainophobia
\<heart disease\> cardiophobia
\<heat\> thermophobia
\<heaven\> uranophobia *or* ouranophobia
\<hell\> hadephobia *or* stygiophobia
\<heredity\> patroiophobia
\<high places\> acrophobia *or* altophobia *or* batophobia *or* hypsophobia *or* hypsiphobia

\<home\> ecophobia *or* oecophobia *or* oikophobia *or* domatophobia
\<homosexuality\> homophobia
\<horses\> hippophobia
\<hospitals\> nosocomephobia
\<hurricanes\> lilapsophobia
\<ice, frost\> cryophobia
\<ideas\> ideophobia
\<illness\> nosemaphobia *or* nosophobia
\<imperfection\> atelophobia
\<infinity\> apeirophobia
\<injury\> traumatophobia
\<inoculation\> trypanophobia *or* vaccinophobia
\<insanity\> lyssophobia *or* maniaphobia
\<insects\> entomophobia
\<insect stings\> cnidophobia
\<itching\> acarophobia
\<Japanese\> Japanophobia
\<jealousy\> zelophobia
\<Jews\> Judeophobia
\<justice\> dikephobia
\<kissing\> philemaphobia *or* philematophobia
\<lakes\> limnophobia
\<learning\> sophophobia
\<lice, parasites\> pediculophobia *or* phthiriophobia
\<light\> photophobia
\<light flashes\> selaphobia
\<lightning\> astraphobia *or* astrapophobia
\<loneliness\> autophobia *or* monophobia *or* eremitophobia
\<love\> philophobia
\<machinery\> mechanophobia
\<magic\> rhabdophobia
\<marriage\> gametophobia *or* gamophobia
\<meat\> carnophobia
\<men\> androphobia
\<meningitis\> meningitophobia
\<menstruation\> menophobia
\<metal\> metallophobia
\<mice\> musophobia *or* murophobia

<microbes> bacillophobia *or* microbiophobia
<mirrors> eisoptrophobia *or* catoptrophobia
<mites> acarophobia
<mobs> ochlophobia
<money> chrometophobia
<monsters> teratophobia
<moon> selenophobia
<mother-in-law> pentheraphobia
<motion> dromophobia *or* kinetophobia *or* kinesophobia
<moving vehicles> ochophobia
<music> musicophobia
<names> onomatophobia
<narrowness> anginophobia
<needles> belonephobia
<newness> cainophobia *or* cainotophobia *or* centophobia
<new things> neophobia
<night> nyctophobia
<noise> ligyrophobia
<nuclear weapons> nucleomitophobia
<nudity> gymnophobia *or* nudophobia
<number 13> triskaidekaphobia
<numbers> arithmophobia *or* numerophobia
<old people, old age> gerontophobia
<one thing> monophobia
<open places> agoraphobia
<opposite sex> sexophobia *or* heterophobia
<other people's opinions> allodoxaphobia
<pain> algophobia *or* odynesphobia
<parasites> parasitophobia
<passing high buildings> batophobia
<peanut butter> arachibutyrophobia
<people> anthropophobia
<philosophy> philosophobia
<pins> enetophobia
<plants> botanophobia
<pleasure> hedonophobia
<poison> toxiphobia *or* toxophobia *or* toxicophobia

<politics> politicophobia
<the Pope> papaphobia
<poverty> peniaphobia
<precipices> cremnophobia
<priests, holy people> hierophobia
<protein> proteinphobia
<punishment> poinephobia
<rabies> hydrophobophobia
<radiation> radiophobia
<rain> ombrophobia
<rectum, rectal disease> rectophobia *or* proctophobia
<relatives> syngenesophobia
<reptiles> batrachophobia *or* herpetophobia
<responsibility> hypegiaphobia
<ridicule> katagelophobia
<riding in cars> hamaxophobia *or* amaxophobia
<rivers> potamophobia
<robbers> harpaxophobia
<ruin, ruins> atephobia
<Russians> Russophobia
<saints> hagiophobia
<sand> eremikophobia
<Satan> Satanophobia
<school> didaskaleinophobia *or* scolionophobia
<sea> thalassophobia
<sex> erotophobia *or* genophobia
<shadows> sciophobia *or* sciaphobia
<sharpness> acrophobia *or* aichurophobia
<shock> hormephobia
<sin> hamartophobia *or* peccatiphobia
<skin> dermatosiophobia *or* dermatophobia
<skin disease> dermatopathophobia
<sleep> hypnophobia *or* noctiphobia
<slime> blennophobia *or* myxophobia
<small things> microphobia
<smell> olfactophobia *or* osmophobia *or* ophresiophobia
<smothering> pnigophobia *or* pnigerophobia

<snakes> ophiciophobia *or* ophiophobia *or* snakephobia
<snow> chionophobia
<soiling> rypophobia
<solitude> isolophobia
<sound> acousticophobia
<sourness> acerophobia *or* acerbophobia
<speech> lalophobia *or* laliophobia *or* glossophobia *or* phonophobia
<speed> tachophobia
<spiders> arachnophobia
<spirits> pneumatophobia
<stairs> climacophobia
<standing> stasophobia
<stars> siderophobia
<stealing> kleptophobia
<stillness, solitude> eremitophobia *or* eremophobia
<string> linonophobia
<sun> heliophobia
<surgery> tomophobia
<swallowing> phagophobia
<symmetry> symmetrophobia
<syphilis> syphilophobia
<taste> geumatophobia
<technology> technophobia
<teeth> odontophobia
<telephone> telephonophobia
<termites> isopterophobia
phronemophobia
<thirteen> tredecaphobia *or* triskaidekaphobia
<thunder> brontophobia *or* tonitrophobia *or* keraunophobia
<thunder and lightning> astraphobia *or* astrapophobia

36 phobias by name

ablutophobia <washing, bathing>
acrophobia *or* altophobia *or* batophobia *or* hypsophobia <high places>
acrophobia <sharpness>
aerophobia <draft>
agoraphobia <open places>
agrizoophobia <wild animals>

<touch> haptophobia *or* haphophobia *or* thixophobia
<travel> hodophobia
<trees> dendrophobia
<trembling> tremophobia
<trichinosis> trichinophobia
<tuberculosis> tuberculophobia *or* phthisiophobia
<tyrants> tyrannophobia
<urine> urophobia
<vegetables> lachanophobia
<vehicles> ochophobia
<venereal disease> venereophobia *or* cypridophobia
<void> kenophobia
<vomiting> emetophobia
<walking> ambulophobia *or* basiphobia
<washing, bathing> ablutophobia
<wasps> spheksophobia
<water> hydrophobia *or* aquaphobia
<waves> cymophobia
<weakness> asthenophobia
<wild animals> agrizoophobia
<wind> ancraophobia
<women> gynephobia *or* feminophobia
<words> logophobia
<work> ergophobia
<worms> vermiphobia *or* helminthophobia
<wound, injury> traumatophobia
<wrinkles> rhytiphobia
<writing> graphophobia
<young girls> parthenophobia

agyrophobia <crossing a street>
ailurophobia *or* aelurophobia *or* galeophobia <cats>
alcoholophobia *or* dipsophobia <alcohol>
alektorophobia <chickens>
algophobia <pain>
allodoxaphobia <other people's opinions>

amaxophobia <being in vehicles>
ancraophobia <wind>
alliumphobia <garlic>
ambulophobia or basiphobia <walking>
androphobia <men>
anemophobia <anemia>
anginophobia <narrowness>
Anglophobia <English>
anthophobia <flowers>
anthropophobia <people>
antlophobia <floods>
apeirophobia <infinity>
apiphobia or melissophobia <bees>
arachibutyrophobia <peanut butter sticking in mouth>
arachnophobia <spiders>
arithmophobia or numerophobia <numbers>
asthenophobia <weakness>
astraphobia or astrapophobia <lightning>
ataxophobia or ataxiophobia <chaos, disorder>
atelophobia <imperfection>
atephobia <ruin, ruins>
aulophobia <flutes>
aurophobia <gold>
automysophobia <being dirty>
autophobia or monophobia or ermitophobia <being alone, loneliness>
aviatophobia <flying>
bacillophobia or microbiophobia <microbes>
bacteriophobia <bacteria>
ballistophobia <bullets>
barophobia <gravity>
bathophobia <depth>
batophobia <passing high buildings>
batrachophobia or herpetophobia <reptiles, frogs>
belonephobia <needles>
bibliophobia <books>
blennophobia or myxophobia <slime>
botanophobia <plants>
bromidrosiphobia or bromidrophobia <body odor>

brontophobia or tonitrophobia or keraunophobia <thunder>
cancerphobia or cancerophobia or carcinophobia <cancer>
cainophobia or cainotophobia <newness>
cardiophobia <heart disease>
carnophobia <meat>
chaetophobia or trichophobia <hair>
cheimaphobia or cheimatophobia or frigophobia <cold>
chionophobia <snow>
cholerophobia <cholera>
chrometophobia <money>
chromophobia <color>
chronophobia <duration, time>
cibophobia or sitophobia or sitiophobia <food>
claustrophobia <enclosed places>
climacophobia <stairs>
clinophobia <going to bed>
cnidophobia <insect stings>
coimetrophobia <cemeteries>
coitophobia <coitus, intercourse>
cometophobia <comets>
coprophobia <feces>
coprostasophobia <constipation>
cremnophobia <precipices>
cryophobia <ice>
crystallophobia or hyalophobia <crystals>
cyberphobia <computers>
cymophobia <waves>
cynophobia <dogs>
decidophobia <decisions>
demonophobia <demons>
demophobia <crowds>
dendrophobia <trees>
dentophobia <dentists>
dermatopathophobia <skin disease>
dermatosiophobia or dermatophobia <skin>
diabetophobia <diabetes>
didaskaleinophobia or scolionophobia <school>
dikephobia <justice>

diplopiaphobia <double vision>
doraphobia <fur>
dromophobia or kinetophobia or kinesophobia <motion>
dystychiphobia <accidents>
ecclesiophobia <church>
ecophobia or oecophobia or oikophobia or domatophobia <home>
eisoptrophobia <mirrors>
electrophobia <electricity>
eleutherophobia <freedom>
emetophobia <vomiting>
enetophobia <pins>
entomophobia <insects>
eosophobia <dawn>
eremikophobia <sand>
eremitophobia or eremophobia <stillness, solitude>
ergophobia <work>
erotophobia or genophobia <sex>
erythrophobia <blushing>
febriphobia <fever>
Francophobia or Gallophobia <French>
gametophobia <marriage>
gephyrophobia <crossing a bridge>
gerascophobia <growing old>
gerontophobia <old people, old age>
Germanophobia or Teutonophobia <Germans>
geumatophobia <taste>
graphophobia <writing>
gymnophobia or nudophobia <nudity>
gynephobia <women>
hadephobia or stygiophobia <hell>
hagiophobia <saints>
hamartophobia or peccatiphobia <sin>
hamaxophobia or amaxophobia <riding in cars>
haptophobia or haphophobia or thixophobia <touch>
harpaxophobia <robbers>
hedonophobia <pleasure>

heliophobia <sun>
helminthophobia <worms>
hemaphobia or hematophobia or hemophobia <blood>
hierophobia <priests, holy people>
hippophobia <horses>
hodophobia <travel>
homichlophobia <fog>
homophobia <homosexuality>
hormephobia <shock>
hydrophobia <water>
hydrophobophobia <rabies>
hygrophobia <dampness>
hypegiaphobia <responsibility>
hypnophobia or noctiphobia <sleep>
iatrophobia <doctors, hospitals>
ichthyophobia <fish>
ideophobia <ideas>
isolophobia <solitude>
isopterophobia <termites>
Japanophobia <Japanese>
Judeophobia <Jews>
kakorraphiaphobia <failure>
katagelophobia <ridicule>
kenophobia <void>
kleptophobia <stealing>
koniophobia or coniophobia or amathophobia <dust>
kopophobia <fatigue>
lachanophobia <vegetables>
lalophobia or laliophobia or glossophobia or phonophobia <speech>
ligyrophobia <noise>
lilapsophobia <hurricanes>
limnophobia <lakes>
linonophobia <string>
logophobia <words>
lyssophobia or maniaphobia <insanity>
mastigophobia <beating>
mechanophobia <machinery>
meningitophobia <meningitis>
menophobia <menstruation>
metallophobia <metal>

microphobia <small things>
monophobia <one thing>
musicophobia <music>
musophobia <mice>
myrmecophobia <ants>
mysophobia <dirt>
necrophobia <corpses>
neophobia <new things>
nephophobia <clouds>
nephophobia *or* pathophobia <disease>
nosemaphobia *or* nosophobia <illness>
nosocomephobia <hospitals>
nucleomitophobia <nuclear weapons>
nyctophobia <night>
obesophobia *or* pocrescophobia <gaining weight>
ochlophobia <mobs>
ochophobia <vehicles>
odontophobia <teeth>
olfactophobia *or* osmophobia *or* ophresiophobia <smell>
ombrophobia <rain>
ommatophobia <eyes>
oneirophobia <dreams>
onomatophobia <names>
ophiciophobia *or* ophiophobia *or* snakephobia <snakes>
ornithophobia <birds>
panphobia *or* pantophobia <everything>
papaphobia <the Pope>
parasitophobia <parasites>
parthenophobia <young girls>
pathophobia <disease>
patroiophobia <heredity>
pediculophobia <lice, parasites>
pedophobia <children>
peniaphobia <poverty>
pentheraphobia <mother-in-law>
phagophobia <swallowing>
phalacrophobia <baldness>
pharmacophobia <drugs>
phasmophobia <ghosts>
phengophobia <daylight, sunlight>
philemaphobia *or* philematophobia <kissing>

philophobia <love>
philosophobia <philosophy>
phobophobia <fear>
photophobia <light>
phronemophobia <thinking>
pneumatophobia <spirits>
pnigophobia *or* pnigerophobia <smothering>
pogonophobia <beards>
poinephobia <punishment>
politicophobia <politics>
potamophobia <rivers>
potophobia <drink>
proteinphobia <protein>
pteronophobia <feathers>
pyrophobia <fire>
radiophobia <radiation>
rectophobia <rectum>
rhabdophobia <magic>
rhytiphobia <wrinkles>
Russophobia <Russians>
rypophobia <soiling>
samhainophobia <Halloween>
Satanophobia <Satan>
scabiophobia <scabies>
sciophobia <shadows>
selaphobia <light flashes>
selenophobia <moon>
sexophobia *or* heterophobia <opposite sex>
siderophobia <stars>
Sinophobia <Chinese>
sophophobia <learning>
spermophobia *or* spermatophobia <germs>
spheksophobia <wasps>
stasophobia <standing>
symmetrophobia <symmetry>
syngenesophobia <relatives>
syphilophobia <syphilis>
tachophobia <speed>
taphophobia <being buried alive>
taurophobia <bulls>
technophobia <technology>
telephonophobia <telephone>
teratophobia <monsters>
thaasophobia <being idle>
thalassophobia <sea>
thanatophobia <death>
theophobia <God>

thermophobia <heat>
tocophobia *or* maieusiophobia *or* maieuticophobia <childbirth>
tomophobia <surgery>
topophobia <certain places>
toxiphobia *or* toxophobia *or* toxicophobia <poison>
traumatophobia <wound, injury>
tredecaphobia *or* triskaidekaphobia <the number thirteen>
tremophobia <trembling>
trichinophobia <trichinosis>
trichopathophobia <hair disease>

trypanophobia *or* vaccinophobia <inoculation>
tuberculophobia *or* phthisiophobia <tuberculosis>
tyrannophobia <tyrants>
uranophobia *or* ouranophobia <heaven>
urophobia <urine>
ursaphobia <bears>
venereophobia <venereal disease>
vermiphobia *or* helminthophobia <worms>
xenophobia <foreigners>
xylophobia <forests>
zelophobia <jealousy>
zoophobia <animals>

128 NERVOUSNESS

NOUNS **1 nervousness, nerves,** nervosity, **disquiet, uneasiness, apprehensiveness,** disquietude, qualmishness, malaise, funny *or* creepy feeling, **qualm, qualms, misgiving;** undue *or* morbid excitability, excessive irritability, state of nerves, case of nerves, spell of nerves, attack of nerves; **agitation, trepidation; fear** 127; panic; **fidgets,** fidgetiness, jitteriness, jumpiness; nail-biting; twitching, tic, vellication; stage fright, buck fever <nf>; nervous stomach, butterflies in one's stomach <nf>

2 <nf terms> **jitters,** willies, **heebie-jeebies,** jimjams, **jumps, shakes,** quivers, trembles, dithers, collywobbles, butterflies, shivers, cold shivers, creeps, sweat, cold sweat, heebie-jeebies; antsyness, ants in one's pants, yips

3 tension, tenseness, tautness, **strain, stress,** stress and strain, mental strain, nervous tension *or* strain, pressure

4 frayed nerves, frazzled nerves, jangled nerves, shattered nerves, raw nerves *or* nerve endings, twanging *or* tingling nerves; neurosis; neurasthenia, nervous prostration, crackup, **nervous breakdown**

5 nervous wreck, wreck, a bundle of nerves

VERBS **6 fidget,** have the fidgets; jitter, have the jitters, etc; **tense up; tremble**

7 lose self-control, go into hysterics; lose courage 491.8; **go to pieces,** have a nervous breakdown, fall apart *or* to pieces, come apart, fall *or* come apart at the seams

8 <nf terms> **crack, crack up,** go haywire, **blow one's cork** *or* mind *or* stack, **flip,** flip one's lid *or*

wig, wig out, freak out, spazz out, go out of one's
skull; come unglued *or* unstuck *or* unhinged, go
up the wall

9 **get on one's nerves,** jangle the nerves, **grate on, jar
on,** put on edge, **set one's teeth on edge, go
against the grain, send one up the wall** <nf>,
drive one crazy; **irritate** 96.14

10 **unnerve, unman, undo, unstring,** unbrace, reduce
to jelly, **demoralize, shake, upset,** psych out <nf>,
dash, knock down *or* flat, **crush,** overcome,
prostrate, freak someone out

ADJS 11 **nervous,** nervy <Brit nf>; **high-strung,**
overstrung, highly strung, all nerves; **uneasy,
apprehensive,** qualmish, nail-biting, white-
knuckle <nf>, frit <Brit nf>; nervous as a cat;
excitable; irritable, edgy, **on edge,** nerves on edge,
on the ragged edge <nf>, unhinged, wired <nf>,
panicky, **fearful, frightened**

12 **jittery** <nf>, **jumpy,** twittery, skittish, skittery,
trigger-happy <nf>, gun-shy; **shaky,** shivery,
quivery, in a quiver; tremulous, tremulant,
trembly; jumpy as a cat on a hot tin roof; **fidgety,**
fidgeting; fluttery, all of a flutter *or* twitter;
twitchy; **agitated;** shaking, trembling, quivering,
shivering; shook up *and* all shook up <nf>

13 **tense,** tensed-up, uptight <nf>, **strained,** stretched
tight, taut, unrelaxed, **under a strain**

14 **unnerved, unmanned, unstrung, undone,** reduced
to jelly, unglued <nf>, panicked, **demoralized,
shaken, upset,** dashed, stricken, **crushed; shot,**
shot to pieces; neurasthenic, prostrate, prostrated,
overcome

15 **unnerving, nerve-racking,** nerve-rending,
nerve-shaking, nerve-jangling, nerve-trying,
nerve-stretching; jarring, grating

ADVS 16 **nervously, shakily,** shakingly, tremulously,
tremblingly, quiveringly

129 UNNERVOUSNESS

NOUNS 1 **unnervousness, nervelessness; sangfroid,
calmness, inexcitability** 106; unshakiness,
untremulousness; **steadiness,** steady-handedness,
steady nerves; no nerves, strong nerves, iron
nerves, nerves of steel, icy nerves; cool head

ADJS 2 **unnervous, nerveless,** without a nerve in
one's body; strong-nerved, iron-nerved, steel-
nerved; coolheaded, **calm, inexcitable** 106.10;
calm, cool, and collected; cool as a cucumber
<nf>; **steady,** steady as a rock, rock-steady,
steady-nerved, steady-handed; unshaky,
unshaken, unquivering, untremulous, without a
tremor; unflinching, unfaltering, unwavering,
unshrinking, unblenching, unblinking; **relaxed,**
unstrained, laid-back

130 EXPECTATION

NOUNS 1 **expectation,** expectance *or* **expectancy,**
state of expectancy; **predictability,**
predictableness; **anticipation, prospect,** thought;
contemplation; likelihood, probability 968;
confidence, presumption, reliance 953.1,
overreliance; certainty 970; imminence 840;
unastonishment 123

2 sanguine *or* cheerful expectation, optimism, eager
expectation, **hope** 124; the light at the end of the
tunnel

3 **suspense,** state of suspense, cliff-hanging *and*
nail-biting <nf>; **waiting,** expectant waiting,
hushed expectancy; uncertainty 971, nervous
expectation; **anxiety, dread, pessimism,**
apprehension 126.1

4 **expectations,** prospects, outlook, hopes, apparent
destiny *or* fate, future prospects; likelihoods,
probabilities; prognosis; accountability,
responsibility

VERBS 5 **expect,** be expectant, **anticipate, have in
prospect,** face, think, **contemplate,** have in
contemplation *or* mind, envision, envisage; **hope**
124.6; presume 951.10; dread; **take for granted;** not
be surprised *or* a bit surprised; foresee 961.5

6 **look forward to,** reckon *or* calculate *or* count on,
predict, foresee; look to, **look for, watch for,** look
out for, watch out for, be on the watch *or* lookout
for, keep a good *or* sharp lookout for; be ready for;
forestall

7 **be expected,** be one's probable fate *or* destiny, be
one's outlook *or* prospect, be in store

8 **await,** wait, wait for, wait on *or* upon, stay *or* tarry
for; have *or* keep an eye out for, lie in wait for, line
up for; wait around *or* about, watch, watch and
wait; **bide one's time,** bide, abide, **mark time;** cool
one's heels <nf>; be in suspense, be on
tenterhooks, be on pins and needles, hold one's
breath, bite one's nails, sweat *or* sweat out *or*
sweat it *or* sweat it out <nf>; **wait up for,** stay up
for, sit up for; cross one's fingers; be on the
waiting list; be on standby, be on call

9 **expect to,** intend, **plan on** 380.6

10 **be as expected,** be as one thought *or* looked for,
turn out that way, come as no surprise; **be just
like one,** be one all over <nf>; **expect it of,** think
that way about, **not put it past** <nf>; **impend,** be
imminent 840.2; lead one to expect 133.12

ADJS 11 **expectant,** expecting, in expectation *or*
anticipation; **anticipative,** anticipant, anticipating,
anticipatory; **holding one's breath; waiting,**
awaiting, waiting for; forewarned, forearmed,
forestalling, ready, prepared, on standby; **looking
forward to,** looking for, watching for, on the watch

or lookout for; gaping, agape, agog, all agog, atiptoe, atingle, **eager;** sanguine, optimistic, hopeful 124.10; sure, confident 953.21/970.21; certain 970.13; unsurprised, not surprised

12 in suspense, on tenterhooks, on pins and needles, on tiptoe, **on edge, with bated breath,** tense, taut, with muscles tense, quivering, keyed-up, biting one's nails; anxious, **apprehensive;** dreading; **suspenseful,** cliff-hanging <nf>

13 expected, anticipated, awaited, predicted, foreseen; taken for granted; presumed 951.14; probable 968.6; **looked-for,** hoped-for; **due, promised;** long-expected, long-awaited, overdue; **in prospect, prospective;** in the cards; **in view,** in one's eye, on the horizon; imminent 840.3

14 to be expected, as expected, up to *or* according to expectation, just as one thought, just as predicted, on schedule, **as one may have suspected,** as one might think *or* suppose; **expected of,** counted on, **taken for granted;** just like one, one all over <nf>, in character

ADVS **15 expectantly,** expectingly; anticipatively, **anticipatingly,** anticipatorily; hopefully 124.13; **with bated breath,** in hushed expectancy, with breathless expectation; with ears pricked up, with eyes *or* ears strained

131 INEXPECTATION

NOUNS **1 inexpectation,** nonexpectation, inexpectance *or* inexpectancy, no expectation, **unanticipation; unexpectedness;** unforeseeableness, unpredictableness, unpredictability; unreadiness, unpreparedness; the unforeseen, the unlooked-for, the last thing one expects; **improbability** 969

2 surprise, surprisal, wonder; **astonishment** 122.1–2; surpriser, startler, shocker, **blow,** staggerer <nf>, **eye-opener,** revelation; **bolt out of** *or* **from the blue,** thunderbolt, thunderclap; **bombshell,** bomb; blockbuster, earthshaker; sudden turn *or* development, *peripeteia* <Gk>, switch; surprise ending, kicker *or* joker *or* catch <nf>; surprise package; surprise party

3 start, shock, jar, jolt, turn, fright

VERBS **4 not expect,** hardly expect, **not anticipate, not look for,** not bargain for, **not foresee,** not think of, not see coming, have no thought of, have no expectation, think unlikely *or* improbable

5 be startled, be taken by surprise, be taken aback, be given a start, be given a turn *or* jar *or* jolt; **start,** startle, **jump,** jump a mile <nf>, jump out of one's skin; **shy,** start aside, flinch

6 be unexpected, come unawares, come as a surprise *or* shock, come out of left field <nf>,

come out of nowhere, appear unexpectedly, turn up, pop up *and* bob up <nf>, drop from the clouds, appear like a bolt out of the blue, come *or* burst like a thunderclap *or* thunderbolt, burst *or* flash upon one, come *or* fall *or* pounce upon, steal *or* creep up on

7 surprise, take by surprise, do the unexpected, spring a surprise <nf>, **open one's eyes,** give one a revelation; **catch** *or* **take unawares,** catch *or* take short, take aback, pull up short, raise some eyebrows, **catch off-guard** 941.7, cross one up <nf>; throw a curve <nf>, bowl over, come from behind, come from an unexpected quarter, come out of the blue, come upon unexpectedly *or* without warning, spring *or* pounce upon; drop a bombshell, drop a brick <nf>; throw *or* knock for a loop <nf>; **blindside** <nf>, spring a mine under, ambush, bushwhack; drop in on <nf>; give a surprise party; **astonish** 122.6

8 startle, shock, electrify, jar, jolt, shake, stun, **stagger, give one a turn** <nf>, give the shock of one's life, make one jump out of his skin, take aback, take one's breath away, throw on one's beam ends, bowl down *or* over <nf>, strike all of a heap <nf>; frighten

ADJS **9 inexpectant,** nonexpectant, unexpecting; **unanticipative,** unanticipating; **unsuspecting, unaware,** unguessing; uninformed, unwarned, unforewarned, unadvised, unadmonished; unready, unprepared; off one's guard 984.8

10 unexpected, unanticipated, unlooked for, unhoped for, unprepared for, undivined, unguessed, unpredicted, **unforeseen;** unforeseeable, unpredictable, off-the-wall <nf>; **improbable** 969.3; contrary to expectation, beyond *or* past expectation, on the contrary, au contraire <Fr>, out of one's reckoning, more than expected, more than one bargained for; out of the blue, dropped from the clouds, out of left field *and* from out in left field <nf>; without warning, unheralded, unannounced; sudden 830.5; out-of-the-way, **extraordinary**

11 surprising, astonishing 122.12; eye-opening, eye-popping <nf>; **startling, shocking,** amazing, electrifying, boggling, staggering, stunning, jarring, jolting

12 surprised, struck with surprise, openmouthed, amazed; **astonished** 122.9; **taken by surprise,** taken unawares, caught short; blindsided <nf>

13 startled, shocked, electrified, jarred, jolted, shaken, shook <nf>, staggered, **given a turn** *or* **jar** *or* **jolt,** taken aback, bowled down *or* over <nf>, struck all of a heap <nf>, able to be knocked down with a feather; speechless, flabbergasted

ADVS **14 unexpectedly,** unanticipatedly, improbably, implausibly, unpredictably, **unforseeably,** *à l'improviste* <Fr>, **by surprise, unawares,** against *or* contrary to all expectation, on the contrary, when least expected, as no one would have predicted, without notice *or* warning, in an unguarded moment, like a thief in the night; **out of a clear sky, out of the blue, like a bolt from the blue;** all of the sudden, suddenly 830.9

15 surprisingly, startlingly, to one's surprise, to one's great surprise; shockingly, staggeringly, stunningly, **astonishingly** 122.16

132 DISAPPOINTMENT

NOUNS **1 disappointment,** sad *or* sore disappointment, bitter *or* cruel disappointment, failed *or* blasted expectation, chagrin; **dashed hope, blighted hope,** betrayed hope, hope deferred, forlorn hope; **dash** <old>, dash to one's hopes; blow, buffet; **frustration,** discomfiture, bafflement, defeat, balk, foiling; **comedown,** setback, **letdown** <nf>; failure, smackdown <nf>, fizzle <nf>, fiasco; **disillusionment** 977; tantalization, mirage, tease; dissatisfaction 108.1; fallen countenance; bad news, bummer <nf>

VERBS **2 disappoint,** defeat expectation *or* hope; **dash,** dash *or* blight *or* blast *or* crush one's hope; **balk,** bilk, **thwart, frustrate, baffle, defeat,** foil, cross; put one's nose out of joint; **let down,** cast down; **disillusion** 977.2; tantalize, tease; dissatisfy; leave in the lurch; burst someone's bubble; fail

3 be disappointing, let one down <nf>, **not come up to expectation,** come to nothing, not live *or* measure up to expectation, go wrong, turn sour, disappoint one's expectations, come *or* fall short; peter out *or* fizzle *or* fizzle out <nf>, not make it *and* not hack it <nf>

4 be disappointed, have hoped for better, not realize one's expectations, fail of one's hopes *or* ambitions, run into a stone wall, be let down; look blue, laugh on the wrong side of one's mouth <nf>; be crestfallen *or* chapfallen *or* disenchanted

ADJS **5 disappointed,** bitterly *or* sorely disappointed; **let down,** betrayed, ill-served, ill done-by; **dashed,** blighted, blasted, crushed; **balked,** bilked, **thwarted, frustrated,** baffled, crossed, dished <Brit>, defeated, foiled; caught in one's own trap; disillusioned 977.5; disenchanted, chagrined, crestfallen, chapfallen, out of countenance; soured; dissatisfied; regretful 113.8

6 disappointing, not up to expectation, falling short, out of the running, not up to one's hopes, second- *or* third-best; tantalizing, teasing; **unsatisfactory,** unsatisfying; disheartening

133 PREMONITION

NOUNS **1 premonition, presentiment,** preapprehension, forefeeling, presage, presagement; **hunch** 934.3, **feeling in one's bones;** prediction 962

2 foreboding, boding; **apprehension, misgiving,** chill *or* quiver along the spine, creeping *or* shudder of the flesh; wind of change

3 omen, portent; augury, auspice, soothsay, prognostic, prognostication; **premonitory sign *or* symptom,** premonitory shiver *or* chill, **foretoken,** foretokening, tokening, betokening, betokenment, foreshowing, prefiguration, presigning <old>, presignifying, presignification, **preindication,** indicant, indication, **sign, token,** type, **promise,** sign of the times; **foreshadowing, adumbration,** foreshadow, shadow

4 harbinger, forerunner, precursor, messenger <old>, **herald,** announcer, *buccinator novi temporis* <L>; presager, premonitor, foreshadower, apparitor

5 <omens> bird of ill omen, owl, raven, stormy petrel, Mother Carey's chicken; gathering clouds, clouds on the horizon, dark *or* black clouds, angry clouds, storm clouds, thundercloud, thunderhead; black cat; broken mirror; rainbow; ring around the moon; shooting star; halcyon bird; woolly bear, groundhog

6 ominousness, portentousness, portent, bodefulness, presagefulness, suggestiveness, significance, **meaning** 518, meaningfulness; fatefulness, fatality, doomfulness, sinisterness, banefulness, balefulness, direness

7 inauspiciousness, unpropitiousness, unfavorableness, unfortunateness, unluckiness, ill-fatedness, ill-omenedness; fatality

8 auspiciousness, propitiousness, favorableness; luckiness, fortunateness, prosperousness, beneficence, benignity, benignancy, benevolence; brightness, cheerfulness, cheeriness; good omen, good auspices, *auspicium melioris aevi* <L>

VERBS **9 foreshow, presage;** omen, be the omen of, auspicate <old>; **foreshadow, adumbrate,** shadow, shadow forth, cast their shadows before; **predict** 962.9; have an intimation, have a hunch <nf>, feel *or* know in one's bones, feel the wind of change

10 forebode, bode, portend, croak; **threaten, menace, lower,** look black, spell trouble; **warn, forewarn,** raise a warning flag, give pause; have a premonition *or* presentiment, apprehend, preapprehend, fear for

11 augur, hint, divine <old>; **foretoken, preindicate,** presignify, presign, presignal, pretypify, **prefigure,** betoken, token, typify, **signify, mean** 518.8, spell,

indicate, point to, look like, **be a sign of,** show signs of

12 promise, suggest, hint, imply, give prospect of, make likely, give ground for expecting, raise expectation, **lead one to expect,** hold out hope, make fair promise, have a lot going for, have *or* show promise, **bid fair, stand fair to**

13 herald, harbinger, forerun, run before; speak of, announce, proclaim, preannounce; give notice, notify, talk about

ADJS **14** augured, **foreshadowed, adumbrated, foreshown; indicated, signified; preindicated,** prognosticated, **foretokened,** prefigured, pretypified, presignified, presigned <old>; presignaled; **presaged; promised, threatened;** predicted 962.14

15 premonitory, forewarning, augural, monitory, warning, presageful, presaging, **foretokening, preindicative,** indicative, prognostic, prognosticative, presignificant, prefigurative; **significant, meaningful** 518.10, speaking; **foreshowing, foreshadowing;** big *or* pregnant *or* heavy with meaning; forerunning, precursory, precursive; intuitive 934.5; predictive 962.11

16 ominous, portentous, portending; **foreboding,** boding, **bodeful; inauspicious, ill-omened,** ill-boding, of ill *or* fatal omen, of evil portent, loaded *or* laden *or* freighted *or* fraught with doom, looming, looming over; fateful, doomful; presageful; apocalyptic; **unpropitious, unpromising, unfavorable, unfortunate, unlucky; sinister,** dark, black, gloomy, somber, dreary; **threatening, menacing, lowering;** bad, evil, ill, untoward; dire, baleful, baneful, **ill-fated,** ill-starred, evil-starred, star-crossed

17 auspicious, of good omen, of happy portent; **propitious, favorable,** favoring, fair, good; **promising,** of promise, full of promise; **fortunate, lucky,** prosperous; benign, benignant, bright, happy, golden, ripe

ADVS **18 ominously, portentously, bodefully, forebodingly;** significantly, meaningly, meaningfully, speakingly, sinisterly; **threateningly, menacingly,** loweringly

19 inauspiciously, unpropitiously, unpromisingly, unfavorably, unfortunately, unluckily

20 auspiciously, propitiously, promisingly, favorably; fortunately, luckily, happily; brightly, fairly

134 PATIENCE

NOUNS **1 patience,** patientness; **tolerance,** toleration, **acceptance; indulgence,** lenience, leniency 427; sweet reasonableness; **forbearance,** forbearing, forbearingness; **sufferance, endurance;**

long-suffering, long-sufferance, longanimity; **stoicism,** fortitude, self-control; patience of Job; waiting game, waiting it out; **perseverance** 360

2 resignation, meekness, humility, humbleness; obedience; amenability; submission, **submissiveness** 433.3; acquiescence, compliance, uncomplainingness; **fatalism,** submission to fate *or* the inevitable *or* necessity; quietude, quietism, passivity, **passiveness** 329.1; *zitzflaysh* <Yiddish>; passive resistance, nonviolent resistance, nonresistance; Quakerism

3 stoic, Spartan, man of iron; Job, Griselda

VERBS **4 be patient,** forbear, bear with composure, **wait,** wait it out, play a waiting game, wait around, wait one's turn, watch for one's moment, keep one's shirt *or* pants on <nf>, not hold one's breath <nf>; contain oneself, possess oneself, possess one's soul in patience; carry on, carry through

5 endure, bear, stand, support, sustain, **suffer, tolerate, abide,** bide, live with; persevere; **bear up under, bear the brunt, bear with, put up with, stand for,** tolerate, carry *or* bear one's cross, take what comes, take the bitter with the sweet, abide with, brook, brave, brave out, hang in there, keep it up

6 <nf terms> **take it,** take it on the chin, take it like a man, not let it get one down, stand the gaff; bite the bullet; hold still *or* stand still for, swallow, stick, **hang in, hang in there, hang tough,** tough *or* stick it out; lump it

7 accept, condone, countenance; overlook, not make an issue of, let go by, let pass; **reconcile oneself to,** resign oneself to, yield *or* submit to, obey; accustom *or* accommodate *or* adjust oneself to, sit through; accept one's fate, lay in the lap of the gods, take things as they come, roll with the punches <nf>; **make the best of it,** make the most of it, make the best of a bad bargain, make a virtue of necessity; submit with a good grace, **grin and bear it,** grin and abide, shrug, shrug it off, slough off, not let it bother one; take in good part, take in stride; rise above

8 take, pocket, swallow, down, stomach, eat, digest, disregard, turn a blind eye, ignore; swallow an insult, pocket the affront, turn the other cheek, take it lying down, turn aside provocation

ADJS **9 patient,** armed with patience, with a soul possessed in patience, patient as Job, Job-like, Griselda-like; **tolerant,** tolerative, tolerating, accepting; understanding, **indulgent,** lenient, **forbearing;** philosophical; **long-suffering,** longanimous; **enduring,** endurant; stoic, stoical, Spartan; disciplined, self-controlled; **persevering;** impassive

10 **resigned,** reconciled; wait-and-see; **meek,** humble; obedient, amenable, **submissive** 433.12; acquiescent, compliant; accommodating, adjusting, adapting, adaptive; unresisting, **passive** 329.6; **uncomplaining,** long-suffering

ADVS 11 **patiently,** enduringly, stoically; **tolerantly, indulgently,** longanimously, leniently, forbearantly, forbearingly, philosophically, more in sorrow than in anger; perseveringly

12 **resignedly, meekly, submissively,** passively, acquiescently, compliantly, uncomplainingly

PHRS 13 Rome wasn't built in a day; all in good time; all things come to him who waits; don't hold your breath; time will tell

135 IMPATIENCE

NOUNS 1 **impatience,** impatientness, unpatientness; breathless impatience; **anxiety, eagerness** 101; tense readiness, **restlessness,** restiveness, ants in one's pants <nf>, prothymia; **disquiet,** disquietude, unquietness, uneasiness, **nervousness** 128; sweat *and* lather *and* stew <nf>, **fretfulness,** fretting, chafing; **impetuousness** 365.2; **haste** 401; excitement 105

2 **intolerance,** intoleration, unforbearance, nonendurance

3 **the last straw,** the straw that breaks the camel's back, the limit, the limit of one's patience, all one can bear *or* stand

VERBS 4 **be impatient,** hardly wait; hasten 401.4,5; itch to, burn to; **champ at the bit, pull at the leash,** not be able to sit down *or* stand still; **chafe, fret, fuss,** squirm; **stew,** sweat, sweat and stew, get into a dither, get into a stew <nf>, work oneself into a lather *or* sweat <nf>, get excited; wait impatiently, sweat it out <nf>, pace the floor; beat the gun, jump the gun <nf>, go off half-cocked, shoot from the hip

5 **have no patience with,** be out of all patience; **lose patience,** run out of patience, be exasperated, call a halt, have had it <nf>, blow the whistle <nf>

ADJS 6 **impatient,** unpatient; breathless; champing at the bit, rarin' to go <nf>; dying, **anxious, eager;** hopped-up *and* in a lather *and* in a sweat *or* stew <nf>, excited 105.18; edgy, **on edge; restless,** restive, unquiet, uneasy, on *shpilkes* <Yiddish>; **fretful,** fretting, chafing, antsy-pantsy *and* antsy <nf>, squirming, squirmy, about to pee *or* piss one's pants <nf>; exasperated; **impetuous** 365.9; **hasty** 401.9

7 **intolerant, unforbearing, unindulgent**

ADVS 8 **impatiently,** breathlessly; **anxiously;** fretfully; restlessly, restively, uneasily; intolerantly; hastily

136 PRIDE

NOUNS 1 **pride,** proudness, pridefulness; **self-esteem, self-respect,** self-confidence, self-reliance, self-consequence, face, independence, self-sufficiency; pardonable pride; obstinate *or* stiff-necked pride, stiff-neckedness; **vanity, conceit** 140.4; haughtiness, swell, **arrogance** 141, hubris; boastfulness 502.1; purse-pride

2 **proud bearing,** pride of bearing, military *or* erect bearing, stiff *or* straight backbone, **dignity,** dignifiedness, **stateliness,** courtliness, grandeur, **loftiness;** pride of place; **nobility,** lordliness, princeliness; **majesty,** regality, kingliness, queenliness; distinction, worthiness, augustness, venerability; **sedateness, solemnity** 111, gravity, *gravitas* <L>, sobriety

3 proudling; stiff neck; egoist 140.5; boaster 502.5, peacock; the proud

VERBS 4 **be proud,** hold up one's head, hold one's head high, stand up straight, hold oneself erect, never stoop; look one in the face *or* eye; stand on one's own two feet, pay one's own way; have one's pride

5 **take pride, pride oneself, preen oneself,** plume oneself on, pique oneself, **congratulate oneself,** hug oneself; **be proud of,** glory in, exult in, **burst with pride**

6 **make proud,** do one's heart good, do one proud <nf>, **gratify, elate,** flush, turn one's head

7 save face, save one's face, preserve one's dignity, guard *or* preserve one's honor, be jealous of one's repute *or* good name, cover one's ass <nf>

ADJS 8 **proud, prideful,** proudful <nf>; **self-esteeming, self-respecting;** self-confident, self-reliant, **independent, self-sufficient;** proudhearted, proud-minded, proud-spirited, proud-blooded; proud-looking; proud as Punch, proud as Lucifer, proud as a peacock; erect, stiff-backed, **stiff-necked;** purse-proud, house-proud

9 **vain, conceited** 140.11; haughty, **arrogant** 141.9; boastful 502.10, egotistic

10 **puffed up,** swollen, bloated, swollen *or* bloated *or* puffed-up with pride; elated, flushed, flushed with pride; bigheaded, swellheaded; egotistical

11 **lofty, elevated,** triumphal, high, high-flown, highfalutin *and* highfaluting <nf>, high-toned <nf>; high-minded, lofty-minded; high-headed, high-nosed <nf>

12 **dignified, stately, imposing, grand, courtly,** magisterial, aristocratic; **noble,** ennobled, lordly, princely; **majestic,** regal, royal, kingly, queenly; worthy, **august, venerable;** statuesque; **sedate, solemn** 111.3, sober, grave

ADVS **13 proudly,** pridefully, **with pride;** self-esteemingly, self-respectingly, self-confidently, self-reliantly, independently, self-sufficiently; erectly, with head erect, with head held high, with nose in air; stiff-neckedly; like a lord, *en grand seigneur* <Fr>

14 dignifiedly, with dignity; nobly, stately, imposingly, loftily, grandly, magisterially; majestically, regally, royally; worthily, augustly, venerably; sedately, solemnly, soberly, gravely

137 HUMILITY

NOUNS **1 humility, humbleness, meekness; lowliness,** lowlihood, poorness, meanness, smallness, ingloriousness, undistinguishedness; unimportance 998; innocuousness 999.9; teachableness 570.5; submissiveness 433.3; **modesty,** unpretentiousness 139.1; plainness, simpleness, homeliness

2 humiliation, mortification <old>, egg on one's face <nf>, **chagrin, embarrassment** 96.4; **abasement,** debasement, letdown, setdown, put-down *and* dump <nf>; **comedown,** descent, deflation, climb-down, wounded *or* injured pride; self-diminishment, **self-abasement, self-abnegation** 652.1; **shame, disgrace;** shamefacedness, shamefastness, hangdog look

3 condescension, condescendence, deigning, lowering oneself, stooping from one's high place

VERBS **4 humiliate, humble;** mortify <old>, **embarrass** 96.15; put out, put out of face *or* countenance; **shame, disgrace,** put to shame, put to the blush, give one a red face; **deflate,** prick one's balloon; take it out of; marginalize; make one feel small *or* this high; do down; bitch-slap <nf>

5 abase, debase, crush, abash, **degrade, reduce,** diminish, **demean,** lower, **bring low,** bring down, trip up, take down, set down, put in one's place, put down, diss <nf>, dump *and* dump on <nf>, knock one off his perch; take down a peg *or* notch *or* two <nf>, make a fool *or* an ass *or* a monkey of one; put down <nf>

6 <nf terms> beat *or* knock *or* **cut one down to size,** take the shine *or* starch out of, take the wind out of one's sails; put one's nose out of joint, put a tuck in one's tail, make one sing small, take down a rung

7 humble oneself, demean oneself, abase oneself, climb down *and* get down from one's high horse <nf>; put one's pride in one's pocket; **eat humble pie,** eat crow *or* dirt, eat one's words, swallow one's pride, lick the dust, take *or* eat shit <nf>; come on bended knee, come hat in hand; go down

on one's knees; pull *or* draw in one's horns *and* sing small <nf>, lower one's note *or* tone, tuck one's tail; come down a peg *or* a peg or two; **deprecate** *or* **depreciate oneself,** diminish oneself, discount oneself, belittle oneself; kiss one's ass <nf> 138.7

8 condescend, deign, vouchsafe; stoop, descend, lower *or* demean oneself, trouble oneself, set one's dignity aside *or* to one side; **patronize;** be so good as to, so forget oneself, dirty *or* soil one's hands; talk down to, talk *de haut en bas* <Fr, from high to low>

9 be humiliated, be put out of countenance; **be crushed, feel small, feel cheap,** look foolish *or* silly, be ready to sink through the floor; **take shame, be ashamed, feel ashamed of oneself,** be put to the blush, have a very red face; bite one's tongue; hang one's head, hide one's face, not dare to show one's face, not have a word to say for oneself; be taken down a rung

ADJS **10 humble, lowly,** low, **poor, mean,** small, inglorious, undistinguished; unimportant 998.16; innocuous; biddable, teachable 570.18; **modest, unpretentious** 139.9, without airs; **plain, simple,** homely; humble-looking, humble-visaged; humblest, lowliest, lowest, least

11 humble-hearted, humble-minded, humble-spirited, poor in spirit; meek, meek-hearted, meek-minded, meek-spirited, lamblike, Christlike; **abject,** submissive 433.12

12 self-abasing, self-abnegating, self-deprecating, self-depreciating 139.10, self-doubting

13 humbled, reduced, diminished, lowered, brought down *or* low, set down, bowed down, in the dust, cut down to size; on one's knees, on one's marrowbones <nf>

14 humiliated, humbled, mortified <old>, **embarrassed, chagrined, abashed, crushed,** out of countenance; blushing, ablush, **red-faced, ashamed,** shamed, ashamed of oneself, shamefaced, shamefast; crestfallen, chapfallen, hangdog; taken down a notch

15 humiliating, humiliative, humbling, chastening, mortifying, **embarrassing,** crushing

ADVS **16 humbly, meekly;** modestly 139.14; with due deference, with bated breath; submissively 433.17; **abjectly,** on bended knee, **on one's knees,** on one's marrowbones <nf>, on all fours, with one's tail between one's legs, hat-in-hand

138 SERVILITY

NOUNS **1 servility, slavishness,** subservience *or* subserviency, menialness, abjectness, **baseness,** meanness; **submissiveness** 433.3; slavery, helotry, helotism, serfdom, peonage

2 obsequiousness, sycophancy, morigeration, fawningness, fawnery, **toadyism,** flunkyism; parasitism, sponging; **ingratiation,** insinuation; **truckling, fawning, toadying,** toadeating, groveling, cringing, **bootlicking** <nf>, back scratching, tufthunting <chiefly Brit old>, flattery; **apple-polishing** <nf>; ass-licking *and* ass-kissing *and* brown-nosing *and* sucking up <nf>; timeserving; obeisance, prostration; mealymouthedness

3 sycophant, flatterer, toady, toad, toadeater, lickspit, lickspittle, **truckler, fawner,** courtier, led captain *and* tufthunter <chiefly Brit old>, kowtower, groveler, cringer, spaniel; flunky, lackey, jackal; timeserver; creature, **puppet,** minion, lap dog, **tool,** cat's-paw, dupe, instrument, faithful servant, slave, helot, serf, peon; mealymouth

4 <nf terms> **apple-polisher, ass-kisser, brown-nose,** brown-noser, brownie, ass-licker, ass-wiper, suck-ass; **backslapper,** backscratcher, clawback, back-patter; **bootlicker,** bootlick; **handshaker; yes-man, stooge;** doormat

5 parasite, barnacle, leech; **sponger,** sponge <nf>, freeloader <nf>, gigolo, smell-feast; beat *and* deadbeat <nf>

6 hanger-on, adherent, dangler, appendage, **dependent, satellite, follower,** cohort, retainer, servant, man, shadow, tagtail, **henchman,** heeler <nf>

VERBS **7 fawn, truckle; flatter; toady,** toadeat; **bootlick** <nf>, lickspittle, lick one's shoes, lick the feet of; **grovel,** crawl, creep, cower, cringe, crouch, stoop, kneel, bend the knee, fall on one's knees, prostrate oneself, throw oneself at the feet of, fall at one's feet, kiss *or* lick *or* suck one's ass *and* brown-nose <nf>, kiss one's feet, kiss the hem of one's garment, lick the dust, make a doormat of oneself; **kowtow,** bow, **bow and scrape**

8 toady to, truckle to, pander to, cater to, cater for <Brit>; **wait on** *or* **upon,** wait on hand and foot, dance attendance, do service, fetch and carry, do the dirty work of, do *or* jump at the bidding of, run after

9 curry favor, court, pay court to, make court to, run after <nf>, dance attendance on; **shine up to,** make up to <nf>; **suck up to** *and* **play up to** *and* act up to <nf>; be a yes-man <nf>, agree to anything; fawn upon, fall over *or* all over <nf>; **handshake** *and* back-scratch *and* **polish the apple** <nf>

10 ingratiate oneself, insinuate oneself, worm oneself in, get into the good graces of, get in with *or* next to <nf>, **get on the good** *or* **right side of,** rub the right way <nf>

11 attach oneself to, pin *or* fasten oneself upon, hang about *or* around, dangle, hang on the skirts of, hang on the sleeve of, become an appendage of, **follow,** follow at heel; follow the crowd, get on the bandwagon, go with the stream, hold with the hare and run with the hounds; latch onto <nf>

12 sponge *and* **sponge on** *and* **sponge off of** <nf>; feed on, fatten on, batten on, live off of, use as a meal ticket; parasitize

ADJS **13 servile, slavish,** subservient, **menial, base,** mean; **submissive** 433.12; under one's thumb

14 obsequious, flattering, sycophantic, sycophantical, morigerous, toadyish, fawning, truckling, ingratiating, smarmy <nf>, toadying, toadeating, **bootlicking** *and* back scratching *and* backslapping *and* ass-licking *and* brown-nosing *or* kiss-ass <nf>; **groveling,** sniveling, cringing, cowering, crouching, crawling; **parasitic,** leechlike, sponging <nf>; timeserving; **abject,** beggarly, hangdog; obeisant, prostrate, on one's knees, on one's marrowbones <nf>, on bended knee; mealymouthed; overattentive; sequacious

ADVS **15 servilely, slavishly,** subserviently, menially, sequaciously; **submissively** 433.17

16 obsequiously, sycophantically, ingratiatingly, fawningly, trucklingly; hat-in-hand, cap-in-hand; **abjectly,** obeisantly, grovelingly, on one's knees; parasitically

139 MODESTY

NOUNS **1 modesty, meekness;** humility 137; **unpretentiousness,** unassumingness, unpresumptuousness, **unostentatiousness,** unambitiousness, unobtrusiveness, unboastfulness

2 self-effacement, self-depreciation, self-deprecation, self-detraction, undervaluing of self, self-doubt, **diffidence;** hiding one's light under a bushel; low self-esteem, weak ego, lack of self-confidence *or* self-reliance, self-distrust; inferiority complex

3 reserve, restraint, constraint, backwardness, retiring disposition; low key, low visibility, low profile; reticence, reluctance, disinclination

4 shyness, timidity, timidness, timorousness, **bashfulness,** shamefacedness, shamefastness, pudicity, pudency, pudibundity *and* pudibundness *and* verecundity <old>; **coyness, demureness,** demurity, skittishness, mousiness; self-consciousness, embarrassment; stammering, confusion; stagefright, mike fright *and* flop sweat <nf>

5 blushing, flushing, coloring, mantling, reddening, crimsoning; **blush, flush,** suffusion, red face

6 shrinking violet, modest violet, mouse

VERBS **7 efface oneself,** depreciate *or* deprecate *or* doubt *or* distrust oneself; have low self-esteem; reserve oneself, retire, shrink, **retire into one's shell, keep in the background,** not thrust oneself forward, **keep a low profile,** keep oneself to oneself, keep one's distance, remain in the shade, take a back seat *and* play second fiddle <nf>, know one's place, hide one's face, hide one's light under a bushel, avoid the limelight, eschew self-advertisement; disincline

8 blush, flush, mantle, **color,** change color, color up, redden, crimson, turn red, have a red face, get red in the face, blush up to the eyes; stammer; squirm; die of embarrassment

ADJS **9 modest, meek;** humble; **unpretentious,** unpretending, **unassuming,** unpresuming, unpresumptuous, **unostentatious,** unassuming, unobtrusive, unimposing, unboastful; unambitious, unaspiring

10 self-effacing, self-depreciative, self-depreciating, self-deprecating; **diffident,** deprecatory, deprecative, self-doubting, unself-confident, unsure of oneself, unself-reliant, self-distrustful, self-mistrustful; low in self-esteem

11 reserved, restrained, constrained; quiet; low-keyed, keeping low visibility *or* a low profile; **backward, retiring, shrinking**

12 shy, timid, timorous, **bashful,** shamefaced, shamefast, pudibund *and* verecund *and* verecundious <old>; **coy, demure,** skittish, mousy; reluctant, disinclined; self-conscious, conscious, confused; stammering, inarticulate

13 blushing, blushful; **flushed,** aflush, red, ruddy, red-faced, red in the face; **sheepish; embarrassed**

ADVS **14 modestly, meekly;** humbly; **unpretentiously,** unpretendingly, **unassumingly,** unpresumptuously, **unostentatiously,** unobtrusively; quietly, without ceremony, *sans façon* <Fr>

15 shyly, timidly, timorously, **bashfully, coyly, demurely,** diffidently; **shamefacedly,** shamefastly, **sheepishly,** blushingly, with downcast eyes

140 VANITY

NOUNS **1 vanity, vainness;** overproudness, overweening pride; **self-importance,** consequentiality, consequentialness, **self-esteem,** high self-esteem *or* self-valuation, positive self image, self-respect, self-assumption, **self-admiration,** self-delight, self-worship, self-endearment, **self-love,** *amour propre* <Fr>, self-infatuation, narcissism, narcism; autoeroticism, autoerotism, self-gratification;

self-satisfaction, self-content, ego trip <nf>, self-approbation, self-congratulation, self-gratulation, self-complacency, **smugness,** complacency, self-sufficiency; vainglory, vaingloriousness; God's gift

2 pride 136; arrogance 141; **boastfulness** 502.1

3 egotism, egoism, egoisticalness, egotisticalness, **ego** <nf>, self-interest, individualism; **egocentricity,** egocentrism, self-centeredness, self-centerment, self-obsession; selfishness 651

4 conceit, conceitedness, self-conceit, self-conceitedness, immodesty, side, self-assertiveness; **stuck-upness** <nf>, chestiness <nf>, swelled-headedness, swelled head, swollen head, big head, large hat size; **cockiness** <nf>, pertness, perkiness; pomposity; obtrusiveness, bumptiousness; egomania, megalomania

5 egotist, egoist, egocentric, individualist; show-off, peacock; narcissist, narcist, Narcissus; **swellhead** <nf>, **braggart** 502.5, know-it-all *or* know-all, smart-ass *and* wise-ass <nf>, smart aleck, no modest violet, vaunter

VERBS **6 be stuck on oneself** <nf>, be impressed *or* overly impressed with oneself; ego-trip *and* be *or* go on an ego trip <nf>; think well of oneself, think one is it *or* one's shit doesn't stink <nf>, get too big for one's breeches, have a swelled head, know it all, have no false modesty, have no self-doubt, love the sound of one's own voice, be blinded by one's own glory, lay the flattering unction to one's soul; fish for compliments; toot one's own horn, **boast** 502.6; be vain as a peacock, give oneself airs 501.14

7 puff up, inflate, swell; go to one's head, turn one's head

ADJS **8 vain, vainglorious,** overproud, overweening; **self-important, self-esteeming,** having high self-esteem *or* self-valuation, self-respecting, self-assuming, consequential; **self-admiring,** self-delighting, self-worshiping, self-loving, self-endeared, self-infatuated, narcissistic, narcistic; autoerotic, masturbatory; **self-satisfied, self-content,** self-contented, self-approving, self-gratulating, self-gratulatory, self-congratulating, self-congratulatory, self-complacent, **smug,** complacent, self-sufficient

9 proud 136.8; arrogant 141.9; boastful 502.10

10 egotistic, egotistical, egoistic, egoistical, self-interested; **egocentric,** egocentristic, self-centered, self-obsessed, narcissistic, narcistic; selfish 651.5; egomaniac

11 conceited, self-conceited, immodest, self-opinionated; **stuck-up** <nf>, **puffed up;** swollen headed, **swelled-headed, big-headed** *and* too big for one's shoes *or* britches *and* biggety *and* **cocky** <nf>, jumped-up <chiefly Brit nf>; pert, perk, perky; peacockish, peacocky; know-all *or* know-it-all, smart-ass *and* wise-ass <nf>, smarty, smart-alecky, smart-ass <nf>, overwise, wise in one's own conceit; aggressively self-confident, obtrusive, bumptious

12 **stuck on oneself** <nf>, impressed with oneself, pleased with oneself, full of oneself, all wrapped up in oneself

ADVS 13 **vainly,** self-importantly; **egotistically,** egoistically; **conceitedly,** self-conceitedly, immodestly; cockily <nf>, pertly, perkily

141 ARROGANCE

NOUNS 1 **arrogance,** arrogantness; overbearingness, overbearing pride, overweening pride, stiff-necked pride, assumption of superiority, domineering, domineeringness; **pride,** proudness; superbia, sin of pride, chief of the deadly sins; **haughtiness, hauteur; loftiness,** Olympian loftiness *or* detachment; **toploftiness** *and* stuckupness *and* uppishness *and* uppityness <nf>, hoity-toitiness, hoity-toity; haughty airs, airs of *de haut en bas*; cornstarchy airs <nf>; high horse <nf>; **condescension,** condescendence, patronizing, patronization, patronizing attitude; purse-pride

2 **presumptuousness,** presumption, overweening, overweeningness, assumption, total self-assurance; hubris; **insolence** 142

3 **lordliness, imperiousness,** masterfulness, magisterialness, **high-and-mightiness,** aristocratic presumption; elitism

4 **aloofness, standoffishness,** offishness <nf>, chilliness, coolness, distantness, remoteness

5 **disdainfulness, disdain,** aristocratic disdain, **contemptuousness, superciliousness,** contumeliousness, cavalierness, you-be-damnedness <nf>

6 **snobbery, snobbishness,** snobbiness, snobbism; **priggishness, priggery,** priggism; snootiness *and* snottiness *and* sniffiness *and* high-hattedness *and* high-hattiness <nf>; tufthunting

7 **snob, prig; elitist; highbrow** *and* egghead <nf>, Brahmin, mandarin; name-dropper, tufthunter <chiefly Brit old>, snoot, cold fish <nf>

VERBS 8 **give oneself airs** 501.14; **hold one's nose in the air, look down one's nose,** toss the head, bridle; mount *or* get on one's high horse *and* ride the high horse <nf>; **condescend, patronize, deign,** vouchsafe, stoop, descend, lower *or* demean oneself, trouble oneself, set one's dignity aside *or* to one side, be so good as to, so forget oneself, dirty *or* soil one's hands; deal with *or* treat *de haut en bas* <Fr, from high to low> *or* *en grand seigneur*

<Fr, like a great lord>, talk down to, talk *de haut en bas;* feel entitled

ADJS 9 **arrogant, overbearing, superior,** domineering, **proud, haughty; lofty, top-lofty** <nf>; high-flown, high-falutin *and* high-faluting <nf>; high-headed; high-nosed *and* **stuck-up** *and* **uppish** *and* uppity *and* **upstage** <nf>; **hoity-toity,** big, big as you please, six feet above contradiction; on one's high horse; **condescending, patronizing,** *de haut en bas* <Fr>; purse-proud

10 **presumptuous,** presuming, assuming, overweening, would-be, self-elect, self-elected, self-appointed, self-proclaimed, *soi-disant* <Fr>; **insolent**

11 **lordly, imperious,** aristocratic, totally self-assured, noble; hubristic; masterful, magisterial, magistral, **high-and-mighty;** elitist; U <Brit nf>; dictatorial 417.16

12 **aloof, standoffish,** standoff, offish <nf>, chilly, cool, distant, remote, above all that; Olympian

13 **disdainful,** dismissive, **contemptuous, supercilious,** contumelious, cavalier, you-be-damned <nf>

14 **snobbish,** snobby, toffee-nosed <Brit nf>, **priggish,** snippy <nf>; **snooty** *and* **snotty** *and* sniffy <nf>; **high-hat** *and* high-hatted *and* high-hatty <nf>

ADVS 15 **arrogantly, haughtily, proudly,** aloofly; **condescendingly, patronizingly,** *de haut en bas* *and* *en grand seigneur* <Fr>; loftily, toploftily <nf>; imperiously, magisterially; Olympianly; **disdainfully, contemptuously,** superciliously, contumeliously; with nose in air, with nose turned up, with head held high, with arms akimbo

16 **presumptuously,** overweeningly, aristocratically; hubristically; **insolently**

17 **snobbishly,** snobbily, **priggishly;** snootily *and* snottily <nf>

142 INSOLENCE

NOUNS 1 **insolence; presumption,** presumptuousness; **audacity, effrontery,** boldness, assurance, hardihood, bumptiousness; hubris; overweening, overweeningness; **contempt** 157, **contemptuousness,** contumely; **disdain** 141.5, *sprezzatura* <Ital>; **arrogance** 141, uppishness *and* uppityness <nf>; obtrusiveness, pushiness <nf>

2 **impudence, impertinence,** flippancy, procacity *and* malapertness <old>, pertness, **sauciness,** sassiness <nf>, **cockiness,** *and* cheekiness <nf>, freshness <nf>, chutzpa *or* hutzpa, **brazenness,** brazenfacedness, brassiness <nf>, face of brass, shamelessness, **rudeness** 505.1, **brashness,** disrespect, disrespectfulness, derision, ridicule 508

3 <nf terms> **cheek,** face, brass, **nerve, gall, chutzpah,** crust, nads <nf>, stones <nf>

4 **sauce** *and* sass *and* lip <nf>, **back talk,** backchat <nf>, mouth

5 <impudent person> malapert <old>; minx, hussy; whippersnapper, puppy, pup, upstart; boldface, brazenface; *chutzpadik* <Yiddish>; swaggerer 503.2

6 <nf terms> **smart aleck,** smarty, smart guy, smartmouth, smart-ass, wise-ass, smarty-pants, ho-dad, wisenheimer, wise guy, know-it-all, saucebox

VERBS 7 **have the audacity, have the cheek; have the gall** *or* a nerve *or* one's nerve <nf>; **get fresh** <nf>, get smart <nf>, forget one's place, **dare, presume,** take liberties, make bold *or* free; hold in contempt 157.3, ridicule, taunt, deride 508.8

8 **sauce** *and* sass <nf>, **talk back,** answer back, lip *and* give one the lip <nf>, mouth off <nf>, provoke

ADJS 9 **insolent, insulting; presumptuous,** presuming, overpresumptuous, overweening; **audacious, bold,** assured, hardy, bumptious; **contemptuous** 157.8, contumelious; **disdainful** 141.13, **arrogant** 141.9, uppish *and* uppity <nf>; hubristic; forward, pushy <nf>, obtrusive, familiar; cool, cold

10 **impudent, impertinent, pert,** malapert *and* procacious <old>, flip <nf>, flippant, **cocky** *and* cheeky *and* **fresh** *and* facy *and* crusty *and* nervy <nf>, *chutzpadik* <Yiddish>; uncalled-for, gratuitous, biggety <nf>; **rude** 505.4,6, **disrespectful,** derisive 508.12, brash, bluff; **saucy,** sassy <nf>; smart *or* smart-alecky <nf>, smart-ass *or* wise-ass <nf>, snot-nosed <nf>

11 **brazen,** brazenfaced, boldfaced, barefaced, brassy <nf>, **bold,** bold as brass <nf>, unblushing, unabashed, aweless, **shameless,** dead *or* lost to shame; swaggering 503.4

ADVS 12 **insolently, audaciously,** bumptiously, contumeliously; **arrogantly** 141.15; **presumptuously,** obtrusively, pushily <nf>; **disdainfully** 141.15

13 **impudently, impertinently,** pertly, procaciously *and* malapertly <old>, flippantly, **cockily** *and* cheekily <nf>, saucily; **rudely** 505.8, brashly, disrespectfully, contemptuously 157.9, derisively 508.15, in a smart-alecky way <nf>, in a smart-ass fashion <nf>

14 **brazenly,** brazenfacedly, **boldly,** boldfacedly, **shamelessly,** unblushingly

143 KINDNESS, BENEVOLENCE

NOUNS 1 **kindness, kindliness,** kindly disposition; **benignity,** benignancy; **goodness, decency,** niceness; **graciousness; kindheartedness,** goodheartedness, warmheartedness, softheartedness, tenderheartedness, kindness *or* goodness *or* warmth *or* softness *or* tenderness of heart, affectionateness, warmth, **lovingkindness,** metta; soul of kindness, kind heart, heart of gold; **brotherhood,** fellow feeling, **sympathy,** fraternal feeling, feeling of kinship; **pity** 145, **mercy, compassion; humaneness,** humanity; charitableness

2 **good nature, good humor,** good disposition, grace, benevolent disposition, good temper, sweetness, sweet temper *or* nature, good-naturedness, good-humoredness, good-temperedness, bonhomie; **amiability,** affability, geniality, cordiality; **gentleness,** mildness, lenity

3 **considerateness, consideration, thoughtfulness,** courteousness, mindfulness, heedfulness, regardfulness, attentiveness, **solicitousness,** solicitude, thought, regard, concern, delicacy, **sensitivity,** tact, tactfulness; indulgence, toleration, leniency 427; complaisance, accommodatingness, **helpfulness,** obligingness, agreeableness

4 **benevolence,** benevolentness, benevolent disposition, well-disposedness, **beneficence, charity,** charitableness, **philanthropy; altruism,** philanthropism, **humanitarianism,** welfarism, do-goodism; utilitarianism, Benthamism, greatest good of the greatest number; **goodwill,** grace, brotherly *or* sisterly, love, charity, Christian charity *or* love, *caritas* <L>, love of mankind, love of man *or* humankind, good will to *or* toward man, love, *agape* <Gk>, flower power; BOMFOG *or* brotherhood of man and fatherhood of God; **bigheartedness,** largeheartedness, greatheartedness; hospitality; **generosity** 485.1; giving 478

5 **welfare; welfare work, social service,** social welfare, social work; child welfare, etc; commonweal, public welfare; welfare state, welfare statism, welfarism; relief, the dole, social security <Brit>

6 **benevolences,** philanthropies, charities; works, **good works,** public service

7 **act of kindness, kindness, favor,** mercy, **benefit,** benefaction, benevolence, benignity, blessing, **service,** turn, break <nf>, **good turn, good** *or* **kind deed,** *mitzvah* <Heb>, office, good *or* kind offices, obligation, grace, act of grace, courtesy, kindly act, labor of love, good work; rescue, relief, largess, donation, alms

8 **philanthropist, altruist,** benevolist, **humanitarian,** man of good will, **do-gooder,** goo-goo *and* bleeding heart <nf>, well-doer, power for good; good Samaritan; well-wisher; welfare worker, social worker, caseworker; welfare statist;

almsgiver, almoner; bodhisattva; Robin Hood, Lady Bountiful; Mr Nice Guy

VERBS **9 be kind,** be good *or* nice, show kindness; treat well, do right by; favor, oblige, accommodate

10 be considerate, consider, respect, regard, think of, **be thoughtful of,** have consideration *or* regard for; remember; be mindful; be at one's service, fuss over one, spoil one <nf>

11 be benevolent, bear good will, wish well, give one's blessing, have one's heart in the right place, have a heart of gold; practice *or* follow the golden rule, do as you would be done by, do unto others as you would have others do unto you; make love not war

12 do a favor, do good, do a kindness, do a good turn, do a good *or* kind deed, do good works, do a *mitzvah* <Heb>, use one's good offices, render a service, confer a benefit; benefit, help 449.11; mean well

ADJS **13 kind, kindly,** kindly-disposed; **benign,** benignant; good as gold, **good, nice, decent; gracious; kindhearted, warm, warmhearted,** softhearted, tenderhearted, good-hearted, tender, loving, affectionate, sweet; **sympathetic,** sympathizing, **compassionate** 145.7, tolerant, merciful; brotherly, fraternal, sisterly; humane, human; charitable, caritative; Christly, Christlike; brotherly

14 good-natured, well-natured, **good-humored, good-tempered,** bonhomous, **sweet, sweet-tempered; amiable, affable, genial, cordial,** congenial; **gentle,** mild, mild-mannered; easy, easy-natured, easy to get along with, able to take a joke, **agreeable;** laid-back

15 benevolent, charitable, beneficent, philanthropic, altruistic, humanitarian; **bighearted,** largehearted, greathearted, freehearted; hospitable; **generous** 485.4; well-disposed; openhanded; almsgiving, eleemosynary; **welfare,** welfarist, welfaristic, welfare statist

16 considerate, thoughtful, mindful, heedful, regardful, solicitous, attentive, delicate, tactful, mindful of others; complaisant, **accommodating,** accommodative, at one's service, **helpful,** agreeable, **obliging,** indulgent, tolerant, lenient 427.7

17 well-meaning, well-meant, well-affected, well-disposed, **well-intentioned**

ADVS **18 kindly,** benignly, benignantly; **good,** nicely, well, favorably; **kindheartedly, warmly,** warmheartedly, softheartedly, tenderheartedly; humanely, humanly; brotherly

19 good-naturedly, good-humoredly, bonhomously; **sweetly; amiably,** affably, genially, cordially; graciously, in good part

20 benevolently, beneficently, charitably, philanthropically, altruistically, bigheartedly, with good will

21 considerately, thoughtfully, mindfully, heedfully, regardfully, tactfully, **sensitively,** solicitously, attentively; well-meaningly, well-disposedly; out of consideration *or* courtesy

144 UNKINDNESS, MALEVOLENCE

NOUNS **1 unkindness, unkindliness;** unbenignity, unbenignness; **unamiability,** uncordiality, ungraciousness, inhospitality, inhospitableness, ungeniality, unaffectionateness; unsympatheticness, uncompassionateness; disagreeableness

2 unbenevolentness, uncharitableness, ungenerousness

3 inconsiderateness, inconsideration, unthoughtfulness, unmindfulness, unheedfulness, **thoughtlessness,** heedlessness, respectlessness, disregardfulness, forgetfulness; **unhelpfulness,** unobligingness, unaccommodatingness; selfishness

4 malevolence, ill will, bad will, bad blood, bad temper, ill nature, ill-disposedness, ill *or* evil disposition; evil eye, stink eye <nf>, *malocchio* <Ital>, whammy <nf>, blighting glance

5 malice, maliciousness, maleficence; malignance *or* **malignancy,** malignity; **meanness** *and* orneriness *and* cussedness *and* bitchiness <nf>, hatefulness, nastiness, invidiousness; **wickedness,** iniquitousness 654.4; deviltry, devilry, devilment; malice prepense *or* aforethought, evil intent; **harmfulness, noxiousness** 1000.5

6 spite, despite; **spitefulness,** cattiness; gloating, unwholesome *or* unholy joy, *Schadenfreude* <Ger>

7 rancor, virulence, venomousness, **venom,** vitriol, gall, spleen, bile; sharp tongue; loathing

8 causticity, causticness, corrosiveness, mordancy, mordacity, bitingness; **acrimony, asperity,** acidity, acidness, acidulousness, acridity, acerbity, **bitterness,** tartness; sharpness, keenness, incisiveness, piercingness, stabbingness, trenchancy

9 harshness, roughness, ungentleness; **severity,** austerity, hardness, sternness, grimness, inclemency; stringency, astringency, asperity

10 heartlessness, unfeeling, unnaturalness, unresponsiveness, insensitivity, coldness, **cold-heartedness,** cold-bloodedness; **hard-heartedness,** hardness, hardness of heart, heart of stone; **callousness,** callosity; obduracy, induration; **pitilessness, unmercifulness** 146.1

11 **cruelty,** cruelness, *sadistic or* insensate cruelty, sadism, wanton cruelty; **ruthlessness** 146.1; inhumaness, **inhumanity,** atrociousness; **brutality,** mindless *or* senseless brutality, brutalness, **brutishness, bestiality, animality,** beastliness; **barbarity,** barbarousness, vandalism; **savagery, viciousness, violence,** fiendishness, heinousness; **child abuse** 389.2, spousal abuse; mental abuse, mental cruelty; truculence, fierceness, ferociousness, **ferocity;** excessive force, piling on <nf>; bloodthirst, bloodthirstiness, bloodlust, bloodiness, bloody-mindedness, sanguineousness; cannibalism; crime against humanity

12 **act of cruelty, atrocity,** cruelty, brutality, bestiality, barbarity, inhumanity; act of terrorism

13 **bad deed, disservice,** ill service, **ill turn,** bad turn

14 **beast, animal, brute, monster,** monster of cruelty, **devil,** devil incarnate; **sadist,** torturer, tormenter; Attila, Torquemada, the Marquis de Sade; malefactor, malfeasor, malfeasant, evildoer, miscreant

VERBS 15 bear malice *or* ill will, malign; do a bad turn; **harshen, dehumanize,** brutalize, bestialize; torture, torment; **have a cruel streak,** go for the jugular, have the killer instinct; have it in for <nf>

ADJS 16 **unkind, unkindly,** ill; **unbenign,** unbenignant; **unamiable,** disagreeable, **uncordial, ungracious,** inhospitable, **ungenial,** unaffectionate, unloving; **unsympathetic,** unsympathizing, **uncompassionate,** uncompassioned

17 **unbenevolent,** unbeneficent, **uncharitable,** unphilanthropic, unaltruistic, ungenerous

18 **inconsiderate, unthoughtful,** unmindful, unheedful, disregardful, **thoughtless,** heedless, respectless, mindless, unthinking, forgetful; **tactless, insensitive;** uncomplaisant; **unhelpful, unaccommodating, unobliging,** disobliging, uncooperative; selfish

19 **malevolent, ill-disposed,** evil-disposed, **ill-natured,** ill-affected, ill-conditioned, ill-intentioned, loathing

20 **malicious,** maleficent, malefic; **malignant,** malign; **mean** *and* **ornery** *and* cussed *and* bitchy <nf>, hateful, nasty, baleful, baneful, invidious; **wicked,** iniquitous 654.16; **harmful, noxious** 1000.12, toxic

21 **spiteful,** despiteful; **catty,** cattish, bitchy <nf>; **snide;** despiteful

22 **rancorous, virulent,** vitriolic; **venomous,** venenate, envenomed

23 **caustic,** mordant, mordacious, corrosive, corroding; **acrimonious,** acrid, acid, acidic, acidulous, acidulent, acerb, acerbate, acerbic, **bitter,** tart; **sharp,** sharpish, keen, incisive, trenchant, **cutting,** penetrating, piercing, biting,

stinging, stabbing, **scathing, scorching,** withering, scurrilous, abusive, thersitical, foulmouthed, harsh-tongued

24 **harsh, rough,** rugged, ungentle; **severe,** austere, **stringent,** astringent, hard, stern, dour, grim, inclement, unsparing

25 **heartless, unfeeling,** unnatural, unresponsive, insensitive, **cold,** cold of heart, coldhearted, **cold-blooded; hard, hardened,** hard of heart, **hard-hearted,** stony-hearted, marble-hearted, flint-hearted; **callous,** calloused; obdurate, indurated; **unmerciful** 146.3

26 **cruel,** cruel-hearted, sadistic; **ruthless** 146.3; **brutal,** brutish, brute, bestial, beastly, animal, animalistic; abusive; **mindless, soulless,** insensate, senseless, subhuman, dehumanized, brutalized; sharkish, wolfish, slavering; **barbarous,** barbaric, uncivilized, unchristian; **savage, ferocious,** feral, mean *and* mean as a junkyard dog <nf>, **vicious,** fierce, **atrocious,** truculent, fell; **inhuman,** inhumane, unhuman; fiendish, fiendlike; demoniac *or* demoniacal, diabolic, diabolical, devilish, satanic, hellish, infernal; **bloodthirsty,** bloody-minded, bloody, sanguineous, sanguinary; cannibalistic, anthropophagous; murderous; Draconian, Tartarean

ADVS 27 **unkindly,** ill; **unbenignly,** unbenignantly; **unamiably,** disagreeably, uncordially, ungraciously, inhospitably, ungenially, unaffectionately, unlovingly; unsympathetically, uncompassionately

28 **unbenevolently,** unbeneficently, **uncharitably,** unphilanthropically, unaltruistically, ungenerously

29 **inconsiderately, unthoughtfully,** thoughtlessly, heedlessly, unthinkingly; unhelpfully, uncooperatively

30 **malevolently, maliciously,** maleficently, **malignantly; meanly** *and* ornerily *and* cussedly *and* bitchily *and* cattily <nf>, hatefully, nastily, invidiously, balefully; **wickedly,** iniquitously 654.19; **harmfully, noxiously** 1000.15, **spitefully,** in spite; with bad intent, with malice prepense *or* aforethought

31 **rancorously, virulently,** vitriolically; venomously, venenately

32 **caustically,** mordantly, mordaciously, corrosively, corrodingly; **acrimoniously,** acridly, acidly, acerbly, acerbically, **bitterly,** tartly; **sharply,** keenly, incisively, trenchantly, **cuttingly,** penetratingly, piercingly, bitingly, **stingingly,** stabbingly, **scathingly,** scorchingly, witheringly, thersitically, scurrilously, abusively

33 **harshly, roughly; severely,** austerely, stringently, sternly, grimly, inclemently, unsparingly

34 heartlessly, soullessly, unfeelingly, callously, cold-heartedly; cold-bloodedly, **in cold blood**

35 **cruelly, brutally,** brutishly, bestially, animalistically, subhumanly, sharkishly, wolfishly, slaveringly; **barbarously, savagely, ferociously,** ferally, **viciously,** fiercely, **atrociously,** truculently, terroristically; **ruthlessly** 146.4; **inhumanely,** inhumanly, unhumanly; fiendishly, diabolically, devilishly

145 PITY

NOUNS **1 pity, sympathy,** feeling, fellow feeling, **commiseration,** condolence, condolences; **compassion, mercy,** empathy, ruth, rue, humanity; **sensitivity; clemency,** quarter, reprieve, mitigation, relief 120, favor, grace; **leniency,** lenity, gentleness; forbearance; **kindness, benevolence** 143; pardon, **forgiveness** 601.1; self-pity; **pathos**

2 compassionateness, mercifulness, ruthfulness, ruefulness, softheartedness, tenderness, tenderheartedness, lenity, gentleness; bowels of compassion *or* mercy; bleeding heart, soft spot

VERBS **3 pity, be** *or* **feel sorry for,** feel sorrow for; **commiserate,** compassionate; open one's heart; **sympathize, sympathize with,** feel for, weep for, lament for, bleed, bleed for, have one's heart bleed for *or* go out to, condole with 147.2

4 have pity, have mercy upon, take pity on *or* **upon;** melt, thaw; relent, forbear, relax, give quarter, spare, temper the wind to the shorn lamb, go easy on *and* let up *or* ease up on <nf>, soften, mitigate, unsteel; **reprieve, pardon,** remit, **forgive** 601.4; put out of one's misery; be cruel to be kind; give a second chance, give a break <nf>

5 <excite pity> **move, touch,** affect, reach, **soften,** unsteel, melt, melt the heart, appeal to one's better feelings; move to tears, sadden, grieve 112.17

6 beg for mercy, ask for pity, cry for quarter, beg for one's life; fall on one's knees, throw oneself at the feet of, throw oneself at someone's mercy

ADJS **7 pitying, sympathetic,** sympathizing, commiserative, condolent, understanding; **compassionate, merciful,** ruthful, rueful, **clement,** gentle, soft, melting, bleeding, tender, **tenderhearted,** softhearted, warmhearted; **humane,** human; lenient, forbearant 427.7; charitable 143.15

8 pitiful, pitiable, pathetic, piteous, touching, moving, affecting, heartrending, grievous, doleful 112.26, sad, heartbreaking, tearjerking <nf>

9 self-pitying, self-pitiful, sorry for oneself

ADVS **10 pitifully,** sympathetically; **compassionately, mercifully,** ruthfully, ruefully, clemently, humanely

146 PITILESSNESS

NOUNS **1 pitilessness, unmercifulness, uncompassionateness,** unsympatheticness, mercilessness, **ruthlessness,** unfeelingness, inclemency, relentlessness, inexorableness, unyieldingness 361.2, unforgivingness; **heartlessness,** heart of stone, hardness, steeliness, flintiness, harshness, induration, vindictiveness, **cruelty** 144.11; remorselessness, unremorsefulness; short shrift, tender mercies

VERBS **2 show no mercy,** give no quarter, turn a deaf ear, be unmoved, claim one's pound of flesh, harden *or* steel one's heart, go by the rule book

ADJS **3 pitiless,** unpitying, unpitiful; blind *or* deaf to pity; **unsympathetic,** unsympathizing; **uncompassionate,** uncompassioned; **merciless, unmerciful,** without mercy, unruing, **ruthless,** dog-eat-dog, vindictive; unfeeling, bowelless, inclement, relentless, inexorable, unyielding 361.9, unforgiving; **heartless,** coldhearted, hard, hard as nails, callous, steely, flinty, harsh, savage, **cruel;** remorseless, unremorseful; out for oneself

ADVS **4 pitilessly,** unsympathetically; mercilessly, **unmercifully, ruthlessly,** uncompassionately, inclemently, relentlessly, inexorably, unyieldingly, unforgivingly; heartlessly, harshly, savagely, cruelly; remorselessly, unremorsefully

147 CONDOLENCE

NOUNS **1 condolence, condolences,** condolement, **consolation,** comfort, balm, soothing words, **commiseration, sympathy,** sharing of grief *or* sorrow

VERBS **2 condole with, commiserate, sympathize with,** feel with, empathize with, express sympathy for, send one's condolences; pity 145.3; **console,** wipe away one's tears, comfort, speak soothing words, bring balm to one's sorrow; sorrow with, share *or* help bear one's grief, grieve *or* weep with, grieve *or* weep for, share one's sorrow

ADJS **3** condoling, condolent, consolatory, comforting, commiserating, commiserative, **sympathetic,** empathic, empathetic; pitying 145.7

148 FORGIVENESS

NOUNS **1 forgiveness,** forgivingness; unresentfulness, unrevengefulness; **condoning,** condonation, condonance, overlooking, disregard; **patience** 134; **indulgence, forbearance,** longanimity, long-suffering; **kindness, benevolence** 143; **magnanimity** 652.2; brooking, **tolerance** 979.4; peace talks

2 pardon, excuse, sparing, **amnesty,** indemnity, exemption, immunity, reprieve, grace; **absolution,** shrift, remission, remission *or* forgiveness of sin; redemption, deliverance; letting go; **exoneration, exculpation** 601.1

VERBS **3 forgive, pardon, excuse,** give *or* grant forgiveness, spare; amnesty, grant amnesty to, grant immunity *or* exemption; hear confession, **absolve,** remit, acquit, give *or* grant absolution, shrive, grant remission; **exonerate, exculpate** 601.4; blot out one's sins, wipe the slate clean, expunge from the record

4 condone 134.7, **overlook, disregard, ignore,** accept, take *and* swallow *and* let go <nf>, pass over, give one another chance, let one off this time *and* let one off easy <nf>, let something go, close *or* shut one's eyes to, turn a blind eye to, **blink** *or* **wink at,** connive at; show mercy; allow for, make allowances for; bear with, endure, regard with indulgence; pocket the affront, leave unavenged, turn the other cheek, bury *or* hide one's head in the sand

5 forget, forgive and forget, dismiss from one's thoughts, think no more of, not give it another *or* a second thought, let it go <nf>, let it pass, **let bygones be bygones;** write off, charge off, charge to experience; bury the hatchet; make peace, make up, shake hands

ADJS **6 forgiving,** sparing, placable, conciliatory; **kind, benevolent** 143.15; **magnanimous, generous** 652.6; **patient** 134.9; **forbearing,** longanimous, long-suffering, stoic; unresentful, unrevengeful; **tolerant** 979.11, more in sorrow than in anger; exonerative

7 forgiven, pardoned, excused, spared, amnestied, reprieved, remitted; overlooked, disregarded, forgotten, not held against one, wiped away, removed from the record, blotted, canceled, **condoned,** indulged; **absolved,** shriven; redeemed, delivered; exonerated, exculpated, acquitted, not guilty, innocent, cleared, absolved, vindicated, off the hook; unresented; unavenged, unrevenged; uncondemned; wiped away, swept clean

149 CONGRATULATION

NOUNS **1 congratulation, congratulations,** congrats <nf>, gratulation, **felicitation,** blessing, **compliment,** pat on the back; good wishes, best wishes; **applause** 509.2, **praise** 509.5, flattery 511

VERBS **2 congratulate,** gratulate, **felicitate,** bless, **compliment,** tender *or* offer one's congratulations *or* felicitations *or* compliments; shake one's hand, pat one on the back; **rejoice with one,** wish one joy; **applaud** 509.10, **praise** 509.12, flatter 511.5

ADJS **3 congratulatory,** congratulant, congratulational; gratulatory, gratulant; **complimentary** 509.16, flattering 511.8

INTERJS **4 congratulations!,** take a bow!, nice going!, **bravo!, well done!,** good show! <Brit>

5 <nf terms> **congrats!, all right!, aw right!, right on!,** way to go!, attaboy!, attagirl!, good deal!, looking good!, nice going!, that's my boy!, that's my girl!, mazel tov!

150 GRATITUDE

NOUNS **1 gratitude, gratefulness, thankfulness, appreciation, appreciativeness;** obligation, sense of obligation *or* indebtedness

2 thanks, thanksgiving, praise, laud, hymn, paean, benediction, eucharist; grace, prayer of thanks; **thank-you;** sincere thanks; **acknowledgment,** cognizance, **credit,** crediting, recognition; bonus, gratuity, tip; thank offering, votary offering

VERBS **3 be grateful, be obliged,** feel *or* be *or* lie under an obligation, be obligated *or* indebted, be in the debt of, give credit *or* due credit; **be thankful,** thank God, thank one's lucky stars, thank *or* bless one's stars; **appreciate,** be appreciative of; never forget; overflow with gratitude; not look a gift horse in the mouth

4 thank, extend gratitude *or* **thanks,** bless; give one's thanks, **express one's appreciation; offer** *or* **give thanks,** tender *or* render thanks, return thanks; acknowledge, make acknowledgments of, credit, recognize, give *or* render credit *or* recognition, give a big hand; fall all over one with gratitude; fall on one's knees; pay tribute

ADJS **5 grateful, thankful; appreciative,** appreciatory, sensible; **obliged, much obliged,** beholden, indebted to, crediting, under obligation, acknowledging, cognizant of; bread-and-butter

INTERJS **6 thanks!, thank you!,** I thank you!, *merci!* <Fr>, *¡gracias!* <Sp>, *grazie!* <Ital>, *danke!* and *danke schön!* <Ger>, gramercy!, *domo* and *domo arrigato* <Japanese>, **much obliged!,** many thanks!, thank you kindly!; thank you very much!, *merci beaucoup!* and *je vous remercie beaucoup!* <Fr>; thanks a lot! *or* a bunch! *or* a heap! <nf>, ta! <Brit>

151 INGRATITUDE

NOUNS **1 ingratitude, ungratefulness, unthankfulness,** thanklessness, unappreciation, **unappreciativeness;** nonacknowledgment, nonrecognition, denial of due *or* proper credit; "benefits forgot"—Shakespeare; grudging *or* halfhearted thanks

2 ingrate, ungrateful wretch, thankless wretch

VERBS **3 be ungrateful,** feel no obligation, **not appreciate,** owe one no thanks; look a gift horse in the mouth; bite the hand that feeds one

ADJS **4 ungrateful, unthankful,** unthanking, thankless, unappreciative, unappreciatory, unmindful, nonrecognitive, unrecognizing, ungracious, discourteous

5 unthanked, unacknowledged, unrecognized, nonrecognized, uncredited, denied due or proper credit, unrequited, unrewarded, forgotten, neglected, unduly or unfairly neglected, ignored, blanked, cold-shouldered; ill-requited, ill-rewarded

152 RESENTMENT, ANGER

NOUNS **1 resentment,** resentfulness; **displeasure,** disapproval, disapprobation, dissatisfaction, **discontent; vexation,** irritation, **annoyance,** aggravation <nf>, exasperation; slow burn <nf>

2 offense, umbrage, pique; glower, scowl, angry look, dirty look <nf>, glare, frown

3 bitterness, bitter resentment, bitterness of spirit, heartburning; **rancor,** virulence, **acrimony,** acerbity, asperity; causticity 144.8; **choler,** gall, bile, spleen, acid, acidity, acidulousness; hard feelings, **animosity** 589.4; soreness, rankling, slow burn <nf>; gnashing of teeth

4 indignation, indignant displeasure, righteous indignation, grievance, grudge

5 anger, wrath, ire, saeva indignatio <L>, mad <nf>; angriness, irateness, wrathfulness, soreness <nf>, "a transient madness"—Horace; infuriation, enragement; vials of wrath, grapes of wrath; **heat,** more heat than light <nf>; pugnacity, aggro <Brit nf>, dancer <nf>

6 temper, dander and Irish <nf>, monkey <Brit nf>; bad temper 110.1

7 dudgeon, high dudgeon; **huff,** pique, pet, tiff, miff and stew <nf>, fret, **fume,** ferment

8 fit, fit of anger, fit of temper, rage, wax <Brit nf>, **tantrum,** temper tantrum; duck or cat fit and **conniption** or conniption fit and snit <nf>, paroxysm, convulsion; agriothymia; stamping one's foot

9 outburst, outburst of anger, burst, **explosion,** eruption, blowup and **flare-up** <nf>, access, blaze of temper; **storm, scene,** high words

10 rage, passion; fury, furor, frenzy; livid or towering rage or passion, blind or burning rage, raging or tearing passion, furious rage; vehemence, violence; the Furies, the Eumenides, the Erinyes; Nemesis; Alecto, Tisiphone, Megaera; steroid rage, roid rage <nf>

11 provocation, affront, offense; casus belli <L>, red rag, red rag to a bull, red flag, sore point, sore spot, tender spot, delicate subject, raw nerve, the quick, where one lives; slap in the face; last straw; incitement

VERBS **12 resent,** be resentful, feel or harbor or nurse resentment, feel hurt, smart, feel sore and have one's nose out of joint <nf>; bear or hold or have a grudge, begrudge, bear malice

13 take amiss, take ill, **take in bad part,** take to heart, not take it as a joke, **mind; take offense, take umbrage,** get miffed or huffy <nf>; be cut or cut to the quick, get one's back up <nf>

14 <show resentment> redden, color, flush, mantle; **growl, snarl,** gnarl, **snap,** show one's teeth, spit; gnash or grind one's teeth; **glower,** lower, scowl, **glare, frown,** give a dirty look <nf>, look daggers; **stew,** stew in one's own juice

15 <be angry> **burn, seethe, simmer,** sizzle, smoke, smolder, steam; be pissed or pissed off or browned off <nf>, be livid, be beside oneself, **fume,** stew <nf>, boil, fret, chafe; foam at the mouth; breathe fire and fury; **rage, storm, rave,** rant, bluster; take on and go on and carry on <nf>, rant and rave, kick up a row or dust or a shindy <nf>; raise Cain or raise hell or raise the devil or raise the roof <nf>, tear up the earth; throw a fit, have a conniption or conniption fit or duck fit or cat fit <nf>, go into a tantrum; stamp one's foot

16 vent one's anger, vent one's rancor or choler or spleen, pour out the vials of one's wrath; **snap at, bite** or **snap one's nose off, bite** or **take one's head off, jump down one's throat;** expend one's anger on, take it out on <nf>

17 <become angry> **anger, lose one's temper,** become irate, forget oneself, let one's angry passions rise; **get one's gorge up,** get one's blood up, **bridle,** bridle up, **bristle,** bristle up, raise one's hackles, get one's back up; reach boiling point, boil over, climb the wall, go through or hit the roof

18 <nf terms> get mad or sore, get one's Irish or dander or hackles up, get one's monkey up <Brit>; **see red, get hot under the collar,** flip out, work oneself into a lather or sweat or stew, get oneself in a tizzy, do a slow burn, blow one's cool

19 flare up, blaze up, fire up, flame up, spunk up, ignite, kindle, take fire

20 fly into a rage or **passion** or **temper,** fly out, fly off at a tangent; **fly off the handle** and **hit the ceiling** and go into a tailspin and have a hemorrhage <nf>; **explode, blow up** <nf>; blow one's top or stack <nf>, blow a fuse or gasket <nf>, flip one's lid or wig <nf>, wig out <nf>; kick or piss up a fuss *or* a row *or* a storm <nf>; jump down someone's throat <nf>, take it out on someone <nf>

21 **offend, give offense, give umbrage,** affront, outrage; grieve, aggrieve; wound, hurt, cut, cut to the quick, hit one where one lives <nf>, **sting,** hurt one's feelings; step *or* tread on one's toes

22 **anger, make angry, make mad,** raise one's gorge *or* choler; make one's blood boil

23 <nf terms> **piss** *or* tee off, tick off, piss, **get one's goat, get one's Irish** *or* back *or* dander *or* hackles up, **make sore,** make one hot under the collar, put one's nose out of joint, burn one up, burn one's ass *or* butt, steam

24 **provoke, incense,** arouse, inflame, embitter; **vex, irritate, annoy, aggravate** <nf>, **exasperate, nettle,** fret, chafe; **pique, peeve** *and* miff <nf>, huff; **ruffle, roil, rile** <nf>, ruffle one's feathers, **rankle;** bristle, put *or* get one's back up, set up, put one's hair *or* fur *or* bristles up; stick in one's craw <nf>; **stir up, work up,** stir one's bile, stir the blood; wave the bloody shirt

25 **enrage, infuriate, madden,** drive one mad, frenzy, lash into fury, work up into a passion, **make one's blood boil**

ADJS 26 **resentful,** resenting; **bitter,** embittered, rancorous, virulent, **acrimonious,** acerb, acerbic, acerbate; caustic; **choleric,** splenetic, acid, acidic, acidulous, acidulent; **sore** <nf>, rankled, burning *and* stewing <nf>

27 **provoked, vexed, piqued; peeved** *and* miffed *and* huffy <nf>, riled, **nettled, irritated, annoyed,** aggravated <nf>, exasperated, put-out; huffed, miffed, peeved, in a snit

28 **angry,** angered, **incensed, indignant, irate,** ireful; **livid,** livid with rage, beside oneself, **wroth, wrathful,** wrathy, **cross,** wrought-up, worked up, riled up <nf>

29 **burning, seething,** simmering, smoldering, sizzling, boiling, **steaming;** flushed with anger

30 <nf terms> **mad, sore,** mad as a hornet *or* as a wet hen *or* as hell, sore as a boil, pissed; **pissed-off** *or* PO'd *or* pissed; teed off *or* TO'd; ticked *or* ticked off, browned-off, waxy *and* stroppy <Brit>, **hot,** het up, **hot under the collar,** burned up, hot and bothered, boiling, boiling *or* hopping *or* fighting *or* roaring mad, fit to be tied, good and mad, steamed, hacked, bent out of shape, in a lather *or* lava *or* pucker, red-assed

31 **in a temper, in a huff, in a pet,** in a snit *or* a stew <nf>; in a wax <Brit nf>, **in high dudgeon**

32 **infuriated,** infuriate, in a rage *or* passion *or* fury; **furious,** fierce, wild, savage; raving mad <nf>, **rabid,** foaming *or* frothing at the mouth; **fuming,** in a fume; **enraged, raging, raving, ranting, storming;** ballistic

ADVS 33 **angrily, indignantly, irately,** wrathfully, infuriatedly, infuriately, furiously, heatedly; **in anger,** in hot blood, in the heat of passion

153 JEALOUSY

NOUNS 1 **jealousy,** *jalousie* <Fr>, jealousness, heartburning, heartburn, **jaundice,** jaundiced eye, green in the eye <nf>, "the jaundice of the soul"—Dryden; "green-eyed monster"—Shakespeare; Othello's flaw, horn-madness; **envy** 154; crime of passion

2 **suspiciousness,** suspicion, doubt, misdoubt, mistrust, distrust, untrust, distrustfulness

VERBS 3 suffer pangs of jealousy, have green in the eye <nf>, be possessive *or* overpossessive, view with a jaundiced eye; **suspect,** distrust, mistrust, doubt, misdoubt; be paranoid

4 make one jealous, put someone's nose out of joint

ADJS 5 **jealous, jaundiced,** jaundice-eyed, yellow-eyed, green-eyed, yellow, green, green with jealousy; horn-mad; invidious, **envious** 154.3; **suspicious,** distrustful

154 ENVY

NOUNS 1 **envy,** enviousness, **covetousness;** emulousness <old>; invidia, deadly sin of envy, **invidiousness;** grudging, grudgingness; resentment, resentfulness; **jealousy** 153; rivalry, competitiveness; meanness, meanspiritedness, ungenerousness; penis envy, class envy

VERBS 2 **envy,** be envious *or* covetous of, **covet,** cast envious eyes, desire for oneself; resent; **grudge, begrudge;** turn green with envy, be jealous, eat one's heart out

ADJS 3 **envious,** envying, **invidious,** green with envy, green-eyed; **jealous** 153.4; **covetous,** desirous of; resentful; **grudging, begrudging;** mean, mean-spirited, ungenerous; stink-eyed, squint-eyed

155 RESPECT

NOUNS 1 **respect, regard,** consideration, appreciation, favor; approbation, approval; **esteem,** estimation, prestige; **reverence, veneration,** awe; **deference,** deferential *or* reverential regard; **honor, homage,** duty; great respect, high regard, high opinion, **admiration;** adoration, breathless adoration, exaggerated respect, worship, hero worship, **idolization;** idolatry, deification, apotheosis; courtesy 504

2 **obeisance,** reverence, homage; **bow, nod, bob,** bend, inclination, inclination of the head, **curtsy,**

salaam, kowtow, scrape, bowing and scraping, making a leg; **genuflection,** kneeling, bending the knee; prostration; salute, salutation, namaste; salaam, kowtow; presenting arms, dipping the colors *or* ensign, standing at attention; red carpet; **submissiveness, submission** 433; **obsequiousness, servility** 138

3 **respects, regards,** *égards* <Fr>; duties, *devoirs* <Fr>; attentions

VERBS 4 **respect,** entertain respect for, accord respect to, **regard, esteem,** hold in esteem *or* consideration, favor, **admire,** think much of, think well of, think highly of, have *or* hold a high opinion of; **appreciate, value,** prize, treasure; **revere, reverence,** hold in reverence, **venerate, honor, look up to, defer to, bow to,** exalt, put on a pedestal, **worship,** hero-worship, deify, apotheosize, **idolize, adore,** worship the ground one walks on, stand in awe of; hold dear

5 **do** *or* **pay homage to,** show *or* demonstrate respect for, pay respect to, pay tribute to, **do** *or* **render honor to, do the honors for; doff one's cap to, take off one's hat to;** salute, present arms, dip the colors *or* ensign, stand at *or* to attention; give the red-carpet treatment, roll out the red carpet; fire a salute

6 **bow, make obeisance, salaam, kowtow,** make one's bow, bow down, **nod,** incline *or* bend *or* bow the head, bend the neck, **bob,** bob down, **curtsy,** bob a curtsy, bend, make a leg, scrape, **bow and scrape; genuflect, kneel,** bend the knee, get down on one's knees, throw oneself on one's knees, fall on one's knees, fall down before, fall at the feet of, prostrate oneself, kiss the hem of one's garment

7 **command respect,** inspire respect, stand high, impress, have prestige, rank high, be widely reputed, be up there *or* way up there <nf>; awe 122.6, overawe

ADJS 8 **respectful, regardful,** attentive; **deferential,** conscious of one's place, dutiful, honorific, ceremonious, appreciative, cap in hand; **courteous** 504.14

9 **reverent,** reverential; admiring, **adoring, worshiping,** worshipful, hero-worshiping, **idolizing,** idolatrous, deifying, apotheosizing; **venerative,** venerational, venerating; awestruck, awestricken, awed, in awe; on bended knee, god-fearing; solemn 111.3

10 **obeisant,** prostrate, on one's knees, on bended knee; **submissive** 433.12; **obsequious;** knowing one's place

11 **respected, esteemed, revered,** reverenced, adored, worshiped, **venerated, honored,** well-thought-of, admired, much-admired, appreciated, valued, prized, in high esteem *or* estimation, highly considered, well-considered, held in respect *or* regard *or* favor *or* consideration, time-honored, prestigious

12 **venerable, reverend, estimable, honorable,** worshipful, august, awe-inspiring, awesome, awful, dreadful; time-honored

ADVS 13 **respectfully,** regardfully, deferentially, reverentially; dutifully

ADVS, PREPS 14 **in deference to,** with due respect, with all respect, **with all due respect** *or* **for,** saving, excusing the liberty, saving your reverence, sir-reverence; out of respect *or* consideration for, out of courtesy to

156 DISRESPECT

NOUNS 1 **disrespect, disrespectfulness,** lack of respect, low estimate *or* esteem, **disesteem,** dishonor, **irreverence; ridicule** 508; **disparagement** 512; **discourtesy** 505; **impudence, insolence** 142; opprobrium; contempt

2 **indignity, affront, offense, injury,** humiliation; scurrility, contempt 157, contumely, despite, flout, flouting, mockery, jeering, jeer, mock, scoff, gibe, taunt, brickbat <nf>; **insult, aspersion,** uncomplimentary remark, snub, slight, slap *or* kick in the face, left-handed *or* backhanded compliment, damning with faint praise; cut, "most unkindest cut of all"—Shakespeare; **outrage, atrocity,** enormity

3 <nf terms> **put-down,** dump, bringdown, brickbat, **dig,** dirty dig, ding, rank-out, rip, shot, slam, go-by

VERBS 4 **disrespect,** not respect, disesteem, hold a low opinion of, rate *or* rank low, hold in low esteem, not care much for, pay a lefthanded *or* backhanded compliment, damn with faint praise, hold in contempt, have no time for; **show disrespect for,** show a lack of respect for, **be disrespectful,** treat with disrespect, turn one's back on, be overfamiliar with; trifle with, make bold *or* free with, take a liberty, take liberties with, play fast and loose with; **ridicule** 508.8; **disparage** 512.8

5 **offend, affront,** give offense to, snub, slight, disoblige, outrage, step *or* tread on one's toes; dishonor, humiliate, treat with indignity; flout, mock, jeer at, scoff at, fleer at, gibe at, taunt, bitch-slap <nf>; **insult,** call names, kick *or* slap in the face, take *or* pluck by the beard; **add insult to injury;** give the cold shoulder, cut dead, spurn

6 <nf terms> **bad-mouth, put down, trash,** give the go-by, rubbish, dump on, dig at, dis *or* diss, rank out, rip *or* rip on, ride, roast, slam, hurl a brickbat

ADJS **7 disrespectful, irreverent,** aweless;
discourteous 505.4; **insolent, impudent;** flippant;
ridiculing, **derisive** 508.12; **disparaging** 512.13

8 insulting, insolent, abusive, offensive,
humiliating, degrading, pejorative, contemptuous
157.8, contumelious, calumnious; blasphemous;
scurrilous, scurrile; backhand, backhanded,
left-handed, cutting; contumacious, outrageous,
atrocious, unspeakable

9 unrespected, disrespected, **unregarded,
unrevered,** unvenerated, unhonored, unenvied;
trivialized

157 CONTEMPT

NOUNS **1 contempt, disdain, scorn,**
contemptuousness, disdainfulness,
superciliousness, snootiness, snottiness,
sniffiness, toploftiness, scornfulness, despite,
contumely, sovereign contempt; snobbishness;
clannishness, cliquishness, exclusiveness,
exclusivity; hauteur, airs, mock, arrogance 141;
ridicule 508; **insult** 156.2; **disparagement** 512

2 snub, rebuff, repulse; **slight,** humiliation,
spurning, spurn, disregard, the go-by <nf>; cut,
cut direct, **the cold shoulder** <nf>; sneer, snort,
sniff; contemptuous dismissal, **dismissal** 908.2,
kiss-off <nf>; **rejection** 372

VERBS **3 disdain, scorn, despise,** contemn, vilipend,
disprize, misprize, rate *or* rank low, be
contemptuous of, feel contempt for, **hold in
contempt,** hold cheap, look down upon, think
little *or* nothing of, feel superior to, be above, hold
beneath one *or* beneath contempt, look with scorn
upon, view with a scornful eye, mock, give one
the fish-eye *or* the beady eye *or* the stink eye *or*
the hairy eyeball <nf>; **put down** *or* dump on
<nf>; deride, **ridicule** 508.8; **insult; disparage**
512.8; thumb one's nose at, sniff at, sneeze at,
snap one's fingers at, sneer at, snort at, curl one's
lip at, shrug one's shoulders at; care nothing for,
couldn't care less about, think nothing of, set at
naught

4 spurn, scout, **turn up one's nose at,** scorn to
receive *or* accept, not want any part of; spit upon

5 snub, rebuff, cut *or* cut dead <nf>, drop, repulse;
high-hat *and* upstage <nf>; **look down one's nose
at,** look cool *or* coldly upon; cold-shoulder *or* turn
a cold shoulder upon *or* **give the cold shoulder**
<nf>, give *or* turn the shoulder <nf>, give the
go by *or* the kiss off <nf>; turn one's back upon,
turn away from, turn on one's heel, set one's face
against, slam the door in one's face, show one his
place, put one in his place, wave one aside; not be
at home to, not receive

6 slight, ignore, pooh-pooh <nf>, make little of,
dismiss, pretend not to see, disregard, overlook,
neglect, pass by, pass up *and* give the go-by <nf>,
leave out in the cold <nf>, take no note *or* notice
of, look right through <nf>, pay no attention *or*
regard to, refuse to acknowledge *or*
recognize

7 avoid 368.6, avoid like the plague, go out of one's
way to avoid, shun, dodge, steer clear of *and* have
no truck with <nf>; **keep one's distance,** keep at a
respectful distance, **keep** *or* **stand** *or* **hold aloof;**
keep at a distance, hold *or* keep at arm's length; **be
stuck-up** <nf>, act holier than thou, give oneself
airs

ADJS **8 contemptuous, disdainful,** supercilious,
snooty, snotty, sniffy, toplofty, toploftical,
scornful, sneering, insulting, withering,
contumelious; snobbish, snobby; clannish,
cliquish, exclusive; stuck-up <nf>, **conceited**
140.11; haughty, **arrogant** 141.9

ADVS **9 contemptuously, scornfully, disdainfully;** in
or with contempt, in disdain, in scorn; sneeringly,
with a sneer, with curling lip

INTERJS **10 bah!,** pah!, phooey!, boo!, phoo!, pish!,
ecch!, yeech!, eeyuck!, eeyuch!, yeeuck!, *feh!*
<Yiddish>

158 SPACE

<indefinite space>

NOUNS **1 space, extent,** extension, spatial extension,
uninterrupted extension, space continuum,
continuum; **expanse,** expansion; spread, breadth;
depth, deeps; height, vertical space; air space;
length; width; **measure,** volume; **dimension,**
proportion, size; **area,** expanse tract, surface,
surface *or* superficial extension; diameter,
circumference; **field,** arena, sphere; capacity;
acreage; **void,** empty space, emptiness,
nothingness; infinite space, infinity, outer space,
wastes of outer space, deep space, depths of outer
space, interplanetary *or* interstellar *or*
intergalactic space

2 range, scope, compass, reach, stretch, expanse;
radius, sweep, carry, fetch, grasp; **gamut, scale,**
register, diapason; **spectrum,** array, tract, range of
motion

3 room, latitude, swing, play, way; spare room,
room to spare, room to swing a cat <nf>,
elbowroom, legroom; **margin, leeway;** breathing
space, sea room, headroom, clearance; windage;
amplitude; headway; living space;

4 open space, clear space; **clearing,** clearance,
glade; open country, wide-open spaces, **terrain,**
prairie, steppe, plain 236; field, glade; wilderness,

back country, boonies *and* boondocks <nf>, outback <Austral>, desert, back o' beyond <Austral nf>; back forty; distant prospect *or* perspective, empty view, far horizon; **territory;** living space, *Lebensraum* <Ger>; national territory, air space

5 **spaciousness, roominess, size** commodiousness, capacity, capaciousness, airiness, amplitude, extensiveness, extent, expanse; stowage, storage; seating capacity, seating

6 **fourth dimension, space-time,** time-space, space-time continuum, continuum, four-dimensional space; four-dimensional geometry, Minkowski world *or* universe; spaceworld; other continuums; **relativity,** theory of relativity, Einstein theory, principle of relativity, principle of equivalence, general theory of relativity, special *or* restricted theory of relativity, continuum theory; time warp; cosmic constant

7 **inner space,** psychological space, the realm of the mind; personal space, room to be, individual *or* private space, space <nf>; semantic space

8 intervening space; distance, interval, gap, remove; break, hiatus, lacuna, pause, interruption, intermission, lapse, blank; duration, period, span, spell, stretch, turn, while

VERBS 9 **extend, reach, stretch,** expand, sweep, spread, run, **go** *or* **go out,** cover, carry, **range,** lie; **reach** *or* stretch *or* thrust out; span, straddle, take in, hold, enclose, encompass, surround, environ, contain, hold; lengthen, widen, deepen, raise

ADJS 10 **spatial,** space, spacial; **dimensional,** proportional; two-dimensional, flat, surface *or* superficial, radial, three-dimensional *or* 3-D, spherical, cubic, volumetric; galactic, intergalactic, interstellar; stereoscopic; fourth-dimensional; space-time, spatiotemporal

11 **spacious, sizeable, roomy, commodious, capacious,** ample; **extensive,** expansive, extended, wide-ranging; far-reaching, extending, spreading, **vast,** vasty, broad, **wide,** deep, high, voluminous, cavernous; airy, lofty; oversized; amplitudinous; widespread **864.13; infinite** 823.3

ADVS 12 **extensively, widely,** broadly, vastly, abroad; **far and wide,** far and near; **right and left,** on all sides, on every side; infinitely

13 **everywhere,** everywheres <nf>, **here, there, and everywhere;** in every place, in every clime *or* region, in all places, in every quarter, in all quarters; **all over,** all round, all over hell *and* all over the map *and* all over the place *and* all over the ballpark *and* all over town <nf>, all over the world, the world over, on the face of the earth, under the sun, throughout the world, throughout

the length and breadth of the land; from end to end, from pole to pole, from here to the back of beyond <Brit nf>, from hell to breakfast <nf>; **high and low,** upstairs and downstairs, inside and out, in every nook and cranny *or* hole and corner; **universally,** in all creation

14 **from everywhere,** everywhence, "from the four corners of the earth"—Shakespeare, from all points of the compass, from every quarter *or* all quarters; everywhere, everywhither, to the four winds, to the uttermost parts of the earth, "unto the ends of the earth"—Bible, to hell and back <nf>

159 LOCATION

NOUNS 1 **location, situation, place, position,** spot, *lieu* <Fr>, placement, emplacement, stead; **whereabouts,** whereabout, ubicity; **area, district, region** 231; **locality, locale,** locus; venue; **abode** 228; **site,** situs; **spot, point,** pinpoint, exact spot *or* point, very spot *or* point, dot; benchmark; *locus classicus* <L>; bearings, coordinates, latitude and longitude, direction; setting, environs, environment; habitat, address

2 **station,** status, **stand, standing,** standpoint, pou sto; **viewpoint,** *optique* <Fr>, point of reference, reference-point, angle, perspective, distance; coign of vantage; **seat, post,** base, footing, ground, venue

3 **navigation,** guidance; dead reckoning, pilotage; coastal navigation; celestial guidance *or* astro-inertial guidance, celestial navigation *or* celo-navigation *or* astronavigation; consolan; loran; radar navigation; radio navigation; orienteering; **position, orientation,** lay, lie, set, **attitude,** aspect, exposure, frontage, **bearing** *or* **bearings,** radio bearing, azimuth; position line *or* line of position; **fix**

4 **place,** stead, lieu

5 **map, chart;** hachure, contour line, isoline, layer tint; **scale,** graphic scale, representative fraction; **legend;** grid line, meridian, parallel, latitude, longitude; inset; index; **projection,** map projection, azimuthal equidistant projection *or* azimuthal projection, conic projection, Mercator projection; **cartography, mapmaking;** chorography, topography, photogrammetry, phototopography; **cartographer, mapmaker, mapper;** chorographer, topographer, photogrammetrist

6 <act of placing> **placement, positioning, emplacement, situation, location, siting,** localization, **locating, placing,** putting; establishment, installation; **allocation,** collocation, **disposition,** assignment, **deployment,** posting, **stationing,** spotting; fixing, fixation,

settling; deposition, reposition, **deposit,** disposal, dumping; **stowage,** storage, warehousing; loading, lading, packing

7 establishment, foundation, settlement, settling, colonization, population, peopling, plantation; lodgment, fixation; anchorage, mooring; **installation,** installment, inauguration, investiture, placing in office, initiation

8 topography, geography, topology; cartography, chorography; surveying, triangulation, navigation, geodesy; geodetic satellite, orbiting geophysical observatory *or* OGO; Global Positioning System *or* GPS; Geographic Information System

VERBS **9 have place,** be there; have its place *or* slot, **belong, go, fit,** fit in

10 be located *or* **situated, lie, be found,** stand, rest, repose; lie in, have its seat in

11 locate, situate, site, place, position; emplace, spot <nf>, **install,** put in place; **allocate,** collocate, **dispose, deploy,** assign; **localize,** narrow *or* pin down; **map, chart,** put on the map *or* chart; put one's finger on, **fix,** assign *or* consign *or* relegate to a place; **pinpoint,** zero in on, home in on, find the spot; find *or* fix *or* calculate one's position, triangulate, survey, find a line of position, **get a fix on** *or* navigational fix, get a bearing, navigate; turn up, track down

12 place, put, set, lay, pose, posit, site, seat, stick <nf>, **station, post;** billet, quarter; **park,** plump down <nf>; **dump**

13 <put violently> **clap,** slap, **thrust, fling, hurl,** throw, cast, chuck, toss; **plump;** plunk *and* plank *and* plop <nf>

14 deposit, repose, reposit, rest, **lay,** lodge; **put down,** set down, lay down

15 load, lade, freight, burden; fill 794.7; **stow,** store, put in storage, warehouse; **pack,** pack away; pile, dump, heap, heap up, stack, mass; bag, sack, pocket

16 establish, fix, plant, ensconce, **site,** pitch, seat, **set,** spot; **found, base,** ground, lay the foundation; **build,** put up, set up; build in; **install, invest,** vest, place in office, put in

17 settle, settle down, sit down, locate, park <nf>, ensconce, ensconce oneself; take up one's abode *or* quarters, make one's home, **reside, inhabit** 225.7; **move,** relocate, change address, establish residence, make one's home, **take up residence,** take residence at, put up *or* live *or* stay at, quarter *or* billet at, move in, hang up one's hat <nf>; take *or* strike root, put down roots, place oneself, plant oneself, get a footing, stand, take one's stand *or* position; **anchor,** drop anchor, come to anchor, moor; **squat;** camp, bivouac; perch, roost, nest, hive, burrow; domesticate, **set up housekeeping,**

keep house; **colonize,** populate, people; **set up in business,** go in business for oneself, set up shop, hang up one's shingle <nf>

ADJS **18 located, placed, sited, situated,** situate, **positioned,** installed, emplaced, spotted <nf>, **set,** seated; **stationed, posted,** deployed, assigned, positioned, prepositioned, oriented; **established,** fixed, in place, **settled,** planted, ensconced, embosomed

19 locational, positional, situational, situal, directional; **cartographic;** topographic, geographic, chorographic, geodetic; navigational; **regional** 231.8

ADVS **20 in place,** in position, in situ, in loco

21 where, whereabouts, in what place, in which place; **whither,** to what *or* which place

22 wherever, where'er, **wheresoever,** wheresoe'er, wheresomever <nf>, whithersoever, wherever it may be; **anywhere,** anyplace <nf>

23 here, hereat, in this place, just here, on the spot; **hereabouts,** hereabout, in this vicinity, near here; somewhere about *or* near; aboard, on board, with *or* among us; **hither,** hitherward, hitherwards, hereto, hereunto, hereinto, to this place

24 there, thereat, in that place, in those parts; thereabout, **thereabouts,** in that vicinity *or* neighborhood; **thither,** thitherward, thitherwards, to that place

25 here and there, in places, in various places, in spots, *passim* <L>

26 somewhere, someplace, in some place, someplace or other

PREPS **27 at, in, on, by; near, next to; with, among,** in the midst of; to, toward; from

28 over, all over, here and there, on *or* in, at about, round about; through, **all through, throughout** 794.17

PHR **29** X marks the spot

160 DISPLACEMENT

NOUNS **1 dislocation, displacement;** disjointing 802.1, disarticulation, unjointing, unhinging, luxation; heterotopia; **shift, removal,** forcible shift *or* removal; knocking off course; eviction; **uprooting,** ripping out, deracination; rootlessness, **disarrangement** 811; incoherence 802.1; discontinuity 813; disruption; Doppler effect *and* red shift *and* violet shift <physics>

2 dislodgment; unplacement, **unseating,** upset, unsaddling, unhorsing, unsettling; **deposal** 447; relocation, translocation, transference, transshipment

3 misplacement, mislaying, misputting, mislocation, malposition, losing

4 displaced person *or* DP, stateless person, homeless person, bag person, Wandering Jew, man without a country, exile, drifter, vagabond, deportee, repatriate; displaced *or* deported population; *déraciné* <Fr>; refugee, evacuee; outcast; waif, stray

VERBS **5** **dislocate, displace, disjoint,** disarticulate, unjoint, luxate, unhinge, put *or* force *or* push out of place, **put** *or* **throw out of joint,** throw out of gear, knock *or* throw off course, disrupt; **disarrange** 811.2

6 **dislodge,** unplace; evict; **uproot,** root up *or* out, deracinate; relocate; depose 447.4, **unseat,** unsaddle, unsettle; **unhorse,** dismount; throw off, buck off

7 **misplace, mislay,** misput, lose, lose track of

ADJS **8** dislocatory, dislocating, heterotopic

9 **dislocated, displaced; disjointed,** unjointed, unhinged; dislodged; out, **out of joint,** out of gear; **disarranged** 810.13

10 **unplaced,** unestablished, unsettled; **uprooted,** deracinated; unhoused, evicted, unharbored, houseless, made homeless, homeless, stateless, exiled, outcast, expatriated; swinging in the wind

11 **misplaced, mislaid,** misput, gone missing *or* astray; **out of place,** out of one's element, like a fish out of water, in the wrong place, in the wrong box *or* pew *and* in the right church but the wrong pew <nf>

12 **eccentric, off-center,** off-balance, unbalanced, uncentered

161 DIRECTION

<compass direction or course>

NOUNS **1** **direction,** directionality; **line,** direction line, line of direction, point, quarter, **aim, way,** track, range, **bearing,** azimuth, compass reading, **heading, course;** current, set; tendency, trend, inclination, bent, tenor, run, drift; **orientation,** lay, lie, lay of the land; steering, helmsmanship, piloting; navigation 182.1,2; line of march

2 <nautical & aviation terms> vector, tack; compass direction, azimuth, compass bearing *or* heading, magnetic bearing *or* heading, relative bearing *or* heading, true bearing *or* heading *or* course; lee side, weather side 218.3

3 **points of the compass,** cardinal points, cardinal directions, half points, quarter points, degrees, compass rose; compass card, lubber line; rhumb, loxodrome; magnetic north, true north, magnetic *or* compass directions, true directions; **north,** northward, nor'; **south,** southward; **east,** eastward, orient, sunrise; **west,** westward, occident, sunset;

southeast, southwest, northeast, northwest; northing, southing, easting, westing

4 **orientation, bearings;** adaptation, adjustment, accommodation, alignment, collimation; disorientation; deviation

VERBS **5** **direct, point, aim, turn, bend, train,** fix, set, determine; point to *or* at, hold on, fix on, sight on; take aim, aim at, turn *or* train upon; directionize, give a push in the right direction; locate; guide, signpost, indicate

6 **direct to,** give directions to, lead *or* conduct to, point out to, show, **show** *or* **point the way,** steer, put on the track, put on the right track, set straight, set *or* put right

7 <have or take a direction> bear, head, turn, point, aim, take *or* hold a heading, lead, go, steer, direct oneself, align oneself; **incline, tend, trend,** set, dispose, verge, tend to go, pilot, navigate

8 go west, wester, go east, easter, go north, go south

9 **head for,** bear for, **go for, make for,** hit *or* hit out for <nf>, **steer for,** hold for, put for, **set out** *or* **off for,** strike out for, take off for <nf>, bend one's steps for, lay for, bear up for, bear up to, make up to, set in towards; set *or* direct *or* shape one's course for, set one's compass for, sail for 182.35; align one's march; **break for,** make a break for <nf>, run *or* dash for, make a run *or* dash for

10 **go directly, go straight,** follow one's nose, go straight on, **head straight for,** vector for, go straight to the point, steer a straight course, follow a course, keep *or* hold one's course, hold steady for, arrow for, cleave to the line, keep pointed; **make a beeline,** go as the crow flies; take the air line, stay on the beam

11 **orient,** orientate, orient *or* orientate oneself, orient the map *or* chart, **take** *or* **get one's bearings,** get the lay *or* lie of the land, see which way the land lies, see which way the wind blows; adapt, adjust, accommodate

ADJS **12** **directional,** azimuthal; **direct, straight,** arrow-straight, ruler-straight, straight-ahead, straightforward, straightaway, straightway; **undeviating,** unswerving, unveering; uninterrupted, unbroken; one-way, unidirectional, irreversible

13 **directable,** aimable, pointable, trainable; **steerable,** dirigible, guidable, leadable; **directed,** guided, aimed; well-aimed *or* -directed *or* -placed, on the mark, on the nose *or* money <nf>; **directional,** directive

14 **northern,** north, northernmost, northerly, northbound, **arctic,** boreal, hyperborean; **southern,** south, southernmost, southerly, southbound, meridional, **antarctic,** austral; **eastern,** east, easternmost *or* eastermost, easterly, eastbound, **oriental; western,** west, westernmost, westerly, westbound, **occidental; northeastern,** northeast, northeasterly; **southeastern,** southeast, southeasterly; **southwestern,** southwest, southwesterly; **northwestern,** northwest, northwesterly; cross-country, downwind, upwind; oblique, axial, parallel

ADVS **15 north,** N, nor', northerly, northward, north'ard, norward, northwards, northwardly; north about

16 south, S, southerly, southward, south'ard, southwards, southwardly; south about

17 east, E, easterly, eastward, eastwards, eastwardly, where the sun rises; eastabout

18 west, W, westerly, westernly, westward, westwards, westwardly, where the sun sets; westabout

19 northeast or NE, nor'east, northeasterly, northeastward, northeastwards, northeastwardly; north-northeast or NNE; northeast by east or NE by E; northeast by north or NE by N

20 northwest or NW, nor'west, northwesterly, northwestward, northwestwards, northwestwardly; north-northwest or NNW; northwest by west or NW by W; northwest by north or NW by N

21 southeast or SE, southeasterly, southeastward, southeastwards, southeastwardly; south-southeast or SSE; southeast by east or SE by E; southeast by south or SE by S

22 southwest or SW, southwesterly, southwestward, southwestwards, southwestwardly; south-southwest or SSW; southwest by south or SW by S

23 directly, direct, straight, straightly, **straightforward,** straightforwards, **undeviatingly,** unswervingly, unveeringly; **straight ahead,** dead ahead; due, dead, due north, etc; right, forthright; in a direct or straight line, in line with, in a line for, **in a beeline, as the crow flies,** straight across; straight as an arrow

24 clockwise, rightward 219.7; **counterclockwise,** anticlockwise, widdershins, leftward 220.6; homeward; landward; seaward; earthward; heavenward; leeward, windward 218.9

25 in every direction, in all directions, in all manner of ways, every which way <nf>, everywhither, **everyway, everywhere,** at every turn, in all directions at once, in every quarter, on every side, all over the place or the ballpark or the map <nf>; around, all round, round about; forty ways or six ways from Sunday <nf>; from every quarter, everywhence; from or to the four corners of the earth, from or to the four winds

PREPS **26 toward,** towards, **in the direction of, to,** up, on, upon; upside <nf>; against, over against, versus; headed for, bound for, on the way to, on the road or high road to, in transit to, en route to, on route to, in passage to

27 through, by, passing by or through, **by way of,** by the way of, **via;** over, around, round about, here and there in, all through

162 PROGRESSION

<motion forwards>

NOUNS **1 progression, progress,** going, going forward; **ongoing,** on-go, go-ahead <nf>, onward course, rolling, rolling on; **advance,** advancing, **advancement, promotion, furtherance,** furthering, preferment; forward motion, forwarding, forwardal; **headway,** way; **leap, jump,** forward leap or jump, quantum jump or leap, leaps and bounds, spring, forward spring; progressiveness, progressivity; **passage,** course, march, career, full career; midpassage, midcourse, midcareer; travel 177; improvement 392

VERBS **2 progress, advance, proceed, go,** go or move forward, step forward, go on, **go ahead,** go along, push ahead, press on, pass on or along, roll on; move, travel; go fast 174.8; **make progress,** come on, **get along,** come along <nf>, **get ahead;** further oneself; **make headway, roll,** gather head, gather way; make strides or rapid strides, cover ground, get over the ground, make good time, make the best of one's way, leap or jump or spring forward, catapult oneself forward; make up for lost time, gain ground, make up leeway, make progress against, stem

3 march on, run on, rub on, **jog on, roll on,** flow on; drift along, go with the stream

4 make or **wend one's way, work** or **weave one's way,** worm or thread one's way, inch forward, feel one's way, muddle along or through, slog toward; go slow 175.6; carve one's way; push or force one's way, fight one's way, go or swim against the current, swim upstream; come a long way, move up in the world; **forge ahead,** drive on or ahead, **push** or **press on** or **onward,** push or press forward, push, crowd; get somewhere, reach toward, raise one's sights

5 advance, further, promote, forward, hasten, contribute to, boost, foster, aid, facilitate, expedite, abet

ADJS **6 progressive,** progressing, advancing, proceeding, **ongoing,** proceeding, oncoming, onward, forward, **forward-looking,** go-ahead <nf>; moving; go-getting <nf>

ADVS **7 in progress,** in mid-progress, in midcourse, in midcareer, in full career; **going on;** by leaps and bounds

8 forward, forwards, onward, onwards, forth, on,
along, **ahead;** on the way to, on the road *or* high
road to, en route to *or* for

163 REGRESSION

<motion backwards>

NOUNS **1 regression,** regress; recession 168;
retrogression, retrocession, retroflexion,
retroflection, reflux, refluence, retrogradation,
retroaction, retrusion, reaction; return, reentry;
setback, backset <nf>, throwback, **rollback;**
back-pedalling, backward motion, backward step;
sternway; **backsliding,** lapse, relapse, recidivism,
recidivation; arrested development

2 retreat, *reculade* <Fr>, motion from, **withdrawal,**
withdrawment, strategic withdrawal, exfiltration;
retirement, fallback, pullout, pullback; advance to
the rear; rout; disengagement; **backing down** *or*
off *or* **out** <nf>; reneging, copping *or* weaseling
out <nf>, resigning, resignation

3 reverse, reversal, reversing, reversion, inversion;
backing, backing up, backup, backflow; **about-face,**
volte-face <Fr>, about-turn, right-about, right-about-
face, turn to the right-about, U-turn, turnaround,
turnabout, swingaround; back track, back trail;
turn of the tide, reflux, refluence; role reversal

4 countermotion, countermovement, counteraction;
recoil, rebound; countermarching

VERBS **5 regress,** go backwards, **recede,** return,
revert; **retrogress,** retrograde, retroflex, retrocede;
pull back, jerk back, reach back, cock <the arm,
fist, etc>; *reculer pour mieux sauter* <Fr>; fall *or*
get *or* go behind, fall astern, lose ground, slip
back; **backslide,** lapse, relapse, recidivate; go
down the tubes *or* drain <nf>

6 retreat, sound *or* beat a retreat, beat a hasty
retreat, **withdraw, retire,** pull out *or* back,
backtrack, exfiltrate, advance to the rear,
disengage; **fall back,** move back, go back, stand
back; run back; **draw back,** draw off; **back out** *or*
out of *and* back off *and* back down *or* back
away<nf>; defer, give ground, give place, take a
back seat, play second fiddle; resign; crawfish *or*
crawfish out <nf>, turn tail <nf>

7 reverse, go into reverse; **back, back up,** backpedal,
back off *or* away, go into reverse; **backwater,** make
sternway; **backtrack,** backtrail, take the back
track; countermarch; reverse one's field; take the
reciprocal course; have second thoughts, think
better of it, cut one's losses, go back to the
drawing board

8 turn back, put back; double, double back, retrace
one's steps; turn one's back upon; **return,** go *or*
come back, go *or* come home

9 turn round *or* **around** *or* **about,** turn, make a
U-turn, turn on a dime, turn tail, **come** *or* **go**
about, put about, fetch about; veer, veer around;
swivel, pivot, pivot about, swing, round, swing
round; wheel, wheel about, double wheel, whirl,
spin; heel, turn upon one's heel; recoil, rebound,
quail

10 about-face, *volte-face* <Fr>, right-about-face, **do an**
about-face *or* a right-about-face *or* an about-turn,
perform a *volte-face,* **face about,** turn *or* face to
the right-about, do a turn to the right-about

ADJS **11 regressive,** recessive; **retrogressive,**
retrocessive, retrograde, retral; retroactive;
reactionary

12 backward, reversed, reflex, **turned around,** back;
wrong-way, wrong-way around, counter, ass-
backwards *and* bassackwards <nf>

ADVS **13 backwards,** backward, retrally, **hindwards,**
hindward, **rearwards,** rearward, arear, astern;
back, away, fro, *à reculons* <Fr>; **in reverse,**
ass-backwards <nf>; against the grain, *à rebours*
<Fr>; counterclockwise, anticlockwise,
widdershins; vice versa

WORD ELEMENTS **14** an-, ana-, re-, retro-

164 DEVIATION

<indirect course>

NOUNS **1 deviation,** deviance *or* deviancy,
deviousness, **departure, digression,** diversion,
divergence, divarication, branching off,
divagation, declination, aberration, aberrancy,
variation, indirection, exorbitation; tangent,
parenthesis; detour, excursion, excursus,
discursion; obliquity, bias, skew, slant;
circuitousness 914; wandering, rambling,
straying, errantry, pererration; drift, drifting,
driftage; turning, shifting, swerving, swinging;
turn, corner, bend, curve, dogleg, crook, hairpin,
zigzag, twist, warp, swerve, **veer,** sheer, sweep;
shift, double; tack, yaw; wandering *or* twisting *or*
zigzag *or* shifting course *or* path, slalom course;
long way around; margin of error

2 deflection, bending, deflexure, flection, flexure;
torsion, distortion, contortion, torture *or*
torturing, twisting, warping; skewness; **refraction,**
diffraction, scatter, diffusion, dispersion;
sidestep, crabwalk

VERBS **3 deviate, depart from, vary, diverge,**
divaricate, branch off, angle, angle off; **digress,**
divagate, turn aside, go out of the way, detour, take
a side road; **swerve, veer,** sheer, curve, **shift, turn,**
trend, bend, heel, bear off; turn right, turn left,
hang a right *or* left <nf>; alter one's course, make a
course correction, change the bearing; tack 182.30

4 stray, go astray, lose one's way, err; go off on a tangent; take a wrong turn *or* turning; drift, go adrift; **wander,** wander off, ramble, rove, straggle, divagate, excurse, pererrate; meander, wind, twist, snake, twist and turn; lose one's bearings

5 deflect, deviate, **divert,** diverge, **bend,** curve, pull, crook, dogleg, hairpin, zigzag; **warp,** bias, twist, distort, contort, torture, skew; refract, diffract, **scatter, diffuse, disperse;** put rudder on

6 avoid, evade, dodge, duck <nf>, turn aside *or* to the side, draw aside, **turn away,** jib, shy, shy off; gee, haw; **sidetrack,** shove aside, shunt, switch; **avert; head off,** turn back 908.3; **step aside,** sidestep, move aside *or* to the side, sidle; **steer clear of,** make way for, get out of the way of; go off, bear off, sheer off, veer off, ease off, edge off; fly off, go *or* fly off at a tangent; glance, glance off

ADJS **7 deviative,** deviatory, deviating, **deviant,** departing, aberrant, aberrational, aberrative, shifting, turning, swerving, veering; **digressive,** discursive, excursive, **circuitous; devious,** indirect, out-of-the-way; errant, erratic, zigzag, doglegged, **wandering,** rambling, roving, winding, twisting, meandering, snaky, serpentine, mazy, labyrinthine, vagrant, stray, desultory, planetary, undirected; out of sync <nf>; off-message

8 deflective, inflective, flectional, diffractive, refractive; refractile, refrangible; deflected, flexed, refracted, diffracted, scattered, diffuse, diffused, dispersed; distorted, skewed, skew; off-course, off-target, wide of the mark

9 avertive, evasive, dodging, dodgy, artful

165 LEADING
<going ahead>

NOUNS **1 leading, heading,** foregoing; anteposition, the lead, *le pas* <Fr>; **preceding,** precedence 814; priority 834.1; front, point, leading edge, cutting edge, forefront, vanguard, bleeding edge, van 216.2; vaunt-courier <old>, herald, precursor 816

VERBS **2 lead, head,** spearhead, stand at the head, stand first, be way ahead <nf>, head the line; take the lead, go in the lead, **lead the way,** break the trail, be the bellwether, lead the pack; be the point *or* point man; lead the dance; **light the way,** show the way, beacon, guide; get before, get ahead *or* in front of, come to the front, come to the fore, lap, outstrip, pace, set the pace; not look back; get *or* have the start, get a head start, steal a march upon; **precede** 814.2, **go before** 816.3

ADJS **3 leading, heading,** precessional, precedent, precursory, foregoing; **first, foremost,** headmost; **preceding,** antecedent 814.4; **prior** 834.4; **chief** 249.14

ADVS **4 before** 814.6, in front, out in front, in the lead, outfront, foremost, headmost, in the the van, in the forefront, in advance 216.12

166 FOLLOWING
<going behind>

NOUNS **1 following,** heeling, **trailing,** tailing <nf>, shadowing; **hounding, dogging,** chasing, **pursuit,** pursual, pursuance; sequence 815; sequel 817; series 812.2

2 follower, successor; shadow *and* tail <nf>; **pursuer,** pursuivant; **attendant** 769.4, **satellite, hanger-on,** dangler, adherent, appendage, dependent, parasite, stooge <nf>, flunky; **henchman,** ward heeler, partisan, supporter, votary, sectary; camp follower, groupy <nf>; fan *and* buff <nf>; courtier, *homme de cour* <Fr>, *cavaliere servente* <Ital>; trainbearer; **public; entourage, following** 769.6; disciple 572.2, discipleship

VERBS **3 follow,** go after *or* behind, come after *or* behind, move behind; **pursue, shadow** *and* **tail** <nf>, **trail,** trail after, follow in the trail of, camp on the trail of, **heel,** follow *or* tread *or* step on the heels of, follow in the steps *or* footsteps *or* footprints of, tread close upon, breathe down the neck of, follow in the wake of, hang on the skirts of, stick like the shadow of, sit on the tail of, tailgate <nf>, go in the rear of, bring up the rear, eat the dust of, take *or* swallow one's dust; tag *and* **tag after** *and* tag along <nf>; string along <nf>; **dog,** bedog, **hound,** chase, chase after, get after, take out *or* take off after, **pursue;** haunt

4 lag, lag behind, straggle, lag back, drag, trail, **trail behind,** hang back *or* behind, loiter, linger, **loiter** *or* **linger behind,** dawdle, get behind; fall behind *or* behindhand, let grass grow under one's feet

ADJS **5 following,** trailing, on the track *or* trail; succeeding 815.4; back-to-back <nf>, consequent, consecutive 812.9

ADVS **6 behind, after,** in the rear, in the train *or* wake of; in back of 217.13

167 APPROACH
<motion towards>

NOUNS **1 approach,** approaching, coming *or* going toward, coming *or* going near, proximation, appropinquation <old>, **access,** accession, nearing; advance, oncoming; **advent, coming,** forthcoming; flowing toward, afflux, affluxion; appulse; nearness 223; imminence 840; approximation 223.1; approach shot

2 **approachability, accessibility, access,** getatableness *and* come-at-ableness <nf>, attainability, openness

VERBS 3 **approach, near, draw near** *or* nigh, go *or* come near, go *or* come toward, come closer *or* nearer, come to close quarters; **close,** close in, close in on, close with; zoom in on; **accost,** encounter, confront; proximate, appropinquate <old>; **advance,** come, **come forward,** come on, come up, bear up, bear down, step up; ease *or* edge *or* sidle up to; bear down on *or* upon, be on a collision course with; gain upon, narrow the gap; approximate 784.7/223.8

ADJS 4 **approaching, nearing,** advancing; attracted to, drawn to; **coming, oncoming, forthcoming,** upcoming, to come, provenient; approximate, proximate, approximative; prospective; near 223.14; imminent 840.3

5 **approachable, accessible,** getatable *and* come-at-able <nf>, attainable, open, easy to find, meet, etc

168 RECESSION
<motion from>

NOUNS 1 **recession,** recedence, receding, retrocedence, ceding; **retreat, retirement, withdrawing, withdrawal;** retraction, retractation, retractility; fleetingness, fugitiveness, fugitivity, evanescence; ebb

VERBS 2 **recede,** retrocede, cede; **retreat, retire, withdraw;** move off *or* away, stand off *or* away, stand out from the shore; go, **go away; die away,** fade away, drift away; erode, wash away; **diminish,** decline, sink, shrink, dwindle, **fade, ebb,** wane; shy away, tail away, tail off; go out with the tide, fade into the distance; pull away, widen the distance

3 **retract,** withdraw, **draw** *or* **pull back,** pull out, draw *or* pull in; draw in one's claws *or* horns; defer, take a back seat, play second fiddle, back-pedal; **shrink,** wince, cringe, flinch, shy, fight shy, duck

ADJS 4 **recessive,** recessional, recessionary; recedent, retrocedent

5 **receding, retreating,** retiring, withdrawing; shy; **diminishing, declining,** sinking, shrinking, eroding, dwindling, **ebbing,** waning; **fading,** dying; fleeting, fugitive, evanescent

6 **retractile,** retractable, retrahent

169 CONVERGENCE
<coming together>

NOUNS 1 **convergence,** converging, confluence, concourse, conflux; mutual approach, approach 167; **meeting,** congress, concurrence, coming together; **concentration,** concentralization,

focalization 208.8, focus 208.4; meeting point, focal point, point of convergence, vanishing point; union, merger; crossing point, crossroads, crossing 170; collision course, narrowing gap; funnel, bottleneck; hub, spokes; asymptote; radius; tangent

VERBS 2 **converge, come together,** approach 167.3, run together, **meet,** unite, connect, merge; **cross, intersect** 170.6; fall in with, link up with; be on a collision course; go toward, narrow the gap, close with, close, close up, close in; funnel; taper, pinch, nip; centralize, center, **come to a center;** center on *or* around, concentralize, concenter, **concentrate,** come *or* tend to a point; **come to a focus** 208.10

ADJS 3 **converging,** convergent; **meeting,** uniting, merging; concurrent, confluent, mutually approaching, approaching; **crossing, intersecting** 170.8; connivent; **focal,** confocal, focusing, focused; centrolineal, centripetal; asymptotic, asymptotical; tangent, tangential, radial, radiating

170 CROSSING

NOUNS 1 **crossing, intercrossing,** intersecting, **intersection;** decussation, chiasma; traversal, transversion; cross section, transection; cruciation; **transit,** transiting; crisscross

2 **crossing,** crossway, **crosswalk, crossroad,** pedestrian crosswalk, zebra *or* zebra crossing <Brit>; *carrefour* <Fr>; **intersection,** intercrossing; level crossing, grade crossing; crossover, overpass, flyover <Brit>, viaduct, undercrossing; traffic circle, rotary, roundabout <Brit>; highway interchange, **interchange,** cloverleaf, spaghetti junction <Brit>

3 **network, webwork, weaving** 740, **meshwork,** tissue, crossing over and under, interlacement, intertwinement, intertexture, texture, reticulum, reticulation, plexus; "Any thing reticulated or decussated, at equal distances, with interstices between the intersections"—Samuel Johnson; crossing-out, cancellation, scrubbing <nf>; **net,** netting; **mesh,** meshes; **web,** webbing; weave, weft; lace, lacery, lacing, lacework; screen, screening; sieve, riddle, raddle; wicker, wickerwork; basketwork, basketry; lattice, latticework; hachure *or* hatchure, hatching, cross-hatching; trellis, trelliswork, treillage; grate, grating; grille, grillwork; **grid,** gridiron; tracery, fretwork, fret, arabesque, filigree; plexus, plexure; reticle, reticule; wattle, wattle and daub

4 **cross,** crux, cruciform; **crucifix,** rood, tree *or* rood tree <old>; X *or* ex, exing, T, Y; **swastika,** gammadion, fylfot, *Hakenkreuz* <Ger>; crossbones; dagger

5 **crosspiece,** traverse, transverse, transversal, transept, transom, cross bitt; diagonal; **crossbar,** crossarm; swingletree, singletree, whiffletree, whippletree; doubletree

VERBS 6 **cross, crisscross,** cruciate; **intersect,** intercross, decussate; **cut across,** crosscut; **traverse,** transverse, lie across; bar, crossbar

7 net, web, mesh; lattice, trellis; grate, grid

ADJS 8 **cross, crossing, crossed; crisscross, crisscrossed; intersecting, intersected,** intersectional; crosscut, cut across; decussate, decussated; chiasmal *or* chiasmic *or* chiastic; secant

9 **transverse,** transversal, traverse; **across,** cross, crossway, **crosswise** *or* crossways, thwart, athwart, overthwart; oblique 204.13

10 **cruciform, crosslike,** cross-shaped, cruciate, X-shaped, cross, crossed; cruciferous

11 **netlike,** retiform, plexiform; **reticulated,** reticular, reticulate; cancellate, cancellated; **netted,** netty; **meshed,** meshy; laced, lacy, lacelike; filigreed; latticed, latticelike; grated, gridded; barred, crossbarred, mullioned; streaked, striped

12 **webbed,** webby, weblike, woven, interwoven, interlaced, intertwined; web-footed, palmiped

ADVS 13 **crosswise** *or* crossways *or* crossway, decussatively; **cross, crisscross, across,** thwart, thwartly, thwartways, **athwart,** athwartwise, overthwart; **traverse,** traversely; **transverse,** transversely, transversally; obliquely 204.21; **sideways** *or* sidewise; contrariwise, contrawise; crossgrained, across the grain, against the grain; athwartship, athwartships

171 DIVERGENCE
<recession from one another>

NOUNS 1 **divergence** *or* divergency, divarication; aberration, deviation 164; **separation,** division, decentralization; centrifugence; **radial, radiating,** radiating out, raying out, beaming out; **spread,** spreading, spreading out, splaying, fanning, fanning out, deployment; ripple effect

2 **radiation,** ray, sunray, radius, spoke; radiance, diffusion, scattering, dispersion, emanation; halo, aureole, glory, corona; ripple effect

3 **forking,** furcation, bifurcation, biforking, trifurcation, divarication, triforking; **branching,** branching off *or* out, **ramification;** arborescence, arborization

4 **fork, prong,** trident; Y, V; **branch, ramification,** stem, offshoot; **crotch,** crutch; **fan, delta; groin,** inguen; furcula, furculum, **wishbone**

VERBS 5 **diverge,** divaricate; aberrate; **separate,** divide, separate off, split off; spread, **spread out,**

outspread, splay, fan out, deploy; go off *or* away, **fly** *or* **go off at a tangent;** part company

6 **radiate,** radiate out, ray, ray out, beam out, diffuse, emanate, spread, disperse, scatter

7 **fork,** furcate, bifurcate, trifurcate, divaricate; **branch,** stem, ramify, branch off *or* out, spread-eagle

ADJS 8 **diverging,** divergent; divaricate, divaricating; palmate, palmated; fanlike, fan-shaped; deltoid, deltoidal, deltalike, delta-shaped; splayed; centrifugal

9 **radiating,** radial, radiate, radiated; rayed, spoked; radiative

10 **forked, forking,** furcate, biforked, bifurcate, bifurcated, forklike, trifurcate, trifurcated, tridentlike, pronged; **crotched,** Y-shaped, V-shaped; **branched, branching;** arborescent, arboreal, arboriform, treelike, tree-shaped, dendriform, dendritic; branchlike, ramous

172 MOTION
<motion in general>

NOUNS 1 **motion; movement,** moving, **momentum; stir,** unrest, restlessness; **going,** running, stirring; **operation,** operating, **working,** ticking; **activity** 330; kinesis, kinetics, kinematics; dynamics; kinesiatrics, kinesipathy, kinesitherapy, kinesiology; **actuation,** motivation; mobilization

2 **course, career,** set, midcareer, **passage, progress,** trend, **advance,** forward motion, going *or* moving on, momentum; **travel** 177; **flow,** flux, flight, **trajectory; stream, current,** run, rush, onrush, ongoing; drift, driftage; backward motion, **regression,** retrogression, sternway, backing, going *or* moving backwards; backflowing, reflowing, refluence, reflux, ebbing, subsiding, withdrawing; downward motion, **descent,** descending, sinking, plunging; upward motion, mounting, climbing, rising, **ascent,** ascending, **soaring,** mounting; oblique *or* crosswise motion; sideward *or* sidewise *or* sideways motion; radial motion, angular motion, axial motion; random motion, Brownian movement; perpetual motion

3 **mobility, motivity,** motility, movableness, movability; **locomotion;** motive power

4 **velocity** 174.1,2, rate, gait, pace, tread, step, stride, clip *and* lick <nf>

VERBS 5 **move, budge, stir;** go, run, flow, stream; **progress,** advance; wend, wend one's way; **back,** back up, regress, retrogress; ebb, subside, wane; **descend,** sink, plunge; **ascend,** mount, rise, climb, soar; go sideways, go crabwise; go round *or* around, circle, rotate, gyrate, spin, whirl; travel; move over, get over; shift, change, shift *or* change place; **speed** 174.8; **hurry** 401.5, do on the fly *or* run

6 **set in motion, move, actuate,** motivate, push, shove, nudge, **drive,** impel, propel; mobilize; dispatch; muster

ADJS 7 **moving, stirring, in motion;** transitional; **mobile,** motive, motile, motor, motorial, motoric; motivational, impelling, propelling, propellant, driving, self-propelled; traveling; **active** 330.17

8 **flowing,** fluent, passing, streaming, flying, **running, going, progressive,** rushing, onrushing; drifting; **regressive,** retrogressive, back, **backward;** back-flowing, refluent, reflowing; descending, sinking, plunging, **downward,** down-trending; ascending, mounting, rising, soaring, **upward,** up-trending; sideward, sidewise, sideways; **rotary,** rotatory, rotational, round-and-round; axial, gyrational, gyratory

ADVS 9 **under way,** under sail, on one's way, on the go *or* move *or* fly *or* run *or* march, **in motion, astir;** from pillar to post

WORD ELEMENTS 10 moto-; -kinesia, kin-, kine-, kino-, kinesi-, kinesio-, kinet-, kineto-

173 QUIESCENCE
<being at rest; absence of motion>

NOUNS 1 **quiescence,** *or* quiescency, **stillness,** silence 51, quietness, **quiet,** quietude, "lucid stillness" —T S Eliot; **calmness,** restfulness, **peacefulness,** imperturbability, passiveness, passivity, "wise passiveness"—Wordsworth, placidness, **placidity, tranquillity, serenity, peace, composure;** quietism, contemplation, satori, nirvana, samadhi, ataraxy *or* ataraxia; **rest, repose,** silken repose, statuelike *or* marmoreal repose; sleep, slumber 22.2

2 **motionlessness, immobility; inactivity, inaction;** fixity, fixation 855.2

3 **standstill, stand,** stillstand; **stop, halt, cessation** 857; dead stop, dead stand, full stop; deadlock, lock, dead set; gridlock, stalemate, stoppage; freeze, strike; running *or* dying down, subsidence, waning, ebbing, wane, ebb

4 **inertness, dormancy; inertia,** *vis inertiae* <L>; passiveness, passivity; suspense, abeyance, latency; torpor, apathy, indifference, indolence, lotus-eating, languor; **stagnation,** stagnancy, **vegetation;** estivation, hibernation; stasis; sloth; deathliness, deadliness; catalepsy, catatonia; entropy

5 **calm, lull,** lull *or* calm before the storm; dead calm, flat calm, oily calm, windlessness, deathlike calm; doldrums, horse latitudes; anticyclone, eye of the hurricane

6 **stuffiness, airlessness, closeness, oppressiveness,** stirlessness, oppression

VERBS 7 **be still, keep quiet,** lie still; **stop moving,** cease motion, freeze *or* seize up, come to a standstill; **rest, repose; remain, stay,** tarry; remain motionless, freeze <nf>; stand, **stand still,** be at a standstill; stand *or* stick fast, stick, stand firm, stay put <nf>; stand like a post; **not stir,** not stir a step, not move a muscle; not breathe, hold one's breath; bide, bide one's time, mark time, tread water, coast; rest on one's oars, put one's feet up, rest and be thankful

8 **quiet,** quieten, **lull, soothe,** quiesce, **calm,** calm down, tranquilize 670.7, pacify, passivize, assuage, pour oil on troubled waters; **stop** 857.7, halt, bring to a standstill; **cease** 857.6, wane, subside, ebb, run *or* die down, die off, dwindle, molder

9 **stagnate, vegetate,** fust <old>; estivate, hibernate; sleep, slumber; smolder, hang fire; **idle**

10 **sit,** set <nf>, **sit down, be seated,** remain seated, remain in situ; perch, roost

11 **becalm,** take the wind out of one's sails

ADJS 12 **quiescent, quiet, still,** stilly <old>, stillish, hushed; quiet as a mouse; waning, subsiding, ebbing, dwindling, moldering; **at rest,** resting, reposing; restful, reposeful, relaxed, sedentary; cloistered, sequestered, sequestrated, isolated, secluded, sheltered; **calm, tranquil, peaceful,** peaceable, pacific, halcyon; **placid, smooth; unruffled, untroubled,** cool, undisturbed, unperturbed, unagitated, unmoved, unstirring, laid-back <nf>; stolid, stoic, stoical, impassive; even-tenored; calm as a mill pond; still as death

13 **motionless, unmoving,** unmoved, moveless, **immobile,** immotive; **still, fixed, stationary, static,** at a standstill; **stock-still,** dead-still; still as a statue, statuelike; still as a mouse; at anchor, riding at anchor; **idle,** unemployed; out of commission, down

14 **inert, inactive, static, dormant,** passive, sedentary; **latent,** unaroused, suspended, abeyant, in suspense *or* abeyance; sleeping, slumbering; estivating, hibernating; smoldering; **stagnant,** standing, foul; **torpid, languorous, languid,** apathetic, phlegmatic, **sluggish,** logy, dopey <nf>, groggy, heavy, leaden, **dull,** flat, slack, tame, **dead,** lifeless; catatonic, cataleptic

15 **untraveled, stay-at-home,** stick-in-the-mud <nf>, home-keeping

16 **stuffy, airless,** breathless, breezeless, windless; **close, oppressive, stifling, suffocating;** stirless, unstirring, not a breath of air, not a leaf stirring; ill-ventilated, unventilated, unvented

17 **becalmed,** in a dead calm

ADVS **18** quiescently, **quietly,** stilly, still; **calmly, tranquilly, peacefully,** serenely; **placidly,** smoothly, unperturbedly, **coolly**

19 motionlessly, movelessly, stationarily, fixedly

20 inertly, inactively, statically, dormantly, passively, latently; stagnantly; **torpidly, languorously, languidly; like a bump on a log; sluggishly,** heavily, dully, coldly, lifelessly, apathetically, phlegmatically; stoically, stolidly, impassively

174 SWIFTNESS

NOUNS **1 velocity, speed; rapidity,** celerity, **swiftness,** fastness, **quickness,** snappiness <nf>, **speediness;** haste 401.1, hurry, flurry, rush, precipitation; **dispatch, expedition, promptness,** promptitude, instantaneousness; flight, flit; lightning speed; fast *or* swift rate, smart *or* rattling *or* spanking *or* lively *or* snappy pace, round pace; relative velocity, angular velocity; air speed, ground speed, speed over the bottom; miles per hour, knots; rpm 915.3; momentum

2 speed of sound, sonic speed, Mach, Mach number, Mach one, Mach two, etc; subsonic speed; supersonic *or* ultrasonic *or* hypersonic *or* transsonic speed; transsonic barrier, sound barrier; escape velocity; speed of light, terminal velocity; warp speed, lightning speed; turbulent flow

3 run, sprint; dash, rush, plunge, headlong rush *or* plunge, **race, scurry, scamper,** scud, scuttle, **spurt,** burst, **burst of speed;** canter, **gallop,** lope; high lope, hand gallop, full gallop; dead run; **trot,** extended trot, dogtrot, jog trot; **full speed,** open throttle, flat-out speed <Brit>, wide-open speed, heavy right foot, maximum speed; **fast-forward;** fast track *or* lane; forced draft *and* flank speed <nautical>

4 acceleration, quickening; pickup, getaway; burst of speed; step-up, speedup; thrust, drive, impetus, kick-start; free fall; flying start; headlong plunge; overtaking; zip *or* zing <nf>

5 speeder, speedster, scorcher *and* hell-driver <nf>, **sprinter,** harrier; flier, goer, stepper; hummer *and* hustler *and* sizzler <nf>; **speed demon** *or* maniac <nf>, **racer, runner;** horse racer, turfman, jockey; Jehu; express messenger, courier

6 <comparisons> lightning, greased lightning <nf>, thunderbolt, flash, streak of lightning, streak, blue streak <nf>, bat out of hell <nf>, light, electricity, thought, wind, shot, bullet, cannonball, rocket, arrow, dart, quicksilver, mercury, express train, jet plane, torrent, eagle, swallow, antelope, courser, gazelle, greyhound, hare, blue darter, striped snake, scared rabbit

7 speedometer, accelerometer; cyclometer; tachometer; Mach meter; knotmeter, log, log line, patent log, taffrail log, harpoon log, ground log; windsock; wind gauge, anemometer

VERBS **8 speed, go fast,** skim, **fly,** flit, fleet, wing one's way, outstrip the wind; **zoom;** make knots, foot; break the sound barrier, go at warp speed; go like the wind, go like a shot *or* flash, go like lightning *or* a streak of lightning, go like greased lightning; **rush, tear,** dash, dart, shoot, hurtle, bolt, fling, **scamper, scurry,** scour, scud, scuttle, scramble, **race,** careen; **hasten,** haste, make haste, **hurry** 401.4, hie, post, kick-start; march in quick *or* double-quick time; **run, sprint, trip,** spring, **bound,** leap; gallop, lope, canter; trot; **make time,** make good time, **cover ground,** get over the ground, **make strides** *or* **rapid strides,** make the best of one's way

9 <nf terms> **barrel,** clip, spank *or* cut along, tear *or* tear along *or* off, bowl along, thunder along, storm along, breeze *or* breeze along, tear up the track *or* road, eat up the track *or* road, scorch, sizzle, rip, zip, whiz, whisk, sweep, brush, nip, zing, fly low, highball, ball the jack, pour it on, boom, shake *or* get the lead out, lollop <Brit>, give it the gun, skedaddle, scoot, step on it, step on the gas, hump *or* hump it, stir one's stumps, hotfoot, hightail, make tracks, step lively, step, step along, carry the mail, hop, hop along, hop it, get, git, go like a bat out of hell, run like a scared rabbit, run like mad, go at full blast, go all out, go flat out, run wide open, go at full tilt *or* steam, let her out, open her up, go hell-bent for election *or* leather, get a move on, give it the gas, go like blazes *or* blue blazes, floor it, let her rip, put the pedal to the metal, tool

10 accelerate, speed up, step up <nf>, **hurry up, quicken; hasten** 401.4; crack on, put on, put on steam, pour on the coal, put on more speed, open the throttle; quicken one's pace; pick up speed, gain ground; race <a motor>, rev <nf>

11 <nautical terms> put on sail, crack *or* pack on sail, crowd sail, press her

12 spurt, make a spurt *or* dash, **dash** *or* dart *or* shoot ahead, rush ahead, put on *or* make a burst of speed; make one's move, plunge

13 overtake, outstrip, overhaul, catch up, **catch up with,** come up with *or* to, gain on *or* upon, pass, lap; outpace, outrun, outsail; leave behind, leave standing *or* looking *or* flatfooted; overwhelm

14 keep up with, keep pace with, run neck and neck

ADJS **15 fast, swift, speedy, rapid; quick,** double-quick, express, **fleet, hasty, expeditious,** hustling, snappy <nf>, rushing, onrushing, dashing, flying, galloping, running, **agile, nimble,** lively, nimble-footed, fleet-footed, light-footed, light-legged, light of heel; winged, eagle-winged; mercurial; quick as lightning, quick as thought, swift as an arrow; **breakneck,** reckless, headlong, precipitate; quick as a wink, quick on the trigger <nf>, hair-trigger <nf>; **prompt** 845.9; rapid-response

16 **supersonic,** transonic, ultrasonic, hypersonic, faster than sound; warp; **high-speed,** high-velocity, high-geared

ADVS 17 **swiftly, rapidly, quickly,** snappily <nf>, **speedily,** with speed, **fast, quick,** apace, amain, on eagle's wings, *ventre à terre* <Fr>; at a great rate, at a good clip <nf>, with rapid strides, with giant strides, *à pas de géant* <Fr>, in seven-league boots, **by leaps and bounds,** trippingly; **lickety-split** *and* lickety-cut <nf>; hell-bent *and* hell-bent for election *and* hell-bent for leather <nf>; **posthaste,** post, **hastily,** expeditiously, promptly, with great *or* all haste, whip and spur, **hand over hand** *or* **fist;** double-quick, in double time, in double-quick time, on the double *or* the double-quick <nf>; in high gear, in high; under press of sail, all sails set, under crowded sails, under press of sail and steam, under forced draft, at flank speed <all nautical>

18 <nf terms> **like a shot, as if shot out of a cannon, like a flash,** like a streak, like a blue streak, like a streak of lightning, like lightning, like greased lightning, **like a bat out of hell, like a scared rabbit,** like a house afire, like sixty, like mad *and* **crazy** *and* fury, like sin, to beat the band *or* the Dutch *or* the deuce *or* the devil

19 **in short order, in no time,** instantaneously, immediately if not sooner, in less than no time, in nothing flat <nf>; in a jiff *or* jiffy <nf>, before you can say Jack Robinson, **in a flash,** in a twink, **in a twinkling,** "in the twinkling of an eye"—Bible, *tout de suite* <Fr>, pronto <nf>, PDQ *or* pretty damn quick <nf>

20 **at full speed,** with all speed, at full throttle, **at the top of one's bent, for all one is worth** <nf>, hit the ground running <nf>, as fast as one's legs will carry one, as fast as one can lay feet to the ground; **at full blast,** at full drive *or* pelt; under full steam, in full sail; **all out** <nf>, flat out <Brit>, **wide open;** full speed ahead

175 SLOWNESS

NOUNS 1 **slowness, leisureliness,** pokiness, slackness, creeping, no hurry; **sluggishness,** sloth, torpor, laziness, idleness, indolence, sluggardy, languor, inertia, inertness, lentitude *or* lentor <old>; deliberateness, deliberation, circumspection, tentativeness, cautiousness, reluctance, foot-dragging <nf>; drawl; gradualism; hesitation, slow start

2 **slow motion, leisurely gait,** snail's *or* tortoise's pace; **creep, crawl; walk,** footpace, dragging *or* lumbering pace, trudge, waddle, saunter, stroll; slouch, shuffle, plod, shamble; limp, claudication, hobble; dogtrot, jog trot; jog, rack; mincing steps; slow march, dead *or* funeral march, largo, andante

3 **dawdling, lingering, loitering, tarrying,** dalliance, **dallying,** dillydallying, shillyshallying, lollygagging, dilatoriness, delaying tactic, delayed action, procrastination 846.5, lag, **lagging,** goofing off <nf>; tardiness, unhurriedness

4 **slowing, retardation,** retardment, **slackening,** flagging, slowing down *or* up; **slowdown,** slowup, **letup, letdown, slack-up, slack-off,** ease-off, ease-up; **deceleration,** negative *or* minus acceleration; **delay** 846.2, **detention, setback, holdup** <nf>, check, arrest, brake, obstruction; lag, drag

5 **slowpoke** *and* slowcoach <nf>, plodder, slow goer, slow-foot, **lingerer, loiterer, dawdler,** dawdle, **laggard,** procrastinator, foot-dragger, lollygagger, stick-in-the-mud <nf>, drone, slug, sluggard, lie-abed, sleepy-head, slow starter, goof-off <nf>, goldbrick <nf>; tortoise, snail; lardass <nf>; Sunday driver

VERBS 6 **go slow** *or* **slowly,** go at a snail's pace, take it slow, get no place fast <nf>; **drag,** drag out; **creep, crawl;** laze, idle; go dead slow, get nowhere fast; inch, inch along; worm, worm along; poke, **poke along;** shuffle *or* stagger *or* totter *or* toddle along *or* toddle off; drag along, drag one's feet, walk, traipse *and* **mosey** <nf>; **saunter, stroll, amble,** waddle, toddle <nf>; jogtrot, dogtrot; limp, hobble, claudicate; *festina lente* <L>

7 **plod,** plug <nf>, peg, shamble, **trudge,** tramp, stump, lumber; plod along, plug along <nf>, schlep <nf>; rub on, jog on, chug on

8 **dawdle, linger, loiter, tarry, delay, dally, dillydally,** shilly-shally, lollygag, waste time, **take one's time,** take one's own sweet time; goof off *or* around <nf>; lag, drag, trail; flag, falter, halt, not get started

9 **slow, slow down** *or* **up, let down** *or* **up, ease off** *or* **up, slack off** *or* **up, slacken,** relax, moderate, taper off, lose speed *or* momentum; **decelerate, retard, delay** 846.8, **detain,** impede, obstruct, arrest, stay, **check,** curb, **hold up, hold back,** keep back, set back, hold in check; draw rein, rein in; throttle down, take one's foot off the gas; idle, barely tick over; brake, **put on the brakes,** put on the drag; reef, take in sail; backwater, backpedal; lose ground; clip the wings; regress

ADJS 10 **slow, leisurely,** slack, moderate, gentle, **easy,** deliberate, go-slow, unhurried, relaxed, gradual, circumspect, tentative, cautious, reluctant, foot-dragging <nf>; **creeping, crawling; poking,** poky, slow-poky <nf>; tottering, staggering, toddling, trudging, **lumbering,** ambling, waddling, shuffling, **sauntering,** strolling; **sluggish,** languid, languorous, lazy, slothful, indolent, idle, slouchy; **slow-going, slow-moving,** slow-creeping, slow-crawling, slow-running, slow-sailing; **slow-footed,** slow-foot, slow-legged, slow-gaited, slow-paced, slow-stepped, easy-paced, slow-winged; snail-paced, snail-like, tortoiselike, turtlelike, "creeping like snail"—Shakespeare; limping, hobbling, hobbled; halting, claudicant, faltering, flagging; slow as slow, slow as molasses *or* molasses in January, slow as death, slower than the seven-year itch <nf>

11 **dawdling, lingering, loitering, tarrying, dallying, dillydallying,** shilly-shallying, lollygagging, procrastinatory *or* procrastinative, dilatory, delaying 846.17, **lagging,** dragging

12 **retarded,** slowed-down, eased, slackened; **delayed, detained,** checked, **arrested,** impeded, set back, backward, behind; late, **tardy** 846.16

ADVS 13 **slowly,** slow, **leisurely,** unhurriedly, relaxedly, easily, moderately, gently; creepingly, crawlingly; pokingly, pokily; **sluggishly,** languidly, languorously, lazily, indolently, idly, deliberately, with deliberation, circumspectly, tentatively, cautiously, reluctantly; **lingeringly,** loiteringly, tarryingly, dilatorily; limpingly, haltingly, falteringly; **in slow motion,** at a funeral pace, with faltering *or* halting steps; at a snail's *or* turtle's pace, "in haste like a snail"—John Heywood; in slow tempo, in march time; with agonizing slowness; in low gear; under easy sail

14 **gradually,** little by little 245.6

PHRS 15 **easy does it,** take it easy, go easy, slack off, slow down

176 TRANSFERAL, TRANSPORTATION

1 **transferal, transfer; transmission,** transference, transmittal, transmittance; transposition, transposal, transplacement; mutual transfer, interchange, metathesis; translocation, transplantation, translation; migration, transmigration; **import, importation; export, exportation;** deportation, extradition, expulsion, **transit,** transition, **passage; communication,** spread, spreading, dissemination, diffusion, contagion, ripple effect; metastasis; transmigration of souls, metempsychosis; passing over; osmosis, diapedesis; transduction, conduction, convection; transfusion, perfusion; transfer of property *or* right 629

2 transferability, conveyability; transmissibility, transmittability; movability, removability; **portability,** transportability; communicability, impartability; deliverability; carrying forward

3 **transportation, conveyance, transport, carrying,** bearing, packing, toting *and* lugging <nf>; **carriage,** carry, **hauling,** haulage, portage, porterage, waft, waftage; **cartage, truckage,** drayage, wagonage; ferriage, lighterage; telpherage; **freightage,** freight, expressage, railway express; **airfreight, air express,** airlift; **package freight,** package service; **shipment, shipping,** transshipment; containerization, cargo-handling; delivery 478.1; travel 177; expressage; public transportation

4 **moving, removal, movement,** relocation, shift, removement, remotion; **displacement,** delocalization

5 people mover, moving sidewalk, automated monorail; conveyor belt; **elevator,** lift <Brit>, escalator 912.4

6 **freight,** freightage; **shipment, consignment,** goods <Brit>; **cargo,** payload; lading, load, pack; **baggage, luggage,** impedimenta

7 **carrier, conveyer;** transporter, hauler, carter, wagoner, drayman, shipper, trucker, common carrier, truck driver, driver; freighter; containerizer; stevedore, cargo handler; expressman, express, messenger, courier; importer, exporter; **bearer, porter,** redcap, skycap, bell boy; bus boy; coolie; litter-bearer, stretcher-bearer; caddie; shield-bearer, gun bearer; water carrier *or* bearer, water boy, bheesty <India>; the Water Bearer, Aquarius; letter carrier 353.5; cupbearer, Ganymede, Hebe; carrier pigeon, homing pigeon

8 **beast of burden; pack** *or* **draft animal,** pack horse *or* mule, sumpter, sumpter horse *or* mule; **horse** 311.13, ass, mule; ox; camel, ship of the desert, dromedary, llama; reindeer; elephant; sledge dog, husky, malamute, Siberian husky

9 <geological terms> **deposit,** sediment; drift, silt, loess, moraine, scree, sinter; alluvium, alluvion, diluvium; detritus, debris

VERBS 10 **transfer, transmit, transpose,** translocate, transplace, metathesize, switch; **transplant,** translate; **pass,** pass over, **hand over,** turn over, carry over, carry forward, make over, consign, assign; **deliver** 478.13; pass on, pass the buck <nf>, hand forward, hand on, relay; **import, export;** deport, extradite, expel, communicate, diffuse, disseminate, spread, impart; expedite; transfuse, perfuse, transfer property *or* right 629

11 **remove, move, relocate, shift,** send, shunt; displace, delocalize, dislodge; **take away,** cart off

or away, carry off *or* away; manhandle; set *or* lay *or* put aside, put *or* set to one side, side

12 transport, convey, freight, conduct, **take; carry, bear,** pack, tote *and* lug <nf>, manhandle; lift, waft, whisk, wing, fly; schlep <nf>

13 haul, cart, truck, bus; **ship,** barge, lighter, ferry; raft, float

14 channel, put through channels; **pipe,** tube, pipeline, flume, **siphon, funnel,** tap

15 send, send off *or* away, send forth; **dispatch,** transmit, remit, consign, forward; expedite; **ship,** ship off, freight, airfreight, embark, containerize, **transship,** pass along, send on; **express,** air-express; express-mail; package-express; **post, mail,** airmail, drop a letter; messenger; export; e-mail; drop-ship

16 fetch, bring, go get, go and get, go to get, **go after,** go fetch, **go for,** call for, pick up; **get,** obtain, procure, secure; **bring back, retrieve;** chase after, run after, shag, fetch and carry

17 ladle, dip, scoop; bail, bucket; **dish,** dish out *or* up; cup; **shovel,** spade, fork; spoon; **pour,** decant

ADJS **18 transferable, conveyable; transmittable,** transmissible, transmissive, consignable, deliverable; **movable,** removable; **portable,** portative; transportable, transportative, transportive, carriageable; roadworthy, seaworthy, airworthy; importable, exportable; conductive, conductional; transposable, interchangeable; **communicable,** contagious, impartable; transfusable; metastatic *or* metastatical, metathetic *or* metathetical; mailable, expressable; assignable 629.5

ADVS **19** by transfer, from hand to hand, from door to door; by freight, by express, by rail, by trolley, by bus, by steamer, by airplane, by mail, by special delivery, by package express, by messenger, by hand; by e-mail

20 on the way, along the way, on the road *or* high road, **en route, in transit,** *in transitu* <L>, on the wing, as one goes; in passing, *en passant* <Fr>; in mid-progress

177 TRAVEL

NOUNS **1 travel,** traveling, going, journeying, touring, moving, **movement, motion, locomotion, transit, progress, passage,** course, crossing; commutation, straphanging; world travel, globe-trotting <nf>; junketing, jaunting; **tourism,** touristry

2 travels, journeys, **journeyings, wanderings,** voyagings, transits, peregrinations, peripatetics, migrations, transmigrations; odyssey

3 wandering, roving, roaming, rambling, gadding, traipsing <nf>, wayfaring, flitting, straying, drifting, gallivanting, peregrination, peregrinity, pilgrimage, errantry, divagation; roam, rove, ramble; **itinerancy,** itineracy **nomadism,** nomadization, gypsydom; vagabonding, vagabondism, vagabondage; **vagrancy,** hoboism, waltzing Matilda <Austral>; bumming <nf>; the open road; wanderyear, *Wanderjahr* <Ger>; **wanderlust**

4 migration, transmigration, passage, trek; run <of fish>, flight <of birds and insects>; swarm, swarming <of bees>; **immigration,** in-migration; **emigration,** out-migration, expatriation; remigration; intermigration

5 journey, trip, *jornada* <Sp>, peregrination, sally, **trek;** road trip; progress, course, run; **tour,** grand tour; tourist season, low season, high season; tourist class; travel agency *or* bureau, holiday company <chiefly Brit>; **conducted tour,** package tour *or* holiday; **excursion, jaunt, junket, outing,** pleasure trip; sight-seeing trip *or* tour, rubberneck tour <nf>; day-trip; round trip, circuit, turn; **cruise,** package cruise, cruise to nowhere; **expedition,** campaign; safari, hunting expedition, hunting trip, stalk, shoot, photography safari; **pilgrimage,** hajj; **voyage** 182.6

6 riding, driving; motoring, automobiling; busing; motorcycling, bicycling, cycling, pedaling, biking <nf>; **horseback riding,** horse-riding, equitation; horsemanship, manège; pony-trekking

7 ride, drive; spin *and* whirl <nf>; joyride <nf>; Sunday drive; airing; lift <nf>, pickup <nf>

8 walking, ambulation, perambulation, pedestrianism, shank's mare *or* pony <nf>, going on foot *or* afoot, footing *or* hoofing, footing it *or* hoofing it; strolling, sauntering, ambling, *flânerie* <Fr>; **tramping, marching, hiking,** backpacking, trail-hiking, footslogging, trudging, treading; lumbering, waddling; toddling, staggering, tottering; **hitchhiking** *and* hitching <nf>, thumbing *and* thumbing a ride <nf>; jaywalking

9 nightwalking, noctambulation, noctambulism; night-wandering, noctivagation; **sleepwalking,** somnambulation, somnambulism; sleepwalk

10 walk, ramble, amble, **hike, tramp,** traipse <nf>; slog, trudge, schlep <nf>; **stroll,** saunter; **promenade;** *passeggiata* <Ital>; jaunt, airing; **constitutional** <nf>, stretch; turn; peripatetic journey *or* exercise, peripateticism; walking tour *or* excursion; **march,** forced march, route march; parade

11 step, pace, stride; footstep, footfall, tread; hoofbeat, clop; hop, jump; skip, hippety-hop <nf>

12 gait, pace, walk, step, stride, tread; saunter, stroll, strolling gait; shuffle, shamble, hobble, limp, hitch, waddle; totter, stagger, lurch; toddle, paddle; slouch, droop, drag; mince, mincing steps, scuttle, prance, flounce, stalk, strut, swagger; slink, slither, sidle; jog; swing, roll; amble, single-foot, rack, piaffer; trot, gallop 174.3; lock step; velocity 174.1,2; slowness 175

13 **march;** quick *or* quickstep march, quickstep, quick time; lockstep; double march, double-quick, double time; slow march, slow time; half step; goose step

14 **leg, limb, shank;** hind leg, foreleg; gamb, jamb <heraldry>; shin, cnemis; ankle, tarsus; hock, gambrel; calf; knee; thigh; popliteal space, ham, drumstick; gigot

15 <nf terms> gams, stems, trotters, hind legs, underpinnings, wheels, shanks, sticks, pins, stumps

16 **gliding, sliding,** slipping, slithering, coasting, sweeping, flowing, sailing; **skating, skiing, tobogganing, sledding,** boarding; glide, slide, slither, sweep, skim, flow

17 **creeping, crawling,** going on all fours; sneaking, stealing, slinking, sidling, gumshoeing *and* pussyfooting <nf>, walking on eggs, padding, prowling, nightwalking; worming, snaking; tiptoeing, tiptoe, tippytoe; creep, crawl, scramble, scrabble; all fours

VERBS 18 **travel, go, move, pass,** fare, wayfare, fare forth, fetch, flit, hie, sashay <nf>, cover ground; **progress** 162.2; move on *or* along, go along; wend, **wend one's way;** betake oneself, direct one's course, bend one's steps *or* course; course, run, flow, stream; roll, roll on; commute, straphang

19 <go at a given speed> go, go at, reach, **make, do,** hit <nf>, clip off <nf>

20 **traverse, cross, travel over** *or* through, pass through, **go** *or* **pass over, cover,** measure, transit, track, range, range over *or* through, course, do, perambulate, peregrinate, overpass, go over the ground; patrol, reconnoiter, scout; sweep, go *or* make one's rounds, scour, scour the country; ply, voyage 182.13

21 **journey, travel,** make *or* take *or* go *or* go on a journey, **take** *or* **make a trip,** fare, **wayfare, gad around or** about, get around *or* about, navigate, trek, jaunt, peregrinate; junket, go on a junket; **tour;** hit the trail <nf>, take the road, go on the road; **cruise, go on a cruise, voyage** 182.13; go abroad, go to foreign places *or* shores, range the world, globe-trot <nf>; travel light, live out of a suitcase; pilgrimage, pilgrim, go on *or* make a pilgrimage; campaign, go overseas, go on an expedition, go on safari; go on a sight-seeing trip, sight-see, rubberneck <nf>

22 **migrate, transmigrate,** trek; flit, take wing; run <of fish>, swarm <of bees>; **emigrate,** out-migrate,

expatriate; **immigrate,** in-migrate; remigrate; intermigrate

23 **wander, roam, rove,** range, nomadize, **gad,** gad around *or* about, follow the seasons, wayfare, flit, traipse <nf>, gallivant, knock around *or* about *and* bat around *or* about <nf>, prowl, **drift, stray,** float around, straggle, **meander, ramble,** stroll, saunter, jaunt, peregrinate, pererrate, divagate, go *or* run about, go the rounds; **tramp,** hobo, bum *or* go on the bum <nf>, vagabond, vagabondize, take to the road, "travel the open road"—Whitman, beat one's way; **hit the road** *or* **trail** <nf>, walk the tracks *and* count ties <nf>, pound the pavement

24 **go for an outing** *or* **airing,** take the air, get some air; go for a walk; go for a ride

25 **go to, repair to,** resort to, hie to, hie oneself to, arise and go to, direct one's course to, turn one's tracks to, make one's way to, set foot in, bend one's steps to, betake oneself to, **visit,** drop in *or* around *or* by, make the scene <nf>

26 **creep, crawl,** scramble, scrabble, grovel, **go on hands and knees,** go on all fours; worm, worm along, worm one's way, snake; inch, inch along; **sneak, steal,** steal along; pussyfoot *and* gumshoe <nf>, slink, sidle, pad, prowl, nightwalk; **tiptoe,** tippytoe, go on tiptoe

27 **walk,** ambulate, peripateticate, pedestrianize, traipse <nf>; **step, tread, pace, stride,** pad; foot, foot it; leg, leg it; hoof it, ankle, go on the heel and toe, ride shank's mare *or* pony <nf>, ride the shoeleather *or* hobnail express, stump it <nf>; peg *or* jog *or* shuffle on *or* along; perambulate; circumambulate; jaywalk; power walk, exercise walk, speed walk, race walk

28 <ways of walking> **stroll,** saunter, *flâner* <Fr>; shuffle, scuff, scuffle, straggle, shamble, slouch; stride, straddle; **trudge, plod,** peg, traipse <nf>, clump, stump, slog, footslog, drag, **lumber, barge;** stamp, stomp <nf>, tromp; swing, roll, lunge; hobble, halt, limp, hitch, lurch; totter, stagger; toddle, paddle; waddle, wobble, wamble, wiggle; link, slither, sidle; stalk; **strut, swagger;** mince, sashay <nf>, scuttle, prance, tittup, flounce, trip, skip, foot; hop, jump, hippety-hop <nf>; jog, jolt; bundle, bowl along; **amble,** pace; singlefoot, rack; piaffe, piaffer

29 **go for a walk, perambulate, take a walk, take one's constitutional** <nf>, take a stretch, stretch the legs; **promenade,** *passeggiare* <Ital>, parade

30 **march,** mush, footslog, **tramp, hike,** backpack, trail-hike; route-march; file, defile, file off; **parade,** go on parade; goose-step, do the goose step; do the lock step

31 **hitchhike** *or* **hitch** <nf>, beat one's way, **thumb** *or*

thumb one's way <nf>, **catch a ride;** hitch *or* hook *or* bum *or* cadge *or* thumb a ride <nf>

32 **nightwalk,** noctambulate; **sleepwalk,** somnambulate, walk in one's sleep

33 **ride, go for a ride** *or* drive; go for a spin <nf>, take *or* go for a Sunday drive; **drive, chauffeur; motor,** taxi; bus; bike *and* cycle *and* wheel *and* pedal <nf>; **motorcycle, bicycle,** mountain bike; BMX, bicycle moto-cross; go by rail, entrain; joyride *or* take a joyride <nf>; catch *or* make a train <nf>

34 **go on horseback, ride, horse-ride** pony-trek; ride bareback; mount, take horse; hack; ride hard, clap spurs to one's horse; trot, amble, pace, canter, gallop, tittup, lope; prance, frisk, curvet, piaffe, caracole

35 **glide, coast, skim,** sweep, flow; **sail, fly,** flit; **slide,** slip, skid, skitter, sideslip, slither, glissade, surf; skate, ice-skate, roller-skate, rollerblade, skateboard; ski; snowboard, board; toboggan, sled, sleigh; bellywhop <nf>

ADJS 36 **traveling, going, moving,** trekking, passing; **progressing; itinerant,** itinerary, circuit-riding; **journeying, wayfaring,** strolling; **peripatetic;** ambulant, ambulatory; ambulative; perambulating, perambulatory; peregrine, peregrinative, pilgrimlike; locomotive; **walking, pedestrian, touring,** on tour, globe-trotting <nf>, globe-girdling, mundivagant <old>; touristic, touristical, touristy <nf>; expeditionary

37 **wandering, roving, roaming,** ranging, **rambling, meandering,** strolling, **straying,** straggling, shifting, flitting, landloping, errant, divagatory, discursive, circumforaneous; **gadding,** traipsing <nf>, gallivanting; **nomad,** nomadic, floating, drifting, gypsyish *or* gypsylike; **transient,** transitory, fugitive, peripatetic; **vagrant,** vagabond, vagabondish; **footloose,** footloose and fancy-free; **migratory,** migrational, transmigrant, transmigratory; viaggiatory

38 **nightwalking,** noctambulant, noctambulous; night-wandering, noctivagant; **sleepwalking,** somnambulant, somnambular

39 **creeping, crawling, on hands and knees, on all fours;** reptant, repent, reptile, reptatorial; **on tiptoe,** on tippytoe, atiptoe, tiptoeing, tiptoe, tippytoe

40 **traveled,** well-traveled, cosmopolitan

41 **wayworn,** way-weary, road-weary, leg-weary, **travel-worn,** travel-weary, travel-tired; travel-sated, travel-jaded; travel-soiled, travel-stained, dusty

ADVS 42 **on the move** *or* go, en route, in transit, on the wing *or* fly; on the run, on the jump <nf>, on the road, on the tramp *or* march; on the gad <nf>, on the bum <nf>

43 **on foot, afoot,** by foot, footback *or* on footback <nf>; on the heel and toe, on *or* by shank's mare *or* pony <nf>

44 **on horseback,** horseback, by horse, mounted, horse-drawn

178 TRAVELER

NOUNS 1 **traveler, goer,** viator, comer and goer, road warrior; **wayfarer, journeyer,** trekker; **tourist,** tourer; **tripper** <Brit>, day-tripper; cicerone, travel *or* tourist guide; **visitor,** visiting fireman <nf>; **excursionist, sightseer,** rubberneck *or* rubbernecker <nf>, looky-loo; **voyager,** cruise-goer, cruiser, sailor, mariner 183; **globe-trotter** <nf>, globe-girdler, world-traveler, cosmopolite; jet set, jet-setter; **pilgrim,** palmer, hajji; **passenger,** fare; **commuter,** straphanger <nf>; transient; passerby; adventurer, alpinist, climber, mountaineer, ecotourist, adventure traveler, adventure athlete; explorer, forty-niner, pioneer, pathfinder, voortrekker, trailblazer, trailbreaker; camper; fellow traveler; astronaut 1075.8

2 **wanderer, rover, roamer,** rambler, stroller, straggler, mover; **gad, gadabout** <nf>, runabout, go-about <nf>; **itinerant,** peripatetic, rolling stone, peregrine, peregrinator, bird of passage, migratory, visitant; **drifter** *and* **floater** <nf>; Wandering Jew, Ahasuerus, Ancient Mariner <Coleridge>, Argonaut, Flying Dutchman, Oisin, Ossian, Gulliver <Swift>, Ulysses, Odysseus <Homer>; wandering scholar, Goliard, *vaganti* <L>; strolling player, wandering minstrel, troubadour

3 **vagabond, vagrant,** vag <nf>; **bum** *or* bummer <nf>, loafer, wastrel, losel <old>, *lazzarone* <Ital>; **tramp,** turnpiker, piker, knight of the road, easy rider, **hobo** *or* bo <nf>, rounder <nf>, stiff *or* bindlestiff <nf>; landloper, sundowner *or* swagman *or* swagsman <Austral nf>; beggar 440.8; **waif,** homeless waif, bag person, dogie, stray, waifs and strays; ragamuffin, tatterdemalion; **gamin,** gamine, urchin, street urchin, dead-end kid <nf>, mudlark, guttersnipe <nf>; beachcomber, loafer, idler; ski bum, beach bum, surf bum, tennis bum; ragman, ragpicker

4 **nomad,** Bedouin, Arab; gypsy, Bohemian, Romany, *zingaro* <Ital>, *Zigeuner* <Ger>, *tzigane* <Fr>

5 **migrant,** migrator, trekker; **immigrant,** in-migrant; migrant *or* migratory worker; **emigrant,** out-migrant, *émigré* <Fr>; expatriate; **evacuee,** *évacué* <Fr>; displaced person *or* DP, stateless person, exile; wetback <nf>

6 **pedestrian, walker,** walkist; foot traveler, foot passenger, hoofer <nf>, footbacker <nf>,

ambulator, peripatetic; **hiker,** backpacker, trailsman, tramper; marcher, footslogger, foot soldier, infantryman, paddlefoot <nf>; **hitchhiker** <nf>; jaywalker; power walker, exercise walker, speed walker, race walker

7 **nightwalker,** noctambulist, noctambule, **sleepwalker,** somnambulist, somnambulator, somnambule

8 **rider, equestrian, horseman,** horserider, horseback rider, horsebacker, *caballero* <Sp>, cavalier, knight, chevalier; horse soldier, cavalryman, mounted policeman; horsewoman, equestrienne; cowboy, cowgirl, puncher *or* cowpuncher *or* cowpoke <nf>, *vaquero* and *gaucho* <Sp>; broncobuster <nf>, buckaroo; postilion, postboy; roughrider; **jockey;** steeplechaser; circus rider, trick rider

9 **driver,** reinsman, whip, Jehu, skinner <nf>; **coachman,** coachy <nf>, *cocher* <Fr>, *cochero* <Sp>, *voiturier* <Fr>, *vetturino* <Ital>, gharry-wallah <India>; stage coachman; charioteer; harness racer; **cabdriver,** cabman, cabby <nf>, hackman, hack *or* hacky <nf>, jarvey <Brit nf>; wagoner, wagonman, drayman, truckman; **carter,** cartman, carman; **teamster;** muleteer, mule skinner <nf>; bullwhacker; elephant driver, mahout; cameleer

10 **driver, motorist,** automobilist; **chauffeur; taxidriver,** cabdriver, cabby <nf>, hackman, **hack** *or* hacky <nf>, hackdriver, pilot <nf>; jitney driver; **truck driver, teamster,** truckman, **trucker; bus driver,** busman, bus jockey <nf>; speeder 174.5, road hog <nf>, Sunday driver, joyrider <nf>; hit-and-run driver; designated driver; backseat driver; new driver, learner

11 cyclist, cycler; **bicyclist,** bicycler, mountain biker, biker; **motorcyclist,** motorcycler, biker <nf>

12 **engineer,** engineman, engine driver <Brit>; hogger *or* hoghead <nf>; Casey Jones; **motorman;** gripman

13 **trainman,** railroad man, **railroader;** conductor, guard <Brit>; brakeman, brakie <nf>; fireman, footplate man <Brit>, stoker; smoke agent *and* bakehead <nf>; switchman; yardman; yardmaster; trainmaster, dispatcher; stationmaster; lineman; baggage man, baggagesmasher <nf>; porter, redcap; trainboy; butcher <nf>; trainspotter

179 VEHICLE
<means of conveyance>

NOUNS 1 **vehicle, conveyance,** carrier, means of carrying *or* transporting, means of transport, medium of transportation, carriage; public transportation; watercraft 180.1, aircraft 181

2 **wagon,** waggon <Brit>, wain; haywagon, milkwagon; dray, van, caravan; covered wagon, prairie schooner, Conestoga wagon, stagecoach

3 **cart,** two-wheeler; oxcart, horsecart, ponycart, dogcart; dumpcart; **handcart,** barrow, wheelbarrow, handbarrow; jinrikisha, ricksha; pushcart

4 **carriage,** four-wheeler, *voiture* <Fr>, gharry <India>; **chaise,** shay <nf>

5 **rig, equipage,** turnout <nf>, coach-and-four; team, pair, span; tandem, random; spike, spike team, unicorn; three-in-hand, four-in-hand, etc; three-up, four-up, etc

6 **baby carriage,** baby buggy <nf>, perambulator, pram <Brit>; go-cart; **stroller,** walker

7 **wheelchair,** Bath chair, push chair

8 **cycle,** wheel <nf>; **bicycle,** bike <nf>, mountain bike, all-terrain bike, touring bike, racing bike, hybrid bike, mountain bike, velocipede; tandem bicycle; **tricycle,** three-wheeler, trike <nf>; BMX; **motorcycle,** motocycle, motorbike, bike *and* iron <nf>; pig <nf>, chopper <nf>, motorscooter, minibike, moped, dirt *or* trail bike; pedicab

9 **automobile** <see list>, **car, auto,** motorcar, motocar, autocar, **machine,** motor, motor vehicle, motorized vehicle, *voiture* <Fr>

10 <nf terms> **jalopy,** banger, bomber, beater, bus, buggy, wheels, tub, tuna wagon, heap, boat, short, crate, wreck, bomb, clunker, junker, junkheap, junkpile

11 **police car, patrol car; prowl car,** squad car, cruiser; **police van,** patrol wagon; wagon *and* paddy wagon *and* Black Maria <nf>, panda car <Brit>

12 **truck** <see list>, lorry <Brit>, *camion* <Fr>; trailer truck, truck trailer, tractor trailer, semitrailer, rig *and* semi <nf>; eighteen-wheeler <nf>; panel truck, van

13 <public vehicles> **commercial vehicle; bus,** omnibus, chartered bus, autobus, motorbus, motor coach, articulated bus, jitney <nf>; express bus, local bus; schoolbus; **cab, taxicab, taxi,** hack <nf>, gypsy cab <nf>; rental car; hired car, limousine, limo *and* stretch limo <nf>; public transportation

14 **train,** railroad train; choo choo *and* choo-choo train <nf>; passenger train, Amtrak; aerotrain; bullet train, *train de haute vitesse* <Fr>; local, way train, milk train, accommodation train; shuttle train, shuttle; express train, express; lightning express, flier, cannonball express <nf>; local express; special, limited; parliamentary train *or* parliamentary <Brit>; freight train, goods train <Brit>, freight, freighter, rattler <nf>; baggage train, luggage train; electric train; cable railroad;

funicular; cog railroad *or* railway, rack-and-pinion railroad; subway, *métro* <Fr>, tube, underground <Brit>; elevated, el <nf>; monorail; streamliner; rolling stock

15 **railway car,** car, waggon <Brit>; baggage car, boxcar, caboose, coach, gondola; diner, dining car *or* compartment; drawing room; freight car; hopper car; flatcar; parlor car; Pullman *or* Pullman car; refrigerator car *or* reefer <nf>; roomette, sleeper *or* sleeping car or *wagon-lit* <Fr>; smoker *or* smoking car *or* compartment

16 **handcar,** go-devil; push car, trolley, truck car, rubble car

17 **streetcar, trolley** *or* trolley car, **tram** *or* tramcar; electric car, electric <nf>; trolley bus, trackless trolley; horsecar, horse box <Brit>; cable car, grip car

18 **tractor,** traction engine; Caterpillar <trademark>, Cat <nf>, tracked vehicle; bulldozer, dozer <nf>

19 **trailer,** trail car; house trailer, mobile home; recreation vehicle *or* RV; truck trailer, **semitrailer,** highway trailer; camp *or* camping trailer, caravan <Brit>; **camper,** camping bus

20 **sled, sleigh,** *traîneau* <Fr>, sledge, dogsled, troika; snowmobile, weasel, skimobile, bombardier <Can>; runner, blade; toboggan, skiboggan

21 **skates,** ice skates, hockey skates, figure skates; roller skates, skateboard, bob skates; **skis, snowshoes**

22 **Hovercraft** <trademark>, hovercar, air-cushion vehicle *or* ACV, cushioncraft, ground-effect machine *or* GEM, captured-air vehicle *or* CAV, captured-air bubble *or* CAB, surface-effect ship

ADJS 23 **vehicular,** transportational; automotive, locomotive

24 **automobiles**

brougham	race car *or* racer *or*
cabriolet	racing car
commercial vehicle	roadster
compact car	runabout
convertible	saloon <Brit>
coupe	sedan
estate car <Brit>	sedan limousine
four-door	sports car
hardtop	station wagon
hatchback	stock car
hybrid	stretch limousine
jeep	*or* limo
limousine *or* limo	tourer <Brit>
luxury	touring car *or* gran
mid-size	turismo
mini-bus	two-door
minicar	two-seater <Brit>

25 **trucks**

articulated vehicle	duck *or* DUKW
big rig	dump truck
fork *or* forklift truck	recreational vehicle
four-by-four *or* 4x4	*or* RV
lorry <Brit>	semitrailer *or* semi
minivan	six-by-six
monster truck	tank truck
panel truck *or* panel	tractor *or* tractor-trailer *or*
van	tractor truck *or* truck
pick-up truck *or* pickup	tractor van

180 SHIP, BOAT

NOUNS 1 **ship,** argosy, cargo ship, container ship, cruise ship, dredge, freighter, liner, merchant ship *or* merchantman, motorship, oceanographic research ship, paddle boat *or* steamer, refrigeration ship, roll-on roll-off ship *or* ro-ro, side-wheeler, supertanker, tanker, trawler, ULCC *or* ultra-large crude carrier, VLCC *or* very large crude carrier, whaler, supercargo; **boat,** ark, canoe, gondola, kayak, lifeboat, motorboat, shell, skiff, whaleboat, workboat; vessel, craft, bottom, bark, argosy, hull, hulk, keel, watercraft; tub *and* bucket *and* rustbucket *and* hooker <nf>, packet; leviathan; "that packet of assorted miseries which we call a ship"—Kipling

2 **steamer, steamboat, steamship;** motor ship

3 **sailboat, sailing vessel,** sailing boat, wind boat, ragboat <nf>, sailing yacht, sailing cruiser, sailing ship, tall *or* taunt ship, sail, sailer, **windjammer** <nf>, windship, windboat; **galley; yacht,** pleasure boat

4 **motorboat, powerboat,** speedboat, stinkpot <nf>; **launch,** motor launch, steam launch, naphtha launch; **cruiser,** power cruiser, **cabin cruiser,** sedan cruiser, outboard cruiser

5 **liner, ocean liner,** ocean greyhound <nf>, passenger steamer, floating hotel *or* palace, luxury liner; **cruise ship**

6 **warship,** war vessel, naval vessel; warship; **man-of-war,** man-o'-war, ship of war, armored vessel; USS *or* United States Ship; HMS *or* His *or* Her Majesty's Ship; line-of-battle ship, ship of the line; aircraft carrier *or* flattop <nf>, assault transport, battle cruiser, battleship, coast guard cutter, communications ship, cruiser, destroyer, destroyer escort, guided missile cruiser, heavy cruiser, patrol boat *or* PT boat, gunboat, hospital ship, minelayer, mine ship, minesweeper; icebreaker

7 **battleship,** battlewagon <nf>, capital ship; **cruiser,** battle-cruiser; **destroyer,** can *or* tin can <nf>

8 **carrier, aircraft carrier,** seaplane carrier, **flattop** <nf>

9 **submarine, sub,** submersible, underwater craft; **U-boat,** *U-boot or Unterseeboot* <Ger>, pigboat <nf>;

nuclear *or* nuclear-powered submarine; Polaris submarine; Trident submarine; hunter-killer submarine

10 **ships, shipping,** merchant *or* mercantile marine, merchant navy *or* fleet, bottoms, tonnage; **fleet,** flotilla, argosy; line; fishing fleet, whaling fleet, etc; **navy** 461.26

11 **float, raft;** balsa, balsa raft, Kon Tiki; life raft, Carling float; boom; pontoon; buoy, life buoy; **life preserver** 397.6; surfboard; cork; bob

12 **rigging,** rig, **tackle,** tackling, **gear; ropework,** roping; service, serving, whipping; standing rigging, running rigging; boatswain's stores; ship chandlery

13 **spar,** timber; **mast,** pole, stick *and* tree <nf>; bare pole

14 **sail, canvas,** muslin, cloth, rag <nf>; **full *or* plain sail,** press *or* crowd of sail; reduced sail, reefed sail; square sail; fore-and-aft sail; luff, leech, foot, earing, reef point, boltrope, clew, cringle, head

15 **oar,** remi-; **paddle,** scull, sweep, pole; steering oar

16 **anchor,** mooring, hook *and* mudhook <nf>; **anchorage,** moorings; **berth,** slip; mooring buoy

ADJS 17 **rigged,** decked, trimmed; square-rigged, fore-and-aft rigged, Marconi-rigged, gaff-rigged, lateen-rigged

18 **seaworthy,** sea-kindly, fit for sea, **snug, bold; watertight,** waterproof; **A1,** A1 at Lloyd's; stiff, tender; weatherly; yare

19 **trim,** in trim; apoise, on an even keel

20 **shipshape,** Bristol fashion, shipshape and Bristol fashion, trim, trig, neat, tight, taut, ataunt, all ataunto, bungup and bilge-free

181 AIRCRAFT

NOUNS 1 **aircraft, airplane,** aeroplane <Brit>, **plane, ship,** fixed-wing aircraft, flying machine <old>, *avion* <Fr>; aerodyne, heavier-than-air craft; kite <Brit nf>; **shuttle, space shuttle,** lifting body; **airplane part; flight instrument,** aircraft instrument; **aircraft engine; piston engine,** radial engine, rotary engine, pancake engine; **jet engine,** fan-jet engine, rocket motor, turbofan, turbojet, turboprop, pulse jet, ramjet, reaction engine *or* motor

2 **propeller plane,** single-prop, double-prop *or* twin-prop, multi-prop; piston plane; turbo-propeller plane, turbo-prop, prop-jet; puddle jumper

3 **jet plane, jet; turbojet,** ramjet, pulse-jet, blowtorch <nf>, single-jet, twin-jet, multi-jet, jet liner, business jet; deltaplanform jet, tailless jet, twin-tailboom jet; jumbo jet; subsonic jet; supersonic jet, supersonic transport *or* SST, Concorde

4 **rocket plane,** repulsor; rocket ship, spaceship 1075.2; rocket 1074.2

5 **rotor plane,** rotary-wing aircraft, rotocraft, rotodyne; gyroplane, gyro, **autogiro,** windmill <nf>; **helicopter,** copter *and* whirlybird *and* chopper *and* eggbeater <nf>

6 **ornithopter,** orthopter, wind flapper, mechanical bird

7 **flying platform,** flying ring, Hiller-CNR machine, flying bedstead *or* bedspring; **Hovercraft** <trademark>, air car, ground-effect machine, air-cushion vehicle, hovercar, cushioncraft; flying crow's nest, flying motorcycle, flying bathtub

8 **seaplane,** waterplane, **hydroplane,** aerohydroplane, aeroboat, **floatplane,** float seaplane; **flying boat,** clipper, boat seaplane; **amphibian,** amphibious aircraft, triphibian

9 **military aircraft, warplane,** battle plane, combat plane; carrier fighter, carrier-based plane, bomber, dive bomber, fighter, helicopter gunship, jet bomber, strategic bomber, jet fighter, jet tanker, night fighter, photo-reconnaissance plane, reconnaissance fighter, spy plane, airborne warning and control systems *or* AWACS plane, Stealth Bomber, Stealth Fighter, tactical support bomber, torpedo bomber, troop carrier *or* transport; amphibian, flying boat; helicopter; suicide plane, kamikaze; bogey, bandit, enemy aircraft; air fleet, air armada; air force 461.29

10 **trainer;** Link trainer; **flight simulator;** dual-control trainer; basic *or* primary trainer, intermediate trainer, advanced trainer; crew trainer, flying classroom; navigator-bombardier trainer, radio-navigational trainer, etc

11 **aerostat,** lighter-than-air craft; **airship,** ship, dirigible balloon, **blimp** <nf>; rigid airship, semirigid airship; **dirigible,** zeppelin, Graf Zeppelin; gasbag, ballonet; hot-air balloon, **balloon,** *ballon* <Fr>

12 **glider,** gliding machine; **sailplane,** soaring plane; rocket glider; student glider; air train, glider train

13 **parachute, chute** <nf>, umbrella <nf>, brolly <Brit nf>; pilot chute, drogue chute; rip cord, safety loop, shroud lines, harness, pack, vent; parachute jump, brolly-hop <Brit nf>, base jump; sky dive; brake *or* braking *or* deceleration parachute; parawing *or* paraglider *or* parafoil

14 **kite,** box kite, Eddy kite, Hargrave *or* cellular kite, tetrahedral kite

182 WATER TRAVEL

NOUNS 1 water travel, travel by water, marine *or* ocean *or* sea travel, **navigation,** navigating, **seafaring, sailing,** steaming, passage-making, voyaging, **cruising,** coasting, gunkholing <nf>; inland navigation; **boating, yachting,** motorboating, canoeing, rowing, sculling; circumnavigation, periplus; navigability

2 <methods> celestial navigation, astronavigation; radio navigation, radio beacon; loran; consolan, shoran; coastal *or* coastwise navigation; dead reckoning; point-to-point navigation; pilotage; sonar, radar, sofar; plane *or* traverse *or* spherical *or* parallel *or* middle *or* latitude *or* Mercator *or* great-circle *or* rhumbline *or* composite sailing; fix, line of position; sextant, chronometer, tables

3 **seamanship,** shipmanship; seamanliness, seamanlikeness; weather eye; sea legs

4 **pilotship,** pilotry, pilotage, **helmsmanship;** steerage; proper piloting

5 embarkation 188.3; disembarkation 186.2

6 **voyage,** ocean *or* sea trip, **cruise,** sail; course, **run, passage; crossing;** shakedown cruise; leg

7 **wake,** track; wash, backwash

8 <submarines> **surfacing,** breaking water; **submergence, dive;** stationary dive, running dive, crash dive

9 **way, progress; headway,** steerageway, sternway, leeway, driftway

10 **seaway, waterway,** fairway, road, channel, ocean *or* sea lane, ship route, steamer track *or* lane; crossing; approaches; navigable water

11 aquatics, **swimming, bathing,** natation, balneation, aquacize; **swim, bathe;** crawl, freestyle, trudgen, Australian crawl, breaststroke, butterfly, sidestroke, dog *or* doggie paddle, backstroke; treading water; floating; diving 367.3; wading; fin; flipper, flapper; fishtail; waterskiing, aquaplaning, surfboarding; surfing; windsurfing, boardsailing; free swimming

12 **swimmer, bather,** natator, merman, fish <nf>; bathing girl, mermaid; bathing beauty; frogman; diver 367.4

VERBS 13 **navigate, sail, cruise,** steam, run, **seafare, voyage,** ply, go on shipboard, go by ship, go on *or* take a voyage; go to sea, sail the sea, sail the ocean blue; **boat, yacht,** motorboat, canoe, row, scull; surf, windsurf, boardsail; steamboat; bear *or* carry sail; cross, traverse, make a passage *or* run; sail round, circumnavigate; coast

14 **pilot,** helm, coxswain, **steer,** guide, be at the helm *or* tiller, direct, manage, handle, run, operate, **conn** *or* cond, be at *or* have the conn; **navigate,** shape *or* chart a course

15 **anchor,** come to anchor, lay anchor, **cast anchor,** let go the anchor, drop the hook; carry out the anchor; kedge, kedge off; **dock, tie up; moor,** pick up the mooring; run out a warp *or* rope; lash, lash and tie; foul the anchor; disembark 186.8

16 **ride at anchor,** ride, lie, rest; ride easy; ride hawse full; lie athwart; set an anchor watch

17 **lay** *or* **lie to,** lay *or* lie by; lie near *or* close to the wind, head to wind *or* windward, be under the sea; lie ahull; lie off, lie off the land; lay *or* lie up

18 **weigh anchor,** up-anchor, bring the anchor home, break out the anchor, cat the anchor, break ground, loose for sea; **unmoor,** drop the mooring, cast off *or* loose *or* away

19 **get under way,** put *or* have way upon, **put** *or* **push** *or* **shove off;** hoist the blue Peter; **put to sea,** put out to sea, go to sea, head for blue water, go off soundings; **sail,** sail away; embark

20 **set sail,** hoist sail, unfurl *or* spread sail, heave out a sail, **make sail,** trim sail; square away, square the yards; **crowd** *or* **clap** *or* **crack** *or* **pack on sail,** put on <more> sail; clap on, crack on, pack on; give her beans <nf>

21 **make way,** gather way, **make headway,** make sternway; make knots, foot; **go full speed ahead,** go full speed astern; go *or* run *or* steam at flank speed

22 run, **run** *or* **sail before the wind,** run *or* sail with the wind, run *or* sail down the wind, make a spinnaker run, sail off the wind, sail free, sail with the wind aft, sail with the wind abaft the beam; tack down wind; run *or* sail with the wind quartering

23 **bring off the wind, pay off,** bear off *or* away, put the helm to leeward, bear *or* head to leeward, pay off the head

24 **sail against the wind,** sail on *or* by the wind, sail to windward, bear *or* head to windward; **bring in** *or* **into the wind,** bring by *or* on the wind, haul the wind *or* one's wind; uphelm, put the helm up; haul, haul off, haul up; **haul to, bring to, heave to;** sail in *or* into the wind's eye *or* the teeth of the wind; sail to the windward of, weather

25 **sail near the wind,** sail close to the wind, lie near *or* close to the wind, sail full and by, hold a close wind, **sail close-hauled,** close-haul; work *or* go *or* beat *or* eat to windward, **beat, ply; luff,** luff up, sail closer to the wind; sail too close to the wind, sail fine, touch the wind, pinch

26 **gain to windward of,** eat *or* claw to windward of, eat the wind out of, have the wind of, be to windward of

27 **chart** *or* **plot** *or* **lay out a course;** shape a course, lay *or* lie a course

28 take *or* follow a course, **keep** *or* **hold the course** *or* **a course,** hold on the course *or* a course, stand on *or* upon a course, stand on a straight course, maintain *or* keep the heading, keep her steady, keep pointed

29 **drift off course, yaw,** yaw off, pay off, bear off, drift, sag; sag *or* bear *or* ride *or* drive to leeward,

make leeway, drive, fetch away; be set by the current, drift with the current, fall down

30 change course, change the heading, bear off *or* away, bear to starboard *or* port; sheer, swerve; **tack,** cast, break, yaw, slew, shift, turn; **cant,** cant round *or* across; **beat, ply; veer, wear, wear ship; jibe** *or* gybe <Brit>, jibe all standing, make a North River jibe; **put about,** come *or* go *or* bring *or* fetch about, beat about, cast *or* throw about; bring *or* swing *or* heave *or* haul round; **about ship,** turn *or* put back, turn on her heel, wind; swing the stern; box off; back and fill; stand off and on; double *or* round a point; miss stays; reroute

31 put the rudder hard left *or* right, put the rudder *or* helm hard over, put the rudder amidships, ease the rudder *or* helm, give her more *or* less rudder

32 veer *or* **wear short,** bring by the lee, **broach to,** lie beam on to the seas

33 <come to a stop> **fetch up, heave to,** haul up, fetch up all standing

34 backwater, back, reverse, go astern; **go full speed astern;** make sternway

35 sail for, put away for, make for *or* toward, make at, **run for,** stand for, head *or* steer toward, lay for, **lay a** *or* **one's course for,** bear up for; bear up to, **bear down on** *or* **upon,** run *or* bear in with, **close with;** make, reach, fetch; heave *or* go alongside; lay *or* go aboard; lay *or* lie in; **put in** *or* into, put into port, approach anchorage

36 sail away from, head *or* steer away from, run from, **stand from,** lay away *or* off from; **stand off,** bear off, put off, shove off, haul off; stand off and on

37 clear the land, bear off the land, lay *or* settle the land, make *or* get sea room

38 make land, reach land; close with the land, stand in for the land; sight land; smell land; make a landfall

39 coast, sail coast-wise, stay in soundings, range the coast, skirt the shore, lie along the shore, **hug the shore** *or* **land** *or* **coast**

40 weather the storm, weather, ride, **ride out,** outride, ride *or* ride out a storm; make heavy *or* bad weather

41 sail into, run down, run in *or* into, **ram; come** *or* **run foul** *or* **afoul of, collide,** fall aboard; nose *or* head into, run prow *or* end *or* head on, run head and head; run broadside on

42 shipwreck, wreck, pile up <nf>, cast away; **go** *or* **run aground,** ground, take the ground, beach, strand, run on the rocks; ground hard and fast

43 careen, list, heel, tip, cant, heave *or* lay down, lie along; be on beam ends

44 capsize, upset, overset, **overturn,** turn over, turn turtle, upset the boat, keel, keel over *or* up; pitchpole, somersault; **sink, founder,** be lost, go

down, go to the bottom, go to Davy Jones's locker; scuttle

45 go overboard, go by the board, go over the board *or* side

46 maneuver, execute a maneuver; heave in together, keep in formation, maintain position, **keep station,** keep pointed, steam in line, steam in line of bearing; convoy

47 <submarines> **surface,** break water; **submerge, dive,** crash-dive, go below; rig for diving; flood the tanks, flood negative

48 <activities aboard ship> lay, lay aloft, lay forward, etc; traverse a yard, brace a yard fore and aft; heave, haul; kedge; warp; boom; heave round, heave short, heave apeak; log, heave *or* stream the log; haul down, board; spar down; ratline down, clap on ratlines; batten down the hatches; unlash, cut *or* cast loose; clear hawse

49 trim ship, trim, trim up; trim by the head *or* stern, put in proper fore-and-aft trim, give greater draft fore and aft, **put on an even keel; ballast,** shift ballast, wing out ballast; break out ballast, break bulk, shoot ballast; **clear the decks,** clear for action, take action stations

50 reduce sail, shorten *or* take in sail, hand a sail, **reef,** reef one's sails; double-reef; lower sail, dowse sail; run under bare poles; snug down; **furl,** put on a harbor furl

51 take bearings, cast a traverse; correct distance and maintain the bearings; run down the latitude, **take a sight,** shoot the sun, bring down the sun; **box the compass; take soundings** 275.9

52 signal, make a signal, speak, hail and speak; dress ship; unfurl *or* hoist a banner, unfurl an ensign, **break out a flag;** hoist the blue Peter; show one's colors, **exchange colors;** salute, dip the ensign

53 row, paddle, ply the oar, **pull, scull, punt;** give way, row away; catch *or* cut a crab *or* lobster <nf>; feather, feather an oar; sky an oar <nf>; row dry <Brit nf>; pace, shoot; ship oars

54 float, ride, drift; **sail, scud, run,** shoot; skim, foot; ghost, glide, slip; ride the sea, plow the deep, walk the waters

55 pitch, toss, tumble, toss and tumble, pitch and toss, **plunge,** hobbyhorse, pound, **rear, rock, roll, reel, swing, sway, lurch, yaw, heave,** scend, **flounder, welter, wallow;** make heavy weather

56 swim, bathe, go in swimming *or* bathing; tread water; **float,** float on one's back, do the deadman's float, dog-paddle; **wade,** go in wading; skinny-dip; aquacize, dive 367.6

ADJS **57 nautical, marine, maritime, naval, navigational; seafaring, seagoing, oceangoing,** seaborne, water-borne; seamanly, seamanlike, **salty** <nf>; pelagic, oceanic 240.8

58 aquatic, water-dwelling, water-living, water-growing, water-loving; **swimming,** balneal, natant, natatory, natatorial; shore, seashore; tidal, estuarine, littoral, grallatorial; riverine; deep-sea 275.14

59 navigable, boatable

60 floating, afloat, awash; water-borne

61 adrift, afloat, unmoored, untied, loose, unanchored, aweigh; cast-off, started

ADVS **62 on board,** on shipboard, on board ship, **aboard,** all aboard, afloat; **on deck,** topside; aloft; in sail; before the mast; athwart the hawse, athwarthawse

63 under way, making way, with steerageway, with way on; **at sea,** on the high seas, off soundings, in blue water; **under sail** or **canvas,** with sails spread; under press of sail or canvas or steam; under steam or power; under bare poles; on or off the heading or course; in soundings, homeward bound

64 before the wind, with the wind, down the wind, running free; off the wind, with the wind aft, with the wind abaft the beam, wing and wing, under the wind, under the lee; on a reach, on a beam or broad reach, with wind abeam

65 against the wind, on the wind, in or into the wind, up the wind, by the wind, head to wind; in or into the wind's eye, in the teeth of the wind

66 near the wind, close to the wind, **close-hauled,** on a beat, full and by

67 coastward, landward, to landward; **coastwise,** coastways

68 leeward, to leeward, alee, downwind; **windward,** to windward, weatherward, aweather, upwind

69 aft, abaft, baft, **astern;** fore and aft

70 alongside, board and board, yardarm to yardarm

71 at anchor, riding at anchor; lying to, hove to; lying ahull

72 afoul, foul, in collision; head and head, head or end or prow on; broadside on

73 aground, on the rocks; hard and fast

74 overboard, over the board or side, by the board; aft the fantail

183 MARINER

NOUNS **1 mariner, seaman, sailor,** sailorman, **navigator, seafarer,** seafaring man, bluejacket, sea or water dog <nf>, Seabee <nf>, crewman, shipman, jack, jacky, jack afloat, jack-tar, **tar, salt** <nf>, gob, swabby, hearty, lobscouser <nf>, matelot <Fr>, windsailor, windjammer; limey or limejuicer <nf>, lascar <India>; common or ordinary seaman, OD; able or able-bodied seaman, AB; deep-sea man, saltwater or bluewater or deepwater sailor; fresh-water sailor; fair-weather sailor; whaler, fisherman, lobsterman; viking, sea rover, buccaneer, privateer, pirate; Jason, Argonaut, Ancient Mariner, Flying Dutchman; Neptune, Poseidon, Varuna, Dylan; **yachtsman, yachtswoman,** cruising sailor, racing sailor; submariner

2 <novice> **lubber, landlubber;** polliwog

3 <veteran> **old salt** and old sea dog and shellback and barnacle-back <nf>; **master mariner**

4 navy man, man-of-war's man, **bluejacket; gob** and swabbie and swabber <nf>; **marine, leatherneck** and gyrene and devil dog or jarhead <nf>, Royal Marine, jolly <Brit nf>; horse marine; boot <nf>; **midshipman,** midshipmate, middy <nf>; cadet, naval cadet; coastguardsman, Naval Reservist, Seabee, frogman

5 boatman, boatsman, boat-handler, **boater,** waterman; **oarsman,** oar, rower, sculler, punter; galley slave; **ferryman,** ferrier; **bargeman,** barger, bargee <Brit>, bargemaster; lighterman, wherryman; **gondolier,** gondoliere <Ital>

6 hand, **deckhand,** deckie <Brit>, roustabout <nf>; stoker, fireman, bakehead <nf>; black gang; wiper, oiler, boilerman; cabin boy; yeoman, ship's writer; purser; ship's carpenter, chips <nf>; ship's cooper, bungs or Jimmy Bungs <nf>; ship's tailor, snip or snips <nf>; steward, stewardess, commissary steward, mess steward, hospital steward; commissary clerk; mail orderly; navigator; radio operator, sparks <nf>; landing signalman; gunner, gun loader, torpedoman; afterguard; complement; watch

7 <ship's officers> **captain,** shipmaster, **master, skipper** <nf>, **commander,** the Old Man <nf>, patron <Fr>; navigator, navigating officer, sailing master; deck officer, officer of the deck or OD; watch officer, officer of the watch; **mate,** first or chief mate, second mate, third mate, boatswain's mate; **boatswain,** bos'n, pipes <nf>; quartermaster; sergeant-at-arms; chief engineer, engine-room officer; naval officer 575.20

8 steersman, helmsman, wheelman, wheelsman, boatsteerer; quartermaster; **coxswain,** cox <nf>; **pilot,** conner, sailing master; harbor pilot, docking pilot

9 longshoreman, wharf hand, dockhand, docker, dockworker, dock-walloper <nf>; **stevedore,** loader; **roustabout** <nf>, lumper

184 AVIATION

NOUNS **1 aviation, aeronautics;** airplaning, skyriding, **flying, flight,** winging; volation, volitation; aeronautism, aerodromics; powered flight, jet flight, subsonic *or* supersonic flight; cruising, cross-country flying; bush flying; **gliding,** sail-planing, soaring, sailing; volplaning; ballooning, balloonery, lighter-than-air aviation; barnstorming <nf>; high-altitude flying; blind *or* instrument flight *or* flying, instrument flight rules *or* IFR; contact flying, visual flight *or* flying, visual flight rules *or* VFR, pilotage; skywriting; cloud-seeding; in-flight training, ground school; **air traffic,** airline traffic, air-traffic control, air-traffic controller; commercial aviation, general aviation, private aviation, private flying; astronautics 1075.1; air show, flying circus

2 air sciences <see list>, aeronautical sciences

3 **airmanship,** pilotship; **flight plan;** briefing, brief, rundown <nf>, debriefing; flight *or* pilot training, flying lessons; washout <nf>

4 air-mindedness, aerophilia; air legs

5 airsickness; aerophobia, aeropathy

6 **navigation,** avigation, aerial *or* air navigation; celestial navigation, astronavigation; electronic navigation, automatic electronic navigation, radio navigation, navar, radar, consolan, tacan, teleran, loran, shoran; omnidirectional range, omni-range, visual-aural range *or* VAR

7 <aeronautical organizations> Civil Aeronautics Administration *or* CAA; Federal Aviation Agency *or* FAA; Bureau of Aeronautics; National Advisory Committee for Aeronautics; Office of Naval Research; Civil Air Patrol; Caterpillar Club; Airline Pilots Association; Air Force 461.29

8 **takeoff,** liftoff, hopoff <nf>; rollout, climb; taxiing, takeoff run, takeoff power, rotation; daisy-clipping *and* grass-cutting <nf>; ground loop; level-off; jet-assisted takeoff *or* JATO, booster rocket, takeoff rocket; catapult, electropult

9 **flight, trip, run; hop** *and* **jump** <nf>; powered flight; solo flight, **solo;** inverted flight; supersonic flight; test flight, **test hop** <nf>; **airlift;** airdrop; scheduled flight; mercy flight; charter flight; connecting flight; non-stop flight; crop-dusting; skywriting; red-eye

10 **air travel,** air transport, air transportation; **airfreight, air cargo; airline travel, airline,** airline service, air service, feeder airline, commuter airline, scheduled airline, charter airline, nonscheduled airline *or* nonsked <nf>, short-hop airline; flying circus; **shuttle,** air shuttle, shuttle service, shuttle trip; air taxi; frequent flier

11 <Air Force> **mission,** flight operation; training mission; gunnery mission; combat rehearsal, **dry run** <nf>; transition mission; reconnaissance mission, reconnaissance, observation flight, search mission; **milk run** <nf>; box-top mission

<nf>; combat flight; **sortie,** scramble <nf>; **air raid;** shuttle raid; bombing mission; bombing, strafing 459.7; **air support** <for ground troops>, **air cover,** cover, umbrella, air umbrella

12 flight formation, formation flying, formation; close formation, loose formation, wing formation; V formation, echelon

13 <maneuvers> acrobatic *or* tactical evolutions *or* maneuvers, acrobatics, **aerobatics;** stunting *and* **stunt flying** <nf>, rolling, crabbing, banking, porpoising, fishtailing, diving; **dive, nose dive, power dive; zoom,** chandelle; stall, whip stall; **glide,** volplane; spiral, split 'S', lazy eight, sideslip, pushdown, pull-up, pull-out; turn, vector in flight *or* VIF

14 **roll, barrel roll,** aileron roll, outside roll, **snap roll**

15 **spin,** autorotation, **tailspin,** flat spin, inverted spin, normal spin, power spin, uncontrolled spin, falling leaf; whipstall

16 **loop,** spiral loop, ground loop, normal loop, outside loop, inverted normal *or* outside loop, dead-stick loop, wingover, looping the loop; Immelmann turn, reverse turn, reversement; flipper turns

17 **buzzing,** flathatting *and* **hedgehopping** <nf>

18 **landing,** coming in <nf>, touching down, touchdown; arrival; landing run, landing pattern; approach, downwind leg, approach leg; holding pattern, stack up <nf>; ballooning in, parachute approach; blind *or* instrument landing, dead-stick landing, glide landing, stall landing, fishtail landing, sideslip landing, level *or* two-point landing, normal *or* three-point landing, Chinese landing <nf>, tail-high landing, tail-low landing, thumped-in landing <nf>, pancake landing, belly landing, crash landing, noseover, nose-up; overflight, overshoot, undershoot; practice landing, bounce drill

19 flying and landing guides marker, pylon; beacon; radio beacon, radio range station, radio marker; fan marker; radar beacon, racon; beam, radio beam; beacon lights; runway lights, high-intensity runway approach lights, sequence flashers, flare path; wind indicator, wind cone *or* sock, air sleeve; instrument landing system *or* ILS; touchdown rate of descent indicator *or* TRODI; ground-controlled approach *or* GCA; talking-down system, talking down

20 **crash, crack-up,** prang <Brit nf>; crash landing; collision, mid-air collision; near-miss, near collision

21 **blackout;** grayout; anoxia; useful consciousness; pressure suit, antiblackout suit

22 **airport, airfield, airdrome,** aerodrome <Brit>, drome, port, air harbor <Can>, aviation field,

landing field, landing, field, airship station; **air terminal, jetport; air base,** air station, naval air station; airpark; **heliport,** helidrome; control tower, island; Air Route Traffic Control Center; baggage pickup, baggage carousel; airside, landside

23 **runway, taxiway,** strip, landing strip, **airstrip, flight strip,** take-off strip; fairway, launching way; stopway; clearway; transition strip; apron; **flight deck,** landing deck; helipad; ramp, apron

24 **hangar,** housing, dock, airdock, shed, airship shed; mooring mast

25 <propulsion> rocket propulsion, rocket power; **jet propulsion,** jet power; turbojet propulsion, pulse-jet propulsion, ram-jet propulsion, resojet propulsion; constant *or* ram pressure, air ram; reaction propulsion, reaction, action and reaction; aeromotor, aircraft engine, power plant

26 **lift,** lift ratio, lift force *or* component, lift direction; aerostatic lift, dynamic lift, gross lift, useful lift, margin of lift

27 **drag,** resistance; drag ratio, drag force *or* component, induced drag, wing drag, parasite *or* parasitic *or* structural drag, profile drag, head resistance, drag direction, cross-wind force

28 **drift,** drift angle; lateral drift, leeway

29 flow, air flow, laminar flow; **turbulence,** turbulent flow, burble, burble point, eddies

30 wash, wake, stream; downwash; backwash, **slipstream,** propeller race, propwash; **exhaust,** jet exhaust, blow wash; **vapor trail,** condensation trail, contrail, vortex

31 <speed> **air speed,** true air speed, operating *or* flying speed, cruising speed, knots, minimum flying speed, hump speed, peripheral speed, pitch speed, terminal speed, sinking speed, get-away *or* take-off speed, landing speed, ground speed, speed over the ground; **speed of sound** 174.2; zone of no signal, Mach cone; **sound barrier,** sonic barrier *or* wall; sonic boom, shock wave, Mach wave

32 <air, atmosphere> **airspace,** navigable airspace; aerosphere; **aerospace;** space, empty space; **weather, weather conditions; ceiling,** ballonet ceiling, service ceiling, static ceiling, absolute ceiling; ceiling and visibility unlimited *or* CAVU; severe clear <nf>; cloud layer *or* cover, ceiling zero; visibility, visibility zero; **overcast,** undercast; fog, soup <nf>; high-pressure area, low-pressure area; trough, trough line; front; **air pocket** *or* **hole,** air bump, pocket, hole, bump; **turbulence;** clear-air turbulence *or* CAT; roughness; head wind, unfavorable wind; tail wind, favorable *or* favoring wind; cross wind; atmospheric tides; jetstream

33 **airway, air lane, air line,** air route, skyway, corridor, flight path, lane, path

34 **course, heading,** vector; compass heading *or* course, compass direction, magnetic heading, true heading *or* course

35 <altitude> altitude of flight, absolute altitude, critical altitude, density altitude, pressure altitude, sextant altitude; clearance; ground elevation

VERBS 36 **fly,** be airborne, wing, take wing, wing one's way, take *or* make a flight, take to the air, take the air, volitate, be wafted; **jet;** aviate, airplane, aeroplane; travel by air, go *or* travel by airline, go by plane *or* air, take to the airways, ride the skies; hop <nf>; **soar,** drift, hover; **cruise; glide,** sailplane, sail, volplane; hydroplane, seaplane; balloon; ferry; airlift; break the sound barrier; navigate, avigate

37 **pilot,** control, be at the controls, **fly,** manipulate, drive <nf>, fly left seat; **copilot,** fly right seat; solo; **barnstorm** <nf>; fly blind, fly by the seat of one's pants <nf>; follow the beam, ride the beam, fly on instruments; fly in formation, take position; peel off

38 **take off,** hop *or* jump off <nf>, become airborne, get off *or* leave the ground, take to the air, go *or* fly aloft, clear; rotate, power off; **taxi**

39 **ascend,** climb, gain altitude, mount; **zoom,** hoick <nf>, chandelle

40 <maneuver> **stunt** <nf>, perform aerobatics; crab, fishtail; **spin,** go into a tailspin; **loop,** loop the loop; **roll,** wingover, spiral, undulate, porpoise, feather, yaw, sideslip, skid, bank, dip, crab, nose down, nose up, pull up, push down, pull out, plow, mush through

41 **dive,** nose-dive, power-dive, go for the deck; lose altitude, settle, dump altitude <nf>

42 **buzz,** flathat *and* **hedgehop** <nf>

43 **land,** set her down <nf>, **alight, light,** touch down; **descend,** come down, dump altitude <nf>, fly down; come in, come in for a landing; **level off,** flatten out; upwind, downwind; overshoot, undershoot; make a dead-stick landing; pancake, thump in <nf>; bellyland, settle down, balloon in; fishtail down; **crash-land;** ditch <nf>; nose up, nose over; talk down

44 **crash, crack up,** prang <Brit nf>, spin in, fail to pull out

45 **stall,** lose power, conk out <nf>; flame out

46 **black out,** gray out

47 **parachute, bail out, jump,** make a parachute jump, hit the silk, make a brollyhop <Brit nf>, sky-dive, base-jump

48 **brief,** give a briefing; debrief

ADJS **49 aviation, aeronautic, aeronautical,** aerial; **aviatorial,** aviational, aviatic; aerodontic, **aerospace,** aerotechnical, aerostatic, aerostatical, aeromechanic, aeromechanical, aerodynamic, aerodynamical, avionic, aeronomic, aerophysical; aeromarine; aerobatic; airworthy, air-minded, air-conscious, aeromedical; air-wise; airsick; air-traffic; subsonic, supersonic, hypersonic; propeller, prop, jet, turbojet

50 flying, airborne, winging, soaring; volant, volitant, volitational, hovering, fluttering; gliding; jet-propelled, rocket-propelled

ADVS **51 in flight, on the wing** or fly, while airborne

52 air or atmospheric sciences

acronomy	aircraft design
aerial photography	aircraft hydraulics
aeroballistics	aviation medicine or
aerocartography	aeromedicine
aerodontia	aviation technology
aerodynamics	avionics
aerogeography	climatology
aerogeology	environmental
aerognosy	science
aerography	hydrostatics
aerology	jet engineering
aeromechanics	kinematics
aerometry	kinetics
aeronautical engineering	meteorology
aeronautical meteorology	micrometeorology
aerophotography	micrometry
aerophysics	photometry
aeroscopy	pneumatics
aerospace research	rocket engineering
aerostatics	rocketry
aerostation	supersonic
aerotechnics	aerodynamics
aerothermodynamics	supersonics

185 AVIATOR

NOUNS **1 aviator, airman, flier, pilot,** air pilot, licensed pilot, private pilot, airline pilot, commercial pilot, aeronaut, flyboy and airplane driver and birdman <nf>; aircrew member; captain, chief pilot; copilot, second officer; flight engineer, third officer; jet pilot, jet jockey <nf>; instructor; test pilot; bush pilot; astronaut 1075.8; cloud seeder, rainmaker; cropduster; barnstormer <nf>; stunt man, stunt flier

2 aviatrix, aviatress, **airwoman,** birdwoman <nf>; stuntwoman

3 military pilot, naval pilot, combat pilot; fighter pilot, bomber pilot, observer, reconnaissance pilot; radarman; **aviation cadet,** air or flying cadet, pilot trainee; flyboy <nf>; ace; air force 461.29

4 crew, aircrew, flight crew; crewman, crewmate, crewmember, aircrewman; **navigator,** avigator;

bombardier; gunner, machine gunner, belly gunner, tail gunner; crew chief; aerial photographer; meteorologist; **flight attendant, steward, stewardess,** hostess, air hostess, purser, stew <nf>

5 ground crew, landing crew, plane handlers; crew chief

6 aircraftsman, aeromechanic, aircraft mechanic, mechanic, grease monkey <nf>, ground engineer; rigger; aeronautical engineer, jet engineer, astronaut 1075.8; ground tester, flight tester; air-traffic controller

7 balloonist, ballooner, hot-air balloonist, aeronaut

8 parachutist, chutist or chuter <nf>, parachute jumper, sports parachutist; sky diver; **paratrooper;** paradoctor, paramedic; jumpmaster

9 <mythological fliers> Daedalus, Icarus

186 ARRIVAL

NOUNS **1 arrival, coming, advent,** approach, appearance, **reaching; attainment, accomplishment, achievement**

2 landing, landfall; docking, mooring, tying up, dropping anchor; **getting off, disembarkation,** disembarkment, debarkation, coming or going ashore; **deplaning,** dropping or weighing anchor

3 return, homecoming, recursion; reentrance, **reentry;** remigration; prodigal's return

4 welcome, hero's welcome, **greetings** 585.3

5 destination, goal, bourn <old>; port, haven, harbor, anchorage, **journey's end;** end of the line, terminus, **terminal,** terminal point, home plate; stop, stopping place, last stop; **airport, air terminal** 184.22

VERBS **6 arrive,** arrive at, arrive in, come, **come or get to,** approach, access, **reach, hit** <nf>; find, **gain,** attain, attain to, accomplish, achieve, make, **make it** <nf>, fetch, fetch up at, get there, reach one's destination, come to one's journey's end, end up; **come to rest,** settle, settle in; **make or put in an appearance, show up** <nf>, turn up, **surface,** pop or bob up and make the scene <nf>; **get in, come in,** blow in <nf>, pull in, roll in; **check in;** clock or punch or ring or time in <nf>, sign in, hit town <nf>; come to hand, be received

7 arrive at, come at, get at, **reach,** arrive upon, **come upon, hit upon,** strike upon, fall upon, light upon, pitch upon, stumble on or upon

8 land, come to land, make a landfall, set foot on dry land; reach or make land, make port; put in or into, put into port; dock, moor, tie up, anchor, drop anchor; go ashore, **disembark,** debark, unboat; **detrain,** debus, **deplane, disemplane;** alight

ADJS **9 arriving,** approaching, entering, **coming,** incoming; inbound, inwardbound; homeward, homeward-bound; immigrant

ADVS **10 arriving,** on arrival *or* arriving

187 RECEPTION

NOUNS **1 reception, taking in,** receipt, receiving; **welcome,** welcoming, cordial welcome, open *or* welcoming arms; hospitality; refuge 1009

2 admission, admittance, acceptance; immission <old>, intromission 191.1; **installation,** installment, instatement, inauguration, initiation; baptism, investiture, ordination; enlistment, enrollment, induction

3 entree, entrée, in <nf>, entry, **entrance** 189, **access,** opening, **open door,** open arms; a foot in the door, opening wedge

4 ingestion; eating 8; **drinking** 8.3, imbibing, imbibition; engorgement, ingurgitation, engulfment; **swallowing,** gulping; swallow, gulp, slurp

5 <drawing in> **suction,** suck, sucking; **inhalation,** inhalement, inspiration, aspiration; snuff, snuffle, sniff, sniffle

6 sorption, **absorption,** adsorption, chemisorption *or* chemosorption, engrossment, digestion, **assimilation,** infiltration; **sponging, blotting;** **seepage,** percolation; **osmosis,** endosmosis, exosmosis, electroosmosis; absorbency; **absorbent,** adsorbent, **sponge, blotter,** blotting paper

7 <bringing in> **introduction; importing,** import, **importation,** investiture, naturalization

8 readmission; reabsorption, resorbence

9 receptivity, receptiveness, welcoming, welcome, invitingness, openness, hospitality, cordiality, recipience *or* recipiency; receptibility, admissibility

VERBS **10 receive, take in; admit, let in,** immit <old>, intromit, give entrance *or* admittance to; **welcome,** bid welcome, give a royal welcome, roll out the red carpet; give an entree, open the door to, give refuge *or* shelter *or* sanctuary to, throw open to; include

11 ingest, eat 8.20, tuck away, put away; imbibe, **drink; swallow, devour,** ingurgitate; **engulf,** engorge; **gulp,** gulp down, swill, swill down, wolf down, gobble

12 draw in, suck, suckle, suck in *or* up, aspirate, pick up; **inhale,** inspire, breathe in; snuff, snuffle, sniff, sniffle, snuff in *or* up, slurp

13 absorb, adsorb, chemisorb *or* chemosorb, **assimilate,** engross, digest, **drink,** imbibe, take up *or* in, drink up *or* in, slurp up, swill up; blot, **blot**

up, soak up, sponge; osmose; infiltrate, filter in; **soak in, seep in,** percolate in; internalize

14 bring in, introduce, import

15 readmit; reabsorb, resorb

ADJS **16 receptive,** recipient; welcoming, open, hospitable, cordial, inviting, invitatory; introceptive; **admissive,** admissory; receivable, receptible, admissible; intromissive, intromittent; ingestive, imbibitory

17 sorbent, **absorbent,** adsorbent, chemisorptive *or* chemosorptive, **assimilative,** digestive; bibulous, imbibitory, thirsty, soaking, blotting; spongy, spongeous; osmotic, endosmotic, exosmotic; resorbent

18 introductory, introductive; **initiatory,** initiative, baptismal

188 DEPARTURE

NOUNS **1 departure, leaving, going,** passing, **parting; exit,** walkout <nf>; egress 190.2; **withdrawal,** removal, retreat 163.2, retirement; evacuation, abandonment, desertion; decampment; escape, flight, getaway <nf>, elopement; exodus, hegira; migration, mass migration; defection, voting with one's feet; checkout

2 start, starting, start-off, setoff, setout, takeoff *and* getaway <nf>, liftoff; the starting gun *or* pistol; break; the green light

3 embarkation, embarkment, boarding; entrainment; enplanement *or* emplanement

4 leave-taking, leave, parting, departure, conge; **send-off,** Godspeed; **adieu,** one's adieus, **farewell,** aloha, **good-bye;** valedictory address, valedictory, valediction, parting words; parting *or* Parthian shot; swan song; viaticum; stirrup cup, one for the road, nightcap <nf>

5 point of departure, starting place *or* **point,** takeoff, **start,** base, baseline, basis; line of departure; starting line *or* post *or* gate, starting blocks, springboard, jumping-off point; stakeboat; port of embarkation

VERBS **6 depart,** make off, begone, be off, take oneself off *or* away, take one's departure, take leave *or* take one's leave, **leave, go, go away, go off, get off** *or* **away,** get under way, come away, go one's way, go *or* get along, be getting along, go on, get on; move off *or* away, move out, march off *or* away; **pull out;** decamp; exit; take *or* break *or* tear oneself away, take oneself off, take wing *or* flight

7 <nf terms> **beat it, split,** scram, amscray, up and go, trot, toddle, stagger along, mosey *or* sashay along, buzz off, buzz along, bug out, bugger off <Brit>, beetle off, fuck off *or* f off, get rolling, hightail it, pull up stakes, check out, clear out, cut out, haul ass, hit the road *or* trail, piss off <chiefly Brit>, get lost, flake off, get going, shove off, push along, push off, get out, get *or* git, get the hell out, make oneself scarce, vamoose, take off, skip, skip out, lam, take it on the lam, powder, take a powder, take a runout powder, skedaddle, absquatulate <old>, clock off

8 **set out, set forth,** put forth, go forth, **sally forth,** sally, issue, issue forth, launch forth, set forward, **set off,** be off, be on one's way, outset, **start, start out** *or* **off, strike out,** get off, get away, get off the dime <nf>; get the green light, break; set sail

9 **quit, vacate,** evacuate, abandon, desert, turn one's back on, walk away from, leave to one's fate, leave flat *or* high and dry; leave *or* desert a sinking ship; **withdraw,** retreat, **beat a retreat,** retire, remove; walk away, abscond, disappear, vanish; **bow out** <nf>, make one's exit; jump ship

10 **hasten off, hurry away; scamper off, dash off,** whiz off, whip off *or* away, nip *and* nip off <nf>, tear off *or* out, **light out** <nf>, dig *or* skin out *and* burn rubber <nf>, vamoose

11 **fling out** *or* **off,** flounce out *or* off

12 **run off** *or* **away,** run along, flee, take to flight, fly, take to one's heels, cut and run *and* hightail *and* make tracks *and* absquatulate <old> <nf>, scarper <Brit nf>; run for one's life; beat a retreat *or* a hasty retreat; run away from 368.10

13 **check out;** clock *and* ring *and* punch out <nf>, sign out

14 **decamp, break camp,** strike camp *or* tent, **pull up stakes**

15 **embark, go aboard,** board, go on board; go on shipboard, take ship; hoist the blue Peter; **entrain,** enplane *or* emplane, embus; weigh anchor, up-anchor, put to sea 182.19

16 say *or* bid good-bye *or* farewell, take leave, make one's adieus; bid Godspeed, give one a send-off *or* a big send-off, see off *or* out, "speed the parting guest"—Pope; drink a stirrup cup, have one for the road

17 **leave home,** go from home; leave the country, emigrate, out-migrate, expatriate, defect; vote with one's feet; burn one's bridges; leave the nest

ADJS 18 **departing, leaving; parting,** last, final, farewell; valedictory; outward-bound

19 **departed, left, gone,** gone off *or* away

ADVS 20 **hence,** thence, whence; off, **away,** forth, out; therefrom, thereof

PREPS 21 **from, away from;** out, out of

INTERJS 22 **farewell!, goodbye!, adieu!, so long!,** see ya!, **I'm outa here** <nf>, cheerio! <Brit>, *au revoir!* <Fr>, *¡adios!* <Sp>, *¡hasta la vista!* <Sp>, *¡hasta luego!* <Sp>, *¡vaya con Dios!* <Sp>, *auf*

Wiedersehen! <Ger>, *addio!* <Ital>, *arrivederci!* and *arrivederla!* <Ital>, *ciao!* <Ital nf>, *do svidanye!* <Russ>, *shalom!* <Heb>, *sayonara!* <Japanese>, *vale!* and *vive valeque!* <L>, aloha!, **until we meet again!,** until tomorrow!, *à demain!* <Fr>, **see you later!,** see you!, tata, toodleoo, I'll be seeing you!, see you around!, we'll see you!, *à bientôt!* <Fr>, *à toute a l'heure!* <Fr>, *a domani* <Ital>; be good!, keep in touch!, come again!; *bon voyage!* <Fr>, pleasant journey!, have a nice trip!, *tsetchem leshalom!* <Heb>, *glückliche Reise!* <Ger>, happy landing!; Godspeed!, peace be with you!, take care!, *pax vobiscum!* <L>; all good go with you!, God bless you!, toodles!

23 **good night!,** nighty-night! <nf>, *bonne nuit!* <Fr>, *gute Nacht!* <Ger>, *¡buenas noches!* <Sp>, *buona notte!* <Ital>, lights out!

189 ENTRANCE

NOUNS 1 **entrance, entry,** access, entree, entrée; **ingress,** ingression; **admission, reception** 187; **ingoing, incoming,** income; **importation,** import, importing; **input, intake; penetration,** interpenetration, injection; infiltration, percolation, seepage, leakage; insinuation; intrusion 214; introduction, **insertion** 191

2 **influx, inflow,** inflooding, incursion, indraft, indrawing, inpour, inrun, inrush; afflux

3 **immigration,** in-migration, incoming population, foreign influx; border-crossing

4 **incomer, entrant,** comer, arrival; **visitor,** visitant; **immigrant,** in-migrant; newcomer 774.4, new girl, new boy, new kid; settler 227.9; **trespasser, intruder** 214.3

5 **entrance,** entry, gate, door, portal, **entranceway,** entryway; **inlet,** ingress, intake, adit, approach, **access,** means of access, in <nf>, way in; a foot in the door, an opening wedge, the camel's nose under the wall of the tent; **opening** 292; **passageway,** corridor, companionway, hall, hallway, passage, way; jetway, jet bridge; gangway, gangplank; **vestibule** 197.19; air lock

6 **porch,** propylaeum, portico, porte-cochere; **portal, threshold,** doorjamb, gatepost, doorpost, lintel; **door, doorway,** French door; **gate, gateway; hatch,** hatchway, scuttle; turnstile

VERBS 7 **enter, go in** *or* **into,** access, cross the threshold, **come in,** find one's way into, put in *or* into; be admitted, gain admission *or* admittance, have an entree, have an in <nf>; **set foot in,** step in, walk in; **get in,** jump in, leap in, hop in; **drop in,** look in, visit, drop by, pop in <nf>; **breeze in,** come breezing in; break *or* burst in, bust *or* come busting in <nf>; **barge in** *or* come barging in *and* wade in <nf>; thrust in, push *or* press in, crowd in, jam in, wedge in, pack in, squeeze in; slip *or* creep in, wriggle *or* worm oneself into, get one's foot in the door, edge in, work in, insinuate oneself, weigh in <nf>; irrupt, intrude 214.5; take in, admit 187.10; insert 191.3

8 **penetrate,** interpenetrate, **pierce,** pass *or* go through, get through, get into, make way into, make an entrance, gain entree; crash <nf>, gatecrash <nf>

9 **flow in,** inpour, **pour in,** inrush, inflow

10 **filter in, infiltrate, seep in,** percolate into, leak in, soak in, perfuse, worm one's way into, insinuate

11 **immigrate,** in-migrate; cross the border

ADJS 12 **entering,** ingressive, **incoming, ingoing;** in, inward; **inbound,** inward-bound; inflowing, influent, inflooding, inpouring, inrushing; invasive, intrusive, irruptive; ingrowing

ADVS 13 **in,** inward, inwards, inwardly; thereinto

PREPS 14 **into, in,** to

190 EMERGENCE

NOUNS 1 **emergence,** coming out, coming forth, coming into view, rising to the surface, surfacing, emerging; **issuing,** issuance, issue; extrusion; **emission,** emitting, giving forth, giving out; emanation; **vent,** venting, discharge; outbreak, breakout

2 **egress,** egression; **exit,** exodus; outgoing, outgo, going out; emersion <astronomy>; **departure** 188; evacuation; extraction 192; exfiltration

3 **outburst** 671.6, ejection 909

4 **outflow,** outflowing; discharge; **outpouring,** outpour; effluence, effusion, exhalation; **efflux,** effluxion, defluxion; **exhaust; runoff, flowoff;** outfall; drainage, drain; gush 238.4

5 **leakage,** leaking, weeping <nf>; **leak; dripping,** drippings, **drip,** dribble, drop, trickle; distillation

6 **exuding,** exudation, transudation; **filtration,** exfiltration, filtering; straining; **percolation,** percolating; leaching, lixiviation; effusion, extravasation; **seepage,** seep; perfusion; **oozing,** ooze; weeping, weep; **excretion** 12

7 **emigration,** out-migration, remigration; exile, expatriation, defection, deportation

8 **export,** exporting, exportation; outgoings

9 **outlet,** egress, **exit,** outgo, outcome, out <nf>, way out; loophole, escape; **opening** 292; outfall, estuary; chute, flume, sluice, weir, floodgate; **vent,** ventage, venthole, port; safety valve; avenue, channel; spout, tap; opening, orifice; debouch; **exhaust;** door 189.6; outgate, sally port; vomitory; emunctory; pore; blowhole, spiracle; fire escape

10 **goer,** outgoer, leaver, departer; **emigrant, émigré,** out-migrant, migrant; colonist; expatriate, defector, refugee, remittance man *or* woman; walk-off <nf>

VERBS 11 **emerge, come out, issue,** issue forth, come into view, extrude, **come forth; surface,** rise to the surface; sally, sally forth, come to the fore; emanate, effuse, arise, come; debouch, disembogue; jump out, leap out, hop out; bail out; **burst forth, break forth, erupt;** break cover, **come out in the open;** protrude

12 **exit,** make an exit, **make one's exit;** egress, **go out,** get out, walk out, march out, run out, pass out, bow out *and* include oneself out <nf>; walk out on, leave cold <nf>; escape; **depart** 188.6

13 **run out,** empty, find vent; **exhaust, drain,** drain out; **flow out,** outflow, outpour, **pour out,** sluice out, well out, gush *or* spout out, spew, flow, pour, well, surge, gush, jet, spout, spurt, vomit forth, blow out, spew out

14 **leak, leak out, drip,** dribble, drop, trickle, trill, distill

15 **exude,** exudate, transude, transpire, reek; **emit, discharge,** give off; **filter,** filtrate, exfiltrate; strain; **percolate;** leach, lixiviate; effuse, extravasate; **seep, ooze;** bleed; weep; excrete 12.12

16 **emigrate,** out-migrate, remigrate; exile, expatriate, defect; deport

17 **export,** send abroad

ADJS 18 **emerging,** emergent; **issuing,** arising, surfacing, coming, forthcoming; emanating, emanent, emanative, transeunt, transient

19 **outgoing, outbound,** outward-bound; **outflowing,** outpouring, effusive, effluent; effused, extravasated

20 exudative, exuding, transudative; percolative; porous, permeable, pervious, oozy, runny, weepy, leaky; excretory 12.19

ADVS 21 **forth; out,** outward, outwards, outwardly

PREPS 22 **out of,** ex; **from; out,** forth

191 INSERTION

<putting in>

NOUNS 1 **insertion, introduction,** insinuation, injection, infusion, perfusion, inoculation, intromission; **entrance** 189; **penetration** 292.3; interjection, interpolation 213.2; graft, grafting, engrafting, transplant, transplantation; infixing, implantation, embedment, tessellation, impactment, impaction; intercalation

2 **insert,** insertion; **inset, inlay;** gore, godet, gusset; **graft,** scion *or* cion; tessera; parentheses; filling, stuffing; inclusion, supplement; blow-in; tampon

VERBS **3 insert, introduce,** insinuate, inject, infuse, perfuse, inoculate, intromit; **enter** 189.7; **penetrate; put in, stick in,** set in, throw in, pop in, tuck in, whip in; slip in, ease in; interject; pot, hole; import; inoculate, vaccinate; intercalate

4 install, instate, inaugurate, initiate, invest, ordain; enlist, enroll, induct, sign up, sign on

5 inset, inlay; embed *or* bed, bed in; dovetail, mount

6 graft, engraft, ingraft, **implant,** imp <old>; bud; inarch

7 thrust in, drive in, run in, plunge in, force in, push in, **ram in,** press in, stuff in, crowd in, squeeze in, cram in, jam in, tamp in, pound in, pack in, poke in, knock in, wedge in, blow in, impact; shoot

8 implant, transplant, bed out; infix 855.9; fit in, **inlay;** tessellate

192 EXTRACTION
<taking or drawing out>

NOUNS **1 extraction, withdrawal,** removal; **drawing, pulling,** drawing out; ripping *or* tearing *or* wresting out, extracting; eradication, **uprooting,** unrooting, deracination; squeezing out, pressing out, expressing, expression; avulsion, evulsion, cutting out, exsection, extirpation, excision, enucleation; extrication, evolvement, disentanglement, unravelment; excavation, mining, quarrying, drilling; dredging; rooting out, uprooting; exit strategy

2 disinterment, exhumation, disentombment, **unearthing,** uncovering, digging out; graverobbing

3 drawing, drafting, sucking, **suction,** aspiration, pipetting; pumping, siphoning, tapping, broaching; milking; drainage, draining, emptying; cupping; bloodletting, bleeding, phlebotomy, venesection

4 evisceration, gutting, **disembowelment,** shelling

5 elicitation, eduction, drawing out *or* forth, bringing out *or* forth; **evocation,** calling forth; arousal, derivation

6 extortion, exaction, claim, demand; **wresting, wrenching, wringing, rending,** tearing, ripping; wrest, wrench, wring; shakedown

7 <obtaining an extract> **squeezing, pressing,** expression; **distillation;** decoction; **rendering,** rendition; **steeping,** soaking, infusion, marinating; concentration

8 extract, extraction; **essence, quintessence, spirit, elixir;** decoction; **distillate,** distillation, sublimate; **concentrate,** concentration; infusion; refinement, purification

9 extractor, separator, excavator, digger, miner; siphon; aspirator, pipette; pump, vacuum pump; press, wringer; corkscrew; forceps, pliers, pincers, tweezers; crowbar; smelter; scoop

VERBS **10 extract, take out,** get out, **withdraw, remove;** pull, draw; **pull out, draw out,** tear out, rip out, wrest out, pluck out, pick out, weed out, rake out; **pry out,** prize out, winkle out <Brit>; **pull up,** pluck up; **root up** *or* **out, uproot,** unroot, eradicate, deracinate, pull *or* pluck out by the roots, pull *or* pluck up by the roots; cut out, excise, exsect; enucleate; gouge out, avulse, evulse; extricate, evolve, disentangle, unravel; free, liberate; **dig up** *or* **out,** grub up *or* out, excavate, **unearth,** mine, quarry; dredge, dredge up *or* out; smelt

11 disinter, exhume, disentomb, unbury, unsepulcher, dig up, excavate, uncover

12 draw off, draft off, draft, draw, draw from; **suck,** suck out *or* up, **siphon off;** pipette; vacuum; pump, pump out; tap, broach; let, let out; bleed; let blood, venesect, phlebotomize, bleed; milk; **drain,** decant; exhaust, empty

13 eviscerate, disembowel, gut, shell

14 elicit, educe, deduce, induce, derive, obtain, procure, secure; **get from,** get out of; **evoke, call up, summon up,** call *or* summon forth, call out; rouse, arouse, stimulate; **draw out** *or* **forth,** bring out *or* forth, pry *or* prize out, winkle out <Brit>, drag out, worm out, bring to light; wangle, wangle out of, worm out of

15 extort, exact, squeeze, claim, demand; **wrest, wring from, wrench from, rend from,** wrest *or* tear from, force out, shake down

16 <obtain an extract> **squeeze** *or* **press out,** express, wring, wring out, bleed; **distill,** distill out, elixirate <old>; **filter,** filter out; decoct; **render,** melt down; refine; **steep,** soak, infuse; **concentrate,** essentialize

ADJS **17 extractive,** eductive; educible; eradicative, uprooting; elicitory, **evocative,** arousing; **exacting,** exactive; **extortionate,** extortionary, extortive

18 essential, quintessential, pure 798.6

193 ASCENT
<motion upwards>

NOUNS **1 ascent,** ascension, levitation, **rise, rising,** uprising, **uprise,** uprisal; **upgoing,** upgo, uphill, upslope, upping; upcoming; **taking off,** leaving the ground, takeoff; **soaring,** zooming, gaining altitude, leaving the earth behind; spiraling *or* gyring up; shooting *or* rocketing up; defying gravity; **jump,** vault, spring, saltation, **leap** 366; mount, **mounting; climb, climbing,** upclimb, anabasis, clamber, escalade; surge, upsurge, upsurgence, upleap, upshoot, uprush; **gush, jet,** spurt, spout, fountain; updraft; upswing, upsweep, bounce; upgrowth; upgrade 204.6; **uplift,** elevation 912; **uptick** <nf>, **increase** 251; surfacing, breaking the surface

2 upturn, uptrend, upcast, upsweep, upbend, upcurve, upsurge

3 stairs, stairway, staircase, *escalier* <Fr>, escalator, flight of stairs, pair of stairs; **steps,** treads and risers; stepping-stones; spiral staircase, winding staircase, cockle stairs <nf>; companionway, companion; stile; back stairs; perron; fire escape; landing, landing stage; ramp, incline

4 ladder, scale; stepladder, folding ladder, rope ladder, fire ladder; hook ladder, extension ladder; Jacob's ladder, companion ladder, accommodation ladder, boarding ladder, loft ladder, side ladder, gangway ladder, quarter ladder, stern ladder, folding ladder, aerial ladder

5 step, stair, footstep, rest, footrest, stepping-stone; **rung, round,** rundle, spoke, stave, scale; doorstep; tread; riser; bridgeboard, string; step stool

6 climber, ascender, upclimber, soarer; mountain climber, **mountaineer,** alpinist, rock climber, rock-jock <nf>, cragsman; steeplejack; stegophilist

7 <comparisons> rocket, skyrocket; lark, skylark, eagle

VERBS **8 ascend, rise, mount,** arise, up, uprise, levitate, upgo, **go up,** rise up, come up; go onwards and upwards; upsurge, **surge,** upstream, upheave; swarm up, upswarm, sweep up; upwind, upspin, spiral, spire, curl upwards; stand up, **rear,** rear up, **tower,** loom; upgrow, grow up

9 shoot up, spring up, jump up, **leap up,** vault up, start up, fly up, pop up, bob up; float up, surface, break water; **gush, jet,** spurt, fountain; upshoot, upstart, upspring, upleap, upspear, rocket, **skyrocket**

10 take off, leave the ground, leave the earth behind, gain altitude, claw skyward; become airborne; **soar,** zoom, fly, plane, kite, fly aloft; aspire; spire, spiral *or* gyre upward; **hover,** hang, poise, float, float in the air; rocket, skyrocket

11 climb, climb up, upclimb, **mount,** clamber, **clamber up,** scramble *or* scrabble up, claw one's way up, struggle up, inch up, shin, shinny *or* shin up <nf>, ramp <nf>, work *or* inch one's way up, climb the ladder; **scale,** escalade, scale the heights; climb over, surmount, go over the top

12 mount, get on, climb on, back; **bestride,** bestraddle; **board,** go aboard, go on board; **get in,** jump in, hop in, pile in <nf>; surmount, remount

13 upturn, turn up, cock up; trend upwards, slope up; upcast, upsweep, upbend, upcurve

ADJS **14 ascending,** in the ascendant, **mounting, rising,** uprising, upgoing, upcoming; ascendant,

ascensional, ascensive, anabatic; **leaping,** springing, saltatory; spiraling, skyrocketing; **upward,** uphill, uphillward, upgrade, upsloping, gradient; uparching, rearing, rampant; climbing, scandent, scansorial; gravity-defying

15 upturned, upcast, uplifted, **turned-up,** retroussé

ADVS **16 up, upward, upwards,** upwith <Scot>; skyward, heavenward; uplong, upalong; upstream, upstreamward; uphill; uphillward; upstairs; up attic *and* up steps <nf>; uptown; up north

INTERJS **17 alley-oop!, upsy-daisy!;** excelsior!, onward and upward!

194 DESCENT
<motion downward>

NOUNS **1 descent, descending,** descension *or* downcome <old>, **comedown,** down; **dropping, falling,** plummeting, **drop, fall, free-fall,** *chute* <Fr>, **downfall,** debacle, **collapse,** crash; **swoop,** stoop, pounce, downrush, downflow, cascade, waterfall, cataract, **downpour,** defluxion; downturn, downcurve, downbend, downward trend, downtrend; declension, declination, inclination; gravitation; abseil, rappel; downgrade 204.5; **down tick; decrease** 252

2 sinkage, lowering, **decline, slump,** subsidence, submergence, lapse, decurrence, downgrade; cadence; **droop, sag,** swag; catenary; downer <nf>

3 tumble, fall, *culbute* <Fr>, cropper *and* spill <nf>, **flop** <nf>; **header** <nf>; **sprawl; pratfall** <nf>; **stumble,** trip; **dive, plunge** 367, belly flop, nosedive; forced landing

4 slide; slip, slippage; **glide,** coast, glissade; glissando; slither; **skid,** sideslip; **landslide,** mudslide, landslip, subsidence; **snowslide,** snowslip <Brit>; **avalanche**

VERBS **5 descend, go** *or* **come down,** down, dip down, lose altitude, dump altitude <nf>; gravitate; **fall, drop,** precipitate, rain, rain *or* pour down, fall *or* drop down; **collapse,** crash; **swoop,** stoop, pounce; **pitch, plunge** 367.6, **plummet;** cascade, cataract; parachute; come down a peg <nf>; **fall off,** drop off; trend downward, down-tick, go downhill

6 sink, go down, sink down, submerge; **set, settle,** settle down; **decline,** lower, **subside,** give way, lapse, cave, cave in; **droop,** slouch, **sag,** swag; **slump,** slump down; flump, flump down; flop *and* flop down <nf>; plump, plop *or* plop down, plunk *or* plunk down <nf>; founder 367.8

7 get down, alight, touch down, **light; land,** settle, perch, come to rest; **dismount, get off,** uphorse; climb down; abseil, rappel

8 **tumble, fall, fall down,** come *or* fall *or* get a cropper <nf>, take a fall *or* tumble, take a flop *or* spill <nf>, precipitate oneself; fall over, tumble over, trip over; **sprawl,** sprawl out, take a pratfall <nf>, spread-eagle <nf>, measure one's length; fall headlong, **take a header** <nf>, nosedive; fall prostrate, fall flat, fall on one's face, fall flat on one's ass <nf>; **fall over,** topple down *or* over; capsize, turn turtle; **topple,** lurch, pitch, **stumble,** stagger, totter, careen, list, tilt, trip, flounder

9 **slide, slip,** slidder <nf>, slip *or* slide down; **glide,** skim, coast, glissade; **slither; skid,** sideslip; avalanche

10 **light upon,** alight upon, settle on; **descend upon, come down on, fall on,** drop on, hit *or* strike upon

ADJS 11 **descending,** descendant, on the descendant; **down,** downward, declivitous; decurrent, deciduous; **downgoing,** downcoming; down-reaching; **dropping, falling, plunging, plummeting,** downfalling; **sinking,** downsinking, foundering, submerging, setting; declining, **subsiding;** collapsing, tumbledown, tottering, drooping, sagging; on the downgrade, downhill 204.16

12 **downcast, downturned;** hanging, down-hanging, collapsed

ADVS 13 **down, downward, downwards,** from the top down, *de haut en bas* <Fr>; adown, below; downright; downhill, downgrade; downstreet; downline; downstream; downstairs; downtown; south, down south

195 CONTAINER

NOUNS 1 **container, receptacle;** receiver 479.3, holder, vessel, utensil; repository, depository, reservoir, store; basin, pot, pan, drinking vessel, cup, glass, bottle, crockery, ladle; cask; box, case, crate, carton; bucket; bottle, can, box, pack, jar; kit; basket; luggage, suitcase, baggage, trunk; cabinet, cupboard; shelf, drawer, locker; frame; compartment; packet; cart, truck

2 **bag, sack,** sac, poke <nf>, bundle; **pocket,** fob; **balloon, bladder;** carryall, pouch; purse, handbag, tote, satchel

196 CONTENTS

NOUNS 1 **contents, content,** what is contained *or* included *or* comprised; **insides** 207.4, innards <nf>, guts, inner workings; **components, constituents, ingredients,** elements, **items, parts, divisions,** subdivisions; **inventory,** index, census, list 871; part 793; whole 792; composition 796; constitution, makeup, embodiment

2 **load, lading, cargo, freight, charge, burden; payload;** boatload, busload, carload, cartload, containerload, shipload, trailerload, trainload, truckload, vanload, wagonload; shipment, stowage, tonnage

3 **lining,** liner; **interlining,** interlineation; inlayer, inside layer, **inlay,** inlaying; **filling,** filler; **packing,** padding, wadding, **stuffing;** facing; doubling, doublure; bushing, bush; wainscot; insole; facing; innards

4 <contents of a container> cup, cupful, etc

5 <essential content> **substance, sum and substance, stuff, material, matter,** medium, building blocks, fabric; **gist, heart, soul, meat, nub;** the nitty-gritty *and* the bottom line *and* the name of the game <nf>, **core,** kernel, marrow, pith, sap, spirit, **essence,** quintessence, elixir, distillate, distillation, distilled essence, nucleus; sine qua non, irreducible *or* indispensable content

6 **enclosure,** the enclosed, yard, corral, pen

VERBS 7 **fill, pack** 794.7, **load; line,** interline, interlineate; inlay; face; wainscot, ceil; **pad,** wad, **stuff;** feather, fur; fill up, top up

197 ROOM

<compartment>

NOUNS 1 **room, chamber,** *chambre* <Fr>, *salle* <Fr>, four walls

2 **compartment,** chamber, space, enclosed space; **cavity,** hollow, hole, concavity; **cell,** cellule; booth, stall, crib, manger; box, pew; **crypt, vault**

3 **nook, corner, cranny, niche, recess,** cove, bay, oriel, alcove; cubicle, roomlet, carrel, hole-in-the-wall <nf>, cubby, **cubbyhole,** snuggery, hidey-hole <nf>

4 **hall;** assembly hall, exhibition hall, convention hall; gallery; meetinghouse, meeting room; **auditorium; concert hall; theater,** music hall; stadium, dome, sports dome, **arena** 463; lecture hall, lyceum, amphitheater; operating theater; dance hall; ballroom, grand ballroom; **chapel** 703.3

5 **parlor, living room, sitting room, morning room, drawing** *or* **withdrawing room, front room,** best room <nf>, foreroom <nf>, **salon,** saloon <old>; sun parlor *or* sunroom, lounge, sun lounge, sunporch, solarium, conservatory

6 **library,** stacks; **study,** studio, *atelier* <Fr>, workroom, den; **office,** workplace, cubicle, cube farm <nf>, home office; **loft,** sail loft

7 **bedroom, boudoir,** chamber, sleeping chamber, **bedchamber,** master bedroom, guest room, sleeping room, cubicle, cubiculum; nursery; dormitory *or* dorm room

8 <private chamber> **sanctum,** sanctum sanctorum, holy of holies, adytum; **den,** retreat, closet, cabinet; cave <nf>

9 <ships> cabin, stateroom; saloon; house, deckhouse, trunk cabin, cuddy, shelter cabin

10 <trains> drawing room, stateroom, parlor car, Pullman car, roomette, bar car

11 **dining room,** *salle à manger* <Fr>, dinette; breakfast room, breakfast nook, dining hall, refectory, mess *or* messroom *or* mess hall, commons, canteen; dining car *or* diner; **restaurant, cafeteria**

12 **playroom,** recreation room, rec room <nf>, family room, game room, **rumpus room** <nf>; **gymnasium**

13 **utility room,** laundry room, sewing room, mud room

14 **kitchen** 11.4, kitchenette, galley, pantry, larder, scullery; **storeroom** 386.6, smoking room 89.13

15 **closet,** clothes closet, wardrobe, cloakroom, walk-in closet; checkroom; linen closet; dressing room, fitting room, pantry

16 **attic,** attic room, **garret, loft,** sky parlor; cockloft, hayloft; storeroom, junk room, lumber room <Brit>

17 **basement; cellar,** cellarage; subbasement; wine cellar, potato cellar, storm cellar, cyclone cellar; coal bin *or* hole, hold, hole, bunker; glory hole; panic room, safe room; man cave

18 **corridor, hall,** hallway; passage, **passageway; gallery,** loggia; arcade, colonnade, pergola, cloister, peristyle; areaway; breezeway

19 **vestibule,** portal, **portico,** entry, entryway, entrance, **entrance hall,** entranceway, **threshold; lobby, foyer;** propylaeum, stoa; narthex, galilee

20 **anteroom,** antechamber; side room, byroom; **waiting room,** transit lounge, *salle d'attente* <Fr>; **reception room,** presence chamber *or* room, audience chamber; throne room; lounge, greenroom, wardroom

21 **porch,** stoop, **veranda,** deck, piazza <nf>, patio, lanai, gallery; sleeping porch

22 **balcony,** gallery, terrace, deck

23 **floor, story,** level, flat; first floor *or* story, ground *or* street floor, *rez-de-chaussée* <Fr>; mezzanine, mezzanine floor, *entresol* <Fr>; clerestory

24 **showroom,** display room, exhibition room, gallery

25 **hospital room; ward,** maternity ward, fever ward, charity ward, prison ward, etc; private room, semi-private room; examining *or* examination room, consulting *or* consultation room, treatment room; **operating room** *or* OR, operating theater, surgery; labor room, delivery room; recovery room; emergency, emergency room; intensive care unit *or* ICU, critical care; pharmacy, dispensary; clinic, nursery; laboratory *or* blood bank; nurses' station

26 **bathroom, lavatory, washroom** 79.10, **water closet** *or* **WC,** closet, **rest room,** privy, john <nf>, comfort station, **toilet** 12.10

27 <for vehicles> **garage,** carport; coach *or* carriage house; carbarn; roundhouse, hangar; boathouse; shed

198 TOP

NOUNS **1** **top,** top side, upper side, upside; surface 206.2; superstratum; topside *or* topsides; upper story, top floor; clerestory; **roof,** ridgepole *or* roofpole; rooftop; ceiling

2 **summit,** top; **tip-top, peak,** pinnacle; **crest, brow;** ridge, edge; **crown,** cap, **tip,** point, spire, pitch; highest pitch, no place higher, **apex,** vertex, **acme,** *ne plus ultra* <Fr>, **zenith, climax,** apogee, pole; **culmination; extremity, maximum, limit,** upper extremity, highest point, very top, top of the world, extreme limit, utmost *or* upmost *or* uppermost height; exosphere, **sky,** heaven *or* heavens, seventh heaven, cloud nine <nf>; meridian, noon, high noon; mountaintop; ninth degree

3 **topping,** icing, frosting; dressing, streusel

4 <top part> **head,** heading, **headpiece,** cap, *caput* <L>, capsheaf, **crown, crest;** topknot; pinhead, nailhead

5 **architectural topping, capital** <see list>, head, crown, cap; bracket capital; cornice; cymatium, clerestory

6 **head,** headpiece, **pate,** poll <nf>, crown, **sconce** *and* **noodle** *and* **noddle** *and* **noggin** *and* **bean** *and* **dome** <nf>; brow, ridge; "the dome of Thought, the palace of the Soul"—Byron

7 **skull,** cranium, pericranium, epicranium; brainpan, brain box *or* case

8 **phrenology,** craniology, metoposcopy, physiognomy; phrenologist, craniologist, metoposcopist, physiognomist

VERBS **9** **top,** top off, **crown, cap,** crest, **head,** tip, peak, surmount; overtop *or* outtop, have the top place *or* spot, overarch; **culminate,** consummate, climax; ice, frost, dress; fill, top up

ADJS **10** **top,** topmost, **uppermost,** upmost, overmost, **highest;** tip-top, tip-crowning, **maximum,** maximal, ultimate; summital, apical, vertical, zenithal, climactic, climactical, **consummate;** acmic, acmatic; meridian, meridional; **head,** headmost, capital, chief, paramount, supreme, preeminent, uber; **top-level,** highest level, top-echelon, top-flight, top-ranking, top-drawer <nf>; peak, pitch, ultimate, maximum, crowning

11 topping, crowning, capping, heading, surmounting, overtopping *or* outtopping, overarching; **culminating,** consummating, perfecting, climaxing

12 topped, headed, **crowned, capped,** crested, plumed, tipped, peaked, roofed

13 topless, headless, crownless

14 cranial; cephalic, encephalic

ADVS **15 atop, on top,** at *or* on the top, topside <nf>; at the top of the tree *or* ladder, on top of the roost *or* heap; on the crest *or* crest of the wave; at the head, at the peak *or* pinnacle *or* summit

PREPS **16 atop, on, upon,** on top of, surmounting, topping; like white on rice

17 capital styles

baroque	Greek Ionic
Byzantine	Ionic
composite	Moorish
Corinthian	Roman Corinthian
Doric	Roman Doric
Gothic	Romanesque
Greek	Roman Ionic
Greek Corinthian	Tuscan

199 BOTTOM

NOUNS **1 bottom,** bottom side, **underside,** nether side, lower side, downside, **underneath,** fundament; belly, underbelly; buttocks 217.4, breech; **rock bottom, bedrock,** bed, hardpan; **grass roots;** substratum, underlayer, lowest level *or* layer *or* stratum, nethermost level *or* layer *or* stratum, basecoat; **nadir,** the pits <nf>; depths, benthos

2 base, basement, **foot,** footing, sole, toe; **foundation** 901.6, core, underpinning, infrastructure; baseboard, mopboard, skirt; wainscot, dado; skeleton, bare bones, chassis, frame, undercarriage, underside; keel, keelson

3 ground covering, **ground,** earth, *terra firma* <L>; **floor,** flooring; parquet; **deck; pavement,** *pavé* <Fr>, paving, surfacing, asphalt, blacktop, macadam, concrete; **cover,** carpet, floor covering; artificial turf, Astroturf <trademark>

4 bed, bottom, floor, ground, **basin, channel,** coulee; riverbed, seabed, ocean bottom 275.4

5 foot, extremity, pes, pedes, *pied* <Fr>, trotter, pedal extremity, dog, tootsy <nf>; **hoof,** ungula, **paw,** pad, pug, *patte* <Fr>; forefoot, forepaw; harefoot, splay-foot, clubfoot, **toe,** digit; **heel, sole,** pedi *or* pedio, instep, arch; pastern; fetlock

VERBS **6 base on, found on, ground on, build on,** bottom on, bed on, set on; root in; **underlie,** undergird; bottom, bottom out, hit bottom

ADJS **7 bottom,** bottommost, **undermost,** nethermost, lowermost, deepest, **lowest; rock-bottom,** bedrock; ground, ground-level

8 basic; basal, basilar, base; **underlying, fundamental,** foundational, essential, elementary, elemental, primary, primal, primitive, rudimentary, original, grass-roots; supporting; radical; nadiral

9 pedal; plantar; footed, hoofed, ungulate, clawed, taloned; toed

200 VERTICALNESS

NOUNS **1 verticalness,** verticality, verticalism; **erectness, uprightness;** stiffness *or* erectness of posture, position of attention, brace; straight up-and-downness, up-and-downness; steepness, sheerness, precipitousness, plungingness, **perpendicularity,** plumbness, aplomb; right-angledness *or* -angularity, squareness, orthogonality; Y-axis

2 vertical, upright, perpendicular, plumb, normal; right angle, orthodiagonal; vertical circle, azimuth circle

3 precipice, cliff, sheer *or* yawning cliff *or* precipice *or* drop, steep, bluff, wall, face, scar; crag; scarp, **escarpment; palisade,** palisades; brink

4 erection, erecting, **elevation; rearing,** raising, **uprearing,** upraising, lofting, uplifting, heaving up *or* aloft; standing on end *or* upright *or* on its feet *or* on its base *or* on its legs *or* on its bottom *or* at attention

5 rising, uprising, ascension, ascending, ascent; vertical height *or* dimension; **gradient,** rise, uprise

6 <instruments> square, T square, try square, set square, carpenter's square; plumb, plumb line, plumb rule, plummet, bob, plumb bob, lead

VERBS **7 stand, stand erect, stand up, stand upright, stand up straight,** be erect, be on one's feet; hold oneself straight *or* stiff, stand ramrod-straight, have an upright carriage; stand at attention *and* brace *and* stand at parade rest <military>

8 rise, arise, ascend, mount, uprise, **rise up, get up,** get to one's feet; **stand up, stand on end; stick up,** cock up; bristle; **rear,** ramp, uprear, rear up, rise on the hind legs; upheave; sit up, sit bolt upright, straighten up; jump up, spring to one's feet

9 erect, elevate, rear, raise, pitch, **set up,** raise *or* lift *or* cast up; raise *or* heave *or* rear aloft; uprear, upraise, uplift, upheave; upright; **upend,** stand on end, stand upright *or* on end; set on its feet *or* legs *or* base *or* bottom

10 plumb, plumb-line, set *à plomb*; **square,** square up

ADJS 11 vertical, upright, bolt upright, ramrod straight, **erect,** upstanding, standing up, stand-up; rearing, rampant; **upended,** upraised, upreared; downright; up-and-down

12 perpendicular, plumb, straight-up-and-down, straight-up, **up-and-down;** sheer, steep, precipitous, plunging; **right-angled,** right-angle, right-angular, orthogonal, orthodiagonal

ADVS 13 vertically, erectly, upstandingly, uprightly, **upright,** up, stark *or* bolt upright; **on end,** up on end, right on end, endwise, endways; on one's feet *or* legs, on one's hind legs <nf>; at attention *and* braced *and* at parade rest <military>

14 perpendicularly, sheer, sheerly; up and down, **straight up and down; plumb,** *à plomb* <Fr>; **at right angles,** square

201 HORIZONTALNESS

NOUNS 1 horizontalness, horizontality; **levelness, flatness,** planeness, planarity, evenness, smoothness, flushness, alignment; unbrokenness, unrelievedness; transom

2 recumbency, recumbence, decumbency *or* decumbence, accumbency; accubation; **prostration,** proneness, procumbency; supineness, reclining, reclination; lying, lounging, **repose** 20; sprawl, loll; shavasana, corpse pose

3 horizontal, plane, level, flat, dead level *or* flat, homaloid; **horizontal** *or* level plane; horizontal *or* level line; horizontal projection; horizontal surface, fascia; horizontal parallax; horizontal axis; horizontal fault; water level, sea level, mean sea level; ground, earth, steppe, **plain, flatland,** prairie, savanna, flats, sea of grass, bowling green, table, billiard table; floor, platform, ledge, terrace

4 horizon, skyline, rim of the horizon; sea line; apparent *or* local *or* visible horizon, sensible horizon, celestial *or* rational *or* geometrical *or* true horizon, artificial *or* false horizon; azimuth

VERBS 5 lie, lie down, lay <nf>, **recline, repose,** lounge, sprawl, loll, drape *or* spread oneself, spread-eagle, splay, lie limply; **lie flat** *or* prostrate *or* prone *or* supine, lie on one's face *or* back, lie on a level, hug the ground *or* deck; **grovel, crawl,** kowtow

6 level, flatten, even, equalize, align, smooth *or* smoothen, level out, smooth out, flush; grade, roll, roll flat, steamroller *or* steamroll; **lay,** lay down *or* out; **raze,** rase, lay level, lay level with the ground; lay low *or* flat; **fell** 913.5; deck <nf>

ADJS 7 horizontal, level, flat, flattened; **even,** smooth, smoothened, smoothed out; table-like, tabular; flush; homaloidal; **plane,** planar, plain; rolled, trodden, squashed, rolled *or* trodden *or* squashed flat, razed; flat as a pancake, flat as a table *or* billiard table *or* bowling green *or* tennis court, flat as a board, level as a plain

8 recumbent, accumbent, procumbent, decumbent; **prostrate, prone,** flat; **supine,** resupine; couchant, *couché* <Fr>; **lying, reclining, reposing,** flat on one's back; sprawling, lolling, lounging; corpselike; sprawled, spread, splay, splayed, draped; groveling, crawling, flat on one's belly *or* nose

ADVS 9 horizontally, flat, flatly, flatways, flatwise; **evenly,** flush; **level, on a level;** lengthwise, lengthways, at full length, on one's back *or* belly *or* nose

202 PENDENCY

NOUNS 1 pendency, pendulousness *or* pendulosity, pensileness *or* pensility; **hanging, suspension,** dangling *or* danglement, suspense, dependence *or* dependency, swinging

2 hang, droop, dangle, swing, fall; **sag,** swag, bag

3 overhang, overhanging, impendence *or* impendency, **projection,** extension, protrusion, beetling, jutting; cantilever

4 pendant, hanger; **hanging,** drape; **lobe,** ear lobe, lobule, lobus, lobation, lappet, wattle; lavalier *or* lavaliere; teardrop; **uvula**

5 suspender, hanger, supporter; **suspenders,** pair of suspenders, braces <Brit>, galluses <nf>

VERBS 6 hang, hang down, fall; **depend,** pend; **dangle,** swing, flap, flop <nf>; flow, drape, cascade; **droop,** lop; nod, weep; **sag,** swag, bag; **trail, drag, draggle,** drabble, daggle

7 overhang, hang over, hang out, **impend,** impend over, **project,** project over, beetle, **jut,** beetle *or* jut *or* thrust over, stick out over

8 suspend, hang, hang up, put up, fasten up; sling; oscillate, swing, sway, hover

ADJS 9 pendent, pendulous, pendulant, pendular, penduline, pensile; **suspended,** hung; **hanging,** pending, depending, dependent; **falling; dangling,** swinging, oscillating, falling loosely; weeping; flowing, cascading

10 drooping, droopy, limp, loose, nodding, floppy <nf>, loppy, lop; **sagging,** saggy, swag, sagging in folds; **bagging,** baggy, ballooning; lop-eared

11 overhanging, overhung, lowering, **impending,** impendent, **pending;** incumbent, superincumbent; **projecting, jutting; beetling,** beetle; beetle-browed; cantilevered

12 lobular, lobar, lobed, lobate, lobated

203 PARALLELISM

<physically parallel direction or state>

NOUNS **1 parallelism,** coextension, nonconvergence, nondivergence, collaterality, concurrence, equidistance; collineation, collimation; alignment; parallelization; parallelotropism; **analogy** 943.1

2 parallel, paralleler; parallel line, parallel dash, parallel bar, parallel file, parallel series, parallel column, parallel trench, parallel vector; parallelogram, parallelepiped *or* parallelepipedon

3 <instruments> parallel rule *or* rules *or* ruler, parallelograph, parallelometer

VERBS **4 parallel,** be parallel, coextend; run parallel, go alongside, go beside, run abreast, run side by side; match, equal

5 parallelize, place parallel to, equidistance; line up, align, realign; collineate, collimate; match; correspond, follow, equate

ADJS **6 parallel,** paralleling, parallelistic; coextending, coextensive, nonconvergent, nondivergent, **equidistant,** equispaced, collateral, concurrent; lined up, aligned; equal, even; parallelogrammical, parallelogrammatical; parallelepipedal; parallelotropic; parallelodrome, parallelinervate; analogous 943.8

ADVS **7 in parallel,** parallelwise, parallelly; side-by-side, alongside, abreast; equidistantly, nonconvergently, nondivergently; collaterally, coextensively

204 OBLIQUITY

NOUNS **1 obliquity,** obliqueness; **deviation** 164, deviance, divergence, digression, divagation, vagary, excursion, skewness, aberration, squint, declination; deflection, deflexure; nonconformity 868; diagonality, crosswiseness, transverseness; indirection, indirectness, deviousness, circumlocution, circuitousness 914; indirect question

2 inclination, leaning, lean, angularity; **slant,** slaunch <nf>, rake, **slope; tilt, tip,** pitch, **list, cant,** swag, sway; leaning tower, tower of Pisa

3 bias, bend, bent, **crook, warp, twist, turn, skew,** slue, veer, sheer, **swerve,** lurch, deflection

4 incline, inclination, **slope, grade,** gradient, pitch, **ramp,** launching ramp, bank, talus, gentle *or* easy slope, glacis; rapid *or* steep slope, stiff climb, scarp, chute; helicline, inclined plane <phys>; **bevel,** bezel, fleam; hillside, side; hanging gardens; shelving beach

5 declivity, descent, dip, drop, fall, falling-off *or* -away, **decline;** hang, hanging; **downgrade, downhill**

6 acclivity, ascent, climb, **rise,** rising, uprise, uprising, rising ground; **upgrade, uphill,** upgo, upclimb, uplift, steepness, precipitousness, abruptness, verticalness 200

7 diagonal, oblique, transverse, bias, bend <heraldry>, oblique line, slash, **slant,** virgule, scratch comma, serial comma, separatrix, solidus, cant; oblique angle *or* figure, rhomboid, rhombus

8 zigzag, zig, zag; zigzaggery, flexuosity, **crookedness,** crankiness; switchback, hairpin, dogleg; chevron; traverse

VERBS **9 oblique, deviate, diverge,** deflect, divagate, **bear off,** digress; angle, **angle off, swerve,** shoot off at an angle, **veer,** sheer, sway, slue, **skew, twist, turn,** bend, bias, dogleg; crook; circumlocute

10 incline, lean; slope, slant, camber, slaunch <nf>, rake, pitch, grade, bank, shelve; **tilt, tip, list, cant,** bevel, careen, keel, sidle, swag, sway; **ascend, rise,** uprise, climb, **go uphill; descend, decline,** dip, drop, fall, fall off *or* away, **go downhill;** retreat

11 cut, cut *or* slant across, cut crosswise *or* transversely *or* diagonally, catercorner, diagonalize, slash, slash across

12 zigzag, zig, zag, **stagger,** crank *or* crankle <old>, wind in and out; traverse

ADJS **13 oblique,** obliquitous; **devious,** deviant, deviative, divergent, digressive, divagational, deflectional, excursive, off course; **indirect,** side, sidelong, roundabout; left-handed, sinister, sinistral; backhand, backhanded; circuitous 914.7

14 askew, skew, skewed; skew-jawed *and* skewgee *and* skew-whiff *and* askewgee *and* agee *and* agee-jawed <nf>; **awry,** wry; askance, askant, asquint, squinting, **cockeyed** <nf>; **crooked** 265.10; slaunchwise *or* slaunchways <nf>; wamperjawed *and* catawampous *and* yaw-ways <nf>, wonky <Brit nf>; wonky

15 inclining, inclined, inclinatory, inclinational; **leaning,** recumbent; **sloping,** sloped, aslope; raking, pitched; **slanting,** slanted, slant, aslant, slantways, slantwise; bias, biased; shelving, shelvy; **tilting,** tilted, atilt, tipped, **tipping,** tipsy, listing, **canting,** careening; sideling, sidelong; out of the perpendicular *or* square *or* plumb, bevel, beveled

16 <sloping downward> **downhill, downgrade; descending,** falling, dropping, dipping; **declining,** declined; declivous, declivitous, declivate

17 <sloping upward> **uphill, upgrade; rising,** uprising, **ascending,** climbing; acclivous, acclivitous, acclinate

18 steep, precipitous, bluff, plunging, abrupt, bold, **sheer,** sharp, rapid; headlong, breakneck; vertical 200.11

19 transverse, crosswise *or* crossways, thwart, athwart, across 170.9; **diagonal,** bendwise; catercorner *or* **catercornered** *or* cattycorner *or* cattycornered *or* kittycorner *or* kittycornered; slant, bias, biased, biaswise *or* biasways

20 crooked, zigzag, zigzagged, zigzaggy, zigzagwise *or* zigzagways, zigged, zagged, dogleg *or* doglegged; flexuous, twisty, hairpin, bendy, curvy, meandering; staggered, crankled <old>; chevrony, chevronwise *or* chevronways <architecture>

ADVS **21 obliquely, deviously,** deviately, **indirectly,** circuitously 914.9; divergently, digressively, excursively, divagationally; **sideways** *or* sidewise, sidelong, sideling, on *or* to one side; at an angle

22 askew, awry; askance, askant, asquint, wonkily

23 slantingly, slopingly, aslant, aslope, atilt, rakingly, tipsily, slopewise, slopeways, slantwise, slantways, aslantwise, on *or* at a slant; slaunchwise *and* slaunchways <nf>; off plumb *or* the vertical; **downhill, downgrade; uphill, upgrade**

24 transversely, crosswise *or* crossways, athwart, across 170.13

25 diagonally, diagonalwise; **on the bias,** bias, biaswise; **cornerwise,** cornerways; catercornerways *or* **catercorner** *or* cattycorner *or* kittycorner

205 INVERSION

NOUNS **1 inversion,** turning over *or* around *or* upside down, the other way round, inverted order; eversion, turning inside out, invagination, intussusception; introversion, turning inward; **reversing, reversal** 858.1, turning front to back *or* side to side; **reversion,** turning back *or* backwards, retroversion, retroflexion, retroflection, revulsion; devolution, atavism; recidivism; **transposition,** transposal; topsy-turvydom *or* topsy-turviness; the world turned upside-down, upside-downness, the tail wagging the dog; pronation, supination, resupination

2 overturn, upset, overset, **overthrow,** upturn, **turnover,** spill <nf>; subversion; **revolution** 860; **capsizing,** capsize, capsizal, turning turtle; **somersault,** somerset, *culbute* <Fr>, cartwheel, handspring; headstand, handstand; turning head over heels

3 <grammatical and rhetorical terms> metastasis, metathesis; anastrophe, chiasmus, hypallage, hyperbaton, hysteron proteron, palindrome, parenthesis, synchysis, tmesis

4 inverse, reverse, converse, opposite 215.5, other side of the coin *or* picture, the flip side *and* B side <nf>; counter, contrary

VERBS **5 invert,** inverse, turn over *or* around *or* upside down; introvert, turn in *or* inward; **turn down; turn inside out,** turn out, evert, invaginate, intussuscept; **revert,** recidivate, relapse, lapse, back-slide; **reverse** 859.4, **transpose,** convert; put the cart before the horse, put in inverted order; turn into the opposite, turn about, flip-flop, turn the tables, turn the scale *or* balance; rotate, revolve, pronate, supinate, resupinate

6 overturn, turn over, turn upside down, turn bottom side up, upturn, **upset,** overset, **overthrow,** subvert, *culbuter* <Fr>; go *or* turn ass over elbows *or* ass over tincups <nf>, turn a somersault, go *or* turn head over heels; **turn turtle, turn topsy-turvy,** topsy-turvy, topsy-turvify, flip-flop; **tip over,** keel over, topple over; **capsize;** careen, set on its beam ends, set on its ears

ADJS **7 inverted,** inversed, back-to-front, **backwards,** retroverted, **reversed, transposed, back side forward, tail first; inside out,** outside in, everted, invaginated, wrong side out, back-to-front; reverted, lapsed, recidivist *or* recidivistic; atavistic; devolutional; **upside-down, topsy-turvy,** ass over elbows *and* ass over tincups *and* arsy-varsy <nf>, bottom-up; **capsized,** head-over-heels; hyperbatic, chiastic, palindromic; resupinate; introverted; flipped, flip-flopped

ADVS **8 inversely, conversely,** contrarily, contrariwise, **vice versa,** the other way around, **backwards,** turned around; **upside down,** over, **topsy-turvy; bottom up,** bottom side up; head over heels, heels over head

206 EXTERIORITY

NOUNS **1 exteriority,** externalness, externality, **outwardness,** outerness; appearance, outward appearance, seeming, mien, **front,** manner; window-dressing, cosmetics; openness; extrinsicality 768; **superficiality, shallowness** 276; extraterritoriality, foreignness

2 exterior, external, **outside; surface,** superficies, covering 295, skin 2.4, outer skin *or* layer, epidermis, integument, envelope, crust, cortex, rind, shell 295.16; exoskeleton; cladding, plating; top, superstratum; **periphery, fringe,** circumference, outline, lineaments, border; **face,** outer face *or* side, facade, **front;** facet; extrados, back; store-front, shop-front, shop-window, street-front

3 outdoors, outside, **the out-of-doors,** the great out-of-doors, the open, **the open air;** outland, hinterland

4 externalization, exteriorization, bringing into the open, show, showing, display, displaying;

projection; **objectification,** actualization, realization

VERBS **5 externalize,** exteriorize, bring into the open, bring out, show, display, exhibit; **objectify,** actualize, project, realize; direct outward

6 scratch the surface; give a lick and a promise, do a cosmetic job, give a once-over-lightly, whitewash, give a nod

ADJS **7 exterior, external;** extrinsic 768.3; **outer, outside, out, outward,** outward-facing, outlying, outstanding; **outermost,** outmost; front, facing; surface, superficial 276.5, epidermic, cortical, cuticular; exoskeletal; cosmetic, merely cosmetic; peripheral, **fringe,** roundabout; apparent, seeming; open 348.10, public 352.17; exomorphic

8 outdoor, out-of-door, out-of-doors, **outside, without-doors; open-air,** alfresco; out and about

9 extraterritorial, exterritorial; extraterrestrial, exterrestrial, extramundane; extragalactic, extralateral, extraliminal, extramural, extrapolar, extrasolar, extraprovincial, extratribal; foreign, outlandish, **alien**

ADVS **10 externally, outwardly,** on the outside, exteriorly; **without, outside, outwards, out;** apparently, to all appearances; openly, publically, to judge by appearances; superficially, on the surface

11 outdoors, out of doors, outside, abroad, withoutdoors; in the open, **in the open air,** alfresco, *en plein air* <Fr>

WORD ELEMENTS **12** e-, ec-, ect-, ecto-, ex-, ef-, epi-, eph-, extra-, hyper-, peripher-, periphero-

207 INTERIORITY

NOUNS **1** interiority, internalness, internality, **inwardness, innerness,** inness; introversion, internalization; **intrinsicality** 767; depth 275

2 interior, inside, inner, inward, internal, intern; inner recess, recesses, **innermost** or **deepest recesses,** penetralia, intimate places, secret place or places; bosom, secret heart, heart, heart of hearts, soul, vitals, vital center; inner self, inner life, inner landscape, inner or interior man, inner nature; intrados; core, center 208.2

3 inland, inlands, **interior,** up-country; **midland,** midlands; heartland; hinterland 233.2; Middle America

4 insides, innards <nf>, inwards, internals; inner mechanism, what makes it tick *and* works <nf>; **guts** <nf>, **vitals, viscera,** *kishkes* <Yiddish>, giblets; entrails, bowels, guts, enteron; tripes *and* stuffings <nf>

VERBS **5** internalize, put in, keep within; introvert, bottle up; enclose, embed, surround, contain, comprise, include, enfold, take to heart, assimilate; introspect; retreat into

ADJS **6 interior, internal, inner, inside, inward;** intestine; **innermost,** inmost, **intimate,** private; visceral, gut <nf>; **intrinsic** 767.7; deep 275.10; central 208.11; indoor; live-in

7 inland, interior, up-country, up-river, landlocked; hinterland; **midland,** mediterranean; Middle American

8 intramarginal, intramural, intramundane, intramontane, intraterritorial, intracoastal, intragroupal; bicoastal

ADVS **9 internally, inwardly,** interiorly, inly, **intimately,** deeply, profoundly, under the surface; **intrinsically** 767.10; centrally

10 in, inside, within; herein, therein, wherein

11 inward, inwards, inwardly, withinward, withinwards; inland, inshore

12 indoors, indoor, withindoors

PREPS **13 in, into; within,** at, inside, **inside of,** in the limits of; to the heart *or* core of

WORD ELEMENTS **14** en-, em-, end-, endo-, ent-, ento-, eso-, infra-, in-, im-, il-, ir-, inter-, intra-, ob-

208 CENTRALITY

NOUNS **1 centrality,** centralness, middleness, central *or* middle *or* mid position; equidistance; centricity, centricality; concentricity; centripetalism

2 center, centrum; **middle** 819, midpoint, **heart, core, nucleus; core of one's being, where one lives; kernel; pith,** marrow, medulla; **nub, hub,** nave, axis, pivot, fulcrum; **navel,** umbilicus, omphalos, belly button <nf>; bull's-eye; dead center; omphalos; "the still point of the turning world"—T S Eliot; storm center, eye of the storm

3 <biological terms> central body, centriole, centrosome, centrosphere, nucleus; pressure point

4 focus, focal point, prime focus, point of convergence; **center of interest** *or* attention, focus of attention; center of consciousness; **center of attraction, centerpiece,** clou, mecca, cynosure; star, key figure; polestar, lodestar; magnet; center of gravity

5 nerve center, ganglion, center of activity, hub, epicenter, hotbed, vital center; control center, guidance center

6 headquarters *or* **HQ,** central station, central office, main office, central administration, seat, base, **base of operations,** center of authority; general headquarters *or* **GHQ,** command post *or* **CP,** company headquarters; where the action is <nf>; home office, central office; homeroom

7 metropolis, capital; art center, cultural center, medical center, shopping center, transportation center, trade center, manufacturing center, tourist center, community center, civic center, etc; capital city; holy place, place of pilgrimage

8 centralization, centering; nucleation; **focalization, focus,** focusing; convergence 169; **concentration,** concentralization, pooling; centralism

VERBS **9 centralize, center,** middle; center round, center on *or* in, pivot on, revolve around

10 focus, focalize, come to a point *or* focus, bring to *or* into focus; bring *or* come to a head, get to the heart of the matter home in on; zero in on, pinpoint; draw a bead on *and* get a handle on <nf>; **concentrate,** concenter, get it together <nf>; **channel,** direct, canalize, channelize; converge 169.2

ADJS **11 central,** centric, **middle** 819; centermost, middlemost, **midmost; equidistant;** centralized, concentrated; umbilical, omphalic; axial, **pivotal, key;** centroidal; centrosymmetric; geocentric, epicentral; halfway

12 nuclear, nucleate, core

13 focal, confocal; converging; centrolineal, centripetal; cynosural; pivotal

14 concentric; homocentric, centric; **coaxial,** coaxal

ADVS **15 centrally,** in the center *or* middle of, at the heart of

209 ENVIRONMENT

NOUNS **1 environment, surroundings, environs,** surround, ambience, entourage, circle, circumjacencies, circumambiencies, **circumstances,** environing circumstances, *alentours* <Fr>; **precincts,** ambit, purlieus, **milieu; neighborhood, vicinity,** vicinage, area; **suburbs,** burbs <nf>, bedroom community; outskirts, outposts, borderlands; borders, boundaries, limits, periphery, perimeter, compass, circuit; **context, situation;** habitat 228; total environment, configuration, gestalt

2 setting, background, backdrop, ground, surround, field, scene, arena, theater, locale, confines; back, rear, hinterland, distance; stage, stage setting, stage set, *mise-en-scène* <Fr>

3 <surrounding influence or condition> **milieu, ambience, atmosphere, climate, air,** aura, spirit, feeling, feel, quality, color, local color, sense, sense of place, note, tone, overtone, undertone, vibrations *or* vibes <nf>

4 <natural or suitable environment> **element,** medium; **the environment**

5 surrounding, encompassment, environment, circumambience *or* circumambiency, circumjacence *or* circumjacency; containment, **enclosure** 212; **encirclement,** cincture, encincture,

circumcincture, circling, girdling, girding; **envelopment,** enfoldment, encompassment, encompassing, compassing, embracement; circumposition; circumflexion; inclusion 772, involvement 898

VERBS **6 surround, environ,** compass, **encompass,** enclose, close; go round *or* around, compass about, outlie; **envelop,** enfold, lap, wrap, enwrap, embrace, enclasp, embosom, embay, involve, invest

7 encircle, circle, ensphere, belt, belt in, zone, cincture, encincture; **girdle,** gird, begird, engird; ring, band; loop; wreathe, wreathe *or* twine around

ADJS **8 environing, surrounding,** encompassing, enclosing; **enveloping,** wrapping, enwrapping, enfolding, embracing; **encircling,** circling; bordering, peripheral, perimetric; circumjacent, circumferential, circumambient, ambient; circumfluent, circumfluous; circumflex; **roundabout,** suburban, neighboring, neighbhorhood

9 environmental, environal; **ecological;** green

10 surrounded, environed, compassed, **encompassed,** enclosed, on all sides, hemmed-in; **enveloped,** wrapped, enfolded, lapped, wreathed

11 encircled, circled, ringed, cinctured, encinctured, belted, girdled, girt, begirt, zoned

ADVS **12 around,** round, **about,** round about, in the neighborhood *or* vicinity *or* vicinage; close, close about

13 all round, all about, on every side, on all sides, on all hands, right and left

WORD ELEMENTS **14** amph-, amphi-, circum-, peri-

210 CIRCUMSCRIPTION

NOUNS **1 circumscription, limiting,** circumscribing, **bounding, demarcation,** delimitation, definition, determination, specification; limit-setting, inclusion-exclusion, circling-in *or* -out, encincture, boundary-marking; containment

2 limitation, limiting, restriction, restricting, confinement 212.1, prescription, proscription, restraint, discipline, moderation, continence; qualification, **hedging;** bounds 211, boundary, cap, limit 211.3; time-limit, time constraint; quota; small space 258.3; proviso, condition

3 patent, copyright, certificate of invention, *brevet d'invention* <Fr>; **trademark, logo** *or* logotype, registered trademark, trade name, service mark; proprietary information

VERBS **4 circumscribe, bound; mark off** *or* mark out, stake out, lay off, rope off; **demarcate,** delimit, delimitate, draw *or* mark *or* set *or* lay out boundaries, circle in *or* out, hedge in, set the limit, mark the periphery; **define**, determine, fix, specify; surround 209.6; enclose 212.5

5 **limit, restrict, restrain, bound, confine,** cap, ground <nf>; straiten, narrow, tighten; specialize; stint, scant; **condition,** qualify, hedge, hedge about; constrain; draw the line, set an end point *or* a stopping place; set a quota; discipline, moderate, contain; restrain oneself, pull one's punches <nf>; **patent, copyright,** register

ADJS 6 **circumscribed,** circumscript; ringed *or* circled *or* hedged about; **demarcated, delimited, defined,** definite, determined, determinate, specific, stated, set, fixed; surrounded 209.10, encircled 209.11

7 **limited, restricted,** bound, **bounded, finite; confined** 212.10, prescribed, proscribed, cramped, strait, straitened, narrow; conditioned, qualified, hedged, capped; disciplined, moderated; **deprived,** in straitened circumstances, pinched, inhibiting, on short commons, on short rations, strapped; patented, registered, protected, copyrighted, proprietary

8 **restricted,** out of bounds, off-limits

9 **limiting, restricting,** defining, determining, determinative, confining; limitative, limitary, restrictive, definitive, exclusive, non-compete; frozen, rationed

10 **terminal,** limital; limitable, terminable

211 BOUNDS

NOUNS 1 **bounds, limits,** boundaries, limitations, **confines, pale,** marches, bourns, verges, edges, outlines, outer markings, skirts, outskirts, **fringes,** metes, metes and bounds; periphery, **perimeter;** coordinates, parameters; **compass, circumference,** circumscription 210

2 **outline, contour,** delineation, lines, lineaments, shapes, figure, figuration, **configuration,** gestalt; **features,** main features; **profile, silhouette;** relief; skeleton, framework, frame, armature

3 **boundary, bound, limit,** limitation, extremity 794.5; **barrier,** block, claustrum; delimitation, hedge, break *or* breakoff point, cutoff, cutoff point, terminus; time limit, time frame, term, deadline, target date, terminal date, time allotment; finish, **end** 820, tail end; **start,** starting line *or* point, mark; **limiting factor,** determinant, limit *or* boundary condition; bracket, brackets, **bookends** <nf>; threshold, limen; upper limit, ceiling, apogee, high-water mark; price cap; lower limit, floor, low-water mark, nadir; **confine,** march, mark, bourn, mete, compass, circumscription; **boundary line, line, border line,**

frontier, division line, interface, break, boundary, line of demarcation *or* circumvallation; county line

4 **border,** limbus, bordure <heraldry>, **edge,** limb, **verge, brink,** brow, **brim, rim, margin,** marge, **skirt, fringe, hem,** list, selvage *or* selvedge, side; **forefront, cutting edge,** front line, new guard, vanguard 216.2; sideline; shore, bank, coast; **lip,** labium, labrum, labellum; flange; ledge; frame, enframement, mat; featheredge; ragged edge

5 **frontier, border, borderland,** border ground, marchland, march, marches; outskirts, outpost, backwoods; frontier post, cow town; iron curtain, bamboo curtain, Berlin wall; Pillars of Hercules; three-mile *or* twelve-mile limit

6 **curb,** kerb <Brit>, curbing; border stone, curbstone, kerbstone <Brit>, edgestone

7 **edging, bordering,** bordure <heraldry>, **trimming,** binding, skirting; fringe, fimbriation, fimbria; **hem,** selvage, list, welt; frill, frilling; beading, flounce, furbelow, galloon, motif, ruffle, valance

VERBS 8 **bound,** circumscribe 210.4, surround 209.6, limit 210.5, enclose 212.5, divide, separate

9 **outline,** contour; **delineate;** silhouette, profile, limn

10 **border, edge, bound, rim, skirt, hem, hem in, ringe,** befringe, lap, list, margin, marge, marginate, march, verge, line, side; **adjoin** 223.9; **frame,** enframe, set off; trim, bind; purl; purfle

ADJS 11 **bordering, fringing,** rimming, skirting; **bounding,** boundary, **limiting,** limit, determining *or* determinant *or* determinative; threshold, liminal, limbic; extreme, terminal; **marginal, borderline,** frontier; coastal, littoral, sea-bordering

12 **bordered,** edged; margined, marged, marginate, marginated; **fringed,** befringed, trimmed, skirted, fimbriate, fimbriated

13 lipped, labial, labiate

14 outlining, delineatory; peripheral, perimetric, perimetrical, circumferential; outlined, **in outline**

ADVS 15 **on the verge, on the brink,** on the borderline, on the point, on the edge, on the ragged edge, at the threshold, at the limit *or* bound; **peripherally,** marginally, at the periphery

16 **thus far,** so far, thus far and no farther

212 ENCLOSURE

NOUNS 1 **enclosure; confinement,** containing, containment, circumscription 210, immurement, walling- *or* hedging- *or* hemming- *or* boxing- *or* fencing-in, circumvallation; **imprisonment,** incarceration, jailing, locking-up, lockdown; **siege,** besieging, beleaguerment, blockade, blockading, cordoning, quarantine, besetment; inclusion 772; **envelopment** 209.5

2 **packaging, packing,** package; boxing, crating, encasement; canning, tinning <Brit>; bottling; **wrapping,** enwrapment, bundling; shrink-wrapping

3 <enclosed place> **enclosure,** close, **confine,** precinct, enclave, pale, paling, list, cincture; jail, detention center; **cloister; pen, coop,** corral, fold; **yard,** park, court, courtyard, curtilage, toft; square, quadrangle, quad <nf>; **field,** delimited field, **arena,** theater, ground; reserve, sanctuary; **container** 195

4 **fence,** fencing, **wall,** boundary 211.3, **barrier;** stone wall; paling, palisade; rail, railing; balustrade, balustrading; moat; arcade

VERBS 5 **enclose,** close in, bound, include, **contain;** compass, encompass; **surround,** encircle 209.7; **shut** or **pen in,** coop in; **fence in,** wall in, wall up, rail in, rail off, screen off, curtain off; **hem** or **hedge in,** box in, pocket; shut or coop or mew up; pen, coop, corral, cage, impound, mew; **imprison,** incarcerate, jail, lock up, lock down; **besiege,** beset, beleaguer, leaguer, cordon, cordon off, quarantine, blockade; yard, yard up; house in; chamber; stable, kennel, shrine, enshrine; **wrap** 295.20

6 **confine, immure;** quarantine; cramp, straiten, encase; cloister, closet, cabin, crib; bury, entomb, coffin, casket; bottle up or in, box up or in

7 **fence, wall,** fence in, fence up; pale, rail, bar; pen up; hem, hem in, hedge, hedge in, hedge out; picket, palisade; bulkhead in

8 parenthesize, bracket, quote, air-quote, precede and follow, bookend

9 **package, pack, parcel;** box, box up, case, encase, crate, carton; can, tin <Brit>; bottle, jar, pot; barrel, cask, tank; sack, bag; basket, hamper; capsule, encyst; contain; **wrap,** enwrap, bundle; shrink-wrap; bandage

ADJS 10 **enclosed,** closed-in; **confined,** bound, immured, cloistered; **imprisoned,** incarcerated, jailed; caged, cramped, restrained, corralled; besieged, beleaguered, leaguered, beset, cordoned, cordoned off, quarantined, blockaded; **shut-in,** pent-up, penned, cooped, mewed, walled- or hedged- or hemmed- or boxed- or fenced-in, fenced, walled, paled, railed, barred; hemmed, hedged

11 enclosing, confining, **cloistered,** cloisterlike, claustral, parietal, surrounding 209.8; limiting 210.9

12 **packed, packaged,** boxed, crated, canned, tinned <Brit>, parceled, cased, encased; bottled; capsuled, encapsuled; **wrapped,** enwrapped, bundled; shrink-wrapped; prepacked; vacuum-packed; bandaged, sheathed

213 INTERPOSITION
<a putting or lying between>

NOUNS 1 **interposition, interposing,** interposal, interlocation, intermediacy, interjacence; **intervention,** intervenience, intercurrence, slipping-in, sandwiching; leafing-in, interleaving, interfoliation, tipping-in; **intrusion** 214

2 **interjection, interpolation,** introduction, throwing- or tossing-in, **injection,** insinuation; intercalation, interlineation; **insertion** 191; interlocution, remark, parenthetical or side or incidental or casual remark, *obiter dictum* <L>, aside, parenthesis; episode; infix, insert

3 **interspersion, interfusion,** interlardment, interpenetration

4 **intermediary,** intermedium, mediary, medium; link, **connecting link,** tie, connection, **go-between,** liaison; middleman, middleperson, broker, agent, wholesaler, jobber, distributor; moderator, **mediator** 466.3

5 **partition, dividing wall,** division, separation, *cloison* <Fr>; **wall, barrier;** panel; paries, parietes; brattice <mining>; bulkhead; diaphragm, midriff, midsection; septum, interseptum, septulum, dissepiment; **border** 211.4, **dividing line,** property line, party wall; **buffer, bumper,** mat, fender, cushion, pad, shock pad, collision mat; buffer state

VERBS 6 **interpose, interject, interpolate,** intercalate, interjaculate; **mediate, go between,** liaise <Brit nf>; **intervene;** put between, sandwich; **insert in,** stick in, introduce in, insinuate in, sandwich in, slip in, inject in, implant in; leaf in, interleaf, tip in, interfoliate; **foist in,** fudge in, work in, drag in, lug in, drag or lug in by the heels, worm in, squeeze in, smuggle in, throw in, run in, thrust in, edge in, wedge in; **intrude** 214.5

7 **intersperse, interfuse,** interlard, interpenetrate; intersow, intersprinkle

8 **partition,** set apart, separate, divide; **wall off,** fence off, screen off, curtain off

ADJS 9 interjectional, interpolative, intercalary; parenthetical, episodic

10 **intervening,** intervenient, **interjacent,** intercurrent; **intermediate,** intermediary, medial, mean, medium, mesne, median, **middle**

11 partitioned, walled; mural; septal, parietal

PREPS 12 **between, betwixt,** 'twixt, betwixt and between <nf>; **among, amongst,** 'mongst; **amid, amidst,** mid, 'mid, midst, 'midst; in the midst of, in the thick of

WORD ELEMENTS 13 medi-, medio-, mes-, meso-; inter-, intra-

14 interjections

adios
ah
aha
ahem
ahoy
alack
alas
all hail
alleluia
aloha
amen
and how
attaboy
avast
aw
aw-shucks
aye
bah
banzai
bleep
boo
boy
bravo
by jingo
cheerio
cheers
chop-chop
ciao
crikey
criminy
cripes
dear
dear me
ditto
duh
eek
egad *or* egads
eh
er
eureka
fiddlesticks
fie
fore
forsooth
gadzooks
gee
gee whillikers
gee whiz
gesundheit
giddyyap
glory
golly
golly gee
golly whillikers
good golly
good gracious
goody
gosh

gracious
gracious me
ha
hallelujah
hark
heads up
hear ye, hear ye
heave-ho
heavens
heavens to Betsy
heigh-ho
hem
hep
here here
hey
hi-hip
ho
ho-hum
holy cow
holy mackerel
holy moly
holy Toledo
hooray
hosanna
hot dog
howdy
hoy
huh
hup
hurrah
huzzah
jeepers
jeepers creepers
jeez
lackaday
lo
lo and behold
Lordy
mama
marry
mazel tov
my gracious
my my
my stars
my word
nah
nay
nerts
nope
nuts
oh
oh boy
oh dear
oh my
okay
okey-doke
okey-dokey
ole

oops
oopsy-daisy
ouch
ow
oy
oyez
peekaboo
phew
phooey
pish
pooh
presto
prithee
prosit
pshaw *or* psha
rah
rah-rah
rats
righto
roger
rot
salud
scram
shaddup
shalom
sheesh
shucks
shush
skoal
tallyho
ten-four
there, there
timber
touch,
touché
tsk
tsk tsk
tush
tut-tut
ugh
uh-huh

uh-oh
uh-uh
um
viva
voila
wahoo
welcome
well
what
whatever
whee
whew
whoa
whoop-de-do
whoopee
whoops
why
wilco
woe is me
wow
wowie
wowie-zowie
yahoo
yea
yeah
yech
yep
yikes
yippee
yo
yo mama
yoicks
yoo-hoo
yuck
yum-yum
yup
zap
zooks
zounds
zowie
zut

214 INTRUSION

NOUNS **1 intrusion,** obtrusion, **interloping;**
interposition 213, interposal, imposition,
insinuation, **interference,** intervention,
interventionism, interruption, injection,
interjection 213.2; **encroachment,** entrenchment,
trespass, trespassing, unlawful entry;
impingement, **infringement,** invasion, incursion,
inroad, influx, irruption, infiltration; entrance 189
 2 meddling, intermeddling; **butting-in** *and* kibitzing
and sticking one's nose in<nf>; **meddlesomeness,**
intrusiveness, forwardness, obtrusiveness;
officiousness, impertinence, presumption,
presumptuousness; inquisitiveness 981.1

3 **intruder, interloper, trespasser;** crasher *and* gate-crasher <nf>, unwelcome *or* uninvited guest; invader, encroacher, infiltrator

4 **meddler,** intermeddler; **busybody, pry,** Paul Pry, prier, Nosey Parker *or* nosey Parker *or* Nosy Parker <nf>, snoop *or* snooper, *yenta* <Yiddish>, **kibitzer** *and* backseat driver <nf>

VERBS **5** **intrude,** obtrude, **interlope;** come between, **interpose** 213.6, insert oneself, **intervene, interfere,** insinuate, impose; **encroach, infringe,** impinge, **trespass,** trespass on *or* upon, trench, entrench, invade, infiltrate; **break in upon,** break in, burst in, charge in, crash in, smash in, storm in; **barge in** <nf>, irrupt, **cut in,** thrust in 191.7, push in, press in, rush in, throng in, crowd in, squeeze in, elbow in, muscle in <nf>; **butt in** *and* **horn in** *and* chisel in *and* muscle in <nf>; appoint oneself; crash *and* crash the gates <nf>; **get in,** get in on, creep in, steal in, sneak in, slink in, slip in; foist in, worm *or* work in, edge in, put in *or* shove in one's oar; **foist oneself upon,** thrust oneself upon; put on *or* upon, impose on *or* upon, put one's two cents in <nf>

6 **interrupt, put in, cut in, break in;** jump in, chime in *and* chip in *and* put in one's two-cents worth <nf>, butt in

7 **meddle, intermeddle,** busybody, not mind one's business; **meddle with, tamper with,** mix oneself up with, inject oneself into, monkey with, fool with *or* around with <nf>, mess with *or* around with <nf>; **pry,** Paul-Pry, snoop, nose, **stick** *or* **poke one's nose in,** stick one's long nose into; have a finger in, have a finger in the pie; kibitz <nf>

ADJS **8** **intrusive,** obtrusive, **interfering,** intervenient, invasive, interruptive

9 **meddlesome,** meddling; **officious,** overofficious, self-appointed, impertinent, presumptuous; **busybody,** busy; pushing, pushy, forward; **prying,** nosy *or* nosey *and* snoopy <nf>; inquisitive 981.5

PHRS **10** <nf terms> **none of your business;** what's it to you?, **mind your own business,** keep your nose out of this, **butt out,** go soak your head, go sit on a tack, go roll your hoop, go peddle your fish, go fly a kite, go chase yourself, go jump in the lake; too many cooks spoil the broth

215 CONTRAPOSITION

<a placing over against>

NOUNS **1** contraposition, anteposition, posing against *or* over against; **opposition,** opposing, opposure; **antithesis,** contrast, ironic *or* contrastive juxtaposition; confronting, **confrontation;** polarity, polar opposition, polarization; **contrariety** 779; contention 457; hostility 451.2

2 **opposites,** antipodes, polar opposites, contraries; **poles,** opposite poles, antipoles, counterpoles, North Pole, South Pole; antipodal points, antipoints; contrapositives <logic>; night and day, black and white; antonyms

3 opposite side, other side, the other side of the picture *or* coin, other face; **reverse, inverse, obverse, converse;** heads, tails <of a coin>; flip side *and* B-side <nf>

VERBS **4** contrapose, **oppose,** contrast, match, **set over against,** pose against *or* over against, put in opposition, set *or* pit against one another; **confront,** face, front, stand *or* lie opposite, stand opposed *or* vis-à-vis; be at loggerheads, be eyeball to eyeball, bump heads, meet head-on; counteract 451.3; contend; subtend; **polarize;** contraposit <logic>

ADJS **5** contrapositive, **opposite,** opposing, **facing,** confronting, confrontational, confrontive, eyeball-to-eyeball, one-on-one, face-to-face; **opposed,** on opposite sides, adversarial, at loggerheads, at daggers drawn, antithetic, antithetical; **reverse, inverse, obverse, converse; antipodal; polar,** polarized one-on-one, up against; love-hate

ADVS **6** **opposite, poles apart,** at opposite extremes; contrary, contrariwise, counter; just opposite, **face-to-face,** vis-à-vis, *front à front* <Fr>, nose to nose, one on one, eyeball-to-eyeball, back to back

PREPS **7** **opposite to,** in opposition to, against, over against; versus, v *or* vs; **facing, across, fronting,** confronting, **in front of;** toward

WORD ELEMENTS **8** ant-, anti-, anth-, cat-, cata-, cath-, kat-, kata-, co-, contra-, counter-, enantio-, ob-

216 FRONT

NOUNS **1** **front, fore,** forepart, forequarter, foreside, forefront, forehand; **priority,** anteriority; front office; **frontier** 211.5; foreland; **foreground;** proscenium; frontage; front page; frontispiece; **preface,** front matter, foreword; prefix; front view, full frontal, front elevation, front seat, front yard; **head,** heading; **face,** façade, frontal; fascia; **false front,** window dressing, display, persona; front man; bold *or* brave front, brave face; facet; obverse <of a coin or medal>, head <of a coin>; lap; front burner

2 **vanguard,** van, point, point man; **spearhead,** advance guard, **forefront, cutting edge,** avant-garde, outguard; scout; **pioneer,** trailblazer; **precursor** 816; **front-runner,** leader, first in line;

front, battlefront, line, front line, forward line, battle line, line of departure, new guard; front rank, first line, first line of battle; **outpost,** farthest outpost; **bridgehead,** beachhead, airhead, railhead; advanced base

3 **prow, bow, stem,** rostrum, figurehead, nose, beak; bowsprit, jib boom; forecastle, forepeak; foredeck; foremast

4 **face,** facies, **visage;** physiognomy, phiz *and* dial <nf>; **countenance,** features, lineaments, favor; mug *and* mush *and* pan *and* kisser *and* map *and* puss <nf>

5 **forehead, brow,** lofty brow

6 **chin,** point of the chin, button <nf>

VERBS 7 be *or* stand in front, **lead, head,** head up; **get ahead of,** steal a march on, take the lead, come to the front *or* fore, forge ahead; be the front-runner, lead, lead the pack *or* field, be first; **pioneer;** front, front for, represent, speak for; spearhead; push the envelope <nf>; trailblaze

8 **confront, front,** affront <old>, **face, meet, encounter,** breast, stem, brave, meet squarely, square up to, come to grips with, head *or* wade into, meet face to face *or* eyeball to eyeball *or* one-on-one, come face to face with, look in the face *or* eye, stare in the face, stand up to, stand fast, hold one's ground, hang tough *and* tough it out *and* gut it out <nf>; call someone's bluff, call *or* bring someone to account; **confront with, face with,** bring face to face with, tell one to one's face, cast *or* throw in one's teeth, present to, **put *or* bring before,** set *or* place before, lay before, put *or* lay it on the line; bring up, bring forward; put it to, put it up to; **challenge,** dare, defy, fly in the teeth of, throw down the gauntlet, ask for trouble, start something, do something about it

9 **front on, face upon, give upon,** face *or* look toward, look out upon, look over, **overlook**

ADJS 10 **front, frontal, anterior; full-face, full-frontal,** physiognomic; **fore, forward,** forehand; foremost, headmost; first, earliest, **pioneering, trail-blazing, advanced,** front-running; **leading,** up-front <nf>, first, chief, head, prime, primary; **confronting,** confrontational, head-on, one-on-one *and* eyeball-to-eyeball <nf>; **ahead, in front,** one up, one jump *or* move ahead

11 **fronting, facing,** looking on *or* out on, opposite

ADVS 12 **before, ahead,** out *or* up ahead, **in front,** in the front, in the lead, in the van, in advance, **in the forefront,** in the foreground; **to the fore,** to the front; foremost, headmost, first; before one's face *or* eyes, under one's nose

13 **frontward,** frontwards, **forward,** forwards, vanward, **headward,** headwards, **onward,** onwards; **facing** 215.7

217 REAR

NOUNS 1 **rear, rear end, hind end,** hind part, hinder part, afterpart, rearward, **posterior, behind,** breech, stern, tail, tail end; **afterpiece,** tailpiece, heelpiece, heel; **back,** back side, reverse <of a coin or medal>, tail <of a coin>; back door, postern, postern door; back seat, rumble seat; hindhead, occiput; wake, train; back burner; tail <of a coin>

2 rear guard, rear, rear area, backyard

3 **back,** dorsum, ridge; dorsal region, lumbar region, backbone; hindquarter; loin

4 **buttocks, rump,** bottom, posterior, derrière; croup, crupper; podex; haunches; gluteal region; nates

5 <nf terms> **ass,** arse *and* bum <chiefly Brit>, behind, backside, buns, **butt, can,** cheeks, hind end, nether cheeks, stern, tail, rusty-dusty, **fanny,** prat, keister, popo, rear, rear end, tuchis *or* tushy *or* tush

6 **tail,** cauda, caudation, caudal appendage; tailpiece, scut <of a hare, rabbit, or deer>, brush <of a fox>, fantail <of fowls>; rattail, rat's-tail; dock, stub; caudal fin; **queue,** cue, **pigtail**

7 **stern,** heel; poop, transom, counter, fantail; sternpost, rudderpost; after mast

VERBS 8 <be behind> **bring up the rear,** come last, **follow,** come after; trail, trail behind, lag behind, draggle, **straggle;** fall behind, fall back, fall astern; **back up, back,** go back, go backwards, regress 163.5, retrogress, get behind; revert 859.4

ADJS 9 **rear,** rearward, **back,** backward, retrograde, **posterior,** postern, tail; after *or* aft; **hind, hinder; hindmost,** hindermost, hindhand, posteriormost, **aftermost,** aftmost, rearmost; latter

10 <anatomy> posterial, dorsal, retral, tergal, lumbar, gluteal, sciatic, occipital

11 **tail,** caudal, caudate, caudated, tailed; taillike, caudiform

12 backswept, swept-back

ADVS 13 **behind, in the rear, in back of;** in the background; behind the scenes; behind one's back; back to back; tandem

14 **after;** aft, abaft, baft, astern; aback

15 **rearward,** rearwards, to the rear, **hindward,** hindwards, **backward,** backwards, posteriorly, retrad, tailward, tailwards

218 SIDE

NOUNS 1 **side, flank, hand;** laterality, sidedness, handedness; unilaterality, unilateralism, bilaterality, bilateralism, etc, multilaterality, many-sidedness; border 211.4; parallelism 203; bank, shore, coast; siding, planking; beam;

broadside; quarter; hip, haunch; cheek, jowl, chop; temple; **profile,** side-view, half-face view; side entrance, side door; sideburns, burnsides

2 **lee side, lee,** leeward; lee shore; lee tide; lee wheel, lee helm, lee anchor, lee sheet, lee tack

3 **windward side, windward,** windwards, weather side, weather, weatherboard; weather wheel, weather helm, weather anchor, weather sheet, weather tack, weather rail, weather bow, weather deck; weather roll; windward tide, weather-going tide, windward ebb, windward flood

VERBS 4 **side, flank;** edge, skirt, border 211.10; stand side by side

5 **go sideways, sidle,** lateral, lateralize, **edge, veer, angle, slant, skew,** sidestep; go crabwise; **sideslip, skid;** make leeway

ADJS 6 **side, lateral;** flanking, skirting, facing, oblique; **beside,** to the side, off to one side; **alongside, parallel** 203.6; next-beside; **sidelong,** sideling, **sidewise,** sideway, **sideways,** sideward, **sidewards,** glancing; leeward, lee; windward, weather; side-by-side; peripheral

7 **sided, flanked,** handed; lateral; **one-sided,** unilateral, unilateralist, **two-sided, bilateral,** bilateralist, etc; dihedral, bifacial; **three-sided, trilateral,** trihedral, triquetrous; **four-sided, quadrilateral,** tetrahedral, etc; **many-sided, multilateral,** multifaceted, polyhedral; left-hand, sinistral, right-hand, dextral

ADVS 8 **laterally,** laterad; **sideways,** sideway, **sidewise, sidewards,** sideward, sideling, sidling, sidelong, aside, crabwise; side-to-side; **edgeways,** edgeway, **edgewise; widthwise, widthways, thwartwise; askance,** askant, asquint, glancingly; broadside, **broadside on,** on the beam; on its side, on its beam ends; on the other hand; right and left

9 **leeward,** to leeward, alee, downwind; **windward,** to windward, weatherward, aweather, upwind

10 **aside,** on one side, **to one side,** to the side, sidelong, on the side, on the one hand, on one hand, on the other hand; **alongside,** in parallel 203.7, side-by-side; nearby, in juxtaposition 223.21; away

PREPS 11 **beside, alongside, abreast,** abeam, by, on the flank of, along by, **by the side of,** along the side of

PHRS 12 **side by side,** cheek to cheek, cheek by cheek, cheek by jowl, shoulder to shoulder, yardarm to yardarm

219 RIGHT SIDE

NOUNS 1 **right side, right,** off side <of a horse or vehicle>, starboard; Epistle side, decanal side; recto <books>; right field; starboard tack; right wing; right-winger, conservative, reactionary

2 **rightness,** dextrality; dexterity, **right-handedness;** dextroversion, dextrocularity, dextroduction; dextrorotation, dextrogyration

3 right-hander; righty <nf>

ADJS 4 **right, right-hand,** dextral, dexter; off, **starboard;** rightmost; dextrorse; dextropedal; dextrocardial; dextrocerebral; dextrocular; **clockwise,** dextrorotary, dextrogyrate, dextrogyratory; right-wing, right-wingish, right-of-center, conservative, reactionary, dry <Brit nf>

5 **right-handed,** dextromanual, dexterous

6 **ambidextrous,** ambidextral, ambidexter; dextrosinistral, sinistrodextral

ADVS 7 **rightward,** rightwards, rightwardly, **right, to the right,** dextrally, dextrad; on the right, dexter; starboard, astarboard

220 LEFT SIDE

NOUNS 1 **left side, left, left hand,** left-hand side, wrong side <nf>, near or nigh side <of a horse or vehicle>, portside, port, larboard; Gospel side, cantorial side, verso <books>; left field; port tack; left wing, left-winger, radical, liberal, progressive

2 **leftness,** sinistrality, **left-handedness;** sinistration; levoversion, levoduction; levorotation, sinistrogyration

3 **left-hander, southpaw** and lefty and portsider <nf>

ADJS 4 **left, left-hand,** sinister, sinistral; near, nigh; **larboard, port;** sinistrorse; sinistrocerebral; sinistrocular; counterclockwise, levorotatory, sinistrogyrate; left-wing, left-wingish, left-of-center, radical, liberal, progressive, wet <Brit nf>

5 **left-handed,** sinistromanual, sinistral, lefty and southpaw <nf>

ADVS 6 **leftward,** leftwards, leftwardly, **left, to the left,** sinistrally, sinister, sinistrad; on the left; larboard, port, aport

221 PRESENCE

NOUNS 1 **presence,** being here or there, hereness, thereness, physical or actual presence, spiritual presence; **immanence,** indwellingness, **inherence;** whereness, **immediacy;** ubiety; availability, accessibility; nearness 223; **occurrence** 831.2, existence 761; manifestness, materialness; presenteeism

2 **omnipresence,** all-presence, **ubiquity;** continuum, plenum; infinity; pluripresence

3 **permeation, pervasion,** penetration; **suffusion,** transfusion, perfusion, diffusion, imbuement;

absorption; **overrunning,** overspreading, ripple effect, overswarming, whelming, overwhelming; saturation

4 **attendance,** frequenting, frequence; participation; number present; turnout *and* box office *and* draw <nf>

5 **attender, visitor,** churchgoer, moviegoer, etc; **patron; fan** *and* buff <nf>, aficionado, supporter; **frequenter,** habitué, haunter; spectator 918; theatergoer; audience 48.6; regular customer, regular

VERBS 6 **be present,** be located *or* situated 159.10, be there, be found, be met with; **occur** 831.5, exist 761.8; lie, stand, remain; fall in the way of; dwell in, indwell, inhere

7 **pervade, permeate,** penetrate; **suffuse,** inform, transfuse, perfuse, diffuse, leaven, imbue; **fill,** extend throughout, leave no void, occupy; **overrun,** overswarm, overspread, bespread, run through, meet one at every turn, whelm, overwhelm; creep *or* crawl *or* swarm with, be lousy with <nf>, teem with; honeycomb

8 **attend, be at,** be present at, find oneself at, **go** *or* **come to; appear** 33.8, turn up, set foot in, show up <nf>, show one's face, make *or* put in an appearance, give the pleasure of one's company, make a personal appearance; materialize; **visit, take in** *and* do *and* catch <nf>; sit in *or* at; be on hand, be on deck <nf>; watch, see; witness, look on, *assister* <Fr>; participate, take part

9 **revisit,** return to, go back to, come again

10 **frequent, haunt,** resort to, hang *and* hang around *and* hang about *and* hang out <nf>

11 **present oneself, report;** report for duty

ADJS 12 **present,** attendant; **on hand,** on deck <nf>, on board, in attendance; **immediate,** immanent, indwelling, inherent, **available, accessible, at hand,** in view, within reach *or* sight *or* call, in place; intrinsic

13 **omnipresent, all-present,** ubiquitous, everywhere; continuous, uninterrupted, infinite

14 **pervasive,** pervading, suffusive, perfusive, diffusive, suffusing

15 **permeated,** saturated, shot through, filled with, perfused, suffused, imbued; honeycombed; crawling, creeping, swarming, teeming, lousy with <nf>

ADVS 16 **here, there**

17 **in person,** personally, bodily, **in the flesh** <nf>, in one's own person, *in propria persona* <L>

PREPS 18 **in the presence of,** in the face of, under the eyes *or* nose of, **before**

PHRS 19 all present and accounted for; standing room only *or* SRO

222 ABSENCE

NOUNS 1 **absence,** nonpresence, awayness; nowhereness, **nonexistence** 762; want, **lack,** total lack, blank, deprivation; nonoccurrence, neverness; **subtraction** 255

2 **vacancy,** vacuity, voidness, **emptiness,** blankness, hollowness, inanition; **bareness,** barrenness, desolateness, bleakness, desertedness; **nonoccupancy,** nonoccupation, vacancy, noninhabitance, nonresidence; job vacancy, opening, open place *or* post, vacant post

3 **void, vacuum,** blank, emptiness, empty space, inanity, vacuity; **nothingness;** *tabula rasa* <L>, clean *or* blank slate; **nothing** 762.2

4 **absence,** nonattendance, **absenting, leaving,** taking leave, **departure** 188; "Say, is not absence death to those who love?"—Pope; running away, fleeing, decamping, bolting, skedaddling, absquatulating *or* absquatulation, abscondence, scarpering <Brit nf>, desertion, defection; **disappearance** 34, escape 369; **absentation,** nonappearance, default, unauthorized *or* unexcused absence; **truancy, hooky** <nf>, French leave, **cut** <nf>; **absence without leave** *or* AWOL; **absenteeism,** truantism, absentation; **leave, leave of absence,** furlough; **vacation,** holiday, paid vacation, paid holiday, paid time off, time off, day off, comp *or* compensation time; authorized *or* excused absence, sick leave; sabbatical

5 **absentee, truant,** no-show, missing person

6 **nobody, no one,** no man, no woman, not one, not a single one *or* person, **not a soul** *or* **blessed soul** *or* **living soul,** never a one, ne'er a one, nary one <nf>, nobody on earth *or* under the sun, nobody present; nonperson, unperson; nonentity

VERBS 7 **be absent, stay away,** keep away, keep out of the way, not come, not show up <nf>, not turn up, turn up missing <nf>, stay away in droves <nf>, fail to appear, default, sit out, include oneself out <nf>

8 **absent oneself, take leave** *or* **leave of absence,** go on leave *or* furlough; **vacation,** go on vacation *or* holiday, take time off, take off from work; slip off *or* away, duck *or* sneak out <nf>, slip out, make oneself scarce <nf>, leave the scene, bow out, exit, vacate, **depart** 188.6, **disappear** 34.2, escape 369.6; defect, desert

9 **play truant, go AWOL,** take French leave; play hooky, cut *or* skip <nf>, cut classes; jump ship

10 <nf terms> **split,** bugger off, fuck off, f off, make tracks, pull up stakes, push along, scarper <Brit>, push off, skedaddle *or* absquatulate <old>, **haul ass,** bag ass, **beat it, blow,** boogie, bug out, cut, **cut**

out, cut and run, peel out, bunk off *or* piss off <Brit>, scram, shove off, vamoose

ADJS **11 absent,** not present, nonattendant, **away, gone,** departed, disappeared, vanished, absconded, out of sight; **missing,** among the missing, wanting, **lacking,** not found, nowhere to be found, omitted, taken away, subtracted, deleted; no longer present *or* with us *or* among us; long-lost; **nonexistent;** conspicuous by its absence

12 nonresident, not in residence, from home, **away from home,** on leave *or* vacation *or* holiday, on sabbatical leave; on tour, on the road; abroad, overseas

13 truant, absent without leave *or* **AWOL**

14 vacant, empty, hollow, inane, **bare, vacuous, void,** without content, with nothing inside, devoid, null, null and void; **blank,** clear, white, bleached; featureless, unrelieved, characterless, bland, insipid; **barren** 891.4

15 available, open, free, **unoccupied,** unfilled, **uninhabited,** unpopulated, unpeopled, untaken, untenanted, tenantless, untended, unmanned, unstaffed; **deserted,** abandoned, forsaken, godforsaken <nf>; untouristed

ADVS **16 absently; vacantly, emptily,** hollowly, vacuously, blankly

17 nowhere, in no place, neither here nor there; nowhither

18 away 188.20, **elsewhere,** somewhere else, not here; elsewhither

PREPS **19** absent, lacking, sans; void of, empty of, free of, **without** 992.17

223 NEARNESS

NOUNS **1 nearness, closeness,** nighness, **proximity,** propinquity, intimacy, immediacy; approximation, approach, convergence; a rough idea <nf>; **vicinity,** vicinage, **neighborhood,** environs, surroundings, surround, setting, grounds, purlieus, confines, precinct; **foreground,** immediate foreground; convenience, handiness, accessibility

2 short distance, short way, little ways, **step,** short step, span, brief span, short piece <nf>, a little, intimate distance; shortcut; short range; close quarters *or* range *or* grips; middle distance; **stone's throw,** spitting distance <nf>, bowshot, gunshot, pistol shot; earshot, earreach, a whoop *and* a whoop and a holler *and* two whoops and a holler <nf>, ace, bit <nf>, **hair, hairbreadth** *or* **hairsbreadth,** finger's breadth *or* width, an inch; inch, millimeter, centimeter; near miss

3 juxtaposition, apposition, adjacency; **contiguity,** contiguousness, conterminousness *or*

coterminousness; butting, abuttal, abutment; adjunction, junction 800.1, connection, union; **conjunction,** conjugation, collocation; appulse, syzygy; perigee, perihelion

4 meeting, meeting up, joining, joining up, **encounter;** juncture; confrontation; rencontre; near-miss, collision course, near thing, narrow squeak *or* brush

5 contact, touch, touching, *attouchement* <Fr>, taction, tangency, contingence; gentle *or* tentative contact, caress, brush, glance, nudge, kiss, rub, graze; impingement, impingence; osculation

6 neighbor, neighborer, next-door *or* immediate neighbor; borderer; abutter, adjoiner; bystander, onlooker, looker-on; tangent; buffer state; ringside seat

VERBS **7 near, come near,** nigh, draw near *or* nigh, **approach** 167.3, come within shouting distance; **converge,** shake hands <nf>; come within an ace *or* an inch

8 be near *or* **around,** be in the vicinity *or* neighborhood, **approximate, approach,** get warm <nf>, come near, have something at hand *or* at one's fingertips; give *or* get a rough idea <nf>

9 adjoin, join, conjoin, **connect,** butt, **abut,** abut on *or* upon, be contiguous, be in contact; **neighbor,** border, **border on** *or* **upon,** verge on *or* upon; lie by, stand by

10 contact, come in contact, touch, feel, impinge, bump up against, hit; osculate; **graze,** caress, kiss, nudge, rub, brush, glance, scrape, sideswipe, skim, skirt, shave; grope *and* feel up *and* cop a feel <nf>; have a near miss, brush *or* graze *or* squeak by

11 meet, encounter; come across, run across, meet up, fall across, cross the path of; **come upon,** run upon, fall upon, light *or* alight upon; come among, fall among; **meet with,** meet up with <nf>, come face to face with, **confront,** meet head-on *or* eyeball to eyeball; **run into, bump into** *and* run smack into <nf>, join up with, come *or* run up against <nf>, run *and* fall foul of; burst *or* pitch *or* pop *or* bounce *or* plump upon <nf>; be on a collision course; reconnect

12 stay near, keep close to; stand by, lie by; go with, march with, follow close upon, breathe down one's neck, tread *or* stay on one's heels, stay on one's tail, tailgate <nf>; hang about *or* around, hang upon the skirts of, hover over; **cling to,** clasp, hug, huddle; hug the shore *or* land, keep hold of the land, stay inshore

13 juxtapose, appose, join 800.5, **adjoin, abut,** butt against, neighbor; bring near, put with, place *or* set side by side

ADJS **14 near, close, nigh,** close-in, nearish, nighish, intimate, cheek-by-jowl, side-by-side, hand-in-hand, arm-in-arm, *bras-dessus-bras-dessous* <Fr>, shoulder-to-shoulder, neck and neck; **approaching,** nearing, approximate *or* approximating, proximate, proximal, propinque <old>; **short-range;** near the mark; warm *or* hot *or* burning <nf>

15 **nearby, handy, convenient,** neighboring, vicinal, propinquant *or* propinquous, ready at hand, easily reached *or* attained; accessible; one-stop; 24-hour

16 **adjacent, next,** immediate, contiguous, **adjoining, abutting; neighboring,** neighbor; in the neighborhood, in the vicinity; **juxtaposed,** juxtapositional, tangential; **bordering,** conterminous *or* coterminous, connecting; **face-to-face** 215.6; end-to-end, endways, endwise; **joined**

17 **in contact,** contacting, **touching, meeting,** contingent; impinging, impingent; tangent, tangential; osculatory; grazing, kissing, glancing, brushing, rubbing, nudging; interfacing, linking

18 **nearer,** nigher, **closer**

19 **nearest,** nighest, **closest,** nearmost, next, immediate

ADVS 20 **near, nigh, close;** hard, at close quarters; **nearby, close by,** hard by, fast by, not far *or* far off, in the vicinity *or* **neighborhood of,** at hand, at close range, **near** *or* **close at hand;** thereabout *or* thereabouts, hereabout *or* hereabouts; nearabout *or* nearabouts *or* nigh about <dial>; **about, around** <nf>, close about, along toward <nf>; at no great distance, only a step; as near as no matter *or* makes no difference <nf>; **within reach** *or* **range,** within call *or* hearing, within earshot *or* earreach, within a whoop *or* two whoops and a holler <nf>, within a stone's throw, a stone's throw away, in spitting distance <nf>, at one's elbow, at one's feet, at one's fingertips, under one's nose, at one's side, within one's grasp; just around the corner, just across the street, next-door, right next door, just next door

21 **in juxtaposition, in conjunction,** in apposition; beside 218.11

22 **nearly, near,** pretty near <nf>, close, **closely; almost,** all but, not quite, as good as, as near as makes no difference; **well-nigh, just about;** nigh, nigh hand

23 **approximately,** approximatively, practically <nf>, for practical purposes *or* all practical purposes, at a first approximation, give or take a little, **more or less;** plus-minus; **roughly,** roundly, in round numbers; **generally,** generally speaking, roughly speaking, say; in the ballpark <nf>

PREPS 24 **near, nigh,** near to, **close to,** near upon, close upon, hard on *or* upon, bordering on *or* upon, **verging on** *or* upon, on the confines of, at the threshold of, **on the brink** *or* **verge of,** on the edge

of, at next hand, at *or* on the point of, on the skirts of; **not far from;** next door to, at one's door; nigh about *or* nearabout *or* nigh on *or* nigh onto <dial>

25 **against,** up against, on, upon, over against, opposite, nose to nose with, vis-à-vis, in contact with

26 **about, around,** just about, circa, c, somewhere about *or* near, near *or* close upon, give or take, near enough to, upwards of <nf>, -ish, -something; **in the neighborhood** *or* **vicinity of**

224 INTERVAL
<space between>

NOUNS 1 **interval, gap, space** 158, intervening *or* intermediate space, **interspace,** distance *or* space between, interstice; **clearance,** margin, leeway, headroom, **room** 158.3; discontinuity 813, jump, leap, interruption; daylight; hiatus, caesura, lacuna, intermission; half space, single space, double space, em space, en space, hair space; time interval, intermission, interim 826

2 **crack, cleft,** cranny, chink, check, craze, chap, **crevice,** fissure, scissure, incision, notch, score, cut, gash, slit, split, **rift,** rent; crack, hairline crack; **opening,** excavation, cavity, concavity, hole; **gap,** gape, **abyss,** abysm, **gulf, chasm,** void 222.3, canyon; **breach, break,** fracture, rupture; fault, flaw; slot, groove, furrow, moat, ditch, trench, dike, ha-ha; joint, seam; **valley**

VERBS 3 **interspace, space,** make a space, make room, set at intervals, dot, scatter 771.4, **space out, separate,** split off, part, dispart, set *or* keep apart

4 **cleave, crack,** check, incise, craze, **cut, cut apart,** gash, slit, **split,** rive, rent, rip open; **open; gap,** breach, break, fracture, rupture; slot, groove, furrow, ditch, trench

ADJS 5 intervallic, intervallary, interspatial, interstitial, discontinuous

6 **interspaced, spaced,** intervaled, **spaced out,** set at intervals, with intervals *or* an interval, interspacial, interstitial; dotted, scattered 771.9, **separated, parted,** disparted, split-off

7 **cleft, cut,** cloven, **cracked,** sundered, rift, riven, rent, chinky, chapped, crazed; **slit, split;** gaping, gappy; hiatal, caesural, lacunar; fissured, fissural, fissile

225 HABITATION
<an inhabiting>

NOUNS 1 **habitation,** inhabiting, inhabitation, habitancy, inhabitancy, **tenancy, occupancy,** occupation, **residence** *or* **residency,** residing, abiding, **living,** nesting, **dwelling,** commorancy

<law>, lodging, staying, stopping, sojourning, staying over; squatting; cohabitation, living together, sharing quarters; living in sin; **abode, habitat** 228

2 **peopling,** peoplement, empeoplement, **population,** inhabiting; **colonization, settlement,** plantation

3 **housing,** domiciliation; lodgment, **lodging,** transient lodging, doss <Brit>, **quartering,** billeting, hospitality; living quarters; **housing development,** subdivision, tract, public housing; housing problem, housing bill

4 **camping,** tenting, **encampment,** bivouacking; camp 228.29

5 **sojourn,** sojourning, sojournment, temporary stay; **stay,** stop; **stopover,** stopoff, stayover, layover

6 **habitability,** inhabitability, **livability**

VERBS 7 **inhabit, occupy,** tenant, move in or into, take up one's abode, make one's home; rent, lease; **reside, live, live in, dwell, lodge, stay,** remain, abide, hang or hang out <nf>, domicile, domiciliate; **room,** bunk, crash <nf>, berth, doss down <Brit>; perch and roost and squat <nf>; nest; room together; cohabit, cohabitate, live together; live in sin

8 **sojourn,** stop, stay, **stop over,** stay over, lay over

9 **people,** empeople, **populate, inhabit,** denizen; colonize, **settle,** settle in, plant

10 **house,** domicile, domiciliate; provide with a roof, have as a guest or lodger, shelter, harbor; **lodge, quarter, put up,** billet, room, bed, berth, bunk; stable

11 **camp,** encamp, tent; pitch, **pitch camp,** pitch one's tent, drive stakes <nf>; bivouac; go camping, camp out, sleep out, rough it

ADJS 12 **inhabited, occupied,** tenanted; **peopled,** empeopled, populated, colonized, settled; populous

13 **resident,** residentiary, **in residence; residing, living, dwelling,** commorant, lodging, **staying,** remaining, abiding, living in; cohabiting, live-in

14 **housed,** domiciled, domiciliated, **lodged,** quartered, billeted; stabled

15 **habitable,** inhabitable, occupiable, lodgeable, tenantable, **livable, fit to live in, fit for occupation;** homelike 228.33

ADVS 16 **at home,** in the bosom of one's family, chez soi <Fr>; in one's element; back home and down home <nf>

226 NATIVENESS

NOUNS 1 **nativeness,** nativity, native-bornness, indigenousness or indigenity, aboriginality, autochthonousness, **nationality;** nativism

2 **citizenship,** native-born citizenship, citizenship by birth, citizenhood, subjecthood; civism; dual citizenship

3 **naturalization,** naturalized citizenship, citizenship by naturalization or adoption, nationalization, adoption, admission, affiliation, **assimilation,** denization; indigenization; Americanization, Anglicization, etc; acculturation, enculturation; papers, citizenship papers; culture shock

VERBS 4 naturalize, grant or confer citizenship, adopt, admit, affiliate, **assimilate;** Americanize, Anglicize, etc; acculturate, acculturize; indigenize, go native <nf>

ADJS 5 **native,** natal, **indigenous,** endemic, autochthonous; mother, maternal, original, aboriginal, primitive; native-born, natural-born, home-grown, homebred, native to the soil or place or heath

6 **naturalized,** adopted, **assimilated;** indoctrinated, Americanized, Anglicized, etc; acculturated, acculturized; indigenized

227 INHABITANT, NATIVE

NOUNS 1 **population, inhabitants,** habitancy, dwellers, **populace, people,** whole people, people at large, citizenry, folk, souls, living souls, body, whole body, warm bodies <nf>; **public,** general public; community, society, **nation,** commonwealth, constituency, body politic, electorate; speech or linguistic community, ethnic or cultural community; colony, commune, neighborhood; nationality; **census,** head count; population statistics, demography, demographics

2 **inhabitant,** inhabiter, habitant; **occupant,** occupier, **dweller, tenant, denizen,** inmate; **resident,** residencer, residentiary, resider; townie; inpatient; resident or live-in maid; writer- or poet- or artist- or composer-in-residence; house detective; incumbent, locum tenens <L>; sojourner; addressee; indweller, inmate

3 **native,** indigene, autochthon, earliest inhabitant, first comer, primitive settler; primitive; **aborigine,** aboriginal; local and local yokel <nf>

4 **citizen, national,** subject; **naturalized citizen,** nonnative citizen, citizen by adoption, immigrant, metic; hyphenated American, hyphenate; **cosmopolitan,** cosmopolite, citizen of the world; active citizen; dual citizen

5 **fellow citizen,** fellow countryman or countrywoman, **compatriot,** congener, **countryman,** countrywoman, landsman <Yiddish>, paesano <Ital>, paisano <Sp>; fellow townsman, home boy and home girl and hometowner <nf>

6 townsman, townswoman, townsperson, towny
and towner *and* townie <nf>, **villager,** oppidan,
city dweller, city person; big-city person, **city
slicker** <nf>; metropolitan, urbanite; suburbanite;
exurbanite; burgher, burgess, *bourgeois* <Fr>;
townspeople, townfolks, townfolk

7 householder, homeowner, house-owner,
proprietor, freeholder, occupier, addressee;
cottager, cotter, cottier, crofter; head of household

8 lodger, roomer, paying guest; **boarder,** board-and-
roomer, **transient,** transient guest *or* boarder;
renter, tenant, leaser *or* lessee, leaseholder,
time-sharer, subleaser *or* sublessee; roommate,
flatmate <Brit>; visitor, guest

9 settler, *habitant* <Canadian & Louisiana Fr>;
colonist, colonizer, colonial, immigrant, incomer,
planter; **homesteader; squatter,** nester; **pioneer;**
sooner; precursor 816

10 wilderness settler *or* hinterlander; **frontiersman,**
mountain man; **backwoodsman,** woodlander,
woodsman, woodman, woodhick <nf>;
mountaineer, hillbilly *and* ridge runner <nf>,
mountain man, brush ape *and* briar-hopper <nf>;
cracker *and* redneck <nf>, desert rat <nf>, clam
digger <nf>, piny <nf>; country gentleman,
ruralist, provincial, rustic, peasant, hayseed, hick,
cottager

11 <regional inhabitants> **Easterner,** eastlander;
Midwesterner; Westerner, westlander;
Southerner, southlander; **Northener,** northlander,
Yankee; Northman; New Englander, Down-Easter
Yankee; Maritimer <Can>

228 ABODE, HABITAT

<place of habitation or resort>

NOUNS **1 abode, habitation, place, dwelling,**
dwelling place, abiding place, place to live, where
one lives *or* resides, where one is at home, roof,
roof over one's head, **residence,** place of residence,
domicile, *domus* <L>; **lodging,** lodgment, lodging
place; seat, nest, living space, houseroom, sleeping
place, place to rest one's head, crash pad <nf>;
native heath, turf, home turf; **address,** permanent
residence; **housing; affordable housing,** low-cost
housing, low-and-middle-income housing, public
housing, public-sector housing, scattersite
housing; council house <Brit>; private housing,
private-sector housing, market-rate
housing

2 home, home sweet home, "the place where, when
you go there, They have to take you in"—Robert
Frost; **fireside, hearth,** hearth and home,
hearthstone, fireplace, *foyer* <Fr>, chimney corner,
ingle, ingleside *or* inglenook; base, nest;

household, ménage; **homestead,** home place,
home roof, roof, rooftree, toft <Brit old>; place
where one hangs one's hat; paternal roof *or*
domicile, family homestead, ancestral halls;
hometown, birthplace, cradle; homeland, native
land, motherland, fatherland; **hominess** *or*
homeyness

3 domesticity; housewifery, **housekeeping,
homemaking;** householding, householdry

4 quarters, living quarters; lodgings, lodging,
lodgment; diggings *and* digs <Brit nf>, pad *and*
crib <nf>, room; **rooms,** berth, roost,
accommodations; **housing** 225.3, shelter,
gîte <Fr>

5 house, dwelling, dwelling house, *casa* <Sp & Ital>;
house and grounds, house and lot, homesite;
building, structure, edifice, fabric, erection, **hall**
197.4; roof; lodge; manor house, hall; town house,
rus in urbe <L>, semidetached house, duplex, row
house; country house, *dacha* <Russ>, country seat;
ranch house, farmhouse, farm, country house;
prefabricated house, modular house; sod house,
adobe house; lake dwelling 241.3; houseboat; cave
or cliff dwelling; penthouse; split-level; parsonage
703.7, **rectory,** vicarage, deanery, manse; official
residence, the White House, Number 10 Downing
Street, the Kremlin; governor's mansion;
presidential palace; embassy, consulate

6 farmstead; ranch, *rancho* and *hacienda* <Sp>, toft
or steading <Brit old>, grange, plantation

7 estate; mansion, palatial residence, stately home
<Brit>, manor house; **villa, château,** *hôtel* <Fr>,
resort, **castle,** tower; **palace,** *palais* <Fr>, *palazzo*
<Ital>, court, great house; ancestral hall *or* seat

8 cottage, cot *or* cote, **bungalow,** box; **cabin,** log
cabin; **second home, vacation home;** chalet, lodge,
snuggery; home away from home, *pied-à-terre*
<Fr>, *casita* <Sp>

9 hut, hutch, **shack, shanty,** crib, hole-in-the-wall
<nf>, **shed; lean-to; booth,** stall; tollbooth *or*
tollhouse, sentry box, gatehouse, porter's lodge;
outhouse, outbuilding; privy; **pavilion,** kiosk;
Quonset hut *or* Nissen hut; hutment

10 <Native American houses> wigwam, tepee *or* tipi,
hogan, wickiup, jacal, longhouse; tupik *and* igloo
<Eskimo>; ajouba

11 hovel, dump <nf>, rathole, hole, sty, pigsty,
pigpen, tumbledown shack; squat

12 summerhouse, arbor, bower, **gazebo,** pergola,
kiosk, alcove, retreat; **conservatory, greenhouse,**
glasshouse <Brit>, lathhouse

13 apartment, flat, tenement, chambers <Brit>, room
or rooms; studio apartment *or* flat; bed-sitter
<Brit>, granny flat, flatlet; **suite,** suite *or* set of
rooms; walkup, cold-water flat; **penthouse;** garden

apartment; duplex apartment; railroad *or* shotgun flat

14 **apartment house, flats, tenement;** duplex, duplex house; tower block; apartment complex; cooperative apartment house *or* co-op <nf>, condominium *or* condo <nf>; high-rise apartment building *or* high rise

15 **inn, hotel,** hostel, hostelry, **tavern,** *posada* <Sp>; tourist hotel, *parador* <Sp>, boutique hotel; resort; **roadhouse,** caravansary *or* caravanserai, guesthouse, bed and breakfast *or* B and B; youth hostel, hospice, elder hostel; **lodging house,** rooming house; **boardinghouse,** *pension* <Fr>, *pensione* <Ital>; **dormitory,** dorm <nf>, fraternity *or* sorority house; bunkhouse; **flophouse** *and* fleabag <nf>, dosshouse <Brit nf>

16 **motel,** motor court, motor inn *or* lodge, motor hotel, auto court; boatel

17 **trailer,** house *or* camp trailer, **mobile home,** motor home, recreational vehicle *or* RV, camper, camper trailer, caravan <Brit>; trailer court *or* camp *or* park, campground

18 **habitat,** home, **range,** environment, surroundings, stamping *or* stomping grounds, locality, native environment; microhabitat, ecosystem, terrain, purlieu

19 **zoo, menagerie,** Tiergarten <Ger>, zoological garden *or* park, marine park, sea zoo, safari park; animal shelter

20 **barn, stable,** stall; **cowbarn,** cowhouse, cowshed, cowbyre, byre; mews; outbuilding

21 **kennel, doghouse;** pound, dog pound; cattery

22 **coop, chicken house** *or* **coop,** henhouse, hencote, hencoop, hennery; brooder

23 **birdhouse, aviary,** bird cage; dovecote, pigeon house *or* loft, columbary; roost, perch, roosting place; rookery, heronry; eyrie

24 vivarium, terrarium, aquarium; fishpond

25 **nest,** nidus; **beehive, apiary,** hive, bee tree, hornet's nest, wasp's nest, vespiary

26 **lair, den,** cave, **hole,** covert, mew, form; **burrow,** tunnel, earth, run, couch, lodge

27 **haunt,** purlieu, **hangout** <nf>, stamping ground *or* stomping ground <nf>; gathering place, rallying point, meeting place, clubhouse, club; casino, gambling house; resort, health resort; **spa,** health spa, yoga retreat, baths, springs, watering place; meditation retreat

28 <disapproved place> **dive** <nf>, **den, lair,** den of thieves; hole *and* dump *and* **joint** <nf>; gyp *or* clip joint <nf>; **whorehouse,** cathouse <nf>, sporting house, brothel, bordello; stews, fleshpots

29 **camp, encampment,** *Lager* <Ger>; bivouac; barrack *or* **barracks,** casern, *caserne* <Fr>, cantonment, lines <Brit>; hobo jungle *or* camp;

detention camp, concentration camp, *Konzentrationslager* <Ger>; campground *or* campsite

30 <deities of the household> lares and penates, Vesta, Hestia

VERBS **31** **keep house,** housekeep <nf>, practice domesticity, maintain *or* run a household

ADJS **32** **residential,** residentiary, residing, in residence; domestic, domiciliary, domal; **home, household,** at home; mansional, manorial, palatial

33 **homelike,** homish, **homey** <nf>, homely; comfortable, friendly, cheerful, peaceful, cozy, snug, intimate; simple, plain, unpretending

34 **domesticated, tame,** tamed, broken; housebroken

229 FURNITURE

NOUNS **1** **furniture,** furnishings, movables, home furnishings, house furnishings, household effects, household goods, office furniture, school furniture, church furniture, library furniture, furnishments <old>; **cabinetmaking,** cabinetwork, cabinetry; **furniture design, furniture style** <see list>; period furniture; **piece of furniture, furniture piece,** chair, couch, sofa, bed, table, desk, cabinet, mirror, clock, screen; **suite, set of furniture,** ensemble, decor

2 **furniture styles and periods**

Adam	Cotswold School
Adapted Colonial	Country Chippendale
Adirondack	Cromwellian *or* Common-
American Chippendale *or*	wealth
Pilgrim	Desornamentado
American Empire	De Stijl
American Jacobean	Directoire
American Moderne	Duncan Phyfe
American Queen Anne	Early American
American Regency *or*	Early Georgian
Directory	Eastlake
American Restoration *or*	Egyptian
Pillar and Scroll	Elizabethan
Anglo-Dutch	Empire
Art Deco	Federal
Art Nouveau	French Provincial
Arts and Crafts	French Renaissance
Baroque	Georgian
Bauhaus	Gothic
Biedermeier	Gothic-Renaissance
Block-front	Hepplewhite
Boston Chippendale	International *or* Interna-
boule *or* boulework	tional Gothic
Byzantine	Italian Renaissance
Chinese Chippendale	Jacobean
Chinoiserie	Japanese
Chippendale	Japonisme
Colonial *or* Campaign	Late Regency
Contemporary	Later Victorian

Louis XIII	Regency
Louis XIV	Renaissance Revival
Louis XV	Restoration *or* Carolean
Louis XVI	Rococo
Mannerist	Rococo Revival *or* Louis
Mission	Philippe *or* Louis XV
Modern	Revival
Modernist	Romano-Byzantine *or*
Morris	Italo-Byzantine *or*
National Romanticism	Romanesque
Naturalistic	Scandinavian Modern
Neoclassical *or* le style	Shaker
antique <Fr>	Sheraton
Neo-Gothic *or* Cathédrale	Spanish Renaissance
Neo-Grec	Stuart
Newport Chippendale	Tudor
New York Chippendale	Turkish
Palladian	Venetian
Pennsylvania Dutch	Victorian
Philadelphia Chippendale	Viking Revival *or*
Pop Art	Dragonesque
Queen Anne	William and Mary

230 TOWN, CITY

NOUNS **1 town,** township; **city, metropolis,** metro, metropolitan area, greater city, megalopolis, supercity, conurbation, urban complex, spread city, urban sprawl *or* spread, Standard Metropolitan Statistical Area *or* SMSA, urban corridor, strip city, **municipality,** urbs <L>, polis <Gk>, city *or* municipal government; ville <Fr>, Stadt <Ger>; **borough, burg** <nf>, bourg, burgh <Scot>; **suburb,** suburbia, burbs <nf>, bedroom community, slurb, stockbroker belt <Brit nf>, garden suburb <Brit>, commuter belt, outskirts, faubourg <Fr>, banlieue <Fr>; exurb, exurbia, bedroom town, streetcar suburb; market town <Brit>; small town; twin town; boom town, ghost town; industrial city; sister city; urbanization, citifying

2 village, hamlet; ham *and* thorp *and* wick <old>; country town, crossroads

3 <nf terms> **one-horse town,** jerkwater town, one-gas-station town, **tank town** *or* station, **whistle-stop,** jumping-off place; **hick town,** rube town, Podunk; hoosier town; wide place in the road

4 capital, capital city, **seat,** seat of government; **county seat** *or* county site, county town *or* shiretown <Brit>

5 town hall, city hall, municipal building; courthouse; police headquarters *or* station, station house, precinct house; firehouse, fire station, station house; county building, county courthouse; community center; school

6 <city districts> East Side *or* End, West Side *or* End; **downtown,** uptown, midtown; city center, main street, city centre <Brit>, urban center, central *or* center city, core, core city, inner city, suburbs, suburbia, burbs <nf>, outskirts, greenbelt, residential district, business district *or* section, shopping center, financial district, residential area; Chinatown, Little Italy, etc; **asphalt** *or* **concrete jungle,** mean streets; **slum** *or* **slums,** the other side *or* the wrong side of the tracks, blighted area *or* neighborhood *or* section, run-down neighborhood, tenement district, shanty-town, hell's kitchen *or* half-acre; favela, tenderloin, red-light district, Bowery, **skid row** *or* skid road <nf>, tin pan alley; combat zone; enterprise zone; **ghetto, inner city,** urban ghetto, barrio

7 block, city block, square

8 square, plaza, place <Fr>, piazza <Ital>, campo <Ital>, **marketplace,** market, mart, rialto, forum, agora

9 circle, circus <Brit>; crescent

10 city planning, urban planning; urban studies, urbanology

ADJS **11 urban, metropolitan, municipal,** metro, burghal, **civic,** oppidan; main-street; citywide; city, town, village; citified; urbane; suburban; interurban; downtown, uptown, midtown; **inner-city,** core, core-city, ghetto; small-town; boom-town

231 REGION

NOUNS **1 region, area, zone,** belt, **territory,** terrain; **place** 159.1; **space** 158; **country** 232, **land** 234, ground, soil; territoriality; territorial waters, twelve- *or* three-mile limit, continental shelf, offshore rights; air space; heartland; hinterland; **district, quarter, section,** sector, department, division; salient, corridor; part, parts; **neighborhood,** vicinity, vicinage, neck of the woods <nf>, stamping ground, turf <nf>, backyard <nf>, purlieu *or* purlieus; premises, confines, precincts, environs, milieu

2 sphere, hemisphere, orb, **orbit,** ambit, circle; **circuit,** judicial circuit, **beat, round,** walk; **realm,** demesne, **domain,** dominion, jurisdiction, bailiwick, niche, forté; border, borderland, march; **province,** precinct, department; **field,** pale, arena

3 zone; climate *or* clime <old>; **longitude,** longitude in arc, longitude in time; meridian, prime meridian; **latitude,** parallel; equator, the line; tropic, Tropic of Cancer, Tropic of Capricorn; tropics, subtropics, Torrid Zone; Temperate *or* Variable Zones; Frigid Zones, Arctic Zone *or*

Circle, Antarctic Zone *or* Circle; horse latitudes, roaring forties; doldrums

4 plot, plot of ground *or* land, parcel of land, plat, **patch, tract, field,** enclosure; lot; air space; block, square; section, forty <sixteenth of a section>, back forty; close, quadrangle, quad, enclave, pale, *clos* <Fr>, croft <Brit>, *kraal* <Africa>; real estate; allotment, holding, claim

5 <territorial divisions> **state, territory, province,** region, duchy, electorate, government, principality; **county,** shire, canton, *oblast* and *okrug* <Russ>, *département* <Fr>, *Kreis* or *Land* <Ger>; **borough, ward,** precinct, riding, *arrondissement* <Fr>; **township,** hundred, commune, wapentake; metropolis, metropolitan area, **city, town** 230; **village,** hamlet; **district,** congressional district, electoral district, precinct; magistracy, soke, bailiwick; shrievalty, sheriffalty, sheriffwick, constablewick <Brit>; archdiocese, archbishopric, stake; **diocese,** bishopric, parish; colony

6 <regions of the world> continent, landmass; **Old World,** the old country; **New World,** America; **Northern Hemisphere,** North America; Central America; **Southern Hemisphere,** South America; Latin America; **Western Hemisphere, Occident,** West; **Eastern Hemisphere, Orient,** Levant, East, eastland; Far East, Mideast *or* Middle East, Near East; Asia, Europe, Eurasia, Asia Major, Asia Minor, Africa; Antipodes, Australia, down under <nf>, Australasia, Oceania; Arctic, Antarctica; Third World

7 <regions of the US> West, westland, wild West, West Coast, Coast, left Coast <nf>; Northwest, Pacific Northwest; Silicon Valley; Sierras; Rockies; Sunbelt; Southwest; Middle West *or* Midwest, Middle America; Great Plains, heartlands, Plains states; North Central region; Rust Belt; East, eastland, East Coast, Eastern Seaboard; Middle Atlantic; Northeast, Southeast; North, northland, Snow Belt, Frost Belt; Appalachia; South, southland, Dixie, Dixieland; Deep South, Old South; Delta, bayous; Bible Belt; borscht belt; Gulf Coast; New England, Down East, Yankeeland <nf>

ADJS **8 regional, territorial, geographical,** areal, sectional, zonal, topographic *or* topographical

9 local, localized, of a place, geographically limited, topical, vernacular, parochial, provincial, insular, limited, confined

10 U.S. state mottoes and nicknames

Alabama "We dare defend our rights"; Heart of Dixie *or* Camellia State

Alaska "North to the future"; The Last Frontier

Arizona "Diat Deus"; Grand Canyon State

Arkansas "Regnat populus"; Land of Opportunity

California "Eureka"; Golden State

Colorado "Nil sine numine"; Centennial State

Connecticut "Qui transtulit sustinet"; Constitution State; Nutmeg State

Delaware "Liberty and independence"; First State *or* Diamond State

District of Columbia "Justitia Omnibus"; Capital City

Florida "In God we trust"; Sunshine State

Georgia "Wisdom, justice, and moderation"; Empire State of the South; Peach State

Hawaii "The life of the land is perpetuated in righteousness"; Aloha State

Idaho "Esto perpetua"; Gem State

Illinois "State sovereignty—national union"; Prairie State

Indiana "Crossroads of America"; Hoosier State

Iowa "Our liberties we prize and our rights we will maintain"; Hawkeye State

Kansas "Ad astra per aspera"; Sunflower State

Kentucky "United we stand, divided we fall"; Bluegrass State

Louisiana "Union, justice and confidence"; Pelican State

Maine "Dirigo"; Pine Tree State

Maryland "Fatti maschii, parole femine"; Old Line State *or* Free State

Massachusetts "Ense petit placidam sub libertate"; Bay State; Colony State

Michigan "Si quaeris peninsulam amoenam"; Great Lake State *or* Wolverine State

Minnesota "L'Etoile du nord"; North Star State *or* Gopher State

Mississippi "Virtute et armis"; Magnolia State

Missouri "Salus populi suprema lex esto"; Show-Me State

Montana "Oro y plato"; Treasure State

Nebraska "Equality before the law"; Cornhusker State

Nevada "All for our country"; Sagebrush State *or* Battle-Born State

New Hampshire "Live free or die"; Granite State

New Jersey "Liberty and prosperity"; Garden State

New Mexico "Crescit eundo"; Land of Enchantment

New York "Excelsior"; Empire State

North Carolina "Esse quam videri"; Tar Heel State *or* Old North State

North Dakota "Liberty and union, now and forever, one and inseparable"; Peace Garden State

Ohio "With God, all things are possible"; Buckeye State

Oklahoma "Labor omnia vincit"; Sooner State

Oregon "The union"; Beaver State

Pennsylvania "Virtue, liberty and independence"; Keystone State

Rhode Island "Hope"; Little Rhody; Ocean State

South Carolina "Dum spiro spero"; Palmetto State

South Dakota "Under God, the people rule"; Coyote State *or* Sunshine State

Tennessee "Agriculture and commerce"; Volunteer State

Texas "Friendship"; Lone Star State
Utah "Industry"; Beehive State
Vermont "Freedom and unity"; Green Mountain State
Virginia "Sic semper tyrannis"; Old Dominion

Washington "Alki"; Evergreen State
West Virginia "Montani semper liberi"; Mountain State
Wisconsin "Forward"; Badger State
Wyoming "Equal rights"; Equality State

11 U.S. Territories and Commonwealths; mottoes

American Samoa "Samoa Muamua le Atua"
Guam "Where America's day begins"
Commonwealth of the Northern Mariana Islands

Commonwealth of Puerto Rico "Joannes est nomen eius"
Virgin Islands

12 Canadian provinces and territories

Alberta
British Columbia
Manitoba
New Brunswick
Newfoundland and Labrador
Northwest Territories

Nova Scotia
Nunavut
Ontario
Prince Edward Island
Quebec
Saskatchewan
Yukon Territory

232 COUNTRY

NOUNS **1 country,** land; **nation,** nationality, **state,** nation-state, sovereign nation *or* state, self-governing state, polity, **body politic; power,** superpower, world power; microstate; **republic,** people's republic, **commonwealth,** commonweal; **kingdom,** sultanate; **empire,** empery; superpower, power; **realm,** dominion, domain; **principality,** principate; duchy, dukedom; grand duchy, archduchy, archdukedom, earldom, county, palatinate, seneschalty; chieftaincy, chieftainry; toparchy, *toparchia* <L>; city-state, *polis* <Gk>, free city; **province,** territory, possession; colony, settlement; protectorate, mandate, mandated territory, mandant, mandatee, mandatory; buffer state; **ally,** military ally, cobelligerent, treaty partner; satellite, puppet regime *or* government; coalition government; free nation *or* country, captive nation, iron curtain country; nonaligned *or* unaligned *or* neutralist nation; developed nation, industrial *or* industrialized nation; underdeveloped nation, third-world nation; federation, confederation, commonwealth, commonweal, bloc, comity, United Nations

2 fatherland, *Vaterland* <Ger>, *patria* <L>, *la patrie* <Fr>, land of our fathers, **motherland,** mother country, **native land,** native soil, one's native heath *or* ground *or* soil *or* place, the old country, country of origin, **birthplace,** cradle; **home, homeland,** home ground, "home is where one starts"—T S Eliot, God's country; the home front

3 United States, United States of America, US, USA, US of A <nf>, **America,** Columbia, the States, Yankeeland <nf>, Land of Liberty, the melting pot; stateside

4 Britain, Great Britain, United Kingdom, the UK, Britannia, Albion, Blighty <Brit nf>, Limeyland <US nf>, Tight Little Island, Land of the Rose, Sovereign of the Seas; British Empire, Commonwealth of Nations, British Commonwealth of Nations, the Commonwealth; perfidious Albion

5 <national personifications> Uncle Sam *or* Brother Jonathan <US>; John Bull <Brit>

6 nationhood, peoplehood, **nationality; statehood, nation-statehood, sovereignty,** sovereign nationhood *or* statehood, independence, self-government, self-determination; internationality, internationalism; **nationalism**

7 native, countryman, countrywoman, citizen, national; nationalist, ultranationalist; patriot

233 THE COUNTRY

NOUNS **1 the country,** agricultural region, farm country, farmland, arable land, grazing region *or* country, rural district, rustic region, province *or* **provinces,** countryside, woodland 310.13, grassland 310.8, woods and fields, meadows and pastures, the soil, grass roots; **the sticks** *and* the tall corn *and* yokeldom *and* hickdom <nf>; cotton belt, tobacco belt, black belt, farm belt, corn belt, fruit belt, wheat belt, citrus belt; dust bowl; highlands, moors, uplands, foothills; lowlands, veld *or* veldt, savanna *or* savannah, plains, prairies, steppes, wide-open spaces

2 hinterland, back country, outback <Austral>, upcountry, boonies *and* boondocks <nf>; **the bush,** bush country, bushveld, **woods,** woodlands, **backwoods,** forests, timbers, the big sticks <nf>, brush; wilderness, wilds, uninhabited region, virgin land *or* territory; **wasteland** 891.2; **frontier,** borderland, outpost; wild West, cow country, cow town

3 rusticity, ruralism, inurbanity, agrarianism, bucolicism, **provincialism,** provinciality, simplicity, pastoral simplicity, unspoiledness; yokelism, hickishness, backwoodsiness; **boorishness,** churlishness, unrefinement, uncultivation; peasantry, gaucherie; agrarian society

4 ruralization, countrification, rustication, pastoralization

VERBS **5 ruralize, countrify, rusticate,** pastoralize; farm 1069.16; return to the soil

ADJS **6 rustic, rural, country, provincial, farm, pastoral, bucolic,** Arcadian, **agrarian,** agrestic, agrestal, proto-industrial; **agricultural** 1069.20; lowland, low-lying, upland, highland, prairie, plains

7 countrified, inurbane; country-born, country-bred, upcountry; farmerish, hobnailed, clodhopping, clodhopperish; **boorish,** clownish, loutish, lumpish, lumpen, cloddish, churlish; **uncouth,** unpolished, uncultivated, uncultured, unrefined; country-style, country-fashion

8 <nf terms> **hick,** hicky, hickified, hicklike, from the sticks, rube, hayseed, yokel, yokelish, down-home, shit-kicking, hillbilly, redneck

9 hinterland, back, **back-country,** up-country, backroad, outback <Austral>, wild, wilderness, virgin; wild-West, cow-country; **waste** 891.4; backwood *or* **backwoods,** back of beyond, backwoodsy; woodland, sylvan

234 LAND

NOUNS **1 land, ground,** landmass, earth, glebe <old>, **sod,** clod, **soil, dirt,** dust, clay, marl, mold <Brit nf>; *terra* <L>, **terra firma,** terra incognita; terrain; **dry land;** arable land; marginal land; grassland 310.8, woodland 310.13; crust, earth's crust, lithosphere; regolith; topsoil, subsoil; alluvium, alluvion; eolian *or* subaerial deposit; **real estate,** real property, landholdings, acres, territory, freehold; region 231; the country 233; earth science 1071

2 shore, coast, *côte* <Fr>; **strand,** *playa* <Sp>, **beach,** beachfront, beachside shingle, plage, lido, riviera, sands, berm; waterside, **waterfront;** shoreline, coastline; foreshore; bank, embankment; riverside; lakefront, lakeshore; **seashore, coast, seacoast, seaside, seaboard,** seabeach, seacliff, seabank, sea margin, oceanfront, oceanside, seafront, shorefront, tidewater, tideland, coastland, littoral, littoral zone; sand dune, sand bar, sandbank, tombolo; wetland, wetlands; **bay,** bayfront, bayside; drowned *or* submerged coast; rockbound coast, ironbound coast; loom of the land

3 landsman, landman, **landlubber**

ADJS **4 terrestrial,** terrene <old>, **earth, earthly,** telluric, tellurian; earthbound; sublunar, subastral; geophilous; terraqueous; fluvioterrestrial

5 earthy, earthen, soily, loamy, marly, gumbo; clayey, clayish; adobe; agrestal

6 alluvial, alluvious, estuarine, fluviomarine

7 coastal, littoral, seaside, shore, shoreside; shoreward; riparian *or* riparial *or* riparious; riverain, riverine; riverside; lakefront, lakeshore; oceanfront, oceanside; seaside, seafront, shorefront, shoreline; beachfront, beachside; bayfront, bayside; tideland, tidal, wetland

ADVS **8 on land,** on dry land, on terra firma; onshore, ashore; alongshore; shoreward; by land, overland

9 on earth, on the face of the earth *or* globe, in the world, in the wide world, in the whole wide world; **under the sun,** under the stars, beneath the sky, under heaven, below, **here below**

235 BODY OF LAND

NOUNS **1 continent, mainland,** main <old>, landform, continental landform, landmass; North America, South America, Africa, Europe, Asia, Eurasia, Eurasian landmass, Australia, Antarctica; subcontinent, India, Greenland; peninsula; **plate,** tectonic plate, crustal plate, crustal segment, Pacific plate, American plate, African plate, Eurasian plate, Antarctic plate, Indian plate; continental divide, continental drift; plate tectonics; Gondwana, Laurasia, Pangaea

2 island, isle; islet, holm, ait <Brit nf>; continental island; oceanic island; volcanic island; **key,** cay; sandbank, sandbar, bar; floating island; **reef,** coral reef, coral head; coral island, atoll; archipelago, island group *or* chain; insularity; islandology

3 continental, mainlander; continentalist

4 islander, islandman, island-dweller, islesman, insular; islandologist

VERBS **5** insulate, isolate, island, enisle; island-hop

ADJS **6 continental,** mainland

7 insular, insulated, isolated; island, islandy *or* islandish, islandlike; islanded, isleted, island-dotted; seagirt; archipelagic *or* archipelagian

236 PLAIN

<open country>

NOUNS **1 plain, plains,** flat country, flatland, **flats,** flat, level; champaign, champaign country, open country, **wide-open spaces; prairie,** grassland 310.8, sea of grass, **steppe, pampas,** *pampa* <Sp>, savanna, tundra, vega, campo, llano, sebkha; **veld,** grass veld, bushveld, tree veld; wold, weald; **moor,** moorland, down, **downs,** lande, **heath,** fell <Brit>; lowland, lowlands, bottomland; basin, playa; sand plain, sand flat, strand flat; tidal flat, salt marsh; salt pan; salt flat, alkali flat; **desert** 891.2; **plateau,** upland, tableland, table, **mesa,** mesilla; peneplain; coastal plain, abyssal plain, tidal plain, alluvial plain, delta, delta plain; flood plain; mare, lunar mare

ADJS 2 champaign, plain, flat, open; campestral *or* campestrian

3 major deserts

An Nafud <Saudi Arabia>	Kyzyl Kum <Uzbekistan, Kazakhstan>
Arabian *or* Eastern <Egypt>	Libyan <Libya, Egypt, Sudan>
Atacama <Chile>	Lut <Iran>
Black Rock <US>	Mojave <US>
Chihuahuan <US, Mex>	Namib <Namibia>
Colorado <US>	Negev <Israel>
Dahna <Saudi Arabia>	Nubian <Sudan>
Dasht-e-Kavir <Iran>	Painted Desert <US>
Dasht-e-Lut <Iran>	Patagonian <Argentina>
Death Valley <US>	Rub' al Khali <Saudi Arabia, Oman, Yemen, UAE>
Eastern *or* Arabian <Egypt>	Sahara <North Africa>
Gibson <Australia>	Shamo *or* Gobi <Mongolia>
Gobi *or* Shamo <Mongolia>	Simpson <Australia>
Great Arabian <Saudi Arabia>	Sinai <Egypt>
Great Australian <Australia>	Sonoran <US>
Great Basin <US>	Sturt Stony <Australia>
Great Indian *or* Thar <India, Pakistan>	Syrian <Syria, Iraq, Jordan, Saudi Arabia>
Great Salt Lake <US>	Takla Makan <China>
Great Sandy <Australia>	Thar *or* Great Indian <India, Pakistan>
Great Victoria <Australia>	Turfan Depression <China>
Iranian <Iran>	Yuma <US, Mex>
Kalahari <South Africa, Nambia, Botswana>	
Kara Kum <Turkmenistan>	

237 HIGHLANDS

NOUNS 1 highlands, uplands, highland, upland, high country, elevated land, dome, **plateau, tableland,** mesa, upland area, downs, downland, piedmont, moor, moorland, **hills, heights,** hill *or* hilly country, downs, wold, foothills, rolling country, **mountains,** mountain *or* mountainous country, high terrain, peaks, range, *massif* <Fr>

2 slope, declivity, steep, versant, incline, rise, talus, brae <Scot>, mountainside, hillside, bank, gentle *or* easy slope, glacis, angle of repose, steep *or* rapid slope, fall line, bluff, cliff, headland, ness, ben <Scot, Ir>; precipice, wall, palisade, scar <Brit>, escarpment, scarp, fault scarp, rim, face; upper slopes, upper reaches, timberline *or* tree line

3 plateau, tableland, high plateau, table, mesa, table mountain, butte, moor, fell <Brit>, hammada

4 hill, down <chiefly Brit>; brae *and* fell <Scot>; **hillock, knob,** butte, kopje, kame, monticle,

monticule, monadnock, **knoll,** hummock, hammock, eminence, rise, mound, swell, barrow, tumulus, kop, tell *or* tel, jebel; **dune,** sand dune; moraine, drumlin; anthill, molehill; **dune,** sand dune, sandhill

5 ridge, ridgeline, *arête* <Fr>, chine, spine, horst, kame, comb <Brit>, esker, os, cuesta, serpent kame, Indian ridge, moraine, terminal moraine; **saddle, hogback,** hog's-back, saddleback, horseback, col, watershed; **pass,** gap, notch, wind gap, water gap

6 mountain <see list>, mount, alp, hump, tor, height, dizzying height, nunatak, dome; **peak, pinnacle, summit** 198.2, mountaintop, point, topmost point *or* pinnacle, **crest,** spine, tor, pike <Brit>, *pic* <Fr>, *pico* <Sp>; crag, spur, cloud-capped *or* cloud-topped *or* snow-clad *or* snow-capped peak, the roof of the world; needle, aiguille, pyramidal peak, horn; fold mountain, fold-belt mountain, alpine chain, fault-block mountain, basin and range; oceanic ridge, oceanic rise; **volcano,** volcanic mountain, volcanic spine, volcanic neck; seamount, submarine mountain, guyot; **mountain range,** range, massif; **mountain system, chain,** mountain chain, cordillera, sierra, cordilleran belt, fold belt; hill heaped upon hill; divide, Continental Divide; mountain-building, orogeny, orogenesis, epeirogeny, folding, faulting, block-faulting, volcanism; isostasy; orography, orology; acrophile

7 valley, vale, glen, dale, dell, hollow, holler <nf>, dip, flume, cleuch *or* corrie <Scot>, cwm <Welsh>; **ravine, gorge, canyon,** box canyon, *arroyo* <Sp>, barranca, bolson, coulee, gully, gulch, combe *or* coomb *or* comb <Brit>, cirque, dingle, rift, rift valley, kloof, donga, graben, draw, wadi, basin, cirque, corrie, hanging valley; **crevasse;** chimney, ditch, chine, clough <Brit>, couloir; **defile,** pass, passage, col; **crater,** volcanic crater, caldera, meteorite *or* meteoritic crater

ADJS 8 hilly, rolling, undulating, upland; **mountainous,** montane, alpine, alpestrine, altitudinous; orogenic, orographic, orological, orometric

9 famous and high mountains

Aconcagua <Argentina 22,834 feet>	Cho Oyu <Nepal-Tibet 26,750 feet>
Annapurna I <Nepal 26,504 feet>	Communism Peak <Tajikistan 24,590 feet>
Annapurna II <Nepal 26,041 feet>	Cook <New Zealand 12,349 feet>
Ararat <Turkey 16,804 feet>	Dhaulagiri <Nepal 26,810 feet>
Ben Nevis <Scotland 4,406 feet>	Elbert <Colorado 14,433 feet>

Elbrus <Russia 18,841 feet>

Erebus <Antarctica 12,450 feet>

Etna <Sicily 10,900 feet>

Everest <Nepal-Tibet 29,028 feet>

Fuji <Japan 12,388 feet>

Gannett Peak <Wyoming 13,804 feet>

Grand Teton <Wyoming 13,766 feet>

Hood <Oregon 11,239 feet>

Jaya <New Guinea 16,500 feet>

Jungfrau <Switzerland 13,642 feet>

K2 or Godwin Austen <Kashmir 28,250 feet>

Kanchenjunga <Nepal-India 28,208 feet>

Kenya <Keny 17,058 feet>

Kilimanjaro <Tanzania 19,340 feet>

Kosciusko <Australia 7,310 feet>

Lhotse I <Nepal-Tibet 27,923 feet>

Lhotse II <Nepal-Tibet 27,560 feet>

Logan <Yukon 19,850 feet>

Makalu I <Nepal-Tibet 27,824 feet>

Manaslu I <Nepal 26,760 feet>

Matterhorn <Switzerland-Italy 14,690 feet>

McKinley <Alaska 20,320 feet>

Mitchell <North Carolina 6,684 feet>

Mont Blanc <France-Italy 15,771 feet>

Monte Rosa <Switzerland 15,203 feet>

Mount Saint Helens <Washington 8,364 feet>

Ojos del Salado <Argentina-Chile 22,572 feet>

Olympus <Greece 9,570 feet>

Pico de Orizaba <Mexico 18,555 feet>

Pikes Peak <Colorado 14,110 feet>

Popocatépetl <Mexico 17,930 feet>

Rainier <Washington 14,410 feet>

Rushmore <South Dakota 6,050 feet>

St. Elias <Alaska-Yukon 18,008 feet>

Teide <Canary Islands 12,198 feet>

Toubaki <Morocco 13,661 feet>

Vesuvius <Italy 3,891 feet>

Vinson Massif <Antarctica 16,864 feet>

Washington <New Hampshire 6,288 feet>

Whitney <California 14,494 feet>

238 STREAM
<running water>

NOUNS **1 stream, waterway, watercourse** 239.2, **channel** 239; meandering stream, flowing stream, lazy stream, racing stream, braided stream; spill stream; adolescent stream; mountain stream; **river;** navigable river, underground or subterranean river, "moving road"—Pascal; dry stream, stream bed, stream channel, stream course, winterbourne, wadi, *arroyo* <Sp>, *donga* <Africa>, *nullah* <India>; **brook,** branch; kill, bourn or bourne, run <Brit nf>, **creek,** crick <nf>; **rivulet,** rill, rillet, **streamlet,** brooklet, runlet, runnel, rundle <nf>, rindle <Brit nf>, beck <Brit>, gill <Brit>, burn <Scot>, sike <Brit nf>; **freshet,** fresh; millstream, race; midstream, midchannel; drainage pattern, watershed; stream action, fluviation

2 headwaters, headstream, headwater, head, riverhead; **source,** fountainhead 886.6

3 tributary, feeder, **branch, fork,** prong <nf>, confluent, confluent stream, affluent, distributary; effluent, anabranch, branch feeder; bayou; billabong <Austral>

4 flow, flowing, **flux,** fluency, profluence, fluid motion or movement; hydrodynamics; **stream, current,** set, trend, tide, water flow; drift, driftage; **course,** onward course, **surge, gush, rush,** onrush, spate, run, race; millrace, mill run; undercurrent, undertow; crosscurrent, crossflow; affluence, afflux, affluxion, confluence, convergence, concourse, conflux; **downflow,** downpour; defluxion; inflow 189.2; outflow 190.4

5 torrent, river, flood, flash flood, wall of water, waterflood, **deluge;** spate, **pour,** freshet, fresh

6 overflow, spillage, spill, spillover, overflowing, overrunning, alluvion, alluvium, **inundation, flood, deluge,** whelming, overwhelming, flush, washout, engulfment, submersion 367.2, cataclysm; the Flood, the Deluge; washout

7 trickle, tricklet, **dribble, drip,** dripping, stillicide <old>, drop, spurtle; percolation, leaching, lixiviation; distillation, condensation, sweating, seeping, seepage

8 lap, swash, wash, slosh, plash, splash; lapping, washing, etc

9 jet, spout, spurt, spurtle, squirt, spit, spew, spray, spritz <nf>; rush, **gush,** flush; **fountain,** fount, font, *jet d'eau* <Fr>; geyser, spouter <nf>

10 rapids, rapid, white water, wild water; ripple, **riffle,** riff <nf>; chute, shoot, sault

11 waterfall, cataract, fall, **falls, Niagara, cascade,** force <Brit>, linn <Scot>, sault; nappe; watershoot

12 eddy, back stream, gurge, **swirl,** twirl, whirl; **whirlpool,** vortex, gulf, **maelstrom;** Maelstrom, Charybdis; countercurrent, counterflow, counterflux, backflow, reflux, refluence, regurgitation, ebb, backwash, backwater, snye <Can>

13 tide, tidal current or stream, tidal flow or flood, **tide race; tidewater;** tideway, tide gate; **riptide,** rip, tiderip, overfalls; direct tide, opposite tide; **spring tide; high tide,** high water, full tide; **low tide,** low water; **neap tide,** neap; lunar tide, solar tide; **flood tide, ebb tide;** rise of the tide, rising tide, flux, flow, flood; ebb, reflux, refluence; ebb and flow, flux and reflux; tidal amplitude, tidal range, intertidal zone, tidal flat, tidal pool; tideland; tide chart or table, tidal current chart; tide gauge, thalassometer

14 wave, billow, surge, **swell,** heave, undulation, lift, rise, send, scend; trough, peak; **sea,** heavy swell, ocean swell, ground swell; **roller,** roll; **comber,** comb; **surf, breakers,** spume; wavelet, **ripple,** riffle; **tidal wave,** tsunami, seismic sea wave, seiche, rogue wave; gravity wave, water wave; tide wave; bore, tidal bore, eagre, traveling wave; **whitecap,** white horse, white foam; rough *or* heavy sea, rough water, broken water, dirty water *or* sea, choppy *or* chopping sea, popple, lop, chop, choppiness, overfall, angry sea; standing wave

15 water gauge, fluviograph, fluviometer; marigraph; Nilometer

VERBS 16 **flow, stream, issue, pour, surge, run, course, rush, gush, flush, flood;** empty into, flow into, join, join with, mingle waters; set, make, trend; flow in 189.9; flow out 190.13; flow back, surge back, ebb, regurgitate; meander

17 **overflow,** flow over, wash over, **run over, well over, brim over,** lap, lap at, lap over, overbrim, overrun, pour out *or* over, **spill, slop, slosh,** spill out *or* over; **cataract, cascade; inundate,** engulf, swamp, sweep, whelm, overwhelm, **flood,** deluge, submerge 367.7

18 **trickle, dribble,** dripple, **drip,** drop, spurtle; **filter,** percolate, leach, lixiviate; distill, condense, sweat; seep, weep; **gurgle** 52.11, murmur

19 **lap, plash, splash, wash, swash, slosh**

20 **jet, spout, spurt,** spurtle, **squirt,** spit, spew, spray, spritz <nf>, play, **gush,** well, surge; vomit, vomit out *or* forth

21 **eddy,** gurge, **swirl,** whirl, purl, reel, spin

22 **billow, surge, swell,** heave, lift, rise, send, scend, toss, popple, **roll,** wave, **undulate; peak,** draw to a peak, be poised; comb, **break,** dash, crash, smash; rise and fall, ebb and flow

ADJS 23 **streamy,** rivery, brooky, creeky; streamlike, riverine, riverlike; fluvial, fluviatile *or* fluviatic, fluviomarine

24 **flowing, streaming, running, pouring,** fluxive, fluxional, coursing, racing, gushing, rushing, onrushing, surging, surgy, torrential, rough, whitewater; **fluent,** profluent, affluent, defluent, decurrent, confluent, diffluent, refluent; tidal; gulfy, vortical; meandering, mazy, sluggish, serpentine

25 **flooded,** deluged, inundated, engulfed, swamped, swept, whelmed, drowned, overwhelmed, afloat, awash; washed, water-washed; in flood, at flood, in spate

26 **major rivers**

Nile <Africa>	Huang Ho *or* Yellow
Amazon <South America>	<China>
Mississippi <North	Congo <Africa>
America>	Amur <Rus>
Ob-Irtysh <Rus>	Lena <Rus>
Yangtze Kiang <China>	Mackenzie <Can>

239 CHANNEL

NOUNS 1 **channel, conduit, duct,** canal, course; **way, passage, passageway;** trough, troughway, troughing; tunnel; ditch, trench 290.2; adit; ingress, entrance 189; egress, exit; **stream** 238; English Channel

2 **watercourse, waterway, aqueduct,** water channel, water gate, water carrier, culvert, **canal;** side-channel, intrariverine channel, snye <Can>; streamway, riverway; **bed,** stream bed, river bed, creek bed, runnel; water gap; dry bed, *arroyo* <Sp>, wadi, winterbourne, *donga* <Africa>, *nullah* <India>, **gully,** gullyhole, gulch; swash, swash channel; race, headrace, tailrace; flume; sluice; spillway; spillbox; irrigation ditch, water furrow; waterworks

3 **gutter, trough,** eave *or* eaves trough; **flume,** chute, shoot; pentrough, penstock; guide

4 <metal founding> gate, ingate, runner, sprue, tedge

5 **drain,** sough <Brit nf>, sluice, scupper; **sink,** sump; piscina; **gutter,** kennel; **sewer,** cloaca, headchute; cloaca maxima

6 **tube; pipe; tubing, piping,** tubulation; tubulure; nipple, pipette, tubulet, tubule; reed, stem, straw; **hose,** hosepipe <Brit>, garden hose, fire hose; sprinkler; pipeline; catheter; **siphon;** tap; efflux tube, adjutage; funnel; snorkel; siamese, siamese connection *or* joint

7 **main,** water main, gas main, fire main

8 **spout,** beak, waterspout, downspout; gargoyle

9 **nozzle,** bib nozzle, pressure nozzle, spray nozzle, nose, snout; **rose,** rosehead; shower head, sprinkler head

10 **valve,** gate; **faucet, spigot, tap;** cock, **petcock,** draw cock, stopcock, sea cock, drain cock, ball cock; bunghole; needle valve; valvule, valvula

11 **floodgate,** flood-hatch, gate, **head gate,** penstock, water gate, **sluice,** sluice gate; tide gate, aboiteau <Can>; weir; **lock,** lock gate, dock gate; air lock

12 **hydrant,** fire hydrant, **plug,** water plug, fireplug

13 air passage, air duct, airway, air shaft, shaft, **air hole,** air tube; speaking tube *or* pipe; **blowhole,** breathing hole, spiracle; nostril; touchhole; spilehole, **vent, venthole,** ventage, ventiduct; **ventilator,** ventilating shaft; transom, louver, louverwork; wind tunnel

14 **chimney, flue,** flue pipe, funnel, **stovepipe, stack, smokestack,** smoke pipe, smokeshaft; Charley Noble; fumarole

VERBS 15 **channel,** channelize, canalize, **conduct, convey,** put through; pipe, tunnel, siphon; trench 290.3; direct 573.8

ADJS 16 **tubular,** tubate, tubiform, tubelike, pipelike; cylindrical; tubed, piped; cannular; tubal

17 **valvular,** valval, valvelike; valved

240 SEA, OCEAN

NOUNS **1 ocean, sea,** ocean sea, great *or* main sea, *thalassa* <Gk>, **main** *or* ocean main, the bounding main, tide, salt sea, salt water, blue water, ocean blue, deep water, open sea, **the brine,** the briny *and* the big pond <nf>, the briny deep, **the deep,** the deep sea, the deep blue sea, drink *and* big drink <nf>, the herring pond <Brit nf>; **high sea, high seas;** the seven seas; hydrosphere; **ocean depths,** ocean deeps and trenches 275.17

2 ocean <see list>; **sea,** tributary sea <see list>, gulf, bay; big pond <nf>

3 spirit of the sea, "the old man of the sea"—Homer, sea devil, Davy, **Davy Jones;** sea god, **Neptune,** Poseidon, Oceanus, Triton, Nereus, Oceanid, Nereid, Thetis, Amphitrite, Calypso; Varuna, Dylan; **mermaid,** siren; merman, seaman, undine, sea nymph, water sprite, sea serpent

4 <ocean zones> pelagic zone, benthic zone, estuarine area, sublittoral, littoral, intertidal zone, splash zone, supralittoral

5 ocean floor, seabed, sea bottom, benthos, Davy Jones's locker; continental shelf, continental slope, submarine canyon, land bridge, abyssal plain, abyssal hill, midoceanic ridge, oceanic ridge, oceanic trench, volcanic island, seamount, guyot, atoll

6 oceanography, thalassography, hydrography, bathymetry; marine biology; aquaculture

7 oceanographer, thalassographer, hydrographer, marine biologist, deep-sea diver, underwater explorer

ADJS **8 oceanic, marine, maritime,** pelagic, thalassic; ocean-going, sea-going, seafaring; undersea, underwater; nautical 182.57; oceanographic, oceanographical, hydrographic, hydrographical, bathymetric, bathymetrical, bathyorographical, thalassographic, thalassographical; terriginous; deep-sea 275.14

ADVS **9 at sea,** on the high seas; afloat 182.62; by water, by sea

10 oversea, overseas, beyond seas, over the water, transmarine, across the sea

11 oceanward, oceanwards, **seaward,** seawards, off; offshore, off soundings, out of soundings, in blue water

WORD ELEMENTS **12** mari-, thalass-, thalasso-; oceano-; bathy-

13 oceans

Antarctic	South Atlantic
Arctic	North Pacific
Indian	Pacific
North Atlantic	South Pacific

14 seas

Adriatic Sea	Gulf of Saint Lawrence
Aegean Sea	Hudson Bay
Amundsen Sea	Inland Sea
Andaman Sea	Ionian Sea
Arabian Sea	Irish Sea
Arafura Sea	Kara Sea
Aral Sea	Laptev Sea
Baffin Bay	Ligurian Sea
Bali Sea	Macassar Strait
Baltic Sea	Mediterranean
Banda Sea	Sea
Barents Sea	Molukka Sea
Bay of Bengal	North Sea
Beaufort Sea	Norwegian Sea
Bellingshausen Sea	Persian Gulf
Bering Sea	Philippine Sea
Black Sea	Red Sea
Caribbean Sea	Ross Sea
Caspian Sea	Sargasso Sea
Celebes Sea	Savu Sea
Ceram Sea	Sea of Azov
China Sea	Sea of Galilee
Chukchi Sea	Sea of Japan
Coral Sea	Sea of Marmara
East China Sea	Sea of Okhotsk
East Siberian Sea	South China Sea
Flores Sea	Sulu Sea
Great Australian Bight	Tasman Sea
Greenland Sea	Timor Sea
Gulf of Alaska	Tyrrhenian Sea
Gulf of California	Weddell Sea
Gulf of Guinea	White Sea
Gulf of Mexico	Yellow Sea

241 LAKE, POOL

NOUNS **1 lake,** landlocked water, loch <Scot>, lough <Ir>, *nyanza* <Africa>, mere, freshwater lake, natural lake; oxbow lake, bayou lake, glacial lake; volcanic lake; mountain lake; salt lake; tarn; inland sea; **pool,** lakelet, **pond,** pondlet, dew pond, linn <Scot>, dike <Brit nf>, *étang* <Fr>; standing water, still water, stagnant water, dead water, bayou; **water** *or* watering hole, water pocket, swimming hole, aquascape; **oasis;** farm pond; fishpond; millpond, millpool; salt pond, salina, tidal pond *or* pool; backwater; **puddle,** plash, sump <nf>; **lagoon,** *laguna* <Sp>; **reservoir,** artificial *or* manmade lake; dam; **well, cistern,** tank, artesian well, flowing well, **spring**

2 lake dweller, lakeside dweller, lacustrian, lacustrine dweller *or* inhabitant, **pile dweller** *or* builder; laker

3 lake dwelling, lacustrine dwelling, **pile house** *or* **dwelling,** stilt house, palafitte; crannog <Scot, Ir>; lake house, lakeside home; lakeside village

4 limnology, limnologist; limnimeter, limnograph

ADJS **5 lakish,** laky, lakelike; lacustrine, lacustral, lacustrian; pondy, pondlike, lacuscular; limnetic, limnologic, limnological, limnophilous; landlocked; lakeside, lake-dwelling

WORD ELEMENTS **6** limn-, limno-, limni-, -limnion

7 major lakes

Aral Sea <Kazakhstan, Uzbekistan>	Manzala <Egypt>
Athabaska <Can>	Maracaibo <Venezuela>
Baikal <Russia>	Mead <US>
Balkhash <Kazakhstan>	Michigan <US>
Bangweulu <Zambia>	Mobutu Sese Seko <Uganda>
Bear <US>	Moosehead <US>
Becharof <US>	Ness <Scot>
Biwa <Japan>	Nettilling <Can>
Caspian Sea <Azerbaijan, Kazakhstan, Turkmenistan, Iran, Rus>	Nicaragua
	Nipigon <Can>
	Nyasa <Malawi, Mozambique, Tanzania>
Chad <Chad, Niger, Nigeria>	Okeechobee <US>
Champlain <US, Can>	Onega <Rus>
Chapala <Mex>	Ontario <US, Can>
Derwent Water <Brit>	Patos <Brazil>
Edward <Uganda, Zaire>	Pontchartrain <US>
Erie <US, Can>	Reindeer <Can>
Eyre <Australia>	Rudolf <Kenya>
Finger Lakes <US>	St. Clair <US, Can>
Flathead <US>	Superior <US, Can>
Gairdner <Australia>	Tahoe <US>
Garda <Italy>	Tanganyika <Tanzania, Congo>
George <US>	Texcoco <Mex>
Great Bear <Can>	Titicaca <Bolivia, Peru>
Great Salt <US>	Torrens <Australia>
Great Slave <Can>	Trasimeno <It>
Huron <US, Can>	Tung-t'ing <China>
Issyk-Kul <Kyrgyzstan>	Turkana <Kenya, Ethiopia>
Katrine <Scot>	Urmia <Iran>
Kioga <Uganda>	Utah <US>
Kivu <Zaire, Rwanda>	Vanem <Swed>
Koko-Nor <China>	Victoria <Tanzania, Uganda>
Ladoga <Rus>	Volta <Ghana>
Lake of the Woods <Can>	Winnebago <US>
Lochy <Scot>	Winnipeg <Can>
Lomond or Loch <Scot>	Yellowstone <US>
Maggiore <It, Switz>	Zurich <Switz>
Malawi <Malawi, Mozambique, Tanzania>	
Manitoba <Can>	

242 INLET, GULF

NOUNS **1 inlet, cove,** creek <Brit>, arm of the sea, arm, armlet, canal, reach, loch <Scot>, **bay, fjord** or fiord, bight; cove; **gulf; estuary,** firth or frith, bayou, mouth, outlet, *boca* <Sp>; **harbor,** natural harbor; bay; road or roads, roadstead; **strait** or straits, kyle <Scot>, **narrow** or **narrows,** euripus, belt, gut, narrow seas; **sound**

ADJS **2** gulfy, gulflike; gulfed, bayed, embayed; estuarine, fluviomarine, tidewater

3 bays and gulfs

Baffin Bay <North America>	Gulf of Lions <Europe>
Bay of Bengal <Asia>	Gulf of Maine <North America>
Bay of Biscay <Europe>	Gulf of Mexico <North America>
Bay of Campeche <North America>	Gulf of Oman <Asia>
Bay of Fundy <North America>	Gulf of Panama <North America>
Bay of Naples <Europe>	Gulf of Siam <Asia>
Bay of Ob <Asia>	Gulf of Sidra <Africa>
Bay of Quinte <North America>	Gulf of St. Lawrence <North America>
Bay of Whales <Antarctica>	Gulf of Suez <Africa>
	Gulf of Thailand <Asia>
Botany Bay <Australia>	Gulf of Tonkin <Asia>
Buzzards Bay <North America>	Gulf of Venezuela <South America>
Cape Cod Bay <North America>	Gulf of Venice <Europe>
Chesapeake Bay <North America>	Hudson Bay <North America>
Delaware Bay <North America>	Humboldt Bay <North America>
Galveston Bay <North America>	James Bay <North America>
Great Australian Bight <Australia>	Massachusetts Bay <North America>
Green Bay <North America>	Montego Bay <North America>
Guanabara Bay <South America>	Narrangasett Bay <North America>
Gulf of Aden <Asia, Africa>	Penobscot Bay <North America>
Gulf of Alaska <North America>	San Diego Bay <North America>
Gulf of Aqaba <Asia, Africa>	San Francisco Bay <North America>
Gulf of Bothnia <Europe>	San Matias Gulf <South America>
Gulf of California <North America>	Tampa Bay <North America>
Gulf of Carpentaria <Australia>	Persian Gulf <Asia>
Gulf of Corinth <Europe>	Table Bay <Africa>
Gulf of Guinea <Africa>	Tasman Bay <Australia>

243 MARSH

NOUNS **1 marsh,** marshland, **swamp,** swampland, wetland, fen, fenland, **morass,** mere or marish <old>, *marais* <Fr>, *maremma* <Ital>, **bog, mire, quagmire,** sump <nf>, wash, baygall; glade, everglade; slough, swale, wallow, hog wallow, buffalo wallow, sough <Brit>; bottom, **bottoms,** bottomland, slob land, holm <Brit>, water meadow, meadow; **moor,** moorland, moss <Scot>, peat bog; salt marsh; quicksand; taiga; mud flat, **mud** 1062.8,9

VERBS **2 mire,** bemire, sink in, **bog,** mire *or* bog down, stick in the mud; stodge

ADJS **3 marshy, swampy,** swampish, **moory,** moorish, fenny, wetland, marish <old>, paludal *or* paludous; **boggy,** boggish, **miry,** mirish, quaggy, quagmiry, spouty, poachy; **muddy** 1062.14; swamp-growing, uliginous

244 QUANTITY

NOUNS **1 quantity,** quantum, amount, **whole** 792; mass, **bulk,** substance, matter, magnitude, amplitude, **extent, sum; measure,** measurement; strength, force, numbers

2 amount, quantity, large amount, small amount, **sum, number,** count, group, total, reckoning, **measure,** parcel, passel <nf>, **part** 793, **portion,** clutch, ration, share, issue, allotment, lot, deal; **batch,** bunch, heap <nf>, pack, mess <nf>, gob *and* chunk *and* hunk <nf>, budget <old>, dose

3 some, somewhat, something; **aught; any,** anything

VERBS **4 quantify,** quantize, **count, number off, enumerate, number** 1017.17, rate, fix; parcel, apportion, mete out, issue, allot, divide 802.18; **increase** 251.4,6, **decrease** 252.6, reduce 252.7; quantitate, **measure** 300.10; set a quota; massify

ADJS **5 quantitative,** quantitive, quantified, quantized, measured; **some,** certain, one; a, an; **any**

ADVS **6 approximately,** nearly, some, about, circa; more or less, *plus ou moins* <Fr>, by and large, upwards of

PREPS **7 to the amount of,** to the tune of <nf>; as much as, all of <nf>, no less than, upwards of

8 indefinite quantities

armful *or* armload	cup *or* cupful
bag *or* bagful	flask *or* flaskful
bargeload	glass *or* glassful
barrel *or* barrelful	handful
basin *or* basinful	jar *or* jarful
basket *or* basketful	keg *or* kegful
bin *or* binful	kettle *or* kettleful
bottle *or* bottleful	lapful
bowl *or* bowlful	mouthful
box *or* boxful	mug *or* mugful
bucket *or* bucketful	pail *or* pailful
bundle	pitcher *or* pitcherful
can *or* canful	planeful *or* planeload
cap *or* capful	plate *or* plateful
carton *or* cartonful	pocketful
case *or* caseful	pot *or* potful
crate *or* crateful	roomful

sack *or* sackful *or* sackload	tankerload
scoop *or* scoopful	teacup *or* teacupful
shovel *or* shovelful	teaspoon *or* teaspoonful
spoon *or* spoonful	thimble *or* thimbleful
tablespoon *or* tablespoonful	truckload
tank *or* tankful	tub *or* tubful

245 DEGREE

NOUNS **1 degree, grade, step,** *pas* <Fr>, leap; round, rung, tread, stair; **point,** mark, peg, tick; **notch,** cut; **plane,** level, plateau; **period,** space, interval; **extent, measure,** amount, ratio, proportion, stint, standard, height, pitch, reach, remove, compass, range, scale, scope, caliber; **shade,** shadow, nuance

2 rank, standing, level, footing, **status,** station; **position,** place, sphere, orbit, echelon; **order,** estate, precedence, condition; rate, rating; **class,** caste; **hierarchy,** power structure

3 gradation, graduation, grading, staging, phasing, tapering, shading; gradualism

VERBS **4 graduate, grade,** calibrate; phase in, phase out, taper off, shade off, scale; **increase** 251, **decrease** 252.6,7; change by degrees

ADJS **5 gradual,** gradational, calibrated, graduated, phased, staged, tapered, scalar; regular, progressive; hierarchic, hierarchical; in scale, calibrated; proportional

ADVS **6 by degrees,** degreewise; **gradually,** gradatim; **step by step,** grade by grade, *di grado in grado* <Ital>, **bit by bit, little by little,** inch by inch, inchmeal, drop by drop; a little, fractionally; a little at a time, by slow degrees, by inches; slowly 175.13

7 to a degree, to some extent, in a way, in a measure, in some measure; somewhat, kind of <nf>, sort of <nf>, rather, pretty, quite, fairly; a little, a bit; slightly, scarcely, in a small degree 248.9, in a limited degree 248.10; very, extremely, to a great extent 247.15, in an extreme degree 247.22

246 MEAN

NOUNS **1 mean, median, middle** 819; **golden mean,** *juste milieu* <Fr>; **medium,** happy medium; middle of the road, middle course, *via media* <L>; middle state *or* ground *or* position *or* echelon *or* level *or* point, midpoint; macrolevel; **average,** balance, par, normal, norm, rule, run, generality; **mediocrity,** averageness, passableness, adequacy; averaging, mediocritization; checks and balances; **center** 208.2

VERBS **2 average,** average out, **split the difference,** take the average, strike a balance, pair off, split down the middle; strike *or* hit a happy medium; keep to the middle, avoid extremes; **do,** just do, pass, barely pass; mediocritize

ADJS **3 medium,** mean, **intermediate,** intermediary, median, medial, mesial, mid-level, middle-echelon; **average,** normal, standard, par for the course; middle-of-the-road, moderate, fence-sitting, middle-ground; **middling, ordinary,** usual, routine, common, mediocre, merely adequate, passing, banal, so-so, vanilla *or* plain vanilla <nf>; **central** 208.11

ADVS **4 mediumly,** medianly; medially, midway 819.5, intermediately, in the mean; **centrally** 208.15

5 on the average, in the long run, over the long haul; taking one thing with another, taking all things together, **all in all, on the whole,** all things considered, on balance; **generally** 864.17

WORD ELEMENTS **6** medi-, mes-, mezzo-, semi-

247 GREATNESS

NOUNS **1 greatness, magnitude,** muchness; **amplitude,** ampleness, fullness, plenitude, great scope *or* compass *or* reach; **grandeur,** grandness; **immensity,** enormousness *or* enormity, **vastness,** vastitude, tremendousness, expanse, boundlessness, infinity 823; stupendousness, formidableness, prodigiousness, humongousness <nf>; **might,** mightiness, strength, power, intensity; **largeness** 257.6, **hugeness,** gigantism, bulk; **superiority** 249

2 glory, eminence, preeminence, majesty, loftiness, prominence, distinction, outstandingness, consequence, notability, high standing, illustriousness; **magnanimity,** nobility, sublimity; **fame,** renown, celebrity; heroism; fifteen minutes of fame

3 quantity 244, **numerousness** 884; **quantities, much, abundance,** copiousness, superabundance, superfluity, profusion, plenty, plenitude; **volume, mass,** mountain, load; peck, bushel; bag, barrel, ton; world, acre, ocean, sea; flood, spate; multitude 884.3, countlessness 823.1

4 lot, lots, deal, no end of, **good** *or* **great deal, considerable,** sight, **heap, pile, stack,** loads, **raft, slew,** whole slew, spate, wad, **batch,** mess, mint, peck, pack, pot, **tidy sum,** quite a little; **oodles, gobs, scads,** bags *and* masses *and* lashings <Brit>

VERBS **5 loom, bulk,** loom large, bulk large, stand out; **tower,** rear, soar, outsoar; **tower above,** rise above, overtop; **exceed, transcend,** outstrip; supersize

ADJS **6 great, grand, considerable,** consequential; **mighty,** powerful, strong, irresistible, intense; main, maximum, **total, full,** plenary, comprehensive, exhaustive; grave, **serious,** heavy, deep

7 large 257.16, **immense, enormous, huge** 257.20; **gigantic,** mountainous, titanic, colossal, mammoth, Gargantuan, gigantesque, monster, monstrous, outsize, sizable, larger-than-life, overgrown, king-size, monumental; **massive,** massy, weighty, bulky, voluminous; **vast,** vasty, boundless, **infinite** 823.3, immeasurable, cosmic, astronomical, galactic; **spacious,** amplitudinous, extensive; **tremendous,** stupendous, awesome, prodigious, ginormous <nf>, humongous <nf>; supersized *or* supersize

8 much, many, beaucoup <nf>, ample, **abundant,** copious, generous, overflowing, superabundant, multitudinous, plentiful, **numerous** 884.6, countless 823.3

9 eminent, prominent, outstanding, standout, high, elevated, towering, soaring, overtopping, exalted, **lofty,** sublime, illustrious; august, majestic, noble, distinguished; **magnificent,** magnanimous, heroic, godlike, superb; famous, renowned, lauded, glorious

10 remarkable, outstanding, extraordinary, **superior** 249.12, **marked,** of mark, signal, conspicuous, **striking; notable,** much in evidence, noticeable, noteworthy; **marvelous,** wonderful, formidable, exceptional, uncommon, astonishing, appalling, humongous <nf>, fabulous, fantastic, incredible, brilliant, egregious

11 <nf terms> **terrific,** terrible, horrible, **dreadful, awful,** fearful, frightful, deadly; **whacking, thumping, rousing,** howling; awesome

12 downright, outright, out-and-out; absolute, utter, perfect, consummate, superlative, surpassing, the veriest, positive, definitive, classical, pronounced, decided, regular <nf>, proper <Brit nf>, precious, profound, stark; **thorough,** thoroughgoing, **complete,** total; **unmitigated,** unqualified, unrelieved, unspoiled, undeniable, unquestionable, unequivocal; **flagrant,** arrant, shocking, shattering, egregious, intolerable, unbearable, unconscionable, glaring, stark-staring, **rank,** crass, gross

13 extreme, radical, out of this world, way *or* far out <nf>, too much <nf>; **greatest,** furthest, **most, utmost,** uttermost, the max <nf>; **ultra,** ultra-ultra; at the height *or* peak *or* limit *or* summit *or* zenith

14 undiminished, unabated, unreduced, unrestricted, unretarded, unmitigated

ADVS **15 greatly, largely,** to a large *or* great extent, in great measure, on a large scale; **much,** muchly <nf>, pretty much, very much, mucho <nf>, jolly well, so, so very much, ever so much, ever so, never so; **considerably,** considerable <nf>; abundantly, plenty <nf>, no end of, no end, not a little, galore <nf>, **a lot,** a deal <nf>, **a great deal,** *beaucoup* <Fr>; **highly,** to the skies; like *or* as all creation <nf>, like *or* as all get-out <nf>, in spades *and* with bells on *and* with bells on one's toes <nf>; **undiminishedly,** unabatedly, unreducedly, unrestrictedly, unretardedly, unmitigatedly

16 **vastly, immensely, enormously, hugely, tremendously,** gigantically, colossally, titanically, prodigiously, stupendously, humongously <nf>

17 **by far, far and away,** far, far and wide, by a long way, by a great deal, by a long shot *or* long chalk <nf>, out and away, by all odds

18 **very, exceedingly,** awfully *and* terribly *and* terrifically <nf>, **quite,** just, so, **really,** real *and* right <nf>, **pretty,** only too, mightily, **mighty** *and* almighty *and* powerfully *and* powerful <nf>

19 <in a positive degree> **positively, decidedly, clearly,** manifestly, unambiguously, patently, **obviously,** visibly, unmistakably, unquestionably, observably, **noticeably,** demonstrably, sensibly, quite; **certainly,** actually, **really, truly,** basically, verily, **undeniably,** indubitably, without doubt, assuredly, **indeed,** for a certainty, for real <nf>, seriously, in all conscience

20 <in a marked degree> **intensely, acutely,** exquisitely, **exceptionally,** surpassingly, superlatively, eminently, preeminently; **remarkably, markedly, notably, strikingly,** signally, emphatically, pointedly, prominently, conspicuously, pronouncedly, impressively, famously, glaringly; **particularly, singularly,** peculiarly; uncommonly, extraordinarily, **unusually; wonderfully,** wondrous, amazingly, magically, surprisingly, astonishingly, marvelously, exuberantly, incredibly, awesomely; **abundantly,** richly, profusely, amply, **generously,** copiously; **magnificently,** splendidly, nobly, worthily, magnanimously

21 <in a distressing degree> **distressingly, sadly, sorely, bitterly,** piteously, grievously, miserably, **cruelly,** woefully, lamentably, balefully, dolorously, shockingly; **terribly, awfully, dreadfully, frightfully, horribly,** abominably, **painfully,** excruciatingly, torturously, **agonizingly,** deathly, deadly, something awful *or* fierce *or* terrible *and* in the worst way <nf>, within an inch of one's life; shatteringly, staggeringly; **excessively,** exorbitantly, extravagantly, **inordinately,** preposterously; **unduly, improperly,** intolerably, unbearably; **inexcusably,** unpardonably, unconscionably; **flagrantly,** blatantly, egregiously;

unashamedly, unabashedly, baldly, nakedly, brashly, openly; **cursedly,** confoundedly, **damnably,** deucedly <nf>, infernally, hellishly

22 <in an extreme degree> **extremely, utterly, totally,** in the extreme, **most,** *à outrance* <Fr, to the utmost>; mondo <nf>; **immeasurably,** incalculably, indefinitely, **infinitely;** beyond compare *or* comparison, **beyond measure,** beyond all bounds, all out <nf>, flat out <Brit nf>, full-on; **perfectly, absolutely,** essentially, fundamentally, radically; **purely, totally,** completely, to the max; unconditionally, with no strings attached, unequivocally, downright, dead; with a vengeance

23 <in a violent degree> **violently,** furiously, hotly, fiercely, severely, **desperately,** madly, **like mad** <nf>; **wildly,** demonically, like one possessed, **frantically,** frenetically, fanatically, uncontrollably

WORD ELEMENTS 24 meg-, mega-, multi-, super-

248 INSIGNIFICANCE

NOUNS 1 **insignificance,** inconsiderableness, unimportance 998, inconsequentialness, inconsequentiality, lowness, pettiness, meanness, triviality, nugacity, nugaciousness; **smallness,** tininess, diminutiveness, minuteness, exiguity *or* exiguousness; **slightness,** moderateness, scantiness, puniness, picayunishness, meanness, meagerness; daintiness, delicacy; **littleness** 258; **fewness** 885; insufficiency 992

2 **modicum,** minim; **minimum; little, bit,** little *or* wee *or* tiny bit <nf>, bite, **particle,** fragment, spot, **speck,** flyspeck, fleck, point, dot, jot, tittle, **iota,** ounce, **dab** <nf>, mote, **mite** <nf> 258.7; whit, ace, **hair,** scruple, groat, farthing, pittance, dole, trifling amount, **smidgen** *and* skosh *and* smitch *and* scooch <nf>, pinch, gobbet, dribble, driblet, dram, drop, drop in a bucket *or* in the ocean, tip of the iceberg; grain, granule, pebble; molecule, **atom;** thimbleful, spoonful, handful, nutshell; trivia, minutiae; dwarf

3 **scrap,** tatter, smithereen <nf>, patch, **stitch, shred,** tag; snip, **snippet,** snick, chip, nip; splinter, sliver, shiver; **morsel,** *morceau* <Fr>, **crumb**

4 **hint,** *soupçon* <Fr>, **suspicion, suggestion,** intimation; tip of the iceberg; **trace, touch, dash,** cast, **smattering,** sprinkling; tinge, tincture; **taste, lick, smack,** sip, sup, **smell;** look, **thought,** idea; **shade,** shadow; gleam, spark, scintilla

5 **hardly anything, mere nothing,** next to nothing, less than nothing, **trifle,** bagatelle, **a drop in the bucket** *or* **in the ocean;** the shadow of a shade, the suspicion of a suspicion

ADJS 6 **insignificant, small, inconsiderable, inconsequential, negligible,** no great shakes, footling, one-horse *and* pint-size *and* vest-pocket <nf>; unimportant, no skin off one's nose *or* ass, **trivial,** trifling, nugacious, nugatory, petty, mean, niggling, piddling, picayune *or* picayunish, of no account, nickel-and-dime *and* penny-ante *and* Mickey-Mouse <nf>; shallow, depthless, cursory, superficial, skin-deep; **little** 258.10, **tiny** 258.11, **weeny, miniature** 258.12, **meager** 992.10, **few** 885.4; **short** 268.8; **low** 274.7

 7 **dainty, delicate, gossamer, diaphanous; subtle,** subtile, tenuous, thin 270.16, rarefied 299.4

 8 **mere, sheer,** stark, bare, barebones, plain, simple, unadorned, unenhanced

ADVS 9 <in a small degree> **scarcely, hardly,** not hardly <nf>, **barely,** only just, by a hair, by an ace *or* a jot *or* a whit *or* an iota, **slightly,** lightly, exiguously, fractionally, scantily, inconsequentially, **insignificantly, negligibly,** imperfectly, minimally, inappreciably, **little; minutely,** meagerly, triflingly, faintly, weakly, feebly; **a little, a bit,** just a bit, to a small extent, on a small scale; ever so little, *tant soit peu* <Fr>, as little as may be

 10 <in a certain or limited degree> **to a degree, to a certain extent, to some degree,** in some measure, to such an extent, *pro tanto* <L>; **moderately,** mildly, **somewhat,** detectably, just visibly, modestly, appreciably, visibly, **fairly,** tolerably, **partially,** partly, part, in part, incompletely, not exhaustively, not comprehensively; **comparatively, relatively; merely,** simply, purely, only; **at least,** at the least, leastwise, at worst, at any rate; **at most,** at the most, at best, at the outside <nf>; in a manner, in a manner of speaking, **in a way,** after a fashion; so far, thus far

 11 <in no degree> **noway,** in your dreams, noways, **nowise,** in no wise, in no case, in no respect, **by no means,** by no manner of means, **on no account, not on any account, not for anything in the world, under no circumstances,** at no hand, nohow <nf>, **not in the least,** not much, **not at all,** never, not by a damn sight <nf>, not by a long shot <nf>; not nearly, **nowhere near; not a bit,** not a bit of it, not a whit, not a speck, not a jot, not an iota, jack squat <nf>

249 SUPERIORITY

NOUNS 1 **superiority, preeminence, greatness** 247, **lead,** pride of place, transcendence *or* transcendency, ascendancy *or* ascendance, prestige, favor, prepotence *or* prepotency, preponderance; predominance *or* predominancy, hegemony; precedence 814, **priority,** prerogative, privilege, right-of-way; **excellence** 999.1, virtuosity, high caliber, inimitability, incomparability; **seniority,** precedence, deanship; clout, pull <nf>; **success** 409, accomplishment 407, **skill** 413

 2 **advantage,** vantage, odds, leg up *and* inside track *and* pole position <nf>; **upper hand,** whip hand, trump hand; start, head *or* flying *or* running start; **edge,** bulge *and* jump *and* drop <nf>; **card up one's sleeve** <nf>, ace in the hole <nf>, something extra *or* in reserve; vantage ground *or* point, coign of vantage, high ground; one-upmanship

 3 **supremacy, primacy,** paramountcy, **first place,** height, acme, zenith, be-all and end-all, summit, top spot <nf>; **sovereignty, rule, hegemony, control** 417.5; kingship, **dominion** 417.6, lordship, imperium, world power; **command,** sway; **mastery,** mastership 417.7; **leadership,** headship, presidency; **authority** 417, directorship, management, jurisdiction, power, say *and* last word <nf>; influence 894; effectiveness; **maximum,** highest, most, *ne plus ultra* <Fr, no more beyond>, the max <nf>; **championship,** crown, laurels, palms, first prize, blue ribbon, new high, record

 4 **superior, chief, head, boss** 575.1, employer, honcho <nf>, commander, **ruler, leader,** dean, *primus inter pares* <L, first among equals>, **master** 575; higher-up <nf>, senior, principal, big shot <nf>; superman, **genius** 413.12; prodigy, nonpareil, paragon, virtuoso, ace, **star, superstar,** champion, winner, top dog *and* top banana <nf>, one in a thousand, one in a million, etc, laureate, fugleman, Cadillac *and* Rolls-Royce *and* Mercedes-Benz <trademark>, A per se, A1, A number 1, standout, money-maker, record-breaker, the greatest *and* whizbang *and* world-beater *and* a tough act to follow <nf>; big fish in a small pond <nf>; alpha male, alpha female; supremist

 5 **the best** 999.8, the top of the line <nf>; the best people, nobility 608; **aristocracy,** barons, top people <nf>, **elite,** cream, crème de la crème, top of the milk, upper crust, upper class, one's betters; **the brass** <nf>, the VIP's <nf>, higher-ups, movers and shakers, lords of creation, ruling circles, **establishment,** power elite, power structure, **ruling class,** bigwigs <nf>, big boys <nf>, authorities, powers that be, officialdom; fast track; happy few, chosen few

VERBS 6 **excel, surpass, exceed, transcend,** get *or* have the ascendancy, get *or* have the edge, have it all over <nf>, overcome, overpass, best, **better,** improve on, perfect, go one better <nf>; **cap, trump; top, tower above** *or* **over, overtop, predominate,** prevail, preponderate, carry the day; **outweigh,** overbalance, overbear

 7 **best, beat, beat out, defeat** 412.6; beat all hollow <nf>, trounce, clobber *and* take to the cleaners

and smoke *and* skin *and* skin alive <nf>, worst, whip *and* lick *and* have it all over *and* cut down to size <nf>; bear the palm, take the cake <nf>, bring home the bacon <nf>; **triumph; win** 411.3

8 **overshadow, eclipse, throw into the shade, top,** extinguish, take the shine out of <nf>; put to shame, show up <nf>, put one's nose out of joint, put down <nf>, fake out <nf>

9 **outdo, outrival,** outvie, outachieve, edge out, **outclass, outshine,** overmatch, outgun <nf>; **outstrip,** outgo, outrange, outreach, outpoint, **outperform;** outplay, overplay, outmaneuver, outwit; outrun, outstep, outpace, outmarch, run rings *or* circles around <nf>; outride, override; outjump, overjump; outleap, overleap

10 **outdistance, distance; pass, surpass,** overpass; **get ahead,** pull ahead, shoot ahead, walk away *or* off <nf>; **leave behind,** leave at the post, leave in the dust, leave in the lurch; **come to the front,** have a healthy lead <nf>, hold the field; steal a march

11 **rule, command, lead,** possess authority 417.13, have the authority, have the say *or* the last word, have the whip hand *and* hold all the aces <nf>; **take precedence, precede** 814.2; **come** *or* **rank first, outrank,** rank, rank out <nf>; **come to the fore,** come to the front, **lead** 165.2; play first fiddle, **star**

ADJS 12 **superior, greater,** better, finer; **higher,** upper, over, super, above; ascendant, in the ascendant, in ascendancy, coming <nf>; **eminent,** outstanding, rare, distinguished, marked, of choice, chosen; **surpassing, exceeding, excellent** 999.12, **excelling, rivaling, eclipsing,** capping, topping, **transcending,** transcendent *or* transcendental, bad <nf>; **ahead,** a cut *or* stroke above, one up on <nf>; more than a match for

13 **superlative, supreme, greatest, best, highest,** veriest, maximal, maximum, most, utmost, outstanding, stickout <nf>; top, topmost, **uppermost,** tip-top, top-level, top-echelon, top-notch *and* top-of-the-line <nf>, **first-rate,** first-class, top of the line, highest-quality, best-quality, far and away the best, the best by a long shot *or* long chalk, head and shoulders above, of the highest type, A1, A number 1, uber

14 **chief, main, principal,** paramount, **foremost,** headmost, **leading, dominant,** crowning, capital, **cardinal;** great, arch, banner, master, magisterial; central, focal, prime, **primary,** primal, first; **preeminent,** supereminent; **predominant,** preponderant, prevailing, hegemonic *or* hegemonical; ruling, overruling; **sovereign** 417.17; topflight, highest-ranking, ranking; **star,** superstar, stellar, world-class

15 **peerless, matchless, champion; unmatched,** unmatchable, makeless <old>, unrivaled,

unparagoned, unparalleled, immortal, **unequaled,** never-to-be-equaled, unpeered, unexampled, unapproached, unapproachable, **unsurpassed, unexcelled;** unsurpassable; inimitable, **incomparable,** beyond compare *or* comparison, apples to oranges, **unique;** without equal *or* parallel, *sans pareil* <Fr>; in a class by itself, *sui generis* <L>, easily first, *facile princeps* <L>; second to none, *nulli secundus* <L>; **unbeatable,** invincible

ADVS 16 **superlatively, exceedingly, surpassingly;** eminently, egregiously, prominently; supremely, paramountly, preeminently, **the most,** transcendently, to crown all, *par excellence* <Fr>; inimitably, incomparably; to *or* in the highest degree, far and away

17 **chiefly, mainly, in the main,** in chief; dominantly, **predominantly; mostly, for the most part; principally, especially, particularly,** peculiarly; **primarily, in the first place,** first of all, **above all; indeed,** even, yea, still more, more than ever, all the more, *a fortiori* <L>; ever so, never so, no end

18 **peerlessly, matchlessly,** unmatchably; unsurpassedly, unsurpassably; inimitably, **incomparably; uniquely,** second to none, *nulli secundus* <L>; **unbeatably,** invincibly

19 **advantageously,** to *or* with advantage, favorably; melioratively, amelioratively, improvingly

WORD ELEMENTS 20 preter-, super-, supra-, sur-, trans-, uber-, ultra-, arch-, prot-

250 INFERIORITY

NOUNS 1 **inferiority, subordinacy,** subordination, secondariness; **juniority,** minority; **subservience, subjection,** servility, lowliness, humbleness, humility; back seat *and* second fiddle <nf>, second *or* third string <nf>, second banana; insignificance

2 **inferior, underling,** understrapper <Brit>, **subordinate,** subaltern, **junior;** secondary, second fiddle *and* second stringer *and* third stringer *and* benchwarmer *and* low man on the totem pole <nf>, loser *and* nonstarter <nf>; lightweight, follower, pawn, cog, flunky, yes-man, creature; lower class *or* orders *or* ranks, lowlife, commonalty; infrastructure *or* commonality, *hoi polloi* <Gk>, masses; satellite; B-list, C-list, D-list; trailer trash, white trash; Eurotrash

3 **inadequacy, mediocrity** 1005, deficiency, imperfection, insufficiency 992; **incompetence** *or* incompetency, maladroitness, unskillfulness 414; **failure** 410; smallness 248.1; littleness 258; meanness, lowness, baseness, pettiness, triviality,

shabbiness, vulgarity 497; **fewness** 885; subnormality

VERBS **4 be inferior, not come up to, not measure up, fall** or **come short, fail** 410.9, not make or hack it and not cut the mustard and not make the cut <nf>, not make the grade; want, leave much to be desired, be found wanting; **not compare,** have nothing on <nf>, **not hold a candle to** <nf>, not approach, not come near; serve, subserve, rank under or beneath, follow, play second fiddle and take a back seat and sit on the bench <nf>

5 bow to, hand it to <nf>, tip the hat to <nf>, yield the palm; retire into the shade; give in <nf>, lose face; submit

ADJS **6 inferior, subordinate,** subaltern, sub, small-scale, **secondary; junior, minor;** second or third string and one-horse and penny-ante and dinky <nf>, second or third rank, third-rate, low in the pecking order, low-rent and downscale <nf>, below the salt; **subservient,** subject, servile, low, **lowly,** humble, modest, scrub; **lesser,** less, lower, low-grade, B-list, C-list, D-list; in the shade, thrown into the shade; **common,** vulgar, **ordinary;** underprivileged, disadvantaged, nothing to write home about, crummy; **beneath one's dignity** or station, infra dig, demeaning; half-assed <nf>

7 inadequate, mediocre, deficient, imperfect, **insufficient; incompetent,** unskillful, maladroit; small, small-time, little, mean, base, petty, trivial, shabby; **not to be compared, not comparable, not a patch on** <nf>; **outclassed,** outshone, not in it and not in the same street or league with <nf>, out of it and out of the picture and **out of the running** and left a mile behind <nf>

8 least, smallest, littlest, slightest, **lowest,** shortest; minimum, minimal, minim; few 885.4; minimalistic

ADVS **9 poorly, incompetently, inadequately,** badly, maladroitly; least of all, at the bottom of the scale, at the nadir, at the bottom of the heap and in the gutter <nf>; beggarly; at a disadvantage

WORD ELEMENTS **10** sub-, hyp-, hypo-

251 INCREASE

NOUNS **1 increase, gain,** augmentation, greatening, **enlargement, amplification, growth,** development, widening, spread, broadening, elevation, **extension,** aggrandizement, access, accession, **increment,** accretion; exponential growth; **addition** 253; **expansion** 259; **inflation,** swelling, ballooning, edema, fattening, tumescence, bloating, dilation; **multiduplication, proliferation,** productiveness 890; accruement, accrual, accumulation; **advance,** appreciation, ascent, mounting, crescendo, waxing, snowballing, **rise** or raise, fattening and boost and hike <nf>, **up** and upping <nf>, buildup; **upturn,** uptick <nf>, uptrend, upsurge, upswing; **leap,** jump; **flood,** surge, gush

2 intensification, heightening, deepening; tightening, turn of the screw; **strengthening,** beefing-up <nf>, enhancement, **magnification,** blowup, blowing up, exaggeration; aggravation, exacerbation, heating-up; **concentration,** condensation, consolidation; **reinforcement,** redoubling; pickup and step-up <nf>, **acceleration,** speedup, accelerando, escalation, upsurge; **boom, explosion,** baby boom, population explosion, information explosion

3 gains, winnings, cut and take <nf>, increase <old>, **profits** 472.3

VERBS **4 increase, enlarge,** aggrandize, **amplify,** amp, **augment, extend,** maximize, **add to; expand** 259.4, **inflate;** lengthen, broaden, fatten, fill out, thicken; **raise,** exalt, boost <nf>, hike and hike up and jack up and jump up and bump up and crank up <nf>, mark up, put up, **up** <nf>; **build, build up;** pyramid, parlay; progress

5 intensify, heighten, deepen, amplify, enhance, **strengthen,** beef up <nf>, aggravate, exacerbate; **exaggerate,** blow up and puff up <nf>, **magnify;** whet, sharpen; **reinforce,** double, redouble, triple; **concentrate,** condense, consolidate; **complicate,** ramify, make complex; give a boost to, **step up** <nf>, accelerate; key up, hop up and soup up and jazz up <nf>; add fuel to the flame or the fire, heat or hot up <nf>

6 grow, increase, advance, appreciate; **spread, widen,** broaden; **gain,** get ahead; wax, swell, balloon, bloat, mount, **rise,** go up, crescendo, snowball, skyrocket, mushroom; **intensify, develop,** gain strength, strengthen; accrue, accumulate; **multiply, proliferate,** breed, teem; run or shoot up, **boom, explode**

ADJS **7 increased, heightened,** raised, elevated, stepped-up <nf>; **intensified,** deepened, reinforced, strengthened, fortified, beefed-up <nf>, tightened, stiffened; **enlarged, extended,** augmented, aggrandized, amplified, **enhanced,** boosted, hiked <nf>, broadened, widened, spread; **magnified, inflated, expanded,** swollen, bloated; **multiplied,** proliferated; **accelerated,** hopped-up and jazzed-up <nf>, cranked up

8 increasing, rising, fast-rising, skyrocketing, meteoric; on the upswing, on the increase, on the rise; crescent, waxing, **growing,** fast-growing, flourishing, burgeoning, blossoming, waxing, swelling, lengthening, **multiplying,** proliferating; spreading, spreading like a cancer or like wildfire, expanding; tightening, intensifying; incremental; **on the increase,** crescendoing, snowballing, mushrooming, growing like a mushroom

ADVS **9 increasingly,** growingly, more, **more and more,** on and on, greater and greater, ever more; in a crescendo

252 DECREASE

NOUNS **1 decrease,** decrescence, decrement, **diminishment,** diminution, **reduction, lessening, lowering,** waning, shrinking *or* shrinkage, withering, withering away, scaling down, scaledown, downsizing, build-down; miniaturization; downplaying, underplaying; depression, damping, dampening; **letup** <nf>, abatement, easing, easing off, slackening; de-escalation; **alleviation,** relaxation, mitigation; attenuation, extenuation, weakening, sagging, dying, dying off *or* away, trailing off, tailing off, tapering off, fade-out, languishment; depreciation, **deflation; deduction** 255.1; subtraction, **abridgment** 268.3; **contraction** 260; simplicity 798

2 decline, declension, **subsidence,** slump <nf>, lapse, **drop,** downtick <nf>; **collapse,** crash; dwindling, wane, ebb; downturn, downtrend, downward trend *or* curve, retreat, remission; **fall, plunge,** dive, decline and fall; decrescendo, diminuendo; catabasis, deceleration, slowdown; leveling off, bottoming out

3 decrement, waste, loss, dissipation, wear and tear, erosion, ablation, wearing away, depletion, corrosion, attrition, consumption, shrinkage, exhaustion; deliquescence, dissolution; extinction, consumption

4 curtailment, retrenchment, cut, cutback, drawdown, rollback, scaleback, pullback; moderation, restraint; abridgment; slash, slashing

5 minimization, minification, making light of, devaluing, undervaluing, **belittling,** belittlement, detraction; abridgment, miniaturization; qualification 959

VERBS **6 decrease, diminish, lessen; let up,** bate, abate; **decline, subside,** shrink, wane, wither, ebb, ebb away, dwindle, languish, sink, sag, die down *or* away, wind down, taper off *and* trail off *or* away *and* tail off *or* away <nf>; **drop,** drop off, dive, take a nose dive, plummet, plunge, fall, fall off, fall away, fall to a low ebb, run low; **waste,** wear, waste *or* wear away, crumble, erode, ablate, corrode, consume, consume away, be eaten away; melt away, deliquesce; become extinct

7 reduce, decrease, diminish, lessen, take from; **lower, depress,** de-escalate, damp, dampen, **step down** *and* tune down *and* phase down *or* out *and* scale back *or* down *and* roll back *or* down <nf>; **downgrade;** depreciate, **deflate; curtail,** retrench; **cut,** cut down *or* back, cut down to size <nf>, trim away, chip away at, whittle away *or* down, pare, pare down, roll back <nf>; deduct 255.9; **shorten** 268.6, abridge; **compress** 260.7, shrink, retrench, downsize; **simplify** 798.4

8 abate, bate, ease; **weaken,** dilute, water, water down, attenuate, extenuate; alleviate, mitigate, slacken, remit; enfeeble, debilitate; tail off, die off

9 minimize, minify, **belittle,** detract from; dwarf, bedwarf; play down, underplay, downplay, de-emphasize, play down, tone down, moderate; hush

ADJS **10 reduced, decreased, diminished, lowered,** dropped, fallen; bated, **abated; deflated,** contracted, shrunk, shrunken; **simplified** 798.9; back-to-basics, no-frills; dissipated, **eroded,** consumed, ablated, **worn;** curtailed, shorn, retrenched, cutback; weakened, attenuated, watered-down, diluted; scaled-down, miniaturized, abridged, pared down; minimized, belittled, on a downer <nf>; **lower,** less, lesser, smaller, shorter; off-peak; downplayed, underplayed, toned down, de-emphasized

11 decreasing, diminishing, lessening, subsiding, declining, languishing, dwindling, waning, on the wane, on the slide, wasting; decrescent, reductive, deliquescent, **contractive;** diminuendo, decrescendo

ADVS **12 decreasingly, diminishingly,** less, **less and less,** ever less; decrescendo, diminuendo; on a declining scale, at a declining rate

253 ADDITION

NOUNS **1 addition,** accession, annexation, affixation, suffixation, prefixation, agglutination, attachment, junction, **joining** 800, adjunction, uniting; **increase** 251; **augmentation, supplementation, complementation,** reinforcement; superaddition, admixture, superposition, superjunction, superfetation, suppletion; juxtaposition 223.3; adjunct 254, add-on, rider, extra, accessory

2 <math terms> plus sign, plus; addend; sum, summation, total, aggregate; subtotal

3 adding, totalizing *or* totalization, toting up, reckoning, computation, calculation, ringing up; **adding machine,** calculator

VERBS **4 add,** add on, plus <nf>, put with, **join** *or* **unite with, bring together, affix, attach,** annex, adjoin, append, conjoin, subjoin, prefix, suffix,

infix, postfix, tag, tag on, **tack on** <nf>, slap on
<nf>, hitch on <nf>, carry over; glue on, paste on,
agglutinate; superpose, superadd; burden,
encumber, saddle with; **complicate,** ornament,
decorate

5 add to, augment, supplement, append; volumize;
increase 251.4; **reinforce,** strengthen, fortify, beef
up <nf>; recruit, swell the ranks of; superadd

6 compute, add up; sum, total, totalize, total up, tot
and tot up *and* tote *and* tote up <nf>, tally,
calculate

7 be added, advene, supervene

ADJS **8 additive,** additional, additory; **cumulative,**
accumulative; summative *or* summational; loaded

9 added, affixed, add-on, **attached,** annexed,
appended, appendant; adjoined, adjunct,
adjunctive, conjoined, subjoined; superadded,
superposed, superjoined

10 additional, supplementary, supplemental; extra,
plus, further, farther, fresh, **more,** new, **other,**
another, ulterior; **auxiliary,** ancillary,
supernumerary, contributory, **accessory,**
collateral, supererogatory; **surplus,** spare,
superfluous

ADVS **11 additionally, in addition, also,** and then
some, even more, more so, and also, and all <nf>,
and so, **as well, too,** else, beside, **besides, to boot,
not to mention, let alone, into the bargain;** on top
of, over, above; **beyond, plus; extra,** on the side
<nf>, for lagniappe; **more, moreover,** *au reste*
<Fr>, *en plus* <Fr>, thereto, farther, further,
furthermore, at the same time, then, again, yet;
similarly, likewise, by the same token, by the same
sign; item; therewith, withal <old>; all included,
altogether; among other things, *inter alia* <L>

PREPS **12 with, plus, including,** inclusive of, **along** *or*
together with, coupled with, **in conjunction with;
as well as,** to say nothing of, not to mention, let
alone; over and above, **in addition to,** added to,
linked to; with the addition of, attended by

CONJS **13 and, also,** and also

PHRS **14 et cetera, etc, and so forth, and so on,** *und
so weiter* <Ger>; et al, *et alii* <L>, and all <nf>, and
others, and other things, *cum multis aliis* <L, with
many others>; and everything else, **and more of the
same, and the rest, and the like;** blah blah blah
blah *and* dah-dah dah-dah dah-dah *and* and
suchlike *or* and all that sort of thing *and* and all
that *and* and all like that *and* and stuff like that *and*
and all that jazz <nf>; yada yada *or* yadda yadda;
and what not *and* and what have you *and* and I
don't know what *and* and God knows what *and* and
then some *and* you name it <nf>; and the following,
et sequens <L>, et seq

WORD ELEMENTS **15** super-, pleo-, pleio-

254 ADJUNCT

<thing added>

NOUNS **1 adjunct, addition,** increase, **increment,**
augmentation, supplementation,
complementation, *additum* <L>, additament,
additory, addendum, addenda <pl>, accession,
fixture; **annex,** annexation; **appendage,**
appendant, pendant, appanage, tailpiece, coda;
undergirding, reinforcement; appurtenance,
appurtenant; **accessory,** attachment; **supplement,**
complement, continuation, extrapolation,
extension; offshoot, side issue, corollary, sidebar
<nf>, side effect, spin-off <nf>, aftereffect;
concomitant, accompaniment 769, **additive,**
adjuvant; leftover, carry-over

2 <written text> **postscript** *or* P.S., **appendix;** rider,
allonge, codicil; **epilogue,** envoi, coda, tail,
afterword; back matter, front matter; note,
marginalia, scholia, commentary, annotation,
footnote; **interpolation,** interlineation; affix,
prefix, suffix, infix; subscript, superscript; enclitic,
proclitic

3 <building> wing, **addition, annex,** extension, ell *or*
L, outhouse, outbuilding

4 extra, bonus, signing bonus, retention bonus,
premium, something extra, extra dash, little extra,
extra added attraction, lagniappe, something into
the bargain, something for good measure, baker's
dozen; peripheral; added value; **padding,** stuffing,
filling; trimming, **frill,** flourish, filigree,
decoration, ornament; bells and whistles <nf>;
superaddition; fillip, wrinkle, twist; the works
<nf>; benefit, perquisite, perk; freebie <nf>

255 SUBTRACTION

NOUNS **1 subtraction, deduction,** subduction,
removal, taking away; abstraction, ablation,
sublation; erosion, abrasion, wearing, wearing
away; refinement, purification; detraction

2 reduction, diminution, decrease 252, build-down,
phasedown, drawdown, decrement, impairment,
cut *or* **cutting,** curtailment, shortening,
truncation; **shrinkage,** depletion, **attrition,**
remission; **depreciation,** detraction,
disparagement, derogation; retraction,
retrenchment; **extraction**

3 excision, abscission, rescission, extirpation;
elimination, exclusion, extinction, eradication,
destruction 395, annihilation, cancellation,
write-off, erasure; circumcision; **amputation,**
mutilation

4 castration, gelding, emasculation, deballing <nf>,
altering *and* fixing <nf>, spaying

5 <written text> **deletion,** erasure, cancellation, omission; editing, blue-penciling, striking or striking out; expurgation, bowdlerization, censoring or censorship; abridgment, abbreviation

6 <math terms> difference; subtrahend, minuend; negative; minus sign, minus

7 <thing subtracted> **deduction,** decrement, minus; refund, rebate

8 <result> **difference, remainder** 256, epact <astronomy>, discrepancy, net, balance, surplus 993.5, deficit, credit; contradistinction

VERBS **9** **subtract, deduct,** subduct, take away, take from, **remove,** withdraw, abstract, debit, dock; **reduce,** shorten, curtail, retrench, lessen, **diminish, decrease,** phase down, impair, bate, abate; **depreciate,** disparage, detract, derogate; **erode,** abrade, eat or wear or rub or shave or file away; **extract,** leach, drain, wash away; thin, thin out, weed; **refine,** purify

10 **excise,** cut out, cut, extirpate, enucleate; **cancel,** write off; **eradicate,** root out, wipe or stamp out, **eliminate,** kill, kill off, liquidate, annihilate, knock off, destroy 395.10, extinguish; **exclude,** except, take out, cancel, cancel out, censor out, bleep out <nf>, rule out, bar, ban; set aside or apart, isolate, pick out, cull; **cut off** or **away,** shear or take or strike or knock or lop off, truncate; minus; **amputate,** mutilate, abscind; **prune,** pare, peel, clip, crop, bob, dock, lop, nip, shear, shave, strip, strip off or away

11 **castrate,** geld, emasculate, eunuchize, neuter, spay, fix or alter <nf>, unsex, desex, deball <nf>; geld, caponize; unman; sterilize

12 <written text> **delete,** erase, expunge, **cancel,** omit; **edit,** edit out, blue-pencil; strike, strike out or off, rub or blot out, cross out or off, kill, cut; void, rescind; **censor,** bowdlerize, expurgate; abridge, abbreviate

ADJS **13** **subtractive, reductive,** deductive, extirpative; ablative, erosive; censorial; removable, eradicable

PREPS **14** **off, from; minus,** less, without, excluding, except or excepting, with the exception of, save, leaving out or aside, barring, exclusive of, not counting, exception taken of, discounting

256 REMAINDER

NOUNS **1** **remainder, remains, remnant,** relict, **residue,** residuum, residual, **rest, balance;** holdover; **leavings, leftovers, oddments; refuse,** odds and ends, scraps, rags, **rubbish, waste,** litter, orts, candle ends; scourings, offscourings; parings, sweepings, filings, shavings, sawdust; chaff, straw, stubble, husks; **debris,** detritus, ruins; end, fag end; stump, butt or butt end, stub, rump; survival, vestige, trace, hint, shadow, afterimage, afterglow; glut; **fossil,** relics

2 **dregs, grounds, lees,** dross, slag, draff, scoria, feces; **sediment, settlings, deposits,** deposition; precipitate, precipitation, sublimate <chem>; alluvium, alluvion, diluvium; overflow; silt, loess, moraine; scum, off-scum, froth; ash, ember, cinder, sinter, clinker; soot, smut

3 **survivor,** heir, successor, inheritor; **widow,** widower, relict, war widow, **orphan;** others, those left

4 **excess** 993, **surplus,** surplusage, overplus, overage; superfluity, redundancy, pleonasm; something for a rainy day

VERBS **5** **remain, be left** or **left over, survive,** subsist, rest, stay

6 **leave,** leave over, leave behind, bequeath

ADJS **7** **remaining, surviving, extant,** vestigial, over, left, **leftover, still around, remnant,** remanent, odd, on the shelf; **spare,** to spare; unused, unconsumed; **surplus,** superfluous; **outstanding,** unmet, unresolved; net; redundant

8 **residual,** residuary; sedimental, sedimentary

257 SIZE, LARGENESS

NOUNS **1** **size, largeness, bigness, greatness** 247, vastness, vastitude, **magnitude,** order of magnitude, amplitude; mass, bulk, **volume,** body; **dimensions, proportions,** dimension, caliber, scantling, proportion; **measure,** measurement 300, gauge, **scale; extent,** extension, expansion, expanse, square footage or yardage etc, **scope,** reach, range, ballpark <nf>, spread, coverage, area, circumference, ambit, girth, diameter, radius, boundary, border, periphery; linear measure or dimension, length, height, procerity <depth>; depth, breadth, width; wheelbase, wingspan

2 **capacity, volume, content,** holding capacity, cubic footage or yardage etc, accommodation, room, space, measure, limit, burden; gallonage, tankage; poundage, tonnage, cordage; stowage; **quantity** 244

3 **full size,** full growth; life size

4 large size, extra large size, economy size, family size, **king size,** California king size, queen size, giant size, plus size

5 **oversize,** outsize; overlargeness, overbigness; **overgrowth,** wild or uncontrolled growth, overdevelopment, sprawl; **overweight,** overheaviness; overstoutness, overfatness, overplumpness, bloat, bloatedness, obesity, chubbiness; gigantism, giantism, titanism;

hyperplasia, hypertrophy, acromegalic gigantism, acromegaly, pituitary gigantism, normal gigantism

6 <large size> **sizableness, largeness, bigness,** greatness, grandness, grandeur, grandiosity; largishness, biggishness; voluminousness, capaciousness, generousness, copiousness, ampleness; tallness, toweringness; broadness, wideness; profundity; extensiveness, expansiveness, comprehensiveness; spaciousness 158.5; bagginess

7 <very large size> **hugeness, vastness,** vastitude; humongousness <nf>; **enormousness, immenseness, enormity, immensity,** tremendousness, **prodigiousness,** stupendousness, mountainousness; **gigantism,** giganticness, giantism, giantlikeness; monumentalism; **monstrousness, monstrosity**

8 corpulence, obesity, stoutness, largeness, bigness, *embonpoint* <Fr>; **fatness,** fattishness, adiposis *or* adiposity, endomorphy, fleshiness, beefiness, meatiness, heftiness, grossness; **plumpness,** buxomness, rotundity, fubsiness <Brit>, tubbiness <nf>, roly-poliness; pudginess, podginess; chubbiness, chunkiness <nf>, stockiness, squattiness, squatness, dumpiness, portliness; paunchiness, bloatedness, puffiness, pursiness, blowziness; middle-age spread; weight problem; hippiness <nf>; steatopygia *or* steatopygy; bosominess, bustiness <nf>

9 bulkiness, bulk, hulkingness *or* hulkiness, **massiveness,** lumpishness, clumpishness; **ponderousness,** cumbrousness, cumbersomeness; clumsiness, awkwardness, unwieldiness, clunkiness <nf>

10 lump, clump, **hunk** *and* **chunk** <nf>, wodge <Brit nf>; **mass,** piece, **gob** *and* glob <nf>, gobbet, dollop, cluster, gobs <nf>; batch, **wad,** heap, block, loaf; pat <of butter>; clod; nugget; **quantity** 244

11 <something large> **whopper** *and* thumper *and* lunker *and* whale *and* jumbo <nf>; monster, hulk; large part, bulk, mass, lion's share, majority, better part

12 <corpulent person> **heavyweight, pig,** porker, heavy <nf>, human *or* man mountain <nf>; big *or* large person; **fat person, fatty** *and* **fatso** <nf>, roly-poly, **tub, tub of lard,** tun, tun of flesh, whale, blimp <nf>, hippo <nf>, **potbelly,** gorbelly <old>, swagbelly, dumpling, lardass <nf>

13 giant <see list>, giantess, **amazon, colossus, titan,** titaness, *nephilim* <Hcb pl>, brute, hulk; long drink of water

14 behemoth, leviathan, monster; mammoth, mastodon; elephant, jumbo <nf>; whale; hippopotamus, hippo <nf>; **dinosaur**

VERBS **15 size, adjust, grade,** group, range, rank, graduate, sort, match; gauge, **measure** 300.10, proportion; **bulk** 247.5; **enlarge** 259.4,5; fatten

ADJS **16 large, sizable, big, great** 247.6, **grand,** tall <nf>, **considerable, goodly,** healthy, tidy <nf>, **substantial,** bumper; as big as all outdoors; numerous 884.6; largish, biggish; large-scale, larger than life; man-sized <nf>; large-size *or* -sized, man-sized, king-size, queen-size, plus-size; economy-size, family-size; good-sized, life-size *or* -sized

17 voluminous, capacious, generous, ample, copious, broad, wide, extensive, expansive, capacious, comprehensive; **spacious**

18 corpulent, stout, fat, overweight, fattish, **obese,** adipose, gross, fleshy, beefy, meaty, hefty, porky, porcine; paunchy, paunched, bloated, puffy, blowzy, distended, swollen, pursy; abdominous, big-bellied, full-bellied, potbellied, gorbellied <old *or* dial>, swag-bellied, pot-gutted *and* pusslegutted <nf>, **plump, buxom,** *zaftig* <Yiddish>, pleasantly plump, full, huggy <nf>, rotund, fubsy <Brit>, **tubby** <nf>, roly-poly; **pudgy,** podgy; thickbodied, thick-girthed, **heavyset, thickset, chubby,** chunky <nf>, fubsy <Brit nf>, **stocky,** squat, squatty, dumpy, square; pyknic, endomorphic; **stalwart, brawny, burly;** lusty, strapping <nf>; **portly,** imposing; full-figured; well-fed, corn-fed, grain-fed; chubby-faced, round-faced, moonfaced; hippy <nf>, full-buttocked, steatopygic *or* steatopygous, fat-assed *and* lard-assed <nf>, broad in the beam <nf>, well-upholstered <nf>; bosomy, full-bosomed, chesty, busty <nf>, top-heavy; plump as a dumpling *or* partridge, fat as a quail, fat as a pig *or* hog, fat as brawn *or* bacon

19 bulky, hulky, hulking, lumpish, lumpy, lumping <nf>, clumpish, lumbering, lubberly; **massive,** massy; elephantine, hippopotamic; **ponderous,** cumbrous, cumbersome; **clumsy,** awkward, **unwieldy;** clunky <nf>

20 huge, immense, vast, enormous, astronomic, astronomical, humongous <nf>, jumbo <nf>, king-size, queen-size, tremendous, prodigious, stupendous, macro, mega, giga; great big, larger than life, Homeric, mighty, **titanic, colossal, monumental,** heroic, heroical, epic, epical, towering, mountainous; profound, abysmal, deep as the ocean *or* as China; **monster,** monstrous; **mammoth,** mastodonic; **gigantic, giant,** giantlike, gigantesque, gigantean; Cyclopean, Brobdingnagian, Gargantuan, Herculean, Atlantean; elephantine, jumbo <nf>; dinosaurian, dinotherian; **infinite** 823.3

21 <nf terms> **whopping, walloping, whaling, whacking,** spanking, slapping, lolloping, thumping, thundering, bumping, banging

22 **full-sized,** full-size, full-scale; **full-grown, full-fledged,** full-blown; full-formed, **life-sized,** large as life, larger than life

23 **oversize,** oversized; **outsize,** outsized, giant-size, **king-size, queen-size,** record-size, extra-large *or* XL, XXL, **overlarge,** overbig, too big; **overgrown,** overdeveloped; **overweight,** overheavy; over-fleshed, overstout, overfat, overplump, overfed, obese

24 this big, so big, yay big <nf>, this size, about this size, of that order

ADVS **25** largely, on a large scale, in a big way; in the large; as can be

WORD ELEMENTS **26** hyper-, macr-, macro-, maxi-, meg-, mega-, megal-, megalo-, super-

27 giants

Abominable Snowman *or* yeti	Galligantus
	Gargantua
Aegir	Godzilla
Alifanfaron	Gog
Antaeus	Goliath
Ascapart	Hercules *or* Heracles
Atlas	Hymir
Balan	Jötunn
Bellerus	King Kong
Big Foot *or* Sasquatch *or* Omah	Magog
	Mimir
Blunderbore	Og
Briareüs	Orion
Brobdingnagian	Pantagruel
Colossus	Patagonian
Cormoran	Paul Bunyan
Cottus	Polyphemus
Cyclops	Titan
Enceladus	Tityus
Ephialtes	Typhon
Ferragus	Ymir

258 LITTLENESS

NOUNS **1 littleness, smallness,** smallishness, **diminutiveness,** miniatureness, slightness, exiguity; puniness, pokiness, dinkiness <nf>; tininess, **minuteness;** undersize; petiteness; dwarfishness, stuntedness, runtiness, shrimpiness; **shortness** 268; **scantiness** 885.1; small scale; compactness, portability; miniaturization, microminiaturization, microscopy, micrography

 2 infinitesimalness; undetectability, inappreciability, evanescence; intangibility, impalpability, tenuousness, imponderability; imperceptibility, invisibility

3 <small space> **tight spot** *and* corner *and* squeeze <nf>, pinch, not enough room to swing a cat <nf>; hole, pigeonhole; hole-in-the-wall; cubby, cubbyhole; dollhouse, playhouse, doghouse; no room to swing a cat

4 <small person or creature> **runt, shrimp** <nf>, wart <nf>, diminutive, wisp, chit, slip, snip, snippet, minikin <old>, **peanut** *and* **peewee** <nf>, wee thing, pipsqueak, squirt, half pint, shorty, fingerling, small fry <nf>, dandiprat *and* tiddler <Brit old>; lightweight, featherweight; bantam, banty <nf>; pony; minnow, mini *and* minny <nf>; mouse, titmouse; nubbin, button

5 <creature small by species or birth> **dwarf,** dwarfling, **midget,** midge, **pygmy,** manikin, homunculus, atomy, micromorph, hop-o'-my-thumb; elf, gnome, brownie, hobbit, leprechaun; Lilliputian, Pigwiggen, Tom Thumb, Thumbelina, Alberich, Alviss, Andvari, Nibelung, Regin

6 miniature, mini; scaled-down *or* miniaturized version; microcosm, microcosmos; baby; doll, puppet, toy; microvolume; Elzevir, Elzevir edition; duodecimo, twelvemo, pocket edition

7 <minute thing> minutia, **minutiae** <pl>, minim, **drop,** droplet, **mite** <nf>, **point,** vanishing point, mathematical point, point of a pin, pinpoint, pinhead, **dot;** mote, fleck, **speck,** flyspeck, jot, tittle, jot nor tittle, iota, **trace,** trace amount, suspicion, *soupçon* <Fr>; **particle,** crumb, scrap, bite, snip, snippet; grain, grain of sand; barleycorn, millet seed, mustard seed; midge, gnat; microbe, **microorganism,** amoeba, bacillus, bacteria, diatom, germ, paramecium, protozoon, zoospore, animalcule, plankton, virus; cell; microchip; pixel

8 atom, atomy, monad; **molecule,** ion; nucleus; **electron,** proton, meson, neutrino, muon, quark, parton, subatomic *or* nuclear particle

VERBS **9 make small, contract** 260.7; **shorten** 268.6; **miniaturize,** minify, minimize, scale down; **reduce** 252.7, scale back

ADJS **10 little, small** 248.6, smallish; **slight,** exiguous; **puny, trifling,** poky, piffling *and* pindling *and* piddling *and* piddly <nf>, paltry, picayune, **dinky** <nf>, negligible; cramped, limited; one-horse, two-by-four <nf>; pintsized <nf>, half-pint; knee-high, knee-high to a grasshopper; petite; short 268.8

11 tiny; teeny *and* teeny-weeny *and* eentsy-weentsy <nf>, wee *and* peewee <nf>, bitty *and* bitsy *and* little-bitty *and* little-bitsy *and* itsy-bitsy *and* itsy-witsy <nf>, dinky <nf>; **minute,** fine

12 miniature, diminutive, minuscule, minuscular, mini, micro, miniaturized, subminiature, minikin <old>, **small-scale,** minimal; pony, bantam, banty

<nf>; **baby,** baby-sized; bite-sized; pocket, pocketsized, pocket-size, **vest-pocket; toy;** handy, compact, portable; duodecimo, twelvemo

13 **dwarf,** dwarfed, dwarfish, **pygmy, midget,** nanoid, elfin; Lilliputian, Tom Thumb; **undersized,** undersize, squat, dumpy; **stunted,** undergrown, runty, pint-size or -sized and sawed-off <nf>; shrunk, shrunken, wizened, shriveled; meager, scrubby, scraggy; rudimentary, rudimental

14 **infinitesimal, microscopic,** ultramicroscopic; evanescent, thin, tenuous; inappreciable; impalpable, imponderable, intangible; imperceptible, indiscernible, invisible, unseeable; atomic, subatomic; molecular; granular, corpuscular, microcosmic<al>; embryonic, germinal

15 **microbic,** microbial, **microorganic;** animalcular, bacterial; microzoic; protozoan, microzoan, amoebic or amoeboid

ADVS 16 **small,** little, **slightly** 248.9, fractionally; **on a small scale,** in a small compass, in a small way, on a minuscule or infinitesimal scale; **in miniature,** in the small; in a nutshell

WORD ELEMENTS 17 micr-, micro-, ultramicr-, ultramicro-; granul-, granulo-, granuli-, chondr-, chondro-; -cle, -ee, -een, -el, -ella, -illa, -et, -ette, -idium, -idion, -ie, -y, -ey, -ium, -kin, -let, -ling, -ock, -sy, -ula, -ule, -ulum, -ulus

259 EXPANSION, GROWTH

<increase in size>

NOUNS 1 **expansion, extension, enlargement, increase** 251, uptick, crescendo, upping, raising, hiking, magnification, aggrandizement, amplification, ampliation <old>, broadening, widening; **spread,** spreading, sprawl, creeping, fanning out, dispersion, ripple effect, sprawl; buildout; **flare,** splay, ramification; deployment; augmentation, **addition** 253; adjunct 254

2 **distension,** stretching; **inflation,** sufflation, blowing up; **dilation,** dilatation, dilating; diastole; **swelling,** swelling 283.4; puffing, puff, puffiness, **bloating,** bloat, **flatulence** or flatulency, flatus, gassiness, windiness; **turgidity,** turgidness, turgescence; tumidness or tumidity, tumefaction; tumescence, intumescence; **swollenness,** bloatedness; dropsy, edema; tympanites, tympany, tympanism

3 **growth, development** 861.1; **bodily development** 14, **maturation,** maturing, coming of age, growing up, upgrowth; vegetation 310.32; reproduction, procreation 78, germination, pullulation; burgeoning, sprouting; budding, gemmation; outgrowth, excrescence; overgrowth 257.5

VERBS 4 <make larger> **enlarge, expand, extend, widen, broaden,** build, build up, aggrandize, **amplify,** crescendo, **magnify, increase** 251.4, augment, add to 253.5, raise, up, scale up, hike or hike up; develop, bulk or bulk up; **stretch, distend, dilate, swell, inflate,** sufflate, **blow up,** puff up, huff, puff, bloat; pump, pump up; rarefy

5 <become larger> **enlarge, expand, extend, increase,** greaten, crescendo, **develop, widen, broaden,** bulk; **stretch, distend, dilate, swell, swell up, swell out, puff up, puff out, pump up, bloat,** tumefy, balloon, fill out; snowball

6 **spread,** spread out, outspread, outstretch; **expand, extend,** widen; open, **open up,** unfold; **flare,** flare out, broaden out, splay; spraddle, sprangle, sprawl; branch, branch out, ramify; fan, fan out, disperse, deploy; spread like wildfire; overrun, overgrow

7 **grow, develop,** wax, **increase** 251; gather, brew; **grow up,** mature, spring up, ripen, come of age, **shoot up,** sprout up, upshoot, upspring, upsprout, upspear, overtop, tower; burgeon, **sprout** 310.34, blossom 310.35, reproduce 78.7, procreate 78.8, grow out of, germinate, pullulate; vegetate 310.34; **flourish, thrive,** grow like a weed; mushroom; outgrow; overgrow, hypertrophy, overdevelop, grow uncontrollably

8 **fatten,** fat, plump, pinguefy and engross <old>, fill out; **gain weight,** gather flesh, take or put on weight, become overweight; chub out <nf>

ADJS 9 **expansive, extensive;** expansional, extensional; expansile, extensile, elastic, stretchy; expansible, inflatable, augmentative; distensive, dilatant; inflationary; developable

10 **expanded, extended, enlarged, increased** 251.7, upped, raised, hiked, **amplified,** ampliate <old>, crescendoed, widened, broadened, built-up, beefed-up <nf>

11 **spread, spreading;** sprawling, sprawly; **outspread, outstretched,** spreadout, stretched-out, drawn-out; open, unfolded, gaping, patulous; widespread, wide-open; flared, spraddled, sprangled, splayed; flaring, flared, flared-out, spraddling, sprangling, splaying; splay; fanned, fanning; fanlike, fan-shaped, fan-shape, flabelliform, deltoid

12 **grown, full-grown, grown-up, mature,** developed, well-developed, fully developed, full-fledged, of age; growing, sprouting, crescent, budding, flowering 310.38, florescent, **flourishing,** blossoming, blooming, burgeoning, fast-growing, thriving; overgrown, hypertrophied, overdeveloped

13 **distended, dilated, inflated,** sufflated, **blown up, puffed up, swollen,** swelled, **bloated,** turgid, tumid, plethoric, incrassate; **puffy,** pursy;

flatulent, gassy, windy, ventose; tumefacient; dropsical, edematous; enchymatous; fat; puffed out, bouffant, bouffed up *and* bouffy <nf>, stuffed

260 CONTRACTION

<decrease in size>

NOUNS **1 contraction,** contracture; systole, syneresis, synizesis, dwindling; **compression,** compressure, pressurizing, pressurization; **compacting,** compaction, compactedness; **condensation, concentration,** consolidation, solidification; **circumscription, narrowing;** reduction, diminuendo, lessening, waning; miniaturization; **decrease** 252; abbreviation, curtailment, shortening 268.3; **constriction,** stricture *or* striction, astriction, strangulation, stenosis, **choking,** choking off, coarctation; bottleneck, chokepoint, hourglass, hourglass figure, nipped *or* wasp waist; neck, cervix, isthmus, narrow place; astringency, constringency; puckering, pursing; knitting, wrinkling

2 squeezing, compression, clamping *or* clamping down, tightening; **pressure,** press, crush; **pinch, squeeze, tweak, nip;** scrunch

3 shrinking, shrinkage, atrophy; **shriveling, withering;** searing, parching, drying *or* drying up; attenuation, thinning; wasting, consumption, emaciation, emaceration <old>; skin and bones; preshrinking, preshrinkage, Sanforizing <trademark>

4 collapse, prostration, cave-in; implosion; **deflation**

5 contractibility, contractility, compactability, **compressibility,** condensability, reducibility; collapsibility; shrinkability

6 contractor, constrictor, clamp, compressor, compacter, condenser, vise, pincer, squeezer; thumbscrew; **astringent,** styptic; alum, astringent bitters, styptic pencil; tourniquet

VERBS **7 contract, compress,** cramp, compact, condense, concentrate, consolidate, solidify; **reduce, decrease** 252; abbreviate, curtail, **shorten** 268.6; miniaturize; **constrict,** constringe, circumscribe, coarct, **narrow,** draw, draw in *or* together; strangle, strangulate, choke, choke off; **pucker,** pucker up, **purse; knit, wrinkle**

8 squeeze, compress, clamp, cramp, cramp up, tighten; roll *or* wad up, roll up into a ball, scrunch, ensphere; **press,** pressurize, crush, appress; tense; **pinch, tweak, nip**

9 shrink, shrivel, wither, sear, parch, dry up; **wizen,** weazen; consume, waste, waste away, attenuate, thin, emaciate, macerate *or* emacerate <old>; preshrink, Sanforize <trademark>

10 collapse, cave, cave in, fall in; telescope; fold, fold

up; implode; **deflate,** let the air out of, take the wind out of, flatten; puncture

ADJS **11 contractive,** contractional, contractible, contractile, compactable; **astringent,** constringent, styptic; **compressible,** condensable, reducible; shrinkable; **collapsible,** foldable; deflationary; consumptive; circumscribable

12 contracted, compressed, cramped, compact *or* compacted, concentrated, condensed, consolidated, solidified, boiled-down; **constricted,** strangled, strangulated, choked, choked off, coarcted, **squeezed,** clamped, nipped, pinched *or* pinched-in, wasp-waisted; puckered, pursed; knitted, wrinkled; miniaturized; scaled-down; shortened, abbreviated

13 shrunk, shrunken; **shriveled,** shriveled up; **withered,** sear, parched, corky, dried-up; **wasted,** wasted away, consumed, emaciated, emacerated, thin, attenuated; **wizened,** wizen, weazened; preshrunk, Sanforized <trademark>

14 deflated, punctured, flat, holed

15 contractions

aren't	she'd
can't	she'll
could've	she's
didn't	should've
doesn't	shouldn't
don't	that's
hadn't	there's
hasn't	they'd
haven't	they'll
he'd	they're
he'll	they've
he's	wasn't
here's	we'd
I'd	we'll
I'll	we're
I'm	we've
I've	weren't
isn't	what's
it'll	who's
it's	won't
let's	would've
might've	wouldn't
mightn't	you'd
mustn't	you'll
oughtn't	you're
shan't	you've

261 DISTANCE, REMOTENESS

NOUNS **1 distance, remoteness,** farness, far-offness, longinquity; **separation,** separatedness, divergence, clearance, margin, leeway; **extent, length,** space 158, **reach,** stretch, range, compass, span, stride, haul, a way, ways *and* piece <nf>; perspective, aesthetic distance, distancing;

astronomical or interstellar or galactic or intergalactic distance, deep space, depths of space, **infinity** 823; **mileage,** light-years, parsecs; aloofness, standoffishness

2 **long way,** good ways <nf>, **great distance, far cry,** far piece <nf>; long step, tidy step, giant step or stride; long run or haul, long road or trail, day's march, miles away; marathon; far cry, long shot; long range; apogee, aphelion

3 the distance, **remote distance, offing; horizon,** the far horizon, where the earth meets the sky, vanishing point, background

4 <remote region> jumping-off place and godforsaken place and God knows where and the middle of nowhere <nf>, the back of beyond, the end of the rainbow, Thule or Ultima Thule, Timbuktu, Siberia, Darkest Africa, the South Seas, Pago Pago, the Great Divide, China, Outer Mongolia, pole, antipodes, end of the earth, North Pole, South Pole, Tierra del Fuego, Greenland, Yukon, Pillars of Hercules, remotest corner of the world, four corners of the earth; outpost, outskirts; hinterland; the sticks and the boondocks and the boonies <nf>; **nowhere;** frontier, outback <Austral>; the moon; outer space

VERBS 5 **reach out, stretch out,** extend, extend out, go or go out, range out, carry out; outstretch, outlie, outdistance, outrange

6 **extend to,** stretch to, stretch away to, **reach to,** lead to, go to, get to, come to, run to, carry to

7 **keep one's distance, distance oneself,** remain at a distance, maintain distance or clearance, keep at a respectful distance, separate oneself, **keep away,** stand off or away; keep away from, keep or stand clear of, **steer clear of** <nf>, hold away from, give a wide berth to, keep a good leeway or margin or offing, keep out of the way of, keep at arm's length, keep a safe distance from, not touch with a ten-foot pole <nf>, keep or stay or stand aloof; maintain one's perspective, keep one's esthetic distance

ADJS 8 **distant,** distal, **remote, removed, far, far-off,** away, **faraway,** way-off, far-flung, at a distance, exotic, separated, apart, asunder; long-distance, long-range

9 **out-of-the-way,** godforsaken, back of beyond, outlying, upcountry; **out of reach, inaccessible,** ungetatable, unapproachable, untouchable, hyperborean, antipodean

10 **thither,** ulterior; **yonder,** yon; **farther, further,** remoter, more distant; outlying

11 transoceanic, transmarine, ultramarine, oversea, overseas; transatlantic, transpacific; tramontane, transmontane, ultramontane, transalpine; transarctic, transcontinental, transequatorial, transpolar, transpontine, transmundane, ultramundane; offshore, overseas

12 **farthest, furthest,** farthermost, farthest off, furthermost, ultimate, extreme, remotest, most distant, terminal

ADVS 13 **yonder,** yon; **in the distance,** in the remote distance; **in the offing,** on the horizon, in the background

14 **at a distance, away, off,** aloof, at arm's length; distantly, remotely

15 **far, far off,** far away, **afar,** afar off, a long way off, a good ways off <nf>, a long cry to, "over the hills and far away"—John Gay, as far as the eye can see, out of sight; clear to hell and gone <nf>

16 **far and wide,** far and near, distantly and broadly, wide, widely, broadly, abroad

17 **apart, away, aside,** wide apart, wide away

18 **out of reach,** beyond reach, **out of range,** beyond the bounds, out-of-the-way, out of the sphere of; out of sight, à perte de vue <Fr>; out of hearing, out of earshot or earreach

19 **wide, clear;** wide of the mark, abroad, all abroad, astray, afield, far afield

PREPS 20 **as far as, to, all the way to,** the whole way to

21 **beyond, past, over, across,** the other or far side of

262 FORM

NOUNS 1 **form, shape, figure;** figuration, **configuration;** formation, **conformation; structure** 266; **build,** make, frame; **arrangement** 808; makeup, format, layout; **composition** 796; cut, set, stamp, type, turn, cast, mold, impression, pattern, matrix, model, mode, modality; archetype, prototype 786.1, Platonic form or idea; style, fashion; aesthetic form, inner form, significant form; art form, genre

2 **contour,** tournure <Fr>, galbe <Fr>; broad lines, silhouette, profile, **outline** 211.2; organization 807.1

3 **appearance** 33, lineaments, features, physiognomy, cut of one's jib

4 <human form> **figure, form,** shape, frame, anatomy, **physique,** build, body-build, person; body 1052.3

5 **forming, shaping,** molding, modeling, fashioning, making, making up, formulation; **formation,** conformation, figuration, configuration; sculpture; morphogeny, morphogenesis; creation

6 <grammatical terms> form, morph, allomorph, morpheme; morphology, morphemics

VERBS 7 **form,** formalize, **shape, fashion,** tailor, frame, figure, **lick into shape** <nf>; work, knead; set, fix; **forge,** drop-forge; **mold,** model, sculpt or sculpture; cast, found; thermoform; stamp, mint; carve, whittle, cut, chisel, hew, hew out;

roughhew, roughcast, rough out, block out, lay out, sketch out; hammer *or* knock out; whomp out *or* up <nf>, cobble up; create; organize 807.4, systematize

8 <be formed> **form,** take form, shape, **shape up, take shape;** materialize

ADJS 9 **formative,** formal, formational, plastic, morphotic; **formed, shaped,** patterned, fashioned, tailored, framed, structured; **forged,** molded, modeled, sculpted; cast, founded; stamped, minted; carved, cut, whittled, chiseled, hewn; roughhewn, roughcast, roughed-out, blocked-out, laid-out, sketched-out; hammered-out, knocked-out, cobbled-up; **made, produced**

10 <biological terms> plasmatic, plasmic, protoplasmic, plastic, metabolic

11 <grammatical terms> morphologic, morphological, morphemic

WORD ELEMENTS 12 morph-, morpho-, -morph, -morphism, -morphy, -form, -iform, -morphic, -morphous

263 FORMLESSNESS

NOUNS 1 **formlessness, shapelessness;** unformedness, amorphousness, amorphism; misshapenness; lack of definition; **chaos** 810.2, confusion, messiness, mess, muddle 810.2, orderlessness, untidiness; **disorder** 810; entropy; anarchy 418.2; **indeterminateness, indefiniteness,** indecisiveness, vagueness, mistiness, haziness, fuzziness, blurriness, unclearness, obscurity; lumpiness, lumpishness

2 unlicked cub, diamond in the rough, raw material

VERBS 3 **deform, distort** 265.5; misshape; unform, unshape; disorder, jumble, mess up, muddle, confuse; obfuscate, obscure, fog up, blur

ADJS 4 **formless, shapeless,** structureless, unstructured, featureless, characterless, nondescript, inchoate, lumpy, lumpish, blobby *and* baggy <nf>, inform; amorphous *or* amorphic, **chaotic, orderless,** disorderly 810.13, unordered, unorganized, confused, anarchic 418.6; kaleidoscopic; **indeterminate, indefinite,** undefined, indecisive, vague, misty, hazy, fuzzy, blurred *or* blurry, unclear, obscure; obfuscatory; unfinished, undeveloped

5 **unformed, unshaped,** unshapen, unfashioned, unlicked; unstructured; uncut, unhewn

264 SYMMETRY

NOUNS 1 **symmetry,** symmetricalness, **proportion,** proportionality, **balance** 790.1, equilibrium; **regularity,** uniformity 781, evenness; equality 790;

finish; harmony, congruity, consistency, conformity 867, **correspondence,** keeping; concord <old>; eurythmy, eurythmics; dynamic symmetry; bilateral symmetry, trilateral symmetry, etc, multilateral symmetry; parallelism 203, polarity; shapeliness

2 symmetrization, regularization, balancing, harmonization; evening, equalization; coordination, integration; **compensation,** playing off, playing off against, posing against *or* over against; counterbalance

VERBS 3 symmetrize, regularize, **balance,** balance off, compensate; harmonize; **proportion,** proportionate; even, even up, equalize; coordinate, integrate; play off, play off against

ADJS 4 **symmetric, symmetrical, balanced,** balanced off, proportioned, eurythmic, harmonious, mirror-image; **regular,** uniform 781.5, even, even-steven <nf>, equal 790.7, equal on both sides, fifty-fifty <nf>, square, squared-off; coequal, coordinate, equilateral, aligned; **well-balanced,** well-set, well-set-up <nf>; finished; enantiomorphic

5 **shapely, well-shaped, well-proportioned,** well-made, **well-formed,** well-favored; comely; trim, trig <old>, neat, spruce, clean, clean-cut, clean-limbed

265 DISTORTION

NOUNS 1 **distortion,** torsion, twist, twistedness, **contortion, crookedness,** tortuosity; asymmetry, unsymmetry, disproportion, lopsidedness, imbalance, irregularity, skewness, **deviation; twist,** quirk, turn, screw, wring, wrench, wrest; **warp,** buckle; knot, gnarl; anamorphosis; anamorphism

2 **perversion, corruption,** misdirection, misrepresentation 350, misinterpretation, misconstruction; **falsification** 354.9; **twisting,** false coloring, bending the truth, **spin,** spin control, slanting, straining, torturing; misuse 389; falsehood, travesty; debasement

3 **deformity,** deformation, **malformation,** malconformation, monstrosity 870.6, teratology, freakishness, misproportion, **misshapenness,** misshape; **disfigurement, defacement;** mutilation, truncation; humpback, hunchback, crookback, camelback, kyphosis; swayback, lordosis; wryneck, torticollis; clubfoot, talipes, flatfoot, splayfoot; knock-knee; bowlegs; valgus; harelip; cleft palate; mutation

4 **grimace, wry face,** wry mouth, rictus, snarl; moue, mow, pout; scowl, frown; squint; tic

VERBS 5 **distort, contort,** turn awry; **twist,** turn, screw, wring, wrench, wrest; writhe; **warp,** buckle, crumple; knot, gnarl; **crook,** bend, spring; put out of kilter

6 pervert, falsify, twist, garble, put a false construction upon, give a spin, give a false coloring, color, varnish, slant, strain, torture; put words in someone's mouth; **bias;** misrepresent 350.3, misconstrue, misinterpret, misrender, misdirect; debase; misuse 389.4; send *or* deliver the wrong signal *or* message, lead up *or* down the garden path; exaggerate

7 deform, malform, misshape, twist, torture, disproportion; **disfigure, deface;** mutilate, truncate; blemish, mar

8 grimace, make a face, make a wry face *or* mouth, pull a face, **screw up one's face,** mug <nf>, mouth, make a mouth, mop, mow, mop and mow; pout

ADJS **9** distortive, contortive, contortional, torsional

10 distorted, contorted, warped, twisted, crooked; tortuous, labyrinthine, buckled, sprung, bent, bowed; cockeyed <nf>, crazy; crunched, crumpled; unsymmetric, unsymmetrical, asymmetric, asymmetrical, nonsymmetric, nonsymmetrical; irregular, deviative, anamorphous; one-sided, lopsided; awry, askew 204.14, off-center, left *or* right of center, off-target; cockeyed

11 falsified, perverted, twisted, garbled, slanted, doctored, biased, crooked; strained, tortured; misrepresented, misquoted; half-true, partially true, falsely colored; creative <nf>

12 deformed, malformed, misshapen, misbegotten, misproportioned, ill-proportioned, ill-made, ill-shaped, **out of shape;** dwarfed, stumpy; bloated; **disfigured,** defaced, blemished, marred; mutilated, truncated; grotesque, **monstrous** 870.13; sway-backed, round-shouldered; bowlegged, bandy-legged, bandy; knock-kneed; rickety, rachitic; club-footed, talipedic; flatfooted, splayfooted, pigeon-toed; pug-nosed, snub-nosed, simous

13 humpbacked, hunchbacked, bunchbacked, crookbacked, crookedbacked, camelback, humped, gibbous, kyphotic

266 STRUCTURE

NOUNS **1 structure, construction,** architecture, tectonics, architectonics, **frame,** make, **build,** fabric, tissue, warp and woof *or* weft, web, weave, texture, contexture, mold, **shape, pattern, plan,** fashion, arrangement, **organization** 807.1; organism, organic structure, **constitution, composition; makeup,** getup <nf>, setup; **formation,** conformation, **format; arrangement** 808, configuration; **composition** 796; making, building, creation, production, forging, fashioning, molding, fabrication, manufacture, shaping, structuring, patterning; anatomy, physique, organic structure; form 262; **morphology,** science of structure; anatomy, histology, zootomy

2 structure, building, edifice, construction, construct, erection, establishment, fabric; house; tower, pile, pyramid, skyscraper, ziggurat; prefabrication, prefab, packaged house; air structure, bubble <nf>, air hall <Brit>; superstructure, structural framework; flat-slab construction, post-and-beam construction, steel-cage construction, steel construction; complex

3 understructure, understruction, underbuilding, undercroft, crypt; **substructure,** substruction; infrastructure, underpinning; spread foundation, footing; fill, backfill

4 frame, framing; braced framing; **framework, skeleton,** fabric, cadre, chassis, shell, armature; lattice, latticework, scaffold; sash, casement, case, casing; window case *or* frame, doorframe; picture frame

VERBS **5 construct, build; structure; organize** 807.4; **form** 262.7; erect, raise, put up

ADJS **6 structural,** formal, morphological, edificial, tectonic, textural; **anatomic,** anatomical, **organic,** organismal, organismic; **structured, patterned,** shaped, formed; **architectural,** architectonic; constructional; superstructural, substructural, infrastructural; organizational

267 LENGTH

NOUNS **1 length,** longness, lengthiness, overall length; wheelbase; **extent,** extension, **measure, span, reach, stretch; distance** 261; footage, yardage, mileage; infinity 823; perpetuity 829; long time 827.4; linear measures; oblongness; longitude

2 a length, piece, portion, part; coil, **strip,** bolt, roll; run

3 line, strip, bar, streak; stripe 517.6; string

4 lengthening, prolongation, elongation, production, protraction; prolixity, prolixness; **extension,** stretching, stretching *or* spinning *or* stringing out, dragging out

VERBS **5 be long, be lengthy, extend,** be prolonged, **stretch,** span; **stretch out,** extend out, reach out; stretch oneself, crane, crane one's neck, rubberneck; stand on tiptoes; outstretch, outreach; sprawl, straggle; last, endure

6 lengthen, prolong, prolongate, **elongate, extend,** expand, produce, **protract,** continue; make prolix;

lengthen out, let out, **draw** or drag or stretch or string or spin out; **stretch,** draw, pull

ADJS **7 long, lengthy;** longish, longsome; tall; **extensive, far-reaching,** fargoing, far-flung; sesquipedalian, sesquipedal; unabridged, full-length; as long as one's arm, a mile long; **time-consuming,** interminable, without end, no end of or to, infinite; long-lasting, enduring, long-range

8 lengthened, prolonged, prolongated, **elongated, extended, protracted; prolix; long-winded; drawn-out,** dragged out, long-drawn-out, stretched or spun or strung out, straggling; **stretched,** drawn, pulled

9 oblong, oblongated, oblongitudinal, **elongated;** rectangular; elliptical; lengthwise, lengthways, longitudinal

ADVS **10** lengthily, extensively, at length, in extenso <L>, ad infinitum <L>, ad nauseam

11 lengthwise or lengthways, longwise or longways, longitudinally, along, in length, at length; **endwise** or endways, endlong; in extenso <L>

268 SHORTNESS

NOUNS **1 shortness, briefness, brevity; succinctness,** curtness, terseness, summariness, compendiousness, compactness; **conciseness** 537; **littleness** 258; transience 828, short time 828.3, instantaneousness 830; banker's hours, French hours

2 stubbiness, stumpiness <nf>, **stockiness, fatness** 257.8, chubbiness, chunkiness <nf>, blockiness, squatness, squattiness, dumpiness; pudginess, podginess; snubbiness; **lowness** 274

3 shortening, abbreviation; reduction; abridgment, condensation, compression, conspectus, epitome, epitomization, summary, summation, summarization, précis, abstract, recapitulation, recap <nf>, wrapup, synopsis, encapsulation; **curtailment,** truncation, retrenchment; telescoping; elision, ellipsis, syncope, apocope; foreshortening; cutback; docking; contraction

4 shortener, cutter, abridger; abstracter, epitomizer or epitomist

5 shortcut, cut, cutoff; shortest way; **beeline,** air line

VERBS **6 shorten, abbreviate, cut; reduce** 260.7; **abridge, condense,** compress, contract, **boil down,** abstract, sum up, summarize, recapitulate, recap <nf>, synopsize, epitomize, encapsulate, capsulize; **curtail,** truncate, retrench; bowdlerize; elide, **cut short,** cut down, cut off short, cut back, take in; **dock,** bob, shear, shave, trim, clip, snub, nip; hem; mow, reap, **crop; prune,** poll, pollard; stunt, check the growth of; telescope; foreshorten

7 take a short cut, short-cut; **cut across,** cut through; **cut a corner,** cut corners; **make a beeline,** take the air line, go as the crow flies

ADJS **8 short, brief, abbreviated,** abbreviatory, "short and sweet"—Thomas Lodge; **concise** 537.6; **curt,** curtal <old>, curtate, decurtate; **succinct, summary,** synoptic, synoptical, compendious, compact; **little** 258.10; **low** 274.7; transient 828.7, instantaneous 830.4

9 shortened, abbreviated; abridged, compressed, condensed, epitomized, digested, abstracted, capsule, capsulized, encapsulated; bowdlerized; nutshell, vest-pocket; **curtailed,** cut short, short-cut, **docked,** bobbed, sheared, shaved, trimmed, clipped, snub, snubbed, nipped; mowed, mown, reaped, **cropped; pruned,** polled, pollarded; elided, elliptic, elliptical; foreshortened

10 stubby, stubbed, stumpy <nf>, undergrown, **thickset, stocky,** blocky, **chunky** <nf>, **fat** 257.18, **chubby,** tubby <nf>, dumpy; **squat,** squatty, squattish; **pudgy,** podgy; pug, **pugged;** snub-nosed; turned-up, retroussé <Fr>

11 short-legged, breviped; short-winged, brevipennate

ADVS **12 shortly, briefly,** summarily, tout court <Fr>, in brief compass, economically, sparely, curtly, succinctly, in a nutshell, in two or a few words; abbreviatedly, for short; **concisely** 537.7, compendiously, synoptically

13 short, abruptly, suddenly 830.9, all of a sudden

269 BREADTH, THICKNESS

NOUNS **1 breadth, width,** broadness, wideness, fullness, amplitude, latitude, distance across or crosswise or crossways, extent, **span, expanse, spread;** beam

2 thickness, the third dimension, distance through, depth; **mass, bulk, body;** corpulence, fatness 257.8, bodily size; **coarseness,** grossness 294.2

3 diameter, bore, caliber; radius, semidiameter; handbreadth, beam

VERBS **4 broaden, widen,** deepen; **expand,** extend, extend to the side or sides; **spread** 259.6, spread out or sidewise or sideways, outspread, outstretch; span

5 thicken, grow thick, thick; incrassate, inspissate; congeal, gel; fatten 259.8

ADJS **6 broad, wide,** deep; broad-scale, wide-scale, wide-ranging, broad-based, exhaustive, comprehensive, in-depth, extensive; spread-out, **expansive;** spacious, **roomy;** ample, full; widespread 864.13; "wide as a church door"—Shakespeare

7 broad of beam, broad-beamed, broad-sterned, beamy, wide-set; wide-body, wide-bodied;

wide-angle, wide-screen; broad-ribbed, wide-ribbed, laticostate; broad-toothed, wide-toothed, latidentate; broad-gauge; broadloom

8 **thick,** three-dimensional; **thickset, heavyset,** thick-bodied, broad-bodied, thick-girthed; **massive, bulky** 257.19, corpulent 257.18; coarse, heavy, gross, crass, fat; full-bodied, full, viscous; **dense** 1045.12; thicknecked, bullnecked

ADVS 9 breadthwise *or* breadthways, in breadth; widthwise *or* widthways; broadwise *or* broadways; broadside, broad side foremost; side-wise *or* -ways; through, depth-wise *or* -ways, in depth

270 NARROWNESS, THINNESS

NOUNS 1 **narrowness, slenderness; closeness,** nearness; **straitness,** restriction, restrictedness, limitation, strictness, confinement, circumscription; crowdedness, incapaciousness, incommodiousness, crampedness; **tightness,** tight squeeze; hair, hairbreadth *or* hairsbreadth; finger's breadth *or* width; narrow gauge

2 **narrowing, tapering,** taper; **contraction** 260, compression; stricture, constriction, strangulation, coarctation

3 <narrow place> narrow, **narrows, strait; bottleneck,** chokepoint; isthmus; channel 239, canal; pass, defile; neck, throat, craw; narrow gauge, single track

4 **thinness, slenderness, slimness, frailty,** slightness, gracility, lightness, airiness, delicacy, flimsiness, wispiness, laciness, paperiness, gauziness, gossameriness, diaphanousness, insubstantiality, ethereality, mistiness, vagueness; light *or* airy texture; **fineness** 294.3; **tenuity, rarity,** subtility, exility, exiguity; **attenuation;** dilution, dilutedness, wateriness 1061.1, weakness

5 **leanness, skinniness,** fleshlessness, slightness, frailness, twigginess, spareness, meagerness, **scrawniness, gauntness,** gangliness, lankness, **lankiness,** gawkiness, **boniness,** skin and bones; haggardness, poorness, paperiness, peakedness <nf>, puniness, "lean and hungry look"— Shakespeare; undernourishment, undernutrition, underweight; hatchet face, lantern jaw

6 **emaciation,** malnutrition, emaceration <old>, attenuation, atrophy, tabes, marasmus, anorexia nervosa

7 <comparisons> paper, wafer, lath, slat, **rail,** rake, splinter, slip, shaving, streak, vein; gruel, soup; shadow, mere shadow; **skeleton**

8 <thin person> **slim, lanky;** twiggy, **shadow, skeleton,** stick, walking skeleton, corpse, barebones, bag *or* stack of bones; rattlebones *or* **spindleshanks** *or* spindlelegs <nf>, gangleshanks

and gammerstang <nf>, lathlegs *and* sticklegs <nf>, **beanpole,** beanstalk, broomstick, clothes pole, stilt; slip, sylph, ectomorph, long drink of water

9 **reducing, slenderizing, slimming down;** weight-watching, calorie-counting; fasting, dieting

10 **thinner,** solvent 1064.4

VERBS 11 **narrow,** constrict, diminish, draw in, go in; restrict, limit, straiten, confine; **taper; contract** 260.7, compress, zip <nf>

12 **thin,** thin down, thin away *or* off *or* out, down; **rarefy,** subtilize, **attenuate;** dilute, water, water down, weaken; undernourish; **emaciate,** emacerate <old>

13 **slenderize, reduce,** reduce *or* lose *or* take off weight, watch one's weight, lose flesh, weight-watch, count calories, diet, crash-diet; slim, **slim down,** thin down

ADJS 14 **narrow, slender;** narrowish, narrowy; close, near; **tight, strait,** isthmic, isthmian; close-fitting; **restricted,** limited, circumscribed, **confined,** constricted; **cramped,** cramp; incapacious, incommodious, crowded; **meager,** scant, scanty; narrow-gauge *or* narrow-gauged, single-track; angustifoliate, angustirostrate, angustiseptal, angustisellate; stenopeic, isthmian

15 **tapered,** taper, tapering, cone- *or* wedge-shaped, attenuated, fusiform, stenosed

16 **thin, slender, slim,** gracile; thin-bodied, thin-set, ectomorphic, narrow- *or* wasp-waisted; **svelte,** slinky, sylphlike, willowy; girlish, boyish; thinnish, slenderish, slimmish; **slight,** slight-made; **frail,** delicate, light, airy, wispy, lacy, gauzy, papery, gossamer, diaphanous, insubstantial, ethereal, misty, vague, flimsy, wafer-thin, **fine; finespun,** thin-spun, fine-drawn, wiredrawn; threadlike, slender as a thread; **tenuous,** subtle, rare, **rarefied;** attenuated, attenuate, **watery, weak,** diluted, watered *or* watered-down, small

17 **lean,** lean-looking, **skinny** <nf>, fleshless, lean-fleshed, thin-fleshed, **spare,** meager, **scrawny,** scraggy, thin-bellied, **gaunt, lank, lanky,** wiry; **gangling** *and* gangly <nf>, gawky, **spindling,** spindly; flat-chested, flat <nf>; **bony, rawboned,** bare-boned, rattleboned <nf>, skeletal, **mere skin and bones, all skin and bones, nothing but skin and bones;** twiggy; **underweight,** undersized, undernourished, spidery, thin *or* skinny as a lath *or* rail; waifish

18 lean-limbed, thin-legged, lath- *or* stick-legged <nf>, spindle-legged *or* shanked <nf>, gangle-shanked <nf>, stilt-legged

19 lean- *or* horse- *or* thin-faced, thin-featured, **hatchet-faced;** wizen- *or* weazen-faced; lean- *or* thin-cheeked; lean- *or* lantern-jawed

20 haggard, poor, puny, **peaked** *and* peaky <nf>,
pinched; gaunt, drawn; shriveled, withered;
wizened, weazeny; emaciated, emaciate,
emacerated, **wasted,** attenuated, corpselike,
skeletal, hollow-eyed, wraithlike, cadaverous;
tabetic, tabid, marantic, marasmic; **starved,**
anorexic, anorectic, starveling, starved-looking;
undernourished, underfed, jejune; worn to a
shadow

21 slenderizing, reducing, slimming

ADVS **22 narrowly,** closely, nearly, **barely,** hardly,
only just, **by the skin of one's teeth**

23 thinly, thin; meagerly, sparsely, sparingly, scantily

271 FILAMENT

NOUNS **1 filament; fiber; thread; strand,** suture;
filature; **hair** 3; artificial fiber, natural fiber,
animal fiber; fibril, fibrilla; cilium, ciliolum;
tendril, cirrus; flagellum; **web,** cobweb, gossamer,
spider *or* spider's web; denier

2 cord, line, rope, wire, braided rope, twisted rope,
flattened-strand rope, wire rope, locked-wire rope,
cable, wire cable; **yarn,** spun yarn, skein, hank;
string, twine; braid; **ligament,** ligature, ligation;
tendon

3 cordage, cording, **ropework,** roping; tackle, tack,
gear, rigging; ship's ropes

4 strip, strap, strop; **lace,** thong; **band,** bandage,
fillet, fascia, taenia; **belt,** girdle; **ribbon,** ribband;
tape, tapeline, tape measure; slat, lath, batten,
spline, strake, plank; ligule, ligula

5 spinner, spinster; silkworm, spider; spinning
wheel, spinning jenny, jenny, mule, mule-jenny;
spinning frame, bobbin and fly frame; spinneret;
rope walk

VERBS **6** <make threads> **spin; braid,** twist

ADJS **7 threadlike,** thready; **stringy,** ropy, wiry;
hairlike 3.23, hairy 3.24; filamentary, filamentous,
filiform; fibrous, fibered, fibroid, fibrilliform;
ligamental; capillary, capilliform; cirrose, cirrous;
funicular, funiculate; flagelliform; taeniate,
taeniform; ligulate, ligular; gossamer, gossamery,
flossy, silky

272 HEIGHT

NOUNS **1 height,** heighth <nf>, vertical *or*
perpendicular distance; **highness, tallness,**
procerity; **altitude, elevation,** ceiling; **loftiness,**
sublimity, exaltation; hauteur, toploftiness 141.1;
eminence, prominence; **stature**

2 height, elevation, eminence, **rise,** raise, **uprise,**
lift, rising ground, vantage point *or* ground;
heights, soaring *or* towering *or* Olympian heights,

aerial heights, dizzy *or* dizzying heights; upmost
or uppermost *or* utmost *or* extreme height; sky,
stratosphere, ether, heaven *or* heavens; **zenith,
apex, acme**

3 highlands 237.1, highland, upland, uplands,
moorland, moors, downs, wold, rolling country

4 plateau, tableland, table, mesa, table mountain,
bench; **hill; ridge; mountain; peak; mountain
range**

5 watershed, water parting, **divide;** Great Divide,
Continental Divide

6 tower; turret, *tour* <Fr>; campanile, bell tower,
belfry; **spire,** church spire; **lighthouse,** light tower;
cupola, lantern; dome; martello, martello
tower; barbican; **derrick,** pole; windmill tower,
observation tower, fire tower, watch tower, control
tower; **mast,** radio *or* television mast, antenna
tower; water tower, standpipe; **spire,** pinnacle;
steeple, *flèche* <Fr>; minaret; stupa, tope, pagoda;
pyramid; pylon; **shaft,** pillar, column; pilaster;
obelisk; monument; colossus; skyscraper

7 <tall person> **longlegs** *and* longshanks *and*
highpockets *and* long drink of water <nf>;
beanpole 270.8; **giant** 257.13; six-footer, seven-
footer, grenadier <Brit>

8 high tide, high water, mean high water, flood tide,
spring tide, flood; storm surge

9 <measurement of height> altimetry, hypsometry,
hypsography; altimeter, hypsometer

VERBS **10 tower, soar,** spire; **rise, uprise, ascend,
mount, rear;** stand on tiptoe

11 rise above, tower above *or* **over,** clear, overtop, o'er
top, outtop, **top, surmount; overlook,** look
down upon *or* over; overhang, beetle; **command,**
dominate, overarch, overshadow, command a view
of; bestride, bestraddle

12 <become higher> **grow,** grow up, upgrow; uprise,
rise *or* **shoot up,** mount, sprout

13 heighten, elevate 912.5

ADJS **14 high,** high-reaching, high-up, **lofty, elevated,**
altitudinous, altitudinal, uplifted *or* upreared,
uprearing, **eminent, exalted, prominent,** supernal,
superlative, sublime; **towering,** towery, **soaring,**
spiring, aspiring, mounting, ascending; towered,
turreted, steepled; **topping,** outtopping *or*
overtopping; overarching, **overlooking, dominating;**
airy, aerial, ethereal; Olympian; monumental,
colossal; high as a steeple; topless; high-set,
high-pitched; high-rise, multistory; **haughty**
141.9/157.8, toplofty

15 skyscraping, **sky-high,** heaven-reaching *or*
-aspiring, heaven-high, heaven-kissing; cloud-
touching *or* -topped *or* –capped, supernal; **mid-air**

16 giant 257.20, gigantic, colossal, statuesque,
amazonian; **tall, lengthy,** long 267.7; **rangy, lanky,**

lank, tall as a maypole; **gangling** *and* gangly <nf>; **long-legged,** long-limbed, leggy

17 **highland,** upland; hill-dwelling, mountain-dwelling

18 **hilly,** knobby, rolling; **mountainous,** mountained, **alpine,** alpen, alpestrine, alpigene; subalpine; monticuline, monticulous

19 **higher,** superior, greater; **over, above;** upper, upmost *or* uppermost, outtopping, overtopping, topmost; highest 198.10

20 altimetric, altimetrical, hypsometrical, hypsographic

ADVS 21 **on high,** high up, high; **aloft,** aloof; **up,** upward, upwards, straight up, to the zenith; **above, over,** o'er, **overhead;** above one's head, over head and ears; skyward, airward, in the air, in the clouds; on the peak *or* summit *or* crest *or* pinnacle; upstairs, abovestairs; tiptoe, on tiptoe; on stilts; on the shoulders of; supra, *ubi supra* <L>, hereinabove, hereinbefore

273 SHAFT

NOUNS 1 **shaft, pole, bar, rod, stick,** scape, scapi-; **stalk, stem;** thill; tongue, wagon tongue; flagstaff; totem pole; Maypole; utility *or* telephone *or* telegraph pole; tent pole

2 **staff,** stave; **cane, stick, walking stick,** handstaff, shillelagh; Malacca cane; baton, marshal's baton, drum-major's baton, conductor's baton; swagger stick, swanking stick; pilgrim's staff, pastoral staff, shepherd's staff, crook; crosier, cross-staff, cross, paterissa; pikestaff, alpenstock; quarterstaff; lituus, thyrsus; **crutch,** crutch-stick

3 **beam, timber,** pole, spar

4 **post, standard, upright;** king post, queen post, crown post; newel; banister, baluster; balustrade, balustrading; gatepost, swinging *or* hinging post, shutting post; doorpost, jamb, doorjamb; signpost, milepost; stile, mullion; stanchion; hitching post, snubbing post, Samson post

5 **pillar, column,** post, pier, pilaster; colonnette, columella; caryatid; atlas, atlantes <pl>; telamon, telamones; **colonnade, arcade,** pilastrade, portico, peristyle

6 **leg,** shank; **stake,** peg; pile, spile, stud; picket, pale, palisade

274 LOWNESS

NOUNS 1 **lowness, shortness,** squatness, squattiness, stumpiness, shallowness, stuntedness; **prostration,** supineness, proneness, recumbency, proneness, reclination, **lying, lying down, reclining;** depression, debasement; subjacency

2 **low tide,** low water, mean low water, dead low water *or* tide, ebb tide, neap tide, neap, low ebb

3 lowland, **lowlands,** bottomland, swale; water meadow, piedmont, foothills, flats, depression

4 **base, bottom** 199, lowest point, nadir, depths; the lowest of the low; lowest *or* underlying level, lower strata, substratum, bedrock

VERBS 5 **lie low, squat, crouch,** lay low <nf>, couch; crawl, grovel, lie prone *or* supine *or* prostrate, hug the earth, lie down; lie under, underlie

6 lower, debase, depress 913.4; flatten

ADJS 7 **low, unelevated, flat, low-lying; short, squat,** squatty, stumpy, runty 258.13; **lowered,** debased, depressed 913.12; demoted; **reduced** 252.10; prone, supine, prostrate *or* prostrated, couchant, crouched, stooped, recumbent, bowed; laid low, knocked flat, decked <nf>; low-set, low-hung; **low-built,** low-rise, low-sized, low-statured, low-bodied; low-level, low-leveled; neap, shallow, shoal; knee-high, knee-high to a grasshopper <nf>; low-necked, low-cut, décolleté

8 **lower,** inferior, **under, nether,** subjacent; down; less advanced; earlier; substrative, rock-bottom; lowest 199.7

ADVS 9 **low,** near the ground; at a low ebb

10 **below,** down below, **under;** infra, hereunder, hereinafter, hereinbelow; thereunder; belowstairs, downstairs, below deck; underfoot; below par, below the mark

PREPS 11 **below, under, underneath, beneath,** neath, at the foot of, at the base of

275 DEPTH

NOUNS 1 **depth, deepness,** profoundness, profundity; deep-downness, extreme innerness, deep-seatedness, deep-rootedness; bottomlessness, plumblessness, fathomlessness; subterraneity, undergroundness; interiority 207; extensiveness, unfathomableness

2 **pit, deep, depth, hole,** hollow, **cavity,** shaft, well, **gulf, chasm, abyss,** abysm, yawning abyss; crater; crevasse; valley; underground, subterrane

3 **depths,** deeps, bowels, bowels of the earth, core; bottomless pit; infernal pit, hell, nether world, underworld; dark *or* unknown *or* yawning *or* gaping depths, unfathomed deeps; outer *or* deep space

4 **ocean depths, the deep sea, the deep,** trench, deep-sea trench <see list>, hadal zone, **the deeps, the depths,** bottomless depths, inner space, abyss; bottom waters; abyssal zone, Bassalia *or* Bassalian realm, bathyal zone, pelagic zone; **seabed,** seafloor, **bottom of the sea,** ocean bottom *or* floor *or* bed, ground, benthos, benthonic

division, benthonic zone; Davy Jones's locker <nf>; Mariana Trench

5 **sounding** or **soundings,** fathoming, depth sounding, probing; **echo sounding,** echolocation; sonar; **depth indicator;** oceanography, bathometry, bathymetry; fathomage, water <depth of water>

6 **draft,** submergence, submersion, sinkage, **displacement**

7 **deepening, lowering, depression;** sinking, sinkage, descent; excavation, digging, mining, tunneling; drilling, probing

VERBS 8 **deepen, lower, depress, sink;** founder; countersink; **dig,** excavate, tunnel, mine, **drill;** pierce to the depths; **dive** 367.6

9 **sound, take soundings,** make a sounding, heave or cast or sling the lead, **fathom, plumb,** plumb-line, plumb the depths, probe

ADJS 10 **deep, profound,** deep-down, penetrating; deepish, deepsome; **deep-going,** deep-lying, deep-reaching; **deep-set,** deep-laid; deep-sunk, deep-sunken, deep-sinking; **deep-seated, deep-rooted,** deep-fixed, deep-settled; deep-cut, deep-engraven; knee-deep, ankle-deep, waist-deep

11 **abysmal,** abyssal, yawning, cavernous, gaping, plunging; **bottomless,** without bottom, soundless, unsounded, plumbless, **fathomless,** unfathomed, unfathomable, rock-bottom; deep as a well, deep as the sea or ocean, deep as hell

12 **underground, subterranean,** subterraneous, hypogeal, buried, deep-buried

13 **underwater,** subaqueous; **submarine, undersea;** submerged, submersed, immersed, buried, engulfed, inundated, flooded, drowned, sunken

14 **deep-sea,** deep-water, blue-water; oceanographic, bathyal; benthic, benthal, benthonic; abyssal, Bassalian; bathyorographic, bathyorographical, bathymetric, bathymetrical; benthopelagic, bathypelagic

15 deepest, deepmost, profoundest; bedrock, rock-bottom

ADVS 16 **deep; beyond one's depth,** out of one's depth; over one's head, over head and ears; at bottom, at the core, at rock bottom

17 **deep-sea trenches and deeps**

Aleutian Trench 25,194 feet	Ionian Basin (Mediterranean) 16,896 feet
Bonin Trench 32,788 feet	
Cayman Trench 24,721 feet	Japan Trench, Ramapo Deep 27,599 feet
Diamantina Fracture, Ob' Trench 22,553 feet	Java or Sunda Trench, Planet Deep 23,376 feet
Eurasia Basin (Arctic Ocean) 17,881 feet	Kermandec Trench 32,963 feet
Guatemala Trench 21,228 feet	Kuril Trench 31,988 feet

Mariana Trench, Challenger Deep 35,840 feet	Puerto Rico Trench, Milwaukee Deep 28,232 feet
North Ryukyu Trench 23,560 feet	Romanche Trench 25,354 feet
Peru-Chile or Atacama Trench, Bartholomew Deep 26,160 feet	Solomon Trench 29,988 feet
	South Sandwich Trench, Meteor Deep 27,313 feet
Philippine Trench, Galathea Deep 32,995 feet	Tonga Trench 35,433 feet
	Verna Trench 21,004 feet
	Yap Trench 27,976 feet

276 SHALLOWNESS

NOUNS 1 **shallowness, depthlessness;** shoalness, shoaliness, no water, no depth; **superficiality,** exteriority, triviality, **cursoriness,** slightness; insufficiency 992; a lick and a promise and once-over-lightly <nf>; **surface,** superficies, skin, rind, epidermis; veneer, gloss; pinprick, scratch, mere scratch

2 **shoal, shallow,** shallows, shallow or shoal water, flat, shelf; **bank, bar,** sandbank, sandbar, tombolo; **reef,** coral reef; ford; wetlands, tidal flats, flats, mud flat

VERBS 3 **shoal,** shallow; fill in or up, silt up

4 **scratch the surface, touch upon,** hardly touch, skim, skim over, skim or graze the surface, hit the high spots and give a lick and a promise and give it once over lightly <nf>, apply a Band-Aid <trademark> <nf>; trivialize, trifle

ADJS 5 **shallow,** shoal, **depthless,** not deep, unprofound; **surface,** on or near the surface, merely surface; **superficial, cursory,** slight, light, cosmetic, merely cosmetic, thin, jejune, trivial; **skin-deep,** epidermal; one-dimensional, trifling, trivial; ankle-deep, knee-deep; shallow-rooted, shallow-rooting; shallow-draft or -bottomed or -hulled

6 shoaly, shelfy; reefy; unnavigable; shallow-sea; neritic

277 STRAIGHTNESS

NOUNS 1 **straightness,** directness, unswervingness, lineality, **linearity,** rectilinearity; verticalness 200; flatness, horizontalness 201; perpendicularity

2 **straight line,** straight, right line, direct line; straight course or stretch, straightaway; **beeline,** air line; **shortcut** 268.5; great-circle course; streamline; edge, side, diagonal, secant, transversal, chord, tangent, perpendicular, normal, segment, directrix, diameter, axis, radius, vector, radius vector <all mathematics>; ray, beeline, plumb line, column

3 **straightedge, rule,** ruler; square, T square, triangle

VERBS 4 be straight, have no turning *or* turns; arrow; go straight, make a beeline

5 **straighten, set** *or* **put straight,** rectify, make right *or* good, square away; **unbend,** unkink, uncurl, unsnarl, disentangle 798.5; straighten up, square up; straighten out, extend; flatten, smooth 201.6; iron, flatten

ADJS 6 **straight;** straight-lined, dead straight, straight as an edge *or* a ruler, ruler-straight, even, right, true, straight as an arrow, arrowlike; straightaway; **rectilinear,** rectilineal; **linear,** lineal, in a line; quasilinear; **direct, undeviating, unswerving,** unbending, undeflected; **unbent, unbowed,** unturned, uncurved, undistorted, uncurled; **uninterrupted, unbroken;** straight-side, straight-front, straight-cut; upright, vertical 200.11; flat, level, smooth, horizontal 201.7; plumb, true, right

ADVS 7 **straight,** straightly, on the straight, unswervingly, undeviatingly, **directly;** straight to the mark; down the alley *and* down the pipe *and* in the groove *and* on the beam *and* on the money <nf>

278 ANGULARITY

NOUNS 1 **angularity,** angularness, crookedness, hookedness; squareness, orthogonality, right-angledness, rectangularity; flection, flexure

2 **angle,** point, bight; vertex, apex 198.2; **corner,** quoin, coin, nook; **crook, hook,** crotchet; **bend,** curve, swerve, veer, inflection, deflection; ell, L; cant; furcation, bifurcation, fork 171.4; zigzag, zig, zag; chevron; elbow, knee, dogleg <nf>; crank; obtuse angle, oblique angle, acute angle, right angle, perpendicular

3 <angular measurement> goniometry; trigonometry; geometry

4 <instruments> goniometer, radiogoniometer; pantometer, clinometer, graphometer, astrolabe; azimuth compass, azimuth circle; theodolite, transit theodolite, transit, transit instrument, transit circle; sextant, quadrant; bevel, bevel square, set square, T-square; protractor, bevel protractor; graduated cylinder

VERBS 5 **angle, crook, hook, bend,** elbow; crank; angle off *or* away, curve, swerve, veer, veer off, slant off, go off on a tangent; furcate, bifurcate, branch, fork 171.7; zigzag, zig, zag

ADJS 6 **angular;** cornered, **crooked, hooked, bent,** flexed, flexural; akimbo, knee-shaped, geniculate, geniculated, doglegged <nf>; crotched, Y-shaped, V-shaped; furcate, furcal, forked 171.10; sharp-

cornered, **sharp, pointed;** zigzag, jagged, serrate, sawtooth *or* saw-toothed; mitered

7 **right-angled, rectangular,** right-angular, right-angle; **orthogonal,** orthodiagonal, orthometric; **perpendicular,** normal

8 **triangular, trilateral,** trigonal, oxygonal, deltoid; wedgeshaped, cuneiform, cuneate, cuneated

9 **quadrangular, quadrilateral,** quadrate, quadriform; **rectangular, square;** foursquare, orthogonal; tetragonal, tetrahedral; **oblong;** trapezoid *or* trapezoidal, rhombic *or* rhombal, rhomboid *or* rhomboidal; **cubic** *or* **cubical,** cubiform, cuboid, cube-shaped, cubed, diced; rhombohedral, trapezohedral

10 pentagonal, hexagonal, heptagonal, octagonal, decagonal, dodecagonal, etc; pentahedral, hexahedral, octahedral, dodecahedral, icosahedral, etc

11 multilateral, multiangular, polygonal; polyhedral, pyramidal, pyramidic; prismatic, prismoid; diamond

279 CURVATURE

NOUNS 1 **curvature,** curving, curvation, arcing; incurvature, incurvation; excurvature, excurvation; decurvature, decurvation; recurvature, recurvity, recurvation; rondure; **arching, vaulting,** arcuation, concameration; aduncity, aquilinity, crookedness, hookedness; sinuosity, sinuousness, tortuosity, tortuousness; circularity 280; convolution 281; rotundity 282, roundness; convexity 283; concavity 284; curvaceousness

2 **curve,** sinus; **bow, arc; crook, hook;** parabola, hyperbola, witch of Agnesi; ellipse; caustic, catacaustic, diacaustic; catenary, festoon, swag; conchoid; lituus; tracery; circle 280.2; curl 281.2; coil, loop, spiral

3 **bend,** bending; **bow,** bowing, oxbow; Cupid's bow; **turn,** turning, sweep, meander, hairpin turn *or* bend, S-curve, U-turn; **flexure,** flex, **flection,** conflexure, inflection, deflection; reflection; geanticline, geosyncline; detour

4 **arch, span, vault,** vaulting, concameration, camber; ogive; apse; **dome,** cupola, geodesic dome, igloo, concha; cove; arched roof, ceilinged roof; **arcade, archway,** arcature; voussoir, keystone, skewback

5 **crescent, semicircle,** scythe, sickle, meniscus; crescent moon, half-moon; lunula, lunule; horseshoe; rainbow

VERBS 6 **curve, turn,** arc, sweep; **crook, hook,** loop; incurve, incurvate; recurve, decurve, bend back, retroflex, detour; sag, swag <nf>; **bend,** flex; deflect, inflect; reflect, reflex; **bow,** embow; **arch,** vault; dome; **hump,** hunch; wind, curl 281.5; round 282.6

ADJS **7 curved,** curve, curvate, curvated, **curving,** curvy, curvaceous <nf>, curvesome, curviform; curvilinear, curvilineal; wavy, undulant, billowy, billowing; sinuous, tortuous, serpentine, mazy, labyrinthine, meandering; **bent,** flexed, flexural, flexuous; incurved, incurving, incurvate, incurvated; recurved, recurving, recurvate, recurvated; geosynclinal, geanticlinal

8 hooked, crooked, aquiline, aduncous; **hook-shaped,** hooklike, uncinate, unciform; hamulate, hamate, hamiform; claw-like, unguiform; down-curving; **hook-nosed,** beak-nosed, parrot-nosed, aquiline-nosed, Roman-nosed, crooknosed, crookbilled; **beaked,** billed; **beak-shaped,** beak-like; bill-shaped, bill-like; rostrate, rostriform, rhamphoid

9 turned-up, upcurving, upsweeping, *retroussé* <Fr>

10 bowed, embowed, bandy; bowlike, bow-shaped, oxbow, Cupid's-bow; **convex, concave** 284.16, convexoconcave; arcuate, arcuated, arcual, arciform, arclike; **arched,** vaulted; **humped,** hunched, humpy, hunchy; gibbous, gibbose; humpbacked 265.13

11 crescent-shaped, crescentlike, crescent, crescentic, crescentiform; meniscoid<al>, menisciform; S-shaped, ess, S, sigmoid; **semicircular,** semilunar; horn-shaped, hornlike, horned, corniform; bicorn, two-horned; sickle-shaped, sickle-like, falcate, falciform; moon-shaped, moonlike, lunar, lunate, lunular, luniform

12 lens-shaped, lenticular, lentiform, lentoid

13 parabolic, parabolical, paraboloid, saucer-shaped; elliptic, elliptical, ellipsoid; bell-shaped, bell-like, campanular, campanulate, campaniform; hyperbolic, domical

14 pear-shaped, pearlike, pyriform, ovipyriform

15 heart-shaped, heartlike; cordate, cardioid, cordiform, obcordate

16 kidney-shaped, kidneylike, reniform, nephroid

17 turnip-shaped, turniplike, napiform

18 shell-shaped, shell-like; conchate, conchiform, conchoidal, cochleated

19 shield-shaped, shieldlike, peltate; scutate, scutiform; clypeate, clypeiform, aspidate

20 helmet-shaped, helmetlike, galeiform, cassideous, galeated

280 CIRCULARITY

NOUNS **1 circularity, roundness,** ring-shape, ringliness, annularity; annulation

2 circle, circus, rondure, **ring,** annulus, O, full circle; **circumference,** radius; **round,** roundel, rondelle; **cycle, circuit;** orbit 1072.16; closed circle *or* arc; vicious circle, eternal return; magic circle, charmed circle, fairy ring; logical circle, circular reasoning, petitio principii; **wheel** 914.5; **disk,** discus, saucer; **loop,** looplet; noose, lasso; crown, diadem, coronet, corona; garland, chaplet, wreath; halo, glory, areola, aureole; annular muscle, sphincter

3 <thing encircling> **band, belt, cincture,** cingulum, **girdle, girth,** girt, zone, fascia, fillet; collar, collarband, neckband; necktie; necklace, bracelet, armlet, torque, wristlet, wristband, anklet; **ring,** earring, nose ring, finger ring; hoop; quoit; zodiac, ecliptic, equator, great circle; round trip

4 rim, felly; **tire**

5 circlet, **ringlet,** roundlet, annulet, eye, **eyelet,** grommet

6 oval, ovule, ovoid; ellipse

7 cycloid; epicycloid; epicycle; hypocycloid; lemniscate; cardioid; Lissajous figure

8 semicircle, half circle, hemicycle; crescent 279.5; quadrant, sextant, sector

9 <music and poetry> **round,** canon; rondo, rondino, rondeau, rondelet

VERBS **10 circle, round;** orbit; **encircle** 209.7, surround, encompass, girdle; make a round trip, circumnavigate

ADJS **11 circular, round,** rounded, circinate, annular, annulate, ring-shaped, ringlike; annulose; disklike, discoid; cyclic, cyclical, cycloid, cycloidal; epicyclic; planetary; coronal, crownlike; orbital; circulatory, circumferential

12 oval, ovate, ovoid, oviform, egg-shaped, obovate, ellipsoid, elliptic, prolate

281 CONVOLUTION

<complex curvature>

NOUNS **1 convolution,** involution, circumvolution, **winding, twisting, turning; meander, meandering;** crinkle, crinkling; circuitousness, circumlocution, circumbendibus, circumambages, ambagiousness, ambages, convolutedness; Byzantinism; tortuousness, tortuosity; torsion, intorsion; sinuousness, **sinuosity,** sinuation, slinkiness; anfractuosity; snakiness; flexuousness, flexuosity; undulation, wave, waving; rivulation; **complexity** 799

2 coil, whorl, roll, **curl,** curlicue, ringlet, pigtail, **spiral,** helix, double helix, volute, volution, involute, evolute, gyre, scroll, turbination; **kink, twist, twirl;** screw, corkscrew, screw thread; tendril, cirrus; whirl, swirl, vortex; intricacy; squiggle; spheroid

3 curler, curling iron; curlpaper, papillote; crimper, crimping iron

VERBS 4 convolve, convolute, **wind, twine,** twirl, **twist, turn, twist and turn, meander,** crinkle; serpentine, snake, slink, worm; screw, corkscrew; whirl, swirl, whorl; scallop; wring; intort; contort; undulate, squiggle, twist and turn

5 **curl, coil;** crisp, kink, crimp, wave

ADJS 6 **convolutional,** convoluted, **winding, twisting,** twisty, **turning, meandering,** meandrous, mazy, labyrinthine; **serpentine,** snaky, anfractuous; roundabout, circuitous, ambagious, circumlocutory; labyrinthine; Byzantine; **sinuous,** sinuose, sinuate; **tortuous,** torsional; tortile; flexular, flexuous, flexuose; involutional, involute, involuted; rivose, rivulose; sigmoidal; wreathy, wreathlike; ruffled, whorled, turbinate

7 **coiled,** tortile, **snakelike, snaky,** snake-shaped, **serpentine,** serpentlike, serpentiform; anguine <old>, anguiform; eellike, eelshaped, anguilliform; wormlike, vermiform, lumbricoid, lumbricine, lumbriciform

8 **spiral,** spiroid, volute, voluted; **helical,** helicoid, helicoidal; anfractuous; screw-shaped, corkscrew, corkscrewy; verticillate, whorled, scrolled; cochlear, cochleate; turbinal, turbinate

9 **curly, curled; kinky,** kinked; **frizzly,** frizzy, frizzled, frizzed; crisp, crispy, crisped

10 **wavy, undulant,** undulatory, undulative, undulating, undulate, undulated; **billowy,** billowing, surgy, rolling

ADVS 11 **windingly, twistingly,** sinuously, tortuously, serpentinely, meanderingly, meandrously; in waves; wavily; **in and out,** round and round

282 SPHERICITY, ROTUNDITY

NOUNS 1 **sphericity, rotundity, roundness,** ball-likeness, rotundness, orbicularness, orbicularity, orbiculation, orblikeness, **sphericalness,** sphericality, globularity, globularness, globosity, globoseness; spheroidity, spheroidicity; belly; cylindricality; convexity 283

2 **sphere; ball,** orb, orbit, **globe,** rondure; geoid; spheroid, globoid, ellipsoid, oblate spheroid, prolate spheroid; spherule, globule, globelet, orblet; glomerulus; **pellet;** boll; **bulb,** bulbil or bulbel, bulblet; knob, knot; **gob,** glob <nf>, blob, gobbet; pill, bolus, **balloon,** bladder, bubble; marble

3 **drop,** droplet; dewdrop, raindrop, teardrop; bead, pearl

4 **cylinder,** cylindroid, pillar, column; barrel, drum, cask; pipe, tube; roll, rouleau, roller, rolling pin; bole, trunk; rung

5 **cone,** conoid, conelet; complex cone, cone of a

complex; funnel; ice-cream cone, cornet <Brit>; pine cone; cop; trumpet; top; traffic cone

VERBS 6 **round; round out, fill out;** cone

7 **ball, snowball;** sphere, spherify, globe, conglobulate; roll; bead; balloon, mushroom

ADJS 8 **rotund, round,** rounded, rounded out, round as a ball; bellied, bellylike; convex, bulging

9 **spherical,** sphereic, spheriform, spherelike, sphere-shaped; **globular, global,** globed, globose, globate, globelike, globe-shaped; orbicular, orbiculate, orbiculated, orbed, orb, orby <old>, orblike; spheroid, spheroidal, globoid, ellipsoid, ellipsoidal; hemispheric, hemispherical; **bulbous,** bulblike, bulging; ovoid, obovoid

10 **beady,** beaded, bead-shaped, bead-like

11 **cylindric, cylindrical,** cylindroid, cylindroidal; **columnar,** columnal, columned, columelliform; **tubular,** tube-shaped; barrel-shaped, drum-shaped

12 **conical,** conic, coned, cone-shaped, conelike; conoid, conoidal; spheroconic; funnel-shaped, funnellike, funnelled, funnelform, infundibuliform, infundibular; bell-shaped

283 CONVEXITY, PROTUBERANCE

NOUNS 1 **convexity,** convexness, convexedness; excurvature, excurvation; camber; gibbousness, gibbosity; tuberousness, tuberosity; **bulging,** bulbousness, bellying, puffing, puffing out

2 **protuberance** or protuberancy, **projection, protrusion, extrusion;** prominence, eminence, salience, boldness, **bulging,** bellying; gibbousness, gibbosity; excrescence or excrescency; tuberousness, tuberosity, puffiness; salient; relief, high relief, *alto-rilievo* <Ital>, low relief, bas-relief, *basso-rilievo* <Ital>, embossment

3 **bulge,** bilge, bow, convex; **bump;** thank-you-ma'am *and* whoopdedoo <nf>, cahot <Can>; speed bump, sleeping policeman <Brit>; hill, mountain; **hump,** hunch; **lump,** clump, bunch, blob; nubbin, nubble, nub; **mole,** nevus; **wart,** papilloma, verruca; **knob,** boss, bulla, button, bulb; stud, jog, joggle, peg, dowel; flange, lip; tab, ear, flap, loop, ring, handle; knot, knur, knurl, gnarl, burl, gall; **ridge,** rib, cost- or costo- or costi-, chine, spine, shoulder; welt, wale; blister, bleb, vesicle <anat>, blain; bubble; condyle; bubo; tubercle or tubercule; beer belly; bandha <Sanskrit>

4 **swelling,** swollenness, edema; **rising, lump, bump,** pimple; pock, furuncle, boil, carbuncle; corn; pustule; dilation, dilatation; turgidity, turgescence or turgescency, tumescence, intumescence; tumor, tumidity, tumefaction; wen, cyst, sebaceous cyst; bunion; distension 259.2

5 **node,** nodule, nodulus, nodulation, nodosity

6 **breast, bosom, bust, chest,** crop, brisket; thorax; pigeon breast; **breasts,** dugs, teats; **nipple,** papilla, pap, mammilla, *mamelon* and *téton* <Fr>; mammillation, mamelonation; mammary gland, udder, bag

7 <nf terms> **tits,** titties, **boobs,** boobies, bubbies, jugs, headlights, **knockers,** knobs, *nénés* <Fr>, bazooms, bags, bazongas, coconuts, hooters; balls

8 **nose,** olfactory organ; **snout, snoot** <nf>, nozzle <nf>, **muzzle; proboscis,** antlia, **trunk; beak,** rostrum; **bill** and pecker <nf>; nib, neb; smeller *and* beezer *and* bugle *and* schnozzle *and* schnoz *and* schnozzola *and* conk <nf>; muffle, rhinarium; nostrils, noseholes <Brit nf>, nares

9 <point of land> **point,** hook, spur, **cape,** tongue, bill; **promontory,** foreland, **headland,** head; naze, ness; **peninsula,** chersonese; **delta; spit,** sandspit; **reef,** coral reef; breakwater 901.4

VERBS 10 **protrude, protuberate, project, extrude; stick out,** jut out, poke out, stand out, shoot out; **stick up,** bristle up, start up, cock up, shoot up

11 **bulge,** bilge, bouge <nf>, **belly,** bag, balloon, **pouch,** pooch <nf>; pout; **goggle,** bug <nf>, pop; **swell, swell up, dilate, distend,** billow; swell out, **belly out,** round out

12 **emboss, boss,** chase, raise; ridge

ADJS 13 **convex,** convexed; excurved, excurvate, excurvated; **bowed,** bowed-out, out-bowed, arched 279.10; gibbous, gibbose; humped 279.10; rotund 282.8

14 **protruding, protrusive,** protrudent; protrusible; **protuberant,** protuberating; **projecting, extruding,** jutting, outstanding; prominent, eminent, salient, bold; prognathous; excrescent, excrescential; protrusile, emissile; sticking out

15 **bulging, swelling,** distended, bloated, potbellied, bellying, pouching; bagging, baggy; rounded, hillocky, hummocky, moutonnée; billowing, billowy, bosomy, ballooning, pneumatic; **bumpy,** bumped; bunchy, bunched; **bulbous,** bulbose; warty, verrucose, verrucated; meniscoid

16 **bulged, bulgy,** bugged-out <nf>; swollen 259.13, turgid, tumid, turgescent, tumescent, tumorous; bellied, ventricose; pouched, pooched <nf>; goggled, goggle; exophthalmic, bug-eyed <nf>, popeyed <nf>

17 **studded, knobbed, knobby,** knoblike, nubbled, nubby, nubbly, torose; **knotty, knotted; gnarled,** knurled, knurly, burled, gnarly; noded, nodal, nodiform; noduled, nodular; nodulated; bubonic; tuberculous, tubercular; tuberous, tuberose

18 **in relief,** in bold *or* high relief, bold, raised, *repoussé* <Fr>; chased, bossed, embossed, bossy

19 **pectoral,** chest, thoracic; pigeon-breasted; mammary, mammillary, mammiform; mammalian, mammate; papillary, papillose, papulous; breasted, bosomed, chested; teated, titted <nf>, nippled; busty, bosomy, chesty

20 **peninsular;** deltaic, deltal

284 CONCAVITY

NOUNS 1 **concavity, hollowness;** incurvature, incurvation; depression, impression; emptiness 222.2

2 **cavity,** concavity, concave; **hollow,** hollow shell, shell; **hole, pit, depression, dip,** sink, fold <Brit>; scoop, pocket, socket; **basin,** trough, **bowl,** punch bowl, cup, container 195; **crater;** antrum; lacuna; alveola, alveolus, alveolation; vug *or* vugg *or* vugh; crypt; armpit; socket; funnel chest *or* breast

3 **pothole, sinkhole,** pitchhole, chuckhole, **mudhole, rut** 290.1

4 **pit, well, shaft,** sump; **chasm, gulf, abyss,** abysm; **excavation,** dig, diggings, workings; mine, quarry

5 **cave, cavern,** cove <Scot>, **hole, grotto,** grot, antre, subterrane; lair 228.26; **tunnel, burrow,** warren; subway; bunker, foxhole, dugout, *abri* <Fr>; sewer

6 **indentation,** indent, indention, indenture, **dent,** dint; gouge, **furrow** 290; sunken part *or* place, **dimple; pit,** pock, pockmark; impression, impress; imprint, print; alveolus, alveolation; honeycomb, Swiss cheese; **notch** 289

7 **recess,** recession, **niche, nook,** inglenook, corner; cove, alcove; bay; pitchhole

8 <hollow in the side of a mountain> combe, cwm <Welsh>, cirque, corrie

9 **valley,** vale, dale, dell, dingle; **glen,** bottom, bottoms, bottom glade, intervale, strath <Scot>, gill <Brit>, cwm <Welsh>, wadi, grove; trench, trough, lunar rill; gap, pass, ravine

10 **excavator, digger;** archaeologist; sapper; **miner;** tunneler, sandhog *and* groundhog <nf>, burrower; gravedigger; dredger; quarryman; driller; steam shovel, navvy <Brit>; dredge, dredger

11 **excavation,** digging; mining; indentation, **engraving**

VERBS 12 <be concave> **sink, dish,** cup, bowl, hollow; retreat, retire; incurve, curve inward

13 **hollow,** hollow out, concave, **dish,** cup, bowl; cave, cave in

14 **indent, dent,** dint, **depress,** press in, stamp, tamp, punch, punch in, impress, imprint; **pit;** pock, pockmark; dimple; honeycomb; **recess,** set back; set in; **notch** 289.4; engrave

15 **excavate, dig,** dig out, **scoop,** scoop out, **gouge,** gouge out, grub, shovel, spade, trowel, dike, delve, scrape, scratch, scrabble; dredge; **trench,** trough,

furrow, groove; **tunnel, burrow;** drive, sink, lower; **mine,** sap; quarry; drill, bore

ADJS **16 concave,** concaved, **incurved,** incurving, incurvate; **sunk,** sunken; retreating, recessed, retiring; **hollow,** hollowed, empty; palm-shaped; dish-shaped, dished, dishing, dishlike, bowl-shaped; bowllike, crater-shaped, craterlike, saucer-shaped; spoon-like; **cupped,** cup-shaped, scyphate; funnel-shaped, infundibular, infundibuliform; funnel-chested, funnel-breasted; boat-shaped, boatlike, navicular, naviform, cymbiform, scaphoid; **cavernous,** cavelike

17 indented, dented, depressed; **dimpled; pitted;** cratered; pocked, pockmarked; honeycombed, alveolar, alveolate, faveolate; **notched** 289.5; **engraved**

285 SHARPNESS

NOUNS **1 sharpness, keenness, edge;** acuteness, acuity; **pointedness,** acumination; thorniness, prickliness, spinosity, spininess, bristliness; mucronation; denticulation, dentition; serration; cornification; acridity 68.1

2 <sharp edge> **edge, cutting edge, honed edge, knife-edge, razor-edge,** saw-edge; jagged edge; featheredge, fine edge; edge tool; sword 462.5

3 point, tip, cusp, vertex; acumination, mucro; **nib,** neb; needle; hypodermic needle, hypodermic syringe; **drill,** borer, auger, bit; prong, tine; **prick, prickle;** sting, acus or aculeus; **tooth** 2.8

4 <pointed projection> **projection,** spur, jag, **snag,** snaggle; **horn,** antler; cornicle; crag, peak, arête; spire, steeple, flèche; **cog, sprocket,** ratchet; sawtooth; harrow, rake; comb, pecten; nail, tack, pin; arrowhead; skewer, spit; tooth, snaggletooth, fang, denticle

5 thorn, bramble, brier, nettle, burr, awn, prickle, sticker <nf>; **spike,** spikelet, spicule, spiculum; **spine;** bristle; quill; **needle,** pine needle; **thistle,** catchweed, cleavers, goose grass, cactus; yucca, Adam's-needle, Spanish bayonet

VERBS **6** come or taper to a point, end in a point, acuminate; prick, prickle, sting, stick, bite; be keen, have an edge, cut, needle; bristle with

7 sharpen, edge, acuminate, aculeate, spiculate, taper; **whet, hone,** oilstone, file, grind; strop, strap; set, reset; **point;** barb, spur, point, file to a point

ADJS **8 sharp, keen, edged, acute,** fine, **cutting,** knifelike, cultrate; sharp-edged, keen-edged, razor-edged, knife-edged, sharp as broken glass; featheredged, fine-edged; acrid 68.6; two-edged, double-edged; sharp-set, sharp as a razor or needle or tack, "sharp as a two-edged sword"— Bible; sharpened, set

9 pointed, pointy, acuminate, acuate, aculeate, aculeated, acute, unbated; tapered, tapering; cusped, cuspate, cuspated, cuspidal, cuspidate, cuspidated; **sharp-pointed; needlelike,** needle-sharp, needle-pointed, needly, acicular, aciculate, aculeiform; mucronate, mucronated; acuminate; toothed; **spiked,** spiky, spiculate; **barbed, tined, pronged; horned,** horny, cornuted, corniculate, cornified, ceratoid; **spined, spiny,** spinous, hispid, acanthoid, acanthous

10 prickly, pricky <nf>, muricate, echinate, acanaceous, acanthous, aculeolate; pricking, stinging; **thorny,** brambly, briery, thistly, nettly, burry; bristly

11 arrowlike, arrowy, arrowheaded; sagittal, sagittate, sagittiform

12 spearlike, hastate; lancelike, lanciform, lanceolate, lanceolar; **spindle-shaped,** fusiform

13 swordlike, gladiate, ensate, ensiform

14 toothlike, dentiform, dentoid, odontoid; **toothed,** toothy, **fanged, tusked,** corniculate, denticulate, cuspidate, muricate; snaggle-toothed, snaggled, jagged; emarginate

15 star-shaped, starlike, star-pointed, stellate, stellular

286 BLUNTNESS

NOUNS **1 bluntness, dullness,** unsharpness, obtuseness, obtundity; bluffness; abruptness; flatness, smoothness; toothlessness, lack of bite or incisiveness

VERBS **2 blunt, dull,** disedge, retund, obtund, **take the edge off,** take the sting or bite out; turn, turn the edge or point of; weaken, repress; draw the teeth or fangs; bate; flatten, smooth

ADJS **3 blunt, dull,** obtuse, obtundent; bluntish, dullish; **unsharp,** unsharpened, unwhetted; **unedged,** edgeless; rounded, faired, smoothed, streamlined; **unpointed,** pointless; blunted, dulled; blunt-edged, dull-edged; blunt-pointed, dull-pointed, blunt-ended; bluff, abrupt; flat

4 toothless, teethless, edentate, edental, edentulous, biteless

287 SMOOTHNESS

NOUNS **1 smoothness, flatness, levelness,** evenness, uniformity, regularity; **sleekness,** glossiness; **slickness,** slipperiness, lubricity, oiliness, greasiness, frictionlessness; silkiness, satininess, velvetiness; glabrousness, glabriety; downiness; suavity 504.5; peacefulness, dead calm

2 polish, gloss, glaze, burnish, varnish, wax, enamel, **shine, luster,** finish; **patina**

3 <smooth surface> smooth, **plane, level, flat;** tennis court, bowling alley *or* green, billiard table *or* ball; slide; glass, ice; marble, alabaster, ivory; silk, satin, velvet, a baby's ass <nf>; mahogany

4 **smoother;** roller, lawn-roller; sleeker, slicker; **polish,** burnish; **abrasive,** abrader, abradant; lubricant; flattener, iron; buffer, sander, burnisher

VERBS 5 **smooth, flatten, plane,** planish, **level,** even, equalize; **dress,** dub, dab; smooth down *or* out, lay; plaster, plaster down; roll, roll smooth; harrow, drag; grade; mow, shave; lubricate, oil, grease

6 **press,** hot-press, **iron, mangle,** calender; roll

7 **polish, shine, burnish, furbish,** sleek, slick, slick down, gloss, glaze, glance, luster; **rub,** scour, **buff;** wax, varnish; finish

8 **grind, file, sand, scrape,** sandpaper, emery, pumice; levigate; abrade; sandblast

9 move smoothly; glide, skate, roll, ski, float, slip, slide, skid, coast

ADJS 10 **smooth;** smooth-textured *or* -surfaced, **even, level, plane, flat,** regular, uniform, **unbroken;** peaceful, still; unrough, unroughened, unruffled, unwrinkled, unrumpled; glabrous, glabrate, glabrescent; downy, peachlike; silky, satiny, velvety, smooth as silk *or* satin *or* velvet, smooth as a billiard ball *or* baby's ass <nf>; leiotrichous, lissotrichous; smooth-shaven 6.17; suave 504.18

11 **sleek, slick, glossy,** shiny, gleaming; silky, silken, satiny, velvety; **polished,** burnished, furbished; buffed, rubbed, finished; varnished, lacquered, shellacked, glazed, *glacé* <Fr>; **glassy,** smooth as glass

12 **slippery,** slippy, **slick,** slithery *and* sliddery <nf>, slippery as an eel; lubricous, lubric, oily, oleaginous, greasy, buttery, soaped, soapy; lubricated, oiled, greased

ADVS 13 **smoothly, evenly,** regularly, uniformly; **like clockwork,** on wheels

288 ROUGHNESS

NOUNS 1 **roughness, unsmoothness, unevenness,** irregularity, ununiformity, nonuniformity 782, inequality; **bumpiness,** pockedness, pockiness, holeyness, lumpiness, knobbliness; **abrasiveness, abrasion,** harshness, asperity; **ruggedness,** rugosity; **jaggedness,** raggedness, cragginess, scraggliness; joltiness, bumpiness; rough air, turbulence; choppiness; tooth; granulation; hispidity, bristliness, spininess, thorniness; nubbiness, nubbliness; scaliness, scabrousness

2 <rough surface> **rough,** broken ground; broken water, chop; **corrugation,** ripple, washboard; serration; gooseflesh, goose bumps, goose

pimples, horripilation; tweed, corduroy, sackcloth; steel wool; sandpaper; potholed road, dirt road

3 **bristle,** barb, barbel, striga, setule, setula, seta; **stubble,** designer stubble; whiskers, five o'clock shadow

VERBS 4 **roughen,** rough, rough up, harshen; coarsen; granulate; gnarl, knob, stud, boss; pimple, horripilate; roughcast, rough-hew

5 **ruffle,** wrinkle, corrugate, crinkle, crumple, corrugate, **rumple; bristle; rub the wrong way, go against the grain,** set on edge

ADJS 6 **rough, unsmooth; uneven,** ununiform, unlevel, inequal, **broken,** irregular, textured; jolty, **bumpy,** rutty, rutted, pitted, pocky, potholed; horripilant, pimply; **corrugated,** ripply, wimpled; **choppy;** ruffled, unkempt; **shaggy,** shagged; **coarse,** rank, unrefined; unpolished; rough-grained, coarse-grained, cross-grained; grainy, granulated; rough-hewn, rough-cast; homespun, linsey-woolsey; bouclé, tweed, tweedy, corduroy

7 **rugged,** ragged, harsh; rugose, rugous, wrinkled, crinkled, crumpled, corrugated; **scratchy, abrasive,** rough as a cob <nf>; **jagged,** jaggy; **snaggy,** snagged, snaggled; scraggy, scragged, scraggly; sawtooth, sawtoothed, serrate, serrated; **craggy,** cragged; **rocky,** gravelly, stony; rockbound, ironbound

8 **gnarled,** gnarly; **knurled,** knurly; **knotted,** knotty, knobbly, nodose, nodular, studded, lumpy

9 **bristly, bristling,** bristled, hispid, hirsute, whiskery; barbellate, whiskered, glochidiate, setaceous, setous, setose; strigal, strigose, strigate, studded; **stubbled,** stubbly; hairy 3.24

10 bristlelike, setiform, aristate, setarious

ADVS 11 **roughly,** rough, in the rough; **unsmoothly,** brokenly, **unevenly,** irregularly, raggedly, choppily, jaggedly; **abrasively**

12 cross-grained, **against the grain,** the wrong way

289 NOTCH

NOUNS 1 **notch, nick,** nock, **cut,** cleft **incision, gash,** hack, blaze, scotch, **score,** kerf, crena, depression, jag; gouge; jog, joggle; **indentation** 284.6

2 **notching, serration,** serrulation, saw, saw tooth *or* teeth; denticulation, dentil, dentil band, dogtooth; crenation, crenelation, crenature, crenulation; **scallop;** rickrack; picot edge, Vandyke edge; deckle edge; cockscomb, crest; pinking shears

3 battlement, crenel, merlon, embrasure, castellation, machicolation; cog, zigzag

VERBS 4 **notch, nick, cut, incise, gash,** nock, slash, chop, crimp, scotch, **score,** blaze, jag, scarify, gouge; **indent** 284.14; **scallop,** crenelate, crenulate, machicolate; serrate, pink, mill, knurl, tooth, picot, Vandyke

ADJS **5 notched, nicked,** incised, incisural, gashed, scotched, scored, chopped, blazed; **indented** 284.17; serrate, serrated, serrulated, **saw-toothed,** saw-edged, sawlike; crenate, crenated, crenulate, crenellated, battlemented, embrasured; scalloped; dentate, dentated, **toothed,** toothlike, tooth-shaped; lacerate, lacerated; **jagged,** jaggy; erose; serrated, serriform

290 FURROW

NOUNS **1 furrow, groove,** scratch, crack, fissure, cranny, chase, chink, score, **cut,** gash, striation, streak, stria, **gouge,** slit, incision; sulcus, sulcation; wrinkle, crinkle, **rut,** ruck <nf>, wheeltrack, well-worn groove; wrinkle 291.3; **corrugation;** flute, fluting; rifling; chamfer, bezel, rabbet, dado; microgroove; **engraving** 713.2
   2 trench, trough, channel, ditch, dike <old>, fosse, **canal,** cut, gutter, conduit, kennel <Brit>; moat; sunk fence, ha-ha; aqueduct 239.2; entrenchment 460.5; canalization; pleat, crimp, goffer

VERBS **3 furrow, groove,** score, scratch, incise, cut, carve, chisel, gash, striate, streak, gouge, slit, crack; plow; rifle; **channel, trough, flute,** chamfer, rabbet, dado; **trench,** canal, canalize, **ditch,** dike <old>, gully, **rut; corrugate,** wrinkle, crinkle; wrinkle 291.6; pleat, crimp, goffer; **engrave** 713.9

ADJS **4 furrowed, grooved,** scratched, scored, incised, cut, gashed, gouged, slit, striated, slotted; **channeled, troughed,** trenched, ditched, plowed; fluted, chamfered, rabbeted, dadoed; rifled; sulcate, sulcated; canaliculate, canaliculated; **corrugated,** corrugate; corduroy, corduroyed, **rutted,** rutty, rimose, wrinkly; wrinkled 291.8, pleated, crimped, goffered, crinkly; **engraved;** ribbed, costate

291 FOLD

NOUNS **1 fold, double,** fold on itself, doubling, doubling over, duplicature; ply; plication, plica, plicature; flection, flexure; **crease,** creasing; crimp; **tuck, gather;** ruffle, frill, ruche, ruching; flounce; lappet; lapel; buckling, geological fold, anticline, syncline; dog-ear
   2 pleat, pleating, plait *or* plat; accordion pleat, box pleat, knife pleat, kick pleat
   3 wrinkle, corrugation, ridge, **furrow** 290, **crease, crimp,** ruck, **pucker,** cockle; **crinkle,** crankle, rimple, ripple, wimple; crumple, rumple; crow's-feet
   4 folding, creasing, infolding, infoldment *or*

enfoldment, envelopment; plication, plicature; paper-folding, origami

VERBS **5 fold,** fold on itself, fold up; **double,** ply, plicate; fold over, double over *or* under, lap, turn over *or* under; **crease, crimp;** crisp; **pleat,** plait, plat <nf>; **tuck, gather,** tuck up, ruck, ruck up; ruffle, ruff, frill; flounce; twill, quill, flute; turn up *or* down, dog-ear; **fold in,** enfold *or* infold, wrap, lap; interfold
   6 wrinkle, corrugate, shirr, ridge, **furrow, crease,** crimp, crimple, cockle, cocker, **pucker, purse; knit;** ruck, ruckle; **crumple,** rumple; **crinkle,** rimple, ripple, wimple

ADJS **7 folded, doubled;** plicate, plicated, plical; **pleated,** plaited; **creased,** crimped; tucked, gathered; flounced, ruffled; twilled, quilled, fluted; dog-eared; foldable, folding, flexural, flexible, flectional, pliable, pliant, willowy
   8 wrinkled, wrinkly; corrugated, corrugate; **creased,** rucked, ruched, **furrowed** 290.4, ridged; cockled, cockly; puckered, puckery; pursed, pursy; knitted, knotted; rugged, rugose, rugous; **crinkled,** crinkly, cranklety <nf>, rimpled, rippled; crimped, crimpy; **crumpled,** rumpled

292 OPENING

NOUNS **1 opening, aperture, hole,** hollow, **cavity** 284.2, **orifice; slot,** split, crack, check, leak, hairline crack; opening up, unstopping, uncorking, clearing, throwing open, laying open, broaching, cutting through; passageway; inlet 189.5; outlet 190.9; **gap,** gape, yawn, hiatus, lacuna, gat, space, interval; **chasm, gulf;** cleft 224.2; fontanel; foramen, fenestra; stoma; pore, porosity; fistula; **disclosure** 351; open space, clearing; window, window of opportunity
   2 gaping, yawning, oscitation, oscitancy, dehiscence, pandiculation; **gape, yawn;** the gapes
   3 hole, perforation, penetration, piercing, empiercement, **puncture,** goring, boring, puncturing, punching, pricking, lancing, broach, transforation, terebration; acupuncture, acupunctuation; trephining, trepanning; **impalement,** skewering, fixing, transfixion, transfixation; bore, borehole, drill hole; ear piercing, body piercing
   4 mouth; maw, oral cavity, gob <nf>, gab <Scot>; **muzzle,** jaw, lips, embouchure; bazoo *or* kisser *or* mug *or* mush *or* trap *or* yap <nf>; **jaws,** mandibles, chops, chaps, jowls; premaxilla
   5 <other body orifices> pore, sweat gland; aural cavity, nasal cavity, nostril; stoma; **anus; asshole** *and* bumhole *and* bunghole <nf>; urethra; vagina
   6 door, doorway 189.6; **entrance, entry** 189.5

7 **window,** casement; **windowpane,** window glass, pane, skylight; window frame, window ledge, window-sill, window bay

8 **porousness,** porosity; sievelikeness, cribriformity, cribrosity; screen, lattice, grate; sieve, strainer, colander; honeycomb; sponge; tea bag; filter, net

9 **permeability, perviousness**

10 **opener;** can opener, tin opener <Brit>; corkscrew, bottle screw, bottle opener, church key <nf>; **key,** clavis; latchkey; passkey, *passe-partout* <Fr>; master key, skeleton key; password, open sesame; key card, smart card; master switch

VERBS 11 **open,** ope <old>, **open up;** lay open, throw open; fly open, spring open, swing open; **tap, broach;** cut open, cut, cleave, split, slit, crack, chink, fissure, crevasse, incise; rift, rive; tear open, rent, tear, rip, rip open, part, dispart, separate, divide, divaricate; spread, spread out, open out, splay, splay out

12 **unclose,** unshut; **unfold,** unwrap, unroll; **unstop, unclog, unblock,** clear, unfoul, free, deobstruct; **unplug,** uncork, uncap; crack; **unlock,** unlatch, undo, unbolt; unseal, unclench, unclutch; **uncover,** uncase, unsheathe, unveil, undrape, uncurtain; **disclose** 351.4, expose, reveal, bare, take the lid off, manifest; gain access

13 **make an opening,** find an opening, make place *or* space, **make way, make room**

14 **breach,** rupture; **break open,** force *or* pry *or* prize open, crack *or* split open, rip *or* tear open; break into, break through; break in, burst in, bust in <nf>, stave *or* stove in, cave in; excavate, dig

15 **perforate, pierce,** empierce, **penetrate, puncture, punch, hole,** prick; **tap, broach; stab, stick,** pink, run through; **transfix,** transpierce, fix, **impale,** spit, skewer; gore, spear, lance, spike, needle; **bore, drill,** auger; **ream,** ream out, countersink, gouge, gouge out; trepan, trephine; punch full of holes, make look like Swiss cheese *or* a sieve, **riddle, honeycomb**

16 **gape,** gap <nf>, **yawn,** oscitate, dehisce, hang open

ADJS 17 **open, unclosed,** uncovered; **unobstructed, unstopped, unclogged;** clear, cleared, free; wide-open, unrestricted; **disclosed** 348.10; bare, exposed, unhidden 348.11, naked, bald; accessible

18 **gaping, yawning,** agape, oscitant, slack-jawed, openmouthed; dehiscent, ringent; ajar, half-open, cracked

19 **apertured,** slotted, **holey;** pierced, **perforated,** perforate, holed; honeycombed, like Swiss cheese, riddled, *criblé* <Fr>, shot through, peppered; windowed, fenestrated; leaky

20 **porous,** porose; poriferous; like a sieve, sievelike, cribose, cribriform; spongy, spongelike; percolating, leachy

21 **permeable, pervious, penetrable,** openable, accessible

22 **mouthlike, oral,** orificial; mandibular, maxillary

INTERJS 23 **open up!,** open sesame!, **gangway!,** passageway!, **make way!,** make a hole!, coming through!, heads up!, say ah!

293 CLOSURE

NOUNS 1 **closure, closing, shutting,** shutting up, occlusion; **shutdown,** shutting down, cloture; **exclusion** 773, shutting out, **ruling out;** blockade, embargo

2 **imperviousness, impermeability, impenetrability,** impassability; imperforation

3 **obstruction, clog, block,** blockade, sealing off, **blockage,** strangulation, choking, choking off, **stoppage,** stop, **bar, barrier, obstacle,** impediment; occlusion; **bottleneck,** chokepoint; **congestion,** jam, traffic jam, gridlock, rush hour; gorge; constipation, obstipation, costiveness; infarct, infarction; embolism, embolus; **blind alley,** blank wall, **dead end,** cul-de-sac, dead-end street, impasse; cecum, blind gut; standstill, deadlock, stalemate

4 **stopper,** stop, **stopple,** stopgap; **plug, cork,** bung, spike, spill, spile, tap, faucet, spigot, valve, check valve, cock, sea cock, peg, pin; lid 295.5; tamper-resistant packaging

5 **stopping, wadding, stuffing,** padding, **packing,** pack, tampon; gland; gasket; bandage, tourniquet; wedge

VERBS 6 **close, shut,** occlude; close up, shut up, contract, constrict, strangle, strangulate, choke, choke off, squeeze, squeeze shut; **exclude** 773.4, shut out, squeeze out; **rule out** 444.3; **fasten,** secure; **lock,** lock up, lock out, key, padlock, latch, bolt, bar, barricade; **seal,** seal up, seal in, seal off; button, button up; snap; zipper, zip up; batten, batten down the hatches; put *or* slap the lid on, **cover;** contain; **shut the door,** slam, clap, bang

7 **stop, stop up;** obstruct, **bar,** stay; **block,** block up; **clog,** clog up, foul, silt up, choke off; **choke,** choke up *or* off; **fill,** fill up; **stuff,** pack, jam; **congest,** stuff up; **plug,** plug up; stopper, stopple, **cork,** bung, spile; cover; **dam,** dam up; stanch; chink; caulk; blockade, barricade, embargo; constipate, obstipate, bind; occlude

8 close shop, **close up** *or* **down,** shut up, **shut down,** go out of business, fold *or* fold up *and* pull an el foldo <nf>, shutter, put up the shutters, discontinue; cease 857.6

ADJS 9 **closed, shut, unopen,** unopened; unvented, unventilated; fastened, secured; **excluded** 773.7, shut-out; **ruled out, barred** 444.7; contracted,

constricted, choked, choked off, choked up,
squeezed shut, strangulated, occluded; blank;
blind, cecal, dead; dead-end, blind-alley, closed-
end, closed-ended; **exclusive,** exclusionary,
closed-door, in-camera, private, closed to the
public; tamper-resistant

10 **unpierced,** pierceless, **unperforated,** imperforate,
intact; **untrodden,** pathless, wayless, trackless

11 **stopped, stopped up; obstructed,** infarcted,
blocked; plugged, plugged up, bunged; **clogged,**
clogged up; foul, fouled; **choked,** choked up,
strangulated, strangled; **full, stuffed,** packed,
jammed, bumper-to-bumper <nf>, jam-packed,
like sardines; **congested,** stuffed up; constipated,
obstipated, costive, bound; silted up

12 **close, tight, compact,** fast, shut fast, **snug,**
staunch, firm; **sealed;** hermetic, hermetical,
hermetically sealed; airtight, dusttight *or*
dustproof, gastight *or* gasproof, lighttight *or*
lightproof, oil-tight *or* oil-proof, raintight *or*
rainproof, smoketight *or* smokeproof, stormtight
or stormproof, watertight *or* waterproof, windtight
or windproof; water-repellant *or* -resistant

13 **impervious, impenetrable, impermeable;**
impassable, unpassable; unpierceable,
unperforable; **punctureproof,** nonpuncturable,
holeproof

294 TEXTURE
<surface quality>

NOUNS **1 texture,** surface texture; **surface; finish,**
feel, touch; intertexture, contexture, constitution,
consistency; **grain,** granular texture, fineness *or*
coarseness of grain; **weave,** woof 740.3, weftage,
wale; **nap,** pile, shag, nub, knub, protuberance 283;
pit, pock, indentation 284.6; structure 266

2 **roughness** 288; irregularity; bumpiness,
lumpiness; **coarseness, grossness, unrefinement,**
coarse-grainedness; cross-grainedness;
graininess, granularity, granulation, grittiness,
grit; pockiness; hardness 1046

3 **smoothness** 287, **fineness, refinement,** fine-
grainedness; **delicacy, daintiness;** filminess,
gossameriness 1029.1; down, **downiness,** fluff,
fluffiness, velvet, velvetiness, fuzz, fuzziness,
peach fuzz, peachiness; pubescence; satin,
satininess; silk, silkiness; softness 1047

VERBS **4 coarsen; grain,** granulate; tooth, **roughen**
288.4; gnarl, knob; rumple, wrinkle; smooth 287.5,
flatten

ADJS **5 textural, textured,** -surfaced

6 **rough** 288.6, **coarse, gross, unrefined, coarse-
grained;** cross-grained; grained, **grainy,** granular,
granulated, gritty, gravelly, gravelish

7 **nappy,** pily, **shaggy,** hairy, hirsute; nubby *or*
nubbly; bumpy, lumpy; studded, knobbed; pocked,
pitted 284.17; woven, matted, ribbed, twilled,
tweedy, woolly; fibrous; frizzly, frizzy

8 **smooth** 287.9; **fine, refined,** attenuate, attenuated,
fine-grained; delicate, dainty; finespun, thin-spun,
fine-drawn, wiredrawn; gauzy, filmy, gossamer,
gossamery 1029.4, **downy,** fluffy, velvety, velutinous,
fuzzy, pubescent; satin, satiny, silky

295 COVERING

NOUNS **1** <act of covering> **covering,** coverage,
obduction; **coating,** cloaking; **screening,** shielding,
hiding, curtaining, **veiling,** clouding, obscuring,
befogging, fogging, fuzzing, masking, mantling,
shrouding, shadowing, blanketing; blocking,
blotting out, eclipse, eclipsing, occultation;
wrapping, enwrapping, enwrapment, sheathing,
envelopment; **overlaying,** overspreading, laying on
or over, superimposition, superposition;
superincumbence; upholstering, upholstery;
plasterwork, stuccowork, brickwork, cementwork,
pargeting; incrustation; geocache, geocaching

2 **cover, covering,** coverage, covert, coverture,
housing, hood, cowl, cowling, **shelter; screen,**
shroud, shield, veil, pall, mantle, curtain, hanging,
drape, drapery, window treatment; **coat,** cloak,
mask, guise; vestment 5.1; camouflage, shroud

3 **skin,** dermis; **cuticle; rind; flesh;** bare skin *or*
flesh, the buff; integument, tegument 206.2,
tegmen, tegmentum, testa; scab; **pelt, hide, coat,
jacket, fell, fleece, fur, hair,** vair <heraldry>;
feathers, plumage; **peel, peeling, rind; skin,**
epicarp; **bark;** cork, phellum; cortex, cortical
tissue, epidermis; periderm, phelloderm;
peridium; dermatogen; protective coloring

4 **overlayer,** overlay; appliqué, **lap, overlap,**
overlapping, imbrication; **flap,** fly, tentfly; shutter

5 **cover, lid, top, cap, screw-top;** operculum; stopper
293.4

6 **roof,** roofing, roofage, top, **housetop,** rooftop;
roof-deck, roof garden, penthouse; roofpole,
ridgepole, rooftree; shingles, slates, tiles; eaves;
ceiling, *plafond* <Fr>, overhead; skylight, lantern,
cupola, dome; widow's walk *or* captain's walk;
canopy, awning, marquee

7 **umbrella,** gamp *or* brolly <Brit nf>, bumbershoot
<nf>; **sunshade, parasol,** beach umbrella

8 **tent,** canvas; top, whitetop, round top, big top;
tentage; tepee, wigwam, yurt

9 **rug, carpet,** floor cover *or* covering; carpeting,
wall-to-wall carpet *or* carpeting; mat; drop cloth,
ground cloth, groundsheet; **flooring,** floorboards,
duckboards; **tiling; pavement,** pavé; tarpaulin

10 **blanket, coverlet,** coverlid <nf>, blankie <nf>, security blanket, space blanket, cover, covers, **spread,** robe, buffalo robe, **afghan,** rug <Brit>; lap robe; **bedspread; bedcover;** counterpane, counterpin <nf>; comfort, **comforter, down comforter,** duvet, continental quilt <Brit>, **quilt,** feather bed, eiderdown; patchwork quilt; **bedding,** bedclothes, clothes; **linen,** bed linen; **sheet,** sheeting, bedsheet, fitted sheet, contour sheet, dust ruffle; **pillowcase,** pillow slip, case, slip, sham; electric blanket

11 horsecloth, **horse blanket;** caparison, housing; **saddle blanket,** saddlecloth

12 **blanket, coating,** coat; **veneer, facing,** veneering, revetment; pellicle, **film, scum,** skin, scale; slick, oil slick; varnish, enamel, lacquer, paint 35.14

13 **plating,** plate, cladding; nickel plate, silver plate, gold plate, copperplate, chromium plate, anodized aluminum; electroplate, electroplating, electrocoating

14 **crust, incrustation** or encrustation, shell; piecrust, pastry shell; lithosphere, stalactite, stalagmite; scale, scab, eschar

15 **shell,** seashell, lorication, lorica, conch; test, testa, episperm, pericarp, elytron, scute, scutum; operculum; exoskeleton; **armor,** mail, **shield; carapace,** plate, chitin, scale, scute; **protective covering,** cortex, thick skin or hide, elephant skin

16 **hull,** shell, pod, capsule, case, **husk, shuck;** cornhusk, corn shuck; bark, jacket; chaff, bran, palea; seed coat; germ

17 **case,** casing, encasement; **sheath,** sheathing

18 **wrapper,** wrapping, gift wrapping, gift wrap, wrap; wrapping paper, tissue paper, waxed paper, aluminum foil, tin foil, plastic wrap, clingfilm <Brit>, cellophane; **binder,** binding; **bandage,** bandaging; **envelope,** envelopment; **jacket,** jacketing; dust jacket or cover

VERBS 19 **cover,** cover up; apply to, **put on,** lay on; **superimpose,** superpose; **lay over,** overlay; **spread over,** overspread; **clothe, cloak,** mantle, muffle, blanket, canopy, cope, cowl, hood, **veil,** curtain, **screen, shield,** screen off, mask, cloud, obscure, fog, befog, fuzz; block, eclipse, occult; film, film over, scum

20 **wrap,** enwrap, wrap up, wrap about or around; **envelop, sheathe;** surround, encompass, lap, smother, enfold, embrace, invest; shroud, enshroud; swathe, swaddle; **box, case,** encase, **crate,** pack, embox; containerize; **package,** encapsulate

21 **top, cap,** tip, crown; put the lid on, cork, stopper, plug; hood, hat, coif, bonnet; roof, roof in or over; ceil; dome, endome

22 **floor; carpet; pave,** causeway, cobblestone, flag, pebble; cement, concrete; **pave, surface,** pave over, repave, resurface; blacktop, tar, asphalt, metal <old>, macadamize

23 **face, veneer,** revet; **sheathe;** board, plank, weatherboard, clapboard, lath; shingle, shake; tile, stone, brick, slate; thatch; glass, glaze, fiberglass; paper, wallpaper; wall in or up

24 **coat,** spread on, **spread with;** smear, **smear on,** besmear, slap on, dab, daub, bedaub, plaster, beplaster; flow on, pour on; lay on, lay it on thick, slather; undercoat, prime; paint, enamel, gild, gloss, lacquer; butter; tar; wallpaper

25 **plaster,** parget, stucco, cement, concrete, mastic, grout, mortar; face, line; roughcast, pebble-dash, spatter-dash

26 **plate,** chromium-plate, copperplate, gold-plate, nickel-plate, silver-plate; **electroplate, galvanize,** anodize

27 **crust, incrust,** encrust; loricate; effloresce; scab, scab over

28 **upholster,** overstuff

29 **re-cover,** reupholster, recap

30 **overlie,** lie over; **overlap,** lap, **lap over,** override, imbricate, jut, shingle; **extend over,** span, bridge, bestride, bestraddle, arch over, overarch, hang over, overhang

ADJS 31 **covered,** covert, under cover; **cloaked,** mantled, blanketed, muffled, canopied, coped, cowled, hooded, **shrouded, veiled,** clouded, obscured, fogged, fogged in; eclipsed, occulted, curtained, **screened,** screened-in, screened-off; shielded, masked; **housed;** tented, under canvas; roofed, roofed-in or -over, domed; walled, walled-in; **wrapped,** enwrapped, jacketed, **enveloped,** sheathed, swathed; **boxed, cased,** encased, encapsuled or encapsulated, **packaged; coated,** filmed, filmed-over, scummed; shelled, loricate, loricated; armored; ceiled; **floored; paved, surfaced;** plastered, stuccoed

32 **cutaneous,** cuticular; skinlike, skinny; skin-deep; **epidermal,** epidermic, dermal, dermic; ectodermal, ectodermic; endermic, endermatic; cortical; epicarpal; testaceous; hairy, furry 3.24; integumental, integumentary, tegumentary, tegumental, tegmental; vaginal; thecal

33 **plated,** chromium-plated, copperplated, gold-plated, nickel-plated, silver-plated; electroplated, galvanized, anodized

34 upholstered, overstuffed

35 **covering, coating;** cloaking, blanketing, shrouding, obscuring, **veiling, screening,** shielding, sheltering; wrapping, **enveloping,** sheathing

36 **overlying,** incumbent, superincumbent, superimposed; **overlapping,** lapping, shingled,

equitant; imbricate, imbricated; spanning, bridging; overarched, overarching

PREPS **37 on, upon, over,** o'er, **above, on top of**

296 LAYER

NOUNS **1 layer,** thickness; **level, tier,** stage, story, floor, gallery, step, ledge, deck, row, landing; **stratum,** strata, seam, *couche* <Fr>, vein, lode, belt, band, **bed, course,** measures; zone; shelf; **overlayer, superstratum,** overstory, topsoil, topcoat; **underlayer, substratum,** understratum, understory, underlay, undercoat; bedding; cultural layer, occupation layer, living floor

2 lamina, lamella; **sheet,** leaf, *feuille* <Fr>, foil; wafer, disk; **plate,** plating, cladding; covering 295, **coat,** coating, veneer, film, patina, scum, membrane, pellicle, sheathe, peel, skin, rind, hide; slick, oil slick; **slice,** cut, rasher, collop, sliver; **slab,** plank, deal <Brit>, slat, tablet, table; panel, pane; **fold,** lap, flap, **ply,** plait; laminate; laminated glass, safety glass; laminated wood, plywood, layered fiberglass; liner

3 flake, flock, floccule, flocculus; **scale, scurf,** dandruff, squama; chip; shaving, paring, swarf

4 stratification, layering, **lamination,** lamellation, sequence; foliation; delamination, exfoliation; desquamation, furfuration; flakiness, scaliness

VERBS **5 layer,** lay down, lay up, **stratify,** arrange in layers *or* levels *or* strata *or* tiers, **laminate;** shingle, sandwich; flake, scale; delaminate, desquamate, exfoliate; interface

ADJS **6 layered,** in layers; **laminated,** laminate, laminous; lamellated, lamellate, lamellar, lamelliform; plated, coated; veneered, faced; two-ply, three-ply, etc; two-level, bilevel, three-level, trilevel, etc; one-story, single story, two-story, double-story, etc; **stratified,** stratiform, straticulate; foliated, foliaceous, leaflike; terraced, multistage

7 flaky, flocculent, floccose; **scaly,** scurfy, squamous, lentiginous, furfuraceous, lepidote; scabby, scabious, scabrous

WORD ELEMENTS **8** strati-, lamin-, lamino-, lamini-, lamell-, lamelli-

297 WEIGHT

NOUNS **1 weight, heaviness, weightiness, ponderousness,** ponderosity, ponderability, leadenness, heftiness *and* heft <nf>; body weight, avoirdupois <nf>, fatness 257.8, beef *and* beefiness <nf>, heft, chunk; poundage, tonnage; deadweight, live weight; gross weight, gr wt; **net weight,** neat weight, nt wt, net, nett <Brit>;

short-weight; underweight; overweight; overbalance, overweightage; **solemnity, gravity** 111.1, 580.1

2 onerousness, **burdensomeness, oppressiveness, deadweight, overburden, cumbersomeness,** cumbrousness; massiveness, massiness <old>, bulkiness 257.9, lumpishness, unwieldiness

3 <sports> bantamweight, featherweight, flyweight, heavyweight, light heavyweight, lightweight, middleweight, cruiser weight, welterweight; catchweight; fighting weight; jockey weight

4 counterbalance 900.4; makeweight; **ballast,** ballasting

5 <physics terms> **gravity, gravitation, G,** supergravity; specific gravity; gravitational field, gravisphere; gravitational pull; graviton; geotropism, positive geotropism, apogeotropism, negative geotropism; G suit, anti-G suit; **mass;** atomic weight, molecular weight, molar weight; quagma

6 weight, paperweight, letterweight; sinker, lead, plumb, plummet, bob; sash weight; sandbag

7 burden, burthen <old>, pressure, **oppression, deadweight;** burdening, saddling, charging, taxing; overburden, overburdening, overtaxing, overweighting, weighing *or* weighting down; charge, **load,** loading, lading, freight, cargo, bale, ballast; cumber, cumbrance, **encumbrance;** incubus; incumbency *or* superincumbency <old>; handicap, drag, millstone; surcharge, overload

8 <systems of weight> avoirdupois weight, troy weight, apothecaries' weight; atomic weight, molecular weight; **pound, ounce, gram** etc, **unit of weight** <see list>

9 weighing, hefting <nf>, balancing; weighing-in, weigh-in, weighing-out, weigh-out; **scale,** weighing instrument

VERBS **10 weigh,** weight; **heft** <nf>, **balance,** weigh in the balance, strike a balance, hold the scales, put on the scales, lay in the scales; **counterbalance; weigh in,** weigh out; be heavy, weigh heavy, lie heavy, have weight, carry weight; **tip the scales,** turn *or* depress *or* tilt the scales, tip the balance

11 weigh on *or* **upon,** rest on *or* upon, bear on *or* upon, lie on, press, press down, press to the ground

12 weight, weigh *or* **weight down;** hang like a millstone; **ballast;** lead, sandbag

13 burden, burthen <old>, **load,** load down *or* up, lade, cumber, **encumber, charge, freight,** tax, handicap, hamper, saddle; **oppress, weigh one down, weigh on** *or* **upon, weigh heavy on,** bear *or* rest hard upon, lie hard *or* heavy upon, press hard upon, be an incubus to; **overburden,** overweight, overtax, **overload** 993.15

14 outweigh, overweigh, overweight, overbalance, **outbalance,** outpoise, overpoise

15 gravitate, descend 194.5, drop, plunge 367.6, precipitate, sink, settle, subside; tend, tend to go, **incline,** point, head, lead, lean

ADJS **16 heavy, ponderous, massive,** massy, weighty, hefty <nf>, bulky, fat 257.18; **leaden,** heavy as lead; deadweight; heavyweight; overweight; **solemn, grave** 111.3/580.8

17 onerous, oppressive, burdensome, incumbent *or* superincumbent, **cumbersome,** cumbrous; massive; lumpish, **unwieldy;** ponderous

18 weighted, weighed *or* **weighted down; burdened, oppressed, laden,** cumbered, **encumbered,** charged, loaded, fraught, freighted, taxed, saddled, hampered; **overburdened,** overloaded, overladen, overcharged, overfreighted, overfraught, overweighted, overtaxed; borne-down, sinking, foundering

19 weighable, ponderable; **appreciable,** palpable, sensible

20 gravitational, mass

ADVS **21 heavily,** heavy, weightily, leadenly; burdensomely, onerously, oppressively; **ponderously,** cumbersomely, cumbrously

22 units of weight or force or mass

assay ton	metric ton *or* MT *or* t
carat *or* c	microgram *or* mcg
carat grain	milligram *or* mg
centigram *or* cg	mole *or* mol
dead-weight ton	myriagram *or* myg
decagram *or* dkg *or*	net ton
decigram *or* dg	newton
displacement ton	ounce *or* ounce
dram *or* dram avoirdupois	avoirdupois *or* oz *or*
or dr	oz av
dram apothecaries' *or*	ounce apothecaries' *or*
dr ap	oz ap
dyne	ounce troy *or* oz t
grain *or* gr	pearl grain
gram *or* g	pennyweight *or* dwt *or* pwt
gram equivalent *or* gram	pound *or* pound avoirdu-
equivalent weight	pois *or* lb *or* lb av
gram molecule *or*	poundal
gram-molecular weight	pound apothecaries'
gross ton	*or* lb ap
hectogram *or* hg	pound troy *or* lb t
hundredweight *or* cwt	quintal *or* q
international carat	scruple *or* s ap
kilogram *or* kilo *or* kg	shipping ton
kiloton	short hundredweight
long hundredweight	short ton *or* st
long ton *or* lt	slug
measurement ton	sthene
megaton	stone *or* st
metric carat	ton *or* tn

298 LIGHTNESS

NOUNS **1 lightness, levity,** unheaviness, lack of weight; **weightlessness; buoyancy,** buoyance, floatability; levitation, ascent 193; **volatility; airiness,** ethereality; foaminess, frothiness, bubbliness, yeastiness; downiness, fluffiness, gossameriness 1029.1; softness, gentleness, delicacy, daintiness, tenderness; light touch, gentle touch; frivolousness 923.1

2 <comparisons> air, ether, feather, down, thistledown, flue, fluff, fuzz, sponge, gossamer, cobweb, fairy, straw, chaff, dust, mote, cork, chip, bubble, froth, foam, spume

3 lightening, easing, **easement, alleviation, relief;** disburdening, **disencumberment,** unburdening, **unloading,** unlading, unsaddling, untaxing, unfreighting; unballasting

4 leavening, fermentation; leaven, ferment

5 <indeterminacy of weight> **imponderableness** *or* imponderability, unweighableness *or* unweighability; imponderables, imponderabilia

VERBS **6 lighten,** make light *or* lighter, reduce weight; unballast; **ease, alleviate, relieve; disburden, disencumber,** unburden, unload, unlade, off-load; **be light,** weigh lightly, have little weight, kick the beam; lose weight

7 leaven, raise, **ferment**

8 buoy, buoy up; float, float high, ride high, waft; **sustain, hold up,** bear up, uphold, upbear, uplift, upraise; refloat

9 levitate, rise, ascend 193.8; hover, **float**

ADJS **10 light,** unheavy, imponderous, lightweight; **weightless; airy, ethereal,** aeriform; **volatile;** frothy, foamy, spumy, spumous, spumescent, bubbly, yeasty; downy, feathery, fluffy, gossamery 1029.4; *soufflé* or *moussé* or *léger* <Fr>; light as air *or* a feather *or* gossamer, etc 298.2; **frivolous** 923.1/109.15; insubstantial

11 lightened, eased, unburdened, disburdened, disencumbered, unencumbered, relieved, alleviated, out from under, breathing easier; mitigated

12 light, gentle, soft, delicate, dainty, tender, **easy**

13 lightweight, bantamweight, featherweight; underweight

14 buoyant, floaty, floatable; floating, supernatant

15 levitative, levitational

16 lightening, easing, alleviating, alleviative, alleviatory, relieving, disburdening, unburdening, disencumbering

17 leavening, raising, **fermenting,** fermentative, working; yeasty, barmy; enzymic, diastatic

18 imponderable, unweighable

299 RARITY

<lack of density>

NOUNS **1 rarity,** rareness; **thinness, tenuousness,** tenuity; **subtlety,** subtility; **fineness,** slightness, flimsiness, **unsubstantiality** or **insubstantiality** 764; **ethereality,** airiness, immateriality, incorporeality, bodilessness, insolidity, low density; **diffuseness,** dispersedness, scatter, scatteredness; "such stuff as dreams are made on"—Shakespeare

2 rarefaction, attenuation, subtilization, etherealization; **diffusion,** dispersion, scattering; **thinning,** thinning-out, dilution, adulteration, watering, watering-down; decompression

VERBS **3 rarefy, attenuate,** thin, thin out; dilute, adulterate, water, water down, cut; subtilize, **etherealize; diffuse,** disperse, scatter; expand 259.4; decompress

ADJS **4 rare,** rarefied; **subtle; thin,** thinned, dilute, attenuated, attenuate; thinned-out, diluted, adulterated, watered, watered-down, cut; **tenuous, fine,** flimsy, slight, **unsubstantial** or **insubstantial** 764; **airy, ethereal,** vaporous, gaseous, windy; **diffused,** diffuse, dispersed, scattered; uncompact, uncompressed, decompressed

5 rarefactive, rarefactional

300 MEASUREMENT

NOUNS **1 measurement, measure;** mensuration, measuring, **gauging;** admeasurement; metage; **estimation,** estimate, rough measure, approximation, ballpark figure <nf>; **quantification,** quantitation, quantization; **appraisal,** appraisement, **stocktaking, assay,** assaying; **assessment,** determination, rating, valuation, evaluation; assizement, assize, sizing up <nf>; **survey,** surveying; triangulation; **instrumentation;** telemetry, telemetering; metric system; metrication; English system of measurement; calibration, correction, computation, calculation

2 measure, measuring instrument, **meter, instrument, gauge,** barometer, **rule, yardstick,** measuring rod or stick, **standard,** norm, canon, **criterion,** test, touchstone, check, benchmark; rule of thumb; **pattern,** model, type, prototype; **scale,** graduated or calibrated scale; meter-reading, reading, readout, value, degree, quantity; parameter

3 extent, quantity 244, degree 245, size 257, distance 261, length 267, breadth 269; **weight** 297

4 <measures> US liquid measure, British imperial liquid measure, US dry measure, British imperial dry measure, apothecaries' measure, linear measure <see list>, square measure, circular measure, cubic measure, volume measure <see list>, area measure <see list>, surface measure, surveyor's measure, land measure, board measure

5 coordinates, Cartesian coordinates, rectangular coordinates, polar coordinates, cylindrical coordinates, spherical coordinates, equator coordinates; latitude, longitude; altitude, azimuth; declination, right ascension; ordinate, abscissa

6 waterline; watermark, tidemark, floodmark, **high-water mark;** load waterline, load line mark, Plimsoll mark or line

7 measurability, mensurability, computability, determinability, quantifiability

8 science of measurement, **mensuration,** metrology

9 measurer, meter, gauger; **geodesist,** geodetic engineer; **surveyor,** land surveyor, quantity surveyor; topographer, cartographer, mapmaker, oceanographer, chorographer; **appraiser, assessor;** assayer; valuer, valuator, evaluator; estimator; quantifier, actuary; timekeeper

VERBS **10 measure, gauge, quantify,** quantitate, quantize, mete <old>, take the measure of, mensurate, triangulate, apply the yardstick to; **estimate,** make an approximation; **assess, rate, appraise, valuate, value,** evaluate, appreciate, prize; **assay;** size or size up <nf>, take the dimensions of; **weigh,** weigh 297.10; survey; plumb, probe, sound, fathom; span, pace, step; calibrate, graduate, grade; divide; caliper; meter; read the meter, take a reading, check a parameter; compute, calculate, reckon

11 measure off, mark off, lay off, set off, rule off; **step off,** pace off or out; **measure out,** mark out, lay out; put at

ADJS **12 measuring, metric, metrical,** mensural, mensurative, mensurational; valuative, valuational; **quantitative,** numerative; approximative, estimative; geodetic, geodetical, geodesic, geodesical, hypsographic, hypsographical, hypsometric, hypsometrical; topographic, topographical, chorographic, chorographical, cartographic, cartographical, oceanographic, oceanographical

13 measured, gauged, metered, **quantified;** quantitated, quantized; **appraised, assessed, valuated,** valued, rated, ranked; **assayed; surveyed,** plotted, mapped, admeasured, triangulated; known by measurement

14 measurable, mensurable, **quantifiable,** numerable, meterable, gaugeable, fathomable, **determinable,** computable, calculable; quantifiable, quantitatable, quantizable; estimable; assessable, appraisable, ratable; appreciable, perceptible, noticeable

ADVS **15 measurably, appreciably, perceptibly, noticeably**

16 linear measures

absolute angstrom	kilometer *or* km
Admiralty mile	land mile
angstrom *or* angstrom unit	league
or a *or* å *or* A *or* Å	light-year
arpent	line
astronomical unit	link *or* li
block	meter *or* m
board foot *or* bd ft	micron *or* µ
cable length	mil
centimeter *or* cm	mile *or* mi
chain *or* Gunter's chain *or*	millimeter *or* mm
chn	millimicron *or*
cubit	micromillimeter
decameter *or* dkm	myriameter *or* mym
decimeter *or* dm	nail
ell	nautical mile *or* naut mi
em	pace
en	palm
fathom *or* fthm	parsec
fingerbreadth *or* finger	perch
foot *or* ft	pica
footstep	point *or* pt
furlong *or* fur	pole *or* p
hand	rod *or* r
handbreadth *or*	statute mile *or* stat mi
handsbreadth	step
hectometer *or* hm	stride
inch *or* in	wavelength
international angstrom	yard *or* yd

17 volume measures

barrel	hectoliter *or* hl
bushel *or* bu	hogshead *or* hhd
centiliter *or* cl	jeroboam
cord *or* cd	jigger
cubic foot *or* yard *or* etc	kiloliter *or* kl
cubic meter	liquid pint *or* quart
cup	*or* etc
decaliter *or* dkl	liter *or* l
decastere *or* dks	magnum
deciliter *or* dl	milliliter *or* ml
drop	minim *or* min
dry pint *or* quart *or* etc	peck *or* pk
fifth	pint *or* pt
finger	pony
fluidounce *or* fl oz	quart *or* qt
fluidram *or* fl dr	stere *or* s
gallon *or* gal	tablespoon *or* tbs
gill *or* gi	teaspoon *or* tsp

18 area measures

acre *or* a *or* ac	rood
are *or* a	section *or* sec
arpent	square inch *or* foot *or* mile
centare *or* ca	*or* etc
hectare *or* ha	square meter *or* kilometer
perch	*or* etc
pole *or* p	

301 YOUTH

NOUNS **1 youth, youthfulness,** youngness, **juvenility,** juvenescence, tenderness, tender age, early years, school age, *jeunesse* <Fr>, jejuneness, prime of life, flower of life, salad days, springtime *or* springtide of life, seedtime of life, flowering time, bloom, florescence, budtime, younger days, school days, golden season of life, heyday of youth *or* of the blood, young blood, early days

2 childhood; boyhood; girlhood, maidenhood *or* maidenhead, puerility; puppyhood, calfhood; subteens, pre-teens

3 immaturity, undevelopment, inexperience, **callowness, unripeness,** greenness, rawness, naiveté, sappiness, freshness, juiciness, dewiness; **minority,** juniority, infancy, nonage

4 childishness, childlikeness, **puerility; boyishness,** boylikeness; **girlishness,** girl-likeness, maidenliness

5 infancy, babyhood, the cradle, the crib, the nursery, incunabula

6 adolescence, maturation, maturement, pubescence, **puberty;** nobility; pre-teen, tweenager

7 teens, teen years *or* age, teenagehood, **awkward age,** age of growing pains <nf>

VERBS **8** make young, youthen, **rejuvenate,** reinvigorate; turn back the clock

ADJS **9 young,** youngling, youngish, **juvenile,** juvenal, juvenescent, **youthful,** youthlike, in the flower *or* bloom of youth, blooming, florescent, flowering, dewy, fresh-faced; young-looking, well-preserved

10 immature, unadult; **inexperienced,** unseasoned, unfledged, new-fledged, fledgling, **callow, unripe,** ripening, unmellowed, **raw, green,** vernal, primaveral, dewy, juicy, sappy, budding, tender, virginal, intact, innocent, naive, ingenuous, **undeveloped,** growing, unformed, unlicked, wet *or* not dry behind the ears, unprepared; **minor,** underage, underaged; unformed

11 childish, childlike, kiddish <nf>, **puerile; boyish,** boylike, beardless; **girlish,** girl-like, maiden, maidenly; puppyish, puppylike, puplike, calflike, coltish, coltlike; knee-high

12 infant, infantile, infantine, **babyish,** baby; dollish, doll-like; kittenish, kittenlike; **newborn,** neonatal; in the cradle *or* crib *or* nursery, in swaddling clothes, in diapers, in nappies <Brit>, in arms, at the breast, tied to mother's apron strings

13 adolescent, pubescent, nubile, pre-teen

14 teenage, teenaged, teenish, **in one's teens;** sweet sixteen <nf>

15 junior, Jr; **younger,** puisne

302 YOUNGSTER

NOUNS **1 youngster,** young person, **youth, juvenile,**
youngling, young'un <nf>, juvenal <old>; **stripling,**
slip, sprig, sapling; fledgling; hopeful, young
hopeful; **minor,** infant; **adolescent,** pubescent;
teenager, teener, teenybopper <nf>, pre-teen,
tweenager <nf>, twenty-something, thirty-
something, young adult; junior, younger,
youngest, baby

2 young people, youth, young, **younger generation,**
rising *or* new generation, baby boomers *or*
boomers, Generation X, Generation Y, young
blood, young fry <nf>, *ragazze* <Ital>; **children,**
tots, childkind; small fry *and* **kids** *and* **little kids**
and little guys <nf>; boyhood, girlhood; babyhood

3 child; nipper, **kid** *and* kiddy *and* kiddo *and* kiddie
<nf>, **little one,** little fellow *or* guy, little bugger
<nf>, shaver *and* little shaver <nf>, little squirt <nf>,
tot, little tot, wee tot, pee-wee, tad *or* little tad,
tyke, mite, chit <nf>, innocent, little innocent,
moppet, poppet; darling, cherub, lamb, lambkin,
kitten, **offspring** 561.3

4 brat, urchin; minx, imp, puck, elf, gamin, little
monkey, **whippersnapper,** young whippersnapper,
enfant terrible <Fr>, little terror, holy terror;
spoiled brat; snotnose kid <nf>; juvenile delinquent,
JD <nf>, punk *and* punk kid <nf>

5 boy, lad, laddie, **youth,** manchild, manling, young
man, *garçon* <Fr>, *muchacho* <Sp>, schoolboy,
schoolkid <nf>, fledgling, hobbledehoy; fellow 76.5;
pup, puppy, whelp, cub, colt; master; sonny, sonny
boy; bud *and* buddy <nf>; bub *and* bubba <nf>;
buck, young buck; schoolboy

6 girl, girlie <nf>, **maid, maiden, lass,** girlchild,
lassie, young thing, young creature, young lady,
damsel in distress, **damsel,** damoiselle, demoiselle,
jeune fille <Fr>, *mademoiselle* <Fr>, *muchacha*
<Sp>, miss, missy, little missy, slip, wench <dial *or*
nf>, colleen <Irish>

7 <nf terms> **gal,** dame, **chick,** tomato, **babe** *or*
baby, **broad,** frail, **doll,** skirt, jill, chit, cutie, filly,
heifer; teenybopper *and* weenybopper <nf>

8 schoolgirl, schoolmaid, schoolmiss, junior miss,
preteen; subdebutante; bobbysoxer <nf>, **tomboy,**
hoyden, romp; piece <nf>, nymphet; virgin, *virgo
intacta* <L>

9 infant, baby, babe, babe in arms, little darling *or*
angel *or* doll *or* cherub, bouncing baby, puling
infant, mewling infant, babykins <nf>, baby
bunting; papoose, *bambino* <Ital>; **toddler;
suckling,** nursling, fosterling, weanling; neonate;
yearling, yearold; premature baby, preemie <nf>,
incubator baby; preschooler; crumbcruncher *and*
-cruncher *and* -grinder *and* -snatcher; rug rat *and*

carpet rat *and* rug ape *and* carpet ape *and*
curtain-climber <nf>

10 <animals> yearling, **fledgling,** birdling, nestling;
chick, chicky, chickling; **pullet,** fry, fryer;
duckling; gosling, cygnet; **kitten,** kit, catling; **pup,**
puppy, whelp; **cub; calf,** dogie, weaner; **colt,** foal,
filly; piglet, pigling, shoat; **lamb,** lambkin; kid,
yeanling; fawn; **tadpole,** polliwog; litter, nest,
brood, clutch, spawn, farrow

11 <plants> **sprout, seedling,** set; sucker, shoot, slip,
offshoot; **twig,** sprig, scion, sapling

12 <insects> **larva, chrysalis,** aurelia, **cocoon,** pupa,
grub; nymph, nympha; wriggler, wiggler;
caterpillar, maggot, grub

303 AGE
<time of life>

NOUNS **1 age,** years, "the measure of my days"—
Bible; time *or* stage of life; lifetime, lifespan, life
expectancy, timespan, longevity; seven ages of
man: infancy, childhood, youth, adolescence,
adulthood, middle age, maturity, old age,
declining years, senility

2 maturity, adulthood, majority, adultness, grown-
upness, maturation, matureness, full growth,
mature age, legal age, voting age, driving age,
drinking age, *legalis homo* <L>; age of consent;
ripeness, ripe age, riper years, full age *or* growth
or bloom, flower of age, **prime, prime of life,** age
of responsibility, age *or* years of discretion, age of
matured powers; **manhood,** man's estate, virility,
toga virilis <L>, masculinity, maleness, manliness;
womanhood, womanness, femininity, femaleness,
womanliness

3 seniority, eldership, deanship, primogeniture

4 middle age, middle life, meridian of life, the
middle years, the wrong side of forty, the
dangerous age, prime of life; change of life,
perimenopause, menopause, climacteric, midlife
crisis

5 old age, oldness, eld <old>, **elderliness,** senectitude,
senescence, agedness, advanced age *or* years;
superannuation, pensionable age, retirement age,
age of retirement; **ripe old age,** the golden years,
advanced years, senior citizenship, hoary age,
hoariness, gray *or* white hairs, grayness; **decline
of life,** declining years, youth deficiency, the vale
of years, threescore years and ten, "the downward
slope"— Seneca, "old age is fifteen years older
than I"—Bernard Baruch, the shady side <nf>;
sunset *or* twilight *or* evening *or* autumn *or*
winter of one's days; **decrepitude,** ricketiness,
infirm old age, infirmity of age, infirmity,
debility, caducity, feebleness; dotage, anecdotage,

second childhood; senility 922.10, anility; **longevity,** long life, length of years, green *or* hale old age

6 maturation, development, growth, ripening, blooming, blossoming, flourishing; **mellowing,** seasoning, tempering; **aging,** senescence

7 change of life, perimenopause, **menopause,** climacteric, grand climacteric, **midlife crisis**

8 geriatrics, gerontology, geriatric medicine

VERBS **9 mature, grow up,** grow, **develop, ripen,** flower, flourish, bloom, blossom; fledge, leave the nest, put up one's hair, not be in pigtails, put on long pants; **come of age,** come to maturity, attain majority, **reach one's majority,** reach twenty-one, reach voting age, reach the age of consent, reach manhood *or* womanhood, write oneself a man, come to *or* into man's estate, put on long trousers *or* pants, assume the toga virilis, come into years of discretion, be in the prime of life, cut one's wisdom teeth *or* eyeteeth <nf>, have sown one's wild oats, settle down; **mellow,** season, temper

10 age, grow old, senesce, get on *or* along, **get on *or* along in years,** grow *or* have whiskers, be over the hill <nf>, turn gray *or* white; **decline,** wane, fade, fail, sink, waste away; **dodder,** totter, shake; wither, wrinkle, shrivel, wizen; **live to a ripe old age,** cheat the undertaker <nf>; be in one's dotage *or* second childhood

11 have had one's day, have seen one's day *or* best days, **have seen better days; show one's age,** show marks of age, have one foot in the grave

ADJS **12 adult, mature, of age,** out of one's teens, big, grown, **grown-up;** old enough to know better; **marriageable,** of marriageable age, marriable, nubile

13 mature, ripe, ripened, of full *or* ripe age, **developed,** fully developed, well-developed, **full-grown,** full-fledged, fully fledged, full-blown, in full bloom, in one's prime; **mellow *or*** mellowed, seasoned, tempered, aged

14 middle-aged, mid-life, *entre deux âges* <Fr>, fortyish, matronly; perimenopausal, menopausal

15 past one's prime, senescent, on the shady side <nf>, overblown, overripe, of a certain age, over the hill <nf>

16 aged, elderly, old, grown old in years, along *or* up *or* advanced *or* on in years, years old, advanced, advanced in life, **at an advanced age, ancient,** geriatric, gerontic; **venerable,** old as Methuselah *or* as God *or* as the hills; patriarchal; hoary, hoar, **gray,** white, gray- *or* white-headed, gray- *or* white-haired, gray- *or* white-crowned, gray- *or* white-bearded, gray *or* white with age; wrinkled, prune-faced <nf>; wrinkly, with crow's feet, marked with the crow's foot

17 aging, growing old, senescent, **getting on *or* along,** getting on *or* along *or* up in years, not as young as one used to be, long in the tooth; **declining,** sinking, waning, fading, wasting, doting

18 stricken in years, decrepit, infirm, weak, debilitated, feeble, geriatric, timeworn, the worse for wear, rusty, moth-eaten *or* mossbacked <nf>, fossilized, wracked *or* ravaged with age, run to seed; **doddering,** doddery, doddered, tottering, tottery, rickety, shaky, palsied; on one's last legs, with one foot in the grave; **wizened,** crabbed, **withered,** shriveled, like a prune, mummylike, papery-skinned; **senile** 922.23, anile

304 ADULT OR OLD PERSON

NOUNS **1 adult, grownup,** mature man *or* woman, grown man *or* woman, big boy *and* big girl <nf>; **man, woman;** major, *legalis homo* <L>; no chicken *and* no spring chicken <nf>

2 old man, elder, oldster <nf>; golden-ager, senior citizen, geriatric, patron; old chap, old party, **old gentleman,** old gent <nf>, codger *and* old codger <nf>, geezer *and* old geezer <nf>, gramps <nf>, gaffer, old duffer <nf>, old dog *and* old-timer <nf>, dotard, veteran, pantaloon, man of the world; **patriarch,** graybeard *or* greybeard, reverend *or* venerable sir; grandfather, grandsire; Father Time, Methuselah, Nestor, Old Paar; sexagenarian, septuagenarian, octogenarian, nonagenarian, centenarian; curmudgeon; eld <nf>

3 old woman, old lady, dowager, granny, old granny, dame, **grandam,** matron, matriarch, trot *and* old trot <nf>; old dame *and* hen *and* girl <nf>; old bag *and* bat *and* battleax *and* witch <nf>; old maid; **crone,** hag, witch, beldam, frump <nf>, old wife; grandmother; woman of the world

4 <old people> the old, older generation, seniors, retirees, over-the-hill gang <nf>; Darby and Joan, Baucis and Philemon

5 senior, Sr, *senex* <L>, **elder,** older; dean, *doyen* <Fr>, *doyenne* <Fr>; father, sire; firstling, first-born, **eldest,** oldest

VERBS **6 mature** 303.9; grow old 303.10

ADJS **7 mature** 303.12; middle-aged 303.14; aged 303.16, older 842.19

305 ORGANIC MATTER

NOUNS **1 organic matter,** animate *or* living matter, all that lives, living nature, organic nature, organized matter; **biology** 1068; **flesh, tissue,** fiber, brawn, plasm; **flora and fauna,** plant and animal life, animal and vegetable kingdom, biosphere, biota, ecosphere, noosphere; force of nature

2 organism, organization, organic being, life-form, form of life, **living being** *or* **thing,** being, animate being, creature, created being, **individual,** genetic individual, physiological individual, morphological individual; zoon, zooid; virus; aerobic organism, anaerobic organism; heterotrophic organism, autotrophic organism; microbe, microorganism

3 biological classification, taxonomy, biotaxy, kingdom, phylum, etc

4 cell, bioplast, cellule; procaryotic cell, eucaryotic cell; plant cell, animal cell; germ cell, somatic cell; corpuscle; unicellularity, multicellularity; germ layer, ectoderm, endoderm, mesoderm; **protoplasm,** energid; trophoplasm; chromatoplasm; germ plasm; cytoplasm; ectoplasm, endoplasm; cellular tissue, reticulum; plasmodium, coenocyte, syncytium

5 organelle; plastid; chromoplast, plastosome; chloroplast; mitochondrion; Golgi apparatus; ribosome; spherosome, microbody; vacuole; central apparatus, cytocentrum; centroplasm; centra body, microcentrum; centrosome; centrosphere; centriole, basal body; pili, cilia, flagella, spindle fibers; aster; kinoplasm; plasmodesmata; cell membrane

6 metaplasm; cell wall, cell plate; structural polysaccharide; bast, phloem, xylem, xyl- *or* xylo-, cellulose, chitin

7 nucleus, cell nucleus; macronucleus, meganucleus; micronucleus; nucleolus; plasmosome; karyosome, chromatin strands; nuclear envelope; chromatin, karyotin; basichromatin, heterochromatin, oxychromatin

8 chromosome; allosome; heterochromosome, sex chromosome, idiochromosome; W chromosome; X chromosome, accessory chromosome, monosome; Y chromosome; Z chromosome; euchromosome, autosome; homologous chromosomes; univalent chromosome, chromatid; centromere; gene-string, chromonema; genome; chromosome complement; chromosome number, diploid number, haploid number; polyploidy

9 genetic material, gene; allele; operon; cistron, structural gene, regulator gene, operator gene; altered gene; deoxyribonucleic acid *or* **DNA;** DNA double helix, superhelix *or* supercoil; nucleotide, codon; ribonucleic acid *or* **RNA;** messenger RNA, mRNA; transfer RNA, tRNA; ribosomal RNA; anticodon; gene pool, gene complex, gene flow, genetic drift; genotype, biotype; **hereditary character,** heredity 560.6; genetic counseling; genetic screening; **recombinant DNA technology,** gene mapping, gene splicing; gene transplantation,

gene transfer, germline insertion; intronizing, intron *or* intervening sequence; exonizing, exon; **genetic engineering,** genetic fingerprinting; designer gene

10 gamete, germ cell, reproductive cell; macrogamete, megagamete; microgamete; planogamete; genetoid; gamone; gametangium, gametophore; gametophyte; germ plasm, idioplasm

11 sperm, spermatozoa, seed, semen, jism *or* gism *and* come *or* cum *and* scum *and* spunk <nf>; seminal *or* spermatic fluid, milt; **sperm cell,** male gamete; spermatozoon, spermatozoid, antherozoid; antheridium; spermatium, spermatiophore *or* spermatophore, spermagonium; pollen; spermatogonium; androcyte, spermatid, spermatocyte

12 ovum, egg, egg cell, female gamete, oösphere; oöcyte; oögonium; ovicell, oöecium; ovule; stirp; ovulation; donor egg

13 spore; microspore; macrospore, megaspore; swarm spore, zoospore, planospore; spore mother cell, sporocyte; zygospore; sporocarp, cystocarp; basidium; sporangium, megasporangium, microsporangium; sporocyst; gonidangium; sporogonium, sporophyte; sporophore; sorus

14 embryo, zygote, oösperm, oöspore, blastula; *Anlage* <Ger>; **fetus,** germ, germen <old>, rudiment; **larva,** nymph

15 egg; ovule; bird's egg; roe, fish eggs, caviar, spawn; **yolk,** yellow, vitellus; white, **egg white,** albumen, glair; eggshell

16 cell division; mitosis; amitosis; metamitosis; eumitosis; endomitosis, promitosis; haplomitosis; mesomitosis; karyomitosis; karyokinesis; interphase, prophase, metaphase, anaphase, telophase, diaster, cytokinesis; **meiosis**

ADJS **17 organic,** organismic; organized; **animate, living,** vital, zoetic; **biological,** biotic; physiological

18 protoplasmic, plasmic, plasmatic; **genetic,** genic, hereditary

19 cellular, cellulous; unicellular, multicellular; corpuscular

20 gametic, gamic, sexual; **spermatic,** spermic, **seminal,** spermatozoal, spermatozoan, spermatozoic; sporal, sporous, sporoid; sporogenous

21 nuclear, nucleal, nucleary, nucleate; multinucleate; nucleolar, nucleolate, nucleolated; **chromosomal;** chromatinic; haploid, diploid, polyploid

22 embryonic, germinal, germinant, germinative, germinational; larval; fetal; in the bud; germiparous

23 egglike, ovicular, eggy; ovular; albuminous, albuminoid; yolked, yolky; oviparous

306 LIFE

NOUNS **1 life, living, vitality,** being alive, having life, animation, animate existence; breath; liveliness, animal spirits, vivacity, spriteliness; long life, longevity; life expectancy, life-span; viability; lifetime 827.5; immortality 829.3; birth 1; existence 761

2 life force, soul, spirit, indwelling spirit, force of life, living force, *vis vitae* or *vis vitalis* <L>, **vital force** or energy, animating force or power or principle, inspiriting force or power or principle, archeus, élan vital, impulse of life, vital principle, **vital spark** or **flame,** spark of life, divine spark, life principle, vital spirit, vital fluid, anima, consciousness; **breath,** life breath, **breath of life,** breath of one's nostrils, divine breath, life essence, essence of life, pneuma; prana, atman, jivatma, jiva; blood, **lifeblood,** heartblood, heart's blood; **heart,** heartbeat, beating heart; seat of life; growth force, bathmism; **life process;** biorhythm, biological clock, internal clock; life cycle

3 the living, the living and breathing, all animate nature, the quick; the quick and the dead

4 living being, human being, living person, entity, living soul, living thing; life on earth; survivor; the quick

5 life cycle, **lifetime,** longevity, life expectancy

6 vivification, vitalization, animation, quickening

7 biosphere, ecosphere, noosphere; biochore, biotype, biocycle

VERBS **8 live,** be alive or animate or vital, have life, exist 761.8, be, breathe, respire, live and breathe, fetch or draw breath, draw the breath of life, walk the earth, subsist

9 come to life, come into existence or being, come into the world, see the light, be incarnated, **be born** or begotten or conceived; quicken; **revive, come to,** come alive, come around, regain consciousness, show signs of life; **awake, awaken;** rise again, live again, rise from the grave, resurge, resurrect, resuscitate, reanimate, return to life

10 vivify, vitalize, energize, animate, quicken, inspirit, invigorate, enliven, imbue or endow with life, give birth to, give life to, put life or new life into, breathe life into, give a new lease on life, bring to life, bring or call into existence or being; conceive; give birth, reproduce

11 keep alive, feed, nourish, provide for, keep body and soul together, endure, survive, persist, last, last out, hang on, hang in <nf>, be spared, come through, continue, carry on, have nine lives; support life; cheat death

ADJS **12 living, alive,** having life, live, very much alive, alive and well, alive and kicking <nf>, conscious, breathing, quick <old>, **animate,** animated, **vital,** viable, zoetic, instinct with life, imbued or endowed with life, vivified, enlivened, inspirited; in the flesh, among the living, in the land of the living, on this side of the grave, still with us, still breathing, above-ground, incarnate; existent 761.13; extant; long-lived, tenacious of life; capable of life or survival, viable

13 life-giving, animating, animative, quickening, vivifying, energizing

307 DEATH

NOUNS **1 death, dying,** somatic death, clinical death, biological death, abiosis, **decease, demise;** brain death; perishing, release, **passing away,** passing, passing over, leaving life, making an end, departure, parting, going, going off or away, exit, ending, **end** 820, end of life, cessation of life, end of the road or line <nf>; **loss of life,** no life, ebb of life, expiration, expiry, **dissolution, extinction,** bane, annihilation, extinguishment, quietus; doom, crack of doom, summons of death, final summons, sentence of death, death knell, knell; **sleep, rest,** eternal rest or sleep, last sleep, last rest; **grave** 309.16; reward, debt of nature, last debt; last muster, last roundup, curtains <nf>, big sleep <nf>; jaws of death, hand or finger of death, shadow or shades of death; clinical death; rigor mortis; near-death experience or NDE; the beyond, the other side, the Great Divide

2 <personifications and symbols> **Death, Grim Reaper,** Reaper; pale horse, pale rider; angel of death, death's bright angel, Azrael; scythe or sickle of Death; **skull,** death's-head, grinning skull, crossbones, skull and crossbones; *memento mori* <L>; white cross; great leveler, thief in the night, Last Summoner; shadow of death, dance of death

3 river of death, Styx, Stygian shore, Acheron; Jordan, Jordan's bank; "valley of the shadow of death"—Bible; Heaven 681; Hell 682

4 early death, early grave, **untimely end,** premature death; sudden death; stroke of death, death stroke; deathblow

5 violent death; killing 308; suffocation, smothering, smotheration <nf>; asphyxiation; choking, choke, strangulation, strangling; drowning, watery grave; fatal accident, accidental death; starvation; liver death, serum death; megadeath; suicide, assisted suicide; murder, assassination; capital punishment, execution

6 natural death; easy or quiet or peaceful death or end, euthanasia, blessed or welcome release; stillbirth

7 dying day, deathday, "the supreme day and the

inevitable hour"—Virgil; final *or* fatal *or* last hour, dying hour, running-out of the sands, deathtime

8 moribundity, extremity, last *or* final extremity; **deathbed;** deathwatch; death struggle, agony, last agony, death agony, death throes, throes of death; last breath *or* gasp, dying breath; **death rattle,** death groan; making an end, passing, passing away, crossing the Styx; extreme unction, last rites

9 **swan song,** *chant du cygne* <Fr>, death song, final words, last words

10 **bereavement** 473.1

11 **deathliness,** deathlikeness, deadliness; **weirdness, eeriness, uncanniness,** unearthliness; ghostliness, ghostlikeness; **ghastliness, grisliness, gruesomeness,** macabreness; paleness, haggardness, wanness, luridness, pallor; cadaverousness, corpselikeness; *facies Hippocratica* <L>, Hippocratic face *or* countenance, mask of death

12 **death rate,** death toll; **mortality,** mortalness, mortality rate; extinction, dissolution, abiosis transience 828; mutability 854.1

13 **obituary,** obit <nf>, death notice, necrology, necrologue; register of deaths, roll of the dead, death roll, mortuary roll, bill of mortality; fatality list, casualty list; martyrology; death toll, body count

14 terminal case; **dying**

15 **corpse,** dead body, dead man *or* woman, dead person, **cadaver, carcass, body;** *corpus delicti* <L>; **stiff** <nf>; **the dead,** the defunct, **the deceased,** the departed, the loved one; **decedent,** the late lamented; **remains,** mortal *or* organic remains, remains, carrion, bones, skeleton, dry bones, relics, reliquiae; dust, ashes, earth, clay, tenement of clay; **carrion,** crowbait, food for worms; **mummy,** mummification; embalmed corpse

16 **dead,** the majority, the great majority; one's fathers, one's ancestors; the choir invisible

17 **autopsy, postmortem, inquest,** postmortem examination, ex post facto examination, necropsy, necroscopy; medical examiner, coroner, pathologist, mortality committee

VERBS **18** **die, decease, succumb, expire, perish,** be taken by death, up and die <nf>, cease to be *or* live, part, depart, quit this world, make one's exit, go, go the way of all flesh, go out, pass, pass on *or* over, **pass away, meet one's death** *or* **end** *or* **fate,** end one's life *or* days, depart this life, "shuffle off this mortal coil"—Shakespeare, put off mortality, lose one's life, fall, be lost, relinquish *or* surrender one's life, resign one's life *or* being, **give up the ghost,** yield the ghost *or* spirit, yield one's breath, take one's last breath, breathe one's last, stop breathing, fall asleep, close one's eyes, take one's

last sleep, pay the debt of *or* to nature, go out with the ebb, "go the way of all earth"—Bible, return to dust *or* the earth

19 <nf terms> **croak,** go west, kick the bucket, kick in, pop off, conk off, conk out, cop it, drop off, step off, go to the wall, go home feet first, knock off, pipe off, kick off, shove off, bow out, pass out, peg out, push up daisies, go for a burton <Brit>, belly up, go belly up, bite the dust, take the last count; flatline; check out, check in, cash in, hand *or* pass *or* cash in one's checks *or* chips; turn up one's toes; slip one's cable; buy the farm *or* the ranch, farm, have one's time *and* have it *and* buy it <Brit>

20 **meet one's Maker,** go to glory, go to kingdom come <nf>, go to the happy hunting grounds, go to *or* reach a better place *or* land *or* life *or* world, go to one's rest *or* reward, go home, go home feet first <nf>, go to one's last home, go to one's long account, go over to *or* join the majority *or* great majority, **be gathered to one's fathers,** join one's ancestors, join the angels, join the choir invisible, die in the Lord, go to Abraham's bosom, pass over Jordan, "walk through the valley of the shadow of death"—Bible, cross the Stygian ferry, give an obolus to Charon; awake to life immortal

21 **drop dead, fall dead,** fall down dead; come to an untimely end; predecease

22 die in harness, die with one's boots on, make a good end, die fighting, die in the last ditch, die like a man

23 die a natural death; die a violent death, be killed; **starve,** famish; smother, **suffocate;** asphyxiate; choke, strangle; **drown,** go to a watery grave, go to Davy Jones's locker <nf>; catch one's death, catch one's death of cold

24 **lay down** *or* **give one's life for one's country, die for one's country,** *"pro patria mori"*—Horace, make the supreme sacrifice, do one's bit

25 be dying, be moribund, be terminal; die out, become extinct

26 be dead, be no more, sleep *or* be asleep with the Lord, sleep with one's fathers *or* ancestors; lie in the grave, lie in Abraham's bosom <nf>

27 **bereave;** leave, leave behind; orphan, widow

ADJS **28** **deathly, deathlike,** deadly; **weird, eerie, uncanny,** unearthly; ghostly, ghostlike; **ghastly, grisly, gruesome, macabre;** pale, deathly pale, wan, lurid, blue, livid, haggard; **cadaverous,** corpselike; mortuary

29 **dead, lifeless,** breathless, without life, inanimate 1055.5, exanimate, without vital functions; **deceased, demised, defunct,** croaked <nf>, departed, departed this life, destitute of life, **gone, passed on,** passed away, gone the way of all flesh, gone west <nf>, extinct, gone before, long gone, dead and gone, done for <nf>, dead and done for

<nf>, no more, finished <nf>, taken off *or* away, released, fallen, bereft of life, gone for a burton <Brit nf>; **at rest,** resting easy <nf>, still, out of one's misery; **asleep,** sleeping, reposing; asleep in Jesus, with the Lord, asleep *or* dead in the Lord; **called home,** out of the world, gone to a better world *or* place *or* land, gone but not forgotten, launched into eternity, gone to glory, taken *or* called by God, at the Pearly Gates, in Abraham's bosom, joined the choir invisible, gone to kingdom come <nf>, with the saints, sainted, numbered with the dead; in the grave, deep-sixed <nf>, six feet under *and* pushing up daisies <nf>; carrion, food for worms; martyred; death-struck, death-stricken, smitten with death; stillborn, dead on arrival, DOA; late, late lamented

30 **stone-dead;** dead as a doornail *and* dead as a dodo *and* dead as a herring *and* dead as mutton <nf>; cold, stone-cold, "as cold as any stone"— Shakespeare, stiff <nf>

31 **drowned,** in a watery grave *or* bier, in Davy Jones's locker

32 **dying, terminal,** expiring, going, slipping, slipping away, sinking, sinking fast, fading, low, despaired of, given up, given up for dead, not long for this world, hopeless, bad, **moribund,** near death, deathlike, perishing, doomed, near one's end, at the end of one's rope <nf>, hanging by a thread, done for <nf>, at the point of death, **at death's door,** at the portals of death, *in articulo mortis* <L>, *in extremis* <L>, in the jaws of death, facing *or* in the face of death; **on one's last legs** <nf>, half-dead, with one foot in the grave, tottering on the brink of the grave; on one's deathbed; at the last gasp; in critical condition, mortally ill, terminal; nonviable, unviable, incapable of life

33 **mortal, perishable,** subject to death, ephemeral, transient 828.7, mutable 854.6

34 **bereaved,** bereft, deprived; widowed; orphan, **orphaned,** parentless, fatherless, motherless

35 **postmortem,** postmortal, postmortuary, postmundane, post-obit, postobituary, **posthumous**

ADVS 36 **deathly, deadly;** to the death, *à la mort* <Fr>

PHRS 37 one's hour is come, one's days are numbered, one's race is run, one's doom is sealed, life hangs by a thread, one's number is up, Death knocks at the door, Death stares one in the face, the sands of life are running out

308 KILLING

NOUNS 1 **killing** <see list>, **slaying, slaughter, dispatch, extermination, destruction, murder,** destruction of life, taking of life, death-dealing, dealing of death, bane; kill; **bloodshed,** bloodletting, blood, gore, flow of blood; mercy killing, euthanasia, negative *or* passive euthanasia; ritual murder *or* killing, immolation, sacrifice, religious sacrifice, crucifixion, martyrdom; *auto-da-fé* <Sp, literally, act of faith>, martyrdom, martyrization; lynching; stoning, lapidation; defenestration; braining; shooting, drive-by shooting; poisoning; execution 604.7; mass killing, biocide, ecocide, genocide; Holocaust; mass murder

2 **homicide, manslaughter; negligent homicide,** unlawful killing; **murder,** bloody murder <nf>, first-degree murder, second-degree murder, capital murder; serial killing; hit *and* bump-off *and* bumping-off *and* rubbing out *and* blowing away *and* wasting <nf>, gangland-style execution, contract murder; kiss of death; foul play; **assassination;** terrorist killing; crime of passion; removal, elimination; liquidation, purge, purging; thuggery, thuggism, thuggee; justifiable homicide

3 **butchery,** butchering, **slaughter,** shambles, occision, slaughtering, hecatomb, holocaust

4 **carnage, massacre, bloodbath, decimation,** saturnalia of blood; **mass murder, mass destruction,** mass extermination, wholesale murder, pogrom, race-murder, genocide, race extermination, ethnic cleansing, **the Holocaust,** the final solution, Roman holiday

5 **suicide,** autocide, self-murder, self-homicide, self-destruction, self-slaughter, death by one's own hand, *felo-de-se* <L>, self-immolation, self-sacrifice; slashing one's wrists, **disembowelment,** ritual suicide, self-immolation, *hara-kiri* and *seppuku* <Japanese>, suttee, sutteeism, kamikaze; car of Jagannath *or* Juggernaut; mass suicide, race suicide, suicide pact; suicide bombing

6 **suffocation,** smothering, smotheration <nf>, **asphyxiation,** asphyxia; **strangulation,** strangling, burking, throttling, stifling, garrote, garroting; **choking,** choke; **drowning**

7 **execution,** capital punishment, death penalty, legalized killing, judicial murder, judicial execution

8 **fatality,** fatal accident, violent death, **casualty,** disaster, calamity; DOA *or* dead-on-arrival

9 **deadliness, lethality,** mortality, fatality; **malignance** *or* malignancy, malignity, **virulence, perniciousness,** banefulness

10 **deathblow,** death stroke, final stroke, fatal *or* mortal *or* lethal blow, *coup de grâce* <Fr>

11 **killer, slayer, slaughterer, butcher,** bloodshedder; massacrer; **manslayer, homicide, murderer,** man-killer, bloodletter, man of blood, Cain; **assassin,** assassinator; **cutthroat,** thug, desperado,

bravo, gorilla <nf>, apache, gunman; professional killer, contract killer, hired killer, hit man *or* button man *or* gun *or* trigger man *or* torpedo *or* gunsel <nf>; **hatchet man;** poisoner; strangler, hangman, garroter, burker; cannibal, maneater, anthropophagus; headhunter; mercy killer, euthanasiast; thrill killer, psychopath, homicidal maniac; serial killer; executioner 604.8; matador; exterminator, eradicator; death squad; terrorist, bomber; poison, pesticide 1001.3

12 <place of slaughter> aceldama, field of blood *or* bloodshed; **slaughterhouse,** butchery <Brit>, shambles, abattoir; bullring, arena, battleground, battlefield; stockyard; gas chamber, concentration camp, death camp, killing fields; Auschwitz, Belsen, etc

VERBS **13 kill, slay, put to death,** deprive of life, bereave of life, **take life,** take the life of, take one's life away, **do away with,** make away with, **put out of the way,** put to sleep, end, **put an end to,** end the life of, hasten someone's end, **dispatch, do to death,** do for, finish, finish off, kill off, take off, **dispose of, exterminate, destroy,** annihilate; **liquidate,** purge; carry off *or* away, remove from life; put down, put away, put to sleep, put one out of one's misery; launch into eternity, send to glory, send to kingdom come <nf>, send to one's last account, send to one's Maker; **martyr,** martyrize; immolate, sacrifice; lynch; cut off, cut down, nip in the bud; poison; chloroform; starve; euthanatize; **execute**

14 <nf terms> **waste, zap,** nuke, rub out, croak, snuff, bump off, knock off, bushwhack, lay out, polish off, blow away, blot out, erase, wipe out, blast, do in, off, hit, ice, gun down, pick off, put to bed with a shovel, scrag, take care of, take out, take for a ride, give the business *or* works, deep-six, get, fix, settle

15 shed blood, spill blood, let blood, bloody one's hands with, dye one's hands in blood, have blood on one's hands, pour out blood like water, wade knee-deep in blood

16 murder, commit murder; **assassinate;** remove, **purge, liquidate,** eliminate, get rid of

17 slaughter, butcher, massacre, decimate, mow down, spare none, take no prisoners, wipe out, wipe off the face of the earth, annihilate, exterminate, liquidate, commit carnage, depopulate, murder *or* kill *or* slay en masse; purge, commit mass murder *or* destruction, murder wholesale, commit genocide, suicide-bomb

18 strike dead, fell, bring down, lay low; drop, drop *or* stop in one's tracks; **shoot,** shoot down, pistol, shotgun, machinegun, gun down, riddle, shoot to death; cut down, cut to pieces *or* ribbons, **put to**

the sword, stab to death, jugulate, cut *or* slash the throat; **deal a deathblow,** give the quietus *or* coup de grâce <Fr>, silence; knock in *or* on the head; **brain,** blow *or* knock *or* dash one's brains out, poleax; **stone,** lapidate, stone to death; defenestrate; blow up, blow to bits *or* pieces *or* kingdom come, frag; disintegrate, vaporize; burn to death, incinerate, burn at the stake

19 strangle, garrote, **throttle, choke,** burke; **suffocate, stifle, smother, asphyxiate,** stop the breath; **drown**

20 condemn to death, sign one's death warrant, strike the death knell of, finger <nf>, give the kiss of death to

21 be killed, get killed, die a violent death, **come to a violent end,** meet with foul play; welter in one's own blood

22 commit suicide, take one's own life, kill oneself, die by one's own hand, do away with oneself, put an end to oneself; blow one's brains out, take an overdose <of a drug>, overdose *or* OD <nf>; commit hara-kiri *or* seppuku; sign one's own death warrant, doom oneself; jump overboard, do oneself in *or* off oneself <nf>

ADJS **23 deadly, deathly,** deathful, **killing, destructive,** death-dealing, death-bringing, feral <old>, fell; savage, brutal; internecine; **fatal, mortal, lethal, malignant,** malign, **virulent, pernicious,** baneful; **life-threatening, terminal;** capital; incurable, terminal, inoperable

24 murderous, slaughterous; cutthroat; redhanded; **homicidal,** man-killing, death-dealing; biocidal, genocidal; suicidal, self-destructive; soul-destroying; cruel; **bloodthirsty,** bloody-minded; **bloody, gory,** sanguinary; psychopathic, pathological

25 types of killing and killers

aborticide *or* feticide <fetus>	homicide <person>
amicicide <friend>	infanticide <infant>
avicide <birds>	insecticide <insects>
biocide <chemical>	mariticide <spouse, especially husband>
ceticide <whales>	matricide <mother>
deicide <god>	microbicide *or* germicide <germs>
ecocide <large area>	
elephanticide <elephants>	ovicide <egg cell>
felicide <cats>	parenticide <parent>
formicicide <ants>	parricide <kinsman>
fratricide <brother>	patricide <father>
fungicide <fungi>	pesticide <pest>
genocide <race or ethnic group>	phytocide <plants>
	prolicide <own child>
giganticide <giant>	regicide <king>
gynecide *or* femicide <woman>	rodenticide <rodent>
	senicide <old person>
herbicide <plants>	sororicide <sister>

spermicide *or* spermaticide *or* spermatozoicide <spermatozoa>
suicide *or* autocide <self>
tauricide <bulls>
tickicide <ticks>

tyrannicide <tyrant>
uxoricide <wife>
vaticide <prophet>
vermicide *or* filaricide <worms>
vespacide <wasps>
viricide <viruses>

309 INTERMENT

NOUNS **1 interment, burial,** burying, inhumation, sepulture, **entombment;** encoffinment, inurning, inurnment, urn burial; primary burial; secondary burial, reburial; disposal of the dead; burial *or* funeral *or* funerary customs; mass burial, burial at sea, military burial, full military rites

2 cremation, incineration, burning, reduction to ashes, pyre, scattering of the ashes

3 embalmment, embalming; mummification

4 last offices, last honors, **last rites,** funeral rites, last duty *or* service, funeral service, funeral ceremony, burial service, graveside service, memorial service, exequies, **obsequies;** Office of the Dead, Memento of the Dead, requiem, requiem mass, dirge <old>; **extreme unction;** viaticum; funeral oration *or* sermon, eulogy; **wake,** deathwatch, Irish wake; lowering the body

5 funeral, burial, burying; funeral procession, cortege; dead march, muffled drum, last post <Brit>, taps; dirge; burial at sea, deep six <nf>

6 knell, passing bell, death bell, funeral ring, tolling, tolling of the knell, funeral hymn, dirge

7 mourner, griever, lamenter, keener; mute, professional mourner; **pallbearer,** bearer; eulogist, eulogizer, elegist, epitaphist, obituarist

8 undertaker, mortician, funeral director; embalmer; gravedigger; sexton

9 mortuary, morgue, deadhouse <old>, charnel house, lichhouse <Brit nf>; ossuary *or* ossuarium; **funeral home** *or* **parlor,** undertaker's establishment; **crematorium,** crematory, cinerarium; pyre, funeral pile; burning ghat

10 hearse, funeral car *or* coach; catafalque

11 coffin, casket, burial case, box, kist <Scot>; wooden kimono *or* overcoat <nf>; **sarcophagus;** mummy case

12 urn, cinerary urn, funerary *or* funeral urn *or* vessel, bone pot, ossuary *or* ossuarium, canopic urn *or* jar *or* vase

13 bier, litter

14 graveclothes, shroud, winding sheet, cerecloth, cerements; pall

15 graveyard, cemetery, burial ground *or* **place,** plot, family plot, burying place *or* ground, *campo santo* <Ital>, boneyard *and* bone orchard <nf>, burial yard, necropolis, god's acre, polyandrium, **memorial park,** city *or* village of the dead; **churchyard,** God's acre, final resting place; garden of remembrance *or* rest; **potter's field;** Golgotha, Calvary; urnfield; lych-gate; columbarium, cinerarium

16 tomb, sepulcher; grave, gravesite, burial, pit, deep six <nf>; resting place; last home, long home, narrow house, house of death, low house, low green tent; **crypt, vault,** burial chamber; ossuary *or* ossuarium; charnel house, bone house; **mausoleum; catacombs;** mastaba; cist grave, box grave, passage grave, shaft grave, beehive tomb; catafalque; **shrine,** reliquary, monstrance, tope, stupa; cenotaph; dokhma, tower of silence; pyramid, mummy chamber; burial mound, tumulus, barrow, cist, cromlech, dolmen, menhir, cairn, tower of silence; grave pit, common grave, mass grave, open grave

17 monument, gravestone 549.12

18 epitaph, inscription, *hic jacet* <L>, here lies, Rest in Peace, RIP; tombstone marking

VERBS **19 inter,** inhume, **bury,** sepulture, inearth <old>, **lay to rest, consign to the grave,** consign to earth, lower the body, lay in the grave *or* earth, lay under the sod, put six feet under <nf>; plant <nf>; tomb, **entomb,** ensepulcher, hearse; enshrine; inurn; encoffin, coffin; hold *or* conduct a funeral

20 cremate, incinerate, burn, reduce to ashes, burn on the pyre

21 lay out; embalm; mummify; lie in state

ADJS **22 funereal,** funeral, funerary, funebrial, funebrous *or* funebrious, *funèbre* <Fr>, feral <old>; burial, mortuary, exequial, obsequial; graveside; sepulchral, tomblike; cinerary; necrological, obituary, epitaphic; **dismal** 112.24; **mournful** 112.26; dirgelike; memorial, eulogistic, elegiac

ADVS **23** beneath the sod, underground, six feet under <nf>; at rest, resting in peace

PHRS **24 RIP,** *requiescat in pace* <L singular>, *requiescant in pace* <L plural>, rest in peace; *hic jacet* <L>, *ci-gît* <Fr>, here lies; "ashes to ashes and dust to dust"—Book of Common Prayer

310 PLANTS

NOUNS **1 plants, vegetation; flora, plant life,** vegetable life; **vegetable kingdom,** plant kingdom; herbage, flowerage, verdure, greenery, greens, green plants; botany 1068.6; vegetation spirit 1069.4

2 growth, stand, crop; plantation, planting; **clump,** tuft, tussock, hassock

3 plant, green plant; **vegetable; weed;** seedling;

cutting; vascular plant, herbaceous plant; seed plant, spermatophyte; gymnosperm; angiosperm, flowering plant; monocotyledon *or* monocot *or* monocotyl; dicotyledon *or* dicot *or* dicotyl; polycotyledon *or* polycot *or* polycotyl; thallophyte, fungus; gametophyte, sporophyte; exotic, hothouse plant, greenhouse plant; ephemeral, annual, biennial, triennial, perennial; evergreen, deciduous plant; cosmopolite; aquatic plant, hydrophyte, amphibian; cultivated plant, garden plant, houseplant, pot plant; food plant, cereal, vegetable, herb; medicinal plant

4 <varieties> **legume,** pulse, vetch, bean, pea, lentil; **herb** <see list>, pot-herb; succulent; **vine** <see list>, grapevine, creeper, ivy, climber, liana; **fern** <see list>, bracken; **moss; wort,** liverwort; **algae; seaweed,** kelp, sea moss, rockweed, gulfweed, sargasso *or* sargassum, sea lentil, wrack, sea wrack; **fungus,** mold, rust, smut, puffball, mushroom, toad-stool; lichen; parasitic plant, parasite, saprophyte, perthophyte, heterophyte, autophyte; plant families; fruits and vegetables

5 **grass,** gramineous *or* graminaceous plant, pasture *or* forage grass, lawn grass, ornamental grass; aftergrass, fog <nf>; **cereal,** cereal plant, farinaceous plant, **grain,** corn <Brit>; sedge; rush, reed, cane, bamboo

6 **turf, sod, sward,** greensward; divot

7 **green, lawn;** artificial turf, Astroturf <trademark>; grassplot, greenyard; grounds; **common, park, village green;** golf course *or* links, fairway; bowling green, putting green; grass court

8 **grassland,** grass; parkland; **meadow,** meadow land, field, mead <old>, swale, lea *or* ley, haugh *or* haughland <Scot>, vega; crop circle; bottomland, water meadow; **pasture,** pastureland, pasturage, pasture land, park <Brit nf>; **range,** grazing, grazing land; **prairie, savanna,** savannah, **steppe,** steppeland, **pampas,** pampa, campo, llano, **veld** *or* veldt, grass veld, plain, range, champaign, campagna; herbage, verdure; moor, moorland, common, heath, downs, downland, wold

9 **shrubbery; shrub, bush;** scrub, bramble, brier, brier bush; topiary

10 **tree** <see list>, timber; shade tree, fruit tree, timber tree; softwood tree, hardwood tree; sapling, seedling; conifer *or* coniferous tree, evergreen; pollard, pollarded tree, standard; deciduous tree, borad-leaved tree; ornamental tree; Christmas tree

11 <tree parts> trunk, bole, gnarl, knot, burl, burr, crown, limb, branch, bough, twig, switch, sprig, spur, leader, leaf, needle, cone, root, tree *or* annual *or* growth ring

12 <tree groupings> **forest,** tree line *or* zone, timberline, jungle, gallery forest, fringing forest, virgin forest, primeval forest, coniferous forest; taiga, woodland, chaparral, plantation, stand, timberland, tree farm, tree nursery, orchard, orangery

13 **woodland, wood, woods, timberland; timber,** stand of timber, **forest,** forest land, forest cover, forest preserve, state *or* national forest; forestry, dendrology, silviculture; afforestation, reforestation; boondocks <nf>; wildwood, **bush,** scrub; bushveld; tree veld; shrubland, scrubland; pine barrens, palmetto barrens; hanger; **park,** parkland, chase <Brit>; park forest; arboretum; conservation land, nature preserve; primeval forest

14 **grove, woodlet;** holt <nf>, hurst, spinney <Brit>, *tope* <India>, shaw <nf>, bosk <old>; **orchard;** wood lot; coppice, copse; *bocage* <Fr>

15 **thicket,** thickset, **copse, coppice,** copsewood, frith <Brit nf>; bosket *or* bosquet <old>, boscage; covert; motte; **brake,** canebrake; chaparral; chamisal; ceja

16 **brush, scrub,** bush, **brushwood,** shrubwood, scrubwood, shrub

17 **undergrowth, underwood, underbrush,** copsewood, undershrubs, boscage, frith <Brit nf>; ground cover, tree litter, leaf litter, leaf mold, covert

18 **foliage, leafage,** leafiness, umbrage, foliation; frondage, frondescence; vernation; greenery

19 **leaf, frond;** leaflet, foliole; ligule; lamina, **blade,** leaf blade, spear, spire, pile, flag; **needle,** pine needle; floral leaf, **petal,** sepal; bract, bractlet, bracteole, spathe, involucre, involucrum, glume, lemma; cotyledon, seed leaf; stipule, stipula; scale leaf, modified leaf

20 **branch,** fork, **limb, bough;** deadwood; **twig, sprig,** switch; spray; **shoot,** offshoot, spear, frond; scion; **sprout,** sprit, slip, burgeon, thallus; sucker; **runner,** stolon, flagellum, sarmentum, sarment; bine; **tendril;** ramage; branchiness, branchedness, ramification

21 **stem, stalk, stock,** axis, *caulis* <L>; **trunk,** bole; spear, spire; straw; reed; cane; culm, haulm <Brit>; caudex; footstalk, pedicel, peduncle; leafstalk, petiole, petiolus, petiolule; seedstalk; caulicle; tigella; funicule, funiculus; stipe, anthrophore, carpophore, gynophore

22 **root,** radix, radicle; rootlet; **taproot,** tap; **rhizome,** rootstock; **tuber,** tubercle, tuberous root, root tuber; **bulb,** bulbil, corm, earthnut; lateral root, prop root, aerial root

23 **bud,** burgeon, gemma; leaf bud, foliage bud; apical bud, terminal bud, axillary bud, lateral bud, resting bud; gemmule, gemmula; plumule, acrospire; leaf bud, flower bud

24 flower <see list>, **posy, blossom, bloom,** blow
<old>; floweret, floret, floscule; **wildflower;** garden
flower, pot plant, cut flowers; **gardening,**
horticulture, floriculture; hortorium; community
garden

25 bouquet, nosegay, posy, boughpot, flower
arrangement; **boutonniere,** buttonhole <Brit>;
corsage; spray; wreath; festoon; **garland,** daisy
chain, chaplet, lei; dried flower, pressed flower

26 flowering, florescence, efflorescence, flowerage,
blossoming, blooming; inflorescence; **blossom,
bloom,** blowing, blow, full blow; unfolding,
unfoldment; anthesis, full bloom

27 <types of inflorescence> flower head; raceme,
corymb, umbel, panicle, cyme, thyrse *or* thyrsus,
verticillaster, spadix, verticillaster; head,
capitulum; spike, spikelet; ament, catkin; strobile,
cone, pine cone; ray flower, disk flower, cymose
inflorescnce

28 <flower parts> petal, perianth, floral envelope;
calyx, epicalyx, sepal; nectary; corolla, corolla
tube, corona; androecium, anther, stamen,
microsporophyll; pistil, gynoecium, ovary, ovule,
micrypyle; style; stigma, carpel, megasporophyll;
receptacle, torus; involucre, bract, whorl, spathe;
pollen, pollen grain, pollen sac, pollen tube

29 ear, spike; auricle; ear of corn, mealie; **cob,**
corncob

30 seed vessel, seedcase, seedbox, pericarp; hull,
husk; **capsule, pod,** cod <nf>, seed pod, seed coat;
pease cod, legume, legumen, boll, burr, follicle,
silique

31 seed; stone, pit, nut; pip; fruit; **grain, kernel,
berry;** flaxseed, linseed; hayseed; bird seed

32 vegetation, growth; germination, pullulation;
burgeoning, sprouting; budding, luxuriation

33 <garden plants> seedling, cutting, bulb, corm,
rhizome, tuber; rock plant, alpine plant, bedding
plant, creeper, ground cover, turf, climber *or*
climbing plant, rambler; annual, biennial,
perennial; herb, flower, woody plant, succulent

VERBS **34 vegetate, grow;** germinate, pullulate; root,
take root, strike root; sprout up, shoot up,
upsprout, upspear; **burgeon,** put forth, burst
forth; **sprout,** shoot; **bud,** gemmate, put forth *or*
put out buds; **leaf,** leave, leaf out, put out *or* put
forth leaves; flourish, luxuriate, riot, grow rank *or*
lush; overgrow, overrun; run to seed, dehisce;
photosynthesize, change color

35 flower, be in flower, **blossom, bloom,** bud, be in
bloom, blow, effloresce, floreate, burst into bloom,
flourish, burgeon

ADJS **36 vegetable,** vegetal, vegetative, vegetational,
vegetarian; **plantlike; herbaceous,** herbal,
herbous, herbose, herby; leguminous, leguminose,

leguminiform; cereal, farinaceous; weedy; fruity,
fruitlike; tuberous, bulbous; rootlike, rhizoid,
radicular, radicated, radiciform; botanic,
botanical; green, grassy, leafy, verdant

37 algal, fucoid, confervoid; phytoplanktonic,
diatomaceous; fungous, fungoid, fungiform

38 floral; flowery, florid <old>; **flowered,** floreate,
floriate, floriated; **flowering, blossoming,
blooming,** abloom, bloomy, florescent, inflorescent,
efflorescent, in flower, in bloom, in blossom;
uniflorous, multiflorous; radiciflorous,
rhizanthous; **garden,** horticultural, hortulan,
floricultural; flowerlike

39 arboreal, arborical, arboresque, arboreous,
arborary, arboraceous; **treelike,** arboriform,
arborescent, dendroid, dendroidal, dendriform,
dendritic; deciduous, nondeciduous; evergreen;
softwood, hardwood; piny *or* piney; coniferous;
citrous; palmate, palmaceous; **bosky,** bushy,
shrubby, scrubby, scrubbly; bushlike, shrublike,
scrublike

40 sylvan, silvan, sylvatic, **woodland, forest,** forestal;
dendrologic, dendrological, silvicultural,
afforestational, reforestational, reforested;
tree-covered; **wooded,** timbered, forested,
afforested, timbered, arboreous; **woody,** woodsy,
bosky, bushy, shrubby, scrubby; copsy, braky;
ligneous, ligniform

41 leafy, leavy <old>, bowery; foliated, foliate, foliose,
foliaged, leaved; **branched,** branchy, branching,
ramified, ramate, ramous *or* ramose; twiggy

42 verdant, verdurous, verdured; **mossy,** moss-
covered, moss-grown; **grassy,** grasslike,
gramineous, graminaceous; turfy, swardy,
turflike, caespitose, tufted; meadowy

43 luxuriant, flourishing, **rank, lush,** riotous,
exuberant; dense, impenetrable, thick, heavy,
gross; jungly, jungled; overgrown, overrun; **weedy,**
unweeded, weed-choked, weed-ridden; gone to
seed

44 perennial, ephemeral; hardy, half-hardy;
deciduous, evergreen

45 herbs

angelica	chicory
anise	chive
balm	cilantro
basil	clover
belladonna	coriander
bergamot	cum(m)in
borage	deadly nightshade
calendula	dill
camomile	fennel
caraway	feverroot
cardamom	figwort
catnip *or* catmint	fraxinella *or* gas plant
chervil	garlic

ginseng
hemp
henbane
horehound
hyssop
licorice
liverwort
mandrake
marjoram
mint
monkshood
mullein
mustard
oregano *or* origanum
parsley

peppermint
rosemary
rue
sage
savory
sesame
sorrel
spearmint
sweet cicely
sweet woodruff
tansy
tarragon
thyme
wintergreen
yarrow

46 vines

air potato
bittersweet
Boston ivy
cissus
clematis
cypress vine
English ivy
grape
greenbrier
honeysuckle
hop
ivy
jasmine
liana

morning glory
paradise flower
poison ivy
stephanotis
sword bean
traveler's-joy
trumpet creeper
trumpet flower
trumpet honeysuckle
velvet bean
Virginia creeper
virgins-bower
wisteria
woodbine

47 ferns

adder's fern
asparagus fern
basket fern
beech fern
bladder fern
boulder fern
bracken
calamite
chain fern
Christmas fern
cliff brake
climbing fern
club moss
cycad
curly grass
grape fern
hart's tongue
holly fern
horsetail
interrupted fern
lady fern
lip fern
lycopod

maidenhair
marsh fern
moonwort
oak fern
osmunda
ostrich fern
polypody
rattlesnake fern
rock brake
seed fern
shield fern
silvery spleenwort
snuffbox
  fern
sword fern
tree fern
tropical fern
true fern
walking fern
wall fern
water clover
wood fern
woodsia

48 trees

abele
acacia
acajou

ailanthus *or* tree of heaven
alder
Aleppo pine

allspice
almond
apple
apricot
ash
aspen
avocado *or* alligator pear
bald cypress
balsa
balsam
banyan
basswood
bay
bayberry
bean
beech
betel palm
birch
bonsai
bo tree
boxwood
Brazil-nut
breadfruit
buckeye
buckthorn
butternut
buttonwood
cabbage tree
cacao
camphor tree
carnauba
carob
cashew
cassia
catalpa
cedar
cherimoya
cherry
chestnut
chinaberry tree *or*
  China tree
chinquapin
Christmas tree
cinnamon
citron
clove
coconut *or* coco
cork oak
cottonwood
cypress
date palm
devilwood
dogwood
dwarf
ebony
elder
elm
eucalyptus
evergreen

ficus
fig
filbert
fir
flame tree
fruit
ginkgo
grapefruit
guava
gum
hardwood
hawthorn
hazel *or* hazelnut
hemlock
henna
hickory
holly
hoptree
hornbeam
horse chestnut
horseradish tree
inkwood
juniper
kola
kumquat
laburnum
lancewood
larch
laurel
lemon
lignum vitae
lime
linden
litchi *or* litchi nut
locust
logwood
loquat *or* Japanese plum
macadamia
madroña *or* madrone
magnolia
mahogany
mango
mangrove
maple
medlar
mesquite
mimosa
monkey puzzle
mountain ash
mulberry
nutmeg
nux vomica
oak
olive
orange
osier
pagoda tree
palm
papaw

papaya
peach
pear
pecan
persimmon
pine
pistachio
pitch pine
plane
plum
poison sumac
pomegranate
pomelo
poplar
quince
raffia palm
rain tree
redwood
rice-paper tree
rosewood
rubber tree
sandalwood
sapodilla
sassafras
satinwood
senna
sequoia
serviceberry
shade tree
shortleaf pine
silver maple
sorrel tree
spruce
sugar maple
sycamore
tamarillo
tamarind

tamarugo
tangerine
teak
thorn tree
thuja
torchwood
tulip tree
tupelo
umbrella tree
upas
varnish tree
walnut
wandoo
wax palm
wax tree
wayfaring tree
weeping willow
western hemlock
whitebeam
white birch
white cedar
white oak
white pine
white poplar
white spruce
whitethorn
wicopy
willow
witch hazel
woollybutt
wychelm
yellow poplar
yellowwood *or*
   gopher wood
yew
ylang-ylang
zebrawood

49 hardwoods

apple
ash
balsa
basswood
beech
birch
black walnut
blackwood
butternut
cherry
chestnut
cottonwood
ebony
elm
gopherwood
gum

hickory
holly
ironwood
lime
magnolia
mahogany
maple
oak
pear
poplar
rosewood
sycamore
walnut
willow
yellowwood
zebrawood

50 softwoods

balsam
basswood
box elder
bristlecone fir

cedar
cypress
Douglas fir
hemlock

Japanese cedar
northern white pine
ponderosa pine
poplar
redwood
spruce

sugar pine
tulipwood
tupelo
white fir
white pine
yellow longleaf pine

51 flowers

acacia
acanthus
African violet
amaranthus
amaryllis
anemone *or* windflower
arbutus
arrowhead
asphodel
aster
autumn crocus
azalea
baby's breath
bachelor's button
begonia
belladonna
bitterroot
bittersweet
black-eyed Susan
bleeding heart
bluebell
bluet
bougainvillea
bridal wreath
broom
buttercup
cactus
calendula
calla lily
camellia
camomile
campanula
candytuft
carnation
cat's-paw
cattail
century plant
chamomile
Chinese lantern
Christmas cactus
Christmas rose
chrysanthemum
cineraria
clematis
clover
cockscomb
columbine
cornel
cornflower
cosmos
cowbell
cowslip

crocus
cyclamen
daffodil
dahlia
daisy
damask rose
dandelion
delphinium
dogtooth violet
Dutchman's-breeches
Easter lily
edelweiss
eglantine
elderflower
fireweed
flax
fleur-de-lis <Fr>
forget-me-not
forsythia
foxglove
foxtail
frangipani
freesia
fuchsia
gardenia
gentian
geranium
gladiolus
globeflower
goldenrod
groundsel
guelder rose
harebell
hawthorn
heather
hepatica
hibiscus
hollyhock
honeysuckle
horehound
hyacinth
hydrangea
hyssop
impatience *or* impatiens
Indian paintbrush
indigo
iris
jack-in-the-pulpit
japonica
jasmine
jonquil
kingcup

laburnum
lady's-slipper
larkspur
lavender
lilac
lily
lily of the valley
lobelia
lotus
love-lies-bleeding
lupine
magnolia
mallow
marguerite
marigold
marshmallow
marsh marigold
mayflower
meadow saffron
Michaelmas daisy
mignonette
milkwort
mimosa
moccasin flower
mock orange
monkshood
moonflower
morning glory
moss rose
motherwort
mullein
musk rose
myrtle
narcissus
nasturtium
oleander
opium poppy
orchid
oxalis
oxeye daisy
pansy
paper-white
   narcissus
passionflower
pennyroyal
peony
periwinkle
petunia
phlox
pink
plumbago
poinsettia
polyanthus
poppy
portulaca
pot marigold
primrose
primula
Queen Anne's lace

ragged robin
ragwort
rambler rose
ranunculus
resurrection
   plant
rhododendron
rose
safflower
shooting star
smilax
snapdragon
snowdrop
spiraea
St. John's wort
stock
strawflower
sunflower
sweet alyssum
sweetbrier
sweet pea
sweet william
tea rose
thistle
tiger lily
trailing arbutus
trillium
trumpet creeper
tulip
twinflower
umbrella
   plant
valerian
Venus's flytrap
verbena
veronica
viburnum
viola
violet
wake-robin
wallflower
water hyacinth
water lily
water milfoil
water pimpernel
wax flower
waxplant
white clover
wisteria
wolfsbane
wood anemone
wood hyacinth
woody nightshade
wood sorrel
yarrow
yellow water
   lily
yucca
zinnia

52 cereal grasses

barley
buckwheat
corn
maize
millet

oats
rice
rye
wheat

53 fruit

apple
apricot
atemoya
avocado
banana
berry
black currant
breadfruit
bullace plum
calmyrna
canistel
cantaloupe
carambola
cherimoya
cherry
citron
clementine
coconut
crabapple
currant
custard apple
damson
date
durian
fig
granadilla
grape
grapefruit
greengage
ground cherry
guava
haw
jackfruit
jujube
kiwi
kumquat
lemon
lime
longan
loquat

mandarin orange
mango
May apple
medlar
melon
muskmelon
navel orange
nectarine
olive
orange
papaya
passion fruit
pawpaw
peach
pear
pepino
Persian melon
persimmon
pineapple
plantain
plum
pomegranate
pomelo
prickly pear
prune
quince
quinoa
raisin
rambutan
sapodilla
sapote
satsuma
sea grape
soursop
tamarillo
tamarind
tangelo
tangerine
tomato
watermelon

54 apples

Anna
Arctic
Arkansas Black
Bailey Sweet
Baldwin
Belmont
Ben Davis
Blue Permain
Braeburn
Bramley

Buckingham
Collins
Cortland
Cox's Orange Pippin
Criterion
Delicious
Dorset Golden
Earliblaze
Early Harvest
Ein Shemer

Empire
English Sweet
Freedom
Gala
Gideon
Golden Delicious
Golden Harvest
Granny Smith
Gravenstein
Green Sweet
Grimes
  Golden
Hubbardston
Ingram
Jersey Black
Jerseymac
Jonared
Jonathan
Lady Sweet
Liberty
Lodi
Longfield
Macoun
macoun
McIntosh
McMahon
Missouri
Monroe
Mutsu
Newton
  Pippin
Northern Spy
Oldenburg
Ortley

Permain
Pippin
Porter
Prima
Priscilla
Rambo
Red Delicious
Redfree
Red Rome
Rhode Island
  Greening
Roman Stem
Rome
Rome Beauty
Roxbury
  Russet
Russet
Saint Lawrence
Sir Prize
Snowapple
Spartan
Starkrimson
Starr
Stayman
Twenty Ounce
Tydeman's Red
Virginia
  Beauty
Wealthy
Williams
Winesap
Winter Banana
Yellow Transparent
York Imperial

55 berries

bilberry
bearberry
blackberry
black raspberry
blueberry
boysenberry
buffalo berry
candleberry
checkerberry
cloudberry
cranberry
currant
dangleberry
dewberry

elderberry
gooseberry
huckleberry
Juneberry
lingonberry
loganberry
mulberry
partridgeberry
raspberry
sala berry
serviceberry
shadberry
strawberry
whortleberry

56 citrus fruit

citron
clementine
grapefruit
kumquat
lemon
lime
mandarin
naartje

orange
ortanique
pomelo
satsuma
shaddock
tangelo
tangerine

57 fruits, bramble

blackberry
boysenberry
cloudberry
loganberry

raspberry
tayberry
wineberry

58 fruits, pome

apple
chokeberry
crabapple
hawthorn
Japanese plum
juneberry
loquat

medlar
pear
quince
rose hip
rowan
service
  tree

59 fruits, stone

apricot
cherry
date
mango
nectarine

olive
peach
plum
pluot

60 fruits, tropical

akee
Asian pear
avocado
banana
breadfruit
camucamu
carambola
cherimoya
coconut
custard apple
durian
feijoya
fig
guarana
guava
horned melon
Indian fig
jaboticaba
jackfruit
Japanese persimmon
jujube

kiwi
litchi *or* lychee
longan
mamoncillo
mango
mangosteen
papaya
passion fruit
pepino
pineapple
plantain
pomegranate
prickly
  pear
rambutan
rose apple
salak
sapodilla
soursop
tamarillo
tamarind

61 grapes

Alicante
Almeria
Cabernet Sauvignon
cardinal
Champion
Chardonnay
Chenin Blanc
Concord
Delaware
Franconian
Hamburgh
Isabella
Italia
Labrusca
Lady Finger

Malaga
Martha
Merlot
Muscadet
Muscat
Pinot Blanc
Pinot Noir
Riesling
seedless
Superb
Thompson seedless
Tokay
White Corinth
Woodbury
zinfandel

62 melons

cantaloupe
casaba
Crenshaw
honeydew
muskmelon
Persian
watermelon
winter melon

63 peaches

Clingstone
Elberta
Freestone
Greensboro
Heath
Late Crawford
Lovell
Mountain Rose
Muir
nectarine
Phillips
Susquehanna
Triumph
Yellow

64 pears

Anjou
Bartlett
Bosc
Clapp Favorite
Comice
Kieffer
Le Conte
Sheldon
Wilder Early
winter nellis

65 vegetables

alfalfa sprout
artichoke
arugula
asparagus
bamboo sprout or shoot
bean
bean sprout
beet
bell pepper
black-eyed pea
Boston lettuce
broad bean
broccoli
Brussels sprout
butter bean
cabbage
cardoon
carrot
cassava
cauliflower
celery
chard
chayote
chickpea
chicory
Chinese cabbage
chive
collard greens
corn
cress
cucumber
dandelion
eggplant
endive
escarole
fennel
garbanzo bean
garlic
glasswort
globe artichoke
gourd
green bean
green pepper
iceberg lettuce
jalapeno pepper
kale
kidney bean
kohlrabi
leek
lentil
lettuce
lima bean
mung bean
mushroom
muskmelon
mustard
navy bean
New Zealand spinach
okra
olive
onion
parsley
parsnip
pea
pepper
petsai
pinto bean
plantain
pokeweed
potato
pumpkin
radiccio
radish
rampion
red bean
red cabbage
red pepper
rhubarb
rice
romaine
rutabaga
sauerkraut
scallion
sea kale
seaweed
shallot
snap bean
snow pea
sorrel
soybean
spinach
squash
string bean
succotash
sugar pea
summer squash
sweet corn
sweet potato
tomato
truffle
turnip
water chestnut
watercress
watermelon
wax bean
white bean
yam
yellow pepper
yellow squash
zucchini

66 vegetables, bulb and stalk

asparagus
broccoli
Brussels sprouts
cardoon
celery
chicory
chive
fennel
finocchio
garlic
globe artichoke
leek
onion
palm hearts
radish
rhubarb
rutabaga
scallion
sea kale
shallot
Swiss
    chard

67 vegetables, leaf

Brussels sprouts
cabbage
celery
chard
chicory
Chinese cabbage
corn salad
cress
dandelion
endive
grape leaf
green cabbage
kale
lettuce
mustard
rhubarb
Romaine
    lettuce
sorrel
spinach
spinach beet
Swiss chard
watercress
white cabbage

68 vegetables, root and tuber

beet
burdock
carrot
celeriac
chervil
Chinese artichoke
ginger
ginseng
gobo
horseradish
Jerusalem artichoke
jicama
kohlrabi
lobok
parsley
parsnip
potato
radish
rutabaga
salsify
skirret
sweet
    potato
taro
turmeric
turnip
wasabi
water chestnut
yam
yuca

69 vegetables, seed

baby corn	mung bean
bean	Navy bean
bean sprouts	pea
black bean	peanut
broad bean	pink bean
chick pea	pinto bean
corn	red bean
English pea	runner bean
fava bean	snow pea
flageolet	soybean
French bean	split green pea
green bean	split yellow pea
green pea	sugar snap pea
kidney bean	sweet corn
legume	sweet pea
lentil	wax bean
lima bean	yellow snap bean

311 ANIMALS, INSECTS

NOUNS **1 animal life, animal kingdom,** brute creation, **fauna,** Animalia <zoology>, animality; animal behavior, biology ; birds, beasts, and fish; the beasts of the field, the fowl of the air, and the fish of the sea; domestic animals, livestock, stock <nf>, cattle; wild animals *or* beasts, beasts of field, wildlife, denizens of the forest *or* jungle *or* wild, furry creatures; predators, beasts of prey; game, big game, small game; animal rights

2 animal, creature, critter <nf>, living being *or* thing, creeping thing; **brute, beast,** varmint <nf>, dumb animal *or* creature, dumb friend, furry friend, four-legged friend, critter <nf>; pet, companion animal, animal companion

3 <varieties> **vertebrate; invertebrate; biped, quadruped; mammal, mammalian, primate** <see list>, warm-blooded animal; chordate; **marsupial,** marsupialian; canine; **feline; rodent,** gnawer; **ungulate; ruminant;** insectivore, herbivore, carnivore, omnivore; cannibal; scavenger; reptile; amphibian; fish; aquatic; bird; cosmopolite; vermin, varmint <nf>; zooid, protist, protozoan; worm, mollusk, gastropod, arthropod, insect, arachnid; parasite, scavenger, predator, grazer; **fungi** <see list>

4 pachyderm; elephant, Jumbo, hathi <India>, "heffalump"—A A Milne; mammoth, woolly mammoth; mastodon; **rhinoceros,** rhino; **hippopotamus,** hippo, river horse; subungulate, proboscidean, Proboscidea

5 <hoofed animals> ungulate, ungulant; odd-toed ungulate, perissodactyl; even-toed ungulate, artiodactyl; **deer, buck, doe, fawn;** red deer, **stag,** hart, hind; roe deer, roe, roebuck; musk deer; fallow deer; hogdeer; white-tailed *or* Virginia deer; mule deer; **elk,** wapiti; **moose; reindeer,** caribou; deerlet; **antelope;** gazelle, kaama, wildebeest *or* gnu, hartebeest, springbok, reebok, dik-dik, eland *or* Cape elk, koodoo; **camel,** dromedary, ship of the desert; **giraffe,** camelopard, okapi; equine, equid; horse; pig, hog, swine; camel, llama; goat, sheep

6 cattle <see list>, kine <old pl>, neat; beef cattle, beef, beeves <pl>; dairy cattle *or* cows; bovine animal, **bovine,** critter <nf>; **cow,** moo-cow *and* bossy <nf>; milk *or* milch cow, milker, milcher, dairy cow; **bull,** bullock, top cow <nf>; **steer,** stot <Brit nf>, **ox,** oxen <pl>; **calf, heifer,** yearling, fatling, stirk <Brit>; **dogie** *and* leppy <W US>; maverick <W US>; hornless cow, butthead *and* muley head <nf>, muley cow; zebu, Brahman; yak; musk-ox; **buffalo,** water buffalo, Indian buffalo, carabao; bison, aurochs, wisent

7 sheep <see list>, jumbuck <Austral>; **lamb,** lambkin, yeanling; teg <Brit>; **ewe,** yow <nf>; ewe lamb; **ram,** tup <Brit>, wether; bellwether; mutton

8 goat; he-goat, buck, **billy goat** *and* billy <nf>; she-goat, doe, **nanny goat** *and* nanny <nf>; **kid,** doeling; mountain goat

9 swine <see list>, **pig, hog,** porker, **shoat,** piggy, piglet, pigling; sucking *or* suckling pig; gilt; **boar, sow;** barrow; wild boar, tusker, razorback; warthog, babirusa

10 horse; horseflesh, hoss <nf>, critter <nf>; **equine,** mount, **nag** <nf>; **steed,** prancer, dobbin; charger, courser, war-horse, destrier <old>; Houyhnhnm <Jonathan Swift>; **colt,** foal, filly; **mare,** brood mare; **stallion, studhorse, stud,** top horse <nf>, entire horse, entire; gelding, purebred horse, thoroughbred, blood horse; wild horse, Przewalsky's horse, tarpan; **pony,** Shetland pony, Shetland, shelty, Iceland pony, Galloway, cob; **bronco,** bronc, range horse, Indian pony, cayuse, mustang; bucking bronco, buckjumper, sunfisher, broomtail; cowcutting horse, stock horse, roping horse, cow pony, circus horse

11 <colored horses> appaloosa, bay, blood bay, bayard, chestnut, liver chestnut, gray, dapple-gray, black, grizzle, roan, sorrel, dun, buckskin, pinto, paint, piebald, skewbald, palomino, seal brown, strawberry roan, calico pony, painted pony

12 <inferior horse> **nag, plug,** hack, jade, crock, garron <Scot & Ir>, crowbait <nf>, scalawag, rosinante; goat *and* stiff *and* dog <nf>; roarer, whistler; balky horse, balker, jughead; rogue; rackabones, scrag, stack of bones

13 workhorse, plow horse, beast of burden; **hunter;** stalking-horse; **saddle horse,** saddler, rouncy <old>, steed, **riding horse,** rider, palfrey, **mount;** remount; polo pony; post-horse; cavalry horse;

driving horse, road horse, roadster, carriage horse, coach horse, gigster; hack, hackney; **draft horse,** dray horse, cart horse, shaft horse, pole horse, thill horse, thiller, fill horse *or* filler <nf>; wheelhorse, wheeler, lead, leader; pack horse, jument <old>, sumpter, sumpter horse, bidet; pit-pony; cow pony; war-horse

14 **race horse; show-horse, gaited horse,** racer, galloper, trotter, pacer, sidewheeler <nf>; stepper, high-stepper, cob, prancer, turf horse, sprinter; ambler, padnag, pad; racker; single-footer; steeplechaser; bangtail <nf>

15 **ass, donkey, burro,** neddy *or* cuddy <Brit nf>, moke <Brit nf>, Rocky Mountain canary <W US>; **jackass,** jack, dickey <Brit nf>; jenny, jenny ass, jennet; **mule,** sumpter mule, sumpter; hinny, jennet

16 **dog** <see list>, **canine, pooch** *and* bow-wow <nf>; **pup, puppy,** puppy dog *and* perp <nf>, **whelp;** bitch, gyp <S US>, slut; toy dog, lap dog; working dog; ratter; watchdog, bandog; sheep dog, shepherd *or* shepherd's dog; hound; Seeing Eye dog, guide dog; guard dog, watchdog; police dog, sled dog; gazehound, sighthound; show dog, fancy dog, toy dog; man's best friend <nf>, bowwow, pooch; kennel, pack of dogs

17 sporting dog, **hunting dog,** hunter, field dog, bird dog, gundog, water dog, hound, courser, setter, pointer, spaniel, retriever

18 **cur, mongrel,** lurcher <Brit>, tyke, **mutt** <nf>; pariah dog

19 **fox,** reynard; **wolf,** timber wolf, lobo <W US>, **coyote,** brush wolf, prairie wolf, medicine wolf <W US>; dingo, jackal, **hyena;** Cape hunting dog, African hunting dog

20 **cat** <see list>, **feline, pussy** *and* **puss** *and* **pussycat** <nf>, domestic cat, house cat, tabby, grimalkin; house cat; **kitten, kitty** *and* kitty-cat <nf>; kit, kitling <Brit nf>; **tomcat,** tom; gib *or* gib-cat <Brit nf>; mouser; ratter; Cheshire cat, Chessycat <nf>; silver cat, Chinchilla cat; blue cat, Maltese cat; tiger cat, tabby cat; tortoise-shell cat, calico cat; alley cat; Morris

21 <wild cats> **big cat, jungle cat; lion,** Leo <nf>, *simba* <Swah>; **tiger,** Siberian tiger; **leopard,** panther, jaguar, cheetah; cougar, painter <S US>, puma, mountain lion, catamount *or* cat-a-mountain; lynx, ocelot; wildcat, bobcat, steppe cat, Pallas's cat

22 <wild animals> **bear,** bar <nf>; guinea pig, cavy; hedgehog, **porcupine,** quill pig <nf>; woodchuck, **groundhog, whistle-pig** <nf>; prairie dog, prairie squirrel; **raccoon,** coon; **opossum,** possum; **weasel,** mousehound <Brit>; **wolverine,** glutton; ferret, monk <nf>; **skunk,** polecat <nf>; zoril,

stink cat <South Africa>, Cape polecat; foumart; **primate, simian; ape; monkey,** chimpanzee, chimp

23 **hare,** leveret, jackrabbit; **rabbit, bunny** *and* bunny rabbit <nf>, lapin; cottontail; Belgian hare, leporide; buck, doe

24 **reptile,** reptilian; **lizard;** saurian, dinosaur; crocodile, crocodilian, alligator, gator <nf>; tortoise, turtle, terrapin; cold-blooded animal, poikilotherm, Reptilia, Squamata, Rhynchocephalia, Crocodilia

25 **serpent, snake,** ophidian; **viper,** pit viper; sea snake

26 **amphibian,** batrachian, croaker, paddock <nf>; **frog,** rani-, tree toad *or* frog, bullfrog; **toad,** hoptoad *or* hoppytoad; newt, salamander; **tadpole, polliwog;** caecilian, apodan, urodele, caudate, salientian, anuran

27 **bird, fowl;** dicky-bird *and* birdy *and* birdie <nf>; fowls of the air, birdlife, avifauna, Aves, feathered friends; baby bird, chick, nestling, fledgling; wildfowl, game bird; waterfowl, water bird, wading bird, diving bird; sea bird; shore bird; migratory bird, migrant, bird of passage; **songbird,** oscine bird, warbler, passerine bird, perching bird; cage bird; flightless bird, ratite; seed-eating bird, insect-eating bird, fruit-eating bird, fish-eating bird; **raptor,** bird of prey; **eagle,** bird of Jove, eaglet; **hawk, falcon; owl,** bird of Minerva, bird of night; peafowl, peahen, **peacock,** bird of Juno; **swan,** cygnet; **pigeon, dove,** squab; stormy *or* storm petrel, Mother Carey's chicken; fulmar, Mother Carey's goose

28 **poultry, fowl,** domestic fowl, barnyard fowl, barn-door fowl, dunghill fowl; **chicken** <see list>, chick, chicky *and* chickabiddy <nf>; **cock, rooster,** chanticleer; **hen,** biddy <nf>, partlet; cockerel, pullet; setting hen, brooder, broody hen; capon, poulard; broiler, fryer, spring chicken, chicklet; roaster, stewing chicken; Bantam, banty <nf>; game fowl; guinea fowl, guinea cock, guinea hen; **goose,** gander, gosling; **duck,** drake, duckling; **turkey,** gobbler, turkey gobbler; turkey-cock, tom, tom turkey; hen turkey; poult

29 marine animal <see list>, denizen of the deep; **whale,** cetacean; **porpoise, dolphin,** sea pig; **sea serpent,** sea snake, Loch Ness monster, sea monster, Leviathan <Bible>; **fish,** game fish, tropical fish, panfish; **shark,** man-eating shark, man-eater; **salmon,** kipper, grilse, smolt, parr, alevin; **minnow** *or* minny <nf>, fry, fingerling; **sponge; plankton,** zooplankton, nekton, benthon, benthos, zoobenthos; **crustacean,** lobster, spiny lobster, **crab,** blueclaw, Dungeness crab, king crab, spider crab, land crab, stone crab, soft-shell crab;

crayfish *or* crawfish *or* crawdaddy; **mollusc,** wentletrap, whelk, snail, cockle, mussel, **clam, oyster,** razor clam, quahog, steamer, toheroa, tridachna *or* giant clam

30 fish; saltwater fish, marine fish, freshwater fish; jawless fish, cyclostome, cartilaginous fish, elasmobranch, selachian, holocephalan, bony fish, lobe-finned fish, crossopterygian, dipnoan, ray-finned fish, teleost fish, flying fish, mouthbreeder, flatfish; food fish, game fish, aquarium fish, tropical fish, fossil fish; shoal, school

31 invertebrate; lower animal, protochordate, echinoderm, arthropod, arachnid, insect, crustacean, myriapod, mollusk, worm, coelenterate, sponge, protozoan *or* protozoon

32 insect, bug; beetle; arthropod; hexapod, myriapod; centipede, chilopod; millipede, diplopod; social insect; **mite; arachnid, spider,** tarantula, black widow spider, daddy longlegs *or* harvestman; **scorpion; tick;** larva, maggot, nymph, **caterpillar;** winged insect, **fly,** gnat, midge, mosquito, dragonfly, butterfly, moth, bee, wasp; creepy-crawly <nf>, pest

33 ant, emmet <nf>, pismire, pissant *and* antymire <nf>; red ant, black ant, fire ant, house ant, agricultural ant, carpenter ant, army ant; slave ant, slave-making ant; **termite,** white ant; queen, worker, soldier

34 bee, honeybee, bumblebee, carpenter bee; queen, queen bee, worker, drone, Africanized bee; **wasp; hornet,** yellow jacket

35 locust, acridian; **grasshopper,** hopper, hoppergrass <nf>; **cricket;** cicada, cicala, dog-day cicada, seventeen-year locust; stick insect, mantis

36 vermin; parasite; **louse,** head louse, body louse, grayback, cootie <nf>; crab, crab louse; weevil; nit; **flea,** sand flea, dog flea, cat flea, chigoe, chigger, jigger, red bug, mite, harvest mite; **roach, cockroach,** *cucaracha* <Sp>; tick, mosquito

37 bloodsucker, parasite; **leech; tick,** wood tick, deer tick; **mosquito,** skeeter <nf>, culex; bedbug, housebug <Brit>

38 worm; earthworm, angleworm, fishworm, night crawler, nightwalker <N US>; measuring worm, inchworm; tapeworm, helminth

ADJS **39 animal,** animalian, animalic, animalistic, animal-like, theriomorphic, zoic, zooidal; zoologic, zoological; **brutish, brutal,** brute, brutelike; **bestial, beastly,** beastlike; **wild,** feral; subhuman, soulless; dumb, "that wants discourse of reason"—Shakespeare; instinctual *or* instinctive, mindless, nonrational; half-animal, half-human, anthropomorphic, therianthropic

40 vertebrate, chordate, mammalian; viviparous; marsupial, cetacean

41 canine, doggish, doggy, doglike; vulpine, foxy, foxlike; lupine, wolfish, wolflike

42 feline, felid, cattish, catty, catlike; kittenish; leonine, lionlike; tigerish, tigerlike

43 ursine, bearish, bearlike

44 rodent, rodential; verminous; mousy, mouselike; ratty, ratlike

45 ungulate, hoofed, hooved; **equine,** hippic, horsy, horselike; **equestrian;** asinine, mulish; bovid, ruminant, "that chew the cud"—Bible; **bovine,** cowlike, cowish; bull-like, bullish, taurine; cervine, deerlike; caprine, caprid, hircine, goatish, goatlike; ovine, sheepish, sheeplike; porcine, swinish, piggish, hoggish

46 elephantlike, elephantine, pachydermous

47 reptile, reptilian, **reptilelike,** reptiloid, reptiliform; reptant, repent, creeping, crawling, slithering; **lizardlike,** saurian; crocodilian; **serpentine,** serpentile, serpentoid, serpentiform, **serpentlike;** snakish, **snaky, snakelike,** colubrine, ophidian, anguine <old>; viperish, viperous, vipery, viperine, viperoid, viperiform, viperlike; amphibian, batrachian, froggy, toadish, salamandrian

48 birdlike, birdy; avian, avicular; gallinaceous, rasorial; oscine, passerine, perching; columbine, columbaceous, dovelike; psittacine; aquiline, hawklike; anserine, anserous, goosy; nidificant, nesting, nest-building; nidicolous, altricial; nidifugous, precocial

49 fishlike, fishy; piscine, pisciform; piscatorial, piscatory; eellike; selachian, sharklike, sharkish

50 invertebrate, invertebral; protozoan, protozoal, protozoic; crustaceous, crustacean; molluscan, molluscoid

51 insectile, insectlike, buggy; verminous; lepidopterous, lepidopteran; weevily

52 wormlike, vermicular, vermiform; wormy

53 planktonic, nektonic, benthonic, zooplanktonic, zoobenthoic

54 primates

angwantibo	colobus
anthropoid ape	drill
ape	entellus
aye-aye	gibbon
baboon	gorilla
Barbary ape	great ape
Bengal monkey	grivet
bonnet monkey *or*	guenon
macaque	guereza
bush baby	hanuman
capuchin	howling monkey *or* howler
chacma	king monkey
chimpanzee	langur

lemur
lion-tailed monkey *or* macaque
loris
macaque
man
mandrill
marmoset
mountain gorilla
orangutan *or* orang
owl monkey
pongid
proboscis monkey
rhesus
saki
siamang
sloth monkey
spider monkey
squirrel monkey
tamarin
tarsier
vervet

55 breeds of cattle

Aberdeen Angus *or* Angus *or* black Angus
Africander
Alderney
Andalusian
Ayrshire
Beefalo
Belted Galloway
Black Angus
Brahman
Brown Swiss
Cattalo
Charolais
Dairy Shorthorn
Devon
Dexter
Durham
Dutch Belted
Egyptian
French Canadian
Fribourg
Galloway
Guernsey
Hereford
Holstein *or* Holstein-Friesian
Icelandic
Jersey
Lincoln Red
Longhorn
Norwegian Red
Polled Durham *or* Shorthorn
Polled Hereford
Red Poll *or* Red Polled
Red Sindhi
Santa Gertrudis
Shetland
Shorthorn
Sussex
Texas Longhorn
Welsh *or* Welsh Black
West Highland

56 breeds of sheep

Abyssinian
American merino
American Rambouillet
American Tunis
Berber
Black-faced Highland
Blackhead Persian
broadtail
Cheviot
Columbia
Corriedale
Corsican
Cotswold
Dorset Down
Hampshire
Karakul
Kerry Hill
Leicester
Lincoln
Merino
Mongolian
Oxford *or* Oxford Down
Panama
Rambouillet
Romanov
Romeldale
Romney
Romney Marsh
Ryeland
Scottish blackface
Shetland
Shropshire
Southdown
Suffolk
Tajik
Targhee
Tibetan
Welsh Mountain
Wensleydale

57 breeds of swine

American Landrace
Berkshire
Cheshire
Chester White
Dorset
Duroc
Duroc Jersey
Hampshire
Hereford
Landrace
large black
large white
Mangalitsa
middle white
National Long White Lop-eared
Poland China
Romagna
Tamworth
Vietnamese Pot-bellied
Wessex saddleback
Yorkshire

58 breeds of dogs

affenpinscher
Afghan hound
Airedale *or* Airedale terrier
Akita
Alaskan malamute
Alsatian
American foxhound
American water spaniel
Australian cattle dog *or* blue heeler
Australian heeler
Australian terrier
Basenji
basset *or* basset hound
beagle
Bedlington terrier
Belgian sheepdog *or* shepherd
Bernese mountain dog
Bichon Frise
black Labrador
Blenheim spaniel
bloodhound *or* sleuth *or* sleuthhound
Border terrier
borzoi
Boston bull *or* terrier
Bouvier des Flandres
boxer
Briard
Brittany spaniel
Brussels griffon
bulldog *or* bull
bull mastiff
bull terrier
cairn terrier
carriage *or* coach dog
Chesapeake Bay retriever
Chihuahua
chow *or* chow chow
clumber spaniel
Clydesdale terrier
cocker spaniel
collie
coonhound
corgi
dachshund *or* sausage dog *or* sausage hound
Dalmatian
Dandie Dinmont
deerhound
Doberman pinscher
elkhound
English bulldog
English cocker spaniel
English foxhound
English setter
English springer spaniel
English toy spaniel
Eskimo dog *or* husky
field spaniel
foxhound
fox terrier
French bulldog
gazelle hound
German shepherd
German shorthaired pointer
German wirehaired pointer
giant schnauzer
golden retriever
Gordon setter
Great Dane
Great Pyrenees
greyhound
griffon
Groenendael
harrier
hound *or* hound-dog <S US>
husky
Irish setter
Irish terrier
Irish water spaniel
Irish wolfhound
Italian greyhound
Jack Russell terrier
Japanese spaniel *or* Japanese Chin
keeshond
kelpie
Kerry blue terrier
King Charles spaniel
Komondor
kuvasz
Labrador retriever
Lakeland terrier

Lhasa apso
malamute
Malinois
Maltese
Manchester terrier
mastiff
Mexican hairless
miniature pinscher
miniature poodle
miniature schnauzer
Newfoundland
Norfolk spaniel
Norwegian elkhound
Norwich terrier
Old English sheepdog
otterhound
papillon
Pekingese
pit bull terrier
pointer
police dog
Pomeranian
poodle
pug or pug dog or mops
puli
rat terrier
retriever
Rhodesian ridgeback
Rottweiler
Russian owtchar
Russian wolfhound
St. Bernard
Saluki
Samoyed
schipperke
schnauzer

Scottish deerhound
Scottish terrier
Sealyham terrier
setter
Shar-Pei
shepherd dog
Shetland sheepdog or
  sheltie
Shih Tzu
Siberian husky
silky terrier
Skye terrier
spaniel
spitz
springer spaniel
Staffordshire bull terrier
Sussex spaniel
terrier
toy poodle
toy spaniel
toy terrier
Vizsla
water spaniel
Weimaraner
Welsh collie
Welsh corgi
Welsh springer
  spaniel
Welsh terrier
West Highland white
  terrier
whippet
wirehaired terrier
wolfhound
yellow Labrador
Yorkshire terrier

59 breeds and varieties of domestic cats

Abyssinian cat
American shorthair
Angora cat
Balinese
blue-point Siamese
Burmese
calico or tortoiseshell
chartreuse cat
Chinese
chocolate-point Siamese
Cornish rex
domestic shorthair cat
Egyptian cat or mau
exotic shorthair
Havana brown
Himalayan
Kashmir

Maine coon
Malayan cat
Maltese
Manx
marmalade cat
Oriental Shorthair
Persian
rex
Russian blue
seal-point
  Siamese
Siamese
Singapura
sphynx
tabby or tabby-cat
tortoiseshell cat
Turkish cat

60 breeds of chickens

Ameraucana
Ancona
Andalusian
Araucana

Australorp
Bantam
Barred Plymouth Rock
Brahma

Buckeye
Buttercup
Campine
Cochin
Cornish
Crevecoeur
Delaware
Dorking
Faverolle
Frizzle
Hamburg
Holland
Houdan
Ixworth
Jersey black giant
Langshan
Leghorn

Minorca
New Hampshire or New
  Hampshire red
Orpington
Plymouth Rock
Rhode Island red
Rhode Island white
Rock
Rock Cornish
Silkie
Spanish
Sultan
Sumatra
Sussex
Turken
white Leghorn
Wyandotte

61 marine animals

cetacean
crustacean
dolphin
dugong
elephant seal
fur seal
harbor seal
manatee
octopus or octopod
phocid
pinniped
porpoise

sea calf
sea cow
sea dog
sea elephant
seal
sea lion
sea urchin
shellfish
sirenian
squid
walrus
whale

62 birds

albatross
auk
avocet
bald eagle
barn owl
bittern
blackbird
blue jay
bluebill
bluebird
bowerbird
bufflehead
bullfinch
bunting
buzzard
canary
cardinal
cassowary
catbird
chaffinch
chickadee
chicken
chicken hawk
chimney swift
cockatoo
condor
coot
cormorant

cowbird
crake
crane
crow
curlew
dipper
diver
dove
duck
dunlin
eagle
egret
emu
falcon
finch
flamingo
flycatcher
frigate bird
frogmouth
fulmar
gannet
gnatcatcher
goldfinch
gooney bird
goose
goshawk
grackle
grebe

greenfinch
grey heron
grouse
guinea fowl
gull
harrier
hawk
heron
honeycreeper
hummingbird
ibis
jackdaw
jaeger
jay
kestrel
king eider
kingfisher
kite
kiwi
lapwing
lark
loon
lovebird
magpie
mallard
man-o-war bird
meadowlark
merlin
mockingbird
mud hen
myna
nighthawk
nightingale
notornis
oriole
osprey
ostrich
ouzel
owl
oystercatcher
parakeet
parrot
partridge
peacock
pelican
penguin
petrel
pewit
pheasant
pigeon
pipit
plover
pochard
prairie chicken
puffin

63 crustaceans

amphipod
barnacle
bass yabby

purple martin
quail
raptor
ratite
raven
razorbill
redpoll
redwing
rhea
roadrunner
robin
rook
sandpiper
sapsucker
scissortail
seabird
seagull
shag
shama
shelduck
shrike
skua
snipe
snowbird
sparrow
song thrush
spoonbill
starling
stork
sunbird
surfbird
swallow
swan
takahe
tern
thrasher
thrush
tit
towhee
turkey
vulture
wader
wagtail
warble
waterfowl
weaverbird
whippoorwill
whitethroat
wigeon
woodcock
woodpecker
wren
yellow finch
yellowbird
yellowhammer

beach flea
branchiopod
brine shrimp

copepod
crab
crawdad
crawfish
crayfish
cumacean
daphnia
fiddler crab
hairy crab
hermit crab
horseshoe crab
isopod
king crab
krill
lobster
mantas shrimp
mussel shrimp
opossum shrimp
ostracod

64 fish

albacore
alewife
alligator gar
amberjack
angelfish
arauana
archerfish
asp
balloonfish
barracuda
basking shark
bass
batfish
beluga
betta
blackfish
blindfish
blowfish
bluefish
bonefish
bowfin
boxfish
bream
brook trout
buffalofish
bullhead
butterfish
butterflyfish
candlefish
capelin
cardinalfish
carp
catfish
cavefish
char
chimaera
chub
cichlid
clingfish

pea crab
pebble crab
prawn
sailor shrimp
sand hopper
sand skater
sea centipede
sea flea
shellfish
shrimp
skeleton louse
soft-shell crab
spider crab
sponge crab
sponge shrimp
stenetrium
tadpole shrimp
water flea
weed shrimp

clown anemone
clownfish
cod
codfish
cowfish
cutlassfish
damselfish
danios
darter
devilfish
devil ray
discus
doctorfish
dogfish
dolphin
dragonfish
eel
electric eel
electric ray
flatfish
flounder
flying fish
frogfish
garpike
giant bass
globefish
goatfish
goby
goldfish
gourami
grayling
grouper
gudgeon
guppy
haddock
hagfish
hake
halibut
hammerhead shark

hatchetfish
headstander
herring
hogfish
ide
kelpfish
killifish
kingfish
koi
lake trout
lanternfish
lionfish
loach
lumpfish
mackerel
manta
marlin
minnow
molly
mudfish
mudskipper
mullet
needlefish
northern pike
oarfish
oscar
paddlefish
paradise fish
parrotfish
perch
pickerel
pike
pikeperch
pipefish
piranha
platyfish
pollack
pompano
porgy
puffer
pupfish
rainbow trout
ray
redfin

redfish
red snapper
sailfish
salmon
salmon trout
sardine
sawfish
sea bass
sea horse
seaperch
sea trout
shad
shark
shiner
skate
smelt
snapper
snook
sole
spearfish
squawfish
stingray
striped bass
sturgeon
sucker
sunfish
surffish
swordfish
swordtail
tang
tarpon
tetra
tigerfish
tiger shark
triggerfish
trout
tuna
weakfish
whitefish
white shark
wimplefish
yellowtail
zander
zebrafish

earthstar
Eumycota
false mildew
false morel
field mushroom
flask fungus
Fungi Imperfecti
gill fungus
green mold
groundwart
inky cap
jelly fungus
lorchel
Mastigomycotina
mildew
milkcap
mold
moniliales
morel
mushroom
mushroom pimple
myxomycetes
Myxomycota
oyster cap
penicillium
phycomycetes
pink gill
pore fungus
powdery mildew

66 insects

acarid
acarine
ant
ant lion
aphid
apple maggot
arachnid
Arachnida
armyworm
bagworm
bark beetle
bedbug
bee
beetle
billbug
black fly
black widow
blackbeetle
bloodworm
boll weevil
bookworm
borer
bug
bumblebee
butterfly
carpet beetle
caterpillar
centipede
chafer

puffball
read bread
  mold
ringstalk
ringworm fungus
roof mushroom
rust
sac fungus
scalecap
sheath mushroom
shell fungus
skin fungus
slime molds
slime mushroom
smoothcap
smut
stinkhorn
thrush fungus
toadstool
tooth fungus
tricholoma
truffle
verticillium
waxy cap
webcap
woodcrust
yeast
zygomycetes
Zygomycota

chigger
chinch bug
click beetle
cockroach
cootie
cricket
cutworm
daddy-longlegs
deer fly
doodlebug
dragonfly
drone
dung beetle
emperor butterfly
false scorpion
firefly
flea
fruit fly
gadfly
glowworm
gnat
grasshopper
grub
gypsy moth
harvestman
honeybee
hornet
horse fly
housefly

65 fungi

agarics
ascomycetes
Ascomycota
aspergillus
basidiomycetes
Basidiomycota
bird's-nest fungus
black bread mold
black mold
blue mold
blue-green mold
boletus
bracket fungus
bread mold

brittlegill
cellular slime molds
chanterelle
club fungus
coral fungus
crumblecap
cup fungus
dead-man's fingers
deathcap
deuteromycetes
Deuteromycota
downy mildew
dung fungus
earth tongue

Japanese bettle
June bug
ladybug
leafhopper
locust
long-horned beetle
looper
louse
maggot
mayfly
mealworm
medfly
midge
mite
mosquito
moth
nit
nymph
opilionid
phalangid
pismire
praying mantis
pseudoscorpion
pupa
queen bee

roach
scale
scorpion
screwworm
silkworm
skipper
snapping beetle
soldier ant
spider
stag beetle
tarantula
tent fly
termite
tick
tiger beetle
tiger moth
wasp
water beetle
water bug
weevil
wireworm
woodworm
woolly bear
worker
yellow jacket

67 mollusks

amphineuran
bivalve
cephalopod
chambered nautilus
chiton
clam
conch
cone
cowry
cuttlefish
gastropod
lamellibranch
lampshell
limpet
murex

mussel
neopilina
octopod
octopus
oyster
rock shell
scallop
scaphopod
shellfish
slug
snail
spider conch
squid
tusk shell
volute

68 reptiles and amphibians

agama
alligator
anaconda
apodan
asp
auratus
basilisk
blindworm
boa
bog turtle
bullfrog
caecilian
caiman
chameleon
chelonid
chicken turtle
Chinese water dragon

cobra
congo snake
constrictor
cricket frog
crocodile
dinosaur
flying dragon
frog
galliwasp
gecko
Gila monster
glass snake
green frog
horned toad
iguana
Komodo dragon
lizard

loggerhead turtle
mamba
marine toad
monitor
mudpuppy
newt
pig frog
python
rainbow snake
rattlesnake
red-eyed tree frog
salamander
serpent

skink
slow worm
snake
snapping turtle
soft-shelled turtle
spring peeper
terrapin
toad
tortoise
tuatara
turtle
viper
waterdog

69 worms

angleworm
annelid
apple pomice worm
armyworm
arrowworm
bearded worm
bloodworm
bollworm
bookworm
cankerworm
clamworm
composting worm
cottonworm
cutworm
dung worm
earthworm
earwom
eelworm
fecal worm
fireworm
fish worm
flatworm
fluke
glowworm
grey worm
hairworm
heligrammite
hookworm
hornworm
horsehair worm
inchworm
leech
looper

lugworm
manure worm
measuringworm
nematode
night crawler
pinworm
platyhelminth
polychaete
red hybrid
redworm
red wiggler
ribbon worm
rotifer
roundworm
sandworm
sea mouse
sea worm
silkworm
stink worm
striped worm
tapeworm
threadworm
tiger worm
tobacco
   hornworm
tomato hornworm
tubeworm
vinegar eel
vinegar worm
webworm
whipworm
wireworm
woodworm

70 animal collective names

<antelopes> herd
<ants> colony
<apes> shrewdness
<asses> pace, herd, drove
<baboons> congress
<badgers> cete
<bass> shoal
<bears> sleuth, sloth
<beavers> colony
<bees> colony, grist, hive,
   hum, swarm

<birds> dissimulation,
   flight, volery
<bison> herd, troop
<boars> singular, sounder
<bovines> herd
<buffalo> herd
<camels> herd, flock
<caterpillars> army
<cats and dogs> rain
<cats> clowder, clutter
<cattle> herd, drove

<chickens> brood, clutch, flock, peep
<clams> bed
<colts> rag
<cows> flink, herd
<cranes> sedge, siege
<crickets> orchestra
<crows> murder
<deers> herd
<dogs> kennel, pack
<doves> dole, dule, flight
<ducks> brace, flock, gaggle, paddling, raft, team
<eagles> convocation
<eels> knot
<eggs> clutch
<elephants> herd, host, parade
<elks> gang, herd
<falcons> cast, passager
<ferrets> business
<finches> charm
<fishes> draught, school, shoal
<foxes> leash, skulk
<frogs> army, knot, colony
<geese> flock, gaggle, skein, wedge
<giraffes> herd
<gnats> cloud, horde
<goats> tribe, trip, herd
<goldfinches> charm
<gorillas> band
<grasshoppers> cluster
<grouses> covey
<hares> down, husk, leap
<hawks> cast, kettle
<hedgehogs> prickle
<hens> brood
<herons> siege
<hippopotami> huddle
<hogs> drift
<horses> harras, herd, pair, stable, team
<hounds> cry, mute, pack
<hummingbirds> hover
<jack rabbits> husk
<jays> band, party
<jellyfish> smack
<kangaroos> mob, troop
<kittens> kindle, kendle, litter
<lapwings> deceit
<larks> ascension, chattering, exaltation
<leopards> leap
<lions> pride
<locusts> host, plague

<magpies> tidings
<mallards> sord, sort
<mares> stud
<martens> richness
<mice> nest
<moles> labor, lobor
<monkeys> tribe, troop
<mules> barren, pack, rake, span
<nightingales> watch
<owls> parliament, wisdom
<oxen> team, yoke, drove, herd
<oysters> bed
<parrots> company
<partridges> covey
<peacocks> muster, ostentation
<penguins> colony
<pheasants> bouquet, covey, nest, nye, nide
<pigeons> flock
<pigs> drove, litter, herd
<plovers> congregation, wing
<polar bears> aurora
<ponies> string
<porpoises> school
<quails> bevy, covey
<rabbits> colony, nest
<racehorses> field
<ravens> conspiracy, unkindness
<reindeers> herd
<rhinoceroses> crash
<seals> pod, herd, school, trip, harem, rookery, spring
<sheeps> drove, flock, herd
<skunks> stench
<slugs> cornucopia
<snakes> bed, slither
<sparrows> host
<squirrels> dray
<starlings> murmuration
<storks> mustering
<swallows> flight
<swans> ballet, bevy, wedge
<swines> drift, sounder
<teal> spring
<tigers> hide, streak
<toads> knot
<trout> hover
<turkeys> rafter
<turtledoves> pitying
<turtles> bale, bevy
<unicorns> blessing

<wasps> pail
<waterfowl> plump
<weasels> gam, sneak
<whales> gam, herd, pod, shoal, surfers

71 animal young names

<antelope> calf
<bear> cub, whelp
<beaver> kit, kitten, pup
<bird> fledgling, nestling
<bison> calf
<bovine> calf
<cat> kit, kitten, kitty, puss, pussy
<cattle> calf, yearling
<chicken> chick, chicklet, pullet, cockerel
<cow> calf, heifer
<deer> fawn
<dog> pup, whelp
<duck> duckling
<eagle> eaglet, fledgling
<elephant> calf
<elk> calf
<falcon> cast
<fish> fingerling, fry
<fox> cub, kit, pup, whelp
<frog> polliwog, tadpole
<giraffe> cub, whelp
<goat> kid
<goose> gosling
<grouse> cheeper, poult
<hare> leveret
<hawk> eyas
<hen> chick, pullet
<hippopotamus> calf

<wolves> pack, rout
<woodchucks> fall
<woodpeckers> descent
<worms> wriggle
<zebras> herd, stripe

<horse> colt, filly, filt, foal, yearling
<kangaroo> joey
<lion> cub, whelp
<monkey> baby
<moose> cub, calf
<owl> owlet
<oyster> spat
<partridge> cheeper
<pig> piglet, shoat, farrow, suckling
<pigeon> squab, squeaker
<quail> cheeper
<rabbit> bunny, kit, leveret
<reindeer> fawn
<rhinoceros> calf
<rooster> cockerel
<sea lion> pup
<seal> calf, pup
<shark> cub
<sheep> lamb, lambkin, cosset, hog, yearling
<swan> cygnet
<swine> piglet, shoat, farrow
<tiger> cub, whelp
<turkey> poult, chick)
<whale> calf
<wolf> cub, whelp
<zebra> colt, foal

312 HUMANKIND

NOUNS **1 humankind, mankind, womankind,** personkind, **man,** human species, **human race,** race of man, human family, the family of man, **humanity,** human beings, mortals, earthlings, mortality, flesh, mortal flesh, clay; generation of man <old>, *le genre humain* <Fr>, homo, genus Homo, **Homo sapiens,** Hominidae, hominids; archaic Homo; **race,** strain, stock, subrace, infrarace, subspecies; **culture** 373.2; ethnic group; ethnicity, ethnicism, roots <nf>; **society,** speech community, **ethnic group;** community, folk, persons, **the people, the populace,** world population; **nationality, nation**

2 <races of humankind> **Caucasoid** *or* **Caucasian** *or* **white race;** Nordic subrace, Alpine subrace, Mediterranean subrace; dolichocephalic people, brachycephalic people; xanthochroi, melanochroi; Archaic Caucasoid *or* archaic white *or* Australoid race; Polynesian race; **Negroid** *or* **black race;** Nilotic race, Melanesian race, Papuan race; Pygmoid race; Bushman race; **Mongoloid** *or* **Mongolian** *or* **yellow race;** Malayan *or* Malaysian *or* brown race; prehistoric races; majority, racial *or* ethnic majority; minority, racial *or* ethnic minority; persons of color

3 **Caucasian, white man** *or* **woman, white person,** paleface *and* ofay *and* the Man *and* Mister Charley *and* whitey *and* honky <nf>; Australian aborigine, blackfellow <Austral>; **Negro, black man** *or* **woman, black,** colored person, person of color, darky *and* spade *and* nigger <nf>; African-American; negritude, Afroism, blackness; pygmy, Negrito, Negrillo; Bushman; **Native American,** Indian, American Indian, Amerindian, Amerind, Red Indian <Brit>, red man *or* woman; injun *and* redskin <nf>; Latino; Mongolian, yellow man *or* woman, **Oriental,** Asian; gook *and* slant-eye <nf>; Malayan, brown man; mixed race, mulatto, quadroon, half-breed

4 **the people** 606, the populace, the population, the public, the world, everyone, everybody

5 **person, human, human being, man, woman, child,** member of the human race *or* family, Adamite, daughter of Eve; **ethnic; mortal,** life, **soul,** living soul; **being,** creature, fellow creature, clay, ordinary clay, flesh and blood, the naked ape, the noble animal; **individual;** personage, **personality, personhood,** individuality; **body;** somebody, one, someone; earthling, groundling, terran, worldling, tellurian; **ordinary person;** head, hand, nose; fellow <nf> 76.5; gal <nf> 77.6

6 **human nature, humanity;** frail *or* fallen humanity, Adam, the generation of Adam, Adam's seed *or* offspring

7 **God's image, lord of creation,** God's creation; homo faber, symbol-using animal; "a reasoning animal"—Seneca, rational animal, animal capable of reason, "this quintessence of dust"—Shakespeare, "the naked ape"—Desmond Morris

8 **humanness, humanity,** mortality; **human nature,** the way you are; **frailty,** human frailty, human fallibility, weakness, **human weakness,** weakness of the flesh, flesh, the weaknesses human flesh is heir to; human equation

9 humanization, humanizing; **anthropomorphism,** pathetic fallacy, anthropopathism, anthropomorphology

10 **anthropology,** science of man; social studies, cultural studies; cultural anthropology, physical anthropology, anthropogeny, anthropography, anthropogeography, human geography, demography, human ecology, anthropometry, craniometry, craniology, ethnology, ethnography, paleoanthropology, paleoethnology; material culture; behavioral science, sociology, social anthropology, social psychology, psychology 92; anatomy; **anthropologist,** ethnologist, ethnographer; sociologist; demographics, population study, population statistics; demographer

11 **humanism;** naturalistic humanism, scientific humanism, secular humanism; religious humanism; Christian humanism, integral humanism; new humanism; anthroposophy

VERBS 12 **humanize,** anthropomorphize, make human, civilize

ADJS 13 **human;** hominal; creaturely, creatural; Adamite *or* Adamitic; **frail, weak,** fleshly, finite, **mortal; only human;** earthborn, of the earth, earthy, tellurian, unangelic; humanistic; man-centered, homocentric, anthropocentric; anthropological, ethnographic, ethnological; demographic, epigraphic; social, societal, sociological

14 **manlike, anthropoid,** humanoid, hominid; anthropomorphic, anthropopathic, therioanthropic

15 **personal, individual,** private, peculiar, idiosyncratic; person-to-person, one-to-one, one-on-one

16 **public, general, common; communal, societal, social;** civic, civil; **national,** state; international, cosmopolitan, supernational, supranational

ADVS 17 **humanly,** mortally, after the manner of men

WORD ELEMENTS 18 anthrop-, anthropo-, homin-, homini-

313 SEASON
<time of year>

NOUNS 1 **season,** time of year, season of the year, **period,** annual period; dry *or* rainy *or* cold season, monsoon; theatrical *or* opera *or* concert season; **social season,** the season; dead *or* off-season; baseball season, football season, basketball season, hunting season, preseason, etc; open season, closed season; seasonality, periodicity 850.2; **seasonableness** 843.1; seasonal affective disorder *or* SAD

2 **spring,** springtide, **springtime,** seedtime *or* budtime, Maytime, Eastertide; *primavera* <Ital>, prime, prime of the year, vernal equinox, "the boyhood of the year"—Tennyson

3 **summer,** summertide, **summertime,** good old summertime; growing season; midsummer; **dog days,** canicular days; the silly season, high summer; summer solstice; estivation

4 **autumn, fall,** fall of the year, fall of the leaf,

harvest, harvest time, harvest home; autumnal equinox

5 **Indian summer,** St Martin's summer, St Luke's summer, little summer of St Luke, St Austin's *or* St Augustine's summer

6 **winter,** wintertide, **wintertime**; midwinter; Christmastime *or* Christmastide, Yule *or* Yuletide; winter solstice; hibernation

7 **equinox,** vernal equinox, autumnal equinox; **solstice,** summer solstice, winter solstice

VERBS 8 summer, winter, overwinter, spend *or* pass the spring, summer, etc; hibernate, estivate

ADJS 9 **seasonal,** in *or* out of season, in season and out of season, off-season; early-season, mid-season, late-season; **spring,** springlike, vernal; **summer,** summery, summerly, summerlike, canicular, aestival; midsummer; **autumn,** autumnal; **winter,** wintry, wintery, hibernal, hiemal, brumal, boreal, arctic 1023.14, winterlike, snowy, icy; midwinter; equinoctial, solstitial, periodic

314 MORNING, NOON

NOUNS 1 **morning,** morn, morningtide, morning time, morntime, matins, morrow <old>, waking time, reveille, get-up time <nf>, **forenoon;** *ante meridiem* <L> *or* **AM,** Ack Emma <Brit old>; this morning, this AM <nf>; early bird; breakfast time

2 Morning, Aurora, Eos; "daughter of the dawn"—Homer

3 **dawn,** the dawn of day, dawning, **daybreak,** dayspring, day-peep, **sunrise, sunup** <nf>, cockcrowing *or* cocklight <Brit nf>, light 1025, first light, daylight, aurora; **break of day,** peep of day, **crack of dawn,** prime, prime of the morning, first blush *or* flush of the morning, brightening *or* first brightening; "the opening eyelids of the morn"—Milton; chanticleer *or* chantecler

4 **foredawn,** twilight, morning twilight, half-light, glow, dawnlight, first light, "the dawn's early light"—Francis Scott Key, crepuscule, aurora; **the small hours;** alpenglow

5 **noon, noonday,** noontide, nooning <nf>, noontime, **high noon, midday,** midsun, meridian, *meridiem* <L>, twelve o'clock, 1200 hours, eight bells; noonlight, "the blaze of noon"—Milton; meridian devil *or* *daemonium meridianum* <L>; lunchtime; sext

ADJS 6 **morning,** matin, matinal, matutinal, **antemeridian;** auroral, dawn, dawning; forenoon

7 **noon,** noonday, noonish, **midday,** meridian, twelve-o'clock, high-noon; noonlit

ADVS 8 **in the morning,** before noon, mornings <nf>; at sunrise, at dawn, at dawn of day, at cockcrow,

at first light, **at the crack** *or* **break of dawn;** with the sun, with the lark

9 at noon, at midday, at twelve-o'clock sharp

315 EVENING, NIGHT

NOUNS 1 **afternoon,** *post meridiem* <L> *or* **PM;** this afternoon, this aft <nf>, this PM <nf>; matinee; siesta

2 **evening,** eve, even, evensong time *or* hour, **eventide,** vesper, crepuscle; **close of day,** decline *or* fall of day, shut of day, gray of the evening, grayness 39, evening's close, when day is done; **nightfall, sunset, sundown,** setting sun, going down of the sun, cockshut *and* cockshut time *and* cockshut light <nf>, retreat; shank of the afternoon *or* evening <nf>, the cool of the evening; "the expiring day"—Dante; cocktail hour, suppertime, dinnertime

3 **dusk,** dusking time *or* -tide, dusk-dark *and* dust-dark *and* dusty-dark <nf>, **twilight,** evening twilight, crepuscule, crepuscular light, gloam, **gloaming,** glooming; duskiness, duskishness, brown of dusk, brownness 40, candlelight, candlelighting, owllight *or* owl's light, cocklight <Brit nf>, "the pale dusk of the impending night"—Longfellow

4 **night, nighttime,** nighttide, lights-out, taps, bedtime, sleepy time <nf>, **darkness** 1027, blackness 38, "empress of silence, and the queen of sleep"—Christopher Marlowe; dark of night

5 eleventh hour, curfew

6 **midnight, dead of night,** hush of night, the witching hour; "the very witching time of night"—Shakespeare; midnight hours, small *or* wee small hours; late-night *or* midnight supper *or* snack

ADJS 7 **afternoon,** postmeridian

8 **evening,** evensong, vesper, vespertine *or* vespertinal, vesperal; **twilight,** twilighty, twilit, crepuscular; **dusk,** dusky, duskish

9 **nocturnal,** night, **nightly,** nighttime; nightlong, all-night; night-fallen; midnight

10 **benighted,** night-overtaken

ADVS 11 **nightly,** nights <nf>, at *or* by night; **overnight,** through the night, all through the night, nightlong, the whole night, all night

WORD ELEMENTS 12 noc-, nocto-, nocti-, nyct-, nycto-, nycti-

316 RAIN

NOUNS 1 **rain, rainfall,** fall, **precipitation,** precip <nf>, moisture, wet, rainwater, raininess; **shower, sprinkle,** flurry, patter, pitter-patter, splatter, intermittent rain *or* showers; streams of rain, sheet of rain, splash *or* spurt of rain, fine rain, light rain, occasional rain *or* showers, April showers, sun shower; **drizzle,** mizzle; **mist,** misty rain, Scotch mist; evening mist; fog drip; blood rain; raindrop, unfrozen hydrometeor; acid rain

2 **rainstorm,** brash *and* scud <Scot>; **cloudburst,** rainburst, burst of rain, torrent of rain, torrential rain *or* downpour; waterspout, spout, rainspout, **downpour,** downflow, downfall, pour, pouring *or* pelting *or* teeming *or* drowning rain, spate <Scot>, plash <nf>, **deluge, flood,** heavy rain, driving *or* gushing rain, drenching *or* soaking rain, drencher, soaker, gullywasher, pluviosity, goosedrownder <nf>, lovely weather for ducks

3 **thunderstorm,** thundersquall, thundergust, thundershower; electric storm

4 **wet weather, raininess,** rainy weather, stormy *or* dirty weather, rainy season, cat-and-dog weather <nf>, spell of rain, wet; rainy day; **rains,** rainy *or* wet season, spring rains, **monsoon;** predominance of Aquarius, reign of St Swithin; flood

5 **rainmaking,** seeding, cloud seeding, nucleation, artificial nucleation; **rainmaker,** rain doctor, cloud seeder; dry ice, silver iodide

6 Jupiter Pluvius, Zeus; Thor

7 **rain gauge,** pluviometer, pluvioscope, pluviograph; ombrometer, ombrograph; udometer, udomograph; hyetometer, hyetometrograph, hyetograph

8 **rainbow,** arc, double rainbow, primary rainbow, seconary rainbow, fogdog, fogbow *or* white rainbow, mistbow *or* seadog

9 <science of precipitation> hydrometeorology, hyetology, hyetography; pluviography, pluviometry, ombrology

VERBS 10 **rain, precipitate,** rain down, fall; weep; **shower,** shower down; **sprinkle,** spit *and* spritz <nf>, spatter, patter, pitter-patter, plash; **drizzle,** mizzle; **pour,** stream, stream down, pour with rain, **pelt,** pelt down, drum, tattoo, come down in torrents *or* sheets *or* buckets *or* curtains, **rain cats and dogs** <nf>, rain tadpoles *or* bullfrogs *or* pitchforks *or* buckets <nf>, "rain daggers with their points downward"—Robert Burton; rainmake, seed clouds

ADJS 11 **rainy, showery;** pluvious *or* pluviose *or* pluvial; **drizzly,** drizzling, mizzly, drippy; **misty,** misty-moisty; torrential, pouring, streaming, pelting, drumming, driving, blinding, cat-and-doggish <nf>; wet

12 pluviometric *or* pluvioscopic *or* pluviographic, ombrometric *or* ombrographic, udometric *or* udographic, hyetometric, hyetographic, hyetometrographic; hydrometeorological, hyetological

317 AIR, WEATHER

NOUNS 1 **air;** ether; ozone <nf>; thin air, rarity

2 **atmosphere;** aerosphere, gaseous envelope *or* environment *or* medium *or* blanket, welkin, lift <nf>; biosphere, ecosphere, noosphere; air mass; atmospheric component, atmospheric gas; atmospheric layer *or* stratum *or* belt <see list>

3 **weather, climate,** clime; **the elements,** forces of nature; microclimate, macroclimate, aerology; weather situation, weather pattern, weather conditions; fair weather, calm weather, halcyon days, good weather; stormy weather 671.4; rainy weather 316.4; windiness 318.14; heat wave, hot weather 1019.7; cold wave, cold weather 1023.3

4 <weather terms> weather map; isobar, isobaric *or* isopiestic line; isotherm, isothermal line; isometric, isometric line; frontal system; high, high-pressure area, ridge; low, low-pressure area; front, wind-shift line, squall line; cold front, polar front, cold sector; warm front; occluded front, occlusion, stationary front; air mass; thermal, downdraft, updraft; cyclone, anticyclone; air pressure, air temperature, heat index, temperature-humidity index, dewpoint; humidity, relative humidity; precipitation; wind speed, wind strength, chill factor, wind-chill factor; ambient temperature; climate change

5 **meteorology,** weather science, aerology, aerography, air-mass analysis, weatherology, climatology, climatography, microclimatology, forecasting, long-range forecasting; barometry; pneumatics 1039.5; anemology 318.15; nephology 319.5 anemometry, anemology, hyetography, nephology, micrometeorology, macrometeorology, mesometeorology, agricultural meteorology, aviation meteorology, maritime meteorology, hydrometeorology, mountain meteorology, planetary meteorology, atmospheric physics

6 **meteorologist,** weather scientist, aerologist, aerographer, weatherologist; climatologist, microclimatologist; **weatherman, weather forecaster,** weather prophet; **weather report,** weather forecast; weather bureau; weather ship; weather station; weather-reporting network

7 weather forecast, forecast, weather report, regional forecast, local forecast, general outlook, travel report, boating report, small craft advisory, long-term forecast, 5-day forecast, storm watch *or* warning, tornado watch *or* warning, hurricane watch *or* warning

8 weather instrument, meteorological *or* aerological instrument; **barometer,** aneroid barometer, glass, weatherglass; barograph, barometrograph, recording barometer, mercury barometer;

thermometer, thermograph; aneroidograph; vacuometer; hygrometer; wind gauge, anemometer, anemograph, wind sock, wind cone, wind sleeve, drogue, weathercock; rain gauge, pluviometer, udometer; weather balloon, radiosonde; weather satellite, weather radar; hurricane-hunter aircraft; weather vane 318.16

9 **ventilation,** cross-ventilation, **airing,** aerage, perflation, refreshment; fanning, **aeration; air conditioning,** central air conditioning, air cooling; oxygenation, oxygenization

10 **ventilator; aerator,** blower; **air conditioner,** air filter, air cooler, ventilating *or* cooling system; blower; heat pump; air passage; fan

VERBS 11 **air,** air out, **ventilate,** cross-ventilate, wind, refresh, freshen; **air-condition,** air-cool; **fan,** winnow; **aerate,** airify, aerify; oxygenate, oxygenize

ADJS 12 **airy,** aery, **aerial,** aeriform, airlike, aeriferous, **pneumatic,** ethereal; exposed, roomy, light; airish, breezy; open-air, alfresco; **atmospheric,** tropospheric, stratospheric

13 **climatal,** climatic, climatical, climatographical, **elemental;** meteorological, meteorologic, aerologic, aerological, aerographic, aerographical, climatologic, climatological; macroclimatic, microclimatic, microclimatologic; barometric, barometrical, baric, barographic; isobaric, isopiestic, isometric; high-pressure, low-pressure; cyclonic, anti-cyclonic; seasonal

14 **atmospheric layers**

boundary layer	mesosphere
chemosphere	outer atmosphere
D layer *or* region	ozone layer *or*
E *or* Heaviside *or* Kennelly-	ozonosphere
Heaviside layer *or* region	stratopause
exosphere	stratosphere
F₁ layer *or* region	substratosphere
F₂ *or* Appleton layer *or*	thermosphere
region	tropopause
ionosphere	troposphere
isothermal region	upper atmosphere
lower atmosphere	Van Allen belt *or* radiation
magnetosphere	belt

318 WIND

<airflow>

NOUNS 1 **wind,** current, **air current,** current of air, **draft,** movement of air, stream, stream of air, flow of air; updraft, uprush; downdraft, downrush, microburst; indraft, inflow, inrush; crosscurrent, crosswind, undercurrent; fall wind, gravity wind, katabatic wind, anabatic wind, head wind, tail wind, following wind; wind aloft; jet stream, upper-atmosphere *or* upper-atmospheric wind, high-altitude wind, gradient wind, geostrophic wind, prevailing wind; surface wind, mountain wind, valley wind; wind shift, wind shear

2 <wind god; the wind personified> Aeolus, Boreas, Aquilo <north wind>; Eurus <east wind>; Zephyr *or* Zephyrus, Favonius <west wind>; Notus, Auster <south wind>; Caurus *or* Caecias <northwest wind>; Afer *or* Africus <southwest wind>; Argestes <northeast wind>

3 **puff,** puff of air *or* wind, breath, breath of air, flatus, waft, capful of wind, whiff, whiffet, stir of air

4 **breeze,** light *or* gentle wind *or* breeze, softblowing wind, **zephyr,** gale <old>, air, light air, moderate breeze; fresh *or* stiff breeze; cool *or* cooling breeze; land breeze; sea breeze, onshore breeze, ocean breeze, cat's-paw

5 **gust,** wind gust, **blast,** blow, flaw, **flurry,** scud <Scot>, squall

6 **hot wind;** snow eater, thawer; chinook, **chinook wind;** simoom, samiel; foehn *or* föhn; khamsin; harmattan; sirocco *or* yugo; solano; Santa Ana; volcanic wind

7 **wintry wind,** winter wind, raw wind, chilling *or* freezing wind, bone-chilling wind, sharp *or* piercing wind, cold *or* icy wind, biting wind, the hawk <nf>, nipping *or* nippy wind, "a nipping and an eager air"—Shakespeare, icy blasts; Arctic *or* boreal *or* hyperboreal *or* hyperborean blast; wind chill *or* wind chill factor

8 **north wind, norther,** mistral, bise, tramontane, Etesian winds, meltemi, vardarac, Papagayo wind; northeaster, **nor'easter,** Euroclydon *or* gregale *or* gregal *or* gregau, bura, Tehuantepec wind, Tehuantepecer; northwester, **nor'wester;** southeaster, **sou'easter;** southwester, **sou'wester,** kite-wind, libeccio; **east wind,** easter, easterly, levanter, sharav; **west wind,** wester, westerly; **south wind,** souther, southerly buster <Austral>

9 **prevailing wind;** polar easterlies; prevailing westerlies, prevailing southwesterlies, prevailing northwesterlies, antitrades; trade winds *or* trades; antitrade winds; doldrums, wind-equator; horse latitudes, roaring forties; intertropical convergence zone *or* ITCZ; equatorial low *or* doldrums

10 <nautical terms> **headwind, beam wind, tailwind,** following wind, fair *or* favorable wind, apparent *or* relative wind, backing wind, veering wind, slant of wind; onshore wind, offshore wind, wind shear

11 **windstorm,** vortex, eddy, big *or* great *or* fresh *or* strong *or* stiff *or* high *or* howling *or* spanking wind, ill *or* dirty *or* ugly wind; storm, storm wind, stormy winds, **tempest,** tempestuous wind; williwaw; **blow,** violent *or* heavy blow; **squall,**

thick squall, black squall, white squall; squall line, wind-shift line, line squall; line storm; equinoctial; **gale,** half a gale, whole gale; tropical cyclone, **hurricane,** typhoon, tropical storm, **blizzard** 1023.8; **thundersquall,** thundergust; wind shear

12 **dust storm, sandstorm,** shaitan, peesash, devil, khamsin, sirocco, simoom, samiel, harmattan

13 **whirlwind,** whirlblast, tourbillon, wind eddy; **cyclone, tornado, twister,** funnel cloud, rotary storm, typhoon, *baguio* <Sp>; sandspout, sand column, dust devil; waterspout, rainspout

14 **windiness,** gustiness; airiness, **breeziness; draftiness**

15 **anemology,** anemometry; **wind direction; wind force, Beaufort scale,** half-Beaufort scale, International scale; wind rose, barometric wind rose, humidity wind rose, hyetal *or* rain wind rose, temperature wind rose, dynamic wind rose; wind arrow, wind marker

16 **weather vane, weathercock,** vane, cock, wind vane, wind indicator, wind cone *or* sleeve *or* sock, anemoscope; anemometer, wind-speed indicator, anemograph, anemometrograph

17 **blower,** bellows; blowpipe, blowtube, blowgun

18 **fan,** flabellum; punkah, thermantidote, electric fan, blower, window fan, attic fan, exhaust fan; ventilator; windsail, windscoop, windcatcher

VERBS 19 **blow, waft; puff,** huff, whiff; whiffle; **breeze;** breeze up, freshen; **gather, brew,** set in, blow up, pipe up, come up, **blow up a storm;** bluster, squall; **storm,** rage, blast, blow great guns, blow a hurricane; blow over

20 **sigh,** sough, whisper, mutter, murmur, **sob, moan,** groan, growl, snarl, **wail, howl,** scream, screech, shriek, **roar,** whistle, pipe, sing, sing in the shrouds

ADJS 21 **windy, blowy; breezy, drafty,** airy, airish; brisk, fresh; **gusty,** blasty, puffy, flawy; **squally;** prevailing; blustery, blustering, blusterous; aeolian, favonian, boreal; ventose

22 **stormy, tempestuous,** raging, storming, angry; turbulent; gale-force, storm-force, hurricane-force; dirty, foul; cyclonic, tornadic, typhonic, typhoonish; inclement; rainy 316.11; cloudy 319.8

23 **windblown,** blown; **windswept,** bleak, raw, exposed

24 anemological, anemographic, anemometric, anemometrical

319 CLOUD

NOUNS 1 **cloud,** high fog; "islands on a dark-blue sea"—Shelley; fleecy cloud, cottony cloud, billowy cloud; **cloud bank,** cloud mass, cloud cover, cloud drift; cloud base; cloudling, cloudlet; cloudscape, cloud band; cloudland, Cloudcuckooland *or* Nephelococcygia <Aristophanes>; macerel sky, buttermilk sky

2 <cloud types> ice cloud, water cloud, storm cloud, thunderhead, thunder cloud; cirrus, cirrocumulus, altostratus, cirrostratus, altocumulus, nimbostratus, stratocumulus *or* cumulostratus, stratus, cumulus, cumulonimbus, nimbus

3 **fog,** pea soup *and* peasouper *and* pea-soup fog <nf>; ground fog, coastal fog, fog drip, dense fog; London fog, London special <Brit nf>, Scotch mist, brume; fog-bank; **smog** <smoke-fog>, smaze <smoke-haze>; frost smoke; mist, drizzling mist, drisk <nf>; haze, gauze, film; vapor 1067

4 **cloudiness,** cloud cover, **haziness, mistiness, fogginess,** nebulosity, nubilation, nimbosity, **overcast,** heavy sky, dirty sky, lowering *or* louring sky

5 nephology, nephelognosy; nephologist

6 nephelometer, nepheloscope

VERBS 7 **cloud,** becloud, encloud, cloud over, overcloud, cloud up, clabber up <nf>, **overcast,** overshadow, shadow, shade, **darken** 1027.9, darken over, nubilate, obnubilate, obscure; **smoke,** oversmoke; **fog,** befog, fog in; smog; **mist,** mist over, mist up, bemist, enmist; **haze**

ADJS 8 **cloudy,** nebulous, nubilous, nimbose, nebulosus, nephological; **clouded,** overclouded, **overcast;** dirty, heavy, lowering *or* louring; dark 1027.13; **gloomy** 1027.14; cloud-flecked; cirrous, cirrose; cumulous, cumuliform, stratous, stratiform, cirrocumiliform, cirrocumuous, altocumuliform, altocumulous, altostratous, cirrostratous, nimbostratous, cumulonimbiform; lenticularis, mammatus, castellatus; thunderheaded, stormy, squally

9 **cloud-covered,** cloud-laden, cloud-curtained, cloud-crammed, cloud-crossed, cloud-decked, cloud-hidden, cloud-wrapped, cloud-enveloped, cloud-surrounded, cloud-girt, cloud-flecked, cloud-eclipsed, **cloud-capped,** cloud-topped

10 **foggy,** soupy *or* pea-soupy <nf>, nubilous; fog-bound, fogged-in; smoggy; hazy, misty; so foggy the seagulls are walking, so thick you can cut it with a knife

11 nephological

320 BUBBLE

NOUNS 1 **bubble,** bleb, **globule;** vesicle, bulla, **blister,** blood blister, fever blister; balloon, bladder 195.2; air bubble, soap bubble

2 foam, froth; spume, sea foam, scud; **spray, surf,** breakers, white water, spoondrift *or* **spindrift; suds, lather,** soap-suds; beer-suds, head; **scum,** off-scum; head, collar; puff, mousse, soufflé, meringue

3 bubbling, bubbliness, **effervescence** *or* effervescency, **sparkle,** spumescence, frothiness, frothing, foaming; **fizz,** fizzle, carbonation; ebullience *or* ebulliency; **ebullition,** boiling; **fermentation,** ferment

VERBS **4 bubble,** bubble up, burble; **effervesce, fizz, fizzle;** hiss, **sparkle; ferment,** work; **foam, froth,** froth up; have a head, foam over; **boil,** seethe, simmer; plop, blubber; guggle, gurgle; bubble over, **boil over**

5 foam, froth, spume, cream; **lather,** suds, sud; scum, mantle; **aerate,** whip, beat, whisk

ADJS **6 bubbly,** burbly, **bubbling,** burbling; **effervescent,** spumescent, **fizzy, sparkling,** *mousseux* <Fr>, *spumante* <Ital>; carbonated; ebullient; puffed, soufflé *or* souffléed, beaten, whipped, chiffon; **blistered,** blistery, blebby, vesicated, vesicular; blistering, vesicant, vesicatory

7 foamy, foam-flecked, **frothy,** spumy, spumous *or* spumose; yeasty, barmy; **sudsy,** suddy, **lathery,** soapy, soapsudsy, soapsuddy; heady, with a head *or* collar on

321 BEHAVIOR

NOUNS **1 behavior, conduct, deportment, comportment, manner, manners, demeanor, mien,** *maintien* <Fr>, **carriage, bearing,** port, poise, posture, guise, **air,** address, presence; tone, style, lifestyle; way of life, habit of life, modus vivendi; **way, way of acting, ways; trait behavior,** behavior trait; methods, **method, methodology; practice,** praxis; procedure, proceeding; **actions,** acts, goings-on, doings, what one is up to, movements, moves, tactics; action, doing 328.1; activity 330; objective *or* observable behavior; motions, gestures, gesticulation, hand-waving; pose, affectation 500; pattern, behavior pattern; Type A behavior, Type B behavior; culture pattern, behavioral norm, folkway, **custom** 373

2 good behavior, sanctioned behavior; good citizenship; good manners, correct deportment, **etiquette** 580.3; **courtesy** 504; social behavior, sociability 582; bad *or* poor behavior, **misbehavior** 322; **discourtesy** 505

3 behaviorism, behavioral science, behavior *or* behavioristic psychology, Watsonian psychology, Skinnerian psychology; social science; behavior modification, behavior therapy ethology, animal behavior, human behavior, social behavior, ethology; behavior modification

VERBS **4 behave, act, do,** go on; **behave oneself, conduct oneself,** manage oneself, **handle oneself,** guide oneself, **comport oneself, deport oneself,** demean oneself, **bear oneself, carry oneself;** acquit oneself, quit oneself <old>; proceed, move, swing into action; **misbehave** 322.4

5 behave oneself, behave, act well, clean up one's act <nf>, act one's age, **be good,** be nice, **do right,** do what is right, do the right *or* proper thing, keep out of mischief, play the game *and* mind one's P's and Q's <nf>, be on one's good *or* best behavior, play one's cards right, set a good example

6 treat, use, do by, deal by, **act *or* behave toward,** conduct oneself toward, act with regard to, conduct oneself vis-à-vis *or* in the face of; **deal with,** cope with, **handle;** respond to

ADJS **7 behavioral;** behaviorist, behavioristic; ethological; **behaved,** behaviored, **mannered,** demeanored

322 MISBEHAVIOR

NOUNS **1 misbehavior, misconduct,** misdemeanor <old>; unsanctioned *or* nonsanctioned behavior; frowned-upon behavior; **naughtiness,** badness; impropriety; venial sin; **disorderly conduct,** disorder, disorderliness, disruptiveness, disruption, **rowdiness,** rowdyism, riotousness, ruffianism, hooliganism, hoodlumism, aggro <Brit nf>; vandalism, trashing; roughhouse, horseplay; discourtesy 505; vice 654; misfeasance, malfeasance, misdoing, delinquency, **wrongdoing** 655

2 mischief, mischievousness; devilment, deviltry, devilry; **roguishness,** roguery, scampishness; **waggery,** waggishness; **impishness,** devilishness, puckishness, elfishness; **prankishness,** pranksomeness; sportiveness, playfulness, *espièglerie* <Fr>; high spirits, youthful spirits; foolishness 923

3 mischief-maker, mischief, **rogue, devil,** knave, **rascal,** rapscallion, scapegrace, **scamp; wag** 489.12; buffoon 707.10; funmaker, joker, jokester, practical joker, prankster, life of the party, **cutup** <nf>; **rowdy,** ruffian, hoodlum, hood <nf>; hooligan; **imp, elf, puck,** pixie, **minx,** bad boy, bugger *and* booger <nf>, little devil, little rascal, little monkey, *enfant terrible* <Fr>

VERBS **4 misbehave,** misdemean <old>, **misbehave oneself, misconduct oneself,** misdemean oneself <old>, behave ill; get into mischief; **act up** *and* make waves *and* **carry on** *and* carry on something scandalous <nf>, sow one's wild oats; **cut up** <nf>, horse around <nf>, roughhouse *and* cut up rough <nf>; rock on; play the fool 923.6

ADJS 5 misbehaving, unbehaving; naughty, bad; improper, not respectable; out-of-order *and* off-base *and* out-of-line <nf>; **disorderly,** disruptive, **rowdy,** rowdyish, **ruffianly**

6 mischievous, mischief-loving, full of mischief, full of the devil *or* old nick; **roguish,** scampish, scapegrace, arch, knavish; **devilish; impish; puckish, elfish,** elvish; **waggish, prankish,** pranky, pranksome, trickish, tricksy; **playful,** sportive, high-spirited, *espiègle* <Fr>; foolish 923.8

ADVS 7 mischievously, roguishly, knavishly, scampishly, devilishly; impishly, puckishly, elfishly; waggishly; prankishly, playfully, sportively, in fun

323 WILL

NOUNS 1 will, volition; choice, determination, **decision** 371.1; **wish, mind, fancy,** discretion, pleasure, **inclination, disposition,** liking, appetence, appetency, **desire** 100; half a mind *or* notion, idle wish, velleity; **appetite, passion, lust, sexual desire** 75.5; animus, **objective, intention** 380; **command** 420; **free choice,** one's own will *or* choice *or* discretion *or* initiative, **free will** 430.6, free hand; conation, conatus; will power, **resolution** 359; final will *or* wishes

VERBS 2 will, wish, see *or* think fit, think good, think proper, **choose to, have a mind to;** have half a mind *or* notion to; **choose, determine, decide** 371.14,16; **resolve** 359.7; command, decree; **desire** 100.14,18

3 have one's will, **have *or* get one's way, get one's wish, have one's druthers** <nf>, **write one's own ticket,** have it all one's way, do *or* go as one pleases, please oneself; assert oneself, take the bit in one's teeth, take charge of one's destiny; stand on one's rights; take the law into one's own hands; have the last word, impose one's will; know one's own mind

ADJS 4 volitional, volitive; willing, voluntary; conative; *ex gratia* <L>; intentional

ADVS 5 at will, at choice, at pleasure, *al piacere* <Ital>, **at one's pleasure,** *a beneplacito* <Ital>, at one's will and pleasure, at one's own sweet will, **at one's discretion,** *à discrétion* <Fr>, *ad arbitrium* <L>; *ad libitum* <L>, ad lib; as one wishes, as it pleases *or* suits oneself, **in one's own way,** in one's own sweet way *or* time <nf>, **as one thinks best,** as it seems good *or* best, as far as one desires; of one's own free will, of one's own accord, on one's own; without coercion, unforced

324 WILLINGNESS

NOUNS 1 willingness, gameness <nf>, readiness; **unreluctance,** unloathness, ungrudgingness; agreeableness, **agreeability,** favorableness; **acquiescence, consent** 441; **compliance,** cooperativeness; receptivity, receptiveness, responsiveness; amenability, tractableness, tractability, docility, biddability, biddableness, pliancy, pliability, malleability; **eagerness,** keenness, promptness, forwardness, alacrity, zeal, zealousness, ardor, enthusiasm, fervor; goodwill, cheerful consent; **willing heart** *or* **mind** *or* **humor, favorable disposition,** positive *or* right *or* receptive mood, willing ear

2 voluntariness, volunteering; **gratuitousness; spontaneity,** spontaneousness, unforcedness; **self-determination,** self-activity, self-action, autonomy, autonomousness, independence, free will 430.6; **volunteerism,** voluntaryism, voluntarism; volunteer; labor of love

VERBS 3 be willing, be game <nf>, be ready; be of favorable disposition, take the trouble, find it in one's heart, find one's heart <old>, have a willing heart; **incline, lean;** look kindly upon; be open to, bring oneself, **agree,** be agreeable to; **acquiesce, consent** 441.2; not hesitate to, would as lief, would as leave <nf>, would as lief as not, not care *or* mind if one does <nf>; **play** *or* **go along** <nf>, do one's part *or* bit, have a good mind to; be eager, be keen, be dying to, fall all over oneself, be spoiling for, be champing at the bit; be Johnny on the spot, step into the breach; **enter with a will,** lean *or* bend over backward, go into heart and soul, go the extra mile, plunge into; **cooperate,** collaborate 450.3; lend *or* give *or* turn a willing ear

4 volunteer, do voluntarily, do ex gratia, **do of one's own accord,** do of one's own volition, **do of one's own free will** *or* **choice;** do independently; put forward, sacrifice oneself; offer

ADJS 5 willing, willinghearted, ready, game <nf>; **disposed, inclined, minded, willed,** fain *and* prone <old>; **well-disposed,** well-inclined, favorably inclined *or* disposed; predisposed; **favorable, agreeable, cooperative; compliant,** content <old>, **acquiescent** 332.13, **consenting** 441.4; **eager;** keen, prompt, quick, alacritous, forward, ready and willing, zealous, ardent, enthusiastic; in the mood *or* vein *or* humor *or* mind, in a good mood; receptive, responsive; amenable, tractable, docile, pliant, in favor

6 ungrudging, ungrumbling, **unreluctant,** unloath, **nothing loath,** unaverse, unshrinking

7 voluntary, volunteer; *ex gratia* <L>, **gratuitous; spontaneous, free, freewill;** offered, proffered;

discretionary, discretional, nonmandatory, **optional,** elective; arbitrary; **self-determined,** self-determining, autonomous, independent, self-active, self-acting; **unsought,** unbesought, **unasked,** unrequested, **unsolicited, uninvited,** unbidden, uncalled-for; **unforced,** uncoerced, unpressured, unrequired, uncompelled; unprompted, uninfluenced; spontaneous

ADVS **8 willingly, with a will,** with good will, with right good will, *de bonne volonté* <Fr>; **eagerly,** with zest, with relish, with open arms, without question, zealously, ardently, enthusiastically; **readily,** promptly, at the drop of a hat <nf>

9 agreeably, favorably, compliantly; lief, lieve <nf>, fain, as lief, as lief as not; **ungrudgingly,** ungrumblingly, **unreluctantly, nothing loath,** without reluctance *or* demur *or* hesitation, unstintingly, unreservedly

10 voluntarily, freely, gratuitously, spontaneously; optionally, electively, by choice; **of one's own accord,** of one's own free will, of one's own volition, without reservation, of one's own choice, at one's own discretion; without coercion *or* pressure *or* compulsion *or* intimidation; independently

325 UNWILLINGNESS

NOUNS **1 refusal** 442, **unwillingness, disinclination,** nolition, **indisposition,** indisposedness, **reluctance,** renitency, renitence, grudgingness, grudging consent; unenthusiasm, lack of enthusiasm *or* zeal *or* eagerness, slowness, backwardness, dragging of the feet *and* foot-dragging <nf>, apathy, indifference; sullenness, sulk, sulks, sulkiness; cursoriness, perfunctoriness; recalcitrance *or* recalcitrancy, disobedience, refractoriness, fractiousness, intractableness, indocility, mutinousness; averseness, aversion, repugnance, antipathy, distaste, disrelish, no stomach for; **obstinacy, stubbornness** 361.1; opposition 451; **resistance** 453; **disagreement,** dissent 456.3

2 demur, demurral, **scruple, qualm,** qualm of conscience, reservation, compunction; **hesitation,** hesitancy *or* hesitance, pause, boggle, **falter;** qualmishness, scrupulousness, scrupulosity; **stickling,** boggling; **faltering;** shrinking; shyness, **diffidence,** modesty, bashfulness, retiring disposition, restraint; recoil; **protest, objection** 333.2

VERBS **3 refuse** 442.3, **be unwilling, would** *or* **had rather not, not care to,** not feel like <nf>, not find it in one's heart to, not have the heart *or* stomach

to; **mind,** object to, draw the line at, be dead set against, **balk at;** grudge, begrudge

4 demur, scruple, have qualms *or* scruples; **stickle, stick at,** boggle, strain; falter, waver; **hesitate,** pause, be half-hearted, **hang back,** hang off, hold off; **fight shy of,** shy at, shy, crane, shrink, recoil, blench, flinch, wince, quail, pull back; make bones about *or* of

ADJS **5 unwilling, disinclined, indisposed,** not in the mood, averse, not feeling like; **unconsenting** 442.6; dead set against, opposed 451.8; **resistant** 453.5; **disagreeing,** differing, at odds 456.16; disobedient, recalcitrant, refractory, fractious, sullen, sulky, indocile, mutinous; cursory, perfunctory; **involuntary, forced**

6 reluctant, renitent, **grudging, loath;** backward, laggard, dilatory, slow, slow to, foot-dragging; unenthusiastic, unzealous, indifferent, apathetic, perfunctory; balky, balking, restive

7 demurring, qualmish, boggling, stickling, hedging, squeamish, **scrupulous; diffident,** shy, modest, bashful; **hesitant,** hesitating, faltering; shrinking

ADVS **8 unwillingly, involuntarily, against one's will,** *à contre coeur* <Fr>; under compulsion *or* coercion *or* pressure; in spite of oneself, *malgré soi* <Fr>

9 reluctantly, grudgingly, sullenly, sulkily; unenthusiastically, perfunctorily; with dragging feet, with a bad *or* an ill grace, **under protest;** with a heavy heart, with no heart *or* stomach; over one's dead body, not on one's life

326 OBEDIENCE

NOUNS **1 obedience** *or* **obediency,** compliance; acquiescence, consent 441; **deference** 155.1, self-abnegation, submission, submissiveness 433.3; servility 138; eagerness *or* readiness *or* willingness to serve, **dutifulness,** duteousness; **service,** servitium, homage, fealty, **allegiance, loyalty,** faithfulness, faith, suit and service *or* suit service, observance <old>, brand loyalty; doglike devotion *or* obedience; **conformity** 867, lockstep; law-abidingness; obeisance, good behavior, best behavior

VERBS **2 obey, mind, heed, keep, observe,** listen *or* hearken to; **comply, conform** 867.3, walk in lockstep; stay in line *and* not get out of line *and* not get off base <nf>, **toe the line** *or* mark, come to heel, fall in, fall in line, obey the rules, follow the book, keep the law, behave, be on one's best behavior, **do what one is told;** do as one says, do the will of, defer to 155.4, do one's bidding, come at one's call, lie down and roll over for <nf>; take orders, attend to orders, do suit and service, follow the lead of; **submit** 433.6,9

ADJS **3 obedient, compliant,** complying, allegiant; **acquiescent,** consenting 441.4, **submissive** 433.12, deferential 155.8, self-abnegating; willing, **dutiful,** duteous; under control; loyal, faithful, devoted; uncritical, unshakeable, doglike; conforming, in conformity; law-abiding

4 at one's command, at one's whim *or* pleasure, at one's disposal, at one's nod, at one's call, **at one's beck and call**

5 henpecked, tied to one's apron strings, on a string, on a leash, in leading strings; wimpish <nf>; milk-toast *or* milquetoast, Caspar Milquetoast; under one's thumb; chicken-pecked

ADVS **6 obediently, compliantly; acquiescently, submissively** 433.17; willingly, **dutifully,** duteously; loyally, faithfully, devotedly; in obedience to, in compliance *or* conformity with

7 at your service *or* command *or* orders, as you please, as you will, as thou wilt <old>

327 DISOBEDIENCE

NOUNS **1 disobedience,** nonobedience, **noncompliance; undutifulness,** unduteousness; willful disobedience; **insubordination,** indiscipline; **unsubmissiveness, intractability,** indocility 361.4, recusancy; **nonconformity** 868; **disrespect** 156; **lawlessness,** waywardness, frowardness, naughtiness; violation, transgression, infraction, infringement, lawbreaking; civil disobedience, passive resistance; uncooperativeness, noncooperation; **dereliction,** deliberate negligence, default, delinquency, nonfeasance

2 defiance, refractoriness, recalcitrance *or* recalcitrancy, recalcitration, defiance of authority, contumacy, **contumaciousness, obstreperousness, unruliness,** restiveness, fractiousness, orneriness *and* feistiness <nf>; wildness 430.3; **obstinacy, stubbornness** 361.1

3 rebelliousness, mutinousness; riotousness; insurrectionism, insurgentism; factiousness, **sedition,** seditiousness; treasonableness, traitorousness, subversiveness, subversion; extremism 611.4

4 revolt, rebellion, revolution, mutiny, insurrection, insurgence *or* insurgency, *émeute* <Fr>, **uprising,** rising, outbreak, general uprising, *levée en masse* <Fr>, **riot,** civil disorder; peasant revolt, *jacquerie* <Fr>; putsch, coup, coup d'état; **strike, general strike;** intifada; resistance movement, resistance; terrorism

5 rebel, revolter; **insurgent,** insurrectionary, insurrecto, **insurrectionist;** malcontent, *frondeur* <Fr>; **insubordinate; mutineer,** rioter, brawler; maverick <nf>, noncooperator, troublemaker, refusenik <nf>, agent provocateur; nonconformist 868.3; agitator 375.11; extremist 611.12; reactionary; revolutionary, revolutionist 860.3; traitor, subversive 357.11; freedom fighter; contra

VERBS **6 disobey,** not mind, not heed, not keep *or* observe, not listen *or* hearken, pay no attention to, **ignore, disregard, defy,** set at defiance, fly in the face of, snap one's fingers at, scoff at, flout, go counter to, set at naught, set naught by, care naught for; be a law unto oneself, step out of line, get off-base <nf>, refuse to cooperate; not conform 868.4, hear a different drummer; **violate,** transgress 435.4; break the law 674.5; thumb one's nose at

7 revolt, rebel, kick over the traces, reluct, reluctate; **rise up,** rise, arise, rise up in arms, mount the barricades; mount *or* make a coup d'état; **mutiny,** mutineer <old>; insurge *and* insurrect <old>, **riot,** run riot; revolutionize, revolution, revolute, subvert, overthrow 852.2; call a general strike, strike 727.5; secede, break away

ADJS **8 disobedient, transgressive,** uncomplying, violative, lawless, wayward, froward, naughty; recusant, nonconforming 868.5; **undutiful,** unduteous; self-willed, willful, obstinate 361.8; **defiant** 454.7; **undisciplined,** ill-disciplined, indisciplined

9 insubordinate, unsubmissive, indocile, **uncompliant, uncooperative,** noncooperative, noncooperating, **intractable** 361.12

10 defiant, refractory, recalcitrant, contumacious, obstreperous, unruly, restive, impatient of control *or* discipline; fractious, ornery *and* feisty <nf>; wild, untamed 430.29

11 rebellious, rebel, breakaway; **mutinous,** mutineering; **insurgent, insurrectionary,** riotous, turbulent; factious, **seditious,** seditionary; revolutionary, revolutional; traitorous, treasonable, subversive; extreme, extremistic 611.20

ADVS **12 disobediently,** uncompliantly, against *or* contrary to order and discipline; **insubordinately, unsubmissively,** indocilely, **uncooperatively;** unresignedly; disregardfully, floutingly, **defiantly;** intractably 361.17; obstreperously, contumaciously, restively, fractiously; **rebelliously,** mutinously; riotously

328 ACTION

<voluntary action>

NOUNS **1 action, activity** 330, act, willed action *or* activity; **acting, doing,** activism, direct action, not words but action, happening; **practice,** actual practice, praxis; **exercise,** drill; **operation,** working, function, functioning; play; **operations,** affairs, workings; **business,** employment, work, occupation; **behavior** 321

2 **performance, execution,** carrying out, enactment; **transaction; discharge, dispatch;** conduct, **handling,** management, administration; **achievement, accomplishment, effectuation, implementation; commission, perpetration;** completion 407.2

3 **act, action, deed, doing,** thing, thing done, overt act; **turn; feat, stunt** and **trick** <nf>; **master stroke,** *tour de force* <Fr>, **exploit,** adventure, **enterprise, initiative,** achievement, accomplishment, **performance,** production, track record <nf>; gesture; effort, endeavor, job, undertaking; **transaction;** dealing, deal <nf>; passage; **operation, proceeding,** process, **step, measure, maneuver, move, movement;** policy, tactics; *démarche* <Fr>, coup, stroke; blow, go <nf>; accomplished fact, *fait accompli* <Fr>, done deal <nf>; overt act <law>; acta, *res gestae* <L>, **doings, dealings,** affairs; **works;** work, handiwork, hand

VERBS **4** **act, serve, function; operate, work, move,** practice, do one's stuff or one's thing <nf>; **move,** proceed; make, play, **behave** 321.4

5 **take action, take steps** or **measures; proceed,** proceed with, go ahead with, go with, go through with; do something, go or swing into action, **do something about, act on** or **upon,** take it on, run with it <nf>, get off the dime or one's ass or one's dead ass <nf>, get with it or the picture <nf>; fish or cut bait, shit or get off the pot *and* put up or shut up *and* put one's money where one's mouth is <nf>; **go,** have a go <chiefly Brit nf>, take a whack or a cut <nf>, lift a finger, **take** or **bear a hand;** play a role or part in; stretch forth one's hand, strike a blow; **maneuver,** make moves <nf>; get a life <nf>

6 **do, effect,** effectuate, **make; bring about,** bring to pass, **bring off, produce, deliver** <nf>, **do the trick,** put across or through; swing or swing it *and* hack it *and* cut it *and* cut the mustard <nf>; **do one's part,** carry one's weight, carry the ball <nf>, hold up one's end or one's end of the bargain; tear off <nf>, **achieve, accomplish,** realize 407.4; **render, pay; inflict, wreak,** do to; **commit, perpetrate;** pull off <nf>; go and do, up and do or take and do <nf>

7 **carry out,** carry through, go through, fulfill, work out; **bring off,** carry off; **put through,** get through; **implement; put into effect, put in** or **into practice,** carry into effect, execute, carry into execution, **translate into action;** suit the action to the word; rise to the occasion, come through <nf>

8 **practice, put into practice, exercise, employ, use; carry on, conduct, prosecute, wage; follow, pursue; engage in,** work at, devote oneself to, **do,** turn to, apply oneself to, employ oneself in; play at; **take up,** take to, **undertake, tackle,** take on, address oneself to, have a go at, turn one's hand to, **go in** or **out for** <nf>, make it one's business, follow as an occupation, set up shop; specialize in 866.4

9 **perform, execute, enact; transact; discharge, dispatch;** conduct, **manage, handle;** legislate, commission; dispose of, take care of, **deal with,** cope with; **make, accomplish,** complete 407.6

ADJS **10** **acting,** performing, practicing, serving, functioning, functional, operating, operative, operational, working, in harness; in action 889.11; behavioral 321.7

329 INACTION
<voluntary inaction>

NOUNS **1** **inaction,** passiveness, **passivity,** passivism; passive resistance, nonviolent resistance; nonresistance, nonviolence; pacifism; neutrality, neutralness, neutralism, **nonparticipation, noninvolvement;** standpattism <nf>; **do-nothingism,** do-nothingness, do-nothing policy; **laissez-faireism,** *laissez-faire* and *laissez-aller* <Fr>; watching and waiting, watchful waiting, waiting game, a wait-and-see attitude, indecision; **inertia,** inertness, **immobility,** dormancy, stagnation, stagnancy, vegetation, stasis, paralysis, standstill; **procrastination; idleness,** indolence, torpor, torpidness, torpidity, sloth; stalemate, logjam; **immobility** 853.1; equilibrium, dead center; **inactivity** 331; **quietude, serenity, quiescence** 173; **quietism,** contemplation, meditation, passive self-annihilation; leisure; contemplative life, *vita contemplativa* <L>; back burner

VERBS **2** **do nothing,** not stir, not budge, **not lift a finger** or **hand,** not move a foot, **sit back, sit on one's hands** <nf>, sit on one's ass or dead ass or butt or duff <nf>, sit on the sidelines, be a sideliner, sit it out, take a raincheck <nf>, fold one's arms, twiddle one's thumbs; **cool one's heels** or **jets** <nf>; **bide one's time, delay,** watch and wait, wait and see, play a waiting game, lie low, tread water <nf>; hang fire, not go off half-cocked; lie or sit back, lie or rest upon one's oars, rest, put one's feet up *and* kick back <nf>, be still 173.7; repose on one's laurels; drift, coast; **stagnate,** vegetate, veg out <nf>, lie dormant, hibernate; lay down on the job <nf>, idle 331.12; not stir, freeze; back-burner

3 **refrain, abstain,** hold, **spare, forbear, forgo,** keep from; hold or stay one's hand, sit by or idly by, sit on one's hands

4 let alone, leave alone, **leave** *or* **let well enough alone;** look the other way, not make waves, not look for trouble, not rock the boat; **let be,** leave be <nf>, let things take their course, let it have its way; leave things as they are; *laisser faire* or *laisser passer* or *laisser aller* <Fr>, live and let live; **take no part in,** not get involved in, **have nothing to do with,** have no hand in, stand *or* hold *or* remain aloof, keep out of; tolerate, sit on the fence

5 let go, let pass, **let slip, let slide** and let ride <nf>; procrastinate, sit tight, defer

ADJS **6 passive; neutral,** neuter; standpat <nf>, **do-nothing;** *laissez-faire* and *laissez-aller* <Fr>; **inert,** like a bump on a log <nf>, immobile, dormant, stagnant, stagnating, vegetative, vegetable, static, stationary, motionless, unmoving, paralyzed, paralytic; procrastinating; **inactive, idle** 331.18; quiescent 173.12; quietist, quietistic, contemplative, meditative

ADVS **7 at a stand** *or* **standstill,** at a halt; as a last resort

PHRS **8** if it ain't broke don't fix it, let sleeping dogs lie; *dolce far niente* <Ital>

330 ACTIVITY

NOUNS **1 activity, action,** activeness; **movement,** motion, **stir; proceedings, doings, goings-on; activism,** political activism, judicial activism, etc; **militancy;** business 724.1

2 liveliness, animation, vivacity, vivaciousness, **sprightliness, spiritedness,** bubbliness, ebullience, effervescence, **briskness, breeziness, peppiness** <nf>; **life, spirit, verve,** energy, adrenalin; pep *and* moxie *and* oomph *and* pizzazz *and* piss and vinegar <nf>, **vim** 17.2

3 quickness, swiftness, speediness, alacrity, celerity, readiness, smartness, sharpness, briskness; **promptness,** promptitude; dispatch, expeditiousness, expedition; **agility, nimbleness, spryness,** springiness

4 bustle, fuss, flurry, flutter, fluster, scramble, ferment, stew, sweat, whirl, swirl, vortex, maelstrom, **stir,** hubbub, hullabaloo, hoo-ha *and* foofaraw *and* flap <nf>, schemozzle <Brit nf>, ado, to-do <nf>, bother, botheration <nf>, pother; fussiness, flutteriness; tumult, commotion, **agitation; restlessness,** unquiet, fidgetiness; **spurt, burst,** fit, spasm

5 busyness, press of business, hive of activity; plenty to do, many irons in the fire, much on one's plate; the battle of life, rat race <nf>

6 industry, industriousness, assiduousness, **assiduity, diligence, application,** concentration, laboriousness, sedulity, **sedulousness,**

unsparingness, relentlessness, zealousness, ardor, fervor, vehemence; **energy,** energeticalness, strenuousness, strenuosity, tirelessness, indefatigability

7 enterprise, enterprisingness, dynamism, **initiative,** aggression, **aggressiveness,** killer instinct, force, forcefulness, pushfulness, pushingness, **pushiness, push, drive, hustle, go,** getup, get-up-and-get *or* **get-up-and-go** <nf>, go-ahead, go-getting, go-to-itiveness <nf>, **up-and-comingness; adventurousness,** venturousness, venturesomeness, adventuresomeness; spirit, gumption *and* spunk <nf>; **ambitiousness** 100.10

8 man *or* **woman of action, doer,** man of deeds; **hustler** *and* self-starter <nf>, bustler; go-getter *and* ball of fire *and* live wire *and* powerhouse *and* human dynamo *and* spitfire <nf>; **workaholic,** overachiever; beaver, busy bee, **eager beaver** <nf>, no slouch <nf>; operator *and* big-time operator *and* wheeler-dealer <nf>; winner <nf>; **activist,** political activist, **militant;** enthusiast 101.4; new broom, take-charge guy <nf>

9 overactivity, hyperactivity; hyperkinesia *or* hyperkinesis; franticness, frenziedness; overexertion, overextension; officiousness 214.2; a finger in every pie

VERBS **10 be busy, have one's hands full,** have many irons in the fire, have a lot on one's plate; not have a moment to spare, not have a moment to call one's own, not be able to call one's time one's own; do it on the run; have other things to do, have other fish to fry; **work, labor, drudge** 725.14; **busy oneself** 724.10,11

11 stir, stir about, **bestir oneself,** stir one's stumps <nf>, get down to business, sink one's teeth into it, take hold, be up and doing

12 bustle, fuss, make a fuss, stir, stir about, rush around *or* about, tear around, hurry about, buzz *or* whiz about, dart to and fro, run *or* go around like a chicken with its head cut off, run around in circles

13 hustle <nf>, **drive,** drive oneself, **push, scramble,** go all out <nf>, **make things hum,** step lively <nf>, make the sparks *or* chips fly <nf>, do one's damnedest <nf>; make up for lost time; press on, drive on; go ahead, forge ahead, shoot ahead, go full steam ahead

14 <nf terms> **hump,** get cutting, break one's neck, bear down on it, put one's back into it, get off the dime, get off one's ass *or* duff *or* dead ass, **hit the ball,** pour it on, lean on it, shake a leg, go to town, get the lead out, floor it, go wild, go gangbusters

15 keep going, keep on, keep on the go, keep on keeping on, keep on trucking <nf>, **carry on,** peg *or* plug away <nf>, **keep at it,** keep moving, keep driving, **keep the pot boiling,** keep the ball rolling; keep busy, **keep one's nose to the grindstone,** stay on the treadmill, burn the candle at both ends

16 make the most of one's time, improve the shining hour, make hay while the sun shines, not let the grass grow under one's feet; get up early

ADJS 17 **active, lively, animated, spirited,** bubbly, ebullient, effervescent, **vivacious, sprightly,** chipper *and* perky <nf>, pert; **spry, breezy, brisk, energetic,** eager, keen, can-do <nf>; smacking, spanking; alive, live, full of life, full of pep *or* go *and* pizzazz *or* moxie <nf>, alive and kicking; **peppy** *and* snappy *and* zingy <nf>; frisky, bouncing, bouncy; mercurial, quicksilver; **activist,** activistic, **militant**

18 **quick, swift, speedy, expeditious, snappy** <nf>, celeritous, alacritous, dispatchful <old>, **prompt,** ready, smart, sharp, quick on the draw *or* trigger *or* upswing <nf>; **agile, nimble, spry,** springy

19 **astir, stirring,** afoot, **on foot;** in full swing

20 **bustling,** fussing, fussy; **fidgety,** restless, fretful, jumpy, unquiet, unsettled 105.23; **agitated, turbulent**

21 **busy,** full of business; **occupied, engaged, employed, working;** at it; **at work,** on duty, on the job, in harness; involved, engagé; **hard at work, hard at it; on the move, on the go,** on the run, **on the hop** *or* **jump** <nf>, on the make <nf>; busy as a bee *or* beaver, busier than a one-armed paper hanger <nf>; up to one's ears *or* elbows *or* neck *or* eyeballs in <nf>; tied up

22 **industrious, assiduous, diligent, sedulous,** laborious, **hardworking,** workaholic; hard, unremitting, unsparing, relentless, zealous, ardent, fervent, vehement; **energetic,** strenuous; never idle; unsleeping; tireless, unwearied, unflagging, indefatigable; stick-to-it-ive <nf>

23 **enterprising, aggressive, dynamic,** activist, proactive, driving, forceful, **pushing,** pushful, **pushy, up-and-coming, go-ahead** *and* **hustling** <nf>, go-getting <nf>; adventurous, venturous, venturesome, adventuresome; **ambitious** 100.28

24 **overactive,** hyperactive, hyper <nf>; hectic, frenzied, frantic, frenetic; hyperkinetic; intrusive, officious 214.9; full of beans <nf>

ADVS 25 **actively, busily;** lively, sprightly, **briskly, breezily, energetically, animatedly, vivaciously, spiritedly,** with life and spirit, with gusto; allegro, allegretto; full tilt, in full swing, all out <nf>; like a house afire

26 **quickly, swiftly, expeditiously,** with dispatch, readily, **promptly; agilely, nimbly, spryly**

27 **industriously, assiduously, diligently, sedulously,** laboriously; unsparingly, relentlessly, zealously,

ardently, fervently, vehemently; **energetically,** strenuously, tirelessly, indefatigably

331 INACTIVITY

NOUNS 1 **inactivity, inaction** 329, inactiveness; lull, suspension; suspended animation; dormancy, hibernation; immobility, motionlessness, quiescence 173; **inertia** 329.1; underactivity; back burner

2 **idleness,** unemployment, nothing to do, otiosity, inoccupation; **leisure,** leisureliness, unhurried ease; idle hands, idle hours, off hours, time on one's hands; "a life of dignified otiosity"— Thackeray; **relaxation,** letting down, unwinding, putting one's feet up, slippered ease

3 **unemployment,** lack of work, joblessness, inoccupation; layoff, furlough; normal unemployment, seasonal unemployment, technological unemployment, cyclical unemployment; unemployment insurance; shutdown, recession, depression

4 **idling, loafing,** lazing, *flânerie* <Fr>, goofing off <nf>, slacking <nf>, goldbricking <nf>; *dolce far niente* <Ital>; trifling; dallying, dillydallying, mopery, dawdling; loitering, tarrying, lingering; lounging, **lolling**

5 **indolence, laziness, sloth,** slothfulness, bone-laziness; laggardness, slowness, dilatoriness, remissness, do-nothingness, faineancy, *fainéantise* <Fr>; inexertion, inertia; **shiftlessness,** do-lessness <nf>; hoboism, vagrancy; spring fever; ergophobia

6 **languor,** languidness, languorousness, languishment <old>, lackadaisicalness, lotus-eating; **listlessness,** lifelessness, inanimation, enervation, slowness, lenitude *or* lentor <old>, **dullness, sluggishness,** heaviness, dopiness <nf>, hebetude, supineness, **lassitude, lethargy,** loginess; kef, nodding; phlegm, **apathy, indifference, passivity;** torpidness, torpor, torpidity; stupor, stuporousness, stupefaction; **sloth,** slothfulness, acedia; **sleepiness, somnolence, oscitancy, yawning, drowsiness** 22.1; **weariness, fatigue** 21; jadedness, satedness 994.2; world-weariness, ennui, boredom 118.3

7 **lazybones,** lazyboots, lazylegs, indolent, lie-abed, slugabed

8 **idler, loafer, lounger,** loller, layabout <Brit nf>, couch potato <nf>, lotus-eater, *flâneur and flâneuse* <Fr>, **do-nothing,** dolittle, *fainéant* <Fr>, goof-off *and* fuck-off *and* goldbrick *and* goldbricker <nf>, clock watcher; **sluggard,** slug, slouch, sloucher, lubber, stick-in-the-mud <nf>, gentleman of leisure; **time waster,** time killer; **dallier, dillydallier,** mope, moper, doodler, diddler

<nf>, **dawdler,** dawdle, laggard, **loiterer,** lingerer; waiter on Providence; trifler, **putterer,** potterer

9 **bum,** stiff <nf>, derelict, skid-row bum, Bowery bum, *lazzarone* <Ital>; beachcomber; **good-for-nothing,** good-for-naught, **ne'er-do-well,** wastrel; drifter, vagrant, hobo, tramp 178.3; beggar 440.8

10 homeless person; street person; shopping-bag lady *or* woman, bag person

11 **nonworker, drone;** cadger, bummer *and* moocher <nf>, **sponger,** freeloader, lounge lizard <nf>, social parasite, parasite, spiv <Brit>; beggar, mendicant, panhandler <nf>; **the unemployed;** the unemployable; the chronically unemployed, discouraged workers, lumpen proletariat; leisure class, rentiers, coupon-clippers, idle rich

VERBS 12 **idle,** do nothing, **laze,** lazy <nf>, take one's ease *or* leisure, take one's time, **loaf, lounge; lie around,** lounge around, loll around, lollop about <Brit nf>, moon, moon around, sit around, sit on one's ass *or* butt *or* duff <nf>, stand *or* hang around, **loiter about** *or* **around,** slouch, slouch around, **bum around** *and* mooch around <nf>; **shirk,** avoid work, **goof off** *and* **lie down on the job** <nf>; sleep at one's post; let the grass grow under one's feet; twiddle one's thumbs, fold one's arms; back-burner

13 **waste time,** consume time, **kill time,** idle *or* trifle *or* fritter *or* fool away time, loiter away *or* loiter out the time, beguile the time, **while away the time,** pass the time, lose time, waste the precious hours, burn daylight <old>; **trifle,** dabble, fribble, footle, putter, potter, piddle, diddle, doodle

14 **dally, dillydally,** piddle, diddle, diddle-daddle, doodle, **dawdle, loiter,** lollygag <nf>, linger, lag, poke, take one's time, hang around *or* about <nf>, kick around <nf>

15 **take it easy,** take things as they come, **drift,** drift with the current, go with the flow, swim with the stream, coast, lead an easy life, **live a life of ease,** eat the bread of idleness, lie *or* rest on one's oars; rest *or* repose on one's laurels, lie back on one's record

16 **lie idle, lie fallow;** aestivate, hibernate, lie dormant; lie *or* lay off, charge *or* recharge one's batteries <nf>; lie up, lie on the shelf; ride at anchor, lay *or* lie by, lay *or* lie to; have nothing to do, have nothing on <nf>

ADJS 17 **inactive,** unactive; stationary, static, at a standstill; sedentary; **quiescent,** motionless 173.13; inanimate

18 **idle,** fallow, otiose; **unemployed, unoccupied,** disengaged, *désœuvré* <Fr>, **jobless, out of work,** out of employ, out of a job, out of harness; free, available, at liberty, at leisure; at loose ends;

unemployable, lumpen; leisure, leisured; off-duty, off-work, off; housebound, shut-in; back-burnered

19 **indolent, lazy,** bone-lazy, **slothful,** workshy, ergophobic; **do-nothing,** *fainéant* <Fr>, **laggard,** slow, **dilatory,** procrastinative, remiss, slack, slacking, lax; easy; **shiftless,** do-less <nf>; **unenterprising,** nonaggressive; good-for-nothing, ne'er-do-well; drony, dronish, spivvish <Brit>, parasitic, cadging, sponging, scrounging

20 **languid, languorous, listless,** lifeless, inanimate, enervated, debilitated, **pepless** <nf>, lackadaisical, slow, wan, **lethargic,** logy, hebetudinous, supine, lymphatic, apathetic, **sluggish,** dopey <nf>, drugged, nodding, droopy, **dull,** heavy, leaden, lumpish, **torpid,** stultified, stuporous, **inert,** stagnant, stagnating, vegetative, vegetable, dormant; phlegmatic, numb, benumbed; moribund, dead, exanimate, dead to the world; sleepy, somnolent 22.21; **pooped** <nf>, weary; jaded, sated 994.6; **blasé,** world-weary, bored; out cold, comatose

332 ASSENT

NOUNS 1 **assent, acquiescence, concurrence, concurring, concurrency, compliance, agreement, acceptance,** accession, agreeance; eager *or* hearty *or* warm assent, welcome; assentation; agreement in principle, general agreement; support; **consent** 441; oral agreement, written agreement

2 **affirmative; yes,** yea, aye, amen, OK, yeah <nf>; nod, nod of assent; thumbs-up; **affirmativeness,** affirmative attitude, yea-saying; **me-tooism;** toadying, automatic agreement, knee-jerk assent, subservience, ass-licking <nf>

3 **acknowledgment, recognition, acceptance;** appreciation; **admission,** confession, concession, allowance; avowal, profession, declaration; shout-out

4 **ratification, endorsement, acceptance, approval, approbation** 509.1, subscription, subscribership, signing-off, imprimatur, **sanction, permission, the OK** *and* the okay *and* **the green light** *and* **the go-ahead** *and* the nod <nf>, **certification, confirmation, validation, authentication,** authorization, warrant; **affirmation,** affirmance; stamp, rubber stamp, seal *or* **stamp of approval;** seal, signet, sigil; **subscription, signature,** John Hancock <nf>; countersignature; visa, *visé* <Fr>; notarization

5 **unanimity,** unanimousness, universal *or* univocal *or* unambiguous assent; **like-mindedness, meeting of minds,** one *or* same mind; total agreement; **understanding,** mutual understanding; **concurrence, consent,** general consent, common

assent *or* consent, consentaneity, **accord,** accordance, **concord,** concordance, **agreement,** general agreement; **consensus,** consensus of opinion <nf>; *consensus omnium* <L>, universal agreement *or* accord, *consensus gentium* <L>, agreement of all, shared sense, sense of the meeting; **acclamation,** general acclamation; unison, harmony, **chorus, concert,** one *or* single voice, one accord; general voice, vox pop, *vox populi* <L>

6 **assenter, consenter, accepter,** covenanter, covenantor; assentator, yea-sayer; **yes-man,** toady, creature, ass-licker *and* ass-kisser *and* brown-nose *and* boot-licker <nf>, fellow traveler, supporter

7 **endorser, subscriber, ratifier,** approver, upholder, certifier, confirmer; **signer,** signatory, the undersigned; seconder; cosigner, cosignatory, party; underwriter, guarantor, insurer; notary, notary public

VERBS 8 **assent,** give *or* yield assent, **acquiesce, consent** 441.2, **comply, accede, agree,** agree to *or* with, have no problem with; find it in one's heart; take kindly to *and* hold with <nf>; **accept,** receive, buy <nf>, take one up on <nf>; **subscribe to,** acquiesce in, abide by; yes, **say 'yes' to; nod,** nod assent, vote for, cast one's vote for, give one's voice for; welcome, hail, cheer, acclaim, applaud, accept in toto

9 **concur, accord,** coincide, **agree, agree with,** agree in opinion; enter into one's view, enter into the ideas *or* feelings of, **see eye to eye, be at one with,** be of one mind with, go with, **go along with,** fall *or* chime *or* strike in with, close with, meet, conform to, side with, join *or* identify oneself with; cast in one's lot, fall in *or* into line, lend oneself to, play *or* go along, take kindly to; **echo,** ditto <nf>, say 'ditto' to, say 'amen' to; join in the chorus, go along with the crowd <nf>, run with the pack, go *or* float *or* swim with the stream *or* current; get on the bandwagon <nf>; rubber-stamp

10 **come to an agreement, agree, concur on, settle on,** agree with, **agree on** *or* **upon, arrive at an agreement, come to an understanding, come to terms, reach an understanding** *or* **agreement** *or* **accord,** strike *or* hammer out a bargain, covenant, get together <nf>; **shake hands on,** shake on it <nf>, seal the deal; come around to

11 **acknowledge, admit, own, confess, allow,** avow, **grant,** warrant, **concede,** yield <old>, defer; **accept, recognize;** agree in principle, express general agreement, go along with, not oppose *or* deny, agree provisionally *or* for the sake of argument; bring oneself to agree, assent grudgingly *or* under protest; let the ayes have it; acknowledge the corn

12 **ratify, endorse,** sign off on, second, support, **certify, confirm, validate, authenticate, accept,** give the nod *or* the green light *or* the go-ahead *or* the OK <nf>, give a nod of assent, give one's imprimatur, permit, give permission, **approve** 509.9; sanction, **authorize,** warrant, accredit; **pass,** pass on *or* upon, give thumbs up <nf>; amen, say amen to; visa, *visé* <Fr>; underwrite, subscribe to; **sign,** undersign, sign on the dotted line, put one's John Hancock on <nf>, initial, put one's mark *or* X *or* cross on; autograph; cosign, countersign; seal, sign and seal, set one's seal, **set one's hand and seal;** affirm, swear and affirm, take one's oath, swear to; rubber stamp <nf>; notarize

ADJS 13 **assenting, agreeing,** acquiescing, **acquiescent, compliant,** consenting, consentient, consensual, submissive, unmurmuring, conceding, concessive, assentatious, **agreed, content**

14 **accepted, approved,** received; acknowledged, admitted, allowed, granted, conceded, recognized, professed, confessed, avowed, warranted; self-confessed; **ratified, endorsed, certified,** confirmed, validated, authenticated; certificatory, confirmatory, validating, warranting; **signed,** sealed, signed and sealed, countersigned, underwritten; stamped; sworn to, notarized, affirmed, sworn and affirmed

15 **unanimous, solid,** consentaneous, **with one consent** *or* **voice;** uncontradicted, unchallenged, uncontroverted, uncontested, unopposed; **concurrent,** concordant, **of one accord; agreeing, in agreement, like-minded, of one mind,** of the same mind; of a piece, **at one,** at one with, agreed on all hands, carried by acclamation

ADVS 16 **affirmatively,** assentingly, in the affirmative

17 **unanimously,** concurrently, consentaneously, **by common** *or* **general consent,** with one consent, **with one accord,** with one voice, without contradiction, *nemine contradicente* <L>, nem con, without a dissenting voice, *nemine dissentiente* <L>, in chorus, in concert, in unison, in one voice, univocally, unambiguously, to a man, **together,** all together, all agreeing, **as one,** as one man, one and all, on all hands; by acclamation

INTERJS 18 **yes, yea,** aye, *oui* <Fr>, *sí* <Sp>, *da* <Russ>, *ja* <Ger>; yes sir, yes ma'am; why yes, *mais oui* <Fr>; **indeed,** yes indeed; **surely, certainly,** assuredly, most assuredly, **right, right you are, exactly, precisely,** just so, absolutely, positively, really, truly, rather <Brit>, quite, to be sure; **all right, right, good,** well and good, good enough, **very well,** *très bien* <Fr>; naturally, *naturellement* <Fr>; **of course,** as you say, **by all means,** by all manner of means; **amen;** hear hear <Brit>

19 <nf terms> **yeah,** yep, yup, uh-huh; yes sirree, same here, likewise, indeedy, yes indeedy, sure, sure thing, sure enough, surest thing you know; right on!, righto!; OK, okay, okey-dokey; Roger, Roger-dodger; fine; you bet!, bet your ass!, you can bet on it!, you can say that again!, you said it!, you better believe it; capeesh?

PHRS **20 so be it,** be it so, so mote it be <old>, so shall it be, *amen* <Heb>; so it is, so is it; agreed, done, that's about the size of it; *c'est bien* <Fr>; that takes care of that, that's that, that's right; that makes two of us

333 DISSENT

NOUNS **1 dissent, dissidence,** dissentience; nonassent, nonconsent, nonconcurrence, nonagreement, agreement to disagree; minority opinion *or* report *or* position; **disagreement, difference, variance,** diversity, disparity; **dissatisfaction, disapproval,** disapprobation, red light, thumbs down; repudiation, **rejection; refusal, opposition** 451; dissension, disaccord 456; **alienation,** withdrawal, dropping out, secession; recusance *or* recusancy, **nonconformity** 868; apostasy 363.2; counterculture, underground, alternative; raspberry *or* Bronx cheer <nf>

2 objection, protest; kick *and* **beef** *and* **bitch** *and* squawk *and* howl <nf>, protestation; **remonstrance, remonstration,** expostulation; **challenge; demur,** demurrer; **reservation, scruple,** compunction, qualm, twinge *or* qualm of conscience; **complaint, grievance; exception;** peaceful *or* nonviolent protest; **demonstration, demo** <nf>, protest demonstration, counterdemonstration, **rally,** march, sit-in, teach-in, boycott, strike, picketing, indignation meeting; grievance committee; **rebellion** 327.4

3 dissenter, dissident, dissentient, recusant; **objector,** demurrer; minority *or* opposition voice; **protester,** protestant, detractor; **separatist,** schismatic; sectary, sectarian, opinionist; nonconformist 868.3, odd man out; apostate 363.5; conscientious objector, passive resister; dissatisfied customer, bellyacher <nf>

VERBS **4 dissent,** dissent from, be in dissent, say nay, **disagree,** discord with, **differ,** not agree, disagree with, agree to disagree *or* differ; divide on, be at variance; **take exception,** withhold assent, **take issue, beg to differ,** raise an objection, rise to a point of order; be in opposition to, oppose, be at odds with; refuse to conform, kick against the pricks, march to *or* hear a different drummer, swim against the tide *or* against the current *or* upstream; **split off,**

withdraw, drop out, secede, separate *or* disjoin oneself, schismatize

5 object, protest, kick *and* **beef** <nf>, put up a struggle *or* fight; **bitch** *and* **beef** *and* **squawk** *and* howl *and* holler *and* put up a squawk *and* raise a howl <nf>; exclaim *or* cry out against, make *or* create *or* raise a stink about <nf>; yell bloody murder <nf>; **remonstrate,** expostulate; raise *or* press objections, raise one's voice against, enter a protest; **complain,** exclaim at, state a grievance, air one's grievances; **dispute, challenge,** call in question; **demur, scruple,** boggle, dig in one's heels; **demonstrate, demonstrate against,** rally, march, sit-in, teach-in, boycott, strike, picket; **rebel** 327.7

ADJS **6 dissenting, dissident,** dissentient, recusant; **disagreeing, differing; opposing** 451.8, in opposition; alienated; counterculture, antiestablishment, underground, alternative; breakaway <Brit>; at variance with, at odds with; schismatic, schismatical, sectarian, sectary; heterodox; nonconforming 868.5; rebellious 327.11; resistant 453.5

7 protesting, protestant; **objecting,** expostulative, expostulatory, remonstrative, remonstrant; under protest

334 AFFIRMATION

NOUNS **1 affirmation,** affirmance, **assertion,** assertation, **asseveration,** averment, **declaration,** vouch <old>, allegation; **avouchment, avowal; position, stand,** stance; profession, **statement, word,** say, saying, say-so <nf>, positive declaration *or* statement, affirmative; manifesto, position paper; statement of principles, **creed** 953.3; **pronouncement, proclamation,** announcement, annunciation, enunciation; proposition, conclusion; predication, predicate; protest, protestation; utterance, dictum, *ipse dixit* <L>; emphasis, stress; admission, confession, disclosure; mission statement

2 affirmativeness; assertiveness, positiveness, absoluteness, speaking out, table-thumping <nf>; definiteness

3 deposition, sworn statement, affidavit, statement under oath, notarized statement, sworn testimony *or* statement, affirmation; **vouching, swearing; attestation;** certification; **testimony;** authentication, validation, verification, vouch <old>; substantiation, proof

4 oath, vow, avow <old>, **word, assurance, guarantee, warrant,** promise, solemn oath *or* affirmation *or* word *or* declaration, word of honor; **pledge** 436.1; Bible oath, ironclad oath; judicial oath, extrajudicial oath, Hippocratic oath; oath of office, official oath; oath of allegiance, loyalty oath, test oath; commitment

VERBS **5 affirm, assert,** assever <old>, asseverate, **aver,** state positively, protest, lay down, avouch, avow, **declare,** say, say loud and clear, say out loud, sound off <nf>, have one's say, speak, speak one's piece *or* one's mind, speak up *or* out, **state,** set down, express, put, put it, put in one's two-cents worth <nf>; **allege,** profess; stand on *or* for; predicate; issue a manifesto *or* position paper, manifesto; announce, **pronounce,** annunciate, enunciate, **proclaim; maintain,** have, **contend,** argue, **insist, hold,** submit, maintain with one's last breath

6 depose, depone; **testify,** take the stand, witness; **warrant, attest,** certify, **guarantee, assure; vouch, vouch for, swear, swear to,** swear the truth, **assert under oath;** make *or* take one's oath, **vow;** swear by bell, book, and candle; call heaven to witness, declare *or* swear to God, swear on the Bible, kiss the book, swear to goodness, hope to die, cross one's heart *or* cross one's heart and hope to die; swear till one is black *or* blue in the face <nf>; corroborate, substantiate

7 administer an oath, **place** *or* **put under oath,** put to one's oath, put upon oath; **swear, swear in,** adjure <old>; charge

ADJS **8 affirmative,** affirming, affirmatory, certifying, certificatory; **assertive,** assertative, assertional; annunciative, annunciatory; enunciative, enunciatory; **declarative,** declaratory; predicative, predicational; **positive,** absolute, emphatic, decided, table-thumping <nf>, unambiguously, unmistakably, loud and clear; attested, corroboratory, substantiating

9 affirmed, asserted, asseverated, avouched, avowed, averred, **declared; alleged,** professed; **stated,** pronounced, announced, annunciated, enunciated; predicated; manifestoed; **deposed,** warranted, **attested, certified,** vouched, **vouched for,** vowed, pledged, **sworn, sworn to;** strongly worded, emphatic, underscored; allegeable

ADVS **10 affirmatively,** assertively, assertorily, declaratively, predicatively; **positively,** absolutely, decidedly, loudly, loud and clear, at the top of one's voice *or* one's lungs; emphatically, with emphasis, pointedly; without fear of contradiction; under oath, on one's honor *or* one's word

335 NEGATION, DENIAL

NOUNS **1 negation,** negating, abnegation; negativeness, negativity, **negativism,** negative attitude, naysaying; **obtusenss,** perversity, orneriness <nf>, cross-grainedness; **negative, no,** nay, nix <nf>; defiance; refusal; unacceptance; pessimism, defeatism; deal breaker

2 denial, disavowal, disaffirmation, disaffirmance, **disownment,** disallowance; disclamation, disclaimer; **renunciation, retraction,** retractation, **repudiation,** recantation; revocation, nullification, annulment, abrogation; abjuration, abjurement, forswearing; **contradiction,** flat *or* absolute contradiction, contravention, contrary assertion, controversion, countering, crossing, gainsaying, impugnment; flat denial, emphatic denial, **refutation, disproof** 958; **apostasy, defection** 363.2; **about-face, reversal** 363.1

VERBS **3 negate,** abnegate, negative; **say 'no',** no, naysay; shake one's head, wag *or* waggle the beard, nix <nf>; refuse, reject

4 deny, not admit, not accept, refuse to admit *or* accept; **disclaim, disown, disaffirm, disavow, disallow,** abjure, forswear, **renounce, retract,** take back, recant; revoke, nullify, **repudiate; contradict,** fly in the face of, cross, assert the contrary, contravene, controvert, impugn, **dispute,** gainsay, **oppose, counter,** go counter to, go contra, contest, take issue with, join issue upon, run counter to; belie, give the lie to, give one the lie direct *or* in his throat; deprecate; **refute** 958.5, **disprove** 958.4; **reverse oneself** 363.6; **defect, apostatize** 363.7

ADJS **5 negative,** negatory, abnegative, negational; **denying, disclaiming,** disowning, disaffirming, disallowing, disavowing, renunciative, renunciatory, repudiative, recanting, abjuratory, revocative *or* revocatory; **contradictory,** contradicting, contradictive, **opposing, contrary,** contra, counter, opposite, nay-saying, refuting, adversative, repugnant; **obtuse,** perverse, ornery <nf>, crossgrained, contrarious <nf>

ADVS **6 negatively, in the negative;** in denial, in contradiction, in opposition; in no way

CONJS **7 neither,** not either, **nor,** nor yet, or not, and not, also not

INTERJS **8 no, nay,** negative, *non* <Fr>, *nein* <Ger>, *nyet* <Russ>; certainly not, absolutely no; no sir, no ma'am, no siree; **not,** not a bit *or* whit *or* jot, I think not, not really; to the contrary, *au contraire* <Fr>, quite the contrary, far from it; no such thing, nothing of the kind *or* sort, not so

9 by no means, by no manner of means; on no account, in no respect, **in no case, under no circumstances, on no condition,** no matter what; **not at all,** not in the least, **never;** in no wise, in no way, noways, noway, nohow <nf>, not even; out of the question, in your dreams; **not for the world,** not for anything in the world, not if one can help it, not if I know it, not at any price, not for love or money, not for the life of me, over one's dead body; a thousand times no; to the contrary, *au contraire* <Fr>, quite the contrary, far from it; God forbid 510.27

10 <nf terms> nope, nix, no dice, unhunh, no sirree; no way, no way José, not on your life, not by a long chalk, not by a long shot *or* sight, not by a darn *or* damn sight, not a bit of it, not much, not a chance, fat chance, nothing doing, forget it, that'll be the day, you've got to be kidding *or* joking

336 IMITATION

NOUNS **1 imitation, copying,** counterfeiting, repetition; **me-tooism** <nf>, emulation, the sincerest form of flattery, following, mirroring, reflection, echo; copycat crime <nf>; **simulation** 354.3, modeling; fakery, forgery, plagiarism, plagiarizing, plagiary; **imposture, impersonation, takeoff** *and* hit-off <nf>, **impression,** burlesque, pastiche, *pasticcio* <Ital>; mimesis; parody, onomatopoeia

2 **mimicry, mockery,** apery, parrotry, mimetism; protective coloration *or* mimicry, aggressive mimicry, aposematic *or* synaposematic mimicry *and* cryptic mimicry <biology>, playing possum

3 **reproduction, duplication, imitation** 784.1, **copy** 785.1, dummy, mock-up, **replica,** facsimile, representation, paraphrase, approximation, model, version, knockoff <nf>, recording, transcript; computer model *or* simulation; parody, burlesque, pastiche, *pasticcio* <Ital>, travesty 508.6

4 **imitator,** simulator, me-tooer <nf>, **impersonator, impostor** 357.6, **mimic,** mimicker, mimer, mime, **mocker;** ventriloquist; mockingbird, cuckoo; **parrot,** polly, poll-parrot *or* polly-parrot, **ape,** aper, monkey; **echo,** echoer, echoist; **copier,** copyist, **copycat** <nf>; **faker, imposter,** counterfeiter, forger, plagiarist; dissimulator, dissembler, deceiver, gay deceiver, hypocrite, phony <nf>, poseur; conformist, sheep, slave to fashion

VERBS **5 imitate, copy, repeat,** ditto <nf>; do like <nf>, do <nf>, act *or* go *or* make like <nf>; **mirror, reflect; echo,** reecho, chorus; **borrow,** steal one's stuff <nf>, take a leaf out of one's book; assume, **affect; simulate;** counterfeit, fake <nf>, hoke *and* hoke up <nf>, forge, plagiarize, crib, lift <nf>; **parody,** pastiche, travesty; **paraphrase,** approximate

6 **mimic, impersonate,** mime, **ape, parrot,** copycat <nf>; do an impression; take off, hit off, hit off on, take off on, send up

7 **emulate, follow,** follow in the steps *or* footsteps of, walk in the shoes of, put oneself in another's shoes, follow in the wake of, follow the example of, follow suit, follow like sheep, jump on the bandwagon, play follow the leader; **copy after,** model after, model on, pattern after, pattern on, shape after, take after, take a leaf out of one's book, take as a model

ADJS **8 imitation, mock, sham,** copied, fake *and* phony <nf>, counterfeit, faux, dummy, forged, plagiarized, unoriginal, ungenuine; **pseudo,** synthetic, synthetical, artificial, man-made, ersatz, hokey *and* hoked-up <nf>, quasi

9 **imitative,** simulative, me-too <nf>, derivative; **mimic,** mimetic, **apish,** parrotlike; **emulative;** echoic, onomatopoetic, onomatopoeic

10 imitable, copiable, duplicable, replicable

ADVS **11** imitatively, apishly, apewise, parrotwise; onomatopoetically; synthetically; quasi

PREPS **12 like, in imitation of,** after, in the semblance of, on the model of, *à la* <Fr>

WORD ELEMENTS **13** quasi-, mim-, ne-, near-, semi-; -ish, -like

337 NONIMITATION

NOUNS **1 nonimitation, originality, novelty,** newness, innovation, freshness, uniqueness; **authenticity;** inventiveness, creativity, creativeness 986.3; idiosyncrasy

2 **original, model** 786, archetype, prototype 786.1, master, **pattern, mold,** pilot model; **innovation,** new departure; original thought; precedent, invention

3 **autograph,** holograph, first edition; genuine article

VERBS **4 originate, invent; innovate; create;** revolutionize; pioneer

ADJS **5 original, novel, unprecedented; unique,** *sui generis* <L>; new, fresh 841.7; underived, **firsthand; authentic, imaginative, creative** 986.18; **avant-garde,** revolutionary; **pioneer,** bellwether, trail-blazing, first in the field; *nouvelle* <Fr>

6 **unimitated,** uncopied, **unduplicated,** unreproduced, unprecedented, unexampled; **archetypal,** archetypical, archetypic, seminal, prototypal 786.9; **prime,** primary, primal, primitive, pristine

338 COMPENSATION

NOUNS **1 compensation, recompense,** repayment, payback, recoup, indemnity, indemnification, measure for measure, rectification, restitution, **reparation; amends,** expiation, atonement, meed

<old>; damage control; **redress,** satisfaction, remedy; commutation, substitution; **offsetting,** balancing, **counterbalancing,** counteraction; payback time; **retaliation** 506, revenge, *lex talionis* <L>

2 **offset,** setoff; **counterbalance,** counterpoise, equipoise, counterweight, makeweight; **balance,** ballast; **trade-off,** equivalent, consideration, something of value, *quid pro quo* <L, something for something>, tit for tat, give-and-take 863.1; retroaction

3 **counterclaim,** counterdemand

VERBS 4 **compensate,** make compensation, make good, set right, restitute, pay back, rectify, **make up for; make amends,** expiate, do penance, atone; **recompense,** pay back, repay, indemnify, cover; **trade off,** give and take; correct, **retaliate** 506.4

5 **offset** 779.4, set off, **counteract,** countervail, **counterbalance,** counterweigh, counterpoise, **balance,** play off against, set against, set over against, equiponderate; recoup, **square,** square up, settle the score

ADJS 6 **compensating, compensatory;** recompensive, amendatory, indemnificatory, reparative, rectifying, retributive; **offsetting,** counteracting *or* counteractive, countervailing, balancing, **counterbalancing,** zero-sum; **expiatory,** penitential; **retaliatory** 506.8

ADVS 7 **in compensation,** in return, back; in consideration, for a consideration

ADVS, CONJS 8 **notwithstanding,** but, all the same <nf>, still, yet, even; **however, nevertheless,** nonetheless; **although,** when, though; howbeit, albeit; **at all events,** in any event, **in any case,** at any rate; **be that as it may,** for all that, even so, **on the other hand,** rather, again, at the same time, all the same, just the same, **however, that may be;** after all, after all is said and done

ADVS, PREPS 9 **in spite of,** spite of <nf>, **despite,** in despite of, with, even with; **regardless of,** regardless, irregardless <nf>, irrespective of, without respect *or* regard to; cost what it may, regardless of cost, at any cost, at all costs, whatever the cost

339 CAREFULNESS
<close or watchful attention>

NOUNS 1 **carefulness, care, heed, concern, regard; attention** 983; **heedfulness,** regardfulness, mindfulness, **thoughtfulness; consideration,** solicitude, caring, loving care, tender loving care, TLC <nf>, caregiving, compassion; circumspectness, circumspection; forethought, anticipation, preparedness; **caution** 494

2 **painstakingness,** painstaking, **pains; diligence,** assiduousness, assiduity, sedulousness, industriousness, industry; **thoroughness,** thoroughgoingness

3 **meticulousness,** exactingness, **scrupulousness,** scrupulosity, **conscientiousness,** punctiliousness, attention to detail, fine-tuning; **particularness,** particularity, circumstantiality; **fussiness, criticalness,** criticality; **finicalness,** finickingness, finickiness, finicality, persnicketiness <nf>; **exactness, exactitude, accuracy, preciseness, precision,** precisionism, precisianism, punctuality, correctness, prissiness; **strictness, rigor,** rigorousness, spit and polish; nicety, niceness, delicacy, detail, subtlety, refinement, minuteness, exquisiteness, elegance

4 **vigilance, wariness,** prudence, **watchfulness,** watching, observance, **surveillance; watch, vigil, lookout;** *qui vive* <Fr>; invigilation, proctoring, monitoring; inspection; watch and ward; custody, custodianship, guardianship, stewardship; **guard,** guardedness, guard duty; **sharp eye, weather eye,** peeled eye, watchful eye, eagle eye, lidless *or* sleepless *or* unblinking *or* unwinking eye

5 **alertness, attentiveness; attention** 983; **wakefulness,** sleeplessness; **readiness,** promptness, promptitude, punctuality; **quickness,** agility, nimbleness; **smartness,** brightness, keenness, sharpness, acuteness, acuity

VERBS 6 **care, mind, heed,** reck, think, consider, regard, pay heed to, take heed *or* thought of; **take an interest,** be concerned; **pay attention** 983.8

7 **be careful, take care** *or* good care, take heed, have a care, exercise care; **be cautious** 494.5; **take pains,** take trouble, **be painstaking,** go to great pains, go to great lengths, go out of one's way, go the extra mile <nf>, bend over backwards <nf>, use every trick in the book, not miss a trick; mind what one is doing *or* about, mind one's business, **mind one's P's and Q's** <nf>; **watch one's step** <nf>, pick one's steps, tread on eggs, tread warily, walk on eggshells, place one's feet carefully, feel one's way; treat gently, **handle with gloves** *or* **kid gloves**

8 **be vigilant,** be watchful, never nod *or* sleep, **be on the watch** *or* **lookout,** be on the *qui vive* <Fr>, keep a good *or* sharp lookout, keep in sight *or* view; **keep watch,** keep watch and ward, keep vigil; **watch, look sharp,** look about one, look with one's own eyes, **be on one's guard,** keep an eye out, sleep with one eye open, have all one's eyes *or* wits about one, keep one's eye on the ball <nf>, keep one's eyes open, keep a weather eye open *and* **keep one's eyes peeled** <nf>, keep the ear to the ground,

keep a nose to the wind; keep alert, **be on the alert; look out, watch out;** look lively *or* alive; stop, look, and listen

9 look after, nurture, foster, **tend, take care of** 1008.19, care for, keep an eye on

ADJS 10 **careful, heedful, regardful, mindful, thoughtful, considerate, caring,** solicitous, loving, tender, curious <old>; circumspect; **attentive** 983.15; **cautious** 494.8

11 **painstaking, diligent, assiduous,** sedulous, **thorough, thoroughgoing,** operose, industrious, elaborate

12 **meticulous, exacting, scrupulous, conscientious,** religious, punctilious, punctual, **particular, fussy, critical, attentive,** scrutinizing; **thorough,** thoroughgoing, thoroughpaced; **finical,** finicking, finicky, high-maintenance; **exact, precise,** precisionistic, precisianistic, persnickety, prissy, **accurate, correct;** close, narrow; **strict,** rigid, **rigorous,** spit-and-polish, exigent, demanding; nice, delicate, subtle, fine, refined, minute, detailed, exquisite

13 **vigilant, wary,** prudent, **watchful,** lidless, sleepless, observant, chary; **on the watch, on the lookout,** *aux aguets* <Fr>; **on guard,** on one's guard, guarded; with open eyes, with one's eyes open, with one's eyes peeled *or* with a weather eye open <nf>; open-eyed, sharp-eyed, keen-eyed, Argus-eyed, eagle-eyed, hawk-eyed; all eyes, all ears, **all eyes and ears;** custodial

14 **alert, on the alert,** on the *qui vive* <Fr>, **on one's toes, on top** *and* **on the job** *and* on the ball <nf>, **attentive; awake,** wakeful, **wide-awake,** sleepless, unsleeping, unblinking, unwinking, unnodding, alive, ready, prompt, quick, agile, nimble, quick on the trigger *or* draw *or* uptake <nf>; **smart, bright, keen, sharp**

ADVS 15 **carefully, heedfully,** regardfully, **mindfully,** thoughtfully, **considerately,** solicitously, tenderly, lovingly; circumspectly; **cautiously** 494.12; **with care,** with great care; **painstakingly, diligently,** assiduously, industriously, sedulously, thoroughly, thoroughgoingly, nine ways to Sunday *and* to a t *or* a turn *and* to a fare-thee-well <nf>

16 **meticulously, exactingly, scrupulously, conscientiously,** religiously, punctiliously, punctually, fussily; strictly, rigorously; exactly, **accurately, precisely, with exactitude, with precision;** nicely, with great nicety, refinedly, minutely, in detail, exquisitely

17 **vigilantly, warily,** prudently, **watchfully,** observantly; **alertly,** attentively; sleeplessly, unsleepingly, unwinkingly, unblinkingly, lidlessly, unnoddingly

340 NEGLECT

NOUNS 1 **neglect,** neglectfulness, **negligence,** inadvertence *or* inadvertency, malperformance, dereliction, *culpa* <L>, culpable negligence, criminal negligence; **remissness,** laxity, laxness, slackness, looseness, laches; unrigorousness, permissiveness; noninterference, *laissez-faire* <Fr>, nonrestriction; **disregard,** airy disregard, slighting; **inattention** 984; **oversight,** overlooking; **omission,** nonfeasance, nonperformance, lapse, failure, **default;** poor stewardship *or* guardianship *or* custody; procrastination 846.5

2 **carelessness, heedlessness, unheedfulness,** disregardfulness, regardlessness, ignorance; unperceptiveness, impercipience, blindness, deliberate blindess; uncaring, unsolicitude, unsolicitousness, **thoughtlessness,** tactlessness, inconsiderateness, **inconsideration;** unthinkingness, unmindfulness, oblivion, forgetfulness; **unpreparedness,** unreadiness, lack of foresight *or* forethought; **recklessness** 493.2; **indifference** 102, *je-m'en-fichisme* and *je-m'en-foutisme* <Fr>; **laziness** 331.5; perfunctoriness; cursoriness, hastiness, offhandedness, casualness; easiness; nonconcern, insouciance; abandon, careless abandon, *sprezzatura* <Ital>

3 **slipshodness,** slipshoddiness, **slovenliness,** slovenry, sluttishness, untidiness, **sloppiness** *and* **messiness** <nf>; haphazardness; slapdash, slapdashness, a lick and a promise <nf>, loose ends; bad job, sad work, botch, slovenly performance; bungling 414.4; procrastination, avoidance

4 **unmeticulousness,** unexactingness, **unscrupulousness,** unrigorousness, **unconscientiousness,** unpunctiliousness, unpunctuality, unparticularness, unfussiness, unfinicalness, **uncriticalness;** inexactness, **inexactitude,** inaccuracy, imprecision, unpreciseness

5 **neglecter,** negligent <old>, ignorer, disregarder; *je-m'en-fichiste* and *je-m'en-foutiste* <Fr>; **procrastinator,** waiter on Providence, Micawber <Dickens>; slacker, shirker, malingerer, dodger, goof off *and* goldbrick <nf>, idler; skimper <nf>, trifler; sloven, slob; bungler 414.8

VERBS 6 **neglect, overlook, disregard,** not heed, not attend to, take for granted, **ignore;** not care for, not take care of; **pass over,** gloss over; **let slip, let slide** <nf>, let the chance slip by, **let go,** let ride <nf>, let take its course; let the grass grow under one's feet; put off till tomorrow; not think *or* consider, not give a thought to, take no thought *or* account of, blind oneself to, turn a blind eye to, leave out of one's calculation; lose sight of, lose track of; **be neglectful** *or* **negligent,** fail in one's duty, **fail,** lapse, **default,** let go by default; not get involved; nod, nod *or* sleep through, sleep <old>, be caught napping, be asleep at the switch <nf>

7 **leave undone,** leave, **let go,** leave half-done, pretermit, **skip,** jump, **miss, omit,** cut *and* blow off <nf>, let be *or* alone, pass over, pass up <nf>, abandon; leave a loose thread, leave loose ends, let dangle, give a lick and a promise; **slack, shirk,** malinger, goof off *and* goldbrick <nf>; trifle; **procrastinate** 846.11

8 **slight;** turn one's back on, turn a cold shoulder to, get *or* give the cold shoulder *and* get *or* give the go-by *and* cold-shoulder <nf>, leave out in the cold; not lift a finger, leave undone; scamp, skimp <nf>; slur, **slur over,** pass over, skate over <Brit>, slubber over, slip *or* **skip over,** dodge, waffle <Brit nf>, fudge, blink, carefully ignore; skim, **skim over,** skim the surface, **touch upon,** touch upon lightly *or* in passing, pass over lightly, go once over lightly, **hit the high spots** *and* **give a lick and a promise** <nf>; **cut corners,** cut a corner

9 **do carelessly,** do by halves, do in a half-assed way <nf>, do in a slip-shod fashion, do anyhow, do in any old way <nf>; botch, **bungle** 414.11; **trifle with,** play *or* play at fast and loose with, mess around *or* about with *and* muck around *or* about with *and* piss around *or* about with <nf>; **do offhand,** dash off, knock off *and* throw off <nf>, **toss off** *or* **out** <nf>; **roughhew,** roughcast, rough out; **knock out** <nf>, hammer *or* pound out, bat out <nf>; toss *or* slap *or* **throw together,** knock together, cobble up, patch together, patch, patch up, fudge up, fake up, whomp up <nf>, lash up <Brit nf>, slap up <nf>; jury-rig

ADJS 10 **negligent, neglectful,** neglecting, derelict, culpably negligent; inadvertent, uncircumspec, ignorant; **inattentive** 984.6; unwary, unwatchful, asleep at the switch, off-guard, unguarded; **remiss,** slack, lax, relaxed, laid-back <nf>, loose, loosey-goosey <nf>, unrigorous, permissive, overly permissive; noninterfering, *laissez-faire* <Fr>, nonrestrictive; slighting; slurring, scamping, skimping <nf>; procrastinating 846.17

11 **careless, heedless, unheeding, unheedful, disregardful,** disregardant, regardless, **unsolicitous, uncaring;** tactless, respectless, **thoughtless, unthinking, inconsiderate,** untactful, undiplomatic, mindless of, **unmindful,** forgetful, oblivious; **unprepared,** unready; **reckless** 493.8; **indifferent** 102.6; lackadaisical; lazy, shirking; perfunctory, cursory, casual, offhand; easygoing, *dégagé* <Fr>, airy, flippant, insouciant, free and easy, free as a bird

12 **slipshod,** slipshoddy, **slovenly,** sloppy *and* **messy** *and* half-assed <nf>, lax, slapdash, shoddy, sluttish, untidy, messy; **clumsy, bungling** 414.20; **haphazard, promiscuous, hit-or-miss,** hit-and-miss; deficient, half-assed <nf>, botched

13 **unmeticulous, unexacting, unpainstaking, unscrupulous,** unrigorous, **unconscientious,** unpunctilious, unpunctual, **unparticular, unfussy, unfinical, uncritical;** inexact, inaccurate, unprecise

14 **neglected,** unattended to, untended, unwatched, unchaperoned, uncared-for; **disregarded,** unconsidered, unregarded, **overlooked, missed,** omitted, passed by, passed over, passed up <nf>, gathering dust, **ignored, slighted,** blanked; unasked, unsolicited; half-done, undone, left undone; deserted, abandoned; in the cold *and* out in the cold <nf>; on the shelf, shelved, pigeonholed, on hold *and* on the back burner <nf>, **put** *or* **laid aside,** sidetracked *and* sidelined <nf>, shunted

15 **unheeded, unobserved, unnoticed, unnoted, unperceived, unseen,** undiscerned, undescried, unmarked, unremarked, unregarded, unminded, unconsidered, unthought-of, unmissed

16 **unexamined, unstudied,** unconsidered, unsearched, unscanned, unweighed, unsifted, unexplored, uninvestigated, unindagated, unconned

ADVS 17 **negligently, neglectfully,** inadvertently; **remissly,** laxly, slackly, loosely; **unrigorously,** permissively; nonrestrictively; **slightingly,** lightly, slurringly; scampingly, skimpingly <nf>

18 **carelessly, heedlessly,** unheedingly, unheedfully, disregardfully, regardlessly, **thoughtlessly, unthinkingly, unsolicitously,** tactlessly, **inconsiderately,** unmindfully, forgetfully; **inattentively, unwarily,** unvigilantly, unguardedly, unwatchfully; **recklessly** 493.11; perfunctorily; once over lightly, cursorily; casually, offhand, offhandedly, airily; clumsily, bunglingly 414.24; **sloppily** *and* **messily** <nf>, sluttishly, shoddily, shabbily; haphazardly, promiscuously, hit or miss *and* hit and miss *and* helter-skelter *and* slapdash *and* anyhow *and* any old way *and* any which way <nf>

19 **unmeticulously, unscrupulously, unconscientiously,** unfussily, **uncritically;** inexactly, inaccurately, unprecisely, imprecisely, unrigorously, unpunctually

341 INTERPRETATION

NOUNS 1 **interpretation, construction, reading,** way of seeing *or* understanding *or* putting; constructionism, strict constructionism, loose constructionism; **diagnosis; definition,** description; **meaning** 518

2 rendering, rendition; text, edited text, diplomatic text, normalized text; **version;** reading, lection, variant, variant reading; **edition,** critical *or* scholarly edition; variorum edition *or* variorum; conflation, composite reading *or* text

3 translation, transcription, transliteration; Englishing; **paraphrase,** loose *or* free translation; decipherment, decoding, code cracking, unscrambling; amplification, restatement, rewording, simplification; metaphrase, literal *or* verbal *or* faithful *or* word-for-word translation; **pony** *and* trot *and* crib <nf>; interlinear, interlinear translation, bilingual text *or* edition; **gloss, glossary;** key, *clavis* <L>; lipreading

4 explanation, explication, unfolding, **elucidation,** illumination, enlightenment, light, **clarification,** *éclaircissement* <Fr>, simplification; take <nf>; **exposition,** expounding, exegesis; **illustration, demonstration,** exemplification; **reason,** rationale; euhemerism, demythologization, allegorization; decipherment, decoding, cracking, unlocking, **solution** 940; editing, emendation; critical revision, rescension, diaskeuasis

5 <explanatory remark> **comment, word of explanation,** explanatory remark; **annotation,** notation, **note,** note of explanation, footnote, gloss, definition, scholium; exegesis; *apparatus criticus* <L>; commentary, commentation <old>; legend, appendix

6 interpretability, interpretableness, construability; **definability, describability;** translatability; **explicability,** explainableness, accountableness

7 interpreter, exegete, exegetist, exegesist, hermeneut; constructionist, strict constructionist, loose constructionist; **commentator,** annotator, scholiast; critic, textual critic, **editor,** diaskeuast, emender, emendator; cryptographer, cryptologist, decoder, decipherer, cryptanalyst, lipreader; **explainer,** lexicographer, definer, **explicator,** exponent, expositor, expounder, clarifier; demonstrator, euhemerist, demythologizer, allegorist; go-between 576.4; **translator,** metaphrast, paraphrast; oneirocritic; guide, *cicerone* <Ital>, dragoman

8 <science of interpretation> exegetics, hermeneutics; tropology; criticism, literary criticism, textual criticism; paleography, epigraphy; cryptology, cryptography, cryptanalysis; lexicography; diagnostics, symptomatology, semiology, semiotics; pathognomy; physiognomics, physiognomy; metoposcopy; oneirology, oneirocriticism

VERBS **9 interpret, diagnose; construe,** put a construction on, **take;** understand, **understand by, take to mean,** take it that; **read; read into,** read between the lines; see in a special light, read in view of, take an approach to

10 explain, explicate, expound, make of, exposit; **give the meaning,** tell the meaning of, **define, describe; spell out,** unfold; **account for,** give reason for; **clarify, elucidate,** clear up, clear the air, **cover** *and* cover the waterfront *or* the territory <nf>, **make clear,** make plain; **simplify,** popularize; **illuminate,** enlighten, give insight, **shed** *or* **throw light upon;** rationalize, euhemerize, demythologize, allegorize; tell *or* show how, show the way; **demonstrate, show, illustrate,** exemplify, represent; get to the bottom of *or* to the heart of, make sense of, make head or tails of; decipher, crack, unlock, find the key to, unravel, demystify, read between the lines, read into, **solve** 940.2; explain oneself; explain away; overinterpret

11 comment upon, commentate, remark upon; **annotate,** gloss; **edit,** make an edition

12 translate, render, transcribe, transliterate, put *or* turn into, transfuse the sense of; construe; disambiguate

13 paraphrase, rephrase, reword, restate, rehash; give a free *or* loose translation

ADJS **14 interpretative,** interpretive, interpretational, exegetic, exegetical, hermeneutic, hermeneutical; constructive, constructional; **diagnostic;** symptomatological, semeiological; tropological; **definitional, descriptive**

15 explanatory, explaining, exegetic, exegetical, **explicative,** explicatory, defining; **expository,** expositive; **clarifying, elucidative, elucidatory; illuminating,** illuminative, enlightening; **demonstrative, illustrative,** exemplificative; glossarial, annotative, critical, editorial, scholiastic; rationalizing, rationalistic, euhemeristic, demythologizing, allegorizing

16 translational, translative; paraphrastic, metaphrastic; literal, word-for-word, verbatim

17 interpretable, construable; definable, describable; translatable, renderable; Englishable <old>; explainable, explicable, accountable; diagnosable

ADVS **18 by interpretation,** as here interpreted, as here defined, according to this reading, **in explanation, to explain; that is,** that is to say, as it were, *id est* <L>, i.e.; **to wit, namely,** *videlicet* <L>, viz, *scilicet* <L>, sc; **in other words,** in words to that effect

342 MISINTERPRETATION

NOUNS **1 misinterpretation, misunderstanding,** *malentente* <Fr>, misintelligence, **misapprehension,** misreading, **misconstruction,** mistaking, malobservation, **misconception; misrendering,** mistranslation, translator's error, eisegesis; misexplanation, misexplication, misexposition; misreading; misapplication; gloss; **perversion, distortion,** wrenching, twisting, contorting, torturing, squeezing, garbling; reversal; abuse of terms, misuse of words, catachresis; misquotation, miscitation; misjudgment 948; **error** 975; misrepresentation; sniglet

VERBS **2 misinterpret, misunderstand,** misconceive, **mistake, misapprehend; misread, misconstrue,** put a false construction on, miss the point, **take wrong, get wrong,** get one wrong, take amiss, take the wrong way; **get backwards,** reverse, have the wrong way round, put the cart before the horse; misapply; misexplain, misexplicate, misexpound; **misrender,** mistranslate; quote out of context; misquote, miscite, give a false coloring, give a false impression *or* idea, gloss; misread; **garble, pervert, distort,** wrench, contort, torture, squeeze, twist the words *or* meaning, stretch *or* strain the sense *or* meaning, misdeem, **misjudge** 948.2; bark up the wrong tree; misrepresent

ADJS **3 misinterpreted, misunderstood, mistaken, misapprehended, misread,** eisegetical, misconceived, **misconstrued; garbled,** misquoted, misrepresented, **perverted, distorted,** catachrestic, catechrestical; backwards, reversed, ass-backwards <nf>

4 misinterpretable, misunderstandable, mistakable

343 COMMUNICATION

NOUNS **1 communication,** communion, congress, **commerce, intercourse;** means of communication, **speaking, speech** 524, utterance, speech act, talking, linguistic intercourse, speech situation, speech circuit, converse, **conversation** 541; signalling; **contact, touch, connection; interpersonal communication, intercommunication,** intercommunion, grokking <nf>, **interplay,** interaction; **exchange,** interchange; answer, response, reply; one-way communication, two-way communication; **dealings,** dealing, **traffic, truck** <nf>; information 551; message 552.4; ESP, telepathy 689.9; writing; correspondence 553; social intercourse 582.4; media studies

2 informing, telling, imparting, impartation, impartment, **conveyance, transmission,** transmittal, transfer, transference, sharing, giving, sending, signaling, letting one in on; notification, alerting, **announcement** 352.2, publication 352, **disclosure** 351

3 communicativeness, talkativeness 540, **sociability** 582; **unreserve,** unreservedness, **unreticence, unrestraint, unconstraint,** unrestriction; **unrepression,** unsuppression; **unsecretiveness,** untaciturnity; candor, **frankness** 644.4; **openness,** plainness, freeness, outspokenness, plainspokenness; **accessibility,** approachability, conversableness; **extroversion,** outgoingness; **uncommunicativeness** 344, reserve, taciturnity

4 communicability, impartability, conveyability, transmittability, transmissibility, transferability; contagiousness

5 communications, electronic communications, communications industry, media, communications medium *or* media, mass communications, communications network; telecommunication 347.1, long-distance communication; radio communication, wire communication, broadcasting, satellite broadcasting, broadband, podcasting; information theory 551.7; signaling

VERBS **6 communicate, be in touch** *or* **contact,** be in connection *or* intercourse, have intercourse, hold communication; **intercommunicate,** interchange, commune with; grok <nf>; commerce with, **deal with, traffic with, have dealings with, have truck with** <nf>; **speak, talk,** be in a speech situation, **converse** 541.8, pass the time of day

7 communicate, impart, tell, lay on one <nf>, **convey, transmit,** transfer, send, send word, deliver *or* send a signal *or* message, **disseminate,** broadcast, pass, **pass on** *or* **along, hand on; report, render, make known,** get across *or* over, let in on; give *or* send *or* leave word; **signal;** share, share with; **leak,** let slip out, **give** 478.12; tell 551.8

8 communicate with, get in touch *or* **contact with, contact** <nf>, **make contact with,** raise, reach, get to, get through to, get hold of, make *or* establish connection, get in connection with; **make advances,** make overtures, **approach,** make up to <nf>; relate to; keep in touch *or* contact with, maintain connection; **answer,** respond *or* reply to, get back to; **question,** interrogate; **correspond,** drop a line; reconnect

ADJS **9 communicational, communicating,** communional; transmissional; speech, **verbal,** linguistic, oral; **conversational** 541.12; **intercommunicational,** intercommunicative, intercommunional, interactional, interactive, interacting, interresponsive, responsive, answering; questioning, interrogative, interrogatory; telepathic

10 communicative, talkative 540.9, gossipy, newsy; **sociable; unreserved, unreticent,** unshrinking, **unrestrained, unconstrained,** unhampered, unrestricted; demonstrative, expansive, effusive;

unrepressed, unsuppressed; unsecretive, unsilent, untaciturn; candid, **frank** 644.17; self-revealing, self-revelatory; **open,** free, outspoken, free-speaking, free-spoken, free-tongued; **accessible, approachable,** conversable, easy to speak to; **extroverted,** outgoing; **uncommunicative** 344.8

11 **communicable, impartable, conveyable, transmittable,** transmissible, transferable; contagious

12 communicatively; verbally, talkatively, by word of mouth, orally, viva voce

344 UNCOMMUNICATIVENESS

NOUNS 1 **uncommunicativeness,** closeness, indisposition to speak, disinclination to communicate; unconversableness, **unsociability** 583; nondisclosure, **secretiveness** 345.1; lack of message *or* meaning, meaninglessness 520; miscommunication

2 **taciturnity, untalkativeness,** unloquaciousness; **silence** 51; **speechlessness,** wordlessness, dumbness, **muteness** 51.2; quietness, quietude; laconicalness, laconism, curtness, shortness, terseness; brusqueness, briefness, brevity, conciseness, economy *or* sparingness of words, pauciloquy <old>

3 **reticence** *or* reticency; **reserve,** reservedness, restraint, low key, **constraint;** guardedness, discreetness, discretion; suppression, repression; subduedness; backwardness, retirement, low profile; **aloofness, standoffishness,** distance, remoteness, **detachment,** withdrawal, withdrawnness, reclusiveness, solitariness; impersonality; **coolness,** coldness, frigidity, iciness, frostiness, chilliness; **inaccessibility, unapproachability; undemonstrativeness,** unexpansiveness, unaffability, uncongeniality; **introversion;** modesty, bashfulness 139.4, pudency; expressionlessness, blankness, impassiveness, impassivity; straight *or* poker face, mask

4 **prevarication, equivocation,** tergiversation, **evasion,** shuffle, fencing, dodging, parrying, waffling *and* tap-dancing <nf>; *suppressio veri* <L>; weasel words

5 **man of few words,** clam <nf>, strong silent type, laconic <old>; Spartan, Laconian; evader, weasel

VERBS 6 **keep to oneself,** keep one's own counsel; not open one's mouth, not say a word, not breathe a word, stand mute, **hold one's tongue** 51.5, clam up <nf>; bite one's tongue; have little to say, refuse comment, say neither yes nor no, waste no words, save one's breath; retire; **keep one's distance,** keep at a distance, keep oneself to oneself, **stand aloof,** hold oneself aloof; keep secret 345.7

7 **prevaricate, equivocate,** waffle <nf>, tergiversate, evade, dodge, sidestep, pussyfoot, say in a roundabout way, parry, duck, weasel *and* weasel out <nf>, palter; hum and haw, **hem and haw,** back and fill; **mince words,** mince the truth, euphemize

ADJS 8 **uncommunicative,** indisposed *or* disinclined to communicate; unconversational, unconversable <old>; **unsociable** 583.5; **secretive** 345.15; meaningless 520.6

9 **taciturn, untalkative,** unloquacious, indisposed to talk; **silent, speechless,** wordless, **mum; mute** 51.12, dumb, quiet; close, **closemouthed,** close-tongued, snug <nf>, **tight-lipped;** close-lipped, tongue-tied, word-bound; **laconic,** curt, brief, terse, brusque, short, concise, **sparing of words,** economical of words, of few words

10 **reticent, reserved,** restrained, nonassertive, low-key, low-keyed, constrained; **suppressed,** repressed; subdued; guarded, discreet; backward, **retiring,** shrinking; **aloof, standoffish,** offish <nf>, standoff, **distant,** remote, removed, **detached,** Olympian, withdrawn; impersonal; **cool,** cold, frigid, icy, frosty, chilled, chilly; **inaccessible, unapproachable,** forbidding; **undemonstrative,** unexpansive, unaffable, uncongenial, ungenial; **introverted;** modest, verecund, verecundious, *pudique* <Fr>, bashful 139.12; expressionless, blank, impassive

11 **prevaricating, equivocal,** tergiversating, tergiversant, waffling <nf>, **evasive,** weaselly, weasel-worded

345 SECRECY

NOUNS 1 **secrecy,** secretness, airtight secrecy, close secrecy; crypticness; the dark; hiddenness, hiding, **concealment** 346; **secretiveness,** closeness; discreetness, discretion, **uncommunicativeness** 344; **evasiveness,** evasion, subterfuge; hugger-mugger, hugger-muggery; Area 51; back channel; down-low

2 **privacy,** retirement, isolation, sequestration, seclusion; incognito, anonymity, **confidentialness,** confidentiality; closed meeting *or* session, executive session, private conference, secret meeting

3 **veil of secrecy, veil,** curtain, pall, wraps; iron curtain, bamboo curtain; wall *or* barrier of secrecy, wall of silence; **suppression,** repression, stifling, smothering; **censorship,** blackout <nf>, **hush-up, cover-up; seal of secrecy,** official secrecy, classification, official classification; security, ironbound security; pledge *or* oath of secrecy

4 stealth, stealthiness, **furtiveness, clandestineness,** clandestinity, clandestine behavior, **surreptitiousness, covertness,** slyness, shiftiness, sneakiness, slinkiness, underhandedness, underhand dealing, undercover *or* underground activity, **covert activity** *or* **operation;** prowl, prowling; stalking; hugger-mugger; counterintelligence; conspiracy, cabal, intrigue; funny business <nf>; secret service, intelligence agency

5 secret, confidence; private *or* personal matter, privity <old>; trade secret; confidential *or* **privileged information** *or* **communication;** doctor-patient *or* lawyer-client confidentiality; seal *or* secret of the confessional; more than meets the eye; deep dark secret; solemn secret; guarded secret, hush-hush matter, classified information, eyes-only *or* top-secret information, restricted information; confession; inside information, inside skinny <nf>; **mystery, enigma** 522.8; the arcane, arcanum, *arcanum arcanorum* <L>; esoterica, cabala, the occult, occultism, hermetism, hermeticism, hermetics; deep *or* profound secret, sealed book, mystery of mysteries; skeleton in the closet *or* cupboard, family secret; sealed orders, state secret

6 cryptography, cryptoanalysis, cryptoanalytics; **code, cipher;** secret language; code book, code word, code name; **secret writing,** coded message, cryptogram, cryptograph; secret *or* invisible *or* sympathetic ink; cryptographer

VERBS **7 keep secret, keep mum, veil,** keep dark; keep it a deep, dark secret; secrete, **conceal;** keep to oneself 344.6, keep *in petto* <Ital>, bosom, keep close, keep snug <nf>, keep back, keep from, **withhold,** hold out on <nf>; not let it go further, keep within these walls, keep within the bosom of the lodge, keep between us; **not tell,** hold one's tongue 51.5, never let on <nf>, make no sign, not breathe *or* whisper a word, clam up <nf>, be the soul of discretion; **not give away** <nf>, **keep it under one's hat** <nf>, keep under wraps <nf>, keep a lid on, keep buttoned up <nf>, keep one's own counsel; play one's cards close to the chest *or* to one's vest; play dumb; clam up; not let the right hand know what the left is doing; keep in ignorance, keep *or* leave in the dark; classify; file and forget; **have secret** *or* **confidential information,** be in on the secret *and* know where the bodies are buried <nf>; anonymize

8 cover up, muffle up; **hush up, hush,** hush-hush, shush, hugger-mugger; **suppress,** repress, **stifle,** muffle, **smother,** squash, quash, squelch, kill, sit on *or* upon, put the lid on <nf>; **censor,** black out <nf>

9 tell confidentially, tell for one's ears only, mention privately, **whisper, breathe, whisper in the ear;** tell one a secret; take aside, see one alone, talk to in private, speak in privacy; say under one's breath

10 code, encode, encipher, cipher

ADJS **11 secret,** close, closed, closet; cryptic, dark; unuttered, unrevealed, undivulged, undisclosed, unspoken, untold; **hush-hush, top secret,** supersecret, eyes-only, classified, restricted, under wraps <nf>, under security *or* security restrictions; **censored,** suppressed, stifled, smothered, hushed-up, under the seal *or* ban of secrecy; **unrevealable, undivulgable, undisclosable, untellable,** unwhisperable, unbreatheable, unutterable; latent, ulterior, concealed, hidden 346.11; arcane, esoteric, occult, cabalistic, hermetic; enigmatic, mysterious 522.18

12 covert, clandestine, quiet, unobtrusive, hugger-mugger, **surreptitious, undercover,** underground, under-the-counter, under-the-table, **cloak-and-dagger** <nf>, backdoor, hole-and-corner <nf>, underhand, **underhanded; furtive, stealthy,** privy, backstairs, **sly, shifty, sneaky,** sneaking, skulking, slinking, slinky, feline

13 private, privy, closed-door; intimate, inmost, innermost, interior, inward, **personal; privileged,** protected; **secluded, sequestered,** isolated, withdrawn, retired; incognito, anonymous

14 confidential, auricular, **inside** <nf>, esoteric; *in petto* <Ital>, close to one's chest *or* vest <nf>, under one's hat <nf>; **off the record,** not for the record, not to be minuted, within these four walls, in the bosom of the lodge, for no other ears, eyes-only, between us; not to be quoted, not for publication *or* release; not for attribution; unquotable, unpublishable, sealed; sensitive, privileged, under privilege

15 secretive, close-lipped, secret, close, dark; discreet; evasive, shifty; **uncommunicative, close-mouthed**

16 coded, encoded; ciphered, enciphered; cryptographic, cryptographical; hieroglyphic

ADVS **17 secretly, in secret,** in *or* up one's sleeve, on the down-low; in the closet; with nobody the wiser; **covertly,** stownlins *and* in hidlings <Scot>, **undercover,** *à couvert* <Fr>, under the cloak of; **behind the scenes,** in the background, in a corner, in the dark, in darkness, behind the veil *or* curtain, behind the veil of secrecy; *sub rosa* <L>, under the rose; underground; *sotto voce* <Ital>, under the breath, with bated breath, in a whisper; off the record

18 surreptitiously, clandestinely, secretively, furtively, stealthily, slyly, shiftily, sneakily, sneakingly, skulkingly, slinkingly, slinkily; by stealth, **on the sly** and **on the quiet** and on the qt <nf>, *à la dérobée* <Fr>, *en tapinois* <Fr>, behind one's back, by a side door, **like a thief in the night,** underhand, underhandedly, under the table, in holes and corners and in a hole-and-corner way <nf>

19 privately, privily, **in private,** in privacy, in privy; apart, aside; **behind closed doors,** *januis clausis* <L>, *à huis clos* <Fr>, *in camera* <L>, in chambers, in secret or closed meeting, in executive session, in private conference

20 confidentially, in confidence, in strict confidence, under the seal of secrecy, **off the record; between ourselves,** strictly between us, *entre nous* <Fr>, *inter nos* <L>, for your ears or eyes only, between you and me, from me to you, between you and me and the bedpost or lamppost <nf>

346 CONCEALMENT

NOUNS **1 concealment, hiding, secretion;** burial, burying, interment, putting away; **cover, covering,** covering up, masking, screening 295.1; mystification, obscuration; darkening, obscurement, clouding 1027.6; hiddenness, concealedness, **covertness,** occultation; eclipse; disappearance; **secrecy** 345; uncommunicativeness 344; invisibility 32; **subterfuge, deception** 356

2 veil, curtain, **cover, screen** 295.2, mask, camouflage; fig leaf; **wraps** <nf>; **cover, disguise**

3 ambush, ambushment, **ambuscade,** *guet-apens* <Fr>; surveillance, shadowing 938.9; lurking hole or place; blind, stalking-horse; booby trap, trap

4 hiding place, hideaway, hideout, hidey-hole <nf>, hiding, concealment, **cover,** secret place; safe house; drop, accommodation address <Brit>; **recess, corner,** dark corner, nook, cranny, niche; **hole,** bolt-hole, foxhole, trench, dugout, lair, den; bomb shelter, storm shelter; **asylum, sanctuary, retreat, refuge** 1009; covert, coverture, undercovert; **cache,** stash <nf>; safe-deposit box, bank vault, safe, lockbox; cubbyhole, cubby, pigeonhole; secret compartment; mother's skirts

5 secret passage, covert way, secret exit; **back way, back door, side door;** bolt-hole, escape route, escape hatch, escapeway; secret staircase, *escalier dérobé* <Fr>, **back stairs; underground,** underground route, underground railroad

VERBS **6 conceal, hide,** ensconce; **cover, cover up,** blind, **screen, cloak, veil,** screen off, curtain, blanket, shroud, enshroud, envelop; **disguise, camouflage, mask,** dissemble; plain-wrap, wrap in plain brown paper; whitewash <nf>; **paper over,** gloss over, varnish, slur over; distract attention from; **obscure,** obfuscate, cloud, becloud, befog, throw out a smoke screen, shade, throw into the shade; **eclipse,** occult; put out of sight, sweep under the rug or carpet, keep under cover, keep under wraps; cover up one's tracks, lay a false scent, hide one's trail; hide one's light under a bushel

7 secrete, hide away, keep hidden, put away, store away, stow away, file and forget, bottle up, lock up, seal up, put out of sight; **keep secret** 345.7; **cache,** stash <nf>, deposit, plant <nf>; **bury;** bosom, embosom <old>

8 <hide oneself> hide, conceal oneself, take cover, hide out <nf>, hide away, **go into hiding,** go to ground; stay in hiding, **lie hid** or **hidden,** lie or lay low <nf>, lie perdue, lie snug or close <nf>, lie doggo and sit tight <nf>, burrow <old>, **hole up** <nf>, **go underground;** play peekaboo or bopeep or hide and seek; keep out of sight, retire from sight, drop from sight, disappear 34.2, crawl or retreat into one's shell, keep or stay in the background, keep a low profile, stay in the shade; **disguise oneself,** masquerade, take an assumed name, assume a cover, change one's identity, go under an alias, remain anonymous, be incognito, go or sail under false colors, wear a mask; leave no address; reinvent oneself

9 lurk, couch; **lie in wait,** lay wait; **sneak, skulk, slink, prowl,** nightwalk, **steal, creep,** pussyfoot <nf>, gumshoe <nf>, tiptoe; stalk, shadow 938.35

10 ambush, ambuscade, **waylay; lie in ambush,** lay wait for, **lie in wait for,** lay for <nf>; stalk; set a trap for, still-hunt

ADJS **11 concealed, hidden, hid,** occult, recondite <old>, blind; **covered** 295.31; **covert, under cover, under wraps** <nf>; code-named; **obscured,** obfuscated, clouded, clouded over, wrapped in clouds, in a cloud or fog or mist or haze, beclouded, befogged; eclipsed, in eclipse, under an eclipse; in the wings; buried; underground; close, secluded, secluse, sequestered; in purdah, under house arrest, incommunicado; **obscure,** abstruse, mysterious 522.18; **secret** 345.11; unknown 930.16, latent 519.5

12 unrevealed, undisclosed, undivulged, **unexposed;** unapparent, **invisible, unseen,** unperceived, unspied, undetected; undiscovered, unexplored, untraced, untracked; unaccounted for, unexplained, unsolved

13 disguised, camouflaged, in disguise; masked, masquerading; **incognito,** incog <nf>, anonymous, unrecognizable; in plain wrapping or plain brown paper <nf>; cryptic, coded, codified

14 in hiding, hidden out, **under cover,** in a dark corner, lying hid, doggo <nf>; in ambush or ambuscade; waiting concealed, lying in wait; in the wings; lurking, skulking, prowling, sneaking, stealing; pussyfooted, pussyfoot, on tiptoe; stealthy, furtive, surreptitious 345.12

15 **concealing, hiding,** obscuring, obfuscatory; covering; unrevealing, nonrevealing, undisclosing

347 COMMUNICATIONS

NOUNS 1 **communications,** signaling, telecommunication, comms <Brit nf>, transmission; electronic communication, electrical communication; satellite communication; wire communication, wireless communication; communications engineering, communications technology; communications engineer; media, communications medium *or* media; communication or information theory 551.7; communication *or* information explosion

2 **telegraph, telegraph recorder,** ticker; **telegraphy,** telegraphics, data transmission; **teleprinter,** Telex <trademark>, teletypewriter; teleprinter exchange *or* telex; wire service; code 345.6; electricity 1032; **key,** interrupter, transmitter, sender; receiver, **sounder**

3 **radio** 1034, **radiotelephony, radiotelegraphy,** wireless <Brit>, wireless telephony, wireless telegraphy; line radio, wire *or* wired radio, wired wireless <Brit>, wire wave communication; radiophotography; digital audio broadcasting *or* DAB; **television** 1035; electronics 1033

4 **telephone, phone** *and* horn <nf>, dog <Brit nf>, telephone set, handset; telephony, telephonics, telephone mechanics, telephone engineering; high-frequency telephony; receiver, telephone receiver, earpiece; mouthpiece, transmitter; telephone extension, extension; wall telephone, desk telephone; dial *or* rotary telephone, touch-tone telephone, push-button telephone, cordless phone; beeper; scrambler; telephone booth, telephone box, call box <Brit>, telephone kiosk <Brit>, public telephone, coin telephone, pay station, pay phone; mobile telephone *or* phone <nf>, cellular *or* cell telephone *or* phone <nf>, car phone, digital phone, flip phone; iPhone <trademark>; SIM *or* SIM card; speakerphone, videophone; speed calling, call forwarding, call waiting, redial, caller ID service; phone card; facsimilie transmission, fax

5 **radiophone, radiotelephone,** wireless telephone, wireless; headset, headphone 50.8

6 **intercom** <nf>, Interphone, intercommunication system

7 **telephone exchange,** telephone office, central office, **central;** automatic exchange, machine-switching office; step-by-step switching, panel switching, crossbar switching, electronic switching

8 **switchboard; PBX** *or* private branch *or* business exchange, private exchange; in *or* A board, out *or* B board

9 **telephone operator, operator,** switchboard operator, telephonist, central <old>; long distance; PBX operator

10 **telephone man;** telephone mechanic; telephonic engineer; lineman *or* linewoman

11 **telephoner,** phoner <nf>, caller, **party,** calling party, subscriber

12 telephone number, **phone number** <nf>, unlisted number, fax number, cell phone number; telephone directory *or* book, phone book <nf>; telephone exchange, exchange; telephone area, area code; calling zone

13 telephone call, **phone call** <nf>, **call, ring** *and* buzz <nf>; local call, toll call, long-distance call; long distance, direct distance nondialing, DDD; trunk call; station-to-station call, person-to-person call; collect call; toll-free call; mobile call; dial tone, busy signal; crank call, nuisance call; conference call, video teleconference, teleconference; hot line; chat *or* talk *or* gab line, messagerie; voicemail, phonemail; electronic mail *or* e-mail *or* email; telemarketing; direct marketing; multilevel marketing, multilevel sales; cold call; ringy-dingy *or* jingle *or* tinkle <nf>

14 **telegram, telegraph, wire** <nf>, telex; **cablegram, cable; radiogram,** radiotelegram; **day letter, night letter;** fast telegram

15 **Telephoto** <trademark>, Wirephoto <trademark>, Telecopier <trademark>, **facsimile, fax** <nf>; telephotograph, radiophotograph

16 **telegrapher,** telegraphist, telegraph operator; **sparks** *and* brass pounder *and* dit-da artist <nf>; radiotelegrapher; wireman, wire chief

17 **line,** wire line, telegraph line, telephone line; private line, direct line; party line; hot line; trunk, trunk line; WATS *or* wide area telecommunications service, WATS line; cable, telegraph cable; transmission line, concentric cable, coaxial cable, co-ax <nf>, fiber cable, fiberoptic cable

18 computer networking, **Internet**, World Wide Web *or* WWW, electronic mail; modem; digital compression; broadband

VERBS 19 **telephone, phone** <nf>, call, call on the phone <nf>, put in *or* make a call, **call up, ring,** ring up, give a ring *or* buzz *or* call *or* tinkle *or* jingle <nf>, buzz <nf>; nonformal; listen in; hold the phone *or* wire; hang up, ring off <Brit>; cold call

20 telegraph, telegram, flash, **wire** *and* send a wire <nf>, telex; **cable;** Teletype; radio; sign on, sign off

ADJS **21 communicational,** telecommunicational, **communications,** communication, signal; **telephonic,** magnetotelephonic, microtelephonic, monotelephonic, thermotelephonic; **telegraphic; Teletype;** Wirephoto, facsimile, fax; phototelegraphic, telephotographic; **radio,** wireless <Brit>; radiotelegraphic; networkable

348 MANIFESTATION

NOUNS **1 manifestation, appearance; expression,** evincement; **indication, evidence,** proof 957, proof positive; embodiment, incarnation, bodying forth, materialization; epiphany, theophany, pneumatophany, avatar; **revelation, disclosure** 351, showing forth; dissemination, **publication** 352

2 display, demonstration, show, showing; presentation, showing forth, presentment, ostentation <old>, **exhibition, exhibit, exposition,** expo, retrospective; production, performance, representation, enactment, projection; opening, unfolding, unfoldment; **showcase,** showcasing, unveiling, exposure, varnishing day, *vernissage* <Fr>

3 manifestness, apparentness, obviousness, plainness, clearness, crystal-clearness, perspicuity, distinctness, microscopical distinctness, patency, patentness, palpability, tangibility; evidentness, evidence <old>, **self-evidence; openness,** openness to sight, overtness; visibility 31; unmistakableness, unquestionability 970.3

4 conspicuousness, prominence, salience *or* saliency, bold *or* high *or* strong relief, boldness, **noticeability,** pronouncedness, strikingness, demonstrativeness, outstandingness; highlighting, spotlighting, featuring; obtrusiveness; **flagrance** *or* flagrancy, arrantness, blatancy, notoriousness, notoriety; ostentation 501; dramatics, theatrics

VERBS **5 manifest, show, exhibit, demonstrate, display,** breathe, unfold, develop; **present,** represent <old>, **evince, evidence; indicate,** give sign *or* token, token, betoken, mean 518.8; **express,** show forth, set forth; show off, showcase, **make plain, make clear;** produce, bring out, roll out, trot out <nf>, bring forth, bring forward *or* to the front, put forward, bring to notice, expose to view, bring to *or* into view; **reveal, divulge, disclose** 351.4; **illuminate, highlight, spotlight, feature,** bring to the fore, place in the foreground, bring out in bold *or* strong *or* high relief; **flaunt,** dangle, wave, **flourish,** brandish, parade; affect, make a show *or* a great show of; perform, enact,

dramatize; **embody,** incarnate, body forth, **materialize**

6 <manifest oneself> **come out, come into the open,** come out of the closet <nf>, come forth, **surface; show one's colors** *or* true colors, wear one's heart upon one's sleeve; **speak up, speak out,** raise one's voice, **assert oneself,** let one's voice be heard, speak one's piece *or* one's mind, **stand up and be counted,** take a stand; open up, show one's mind, have no secrets; **appear, materialize**

7 be manifest, be there for all to see, make an appearance, be no secret *or* revelation, **surface,** lie on the surface, be seen with half an eye; need no explanation, **speak for itself,** tell its own story *or* tale; **go without saying,** *aller sans dire* <Fr>; **leap to the eye,** *sauter aux yeux* <Fr>, **stare one in the face,** hit one in the eye, strike the eye, glare, shout; come across, project; stand out, stick out, stick out a mile, stick out like a sore thumb, hang out <nf>

ADJS **8 manifest, apparent, evident, self-evident,** axiomatic, indisputable, **obvious, plain, clear,** perspicuous, distinct, palpable, patent, tangible; **visible, perceptible, perceivable, discernible,** seeable, observable, **noticeable, much in evidence; to be seen,** easy to be seen, plain to be seen; plain as day, plain as the nose on one's face, plain as a pikestaff, big as life, big as life and twice as ugly; **crystal-clear,** clear as crystal; **express, explicit, unmistakable,** not to be mistaken, open-and-shut <nf>; self-explanatory, self-explaining; **indubitable** 970.15

9 manifesting, manifestative, showing, displaying, showcasing, demonstrating, **demonstrative,** presentational, expository, expositional, exhibitive, exhibitional, **expressive;** evincive, evidential; **indicative,** indicatory; appearing, incarnating, incarnational, materializing; epiphanic, theophanic, angelophanic, Satanophanic, Christophanic, pneumatophanic; **revelational,** revelatory, **disclosive** 351.10; promulgatory 352.18; histrionic

10 open, overt, open to all, open as day, out of the closet <nf>; unclassified; **revealed, disclosed, exposed;** made public; bare, bald, naked

11 unhidden, unconcealed, unscreened, uncurtained, unshaded, veilless; **unobscure,** unobscured, undarkened, unclouded; **undisguised,** uncamouflaged

12 conspicuous, noticeable, notable, ostensible, **prominent, bold, pronounced, salient,** in relief, in bold *or* high *or* strong relief, **striking, outstanding,** in the foreground, sticking *or* hanging out <nf>; highlighted, spotlighted, featured; obtrusive; **flagrant,** arrant, blatant, notorious; **glaring,** staring, stark-staring

13 manifested, demonstrated, exhibited, shown, displayed, showcased; **manifestable,** demonstrable, exhibitable, displayable

ADVS **14 manifestly, apparently, evidently, obviously, patently, plainly, clearly,** distinctly, **unmistakably,** expressly, explicitly, palpably, tangibly; **visibly, perceptibly,** perceivably, discernibly, observably, **noticeably**

15 openly, overtly, before one, **before one's eyes** *or* very eyes, under one's nose <nf>; to one's face, face-to-face; **publicly,** in public; **in the open,** out in the open, in open court, **in plain sight,** in broad daylight, in the face of day *or* heaven, for all to see, in public view, in plain view, in the marketplace; aboveboard, on the table

16 conspicuously, prominently, noticeably, ostensibly, **notably, markedly, pronouncedly, saliently, strikingly, boldly, outstandingly;** obtrusively; arrantly, flagrantly, blatantly, notoriously; glaringly, staringly

349 REPRESENTATION, DESCRIPTION

NOUNS **1 representation, delineation,** presentment, drawing, **portrayal, portraiture, depiction,** depictment, rendering, rendition, characterization, charactering <old>, picturization, figuration, limning, imaging; prefigurement; **illustration,** exemplification, demonstration; projection, **realization**, manifestation, presentment; imagery, iconography; **art** 712; **drama** 704.1; conventional representation, plan, diagram, schema, schematization, **blueprint, chart, map;** conceptual model; drawing, sketch; mind map; visual; **notation,** mathematical notation, musical notation, score, tablature; dance notation, Laban dance notation system *or* labanotation, choreography; symbolization; **writing,** script, written word, text; **writing system; alphabet,** syllabary; alphabetic symbol, syllabic symbol, letter, ideogram, pictogram, logogram, logograph, hieroglyphic *or* hieroglyph, rune; printing 548; **symbol**

2 description, portrayal, portraiture, **depiction,** rendering, rendition, **delineation,** limning, **representation** 349; imagery; stream of consciousness; **word painting** *or* **picture, picture, portrait, image,** photograph; evocation, impression; **sketch,** vignette, cameo; **characterization,** character, character sketch, profile; vivid description, exact description, realistic *or* naturalistic description, slice of life, *tranche de vie* <Fr>, graphic account; specification, particularization, particulars, details, itemization, catalog, cataloging; **narration;** version; air quotes

3 account, recounting, statement, report, word, statement of fact; play-by-play description, blow-by-blow account *or* description; case study *or* history

4 impersonation, personation; mimicry, mimicking, mime, miming, pantomime, pantomiming, aping, dumb show; air guitar; mimesis, **imitation** 336; personification, embodiment, incarnation, realization; **characterization,** portrayal; **acting,** playing, dramatization, enacting, enactment, performing, performance; **posing,** masquerade

5 image, likeness; resemblance, semblance, similitude, simulacrum; **effigy,** icon, idol; **copy** 785, fair copy; **picture; portrait,** likeness; **photograph** 714.3; **perfect** *or* **exact likeness, duplicate, double,** clone; replica, facsimile; match, fellow, mate, companion, **twin;** living image, very image, very picture, living picture, dead ringer <nf>, spitting image *or* spit and image <nf>, eidetic image; miniature, model; **reflection,** shadow, mirroring; trace, tracing; rubbing

6 figure, figurine; doll, dolly <nf>; teddy bear; **puppet, marionette,** *fantoche* <Fr>, *fantoccino* and *fantoccio* <Ital>, hand puppet, glove puppet; **mannequin** *or* manikin, model, dummy, working model, lay figure; wax figure, waxwork; scarecrow, corn dolly <Brit>, woman *or* man of straw, snowman, snowwoman, gingerbread woman *or* man, scarecrow, robot, automaton; **sculpture, bust, statue, statuette,** statuary, monument <old>; portrait bust *or* statue; death mask, life mask; carving, wood carving; figurehead

7 representative, representation, **type, specimen,** typification, embodiment, type specimen; **cross section;** exponent; **example** 786.2, exemplar; exemplification, typicality, typicalness, representativeness; epitome, quintessence, figuration; mother of all <nf>

VERBS **8 represent, delineate, depict,** render, characterize, hit off, character <old>, **portray, picture,** picturize, limn, draw, paint 712.19; **register,** convey an impression of; take *or* catch a likeness, capture; **notate, write,** print, map, chart, diagram, schematize; trace, trace out, trace over; rub, take a rubbing; record, photograph, film, shoot, scan; **symbolize** 517.18

9 describe, portray, picture, render, **depict, represent, delineate,** limn, **paint,** draw; evoke, bring to life, make one see, define; outline, sketch; **characterize,** character; **express,** set forth, give words to; **write** 547.19

10 go for *or* **as, pass for** *or* **as, count for** *or* **as,** answer for *or* as, stand in the place of, be taken as, be regarded as, be the equivalent of; **serve as,** be accepted for

11 image, mirror, hold the mirror up to nature, reflect, figure; **embody,** body forth, incarnate, **personify,** personate, impersonate; **illustrate,** demonstrate, exemplify; project, realize; shadow, shadow forth; **prefigure, pretypify,** foreshadow, adumbrate

12 impersonate, personate; **mimic,** mime, pantomime, take off, do *or* give an impression of, mock; ape, copy; **pose as, masquerade as,** affect the manner *or* guise of, pass for, pretend to be, represent oneself to be; **act,** enact, perform, do; **play, act as,** act *or* play a part, act the part of, act out, role-play, portray

ADJS **13 representational, representative, depictive, delineatory, resemblant; illustrative,** illustrational; pictorial, graphic, vivid; ideographic, pictographic, figurative; **representing, portraying,** limning, illustrating; **typifying, symbolizing,** symbolic, personifying, incarnating, embodying; imitative, mimetic, simulative, apish, mimish; echoic, onomatopoeic

14 descriptive, depictive, expositive, **representative,** representational, **delineative; expressive, vivid, graphic,** well-drawn, detailed; realistic, naturalistic, true to life, lifelike, real-life, faithful; evocative

15 typical, typic, typal; exemplary, sample; **characteristic,** distinctive, distinguishing, quintessential; **realistic, naturalistic; natural, normal,** usual, regular, par for the course <nf>; **true to type, true to form,** the nature of the beast <nf>

ADVS **16 descriptively,** representatively; **expressively, vividly, graphically;** faithfully, realistically, naturalistically

350 MISREPRESENTATION

NOUNS **1 misrepresentation, perversion, distortion,** deformation, garbling, twisting, slanting; inaccuracy; **coloring,** miscoloring, **false coloring;** false pretenses; **falsification** 354.9, **spin,** spin control, disinformation; misteaching 569; injustice, unjust representation; misdrawing, mispainting; misstatement, misreport, misquotation, misinformation; misdirection, misguidance, nonrepresentationalism, nonrealism, abstractionism, expressionism, calculated distortion; overstatement, exaggeration, hyperbole, overdrawing; understatement, litotes, conservative estimate; adulteration, forgery, counterfeiting; cover-up, whitewash

2 bad *or* poor likeness, **daub,** botch; scribble, scratch, hen tracks *or* scratches <nf>; distortion, distorted image, false image, anamorphosis,

astigmatism; **travesty,** parody, **caricature, burlesque,** gross exaggeration

VERBS **3 misrepresent, belie,** give a wrong idea, pass *or* pawn *or* foist *or* fob off as, send *or* deliver the wrong signal *or* message; put in a false light, **pervert, distort, garble, twist,** warp, deform, wrench, slant, put a spin on, twist the meaning of; **color,** miscolor, pervert, **give a false coloring,** put a false construction *or* appearance upon, slant, falsify 354.16; misteach 569.3; **disguise,** camouflage; misstate, misreport, misquote, put words into one's mouth, quote out of context; overstate, exaggerate, overdraw, blow up, blow out of all proportion, overemphasize; understate; **travesty,** parody, **caricature, burlesque;** misinform, disinform

4 misdraw, mispaint; overdraw, daub, botch, butcher, scribble, scratch

351 DISCLOSURE

NOUNS **1 disclosure,** disclosing; **revelation,** revealment, revealing, making public, publicizing, broadcasting, announcement, breaking news; apocalypse; discovery, discovering; manifestation 348; unfolding, unfoldment, **uncovering,** unwrapping, uncloaking, taking the wraps off, taking from under wraps, removing the veil, **unveiling, unmasking; exposure,** exposition, **exposé; baring,** stripping, stripping *or* laying bare; outing <nf>; **showing up**

2 divulgence, divulging, divulgement, divulgation, evulgation <old>, letting out, full report; **betrayal,** unwitting disclosure, indiscretion; leak, communication leak; **giveaway** *and* dead giveaway <nf>; telltale, telltale sign, obvious clue; **blabbing** *and* blabbering <nf>, babbling; **tattling;** state's evidence

3 confession, confessing, shrift, **acknowledgment, admission,** concession, avowal, self-admission, self-concession, self-avowal, owning, owning up *and* coming clean <nf>, unbosoming, unburdening oneself, getting a load off one's mind <nf>, fessing up <nf>, making a clean breast, baring one's breast; rite of confession

VERBS **4 disclose, reveal, let out, show,** impart, discover, develop <old>, **leak,** let slip out, let the cat out of the bag *and* spill the beans <nf>; manifest 348.5; unfold, unroll; **open,** open up, lay open, break the seal, bring into the open, get out in the open, bring out of the closet; **expose, show up; bare,** strip *or* lay bare, blow the lid off *and* blow wide open *and* rip open *and* crack wide open <nf>; take the lid off, **bring to light,** bring into the open, hold up to view; hold up the mirror to;

unmask, dismask, tear off the mask, **uncover,** unveil, take the lid off <nf>, ventilate, take out from under wraps, take the wraps off, lift *or* draw the veil, raise the curtain, let daylight in, shine some light on, unscreen, uncloak, undrape, unshroud, unfurl, unsheathe, unwrap, unpack, unkennel; put one wise *and* clue one in *and* bring one up to speed <nf>, put one in the picture <chiefly Brit nf>, open one's eyes

5 **divulge,** divulgate, evulgate <old>; **reveal, make known, tell,** breathe, utter, vent, ventilate, air, give vent to, **give out, let out** <Brit>, let get around, out with <nf>, come out with; break it to, **break the news;** let in on *or* to, **confide,** confide to, let one's hair down <nf>, unbosom oneself, let into the secret; **publish** 352.10

6 **betray,** inform, **inform on** 551.12, talk *and* peach <nf>; rat *and* stool *and* sing *and* squeal <nf>, turn state's evidence; leak <nf>, spill <nf>, **spill the beans** <nf>; **let the cat out of the bag** <nf>, speak before one thinks, be unguarded *or* indiscreet, kiss and tell, **give away** *and* give the show away *and* give the game away <nf>, betray a confidence, tell secrets, reveal a secret; have a big mouth *or* bazoo <nf>, **blab** *or* blabber <nf>; babble, **tattle,** tell *or* tattle on, tell tales, **tell tales out of school;** talk out of turn, let slip, let fall *or* drop; **blurt, blurt out**

7 **confess,** break down and confess, **admit, acknowledge,** tell all, avow, concede, grant, **own, own up** <nf>, let on, implicate *or* incriminate oneself, come clean <nf>; spill *and* spill it *and* spill one's guts <nf>; **tell the truth,** tell all, admit everything, let it all hang out <nf>, throw off all disguise; **plead guilty,** own oneself in the wrong, cop a plea <nf>; **unbosom oneself, make a clean breast, get it off one's chest** <nf>, **get it out of one's system** <nf>, disburden *or* unburden one's mind *or* conscience *or* heart, **get a load off one's mind** <nf>, fess up <nf>; out with it *and* spit it out *and* open up <nf>; throw oneself on the mercy of the court; **reveal oneself,** show one's colors *or* true colors, come out of the closet <nf>, show one's hand *or* cards, put *or* lay one's cards on the table

8 **be revealed, become known, surface, come to light,** appear, manifest itself, come to one's ears, transpire, **leak out, get out, come out,** out, come home to roost, come out in the wash, break forth, show its face; show its colors, be seen in its true colors, stand revealed; blow one's cover <nf>

ADJS 9 **revealed, disclosed** 348.10

10 **disclosive, revealing,** revelatory, revelational, clueful; **disclosing,** showing, exposing, betraying; kiss-and-tell; eye-opening; **talkative** 343.10/540.9; admitted, confessed, self-confessed

11 confessional, admissive

352 PUBLICATION

NOUNS 1 **publication, publishing, promulgation,** evulgation, **propagation, dissemination, diffusion, broadcast, broadcasting, spread, spreading,** spreading abroad, divulgence, disclosure, **circulation,** ventilation, airing, noising, bandying, bruiting, bruiting about, spreading the word; **display;** issue, issuance; telecasting, videocasting, podcasting, blogging; printing 548; book, periodical 555

2 **announcement,** annunciation, enunciation; **proclamation,** pronouncement, pronunciamento; edict, decree; **report,** communiqué, **declaration, statement;** public declaration *or* statement, program, programma, **notice, notification,** public notice; speech; circular, encyclical, encyclical letter; manifesto, position paper; broadside; rationale; white paper, white book; ukase, edict 420.4; bulletin board, notice board

3 **press release,** release, handout, bulletin, official bulletin, notice, public service announcement

4 **publicity, publicness, notoriety, fame,** famousness, renown, notoriousness, infamy, notice, public notice *or* recognition, **celebrity,** *réclame and éclat* <Fr>; **limelight** *and* **spotlight** <nf>, daylight, bright light, glare, public eye *or* consciousness, **exposure, currency,** common *or* public knowledge, widest *or* maximum dissemination, public forum; **ballyhoo** *and* hoopla <nf>; report, public report; cry, hue and cry; **public relations** *or* PR, flackery <nf>; **publicity story,** press notice; propaganda; **writeup, puff** <nf>, **plug** <nf>, **blurb** <nf>, hype <nf>; photo opportunity, photo op <nf>; name in bright lights <nf>

5 **promotion, buildup** *and* promo <nf>, flack <nf>, publicization, publicizing, promoting, advocating, advocacy, bruiting, drumbeating, tub-thumping, press-agentry; **advertising,** salesmanship 734.2, Madison Avenue, hucksterism <nf>; advertising campaign; advertising agency; advertising medium *or* media; advocacy, advocacy group; product placement

6 **advertisement, ad** <nf>, advert <Brit nf>, notice; **commercial,** message, important message, message *or* words from the sponsor; spot commercial *or* spot, network commercial; infomercial; reader, reading notice; display ad; want ad <nf>, classified ad; personal ad; spread, two-page spread, testimonial; advertorial; trailer; teaser; website ad, banner ad; Yellow Pages; bumper sticker; ad creep

7 **poster, bill, placard, sign,** show card, banner, *affiche* <Fr>; **signboard, billboard,** highway sign,

hoarding <Brit>; sandwich board; marquee; bulletin board

8 advertising matter, promotional material, public relations handout *or* release, **literature** <nf>; **leaflet, leaf, folder, handbill, bill, flier, throwaway, handout, circular,** pamphlet, brochure, broadside, broadsheet; insert *or* insertion, blow-in

9 publicist, publicizer, public relations person, public relations officer, PR person, flack *and* pitchman *or* pitchperson <nf>, public relations specialist, **publicity man** *or* agent, **press agent,** agent, flack <nf>, imagemaker; **advertiser; adman** *and* huckster *and* pitchman <nf>; ad writer <nf>, copywriter, blurb writer; **promoter, booster** <nf>, plugger <nf>; **ballyhooer** *or* **ballyhoo man** <nf>; **barker,** spieler <nf>, skywriter; billposter; sign-painter; sandwich boy *or* man; spin doctor

VERBS **10 publish, promulgate, propagate, circulate,** circularize, **diffuse, disseminate,** distribute, **broadcast,** televise, telecast, videocast, air, **spread,** spread around *or* about, spread far and wide, publish abroad, **pass the word around,** bruit, **bruit about, advertise,** repeat, retail, put about, **bandy about, noise about,** cry about *or* abroad, noise *or* sound abroad, bruit abroad, set news afloat, **spread a report; rumor,** launch a rumor, voice <old>, whisper, buzz, **rumor about,** whisper *or* buzz about

11 make public, go public with <nf>; bring *or* lay *or* drag before the public, **display,** take one's case to the public, **give** *or* **put out,** give to the world, **make known; divulge** 351.5; **ventilate,** air, give air to, bring into the open, get out in the open, open up, broach, give vent to

12 announce, annunciate, enunciate; **declare, state,** declare roundly, affirm, pronounce, give notice; **say,** make a statement, send a message *or* signal; **report,** make an announcement *or* a report, issue a statement, publish *or* issue a manifesto, present a position paper, issue a white paper, hold a press conference

13 proclaim, cry, cry out, **promulgate,** give voice to; **herald,** herald abroad; **blazon,** blaze, blaze *or* blazon about *or* abroad, blare, blare forth *or* abroad, thunder, declaim, shout, trumpet, trumpet *or* thunder forth, announce with flourish of trumpets *or* beat of drum; shout from the housetops, proclaim at the crossroads *or* market cross, proclaim at Charing Cross <Brit>

14 issue, bring out, put out, get out, launch, get off, emit, put *or* give *or* send forth, offer to the public, pass out

15 publicize, give publicity; go public with <nf>; bring *or* drag into the limelight, throw the spotlight on <nf>; **advertise, promote,** build up,

cry up, sell, puff <nf>, **boost** <nf>, **plug** <nf>, **ballyhoo** <nf>; put on the map, make a household word of, establish; bark *and* spiel <nf>; make a pitch for *and* beat the drum for *and* thump the tub for <nf>; **write up,** give a write-up, press-agent <nf>; circularize; bulletin; bill; **post bills,** post, post up, placard; skywrite

16 <be published> **come out, appear,** break, hit the streets <nf>, **issue,** go *or* come forth, find vent, **see the light,** see the light of day, become public; **circulate, spread,** spread about, have currency, **get around** *or* about, get abroad, get afloat, get exposure, go *or* fly *or* buzz *or* blow about, **go the rounds,** pass from mouth to mouth, be on everyone's lips, go through the length and breadth of the land; spread like wildfire; blog

ADJS **17 published, public,** made public, **circulated,** in circulation, promulgated, propagated, **disseminated,** issued, spread, diffused, distributed; in print; **broadcast,** telecast, televised; **announced,** proclaimed, declared, **stated,** affirmed; **reported,** brought to notice; common knowledge, common property, current; **open,** accessible, open to the public; hot off the press

18 publicational, promulgatory, propagatory; proclamatory, annunciatory, enunciative; declarative, declaratory; heraldic; promotional; on-message

ADVS **19 publicly, in public; openly** 348.15; in the public eye, in the glare of publicity, in the limelight *or* spotlight <nf>, reportedly

353 MESSENGER

NOUNS **1 messenger,** message-bearer, **dispatch-bearer,** commissionaire <Brit>, nuncio <old>, **courier,** diplomatic courier, carrier, **runner,** express <Brit>, dispatch-rider, pony-express rider, post <old>, postboy, postrider, **estafette** <Fr>; bicycle *or* motorcycle messenger; **go-between** 576.4; **emissary** 576.6; Mercury, Hermes, Iris, Pheidippides, Paul Revere; post office, courier service, package service, message service *or* center; answering service

2 herald, harbinger, forerunner, vaunt-courier; evangel, evangelist, bearer of glad tidings; herald angel, Gabriel, **buccinator** <L>

3 announcer, annunciator, enunciator; nunciate <old>; **proclaimer; crier, town crier,** bellman

4 errand boy, office boy, messenger-boy, copyboy; bellhop <nf>, bellboy, bellman, callboy, caller

5 postman, mailman, mail carrier, letter carrier; postmaster, postmistress; postal clerk

6 <mail carriers> carrier pigeon, carrier, homing pigeon, homer <nf>; pigeon post; post-horse, poster; post coach, mail coach; post boat, packet boat *or* ship, mail boat, mail packet, mailer <old>; mail train, mail car, post car, post-office car, railway mail car; mail truck; mailplane; electronic mail

354 FALSENESS

NOUNS **1 falseness, falsehood,** falsity, inveracity, untruth, **truthlessness, untrueness; fallaciousness,** fallacy, **erroneousness** 975.1; false negative, false positive

2 spuriousness, phoniness <nf>, bogusness, **ungenuineness, unauthenticity,** unrealness, artificiality, factitiousness, syntheticness

3 sham, fakery, faking, falsity, feigning, pretending; feint, pretext, **pretense,** hollow pretense, **pretension, false pretense** *or* **pretension;** humbug, humbuggery; **bluff,** bluffing, four-flushing <nf>; speciousness, meretriciousness; cheating, fraud; imposture; deception, delusion 356.1; acting, playacting; representation, **simulation,** simulacrum; dissembling, **dissemblance, dissimulation;** seeming, semblance, appearance, face, ostentation, **show, false show,** outward show, false air; window dressing, front, **false front, façade,** gloss, varnish; gilt; color, coloring, false color; masquerade, facade, disguise; posture, pose, posing, attitudinizing; mannerism, affectation 500

4 falseheartedness, falseness, doubleheartedness, doubleness of heart, doubleness, **duplicity, two-facedness,** double-facedness, **double-dealing,** ambidexterity; double standard; **dishonesty,** improbity, lack of integrity, Machiavellianism, bad faith; low cunning, **cunning,** artifice, wile 415.3; **deceitfulness** 356.3; faithlessness, treachery 645.6

5 insincerity, uncandidness, uncandor, **unfrankness,** disingenuousness, indirectness; emptiness, hollowness; mockery, hollow mockery; crossed fingers, tongue in cheek, unseriousness; halfheartedness; sophistry, jesuitry, jesuitism, casuistry 936.1

6 hypocrisy, hypocriticalness; Tartuffery, Tartuffism, Pecksniffery, pharisaism, **sanctimony** 693, sanctimoniousness, religiosity, false piety, ostentatious devotion, pietism, Bible-thumping <nf>; **mealymouthedness, unctuousness,** oiliness, smarminess *or* smarm <nf>; cant, mummery, snuffling <old>, **mouthing; lip service;** tokenism; token gesture, empty gesture; smooth tongue, smooth talk, sweet talk *and* soft soap <nf>; crocodile tears

7 quackery, chicanery, quackishness, quackism, **mountebankery, charlatanry,** charlatanism; **imposture; humbug,** humbuggery

8 untruthfulness, dishonesty, falsehood, **unveracity,** unveraciousness, truthlessness, **mendaciousness, mendacity;** credibility gap; **lying, fibbing,** fibbery, pseudology; pathological lying, habitual lying, mythomania, *pseudologia phantastica* <L>

9 deliberate falsehood, disinformation, falsification, disinforming, falsifying; confabulation; **perversion, distortion,** straining, **bending; misrepresentation,** misconstruction, misstatement, coloring, false coloring, miscoloring, slanting, imparting a spin <nf>; tampering, cooking *and* fiddling <nf>; stretching, fictionalization, **exaggeration** 355; **prevarication,** equivocation 344.4; **perjury,** false swearing, oath breaking, false oath, false plea

10 fabrication, invention, concoction, disinformation; canard, base canard; **forgery; fiction,** figment, **myth,** legend, fable, story, romanticized version, extravaganza; old wives' tale, unfact

11 lie, falsehood, falsity, **untruth,** false statement, untruism, mendacity, **prevarication, fib,** taradiddle *or* tarradiddle <nf>, flimflam *or* flam, a crock *and* a crock of shit <nf>, *blague* <Fr>; **fiction,** pious fiction, legal fiction; **story** <nf>, **trumped-up story,** farrago; **yarn** <nf>, **tale,** fairy tale <nf>, ghost story; farfetched story, tall tale *and* **tall story** <nf>, **cock-and-bull story,** fish story <nf>, flight of fancy; exaggeration 355; half-truth, stretching of the truth, slight stretching, white lie, little white lie; *suggestio falsi* <L>; partial truth; propaganda, rumor, gossip, empty talk; a pack of lies

12 monstrous lie, consummate lie, deep-dyed falsehood, out-and-out lie, **whopper** <nf>, gross *or* flagrant *or* shameless falsehood, downright lie, **barefaced lie, dirty lie** <nf>, big lie; **slander, libel** 512.3; the big lie; bullshit *or* load of crap <nf>

13 fake, fakement *and* put-up job <nf>, **phony** <nf>, **rip-off** <nf>, **sham, mock, imitation,** simulacrum, dummy; paste, tinsel, *clinquant* <Fr>, pinchbeck, shoddy, junk; **counterfeit, forgery;** put-up job *and* frame-up <nf>, put-on <nf>; **hoax, cheat, fraud, swindle** 356.8; whited sepulcher, whitewash job <nf>; impostor 357.6

14 humbug, humbuggery; **bunk** <nf>, **bunkum;** hooey *and* hoke *and* **hokum** <nf>, **bosh** <nf>, bull *and* **bullshit** *and* crap <nf>, baloney <nf>, flimflam, flam, smoke and mirrors <nf>, claptrap, moonshine, eyewash, hogwash, gammon <Brit nf>, *blague* <Fr>, jiggery-pokery <Brit>

VERBS **15** ring false, **not ring true**

16 falsify, belie, misrepresent, miscolor; misstate, misquote, misreport, miscite; overstate, understate; **pervert, distort,** strain, warp, **slant, twist,** warp, stretch the truth, impart spin <nf>; garble; put a false appearance upon, give a false coloring, falsely color, give a color to, **color, gild,** gloss, gloss over, whitewash, varnish, paper over <nf>; fudge <nf>, dress up, titivate, embellish, embroider, trick or prink out; deodorize, make smell like roses; **disguise, camouflage, mask;** propagandize, gossip

17 **tamper with, manipulate, fake, juggle,** sophisticate, **doctor** and **cook** <nf>, rig, cook or juggle the books or the accounts <nf>; pack, stack; **adulterate;** retouch; **load; salt,** plant <nf>, salt a mine

18 **fabricate, invent, manufacture, trump up, make up, hatch, concoct, cook up** and make out of whole cloth <nf>, fictionalize, mythologize, fudge <nf>, fake, hoke up <nf>; **counterfeit, forge;** fantasize, fantasize about

19 **lie, tell a lie,** falsify, speak falsely, speak with forked tongue <nf>, be untruthful, trifle with the truth, deviate from the truth, **fib, story** <nf>; **stretch the truth,** strain or bend the truth; draw the longbow; **exaggerate** 355.3; lie flatly, lie in one's throat, lie through one's teeth, lie like a trooper, **prevaricate,** misstate, equivocate 344.7; **deceive, mislead,** tell a white lie; bullshit <nf>

20 swear falsely, forswear oneself <old>, perjure, **perjure oneself, bear false witness**

21 **sham, fake** <nf>, **feign, counterfeit, simulate,** put up <nf>, gammon <Brit nf>; **pretend,** make a pretense, **make believe, make a show of,** make like <nf>, make as if or as though; go through the motions <nf>; let on, let on like <nf>; **affect,** profess, **assume,** put on; **dissimulate, dissemble,** cover up; **act, play,** play-act, **put on an act** or a charade <nf>, act or play a part; **put up a front** <nf>, put on a front or false front <nf>; four-flush <nf>, **bluff,** pull or put up a bluff <nf>; **play possum** <nf>, roll over and play dead

22 **pose as, masquerade as,** impersonate, pass for, assume the guise or identity of, set up for, act the part of, represent oneself to be, claim or pretend to be, **make false pretenses,** go under false pretenses, **sail under false colors**

23 be hypocritical, act or play the hypocrite; cant, be holier than the Pope or thou, reek of piety; shed crocodile tears, snuffle <old>, snivel, mouth; give mouth honor, render or give lip service; sweet-talk, soft-soap, blandish 511.5

24 play a double game or role, play both ends against the middle, work both sides of the street, have it both ways at once, have one's cake and eat it too, run with the hare and hunt with the hounds <Brit>; two-time <nf>

ADJS **25 false, untrue, truthless, not true,** void or devoid of truth, contrary to fact, in error, **fallacious, erroneous** 975.16; unfounded 936.13; disinformative

26 **spurious, ungenuine, unauthentic,** supposititious, bastard, **pseudo, quasi,** apocryphal, **fake** <nf>, **phony** <nf>, **sham, mock, counterfeit,** colorable, **bogus,** queer <nf>, dummy, **make-believe,** so-called, **imitation** 336.8; not what it's cracked up to be <nf>; **falsified;** dressed up, titivated, embellished, embroidered; garbled; twisted, distorted, warped, perverted, slanted; half-true, falsely colored; **simulated, faked, feigned,** colored, fictitious, fictive, **counterfeited, pretended, affected, assumed, put-on; artificial, synthetic,** ersatz; unreal; factitious, unnatural, man-made; illegitimate; soi-disant <Fr>, self-styled; pinchbeck, brummagem <Brit>, tinsel, shoddy, tin, junky

27 **specious, meretricious,** gilded, tinsel, **seeming,** apparent, colored, colorable, plausible, **ostensible**

28 **quack, quackish; charlatan, charlatanish,** charlatanic

29 **fabricated,** invented, manufactured, **concocted, hatched, trumped-up, made-up,** put-up, cooked-up <nf>; **forged;** fictitious, fictional, fictionalized, figmental, **mythical,** fabulous, legendary; fantastic, fantasied, fancied, legendary

30 **tampered with, manipulated, cooked** and **doctored** <nf>, juggled, **rigged,** engineered; packed

31 **falsehearted, false,** false-principled, false-dealing; double, duplicitous, ambidextrous, **double-dealing,** doublehearted, double-minded, double-tongued, double-faced, **two-faced,** Janus-faced; Machiavellian, dishonest; **crooked, deceitful;** creative, artful, cunning, crafty 415.12; faithless, perfidious, treacherous 645.21

32 **insincere, uncandid, unfrank, mealymouthed, unctuous, oily,** disingenuous, ungenuine, pseudo, smarmy <nf>; dishonest; **empty, hollow;** tongue in cheek, unserious; sophistic or sophistical, jesuitic or jesuitical, casuistic 936.10

33 **hypocritic** or hypocritical, canting, Pecksniffian, pharisaic, pharisaical, pharisean, **sanctimonious, goody-goody** <nf>, goody two-shoes, holier-than-the-Pope, holier-than-thou, simon-pure; artificial, dissembling, phony

34 **untruthful, dishonest, unveracious,** unveridical, truthless, **lying, mendacious,** untrue; perjured, forsworn; prevaricating, equivocal 344.11

ADVS **35 falsely, untruly,** truthlessly; **erroneously** 975.20; **untruthfully,** unveraciously; mendaciously; **spuriously,** ungenuinely; artificially, synthetically; unnaturally, factitiously; speciously, seemingly, apparently, plausibly, ostensibly; nominally, in name only

36 insincerely, uncandidly, unfrankly; emptily, hollowly; unseriously; ambiguously; **hypocritically,** mealy-mouthedly, unctuously

355 EXAGGERATION

NOUNS **1 exaggeration,** exaggerating; **overstatement,** big *or* tall talk <nf>, bullshit <nf>, jive <nf>, **hyperbole,** hyperbolism; **superlative; extravagance,** profuseness, **prodigality** 486, overdoing it, going too far, overshooting; **magnification, enlargement,** amplification <old>, dilation, dilatation, **inflation,** expansion, blowing up, puff, puffing up, aggrandizement, embellishment, elaboration, embroidery; **stretching, heightening,** enhancement; overemphasis, overstressing; overestimation 949; exaggerated lengths, **extreme,** extremism, stretch, exorbitance, inordinacy, **overkill, excess** 993; burlesque, travesty, caricature; crock <nf>, whopper, tall story; sensationalism, puffery *and* ballyhoo <nf>, touting, huckstering; grandiloquence 545; painting *or* gilding the lily; to-do *and* hype *and* hoopla <nf>

2 overreaction, much ado about nothing, fuss, uproar, commotion, storm *or* tempest in a teapot, making a mountain out of a molehill

VERBS **3 exaggerate,** hyperbolize; **overstate,** overspeak <old>, overreach, **overdraw,** overcharge; overstress, overemphasize; **overdo, carry too far, go to extremes;** push to the extreme, indulge in overkill, overestimate 949.2; gild the lily; overpraise, oversell, tout, puff *and* ballyhoo *and* hype <nf>; **stretch,** stretch the truth, stretch the point, draw the longbow, embellish; **magnify, inflate,** amplify <old>; aggrandize, build up; pile *or* lay it on *and* pour *or* spread *or* lay it on thick *and* lay it on with a trowel <nf>; talk big <nf>, talk in superlatives, deal in the marvelous, make much of; **overreact,** make a Federal case out of it <nf>, something out of nothing, make a mountain out of a molehill, create a tempest in a teapot *or* teacup, make too much of, cry over spilt milk; caricature, travesty, burlesque, ham, ham it up

ADJS **4 exaggerated,** hyperbolical, **magnified,** amplified <old>, **inflated,** aggrandized, stylized, embroidered, embellished, varnished; **stretched,** disproportionate, **blown up out of all proportion,** blown out of proportion, overblown; overpraised, oversold, overrated, touted, puff *and* puffed *and* ballyhooed <nf>, hyped <nf>; overemphasized, **overemphatic, overstressed; overemphatic, overstressed; overstated, overdrawn; overdone,**

overwrought, a bit thick; caricatural, melodramatic, farfetched, too much <nf>, over the top; overestimated 949.3; overlarge, overgreat; **extreme,** pushed to the extreme, exorbitant, inordinate, **excessive** 993.16; **superlative, extravagant,** profuse, **prodigal** 486.8; high-flown, grandiloquent 545.8; overexposed

5 exaggerating, exaggerative, hyperbolical

356 DECEPTION

NOUNS **1 deception,** calculated deception, **deceptiveness, subterfuge,** gimmickry *or* gimmickery, **trickiness; falseness** 354; fallaciousness, fallacy; self-deception, fond illusion, wishful thinking, willful misconception; vision, hallucination, phantasm, mirage, will-o'-the-wisp, **delusion,** delusiveness, illusion 976; deceiving, **victimization, dupery;** bamboozlement <nf>, hoodwinking; swindling, defrauding, conning, flimflam *or* flimflammery <nf>; **fooling,** befooling, tricking, **kidding** *and* putting on <nf>; spoofing *and* spoofery <nf>; bluffing; circumvention, overreaching, outwitting; ensnarement, entrapment, enmeshment, entanglement; smoke and mirrors

2 misleading, misguidance, misdirection; bum steer <nf>; misinformation 569.1

3 deceit, deceitfulness, guile, falseness, insidiousness, **underhandedness; shiftiness, furtiveness,** surreptitiousness, indirection; **hypocrisy** 354.6; **falseheartedness, duplicity** 354.4; **treacherousness** 645.6; **artfulness,** craft, guile, **cunning** 415; sneakiness 345.4; sneak attack; funny business

4 chicanery, chicane, **skulduggery** <nf>, knavery, **trickery,** dodgery, pettifogging, pettifoggery, *supercherie* <Fr>, **artifice,** sleight, machination; **sharp practice, underhand dealing, foul play;** connivery, connivance, collusion, conspiracy, covin <law>; fakery, charlatanism, mountebankery, quackery

5 juggling, jugglery, **trickery,** dirty pool <nf>, *escamotage* <Fr>, prestidigitation, conjuration, **legerdemain, sleight of hand,** smoke and mirrors <nf>; mumbo jumbo, **hocus-pocus,** hanky-panky *and* monkey business *and* hokey-pokey <nf>, nobbling *and* jiggery-pokery <Brit nf>, shenanigans <nf>

6 trick, artifice, device, ploy, gambit, stratagem, scheme, **design,** *ficelle* <Fr>, **subterfuge,** blind, **ruse, wile,** chouse <nf>, shift, **dodge,** artful dodge, sleight, pass, feint, fetch, chicanery; **bluff;** gimmick, joker, catch; curve, curve-ball, googly *or* bosey *or* wrong'un <Brit nf>; **dirty trick,** dirty deal, fast deal, scurvy trick; sleight of hand, sleight-of-hand trick, hocus-pocus <old>; juggle, juggler's trick; **bag of tricks,** tricks of the trade

7 **hoax, deception,** spoof <nf>, **humbug,** flam, **fake** *and* fakement, **rip-off** <nf>, **sham;** mare's nest; put-on <nf>

8 **fraud, fraudulence** *or* fraudulency, **dishonesty; imposture; imposition, cheat, cheating,** cozenage, **swindle,** dodge, fishy transaction, piece of sharp practice; customer-gouging, insider-trading, short weight, chiseling; **gyp joint** <nf>; **racket** <nf>, illicit business 732; **graft** <nf>, grift <nf>; bunco; cardsharping; ballot-box stuffing, gerrymandering

9 <nf terms> **gyp,** diddle, diddling, scam, flimflam flam, ramp <Brit>, snow job, song and dance, number, bill of goods, burn, the business, dipsy-doodle, double cross, fiddle, hosing, the old army game, reaming, suckering, sting, con, ripoff

10 **confidence game, con game** <nf>, **skin game** <nf>, **bunco game; shell game,** thimblerig, thimblerigging; bucket shop, boiler room <nf>; goldbrick; bait-and-switch, the wire, the pay-off, the rag, pastposting

11 **cover, disguise, camouflage,** protective coloration; **false colors, false front** 354.3; **incognito;** smoke screen; **masquerade,** masque, mummery; **mask,** visor, vizard, vizard mask <old>, false face, domino, domino mask; red herring, diversion

12 **trap, gin; pitfall,** trapfall, deadfall; flytrap, mousetrap, mole trap, rattrap, bear trap; deathtrap, firetrap; Venus's flytrap, Dionaea; Catch-22; spring gun, set gun; baited trap; **booby trap, mine; decoy** 357.5; hidden danger

13 **snare,** springe; noose, lasso, lariat; bola; **net,** trawl, dragnet, seine, purse seine, pound net, gill net; cobweb; **meshes, toils; fishhook, hook,** sniggle; **bait,** ground bait; lure, fly, jig, squid, plug, wobbler, spinner; lime, birdlime

VERBS 14 **deceive, beguile, trick, hoax, dupe,** gammon, **gull,** pigeon, play one for a fool *or* sucker, **bamboozle** *and* snow *and* **hornswoggle** *and* diddle *and* scam <nf>, nobble <Brit nf>, **humbug, take in,** put on *and* hocus-pocus <nf>, string along, **put something over** *or* **across,** slip one over on <nf>, pull a fast one on; **play games** <nf>; **delude,** mock; **betray,** let down, leave in the lurch, leave holding the bag, play one false, **double-cross** <nf>, cheat on; two-time <nf>; juggle, conjure; **bluff;** cajole, **circumvent,** get around, forestall; **overreach,** outreach, outwit, outmaneuver, outsmart

15 **fool,** befool, make a fool of, practice on one's credulity, **pull one's leg,** make an ass of; **trick; spoof** *and* **kid** *and* put one on <nf>; **play a trick on,** play a practical joke upon, send on a fool's errand; fake one out <nf>; sell one a bill of goods, give one a snow job

16 **mislead, misguide, misdirect,** lead astray, lead up the garden path; **give a bum steer** <nf>; fake someone out, feed one a line <nf>, throw off the scent, throw off the track *or* trail, put on a false scent, drag *or* draw a red herring across the trail; throw one a curve *or* curve ball <nf>, bowl a googly *or* bosey *or* wrong 'un <Brit nf>; misinform 569.3

17 **hoodwink,** blindfold, blind, blind one's eyes, blear the eyes of <old>, throw dust in one's eyes, **pull the wool over one's eyes**

18 **cheat, victimize, gull,** pigeon, fudge, **swindle, defraud,** practice fraud upon, euchre, **con,** finagle, **fleece,** mulct, fob <old>, **bilk,** cozen, cog <old>, chouse, **cheat out of, do out of,** chouse out of, beguile of *or* out of; obtain under false pretenses; live by one's wits; bunco, play a bunco game; sell gold bricks <nf>; shortchange, shortweight, skim off the top; stack the cards *or* deck, pack the deal <nf>, deal off the bottom of the deck, play with marked cards; cog the dice, load the dice; thimblerig; crib <nf>; throw a fight *or* game <nf>, take a dive <nf>

19 <nf terms> **gyp, clip, scam,** rope in, hose, shave, beat, rook, flam, flimflam, diddle, dipsy-doodle, do a number on, hustle, fuck, screw, have, pull something, pull a trick *or* stunt, give the business, ramp <Brit>, stick, sting, burn, gouge, chisel, hocus, hocus-pocus, play *or* take for a sucker, make a patsy of, do, run a game on, slicker, take for a ride

20 **trap,** entrap, gin, catch, catch out, catch in a trap; catch unawares, ambush; **ensnare, snare,** hook, **hook in,** sniggle, noose; inveigle; net, mesh, enmesh, snarl <old>, ensnarl, wind, tangle, entangle, entoil, enweb; trip, trip up; **set** *or* **lay a trap for,** bait the hook, spread the toils; lime, birdlime; **lure,** allure, **decoy** 377.3

ADJS 21 **deceptive, deceiving, misleading,** beguiling, **false, fallacious,** delusive, delusory; hallucinatory, illusive, **illusory;** tricky, trickish, tricksy <old>, catchy; **fishy** <nf>, questionable, dubious; delusional

22 **deceitful, false; fraudulent, sharp, guileful, insidious,** slick, slippery, slippery as an eel, **shifty, tricky,** trickish, cute, finagling, chiseling <nf>; underhand, **underhanded, furtive, surreptitious,** indirect; collusive, covinous; **falsehearted, two-faced; treacherous** 645.21; sneaky 345.12; **cunning,** artful, gimmicky <nf>, **wily, crafty** 415.12; calculating, scheming, double-dealing

ADVS 23 **deceptively,** beguilingly, **falsely,** fallaciously, delusively, **trickily, misleadingly,** with intent to deceive; **under false colors,** under cover of, under the garb of, in disguise

24 **deceitfully, fraudulently, guilefully,** insidiously, **shiftily, trickily; underhandedly,** furtively, surreptitiously, indirectly, like a thief in the night; **treacherously** 645.25

357 DECEIVER

NOUNS 1 **deceiver, deluder,** duper, misleader, **beguiler, bamboozler** <nf>; actor, playactor <nf>, role-player; **dissembler,** dissimulator; confidence man; **double-dealer,** Machiavelli, Machiavel, Machiavellian; dodger, Artful Dodger <Charles Dickens>, **counterfeiter, forger, faker;** plagiarizer, plagiarist; entrancer, **enchanter,** charmer, befuddler, hypnotizer, mesmerizer; **seducer,** Don Juan, Casanova; tease, teaser; jilt, jilter; gay deceiver; **fooler, joker,** jokester, **hoaxer,** practical joker; spoofer *and* **kidder** *and* ragger *and* leg-puller <nf>

2 **trickster,** tricker; **juggler,** sleight-of-hand performer, magician, illusionist, conjurer, **prestidigitator,** *escamoteur* <Fr>, manipulator

3 **cheat, cheater;** two-timer <nf>; **swindler, defrauder,** cozener, juggler; **sharper, sharp,** spieler, pitchman, pitchperson; **confidence man, confidence trickster, horse trader,** horse coper <Brit>; **cardsharp,** cardsharper; thimblerigger; shortchanger; **shyster** *and* pettifogger <nf>; land shark, land pirate, land grabber, mortgage shark; carpetbagger; crimp

4 <nf terms> **gyp,** gypper, gyp artist, flimflammer, flimflam man, blackleg, chiseler, bilker, fleecer, diddler, crook, sharpie, shark, jackleg, slicker, con man, con artist, bunco, bunco artist, bunco steerer, scammer, clip artist, smoothie, dipsy-doodle, hustler, hoser

5 **shill,** decoy, **come-on man** <nf>, plant, capper, stool pigeon, stoolie <nf>; *agent provocateur* <Fr>

6 **impostor, ringer; impersonator; pretender;** sham, shammer, **humbug,** *blagueur* <Fr>, **fraud** <nf>, **fake** *and* **faker** *and* **phony** <nf>, **fourflusher** <nf>, bluff, bluffer; **charlatan, quack,** quacksalver, quackster, **mountebank,** saltimbanco; **wolf in sheep's clothing,** ass in lion's skin, jackdaw in peacock's feathers; poser, poseur; malingerer

7 **masquerader,** masker; **impersonator,** personator; mummer, guiser <Scot>, guisard; incognito, incognita

8 **hypocrite, phony** <nf>, sanctimonious fraud, pharisee, whited sepulcher, **canter,** snuffler, mealy-mouth, dissembler, dissimulator, pretender, poseur, poser; Tartuffe <Molière>, Pecksniff *and* Uriah Heep <Charles Dickens>, Joseph Surface <Richard B Sheridan>; false friend, fair-weather friend; summer soldier; cupboard lover

9 **liar, fibber,** fibster, fabricator, fabulist, pseudologist; falsifier; **prevaricator,** equivocator, evader, mudger <Brit nf>, waffler <nf>, palterer; **storyteller;** yarner *and* yarn spinner *and* spinner of yarns <nf>, double-talker; Ananias; Satan, Father of Lies; Baron Münchausen; Sir John Mandeville; consummate liar, "liar of the first magnitude"—Congreve; *menteur à triple étage* <Fr>, dirty liar; pathological liar, mythomane, mythomaniac, pseudologue, confirmed *or* habitual liar, consummate liar; **perjurer,** false witness; slanderer, libeler, libelant; bullshitter <nf>

10 **traitor,** treasonist, **betrayer, quisling, rat** <nf>, serpent, snake, cockatrice, **snake in the grass, double-crosser** <nf>, double-dealer; double agent; trimmer, time-server; turncoat 363.5; informer 551.6; archtraitor; Judas, Judas Iscariot, Benedict Arnold, Quisling, Brutus; **schemer, plotter,** intriguer, *intrigant* <Fr>, conspirer, **conspirator,** conniver, machinator; pseud <nf>, two-timer <nf>

11 **subversive; saboteur, fifth columnist,** crypto; security risk; **collaborationist,** collaborator, fraternizer; fifth column, underground; Trojan horse; renegade

358 DUPE

NOUNS 1 **dupe, gull,** gudgeon, *gobe-mouches* <Fr>; **victim;** gullible *or* dupable *or* credulous person, trusting *or* simple soul, innocent, *naïf* <Fr>, babe, babe in the woods; greenhorn; toy, plaything; monkey; **fool** 924; stooge, **cat's-paw**

2 <nf terms> **sucker, patsy,** pigeon, chicken, fall guy, doormat, mug <Brit>, fish, jay <chiefly Brit>, easy mark, sitting duck, juggin <chiefly Brit>, pushover, cinch, mark, vic, easy pickings, greeny, greener, chump, boob, schlemiel, sap, saphead, prize sap, easy touch, soft touch, hornswoggler

359 RESOLUTION

NOUNS 1 **resolution,** resolve, resolvedness, **determination, decision,** fixed *or* firm resolve, will, purpose; **resoluteness, determinedness,** determinateness, decisiveness, decidedness, **purposefulness;** definiteness, closure; **earnestness, seriousness,** sincerity, devotion, dedication, commitment, total commitment; "the native hue of resolution"—Shakespeare; single-mindedness, relentlessness, persistence, tenacity, perseverance 360; self-will, obstinacy 361; control freak

2 firmness, firmness of mind *or* spirit, fixity of purpose, **staunchness,** settledness, steadiness, constancy, steadfastness, fixedness, unshakableness; **stability** 855; concentration; flintiness, steeliness; inflexibility, rigidity, unyieldingness 361.2; trueness, loyalty 644.7

3 pluck, spunk <nf>, **mettle, backbone** <nf>, **grit,** true grit, spirit, **stamina, guts** *and* moxie <nf>, pith <old>, bottom, **toughness** <nf>; clenched teeth, gritted teeth; pluckiness, spunkiness <nf>, **gameness,** feistiness <nf>, mettlesomeness; courage 492

4 willpower, will, power, **strong-mindedness,** strength of mind, strength *or* fixity of purpose, strength, fortitude, **moral fiber; iron will,** will of iron *or* steel; a will *or* mind of one's own, law unto oneself; the courage of one's convictions, moral courage

5 self-control, self-command, self-possession, strength of character, self-mastery, self-government, self-domination, **self-restraint,** self-conquest, self-discipline, **self-denial;** control, restraint, constraint, discipline; composure, possession, aplomb; **independence** 430.5

6 self-assertion, self-assertiveness, forwardness, **nerve** *and* pushiness <nf>, importunateness, importunacy; self-expression, self-expressiveness

VERBS **7 resolve, determine, decide, will, purpose, make up one's mind,** make *or* take a resolution, make a point of; **settle,** settle on, fix, seal; conclude, come to a determination *or* conclusion *or* decision, determine once for all

8 be determined, be resolved, attain closure; **have a mind** *or* **will of one's own,** know one's own mind; **be in earnest, mean business** <nf>, mean what one says; have blood in one's eyes *and* be out for blood <nf>, **set one's mind** *or* **heart upon;** put one's heart into, devote *or* commit *or* dedicate oneself to, give oneself up to; buckle oneself, buckle down, buckle to; steel oneself, brace oneself, grit one's teeth, set one's teeth *or* jaw; put *or* lay *or* set one's shoulder to the wheel; take the bull by the horns, take the plunge, cross the Rubicon; nail one's colors to the mast, burn one's bridges *or* boats, go for broke *and* shoot the works <nf>, kick down the ladder, throw away the scabbard; never say die, die hard, die fighting, die with one's boots on

9 remain firm, stand fast *or* **firm, hold out,** hold fast, get tough <nf>, **take one's stand,** set one's back against the wall, **stand** *or* **hold one's ground,** keep one's footing, hold one's own, hang in *and* hang in there *and* hang tough <nf>, dig in, dig one's heels in; **stick to one's guns,** stick, stick with it, stick fast, stick to one's colors, adhere to one's

principles; not listen to the voice of the siren; take what comes, stand the gaff; **put one's foot down** <nf>, stand no nonsense

10 not hesitate, think nothing of, think little of, **make no bones about** <nf>, have *or* make no scruple of <old>, **stick at nothing,** stop at nothing; not look back; go the whole hog <nf>, carry through, face out; go the whole nine yards <nf>

ADJS **11 resolute, resolved, determined,** bound *and* bound and determined <nf>, **decided,** decisive, **purposeful;** definite; **earnest, serious,** sincere; devoted, dedicated, committed, wholehearted; single-minded, relentless, persistent, tenacious, persevering; **obstinate** 361.8

12 firm, staunch, standup <nf>, fixed, settled, steady, steadfast, constant, set *or* sot <nf>, flinty, steely; unshaken, not to be shaken, unflappable <nf>; undeflectable, **unswerving,** not to be deflected; immovable, unbending, inflexible, **unyielding** 361.9; true, committed, loyal 644.20

13 unhesitating, unhesitant, **unfaltering,** unflinching, unshrinking; stick-at-nothing <nf>

14 plucky, spunky *and* feisty *and* gutty *or* gutsy <nf>, gritty, **mettlesome,** dauntless, **game,** game to the last *or* end; **courageous** 492.16

15 strong-willed, strong-minded, firm-minded; **self-controlled,** controlled, self-disciplined, self-restrained; **self-possessed; self-assertive,** self-asserting, forward, pushy <nf>, importunate; self-expressive; **independent**

16 determined upon, resolved upon, decided upon, intent upon, fixed upon, settled upon, **set on,** dead set on <nf>, sot on <nf>, **bent on,** hell-bent on <nf>; obsessed

ADVS **17 resolutely, determinedly, decidedly,** decisively, resolvedly, **purposefully, with a will;** firmly, steadfastly, steadily, fixedly, with constancy, staunchly; **seriously,** in all seriousness, **earnestly,** in earnest, in good earnest, sincerely; devotedly, with total dedication, committedly; hammer and tongs, tooth and nail, *bec et ongles* <Fr>; heart and soul, with all one's heart *or* might, wholeheartedly; **unswervingly;** singlemindedly, relentlessly, persistently, tenaciously, like a bulldog, like a leech, perseveringly; **obstinately, unyieldingly, inflexibly** 361.15

18 pluckily, spunkily *and* feistily *and* gutsily <nf>, mettlesomely, **gamely,** dauntlessly, manfully, like a man; on one's mettle; **courageously, heroically** 492.22

19 unhesitatingly, unhesitantly, **unfalteringly,** unflinchingly, unshrinkingly

PHRS **20 come what may, venga lo que venga** <Sp>, *vogue la galère* <Fr>, **cost what it may,** *coûte que coûte* <Fr>, whatever the cost, at any price *or* cost *or* sacrifice, at all risks *or* hazards, **whatever may happen,** *ruat caelum* <L>, though the heavens may fall, at all events, live or die, survive or perish, sink or swim, rain or shine, come hell or high water; in some way or other

360 PERSEVERANCE

NOUNS **1 perseverance, persistence** *or* persistency, insistence *or* insistency, singleness of purpose; **resolution** 359; **steadfastness, steadiness,** stability 855; **constancy, permanence** 853.1; loyalty, fidelity 644.7; **single-mindedness,** concentration, undivided *or* unswerving attention, engrossment, preoccupation 983.3; **endurance, stick-to-itiveness** <nf>, staying power, bitterendism, **pertinacity,** pertinaciousness, **tenacity,** tenaciousness, **doggedness,** unremittingness, relentlessness, dogged perseverance, bulldog tenacity, unfailing *or* leechlike grip; plodding, plugging, slogging; bidding war; **obstinacy, stubbornness** 361.1; **diligence,** application, sedulousness, sedulity, industry, industriousness, hard work, assiduousness, assiduity, unflagging efforts; **tirelessness, indefatigability, stamina; patience,** patience of Job 134.1

VERBS **2 persevere, persist, carry on,** go on, **keep on,** keep up, keep at, **keep at it,** keep going, keep driving, keep trying, try and try again, **keep the ball rolling,** keep the pot boiling, keep up the good work; not take 'no' for an answer; not accept compromise *or* defeat; **endure,** last, **continue** 827.6

3 keep doggedly at, **plod,** drudge, slog *or* slog away, soldier on, put one foot in front of the other, peg away *or* at *or* on; **plug,** plug at, plug away *or* along; pound *or* hammer away; **keep one's nose to the grindstone**

4 stay with it, hold on, hold fast, **hang on,** hang on like a bulldog *or* leech, **stick to one's guns;** not give up, **never say die,** not give up the ship, not strike one's colors; come up fighting, come up for more; **stay it out, stick out, hold out;** hold up, last out, **bear up,** stand up; **live with it,** live through it; stay the distance *or* the course; sit tight, be unmoved *or* unmoveable; brazen it out

5 prosecute to a conclusion, **go through with it, carry through, follow through, see it through,** see it out, follow out *or* up; go through with it, go to the bitter end, go the distance, go all the way, go to any length, go to any lengths; **leave no stone unturned,** leave no avenue unexplored, overlook nothing, exhaust every move; move heaven and earth, go through fire and water

6 die trying, die in the last ditch, die in harness, **die with one's boots on** *or* die in one's boots, die at one's post, die in the attempt, die game, die hard, **go down with flying colors**

7 <nf terms> **stick,** stick to it, stick with it, stick it, stick it out, hang on for dear life, hang in, hang in there, hang tough, tough it out, keep on trucking, keep on keeping on; **go the limit,** go the whole hog, go the whole nine yards, go all out, shoot the works, go for broke, go through hell and high water; work one's ass *or* butt *or* tail off

ADJS **8 persevering,** perseverant, **persistent,** persisting, insistent; **enduring,** permanent, **constant, lasting;** continuing 856.7; **stable, steady, steadfast** 855.12; immutable, inalterable; **resolute** 359.11; **diligent, assiduous, sedulous,** industrious; dogged, plodding, slogging, plugging; **pertinacious, tenacious, stick-to-itive** <nf>; loyal, faithful 644.20; **unswerving,** unremitting, unabating, unintermitting, uninterrupted; single-minded, utterly attentive; rapt, preoccupied 983.17; **unfaltering, unwavering,** unflinching; relentless, **unrelenting; obstinate,** high-maintenance, **stubborn** 361.8; **unrelaxing,** unfailing, **untiring,** unwearying, unflagging, never-tiring, **tireless,** weariless, **indefatigable,** unwearied, unsleeping, undrooping, unnodding, unwinking, sleepless; undiscouraged, undaunted, indomitable, unconquerable, invincible, game to the last *or* to the end, hanging in there; **patient,** patient as Job 134.9

ADVS **9 perseveringly, persistently,** persistingly, insistently; **resolutely** 359.17; loyally, faithfully, devotedly 644.25; **diligently,** industriously, assiduously, sedulously; **doggedly,** sloggingly, ploddingly; pertinaciously, tenaciously; unremittingly, unabatingly, unintermittingly, uninterruptedly; unswervingly, unwaveringly, unfalteringly, unflinchingly; relentlessly, unrelentingly; **indefatigably, tirelessly,** wearilessly, untiringly, unwearyingly, unflaggingly, unrestingly, unsleepingly; **patiently**

10 through thick and thin, through fire and water, come hell or high water, through evil report and good report, rain or shine, fair or foul, in sickness and in health; **come what may** 359.20, **all the way, down to the wire,** to the bitter end

361 OBSTINACY

NOUNS **1 obstinacy,** obstinateness, pertinacity, restiveness, **stubbornness, willfulness,** self-will, hardheadedness, **headstrongness,** strongheadedness; mind *or* will of one's own, set *or* fixed mind, inflexible will; **perseverance** 360, **doggedness, determination,** tenaciousness, tenacity, bitterendism; **bullheadedness, pigheadedness, mulishness; obduracy,** unregenerateness; stiff neck, stiff-neckedness; sullenness, sulkiness; balkiness; uncooperativeness; dogmatism, opinionatedness 970.6; overzealousness, fanaticism 926.11; intolerance, bigotry 980; bloody-mindedness <Brit>

2 **unyieldingness,** unbendingness, stiff temper, **inflexibility,** inelasticity, impliability, ungivingness, **obduracy,** toughness, **firmness,** stiffness, adamantness, rigorism, **rigidity,** strait-lacedness or straight-lacedness, stuffiness; **hard line,** hard-bittenness, hard-nosedness <nf>; fixity; unalterability, unchangeability, immutability, immovability; irreconcilability, uncompromisingness, **intransigence** or intransigency, intransigeance <Fr>, intransigentism; **implacability,** inexorability, **relentlessness,** unrelentingness; sternness, grimness, dourness, flintiness, **steeliness**

3 **perversity,** perverseness, **contrariness, wrongheadedness, waywardness,** forwardness, difficultness, crossgrainedness, cantankerousness, feistiness and orneriness and cussedness <nf>; sullenness, sulkiness, dourness, stuffiness; irascibility 110.2

4 **ungovernability, unmanageability,** uncontrollability; indomitability, untamableness, **intractability,** refractoriness, shrewishness; incorrigibility; **unsubmissiveness,** unbiddability <Brit>, **indocility;** irrepressibility, insuppressibility; unmalleability, unmoldableness; recidivism; **recalcitrance** or recalcitrancy, contumacy, contumaciousness; **unruliness,** obstreperousness, restiveness, fractiousness, wildness; defiance 454; resistance 453

5 **unpersuadableness,** deafness, blindness; closed-mindedness; positiveness, dogmatism 970.6

6 <obstinate person> **mule** and donkey <nf>, ass, perverse fool; bullethead, pighead; hardnose <nf>, hardhead, hammerhead <nf>, hard-liner; standpat and **standpatter, stickler; intransigent,** maverick; dogmatist, positivist, bigot, fanatic, purist; **diehard, bitter-ender,** last-ditcher; conservative; stick-in-the-mud

VERBS 7 **balk, stickle;** hold one's ground, not budge, dig one's heels in, **stand pat** <nf>, **not yield an inch,** stick to one's guns; hold out; stand firm; take no denial, not take 'no' for an answer; take the bit in one's teeth; die hard; cut off one's nose to spite one's face; **persevere** 360.2; turn a deaf ear

ADJS 8 **obstinate, stubborn, pertinacious, restive; willful, self-willed,** strong-willed, hardheaded, **headstrong,** strongheaded, entêté <Fr>; **dogged,** bulldogged, **tenacious, perserving; bullheaded,** bulletheaded, **pigheaded, mulish** <nf>, stubborn as a mule; set, **set in one's ways,** case-hardened, stiff-necked; sullen, sulky; balky, balking; unregenerate, uncooperative; bigoted, intolerant 980.11, overzealous, fanatic, fanatical 926.32; dogmatic, opinionated 970.22

9 **unyielding, unbending, inflexible, hard, hard-line,** inelastic, impliable, ungiving, **firm, stiff,** rigid, rigorous, stuffy; rock-ribbed, rock-hard, rock-like; **adamant,** adamantine; unmoved, unaffected; **immovable,** not to be moved; **unalterable,** unchangeable, immutable; **uncompromising,** intransigent, irreconcilable, hard-shell and hard-core <nf>; implacable, inexorable, **relentless,** unrelenting; stern, grim, dour; iron, cast-iron, flinty, steely

10 **obdurate,** tough, **hard,** hard-set, hard-mouthed, hard-bitten, hard-nosed and hard-boiled <nf>

11 **perverse, contrary, wrongheaded, wayward, froward, difficult,** cross-grained, cantankerous, feisty, ornery <nf>; sullen, sulky, stuffy; irascible 110.19

12 **ungovernable, unmanageable, uncontrollable, indomitable,** untamable, **intractable, refractory;** shrewish; **incorrigible, unreconstructed; unsubmissive,** unbiddable <Brit>, **indocile;** irrepressible, insuppressible; unmalleable, unmoldable; recidivist, recidivistic; **recalcitrant,** contumacious; obstreperous, **unruly, restive,** wild, fractious, breachy <nf>; beyond control, out of hand; **resistant, resisting** 453.5; **defiant** 454.7; irascible; like a hog on ice <nf>

13 **unpersuadable,** deaf, blind; closed-minded; positive; dogmatic 970.22

ADVS 14 **obstinately, stubbornly,** pertinaciously; willfully, headstrongly; **doggedly,** tenaciously; **bullheadedly,** pigheadedly, mulishly; unregenerately; uncooperatively; with set jaw, with sullen mouth, with a stiff neck

15 **unyieldingly, unbendingly, inflexibly, adamantly,** obdurately, **firmly,** stiffly, rigidly, rigorously; unalterably, unchangeably, immutably, immovably, unregenerately; uncompromisingly, intransigently, irreconcilably; implacably, inexorably, relentlessly, unrelentingly; sternly, grimly, dourly

16 **perversely, contrarily,** contrariwise, waywardly, wrongheadedly, frowardly, crossgrainedly, cantankerously, feistily, sullenly, sulkily

17 **ungovernably, unmanageably, uncontrollably,** indomitably, untamably, intractably; shrewishly; incorrigibly; unsubmissively; irrepressibly, insuppressibly; contumaciously; unrulily, obstreperously, restively, fractiously

362 IRRESOLUTION

NOUNS **1 irresolution, indecision,** unsettlement, unsettledness, irresoluteness, undeterminedness, **indecisiveness,** undecidedness, infirmity of purpose; mugwumpery, mugwumpism, fence-sitting, fence-straddling; double-mindedness, **ambivalence,** ambitendency; dubiety, dubiousness, **uncertainty** 971; **instability, inconstancy,** changeableness 854; capriciousness, mercuriality, fickleness 364.3; change of mind, second thoughts, tergiversation 363.1; fence-sitting

2 vacillation, fluctuation, oscillation, pendulation, mood swing, **wavering,** wobbling, waffling <nf>, shilly-shally, **shilly-shallying,** blowing hot and cold; equivocation 344.4; second thoughts; back-pedaling, reversal, about-face

3 hesitation, hesitance, **hesitancy,** hesitating, holding back, dragging one's feet; falter, faltering, shilly-shally, shilly-shallying; diffidence, tentativeness, caution, cautiousness

4 weak will, weak-mindedness; feeblemindedness <old>, **weakness,** feebleness, faintness, faintheartedness, **frailty, infirmity; wimpiness** or wimpishness <nf>, spinelessness, invertebracy; abulia; fear 127; cowardice 491; **pliability** 1047.2

5 vacillator, shillyshallyer, shilly-shally, **waverer,** wobbler, butterfly; mugwump, fence-sitter, fence-straddler; equivocator, tergiversator, prevaricator; ass between two bundles of hay; yo-yo <nf>, flip-flopper <nf>; **wimp** <nf>, weakling, jellyfish, Milquetoast; quitter; don't know

VERBS **6 not know one's own mind,** not know where one stands, **be of two minds,** have two minds, have mixed feelings, be in conflict, be conflicted <nf>; stagger, stumble, boggle

7 hesitate, pause, falter, hang back, hover; procrastinate; shilly-shally, hum and haw, **hem and haw;** wait to see how the cat jumps or the wind blows, scruple, jib, demur <old>, stick at, stickle, strain at; think twice about, stop to consider, ponder, wrinkle one's brow; debate, deliberate, see both sides of the question, balance, weigh one thing against another, consider both sides of the question, weigh the pros and cons; be divided, come down squarely in the middle, sit on or straddle the fence, fall between two stools; yield, back down 433.7; retreat, withdraw 163.6, wimp or chicken or cop out <nf>; pull back, drag one's feet; **flinch, shy away from, shy** 903.7, back off <nf>; fear; not face up to, hide one's head in the sand

8 vacillate, waver, waffle <nf>, **fluctuate,** pendulate, oscillate, wobble, wobble about, teeter, totter

<old>, dither, swing from one thing to another, **shilly-shally,** back and fill, keep off and on, will and will not, keep or leave hanging in midair; blow hot and cold 364.4; **equivocate** 344.7, fudge and mudge <Brit nf>; change one's mind, tergiversate; vary, **alternate** 854.5; shift, change horses in midstream, **change** 852.7

ADJS **9 irresolute,** irresolved, **unresolved; undecided, indecisive, undetermined,** unsettled, infirm of purpose; dubious, **uncertain** 971.16; at loose ends, at a loose end; **of two minds,** in conflict, double-minded, ambivalent, ambitendent; changeable, mutable 828.7; capricious, mercurial, fickle 364.6; mugwumpian, mugwumpish, fence-sitting, fence-straddling

10 vacillating, vacillatory, waffling <nf>, oscillatory, wobbly, **wavering, fluctuating,** pendulating, oscillating, **shilly-shallying,** shilly-shally; inconsistent

11 hesitant, hesitating, pikerish; faltering; shilly-shallying; diffident, tentative, timid, cautious; scrupling, jibbing, demurring <old>, sticking, straining, stickling

12 weak-willed, weak-minded, feebleminded <old>, weak-kneed, **weak,** wimpy or wimpish <nf>, feeble, fainthearted, **frail, faint, infirm,** feeble; **spineless,** invertebrate; without a will of one's own, unable to say 'no'; abulic; afraid, **chicken** and chicken-hearted and chicken-livered <nf>, cowardly 491.10; like putty, **pliable** 1047.9

ADVS **13 irresolutely,** irresolvedly, **undecidedly, indecisively, undeterminedly; uncertainly;** hesitantly, hesitatingly, falteringly; waveringly, vacillatingly, shilly-shally, shilly-shallyingly

363 CHANGING OF MIND

NOUNS **1 reverse, reversal,** flip and flip-flop and U-turn <nf>, turnabout, turnaround, **about-face,** about turn <Brit>, volte-face <Fr>, right-about-face, right-about turn <Brit>, right-about, a turn to the right-about; tergiversation, tergiversating; **change of mind;** second thoughts, better thoughts, afterthoughts, mature judgment; paradigm shift

2 apostasy, recreancy; **treason,** misprision of treason, betrayal, turning traitor, turning one's coat, changing one's stripes, ratting <nf>, going over, joining or going over to the opposition, siding with the enemy; **defection;** bolt, bolting, secession, breakaway; **desertion** 370.2; **recidivism,** recidivation, relapse, backsliding 394.2; faithlessness, **disloyalty** 645.5

3 recantation, withdrawal, disavowal, denial, reneging, **unsaying, repudiation,** palinode, palinody, **retraction,** retractation; **disclaimer,**

disclamation, **disownment,** disowning, abjurement, abjuration, **renunciation,** renouncement, forswearing; expatriation, self-exile

4 timeserver, timepleaser <old>, temporizer, opportunist, trimmer, weathercock; mugwump; chameleon, Vicar of Bray

5 apostate, turncoat, turnabout, **recreant, renegade,** renegado, renegate *or* runagate <old>, **defector,** tergiversator, tergiversant; **deserter,** turntail, quisling, fifth columnist, collaborationist, collaborator, **traitor** 357.10; strikebreaker; **bolter, seceder,** secessionist, **separatist,** schismatic; **backslider,** recidivist; reversionist; convert, proselyte

VERBS **6 change one's mind** *or* **song** *or* **tune** *or* **note,** sing a different tune, dance to another tune; come round, wheel, do an about-face, reverse oneself, do a flip-flop *or* U-turn <nf>, go over, change sides; swing from one thing to another; think better of it, have second thoughts, be of another mind; bite one's tongue

7 apostatize *or* apostacize, go over, change sides, switch, switch over, change one's allegiance, **defect; turn one's coat,** turn cloak; desert *or* leave a sinking ship; secede, break away, bolt, fall off *or* away; desert

8 recant, retract, repudiate, withdraw, take back, unswear, renege, welsh <nf>, **abjure, disavow, disown; deny,** disclaim, unsay, unspeak; **renounce, forswear, eat one's words,** eat one's hat, swallow, eat crow, eat humble pie; **back down** *or* **out,** climb down, crawfish out <nf>, backwater, weasel

9 be a timeserver, trim, temporize, change with the times; sit on *or* straddle the fence

ADJS **10 timeserving, trimming, temporizing;** supple, neither fish nor fowl

11 apostate, recreant, renegade, tergiversating, tergiversant; **treasonous, treasonable, traitorous,** forsworn; collaborating; faithless, **disloyal** 645.20

12 repudiative, repudiatory; abjuratory, renunciative, renunciatory; schismatic; **separatist,** secessionist, breakaway <nf>; **opportunistic,** mugwumpian, mugwumpish, fence-straddling, fence-sitting

364 CAPRICE

NOUNS **1 caprice, whim,** *capriccio* <Ital>, *boutade* <Fr>, humor, **whimsy,** freak, whim-wham; **fancy,** fantasy, **conceit, notion,** flimflam, toy, freakish inspiration, crazy idea, fantastic notion, fool notion <nf>, harebrained idea, brainstorm, **vagary,** megrim; **fad, craze, passing fancy,** next big thing; **quirk, crotchet,** crank, kink; maggot,

maggot in the brain, bee in one's bonnet <nf>, flea in one's nose <nf>

2 capriciousness, caprice, **whimsicalness,** whimsy, whimsicality; humorsomeness, **fancifulness,** fantasticality, **freakishness;** crankiness, crotchetiness, quirkiness; **moodiness,** temperamentalness, prima-donnaism; petulance 110.6; **arbitrariness,** motivelessness

3 fickleness, flightiness, skittishness, inconstancy, **lightness, levity,** *légèreté* <Fr>; flakiness <nf>; volatility, mercurialness, mercuriality, erraticism; **mood swing;** faddishness, faddism; **changeableness** 854; unpredictability 971.1; unreliability, undependability 645.4; coquettishness; frivolousness 922.7; purposelessness, motivelessness

VERBS **4 blow hot and cold,** keep off and on, have as many phases as the moon, chop and change, **fluctuate** 854.5, vacillate 362.8, flip-flop <nf>; act on impulse

ADJS **5 capricious, whimsical,** freakish, humorsome, vagarious; **fanciful, notional,** fantasied <old>, fantastic *or* fantastical, maggoty, **crotchety,** kinky, harebrained, cranky, flaky <nf>, quirky; wanton, wayward, vagrant; **arbitrary, unreasonable,** motiveless; **moody, temperamental,** prima-donnaish; petulant 110.22; unrestrained

6 fickle, flighty, skittish, **light;** coquettish, flirtatious, toying; versatile, **inconstant,** erratic, **changeable** 854.7; vacillating 362.10; volatile, mercurial, quicksilver; faddish; **scatterbrained** 985.16, unpredictable; **impulsive;** idiosyncratic; unreliable, undependable 645.19; polytropic

ADVS **7 capriciously, whimsically,** fancifully, at one's own sweet will <nf>; **flightily, lightly;** arbitrarily, unreasonably, without rhyme or reason

365 IMPULSE

NOUNS **1 impulse;** natural impulse, blind impulse, irresistible impulse, **instinct,** urge, drive; vagrant *or* fleeting impulse; involuntary impulse, reflex, knee jerk, automatic response; gut response *or* reaction <nf>; **notion, fancy; sudden thought,** flash, inspiration, brainstorm, brain wave, quick hunch; impulse buy

2 impulsiveness, impetuousness, impulsivity, impetuousity; **hastiness,** overhastiness, haste, quickness, suddenness; **precipitateness,** precipitance, precipitancy, precipitation; hair-trigger; **recklessness, rashness** 493; impatience 135

3 thoughtlessness, unthoughtfulness, **heedlessness** 984.1, **carelessness,** inconsideration, inconsiderateness; **negligence** 102.2, caprice 364

4 unpremeditation, indeliberation, **undeliberateness,** uncalculatedness, undesignedness, **spontaneity, spontaneousness,** unstudiedness; involuntariness 963.5; snap judgment *or* decision; snap shot, offhand shot

5 improvisation, extemporization, improvision, improvising, extempore <old>, **impromptu, ad-lib,** ad-libbing *and* playing by ear <nf>, **ad hoc measure** *or* solution, adhocracy <nf>, ad hockery *or* hocery *or* hocism <nf>; extemporaneousness, extemporariness; temporary measure *or* arrangement, pro tempore measure *or* arrangement, **stopgap, makeshift,** jury-rig; cannibalization; bricolage; jam session; thinking on one's feet

6 improviser, improvisator, *improvvisatore and improvvisatrice* <Ital>, **extemporizer,** ad-libber <nf>; cannibalizer; bricoleur; creature of impulse

VERBS **7 act on the spur of the moment,** obey one's impulse, let oneself go; shoot from the hip <nf>, be too quick on the trigger *or* the uptake *or* the draw; **blurt out,** come out with, let slip out, say what comes uppermost, say the first thing that comes into one's head *or* to one's mind; be unable to help oneself; impulse-buy; reinvent oneself

8 improvise, extemporize, improvisate, improv *and* tapdance *and* talk off the top of one's head <nf>, speak off the cuff, think on one's feet, invent, make it up as one goes along, play it by ear <nf>, throw away *or* depart from the prepared text, throw away the speech, scrap the plan, **ad-lib** <nf>, **do offhand,** wing it <nf>, vamp, fake <nf>, play by ear <nf>; **dash off, strike off,** knock off, throw off, toss off *or* out; make up, whip up, **cook up,** run up, rustle up *or* whomp up <nf>, slap up *or* together *and* throw together <nf>, lash up <Brit>, cobble up; jury-rig; rise to the occasion; cannibalize

ADJS **9 impulsive, impetuous, hasty,** overhasty, quick, sudden, snap; quick on the draw *or* trigger *or* uptake, hair-trigger; **precipitate,** headlong; **reckless, rash** 493.7; impatient 135.6

10 unthinking, unreasoning, unreflecting, uncalculating, unthoughtful, **thoughtless, inadvertent,** reasonless, **heedless, careless,** inconsiderate; unguarded; arbitrary, capricious 364.5

11 unpremeditated, unmeditated, **uncalculated,** undeliberated, **spontaneous, undesigned, unstudied;** unintentional, unintended, inadvertent, unwilled, **indeliberate,** undeliberate, collateral; **involuntary,** reflex, reflexive, knee-jerk <nf>, acting out, automatic, goose-step, lockstep; gut <nf>, unconscious; **unconsidered,** unadvised, snap, casual, offhand, throwaway <nf>; **ill-considered,** ill-advised, ill-devised; act-first-and-think-later

12 extemporaneous, extemporary, extempore, **impromptu,** unrehearsed, **improvised,** improvisatory, improvisatorial, improviso, *improvisé* <Fr>; **ad-lib,** *ad libitum* <L>; **ad-hoc,** stopgap, makeshift, jury-rigged; **offhand,** off the top of one's head *and* off-the-cuff <nf>, **spur-of-the-moment, quick and dirty** <nf>; catch-as-catch-can; potluck

ADVS **13 impulsively, impetuously, hastily,** suddenly, quickly, **precipitately,** headlong; **recklessly, rashly** 493.10

14 on impulse, on a sudden impulse, **on the spur of the moment; without premeditation,** unpremeditatedly, uncalculatedly, undesignedly; unthinkingly, unreflectingly, unreasoningly, unthoughtfully, thoughtlessly, heedlessly, carelessly, inconsiderately, unadvisedly; unintentionally, inadvertently, without willing, indeliberately, involuntarily

15 extemporaneously, extemporarily, extempore, *à l'improviste* <Fr>, **impromptu, ad lib, offhand,** out of hand; at *or* on sight; by ear, off the hip *and* off the top of one's head *and* off the cuff <nf>; at short notice

366 LEAP

NOUNS **1 leap, jump, hop, spring, skip, bound,** bounce; **pounce;** upleap, upspring, jump-off; **hurdle; vault,** pole vault; demivolt, curvet, capriole; jeté, grand jeté, tour jeté, saut de basque; jig, galliard, lavolta, Highland fling, morris; standing *or* running *or* flying jump; long jump, broad jump, standing *or* running broad jump; high jump, standing *or* running high jump; leapfrog; jump shot; handspring; buck, buckjump; ski jump, jump turn, geländesprung, gelände jump; steeplechase; hippety-hop <nf>; jump-hop; hop, skip, and jump

2 caper, dido <nf>, **gambol, frisk,** curvet, cavort, capriole; **prance,** caracole; *gambade* <Fr>, gambado; falcade

3 leaping, jumping, bouncing, bounding, hopping, capering, cavorting, prancing, skipping, **springing,** saltation; **vaulting,** pole vaulting; **hurdling,** the hurdles, hurdle race, timber topping <nf>, steeplechase; leapfrogging; bungee-jumping

4 jumper, leaper, hopper; broad jumper, high jumper; **vaulter,** pole vaulter; **hurdler,** hurdle racer, timber topper <nf>; jumping jack; bucking bronco, buckjumper, sunfisher <nf>; jumping bean; kangaroo, gazelle, stag, jackrabbit, goat, frog, grasshopper, flea; salmon

VERBS **5 leap, jump, vault, spring, skip, hop, bound,** bounce; upleap, upspring, updive; leap over, jump over, etc; overleap, overjump, overskip, leapfrog; **hurdle,** clear, negotiate; curvet, capriole; buck, buckjump; ski jump; steeplechase; start, start up, start aside; **pounce,** pounce on *or* upon; hippety-hop <nf>

6 caper, cut capers, cut a dido <nf>, curvet, cavort, capriole, **gambol,** gambado, **frisk,** flounce, **trip, skip,** bob, bounce, jump about; **romp,** ramp <nf>; **prance;** caracole

ADJS **7 leaping, jumping,** springing, hopping, skipping, prancing, bouncing, bounding; saltant, saltatory, saltatorial

367 PLUNGE

NOUNS **1 plunge, dive, pitch, drop, fall;** free-fall; header <nf>; **swoop, pounce,** stoop; swan dive, gainer, jackknife, cannonball; belly flop *and* belly buster *and* belly whopper <nf>; nose dive, power dive; parachute jump, sky dive; bungee jump; crash dive, stationary dive, running dive

2 submergence, submersion, immersion, immergence, engulfment, **inundation,** burial; **dipping, ducking,** dousing, sousing, dunking <nf>, sinking; **dip, duck, souse;** baptism

3 diving, plunging; skydiving; bungee jumping; fancy diving, high diving; scuba diving, snorkeling, skin diving, pearl diving, deep-sea diving

4 diver, plunger; high diver; bungee jumper; parachute jumper, jumper, sky diver, sport jumper, paratrooper, smoke jumper, paramedic; skin diver, snorkel diver, scuba diver, free diver, pearl diver, deep-sea diver, frogman

5 <diving equipment> diving bell, diving chamber, bathysphere, bathyscaphe, benthoscope, aquascope; submarine 180.9; diving boat; scuba *or* self-contained underwater breathing apparatus, Aqua-Lung <trademark>; Scuba; diving goggles, diving mask, swim fins; wet suit; air cylinder; diving suit; diving helmet, diving hood; snorkel, periscope

VERBS **6 plunge, dive, pitch, plummet, drop, fall;** skydive; bungee jump; free-fall; plump, plunk, plop; swoop, swoop down, stoop, **pounce,** pounce on *or* upon; nose-dive, make *or* take a nose dive; parachute, sky-dive; skin-dive; sound; take a header <nf>

7 submerge, submerse, immerse, immerge, merge, **sink,** bury, engulf, **inundate,** deluge, drown, overwhelm, whelm; **dip, duck, dunk** <nf>, douse, souse, plunge in water; baptize

8 sink, scuttle, send to the bottom, send to Davy Jones's locker; **founder, go down,** go to the bottom, sink like lead, go down like a stone; get out of one's depth

ADJS **9 submersible,** submergible, immersible, sinkable; immersive

368 AVOIDANCE

NOUNS **1 avoidance, shunning; forbearance,** refraining; hands-off policy, **nonintervention,** noninvolvement, neutrality; **evasion,** elusion; side-stepping, getting around <nf>, **circumvention;** prevention, forestalling, forestallment; **escape** 369; evasive action, the runaround <nf>; zigzag, jink *and* juke <nf>, slip, dodge, duck, side step, shy; shunting off, sidetracking; bypassing; evasiveness, elusiveness; **equivocation** 344.4, waffle <nf>, fudging, fudge and mudge <Brit nf>; avoiding reaction, defense mechanism *or* reaction; safe distance, wide berth; cold shoulder, snub; abstinence; shyness

2 shirking, slacking, goldbricking <nf>, cop-out <nf>, soldiering, goofing *and* goofing off *and* fucking off <nf>; clock-watching; **malingering,** skulking <Brit>; passivity; **dodging,** ducking; welshing <nf>; truancy; tax evasion, tax dodging

3 shirker, shirk, **slacker,** eye-servant *or* eye-server <old>, goof-off <nf>, soldier *or* old soldier, **goldbricker,** goldbrick <nf>; clock watcher; **welsher** <nf>; **malingerer,** skulker *or* skulk <Brit>; truant; tax dodger *or* evader

4 flight, fugitation, exit, quick exit, making oneself scarce *and* getting the hell out <nf>, bolt, scarpering <Brit nf>, disappearing act <nf>, hasty retreat; **running away, decampment,** bugging out <nf>; skedaddle *and* skedaddling *and* scramming *and* absquatulation <old> <nf>; **elopement;** disappearance 34; French leave, absence without leave *or* AWOL; desertion 370.2; hegira; truancy, hooky *or* hookey

5 fugitive, fleer, person on the run, **runaway,** runagate, **bolter,** skedaddler <nf>; **absconder, eloper; refugee, evacuee,** boat person, émigré <Fr>; **displaced person** *or* DP, stateless person; **escapee** 369.5; illegal immigrant, wetback <nf>, day-crosser; draft dodger; truant, absentee; deserter

VERBS **6 avoid, shun, fight shy of, shy away from,** keep from, **keep away from, circumvent,** keep clear of, avoid like the plague, **steer clear of** <nf>, give a miss to <nf>, skate around <Brit nf>, keep *or* get out of the way of, **give a wide berth,** keep remote from, stay detached from; make way for, give place to; **keep one's distance,** keep at a respectful distance, keep *or* stand *or* hold aloof;

give the cold shoulder to <nf>, have nothing to do with, have no association with, not give the time of day, **have no truck with** <nf>; not meddle with, let alone, let well enough alone, keep hands off, not touch, not touch with a ten-foot pole, back off; turn away from, turn one's back upon, slam the door in one's face

7 **evade, elude,** beg, **get out of,** shuffle out of, skirt, **get around** <nf>, circumvent; take evasive action; give one the run-around; ditch *and* shake *and* shake off <nf>, get away from, give the runaround *or* the slip <nf>; throw off the scent; play at hide and seek; lead one a chase *or* merry chase, lead one a dance *or* pretty dance; escape 369.6

8 **dodge, duck; take evasive action,** juke *and* jink <nf>, zig-zag; throw off the track *or* trail; shy, shy off *or* away; swerve, sheer off; pull away *or* clear; pull back, shrink, recoil 903.6,7; **sidestep,** step aside; parry, fence, ward off; have an out *or* escape hatch; shift, shift *or* put off; **hedge,** pussyfoot <nf>, be *or* sit on the fence, beat around *or* about the bush, hem and haw, beg the question, tapdance <nf>, dance around, equivocate 344.7, fudge and mudge <Brit nf>

9 **shirk, slack, lie *or* rest upon one's oars,** not pull fair, not pull one's weight; **lie down on the job** <nf>; soldier, duck duty, **goof off** *and* dog it <nf>, **goldbrick** <nf>; **malinger,** skulk <Brit>; **get out of,** sneak *or* slip out of, slide out of, pass the buck, cop out <nf>, dodge, duck; welsh <nf>

10 **flee, fly, take flight,** take to flight, take wing, fugitate, **run, cut and run** <nf>, make a precipitate departure, **run off** *or* **away,** run away from, bug out <nf>, **decamp,** pull up stakes, **take to one's heels,** make off, **depart** 188.6, do the disappearing act, make a quick exit, **beat a retreat** *or* **a hasty retreat, turn tail,** show the heels, show a clean *or* light pair of heels; **run for it,** "show it a fair pair of heels and run for it"—Shakespeare, **bolt, run for one's life;** make a run for it; advance to the rear, make a strategic withdrawal; **take French leave,** go AWOL, slip the cable; **desert; abscond,** levant <Brit>, **elope,** run away with; skip *or* jump bail; play hooky *or* hookey

11 <nf terms> **beat it, blow, scram,** bug off, lam, book, air out, shemozzle *and* bugger off <Brit>, **take it on the lam,** take a powder *or* runout powder, make tracks, cut ass, cut and run, peel out, **split,** skin out, **skip,** skip out, duck out, duck and run, dog it, vamoose, absquatulate *and* skedaddle <old>, **clear out,** make oneself scarce, get the hell out, make a break for it, warp out, scram

12 **slip away, steal away, sneak off,** shuffle off, slink off, slide off, slither off, skulk away, mooch off *and* duck out <nf>, slip out of

13 **not face up to,** hide one's head in the sand, not come to grips with, put off, procrastinate, temporize, waffle <nf>

ADJS **14** **avoidable, escapable,** eludible; evadable; preventable

15 **evasive, elusive,** elusory; **shifty,** slippery, slippery as an eel; cagey <nf>; shirking, malingering

16 **fugitive, runaway,** in flight, on the lam <nf>, hot <nf>; disappearing 34.3

369 ESCAPE

NOUNS **1** **escape; getaway** *and* break *and* breakout <nf>; **deliverance; delivery,** riddance, **release,** setting-free, freeing, freedom, **liberation, extrication, rescue;** emergence, issuance, issue, outlet, vent; **leakage,** leak; jailbreak, prisonbreak, break, breakout; evasion 368.1; **flight** 368.4; retreat; French leave; hooky; elopment; escapology; escapism

2 **narrow escape,** hairbreadth escape, **close call** *or* **shave** <nf>, **near miss,** near go *or* thing <Brit nf>, near *or* narrow squeak <Brit nf>, close *or* tight squeeze <nf>, squeaker <nf>

3 bolt-hole, escape hatch, fire escape, life net, lifeboat, life raft, life buoy, lifeline, sally port, slide, inflatable slide, ejection *or* ejector seat, emergency exit, escapeway, back door, trapdoor, escape hatch, secret passage

4 **loophole, way out,** way of escape, hole to creep out of, escape hatch, escape clause, saving clause, technicality; pretext 376; **alternative,** choice 371

5 **escapee,** escaper, evader; escape artist; escapologist; runaway, **fugitive** 368.5; escapist, Houdini

VERBS **6** **escape,** make *or* effect one's escape, make good one's escape; **get away, make a getaway** <nf>; **free oneself,** deliver oneself, gain one's liberty, **get free, get clear of,** bail out, **get out, get out of,** get well out of; **break loose,** cut loose, break away, break one's bonds *or* chains, slip the collar, shake off the yoke; **jump** *and* **skip** <nf>; **break jail** *or* **prison,** escape prison, fly the coop <nf>; leap over the wall; evade 368.7; flee 368.10; vamoose, take it on the lam

7 **get off, go free,** win freedom, go at liberty, **go scot free,** escape with a whole skin, escape without penalty, walk *and* beat the rap <nf>; **get away with** <nf>, get by, get by with, get off easy *or* lightly, get away with murder <nf>, **get off cheap;** cop a plea *and* cop out <nf>, get off on a technicality

8 scrape *or* squeak through, squeak by, escape with *or* by the skin of one's teeth, have a close call *or* close shave <nf>

9 **slip away, give one the slip,** slip through one's hands *or* fingers; slip *or* sneak through; **slip out of,** slide out of, crawl *or* creep out of, sneak out of, wiggle *or* squirm *or* shuffle *or* wriggle *or* worm out of, find a loophole, elude

10 **find vent,** issue forth, come forth, exit, **emerge, issue,** debouch, erupt, break out, break through, come out, run out, **leak out,** ooze out

ADJS 11 **escaped, loose,** on the loose, disengaged, out of, well out of; fled, flown; fugitive, runaway; free as a bird, scot-free, at large, **free**

370 ABANDONMENT

NOUNS 1 **abandonment, forsaking, leaving,** jilting; jettison, jettisoning, throwing overboard *or* away *or* aside, casting away *or* aside; **withdrawal,** evacuation, pulling out, absentation; cessation 857; disuse, desuetude

2 **desertion, defection,** ratting <nf>; dereliction, decampment; **secession,** bolt, breakaway, walkout; betrayal 645.8; schism, apostasy 363.2; deserter 363.5

3 <giving up> **relinquishment, surrender, resignation, renouncement,** renunciation, abdication, waiver, abjurement, abjuration, ceding, cession, handing over, standing *or* stepping down, **yielding, forswearing; withdrawing, dropping out** <nf>

4 **derelict,** castoff; jetsam, flotsam, lagan, **flotsam and jetsam;** waifs and strays; **rubbish, junk,** trash, refuse, waste, waste product, solid waste; liquid waste, wastewater; **dump,** dumpsite, garbage dump, landfill, sanitary landfill, junkheap, junkpile, scrap heap, midden; abandonee, waif, throwaway, orphan, dogie <nf>; **castaway;** foundling; wastrel, reject, deselect, **discard** 390.3

VERBS 5 **abandon, desert, forsake; quit, leave,** leave behind, take leave of, depart from, absent oneself from, turn one's back upon, turn one's tail upon, say goodbye to, bid a long farewell to, walk away, **walk** *or* **run out on** <nf>, **leave flat** *and* leave high and dry *or* holding the bag *or* in the lurch <nf>, leave one to one's fate, throw to the wolves <nf>; **withdraw, back out, drop out** <nf>, pull out, stand down <nf>; **go back on, go back on one's word;** cry off <Brit>, beg off, renege; **vacate,** evacuate; quit cold *and* leave flat <nf>, toss aside; jilt, throw over <nf>; maroon; **jettison; junk,** deep-six <nf>, **discard** 390.7; let fall into disuse *or* desuetude

6 **defect, secede, bolt,** break away; pull out <nf>, withdraw one's support, decamp; sell out *and* sell down the river <nf>, **betray** 645.14; turn one's back on; apostatize

7 **give up, relinquish, surrender, yield,** yield up, waive, **forgo, resign, renounce,** throw up,

abdicate, **abjure, forswear, give up on, have done with,** give up as a bad job, cede, hand over, lay down, wash one's hands of, **write off,** drop, drop all idea of, drop like a hot potato; **cease** 857.6, **desist from,** leave off, give over; hold *or* stay one's hand, cry quits, acknowledge defeat, **throw in the towel** *or* **sponge** 433.8

ADJS 8 **abandoned, forsaken, deserted,** left; untouristed; disused; **derelict,** castaway, jettisoned; marooned; junk, junked, discarded 390.11

371 CHOICE

NOUNS 1 **choice, selection, election,** preference, decision, **pick, choosing,** free choice; alternativity; co-option, co-optation; **will,** volition, free will 430.6,7; preoption, first choice; the best 999.8

2 **option, discretion, pleasure,** will and pleasure; optionality; possible choice, alternative, alternate choice, possible action

3 **dilemma,** Scylla and Charybdis, quandary, fix, bind, the devil and the deep blue sea; *embarras de choix* <Fr>; choice of Hercules; Hobson's choice, **no choice,** only choice, zero option; limited choice, positive discrimination <Brit>, affirmative action; lesser of two evils

4 **adoption, embracement,** acceptance, espousal; affiliation

5 **preference, predilection,** proclivity, bent, affinity, prepossession, predisposition, partiality, inclination, leaning, tilt, penchant, bias, tendency, taste, favoritism; favor, fancy, preferment; prejudice; personal choice, particular choice <old>, druthers <nf>; chosen kind *or* sort, style, one's cup of tea <nf>, type, bag *and* thing <nf>; way of life, lifestyle

6 **vote,** voting, **suffrage,** franchise, enfranchisement, voting right, right to vote; **voice, say;** representation; **poll,** polling, canvass, canvassing, division <Brit>, counting heads *or* noses *or* hands, exit poll; **ballot,** balloting, secret ballot, absentee ballot; ballot-box, voting machine; **plebiscite,** plebiscitum, **referendum;** yeas and nays, yea, aye, yes, nay, no; voice vote, *viva voce* vote; rising vote; hand vote, show of hands; absentee vote, proxy; casting vote, deciding vote; write-in vote, write-in; faggot vote <Brit old>; graveyard vote; single vote, plural vote; transferable vote, nontransferable vote; direct vote; Hare system, list system, cumulative voting, preferential voting, proportional representation; straw vote *or* poll; informal vote, record vote, snap vote

7 **selector,** chooser, optant, elector, balloter, **voter;** delegate, superdelegate; **electorate;** electoral college

8 **nomination, designation,** naming, proposal

9 **election, appointment;** political election; caucus; primary election, general election

10 **selectivity,** selectiveness, picking and choosing; **choosiness** 495.1; eclecticism; discretion, **discrimination** 944

11 **eligibility, qualification, fitness,** fittedness, **suitability,** acceptability, worthiness, desirability; competency

12 **elect,** elite, the chosen, the cream, crème de la crème; president-elect

VERBS 13 **choose, elect,** pick, go with <nf>, opt, opt for, co-opt, make or take one's choice, make choice of, have one's druthers <nf>, use or take up or exercise one's option, exercise one's discretion; **shop around** <nf>, pick and choose

14 **select,** make a selection; **pick,** handpick, **pick out, single out,** choose, like, choose out, smile on, give the nod <nf>, jump at, seize on; extract, excerpt; **decide between, choose up sides** <nf>, cull, glean, winnow, sift; side with; cherry-pick, separate the wheat from the chaff or tares, separate the sheep from the goats

15 **adopt;** approve, ratify, pass, carry, endorse, sign off on <nf>; **take up, go in for** <nf>; accept, take on up on <nf>, **embrace,** advance, espouse; affiliate

16 **decide upon, determine upon,** settle upon, fix upon, resolve upon; make or take a decision, **make up one's mind**

17 **prefer,** have preference, **favor, like better** or **best,** wish, prefer to, set before or above, regard or honor before; rather <nf>, **had** or **have rather,** would rather, choose rather, had sooner, had or would as soon; think proper, see or think fit, think best, please; tilt or incline or lean or tend toward, have a bias or partiality or penchant

18 **vote, cast one's vote,** ballot, cast a ballot; go to the polls; have a say or a voice; hold up one's hand, exercise one's suffrage or franchise, stand up and be counted; plump or plump for <Brit>; divide <Brit>; **poll,** canvass

19 **nominate, name, designate;** put up, propose, submit, name for office; run, run for office

20 **elect, vote in,** place in office; **appoint**

21 **put to choice,** offer, present, set before; put to vote, have a show of hands

ADJS 22 **elective;** volitional, voluntary, volitive; **optional,** discretional; **alternative,** disjunctive

23 **selective,** selecting, choosing; eclectic or eclectical; elective, electoral; appointing, appointive, constituent; adoptive; exclusive, discriminating 944.7; **choosy** <nf>, particular 495.9

24 **eligible, qualified, fit,** fitted, **suitable,** acceptable, admissible, worthy, desirable; with voice, with vote, with voice and vote, enfranchised

25 **preferable,** of choice or preference, **better,** preferred, **to be preferred,** more desirable, favored; handpicked; preferential, preferring, favoring; not to be sniffed or sneezed at <nf>

26 **chosen, selected, picked;** select, elect; handpicked, singled-out; **adopted,** accepted, embraced, espoused, approved, ratified, passed, carried; **elected,** unanimously elected, elected by acclamation; appointed; **nominated,** designated, named

ADVS 27 **at choice, at will,** at one's will and pleasure, at one's pleasure, electively, at one's discretion, at the option of, if one wishes; on approval; **optionally;** alternatively

28 **preferably, by choice** or **preference,** in preference; by vote, by election or suffrage; **rather than,** sooner than, first, sooner, rather, before

CONJS 29 or, either...or; and/or

PHRS 30 one man's meat is another man's poison, there's no accounting for taste

372 REJECTION

NOUNS 1 **rejection, repudiation;** abjurement, abjuration, **renouncement** 370.3, renunciation; disownment, disavowal, disclamation, **recantation** 363.3; **exclusion,** exception 773.1; **disapproval, nonacceptance,** zero tolerance, nonapproval, declining, declination, veto, **refusal** 442; contradiction, **denial** 335.2; passing by or up <nf>, ignoring, nonconsideration, discounting, dismissal, disregard 984.1; throwing out or away, putting out or away, chucking and chucking out <nf>, heave-ho; discard 390.3; turning out or away, repulse, a flea in one's ear, rebuff 908.2; **spurning,** kiss-off and brush-off <nf>, cold shoulder, despising, despisal, contempt 157; scorn, disdain; bum's rush <nf>; excommunication

VERBS 2 **reject, repudiate,** abjure, forswear, **renounce** 370.7, **disown, disclaim, recant;** vote out; except, **exclude** 773.4, deselect, include out <nf>, close out, close the door on, leave out in the cold, cut out, blackball, blacklist; **disapprove, decline, refuse** 442.3; contradict, **deny** 335.4; pass by or up <nf>, waive, ignore, not hear of, wave aside, brush away or aside or off, refuse to consider, discount, **dismiss,** dismiss out of hand; **disregard** 984.2; throw out or away, chuck and chuck out <nf>, **discard** 390.7; turn out or away, shove away, push aside, repulse, repel, slap or smack down <nf>, rebuff 908.2, send away with a flea in one's ear, show the door, send about one's business, send packing, excommunicate;

turn one's back on; **spurn, disdain,** scorn, contemn, make a face at, turn up one's nose at, look down one's nose at, raise one's eyebrows at, **despise** 157.3

ADJS **3 rejected, repudiated; renounced,** forsworn, **disowned; denied,** refused; excluded, excepted; **disapproved, declined;** ignored, blanked, discounted, not considered, **dismissed,** dismissed out of hand; **discarded;** repulsed, rebuffed; **spurned,** snubbed, **disdained, scorned,** contemned, **despised;** out of the question, not to be thought of, declined with thanks; discarded; excommunicated

4 rejective; renunciative, abjuratory; declinatory; dismissive; contemptuous, despising, **scornful,** disdainful

373 CUSTOM, HABIT

NOUNS **1 custom, convention,** use, **usage,** standard usage, standard behavior, **wont,** wonting, **way,** established way, time-honored practice, **tradition,** standing custom, **folkway,** manner, **practice,** praxis, prescription, **observance,** ritual, rite, consuetude, **mores;** institution; unwritten law, consuetude; proper thing, what is done, **social convention** 579; bon ton, **fashion** 578; manners, protocol, etiquette 580.3; way of life, lifestyle; conformity 867; **generalization** 864.1, labeling, stereotyping

2 culture, society, civilization; trait, culture trait; key trait; complex, culture complex, trait-complex; culture area; culture center; shame culture, memory culture; **folkways, mores,** system of values, **ethos, culture pattern;** cultural change; cultural lag; culture conflict; acculturation, enculturation; culture contact <Brit>, cultural drift; ancient wisdom

3 habit, habitude, **custom, second nature,** matter of course; use, **usage,** trick, wont, **way,** practice, praxis; bad habit; stereotype; "the petrifaction of feelings"—L E Landon; pattern, **habit pattern;** stereotyped behavior; force of habit; creature of habit; knee-jerk reaction <nf>, automatism 963.5; peculiarity, characteristic 865.4

4 rule, norm, procedure, **common practice,** the way things are done, form, prescribed or set form; common or ordinary run of things, matter of course, par for the course <nf>; standard operating procedure or SOP, standard procedure, drill, standing orders

5 routine, run, ritual, round, beat, track, beaten path or track; pattern, custom; jog trot, **rut, groove,** well-worn groove; **treadmill,** squirrel cage, hamster wheel, hedonic treadmill; the

working day, nine-to-five, the grind or the daily grind <nf>; **red tape,** redtapeism, **bureaucracy,** bureaucratism, chinoiseries <Fr>

6 customariness, accustomedness, wontedness, **habitualness; inveteracy,** inveterateness, confirmedness, settledness, fixedness; commonness, prevalence 864.2

7 habituation, accustoming; conditioning, seasoning, training; **familiarization,** naturalization <old>, breaking-in <nf>, orientation, adaptation; **domestication, taming,** breaking, housebreaking; acclimation, acclimatization; **inurement,** hardening, case hardening, seasoning, assuetude, assuefaction; adaption, adjustment, accommodation 867.1

8 addiction 87.1; **addict** 87.21

VERBS **9 accustom, habituate,** wont; **condition,** season, **train;** familiarize, naturalize <old>, break in <nf>, orient, orientate; **domesticate,** domesticize, **tame,** break, gentle, housebreak; put through the mill; acclimatize, acclimate; inure, harden, case harden; adapt, adjust, accommodate 788.7; confirm, fix, establish 855.9; acculturate, enculturate

10 become a habit, take root, become fixed, **grow on one,** take hold of one, take one over

11 be used to, be wont, wont, **make a practice of;** get used to, get into the way of, get the knack of, get the hang of <nf>, **take to,** accustom oneself to, make a practice of; catch oneself doing; contract or fall into a habit, addict oneself to

12 get in a rut, be in a rut, move or travel in a groove or rut, run on in a groove, follow the beaten path or track

ADJS **13 customary, wonted,** consuetudinary; traditional, time-honored, immemorial; familiar, everyday, ordinary, **usual; established,** received, accepted, handed down, time-honored; set, prescribed, prescriptive; **normative, normal; standard,** regular, stock, regulation; prevalent, prevailing, widespread, obtaining, generally accepted, popular, **current** 864.12; **conventional** 579.5, orthodox; inside the box; conformist, conformable 867.5

14 habitual, regular, frequent, constant, persistent; repetitive, recurring, recurrent; stereotyped; knee-jerk <nf>, goose-step, lockstep, automatic 963.14; **routine,** usual, nine-to-five, workaday, well-trodden, well-worn, beaten; trite, hackneyed 117.9; predictable

15 accustomed, wont, wonted, used to; conditioned, trained, seasoned; experienced, **familiarized,** naturalized <old>, broken-in, run-in <nf>, oriented, orientated; acclimated, acclimatized; inured, hardened, case-hardened; adapted, adjusted, accommodated; housebroken, potty-trained

16 **used to, familiar with,** conversant with, **at home in** *or* **with,** no stranger to, an old hand at, *au fait* <Fr>

17 **habituated,** *habitué* <Fr>; **in the habit of,** used to; never free from; **in a rut**

18 **confirmed, inveterate, chronic, established,** long-established, **fixed, settled, rooted,** thorough; incorrigible, irreversible; **deep-rooted,** deep-set, deep-settled, **deep-seated,** deep-fixed, deep-dyed; **infixed, ingrained,** fast, dyed-in-the-wool, inveterate; implanted, inculcated, instilled; set, **set in one's ways,** settled in habit; addicted, given

ADVS 19 **customarily,** conventionally, accustomedly, wontedly; normatively, normally, **usually; as is the custom;** as is usual, *comme d'habitude* <Fr>; as things go, as the world goes

20 **habitually, regularly,** routinely, frequently, persistently, repetitively, recurringly; **inveterately, chronically;** from habit, **by** *or* **from force of habit,** as is one's wont

374 UNACCUSTOMEDNESS

NOUNS 1 **unaccustomedness, newness,** unwontedness, disaccustomedness, unusedness, unhabituatedness; shakiness <nf>; **unfamiliarity,** unacquaintance, unconversance, unpracticedness, newness to; inexperience 414.2; ignorance 930

VERBS 2 **disaccustom, cure, break off,** stop, **wean**

3 **break the habit, cure oneself of,** disaccustom oneself, kick a habit <nf>, wean oneself from, break the pattern, break one's chains *or* fetters; **give up,** leave off, **abandon,** drop, stop, discontinue, kick *and* shake <nf>, throw off, rid oneself of; get on the wagon, swear off 668.8

ADJS 4 **unaccustomed, new,** disaccustomed, **unused, unwonted,** unwont, wontless; uninured, unseasoned, untrained, unhardened; shaky <nf>, tyronic; unhabituated, **not in the habit of;** out of the habit of, rusty; unweaned; **unused to, unfamiliar with,** not used to, unacquainted with, unconversant with, unpracticed, new to, a stranger to; cub, greenhorn; inexperienced 414.17; ignorant 930.11

375 MOTIVATION, INDUCEMENT

NOUNS 1 **motive, reason, cause,** source, spring, mainspring; matter, score, consideration; **ground, basis** 886.1; sake; **aim, goal** 380.2, end, end in view, telos, final cause; **ideal,** principle, **ambition,** aspiration, inspiration, guiding light *or* star, lodestar; impetus; calling, vocation; intention 380;

ulterior motive, hidden agenda; rationale, rational motive, justification, driving force

2 **motivation,** moving, **actuation, prompting, stimulation,** animation, triggering, setting-off, setting in motion, getting under way; direction, inner-direction, other-direction; **influence** 894; hot button; carrot

3 **inducement,** enlistment, engagement, solicitation, **persuasion,** suasion; exhortation, hortation, preaching, preachment; **selling,** sales talk, salesmanship, hard sell, high pressure, hawking, huckstering, flogging <Brit>; jawboning *and* arm-twisting <nf>; **lobbying; coaxing,** wheedling, working on <nf>, cajolery, cajolement, conning, snow job *and* smoke and mirrors <nf>, nobbling <Brit nf>, blandishment, sweet talk *and* soft soap <nf>, soft sell <nf>; **allurement** 377

4 **incitement,** incitation, **instigation, stimulation, arousal, excitement, agitation, inflammation,** excitation, fomentation, eggement, firing, stirring, stirring-up, impassioning, whipping-up, rabble-rousing; waving the bloody shirt, rallying cry; **provocation,** irritation, exasperation; pep talk, pep rally

5 **urging, pressure,** pressing, pushing, entreaty, plea, advocacy; **encouragement,** abetment; **insistence,** instance; **goading, prodding,** exhortation, goosing <nf>, spurring, pricking, needling

6 **urge,** urgency; impulse, impulsion, compulsion; press, **pressure, drive,** push; sudden *or* rash impulse; constraint, exigency, stress, pinch

7 **incentive, inducement, encouragement,** persuasive, **invitation, provocation, incitement; stimulus, stimulation,** stimulative, fillip, whet; carrot; reward, payment 624; **profit** 472.3; bait, **lure** 377.3; palm oil <nf>, greased palm <nf>, bribe 378.2; sweetening *and* sweetener <nf>, flattery, interest, percentage, what's in it for one <nf>; offer one cannot refuse; payola <nf>, pork barrel <nf>; perk <nf>

8 **goad, spur, prod,** prick <old>, sting, **gadfly;** oxgoad; rowel; whip, lash, gad <nf>, crack of the whip

9 **inspiration, infusion,** infection; fire, firing, spark, sparking; **animation, exhilaration,** enlivenment; afflatus, divine afflatus; genius, animus, moving *or* animating spirit; muse; the Muses; guiding light, angel

10 **prompter, mover, prime mover,** motivator, impeller, energizer, galvanizer, inducer, **actuator, animator,** moving spirit, mover and shaker <nf>; **encourager,** abettor, **inspirer,** firer, spark, sparker, spark plug <nf>; persuader, salesperson, brainwasher, spin doctor <nf>; **stimulator, gadfly;**

tempter 377.4; coaxer, coax <nf>, wheedler, cajoler, pleader

11 **instigator, inciter,** exciter, urger, motivator; **provoker,** *provocateur* <Fr>, *agent provocateur* <Fr>, catalyst; **agitator, fomenter,** inflamer; agitprop; **rabble-rouser,** rouser, **demagogue; firebrand, incendiary; seditionist,** seditionary; lobbyist, activist; **troublemaker,** makebate <old>, mischief-maker, ringleader; tactician, strategist; pressure group, special-interest group

VERBS 12 **motivate, move,** set in motion, **actuate,** move to action, **impel,** propel; **stimulate,** energize, galvanize, **animate, spark;** promote, foster; force, compel 424.4; ego-involve

13 **prompt, provoke, evoke, elicit, call up,** summon up, muster up, call forth, **inspire;** bring about, **cause**

14 **urge, press, push,** work on <nf>, twist one's arm <nf>; **sell,** flog <Brit>; **insist,** push for, not take no for an answer, **importune, nag, pressure, high-pressure,** browbeat, bring pressure to bear upon, throw one's weight around, throw one's weight into the scale, jawbone *and* build a fire under <nf>, talk round *or* around; grind in; **lobby,** pitch <nf>; hype <nf>; **coax,** wheedle, cajole, blandish, plead with, sweet-talk *and* soft-soap <nf>, **exhort,** call on *or* upon, advocate, recommend, put in a good word, buck for *and* hype <nf>; insist, insist upon

15 **goad, prod,** poke, nudge, prod at, goose <nf>, **spur** *or* spur on, encourage, prick, sting, needle; whip, lash; pick at *or* on, nibble at, nibble away at

16 **urge on** *or* **along, egg on** <nf>, hound on, hie on, hasten on, hurry on, speed on; **goad on, spur on,** drive on, whip on *or* along; cheer on, root on <nf>, root from the sidelines <nf>; aid and abet

17 **incite, instigate, put up to** <nf>; set on, sic on; **foment,** ferment, **agitate, arouse, excite, stir up,** work up, whip up, turn on; rally; **inflame,** incense, **fire,** heat, heat up, impassion; **provoke,** pique, whet, tickle; nettle; lash into a fury *or* frenzy; wave the bloody shirt; pour oil on the fire, feed the fire, add fuel to the flame, fan, fan the flame, blow the coals, stir the embers

18 **kindle,** enkindle, **fire, spark, spark off, trigger, trigger off, touch off,** set off, light the fuse, **enflame,** set afire *or* on fire, turn on <nf>

19 **rouse, arouse,** raise, raise up, **waken, awaken,** wake up, turn on <nf>, charge *or* psych *or* pump up <nf>, stir, **stir up,** set astir, **pique**

20 **inspire,** inspirit, spirit, spirit up; **fire, fire one's imagination; animate, exhilarate,** enliven; **infuse, infect,** inject, inoculate, imbue, inform

21 **encourage, hearten, embolden,** give encouragement, pat *or* clap on the back, stroke

<nf>; **invite,** ask for; **abet,** aid and abet, countenance, keep in countenance; **foster, nurture,** nourish, feed

22 **induce, prompt, move one to, influence, sway,** incline, **dispose,** carry, bring, lead, **lead one to; lure; tempt;** determine, decide; enlist, procure, engage <old>, interest in, get to do

23 **persuade, prevail on** *or* **upon,** prevail with, **sway,** convince, lead to believe, **bring round,** bring to reason, bring to one's senses; **win, win over,** win around, bring over, draw over, gain, gain over; **talk over, talk into,** argue into, out-talk <nf>; wangle, wangle into; hook and hook in <nf>, con *and* do a snow job on <nf>, nobble <Brit nf>, sell *and* sell one on <nf>, **charm, captivate;** wear down, overcome one's resistance, arm-twist *and* twist one's arm <nf>, put the screws to; **bribe** 378.3, grease *or* oil *or* cross one's palm <nf>; brainwash

24 **persuade oneself, make oneself easy about,** make sure of, make up one's mind; follow one's conscience; be persuaded, rest easy, come around, buy <nf>

ADJS 25 **motivating, motivational, motive, moving, animating, actuating, impelling, driving,** impulsive, inducive, directive; **urgent, pressing, driving;** compelling; causal, causative; goal-oriented

26 **inspiring, inspirational,** inspiriting; infusive; animating, exhilarating, enlivening

27 **provocative, provoking,** piquant, **exciting,** challenging, prompting, **rousing, stirring, stimulating,** stimulant, stimulative, stimulatory, energizing, electric, galvanizing, galvanic; **encouraging,** inviting, **alluring;** enticing; addictive

28 **incitive,** inciting, incentive; **instigative,** instigating; **agitative,** agitational; **inflammatory, incendiary,** fomenting, rabble-rousing

29 **persuasive,** suasive, persuading; wheedling, cajoling; hortative, hortatory; exhortative, exhortatory; hard-selling

30 **moved, motivated, prompted, impelled, actuated;** stimulated, animated; minded, inclined, of a mind to, with half a mind to; inner-directed, other-directed; soft <nf>

31 **inspired, fired,** afire, on fire

376 PRETEXT

NOUNS 1 **pretext, pretense, pretension,** lying pretension, **show,** ostensible *or* announced *or* public *or* professed motive; **front,** facade, ruse, **sham** 354.3; **excuse,** apology, protestation, poor excuse, lame excuse; **occasion,** mere occasion; put-off <nf>; handle, peg to hang on, leg to stand on, *locus standi* <L>; **subterfuge,** refuge, device, stratagem, feint, dipsy-doodle <nf>, swiftie, **trick** 356.6; dust thrown in the eye, smoke screen, **screen, cover,** stalking-horse, **blind;** guise, semblance; mask, cloak, veil; **cosmetics,** mere cosmetics, gloss, varnish, color, coat of paint, whitewash <nf>; spit and polish; **cover,** cover-up, cover story, alibi; band-aid

2 **claim,** profession, allegation

VERBS 3 pretext, make a pretext of, take as an excuse *or* reason *or* occasion, urge as a motive, **pretend,** make a pretense of; put up a front *or* false front; **allege, claim,** profess, purport, avow; protest too much

4 **hide under,** cover oneself with, shelter under, take cover under, wrap oneself in, cloak *or* mantle oneself with, take refuge in; conceal one's motive with; **cover,** cover up, gloss *or* varnish over, apply a coat of paint *or* whitewash, stick on a band-aid

ADJS 5 **pretexted, pretended, alleged, claimed, professed, purported,** avowed; **ostensible,** hypocritical, **specious;** so-called, in name only

ADVS 6 **ostensibly, allegedly,** purportedly, professedly, avowedly; for the record, for public consumption; under the pretext of, **as a pretext,** as an excuse, as a cover *or* a cover-up *or* an alibi

377 ALLUREMENT

NOUNS 1 **allurement, allure, enticement, inveiglement,** invitation, come-hither <nf>, blandishment, cajolery; inducement 375.7; **temptation,** tantalization; **seduction,** seducement; **beguilement,** beguiling; **fascination, captivation,** enthrallment, entrapment, snaring; **enchantment,** witchery, bewitchery, bewitchment; **attraction, interest, charm, glamour, appeal,** magnetism; charisma; star quality; wooing; flirtation

2 **attractiveness, allure,** charmingness, bewitchingness, impressiveness, **seductiveness,** winsomeness, winning ways, winningness; **sexiness,** sex appeal *or* SA <nf>

3 **lure,** charm, **come-on** <nf>, attention-getter *or* -grabber, **attraction, draw** *or* drawer *or* crowd-drawer, crowd-pleaser, headliner; clou, hook *and* gimmick <nf>, drawing card, drawcard; **decoy,** decoy duck; **bait,** ground bait, baited trap, baited hook; **snare,** trap; **endearment** 562; the song of the Sirens, the voice of the tempter, honeyed words; forbidden fruit

4 **tempter, seducer, enticer,** inveigler, **charmer,** enchanter, fascinator, tantalizer, teaser; coquette, flirt; Don Juan; Pied Piper of Hamelin; **temptress,** enchantress, seductress, **siren;** Siren, Circe,

Lorelei, Parthenope; **vampire,** vamp <nf>, *femme fatale* <Fr>

VERBS 5 **lure,** allure, **entice, seduce, inveigle, decoy,** draw, **draw on, lead on;** come on to *and* give the come-on *and* give a come-hither look *and* bat the eyes at *and* make goo-goo eyes at <nf>, flirt with, flirt; **woo;** coax, cajole, blandish; **ensnare;** draw in, suck in *and* rope in <nf>; bait, offer bait to, bait the hook, angle with a silver hook

6 **attract, interest, appeal, engage,** impress, charismatize, fetch <nf>, catch *or* get one's eye, command one's attention, rivet one, attract one's interest, be attractive, take *or* tickle one's fancy; **invite,** summon, beckon; **tempt, tantalize, titillate,** tickle, **tease,** whet the appetite, make one's mouth water, dangle before one

7 **fascinate, captivate, charm,** becharm, spell, spellbind, cast a spell, put under a spell, **beguile, intrigue, enthrall,** infatuate, **enrapture, transport, enravish, entrance, enchant,** witch, **bewitch,** voodoo; carry away, sweep off one's feet, turn one's head, knock one's socks off <nf>; hypnotize, mesmerize; vamp <nf>; charismatize

ADJS 8 **alluring, fascinating, captivating, riveting, charming, glamorous,** glam <nf>, exotic, **enchanting,** spellful, spellbinding, **entrancing,** ravishing, **enravishing, intriguing, enthralling,** witching, **bewitching; attractive, interesting, appealing,** dishy <Brit nf>, sexy <nf>, engaging, taking, eye-catching, catching, fetching, winning, winsome, prepossessing; exciting; charismatic; **seductive,** seducing, **beguiling, enticing, inviting,** come-hither <nf>; flirtatious, coquettish; coaxing, cajoling, blandishing; **tempting, tantalizing,** teasing, titillating, titillative, tickling; **provocative,** *provoquant* <Fr>; appetizing, mouth-watering, piquant; **irresistible;** siren, sirenic; hypnotic, mesmeric

ADVS 9 **alluringly, fascinatingly,** captivatingly, charmingly, enchantingly, entrancingly, enravishingly, intriguingly, beguilingly, glamorously, bewitchingly; attractively, appealingly, engagingly, winsomely; **enticingly, seductively,** with bedroom eyes <nf>; **temptingly,** provocatively; **tantalizingly,** teasingly; piquantly, appetizingly; irresistibly; hypnotically, mesmerically

378 BRIBERY

NOUNS 1 **bribery,** bribing, subornation, **corruption, graft,** bribery and corruption

2 **bribe,** bribe money, sop, sop to Cerberus, gratuity, gratification <old>, payoff <nf>, boodle <nf>; hush money <nf>; payola <nf>; protection

VERBS **3 bribe,** throw a sop to; grease *and* **grease the palm** *or* **hand** *and* oil the palm *and* tickle the palm <nf>; **purchase;** buy *and* **buy off** *and* pay off <nf>; suborn, **corrupt,** tamper with; reach *and* get at *and* get to <nf>; approach, try to bribe; **fix, take care of**

ADJS **4 bribable,** corruptible, purchasable, buyable; approachable; fixable; on the take *and* on the pad <nf>; **venal, corrupt,** bought and paid for, in one's pocket

379 DISSUASION

NOUNS **1 dissuasion,** talking out of <nf>, remonstrance, expostulation, admonition, monition, dehortation, **warning,** caveat, **caution,** cautioning; intimidation, **determent,** deterrence, scaring *or* frightening off, turning around; contraindication

2 deterrent, determent; **discouragement,** disincentive, chilling effect, demotivation; deflection, roadblock, obstacle, red light, closed door; damp, damper, **wet blanket,** cold water, chill; alienation, disaffection

VERBS **3 dissuade,** convince to the contrary, convince otherwise, **talk out of** <nf>; contraindicate; unconvince, unpersuade; remonstrate, expostulate, admonish, cry out against; **warn, warn off** *or* **away, caution;** enter a caveat; **intimidate,** scare *or* frighten off, daunt, cow; turn around

4 disincline, indispose, disaffect, disinterest; **deter,** repel, turn from, turn away *or* aside; divert, deflect; distract, put off *and* turn off <nf>; wean from; **discourage; pour** *or* **dash** *or* **throw cold water on,** throw *or* lay a wet blanket on, be a wet blanket, damp, dampen, demotivate, **cool, chill,** quench, blunt; nip in the bud; take the starch out of, take the wind out of one's sails

ADJS **5 dissuasive,** dissuading, disinclining, unwilling, **discouraging; deterrent,** off-putting, repellent, disenchanting; expostulatory, admonitory, monitory, cautionary; intimidating

380 INTENTION

NOUNS **1 intention, intent,** intendment, mindset, **aim,** effect, meaning, view, study, animus, **point, purpose,** function, set *or* settled *or* fixed purpose; sake; **design, plan, project,** idea, notion; **quest,** pursuit; **proposal,** prospectus; **resolve,** resolution, mind, will; **motive** 375.1; determination 359.1; desideratum, desideration, **ambition,** aspiration, **desire** 100; striving, nisus

2 objective, object, aim, end, goal, destination, mark, object in mind, **end in view,** telos, final cause, ultimate aim *or* purpose, mission; end in itself; **target,** butt, bull's-eye, quintain; quarry, prey, game; reason for being, *raison d'être* <Fr>; by-purpose, by-end; "the be-all and the end-all"—Shakespeare; teleology

3 intentionality, deliberation, deliberateness, directedness; express intention, expressness, **premeditation, predeliberation,** preconsideration, **calculation, calculatedness, predetermination,** preresolution, forethought, aforethought, calculated risk

VERBS **4 intend, purpose, plan,** purport, **mean,** think, **propose; resolve,** determine 359.7; project, **design,** destine; **aim,** aim at, take aim at, draw a bead on, set one's sights on, have designs on, go for, drive at, aspire to *or* after, be after, set before oneself, purpose to oneself, have every intention; harbor a design; **desire** 100.14

5 contemplate, meditate; envisage, envision, **have in mind, have in view;** have an eye to, have every intention, have a mind *or* notion, have half a mind *or* notion, have a good *or* great mind *or* notion

6 plan, plan on, figure on, plan for *or* out, count on, figure out, calculate, calculate on, reckon, do the math, reckon *or* bargain on, bargain for, bank on *or* upon, make book on <nf>, expect, foresee

7 premeditate, calculate, preresolve, predetermine, predeliberate, preconsider, direct oneself, forethink, work out beforehand; plan; plot, scheme

ADJS **8 intentional, intended,** proposed, purposed, telic, **projected, designed,** of design, aimed, aimed at, **meant, purposeful,** purposive, **willful, voluntary, deliberate;** deliberated; on-message; considered, studied, advised, **calculated, contemplated, envisaged,** envisioned, meditated, **conscious,** knowing, witting; planned; teleological

9 premeditated, predeliberated, preconsidered, predetermined, preresolved, prepense, aforethought, foremeant

ADVS **10 intentionally, purposely,** purposefully, purposively, pointedly, **on purpose,** with purpose, prepensely, with a view *or* an eye to, **deliberately, designedly, willfully, voluntarily,** of one's own accord *or* one's own free will; **wittingly, consciously, knowingly;** advisedly, calculatedly, contemplatedly, meditatedly, premeditatedly, **with premeditation, with intent,** with full intent, **by design,** with one's eyes open; with malice aforethought, in cold blood

PREPS, CONJS **11 for, to; in order to** *or* **that,** so, **so that, so as to; for the purpose of,** to the end that, with the intent that, with the view of, with a view to, with an eye to; in contemplation of, in consideration of; **for the sake of**

381 PLAN

NOUNS **1 plan, scheme, design,** method, **program,** device, contrivance, game, envisagement, conception, enterprise, **idea, notion;** organization, rationalization, systematization, schematization; charting, mapping, graphing, blueprinting; **planning,** calculation, figuring; planning function; long-range planning, long-range or long-term plan; **master plan,** the picture and the big picture <nf>; approach, attack, plan of attack; way, procedure; **arrangement,** prearrangement, system, disposition, layout, setup, lineup; **schedule,** timetable, time-scheme, time frame; agenda, order of the day, dance card; deadline; plan of work; **schema,** schematism, scheme of arrangement; blueprint, **guideline, guidelines,** program of action; methodology; working plan, ground plan, tactical plan, strategic plan; tactics, **strategy,** game plan <nf>; mission statement; contingency plan; operations research; **intention** 380; forethought, foresight 961; back room; mise en place; Plan A, Plan B

2 project, projection, scheme; proposal, prospectus, proposition; scenario, **game plan** <nf>

3 diagram, plot, chart, blueprint, graph, bar graph, pie or circle graph or chart, area graph; flow diagram, flow chart; **table; design, pattern,** copy <old>, cartoon; **sketch, draft, drawing,** working drawing, rough; brouillon and ébauche and esquisse <Fr>; **outline, delineation,** skeleton, figure, profile; house plan, ground plan, ichnography; elevation, projection; **map, chart** 159.5

4 policy, polity, principles, guiding principles; **procedure,** course, line, plan of action; creed 953.3; **platform,** party line; position paper; formula; rule

5 intrigue, web of intrigue, **plot, scheme,** deep-laid plot or scheme, underplot, game or little game <nf>, secret plan, trick, stratagem, finesse, method; counterplot; **conspiracy,** confederacy, covin, complot <old>, cabal; **complicity, collusion, connivance; artifice** 415.3; **contrivance,** contriving; **scheming,** schemery, plotting; finagling <nf>, **machination,** manipulation, **maneuvering,** engineering, rigging; frame-up <nf>; wire-pulling <nf>; inside job; expedient, last resort, eleventh-hour rescue; way out, loophole

6 planner, designer, deviser, contriver, framer, projector; enterpriser, entrepreneur; intrapreneur; organizer, promoter, developer, engineer; expediter, facilitator, animator; **policymaker, decision-maker; architect, tactician, strategist, strategian,** mastermind, brains <nf>

7 schemer, plotter, counterplotter, finagler <nf>, Machiavelli; **intriguer,** intrigant and intrigante <Fr>, cabalist; **conspirer, conspirator,** coconspirator, **conniver;** maneuverer, machinator, operator <nf>, opportunist, pot-hunter, exploiter; wire-puller <nf>, wangler

VERBS **8 plan, devise, contrive, design,** frame, shape, cast, concert, lay plans; organize, rationalize, systematize, schematize, methodize, configure, pull together, sort out; **arrange,** prearrange, make arrangements, set up, work up, work out; **schedule;** lay down a plan, shape or mark out a course; program; **calculate,** figure; **project,** cut out, make a projection, forecast <old>, plan ahead; intend 380.4

9 plot, scheme, intrigue, be up to something; **conspire, connive,** collude, complot <old>, cabal; **hatch, hatch up,** cook up <nf>, brew, concoct, hatch or lay a plot; **maneuver,** machinate, finesse, operate <nf>, engineer, rig, wangle <nf>, angle, finagle <nf>; frame or frame up <nf>; counterplot, countermine

10 plot; map, chart 159.11, **blueprint; diagram,** graph; **sketch,** sketch in or out, draw up a plan; map out, plot out, **lay out,** set out, mark out; lay off, mark off; design a prototype

11 outline, line, **delineate,** chalk out, brief; **sketch, draft,** trace; block in or out; rough in, rough out; chalk out

ADJS **12 planned, devised, designed,** shaped, set, **blueprinted,** charted, mapped, **contrived; plotted;** premeditated; arranged; organized, rationalized, systematized, schematized, methodized, strategized; worked out, calculated, figured; **projected; scheduled,** on the agenda, in the works, in the pipeline <nf>, on the calendar, on the docket, on the anvil, on the carpet, on the tapis <old>, sur le tapis <Fr>; tactical, **strategic**

13 scheming, calculating, designing, contriving, plotting, intriguing; resourceful; manipulatory, **manipulative;** opportunist, **opportunistic;** Machiavellian, Byzantine; **conniving,** connivent <old>, wangling, conspiring, conspiratorial, collusive; stratagemical

14 schematic, diagrammatic

382 PURSUIT

NOUNS **1 pursuit,** pursuing, pursuance, prosecution <old>; **quest,** seeking, hunting, searching, all-points bulletin; **following,** follow, follow-up;

tracking, trailing, tracking down, dogging, hounding, shadowing, stalking, tailing <nf>; **chase,** hot pursuit; hue and cry; all points bulletin *or* APB, dragnet, manhunt; wild-goose chase; trainspotting, aircraft spotting

2 hunting, gunning, shooting, venery, cynegetics, sport, sporting; **hunt, chase,** chevy *or* chivy <Brit>, *shikar* <India>, coursing; blood sport; fox hunt, fox hunting; hawking, falconry; stalking, still hunt

3 fishing, fishery; **angling,** piscatology <old>, halieutics; fly-fishing, saltwater fishing, ice fishing, competitive fishing

4 pursuer, pursuant, **chaser,** follower; hunter, quester, **seeker,** tracker, trailer, tail <nf>

5 hunter, huntsman, sportsman, **Nimrod;** huntress, sportswoman; stalker; courser; trapper; big game hunter, *shikari* <India>, white hunter; jacklighter, jacker; gamekeeper; beater, whipper-in; falconer; gundog; poacher

6 fisher, fisherman, angler, *piscator* <L>, piscatorian, piscatorialist; Waltonian; dibber, dibbler, troller, trawler, trawlerman, dragger, jacker, jigger, bobber, guddler, tickler, drifter, drift netter, whaler, clam digger, lobsterman, etc

7 quarry, game, prey, venery, beasts of venery, victim, the hunted; kill; big game, small game

VERBS **8 pursue,** prosecute <old>, **follow,** follow up, **go after,** take out *or* off after <nf>, bay after, run after, run in pursuit of, make after, go in pursuit of; raise the hunt, raise the hue and cry, hollo after; **chase, give chase,** chivy; hound, dog; **quest,** quest after, **seek,** seek out, hunt, **search** 938.31, send out a search party; trawl

9 hunt, go hunting, hunt down, chase, run, *shikar* <India>, sport; engage in a blood sport; shoot, gun; course; ride to hounds, follow the hounds; **track,** trail; **stalk,** prowl after, still-hunt; poach; hound, dog; hawk, falcon; fowl; flush, start; drive, beat; jack, jacklight; trap, ensnare

10 fish, go fishing, **angle;** cast one's hook *or* net; bait the hook; shrimp, whale, clam, grig, still-fish, fly-fish, troll, bob, dap, dib *or* dibble, gig, jig, etc; reel in

ADJS **11 pursuing,** pursuant, following; **questing,** in quest of, **seeking, searching** 938.38; **in pursuit,** in hot pursuit, in full cry, tailing, chasing, trailing; hunting, cynegetic, fishing, piscatory, piscatorial, halieutic, halieutical

PREPS **12 after, in pursuit** *or* **pursuance of,** in search of, on the lookout for, in the market for, out for; on the track *or* trail of, on the scent of

INTERJS **13** <hunting cries> view halloo!, yoicks! <old>; so-ho!, tallyho!, tallyho over!, tallyho back!

383 ROUTE, PATH

NOUNS **1 route, path, way, itinerary, course,** track, run, line, road; trajectory, traject, *trajet* <Fr>; direction; circuit, tour, orbit; walk, beat, round; trade route, traffic lane, **sea lane,** shipping lane, **air lane,** flight path; path of least resistance, primrose path, garden path; shortcut, detour; line of advance, line of retreat; scenic route

2 path, track, trail, pathway, footpath, footway, *piste* <Fr>; walkway, catwalk, skybridge *or* skywalk *or* flying bridge *or* walkway; **sidewalk, walk,** fastwalk, *trottoir* <Fr>, foot pavement <Brit>; boardwalk; hiking trail; public walk, promenade, esplanade, alameda, parade, *prado* <Sp>, mall; towpath *or* towing path; bridle path *or* road *or* trail *or* way; bicycle path; berm; run, runway; beaten track *or* path, rut, groove; garden path

3 passageway, pass, passage, defile; avenue, artery; corridor, aisle, aisleway, **alley, lane,** back alley; **channel, conduit** 239.1; ford, ferry, traject, *trajet* <Fr>; opening, aperture; access, right of way, approach, inlet 189.5; exit, outlet 190.9; connection, communication; covered way, gallery, arcade, portico, colonnade, cloister, ambulatory; underpass, overpass, flyover <Brit>; tunnel, railroad tunnel, vehicular tunnel; junction, interchange, **intersection** 170.2

4 byway, bypath, byroad, by-lane, bystreet, side road, side street; **bypass, detour,** roundabout way; bypaths and crooked ways, side path; back way, back stairs, back door, side door; back road, back street

5 road <see list>, highway, roadway, carriageway <Brit>, right-of-way; **street** <see list>

6 pavement, paving; macadam, blacktop, bitumen, asphalt, tarmacadam, tarmac, tarvia, bituminous macadam; cement, concrete; tile, brick, paving brick; stone, paving stone, pavestone, flag, flagstone, flagging; cobblestone, cobble; road metal <Brit>; gravel; washboard; curbstone, kerbstone <Brit>, edgestone; curb, kerb <Brit>, curbing; gutter, kennel <Brit>

7 railway <see list>, **railroad,** rail, line, track, trackage, railway *or* railroad *or* rail line; subway; junction; terminus, terminal, the end of the line; roadway, roadbed, embankment; bridge, trestle

8 cableway, ropeway, wireway, wire ropeway, cable *or* rope railway, funicular *or* funicular railway; monorail; *téléphérique* <Fr>, telpher, telpherway, telpher ropeway, telpher line *or* railway; ski lift, chair lift, gondola, aerial tramway, tram

9 bridge, span, viaduct; cantilever bridge, clapper bridge, drawbridge, footbridge, pontoon bridge, rope bridge, skybridge *or* skywalk *or* flying bridge *or* walkway, suspension bridge, toll bridge, floating bridge, covered bridge, aqueduct; overpass, overcrossing, overbridge *or* flyover <Brit>; stepping-stone, stepstone, catwalk; Bifrost

10 roads, highways

access road	king's *or* queen's highway
arterial highway	limited access highway
artery	main road *or* main
Autobahn <Ger>	drag <nf>
autoroute <Fr>	motorway <Brit>
autostrada <Ital>	parkway
beltway *or* circumferential	pavé <Fr>
or ring road *or* belt	pike
highway	post road
big road <S US>	private road
busway	shunpike
camino real <Sp>	skyway
causeway	speedway
country road	superhighway
dirt road	switchback
divided *or* dual highway	throughway *or*
expressway	thruway
freeway	toll road
highroad <Brit>	trunk road
interstate highway	turnpike

11 streets, alleys

alley *or* alleyway	drive
avenue	lane
blind alley	mews
boulevard	one-way street
close <Brit>	place
court	row
crescent	thoroughfare
cul-de-sac	vennel <Scot>
dead-end street	wynd <Scot>

12 railways

cable railway	métro <Fr>
cog railway	monorail
electric railway	rack *or* rack-and-pinion
elevated railway or	railway
elevated *or* el or	scenic railroad
L <nf>	subway
funicular railway	tram *or* tramline *or*
gravity-operated railway *or*	tramway *or* tramroad
gravity railroad	<Brit>
inclined railroad	trolley *or* streetcar line
light-rail rapid-transit	trunk *or* trunk line
system	underground *or* tube
mainline	<Brit>

384 MANNER, MEANS

NOUNS 1 manner, way, wise, **means, mode,** modality, form <old>, **fashion, style,** tone, guise <old>; **method,** methodology, **system;** algorithm <math>; **approach,** attack, tack; **technique, procedure, process,** proceeding, measures, steps, course, practice; order; lines, line, line of action; *modus operandi* <L>, mode of operation *or* MO, manner of working, mode of procedure; **routine;** the way of, the how, the how-to, the drill <Brit>

2 means, ways, **ways and means,** means to an end; **wherewithal,** wherewith; funds 728.14; **resources,** disposable resources, capital 728.15; bankroll <nf>; stock in trade, inventory, stock, supply 386; power, capacity, ability 18.2; power base, constituency, backing, support; recourses, resorts, devices; tools of the trade, tricks of the trade, bag of tricks

3 instrumentality, agency; machinery, **mechanism,** modality; gadgetry <nf>; mediation, going between, intermediation, service; **expedient,** recourse, resort, device 995.2

4 instrument, tool, implement, appliance, device; contrivance, makeshift, lever, mechanism; **vehicle, organ; agent** 576; medium, mediator, intermedium, intermediary, intermediate, interagent, liaison, go-between 576.4; expediter, facilitator, animator; midwife, servant, slave, handmaid, handmaiden, *ancilla* <L>; **cat's-paw, puppet, dummy, pawn,** creature, minion, stooge <nf>; stalking horse; toy, plaything; gadget, contrivance; dupe 358

VERBS 5 use, utilize, adopt, effect; **approach, attack;** proceed, practice, go about; routinize

6 find means, find a way, provide *or* have the wherewithal, develop a method; enable, facilitate; get by hook or by crook, obtain by fair means or foul; beg, borrow, or steal; think laterally; network

7 be instrumental, **serve, subserve,** serve one's purpose, come in handy, stand in good stead, fill the bill; minister to, act for, act in the interests of, **promote, advance, forward, assist,** facilitate; mediate, go between; liaise

ADJS 8 modal; **instrumental, implemental;** agential, agentive, agentival; effective, efficacious; **useful,** utile, handy, employable, **serviceable; helpful,** conducive, forwarding, favoring, promoting, assisting, facilitating; subservient, ministering, ministerial; mediating, mediatorial, intermediary

ADVS 9 how, in what way *or* **manner,** by what mode *or* means; to what extent; in what condition; by what name; at what price; after this fashion, in this way, in such wise, along these lines; **thus, so,** just so, thus and so; as, like, on the lines of

10 anyhow, anyway, anywise, anyroad <Brit nf>, in any way, **by any means, by any manner of means;** in any event, at any rate, leastways <nf>, in any case; **nevertheless, nonetheless, however, regardless,** irregardless <nf>; at all, nohow <nf>

11 somehow, in some way, in some way or other, someway <nf>, by some means, **somehow or**

other, somehow or another, in one way or another, in some such way, after a fashion; no matter how, **by hook or by crook,** by fair means or foul

12 herewith, therewith, wherewith, wherewithal; whereby, thereby, hereby

PREPS 13 **by means of, by** *or* **through the agency of,** by *or* through the good offices of, through the instrumentality of, by the aid of, thanks to, by use of, **by way of,** by dint of, by the act of, through the medium of, by *or* in virtue of, at the hand of, at the hands of; **with, through,** by, per

PHRS 14 it isn't what you do, it's how you do it; there's more than one way to skin a cat

385 PROVISION, EQUIPMENT

NOUNS 1 **provision,** providing; **equipment, accouterment,** fitting out, outfitting; **supply,** supplying, finding; **furnishing,** furnishment; chandlery, **retailing, selling** 734.2; **logistics;** procurement 472.1; investment, endowment, subvention, subsidy, subsidization; provisioning, victualing, purveyance, catering; armament; resupply, replenishment, reinforcement; supply line, line of supply; **preparation** 405

2 **provisions, supplies** 386.1; provender 10.4; **merchandise** 735; basics

3 **accommodations,** accommodation, facilities; **lodgings;** bed, board, full board; **room and board,** bed and board; **subsistence,** keep, fostering

4 **equipment,** matériel, equipage, munitions; **furniture, furnishings,** furnishments <old>; **fixtures, fittings, appointments, accouterments, appurtenances,** trappings, installations, plumbing; **appliances,** utensils, **conveniences; outfit, apparatus, rig,** machinery; stock-in-trade; **plant,** facility, facilities; paraphernalia, harness, things, **gear, stuff** <nf>, impedimenta <pl>, **tackle;** rigging; armament, munition; **kit,** duffel, effects, personal effects; government issue, military issue

5 **harness,** caparison, trappings, **tack,** tackle

6 **provider, supplier,** furnisher; donor 478.11; patron; **purveyor,** provisioner, distributor, middleman; **caterer,** victualler, sutler; *vivandier* or *vivandière* <Fr>; chandler, retailer, merchant 730.2; commissary, commissariat, quartermaster, shopkeeper, storekeeper, merchant, stock clerk, steward, manciple; grocer, vintner; procurer; megastore

VERBS 7 **provide, supply,** find, dish up *and* rustle up *and* offer up <nf>, **furnish;** accommodate; invest, endow, fund, subsidize; donate, give, afford, contribute, kick in <nf>, yield, present 478.12; make available; stock, store; provide for, make

provision *or* due provision for, plenish; prepare 405.6; support, maintain, keep; fill, fill up; replenish, restock, recruit

8 **equip, furnish, outfit,** gear, **prepare, fit,** fit up *or* out, fix up <nf>, **rig,** rig up *or* out, set up, **turn out,** appoint, accouter, clothe, dress; arm, heel <nf>, munition; man, staff

9 **provision,** provender, cater, victual, plenish <old>, serve, cook for; provide a grubstake <nf>; **board,** feed; forage; fuel, gas, gas up, fill up, top off, coal, oil, bunker; **purvey,** sell 734.8

10 **accommodate,** furnish accommodations; house, lodge 225.10; **put up,** take in, board

11 **make a living,** earn a living *or* livelihood, **make** *or* **earn one's keep**

12 **support oneself,** make one's way; **make ends meet, keep body and soul together, keep the wolf from the door,** keep *or* hold one's head above water, keep afloat; **survive, subsist, cope, eke out,** make out, scrape along, manage, get by

ADJS 13 **provided, supplied, furnished,** provisioned, purveyed, catered; perquisited; invested, endowed; **equipped, fitted,** fitted out, outfitted, rigged, accoutered; armed, heeled <nf>; staffed, manned; readied, in place, **prepared** 405.16

14 **well-provided, well-supplied, well-furnished,** well-stocked, well-found; **well-equipped, well-fitted,** well-appointed; well-armed

386 STORE, SUPPLY

NOUNS 1 **store, hoard, treasure,** treasury; plenty, plenitude, abundance, cornucopia; heap, mass, stack, pile, dump, rick; **collection, accumulation,** cumulation, **amassment,** budget, **stockpile; backlog;** repertory, repertoire; stock-in-trade; **inventory, stock,** supply on hand; lock, stock, and barrel; **stores, supplies, provisions,** provisionment, rations; larder, commissariat, commissary; munitions; matériel; material, materials 1054

2 **supply, fund, resource, resources; means, assets,** liquid assets, balance, pluses <nf>, black-ink items, financial resources, **capital,** capital goods, capitalization, available means *or* resources *or* funds, cash flow, stock in trade; venture capital; backing, support; grist, grist for the mill; holdings, property 471; labor resources

3 **reserve, reserves,** reservoir, resource; proved *or* proven reserve; **stockpile, cache,** backup, reserve supply, store, standby, safeguard, something in reserve *or* in hand, something to fall back on, reserve fund, emergency funds, **nest egg, savings,** petty cash, sinking fund; trust fund; proved reserves; backlog, unexpended balance; ace in the

hole <nf>, a card *or* ace up one's sleeve; spare *or* replacement part

4 **source of supply,** source, staple, resource; well, fountain, fount, font <old>, spring, wellspring; mine, **gold mine, bonanza,** luau <nf>; quarry, lode, vein; oilfield, oil well, oil rig; cornucopia

5 **storage, stowage;** preservation, conservation, safekeeping, warehousing; cold storage, cold store, dry storage, dead storage; storage space, shelf-room; custody, guardianship 1008.2; sequestration, escrow

6 **storehouse, storeroom,** stockroom, box room <Brit>, lumber room, store, storage, **depository, repository,** conservatory <old>, reservoir, repertory, depot, supply depot, supply base, magazine, *magasin* <Fr>, warehouse, megastore, big-box store, godown <Asia>; bonded warehouse, entrepôt; dock; hold, cargo dock; attic, loft, cellar, basement; closet, cupboard; wine cellar, larder; shed, stable, garage; **treasury,** treasure house, treasure room, exchequer, coffers; bank, vault 729.13, strongroom, strongbox; **archives, library,** stack room; armory, arsenal, dump; lumberyard; drawer, shelf; bin, bunker, bay, crib; rack, rick; vat, tank; elevator; crate, box; chest, **locker,** hutch; bookcase, stack; sail locker, chain locker, lazaret, lazaretto, glory hole

7 **garner, granary,** grain bin, elevator, grain elevator, **silo;** mow, haymow, hayloft, hayrick; crib, corncrib

8 **larder, pantry,** buttery <nf>; spence <Brit nf>, stillroom <Brit>; root cellar; dairy, dairy house *or* room

9 **museum; gallery,** art gallery, picture gallery, pinacotheca; science museum, natural history museum; salon; waxworks; museology, curatorship

VERBS 10 **store, stow,** lay in store; **lay in,** lay in a supply *or* stock *or* store, store away, stow away, **put away, lay away,** put *or* lay by, pack away, bundle away, lay down, stow down, salt down *or* away *and* sock away *and* squirrel away <nf>; **deposit,** reposit, lodge; **cache,** stash <nf>, bury away; **bank,** coffer, hutch <old>; warehouse, reservoir; file, file away

11 **store up, stock up, lay up,** put up, **save up,** hoard up, treasure up, garner up, **heap up,** pile up, build up a stock *or* an inventory, provision; **accumulate,** cumulate, **collect, amass, stockpile;** backlog; garner, gather into barns; **hoard,** treasure, save, keep, hold, squirrel, squirrel away; hide, secrete 346.7

12 **reserve, save, conserve, keep,** retain, husband, husband one's resources, keep *or* hold back, withhold; **keep in reserve,** keep in store, keep on hand, keep by one; sequester, put in escrow;

preserve 397.7; **set** *or* **put aside,** set *or* put apart, put *or* lay *or* set by; save up, save to fall back upon, keep as a nest egg, **save for a rainy day,** provide for *or* against a rainy day

13 **have in store** *or* **reserve,** have to fall back upon, have something to draw on, have something laid by, have something laid by for a rainy day, have something up one's sleeve

ADJS 14 **stored, accumulated,** amassed, laid up, stocked; gathered, garnered, collected, heaped, piled; **stockpiled;** backlogged; **hoarded,** treasured

15 **reserved, preserved, saved,** conserved, put by *or* aside, kept, retained, held, filed, withheld, held back, kept *or* held in reserve; in storage, warehoused, mothballed; bottled, pickled, canned, refrigerated, frozen; spare

ADVS 16 **in store,** in stock, in supply, **on hand**
17 **in reserve,** back, aside, by

387 USE

NOUNS 1 **use, employment,** utilization, employ <old>, **usage; exercise, exertion,** active use, wear; good use; ill use, wrong use, misuse 389; hard use, hard *or* rough usage; hard wear, heavy duty; **application,** appliance, deployment; expenditure, expending, using up, exhausting, dissipation, dissipating, **consumption** 388

2 **usage, treatment, handling,** management; way *or* means of dealing; stewardship, custodianship, guardianship, care

3 **utility, usefulness, usability, use,** utilizability, avail, good, advantage, benefit, added value, **serviceability,** service, **helpfulness,** functionality, profitability, applicability, availability, **practicability,** practicality, practical utility, operability, **effectiveness,** efficacy, efficiency; readiness, availability; instrumentality; ultimate purpose

4 **benefit, use, service, avail, profit, advantage,** point, percentage *and* mileage <nf>, what's in it for one <nf>, convenience; interest, behalf, behoof; **value, worth,** fruitfulness; commonweal, public good

5 **function, use, purpose, role,** part, point, end use, immediate purpose, ultimate purpose, operational purpose, operation; work, duty, office

6 **functionalism, utilitarianism;** pragmatism, pragmaticism; functional design, functional furniture *or* housing, etc

7 <law terms> usufruct, imperfect usufruct, perfect usufruct, right of use, user, enjoyment of property; *jus primae noctis* <L>, *droit du seigneur* <Fr>; disposal; possession

8 **utilization,** using, making use of, making instrumental, using as a means *or* tool; **employment,** employing; **management,** manipulation, handling, working, operation, **exploitation,** recruiting, recruitment, calling upon, calling into service; mobilization, mobilizing

9 **user,** employer; **consumer,** enjoyer, exploiter; customer, client; end user

VERBS 10 **use, utilize, make use of,** do with; **employ,** practice, ply, work, manage, handle, manipulate, operate, **wield,** play, exercise; **have *or* enjoy the use of;** exercise, exert; reuse, repurpose

11 **apply, put to use *or* good use,** carry out, put into execution, **put into practice *or* operation,** put in force, enforce; bring to bear upon

12 **treat, handle,** manage, use, **deal with, cope with,** come to grips with, take on, tackle <nf>, contend with, do with; steward, care for

13 **spend,** consume, expend, **pass,** employ, **put in;** devote, bestow, give to *or* give over to, devote *or* consecrate *or* dedicate to; while, while away, wile; dissipate, **exhaust, use up**

14 **avail oneself of, make use of, resort to, put to use *or* good use,** have recourse to, **turn to,** look to, recur to, refer to, take to <nf>, betake oneself to; revert to, fall back on *or* upon, rely on; convert *or* turn to use, put in *or* into requisition, press *or* enlist into service, lay under contribution, impress, **call upon,** call *or* bring into play, draw on *or* upon, recruit, muster; pick someone's brains

15 **take advantage of, avail oneself of, make the most of,** use to the full, make good use of, maximize, improve, **turn to use *or* profit *or* account *or* good account,** turn to advantage *or* good advantage, use to advantage, put to advantage, find one's account *or* advantage in; improve the occasion 843.8; **profit by, benefit from,** reap the benefit of; **exploit, capitalize on, make capital of,** make a good thing of <nf>, make hay <nf>, **trade on,** cash in on <nf>, play on, play off against; make the best of, make a virtue of necessity, "make necessity a virtue"—Quintilian

16 <take unfair advantage of> **exploit, take advantage of, use,** make use of, **use for one's own ends;** make a paw *or* cat's-paw of, make a pawn of, sucker *and* play for a sucker <nf>; **manipulate,** work on, work upon, stroke, play on *or* upon; play both ends against the middle; **impose upon,** presume upon; use ill, ill-use, abuse, misuse 389.4; batten on; milk, bleed, bleed white <nf>; drain, suck the blood of *or* from, suck dry; exploit one's position, feather one's nest <nf>, **profiteer;** abuse

17 **avail,** be of use, be of service, serve, **suffice, do,** answer, **answer *or* serve one's purpose,** serve one's

need, fill the bill *and* do the trick <nf>, suit one's purpose; bestead <old>, **stand one in stead *or* good stead,** be handy, come in handy, stand one in hand <nf>; advantage, be of advantage *or* service to; **profit, benefit,** pay *and* pay off <nf>, give good returns, yield a profit, bear fruit

ADJS 18 **useful,** employable, of use, of service, **serviceable,** commodious <old>; good for; **helpful,** of help 449.21; **advantageous, to one's advantage *or* profit, profitable,** remuneratory, bankable, beneficial 999.12; **practical,** banausic, pragmatical, **functional, utilitarian,** of general utility *or* application, commodious; fitting, proper, appropriate, expedient 995.5; well-used, well-thumbed; reusable, recyclable

19 **using, exploitive,** exploitative, manipulative, manipulatory

20 **handy, convenient; available,** accessible, **ready, at hand,** to hand, **on hand,** on tap, on deck <nf>, on call, at one's call *or* beck and call, at one's elbow, at one's fingertips, just around the corner, at one's disposal; versatile, adaptable, all-around <nf>, of all work; crude but effective, quick and dirty <nf>; to the purpose; fast-food, convenience; one-stop

21 **effectual, effective,** active, efficient, efficacious, operative; instrumental; subsidiary, subservient

22 **valuable,** of value, all for the best, all to the good, **profitable,** bankable, yielding a return, well-spent, **worthwhile,** rewarding; gainful, remunerative, moneymaking, lucrative

23 **usable, utilizable; applicable,** appliable, employable, serviceable; practical, operable; **reusable,** recyclable; **exploitable;** manipulable, pliable, compliant 433.12; at one's service

24 **used, employed,** exercised, exerted, **applied;** previously owned *or* pre-owned, secondhand 842.18

25 **in use, in practice,** in force, in effect, in service, in operation, in commission

ADVS 26 **usefully,** to good use; **profitably, advantageously, to advantage,** to profit, to good effect; effectually, effectively, efficiently; serviceably, functionally, **practically;** handily, conveniently; by use of, by dint of

388 CONSUMPTION

NOUNS 1 **consumption, consuming, using *or* eating up;** burning up; absorption, assimilation, digestion, ingestion, **expenditure,** expending, spending; squandering, wastefulness 486.1; finishing; **depletion,** drain, exhausting, **exhaustion,** impoverishment; **waste,** wastage, wasting away, erosion, ablation, wearing down, wearing away, attrition; throwing away

2 consumable, consumable item *or* **goods;**
nonrenewable *or* nonreusable *or* nonrecyclable
item *or* resource; **throwaway,** throwaway item,
disposable goods *or* item; throwaway culture *or*
psychology, instant obsolescence

VERBS **3 consume, spend, expend, use up;** absorb,
assimilate, digest, ingest, eat, **eat up,** swallow,
swallow up, gobble, gobble up; burn up; **finish,**
finish off; **exhaust, deplete,** impoverish, drain,
drain of resources; suck dry, bleed white <nf>,
suck one's blood; wear away, erode, erode away,
ablate; waste away; **throw away, squander**
486.3

4 be consumed, be used up, waste; **run out, give
out,** peter out <nf>; run dry, dry up

ADJS **5 used up, consumed,** eaten up, burnt up;
finished, gone; unreclaimable, irreplaceable;
nonrenewable, nonrecyclable, nonreusable; **spent,**
exhausted, maxed-out, effete, dissipated, depleted,
impoverished, drained, worn-out; worn away,
eroded, ablated; **wasted** 486.9

6 consumable, expendable, spendable; exhaustible;
replaceable; disposable, throwaway, no-deposit,
no-deposit-no-return

389 MISUSE

NOUNS **1 misuse, misusage, abuse,** wrong use;
misemployment, misapplication; mishandling,
mismanagement, poor stewardship; corrupt
administration, malversation, breach of public
trust, maladministration; diversion, defalcation,
misappropriation, conversion, **embezzlement,**
peculation, pilfering, fraud; perversion,
prostitution; profanation, violation, pollution,
fouling, befoulment, desecration, defilement,
debasement; malpractice, abuse of office,
malversation, misconduct, malfeasance,
misfeasance

**2 mistreatment, ill-treatment, maltreatment,
ill-use,** ill-usage, **abuse,** verbal abuse; **molesting,
molestation,** child abuse *or* molestation; spousal
abuse; self-abuse; **violation,** outrage, violence,
injury, atrocity; cruel and unusual punishment;
overuse

3 persecution, oppression, harrying, hounding,
tormenting, bashing <nf>, harassment, nobbling
<Brit nf>, victimization, torture; **witch-hunting,**
witch-hunt, red-baiting <nf>, McCarthyism;
Spanish inquisition; open season, piling
on <nf>

VERBS **4 misuse, misemploy, abuse, misapply;
mishandle,** mismanage, maladminister; divert,
misappropriate, expropriate, convert, defalcate
<old>, embezzle, defraud, pilfer, peculate, feather

one's nest <nf>; pervert, prostitute; profane,
violate, pollute, foul, foul one's own nest, spoil,
befoul, desecrate, defile, debase; verbally abuse,
bad-mouth; misuse *or* abuse power

5 mistreat, maltreat, ill-treat, ill-use, abuse, injure,
molest; do wrong to, do wrong by; outrage,
do violence to, do one's worst to; mishandle,
manhandle; buffet, batter, bruise, **savage,**
manhandle, maul, knock about, rough, rough up;
pollute; overuse, overwork, overtax

6 <nf terms> **screw,** screw over, shaft, kick around,
stiff, give the short *or* the shitty end of the stick,
fuck, fuck over

7 persecute, oppress, **torment,** victimize, play cat
and mouse with, **harass,** get *or* keep after, get *or*
keep at, harry, hound, beset, nobble <Brit nf>;
pursue, hunt

ADVS **8** on one's back *and* on one's case *and* in one's
face <nf>

390 DISUSE

NOUNS **1 disuse,** disusage, desuetude; **nonuse,
nonemployment; abstinence, abstention;** neglect;
inusitation; nonprevalence, unprevalence;
obsolescence, obsoleteness, obsoletism,
obsoletion, planned obsolescence;
superannuation, retirement, pensioning off, early
retirement; redundancy <Brit>

2 discontinuance, cessation, desisting, desistance;
abdication, relinquishment, forebearance,
resignation, renunciation, renouncement,
abjurement, abjuration; waiver, nonexercise;
abeyance, suspension, back burner *and* cold
storage <nf>, limbo, bardo; **phaseout,
abandonment** 370

3 discard, discarding, jettison, deep six <nf>,
disposal, dumping, **waste disposal,** solid waste
disposal, burning, incineration, ocean burning *or*
incineration; compacting; **scrapping, junking**
<nf>; removal, elimination 773.2; **rejection** 372;
reject, throwaway, castaway, castoff, remains,
rejectamenta <pl>; **refuse** 391.4

VERBS **4 cease to use; abdicate, relinquish;
discontinue, disuse,** quit, stop, drop <nf>, give up,
give over, lay off <nf>, **phase out,** phase down, put
behind one, let go, leave off, come off <nf>, cut
out, desist, desist from, have done with; waive
<old>, resign, renounce, abjure, neglect; nol-pros,
not pursue *or* proceed with; decommission, put
out of commission

5 not use, do without, dispense with, **let alone,** not
touch, hold off; **abstain, refrain,** forgo, forbear,
spare, waive; keep *or* hold back, reserve, save, save
up, sock *or* squirrel away, tuck away, put under the

mattress, hoard; keep in hand, have up one's sleeve; see the last of

6 **put away,** lay away, **put aside,** lay *or* set *or* wave *or* cast *or* push aside, sideline <nf>, put *or* lay *or* set by; stow, store 386.10; **pigeonhole, shelve,** put on the shelf, put in mothballs; **table,** lay on the table; table the motion, pass to the order of the day; put on hold *or* on the back burner <nf>, postpone, delay 846.8

7 **discard, reject, throw away, throw out,** chuck *or* chuck away *and* shit-can *and* eighty-six <nf>, cast, cast off *or* away *or* aside; **get rid of,** get quit of, get shut *or* shet of <nf>, rid oneself of, shrug off, **dispose of,** slough, **dump, ditch** <nf>, **jettison, throw** *or* **heave** *or* **toss overboard,** deep-six <nf>, throw out the window, throw *or* cast to the dogs, cast to the winds; sell off *or* out; throw over, jilt; part with, give away; throw to the wolves, write off, walk away from, **abandon** 370.5; remove, **eliminate** 773.5

8 **scrap, junk** <nf>, consign to the scrap heap, throw on the junk heap <nf>; superannuate, retire, pension off, put out to pasture *or* grass

9 **obsolesce,** fall into disuse, go out, pass away; be superseded; superannuate

ADJS 10 **disused, abandoned,** deserted, **discontinued,** done with, derelict; out, **out of use;** old; relinquished, resigned, renounced, abjured; decommissioned, out of commission; **outworn,** worn-out, past use, not worth saving; **obsolete,** obsolescent, life-expired, superannuated, superannuate; superseded, outdated, out-of-date, outmoded, desuete; retired, pensioned off; on the shelf; written off <nf>; antique, antiquated, old-fashioned, old

11 **discarded,** rejected, **castoff,** castaway, scrapped, junked

12 **unused,** unutilized, **unemployed,** unapplied, unexercised; in abeyance, suspended; waived; **unspent,** unexpended, unconsumed; held back, held out, put by, put aside, saved, held in reserve, in hand, spare, to spare, extra, reserve; stored 386.14; untouched, unhandled; untapped; untrodden, unbeaten; **new,** brand-new, original, pristine, virgin, fresh, fresh off the assembly line, mint, in mint condition, factory-fresh; underused, underutilized

391 USELESSNESS

NOUNS 1 **uselessness,** inutility; **needlessness,** unnecessity; unserviceability, **unusability,** unemployability, inoperativeness, inoperability, disrepair; unhelpfulness; inapplicability, unsuitability, unfitness; functionlessness;

otioseness, otiosity; redundancy, tautology; **superfluousness** 993.4; excess baggage

2 **futility,** vanity, emptiness, hollowness; **fruitlessness,** bootlessness, unprofitableness, profitlessness, unprofitability, otiosity, worthlessness, valuelessness; triviality, nugacity, nugaciousness; unproductiveness 891; **ineffectuality,** ineffectiveness, inefficacy 19.3; **impotence** 19.1; effeteness; **pointlessness,** meaninglessness, purposelessness, aimlessness, fecklessness; the absurd, absurdity; inanity, fatuity; vicious circle *or* cycle; **rat race** <nf>

3 **labor in vain,** labor lost, labor for naught; labor of Sisyphus, work of Penelope, Penelope's web; **wild-goose chase,** snipe hunt, bootless errand; waste of energy, waste of labor, waste of breath, waste of time, waste of effort *or* wasted effort, wasted breath, wasted labor; red herring; fool's errand; blind alley

4 **refuse, waste,** wastage, waste matter, waste stream, waste product, solid waste, liquid waste, wastewater, effluent, sewage, sludge; incinerator ash; industrial waste, hazardous waste, toxic waste, atomic waste, dumping; hazardous materials; medical waste; **offal; leavings,** sweepings, dust <Brit>, **scraps,** orts; **garbage,** gash <nf>, swill, pig-swill, slop, slops, hogwash <nf>; bilgewater; draff, lees, **dregs** 256.2; **offscourings,** scourings, rinsings, dishwater; parings, raspings, filings, shavings; **scum;** chaff, stubble, husks; weeds, tares; deadwood; rags, bones, wastepaper, shard, potsherd; scrap iron; slag, culm, slack

5 **rubbish, rubble, trash, junk** <nf>, shoddy, riffraff, raff <Brit nf>, **scrap,** dust <Brit>, **debris, litter,** lumber, clamjamfry <Scot>, truck <nf>

6 **trash pile,** rubbish heap, junkheap *and* junkpile <nf>, scrap heap, dustheap, dustbin, midden, kitchen midden; wasteyard, **junkyard** <nf>, scrapyard, **dump,** dumpsite, garbage dump, landfill, sanitary landfill, toxic waste dump, dumping; garbology

7 wastepaper basket, wastebasket, shitcan <nf>; litter basket, litter bin; garbage bag, garbage can, wastebin, dustbin <Brit>, trash can; Dumpster <trademark>, skip <Brit>; waste disposal unit, compactor, garbage grinder <nf>; compost, compost heap; circular file <nf>, file 13 <nf>

VERBS 8 **be useless, be futile, make no difference, cut no ice;** die aborning; **labor in vain, go on a wild-goose chase,** run in circles, go around in circles, fall by the wayside, spin one's wheels *and* bang one's head against a brick wall <nf>, beat the air, lash the waves, tilt at windmills, sow the sand, bay at the moon, waste one's effort *or* breath, preach *or* speak to the winds, beat *or* flog a dead horse, roll the stone of Sisyphus, carry coals to Newcastle, milk the ram, milk a he-goat into a sieve, pour water into a sieve, hold a farthing candle to the sun, look for a needle in a haystack, lock the barn door after the horse is stolen; attempt the impossible, spin one's wheels

ADJS **9 useless,** of no use, no go <nf>; **aimless,** meaningless, **purposeless,** of no purpose, **pointless,** feckless; **unavailing,** of no avail, failed; ineffective, **ineffectual** 19.15; impotent 19.13; **superfluous** 993.17; frustaneous; dud

10 needless, unnecessary, unessential, nonessential, **unneeded, uncalled-for,** unrequired; unrecognized, neglected; tautological, tautologic, redundant

11 worthless, valueless, good-for-nothing, good-for-naught, no-good *or* NG <nf>, no-account <nf>, dear at any price, worthless as tits on a boar <nf>, not worth a dime *or* a red cent *or* a hill of beans *or* shit *or* bubkes <nf>, not worth the paper it's written on, not worthwhile, not worth having, not worth mentioning *or* speaking of, not worth a thought, not worth a rap *or* a continental *or* a damn, not worth the powder to blow it to hell, not worth the powder and shot, not worth the pains *or* the trouble, of no earthly use, fit for the junkyard <nf>; trivial, penny-ante <nf>, nugatory, nugacious; **junk** *and* **junky** <nf>; **cheap,** shoddy, trashy, **shabby**

12 fruitless, gainless, profitless, bootless, otiose, **unprofitable,** unremunerative, nonremunerative; uncommercial; **unrewarding,** rewardless; abortive; barren, sterile, unproductive 891.4

13 vain, futile, hollow, empty, "weary, stale, flat, and unprofitable"—Shakespeare, idle, unavailing; absurd; inane, fatuous, fatuitous

14 unserviceable, unusable, unemployable, inoperative, inoperable, unworkable; out of order, out of whack *and* on the blink *and* on the fritz <nf>, in disrepair; **unhelpful,** unconducive; inapplicable; unsuitable, unfit; functionless, nonfunctional, otiose, nonutilitarian; kaput

ADVS **15 uselessly; needlessly,** unnecessarily; bootlessly, fruitlessly; **futilely, vainly;** purposelessly, to little purpose, to no purpose, **aimlessly, pointlessly,** fecklessly; tautologically

392 IMPROVEMENT

NOUNS **1 improvement, betterment,** bettering, change *or* turn for the better; melioration, **amelioration;** sea change; **mend,** mending, **amendment; progress,** progression, headway; breakthrough, quantum jump *or* leap; **advance,** advancement; upward mobility; **promotion, furtherance,** preferment; **rise,** ascent, **lift, uplift,**

uptick <nf>, upswing, uptrend, upbeat, edification; **increase** 251, upgrade, upping *and* boost *and* pickup <nf>; gentrification; **enhancement, enrichment,** good influence; euthenics, eugenics; **restoration,** revival, retro, recovery, comeback

2 development, refinement, elaboration, **perfection;** beautification, embellishment; maturation, coming-of-age, ripening, evolution, seasoning

3 cultivation, culture, refinement, polish, civility; cultivation of the mind; **civilization;** acculturation; enculturation, socialization; enlightenment, Age of Enlightenment, Age of Reason; education 928.4

4 revision, revise, revisal; revised edition; **emendation, amendment, correction, corrigenda, rectification;** editing, redaction, recension, revampment, blue-penciling; **rewrite,** rewriting, rescript, rescription <old>; **polishing,** touching up, putting on the finishing touches, putting the gloss on, finishing, perfecting, tuning, fine-tuning; retrofitting

5 reform, reformation; regeneration 858.2; **transformation; conversion** 858; makeover; reformism, meliorism; gradualism, Fabianism, revisionism; utopianism; progressiveness, progressivism, progressism; radical reform, extremism, radicalism 611.4; revolution 860; quiet revolution; perestroika

6 reformer, reformist, meliorist; gradualist, Fabian, revisionist; utopian, utopist; progressive, progressivist, progressionist, progressist; resister, passive resister; radical, extremist 611.12; revolutionary 860.3; comeback kid

VERBS **7** <get better> **improve, grow better,** look better, show improvement, **mend,** amend <old>, meliorate, ameliorate; **look up** *or* **pick up** *or* **perk up** <nf>; **develop,** shape up; **advance, progress, make progress, make headway, gain,** gain ground, go forward, get *or* go ahead, come on, come along *and* come along nicely <nf>, get along; make strides *or* rapid strides, take off *and* skyrocket <nf>, make up for lost time, turn around; straighten up and fly right <nf>; make the grade, graduate

8 rally, come about *or* round, come back, **take a favorable turn,** get over <nf>, take a turn for the better, gain strength; come a long way <nf>; **recuperate, recover** 396.20

9 improve, better, change for the better, make an improvement; transform, transfigure; vet; improve upon, refine upon, **mend, amend,** emend; meliorate, **ameliorate; advance, promote,** foster, favor, nurture, forward, bring forward; **lift,** elevate, **uplift,** raise, boost <nf>; upgrade; gentrify; **enhance, enrich,** fatten, lard <old>; make one's way, better oneself; be the making of; **reform,** put *or* set straight; reform oneself, turn over a new leaf, mend one's ways, straighten out, straighten oneself out, go straight <nf>; get it together *and* get one's ducks in a row <nf>; **civilize,** acculturate, socialize; enlighten, edify; **educate**

10 **develop,** elaborate; beautify, embellish; **cultivate;** come of age, come into its own, mature, ripen, evolve, season; gild the lily; formulate

11 **perfect, touch up,** finish, put on the finishing touches, polish *or* polish up, fine down, fine-tune <nf>, tone up, **brush up, furbish,** furbish up, spruce, **spruce up,** freshen, vamp, vamp up, rub up, brighten up, shine <nf>; retouch; **revive, renovate** 396.17; **repair, fix** 396.14; retrofit; streamline

12 **revise,** redact, recense, **revamp, rewrite,** redraft, **rework,** work over, retool; **emend, amend,** emendate, **rectify,** correct; **edit,** blue-pencil; straighten out; autocorrect

ADJS 13 **improved, bettered;** changed for the better, advanced, ameliorated, enhanced, enriched, touched up; developed, perfected; beautified, embellished; upgraded; gentrified; **reformed; transformed,** transfigured, converted; **cultivated,** cultured, **refined,** polished, emended, civilized; **educated** 928.18

14 **better,** better off, better for, all the better for; before-and-after

15 **improving, bettering;** meliorative, ameliorative, amelioratory, medial; progressive, progressing, advancing, ongoing; mending, **on the mend;** on the lift *or* rise *or* upswing *or* upbeat *or* upgrade <nf>, looking up <nf>

16 **emendatory, corrective;** revisory, revisional; reformatory, reformative, reformational; **reformist,** reformistic, progressive, progressivist, melioristic; gradualistic, Fabian, revisionist; utopian; radical 611.20; revolutionary 860.5

17 **improvable,** ameliorable, corrigible, revisable, perfectible; **emendable** 396.25; curable

393 IMPAIRMENT

NOUNS 1 **impairment, damage, injury, harm,** mischief, scathe, **hurt, detriment,** loss, weakening, sickening; **worsening,** disimprovement; disablement, incapacitation; collateral damage; encroachment, inroad, infringement 214.1; **disrepair, dilapidation,** ruinousness; breakage; **breakdown, collapse,** crash *and* crack-up <nf>; **malfunction,** glitch <nf>; bankruptcy; hurting, spoiling, ruination; sabotage, monkey-wrenching <nf>; mayhem, mutilation, crippling, hobbling,

hamstringing, laming, maiming; destruction 395; the skids <nf>

2 **corruption, pollution, contamination,** vitiation, **defilement,** fouling, befouling; **poisoning,** envenoming; infection, festering, suppuration; **perversion,** prostitution, misuse 389; denaturing, adulteration

3 **deterioration, decadence** *or* decadency, **degradation, debasement,** derogation, deformation; **degeneration,** degeneracy, degenerateness, effeteness; etiolation, loss of tone, failure of nerve; depravation, depravedness; **retrogression,** retrogradation, retrocession, **regression;** devolution, involution; demotion 447; downward mobility; **decline,** declination, declension, worsening, comedown, **descent,** downtick <nf>, downtrend, downward trend, downturn, depreciation, **decrease** 252, **drop, fall, plunge,** free-fall, falling-off, lessening, slippage, slump, lapse, fading, dying, failing, failure, wane, ebb; loss of morale; shadow of one's former self

4 **waste,** wastage, **consumption;** withering, wasting, wasting away, atrophy, wilting, marcescence; emaciation 270.6

5 **wear,** use, hard wear; **wear and tear; erosion, weathering,** ablation, ravages of time, attrition

6 **decay, decomposition, disintegration, dissolution,** resolution, degradation, biodegradation, breakup, disorganization, **corruption, spoilage, dilapidation; corrosion,** oxidation, oxidization, rust; mildew, mold 1001.2; degradability, biodegradability; radioactive decay

7 **rot, rottenness, foulness, putridness,** putridity, rancidness, rancidity, rankness, **putrefaction,** putrescence, spoilage, decay, decomposition, moldering; carrion; dry rot, wet rot

8 **wreck, ruins, ruin, total loss;** hulk, carcass, skeleton; mere wreck, wreck of one's former self, perfect wreck; nervous wreck; rattletrap

VERBS 9 **impair, damage,** endamage, **injure, harm, hurt,** irritate; **worsen,** make worse, disimprove, deteriorate, put *or* set back, aggravate, exacerbate, embitter; **weaken; dilapidate;** add insult to injury, rub salt in the wound

10 **spoil, mar,** botch, **ruin, wreck,** blight, **play havoc with; destroy** 395.10; pollute

11 <nf terms> **screw up, foul up,** fuck up, bitch up, **blow,** louse up, queer, snafu, snarl up, balls up <Brit>, bugger, bugger up, gum up, ball up, bollix, bollix up, **mess up,** hash up, muck up; play hob with, play hell with, play merry hell with, play the devil with, rain on one's picnic *or* parade; upset the apple cart, cook, sink, shoot down in flames; **total;** pulverize

12 corrupt, debase, degrade, degenerate, **deprave, debauch, defile,** violate, desecrate, profane, deflower, ravish, ravage, despoil; **contaminate,** confound, **pollute, vitiate, poison, infect, taint;** canker, ulcerate; **pervert,** warp, twist, distort; prostitute, misuse 389.4; denature; **cheapen,** devalue; coarsen, vulgarize, drag in the mud; adulterate, alloy, water, water down

13 <inflict an injury> **injure, hurt;** draw blood, wound, scotch <old>; **traumatize;** stab, stick, pierce, puncture; cut, incise, slit, slash, gash, scratch; abrade, eat away at, scuff, scrape, chafe, fret, gall, bark, skin; break, fracture, rupture; crack, chip, craze, check; lacerate, claw, tear, rip, rend; run; frazzle, fray; burn, scorch, scald; mutilate, maim, rough up <nf>, make mincemeat of, maul, batter, savage; sprain, strain, wrench; bloody; **blemish** 1004.4; **bruise, contuse,** bung *and* bung up <nf>; **buffet,** batter, bash <nf>, maul, pound, beat, beat black and blue; give a black eye; play havoc with

14 cripple, lame, maim; **hamstring,** hobble; wing; emasculate, castrate; incapacitate, **disable** 19.9

15 undermine, sap, mine, sap the foundations of, honeycomb; sabotage, monkey-wrench *and* throw *or* toss a monkey-wrench in the works <nf>, subvert

16 deteriorate, sicken, worsen, get *or* **grow worse,** get no better fast <nf>, disimprove, **degenerate;** slip back, **retrogress,** retrograde, regress, relapse, fall back; jump the track; go to the bad 395.24; let oneself go, let down, slacken; be the worse for, be the worse for wear *and* have seen better days <nf>

17 decline, sink, fail, fall, slip, fade, die, wane, ebb, subside, lapse, **run down,** go down, **go downhill, fall away, fall off,** go off <nf>, slide, slump, hit a slump, take a nose dive <nf>, go into a tailspin, take a turn for the worse; hit the skids <nf>; reach the depths, hit *or* touch bottom, hit rock bottom, have no lower to go

18 languish, pine, droop, flag, wilt; fade, fade away; **wither, shrivel,** shrink, diminish, wither *or* die on the vine, **dry up,** desiccate, wizen, wrinkle, sear; retrograde, retrogress

19 waste, waste away, wither away, atrophy, consume, consume away, erode away, emaciate, pine away; trickle *or* dribble away; run to waste, run to seed

20 wear, wear away, wear down, wear off; abrade, fret, whittle away, rub off; fray, frazzle, tatter, wear ragged; **wear out;** weather, erode, ablate

21 corrode, erode, eat, gnaw, eat into, eat away, nibble away, gnaw at the root of; canker; **oxidize, rust**

22 decay, decompose, disintegrate; biodegrade; go *or* fall into decay, go *or* fall to pieces, break up, crumble, crumble into dust; **spoil,** corrupt, canker, **go bad; rot, putrefy,** putresce; fester, suppurate, rankle <nf>; **mortify,** necrose, gangrene, sphacelate; mold, molder, molder away, rot away, rust away, mildew; gangrene

23 break, break up, fracture, **come apart,** come unstuck, **come** *or* **fall to pieces, fall apart, disintegrate;** burst, rupture; crack, split, fissure; snap; break open, give way *or* away, start, spring a leak, come apart at the seams, come unstuck <nf>

24 break down, founder, collapse; crash <nf>, cave *or* fall in, come crashing *or* tumbling down, topple, topple down *or* over, tremble *or* nod *or* totter to one's fall; totter, sway

25 get out of order, malfunction, get out of gear; get out of joint; go wrong

26 <nf terms> **get out of whack,** get out of kilter, get out of commission, go kaput, **go on the blink** *or* **fritz, go haywire,** fritz out, go blooey *or* kerflooey, give out, **break down,** pack up <Brit>, conk out

ADJS **27 impaired, damaged, hurt, injured, harmed; deteriorated, worsened,** cut to the quick, aggravated, exacerbated, irritated, embittered; weakened; **worse,** worse off, the worse for, all the worse for; imperfect; lacerated, mangled, cut, split, rent, torn, slit, slashed, mutilated, chewed-up; **broken** 802.24, **shattered, smashed,** in bits, in pieces, in shards, burst, busted <nf>, ruptured, sprung; cracked, chipped, crazed, checked; burned, scorched, scalded; **damaging, injurious,** traumatic, degenerative

28 spoiled *or* spoilt, **marred,** botched, blighted, **ruined,** wrecked; **destroyed** 395.28

29 <nf terms> **queered, screwed up, fouled up,** loused up, snafued, buggered, buggered up, gummed up, snarled up, balled up, bollixed up, **messed up,** hashed up, mucked up, botched up; beat up, clapped-out <Brit>; **totaled,** kaput, finished, packed-up <Brit>, done for, done in, cooked, sunk, shot

30 crippled, game <nf>, bad, handicapped, maimed; **lame, halt,** halting, hobbling, limping; knee-sprung; hamstrung; spavined; **disabled, incapacitated,** challenged; emasculated, castrated

31 worn, well-worn, deep-worn, worn-down, the worse for wear, dog-eared; timeworn; shopworn, shopsoiled <Brit>, shelfworn; worn to the stump, worn to the bone; **worn ragged,** worn to rags, worn to threads; **threadbare,** bare, sere <old>

32 shabby, shoddy, seedy, scruffy, **tacky** <nf>, dowdy, tatty, ratty, holey, full of holes; raggedy, raggedy-ass <nf>, **ragged, tattered, torn;** patchy; **frayed,**

frazzled; in rags, in tatters, in shreds; **out at the elbows,** out at the heels, **down-at-heel** *or* **-heels, down-at-the-heel** *or* **-heels**

33 **dilapidated, ramshackle,** decrepit, shacky, tottery, slummy <nf>, **tumbledown, broken-down, run-down,** in ruins, ruinous, ruined, derelict, gone to wrack and ruin, the worse for wear; **battered,** beaten up, **beat-up** <nf>

34 **weatherworn, weather-beaten, weathered,** weather-battered, weather-wasted, weather-eaten, weather-bitten, weather-scarred; eroded; **faded,** washed-out, bleached, blanched, etiolated

35 **wasted,** atrophied, shrunken; **withered,** sere, shriveled, wilted, wizened, dried-up, desiccated; wrinkled, wrinkled like a prune; brittle, papery, parchmenty; **emaciated** 270.20; starved, worn to a shadow, reduced to a skeleton, skin and bones, "worn to the bones"—Shakespeare

36 **worn-out, used up** <nf>, worn to a frazzle, frazzled, fit for the dust hole *or* wastepaper basket; **exhausted, tired,** fatigued, pooped <nf>, **spent,** effete, etiolated, played out, maxed-out, *ausgespielt* <Ger>, shotten <nf>, jaded, emptied, done *and* done up <nf>; **run-down,** dragged-out <nf>, laid low, at a low ebb, in a bad way, far-gone, on one's last legs

37 **in disrepair, out of order, malfunctioning,** out of working order, out of condition, out of repair, inoperative; out of tune, out of gear; out of joint; **broken** 802.24

38 <nf terms> **out of whack** *or* **kilter** *or* kelter *or* sync *or* commission, on the fritz, fritzed, on the blink, blooey, kerflooey, haywire, wonky <Brit>

39 **putrefactive,** putrefacient, rotting; **septic;** saprogenic, saprogenous; saprophilous, saprophytic, saprobic

40 **decayed, decomposed; spoiled, corrupt,** peccant, bad, **gone bad; rotten, rotting, putrid, putrefied, foul;** putrescent, **mortified,** necrosed, necrotic, sphacelated, gangrened, gangrenous; carious; cankered, ulcerated, festering, suppurating, suppurative; rotten at *or* to the core

41 **tainted, off,** blown, frowy <nf>; **stale; sour,** soured, turned; **rank,** reechy <old>, **rancid,** strong <nf>, **high,** gamy

42 **blighted, blasted, ravaged,** despoiled, blown, flyblown, wormy, weevily, maggoty; **moth-eaten, worm-eaten; moldy,** moldering, **mildewed,** smutty, smutted; **musty, fusty,** frowzy *or* frowsy, frowsty <Brit>

43 **corroded, eroded,** eaten; **rusty,** rust-eaten, rust-worn, rust-cankered

44 **corrupting, corruptive;** corrosive, corroding; erosive, eroding, **damaging, injurious** 1000.12; pollutive

45 deteriorating, worsening, disintegrating, coming apart *or* unstuck, crumbling, cracking, fragmenting, going to pieces; **decadent, degenerate,** effete; **retrogressive,** retrograde, regressive, from better to worse; **declining, sinking, failing,** falling, waning, subsiding, **slipping,** sliding, slumping; **languishing, pining,** drooping, flagging, wilting; ebbing, draining, dwindling; **wasting,** fading, fading fast, **withering,** shriveling; tabetic, marcescent

46 **on the wane, on the decline,** on the downgrade, on the downward track, on the skids <nf>; tottering, nodding to its fall, on the way out

47 degradable, biodegradable, decomposable, putrefiable, putrescible

ADVS 48 out of the frying pan into the fire, from better to worse; for the worse

394 RELAPSE

NOUNS 1 **relapse, lapse,** falling back; **reversion, regression** 859.1; **reverse, reversal,** backward deviation, devolution, **setback,** backset; **return,** recurrence, renewal, recrudescence; throwback, atavism; recadency

2 **backsliding,** backslide; **fall, fall from grace;** lapsing, recidivism, recidivation; apostasy 363.2

3 **backslider,** recidivist, reversionist; apostate 363.5

VERBS 4 **relapse, lapse, backslide,** slide back, lapse back, **slip back,** sink back, **fall back,** have a relapse, devolve, **return to, revert to,** recur to, yield again to, fall again into, recidivate; revert, **regress** 859.4; **fall, fall from grace**

ADJS 5 **relapsing, lapsing, lapsarian, backsliding,** recidivous; recadent; recrudescent; **regressive** 859.7; apostate 363.11

395 DESTRUCTION

NOUNS 1 **destruction, ruin, ruination,** rack, **rack and ruin,** blue ruin <nf>; perdition, damnation, eternal damnation; universal ruin; **wreck;** devastation, ravage, havoc, holocaust, firestorm, hecatomb, carnage, shambles, slaughter, bloodbath, **desolation; waste, consumption;** decimation; **dissolution, disintegration,** breakup, disruption, disorganization, undoing, lysis; vandalism, depredation, spoliation, despoliation, despoilment; the road to ruin *or* wrack and ruin; iconoclasm

2 **end, fate, doom,** death, death knell, bane, deathblow, death warrant, *coup de grâce* <Fr>, final blow, quietus, cutoff, end of the world, eschaton, apocalypse

3 fall, downfall, prostration; **overthrow, overturn, upset, upheaval,** *bouleversement* <Fr>; convulsion, **subversion,** sabotage, monkey-wrenching <nf>

4 debacle, disaster, cataclysm, catastrophe; breakup, breaking up; **breakdown, collapse; crash,** meltdown, smash, **smashup,** crack-up <nf>; **wreck,** wrack, shipwreck; cave-in, cave; washout; total loss, big one

5 demolition, demolishment; wrecking, wreckage, leveling, razing, flattening, smashing, tearing down, bringing to the ground; **dismantlement,** disassembly, unmaking; hatchet job

6 extinction, extermination, elimination, eradication, extirpation; rooting out, deracination, uprooting, tearing up root and branch; **annihilation,** extinguishment, **snuffing out; abolition,** abolishment; annulment, **nullification,** voiding, **negation; liquidation, purge; suppression;** choking, choking off, suffocation, stifling, strangulation; silencing; nuclear winter

7 obliteration, erasure, effacement, deletion, expunction, blot <old>, blotting, **blotting out, wiping out;** washing out *and* scrubbing <nf>, cancellation, cancel; deletion; annulment, abrogation; palimpsest, clean slate, tabula rasa

8 destroyer, ruiner, wrecker, bane, wiper-out, demolisher; **vandal,** hun; exterminator, annihilator; **iconoclast,** idoloclast; biblioclast; nihilist; terrorist, syndicalist; **bomber,** dynamiter, dynamitard; burner, arsonist; loose cannon

9 eradicator, expunger; **eraser,** rubber, India rubber, sponge; extinguisher

VERBS **10 destroy,** deal *or* unleash destruction, unleash the hurricane, nuke <nf>; **ruin,** ruinate <nf>, bring to ruin, lay in ruins, play *or* raise hob with; throw into disorder, turn upside-down, upheave; **wreck,** wrack, shipwreck; damn, seal the doom of, **condemn,** confound; **devastate, desolate,** waste, **lay waste, ravage,** havoc, wreak havoc, despoil, depredate; vandalize; **decimate;** devour, consume, engorge, gobble, gobble up, swallow up; gut, gut with fire, incinerate, vaporize, ravage with fire and sword; dissolve, lyse

11 do for, fix <nf>, settle, sink, cook *and* cook one's goose *and* cut one down to size *and* cut one off at the knees *and* pull the plug on *and* pull the rug out from under <nf>, dish, scuttle, put the kibosh on *and* put the skids under <nf>, do in, **undo,** knock in *or* on the head, poleax, torpedo, knock out, clobber, KO *and* banjax <nf>, deal a knockout blow to, zap *and* shoot down *and* shoot down in flames <nf>; break the back of; make short work of; hamstring; **defeat** 412.6

12 put an end to, make an end of, **end, finish,** finish off <nf>, put paid to <Brit>, give the *coup de grâce* <Fr> to, give the quietus to, deal a deathblow to, dispose of, get rid of, do in, do away with; cut off, take off, be the death of, sound the death knell of; put out of the way, put out of existence, **slaughter,** make away with, off *and* waste *and* blow away <nf>, kill off, strike down, **kill** 308.13; nip, nip in the bud; cut short; scrub <nf>

13 abolish, nullify, void, abrogate, annihilate, annul, tear up, repeal, revoke, negate, negative, invalidate, **undo, cancel,** cancel out, bring to naught, put *or* lay to rest

14 exterminate, eliminate, eradicate, deracinate, **extirpate, annihilate; wipe out** <nf>; cut out, root up *or* out, uproot, pull *or* pluck up by the roots, cut up root and branch, strike at the root of, lay the ax to the root of; **liquidate,** vaporize, **purge;** remove, sweep away, wash away; wipe off the map <nf>, leave no trace

15 extinguish, quench, snuff out, put out, stamp *or* trample out, trample underfoot; **smother,** choke, stifle, strangle, suffocate; silence; **suppress, quash,** squash *and* squelch <nf>, **quell,** put down

16 obliterate, expunge, efface, erase, raze <old>, blot, sponge, **wipe out,** wipe off the map, rub out, **blot out,** sponge out, wash away; cancel, strike out, cross out, scratch, scratch out, rule out; blue-pencil; **delete** *or* dele, kill; leave on the cutting-room floor <nf>

17 demolish, wreck, total *and* rack up <nf>, undo, unbuild, unmake, **dismantle, disassemble; take apart, tear apart, tear asunder, rend, take** *or* **pull** *or* **pick** *or* **tear to pieces,** pull in pieces, tear to shreds *or* rags *or* tatters; sunder, cleave, **split; disintegrate, fragment,** break to pieces, make mincemeat of, reduce to rubble, atomize, pulverize, **smash,** shatter 802.13

18 blow up, blast, spring, explode, blow to pieces *or* bits *or* smithereens *or* kingdom come, bomb, bombard, blitz; mine; self-destruct

19 raze, rase, **fell, level,** flatten, smash, prostrate, raze to the ground *or* dust; steamroller, bulldoze; **pull down, tear down, take down,** bring down, bring down about one's ears, bring tumbling *or* crashing down, break down, throw down, cast down, beat down, knock down *or* over; cut down, chop down, mow down; blow down; burn down

20 overthrow, overturn; upset, overset, upend, **subvert,** throw down *or* over; undermine, honeycomb, **sap,** sap the foundations, weaken

21 overwhelm, whelm, swamp, engulf; inundate

22 <be destroyed> fall, fall to the ground, tumble,

come tumbling *or* crashing down, topple, tremble *or* nod to its fall, bite the dust <nf>; **break up,** crumble, crumble to dust, disintegrate, go *or* fall to pieces; go by the board, go out the window *or* up the spout <nf>, go down the tube *or* tubes <nf>; self-destruct

23 **perish, expire, succumb, die, cease, end,** come to an end, go, pass, **pass away, vanish, disappear,** fade away, run out, peg *or* conk out <nf>, come to nothing *or* naught, be no more, be done for; be all over with, be all up with <nf>

24 **go to ruin, go to rack and ruin,** go to rack and manger <old>, **go to the bad,** go wrong, **go to the dogs** *or* **pot** <nf>, go *or* run to seed, go to hell in a handbasket <nf>, go to the deuce *or* devil <nf>, go to hell <nf>, go to the wall, go to perdition *or* glory <nf>; go up <nf>, go under; **go to smash,** go to shivers, go to smithereens <nf>

25 **drive to ruin,** drive to the bad, **force to the wall,** drive to the dogs <nf>, hound *or* harry to destruction

ADJS 26 **destructive,** destroying; **ruinous,** ruining; demolishing, demolitionary; **disastrous, calamitous, cataclysmic,** cataclysmal, **catastrophic;** fatal, fateful, doomful, baneful; bad news <nf>; **deadly;** consumptive, consuming, withering; **devastating, desolating,** ravaging, wasting, wasteful, spoliative, depredatory; vandalic, vandalish, vandalistic; subversive, subversionary; nihilist, nihilistic; suicidal, self-destructive; fratricidal, internecine, internecive

27 **exterminative,** exterminatory, **annihilative, eradicative,** extirpative, extirpatory; all-destroying, all-devouring, all-consuming

28 **ruined, destroyed, wrecked, blasted, undone,** down-and-out, broken, bankrupt; spoiled; irremediable 125.15; fallen, overthrown; **devastated, desolated, ravaged,** blighted, wasted; ruinous, in ruins, gutted; gone to rack and ruin; obliterated, annihilated, liquidated, vaporized; doomed, not long for this world

29 <nf terms> **shot, done for,** done in, finished, *ausgespielt* <Ger>, kaput; gone to pot, gone to the dogs, gone to hell in a handbasket, phut, belly up, blooey, kerflooey, dead in the water, washed up, all washed up, history, **dead meat, down the tube** *or* **tubes,** zapped, nuked, tapped out, wiped out, rubbed out, bust

396 RESTORATION

NOUNS 1 **restoration,** restoral, **restitution, reestablishment, redintegration, reinstatement,** reinstation, reformation <old>, reinvestment, reinvestiture, instauration, reversion, reinstitution, reconstitution, recomposition; replacement; **rehabilitation,** redevelopment, reconversion, reactivation, reenactment; improvement 392; return to normal

2 **reclamation, recovery, retrieval,** salvage, salving; redemption, salvation

3 **revival,** revivification, revivescence *or* revivescency, **renewal,** resurrection, resuscitation, restimulation, reanimation, resurgence, recrudescence, comeback; retro; **refreshment** 9; second wind; renaissance, renascence, **rebirth,** new birth; **rejuvenation,** rejuvenescence, second youth, new lease on life; **regeneration,** regeneracy, regenerateness; regenesis, palingenesis, reanimation, reincarnation; new hope, second chance

4 **renovation, renewal;** refreshment; **redecorating; reconditioning,** furbishment, refurbishment, refurbishing; retread *and* retreading <nf>; face-lifting *or* face-lift; slum clearance, urban renewal; remodeling; overhauling

5 **reconstruction, re-creation, remaking,** recomposition, remodeling, **rebuilding,** refabrication, refashioning; reassembling, reassembly; reformation; restructuring, perestroika

6 **reparation, repair,** repairing, **fixing, mending,** making *or* setting right, repairwork; servicing, maintenance; **overhaul,** overhauling; troubleshooting <nf>; **rectification, correction, remedy;** damage control; **redress,** making *or* setting right, amends, satisfaction, compensation, **recompense;** emendation

7 **cure, curing, healing, remedy** 86; **therapy** 91

8 **recovery, rally, comeback** <nf>, return, upturn; **recuperation, convalescence**

9 **restorability, reparability,** curability, recoverability, reversibility, remediability, retrievability, redeemability, salvageability, corrigibility

10 **mender, fixer,** doctor <nf>, restorer, renovator, repairer, **repairman, repairwoman,** handyman, maintenance man *or* woman, **serviceman, servicewoman;** trouble man *and* troubleshooter <nf>; Mr Fixit *and* little Miss Fixit <nf>; **mechanic** *or* mechanician; tinker, tinkerer; cobbler; salvor, salvager

VERBS 11 **restore, put back, replace, return,** place in *status quo ante;* **reestablish,** redintegrate, reform <old>, reenact, **reinstate,** restitute; **reinstall,** reinvest, revest, reinstitute, reconstitute, recompose, recruit, **rehabilitate,** redevelop; reintegrate, reconvert, reactivate; make as good as new; refill, replenish; give back 481.4

12 redeem, reclaim, recover, retrieve; ransom; rescue; salvage, salve; recycle; win back, **recoup**

13 remedy, rectify, correct, right, patch up, emend, amend, **redress,** make good *or* right, **put right,** set right, put *or* set to rights, put *or* set straight, set up, heal up, knit up, make all square; pay reparations, give satisfaction, requite, restitute, recompense, compensate, remunerate

14 repair, mend, fix, fix up <nf>, do up, doctor <nf>, put in repair, put in shape, set to rights, put in order *or* condition; **condition, recondition,** commission, put in commission, ready; **service, overhaul;** patch, **patch up;** tinker, tinker up, fiddle, fiddle around; cobble; sew up, darn; recap, retread

15 cure, work a cure, recure <old>, **remedy, heal, restore to health,** heal up, knit up, bring round *or* around, pull round *or* around, give a new *or* fresh lease on life, make better, make well, fix up, pull through, set on one's feet *or* legs; snatch from the jaws of death

16 revive, revivify, renew, recruit; **reanimate,** reinspire, **regenerate, rejuvenate, revitalize,** put *or* breathe new life into, restimulate; **refresh** 9.2; **resuscitate,** bring to, bring round *or* around; recharge; **resurrect,** bring back, call back, recall to life, raise from the dead; rewarm, warm up *or* over; **rekindle,** relight, reheat the ashes, stir the embers; restore to health

17 renovate, renew; recondition, refit, revamp, furbish, refurbish; refresh, face-lift; fix up, upgrade

18 remake, reconstruct, remodel, recompose, reconstitute, re-create, **rebuild,** refabricate, re-form, refashion, reassemble

19 recuperate, recruit, **gain strength,** recruit *or* renew one's strength, catch one's breath, **get better; improve** 392.7; **rally, pick up,** perk up *and* brace up <nf>, bounce back, take a new *or* fresh lease on life; **take a favorable turn,** turn the corner, be out of the woods, take a turn for the better; **convalesce;** sleep it off

20 recover, rally, revive, get well, get over, pull through, pull round *or* around, come round *or* around <nf>, come back <nf>, make a comeback <nf>; get about, get back in shape <nf>, be oneself again, feel like a new person; **survive,** weather the storm, live through; **come to,** come to oneself, show signs of life; come up smiling <nf>, get one's second wind; come *or* pull *or* snap out of it <nf>

21 heal, heal over, close up, scab over, cicatrize, granulate; heal *or* right itself; **knit, set**

ADJS **22 tonic, restorative, restitutive,** restitutory, restimulative; analeptic; reparative, reparatory; sanative; remedial, **curative** 86.39

23 recuperative, recuperatory; reviviscent; **convalescent;** buoyant, resilient, elastic

24 renascent, redivivus, redux, resurrected, renewed, revived, reborn, resurgent, recrudescent, reappearing, phoenix-like; like new; oneself again

25 remediable, curable; medicable, treatable; emendable, amendable, **correctable,** rectifiable, corrigible; **improvable,** ameliorable; **reparable,** repairable, **mendable, fixable;** restorable, recoverable, salvageable, retrievable, reversible, reclaimable, recyclable, redeemable; renewable; sustainable

397 PRESERVATION

NOUNS **1 preservation,** preserval, **conservation, saving, salvation,** salvage, **keeping, safekeeping,** maintenance, upkeep, support, service; custody, custodianship, guardianship, curatorship; protectiveness, protection 1008; conservationism, environmental conservation, environmentalism, ecology; nature conservation *or* conservancy, soil conservation, forest conservation, forest management, wildlife conservation, stream conservation, water conservation, wetlands conservation; salvage; self-preservation

2 food preservation; storage, retention; **curing,** seasoning, salting, brining, pickling, marinating, corning; **drying,** dry-curing, jerking; dehydration, anhydration, evaporation, desiccation; **smoking,** fuming, smoke-curing, kippering; **refrigeration,** freezing, quick-freezing, blast-freezing, deep-freezing; freeze-drying, lyophilization; irradiation; **canning,** tinning <Brit>; bottling, processing, packaging; irradiation, sterilization

3 embalming, mummification; taxidermy, stuffing; tanning

4 preservative, preservative medium; salt, brine, vinegar, formaldehyde, formalin *or* formol, embalming fluid, food additive, MSG *or* monosodium glutamate

5 preserver, saver, conservator, keeper, safekeeper; taxidermist; lifesaver, rescuer, deliverer, savior; **conservationist,** preservationist; National Wildlife Service, Audubon Society, Sierra Club, Nature Conservancy; **ranger, forest ranger,** Smokey the Bear, fire warden, game warden

6 life preserver, life jacket, life vest, life belt, cork jacket, Mae West <nf>; life buoy, life ring, buoy, flotation device, floating cushion; man-overboard buoy; water wings; breeches buoy; lifeboat, life raft, rubber dinghy <Brit>; life net; lifeline; safety belt; **parachute;** ejection seat *or* ejector seat, ejection capsule

7 preserve, reserve, reservation; park, paradise; national park, state park; national seashore; forest preserve *or* reserve, arboretum; national *or* state forest; wilderness preserve; Indian reservation; **refuge, sanctuary** 1009.1, game preserve *or* reserve, bird sanctuary, wildlife sanctuary *or* preserve; museum, library 558, archives 549.2, bank, store 386; protected area

VERBS **8 preserve, conserve, save,** spare; **keep,** keep safe, keep inviolate *or* intact; patent, copyright, register; not endanger, not destroy; not use up, not waste, not expend; **guard, protect** 1008.18; **maintain, sustain,** uphold, support, **keep up,** keep alive

9 preserve, cure, season, salt, brine, marinate *or* marinade, pickle, corn, **dry, dry-cure,** jerk, dry-salt; dehydrate, anhydrate, evaporate, desiccate; vacuum-pack; **smoke,** fume, **smoke-cure,** smoke-dry, kipper; **refrigerate,** freeze, quick-freeze, blast-freeze, keep on ice; freeze-dry, lyophilize; irradiate

10 embalm, mummify; stuff; tan

11 put up, put by, do up; **can,** tin <Brit>, bottle

ADJS **12 preservative,** preservatory, conservative, conservatory; custodial, curatorial; **conservational,** conservationist; preserving, conserving, saving, salubrious, keeping, eco-friendly, environment-friendly; **protective** 1008.23

13 preserved, conserved, **kept,** saved, spared; protected 1008.21; **untainted, unspoiled;** intact, all in one piece, undamaged 1002.8; **well-preserved,** well-conserved, **well-kept,** in a good state of preservation, none the worse for wear; embalmed, laid up in lavender, mummified, stuffed

398 RESCUE

NOUNS **1 rescue, deliverance,** delivery, **saving;** lifesaving; **extrication, release, freeing, liberation** 431; **bailout; salvation,** salvage, **redemption,** ransom; **recovery, retrieval;** good riddance; 911

2 rescuer, lifesaver, lifeguard; coast guard, lifesaving service, air-sea rescue; emergency medical technician *or* EMT; savior 592.2; lifeboat; salvager, salvor; savior; emancipator

VERBS **3 rescue,** come to the rescue, **deliver, save,** be the saving of, save by the bell, **redeem,** ransom, **salvage; recover, retrieve** 481.6; **free,** set free, **release, extricate,** extract, **liberate** 431.4; snatch from the jaws of death; save one's bacon *and* save one's neck *or* ass *and* bail one out <nf>

ADJS **4 rescuable, savable;** redeemable; deliverable, extricable; salvageable; fit for release

399 WARNING

NOUNS **1 warning, caution,** caveat, **admonition,** monition, admonishment; **notice,** notification;

word to the wise, word of advice, *verbum sapienti* <L>, verb sap, enough said; **hint,** broad hint, measured words, flea in one's ear <nf>, little birdy <nf>, kick under the table; tip-off <nf>; **lesson,** object lesson, **example,** deterrent example, warning piece; moral, moral of the story; **alarm** 400; code red; final warning *or* notice, ultimatum; **threat** 514

2 forewarning, prewarning, **premonition,** precautioning; advance warning *or* notice, plenty of notice, prenotification; presentiment, hunch *and* funny feeling <nf>, **foreboding; portent;** evil portent

3 warning sign, premonitory sign, danger sign; preliminary sign *or* signal *or* token; **symptom,** early symptom, premonitory symptom, prodrome, prodroma, prodromata <pl>; **precursor** 816; **omen** 133.3,5; **handwriting on the wall;** straw in the wind; gathering clouds, clouds on the horizon; thundercloud, thunderhead; falling barometer *or* glass; storm *or* stormy petrel, **red light,** red flag, Very lights; quarantine flag, yellow flag, yellow jack; death's-head, skull *and* crossbones; **high sign** <nf>, **warning signal, alert,** red alert; siren, klaxon, tocsin, alarm bell, burglar alarm, car horn, fog horn; tattoo; early warning system

4 warner, cautioner, admonisher, monitor; prophet *or* messenger of doom, Cassandra, Jeremiah, Nostradamus, Ezekiel; **lookout, lookout man; sentinel, sentry; signalman,** signaler, flagman; lighthouse keeper

VERBS **5 warn, caution, advise, admonish; give warning,** give fair warning, utter a caveat, address a warning to, put a flea in one's ear <nf>, drop a hint, have a word with one, say a word to the wise; tip *and* tip off <nf>; notify, put on notice, give notice *or* advance notice *or* advance word; tell once *and* for all; issue an ultimatum; **threaten** 514.2; **alert,** warn against, put on one's guard, warn away *or* off; **give the high sign** <nf>; **put on alert,** cry havoc, sound the alarm 400.3

6 forewarn, prewarn, precaution, premonish; prenotify, tell in advance, give advance notice; **portend, forebode;** give a head's up

ADJS **7 warning,** cautioning, **cautionary; monitory,** monitorial, admonitory, admonishing, minatory; notifying, notificational, exemplary, deterrent

8 forewarning, premonitory; portentous, foreboding 133.16; **precautionary,** precautional; en garde; precursive, precursory, forerunning, prodromal, prodromic

400 ALARM

NOUNS **1 alarm,** alarum, alarm signal *or* bell, **alert;** hue and cry; **red light,** danger signal, amber light, caution signal; **alarm button,** panic button <nf>, nurse's signal; **beeper,** buzzer; note of alarm; air-raid alarm; all clear; tocsin, alarm bell; signal of distress, SOS, Mayday, upside-down flag, flare; *sécurité* <Fr>, notice to mariners; storm warning, storm flag *or* pennant *or* cone, hurricane watch *or* warning *or* advisory, gale warning, small-craft warning *or* advisory, tornado watch *or* warning, winter storm watch *or* advisory, winter weather advisory, severe thunderstorm watch *or* warning; fog signal *or* alarm, foghorn, fog bell; burglar alarm; car alarm; fire alarm, fire bell, fire flag, still alarm; siren, whistle, horn, klaxon, hooter <Brit>; police whistle, watchman's rattle; alarm clock; five-minute gun, two-minute gun; lighthouse, beacon; blinking light, flashing light, occulting light

2 **false alarm,** cry of wolf; bugbear, bugaboo; bogy; flash in the pan *and* dud <nf>; false positive

VERBS 3 **alarm, alert, arouse,** put on the alert; **warn** 399.5; fly storm warnings; **sound the alarm,** give *or* raise *or* beat *or* turn in an alarm, ring *or* sound the tocsin, cry havoc, raise a hue *and* cry; give a false alarm, cry before one is hurt, **cry wolf;** frighten *or* scare out of one's wits *or* to death, **frighten,** startle 131.8

ADJS 4 **alarmed, aroused;** alerted; frit <Brit nf>, frightened to death *or* out of one's wits, **frightened; startled** 131.13

401 HASTE

<rapidity of action>

NOUNS 1 **haste, hurry, scurry, rush, race,** speed, dash, drive, scuttle, scamper, **scramble,** hustle <nf>, **bustle,** flutter, **flurry,** hurry-scurry, helter-skelter; no time to be lost; shotgun approach; express lane

2 **hastiness, hurriedness,** quickness, swiftness, expeditiousness, alacrity, promptness 330.3; **speed** 174.1; furiousness, feverishness; **precipitousness,** precipitance *or* precipitancy, precipitation; rapidity; suddenness, abruptness; **impetuousness** 365.2, impetuosity, **impulsiveness, rashness** 493, impulsivity; eagerness, zealousness, **overeagerness, overzealousness**

3 **hastening, hurrying,** festination, speeding, forwarding, quickening, hotfooting, **acceleration;** forced march, double time, double-quick time, double-quick; fast-forward; skedaddle <nf>

VERBS 4 **hasten,** haste, **hurry, accelerate, speed,** speed up, **hurry up,** hustle up <nf>, **rush,** quicken, hustle <nf>, bustle, bundle, precipitate, forward; **dispatch, expedite; whip,** whip along, spur, **urge** 375.14,16; push, press; crowd, stampede; **hurry on,** hasten on, drive on, hie on, push on, press on;

hurry along, lollop <chiefly Brit>, rush along, speed along, **speed on its way; push through,** railroad <nf>, steamroll

5 **make haste, hasten,** festinate, **hurry, hurry up, race, run,** post, **rush, chase, tear, dash,** spurt, leap, plunge, **scurry,** hurry-scurry, **scamper, scramble, scuttle, hustle** <nf>, bundle, **bustle;** bestir oneself, move quickly 174.9; make for, hurry on, dash on, press *or* push on, crowd; double-time, go at the double; break one's neck *or* fall all over oneself <nf>; lose no time, not lose a moment; rush through, romp through, hurry through; dash off; make short *or* fast work of, make the best of one's time *or* way, think on one's feet, make up for lost time; do on the run *or* on the fly

6 <nf terms> **step on it, snap to it,** hop to it, hotfoot, bear down on it, shake it up, **get moving** *or* **going,** get a move on, get cracking <chiefly Brit>, get *or* shake the lead out, get the lead out of one's ass, get one's ass in gear, give it the gun, hump, hump it, hump oneself, shag ass, tear ass, **get a hustle** *or* **wiggle on,** stir one's stumps, not spare the horses, barrel along, tear off, make tracks

7 **rush into, plunge into,** dive into, plunge, plunge ahead *or* headlong, cannonball; **not stop to think,** go off half-cocked *or* at half cock <nf>, leap before one looks, cross a bridge before one comes to it

8 **be in a hurry,** be under the gun <nf>, have no time to lose *or* spare, not have a moment to spare, hardly have time to breathe, work against time *or* the clock, work under pressure, have a deadline, do at the last moment

ADJS 9 **hasty, hurried,** festinate, **quick,** flying, **expeditious,** prompt 330.18; quick-and-dirty <nf>, **immediate,** instant, on the spot, precipitant; onrushing, **swift, speedy; urgent;** furious, feverish; slap-bang, slapdash, **cursory,** passing, cosmetic, snap <nf>, superficial; spur-of-the-moment, last-minute

10 **precipitate,** precipitant, precipitous; **sudden,** abrupt; **impetuous, impulsive, rash;** headlong, breakneck; breathless, panting

11 **hurried, rushed,** pushed, pressed, railroaded, crowded, **pressed for time,** hard-pushed *or* -pressed, hard-run; double-time, double-quick, on *or* at the double; fool-hasty

ADVS 12 **hastily, hurriedly, quickly; expeditiously,** promptly, with dispatch; all in one breath, in one word, in two words; apace, amain, hand over fist, **immediately,** instantly, in a second *or* split second *or* jiffy, at once, as soon as possible *or* **ASAP; swiftly, speedily,** on *or* at fast-forward; with haste, with great *or* all haste, in *or* with a rush, in a mad rush, at fever pitch; furiously, feverishly, in a sweat *or* lather of haste, hotfoot; by forced marches; **helter-skelter, hurry-scurry,** pellmell; slapdash, cursorily, superficially, on the run *or* fly, in passing, on the spur of the moment

13 **posthaste,** in posthaste; post, express; by express, by airmail, by return mail, by express mail; by cable, by telegraph, by fax

14 **in a hurry, in haste,** in hot haste, in all haste; in short order; against time, against the clock

15 **precipitately,** precipitantly, precipitously, slap-bang; **suddenly,** abruptly; **impetuously, impulsively, rashly; headlong,** headfirst, headforemost, head over heels, heels over head <old>, *à corps perdu* <Fr>

INTERJS 16 **make haste!,** make it quick!, **hurry up!; now!; at once!,** rush!, immediate!, **urgent!,** instanter!; **step lively!,** look alive!, on the double!

17 <nf terms> **step on it!,** snap to it!, **make it snappy!, get a move on!,** get a wiggle on!, **chop-chop!, shake a leg!,** stir your stumps!, get the lead out!, **get moving!, get going!,** get cracking!, get with it!, hop to it!, move your tail!, move your fanny!, get on the ball!, don't spare the horses!

402 LEISURE

NOUNS 1 **leisure, ease, convenience,** freedom; retirement, semiretirement; rest, repose 20; **free time, spare time,** goof-off time <nf>, downtime, odd moments, idle hours; time to spare *or* burn *or* kill, time on one's hands, time at one's disposal *or* command, time to oneself; time, one's own sweet time <nf>; breathing room; all the time in the world; time off, holiday, vacation, furlough, sabbatical, leave; break, recess, breather, coffee break; day of rest; letup <nf>; couch potato

2 **leisureliness, unhurriedness,** unhastiness, hastelessness, relaxedness; *dolce far niente* <Ital>; **inactivity** 331; **slowness** 175; otiosity; deliberateness, deliberation; contentment

VERBS 3 **have time,** have time enough, have time to spare, have plenty of time, have nothing but time, be in no hurry; lounge, loll

4 **take one's leisure,** take one's ease, **take one's time, take one's own sweet time** <nf>, do at one's leisure *or* convenience *or* pleasure; go slow 175.6; ride the gravy train *and* lead the life of Riley <nf>, take time to smell the flowers *or* roses; put one's feet up, be a couch potato

ADJS 5 **leisure, leisured;** idle, unoccupied, free, open, spare; retired, semiretired, unemployed, in retirement; otiose; on vacation, on holiday; after-dinner

6 **leisurely, unhurried,** laid-back <nf>, unhasty, hasteless, easy, relaxed; sluggish, lazy; deliberate; inactive 331.17; **slow** 175.10

ADVS 7 **at leisure, at one's leisure, at one's convenience,** at one's own sweet time <nf>, when one gets around to it, when it is handy, when one has the time, when one has a minute to spare, when one has a moment to call one's own

INTERJS 8 easy does it!, take it easy!

403 ENDEAVOR

NOUNS 1 **endeavor,** effort, striving, struggle, strain; **all-out effort,** best effort, college try *or* old college try <nf>, valiant effort; **exertion** 725; determination, resolution 359; **enterprise** 330.7

2 **attempt, trial, effort, essay,** assay <old>, first attempt, *coup d'essai* <Fr>; **endeavor, undertaking;** approach, move; coup, stroke 328.3, step; gambit, offer, **bid,** strong bid; experiment, tentative; tentation, trial and error

3 <nf terms> **try, whack, fling, shot, crack,** bash, belt, go, stab, leap, lick, rip, ripple, cut, hack, smack; last shot, swan song

4 **one's best, one's level best, one's utmost,** one's damndest *or* darndest <nf>, one's best effort *or* endeavor, the best one can, the best one knows how, all one can do, all one's got, all one's got in one, one's all <nf>, the top of one's bent, as much as in one lies

VERBS 5 **endeavor, strive, struggle,** strain, sweat, sweat blood, labor, get one's teeth into, come to grips with, take it on, make an all-out effort, move heaven *and* earth, **exert oneself,** apply oneself, use some elbow grease <nf>; spend oneself; seek, study, aim; resolve, be determined 359.8

6 **attempt, try, essay,** assay, offer; try one's hand *or* wings, try it on <chiefly Brit>, set about; **undertake** 404.3, **approach,** come to grips with, engage, take the bull by the horns; venture, venture on *or* upon, chance; **make an attempt *or* effort,** lift a finger *or* hand

7 <nf terms> **tackle, take on, make a try, give a try,** have a go <chiefly Brit>, take a shot *or* stab *or* crack *or* try *or* whack at; try on for size, **go for it,** go for the brass ring, **have a fling *or* go at,** give a fling *or* a go *or* a whirl, **make a stab at,** have a shot *or* stab *or* crack *or* try *or* whack at

8 **try to,** try and <nf>, **attempt to, endeavor to,** strive to, seek to, study to, aim to, venture to, dare to, pretend to

9 **try for, strive for,** strain for, struggle for, contend for, pull for <nf>, bid for, make a bid *or* strong bid for, make a play for <nf>

10 **see what one can do,** see what can be done, see if one can do, do what one can, use one's endeavor; try anything once; **try one's hand,** try one's luck, tempt fate; make a cautious *or* tentative move,

experiment, feel one's way, test the waters, run it up the flagpole <nf>

11 **make a special effort, go out of the way,** go out of one's way, take special pains, **put oneself out,** put oneself out of the way, lay oneself out *and* fall *or* bend *or* lean over backward <nf>, fall all over oneself, trouble oneself, **go to the trouble,** take trouble, **take pains,** redouble one's efforts

12 **try hard, push** <nf>, make a bold push, **put one's back to *or* into,** put one's heart into, try until one is blue in the face, die trying, **try and try;** try, try again; exert oneself 725.9

13 **do one's best *or* level best, do one's utmost,** try one's best *or* utmost, **do all *or* everything one can,** do the best one can, **do the best one knows how,** do all in one's power, do as much as in one lies, do what lies in one's power, do one's damnedest <nf>; put all one's strength into, put one's whole soul in, **strain every nerve; give it one's all**, go flat out <nf>; go for broke; be on one's mettle, **die trying**

14 <nf terms> **knock oneself out, break one's neck,** break *or* bust one's balls, bust a gut, bust one's ass *or* hump, rupture oneself, do it *or* know why not, do it *or* break a leg, do it *or* bust a gut, do *or* try one's damndest *or* darndest, go all out, go the limit, go for broke, shoot the works, give it all one's got, give it one's best shot, go for it

15 **make every effort, spare no effort or pains, go all lengths, go to great lengths,** go the whole length, go through fire *and* water, not rest, not relax, not slacken, move heaven *and* earth, leave no stone unturned, leave no avenue unexplored

ADJS 16 trial, tentative, experimental; venturesome, willing; determined, resolute 359.11; utmost, damndest

ADVS 17 **out for,** out to, trying for, **on the make** <nf>

18 **at the top of one's bent,** to one's utmost, as far as possible

404 UNDERTAKING

NOUNS 1 **undertaking, enterprise, operation,** work, **venture, project,** proposition *and* deal <nf>; matter at hand; **program, plan** 381; **affair, business, matter, task** 724.2, concern, interest; **initiative,** effort, attempt 403.2; **action** 328.3; **engagement, contract, obligation,** mission statement, **commitment** 436.2; *démarche* <Fr>

2 **adventure, emprise, mission;** quest, pilgrimage; expedition, exploration, escapade

VERBS 3 **undertake, assume,** accept, **take on, take upon oneself,** take in hand, take upon one's shoulders, take up, sign up, go with, **tackle,** attack; engage *or* contract *or* obligate *or* commit oneself;

put *or* set *or* **turn one's hand to, engage in, devote oneself to, apply oneself to,** betake oneself to <old>, address oneself to, give oneself up to; join oneself to, associate oneself with, take in hand, **come aboard** <nf>; busy oneself with 724.11; **take up,** move into, go into, **go in *or* out for** <nf>, **enter on *or* upon,** proceed to, embark in *or* upon, **venture upon,** go upon, launch, set forward, get going, get under way, initiate; set about, go about, lay about, go to do; **go *or* swing into action, set to, turn to, buckle to, fall to; pitch into** <nf>, plunge into, fall into, **launch into *or* upon;** go at, set at, have at <nf>, knuckle *or* buckle down to; put one's hand to the plow, put *or* lay one's shoulder to the wheel; take the bull by the horns; **endeavor, attempt**; dare, take a shot at

4 **have in hand, have one's hands in,** have on one's hands *or* shoulders

5 **be in progress *or* process,** be on the anvil, be in the fire, be in the works *or* hopper *or* pipeline <nf>, **be under way**

6 **bite off more than one can chew** <nf>, take on too much, overextend *or* overreach oneself, have too many irons in the fire, have too much on one's plate, stretch oneself too thin

ADJS 7 **undertaken, assumed,** accepted, **taken on** <nf>; **ventured,** attempted, chanced; **in hand,** on the anvil, in the fire, **in progress *or* process,** on one's plate, in the works *or* hopper *or* pipeline <nf>, on the agenda, **under way**; contractual

8 **enterprising,** venturesome, adventurous, plucky, keen, eager; resourceful, ambitious; pioneering, ground-breaking; avant-garde

405 PREPARATION

NOUNS 1 **preparation,** preparing, prep *and* prepping <nf>, **readying,** getting *or* making ready, makeready, taking measures; warm-up, getting in shape *or* condition; mobilization; walk-up, **run-up; prearrangement** 965, lead time, advance notice, warning, advance warning, alerting; **planning** 381.1; trial, dry run, **tryout** 942.3; **provision, arrangement;** preparatory *or* preliminary act *or* measure *or* step; **preliminary, preliminaries;** clearing the decks <nf>; **grounding,** propaedeutic, preparatory study *or* instruction, preparatory *or* prep school; basic training, familiarization, briefing; prerequisite; processing, treatment, pretreatment; equipment 385; training 568.3; manufacture; **spadework,** groundwork, foundation 901.6; pioneering, trailblazing, pushing the envelope <nf>; all-nighter

2 **fitting,** checking the fit, fit, fitting out; **conditioning; adaptation, adjustment,** tuning;

qualification, capacitation, enablement; **equipment, furnishing** 385.1

3 <a preparation> **concoction,** decoction, *decoctum* <L>, brew, **confection;** solution; **composition, mixture** 797.5, combination 805

4 **preparedness, readiness; fitness,** fittedness, suitedness, suitableness, **suitability;** condition, trim; **qualification,** qualifiedness, credentials, record, track record <nf>; **competence** *or* competency, **ability, capability, proficiency,** mastery; ripeness, maturity, seasoning, fitness, tempering; emergency preparedness

5 **preparer,** preparator, preparationist; trainer, coach, instructor, mentor, teacher, tutor; **trailblazer, pathfinder; forerunner** 816.1; **paver of the way,** pioneer

VERBS 6 **prepare, make** *or* **get ready,** prep <nf>, do the prep work, trim <old>, **ready, fix** <nf>; provide <old>, **arrange; make preparations** *or* **arrangements,** take measures, sound the note of preparation, clear the decks <nf>, clear for action, settle preliminaries, tee up <nf>; mobilize, marshal, deploy, marshal *or* deploy one's forces *or* resources; **prearrange; plan; try out** 942.8; fix *or* ready up <nf>, put in *or* into shape; dress; treat, pretreat, process; cure, tan, taw; map out, sketch out, outline

7 **make up, get up, fix up** *and* rustle up <nf>; **concoct,** decoct, brew; **compound, compose, put together, mix;** make

8 **fit, condition, adapt, adjust,** suit, tune, attune, put in tune *or* trim *or* working order; customize; **qualify,** enable, capacitate; **equip,** fit out, supply, **furnish** 385.7,8

9 **prime, load,** charge, cock, set, precondition; wind, wind up; steam up, get up steam, warm up

10 **prepare to, get ready to,** get set for <nf>, fix to <nf>; be about to, be on the point of; ready oneself to, hold oneself in readiness

11 **prepare for, provide for,** arrange for, make arrangements *or* dispositions for, look to, look out for, see to, **make provision** *or* **due provision for;** provide against, make sure against, forearm, **provide for** *or* **against a rainy day,** prepare for the evil day; lay in provisions, lay up a store, keep as a nest egg, save to fall back upon, lay by, husband one's resources, salt *or* squirrel something away; set one's house in order, line up one's ducks

12 **prepare the way, pave the way,** smooth the path *or* road, **clear the way,** open the way, open the door to; build a bridge; **break the ice;** pioneer, go in advance, be the point, push the envelope, **blaze the trail; prepare the ground,** cultivate the soil, sow the seed; do the spadework, lay the groundwork *or* foundation, lay the first stone, provide the basis; lead up to

13 **prepare oneself,** brace oneself, **get ready, get set** <nf>, put one's house in order, strip for action, get into shape *or* condition, roll up one's sleeves, spit on one's hands, limber up, warm up, flex one's muscles, gird up one's loins, buckle on one's armor, get into harness, shoulder arms; sharpen one's tools, whet the knife *or* sword; psych oneself up <nf>; do one's homework; get one's house in order; **run up to,** build up to, gear up, tool up, rev up

14 **be prepared, be ready,** stand by, stand ready, hold oneself in readiness, "put your trust in God, my boys, and keep your powder dry"—Cromwell

15 <be fitted> **qualify, measure up,** meet the requirements, check out <nf>, have the credentials *or* qualifications *or* prerequisites; be up to *and* be just the ticket *and* fill the bill <nf>

ADJS 16 **prepared, ready,** well-prepared, prepped <nf>, in readiness *or* ready state, all ready, good *and* ready, prepared *and* ready; psyched *or* pumped up <nf>, eager, keen, champing at the bit; alert, vigilant 339.13; **ripe, mature; set** *and* **all set** <nf>, on the mark *and* teed up <nf>; about to, fixing to <nf>; **prearranged; planned; primed,** loaded, cocked, **loaded for bear** <nf>; familiarized, briefed, informed, put into the picture <Brit nf>; groomed, coached; ready for anything; in the saddle, booted *and* spurred; armed *and* ready, in arms, up in arms, **armed** 460.14; in battle array, mobilized; **provided, equipped** 385.13; dressed; treated, pretreated, processed; cured, tanned, tawed; **readied, available** 221.12

17 **fitted, adapted, adjusted, suited; qualified, fit, competent, able, capable,** proficient; customized; checked out <nf>; well-qualified, well-fitted, well-suited

18 **prepared for, ready for,** alert for, set *or* all set for <nf>; loaded for, primed for; up for <nf>; equal to, up to

19 **ready-made,** ready-formed, ready-mixed, ready-furnished, ready-dressed; ready-built, prefabricated, prefab <nf>, preformed; ready-to-wear, ready-for-wear, off-the-rack; ready-cut, cut-and-dried; convenient, convenience, fast-food; ready-to-cook, precooked, oven-ready; instant

20 **preparatory,** preparative; propaedeutic; prerequisite; provident, provisional

ADJS, ADVS 21 **in readiness, in store, in reserve;** in anticipation

22 **in preparation,** in course of preparation, **in progress** *or* **process,** under way, **going on,** in embryo, **in production,** on stream, under

construction, **in the works** or hopper or pipeline
<nf>, on the way, **in the making, in hand,** on the
anvil, on the fire, in the oven; under revision;
brewing, forthcoming

23 afoot, on foot, afloat, astir

PREPS **24** in preparation for, against, for; in order to;
ready for, set for and fixing to <nf>

406 UNPREPAREDNESS

NOUNS **1 unpreparedness, unreadiness,**
unprovidedness, nonpreparedness,
nonpreparation, lack of preparation; vulnerability
1006.4; extemporaneousness, improvisation, ad lib
<nf>, planlessness, disorganization; **unfitness,**
unfittedness, unsuitedness, unsuitableness,
unsuitability, unqualifiedness, unqualification,
lack of credentials, poor track record <nf>,
disqualification, incompetence or incompetency,
incapability; rustiness

2 improvidence, thriftlessness, unthriftiness, poor
husbandry, lax stewardship; **shiftlessness,**
fecklessness, thoughtlessness, heedlessness;
happy-go-luckiness; hastiness 401.2; negligence
340.1

3 <raw or original condition> **naturalness,**
inartificiality; **natural state,** nature, **state of
nature,** nature in the raw; pristineness, intactness,
virginity; defenselessness; natural man,
"unaccommodated man"—Shakespeare;
artlessness 416

4 undevelopment, nondevelopment; **immaturity,**
immatureness, callowness, unfledgedness,
cubbishness, **rawness, unripeness, greenness;
unfinish,** unfinishedness, unpolishedness,
unrefinement, uncultivation; crudity, crudeness,
rudeness, coarseness, roughness, the rough;
oversimplification, oversimplicity, simplism,
reductionism

5 raw material; crude, crude stuff <nf>; ore, rich
ore, rich vein; unsorted or unanalyzed mass;
rough diamond, **diamond in the rough;** unlicked
cub; **virgin soil,** untilled ground

VERBS **6 be unprepared** or **unready,** not be ready,
lack preparation; go off half-cocked or at half cock
<nf>; be taken unawares or aback, be blindsided
<nf>, be caught napping, be caught with one's
pants down <nf>, be surprised, drop one's guard;
extemporize, improvise, ad-lib and play by ear
<nf>; have no plan, be innocent of forethought;
improvise

7 make no provision, take no thought of tomorrow
or the morrow, seize the day, carpe diem <L,
Horace>, let tomorrow take care of itself, live for
the day, live like the grasshopper, live from hand

to mouth; "eat, drink, and be merry"—Bible; make
it up as one goes along

ADJS **8 unprepared, unready,** unprimed; surprised,
caught short, caught napping, caught with one's
pants down <nf>, taken by surprise, taken aback,
taken unawares, blindsided <nf>, caught off
balance, caught off base <nf>, tripped up;
unarranged, unorganized, haphazard; makeshift,
rough-and-ready, **extemporaneous,** extemporized,
improvised, ad-lib and off the top of one's head
<nf>; spontaneous, ad hoc; impromptu, snap <nf>;
unmade, unmanufactured, unconcocted,
unhatched, uncontrived, undevised, unplanned,
unpremeditated, undeliberated, unstudied; hasty,
precipitate 401.10; unbegun

9 unfitted, unfit, ill-fitted, unsuited, unadapted,
unqualified, disqualified, incompetent, incapable;
unequipped, unfurnished, unarmed, ill-equipped,
ill-furnished, **unprovided,** ill-provided 992.12

10 raw, crude; uncooked, unbaked, unboiled;
underdone, undercooked, rare, red; half-baked

11 immature, unripe, underripe, unripened,
impubic, **raw, green,** callow, wet behind the ears,
cub, cubbish, unfledged, fledgling, unseasoned,
unmellowed, vulnerable; ungrown, half-grown,
adolescent, juvenile, puerile, boyish, girlish,
inchoate; undigested, ill-digested; half-baked
<nf>; half-cocked and at half cock <nf>, wet
behind the ears

12 undeveloped, unfinished, unlicked, unformed;
unfashioned, unwrought, unlabored, unworked,
unprocessed, untreated; unblown; uncut, unhewn;
underdeveloped; backward, arrested, stunted;
**crude, rude, coarse, unpolished, unrefined;
uncultivated, uncultured; rough,** roughcast,
roughhewn, **in the rough; rudimentary,**
rudimental; embryonic, in embryo, fetal, in ovo
<L>; **oversimple, simplistic,** reductive,
reductionistic, unsophisticated; untrained; rusty,
unpracticed; scratch <nf>

13 <in the raw or original state> **natural, native, in a
state of nature,** in the raw; inartificial, artless
416.5; virgin, virginal, pristine, untouched,
unsullied

14 fallow, untilled, uncultivated, unsown, unworked

15 improvident, prodigal, unproviding; **thriftless,
unthrifty,** uneconomical; grasshopper; hand-to-
mouth; **shiftless, feckless, thoughtless, heedless;**
happy-go-lucky; negligent 340.10

407 ACCOMPLISHMENT

<act of accomplishing; entire performance>

NOUNS **1 accomplishment, achievement, fulfillment,
performance, execution, effectuation,**

implementation, carrying out *or* through, **discharge, dispatch, consummation, realization, attainment,** production, fruition; **success** 409; track record *or* track <nf>; *fait accompli* <Fr>, accomplished fact, done deal <nf>; mission accomplished

2 completion, completing, **finish,** finishing, **conclusion, end,** ending, **termination,** terminus, **close, windup** <nf>, rounding off *or* out, topping off, wrapping up, wrap-up, finalization; **perfection,** culmination 1002.3; ripeness, maturity, maturation, full development; tipping point

3 finishing touch, final touch, last touch, last stroke, final *or* finishing stroke, finisher <nf>, craftsmanship, icing the cake, the icing on the cake; copestone, capstone, crown, crowning of the edifice; capper <nf>, climax 198.2

VERBS **4 accomplish, achieve, effect, effectuate, compass, consummate, do, execute, produce, deliver, make,** enact, **perform, discharge, fulfill, realize, attain,** run with *and* hack *and* swing <nf>; **work,** work out; **dispatch, dispose of,** knock off <nf>, polish off <nf>, take care of <nf>, **deal with,** put away, make short work of; succeed, manage 409.12; come through *and* do the job <nf>, **do** *or* **turn the trick** <nf>

5 bring about, bring to pass, bring to effect, **bring to a happy issue; implement, carry out, carry through,** carry into execution; **bring off, carry off, pull off** <nf>; **put through,** get through, **put over** *or* **across** <nf>; come through with <nf>

6 complete, perfect, finish, finish off, conclude, terminate, end, bring to a close, carry to completion, prosecute to a conclusion; **get through, get done;** come off of, get through with, get it over, get it over with, **finish up;** clean up *and* wind up *and* button up *and* sew up *and* wrap up *and* mop up <nf>, close up *or* out; put the lid on *and* call it a day <nf>; **round off** *or* **out, wind up** <nf>, **top off;** top out, crown, cap 198.9; climax, culminate; give the finishing touches *or* strokes, **put the finishing touches or strokes on,** lick *or* whip into shape, finalize, put the icing on the cake; autocomplete

7 do to perfection, do up brown <nf>, **do to a turn,** do to a T *or* to a frazzle *or* down to the ground <nf>, not do by halves, do oneself proud <nf>, use every trick in the book, leave no loose ends, leave nothing hanging; go all lengths, go to all lengths, go the whole length *or* way, go the limit *and* go whole hog *and* go all out *and* shoot the works *and* go for broke <nf>

8 ripen, ripe <nf>, **mature,** maturate; bloom, blow, blossom, flourish; come to fruition, bear fruit; **mellow;** grow up, reach maturity, reach its season;

come *or* draw to a head; bring to maturity, bring to a head

ADJS **9 completing,** completive, completory, **finishing,** consummative, culminating, terminative, conclusive, **concluding,** fulfilling, finalizing, crowning; ultimate, **last, final,** terminal

10 accomplished, achieved, effected, effectuated, implemented, **consummated, executed, discharged, fulfilled, realized,** consummate, compassed, **attained; dispatched, disposed of,** set at rest; wrought, wrought out

11 completed, done, finished, concluded, terminated, ended, finished up; signed, sealed, *and* delivered; cleaned up *and* wound up *and* sewed *or* sewn up *and* wrapped up *and* mopped up <nf>; washed up <nf>, **through,** done with; all over with, all said *and* done, all over but the shouting; perfective

12 complete, perfect, consummate, polished; exhaustive, thorough 794.10; fully realized

13 ripe, mature, matured, maturated, seasoned; blooming, abloom; **mellow,** full-grown, fully developed

ADVS **14 to completion,** to the end, down-the-line, to the full, to the limit; to a turn, to a T <nf>, to a finish, to a frazzle <nf>

INTERJS **15** so much for that!, that's that!, *voilà!* <Fr>

408 NONACCOMPLISHMENT

NOUNS **1 nonaccomplishment, nonachievement, nonperformance,** inexecution, nonexecution, nondischarging, **noncompletion,** nonconsummation, nonfulfillment, unfulfillment; nonfeasance, omission; **neglect** 340; loose ends, rough edges; endless task, work of Penelope, Sisyphean labor *or* toil *or* task; **disappointment** 132; **failure** 410

VERBS **2** neglect, leave undone 340.7, fail 410.9; be disappointed 132.4

ADJS **3 unaccomplished, unachieved, unperformed,** unexecuted, undischarged, unfulfilled, unconsummated, unrealized, unattained; **unfinished, uncompleted, undone;** open-ended; **neglected** 340.14; **disappointed** 132.5

409 SUCCESS

NOUNS **1 success, successfulness,** fortunate outcome, prosperous issue, favorable termination; **prosperity** 1010; accomplishment 407; **victory** 411; the big time

2 sure success, foregone conclusion, sure-fire proposition <nf>; **winner** *and* **natural** <nf>;

shoo-in *and* **sure thing** *and* sure bet *and* **cinch** *and* lead-pipe cinch <nf>

3 **great success, triumph,** resounding triumph, brilliant success, striking success, **meteoric** success; flying colors; **stardom; success story**; best seller; brief *or* momentary success, nine days' wonder, flash in the pan, fad, next big thing

4 <nf terms> smash, hit, smash hit, gas, gasser, blast, boffo, showstopper, barn-burner, howling *or* roaring success, one for the book, wow, wowser, sensation, overnight sensation, sensaysh, phenom, sockeroo

5 **score, hit, bull's-eye;** goal, touchdown; slam, grand slam; strike; hole, hole in one; home run, homer <nf>

6 <successful person> **winner,** star, star in the firmament, success, superstar *and* megastar <nf>; prizewinner, lottery winner; phenom *and* comer <nf>, whiz kid, VIP; **victor** 411.2

VERBS 7 **succeed, prevail,** be successful, be crowned with success, meet with success, do very well, do famously, deliver, come through *and* make a go of it <nf>; **go, come off,** go off; **prosper** 1010.7; fare well, work well, do *or* work wonders, go to town *or* go great guns <nf>; make a hit <nf>, click *and* connect <nf>, **catch on** *and* take <nf>, catch fire, have legs <nf>; **go over** *and* go over big *or* with a bang <nf>; pass, graduate, qualify, win one's spurs *or* wings, get one's credentials, be blooded; pass with flying colors

8 **achieve one's purpose, gain one's end** *or* **ends,** secure one's object, attain one's objective, do what one set out to do, reach one's goal, bring it off, pull it off *and* hack it *and* swing it <nf>; make one's point; play it *or* handle it just right <nf>, not put a foot wrong, play it like a master

9 **score a success,** score, notch one up <nf>, hit it, hit the mark, ring the bell <nf>, turn up trumps, break the bank *or* make a killing <nf>, hit the jackpot <nf>

10 **make good, come through, achieve success,** make a success, have a good thing going <nf>, **make it** <nf>, get into the zone *or* bubble <nf>, wing *and* cruise, <nf>, hit one's stride, **make one's mark, give a good account of oneself,** bear oneself with credit, do all right by oneself *and* **do oneself proud,** make out like a bandit <nf>; **advance, progress,** make one's way, make headway, **get on,** come on <nf>, **get ahead** <nf>; go places, **go far;** rise, **rise in the world,** work one's way up, step up, come *or* move up in the world, claw *or* scrabble one's way up, mount the ladder of success, pull oneself up by one's bootstraps; **arrive,** get there <nf>, make the scene <nf>; come out on top, come out on top of the heap <nf>; **be a success,** have it

made *or* hacked *or* wrapped up <nf>, have the world at one's feet, eat *or* live high on the hog <nf>; **make a noise in the world** <nf>, cut a swath, set the world *or* river *or* Thames on fire; break through, score *or* make a breakthrough

11 **succeed with,** crown with success; **make a go of it; accomplish,** compass, **achieve** 407.4; **bring off, carry off, pull off** <nf>, turn *or* do the trick <nf>, **put through,** bring through; **put over** *or* **across** <nf>; get away with it *and* get by <nf>

12 **manage, contrive, succeed in; make out, get on** *or* **along** <nf>, come on *or* along <nf>, go on; **scrape along,** worry along, **muddle through** <Brit>, get by, **manage somehow; make it** <nf>, **make the grade,** cut the mustard *and* hack it <nf>; **clear,** clear the hurdle; **negotiate** <nf>, **engineer; swing** <nf>, put over <nf>, put through

13 **win through, win out** <nf>, come through <nf>, rise to the occasion, beat the game *and* beat the system <nf>; **triumph** 411.3; weather out, **weather the storm,** live through, keep one's head above water; come up fighting *or* smiling, not know when one is beaten, **persevere** 360.2

ADJS 14 **successful,** succeeding, crowned with success; **prosperous,** fortunate 1010.14; **triumphant;** ahead of the game, out in front, on top, sitting on top of the world *and* sitting pretty <nf>, on top of the heap <nf>; assured of success, surefire, made; coming *and* on the up-and-up <nf>

ADVS 15 **successfully,** swimmingly <nf>, well, to some purpose, to good purpose; beyond all expectation, beyond one's fondest dreams, from rags to riches, with flying colors

410 FAILURE

NOUNS 1 **failure, unsuccessfulness,** unsuccess, successlessness, nonsuccess; no go <nf>; ill success; futility, uselessness 391; **defeat** 412; losing game, **no-win situation;** nonaccomplishment 408; **bankruptcy** 625.3

2 <nf terms> **flop,** flopperoo, megaflop, gigaflop, **bust,** frost, **fizzle,** lemon, clinker, dud, non-starter, **loser, washout,** turkey, bomb, flat failure, dull thud, total loss, black mark; game over; the pits

3 **collapse, crash,** smash, comedown, breakdown, derailment, **fall,** pratfall <nf>, stumble, tumble, **downfall,** cropper <chiefly Brit nf>; nose dive *and* tailspin <nf>; deflation, bursting of the bubble, letdown, **disappointment** 132

4 **miss,** near-miss; **slip, slipup** <nf>, slip 'twixt cup *and* lip; **error, mistake** 975.3

5 **abortion, miscarriage,** miscarrying, abortive attempt, vain attempt; wild-goose chase, merry chase; **misfire, flash in the pan,** wet squib,

malfunction, glitch <nf>; **dud** <nf>; **flunk** <nf>, **washout** <nf>

6 fiasco, botch, botch-up, cock-up *and* balls-up <Brit nf>, bungle, hash, mess, muddle, foozle *and* bollix *and* bitch-up *and* screw-up *and* fuck-up <nf>

7 <unsuccessful person> **failure**, flash in the pan; bankrupt 625.4

8 <nf terms> **loser, non-starter,** born loser, **flop,** washout, false alarm, **dud,** also-ran, bum, dull tool, bust, schlemiel, turkey, hopeless case; underdog

VERBS **9 fail,** be unsuccessful, fail of success, not work *and* not come off <nf>, come to grief, **lose,** not make the grade, go nowhere, be found wanting, not come up to the mark; not pass, **flunk** *and* **flunk out** <nf>; go to the wall, **go on the rocks;** labor in vain 391.8; come away empty-handed; tap out <nf>, go bankrupt 625.7

10 <nf terms> **lose out,** get left, **not make it,** not hack it, not get to first base, drop the ball, go for a Burton *and* come a cropper <Brit>, **flop,** flummox, fall flat on one's ass, lay an egg, go over like a lead balloon, draw a blank, bomb, drop a bomb; fold, fold up; take it on the chin, take the count; crap out; strike out, fan, whiff

11 sink, founder, go down, go under <nf>, go south; **slip,** go downhill, be on the skids <nf>

12 fall, fall down <nf>, fall *or* drop by the wayside, fall flat, fall flat on one's face; fall down on the job <nf>; **fall short, fall through,** fall to the ground; fall between two stools; **fall dead; collapse,** fall in; **crash,** go to smash <nf>

13 come to nothing, hang up *and* get nowhere <nf>; **poop out** *and* go phut <nf>; be all over *or* up with; fail miserably *or* ignominiously; fizz out *and* **fizzle** *and* **fizzle out** *and* peter out *and* poop out <nf>; **misfire,** flash in the pan, hang fire; **blow up, blow up in one's face, explode, end** *or* **go up in smoke,** go up like a rocket *and* come down like a stick

14 miss, miss the mark, miss one's aim; slip, slip up <nf>; goof <nf>, blunder, foozle <nf>, **err** 975.9; **botch, bungle** 414.11; waste one's effort, run around in circles, spin one's wheels

15 miscarry, abort, be stillborn, die aborning; **go amiss,** go astray, **go wrong,** go on a wrong tack, take a wrong turn, derail, go off the rails

16 stall, stick, die, go dead, **conk out** <nf>, sputter *and* stop, run out of gas *or* steam, come to a shuddering halt, come to a dead stop

17 flunk *or* **flunk out** <nf>; **fail,** pluck *and* plough <Brit nf>, bust *and* wash out <nf>, bomb <nf>, flush it <nf>

ADJS **18 unsuccessful,** successless, failing; failed, manqué <Fr>, stickit <Scot>; **unfortunate** 1011.14; **abortive,** miscarrying, miscarried, stillborn, died aborning; fruitless, bootless, no-win <nf>, futile, useless 391.9; lame, **ineffectual,** ineffective, inefficacious, of no effect; malfunctioning, glitchy <nf>

ADVS **19 unsuccessfully,** successlessly, **without success;** fruitlessly, bootlessly, ineffectually, ineffectively, inefficaciously, lamely; to little *or* no purpose, **in vain**

411 VICTORY

NOUNS **1 victory, triumph, conquest,** subduing, subdual; a feather in one's cap <nf>; total victory, grand slam; **championship,** crown, laurels, cup, trophy, belt, blue ribbon, first prize, flying colors; V-for-victory sign *or* V-sign, raised arms; victory lap; **winning,** win <nf>; knockout *or* KO <nf>; easy victory, walkover *and* walkaway <nf>, pushover *and* picnic <nf>; runaway victory, laugher *and* romp *and* shellacking <nf>; landslide victory, landslide; Pyrrhic victory, Cadmean victory; moral victory; winning streak <nf>; winning ways, triumphalism; **success** 409; ascendancy 417.6; mastery 612.2

2 victor, winner, victress, victrix, triumpher; **conqueror,** defeater, **vanquisher,** subduer, subjugator, *conquistador* <Sp>; top dog <nf>; master, master of the situation; hero, conquering hero; champion, champ *and* number one <nf>; easy winner, sure winner, shoo-in <nf>; pancratiast; runner-up

VERBS **3 triumph, prevail, be victorious,** come out ahead, come out on top <nf>, clean up, chain victory to one's car; **win, gain, capture, carry;** win out <nf>, **win through,** carry it, carry off *or* away; **win** *or* **carry** *or* **gain the day,** win the battle, come out first, finish in front, make a killing <nf>, remain in possession of the field; get *or* have the last laugh; **win the prize,** win the palm *or* bays *or* laurels, bear the palm, take the cake <nf>, win one's spurs *or* wings; fluke *and* win by a fluke <nf>; **win by a nose** *and* nose out *and* edge out <nf>; **succeed;** break the record, set a new mark <nf>

4 win hands down *and* win going away <nf>, win in a canter *and* walk *and* waltz <nf>, romp *or* breeze *or* waltz home <nf>, **walk off** *or* **away with,** waltz off with <nf>, walk off with the game, **walk over** <nf>; have the game in one's own hands, have it all one's way; **take** *or* **carry by storm,** sweep aside all obstacles, sweep, carry all before one, make short work of

5 defeat 412.6, **triumph over, prevail over,** best, **beat** <nf>, **get the better** *or* **best of; surmount, overcome,** outmatch, rise above

6 gain the ascendancy, come out on top <nf>, **get the advantage, gain the upper** *or* **whip hand,** dominate the field, get the edge on *or* jump on *or* drop on <nf>, get a leg up on <nf>, get a stranglehold on

ADJS **7 victorious, triumphant,** triumphal, **winning, prevailing;** conquering, vanquishing, defeating, overcoming; ahead of the game, ascendant, in the ascendant, in ascendancy, sitting on top of the world *and* sitting pretty <nf>, dominant 612.17; successful; flushed with success *or* victory

8 undefeated, unbeaten, unvanquished, unconquered, unsubdued, unquelled, unbowed

ADVS **9 triumphantly,** victoriously, **in triumph;** by a mile

412 DEFEAT

NOUNS **1 defeat; beating,** drubbing, thrashing; clobbering *and* hiding *and* lathering *and* whipping *and* lambasting *and* trimming *and* licking <nf>, trouncing; **vanquishment, conquest, conquering,** mastery, subjugation, subduing, subdual; **overthrow,** overturn, overcoming; **fall, downfall,** collapse, smash, crash, **undoing, ruin,** debacle, derailing, derailment; **destruction** 395; deathblow, quietus; Waterloo; failure 410

2 discomfiture, rout, repulse, rebuff; **frustration,** bafflement, confusion; **checkmate,** check, balk, foil <old>; **reverse,** reversal, **setback**

3 utter defeat, total defeat, overwhelming defeat, crushing defeat, smashing defeat, decisive defeat; no contest; **smearing** *and* **pasting** *and* creaming *and* **clobbering** *and* **shellacking** *and* whopping *and* whomping <nf>; whitewash *or* **whitewashing** <nf>, **shutout**

4 ignominious defeat, abject defeat, inglorious defeat, disastrous defeat, utter rout, bitter defeat, stinging defeat, embarrassing defeat

5 loser, defeatee <nf>; the vanquished; good loser, game loser, sport *or* **good sport** <nf>; poor sport, poor loser; **underdog, also-ran;** booby *and* duck <nf>; stooge *and* fall guy <nf>; victim 96.11

VERBS **6 defeat, worst, best, get the better** *or* **best of,** be too good for, be too much for, be more than a match for; **outdo,** outgeneral, outmaneuver, outclass, outshine, outpoint, outsail, outrun, outfight, etc; **triumph over; knock on the head,** deal a deathblow to, put *hors de combat*; undo, ruin, destroy 395.10; beat by a nose *and* nose out *and* edge out <nf>

7 overcome, surmount; **overpower, overmaster,** overmatch; **overthrow, overturn,** overset; put the skids to <nf>; **upset,** trip, trip up, lay by the heels, send flying *or* sprawling; silence, floor, deck, make bite the dust; overcome oneself, master oneself; kick the habit <nf>

8 overwhelm, whelm, snow under <nf>, overbear, defeat utterly, deal a crushing *or* smashing defeat; **discomfit, rout, put to rout,** put to flight, scatter, stampede, panic; confound; put out of court

9 <nf terms> **clobber, trim, skin alive, beat,** skunk, drub, massacre, marmelize <Brit>, lick, whip, thrash, knock off, trim, hide, cut to pieces, run rings *or* circles around, throw for a loss, lather, trounce, **lambaste,** skin alive; fix, settle, settle one's hash, make one say 'uncle,' do in, lick to a frazzle, beat all hollow, beat one's brains out, cook one's goose, make hamburger *or* mincemeat out of, mop up the floor with, sandbag, banjax, bulldoze, steamroller, **smear,** paste, cream, **shellac,** whup, whop, whomp, shut out

10 conquer, vanquish, quell, **suppress, put down, subdue, subjugate,** put under the yoke, master; **reduce,** prostrate, fell, **flatten, break, smash, crush, humble,** bend, **bring one to his knees;** roll *or* trample in the dust, tread *or* trample underfoot, trample down, ride down, ride *or* run roughshod over, override; have one's way with

11 thwart, frustrate, dash, check, deal a check to, checkmate 1012.15

12 lose, lose out <nf>, lose the day, come off second best, **get** *or* **have the worst of it, meet one's Waterloo; fall,** succumb, tumble, bow, go down, go under, **bite** *or* **lick the dust,** take the count <nf>; snatch defeat from the jaws of victory; throw in the towel, say 'uncle'; have enough

ADJS **13 lost,** unwon

14 defeated, worsted, bested, outdone; beaten, discomfited, put to rout, **routed,** scattered, stampeded, panicked; confounded; **overcome, overthrown,** upset, overturned, overmatched, **overpowered, overwhelmed,** whelmed, **overmastered,** overborne, overridden; **fallen,** down; floored, silenced; **undone, done for** <nf>, **ruined,** kaput *and* on the skids <nf>, *hors de combat* <Fr>; all up with <nf>

15 <nf terms> **beat, clobbered, licked, whipped,** trimmed, sandbagged, banjaxed, done in, lathered, creamed, shellacked, trounced, lambasted, settled, fixed; skinned alive; thrown for a loss

16 shut out, skunked *and* blanked *and* whitewashed <nf>, scoreless, not on the scoreboard

17 conquered, vanquished, quelled, suppressed, put down, **subdued, subjugated,** mastered; **reduced,** prostrate *or* prostrated, felled, **flattened,** smashed, **crushed,** broken; **humbled,** brought to one's knees

18 irresistible, overpowering, overcoming,

overwhelming, overmastering, overmatching, avalanchine

413 SKILL

NOUNS **1 skill,** skillfulness, **expertness, expertise, proficiency,** callidity <old>, craft, moxie <nf>, **cleverness; dexterity,** dexterousness *or* dextrousness; **adroitness,** address, **adeptness,** deftness, handiness, hand, practical ability; coordination, timing; quickness, readiness; **competence,** capability, capacity, ability; efficiency; **facility, prowess;** grace, style, finesse; **tact, tactfulness, diplomacy;** *savoir-faire* <Fr>; **artistry;** artfulness; **craftsmanship,** workmanship, artisanship; **know-how** *and* savvy *and* bag of tricks <nf>; technical skill, **technique, touch,** technical brilliance, technical mastery, **virtuosity,** bravura, wizardry; brilliance 920.2; cunning 415; **ingenuity,** ingeniousness, resource, resourcefulness, wit; **mastery,** mastership, **command,** control, grip; steady hand; marksmanship, seamanship, airmanship, horsemanship, etc

2 agility, nimbleness, spryness, lightness, featliness
3 versatility, ambidexterity, many-sidedness, all-roundedness <nf>, Renaissance versatility; **adaptability,** adjustability, flexibility; broad-gauge, many hats; Renaissance man *or* woman
4 talent, flair, strong flair, **gift, endowment,** dowry, dower, natural gift *or* endowment, **genius,** instinct, **faculty,** bump <nf>; **power, ability, capability, capacity,** potential; caliber; **forte,** speciality, métier, long suit, strong point, strong suit, strength; **equipment, qualification;** talents, powers, naturals <old>, parts; the goods *and* the stuff *and* the right stuff *and* what it takes *and* the makings <nf>
5 aptitude, inborn *or* innate aptitude, innate ability, genius, aptness, felicity, flair; **bent, turn,** propensity, **leaning,** inclination, tendency; turn for, capacity for, gift for, genius for; feeling for, good head for, an eye for, an ear for, a hand for, a way with
6 knack, art, hang, trick, way; **touch,** feel
7 art, science, craft; skill; technique, technic, **technics,** technology, technical knowledge *or* skill, technical know-how <nf>; **mechanics,** mechanism; method
8 accomplishment, acquirement, attainment; finish; coup, feat, clincher, classic; hit, smash hit
9 experience, practice, practical knowledge *or* skill, hands-on experience <nf>, field-work; background, past experience, seasoning, tempering; backstory; **worldly wisdom,** knowledge of the world, episteme, **sophistication;** sagacity 920.4

10 masterpiece, masterwork, *chef d'œuvre* <Fr>; **master stroke,** *coup de maître* <Fr>; **feat,** *tour de force* <Fr>, *pièce de résistance* <Fr>, magnum opus, classic, treasure, work of art, epic, crème de la crème, artistry
11 expert, adept, proficient, genius; **artist, craftsman,** artisan, skilled workman, journeyman; technician; seasoned *or* experienced hand; shark *or* sharp *or* sharpy *and* no slouch *and* tough act to follow <nf>; graduate; **professional, pro** <nf>; **jack-of-all-trades,** all-rounder, Renaissance man *or* woman, handy man; wordsmith <etc.>; **authority,** maven <nf>, know-it-all <nf>; professor; **consultant,** expert consultant, specialist, attaché, technical adviser; counselor, adviser, mentor; boffin <Brit nf>, pundit, savant 929.3; diplomatist, diplomat; politician, statesman, statesperson, elder statesman; connoisseur, cognoscente; *cordon bleu* <Fr>; marksman, crack shot, dead shot; walking encyclopedia <nf>, illuminati
12 talented person, talent, man *or* woman of parts, gifted person, prodigy, natural <nf>, **genius,** mental genius, intellectual genius, intellectual prodigy, mental giant; rocket scientist *and* brain surgeon <nf>; phenom <nf>; gifted child, **child prodigy,** wunderkind, whiz kid *and* boy wonder <nf>; polymath; one-trick pony
13 master, past master, grand master; master hand, world-class performer, champion, **good hand,** dab hand <Brit nf>, skilled *or* practiced hand, practitioner, specialist; first chair; **prodigy; wizard,** magician; **virtuoso;** maestro; **genius,** man *or* woman of genius, paragon; mastermind; master spirit, mahatma, sage 920.17
14 <nf terms> **ace, star, superstar, crackerjack,** dab, great, all-time great, topnotcher, first-rater, whiz, flash, hot stuff, pisser, piss-cutter, pistol, no slouch, world-beater, hot rock, the one who wrote the book, right person for the job, smart cookie; geek, nerd
15 champion, champ <nf>, victor, title-holder, world champion; **record holder,** world-record holder; laureate; medal winner, Olympic medal winner, medalist, award winner, prizeman, prizetaker, **prizewinner,** titleholder; most valuable player *or* MVP; hall of famer
16 veteran, vet <nf>, seasoned *or* grizzled veteran, **old pro** <nf>; **old hand, old-timer** <nf> one of the old guard, old stager <Brit>; old campaigner, war-horse *or* old war-horse <nf>; salt *and* old salt *and* old sea dog <nf>, shellback <nf>
17 sophisticate, man of experience, **man of the world;** slicker *and* city slicker <nf>; man-about-

town; **cosmopolitan,** cosmopolite, citizen of the world

VERBS 18 excel in *or* **at, shine in** *or* at <nf>, be master of; write the book <nf>, have a good command of, feel comfortable with, be at home in; **have a gift** *or* **flair** *or* **talent** *or* **bent** *or* **faculty** *or* **turn for,** have a bump for <nf>, be a natural *and* be cut out *or* born to be <nf>, **have a good head for,** have an ear for, have an eye for, be born for, show aptitude *or* talent for, have something to spare; have the knack *or* touch, have a way with, have the right touch, have the hang of it, have a lot going for one <nf>, be able to do it blindfolded *or* standing on one's head <nf>; have something *or* plenty on the ball <nf>

19 know backwards *and* **forwards, know one's stuff** *or* **know one's onions** <nf>, **know the ropes** *and* **know all the ins** *and* **outs** <nf>, know from A to Z *or* alpha to omega, know like the back of one's hand *or* a book, know from the ground up, know all the tricks *or* moves, know all the tricks of the trade, know all the moves of the game; **know what's what, know a thing or two, know what it's all about, know the score** *and* know all the answers <nf>, "know a hawk from a handsaw"— Shakespeare; have savvy <nf>; **know one's way about,** know the ways of the world, have been around <nf>, have been around the block <nf>, have been through the mill <nf>, have cut one's wisdom teeth *or* eyeteeth <nf>, be long in the tooth, **not be born yesterday;** get around <nf>

20 exercise skill, handle oneself well, demonstrate one's ability, **strut one's stuff** *and* hotdog *and* grandstand *and* showboat <nf>, show expertise; cut one's coat according to one's cloth, play one's cards well

21 be versatile, double in brass *and* wear more than one hat <nf>

ADJS 22 skillful, good, goodish, excellent, **expert, proficient; dexterous,** callid <old>, good at, **adroit, deft, adept, coordinated,** well-coordinated, **apt,** no mean, **handy;** quick, ready; **clever,** cute *and* slick *and* slick as a whistle <nf>, neat, clean; fancy, graceful, stylish; some *or* quite some *or* quite a *or* every bit a <nf>; **masterly, masterful;** magistral, magisterial; authoritative, consummate, professional; the compleat *or* the complete; crack *or* crackerjack <nf>, ace, first-rate, supreme; whiz-kid <nf>; **virtuoso,** bravura, technically superb; **brilliant** 920.14; cunning 415.12; tactful, diplomatic, politic, statesmanlike; **ingenious,** resourceful, daedal, Daedalian; **artistic; workmanlike, well-done**

23 agile, nimble, spry, sprightly, fleet, featly, peart <nf>, light, graceful, nimble-footed, light-footed, sure-footed; nimble-fingered, neat-fingered, neat-handed

24 competent, capable, able, efficient, qualified, fit, fitted, suited, worthy; journeyman; fit *or* fitted for; **equal to, up to;** up to snuff <nf>, up to the mark <nf>, *au fait* <Fr>; well-qualified, well-fitted, well-suited

25 versatile, ambidextrous, two-handed, **all around** <nf>, broad-gauge, **well-rounded, many-sided,** generally capable; **adaptable,** adjustable, flexible, resourceful, supple, ready for anything; amphibious

26 skilled, accomplished; practiced; professional, career; trained, coached, prepared, primed, finished; at one's best, at concert pitch; initiated, initiate; technical; conversant

27 skilled in, proficient in, adept in, versed in, **good at,** expert at, **handy at, a hand** *or* **good hand at,** master of, strong in, at home in; **up on,** well up on, well-versed 928.20

28 experienced, practiced, mature, matured, ripe, ripened, **seasoned,** tried, well-tried, tried *and* true, **veteran,** old, an old dog at <nf>; sagacious 920.16; **worldly, worldly-wise,** world-wise, wise in the ways of the world, knowing, shrewd, **sophisticated,** cosmopolitan, cosmopolite, blasé, dry behind the ears, not born yesterday, long in the tooth; been there done that <nf>

29 talented, gifted, endowed, with a flair; born for, made for, cut out for <nf>, with an eye for, with an ear for, with a bump for <nf>

30 well-laid, well-devised, well-contrived, well-designed, well-planned, well-worked-out; well-invented, *ben trovato* <Ital>; **well-weighed, well-reasoned,** well-considered, well-thought-out, thought-out; **cunning, clever**

ADVS 31 skillfully, expertly, proficiently, excellently, well; **cleverly,** neatly, ingeniously, resourcefully; cunningly 415.13; **dexterously, adroitly, deftly, adeptly,** aptly, handily; agilely, nimbly, featly, spryly; **competently, capably, ably,** efficiently; **masterfully;** brilliantly, superbly, with genius, with a touch of genius; **artistically,** artfully; with skill, with consummate skill, with finesse

414 UNSKILLFULNESS

NOUNS 1 unskillfulness, skill-lessness, **inexpertness, unproficiency, uncleverness;** unintelligence 922; inadeptness, **undexterousness,** indexterity, **undeftness;** inefficiency; **incompetence** *or* incompetency, **inability, incapability, incapacity,** inadequacy; ineffectiveness, **ineffectuality; mediocrity,** pedestrianism; **inaptitude,** inaptness, unaptness, ineptness, maladroitness; unfitness, unfittedness; untrainedness, unschooledness; thoughtlessness, inattentiveness; maladjustment; rustiness <nf>, nonuse

2 inexperience, unexperience, unexperiencedness, unpracticedness; **rawness, greenness,** unripeness, callowness, unfledgedness, unreadiness, immaturity; ignorance 930; **unfamiliarity,** unacquaintance, unacquaintedness, unaccustomedness; rawness, greenness, **amateurishness,** amateurism, unprofessionalness, unprofessionalism

3 clumsiness, awkwardness, bumblingness, **maladroitness, unhandiness,** left-handedness, heavy-handedness, fumblitis *and* ham-handedness <nf>, ham-fistedness <Brit nf>; handful of thumbs; **ungainliness,** uncouthness, **ungracefulness,** gracelessness, inelegance; **gawkiness,** gawkishness; **lubberliness, oafishness,** loutishness, boorishness, clownishness, lumpishness; **cumbersomeness,** hulkiness, **ponderousness; unwieldiness, unmanageability**

4 bungling, blundering, boggling, **fumbling,** malperformance, muffing, **botching,** botchery, blunderheadedness; **sloppiness, carelessness** 340.2; too many cooks

5 bungle, blunder, botch, flub, boner *and* bonehead play <nf>, boggle, bobble *and* boo-boo *and* screw-up *and* ball-up *and* fuck-up *and* foul-up <nf>, foozle <nf>, bevue; **fumble, muff,** fluff, flop, miscue <nf>, misfire, mishit; **slip,** trip, stumble; *gaucherie and étourderie and balourdise* <Fr>; **hash** *and* **mess** <nf>; bad job, sad work, clumsy performance, poor show *or* performance; off day; **error, mistake** 975.3

6 mismanagement, mishandling, misdirection, misguidance, misconduct, **misgovernment,** misrule; misadministration, maladministration; malfeasance, malpractice, misfeasance, wrongdoing 655; nonfeasance, omission, **negligence,** neglect 340.6; bad policy, impolicy, inexpedience *or* inexpediency 996

7 incompetent, incapable; dull tool, mediocrity, duffer *and* hacker <nf>, no great shakes, no prize, no prize package, no brain surgeon, no rocket scientist; no conjuror; one who will not set the Thames on fire <Brit>; greenhorn 930.7

8 bungler, blunderer, blunderhead, boggler, slubberer, bumbler, hack, **fumbler, botcher;** bull in a china shop, ox; lubber, lobby, **lout, oaf,** gawk, boor, **clown,** slouch; clodhopper, clodknocker, bumpkin, yokel, geek; **clod,** clot <Brit>, **dolt,** sad sack, blockhead 924.4; awkward squad; blind leading the blind

9 <nf terms> goof, goofer, goofball, goofus, foul-up, fuck-up, screw-up, bobbler, bonehead, dub, jerk,

bozo, foozler, clumsy, fumble-fist, klutz, **butterfingers,** muff, muffer, stumblebum, stumblebunny, duffer, lummox, **slob,** lump; gowk <Brit>, rube, hick

VERBS 10 not know how, not have the knack, not have it in one <nf>; not be up to <nf>; not be versed; muddle along, pedestrianize; show one's ignorance, not have a clue <nf>

11 bungle, blunder, bumble, boggle, bobble, **muff,** muff one's cue *or* lines, **fumble,** be all thumbs, have a handful of thumbs; **flounder,** muddle, lumber; stumble, **slip,** trip, trip over one's own feet, get in one's own way, miss one's footing, miscue; commit a faux pas, commit a gaffe; blunder on *or* upon *or* into; blunder away, be not one's day; **botch,** mar, **spoil, butcher, murder,** make sad work of; play havoc with, play mischief with

12 <nf terms> goof, pull a boner, bobble, lay an egg, put *or* stick one's foot in it, stub one's toe, step on one's schvantz *or* pecker, drop the ball, drop a pop-up, drop a brick, bonehead into it; **blow,** blow it, bitch, bitch up, hash up, **mess up,** flub, flub the dub, **make a mess** *or* **hash of,** make a faux pas, foul up, fuck up, goof up, bollix up, **screw up, louse up, gum up,** gum up the works, bugger, bugger up, play the deuce *or* devil *or* hell *or* merry hell with; go at it ass-backwards; put one's foot in one's mouth; self-destruct

13 mismanage, mishandle, misconduct, misdirect, misguide, **misgovern, misrule;** misadminister, maladminister; be negligent 340.6

14 not know what one is about, not know one's interest, lose one's touch, make an ass of oneself, **make a fool of oneself,** lose face, stultify oneself, have egg on one's face, put oneself out of court, stand in one's own light, not know on which side one's bread is buttered, not know one's ass from one's elbow *or* a hole in the ground, kill the goose that lays the golden egg, cut one's own throat, dig one's own grave, behave self-destructively, **play with fire,** burn one's fingers, jump out of the frying pan into the fire, lock the barn door after the horse is stolen, **count one's chickens before they are hatched,** buy a pig in a poke, aim at a pigeon and kill a crow, **put the cart before the horse,** put a square peg into a round hole, paint oneself into a corner, run before one can walk

ADJS 15 unskillful, skill-less, artless, **inexpert, unproficient, unclever;** inefficient; **undexterous, undeft, inadept, unfacile; unapt, inapt, inept,** hopeless, half-assed *and* clunky <nf>, **poor;** mediocre, pedestrian; thoughtless, inattentive; unintelligent 922.13

16 unskilled, unaccomplished, untrained, untaught, unschooled, untutored, uncoached, unimproved, uninitiated, **unprepared,** unprimed, unfinished, unpolished; **untalented, ungifted, unendowed; amateurish,** unprofessional, unbusinesslike, semiskilled

17 **inexperienced,** unexperienced, unversed, unconversant, **unpracticed;** undeveloped, unseasoned; **raw, green,** green as grass, unripe, callow, unfledged, immature, unmatured, fresh, wet behind the ears, not dry behind the ears, in training, **untried;** unskilled in, unpracticed in, unversed in, unconversant with, unaccustomed to, unused to, unfamiliar *or* unacquainted with, new to, uninitiated in, a stranger to, a novice *or* tyro at; 930.11; semiskilled

18 **out of practice,** out of training *or* form, soft <nf>, out of shape *or* condition, stiff, **rusty;** gone *or* run to seed *and* over the hill *and* not what one used to be <nf>, losing one's touch, slipping, on the downgrade

19 **incompetent, incapable, unable, inadequate, unequipped, unqualified,** ill-qualified, out of one's depth, outmatched, **unfit, unfitted,** unadapted, not equal *or* up to, not cut out for <nf>; ineffective, **ineffectual;** unadjusted, maladjusted

20 **bungling, blundering,** blunderheaded, bumbling, fumbling, mistake-prone, accident-prone; **clumsy, awkward, uncoordinated,** maladroit, unhandy, left-hand, left-handed, heavy-handed, ham-handed <nf>, ham-fisted *and* cack-handed <Brit nf>, clumsy-fisted, butterfingered <nf>, **all thumbs,** fingers all thumbs, with a handful of thumbs; stiff; **ungainly,** uncouth, **ungraceful,** graceless, inelegant, *gauche* <Fr>; **gawky,** gawkish; **lubberly, loutish, oafish,** boorish, clownish, lumpish, slobbish <nf>; **sloppy, careless** 340.11; **ponderous, cumbersome,** lumbering, hulking, hulky; **unwieldy**

21 **botched, bungled,** fumbled, muffed, spoiled, **butchered,** murdered; **ill-managed,** ill-done, ill-conducted, ill-devised, ill-contrived, ill-executed; mismanaged, misconducted, **misdirected, misguided;** impolitic, ill-considered, ill-advised; negligent 340.10

22 <nf terms> **goofed-up, bobbled,** bitched, bitched-up, hashed-up, **messed-up, fouled-up, fucked-up, screwed-up, bollixed-up, loused-up,** gummed-up, buggered, buggered-up, snafued; clunky, half-assed; ass-backwards

ADVS 23 **unskillfully, inexpertly, unproficiently, uncleverly;** inefficiently; **incompetently, incapably,** inadequately, unfitly; **undexterously, undeftly, inadeptly,** unfacilely; **unaptly, inaptly, ineptly,** poorly

24 **clumsily, awkwardly; bunglingly, blunderingly; maladroitly,** unhandily; ungracefully, gracelessly, inelegantly, uncouthly; **ponderously,** **cumbersomely,** lumberingly, hulkingly, hulkily; ass-backwards <nf>

415 CUNNING

NOUNS 1 **cunning,** cunningness, **craft, craftiness,** callidity <old>, **artfulness, art, artifice, wiliness,** wiles, guile, **slyness,** insidiousness, suppleness <Scot>, **foxiness,** slipperiness, shiftiness, trickiness; low cunning, animal cunning; gamesmanship *and* one-upmanship <nf>; **canniness, shrewdness,** sharpness, acuteness, astuteness, **cleverness** 413.1; **resourcefulness, ingeniousness, wit,** inventiveness, readiness; subtlety, subtleness, Italian hand, fine Italian hand, finesse, restraint; acuteness, cuteness *and* cutification <nf>; Jesuitism, Jesuitry, **sophistry** 936; satanic cunning, the cunning of the serpent; sneakiness, concealment, **stealthiness, stealth** 345.4; cageyness <nf>, wariness 494.2

2 **Machiavellianism,** Machiavellism; realpolitik; **politics, diplomacy,** diplomatics; jobbery, jobbing

3 **stratagem, artifice,** art <old>, **craft, wile,** strategy, maneuver, **device,** wily device, **contrivance, expedient, design, scheme, trick,** cute trick, fetch, fakement <nf>, gimmick <nf>, **ruse, red herring, shift,** tactic, **maneuver, stroke,** stroke of policy, master stroke, **move,** coup, gambit, **ploy, dodge,** artful dodge; **game,** little game, racket *and* grift <nf>; **plot,** conspiracy, **intrigue;** sleight, feint, jugglery; method in one's madness; **subterfuge,** blind, dust in the eyes; chicanery, knavery, deceit, trickery 356.4

4 **machination, manipulation, wire-pulling** <nf>; influence, political influence, behind-the-scenes influence *or* pressure; **maneuvering,** maneuvers, tactical maneuvers; **tactics,** devices, expedients, gimmickry <nf>; web of deceit

5 **circumvention,** getting round *or* around; **evasion,** elusion, the slip <nf>, pretext; the runaround *and* buck-passing *and* passing the buck <nf>; **frustration, foiling, thwarting** 1012.3; **outwitting,** outsmarting, outguessing, **outmaneuvering**

6 **slyboots,** sly dog <nf>, **fox,** reynard, dodger, Artful Dodger <Charles Dickens>, crafty rascal, smooth *or* slick citizen <nf>, smooth *or* cool customer <nf>, smooth operator, slickster, smoothy *or* smoothie, glib tongue, smooth *or* sweet talker, smoothie <nf>, charmer; **trickster,** shyster <nf>, shady character, Philadelphia lawyer <nf>; horse trader, Yankee horse trader, wheeler-dealer; **swindler** 357.3

7 **strategist, tactician; maneuverer, machinator, manipulator, wire-puller** <nf>; calculator, schemer, **intriguer**

8 **Machiavellian,** Machiavel, Machiavellianist; **diplomat,** diplomatist, **politician** 610; political realist; influence peddler; powerbroker, kingmaker; power behind the throne, gray eminence, *éminence grise* <Fr>

VERBS 9 **live by one's wits,** fly by the seat of one's pants, play a deep game; use one's fine Italian hand, finesse; shift, dodge, twist and turn, zig and zag; have something up one's sleeve, hide one's hand, cover one's path, have an out *or* a way out *or* an escape hatch; **trick, deceive** 356.14

10 **maneuver, manipulate,** pull strings *or* wires; **machinate, contrive,** angle <nf>, **jockey, engineer;** play games <nf>; **plot, scheme, intrigue; finagle, wangle;** gerrymander; know a trick or two

11 **outwit, outfox, outsmart,** outguess, outfigure, **outmaneuver,** outgeneral, outflank, outplay, be one up on; get the better *or* best of, go one better, know a trick worth two of that; play one's trump card; **overreach,** outreach; **circumvent,** get round *or* around, **evade,** stonewall <nf>, **elude, frustrate, foil,** give the slip *or* runaround <nf>; pass the buck <nf>; pull a fast one <nf>, steal a march on; make a fool of, make a sucker *or* patsy of <nf>; be too much for, be too deep for; throw a curve <nf>, **deceive, victimize** 356.18

ADJS 12 **cunning, crafty, artful, wily,** callid <old>, guileful, **sly,** insidious, **shifty,** pawky <Brit>, arch, **smooth, slick** *and* slick as a whistle <nf>, **slippery,** snaky, serpentine, **foxy,** vulpine, feline, no flies on <nf>; **canny, shrewd,** knowing, sharp, razor-sharp, cute *or* cutesy *or* cutesy-poo <nf>, acute, astute, **clever;** resourceful, ingenious, inventive, ready; subtle; Jesuitical, **sophistical** 936.10; **tricky,** trickish, tricksy <old>, gimmicky <nf>; **Machiavellian,** Machiavellic, politic, diplomatic; strategic, tactical; deep, deep-laid; cunning as a fox *or* serpent, crazy like a fox <nf>, slippery as an eel, too clever by half; sneaky, clandestine, **stealthy** 345.12; cagey <nf>, wary 494.9**; scheming, designing; manipulative,** manipulatory; **deceitful**

ADVS 13 **cunningly, craftily, artfully,** wilily, guilefully, insidiously, shiftily, foxily, trickily, smoothly, slick <nf>; **slyly,** on the sly; **cannily, shrewdly,** knowingly, astutely, **cleverly;** subtlely; cagily <nf>, warily 494.13; diplomatically

416 ARTLESSNESS

NOUNS 1 **artlessness, ingenuousness, guilelessness; simplicity,** simpleness, plainness; simpleheartedness, simplemindedness; **unsophistication,** unsophisticatedness; *naïveté* <Fr>, naivety, naiveness, childlikeness; **innocence;** trustfulness, trustingness, unguardedness, unwariness, unsuspiciousness; **openness,** openheartedness, sincerity, **candor** 644.4; **integrity,** single-heartedness, single-mindedness, singleness of heart; directness, bluffness, bluntness, outspokenness

2 **naturalness,** naturalism, nature; state of nature; unspoiledness; **unaffectedness,** unaffectation, **unassumingness,** unpretendingness, unpretentiousness, undisguise; **inartificiality,** unartificialness, genuineness

3 **simple soul,** unsophisticate, naïf, **ingenue, innocent,** pure heart, **child,** mere child, infant, **babe,** baby, newborn babe, babe in the woods, lamb, dove; child of nature, noble savage; primitive; yokel, rube *and* hick <nf>; oaf, lout 924.5; dupe 358

VERBS 4 wear one's heart on one's sleeve, look one in the face, have no affectations

ADJS 5 **artless, simple,** plain, **guideless;** simplehearted, simpleminded; **ingenuous,** *ingénu* <Fr>; **unsophisticated, naive;** childlike, born yesterday; **innocent,** innocuous**;** trustful, trusting, unguarded, unwary, unreserved, confiding, unsuspicious, on the up and up; **open,** openhearted, sincere, candid, **frank** 644.17; single-hearted, single-minded; direct, bluff, blunt, outspoken

6 **natural,** naturelike, native; in the state of nature; primitive, primal, pristine, unspoiled, untainted, uncontaminated; **unaffected, unassuming, unpretending,** unpretentious, unfeigning, undisguising, undissimulating, undissembling, undesigning; **genuine, inartificial,** unartificial, unadorned, unvarnished, unembellished, uncontrived; homespun; **pastoral, rural,** arcadian, bucolic

ADVS 7 **artlessly, ingenuously, guilelessly;** simply, plainly; naturally, genuinely; naïvely; openly, openheartedly

417 AUTHORITY

NOUNS 1 **authority, prerogative, right, power,** faculty, competence *or* competency; **mandate,** popular authority *or* mandate, people's mandate, electoral mandate; regality, royal prerogative; constituted authority, vested authority; inherent authority; legal *or* lawful *or* rightful authority, legitimacy, law, eminent domain, divine right; derived *or* delegated authority, vicarious authority, indirect authority, constituted *or* invested authority, inherent authority; **the say** *and* **the say-so** <nf>; the man <nf>, Big Brother; rubber stamp; divine right, *jus divinum* <L>; absolute power, absolutism 612.8

2 **authoritativeness, authority, power,** powerfulness, magisterialness, **potency** *or* potence, puissance, **strength,** might, mightiness, string pulling, wire pulling, clout <nf>

3 **authoritativeness, masterfulness, lordliness,** magistrality, magisterialness; **arbitrariness,** peremptoriness, imperativeness, **imperiousness,** autocraticalness, high-handedness, dictatorialness, overbearingness, overbearance, overbearing, domineering, domineeringness, tyrannicalness, authoritarianism, bossism <nf>

4 **prestige, authority, influence,** influentialness; pressure, **weight,** weightiness, moment, **consequence;** eminence, **stature,** rank, seniority, preeminence, priority, precedence; **greatness** 247; **importance, prominence** 997.2

5 **governance, authority, jurisdiction, control, command, power, rule, reign,** regnancy, **dominion, sovereignty,** empire, empery, raj <India>, imperium, **sway; government** 612; administration, disposition 573.3; **control, grip,** claws, **clutches,** hand, hands, iron hand, talons

6 **dominance** *or* dominancy, **dominion, domination; preeminence, supremacy, superiority** 249; **ascendance** *or* **ascendancy; upper** *or* **whip hand, sway; sovereignty,** suzerainty, suzerainship, **overlordship;** primacy, principality, **predominance** *or* predominancy, predomination, prepotence *or* prepotency, hegemony; preponderance; balance of power; eminent domain

7 **mastership,** masterhood, masterdom, **mastery; leadership, headship, lordship;** hegemony; supervisorship, directorship 573.4; hierarchy, nobility, aristocracy, **ruling class** 575.15; chair, chairmanship; chieftainship, chieftaincy, chieftainry, chiefery; presidentship, presidency; premiership, prime-ministership, prime-ministry; governorship; princeship, princedom, principality; rectorship, rectorate; suzerainty, suzerainship; regency, regentship; prefectship, prefecture; proconsulship, proconsulate; provostship, provostry; protectorship, protectorate; seneschalship, seneschalsy; pashadom, pashalic; sheikhdom; emirate, viziership, vizierate; magistrateship, magistrature, magistracy; mayorship, mayoralty; sheriffdom, sheriffcy, sheriffalty, shrievalty; consulship, consulate; chancellorship, chancellery, chancellorate; seigniory; tribunate, aedileship; deanship, decanal authority, deanery; patriarchate, patriarchy <old>; bishopric, episcopacy; archbishopric, archiepiscopacy, archiepiscopate; metropolitanship, metropolitanate; popedom, popeship, popehood, papacy, pontificate, pontificality; dictatorship,

dictature; chess master, grand master, past master

8 **sovereignty, royalty,** regnancy, **majesty,** empire, empery, imperialism, **emperorship; kingship,** kinghood; queenship, queenhood; kaisership, kaiserdom; czardom; rajaship; sultanship, sultanate; caliphate; the throne, the Crown, the purple; royal insignia 647.3

9 **scepter, rod, staff,** wand, staff *or* rod *or* wand of office, baton, mace, truncheon, fasces; crosier, crook, cross-staff; caduceus; gavel; mantle; chain of office; portfolio

10 <seat of authority> saddle <nf>, **helm, driver's seat** <nf>; office of power, high office; seat, **chair,** bench; woolsack <Brit>; seat of state, seat of power; curule chair; dais; chairmanship, directorship, chieftainship, presidency, premiership, secretariat, governorship, mayoralty; consulate, proconsulate, prefecture, magistry; supremist

11 **throne,** royal seat; musnud *or* gaddi <India>; Peacock throne

12 <acquisition of authority> accession; succession, rightful *or* legitimate succession; **usurpation,** arrogation, assumption, taking over, seizure, seizure of power, takeover, coup d'etat, coup, revolution, overthrowing; anointment, anointing, consecration, coronation; selection, **delegation,** deputation, devolution, devolvement, assignment, nomination, **appointment; election,** mandate; **authorization,** empowerment, permission, grant, sanction, warrant, license, charter; consignation; job sharing

VERBS 13 **possess** *or* **wield** *or* **have authority, have power,** have the power, have in one's hands, have the right, have the say *or* say-so <nf>, have the whip hand, wear the crown, hold the prerogative, have the mandate; exercise sovereignty; be vested *or* invested, carry authority, have clout <nf>, have what one says go, have one's own way; show one's authority, crack the whip, throw one's weight around *and* ride herd <nf>, have under one's thumb, wear the pants, have over a barrel <nf>; **rule** 612.13, **control,** govern; supervise 573.10

14 **take command, take charge, take over,** take the helm, take the reins of government, take the reins into one's hand, take office, gain authority, get the power into one's hands, gain *or* get the upper hand, lead, take the lead; ascend *or* mount *or* succeed *or* accede to the throne, call the shots <nf>; **assume command,** assume, **usurp,** arrogate, seize; usurp *or* seize the throne *or* crown *or* mantle, usurp the prerogatives of the crown; seize power, execute a *coup d'état*

ADJS 15 **authoritative,** clothed *or* vested *or* invested with authority, **commanding, imperative; governing, controlling,** definitive, **ruling** 612.17; **preeminent, supreme,** administrative, managerial, bureaucratic, ruling, leading, **superior** 249.12; **powerful, potent,** puissant, mighty; dominant, ascendant, hegemonic, hegemonistic; **influential, prestigious, weighty,** momentous, consequential, eminent, substantial, considerable; great 247.6; important, prominent; ranking, senior; authorized, empowered, duly constituted, competent; **official,** *ex officio* <L>; authoritarian; absolute, autocratic, monocratic; **totalitarian**

16 **imperious,** imperial, **masterful,** authoritative, feudal, aristocratic, **lordly,** magistral, **magisterial,** commanding; arrogant 141.9; **arbitrary, peremptory,** imperative; absolute, absolutist, absolutistic; **dictatorial, authoritarian; bossy** <nf>, **domineering, high-handed, overbearing,** overruling, imperious; autocratic, monocratic, **despotic, tyrannical;** tyrannous, grinding, oppressive 98.24; repressive, suppressive 428.11; strict, severe 425.6

17 **sovereign; regal, royal, majestic,** purple; **kinglike, kingly,** "every inch a king"—Shakespeare; **imperial,** imperious *or* imperatorious <old>; imperatorial; monarchic *or* monarchical, monarchal, monarchial; tetrarchic; princely, princelike; **queenly,** queenlike; dynastic

ADVS 18 **authoritatively,** with authority, by virtue of office; **commandingly, imperatively; powerfully, potently,** puissantly, mightily; **influentially, weightily,** momentously, consequentially; **officially,** *ex cathedra* <L>

19 **imperiously, masterfully,** magisterially; **arbitrarily, peremptorily; autocratically, dictatorially, high-handedly, domineeringly, overbearingly, despotically, tyrannically**

20 **by authority of,** in the name of, in *or* by virtue of, by the power vested in

21 **in authority,** in power, in charge, in control, in **command,** at the reins, at the head, **at the helm,** at the wheel, **in the saddle** *or* driver's seat <nf>, on the throne

418 LAWLESSNESS
<absence of authority>

NOUNS 1 **lawlessness; licentiousness,** license, uncontrol, anything goes, unrestraint 430.3; indiscipline, insubordination, mutiny, disobedience 327; permissiveness; **irresponsibility,** unaccountability; willfulness, unchecked *or* rampant will; interregnum, power vacuum; defiance of authority, lack of authority, breakdown

of authority, breakdown of law and order; overthrow, coup, coup d'etat

2 **anarchy,** anarchism; **disorderliness, unruliness,** misrule, **disorder,** disruption, disorganization, confusion, arrogation, unruliness, riot, **turmoil, chaos,** primal chaos, tohubohu; antinomianism; **nihilism;** syndicalism *and* anarcho-syndicalism *and* criminal syndicalism <old>, lynch law, mob rule *or* law, mobocracy, ochlocracy; **law of the jungle;** dog eat dog; subversion, sedition, unrestraint, insubordination, disobedience, revolution 860; rebellion 327.4

3 **anarchist,** anarch; antinomian; **nihilist,** syndicalist *and* anarcho-syndicalist <old>; subversive, seditionary; revolutionist 860.3; mutineer, rebel 327.5

VERBS 4 **reject** *or* **defy authority,** usurp power *or* authority, enthrone one's own will; **take the law in one's own hands,** act on one's own responsibility; do *or* go as one pleases, indulge oneself; be a law unto oneself, answer to no man, undermine, arrogate; resist control; overthrow, depose, topple; "swear allegiance to the words of no master"—Horace

ADJS 5 **lawless; licentious, ungoverned,** undisciplined, unrestrained; permissive; insubordinate, mutinous, disobedient 327.8; **uncontrolled,** uncurbed, unbridled, unchecked, rampant, untrammeled, unreined, unrestrained, reinless, anything goes; **irresponsible,** wildcat, unaccountable; selfwilled, willful, headstrong, heady, defiant; rebellious, riotous, seditious, insurgent

6 **anarchic, anarchical,** anarchial, anarchistic; **unruly, disorderly,** disorganized, chaotic; antinomian; **nihilistic,** syndicalistic, ochlocratic, mobocratic; every man for himself, ungovernable

ADVS 7 **lawlessly,** licentiously; anarchically, chaotically

419 PRECEPT

NOUNS 1 **precept,** prescript, **prescription, teaching; instruction, direction, charge,** commission, injunction, dictate; **order,** command 420

2 **rule, law, canon, maxim,** dictum, moral, moralism; **norm, standard;** formula, form; rule of action *or* conduct, moral precept; commandment, *mitzvah* <Heb>; sutra; **tradition;** ordinance, imperative, **regulation,** reg <nf>, *règlement* <Fr>; **principle,** principium, settled principle, general principle *or* truth, tenet, convention; **guideline,** ground rule, rubric, protocol, working rule, working principle, standard procedure; guiding principle, golden rule, caveat emptor; **code;** gold standard

3 formula, form <old>, **recipe,** receipt; **prescription;** formulary

ADJS **4 preceptive,** didactic, didactive, instructive, moralistic, **prescriptive;** prescript, prescribed, mandatory, hard-and-fast, binding, dictated; formulary, standard, regulation, official, authoritative, canonical, statutory, rubric, rubrical, protocolary, protocolic; **normative; conventional;** traditional

420 COMMAND

NOUNS **1 command, commandment, order,** direct order, command decision, **bidding,** behest, hest <old>, imperative, **dictate,** dictation, **will, pleasure,** say-so <nf>, word, word of command, *mot d'ordre* <Fr>; special order; **authority** 417
2 injunction, charge, commission, **mandate**
3 direction, directive, instruction, rule, regulation; prescript, prescription, **precept** 419; general order
4 decree, decreement <old>, decretum, decretal, rescript, fiat, **edict,** *edictum* <L>; **law** 673.3; **rule, ruling,** dictum, ipse dixit; ordinance, *ordonnance* <Fr>, appointment <old>; **proclamation,** pronouncement, pronunciamento, **declaration,** ukase; bull, brevet <old>; decree-law, *décret-loi* <Fr>; *senatus consultum* <L>, senatus consult; diktat
5 summons, bidding, beck, call, calling, nod, **beck and call,** preconization; **convocation,** convoking; evocation, calling forth, invocation; requisition, indent <chiefly Brit>
6 court order, injunction, legal order, warrant, subpoena, citation, injunction, interdict *or* interdiction
7 process server, summoner
VERBS **8 command, order, dictate, direct, instruct,** mandate, **bid, enjoin, charge,** commission, call on *or* upon; issue a writ *or* an injunction; **decree, rule, ordain,** promulgate; give an order *or* a direct order, issue a command, say the word, give the word *or* word of command; call the shots *or* tune *or* signals *or* play <nf>; order about *or* around; **speak, proclaim, declare,** pronounce 352.12
9 prescribe, require, demand, dictate, impose, lay down, set, fix, appoint, make obligatory *or* mandatory; decide once and for all, carve in stone, set in concrete <nf>; authorize 443.11
10 lay down the law, put one's foot down <nf>, read the riot act, lower the boom <nf>, set the record straight
11 summon, call, demand, preconize; call for, send for *or* after, bid come; **cite, summons** <nf>, **subpoena,** serve; page; convoke, convene, call together; call away; muster, invoke, conjure; order

up, summon up, muster up, call up, conjure up, magic *or* magic up <Brit>; evoke, call forth, summon forth, call out; recall, call back, call in; requisition, indent <chiefly Brit>
ADJS **12 mandatory,** mandated, **imperative, compulsory,** prescript, prescriptive, **obligatory,** must <nf>; dictated, imposed, required, entailed, decretory; decisive, final, peremptory, absolute, eternal, written, hard-and-fast, carved in stone, set in concrete <nf>, ultimate, conclusive, binding, irrevocable, without appeal
13 commanding, imperious, imperative, jussive, peremptory, abrupt; **directive, instructive; mandating,** dictating, compelling, obligating, **prescriptive,** preceptive; decretory, decretive, decretal; **authoritative** 417.15
ADVS **14 commandingly, imperatively,** peremptorily
15 by order *or* **command,** at the word of command, as ordered *or* required, to order; mandatorily, compulsorily, obligatorily

421 DEMAND

NOUNS **1 demand, claim, call; requisition,** requirement, stated requirement, order, rush order, indent <chiefly Brit>; seller's market, land-office business; strong *or* heavy demand, draft, drain, levy, tax, taxing; imposition, impost, tribute, duty, dun, contribution; insistent demand, rush; exorbitant *or* extortionate demand, exaction, extortion, blackmail; **ultimatum,** nonnegotiable demand; notice, warning 399
2 stipulation, provision, proviso, condition; **terms;** exception, reservation; **qualification** 959
3 <nf terms> catch, **Catch-22** 356.12, kicker, zinger, snag, joker; strings, strings attached; ifs, ands, *and* buts; whereases, howevers, howsomevers
4 insistence, exigence, importunity, importunateness, importunacy, **demandingness,** pertinaciousness, pertinacity; pressure, pressingness, **urgency, exigency** 997.4; **persistence** 360.1
VERBS **5 demand, ask, ask for,** make a demand; **call for,** call on *or* upon one for, appeal to one for; call out for, cry *or* cry out for, clamor for; **claim, challenge, require;** levy, **impose,** impose on one for; **exact, extort,** squeeze, screw; blackmail; requisition, make *or* put in **requisition,** dun, indent <chiefly Brit>, **confiscate; order,** put in *or* place an order, order up; deliver *or* issue an ultimatum; warn 399.5
6 claim, pretend to, lay claim to, stake a claim <nf>, put *or* have dibs on <nf>, assert *or* vindicate a claim *or* right *or* title to; have going for it *or* one <nf>; **challenge**

7 stipulate, stipulate for, specifically provide, set conditions *or* terms, make reservations; **qualify** 959.3

8 insist, insist on *or* **upon,** stick to <nf>, set one's heart *or* mind upon; **take one's stand upon,** stand on *or* upon, put *or* lay it on the line <nf>, make no bones about it; stand upon one's rights, **put one's foot down** <nf>; brook *or* take no denial, not take no for an answer; **maintain, contend,** assert; urge, press 375.14; **persist** 360.2

ADJS **9 demanding, exacting,** exigent; draining, taxing, exorbitant, extortionate, grasping; **insistent,** instant, **importunate,** urgent, pertinacious, pressing, loud, clamant, crying, clamorous; persistent

10 claimed, spoken for; requisitioned; requisitorial, requisitory

ADVS **11 demandingly, exactingly,** exigently; exorbitantly, extortionately; **insistently, importunately, urgently,** pressingly, clamorously, loudly, clamantly

12 on demand, at demand, **on call,** upon presentation

422 ADVICE

NOUNS **1 advice, counsel, recommendation, suggestion,** rede <Brit>; proposition, proposal; advising, advocacy; **direction, instruction,** guidance, briefing; **exhortation,** hortation <old>, enjoinder, expostulation, remonstrance; **sermons,** sermonizing, preaching, preachiness; **admonition,** monition, monitory *or* monitory letter, caution, caveat, **warning** 399; **idea,** thought, opinion 953.6, precept; consultancy, consultantship, **consultation,** parley 541.5, advisement; council 423; **counseling;** guidance counseling, educational counseling, vocational guidance; mentorship; constructive criticism

2 piece of advice, **word of advice, word to the wise,** words of wisdom, pearls of wisdom, *verbum sapienti* <L>, verb *or* verbum sap <nf>, word in the ear, maxim, **hint, broad hint, flea in the ear** <nf>, **tip** <nf>, one's two cents' worth <nf>, intimation, insinuation; ear worm <nf>

3 adviser, advisor, counsel, counselor, consultant, professional consultant, expert, maven <nf>, boffin <Brit nf>; instructor, guide, **mentor,** nestor, orienter; confidant *or* confidante, personal adviser; admonisher, monitor, Dutch uncle; Polonius <Shakespeare>, preceptist; **teacher** 571; meddler, buttinsky *and* yenta *and* kibitzer *and* backseat driver <nf>; advocate; brain trust

4 advisee, counselee; client

VERBS **5 advise, counsel, recommend, suggest, advocate,** propose, submit, propound; instruct, coach, guide, direct, brief; prescribe; weigh in with advice <nf>, give a piece of advice, give a hint *or* broad hint, hint at, intimate, insinuate, put a flea in one's ear <nf>, have a word with one, speak words of wisdom; meddle, kibitz <nf>; confer, consult with 541.10

6 admonish, exhort, expostulate, remonstrate, preach; **enjoin, charge,** call upon one to; caution, issue a caveat, wag one's finger <nf>; advise against, warn away, warn off, **warn** 399.5, dissuade; move, prompt, **urge, incite, encourage, induce, persuade** 375.23; **implore** 440.11

7 take *or* **accept advice, follow advice,** follow, follow implicitly <nf>, buy *or* buy into <nf>; go along with <nf>; consult, confer; solicit advice, desire guidance, implore counsel; **be advised by;** refer to, have at one's elbow, take one's cue from; seek a second opinion; put heads together *or* have a powwow with <nf>, huddle

ADJS **8 advisory,** recommendatory; **consultative,** consultatory, consultive; directive, instructive; **admonitory,** monitory, monitorial, cautionary, **warning** 399.7; **expostulative,** expostulatory, **remonstrative,** remonstratory, remonstrant; **exhortative,** exhortatory, hortative, hortatory, preachy <nf>, **didactic,** moralistic, sententious

PHRS **9 too many cooks spoil the broth,** another country heard from

423 COUNCIL

NOUNS **1 council,** conclave, *concilium* <L>, deliberative *or* advisory body, **assembly;** deliberative assembly, consultative assembly; chamber, house; **board,** court, bench, panel; **full assembly,** plenum, plenary session; **congress,** diet, synod, senate, soviet; **legislature** 613; **cabinet,** divan, council of ministers, council of state, US Cabinet, British Cabinet; kitchen cabinet, camarilla; staff; junta, directory; Sanhedrin; privy council; common council, county council, parish council, borough *or* town council, city *or* municipal council, village council; brain trust <nf>, brains trust <Brit nf>, group *or* corps *or* body of advisers, inner circle; council of war; council fire, syndicate, **association** 617, **conference** 541.5; **assembly** 770.2; **tribunal** 595

2 committee, subcommittee, standing committee; select committee, special committee, ad hoc committee; committee of one

3 forum, conference, discussion group, buzz session <nf>, **round table, panel;** open forum, colloquium, symposium; town meeting; board meeting; **powwow** <nf>; working lunch, power lunch, power breakfast

4 ecclesiastical council, chapter, classis, conclave,

conference, caucus, congregation, consistory, convention, convocation, presbytery, session, synod, vestry; parochial council, parochial church council; diocesan conference, diocesan court; provincial court, plenary council; ecumenical council; Council of Nicaea, Council of Trent, Lateran Council, Vatican Council, Vatican Two; conciliarism

ADJS **5 conciliar,** council, councilmanic, aldermanic; **consultative, deliberative, advisory;** synodal, synodic, synodical

ADVS **6 in council, in conference, in consultation, in a huddle** <nf>, in conclave; **in session,** sitting

424 COMPULSION

NOUNS **1 compulsion, obligation,** obligement; **command** 420; **necessity** 963; **inevitability** 963.7; **irresistibility, compulsiveness; forcing,** enforcement; command performance; **constraint,** coaction; **restraint** 428; obsession; self-determination

2 force, *ultima ratio* <L>; **brute force,** naked force, rule of might, big battalions, **main force,** physical force; the right of the strong, the law of the jungle; **tyranny** 612.9; steamroller <nf>, irresistible force

3 coercion, coercing, intimidation, scare tactics, headbanging *and* arm-twisting <nf>, **duress; the strong arm** *and* strong-arm tactics <nf>, a pistol *or* gun to one's head, the sword, the mailed fist, the bludgeon, the boot in the face, the jackboot, the big stick, the club, *argumentum baculinum* <L>; terrorism; **pressure, high pressure,** high-pressure methods; **violence** 671; impressment

VERBS **4 compel, force, make;** have, cause, cause to; **constrain, bind,** tie, tie one's hands; **restrain** 428.7; enforce, **drive,** impel; dragoon, use force upon, force one's hand, hold a pistol *or* gun to one's head; browbeat

5 oblige, necessitate, require, exact, demand, dictate, impose, call for; take *or* brook no denial; leave no option *or* escape, admit of no option

6 press; bring pressure to bear upon, put pressure on, bear down on, bear against, bear hard upon, put under duress

7 coerce, use violence, terrorize, ride roughshod, intimidate, bully, bludgeon, blackjack; hijack, shanghai, dragoon, carjack

8 <nf terms> **twist one's arm, arm-twist, twist arms, knock or bang heads, knock** *or* bang heads together, strong-arm, steamroller, bulldoze, **pressure,** high-pressure, lean on, squeeze; put the screws on *or* to, get one over a barrel *or* under one's thumb, hold one's feet to the fire, turn on the heat; pull rank; ram *or* cram down one's throat

9 be compelled, be coerced, have to 963.10; be stuck with <nf>, can't help but

ADJS **10 compulsory, compulsive,** compulsatory, **compelling; pressing, driving,** imperative, imperious; constraining, coactive; **restraining** 428.11; **irresistible**

11 obligatory, compulsory, imperative, mandatory, required, dictated, **binding;** involuntary; **necessary** 963.12; **inevitable** 963.15

12 coercive, forcible; steamroller *and* bulldozer *and* sledgehammer *and* strong-arm <nf>; terroristic, violent

ADVS **13 compulsively,** compulsorily, **compellingly,** imperatively, imperiously

14 forcibly, by force, by main force, by *force majeure,* by a strong arm; by force of arms, *vi et armis* <L>, at gunpoint, with a pistol *or* gun to one's head, at the point of a gun, at the point of the sword *or* bayonet, at bayonet point

15 obligatorily, compulsorily, mandatorily, by stress of, under press of; under the lash *or* gun; of necessity

425 STRICTNESS

NOUNS **1 strictness, severity, harshness, stringency,** astringency, **hard line; discipline,** strict *or* tight *or* rigid discipline, regimentation, spit and polish; **austerity, sternness,** grimness, ruggedness, **toughness** <nf>; **belt-tightening;** Spartanism; authoritarianism; demandingness, exactingness; **meticulousness** 339.3

2 firmness, rigor, rigorousness, rigidness, rigidity, stiffness, **hardness,** obduracy, obdurateness, **inflexibility,** inexorability, unyieldingness, unbendingness, impliability, unrelentingness, **relentlessness; uncompromisingness;** stubbornness, obstinacy 361; purism; precisianism, puritanism, fundamentalism, orthodoxy

3 firm hand, iron hand, heavy hand, strong hand, tight hand, tight rein; tight *or* taut ship

VERBS **4 hold** *or* **keep a tight hand upon,** keep a firm hand on, keep a tight rein on, rule with an iron hand, rule with a rod of iron, knock *or* bang heads together <nf>; regiment, discipline; run a tight *or* taut ship, ride herd, keep one in line; maintain the highest standards, not spare oneself nor anyone else, go out of one's way, go the extra mile <nf>

5 deal hardly *or* **harshly with,** deal hard measure to, lay a heavy hand on, bear hard upon, **take a hard line,** not pull one's punches <nf>

ADJS **6 strict, exacting,** exigent, demanding, not to be trifled with, **stringent,** astringent; disciplined, spit-and-polish; **severe, harsh,** dour, unsparing; **stern, grim, austere,** rugged, **tough** <nf>; Spartan,

Spartanic; **hard-line,** authoritarian 417.16; **meticulous** 339.12

7 **firm, rigid, rigorous,** rigorist, rigoristic, stiff, **hard,** iron, steel, steely, hard-shell, obdurate, **inflexible,** ironhanded, inexorable, dour, **unyielding,** unbending, impliable, **relentless,** unrelenting, procrustean; **uncompromising;** stubborn, obstinate 361.8; purist, puristic; puritan, puritanic, puritanical, fundamentalist, orthodox; ironbound, rockbound, musclebound, ironclad <nf>; straitlaced, hidebound

ADVS 8 **strictly, severely, stringently, harshly; sternly,** grimly, **austerely,** ruggedly, toughly <nf>

9 **firmly, rigidly, rigorously,** stiffly, stiff, hardly, obdurately, **inflexibly,** impliably, inexorably, unyieldingly, unbendingly; **uncompromisingly, relentlessly,** unrelentingly; ironhandedly, with a firm *or* a strong *or* a heavy *or* a tight *or* an iron hand

426 LAXNESS

NOUNS 1 **laxness, laxity, slackness, looseness,** relaxedness; loosening, relaxation; imprecision, sloppiness <nf>, carelessness, remissness, negligence 340.1; indifference 102; weakness 16; impotence 19; unrestraint 430.3

2 **unstrictness,** nonstrictness, undemandingness, unsevereness, unharshness; leniency 427; **permissiveness,** overpermissiveness, overindulgence, **softness;** unsternness, unaustereness; easygoingness, easiness; **flexibility,** pliancy; latitude, lenience

VERBS 3 **hold a loose rein, give free rein to,** give the reins to, **give one his head,** give a free course to, give rope enough to; permit all *or* anything

ADJS 4 **lax, slack, loose,** relaxed; imprecise, sloppy <nf>, careless, slipshod; remiss, negligent 340.10; indifferent 102.6; weak 16.12; impotent 19.13; untrammeled, unrestrained

5 **unstrict,** undemanding, **unexacting; unsevere, unharsh; unstern,** unaustere; lenient 427.7; **permissive,** overpermissive, overindulgent, **soft;** easy, easygoing, laid-back <nf>, low-maintenance, concessory; **flexible,** pliant, yielding

427 LENIENCY

NOUNS 1 **leniency** *or* lenience, lenientness, lenity; **clemency,** clementness, **mercifulness,** mercy, **humaneness,** humanity, pity, **compassion** 145.1; **mildness, gentleness,** tenderness, softness, moderateness; **easiness,** easygoingness; laxness 426; **forebearance,** forbearing, patience 134; acceptance, concession, **tolerance** 979.4; kid gloves, kid-glove treatment, light hand *or* rein

2 **compliance, complaisance,** obligingness, accommodatingness, **agreeableness;** affability, graciosity, graciousness, generousness, decency, amiability; kindness, kindliness, benignity, **benevolence** 143

3 **indulgence, humoring,** obliging; favoring, gratification, pleasing; **pampering,** cosseting, **coddling,** mollycoddling, petting, **spoiling; permissiveness,** overpermissiveness, overindulgence, acquiescence; sparing the rod; laissez faire

4 **spoiled child** *or* **brat,** *enfant gâté* <Fr>, pampered darling, mama's boy, mollycoddle, sissy; *enfant terrible* <Fr>, naughty child, holy terror

VERBS 5 **be** *or* **go easy on,** ease up on, handle with kid *or* velvet gloves, use a light hand *or* rein, slap one's wrist, spare the rod, let off the hook; **tolerate,** bear with 134.5

6 **indulge, humor, oblige;** favor, please, gratify, satisfy, **cater to; give way to,** yield to, let one have his own way; **pamper,** cosset, **coddle,** mollycoddle, pet, make a lap dog of, **spoil;** spare the rod; make few demands

ADJS 7 **lenient, mild, gentle,** mild-mannered, tender, humane, compassionate, **clement,** merciful 145.7; soft, moderate, **easy,** easygoing; lax 426.4; forgiving 148.6; **forebearing, forbearant,** patient 134.9; accepting, **tolerant** 979.11

8 **indulgent, compliant,** complaisant; **obliging, accommodating, agreeable,** amiable, gracious, generous, magnanimous, benignant, affable, decent, kind, kindly, benign, benevolent 143.15; **hands-off** <nf>, permissive, overpermissive, overindulgent, spoiling

9 **indulged, pampered, coddled, spoiled,** spoiled rotten <nf>

428 RESTRAINT

NOUNS 1 **restraint, constraint; inhibition;** legal restraint, injunction, enjoining, enjoinder, interdict, veto; **control, curb, check,** rein, arrest, arrestation; **retardation,** deceleration, slowing down; cooling *and* cooling off *and* cooling down <nf>; retrenchment, curtailment; self-control 359.5; **hindrance** 1012; rationing; thought control; restraint of trade, monopoly, protection, protectionism, protective tariff, tariff wall; clampdown *and* crackdown <nf>, proscription, **prohibition** 444

2 **suppression, repression,** oppression; **subdual,** quelling, putting down, shutting *or* closing down, smashing, crushing; quashing, squashing *and* squelching <nf>; smothering, stifling, suffocating, strangling, throttling; extinguishment, quenching; **censorship,** censoring, bleeping *or* bleeping out <nf>, blue laws

3 **restriction, limitation, confinement;** Hobson's choice, no choice, zero option; circumscription 210; stint, cramping, cramp; qualification 959

4 **shackle,** restraint, **restraints, fetter, hamper,** trammel, trammels, **manacle,** gyves, bond, **bonds,** irons, chains, ball and chain; stranglehold; **handcuffs,** cuffs, bracelets <nf>; stocks, bilbo, pillory; **tether,** spancel, leash, lead <chiefly Brit>, leading string; **rein;** hobble, hopple; strait-jacket, strait-waistcoat <Brit>, camisole; yoke, collar; bridle, halter; **muzzle, gag;** electronic ankle bracelet *and* offender's tag *and* monitor; iron rule, iron hand

5 **lock,** bolt, bar, padlock, catch, safety catch; barrier 1012.5

6 restrictionist, protectionist, monopolist; censor; screw <nf>

VERBS 7 **restrain, constrain, control, govern,** guard, contain, keep under control, put *or* lay under restraint; **inhibit,** straiten <old>; enjoin, clamp *or* crack down on <nf>, proscribe, prohibit 444.3; **curb, check, arrest, bridle,** get under control, rein, snub, snub in; **retard,** slow down, decelerate; **cool** *and* **cool off** *and* **cool down** <nf>; retrench, curtail; hold, **hold in,** keep, withhold, hold up <nf>, **keep from;** hinder 1012.10; **hold back, keep back,** pull, set back; **hold in, keep in,** pull in, rein in; **hold** *or* **keep in check, hold at bay,** hold in leash, tie one down, tie one's hands; hold fast, keep a tight hand on; restrain oneself, not go too far, not go off the deep end <nf>

8 suppress, repress, stultify; **keep down,** hold down, keep under; **close** *or* shut down; **subdue, quell, put down,** smash, **crush; quash, squash** *and* **squelch** <nf>; **extinguish,** quench, stanch, damp down, pour water on, dash *or* pour cold water on, drown, kill; **smother, stifle,** suffocate, asphyxiate, strangle, throttle, choke off, **muzzle, gag;** censor, bleep *or* bleep out <nf>, silence; sit on *and* sit down on *and* slap *or* smack down <nf>; jump on *and* crack down on *and* clamp down on <nf>, put *or* keep the lid on <nf>; bottle up, cork, cork up

9 **restrict, limit, narrow, confine,** tighten; ground, restrict to home, barracks, bedroom, quarters, etc; circumscribe 210.4; keep in *or* within bounds, keep from spreading, localize; **cage in,** hem, hem in, box, box in *or* up; **cramp,** stint, cramp one's style; qualify 959.3

10 **bind, restrain, tie,** tie up, put the clamps on, **strap,** lash, leash, pinion, fasten, secure, make fast; **hamper, trammel,** entrammel; rope; **chain,** enchain; **shackle, fetter, manacle,** gyve, **put in irons; handcuff, tie one's hands; tie hand and foot,** hog-tie <nf>; straitjacket; hobble, hopple, fetter, leash, put on a lead <chiefly Brit>, spancel; tether, picket, moor, anchor; tie down, pin down,

peg down; get a stranglehold on, put a half nelson on <nf>; **bridle;** gag, muzzle

ADJS 11 **restraining, constraining; inhibiting,** inhibitive; **suppressive, repressive,** oppressive, stultifying; controlling, on top of <nf>, prohibitive

12 **restrictive,** limitative, restricting, **narrowing, limiting, confining,** cramping; censorial

13 **restrained, constrained, inhibited,** pent up; guarded; controlled, curbed, bridled; **under restraint,** under control, in check, under discipline; grounded, out of circulation; slowed down, retarded, arrested, in remission; in *or* on leash, in leading strings

14 **suppressed, repressed; subdued,** quelled, put down, smashed, crushed; quashed, squashed *and* squelched <nf>; smothered, stifled, suffocated; censored

15 **restricted, limited, confined;** circumscribed 210.6, hemmed in, hedged in *or* about, boxed in; landlocked; **shut-in,** stormbound, weatherbound, windbound, icebound, snowbound; cramped, stinted; qualified 959.10; under arrest, up the river <nf>, doing time <nf>, in the big house <nf>

16 **bound, tied,** bound hand *and* foot, tied up, tied down, strapped, hampered, trammeled, shackled, handcuffed, fettered, manacled, tethered, leashed; **in bonds,** in irons *or* chains, ironbound

429 CONFINEMENT

NOUNS 1 **confinement,** locking-up, lockup, lockdown, caging, penning, putting behind barriers, impoundment, **restraint,** restriction; check, **restraint, constraint** 428.1

2 **quarantine, isolation,** cordoning off, segregation, separation, sequestration, seclusion; walling in *or* up *or* off; sanitary cordon, *cordon sanitaire* <Fr>, cordon; quarantine flag, yellow flag, yellow jack

3 **imprisonment, jailing,** incarceration, **internment,** immurement, immuration; **detention, captivity,** detainment, duress, durance, durance vile; close arrest, house arrest; term of imprisonment; preventive detention; minimum- *or* maximum-security imprisonment *or* detention; lockdown, solitary confinement

4 **commitment,** committal, consignment; recommitment, remand; mittimus <law>; institutionalization

5 **custody,** custodianship, keep <old>, **keeping, care, change, ward,** guarding, hold, protective *or* preventive custody; protection, safekeeping 1008.1

6 **arrest,** arrestment, arrestation, pinch *and* bust *and* collar <nf>; **capture, apprehension, seizure,** netting <nf>; house arrest, protective *or* preventive custody

7 **place of confinement,** close quarters, not enough

room to swing a cat; limbo, bardo, hell, purgatory; pound, pinfold *or* penfold; **cage; enclosure,** pen, coop 212.3

8 prison, prison house, correctional *or* correction facility, minimum- *or* maximum-security facility, **penitentiary,** pen <nf>, keep, penal institution, bastille, state prison, federal prison; house of detention *or* correction, detention center, detention home; **jail, gaol** <Brit>, jailhouse, lockup, bridewell <Brit>, county jail, city jail; maximum- *or* minimum-security prison; **military prison, guardhouse, stockade, brig; dungeon,** oubliette, black hole; **reformatory,** house of correction, reform school, training school, industrial school, borstal *or* borstal institution <Brit>; debtor's prison *and* sponging house <old>; **prison camp,** internment camp, detention camp, labor camp, forced-labor camp, gulag, **concentration camp;** prisoner-of-war camp *or* stockade, POW camp, prison farm; cell; bullpen; solitary confinement, the hole <nf>, solitary; **cell,** prison *or* jail cell; detention center, **detention cell,** holding cell, lockup; tank *and* drunk tank <nf>; cellblock, cellhouse; condemned cell, death cell, death house *or* row, jail cell; penal settlement *or* colony, Devil's Island, Alcatraz; halfway house, reformatory, reform school, detension home

9 <nf terms> **slammer, slam, jug,** can, coop, cooler, hoosegow, stir, clink, pokey *or* poky, nick *and* quod *and* chokey <Brit>, hoosegow; **joint,** big house, big school, big cage, big joint, brig, tank, icebox

10 jailer, gaoler <Brit>, correctional *or* correction *or* corrections officer; **keeper, warder,** prison guard, **turnkey,** bull *and* screw <nf>; **warden,** governor <Brit>, commandant, principal keeper; custodian, caretaker, guardian 1008.6; **guard** 1008.9

11 prisoner, captive, inmate, *détenu* <Fr>, cageling; arrestee; **convict,** con <nf>; **jailbird** <nf>, gaolbird <Brit nf>, stir bird <nf>, lifer, collar, yardbird, lag *or* lagger <Brit>; **detainee; internee; prisoner of war** *or* POW; enemy prisoner of war *or* EPWS; political prisoner, prisoner of conscience, political detainee, terror suspect; lifer <nf>; trusty *or* trustee; condemned prisoner; parolee, ticket-of-leave man *or* ticket-of-leaver <Brit>; ex-convict; chain-gang member, hostage

VERBS 12 confine, shut in, shut away, coop in, hem in, fence in *or* up, wall in *or* up, rail in; **shut up, coop up, pen up,** box up, mew up, bottle up, cork up, seal up, **impound;** pen, coop, pound <old>, crib, mew, cloister, immure, cage, cage in, encage, **enclose** 212.5; **hold, keep in,** hold *or* keep in custody, **detain,** keep in detention, constrain, ground, **restrain,** hold in restraint; check, inhibit 428.7; restrict 428.9; shackle 428.10

13 quarantine, isolate, segregate, separate, seclude; **cordon, cordon off,** seal off, rope off, wall off, set up barriers, put behind barriers

14 imprison, incarcerate, intern, immure; **jail,** gaol <Brit>, jug <nf>, put under security, put behind bars, put away, put *or* throw into jail, throw under the jailhouse <nf>; throw *or* cast in prison, clap up, clap in jail *or* prison, send up the river <nf>, send to the big house <nf>; **lock up,** lock in, bolt in, put *or* keep under lock *and* key; hold captive, hold prisoner, hold in captivity; hold under close *or* house arrest, throw in the tank *or* cooler

15 arrest, make an arrest, put under arrest, pick up; catch flat-footed; catch with one's pants down *or* hand in the till <nf>, catch one in the act *or* red-handed *or* in flagrante delicto, catch *or* have one dead to rights; run down, run to earth, **take captive, take prisoner, apprehend, capture,** seize, net <nf>, lay by the heels, **take into custody,** entrap

16 <nf terms> **bust, pinch,** make a pinch, nab, collar, nick, pull in, **run in,** collar

17 commit, consign, commit to prison, send to jail, send up *and* send up the river <nf>; commit to an institution, institutionalize; recommit, remit, remand

18 be imprisoned, do *or* **serve time** <nf>; pay one's debt to society, land in the cooler, lag <Brit>

ADJS 19 confined, in confinement, **shut-in,** pent, **pent-up,** penned in, kept in, under restraint, held, in detention; impounded; grounded, out of circulation; **detained;** restricted 428.15; cloistered, enclosed 212.10

20 quarantined, isolated, segregated, separated; cordoned, cordoned *or* sealed *or* roped off

21 jailed, jugged <nf>, **imprisoned, incarcerated, interned,** immured; **in prison,** in stir <nf>, in captivity, captive, **behind bars,** locked up, under lock *and* key, in durance vile, serving a sentence; doing time, on the inside, on ice, in the cooler, up the river, in the big house

22 under arrest, in custody, in hold, in charge <Brit>, under *or* in detention; under close arrest, under house arrest

430 FREEDOM

NOUNS 1 freedom, liberty; license, loose <old>; run *and* the run of <nf>, "the right to live as we wish"—Epictetus; **civil liberty,** the Four Freedoms <F D Roosevelt>: freedom of speech *and* expression, freedom of worship, freedom from want, freedom from fear; freedom of movement; constitutional freedom; lack of censorship; academic freedom; artistic license, poetic license

2 right, rights, civil rights, civil liberties,

constitutional rights, legal rights; Bill of Rights, Petition of Right, Declaration of Right, Declaration of the Rights of Man, Magna Charta *or* Carta; **unalienable rights, human rights,** natural rights, "life, liberty, and the pursuit of happiness"— Thomas Jefferson; diplomatic immunity

3 **unrestraint, unconstraint,** noncoercion, nonintimidation; **unreserve,** irrepressibleness, irrepressibility, uninhibitedness, exuberance 109.4; **immoderacy, intemperance,** incontinence, uncontrol, unruliness, indiscipline; **abandon,** abandonment, **licentiousness,** wantonness, riotousness, wildness, permissiveness, unstrictness, **laxness** 426; one's own way, one's own devices

4 **latitude, scope, room,** range, way, field, maneuvering space *or* room, room to swing a cat <nf>; **margin,** clearance, **space,** open space *or* field, elbowroom, breathing space *or* room, **leeway** <nf>, sea room, wide berth; **tolerance; free scope,** full *or* ample scope, **free hand,** free play, free course; **carte blanche,** blank check; no holds barred; swing, play, full swing; rope, long rope *or* tether, rope enough to hang oneself

5 **independence, self-determination, self government,** self-direction, autonomy, home rule; autarky, autarchy, self-containment, self-sufficiency; **individualism,** rugged individualism, individual freedom; **self-reliance,** self-dependence; inner-direction; no allegiance; singleness, bachelorhood; independent means

6 **free will,** free choice, **discretion,** option, choice, say, say-so *and* druthers <nf>, free decision; **full consent;** absolute *or* unconditioned *or* noncontingent free will

7 **own free will, own account, own accord, own hook** *and* own say-so <nf>, own discretion, own choice, **own initiative,** personal initiative, own responsibility, personal *or* individual responsibility, own volition, own authority, own power; own way, own sweet way <nf>; law unto oneself

8 **exemption,** exception, **immunity; release,** discharge; **franchise, license,** charter, patent, liberty; diplomatic immunity, congressional *or* legislative immunity; special case *or* privilege; grandfather clause, grandfathering; privilege; permission 443

9 **noninterference, nonintervention; isolationism; laissez-faireism,** let-alone principle *or* doctrine *or* policy, deregulation; *laissez-faire* and *laissez-aller* <Fr>; liberalism, free enterprise, free competition, self-regulating market; open market; capitalism 611.8; free trade; noninvolvement, nonalignment, neutrality

10 **liberalism,** libertarianism, latitudinarianism; broad-mindedness, open-mindedness, toleration, tolerance; unbigotedness 979.1; libertinism, **freethinking,** free thought; liberalization, **liberation** 431; nonconformity

11 **freeman,** freewoman; citizen, free citizen, burgess, bourgeois; franklin; emancipated *or* manumitted slave, freedman, freedwoman; deditician

12 **free agent, independent, free lance; individualist,** rugged individualist; free spirit; **liberal,** libertarian, latitudinarian; libertine, freethinker; free trader; **nonpartisan,** neutral, undecided, mugwump; isolationist; nonaligned nation; third world, third force, developing world; indie <nf>; lone wolf <nf>, loner, nonconformist, one-man band

VERBS 13 **liberalize,** ease; **free, liberate** 431.4

14 **exempt, free, release,** discharge, **let go** *and* **let off** <nf>, set at liberty, spring <nf>; **excuse,** spare, except, grant immunity, make a special case of; grandfather; **dispense,** dispense from, give dispensation from; dispense with, save the necessity; remit, remise; absolve 601.4

15 **give a free hand,** let one have his head, **give one his head; give the run of** <nf>, give the freedom of; give one leeway <nf>, give full play; give one scope *or* space *or* room; **give rein** *or* **free rein to,** give the reins to, give bridle to, give one line, give one rope; **give one carte blanche, give one a blank check;** let go one's own way, let one go at will

16 **not interfere, leave** *or* **let alone, let be,** leave *or* let well enough alone, let sleeping dogs lie; **keep hands off,** not tamper, not meddle, not involve oneself, not get involved, let it ride <nf>, let nature take its course; live *and* let live, leave one to oneself, leave one in peace; mind one's own business; tolerate; **decontrol, deregulate**

17 <nf terms> **get off one's back** *or* **one's case** *or* **one's tail,** get out of one's face *or* hair, **butt out, back off,** leave be, call off the dogs, keep one's nose out, get lost, take a walk, not cramp someone's style

18 **be free,** feel free, feel free as a bird, feel at liberty; **go at large,** breathe free, breathe the air of freedom; **have free scope,** have one's druthers <nf>, have a free hand, have the run of <nf>; be at home, feel at home; be freed, be released; be exonerated, go *or* get off scot-free, walk

19 **let oneself go,** let go, let loose *and* cut loose *and* let one's hair down <nf>, **give way to,** open up, let it all hang out <nf>; go all out, go flat out <Brit>, pull out all the stops; go unrestrained, run wild, have one's fling, sow one's wild oats

20 **stand on one's own two feet, shift for oneself, fend for oneself,** stand on one's own, strike out for oneself, trust one's good right arm, look out for number one <nf>; **go it alone, be one's own man,** pull a lone oar, play a lone hand <nf>, **paddle**

one's own canoe <nf>; suffice to oneself, do for oneself, make *or* pay one's own way; ask no favors, ask no quarter; **be one's own boss** <nf>, call no man master, answer only to oneself, ask leave of no man; **go one's own way,** take one's own course; do on one's own, don one's own thing, do on one's own initiative, do on one's own hook *or* say-so <nf>, do in one's own sweet way <nf>; **have a will of one's own,** have one's own way, do what one likes *or* wishes *or* chooses, do as one pleases, **go as one pleases,** please oneself <nf>, **suit oneself;** have a free mind; free-lance, be a free agent

ADJS **21 free; at liberty, at large,** on the loose, **loose,** unengaged, disengaged, detached, unattached, uncommitted, uninvolved, clear, in the clear, go-as-you-please, easygoing, footloose, footloose *and* fancy-free, free *and* easy; free as air, free as a bird, free as the wind; scot-free; **freeborn; freed, liberated, emancipated,** manumitted, released, uncaged, sprung <nf>

22 independent, self-dependent; free-spirited, freewheeling, free-floating, free-standing; **self-determined,** self-directing, one's own man; freelance; inner-directed, **individualistic;** self-governed, **self-governing, autonomous,** sovereign; stand-alone, self-reliant, self-sufficient, self-subsistent, self-supporting, self-contained, autarkic, autarchic; nonpartisan, neutral, **nonaligned;** third-world, third-force

23 free-acting, free-going, free-moving, free-working; freehand, freehanded; **free-spoken,** outspoken, **plain-spoken, open, frank,** direct, candid, blunt 644.17

24 unrestrained, unconstrained, unforced, uncompelled, uncoerced; unmeasured, **uninhibited, unsuppressed, unrepressed, unreserved,** go-go <nf>, exuberant 109.14; **uncurbed, unchecked, unbridled,** unmuzzled; **unreined,** reinless; **uncontrolled,** unmastered, unsubdued, ungoverned, **unruly;** out of control, out of hand, out of one's power; **abandoned,** intemperate, immoderate, **incontinent, licentious,** loose, wanton, rampant, riotous, wild; irrepressible; lax 426.4

25 nonrestrictive, unrestrictive; **permissive,** hands-off <nf>; indulgent 427.8; lax 426.4; **liberal,** libertarian, latitudinarian; broad-minded, open-minded, tolerant; unbigoted 979.8; libertine; freethinking

26 unhampered, untrammeled, unhandicapped, unimpeded, unhindered, unprevented, unclogged, unobstructed; clear, unencumbered, unburdened, unladen, unembarrassed, disembarrassed; free-ranging, free-range

27 unrestricted, unconfined, uncircumscribed, unbound <old>, unbounded, unmeasured;

unlimited, limitless, illimitable; unqualified, unconditioned, **unconditional,** without strings, no strings, no strings attached; **absolute,** perfect, unequivocal, full, plenary; open-ended, open, **wide-open** <nf>; permissive; decontrolled, deregulated

28 unbound, untied, **unfettered,** unshackled, unchained; unmuzzled, ungagged; uncensored; declassified

29 unsubject, ungoverned, unenslaved, **unenthralled;** unvanquished, unconquered, unsubdued, unquelled, **untamed,** unbroken, undomesticated, unreconstructed

30 exempt, immune; exempted, **released, excused,** excepted, let off <nf>, spared; grandfathered; **privileged, licensed,** favored, chartered; permitted; dispensed; **unliable,** unsubject, irresponsible, unaccountable, unanswerable

31 quit, clear, free, rid; free of, clear of, quit of, rid of, shut of, shed of <nf>

ADVS **32 freely,** free; **without restraint,** without stint, **unreservedly,** with abandon; outright

33 independently, alone, by oneself, all by one's lonesome <nf>, under one's own power *or* steam, **on one's own** *and* **on one's own hook** <nf>, on one's own initiative, on one's own bottom <old>; **on one's own account** *or* **responsibility,** on one's own say-so <nf>; **of one's own free will, of one's own accord,** of one's own volition, at one's own discretion

431 LIBERATION

NOUNS **1 liberation, freeing,** setting free, setting at liberty; **deliverance, delivery; rescue** 398; **emancipation,** disenthrallment, manumission; enfranchisement, affranchisement; Emancipation Proclamation; Nineteenth Amendment; Equal Rights Amendment; women's liberation; gay liberation; women's *or* gay *or* men's lib <nf>

2 release, freeing, unhanding, **loosing,** unloosing; unbinding, untying, unbuckling, unshackling, unfettering, unlashing, unstrapping, untrussing *and* unpinioning <old>, unmanacling, **unleashing,** unchaining, untethering, unhobbling, unharnessing, unyoking, unbridling; unmuzzling, ungagging; unlocking, unlatching, unbolting, unbarring, unpenning, uncaging; **discharge, dismissal;** parole, bail; convict release, springing <nf>; demobilization, separation from the service

3 extrication, freeing, releasing, clearing; **disengagement, disentanglement,** untangling, unsnarling, unraveling, disentwining, disinvolvement, unknotting, disembarrassment, disembroilment; dislodgment, breaking out *or* loose, busting out *or* loose <nf>

VERBS **4 liberate, free, deliver, set free,** set at
liberty, set at large; **emancipate,** manumit,
disenthrall; enfranchise, affranchise; **rescue** 398.3

5 release, unhand, let go, let loose, turn loose, cast
loose, let out, let off, let go free, let off the hook;
discharge, dismiss; let out on bail, grant bail to,
go bail for <nf>; parole, put on parole; release
from prison, spring <nf>; demobilize, separate
from the service

6 loose, loosen, let loose, cut loose *or* free, unloose,
unloosen; **unbind, untie,** unstrap, unbuckle,
unlash, untruss *and* unpinion <old>; **unfetter,
unshackle,** unmanacle, unchain, unhandcuff,
untie one's hands; **unleash,** untether, unhobble;
unharness, unyoke, unbridle; unmuzzle, ungag;
unlock, unlatch, unbolt, unbar; unpen, uncage

7 extricate, free, release, clear, get out; **disengage,**
disentangle, untangle, unsnarl, unravel,
disentwine, disinvolve, unknot, detangle,
disembarrass, disembroil; dislodge, break out *or*
loose, cut loose, tear loose

8 free oneself from, deliver oneself from, **get free of,**
get quit of, **get rid of,** get clear of, **get out of,** get
well out of, get around, extricate oneself, get out of
a jam <nf>; **throw off, shake off;** break out, bust
out <nf>, go over the wall <nf>, **escape** 369.6;
wriggle out of

9 go free, go scot free, go at liberty, **get off,** get off
scot-free, get out of, beat the rap *and* walk <nf>

ADJS **10 liberated, freed, emancipated, released;**
delivered, rescued, ransomed, redeemed;
extricated, unbound, untied, unshackled, etc; free
430.21; scot-free; on parole, out on bail

432 SUBJECTION

NOUNS **1 subjection, subjugation; domination** 612.2;
restraint, control 428.1; **bondage, captivity; thrall,
thralldom,** enthrallment; **slavery,** enslavement,
master-slave relationship; **servitude,** compulsory
or involuntary servitude, servility, bond service,
indentureship; **serfdom,** serfhood, villenage,
vassalage; helotry, helotism; debt slavery,
peonage; feudalism, feudality; absolutism, tyranny
612.8,9; deprivation of freedom,
disenfranchisement, disfranchisement

2 subservience *or* subserviency, subjecthood,
subordinacy, **subordination,** juniority, **inferiority;**
lower status, subordinate role, satellite status;
back seat *and* second fiddle *and* hind tit <nf>;
service, servitorship 577.12

3 dependence *or* dependency, codependency,
contingency, tutelage, chargeship, wardship;
apprenticeship; clientship, clientage

4 subdual, quelling, conquest, crushing, trampling

or treading down, reduction, **humbling,
humiliation;** breaking, taming, domestication,
gentling; conquering 412.1; **suppression** 428.2

5 subordinate, junior, secondary, second-in-
command, lieutenant, **inferior; underling,**
understrapper, low man on the totem pole <nf>,
errand boy, flunky, gofer <nf>, grunt <nf>;
assistant, personal assistant, undersecretary,
helper 616.6; strong right arm, **right-hand man**
616.7; **servant, employee** 577

6 dependent, charge, ward, client, protégé,
encumbrance; pensioner, pensionary; public
charge, ward of the state; child; foster child;
dependency *or* dependent state, client state,
satellite *or* satellite state, puppet government,
creature; hanger-on, parasite

7 subject, vassal, liege, liege man, liege subject,
homager; **captive; slave,** servant, chattel, chattel
slave, **bondsman,** bondman, **bondslave,** theow,
thrall; indentured servant; laborer, esne;
bondwoman, bondswoman, bondmaid; odalisque,
concubine; galley slave; **serf,** helot, villein; churl;
debt slave, **peon;** conscript

VERBS **8 subjugate, subject, subordinate; dominate**
612.14; disfranchise, disenfranchise, divest *or*
deprive of freedom; **enslave,** enthrall, hold in
thrall, make a chattel of; take captive, lead captive
or into captivity; **hold in subjection,** hold in
bondage, **hold captive,** hold in captivity; **hold
down,** keep down, keep under; **keep *or* have under
one's thumb,** have tied to one's apron strings, hold
in leash, hold in leading strings, hold in swaddling
clothes, hold *or* keep at one's beck *and* call;
vassalize, make dependent *or* tributary; peonize

9 subdue, master, overmaster, **quell, crush, reduce,**
beat down, **break,** break down, overwhelm; tread
underfoot, trample on *or* down, trample
underfoot, roll in the dust, trample in the dust,
drag at one's chariot wheel; oppress, **suppress**
428.8; make one give in *or* say 'uncle' <nf>,
conquer 412.10; kick around <nf>, tyrannize 612.15;
unman 19.12; bring low, **bring to terms, humble,**
humiliate, take down a notch *or* peg, bend, **bring
one to his knees, bend to one's will**

10 have subject, twist *or* turn *or* wind around one's
little finger, make lie down *and* roll over, have
eating out of one's hand, **lead by the nose,** make a
puppet of, make putty of, make a sport *or*
plaything of; use as a doormat, treat like dirt
under one's feet, walk all over

11 domesticate, tame, break, bust *and* gentle <nf>,
break in, break to harness; housebreak

12 depend on, be at the mercy of, be the sport *or*
plaything *or* puppet of, be putty in the hands of;
not dare to say one's soul is one's own; eat out of

one's hands; **play second fiddle, suck hind tit** <nf>, take a back seat; pay tribute

ADJS 13 subject, dependent, tributary, client; **subservient, subordinate, inferior;** servile; liege, **vassal,** feudal, feudatory

14 subjugated, subjected, **enslaved, enthralled, in thrall, captive,** bond, unfree; disenfranchised, disfranchised, **oppressed, suppressed** 428.14; **in subjection, in bondage, in captivity,** in slavery, in bonds, in chains; under the lash, under the heel; **in one's power,** in one's control, in one's hands *or* clutches, in one's pocket, **under one's thumb,** at one's mercy, under one's command *or* orders, at one's beck and call, at one's feet, at one's pleasure; **subordinated,** playing second fiddle; at the bottom of the ladder, sucking hind tit <nf>

15 subdued, quelled, crushed, broken, reduced, mastered, overmastered, humbled, humiliated, brought to one's knees, brought low, made to grovel; **tamed, domesticated,** broken to harness, gentled; housebroken *or* housebroke

16 downtrodden, downtrod <old>, kept down *or* under, ground down, overborne, trampled, **oppressed; abused,** misused; **henpecked, browbeaten,** led by the nose, in leading strings, tied to one's apron strings, ordered *or* kicked around <nf>, regimented, tyrannized; slavish, servile, submissive 433.12; unmanned 19.19; treated like dirt under one's feet, treated like shit <nf>

PREPS 17 under, below, beneath, underneath, subordinate to; at the feet of; under the heel of; at the beck and call of, at the whim *or* pleasure of

433 SUBMISSION

NOUNS 1 submission, submittal, **yielding; compliance,** com**plaisance, acquiescence, acceptance;** going along with <nf>, **assent** 332; **consent** 441; **obedience** 326; subjection 432; **resignation,** resignedness, stoicism, philosophical attitude; **deference,** homage, kneeling, obeisance; **passivity, unassertiveness,** passiveness, supineness, longanimity, long-suffering, long-sufferance <old>, nonresistance, nonopposition, nonopposal, quietness, nondissent, quietude, quietism; **cowardice** 491

2 surrender, capitulation; renunciation, giving over, abandonment, relinquishment, **cession;** giving up *or* in, backing off *or* down <nf>, retreat, recession, recedence, caving in <nf>, giving up the fort, the white flag <nf>, throwing in the towel *or* sponge <nf>

3 submissiveness, docility, tractability, prostration, biddability, yieldingness, compliableness <old>, pliancy, pliability, flexibility, malleability,

moldability, ductility, plasticity, facility; agreeableness, agreeability; subservience, **servility** 138

4 manageability, governability, controllability, manipulability, manipulatability, corrigibility, untroublesomeness; **tameness,** housebrokenness; tamableness, domesticability; milk-toast, milquetoast, Caspar Milquetoast

5 meekness, gentleness, tameness, mildness, mild-manneredness, peaceableness, lamblikeness, dovelikeness, spinelessness; **self-abnegation, humility** 137

VERBS 6 submit, comply, take, accept, go along with <nf>, suffer, bear, brook, **acquiesce,** be agreeable, accede, **assent** 332.8; **consent** 441.2; relent, **succumb,** resign, resign oneself, give oneself up, not resist; take one's medicine, swallow the pill, face the music, face the facts; **bite the bullet; knuckle down** *or* **under,** knock under <old>, take it, swallow it; jump through a hoop, dance to another's tune; take it lying down; put up with it, grin and bear it, make the best of it, take the bitter with the sweet, shrug, shrug off, live with it; obey 326.2

7 yield, cede, give way, give ground, back down, give up, give in, cave in <nf>, withdraw from *or* quit the field, break off combat, cease resistance, have no fight left

8 surrender, give up, capitulate, acknowledge defeat, **cry quits,** cry pax <Brit>, **say 'uncle'** <nf>, beg a truce, pray for quarter, implore mercy, throw **in the towel** *or* **sponge** <nf>, show *or* wave the white flag, lower *or* haul down *or* strike one's flag *or* colors, throw down *or* lay down *or* deliver up one's arms, hand over one's sword, yield the palm, ask for mercy, pull in one's horns <nf>, come to terms; renounce, abandon, relinquish, **cede,** give over, hand over

9 submit to, yield to, defer to, bow to, give way to, knuckle under to, succumb to

10 bow down, bow, bend, stoop, crouch, **bow one's head,** bend the neck, bow submission; genuflect, curtsy; **bow to,** bend to, knuckle to <nf>, bend *or* bow to one's will, bend to one's yoke; kneel to, **bend the knee to, fall on one's knees before,** crouch before, **fall at one's feet,** throw oneself at the feet of, prostrate oneself before, **truckle to,** cringe to, cave in; **kowtow,** bow *and* scrape, grovel, do obeisance *or* homage; kiss ass <nf>; take the line of least resistance

11 eat dirt, eat crow, eat humble pie, lick the dust, kiss the rod, take it on the chin

ADJS 12 submissive, compliant, compliable <old>, complaisant, complying, **acquiescent,** consenting 441.4; **assenting,** accepting, agreeable; subservient, abject, **obedient** 326.3; servile; **resigned,**

uncomplaining; unassertive; **passive,** supine, **unresisting,** nonresisting, unresistant, nonresistant, nonresistive, long-suffering, longanimous, nonopposing, nondissenting

13 **docile, tractable,** biddable, unmurmuring, **yielding,** pliant, pliable, flexible, malleable, moldable, ductile, plastic, facile <old>, like putty in one's hands

14 **manageable, governable, controllable,** manipulable, manipulatable, handleable, corrigible, restrainable, untroublesome; domitable, tamable, domesticable; milk-toast *or* milquetoast

15 **meek, gentle, mild,** mild-mannered, peaceable, pacific, quiet; **subdued, chastened, tame,** tamed, broken, housebroken, domesticated; lamblike, gentle as a lamb, dovelike; humble; spineless, soft, weak-kneed

16 **deferential, obeisant; subservient, obsequious,** servile 138.13; crouching, prostrate, prone, on one's belly, on one's knees, on one's marrowbones <nf>, on bended knee, bowed, bowing

ADVS 17 **submissively, compliantly,** complaisantly, acquiescently, agreeably; **obediently** 326.6; **resignedly,** uncomplainingly, with resignation; **passively,** supinely, unresistingly, unresistantly, nonresistively

18 **docilely, tractably,** biddably, **yieldingly,** pliantly, pliably, malleably, flexibly, plastically, facilely <old>

19 **meekly, gently, tamely, mildly,** peaceably, pacifically, quietly, like a lamb

434 OBSERVANCE

NOUNS 1 **observance,** observation, honoring; **keeping,** adherence, heeding; compliance, conformance, conformity, accordance; **faith,** faithfulness, fidelity; **respect, deference** 155.1; **performance, practice,** execution, discharge, carrying out *or* through; dutifulness 641.2, acquittal *or* acquittance <old>, fulfillment, satisfaction; heed, care 339.1; obeying the law

VERBS 2 **observe, keep, heed, follow,** keep the faith; regard, defer to, **respect** 155.4, attend to, **comply with,** conform to; hold by, **abide by,** adhere to; **live up to,** act up to, practice what one preaches, **be faithful to,** keep faith with, do justice to, do the right thing by; **fulfill,** fill, meet, satisfy; **make good,** keep *or* make good one's word *or* promise, be as good as one's word, redeem one's pledge, stand to one's engagement; keep to the spirit of, keep faith with; obey the law

3 **perform, practice,** do, execute, discharge, carry out *or* through, carry into execution, do one's duty 641.10, do one's office, fulfill one's role, discharge one's function; honor one's obligations

ADJS 4 **observant,** respectful 155.8, regardful, mindful; **faithful,** devout, devoted, true, loyal, constant; dutiful 641.13, duteous; as good as one's word; **practicing,** active; compliant, conforming; punctual, punctilious, scrupulous, meticulous, conscientious 339.12; obedient; sabbatarian

435 NONOBSERVANCE

NOUNS 1 **nonobservance,** inobservance, unobservance, nonadherence; nonconformity, disconformity, **nonconformance, noncompliance;** apostasy; inattention, indifference, **disregard** 984.2; laxity 426.1; **nonfulfillment, nonperformance,** nonfeasance, failure, **dereliction, delinquency,** omission, default, slight, oversight; **negligence; neglect** 340, laches; abandonment 370; lack of ceremony

2 **violation, infraction, breach,** breaking; **infringement, transgression, trespass,** contravention; offense 674.4; breach of promise, breach of contract, breach of trust *or* faith, bad faith, breach of privilege; breach of the peace

VERBS 3 **disregard,** lose sight of, pay no regard to; **neglect** 340.6; renege, abandon 370.5; defect 858.13; do one's own thing <nf>

4 **violate, break, breach; infringe, transgress, trespass,** contravene, trample on *or* upon, trample underfoot, do violence to, make a mockery of, outrage; defy, set at defiance, flout, set at naught, set naught by; take the law into one's own hands; break one's promise, break one's word

ADJS 5 **nonobservant,** inobservant, unobservant, nonadherent; nonconforming, unconforming, noncompliant, uncompliant; inattentive, **disregardful** 984.6; **negligent** 340.10; unfaithful, untrue, unloyal, inconstant, lapsed, renegade 858.20/363.11; contemptuous

436 PROMISE

NOUNS 1 **promise, pledge,** solemn promise, troth, plight, faith, parole, **word, word of honor,** debt of honor, solemn declaration *or* word; **oath, vow;** avouch, avouchment; **assurance, guarantee,** warranty, personal guarantee; entitlement

2 **obligation, commitment, agreement, engagement,** undertaking, recognizance, feasance; **understanding,** gentlemen's agreement, unwritten agreement, handshake; verbal agreement, nonformal agreement, pactum <law>; tacit *or* unspoken agreement; **contract** 437.1, covenant, bond; designation, committal, earmarking; promissory note

3 **betrothal,** betrothment, intention, espousal,

engagement, handfasting *and* affiance <old>, troth, marriage contract *or* vow, plighted troth *or* faith *or* love, exchange of vows; banns, banns of matrimony; prenuptial agreement *or* contract, prenup <nf>

VERBS **4 promise,** give *or* make a promise, hold out an expectation; **pledge,** plight, troth, **vow; give one's word,** pledge *or* pass one's word, give one's parole, **give one's word of honor,** plight one's troth *or* faith, pledge *or* plight one's honor; cross one's heart *and* cross one's heart *and* hope to die <nf>, **swear;** vouch, avouch, **warrant, guarantee, assure;** underwrite, countersign

5 commit, engage, undertake, obligate, bind, **agree to,** say yes, answer for, be answerable for, take on oneself, be responsible for, be security for, go bail for, accept obligation *or* responsibility, bind oneself to, put oneself down for; have an understanding; enter into a gentlemen's agreement; take the vows *or* marriage vows; shake hands on, shake on it; contract, sign on the dotted line; designate, commit, earmark

6 be engaged, affiance, betroth, troth, plight one's troth, say 'I do'; **contract,** contract an engagement, pledge *or* promise in marriage; read *or* publish the banns

ADJS **7 promissory,** votive; under *or* upon oath, on one's word, on one's word of honor, on the Book, under hand and seal, avowed

8 promised, pledged, bound, committed, compromised, **obligated; sworn,** warranted, **guaranteed,** assured, underwritten, cosigned; contracted 437.11; **engaged, plighted, affianced, betrothed,** intended

ADVS **9** on one's honor *or* word *or* word of honor *or* parole; solemnly

437 COMPACT

NOUNS **1 compact, pact, contract,** legal contract, valid contract, **covenant,** convention, transaction, paction <Scot>, accord, **agreement,** mutual agreement, agreement between *or* among parties, signed *or* written agreement, formal agreement, legal agreement, undertaking, stipulation; adjustment, accommodation; **understanding, arrangement, bargain,** dicker *and* **deal** <nf>, informal agreement; **settlement,** negotiated settlement; **labor contract, union contract** 727.3, wage contract, employment contract, collective agreement; deed; cartel, consortium; **protocol;** bond, binding agreement, ironclad agreement, covenant of salt; gentleman's *or* gentlemen's agreement; prenuptial agreement; licensing agreement; promise 436

2 treaty, international agreement, entente *or* entente cordiale <Fr>, concord, concordat, cartel, convention, consortium, protocol, paction, capitulation; **alliance, league;** nonaggression pact, mutual-defense treaty; trade agreement; arms control agreement; NATO *or* North Atlantic Treaty Organization; SEATO *or* Southeast Asia Treaty Organization; Warsaw Pact

3 signing, **signature,** sealing, closing, conclusion, solemnization; handshake

4 execution, completion; transaction; carrying out, discharge, fulfillment, prosecution, effectuation; enforcement; observance 434

VERBS **5 contract,** compact, **covenant, bargain, agree, engage,** undertake, commit, mutually commit, make a deal <nf>, do a deal <Brit nf>, stipulate, agree to, bargain for, contract for; preset, prearrange, **promise** 436.4; subcontract, outsource; cut a deal <nf>

6 treat with, negotiate, bargain, make terms, sit down with, sit down at the bargaining table

7 sign, shake hands *or* shake <nf>, affix one's John Hancock <nf>, seal, formalize, make legal *and* binding, solemnize; agree on terms, come to terms, come to an agreement 332.10; strike a bargain 731.18; plea-bargain

8 arrange, settle; adjust, fine-tune, accommodate, reshuffle, rejigger <nf>, **compose,** fix, make up, straighten out, put *or* set straight, work out, sort out *and* square away <nf>; **conclude,** close, **close with,** settle with

9 execute, complete, transact, promulgate, make; close a deal; make out, fill out; **discharge, fulfill,** render, administer; **carry out,** carry through, put through, prosecute; effect, effectuate, set in motion, implement; enforce, put in force; **abide by, honor, live up to,** adhere to, live by, **observe** 434.2

ADJS **10** contractual, covenantal, conventional, consensual

11 contracted, compacted, **covenanted, agreed upon, bargained for,** agreed <Brit>, stipulated; engaged, undertaken; **promised** 436.8; arranged, settled; under hand and seal, **signed,** sealed, signed sealed and delivered; ratified

ADVS **12 contractually, as agreed upon, as promised,** as contracted for, by the terms of the contract, according to the contract *or* bargain *or* agreement

438 SECURITY

<thing given as a pledge>

NOUNS **1 security, surety,** indemnity, **guaranty, guarantee, warranty, insurance,** warrant, assurance, underwriting; **obligation** 436.2, full faith *and* credit; **bond,** tie; stocks and bonds 738.1; national security

2 **pledge, gage,** *pignus* or *vadium* <L>; undertaking; **earnest,** earnest money, god's penny, handsel; escrow; token payment; pawn, hock <nf>; **bail,** bond, vadimonium; replevin, replevy, recognizance; mainprise; hostage, surety

3 **collateral,** collateral security or warranty; deposit, stake, forfeit; indemnity, IOU; caution money, caution; margin; cosigned promissory note; cosignage

4 **mortgage,** mortgage deed, deed of trust, lien, security agreement, real estate loan; vadium mortuum or mortuum vadium; dead pledge; vadium vivum, living pledge, antichresis; hypothec, hypothecation, bottomry, bottomry bond; adjustment mortgage, blanket mortgage, chattel mortgage, closed mortgage, participating mortgage, installment mortgage, leasehold mortgage, trust mortgage, reverse mortgage, jumbo mortgage; first mortgage, second mortgage, third mortgage; adjustable-rate mortgage or ARM, variable-rate mortgage or VRM, fixed-rate mortgage; equity loan; reverse equity

5 **lien,** general lien, particular lien; pignus legale, common-law lien, statutory lien, judgment lien, pignus judiciale, tax lien, mechanic's lien; mortgage bond

6 **guarantor,** warrantor, guaranty, guarantee; mortgagor; insurer, underwriter; sponsor, surety; godparent, godfather, godmother; bondsman, bailsman, mainpernor

7 **warrantee,** mortgagee; insuree, policyholder; godchild, godson, goddaughter

8 guarantorship, **sponsorship,** sponsion

VERBS 9 **secure, guarantee, guaranty, warrant, assure, insure,** ensure, bond, certify; countersecure; stand surety; **sponsor,** be sponsor for, sign for, sign one's note, **back,** stand behind or back of, stand up for; **endorse;** indemnify, countersign; sign, cosign, **underwrite,** undersign, subscribe to; confirm, attest

10 **pledge,** impignorate and handsel <old>, **deposit, stake,** post, put in escrow, **put up,** put up as collateral, lay out or down; **pawn,** put in pawn, spout or put up the spout <old>, **hock** and **put in hock** <nf>; mortgage, hypothecate, bottomry, bond; **put up** or **go bail,** bail out

ADJS 11 **secured,** covered, **guaranteed, warranted,** certified, **insured,** ensured, **assured;** certain, sure 970.13

12 **pledged,** staked, posted, deposited, in escrow, **put up,** put up as collateral; on deposit, at stake; as earnest; **pawned,** in pawn, **in hock** <nf>, hocked, up the spout <old>

13 **in trust,** held in trust, held in pledge, fiduciary; in escrow; mortgaged

439 OFFER

NOUNS 1 **offer,** offering, proffer, presentation, **bid,** submission; **advance, overture,** approach, invitation, come-on <nf>; hesitant or tentative or preliminary approach, feeling-out, **feeler** <nf>; asking price; **counteroffer, counterproposal**

2 **proposal, proposition, suggestion,** instance; **motion,** resolution; sexual advance or approach or invitation or overture, indecent proposal, pass <nf>, improper suggestion; request 440

3 **ultimatum,** last or final word or offer, firm bid or price, sticking point, ultimation

VERBS 4 **offer, proffer, present,** tender, offer up, **put up, submit, extend,** prefer <old>, **hold out,** hold forth, place in one's way, lay at one's feet, put or place at one's disposal, put one in the way of

5 **propose, submit,** prefer; **suggest,** recommend, **advance,** commend to attention, **propound, pose, put forward,** bring forward, put or set forth, put it to, put or set or lay or bring before, dish up and come out or up with <nf>; put a bee in one's bonnet, put ideas into one's head; **bring up, broach, moot,** introduce, open up, launch, start, kick off <nf>; **move, make a motion,** offer a resolution; postulate 951.12

6 **bid,** bid for, make a bid

7 **make advances,** approach, overture, **make an overture,** throw or fling oneself at one <nf>; **solicit, importune**

8 <nf terms> **proposition, come on to,** hit on, put or make a move on, jump one's bones, make or throw a pass, george, **make a play for,** play footsie with, pitch, mash <old>

9 **urge upon, press upon,** ply upon, push upon, force upon, thrust upon; **press, ply;** insist

10 **volunteer, come** or **step forward, offer** or **proffer** or **present oneself,** be at one's service, not wait to be asked, not wait for an invitation, need no prodding, step into the breach, be Johnny-on-the-spot <nf>

440 REQUEST

NOUNS 1 **request,** asking; the touch <nf>; desire, wish, expressed desire; **petition,** petitioning, impetration, address; **application; requisition,** indent <Brit>; demand 421; special request

2 **entreaty, appeal, plea, bid,** suit, call, cry, clamor, cri du cœur <Fr>, beseeching, impetration, obtestation; **supplication, prayer,** rogation, **beseechment,** imploring, imploration, obsecration, obtestation, adjuration, imprecation; **invocation,** invocatory plea or prayer; act of contrition

3 **importunity,** importunateness, urgency, pressure,

high pressure *and* hard sell <nf>; **urging, pressing, plying;** buttonholing; dunning; teasing, pestering, plaguing, nagging, nudging <nf>; **coaxing,** wheedling, cajolery, cajolement, blandishment

4 **invitation, invite** *and* **bid** <nf>, engraved invitation, bidding, biddance, **call,** calling, **summons**

5 **solicitation, canvass, canvassing; suit,** addresses; **courting, wooing;** fund-raising; the touch <nf>

6 **beggary,** mendicancy, mendicity; **begging,** cadging, scrounging; mooching *and* bumming *and* panhandling <nf>

7 **petitioner, supplicant,** suppliant, suitor; **solicitor** 730.6; **applicant,** solicitant, claimant; aspirant, seeker, wannabee <nf>; candidate, postulant; bidder

8 **beggar, mendicant,** scrounger, **cadger; bum** *and* bummer *and* **moocher** *and* **panhandler** *and* sponger <nf>; *schnorrer* <Yiddish>; hobo, tramp 178.3; loafer 331.8; mendicant friar; mendicant order

VERBS 9 **request, ask,** make a request, **beg leave,** make bold to ask; **desire,** wish, wish for, express a wish for, crave; **ask for,** order, put in an order for, bespeak, call for, trouble one for; whistle for <nf>; **requisition,** make *or* put in a requisition, indent <Brit>; make application, apply for, file for, put in for; demand 421.5; pop the question <nf>

10 **petition,** present *or* prefer a petition, sign a petition, circulate a petition; **pray,** sue; **apply to, call on** *or* **upon;** memorialize

11 **entreat, implore, beseech, beg,** crave, **plead, appeal, pray, supplicate,** impetrate, obtest; adjure, conjure; invoke, imprecate <old>, **call on** *or* **upon,** cry on *or* upon, **appeal to,** cry to, run to; go cap *or* hat in hand to; kneel to, go down on one's knees to, fall on one's knees to, go on bended knee to, throw oneself at the feet of, get *or* come down on one's marrow-bones <nf>; **plead for,** clamor for, cry for, cry out for; call for help

12 **importune, urge, press,** pressure <nf>, prod, prod at, apply *or* exert pressure, push, **ply;** dun; **beset, buttonhole,** besiege, take *or* grasp by the lapels; work on <nf>, tease, pester, plague, nag, nag at, make a pest *or* nuisance of oneself, try one's patience, bug <nf>, nudge; coax, wheedle, cajole, blandish, flatter, soft soap <nf>

13 **invite, ask, call, summon, call in, bid come,** extend *or* issue an invitation, request the presence of, request the pleasure of one's company, send an engraved invitation

14 **solicit, canvass; court, woo,** address, sue, sue for, pop the question <nf>, propose; **seek, bid for,** look for; **fish for,** angle for; pass the hat

15 beg, **scrounge, cadge; mooch** *and* **bum** *and* **panhandle** <nf>; **hit** *and* hit up *and* **touch** *and* put

the touch on *and* make a touch <nf>; pass the hat <nf>

ADJS 16 **supplicatory, suppliant,** supplicant, supplicating, **prayerful,** precative; **petitionary; begging,** mendicant, cadging, scrounging, mooching <nf>; on one's knees *or* bended knees, on one's marrow-bones <nf>; with joined *or* folded hands

17 **imploring, entreating, beseeching, begging, pleading, appealing,** precatory, precative, adjuratory

18 **importunate; teasing,** pesty, pesky <nf>, pestering, plaguing, nagging, dunning; **coaxing,** wheedling, cajoling, flattering, soft-soaping <nf>; **insistent, demanding, urgent**

19 **invitational,** inviting, invitatory

INTERJS 20 **please,** prithee <old>, pray, do, **pray do,** puhleez! <nf>; be so good as to, be good enough, have the goodness; will you, may it please you; **if you please,** *s'il vous plaît* <Fr>; I beg you, *je vous en prie* <Fr>; for God's *or* goodness *or* heaven's *or* mercy's sake; be my guest, feel free; gimme a break!, cut me some slack!

441 CONSENT

NOUNS 1 **consent, assent, agreement,** accord <old>, acceptance, approval, blessing, approbation, sanction, **endorsement,** ratification, backing; affirmation, affirmative, affirmative voice *or* vote, yea, aye, **nod** *and* **okay** *and* **OK** <nf>, okey-dokey <nf>, go-ahead <nf>, green light <nf>; **leave, permission** 443; **willingness,** readiness, promptness, promptitude, eagerness, unreluctance, unloathness, ungrudgingness, tacit *or* unspoken *or* silent *or* implicit consent, **connivance; acquiescence, compliance;** submission 433

VERBS 2 **consent, assent,** give consent, yield assent, be willing, be amenable, be persuaded, accede to, accord to *and* grant <old>, say yes *or* aye *or* yea, vote affirmatively, vote aye, **nod, nod assent; accept, play** *or* **go along** <nf>, **agree to, sign off on** <nf>, go along with <nf>; be in accord with, be in favor of, take kindly to, **approve of,** hold with; **approve,** give one's blessing to, **okay** *or* **OK** <nf>; sanction, **endorse, ratify;** consent to silently *or* by implication *or* in petto <Ital>; **wink at, connive at; be willing,** turn a willing ear; deign, condescend; have no objection, not refuse; permit 443.9

3 **acquiesce, comply, comply with,** fall in with, take one up on <nf>, be persuaded, come round *or* around, come over, come to <nf>, see one's way clear to; **submit** 433.6,9

ADJS 4 **consenting, assenting,** affirmative, amenable,

persuaded, approving, agreeing, favorable, accordant, consentient, consentual, consentant; sanctioning, endorsing, ratifying; **acquiescent, compliant,** compliable <old>; submissive 433.12; **willing, agreeable,** content; ready, prompt, eager, unreluctant, unloath, nothing loath, unmurmuring, ungrudging, unrefusing; permissive 443.14

ADVS **5 consentingly, assentingly,** affirmatively, approvingly, favorably, positively, agreeably, accordantly; acquiescently, compliantly; willingly 324.8; **yes** 332.18

442 REFUSAL

NOUNS **1 refusal, rejection,** turndown, turning down; thumbs-down <nf>, *pollice verso* <L>; nonconsent, nonacceptance, zero tolerance; **declining,** declination, declension, declinature; **denial,** disclamation, disclaimer, disallowance; decertification, disaccreditation; **repudiation** 372.1; disagreement, dissent 333; recantation 363.3; contradiction 335.2; negation, abnegation, negative, negative answer, nay, no, nix <nf>; unwillingness 325; disobedience 327; noncompliance, noncooperation, nonobservance 435; withholding, holding back, retention, deprivation

2 repulse, rebuff, peremptory *or* flat *or* point-blank refusal, summary negative; a flea in one's ear; kiss-off *and* slap in the face *and* kick in the teeth <nf>; short shrift

VERBS **3 refuse, decline,** not consent, refuse consent, **reject, turn down** <nf>, decline to accept, **not have,** not buy <nf>; not hold with, not think *or* hear of; **say no,** say nay, vote nay, vote negatively *or* in the negative, side against, disagree, beg to disagree, dissent 333.4; shake one's head, negative, negate; vote down, **turn thumbs down on;** be unwilling 325.3; turn one's back on, turn a deaf ear to, set oneself against, set one's face against, be unmoved, harden one's heart, resist entreaty *or* persuasion; stand aloof, not lift a finger, have nothing to do with, wash one's hands of; hold out against; put *or* set one's foot down, refuse point-blank *or* summarily; decline politely *or* with thanks, beg off; **repudiate,** disallow, disclaim 372.2; decertify, disaccredit

4 deny, withhold, hold back; grudge, begrudge; close the hand *or* purse; deprive one of; **renege**

5 repulse, rebuff, repel, kiss one off *and* slap one in the face *and* kick one in the teeth <nf>, send one away with a flea in one's ear, give one short shrift, shut *or* slam the door in one's face, turn one away; slap *or* smack one down <nf>; deny oneself to, refuse to receive, not be at home to, cut, **snub** 157.5; not want anything to do with

ADJS **6 unconsenting,** nonconsenting, **negative; unwilling** 325.5; **uncompliant,** uncomplying, uncomplaisant, inacquiescent, uncooperative; disobedient; rejective, declinatory; deaf to, not willing to hear of; dissenting

PHRS **7 I refuse, I won't,** I will not, I will do no such thing; over my dead body, far be it from me, not if I can help it, not likely, not on your life, count me out, include me out, I'm not taking any, I won't buy it, it's no go, like hell I will, I'll be hanged if I will, try and make me, you have another guess coming, you should live so long, I'll see you in hell first, nothing doing <nf>; out of the question, not to be thought of, impossible; **no,** by no means, **no way, no way José, there's no way;** in a pig's eye *or* ear *or* ass, my eye *or* ass; you've got to be kidding

443 PERMISSION

NOUNS **1 permission, leave, allowance,** vouchsafement; **consent** 441; permission to enter, admission, ticket, ticket of admission; implied consent, clearance; approbation, blessing; **license,** liberty 430.1; **okay** *and* **OK** *and* **nod** *and* **go-ahead** *and* **green light** *and* **go sign** *and* **thumbs-up** <nf>; special permission, charter, patent, dispensation, release, waiver; zoning variance, variance

2 sufferance, tolerance, toleration, **indulgence;** leniency; winking, overlooking, connivance; permissiveness; dispensation, exemption

3 authorization, authority, sanction, licensing, countenance, **warrant,** warranty, fiat; empowerment, enabling, entitlement, enfranchisement, certification; clearance, security clearance; ratification 332.4; legalization, legitimation, decriminalization

4 carte blanche, blank check <nf>, freedom, **full authority,** full power, free hand, open mandate

5 grant, concession; charter, franchise, liberty, diploma, patent, letters patent, brevet; royal grant

6 permit, license, warrant; building permit, learner's permit, work permit; driver's license, marriage license, hunting license, fishing license, gaming license, etc; nihil obstat, imprimatur; credentials

7 pass, passport, safe-conduct, safeguard, protection; visa, entry visa, exit visa; green card; **clearance,** clearance papers; bill of health, clean bill of health, pratique, full pratique

8 permissibility, permissibleness, **allowableness; admissibility,** admissibleness; justifiableness, warrantableness, sanctionableness; **validity,** legitimacy, lawfulness, licitness, legality

VERBS **9 permit, allow, admit, let,** leave <nf>, give

permission, give leave, make possible; **allow** *or* **permit of;** give *or* leave room for, open the door to; consent 441.2; **grant,** accord, vouchsafe; **okay** *and* **OK** *and* **give the nod** *or* **go-ahead** *or* **green light** *or* **go sign** <nf>, say *or* give the word <nf>; dispense, release, waive

10 **suffer, countenance,** have, **tolerate, condone,** brook, endure, stomach, bear, bear with, put up with, stand for, hear of *and* go along with <nf>; indulge 427.6; **wink at,** blink at, overlook, connive at; leave the door *or* way open to

11 **authorize, sanction, warrant;** give official sanction *or* warrant, legitimize, validate, legalize; empower, give power, enable, entitle; **license; privilege;** charter, patent, enfranchise, franchise; accredit, certificate, certify; ratify 332.12; **legalize,** legitimate, legitimize, decriminalize

12 **give carte blanche,** issue *or* accord *or* give a blank check <nf>, give full power *or* authority, give an open mandate *or* invitation, give free rein, give a free hand, leave alone, leave it to one; permit all *or* anything, open the floodgates, remove all restrictions, let someone get away with murder <nf>

13 **may,** can, have permission, **be permitted or allowed**

ADJS 14 **permissive,** admissive, permitting, allowing; consenting 441.4; **unprohibitive,** nonprohibitive; tolerating, obliging, tolerant; suffering, **indulgent,** soft, liberal, **lenient** 427.7; hands-off <nf>; lax 426.4; easy come easy go <nf>

15 **permissible, allowable, admissible;** justifiable, warrantable, sanctionable; licit, **lawful, legitimate, legal,** legitimized, legalized, legitimated, decriminalized, legit <nf>

16 **permitted, allowed,** allowable, admitted; tolerated, on sufferance; unprohibited, unforbidden, unregulated, unchecked; unconditional, without strings

17 **authorized,** empowered, entitled; **warranted, sanctioned; licensed, privileged;** chartered, patented; franchised, enfranchised; accredited, certificated

ADVS 18 **permissively,** admissively; **tolerantly, indulgently**

19 **permissibly, allowably,** admissibly; with permission, by one's leave; licitly, lawfully, legitimately, legally

PHRS 20 **by your leave,** with your permission, if you please, with respect, may I?

444 PROHIBITION

NOUNS 1 **prohibition, forbidding,** forbiddance; **ruling out, disallowance,** denial, rejection 372; refusal 442; **repression, suppression** 428.2; **ban,** embargo, enjoinder, injunction, prohibitory injunction, **proscription,** inhibition, **interdict,** *interdictum* <L>, interdiction; index, *Index Expurgatorius* and *Index Librorum Prohibitorum* <L>; gag order; **taboo;** thou-shalt-not *and* don't *and* no-no <nf>; law, statute 673.3; preclusion, exclusion, **prevention** 1012.2; forbidden fruit, contraband; sumptuary law *or* ordinance; zoning, zoning law, restrictive convenant; **forbidden ground** *or* **territory,** no-man's land <nf>, no-fly zone; curfew; restriction, circumscription

2 **veto,** negative <old>; absolute veto, qualified *or* limited *or* negative veto, countermand, suspensive *or* suspensory veto, item veto, pocket veto; **thumbs-down** <nf>, red light <nf>, *pollice verso* <L>; blacklist

VERBS 3 **prohibit, forbid; disallow, rule out** *or* **against,** forfend; deny; **reject** 372.2; say no to, **refuse** 442.3; **bar,** debar, preclude, exclude, exclude from, shut out, shut *or* close the door on, **prevent** 1012.14; **ban,** put under the ban, **outlaw,** criminalize, proscribe; **repress, suppress** 428.8; **enjoin,** put under an injunction, issue an injunction against, issue a prohibitory injunction; **proscribe,** inhibit, **interdict,** put *or* lay under an interdict *or* interdiction; put on the Index; embargo, **lay** *or* **put an embargo on; taboo;** outlaw, criminalize,

4 **not permit** *or* **allow, not have, not suffer** *or* **tolerate,** not endure, not stomach, not bear, not bear with, **not countenance,** not brook, brook no, not condone, not accept, not put up with, not go along with <nf>; not stand for *and* not hear of <nf>, put *or* set one's foot down on <nf>

5 **veto,** put one's veto upon, decide *or* rule against, **turn thumbs down on** <nf>, **negative,** kill, nix <nf>

ADJS 6 **prohibitive,** prohibitory, prohibiting, **forbidding;** inhibitive, inhibitory, **repressive, suppressive** 428.11; proscriptive, interdictive, interdictory; preclusive, exclusive, **preventive** 1012.19

7 **prohibited, forbidden,** forbade, forbid, *verboten* <Ger>, **barred; vetoed; unpermissible,** nonpermissible, not permitted *or* allowed, unchartered, **unallowed;** disallowed, ruled out, contraindicated; beyond the pale, off limits, out of bounds; unauthorized, **unsanctioned,** unlicensed; banned, under the ban, **outlawed,** contraband; taboo, untouchable; **illegal,** unlawful, illicit

445 REPEAL

NOUNS 1 **repeal, revocation,** revoke, revokement; reneging, renigging *and* going back on *and* welshing <nf>, **rescinding,** rescindment, rescission, **reversal, striking down, abrogation,** cassation; suspension; waiving, **waiver, setting**

aside; **countermand,** counterorder; **annulment,**
nullification, withdrawal, **invalidation,** voiding,
voidance, vacation, vacatur, defeasance;
cancellation, canceling, cancel, write-off;
abolition, abolishment; **recall,** retraction,
recantation 363.3

VERBS **2 repeal, revoke, rescind, reverse, strike
down, abrogate;** renege, renig *and* go back on
and welsh <nf>; suspend; **waive, set aside;
countermand,** counterorder; **abolish,** do away
with; **cancel,** write off; **annul,** nullify, disannul,
withdraw, **invalidate,** void, vacate, make void,
declare null *and* void; **overrule,** override; **recall,**
retract, recant; unwish

ADJS **3 repealed, revoked, rescinded,** struck down,
set aside; **invalid,** void, **null and void**

446 PROMOTION

NOUNS **1 promotion, preferment, advancement,
advance,** step-up *and* upping <nf>, rise, elevation,
upgrading, jump, step up, step up the ladder,
furtherance; **raise, boost** <nf>; kicking *or*
bumping upstairs <nf>; exaltation,
aggrandizement; ennoblement, knighting;
graduation, passing; pay raise

VERBS **2 promote, advance,** prefer <old>, up *and*
boost <nf>, elevate, upgrade, jump; kick *or* bump
upstairs <nf>, furthering; **raise;** exalt, aggrandize;
ennoble, knight; pass, graduate; raise one's pay, up
or boost one's pay <nf>

447 DEMOTION, DEPOSAL

NOUNS **1 demotion,** degrading, degradation,
disgrading, downgrading, debasement;
abasement, humbling, humiliation, casting down;
reduction, bump *and* bust <nf>; stripping of rank,
depluming, displuming

2 deposal, deposition, removal, displacement,
outplacement, supplanting, supplantation,
replacement, deprivation, **ousting,** unseating;
cashiering, firing <nf>, **dismissal** 909.5; pink slip
<nf>, walking papers <nf>; reduction in forces *or*
RIF; forced resignation; kicking upstairs <nf>;
superannuation, pensioning off, putting out to
pasture, **retirement,** the golden handshake *or*
parachute <nf>; **suspension;** impeachment; purge,
liquidation; overthrow, overthrowal;
dethronement, disenthronement, discrownment;
disbarment, disbarring; unfrocking, defrocking,
unchurching; deconsecration, expulsion,
excommunication 909.4

VERBS **3 demote, degrade,** disgrade, downgrade,
debase, abase, humble, humiliate, **lower, reduce,**
bump *and* bust <nf>; strip of rank, cut off one's
spurs, deplume, displume; force out

4 depose, remove from office, send to the showers
and give the gate <nf>, divest *or* deprive *or* strip of
office, **remove,** displace, outplace, supplant,
replace; **oust; suspend; cashier,** drum out, strip of
rank, **break,** bust <nf>; give a pink slip, hand one's
walking papers; **dismiss** 909.19; **purge, liquidate;
overthrow; retire,** superannuate, pension, pension
off, put out to pasture, give the golden handshake
or parachute <nf>; kick upstairs <nf>; **unseat,**
unsaddle; **dethrone,** disenthrone, unthrone,
uncrown, discrown; **disbar; unfrock,** defrock,
unchurch; strike off the roll, read out of; **expel,**
excommunicate 909.17; deconsecrate

448 RESIGNATION, RETIREMENT

NOUNS **1 resignation,** demission, **withdrawal,
retirement,** pensioning, pensioning off, golden
handshake *or* parachute <nf>, superannuation,
emeritus status, retiracy; **abdication;** voluntary
resignation; forced resignation, forced retirement,
early retirement, deposal 447; relinquishment 370.3

VERBS **2 resign,** demit, **quit,** leave, **vacate,** withdraw
from; **retire,** superannuate, be superannuated, be
pensioned *or* pensioned off, be put out to pasture,
get the golden handshake *or* parachute <nf>;
relinquish, give up 370.7; retire from office, stand
down, stand *or* step aside, give up one's post, hang
up one's spurs <nf>; **tender *or* hand in one's
resignation,** send in one's papers, turn in one's
badge *or* uniform; **abdicate,** renounce the throne,
give up the crown; pension off 447.4; be invalided out

ADJS **3 retired,** in retirement, superannuated, on
pension, pensioned, pensioned off, emeritus,
emerita <fem>

449 AID

NOUNS **1 aid, help, assistance, support, succor,
relief, comfort,** ease, remedy; mutual help *or*
assistance; **service, benefit** 387.4; ministry,
ministration, office, offices, good offices; yeoman's
service; therapy 91; protection 1008; **bailout** <nf>,
rescue 398; means to an end

2 assist, helping hand, hand, lift; boost *and* leg up
<nf>; help in time of need; **support group,**
self-help group, Alcoholics Anonymous *or* AA,
Gamblers Anonymous, etc, 12-step group; tough
love, intervention; social assistance, counsel,
guidance, moral support, constructive criticism,
tender loving care *or* TLC

3 support, maintenance, sustainment, sustentation,
sustenance, subsistence, provision, total support,

meal ticket <nf>; **keep, upkeep; livelihood, living,** meat, bread, daily bread; **nurture, fostering,** nurturance, nourishment, nutriture <old>, mothering, parenting, rearing, fosterage, foster-care, **care, caring,** care-giving, tender loving care or TLC <nf>; manna, manna in the wilderness; economic support, price support, subsidy, subsidization, subvention, endowment, boost; **support services, social services,** welfare, relief, succor; technical support or tech support

4 **patronage, fosterage, tutelage, sponsorship, backing, auspices,** aegis, coattails <nf>, care, guidance, **championing, championship,** seconding; interest, advocacy, encouragement, **backing, abetment;** countenance, **favor, goodwill,** charity, **sympathy,** handout <nf>

5 **furtherance, helping along, advancement,** advance, **promotion, forwarding,** facilitation, speeding, easing or smoothing of the way, clearing of the track, greasing of the wheels, expedition, expediting, rushing; preferment, special or preferential treatment; tailwind

6 **self-help,** self-helpfulness, **self-support,** self-sustainment, self-improvement; independence 430.5

7 helper, assistant 616.6; benefactor 592; facilitator, animator

8 **reinforcements, support, relief,** auxiliaries, reserves, reserve forces, staff

9 **facility, accommodation, appliance, convenience,** amenity, appurtenance; advantage; labor-saving device, time-saving device

10 **helpfulness,** aidfulness <old>, cooperation, goodwill, charity; serviceability, utility, **usefulness** 387.3; **advantageousness,** profitability, favorableness, beneficialness 999.1

VERBS 11 **aid, help, assist,** comfort, abet <old>, succor, relieve, **ease,** doctor, remedy; be of some help, put one's oar in <nf>; do good, do a world of good, **benefit, avail** 999.10; **favor, befriend; give help,** render assistance, offer or proffer aid, come to the aid of, rush or fly to the assistance of, lend aid, **give** or **lend** or **bear a hand** or **helping hand,** stretch forth or hold out a helping hand, boost, cater for <chiefly Brit>; take by the hand, take in tow; **give an assist, give a leg up** or lift or boost <nf>, help a lame dog over a stile; **save,** redeem, bail out <nf>, **rescue** 398.3; protect 1008.18; set up, put on one's feet; give new life to, resuscitate, rally, reclaim, revive, **restore** 396.11,15; be the making of, set one up in business; see one through

12 **support, lend support,** give or furnish or afford support; **maintain, sustain, keep,** upkeep <Brit>; **uphold,** hold up, bear, upbear, **bear up,** bear out, reinforce, undergird, bolster, **bolster up,** buttress, shore, shore up, prop, prop up, crutch;

finance, fund, subsidize, subvention, subventionize; comp and pick up the tab or check <nf>, give new life to

13 **back, back up, stand behind, stand back of** or in back of, get behind, get in behind, get in back of; stand by, stick by and **stick up for** <nf>, **champion; second, take the part of,** take up or adopt or espouse the cause of, take under one's wing, **go to bat for** <nf>, take up the cudgels for, run interference for <nf>, **side with,** take sides with, associate oneself with, join oneself to, align oneself with, ally with, come down or range oneself on the side of, find time for

14 **abet, aid** and **abet, encourage,** hearten, embolden, comfort <old>; advocate, hold a brief for <nf>, countenance, keep in countenance, **endorse, lend oneself to,** lend one's countenance to, lend one's favor or support to, lend one's offices, put one's weight in the scale, plump for and thump the tub for <nf>, lend one's name to, give one's support or countenance to, give moral support to, hold one's hand, make one's cause one's own, weigh in for <nf>; subscribe <Brit>, **favor, go for** <nf>, smile upon, shine upon

15 **patronize, sponsor,** take up, endow, finance

16 **foster, nurture,** nourish, mother, care for, lavish care on, feed, parent, rear, sustain, cultivate, **cherish;** pamper, coddle, cosset, fondle <old>; **nurse,** suckle, cradle; dry-nurse, wet-nurse; spoon-feed; take in hand

17 **be useful, further, forward, advance, promote,** stand in good stead, encourage, **boost** <nf>, favor, advantage, **facilitate,** set or put or push forward, give an impulse to; speed, expedite, quicken, hasten, lend wings to; conduce to, make for, contribute to

18 **serve, lend** or **give oneself,** render service to, do service for, **work for, labor in behalf of; minister to,** cater to, do for <Brit>; attend 577.13; pander to

19 **oblige, accommodate, favor,** do a favor, do a service

ADJS 20 **helping,** assisting, serving, promoting; **assistant, auxiliary,** adjuvant, subservient, subsidiary, ancillary, accessory; ministerial, ministering, ministrant; fostering, nurtural; care, caring, care-giving; instrumental

21 **helpful, useful,** utile, aidful <old>; **profitable, salutary,** good for, **beneficial** 999.12; remedial, therapeutic; **serviceable, useful** 387.18; **contributory,** contributing, conducive, **constructive, positive,** promotional, furthersome <old>; at one's service, at one's command, at one's beck and call; right-hand; adjuvant

22 **favorable, propitious;** kind, kindly, kindly-disposed, all for <nf>, **well-disposed,** well-affected,

well-intentioned, well-meant, **well-meaning;** benevolent, beneficent, benign, benignant; friendly, amicable, neighborly; cooperative

23 self-helpful, self-helping, self-improving; **self-supporting, self-sustaining;** self-supported, self-sustained; independent

ADVS 24 **helpfully,** helpingly; **beneficially,** favorably, profitably, advantageously, to advantage, to the good; serviceably, **usefully**

PREPS 25 helped by, with the help or assistance of, by the aid of; **by means of**

26 **for, on** or **in behalf of,** in aid of <chiefly Brit>, in the name of, on account of, **for the sake of,** in the service of, in furtherance of, in favor of; remedial of

27 **behind, back of** <nf>, supporting, **in support of**

450 COOPERATION

NOUNS 1 **cooperation, collaboration, coaction,** concurrence, synergy, synergism; support, backup; **consensus, commonality; community,** harmony, concordance, concord, fellowship, fellow feeling, solidarity, concert, united front, **teamwork;** pulling or working together, communal or community activity, joining of forces, pooling, pooling of resources, joining of hands; bipartisanship, **mutualism,** mutuality, mutual assistance, coadjuvancy; **reciprocity;** back-scratching, give and take; joint effort, common effort, combined or joint operation, common enterprise or endeavor, collective or united action, mass action; job-sharing; coagency; coadministration, cochairmanship, codirectorship; duet, duumvirate; trio, triumvirate, troika; quartet, quintet, sextet, septet, octet; government by committee, coalition government; symbiosis, commensalism; **cooperativeness,** collaborativeness, team spirit, morale, esprit, *esprit de corps* <Fr>; communism, communalism, communitarianism, collectivism; quislingism; ecumenism, ecumenicism, ecumenicalism; **collusion,** complicity; networking

2 **affiliation, alliance, allying, alignment, association,** consociation, combination, union, unification, **coalition,** fusion, merger, coalescence, coadunation, amalgamation, **league, federation, confederation,** confederacy, consolidation, incorporation, inclusion, integration; hookup and tie-up and tie-in <nf>; **partnership,** copartnership, copartnery <old>, cahoots <nf>; colleagueship, **collegialism, collegiality; fraternity,** confraternity, fraternization, fraternalism; sorority; **fellowship,** sodality; comradeship, camaraderie, freemasonry, communalism, ecumenicism; adfiliation; reaffiliation

VERBS 3 **cooperate, collaborate,** do business and **play ball** <nf>, coact, concur; concert, harmonize, concord; join, band, league, **associate, affiliate,** ally, **combine, unite,** fuse, merge, coalesce, amalgamate, federate, confederate, consolidate; synergize; hook up and tie up and tie in <nf>; partner, be in league, **go into partnership with,** go partners <nf>, go or be in cahoots with; **join together,** club together, league together, band together; **work together,** get together and team up and buddy up <nf>, work as a team, act together, act in concert, **pull together; hold together, hang together,** keep together, **stand together,** stand shoulder to shoulder; lay or put or get heads together; **close ranks,** make common cause, throw in together <nf>, unite efforts, join in, pitch in; network; reciprocate; conspire, collude, aid and abet, stonewall

4 **side with,** take sides with, **unite with; join, join with,** join up with and get together with and team up with <nf>, strike in with <old>; **throw in with** and string along with and swing in with <nf>, **go along with; line up with** <nf>, align with, align oneself with, range with, range oneself with, stand up with, stand in with; **join hands with,** be hand in glove with, go hand in hand with; act with, take part with, **go in with;** cast in one's lot with, join one's fortunes with, stand shoulder to shoulder with, be cheek by jowl with, sink or swim with, stand or fall with; **close ranks with,** fall in with, make common cause with, pool one's interests with; enlist under the banner of, rally round, flock to

ADJS 5 **cooperative, cooperating,** cooperant, **hand in glove;** in cahoots <nf>; **collaborative,** coactive, coacting, coefficient, synergetic, synergic, synergical, synergistic or synergistical; **fellow;** concurrent, concurring, concerted, **in concert; consensus,** consensual, agreeing, in agreement, of like mind; harmonious, harmonized, concordant, **common, communal,** collective; **mutual,** reciprocal; **joint, combined** 805.5; coadjuvant, coadjutant, symbiotic, symbiotical, commensal; complicit, complicitous; uncompetitive, noncompetitive, communalist, communalistic, communist, communistic, communitarian, collective, collectivist, collectivistic, ecumenic or ecumenical; **conniving, collusive**

ADVS 6 **cooperatively,** cooperatingly, coactively, coefficiently, concurrently; in consensus, consensually; **jointly,** combinedly, **conjointly,** concertedly, in concert with; harmoniously, concordantly; communally, collectively, **together;** as one, with one voice, unanimously, in chorus, in unison, as one man, en masse; **side by side, hand in hand, hand in glove, shoulder to shoulder, back to back,** "all for one, one for all"—Dumas père

7 in cooperation, in collaboration, in partnership, in cahoots <nf>, **in collusion,** in league

PREPS **8 with, in cooperation with,** etc

451 OPPOSITION

NOUNS **1 opposition,** opposing, opposure, crossing, oppugnancy, bucking <nf>, standing against; contraposition 779.1; **resistance 453; noncooperation; contention** 457; negation 335; **rejection** 372, refusal; **counteraction,** counterworking 900.1; refusal 442; **contradiction,** challenge, contravention, contraversion, rebutment, rebuttal, denial, impugnation, impugnment; countercurrent, head wind; crosscurrent, undercurrent, undertow; unfriendliness, stiff opposition; contest, pageant, grudge match; line in the sand

2 hostility, antagonism, oppugnancy, oppugnance *and* oppugnation <old>, **antipathy,** enmity, bad blood, inimicalness; **contrariness, contrariety,** orneriness <nf>, repugnance *or* repugnancy, perverseness, **obstinacy** 361; fractiousness, refractoriness, recalcitrance 327.2; uncooperativeness, noncooperation, negativeness, **obstructionism,** traversal, bloody-mindedness <Brit>; **friction, conflict,** clashing, **collision,** cross-purposes, dissension, disaccord 456; latent hostility; rivalry, vying, competition 457.2; polarity

VERBS **3 oppose, counter, cross,** go *or* act in opposition to, **go against,** run against, strive against, **run counter to,** fly in the face of, fly in the teeth of, conflict with, butt heads; kick out against, make waves <nf>, **protest** 333.5; set oneself against, set one's face *or* heart against; be *or* play at cross-purposes, **obstruct,** traverse, sabotage; **take issue with, take one's stand against,** lift *or* raise a hand against, declare oneself against, stand and be counted against, side against, vote against, vote nay, veto; make a stand against, make a dead set against; join the opposition; not put up with, not abide, not be content with; counteract, counterwork, countervail 900.6; **resist,** withstand 453.3

4 contend against, militate against, **contest, combat, battle, clash with, clash, fight against,** **strive against,** struggle against, labor against, **take on** <nf>, grapple with, join battle with, close with, come to close quarters with, go the the mat with <nf>, antagonize <old>, **fight, buck** <nf>, **counter;** buffet, beat against, beat up against, breast, stem, breast *or* stem the tide *or* current *or* flood, breast the wave, buffet the waves; rival, compete with *or* against, vie with *or* against; fight back, **resist, offer resistance** 453.3

5 confront, affront, front, go eyeball-to-eyeball *or* one-on-one with <nf>, take on, tackle, **meet, face, meet head-on; encounter**

6 contradict, cross, traverse, contravene, controvert, rebut, deny, **gainsay;** challenge, contest; oppugn, call into question; **belie,** be contrary to, come in conflict with, negate 335.3; **reject** 372.2

7 be against, be agin <nf>, reject; discountenance 510.11; not hold with, not have anything to do with; have a crow to pluck *or* pick, have a bone to pick

ADJS **8 oppositional, opponent, opposing, opposed; anti** <nf>, contra, confrontational, confrontive; at odds, at loggerheads; **adverse, adversary,** adversarial, adversative, oppugnant, antithetic, antithetical, repugnant, con <nf>, **set** *or* **dead set against; contrary, counter; negative; opposite,** oppositive, death on; overthwart <old>, cross; **contradictory;** unfavorable, unpropitious 133.19; **hostile, antagonistic,** unfriendly, enemy, inimical, alien, antipathetic, antipathetical, unsympathetic, averse; fractious, refractory, recalcitrant 327.10; uncooperative, noncooperative, **obstructive,** bloody-minded <Brit>; ornery <nf>, perverse, obstinate 361.8; **conflicting, clashing,** dissentient, disaccordant 456.15; rival, competitive

ADVS **9 in opposition, in confrontation,** eyeball-to-eyeball *and* one-on-one <nf>, head-on, **at variance, at cross-purposes, at odds,** at issue, at war with, up in arms, with crossed bayonets, at daggers drawn, at daggers, in hostile array, poised against one another; contra, contrariwise, counter, cross, athwart; against the tide *or* wind *or* grain

PREPS **10 opposed to, adverse to,** counter to, **in opposition to,** in conflict with, at cross-purposes with; **against,** agin <nf>, dead against, athwart; **versus,** vs; **con,** contra, face to face with, *vis-à-vis* <Fr>

452 OPPONENT

NOUNS **1 opponent, adversary, antagonist, assailant, foe,** foeman, enemy, archenemy; adverse *or* opposing party, opposite camp, opposite *or* opposing side, **the opposition,** the loyal opposition, unfriendly <nf>; **combatant** 461

2 competitor, contestant, contender, corrival, vier, player, entrant; **rival,** arch-rival; emulator; the field; finalist, semifinalist, etc

3 oppositionist, opposer; obstructionist, obstructive, negativist, naysayer, wet noodle <nf>; contra; **objector, protester,** dissident, dissentient; **resister;** noncooperator; **disputant,** litigant, plaintiff, defendant; quarreler, irritable man, curmudgeon, scrapper <nf>, wrangler, brawler;

die-hard, bitter-ender, last-ditcher, intransigent, irreconcilable

453 RESISTANCE

NOUNS **1 resistance,** withstanding, countering, renitence *or* renitency, repellence *or* repellency; **defiance** 454; **opposing, opposition** 451; **stand; repulsion,** repulse, rebuff; **objection, protest,** remonstrance, **dispute,** challenge, **demur; complaint;** dissentience, **dissent** 333; reaction, hostile *or* combative reaction, rebellion, **counteraction** 900; revolt 327.4; recalcitrance *or* recalcitrancy, recalcitration, fractiousness, refractoriness 327.2; **reluctance** 325.1; **obstinacy** 361; passive resistance, noncooperation; uncooperativeness, negativism; obstinacy; resistance movement, passive resistance, civil disobedience, mutiny, insurrection, insurgence

VERBS **2 resist, withstand; stand; endure** 134.5; **stand up, bear up, hold up, hold out; defy** 454.3, tell one where to get off <nf>, throw down the gauntlet; be obstinate; be proof against, bear up against; **repel,** repulse, rebuff

3 offer resistance, fight back, bite back, not turn the other cheek, show fight, lift *or* raise a hand, stand *or* hold one's ground, **withstand,** stand, **take one's stand,** make a stand, make a stand against, take one's stand against, square off *and* put up one's dukes <nf>, **stand up to,** stand up against, stand at bay; front, **confront,** meet head-on, fly in the teeth *or* face of, **face up to,** face down, face out; **object, protest,** remonstrate, **dispute,** challenge, **complain,** complain loudly, exclaim at; **dissent** 333.4; revolt, mutiny; make waves <nf>; make a determined resistance; kick against, kick out against, recalcitrate; put up a fight *or* struggle <nf>, not take lying down, hang tough *and* tough it out <nf>; **revolt** 327.7; **oppose** 451.3; **contend with** 457.17; **strive against** 451.4

4 stand fast, stand *or* **hold one's ground,** stand firm, make a resolute stand, **hold one's own,** remain firm, stick *and* stuck fast <nf>, **stick to one's guns, stay it out, stick it out** <nf>, **hold out,** not back down, not give up, not submit, **never say die; fight to the last ditch,** die hard, sell one's life dearly, go down with flying colors, refuse to bow down

ADJS **5 resistant, resistive,** resisting, renitent, up against, **withstanding,** repellent; obstructive, retardant, retardative; **unyielding,** unsubmissive 361.12; hard-shell, hard-nosed; rebellious 327.11; **proof against; objecting, protesting,** disputing, disputatious, complaining, dissentient, dissenting 333.6; recalcitrant, fractious, obstinate, refractory 327.10; **reluctant** 325.6; noncooperative,

uncooperative; up in arms, on the barricades, not lying down; immune

454 DEFIANCE

NOUNS **1 defiance,** defying, defial <old>; **daring,** daringness, **audacity,** boldness, bold front, brash bearing, brashness, brassiness <nf>, brazenness, bravado, insolence; bearding, beard-tweaking, nose-tweaking; **arrogance** 141; **sauciness,** sauce, **cheekiness** *or* cheek <nf>, rebelliousness, pertness, impudence, impertinence; bumptiousness, cockiness; **contempt,** contemptuousness, derision, **disdain,** disregard, despite; **risk-taking,** tightrope walking, funambulism; disobedience, insubordination

2 challenge, dare, double dare, threat, taunt; fighting words; **defy** *or* defi; gage, gage of battle, gauntlet, glove, chip on one's shoulder, slap of the glove, invitation *or* bid to combat, call to arms; war cry, war whoop, battle cry, rebel yell; back talk, insult

VERBS **3 defy,** bid defiance, hurl defiance, snarl *or* shout *or* scream defiance; **dare,** double-dare, outdare; **challenge,** call out, throw *or* fling down the gauntlet *or* glove *or* gage, stand up to, knock the chip off one's shoulder, cross swords; oppose, protest; beard, beard the lion in his den, face, face out, look in the eye, stare down, stare out <Brit>, **confront, affront,** front, say right to one's face, square up to, go eyeball-to-eyeball *or* one-on-one with <nf>; tweak the nose, pluck by the beard, slap one's face, double *or* shake one's fist at; give one the finger; **ask for it** <nf>, ask *or* look for trouble, make something of it <nf>, show fight, show one's teeth, bare one's fangs; dance the war dance; **brave** 492.10; be insubordinate

4 flout, disregard, **slight,** slight over, treat with contempt, set at defiance, fly in the teeth *or* face of, **snap one's fingers at; thumb one's nose at,** cock a snook at, bite the thumb at; **disdain, despise, scorn** 157.3; laugh at, laugh to scorn, laugh out of court, laugh in one's face; hold in derision, scout, scoff at, **deride** 508.8; give someone lip <nf>, sass <nf>

5 show *or* **put up a bold front,** bluster, throw out one's chest, strut, crow, look big, stand with arms akimbo, gasconade

6 take a dare, accept a challenge, **take one up on** *and* **call one's bluff** <nf>; **start something,** take up the gauntlet

ADJS **7 defiant,** defying, challenging; **daring, bold,** brash, brassy <nf>, brazen, **audacious,** insolent; arrogant 141.9; saucy, cheeky <nf>, pert, impudent, impertinent; stubborn, obstinate; bumptious, cocky, sassy; **contemptuous,** disdainful, derisive, disregardful, greatly daring, regardless of consequences; obstreperous

ADVS **8 in defiance of,** in the teeth of, in the face of, under one's very nose

455 ACCORD
<harmonious relationship>

NOUNS **1 accord,** accordance, **concord,** concordance, **harmony,** symphony, sync <nf>; **rapport;** good vibrations <nf>, good vibes <nf>, good karma; amity 587.1; frictionlessness; *rapprochement* <Fr>; **sympathy,** empathy, identity, feeling of identity, fellow feeling, **fellowship,** kinship, togetherness, **affinity; agreement, understanding, like-mindedness, congruence;** congeniality, **compatibility; oneness,** unity, unison, union; **community,** communion, community of interests, meeting of the minds; solidarity, team spirit, esprit, *esprit de corps* <Fr>; mutuality, sharing, reciprocity, mutual supportiveness; bonds of harmony, ties of affection, cement of friendship; happy family; peace 464; **love,** agape <Gk>, charity, *caritas* <L>, brotherly love; correspondence 788.1

VERBS **2 get along,** harmonize, **agree with, agree, get along with,** get on with, cotton to *or* hit it off with <nf>, harmonize with, **be in harmony with,** be in tune with, fall *or* chime in with, blend in with, go hand in hand with, **be at one with;** sing in chorus, be on the same wavelength <nf>, see eye to eye; **sympathize,** empathize, identify with, respond to, understand one another, enter into one's views, enter into the ideas *or* feelings of; accord, correspond 788.6; reciprocate, interchange 863.4

ADJS **3 in accord,** accordant <old>, **harmonious, in harmony,** congruous, congruent, in tune, attuned, agreeing, in concert, **in rapport,** *en rapport* <Fr>, amicable 587.15,18; frictionless; **sympathetic,** simpatico <nf>, empathic, empathetic, **understanding; like-minded,** akin, of the same mind, of one mind, at one, united, together; concordant, corresponding 788.9; agreeable, congenial, **compatible; peaceful** 464.9

456 DISACCORD
<unharmonious relationship>

NOUNS **1 disaccord, discord,** discordance *or* discordancy, asynchrony, **unharmoniousness,** inharmoniousness, disharmony, inharmony, incongruence, incongruency, disaffinity, incompatibility, incompatibleness; culture gap, generation gap, gender gap; noncooperation; **conflict,** open conflict *or* war, **friction,** rub; jar,

jarring, jangle, clash, clashing; touchiness, strained relations, tension; bad blood; **unpleasantness;** mischief; **contention** 457; **enmity** 589; Eris, Discordia; the Apple of Discord

2 disagreement, difficulty, misunderstanding, difference, difference of opinion, agreement to disagree, **variance,** division, dividedness; cross-purposes; polarity of opinion, polarization; credibility gap, **disparity** 789.1

3 dissension, dissent, dissidence, flak <nf>; bickering, infighting, faction, factiousness, partisanship, partisan spirit; **divisiveness; quarrelsomeness;** litigiousness; pugnacity, bellicosity, combativeness, **aggressiveness,** contentiousness, belligerence; feistiness <nf>, **touchiness, irritability,** shrewishness, irascibility 110.2

4 falling-out, breach of friendship, parting of the ways, bust-up <nf>; **alienation, estrangement, disaffection,** disfavor; **breach, break, rupture, schism, split, rift,** cleft, **disunity, disunion, disruption,** separation, cleavage, divergence, division, dividedness; division in the camp, house divided against itself; open rupture, breaking off of negotiations, recall of ambassadors

5 quarrel, open quarrel, dustup, **dispute, argument,** polemic, argy-bargy *and* slanging match <Brit>, fliting <old>, lovers' quarrel, **controversy,** altercation, **fight, squabble, contention,** strife, **tussle,** bicker, wrangle, snarl, **tiff, spat,** fuss; **breach of the peace; fracas,** donnybrook *or* donnybrook fair, brouhaha; dissent; broil, embroilment, imbroglio; words, sharp words, war of words, logomachy; **feud,** blood feud, vendetta; brawl 457.5; turf war

6 <nf terms> **row, rumpus,** row-de-dow, ruckus, ruction, brannigan, shindy, foofooraw, hoo-ha, barney *and* shemozzle <Brit>, set-to, run-in, **scrap, hassle,** rhubarb; knock-down-and-drag-out, knock-down-and-drag-out quarrel *or* fight; the dozens; handbags at dawn, handbag situation

7 bone of contention, apple of discord, sore point, tender spot, delicate *or* ticklish issue, rub, beef <nf>; **bone to pick,** crow to pluck *or* pick *or* pull; *casus belli* <L>, grounds for war

VERBS **8 disagree, differ,** differ in opinion, hold opposite views, disaccord, **be at variance,** not get along, pull different ways, be at cross-purposes, have no measures with, misunderstand one another; **conflict, clash,** collide, jostle, jangle, jar; live like cat *and* dog, live a cat-and-dog life

9 have a bone to pick with, have a crow to pluck with *or* pick with *or* pull with, have a beef with <nf>

10 fall out, have a falling-out, **break with, split,** separate, **diverge,** divide, agree to disagree, **part company,** come to *or* reach a parting of the ways

11 quarrel, dispute, oppugn, flite <old>, altercate, **fight, squabble,** tiff, spat, **bicker, wrangle,** spar, broil, have words, set to, join issue, make the fur fly; cross swords, **feud, battle; brawl; be quarrelsome** *or* contentious, be thin-skinned, be touchy *or* sensitive, get up on the wrong side of the bed

12 <nf terms> **row, scrap, hassle,** make *or* kick up a row; mix it up, lock horns, bump heads

13 pick a quarrel, fasten a quarrel on, look for trouble, pick a bone with, pluck a crow with; have a chip on one's shoulder; add insult to injury

14 sow dissension, stir up trouble, make *or* borrow trouble; **alienate, estrange,** separate, **divide, disunite,** disaffect, **come between; irritate, provoke,** aggravate; **set at odds,** set at variance; **set against,** pit against, **sic on** *or* **at, set on,** set by the ears, set at one's throat; add fuel to the fire *or* flame, fan the flame, pour oil on the blaze, light the fuse, stir the pot <nf>

ADJS **15 disaccordant, unharmonious,** inharmonious, disharmonious, out of tune, asynchronous, unsynchronized, out of sync <nf>, **discordant,** out of accord, dissident, dissentient, **disagreeing, differing; conflicting,** clashing, colliding; like cats *and* dogs; **divided,** faction-ridden, fragmented

16 at odds, at variance, at loggerheads, at square <old>, at cross-purposes; at war, at strife, at feud, at swords' points, at daggers *or* at daggers drawn, up in arms

17 partisan, polarizing, **divisive,** factional, factious; **quarrelsome,** bickering, disputatious, wrangling, eristic, eristical, polemical; litigious, pugnacious, combative, **aggressive,** bellicose, belligerent; feisty <nf>, touchy, irritable, shrewish, **irascible** 110.19

457 CONTENTION

NOUNS **1 contention, contest,** contestation, combat, **fighting, conflict, strife, war, struggle,** blood on the floor, cut *and* thrust; fighting at close quarters, infighting; **warfare** 458; **hostility,** enmity 589; **quarrel, altercation, controversy,** dustup, polemic, debate, forensics, **argument, dispute, disputation;** litigation; words, war of words, paper war, logomachy; **fighting,** scrapping *and* hassling <nf>; **quarreling, bickering, wrangling, squabbling;** oppugnancy, contentiousness, disputatiousness, litigiousness, **quarrelsomeness** 456.3; cat-and-dog life; Kilkenny cats; **competitiveness,** vying, rivalrousness, competitorship; cold war; bone of contention

2 competition, rivalry, trying conclusions *or* the issue, vying, emulation, jockeying <nf>; cutthroat competition; run for one's money; **sportsmanship,** gamesmanship, lifemanship, one-upmanship, competitive advantage; rat race <nf>; feeding frenzy <nf>

3 contest, engagement, encounter, match, matching, meet, meeting, derby, pissing match *or* contest <nf>, **trial, test,** *concours* and *rencontre* <Fr>; **close contest, hard contest,** closely fought contest, close *or* tight one, horse race *and* crapshoot <nf>; fight, bout, go <nf>, tussle; joust, tilt; tournament, tourney; rally; **game** 743.9; **games,** Olympic games, Olympics, gymkhana; cookoff, Bake-Off <trademark>; spelling bee

4 fight, battle, fray, affray, combat, action, conflict, embroilment; gun battle; **clash; brush, skirmish,** scrimmage; tussle, **scuffle, struggle,** scramble, shoving match; exchange of blows, *passage d'armes* <Fr>, passage at *or* of arms, clash of arms; **quarrel** 456.5; pitched battle; battle royal; unarmed combat; **fistfight,** punch-out *and* duke-out <nf>, punch-up <Brit nf>; **hand-to-hand fight,** stand-up fight <nf>, running fight *or* engagement; tug-of-war; bull-fight, tauromachy; dogfight, cockfight; street fight, rumble <nf>; air *or* aerial combat, sea *or* naval combat, ground combat, armored combat, infantry combat, fire fight, hand-to-hand combat, house-to-house combat; **internal struggle,** intestine *or* internecine struggle *or* combat; rhubarb <nf>

5 free-for-all, knock-down-and-drag-out <nf>, **brawl,** broil, melee, scrimmage, **fracas,** riot

6 death struggle, life-and-death *or* **life-or-death struggle, struggle** *or* **fight** *or* **duel to the death,** *guerre à mort* and *guerre à outrance* <Fr>, all-out war, total war, last-ditch fight, fight to the last ditch, fight with no quarter given

7 duel, single combat, monomachy, satisfaction, **affair of honor,** *affaire d'honneur* <Fr>

8 fencing, swordplay; swordsmanship, dueling

9 boxing 754, **fighting,** noble *or* manly art of self-defense, **fisticuffs, pugilism, prize-fighting,** the fights <nf>, the ring; **boxing match, prizefight,** spar, bout; shadowboxing; close fighting, infighting, the clinches <nf>; Chinese boxing; savate

10 wrestling, rassling <nf>, grappling, *sumo* <Japanese>; **martial arts;** catch-as-catch-can; wrestling match, wrestling meet; Greco-Roman wrestling, Cornish wrestling, Westmorland wrestling, Cumberland wrestling; professional wrestling

11 racing, track, track sports; **horse racing** 757, the turf, the sport of kings; dog racing, automobile racing 756

12 race, contest of speed *or* fleetness; derby; **horse race; automobile race,** off-road race; **heat, lap,** bell lap, victory lap; footrace, run, running event;

torch race; match race, obstacle race, three-legged race, sack race, potato race; walk; ride *and* tie; endurance race, motorcycle race, bicycle race; boat race, yacht race, regatta; air race; dog race

VERBS **13 contend, contest,** jostle; **fight, battle, combat, war, declare** *or* **go to war,** take *or* take up arms, put up a fight <nf>, open hostilities, call to arms; wage war; **strive, struggle,** scramble, go for the brass ring; make the fur *or* feathers fly, **tussle, scuffle; quarrel** 456.11; clash, collide; **wrestle,** rassle <nf>, grapple, grapple with, go to the mat with; **come to blows,** close, try conclusions, **mix it up** *and* go toe-to-toe <nf>, exchange blows *or* fisticuffs, **box,** spar, give *and* take, give one a knuckle sandwich <nf>; cut *and* thrust, **cross swords, fence,** thrust *and* parry; **joust, tilt, tourney,** run a tilt *or* a tilt at, break a lance with; **duel,** fight a duel, give satisfaction; feud; skirmish; fight one's way; fight the good fight; **brawl,** broil; **riot;** do a job on <nf>

14 lift *or* **raise one's hand against;** make war on; draw the sword against, take up the cudgels, couch one's lance; square up *or* off <nf>, come to the scratch; have at, jump; lay on, lay about one; **pitch into** *and* **sail into** *and* light into *and* lay into *and* rip into <nf>, strike the first blow, draw first blood; **attack** 459.14

15 encounter, come *or* **go up against,** fall *or* run foul *or* afoul of; close with, come to close quarters, bring to bay, meet *or* fight hand-to-hand

16 engage, take on <nf>, go against *or* up against, close with, try conclusions with, enter the ring *or* arena with, put on the gloves with, match oneself against; **join issue** *or* **battle, do** *or* **give battle,** engage in battle *or* combat

17 contend with, engage with, cope with, **fight with, strive with, struggle with,** wrestle with, grapple with, bandy with <old>, try conclusions with, measure swords with, tilt with, **cross swords with;** exchange shots, shoot it out with <nf>; **lock horns** *and* **bump heads** <nf>, fall *or* go to loggerheads <old>; **tangle with** *and* **mix it up with** <nf>, have a brush with; have it out, fight *or* battle it out, settle it; **fight** *or* **go at it hammer and tongs** *or* tooth and nail, fight it out, duke it out <nf>, fight like devils, ask *and* give no quarter, make blood flow freely, battle *à outrance,* fight to the death, fight to the finish

18 compete, contend, vie, try conclusions *or* the issue, jockey <nf>; **compete with** *or* **against, vie with, challenge,** cope <old>, enter into competition with, give a run for one's money, **meet;** try *or* test one another; **rival,** emulate, outvie; keep up with the Joneses

19 race, race with, run a race; horse-race, boat-race, etc

20 contend for, strive for, struggle for, fight for, vie for; stickle for, stipulate for, hold out for, make a point of

21 dispute, contest, oppugn, take issue with; **fight over, quarrel over, wrangle over, squabble over,** bicker over, strive *or* contend about

ADJS **22 contending,** contesting; **contestant,** disputant; striving, struggling; fighting, battling, warring; **warlike; quarrelsome** 456.17

23 competitive, competitory, competing, **vying,** rivaling, **rival,** rivalrous, emulous, in competition, in rivalry; **cutthroat**

458 WARFARE

NOUNS **1 war, warfare, warring, warmaking,** art of war, **combat, fighting,** *la guerre* <Fr>; armed conflict, armed combat, military operation, the sword, arbitrament of the sword, appeal to arms *or* the sword, resort to arms, force *or* might of arms, bloodshed; **state of war, hostilities,** belligerence *or* belligerency, open war *or* warfare *or* hostilities; **hot war, shooting war;** total war, **all-out war; wartime; battle** 457.4; **attack** 459; **war zone, theater of operations;** trouble spot; warpath; localized war, major war, world war, atomic war, nuclear war, civil war, chemical war, biological war, bacteriological warfare, war of independence, naval war; offensive warfare, preventive warfare, psychological warfare; static warfare, trench warfare, guerrilla warfare; nuclear winter; limited war

2 battle array, order of battle, **disposition, deployment, marshaling;** open order; close formation; echelon

3 campaign, war, **drive, expedition,** battle plan, hostile expedition; **crusade,** holy war, jihad

4 operation, action; **movement; mission; operations,** military operations, land operations, naval *or* sea operations, air operations; combined operations, joint operations, coordinated operations; active operations, amphibious operations, airborne operations, fluid operations, major operations, minor operations, night operations, overseas operations; war plans, staff work; logistic; war game, dry run, kriegspiel, maneuver, maneuvers; **strategy, tactics, battle**

5 military science, art *or* rules *or* science of war, military affairs, military strategy, military tactics, military operations; siegecraft; warcraft, war, **arms,** profession of arms; **generalship,** soldiership, chivalry, knighthood, knightly skill

6 declaration of war, challenge; defiance 454

7 call to arms, call-up, call to the colors, **rally; mobilization; muster,** levy; conscription, recruitment; **rallying cry,** slogan, watchword, catchword, exhortation; battle cry, war cry, war whoop, rebel yell; banzai, gung ho, St George, Montjoie, Geronimo, go for broke; **bugle call, trumpet call,** clarion, clarion call; remember the Maine *or* the Alamo *or* Pearl Harbor; battle orders, military orders

8 **service, military service;** active service *or* duty; military duty, military obligation, compulsory service, conscription, draft, impressment; selective service, national service <Brit>; reserve status; recruiting, recruitment; enlisting, volunteering

9 **militarization,** activation, **mobilization;** war *or* wartime footing, national emergency; **war effort, war economy;** martial law, suspension of civil rights; garrison state, military dictatorship; remilitarization, reactivation; arms race; war clouds, war scare

10 **warlikeness,** unpeacefulness, war *or* warlike spirit, ferocity, fierceness; **hard line; combativeness, contentiousness; hostility, antagonism;** unfriendliness 589.1; aggression, **aggressiveness;** aggro <Brit nf>; belligerence *or* belligerency, **pugnacity,** pugnaciousness, **bellicosity, bellicoseness, truculence,** fight <nf>; chip on one's shoulder <nf>; militancy, **militarism,** martialism, militaryism; saber rattling; **chauvinism, jingoism,** hawkishness <nf>, **warmongering;** waving of the bloody shirt; warpath; war fever; oppugnancy, **quarrelsomeness** 456.3

11 <rallying devices *and* themes> battle flag, banner, colors, gonfalon, bloody shirt, bluidy sark <Scot>, fiery cross *or* crostarie, atrocity story, enemy atrocities; martial music, war song, battle hymn, national anthem, military band; national honor, face; foreign threat, totalitarian threat, Communist threat, colonialist *or* neocolonialist *or* imperialist threat, Western imperialism, yellow peril; expansionism, manifest destiny; independence, self-determination

12 war-god, Mars, Ares, Odin *or* Woden *or* Wotan, Tyr *or* Tiu *or* Tiw; war-goddess, Athena, Minerva, Bellona, Enyo, Valkyrie

VERBS 13 **war, wage war, make war, carry on war** *or* **hostilities,** engage in hostilities, wield the sword; battle, **fight;** spill *or* shed blood

14 **make war on,** levy war on; **attack** 459.14,17; **declare war, challenge,** combat, attack, throw *or* fling down the gauntlet; defy 454.3; open hostilities, plunge the world into war; launch a holy war on, go on a crusade against

15 **go to war,** break *or* breach the peace, take up the gauntlet, **go on the warpath, rise up in arms, take** *or* **resort to arms,** take arms, take up arms, take up the cudgels *or* sword, fly *or* appeal to the sword, unsheathe one's weapon, come to cold steel; take the offensive, take the field

16 **campaign,** undertake operations, open a campaign, make an expedition, go on a crusade

17 **serve,** do duty; fulfill one's military obligation, wear the uniform; **soldier,** see *or* do active duty; **bear arms,** carry arms, shoulder arms, shoulder a gun, defend, protect; see action *or* combat, hear shots fired in anger

18 **call to arms, call up,** call to the colors, **rally; mobilize; muster,** levy; **conscript, recruit;** sound the call to arms, give the battle cry, wave the bloody shirt, beat the drums, blow the bugle *or* clarion

19 **militarize, activate, mobilize,** go on a wartime footing, put on a war footing, call to the colors, gird *or* gird up one's loins, muster one's resources; reactivate, remilitarize, take out of mothballs *and* retread <nf>

ADJS 20 **warlike, militant,** fighting, warring, battling; **martial, military,** soldierly, soldierlike; **combative, contentious,** gladiatorial; trigger-happy <nf>; **belligerent, pugnacious,** pugilistic, **truculent, bellicose,** scrappy <nf>, full of fight; **aggressive,** offensive; fierce, ferocious, savage, bloody, bloody-minded, bloodthirsty, sanguinary, sanguineous; **unpeaceful,** unpeaceable, unpacific; **hostile, antagonistic,** agonistic, **enemy,** inimical; unfriendly 589.9; **quarrelsome** 456.17; paramilitary, mercenary, soldierlike; don't ask don't tell

21 **militaristic, warmongering,** war-loving, warlike, saber-rattling, battle-hungry; **chauvinistic,** chauvinist, **jingoistic,** jingoist, jingoish, jingo, crusading; **hard-line, hawkish** <nf>, of the war party

22 **embattled,** battled, **engaged,** at grips, in combat, on the warpath, on the offensive; **arrayed, deployed,** ranged, in battle array, in the field; **militarized; armed** 460.14; war-ravaged, war-torn

ADVS 23 **at war, up in arms;** in the midst of battle, in the thick of the fray *or* combat; in the cannon's mouth, at the point of the gun; at swords' points, at the point of the bayonet *or* sword

24 **wars**

American Civil War <1861-65>	English Civil War <1642-46>
American Revolution *or* War of Independence *or* Revolutionary War <1775-83>	Franco-Prussian War <1870-71>
	French and Indian War <1754-63>
Arab-Israeli War <1948-49, 1956, 1967, 1973-74, 1982>	French Revolution <1789-99>
Balkan Wars <1912-13>	Gallic War <58-50 BC>
Boer Wars <1880-81, 1899-1902>	Greco-Persian Wars <492-449 BC>
Crimean War <1853-56>	Gulf War <1980-88>
Crusades <11th-13th centuries>	Hundred Years' War <1337-1453>

Indian Wars <1622-75, 1840-80s>
Iran-Iraq War <1980-90>
Iraq War or Operation Iraqi Freedom <2003->
Italian Wars of Independence <1848-49, 1859-60>
Korean War <1950-53>
Kosovo Crisis <1998-99>
Mexican Civil War <1910-20>
Mexican War <1846-48>
Napoleonic Wars <1793-1815>
Norman Conquest <1066>
Opium Wars <1839-42, 1856-60>
Peloponnesian Wars <431-404 BC>
Persian Gulf War <1990-91>
Punic Wars <264-241 BC, 218-201 BC>
Russian Revolution or Russian Civil War <1918-20>
Russo-Finnish War or Winter War <1939-40>
Russo-Japanese War <1904-05>
Samnite Wars <343-341, 326-304, 298-290 BC>
Seven Weeks' War <1866>
Seven Years' War <1756-63>
Sino-Japanese Wars <1894-95, 1937-45>
Six-Day War <1967>
Spanish-American War <1898>
Spanish Civil War <1936-39>
Taiping Rebellion <1850-64>
Thirty Years' War <1618-48>
Vietnam War or War in Southeast Asia <1955-75>
War of 1812 <1812-14>
War of the Austrian Succession <1740-48>
War of the Polish Succession <1733-38>
War of the Spanish Succession <1701-14>
Wars of the Roses <1455-85>
World War I or Great War or War of the Nations <1914-18>
World War II <1939-45>
Yom Kippur War <1973>

459 ATTACK

NOUNS **1 attack, assault,** assailing, assailment; offense, **offensive; aggression; onset, onslaught; strike;** surgical strike, first strike, preventive war; descent on or upon; **charge,** rush, dead set at, run at or against; **drive, push** <nf>; **sally, sortie;** infiltration; *coup de main* <Fr>; frontal attack or assault, head-on attack, flank attack; mass attack, kamikaze attack; banzai attack or charge, suicide attack or charge; hit-and-run attack; breakthrough; **counterattack, counteroffensive;** amphibious attack; gas attack; diversionary attack, diversion; assault *and* battery, simple assault, mugging <nf>, aggravated assault, aggravated battery, armed assault, unprovoked assault, **preemptive strike; blitzkrieg, blitz,** lightning attack, lightning war, panzer warfare, sudden or devastating or crippling attack, deep strike, shock tactics; atomic or thermonuclear attack, first-strike capacity, megadeath, overkill; nuclear winter; land attack, air attack, combined attack, terrorist attack, bioterror, biowarfare; personal attack

2 surprise attack, surprise, surprisal, unforeseen attack, **sneak attack** <nf>; Pearl Harbor; stab in the back; shock tactics

3 thrust, pass, lunge, swing, cut, stab, jab; feint; home thrust

4 raid, foray, razzia; **invasion, incursion,** inroad, irruption; **air raid, air strike,** air attack, shuttle raid, fire raid, saturation raid; escalade, scaling, boarding, **tank** or **armored attack,** panzer attack

5 siege, besiegement, beleaguerment; encompassment, investment, encirclement, envelopment; blockading, blockade; cutting of supply lines; vertical envelopment; pincer movement

6 storm, storming, taking by storm, overrunning

7 bombardment, bombing, air bombing, strategic bombing, tactical bombing, saturation bombing; strafing; terrorist attack; suicide bombing

8 gunfire, fire, firing, musketry, **shooting,** fireworks or gunplay <nf>; gunfight, shoot-out; **firepower,** offensive capacity, bang <nf>

9 volley, salvo, burst, spray, strafe, **fusillade,** rapid fire; cross fire; drumfire, **cannonade,** cannonry, **broadside,** enfilade; **barrage, artillery barrage;** sharpshooting, sniping

10 stabbing, piercing, sticking <nf>; **knifing,** bayonetting; the sword; **impalement, transfixion**

11 stoning, lapidation

12 assailant, assailer, **attacker;** assaulter, mugger <nf>; **aggressor;** invader, raider; warrior; terrorist

13 zero hour, H-hour; D-day, target day

VERBS **14 attack, assault, assail,** harry, assume or take the offensive; commit an assault upon; **strike, hit, pound; go at, come at,** have at, **launch out against,** make a set or dead set at; **fall on** or **upon, set on** or **upon, descend on** or upon, come down on, swoop down on; pounce upon; **lift** or **raise a hand against,** draw the sword against, take up arms or the cudgels against; **lay hands on,** lay a hand on, bloody one's hands with; gang up on, attack in force; surprise, **ambush; blitz,** attack or hit like lightning

15 <nf terms> **pitch into, light into, lambaste,** pile into, sail into, wade into, lay into, plow into, tie into, rip into; **let one have it,** let one have it with both barrels, kick ass; **land on,** land on like a ton of bricks, climb all over, crack down on, lower the boom on, tee off on; **mug,** jump, bushwhack, sandbag, scrag, swipe at, lay at, **go for, go at;** blindside, blind-pop, sucker-punch; **take a swing** or **crack** or **swipe** or **poke** or punch or **shot at**

16 lash out at, strike out at, hit out at, let drive at, let fly at; **strike at,** hit at, poke at, thrust at, **swing at,** swing on, make a thrust or pass at, lunge at, aim or deal a blow at, flail at, flail away at, take a fling or shy at; cut and thrust; smite; feint

17 launch an attack, kick off an attack, mount an

attack, **push, thrust,** mount *or* open an offensive, **drive; advance against** *or* **upon, march upon** *or* **against,** bear down upon; **infiltrate; strike;** flank; press the attack, follow up the attack; **counterattack,** retaliate, take on

18 **charge,** rush, **rush at, fly at,** run at, dash at, make a dash *or* rush at; tilt at, go full tilt at, make *or* run a tilt at, ride full tilt against; **jump off,** go over the top <nf>

19 **besiege, lay siege to,** encompass, surround, **encircle,** envelope, invest, hem in, set upon on all sides, get in a pincers, close the jaws of the pincers *or* trap; **blockade; beset, beleaguer, harry, harass,** drive *or* press one hard; soften up

20 **raid,** foray, make a raid; **invade,** inroad, make an inroad, make an irruption into; escalade, scale, scale the walls, board; storm, take by storm, overwhelm, inundate

21 **pull a gun on,** draw a gun on; **get the drop on** *and* **beat to the draw** <nf>

22 **pull the trigger, fire upon,** fire at, **shoot at,** pop at *and* take a pop at <nf>, take *or* fire *or* let off a shot at, blaze away at <nf>; **open fire,** commence firing, open up on <nf>; aim at, take aim at, level at <old>, zero in on, take dead aim at, draw a bead on; **snipe,** snipe at; **bombard, blast, strafe, shell,** cannonade, mortar, barrage, blitz; pepper, fusillade, fire a volley; rake, enfilade; pour a broadside into; cannon; **torpedo; shoot**

23 **bomb,** drop a bomb, lay an egg <nf>; dive-bomb, glide-bomb, skip-bomb, pattern-bomb, suicide-bomb, etc; atom-bomb, hydrogen-bomb; nuke <nf>, plaster <nf>

24 **mine,** plant a mine, trigger a mine

25 **stab, stick** <nf>, **pierce,** plunge in; **run through, impale,** spit, **transfix,** transpierce; **spear,** lance, poniard, bayonet, saber, sword, put to the sword; **knife,** dirk, dagger, stiletto; spike; cut down

26 **gore,** horn, tusk

27 **pelt, stone,** lapidate <old>, pellet; brickbat *or* egg <nf>, chuck

28 **hurl at, throw at, cast at,** heave at, fling at, sling at, toss at, shy at, fire at, let fly at; hurl against, hurl at the head of

ADJS 29 **attacking,** assailing, assaulting, charging, driving, thrusting, advancing; **invading,** invasive, invasionary, incursive, incursionary, irruptive, storming

30 **offensive, combative,** on the offensive *or* attack; **aggressive;** militant, hawkish, on the warpath

ADVS 31 **under attack, under fire;** under siege; counterattacking

INTERJS 32 **attack!,** advance!, **charge!,** over the top!, up *and* at 'em!, have at them!, give 'em hell!, let 'em have it!, fire!, open fire!; banzai!, Geronimo!

460 DEFENSE

NOUNS 1 **defense,** defence <Brit>, **guard,** ward; **protection** 1008; resistance 453; self-defense, self-protection, self-preservation; deterrent capacity; defense in depth; the defensive; covering one's ass *or* rear-end <nf>; defenses, psychological defenses, ego defenses, defense mechanism, escape mechanism, avoidance reaction, negative taxis *or* tropism; bunker atmosphere *or* mentality; siege mentality

2 **military defense, national defense,** defense capability; Air Defense Command; **civil defense;** CONELRAD *or* control of electromagnetic radiation for civil defense, Emergency Broadcast System *or* EBS, Civil Defense Warning System; radar defenses, distant early warning *or* DEW Line; antimissile missile, antiballistic-missile system *or* ABM; strategic defense initiative *or* Star Wars

3 **armor,** armature; armor plate; body armor, suit of armor, plate armor; panoply, harness; **mail,** chain mail, chain armor; bulletproof vest; **battlegear; protective covering,** cortex, **thick skin,** carapace, shell 295.15; spines, needles; human shield

4 **fortification,** work, defense work, **bulwark, rampart, fence,** earthwork, stockade, **barrier** 1012.5; **enclosure** 212.3

5 **entrenchment, trench,** ditch, fosse; **moat; dugout,** *abri* <Fr>; **bunker; foxhole,** slit trench; approach trench, communication trench, fire trench, gallery, parallel, coupure; tunnel, fortified tunnel; undermining, sap, single *or* double sap, flying sap; mine, countermine

6 **stronghold,** hold, safehold, fasthold, strong point, **fastness,** keep, ward, **bastion,** donjon, **citadel, castle,** tower, tower of strength; mote *or* motte; **fort, fortress,** post; **bunker, pillbox,** blockhouse, garrison *or* trenches *or* barricades; garrison house; acropolis; peel, peel tower; rath; martello tower, martello; **bridgehead, beachhead;** safeguard

7 **defender, champion, advocate; upholder; guardian angel,** angel <nf>; **supporter** 616.9; vindicator, apologist; **protector** 1008.5; **guard** 1008.9; henchman; paladin, knight, white knight; guard dog, attack dog, junkyard dog

VERBS 8 **defend, guard, shield,** screen, secure, guard against, ward; defend tooth *and* nail *or* to the death *or* to the last breath; **safeguard, protect** 1008.18; stand by the side of, flank; **advocate, champion** 600.10; **defend oneself,** cover one's ass *or* rear-end <nf>, CYA *or* cover your ass <nf>

9 **fortify,** embattle *or* battle <old>; **arm; armor,** armor-plate; **man;** garrison, man the garrison *or*

trenches *or* barricades; **barricade, blockade;** bulwark, wall, palisade, fence; castellate, crenellate; bank; entrench, **dig in;** mine; beef up

10 **fend off, ward off, stave off, hold off, fight off,** keep off, beat off, parry, fend, counter, turn aside; **hold** *or* **keep at bay,** keep at arm's length; **hold the fort, hold the line,** stop, check, block, hinder, obstruct; **repel, repulse, rebuff, drive back,** put back, push back; avert; go on the defensive, fight a holding *or* delaying action, fall back to prepared positions

ADJS 11 **defensive,** defending, **guarding,** shielding, screening; **protective** 1008.23; self-defensive, self-protective, self-preservative

12 **fortified,** battlemented, embattled *or* battled <old>, entrenched; castellated, crenellated, casemated, machicolated; secured, protected

13 **armored,** armor-plated; in armor, panoplied, armed cap-a-pie, armed at all points, in harness; mailed, mailclad, ironclad; loricate, loricated

14 **armed,** heeled *and* carrying *and* gun-toting <nf>; accoutered, **in arms,** bearing *or* wearing *or* carrying arms, under arms, sword in hand; **well-armed,** heavy-armed, full-armed, bristling with arms, **armed to the teeth;** light-armed; **garrisoned,** manned

15 **defensible, defendable, tenable**

ADVS 16 **defensively, in defense,** in self-defense; **on the defensive,** on guard; **at bay,** *aux abois* <Fr>, with one's back to the wall

461 COMBATANT

NOUNS 1 **combatant, fighter, battler,** scrapper <nf>; **contestant, contender, competitor, rival,** adversary, opponent, agonist; disputant, wrangler, squabbler, bickerer, quarreler; struggler, tussler, scuffler; brawler, rioter; feuder; **belligerent,** militant; gladiator; jouster, tilter; knight, belted **knight;** swordsman, blade, sword, *sabreur* or *beau sabreur* <Fr>; fencer, foilsman, swordplayer <old>; duelist, dueler; gamecock, fighting cock; **tough,** rough, rowdy, **ruffian,** thug, **hoodlum, hood** <nf>, hooligan, streetfighter, bully, bullyboy, bravo; gorilla *and* goon *and* plug-ugly *and* skinhead <nf>; hatchet man *and* enforcer <nf>, strong-arm man, strong arm, strong-armer; fire-eater, swaggerer, swashbuckler

2 **boxer, pugilist,** pug *or* palooka <nf>; **street fighter,** scrapper, pit bull

3 **wrestler,** rassler *and* grunt-and-groaner <nf>, grappler, scuffler, matman

4 **bullfighter,** toreador, *torero* <Sp>; banderillero, picador, matador

5 **militarist, warmonger,** war dog *or* hound, war hawk, **hawk** <nf>; **chauvinist, jingo,** jingoist, hard-liner; conquistador, privateer, pirate, buccaneer; terrorist

6 **military man** *or* **woman, serviceman, servicewoman,** navy man *or* woman; air serviceman *or* servicewoman; **soldier, warrior,** brave, fighting man, legionary, hoplite, **man-at-arms,** rifleman, rifle; ninja; **cannon fodder,** food for powder, trooper, militiaman; warrioress, Amazon; spearman, pikeman, halberdier; military training, boot camp

7 <common soldiers> **GI,** GI Joe, dough *and* doughfoot *and* Joe Tentpeg *and* John Dogface *and* grunt <nf>, **doughboy, Yank;** Tommy Atkins *or* Tommy *or* Johnny *or* swaddy <Brit>; redcoat; poilu <Fr>; Aussie *and* Anzac *and* digger <Austral>; jock <Scot>; Fritz, Jerry, Heinie, Hun, Boche, Kraut, krauthead <Ger soldier>; Janissary <Turkish soldier>; sepoy <India>; askari <Africa>; weekend warrior

8 **enlisted man,** noncommissioned officer 575.19; **common soldier, private, private soldier,** buck private <nf>; private first class *or* pfc

9 **infantryman, foot soldier;** light infantryman, chasseur, *Jäger* <Ger>, Zouave; rifleman, rifle, musketeer; fusileer, carabineer; **sharpshooter,** marksman, expert rifleman, *bersagliere* <Ital>; **sniper;** grenadier

10 <nf terms> **grunt, dogface,** footslogger, paddlefoot, doughfoot, blisterfoot, crunchie, line doggie, groundpounder

11 **artilleryman,** artillerist, **gunner,** guns <nf>, cannoneer, machine gunner; **bomber,** bomb thrower, bombardier

12 **cavalryman,** mounted infantryman, **trooper;** dragoon, light *or* heavy dragoon; lancer, lance, uhlan, hussar; cuirassier; spahi; cossack

13 **tanker,** tank corpsman, tank crewman

14 **engineer,** combat engineer, pioneer, Seabee; sapper, sapper *and* miner

15 **elite troops, shock troops,** storm troops; rapid deployment force *or* RDF; commandos, rangers, Special Forces, special ops, Green Berets, marines, paratroops; guardsmen, guards, household troops; Life Guards, Horse Guards, Foot Guards, Grenadier Guards, Coldstream Guards, Scot Guards, Irish Guards; Swiss Guards

16 **irregular,** casual; **guerrilla,** partisan, franctireur; **bushfighter,** bushwhacker <nf>; underground, resistance, maquis; Vietcong *or* VC, Charley <nf>; SWAPO *or* South West African People's Organization guerrilla; Shining Path Guerrilla; Contra; *maquisard* <Fr>, underground *or* resistance fighter, freedom fighter; terrorist

17 **mercenary, hireling,** *condottiere* <Ital>, free lance, free companion, **soldier of fortune,** adventurer; gunman, gun, hired gun, hired killer, professional killer; terrorist

18 **recruit, rookie** <nf>, **conscript,** drafted man, **draftee, inductee, selectee, enlistee,** enrollee, trainee, boot <nf>; **raw recruit,** tenderfoot; awkward squad <nf>; draft, levy

19 **veteran, vet** <nf>, campaigner, old campaigner, old soldier, old trooper, war-horse <nf>, Veterans of Foreign Wars *or* VFW member, American Legion member

20 **defense forces, services, the service, armed forces,** armed services, fighting machine; **the military,** the military establishment; professional forces, standing forces, regular forces, reserve forces, volunteer forces; combat troops, support troops

21 **branch, branch of the service, corps** <see list>; **service, arm of the service,** Air Force, Army, Navy, Marine Corps, Coast Guard, Merchant Marine

22 <military units> **unit, organization,** tactical unit, **outfit** <nf>; **army,** field army, army group, corps, army corps, **division,** infantry division, armored division, airborne division, triangular division, pentomic division, Reorganization Objective Army Division *or* ROAD; **regiment, battle group,** battalion, garrison, **company,** troop, brigade, legion, phalanx, cohort, **platoon,** section, **battery,** maniple; **combat team,** combat command; **task force;** commando unit, combat team; **squad,** squadron; detachment, detail, section, posse, unit, detachment; kitchen police *or* KP; column, flying column; rank, file; train, field train; cadre

23 **army,** this man's army <nf>, **soldiery, forces,** armed forces, **troops, host,** array, legions; ranks, rank *and* file; **standing army, regular army,** active forces, regulars, professional *or* career soldiers; the line, troops of the line; line of defense, first *or* second line of defense; ground forces, ground troops; storm troops, assault troops; **airborne troops,** paratroops; ski troops, mountain troops; occupation force; elite troops

24 **militia,** organized militia, national militia, mobile militia, territorial militia, reserve militia, citizen's army; home reserve; **National Guard,** Air National Guard, state guard; home guard <chiefly Brit>; minutemen, trainband, yeomanry

25 **reserves,** auxiliaries, **second line of defense,** reinforcements, ready reserves, landwehr, army reserves, home reserves, territorial reserves, territorial *or* home defense army <Brit>, supplementary reserves, organized reserves; US Army Reserve, US Naval Reserve, US Marine Corps Reserve, US Air Force Reserve, US Coast Guard Reserve, National Guard; ready reserves, standby reserves, retired reserves

26 **volunteers, enlistees,** volunteer forces, volunteer army, volunteer militia, volunteer navy

27 **navy,** naval forces, **first line of defense; fleet,** flotilla, argosy, armada, squadron, escadrille, division, task force, task group; amphibious force; mosquito fleet; support fleet, destroyer fleet, auxiliary fleet, reserve fleet, mothball fleet; United States Navy *or* USN; Royal Navy *or* RN; marine, mercantile *or* merchant marine, merchant navy, merchant fleet; naval militia; naval reserve; coast guard; Seabees, Naval Construction Battalion; admiralty; gunboat diplomacy

28 **marines,** sea soldiers, Marine Corps, Royal Marines; **leathernecks** *and* devil dogs *and* gyrenes <nf>, jollies <Brit nf>

29 **air force,** air corps, air service, air arm; US Air Force *or* USAF; strategic air force, tactical air force; squadron, escadrille, flight, wing

30 **war-horse, charger,** courser, trooper

31 **US Army branches and corps**

Adjutant General Corps	Finance Corps
Air Defense Artillery	General Staff Corps
Armored Corps	Infantry Corps
Army Air Corps	Judge Advocate General
Army Digitization Office	Corps
Army Nurse Corps	Medical Service Corps
Army Research Laboratory	Military Police Corps
Army Service Corps	Ordnance Corps
Chemical Corps	Quartermaster Corps
Corps of Cadets <West	Signal Corps
Point>	Special Operations
Corps of Engineers	Command
Dental Command	Transportation Corps

32 **US Air Force branches and corps**

Air Combat Command	Reserve Command
Air Education and	Reserve Officer Training
Training Command	Corps
Air National Guard	Space Command
Materiel Command	Special Operations
Mobility Command	Command

462 ARMS

NOUNS 1 arms, weapons, deadly weapons, instruments of destruction, offensive weapons, **military hardware,** matériel, **weaponry, armament, munitions, ordnance,** munitions of war, *apparatus belli* <L>; musketry; missilery; small arms; side arms; stand of arms; conventional weapons, nonnuclear weapons; **nuclear weapons,** atomic weapons, thermonuclear weapons, A-weapons, strategic nuclear weapon, tactical nuclear weapon; bacteriological *or* biological weapon, chemical weapon; weapons of mass destruction; arms industry, arms maker, military-industrial complex; natural weapon; secret weapon

2 **armory, arsenal,** magazine, dump; ammunition depot, ammo dump <nf>, arms depot; park, gun park, artillery park, park of artillery; atomic arsenal, thermonuclear arsenal, gun room, powder barrel *or* keg

3 **ballistics, gunnery,** musketry, artillery; rocketry, missilery; archery

4 **fist, clenched fist; brass knuckles;** knucks *and* brass knucks <nf>, knuckles, knuckle-dusters; club, bludgeon, blackjack, truncheon, billy, blunt instrument, etc

5 **sword, blade,** cutlass, saber, rapier, foil, bayonet, machete; steel, **cold steel;** Excalibur; **knife,** switchblade, bowie knife, Swiss Army knife, box cutter; **dagger; axe**

6 **arrow, shaft, dart,** reed, **bolt;** quarrel; chested arrow, footed arrow, bobtailed arrow; arrowhead, barb; flight, volley

7 **bow,** longbow, carriage bow; **bow and arrow;** crossbow, arbalest

8 **spear,** throwing spear, javelin, lance, harpoon, sharp weapon

9 **sling, slingshot;** throwing-stick, throw stick, spear-thrower, atlatl, wommera; **catapult,** arbalest, ballista, trebuchet

10 **gun, firearm;** shooting iron *and* gat *and* rod *and* heater *and* piece <nf>; shoulder weapon *or* gun *or* arm; gun make; gun part; stun gun; automatic, BB gun, blunderbuss <old>, Bren, Browning automatic rifle, burp gun <nf>, carbine, derringer, flintlock, forty-five *or* .45, forty-four *or* .44, Gatling gun, handgun, machine gun, musket, pistol, piece *or* equalizer <nf>, automatic, semiautomatic, repeater, revolver, rifle, Saturday night special, sawed-off shotgun, shotgun, six-gun *or* six-shooter <nf>, submachine gun, thirty-eight *or* .38, thirty-thirty *or* .30-30, thirty-two *or* .32, Thompson submachine gun *or* tommy gun <nf>, twenty-two *or* .22, Uzi submachine gun, zip gun

11 **artillery, cannon,** guns, cannonry, ordnance, engines of war, Big Bertha, howitzer; field artillery; heavy artillery, heavy field artillery; self-propelled artillery; siege artillery; bombardment weapons; breakthrough weapons; siege engine; mountain artillery, coast artillery, trench artillery, anti-aircraft artillery, flak <nf>; battery

12 **antiaircraft gun** *or* AA gun, ack-ack <nf>, pom-pom <nf>, *Fliegerabwehrkanone* <Ger>, skysweeper, Bofors, Oerlikon

13 **ammunition, ammo** <nf>, **powder and shot,** iron rations <nf>, round, live ammunition

14 **explosive,** high explosive; cellulose nitrate, cordite, dynamite, gelignite, guncotton, gunpowder, nitroglycerin *or* nitroglycerine, plastic explosive *or* plastique, powder, trinitrotoluene *or* trinitrotoluol *or* TNT

15 **fuse, detonator,** exploder; **cap,** blasting cap, percussion cap, mercury fulminate, fulminating mercury; electric detonator *or* exploder; detonating powder; **primer,** priming; primacord

16 **charge, load;** blast; warhead, payload

17 **cartridge,** cartouche, **shell;** ball cartridge; clip, blank cartridge, dry ammunition

18 **missile, projectile,** bolt; brickbat, stone, rock, alley apple *and* Irish confetti <nf>; boomerang; bola; throwing-stick, throw stick, waddy <Austral>; **ballistic missile,** cruise missile, Exocet missile, surface-to-air missile *or* SAM, surface-to-surface missile, Tomahawk missile; **rocket** 1074.2-6,14; **torpedo**

19 **shot; ball,** cannonball, rifle ball, minié ball; **bullet,** slug, pellet; buckshot; dumdum bullet, expanding bullet, explosive bullet, manstopping bullet, manstopper, copkiller *or* Teflon bullet <trademark>; tracer bullet, tracer; **shell,** high-explosive shell, **shrapnel**

20 **bomb,** bombshell, device <nf>; antipersonnel bomb, atomic bomb *or* atom bomb *or* A-bomb, atomic warhead, hydrogen bomb *or* H-bomb, nuclear bomb, blockbuster, depth charge *or* depth bomb *or* ash can <nf>, fire bomb *or* incendiary bomb *or* incendiary, grenade, hand grenade, pineapple <nf>, letter bomb, Molotov cocktail, napalm bomb, neutron bomb, nuclear warhead, pipe bomb, plastic *or* plastique bomb, plutonium bomb, smart bomb, stench *or* stink bomb, time bomb; clean bomb, dirty bomb; **mine,** landmine; booby trap

21 **launcher,** projector, bazooka; rocket launcher, grenade launcher, hedgehog, mine thrower, *Minenwerfer* <Ger>, **mortar**

22 non-lethal weapon, riot control agent; stun gun, Taser <trademark>, pepper spray, water cannon; rubber bullet, plastic bullet; minimal force, controlled force, soft kill, mission kill

463 ARENA

NOUNS 1 **arena, scene of action, site,** scene, setting, background, **field, ground,** terrain, sphere, place, locale, milieu, precinct, purlieu; course, range, walk <old>; campus; **theater,** stage, stage set *or* setting, scenery; **platform; forum,** agora, marketplace, open forum, public square;

amphitheater, circus, **hippodrome, coliseum,** colosseum, **stadium, bowl; hall, auditorium;** gymnasium, gym <nf>, palaestra; **lists,** tiltyard, tilting ground; floor, **pit,** cockpit; bear garden; **ring,** prize ring, boxing ring, canvas, squared circle <nf>, wrestling ring, mat, bull ring; parade ground; athletic field, field, playing field; covered stadium; domed stadium; stamping ground, turf, bailiwick 894.4

2 **battlefield, battleground,** battle site, **field,** combat area, **field of battle;** field of slaughter, field of blood *or* bloodshed, aceldama, killing ground *or* field, shambles; **battlefront, the front,** front line, line, enemy line *or* lines, firing line, battle line, line of battle; battle zone, war zone, combat zone; **theater, theater of operations,** theater *or* seat of war; beachhead, bridgehead; communications zone, zone of communications; no-man's-land; demilitarized zone *or* DMZ; jump area *or* zone, landing beach

3 **campground,** camp, campsite, camping ground *or* area, encampment, bivouac, tented field

464 PEACE

NOUNS 1 **peace,** *pax* <L>; **peacetime,** state of peace, peaceable kingdom, the storm blown over; freedom from war, cessation of combat, exemption from hostilities, public tranquillity, peace movement; **harmony,** concord, accord 455; universal peace, lasting peace, Pax Romana

2 **peacefulness, tranquillity, serenity, calmness, quiet,** peace and quiet, quietude, quietness, quiescence, quiet life, restfulness, rest, stillness, silence; order, orderliness, law and order, imposed peace; no hassle <nf>

3 **peace of mind,** peace of heart, peace of soul *or* spirit, peace of God, "peace which passeth all understanding"—Bible; ataraxia, shanti

4 **peaceableness, unpugnaciousness,** uncontentiousness, nonaggression; irenicism, dovelikeness, dovishness <nf>, **pacifism,** pacificism; peaceful coexistence; **nonviolence,** ahimsa; line of least resistance; meekness, lamblikeness 433.5

5 **noncombatant,** nonbelligerent, nonresistant, nonresister; **civilian,** citizen

6 **pacifist,** pacificist, peacenik <nf>, **peace lover, dove,** *and* dove of peace <nf>; pacificator, peacemaker, bridgebuilder; peacemonger; **conscientious objector,** passive resister, conchie <nf>

7 **peace treaty,** peace agreement, nonaggression

pact, disarmament treaty, arms reduction, arms control; test ban; deescalation; amnesty, pardon, forgiveness, burying the hatchet <nf>

VERBS 8 **keep the peace,** remain at peace, wage peace; refuse to shed blood, keep one's sword in its sheath; forswear violence, beat one's swords into plowshares; pursue the arts of peace, pour oil on troubled waters; make love not war; defuse

ADJS 9 **pacific, peaceful, peaceable; tranquil, serene;** idyllic, pastoral; halcyon, soft, piping, **calm, quiet,** quiet as a lamb, quiescent, still, restful, **untroubled,** orderly, **at peace;** concordant 455.3; bloodless; peacetime; postwar, postbellum

10 **unbelligerent, unhostile,** unbellicose, **unpugnacious, uncontentious,** unmilitant, unmilitary, nonaggressive, noncombative, nonmilitant; noncombatant, civilian, **antiwar, pacific, peaceable,** peace-loving, dovelike; meek, passive, lamblike 433.15; pacifistic, pacifist, irenic; nonviolent; conciliatory 465.12

INTERJS 11 **peace!, peace be with you!,** peace be to you!, *pax vobiscum!* and *pax tecum!* <L>; *shalom!* or *shalom aleichem!* <Hebrew>, *salaam aleikum!* <Arabic>; go in peace!, *vade in pace!* <L>

465 PACIFICATION

NOUNS 1 **pacification, peacemaking,** irenics, peacemongering, **conciliation, propitiation, placation, appeasement, mollification,** dulcification; **calming, soothing,** tranquilization; détente, relaxation of tension, easing of relations; mediation 466; placability; peacekeeping force, United Nations peacekeeping force

2 **peace offer,** offer of parley, parley, peace overture; peace feelers; **peace offering,** propitiatory gift; **olive branch; white flag,** truce flag, flag of truce; calumet, peace pipe, **pipe of peace;** downing of arms, hand of friendship, empty hands, outstretched hand; **cooling off, cooling-off period;** peace sign; compensation, reparation, atonement, restitution; amnesty, pardon, mercy, leniency, clemency; dove, lamb

3 **reconciliation,** reconcilement, rapprochement <Fr>, reunion, shaking of hands, making up *and* kissing *and* making up <nf>

4 **adjustment,** accommodation, resolution, composition *or* settlement of differences, compromise, arrangement, settlement, terms; consensus building, consensus seeking

5 **truce, armistice, peace; pacification,** treaty of peace, suspension *or* end of hostilities, **cease-fire,**

cessation, stand-down, breathing spell, cooling-off period, lull in hostilities; Truce *or* Peace of God, Pax Dei, Pax Romana; temporary truce, temporary arrangement, *modus vivendi* <L>; hollow truce, *pax in bello* <L>; demilitarized zone, buffer zone, neutral territory; uneasy truce; peacekeeping mission

6 disarmament, reduction of armaments; unilateral disarmament; **demilitarization,** deactivation, disbanding, disbandment, **demobilization,** mustering out, reconversion, decommissioning; civilian life, mufti *and* civvy street <Brit>; defense cuts, arms reduction, arms control; test ban

VERBS **7 pacify, conciliate, placate, propitiate, appease, mollify,** dulcify; **calm, settle, soothe,** tranquilize 670.7; smooth, smooth over *or* out, smooth down, smooth one's feathers; allay, lay, lay the dust; pour oil on troubled waters, pour balm on, take the edge off of, take the sting out of; cool <nf>, defuse; clear the air

8 reconcile, bring to terms, bring together, reunite, heal the breach; bring about a détente; **harmonize,** restore harmony, put in tune; **iron** *or* **sort out,** adjust, settle, compose, accommodate, arrange matters, settle differences, resolve, compromise; **patch things up,** make up <nf>, fix up <nf>, patch up a friendship *or* quarrel, smooth it over; weave peace between, mediate 466.6

9 make peace, cease hostilities, cease fire, stand down, raise a siege; **cool it** *and* **chill out** <nf>, **bury the hatchet, smoke the peace pipe;** negotiate a peace, dictate peace; make a peace offering, hold out the olive branch, hoist *or* show *or* wave the white flag; make the world a safer place, make the lion lie down with the lamb; turn the other cheek

10 make up *and* **kiss and make up** *and* make it up *and* make matters up <nf>, **shake hands,** come round, come together, come to an understanding, **come to terms,** let the wound heal, let bygones be bygones, forgive and forget, put it all behind one, settle *or* compose one's differences, meet halfway, compromise

11 disarm, lay down one's arms, unarm, turn in one's weapons, down *or* ground one's arms, put down one's gun, sheathe the sword, turn swords into plowshares; **demilitarize,** deactivate, **demobilize, disband,** reconvert, decommission

ADJS **12 pacificatory, pacific,** irenic, **conciliatory,** reconciliatory, **propitiatory,** propitiative, **placative,** placatory, **mollifying, appeasing; pacifying, soothing** 670.15, appeasable

13 pacifiable, placable, appeasable, propitiable

ADVS **14 pacifically, peaceably; with no hard feelings**

466 MEDIATION

NOUNS **1 mediation,** mediating, intermediation, **intercession; intervention,** interposition, putting oneself between, moderation, stepping in, declaring oneself in, involvement, interagency; interventionism; diplomacy, statesmanship; troubleshooting, good offices; peacekeeping mission

2 arbitration, arbitrament, compulsory arbitration, binding arbitration; nonbinding arbitration; umpirage, refereeship, mediatorship

3 mediator, intermediator, intermediate agent, intermediate, intermedium, **intermediary,** interagent, internuncio, mediatrix; **medium; intercessor,** interceder; ombudsman; intervener, **intervenor;** interventionist; **go-between,** liaison, **middleman** 576.4; connection <nf>; front *and* front man <nf>; deputy, agent 576; **spokesman, spokeswoman,** spokesperson, spokespeople; **mouthpiece; negotiator,** negotiant, negotiatress *or* negotiatrix; Little Miss Fixit; troubleshooter; spin doctor <nf>; harmonizer

4 arbitrator, arbiter, impartial arbitrator, third party, unbiased observer; **moderator,** moderating influence; **umpire, referee, judge;** armchair quarterback; magistrate 596.1

5 peacemaker, make-peace, reconciler, smoother-over, peace negotiator, mediator; **pacifier,** pacificator, peace lover, pacifist; peacekeeper, United Nations peacekeeping force; **conciliator,** propitiator, **appeaser;** marriage counselor, family counselor; guidance counselor; patcher-up

VERBS **6 mediate,** intermediate, **intercede,** go between; **intervene,** interpose, step in, step into the breach, declare oneself a party, involve oneself, put oneself between disputants, use one's good offices, act between; butt in *and* put one's nose in <nf>; represent 576.14; **negotiate,** bargain, **treat with,** make terms, meet halfway; **arbitrate,** moderate; **umpire, referee,** judge, officiate

7 settle, arrange, compose, patch up, adjust, straighten out, bring to terms *or* an understanding; make peace 465.9; reconcile, conciliate

ADJS **8 mediatory,** mediatorial, mediative, mediating, arbitral, going *or* coming between; intermediatory, intermediary, intermedial, intermediate, **middle,** intervening, mesne, interlocutory; interventional, arbitrational, arbitrative; **intercessory,** intercessional; diplomatic; pacificatory 465.12

467 NEUTRALITY

NOUNS **1 neutrality, neutralism,** strict neutrality; noncommitment, noninvolvement; **independence, nonpartisanism, unalignment, nonalignment;** anythingarianism *or* nothingarianism <nf>; mugwumpery, mugwumpism, fence-sitting *or* -straddling, fence <nf>, trimming; **evasion, cop-out** <nf>, abstention; **impartiality** 649.3, coexistence, avoidance; nonintervention, nonaggression

2 indifference, indifferentness, Laodiceanism; passiveness 329.1; apathy 94.4, phlegm, disinterest

3 middle course *or* **way,** *via media* <L>; middle ground, neutral ground *or* territory, center; meeting ground, interface; gray area, penumbra, compromise; **middle of the road,** sitting on *or* straddling the fence <nf>; medium, **happy medium;** mean, **golden mean;** moderation, moderateness 670.1; compromise 468; halfway measures, half measures, half-and-half measures

4 neutral, neuter; **independent, nonpartisan;** mugwump, fence-sitter *or* -straddler, trimmer; anythingarian *and* nothingarian <nf>; unaligned *or* nonaligned nation, third force, third world; game face

VERBS **5 remain neutral,** stand neuter, hold no brief, **keep in the middle of the road, straddle** *or* **sit on the fence** *and* sit out *and* sit on the sidelines <nf>, trim; **evade,** evade the issue, duck the issue *and* waffle *and* cop out <nf>, abstain

6 steer a middle course, hold *or* keep *or* preserve a middle course, walk a middle path, follow the via media, strike *or* preserve a balance, stay on an even keel, **strike** *or* **keep a happy medium,** keep the golden mean, steer between *or* avoid Scylla *and* Charybdis; be moderate 670.5

ADJS **7 neutral,** neuter; noncommitted, uncommitted, noninvolved, uninvolved; anythingarian *and* nothingarian <nf>; **indifferent,** Laodicean; tolerant; passive 329.6; apathetic 94.13; neither one thing nor the other, neither hot nor cold, inert; even, half-and-half, fifty-fifty <nf>; **on the fence** *or* **sidelines** <nf>; **middle-of-the-road,** centrist, center, moderate, midway; **independent, nonpartisan; unaligned,**

nonaligned, third-force, third-world; **impartial** 649.9

468 COMPROMISE

<mutual concession>

NOUNS **1 compromise,** composition, adjustment, accommodation, settlement, mutual concession, give-and-take; abatement of differences; bargain, deal <nf>, arrangement, understanding; **concession,** giving way, yielding; surrender, desertion of principle, evasion of responsibility, cop-out <nf>; middle ground, happy medium; meeting halfway; trade-off; face-saver

VERBS **2 compromise,** make *or* reach a compromise, compound, compose, accommodate, adjust, settle, make an adjustment *or* arrangement, **make a deal** <nf>, do a deal <Brit nf>, come to an understanding, strike a bargain, do something mutually beneficial; plea-bargain; strike a balance, take the mean, **meet halfway,** split the difference, go fifty-fifty <nf>, give *and* take; play politics; steer a middle course 467.6; **make concessions,** make trade-off, give way, yield, wimp *or* chicken out <nf>; **surrender** 433.8, desert one's principles, evade responsibility, sidestep, duck responsibility *and* cop out *and* punt <nf>

PHRS **3** half a loaf is better than none; you can't win them all

469 POSSESSION

NOUNS **1 possession,** possessing, outright possession, free-and-clear possession; **owning,** having title to; seisin, nine points of the law, *de facto* possession, **de jure** possession, lawful *or* legal possession; property rights, proprietary rights; **title,** absolute title, free-and-clear title, original title; derivative title; adverse possession, squatting, squatterdom, **squatter's right; claim,** legal claim, lien; usucapion, usucaption <old>, prescription; **occupancy,** occupation; **hold, holding, tenure; tenancy,** tenantry, **lease,** leasehold, sublease, underlease, undertenancy; gavelkind; villenage, villein socage, villeinhold; socage, free socage; burgage; frankalmoign, lay fee; tenure in chivalry, knight service; fee fief, fiefdom, feud, feodum; freehold, alodium; fee simple, fee tail, fee simple absolute, fee simple conditional, fee simple defeasible *or* fee simple determinable; fee position; dependency, colony, mandate; prepossession <old>, preoccupation, preoccupancy; chose in possession, bird in hand, nine tenths of the law <nf>; **property** 471

2 ownership, title, possessorship, *dominium* <L>, **proprietorship,** proprietary, **property right** *or* rights; lordship, **overlordship,** seigniory; **dominion, sovereignty** 417.5; landownership, landowning, landholding, land tenure; nationalization, public domain, state ownership

3 monopoly, monopolization; **corner** *and* cornering *and* a corner on <nf>; exclusive possession; engrossment, forestallment

VERBS **4 possess, have, hold,** have and hold, possess outright *or* free *and* clear, **occupy, fill, enjoy,** boast; be possessed of, have tenure of, have in hand, be seized of, have in one's grip *or* grasp, have in one's possession, be enfeoffed of; **command,** have at one's command *or* pleasure *or* disposition *or* disposal, have going for one <nf>; claim, usucapt; squat, squat on, claim squatter's rights

5 own, have title to, have for one's own *or* very own, have to one's name, call one's own, have the deed for, hold in fee simple, etc

6 monopolize, hog *and* grab all of *and* gobble up <nf>, call one's own, take it all, have all to oneself, have exclusive possession of *or* exclusive rights to; engross, forestall, tie up; **corner** *and* get a corner on *and* corner the market <nf>

7 belong to, pertain to, appertain to; vest in

ADJS **8 possessed, owned,** held; in seisin, in fee, in fee simple, **free and clear; own,** of one's own, in one's name; **in one's possession, in hand,** in one's grip *or* grasp, at one's command *or* disposal; on hand, by one, in stock, in store

9 possessing, having, holding, having *and* holding, **occupying, owning; in possession of, possessed of,** seized of, master of; tenured; enfeoffed; endowed with, blessed with; worth; propertied, property-owning, landed, landowning, landholding

10 possessive, possessory, **proprietary**

11 monopolistic, monopolist, monopolizing, hogging *or* hoggish <nf>; exclusive

ADVS **12 free and clear, outright;** bag and baggage; by fee simple, etc

470 POSSESSOR

NOUNS **1 possessor, holder,** keeper, haver, enjoyer; a have <nf>

2 proprietor, proprietary, **owner;** *rentier* <Fr>; titleholder, deedholder; proprietress, proprietrix; **master, mistress, lord; landlord, landlady;** lord *or* lady of the manor <Brit>, man *or* lady of the house, mesne lord, mesne, feudatory, feoffee; squire, country gentleman; householder;

beneficiary, cestui, cestui que trust, cestui que use

3 landowner, landholder, property owner, propertied *or* landed person, man of property, freeholder; landed interests, landed gentry, slumlord, rent gouger; absentee landlord

4 tenant, occupant, occupier, incumbent, **resident; lodger,** roomer, boarder, paying guest; **renter,** hirer <Brit>, rent-payer, **lessee,** leaseholder; subtenant, sublessee, underlessee, undertenant; tenant at sufferance, tenant at will; tenant from year to year, tenant for years, tenant for life; squatter; homesteader; squatter

5 trustee, fiduciary, holder of the legal estate; depository, depositary

471 PROPERTY

NOUNS **1 property, properties, possessions, holdings,** havings, goods, chattels, goods *and* chattels, **effects,** estate and effects, what one can call one's own, what one has to one's name, all one owns *or* has, all one can lay claim to, one's all; household possessions *or* effects, lares *and* penates; hereditament, corporeal hereditament, incorporeal hereditament; acquest; acquisitions, receipts 627; **inheritance** 479.2; public property, common property

2 belongings, appurtenances, trappings, paraphernalia, appointments, accessories, perquisites, appendages, appanages, choses local; **things,** material things, mere things; consumer goods; choses, choses in possession, choses in action; **personal effects,** personal property, chattels personal, movables, choses transitory; what one can call one's own, what has to one's name

3 impedimenta, luggage, dunnage, baggage, bag and baggage, traps, tackle, apparatus, truck, gear, kit, outfit, duffel

4 estate, interest, equity, stake, part, percentage; **right, title** 469.1, **claim,** holding; use, trust, benefit; absolute interest, vested interest, contingent interest, beneficial interest, equitable interest; easement, right of common, common, right of entry; limitation; settlement, strict settlement; copyright, patent

5 freehold, estate of freehold; alodium, alod; frankalmoign, lay fee, tenure in *or* by free alms, appanage; mortmain, dead hand; leasehold

6 real estate, realty, real property, land *and* buildings, chattels real, tenements; immoveables; *praedium* <L>, landed property *or* estate, **land, lands,** property, grounds, acres; lot, lots, parcel, plot, plat, quadrat; demesne, domain <old>; messuage, manor, honor, toft <Brit>

7 **assets, means, resources,** total assets *or* resources; stock, stock-in-trade; worth, net worth, what one is **worth;** circumstances, funds 728.14; wealth 618; **material assets,** tangible assets, tangibles; intangible assets, intangibles; current assets, deferred assets, fixed assets, frozen assets, liquid assets, quick assets, assets *and* liabilities, net assets; assessed valuation

ADJS **8** **propertied,** proprietary; **landed;** copyrighted, patented

9 real, praedial; manorial, seignioral, seigneurial; feudal, feudatory, feodal; patrimonial

10 freehold, leasehold, copyhold; allodial

472 ACQUISITION

NOUNS **1** **acquisition,** gaining, getting, getting hold of <nf>, coming by, **acquirement, obtainment,** obtention, **attainment,** securement, winning, realization; trover; accession; addition 253; **procurement,** procural, procurance, procuration; **earnings,** making, pulling *or* dragging *or* knocking down <nf>, moneymaking, breadwinning, moneygetting, moneygrubbing

2 **collection, gathering,** gleaning, bringing together, assembling, putting *or* piecing together, **accumulation,** cumulation, **amassment,** accretion, heaping up, grubbing

3 **gain, profit,** percentage <nf>, get <Brit nf>, **take** *or* take-in *and* piece *and* slice *and* end *and* rakeoff *and* skimmings <nf>; **gains, profits, earnings, winnings, return, returns, proceeds, bottom line** <nf>, ettings, makings; **income** 624.4; **receipts** 627; **fruits,** pickings, gleanings; **booty, spoils** 482.11; pelf, lucre, filthy lucre; perquisite, perk *or* perks; **pile** *and* bundle *and* cleanup *and* killing *and* haul *and* mint <nf>; net *or* neat profit, clean *or* clear profit, net; gross profit, gross; paper profits; capital gains; interest, dividends; net profit, net revenue; getting ahead; hoard, store 386; wealth 618

4 **profitableness, profitability,** gainfulness, remunerativeness, rewardingness, bang for the buck <nf>

5 **yield, output,** make, production; **proceeds,** produce, product; **crop, harvest,** fruit, vintage, bearing; second crop, aftermath; bumper crop

6 **find,** finding, **discovery; trove,** *trouvaille* <Fr>; treasure trove, buried treasure; **windfall,** windfall money, windfall profit, found money, easy money, money in the bank, **bonus, gravy** <nf>, bunce <Brit nf>

7 **godsend, boon, blessing;** manna, manna from heaven, loaves and fishes, gift from on high; piece of luck

VERBS **8** **acquire, get, gain, obtain, secure, procure; win,** score; **earn,** make; **reap, harvest;** contract; take, catch, capture; **net;** come *or* enter into possession of, **come into, come by,** come in for, be seized of; draw, derive

9 <nf terms> **grab, latch** *or* glom on to, corral, bag, get *or* lay hold of, rake in *or* up *or* off, skim *or* skim off, catch, collar, cop, dig up, grub up, round up, drum up, get *or* lay one's hands, get *or* lay one's mitts on, get one's fingers *or* hands on, get one's hooks into, snag, snaffle, scratch together, hook, land, throw together, nab, pick up, nail, scare *or* scrape up; take home, pull *or* drag *or* knock down

10 **take possession, appropriate, take up,** take over, make one's own, move in *or* move in on <nf>, annex

11 **collect, gather, glean,** harvest, **pick, pluck,** cull, **take up,** pick up, get *or* gather in, gather to oneself, bring *or* get together, scrape together, scare up <nf>; heap up, amass, assemble, accumulate 386.11

12 **profit, make** *or* draw *or* realize *or* **reap profit, come out ahead, make money;** rake it in *and* coin money *and* make a bundle *or* pile *or* killing *or* mint *and* clean up <nf>, laugh all the way to the bank; gain by, **capitalize on,** commercialize, make capital out of, **cash in on** *and* make a good thing of <nf>, turn to profit *or* account, **realize on,** make money by, obtain a return, turn a penny *or* an honest penny; **gross, net; realize, clear;** kill two birds with one stone, turn to one's advantage; make a fast *or* quick buck <nf>; line one's pockets

13 **be profitable,** pay, repay, pay off <nf>, yield a profit, show a percentage, be gainful, be worthwhile *or* worth one's while, be a good investment show a profit, pay interest; roll in <nf>

ADJS **14** **obtainable, attainable, available,** accessible, to be had

15 **acquisitive,** acquiring; grasping, hoggy *and* grabby <nf>; greedy 100.27

16 **gainful,** productive, **profitable, remunerative, remuneratory, lucrative,** fat, **paying,** well-paying, high-yield, high-yielding, bankable; advantageous, worthwhile, rewarding; banausic, moneymaking, breadwinning

ADVS **17** **profitably, gainfully,** remuneratively, lucratively, **at a profit,** in the black; for money; advantageously, to advantage, to profit, to the good

473 LOSS

NOUNS 1 loss, losing, privation, getting away, losing hold of; **deprivation, bereavement,** taking away, stripping, dispossession, despoilment, despoliation, spoliation, robbery; setback, reversal; divestment, denudation; **sacrifice, forfeit, forfeiture,** giving up or over, denial; nonrestoration; **expense, cost, debit;** detriment, injury, damage; **destruction, ruin,** perdition, total loss, dead loss; collateral damage; losing streak <nf>; **loser** 412.5

2 waste, wastage, **exhaustion, depletion,** sapping, depreciation, dissipation, diffusion, **wearing, wearing away, erosion,** ablation, leaching away; molting, shedding, casting or sloughing off; **using, using up, consumption, expenditure, drain;** stripping, clear-cutting; impoverishment, shrinkage; leakage, evaporation; decrement, decrease 252

3 losses, losings; red ink; net loss, bottom line <nf>; diminishing returns; going to the wall or going belly up <nf>

VERBS 4 lose, incur loss, **suffer loss,** undergo privation or deprivation, be bereaved or bereft of, have no more, meet with a loss; drop and kiss good-bye <nf>; let slip, let slip through one's fingers; **forfeit,** default; **sacrifice; miss,** wander from, go astray from; **mislay,** misplace; lose out; **lose everything,** go broke and lose one's shirt and take a bath or to the cleaners and tap out and go to Tap City <nf>; have a setback or reversal

5 waste, deplete, depreciate, dissipate, wear, wear away, erode, ablate, consume, drain, **shrink,** dribble away; **molt, shed,** cast or slough off; decrease 252.6; squander 486.3; labor in vain

6 go to waste, come to nothing, come to naught, go up in smoke and go down the drain <nf>; run to waste, go to pot <nf>, run or go to seed, go down the tubes <nf>, go to the dogs <nf>; dissipate, leak, leak away, scatter to the winds

ADJS 7 lost, gone; forfeited, forfeit; by the board, out the window and down the drain or tube <nf>; **nonrenewable,** irreclaimable; long-lost; lost to; wasted, consumed, depleted, dissipated, diffused, **expended; worn away, eroded,** ablated, used, used up, shrunken; stripped, clear-cut; squandered 486.9; irretrievable 125.15; astray; the worse for wear

8 bereft, bereaved, divested, denuded, **deprived of,** shorn of, parted from, bereaved of, stripped of, dispossessed of, despoiled of, robbed of; **out of,** minus <nf>, wanting, lacking; cut off, cut off without a cent; out-of-pocket; **penniless, destitute,** broke and cleaned out and tapped out and wiped out and bust and belly up <nf>

ADVS 9 at a loss, unprofitably, to the bad <nf>; in the red <nf>; out, out-of-pocket

474 RETENTION

NOUNS 1 retention, retainment, **keeping, holding, maintenance, preservation;** prehension; keeping or holding in, **bottling** or corking up <nf>, locking in, suppression, repression, inhibition, retentiveness, retentivity; **tenacity** 803.3; adhesion; tenaciousness; detention

2 hold, purchase, grasp, grip, clutch, clamp, clinch, clench; seizure 480.2; bite, nip, toothhold; **cling,** clinging; toehold, foothold, footing; **clasp, hug, embrace,** bear hug, squeeze; grapple; handhold, firm hold, tight grip, iron grip, grip of iron or steel, death grip, stranglehold

3 <wrestling holds> half nelson, full nelson, quarter nelson, three-quarter nelson, stranglehold, toehold, flying mare, body slam, lock, hammerlock, headlock, scissors, bear hug, pin, fall

4 clutches, claws, talons, pounces, unguals; **nails,** fingernails; **pincers,** nippers, chelae; **tentacles; fingers,** digits, hooks <nf>; **hands,** paws and meathooks and mitts <nf>; palm; prehensile tail; **jaws,** mandibles, maxillae; **teeth,** fangs

VERBS 5 retain, keep, save, save up, pocket and hip-pocket <nf>; **maintain, preserve;** keep or hold in, **bottle** or cork up <nf>, lock in, suppress, repress, inhibit, keep to oneself; persist in; hold one's own, hold one's ground; get a foot hold

6 hold, grip, grasp, clutch, clip, **clinch, clench;** bite, nip; grapple; **clasp, hug, embrace; cling, cling to,** cleave to, stick to, adhere to, freeze to; **hold on to,** hold fast or tight, hang on to, keep a firm or tight hold on; **hold on, hang on** <nf>, hold on like a bulldog, stick like a leech, cling like a winkle, hang on for dear life; keep hold of, never let go, not part with; **seize** 480.14

7 hold, keep, harbor, bear, have, have and hold, hold on to; **cherish,** fondle, entertain, treasure, treasure up; **foster, nurture, nurse;** embrace, hug, clip <Brit nf>, cling to; bosom or embosom <old>, take to the bosom

ADJS 8 retentive, retaining, keeping, holding, gripping, grasping; **tenacious,** clinging; viselike; anal

9 prehensile, raptorial; fingered, digitate or digitated, digital; clawed, taloned, jawed, toothed, dentate, fanged

ADVS 10 for keeps <nf>, to keep, **for good,** for good and all, for always; forever 829.12

475 RELINQUISHMENT

NOUNS **1 relinquishment, release,** giving up, letting go, dispensation; **disposal,** disposition, riddance, getting rid of, dumping 390.3; **renunciation,** forgoing, forswearing, swearing off, abstinence, resignation, abjuration, **abandonment** 370; recantation, retraction 363.3; **surrender,** cession, handover, turning over, **yielding;** sacrifice; abdication; derequisition

2 waiver, quitclaim, disclaimer, deed of release

VERBS **3 relinquish, give up,** render up, **surrender, yield,** cede, hand or turn over, cough up <nf>; take one's hands off, loose one's grip on; spare; resign, vacate; drop, **waive,** dispense with; **forgo,** do without, get along without, forswear, abjure, **renounce,** swear off; walk away from, **abandon** 370.5; recant, retract; disgorge, throw up; have done with, wash one's hands of, pack it in; **part with,** give away, dispose of, ditch <nf>, rid oneself of, get rid of, see the last of, dump 390.7; kiss goodbye or off <nf>; **sacrifice,** make a sacrifice, forfeit; quitclaim; sell off

4 release, let go, leave go <nf>, **let loose of,** unhand, unclutch, unclasp, relax one's grip or hold

ADJS **5 relinquished,** released, disposed of; waived, dispensed with; forgone, forsworn, renounced, abjured, **abandoned** 370.8; recanted, retracted; **surrendered,** ceded, yielded; sacrificed, forfeited

476 PARTICIPATION

NOUNS **1 participation, partaking, sharing,** having a part or share or voice, contribution, association; **involvement,** engagement; complicity; **voting** 609.18, **suffrage** 609.17; **power-sharing;** partnership, copartnership, copartnery, joint control, cochairmanship, joint chairmanship; joint tenancy, cotenancy; joint ownership, condominium or condo, cooperative or coop; communal ownership, commune

2 communion, community, communal effort or enterprise, **cooperation,** cooperative society, intercommunion; social life, socializing; **collectivity,** collectivism, collective enterprise, collective farm, kibbutz, kolkhoz; **democracy,** participatory democracy, town meeting, self-rule; collegiality; common ownership, public ownership, state ownership, communism, socialism 611.6; profit sharing; sharecropping

3 communization, communalization, **socialization, nationalization, collectivization**

4 participator, participant, partaker, player, sharer; party, **a party to,** accomplice, accessory; partner, copartner; cotenant; shareholder

VERBS **5 participate, take part, partake, contribute,** chip in, involve or engage oneself, get involved; **have or take a hand in,** get in on, have a finger in, have a finger in the pie, have to do with, have a part in, be an accessory to, be implicated in, be a party to, be a player in; **participate in,** partake of or in, **take part in,** take an active part in, **join, join in,** figure in, make oneself part of, join oneself to, associate oneself with, play or perform a part in, play a role in, get in the act <nf>; **join up,** sign on, enlist, volunteer, answer the call; climb on the bandwagon; **have a voice in,** help decide, be in on the decisions, **vote,** have suffrage, be enfranchised; **enter into,** go into; make the scene <nf>; sit in, sit on; bear a hand, pull an oar; come out of one's shell

6 share, share in, come in for a share, **go shares,** be partners in, have a stake in, have a percentage or piece of <nf>, partake in, **divide with, divvy up with** <nf>, halve, go halves; go halvers and **go fifty-fifty** and go even stephen <nf>, split the difference, **share and share alike;** do one's share or part, pull one's weight; cooperate 450.3; apportion 477.6

7 communize, communalize, **socialize, collectivize, nationalize**

ADJS **8 participating, participative,** participant, participatory; hands-on, involved, engaged, **in or in on** <nf>; implicated, accessory; partaking, sharing

9 communal, common, general, public, collective, popular, social, societal; **mutual,** commutual <old>, reciprocal, associated, **joint,** conjoint, **in common,** share and share alike; **cooperative** 450.5; power-sharing, profit-sharing; collectivistic, **communistic,** socialistic 611.22

477 APPORTIONMENT

NOUNS **1 apportionment, apportioning, portioning, division,** divvy <nf>, partition, repartition, partitionment, partitioning, parceling, budgeting, rationing, **dividing, sharing,** share-out, sharing out, splitting, cutting, slicing, cutting the pie and divvying up <nf>; reapportionment

2 distribution, dispersion, **disposal,** disposition; dole, doling, doling or parceling out, giving out, passing around; **dispensation,** administration, issuance; disbursal, disbursement, paying out; redistribution; maldistribution; dealing, dispensing, divvying <nf>

3 allotment, assignment, appointment, setting aside, **earmarking,** tagging; underallotment, overallotment; appropriation; **allocation;** misallocation; reallocation

4 dedication, commitment, devoting, devotion, consecration

5 portion, share, interest, part, stake, stock, **piece,** bit, segment; **bite** *and* **cut** *and* **slice** *and* **chunk** *and* slice *and* piece of the pie *or* melon <nf>, piece of the action <nf>, **lot, allotment, end** <nf>, **proportion, percentage,** measure, quantum, **quota,** deal *or* dole <old>, ratio, meed, moiety, mess, helping; contingent; dividend; **commission,** rake-off <nf>; equal share, half; **lion's share,** bigger half, big end <nf>; small share, modicum; **allowance, ration, budget; load, work load;** fate, destiny 964.2

VERBS **6 apportion, portion, parcel, partition, part, divide,** share; share with, cut *or* deal one in <nf>, share *and* share alike, divide with, go halvers *or* fifty-fifty *or* even stephen with <nf>; divide into shares, **share out** *or* **around,** divide up, divvy *or* divvy up *or* out <nf>, **split,** split up, carve, cut, slice, carve up, slice up, cut up, cut *or* slice the pie *or* melon <nf>; divide *or* split fifty-fifty

7 proportion, proportionate, **prorate,** divide *pro rata,* appropriate

8 parcel out, portion out, measure out, serve out, spoon *or* ladle *or* dish out, **deal out, dole out, hand out, mete out,** ration out, give out, hand around, pass around; mete, dole, deal; **distribute,** disperse; **dispense,** dispose <old>, issue, administer; disburse, pay out

9 allot, lot, **assign, appoint, set,** detail; **allocate,** make assignments *or* allocations, schedule; **set apart** *or* **aside, earmark,** tag, mark out for; demarcate, set off, mark off, portion off; assign to, appropriate to *or* for; reserve, restrict to, restrict 210.5; **ordain, destine, fate**

10 budget, ration; allowance, put on an allowance; divvy <nf>

11 dedicate, commit, devote, consecrate, set apart

ADJS **12 apportioned,** portioned out, parceled, allocated, etc; **apportionable,** allocable, divisible, divvied <nf>, distributable, committable, appropriable, dispensable, donable, severable

13 proportionate, proportional; prorated, *pro rata* <L>; half; halvers *or* fifty-fifty *or* even stephen <nf>, half-and-half, equal; **distributive,** distributional; **respective,** particular, per head, per capita, several

ADVS **14 proportionately, in proportion,** *pro rata* <L>; **distributively; respectively,** severally, each to each; share *and* share alike, in equal shares, half-and-half; fifty-fifty *and* even stephen <nf>

478 GIVING

NOUNS **1 giving, donation,** bestowal, bestowment; **endowment,** gifting <nf>, **presentation,** presentment; **award,** awarding; grant, granting; accordance, vouchsafement <old>; conferment, conferral; investiture; **delivery,** deliverance, surrender; **concession,** communication, impartation, impartment; **contribution,** subscription; tithing; accommodation, supplying, furnishment, provision 385; **offer** 439; **liberality** 485

2 commitment, consignment, assignment, **delegation,** relegation, commendation, remanding, **entrustment;** enfeoffment, infeudation *or* infeodation; labor of love

3 charity, almsgiving; philanthropy 143.4

4 gift, present, presentation, *cadeau* <Fr>, **offering,** fairing <Brit>; tribute, **award;** free gift, freebie *and* gimme <nf>, gift horse; oblation 696.7; handsel; box <Brit>; Christmas present *or* gift, birthday present *or* gift; peace offering; a little something; dowry; treat; goody bag

5 gratuity, largess, bounty, liberality, donative, sportula; perquisite, perks <Brit nf>; consideration, fee <old>, **tip,** *pourboire* <Fr>, *Trinkgeld* <Ger>, sweetener, inducement; grease *and* salve *and* palm oil <nf>; **premium, bonus,** something extra, **gravy** <nf>, bunce <Brit nf>, lagniappe; baker's dozen; honorarium; incentive pay, time and a half, double time; bribe 378.2; slush fund

6 donation, donative; **contribution, subscription; alms,** pittance, **charity, dole, handout** <nf>, alms fee, widow's mite, **pledge;** Peter's pence; **offering,** offertory, votive offering, collection; tithe

7 benefit, benefaction, benevolence, **blessing, favor, boon,** grace; manna, manna from heaven

8 subsidy, subvention, subsidization, support, price support, depletion allowance, tax benefit *or* write-off; **grant,** grant-in-aid, bounty; **allowance, stipend,** allotment; **aid,** assistance, financial assistance, financial aid; **help,** pecuniary aid; scholarship, fellowship; honorarium; **welfare,** public welfare, public assistance, relief, relief *or* welfare payments, welfare aid, dole, aid to dependent children, bailout, food stamps, meal ticket; guaranteed annual income; alimony, palimony; annuity; pension, old age insurance, retirement benefits, social security, remittance; unemployment insurance; golden handcuffs; handout <nf>

9 endowment, investment, **settlement,** foundation; fund; charitable foundation; **dowry,** *dot* <Fr>, portion, marriage portion, marriage money; **dower,** widow's dower; jointure, legal jointure, thirds; appanage; community chest; charity event, fund-raiser, telethon

10 bequest, bequeathal, **legacy,** devise; inheritance 479.2; **will, testament,** last will and testament, living will; probate, attested copy; codicil

11 giver, donor, donator, gifter <nf>, presenter, bestower, conferrer, grantor, awarder, imparter, vouchsafer; fairy godmother, Lady Bountiful, Santa Claus, Robin Hood, sugar daddy <nf>; cheerful giver; **contributor, subscriber,** supporter, backer, financer, funder, angel <nf>; subsidizer; patron, patroness, Maecenas; tither; almsgiver, almoner; **philanthropist** 143.8, humanitarian; assignor, consignor; settler; testate, testator, testatrix; feoffor; good neighbor, good Samaritan

VERBS **12 give, present, donate,** slip <nf>, let have; **bestow, confer, award, allot, render,** bestow on; impart, let one know, communicate; **grant,** accord, **allow,** vouchsafe, yield, afford, make available; **tender,** proffer, offer, extend, come up with <nf>; **issue, dispense,** administer; serve, help to; distribute; deal, dole, mete; **give out, deal out, dole out, mete out, hand** or dish or shell out <nf>, fork out or over or up <nf>; make a present of, gift or gift with <nf>, give as a gift; **give generously,** give the shirt off one's back; be generous or liberal with, give freely; pour, shower, rain, snow, heap, lavish 486.3; give in addition or as lagniappe, give into the bargain; regift

13 deliver, hand, pass, reach, forward, render, put into the hands of; transfer; **hand over,** give over, deliver over, fork over <nf>, **pass over, turn over,** come across with <nf>; hand out, give out, pass out, distribute, circulate; hand in, give in; **surrender,** resign

14 contribute, subscribe, chip in and kick in and pony up and pay up <nf>, give one's share or fair share; put oneself down for, pledge; contribute to, give to, donate to, gift and gift with <nf>; put something in the pot, sweeten the kitty

15 furnish, supply, provide, afford, provide for; **make available to,** put one in the way of; **accommodate with,** favor with, indulge with; **heap upon,** pour on, shower down upon, **lavish upon**

16 commit, consign, assign, delegate, relegate, confide, commend, remit, remand, give in charge; **entrust,** trust, give in trust; enfeoff, infeudate

17 endow, invest, vest; endow with, favor with, bless with, grace with, vest with; **settle on** or **upon; dower;** philanthropize, aid, benefit, relieve

18 bequeath, will, will and bequeath, **leave, devise, will to,** hand down, hand on, pass on, transmit, provide for; **make a will,** draw up a will, execute a will, make a bequest, write one's last will and testament, write into one's will; add a codicil; entail

19 subsidize, finance, bankroll and greenback <nf>, fund; angel <nf>; **aid, assist, support, help,** pay

the bills, pick up the check or tab and spring for and pop for <nf>; pension, pension off

20 thrust upon, force upon, press upon, push upon, obtrude on, ram or cram down one's throat

21 give away, dispose of, part with, sacrifice, spare

ADJS **22** philanthropic, philanthropical, eleemosynary, **charitable** 143.15; giving, generous to a fault, liberal, **generous** 485.4; openhanded

23 giveable, presentable, bestowable; impartable, communicable; bequeathable, devisable; allowable; committable; fundable

24 given, allowed, accorded, granted, vouchsafed, bestowed, etc; gratuitous 634.5; God-given, providential

25 donative, contributory; concessive; testate, testamentary; intestate

26 endowed, dowered, subsidized, invested; dower, dowry, dotal; subsidiary, stipendiary, pensionary

ADVS **27** as a gift, gratis, on one, on the house, free, all-expense-paid; to his heirs, to the heirs of his body, to his heirs and assigns, to his executors or administrators and assigns

479 RECEIVING

NOUNS **1 receiving, reception,** receival, **receipt, getting, taking; acquisition** 472; derivation; **assumption, acceptance;** admission, admittance; **reception** 187

2 inheritance, heritance <old>, **heritage, patrimony, birthright, legacy, bequest,** bequeathal; reversion; entail; heirship; **succession,** line of succession, mode of succession, law of succession; primogeniture, ultimogeniture, postremogeniture, borough-English, coheirship, coparcenary, gavelkind; hereditament, corporeal or incorporeal hereditament; **heritable; heirloom**

3 recipient, receiver, accepter, getter, taker, acquirer, obtainer, procurer, donee; payee, endorsee; addressee, consignee; holder, trustee; **hearer,** viewer, beholder, audience, auditor, listener, looker, spectator; the receiving end; charity case; receiver of stolen property, fence <nf>

4 beneficiary, allottee, **donee, grantee,** patentee; **assignee, assign; devisee, legatee,** legatary <old>; trustee; feoffee; almsman, almswoman; stipendiary; pensioner, pensionary; annuitant

5 heir, heritor, inheritor, heres <L>; **heiress,** inheritress, inheritrix; coheir, joint heir, fellow heir, coparcener; heir expectant; **heir apparent,** apparent heir; **heir presumptive,** presumptive heir; statutory next of kin; legal heir, heir at law, heir general; heir by destination; heir of the body; heir in tail, heir of entail; fideicommissary heir, fiduciary heir; reversioner; remainderman; **successor,** next in line

VERBS **6 receive, get, gain, secure,** have, come by, be in receipt of, be on the receiving end; **obtain, acquire** 472.8; admit, accept, take, take off one's hands; **take in** 187.10; assume, take on, take over; **derive, draw,** draw or derive from; have an income of, drag down and pull down and rake in <nf>, have coming in, take home; accept stolen property, fence <nf>

7 inherit, be heir to, **come into,** come in for, come by, fall or step into; step into the shoes of, succeed to

8 be received, come in, come to hand, pass or fall into one's hands, go into one's pocket, come or fall to one, fall to one's share or lot; **accrue,** accrue to

ADJS **9 receiving,** on the receiving end; **receptive,** recipient 187.16

10 received, accepted, admitted, recognized, approved

480 TAKING

NOUNS **1 taking,** possession, taking possession, taking away; **claiming,** staking one's claim; **acquisition** 472; **reception** 479.1; **theft** 482; bumming or mooching <nf>; moonlight requisition

2 seizure, seizing, grab, grabbing, snatching, snatch; **kidnapping, abduction,** forcible seizure; power grab <nf>, coup, coup d'état, seizure of power; hold 474.2; **catch,** catching; **capture,** collaring <nf>, nabbing <nf>; **apprehension,** prehension; **arrest,** arrestation, taking into custody; picking up and taking in and running in <nf>; dragnet

3 sexual possession, taking; sexual assault, ravishment, **rape,** violation, indecent assault, date rape or acquaintance rape, serial rape or gang bang <nf>; statutory rape; defloration, deflowerment, devirgination

4 appropriation, taking over, takeover <nf>, **adoption, assumption, usurpation,** arrogation; requisition, indent <Brit>; preoccupation, prepossession, preemption; **conquest,** occupation, subjugation, enslavement, colonization; infringement of copyright, plagiarism

5 attachment, annexation, annexure <Brit>; **confiscation,** sequestration; impoundment; **commandeering, impressment;** expropriation, nationalization, socialization, communalization, communization, collectivization; levy; distraint, distress; garnishment; execution; eminent domain, angary, right of eminent domain, right of angary

6 deprivation, deprival, privation, divestment, bereavement; relieving, disburdening, disburdenment; curtailment, abridgment <old>; disentitlement

7 dispossession, disseisin, expropriation; reclaiming, repossessing, **repossession,** foreclosure; **eviction** 909.2; disendowment; **disinheritance,** disherison, disownment

8 extortion, shakedown <nf>, **blackmail,** bloodsucking, vampirism; protection racket; badger game

9 rapacity, rapaciousness, ravenousness, sharkishness, wolfishness, **predaciousness,** predacity; pillaging, looting

10 take, catch, bag, capture, seizure, **haul;** booty 482.11; hot property

11 taker; partaker; **catcher, captor,** capturer; appropriator, expropriator

12 extortionist, extortioner, **blackmailer,** racketeer, shakedown artist <nf>, **bloodsucker,** leech, **vampire; predator,** raptor, bird of prey, beast of prey; harpy; vulture, shark; profiteer; rack-renter; kidnapper, abductor

VERBS **13 take,** possess, take possession; **get,** get into one's hold or possession; pocket, palm; draw off, drain off; skim and skim off and take up front <nf>; **claim,** stake one's claim, enforce one's claim; partake; **acquire** 472.8; **receive** 479.6; **steal** 482.13

14 seize, take or get hold of, **lay hold of,** catch or grab hold of, glom or latch on to <nf>, **get** or **lay hands on,** clap hands on <nf>, put one's hands on, get into one's grasp or clutches; get one's fingers or hands on, get between one's finger and thumb; **grab, grasp, grip,** gripe <old>, **grapple, snatch,** snatch up, nip, nail <nf>, **clutch,** claw, clinch, clench; **clasp, hug, embrace;** snap up, nip up, whip up, catch up; pillage, loot; take by assault or storm; **kidnap, abduct,** snatch <nf>, carry off; shanghai; take by the throat, throttle

15 possess sexually, take; **rape,** commit rape, commit date or acquaintance rape, ravish, violate, assault sexually, lay violent hands on, have one's will of; deflower, deflorate, devirginate

16 seize on or **upon,** fasten upon; spring or pounce upon, jump <nf>, swoop down upon; **catch at, snatch at,** snap at, jump at, make a grab for, scramble for

17 catch, take, catch flatfooted, land and nail <nf>, hook, **snag, snare,** sniggle, spear, harpoon; ensnare, enmesh, entangle, tangle, foul, tangle up with; **net,** mesh; **bag,** sack; **trap,** entrap; lasso, rope, noose

18 capture, apprehend, collar <nf>, run down, run to earth, **nab** <nf>, grab <nf>, lay by the heels, take prisoner; **arrest,** place or put under arrest, take into custody; pick up or take in or run in <nf>

19 **appropriate, adopt, assume, usurp,** arrogate, accroach; requisition, indent <Brit>; **take possession of,** possess oneself of, take for oneself, arrogate to oneself, take up, **take over, help oneself to,** make use of, make one's own, make free with, dip one's hands into; take it all, take all of, hog <nf>, monopolize, sit on; preoccupy, prepossess, preempt; jump a claim; **conquer,** overrun, occupy, subjugate, enslave, colonize; squat on; bum or mooch <nf>

20 **attach, annex; confiscate,** sequester, sequestrate, impound; **commandeer,** press, **impress;** expropriate, nationalize, socialize, communalize, communize, collectivize; exercise the right of eminent domain, exercise the right of angary; levy, distrain, replevy, replevin; garnishee, garnish

21 **take from,** take away from, **deprive of,** do out of <nf>, relieve of, disburden of, lighten of, ease of; **deprive, bereave, divest;** tap, milk, mine, drain, bleed, curtail, abridge <old>; cut off; disentitle

22 **wrest,** wring, wrench, **rend, rip; extort, exact,** squeeze, screw, **shake down** <nf>, **blackmail,** levy blackmail, badger and play the badger game <nf>; **force from, wrest from, wrench from, wring from, tear from, rip from, rend from,** snatch from, pry loose from

23 **dispossess,** disseise, expropriate, foreclose; evict 909.15; disendow; **disinherit,** disherison, **disown,** cut out of one's will, **cut off,** cut off with a shilling, cut off without a cent

24 **strip,** strip bare or clean, **fleece** <nf>, **shear,** denude, skin and pluck <nf>, flay, **despoil, divest,** pick clean, pick the bones of; deplume, displume; **milk; bleed, bleed white;** exhaust, drain, dry, suck dry; **impoverish,** beggar; clean out and take to the cleaners <nf>; eat out of house and home

ADJS 25 **taking, catching;** private, deprivative; confiscatory, annexational, expropriatory; **thievish** 482.21; ripoff <nf>

26 **rapacious, ravenous,** ravening, vulturous, vulturine, sharkish, **wolfish,** lupine, predacious, **predatory,** raptorial; vampirish, **bloodsucking,** parasitic; **extortionate; grasping,** graspy, grabby <nf>, **insatiable** 100.27; all-devouring, all-engulfing

481 RESTITUTION

NOUNS 1 **restitution, restoration,** restoring, giving back, sending back, remitting, remission, **return,** redress; reddition <old>; extradition, rendition; repatriation; recommitment, remandment, remand; satisfaction

2 **reparation, recompense,** paying back, squaring <nf>, repayment, reimbursement, refund, remuneration, **compensation, indemnification;** retribution, **atonement,** redress, satisfaction, **amends,** making good, **requital;** conscience money

3 **recovery,** regaining; **retrieval,** retrieve; **recuperation,** recoup, recoupment; **retake,** retaking, recapture; **repossession,** resumption, reoccupation; **reclamation,** reclaiming; **redemption,** ransom, salvage, trover; replevin, replevy; **revival, restoration** 396, retro

VERBS 4 **restore, return, give back,** restitute, hand back, put back; take back, bring back; put the genie back into the bottle, put the toothpaste back into the tube; **remit,** send back; repatriate; extradite; recommit, remand; requite

5 **make restitution,** make reparation, **make amends,** make good, make up for, atone, give satisfaction, redress, **recompense,** pay back, square <nf>, repay, reimburse, refund, remunerate, **compensate, requite,** indemnify, make it up; pay damages, pay reparations; pay conscience money; overcompensate

6 **recover, regain, retrieve,** recuperate, **recoup, get back,** come by one's own; **redeem,** ransom; **reclaim; repossess,** resume, reoccupy; **retake,** recapture, take back; replevin, replevy; revive, renovate, **restore** 396.11,15

ADJS 7 **restitutive,** restitutory, **restorative;** compensatory, indemnificatory, retributive, reparative, reparatory; reversionary, reversional, revertible; redeeming, redemptive, redemptional; reimbursable

ADVS 8 **in restitution,** in reparation, in recompense, in compensation, to make up for, in return for, in retribution, in requital, in amends, in atonement, to atone for

482 THEFT

NOUNS 1 **theft, thievery,** stealage, **stealing,** thieving, **purloining;** swiping and lifting and snatching and snitching and pinching <nf>; conveyance <old>, **appropriation,** conversion, liberation and annexation <nf>; **pilfering,** pilferage, **filching,** scrounging <nf>; abstraction; sneak thievery; shoplifting, boosting <nf>; poaching; **graft;** embezzlement 389.1; **fraud, swindle** 356.8

2 **larceny,** petit or petty larceny, petty theft, grand larceny, grand theft, simple larceny, mixed or aggravated larceny; automobile theft

3 **theft, robbery,** robbing; bank robbery; banditry, highway robbery; **armed robbery, holdup,** assault and robbery, **mugging,** push-in job or crime; purse

snatching; **pocket picking** *or* pick-pocketing, jostling; **hijacking,** asportation <old>; carjacking; cattle stealing, **cattle rustling** *and* cattle lifting <nf>; **extortion** 480.8; identity theft

4 <nf terms> **heist, stickup,** job, stickup job, bag job, boost, hustle, pinch, swipe, lift, burn, knockover, **ripoff;** sticky fingers

5 **burglary,** burglarizing, housebreaking, **breaking and entering,** break and entry, break-in, unlawful entry; second-story work <nf>; safebreaking, **safecracking, safeblowing**

6 **plundering, pillaging, looting, sacking,** freebooting, ransacking, rifling, spoiling, **despoliation,** despoilment, despoiling; rapine, spoliation, depredation, direption <old>, **raiding,** ravage, ravaging, ravagement, rape, ravishment; **pillage, plunder,** sack; brigandage, brigandism, banditry; **marauding,** foraging; raid, foray, razzia

7 **piracy, buccaneering, privateering, freebooting;** letters of marque, letters of marque and reprisal; **air piracy,** airplane hijacking, skyjacking; carjacking

8 **plagiarism,** plagiarizing, plagiary, **piracy,** literary piracy, appropriation, borrowing, cribbing; infringement; infringement of copyright; autoplagiarism; cribbing <nf>; crib *or* cheat sheet

9 **abduction, kidnapping, snatching** <nf>; **shanghaiing,** impressment, crimping

10 **grave-robbing,** body-snatching <nf>, resurrectionism

11 **booty,** spoil, **spoils, loot, swag** <nf>, ill-gotten gains, **plunder,** prize, haul, take, pickings, stealings, stolen goods, hot goods *or* items <nf>; **boodle** *and* squeeze *and* **graft** <nf>; perquisite, perks <Brit nf>, pork barrel, spoils of office, public trough; till, public till; blackmail; hot property

12 **thievishness,** larcenousness, taking ways <nf>, light fingers, sticky fingers; kleptomania, bibliokleptomania, etc

VERBS 13 **steal, thieve, purloin, appropriate, take,** snatch, palm, **make off with,** walk off with, run off *or* away with, abstract, disregard the distinction between *meum* and *tuum*; have one's hand in the till; **pilfer, filch,** shoplift; poach; rustle; **embezzle** 389.4; defraud, swindle; **extort** 480.22

14 **rob,** commit robbery; pick pockets, jostle; hold up, stick someone up

15 **burglarize,** burgle <nf>, commit burglary, housebreak; crack *or* blow a safe

16 <nf terms> **swipe, pinch,** bag, **lift,** hook, crib, **cop,** nip, snitch, snare, boost, annex, borrow, burn, clip, **rip off,** nick *and* nobble <Brit>; **heist, knock**

off *or* **over,** tip over; **stick up; mug;** roll, jackroll; do a job; cook the books; case the joint

17 **plunder, pillage, loot, sack,** ransack, rifle, freeboot, spoil, spoliate, despoil, depredate, prey on *or* upon, **raid,** reive <Scot>, ravage, ravish, raven, sweep, gut; **fleece** 480.24; maraud, foray, forage

18 **pirate,** buccaneer, privateer, freeboot

19 **plagiarize, pirate,** borrow *and* crib <nf>, appropriate; **pick one's brains;** infringe a copyright

20 **abduct,** abduce, spirit away, **carry off** *or* **away,** magic away <Brit>, run off *or* away with; **kidnap,** snatch <nf>, hold for ransom; skyjack, hijack, carjack; **shanghai,** crimp, impress

ADJS 21 **thievish, thieving, larcenous, light-fingered, sticky-fingered;** kleptomaniacal, burglarious; brigandish, piratical, piratelike; fraudulent

22 **plunderous, plundering, looting,** pillaging, ravaging, marauding, spoliatory; predatory, predacious

23 **stolen,** pilfered, purloined, ripped off; pirated, plagiarized; hot <nf>

483 THIEF

NOUNS 1 **thief, robber,** stealer, purloiner, lifter <nf>, *ganef* <Yiddish>, **crook** <nf>; larcenist, larcener; **pilferer, filcher,** petty thief, chicken thief; sneak thief, prowler; shoplifter, booster <nf>; poacher; **grafter,** petty grafter; jewel thief; **swindler,** con man 357.3,4; land pirate, land shark, land-grabber; grave robber, body snatcher, resurrectionist, ghoul; embezzler, peculator, white-collar thief; den of thieves

2 **pickpocket,** cutpurse, fingersmith *and* dip <nf>; **purse snatcher;** light-fingered gentry

3 **burglar,** yegg *and* cracksman <nf>; housebreaker, cat burglar, cat man, second-story thief *or* worker; **safecracker,** safebreaker, safeblower; pete blower *or* pete man *or* peterman <nf>

4 **bandit, brigand,** dacoit; **gangster** *and* mobster <nf>, goodfella <nf>; racketeer; **thug, hoodlum** 593.4

5 **robber, holdup man** *and* stickup man <nf>; highwayman, highway robber, footpad, road agent, bushranger <Austral>; **mugger** <nf>, sandbagger; train robber; bank robber, **hijacker** <nf>

6 **plunderer, pillager, looter, marauder,** rifler, sacker, spoiler, despoiler, spoliator, depredator, **raider,** moss-trooper, free-booter rapparee, reiver <Scot>, forayer, forager, ravisher, ravager; wrecker

7 **pirate, corsair, buccaneer, privateer,** sea rover, rover, picaroon; viking, sea king; Blackbeard,

Captain Kidd, Jean Lafitte, Henry Morgan;
Captain Hook, Long John Silver; air pirate,
airplane hijacker, skyjacker; hijacker, carjacker;
record pirate, video pirate, bootlegger

8 cattle thief, abactor, rustler *and* **cattle rustler**
<nf>; poacher

9 **plagiarist,** plagiarizer, cribber <nf>, pirate,
literary pirate, copyright infringer

10 abductor, kidnapper; shanghaier, snatcher *and*
baby-snatcher <nf>; crimp, crimper

11 <famous thieves> Barabbas, Robin Hood, Jesse
James, Clyde Barrow, John Dillinger, Claude
Duval, Jack Sheppard, Willie Sutton, Dick Turpin,
Jonathan Wild; Autolycus, Macheath, Thief of
Baghdad, Jean Valjean, Jimmy Valentine, Raffles,
Bill Sikes

484 PARSIMONY

NOUNS 1 **parsimony,** parsimoniousness; frugality
635.1; **stinting, pinching, scrimping,** skimping,
cheeseparing; economy, economy of means,
economy of assumption, law of parsimony,
Ockham's razor, elegance

2 **niggardliness,** penuriousness, **meanness,**
minginess, shabbiness, sordidness

3 **stinginess, ungenerosity, illiberality, cheapness,
chintziness** *and* tightness *and* narrowness <nf>,
tight purse strings, nearness, closeness,
closefistedness, closehandedness <old>,
tightfistedness, hardfistedness, **miserliness,**
penny-pinching, hoarding, austerity; **avarice** 100.8

4 **niggard, tightwad** *and* **cheapskate** <nf>, **miser,**
hard man with a buck <nf>, **skinflint,** scrooge,
penny pincher, moneygrubber <nf>, pinchfist,
pinchgut <old>, churl, curmudgeon <old>,
muckworm, save-all <nf>, Silas Marner

VERBS 5 **stint, scrimp, skimp, scamp,** scant, screw,
pinch, starve, famish; **pinch pennies,** rub the
print off a dollar bill, rub the picture off a nickel;
live upon nothing; grudge, begrudge

6 **withhold,** hold back, hold out on <nf>

ADJS 7 **parsimonious, sparing,** cheeseparing, **stinting,
scamping, scrimping,** skimping; frugal 635.6; too
frugal, overfrugal, frugal to excess; penny-wise,
penny-wise and pound-foolish; austere

8 **niggardly,** niggard, pinchpenny, penurious,
grudging, mean, mingy, shabby, sordid

9 **stingy, illiberal, ungenerous, chintzy, miserly,**
save-all, **cheap** *and* **tight** *and* narrow <nf>, **near,
close, closefisted,** closehanded <old>, tightfisted,
pinchfisted, hardfisted; near as the bark on a tree;
pinching, **penny-pinching; avaricious** 100.27

ADVS 10 **parsimoniously,** stintingly, scrimpingly,
skimpingly

11 **niggardly, stingily,** illiberally, ungenerously,
closefistedly, tightfistedly; meanly, shabbily,
sordidly

485 LIBERALITY

NOUNS 1 **liberality,** liberalness, freeness, freedom;
generosity, generousness, largeness,
unselfishness, munificence, largess *or* largesse,
charity; bountifulness, bounteousness,
bounty; hospitality, welcome, graciousness;
openhandedness, freehandedness, open *or* free
hand, easy purse strings; **givingness;** openheartedness, bigheartedness, largeheartedness,
greatheartedness, freeheartedness; open heart,
big *or* large *or* great heart, heart of gold;
magnanimity 652.2

2 **cheerful giver,** free giver; contributor; Lady
Bountiful; Santa Claus; philanthropist; almsgiver,
altruist

VERBS 3 **give freely,** give cheerfully, give with an
open hand, give with both hands, put one's hands
in one's pockets, open the purse, loosen *or* untie
the purse strings; **spare no expense,** spare
nothing, not count the cost, let money be no
object; **heap upon,** lavish upon, shower down
upon; give the coat *or* shirt off one's back, give
more than one's share, **give until it hurts;** give of
oneself, give of one's substance, not hold back,
offer oneself; tip well; keep the change!

ADJS 4 **liberal, free,** free with one's money, free-
spending; **generous, munificent,** large, princely,
handsome; **unselfish,** ungrudging; **unsparing,
unstinting,** stintless, unstinted; **bountiful,**
bounteous, **lavish,** profuse; hospitable, gracious;
openhanded, freehanded, open; **giving;**
openhearted, **bighearted,** largehearted,
greathearted, freehearted; **magnanimous** 652.6

ADVS 5 **liberally, freely; generously, munificently,**
handsomely; **unselfishly,** ungrudgingly;
unsparingly, unstintingly; bountifully,
bounteously, **lavishly,** profusely; hospitably,
graciously; **openhandedly,** freehandedly;
openheartedly, bigheartedly, largeheartedly,
greatheartedly, freeheartedly; with open hands,
with both hands, with an unsparing hand,
without stint

486 PRODIGALITY

NOUNS 1 **prodigality, overliberality,**
overgenerousness, overgenerosity; profligacy,
extravagance, pound-foolishness, recklessness,
reckless spending *or* expenditure, overspending,
frittering away; incontinence, intemperance 669;

lavishness, profuseness, profusion; **wastefulness, waste; dissipation, squandering,** squandermania; *carpe diem* <L>; slack *or* loose purse strings, leaking purse; conspicuous consumption *or* waste; splurge, spree

2 **prodigal, wastrel,** waster, **squanderer; spendthrift,** wastethrift, spender, spendall, big spender <nf>; Diamond Jim Brady; prodigal son; last of the big spenders

VERBS 3 **squander, lavish,** slather, blow <nf>, play ducks *and* drakes with; **dissipate,** scatter <old>, sow broadcast, scatter to the winds, fritter away; **run through,** go through; **throw away,** throw one's money away, throw money around, **spend money like water,** hang the expense, let slip *or* flow through one's fingers, spend as if money grew on trees, spend money as if it were going out of style, spend like a drunken sailor; gamble away; burn the candle at both ends; seize the day, live for the day, let tomorrow take care of itself

4 **waste, consume, spend, expend, use up, exhaust;** deplete, drain, suck dry, milk dry; misuse, abuse; lose; spill, pour down the drain *or* rathole; pour water into a sieve, cast pearls before swine, kill the goose that lays the golden egg, *manger son blé en herbe* <Fr>, throw out the baby with the bath water; waste effort, labor in vain

5 **fritter away,** fool away, fribble away, dribble away, drivel away, **trifle away,** dally away, potter away, piss away <nf>, muddle away, diddle away <nf>, squander in dribs *and* drabs; idle away, while away

6 **misspend,** misapply, **throw good money after bad,** throw the helve after the hatchet, throw out the baby with the bathwater, cast pearls before swine

7 **overspend,** spend more than one has, spend what one hasn't got, lavish; overdraw, overdraw one's account, live beyond one's means, have champagne tastes on a beer budget

ADJS 8 **prodigal, extravagant, lavish,** profuse, **overliberal,** overgenerous, overlavish, **spendthrift, wasteful,** profligate, dissipative; incontinent, intemperate 669.7; pound-foolish, penny-wise *and* pound-foolish; easy come, easy go

9 **wasted, squandered, dissipated,** consumed, spent, used, lost; **gone to waste,** run *or* gone to seed; down the drain *or* spout *or* rathole <nf>; misspent

487 CELEBRATION

NOUNS 1 **celebration,** celebrating; **observance,** formal *or* solemn *or* ritual observance, **solemnization;** marking *or* honoring the occasion; **commemoration,** memorialization, remembrance, memory; jubilee; red-letter day, **holiday** 20.4;

anniversary; **festivity** 743.3,4; **revel** 743.6; rejoicing 116; **ceremony,** rite 580.4; religious rites 701; ovation, triumph; **tribute;** testimonial, testimonial banquet *or* dinner; toast; roast; **salute;** salvo; flourish of trumpets, fanfare, fanfaronade; dressing ship; high-five; binge *or* bender <nf>, blowout <nf>; ladies' night; **party,** afterparty

VERBS 2 **celebrate, observe, keep, mark,** solemnly mark, **honor; commemorate,** memorialize; **solemnize,** signalize, hallow, mark with a red letter; party, party down <nf>, hold jubilee, jubilize, jubilate, maffick <Brit nf>; **make merry,** make whoopie; binge <nf>; kill the fatted calf; sound a fanfare, blow the trumpet, beat the drum, fire a salute; dress ship; high-five

ADJS 3 **celebrative,** celebratory, celebrating, partying; **commemorative,** commemorating; memorial; solemn; festive, festal, gala

ADVS 4 **in honor of, in commemoration of,** in memory *or* remembrance of, to the memory of

5 **anniversaries and holidays**

Admission Day	Citizenship Day
Alaska Day	Columbus Day
Advent	Commonwealth Day
All Saints' Day	Confederate Memorial
All Souls' Day	Day
Allhallows	Confucius's birthday
American Indian Day	Constitution Day
Annunciation	Corpus Christi
Anzac Day	Dasara
April Fools' Day or All	Day of the Dead or Dia de
Fools' Day	los Muertos
Arab League Day	Decoration Day
Arbor Day	Dhammacakka
Armed Forces Day	Discovery Day
Armistice Day	Diwali
Ascension Day	Dominion Day
Ash Wednesday	Double Ten
Assumption Day	Durga Puja or Navratri
Australia Day	Dusshera
autumnal equinox	Earth Day
Bairam	Easter
Baisakhi	Easter Monday
Bastille Day	Eid
birthday	Eid ul-Adha
Bodhi Day	Eid ul-Fitr
Bon	Election Day
Boxing Day	Emancipation Day
Buddha's birthday	Emperor's birthday
Canada Day	Empire Day
Candlemas	engagement anniversary
Carnival	Epiphany
Chinese New Year	Father's Day
Christmas Eve	feast day
Christmas or Xmas	Flag Day
Chusuk	Fourth of July
Cinco de Mayo	Good Friday

Grandparents' Day
Groundhog Day
Guru Gobind Singh's
   Birthday
Guru Nanak's Birthday
Guy Fawkes Day
Halloween
Hanukkah
High Holy Day
Holi
Holi Mohalla
Holy Innocents' Day
Human Rights Day
'Id al-Adha
Ides of March
Immaculate Conception
Inauguration Day
Independence Day
Islamic New Year's Day
Janmashtami
Karwa Chauth
Kenyatta Day
Kuhio Day
Kwanza or Kwanzaa
Labor Day
Lag b'Omer
Lailat ul-Bara'h
Lailat ul-Isra wal Mi'raj
Lailat ul-Qadr
Lammas
Lantern Festival
Lent
Lincoln's birthday
Lunar New Year
Mahashivaratri
Mardi Gras
Martin Luther
   King Jr. Day
Martinmas
Martyrdom of Guru Arjan
Martyrdom of Guru Tegh
   Bahadur
Maundy Thursday
May Day
Memorial Day
Mexican Independence
   Day
Michaelmas
Midsummer Day
Moharram
Mother's Day
Muhammad's birthday
Muhrarran
Nag Panchami
National Day
National Unity Day

Navaratri
New Year's Day
New Year's Eve
Noel
Oktoberfest
Omisoka
Pagan Sabbats
Palm Sunday
Pan American Day
Passover or Pesach
Pentecost
Pesach or Passover
Posadas
President's Day
Purim
Queen's birthday
Queensland Day
Raksha Bandhan
Rama Naumi
Ramadan
Reformation Sunday
Remembrance Day
Republic Day
retirement anniversary
Rosh Hashanah
Sadie Hawkins Day
Saint Patrick's Day
Saint Valentine's Day
Santa Lucia Day
Shavuot or Shavuoth
Shrove Tuesday
Shrovetide
Spring Bank Holiday
Sukkoth or Sukkot or
   Succoth
summer solstice
Tet
Thanksgiving
Trinity Sunday
Twelfth Night
United Nations Day
V-E Day
vernal equinox
Vesak
Veterans' Day
Victoria Day
V-J Day
Walpurgis
Washington's birthday
wedding anniversary
Whitsunday
Whitsuntide
winter solstice
World Health Day
Yom Kippur or Day of
   Atonement

6 birthday flowers and birthstones

January: carnation,
   snowdrop; garnet

February: violet, primrose;
   amethyst

March: jonquil, violet;
   jasper, bloodstone,
   aquamarine
April: daisy, sweet pea;
   sapphire, diamond
May: hawthorn, lily of the
   valley; agate, emerald
June: rose, honeysuckle;
   emerald, pearl,
   moonstone, alexandrite
July: larkspur, water lily;
   onyx, ruby
August: gladiolus, poppy;

carnelian, sardonyx,
   peridot
September: morning glory,
   aster; chrysolite,
   sapphire
October: calendula,
   cosmos; aquamarine,
   opal, tourmaline
November: chrysanthe-
   mum; topaz
December: narcissus,
   holly, poinsettia; ruby,
   turquoise, zircon

7 wedding anniversaries

1st: paper
2nd: cotton
3rd: leather
4th: linen or silk, fruit or
   flowers
5th: wood
6th: iron, sugar or candy
7th: wool or copper
8th: bronze or pottery
9th: pottery or willow
10th: tin or aluminum
11th: steel
12th: linen or silk
13th: lace
14th: ivory
15th: crystal

16th: tungsten
17th: turquoise
18th: bismuth
19th: bismuth or china
20th: china
25th: silver
30th: pearl
35th: coral
40th: ruby
45th: sapphire
50th: gold
55th: emerald
60th: diamond
65th: star sapphire
70th: platinum
75th: diamond

488 HUMOROUSNESS

NOUNS **1 humorousness, funniness,** amusingness, laughableness, laughability, hilarity, hilariousness; wittiness 489.2; **drollness,** drollery; **whimsicalness,** quizzicalness; **ludicrousness, ridiculousness, absurdity,** absurdness, quaintness, eccentricity, incongruity, bizarreness, bizarrerie; richness, pricelessness <nf>; the funny side; barrel of laughs

2 comicalness, comicality, funiosity; farcicalness, **farcicality,** slapstick quality, broadness

3 bathos; anticlimax, comedown, shaggy dog story

ADJS **4 humorous, funny, amusing; witty** 489.15; **droll, whimsical,** quizzical; **laughable,** risible, good for a laugh; **ludicrous, ridiculous, hilarious, absurd,** quaint, eccentric, incongruous, bizarre

5 <nf terms> **funny ha-ha,** priceless, too funny *or* too killing for words, hardy-har *or* hardy-har-har *or* har-har-har, rich, hysterical

6 comic *or* **comical; farcical,** slapstick, broad; **burlesque** 508.14; tragicomic, serio-comic, mock-heroic

ADVS **7 humorously, amusingly,** funnily, **laughably;** wittily 489.18; drolly, whimsically, quizzically;

comically, farcically, broadly; **ludicrously, ridiculously, absurdly,** quaintly, eccentrically, incongruously, bizarrely

489 WIT, HUMOR

NOUNS 1 **wit, humor,** pleasantry, *esprit* <Fr>, salt, spice *or* savor of wit; Attic wit *or* salt, Atticism; ready wit, quick wit, nimble wit, agile wit, pretty wit; dry wit, dry humor, subtle wit; **comedy** 704.6; black humor, dark humor, sick humor, gallows humor; **satire,** sarcasm, irony; Varonnian satire, Menippean satire; **parody, lampoon,** lampoonery, travesty, **caricature, burlesque,** squib, takeoff, spoof; **farce,** mere farce; **slapstick,** slapstick humor, broad humor, black humor; visual humor, cartoon, comic strip, the funnies; stand-up comedy

2 **wittiness, humorousness** 488, **funniness;** facetiousness, pleasantry, **jocularity,** jocoseness, jocosity; **joking,** japery, joshing <nf>; smartness, cleverness, brilliance; pungency, saltiness; keenness, sharpness; keen-wittedness, quick-wittedness, nimble-wittedness

3 **drollery,** drollness; **whimsicality,** whimsicalness, humorsomeness, antic wit

4 **waggishness, waggery;** roguishness 322.2; **playfulness,** sportiveness, **levity, frivolity,** flippancy, merriment 109.5; **prankishness,** pranksomeness; trickery, trickiness, tricksiness, trickishness

5 **buffoonery,** buffoonism, clownery, clowning, clowning around, harlequinade; **clownishness,** buffoonishness; **foolery,** fooling, **tomfoolery;** horseplay; shenanigans *and* monkey tricks *and* monkeyshines <nf>, funny business; **banter** 490

6 **joke, jest, gag** *and* one-liner <nf>, **wheeze,** jape; **fun, sport, play,** kidding; story, yarn, **funny story,** good story; dirty story *or* joke, blue story *or* joke, *double entendre* <Fr>; one-liner; shaggy-dog story; sick joke <nf>; ethnic joke; capital joke, good one, laugh, belly laugh, rib tickler, sidesplitter, thigh-slapper, howler, wow, hoot, scream, riot, panic; visual joke, sight gag <nf>; standing joke; **point,** punch line, gag line, tag line; cream of the jest; jest-book

7 **witticism, pleasantry,** *plaisanterie* and *boutade* <Fr>; **play of wit,** *jeu d'esprit* <Fr>; **crack** *and* smart crack *and* **wisecrack** <nf>; **quip,** conceit, bright *or* happy thought, bright *or* brilliant idea; **mot, bon mot,** smart saying, stroke of wit, one-liner *and* zinger <nf>; epigram, turn of thought, aphorism, apothegm; flash of wit, scintillation; sound bite; **sally,** flight of wit; **repartee,** backchat, retort, riposte, snappy

comeback <nf>; facetiae <pl>, quips *and* cranks; **gibe, dirty** *or* **nasty crack** <nf>; persiflage 490.1

8 **wordplay, play on words,** *jeu de mots* <Fr>, missaying, corruption, paronomasia, *calembour* <Fr>, abuse of terms; **pun,** punning; equivoque, equivocality; anagram, logogram, logogriph, metagram; acrostic, double acrostic; amphiboly, amphibologism; palindrome; spoonerism; malapropism; Tom Swifty

9 **old joke,** old wheeze *or* turkey, **trite joke,** hoary-headed joke, joke with whiskers; **chestnut** *and* corn *and* **corny joke** *and* oldie <nf>; Joe Miller, Joe Millerism; twice-told tale, retold story, warmed-over cabbage <nf>

10 **prank, trick, practical joke,** waggish trick, *espièglerie* <Fr>, antic, caper, frolic; **monkeyshines** *and* **shenanigans** <nf>, leg-pull

11 **sense of humor, risibility,** funny bone

12 **humorist, wit, funnyman, comic,** *bel-esprit* <Fr>, life of the party; **joker,** jokester, gagman <nf>, **jester,** court jester, **quipster, wisecracker** *and* gagster <nf>; wag, wagwit; zany, madcap, cutup <nf>; **prankster; comedian,** stand-up comic *or* comedian, banana <nf>, straight man; **clown** 707.10; punster, punner; epigrammatist; satirist; ironist; burlesquer, caricaturist, cartoonist, parodist, lampooner; reparteeist; witling; gag writer <nf>, jokesmith

VERBS 13 **joke, jest, wisecrack** *and* crack wise <nf>, utter a mot, **quip,** jape, josh <nf>, fun <nf>, make fun, **kid** *or* **kid around** <nf>; **make a funny** <nf>; **crack a joke,** get off a joke, tell a good story; pun, play on words; scintillate, sparkle; **make fun of,** gibe at, fleer at, mock, scoff at, poke fun at, send up, take off, lampoon, make the butt of one's humor, be merry with; ridicule 508.8

14 **trick, play a practical joke,** play tricks *or* pranks, **play a joke** *or* **trick on,** make merry with; **clown around,** pull a stunt *or* trick; pull one's leg *and* put one on <nf>

ADJS 15 **witty, amusing,** *spirituel* <Fr>; **humorous** 488.4, **comic, comical, farcical** 488.6; **funny; jocular,** joky <nf>, **joking, jesting, jocose, tongue-in-cheek; facetious,** joshing <nf>, **whimsical, droll,** humorsome; smart, clever, brilliant, scintillating, sparkling, sprightly; keen, sharp, rapier-like, pungent, pointed, biting, mordant; teasing; satiric, **satirical, sarcastic, ironic,** ironical; salty, salt, Attic; **keen-witted, quick-witted, nimble-witted,** dry-witted; smart

16 **clownish,** buffoonish

17 **waggish;** roguish 322.6; **playful, sportive; prankish,** pranky, pranksome; tricky, trickish, tricksy

ADVS 18 **wittily, humorously; jocularly, jocosely; facetiously; whimsically, drolly**

19 in fun, in sport, in play, in jest, in joke, as a joke, jokingly, jestingly, with tongue in cheek; for fun, for sport

490 BANTER

NOUNS **1 banter, badinage, persiflage, pleasantry, fooling, fooling around, kidding** and **kidding around** <nf>, **raillery,** rallying, **sport,** good-natured banter, harmless teasing; ridicule 508; exchange, give-and-take; side-talk, **byplay,** asides; flyting, slanging, the dozens <nf>

2 bantering, twitting, chaffing, joking, jesting, japing, **fooling, teasing,** hazing; playing the dozens <nf>, backchat

3 <nf terms> **kidding,** joshing, jollying, jiving, fooling around; **ribbing,** ragging, razzing, **roasting**

4 banterer, *persifleur* <Fr>, **chaffer, twitter; kidder** and josher <nf>

VERBS **5 banter, twit, chaff,** rally, **joke, jest,** jape, **tease,** haze; have a slanging match, play the dozens <nf>, backchat

6 <nf terms> **kid,** jolly, josh, fool around, jive, rub, put on; **razz, roast,** ride, needle

ADJS **7 bantering, chaffing, twitting; jollying** and **kidding** and joshing etc <nf>, **fooling, teasing,** quizzical

491 COWARDICE

NOUNS **1 cowardice, cowardliness; fear** 127; **faintheartedness,** faintheart, weakheartedness, chickenheartedness, henheartedness, pigeonheartedness; **yellowness,** white-liveredness and lily-liveredness and chicken-liveredness <nf>, weak-kneedness; weakness, softness; unmanliness, unmanfulness; timidness, **timidity,** timorousness, milksoppiness, milksoppishness, milksopism, cowardship

2 uncourageousness, unvaliantness, unvalorousness, unheroicness, ungallantness, unintrepidness; **plucklessness, spunklessness** and gritlessness and gutlessness <nf>, spiritlessness, heartlessness; defeatism

3 dastardliness, pusillanimousness, **pusillanimity, poltroonery,** poltroonishness, poltroonism, baseness, abjectness, **cravenness;** desertion under fire, bugout and skedaddling <nf>, lack of moral fiber

4 cold feet <nf>, weak knees, **faintheart,** chicken heart, **yellow streak** <nf>, white feather; gutlessness

5 coward, jellyfish, invertebrate, faintheart, **weakling,** weak sister <nf>, milksop, milquetoast, mouse, **sissy, wimp** <nf>, baby, **big baby, chicken** <nf>; namby-pamby; **yellow-belly,** and white-liver and lily-liver and chicken-liver <nf>, jellyfish, white feather; fraid-cat and **fraidy-cat** and scaredy-cat <nf>; funk and funker <nf>

6 dastard, craven, poltroon, recreant, caitiff, arrant coward; sneak; deserter

VERBS **7 dare not; have a yellow streak** <nf>, have cold feet <nf>, be unable to say 'boo' to a goose

8 lose one's nerve, lose courage, **get cold feet** <nf>, **show the white feather;** falter, boggle, funk <nf>, **chicken** <nf>; put one's tail between one's legs, back out, funk out <nf>, **wimp** or **chicken out** <nf>, have no stomach for; desert under fire, turn tail, bug out and skedaddle <nf>, **run scared** <nf>, scuttle, retreat

9 cower, quail, cringe, crouch, skulk, sneak, slink

ADJS **10 cowardly,** coward; **afraid, fearful** 127.23; timid, timorous, overtimorous, overtimid, rabbity and mousy <nf>; **fainthearted,** weakhearted, chicken-hearted, henhearted, pigeonhearted; white-livered and lily-livered and chicken-livered and milk-livered <nf>; **yellow** and yellow-bellied and with a yellow streak <nf>; **weak-kneed, chicken** <nf>, afraid of one's shadow; weak, soft; **wimpy** or wimpish <nf>, unmanly, unmanful, sissy, sissified; milksoppy, milksoppish; panicky, panic-prone, funking and funky <nf>; daunted, dismayed, unmanned, cowed, intimidated

11 uncourageous, unvaliant, unvalorous, unheroic, ungallant, **unintrepid, undaring,** unable to say 'boo' to a goose; unsoldierlike, unsoldierly; **pluckless,** spunkless and gritless <nf>, gutless <nf>, spiritless, heartless

12 dastardly, dastard; hit-and-run; **poltroonish,** poltroon; **pusillanimous,** base, craven, recreant, caitiff; dunghill, dunghilly

13 cowering, quailing, cringing; skulking, sneaking, slinking, sneaky, slinky

ADVS **14 cravenly,** poltroonishly, like a coward, **cowardly, uncourageously,** unvaliantly, unvalorously, unheroically, ungallantly, unintrepidly, undaringly; plucklessly, spunklessly and gritlessly <nf>, spiritlessly, heartlessly; faintheartedly, weakheartedly, chickenheartedly; wimpishly

492 COURAGE

NOUNS **1 courage,** courageousness, **nerve,** pluck, **bravery,** braveness, ballsiness and gutsiness or guttiness <nf>, **boldness,** nerves of steel, **valor,** valorousness, valiance, valiancy, **gallantry,** conspicuous gallantry, gallantry under fire or beyond the call of duty, gallantness, **intrepidity,** intrepidness, **prowess,** virtue; doughtiness, stalwartness, stoutness, stoutheartedness, lionheartedness, greatheartedness; **heroism,** heroicalness; chivalry, chivalrousness, knightliness; military *or* martial spirit, fighting spirit, soldierly quality *or* virtues; **manliness,** manfulness, **manhood,** virility, machismo; Dutch courage <nf>, pot-valor, bold front, bravado

2 **fearlessness,** dauntlessness, **undauntedness, unfearfulness,** unfearingness, unafraidness, **unapprehensiveness; confidence** 970.5; untimidness, untimorousness, unshrinkingness, unshyness, unbashfulness

3 <nf terms> **balls, guts,** intestinal fortitude, spunk, brass balls, cojones, moxie, spizzerinctum, **backbone,** chutzpah

4 **daring,** derring-do, deeds of derring-do; **bravado,** bravura; **audacity,** audaciousness, overboldness; **venturousness,** venturesomeness, risk-taking, tightrope walking, funambulism; **adventurousness,** adventuresomeness, enterprise; foolhardiness 493.3

5 **fortitude, hardihood,** hardiness; **pluckiness; spunkiness** *and* grittiness *and* nerviness <nf>, mettlesomeness; **gameness,** gaminess; grit, **stamina,** toughness, pith <old>, **mettle,** bottom; heart, spirit, stout **heart,** heart of oak; **resolution** 359, resoluteness, tenaciousness, tenacity, pertinaciousness, pertinacity, bulldog courage, true grit, stiff upper lip

6 **exploit, feat, deed, enterprise, achievement, adventure,** act of courage, gest, **bold stroke,** heroic act *or* deed; prowess; heroics; aristeia

7 <brave person> **hero, heroine;** brave, stalwart, gallant, valiant, man *or* woman of courage *or* mettle, a man, valiant knight, good soldier, warrior, knight in shining armor; tragic hero, unsung hero; demigod, paladin; demigoddess; the brave; decorated hero; Hector, Achilles, Roland, David; lion, **tiger,** bulldog, fighting cock, gamecock; he-man; daredevil, stunt person

8 **encouragement, heartening, inspiration,** inspiriting, inspiritment, emboldening, assurance, reassurance, pat *or* clap on the back, bucking up

VERBS 9 **dare, venture, make bold to,** make so bold as to, take risks, walk the tightrope, **have the nerve, have the guts** *or* the balls <nf>, have the courage of one's convictions, be a man; defy 454.3

10 **brave, face, confront,** affront, front, look one in the eye, say to one's face, **face up to,** meet, **meet head-on** *or* boldly, square up to, stand up to *or* against, go eyeball-to-eyeball *or* one-on-one with <nf>; set at defiance 454.4; speak up, speak out, stand up and be counted; not flinch *or* shrink from, bite the bullet <nf>, look full in the face, put

a bold face upon, show *or* present a bold front; head into, face up, come to grips with, grapple with; face the music <nf>; **brazen,** brazen out *or* through; beard, "beard the lion in his den"—Sir Walter Scott; put one's head in the lion's mouth, fly into the face of danger, take the bull by the horns, march up to the cannon's mouth, bell the cat, go through fire and water, court disaster, go in harm's way, throw caution to the wind, run the gauntlet, take one's life in one's hands, put one's ass *or* life on the line <nf>

11 **outbrave, outdare; outface,** face down, face out; **outbrazen,** brazen out; **outlook, outstare,** stare down, stare out <Brit>, stare out of countenance

12 **steel oneself, get up nerve,** nerve oneself, muster *or* summon up *or* gather courage, pluck up heart, screw up one's nerve *or* courage, stiffen one's backbone <nf>

13 **take courage, take heart,** pluck up courage, take heart of grace; **brace** *or* **buck up** <nf>

14 keep up one's courage, bear up, **keep one's chin up** <nf>, keep one's pecker up <Brit nf>, **keep a stiff upper lip** <nf>, hold up one's head, take what comes; hang in *or* hang in there *or* hang tough *or* stick it out <nf>, stick to one's guns, grin and bear it

15 **encourage, hearten, embolden, nerve,** pat *or* clap on the back, **assure, reassure,** bolster, support, cheer on, root for; **inspire,** inspirit; incite, exhort; buck *or* brace up <nf>; put upon one's mettle, make a man of; cheer 109.7

ADJS 16 **courageous, plucky, brave, bold, valiant, valorous, gallant, intrepid,** doughty, **hardy,** stalwart, stout, stouthearted, ironhearted, lionhearted, greathearted, bold-spirited, bold as a lion; **heroic,** herolike; **chivalrous,** chivalric, knightly, knightlike, soldierly, soldierlike; **manly,** manful, virile, macho

17 **resolute, tough, game; spirited,** spiritful, red-blooded, **mettlesome;** bulldoggish, tenacious, pertinacious

18 <nf terms> **ballsy,** gutsy, gutty, nervy, stand-up, dead game, gritty, spunky, nervy

19 **unafraid, unfearing, unfearful; unapprehensive,** undiffident; **confident** 970.21; **fearless, dauntless,** aweless, dreadless, **unfrightened,** unscared, unalarmed, unterrified; **untimid,** untimorous, unshy, unbashful

20 **undaunted, undismayed,** uncowed, unintimidated, unappalled, unabashed, unawed; **unflinching, unshrinking,** unquailing, unbowed, uncringing, unwincing, unblenching, unblinking

21 **daring, audacious,** overbold; **adventurous, venturous, venturesome,** adventuresome, enterprising; foolhardy 493.9

ADVS **22 courageously, bravely, boldly, heroically, valiantly,** valorously, **gallantly, intrepidly,** doughtily, stoutly, hardily, stalwartly; **pluckily, spunkily** <nf>, gutsily <nf>, **resolutely, gamely,** tenaciously, pertinaciously, bulldoggishly, **fearlessly,** unfearingly, unfearfully; **daringly,** audaciously; chivalrously, knightly, yeomanly; like a man, like a soldier

493 RASHNESS

NOUNS **1 rashness, brashness,** brazen boldness, **incautiousness,** overboldness, **imprudence, indiscretion,** injudiciousness, improvidence; irresponsibility; **unwariness,** unchariness; overcarelessness; overconfidence, oversureness, overweeningness; **impudence,** insolence 142; **gall** *and* brass *and* cheek *and* chutzpah <nf>; hubris; **temerity,** temerariousness; heroics

2 recklessness, devil-may-careness; heedlessness, **carelessness** 340.2; **impetuousness** 365.2, impetuosity, hotheadedness; **haste** 401, **hastiness,** hurriedness, overeagerness, overzealousness, overenthusiasm; **furiousness,** desperateness, wantonness, wildness, wild oats; frivolity; **precipitateness,** precipitousness, precipitance, precipitancy, precipitation

3 foolhardiness, harebrainedness; **audacity,** audaciousness; more guts than brains <nf>, *courage fou* <Fr>; forwardness, boldness, **presumption,** presumptuousness; **daring,** daredeviltry, daredevilry, fire-eating; playing with fire, flirting with death, courting disaster, stretching one's luck, going for broke <nf>, brinkmanship, tightrope walking, funambulism; adventurousness

4 daredevil, devil, **madcap,** madbrain, wild man, hotspur, hellcat, rantipole, harumscarum *and* fire-eater <nf>; **adventurer,** adventuress, adventurist; brazen-face

VERBS **5** be rash, be reckless, carry too much sail, sail too near the wind, throw caution to the wind, go out of one's depth, go too far, go to sea in a sieve, take a leap in the dark, buy a pig in a poke, count one's chickens before they are hatched, catch at straws, lean on a broken reed, put all one's eggs in one basket, live in a glass house; go out on a limb <nf>, leave oneself wide open <nf>, drop one's guard, stick one's neck out *and* ask for it <nf>

6 court danger, ask for it, ask for trouble, mock *or* defy danger, go in harm's way, thumb one's nose at the consequences, **tempt fate** *or* **the gods** *or* **S,** tweak the devil's nose, bell the cat, play a desperate game, ride for a fall; play with fire, flirt

with death, stretch one's luck, march up to the cannon's mouth, put one's head in a lion's mouth, beard the lion in his den, sit on a barrel of gunpowder, sleep on a volcano, play Russian roulette, playing with a loaded pistol *or* gun, working without a net; risk all, go for broke *and* shoot the works <nf>

ADJS **7 rash, brash, incautious,** overbold, **imprudent, indiscreet,** injudicious, improvident; ill-considered; irresponsible; **unwary, unchary;** overcareless; overconfident, oversure, overweening, **impudent,** insolent, brazenfaced, brazen; hubristic; temerarious

8 reckless, devil-may-care; careless 340.11; **impetuous,** hotheaded; **hasty** 401.9, hurried, overeager, overzealous, overenthusiastic; **furious,** desperate, mad, wild, wanton, harum-scarum <nf>; precipitate, **precipitous, precipitant; headlong, breakneck;** slapdash, slap-bang; accident-prone; asking for it

9 foolhardy, harebrained, madcap, **wild,** wild-ass <nf>, madbrain, madbrained; **audacious;** forward, bold, **presumptuous; daring,** daredevil, risk-taking, fire-eating, death-defying; adventurous; frivolous, flippant

ADVS **10 rashly, brashly, incautiously, imprudently, indiscreetly,** injudiciously, improvidently; **unwarily,** uncharily; overconfidently, overweeningly, **impudently,** insolently, **brazenly,** hubristically, temerariously

11 recklessly, happen what may; heedlessly, **carelessly** 340.18; **impetuously,** hotheadedly; **hastily,** hurriedly, overeagerly, overzealously, overenthusiastically; **furiously,** desperately, wildly, wantonly, **madly,** like mad *or* crazy *and* like there was no tomorrow <nf>; **precipitately,** precipitiously, precipitantly; **headlong,** headfirst, headforemost, **head over heels,** heels over head, *à corps perdu* <Fr>; slapdash, slap-bang *or* slam-bang <nf>; helter-skelter, ramble-scramble <nf>, hurry-scurry, holus-bolus

12 foolhardily, daringly, audaciously, presumptuously, harebrainedly

494 CAUTION

NOUNS **1 caution, cautiousness;** slowness to act *or* commit oneself *or* make one's move; **care, heed, solicitude; carefulness, heedfulness,** mindfulness, regardfulness, thoroughness; paying mind *or* attention; **guardedness;** uncommunicativeness 344; **gingerliness, tentativeness,** hesitation, hesitancy, unprecipitateness; slow *and* careful steps, deliberate stages, wait-and-see attitude *or* policy; **prudence,** prudentialness, **circumspection,** discretion, canniness <Scot>; **coolness, judiciousness** 920.7; calculation, **deliberateness,** deliberation, careful consideration, prior consultation; **safeness,** safety first, no room for error; **hedge, hedging,** hedging one's bets, cutting one's losses; designated driver

2 **wariness, chariness, cageyness** *and* **leeriness** <nf>; **suspicion,** suspiciousness; **distrust,** distrustfulness, mistrust, mistrustfulness; reticence, skepticism, second thoughts, reservation

3 **precaution,** precautiousness; **forethought, foresight,** foresightedness, forehandedness, forethoughtfulness; **providence,** provision, nest egg, forearming; precautions, steps, measures, steps and measures, preventive measure *or* step; **safeguard,** protection 1008, preventive measure, safety net, safety valve, sheet anchor; **insurance;** rainy-day policy; lemon law

4 **overcaution, overcautiousness, overcarefulness,** overwariness; unadventurousness

VERBS 5 **be cautious, be careful;** think twice, give it a second thought; make haste slowly, take it easy *or* slow <nf>; put the right foot forward, take one step at a time, pick one's steps, go step by step, feel one's ground *or* way; pussyfoot, tiptoe, go *or* walk on tiptoe, walk on eggs *or* eggshells *or* thin ice; pull *or* draw in one's horns; doubt, have second thoughts

6 **take precautions, take steps** *or* **measures,** take steps and measures; **prepare** *or* **provide for** *or* **against,** forearm; **guard against, make sure against,** make sure; **play safe** <nf>, anticipate; keep on the safe side; leave no stone unturned, forget *or* leave out nothing, overlook no possibility, leave no room *or* margin for error, leave nothing to chance, consider every angle; **look before one leaps;** see how the land lies *or* the wind blows, see how the cat jumps <nf>; clear the decks, batten down the hatches, shorten sail, reef down, tie in *or* tuck in *or* take in a reef, get out a sheet-anchor, have an anchor to windward; hedge, provide a **hedge,** hedge one's bets, cut one's losses; take out insurance; keep something for a rainy day; provide for

7 **beware, take care, have a care,** take heed, take heed at one's peril; keep at a respectful distance, keep out of harm's way; mind, mind one's business; **be on one's guard,** be on the watch *or* lookout, be on the *qui vive*; **look out, watch out** <nf>; **look sharp,** keep one's eyes open, keep a weather eye out *or* open <nf>, keep one's eye peeled <nf>, **watch one's step** <nf>, look about one, look over one's shoulder, keep tabs on <nf>; stop, look, and listen; not stick one's neck out <nf>, not go out on a limb <nf>, not expose oneself, not be too visible, **keep a low profile,** lie low, stay in the background, blend with the scenery; not blow one's cover <nf>; hold one's tongue 51.5

ADJS 8 **cautious, careful,** heedful, mindful, alert, regardful, **thorough; prudent, circumspect,** slow to act *or* commit oneself *or* make one's move, noncommittal, uncommitted; canny <Scot>; sly, crafty, scheming; **discreet, politic, judicious** 920.19, Polonian, Macchiavelian; unadventurous, no-risk, unenterprising, undaring; **gingerly; guarded,** on guard, on one's guard; uncommunicative 344.8; **tentative,** hesitant, unprecipitate, cool; **deliberate;** safe, on the safe side, leaving no stone unturned, forgetting *or* leaving out nothing, overlooking no possibility, leaving no room *or* margin for error

9 **wary, chary, cagey** <nf>, **leery** <nf>, **suspicious,** suspecting, **distrustful,** mistrustful, shy; guarded, on guard; cautionary

10 **precautionary,** precautious, precautional; **preventive,** preemptive, prophylactic; **forethoughtful,** forethoughted, **foresighted,** foreseeing, forehanded; **provident,** provisional; anticipatory

11 **overcautious, overcareful,** overwary, unadventurous

ADVS 12 **cautiously, carefully,** heedfully, mindfully, regardfully; **prudently, circumspectly,** cannily, pawkily <Brit>, **discreetly,** judiciously; **gingerly,** guardedly, easy <nf>, with caution, with care

13 **warily, charily,** cagily <nf>; **askance,** askant, suspiciously, leerily <nf>, distrustfully

INTERJS 14 careful!, be careful!, **take care!,** have a care!, **look out!, watch out!, watch your step!,** watch it!, take heed!, steady!, look sharp!, easy!, take it easy!, easy does it!, go easy!

495 FASTIDIOUSNESS

NOUNS 1 **fastidiousness, particularity,** particularness; **scrupulousness,** scrupulosity; punctiliousness, punctilio, spit and polish; preciseness, precision; **meticulousness, conscientiousness,** criticalness; taste 496; **sensitivity, discrimination** 944, discriminatingness, discriminativeness; **selectiveness,** selectivity, pickiness <nf>, choosiness; **strictness** 339.3, **perfectionism,** precisianism, **purism; puritanism, priggishness, prudishness, prissiness** <nf>, propriety, straitlacedness, censoriousness, judgmentalness

2 **finicalness,** finickiness, finickingness, finicality; **fussiness,** pernicketiness *or* persnicketiness <nf>; squeamishness, queasiness

3 **nicety,** niceness, **delicacy,** delicateness, daintiness, exquisiteness, fineness, refinement, **subtlety**

4 overfastidiousness, **overscrupulousness, overparticularity, overconscientiousness,** overmeticulousness, overniceness, **overnicety; overcriticalness,** hypercriticism, hairsplitting; overrefinement, oversubtlety, supersubtlety; oversquamishness, oversensitivity, hypersensitivity, morbid sensibility

5 **exclusiveness,** exclusivity, selectness, selectiveness, selectivity; **cliquishness,** clannishness; **snobbishness,** snobbery, snobbism; quiddity

6 **perfectionist,** precisian, precisianist, stickler, nitpicker <nf>, captious critic 946.7

7 **fussbudget, fusspot** <nf>, fuss, fusser, **fuddy-duddy** <nf>, granny, old woman, old maid; Mrs Grundy

VERBS 8 **be hard to please,** want everything just so, **fuss,** fuss over; pick *and* choose; **turn up one's nose,** look down one's nose, disdain, scorn, spurn; not dirty *or* soil one's hands

ADJS 9 **fastidious, particular, scrupulous, meticulous, conscientious,** exacting, precise, punctilious, spit-and-polish; **sensitive, discriminating** 944.7, discriminative; **selective,** picky <nf>, choosy, choicy <nf>; critical; **strict** 339.12, perfectionistic, precisianistic, puristic; puritanic, puritanical, priggish, prudish, prissy, proper, strait-laced, censorious, judgmental

10 **finical, finicky,** finicking, finikin; **fussy,** fuss-budgety <nf>; **squeamish,** pernickety *and* persnickety <nf>, difficult, hard to please

11 **nice, dainty, delicate,** *délicat* <Fr>, picture-perfect, fine, refined, exquisite, **subtle**

12 **overfastidious,** queasy, **overparticular, overscrupulous, overconscientious,** overmeticulous, **overnice,** overprecise; **overcritical,** hypercritical, ultracritical, hairsplitting; overrefined, oversubtle, supersubtle; oversquamish, oversensitive, hypersensitive, morbidly sensitive; **compulsive,** anal, anal-compulsive

13 **exclusive,** selective, **select,** elect, elite; **cliquish,** clannish; **snobbish,** snobby; quiddative

ADVS 14 **fastidiously, particularly, scrupulously, meticulously, conscientiously,** critically, punctiliously; discriminatingly, discriminatively, selectively; **finically,** finickily, finickingly; **fussily; squeamishly,** queasily; refinedly, subtly

496 TASTE, TASTEFULNESS

NOUNS 1 **taste, good taste,** sound critical judgment, discernment *or* appreciation of excellence, preference for the best, *goût raffiné* <Fr>; **tastefulness,** quality, excellence, choiceness, **elegance,** grace, gracefulness, gracility, graciousness, graciosity, gracious living; propriety; **refinement,** finesse, **polish, culture, cultivation,** civilizedness, refined *or* cultivated *or* civilized taste, finish; niceness, nicety, delicacy, daintiness, **subtlety, sophistication; discrimination** 944, fastidiousness 495; acquired taste, connoisseurship, "caviare to the general"—Shakespeare; etiquette

2 **decorousness, decorum,** decency, properness, propriety, rightness, right thinking, **seemliness,** becomingness, fittingness, fitness, appropriateness, suitability, meetness, happiness, felicity; gentility, genteelness; civility, urbanity 504.1

3 **restraint,** restrainedness, **understatement,** unobtrusiveness, quietness, subduedness, quiet taste; simplicity 499.1; subtlety

4 aesthetic *or* **artistic taste,** virtuosity, virtu, **expertise,** expertism, connoisseurship; dilettantism; fine art of living; epicurism, epicureanism; gastronomy, *friandise* <Fr>; aesthetics

5 **aesthete,** person of taste, lover of beauty

6 **connoisseur,** *connaisseur* <Fr>, *cognoscente* <Ital>; **judge,** good judge, **critic, expert,** authority, maven <nf>, arbiter, arbiter of taste, *arbiter elegantiarum* <L>, tastemaker, trend-setter; **epicure,** epicurean; **gourmet, gourmand,** *bon vivant* <Fr>, good *or* refined palate; oenophile, wine lover; virtuoso; dilettante, amateur; culture vulture <nf>; collector; gentleperson

ADJS 7 **tasteful, in good taste,** in the best taste; excellent, of quality, of the best, of the first water; **aesthetic,** artistic, pleasing, well-chosen, choice, of choice; pure, chaste; classic *or* classical, Attic, restrained, understated, unobtrusive, conservative, quiet, subdued, simple, low-key, unaffected 499.7

8 **elegant,** graceful, gracile, gracious; **refined, polished, cultivated,** civilized, **cultured;** nice, fine, delicate, dainty, **subtle, sophisticated, discriminating** 944.7, fastidious 495.9, sensitive, U <nf>

9 **decorous,** decent, proper, right, right-thinking, **seemly, becoming,** fitting, appropriate, suitable, meet, happy, felicitous; genteel; civil, urbane 504.14

ADVS 10 **tastefully, with taste,** in good taste, in the best taste; aesthetically, artistically; elegantly, gracefully; decorously, genteelly, decently, properly, seemly, becomingly; quietly, unobtrusively; simply 499.10

497 VULGARITY

NOUNS **1 vulgarity,** vulgarness, vulgarism, commonness, meanness; **inelegance** or **inelegancy, indelicacy, impropriety, indecency, indecorum,** indecorousness, unseemliness, unbecomingness, unfittingness, inappropriateness, unsuitableness, unsuitability; ungentility; **untastefulness,** tastelessness, unaestheticness, unaestheticism, tackiness; low or bad or poor taste, *mauvais goût* <Fr>; vulgar taste, bourgeois taste, Babbittry, philistinism; popular taste, pop culture and pop <nf>; campiness, camp, high or low camp; baseness, kitsch

2 coarseness, grossness, *grossièreté* <Fr>, **rudeness, crudeness,** crudity, **crassness,** rawness, roughness, **earthiness;** ribaldness, ribaldry; raunchiness <nf>, **obscenity** 666.4; meretriciousness, **loudness** <nf>, **gaudiness** 501.3

3 unrefinement, uncouthness, uncultivation, uncultivatedness, unculturedness; uncivilizedness, wildness; impoliteness, incivility, ill breeding 505.1; **barbarism,** barbarousness, barbarity, philistinism, Gothicism; **savagery,** savagism; **brutality,** brutishness, bestiality, animality, **mindlessness;** Neanderthalism, troglodytism

4 boorishness, churlishness, carlishness, **loutishness,** lubberliness, lumpishness, cloddishness, clownishness, yokelism; ruffianism, rowdyism, hooliganism; parvenuism, arrivism, upstartness; roughness

5 commonness, commonplaceness, ordinariness, homeliness; **lowness, baseness, meanness; ignobility,** plebeianism

6 vulgarian, low or vulgar or ill-bred fellow, mucker <nf>, guttersnipe <nf>, *épicier* <Fr>; Babbitt, Philistine, bourgeois; *parvenu* and *arriviste* and *nouveau riche* <Fr>, upstart; bounder <nf>, cad, **boor,** churl, clown, **lout,** yahoo, redneck <nf>, looby, peasant, groundling, yokel; rough, **ruffian,** roughneck <nf>, **rowdy,** hooligan; vulgarist, ribald; guttermouth; rascal, rapscallion; vulgus, hoi polloi, rabble, riffraff, great unwashed, scum, huddled masses

7 barbarian, savage, Goth, animal, brute; Neanderthal, troglodyte

8 vulgarization, coarsening; popularization; *haute vulgarisation* <Fr>; dumbing down <nf>

VERBS **9** vulgarize, coarsen; popularize; dumb down <nf>; **pander;** commercialize

ADJS **10 vulgar, inelegant, indelicate, indecorous, indecent, improper, unseemly,** unbeseeming, unbecoming, unfitting, inappropriate, unsuitable, **ungenteel,** undignified, discourteous; **untasteful,** tasteless, in bad or poor taste, tacky and chintzy and Mickey Mouse <nf>, gauche, garish; **offensive,** offensive to gentle ears

11 coarse, gross, rude, crude, crass, raw, rough, **earthy;** ribald; raunchy <nf>, **obscene** 666.9; meretricious, **loud** <nf>, **gaudy** 501.20; cacological, solecistic

12 unrefined, unpolished, uncouth, unkempt, uncombed, unlicked; **uncultivated, uncultured; uncivilized,** noncivilized; impolite, uncivil, ill-bred 505.6; **wild,** untamed; **barbarous,** barbaric, barbarian, infra dig; outlandish, Gothic; primitive; **savage, brutal,** brutish, bestial, animal, **mindless;** Neanderthal, troglodytic; wild-and-woolly, rough-and-ready

13 boorish, churlish, carlish, **loutish,** redneck <nf>, lubberly, lumpish, cloddish, clownish, loobyish, yokelish; rowdy, **rowdyish, ruffianly,** roughneck <nf>, hooliganish, raffish, raised in a barn

14 common, commonplace, ordinary; plebeian; homely, homespun; **general, public, popular,** pop <nf>; vernacular; Babbittish, Philistine, bourgeois; campy, high-camp, low-camp, kitschy

15 low, base, mean, ignoble, vile, scurvy, sorry, scrubby, beggarly; low-minded, base-minded

ADVS **16 vulgarly, uncouthly, inelegantly,** indelicately, indecorously, indecently, improperly, unseemly, untastefully, offensively; **coarsely, grossly, rudely, crudely,** crassly, roughly; ribaldly

498 ORNAMENTATION

NOUNS **1 ornamentation, ornament; decoration,** decor; **adornment, embellishment,** embroidery, elaboration; nonfunctional addition or adjunct; garnish, garnishment, garniture; trimming, trim; flourish; emblazonment, emblazonry; illumination; **color,** color scheme, color pattern, color compatibility, color design, color arrangement; **arrangement,** flower arrangement, floral decoration, furniture arrangement; table setting or decoration; window dressing; **interior decoration** or decorating, room decoration, interior design; feng shui; **redecoration, refurbishment** 396.4, redoing

2 ornateness, elegance, fanciness, fineness, **elaborateness; ostentation** 501; richness, luxuriousness, luxuriance; **floweriness,** floridness, floridity; dizenment <old>, **bedizenment; gaudiness, flashiness** 501.3; flamboyance or flamboyancy, chi-chi; **overelegance,** overelaborateness, overornamentation, busyness; clutteredness; baroqueness, baroque, rococo, arabesque, moresque, chinoiserie

3 finery, frippery, gaudery, gaiety, bravery, trumpery, folderol, trickery, chiffon, trappings, festoons, superfluity; **frills,** frills and furbelows, bells and whistles *and* gimmickry *and* Mickey Mouse *and* glitz <nf>, **frillery,** frilling, frilliness; foofaraw <nf>, fuss <nf>, froufrou; gingerbread; tinsel, clinquant, pinchbeck, paste; gilt, gilding

4 trinket, gewgaw, **knickknack** *or* nicknack, knack <old>, **gimcrack,** kickshaw, doodad, whim-wham, **bauble,** fribble, bibelot, toy, gaud; bric-a-brac; sequin

5 jewelry, bijouterie, ice <nf>; costume jewelry, glass, paste, junk jewelry <nf>; bling *or* bling-bling <nf>

6 jewel, bijou, **gem,** stone, precious stone; rhinestone; pin, brooch, stickpin, breastpin, scatter pin, chatelaine; cuff-link, tie clasp *or* clip, tie bar, tiepin *or* scarfpin, tie tack *or* tie tac; **ring,** band, wedding band, engagement ring, promise ring, mood ring, signet ring, school *or* class ring, circle, earring, nose ring; bracelet, wristlet, wristband, armlet, anklet; chain, necklace, torque; locket; beads, chaplet, wampum; bangle; charm; fob; crown, coronet, diadem, tiara; laurel

7 motif, ornamental motif, **figure, detail,** form, touch, repeated figure; **pattern, theme,** design, ornamental theme, ornamental *or* decorative composition; foreground detail, background detail; **background,** setting, foil, **style,** ornamental *or* decorative style, national style, **period style**

VERBS **8 ornament, decorate, adorn, dress, trim, garnish,** array, **deck,** bedeck, dizen <old>, bedizen; prettify, **beautify; redecorate,** refurbish, redo; gimmick *or* glitz *or* sex up <nf>; **embellish, furbish,** embroider, enrich, grace, set off *or* out, paint, color, blazon, emblazon, paint in glowing colors; **dress up; spruce up** *and* gussy up *and* doll up *and* fix up <nf>, **primp up,** prink up, prank up, trick up *or* out, deck out, bedight <old>, fig out; primp, prink, prank, preen; smarten, smarten up, dandify, titivate, give a face lift

9 figure, filigree; **spangle, bespangle;** bead; tinsel; jewel, bejewel, gem, diamond; pavé; ribbon, beribbon; flounce; flower, garland, wreathe; feather, plume; flag; illuminate; paint 35.14; engrave

ADJS **10 ornamental, decorative,** adorning, embellishing

11 ornamented, adorned, decorated, embellished, bedecked, decked out, tricked out, garnished, trimmed, dizened <old>, bedizened; figured; flowered; festooned, befrilled, wreathed; spangled, bespangled, spangly; jeweled, bejeweled; beaded; studded; plumed, feathered; beribboned

12 ornate, elegant, fancy, fine, chichi, pretty-pretty; picturesque; **elaborate,** overornamented, overornate, overelegant, etc, labored, high-wrought; **ostentatious** 501.18; glitzy, flashy; **rich, luxurious,** luxuriant; **flowery,** florid; flamboyant, fussy, frilly, frilled, flouncy, gingerbread *or* gingerbready; **overelegant,** overelaborate, overlabored, overworked, overwrought, overornamented, busy; cluttered; **baroque,** rococo, arabesque, moresque, gilded; gimmicked-*or* glitzed- *or* sexed-up <nf>

499 PLAINNESS

<unaffectedness>

NOUNS **1 plainness, simplicity** 798, **simpleness, ordinariness, commonness, commonplaceness,** homeliness, prosaicness, prosiness, matter-of-factness; **purity,** chasteness, classic *or* classical purity, Attic simplicity

2 naturalness, inartificiality; **unaffectedness,** unassumingness, **unpretentiousness;** directness, straightforwardness; innocence, naïveté, chasteness

3 unadornment, unembellishment, unadornedness, unornamentation; **no frills,** no nonsense, back-to-basics; **uncomplexity,** uncomplication, uncomplicatedness, **unsophistication,** unadulteration; bareness, baldness, nakedness, nudity, starkness, undress, beauty unadorned

4 inornateness, unelaborateness, unfanciness, unfussiness; **austerity,** severity, starkness, Spartan simplicity

VERBS **5 simplify** 798.4; chasten, restrain, purify; put in words of one syllable, spell out

ADJS **6 simple** 798.6, **plain, ordinary, nondescript, common, commonplace, prosaic,** prosy, **matter-of-fact, homely, homespun,** everyday, vanilla <nf>, conventional, workday, workaday, household, garden, common- *or* garden-variety; pure, **pure and simple,** chaste, classic *or* classical, Attic

7 natural, native; **inartificial,** unartificial; **unaffected, unpretentious,** unpretending, unassuming, unfeigning, direct, straightforward, honest, candid; innocent, naive

8 unadorned, undecorated, unornamented, unembellished, ungarnished, unfurbished, unvarnished, untrimmed; olde *and* olde-worlde <nf>; back-to-basics, no-frills, no-nonsense, vanilla *or* plain-vanilla *and* white-bread *or* white-bready <nf>; back-to-nature; **uncomplex,** uncomplicated, **unsophisticated,** unadulterated; **undressed,** undecked, unarrayed; bare, bald, blank, naked, nude

9 inornate, unornate, **unelaborate,** unfancy, unfussy; austere, monkish, cloistral, severe, stark, Spartan

ADVS **10 plainly, simply,** ordinarily, commonly, commonplacely, prosaically, matter-of-factly

11 unaffectedly, naturally, unpretentiously, unassumingly, directly, straightforwardly

500 AFFECTATION

NOUNS **1 affectation, affectedness; pretension, pretense, airs,** pretentiousness, putting on airs, put-on <nf>; **show, false show,** mere show; front, false front <nf>, **facade,** mere facade, **image,** public image; feigned belief, **hypocrisy** 354.6; la-di-da <nf>, phoniness <nf>, sham 354.3; artificiality, unnaturalness, insincerity; prunes *and* prisms, airs *and* graces; stylishness, mannerism

2 mannerism, *minauderie* <Fr>, **trick of behavior,** trick, **quirk,** habit, peculiarity, peculiar trait, idiosyncrasy, trademark

3 posing, pose, posturing, attitudinizing, attitudinarianism; peacockery, peacockishness; pompousness; putting on airs

4 foppery, foppishness, dandyism, coxcombry, puppyism, conceit

5 overniceness, overpreciseness, **overrefinement, elegance,** exquisiteness, preciousness, preciosity; goody-goodyism *and* goody-goodness <nf>; purism, formalism, formality, pedantry, precisionism, precisianism; euphuism; euphemism

6 prudery, prudishness, prissiness, priggishness, primness, smugness, stuffiness <nf>, old-maidishness, **straitlacedness,** stiff-neckedness, hidebound, narrowness, censoriousness, sanctimony, sanctimoniousness, **puritanism,** puritanicalness; **false modesty,** overmodesty, demureness, *mauvaise honte* <Fr>

7 phony *and* **fake** *and* **fraud** <nf> 354.13; affecter; mannerist; **pretender,** actor, playactor <nf>, performer; paper tiger, hollow man, straw man, man of straw, empty suit <nf>

8 poser, poseur, striker of poses, **posturer,** posturist, posture maker, attitudinarian, attitudinizer, bluffer

9 dandy, fop, coxcomb, macaroni, gallant, dude *and* swell *and* sport <nf>, ponce *and* toff <Brit nf>, exquisite, blood, fine gentleman, puppy, jackanapes, jack-a-dandy, fribble, clotheshorse, fashion plate; beau, Beau Brummel, spark, blade, ladies' man, lady-killer <nf>, masher, cocksman <nf>; man-about-town, boulevardier

10 fine lady, *grande dame* and *précieuse* <Fr>; belle, toast

11 prude, prig, priss, puritan, bluenose, goody-goody <nf>, goody two-shoes, wowser <Brit nf>, old maid; Victorian, mid-Victorian

VERBS **12 affect, assume, put on,** assume *or* put on airs, wear, **pretend, simulate, counterfeit, sham, fake** <nf>, **feign,** make out like <nf>, make a show of, play, playact <nf>, act *or* play a part, play a scene, do a bit <nf>, put up a front <nf>, dramatize, histrionize, show off, play to the gallery, lay it on thick <nf>, overact, ham *and* ham it up *and* chew up the scenery *and* emote <nf>, tug at the heartstrings

13 pose, posture, attitudinize, peacock, strike a pose, strike an attitude, pose for effect

14 mince, mince it, prink <Brit nf>; **simper,** smirk, bridle

ADJS **15 affected, pretentious,** la-di-da, posy <Brit nf>; mannered, *maniéré* <Fr>; **artificial, unnatural,** insincere; theatrical, stagy, histrionic; overdone, overacted, hammed up <nf>

16 assumed, put-on, pretended, simulated, **phony** *and* **fake** *and* **faked** <nf>, feigned, counterfeited; spurious, sham; deceptive, specious; hypocritical

17 foppish, dandified, dandy, coxcombical, conceited, chichi, pompous

18 <affectedly nice> overnice, overprecise, precious, *précieuse* <Fr>, exquisite, **overrefined, elegant,** mincing, simpering, namby-pamby; **goody-goody** *and* goody good-good <nf>; puristic, formalistic, pedantic, precisionistic, precisian, precisianistic, euphuistic, euphemistic

19 prudish, priggish, prim, prissy, smug, stuffy <nf>, old-maidish, **overmodest,** demure, **straitlaced,** stiff-necked, hide-bound, narrow, censorious, po-faced <Brit>, sanctimonious, **puritanical,** Victorian, mid-Victorian

ADVS **20 affectedly, pretentiously;** elegantly, mincingly; for effect, for show

21 prudishly, priggishly, primly, smugly, stuffily <nf>, straitlacedly, stiffneckedly, puritanically

501 OSTENTATION

NOUNS **1 ostentation,** ostentatiousness, ostent; **pretentiousness, pretension, pretense;** loftiness, lofty affectations, **triumphalism**

2 pretensions, vain pretensions; **airs,** lofty airs, airs *and* graces, vaporing, highfalutin *or* highfaluting ways <nf>, side, swank <nf>, delusions of grandeur

3 showiness, flashiness, flamboyance, panache, dash, jazziness <nf>, jauntiness, sportiness <nf>, gaiety, glitter, glare, dazzle, dazzlingness; extravaganza; **gaudiness,** gaudery, glitz *and* gimmickry *and* razzmatazz *and* razzledazzle <nf>, **tawdriness,** meretriciousness; gorgeousness, colorfulness; loudness <nf>, **blatancy,** flagrancy, shamelessness, brazenness, luridness, extravagance, sensationalism, obtrusiveness, vulgarness, crudeness, extravagation

4 display, show, demonstration, manifestation, **exhibition, parade,** *étalage* <Fr>; **pageantry,** pageant, **spectacle,** gala; vaunt, fanfaronade, blazon, flourish, flaunt, flaunting; daring, brilliancy, éclat, bravura, flair; dash *and* splash *and* splurge <nf>; figure; showmanship, **exhibitionism,** showing-off, fuss and feathers; theatrics, histrionics, dramatics, staginess, camp; false front, **sham** 354.3

5 grandeur, grandness, grandiosity, **magnificence,** gorgeousness, **splendor,** splendidness, splendiferousness, resplendence, brilliance, glory; nobility, proudness, **state, stateliness, majesty;** impressiveness, imposingness; **sumptuousness, elegance, elaborateness, lavishness, luxuriousness;** ritziness *or* poshness *or* plushness *or* swankness *or* swankiness <nf>; **luxury,** barbaric *or* Babylonian splendor

6 pomp, circumstance, pride, **state,** solemnity, formality; **pomp and circumstance,** "pride, pomp, and circumstance"—Shakespeare; heraldry

7 pompousness, pomposity, pontification, pontificality, **stuffiness** <nf>, **self-importance,** inflation; grandiloquence, bombast, turgidity, orotundity

8 swagger, strut, swank <nf>, bounce, brave show; swaggering, strutting; swash, **swashbucklery,** swashbuckling, swashbucklering; peacockishness, peacockery

9 stuffed shirt <nf>, blimp <nf>, Colonel Blimp; bloated aristocrat

10 strutter, swaggerer, swanker <Brit>, swash, swasher, **swashbuckler,** peacock, miles gloriosus

11 show-off <nf>, **exhibitionist,** flaunter; **grandstander** *or* grandstand player *or* hot dog *or* **hotshot** *or* showboat <nf>

VERBS **12 put** *or* **thrust oneself forward,** come forward, step to the front *or* fore, step into the limelight, take center stage, attract attention, make oneself conspicuous

13 cut a dash, make a show, put on a show, make one's mark, cut a swath, cut *or* **make a figure;** make a splash *or* a **splurge** <nf>; splurge *and* splash <nf>; shine, glitter, glare, dazzle

14 give oneself airs, put on airs, put on, put on side, put on the dog <nf>, put up a front <nf>, put on the ritz *and* ritz it <nf>, look big, **swank** <nf>, swell, swell it, act the grand seigneur; pontificate, play the pontiff

15 strut, swagger, swank <Brit>, prance, stalk, peacock, swash, swashbuckle

16 show off <nf>, **grandstand** *and* hotdog *and* showboat <nf>, play to the gallery *or* galleries <nf>, please the crowd, ham it up; exhibit *or* parade one's wares <nf>, strut one's stuff <nf>, go through one's paces, show what one has

17 flaunt, vaunt, **parade, display, demonstrate,** manifest, make a great show of, **exhibit,** air, put forward, put forth, hold up, flash *and* sport <nf>; advertise; **flourish,** brandish, wave; dangle, dangle before the eyes; emblazon, blazon forth; trumpet, trumpet forth

ADJS **18 ostentatious, pretentious,** posy <Brit nf>; **ambitious,** vaunting, **lofty, highfalutin** *and* highfaluting <nf>, **high-flown,** high-flying; **high-toned,** tony <nf>, **fancy,** classy *or* glitzy *or* flossy <nf>; Gatsbyesque

19 showy, flaunting, flashy, snazzy, flashing, glittering, **jazzy** *and* **glitzy** *and* gimmicky *and* splashy *and* splurgy <nf>; camp; exhibitionistic, showoffy <nf>, bravura; **gay,** jaunty, rakish, **dashing;** gallant, brave, daring; **sporty** *or* dressy <nf>; **frilly, flouncy,** frothy, chichi

20 gaudy, tawdry; gorgeous, colorful; **garish, loud** <nf>, **blatant, flagrant,** shameless, **brazen,** brazenfaced, lurid, extravagant, sensational, **spectacular,** glaring, flaring, flaunting, screaming <nf>, obtrusive, vulgar, crude; meretricious, low-rent *and* low-ride *and* tacky <nf>

21 grandiose, grand, magnificent, splendid, splendiferous, splendacious <nf>, **glorious,** superb, fine, superfine, fancy, superfancy, swell <nf>; **imposing, impressive,** larger-than-life, awful, awe-inspiring, awesome; **noble, proud, stately, majestic,** princely; **sumptuous, elegant, elaborate, luxurious,** luxuriant, extravagant, deluxe; executive *and* plush *and* posh *and* ritzy *and* swank *and* swanky <nf>, Corinthian; palatial, Babylonian

22 pompous, stuffy <nf>, **self-important,** impressed with oneself, pontific, pontifical; **inflated, swollen,** bloated, tumid, turgid, flatulent, gassy <nf>, stilted; grandiloquent, **bombastic** 545.9; solemn 111.3, formal

23 strutting, swaggering; swashing, **swashbuckling,** swashbucklering; peacockish, peacocky; too big for one's britches

24 theatrical, theatric, stagy, dramatic, histrionic; spectacular

ADVS **25 ostentatiously, pretentiously, loftily;** with flourish of trumpet, with beat of drum, with flying colors

26 showily, flauntingly, flashily, with a flair, glitteringly; gaily, jauntily, **dashingly;** gallantly, bravely, daringly

27 gaudily, tawdrily; gorgeously, colorfully; **garishly, blatantly, flagrantly,** shamelessly, **brazenly,** brazenfacedly, luridly, sensationally, **spectacularly,** glaringly, flaringly, obtrusively

28 **grandiosely, grandly, magnificently, splendidly,** splendiferously, splendaciously <nf>, gloriously, superbly; nobly, proudly, majestically; imposingly, impressively; **sumptuously, elegantly,** elaborately, luxuriously, **extravagantly;** palatially

29 **pompously, pontifically,** stuffily <nf>, **self-importantly;** stiltedly; **bombastically** 545.12

502 BOASTING

NOUNS 1 boasting, bragging, vaunting; **boastfulness, braggadocio, braggartism; boast, brag,** vaunt; side, bombast, bravado, vauntery, fanfaronade, blowing-off or blowing or tooting one's own horn <nf>, gasconade, gasconism, rodomontade, fanfaronade; bluster, swagger 503.1; vanity, conceit 140.4; jactation, jactitation; heroics

2 <nf terms> **big talk,** fine talk, fancy talk, tall talk, highfalutin or highfaluting, **hot air,** gas, bunk, bunkum, **bullshit;** tall story, fish story; bragging rights

3 **self-approbation,** self-praise, self-laudation, self-gratulation, self-applause, self-boosting, self-puffery, self-vaunting, self-advertising, self-advertisement, self-adulation, self-glorification, self-dramatizing, self-dramatization, self-promoting, self-promotion; **vainglory,** vaingloriousness

4 **crowing,** exultation, elation, triumph, jubilation; **gloating**

5 **braggart, boaster,** brag, braggadocio, exaggerator, hector, fanfaron, Gascon, gasconader, miles gloriosus; **blowhard** and blower and big mouth and bullshitter and bullshit artist and hot-air artist and gasbag and windbag and big bag of wind and windjammer and windy <nf>; blusterer 503.2, panjandrum; Texan, Fourth-of-July orator; Braggadocchio <Spenser>, Captain Bobadil <Ben Jonson>, Thraso <Terence>, Parolles <Shakespeare>; swashbuckler, rushbuckler

VERBS 6 boast, brag, make a boast of, vaunt, flourish, gasconade, vapor, puff, draw the longbow, advertise oneself, **blow one's own trumpet, toot one's own horn,** sing one's own praises, exaggerate one's own merits; bluster, swagger 503.3; speak for Buncombe

7 <nf terms> **blow,** blow off, mouth off, **blow hard, talk big,** sound off, blow off and toot or blow one's own horn, **bullshit,** shoot the shit, spread oneself, lay it on thick, brag oneself up

8 **flatter oneself,** conceit oneself, **congratulate oneself,** hug oneself, shake hands with oneself, form a mutual admiration society with oneself,

pat oneself on the back, take merit to oneself; think one's shit doesn't stink <nf>

9 **exult,** triumph, glory, delight, joy, jubilate; **crow** or crow over, crow like a rooster or cock; gloat, gloat over

ADJS 10 boastful, boasting, braggart, bragging, thrasonical, thrasonic, big-mouthed <nf>, vaunting, vaporing, gasconading, Gascon, fanfaronading, fanfaron; vain, pompous, conceited 140.11; **vainglorious**

11 **self-approving,** self-approbatory, self-praising, self-gratulating, self-boosting, self-puffing, self-adulating, self-adulatory, self-glorifying, self-glorying, self-glorious, self-lauding, self-laudatory, self-congratulatory, self-applauding, self-flattering, self-vaunting, self-advertising, self-dramatizing, self-promoting

12 **inflated, swollen, windy** and gassy <nf>, **bombastic,** high-swelling, **high-flown, highfalutin** and highfaluting <nf>, **pretentious,** extravagant, big, tall <nf>, hyped <nf>

13 **crowing,** exultant, exulting, elated, elate, jubilant, **triumphant, flushed,** cock-a-hoop, in high feather; **gloating**

ADVS 14 boastfully, boastingly, braggingly, vauntingly, vaingloriously; **self-approvingly,** self-praisingly, etc

15 **exultantly,** exultingly, elatedly, jubilantly, triumphantly, triumphally, in triumph; **gloatingly**

503 BLUSTER

NOUNS 1 bluster, blustering, hectoring, bullying, **swagger,** swashbucklery, side; **bravado,** rant, rodomontade, fanfaronade; sputter, splutter; fuss, bustle, fluster, flurry; bluff, bluster and bluff; intimidation 127.6; **boastfulness** 502.1

2 **blusterer, swaggerer,** swasher, swashbuckler, fanfaron, bravo, **bully,** bullyboy, bucko, roisterer, cock of the walk, vaporer, blatherskite <nf>; ranter, raver, hectorer, hector, Herod; slanger <Brit>; bluff, bluffer; **braggart** 502.5

VERBS 3 bluster, hector; **swagger,** swashbuckle; bully; bounce, vapor, roister, rollick, gasconade, kick up a dust <nf>; sputter, splutter; rant, rage, rave, rave on, storm, "out herod Herod"—Shakespeare; slang <Brit>; bluff, bluster and bluff, put up a bluff <nf>; intimidate; shoot off one's mouth, sound off, bogart <nf>, **brag** 502.6

ADJS 4 blustering, blustery, blusterous, hectoring, **bullying, swaggering,** swashing, swashbuckling, boisterous, roisterous, roistering, rollicking; ranting, raging, raving, storming; tumultuous; noisy, "full of sound and fury"—Shakespeare

504 COURTESY

NOUNS **1 courtesy,** courteousness, common courtesy, **politeness, civility,** *politesse* <Fr>, amenity, agreeableness, urbanity, comity, affability; graciousness, **gracefulness;** complaisance; **thoughtfulness, considerateness** 143.3, **tactfulness,** tact, consideration, **solicitousness, solicitude; respect,** respectfulness, deference; civilization, quality of life

2 gallantry, gallantness, **chivalry,** chivalrousness, knightliness; courtliness, courtly behavior *or* politeness; *noblesse oblige* <Fr>

3 manneliness, manners, good manners, excellent *or* exquisite manners, good *or* polite deportment, good *or* polite behavior, *bienséance* <Fr>; *savoir-faire* and *savoir-vivre* <Fr>; decency; correctness, correctitude, **etiquette** 580.3

4 good breeding, breeding; refinement, finish, polish, culture, cultivation; gentility, gentleness, genteelness, elegance; gentlemanliness, gentlemanlikeness, ladylikeness

5 suavity, suaveness, smoothness, smugness, blandness; **unctuousness,** oiliness, oleaginousness, smarm *or* smarminess <nf>; **glibness,** slickness <nf>, fulsomeness; sweet talk, fair words, soft words *or* tongue, sweet *or* honeyed words *or* tongue, incense; soft soap *and* butter <nf>

6 courtesy, civility, amenity, urbanity, attention, polite act, act of courtesy *or* politeness, graceful gesture, pleasantry; old-fashioned courtesy *or* civility, courtliness

7 amenities, courtesies, civilities, gentilities, graces, elegancies; dignities; formalities, ceremonies, rites, rituals, observances

8 regards, compliments, respects, *égards* and *devoirs* <Fr>; **best wishes,** one's best, good wishes, best regards, kind *or* kindest regards, love, best love; greetings 585.3; remembrances, kind remembrances; compliments of the season

9 gallant, cavalier, chevalier, **knight**

10 "the very pink of courtesy"—Shakespeare, "the very pineapple of politeness"—R B Sheridan

VERBS **11 mind one's manners,** mind one's P's and Q's <nf>; keep a civil tongue in one's head; mend one's manners; observe etiquette, observe *or* follow protocol; be polite, be considerate

12 extend courtesy, do the honors, pay one's respects, make one's compliments, present oneself, pay attentions to, do service, wait on *or* upon

13 give one's regards *or* **compliments** *or* love, give one's best regards, give one's best, send one's regards *or* compliments *or* love; wish one joy, wish one luck, bid Godspeed

ADJS **14 courteous, polite, civil, urbane, gracious,** graceful, agreeable, affable, fair; complaisant; obliging, accommodating; **thoughtful, considerate,** tactful, solicitous; respectful, deferential, attentive

15 gallant, chivalrous, chivalric, knightly; **courtly; formal,** ceremonious; old-fashioned, old-world

16 mannerly, well-mannered, good-mannered, **well-behaved,** well- *or* fair-spoken; **correct,** correct in one's manners *or* behavior; housebroken <nf>

17 well-bred, highbred, **well-brought-up; cultivated, cultured, polished, refined, genteel,** gentle; gentlemanly, gentlemanlike, ladylike

18 suave, smooth, smug, bland, **glib, unctuous,** oily, oleaginous, smarmy <nf>, soapy *and* buttery <nf>, fulsome, ingratiating, disarming; suave-spoken, fine-spoken, fair-spoken, soft-spoken, smooth-spoken, smooth-tongued, oily-tongued, honey-tongued, honey-mouthed, sweet-talking

ADVS **19 courteously, politely, civilly,** urbanely, mannerly; **gallantly, chivalrously,** courtly, knightly; **graciously,** gracefully, with a good grace; complaisantly, complacently; out of consideration *or* courtesy; obligingly, accommodatingly; respectfully, attentively, deferentially

505 DISCOURTESY

NOUNS **1 discourtesy,** discourteousness; **impoliteness,** unpoliteness; **rudeness, incivility,** inurbanity, gall, **ungraciousness, ungallantness,** uncourtesy, uncourtliness, ungentlemanliness, **unmannerliness,** mannerlessness, bad *or* ill manners, **ill breeding,** conduct unbecoming a gentleman, caddishness; inconsiderateness, inconsideration, unsolicitousness, unsolicitude, tactlessness, **insensitivity; grossness, crassness,** gross *or* crass behavior, **boorishness, vulgarity, coarseness, crudeness,** offensiveness, loutishness, nastiness

2 disrespect, disrespectfulness 156.1; **insolence** 142; criminal contempt

3 gruffness, brusqueness, *brusquerie* <Fr>, **curtness,** shortness, sharpness, abruptness, bluntness, brashness; **harshness,** roughness, severity; truculence, aggressiveness; **surliness,** crustiness, bearishness, beastliness, churlishness, crustiness

ADJS **4 discourteous,** uncourteous; **impolite,** unpolite, inurbane; **rude, uncivil, ungracious, ungallant,** uncourtly, inaffable, uncomplaisant, unaccommodating; disrespectful; **insolent;** impertinent

5 unmannerly, unmannered, mannerless, **ill-mannered, ill-behaved,** ill-conditioned, bad-mannered

6 **ill-bred, ungenteel,** ungentle, caddish; **ungentlemanly,** ungentlemanlike; **unladylike,** unfeminine; **vulgar, boorish, unrefined** 497.12, **inconsiderate, unsolicitous, tactless, insensitive; gross,** offensive, crass, **coarse, crude,** loutish, nasty

7 **gruff, brusque, curt,** short, sharp, snippy <nf>, abrupt, **blunt,** bluff, brash, cavalier; **harsh,** rough, severe; truculent, aggressive; **surly,** crusty, bearish, beastly, churlish; vituperative

ADVS 8 **discourteously, impolitely, rudely,** uncivilly, ungraciously, ungallantly, ungenteelly, caddishly; inconsiderately, unsolicitously, tactlessly, insensitively

9 **gruffly, brusquely, curtly,** shortly, sharply, snippily <nf>, abruptly, bluntly, bluffly, brashly, cavalierly; harshly, crustily, bearishly, churlishly, **boorishly,** nastily

506 RETALIATION

NOUNS 1 **retaliation, reciprocation,** exchange, interchange, give-and-take; **retort, reply,** return, comeback <nf>; counter, counterblow, counterstroke, counterblast, counterpunch, recoil, boomerang, backlash

2 **reprisal, requital, retribution; recompense, compensation** 338, **reward,** comeuppance <nf>, desert, deserts, **just deserts,** what is merited, what is due *or* condign, what's coming to one *and* a dose of one's own medicine <nf>; quittance, return of evil for evil; **revenge** 507; **punishment** 604

3 **tit for tat, measure for measure,** like for like, quid pro quo, something in return, blow for blow, a Roland for an Oliver, a game two can play, **an eye for an eye,** a tooth for a tooth, "eye for eye, tooth for tooth, hand for hand, foot for foot"—Bible, law of retaliation *or* equivalent retaliation, *lex talionis* <L>, talion; game at which two can play

VERBS 4 **retaliate, retort,** counter, **strike back,** hit back at <nf>, give in return; **reciprocate,** give in exchange, give *and* take; **get** *or* **come back at** <nf>, turn the tables upon; fight fire with fire, return the compliment

5 **requite,** quit, make requital *or* reprisal *or* retribution, get satisfaction, recompense, compensate, make restitution, indemnify, reward, redress, make amends, **repay,** pay, **pay back,** pay off; **give one his comeuppance** <nf>, give one his desserts *or* just desserts, serve one right, give one what is coming to him <nf>

6 **give in kind,** cap, match, give as good as one gets *or* as was sent; repay in kind, **pay one in one's own coin** *or* **currency, give one a dose of one's own medicine** <nf>; return the like, return the compliment; return like for like, **return evil for** evil; return blow for blow, **give one tit for tat,** give a quid pro quo, give as good as one gets, give measure for measure, give *or* get an eye for an eye *and* a tooth for a tooth, follow *or* observe the *lex talionis*

7 **get even with** <nf>, even the score, **settle** *or* **settle up with, settle** *or* **square accounts** *and* settle the score *and* fix <nf>, pay off old scores, pay back in full measure, be *or* make quits; fix one's wagon <nf>, **take revenge** 507.4; **punish** 604.10

ADJS 8 **retaliatory,** retaliative; **retributive,** retributory; reparative, compensatory, restitutive, recompensing, recompensive, reciprocal; punitive; recriminatory, like for like; revengeful, vindictive

ADVS 9 **in retaliation, in exchange,** in reciprocation; **in return,** in reply; **in requital, in reprisal,** in retribution, in reparation, in amends; **in revenge,** *en revanche* <Fr>

PHRS 10 what goes around comes around, one's chickens come home to roost; the shoe is on the other foot

507 REVENGE

NOUNS 1 **revenge, vengeance, avengement,** sweet revenge, getting even, evening of the score; **wrath;** revanche, revanchism; **retaliation, reprisal** 506.2; vendetta, feud, blood feud; the wrath of God

2 **revengefulness, vengefulness, vindictiveness,** rancor, grudgefulness, irreconcilableness, unappeasableness, implacableness, implacability

3 **avenger, vindicator;** revanchist; Nemesis, the Furies, the Erinyes, the Eumenides

VERBS 4 **revenge, avenge, take** *or* **exact revenge,** have one's revenge, wreak one's vengeance; **retaliate, even the score, get even with** 506.7; launch a vendetta

5 **harbor revenge,** breathe vengeance; have accounts to settle, have a crow to pick *or* pluck *or* pull with; nurse one's revenge, brood over, dwell on *or* upon, keep the wound open, wave the bloody shirt

6 **reap** *or* **suffer** *or* **incur vengeance** *or* revenge; sow the wind and reap the whirlwind; live by the sword and die by the sword

ADJS 7 **revengeful, vengeful,** avenging; **vindictive,** vindicatory; revanchist; **punitive,** punitory, **wrathful,** rancorous, grudgeful, irreconcilable, unappeasable, implacable, unwilling to forgive and forget, unwilling to let bygones be bygones; **retaliatory** 506.8

508 RIDICULE

NOUNS 1 **ridicule, derision, mockery, raillery,** rallying, chaffing; panning *and* razzing *and* roasting *and* ragging <nf>, **scoffing, jeering, sneering,** snickering, sniggering, smirking, grinning, leering, fleering, snorting, levity, flippancy, smartness, smart-aleckiness *and* joshing <nf>, fooling, japery, twitting, taunting, booing, hooting, catcalling, hissing; **banter** 490

2 **gibe, scoff, jeer,** fleer, flout, mock, barracking <Brit>, **taunt, twit,** quip, jest, jape, put-on *and* leg-pull <nf>, foolery; **insult** 156.2; scurrility, caustic remark; **cut,** cutting remark, verbal thrust; gibing retort, rude reproach, short answer, back answer, comeback <nf>, parting shot, Parthian shot

3 **boo,** booing, **hoot, catcall; Bronx cheer** *and* **raspberry** *and* razz <nf>; **hiss, hissing,** the bird <nf>

4 scornful laugh *or* smile, snicker, snigger, **smirk,** sardonic grin, leer, fleer, **sneer,** snort

5 **sarcasm, irony, cynicism, satire,** satiric wit *or* humor, invective, innuendo; causticity 144.8

6 **burlesque, lampoon,** squib, **parody, satire, farce,** mockery, imitation, wicked imitation *or* pastiche, takeoff <nf>, black humor, **travesty, caricature**

7 **laughingstock,** jestingstock, gazingstock, derision, mockery, **figure of fun,** byword, byword of reproach, jest, joke, **butt,** target, stock, goat <nf>, toy, game, **fair game,** victim, dupe, fool, everybody's fool, monkey, mug <Brit nf>

VERBS 8 **ridicule, deride,** ride <nf>, make a laughingstock *or* a mockery of; roast <nf>, **insult** 156.5; **make fun** *or* game of, **poke fun at,** make merry with, put one on *and* pull one's leg <nf>; **laugh at,** laugh in one's face, grin at, smile at, snicker *or* snigger at; **laugh to scorn,** hold in derision, laugh out of court, hoot down; point at, point the finger of scorn; pillory

9 **scoff, jeer,** gibe, barrack <Brit>, **mock, revile, rail at, rally,** chaff, **twit, taunt,** jape, flout, scout, have a fling at, cast in one's teeth; cut at; jab, jab at, dig at, take a dig at; pooh, **pooh-pooh;** sneer, **sneer at,** fleer, curl one's lip

10 **boo, hiss, hoot,** catcall, give the raspberry *or* Bronx cheer <nf>, razz, give the bird <nf>, whistle at

11 **burlesque, lampoon, satirize, parody, caricature,** travesty, hit *or* take off on

ADJS 12 **ridiculing, derisive,** derisory; **mocking,** railing, rallying, chaffing; panning *and* razzing *and* roasting *and* ragging <nf>, **scoffing,** jeering, sneering, snickering, sniggering, smirky, smirking, grinning, leering, fleering, snorting, flippant, smart, smart-alecky *and* smart-ass *and* wise-ass <nf>; joshing *and* jiving <nf>, fooling, japing, twitting, taunting, booing, hooting, catcalling, hissing, bantering, kidding, teasing, quizzical

13 **satiric, satirical; sarcastic, ironic, ironical, sardonic, cynical,** Rabelaisian, dry; caustic

14 **burlesque, farcical, broad,** slapstick; parodic, caricatural, macaronic, doggerel

ADVS 15 **derisively, mockingly, scoffingly,** jeeringly, sneeringly, "with scoffs and scorns and contumelious taunts"—Shakespeare

509 APPROVAL

NOUNS 1 **approval, approbation; sanction,** acceptance, countenance, **favor; admiration, esteem, respect** 155; endorsement, support, backing, vote, favorable vote, yea vote, yea, voice, adherence, blessing, seal of approval, nod *or* nod of approval, wink, stamp of approval, **OK** 332.4, rubber stamp, green light, go-ahead, thumbs up

2 **applause,** plaudit, éclat, **acclaim, acclamation; popularity;** clap, handclap, **clapping,** handclapping, clapping of hands; **cheer** 116.2; burst of applause, peal *or* thunder of applause; **round of applause, hand, big hand; ovation,** standing ovation; encore

3 **commendation,** good word, acknowledgment, recognition, appreciation; boost *and* buildup <nf>; **puff,** promotion; citation, accolade, kudos; good review; **blurb** *and* **plug** *and* promo *and* hype <nf>; honorable mention

4 **recommendation,** recommend <Brit nf>, letter of recommendation; **advocacy,** advocating, advocation, patronage; **reference, credential,** letter of reference, voucher, **testimonial;** character reference, character, certificate of character, good character; letter of introduction

5 **praise,** bepraisement; **laudation,** laud; **glorification,** glory, exaltation, extolment, magnification, **honor; eulogy,** éloge *and* hommage <Fr>, eulogium; **encomium,** accolade, kudos, panegyric; paean; **tribute,** homage, meed of praise; congratulation 149.1; flattery 511; overpraise, excessive praise, idolizing, idolatry, deification, apotheosis, adulation, lionizing, hero worship

6 **compliment,** polite commendation, complimentary *or* flattering remark, flattery, pat on the back, stroke <nf>; **bouquet** *and* posy <nf>, trade-last <old nf>

7 **praiseworthiness, laudability,** laudableness, commendableness, estimableness, meritoriousness, exemplariness, admirability

8 commender, eulogist, eulogizer; **praiser,** lauder, laudator, extoller, encomiast, panegyrist, **booster** <nf>, puffer, promoter, champion; plugger *and* tout *and* touter <nf>; **applauder,** claqueur <Fr>; claque; rooter *and* fan *and* buff <nf>, adherent; admirer; appreciator; **flatterer** 138.3, 511.4, fan club

VERBS 9 approve, approve of, think well of, take kindly to; **sanction, accept; admire, esteem, respect** 155.4; endorse, bless, sign off on <nf>, OK 332.12; countenance, keep in **countenance;** hold with, uphold; **favor,** be in favor of, view with favor, take kindly to

10 applaud, acclaim, hail; clap, clap one's hands, give a hand *or* big hand, have *or* hear a hand *or* big hand for, hear it for <nf>; **cheer** 116.6; root for <nf>, cheer on; encore; cheer *or* applaud to the very echo; huzzah; raise the roof <nf>

11 commend, speak well *or* **highly of,** speak in high terms of, speak warmly of, have *or* say a good word for; boost *and* give a boost to <nf>, puff, promote, cry up; plug *and* tout *and* hype; pour *or* spread *or* lay it on thick <nf>; **recommend, advocate,** put in a word *or* good word for, support, back, lend one's name *or* support *or* backing to, make a pitch for <nf>; condone, bless

12 praise, bepraise, talk one up <nf>; **laud,** belaud; **eulogize,** panegyrize, pay tribute, salute, hand it to one <nf>; **extol, glorify,** magnify, exalt, bless; cry up, blow up, puff, puff up; boast of, brag about <nf>, make much of; celebrate, emblazon, sound *or* resound the praises of, ring one's praises, sing the praises of, trumpet, hype <nf>; praise to the skies, *porter aux nues* <Fr>; flatter 511.5; overpraise, praise to excess, idolize, deify, apotheosize, adulate, lionize, hero-worship; put on a pedestal

13 espouse, join *or* associate oneself with, take up, take for one's own; **campaign for, crusade for,** put on a drive for, take up the cudgels for, push for <nf>; carry the banner of, march under the banner of; beat the drum for, thump the tub for; lavish oneself on, fight the good fight for; devote *or* dedicate oneself to, spend *or* give *or* sacrifice oneself for

14 compliment, pay a compliment, make one a compliment, give a bouquet *or* posy <nf>, say something nice about; hand it to *and* have to hand it to <nf>, pat on the back, take off one's hat to, doff one's cap to, congratulate 149.2

15 meet with approval, find favor with, **pass muster,** recommend itself, do credit to; redound to the honor of; ring with the praises of

ADJS 16 approbatory, approbative, commendatory, complimentary, laudatory, acclamatory, felicitous, eulogistic, panegyric, panegyrical, encomiastic, **appreciative, appreciatory; admiring, regardful, respectful** 155.8; flattering 511.8

17 approving, favorable, favoring, in favor of, **pro,** well-disposed, well-inclined, supporting, backing, **advocating;** promoting, promotional; touting *and* puffing *and* hyping <nf>; recommending

18 uncritical, uncriticizing, **uncensorious,** unreproachful; overpraising, overappreciative, unmeasured *or* excessive in one's praise, idolatrous, adulatory, lionizing, hero-worshiping, fulsome; knee-jerk <nf>

19 approved, favored, backed, advocated, supported; favorite; **accepted,** received, admitted; **recommended,** bearing the seal of approval, highly touted <nf>, **admired** 155.11, **applauded,** well-thought-of, in good odor, **acclaimed,** cried up; **popular;** given a blessing

20 praiseworthy, worthy, **commendable,** estimable, **laudable,** admirable, meritorious, creditable; exemplary, model, unexceptionable; deserving, well-deserving; beyond all praise, *sans peur et sans reproche* <Fr>; **good** 999.12,13

PREPS 21 in favor of, for, pro, all for

INTERJS 22 bravo!, bravissimo!, **well done!,** *¡ole!* <Sp>, *bene!* <Ital>, hear, hear!, aha!; hurrah!; **good!,** fine!, excellent!, whizzo! <Brit>, great!, beautiful!, swell!, good for you!, good enough!, not bad!, now you're talking!; way to go, attaboy!, attababy!, attagirl!, attagal!, good boy!, good girl!; that's the idea!, that's the ticket!; encore!, bis!, take a bow!, three cheers!, one cheer more!, **congratulations!** 149.4

23 hail!, all hail!, *ave!* <L>, *vive!* <Fr>, *viva!* or *evviva!* <Ital>, live live!, long life to!, glory be to!, honor be to!

510 DISAPPROVAL

NOUNS 1 disapproval, disapprobation, disfavor, disesteem, disrespect 156; dim view, poor *or* low opinion, low estimation, adverse judgment; **displeasure,** distaste, **dissatisfaction,** discontent, discontentment, discontentedness, disgruntlement, indignation, **unhappiness;** doghouse <nf>; disillusion, disillusionment, disenchantment, disappointment; disagreement, **opposition** 451, opposure; rejection, thumbs-down, exclusion, ostracism, blackballing, blackball, ban; **complaint, protest,** objection, **dissent** 333

2 deprecation, discommendation, dispraise, denigration, disvaluation; **ridicule** 508; depreciation, disparagement 512; **contempt** 157

3 censure, reprehension, stricture, reprobation, **blame, denunciation,** denouncement, decrying, decrial, bashing *and* trashing <nf>, impeachment, arraignment, indictment, **condemnation,** damnation, fulmination, anathema; castigation, flaying, skinning alive <nf>, fustigation, excoriation; pillorying

4 criticism, adverse criticism, harsh *or* hostile criticism, flak <nf>, bad notices, bad press, panning, brickbat, animadversion, imputation, reflection, **aspersion,** stricture, obloquy; **knock** *and* **swipe** *and* **slam** *and* **rap** *and* hit <nf>, roasting <nf>, home thrust; minor *or* petty criticism, niggle, cavil, quibble, exception, nit <nf>; **censoriousness,** reproachfulness, priggishness; **faultfinding,** taking exception, carping, caviling, pettifogging, quibbling, captiousness, niggling, nitpicking, pestering, nagging; hypercriticism, hypercriticalness, overcriticalness, hairsplitting, trichoschistism

5 **reproof,** reproval, reprobation, a flea in one's ear; **rebuke, reprimand, reproach,** reprehension, **scolding, chiding,** rating, **upbraiding,** objurgation; **admonishment, admonition; correction,** castigation, chastisement, spanking, rap on the knuckles; lecture, lesson, sermon; **disrecommendation,** low rating, adverse report, wolf ticket

6 <nf terms> piece *or* bit of one's mind, **talking-to,** speaking-to, roasting, raking-down, **raking-over,** raking over the coals, dressing, dressing-down, set-down; **bawling-out,** cussing-out, **calling-down,** jacking-up, going-over, chewing-out, chewing, reaming-out, reaming, ass-chewing, ass-reaming, what-for, ticking-off

7 **berating,** rating, tongue-lashing; **revilement, vilification,** blackening, **execration, abuse, vituperation,** invective, contumely, hard *or* cutting *or* bitter words; **tirade, diatribe,** jeremiad, screed, philippic; **attack, assault,** onslaught, assailing; **abusiveness; acrimony**

8 **reproving look,** dirty *or* nasty look <nf>, black look, frown, scowl, glare; hiss, boo; Bronx cheer *or* raspberry <nf>

9 **faultfinder,** disapprover, *frondeur* <Fr>, momus, basher *and* tracher *and* boo-bird <nf>; **critic** 946.7, criticizer, **nitpicker** <nf>, smellfungus, belittler, censor, censurer, castigator, carper, caviler, quibbler, pettifogger, detractor, cynic; **scold,** common scold; kvetch, **complainer** 108.3

VERBS 10 **disapprove, disapprove of,** not approve, raise an objection, go *or* side against, go contra; **disfavor, view with disfavor, raise one's eyebrows, frown at** *or* **on,** look black upon, look askance at, make a wry face at, grimace at, **turn up one's nose at,** shrug one's shoulders at; **take a dim view of** <nf>, not think much of, think ill of, think little of, have no respect for, have a low opinion of, not take kindly to, not hold with, hold no brief for *and* not sign off on <nf>; not hear of, not go for *and* not get all choked up over *and* be turned off by <nf>; not want *or* have any part of, wash one's hands of, dissociate oneself from; **object to,** take exception to; **oppose** 451.3, set

oneself against, set one's face *or* heart against; **reject,** categorically reject, disallow, not hear of; **turn thumbs down on** *and* thumb down <nf>, vote down, veto, frown down, exclude, ostracize, blackball, ban; say no to, shake one's head at; **dissent from, protest, object** 333.4,5; turn over in one's grave

11 **discountenance,** not countenance, **not tolerate,** not brook, not condone, not suffer, not abide, not endure, not bear with, not put up with, **not stand for** <nf>

12 **deprecate,** discommend, dispraise, disvalue, not be able to say much for, denigrate, **fault,** faultfind, find fault with, put down <nf>, pick at *or* on, pick holes in, pick to pieces; **ridicule** 508.8; **depreciate, disparage** 512.8; **hold in contempt,** disdain, **despise** 157.3

13 **censure,** reprehend; **blame,** lay *or* cast blame upon; **bash** *and* trash *and* rubbish <nf>; **reproach,** impugn; **condemn,** damn, take out after; damn with faint praise; fulminate against, anathematize, anathemize, put on the Index; **denounce,** denunciate, **accuse** 599.7,9, **decry,** cry down, impeach, arraign, indict, call to account, exclaim *or* declaim *or* inveigh against, peg away at, cry out against, cry out on *or* upon, cry shame upon, raise one's voice against, raise a hue *and* cry against, shake up <old>; reprobate, hold up to reprobation; animadvert on *or* upon, reflect upon, cast reflection upon, cast a reproach *or* slur upon, complain against; throw a stone at, cast *or* throw the first stone

14 **criticize; pan** *and* **knock** *and* **slam** *and* hit *and* rap *and* take a rap *or* swipe at <nf>, snipe at, strike out at, tie into *and* tee off on *and* rip into *and* open up on *and* plow into <nf>; belittle

15 **find fault,** take exception, fault-find, pick holes, cut up, **pick** *or* **pull** *or* tear apart, pick *or* pull *or* **tear to pieces; tear down, carp, cavil,** quibble, **nitpick,** pick nits, pettifog, catch at straws

16 **nag,** niggle, **carp at, fuss at, fret at,** yap *or* pick at <nf>, peck at, nibble at, **pester, henpeck, pick on** <nf>, bug *and* hassle <nf>

17 **reprove, rebuke, reprimand,** reprehend, put a flea in one's ear, **scold, chide,** rate, **admonish, upbraid,** objurgate, have words with, take a hard line with; **lecture,** read a lesson *or* lecture to; **correct,** rap on the knuckles, **chastise,** spank, turn over one's knees; **take to task,** call to account, bring to book, call on the carpet, read the riot act, give one a tongue-lashing, tonguelash; take down, set down, set straight, straighten out

18 <nf terms> **call down** *or* **dress down, speak** *or* **talk to, tell off,** tell a thing *or* two, pin one's ears back, **give a piece** *or* **bit of one's mind, rake** *or* **haul over**

the coals, rake up one side *and* down the other, give it to, let one have it, let one have it with both barrels, trim, come down on *or* down hard on, jump on *or* all over *or* down one's throat; give one a hard time *or* what for; **bawl out,** give a bawling out, chew, **chew out,** chew ass, ream, ream out, ream ass, cuss out, jack up, sit on *or* upon, lambaste, give a going-over, tell where to get off; give the deuce *or* devil, give hell, give hail Columbia

19 **berate,** rate, betongue, jaw <nf>, clapper-claw <nf>, **tongue-lash, rail at,** rag, thunder *or* fulminate against, rave against, yell at, bark *or* yelp at; **revile, vilify,** blacken, **execrate, abuse,** vituperate, load with reproaches

20 <*criticize or reprove severely*> **attack, assail; castigate, flay,** skin alive <nf>, lash, slash, excoriate, fustigate, scarify, scathe, **roast** <nf>, scorch, blister, trounce; lay into <nf>

ADJS 21 **disapproving, disapprobatory,** unapproving, turned-off, **displeased, dissatisfied,** less than pleased, discontented, disgruntled, indignant, **unhappy;** disillusioned, disenchanted, disappointed; **unfavorable,** low, poor, **opposed** 451.8, **opposing, con,** against, agin <nf>, dead set against, death on, down on, **dissenting** 333.6; **uncomplimentary;** unappreciative

22 **condemnatory, censorious,** censorial, damnatory, **denunciatory, reproachful,** blameful, reprobative, objurgatory, po-faced <Brit>, priggish, judgmental; deprecative, deprecatory; **derisive, ridiculing, scoffing** 508.12; **depreciative, disparaging** 512.13; **contemptuous** 157.8; invective, inveighing; reviling, vilifying, blackening, execrating, execrative, execratory, abusive, vituperative

23 **critical, faultfinding,** carping, picky *and* nitpicky <nf>, caviling, quibbling, pettifogging, captious, cynical; nagging, niggling; hypercritical, ultracritical, overcritical, hairsplitting, trichoschistic; abusive

24 **unpraiseworthy, illaudable; uncommendable,** discommendable, not good enough; objectionable, exceptionable, unacceptable, not to be thought of, beyond the pale

25 **blameworthy,** blamable, to blame, at fault, much at fault; **reprehensible,** censurable, reproachable, reprovable, open to criticism *or* reproach; **culpable,** chargeable, impeachable, accusable, indictable, arraignable, imputable

ADVS 26 **disapprovingly, askance,** askant, **unfavorably;** censoriously, critically, reproachfully, rebukingly; captiously

INTERJS 27 **God forbid!,** Heaven forbid!, Heaven forfend!, forbid it Heaven!; by no means!, not for the world!, not on your life!, over my dead body!, not if I know it!, nothing doing!, no way!, *and* no way José! <nf>, perish the thought!, I'll be hanged *or* damned if!, **shame!,** for shame!, tuttut!

511 FLATTERY

NOUNS 1 **flattery, adulation; praise** 509.5; **blandishment,** palaver, **cajolery,** cajolement, wheedling, inveiglement; **blarney** *and* bunkum *and* **soft soap** *and* soap *or* butter salve <nf>, oil, grease, eyewash <nf>; strokes *and* stroking *and* ego massage <nf>, sweet talk, fair *or* sweet *or* honeyed words, soft *or* honeyed phrases, incense, pretty lies, sweet nothings; trade-last <old nf>, **compliment** 509.6; ass-kissing <nf>, ingratiation, **fawning, sycophancy** 138.2

2 **unction,** "that flattering unction"—Shakespeare; **unctuousness,** oiliness, sliminess; slobber, gush, smarm *and* smarminess <nf>; flattering tongue; insincerity 354.5

3 **overpraise,** overprizing, excessive praise, overcommendation, overlaudation, overestimation; idolatry 509.5

4 **flatterer,** *flatteur* <Fr>, adulator, courtier; **cajoler, wheedler; backslapper,** back-scratcher, yes-man, bootlicker; blarneyer *and* soft-soaper <nf>; ass-kisser <nf>, brown-noser, **sycophant** 138.3

VERBS 5 **flatter,** adulate, conceit; **cajole,** wheedle, **blandish,** palaver; slaver *or* slobber over, beslobber, beslubber; oil the tongue, lay the flattering unction to one's soul, make fair weather; **praise, compliment** 509.14, praise to the skies; scratch one's back, kiss ass <nf>, fawn upon 138.9

6 <nf terms> **soft-soap,** butter, honey, **butter up,** soften up; stroke <nf>, massage the ego <nf>; **blarney,** jolly, pull one's leg; lay it on <nf>, pour *or* spread *or* lay it on thick *or* with a trowel <nf>, overdo it, soap, oil; string along, kid along; play up to, get around; suck up to

7 **overpraise,** overprize, overcommend, overlaud; overesteem, overestimate, overdo it, protest too much; idolize 509.12, put on a pedestal; puff

ADJS 8 **flattering, adulatory; complimentary** 509.16; **blandishing, cajoling, wheedling,** blarneying *and* soft-soaping <nf>; fair-spoken, fine-spoken, smooth-spoken, smooth-tongued, **mealymouthed,** honey-mouthed, honey-tongued, honeyed, oily-tongued; fulsome, slimy, slobbery, gushing, protesting too much, smarmy <nf>, insinuating, oily, buttery <nf>, soapy <nf>, soft-soaping <nf>, **unctuous,** smooth, bland; insincere, hypocritical, tongue-in-cheek; courtly, courtierly; **fawning, sycophantic, obsequious**

512 DISPARAGEMENT

NOUNS **1 disparagement, faultfinding, depreciation, detraction,** deprecation, derogation, bad-mouthing *and* running down *and* knocking *and* putting down <nf>, **belittling;** sour grapes; slighting, minimizing, faint praise, lukewarm support, discrediting, decrying, decrial; **disapproval** 510; **contempt** 157; indignity, disgrace, comedown <nf>

2 defamation, malicious defamation, defamation of character, smear campaign, injury of *or* to one's reputation; **vilification,** revilement, defilement, blackening, denigration; smear, character assassination, *ad hominem* <L> *or* personal attack, name-calling, smear word; **muckraking, mudslinging**

3 slander, scandal, libel, traducement; calumny, calumniation; backbiting, cattiness *and* bitchiness <nf>

4 aspersion, slur, **remark, reflection,** imputation, **insinuation,** suggestion, sly suggestion, innuendo, whispering campaign; disparaging *or* uncomplimentary remark; poison-pen letter, hatchet job

5 lampoon, send-up <nf>, take-off, pasquinade, ridicule, pasquin, pasquil, squib, lampoonery, **satire,** malicious parody, **burlesque** 508.6; caricature

6 disparager, depreciator, decrier, detractor, basher *and* trasher *and* boo-bird <nf>, belittler, debunker, deflater, slighter, derogator, **knocker** <nf>, hatchet man; **slanderer,** libeler, defamer, backbiter; calumniator, traducer; **muckraker, mudslinger,** social critic; **cynic,** railer, Thersites, "A man who knows the price of everything, and the value of nothing"—Oscar Wilde

7 lampooner, lampoonist, **satirist,** pasquinader; poison-pen writer

VERBS **8 disparage, depreciate, belittle,** slight, minimize, make little of, degrade, debase, **run** *or* **knock down** <nf>, **put down** <nf>, sell short; **discredit,** bring into discredit, reflect discredit upon, disgrace; detract from, derogate from, cut down to size <nf>; **decry,** cry down; speak ill of; speak slightingly of, not speak well of; disapprove of 510.10; hold in contempt 157.3; submit to indignity *or* disgrace, bring down, bring low

9 defame, malign, bad-mouth *and* poor-mouth <nf>; **asperse, cast aspersions on,** cast reflections on, injure one's reputation, damage one's good name, give one a black eye <nf>; **slur,** cast a slur on, do a number *or* a job on <nf>, tear down

10 vilify, revile, defile, sully, soil, smear, smirch, besmirch, bespatter, tarnish, **blacken,** denigrate, blacken one's good name, give a black eye <nf>; **call names,** give a bad name, give a dog a bad name, stigmatize 661.9; **muckrake, throw mud at,** mudsling, heap dirt upon, drag through the mud *or* the gutter; engage in personalities

11 slander, libel; calumniate, traduce; stab in the back, backbite, speak ill of behind one's back

12 lampoon, satirize, pasquinade; parody, send up <nf>, take off; dip the pen in gall, **burlesque** 508.11

ADJS **13 disparaging, derogatory,** derogative, **depreciatory,** depreciative, deprecatory, slighting, belittling, minimizing, detractory, pejorative, back-biting, catty *and* bitchy <nf>, contumelious, contemptuous, derisive, derisory, ridiculing 508.12; **snide,** insinuating; censorious; **defamatory,** vilifying, **slanderous, scandalous, libelous;** calumnious, calumniatory; **abusive,** scurrilous, scurrile <old>

513 CURSE

NOUNS **1 curse, malediction,** malison, damnation, denunciation, commination, imprecation, execration; blasphemy; anathema, fulmination, thundering, excommunication; ban, proscription; hex, evil eye, *malocchio* <Ital>, jinx, whammy *or* double whammy <nf>; ill wishes

2 vilification, abuse, revilement, **vituperation, invective,** opprobrium, obloquy, contumely, calumny, scurrility, blackguardism; **disparagement** 512; slanging match <nf>

3 cursing, cussing <nf>, **swearing, profanity,** profane swearing, foul *or* profane *or* obscene *or* blue *or* bad *or* strong *or* unparliamentary *or* indelicate language, vulgar language, vile language, colorful language, unrepeatable expressions, dysphemism, billingsgate, ribaldry, evil speaking, **dirty language** *or* **talk** <nf>, **obscenity,** scatology, coprology, **filthy language, filth;** foul mouth, dirty mouth <nf>

4 oath, profane oath, curse; cuss *or* cuss word *and* dirty word *and* four-letter word *and* **swearword** <nf>, profanity, bad word, naughty word, no-no <nf>, foul invective, **expletive, epithet,** dirty name <nf>, dysphemism, obscenity, vulgarity; F-word

VERBS **5 curse, accurse, damn,** darn, **confound,** blast, anathematize, fulminate *or* thunder against, execrate, imprecate, proscribe; excommunicate; call down evil upon, call down curses on the head of; put a curse on; curse up hill *and* down dale; curse with bell, book, *and* candle; blaspheme; hex, give the evil eye, put a whammy on <nf>

6 curse, swear, cuss <nf>, curse *and* swear, execrate, rap out *or* rip out an oath, take the Lord's name in vain; swear like a trooper, cuss like a sailor, make the air blue, swear till one is blue in the face; **talk dirty** <nf>, scatologize, coprologize, dysphemize, use strong language; blaspheme, profane

7 **vilify, abuse, revile,** vituperate, blackguard, call names, epithet, epithetize; **swear at,** damn, cuss out <nf>

ADJS 8 **cursing, maledictory,** imprecatory, **damnatory,** denunciatory, epithetic, epithetical; **abusive,** vituperative, contumelious; calumnious, calumniatory; execratory, comminatory, fulminatory, excommunicative, excommunicatory; **scurrilous,** scurrile <old>; blasphemous, **profane, foul, foulmouthed, vile,** thersitical, **dirty** <nf>, **obscene,** dysphemistic, scatologic, scatological, coprological, toilet, sewer, cloacal; ribald, Rabelaisian, raw, risqué

9 **cursed,** accursed, bloody <Brit nf>, **damned, damn, damnable,** goddamned, goddamn, **execrable**

10 <euphemisms> **darned,** danged, **confounded,** deuced, blessed, **blasted,** dashed, blamed, goshdarn, doggone or doggoned, goldarned, goldanged, dadburned; blankety-blank; ruddy <Brit>

INTERJS 11 damn!, damn it!, God damn it! or goddam it!, confound it!, dagnabbit!, hang it!, devil take!, a plague upon!, a pox upon!, *parbleu!* <Fr>, *verdammt!* <Ger>, go to hell!

12 <euphemistic oaths> darn!, dern!, dang!, dash!, drat!, blast!, doggone!, goldarn!, goldang!, golding!, gosh-darn!, cripes!, crikey! <Brit>, golly!, gosh!, heck!, bugger it! <Brit>, goodness!, goodness gracious!, jeepers!, gee whillikers! gee whiz!

514 THREAT

NOUNS 1 **threat, menace,** threateningness, threatfulness, promise of harm, knife poised at one's throat, arrow aimed at one's heart, sword of Damocles; imminent threat, powder keg, timebomb, imminence 840; **foreboding; warning** 399; saber-rattling, muscle-flexing, woofing <nf>, bulldozing, scare tactics, **intimidation** 127.6, arm-twisting <nf>; denunciation, commination; veiled or implied threat, idle or hollow or empty threat; bomb threat

VERBS 2 **threaten, menace,** bludgeon, bulldoze, put the heat or screws or squeeze on <nf>, lean on <nf>; hold a pistol to one's head, terrorize, **intimidate,** twist one's arm and arm-twist <nf>; utter threats against, shake or double or clench one's fist at; hold over one's head; denounce, comminate; **lower,** spell or mean trouble, look

threatening, loom, loom up; **be imminent** 840.2; **forebode** 133.10; **warn** 399.5

ADJS 3 **threatening, menacing,** threatful, minatory, minacious; **lowering; imminent** 840.3; **ominous,** foreboding 133.16; denunciatory, comminatory, abusive; fear-inspiring, **intimidating,** bludgeoning, muscle-flexing, saber-rattling, bulldozing, browbeating, bullying, hectoring, blustering, terrorizing, terroristic

ADVS 4 under duress or threat, under the gun, at gunpoint or knifepoint

515 FASTING

NOUNS 1 **fasting,** abstinence from food; abstemiousness, starvation; punishment of Tantalus; religious fasting; hunger strike; anorexia nervosa, bulimia nervosa

2 **fast,** lack of food; spare or meager diet, Lenten diet, Lenten fare; prison fare; short commons or rations, military rations, K rations; starvation diet, water diet, crash diet, bread and water, bare subsistence, bare cupboard; xerophagy, xerophagia; Barmecide or Barmecidal feast

3 **fast day,** *jour maigre* <Fr>; Lent, Good Friday, Quadragesima; Yom Kippur, Tishah B'Av or Ninth of Av; Ramadan; meatless day, fish day, day of abstinence

VERBS 4 **fast,** not eat, go hungry, eat nothing, eat like a bird, dine with Duke Humphrey; eat sparingly, eat less, count calories

ADJS 5 **fasting,** uneating, unfed; abstinent, abstemious; keeping Lent, **Lenten,** quadragesimal; underfed

516 SOBRIETY

NOUNS 1 **sobriety, soberness;** unintoxicatedness, uninebriatedness, undrunkenness; abstinence, abstemiousness; temperance 668; clear head; prohibition, temperance society; nondrinker, teetotaler

VERBS 2 **sober up,** sober off; sleep it off; bring one down, take off a high <nf>; dry out, clear one's head, detoxify; give up alcohol, go on the wagon

ADJS 3 **sober,** in one's sober senses, in one's right mind, in possession of one's faculties; clearheaded; **unintoxicated, uninebriated,** uninebriate, uninebrious, not drunk, undrunk, undrunken, untipsy, unfuddled; stone-cold sober <nf>, **sober as a judge;** able to walk the chalk, able to walk the chalk mark or line <nf>; nondrinking, off the bottle, dry, straight, on the wagon <nf>, temperate 668.9, abstinent

4 unintoxicating, nonintoxicating, uninebriating; **nonalcoholic, soft**

517 SIGNS, INDICATORS

NOUNS **1 sign,** telltale sign, sure sign, tip-off <nf>, **index,** indicant, **indicator,** signal <old>, measure; tip of the iceberg; **symptom;** note, keynote, **mark, earmark,** hallmark, **badge,** device, banner, stamp, signature, sigil, seal, trait, **characteristic,** character, peculiarity, idiosyncrasy, **property,** differentia; image, picture, **representation,** representative; **insignia** 647; notation; reference sign

2 symbol, emblem, icon, token, cipher <old>, type; **allegory; symbolism, symbology,** iconology, iconography, charactery; conventional symbol; symbolic system; **symbolization;** semiotics, semiology; **ideogram,** logogram, pictogram; **logo** <nf>, logotype; **totem,** totem pole; love knot; symbol list

3 indication, signification, identification, differentiation, denotation, **designation,** denomination; characterization, highlighting; **specification,** naming, pointing, pointing out *or* to, fingering <nf>, picking out, selection; symptomaticness, indicativeness; **meaning** 518; hint, suggestion 551.4; **expression, manifestation** 348; show, showing, disclosure 351

4 pointer, index, **lead; direction, guide;** fist, index finger *or* mark, finger, arm; **arrow;** hand, hour hand, minute hand, gauge, **needle,** compass needle, lubber line; **signpost,** guidepost, finger post, direction post; milepost; blaze; guideboard, signboard 352.7

5 mark, marking; watermark; **scratch,** scratching, engraving, graving, **score,** scotch, cut, hack, gash, blaze; bar code; nick, notch 289; **scar,** cicatrix, scarification, cicatrization; **brand, earmark; stigma; stain, discoloration** 1004.2; blemish, macula, **spot,** blotch, splotch, flick, patch, splash; mottle, dapple; **dot,** point; polka dot; tittle, jot; **speck, speckle,** fleck; tick, **freckle,** lentigo, mole; **birthmark,** strawberry mark, port-wine stain, vascular nevus, nevus, hemangioma; beauty mark *or* spot; caste mark; **check,** checkmark; prick, puncture; tattoo, tattoo mark

6 line, score, **stroke,** slash, virgule, diagonal, **dash, stripe, strip, streak, striation,** striping, streaking, bar, band; squiggle; hairline; dotted line; lineation, delineation, sublineation, **underline,** underlining, underscore, underscoring; hatching, cross-hatching, hachure

7 print, imprint, impress, impression; dint, dent, indent, indentation, indention, concavity;

sitzmark; **stamp,** seal, sigil, signet; colophon; **fingerprint,** finger mark, thumbprint, thumbmark, dactylogram, dactylograph; **footprint,** footmark, footstep, step, vestige; hoofprint, hoofmark; pad, paw print, pawmark, pug, pugmark; claw mark; fossil print *or* footprint, ichnite, ichnolite; **bump,** boss, stud, pimple, lump, excrescence, convexity, embossment; ecological footprint

8 track, trail, path, course, *piste* <Fr>, **line, wake;** vapor trail, contrail, condensation trail; **spoor,** signs, traces, **scent**

9 clue, cue, key, tip-off <nf>, telltale, smoking gun <nf>, straw in the wind; **trace, vestige, spoor,** scent, whiff; **lead** *and* hot lead <nf>; catchword, cue word, key word; **evidence** 957; **hint, intimation, suggestion** 551.4

10 marker, mark; bookmark; **landmark,** seamark; bench mark; **milestone,** milepost; cairn, menhir, catstone; **lighthouse,** lightship, tower, Texas tower; platform, watchtower, pharos; buoy, aid to navigation, bell, gong, lighted **buoy,** nun, can, spar buoy, wreck buoy, junction buoy, special-purpose buoy; seamark, watermark, tidemark; **monument** 549.12

11 identification, identification mark; **badge,** identification badge, identification tag, dog tag <military>, passport, personal identification number *or* PIN number *or* PIN, **identity card** *or* **ID card** *or* **ID;** Social Security number, driver's license number; card, business card, calling card, visiting card, *carte de visite* <Fr>, press card; letter of introduction; signature, initials, monogram, calligram; credentials; serial number; countersign, countermark; theme, theme tune *or* song; **criminal identification,** forensic tool, DNA print, genetic fingerprint, voiceprint; fingerprint 517.7; dental record

12 password, watchword, countersign; token; open sesame; secret grip; shibboleth

13 label, tag; ticket, docket <Brit>, tally; stamp, sticker; seal, sigil, signet; cachet; stub, counterfoil; **token,** check; **brand, brand name, trade name,** trademark name; **trademark,** registered trademark; government mark, government stamp, broad arrow <Brit>; **hallmark,** countermark; price tag; plate, bookplate, book stamp, colophon, *ex libris* <L>, logotype *or* logo; International Standard Book Number *or* ISBN; masthead, imprint, title page; letterhead, billhead; running head *or* title

14 gesture, gesticulation; motion, movement; carriage, bearing, posture, poise, pose, stance, way of holding oneself; body language, kinesics; beck, beckon; shrug; charade, dumb show, **pantomime;** sign language, signing, gesture language; dactylology, deaf-and-dumb alphabet; hand signal; chironomy

15 signal, sign; high sign *and* the wink *and* the nod <nf>; wink, flick of the eyelash, glance, leer; look in one's eyes, tone of one's voice; nod; nudge, elbow in the ribs, poke, kick, touch; **alarm** 400; **beacon,** signal beacon, marker beacon, radio beacon, lighthouse beacon; signal light, signal lamp *or* lantern *or* light; blinker; signal fire, beacon fire, watch fire, balefire, smoke signal; **flare,** parachute flare; rocket, signal rocket, Roman candle; signal gun, signal shot; signal siren *or* whistle, signal bell, bell, signal gong, **police whistle,** watchman's rattle; fog signal *or* alarm, fog bell, **foghorn,** diaphone, fog whistle; **traffic signal,** traffic light, red *or* stop light, amber *or* caution light, green *or* go light; heliograph; signal flag; **semaphore,** semaphore telegraph, semaphore flag; **wigwag,** wigwag flag; international alphabet flag, international numeral pennant; red flag; white flag; yellow flag, quarantine flag; blue peter; pilot flag *or* jack; signal post, signal mast, signal tower; telecommunications

16 call, summons; whistle; moose call, bird call, duck call, hog call, goose call, crow call, hawk call, dog whistle; **bugle call,** trumpet call, fanfare, flourish; **reveille, taps,** last post <Brit>; alarm, alarum; **battle cry,** war cry, war whoop, rebel yell, rallying cry; call to arms; Angelus, Angelus bell

VERBS 17 signify, betoken, stand for, identify, differentiate, note <old>, speak of, talk, **indicate,** be indicative of, be an indication of, be significant of, connote, denominate, argue, bespeak, be symptomatic *or* diagnostic of, symptomize, **characterize, mark,** highlight, be the mark *or* sign of, give token, **denote, mean** 518.8; testify, give evidence, bear witness to; **show, express, display, manifest** 348.5, **hint,** suggest 551.10, reveal, **disclose** 351.4; entail, involve 772.4

18 designate, specify; denominate, name, denote; stigmatize; **symbolize, stand for,** typify, be taken as, symbol, emblematize, figure <old>; **point to,** refer to, advert to, allude to, make an allusion to; pick out, select; **point out,** point at, put *or* lay one's finger on, finger <nf>

19 mark, make a mark, put a mark on; pencil, chalk; mark out, demarcate, delimit, define; **mark off, check, check off,** tick, tick off, chalk up; punctuate, point; **dot, spot,** blotch, splotch, dash, **speck, speckle,** fleck, freckle; mottle, dapple; blemish; **brand,** stigmatize; **stain, discolor** 1004.6; stamp, seal, punch, impress, imprint, **print, engrave; score, scratch,** gash, scotch, scar, scarify, cicatrize; nick, notch 289.4; **blaze,** blaze a trail;

line, seam, trace, **stripe, streak, striate;** hatch; **underline, underscore;** prick, puncture, tattoo, riddle, pepper

20 label, tag, tab, ticket; stamp, seal; **brand, earmark;** hallmark; bar-code

21 gesture, gesticulate; motion, motion to; use body language; beckon, wiggle the finger at; wave the arms, wig-wag, saw the air; shrug, shrug the shoulders; pantomime, mime, mimic, imitate, ape, take off

22 signal, signalize, sign, give a signal, make a sign; speak; flash; **give the high sign** *or* **the nod** *or* a high five <nf>; nod; nudge, poke, kick, dig one in the ribs, touch; wink, glance, raise one's eyebrows, leer; hold up the hand; wave, wave the hand, wave a flag, **flag,** flag down; **unfurl a flag,** hoist a banner, break out a flag; **show one's colors,** exchange colors; **salute,** dip; dip a flag, hail, hail *and* speak; half-mast; give *or* sound an alarm, raise a cry; beat the drum, sound the trumpet

ADJS 23 indicative, indicatory, signifying; connotative, indicating, signifying, signalizing; **significant,** significative, meaningful; symptomatic, symptomatologic, symptomatological, diagnostic, pathognomonic, pathognomonical; evidential, **designative,** denotative, denominative, naming; **suggestive,** implicative; **expressive,** demonstrative, exhibitive, telltale; representative; identifying, identificational; individual, peculiar, idiosyncratic; **emblematic, symbolic,** emblematical, symbolical; symbolistic, symbological, typical; figurative, figural, metaphorical; ideographic; semiotic, semantic; nominal, diagrammatic

24 marked, designated, flagged; signed, signposted; monogrammed, individualized, personal; own-brand, own-label; punctuated

25 gestural, gesticulative, gesticulatory; kinesic; pantomimic, **in pantomime,** in dumb show

518 MEANING

NOUNS 1 meaning, significance, signification, *significatum* <L>, *signifié* <Fr>, point, **sense,** idea, **purport, import,** where one is coming from <nf>; **reference, referent;** intension, extension; **denotation;** dictionary meaning, lexical meaning; emotive *or* affective meaning, undertone, overtone, coloring; relevance, bearing, **relation,** pertinence *or* pertinency; **substance, gist,** pith, core, spirit, essence, gravamen, last word, name of the game *and* meat *and* potatoes *and* bottom line <nf>; **drift,** tenor; sum, sum *and* substance; **literal meaning, true** *or* **real meaning, unadorned**

meaning; **secondary meaning, connotation** 519.2; more than meets the eye, what is read between the lines; effect, force, impact, consequence, practical consequence, response; shifted *or* displaced meaning, implied meaning, **implication** 519.2; Aesopian *or* Aesopic meaning, Aesopian *or* Aesopic language; totality of associations *or* references *or* relations, value; syntactic *or* structural meaning, grammatical meaning; symbolic meaning; metaphorical *or* transferred meaning; semantic content, deep structure; semantic field, semantic domain, semantic cluster; range *or* span of meaning, scope; topic, subject matter

2 intent, intention, purpose, point, **aim, object,** end, **design,** plan; value, worth, use

3 explanation, definition, construction, sense-distinction, **interpretation** 341

4 acceptation, acception, accepted *or* received meaning; **usage,** acceptance

5 meaningfulness, suggestiveness, expressiveness, pregnancy; **significance,** significancy, significantness; intelligibility, interpretability, readability; pithiness, meatiness, sententiousness; importance, import

6 <units> sign, symbol, significant, type, token, icon, verbal icon, lexeme, sememe, morpheme, glosseme, **word,** term, phrase, utterance, lexical form *or* item, linguistic form, semantic *or* semiotic *or* semasiological unit; text; synonym, antonym; derivation, etymology

7 semantics, semiotic, semiotics, significs, semasiology, semiology, linguistics; lexicology

VERBS 8 mean, signify, denote, connote, import, spell, have the sense of, be construed as, have the force of; be talking *and* be talking about <nf>; **stand for, symbolize; imply,** suggest, argue, breathe, bespeak, betoken, **indicate; refer to; mean something,** mean a lot, have impact, come home, hit one where one lives *and* hit one close to home <nf>; get across, convey

9 intend, have in mind, seek to communicate

ADJS 10 meaningful, meaning, **significant,** significative; literal, explicit; **denotative, connotative,** denotational, connotational, intensional, extensional, associational; **referential; symbolic, metaphorical,** figurative, allegorical, idiomatic; transferred, extended; intelligible, interpretable, definable, readable; **suggestive,** indicative, **expressive; pregnant,** full of meaning, loaded *or* laden *or* fraught *or* freighted *or* heavy with significance, articulate; **pithy, meaty,** sententious, substantial, full of substance; pointed, full of point

11 meant, implied 519.7, **intended**

12 semantic, semantological, semiotic, semasiological, semiological; linguistic; lexological; **symbolic,** signification, iconic, lexemic, sememic, glossematic, morphemic, **verbal,** phrasal, lexical, philological; structural

ADVS 13 meaningfully, meaningly, **significantly;** suggestively, indicatively; **expressively**

519 LATENT MEANINGFULNESS

NOUNS 1 latent meaningfulness, latency, latentness, delitescence, latent content; **potentiality,** virtuality, possibility; dormancy 173.4

2 implication, connotation, import, latent *or* underlying *or* implied meaning, ironic suggestion *or* implication, more than meets the eye, what is read between the lines; meaning 518; **suggestion,** allusion; coloration, tinge, undertone, overtone, undercurrent, more than meets the eye *or* ear, something between the lines, intimation, touch, nuance, innuendo; **code word,** weasel word; **hint** 551.4; **inference, supposition,** presupposition, assumption, presumption; secondary *or* transferred *or* metaphorical sense; innuendo; undermeaning, undermention, subsidiary sense, subsense, **subtext;** Aesopian *or* Aesopic meaning, cryptic *or* hidden *or* esoteric *or* arcane meaning, occult meaning; **symbolism, allegory**

VERBS 3 be latent, underlie, lie under the surface, lurk, lie hid *or* low, lie beneath, hibernate, lie dormant, smolder; be read between the lines; make no sign, escape notice

4 imply, implicate, involve, import, connote, entail 772.4; mean 518.8; **suggest,** lead one to believe, bring to mind; **hint, insinuate, infer, intimate** 551.10; **allude to,** point to from afar, point indirectly to; write between the lines; allegorize; **suppose, presuppose,** assume, presume, take for granted; mean to say *or* imply *or* suggest

ADJS 5 latent, lurking, lying low, delitescent, **hidden** 346.11, obscured, obfuscated, veiled, muffled, covert, occult, mystic <old>, cryptic; esoteric; **underlying, under the surface,** submerged; **between the lines;** hibernating, sleeping, dormant 173.14; **potential,** unmanifested, virtual, possible

6 suggestive, allusive, allusory, **indicative, inferential; insinuating,** insinuative, insinuatory; ironic; **implicative,** implicatory, implicational; referential

7 implied, implicated, inferred, involved; **meant,** indicated; **suggested, intimated, insinuated, hinted; inferred, supposed,** assumed, presumed, presupposed, reputative; hidden, arcane, esoteric, **cryptic,** Aesopian *or* Aesopic

8 tacit, implicit, implied, understood, taken for granted

9 unexpressed, unpronounced, **unsaid, unspoken,
unuttered,** undeclared, unbreathed, unvoiced,
wordless, silent; **unmentioned,** untalked-of,
untold, unsung, unproclaimed, unpublished;
unwritten, unrecorded
10 symbolic, symbolical, allegoric, allegorical,
figural, figurative, tropological, **metaphoric,**
metaphorical, anagogic, anagogical
ADVS **11 latently,** underlyingly; **potentially,** virtually
12 suggestively, allusively, inferentially,
insinuatingly; impliedly; by suggestion, by
allusion, etc
13 tacitly, implicitly, unspokenly, wordlessly, silently

520 MEANINGLESSNESS

NOUNS **1 meaninglessness,** unmeaningness,
senselessness, nonsensicality; **insignificance,**
unsignificancy, irrelevance; **noise,** mere noise,
static, empty sound, talking to hear oneself talk,
phatic communion; inanity, emptiness, nullity; "a
tale told by an idiot, full of sound and fury,
signifying nothing"—Shakespeare;
purposelessness, aimlessness, futility; dead letter;
no bearing
2 nonsense, stuff and nonsense, pack of nonsense,
folderol, balderdash, niaiserie <Fr>, flummery,
trumpery, **rubbish,** trash, narrishkeit <Yiddish>,
vaporing, fudge; **humbug,** gammon, hocus-pocus;
fandangle; rant, claptrap, fustian, rodomontade,
bombast, absurdity 923.3; stultiloquence, **twaddle,**
twiddle-twaddle, fiddle-faddle, fiddledeedee,
fiddlesticks, **blather, babble,** babblement, bibble-
babble, **gabble,** gibble-gabble, **blabber, gibber,
jabber,** prate, prattle, palaver, rigmarole or
rigamarole, galimatias, skimble-skamble, drivel,
drool; **gibberish,** jargon, mumbo jumbo, **double-
talk,** evasion, equivoke, ambiguity, amphigory,
gobbledygook <nf>; glossolalia, speaking in
tongues; logorrhea
3 <nf terms> **bullshit,** shit, crap or crapola,
horseshit, horsefeathers, bull, poppycock, bosh,
tosh <Brit>, applesauce, bunkum, bunk, garbage,
guff, hogwash, jive, bilge, piffle, moonshine,
flapdoodle, a crock or a crock of shit, claptrap,
tommyrot, rot, hogwash, malarkey, double Dutch,
hokum, hooey, bushwa, balls <Brit>, blah-blah-
blah, baloney, blarney, tripe, hot air, gas, wind,
waffle <Brit>, yada yada
VERBS **4 be meaningless, mean nothing,** signify
nothing, not mean a thing, not convey anything;
not make sense, not figure <nf>, not compute; **not
register,** not ring any bells
5 talk nonsense, twaddle, piffle, waffle <Brit>,
blather, blether, **blabber, babble, gabble,** gibble-

gabble, **jabber, gibber,** prate, **prattle,** rattle, spiel
<nf>; talk through one's hat; gas and bull and
bullshit and throw the bull and shoot off one's
mouth and shoot the bull <nf>; **drivel,** vapor,
drool, run off at the mouth <nf>; speak in
tongues; not mean what one says
ADJS **6 meaningless,** unmeaning, **senseless,**
purportless, importless, nondenotative,
nonconnotative; **insignificant,** unsignificant;
empty, inane, null; phatic, garbled, scrambled;
purposeless, aimless, designless, **without rhyme
or reason**
7 nonsensical, silly, poppycockish <nf>; **foolish,
absurd;** twaddling, twaddly; rubbishy, trashy;
skimble-skamble; Pickwickian
ADVS **8 meaninglessly,** unmeaningly,
nondenotatively, nonconnotatively, **senselessly,
nonsensically;** insignificantly, unsignificantly;
purposelessly, aimlessly

521 INTELLIGIBILITY

NOUNS **1 intelligibility, comprehensibility,
apprehensibility,** prehensibility, graspability,
understandability, understandableness,
knowability, cognizability, scrutability,
penetrability, fathomableness, decipherability;
recognizability, readability, interpretability;
articulateness; open book
2 clearness, clarity; plainness, distinctness,
microscopical distinctness, explicitness,
clear-cutness, definition; **lucidity,** limpidity,
pellucidity, crystal or crystaline clarity, crystallinity,
perspicuity, perspicuousness, transpicuity,
transparency; **simplicity,** straightforwardness,
directness, literalness; unmistakableness,
unequivocalness, unambiguousness, unambiguity;
coherence, connectedness, consistency, structure;
plain language, plain style, plain English, plain
speech, unadorned style; clear, plaintext,
unencoded text; lowest common denominator
3 legibility, decipherability, **readability**
VERBS **4 be understandable, make sense;** be plain
or clear, be obvious, be self-evident, be self-
explanatory; **speak for itself,** tell its own tale,
speak volumes, have no secrets, put up no
barriers; read easily
5 <be understood> **get over** or **across** <nf>, come
through, **register** <nf>, **penetrate, sink in,** soak in;
dawn on, be glimpsed; become apparent
6 make clear, make it clear, **let it be understood,**
make crystal-clear, make oneself understood, get
or put over or across <nf>; **simplify,** put in plain
words or plain English, put in words of one
syllable, spell out <nf>; elucidate, **explain,** define,

demonstrate, explicate, **clarify** 341.10; illuminate, enlighten; put one in the picture <Brit>; disambiguate; demystify, descramble; **decode, decipher;** make available to all, popularize, vulgarize

7 **understand, comprehend, apprehend,** have, **know, conceive, realize,** appreciate, have no problem with, ken <Scot>, savvy <nf>, sense, make sense out of, make something of, make out, make heads or tails of; **fathom, follow; grasp, seize,** get hold of, grasp *or* seize the meaning, be seized of, take, **take in,** catch, **catch on,** get the meaning of, latch onto; **master, learn** 570.6; **assimilate, absorb, digest**

8 <nf terms> **read one loud and clear,** read, read one, dig, get the idea, be with one, be with it, get the message, get the word, get the picture, get up to speed, get into *or* through one's head *or* thick head, get, get it, catch *or* get the drift, have it taped, have it down pat, see where one is coming from, hear loud and clear, hear what one is saying, grok, have hold of, get the hang of, get *or* have a fix on, know like the back *or* palm of one's hand, know inside out

9 **perceive, see, discern, make out,** descry; see the light, see daylight <nf>, wake up, wake up to, tumble to <nf>, come alive; **see through,** see to the bottom of, penetrate, see into, pierce, plumb; see at a glance, see with half an eye; get *or* have someone's number *and* read someone like a book <nf>

ADJS 10 **intelligible, comprehensible, apprehensible,** prehensible, graspable, **knowable,** cognizable, scrutable, **fathomable,** decipherable, plumbable, penetrable, interpretable; **understandable,** easily understood, easy to understand, exoteric; readable; articulate

11 **clear, crystal-clear,** clear as crystal, clear as day, clear as the nose on one's face; **plain, distinct,** microscopically distinct, plain as pikestaffs; **definite,** defined, well-defined, **clear-cut,** clean-cut, crisp, obvious, made easy; **direct, literal;** simple, **straightforward; explicit, express;** **unmistakable, unequivocal,** univocal, unambiguous, unconfused; **loud and clear** <nf>; **lucid,** pellucid, limpid, crystal-clear, crystalline, perspicuous, transpicuous, **transparent,** translucent, luminous; **coherent,** connected, consistent

12 **legible, decipherable, readable,** fair; uncoded, unenciphered, in the clear, clear, plaintext

ADVS 13 **intelligibly, understandably, comprehensibly,** apprehensibly; articulately; **clearly, lucidly,** limpidly, pellucidly, perspicuously, **simply, plainly, distinctly,** definitely; **coherently;**

explicitly, expressly; unmistakably, unequivocally, unambiguously; in plain terms *or* words, in plain English, in no uncertain terms, in words of one syllable

14 **legibly,** decipherably, readably, fairly

522 UNINTELLIGIBILITY

NOUNS 1 **unintelligibility, incomprehensibility,** inapprehensibility, ungraspability, unseizability, **ununderstandability,** inconceivability, unknowability, incognizability, inscrutability, impenetrability, unfathomableness, unsearchableness, numinousness; **incoherence,** unconnectedness, ramblingness; inarticulateness; **ambiguity** 539, equivocation

2 **abstruseness,** reconditeness; crabbedness, crampedness, knottiness; **complexity,** intricacy, **complication** 799.1; **hardness, difficulty; profundity,** profoundness, deepness; esotericism, esotery

3 **obscurity,** obscuration, obscurantism, obfuscation, mumbo jumbo <nf>, mystification; perplexity; **unclearness,** unclarity, unplainness, opacity; **vagueness,** indistinctness, indeterminateness, fuzziness, shapelessness, amorphousness; murkiness, murk, mistiness, mist, fogginess, fog, darkness, dark

4 **illegibility,** unreadability; undecipherability, indecipherability; invisibility; scribble, scrawl, hen track <nf>

5 **unexpressiveness,** inexpressiveness, **expressionlessness,** impassivity; uncommunicativeness; straight face, deadpan <nf>, poker face <nf>

6 **inexplicability,** unexplainableness, uninterpretability, indefinability, undefinability, unaccountableness; insolvability, inextricability; **enigmaticalness,** mysteriousness, mystery, strangeness, weirdness

7 <something unintelligible> Greek, Choctaw, double Dutch; gibberish, babble, jargon, garbage, gubbish, gobbledygook, noise, Babel; scramble, jumble, garble, muddle; purple prose; argot, cant, slang, secret language, Aesopian *or* Aesopic language, code, cipher, cryptogram; glossolalia, gift of tongues; enigma, riddle; double meaning

8 **enigma, mystery, puzzle,** puzzlement; Chinese puzzle, crossword puzzle, word game, jigsaw puzzle, Sudoku; **problem,** puzzling *or* baffling problem, why; question, question mark, vexed *or* perplexed question, enigmatic question, sixty-four dollar question <nf>; **perplexity;** obscure point; knot, knotty point, crux, point to be solved; **puzzler,** poser, brain twister *or* teaser <nf>, sticker

<nf>; mind-boggler, **floorer** or **stumper** <nf>; nut to crack, **hard** or **tough nut to crack;** tough proposition <nf>

9 **riddle, conundrum,** paradox, charade, rebus; brainteaser, Chinese puzzle, tangram, acrostic, logogriph, anagram; riddle of the Sphinx, squaring of the circle; Sudoku, crossword

VERBS 10 **be incomprehensible, not make sense,** be too deep, go over one's head, defy comprehension, be beyond one, beat one <nf>, elude or escape one, lose one, need explanation or clarification or translation, be Greek to, pass comprehension or understanding, not penetrate, make one's head swim; **baffle, perplex** 971.13, riddle, be sphinxlike, speak in riddles; speak in tongues; talk double Dutch, babble, gibber, ramble, drivel, mean nothing

11 **not understand, be unable to comprehend,** not have the first idea, not get or not get it <nf>, be unable to get into or through one's head or thick skull; be out of one's depth, be at sea, be lost; **not know what to make of,** make nothing of, not have the slightest idea, not be able to account for, not make head or tail of, not register; be unable to see, not see the wood for the trees; go over one's head, escape one; give up, pass <nf>; rack one's brains

12 **make unintelligible, scramble,** jumble, garble, mix up; encode, encipher; **obscure,** obfuscate, mystify, shadow; **complicate** 799.3

ADJS 13 **unintelligible, incomprehensible,** inapprehensible, ungraspable, unseizable, **ununderstandable,** unknowable, incognizable; **unfathomable, inscrutable,** impenetrable, unsearchable, numinous; **ambiguous,** equivocal; **incoherent,** unconnected, rambling; **inarticulate; past comprehension,** beyond one's comprehension, beyond understanding; Greek to one; ultracrepidarian

14 **hard to understand, difficult, hard,** tough <nf>, beyond one, **over one's head,** beyond or out of one's depth; knotty, cramp, crabbed; intricate, **complex,** overtechnical, perplexed, **complicated** 799.4; **scrambled,** jumbled, **garbled;** Johnsonian

15 **obscure,** obscured, obfuscated; **vague, indistinct,** indeterminate, undiscernible, fuzzy, shapeless, amorphous or amorphic, obfuscatory; unclear, unplain, opaque, muddy, **clear as mud** and clear as ditch water <nf>; **dark, dim,** blind <old>, shadowy; **murky,** cloudy, foggy, fogbound, hazy, misty, nebulous

16 **recondite, abstruse,** abstract, transcendental; **profound, deep; hidden** 346.11; arcane, **esoteric,** occult; **secret** 345.11

17 **enigmatic,** enigmatical, cryptic, cryptical; sphinxlike; **perplexing, puzzling;** riddling; logogriphic, anagrammatic, mysterious

18 **inexplicable, unexplainable,** uninterpretable, undefinable, indefinable, funny, funny peculiar <nf>, **unaccountable; insolvable,** unsolvable, insoluble, inextricable; mysterious, mystic, mystical, shrouded or wrapped or enwrapped in mystery

19 **illegible, unreadable, unclear; undecipherable,** indecipherable

20 **inexpressive,** unexpressive, impassive, po-faced <Brit>; uncommunicative; **expressionless; vacant, empty, blank;** glassy, glazed, glazed-over, fishy, wooden; deadpan, poker-faced <nf>

ADVS 21 **unintelligibly, incomprehensibly,** inapprehensibly, unununderstandably

22 **obscurely, vaguely, indistinctly,** indeterminately; **unclearly,** unplainly; illegibly

23 reconditely, **abstrusely;** esoterically, occultly

24 **inexplicably, unexplainably,** undefinably, bafflingly, **unaccountably, enigmatically; mysteriously,** mystically

25 **expressionlessly, vacantly, blankly, emptily,** woodenly, glassily, fishily

PREPS 26 **beyond,** past, above; **too deep for**

PHRS 27 **I don't understand, I can't see,** I don't see how or why, **it beats me** <nf>, you've got me <nf>, **it's beyond me,** it's too deep for me, it has me guessing, I don't have the first or foggiest idea, it's Greek to me, I'm clueless <Brit>; **I give up,** I pass <nf>

523 LANGUAGE

NOUNS 1 **language** <see list>, speech, tongue, *lingua* <L>, spoken language, natural language; **talk, parlance, locution,** phraseology, **idiom, lingo** <nf>; dialect; idiolect, personal usage, individual speech habits or performance, parole; code or system of oral communication, individual speech, competence, langue; **usage,** use of words; **language type; language family, subfamily, language group;** area language, regional language; world language, universal language; words, lexicon; foreign language

2 **dead language,** ancient language, lost language; archaic language, archaism, archaic speech; parent language; classical language; living language, vernacular; sacred language or tongue

3 **mother tongue,** native language or tongue, natal tongue, native speech, vernacular, first language

4 **standard language,** standard or prestige dialect, acrolect; national language, official language; educated speech or language; literary language, written language, formal written language, formal language; classical language; correct or good English, **Standard English, the King's** or **Queen's**

English, Received Standard, Received Pronunciation

5 **nonformal language** *or* **speech,** nonformal standard speech, informal language, **spoken language, colloquial language** *or* **speech,** vernacular language *or* speech, vernacular; **slang;** colloquialism, colloquial usage, conversationalism, vernacularism; ordinary language *or* speech; nonformal English, conversational English, colloquial English, English as it is spoken

6 **substandard** *or* nonstandard language *or* **speech,** nonformal language *or* speech; vernacular language *or* speech, **vernacular,** demotic language *or* speech, vulgate, vulgar tongue, common speech, low language; uneducated speech, illiterate speech; substandard usage; basilect; **nonformal**

7 **dialect,** idiom; class dialect; regional *or* local dialect; idiolect; subdialect; folk speech *or* dialect, patois; **provincialism, localism, regionalism,** regional accent 524.8; Canadian French, French Canadian; Pennsylvania Dutch, Pennsylvania German; Yankee, New England dialect; Brooklynese; Southern dialect *or* twang; Black English, Afro-Americanese; Cockney; Yorkshire; Midland, Midland dialect; Anglo-Indian; Australian English; Gullah; Acadian, Cajun; dialect atlas, linguistic atlas; isogloss, bundle of isoglosses; speech community; linguistic community; linguistic ambience; speech *or* linguistic island, relic area; click language

8 <idioms> Anglicism, Briticism, Englishism; Americanism, Yankeeism; Westernism, Southernism; Gallicism, Frenchism; Irishism, Hibernicism; Canadianism, Scotticism, Germanism, Russianism, Latinism, etc

9 **jargon, lingo** <nf>, **slang, cant, argot, patois, patter, vernacular;** vocabulary, terminology, nomenclature, phraseology; gobbledygook, mumbo jumbo, gibberish; **nonformal;** taboo language, vulgar language; obscene language, scatology; doublespeak, bizspeak, mediaspeak, policyspeak, technospeak, technobabble, ecobabble, etc; shoptalk

10 <jargons> Academese, cinemese, collegese, constablese, ecobabble, economese, sociologese, legalese, pedagese, societyese, stagese, telegraphese, Varietyese, Wall Streetese, journalese, newspaperese, newspeak, officialese, federalese, Pentagonese, Washingtonese, medical Greek, medicalese, businessese *or* businessspeak, computerese, technobabble, technospeak, psychobabble; Yinglish, Franglais, Spanglish; Eurojargon; man-talk, bloke-talk <Brit nf>, woman-talk, hen-talk <nf>; shoptalk; pig Latin; glossolalia

11 **lingua franca,** international language, jargon, **pidgin,** trade language; auxiliary language, interlanguage; creolized language, creole language, creole; koine; diplomatic language, business language, language *or* linguistic universal; pidgin English, talkee-talkee, Bêche-de-Mer, Beach-la-mar; Kitchen Kaffir; Chinook *or* Oregon Jargon; Sabir; Esperanto; artificial language, sign language, sign, American Sign Language *or* ASL *or* Ameslan; Morse code, cryptography, cryptanalysis; computer language; shorthand, stenography

12 language family; Indo-European, Indo-Iranian, Anatolian, Hellenic, Tocharian, Italic, Celtic, Germanic, Baltic, Slavic; Finno-Ugric; Afroasiatic *or* Hamito-Semitic; Sino-Tibetan; Austronesian

13 **linguistics,** linguistic science, science of language; glottology, glossology <old>; linguistic analysis; linguistic terminology, metalanguage; **philology;** paleography; speech origins, language origins, bowwow theory, dingdong theory, pooh-pooh theory; language study, foreign-language study, linguistic theory

14 **language element,** morpheme, phoneme, grapheme; letter, alphabet, word, phrase, sentence; grammar, syntax, part of speech; context clue

15 **linguist,** linguistic scientist, linguistician, linguistic scholar; philologist, philologer, philologian; philologaster; **grammarian,** grammatist; grammaticaster; **etymologist,** etymologer; **lexicologist; lexicographer,** glossographer, glossarist; phoneticist, phonetician, phonemicist, phonologist, orthoepist; dialectician, dialectologist; semanticist, semasiologist; paleographer; logophile; morphologist, orthographer

16 **polyglot,** linguist, **bilingual** *or* diglot, trilingual, multilingual

17 **colloquializer;** jargonist, jargoneer, jargonizer; slangster

VERBS 18 **speak, talk,** use language, communicate orally *or* verbally; use nonformal speech *or* style, colloquialize, vernacularize; jargon, jargonize, cant; patter; utter, verbalize, articulate

ADJS 19 **linguistic,** lingual, glottological, glossological <old>; descriptive, structural, glottochronological, lexicostatistical, psycholinguistic, sociolinguistic, metalinguistic; **philological;** lexicological, lexicographic, lexicographical; syntactic, syntactical, **grammatical;** grammatic, semantic 518.12; phonetic 524.30, phonemic, phonological; morphological;

morphophonemic, graphemic, paleographic, paleographical

20 vernacular, colloquial, conversational, unliterary, nonformal, informal, demotic, spoken, vulgar, vulgate; unstudied, familiar, common, everyday; jargonistic; **substandard,** nonformal, uneducated, low

21 jargonish, jargonal; **slang,** slangy; taboo, four-letter, obscene, vulgar; scatological; rhyming slang

22 idiomatic; dialect, dialectal, dialectological; provincial, regional, local

WORD ELEMENTS **23** lingu-, linguo-, lingui-, gloss-, glosso-, glott-, glotto-

24 types of language

affixing	inflectional or inflected
agglutinative	isolating
analytic	monosyllabic
body	polysyllabic
click	polysynthetic
contact or pidgin	polytonic
endangered	symbolic
fusional	synthetic
incorporative	tonal or tone

524 SPEECH

<utterance>

NOUNS **1 speech, talk,** the power *or* faculty of speech, the verbal *or* oral faculty, talking, speaking, **discourse,** colloquy, oral communication, vocal *or* voice *or* viva-voce communication, communication, verbal intercourse; **palaver, prattle, gab** and jaw-jaw <nf>; rapping and yakking and yakkety-yak <nf>; **words, accents;** chatter 540.3; conversation 541; elocution 543.1; **language** 523; "the mirror of the soul"—Publilius Syrus

2 utterance, speaking, *parole* <Fr>, spoken language, vocalization, locution <old>, phonation, phonetics; **speech act,** linguistic act *or* behavior; string, utterance string, sequence of phonemes, expression; **voice, tongue,** vocalism, parlance; word of mouth, parol, the spoken word; vocable, **word** 526

3 remark, statement, earful *and* crack *and* one's two cents' worth <nf>, **word, say, saying, utterance, observation, reflection, expression; note,** thought, **mention; assertion,** averment, allegation, affirmation, pronouncement, position, dictum; **declaration;** interjection, exclamation; question 938.10; answer 939; address, greeting, apostrophe; sentence, phrase; subjoinder, Parthian shot

4 articulateness, articulacy, oracy, readiness *or* facility of speech; eloquence 544; way with words, word power

5 articulation, uttering, phonation, voicing, giving voice, **vocalization; pronunciation, enunciation,** utterance; **delivery, attack**

6 intonation, inflection, modulation; intonation pattern *or* contour, intonation *or* inflection of voice, speech tune *or* melody; suprasegmental, suprasegmental phoneme; **tone, pitch;** pitch accent, tonic accent

7 manner of speaking, way of saying, mode of expression *or* speech; **tone of voice, voice,** *voce* <Ital>, **tone;** speaking voice, voice quality, vocal style, **timbre;** voice qualifier; paralinguistic communication

8 accent, regional accent, brogue, twang, burr, drawl, broad accent, trill, whine, nasality, stridor; **foreign accent;** guttural accent, clipped accent; broken English; speech impediment, speech defect; speech community, isogloss

9 pause, juncture, open juncture, close juncture; terminal, clause terminal, rising terminal, falling terminal; sandhi; word boundary, clause boundary; pause

10 accent, accentuation, stress accent; **emphasis, stress, word stress;** ictus, beat, rhythmical stress; rhythm, rhythmic pattern, **cadence;** prosody, prosodics, metrics; stress pattern; level of stress; primary stress, secondary stress, tertiary stress, weak stress

11 vowel quantity, **quantity,** mora; long vowel, short vowel, full vowel, reduced vowel

12 speech sound, phone, vocable, phonetic unit *or* entity; puff of air, aspiration; stream of air, airstream, glottalic airstream; articulation, manner of articulation; **stop,** plosive, explosive, mute, check, occlusive, **affricate,** continuant, **liquid,** lateral, **nasal;** point *or* place of articulation; voice, voicing; sonority; aspiration, palatalization, labialization, pharyngealization, glottalization; surd, voiceless sound; sonant, voiced sound; **consonant; semivowel,** glide, transition sound; velar, guttural, voiced consonant, frictionless continuant, labial, labio-dental, labio-nasal, spirant, sibilant, aspirate, glottal stop, fricative, sonant, polyphone; vocalic, syllabic nucleus, syllabic peak, peak; vocoid; **vowel;** monophthong, diphthong, triphthong; **syllable; phoneme,** segmental phoneme, morphophoneme, digraph; modification, assimilation, dissimilation; **allophone;** parasitic vowel, epenthetic vowel, svarabhakti vowel, prothetic vowel; vowel gradation, vowel mutation; doubletalk

13 phonetics, articulatory phonetics, acoustic phonetics; phonology; morphophonemics, morphophonology; orthoepy; sound *or* phonetic law; pronunciation; phonography; sound shift,

Lautverschiebung <Ger>; umlaut, mutation, ablaut, gradation; rhotacism, betacism; Grimm's law, Verner's law, Grassmann's law

14 **phonetician,** phonetist, phoneticist; orthoepist

15 **ventriloquism,** ventriloquy; **ventriloquist**

16 talking machine, sonovox, voder, vocoder

17 **talker, speaker,** sayer, utterer, patterer; chatterbox 540.4; conversationalist 541.7

18 **vocal** *or* **speech organ,** articulator, voice, mouth; tongue, apex, tip, blade, dorsum, back; vocal cords *or* bands, vocal processes, vocal folds; voice box, larynx, Adam's apple; syrinx; arytenoid cartilages; glottis, vocal chink, epiglottis; lips, teeth, palate, hard palate, soft palate, velum, alveolus, teeth ridge, alveolar ridge, uvula; nasal cavity, oral cavity; pharynx, throat *or* pharyngeal cavity

VERBS 19 **speak, talk; patter** *or* **gab** *or* wag the tongue <nf>; mouth; chatter 540.5; converse 541.8; declaim 543.10

20 <nf terms> **yak,** yap, yakkety-yak, gab, spiel, chin, jaw, shoot off one's face *or* mouth, shoot *or* bat the breeze, beat *or* bat one's gums, bend one's ear, make chin music, rattle away, talk a blue streak, talk someone's ear *or* head off, flap one's jaw, natter <Brit>, spout off, sound off

21 **speak up, speak out, speak one's piece** *or* **one's mind, pipe up, open one's mouth,** open one's lips, say out, say loud *and* clear, say out loud, sound off, lift *or* raise one's voice, break silence, find one's tongue; take the floor; put in a word, get in a word edgewise *or* edgeway; **have one's say,** put in one's two cents worth <nf>, relieve oneself, get a load off one's mind <nf>, give vent *or* voice to, pour one's heart out

22 **say, utter, breathe,** sound, **voice,** vocalize, phonate, **articulate, enunciate, pronounce,** lip, give voice, give tongue, give utterance; whisper; **express,** give expression, verbalize, put in words, find words to express; **word,** formulate, put into words, couch, phrase 532.4; **present,** deliver; **emit,** give, raise, **let out,** out with, come *or* give out with, put *or* set forth, pour forth; throw off, fling off; chorus, chime; **tell, communicate** 343.6,7; **convey, impart, disclose** 351.4

23 **state, declare, assert,** aver, affirm, asserverate, allege; **say,** make a statement, send a message; **announce,** tell the world; **relate, recite;** quote; proclaim, nuncupate

24 **remark, comment, observe, note; mention,** speak <old>, let drop *or* fall, say by the way, make mention of; refer to, allude to, touch on, make reference to, call attention to; muse, reflect; opine <nf>; interject; blurt, blurt out, exclaim

25 <utter in a certain way> murmur, mutter, mumble, whisper, breathe, buzz, sigh; gasp, pant; exclaim, yell 59.6; sing, lilt, warble, chant, coo, chirp; pipe, flute; squeak; cackle, crow; bark, yelp, yap; growl, snap, snarl; hiss, sibilate; grunt, snort; roar, bellow, blare, trumpet, bray, blat, bawl, thunder, rumble, boom; scream, shriek, screech, squeal, squawk, yawp, squall; whine, wail, keen, blubber, sob; drawl, twang

26 **address, speak to, talk to,** bespeak, beg the ear of; **appeal to,** invoke; apostrophize; **approach; buttonhole,** take by the button *or* lapel; take aside, talk to in private, closet oneself with; **accost, call to, hail,** halloo, greet, salute, speak, speak fair

27 **pass one's lips, escape one's lips,** fall from the lips *or* mouth

28 inflect, modulate, intonate

ADJS 29 **speech; language, linguistic,** lingual; **spoken, uttered, said,** vocalized, **voiced, verbalized, pronounced, sounded, articulated, enunciated;** vocal, voiceful; **oral, verbal, unwritten,** *viva voce* <L>, nuncupative, parol

30 **phonetic,** phonic; articulatory, acoustic; intonated; pitched, pitch, **tonal,** tonic, oxytone, oxytonic, paroxytonic, barytone; **accented, stressed,** strong, heavy; unaccented, unstressed, weak, light, pretonic, atonic, posttonic; articulated; stopped, muted, checked, occlusive, nasal, nasalized, twangy, continuant, liquid, lateral, affricated; alveolabial, alveolar, alveolingual, etc; low, high, mid, open, broad, close; front, back, central; wide, lax, tense, narrow; voiced, sonant, voiceless, surd; rounded, unrounded, flat; aspirated; labialized; palatalized, soft, *mouillé* <Fr>; unpalatalized, hard; pharyngealized, glottalized; velar, guttural; burring, frictionless, labial, spirant, sibilant, fricative, polyphonic, polyphonous, digraphic; **consonant,** consonantal, semivowel, glide, **vowel;** vowellike, vocoid, vocalic, syllabic; monophthongal, diphthongal, triphthongal; **phonemic,** allophonic; assimilated, dissimilated

31 **speaking, talking;** articulate, talkative 540.9; **eloquent** 544.8, well-spoken; true-speaking, clean-speaking, plain-speaking, plain-spoken, **outspoken,** free-speaking, free-spoken, loud-speaking, loud-spoken, soft-speaking, soft-spoken; English-speaking, etc

32 ventriloquial, ventriloquistic

ADVS 33 **orally, vocally, verbally, by word of mouth,** *viva voce* <L>; from the lips of, from his own mouth

525 IMPERFECT SPEECH

NOUNS 1 **speech defect,** speech impediment, speech difficulty, impairment of speech; dysarthria, dysphasia, dysphrasia; dyslalia, dyslogia; idioglossia, idiolalia; **broken speech,** cracked *or* broken voice, broken tones *or* accents; indistinct *or* blurred *or* muzzy speech; loss of voice, aphonia; **nasalization,** nasal tone *or* accent, **twang,** nasal twang, talking through one's nose; **falsetto,** childish treble, artificial voice; **shake, quaver,** tremor; **lisp,** lisping; hiss, sibilation, lallation; **croak,** choked voice, hawking voice; crow; harshness, dysphonia, hoarseness 58.2; voicelessness, loss of voice

2 **inarticulateness,** inarticulacy, inarticulation; thickness of speech

3 **stammering, stuttering,** hesitation, faltering, traulism, dysphemia, *balbuties* <L>; palilalia; stammer, stutter

4 **mumbling, muttering,** maundering; unintelligible speech; droning, drone; mumble, mutter; jabber, jibber, gibber, gibbering, gabble; whispering, whisper, susurration; mouthing; murmuring

5 **mispronunciation,** misspeaking, cacology, cacoepy; lallation, lambdacism, paralambdacism; rhotacism, pararhotacism; gammacism; mytacism; **corruption,** language pollution

6 **aphasia, agraphia;** aphrasia, aphrasia paranoica; **aphonia,** loss of speech, aphonia clericorum, hysterical aphonia, stage fright, aphonia paralytica, aphonia paranoica, spastic aphonia, mutism, muteness 51.2; voiceless speech, sign language

VERBS **7** **speak poorly,** talk incoherently, be unable to put two words together; have an impediment in one's speech, have a bone in one's neck *or* throat; speak thickly; **croak; lisp; shake, quaver; drawl;** mince, clip one's words; lose one's voice, get stage fright, clank *or* clank up *and* freeze <nf>, be struck dumb

8 **stammer, stutter,** stammer out; hesitate, falter, halt, mammer <Brit nf>, stumble; hem, haw, hum, **hum and haw, hem and haw**

9 **mumble, mutter,** maunder; drone, drone on; swallow one's words, speak drunkenly *or* incoherently; jabber, gibber, gabble; splutter, sputter; blubber, sob; whisper, susurrate; murmur; babble; mouth

10 nasalize, whine, **speak through one's nose,** twang, snuffle

11 **mispronounce,** misspeak, missay, **murder the King's** *or* **Queen's English**

ADJS **12** <imperfectly spoken> inarticulate, indistinct, blurred, muzzy, unintelligible; **mispronounced; shaky,** shaking, **quavering,** breaking, cracked, tremulous, titubant; **drawling,** drawly; **lisping; throaty, guttural,** thick, velar; stifled, choked, choking, strangled; **nasal, twangy,**

breathy, adenoidal, snuffling; croaking, hawking; harsh, dysphonic, hoarse 58.15

13 **stammering, stuttering,** halting, hesitating, faltering, stumbling, balbutient; **aphasic;** aphrasic; aphonic, dumb, **mute** 51.12

526 WORD

NOUNS **1** **word,** free form, minimum free form, semanteme, **term,** name, expression, locution, linguistic form, lexeme; written unit; content word, function word; *logos* <Gk>, *verbum* <L>; verbalism, vocable, utterance, articulation; **usage;** syllable, polysyllable; homonym, homophone, homograph; monosyllable; synonym; metonym; antonym; easy word, hard word

2 **root,** etymon, primitive; eponym; derivative, derivation; cognate; doublet

3 **morphology,** morphemics; morphophonemics; **morpheme;** morph, allomorph; bound morpheme *or* form, free morpheme *or* form; difference of form, formal contrast; accidence; **inflection,** conjugation, declension; paradigm; derivation, word-formation; formative; root, radical; theme, stem; word element, combining form; **affix, suffix, prefix,** infix; proclitic, enclitic; affixation, infixation, suffixation, prefixation; morphemic analysis, immediate constituent *or* IC analysis, cutting; morphophonemic analysis

4 **word form,** formation, construction; back formation; clipped word; spoonerism; **compound;** *tatpurusha, dvandva, karmadharaya, dvigu, avyayibhava, bahuvrihi* <all Skt>; endocentric compound, exocentric compound; acronym, acrostic; paronym, conjugate; proclitic, enclitic

5 **technical term,** technicality; jargon word; jargon 523.9,10

6 **barbarism, corruption, vulgarism, impropriety,** taboo word, dirty word *and* four-letter word <nf>, swearword, naughty word, bad word, obscenity, expletive; **colloquialism, slang, localism** 526.6

7 **loan word,** borrowing, borrowed word, paronym; loan translation, calque; foreignism

8 **neologism,** neology, neoterism, new word *or* term, newfangled expression; **coinage;** new sense *or* meaning; **nonce word;** ghost word *or* name

9 **catchword,** catch phrase, shibboleth, slogan, cry; **pet expression,** byword, cliché; **buzzword,** vogue word, fad word, in-word; euphemism, **code word;** commonplace, hackneyed expression

10 long word, hard word, jawbreaker *or* jawtwister *and* two-dollar *or* five-dollar word <nf>, polysyllable; sesquipedalian, sesquipedalia <pl>; lexiphanicism, grandiloquence 545

11 hybrid word, **hybrid;** macaronicism, macaronic; hybridism, contamination; blendword, blend, portmanteau word, portmanteau, portmantologism, telescope word, **counterword;** ghost word

12 **archaism,** archaicism, antiquated word *or* expression; obsoletism, obsolete

13 **vocabulary, lexis, words, word stock,** wordhoard, stock of words; phraseology; **thesaurus,** Roget's; lexicon

14 **lexicology; lexicography,** lexigraphy, glossography; onomastics 527.1, toponymics; **meaning** 518, semantics, semasiology; denotation, connotation

15 **etymology, derivation, origin,** word origin, word history, semantic history, etymon; historical linguistics, comparative linguistics; eponymy; folk etymology

16 echoic word, onomatopoeic word, onomatope; onomatopoeia; bowwow theory

17 **neologist, word-coiner,** neoterist; phraser, phrasemaker, phrasemonger; word nerd

ADJS 18 **verbal,** vocabular, vocabulary

19 lexical, lexicologic, lexicological; lexigraphic, lexigraphical, **lexicographical,** lexicographic; glossographic, glossographical; etymological, etymologic, derivational; onomastic, onomatologic; onomasiological; echoic, onomatopoeic; conjugate, paronymous, paronymic

20 neological, neoterical

21 **morphological,** morphemic; morphophonemic; inflective, inflectional, paradigmatic, derivational; affixal, prefixal, infixal, suffixal

WORD ELEMENTS 22 log-, logo-, onomato-, -onym, -onymy

527 NOMENCLATURE

NOUNS 1 **nomenclature, terminology,** orismology, glossology <old>, vocabulary, lexicon; onomatology, onomastics; toponymics, toponymy, place-names, place-naming; antonomasia; orismology; polyonymy; **taxonomy,** classification, systematics, cladistics, biosystematics, cytotaxonomy, binomial nomenclature, binomialism, Linnaean method, trinomialism; kingdom, phylum, class, order, family, genus, species

2 **naming, calling, denomination,** appellation, designation, designating, styling, terming, definition, identification; **christening,** baptism; dubbing; nicknaming

3 **name, appellation,** appellative, **denomination, designation, style,** heading, *nomen* <L>, cognomen, cognomination, full name; proper name *or* noun; moniker *and* handle <nf>; **title,** honorific; empty title *or* name; **label, tag; epithet,** byword; **scientific name,** trinomen, trinomial name, binomen, binomial name; *nomen nudum* <L>, hyponym; tautonym; typonym; middle name; eponym; namesake; secret name, cryptonym, euonym, password; professional title; title of respect *or* address; military title; place name, toponym; trade name, trademark

4 **first name,** forename, **Christian name, given name,** baptismal name; **middle name**

5 **surname, last name, family name, cognomen,** byname; **maiden name;** married name; patronym, matronym

6 <Latin terms> *praenomen, nomen, agnomen, cognomen*

7 **nickname, sobriquet,** byname, cognomen; epithet, agnomen; **pet name,** diminutive, hypocoristic, affectionate name

8 **alias, pseudonym,** anonym, **assumed name,** false *or* fictitious name, *nom de guerre* <Fr>; pen name, nom de plume; stage name, nom de théâtre <Fr>, professional name; John Doe, Jane Doe, Richard Roe

9 **misnomer,** wrong name

10 **signature,** sign manual, **autograph, hand, John Hancock** <nf>; mark, mark of signature, cross, christcross, X; initials; subscription; countersignature, countersign, countermark, counterstamp; endorsement; visa, *visé* <Fr>; monogram, cipher, device; seal, sigil, signet

VERBS 11 **name, denominate,** nominate, **designate, call, term, style, dub,** color <nf>; specify; define, identify; title, entitle; **label, tag; nickname; christen,** baptize

12 **misname,** misnomer, **miscall,** misterm, misdesignate

13 **be called, be known by** *or* as, go by, go as, **go by the name of,** go *or* pass under the name of, bear the name of, rejoice in the name of; go under an assumed *or* a false name, have an alias

ADJS 14 **named, called,** yclept <old>, **styled, titled,** denominated, denominate <old>, **known as,** known by the name of, designated, termed, dubbed, identified as; christened, baptized; what one may well *or* fairly *or* properly *or* fitly call

15 **nominal,** cognominal; **titular, in name only,** nominative, formal; so-called, quasi; would-be, *soi-disant* <Fr>; **self-called, self-styled,** self-christened; honorific; agnominal, epithetic, epithetical; hypocoristic, diminutive; by name, by whatever name, under any other name; **alias,** a k a *or* also known as

16 denominative, nominative, appellative; eponymous, eponymic

17 **terminological,** nomenclatural, orismological; onomastic; toponymic, toponymous; taxonomic, classificatory, binomial, Linnaean, trinomial
WORD ELEMENTS 18 onomato-, -onym, -onymy

528 ANONYMITY

NOUNS 1 **anonymity, anonymousness, namelessness; incognito;** cover, cover name; code name; anonym; unknown quantity, no-name; Unknown Soldier; Anon.
  2 **what's-its-name** *and* **what's-his-name** *and* what's-his-face *and* what's-her-name *and* **what-you-may-call-it** *and* whatchamacallit *and* what-you-may-call-'em *and* what-d'ye-call-'em *and* what-d'ye-call-it *and* whatzit <nf>; *je ne sais quoi* <Fr>, I don't know what; such-and-such; **so-and-so,** certain person, X *or* Mr X; you-know-who
ADJS 3 **anonymous, anon; nameless, unnamed,** unidentified, undesignated, unspecified, innominate, without a name, **unknown;** undefined; unacknowledged; **incognito;** cryptonymous, cryptonymic; lesser-known

529 PHRASE

NOUNS 1 **phrase, expression, locution, utterance,** usage, term, verbalism; **word-group,** fixed expression, construction, endocentric construction, headed group, syntagm; syntactic structure; noun phrase, compound noun, verb phrase, verb complex, adverbial phrase, adjectival phrase, prepositional phrase; conditional phrase; phrasal verb; **collocation; clause,** coordinate clause, subordinate clause, independent clause; **sentence,** period, periodic sentence; **paragraph; idiom,** idiotism, phrasal idiom; turn of phrase *or* expression, peculiar expression, manner *or* way of speaking; set phrase *or* term; conventional *or* common *or* standard phrase; phraseogram, phraseograph; maxim, adage, moral, proverb, slogan, motto, quotation, quote, sound bite
  2 **diction, phrasing;** phraseology, choice of words, wording
  3 **phraser, phrasemaker,** phrasemonger, phraseman
ADJS 4 **phrasal,** phrase; phrasey
  5 in set phrases *or* terms, in good set terms, in round terms

530 GRAMMAR

NOUNS 1 **grammar,** rules of language, linguistic structure, syntactic structure, sentence structure; "the rule and pattern of speech"—Horace; grammaticalness, well-formedness, grammaticality, grammatical theory; **traditional grammar, school grammar;** descriptive grammar, **structural grammar;** case grammar; phrase-structure grammar; generative grammar, **transformational grammar, transformational generative grammar;** comparative grammar; tagmemic analysis; glossematics; stratificational grammar; **parsing,** construing, grammatical analysis; **morphology** 526.3; **phonology** 524.13, good grammar, good English, Standard English, correct grammar; style guide *or* sheet
  2 **syntax, structure, syntactic structure,** word order, word arrangement; syntactics, syntactic analysis; immediate constituent analysis *or* IC analysis, cutting; phrase structure; surface structure, shallow structure, deep structure, underlying structure; levels, ranks, strata; tagmeme, form-function unit, slot, filler, slot *and* filler; **function, subject, predicate, complement, object,** direct object, indirect object, **modifier,** qualifier, sentence *or* construction modifier, appositive, attribute, attributive; inflection, diminuitive, intensive, formative; asyndeton, syndeton, apposition, hypotaxis, parataxis
  3 **part of speech,** form class, major form class, function class; function *or* empty *or* form word; **adjective,** adjectival, attributive, derived adjective; **adverb,** adverbial; **preposition;** verbal adjective, gerundive; **participle,** present participle, past participle, perfect participle; **conjunction** <see list>, subordinating conjunction, coordinating conjunction, conjunctive adverb, adversative conjunction, copula, copulative, copulative conjunction, correlative conjunction, disjunctive, disjunctive conjunction; **interjection,** exclamatory noun *or* adjective; **particle**
  4 **verb,** transitive, transitive verb, intransitive, intransitive verb, impersonal verb, neuter verb, deponent verb, defective verb, reflexive verb, irregular verb; predicate; finite verb; linking verb, copula; helping verb; verbal, verbid, nonfinite verb form; **infinitive; auxiliary verb,** auxiliary, modal auxiliary; phrasal verb; verb phrase, phrasal verb; present participle, past participle, perfect participle
  5 **noun, pronoun,** substantive, substantival, common noun, proper noun, concrete noun, abstract noun, collective noun, quotation noun, compound noun, possessive noun, hypostasis, adherent noun, adverbial noun, attributive noun; verbal noun, gerund; nominal; noun phrase; mass noun, count noun
  6 **article,** definite article, indefinite article; determiner, noun determiner, determinative, post-determiner

7 **person;** first person; second person, proximate; third person; fourth person, obviative

8 number; singular, dual, trial, plural

9 **case;** common case, subject case, nominative; object *or* objective case, accusative, dative, possessive case, genitive; local case, locative, essive, superessive, inessive, adessive, abessive, lative, allative, illative, sublative, elative, ablative, delative, terminative, approximative, prolative, perlative, translative; comitative, instrumental, prepositional, vocative; oblique case

10 **gender,** masculine, feminine, neuter, common gender; grammatical gender, natural gender; animate, inanimate

11 **mood,** mode; indicative, subjunctive, imperative, conditional, potential, obligative, permissive, optative, jussive

12 **tense; present;** historical present; **past,** preterit *or* preterite; aorist; imperfect; future; **perfect,** present perfect, future perfect; past perfect, **pluperfect;** progressive tense, durative; point tense

13 **aspect;** perfective, imperfective, inchoative, iterative, frequentative, desiderative

14 **voice;** active voice, active, passive voice, passive; middle voice, middle; medio-passive; reflexive

15 **punctuation,** punctuation marks <see list>; diacritical mark *or* sign <see list>, accent; reference mark <see list>, reference; point, tittle; stop, end stop

VERBS 16 grammaticize; **parse,** analyze; inflect, **conjugate, decline; punctuate,** mark, point; parenthesize, hyphenate, bracket; diagram, notate

ADJS 17 **grammatical, syntactical,** formal, structural; correct, well-formed; tagmemic, glossematic; **functional;** substantive, nominal, pronominal; verbal, transitive, intransitive; linking, copulative; attributive, adjectival, adverbal, participial; prepositional, post-positional; conjunctive

18 conjunctions

according as	as though
afore	as well as
after	because
against	before
albeit	being
also	both
although	but
an	'cause
and	considering
and/or	directly
as	either
as far as	ere
as how	ergo
as if	except
as long as	excepting
as soon as	for

for and	still less
forasmuch as	supposing
fore	syne
gin	than
how	that
howbeit	then
however	tho
if	though
immediately	till
in case	unless
in order	unlike
that	until
inasmuch as	well
insofar as	what
insomuch as	when
instantly	whence
lest	whenever
let alone	whensoever
like	where
much as	whereabout
much less	whereabouts
nay	whereas
neither	whereat
never mind	whereby
nor	wherefore
notwithstanding	wherefrom
now	wherein
once	whereinto
once that	whereof
only	whereon
or	whereso
other than	wheresoever
otherwise	wherethrough
plus	whereto
provided	whereunder
providing	whereunto
rather than	whereupon
save	wherever
saving	wherewith
seeing	whether
since	while
so	whilst
sobeit	whither
so long as	why
so that	without
still	yet

19 **prepositions**

a	against
à la	agin
abaft	aloft
aboard	along
about	alongside
above	amid
absent	amidst
according to	among
across	amongst
adown	an
afore	anent
after	apart from

après
apropos
around
as
as of
as per
as regards
as to
as well as
aside
aside from
aslant
astraddle
astride
at
athwart
atop
bar
barring
batting
because
because of
before
behind
below
ben <Scot>
beneath
beside
besides
between
betwixt
beyond
but
but for
by
chez
circa
concerning
considering
contra
contrary to
cross
cum
despite
down
due to
during
ere
ex
except
except for
excepting
excluding
exclusive of
failing
following
for
forby or forbye
fore

forth
foul of
frae <Scot>
fro
from
given
hear
in
in between
in memoriam
in re
including
inclusive of
inside
inside of
instead of
into
irrespective of
less
like
malgré <Fr>
maugre
mid
midst
minus
modulo
near
neath
next
next to
nigh
notwithstanding
o'
o'er
of
off
off of
on
onto
opposite
or
out
out of
outside
outside of
outwith <Scot>
over
over against
over and above
owing to
pace
past
pending
per
plus
preparatory to
previous to
prior to
pro

pursuant to
qua
rather than
re
regarding
regardless of
relative to
respecting
round
sans
save
saving
since
subsequent to
syne <Scot>
than
thanks to
the
thorough
thro
throughout
thru
thwart
till
times
to
together with

20 pronouns

all
another
any
anybody
anyone
anything
both
each
each other
either
few
he
her
hers
herself
him
himself
his
how
I
it
its
itself
many
me
mine
most
much
my
myself

touching
toward
'tween *or*
  tween
twixt
under
underneath
unless
unlike
until
unto
up
up and down
up to
upon
upside
versus
via
vice
vis-à-vis
wanting
while
with
withal
within
without
worth

neither
no one
nobody
none
nothing
one
one another
other
our
ours
ourselves
several
she
some
somebody
someone
something
that
their
theirs
them
themselves
these
they
this
those
us
we
what
whatever

when	whomever
where	whose
which	why
whichever	you
who	your
whoever	yours
whom	yourself

21 diacritical marks

acute accent <´>	hacek <Cz> or wedge <^>
breve or caron <˘>	krozek <°>
cedilla <,>	ligature <æ>
circumflex accent <ˆ, or ˜>	macron <‾>
diaeresis or umlaut <¨>	schwa < >
grave accent <`>	tilde <~>

22 punctuation marks

ampersand <&>	interrobang <!?>
angle brackets <<>>	parentheses or parens <nf>
apostrophe <'>	<()>
braces <[]>	period, full stop <Brit>,
brackets or square	point, decimal point,
brackets <[]>	dot <.>
colon <:>	question mark or interro-
comma <,>	gation mark or point <?>
ellipsis, suspension periods	quotation marks, quotes
< . . . > or <***>	<"">
em dash <—>	semicolon <;>
en dash <–>	single quotation marks,
exclamation mark or	single quotes <''>
point <!>	virgule, diagonal,
guillemets <<< >>>	solidus, slash
hyphen <->	mark </>

23 reference marks

asterisk, star <*>	index or fist <☞>
asterism <***>	leaders <......>
bullet or centered dot <·>	obelus <÷>
caret <>	paragraph <¶>
dagger or obelisk <†>	parallels <‖>
ditto mark <">	prime <'>
double dagger or diesis <‡>	section <§>
double prime <">	swung dash <~>

531 UNGRAMMATICALNESS

NOUNS **1 ungrammaticalness,** bad or faulty grammar, faulty syntax; lack of concord or agreement, incorrect usage, faulty reference, misplaced or dangling modifier, shift of tense, shift of structure, anacoluthon, faulty subordination, faulty comparison, faulty coordination, faulty punctuation, lack of parallelism, sentence fragment, comma fault, comma splice; abuse of terms, corruption of speech, broken speech

2 solecism, ungrammaticism, **misusage, missaying, misconstruction,** barbarism, infelicity; corruption; antiphrasis, spoonerism, malapropism 975.7

VERBS **3** solecize, commit a solecism, use faulty or inadmissable or inappropriate grammar, ignore or disdain or violate grammar, murder the King's or Queen's English, break Priscian's head <old>

ADJS **4 ungrammatic, ungrammatical,** solecistic, solecistical, **incorrect,** barbarous; faulty, erroneous 975.16; infelicitous, improper 789.7; careless, slovenly, slipshod 810.15; loose, imprecise 975.17

532 DICTION

NOUNS **1 diction,** words, wordage, verbiage, word-usage, **usage,** usus loquendi <L>, use or choice of words, formulation, way of putting or couching, word garment, word dressing; **rhetoric,** speech, talk <nf>; **language,** dialect, parlance, locution, expression, **grammar** 530; **idiom;** composition

2 style; mode, manner, strain, vein; fashion, way; **rhetoric; manner of speaking,** mode of expression, literary style, style of writing, command of language or idiom, form of speech, expression of ideas; feeling for words or language, way with words, sense of language, Sprachgefühl <Ger>; gift of gab or of the gab <nf>, blarney or the blarney <nf>; the power or grace of expression; linguistic tact or finesse; personal style; mannerism, trick, pecularity; affectation; "a certain absolute and unique manner of expressing a thing"—Walter Pater; editorial style; inflation, exaggeration, grandiloquence 545; the grand style, the sublime style, the sublime; the plain style; **stylistics,** stylistic analysis

3 stylist, master of style; rhetorician, rhetor, rhetorizer <old>; mannerist; wordsmith; phrasemonger

VERBS **4 phrase, express,** find a phrase for, give expression or words to, **word,** state, **frame,** conceive, style, couch, **put in or into words,** clothe or embody in words, couch in terms, express by or in words, find words to express, find words for; put, present, set out; **formulate,** formularize; paragraph; rhetorize <old>

ADJS **5 phrased,** expressed, worded, formulated, styled, put, presented, couched; stylistic, overdone

533 ELEGANCE
<of language>

NOUNS **1 elegance,** elegancy; **grace,** gracefulness, gracility; **taste,** tastefulness, good taste; **correctness,** seemliness, comeliness, **propriety,** aptness, fittingness; **refinement,** precision, exactitude, lapidary quality, finish; **discrimination,** choice; **restraint; polish, finish,** terseness, neatness; smoothness, flow, **fluency; felicity,** felicitousness, **ease;** clarity, clearness, lucidity, limpidity, pellucidity, perspicuity; distinction, dignity; **purity,** chastity, chasteness; **plainness,** straightforwardness, directness, **simplicity,** naturalness, unaffectedness, Atticism, unadorned simplicity, gracility, Attic quality; classicism, classicalism; well-rounded *or* well-turned periods, flowing periods; the right word in the right place, right word at the right time, *mot juste* <Fr>; fittingness, appropriateness; classicism, Atticism

2 **harmony, proportion,** symmetry, **balance,** equilibrium, order, orderedness, measure, measuredness, concinnity; rhythm; **euphony,** sweetness, beauty

3 <affected elegance> **affectation,** affectedness, studiedness, **pretentiousness, mannerism,** posiness <Brit>, preciosity, manneredness, artifice, artfulness, **artificiality,** unnaturalness; **euphuism,** Gongorism, Marinism; **preciousness,** preciosity; euphemism; purism; overelegance, overelaboration, overniceness, overrefinement, hyperelegance, etc

4 purist, classicist, Atticist, plain stylist

5 euphuist, Gongorist, Marinist, *précieux* and *précieuse* <Fr>; phrasemaker, phrasemonger

ADJS 6 **elegant, tasteful, graceful, polished,** finished, round, terse; neat, trim, **refined, exact,** lapidary *or* lapidarian; **restrained; clear,** lucid, limpid, pellucid, perspicuous; **simple, unaffected, natural,** unlabored, fluent, flowing, **easy; pure,** chaste; **plain,** straightforward, direct, unadorned, gracile, no-frills *and* vanilla *and* plain vanilla <nf>; classic, classical; Attic, Ciceronian, Augustan

7 **appropriate, fit, fitting,** just <old>, **proper, correct, seemly,** comely; **felicitous,** happy, **apt, well-chosen; well-put,** well-expressed, inspired

8 **harmonious, balanced,** symmetrical, orderly, ordered, measured, concinnate, concinnous; **euphonious,** euphonic, euphonical <old>, sweet; **smooth,** tripping, smooth-sounding, fluent, flowing, fluid; classical

9 <affectedly elegant> **affected,** euphuistic, euphuistical; elaborate, elaborated; **pretentious, mannered, artificial, unnatural,** posy <Brit>, studied; precious, *précieux* or *précieuse* <Fr>, deluxe, overnice, overrefined, overelegant, overelaborate, hyperelegant, etc; Gongoristic, Gongoresque, Marinistic

534 INELEGANCE
<of language>

NOUNS 1 **inelegance,** inelegancy; inconcinnity <old>, infelicity; **clumsiness,** cumbrousness, clunkiness *and* klutziness <nf>, leadenness, heavy-handedness, ham-handedness, ham-fistedness <chiefly Brit>, heavy-footedness, heaviness, stiltedness, **ponderousness,** unwieldiness; sesquipedalianism, sesquipedality; turgidity, bombasticness, pompousness 545.1; **gracelessness,** ungracefulness; **tastelessness,** bad taste, impropriety, indecorousness, unseemliness; incorrectness, impurity; **vulgarity,** vulgarism, Gothicism <old>, barbarism, barbarousness, **coarseness, unrefinement,** roughness, grossness, rudeness, crudeness, uncouthness; turgidity; dysphemism; solecism; cacology, poor diction; cacophony, uneuphoniousness, harshness; loose *or* slipshod construction, ill-balanced sentences; lack of finish *or* polish

ADJS 2 **inelegant, clumsy, clunky** *and* **klutzy** <nf>, heavy-handed, heavy-footed, ham-handed, ham-fisted <chiefly Brit>, graceless, ungraceful, inconcinnate *and* inconcinnous <old>, infelicitous, unfelicitous; **tasteless,** in bad taste, offensive to ears polite; **incorrect, improper; indecorous, unseemly,** uncourtly, undignified; **unpolished, unrefined;** impure, unclassical; **vulgar,** barbarous, barbaric, rude, **crude, uncouth,** Doric, outlandish; low, gross, **coarse,** dysphemistic, doggerel; cacologic, cacological, cacophonous, uneuphonious, harsh, ill-sounding; solecistic

3 **stiff, stilted, formal,** Latinate, *guindé* <Fr>, **labored,** ponderous, elephantine, lumbering, cumbrous, leaden, heavy, unwieldy, sesquipedalian, inkhorn, turgid, bombastic, pompous 545.8; **forced,** awkward, cramped, halting; crabbed

535 PLAIN SPEECH

NOUNS 1 **plain speech,** plain speaking, plain-spokenness, plain style, unadorned style, gracility, **plain English,** plain words, common speech, vernacular, household words, words of one syllable; plainness, simpleness, simplicity; "more matter with less art"—Shakespeare; soberness, restrainedness; severity, austerity; spareness, leanness, baldness, bareness, starkness, unadornedness, naturalness, unaffectedness; **directness, straightforwardness,** calling a spade a spade, mincing no words, making no bones about it <nf>; unimaginativeness, prosaicness, matter-of-factness, prosiness, unpoeticalness; homespun, rustic style; **candor,** frankness, openness

VERBS 2 **speak plainly,** waste no words, **call a spade a spade,** come to the point, lay it on the line, not beat about the bush, mince no words, make no bones about it *and* talk turkey <nf>

ADJS **3 plain-speaking,** simple-speaking; **plain,** common; plain-spoken; simple, unadorned, unvarnished, pure, neat; sober, severe, austere, ascetic, spare, lean, bald, bare, stark, Spartan; **natural, unaffected;** direct, straightforward, woman-to-woman, man-to-man, one-on-one; commonplace, homely, homespun, rustic; **candid,** up-front <nf>, plain-spoken, frank, straight-out <nf>, open; **prosaic,** prosing, prosy; unpoetical, unimaginative, dull, dry, matter-of-fact; point-blank

ADVS **4 plainly, simply,** naturally, unaffectedly, matter-of-factly; in plain words, plain-spokenly, **in plain English,** in words of one syllable; **directly,** point-blank, to the point; candidly, frankly

PHRS **5** read my lips, I'll spell it out

536 FIGURE OF SPEECH

NOUNS **1 figure of speech** <see list>, **figure, image,** trope, turn of expression, manner *or* way of speaking, ornament, device, flourish, flower; purple passage; imagery, nonliterality, nonliteralness, figurativeness, figurative language; figured *or* florid *or* flowery style, Gongorism, floridity, euphuism

VERBS **2** metaphorize, figure <old>; similize; personify, personalize; symbolize

ADJS **3 figurative,** tropologic, tropological; **metaphorical,** trolatitious; allusive, referential; mannered, figured, ornamented, **flowery** 545.11

ADVS **4 figuratively,** tropologically; **metaphorically;** symbolically; **figuratively speaking,** so to say *or* speak, in a manner of speaking, **as it were**

5 figures of speech (literary devices)

adynaton	aposiopesis
agnomination	apostrophe
alliteration	auxesis
allusion	catachresis
anacoluthon	chiasmus
anadiplosis	circumlocution
analogy	climax
anaphora	congeries
anapodoton	conversion
anastrophe	correctio
antanaclasis	ecphonesis
anthimeria	ellipsis
antimetabole	emphasis
antiphrasis	enallage
antisthecon	epanalepsis
antithesis	epanaphora
antonomasia	epanodos
aphaersis	epanorthosis
apocope	epenthesis
apophasis	epidiplosis
aporia	epiphora
epistrophe	paradox
epizeuxis	paragoge
eroteme	paralepsis
exclamation	paregmenon
gemination	parenthesis
gradatio	periphrasis
hendiadys	personification
hypallage	pleonasm
hyperbaton	ploce
hyperbole	polyptoton
hypozeugma	polysyndeton
hypozeuxis	preterition
hysteron proteron	prolepsis
inversion	prosopopoeia
irony	prosthesis
isocolon	regression
kenning	repetition
litotes	rhetorical question
malapropism	sarcasm
meiosis	scesis onamaton
metalepsis	simile, similitude
metaphor	spoonerism
metathesis	syllepsis
metonymy	symploce
mixed metaphor	syncope
occupatio	synecdoche
onomatopoeia, onomatopy	tautology
oxymoron	Wellerism
paradiastole	zeugma

537 CONCISENESS

NOUNS **1 conciseness,** concision, briefness, brachylogy, **brevity,** "the soul of wit"—Shakespeare; shortness, compactness; **curtness,** brusqueness, **crispness, terseness,** summariness; compression; taciturnity 344.2, reserve 344.3; **pithiness,** succinctness, pointedness, sententiousness; compendiousness; heart of the matter

2 laconicness, laconism, laconicism, economy of language *or* words; laconics; Atticism; commatism

3 aphorism, epigram 974.1; **abridgment** 557

4 abbreviation, shortening, clipping, cutting, pruning, truncation; ellipsis, aposiopesis, contraction, syncope, apocope, elision, crasis, syneresis <all rhetoric>

VERBS **5 be brief, come to the point,** get to the bottom line *or* the nitty-gritty <nf>, **make a long story short,** cut the matter short, cut the shit <nf>, be telegraphic, waste no words, put it in few words, give more matter *and* less art; shorten, condense, **abbreviate** 268.6

ADJS **6 concise, brief, short,** "short and sweet"—Thomas Lodge; **condensed, compressed,** tight, close, compact; compendious 268.8; curt, brusque, **crisp, terse,** summary; taciturn 344.9; reserved

344.10; **pithy, succinct; laconic,** Spartan; **abridged, abbreviated,** vest-pocket, synopsized, shortened, clipped, cut, pruned, contracted, truncated, docked; elliptic, syncopic, aposiopestic; telegraphic; sententious, epigrammatic, epigrammatical, gnomic, aphoristic *or* aphoristical, **pointed,** to the point; brachylogous; encapsuled

ADVS **7 concisely, briefly,** shortly, standing on one leg; laconically; curtly, brusquely, crisply, tersely, summarily; pithily, succinctly, pointedly; sententiously, aphoristically, epigrammatically

8 in brief, in short, for short, *tout court* <Fr>; in substance, in epitome, in outline; **in a nutshell,** in a capsule; **in a word,** in two words, in a few words, without wasting *or* mincing words; **to be brief,** to the point, to sum up, to come to the point, to cut the matter short, **to make a long story short**

538 DIFFUSENESS

NOUNS **1 diffuseness,** diffusiveness, diffusion; shapelessness, **formlessness** 263, amorphousness, blobbiness <nf>, unstructuredness; obscurity 522.3

2 wordiness, verbosity, verbiage, verbalism, verbality; **prolixity, long-windedness,** longiloquence, loquacity; flow *or* flux of words, cloud of words; profuseness, **profusiveness,** profusion; **effusiveness,** effusion, gush, gushing; outpour, tirade; logorrhea, verbal diarrhea, diarrhea of the mouth, **talkativeness** 540; **copiousness, exuberance,** rampancy, amplitude, extravagance, prodigality, fertility, fecundity, rankness, teemingness, prolificity, prolificacy, productivity, abundance, overflow, fluency <old>; superfluity, superflux, superabundance, overflow, inundation; **redundancy,** pleonasm, repetitiveness, reiterativeness, reiteration, iteration, tautology, macrology, double-talk; repetition for effect *or* emphasis, palilogy

3 discursiveness, desultoriness, digressiveness, aimlessness; **rambling,** maundering, meandering, wandering, roving

4 digression, departure, deviation, **discursion,** excursion, excursus, sidetrack, side path, side road, byway, bypath; episode; rambling; segue

5 circumlocution, roundaboutness, circuitousness, ambages <old>; deviousness, obliqueness, **indirection;** periphrase, periphrasis; ambagiousness

6 amplification, expatiation, enlargement, expansion, dilation, dilatation, dilating; **elaboration, laboring; development,** explication, unfolding, working-out, fleshing-out, detailing, filling in the empty places, filler, padding

VERBS **7 amplify, expatiate, dilate, expand,** enlarge, **enlarge upon,** expand on, **elaborate;** relate *or* rehearse in extenso; detail, particularize; **develop,** open out, fill in, flesh out, evolve, unfold; work out, explicate; descant, relate at large

8 protract, extend, spin out, string out, draw out, stretch out, go on *or* be on about, **drag out,** run out, drive into the ground <nf>; pad, fill out; perorate; **speak at length,** spin a long yarn, never finish; verbify, chatter, talk one to death 540.6

9 digress, wander, **get off the subject, wander from the subject,** get sidetracked, excurse, ramble, maunder, stray, go astray; depart, **deviate,** turn aside, jump the track; **go off on a tangent,** go up blind alleys; segue

10 circumlocute <nf>, say in a roundabout way, talk in circles, **go round about,** go around *and* around, **beat around** *or* **about the bush,** go round Robin Hood's barn; periphrase

ADJS **11 diffuse,** diffusive; **formless** 263.4, unstructured; **profuse,** profusive; **effusive,** gushing, gushy; copious, exuberant, extravagant, prodigal, fecund, teeming, prolific, productive, abundant, superabundant, overflowing; **redundant,** pleonastic, repetitive, reiterative, iterative, tautologous, parrotlike

12 wordy, verbose; talkative 540.9; **prolix,** windy <nf>, **long-winded,** longiloquent; **protracted,** extended, *de longue haleine* <Fr>, lengthy, long, **long-drawn-out,** long-spun, spun-out, endless, unrelenting; padded, filled out

13 discursive, aimless, loose; **rambling, maundering, wandering,** peripatetic, roving, deviating; excursive, discursive, **digressive,** deviative, **desultory,** episodic; by the way; sidetracked

14 circumlocutory, circumlocutional, **roundabout, circuitous,** ambagious <old>, oblique, indirect; periphrastic

15 expatiating, dilative, dilatative, enlarging, amplifying, expanding; **developmental;** garrulous

ADVS **16 at length,** *ad nauseam* <L>, at large, in full, *in extenso* <L>, in detail, on and on

539 AMBIGUITY

NOUNS **1 ambiguity,** ambiguousness; **equivocalness,** equivocacy, equivocality; **double meaning,** amphibology, multivocality, polysemy, polysemousness; punning, paronomasia; double reference, double entendre; twilight zone, gray area; six of one *and* half dozen of the other; inexplicitness, uncertainty 971; irony, contradiction, oxymoron, enantiosis; levels of meaning, richness of meaning, complexity of meaning

2 <ambiguous word *or* expression> **ambiguity,** equivoque, **equivocal,** equivocality; equivocation, amphibology, double entendre; counterword, portmanteau word; polysemant; weasel word; squinting construction; pun 489.8

VERBS 3 equivocate, weasel; ironize; have mixed feelings, be uncertain 971.9

ADJS 4 **ambiguous, equivocal,** equivocatory, dilogical; multivocal, polysemous, polysemantic, amphibolous, amphibological; two-edged, two-sided, either-or, betwixt and between; bittersweet, mixed; inexplicit, uncertain 971.16; ironic; obscure, mysterious, funny, funny peculiar <nf>, enigmatic 522.17

540 TALKATIVENESS

NOUNS 1 **talkativeness, loquacity,** loquaciousness; overtalkativeness, loose tongue, runaway tongue, big mouth <nf>; gabbiness *and* windiness *and* gassiness <nf>; **garrulousness,** garrulity; **long-windedness, prolixity, verbosity** 538.2; multiloquence, multiloquy; **volubility, fluency, glibness;** fluent tongue, flowing tongue, **gift of gab** <nf>; openness, candor, frankness 644.4; effusion, gush, slush; gushiness, **effusiveness, communicativeness;** flow *or* flux *or* spate of words; *flux de bouche* and *flux de mots* and *flux de paroles* <Fr>; **communicativeness** 343.3; gregariousness, sociability, conversableness 343.3

2 **logomania, logorrhea, diarrhea of the mouth, verbal diarrhea,** *cacoëthes loquendi* and *furor loquendi* <L>, blathering, gift of gab

3 **chatter, jabber,** gibber, **babble,** babblement, prate, **prating, prattle, palaver,** small talk, chat, natter <Brit>, **gabble, gab** and jaw-jaw <nf>, **blab, blabber,** blather, blether, blethers <Scot>, clatter, clack, cackle, talkee-talkee; *caquet* and *caqueterie* and *bavardage* <Fr>, twaddle, twattle, **gibble-gabble, bibble-babble, chitter-chatter, prittle-prattle, tittle-tattle,** mere talk, idle talk *or* chatter; **guff** and **gas** and **hot air** and blah-blah and yak and yakkety-yak and blah-blah-blah <nf>; watercooler moment; **gossip;** nonsense 520.2

4 **chatterer, chatterbox, babbler, jabberer, prater, prattler, gabbler,** gibble-gabbler, **gabber** <nf>, **blabberer, blabber,** blatherer, patterer, word-slinger, *moulin à paroles* <Fr>, blab, rattle, bigmouth; magpie, jay, informer; **windbag** *and* gasbag *and* windjammer *and* hot-air artist *and* motor-mouth *and* ratchet-jaw *and* blabbermouth<nf>; idle chatterer, talkative person, **big** *or* **great talker** <nf>, nonstop talker, spendthrift of one's tongue

VERBS 5 **chatter, chat, prate, prattle, patter,** palaver, **babble, gab** <nf>, natter <Brit>, **gabble, gibble-gabble,** tittle-tattle, **jabber,** gibber, **blab, blabber, blather,** blether, clatter, twaddle, twattle, rattle, clack, haver <Brit>, dither, spout *or* **spout off** <nf>, hold forth, pour forth, spin out, **gush,** have a big mouth <nf>, love the sound of one's own voice, talk to hear one's head rattle <nf>; **jaw** *and* **gas** *and* yak *and* **yakkety-yak** *and* run off at the mouth *and* beat one's gums <nf>, **shoot off one's mouth** *or* **face** <nf>; reel off; **talk on,** talk away, **go on** <nf>, run on, rattle on, run on like a mill race; ramble on; talk oneself hoarse, talk till one is blue in the face, talk oneself out of breath; **talk too much; gossip;** talk nonsense 520.5

6 <nf terms> **talk one to death, talk one's head** *or* **ear off,** talk one deaf *and* dumb, talk one into a fever, talk the hind leg off a mule, like the sound of one's own voice, oil one's tongue, talk till one is blue in the face

7 **outtalk,** outspeak, **talk down,** outlast; filibuster

8 be loquacious *or* garrulous, be a windbag *or* gasbag <nf>; have a big mouth *or* bazoo <nf>

ADJS 9 **talkative, loquacious, talky,** big-mouthed <nf>, long-tongued, overtalkative, garrulous, running on, chatty; gossipy, newsy; gabby *and* windy *and* gassy <nf>, all jaw <nf>; multiloquent, multiloquious; **longwinded, prolix, verbose** 538.12; **voluble, fluent; glib,** flip <nf>, smooth; candid, frank 644.17; **effusive,** gushy; expansive, **communicative;** conversational; gregarious, sociable

10 **chattering, prattling, prating,** gabbling, jabbering, gibbering, babbling, blabbing, blabbering, blathering, babblative

ADVS 11 **talkatively, loquaciously,** garrulously; **volubly, fluently,** glibly; effusively, expansively, gushingly

541 CONVERSATION

NOUNS 1 **conversation, converse,** conversing, rapping <nf>; interlocution, colloquy; **exchange;** verbal intercourse, conversational interchange, interchange of speech, give-and-take, cross-talk, rapping <nf>, **repartee,** backchat; **discourse,** colloquial discourse; **communion, intercourse,** social intercourse, **communication** 343

2 **talk, palaver, speech, words;** confabulation, **confab** <nf>, banter, repartee; **chinfest** *and* **chinwag** *and* **talkfest** *and* **bull session** <nf>; **dialogue,** duologue, trialogue; **interview,** question-and-answer session, audience, audition, interlocution; interrogation, examination

3 chat, cozy chat, friendly chat or talk, **little talk,** coze, causerie, **visit** <nf>, gam, *tête-à-tête* <Fr>, **heart-to-heart talk** or heart-to-heart; pillow-talk, intimate discourse, backchat

4 chitchat, chitter-chatter, tittle-tattle, **small talk,** by-talk, cocktail-party chitchat, beauty-parlor chitchat, tea-table talk, table talk, idle chat or talk, gossip, backchat

5 conference, congress, convention, parley, palaver, confab <nf>, confabulation, **conclave, powwow, huddle** <nf>, **consultation,** colloquium, *pourparler* <Fr>, **meeting;** session, sitting, sit-down <nf>, séance; exchange or interchange of views; **council,** council of war; **discussion; interview, audience; news conference,** press conference; photo opportunity, photo op <nf>; high-level talk, conference at the summit, summit, summit conference; summitry; negotiations, bargaining, bargaining session; confrontation, eyeball-to-eyeball encounter <nf>; teleconference; council fire; conference table, negotiating table

6 discussion, debate, debating, **deliberation, nonformalogue,** exchange of views, canvassing, ventilation, airing, review, **treatment, consideration,** investigation, **examination, study, analysis,** logical analysis; logical discussion, dialectic; buzz session <nf>, rap or rap session <nf>; **panel,** panel discussion, open discussion, joint discussion, symposium, colloquium, conference, seminar; **forum,** open forum, town meeting; polemics

7 conversationalist, converser, conversationist; talker, discourser, verbalist, confabulator; colloquist, colloquialist, collocutor; conversational partner; interlocutor, interlocutress or interlocutrice or interlocutrix; parleyer, palaverer; dialogist; Dr Johnson; interviewer, examiner, interrogator, cross-examiner; chatterer

VERBS **8 converse, talk together, talk** or **speak with,** converse with, strike up a conversation, visit with <nf>, discourse with, **commune with,** communicate with, take counsel with, commerce with, **have a talk with,** have a word with, **chin** <nf>, **chew the rag** or **fat** <nf>, **shoot the breeze** <nf>, hold or carry on or join in or engage in a conversation, exchange words; confabulate, confab <nf>, parley; colloque, colloquize; **bandy words; communicate** 343.6,7

9 chat, visit <nf>, gam, coze, pass the time of day, touch base with, have a friendly or cozy chat; **have a little talk,** have a heart-to-heart, let one's hair down; talk with one in private, talk tête-à-tête, be closeted with, make conversation or talk, engage in small talk; prattle, prittle-prattle, tittle-tattle; **gossip**

10 confer, hold a conference, parley, palaver, powwow, hold talks, hold a summit, sit down together, meet around the conference table, **go into a huddle** <nf>, deliberate, take counsel, counsel, **lay** or **put heads together;** collogue; **confer with,** sit down with, **consult with, advise with, discuss with, take up with,** reason with; **discuss,** talk over; **consult,** refer to, call in; compare notes, exchange observations or views; have conversations; negotiate, bargain

11 discuss, debate, reason, deliberate, deliberate upon, exchange views or opinions, talk, **talk over, hash over** <nf>, talk of or about, rap <nf>, exchange ideas, colloquize, comment upon, reason about, discourse about, **consider, treat,** dissertate on, handle, deal with, take up, **go into, examine,** investigate, talk out, brainstorm, **analyze,** sift, **study,** canvass, review, pass under review, controvert, ventilate, air, thrash or thresh out, hammer out, reason the point, consider the pros and cons; **kick** or **knock around** <nf>; talk shop, talk turkey

ADJS **12** conversational, colloquial, confabulatory, interlocutory; communicative; chatty, chitchatty, cozy

ADVS **13** conversationally, colloquially; *tête-à-tête* <Fr>

542 SOLILOQUY

NOUNS **1 soliloquy,** monology, self-address; **monologue;** aside; solo; monodrama; monody; interior monologue, stream of consciousness, apostrophe, aside; one-man or –woman show

2 soliloquist, soliloquizer, Hamlet; monodist, **monologist**

VERBS **3 soliloquize,** monologize; **talk to oneself,** say to oneself, tell oneself, think out loud or aloud; address the four walls, talk to the wall; have an audience of one; say aside, apostrophize; do all the talking, monopolize the conversation, hold forth without interruption

ADJS **4** soliloquizing, monologic, monological, self-addressing; apostrophic; soloistic; monodramatic; thinking aloud, talking to oneself

543 PUBLIC SPEAKING

NOUNS **1 public speaking, declamation, speechmaking, speaking,** speechification <nf>, lecturing, speeching; after dinner speaking; **oratory,** platform oratory or speaking; campaign oratory, stump speaking, the stump, the hustings <Brit>; the soap box; **elocution; rhetoric,** art of public speaking; **eloquence** 544; forensics, debating; speechcraft, wordcraft; **preaching,** pulpit oratory, Bible-thumping <nf>, the pulpit, homiletics; demagogism, demagogy <chiefly Brit>, demagoguery, rabble-rousing; **pyrotechnics**

2 **speech,** speeching, speechification <nf>, **talk, oration, address,** declamation, harangue; public speech *or* address, formal speech, set speech, prepared speech *or* text; welcoming address, farewell address; campaign speech, stump speech, stump oratory; soapbox oratory, tub-thumping <nf>; say; **tirade,** screed, **diatribe,** jeremiad, philippic, invective; after-dinner speech; funeral oration, eulogy; allocution, exhortation, hortatory address, forensic, forensic address; **recitation,** recital, reading; salutatory, salutatory address; valediction, valedictory, valedictory address; inaugural address, inaugural; chalk talk <nf>; pep talk <nf>; pitch, sales talk 734.5; talkathon, filibuster; peroration; debate

3 **lecture,** prelection, **discourse; sermon,** sermonette, homily, religious *or* pulpit discourse, talk; preachment, preaching, preachification <nf>; **evangelism,** televison *or* TV evangelism; travel talk, travelogue

4 **speaker, talker, public speaker, speechmaker,** speecher, speechifier <nf>, spieler *and* jawsmith <nf>; after-dinner speaker, keynote speaker; **spokesperson,** spokesman, spokeswoman; **demagogue,** rabble-rouser; declaimer, ranter, tub-thumper <nf>, haranguer, spouter <nf>; valedictorian, salutatorian; panelist, debater

5 **lecturer,** praelector, discourser, reader, professor; **preacher;** sermonizer, sermonist, sermoner, homilist <old>, pulpitarian, pulpiteer <nf>, Boanerges, hellfire preacher; **evangelist,** televison *or* TV evangelist, televangelist; **expositor,** expounder; chalk talker <nf>

6 **orator, public speaker,** platform orator *or* speaker; rhetorician, rhetor; silver-tongued orator, **spellbinder;** Demosthenes, Cicero, Franklin D Roosevelt, Winston Churchill, William Jennings Bryan, Martin Luther King; **soapbox orator,** soapboxer, stump orator

7 **elocutionist,** elocutioner; **recitationist,** reciter, diseur, diseuse; reader; improvisator, *improvvisatore* <Ital>

8 **rhetorician,** teacher of rhetoric, rhetor, elocutionist; speech-writer

VERBS 9 **make a speech, give a talk, deliver an address,** speechify <nf>, **speak, talk, discourse; address;** stump <nf>, go on *or* take the stump; platform, soapbox; take the floor

10 **declaim,** hold forth, **orate,** elocute <nf>, spout <nf>, spiel <nf>, mouth; **harangue, rant,** "out-herod Herod"—Shakespeare, tub-thump,

perorate, rodomontade; **recite,** read; debate; demagogue, rabble-rouse

11 **lecture,** prelect, read *or* deliver a lectue; **preach,** Bible-thump *and* preachify <nf>, **sermonize,** read a sermon

ADJS 12 **declamatory, elocutionary, oratorical, rhetorical,** forensic; eloquent 544.8; demagogic, demagogical

544 ELOQUENCE

NOUNS 1 **eloquence, rhetoric, silver tongue,** eloquent tongue, facundity; disertitude; **articulateness;** gift of gab <nf>, **glibness,** smoothness, slickness; **felicitousness,** felicity; **oratory** 543.1; expression, **expressiveness,** command of words *or* language, gift of gab *or* of the gab <nf>, gift of expression, vividness, graphicness; pleasing *or* effective style; **meaningfulness** 518.5

2 **fluency,** flow; **smoothness, facility, ease; grace,** gracefulness, poetry; **elegance** 533

3 **vigor, force,** power, strength, vitality, drive, sinew, sinewiness, nervousness, nervosity, vigorousness, forcefulness, effectiveness, impressiveness, pizzazz *and* punch *and* clout <nf>; incisiveness, trenchancy, cuttingness, poignancy, bitingness, bite, mordancy; strong language

4 **spirit,** pep <nf>, liveliness, raciness, sparkle, vivacity, dash, verve, vividness; piquancy, poignancy, pungency

5 **vehemence, passion,** impassionedness, enthusiasm, **ardor,** ardency, **fervor,** fervency, fire, fieriness, glow, warmth, heat

6 **loftiness,** elevation, sublimity; grandeur, **nobility,** stateliness, majesty, gravity, *gravitas* <L>, solemnity, **dignity**

VERBS 7 **have the gift of gab** *or* **of the gab** <nf>, have a tongue in one's head; **spellbind;** shine

ADJS 8 **eloquent, silver-tongued,** silver; well-speaking, well-spoken, **articulate,** facund; **glib, smooth,** smooth-spoken, smooth-tongued, **slick; felicitous;** facile, slick as a whistle <nf>, spellbinding; Demosthenic, Demosthenian; Ciceronian

9 **fluent, flowing,** tripping; **smooth,** pleasing, facile, **easy, graceful, elegant** 533.6

10 **expressive, graphic, vivid,** suggestive, imaginative; well-turned; meaningful 518.10

11 **vigorous,** strong, **powerful,** imperative, **forceful,** forcible, vital, driving, sinewy, sinewed, punchy *and* full of piss and vinegar *and* zappy <nf>, **striking, telling, effective,** impressive; incisive, trenchant, cutting, biting, piercing, poignant, penetrating, slashing, mordant, acid, corrosive; sensational

12 spirited, lively, peppy *and* gingery <nf>, racy, sparkling, vivacious; piquant, poignant, pungent

13 vehement, emphatic, **passionate, impassioned,** enthusiastic, **ardent,** fiery, **fervent,** burning, glowing, warm; urgent, stirring, exciting, stimulating, provoking

14 lofty, elevated, sublime, grand, majestic, noble, stately, grave, solemn, dignified; serious, weighty; moving, inspiring

ADVS **15 eloquently; fluently,** smoothly, glibly, trippingly on the tongue; **expressively,** vividly, graphically; **meaningfully** 518.13; **vigorously,** powerfully, forcefully, spiritedly; tellingly, strikingly, effectively, impressively; **vehemently, passionately,** ardently, fervently, warmly, glowingly, in glowing terms

545 GRANDILOQUENCE

NOUNS **1 grandiloquence,** magniloquence, lexiphanicism, **pompousness,** pomposity, orotundity; **rhetoric,** mere rhetoric, rhetoricalness; high-flown diction, big *or* tall talk <nf>; grandioseness, grandiosity; loftiness, stiltedness; fulsomeness; **pretentiousness,** pretension, **affectation** 533.3; ostentation; **flamboyancy,** showiness, flashiness, gaudiness, meretriciousness, bedizenment, **glitz** <nf>, garishness; sensationalism, luridness, Barnumism; **inflation, inflatedness,** swollenness, turgidity, turgescence, flatulence *or* flatulency, tumidness, tumidity; sententiousness, pontification; swollen phrase *or* diction, swelling utterance; platitudinous ponderosity, polysyllabic profundity, pompous prolixity; Johnsonese; prose run mad; convolution, tortuosity, tortuousness, ostentatious complexity *or* profundity

2 bombast, bombastry, pomposity, **fustian,** highfalutin <nf>, **rant,** rodomontade; **hot air** <nf>; balderdash, gobbledygook <nf>, purple prose, claptrap

3 high-sounding words, lexiphanicism, hard words; **sesquipedalian word,** big *or* long word, twodollar *or* five-dollar word <nf>, **jawbreaker,** jawtwister, mouthful; antidisestablishmentarianism, honorificabilitudinitatibus <Shakespeare>, pneumonoultramicroscopicsilicovolcanoconiosis; polysyllabism, sesquipedalianism, sesquipedality; Latinate diction; academese, technical jargon; puff piece

4 ornateness, floweriness, floridness, floridity, lushness, luxuriance; flourish, flourish of rhetoric, flowers of speech *or* rhetoric, **purple patches** *or* **passages,** beauties, fine writing; **ornament,** ornamentation, **adornment, embellishment,**
elegant variation, **embroidery, frill,** colors *or* colors of rhetoric <old>, figure, **figure of speech** 536

5 phrasemonger, rhetorician; phraseman, phrasemaker, fine writer, wordspinner; euphuist, Gongorist, Marinist; pedant

VERBS **6 talk big** <nf>, talk highfalutin <nf>, phrasemake, **pontificate, blow** <nf>, **vapor,** Barnumize; inflate, bombast, lay *or* pile it on <nf>, lay it on thick *and* lay it on with a trowel <nf>; smell of the lamp

7 ornament, decorate, adorn, embellish, embroider, enrich; overcharge, overlay, overload, load with ornament, festoon, weight down with ornament, flourish <old>; **gild,** gild the lily, trick out, varnish; paint in glowing colors, tell in glowing terms; "to gild refined gold, to paint the lily, to throw a perfume on the violet"—Shakespeare; elaborate, convolute, involve

ADJS **8 grandiloquent,** magniloquent, **pompous, orotund; grandiose;** fulsome; lofty, elevated, tall <nf>, **stilted; pretentious, affected** 533.9; overblown, overdone, overwrought; **showy, flashy, ostentatious,** gaudy, glitzy <nf>, meretricious, flamboyant, flaming, bedizened, flaunting, garish; lurid, sensational, sensationalistic; **high-flown, high-falutin** <nf>, high-flying; high-flowing, **high-sounding, big-sounding,** great-sounding, grandisonant <old>, sonorous; **rhetorical,** declamatory; **pedantic,** inkhorn, lexiphanic <old>; sententious, Johnsonian; convoluted, tortuous, labyrinthine, overelaborate, overinvolved; euphuistic, Gongoresque

9 bombastic, fustian, mouthy, **inflated, swollen,** swelling, turgid, turgescent, tumid, tumescent, flatulent, windy *and* gassy <nf>; overadorned, fulsome

10 sesquipedalian, sesquipedal, polysyllabic, jawbreaking *and* jawtwisting <nf>

11 ornate, purple <nf>, colored, **fancy;** adorned, **embellished, embroidered,** lavish, decorated, festooned, overcharged, overloaded, befrilled, flashy; **flowery, florid,** lush, luxuriant; figured, **figurative** 536.3

ADVS **12 grandiloquently,** magniloquently, **pompously,** grandiosely, fulsomely, loftily, stiltedly, pretentiously; **ostentatiously,** showily; **bombastically,** turgidly, tumidly, flatulently, windily <nf>

13 ornately, fancily; **flowerily,** floridly

546 LETTER

NOUNS **1 letter, written character, character, sign, symbol,** graph, digraph, grapheme, allograph, alphabetic character *or* symbol, phonetic character *or* symbol; diacritic, diacritical mark, vowel point; logographic *or* lexigraphic character *or* symbol; ideographic *or* ideogrammic *or* ideogrammatic character *or* symbol; initial; syllabic character *or* symbol, syllabic, syllabogram; pictographic character *or* symbol; cipher, device; monogram; graphy, *mater lectionis* <L>; **writing** 547

2 <phonetic *and* ideographic symbols> **phonogram;** phonetic symbol; **logogram,** logograph, grammalogue; word letter; **ideogram,** ideograph, phonetic, radical, determinative; **pictograph,** pictogram; **hieroglyphic,** hieroglyph, hieratic symbol, demotic character; **rune,** runic character *or* symbol; **cuneiform, character;** wedge, arrowhead, ogham; kana, hiragana, katakana; kanji; **shorthand** 547.8; hieroglyphics

3 **writing system, script, letters; alphabet,** letters of the alphabet, **ABC's;** christcross-row; **phonetic alphabet,** International Phonetic Alphabet *or* IPA; Initial Teaching Alphabet; phonemic alphabet; phonetic alphabet; runic alphabet, futhark *or* futharc; alphabetism; **syllabary;** alphabetics, alphabetology, graphemics; paleography; speech sound 524.12

4 **spelling,** orthography; phonetic spelling *or* respelling, phonetics, phonography; normalization; spelling reform; spelling match *or* bee, spelldown; bad spelling, cacography; spelling pronunciation

5 **lettering,** initialing; **inscription,** epigraph, graffito, printing, calligraphy; handwriting; alphabetization; transliteration, romanization, pin-yin *or* pinyin, Wade-Giles system; transcription; phonetic transcription, phonography, lexigraphy

VERBS 6 **letter, initial, inscribe,** character, sign, mark; **capitalize; alphabetize,** alphabet; transliterate, transcribe

7 **spell,** orthographize; spell *or* respell phonetically; spell out, write out, trace out; spell backward; outspell, spell down; syllabify, syllabize, syllable, syllabicate

ADJS 8 **literal, lettered; alphabetic, alphabetical;** abecedarian; graphemic, allographic; large-lettered, majuscule, majuscular, uncial; **capital,** capitalized, upper-case; small-lettered, minuscule, minuscular, lower-case; logographic, logogrammatic, lexigraphic, ideographic, ideogrammic, ideogrammatic, pictographic; transliterated, transcribed; orthographic, spelled; symbolical, phonogramic, phonographic, cuneiform, cuneal, hieroglyphic, hieroglyphical

547 WRITING

NOUNS 1 **writing,** scrivening *or* scrivenery <old>, inscription, lettering; engrossment; pen, **pen-and-ink;** inkslinging *and* ink spilling <nf>, pen *or* pencil driving *or* pushing <nf>; **typing, typewriting;** macrography, micrography; stroke *or* dash of the pen, *coup de plume* <Fr>; secret writing, cryptography 345.6; **alphabet, writing system** 546.3; texting

2 **authorship, writing,** authorcraft, pencraft, wordsmanship, **composition,** the art of composition, inditing, inditement; one's pen; **creative writing,** literary art, verbal art, literary composition, literary production, verse-writing, short-story writing, novel-writing, playwriting, drama-writing; essay-writing; **expository writing;** technical writing; journalism, newspaper writing, investigative reporting, editorial-writing, feature-writing, rewriting; magazine writing; citizen journalism; blogging; content creation; **songwriting,** lyric-writing, libretto-writing; artistry, literary power, literary artistry, literary talent *or* flair, skill with words *or* language, facility in writing, ready pen; **writer's itch,** graphomania, scribblemania, graphorrhea, *cacoëthes scribendi* <L>; automatic writing; writer's cramp, graphospasm

3 **handwriting, hand, script,** fist <nf>, chirography, **calligraphy,** autography; **manuscript,** scrive <Scot>; **autograph,** holograph; **penmanship,** penscript, pencraft; stylography; graphology, graphanalysis, graphometry; paleography

4 handwriting style; **printing,** handprinting, block letter, **lettering; stationery; writing materials,** paper, foolscap, note paper, pad, papyrus, parchment, tracing paper, typing paper, vellum

5 <good writing> **calligraphy,** fine writing, elegant penmanship, **good hand,** fine hand, good fist <nf>, fair hand, copybook hand

6 <bad writing> **cacography, bad hand,** poor fist <nf>, cramped *or* crabbed hand, botched writing, childish scrawl, illegible handwriting, griffonage <Fr>

7 **scribbling,** scribblement; **scribble,** scrabble, **scrawl, scratch,** *barbouillage* <Fr>; *pattes de mouche* <Fr>, hen tracks *and* hen scratches <nf>, pothookery, pothooks, pothooks *and* hangers

8 **stenography, shorthand,** brachygraphy, tachygraphy; speedwriting; phonography, stenotype; contraction

9 **letter, written character** 546.1; **alphabet, writing system** 546.3; punctuation marks 530.22

10 <written matter> **writing, the written word; piece;** piece of writing, text, screed; **copy, matter;** printed

matter, literature, reading matter; the written word, *literae scriptae* <L>; nonfiction; fiction 722; composition, work, opus, production, literary production, literary artefact *or* artifact, lucubration, brainchild; essay, article 556.1; poem; play 704.4; letter 553.2; **document** 549.5,8; **paper,** parchment, scroll; **script,** scrip, scrive <Scot>; **penscript, typescript; manuscript** *or* MS *or* Ms *or* ms, holograph, autograph; **draft,** first draft, second draft, etc, recension, **version;** edited version, finished version, final draft; transcription, transcript, fair copy, engrossment; flimsy; original, author's copy; camera-ready copy; printout, computer printout, hard copy; gray literature; blog, post

11 <ancient manuscript> **codex;** scroll; palimpsest, *codex rescriptus* <L>; papyrus, parchment

12 **literature, letters, belles lettres,** polite literature, humane letters, *litterae humaniores* <L>, republic of letters, writing; **work, literary work, text, literary text; works, complete works, oeuvre, canon, literary canon, author's canon;** serious literature; **classics,** ancient literature; medieval literature, Renaissance literature, etc; national literature, English literature, French literature, etc; contemporary literature; underground literature; pseudonymous literature; folk literature, oral history; travel literature; wisdom literature; erotic literature, erotica; pornographic literature, pornography, porn *and* hard porn *and* soft porn <nf>, obscene literature, scatological literature; Weblog, blog, bulletin board; popular literature, pop literature <nf>; kitsch

13 **writer, scribbler** <nf>, **penman,** pen, penner; pen *or* pencil driver *or* pusher <nf>, word-slinger, **inkslinger** *and* ink spiller <nf>, knight of the plume *or* pen *or* quill <nf>; **scribe, scrivener, amanuensis, secretary,** recording secretary, **clerk,** administrative assistant; letterer; **copyist,** copier, transcriber; chirographer, calligrapher

14 **writing expert,** graphologist, handwriting expert, graphometrist; paleographer

15 **author, writer,** scribe <nf>, composer, inditer; authoress, penwoman; **creative writer,** *littérateur* <Fr>, literary artist, literary craftsman *or* artisan *or* journeyman, belletrist, man of letters, literary man, literary lion; wordsmith, word painter; free lance, free-lance writer; ghostwriter, ghost <nf>; collaborator, coauthor; prose writer, logographer; fiction writer, fictioneer <nf>; story writer, **short story writer;** storyteller; **novelist;** novelettist; diarist; **newspaperman; annalist; poet** 720.11; **dramatist,** humorist 489.12; scriptwriter, scenario writer, scenarist, script doctor; nonfiction writer; article writer, magazine writer; **essayist;** monographer; reviewer, critic, literary critic, music critic, art critic, drama critic, dance critic; columnist; pamphleteer; technical writer; copywriter, advertising writer; compiler, list-maker, encyclopedist, bibliographer; blogger

16 **hack writer,** hack, literary hack, Grub Street writer <Brit>, **penny-a-liner, scribbler** <nf>, **potboiler** <nf>; blogger

17 **stenographer,** brachygrapher, tachygrapher; phonographer, stenotypist

18 **typist,** keyboarder; texter; printer

VERBS 19 **write, pen, pencil,** drive *or* push the pen *or* pencil <nf>; stain *or* spoil paper <nf>, shed *or* spill ink <nf>, **scribe,** scrive <Scot>; inscribe, scroll; superscribe; enface; take pen in hand; **put in writing,** put in black and white; **draw up, draft, write out,** make out; write down, record 549.15; take down in shorthand; **type; transcribe,** copy out, engross, make a fair copy, copy; trace; **rewrite, revise, edit,** recense, make a recension, make a critical revision; highlight

20 **scribble,** scrabble, **scratch, scrawl,** make hen tracks *or* hen *or* chicken scratches <nf>, doodle

21 **write,** author, **compose, indite,** formulate, produce, prepare; dash off, knock off *or* out <nf>, throw on paper, pound *or* crank *or* grind *or* churn out; free-lance; collaborate, coauthor; ghostwrite, ghost <nf>; novelize; scenarize; pamphleteer; editorialize; blog

ADJS 22 **written,** penned, penciled, lettered, literal, graphical, typed; **inscribed;** engrossed; **in writing, in black and white,** on paper; scriptural, scriptorial, graphic; calligraphic, chirographic, chirographical; stylographic, stylographical; manuscript, autograph, autographic, holograph, holographic, holographical, in one's own hand, under one's hand; **longhand,** in longhand, in script, handwritten; **shorthand,** in shorthand; italic, italicized; cursive, running, flowing; graphologic, graphological, graphometric, graphometrical; graphoanalytic, graphoanalytical; typewritten; printed

23 **scribbled,** scrabbled, **scratched, scrawled; scribbly, scratchy, scrawly**

24 **literary,** belletristic, lettered, classical

25 auctorial, authorial; polygraphic; graphomaniac, graphomaniacal, scribblemaniac, scribblemaniacal, scripturient <old>

26 **alphabetic,** ideographic, etc

27 stenographic, stenographical; **shorthand,** in shorthand

28 **clerical, secretarial**

WORD ELEMENTS 29 grapho-, -graphy, -graphia; -graph, -gram; -grapher

548 PRINTING

NOUNS **1 printing,** publishing, publication, photographic reproduction, photochemical process, phototypography, phototypy; **photoengraving; letterpress,** relief printing, **typography,** letterpress photoengraving; zincography, photozincography; line engraving, halftone engraving; stereotypy; wood-block printing, xylotypography, chromoxylography; intaglio printing, **gravure;** rotogravure, rotary photogravure; planographic printing, planography, **lithography,** typolithography, photolithography, lithogravure, lithophotogravure; **offset printing,** offset lithography, offset, dry offset, photo-offset; photogelatin process, albertype, collotype; electronography, electrostatic printing, onset, xerography, xeroprinting; stencil, mimeograph, silk-screen printing; color printing, chromotypography, chromotypy, two-color printing, three-color printing; book printing, job printing, sheetwork; history of printing, palaeotypography; photography 714; **graphic arts, printmaking** 713.1

2 composition, typesetting, setting, composing; hand composition, machine composition; hot-metal typesetting, cold-type typesetting, photosetting, photocomposition; imposition; justification; composing stick, galley chase, furniture, quoin; typesetting machine, phototypesetter, phototypesetting machine; computer composition, computerized typesetting; composition tape; line of type, slug; layout, dummy

3 print, imprint, stamp, impression, impress, letterpress; reprint, reissue; offprint; offcut; offset, setoff, mackle; duplicate, facsimile, carbon copy, repro <nf>

4 copy, printer's copy, manuscript, typescript; **camera-ready copy; matter;** composed matter, live matter, dead matter, standing matter

5 proof, proof sheet, pull <Brit>, trial impression; galley, **galley proof,** slip; page proof, foundry proof, plate proof, stone proof, press proof, cold-type proof, color proof, computer proof, engraver's proof, reproduction *or* repro proof, blueprint, blue <nf>, vandyke, progressive proof; author's proof; revise

6 type, key in *or* key, **print, stamp, letter; type size;** type body *or* shank *or* stem, body, shank, stem, shoulder, belly, back, bevel, beard, feet, groove, nick, face, counter; ascender, descender, serif; lower case, minuscule; upper case, majuscule; capital, cap <nf>, small capital, small cap <nf>; ligature, logotype; bastard type, bottle-assed type,

fat-faced type; **pi;** type lice; **font; face,** typeface; type class, roman, sans serif, script, italic, black letter; case, typecase; point, pica; en, em; typefounders, typefoundry

7 space, spacing, patent space, justifying space, justification space; spaceband, slug; quadrat, quad; em quad, en quad; em, en; three-em space, thick space; four-em space, five-em space, thin space; hair space

8 printing surface, plate, printing plate; typeform, locked-up page; duplicate plate, electrotype, stereotype, plastic plate, rubber plate; zincograph, zincotype; **printing equipment**

9 presswork, makeready; **press, printing press,** printing machine <Brit>; platen press, flatbed cylinder press, cylinder press, rotary press, web press, rotogravure press; bed, platen, web

10 printed matter; reading matter, text, letterpress <Brit>; advertising matter; advance sheets

11 press, printing office, print shop, printery, printers; publishers, **publishing house; pressroom,** composing room, proofroom

12 printer, printworker; **compositor, typesetter,** typographer, Linotyper; keyboarder; stoneman, makeup man; proofer; stereotyper, stereotypist, electrotyper; apprentice printer, devil, printer's devil; **pressman**

13 proofreader, reader, printer's reader <Brit>, copyholder; **copyreader,** copy editor

VERBS **14 print; imprint, impress, stamp,** enstamp <old>; engrave; run, run off, strike; **publish, issue, put in print, bring out, put out, get out;** put to press, put to bed, see through the press; prove, proof, prove up, make *or* pull a proof, pull; overprint; reprint, reissue; mimeograph, hectograph; multigraph

15 autotype, electrotype, Linotype <trademark>, monotype, palaeotype, stereotype; keyboard

16 compose, set, set in print; **make up,** impose; justify, overrun; pi, pi a form

17 copy-edit; proofread, read, read *or* correct copy; vet

18 <be printed> go to press, come off press, come out, appear in print

ADJS **19 printed, in print;** typeset

20 typographic, typographical; phototypic, phototypographic; chromotypic, chromotypographic; stereotypic, palaeotypographical; **boldface,** bold-faced, blackface, black-faced, full-faced; **lightface,** light-faced; **upper-case, lower-case**

549 RECORD

NOUNS **1 record, recording,** documentation, written word; **chronicle, annals,** history, story; roll, **rolls,** pipe roll <Brit>; account; register, registry, rota, roster, scroll, catalog, inventory, table, list 871, dossier, portfolio; letters, correspondence; **vestige, trace,** memorial, token, relic, remains; herstory <nf>; listmaking, glazomania

2 **archives**, public records, government archives, government papers, presidential papers, historical documents, historical records, memorabilia; clipping; cartulary; biographical records, life records, biographical material, papers, ana; parish rolls or register or records

3 **registry**, registrar, registry office; archives, files; chancery; National Archives, Library of Congress; Somerset House <Brit>

4 **memorandum, memo** <nf>, memoir, *aide-mémoire* <Fr>, memorial; **reminder** 989.5; **note, notation,** annotation, jotting, docket, marginal note, marginalia, scholium, scholia, adversaria, footnote; jottings; **entry,** register, **registry,** item; **minutes;** inscription, personal note

5 **document,** official document, legal document, legal paper, legal instrument, **instrument,** writ, **paper,** parchment, scroll, roll, **writing,** script, scrip; holograph, chirograph; **papers,** ship's papers; docket, **file,** personal file, **dossier;** blank, form; deed, title deed, muniments; registration document, insurance papers; attachment

6 **certificate,** certification, **ticket; authority,** authorization; **credential, voucher, warrant,** warranty, testimonial, charter; note; **affidavit,** sworn statement, notarized statement, deposition, witness, attestation, *procès-verbal* <Fr>; **visa,** *visé* <Fr>; passport; **bill of health,** clean bill of health; navicert <Brit>; **diploma,** sheepskin <nf>; certificate of proficiency, testamur <Brit>; birth certificate, death certificate, marriage certificate

7 **report, bulletin, brief, statement, account,** accounting; account rendered, *compte rendu* <Fr>; **minutes,** the record, proceedings, transactions, acta; official report, annual report; report card, transcript; **yearbook,** annual; **returns,** census report or returns, election returns, tally; case history; book report

8 <official documents> state paper, white paper; blue book, green book, Red Book <Brit>, white book, yellow book, *livre jaune* <Fr>; gazette, official journal, Congressional Record, Hansard

9 <registers> genealogy, pedigree, studbook; Social Register, blue book; directory; Who's Who; Lloyd's Register

10 <recording media> bulletin board, notice board; scoresheet, scorecard, scoreboard; **tape,** magnetic tape, magnetic track, magnetic storage, cassette tape, videotape, ticker tape; **computer disk,** magnetic disk, diskette, floppy disk or floppy, hard disk, disk cartridge, CD-ROM, laser disk, optical disk; memory; computer file, database; compact disk or CD, multimedia CD, laser disk, DVD; phonograph record, disc or disk, platter <nf>; film, motion-picture film; slip, card, index card, filing card; library catalog, catalog card; microcard, microfiche, microdot, microfilm; **file** 871.3; recording instrument, photocopier, camera, videocamera, camcorder, recorder, tape recorder, wiretap, bug <nf>, answering machine, videocassette recorder or VCR, flight recorder, black box; voice recognition

11 <record books> **notebook, pocketbook,** pocket notebook, blankbook; loose-leaf notebook, spiral notebook; **memorandum book,** memo book <nf>, commonplace book, adversaria; address book, directory; workbook; **blotter,** police blotter; docket, court calendar; **calendar,** desk calendar, appointment calendar, appointment schedule, engagement book, agenda, agenda book, Filofax <trademark>, datebook; Moleskine <trademark>; **tablet,** table <old>, writing tablet; diptych, triptych; pad, **scratch pad,** notepad; Post-it Note <trademark>, sticky <nf>; **scrapbook,** memory book, **album; diary, journal,** daybook; **log,** ship's log, **logbook; account book, ledger,** daybook; **cashbook,** petty cashbook; checkbook; Domesday Book; catalog, classified catalog, index; yearbook, annual; guestbook, guest register, register, registry; cartulary or chartulary; art journal; blog, online journal

12 **monument,** monumental or memorial record, **memorial;** necrology, obituary, **memento,** remembrance, testimonial; cup, trophy, prize, ribbon, plaque; **marker;** inscription; **tablet,** stone, hoarstone <Brit>, boundary stone, memorial stone; **pillar,** stele or stela, shaft, column, memorial column, rostral column, manubial column; cross; war memorial; arch, memorial arch, triumphal arch, victory arch; memorial statue, bust; monolith, obelisk, **pyramid; tomb,** grave 309.16**;** tomb of unknown soldier; **gravestone, tombstone;** memorial tablet, brass; headstone, footstone; mausoleum; cenotaph; cairn, mound, barrow, cromlech, dolmen, megalith, menhir, cyclolith, earthwork, mound; **shrine,** reliquary, tope, stupa

13 recorder, registrar 550.1, blogger, listmaker

14 **registration, register, registry; recording,** record keeping, recordation; archiving; minuting, **enrollment,** matriculation, enlistment; impanelment; **listing, tabulation, cataloging,** inventorying, indexing; chronicling; **entry,** insertion, entering, posting; docketing, inscribing, **inscription; booking, logging;** recording instruments

VERBS **15 record,** put or place upon record; **inscribe,** enscroll; **register, enroll,** matriculate, check in; impanel; poll; **file,** index, catalog, calendar, **tabulate, list,** docket; **chronicle,** document; minute, put in the minutes or on the record, spread on the record; commit to or preserve in an archive, archive; **write,** commit or reduce to writing, put in writing, put in black and white, put on paper; **write out; make out,** fill out; **write up,** chalk, chalk up; **write down, mark down, jot down, put down, set down, take down; note,** note down, make a note, make a memorandum; **post,** post up; **enter,** make an entry, insert, write in; **book, log;** cut, carve, grave, engrave, incise; put on tape, tape, tape-record; capture on film; record, cut; videotape; keyboard, key; diarize

ADJS **16 recording,** recordative <old>, registrational; certificatory

17 recorded, registered; inscribed, written down, down; **filed,** indexed, enrolled, **entered,** logged, booked, posted; documented, chronicled; minuted; **on record,** on file, on the books; official, legal, of record; in black and white; duly noted

18 documentary, documentational, documental, archival, archived; epigraphic, inscriptional; necrological, obituary; testimonial

550 RECORDER

NOUNS **1 recorder,** recordist, record keeper; **registrar,** register, prothonotary; archivist, documentalist; master of the rolls <Brit>, *custos rotulorum* <L>; librarian, cybrarian; **clerk,** record clerk, penpusher <nf>, filing clerk; town or municipal clerk, county clerk; bookkeeper, accountant, tax preparer; **scribe,** scrivener; **secretary,** amanuensis; **stenographer** 547.17; notary, notary public; marker; scorekeeper, scorer, official scorer, timekeeper; engraver, stonecutter; reporter

2 annalist, genealogist, chronicler; cliometrician; historian

551 INFORMATION

NOUNS **1 information,** info <nf>, gen <Brit nf>, **facts, data, knowledge** 928; public knowledge, open secret, common knowledge; general information; news, factual information, hard information; **evidence, proof** 957; **enlightenment,** light; incidental information, sidelight; **acquaintance,** familiarization, briefing; **instruction** 568.1; **intelligence,** intel <nf>; **the dope** and the goods and **the scoop** and the skinny and the straight skinny and the inside skinny

<nf>, the know <nf>, the gen <Brit>; transmission, **communication** 343; **report, word,** message, presentation, account, **statement,** mention; white paper, white book, blue book, command paper <Brit>; dispatch, bulletin, communiqué, handout <nf>, fact sheet, release; publicity, promotional material, broadside; **notice,** notification; notice board, bulletin board; announcement, publication 352; directory, guidebook 574.10; trivia; current events, current affairs; information processing; information overload; bullet points

2 inside information, private or confidential information; **the lowdown** and **inside dope** and inside wire and **hot tip** and dirt and poop <nf>; insider; pipeline <nf>; privileged information, classified information; insider trading

3 tip and tip-off and **pointer** <nf>, clue, cue; steer <nf>; **advice;** whisper, passing word, **word to the wise,** word in the ear, bug in the ear <nf>, bee in the bonnet <nf>; warning, caution, monition, alerting, sound bite; aside

4 hint, gentle hint, **intimation, indication, suggestion, mere** or **faint suggestion, suspicion, inkling,** whisper, **glimmer, glimmering; cue, clue,** index, **symptom, sign,** spoor, track, scent, sniff, whiff, telltale, tip-off <nf>; **implication, insinuation, innuendo;** broad hint, gesture, signal, nod, wink, look, nudge, kick, prompt; disguised message, backward masking; rumor, leak, gossip

5 informant, informer, source, teller, interviewee, enlightener, deep throat <nf>; **adviser,** monitor; **reporter,** notifier, **announcer,** annunciator; spokesperson, spokespeople, spokeswoman, spokesman, press secretary, press officer, information officer, mouthpiece, messenger, correspondent; spin doctor <nf>; communicator, communicant, publisher; **authority,** witness, expert witness; **tipster** <nf>, **tout** <nf>; newsmonger, gossipmonger; **information medium** or **media, mass media,** print media, electronic media, the press, radio, television; channel, the grapevine; information network, network; information center; public relations officer or person; agent, handler; infopreneur

6 informer, betrayer, double-crosser <nf>, delator <old>; fifth columnist; **snitch** and snitcher <nf>; whistle-blower <nf>; **tattler, tattletale, telltale, talebearer; blab** or blabber or blabberer or blabbermouth <nf>; **squealer** and preacher and **stool pigeon** and stoolie and **fink** and rat <nf>, nark <Brit nf>; spy 576.9; mole; grapevine, channel

7 information technology or IT, information or communication theory; data storage or retrieval, information retrieval, EDP or electronic data processing, data processing, information processing; signal, noise; encoding, decoding; bit; redundancy, entropy; channel; information *or* communication explosion, information superhighway

VERBS **8 inform, tell, speak on** *or* **for,** apprise, **advise, advertise,** advertise of, **give word,** mention to, **acquaint, enlighten,** familiarize, brief, verse, give the facts, give an account of, give by way of information; **instruct,** educate; possess *or* seize one of the facts; **let know, have one to know, give** *or* **lead one to believe** *or* **understand;** tell once *and* for all; notify, give notice *or* notification, serve notice; **communicate** 343.6,7; bring *or* send *or* leave word; **report** 552.11; **disclose** 351.4; put in a new light, shed new *or* fresh light upon; announce, broadcast, convey, break the news

9 post *and* **keep posted** <nf>; wise up *and* clue *or* fill in *and* bring up to speed *or* date *and* put in the picture <nf>

10 hint, intimate, suggest, insinuate, imply, indicate, adumbrate, lead *or* leave one to gather, justify one in supposing, give *or* drop *or* throw out a hint, give an inkling of, signal, suggest, **hint at; leak,** let slip out; allude to, make an allusion to, glance at <old>; **prompt,** give the cue, put onto; put in *or* into one's head, put a bee in one's bonnet

11 tip *and* tip off *and* **give one a tip** <nf>, alert; **give a pointer to** <nf>; put hep *or* hip <nf>, **let in on,** let in on the know <nf>; let next to *and* put next to *and* **put on to** *and* put on to something hot <nf>; **confide,** confide to, entrust with information, give confidential information, mention privately *or* confidentially, whisper, buzz, breathe, whisper in the ear, **put a bug in one's ear** <nf>

12 inform on *or* **against, betray; tattle;** turn informer; testify against, **bear witness against;** turn state's evidence, turn king's *or* queen's evidence <Brit>

13 <nf terms> **sell one out** *or* **down the river,** tell on, blab, snitch, squeal, peach <old>, sell out, sing, rat, stool, fink, nark, finger, put the finger on, blow the whistle, shop <Brit>, dime, drop a dime, spill one's guts, spill the beans, squawk, weasel, let the cat out of the bag, sell down the river

14 learn, come to know, be informed *or* **apprised of,** have it reported, get the facts, **get wise to** <nf>, **get hep to** *and* **next to** *and* **on to** <nf>, find out, get word; become conscious *or* aware of, become alive *or* awake to, awaken to, tumble to <nf>, open one's eyes to; realize, get wind of; overhear

15 know 928.12, be informed *or* apprised, have the facts, be in the know <nf>, **come to one's knowledge,** come to *or* reach one's ears; be told, **hear, overhear,** hear tell of *and* hear say <nf>; get scent *or* wind of; **know well** 928.13; have inside

information, know where the bodies are buried <nf>

16 keep informed, keep posted <nf>, stay briefed, **keep up on,** keep up to date *or* au courant, keep abreast of the times; **keep track of,** keep count *or* account of, keep watch on, keep tab *or* tabs on <nf>, keep a check on, keep an eye on

ADJS **17 informed** 928.18–20; informed of, enlightened, briefed, in the know 928.16, clued-in *or* clued-up <nf>

18 informative, informing, informational, informatory; illuminating, **instructive, enlightening;** educative, educational; advisory, monitory; **communicative**

19 telltale, tattletale, kiss-and-tell

ADVS **20** from information received, according to reports *or* rumor, from notice given, as a matter of general information, by common report, from what one can gather, as far as anyone knows

552 NEWS

NOUNS **1 news, tidings, intelligence, information, word,** advice; happenings, current affairs, hard news; newsiness <nf>; newsworthiness; a nose for news; **journalism,** reportage, coverage, news coverage, news gathering; **the press,** the fourth estate, the press corps, print journalism, electronic journalism, investigative journalism, broadcast journalism, broadcast news, radio journalism, television journalism; **news medium** *or* **media,** newspaper, newsletter, newsmagazine, radio, television, press association, news service, news agency, press agency, wire service, telegraph agency; press box, press gallery; yellow press, tabloid press; pack journalism; alternative press; newsserver, multimedia; Internet forum

2 good news, good word, **glad tidings;** gospel, evangel; bad news

3 news item, piece *or* budget of news; **article, story,** piece, account; copy; scoop *and* beat <nf>, exclusive; interview; breaking story, newsbreak; feature story; follow-up, sidebar; column, editorial; spot news; photo opportunity; outtake; sound bite; media hype <nf>; factoid, data point

4 message, dispatch, word, communication, communiqué, advice, press *or* news release, release; press conference, news conference; express <Brit>; embassy, embassage <old>; **letter** 553.2; **telegram** 347.14; pneumatogram, *petit bleu* <Fr>; text message, instant message

5 bulletin, news report, **flash,** brief *or* news brief, update, newsfeed

6 report, rumor, flying rumor, unverified *or* unconfirmed report, **hearsay,** *on-dit* <Fr>,

scuttlebutt *and* latrine rumor <nf>; **talk, whisper, buzz, rumble,** bruit, cry; idea afloat, news stirring; **common talk,** town talk, **talk of the town,** topic of the day, *cause célèbre* <Fr>; **grapevine; canard,** roorback

7 **gossip,** gossiping, gossipry, gossipmongering, newsmongering, mongering, back-fence gossip <nf>; **talebearing,** taletelling; **tattle,** tittle-tattle, chitchat, **talk,** idle talk, small talk, by-talk; "putting two and two together, and making it five"—Pascal; piece of gossip, groundless rumor, tale, story

8 **scandal, dirt** <nf>, **malicious gossip;** juicy morsel, tidbit, choice bit of dirt <nf>; **scandalmongering;** gossip column; character assassination, **slander** 512.3; whispering campaign

9 **newsmonger, rumormonger, scandalmonger, gossip,** gossipmonger, gossiper, *yenta* <Yiddish>, quidnunc, **busybody,** tabby <nf>; **talebearer,** taleteller, telltale, **tattletale** <nf>, tattler, tittle-tattler; gossip columnist; reporter, newspaperman, newsperson, cub reporter

10 <secret news channel> **grapevine, grapevine telegraph,** channel, bush telegraph <Austral>; **pipeline;** a litle bird *or* birdie; informer, leak; insider information; contact

VERBS 11 **report,** give a report, give an account of, tell, relate, rehearse <old>; write up, make out *or* write up a report, publicize; editorialize; gather the news, newsgather; dig *or* dig up dirt <nf>; bring word, tell the news, break the news, give tidings of; bring glad tidings, give the good word; announce 352.12; put around, spread, **rumor** 352.10; clue in *or* clue up <nf>, **inform** 551.8

12 **gossip,** talk over the back fence <nf>; **tattle,** tittle-tattle; clatter <Scot>, **talk;** retail gossip, **dish the dirt** <nf>, tell idle tales

ADJS 13 **newsworthy,** front-page, with news value, newsy, informative; reportorial

14 **gossipy,** gossiping, newsy; **talebearing,** taletelling; tabloidesque

15 **reported, rumored,** whispered; rumored about, talked about, whispered about, bruited about, bandied about; **in the news, in circulation, in the air, going around,** going about, going the rounds, **current, rife,** afloat, in every one's mouth, on all tongues, on the street, all over the town, hot off the press; made public 352.17

ADVS 16 reportedly, allegedly, as they say, as it is said, **as the story goes** *or* runs, as the fellow says <nf>, it is said

553 CORRESPONDENCE

NOUNS 1 **correspondence, letter writing,** written communication, exchange of letters, epistolary intercourse *or* communication; personal correspondence, business correspondence; mailing, mass mailing; electronic mail, e-mail; text messaging *or* texting, instant messaging

2 **letter** <see list>, **epistle, message, communication, dispatch, missive,** favor <old>; personal letter, business letter; **note, line,** chit, billet <old>; **reply, answer, acknowledgment,** rescript

3 **card, postcard, postal card,** lettercard <Brit>; picture postcard

4 **mail, post** <chiefly Brit>, **postal services,** letter bag; post day <Brit>; domestic mail, general delivery, snail mail <nf>, airmail, surface mail, express mail, priority mail, special handling, special delivery, first- *or* second- *or* third—*or* fourth-class mail, parcel post, registered mail, certified mail, insured mail, metered mail; mailing list; junk mail <nf>; direct mail, direct-mail advertising *or* selling, mail-order selling; mail solicitation; fan mail; electronic mail, e-mail; text message, instant message; Pony Express <old>

5 **postage;** stamp, postage stamp; frank; postmark, cancellation; postage meter

6 **mailbox,** postbox *and* letter box <chiefly Brit>, pillar box <Brit>; letter drop, mail drop; mailing machine *or* mailer; mailbag, postbag <Brit>; e-mail box, voicemail box

7 **postal service, postal system; post office** *or* **PO,** general post office *or* GPO, sorting office, dead-letter office, sea post office, mailboat; postmaster, **mailman, postman,** mail carrier, letter carrier; mail clerk, post-office *or* postal clerk; messenger, courier; postal union; electronic mail service

8 **correspondent, letter writer,** writer, communicator; pen pal <nf>; addressee

9 **address,** name *and* address, direction <old>, **destination,** superscription; zone, zip code *or* ZIP, zip plus four, postal code *or* postcode; letterhead, billhead; drop, accommodation address <Brit>; e-mail address

VERBS 10 **correspond,** correspond with, **communicate with, write, write to,** write a letter, send a letter to, send a note, **drop a line** <nf>; use the mails; keep up a correspondence, exchange letters

11 **reply, answer, acknowledge,** respond; reply by return mail

12 **mail, post,** dispatch, send, forward; airmail

13 **address, direct,** superscribe

ADJS 14 epistolary; **postal,** post; letter; mail-order, direct-mail; mail-in; mailable; send-in, sendable

PHRS 15 please reply, RSVP *or* *répondez s'il vous plaît* <Fr>

16 kinds of letters

aerogram	letter of intent
air letter	letter of introduction
airgraph <Brit>	letter of marque
apostolic *or* papal brief	letter of
bull	recommendation
chain letter	letter of request
circular letter	letter of resignation
cover letter	letter overt
dead letter	letter patent
Dear John	letter rogatory
dimissory letter *or*	letter testamentary
dimissorial	love letter *or* billet
drop letter	doux <Fr>
encyclical	market letter
encyclical letter	memorandum *or* memo
epistle	monitory *or* monitory
fan letter	letter
form letter	newsletter
invitation	open letter
letter credential	paschal letter
letter of condolence	pastoral letter
letter of credence	pink slip
letter of credit	poison-pen letter
letter of delegation	round robin

554 BOOK

NOUNS 1 book, volume, tome; publication, writing, **work, opus, production; title;** opusculum, opuscule; **trade book; textbook,** schoolbook, reader, grammar; **reference book,** playbook; songbook 708.28; notebook 549.11; storybook, **novel; best seller** *or* bestseller; coffee-table book; nonbook; **children's book,** juvenile book, juvenile; picture book; coloring book, sketchbook; prayer book, psalter, psalmbook; **classic,** the book, the bible, magnum opus, great work, standard work, definitive work

2 publisher, book publisher; publishing house, press, small press, vanity press; **editor,** trade editor, reference editor, juvenile editor, textbook editor, dictionary editor, college editor, line editor; acquisitions editor, executive editor, managing editor, editor-in-chief; picture editor; packager; copy editor *or* copyeditor, fact checker, proofreader; production editor, permissions editor; **printer,** book printer, typesetter, compositor; **bookbinder,** bibliopegist; **bookdealer, bookseller,** book agent, book salesman; book packager; book manufacturer, press

3 book, printed book, bound book, bound volume, cased book, casebound book, cloth bound book, clothback, leather-bound book; manufactured book, finished book; packaged book; **hardcover,** hardcover book, hardbound, hardbound book, hard book; **paperback,** paper-bound book; pocket book, soft-cover, soft-bound book, limp-cover book; self-published book; electronic book, e-book

4 volume, tome; folio; quarto *or* 4to; octavo *or* 8vo; twelvemo *or* 12mo; sextodecimo *or* sixteenmo *or* 16mo; octodecimo *or* eighteenmo *or* 18mo; imperial, super, royal, medium, crown; trim size

5 edition, issue; volume, number; **printing,** impression, press order, print order, print run; copy; series, set, boxed set, collection, library; library edition; back number; **trade edition,** subscription edition, subscription book; school edition, text edition

6 rare book, early edition; first edition; signed edition; Elzevir, Elzevir book *or* edition; Aldine, Aldine book *or* edition; manuscript, scroll, codex; incunabulum, cradle book

7 compilation, omnibus; symposium; collection, collectanea, miscellany; collected works, selected works, complete works, corpus, *œuvres* <Fr>, canon; **miscellanea,** analects; ana; chrestomathy, delectus; compendium, **anthology,** composition, garland, florilegium; flowers, beauties; garden; *Festschrift* <Ger>; quotation book; album, photograph album; scrapbook; yearbook; display, exhibition; series, serialization

8 handbook, manual, enchiridion, vade mecum, gradus, how-to book <nf>; **cookbook,** cookery book <Brit>; nature book, field guide; travel book, **guidebook** 574.10; sports book

9 reference book, work of reference; **encyclopedia,** cyclopedia; **concordance; catalog;** calendar; index; classified catalog, catalogue raisonné <Fr>, dictionary catalog; **directory,** city directory; telephone directory, telephone book, phone book <nf>; **atlas, gazetteer;** studbook; source book, casebook; record book 549.11; **language reference book** <see list>; **dictionary,** lexicon, wordbook, Webster's; glossary, gloss, **vocabulary,** onomasticon, nomenclator; **thesaurus, Roget's,** storehouse *or* treasury of words, synonomicon; **almanac**

10 textbook, text, schoolbook, manual, manual of instruction; **primer,** alphabet book, abecedary, abecedarium; hornbook, battledore; gradus, exercise book, workbook; **grammar, reader;** spelling book, speller, casebook

11 booklet, pamphlet, brochure, chapbook, leaflet, folder, tract; circular 352.8; comic book

12 makeup, design; front matter, preliminaries, text, back matter; head, fore edge, back, tail; page, leaf, folio; type page; trim size; flyleaf, endpaper, endleaf, endsheet, signature; recto, verso *or* reverso; title page, half-title page; title, bastard title, binder's title, subtitle, running title; copyright page, imprint, printer's imprint, imprimatur, colophon; catchword, catch line; dedication, inscription; acknowledgments, preface, foreword, introduction; contents, contents page, table of contents; appendix, notes, glossary; errata; bibliography; index

13 **part, section,** book, volume; article; serial, installment, *livraison* <Fr>; fascicle; **passage,** phrase, clause, verse, paragraph, chapter, column

14 **bookbinding,** bibliopegy; **binding, cover, book cover,** case, bookcase, hard binding, soft binding, mechanical binding, spiral binding, comb binding, plastic binding; library binding; headband, footband, tailband; **jacket, book jacket, dust jacket,** dust cover, wrapper; slipcase, slipcover; book cloth, binder's cloth, binder's board, binder board; folding, tipping, gathering, collating, sewing; **signature;** collating mark, niggerhead; Smyth sewing, side sewing, saddle stitching, wire stitching, stapling, perfect binding; smashing, gluing-off, trimming, rounding, backing, lining, lining-up; casemaking, stamping, casing-in

15 <bookbinding styles> Aldine, Arabesque, Byzantine, Canevari, cottage, dentelle, Etruscan, fanfare, Grolier, Harleian, Jansenist, Maioli, pointillé, Roxburgh

16 **bookstore, bookshop,** *librairie* <Fr>, bookseller, book dealer; **bookstall,** bookstand; **book club;** bibliopole; online bookseller

17 **bookholder, bookrest,** book support, **book end; bookcase,** revolving bookcase *or* bookstand, bookrack, bookstand, **bookshelf;** stack, bookstack; book table, book tray, book truck; folder, folio; **portfolio**

18 **booklover,** philobiblist, bibliophile, bibliolater, book collector, bibliomane, bibliomaniac, bibliotaph; **bookworm,** bibliophage; book-stealer; biblioklept; word nerd

19 **bibliology,** bibliography; bookcraft, bookmaking, book printing, book production, book manufacturing, bibliogenesis, bibliogony; bookselling, bibliopolism

ADJS 20 **bibliological,** bibliographical; bibliothecal, bibliothecary; bibliopolic; bibliopegic

21 **reference books**

almanac	directory
atlas	encyclopedia
bilingual dictionary	encyclopedic dictionary
biographical dictionary	etymological dictionary *or*
children's dictionary	etymologicon
college dictionary	foreign-language dictionary
concordance	geographical dictionary *or*
desk dictionary	gazetteer
dialect dictionary	glossary
dictionary of quotations	guidebook
handbook	school dictionary
how-to book	specialized *or* special-
idiom dictionary	subject dictionary
index	synonym dictionary
lexicon	telephone directory *or*
list book	book
manual	thesaurus
reverse dictionary	unabridged dictionary
rhyming dictionary	usage dictionary
Roget's Thesaurus	vade mecum

555 PERIODICAL

NOUNS 1 **periodical, serial, journal,** gazette; ephemeris; **magazine,** book *and* zine <nf>, webzine; pictorial; review; organ, **house organ; trade journal,** trade magazine; academic journal; daily, weekly, biweekly, bimonthly, fortnightly, monthly, quarterly, seasonal; annual, yearbook; newsletter; daybook, diary 549.11

2 **newspaper,** news, **paper,** sheet *or* rag <nf>, **gazette,** daily newspaper, daily, weekly newspaper, weekly, local paper, neighborhood newspaper, national newspaper; newspaper of record; **tabloid,** scandal sheet, extra, special, extra edition, special edition, Sunday paper, early edition, late edition; magazine section, comics, color supplement; online edition

3 **the press,** journalism, the public press, **the fourth estate;** print medium, the print media, print journalism, the print press, the public print; Fleet Street <Brit>; **wire service,** newswire; **publishing, newspaper publishing, magazine publishing; the publishing industry, communications,** mass media, the communications industry, public communication; satellite publishing; reportage, coverage, legwork

4 **journalist, newspaperman, newspaperwoman, newsman, newswoman,** journo <Brit nf>, newspeople, inkstained wretch, pressman <Brit>, newswriter, gazetteer <old>, gentleman *or* representative of the press; **reporter,** newshawk *and* newshound <nf>; leg man <nf>; interviewer; investigative reporter *or* journalist; **cub reporter; correspondent, foreign correspondent,** war correspondent, special correspondent, stringer; publicist; rewriter, **rewrite man;** reviser, diaskeuast; **editor,** subeditor, managing editor, city editor, news editor, sports editor, woman's editor, feature editor, **copy editor,** copyman, copy chief, slotman; reader, **copyreader;** editorial writer, leader writer <Brit>; **columnist,** paragrapher, paragraphist; freelance reporter; **photographer, news photographer,** photojournalist; paparazzo; press baron; press corps

ADJS **5 journalistic,** journalese <nf>; **periodical,**
serial; magazinish, magaziny; newspaperish,
newspapery; **editorial; reportorial**

556 TREATISE

NOUNS **1 treatise,** piece, treatment, handling,
tractate, tract; contribution; examination, survey,
inquiry, **discourse, discussion,** disquisition,
descant, exposition, screed; homily; memoir;
dissertation, thesis; essay, theme; pandect;
excursus; **study,** lucubration, étude; **paper,**
research paper, term paper, position paper;
sketch, outline, aperçu; causerie; **monograph,**
research monograph; *morceau* <Fr>, paragraph,
note; preliminary study, introductory study, first
approach, prolegomenon; **article,** feature, special
article

2 commentary, commentation <old>; **comment,**
remark; criticism, critique, *compte-rendu critique*
<Fr>, analysis; **review,** critical review, **report,**
notice, **write-up** <nf>; **editorial,** leading article *or*
leader <Brit>; gloss, running commentary, Op-Ed
column

3 discourser, discusser, disquisitor, dissertator,
doctoral candidate, expositor, descanter;
symposiast, discussant; essayist; monographer,
monographist; tractation, tractator <old>; **writer,**
author 547.15; scholar

4 commentator, commenter; expositor, expounder,
exponent; annotator, scholiast; glossarist,
glossographer; **critic; reviewer,** book reviewer;
editor; editorial writer, editorialist, leader writer
<Brit>; news analyst; publicist

VERBS **5 write upon,** touch upon, **discuss, treat,**
treat of, deal with, take up, handle, go into,
inquire into, survey; discourse, dissert, dissertate,
descant, develop at thesis; **comment upon,**
commentate, remark upon, annotate; expound;
criticize, review, write up

ADJS **6** dissertational, disquisitional, discoursive,
discursive; expository, expositorial, expositive,
exegetical; essayistic; monographic,
commentative, commentatorial, annotative;
critical, interpretive *or* interpretative; editorial

557 ABRIDGMENT

NOUNS **1 abridgment,** compendium, compend,
abrégé <Fr>, **condensation,** short *or* shortened
version, condensed version, potted version <Brit>,
abbreviation, abbreviature, diminution, brief,
digest, **abstract,** epitome, **précis, capsule,** nutshell
or capsule version, capsulization, encapsulation,
sketch, thumbnail sketch, **synopsis,** conspectus,

syllabus, *aperçu* <Fr>, **survey, review,** overview,
pandect, bird's-eye view; **outline,** skeleton, draft,
blueprint, prospectus; topical outline; head, rubric

2 summary, résumé, curriculum vitae *or* CV,
recapitulation, recap <nf>, rundown, run-
through; **summation;** review; sum, substance,
sum *and* substance, **wrapup** <nf>; pith, meat, gist,
drift, core, essence, main point 997.6

3 excerpt, extract, selection, extraction, excerption,
snippet; passage, selected passage; **clip** <nf>, film
clip, outtake, sound bite <nf>

4 excerpts, *excerpta* <L>, **extracts, gleanings,**
cuttings, clippings, snippets, selections; flowers,
florilegium, **anthology;** compendium, treasury;
ephemera; fragments; analects; **miscellany,**
miscellanea; **collection,** collectanea; ana

VERBS **5 abridge, shorten** 268.6, **condense, cut, clip;**
summarize, synopsize, wrap up <nf>; **outline,**
sketch, sketch out, hit the high spots; capsule,
capsulize, encapsulate; **put in a nutshell**

ADJS **6 abridged,** condensed; shortened, clipped,
abstracted, abbreviated, truncated, compressed;
nutshell, compendious, **brief** 268.8

ADVS **7 in brief,** in summary, in sum, to the point,
laconically, in a nutshell 537.8

558 LIBRARY

NOUNS **1 library,** book depository; learning center;
media center, media resource center, information
center; **public library,** town *or* city *or* municipal
library, county library, state library; school
library, community college library, college library,
university library; **special library,** medical library,
law library, art library, etc; **circulating library,**
lending library <Brit>; rental library; **book**
wagon, bookmobile; bookroom, bookery <old>,
bibliothèque <Fr>, bibliotheca <L>, athenaeum;
reading room; **national library,** Bibliothèque
Nationale, Bodleian Library, British Library,
Deutsche B_cherei, Library of Congress; carrel;
interlibrary loan

2 librarianship, professional librarianship; **library**
science, information science, library services,
library and information services, library and
information studies; cybrarianship

3 librarian, professional librarian, library
professional; **director, head librarian, chief**
librarian; head of service; library services
director; cybrarian

4 bibliography, annotated bibliography; **index;**
Books in Print, Paperbound Books in Print;
publisher's catalog, publisher's list, backlist;
National Union Catalog, Library of Congress
Catalog, General Catalogue of Printed Books

<Brit>, Union List of Serials; **library catalog,** computerized catalog, on-line catalog, integrated online system; CD-ROM workstation

559 RELATIONSHIP BY BLOOD

NOUNS **1 blood relationship,** blood, ties of blood, consanguinity, common descent *or* ancestry, biological *or* genetic relationship, **kinship,** kindred, **relation, relationship,** sibship; propinquity; cognation; agnation, enation; filiation, affiliation; alliance, connection, **family connection** *or* tie; motherhood, maternity; fatherhood, paternity; patrocliny, matrocliny; patrilineage, matrilineage; patriliny, matriliny; patrisib, matrisib; brotherhood, brothership, fraternity; sisterhood, sistership; cousinhood, cousinship; parental unit <nf>; **ancestry** 560

2 kinfolk *and* **kinfolks** <nf>, **kinsmen, kinsfolk, kindred,** kinnery <nf>, **kin,** kith *and* kin, **family, relatives, relations, people,** immediate family, folks <nf>, connections; **blood relation** *or* **relative,** flesh, blood, flesh *and* blood, uterine kin, consanguinean; cognate; agnate, enate; kinsman, kinswoman, sib, sibling; german; near relation, distant relation; next of kin; collateral relative, collateral; distaff *or* spindle side, distaff *or* spindle kin; sword *or* spear side, sword *or* spear kin; **tribesman,** tribespeople, clansman *or* -woman; **ancestry** 560, **posterity** 561

3 brother, bub *and* bubba *and* bro *and* bud *and* buddy <nf>, frater; brethren 700.1; **sister,** sis *and* sissy <nf>; sistern <nf>; kid brother *or* sister; blood brother *or* sister, uterine brother *or* sister, brother- *or* sister-german; half brother *or* sister, foster brother *or* sister, stepbrother *or* stepsister; **aunt,** auntie <nf>; **uncle,** unc *and* uncs *and* nunks *and* nunky *and* nuncle <nf>, **nephew, niece; cousin,** cousin-german; first cousin, second cousin, etc; cousin once removed, cousin twice removed, etc; country cousin; great-uncle, granduncle; great-granduncle; great-aunt, grandaunt; great-grandaunt; grandnephew, grandniece; **father, mother; son, daughter** 561.3

4 race, people, folk, family, house, clan, tribe, nation; patriclan, matriclan, deme, sept, gens, phyle, phratry, totem; **lineage,** line, blood, strain, stock, stem, species, stirps, **breed,** brood, kind; plant *or* animal kingdom, class, order, etc 809.5; **ethnicity,** tribalism, clannishness, roots <nf>

5 family, fam <nf>, brood, nuclear family, binuclear family, extended family, one-parent *or* single-parent family; **house, household,** hearth, hearthside, ménage, people, **folk,** homefolk, folks

and homefolks <nf>; kin, relatives, relations; **children,** issue, descendants, progeny, **offspring,** litter, get, kids <nf>

ADJS **6 related, kindred, akin;** consanguineous *or* consanguinean *or* consanguineal, consanguine, by *or* of the blood; **biological,** genetic; **natural, birth,** by birth; cognate, uterine, agnate, enate; sib, sibling; allied, affiliated, congeneric; german, germane; collateral; foster, novercal; patrilineal, matrilineal; patroclinous, matroclinous; patrilateral, matrilateral; avuncular; intimately *or* closely related, remotely *or* distantly related

7 racial, ethnic, tribal, national, family, clannish, totemic, **lineal; ethnic;** phyletic, phylogenetic, genetic; gentile, gentilic

WORD ELEMENTS **8** adelpho-, phyl-

560 ANCESTRY

NOUNS **1 ancestry,** progenitorship; parentage, parenthood; grandparentage, grandfatherhood, grandmotherhood

2 paternity, fatherhood, fathership; natural *or* birth *or* biological fatherhood; fatherliness, paternalness; adoptive fatherhood

3 maternity, motherhood, mothership; natural *or* birth *or* biological motherhood; motherliness, maternalness; adoptive motherhood; surrogate motherhood

4 lineage, line, bloodline, descent, descendancy, line of descent, ancestral line, succession, **extraction,** derivation, birth, **blood,** breed, **family, house, strain,** sept, **stock,** race, stirps, seed; direct line, phylum; **branch,** stem; filiation, affiliation, apparentation; side, father's side, mother's side; enate, agnate, cognate; male line, spear *or* sword side; female line, distaff *or* spindle side; consanguinity, ancestry 560.1

5 genealogy, pedigree, stemma, *Stammbaum* <Ger>, genealogical tree, **family tree,** tree; genogram; descent, lineage, line, bloodline, ancestry

6 heredity, heritage, inheritance, birth; patrocliny, matrocliny; endowment, inborn capacity *or* tendency *or* susceptibility *or* predisposition; diathesis; inheritability, heritability, hereditability; Mendel's law, Mendelism *or* Mendelianism; Weismann theory, Weismannism; Altmann theory, De Vries theory, Galtonian theory, Verworn theory, Wiesner theory; **genetics,** genetic engineering, genetic fingerprinting, pharmacogenetics, genesiology, eugenics; **gene,** factor, inheritance factor, determiner, determinant; **character,** dominant *or* recessive character, allele *or* allelomorph; germ cell, germ plasm; **chromosome;** sex chromosome, X chromosome, Y chromosome;

chromatin, chromatid; genetic code; DNA, RNA, replication

7 **ancestors, antecedents, predecessors,** ascendants, **fathers, forefathers, forebears,** progenitors, primogenitors; **grandparents,** grandfathers; patriarchs, elders

8 **parent, progenitor, ancestor,** procreator, begetter; natural *or* birth *or* biological parent; grandparent; ancestress, progenitress, progenitrix; stepparent; adoptive parent; surrogate parent; empty-nester

9 **father, sire,** genitor, paternal ancestor, pater <nf>, the old man <nf>, governor <nf>, abba <Heb>; patriarch, paterfamilias; stepfather; foster father, adoptive father; birth father

10 <nf terms> **papa,** pa, pap, pappy, **pop,** pops, **dad, daddy,** daddums, daddyo, big daddy, the old man, the governor, pater

11 **mother,** genetrix, dam, maternal ancestor, matriarch, materfamilias; stepmother; foster mother, adoptive mother; birth mother

12 <nf terms> **mama,** mater, the old woman, mammy, mam, **ma, mom, mommy,** mummy, mumsy, mimsy, motherkin, motherkins

13 **grandfather,** grandsire; old man 304.2; great-grandfather

14 <nf terms> **grandpa,** grampa, gramper, gramp, gramps, grandpapa, grandpap, grandpappy, **granddad,** granddaddy, granddada, granfer, gramfer, granther, pop, grandpop

15 **grandmother,** grandam; great-grandmother

16 <nf terms> **grandma,** granma, old woman 304.3; grandmamma, grandmammy, **granny,** grammy, gammy, grannam, gammer

ADJS 17 **ancestral,** ancestorial, patriarchal; patrifocal; **parental,** parent; **paternal,** fatherly, fatherlike; **maternal,** motherly, motherlike; matrifocal; grandparental; grandmotherly, grandmaternal; grandfatherly, grandpaternal

18 **lineal,** family, familial, genealogical; kindred, akin; enate *or* enatic, agnate *or* agnatic, cognate *or* cognatic; direct, in a direct line; phyletic, phylogenetic; diphyletic

19 **hereditary,** patrimonial, **inherited, innate;** genetic, genic; patroclinous, matroclinous

20 **inheritable,** heritable, hereditable

561 POSTERITY

NOUNS 1 **posterity, progeny, issue, offspring,** fruit, seed, brood, breed, family; **descent,** succession; lineage 560.4, blood, bloodline; **descendants,** heirs, inheritors, sons, **children, kids** <nf>, little ones, little people <nf>, treasures, hostages to fortune, youngsters, younglings; grandchildren, great-grandchildren; new *or* young *or* rising generation

2 <of animals> **young, brood,** get, **spawn,** spat, fry; **litter,** farrow <of pigs>; clutch, hatch

3 **descendant; offspring, child, scion; son,** son *and* heir, a chip off the old block, sonny; **daughter,** heiress; grandchild, grandson, granddaughter; stepchild, stepson, stepdaughter; foster child; adopted child

4 <derived *or* collateral descendant> **offshoot,** offset, **branch,** sprout, shoot, filiation

5 **bastard,** illegitimate, illegitimate *or* bastard child, whoreson, by-blow, child born out of wedlock *or* without benefit of clergy *or* on the wrong side of the blanket, natural *or* love child, *nullius filius* <L>; illegitimacy, bastardy, bar *or* bend sinister; hellspawn

6 sonship, sonhood; daughtership, daughterhood

ADJS 7 **filial,** sonly, sonlike; **daughterly,** daughterlike

562 LOVEMAKING, ENDEARMENT

NOUNS 1 **lovemaking,** dalliance, amorous dalliance, billing and cooing; **fondling, caressing,** hugging, kissing; cuddling, snuggling, nestling, nuzzling; bundling; sexual intercourse 75.7

2 <nf terms> **making out, necking, petting,** spooning, smooching, lollygagging, canoodling, playing kissy-face *or* kissy-kissy *or* kissy-poo *or* kissy-huggy *or* lickey-face *or* smacky-lips, pitching *or* flinging woo, sucking face, swapping spit

3 **embrace, hug, squeeze,** fond embrace, embracement, clasp, enfoldment, bear hug <nf>

4 **kiss,** buss, smack, smooch <nf>, **osculation;** French kiss, soul kiss; fish-kiss; air-kiss

5 **endearment; caress,** pat; sweet talk, soft words, honeyed words, sweet nothings; line <nf>, blandishments, artful endearments; love call, mating call, wolf whistle

6 <terms of endearment> **darling, dear,** deary, **sweetheart, sweetie, sweet,** sweets, sweetkins, **honey,** hon, honeybun, honey-bunny, honeybunch, honey child, sugar, love, lover, precious, precious heart, pet, petkins, babe, **baby, doll,** baby-doll, cherub, angel, chick, chickabiddy, buttercup, duck, duckling, ducks, lamb, lambkin, snookums, poppet <Brit>

7 **courtship, courting, wooing;** court, suit, suing, amorous pursuit, addresses; gallantry; serenade

8 **proposal,** marriage proposal, offer of marriage, popping of the question; engagement 436.3

9 **flirtation, flirtiness, coquetry,** dalliance; flirtatiousness, coquettishness, coyness; sheep's eyes, goo-goo eyes <nf>, puppy-dog eyes <nf>, amorous looks, coquettish glances, come-hither look; ogle, side-glance; bedroom eyes <nf>

10 **philandering,** philander, lady-killing <nf>; lechery, licentiousness, unchastity 665

11 **flirt, coquette,** gold digger *and* vamp <nf>; strumpet, whore 665.14,16

12 **philanderer,** philander, woman chaser, **ladies' man,** heartbreaker, rake, cad, man of the world; masher, lady-killer, wolf, skirt chaser, man on the make *and* make-out artist <nf>; libertine, lecher, cocksman <nf>, seducer 665.12, gigolo, Casanova, Don Juan, Lothario; male prostitute, stud; roving eye

13 **love letter,** billet-doux, mash note <nf>; valentine

VERBS 14 **make love,** bill *and* coo; dally, toy, trifle, wanton, make time; sweet-talk <nf>, whisper sweet nothings; go steady, keep company; copulate

15 <nf terms> **make out, neck,** pet, spoon, smooch, lollygag, canoodle, pitch *or* fling woo, play kissy-face *or* kissy-kissy *or* kissy-huggy *or* kissy-poo *or* lickey-face *or* smacky-lips, suck face, swap spit

16 **caress, pet,** pat; feel *or* feel up <nf>, **fondle,** dandle, coddle, cocker, cosset; pat on the head *or* cheek, chuck under the chin

17 **cuddle, snuggle, nestle,** nuzzle; lap; bundle

18 **embrace, hug, clasp, press, squeeze** <nf>, fold, **enfold,** bosom, embosom, put *or* throw one's arms around, take to *or* in one's arms, fold to the heart, press to the bosom

19 **kiss, osculate,** buss, smack, smooch <nf>; blow a kiss

20 **flirt, coquet; philander,** gallivant, play the field <nf>, run *or* play around, sow one's oats; **make eyes at, ogle,** eye, cast coquettish glances, cast sheep's eyes at, make goo-goo eyes at <nf>, *faire les yeux doux* <Fr>, look sweet upon <nf>; play hard to get

21 **court, woo,** sue, press one's suit, **pay court *or* suit to,** make suit to, cozy up to <nf>, eye up *and* chat up <Brit nf>, pay one's court to, address, pay one's addresses to, pay attention to, lay siege to, fling oneself at, throw oneself at the head of; **pursue,** follow; chase <nf>; set one's cap at *or* for <nf>; serenade; spark <nf>, squire, esquire, beau, sweetheart <nf>, swain

22 **propose, pop the question** <nf>, ask for one's hand; become engaged

ADJS 23 amatory, amative; sexual 75.25; caressive; **flirtatious,** flirty; **coquettish,** coy, come-hither

563 MARRIAGE

NOUNS 1 **marriage, matrimony, wedlock, married status,** holy matrimony, holy wedlock, match, matching, match-up, splicing <nf>, union, matrimonial union, alliance, marriage sacrament, sacrament of matrimony *or* marriage, bond *or* state of matrimony, wedding knot, conjugal bond *or* tie *or* knot, conjugality, nuptial bond *or* tie *or* knot, one flesh, alliance; married state *or* status, wedded state *or* status, wedded bliss, conjugal bliss, weddedness, wifehood, coverture, husbandhood, spousehood; coverture, cohabitation; bed, marriage bed, bridal bed, bridebed; living as man and wife, common-law marriage; tying the knot *and* getting hitched *and* getting spliced <nf>; intermarriage, mixed marriage, interfaith marriage, interracial marriage; remarriage; arranged marriage; lesbian marriage, homosexual marriage, gay marriage, civil union; miscegenation; misalliance, *mésalliance* <Fr>

2 **marriageability,** marriageableness, nubility, ripeness; age of consent

3 **wedding, marriage,** marriage *or* wedding ceremony, nuptial mass; church wedding, civil wedding, civil ceremony, courthouse wedding; espousement, bridal; banns; wedding bells, **nuptials,** spousals, espousals, marriage vows, hymeneal rites, wedding service; commitment ceremony; *chuppah* <Heb>, wedding canopy; white wedding; wedding song, marriage song, nuptial song, prothalamium, epithalamium, epithalamy, hymen, hymeneal; wedding veil, saffron veil *or* robe; bridechamber, bridal suite, nuptial apartment; **honeymoon;** forced marriage, shotgun wedding; Gretna Green wedding, elopement; wedding planner

4 **wedding party;** wedding attendant, usher; **best man,** bridesman, groomsman; paranymph; **bridesmaid,** bridemaiden, maid *or* matron of honor; attendant, flower girl, train bearer, ring bearer

5 **newlywed; bridegroom, groom; bride,** plighted bride, blushing bride; war bride, GI bride <nf>; honeymooner

6 **spouse,** espouser, espoused, **mate,** yokemate, partner, consort, **better half** <nf>, other half <nf>, one's promised, one's betrothed, soul mate, helpmate, helpmeet; old ball and chain <nf>

7 **husband, married man,** man, benedict, goodman <old>, old man <nf>, hubby <nf>

8 **wife, married woman,** wedded wife, goodwife *or* goody <old>, squaw, woman, lady, matron, old lady *and* old woman *and* little woman *and* ball and chain <nf>, feme, feme covert, **better half** <nf>, **helpmate,** helpmeet, rib, wife of one's bosom; wife in name only; wife in all but name, concubine, common-law wife; blushing bride, war bride, GI bride

9 **married couple,** wedded pair, bridal pair, happy couple, **man and wife,** husband and wife, man and

woman, *vir et uxor* <L>, one flesh, Mr. and Mrs.;
newlyweds, **bride and groom**, honeymooners

10 **harem, seraglio,** serai, gynaeceum; zenana, purdah

11 **monogamist,** monogynist; **bigamist;** digamist,
deuterogamist; trigamist; **polygamist,** polygynist,
polyandrist; Bluebeard

12 **matchmaker, marriage broker,** matrimonial
agent, *shadchan* <Yiddish>; matrimonial agency
or bureau; go-between; dating agency *or* service,
lonely hearts club, computer dating

13 <god> Hymen; <goddesses> Hera, Teleia; Juno,
Pronuba; Frigg

VERBS 14 <join in marriage> **marry,** wed, nuptial,
join, unite, hitch *and* **splice** <nf>, couple, match,
match up, make *or* arrange a match, join together,
unite in marriage, join *or* unite in holy wedlock *or*
matrimony, tie the knot, tie the nuptial *or* wedding
knot, celebrate a marriage, make one, pronounce
man and wife; give away, give in marriage; marry
off, find a mate for, find a husband *or* wife for

15 <get married> **marry, wed,** contract matrimony,
say "I do", mate, couple, espouse, wive, **take to
wife,** take a wife *or* husband, **get hitched** *or*
spliced <nf>, tie the knot, become one, be made
one, pair off, give one's hand to, bestow one's hand
upon, lead to the altar, take for better *or* for worse;
make an honest man *or* woman of; remarry,
rewed; intermarry, interwed, miscegenate

16 **honeymoon,** go on a honeymoon, consummate
one's marriage; second-honeymoon

17 **cohabit,** cohabitate, live together, live as man and
wife, share one's bed and board; shack up <nf>

ADJS 18 **matrimonial, marital, conjugal, connubial,
nuptial,** wedded, married, hymeneal; epithalamic;
spousal; husbandly, uxorious; bridal, wifely,
uxorial; premarital, concubinal, concubinary

19 **monogamous,** monogynous, monandrous;
bigamous, digamous; **polygamous,** polygynous,
polyandrous; morganatic; miscegenetic

20 **marriageable,** nubile, eligible, ripe, of age, of
marriageable age

21 **married, wedded,** newlywed, espoused, one, one
bone and one flesh, mated, matched, coupled,
partnered, paired, hitched *and* spliced *and*
hooked <nf>

WORD ELEMENTS 22 -gamy; -gamous

564 RELATIONSHIP BY MARRIAGE

NOUNS 1 **marriage relationship,** affinity, marital
affinity, connection, family connection, marriage
connection, matrimonial connection

2 **in-laws** <nf>, **relatives-in-law;** brother-in-law,
sister-in-law, father-in-law, mother-in-law,
son-in-law, daughter-in-law

3 stepfather, stepmother; stepbrother, stepsister;
stepchild, stepson, stepdaughter

ADJS 4 **affinal,** affined, by marriage

565 CELIBACY

NOUNS 1 **celibacy, singleness,** singlehood, single
blessedness, single *or* unmarried *or* unwed state
or condition; **bachelorhood,** bachelordom,
bachelorism, bachelorship; **spinsterhood,**
maidenhood, maidenhead, **virginity,** maiden *or*
virgin state, chastity, chasteness; **monasticism,**
monachism, spiritual marriage, holy orders, the
veil; misogamy, misogyny; self-restraint, self-
denial; sexual abstinence *or* abstention, continence
664.3

2 **celibate,** *célibataire* <Fr>; monk, monastic, lama,
bhikkhu, priest, nun, cenobite, eremite; virgin,
vestal; misogamist, misogynist; unmarried,
single <nf>

3 **bachelor,** bach *and* old bach <nf>, single *or*
unmarried man, confirmed bachelor, **single man,**
unattached male; misogamist

4 **single** *or* unmarried woman, spinster, spinstress,
old maid, maid, maiden, bachelor girl, single girl,
lone woman, maiden lady, feme sole, unattached
female; **virgin,** virgo intacta, cherry <nf>; vestal,
vestal virgin

VERBS 5 **be unmarried, be single, live alone,** enjoy
single blessedness, **bach** *and* **bach it** <nf>, keep
bachelor quarters, keep one's freedom, sit on the
shelf <nf>

ADJS 6 **celibate,** celibatic; **monastic,** monachal,
monkish, cenobitic, nunnish; misogamic,
misogynous; sexually abstinent *or* continent,
abstinent, abstaining; self-restrained

7 **unmarried, unwedded, unwed, single,** sole,
spouseless, wifeless, husbandless, unmated,
mateless; **bachelorly,** bachelorlike; **spinsterly,**
spinsterish, spinsterlike; **old-maidish,** old-
maidenish; maiden, maidenly; virgin, virginal;
independent, unattached, fancy-free; on the
shelf <nf>

566 DIVORCE, WIDOWHOOD

NOUNS 1 **divorce,** divorcement, grasswidowhood,
civil divorce, **separation,** legal *or* judicial
separation, separate maintenance; interlocutory
decree; dissolution of marriage; divorce decree,
decree nisi, decree absolute; annulment, decree of
nullity; nonconsummation of marriage,
estrangement, living apart, desertion; broken
marriage, broken home; breakup, split-up, split,
marriage on the rocks <nf>

2 divorcé, divorced person, divorced man, divorced woman, *divorcée* <Fr>, free man *or* woman; divorcer; grass widow, grass widower

3 widowhood, viduity <old>; **widowerhood,** widowership; weeds, widow's weeds

4 widow, widow woman <nf>, relict; dowager, queen dowager *or* dowager queen, merry widow, war widow; **widower,** widowman <nf>

VERBS **5 divorce, separate,** part, split up *and* split the sheets <nf>, unmarry, put away, obtain a divorce, dissolve one's marriage, come to a parting of the ways, untie the knot, sue for divorce, file for divorce; have one's marriage annulled; grant a divorce, grant a final decree; grant an annulment, grant a decree of nullity, annul a marriage, put asunder, regain one's freedom; break up, split up, split, sunder; separate, live apart, part, be estranged; desert, abandon, leave, walk out

6 widow, bereave, make a widow

ADJS **7** widowly, widowish, widowlike; **widowed,** widowered; **divorced;** separated, legally separated, split, estranged; on the rocks <nf>

567 SCHOOL

NOUNS **1 school** <see list>, **educational institution,** teaching institution, academic *or* scholastic institution, teaching and research institution, **institute, academy,** seminary, *Schule* <Ger>, *école* <Fr>, *escuela* <Sp>; alternative school; magnet school

2 preschool, prekindergarten, pre-K, infant school <Brit>, nursery, **nursery school;** day nursery, **day-care center,** crèche; playschool; **kindergarten**

3 elementary school, grade school *or* graded school, the grades; **primary school;** junior school <Brit>; **grammar school;** folk school, *Volksschule* <Ger>, home schooling

4 secondary school, middle school, **academy,** *Gymnasium* <Ger>; *lycée* <Fr>, lyceum; **high school,** high <nf>; **junior high school,** junior high <nf>, intermediate school; **senior high school,** senior high <nf>; **preparatory school,** prep school <nf>, public school <Brit>, seminary; **grammar school** <Brit>, Latin school, *Progymnasium* <Ger>; *Realschule* <Ger>; *Realgymnasium* <Ger>; charter school

5 college, university, institution *or* institute of higher education or learning, degree-granting institution; tertiary school, graduate school, post graduate school, coeducational school; academe, academia, the groves of Academe, **the campus,** the halls of learning or ivy, ivied halls; alma mater; women's college; polytechnic, adult education,

correspondence course; distance learning, distance education, e-learning, online degree, virtual classroom; professional development

6 service school, service academy <see list>, military academy, naval academy

7 art school, performing arts school, music school, conservatory, arts conservatory, school of the arts, dance school

8 religious school <see list>, parochial school, church-related school, church school; Sunday school

9 reform school, reformatory, correctional institution, industrial school, training school; borstal *or* borstal school *or* remand school <Brit>

10 schoolhouse, school building; little red schoolhouse; classroom building; portable classroom; hall; campus

11 schoolroom, classroom; recitation room; lecture room *or* hall; auditorium, assembly hall; theater, amphitheater

12 governing board, board; board of education, school board; college board, board of regents, board of trustees, board of visitors

ADJS **13 scholastic, academic,** institutional, **school,** classroom; **collegiate; university;** preschool; interscholastic, intercollegiate, extramural; intramural

14 schools

academy	medical school
adult-education school	military school *or* academy
alternate *or* alternative school	night school
boarding school	open-classroom school
business college *or* school	polytechnic school *or* polytechnic <chiefly Brit>
charm school	preparatory school *or* prep school <nf>
community college	preschool
comprehensive school	primary school
conservatory	private school
correspondence school	public school
country day school	reformatory school
day school	school of continuing education *or* continuation school
distance learning institution	
elementary *or* grade school	secondary school *or* high school *or* senior high school
extension school *or* program	
finishing school	secretarial school
graduate school	special needs school
gymnasium	state school
institute	summer school
junior college	technical school *or* technical college *or* tech <nf>
junior high school *or* junior school *or* middle school *or* intermediate school	
	university extension
law school	vocational *or* trade school
lyceum *or* lycée	women's college

15 religious schools

bible institute
bible school
Catholic school
church school
convent school
denominational school
divinity school
Hebrew school *or* heder
  <Yiddish>
madrasah
mesivta
parish school
parochial school

religious *or* parochial
  school
Sabbath school
schola cantorum
scholasticate
seminary
Sunday school
Talmud Torah
theological seminary *or*
  school
vacation church
  school
yeshiva

568 TEACHING

NOUNS **1 teaching, instruction, education, schooling, tuition; edification, enlightenment,** illumination; tutelage, tutorage, tutorship; tutoring, coaching, direction, training, preparation, private teaching, teacher 571; spoon-feeding; direction, guidance; **pedagogy,** pedagogics, didactics, didacticism; scholarship; catechization; computer-aided instruction, programmed instruction; home schooling; self-teaching, self-instruction; distance education; information 551; reeducation 858.4; **school** 567; **formal education,** coursework, schoolwork

2 inculcation, indoctrination, catechization, inoculation, **implantation,** infixation, infixion, **impression, instillment,** instillation, impregnation, **infusion,** imbuement; absorption and regurgitation; dictation; conditioning, brainwashing; reindoctrination 858.5

3 training, preparation, readying <nf>, **conditioning, grooming,** cultivation, development, improvement; **discipline;** breaking, housebreaking; **upbringing, bringing-up,** fetching-up <nf>, **rearing, raising, breeding, nurture,** nurturing, fostering; **practice,** rehearsal, **exercise, drill,** drilling; **apprenticeship,** in-service training, on-the-job training; work-study; military training, basic training; manual training, sloyd; vocational training *or* education; **liberal arts,** arithmetic, astronomy, geometry, grammar, logic, music, rhetoric

4 preinstruction, pre-education; **priming,** cramming <nf>

5 elementary education, nursery school, preschool, primary education, home schooling; **initiation, introduction,** propaedeutic; **rudiments,** grounding, first steps, elements, **ABC's, basics;** reading, writing, and arithmetic, **three R's;** primer, hornbook, abecedarium, abecedary

6 instructions, directions, orders; briefing, final instructions

7 lesson, teaching, instruction, lecture, lecture-demonstration, harangue, **discourse,** disquisition, exposition, **talk,** homily, **sermon,** preachment; chalk talk <nf>; skull session <nf>; **recitation,** recital; **assignment, exercise,** task, set task, homework; moral, morality, moral compass, moralization, moral lesson; object lesson

8 study, branch of learning, branch of knowledge; **discipline,** subdiscipline; **field, specialty,** academic specialty, area; **course,** course of study, **curriculum,** syllabus, module, department; **subject;** major, minor; requirement *or* required course, elective course, core curriculum; refresher course; summer *or* summer-session course, intersession course; crash course; gut course <nf>; correspondence course; distance-learning course; **seminar,** proseminar; professional development

9 physical education, physical culture, gymnastics, calisthenics, eurythmics

VERBS **10 teach, instruct,** give instruction, give lessons in, **educate, school; edify, enlighten,** civilize, illumine; **direct, guide;** get across, **inform** 551.8; **show,** show how, show the ropes, demonstrate; give an idea of; put in the right, set right; improve one's mind, enlarge *or* broaden the mind; sharpen the wits, open the eyes *or* mind; teach a lesson, give a lesson to; **ground,** teach the rudiments *or* elements *or* basics; catechize; teach an old dog new tricks; reeducate 858.14

11 tutor, coach, mentor, direct; **prime, cram** <nf>, cram with facts, stuff with knowledge

12 inculcate, indoctrinate, catechize, inoculate, **instill, infuse,** imbue, impregnate, **implant,** infix, impress; **impress upon the mind** *or* **memory,** urge on the mind, beat into, beat *or* knock into one's head, grind in, drill into, drum into one's head *or* skull; **condition, brainwash, program**

13 train; drill, exercise; practice, rehearse; keep in practice, keep one's hand in; **prepare,** ready, **condition, groom,** fit, put in tune, form, **lick into shape** <nf>; **rear, raise, bring up,** fetch up <nf>, bring up by hand, **breed; cultivate,** develop, improve; **nurture, foster,** nurse; **discipline,** take in hand; put through the mill *or* grind <nf>; break, break in, housebreak, house-train <Brit>; put to school, send to school, apprentice

14 preinstruct, pre-educate; **initiate,** introduce

15 give instructions, give directions; **brief,** give a briefing

16 expound, exposit; explain 341.10; **lecture, discourse,** harangue, hold forth, give *or* read a lesson; **preach,** sermonize; **moralize,** point a moral

17 assign, give *or* make an assignment, give homework, set a task, set hurdles; lay out a course, make a syllabus

ADJS **18 educational,** educative, educating, educatory, teaching, **instructive,** instructional, **tuitional,** tuitionary; **cultural, edifying, enlightening,** illuminating; informative, informational; edifying; didactic, preceptive; self instructional, self-teaching, autodidactic; lecturing, preaching, hortatory, exhortatory, homiletic, homiletical; initiatory, introductory, propaedeutic; **disciplinary;** coeducational; remedial

19 scholastic, academic, schoolish, pedantic, donnish <Brit>; **scholarly; pedagogical;** collegiate, graduate, professional, doctoral, graduate-professional, postgraduate; interdisciplinary, cross-disciplinary, transdisciplinary; curricular, intramural, extramural, varsity

20 extracurricular, extraclassroom; nonscholastic, noncollegiate

569 MISTEACHING

NOUNS **1 misteaching,** misinstruction; **misguidance,** misdirection, misleading; sophistry 935; perversion, corruption; mystification, obscuration, obfuscation, obscurantism; **misinformation,** misknowledge; the blind leading the blind; college of Laputa

2 propaganda; propagandism, indoctrination; brainwashing; **propagandist,** agitprop; **disinformation;** war of nerves

VERBS **3 misteach,** misinstruct, miseducate; **misinform;** misadvise, **misguide,** misdirect, **mislead;** pervert, corrupt; mystify, obscure, obfuscate

4 propagandize, carry on a propaganda; indoctrinate; **disinform,** brainwash

ADJS **5 mistaught,** misinstructed; **misinformed;** misadvised, **misguided,** misdirected, **misled**

6 misteaching, misinstructive, miseducative, **misinforming; misleading,** misguiding, misdirecting; obscuring, mystifying, obfuscatory; propagandistic, indoctrinational; disinformational

570 LEARNING

NOUNS **1 learning,** intellectual acquirement *or* acquisition *or* attainment, stocking *or* storing the mind, mental cultivation, mental culture, improving *or* broadening the mind, acquisition of knowledge, scholarship; **mastery,** mastery of skills; **self-education,** self-instruction; **knowledge, erudition** 928.5; education 568.1; memorization 989.3; cultural literacy; professional student

2 absorption, ingestion, imbibing, assimilation, taking-in, getting, getting hold of, getting the hang of <nf>, soaking-up, digestion; aha moment

3 study, studying, application, conning; **reading, perusal;** restudy, restudying, brushing up, boning up <nf>; **review; contemplation** 931.2; **inspection** 938.3; **engrossment; brainwork, headwork,** lucubration, mental labor; exercise, **practice, drill;** grind *and* grinding *and* boning <nf>, boning up <nf>; **cramming** *and* cram <nf>, swotting <Brit nf>; extensive study, wide reading; subject 568.8

4 studiousness, scholarliness, scholarship; bookishness, diligence 330.6; learnedness, intellectuality, literacy, polymathy, erudition

5 teachableness, teachability, educability, trainableness; **aptness, aptitude,** quickness, **readiness; receptivity,** mind like a blotter, ready grasp, quick mind, quick study; **willingness, motivation,** hunger *or* thirst for learning, willingness to learn, curiosity, inquisitiveness; docility, **malleability,** moldability, pliability, facility, plasticity, **impressionability,** susceptibility, formability; brightness, cleverness, quickness, readiness, **intelligence** 920

VERBS **6 learn,** get, get hold of <nf>, get into one's head, get through one's thick skull <nf>; **gain knowledge,** pick up information, gather *or* collect *or* glean knowledge *or* learning; stock *or* store the mind, improve *or* broaden the mind; stuff *or* cram the mind; burden *or* load the mind; **find out, ascertain, discover,** find, determine, figure out; **become informed,** gain knowledge *or* understanding of, acquire information *or* intelligence about, research, become aware of, **learn about, find out about,** do the math; acquaint oneself with, make oneself acquainted with, become acquainted with; be informed 551.14

7 absorb, acquire, take in, ingest, imbibe, get by osmosis, **assimilate, digest, soak up,** drink in; **soak in, seep in,** percolate in

8 memorize 989.16, get by rote; fix in the mind 989.17

9 master, attain mastery of, make oneself master of, **gain command of, become adept in,** become familiar *or* conversant with, become versed *or* well-versed in, **get up in** *or* **on,** gain a good *or* thorough knowledge of, **learn all about, get down pat** <nf>, get down cold <nf>, get taped <Brit nf>, get to the bottom *or* heart of; **get the hang** *or* **knack of; learn the ropes,** learn the ins and outs; know well 928.13

10 learn by experience, learn by doing, **live and learn,** go through the school of hard knocks, learn the hard way <nf>; teach *or* school oneself; **learn a lesson,** be taught a lesson

11 be taught, receive instruction, be tutored, be instructed, undergo schooling, pursue one's education, attend classes, go to *or* attend school, take lessons, be mentored, matriculate, enroll, register; **train,** prepare oneself, ready oneself, go into training; serve an apprenticeship; apprentice, apprentice oneself to; **study with,** read with, sit at the feet of, learn from, have as one's master; monitor, audit

12 **study,** regard studiously, apply oneself to, con, crack a book *and* hit the books <nf>; **read, peruse,** go over, read up *or* read up on, have one's nose in a book <nf>; restudy, **review; contemplate** 931.12; **examine** 938.21; give mind to 983.5; **pore over,** vet <Brit nf>; be highly motivated, hunger *or* thirst for knowledge; bury oneself in, wade through, plunge into, throw oneself into; **dig** *and* **grind** *and* **bone** *and* bone up on <nf>, swot <Brit nf>; lucubrate, elucubrate, **burn the midnight oil;** make a study of; **practice, drill**

13 **browse, scan, skim, dip into,** thumb over *or* through, run over *or* through, glance *or* run the eye over *or* through, turn over the leaves, have a look at, hit the high spots, graze

14 **study up, get up,** study up on, read up on, get up on; **review, brush up,** polish up <nf>, rub up, **cram** *or* cram up <nf>, **bone up** <nf>; pull an all-nighter

15 **study to be, study for, read for,** read law, etc; **specialize in, go in for,** make one's field; major in, minor in

ADJS 16 educated, **learned** 927.21,22; knowledgeable, erudite; literate, numerate; self-taught, self-instructed, autodidactic

17 **studious,** devoted to studies, **scholarly,** scholastic, academic, professorial, tweedy, donnish <Brit>; owlish; rabbinic, mandarin; pedantic, dryasdust; bookish 928.22; diligent 330.22

18 **teachable, instructable, educable,** schoolable, trainable; **apt,** quick, **ready,** ripe for instruction; **receptive, willing,** motivated; hungry *or* thirsty for knowledge; docile, **malleable, moldable,** pliable, facile, plastic, **impressionable,** susceptible, formable; bright, clever, **intelligent** 920.12

571 TEACHER

NOUNS 1 **teacher, instructor, educator,** preceptor, **mentor; master,** maestro; **pedagogue,** pedagogist, educationist, educationalist, tutor; schoolman; **schoolteacher, schoolmaster,** schoolkeeper; abecedarian <old>, certified *or* licensed teacher; **professor, academic,** member of academy; don <Brit>, fellow; guide 574.7, docent; rabbi, *melamed* <Heb>, pandit, pundit, guru, *mullah* <Persian>, *starets* <Russ>, acharya <Sanskrit>; home tutor, private tutor, mentor

2 <woman teachers> instructress, educatress, preceptress, **mistress; schoolmistress;**

schoolma'am *or* schoolmarm, dame, schooldame; **governess,** duenna

3 <academic ranks> professor, associate professor, assistant professor, instructor, tutor, associate, assistant, lecturer, reader <Brit>; visiting professor; emeritus, professor emeritus, retired professor

4 teaching fellow, teaching assistant *or* TA; paraeducator; teaching intern, fellow, intern; practice teacher, apprentice teacher, student *or* pupil teacher; teacher's aide, paraprofessional; monitor, proctor, prefect, praepostor <Brit>; student assistant, graduate assistant

5 **tutor,** tutorer; **coach,** coacher; **private instructor,** *Privatdocent* *or* *Privatdozent* <Ger>; crammer <Brit nf>

6 **trainer, handler, groomer;** driller, drillmaster; **coach,** athletic coach

7 **lecturer,** lector, **reader** <Brit>, praelector, **preacher,** homilist

8 **principal, headmaster,** headmistress, vice-principal; president, chancellor, vice-chancellor, rector, provost, master; **dean,** academic dean, dean of the faculty, dean of women, dean of men; administrator, educational administrator; administration; department head *or* chair

9 **faculty,** staff <Brit>, faculty members, professorate, professoriate, professors, professordom, teaching staff

10 **instructorship, teachership,** preceptorship, schoolmastery; **tutorship,** tutorhood, tutorage, tutelage; **professorship,** professorhood, professorate, professoriate; **chair,** endowed chair; lectureship, readership <Brit>; fellowship, research fellowship; assistantship

ADJS 11 **pedagogic, pedagogical,** preceptorial, tutorial; **teacherish,** teachery, teacherlike, teachy, **schoolteacherish,** schoolteachery, **schoolmasterish,** schoolmasterly, schoolmastering, schoolmasterlike; schoolmistressy, schoolmarmish <nf>; **professorial,** professorlike, academic, tweedy, donnish <Brit>; pedantic 928.22

572 STUDENT

NOUNS 1 **student, pupil, scholar,** learner, studier, educatee, **trainee,** *élève* <Fr>; tutee; inquirer; mature student, adult-education *or* continuing education student; self-taught person, autodidact; auditor; **reader,** reading enthusiast, great reader, printhead <nf>; bookworm, researcher; opsimath

2 **disciple, follower,** apostle; convert, proselyte 858.7; **discipleship,** disciplehood, pupilage, tutelage, studentship, followership

3 schoolchild, school kid <nf>; **schoolboy,** school
lad; **schoolgirl;** day-pupil, day boy, day girl;
preschool child, preschooler, nursery school child,
infant <Brit>; kindergartner, grade schooler,
primary schooler, intermediate schooler;
secondary schooler, prep schooler, preppie <nf>,
high schooler; schoolmate, schoolfellow, fellow
student, classmate
4 special *or* exceptional student, gifted student;
special education *or* special ed <nf> student;
learning disabled *or* LD student; learning impaired
student; slow learner, underachiever; handicapped
or retarded student; emotionally disturbed
student; culturally disadvantaged student
5 college student, collegian, collegiate, university
student, **varsity student** <Brit nf>, college boy *or*
girl; co-ed <nf>; seminarian, seminarist; *bahur*
<Heb>, *yeshiva bocher* <Yiddish>
6 undergraduate, undergrad <nf>, cadet,
midshipman; underclassman, **freshman,** freshie
<nf>, plebe, **sophomore,** soph <nf>;
upperclassman, junior, senior
7 <Brit terms> commoner, pensioner, sizar, servitor
<old>, exhibitioner, fellow commoner; sophister
and questionist <old>; wrangler, optime; passman;
muggle
8 graduate, grad <nf>; **alumnus,** alumni, alumna,
alumnae; old boy <Brit>; **graduate student,** grad
student <nf>, master's degree candidate, doctoral
candidate; **postgraduate,** postgrad <nf>; degrees;
college graduate, college man *or* woman, educated
man *or* woman, educated class; meritocracy
9 novice, novitiate *or* noviciate, **tyro,** abecedarian,
alphabetarian, **beginner** 818.2, entrant, **neophyte,**
tenderfoot *and* **greenhorn** <nf>, freshman,
fledgling; newbie; Bambi; catechumen, initiate,
debutant; new boy <Brit>, newcomer 774.4;
ignoramus 930.7; **recruit, raw recruit,** inductee,
rookie *and* yardbird <nf>, boot; **probationer,**
probationist, postulant; **apprentice,** articled clerk
10 nerd *or* egghead *or* grind *or* greasy grind <nf>,
swotter *or* mugger <Brit nf>; bookworm 929.4
11 class, form <Brit>, **grade;** track; year
ADJS **12 studentlike,** schoolboyish, schoolgirlish;
undergraduate, graduate, postgraduate; **collegiate,**
college-bred; sophomoric; sophomorical;
autodidactic; **studious** 570.17; **learned, bookish**
928.22; exceptional, gifted, special
13 probationary, probational, on probation; in
detention

573 DIRECTION, MANAGEMENT

NOUNS **1 direction, management, managing,**
managery <old>, handling, **running** <nf>,
conduct; governance, **command, control,**
chiefdom, government 612, governance,
controllership; **authority** 417; **regulation,** ordering,
husbandry; manipulation, orchestration;
guidance, lead, leading; steering, navigation,
pilotage, conning, the conn, the helm, the wheel
2 supervision, superintendence, intendance *or*
intendancy, heading, heading up *and* **bossing** *and*
running <nf>; **surveillance,** oversight, eye; **charge,**
care, auspices, jurisdiction; responsibility,
accountability 641.2
3 administration, executive function *or* role,
command function, say-so *and* last word <nf>;
decision-making; disposition, disposal,
dispensation; officiation; lawmaking, legislation,
regulation
4 directorship, leadership, managership, directorate,
headship, governorship, chairmanship,
convenership <Brit>, presidency, premiership,
generalship, captainship; mastership 417.7;
dictatorship, sovereignty 417.8; superintendence *or*
superintendency, intendancy, foremanship,
overseership, supervisorship; stewardship, custody,
guardianship, shepherding, proctorship; personnel
management; collective leadership
5 helm, conn, rudder, tiller, wheel, steering wheel;
reins; joystick; remote control *or* remote
6 domestic management, housekeeping,
homemaking, housewifery, ménage, husbandry
<old>; domestic economy, home economics
7 efficiency engineering, scientific management,
bean-counting <nf>, industrial engineering,
management engineering, management
consulting; management theory; efficiency expert,
management consultant; time and motion study,
time-motion study, time study; therblig
VERBS **8 direct, manage, regulate, conduct, carry**
on, handle, run <nf>, be in charge; **control,**
command, head, govern 612.11, rule, **boss** *and*
head up *and* pull the strings *and* **mastermind** *and*
quarterback *and* call the signals <nf>; **order,**
prescribe; organize; lay down the law, make the
rules, call the shots *or* tune <nf>; **head,** head up,
office, captain, skipper <nf>; **lead,** take the lead,
lead on; manipulate, maneuver, engineer; take
command 417.14; be responsible for; hold the purse
strings <nf>
9 guide, steer, drive, run <nf>; herd, counsel,
advise, shepherd; channel; **pilot,** take the helm *or*
wheel, be at the helm *or* wheel *or* tiller *or* rudder,
hold the reins, **be in the driver's seat** <nf>; emcee
10 supervise, superintend, boss, oversee, overlook,
ride herd on <nf>, crack the whip <nf>, stand over,
keep an eye on *or* upon, keep in order; cut work
out for; straw-boss <nf>; take care of 1008.19

11 administer, administrate; **officiate; preside,** preside over, preside at the board; chair, chairman, occupy the chair, take the chair

ADJS **12 directing, directive,** directory, directorial; **managing, managerial; commanding, controlling, governing** 612.17; regulating, regulative, regulatory; **head, chief;** leading, guiding

13 supervising, supervisory, overseeing, **superintendent, boss; in charge** 417.21, in the driver's seat *and* holding the reins <nf>

14 administrative, administrating; ministerial, **executive; officiating, presiding**

ADVS **15** in the charge of, in the hands of, in the care of; **under the auspices of,** under the aegis of; in one's charge, on one's hands, under one's care, under one's jurisdiction

574 DIRECTOR

NOUNS **1 director,** *directeur* <Fr>, director general, **governor,** rector, **manager, administrator,** intendant, **conductor;** person in charge, responsible person, key person; ship's husband, supercargo; impresario, producer; deputy, agent 576

2 superintendent; supervisor, foreman, monitor, **head,** headman, overman, **boss,** chief, gaffer *and* ganger <Brit nf>, taskmaster; sirdar <India>, **overseer,** overlooker; inspector, surveyor; proctor; subforeman, **straw boss** <nf>; slave driver; boatswain; floorman, floorwalker, floor manager; noncommissioned officer 575.19; controller, comptroller, auditor; department head; chief cook and bottle washer <nf>

3 executive, officer, official, pinstriper <nf>, employer, company official; suit <nf>; **president,** prexy <nf>, chief executive officer *or* CEO, chief executive, chief operating officer *or* COO, managing director, director; provost, prefect, warden, archon; policy-maker, agenda-setter; magistrate; **chairman of the board; chancellor,** vice-chancellor; vice-president *or* VP *or* veep <nf>; secretary; treasurer; dean; executive officer, executive director, executive secretary; **management,** the administration 574.11

4 steward, bailiff <Brit>, reeve <old>, factor <Scot>, seneschal; majordomo, butler, housekeeper, *maître d'hôtel* <Fr>; master of ceremonies *or* MC *and* emcee <nf>, master of the revels; proctor, procurator, attorney; guardian, custodian 1008.6, executor; curator, librarian; croupier; factor

5 chairman, chairwoman, **chair,** chairperson, convener <Brit>, speaker, presiding officer; co-chairman, etc

6 leader, conductor <old>; file leader, fugleman; pacemaker, pacesetter, honcho; bellwether, bell mare, bell cow, Judas goat; standard-bearer, torchbearer; **leader of men,** born leader, charismatic leader *or* figure, inspired leader; messiah, Mahdi; führer, duce; forerunner 816.1; ringleader 375.11; precentor, coryphaeus, choragus, symphonic conductor, choirmaster 710.18

7 guide, guider; **shepherd,** herd, herdsman, drover, cowherd, goatherd, etc; tour guide, tour director *or* conductor, cicerone, mercury <old>, courier, dragoman; **pilot,** river pilot, navigator, **helmsman,** timoneer, steerman, steerer, coxswain, boatsteerer, boatheader; automatic pilot, Gyropilot; pointer, fingerpost <Brit>, guidepost 517.4; leader, motivator, pacesetter, standard-bearer

8 guiding star, guiding light, cynosure <old>, **polestar,** polar star, lodestar, Polaris, **North Star**

9 compass, magnetic compass, gyrocompass, gyroscopic compass, gyrostatic compass, Gyrosin compass, surveyor's compass, mariner's compass; needle, magnetic needle; direction finder, radio compass, radio direction finder *or* RDF

10 directory, guidebook, handbook, Baedeker; city directory, business directory; telephone directory, telephone book, phone book <nf>, classified directory, Yellow Pages; **bibliography;** catalog, index, handlist, checklist, finding list; itinerary, road map, roadbook; gazetteer, reference book

11 directorate, directory, **management, the administration,** the brass *and* top brass <nf>, the people upstairs *and* the people in the front office <nf>, executive hierarchy; the executive, executive arm *or* branch; middle management; **cabinet; board,** governing board *or* body, board of directors, board of trustees, board of regents; steering committee, executive committee, interlocking directorate; cadre, executive council; infrastructure; council 423

575 MASTER

NOUNS **1 master, lord, lord and master,** overlord, seigneur, paramount, lord paramount, liege, liege lord, lord of the manor, *padrone* <Ital>, *patron and chef* <Fr>, patroon; **chief, boss,** sahib <India>, *bwana* <Swah>; employer; husband, man of the house, master of the house, goodman <old nf>, paterfamilias; patriarch, elder; teacher, rabbi, guru, starets; church dignitary, ecclesiarch

2 mistress, governess, dame <old>, madam; **matron, housewife,** homemaker, goodwife <Scot>, mistress *or* lady of the house, chatelaine; housemistress, housemother; rectoress, abbess, mother superior; great lady, first lady; materfamilias, matriarch, dowager

3 **chief,** principal, headman; **master,** dean, doyen, doyenne; high priest <nf>, superior, senior; **leader** 574.6; important person, personage 997.8; owner, landowner

4 <nf terms> **top dog,** boss man, big boy, Big Daddy, big cheese, kingpin, kingfish, el supremo, honcho *or* head honcho, top banana, big enchilada, bigwig, big gun, top gun, big shot, big wheel, VIP, himself, herself, man *or* woman upstairs, cock of the walk; queen bee, heavy momma, Big Momma, old man, quarterback, ringmaster, skipper, high priest

5 **figurehead,** nominal head, dummy, lay figure, front man *and* front <nf>, stooge *and* Charlie McCarthy <nf>, puppet, creature; straw man, lame duck

6 **governor, ruler; captain, master, commander,** commandant, commanding officer, intendant, castellan, chatelain, chatelaine; **director, manager, executive** 574.3

7 **head of state, chief of state,** leader; **premier, prime minister, chancellor,** grand vizier, dewan <India>; doge; **president,** chief executive, POTUS <nf>, the man in the White House

8 **potentate, sovereign, monarch,** absolute monarch, **ruler, prince,** dynast, **crowned head, emperor,** *imperator* <L>, king-emperor, **king,** anointed king, majesty, royalty, royal, royal personage, emperor, etc; petty king, tetrarch, kinglet; grand duke; paramount, lord paramount, suzerain, overlord, overking, high king; **chief, chieftain,** high chief; prince consort 608.7

9 <rulers> **caesar,** kaiser, **czar;** Holy Roman Emperor; Dalai Lama; **pharaoh;** pendragon, rig, ardri; **mikado,** tenno; shogun, tycoon; khan *or* cham; shah, padishah; negus; bey; sheikh; sachem, sagamore; Inca; cacique; kaid

10 <Muslim rulers> **sultan,** Grand Turk, grand seignior; caliph, imam; hakim; khan *or* cham; nizam, nabab; emir; Great Mogul, Mogul

11 **sovereign queen, sovereign princess, princess, queen,** queen regent, queen regnant, **empress,** czarina, *Kaiserin* <Ger>; rani *and* maharani <India>; grand duchess; queen consort

12 **regent,** protector, prince regent, queen regent

13 <regional governors> **governor,** governor-general, lieutenant governor; **viceroy,** vice-king, exarch, proconsul, khedive, stadtholder, vizier; nabob *and* nabab *and* subahdar <India>; gauleiter; eparch; palatine; tetrarch; burgrave; collector; hospodar, vaivode; dey, bey *or* beg, beglerbeg, wali *or* vali, satrap; provincial; warlord; military governor

14 **tyrant, despot,** warlord; **autocrat,** autarch; oligarch; absolute ruler *or* master *or* monarch, omnipotent *or* all-powerful ruler; **dictator,** duce, führer, commissar, pharaoh, caesar, czar; usurper, arrogator; **oppressor, hard master,** driver, **slave driver,** Simon Legree <Harriet B Stowe>; **martinet, disciplinarian,** stickler, tin god, petty tyrant

15 **the authorities, the powers that be,** ruling class *or* classes, the lords of creation, **the Establishment,** the interests, the power elite, **the power structure; they,** them; the inner circle; the ins *and* the in-group *and* those on the inside <nf>; **management, the administration;** higher echelons, top brass <nf>; higher-ups *and* the people upstairs *or* in the front office <nf>; **the top** <nf>, the corridors of power; prelacy, hierarchy; ministry; **bureaucracy, officialdom;** directorate 574.11

16 **official, officer,** officiary, functionary, *fonctionnaire* <Fr>, apparatchik; **public official,** public servant; officeholder, office-bearer *and* placeman <Brit>; government *or* public employee; **civil servant; bureaucrat,** politician, mandarin, red-tapist, *rond-de-cuir* <Fr>; petty tyrant, jack-in-office; The Man <nf>,

17 <public officials> **minister,** secretary, secretary of state <Brit>, undersecretary, cabinet minister, cabinet member, minister of state <Brit>; chancellor; warden; archon; magistrate; syndic; commissioner; commissar; county commissioners; city manager, mayor, *maire* <Fr>, lord mayor, burgomaster; headman, induna <Africa>; **councilman,** councilwoman, councillor, city councilman, elder, city father, alderman, alderperson, bailie <Scot>, selectman; supervisor, county supervisor; reeve, portreeve; legislator 610.3

18 **commissioned officer, officer,** military leader, military officer; top brass *and* the brass <nf>; **commander in chief,** generalissimo, captain general; hetman, sirdar, commanding officer, commandant; general of the army, general of the air force, five-star general <nf>, marshal, *maréchal* <Fr>, field marshal; general officer, **general,** four-star general <nf>; lieutenant general, three-star general <nf>; major general, two-star general <nf>, brigadier general, one-star general <nf>, brigadier <Brit>; field officer; **colonel,** chicken colonel <nf>; lieutenant colonel; **major;** company officer; **captain; lieutenant,** first lieutenant; second lieutenant, shavetail <nf>, subaltern *and* sublieutenant <Brit>; warrant officer, chief warrant officer; **commander,** commandant, the Old Man <nf>; **commanding officer** *or* CO; executive officer, exec <nf>; chief of staff; aide, aide-de-camp *or* ADC; officer of the day *or* OD, orderly officer <Brit>; staff officer; senior officer, junior officer; brass hat <nf>; air marshal

19 Army noncommissioned officer, noncom *or* NCO
<nf>; centurion; sergeant, sarge <nf>, havildar
<India>; sergeant major of the Army, command
sergeant major, sergeant major, first sergeant, top
sergeant *and* topkick *and* first man <nf>,
master sergeant, sergeant first class, technical
sergeant, staff sergeant, sergeant, specialist seven,
platoon sergeant, mess sergeant, color sergeant,
acting sergeant, lance sergeant <Brit>; **corporal,**
acting corporal, lance corporal <Brit>, lance-jack
<Brit nf>; **Air Force noncommissioned officer,**
chief master sergeant of the Air Force, chief
master sergeant, senior master sergeant, master
sergeant, technical sergeant, staff sergeant,
sergeant, airman first class

20 Navy *or* **naval officer; fleet admiral,** navarch,
admiral, vice admiral, rear admiral, **commodore,**
captain, commander, lieutenant commander,
lieutenant, lieutenant junior grade, ensign;
warrant officer; Navy *or* naval noncommissioned
officer, master chief petty officer of the Navy,
master chief petty officer, senior chief petty
officer, chief petty officer, petty officer first class,
petty officer second class, petty officer third class;
Marine Corps noncommissioned officer, sergeant
major of the Marine Corps, sergeant major,
master gunnery sergeant, first sergeant, master
sergeant, gunnery sergeant, staff sergeant,
sergeant, corporal, lance corporal

21 <heraldic officials> herald, king of arms, king at
arms, earl marshal; Garter, Garter King of Arms,
Clarenceux, Clarenceux King of Arms, Norroy and
Ulster, Norroy and Ulster King of Arms, Norroy,
Norroy King of Arms, Lyon, Lyon King of Arms;
College of Arms

576 DEPUTY, AGENT

NOUNS **1 deputy, proxy, representative, substitute,**
sub <nf>, vice, vicegerent, **alternate,** backup *and*
stand-in <nf>, body double, alternative, alter ego,
surrogate, procurator, secondary, understudy,
pinch hitter <nf>, utility man *or* woman, scrub
<nf>, reserve, the bench <nf>; assistant, right
hand, second in command, number two, executive
officer, exponent, advocate, pleader, paranymph,
attorney, champion; **lieutenant;** aide; vicar, vicar
general; locum tenens *or* locum <chiefly Brit>;
amicus curiae; **puppet,** dummy, creature, cat's-
paw, figurehead; stunt man *or* woman; ghost
writer

2 delegate, legate, appointee; **commissioner,**
commissary, *commissionaire* <Fr>, commissar;
messenger, herald, **emissary, envoy; minister,**
secretary

3 agent, instrument, implement, implementer,
trustee, broker; expediter, facilitator; **tool;**
steward 574.4; **functionary; official** 575.16; clerk,
secretary; amanuensis; factor, consignee; puppet,
cat's-paw; dupe 358

4 go-between, middleman, intermediary, medium,
intermedium, intermediate, interagent,
internuncio, broker; connection <nf>, **contact;**
negotiator, negotiant; interpleader; arbitrator,
mediator 466.3

5 spokesman, spokeswoman, spokesperson,
spokespeople, official spokesman *or* -woman *or*
-person, press officer, speaker, voice, mouthpiece
<nf>; spin doctor <nf>; herald; messenger;
proloctor, prolocutress *or* prolocutrix; reporter,
rapporteur

6 diplomat, diplomatist, diplomatic agent,
diplomatic <old>; **emissary, envoy, legate,**
minister, foreign service officer; **ambassador,**
ambassadress, ambassador-at-large; envoy
extraordinary, plentipotentiary, **minister**
plenipotentiary; nuncio, internuncio, apostolic
delegate; vice-legate; resident, minister resident;
chargé d'affaires, chargé, chargé d'affaires ad
interim; secretary of legation, chancellor <Brit>;
attaché, commercial attaché, military attaché,
consul, consul general, vice-consul, consular
agent; career diplomat

7 foreign office, foreign service, diplomatic service;
diplomatic mission, diplomatic staff *or* corps,
corps diplomatique <Fr>; **embassy, legation;**
consular service

8 vice-president, vice-chairman, vice-governor, vice-
director, vice-master, vice-chancellor, vice-
premier, vice-warden, vice-consul, vice-legate;
vice-regent, viceroy, vicegerent, vice-king,
vice-queen, vice-reine, etc

9 secret agent, operative, cloak-and-dagger
operative, **undercover man,** inside man <nf>; **spy,**
espionage agent; counterspy, double agent;
spotter; scout, reconnoiterer; **intelligence agent** *or*
officer; military-intelligence man, naval-
intelligence man; spymaster; spy-catcher <nf>,
counterintelligence agent; agent provocateur;
codetalker, windtalker

10 detective, operative, investigator, sleuth, Sherlock
Holmes <A Conan Doyle>; police detective, Bow
Street runner *or* officer <Brit old>,
plainclothesman; private detective *or* dick, private
investigator *or* PI, inquiry agent <Brit>; hotel
detective, house detective, house dick <nf>, store
detective; arson investigator; narcotics agent, narc
<nf>; FBI agent *or* G-man <nf>; treasury agent *or*
T-man <nf>; Federal *or* fed <nf>; Federal Bureau
of Investigation *or* FBI; Secret Service

11 <nf terms> **dick,** gumshoe, gumshoe man, hawkshaw, sleuthhound, beagle, flatfoot, tec; eye, private eye; skip tracer, spotter

12 secret service, intelligence service, intelligence bureau *or* department; intelligence, military intelligence, naval intelligence; Central Intelligence Agency *or* CIA; **counterintelligence**

13 <group of delegates> **delegation, deputation, commission, mission**, legation; committee, subcommittee

VERBS **14 represent, act for,** act on behalf of, substitute for, appear for, answer for, speak for, be the voice of, give voice to, be the mouthpiece of <nf>, hold the proxy of, hold a brief for, act in the place of, stand in the stead of, serve in one's stead, pinch-hit for <nf>; understudy, double for *and* stand in for *and* back up <nf>, substitute for; front for <nf>; deputize, commission; ghostwrite *or* ghost

15 deputize, depute, authorize, empower, charge, designate, nominate

ADJS **16 deputy,** deputative; **acting,** representative

17 diplomatic, ambassadorial, consular, ministerial, plenipotentiary

ADVS **18** by proxy, indirectly; on behalf of 862.12

577 SERVANT, EMPLOYEE

NOUNS **1 retainer,** dependent, follower; myrmidon, yeoman; vassal, liege, liege man, henchman, feudatory, homager; inferior, **underling, subordinate,** understrapper; **minion,** creature, hanger-on, lackey, flunky, stooge <nf>, drudge; peon, serf, bond servant, thrall, vassal, slave 432.7

2 servant, servitor, help, paid helper; **domestic,** domestic help, domestic servant, house *or* household servant; live-in help, day help; **menial,** drudge, slavey <nf>; scullion, turnspit; humble servant

3 employee; pensioner, **hireling, mercenary,** myrmidon; wage earner, staff member; hired man, hired hand, man *or* girl Friday, right-hand man, go-to guy, point man *or* person, assistant 616.6; worker 726, subordinate, subaltern; white-collar worker, nonmanual worker, skilled worker, semiskilled worker, unskilled worker, blue-collar worker, manual worker, laborer; part-time worker, freelance worker; hourly worker; officer worker, assistant, administrative assistant, secretary, clerk, messenger, runner, gofer

4 man, manservant, serving man, gillie <Scot>, **boy,** *garçon* <Fr>, houseboy, houseman; butler; valet, *valet de chambre* <Fr>, gentleman, gentleman's gentleman; driver, chauffeur, coachman;

gardener; handyman, odd-job man; lord-in-waiting, lord of the bedchamber, equerry; bodyguard, chaperon

5 attendant, tender, usher, server, squire, yeoman; errand boy *or* girl, gofer <nf>, office boy *or* girl, copyboy; page, footboy; concierge; bellboy, bellman, bellhop; cabin boy, purser; porter, redcap; printer's devil; chore boy; caddie; bootblack, boots <Brit>, shoeshine boy, shoeblack; trainbearer; cupbearer, Ganymede, Hebe; orderly, batman <Brit>; **cabin** *or* **flight attendant, steward, stewardess, hostess,** airline stewardess *or* hostess, stew <nf>, cabin crew, skycap; hat-check girl, cloakroom attendant; salesclerk *or* clerk, salesperson, sales associate, shop assistant <Brit>

6 lackey, flunky, livery *or* liveried servant; **footman,** *valet de pied* <Fr>

7 waiter, waitress, waitperson, waitron; carhop; counterman, soda jerk <nf>; busboy; headwaiter, *maître d'hôtel* <Fr>, maître d' <nf>; hostess; wine steward, sommelier; bartender, barkeeper *or* barkeep, barman, barmaid

8 maid, maidservant, servitress, **girl,** servant girl, *bonne* <Fr>, serving girl, wench, biddy <nf>, hired girl; lady-help <Brit>, au pair girl, ayah <India>, amah <China>; live-in maid, live-out maid; **handmaid,** handmaiden; personal attendant; **lady's maid,** waiting maid *or* woman, gentlewoman, abigail, soubrette; lady-in-waiting, maid-in-waiting, lady of the bedchamber; companion; chaperon; betweenmaid *or* tweeny <Brit>; duenna; parlormaid; kitchenmaid, scullery maid; cook; housemaid, chambermaid, *femme de chambre* or *fille de chambre* <Fr>, upstairs maid; nursemaid 1008.8

9 factotum, do-all <old>, general servant <Brit>, man of all work; maid of all work, domestic drudge, slavey <nf>, Mister Fix-it, handyman

10 major-domo, steward, house steward, **butler,** chamberlain, *maître d'hôtel* <Fr>, seneschal; **housekeeper**

11 staff, personnel, employees, help, hired help, occasional help, the help, **crew, gang,** men, force, servantry, retinue 769.6

12 service, servanthood, servitude <old>, servitorship, *servitium* <L>; **employment, employ; ministry, ministration, attendance,** tendance; serfdom, peonage, thralldom, slavery 432.1

VERBS **13 serve, work for,** be in service, serve one's every need; minister *or* administer to, pander to, do service; **help** 449.11; **care for,** do for <nf>, **look after,** wait on hand and foot, take care of; **wait, wait on** *or* **upon, attend,** tend, attend on *or* upon, dance attendance upon; make oneself useful; lackey, valet, maid, chore; drudge 725.14

ADJS 14 serving, servitorial, servitial, **ministering,** waiting, waiting on, **attending,** attendant; in the train of, in one's pay *or* employ; helping 449.20; **menial, servile**

578 FASHION

NOUNS 1 fashion, style, mode, vogue, trend, prevailing taste; proper thing, ton, bon ton; design; custom 373; convention 579.1,2; the swim <nf>, current *or* stream of fashion; height of fashion; the new look, the season's look; high fashion, *haute couture* <Fr>, designer label; flavor of the month, flavor of the week; personal style, signature

2 fashionableness, chic, ton, bon ton, fashionability, **stylishness, modishness,** voguishness; with-itness <nf>; **popularity,** prevalence, currency 864.2

3 smartness, chic, elegance; style-consciousness, clothes-consciousness; **spruceness, nattiness,** neatness, trimness, sleekness, **dapperness,** jauntiness; sharpness *and* spiffiness *and* classiness *and* niftiness <nf>; swankness *and* **swankiness** <nf>; foppery, foppishness, coxcombry, dandyism; hipness <nf>

4 the rage, the thing, **the last word** <nf>, *le dernier cri* <Fr>, **the latest thing,** the in thing *and* the latest wrinkle <nf>

5 fad, craze, rage; wrinkle <nf>; new take <nf>, next big thing, new new thing; novelty 841.2; faddishness, faddiness <nf>, faddism; **faddist;** the bandwagon, me-tooism

6 society, *société* <Fr>, fashionable society, **polite society, high society,** high life, *beau monde* and *haut monde* <Fr>, good society; best people, people of fashion, right people; *monde* <Fr>, world of fashion, Vanity Fair; **smart set** <nf>; the Four Hundred, **upper crust** *and* upper cut <nf>; **cream of society,** *crème de la crème* <Fr>, cream of the crop, elite, carriage trade; café society, jet set, beautiful people, in-crowd, glitterati <nf>; *jeunesse dorée* <Fr>; drawing room, salon; social register; fast track

7 person of fashion, fashionable, man-about-town, man *or* woman of the world, nob, *mondain or mondaine* <Fr>; leader *or* arbiter of fashion, tastemaker, trendsetter, tonesetter, *arbiter elegantiae* <L>, arbiter of fashion; ten best-dressed, fashion plate, clotheshorse, sharpy <nf>, snappy dresser; Beau Brummel, fop, dandy 500.9; **socialite; clubwoman,** clubman; salonist, salonnard; jet setter; swinger <nf>; **debutante,** subdebutante, deb *and* subdeb <nf>, Sloane Ranger <Brit nf>; rag trade <nf>

VERBS 8 catch on, become popular, **become the rage,** catch *or* take fire

9 be fashionable, be the style, be the rage, be the thing; have a run; cut a figure in society <nf>, give a tone to society, set the fashion *or* style *or* tone; dress to kill

10 follow the fashion, get in the swim <nf>, get *or* climb *or* jump on the bandwagon <nf>, join the parade, follow the crowd, go with the stream *or* tide *or* current *or* flow; keep in step, do as others do; keep up, **keep up appearances,** keep up with the Joneses

ADJS 11 fashionable, in fashion, smart, in style, in vogue; all the rage, all the thing; **popular,** prevalent, current 864.12; **up-to-date,** up-to-datish, up-to-the-minute, happening <nf>, switched-on *and* hip *and* with-it *and* in <nf>, trendy <nf>, newfashioned, modern, mod <nf>, new 841.7,9,10,12–14; **in the swim;** sought-after, much sought-after

12 stylish, modish, voguish, vogue; dressy <nf>; *soigné or soignée* <Fr>; *à la mode* <Fr>, in the mode

13 chic, smart, elegant; style-conscious, clothes-conscious; **well-dressed,** well-groomed, *soigné or soignée* <Fr>, dressed to advantage, all dressed up, dressed to kill, dressed to the teeth, dressed to the nines, well-turned-out; **spruce, natty,** neat, trim, sleek, smug, trig, tricksy <old>; **dapper,** dashing, jaunty, braw <Scot>; sharp *and* spiffy *and* classy *and* nifty *and* snazzy <nf>; **swank** *or* **swanky** <nf>, posh <nf>, ritzy <nf>, swell *and* nobby <nf>; genteel; exquisite, *recherché* <Fr>; cosmopolitan, sophisticated

14 ultrafashionable, ultrastylish, ultrasmart; chichi; foppish, dandified, dandyish, dandiacal

15 trendy <nf>, **faddish,** faddy <nf>, groovy

16 socially prominent, in society, high-society, elite; café-society, jet-set; lace-curtain, silk-stocking

ADVS 17 fashionably, stylishly, modishly, *à la mode* <Fr>, in the latest style *or* mode

18 smartly, dressily, chicly, elegantly, exquisitely; **sprucely, nattily,** neatly, trimly, sleekly; **dapperly,** jauntily, dashingly, swankly *or* swankily <nf>; foppishly, dandyishly

579 SOCIAL CONVENTION

NOUNS 1 social convention, convention, conventional usage, what is done, what one does, **social usage, form, formality; custom** 373; **conformism, conformity** 867; **propriety, decorum,** decorousness, correctness, *convenance* and *bienséance* <Fr>, decency, seemliness, civility <old>, good form, etiquette 580.3; **conventionalism, conventionality, Grundyism; Mrs Grundy**

2 the conventions, the proprieties, the mores, the right things, accepted *or* sanctioned conduct, what is done, civilized behavior; **dictates of society,** dictates of Mrs Grundy

3 conventionalist, Grundy, Mrs Grundy; conformist 867.2

VERBS **4 conform,** observe the proprieties, play the game, follow the rule 867.4, fall in or into line

ADJS **5 conventional, decorous,** orthodox, **correct,** right, **right-thinking, proper,** decent, seemly, meet; **accepted, recognized,** acknowledged, received, admitted, approved, being done; *comme il faut* and *de rigueur* <Fr>; **traditional, customary;** formal 580.7; conformable 867.5

ADVS **6 conventionally,** decorously, orthodoxly; **customarily, traditionally;** correctly, properly, as is proper, as it should be, *comme il faut* <Fr>; according to use *or* custom, according to the dictates of society *or* Mrs Grundy

580 FORMALITY

NOUNS **1 formality, form, formalness; ceremony,** ceremonial, **ceremoniousness; the red carpet; ritual,** rituality; extrinsicality, impersonality 768.1; formalization, stylization, conventionalization; **stiffness, stiltedness,** primness, prissiness, rigidness, starchiness, buckram <old>, **dignity,** gravity, weight, *gravitas* <L>, weighty dignity, staidness, reverend seriousness, **solemnity** 111; **pomp** 501.6; pomposity 501.7

2 formalism, ceremonialism, ritualism; legalism; pedantry, pedantism, pedanticism; precisianism, preciseness, preciousness, preciosity, purism; punctiliousness, punctilio, scrupulousness; overrefinement

3 etiquette, social code, rules *or* code of conduct; **formalities,** social procedures, social conduct *or* convention, what is done, what one does; **manners,** good manners, exquisite manners, quiet good manners, **politeness,** *politesse* <Fr>, natural politeness, comity, civility 504.1; **amenities,** decencies, civilities, elegancies, **social graces, mores, proprieties;** decorum, good form; **courtliness,** elegance 533; **protocol,** diplomatic code; punctilio, point of etiquette; convention, social usage; table manners

4 <ceremonial function> **ceremony,** ceremonial; **rite, ritual, formality; solemnity, service, function,** office, **observance,** performance; **exercise,** exercises; **celebration,** solemnization; **liturgy,** religious ceremony; **rite of passage,** *rite de passage* <Fr>; convocation; commencement, commencement exercises; graduation, graduation exercises; baccalaureate service; inaugural, inauguration; initiation; formal, ball; wedding; funeral; set piece; empty formality or ceremony, mummery

VERBS **5 formalize,** ritualize, solemnize, **celebrate,** dignify; **observe;** conventionalize, stylize

6 stand on ceremony, observe the formalities, follow protocol, do things by the book

ADJS **7 formal,** formulary; formalist, formalistic; legalistic; pedantic, pedantical; official, stylized, conventionalized; extrinsic, outward, impersonal 768.3; surface, **superficial, nominal** 527.15

8 ceremonious, ceremonial; red-carpet; ritualistic, ritual; hieratic, hieratical, sacerdotal, liturgic; **grave, solemn** 111.3; **pompous** 501.22; **stately** 501.21; well-mannered 504.16; **conventional,** decorous 579.5

9 stiff, stilted, prim, prissy, rigid, starch, starchy, starched; buckram *and* in buckram <old>

10 punctilious, scrupulous, precise, precisian, precisionist, precious, puristic; by-the-book; exact, **meticulous** 339.12; **orderly, methodical** 807.6

ADVS **11 formally,** in due form, in set form; **ceremoniously, ritually,** ritualistically; **solemnly** 111.4; for form's sake, *pro forma* <L>, **as a matter of form**; by the book

12 stiffly, stiltedly, starchly, primly, rigidly

581 INFORMALITY

NOUNS **1 informality, informalness, unceremoniousness; casualness,** offhandedness, **ease, easiness,** easygoingness; **relaxedness;** affability, graciousness, cordiality, sociability 582; Bohemianism, unconventionality 868.2; **familiarity; naturalness,** simplicity, plainness, homeliness, homeyness, folksiness <nf>, common touch, **unaffectedness,** unpretentiousness 499.2; unconstraint, unconstrainedness, looseness; irregularity; lack of convention, freedom, license

VERBS **2 not stand on ceremony,** let one's hair down <nf>, be oneself, be at ease, feel at home, come as you are; relax

ADJS **3 informal, unceremonious; casual, offhand,** offhanded, throwaway <nf>, unstudied, easy, easygoing, free and easy, loose, nonformal; *dégagé* <Fr>; **relaxed;** affable, gracious, cordial, sociable; Bohemian, unconventional 868.6, nonconformist; **familiar; natural,** simple, plain, homely, homey, down-home *and* folksy <nf>, *haymish* <Yiddish>; **unaffected, unassuming** 499.7; unconstrained, loose; irregular; unofficial

ADVS **4 informally, unceremoniously,** without ceremony, *sans cérémonie* and *sans façon* <Fr>; **casually,** offhand, offhandedly; relaxedly; familiarly; **naturally,** simply, plainly; **unaffectedly,** unassumingly 499.11; unconstrainedly, unofficially; *en famille* <Fr>

582 SOCIABILITY

NOUNS **1 sociability,** sociality, sociableness, fitness *or* fondness for society, socialmindedness, **gregariousness, affability,** companionability, compatibility, geniality, *Gemütlichkeit* <Ger>, **congeniality;** hospitality 585; clubbability <nf>, clubbishness, clubbiness, clubbism; intimacy, familiarity; amiability, **friendliness** 587.1; **communicativeness** 343.3; social grace, civility, urbanity, courtesy 504

2 camaraderie, comradery, comradeship, **fellowship, good-fellowship;** male bonding; consorting, hobnobbing, hanging *and* hanging out <nf>

3 conviviality, joviality, jollity, gaiety, heartiness, cheer, good cheer, festivity, partying, merrymaking, merriment, revelry

4 social life, social intercourse, social activity, **intercourse, communication, communion,** intercommunion, **fellowship,** intercommunication, **community,** collegiality, commerce, congress, converse, conversation, social relations

5 social circle *or* **set,** social class, one's crowd *or* set, clique, coterie, crowd <nf>; **association** 617

6 association, consociation, affiliation, bonding, social bonding, **fellowship, companionship, company, society;** fraternity, **fraternization;** membership, participation, partaking, sharing, cooperation 450

7 visit, social call, call; formal visit, duty visit, required visit; exchange visit; flying visit, look-in; visiting, visitation; round of visits; social round, social whirl, mad round; play date

8 appointment, engagement, date <nf>, double date *and* blind date <nf>; arrangement, interview, meeting, meet; fix-up; engagement book, agenda book, personal digital assistant

9 rendezvous, tryst, assignation, meeting; blind date; trysting place, meeting place, place of assignation; assignation house; love nest <nf>

10 social gathering, social, sociable, social affair, social hour, hospitality hour, affair, gathering, get-together <nf>; function; **reception,** at home, salon, levee, soiree; matinee; reunion, family reunion; wake

11 party, <see list> **entertainment,** celebration, fete, bash, party time, **festivity** 743.3,4

12 <nf terms> **brawl, bash,** blast, clambake, wingding, hoodang, blowout, shindig, shindy, do *and* beanfeast *and* knees-up *and* rave *and* rave-up <Brit>

13 tea, afternoon tea, five-o'clock tea, high tea, cream tea

14 bee, quilting bee, raising bee, husking bee, cornhusking, corn shucking, husking

15 debut, coming out <nf>, presentation

16 <sociable person> joiner, mixer *and* **good mixer** <nf>, good *or* pleasant company, excellent companion, life of the party, social butterfly, bon vivant; man-about-town, playboy, social lion, habitué; clubman, clubwoman; salonnard, salonist

VERBS **17 associate with,** assort with, sort with, consort with, hobnob with, fall in with, socialize, interact, go around with, **mingle with, mix with, touch** *or* **rub elbows** *or* **shoulders with,** eat off the same trencher; **fraternize,** fellowship, join in fellowship; **keep company with,** bear one's company, walk hand in hand with; **join; flock together,** herd together, club together

18 <nf terms> **hang with,** hang out *or* around with, clique, clique with, gang up with, run *or* run around with, chum, chum together, pal, pal with, pal up *or* around with; take *or* tie up with, hook up with

19 visit, make *or* pay a visit, **call on** *or* **upon, drop in,** run *or* stop in, look in, look one up, see, stop off *or* over <nf>, drop *or* run *or* stop by, drop around *or* round; leave one's card; exchange visits

20 have *or* give a party, entertain

21 <nf terms> **throw a party; party,** have fun, live it up, have a ball, ball, boogie, jam, kick up one's heels, make whoopee, whoop it up

ADJS **22 sociable, social,** social-minded, fit for society, fond of society, **gregarious, affable; companionable,** companionate, compatible, genial, *gemütlich* <Ger>, **congenial;** hospitable 585.11; neighborly; clubby, clubbable <nf>, clubbish; **communicative** 343.10; amiable, **friendly;** civil, urbane, courteous 504.14

23 convivial, boon, free and easy, hail-fellow-well-met; **jovial, jolly,** hearty, festive, gay

24 intimate, familiar, cozy, chatty, *tête-à-tête* <Fr>; man-to-man, woman-to-woman

ADVS **25 sociably,** socially, gregariously, affably; friendlily, companionably, arm in arm, hand in hand, hand in glove

26 types of parties

at-home	garden party
baby shower	hen party
ball	housewarming
birthday party	ladies' *or* men's night out
cocktail party	masked ball *or* bal masqué
coffee party *or* kaffee	<Fr>
klatsch *or* coffee klatsch	masquerade party *or*
dinner party	mask *or* masque *or*
fête champêtre <Fr>	masquerade

open house	social
pajama party	soiree
rave	stag *or* stag party <nf>
shindig *or* shindy	surprise party
shower	tea party
smoker <nf>	*thé dansante* <Fr>

583 UNSOCIABILITY

NOUNS **1 unsociability,** insociability, unsociableness, dissociability, dissociableness; **ungregariousness,** uncompanionability; unclubbableness *or* unclubbability <nf>, ungeniality, **uncongeniality;** incompatibility, social incompatibility; **unfriendliness** 589.1; **uncommunicativeness** 344; sullenness, mopishness, moroseness; self-sufficiency, self-containment; autism, catatonia; bashfulness 139.4

2 aloofness, standoffishness, offishness, withdrawnness, **remoteness,** distance, detachment; **coolness,** coldness, frigidity, chill, chilliness, iciness, frostiness; cold shoulder; inaccessibility, unapproachability; private world

3 seclusiveness, **seclusion** 584; exclusiveness, exclusivity

VERBS **4 keep to oneself,** keep oneself to oneself, not mix *or* mingle, enjoy *or* prefer one's own company, stay at home, shun companionship, be a poor mixer, **stand aloof,** hold oneself aloof *or* apart, keep one's distance, keep at a distance, keep in the background, retire, retire into the shade, creep into a corner, seclude oneself, stay in one's shell; have nothing to do with 586.5, be unfriendly, not give one the time of day

ADJS **5 unsociable,** insociable, dissociable, unsocial; **ungregarious,** nongregarious; **uncompanionable,** ungenial, uncongenial; incompatible, socially incompatible; unclubbable <nf>; **unfriendly** 589.9; **uncommunicative** 344.8; sullen, mopish, mopey, morose; close, snug; self-sufficient, self-contained; autistic, catatonic; bashful 139.12

6 aloof, standoffish, offish, standoff, **distant, remote,** withdrawn, removed, detached, Olympian; **cool,** cold, cold-fish, frigid, chilly, icy, frosty; seclusive; exclusive; inaccessible, unapproachable; tight-assed <nf>

584 SECLUSION

NOUNS **1 seclusion,** reclusion, **retirement, withdrawal, retreat,** recess; renunciation *or* forsaking of the world; cocooning; **sequestration,** quarantine, separation, detachment, apartness; segregation, apartheid, Jim Crow; **isolation,** "splendid isolation"—Sir William Goschen; ivory tower, ivory-towerism, ivory-towerishness; **privacy,** privatism, **secrecy;** rustication; privatization; isolationism; opt-out

2 hermitism, hermitry, eremitism, anchoritism, anchoretism, cloistered monasticism

3 solitude, solitariness, **aloneness,** loneness, singleness; **loneliness, lonesomeness**

4 forlornness, desolation; friendlessness, kithlessness, fatherlessness, motherlessness, homelessness, rootlessness; helplessness, defenselessness; abandonment, desertion

5 recluse, loner, solitaire, solitary, solitudinarian; **shut-in,** invalid, bedridden invalid; cloistered monk *or* nun; **hermit,** eremite, anchorite, anchoret; marabout; hermitess, anchoress; **ascetic;** closet cynic; stylite, pillarist, pillar saint; Hieronymite, Hieronymian; Diogenes, Timon of Athens, St Simeon Stylites, St Anthony, desert saints, desert fathers; outcast, pariah 586.4; **stay-at-home, homebody; isolationist,** seclusionist; ivory-towerist, ivory-towerite; one-man band

6 retreat 1009.5, **hideaway, cell, ivory tower,** hidey-hole <nf>, lair, sanctum, sanctum sanctorum, inner sanctum

VERBS **7 seclude oneself, go into seclusion, retire, go into retirement,** retire from the world, abandon *or* forsake the world, live in retirement, lead a retired life, lead a cloistered life, sequester *or* sequestrate oneself, be *or* remain incommunicado, shut oneself up, live alone, live apart, retreat to one's ivory tower; stay at home; rusticate; take the veil; cop out <nf>, opt out *or* drop out of society

ADJS **8 secluded, seclusive, retired, withdrawn; isolated,** shut off, insular, **separate,** separated, **apart,** detached, removed; segregated, quarantined; **remote, out-of-the-way,** up-country, in a backwater, out-of-the-world, out-back *and* back of beyond <Austral>; **unfrequented,** unvisited, off the beaten track; untraveled

9 private, privatistic, reclusive; ivory-towered, ivory-towerish

10 recluse, reclusive, sequestered, cloistered, sequestrated, shut up *or* in; hermitlike, hermitic, hermitical, eremitic, eremitical, hermitish; anchoritic, anchoritical; stay-at-home, domestic; homebound

11 solitary, alone; in solitude, by oneself, all alone; **lonely, lonesome, lone;** lonely-hearts

12 forlorn, lorn; **abandoned, forsaken, deserted, desolate,** godforsaken <nf>, friendless, unfriended, kithless, fatherless, motherless, homeless; helpless, defenseless; outcast 586.10

ADVS **13 in seclusion, in retirement,** in retreat, in solitude; in privacy, in secrecy; "far from the madding crowd's ignoble strife"—Thomas Gray

585 HOSPITALITY, WELCOME

NOUNS 1 **hospitality,** hospitableness, receptiveness; honors *or* freedom of the house; **cordiality,** amiability, graciousness, **friendliness,** neighborliness, geniality, heartiness, bonhomie, **generosity,** liberality, openheartedness, warmth, warmness, warmheartedness; open door

2 **welcome,** welcoming, **reception,** *accueil* <Fr>; cordial *or* warm *or* hearty welcome, pleasant *or* smiling reception, the glad hand <nf>, **open arms; embrace, hug;** welcome mat

3 **greetings, salutations,** salaams; **regards,** best wishes 504.8

4 **greeting, salutation,** salute, salaam; **hail, hello,** how-do-you-do; accost, address; nod, bow, bob; curtsy 155.2; wave; handshake, handclasp; namaste; open arms, embrace, hug, kiss; smile, smile *or* nod of recognition, nod

5 **host,** mine host; hostess, receptionist, greeter; landlord 470.2

6 **guest, visitor,** visitant; **caller,** company; invited guest, invitee; frequenter, habitué, haunter; uninvited guest, gate-crasher <nf>; moocher *and* freeloader <nf>; guest list

VERBS 7 **receive, admit,** accept, take in, let in, open the door to; **be at home to,** have the latchstring out, keep a light in the window, put out the welcome mat, keep the door open, keep an open house, keep the home fires burning

8 **entertain,** entertain guests, guest; host, preside, do the honors <nf>; give a party, throw a party <nf>; spread oneself <nf>

9 **welcome,** make welcome, bid one welcome, bid one feel at home, make one feel welcome *or* at home *or* like one of the family, do the honors of the house, give one the freedom of the house, hold out the hand, extend the right hand of friendship; glad hand *and* give the glad hand *and* glad eye <nf>; **embrace, hug, receive** *or* **welcome with open arms;** give a warm reception to, "kill the fatted calf"—Bible, roll out the red carpet, give the red-carpet treatment, receive royally, make feel like a king *or* queen

10 **greet, hail, accost,** address; **salute,** make one's salutations; **bid** *or* **say hello,** bid good day *or* good morning, etc; exchange greetings, **pass the time of day; give one's regards** 504.13; shake hands, shake *and* give one some skin *and* give a high *or* a low five <nf>, press the flesh <nf>, press *or* squeeze one's hand; nod to, bow to; curtsy 155.6; tip the hat to, lift the hat, touch the hat *or* cap; take one's hat off to, uncover; pull *or* tug at the forelock; kiss, greet with a kiss, kiss hands *or* cheeks

ADJS 11 **hospitable, receptive,** welcoming; **cordial,** amiable, gracious, **friendly,** neighborly, genial, hearty, open, openhearted, warm, warmhearted; **generous,** liberal

12 **welcome,** welcome as the roses in May, wanted, desired, wished-for; **agreeable,** desirable, acceptable; **grateful,** gratifying, pleasing

ADVS 13 **hospitably,** with open arms; friendlily

INTERJS 14 **welcome!,** *soyez le bienvenu!* <Fr>, *bien venido!* <Sp>, *benvenuto!* <Ital>, *Willkommen!* <Ger>; glad to see you!

15 **greetings!,** salutations!, **hello!,** hullo!, hail!, hey! *or* heigh!, **hi!,** aloha!, *hola!* <Sp>; **how do you do?, how are you?,** *comment allez-vous?* and *comment ça va?* <Fr>, *¿cómo está usted?* <Sp>, *come sta?* <Ital>, *wie geht's?* <Ger>; **good morning!,** top of the morning!, *guten Morgen!* <Ger>; good day!, *bon jour!* <Fr>, *buenos días!* <Sp>, *buon giorno!* <Ital>, *guten Tag!* <Ger>; **good afternoon!,** *buenas tardes!* <Sp>; **good evening!,** *bon soir!* <Fr>, *buona sera!* <Ital>, *guten Abend!* <Ger>

16 <nf terms> **howdy!,** howdy-do!, how-de-do!, how-do-ye-do!, how-d'ye-do!, how you doin'?, hi ya!; how's things?, how's tricks?, how goes it?, how's every little thing?, how's the world treating you?, **yo!,** ahoy!, hey!; long time no see!

17 **greetings and farewells**

a bientot <Fr>	check
a demain <Fr>	cheerio
a toute a l'heure <Fr>	cheers
adieu <Fr>	chin-chin
adios <Sp>	ciao <It>
ahoy	come again
all hail	das vedanya <Rus>
aloha	enjoy
arrivederci <It>	fare thee well
au revoir <Fr>	farewell
Auf Wiedersehen	g'day
<Ger>	glad to see you
ave	God be with you
be good	God bless
be seeing you	Godspeed
bless you	good afternoon
bon matin <Fr>	good day
bon soir <Fr>	good evening
bon voyage	good luck
bonjour <Fr>	good morning
bonne nuit <Fr>	good night
buenas noches <Sp>	good to see you
buenas tardes <Sp>	good to see you
buenos dias <Sp>	good-bye
buon giorno <It>	greetings
buona notte <It>	gute Nacht <Ger>
buona sera <It>	guten Abend <Ger>
bye	guten Morgen <Ger>
bye-bye	guten Tag <Ger>
catch you later	hail

hallo
halloo
happy trails
hasta la vista <Sp>
hasta luego <Sp>
hasta manana <Sp>
have a good one
have a nice day
hello
hello there
hey
hey-ho
hi
hi ya
hi, there
hola <Sp>
how are you?
how do you do?
how do?
how goes it?
how you be?
how you been?
how you doing?
howdy
howdy-do
howdy-doody
how's by you?
how's everything?
how's it going?
how's the world treating
  you?
how's things?
hullo
knoban wa <Japanese>

konichiwa <Japanese>
later
later on
manana <Sp>
many happy returns
namaste
over
over and out
pax <L>
peace
pip-pip
¿qué pasa? <Sp>
regards
roger
salaam
salud <Sp>
salutations
sayonara <Japanese>
see ya
see you later
see you later, alligator
see you soon
shake
shalom <Jewish>
take care
take it easy
ten-four
toodleoo
toodles
welcome
what it is?
what's happening?
wie gehts? <Ger>
yo

586 INHOSPITALITY

NOUNS **1 inhospitality,** inhospitableness, unhospitableness, unreceptiveness; **uncordialness,** ungraciousness, **unfriendliness,** unneighborliness; nonwelcome, nonwelcoming

2 unhabitability, uninhabitability, unlivability

3 ostracism, ostracization, thumbs down; **banishment** 909.4; **proscription, ban;** boycott, boycottage; **blackball,** blackballing, blacklist; **rejection** 442.1

4 outcast, social outcast, outcast of society, **castaway, derelict,** Ishmael; **pariah, untouchable,** leper; outcaste; *déclassé* <Fr>; **outlaw; expellee, evictee; displaced person** or **DP; exile, expatriate,** man without a country; undesirable; *persona non grata* <L>, unacceptable person

VERBS **5 have nothing to do with,** have no truck with <nf>, refuse to associate with, steer clear of <nf>, **spurn, turn one's back upon,** not give one the time of day <nf>; deny oneself to, refuse to receive, not be at home to; shut the door upon

6 ostracize, turn thumbs down, disfellowship; **reject** 442.3, **exile, banish** 909.17; **proscribe, ban, outlaw** 444.3, put under the ban, criminalize; **boycott, blackball,** blacklist

ADJS **7 inhospitable,** unhospitable; **unreceptive,** closed; **uncordial,** ungracious, **unfriendly,** unneighborly

8 unhabitable, uninhabitable, nonhabitable, unoccupiable, untenantable, **unlivable, unfit to live in,** not fit for man or beast

9 unwelcome, unwanted; unagreeable, undesirable, unacceptable; **uninvited,** unasked, unbidden

10 outcast, cast-off, castaway, derelict; outlawed 444.7, outside the pale, outside the gates; **rejected, disowned; abandoned, forsaken**

587 FRIENDSHIP

NOUNS **1 friendship, friendliness; amicability,** amicableness, amity, peaceableness, unhostility; **amiability,** amiableness, **congeniality,** well-affectedness; neighborliness, neighborlikeness; peaceableness; sociability 582; **affection, love** 104; **loving kindness, kindness** 143

2 fellowship, companionship, comradeship, colleagueship, chumship <nf>, palship <nf>, circle of friends, freemasonry, consortship, boon companionship; comradery, camaraderie, male bonding; **brotherhood, fraternity,** fraternalism, fraternization, sodality, confraternity; **sisterhood, sorority;** brotherliness, sisterliness; community of interest, *esprit de corps* <Fr>; chumminess <nf>

3 good terms, good understanding, good footing, friendly relations; **harmony,** compatibility, sympathy, fellow feeling, bonding, understanding, **rapport** 455.1, rapprochement; **favor, goodwill, good graces, regard,** respect, mutual regard or respect, favorable regard, the good or right side of <nf>, esprit de corps; an in <nf>; entente, entente cordiale, hands across the sea

4 acquaintance, acquaintedness, close acquaintance, acquaintanceship; **introduction,** presentation, knockdown <nf>

5 familiarity, intimacy, intimate acquaintance, closeness, nearness, inseparableness, inseparability; affinity, special affinity, mutual affinity; chumminess <nf>, palliness or palsiness or palsy-walsiness <nf>, mateyness <Brit nf>; togetherness; conversance

6 cordiality, geniality, heartiness, bonhomie, ardency, warmth, warmness, affability, warmheartedness; hospitality 585

7 devotion, devotedness; dedication, commitment; fastness, steadfastness, firmness, constancy, staunchness; triedness, trueness, true-blueness, tried-and-trueness

8 cordial friendship, warm *or* ardent friendship, close friendship, passionate friendship, devoted friendship, bosom friendship, intimate *or* familiar friendship, sincere friendship, beautiful friendship, fast *or* firm friendship, staunch friendship, loyal friendship, lasting friendship, undying friendship, cross-sex friendship

VERBS 9 **be friends,** have the friendship of, have the ear of; be old friends *or* friends of long standing, be long acquainted, go way back; **know, be acquainted with;** associate with; cotton to *and* hit it off <nf>, get on well with, hobnob with, fraternize with, keep company with, go around with; be close friends with, be best friends, be buddies, be inseparable; **be on good terms,** enjoy good *or* friendly relations with; keep on good terms, have an in with <nf>

10 **befriend, make** *or* **win friends,** gain the friendship of, **strike up a friendship,** get to know one another, take up with <nf>, shake hands with, **get acquainted,** make *or* scrape acquaintance with, pick up an acquaintance with; win friends, win friends and influence people; break the ice; warm to

11 <nf terms> **be buddy-buddy** *or* **palsy-walsy with,** click, have good *or* great chemistry, team up; **get next to, get palsy** *or* **palsy-walsy with,** get cozy with, cozy *or* snuggle up to, get close to, get chummy with, buddy *or* pal up with, play footsie with

12 **cultivate,** cultivate the friendship of, **court,** pay court to, pay addresses to, seek the company of, **run after** <nf>, **shine up to,** make up to <nf>, play up to *and* suck up to <nf>, hold out *or* extend the right of friendship *or* fellowship; **make advances,** approach, break the ice

13 **get on good terms with, get into favor,** win the regard of, **get in the good graces of, get in good with,** get in with *or* on the in with *and* get next to <nf>, **get on the good** *or* **right side of** <nf>; stay friends with, keep in with <nf>

14 **introduce, present, acquaint,** make acquainted, give an introduction, give a knockdown <nf>, do the honors <nf>

ADJS 15 **friendly,** friendlike; **amicable, peaceable,** unhostile; **harmonious** 455.1; **amiable, congenial,** *simpático* <Sp>, *simpatico* <Ital>, *sympathique* <Fr>, pleasant, agreeable, favorable, well-affected, well-disposed, well-intentioned, well-meaning, well-meant, well-intended; brotherly, fraternal, confraternal; sisterly; neighborly, neighborlike; sociable; kind 143.13

16 **cordial, genial,** gracious, courteous, hearty, ardent, warm, warmhearted, affable; compatible, cooperative; welcoming, receptive, hospitable 585.11

17 **friends with,** friendly with, at home with; **acquainted**

18 **on good terms,** on a good footing, on friendly *or* amicable terms, **on speaking terms,** on a first-name basis, on visiting terms; **in good with,** in with *and* on the in with *and* in <nf>, **in favor, in one's good graces,** in one's good books, on the good *or* right side of <nf>, regarded highly by, on a first-name basis with, in with <nf>

19 **familiar, intimate, close,** near, inseparable, on familiar *or* intimate terms, favorite, affectionate; just between the two, one-on-one, man-to-man, woman-to-woman; hand-in-hand, hand and glove *or* hand in glove; **thick, thick as thieves** <nf>; demonstrative, backslapping, effusive

20 **chummy** <nf>, matey <Brit nf>; pally *and* palsy *and* palsy-walsy *and* buddy-buddy <nf>; companionable

21 **devoted,** dedicated, committed, **fast,** steadfast, supportive, constant, faithful, staunch, firm; tried, true, **tried and true,** true-blue, loyal, tested, trusty, trustful, trustworthy

ADVS 22 **amicably,** friendly, friendlily, friendliwise; **amiably, congenially,** pleasantly, agreeably, favorably; **cordially, genially,** heartily, ardently, warmly, with open arms; familiarly, intimately; arm in arm, hand in hand, hand in glove

588 FRIEND

NOUNS 1 **friend, acquaintance,** close acquaintance; confidant, confidante, repository; **intimate,** familiar, **close friend,** intimate *or* familiar friend; **bosom friend,** friend of one's bosom, inseparable friend, **best friend;** alter ego, other self, shadow; brother, fellow, fellowman, fellow creature, neighbor; mutual friend; **sympathizer,** well-wisher, partisan, advocate, favorer, backer, **supporter** 616.9; casual acquaintance; pickup <nf>; lover 104.12; girlfriend, boyfriend; live-in lover, POSSLQ *or* person of opposite sex sharing living quarters, significant other

2 **good friend, best friend,** great friend, **devoted friend,** warm *or* ardent friend, **faithful friend,** trusted *or* trusty friend, *fidus Achates* <L>, constant friend, staunch friend, fast friend; friend in need, friend indeed

3 **companion, fellow,** fellow companion, **comrade,** *camarade* <Fr>, amigo <nf>, mate <Brit>, comate, company, **associate** 616, peer, consociate, compeer, confrere, consort, **colleague, partner,** copartner, side partner, **crony,** old crony, gossip; girlfriend <nf>; **roommate,** chamberfellow; flatmate;

bunkmate, bunkie <nf>; bedfellow, bedmate; **schoolmate,** schoolfellow, classmate, classfellow, school companion, school chum, fellow student *or* pupil; **playmate,** playfellow; **teammate,** yokefellow, yokemate; workmate, workfellow 616.5; shipmate; messmate; confederate, comrade in arms; homeboy <nf>

4 <nf terms> **pal, buddy,** bud, buddy-boy, bosom buddy, asshole buddy, main man, home boy, goombah, landsman, paesan, paesano, pally, palsy-walsy, road dog, walkboy, cobber <Austral>, pardner, pard, sidekick, tillicum, **chum,** ace, mate *and* butty <Brit>, my man

5 **boon companion,** boonfellow; **good fellow,** jolly fellow, hearty, *bon vivant* <Fr>; pot companion

6 <famous friendships> Achilles and Patroclus, Castor and Pollux, Damon and Pythias, David and Jonathan, Diomedes and Sthenelus, Epaminondas and Pelopidas, Hercules and Iolaus, Nisus and Euryalus, Pylades and Orestes, Theseus and Pirithoüs, Christ and the beloved disciple; the Three Musketeers

589 ENMITY

NOUNS 1 **enmity, unfriendliness,** inimicality; **uncordiality,** unamiability, ungeniality, disaffinity, incompatibility, incompatibleness; personal conflict, strain, **tension;** coolness, coldness, chilliness, chill, frost, frostiness, iciness, the freeze; inhospitality 586, unsociability 583

2 **disaccord** 456; ruffled feelings, strained relations, alienation, **disaffection, estrangement** 456.4

3 **hostility, antagonism, repugnance, antipathy,** spitefulness, spite, despitefulness, bellicosity, malice, malevolence, malignity, **hatred, hate** 103; dislike; **conflict, contention** 457, collision, clash, clashing, **friction;** quarrelsomeness 456.3; belligerence, intolerance; state of war

4 **animosity,** animus; **ill will,** ill feeling, bitter feeling, **hard feelings,** no love lost; **bad blood,** ill blood, feud, blood feud, vendetta; **bitterness,** sourness, soreness, **rancor,** resentment, acrimony, virulence, venom, vitriol

5 **grudge, spite,** crow to pick *or* pluck *or* pull, bone to pick; peeve *and* pet peeve <nf>; peevishness

6 **enemy, foe,** foeman, **adversary, antagonist,** unfriendly <nf>; bitter enemy; sworn enemy; open enemy; secret enemy; public enemy, public enemy number one; archenemy, devil; the other side, the opposition, opponent, rival; **bane** 395.8, bête noire; no friend

VERBS 7 **antagonize,** set against, make enemies, set at odds, set at each other's throat, sick on each other <nf>; aggravate, exacerbate, heat up,

provoke, envenom, **embitter,** infuriate, irritate, madden; divide, disunite, **alienate,** estrange 456.14; be alienated *or* estranged, draw *or* grow apart

8 **bear ill will,** bear malice, have it in for <nf>, hold it against, be down on <nf>; **bear** *or* **harbor** *or* **nurse a grudge,** owe a grudge, have a bone to pick with; no love is lost between; have a crow to pick *or* pluck *or* pull with; pick a quarrel; take offense, take umbrage; scorn, **hate** 103.5

ADJS 9 **unfriendly, inimical, unamicable; uncordial,** unamiable, ungenial, incompatible; strained, tense; discordant, unharmonious; cool, cold, chill, chilly, frosty, icy; inhospitable 586.7; unsociable 583.5

10 **hostile, antagonistic,** repugnant, antipathetic, set against, ill-disposed, acrimonious, snide, spiteful, despiteful, malicious, malevolent, malignant, hateful, full of hate *or* hatred; virulent, **bitter,** sore, sour, rancorous, acrid, caustic, venomous, vitriolic; conflicting, clashing, colliding; resentful, grudging, peevish; quarrelsome 456.17, contentious; **provocative,** off-putting; belligerent, bellicose

11 **alienated, estranged,** pffft <nf>, disaffected, separated, divided, disunited, torn, at variance; irreconcilable; distant; not on speaking terms

12 **at outs, on the outs** <nf>, at enmity, at variance, **at odds,** at loggerheads, at cross-purposes, at sixes and sevens, at each other's throats, at swords points, at daggers drawn, at war; on bad terms, in bad with <nf>

13 **on bad terms,** not on speaking terms, on the outs; in bad with <nf>, in bad odor with, in one's bad *or* black books, on one's shitlist *or* drop-dead list <nf>

ADVS 14 **unamicably,** inimically; **uncordially,** unamiably, ungenially; coolly, coldly, chillily, frostily; **hostilely, antagonistically**

590 MISANTHROPY

NOUNS 1 **misanthropy,** misanthropism, people-hating, Timonism, cynicism, antisociality, antisocial sentiments *or* attitudes; unsociability 583; **man-hating,** misandry; **woman-hating,** misogyny; **sexism,** sex discrimination, sexual stereotyping, male *or* female chauvinism

2 **misanthrope,** misanthropist, people-hater, cynic, Timon, Timonist; **man-hater,** misandrist; **woman-hater,** misogynist; **sexist,** male *or* female chauvinist, chauvinist

ADJS 3 **misanthropic,** people-hating, Timonist, Timonistic, cynical, **antisocial;** unsociable 583.5; **man-hating,** misandrist; **woman-hating,**

misogynic, misogynistic, misogynous; **sexist,**
male- *or* female-chauvinistic, chauvinistic

591 PUBLIC SPIRIT

NOUNS 1 **public spirit,** social consciousness *or*
responsibility; **citizenship, good citizenship,**
citizenism, civism; altruism

2 **patriotism,** love of country; "the last refuge of a
scoundrel"—Samuel Johnson; **nationalism,**
nationality, ultranationalism superpatriotism;
Americanism, Anglicism, Briticism, etc;
chauvinism, jingoism, overpatriotism; patriotics,
flag-waving; saber-rattling

3 **patriot;** nationalist; ultranationalist; **chauvinist,**
chauvin, **jingo,** jingoist; patrioteer <nf>, flag
waver, superpatriot, hard hat <nf>, hundred-
percenter, hundred-percent American; hawk

ADJS 4 **public-spirited, civic; patriotic; nationalistic;**
ultranationalist, ultranationalistic; overpatriotic,
superpatriotic, flagwaving, **chauvinist,**
chauvinistic, jingoist, jingoistic; hawkish

592 BENEFACTOR

NOUNS 1 **benefactor,** benefactress, **benefiter,**
succorer, befriender; ministrant, ministering
angel; Samaritan, **good Samaritan; helper,** aider,
assister, help, aid, helping hand; Johnny-on-the-
spot <nf>, jack-at-a-pinch <old Brit nf>, fairy
godmother; **patron, backer** 616.9, angel *and* cash
cow <nf>; **good person** 659

2 **savior, redeemer,** deliverer, **liberator,** rescuer,
freer, **emancipator,** manumitter

VERBS 3 **benefit, aid,** assist, succor; befriend, take
under one's wing; back, support; save the day, save
one's neck *or* skin *or* bacon

ADJS 4 benefitting, aiding, befriending, assisting;
backing, supporting; saving, salving, salvational,
redemptive, redeeming; liberating, freeing,
emancipative, emancipating, manumitting

ADVS 5 by one's aid *or* good offices, with one's
support, on one's shoulders *or* coattails

PREPS 6 with *or* by benefit of, with *or* by the aid of

593 EVILDOER

NOUNS 1 **evildoer, wrongdoer,** worker of ill *or* evil,
malefactor, malfeasant, malfeasor, misfeasor,
malevolent, public enemy, **sinner, villain,**
villainess, transgressor, delinquent, culprit; bad *or*
bad guy *and* baddy *and* meany *and* wrongo *and*
black hat <nf>, wrong'un <Brit nf>, villain;
criminal, outlaw, felon, **crook** <nf>, lawbreaker,
perpetrator, perp <nf>, gangster *and* mobster <nf>;

racketeer, thief, robber, burglar, rapist, murderer,
con; terrorist; **bad person** 660; deceiver 357

2 **troublemaker, mischief-maker;** holy terror;
agitator 375.11

3 **ruffian,** rough, bravo, **rowdy, thug,** desperado,
cutthroat, kill-crazy animal, mad dog; gunman;
bully, bullyboy, bucko; devil, hellcat, hell-raiser;
killer; gang member, gangster

4 <nf terms> **roughneck, tough,** bruiser, mug,
mugger, bimbo, bozo, ugly customer, **hoodlum,**
hood, hooligan, gorilla, ape, plug-ugly, strong-arm
man, muscle man, **goon;** gun, gunsel, trigger man,
rodman, torpedo, hatchet man; hellion, terror,
holy terror, shtarker, ugly customer

5 **savage, barbarian, brute, beast, animal,** tiger,
shark, hyena; wild man; cannibal, man-eater,
anthropophagite; **wrecker, vandal,** nihilist,
destroyer

6 **monster, fiend,** fiend from hell, **demon, devil,** devil
incarnate, hellhound, hellkite; **vampire,** lamia,
harpy, ghoul; werewolf, ape-man; ogre, ogress;
Frankenstein's monster

7 **witch, hag, vixen,** hellhag, hellcat, she-devil,
virago, brimstone, termagant, grimalkin, Jezebel,
beldam, she-wolf, tigress, wildcat, bitch-kitty
<nf>, siren, fury

594 JURISDICTION
<administration of justice>

NOUNS 1 **jurisdiction,** legal authority *or* power *or*
right *or* sway, the confines of the law; original *or*
appellate jurisdiction, exclusive *or* concurrent
jurisdiction, civil *or* criminal jurisdiction,
common-law *or* equitable jurisdiction, *in rem*
jurisdiction, *in personam* jurisdiction, subject-
matter juristiction, territorial jurisdiction;
voluntary jurisdiction; mandate, cognizance

2 **judiciary,** judicial *or* legal *or* court system,
judicature, judicatory, court, the courts; criminal-
justice system; **justice,** the wheels of justice,
judicial process; judgment 946

3 **magistracy,** magistrature, magistrateship;
judgeship, justiceship; mayoralty, mayorship

4 **bureau, office, department;** secretariat, ministry,
commissariat; municipality, bailiwick,
constabulary, constablery, sheriffry, sheriffalty,
shrievalty; constablewick, sheriffwick

VERBS 5 **administer justice,** administer,
administrate; preside, preside at the board; **sit in**
judgment 598.18, **judge** 946.8

ADJS 6 **jurisdictional,** jurisdictive; **judicatory,**
judicatorial, judicative, **juridic** *or* **juridical;** jural,
jurisprudential, **judicial, judiciary;** magisterial;
forensic

595 TRIBUNAL

NOUNS **1 tribunal, forum, board,** curia, Areopagus; judicature, judicatory, judiciary 594.2; council 423; inquisition, the Inquisition

2 court, law court, court of law *or* **justice,** court of arbitration, legal tribunal, judicature; **United States court** <see list>, federal court; **British court** <see list>, Crown court; high court, trial court, court of record, superior court, inferior court; criminal court, civil court

3 <ecclesiastical courts> Papal Court, Curia, Rota, Sacra Romana Rota, Court of Arches *and* Court of Peculiars <Brit>

4 military court, court-martial, general *or* special *or* summary court-martial, drumhead court-martial; naval court, captain's mast

5 seat of justice, judgment seat, mercy seat, siege of justice <old>; **bench;** woolsack <Brit>

6 courthouse, court; county *or* town hall, town house; **courtroom;** jury box; bench, bar; witness stand *or* box, dock

ADJS **7 tribunal, judicial,** judiciary, court, curial; appellate

8 United States courts

Court of Private Land Claims	Territorial court
Federal Court of Claims	United States Circuit Court of Appeals
Supreme Court *or* United States Supreme Court	United States District Court

9 British courts

Board of Green Cloth Council	Court of the Duchy of Lancaster
court of admiralty	Green Cloth
Court of Appeal	High Court
court of attachments	High Court of Appeal
Court of Common	High *or* Supreme Court of
Court of Common Bank	Judicature
Court of Common Pleas	High Court of Justice
Court of Criminal Appeal	Judicial Committee of the Privy Council
Court of Divorce and Matrimonial Causes	Lords Justices' Court
Court of Exchequer	Palatine Court
Court of Exchequer Chamber	Rolls Court
	Stannary Court
court of piepoudre *or* dustyfoot	superior courts of Westminster
Court of Queen's *or* King's Bench	Teind Court <Scot>
	Vice Chancellor's Court
Court of Session <Scot>	Wardmote *or* Wardmote Court
	Woodmote

officer, beak <Brit nf>; **justice of the peace** *or* **JP;** arbiter, arbitrator, moderator; umpire, referee; his *or* her honor, your honor, his *or* her worship, his lordship; Mr Justice; critic 946.7; **special judge** <see list>

2 <historical> tribune, praetor, ephor, archon, syndic, podesta; Areopagite; justiciar, justiciary; dempster, deemster, doomster, doomsman

3 <Muslim> mullah, ulema, hakim, mufti, cadi

4 Chief Justice, Associate Justice, Justice of the Supreme Court; Lord Chief Justice, Lord Justice, Lord Chancellor, Master of the Rolls, Baron of the Exchequer; Judge Advocate General

5 Pontius Pilate, Solomon, Minos, Rhadamanthus, Aeacus

6 jury <see list>, **panel,** jury of one's peers, country, twelve men in a box, twelve good men and true; inquest; jury panel, jury list, venire facias; hung *or* deadlocked jury; grand jury, petit jury, common jury, special jury *or* blue-ribbon jury *or* struck jury

7 juror, juryman, jurywoman, venire-man *or* -woman, talesman; foreman of the jury, foreman *or* foreperson; grand-juror, grand-juryman; petit-juror, petit-juryman; recognitor

8 judges

amicus curiae	justiciar
assessor *or* legal assessor	lay judge
associate justice	magistrate
bankruptcy judge	master
barmaster <Brit>	military judge
chancellor	ombudsman
chief justice	ordinary *or* judge ordinary
circuit judge	police judge *or* justice *or*
district judge	magistrate *or* PJ
hearing officer	presiding judge *or* officer
judge advocate general *or* JAG	probate judge
	puisne judge *or* justice
judge *or* justice of assize	recorder
jurat	tax judge
justice in eyre	trial judge
justice of the peace	vice-chancellor

9 juries

blue-ribbon jury *or* panel	jury of the vicinage
common jury	petit jury *or* petty jury *or*
coroner's jury	traverse jury
elisor jury	police jury
grand jury	pyx jury
Jedburgh jury <Scot>	sheriff's jury
jury of inquest	special jury
jury of matrons *or* women	struck jury
	trial jury

596 JUDGE, JURY

NOUNS **1 judge, magistrate, justice,** adjudicator, bencher, man *or* woman on the bench, presiding

597 LAWYER

NOUNS **1 lawyer, attorney, attorney-at-law,** barrister, barrister-at-law, **counselor,** counselor-at-law,

counsel, legal counsel *or* counselor, legal adviser, law officer, legal expert, **solicitor, advocate, pleader;** member of the bar, legal practitioner, officer of the court; smart lawyer, pettifogger, Philadelphia lawyer; Juris Doctor *or* Jur.D., proctor, procurator; friend at *or* in court, amicus curiae; deputy, agent 576; intercessor 466.3; sea lawyer, latrine *or* guardhouse lawyer <nf>, self-styled lawyer, legalist; public prosecutor, public defender, defense lawyer *or* attorney, prosecuting attorney, trial lawyer *or* attorney; judge advocate, district attorney *or* DA, attorney general

2 legist, jurist, jurisprudent, jurisconsult; law member of a court-martial

3 <nf terms> **shyster, mouthpiece, ambulance chaser,** lip, fixer, legal eagle, ambulance chaser

4 **bar,** legal profession, members of the bar; representation, counsel, pleading, attorneyship; **practice,** legal practice, criminal practice, corporate practice, etc; legal-aid *or* pro bono practice; **law firm,** legal firm, partnership

VERBS 5 **practice law,** practice at the bar; be admitted to the bar; take silk <Brit>

ADJS 6 **lawyerly,** lawyerlike, barristerial; representing, of counsel

598 LEGAL ACTION

NOUNS 1 **lawsuit, suit,** suit in *or* at law; countersuit; **litigation, prosecution, action, legal action,** proceedings, legal proceedings, legal process, legal procedure, due process, course of law; legal remedy; **case, court case,** cause, cause in court, legal case; **judicial process;** claim, counterclaim; test case; one's day in court

2 **summons, subpoena,** writ of summons; **writ, warrant**

3 **arraignment, indictment, impeachment; complaint, charge** 599.1; presentment; information; bill of indictment, true bill; **bail** 438.2

4 **jury selection, impanelment,** venire, venire facias, venire facias de novo, jury service, sequestration

5 **trial, jury trial,** trial by jury, trial at the bar, trial by law, **hearing, inquiry, inquisition,** inquest, assize; court-martial; **examination,** cross-examination; retrial; mistrial; change of venue; civil trial, criminal trial, bench trial

6 **pleadings,** arguments at the bar; **plea,** pleading, argument; **defense,** statement of defense; demurrer, general *or* special demurrer; refutation 958.2; rebuttal 939.2

7 **declaration, statement,** allegation, allegation *or* statement of facts, procès-verbal; **deposition,** affidavit; claim; complaint; bill, bill of complaint; libel, narratio; nolle prosequi, nol pros; nonsuit

8 **testimony; evidence** 957; , cross-examination, direct examination; **argument,** presentation of the case; resting of the case; **summing up,** summation, closing arguments, jury instructions, charge to the jury, charging of the jury

9 **judgment, decision,** landmark decision; **verdict,** directed verdict, special verdict, sealed verdict, **sentence** 946.5; acquittal 601; condemnation 602, penalty 603

10 **appeal,** appeal motion, application for retrial, appeal to a higher court; writ of error; certiorari, writ of certiorari

11 **litigant, litigator,** litigationist; suitor, **party,** party to a suit, suitor; injured *or* aggrieved party, **plaintiff** 599.5; **defendant** 599.6; witness; accessory, accessory before *or* after the fact; panel, parties litigant

12 <legal terms> motion for summary judgment, search warrant, bench warrant, discovery, written interrogatories, witness list, plea bargaining, objection, perjury

VERBS 13 **sue, litigate, prosecute,** go into litigation, **bring suit,** put in suit, sue *or* prosecute at law, **go to law,** seek in law, appeal to the law, seek justice *or* legal redress, implead, **bring action against,** bring legal action, start an action, prosecute a suit against, take *or* institute legal proceedings against; law *or* have the law in <nf>; take to court, bring into court, hale *or* haul *or* drag into court, bring a case before the court *or* bar, bring before a jury, bring to justice, bring to trial, **put on trial,** bring to the bar, take before the judge; set down for hearing; implead, seek legal protection

14 **summons, issue a summons,** subpoena

15 **arraign, indict, impeach,** cite, serve notice on, find an indictment against, present a true bill, claim, prefer *or* file a claim, have *or* pull up <nf>, bring up for investigation; press charges, **prefer charges** 599.7

16 **select** *or* **impanel a jury,** impanel, panel

17 **call to witness,** bring forward, put on the stand; swear in 334.7; take oath; take the stand, testify

18 **try,** try a case, conduct a trial, bring to trial, put on trial, **hear,** give a hearing to, sit on; charge the jury, deliver one's charge to the jury; **judge, sit in judgment**

19 **plead, enter a plea** *or* **pleading,** implead, conduct pleadings, argue at the bar; **plead** *or* **argue one's case,** stand trial, present one's case, make a plea, tell it to the judge <nf>; hang the jury <nf>; rest, rest one's case; sum up one's case; throw oneself on the mercy of the court

20 **bring in a verdict,** judge, **pass** *or* **pronounce sentence** 946.13; acquit 601.4; convict 602.3; penalize 603.4

ADJS 21 litigious, litigant, litigatory, litigating; causidical, lawyerly; litigable, actionable, justicble, prosecutable; prosecutorial; **moot,** sub judice; unactionable, unprosecutable, unlitigable, frivolous, without merit

PHRS 22 in litigation, in court, in chancery, in jeopardy, **at law,** litigated, coram judice, brought before the court *or* judge, at bar, at the bar, **on trial,** up for investigation *or* hearing, before the court *or* bar *or* judge

599 ACCUSATION

NOUNS 1 accusation, accusal, finger-pointing <nf>, **charge, complaint,** plaint, count, **blame, imputation,** delation, reproach, taxing; **accusing, bringing of charges,** laying of charges, bringing to book; **denunciation,** denouncement; **impeachment, arraignment, indictment,** bill of indictment, true bill; **allegation,** allegement; **imputation,** ascription; **insinuation, implication, innuendo,** veiled accusation, unspoken accusation; information, information against, bill of particulars; charge sheet; specification; gravamen of a charge; prosecution, suit, lawsuit 598.1

2 incrimination, crimination, **inculpation,** implication, **citation,** involvement, impugnment; attack, assault; **censure** 510.3

3 recrimination, retort, countercharge

4 trumped-up charge, false witness; **put-up job** *and* **frame-up** *and* **frame** <nf>; false charge

5 accuser, accusant, accusatrix; incriminator, delator, allegator, impugner; informer 551.6; impeacher, indictor; **plaintiff, complainant,** claimant, appellant, petitioner, libelant, suitor, **party,** party to a suit, pursuer; **prosecutor,** the prosecution; hostile witness

6 accused, defendant, respondent, codefendant, corespondent, libelee, appellee, suspect, culprit, prisoner, prisoner before the court, accused person; prime suspect

VERBS 7 accuse, bring accusation; **charge, press charges, prefer** *or* **bring charges,** lay charges; complain, **lodge a complaint,** lodge a plaint; **impeach, arraign, indict,** bring in *or* hand up an indictment, return a true bill, article, **cite,** cite on several counts; book; **denounce,** denunciate; **finger** *and* point the finger at *and* put *or* lay the finger on <nf>, throw the book at <nf>, **testify against** 551.12; **impute,** ascribe; allege, insinuate, imply; bring to book; tax, task, take to task *or* account; **reproach,** twit, taunt with; report, put on report

8 blame, blame on *or* upon <nf>, lay on, hold against, **put** *or* **place** *or* lay the blame on, lay *or* cast blame upon, place *or* fix the blame *or* responsibility for; fasten on *or* upon, pin *or* hang on <nf>

9 accuse of, charge with, tax *or* task with, saddle with, lay to one's charge, place to one's account, lay at one's door, bring home to, cast *or* throw in one's teeth, throw up to one, throw *or* thrust in the face of

10 incriminate, criminate, **inculpate,** implicate, involve; cry out against, cry out on *or* upon, cry shame upon, raise one's voice against; attack, assail, impugn; **censure** 510.13; throw a stone at, cast *or* throw the first stone

11 recriminate, countercharge, retort an accusation

12 trump up a charge, bear false witness; frame *and* frame up *and* set up *and* put up a job on <nf>, plant evidence

ADJS 13 accusing, accusatory, accusatorial, accusative, pointing to; imputative, denunciatory; recriminatory; prosecutorial; **condemnatory**

14 incriminating, incriminatory, criminatory; delatorian; inculpative, inculpatory

15 accused, charged, blamed, tasked, taxed, reproached, **denounced, impeached, indicted, arraigned; under a cloud** *or* a cloud of suspicion, under suspicion; incriminated, recriminated, inculpated, implicated, involved, in complicity; **cited,** impugned; under attack, under fire

600 JUSTIFICATION

NOUNS 1 justification, vindication; clearing, clearing of one's name *or* one's good name, clearance, purging, purgation, destigmatizing, destigmatization, **exculpation** 601.1; no bill, failure to indict; explanation, rationalization; reinstatement, restitution, restoration, **rehabilitation**

2 defense, plea, pleading; argument, statement of defense; answer, reply, counterstatement, response, riposte; grounds; **refutation** 958.2, **rebuttal** 939.2; demurrer, general *or* special demurrer; denial, objection, exception; **special pleading;** self-defense, plea of self-defense, Nuremberg defense, the devil-made-me-do-it defense, blame-the-victim defense

3 apology, apologia, apologetic; amende

4 excuse, cop-out *and* **alibi** *and* **out** <nf>; lame excuse, poor excuse, likely story, sob story; escape hatch, way out; credibility gap

5 extenuation, mitigation, palliation, softening; extenuative, palliative, saving grace; **whitewash, whitewashing,** decontamination; gilding, gloss, varnish, color, putting the best color on; qualification, allowance; extenuating circumstances, mitigating circumstances, diminished responsibility; five second rule; dichaeologia

6 warrant, reason, good reason, **cause,** call, **right, basis,** substantive *or* material basis, **ground, grounds,** foundation, substance

7 justifiability, vindicability, defensibility; explainability, explicability; **excusability,** pardonableness, forgivableness, remissibility, veniality; warrantableness, allowableness, admissibility, reasonableness, reasonability, legitimacy

8 justifier, vindicator; defender, pleader; **advocate,** successful advocate *or* defender, proponent, **champion; apologist,** apologizer, apologetic, excuser; whitewasher

VERBS **9 justify, vindicate,** do justice to, make justice *or* right prevail; fail to indict, no-bill; **warrant,** account for, show sufficient grounds for, give good reasons for; **rationalize,** explain; cry sour grapes, "make a virtue of necessity"— Shakespeare; get off the hook <nf>, find an out, **exculpate** 601.4; **clear,** clear one's name *or* one's good name, purge, destigmatize, reinstate, restore, rehabilitate

10 defend, offer *or* say in defense, allege in support *or* vindication, **support, uphold, sustain, maintain,** assert, stick up for; **answer,** reply, respond, riposte, counter; refute 958.5, **rebut** 939.5; **plead for,** make a plea, offer as a plea, plead one's case *or* cause, put up a front *or* a brave front; **advocate,** champion, go to bat for <nf>, espouse, join *or* associate oneself with, stand *or* stick up for, speak up for, contend for, speak for, argue for, urge reasons for, put in a good word for

11 excuse, alibi <nf>, offer excuse for, give as an excuse, cover with excuses, **explain,** offer an explanation; plead ignorance *or* insanity *or* diminished responsibility; **apologize for,** make apology for; alibi out of <nf>, crawl *or* worm *or* squirm out of, lie out of, have an out *or* alibi *or* story <nf>

12 extenuate, mitigate, palliate, soften, lessen, diminish, **ease,** mince; **soft-pedal;** slur over, ignore, pass by in silence, give the benefit of the doubt, not hold it against one, **explain away, gloss** *or* **smooth over,** put a gloss upon, put a good face upon, varnish, **white-wash,** color, lend a color to, put the best color *or* face on, show in the best colors, show to best advantage; **allow for,** make allowance for; give the Devil his due

ADJS **13 justifying,** justificatory; **vindicative,** vindicatory, rehabilitative; refuting 958.6; defensive; **excusing,** excusatory; **apologetic, apologetical; extenuating,** extenuative, **palliative**

14 justifiable, vindicable, defensible; excusable, pardonable, forgivable, expiable, remissible, exemptible, venial; **condonable,** dispensable; **warrantable,** allowable, admissible, reasonable, colorable, legitimate; innocuous, unobjectionable, inoffensive

601 ACQUITTAL

NOUNS **1 acquittal,** acquittance, acquitment; **exculpation,** disculpation, verdict of acquittal *or* not guilty; **exoneration, absolution, vindication, remission,** compurgation, purgation, purging; **clearing,** clearance, destigmatizing, destigmatization, quietus; **pardon, excuse, forgiveness, free pardon; discharge, release, dismissal,** setting free; quashing of the charge *or* indictment; assoilment; grace

2 exemption, immunity, impunity, nonliability, dispensation, waiver; diplomatic immunity; **amnesty,** indemnity, nonprosecution, non prosequitur, nolle prosequi; stay; dispensation; freedom

3 reprieve, respite, grace, remit

VERBS **4 acquit, clear, exculpate, exonerate, absolve,** give *or* grant absolution, bring in *or* return a verdict of not guilty; **vindicate,** justify; **pardon, excuse, forgive,** show mercy; remit, grant remission, remit the penalty of; amnesty, grant or extend amnesty; **discharge, release, dismiss, free, set free,** let off <nf>, let go, let off scot-free, spare; quash the charge *or* indictment, withdraw the charge; **exempt,** grant immunity, exempt from, dispense from; clear the skirts of, shrive, purge; blot out one's sins, wipe the slate clean; **whitewash,** decontaminate; destigmatize; non-pros; assoil

5 reprieve, respite, give *or* grant a reprieve; stay

602 CONDEMNATION

NOUNS **1 condemnation, damnation, doom,** guilty verdict, verdict of guilty; proscription, excommunication, anathematizing; **denunciation,** denouncement; **censure** 510.3; **conviction; sentence, judgment,** rap <nf>; capital punishment, corporal punishment, death penalty, death sentence, death warrant, burning at the stake; curse

2 attainder, attainture, attaintment; bill of attainder, civil death

VERBS **3 condemn, damn, doom; denounce,** denunciate; **censure** 510.13; **convict,** find guilty, bring home to; proscribe, excommunicate, anathematize; blacklist, put on the Index;

reprobate; pronounce judgment 946.13; **sentence, pronounce sentence, pass sentence on;** penalize 603.4; attaint; sign one's death warrant

4 stand condemned, be convicted, be found guilty

ADJS **5 condemnatory, damnatory,** denunciatory, proscriptive; **censorious**

6 convicted, condemned, guilty, blameworthy, liable, sentenced

603 PENALTY

NOUNS **1 penalty,** penalization, penance, penal retribution; **sanctions,** penal *or* punitive measures; **punishment** 604; **reprisal** 506.2, retaliation 506, compensation, price; the devil to pay

2 handicap, disability, **disadvantage** 1012.6

3 fine, monetary *or* financial penalty, mulct, amercement, sconce, **damages,** punitive damages, compensatory damages; distress, distraint; forfeit, forfeiture; escheat, escheatment

VERBS **4 penalize,** put *or* impose *or* inflict a penalty *or* sanctions on; **punish** 604.10; **handicap,** put at a disadvantage

5 fine, mulct, amerce, sconce, estreat, pillory; distrain, levy a distress; award damages

ADVS **6 on pain of,** under *or* upon pain of, **on** *or* **under penalty of**

604 PUNISHMENT

NOUNS **1 punishment,** punition, **chastisement, chastening, correction, discipline,** disciplinary measure *or* action, **castigation,** infliction, scourge, ferule, what-for <nf>; pains, pains and punishments; pay, payment; crime fighting; **retribution,** retributive justice, nemesis; judicial punishment; punishment that fits the crime, condign punishment, well-deserved punishment; **penalty,** penal retribution; penalization; penology; cruel and unusual punishment; judgment; what's coming to one, **just desserts, desserts**

2 <forms of punishment> penal servitude, jailing, imprisonment, incarceration, confinement; hard labor, rock pile, chain gang, labor camp; galleys; torture, torment, martyrdom; the gantlet, keelhauling, tar-and-feathering, railriding, picketing, the rack, impalement, dismemberment; walking the plank; house arrest; exile

3 slap, smack, whack, whomp, **cuff, box,** buffet, belt; blow 902.4; **rap on the knuckles,** box on the ear, slap in the face; slap on the wrist, token punishment

4 corporal punishment, whipping, beating, thrashing, spanking, flogging, paddling, flagellation, scourging, flailing, trouncing,

basting, bastinado, drubbing, buffeting, belaboring; **lashing, lacing,** stripes; horsewhipping, strapping, belting, rawhiding, cowhiding; **switching; clubbing,** cudgeling, caning, truncheoning, fustigation, bastinado; pistol-whipping; battery; dusting

5 <nf terms> **licking,** larruping, walloping, whaling, lathering, leathering, **hiding, tanning, dressing-down,** chewing out; **paddling,** swingeing; grounding

6 <old nf terms> strap oil, hazel oil, hickory oil, birch oil; dose of strap oil, etc

7 capital punishment, execution; legal *or* judicial murder, extreme penalty, death sentence *or* penalty *or* warrant; **hanging,** the gallows, the rope *or* noose; summary execution; **lynching,** necktie party *or* sociable <nf>, vigilanteism, vigilante justice; the necklace; **crucifixion,** impalement; **electrocution,** the chair <nf>, the hot seat <nf>; gassing, the gas chamber; lethal injection; **decapitation,** decollation, beheading, the guillotine, the ax, the block; **strangling,** strangulation, garrote; **shooting,** fusillade, firing squad; **burning,** burning at the stake; **poisoning,** hemlock; stoning, lapidation; drowning; defenestration

8 punisher, discipliner, chastiser, chastener; **executioner,** executionist, deathsman <old>, Jack Ketch <Brit>; **hangman; lyncher;** electrocutioner; headsman, **beheader,** decapitator; strangler, garroter; sadist, torturer; hatchet man, hit man <nf>

9 penologist; jailer 429.10

VERBS **10 punish, chastise, chasten, discipline, correct, castigate, penalize,** reprimand; **take to task,** bring to book, bring *or* call to account; deal with, settle with, settle *or* square accounts, **give one his desserts** *or* **just desserts,** serve one right; inflict upon, visit upon; teach *or* give one a lesson, make an example of; pillory; masthead; reduce to the ranks

11 <nf terms> **attend to,** do for, take care of, serve one out, **give it to,** take *or* have it out of; pay, pay out, **fix, settle,** fix one's wagon, settle one's hash, settle the score, give one his gruel, make it hot for one, **give one his comeuppance;** lower the boom, put one through the wringer, come down on *or* down hard on, throw the book at, throw to the wolves; **give what-for,** give a going-over, climb one's frame, let one have it, tell off, light into, lay into, land on, mop *or* wipe up the floor with, skin live, have one's hide

12 slap, smack, whack, thwack, whomp, **cuff, box,** buffet; strike 902.13; slap the face, box the ears, give a rap on the knuckles

13 **whip,** give a whipping *or* beating *or* thrashing, **beat, thrash, spank, flog,** scourge, flagellate, flay, flail, whale; **smite,** thump, trounce, baste, **pummel,** pommel, **drub, buffet, belabor,** lay on; **lash, lace,** cut, stripe; horsewhip; knout; **strap,** belt, rawhide, cowhide; **switch,** birch, give the stick; **club, cudgel,** cane, truncheon, fustigate, bastinado; pistol-whip

14 **thrash soundly, batter,** bruise

15 <nf terms> **beat up,** rough up, clobber, marmelize <Brit>, work over, lick, larrup, wallop, whop, swinge, beat one's brains out, whale, whale the tar out of, beat *or* kick the shit out of, beat to a jelly, **beat black and blue, knock one's lights out, nail,** welt, trim, flax, lather, leather, **hide,** tan, **tan one's hide,** dress down, **kick ass,** give a dressing-down, knock head, knock heads together; **paddle; lambaste, clobber,** dust one's jacket, give a dose of birch oil *or* strap oil *or* hickory oil *or* hazel oil, take it out of one's hide *or* skin

16 **torture,** put to the question; rack, put on *or* to the rack; dismember, tear limb from limb; draw and quarter, break on the wheel, tar and feather, ride on a rail, picket, keelhaul, impale, grill, thumbscrew, persecute, work over

17 **execute, put to death,** inflict capital punishment; **electrocute,** burn *and* fry <nf>; send to the gas chamber; **behead, decapitate,** decollate, guillotine, bring to the block; **crucify; shoot,** execute by firing squad; burn, **burn at the stake; strangle,** garrote, bowstring; stone, lapidate; defenestrate; send to the hot seat <nf>

18 **hang,** hang by the neck; **string up** *and* scrag *and* stretch <nf>; gibbet, noose, neck, bring to the gallows; **lynch;** hang, draw, and quarter

19 **be hanged,** suffer hanging, **swing,** dance upon nothing, kick the air *or* wind *or* clouds

20 **be punished, suffer,** suffer for, **suffer the consequences** *or* **penalty,** get it *and* **catch it** <nf>, get *or* catch it in the neck <nf>, catch hell *or* the devil <nf>, get *or* take a licking *or* shellacking <nf>; **get one's desserts** 639.6; get it coming and going <nf>, be doubly punished, sow the wind and reap the whirlwind; get hurt, get one's fingers burned, have *or* get one's knuckles rapped

21 **take one's punishment,** bow one's neck, take the consequences, **take one's medicine** *or* what is coming to one, swallow the bitter pill *or* one's medicine, pay the piper, face the music <nf>, stand up to it, make one's bed and lie on it, get what one is asking for; take the rap <nf>, take the fall <nf>

22 **deserve punishment, have it coming** <nf>, be for it *or* in for it, be heading for a fall, be cruising for a bruising <nf>

ADJS 23 **punishing, chastising,** chastening, corrective, disciplinary, correctional; retributive; grueling <nf>; **penal, punitive,** punitory, inflictive; castigatory; baculine; penological; capital; corporal

605 INSTRUMENTS OF PUNISHMENT

NOUNS 1 **whip, lash, scourge,** flagellum, strap, thong, rawhide, cowhide, blacksnake, kurbash, sjambok, belt, razor strap; knout; bullwhip, bullwhack; horsewhip; crop; quirt; rope's end; cat, cat-o'-nine-tails; whiplash; bastinado

2 **rod, stick, switch; paddle,** ruler, ferule, pandybat; birch, rattan; cane; club

3 <devices> **pillory, stocks,** finger pillory; cucking stool, ducking stool, trebuchet; whipping post, branks, triangle *or* triangles, wooden horse, treadmill, crank

4 <instruments of torture> **rack,** wheel, Iron Maiden of Nuremberg; screw, thumbscrew; boot, iron heel, scarpines; Procrustean bed *or* bed of Procrustes

5 <instruments of execution> **scaffold; block, guillotine,** ax, maiden; **stake; cross; gallows,** gallows-tree, gibbet, tree, drop; **hangman's rope, noose,** rope, halter, hemp, hempen collar *or* necktie *or* bridle <nf>; **electric chair,** death chair, the chair <nf>, hot seat <nf>; **gas chamber,** lethal chamber, death chamber; the necklace, the needle

606 THE PEOPLE
<the population>

NOUNS 1 **the people, the populace, the public,** the general public, people in general, everyone, everybody; **the population,** the citizenry, the whole people, the polity, the body politic; **the community, the commonwealth, society,** the society, the social order *or* fabric, the nation; the commonalty *or* commonality, commonage, commoners, commons, demos <Gk>; **common people, ordinary people** *or* **folk, persons, folk, folks,** gentry; the common sort, plain people *or* folks, the common run <nf>, the rank and file, the boy *or* girl next door, Brown Jones and Robinson, John Q. Public, Middle America; Tom, Dick, and Harry; the salt of the earth, Everyman, Everywoman, the man *or* woman in the street, the common man, you and me, John Doe, Joe Sixpack *or* Joe Schmo <nf>, *vulgus* <L>, the third estate; **the upper class; the middle class; the lower class;** demography, demographics; social anthropology

2 **the masses, the hoi polloi,** *hoi polloi* <Gk>, the many, **the multitude,** the crowd, **the mob,** the

horde, the million, "the booboisie"—H L Mencken, **the majority,** the mass of the people, the herd, the great unnumbered, the great unwashed, **the vulgar** or **common herd,** vulgar masses; *profanum vulgus* and *ignobile vulgus* and *mobile vulgus* <L>; audience, followers

3 rabble, rabblement, rout, ruck, common ruck, canaille, *racaille* <Fr>, ragtag <nf>, **ragtag and bobtail;** rag, tag, and bobtail; **riffraff, trash,** raff, chaff, **rubbish,** dregs, sordes, offscourings, off-scum, **scum, scum of the earth, dregs** or **scum** or **off-scum** or **offscourings of society,** swinish multitude, vermin, cattle; colluvies

4 the underprivileged, the disadvantaged, the poor, ghetto-dwellers, slum-dwellers, welfare cases, chronic poor, underclass, depressed class, poverty subculture, the wretched of the earth, outcasts, the homeless, the dispossessed, bag people, the powerless, the unemployable, lumpen, the lumpenproletariat or lumpenprole <nf>, lower orders, second-class citizens, the have-nots, small potatoes

5 common man, commoner, little man, **little fellow, average man,** ordinary man, typical man, **man in the street,** one of the people, man of the people, man in the street, regular guy, regular joe, Everyman, ham-and-egger; **plebeian,** pleb <slang>; **proletarian,** prole <Brit nf>, *roturier* <Fr>; ordinary or average Joe and Joe Doakes and Joe Sixpack <nf>, John Doe, Jane Doe, John Smith, Mr or Mrs Brown or Smith, Joe Blow, John Q. Public, Mr. Nobody; nonentity; muggle; bourgeois

6 peasant, countryman, countrywoman, **provincial,** son of the soil, tiller of the soil; **peon,** hind, fellah, muzhik, serf, villein, churl; **farmer** 1069.5, **hick** and yokel and rube and hayseed and shit-kicker <nf>, **bumpkin,** country bumpkin, rustic, clod, **clodhopper** <nf>, hillbilly and woodhick <nf>, **boor,** clown, lout, looby; townie

7 upstart, parvenu, adventurer, sprout <nf>; *bourgeois gentilhomme* <Fr>, would-be gentleman; *nouveau riche* and *nouveau roturier* <Fr>, *arriviste* <Fr>, **newly-rich,** pig in clover <nf>; **social climber,** climber, name-dropper, tufthunter, status seeker

ADJS **8 populational,** population; **demographic,** demographical; national, societal; **popular,** public, mass, grass-roots, cultural, **common,** common as dirt, commonplace, communal, folk, tribal, **plain, ordinary, lowly,** low, mean, base; **humble,** homely; rank-and-file, provincial, of the people; second-class, **lowborn,** lowbred, baseborn, earthborn, earthy, of humble birth, plebeian; third-estate; ungenteel, shabby-genteel, uncultured; **vulgar,**

rude, coarse, below the salt; **parvenu, upstart,** risen from the ranks, jumped-up <nf>; newly-rich, *nouveau-riche* <Fr>; non-U <Brit>

607 SOCIAL CLASS AND STATUS

NOUNS **1 class, social class, economic class,** social group or grouping, status group, accorded status, social category, order, grade, caste, estate, rank; **status, social status, economic status,** socioeconomic status or background, standing, footing, prestige, rank, ranking, place, station, position, level, degree, stratum; **social structure, hierarchy,** pecking order, social stratification, social system, social gamut, social differentiation, social pyramid, class structure, class distinction, status system, power structure, ranking, stratification, social network, ordering, social scale, gradation, division, social inequality, inequality, haves and have-nots; **social bias, class conflict,** class identity, class difference, class prejudice, class struggle, class politics; ageism; **mobility, social mobility,** upward mobility, downward mobility, vertical mobility, horizontal mobility; social justice

2 upper class, upper classes, aristocracy, patriciate, second estate, ruling class, ruling circles, elite, elect, the privileged, the classes, the quality, the better sort, upper circles, upper cut and upper crust and crust and cream <nf>, upper-income group or higher-income group, gentlefolk, gentility, lords of creation; **high society,** high life, the Four Hundred, bon ton, *haut monde* <Fr>, First Families of Virginia or FFV; Social Register, Bluebook; nobility, gentry 608; status symbol; social ladder

3 aristocracy, aristocratic status, aristocraticalness, aristocraticness, high status, high rank, quality, high estate, gentility, social distinction, social prestige; **birth,** high birth, distinguished ancestry or descent or heritage or blood, blue blood, silk stocking

4 aristocrat, patrician, Brahmin, blue-blood, thoroughbred, member of the upper class, socialite, swell and upper-cruster <nf>, grandee, grand dame, dowager, magnifico, lord of creation; **gentleman, lady,** person of breeding; trophy wife <nf>; debutante

5 middle class, middle order or orders, lower middle class, upper middle class, bourgeoisie, educated class, professional class, middle-income group, white-collar workers, salaried workers; suburbia; Middle America, silent majority; white bread <nf>; third estate

6 bourgeois, member of the middle class, white-collar worker 726.2, salaried worker; pillar of society, solid citizen

7 **lower class, lower classes,** lower orders, plebeians, plebs, workers, working class, working people, proletariat, proles <Brit nf>, rank and file, grass roots, laboring class *or* classes, toilers, toiling class *or* classes, the other half, low-income group, wage-earners, hourly worker, blue-collar worker; bottom feeder

8 **the underclass, the underprivileged**

9 **worker** 726.2, **workman, working man, working woman,** working girl, proletarian, laborer, laboring man, toiler, stiff *and* working stiff <nf>, artisan, mechanic, industrial worker, factory worker; grunt worker or grunt <nf>

ADJS 10 **upper-class, aristocratic, patrician, upscale;** gentle, genteel, of gentle blood; gentlemanly, gentlemanlike; ladylike, quite the lady; **wellborn, well-bred, blue-blooded,** of good breed; **thoroughbred,** purebred, pure-blooded, *pur sang* <Fr>, full-blooded; **highborn,** highbred; born to the purple, "to the manner born"—Shakespeare, born with a silver spoon in one's mouth; **high-society,** socialite, hoity-toity <nf>, posh; **middle-class, bourgeois,** *petit-bourgeois* <Fr>, petty-bourgeois, suburban, white-bread <nf>; **working class, blue collar,** proletarian, lower-class, born on the wrong side of the tracks; **class-conscious; mobile, socially mobile,** upwardly mobile, downwardly mobile, vertically mobile, horizontally mobile, déclassé

608 ARISTOCRACY, NOBILITY, GENTRY
<noble rank or birth>

NOUNS 1 **aristocracy, nobility,** titled aristocracy, hereditary nobility, noblesse; **royalty; elite,** upper class, elect, the classes, **upper classes** *or* circles, upper cut *and* **upper crust** <nf>, upper ten <Brit nf>, **upper ten thousand,** the Four Hundred, Social Register <trademark>, high society, high life, *haut monde* <Fr>; old nobility, *ancienne noblesse* <Fr>, *noblesse de robe* and *noblesse d'épée* <Fr>, *ancien régime* <Fr>; First Families of Virginia *or* FFV; **peerage,** baronage, lords temporal and spiritual; baronetage; knightage, chivalry; gentlefolk, beau monde, jet set

2 **nobility, nobleness, aristocracy,** aristocraticalness; **gentility,** genteelness; quality, rank, virtue, distinction; birth, high *or* noble birth, ancestry, high *or* honorable descent; lineage, pedigree; blood, **blue blood;** royalty 417.8

3 **gentry,** gentlefolk, gentlefolks, gentlepeople, better sort; lesser nobility, *petite noblesse* <Fr>; *samurai* <Japanese>; landed gentry, squirearchy

4 **nobleman, noble, gentleman; peer; aristocrat, patrician,** Brahman, **blue blood,** titled person, thoroughbred, silk-stocking, lace-curtain, swell *and* upper-cruster <nf>, life peer; **grandee,** magnifico, magnate, optimate; **lord,** laird <Scot>, lordling; seignior, seigneur, *hidalgo* <Sp>; **duke,** grand duke, archduke, marquis, **earl, count,** viscount, **baron,** daimio, **baronet;** squire; esquire, armiger; palsgrave, waldgrave, margrave, landgrave; jet-setter, patrician

5 **knight, cavalier,** chevalier, *caballero* <Sp>, *Ritter* <Ger>; **knight-errant,** knight-adventurer; companion; bachelor, knight bachelor; baronet, knight baronet; banneret, knight banneret; Bayard, Gawain, Lancelot, Sidney, Sir Galahad, Don Quixote

6 **noblewoman, peeress, gentlewoman; lady,** dame, *doña* <Sp>, khanum; **duchess,** grand duchess, archduchess, marchioness, marquise, viscountess, **countess, baroness,** margravine

7 **prince,** *Prinz* and *Fürst* <Ger>, knez, atheling, sheikh, sherif, mirza, khan, emir, shahzada <India>; princeling, princelet; crown prince, heir apparent; heir presumptive; prince consort; prince regent; **king;** princes of India; Muslim rulers 575.10

8 **princess,** *princesse* <Fr>, *infanta* <Sp>, rani *and* maharani *and* begum *and* shahzadi *and* kumari *or* kunwari *and* raj-kumari *and* malikzadi <India>; crown princess; **queen** 575.11

9 <rank or office> lordship, ladyship; dukedom, marquisate, earldom, barony, baronetcy; viscountship, viscountcy, viscounty; knighthood, knight-errantship; seigniory, seigneury, seignioralty; pashaship, pashadom; peerage; princeship, princedom; kingship, queenship 417.8

ADJS 10 **noble,** ennobled, titled, of rank, high, exalted; **aristocratic, patrician; gentle,** genteel, of gentle blood; gentlemanly, gentlemanlike; ladylike, quite the lady; knightly, chivalrous; ducal, archducal; princely, princelike; **regal** 417.17, kingly, kinglike, "every inch a king"—Shakespeare; queenly, queenlike; titled

11 **wellborn, well-bred, blue-blooded,** well-connected, of good breed; **thoroughbred,** purebred, pure-blooded, *pur sang* <Fr>, full-blooded; **highborn,** highbred; born to the purple, high-caste, of good family; classy <nf>, U <Brit>

609 POLITICS

NOUNS 1 **politics,** polity, the art of the possible; practical politics, *Realpolitik* <Ger>; empirical politics; **party** *or* **partisan politics, partisanism; politicization;** reform politics; multiparty politics;

power politics, *Machtpolitik* <Ger>; machine politics, bossism <nf>, Tammany Hall, Tammanism <nf>; confrontation *or* confrontational *or* confro politics; **interest politics,** single-issue politics, interest-group politics, pressure-group politics, PAC *or* political action committee politics; consensus politics; fusion politics; career politics; petty politics, peanut politics <nf>; pork-barrel politics; kid-glove politics <nf>; silk-stocking politics <nf>; ward politics; electronic *or* technological politics; public affairs, civic affairs

2 **political science,** poli-sci <nf>, **politics, government, civics;** political philosophy, political theory; political behavior; political economy, comparative government, international relations, public administration; political geography, geopolitics, *Geopolitik* <Ger>; realpolitik

3 **statesmanship, statecraft,** political *or* governmental leadership, national leadership; transpartisan *or* suprapartisan leadership; kingcraft, queencraft; senatorship

4 **policy, polity,** public policy; line, **party line,** party principle *or* doctrine *or* philosophy, **position,** bipartisan policy; noninterference, nonintervention, *laissez-faire* <Fr>, laissez-faireism; free enterprise; go-slow policy; government control, governmentalism; planned economy, managed currency, price supports, pump-priming <nf>; autarky, economic self-sufficiency; free trade; protection, protectionism; bimetallism; strict constructionism; localism, sectionalism, states' rights, nullification; political correctness

5 **foreign policy, foreign affairs;** world politics; **diplomacy,** diplomatic *or* diplomatics <old>; shirt-sleeve diplomacy; shuttle diplomacy; dollar diplomacy, dollar imperialism; gunboat diplomacy; brinkmanship; **nationalism, internationalism;** expansionism, imperialism, manifest destiny, colonialism, neocolonialism; spheres of influence; balance of power; containment; deterrence; militarism, preparedness; tough policy, the big stick <nf>, twisting the lion's tail; brinksmanship; nonresistance, isolationism, neutralism, coexistence, peaceful coexistence; détente; compromise, appeasement; peace offensive; good-neighbor policy; open-door policy, open door; diplomatic doctrine; Monroe Doctrine; Truman Doctrine; Eisenhower Doctrine; Nixon Doctrine

6 **program;** Square Deal <Theodore Roosevelt>, New Deal <Franklin D Roosevelt>, Fair Deal <Harry S Truman>, New Frontier <John F Kennedy>, Great Society <Lyndon B Johnson>; austerity program; Thatcherism <Brit>

7 **platform,** party platform, **program,** declaration of policy; **plank; issue;** keynote address, keynote speech; position paper

8 **political convention, convention;** conclave, powwow <nf>; national convention, quadrennial circus <nf>; state convention, county convention, preliminary convention, nominating convention; constitutional convention

9 **caucus,** legislative *or* congressional caucus, packed caucus; secret caucus

10 **candidacy,** candidature <chiefly Brit>, **running, running for office,** throwing *or* tossing one's hat in the ring <nf>, standing *or* standing for office <Brit>

11 **nomination,** caucus nomination, direct nomination, petition nomination; acceptance speech

12 **electioneering,** campaigning, politicking <nf>, **stumping** *and* **whistle-stopping** <nf>; **rally,** clambake <nf>; campaign dinner, fund-raising dinner

13 **campaign,** all-out campaign, hard-hitting campaign, hoopla *or* hurrah campaign <nf>; **canvass, solicitation;** front-porch campaign; grass-roots campaign; stump excursion *and* stumping tour *and* whistle-stop campaign <nf>; TV *or* media campaign; campaign commitments *or* promises; campaign fund, campaign contribution; campaign button

14 **smear campaign,** mudslinging campaign, negative campaign; **whispering campaign;** muckraking, **mudslinging** *and* **dirty politics** *and* **dirty tricks** *and* dirty pool <nf>, character assassination; political canard, roorback; last-minute lie

15 **election,** general election, by-election; congressional election, presidential election; partisan election, nonpartisan election; **primary,** primary election; direct primary, open primary, closed primary, nonpartisan primary, mandatory primary, optional primary, preference primary, presidential primary, presidential preference primary, runoff primary; caucus 609.9; runoff, runoff election; disputed *or* contested election; referendum; close election, horse race *and* toss-up <nf>

16 **election district, precinct, ward, borough;** congressional district; safe district; swing district <nf>; close borough *and* pocket borough *and* rotten borough <Brit>; gerrymander, gerrymandered district, shoestring district; silk-stocking district *or* ward; single-member district *or* constituency; body politic

17 **suffrage, franchise, the vote,** right to vote;

universal suffrage, manhood suffrage, woman *or* female suffrage; suffragism, suffragettism; suffragist, woman-suffragist, suffragette; household franchise; one man one vote

18 **voting,** going to the polls, casting one's ballot; preferential voting, preferential system, alternative vote; proportional representation *or* PR, cumulative system *or* voting, Hare system, list system; single system *or* voting, single transferrable vote; plural system *or* voting; single-member district 609.16; absentee voting; proxy voting, card voting; voting machine; election fraud, colonization, floating, repeating, ballot-box stuffing; **vote** 371.6

19 **ballot, slate, ticket,** proxy <nf>; straight ticket, split ticket; Australian ballot; office-block ballot; Indiana ballot, party-column ballot; absentee ballot; long ballot, blanket ballot, jungle ballot <nf>; short ballot; nonpartisan ballot; sample ballot; party emblem

20 **polls,** poll, polling place, polling station <Brit>, balloting place; voting booth, polling booth; ballot box; voting machine; pollbook

21 **returns,** election returns, **poll,** count, official count; **recount;** landslide, tidal wave

22 **electorate,** electors; **constituency,** constituents; electoral college

23 **voter, elector, balloter;** registered voter; fraudulent voter, floater, repeater, ballot-box stuffer; proxy

24 **political party** <see list>, **party,** major party, minor party, third party, splinter party; party in power, opposition party, loyal opposition; **fraction, camp; machine,** political *or* party machine, Tammany Hall; city hall; one-party system, two-party system, multiple party system, multiparty system; right, left, center; new left; right-wing *or* left-wing conspiracy; popular front; bloc, coalition

25 **partisanism,** partisanship, partisanry; Republicanism; Conservatism, Toryism; Liberalism; Whiggism, Whiggery

26 **nonpartisanism, independence,** neutralism; mugwumpery, mugwumpism

27 **partisan, party member,** party man *or* woman; regular, stalwart, loyalist, wheelhorse, party wheelhorse; heeler, ward heeler, **party hack;** party faithful; right-winger, left-winger; Democrat, Republican

28 **nonpartisan, independent, neutral, mugwump,** undecided *or* uncommitted voter, centrist; swing vote; superdelegate

29 **political influence, wire-pulling** <nf>; **social pressure, public opinion, special-interest pressure,** group pressure; **influence peddling;**

lobbying, lobbyism; **logrolling,** back scratching; political corruption

30 **wire-puller** <nf>; **influence peddler,** four-percenter, power broker, fixer <nf>, five-percenter <nf>; logroller

31 **pressure group,** interest group, special-interest group, political action committee *or* PAC, single-issue group; **special interest;** vested interest; financial interests, farm interests, labor interests, etc; minority interests, ethnic vote, black vote, etc; **Black Power,** White Power, Polish Power, etc

32 **lobby,** legislative lobby, special-interest lobby; **lobbyist,** registered lobbyist, lobbyer, parliamentary agent <Brit>

33 **front, movement,** coalition, political front; popular front, people's front, communist front, etc; grass-roots movement, ground swell, the silent majority; youth crusade *or* movement

34 <political corruption> **graft,** boodling <nf>, jobbery; pork-barrel legislation *or* pork-barreling; political intrigue

35 **spoils of office; graft,** boodle <nf>; slush fund <nf>; campaign fund, campaign contribution; public tit *and* public trough <nf>; spoils system; cronyism, nepotism

36 **political patronage, patronage, favors of office, pork** *and* **pork barrel** <nf>, plum, melon <nf>

37 **political** *or* **official jargon; officialese** *and* federalese *and* Washingtonese *and* gobbledygook <nf>; bafflegab <nf>; political doubletalk, doublespeak, bunkum <nf>; pussyfooting; pointing with pride and viewing with alarm; new world order

VERBS 38 **politick** <nf>, politicize; look after one's fences *and* mend one's fences <nf>; caucus; gerrymander, lobby

39 **run for office,** run; **throw** *or* **toss one's hat in the ring** <nf>, go into politics, announce for, enter the lists *or* arena, stand *and* stand for office <Brit>; contest a seat <Brit>; take the field

40 **electioneer, campaign; stump** *and* take the stump *and* take to the stump *and* stump the country *and* take to the hustings *and* hit the campaign trail *and* **whistle-stop** <nf>; **canvass,** go to the voters *or* electorate, solicit votes, ring doorbells; shake hands and kiss babies

41 **support, back** *and* **back up** <nf>, come out for, **endorse;** go with the party, follow the party line; **get on the bandwagon** <nf>; **nominate, elect, vote** 371.18,20

42 **hold office,** hold *or* occupy a post, fill an office, be the incumbent, be in office, be elected, be voted in

ADJS 43 **political,** politic; governmental, civic; geopolitical; statesmanlike; diplomatic; suffragist; politico-commercial, politico-diplomatic, politico-ecclesiastical, politico-economic, politico-ethical, politico-geographical, politico-judicial, politico-military, politico-moral, politico-religious, politico-scientific, politico-social, politico-theological; politically correct

44 partisan, party; bipartisan, biparty, two-party

45 nonpartisan, independent, neutral, mugwumpian *and* mugwumpish <nf>, **on the fence**

WORD ELEMENT **46** politico-

47 political parties

American Labor Party	New Democratic Party
American Party *or*	<Can>
Know-Nothing Party	People's *or* Populist Party
Anti-Masonic Party	Plaid Cymru <Wales>
Anti-Monopoly Party	Populist/America First
Bull Moose Party	Party <US>
Citizens Party <US>	Progressive Party
Communist Party	Progressive Conservative
Conservative Party	Party <US>
Conservative Union Party	Progressive Democrat
<Can>	Party <Ir>
Constitutional Union Party	Prohibition Party
Democratic Party <US>	Republican Party *or* GOP
Democratic-Republican	*or* Grand Old Party <US>
Party	Scottish National Party
Farmer-Labor Party	Sinn Fein <N Ir>
Federalist Party <US>	Social and Liberal
Fianna Fail <Ir>	Democratic Party <Brit>
Fine Gael <Ir>	Social Democratic and
Free Soil Party	Labour Party <N Ir>
Green Party	Social Democratic Party *or*
Greenback Party	SDP <Brit>
Labour Party <Brit>	Socialist Labor Party <US>
Liberal Democrat Party	Socialist Party
<Brit>	Socialist Workers Party
Liberal Party	States' Rights Democratic
Liberal Republican Party	Party *or* Dixiecrats <US>
Libertarian Party <US>	Tory Party <Brit>
Militant Tendency <Brit>	Ulster Democratic Unionist
National Republican Party	Party <N Ir>
National Front <Brit>	US Labor Party
New Alliance Party <US>	Whig Party

610 POLITICIAN

NOUNS **1 politician,** politico, political leader, professional politician; party leader, party boss *and* party chieftain <nf>; machine *or* clubhouse politician, **political hack,** Tammany man <old>; **pol** <nf>; old campaigner, war-horse; wheelhorse; reform politician, reformer, advocate; campaigner

2 statesman, stateswoman, statesperson, solon, public man *or* woman, national leader; elder statesman; ruler; governor, executive, administrator, leader; president, vice president; prime minister, premier

3 legislator, lawmaker, legislatrix, solon, lawgiver; solon; **congressman,** congresswoman, Member of Congress; **senator; representative;** Speaker of the House; majority leader, minority leader; floor leader; whip, party whip; Member of Parliament *or* MP; state senator, assemblyman, assemblywoman, chosen, freeholder, councilman, alderman, alderperson, selectman, selectperson, city father

4 <petty politician> **two-bit** *or* **peanut politician** <nf>, politicaster, statemonger <old>, political dabbler; **hack,** political hack, **party hack**

5 <corrupt politician> **dirty** *or* **crooked politician** *and* jackleg politician <nf>; **grafter,** boodler <nf>; spoilsman, spoilsmonger; influence peddler 609.30

6 <political intriguer> strategist, machinator, gamesman, wheeler-dealer <nf>; operator *and* finagler *and* **wire-puller** <nf>; **logroller,** pork-barrel politician; Machiavellian; behind-the-scenes operator, gray eminence, *éminence grise* <Fr>, power behind the throne, kingmaker <nf>, **powerbroker** 894.6

7 <political leader> **boss** <nf>, higher-up *or* man higher up <nf>, cacique *and* sachem <old>; keynoter <nf>, policy maker; standard-bearer; ringleader 375.11; **big shot** 997.9

8 henchman, cohort, hanger-on, buddy *and* sidekick <nf>; heeler *and* **ward heeler** <nf>; hatchet man; partner in crime

9 candidate, aspirant, hopeful *and* political hopeful *and* wannabee <nf>, office seeker *or* hunter, baby kisser <nf>; running mate; leading candidate, head of the ticket *or* slate; **dark horse;** stalking-horse; favorite son; presidential timber; defeated candidate, also-ran *and* dud <nf>

10 campaigner, electioneer, **stumper** <nf>, whistle-stopper <nf>, stump speaker *or* orator <nf>

11 officeholder, office-bearer <Brit>, jack-in-office, elected official, public servant, public official, **incumbent;** holdover, lame duck; new broom <nf>; president-elect; ins, the powers that be

12 political worker, committeeman, committeewoman, precinct captain, precinct leader, district leader; party chairperson, state chairperson, national chairperson, chairperson of the national committee; speechwriter; political philosopher

VERBS **13** go into politics; **run,** get on the ticket, run for office; **campaign,** stump

ADJS **14 statesmanlike,** statesmanly

611 POLITICO-ECONOMIC PRINCIPLES

NOUNS **1 conservatism, conservativeness, rightism;** standpattism <nf>, unprogressiveness, backwardness; **ultraconservatism, reaction,** arch-conservative, reactionism, reactionarism, reactionaryism, reactionariness, die-hardism <nf>

2 **moderatism, moderateness**, middle-of-the-roadism; middle of the road, moderate position, via media, **center,** centrism; third force, nonalignment

3 **liberalism, progressivism, leftism; left, left wing,** progressiveness

4 **radicalism, extremism,** ultraism; radicalization; revolutionism; ultraconservatism 611.1; extreme left, extreme left wing, left-wing extremism, loony left <Brit nf>; New Left, Old Left; Jacobinism, sans-culottism, *sans-culotterie* <Fr>; **anarchism, nihilism,** syndicalism *and* anarcho-syndicalism *and* criminal syndicalism <old>; extreme rightism, radical rightism, know-nothingism; extreme right, extreme right wing; social Darwinism; laissez-faireism 329.1; **royalism, monarchism;** Toryism, Bourbonism

5 **communism, Bolshevism, Marxism,** Marxism-Leninism, Leninism, Trotskyism, Stalinism, Maoism, Titoism, Castroism, revisionism; Marxian socialism; dialectical materialism; democratic centralism; dictatorship of the proletariat; **Communist Party;** Communist International, Comintern; Communist Information Bureau, Cominform; iron curtain 1012.5

6 **socialism,** collective ownership, collectivization, public ownership; **collectivism;** creeping socialism; state socialism, *Staatsozialismus* <Ger>; guild socialism; Fabian socialism, Fabianism; utopian socialism; Marxian socialism; Marxism 611.5; phalansterism; Owenism; Saint-Simonianism, Saint-Simonism; **nationalization**

7 **welfarism,** welfare statism; womb-to-tomb security, cradle-to-grave security; social welfare; social security, social insurance; old-age and survivors insurance; unemployment compensation, unemployment insurance; workmen's compensation, workmen's compensation insurance; health insurance, Medicare, Medicaid, state medicine, **socialized medicine;** sickness insurance; public assistance, **welfare, relief,** welfare payments, aid to dependent children *or* ADC, old-age assistance, aid to the blind, aid to the permanently and totally disabled; guaranteed income, guaranteed annual income; welfare state; welfare capitalism

8 **capitalism,** capitalistic system, **free enterprise,** private enterprise, free-enterprise economy, free-enterprise system, free economy; finance capitalism; *laissez-faire* <Fr>, laissez-faireism; private sector; private ownership; state capitalism; **individualism,** rugged individualism

9 **conservative,** conservatist, **rightist, rightwinger;** dry <Brit nf>, "the leftover progressive of an earlier generation" —Edmund Fuller; standpat *and* standpatter <nf>; hard hat; social Darwinist; ultraconservative, arch-conservative, extreme right-winger, **reactionary,** reactionarist, reactionist, diehard; **royalist, monarchist,** Bourbon, Tory, imperialist; **right, right wing; radical right**

10 **moderate,** moderatist, moderationist, **centrist,** middle-of-the-roader <nf>; independent; center

11 **liberal,** liberalist, wet <Brit nf>, **progressive,** progressivist, **leftist, left-winger;** welfare stater; Lib-Lab <Brit nf>; **left**

12 **radical, extremist,** ultra, ultraist; **revolutionary,** revolutionist; subversive; extreme left-winger, left-wing extremist, **red** <nf>, Bolshevik; yippie; Jacobin, sansculotte; **anarchist,** nihilist; mild radical, parlor Bolshevik <nf>, pink *and* parlor pink *and* pinko <nf>; lunatic fringe

13 **Communist,** Bolshevist; Bolshevik, **Red** *and* commie *and* bolshie <nf>; Marxist, Leninist, Marxist-Leninist, Trotskyite *or* Trotskyist, Stalinist, Maoist, Titoist, Castroite, revisionist; card-carrying Communist, avowed Communist; fellow traveler, Communist sympathizer, comsymp <nf>

14 **socialist,** collectivist; social democrat; state socialist; Fabian, Fabian socialist; Marxist 611.13; utopian socialist; Fourierist, phalansterian; Saint-Simonian; Owenite

15 **capitalist;** coupon-clipper <nf>; rich man 618.7

VERBS 16 **politicize;** democratize, republicanize, socialize, communize; nationalize 476.7; deregulate, privatize, denationalize; radicalize

ADJS 17 **conservative, right-wing,** right of center, dry <Brit nf>; old-line, die-hard, unreconstructed, standpat <nf>, unprogressive, nonprogressive; ultraconservative, **reactionary,** reactionist

18 **moderate,** centrist, middle-of-the-road <nf>, independent

19 **liberal, liberalistic,** liberalist, wet <Brit nf>, bleeding-heart <nf>; **progressive,** progressivistic; **leftist, left-wing,** on the left, left of center

20 **radical, extreme, extremist,** extremistic, ultraist, ultraistic; revolutionary, revolutionist; subversive; ultraconservative 611.17; extreme left-wing, **red** <nf>; anarchistic, nihilistic, syndicalist *and* anarcho-syndicalist <old>; mildly radical, pink <nf>

21 **Communist, communistic,** Bolshevik, Bolshevist, commie *and* bolshie *and* Red <nf>; **Marxist,** Leninist, Marxist-Leninist, Trotskyite *or* Trotskyist, Stalinist, Maoist, Titoist, Castroite; revisionist

22 **socialist, socialistic,** collectivistic; social-democratic; Fabian; Fourieristic, phalansterian; Saint-Simonian

23 **capitalist, capitalistic,** bourgeois, individualistic, nonsocialistic, free-enterprise, private-enterprise

612 GOVERNMENT

NOUNS 1 **government,** governance, **discipline, regulation; direction, management, administration,** dispensation, disposition, oversight, **supervision** 573.2; **regime,** regimen; **rule, sway, sovereignty, reign,** regnancy, regency; empire, empery, dominion, dynasty, regime, regimen; social order, civil government, political government, political system; form *or* system of government, political organization, polity, political party; local government, state government, national government, world government, international government

2 **control, mastery, mastership, command, power, jurisdiction, dominion, domination; hold, grasp,** grip, gripe, command; hand, hands, iron hand, clutches; talons, claws; helm, reins of government

3 **the government, the authorities; the powers that be,** national government, central government, the Establishment; the corridors of power, government circles; Uncle Sam, Washington; John Bull, the Crown, His *or* Her Majesty's Government, Whitehall

4 <kinds of government> **federal government,** federation, federalism; **constitutional government,** majority rule; **republic,** commonwealth; **democracy,** representative government, representative democracy, direct *or* pure democracy, town-meeting democracy; "government of the people, by the people, for the people"—Lincoln; **parliamentary government;** social democracy, welfare state; mob rule, tyranny of the majority, mobocracy <nf>, ochlocracy; minority government; pantisocracy; aristocracy, hierarchy, oligarchy, elitism, plutocracy, minority rule; feudal system; monarchy, monarchical government, absolute monarchy, constitutional monarchy, limited monarchy, kingship, queenship; dictatorship, tyranny, autocracy, autarchy; dyarchy, duarchy, duumvirate; triarchy, triumvirate; **totalitarian government** *or* regime, totalitarianism, police state, despotism; **fascism, communism;** stratocracy, demagogy, **military government,** militarism, garrison state; martial law, rule of the sword; regency; hierocracy, theocracy, thearchy; patriarchy, patriarchate; gerontocracy; technocracy, meritocracy;

autonomy, **self-government,** autarchy, self-rule, self-determination, home rule; heteronomy, dominion rule, colonial government, colonialism, neocolonialism; provisional government; coalition government; tribalism, tribal system, clan system; isocracy, egalitarianism; caretaker government, interregnum, provisional government, coalition government

5 <government by women> matriarchy, matriarchate, gynarchy, gynocracy, gynecocracy; petticoat government

6 **supranational government,** supergovernment, **world government,** World Federalism; League of Nations, United Nations 614

7 <principles of government> democratism, power-sharing, republicanism; constitutionalism, rule of law, parliamentarism, parliamentarianism; monarchism, royalism; feudalism, feudality; imperialism; fascism, neofascism, Nazism, national socialism; statism, governmentalism; collectivism, communism 611.5, socialism 611.6; federalism; centralism; pluralism; politico-economic principles 611; glasnost

8 **absolutism, dictatorship, despotism,** tyranny, autocracy, autarchy, monarchy, absolute monarchy; **authoritarianism;** totalitarianism; one-man rule, one-party rule; Caesarism, Stalinism, kaiserism, czarism; benevolent despotism, paternalism

9 **despotism, tyranny, fascism,** domineering, domination, oppression; heavy hand, high hand, iron hand, iron heel *or* boot; big stick, *argumentum baculinum* <L>; **terrorism,** reign of terror; thought control

10 **officialism, bureaucracy;** beadledom, bumbledom; **red-tapeism** *and* red-tapery *and* **red tape** <nf>; federalese, official jargon 609.37

VERBS 11 **govern, regulate; wield authority** 417.13; **command,** officer, captain, **head, lead,** be master, be at the head of, **preside over,** chair; **direct, manage, supervise, administer,** administrate 573.11; discipline; stand over

12 **control, hold in hand,** have in one's power, be in power, have power, gain a hold upon; hold the reins, hold the helm, call the shots *or* tune *and* be in the driver's seat *or* saddle <nf>; direct, have control of, **have under control, have in hand** *or* **well in hand;** be master of the situation, have it all one's own way, have the game in one's own hands, hold all the aces <nf>; pull the strings *or* wires

13 **rule, sway,** hold sway, **reign,** bear reign, have the sway, wield the scepter, wear the crown, sit on the throne; rule over, overrule

14 dominate, predominate, preponderate, prevail; **have the ascendancy, have the upper** *or* **whip hand,** get under control, have on the hip <old>; **master,** have the mastery of; bestride; dictate, lay down the law; **rule the roost** *and* wear the pants *and* crack the whip *and* ride herd <nf>; take the lead, play first fiddle; **lead by the nose, twist** *or* **turn around one's little finger; keep under one's thumb,** bend to one's will

15 domineer, domineer over, **lord it over;** browbeat, order around, henpeck <nf>, intimidate, bully, cow, bulldoze <nf>, walk over, walk all over; castrate, unman; daunt, terrorize; **tyrannize,** tyrannize over, push *or* kick around <nf>, despotize; **grind,** grind down, break, **oppress,** suppress, repress, weigh *or* press heavy on; keep under, keep down, beat down, clamp down on <nf>; overbear, overmaster, overawe; override, ride over, trample *or* stamp *or* tread upon, trample *or* tread down, **trample** *or* **tread underfoot,** keep down, crush under an iron heel, **ride roughshod over;** hold *or* keep a tight hand upon, rule with a rod of iron, rule with an iron hand *or* fist; enslave, subjugate 432.8; compel, coerce 424.7

ADJS **16 governmental,** gubernatorial; **political, civil,** civic; **official,** bureaucratic, administrative; democratic, republican, fascist, fascistic, oligarchal, oligarchic, oligarchical, aristocratic, aristocratical, theocratic, **federal,** federalist, federalistic, **constitutional,** parliamentary, parliamentarian; monarchic *or* monarchical, monarchial, monarchal <old>; autocratic, monocratic, absolute; **authoritarian;** despotic, **dictatorial; totalitarian;** pluralistic; paternalistic, patriarchal, patriarchic, patriarchical; matriarchal, matriarchic, matriarchical; heteronomous; autonomous, self-governing, self-ruling, autarchic; executive, presidential; gubernatorial

17 governing, controlling, regulating, regulative, regulatory, **commanding; ruling, reigning, sovereign,** regnant, regnal, titular; **master, chief,** general, **boss, head; dominant, predominant,** predominate, preponderant, preponderate, prepotent, prepollent, prevalent, **leading, paramount, supreme,** number one <nf>, hegemonic, hegemonistic; ascendant, in the ascendant, in ascendancy; at the head, in chief; in charge 417.21

18 executive, administrative, ministerial; official, bureaucratic; **supervisory, directing, managing** 573.12

ADVS **19 under control, in hand,** well in hand; **in one's power,** under one's control

WORD ELEMENTS **20** -archy, -cracy, -ocracy

613 LEGISLATURE, GOVERNMENT ORGANIZATION

NOUNS **1 legislature** <see list>, legislative body; **parliament, congress, assembly,** general assembly, house of assembly, legislative assembly, **national assembly, chamber of deputies,** federal assembly, diet, soviet, court; unicameral legislature, bicameral legislature; legislative chamber, **upper chamber** *or* **house** <see list>, **lower chamber** *or* **house** <see list>; state legislature, state assembly; provincial legislature, provincial parliament; city council, city board, board of aldermen, common council, commission; representative town meeting, town meeting

2 United States Government, Federal Government; Cabinet <see list>; Executive Department, executive branch; government agency; legislature; Congress, Senate, Upper House, Senate committee; House of Representatives, House, Lower House, House of Representatives committee; Supreme Court

3 cabinet, ministry, British cabinet <see list>, **council,** advisory council, council of state, privy council, divan; shadow cabinet; kitchen cabinet, camarilla

4 capitol, statehouse; courthouse; city hall

5 legislation, lawmaking, legislature <old>; **enactment,** enaction, constitution, passage, passing; **resolution,** concurrent resolution, joint resolution; act 673.3

6 <legislative procedure> introduction, first reading, committee consideration, tabling, filing, second reading, deliberation, **debate,** third reading, **vote,** division, roll call; **filibustering,** filibuster, talkathon <nf>; cloture 857.5; **logrolling;** steamroller methods; guillotine <Brit>

7 veto, executive veto, absolute veto, qualified *or* limited veto, suspensive *or* suspensory veto, item veto, pocket veto; veto power; veto message; senatorial courtesy

8 referendum, constitutional referendum, statutory referendum, optional *or* facultative referendum, compulsory *or* mandatory referendum; **mandate; plebiscite,** plebiscitum; initiative, direct initiative, indirect initiative; recall

9 bill, omnibus bill, hold-up bill, companion bills amendment; **clause, proviso;** enacting clause, dragnet clause, escalator clause, saving clause; **rider;** joker <nf>; **calendar, motion;** question, previous question, privileged question

VERBS **10 legislate,** make *or* enact laws, **enact, pass,** constitute, ordain, put in force; **put through, jam** *or* **steamroller** *or* **railroad through** <nf>, lobby through; table, pigeonhole; take the floor, get the floor, have the floor; yield the floor; **filibuster; logroll,** roll logs; **veto, pocket, kill; decree** 420.8

ADJS **11 legislative,** legislatorial, lawmaking; deliberative; **parliamentary, congressional;** senatorial; bicameral, unicameral

12 legislatures

Althing <Iceland>
bicameral legislature <Bosnia and Herzegovina, Haiti, Kazakhstan, Russia>
Assembly of the Republic <Portugal>
Chamber of Deputies <Luxembourg>
Congress <Argentina, Colombia, Liberia, Mexico, Philippines, Uruguay, US, Venezuela>
Cortes <Spain>
Diet <Japan>
Eduskunta <Finland>
Federal Assembly <Switzerland, Yugoslavia>
Federal Parliament <Australia>
Folketing <Denmark>
Grand National Assembly <Turkey>
Great and General Council <San Marino>
Great People's Khural <Mongolia>
House of Assembly <Bahamas, Kiribati>
House of Representatives <Cyprus, Gambia, Malta, Sierra Leone>
Knesset <Israel>
Landtag <Liechtenstein>
Legislative Assembly <Costa Rica, Tonga>
National Assembly <Benin, Bhutan, Bulgaria, Cameroon, Cuba, El Salvador, Gabon, Guyana, Haiti, Hungary, Ivory Coast, Kenya, Kuwait, Macedonia, Malawi, Mauritius, Morocco, Nicaragua, Pakistan, Panama, Rwanda, Senegal, South Korea, Sri Lanka, Suriname, Tanzania, Tunisia, Uganda, Zambia>

National Congress <Bolivia, Brazil, Chile, Ecuador, Honduras, Micronesia>
National Council <Monaco>
Oireachtas <Ireland>
Parliament <Afghanistan, Algeria, Andorra, Austria, Azerbaijan, Barbados, Belgium, Botswana, Canada, Czech Republic, Estonia, Ethiopia, Fiji, France, Germany, Ghana, Greece, Guinea, India, Italy, Jamaica, Jordan, Malaysia, Maldives, Mali, Moldova, Nauru, Nepal, Netherlands, New Zealand, Palau, Papua New Guinea, Romania, Sierra Leone, Singapore, Slovakia, Slovenia, South Africa, Swaziland, Taiwan, Tajikistan, Trinidad and Tobago, Turkmenistan, Tuvalu, Ukraine, United Kingdom, Yemen, Zimbabwe>
People's Assembly <Albania, Egypt, Seychelles>
People's Consultative Assembly <Indonesia>
People's Council <Syria>
Riksdag <Sweden>
Sejm <Poland>
Storting <Norway>
Supreme Assembly <Uzbekistan>
Supreme Military Council <Equatorial Guinea>
Supreme People's Assembly <North Korea>
unicameral legislature <Comoros, Djibouti, Dominican Republic, Georgia, Guatemala, Guinea-Bissau, Namibia, Peru, United Arab Emirates, Vanuatu>

13 upper houses

Bundesrat <Austria, Germany>
Federation Council <Russia>

House of Councilors <Japan>
House of Lords <United Kingdom>
Lagting <Norway>
Rajya Sabha <India>
Standerat <Switzerland>
Senate <Australia, Barbados, Belgium, Brazil, Canada, Chile, Colombia, Czech Republic, Dominican Republic, Ecuador, Ethiopia, Fiji, France, Iran, Ireland, Italy, Jamaica, Liberia, Malagasy Republic, Malaysia, Mexico, Nicaragua, Paraguay, Philippines, Rhodesia, South Africa, Swaziland, Trinidad and Tobago, US, Venezuela>

14 lower houses

Bundestag <Germany>
Chamber of Deputies <Brazil, Chile, Czech Republic, Dominican Republic, Ecuador, Ethiopia, Italy, Jordan, Mexico, Nicaragua, Paraguay, Venezuela>
Chamber of Representatives <Belgium, Colombia>
Dáil Eireann <Ireland>
House of Assembly <Barbados, Rhodesia, South Africa, Swaziland>

House of Commons <Canada, United Kingdom>
House of Representatives <Australia, Fiji, Jamaica, Japan, Liberia, Malaysia, Philippines, US>
Lok Sabha <India>
National Assembly <France, Laos, Malagasy Republic, Portugal, Turkey>
Nationalrat <Austria>
Odelsting <Norway>
State Duma <Russia>

15 US Cabinet

Attorney General
Secretary of Agriculture
Secretary of Commerce
Secretary of Defense
Secretary of Education
Secretary of Energy
Secretary of Health and Human Services

Secretary of Housing and Urban Development
Secretary of Labor
Secretary of State
Secretary of the Interior
Secretary of the Treasury
Secretary of Transportation
Secretary of Veterans' Affairs

16 British Cabinet and Ministries

Chancellor of the Exchequer
Chief Secretary to the Treasury
Deputy Prime Minister
Chancellor of the Duchy of Lancaster
First Lord of the Admiralty
First Lord of the Treasury
First Secretary of State
Home Secretary <Home Office>
Lord Chancellor
Lord President of the Council
Lord Privy Seal
Minister of Agriculture, Fisheries, and Food
Minister of Defence
Minister of Housing and Local Government

Minister of Public Service and Science
Minister of State <Cabinet Office>
Minister of Technology
Minister of Transport
Paymaster-General
President of the Board of Education
President of the Board of Trade
Prime Minister
Secretary of State for Culture, Media and Sport
Secretary of State for Defence
Secretary of State for Economic Affairs
Secretary of State for Education and Science

Secretary of State for
Education and
Employment
Secretary of State for
Environment
Secretary of State for
Foreign Affairs
Secretary of State for
Foreign and Common-
wealth Affairs
Secretary of State for
Health

Secretary of State for
National Heritage
Secretary of State for
Northern Ireland
Secretary of State for
Scotland
Secretary of State for
Social Security
Secretary of State for
Trade and Industry
Secretary of State for
Wales

614 UNITED NATIONS, INTERNATIONAL ORGANIZATIONS

NOUNS **1 United Nations** or **UN;** League of Nations
 2 <United Nations organs> Secretariat; General
Assembly; Security Council; Trusteeship Council;
International Court of Justice; **United Nations
agency** <see list>, Economic and Social Council or
ECOSOC, ECOSOC commission
 3 international organization, non-UN international
organization
 4 United Nations agencies

Food and Agricultural
Organization or FAO
General Agreement on
Tariffs and Trade or GATT
Industrial Development
Organization or UNIDO
International Atomic
Energy Agency or IAEA
International Civil Aviation
Organization or ICAO
International Development
Association or IDA
International Finance
Corporation or IFO
International Fund for
Agricultural Develop-
ment or IFAD
International Labor
Organization or ILO
International Maritime
Organization or IMO
International Monetary
Fund or the Fund
International Telecommu-
nication Union or ITU

United Nations Children's
Fund or UNICEF
United Nations
Educational,
Scientific and Cultural
Organization or
UNESCO
United Nations Relief and
Works Agency or
UNRWA
Universal Postal Union or
UPU
World Bank or Interna-
tional Bank for
Reconstruction and
Development
World Health Organization
or WHO
World Intellectual
Property Organization
or WIPO
World Meteorological
Organization or WMO
World Trade Organization
or WTO

615 COMMISSION

NOUNS **1 commission,** commissioning, **delegation,**
devolution, devolvement, vesting, investing,
investment, investiture; **deputation;** commitment,
entrusting, entrustment, **assignment,**
consignment, consignation; **errand, task, office;**

care, cure, **responsibility,** purview, jurisdiction;
mission, legation, embassy; **authority** 417;
authorization, empowerment, power to act, full
power, plenipotentiary power, vicarious or
delegated authority; **warrant,** license, **mandate,
charge, trust,** brevet, exequatur; **agency,**
agentship, factorship; regency, regentship;
lieutenancy; trusteeship, executorship; **proxy,**
procuration, **power of attorney**
 2 **appointment, assignment,** designation,
nomination, naming, selection, tabbing <nf>;
ordainment, ordination; posting, transferral
 3 **installation,** installment, **instatement,** induction,
placement, **inauguration,** investiture, taking
office; **accession,** accedence; coronation,
crowning, enthronement
 4 **engagement, employment, hiring, appointment,**
taking on <nf>, recruitment, recruiting; executive
recruiting, executive search; retaining,
retainment, briefing <Brit>; preengagement,
bespeaking; reservation, booking; exercise,
function
 5 executive search agency or firm; executive recruiter,
executive recruitment consultant, executive
development specialist; **headhunter** and body
snatcher and flesh peddler and talent scout <nf>
 6 **rental, rent; lease,** let <Brit>; hire, hiring;
sublease, subrent; **charter,** bareboat charter;
lend-lease
 7 **enlistment, enrollment; conscription, draft,
drafting, induction,** impressment, press; call,
draft call, call-up, summons, call to the colors,
letter from Uncle Sam <nf>; **recruitment,**
recruiting; **muster,** mustering, mustering in, levy,
levying; mobilization; selective service,
compulsory military service
 8 indenture, binding over; **apprenticeship**
 9 **assignee, appointee,** selectee, nominee, candidate;
licensee, licentiate; deputy, agent 576
VERBS **10 commission, authorize,** empower,
accredit; **delegate,** devolute, devolve, devolve upon,
vest, invest; depute, **deputize; assign,** consign,
commit, charge, entrust, give in charge; license,
charter, warrant; detail, detach, post, transfer,
send out, mission, send on a mission
 11 appoint, assign, designate, **nominate,** name,
select, tab <nf>, elect; **ordain,** ordinate <old>
 12 install, instate, induct, **inaugurate,** invest, put in,
place, **place in office;** chair; crown, throne,
enthrone, anoint
 13 be instated, take office, accede; take or mount the
throne; attain to
 14 employ, hire, give a job to, take into employment,
take into one's service, take on <nf>, recruit,
headhunt <nf>, **engage,** sign up or on <nf>; retain,

brief <Brit>; bespeak, preengage; sign up for <nf>, **reserve,** book

15 **rent, lease, let** <Brit>, hire, job, **charter; sublease, sublet,** underlet

16 **rent out, rent; lease,** lease out; let *and* let off *and* let out <Brit>; **hire out,** hire; charter; **sublease, sublet,** underlet; lend-lease, lease-lend; lease-back; farm, farm out; job

17 **enlist,** list <old>, **enroll, sign up** *or* **on** <nf>; **conscript, draft, induct,** press, impress, commandeer; detach, detach for service; summon, call up, call to the colors; **mobilize,** call to active duty; **recruit, muster,** levy, raise, muster in; join 617.14

18 indenture, article, bind, bind over; **apprentice**

ADJS 19 **commissioned, authorized, accredited;** delegated, deputized, appointed; devolutionary

20 **employed, hired, hireling, paid,** mercenary; rented, leased, let <Brit>; sublet, underlet, subleased; chartered

21 **indentured,** articled, bound over; **apprenticed, apprentice,** prentice *or* 'prentice

ADVS 22 **for hire,** for rent, to let, to lease

616 ASSOCIATE

NOUNS 1 **associate, confederate,** consociate, **colleague,** fellow member, **companion, fellow,** bedfellow, **crony,** consort, cohort, compeer, compatriot, confrere, brother, brother-in-arms, **ally,** adjunct, coadjutor; comrade in arms, **comrade** 588.3

2 **partner,** pardner *or* pard <nf>, copartner, side partner, buddy <nf>, **sidekick** *and* sidekicker <nf>; **mate; business partner,** nominal *or* holding-out *or* ostensible *or* quasi partner, general partner, special partner, silent partner, secret partner, dormant *or* sleeping partner

3 **accomplice,** cohort, confederate, fellow conspirator, coconspirator, partner *or* accomplice in crime; *particeps criminis* and *socius criminis* <L>; **accessory,** accessory before the fact, accessory after the fact; **abettor**

4 **collaborator,** cooperator; coauthor; **collaborationist;** quisling, partner in crime

5 **co-worker, workfellow, workmate, fellow worker, buddy** <nf>, butty <Brit nf>; **teammate, yokefellow,** yokemate; benchfellow, shopmate

6 **assistant, helper,** auxiliary, aider, **aid,** aide, paraprofessional; **help, helpmate, helpmeet;** deputy, **agent** 576; **attendant, second,** acolyte; best man, groomsman, paranymph; **servant, employee** 577; adjutant, aide-de-camp; lieutenant, executive officer; coadjutant, coadjutor, coadjutress, coadjutrix; sidesman <Brit>; supporting actor *or*

player; supporting instrumentalist, sideman; suffragan; special assistant

7 **right-hand man** *or* **woman, right hand,** strong right hand *or* arm, **man** *or* **gal Friday,** fidus Achates, second self, alter ego, confidant; Boswell

8 **follower, disciple,** adherent, votary; **man, henchman,** camp follower, hanger-on, devotee, satellite, creature, lackey, flunky, stooge <nf>, jackal, minion, myrmidon, yes-man <nf>, sycophant 138.3; goon <nf>; thug 593.3; puppet, cat's-paw; dummy, figurehead

9 **supporter, upholder,** maintainer, sustainer; support, **mainstay, standby** <nf>, stalwart, reliance, dependence; **abettor, seconder,** second; endorser, sponsor; **backer, promoter,** angel <nf>, rabbi <nf>; **patron,** Maecenas; friend at *or* in court; **champion,** defender, apologist, **advocate,** exponent, **protagonist; well-wisher,** favorer, encourager, sympathizer; **partisan,** sider <old>, sectary, votary; **fan** *and* buff <nf>, aficionado, **admirer,** lover

617 ASSOCIATION

NOUNS 1 **association, society,** body, organization; **alliance, coalition, league, union;** council; **bloc,** axis; **partnership; federation, confederation,** confederacy; grouping, assemblage 770; **combination,** combine; *Bund* and *Verein* <Ger>; **unholy alliance, gang** *and* **ring** *and* mob <nf>; machine, **political machine;** economic community, common market, free trade area, customs union; credit union; cooperative, cooperative society, consumer cooperative, Rochdale cooperative; syndicate, guild; college, **group,** corps, band 770.3; labor union 727

2 **community, society, commonwealth,** social system; body; **kinship group, clan,** sept <Scot>, moiety, clan, tribe, totemic *or* totemistic group, phyle, phratry *or* phratria, gens, caste, subcaste, endogamous group; **family,** extended family, nuclear family, binuclear family; order, **class, social class** 607.1, economic class; colony, settlement; **commune,** ashram

3 **fellowship,** sodality; **society,** guild, order; **brotherhood, fraternity,** confraternity, confrerie, fraternal order *or* society; **sisterhood, sorority; club,** country club, lodge; peer group; secret society, **cabal**

4 **party, interest, camp, side;** interest group, lobby, pressure group, ethnic group; minority group, vocal minority; political action committee *or* PAC; silent majority; **faction,** division, **sect,** wing, **caucus,** splinter, splinter group, breakaway group, offshoot; **political party** 609.24

5 **school, sect,** class, order; **denomination, communion,** confession, faith, church; **persuasion, ism; disciples, followers,** adherents

6 **clique, coterie, set, circle,** ring, junto, junta, cabal, camarilla, **clan,** group, grouping, cult; **crew** *and* mob *and* **crowd** *and* **bunch** *and* outfit <nf>; cell; cadre, cohort, inner circle; closed *or* charmed circle; ingroup, in-crowd, popular crowd, we-group; elite, elite group; leadership group; **old-boy network;** peer group, age group

7 **team, outfit,** squad, string, corps; eleven, nine, eight, five, etc; **crew,** rowing crew; varsity, first team, first string; bench, reserves, second team, second string, third string; platoon, troupe; complement; **cast,** company

8 **organization,** establishment, **foundation, institution, institute**

9 **company, firm, business firm, concern, house,** *compagnie* <Fr>, *compañía* <Sp>, *Aktiengesellschaft* <Ger>, *aktiebolag* <Swed>; **business, industry, enterprise,** business establishment, commercial enterprise; **trust, syndicate, cartel,** combine, pool, consortium, plunderbund <nf>; combination in restraint of trade; chamber of commerce, junior chamber of commerce; trade association

10 **branch, organ, division,** wing, arm, offshoot, **affiliate; chapter,** lodge, post; chapel; **local;** branch office; virtual office

11 **member,** affiliate, belonger, insider, initiate, one of us, cardholder, card-carrier, card-carrying member; **enrollee,** enlistee; **associate,** socius, **fellow;** brother, sister; comrade; honorary member; life member; member in good standing, dues-paying member; charter member; clubman, clubwoman, clubber <nf>; fraternity man, fraternity *or* frat brother, Greek <nf>, sorority woman; sorority sister, guildsman; committeeman; conventionist, conventioner, conventioneer; joiner <nf>; pledge

12 **membership,** members, associates, affiliates, body of affiliates, constituency

13 **partisanism,** partisanship, **partiality; factionalism, sectionalism,** faction; sectarianism, denominationalism; **cliquism,** cliquishness, cliqueyness; **clannishness,** clanship; exclusiveness, exclusivity; ethnocentricity; party spirit, *esprit de corps* <Fr>; the old college spirit

VERBS 14 join, join up <nf>, **enter, go into,** come into, get into, make oneself part of, swell the ranks of; **enlist, enroll, affiliate, sign up** *or* **on** <nf>, take up membership, take out membership; inscribe oneself, put oneself down; associate oneself with, affiliate with, league with, team *or* team up with;

sneak in, creep in, insinuate oneself into; **combine, associate** 805.4

15 **belong,** hold membership, be a member, be on the rolls, be inscribed, subscribe, hold *or* carry a card, be in <nf>

ADJS 16 associated, corporate, incorporated; **combined** 805.5; non-profit-making, non-profit, not-for-profit

17 **associational, social, society, communal;** organizational; coalitional; sociable

18 **cliquish,** cliquey, **clannish;** ethnocentric; exclusive

19 **partisan,** party; **partial,** interested; **factional, sectional,** sectarian, sectary, denominational

ADVS 20 in association, conjointly 450.6

618 WEALTH

NOUNS 1 wealth, riches, opulence *or* opulency 991.2, **luxuriousness** 501.5; richness, wealthiness; **prosperity,** prosperousness, **affluence,** comfortable *or* easy circumstances, independence; **money,** lucre, pelf, gold, mammon; **substance, property, possessions,** material wealth; **assets** 728.14; **fortune, treasure,** handsome fortune; full *or* heavy *or* well-lined *or* bottomless *or* fat *or* bulging purse, deep pockets <nf>; *embarras de richesses* <Fr>, money to burn <nf>; high income, six-figure income; high tax bracket, upper bracket; old money, new money

2 **large sum,** good sum, tidy sum *and* **pretty penny, king's ransom;** heaps of gold; thousands, millions, cool million, billion, etc

3 <nf terms> **bundle, big bucks,** megabucks, gigabucks, big money, serious money, gobs, heaps, heavy lettuce, heavy jack, heavy money, important money, pot, potful, power, mint, barrel, raft, load, **loads,** pile, wad, wads, nice hunk of change, packet <Brit>, long green, deep pockets

4 <rich source> **mine,** mine of wealth, **gold mine,** bonanza, luau <nf>, lode, rich lode, mother lode, pot of gold, Eldorado, Golconda, Seven Cities of Cibola; gravy train <nf>; rich uncle; golden goose; cash cow <nf>

5 **the golden touch,** Midas touch; philosophers' stone; Pactolus

6 **the rich, the wealthy,** the well to do, the well off, the haves <nf>, privileged class; jet set, glitterati, country-club set, beau monde; **plutocracy,** timocracy

7 **rich man** *or* **woman,** wealthy man *or* woman, warm man *or* woman <Brit nf>, **moneyed man** *or* **woman,** man *or* woman of wealth, **man** *or* **woman of means** *or* **substance,** fat cat <nf>, richling, deep pocket *and* moneybags *and* Mr Moneybags <nf>, tycoon, magnate, baron, Daddy Warbucks

<Harold Gray>, coupon-clipper, **nabob; capitalist, plutocrat,** bloated plutocrat; **millionaire,** multimillionaire, megamillionaire, millionairess, multibillionaire, multimillionairess, billionaire; parvenu; vulgarian; nouveau riche

8 Croesus, Midas, Plutus, Timon of Athens; Rockefeller, Vanderbilt, Whitney, DuPont, Ford, Getty, Rothschild, Onassis, Hughes, Hunt, Trump; Sergey Brin and Larry Page, Bill Gates, Warren Buffett

VERBS 9 **enrich, richen;** endow

10 **grow rich, get rich,** fill or line one's pockets, feather one's nest, **make or coin money,** have a gold mine, have the golden touch, **make a fortune,** make one's pile <nf>; **strike it rich;** come into money; make good, get on in the world, do all right by oneself and rake it in <nf>; hit the jackpot, clean up <nf>

11 **have money,** command money, **be loaded** and have deep pockets <nf>, have the wherewithal, have means, have independent means; **afford,** well afford

12 **live well,** live high, live high on the hog <nf>, **live in clover,** live the life of Riley, roll or wallow in wealth, roll or live in the lap of luxury; have all the money in the world, have a mint, have money to burn <nf>

13 worship mammon, worship the golden calf, worship the almighty dollar

ADJS 14 **wealthy, rich, affluent,** affluential, **moneyed** or **monied,** in funds or cash, **well-to-do,** well-to-do in the world, **well-off, well-situated, prosperous,** comfortable, provided for, well provided for, fat, **flush,** flush with or of money, abounding in riches, worth a great deal, in clover, frightfully rich, rich as Croesus; independent, independently rich, independently wealthy; **luxurious** 501.21; **opulent** 991.7; privileged, born with a silver spoon in one's mouth; higher-income, upper-income, well-paid

15 <nf terms> **loaded, well-heeled, filthy rich,** warm <Brit>, flush, in the money or dough or chips or gravy, well-fixed, worth a bundle, made of money, **rolling in money,** rolling or wallowing in it, disgustingly rich, big-rich, rich-rich, oofy, lousy rich, upscale

619 POVERTY

NOUNS 1 **poverty,** poorness, impecuniousness, impecuniosity; **straits,** dire straits, difficulties, **hardship** 1011.1; financial distress or embarrassment, **embarrassed** or **reduced** or **straitened circumstances,** tight squeeze, hard pinch, crunch <nf>, cash or credit or budget crunch

<nf>; cash-flow shortage, cash-flow blowout <nf>; slender or narrow means, insolvency, light purse; unprosperousness; broken fortune; genteel poverty; vows of poverty, voluntary poverty

2 **indigence, penury, pennilessness,** penuriousness, moneylessness; **pauperism,** pauperization, **impoverishment,** grinding or crushing poverty, chronic pauperism; subsistence level, poverty line; **beggary,** beggarliness, mendicancy; **destitution, privation, deprivation; neediness, want,** need, lack, pinch, gripe, necessity, dire necessity, disadvantagedness, necessitousness, **homelessness; hand-to-mouth existence,** bare subsistence, wolf at the door, bare cupboard, empty purse or pocket

3 **the poor, the needy,** the have-nots <nf>, the down-and-out, the disadvantaged, the underprivileged, the distressed, the underclass; the urban poor, ghetto-dwellers, barrio-dwellers; welfare rolls, welfare clients, welfare families; the homeless, the ranks of the homeless, bag people; the other America; the forgotten man; depressed population, depressed area, chronic poverty area; underdeveloped nation, Third World, developing world; cardboard city

4 **poor person,** poorling, poor devil, down-and-out or down-and-outer, **pauper,** indigent, penniless man, hard case, starveling; homeless person, bag woman or lady, bag person, shopping-bag lady, shopping-cart woman or lady, street person, skell <nf>; hobo, bum; **beggar** 440.8; welfare client; almsman, almswoman, charity case, casual; bankrupt 625.4

VERBS 5 **be poor,** be hard up <nf>, find it hard going, have seen better days, be on one's uppers, be pinched or strapped, **be in want,** want, need, lack; **starve,** not know where one's next meal is coming from, **live from hand to mouth,** eke out or squeeze out a living; **not have a penny or sou,** not have a penny to bless oneself with, not have one dollar to rub against another; sing for one's supper; go on welfare, use food stamps

6 **impoverish,** reduce, **pauperize, beggar;** eat out of house and home; cut off without a penny; **bankrupt** 625.8

ADJS 7 **poor, ill off,** badly or poorly off, hard up <nf>, downscale, impecunious, **unmoneyed; unprosperous;** reduced, in reduced circumstances; **straitened, in straitened circumstances,** narrow, in narrow circumstances, feeling the pinch, strapped, **financially embarrassed** or distressed, **pinched,** squeezed, put to one's shifts or last shifts, at the end of one's rope, on the edge or ragged edge <nf>, down to bedrock, in Queer Street; short,

short of money or **funds** or **cash,** out-of-pocket; unable to make ends meet, unable to keep the wolf from the door; poor as a church mouse; house-poor; land-poor

8 **indigent, poverty-stricken; needy,** necessitous, **in need, in want,** disadvantaged, deprived, underprivileged; **beggared,** beggarly, mendicant; **impoverished, pauperized,** starveling; ghettoized; bereft, bereaved; stripped, fleeced; **down at heels,** down at the heel, on or down on one's uppers, out at the heels, out at elbows, in rags; on welfare, on relief, on the bread line, on the dole <Brit>

9 **destitute, down-and-out,** in the gutter; **penniless,** moneyless, fortuneless, out of funds, **without a sou,** without a penny to bless oneself with, without one dollar to rub against another; insolvent, in the red, **bankrupt** 625.11; homeless; propertyless, landless

10 <nf terms> **broke, dead broke,** bust, busted, dirt poor, **flat, flat broke,** flat on one's ass, flat-ass, down for the count, belly up, stone or stony broke, stony, **strapped,** skint <Brit>, hurting, beat, oofless; down to one's last penny or cent, cleaned out, tapped out, Tap City, oofless, wasted, wiped out, without a pot to piss in

620 LENDING

NOUNS 1 **lending, loaning;** moneylending, lending at interest; advance, advancing, advancement; **usury,** loan-sharking and shylocking <nf>; pawnbroking, hocking; **interest,** interest rate, lending rate, the price of money; points, mortgage points

2 **loan,** the lend <nf>, **advance,** accommodation; lending on security; lend-lease

3 **lender, loaner;** loan officer; commercial banker; **moneylender,** moneymonger; money broker; banker 729.11; **usurer,** shylock and loan shark <nf>; **pawnbroker;** uncle <nf>; mortgagee, mortgage holder; creditor; financier

4 **lending institution,** savings and loan association or thrift or thrift institution or savings institution; savings and loan or thrift industry; building society <Brit>; finance company or corporation, loan office, mortgage company; commercial bank, **bank** 729.13; **credit union; pawnshop, pawnbroker,** pawnbrokery, **hock shop** <nf>, mont-de-piété <Fr>, sign of the three balls; World Bank

VERBS 5 **lend, loan, advance,** accommodate with; loan-shark <nf>; float or negotiate a loan; lend-lease, lease-lend; give credit

ADJS 6 **loaned, lent,** on loan, on credit

ADVS 7 **on loan,** on security; in advance

621 BORROWING

NOUNS 1 **borrowing,** money-raising; touching or hitting or hitting up <nf>; financing, mortgaging; installment buying, installment plan, hire purchase <Brit>; debt, debtor 623.4; debt counseling

2 **adoption, appropriation, taking,** deriving, **derivation, assumption; imitation,** simulation, copying, mocking; borrowed plumes; a leaf from someone else's book; adaptation; plagiarism, plagiary, pastiche, pasticcio; infringement, pirating; cribbing, lifting

VERBS 3 **borrow,** borrow the loan of, get on credit or trust, get on tick and get on the cuff <nf>; get a loan, float or negotiate a loan, go into the money market, **raise money; touch** and hit up and hit one for and put the arm or bite or touch on <nf>; run into debt 623.6; pawn 438.10

4 **adopt, appropriate,** take, take on, take over, assume, make use of, take a leaf from someone's book, derive from; **imitate,** simulate, copy, mock, steal one's stuff <nf>; plagiarize, steal; pirate, infringe, crib, lift; adapt, parody

622 FINANCIAL CREDIT

NOUNS 1 **credit, trust,** tick <nf>; borrowing power or capacity; commercial credit, cash credit, bank credit, book credit, tax credit, investment credit; credit line, line of credit; installment plan, installment credit, consumer credit, store credit, hire purchase plan <Brit>, never-never <Brit nf>; **credit standing,** standing, **credit rating,** rating, Dun and Bradstreet rating, solvency 729.7; credit squeeze, insolvency; credit risk; credit bureau or agency; credit insurance, credit life insurance; credit union, cooperative credit union

2 **account,** credit account, charge account; bank account, savings account, checking account; share account; bank balance; expense account; current or open account; installment plan

3 **credit instrument;** paper credit; **letter of credit,** lettre de créance <Fr>, circular note; credit slip, credit memorandum, deposit slip, certificate of deposit; share certificate; negotiable instrument 728.11; **credit card,** plastic <nf>, plastic money or credit, bank card, affinity card, custom credit card, gold card, platinum card, charge card, charge plate; debit card; smart card, supersmart card; phonecard; automated teller machine or ATM, cash machine

4 **creditor,** creditress; debtee; mortgagee, mortgage-holder; note-holder; credit man; bill collector, collection agent; loan shark; pawnbroker; dunner, dun

VERBS **5 credit, credit with; credit to one's account,** place to one's credit *or* account

6 give *or* **extend credit** *or* a line of credit; sell on credit, trust, entrust; give tick <nf>; carry, carry on one's books

7 receive credit, take credit, **charge,** charge to one's account, keep an account with, go on tick <nf>, buy on credit, buy on the cuff <nf>, buy on the installment plan, buy on time, defer payment, put on layaway; go in hock for <nf>; have one's credit good for

ADJS **8 credited,** of good credit, **well-rated**

ADVS **9 to one's credit** *or* **account,** to the credit *or* account of, to the good

10 on credit, on account, on trust, on tick *and* **on the cuff** <nf>; on terms, on good terms, on easy terms, on budget terms, in installments, on time

623 DEBT

NOUNS **1 debt, indebtedness,** indebtment, **obligation, liability,** financial commitment, due, **dues,** score, pledge, unfulfilled pledge, amount due, outstanding debt; **bill, bills,** chits <nf>, **charges;** floating debt; funded debt, unfunded debt; accounts receivable; accounts payable; borrowing 621; maturity; bad debts, uncollectibles, frozen assets; **national debt,** public debt; deficit, national deficit; megadebt <nf>; debt explosion

2 arrears, arrear, arrearage, back debts, back payments; the red; **deficit,** default, deferred payments; cash *or* credit crunch <nf>; overdraft, bounced *or* bouncing check, rubber check <nf>; dollar gap, unfavorable trade balance *or* balance of payments; deficit financing

3 interest, premium, price, rate; interest rate, rate of interest, prime interest rate *or* **prime rate,** bank rate, lending rate, borrowing rate, the price of money; discount rate; annual percentage rate *or* APR; **usury** 620.1, excessive *or* exorbitant interest; points, mortgage points; simple interest, compound interest; net interest, gross interest; compensatory interest; lucrative interest; penal interest

4 debtor, borrower; mortgagor; insolvent

VERBS **5 owe, be indebted,** be obliged *or* obligated for, be financially committed, lie under an obligation, be bound to pay, owe money

6 go in debt, get into debt, run into debt, plunge into debt, incur *or* contract a debt, go in hock <nf>, be overextended, **run up a bill** *or* a score *or* an account *or* a tab; run *or* show a deficit, operate at a loss; borrow; overspend, overdraw

7 mature, accrue, fall due

ADJS **8 indebted, in debt,** plunged in debt, in difficulties, embarrassed, in embarrassed circumstances, in the hole *and* in hock <nf>, in the red, in dire straits, **insolvent,** encumbered, mortgaged, mortgaged to the hilt, tied up, involved; deep in debt, involved *or* deeply involved in debt, burdened with debt, head over heels *or* up to one's ears in debt <nf>; cash poor

9 chargeable, obligated, liable, pledged, responsible, answerable for

10 due, owed, owing, payable, receivable, redeemable, mature, **outstanding, unpaid,** in arrear *or* arrears, back

624 PAYMENT

NOUNS **1 payment, paying,** paying off, paying up <nf>, payoff; **defrayment,** defrayal; paying out, doling out, **disbursal** 626.1; **discharge, settlement, clearance, liquidation, amortization, amortizement,** retirement, satisfaction; quittance; acquittance *or* acquitment *or* acquittal <old>; **debt service, interest payment,** sinking-fund payment; **remittance;** installment, installment plan, lay-away plan; hire purchase *or* hire purchase plan *or* never-never <Brit>; regular payments, monthly payments, weekly payments, quarterly payments, etc; down payment, deposit, earnest, earnest money, binder; god's penny; the King's shilling <Brit>; **cash,** hard cash, spot cash, cash payment, cash on the nail *and* cash on the barrelhead <nf>; pay-as-you-go; prepayment; **postponed** *or* **deferred payment,** contango *or* carryover *and* continuation *and* backwardation <Brit>; payment in kind; accounts receivable, receivables

2 reimbursement, recoupment, recoup, return, restitution, settlement; payment in lieu; **refund,** refundment; kickback <nf>; payback, chargeback, **repayment** 481.2

3 recompense, remuneration, compensation; requital, requitement, quittance, **retribution, reparation, redress,** satisfaction, **atonement, amends,** return, restitution 481; blood money, wergild <old>; **indemnity,** indemnification; price, consideration; **reward,** meed, guerdon; honorarium; workmen's compensation *or* comp <nf>, solatium, damages, smart money; salvage

4 pay, payment, remuneration, compensation, total compensation, wages plus fringe benefits, financial package, pay and allowances, financial remuneration; rate of pay; **salary, wage, wages, income, earnings,** hire; real wages, purchasing power; payday, pay check, pay envelope, pay packet <Brit>; take-home pay *or* income, wages after taxes, pay *or* income *or* wages after deductions, net income *or* wages *or* pay *or* earnings, taxable income; gross income; living wage; minimum wage, base pay; portal-to-portal pay; severance pay, discontinuance *or* dismissal wage, golden parachute; wage scale; escalator plan, escalator clause, sliding scale; guaranteed income, guaranteed annual income, negative income tax; fixed income; wage freeze, wage rollback, wage reduction, wage control; guaranteed annual wage, guaranteed income plan; overtime pay; danger money, combat pay, flight pay; back pay; strike pay; **payroll;** golden handcuffs; royalty, advance

5 **fee, stipend, allowance,** emolument, tribute, honorarium; **reckoning,** account, bill; assessment, scot; initiation fee, footing <old>; retainer, retaining fee; hush money, blackmail; blood money; mileage

6 <extra pay or allowance> **bonus, premium, fringe benefit** *or* **benefits,** bounty, perquisite, perquisites, perks <nf>, gravy <nf>, lagniappe, solatium; **tip** 478.5; overtime pay; bonus system; health insurance, life insurance, disability insurance; profit-sharing; holidays, vacation time, flextime *or* flexitime; pension program

7 **dividend; royalty; commission,** rake-off *and* cut <nf>

8 <the bearing of another's expense> **treat,** standing treat, picking up the check *or* tab <nf>; paying the bills, maintenance; child support, support 449.3; subsidy 478.8

9 **payer,** remunerator, compensator, recompenser; paymaster, purser, bursar, cashier, treasurer 729.12; defrayer; liquidator; **taxpayer, ratepayer** <Brit>

VERBS 10 **pay,** render, tender; **recompense, remunerate, compensate, reward,** guerdon, indemnify, satisfy; salary, fee; remit; prepay; pay by *or* in installments, pay on, pay in; make payments to *or* towards *or* on

11 **repay,** pay back, restitute, **reimburse,** recoup; **requite,** quit, **atone,** redress <old>, **make amends,** make good, make up for, make up to, make restitution, make reparation 481.5; pay in kind, pay one in his own coin, give tit for tat; **refund,** kick back <nf>

12 **settle with,** reckon with, account with <old>, pay out, **settle** *or* **square accounts with,** square oneself with, get square with, **get even with,** get quits with; even the score <nf>, wipe *or* clear off old scores, pay old debts, clear the board

13 **pay in full, pay off, pay up** <nf>, **discharge, settle,** square, **clear, liquidate, amortize,** retire, take up, lift, take up and pay off, honor, acquit oneself of <old>; satisfy; meet one's obligations *or*

commitments, redeem, redeem one's pledge *or* pledges, tear up *or* burn one's mortgage, have a mortgage-burning party, settle *or* square accounts, make accounts square, strike a balance; pay the bill, pay the shot

14 **pay out, fork out** *or* **over** <nf>, **shell out** <nf>; **expend** 626.5

15 **pay over,** hand over; ante, **ante up,** put up; put down, lay down, lay one's money down, show the color of one's money

16 <nf terms> **kick in, fork over,** pony up, pay up, cough up, stump up <Brit>, come across, come through with, come across with, come down with, come down with the needful, plank down, plunk down, post, tickle *or* grease the palm, cross one's palm with, lay on one; pay to the tune of

17 **pay cash,** make a cash payment, cash, **pay spot cash, pay cash down,** pay cash on the barrelhead <nf>, plunk down the money *and* put one's money on the line <nf>, pay at sight; pay in advance; pay as you go; pay cash on delivery *or* pay COD

18 **pay for,** pay *or* stand the costs, **bear the expense** *or* **cost,** pay the piper <nf>; **finance, fund** 729.16; **defray,** defray expenses; pay the bill, **foot the bill** *and* pick up the check *or* tab *and* spring *or* pop for <nf>; honor a bill, acknowledge, redeem; pay one's way; pay one's share, chip in <nf>, go Dutch <nf>, Dutch-treat, go halvsies <nf>

19 **treat,** treat to, **stand treat,** go treat, stand to <nf>, pick up the check *or* tab <nf>, pay the bill, set up, blow to <nf>; stand drinks; maintain, support 449.12; subsidize 478.19

20 **be paid, draw wages,** be salaried, work for wages, be remunerated, collect for one's services, **earn,** get an income, pull down *and* drag down <nf>

ADJS 21 **paying, remunerative, remuneratory; compensating,** compensative, compensatory, disbursing; retributive, retributory; **rewarding,** rewardful; lucrative, moneymaking, profitable, gainful; repaying, satisfying, reparative; bankable

22 **paid, paid-up,** discharged, settled, liquidated, acquitted <old>, paid in full, receipted, remitted; **spent, expended;** salaried, waged, hired; compensated; prepaid, postpaid

23 **unindebted,** unowing, **out of debt,** above water, out of the hole *or* the red <nf>, **clear,** all clear, free and clear, all straight; solvent 729.18

ADVS 24 **in compensation,** as compensation, in recompense, for services rendered, for professional services, **in reward,** in requital, in reparation, in retribution, in restitution, in exchange for, **in amends,** in atonement, to atone for

25 **cash,** cash on the barrelhead <nf>, strictly cash; **cash down, money down,** down; cash on delivery *or* **COD;** on demand, on call; pay-as-you-go

625 NONPAYMENT

NOUNS **1 nonpayment, default, delinquency,** delinquence <old>, nondischarge of debts, nonremittal, failure to pay; defection; protest, repudiation; dishonor, dishonoring; bad debt, uncollectible, dishonored *or* protested bill; tax evasion; creative accounting

2 moratorium, grace period; embargo, freeze; **write-off,** cancellation, obliteration 395.7

3 insolvency, bankruptcy, receivership, Chapter 11, **failure; crash,** collapse, bust <nf>, ruin; run on a bank; insufficient funds, overdraft, overdrawn account, not enough to cover, bounced *or* bouncing check, bad check, kited *or* rubber check; Chapter 7, Chapter 13

4 insolvent, insolvent debtor; **bankrupt,** failure; **loser,** heavy loser, lame duck <nf>

5 defaulter, delinquent, nonpayer; **welsher** <nf>, levanter; tax evader, tax dodger *or* cheat <nf>

VERBS **6 not pay;** dishonor, repudiate, disallow, protest, stop payment, refuse to pay; **default, welsh** <nf>, levant; button up one's pockets, draw the purse strings; **underpay;** bounce *or* kite a check <nf>

7 go bankrupt, go broke <nf>, go into receivership, become insolvent *or* bankrupt, **fail,** break, bust <nf>, crash, collapse, **fold, fold up,** belly up *and* go up *and* go belly up *and* **go under** <nf>, shut down, shut one's doors, go out of business, **be ruined,** go to ruin, go on the rocks, go to the wall, go to pot <nf>, go to the dogs, go bust <nf>; take a bath *and* be taken to the cleaners *and* be cleaned out *and* lose one's shirt *and* tap out <nf>

8 bankrupt, ruin, break, bust *and* wipe out <nf>; put out of business, drive to the wall, scuttle, sink; impoverish 619.6

9 declare a moratorium; write off, forgive, absolve, **cancel,** nullify, wipe the slate clean; wipe out, obliterate 395.16

ADJS **10 defaulting,** nonpaying, **delinquent;** behindhand, in arrear *or* arrears, in hock, in the red

11 insolvent, bankrupt, in receivership, in the hands of receivers, belly-up <nf>, broken, **broke** *and* busted <nf>, **ruined,** failed, out of business, unable to pay one's creditors, unable to meet one's obligations, illiquid, on the rocks; destitute 619.9

12 unpaid, unremunerated, uncompensated, unrecompensed, **unrewarded,** unrequited; underpaid

13 unpayable, irredeemable, inconvertible

626 EXPENDITURE

NOUNS **1 expenditure, spending,** expense, disbursal, **disbursement;** debit, debiting; budgeting, scheduling; costing, costing-out; **payment** 624; deficit spending; **use** 387; **consumption** 388

2 spendings, disbursements, payments, outgoings, outgo, outflow, **outlay,** money going out; capital outlay *or* expenditure

3 expenses, costs, charges, disbursals, **liabilities**, damages <nf>; **expense, cost,** burden of expenditure; budget, budget item, budget line, line item; **overhead,** operating expense *or* expenses *or* costs *or* budget, general expenses; expense account, swindle sheet <nf>; business expenses, nonremunerated business expenses, out-of-pocket expenses; direct costs, indirect costs; distributed costs, undistributed costs; material costs; labor costs; carrying charge; unit cost; replacement cost; prime cost; cost of living, cost-of-living index, cost-of-living allowance *or* COLA, inflation

4 spender, expender, expenditor, disburser, buyer, purchaser; spend-all, spendthrift

VERBS **5 spend, expend, disburse, pay out,** fork out *or* over <nf>, shell out <nf>, **lay out,** outlay; go to the expense of; **pay** 624.10; put one's hands in one's pockets, open the purse, loosen *or* untie the purse strings *and* throw money around <nf>, go on a spending spree, splurge, spend money like a drunken sailor *and* spend money as if it were going out of style <nf>, go *or* run through, be out of pocket, **squander** 486.3; **invest,** sink money in <nf>, put out; throw money away; **incur costs** *or* **expenses;** budget, schedule, cost, cost out; **use** 387.10; **consume**

6 be spent, burn in one's pocket, burn a hole in one's pocket

7 afford, well afford, spare, spare the price, bear, stand, support, endure, undergo, meet the expense of, swing

627 RECEIPTS

NOUNS **1 receipts,** receipt, **income, revenue, profits, earnings, returns, proceeds,** avails <old>, **take,** takings, intake, take *or* take-in <nf>, get <Brit nf>; credit, credits; gains 472.3; gate receipts, gate, box office; net receipts, net; gross receipts, gross; national income; net income, gross income, gross profit margin; earned income, take-home pay, unearned income; **dividend** 738.7, dividends, payout, payback; interest; royalties, commissions; receivables; disposable income; make, produce, **yield, output** 893.2, bang for the buck <nf>, fruits, first fruits; bonus, premium; income; legacy; winnings

2 <written acknowledgment> **receipt, acknowledgment, voucher,** warrant <Brit>; canceled check, bank statement; proof of

purchase; **receipt in full,** receipt in full of all
demands, release, acquittance, quittance,
discharge

VERBS **3 receive** 479.6, **pocket, acquire** 472.8,9; earn;
accrue; acknowledge receipt of, receipt, mark paid

4 yield, bring in, afford, pay, pay off <nf>, **return;
gross, net**

628 ACCOUNTS

NOUNS **1 accounts; outstanding accounts,**
uncollected *or* unpaid accounts; **accounts
receivable,** receipts, assets; **accounts payable,**
expenditures, liabilities; **budget,** budgeting;
costing out

2 account, reckoning, tally, rendering-up, score;
account current; account rendered, *compte rendu*
<Fr>, account stated; balance, trial balance

3 statement, bill, itemized bill, bill of account,
account, reckoning, check, *l'addition* <Fr>, score
or tab <nf>; **dun; invoice,** manifest, bill of lading

4 account book, ledger, journal, daybook; **register,**
registry, **record book,** books; inventory, catalog;
log, logbook; **cashbook; bankbook,** passbook;
balance sheet; cost sheet, cost card

5 entry, item, line item, minute, note, notation;
single entry, double entry; **credit, debit**

6 accounting, accountancy, bookkeeping, double-
entry bookkeeping *or* accounting, single-entry
bookkeeping *or* accounting; comptrollership *or*
controllership; business *or* commercial *or*
monetary arithmetic; cost accounting, costing
<Brit>, cost system, cost-accounting system;
audit, auditing; stocktaking, inspection of books

7 accountant, bookkeeper; tax preparer**; clerk,**
actuary <old>, registrar, recorder, journalizer;
calculator, reckoner; cost accountant, cost
keeper; certified public accountant *or* CPA;
chartered accountant *or* CA <Brit>; **auditor,** bank
examiner; bank accountant; actuary; accountant
general; comptroller *or* controller; statistician;
investment manager, money manager; financial
advisor

VERBS **8 keep accounts, keep books,** make up *or*
cast up *or* render accounts; make an entry, enter,
post, post up, journalize, book, docket, log, note,
minute; **credit, debit;** charge off, write off;
capitalize; carry, carry on one's books; carry over;
balance, balance accounts, balance the books,
strike a balance; close the books, close out

9 take account of, take stock, overhaul; **inventory;
audit,** examine *or* inspect the books

10 falsify accounts, garble accounts, cook *or* doctor
accounts <nf>, cook the books <nf>, salt, fudge;
surcharge

11 bill, send a statement; **invoice;** call, call in,
demand payment, **dun**

ADJS **12** accounting, bookkeeping; budget, budgetary

629 TRANSFER OF PROPERTY OR RIGHT

NOUNS **1 transfer,** transference; **conveyance,**
conveyancing; **giving** 478; **delivery,** deliverance;
assignment, assignation; **consignment,**
consignation; conferment, conferral, settling,
settlement; vesting; bequeathal 478.10; **sale** 734;
surrender, cession; transmission, transmittal;
disposal, disposition, deaccession, deaccessioning;
demise; alienation, abalienation; amortization,
amortizement; enfeoffment; deeding; bargain and
sale; lease and release; **exchange,** barter, trading;
entailment

2 devolution, succession, reversion; shifting use,
shifting trust

VERBS **3 transfer, convey, deliver,** hand, pass,
negotiate; **give** 478.12-14,16,21; **hand over, turn
over, pass over; assign, consign,** confer, settle,
settle on; cede, surrender; bequeath 478.18; entail;
sell 734.8,11,12, sell off, deaccession; **make over,
sign over,** sign away; transmit, **hand down, hand
on, pass on,** devolve upon; demise; alienate, alien,
abalienate, amortize; enfeoff; **deed,** deed over,
give title to; **exchange,** barter, trade, trade away

4 change hands, change ownership; devolve, pass
on, descend, succeed <old>

ADJS **5 transferable, conveyable,** negotiable,
alienable; **assignable,** consignable; devisable,
bequeathable; heritable, inheritable

630 PRICE, FEE

NOUNS **1 price, cost, expense,** expenditure, **charge,**
damage *and* score *and* tab <nf>; rate, figure,
amount; **quotation,** quoted price, price tag *and*
ticket *and* **sticker** <nf>; **price list,** price range,
prices current; stock market quotations; standard
price, asking price, list price, sale price, selling
price, market price

2 worth, value, account, rate; face value, face; par
value; market value; street value; fair value; net
worth; conversion factor *or* value; monetary value;
money's worth, pennyworth, value received; bang
for the buck <nf>; going rate; trade-in price

3 valuation, evaluation, value-setting, value-fixing,
pricing, price determination, **assessment,
appraisal,** appraisement, estimation, rating, bond
rating; unit pricing, dual pricing

4 price index, business index; wholesale price index;
consumer price *or* retail price index; cost-of-living
index; stock market index; price level; price

ceiling, ceiling price, ceiling, top price; floor price, floor, bottom price; demand curve; rising prices, **inflation,** inflationary spiral

5 **price controls,** price-fixing, valorization; managed prices, fair-trading, fair trade, fair-trade agreement; **price supports,** rigid supports, flexible supports; price freeze; rent control; prix fixe

6 **fee, dues, toll, charge, charges, demand, exaction,** exactment, scot, shot, scot and lot; hire; **fare,** carfare; user fee; airport fee *or* charge; license fee; entrance *or* entry *or* admission fee, admission; cover charge; portage, towage; wharfage, anchorage, dockage; pilotage; storage, cellarage; brokerage; salvage; service fee *or* charge; commission, cut

7 freightage, freight, haulage, carriage, cartage, drayage, expressage, lighterage; poundage, tonnage

8 **rent, rental;** rent-roll; rent charge; rack rent, quitrent; ground rent, wayleave rent

9 **tax, taxation, duty, tribute,** taxes, rates <Brit>, contribution, **assessment, revenue enhancement,** cess <Brit>, **levy, toll, impost,** imposition; tax code, tax law; **tithe;** indirect taxation, direct taxation; **tax burden,** overtaxation, undertaxation; bracket *or* tax-bracket creep; progressive taxation, graduated taxation; regressive taxation; tax withholding; tax return, separate returns, joint return; tax evasion *or* avoidance; tax haven *or* shelter; **tax deduction, deduction; tax write-off,** write-off, tax relief; tax exemption, tax-exempt status; tax structure, tax base; taxable income *or* goods *or* land *or* property, ratables

10 **tax collector,** taxer, taxman, publican; collector of internal revenue, internal revenue agent, revenuer; tax farmer, farmer; assessor, **tax assessor;** exciseman <Brit>, revenuer; Internal Revenue Service *or* IRS; Inland Revenue *or* IR <Brit>; **customs agent; customs,** US Customs Service, Bureau of Customs and Excise <Brit>; customhouse; taxpayer

VERBS 11 **price,** set *or* name a price, fix the price of; place a value on, **value, evaluate,** valuate, **appraise, assess, rate,** prize, apprize; quote a price; set an arbitrary price on, control *or* manage the price of, valorize; mark up, mark down, **discount;** fair-trade; reassess

12 **charge, demand, ask,** require; overcharge, undercharge; **exact, assess, levy, impose; tax,** assess a tax upon, slap a tax on <nf>, lay *or* put a duty on, make dutiable, subject to a tax *or* fee *or* duty, collect a tax *or* duty on; tithe; prorate, assess *pro rata;* charge for, stick for <nf>

13 **cost, sell for, fetch, bring,** bring in, stand one *and* set *or* move one back <nf>, knock one back <Brit

nf>; **come to,** run to *or* into, **amount to,** mount up to, come up to, total up to

ADJS 14 **priced, valued,** evaluated, assessed, appraised, rated, prized; **worth,** valued at; good for; ad valorem, pro rata

15 **chargeable, taxable,** ratable <Brit>, assessable, dutiable, leviable, declarable; tithable

16 tax-free, nontaxable, nondutiable, tax-exempt; deductible, tax-deductible; duty-free

ADVS 17 **at a price,** for a consideration; to the amount of, to the tune of *and* in the neighborhood of <nf>

631 DISCOUNT

NOUNS 1 **discount, cut, deduction,** price reduction, slash, abatement, reduction, price reduction, price-cutting, price-cut, rollback <nf>; underselling; **rebate,** rebatement; bank discount, cash discount, chain discount, time discount, trade discount; write-off, charge-off; **depreciation; allowance,** concession; setoff; drawback, **refund,** kickback <nf>; **premium,** percentage, agio; trading stamp; bank rate, bank discount

VERBS 2 **discount, cut, deduct,** bate, abate; **take off,** write off, charge off; knock down <nf>; **depreciate,** reduce; sell at a loss; **allow,** make allowance; rebate, **refund,** kick back <nf>; take a premium *or* percentage

ADVS 3 **at a discount,** at a reduction, at a reduced rate, below par, below *or* under cost; cost-efficient

632 EXPENSIVENESS

NOUNS 1 **expensiveness, costliness, dearness,** high *or* great cost, highness, stiffness *or* **steepness** <nf>, priceyness; **richness, sumptuousness,** sumptuosity, **luxuriousness;** pretty penny <nf>

2 **preciousness, dearness, value,** high *or* great value, **worth,** extraordinary worth, price *or* great price <old>, **valuableness; pricelessness, invaluableness**

3 **high price,** high *or* big price tag *and* big ticket *and* big sticker price <nf>, **fancy price,** good price, steep *or* stiff price <nf>, luxury price, a pretty penny *or* an arm and a leg <nf>, exorbitant *or* unconscionable *or* extortionate price; famine price, scarcity price; rack rent; bracket creep; inflationary prices, rising *or* soaring *or* spiraling prices, soaring costs; sellers' market; **inflation,** cost *or* cost-push inflation *or* cost-push, demand-pull inflation, inflationary trend *or* pressure, hot economy, inflationary spiral, inflationary gap; reflation; stagflation, slumpflation

4 exorbitance, exorbitancy <old>, **extravagance,** excess, **excessiveness,** inordinateness, immoderateness, immoderation, undueness, unreasonableness, outrageousness, preposterousness; unconscionableness, extortionateness

5 overcharge, surcharge, overassessment; gouging *or* price-gouging; **extortion,** extortionate price; **holdup** *and* armed robbery *and* highway robbery <nf>; profiteering, rack-rent; ripoff <nf>

VERBS **6 cost much,** cost money *and* cost you <nf>, be dear, cost a pretty penny *or* an arm and a leg *or* a packet <nf>, **run into money;** be overpriced, price out of the market

7 overprice, set the price tag too high; **overcharge,** surcharge, overtax; **hold up** *and* **soak** *and* **stick** *and* **sting** *and* **clip** <nf>, **make pay through the nose, gouge;** commit highway robbery; victimize, rip off, swindle 356.18; exploit, skin <nf>, **fleece,** screw *and* put the screws to <nf>, bleed, bleed white; profiteer; rack *or* rack up the rents, rack rent; double-charge; profiteer

8 overpay, overspend, pay too much, pay more than it's worth, **pay dearly,** pay exorbitantly, pay, **pay through the nose,** be had *or* taken <nf>

9 inflate, heat *or* heat up the economy; reflate

ADJS **10 precious, dear, valuable,** worthy, rich, golden, of great price <old>, worth a pretty penny <nf>, worth a king's ransom, worth its weight in gold, good as gold, precious as the apple of one's eye; **priceless, invaluable,** inestimable, without *or* **beyond price,** not to be had for love or money, not for all the tea in China

11 expensive, dear, costly, of great cost, dear-bought, **high, high-priced,** premium, at a premium, top; big ticket <nf>, **fancy** *and* stiff *and* steep <nf>, pricey; beyond one's means, not affordable, more than one can afford, sky-high; unpayable; upmarket, upscale <nf> rich, sumptuous, executive *and* posh <nf>, **luxurious** 501.21, gold-plated

12 overpriced, grossly overpriced, **exorbitant, excessive, extravagant, inordinate, immoderate,** undue, unwarranted, unreasonable, fancy, unconscionable, outrageous, preposterous, out of bounds, out of sight <nf>, **prohibitive; extortionate,** cutthroat, **gouging, usurious,** exacting; **inflationary,** spiraling, skyrocketing, mounting; stagflationary, slumpflationary; reflationary

ADVS **13 dear, dearly;** at a high price, at great cost, at a premium, at a great rate, at heavy cost, at great expense

14 preciously, valuably, worthily; pricelessly, invaluably, inestimably

15 expensively, richly, sumptuously, luxuriously

16 exorbitantly, excessively, grossly, **extravagantly, inordinately,** immoderately, unduly, unreasonably, unconscionably, outrageously, preposterously; **extortionately,** usuriously, gougingly

633 CHEAPNESS

NOUNS **1 cheapness, inexpensiveness,** affordableness, affordability, reasonableness, modestness, moderateness, nominalness; drug *or* glut on the market; shabbiness, shoddiness 998.2

2 low price, nominal price, reasonable price, modest *or* manageable price, sensible price, moderate price; low *or* nominal *or* reasonable charge; bargain prices, budget prices, economy prices, easy prices *or* terms, popular prices, rock-bottom prices; buyers' market; low *or* small price tag *and* low sticker price *and* low tariff <nf>; **reduced price,** cut price, sale price; cheap *or* reduced rates; bargain rate; cut price *or* rate

3 bargain, advantageous purchase, **buy** <nf>, **good buy, steal** <nf>; money's worth, pennyworth, good pennyworth; special offer; loss leader

4 cheapening, depreciation, devaluation, reduction, lowering; deflation, deflationary spiral, cooling *or* cooling off of the economy; **buyers' market; decline,** plummet, plummeting, plunge, dive, nose dive *and* slump *and* sag <nf>, free fall; price fall, break; **price cut** *or* **reduction,** cut, slash, **markdown;** oversupply

VERBS **5 be cheap,** cost little, not cost anything *and* cost nothing *and* next to nothing <nf>; **go dirt cheap** *or* for a song *or* for nickels and dimes *or* for peanuts <nf>, buy at a bargain, buy for a mere nothing; get one's money's worth, get a good pennyworth; buy at wholesale prices *or* at cost

6 cheapen, depreciate, devaluate, lower, reduce, devalue, **mark down, cut prices, cut,** slash, shave, trim, pare, underprice, knock the bottom out of <nf>, knock down <nf>; deflate, cool *or* cool off the economy; beat down; come down *or* fall in price; **fall,** decline, plummet, dive, nose-dive <nf>, drop, crash, head for the bottom, plunge, sag, slump, break, give way; reach a new low; unload

ADJS **7 cheap, inexpensive,** unexpensive, **low, low-priced,** bargain, frugal, reasonable, sensible, manageable, modest, moderate, affordable, to fit the pocketbook, budget, easy, economy, economic, economical; within means, within reach *or* easy reach; nominal, token; austere; worth the money, well worth the money; cheap *or* good at the price, cheap at half the price; shabby, shoddy, cheapo <nf>; deflationary

8 dirt cheap, cheap as dirt, dog-cheap <nf>, **a dime a dozen,** bargain-priced, bargain-basement, five-and-ten, dime-store

9 reduced, cut, cut-price, slashed, **marked down;** cut-rate; half-price; priced to go; giveaway, sacrificial; **lowest,** rock-bottom, bottom; deep-discount

ADVS **10 cheaply, cheap,** on the cheap <Brit nf>; **inexpensively,** reasonably, moderately, nominally; **at a bargain,** à bon marché <Fr>, for a song *or* mere song <nf>, for pennies *or* nickels and dimes *or* peanuts <nf>, at small cost, at a low price, at budget prices, at piggy-bank prices, at a sacrifice; at cost *or* cost price, at prime cost, wholesale, at wholesale; at reduced rates

634 COSTLESSNESS
<absence of charge>

NOUNS **1 costlessness,** gratuitousness, gratuity, **freeness,** expenselessness, complimentariness, no charge; free ride <nf>; freebie *and* gimme <nf>; labor of love; **gift** 478.4

2 complimentary ticket, pass, comp <nf>, free pass *or* ticket, paper <nf>, free admission, guest pass *or* ticket, Annie Oakley <nf>; discount ticket, twofer <nf>

3 freeloader, free rider, pass holder, deadhead <nf>, sponger

VERBS **4 give, present** 478.12, comp <nf>; freeload, sponge

ADJS **5 gratuitous, gratis, free, free of charge,** for free, for nothing, free for nothing, free for the asking, free gratis *and* free gratis for nothing <nf>, for love, free as air; freebie *and* freebee *and* freeby <nf>; costless, expenseless, untaxed, without charge, free of cost *or* expense, all-expense-paid; no charge; unbought, unpaid-for; **complimentary, on the house, comp** <nf>, given 478.24; giftlike; eleemosynary, charitable 143.15

ADVS **6 gratuitously, gratis, free, free of charge,** for nothing, for the asking, at no charge, without charge, with the compliments of the management, as our guest, on the house

635 THRIFT

NOUNS **1 thrift, economy, thriftiness,** economicalness, savingness, sparingness, unwastefulness, **frugality,** frugalness; tight purse strings; parsimony, **parsimoniousness** 484.1; false economy; carefulness, care, chariness, canniness; **prudence,** providence, forehandedness; **husbandry,** management, good management *or* stewardship, custodianship, prudent *or* prudential

administration; **austerity,** austerity program, belt-tightening; economic planning; economy of means 484.1

2 economizing, economization, reduction of spending or government spending; **cost-effectiveness; saving,** scrimping, skimping <nf>, scraping, sparing, cheeseparing; **retrenchment, curtailment,** reduction of expenses, cutback, rollback, slowdown, cooling, cooling off *or* down, low growth rate; reduction in forces *or* RIF; budget, spending plan

3 economizer, economist <old>, **saver,** string-saver, skimper

VERBS **4 economize, save,** make *or* enforce economies; **scrimp, skimp** <nf>, **scrape,** scrape and save; **manage, husband,** husband one's resources, conserve; budget; live frugally, get along on a shoestring, get by on little; keep within compass <old>, keep *or* stay within one's means *or* budget, balance income with outgo, live within one's income, make ends meet, cut one's coat according to one's cloth, keep *or* stay ahead of the game; put something aside, **save up,** save for a rainy day, have a nest egg; supplement *or* eke out one's income

5 retrench, cut down, cut *or* pare down expenses, **curtail expenses; cut corners, tighten one's belt,** cut back, roll back, take a reef, slow down

ADJS **6 economical, thrifty, frugal,** economic, unwasteful, conserving, **saving,** economizing, spare, **sparing;** Scotch; **prudent,** prudential, provident, forehanded; careful, chary, canny; scrimping, skimping <nf>, cheeseparing, austere; penny-wise; **parsimonious** 484.7; **cost-effective, cost-efficient; efficient,** labor-saving, time-saving, money-saving

ADVS **7 economically, thriftily, frugally,** husbandly <old>; **cost-effectively, cost-efficiently;** prudently, providently; carefully, charily, cannily; sparingly, with a sparing hand

636 ETHICS

NOUNS **1 ethics, principles,** standards, norms, principles of conduct *or* behavior, principles of professional practice; **morals,** moral principles; code, ethical *or* moral code, **ethic,** code of morals *or* ethics, ethical system, value system, values, axiology; **norm,** behavioral norm, normative system; moral climate, **ethos,** *Zeitgeist* <Ger>; Ten Commandments, decalogue; social ethics, professional ethics, bioethics, medical ethics, legal ethics, business ethics, etc

2 ethical *or* moral philosophy, ethonomics, aretaics, eudaemonics, casuistry, deontology, empiricism, evolutionism, hedonism, ethical formalism, intuitionism, perfectionism, Stoicism, utilitarianism, categorical imperative, golden rule; egoistic ethics, altruistic ethics; Christian ethics; situation ethics; comparative ethics

3 **morality, morals,** morale; virtue 653; ethicality, ethicalness; scruples, good conscience, moral fiber, moral compass

4 **amorality,** unmorality; amoralism; moral delinquency, moral turpitude

5 **conscience,** grace, **sense of right and wrong,** moral sense, sense of right and wrong; inward monitor, inner arbiter, moral censor, censor, ethical self, superego; **voice of conscience,** still small voice within, wee small voice, guardian *or* good angel; inner light, light within; tender conscience; clear *or* clean conscience; social conscience; conscientiousness 644.2; twinge of conscience 113.2

ADJS 6 **ethical, moral,** moralistic; ethological; axiological

637 RIGHT

NOUNS 1 **right,** rightfulness, rightness; what is right *or* proper, what should be, what ought to be, the seemly, the thing, the right *or* proper thing, the right *or* proper thing to do, what is done

2 **propriety, decorum, decency,** good behavior *or* conduct, correctness, correctitude, rightness, properness, decorousness, goodness, goodliness, niceness, seemliness, cricket <Brit nf>; fitness, fittingness, appropriateness, expediency, suitability 995.1; normativeness, normality; proprieties, decencies; rightmindedness, **righteousness** 653.1

ADJS 3 **right,** rightful; fit, suitable 995.5; **proper, correct, decorous,** good, nice, decent, seemly, **due, appropriate,** fitting, condign, **right and proper,** as it should be, as it ought to be, expedient, up to par, *comme il faut* <Fr>; kosher *and* according to Hoyle <nf>; in the right; normative, normal; rightminded, right-thinking, **righteous**

ADVS 4 **rightly, rightfully,** right; **by rights,** by right, with good right, **as is right** *or* **only right; properly,** correctly, as is proper *or* fitting, **duly, appropriately,** fittingly, condignly, **in justice,** in equity; in reason, in all conscience

638 WRONG

NOUNS 1 **wrong,** wrongfulness, wrongness; **impropriety, indecorum;** incorrectness, improperness, indecorousness, unseemliness; unfitness, unfittingness, inappropriateness,

unsuitableness, unsuitability 996.1; infraction, violation, delinquency, criminality, illegality, unlawfulness; abnormality, deviance *or* deviancy, aberrance *or* aberrancy; sinfulness, wickedness, unrighteousness; **dysfunction,** malfunction, out of order; maladaptation, maladjustment; malfeasance, malversation, malpractice; malformation

2 **abomination, horror,** terrible thing; **scandal, disgrace, shame, pity,** atrocity, profanation, desecration, violation, sacrilege, infamy, ignominy

ADJS 3 **wrong, wrongful; improper, incorrect, indecorous,** undue, unseemly; unfit, unfitting, inappropriate, unsuitable 996.5; delinquent, criminal, illegal, unlawful; fraudulent, creative <nf>; abnormal, deviant, aberrant; **dysfunctional,** out of order; **evil, sinful, wicked, unrighteous;** not the thing, hardly the thing, not done, not cricket <Brit>; **off-base** *and* **out-of-line** *and* **off-color** *and* off the beam <nf>; abominable, terrible, scandalous, disgraceful, immoral, shameful, shameless, atrocious, sacrilegious, infamous, ignominious; maladapted, maladjusted, unjust

ADVS 4 **wrongly, wrongfully,** wrong; **improperly,** incorrectly, indecorously; unjustly

WORD ELEMENTS 5 mis-, dis-; dys-, caco-

639 DUENESS

NOUNS 1 **dueness, entitlement,** entitledness, deservingness, deservedness, meritedness, expectation, just *or* justifiable expectation, expectations, outlook, prospect, prospects; **justice** 649

2 **due,** one's due, what one merits *or* is entitled to, what one has earned, what is owing, what one has coming, what is coming to one, acknowledgment, cognizance, recognition, credit, crediting; **right**

3 **desserts,** just desserts, deservings, merits, dues, due reward *or* punishment, **comeuppance** <nf>, all that is coming to one, what's coming to one; the wrath of God; retaliation 506, vengeance 507.1

VERBS 4 **be due,** be one's due, **be entitled to,** have a right or title to, have a rightful claim to *or* upon, claim as one's right, **have coming,** come by honestly

5 **deserve, merit,** earn, rate *and* be in line for <nf>, **be worthy of,** be deserving, richly deserve

6 **get one's desserts,** get one's dues, **get one's comeuppance** *and* get his *or* hers <nf>, get what is coming to one; get justice; serve one right, be rightly served; get for one's pains, reap the fruits *or* benefit of, reap where one has sown, come into one's own

ADJS 7 **due, owed, owing,** payable, redeemable, coming, **coming to**

8 rightful, condign, appropriate, proper; fit, becoming 995.5; **fair, just** 649.7

9 warranted, justified, entitled, qualified, worthy; **deserved, merited,** richly deserved, earned, well-earned

10 due, entitled to, with a right to; **deserving, meriting, meritorious, worthy of;** attributable, ascribable

ADVS **11 duly,** rightfully, condignly, as is one's due *or* right

PHRS **12** what's sauce for the goose is sauce for the gander; give the devil his due; give credit where credit is due; he's made his bed let him lie in it; let the punishment fit the crime

640 UNDUENESS

NOUNS **1 undueness, undeservedness,** undeservingness, unentitledness, unentitlement, unmeritedness, unwarrantedness; disentitlement; lack of claim *or* title, false claim *or* title, invalid claim *or* title, no claim *or* title, empty claim *or* title; unearned increment; **inappropriateness** 996.1; **impropriety** 638.1; **excess** 993

2 presumption, assumption, **imposition; license,** licentiousness, **undue liberty,** liberties, familiarity, **presumptuousness,** freedom *or* liberty abused, hubris; lawlessness 418; injustice 650

3 usurpation, arrogation, seizure, unlawful seizure, **appropriation,** assumption, adoption, infringement, encroachment, invasion, trespass, trespassing; playing God

4 usurper, arrogator, pretender

VERBS **5 not be entitled to,** have no right *or* title to, have no claim upon, not have a leg to stand on

6 presume, assume, venture, hazard, dare, pretend, attempt, **make bold** *or* so bold, make free, **take the liberty,** take upon oneself, go so far as to

7 presume on *or* **upon, impose on** *or* **upon,** encroach upon, obtrude upon; **take liberties,** take a liberty, overstep, overstep one's rights *or* bounds *or* prerogatives, make free with *or* of, abuse one's rights, abuse a privilege, give an inch and take an ell; take for granted, presuppose; **inconvenience,** bother, trouble, cause to go out of one's way

8 <take to oneself unduly> **usurp, arrogate,** seize, grab *and* latch on to <nf>, **appropriate,** assume, adopt, take over, arrogate *or* accroach to oneself, pretend to, infringe, encroach, invade, trespass; play God

ADJS **9 undue, unowed, unowing,** not coming, not outstanding; **undeserved, unmerited,** unearned; **unwarranted, unjustified,** unprovoked; unentitled, undeserving, unmeriting, nonmeritorious, unworthy; preposterous, outrageous

10 inappropriate 996.5; **improper** 638.3; **excessive** 993.16

11 presumptuous, presuming, licentious; hubristic 493.7

PHRS **12** give him an inch he'll take a mile; let a camel get his nose under the tent and he'll come in

641 DUTY

<moral obligation>

NOUNS **1 duty, obligation,** charge, **onus, burden,** mission, devoir, must, ought, imperative, bounden duty, proper *or* assigned task, what ought to be done, what one is responsible for, where the buck stops <nf>, deference, respect 155, fealty, allegiance, loyalty, homage; devotion, dedication, **commitment;** self-commitment, self-imposed duty; **business** 724.1, function, province, place 724.3; ethics 636; line of duty; call of duty; duties and responsibilities, assignment, work-load; burden of proof; civic duty

2 responsibility, incumbency; **liability, accountability,** accountableness, answerability, answerableness, amenability; product liability; **responsibleness, dutifulness,** duteousness, devotion *or* dedication to duty, sense of duty *or* obligation, code of honor, inner voice

VERBS **3 should, ought to,** had best, had better, be expedient

4 behoove, become, befit, beseem, be bound, be obliged *or* obligated, be under an obligation; **owe it to,** owe it to oneself; must

5 be the duty of, be incumbent on *or* **upon,** be his *or* hers to, fall to, stand on *or* upon, be a must *or* an imperative for, duty calls one to

6 be responsible for, answer for, stand responsible for, **be liable for,** be answerable *or* accountable for; be on the hook for *and* take the heat *or* rap for <nf>

7 be one's responsibility, be one's office, be one's charge *or* mission, be one's concern, **rest with,** lie upon, devolve upon, rest on the shoulders of, lie on one's head *or* one's door *or* one's doorstep, fall to one *or* to one's lot

8 incur a responsibility, become bound to, become sponsor for

9 take *or* **accept the responsibility, take upon oneself,** take upon one's shoulders, commit oneself; be where the buck stops <nf>; **answer for,** respect *or* defer to one's duty; sponsor, be *or* stand sponsor for; do at one's own risk *or* peril; **take the blame,** be in the hot seat *or* on the spot *and* take the heat *or* rap for <nf>

10 do one's duty, perform *or* fulfill *or* discharge one's duty, do what one has to do, pay one's dues <nf>, **do what is expected,** do the needful, do the right thing, do justice to, **do** or **act one's part,** play one's proper role; answer the call of duty, do one's bit or part; walk the walk

11 **meet an obligation,** satisfy one's obligations, stand to one's engagement, stand up to, **acquit oneself, make good,** redeem one's pledge

12 **obligate, oblige, require,** make incumbent or imperative, tie, **bind,** pledge, commit, saddle with, put under an obligation; call to account, hold responsible or accountable or answerable

ADJS 13 **dutiful, duteous;** moral, ethical; conscientious, scrupulous, observant; obedient 326.3; deferential, respectful 155.8

14 **incumbent on** or **upon,** chargeable to, behooving

15 **obligatory, binding, imperative,** imperious, peremptory, mandatory, compulsory, must, *de rigueur* <Fr>; **necessary,** required 963.13

16 **obliged, obligated,** obligate, **under obligation; bound, duty-bound,** in duty bound, tied, pledged, committed, saddled, beholden, bounden; **obliged to,** beholden to, bound or bounden to, **indebted to**

17 **responsible, answerable; liable, accountable,** incumbent, amenable, unexempt from, chargeable, on one's head, at one's doorstep, on the hook <nf>; responsible for, at the bottom of; to blame

ADVS 18 **dutifully, duteously, in the line of duty,** as in duty bound; beyond the call of duty

642 PREROGATIVE

NOUNS 1 **prerogative, right, due,** droit; power, authority, prerogative of office; faculty, appurtenance; **claim,** proper claim, demand, **interest, title,** pretension, pretense, prescription; birthright; natural right, presumptive right, inalienable right, exclusive right; divine right; vested right or interest; property right; conjugal right; royal charter

2 **privilege, license, liberty, freedom, immunity;** franchise, patent, copyright, grant, warrant, blank check, carte blanche; favor, indulgence, **special favor,** dispensation

3 **human rights,** rights of man; constitutional rights, rights of citizenship, **civil rights** 430.2, civil liberties; rights of minorities, minority rights; gay rights; Bill of Rights

4 **women's rights,** rights of women; **feminism, women's liberation,** women's lib <nf>, womanism, women's movement or liberation movement, sisterhood

5 women's rightist, **feminist,** women's liberationist, women's liberation advocate or adherent or

activist, womanist, women's libber *and* libber <nf>; suffragette, suffragist

VERBS 6 have or claim or assert a right, exercise a right; defend a right

643 IMPOSITION

<a putting or inflicting upon>

NOUNS 1 **imposition, infliction,** laying on or upon, charging, taxing, tasking; burdening, weighting or weighting down, freighting, loading or loading down, heaping on or upon, imposing an onus; **exaction, demand** 421; unwarranted demand, obtrusiveness, presumptuousness 142.1; inconvenience, trouble, bother, pain <nf>; inconsiderateness 144.3

2 administration, giving, bestowal; applying, application, dosing, dosage, meting out, prescribing; **forcing,** forcing on or upon, enforcing; regimentation

3 charge, duty, tax, task; **burden,** weight, freight, cargo, load, onus

VERBS 4 **impose, impose on** or **upon, inflict on** or **upon, put on** or **upon, lay on** or **upon,** enjoin; **put, place, set, lay,** put down; **levy, exact, demand** 421.1; **tax,** task, **charge,** burden with, weight or freight with, weight down with, yoke with, **fasten upon,** saddle with, stick with <nf>; subject to

5 **inflict, wreak, do to,** bring, bring upon, bring down upon, bring on or down on one's head, visit upon

6 **administer, give, bestow; apply, put on** or **upon,** lay on or upon, dose, dose with, dish out <nf>, mete out, prescribe, regiment; **force, force upon,** impose by force or main force, strongarm <nf>, force down one's throat, enforce upon

7 **impose on** or **upon, take advantage of** 387.16; **presume upon** 640.7; **deceive,** play or work on, out on or upon, put over or across <nf>; palm or pass or fob off on, fob or foist on; shift the blame or responsibility, **pass the buck** <nf>

ADJS 8 **imposed, inflicted,** piled or heaped on; burdened with, stuck with <nf>; self-inflicted; exacted, demanded

644 PROBITY

NOUNS 1 **probity,** truthfulness, assured probity, **honesty, integrity, rectitude, uprightness,** upstandingness, erectness, **virtue,** virtuousness, **righteousness, goodness;** cleanness, **decency; honor,** honorableness, worthiness, estimableness, reputability, nobility; unimpeachableness, unimpeachability, irreproachableness, irreproachability, blamelessness; immaculacy, unspottedness, stainlessness, pureness, purity;

respectability; principles, high principles, high ideals, high-mindedness; **character,** good *or* sterling character, moral strength, moral excellence; **fairness,** justness, justice 649; gentrification

2 **conscientiousness, scrupulousness,** scrupulosity, **scruples,** punctiliousness, meticulousness; scruple, point of honor, punctilio; qualm 325.2; twinge of conscience 113.2; overconscientiousness, overscrupulousness; fastidiousness 495

3 **honesty, veracity,** veraciousness, verity, **truthfulness,** truth, veridicality, truth-telling, truth-speaking; truth-loving; credibility, absolute credibility; objectivity

4 **candor, candidness, frankness,** plain dealing; sincerity, genuineness, authenticity; ingenuousness; artlessness 416; **openness,** openheartedness; freedom, freeness; **unreserve,** unrestraint, unconstraint; **forthrightness, directness, straightforwardness; outspokenness,** plainness, plainspokenness, plain speaking, plain speech, roundness, broadness; **bluntness,** bluffness, brusqueness

5 **undeceptiveness, undeceitfulness, guilelessness**

6 **trustworthiness,** faithworthiness, trustiness, trustability, **reliability, dependability,** dependableness, sureness; answerableness, responsibility 641.2; unfalseness, unperfidiousness, untreacherousness; incorruptibility, inviolability

7 **fidelity, faithfulness, loyalty,** faith; **constancy, steadfastness,** staunchness, firmness; trueness, troth, true blue; good faith, *bona fides* <L>, *bonne foi* <Fr>; **allegiance, fealty, homage;** bond, tie; attachment, adherence, adhesion; devotion, devotedness

8 **person** *or* **man** *or* **woman of honor,** man of his word, woman of her word; gentleman, *gentilhomme* <Fr>, *galantuomo* <Ital>; **honest man,** good man; **lady, real lady; honest woman, good woman;** salt of the earth; square *or* straight shooter *and* straight arrow <nf>; true blue, truepenny; trusty, faithful

VERBS **9** **keep faith,** not fail, **keep one's word** *or* **promise,** keep troth, show good faith, be as good as one's word, one's word is one's bond, redeem one's pledge, play by the rules, acquit oneself, make good; practice what one preaches

10 shoot straight <nf>, draw a straight furrow, **put one's cards on the table,** level with one <nf>, play it straight <nf>, shoot from the hip <nf>

11 **speak** *or* **tell the truth,** speak *or* tell true, paint in its true colors, tell the truth and shame the devil; tell the truth, the whole truth, and nothing but the truth, stick to the facts

12 **be frank, speak plainly,** speak out, speak one's mind, say what one thinks, **call a spade a spade,** tell it like it is, make no bones about it, not mince words

ADJS **13** **honest, upright,** uprighteous, **upstanding,** erect, right, **righteous, virtuous, good,** clean, squeaky-clean <nf>, **decent; honorable,** full of integrity, **reputable,** estimable, creditable, worthy, noble, sterling, manly, yeomanly; Christian <nf>; unimpeachable, beyond reproach, irreproachable, squeaky-clean <nf>, blameless, immaculate, spotless, stainless, unstained, unspotted, unblemished, untarnished, unsullied, undefiled, pure; **respectable,** highly respectable; **ethical, moral; principled, high-principled,** high-minded, right-minded; uncorrupt, uncorrupted, inviolate; truehearted, true-blue, true-souled, true-spirited; true-dealing, true-disposing, true-devoted; **law-abiding,** law-loving, law-revering; **fair, just** 649.7

14 **straight, square,** foursquare, straight-arrow <nf>, honest and aboveboard, right as rain; **fair and square; square-dealing,** square-shooting, straight-shooting, up-and-up, **on the up-and-up** *and* **on the level,** *and* on the square <nf>; **aboveboard, open and aboveboard;** bona fide, good-faith; authentic, all wool and a yard wide, veritable, genuine; single-hearted; honest as the day is long

15 **conscientious,** tender-conscienced; **scrupulous,** careful 339.10; punctilious, punctual, meticulous, religious, strict, nice; fastidious 495.9; overconscientious, overscrupulous

16 **honest, veracious, truthful,** true, true to one's word, veridical; truth-telling, truth-speaking, truth-declaring, truth-passing, truth-bearing, truth-loving, truth-seeking, truth-desiring, truth-guarding, truth-filled; true-speaking, true-meaning, true-tongued

17 **candid, frank, sincere,** genuine, ingenuous, frankhearted; **open,** openhearted, transparent, open-faced; artless 416.5; **straightforward, direct,** up-front *and* straight <nf>, **forthright,** downright, straight-out <nf>, straight-from-the-shoulder; plain, broad, round; **unreserved,** unrestrained, unconstrained, unchecked; unguarded, uncalculating; free; **outspoken, plain-spoken,** free-spoken, free-speaking, free-tongued; explicit, unequivocal; **blunt,** bluff, brusque; heart-to-heart

18 **undeceptive, undeceitful, undissembling,** undissimulating, undeceiving, undesigning, uncalculating; **guileless,** unbeguiling, unbeguileful; unassuming, unpretending, unfeigning, undisguising, unflattering; undissimulated, undissembled; unassumed, unaffected, unpretended, unfeigned, undisguised, unvarnished, untrimmed

19 trustworthy, trusty, trustable, faithworthy, **reliable, dependable, responsible,** straight <nf>, sure, to be trusted, **to be depended** or **relied upon,** to be counted or reckoned on, as good as one's word; tried, true, **tried and true,** tested, proven; unfalse, unperfidious, untreacherous; incorruptible, inviolable

20 faithful, loyal, devoted, allegiant; **true, true-blue,** true to one's colors; **constant, steadfast,** unswerving, steady, consistent, stable, unfailing, staunch, firm, solid

ADVS **21 honestly, uprightly, honorably,** upstandingly, erectly, **virtuously, righteously, decently,** worthily, reputably, nobly; unimpeachably, irreproachably, blamelessly, immaculately, unspottedly, stainlessly, purely; high-mindedly, morally; **conscientiously, scrupulously,** punctiliously, meticulously, fastidiously 495.14

22 truthfully, truly, veraciously; to tell the truth, to speak truthfully; in truth, in sooth <old>, of a truth, with truth, in good or very truth; objectively

23 candidly, frankly, sincerely, genuinely, in all seriousness or soberness, from the heart, in all conscience; in plain words or English, straight from the shoulder, not to mince the matter, not to mince words, without equivocation, with no nonsense, all joking aside or apart; **openly,** openheartedly, **unreservedly,** unrestrainedly, unconstrainedly, **forthrightly, directly, straightforwardly, outspokenly, plainly,** plain-spokenly, uninhibitedly, broadly, roundly, **bluntly,** bluffy, brusquely

24 trustworthily, trustily, **reliably, dependably, responsibly;** undeceptively, undeceitfully, guilelessly; incorruptibly, inviolably

25 faithfully, loyally, devotedly; **constantly, steadfastly,** steadily, responsibly, consistently, unfailingly, unswervingly, staunchly, firmly; in or with good faith, *bona fide* <L>

645 IMPROBITY

NOUNS **1 improbity,** untruthfulness, **dishonesty,** dishonor; **unscrupulousness,** unconscientiousness; **corruption,** corruptness, corruptedness; **crookedness,** criminality, feloniousness, **fraudulence** or fraudulency, underhandedness, unsavoriness, fishiness and shadiness <nf>, indirection, shiftiness, slipperiness, deviousness, evasiveness, unstraightforwardness, trickiness

2 knavery, roguery, rascality, rascalry, **villainy,** reprobacy, scoundrelism; chicanery 356.4; knavishness, roguishness, scampishness, villainousness, charlatanism; **baseness, vileness,** degradation, turpitude, moral turpitude

3 deceitfulness; falseness 354; perjury, forswearing, untruthfulness 354.8, credibility gap; inveracity; mendacity, mendaciousness; **insincerity,** unsincereness, uncandidness, uncandor, unfrankness, disingenuousness; hypocrisy; sharp practice 356.4; fraud 356.8; artfulness, craftiness 415.1; intrigue

4 untrustworthiness, unfaithworthiness, untrustiness, **unreliability, undependability,** irresponsibility

5 infidelity, unfaithfulness, unfaith, faithlessness, cheating, trothlessness; **inconstancy, unsteadfastness,** fickleness; **disloyalty,** unloyalty; **falsity,** falseness, untrueness; disaffection, recreancy, dereliction; bad faith, *mala fides* <L>, Punic faith; breach of promise, breach of trust or faith, barratry; breach of confidence

6 treachery, treacherousness; **perfidy,** perfidiousness, falseheartedness 354.4, two-facedness, doubleness, sycophancy, false face; **duplicity, double-dealing,** foul play, dirty work and dirty pool and dirty trick and dirty game <nf>; broken promise, breach of promise, breach of faith

7 treason, petty treason, misprision of treason, high treason; lese majesty, sedition; quislingism, fifth-column activity; collaboration, fraternization; subversion, subversiveness, subversivism

8 betrayal, betrayment, letting down <nf>, **double cross** and sellout <nf>, Judas kiss, kiss of death, stab in the back

9 corruptibility, venality, bribability, purchasability

10 criminal 660.9, perpetrator, perp <nf>, scoundrel 660.3, traitor 357.10, deceiver 357

VERBS **11** <be dishonest> live by one's wits; shift, shift about, evade; deceive; cheat; falsify; lie; sail under false colors, put on a false face, pass oneself off as

12 be unfaithful, not keep faith or troth, **go back on** <nf>, **fail,** break one's word or promise, renege, go back on one's word <nf>, break faith, betray, perjure or forswear oneself; forsake, desert 370.5; pass the buck <nf>; shift the responsibility or blame; cheat and cheat on and two-time <nf>

13 play one false, prove false; **stab one in the back,** backstab, knife one <nf>; bite the hand that feeds one; play dirty pool <nf>; shift or move the goalposts and change the rules <nf>; bamboozle

14 betray, double-cross and two-time <nf>, sell out and sell down the river <nf>, turn in; **mislead,** lead one down the garden path; let down; inform on 551.12

15 act the traitor, turn against, go over to the enemy, turn one's coat, sell oneself, sell out <nf>; collaborate, fraternize

ADJS **16 dishonest, dishonorable; unconscientious,** unconscienced, conscienceless, unconscionable, shameless, without shame or remorse, **unscrupulous, unprincipled,** unethical, immoral, amoral; **corrupt,** corrupted, rotten, bottom-dwelling; **crooked, criminal,** felonious, **fraudulent,** creative <nf>, underhand, underhanded; shady <nf>, up to no good, not kosher <nf>, unsavory, dark, sinister, insidious, indirect, slippery, devious, tricky, shifty, evasive, unstraightforward; fishy <nf>, questionable, suspicious, doubtful, dubious, hinky <nf>; ill-gotten, ill-got

17 knavish, roguish, scampish, rascally, scoundrelly, blackguardly, villainous, reprobate, recreant, **base, vile,** degraded; **infamous, notorious**

18 deceitful; falsehearted; perjured, forsworn, untruthful 354.34; **insincere,** unsincere, uncandid, unfrank, disingenuous; artful, crafty 415.12; calculating, scheming; **tricky,** cute and dodgy <nf>, slippery as an eel

19 untrustworthy, unfaithworthy, untrusty, trustless, **unreliable, undependable,** fly-by-night, irresponsible, unsure, not to be trusted, not to be depended or relied upon

20 unfaithful, faithless, of bad faith, trothless; **inconstant, unsteadfast,** fickle; **disloyal,** unloyal; false, **untrue,** not true to; disaffected, recreant, derelict, barratrous; two-timing <nf>

21 treacherous, perfidious, falsehearted; **shifty,** slippery, tricky; **double-dealing,** double, ambidextrous; **two-faced**

22 traitorous, turncoat, double-crossing and two-timing <nf>, betraying; Judas-like, Iscariotic; **treasonable,** treasonous; quisling, quislingistic, fifth-column, Trojan-horse; subversive, seditious

23 corruptible, venal, bribable, purchasable, on the pad <nf>, mercenary, hireling

ADVS **24 dishonestly, dishonorably; unscrupulously,** unconscientiously; **crookedly,** criminally, feloniously, **fraudulently,** underhandedly, like a thief in the night, insidiously, deviously, shiftily, evasively, fishily <nf>, suspiciously, dubiously, by fair means or foul; **deceitfully;** knavishly, roguishly, villainously; basely, vilely; infamously, notoriously

25 perfidiously, falseheartedly; **unfaithfully,** faithlessly; **treacherously;** traitorously, treasonably

646 HONOR

<token of esteem>

NOUNS **1 honor,** great honor, distinction, glory, credit, ornament

2 award, reward, prize; first prize, second prize, etc; blue ribbon; consolation prize; booby prize; Nobel Prize, Pulitzer Prize; sweepstakes; jackpot; Oscar, Academy Award, Emmy, Tony; gold medal; Olympic Gold or Silver or Bronze medal

3 trophy, laurel, **laurels,** bays, palm, palms, crown, chaplet, wreath, garland, **feather in one's cap** <nf>; civic crown or garland or wreath; **cup,** loving cup, pot <nf>; America's Cup, Old Mug; **belt,** championship belt, black belt, brown belt, etc; banner, flag

4 citation, eulogy, mention, honorable mention, kudos, **accolade, tribute, praise** 511.1

5 decoration, decoration of honor, order, ornament; ribbon, riband; blue ribbon, *cordon bleu* <Fr>; red ribbon, red ribbon of the Legion of Honor; cordon, grand cordon; garter; star, gold star

6 medal, military honor <see list>, order, medallion; military medal, service medal, war medal, soldier's medal; lifesaving medal, Carnegie hero's medal; police citation, departmental citation; spurs, stripes, pips, star, gold star

7 scholarship, fellowship; grant

VERBS **8 honor, do honor,** pay regard to, give or pay or render honor to, **recognize; cite; decorate,** pin a medal on; crown, crown with laurel; hand it to or take off one's hat to one <nf>, pay tribute, praise 511.5; give credit where credit is due; give one the red carpet treatment, roll out the red carpet

ADJS **9 honored, distinguished;** laureate, crowned with laurel

10 honorary, honorific, honorable

ADVS **11 with honor,** with distinction; *cum laude, magna cum laude, summa cum laude, insigne cum laude, honoris causa* <all L>

12 military honors

Air Medal	Distinguished Service
Bronze Star Medal	Order
Congressional Medal of	Distinguished Unit
Honor	Citation
Croix de Guerre <France>	Médaille Militaire
Distinguished Conduct	<France>
Medal	Medal of Honor
Distinguished Flying	Military Cross
Cross	Navy Cross
Distinguished Service	Order of the Purple Heart
Cross	Silver Star Medal
Distinguished Service	Unit Citation
Medal	Victoria Cross <Britain>

647 INSIGNIA

NOUNS **1 insignia, regalia,** ensign, **emblem, badge, symbol,** logo <nf>, marking, attribute; badge of office, mark of office, chain, chain of office, collar; wand, verge, *fasces* <L>, **mace, staff, baton;** livery, uniform, mantle, dress; tartan, tie, old school tie, regimental tie, club tie; ring, school ring, class ring; pin, button, lapel pin or button; cap and gown, mortarboard; cockade; brassard; figurehead, eagle; cross 170.4, skull and crossbones, swastika, hammer and sickle, rose, thistle, shamrock, fleur-de-lis, caduceus; medal, **decoration** 646.5; **heraldry,** armory, blazonry, sigillography, sphragistics

2 <heraldry terms> heraldic device, achievement, bearings, coat of arms, arms, armorial bearings, armory, blazonry, blazon; hatchment; shield, escutcheon, scutcheon, lozenge; charge, field; crest, torse, wreath, garland, bandeau, chaplet, mantling, helmet; crown, coronet; device, motto; pheon, broad arrow; animal charge, lion, unicorn, griffin, yale, cockatrice, falcon, alerion, eagle, spread eagle; marshaling, quartering, impaling, impalement, dimidiating, differencing, difference; ordinary, bar, bend, bar sinister, bend sinister, baton, chevron, chief, cross, fess, pale, paly, saltire; subordinary, billet, bordure, canton, flanch, fret, fusil, gyron, inescutcheon, mascle, orle, quarter, rustre, tressure; fess point, nombril point, honor point; cadency mark, file, label, crescent, mullet, martlet, annulet, fleur-de-lis, rose, cross moline, octofoil; tincture, gules, azure, vert, sable, purpure, tenne; metal, or, argent; fur, ermine, ermines, erminites, erminois, pean, vair; heraldic officials 575.21; Hershey bar or pip or hash mark <nf>

3 <royal insignia> **regalia**; scepter, rod, rod of empire; orb; armilla; purple, ermine, robe of state or royalty, robes of office; purple pall; crown, royal crown, coronet, tiara, diadem; cap of maintenance or dignity or estate, triple plume, Prince of Wales's feathers; uraeus; seal, signet, great seal, privy seal; throne; badge of office

4 <ecclesiastical insignia> tiara, triple crown; ring, keys; miter, crosier, crook, pastoral staff; pallium; cardinal's hat, red hat

5 <military insignia> insignia of rank, grade insignia, chevron, stripe; star, bar, eagle, spread eagle, chicken <nf>, pip <Brit>, oak leaf; branch of service insignia, insignia of branch or arm; unit insignia, organization insignia, shoulder patch, patch; shoulder sleeve insignia, badge, aviation badge or wings; parachute badge, submarine badge; service stripe, hash mark <nf>, overseas bar, Hershey bar <nf>; epaulet

6 <national insignia> American eagle, British lion and unicorn, Canadian maple leaf, English rose, French fleur-de-lis, Irish shamrock, Japanese rising sun, Nazi swastika, Roman eagle, Russian bear, Scottish thistle, Soviet hammer and sickle, Swiss cross, Welsh leek or daffodil

7 **flag, banner,** oriflamme, **standard,** gonfalon or gonfanon, guidon, *vexillum* <L>, *labarum* <L>; **pennant,** pennon, pennoncel, banneret or bannerette, banderole, swallowtail, burgee, ensign, **streamer; bunting;** coachwhip, long pennant; **national flag, colors;** royal standard; **ensign,** merchant flag, jack, Jolly Roger, black flag; house flag; <US> Old Glory, Stars and Stripes, Star-Spangled Banner, red, white, and blue; <Confederacy> Stars and Bars; <France> tricolor, *le drapeau tricolore* <Fr>; <Britain> Union Jack, Union Flag, white or red or blue ensign; yellow flag, white flag; vexillology; signal 517.15

648 TITLE

<appellation of dignity or distinction>

NOUNS 1 **title, honorific, honor,** title of honor; **handle** and handle to one's name <nf>; courtesy title

2 <honorifics> Excellency, Eminence, Reverence, Grace, Honor, Worship, Your or His or Her Excellency; Lord, My Lord, milord, Lordship, Your or His Lordship; Lady, My Lady, milady, Ladyship, Your or Her Ladyship; Highness, Royal Highness, Imperial Highness, Serene Highness, Your or His or Her Highness; Majesty, Royal Majesty, Imperial Majesty, Serene Majesty, Your or His or Her Majesty

3 Sir, sire, sirrah; Esquire; Master, Mister 76.7; mirza, effendi, sirdar, emir, khan, sahib

4 Mistress, Ms, madame 77.8

5 <ecclesiastical titles> Reverend, His Reverence, His Grace; Monsignor; Holiness, His Holiness; Dom, Brother, Sister, Father, Mother; Rabbi

6 **degree, academic degree** <see list>; **bachelor,** baccalaureate, *baccalaureus* <L>, bachelor's degree; **master,** master's degree; **doctor,** doctorate, doctor's degree, doctoral degree; terminal degree

ADJS 7 **titular,** titulary; honorific; honorary

8 the Noble, the Most Noble, the Most Excellent, the Most Worthy, the Most Worshipful; the Honorable, the Most Honorable, the Right Honorable; the Reverend, the Very Reverend, the Right Reverend, the Most Reverend

9 **academic degrees**

AA or Associate of Arts	AM or Master of Arts
AAS or Associate in	<Artium Magister>
Applied Science	AMusD or Doctor of
AB or Bachelor of Arts	Musical Arts
<Artium Baccalaureus>	AN or Associate in Nursing
ABLS or Bachelor of Arts	ArtsD or Doctor of Arts
in Library Science	AS or Associate of Science
AdjA or Adjunct in Arts	BA or Bachelor of Arts

BAE or Bachelor of Arts in Education
BAN or Bachelor of Arts in Nursing
BBA or Bachelor of Business Administration
BCE or Bachelor of Chemical Engineering
BCL or Bachelor of Civil Law
BD or Bachelor of Divinity
BFA or Bachelor of Fine Arts
BLitt or Blit or Bachelor of Literature
BMus or Bachelor of Music
BNS or Bachelor of Naval Science
BPhil or Bachelor of Philosophy
BS or Bachelor of Science
BSArch or Bachelor of Science in Architecture
ChD or Doctor of Chemistry
DD or Doctor of Divinity
DDS or Doctor of Dental Surgery
DEd or Doctor of Education
DJ or Djur or Doctor of Jurisprudence
DJS or D.Jur.Sc. or Doctor of Juridical Science
DLit or Dlitt or Doctor of Letters
DMD or Doctor of Dental Medicine
DMin or Doctor of Ministry
DMus or Doctor of Music
DO or Doctor of Osteopathy
DPH or Doctor of Public Health
DPhil or Doctor of Philosophy <Brit>
DS or Doctor of Science
DSC or Doctor of Surgical Chiropody
EdD or Doctor of Education
EdS or Education Specialist
JCD or Doctor of Canon Law

JD or Doctor of Jurisprudence
LittD or Doctor of Letters
LLB or Bachelor of Laws
LLD or Doctor of Laws
LLM or Master of Laws
MA or Master of Arts
MALS or Master of Arts in Library Science
MArch or Master of Architecture
MAT or Master of Arts in Teaching
MB or Bachelor of Medicine <Brit>
MBA or Master in Business Administration
MD or Doctor of Medicine
MDiv or Master of Divinity
MEd or Master of Education
MFA or Master of Fine Arts
MLitt or Master of Literature
MLS or Master of Library Science
MPhil or Master of Philosophy
MRE or Master of Religious Education
MS or Master of Science
MSW or Master of Social Work
MusD or Doctor of Music
OD or Doctor of Optometry
PharD or PharmD or Doctor of Pharmacy
PhD or Doctor of Philosophy
SB or Bachelor of Science
ScD or SD or Doctor of Science
SM or Master of Science
STD or Doctor of Sacred Theology
ThB or Bachelor of Theology
ThD or Doctor of Theology
ThM or Master of Theology
VMD or Doctor of Veterinary Medicine

649 JUSTICE

NOUNS **1 justice, justness; equity,** equitableness, level playing field <nf>; **evenhandedness,** measure for measure, give-and-take; balance, equality 790; **right, rightness,** rightfulness, meetness, properness, propriety, what is right; dueness 639; justification, **justifiableness,** justifiability, warrantedness, warrantability, defensibility; poetic justice; retributive justice, nemesis; summary justice, drumhead justice, rude justice; scales of justice; lawfulness, legality 673

2 **fairness,** fair-mindedness, candor; the fair thing, the right or proper thing, the handsome thing <nf>; level playing field, **square deal** and **fair shake** <nf>; **fair play,** cricket <nf>; sportsmanship, good sportsmanship, sportsmanliness, sportsmanlikeness

3 **impartiality,** detachment, **dispassion,** loftiness, Olympian detachment, **dispassionateness, disinterestedness,** disinterest, unbias, unbiasedness, a fair field and no favor; **neutrality** 467; selflessness, unselfishness 652

4 <personifications> Justice, Justitia, blind or blindfolded Justice; Rhadamanthus, Minos; <deities> Jupiter Fidius, Deus Fidius; Fides, Fides publica Romani, Fides populi Romani; Nemesis, Dike, Themis; Astraea

VERBS **5 be just, be fair,** do the fair thing, do the handsome thing <nf>, do right, be righteous, do it fair and square, do the right thing by; **do justice to,** see justice done, see one righted or redressed, redress a wrong or an injustice, remedy an injustice, serve one right, shoot straight with and **give a square deal** or **fair shake** <nf>; give the Devil his due; give and take; bend or lean over backwards, go out of one's way, go the extra mile <nf>

6 **play fair, play the game** <nf>, be a good sport, show a proper spirit; judge on its own merits, hold no brief

ADJS **7 just, fair,** square, **fair and square; equitable,** balanced, level <nf>, **even,** evenhanded; **right, rightful;** justifiable, justified, warranted, warrantable, defensible; **due** 639.7,10, deserved, merited; meet, meet and right, right and proper, fit, **proper, good,** as it should or ought to be; lawful, legal 673.11

8 fair-minded; **sporting,** sportsmanly, sportsmanlike; square-dealing and square-shooting <nf>

9 **impartial, impersonal, evenhanded,** equitable, **dispassionate, disinterested,** detached, objective, lofty, Olympian; **unbiased,** uninfluenced, unswayed; **neutral** 467.7; selfless, unselfish 652.5

ADVS **10 justly, fairly,** fair, in a fair manner; rightfully, rightly, duly, deservedly, meetly, properly; **equitably, equally, evenly,** upon even terms; justifiedly, justifiably, warrantably, warrantedly; **impartially, impersonally, dispassionately, disinterestedly,** without distinction, without regard or respect to persons, without fear or favor

11 in justice, in equity, in reason, in all conscience, in all fairness, **to be fair,** as is only fair *or* right, as is right *or* just *or* fitting *or* proper

650 INJUSTICE

NOUNS **1 injustice, unjustness; inequity,** iniquity, inequitableness, iniquitousness; inequality 791, inequality of treatment *or* dealing; **wrong, wrongness,** wrongfulness, unmeetness, improperness, **impropriety;** undueness 640; what should not be, what ought not *or* must not be; unlawfulness, illegality 674

2 unfairness; unsportsmanliness, **unsportsmanlikeness;** foul play, foul, a hit below the belt, dirty pool <nf>

3 partiality, onesidedness; bias, leaning, inclination, tendentiousness; undispassionateness, undetachment, interest, involvement, **partisanism,** partisanship, *parti pris* <Fr>, *Tendenz* <Ger>; unneutrality; **slant,** angle, spin <nf>; **favoritism,** preference, nepotism; unequal *or* preferential treatment, discrimination, unjust legal disability, inequality

4 injustice, wrong, injury, grievance, disservice; raw *or* rotten deal *and* bad rap <nf>; imposition; mockery *or* miscarriage of justice; great wrong, grave *or* gross injustice; atrocity, outrage

5 unjustifiability, unwarrantability, indefensibility; **inexcusability,** unconscionableness, **unpardonability,** unforgivableness, inexpiableness, irremissibility

VERBS **6** not play fair, hit below the belt, give a raw deal *or* rotten deal *or* bad rap <nf>

7 do one an injustice, wrong, do wrong, do wrong by, **do one a wrong,** do a disservice; do a great wrong, do a grave *or* gross injustice, commit an atrocity *or* outrage

8 favor, prefer, show preference, **play favorites,** treat unequally, discriminate; **slant,** angle, put on spin <nf>

ADJS **9 unjust, inequitable,** unequitable, iniquitous, **unbalanced, discriminatory, uneven, unequal** 791.4; **wrong, wrongful,** unrightful; **undue** 640.9, unmeet, undeserved, unmerited; unlawful, illegal 674.6

10 unfair, not fair; **unsporting,** unsportsmanly, **unsportsmanlike,** not done, not kosher <nf>, not cricket <Brit nf>; **dirty** <nf>, foul, below the belt; sexist

11 partial, interested, involved, **partisan,** unneutral, **one-sided,** all on *or* way over to one side, undetached, unobjective, **undispassionate, biased,** tendentious, tendential, warped, influenced, swayed, slanted

12 unjustifiable, unwarrantable, unallowable, unreasonable, indefensible; **inexcusable,** unconscionable, **unpardonable, unforgivable,** inexpiable, irremissible

ADVS **13 unjustly, unfairly;** wrongfully, wrongly, undeservedly; inequitably, iniquitously, unequally, unevenly; partially, interestedly, one-sidedly, undispassionately; **unjustifiably, unwarrantably,** unallowably, unreasonably, indefensibly; inexcusably, unconscionably, unpardonably, unforgivably, inexpiably, irremissibly

651 SELFISHNESS

NOUNS **1 selfishness,** selfism, **self-seeking,** self-serving, self-pleasing, **self-indulgence,** hedonism; self-advancement, self-promotion, self-advertisement; **careerism,** personal ambition; **narcissism, self-love,** self-devotion, self-jealousy, **self-consideration,** self-solicitude, self-sufficiency, self-absorption, ego trip, self-occupation; self-containment, self-isolation; autism, catatonia, remoteness 583.2; **self-interest,** self-concern, self-interestedness, interest; self-esteem, self-admiration 140.1; **self-centeredness, self-obsession, narcissism, egotism** 140.3; **avarice, greed,** graspingness, grabbiness <nf>, acquisitiveness, possessiveness, covetousness; **individualism** 430.5, personalism, privatism, private *or* personal desires, private *or* personal aims; looking out for number one; me generation, entitlement generation

2 ungenerousness, unmagnanimousness, illiberality, meanness, smallness, littleness, paltriness, minginess, pettiness; **niggardliness, stinginess** 484.3

3 self-seeker, self-pleaser, self-advancer; member of the me generation, member of the entitlement generation; **narcissist, egotist** 140.5; timepleaser, timeserver, temporizer; fortune hunter, moneygrubber, tufthunter, name-dropper; self-server, careerist; opportunist; monopolist, hog, road hog; dog in the manger; **individualist,** loner *and* lone wolf <nf>

VERBS **4 please oneself,** gratify oneself; ego-trip *and* be *or* go on an ego trip <nf>, be full of oneself; indulge *or* pamper *or* coddle oneself, consult one's own wishes, look after one's own interests, know which side one's bread is buttered on, take care of *or* look out for number one *or* numero uno <nf>, think only of oneself, want everything, have one's cake and eat it; covet; monopolize, hog

ADJS **5 selfish, self-seeking, self-serving,** self-advancing, self-promoting, self-advertising, careerist, opportunistic, ambitious for self,

self-indulgent, self-pleasing, hedonistic, self-jealous, self-sufficient, **self-interested,** self-considerative, self-besot, self-devoted, self-occupied, self-absorbed, wrapped up in oneself, self-contained, autistic, remote 583.6; self-esteeming, self-admiring 140.8; **self-centered, self-obsessed, narcissistic, egotistical** 140.10; possessive; **avaricious, greedy,** covetous, grasping, graspy *and* grabby <nf>, acquisitive; **individualistic,** personalistic, privatistic

6 **ungenerous, illiberal,** unchivalrous, mean, small, little, paltry, mingy, petty; **niggardly, stingy** 484.9

ADVS 7 **selfishly, for oneself,** in one's own interest, from selfish *or* interested motives, to gain some private ends

652 UNSELFISHNESS

NOUNS 1 **unselfishness, selflessness;** self-subjection, self-subordination, self-suppression, self-abasement, self-effacement; **humility** 137; modesty 139; self-neglect, self-neglectfulness, self-forgetfulness; **self-renunciation,** self-renouncement; **self-denial,** self-abnegation, self-effacement; **self-sacrifice,** sacrifice, self-immolation, self-devotion, devotion, dedication, commitment, consecration; disinterest, disinterestedness; unpossessiveness, unacquisitiveness; **altruism** 143.4; martyrdom

2 **magnanimity,** magnanimousness, greatness of spirit *or* soul, **generosity,** generousness, openhandedness, **liberality,** liberalness; **bigness, bigheartedness,** greatheartedness, largeheartedness, big *or* large *or* great heart, greatness of heart; noble-mindedness, **high-mindedness, idealism; benevolence** 143.4; **nobleness,** nobility, princeliness, greatness, **loftiness,** elevation, exaltation, sublimity; chivalry, chivalrousness, knightliness, errantry, knight-errantry; heroism; consideration, considerateness, compassion

VERBS 3 not have a selfish bone in one's body, think only of others; be generous to a fault; put oneself out, go out of the way, lean over backwards; sacrifice, make a sacrifice; subject oneself, subordinate oneself, abase oneself; show compassion; take a backseat

4 observe the golden rule, do as one would be done by, do unto others as you would have others do unto you

ADJS 5 **unselfish, selfless;** self-unconscious, self-forgetful, self-abasing, self-effacing; **altruistic** 143.15, **humble; unpretentious, modest** 139.9; self-neglectful, self-neglecting; **self-denying,** self-renouncing, self-abnegating, self-abnegatory,

self-effacing; **self-sacrificing,** self-immolating, sacrificing, self-devotional, self-devoted, devoted, dedicated, committed, consecrated, unsparing of self, disinterested; unpossessive, unacquisitive; ready to die for, martyred

6 **magnanimous,** great-souled *or* -spirited; **generous,** generous to a fault, openhanded, **liberal; big, bighearted,** greathearted, largehearted, great of heart *or* soul; noble-minded, **high-minded, idealistic,** public-spirited; **benevolent** 143.15, **noble,** princely, handsome, great, high, elevated, **lofty,** exalted, sublime; chivalrous, knightly; heroic

ADVS 7 **unselfishly, altruistically,** forgetful of self; for others

8 **magnanimously, generously,** openhandedly, **liberally; bigheartedly,** greatheartedly, largeheartedly; **nobly,** handsomely; chivalrously, knightly

653 VIRTUE

<moral goodness>

NOUNS 1 **virtue, virtuousness, goodness, righteousness,** rectitude, right conduct *or* behavior, the straight and narrow, the right thing, integrity; probity 644; **morality,** moral fiber *or* rectitude *or* virtue *or* excellence, morale; **saintliness,** saintlikeness, angelicalness; **godliness** 692.2; aretaics

2 **purity,** immaculacy, immaculateness, spotlessness, unspottedness; upstandingness; **uncorruptness,** uncorruptedness, incorruptness; angel, saint, good egg <nf>; **unsinfulness, sinlessness,** unwickedness, uniniquitousness; undegenerateness, undepravedness, undissoluteness, undebauchedness; **chastity** 664; guiltlessness, innocence 657

3 **cardinal virtues,** natural virtues; prudence, justice, temperance, fortitude; theological virtues *or* supernatural virtues; faith, hope, charity *or* love

VERBS 4 **be good,** do no evil, do the right thing; keep in the right path, walk the straight path, follow the straight and narrow, keep on the straight and narrow way *or* path, fly right, resist temptation; fight the good fight

ADJS 5 **virtuous, good, moral; upright, honest** 644.13,14,16; **righteous,** just, straight, rightminded, right-thinking; **angelic,** seraphic; **saintly,** saintlike; **godly** 692.9; irreproachable; goody-goody

6 **chaste, immaculate, spotless, pure** 664.4; **clean,** squeaky-clean <nf>; guiltless, **innocent** 657.6; pure as the driven snow

7 uncorrupt, uncorrupted, incorrupt, incorrupted; **unsinful,** sinless; **unwicked,** uniniquitous, unerring, unfallen; undegenerate, undepraved, undemoralized, undissolute, undebauched

654 VICE

<*moral badness*>

NOUNS **1 vice,** viciousness; criminality, **wrongdoing** 655; **immorality,** unmorality, **evil; amorality** 636.4; **unvirtuousness,** ungoodness; **unrighteousness, ungodliness,** unsaintliness, unangelicalness; **uncleanness, impurity, unchastity** 665, fallenness, fallen state, lapsedness; waywardness, wantonness, prodigality; delinquency, moral delinquency; peccability; backsliding, recidivism; **evil nature, carnality** 663.2

2 vice, weakness, weakness of the flesh, **flaw,** moral flaw *or* blemish, **frailty, infirmity; failing,** failure; weak point, weak side, foible; bad habit, besetting sin; **fault, imperfection** 1003; laxity, lack of principle

3 iniquity, evil, bad, wrong, error, obliquity, villainy, knavery, reprobacy, peccancy, **abomination, atrocity, infamy,** shame, disgrace, scandal, unforgivable *or* cardinal *or* mortal sin, **sin** 655.2; seven deadly sins, pride, covetousness *or* avarice, lust, anger, gluttony, envy, sloth

4 wickedness, badness, naughtiness, **evilness, viciousness, sinfulness, iniquitousness,** wicked ways; **baseness,** rankness, **vileness,** foulness, arrantness, nefariousness, **heinousness,** infamousness, villainousness, flagitiousness; fiendishness, hellishness; devilishness, devilry, deviltry; bad egg <nf>

5 turpitude, moral turpitude; corruption, corruptedness, corruptness, rottenness, moral pollution *or* pollutedness, lack *or* absence of moral fiber; **decadence** *or* decadency, debasement, **degradation,** demoralization, abjection; **degeneracy,** degenerateness, degeneration, reprobacy, **depravity,** depravedness, depravation, corruption, perversion; **dissoluteness, profligacy;** abandonment, abandon; notoriety

6 obduracy, hardheartedness, hardness, callousness, heartlessness, hardness of heart, heart of stone

7 sewer, gutter, pit, sink, sink of corruption, sinkhole; **den of iniquity, den, fleshpot,** hellhole; hole *and* joint *and* the pits <nf>; Sodom, Gomorrah, Babylon; **brothel** 665.9; road to hell; hellhole

VERBS **8 do wrong, sin** 655.5; misbehave, misdemean *and* misdo <old>

9 go wrong, stray, go astray, **err,** deviate, deviate from the path of virtue, leave the straight and narrow, step out of line, get or go off base <nf>; **fall,** fall from grace, **lapse,** slip, trip; **degenerate; go to the bad** 395.24, go to the dogs; **relapse,** recidivate, backslide 394.4

10 corrupt; sully, soil, defile; demoralize, vitiate; mislead; seduce, tempt

ADJS **11** vice-prone, vice-laden, vicious, **steeped in vice; immoral,** unmoral; **amoral,** nonmoral; unethical

12 unvirtuous, virtueless, ungood; **unrighteous, ungodly,** unsaintly, unangelic; morally weak, lax; **unclean, impure,** spotted, flawed, blemished, maculate <old>, **unchaste** 665.23; fleshly, carnal 663.6, wayward, wanton, prodigal; erring, **fallen, lapsed,** postlapsarian; frail, weak, infirm; Adamic; peccable; **relapsing, backsliding,** recidivist, recidivistic; of easy virtue 665.26

13 diabolic, diabolical, devilish, demonic, demoniac, demoniacal, **satanic,** Mephistophelian; **fiendish,** fiendlike; **hellish,** hellborn, **infernal**

14 corrupt, corrupted, vice-corrupted, polluted, morally polluted, rotten, tainted, contaminated, vitiated; warped, perverted; **decadent,** debased, degraded, reprobate, **depraved, debauched,** debaucherous, **dissolute, degenerate,** profligate, abandoned, gone to the bad *or* dogs, sunk *or* steeped in iniquity, rotten at *or* to the core, in the sewer *or* gutter

15 evil-minded, evilhearted, **blackhearted; base-minded,** low-minded; low-thoughted, dirty *or* dirty-minded <nf>; crooked

16 wicked, evil, vicious, bad, naughty, wrong, sinful, iniquitous, peccant, reprobate; dark, black; **base, low, vile,** foul, rank, flagrant, arrant, nefarious, **heinous,** villainous, criminal, up to no good, knavish, flagitious; abominable, atrocious, monstrous, unspeakable, execrable, damnable; shameful, disgraceful, scandalous, **infamous, unpardonable,** unforgivable; **improper,** reprehensible, blamable, blameworthy, unworthy

17 hardened, hard, case-hardened, obdurate, inured, indurated; **callous,** calloused, **seared; hardhearted,** heartless; **shameless,** lost to shame, blind to virtue, lost to all sense of honor, conscienceless, unblushing, **brazen**

18 irreclaimable, irredeemable, unredeemable, unregenerate, **irreformable,** incorrigible, past praying for; shriftless, graceless, **lost**

ADVS **19 wickedly, evilly, sinfully, iniquitously,** peccantly, **viciously;** basely, vilely, foully, rankly, arrantly, flagrantly, flagitiously

655 WRONGDOING

NOUNS **1 wrongdoing, evildoing, wickedness,** misdoing <old>, wrong conduct, **misbehavior** 322, **misconduct,** misdemeaning, misfeasance, malfeasance, malversation, **malpractice,** evil courses, machinations of the devil; **sin; crime, criminality,** lawbreaking, feloniousness, trespass, offense, transgression, infringement, infraction, breach, encroachment; criminal tendency; habitual criminality, criminosis; viciousness, **vice** 654; misprision, negative *or* positive misprision, misprision of treason *or* felony

2 **misdeed, misdemeanor,** misfeasance, malfeasance, malefaction, criminal *or* guilty *or* sinful act, **offense,** injustice, injury, **wrong, iniquity, evil,** peccancy, *malum* <L>; tort; **error, fault,** breach; **impropriety,** slight *or* minor wrong, venial sin, **indiscretion,** peccadillo, misstep, trip, slip, lapse; **transgression,** trespass; **sin; cardinal** *or* **deadly** *or* **mortal sin,** grave *or* heavy sin, unutterable sin, unpardonable *or* unforgivable *or* inexpiable sin, original sin, capital sin, carnal sin; sin against the Holy Ghost; sin of commission; sin of omission, nonfeasance, omission, failure, dereliction, delinquency; **crime, felony;** capital crime; white-collar crime, execu-crime; computer crime; copycat crime <nf>; war crime, crime against humanity, genocide, terrorism; **outrage, atrocity,** enormity

3 **original sin,** fall from grace, fall, fall of man, fall of Adam *or* Adam's fall, sin of Adam; **cardinal sins,** lust, gluttony, greed, sloth, wrath, envy, pride

VERBS 4 **do wrong,** do amiss, misdo <old>, misdemean oneself, **misbehave** 322.4, **err,** offend; **sin,** commit sin; **transgress,** trespass

ADJS 5 **wrongdoing, evildoing,** malefactory, malfeasant; **wrong,** iniquitous, **sinful, wicked** 654.16; **criminal,** felonious, criminous <old>; crime-infested, crime-ridden

656 GUILT

NOUNS 1 **guilt, guiltiness; criminality,** peccancy; guilty *or* wrongful *or* criminal involvement; **culpability,** reprehensibility, blamability, blameworthiness; chargeability, answerability, much to answer for; censurability, censurableness, reproachability, reproachableness, reprovability, reprovableness, inculpation, implication, involvement, complicity, impeachability, impeachableness, indictability, indictableness, arraignability, arraignableness; bloodguilt *or* -guiltiness, red-handedness, dirty hands, red *or* bloody hands, "hangman's hands"—Shakespeare; much to answer for; **ruth,** ruefulness, remorse, guilty conscience, guilt feelings; onus, burden

VERBS 2 **be guilty,** look guilty, have no alibi, look like the cat that swallowed the canary, blush, stammer; have on one's hands *or* to one's

discredit, have much to answer for; have a red face; be caught in the act *or* flatfooted *or* redhanded, be caught with one's pants down *or* with one's hand in the till *or* with one's hand in the cookie jar <nf>; guilt someone <nf>

ADJS 3 **guilty,** guilty as hell, peccant, **criminal, to blame, at fault,** faulty, in the wrong, on one's head; **culpable,** reprehensible, censurable, reproachable, reprovable, inculpated, implicated, involved, impeachable, indictable, arraignable; red-handed, bloodguilty; caught in the act *or* flatfooted *or* red-handed, caught with one's pants down *or* with one's hand in the till *or* with one's hand in the cookie jar <nf>

ADVS 4 **red-handed,** red-hand, **in the act,** in the very act, *in flagrante delicto* <L>

5 **guilty,** shamefacedly, sheepishly, with a guilty conscience

657 INNOCENCE

NOUNS 1 **innocence,** innocency, innocentness; unfallen *or* unlapsed *or* prelapsarian state, state of grace; unguiltiness, **guiltlessness,** faultlessness, blamelessness, reproachlessness, **sinlessness,** offenselessness; **spotlessness,** stainlessness, taintlessness, unblemishedness; **purity,** cleanness, cleanliness, whiteness, immaculateness, immaculacy, impeccability; clean hands, clean slate, clear conscience, nothing to hide

2 childlikeness 416.1; lamblikeness, dove-likeness, angelicness; unacquaintance with evil, uncorruptedness, incorruptness, pristineness, undefiledness; naiveté

3 **inculpability,** unblamability, unblamableness, **unblameworthiness,** irreproachability, irreproachableness, impeccability, impeccableness, unexceptionability, unexceptionableness, **irreprehensibility,** irreprehensibleness, uncensurability, uncensurableness, unimpeachability, unimpeachableness, unindictableness, unarraignableness

4 **innocent,** baby, babe, babe in arms, newborn babe, infant, babe in the woods, child, mere child, lamb, dove, angel; virgin

VERBS 5 know no wrong, have clean hands, have a clear conscience, look as if butter would not melt in one's mouth; have nothing to hide

ADJS 6 **innocent;** unfallen, unlapsed, prelapsarian; **unguilty,** not guilty, **guiltless, faultless, blameless,** reproachless, **sinless,** offenseless, with clean hands; clear, in the clear; without reproach, *sans reproche* <Fr>; innocent as a lamb, lamblike, dovelike, angelic, childlike 416.5; unacquainted with *or* untouched by evil, uncorrupted, incorrupt, pristine, undefiled; innocuous

7 **spotless,** stainless, taintless, unblemished, unspotted, **untainted, unsoiled, unsullied, undefiled,** wemless; **pure, clean, immaculate,** impeccable, white, pure *or* white as driven snow, squeaky-clean <nf>

8 **inculpable,** unblamable, unblameworthy, **irreproachable,** beyond reproach, irreprovable, **irreprehensible,** uncensurable, unimpeachable, unindictable, unarraignable, unobjectionable, unexceptionable, above suspicion, squeaky-clean <nf>, with clean hands

ADVS 9 **innocently, guiltlessly, unguiltily,** with a clear conscience; **unknowingly,** unconsciously, unawares

658 ATONEMENT

NOUNS 1 **atonement, reparation, amends,** making amends, **restitution, propitiation, expiation, redress, recompense,** compensation, setting right, making right *or* good, making up, squaring, redemption, reclamation, satisfaction, quittance; making it quits; indemnity, indemnification; compromise, composition; expiatory offering *or* sacrifice, piaculum, peace offering; eye for an eye, measure for measure; conciliation, propitiation

2 **apology, excuse,** regrets; acknowledgment, penitence, contrition, breast-beating, *mea culpa* <L>, confession 351.3; abject apology

3 **penance,** penitence, repentance; penitential act *or* exercise, **mortification,** maceration, flagellation, lustration; sacrifice, offering, peace offering; **asceticism** 667, **fasting** 515; **purgation,** purgatory; **sackcloth and ashes;** hair shirt; **Lent;** Day of Atonement, Yom Kippur

VERBS 4 **atone, atone for, propitiate, expiate,** compensate, restitute, recompense, redress, redeem, repair, satisfy, give satisfaction, **make amends, make reparation** *or* **compensation** *or* **expiation** *or* **restitution,** make good *or* right, rectify, set right, **make up for,** make matters up, square, square things, make it quits, pay the forfeit *or* penalty, pay one's dues <nf>, pay back, wipe off old scores; wipe the slate clean; set one's house in order; live down, unlive; reconcile, propitiate

5 **apologize, beg pardon, ask forgiveness,** beg indulgence, express regret; take back; get *or* fall down on one's knees, get down on one's marrowbones <nf>, come hat in hand; confess, admit

6 **do penance,** flagellate oneself, mortify oneself, mortify one's flesh, make oneself miserable, shrive oneself, purge oneself, cleanse oneself of guilt, stand in a white sheet, repent in sackcloth and ashes, wear a hair shirt, wear sackcloth *or* sackcloth and ashes; receive absolution; regret, show remorse *or* compunction

ADJS 7 **atoning, propitiatory, expiatory,** piacular, reparative, reparatory, restitutive, restitutory, restitutional, redressing, recompensing, compensatory, compensational, righting, squaring, conciliatory; redemptive, redeeming, reclamatory, satisfactional; **apologetic, apologetical;** repentant, repenting; **penitential,** purgative, purgatorial; lustral, lustrative, lustrational, cleansing, purifying; ascetic

659 GOOD PERSON

NOUNS 1 good person, fine person, good *or* fine man *or* woman *or* child, worthy, prince, nature's nobleman *or* -woman, man *or* woman after one's own heart; *persona grata* <L>, acceptable person; **good fellow,** capital fellow, **good sort,** right sort, a decent sort of fellow, good lot <Brit nf>, no end of a fellow; real person, real man *or* woman, mensch <nf>, cool cat <nf>; **gentleman,** perfect gentleman, a gentleman and a scholar; **lady,** perfect lady; **gem,** jewel, pearl, diamond; rough diamond, diamond in the rough; honest man 644.8

2 <nf terms> **good guy,** crackerjack, brick, trump, good egg, stout fellow, nice guy, Mr Nice Guy, good Joe, likely lad, no slouch, doll, living doll, pussycat, **sweetheart, sweetie**

3 **good** *or* **respectable citizen,** excellent *or* exemplary citizen, good neighbor, burgher, taxpayer, **pillar of society,** pillar of the church, salt of the earth; Christian *and* true Christian <nf>

4 **paragon, ideal,** beau ideal, nonpareil, person to look up to, *chevalier sans peur et sans reproche* <Fr>, **good example, role model,** shining example, gold standard; exemplar, epitome; **model, pattern, standard,** norm, mirror; *Übermensch* <Ger; Nietzsche>; **standout,** one in a thousand *or* ten thousand, man of men, a man among men, woman of women, a woman among women

5 **hero, god, demigod,** phoenix; **heroine, goddess,** demigoddess; **idol;** fairy godmother

6 holy man; great soul, mahatma; guru, *rishi* <Skt>; *starets* <Russ>; saint, angel 679

660 BAD PERSON

NOUNS 1 bad person, bad man *or* woman *or* child, unworthy *or* disreputable person, unworthy, disreputable, **undesirable,** *persona non grata* <L>, unacceptable *or* unwanted *or* objectionable person, baddy *and* wrongo *and* bad news <nf>; bad egg, bad example

2 **wretch,** mean *or* miserable wretch, **beggarly fellow, beggar, blighter** <Brit nf>; **bum** *and* bummer *and* lowlifer *and* lowlife *and* **mucker** <nf>, caitiff, budmash <India>, pilgarlic; devil, **poor devil,** *pauvre diable* <Fr>, poor creature, *mauvais sujet* <Fr>; **sad case,** sad sack *and* sad sack of shit <nf>; **good-for-nothing, good-for-naught, no-good** <nf>, **ne'er-do-well,** wastrel, *vaurien* <Fr>, worthless fellow; **derelict,** skid-row bum, Bowery bum, tramp, hobo, beachcomber, **drifter,** drunkard, vagrant, vag <nf>, vagabond, truant, stiff *and* bindlestiff <nf>, swagman *or* sundowner <Austral>; human wreck; trailer trash, white trash

3 **rascal,** precious rascal, rogue, knave, **scoundrel,** villain, blackguard, **scamp, scalawag** <nf>, spalpeen <Ir>, rapscallion, **devil;** shyster; sneak

4 **reprobate,** recreant, **miscreant,** bad *or* sorry lot <Brit nf>, bad egg *and* wrongo *and* wrong number <nf>, bad'un *or* wrong'un <Brit nf>; scapegrace, black sheep; lost soul, lost sheep, *âme damnée* <Fr>, backslider, recidivist, fallen angel; degenerate, pervert; profligate, **lecher** 665.11; trollop, **whore** 665.14,16; **pimp** 665.18

5 <nf terms> **asshole, prick, bastard, son of a bitch** *or* SOB, **jerk, horse's ass,** creep, motherfucker, mother, dork, **shit,** turd, birdturd, shithead, shitface, cuntface, dickhead, fart, **louse, meanie, heel, shitheel, rat,** rat bastard, **stinker,** stinkard, pill, bugger, dirtbag, dweeb, twerp, sleaze, sleazoid, sleazebag, bad lot <Brit>; **hood, hooligan** 593.4

6 beast, **animal; cur,** dog, hound, whelp, mongrel; **reptile,** viper, serpent, snake; vermin, varmint <nf>, hyena; **swine,** pig; **skunk,** polecat; insect, worm

7 cad, bounder *and* rotter <nf>

8 **wrongdoer, malefactor, sinner,** transgressor, delinquent; malfeasor, misfeasor, nonfeasor; misdemeanant, misdemeanist; **culprit, offender; evil person, evil man** *or* **woman** *or* **child, evildoer** 593

9 **criminal, felon, perpetrator, crook** *and* perp <nf>, public enemy, **lawbreaker,** scofflaw; **gangster** *and* mobster *and* wiseguy <nf>, **racketeer; swindler** 357.3; thief 483; thug 593.3; **desperado,** desperate criminal; **outlaw,** fugitive, **convict,** jailbird, gaolbird <Brit>; gallows bird <nf>; **traitor,** betrayer, quisling, Judas, double-dealer, two-timer <nf>, **deceiver** 357; stalker

10 **the underworld,** gangland, gangdom, **organized crime,** organized crime family, the rackets, the mob, the syndicate, the Mafia, Cosa Nostra, Black Hand; **gangsterism; gangster,** ganglord, gangleader, caporegime *or* capo, button man, soldier

11 **the wicked,** the bad, the evil, the unrighteous, the reprobate; sons of men, sons of Belial, sons *or* children of the devil, limbs *or* get *or* imps of Satan, children of darkness; **scum of the earth,** dregs of society

661 DISREPUTE

NOUNS 1 **disrepute, ill repute,** bad repute, bad *or* poor reputation, evil repute *or* reputation, ill fame, shady *or* unsavory reputation, **bad name,** bad odor, bad report, bad character; **disesteem, dishonor,** public dishonor, **discredit; disfavor,** ill-favor; disapprobation 510.1

2 **disreputability,** disreputableness, **notoriety;** discreditableness, dishonorableness, unsavoriness, **unrespectability;** disgracefulness, **shamefulness**

3 **baseness, lowness, meanness, crumminess** <nf>, poorness, pettiness, paltriness, smallness, littleness, pokiness, cheesiness <nf>, beggarliness, **shabbiness, shoddiness, squalor,** scrubbiness, scumminess, scabbiness, scurviness, scruffiness, shittiness <nf>; **abjectness, wretchedness,** miserableness, despicableness, contemptibleness, contemptibility, abominableness, execrableness, obnoxiousness; **vulgarity,** tastelessness, crudity, crudeness, tackiness *and* chintziness <nf>; **vileness** 98.2, foulness, rankness, fulsomeness, grossness, nefariousness, heinousness, **atrociousness,** monstrousness, enormity; degradation, debasement, depravity

4 **infamy,** infamousness; **ignominy,** ignominiousness; ingloriousness, **ignobility,** odium, obloquy, opprobrium; depluming, displuming, loss of honor *or* name *or* repute *or* face; degradation, comedown <nf>, **demotion** 447

5 **disgrace, scandal, humiliation; shame,** dirty shame *and* low-down dirty shame <nf>, crying *or* burning shame; **reproach,** byword, byword of reproach, a disgrace to one's name

6 **stigma,** stigmatism, onus; **brand,** badge of infamy; **slur,** reproach, censure, reprimand, imputation, aspersion, reflection, stigmatization; pillorying; **black eye** <nf>, black mark; **disparagement** 512; **stain, taint,** attaint, **tarnish,** blur, **smirch,** smutch *or* smooch, smudge, **smear,** spot, blot, blot on *or* in one's escutcheon *or* scutcheon; bend *or* bar sinister <heraldry>; baton *and* champain *and* point champain <heraldry>; mark of Cain; broad arrow <Brit>; shady past

VERBS 7 **incur disgrace,** incur disesteem *or*

dishonor *or* discredit, get a black eye <nf>, be shamed, earn a bad name *or* reproach *or* reproof, forfeit one's good opinion, fall into disrepute, seal one's infamy; lose one's good name, **lose face,** lose countenance, lose credit, **lose caste; disgrace oneself,** lower oneself, demean oneself, drag one's banner in the dust, degrade *or* debase oneself, act beneath oneself, dirty *or* soil one's hands, get one's hands dirty, sully *or* lower oneself, derogate, stoop, descend, ride to a fall, fall from one's high estate, fall from grace *or* favor, foul one's own nest; **scandalize,** make oneself notorious, put one's good name in jeopardy; compromise oneself; raise eyebrows, cause eyebrows to raise, cause tongues to wag

8 **disgrace, dishonor, discredit,** reflect discredit upon, bring into discredit, reproach, cast reproach upon, be a reproach to; **shame, put to shame,** impute shame to, hold up to shame; hold up to public shame *or* public scorn *or* public ridicule, pillory, bring shame upon, **humiliate** 137.4; **degrade, debase** 447.3, deplume, displume, defrock, unfrock, bring low

9 **stigmatize, brand; stain, besmirch,** smirch, tarnish, taint, attaint, blot, **blacken, smear,** bespatter, desecrate, **sully,** soil, defile, vilify, **slur,** cast a slur upon, blow upon; disapprove 510.10; **disparage, defame** 512.9; censure, reprimand, **give a black eye** <nf>, give a black mark, put in one's bad *or* black books; give a bad name, give a dog a bad name; expose, expose to infamy; pillory, gibbet; burn *or* hang in effigy; **skewer,** impale, crucify

ADJS 10 **disreputable, discreditable, dishonorable,** unsavory, shady, **seamy, sordid; unrespectable, ignoble, ignominious, infamous,** inglorious; notorious; unpraiseworthy; derogatory 512.13

11 **disgraceful, shameful,** pitiful, deplorable, opprobrious, sad, sorry, too bad; degrading, debasing, demeaning, beneath one, beneath one's dignity, *infra indignitatem* <L>, infra dig <nf>, unbecoming, unworthy of one; cheap, gutter; **humiliating,** humiliative; **scandalous,** shocking, outrageous

12 **base, low,** low rent *and* low ride *and* low-down *and* cotton-picking <nf>, **mean,** crummy <nf>, poor, petty, paltry, small, little, **shabby, shoddy, squalid,** lumpen, scrubby, scummy, scabby, **scurvy,** scruffy, mangy <nf>, measly *and* cheesy <nf>, poky, beggarly, **wretched, miserable,** abject, **despicable, contemptible,** abominable, execrable, obnoxious, **vulgar,** tasteless, crude, **tacky** *and* chintzy <nf>; **disgusting, odious** 98.18, vile, foul, **dirty,** rank, fulsome, gross, flagrant, grave, arrant, nefarious, heinous, reptilian, **atrocious,** monstrous,

unspeakable, unmentionable; degraded, debased, depraved

13 **in disrepute,** in bad repute, in bad odor; **in disfavor,** in discredit, **in bad** <nf>, in one's bad *or* black books, out of favor, out of countenance, at a discount; **in disgrace,** in Dutch *and* **in the doghouse** <nf>, under a cloud; scandal-plagued *or* -ridden; stripped of reputation, disgraced, discredited, dishonored, shamed, loaded with shame, unable to show one's face; **in trouble**

14 **unrenowned,** renownless, nameless, inglorious, **unnotable, unnoted,** unnoticed, unremarked, **undistinguished, unfamed,** uncelebrated, unsung, unhonored, unglorified, unpopular; no credit to; **unknown,** little known, obscure, unheard-of, *ignotus* <L>

ADVS 15 **disreputably, discreditably, dishonorably, unrespectably, ignobly, ignominiously, infamously,** ingloriously

16 **disgracefully, scandalously,** shockingly, deplorably, outrageously; **shamefully,** to one's shame, to one's shame be it spoken

17 **basely, meanly,** poorly, pettily, **shabbily, shoddily,** scurvily, **wretchedly, miserably,** abjectly, **despicably, contemptibly,** abominably, execrably, obnoxiously, **odiously** 98.26, **vilely,** foully, grossly, flagrantly, arrantly, nefariously, heinously, **atrociously,** monstrously

662 REPUTE

NOUNS 1 **repute, reputation; name,** character, figure; **fame,** famousness, **renown, kudos,** report, glory; éclat, **celebrity, popularity,** recognition, a place in the sun; popular acceptance *or* favor, vogue; **acclaim, public acclaim,** réclame, **publicity; notoriety,** notoriousness, talk of the town; **exposure;** play *and* air-play <nf>

2 **reputability,** reputableness; good reputation, good name, **good** *or* **high repute,** good report, good track record <nf>, good odor, face, fair name, name to conjure with; good reference; good color

3 **esteem,** estimation, **honor, regard, respect,** approval, approbation, account, favor, consideration, **credit,** credibility, points *and* Brownie points <nf>

4 **prestige, honor; dignity; rank, standing,** stature, high place, eminence, position, station, face, **status**

5 **distinction, mark, note; importance, consequence,** significance; **notability, prominence, eminence, preeminence, greatness,** conspicuousness, outstandingness; **stardom;** elevation, exaltation, exaltedness, loftiness, high and mightiness <nf>; nobility, grandeur, sublimity; excellence 999.1, supereminence 999.2

6 illustriousness, luster, brilliance *or* brilliancy, radiance, splendor, resplendence *or* resplendency, refulgence *or* refulgency, refulgentness, **glory,** blaze of glory, nimbus, halo, aura, envelope; charisma, mystique, glamour, numinousness, magic; cult of personality, personality cult; claim to fame; fifteen minutes of fame

7 <posthumous fame> **memory, remembrance,** blessed *or* sacred memory, legend, heroic legend *or* myth; **immortality,** lasting *or* undying fame, niche in the hall of fame, secure place in history; immortal name

8 glorification, ennoblement, dignification, **exaltation,** elevation, enskying, enskyment, magnification, aggrandizement; enthronement; immortalization, enshrinement; beatification, canonization, sainting, sanctification; **deification, apotheosis;** lionization

9 celebrity, man *or* woman of mark *or* note, person of note *or* consequence, **notable, notability, luminary, great man** *or* **woman,** eminence, master spirit, worthy, name, **big name,** figure, public figure, **somebody; important person, VIP** *and* **standout** <nf>, personage 997.8, one in a hundred *or* thousand *or* million etc; cynosure, model, very model, ideal type, **idol,** popular idol, tin god *or* little tin god <nf>; lion, social lion, pillar of the community; hero, heroine, popular hero, pop hero <nf>, folk hero, superhero; **star, superstar,** megastar, hot stuff <nf>; cult figure *or* hero; **immortal;** luminaries, galaxy, pleiad, constellation; celebutante; semicelebrity; favorite

VERBS 10 be somebody, be something, **impress,** charismatize; **figure,** make *or* cut a figure, cut a dash *and* make a splash <nf>, **make a noise in the world,** make *or* leave one's mark; live, **flourish; shine,** glitter, gleam, glow

11 gain recognition, be recognized, get a reputation, **make a name** *or* make a name for oneself, make oneself known, come into one's own, come to the front *or* fore, come into vogue; **burst onto the scene,** become an overnight celebrity, come onto the scene <nf>, come out of the woods *or* out of nowhere *or* out of left field <nf>; make points *or* Brownie points <nf>

12 honor, confer *or* bestow honor upon; **dignify,** adorn, grace; **distinguish,** signalize, confer distinction on, give credit where credit is due

13 glorify, glamorize; **exalt,** elevate, ensky, raise, uplift, set up, **ennoble,** aggrandize, magnify, exalt to the skies; crown; throne, enthrone; immortalize, enshrine, hand one's name down to posterity, make legendary; beatify, canonize, saint, sanctify; **deify,** apotheosize, apotheose; **lionize**

14 reflect honor, lend credit *or* distinction, shed a luster, redound to one's honor, give one a reputation

ADJS 15 reputable, highly reputed, of repute, **estimable, esteemed,** much *or* highly esteemed, **honorable,** honored; **meritorious,** worth one's salt, noble, worthy, creditable; respected, respectable, highly respectable; revered, reverend, venerable, venerated, worshipful; **well-thought-of,** highly regarded, held in esteem, in good odor, in favor, in high favor; in one's good books; prestigious

16 distinguished, distingué; **noted, notable,** marked, of note, of mark; **famous,** famed, honored, **renowned, celebrated, popular,** in favor, acclaimed, much acclaimed, sought-after, hot *and* world-class <nf>, **notorious, well-known,** best-known, in everyone's mouth, on everyone's tongue *or* lips, talked-of, talked-about; far-famed, far-heard; fabled, legendary, mythical

17 prominent, conspicuous, outstanding, stickout <nf>, much in evidence, to the front, in the limelight <nf>; **important,** consequential, significant

18 eminent, high, exalted, elevated, enskyed, lofty, sublime, held in awe, awesome; immortal; **great,** big <nf>, **grand;** excellent 999.12,13,15, supereminent, mighty, high and mighty <nf>; glorified, ennobled, magnified, aggrandized; enthroned, throned; immortalized, shrined, enshrined; beatified, canonized, sainted, sanctified; **idolized, godlike, deified,** apotheosized

19 illustrious, lustrous, glorious, brilliant, radiant, splendid, splendorous, splendrous, splendent, resplendent, bright, shining; charismatic, glamorous, numinous, magic, magical

ADVS 20 reputably, estimably, honorably, nobly, respectably, worthily, creditably

21 famously, notably, notedly, notoriously, popularly, celebratedly; **prominently, eminently,** conspicuously, outstandingly; **illustriously,** gloriously

663 SENSUALITY

NOUNS 1 sensuality, sensualness, sensualism; appetitiveness, appetite; **voluptuousness,** luxuriousness, luxury; **unchastity** 665; **pleasure-seeking;** sybaritism; **self-indulgence, hedonism,** Cyrenaic hedonism, Cyrenaicism, ethical hedonism, psychological hedonism, hedonics, hedonic calculus; epicurism, epicureanism; pleasure principle, *Lustprinzip* <Ger>; **instant gratification;** sensuousness 24.1

2 carnality, carnal-mindedness; **fleshliness,** flesh;

animal *or* carnal nature, the flesh, the beast, Adam, the Old Adam, the offending Adam, fallen state *or* nature, lapsed state *or* nature, postlapsarian state *or* nature; **animality, animalism, bestiality,** beastliness, brutishness, **brutality;** coarseness, grossness; swinishness; **earthiness,** unspirituality, nonspirituality, materialism; erotica

3 **sensualist, voluptuary, pleasure-seeker,** sybarite, Cyrenaic, Sardanapalus, Heliogabalus, **hedonist,** *bon vivant* <Fr>, carpet knight; epicure, epicurean; gourmet, gourmand; swine

VERBS 4 sensualize, carnalize, coarsen, brutify; *carpe diem* <L, seize the day>, live for the moment

ADJS 5 **sensual,** sensualist, sensualistic; appetitive; **voluptuous,** luxurious; **unchaste** 665.23, **hedonistic, pleasure-seeking,** pleasure-bent, bent on pleasure, luxury-loving, hedonic, epicurean, sybaritic; Cyrenaic; sensory, sensuous

6 **carnal,** carnal-minded, **fleshly,** bodily, physical; Adamic, fallen, lapsed, postlapsarian; animal, animalistic; **brutish, brutal,** brute; **bestial,** beastly, beastlike; Circean; coarse, gross; swinish; orgiastic; **earthy,** unspiritual, nonspiritual, material, materialistic

664 CHASTITY

NOUNS 1 **chastity, virtue,** virtuousness, honor; **purity,** cleanness, cleanliness; whiteness, snowiness; **immaculacy,** immaculateness, spotlessness, stainlessness, taintlessness, blotlessness, unspottedness, unstainedness, unblottedness, untaintedness, unblemishedness, unsoiledness, unsulliedness, undefiledness, untarnishedness; uncorruptness; sexual innocence, innocence 657

2 **decency, seemliness, propriety, decorum,** decorousness, elegance, delicacy; **modesty,** shame, pudicity, pudency

3 **continence** *or* continency; abstemiousness, abstaining, abstinence 668.2; celibacy; **virginity,** intactness, maidenhood, maidenhead; Platonic love; marital fidelity *or* faithfulness

ADJS 4 **chaste, virtuous; pure,** purehearted, pure in heart; **clean,** cleanly; **immaculate, spotless,** blotless, stainless, taintless, white, snowy, pure *or* white as driven snow; **unsoiled, unsullied, undefiled,** untarnished, unstained, unspotted, untainted, unblemished, unblotted, uncorrupt; sexually innocent, innocent 657.6

5 **decent, modest, decorous,** delicate, elegant, proper, becoming, seemly

6 **continent;** abstemious, abstinent 668.10; celibate; virginal, **virgin,** maidenly, vestal, intact; Platonic

7 **undebauched, undissipated, undissolute,** unwanton, unlicentious

665 UNCHASTITY

NOUNS 1 **unchastity,** unchasteness; unvirtuousness; **impurity,** uncleanness, uncleanliness, taintedness, soiledness, sulliedness; **indecency** 666

2 **incontinence,** uncontinence; intemperance 669; unrestraint 430.3

3 **profligacy, dissoluteness, licentiousness,** license, unbridledness, wildness, fastness, rakishness, gallantry, **libertinism,** libertinage; **dissipation, debauchery,** debauchment; venery, wenching, whoring, womanizing

4 **wantonness, waywardness; looseness,** laxity, lightness, loose morals, easy virtue, whorishness, chambering, **promiscuity,** sleeping around *and* swinging <nf>

5 **lasciviousness, lechery, lecherousness, lewdness,** bawdiness, **dirtiness,** salacity, salaciousness, **carnality,** animality, fleshliness, **sexuality, sexiness, lust, lustfulness; obscenity** 666.4; **prurience** *or* pruriency, sexual itch, concupiscence, lickerishness, libidinousness, randiness, horniness <nf>, lubricity, lubriciousness, **sensuality,** eroticism, goatishness; satyrism, satyriasis, gynecomania; nymphomania, *furor uterinus* <L>, hysteromania, uteromania, clitoromania; erotomania, eroticomania, aphrodisiomania

6 **seduction,** seducement, **betrayal; violation,** abuse; **debauchment, defilement,** ravishment, ravage, despoilment, fate worse than death; priapism; defloration, deflowering; **rape,** sexual *or* criminal assault; date *or* acquaintance rape

7 <illicit sexual intercourse> **adultery,** criminal conversation *or* congress *or* cohabitation, extramarital *or* premarital sex, extramarital *or* premarital relations, extracurricular sex *or* relations <nf>, **fornication;** free love, free-lovism; **incest;** concubinage; cuckoldry

8 **prostitution, harlotry,** whoredom, **street-walking;** soliciting, solicitation; Mrs Warren's profession; whoremonging, whoremastery, pimping, pandering

9 **brothel, house of prostitution,** house of assignation, house of joy *or* ill repute *or* ill fame, **whorehouse,** bawdyhouse, massage parlor, sporting house, disorderly house, **cathouse, bordello,** bagnio, stew, dive, den of vice, den *or* sink of iniquity, crib, joint; panel house *or* den; red-light district, tenderloin, stews, street of fallen women

10 **libertine, swinger** <nf>, **profligate, rake,** rakehell,

rip <nf>, **roué,** wanton, womanizer, cocksman <nf>, walking phallus, debauchee, rounder <old>, **wolf** <nf>, woman chaser, skirt chaser <nf>, gay dog, gay deceiver, gallant, philanderer, lover-boy <nf>, lady-killer, Lothario, Don Juan, Casanova

11 **lecher, satyr, goat,** old goat, **dirty old man;** whorer *or* whoremonger <old>, whoremaster, whorehound <nf>; Priapus; gynecomaniac; erotomaniac, eroticomaniac, aphrodisiomaniac

12 **seducer, betrayer,** deceiver; **debaucher, ravisher,** ravager, violator, despoiler, defiler; raper, **rapist**

13 **adulterer, cheater, fornicator; adulteress,** fornicatress, fornicatrix

14 **strumpet, trollop, wench, hussy, slut, jade, baggage,** *cocotte* <Fr>, grisette; **tart** *and* **chippy** *and* **floozy** *and* broad <nf>, bitch, drab, trull, quean, harridan, Jezebel, harlot, wanton, whore <nf>, bad woman, **loose woman,** easy woman <nf>, easy lay <nf>, woman of easy virtue, frail sister; pickup; nymphomaniac, nymphet, nympho <nf>, hysteromaniac, uteromaniac, clitoromaniac; nymphet

15 **demimonde,** demimondaine, demirep; **courtesan,** adventuress, **seductress,** femme fatale, vampire, vamp, temptress; hetaera, houri, harem girl, odalisque; Jezebel, Messalina, Delilah, Thais, Phryne, Aspasia, Lais

16 **prostitute, harlot, whore,** *fille de joie* <Fr>, daughter of joy, lady of the evening, call girl *and* B-girl <nf>, **scarlet woman,** unfortunate woman, painted woman, fallen woman, erring sister, **streetwalker,** hustler *and* **hooker** <nf>, woman of the town, *poule* <Fr>, stew, meretrix, Cyprian, Paphian; white slave

17 **mistress,** woman, **kept woman,** kept mistress, **paramour,** concubine, doxy, playmate, spiritual *or* unofficial wife; live-in lover <nf>; other woman <nf>

18 **procurer, pimp,** pander *or* panderer, *maquereau* <Fr>, mack *or* mackman, ponce <Brit nf>; **bawd; gigolo,** fancy man; procuress, **madam** <nf>; white slaver

VERBS 19 **be promiscuous,** sleep around *and* swing <nf>; **debauch, wanton,** rake, chase women, womanize, whore, sow one's wild oats; **philander; dissipate** 669.6; fornicate, **cheat, commit adultery,** get a little on the side <nf>; grovel, wallow, wallow in the mire

20 **seduce, betray, deceive,** mislead, lead astray, lead down the garden *or* the primrose path; **debauch, ravish,** ravage, despoil, ruin; deflower, pop one's cherry <nf>; **defile,** soil, sully; **violate,** abuse; **rape,** force

21 **prostitute oneself,** sell *or* peddle one's ass <nf>, streetwalk; pimp, procure, pander

22 **cuckold;** wear horns, wear the horn

ADJS 23 **unchaste, unvirtuous,** unvirginal; **impure, unclean; indecent** 666.5; soiled, sullied, smirched, besmirched, defiled, tainted, maculate

24 **incontinent,** uncontinent; **orgiastic;** intemperate 669.7; unrestrained

25 **profligate, licentious,** unbridled, untrammeled, uninhibited, free; **dissolute, dissipated, debauched,** abandoned; **wild, fast,** gallant, gay, rakish; rakehell, rakehellish, rakehelly

26 **wanton, wayward,** Paphian; **loose,** lax, slack, loose-moraled, of loose morals, of easy virtue, easy <nf>, **light,** no better than she should be, whorish, chambering, **promiscuous**

27 freeloving; **adulterous,** illicit, extramarital, premarital; incestuous

28 **prostitute, prostituted, whorish, harlot,** scarlet, fallen, meretricious, streetwalking, hustling <nf>, on the town *or* streets, on the *pavé,* in the life

29 **lascivious, lecherous, sexy, salacious, carnal,** animal, **sexual, lustful,** ithyphallic, **hot,** horny *and* sexed-up *and* hot to trot <nf>; prurient, itching, itchy <nf>; concupiscent, lickerish, libidinous, randy, horny <nf>, lubricious; **lewd, bawdy,** adult, X-rated, hard, pornographic, porno <nf>, **dirty, obscene** 666.9; erotic, **sensual,** fleshly; goatish, satyric, priapic, gynecomaniacal; nymphomaniacal, hysteromaniacal, uteromaniacal, clitoromaniacal; erotomaniacal, eroticomaniacal, aphrodisiomaniacal

666 INDECENCY

NOUNS 1 **indecency, indelicacy,** inelegance *or* inelegancy, **indecorousness,** indecorum, **impropriety** 638.1, inappropriateness, unseemliness, indiscretion, indiscreetness; **unchastity** 665

2 **immodesty,** unmodestness, impudicity; exhibitionism; **shamelessness,** unembarrassedness; **brazenness** 142.2, brassiness, pertness, forwardness, boldness, procacity, bumptiousness; **flagrancy,** notoriousness, scandal, scandalousness

3 **vulgarity** 497, **uncouthness, coarseness, crudeness, grossness,** rankness, rawness, raunchiness <nf>; **earthiness,** frankness; **spiciness, raciness,** saltiness

4 **obscenity, dirtiness,** bawdry, raunch <nf>, **ribaldry, pornography,** porno *and* porn <nf>, hard *or* hard-core pornography, soft *or* soft-core pornography, salacity, **smut, dirt, filth; lewdness, bawdiness,** salaciousness, **smuttiness, foulness, filthiness,** nastiness, vileness, offensiveness; scurrility, fescenninity; Rabelaisianism; erotic art

or literature, pornographic art or literature; sexploitation; blue movie *and* dirty movie *and* porno film *and* skin flick <nf>, adult movie, stag film <nf>, X-rated movie; pornographomania, erotographomania, iconolagny, erotology; **dirty talk, scatology** 523.9

ADJS **5 indecent, indelicate, inelegant, indecorous, improper,** inappropriate, **unseemly, unbecoming,** indiscreet

6 immodest, unmodest; exhibitionistic; **shameless,** unashamed, unembarrassed, unabashed, unblushing, **brazen,** brazenfaced, brassy; **forward,** bold, pert, procacious <old>, bumptious; **flagrant,** notorious, scandalous

7 risqué, risky, **racy,** salty, spicy, **off-color,** suggestive, scabrous

8 vulgar, uncouth, coarse, gross, rank, raw, broad, low, foul, gutter; **earthy,** frank, pulling no punches

9 obscene, lewd, adult, bawdy, ithyphallic, **ribald, pornographic, salacious,** sultry <nf>, lurid, **dirty, smutty,** raunchy <nf>, blue, smoking-room, impure, unchaste, unclean, **foul, filthy, nasty,** vile, fulsome, offensive, unprintable, unrepeatable, not fit for mixed company; scurrilous, scurrile, Fescennine; **foulmouthed,** foul-tongued, foul-spoken; Rabelaisian

667 ASCETICISM

NOUNS **1 asceticism,** ascetism, **austerity, self-denial,** self-abnegation, **rigor; puritanism,** eremitism, anchoritism, anchorite *or* anchoritic monasticism, monasticism, monachism; austerity; Sabbatarianism; Albigensianism, Waldensianism, Catharism; Yoga; mortification, self-mortification, maceration, flagellation; **abstinence** 668.2; belt-tightening, fasting 515; voluntary poverty, mendicantism, Franciscanism; Trappism

2 ascetic, puritan, Sabbatarian; Albigensian, Waldensian, Catharist; **abstainer** 668.4; anchorite, **hermit** 584.5; yogi, yogin; sannyasi, bhikshu, dervish, fakir, flagellant, Penitente; Buddha, bodhi; eremite; mendicant, Franciscan, Discalced *or* barefooted Carmelite; Trappist

VERBS **3** deny oneself; abstain, tighten one's belt; flagellate oneself, wear a hair shirt, make oneself miserable

ADJS **4 ascetic, austere,** self-denying, self-abnegating, **rigorous, rigoristic; puritanical,** eremitic, anchoritic, Sabbatarian, **penitential;** Albigensian, Waldensian, Catharist; **abstinent** 668.10; mendicant, discalced, barefoot, wedded to poverty, Franciscan; Trappist; flagellant; eremitic, eremitical

668 TEMPERANCE

NOUNS **1 temperance,** temperateness, **moderation,** moderateness, middle way, sophrosyne; golden mean, via media, *juste milieu* <Fr>; nothing in excess, sobriety, soberness, frugality, forbearance, abnegation; renunciation, renouncement, forgoing; denial, **self-denial;** restraint, constraint, **self-restraint; self-control,** self-reining, self-mastery, **discipline,** self-discipline

2 abstinence, abstention, abstainment, **abstemiousness,** refraining, refrainment, avoidance, eschewal, denying *or* refusing oneself, saying no to, passing up <nf>; **total abstinence, teetotalism,** nephalism, Rechabitism; the pledge; Encratism, Shakerism; Pythagorism, Pythagoreanism; sexual abstinence, celibacy 565; chastity 664; gymnosophy; Stoicism; vegetarianism, veganism, fruitarianism; plain living, spare diet, simple diet; Spartan fare, Lenten fare; fish day, banyan day; fast 515.2,3; **continence** 664.3; **asceticism** 667; smokeout

3 prohibition, prohibitionism; Eighteenth Amendment, Volstead Act

4 abstainer, abstinent; **teetotaler,** teetotalist, sobersides <nf>; nephalist, Rechabite, hydropot, water-drinker; vegetarian, vegan, fruitarian, pescetarian; banian, banya; gymnosophist; Pythagorean, Pythagorist; Encratite, Apostolici, Shaker; **ascetic** 667.2; nonsmoker, nondrinker, etc; moderationist

5 prohibitionist, dry <nf>; Anti-Saloon League; Women's Christian Temperance Union *or* WCTU

VERBS **6 restrain oneself,** constrain oneself, curb oneself, hold back, **avoid excess; limit oneself, restrict oneself; control oneself,** control one's appetites, repress *or* inhibit one's desires, contain oneself, discipline oneself, master oneself, exercise self-control *or* self-restraint, keep oneself under control, keep in *or* within bounds, keep within compass *or* limits, know when one has had enough, **deny** *or* refuse oneself, **say no** *or* just say no; live plainly *or* simply *or* frugally; mortify oneself, mortify the flesh, control the fleshy lusts, control the carnal man *or* the old Adam; eat to live, not live to eat; eat sparingly, diet; tighten one's belt

7 abstain, abstain from, refrain, **refrain from, forbear, forgo,** spare, withhold, hold back, **avoid, shun,** eschew, **pass up** <nf>, **keep from,** keep or stand *or* hold aloof from, have nothing to do with, take no part in, have no hand in, **let alone,** let well enough alone, let go by, **deny oneself,** do without, go without, make do without, not *or* never touch, keep hands off; fast

8 **swear off, renounce,** forswear, **give up,** abandon, stop, discontinue; take the pledge, get on the wagon *or* water wagon <nf>, go on the wagon <nf>; **kick** and kick the habit <nf>, dry out

ADJS 9 **temperate, moderate,** sober, frugal, restrained, **sparing,** stinting, measured

10 **abstinent,** abstentious, **abstemious;** teetotal, sworn off, on the wagon *or* water wagon <nf>; nephalistic, Rechabite; Encratic, Apostolic, Shaker; Pythagorean; sexually abstinent, celibate, chaste; Stoic; fasting; vegetarian, veganistic, vegan, fruitarian; Spartan, Lenten; maigre, meatless; **continent** 664.6; **ascetic**

11 prohibitionist, antisaloon, dry <nf>

ADVS 12 **temperately, moderately, sparingly,** stintingly, frugally, in moderation, within compass *or* bounds

669 INTEMPERANCE

NOUNS 1 **intemperance,** intemperateness, **indulgence, self-indulgence,** self-absorption; instant gratification; **overindulgence,** overdoing; **unrestraint,** unconstraint, indiscipline, uncontrol; **immoderation,** immoderacy, immoderateness; inordinacy, inordinateness; **excess, excessiveness,** too much, too-muchness <nf>; addiction; prodigality, extravagance; crapulence *or* crapulency, crapulousness; **incontinence** 665.2; **swinishness, gluttony** 672; **drunkenness** 88.1

2 **dissipation, licentiousness; riotous living,** free living, high living <nf>, fast *or* killing pace, fast lane <nf>, burning the candle at both ends; **debauchery,** debauchment; **carousal** 88.5, carousing, carouse; **debauch, orgy,** saturnalia; hedonism, sybaritism

3 **dissipater,** rounder <old>, free liver, high liver <nf>; nighthawk and nightowl <nf>; debauchee; **playboy,** partyer, partygoer, party girl, party animal; pleasure-seeker

VERBS 4 **indulge,** indulge oneself, indulge one's appetites, "indulge in easy vices"—Samuel Johnson, deny oneself nothing *or* not at all; **give oneself up to,** give free course to, give free rein to; live well *or* high, live high on the hog <nf>, live it up <nf>, live off the fat of the land; indulge in, luxuriate in, wallow in; roll in; look out for number one

5 **overindulge, overdo, carry to excess,** carry too far, go the limit, go whole hog <nf>, know no limits, not know when to stop, bite off more than one can chew, spread oneself too thin; dine not wisely but too well; live above *or* beyond one's means; binge <nf>

6 **dissipate,** plunge into dissipation, **debauch, wanton, carouse,** run riot, live hard *or* fast, squander one's money in riotous living, burn the candle at both ends, keep up a fast *or* killing pace, not know when to stop, sow one's wild oats, have one's fling, **party** <nf>, "eat, drink, and be merry"—Bible

ADJS 7 **intemperate, indulgent, self-indulgent; overindulgent,** overindulging, unthrifty, unfrugal, **immoderate,** inordinate, **excessive,** too much, prodigal, extravagant, extreme, unmeasured, unlimited; crapulous, crapulent; undisciplined, uncontrolled, unbridled, unconstrained, uninhibited, **unrestrained; incontinent** 665.24; **swinish, gluttonous** 672.6; bibulous; party-hearty

8 **licentious, dissipated, riotous, dissolute, debauched;** free-living, high-living <nf>

9 **orgiastic,** saturnalian, corybantic

ADVS 10 **intemperately,** prodigally, **immoderately,** inordinately, excessively, **in** *or* **to excess,** to extremes, beyond all bounds *or* limits, without restraint; high, high on the hog <nf>

670 MODERATION

NOUNS 1 **moderation,** moderateness; **restraint,** constraint, control; **judiciousness,** prudence; steadiness, evenness, balance, equilibrium, **stability** 855; **temperateness,** temperance, sobriety; self-abnegation, self-restraint, self-control, self-denial; abstinence, continence, abnegation; **mildness,** lenity, gentleness; calmness, serenity, tranquillity, repose, calm, cool <nf>; unexcessiveness, unextremeness, unextravagance, nothing in excess, *meden agan* <Gk>; **happy medium, golden mean,** *juste-milieu* <Fr>, middle way *or* path, *via media* <L>, balancing act <nf>; moderationism, **conservatism** 853.3; **nonviolence,** pacifism, pacification, peace movement, ahimsa; impartiality, neutrality, dispassion; irenics, ecumenism

2 modulation, **abatement,** remission, **mitigation,** diminution, defusing, de-escalation, **reduction,** lessening, falling-off; **relaxation,** relaxing, slackening, **easing,** loosening, letup and letdown <nf>; **alleviation,** assuagement, allayment, palliation, leniency, relenting, lightening, **tempering, softening,** moderating, moderative, subdual; **deadening, dulling,** damping, blunting; drugging, narcotizing, sedating, sedation; **pacification, tranquilization,** tranquilizing, mollification, demulsion, dulcification, **quieting,** quietening, lulling, **soothing, calming,** hushing

3 **moderator, mitigator,** modulator, stabilizer, temperer, assuager; **mediator, bridge-builder,**

calming *or* restraining hand, wiser head; **alleviator,** alleviative, palliative, lenitive; **pacifier, soother,** comforter, peacemaker, pacificator, dove of peace, mollifier; **drug,** anodyne, dolorifuge, soothing syrup, **tranquilizer,** calmative; **sedative** 86.12; balm, salve; cushion, shock absorber

4 **moderate,** moderatist, moderationist, middle-of-the-roader, **centrist,** neutral, compromiser; **conservative** 853.4

VERBS 5 **be moderate, keep within bounds,** keep within compass; practice self-control *or* self-denial, live within one's means, live temperately, do nothing in excess, strike a balance, strike *or* keep a happy medium, seek the golden mean, steer *or* preserve an even course, keep to the middle path *or* way, steer *or* be between Scylla and Charybdis; keep the peace, not resist, espouse *or* practice nonviolence, be pacifistic; not rock the boat *and* not make waves *or* static <nf>; cool it *and* keep one's cool <nf>, keep one's head *or* temper; sober down, settle down; remit, relent; take in sail; go out like a lamb; be conservative 853.6

6 **moderate, restrain,** constrain, control, **keep within bounds; modulate, mitigate,** defuse, abate, weaken, **diminish, reduce,** de-escalate, slacken, lessen, slow down; **alleviate,** assuage, allay, lay, lighten, palliate, extenuate, **temper,** attemper, lenify; **soften, subdue,** tame, hold in check, keep a tight rein, chasten, underplay, play down, downplay, de-emphasize, tone *or* tune down; turn down the volume, lower the voice; **drug,** narcotize, sedate, tranquilize, deaden, dull, blunt, obtund, take the edge off, take the sting *or* bite out; smother, suppress, stifle; **damp, dampen,** bank the fire, reduce the temperature, throw cold water on, throw a wet blanket on; sober, sober down *or* up; clear the air

7 **calm,** calm down, **stabilize, tranquilize, pacify,** mollify, appease, dulcify; **quiet,** hush, still, rest, compose, **lull, soothe,** gentle, rock, cradle, rock to sleep; cool, **subdue,** quell; ease, steady, smooth, smoothen, smooth over, smooth down, even out; keep the peace, be the dove of peace, pour oil on troubled waters, pour balm into

8 **cushion,** absorb the shock, **soften the blow,** break the fall, deaden, damp *or* dampen, soften, suppress, neutralize, offset; show pity *or* mercy *or* consideration *or* sensitivity, temper the wind to the shorn lamb

9 **relax,** unbend; ease, **ease up,** ease off, **let up,** let down; abate, bate, remit, mitigate; **slacken,** slack, slake, slack off, slack up; loose, **loosen;** unbrace, unstrain, unstring

ADJS 10 **moderate, temperate,** sober; **mild,** soft, bland, **gentle,** tame; mild as milk *or* mother's milk, mild as milk and water, gentle as a lamb;

nonviolent, peaceable, peaceful, pacifistic; **judicious, prudent**

11 **restrained,** constrained, limited, controlled, **stable,** in control, in hand; tempered, **softened,** hushed, **subdued,** quelled, chastened

12 **unexcessive,** unextreme, unextravagant, **conservative;** reasonable

13 **equable,** even, low-key *or* low-keyed, **cool,** even-tempered, level-headed, dispassionate; tranquil, reposeful, serene, calm 173.12

14 **mitigating,** assuaging, abating, **diminishing, reducing,** lessening, allaying, **alleviating, relaxing, easing;** tempering, **softening,** chastening, **subduing;** deadening, dulling, blunting, damping, dampening, cushioning

15 **tranquilizing,** pacifying, mollifying, appeasing; cooling-off; **calming,** lulling, gentling, rocking, cradling, hushing, quietening, stilling; **soothing,** soothful, restful; dreamy, drowsy

16 **palliative, alleviative,** alleviatory, assuasive, lenitive, **calmative,** calmant, **narcotic, sedative,** demulcent, anodyne; antiorgastic, anaphrodisiac

ADVS 17 **moderately, in moderation,** restrainedly, subduedly, in *or* within reason, within bounds *or* compass, in balance; **temperately,** soberly, prudently, judiciously, dispassionately; composedly, calmly, coolly, evenly, steadily, equably, tranquilly, serenely; soothingly, conservatively

671 VIOLENCE
<vehement action>

NOUNS 1 **violence, vehemence, virulence, venom, furiousness, force, rigor,** roughness, harshness, ungentleness, extremity, impetuosity, inclemency, **severity, intensity,** acuteness, **sharpness; acrimony** 17.5; fierceness, ferociousness, ferocity, furiousness, viciousness, insensateness, savagery, destructiveness, **destruction, vandalism; terrorism, barbarity, brutality, atrocity,** inhumanity, bloodlust, killer instinct, murderousness, malignity, mercilessness, pitilessness, mindlessness, animality, brutishness; **rage,** raging, **anger** 152

2 **turbulence, turmoil,** chaos, upset, **fury, furor,** *furore* <Ital>, **rage, frenzy, passion,** fanaticism, zealousness, zeal, tempestuousness, storminess, wildness, tumultuousness, **tumult, uproar,** racket, cacophony, pandemonium, hubbub, **commotion, disturbance, agitation,** bluster, broil, brawl, embroilment, brouhaha, fuss, flap <Brit nf>, **row, rumpus,** ruckus <nf>, foofaraw <nf>, **ferment,** fume, boil, boiling, seething, ebullition, fomentation; all hell let loose

3 **unruliness, disorderliness,** obstreperousness, Katy-bar-the-door <nf>; **riot, rioting;** looting, pillaging, plundering, rapine; wilding <nf>; laying waste, sowing with salt, sacking; scorched earth; **attack** 459, **assault,** onslaught, battering; **rape, violation,** forcible seizure; **killing** 308, butchery, massacre, slaughter

4 **storm, tempest,** squall, line squall, **tornado, cyclone, hurricane,** tropical cyclone, typhoon, storm-center, tropical storm, eye of the storm *or* hurricane, war of the elements; stormy weather, rough weather, foul weather, dirty weather; rainstorm 316.2; thunderstorm 316.3; windstorm 318.11; **snowstorm** 1023.8; **firestorm**

5 **upheaval, convulsion,** cataclysm, catastrophe, disaster; meltdown; **fit,** spasm, **paroxysm,** apoplexy, stroke; climax; **earthquake,** quake, temblor, diastrophism, epicenter, shock wave; tidal wave, *tsunami* <Japanese>

6 **outburst, outbreak, eruption,** debouchment, eructation, belch, spew; **burst,** dissilience *or* dissiliency; meltdown, atomic meltdown; **torrent,** rush, gush, spate, cascade, spurt, jet, rapids, **volcano,** volcan, burning mountain

7 **explosion, discharge, blowout,** blowup, detonation, fulmination, **blast, burst, report** 56.1; flash, flash *or* flashing point, flare, flare-up, fulguration; bang, boom 56.4; backfire

8 **concussion, shock, impact,** crunch, smash; percussion, repercussion

9 <violent person> berserk *or* berserker; **hothead,** hotspur; **devil, demon, fiend, brute,** hellhound, hellcat, hellion, hell-raiser; **beast,** wild beast, tiger, dragon, mad dog, wolf, monster, mutant, savage; **rapist, mugger, killer;** Mafioso, hit man <nf>, contract killer, hired killer, hired gun; **fury,** virago, vixen, termagant, beldam, she-wolf, tigress, witch; firebrand, revolutionary 860.3, **terrorist,** incendiary, bomber, guerrilla, suicide bomber

10 <nf terms> **goon, gorilla,** ape, knuckle dragger, muscle man, plug-ugly, shtarker, cowboy, bimbo, bozo, bruiser, hardnose, tough guy, tough, hoodlum, hood, meat-eater, gunsel, terror, holy terror, fire-eater, spitfire, tough *or* ugly customer

VERBS 11 **rage, storm, rant, rave,** roar; **rampage,** ramp, **tear,** tear around; go *or* carry on <nf>; come in like a lion; **destroy, wreck,** wreak havoc, ruin; sow chaos *or* disorder; **terrorize,** sow terror, vandalize, barbarize, brutalize; **riot,** loot, burn, pillage, sack, lay waste; **slaughter, butcher; rape,** violate; **attack, assault,** batter, savage, mug, maul, hammer; go for the jugular

12 **seethe, boil, fume,** foam, simmer, stew, ferment, stir, churn, see red

13 **erupt, burst forth** *or* **out, break out, blow out** *or* **open,** eruct, belch, **vomit,** spout, spew, disgorge, **discharge,** eject, throw *or* hurl forth

14 **explode, blow up, burst,** go off, go up, blow out, blast, bust <nf>; **detonate,** fulminate; **touch off,** trigger, trip, set off, let off; **discharge,** fire, shoot; backfire; melt down

15 **run amok, go berserk, go on a rampage,** cut loose, run riot, run wild

ADJS 16 **violent, vehement, virulent, venomous, severe, rigorous, furious, fierce, intense,** sharp, acute, keen, cutting, splitting, piercing; **destructive;** rough, bruising, tough <nf>; **drastic,** extreme, outrageous, excessive, exorbitant, unconscionable, intemperate, immoderate, extravagant; acrimonious 17.14; on the warpath

17 **unmitigated, unsoftened, untempered,** unallayed, unsubdued, unquelled; unquenched, unextinguished, unabated; unmixed, unalloyed; **total**

18 **turbulent, tumultuous, raging, chaotic,** hellish, anarchic, **storming,** stormy, **tempestuous,** troublous, **frenzied, wild, wild-eyed, frantic, furious,** infuriate, insensate, **mad,** demented, insane, enraged, ravening, raving, slavering; **angry; blustering,** blustery, blusterous; **uproarious,** rip-roaring <nf>; pandemoniac

19 **unruly, disorderly,** obstreperous; **unbridled; riotous,** wild, rampant; **terroristic,** anarchic, nihilistic, revolutionary 860.5

20 **boisterous, rampageous, rambunctious** <nf>, on the rampage, rumbustious, roisterous, wild, rollicking, **rowdy,** rough, hoody <nf>, harum-scarum <nf>; knockabout, rough-and-tumble, knock-down-and-drag-out <nf>

21 **savage, fierce, ferocious, vicious, murderous, cruel, atrocious, mindless, brutal,** brutish, **bestial,** insensate, monstrous, mutant, inhuman, pitiless, ruthless, merciless, bloody, sanguinary, kill-crazy <nf>; malign, malignant; feral, ferine; **wild,** untamed, tameless, undomesticated, ungentle; **barbarous,** barbaric, **uncivilized,** noncivilized

22 **fiery, heated, inflamed,** flaming, scorching, hot, red-hot, white-hot; **fanatic, zealous,** totally committed, hard-core, hard-line, ardent, passionate; **hotheaded**

23 **convulsive,** cataclysmic, disastrous, upheaving; seismic; **spasmodic,** paroxysmal, spastic, jerky, herky-jerky <nf>; orgasmic

24 **explosive,** bursting, detonating, explosible, explodable, fulminating, fulminant, fulminatory; cataclysmic; dissilient; **volcanic,** eruptive

ADVS 25 **violently, vehemently, virulently,**

venomously, rigorously, severely, fiercely,
drastically; **furiously,** wildly, madly, **like mad,** like
fury <nf>, like blazes; all to pieces, with a
vengeance

26 turbulently, tumultuously, riotously, uproariously,
stormily, tempestuously, troublously, **frenziedly,**
frantically, furiously, ragingly, enragedly, madly;
angrily 152.33

27 savagely, fiercely, ferociously, atrociously,
viciously, murderously, brutally *or* brutishly,
mindlessly, bestially, barbarously, inhumanly,
insensately, ruthlessly, pitilessly, mercilessly;
tooth and nail, tooth and claw, *bec et*
ongles <Fr>

672 GLUTTONY

NOUNS **1 gluttony,** gluttonousness, **greed,**
greediness, voraciousness, voracity, ravenousness,
edacity, crapulence *or* crapulency, gulosity,
rapacity, insatiability; omnivorousness; big
appetite, **piggishness, hoggishness,** swinishness;
overindulgence, overeating; eating disorder,
polyphagia, hyperphagia, bulimia, bulimia
nervosa, binge-purge syndrome, binging <nf>;
intemperance 669

2 epicurism, epicureanism, gourmandise;
gastronomy

3 glutton, greedy eater, big *or* hearty *or* good eater
<nf>, trencherman, trencherwoman, belly-god,
gobbler, greedygut *or* greedyguts <nf>, gorger,
gourmand, gourmandizer, gormand, gormandizer,
guttler, cormorant, bon vivant; animal, **hog** *and*
pig *and* chow hound *and* khazer *and* gobbler *and*
wolf <nf>; omnivore; binger

VERBS **4 gluttonize,** gormandize, **indulge one's**
appetite, live to eat, love to eat; **gorge,** engorge,
glut, cram, stuff, batten, guttle, guzzle, **devour,**
raven, bolt, gobble, gulp, **wolf,** gobble *or* gulp *or*
bolt *or* wolf down, eat like a horse, tuck into, stuff
oneself *and* hog it down *and* eat one's head off *and*
fork *or* shovel it in <nf>, eat one out of house and
home, wipe the plate clean

5 overeat, overgorge, **overindulge, make a pig** *or*
hog of oneself, pig out *or* pork out *or* scarf out
<nf>; glut oneself, stuff oneself

ADJS **6 gluttonous, greedy,** voracious, ravenous,
edacious, esurient, rapacious, insatiable,
polyphagic, bulimic, hyperphagic, Apician;
piggish, hoggish, swinish; crapulous, crapulent;
intemperate 669.7; omnivorous, all-devouring;
gorging, cramming, glutting, guttling, stuffing,
guzzling, wolfing, bolting, **gobbling, gulping,**
gluttonizing; binging <nf>

7 overfed, overgorged, overindulged

ADVS **8 gluttonously, greedily,** voraciously,
ravenously, edaciously; **piggishly, hoggishly,**
swinishly

673 LEGALITY

NOUNS **1 legality, legitimacy, lawfulness,**
legitimateness, licitness, rightfulness, validity,
scope, applicability; **jurisdiction** 594; actionability,
justiciability, **constitutionality,** constitutional
validity; letter of the law; legal process, legal form,
due process; legalism, constitutionalism; **justice**
649

2 legalization, legitimation, legitimatization,
decriminalization; money-washing *or* -laundering;
validation; authorization, sanction; legislation,
enactment, authority, license, warrant

3 law, *lex* and *jus* <L>, **statute,** rubric, **canon,**
institution; **ordinance; act, enactment, measure,**
legislation; **rule, ruling; prescript,** prescription;
regulation, *règlement* <Fr>, reg <nf>; **dictate,**
dictation; form, formula, formulary, formality;
standing order; bylaw; **edict, decree** 420.4; **bill;**
manifesto, order, standing order, rescript, precept

4 law, legal system, system of laws, legal branch *or*
specialty

5 code, digest, pandect, capitulary, **body of law,**
corpus juris, legal code, code of laws, digest of law;
codification; civil code, penal code; Justinian Code;
Napoleonic code, *Code Napoléon* <Fr>; lawbook,
statute book, compilation; Blackstone; Uniform
Code of Military Justice; written law, unwritten
law, statute law, common law, private law,
international law, military law, commercial law,
contracts law, criminal law, civil law, labor law,
constitutional law; law of the land; canon

6 constitution, written constitution, unwritten
constitution; law and equity; charter, codification,
codified law; constitutional amendment; Bill of
Rights, constitutional guarantees; constitutional
interpretation

7 jurisprudence, law, legal science; nomology,
nomography; **forensic science,** science of law,
forensic *or* legal medicine, medical jurisprudence,
medico-legal medicine; forensic psychiatry;
forensic *or* legal chemistry, criminology,
constitutionalism, penology

8 <codes of law> Constitution of the U.S., Bill of
Rights; Corpus Juris Civilis, Codex Juris Canonici,
Digest *or* Pandects of Justinian; Law of Moses,
Ten Commandments, Pentateuch, Torah, Koran *or*
Qur'an, the Bible; Code of Hammurabi, Magna
Carta, Napoleonic Code

VERBS **9 legalize, legitimize,** legitimatize,
legitimate, make legal, declare lawful,

decriminalize; wash *or* launder money; validate; **authorize, sanction,** license, warrant; constitute, ordain, establish, put in force; prescribe, formulate; regulate, make a regulation, bring within the law; **decree; legislate, enact; enforce; litigate** 598.13, take legal action

10 **codify,** digest; compile, publish

ADJS 11 **legal, legitimate,** legit *and* kosher <nf>, competent, by right, de jure, **licit, lawful,** rightful, according to law, within the law; **actionable,** litigable, justiciable, within the scope of the law; **enforceable,** legally binding; **judicial,** juridical; **authorized, sanctioned,** valid, applicable, warranted; **constitutional;** statutory, statutable; legalized, legitimized, decriminalized; **legislative, lawmaking;** lawlike; **just** 649.7

12 jurisprudent, jurisprudential; **legalistic; forensic;** nomistic, nomothetic; criminological

ADVS 13 **legally, legitimately, licitly, lawfully,** by law, *de jure* <L>, in the eyes of the law, within the law

674 ILLEGALITY

NOUNS 1 **illegality, unlawfulness, illicitness, lawlessness,** wrongfulness; unauthorization, impermissibility, **unconstitutionality;** legal *or* technical flaw, legal irregularity; **outlawry; anarchy,** collapse *or* breakdown *or* paralysis of authority, anomie; illicit business 732

2 **illegitimacy, illegitimateness,** illegitimation; **bastardy,** bastardism; bend *or* bar sinister, baton

3 **lawbreaking, violation,** breach *or* violation of law, infringement, contravention, infraction, **transgression,** trespass, trespassing, offense, breach, nonfeasance, encroachment; vice, fraud; crime, **criminality,** criminalism, habitual criminality, delinquency; flouting *or* making a mockery of the law

4 **offense, wrong,** illegality; **violation** 435.2; **wrongdoing** 655; much to answer for; **crime, felony; misdemeanor;** tort; delict, delictum

VERBS 5 **break** *or* **violate the law,** breach the law, infringe, contravene, infract, violate 435.4, **transgress, trespass,** disobey the law, offend against the law, flout the law, make a mockery of the law, fly in the face of the law, set the law at defiance, snap one's fingers at the law, set the law at naught, circumvent the law, disregard the law, **take the law into one's own hands,** twist *or* torture the law to one's own ends *or* purposes; commit a crime; have much to answer for; live outside the law

ADJS 6 **illegal, unlawful, illegitimate, illicit,** nonlicit, nonlegal, lawless, wrongful, fraudulent, creative <nf>, **against the law; unauthorized,** unallowed,

impermissible, unwarranted, unwarrantable, unofficial, unlicensed; unstatutory, instatutory, injudicial, extrajudicial; **unconstitutional,** nonconstitutional; flawed, irregular, contrary to law; actionable, chargeable, justiciable, litigable; triable, punishable; **criminal, felonious; outlaw, outlawed; contraband,** bootleg, black-market; under-the-table, under-the-counter; unregulated, unchartered; anarchic, anarchistic, anomic

7 **illegitimate, spurious,** false; **bastard,** misbegot, **misbegotten,** miscreated, gotten on the wrong side of the blanket, baseborn, born out of wedlock, without benefit of clergy

ADVS 8 **illegally, unlawfully, illegitimately, illicitly;** impermissibly; criminally, feloniously; contrary to law, in violation of law, against the law

675 RELIGIONS, CULTS, SECTS

NOUNS 1 **religion,** religious belief *or* faith, **belief, faith,** teaching, doctrine, creed, credo, dogma, theology 676, orthodoxy 687; system of beliefs, belief system; persuasion, tradition

2 **cult, ism;** cultism; **mystique**

3 **sect** <see list>, sectarism, religious order, **denomination, persuasion,** faction, **church,** communion, community, group, fellowship, affiliation, order, school, party, society, body, organization; branch, variety, version, segment; offshoot; **schism,** division

4 **sectarianism,** sectarism, **denominationalism,** partisanism, the clash of creeds; schismatism; syncretism, eclecticism

5 **theism; monotheism; polytheism,** multitheism, myriotheism; **ditheism,** dyotheism, dualism; **tritheism;** tetratheism; **pantheism,** cosmotheism, theopantism, acosmism; physitheism, psychotheism, animotheism; physicomorphism; hylotheism; anthropotheism, anthropomorphism; anthropolatry; allotheism; monolatry, henotheism; autotheism; zootheism, theriotheism; **deism**

6 **animism, animistic religion** *or* cult; voodooism, voodoo, hoodoo, wanga, juju, jujuism, obeah, obeahism; shamanism; fetishism, totemism; nature worship, naturism; primitive religion

7 **Christianity** <see list>, Christianism, Christendom; Latin *or* Roman *or* Western Christianity; Eastern *or* Orthodox Christianity; Protestant Christianity; Judeo-Christian religion *or* tradition *or* belief; fundamentalism, Christian fundamentalism

8 **Catholicism,** Catholicity; **Roman Catholicism,** Romanism, Rome; papalism; popery *and* popeism *and* papism *and* papistry <nf>; ultramontanism; Catholic Church, **Roman Catholic Church,** Church

of Rome; Eastern Rites, Uniate Rites, Uniatism, Alexandrian *or* Antiochian *or* Byzantine Rite

9 Orthodoxy; **Eastern Orthodox Church, Holy Orthodox Catholic Apostolic Church,** Greek Orthodox Church, Russian Orthodox Church; patriarchate of Constantinople, patriarchate of Antioch, patriarchate of Alexandria, patriarchate of Jerusalem

10 **Protestantism,** Reform, Reformationism; Evangelicalism; Zwinglianism; dissent 333; apostasy 363.2; new theology

11 **Anglicanism;** High-Churchism, Low-Churchism; Anglo-Catholicism; Church of England, Established Church; High Church, Low Church; Broad Church, Free Church

12 **Judaism;** Hebraism, Hebrewism; Israelitism; Orthodox Judaism, Conservative Judaism, Reform Judaism, Reconstructionism; Hasidism; rabbinism, Talmudism; Pharisaism; Sadduceeism; Karaism *or* Karaitism

13 **Islam, Muslimism,** Islamism, Moslemism, Muhammadanism, Mohammedanism; Sufism, Wahabiism, Sunnism, Shi'ism, Druzism; Black Muslimism; Muslim fundamentalism, militant Muslimism

14 <other religions> **Christian Science; Mormonism;** New Thought, Higher Thought, Practical Christianity, Mental Science, Divine Science Church; Buddhism, Zen Buddhism; Hinduism; Sikhism; Shintoism; Jainism; Rastafarianism; Zoroastrianism; Confucianism; Taoism

15 **religionist,** religioner; zealot, iconoclast; **believer** 692.4; worshiper; cultist

16 **theist; monotheist; polytheist,** multitheist, myriotheist; ditheist, dualist; tritheist; tetratheist; **pantheist,** cosmotheist; psychotheist; physitheist; hylotheist; anthropotheist; anthropolater; allotheist; henotheist; autotheist; zootheist, theriotheist; **deist**

17 **Christian,** Nazarene, Nazarite; practicing Christian; Christian sectarian

18 **sectarian,** sectary, **denominationalist,** factionist, schismatic

19 **Catholic,** Roman Catholic *or* RC <nf>, Romanist, papist <nf>; ultramontane; Eastern-Rite Christian, Uniate

20 **Protestant,** non-Catholic, Reformed believer, Reformationist, Evangelical; Zwinglian; dissenter 333.3; apostate 363.5; Anglican, Episcopalian, Unitarian, born-again Christian

21 **Jew, Hebrew,** Judaist, Israelite; Orthodox *or* Conservative *or* Reform Jew, Reconstructionist; Hasid; Zionist; Essene; Rabbinist, Talmudist; Pharisee; Sadducee; Karaite

22 **Mormon,** Latter-day Saint, Josephite <nf>

23 **Muslim,** Muhammadan *and* Mohammedan <nf>, Mussulman, Moslem, Islamite; Shi'ite, Shia, Sectary; Motazilite, Sunni, Sunnite, Wahhabi, Sufi, Druze; dervish; abdal; Black Muslim; Muslim fundamentalist *or* militant

24 **Christian Scientist,** Christian Science Practitioner; Buddhist, Zen Buddhist; Hindu; Sikh; Shintoist; Jainist; Rastafarian; Zoroastrian; Confucianist; Taoist

ADJS **25** **religious, theistic; monotheistic; polytheistic,** ditheistic, tritheistic; **pantheistic,** cosmotheistic; physicomorphic; anthropomorphic, anthropotheistic; **deistic;** theophoric

26 **sectarian,** sectary, **denominational,** schismatic, schismatical

27 **nonsectarian, undenominational, nondenominational;** interdenominational

28 **Protestant,** non-Catholic, Reformed, Reformationist, Evangelical; Lutheran, Calvinist, Calvinistic, Zwinglian; dissentient 333.6; apostate 363.11

29 **Catholic; Roman Catholic** *or* RC <nf>, Roman; Romish *and* popish *and* papish *and* papist *and* papistical <nf>; ultramontane

30 **Jewish, Hebrew,** Judaic, Judaical, Israelite, Israelitic, Israelitish; Orthodox, Conservative, Reform, Reconstructionist; Hasidic

31 **Muslim, Islamic,** Moslem, Islamitic, Islamistic, Muhammadan, Mohammedan; Shiite, Sunni, Sunnite

32 <Oriental> Buddhist, Buddhistic; Brahmanic, Brahmanistic; Vedic, Vedantic; Confucian, Confucianist; Taoist, Taoistic, Shintoist, Shintoistic; Zoroastrian, Zarathustrian, Parsee

33 **religions and sects**

anthroposophy	Islam
Babism *or* Babi	Jainism
Baha'i *or* Bahaism	Jodo Buddhism
Brahmanism	Judaism
Brahmoism	Lamaism
Buddhism	Lingayat Hinduism
Ch'an Buddhism	Magianism
Chen Yen Buddhism	Mahayana Buddhism
Ching-t'u Buddhism	Mandaeism
Christianity	Mithraism
Confucianism	Nichiren Buddhism
Conservative Judaism	Orphism
Dakshincharin Hinduism	Orthodox Judaism
Eleusinianism	Parsiism *or* Parsism
Ethical Culture	Rastafarianism
Gnosticism	Reconstructionism
gymnosophy	Reform Judaism
Hare Krishna	reincarnationism
Hasidism	Rosicrucianism
Hinduism	Sabaeanism
Hinayana Buddhism	Saivism

Shaivite Hinduism
Shamanism
Shiite Muslimism
Shin Buddhism
Shingon Buddhism
Shinto *or* Shintoism
Sikhism
Soka Gakkai Buddhism
Sufism
Sunni Muslimism
Taoism
Tendai Buddhism
Theosophy

Theravada Buddhism
T'ien-t'ai Buddhism
Unitarianism
Vaishnavite Hinduism
Vajrayana Buddhism
Vamacharin
  Hinduism
Vedanta *or* Vedantism
Wahabiism
Yoga *or* Yogism
Zen *or* Zen Buddhism
Zoroastrianism *or*
  Zoroastrism

34 Christian denominations

Adventism *or* Second
  Adventism
African Methodist
  Episcopal church
African Methodist
  Episcopal Zion church
Amish
Anabaptism
Anglicanism
Anglo-Catholicism
antinomianism
Arianism
Assemblies of God
Athanasianism
Baptist church
Boehmenism
Calvinism
Catholicism
Christadelphian
Christian Science *or*
  Church of Christ,
  Scientist
Churches of Christ
Churches of God
Churches of the Brethren
Churches of the
  Nazarene
Congregationalism
Coptic Church
Eastern Orthodox
Episcopalianism
Erastianism
Evangelicanism
Greek Orthodox
homoiousianism
homoousianism
Jansenism

Jehovah's Witness
latitudinarianism
Laudism *or* Laudianism
Liberal Catholicism
Lutheranism
Mennonitism
Methodism
Moral Rearmament
Mormonism
New Thought
Origenism
Orthodox Christianity
Oxford Movement
Pentecostal church
Practical Christianity
Presbyterianism
Puritanism
Puseyism
Quakerism *or* Society of
  Friends
quietism
Roman Catholicism
Rosicrucianism
Russian Orthodox
Sabellianism
Salvation Army
Seventh-Day Adventist
Socinianism
Stundism
Swedenborgianism
Tractarianism
Trinitarianism
Ubiquitarianism
Uniatism
Unification church
Universalism
Wesleyanism *or* Wesleyism

676 THEOLOGY

NOUNS **1 theology** <see list>, **religion, divinity;**
theologism; doctrinism, doctrinalism; religious
studies, religious education

2 doctrine, dogma 953.2; **creed,** credo; credenda,

articles of religion *or* faith; Apostles' Creed,
Nicene Creed, Athanasian Creed; Catechism

3 theologian, theologist, theologizer, theologer,
theologician, theologue; **divine;** scholastic,
schoolman; theological *or* divinity student,
theological, theologue; canonist

ADJS **4 theological, religious; divine;** doctrinal,
doctrinary, ecclesiological; canonic *or* canonical;
physicotheological

5 kinds and branches of theology

angelology
apologetics
Buddhist theology
canonics
Christian theology
Christology
covenant theology
crisis theology
demonology
doctrinal theology
dogmatics *or* dogmatic
  theology
eschatology
existential theology
feminist theology
fideism
hagiology
hierography *or*
  hagiography
hierology
Islamic theology
Judaism theology
liberation theology

Mercersburg theology
natural *or* rational theology
neoorthodoxy *or*
  neoorthodox theology
nonformalogical theology
patristics *or* patristic
  theology
phenomenological
  theology
philosophical theology
physicotheology
rationalism
sacerdotalism
school theology *or*
  scholastic theology
secularism
sophiology
soteriology *or* Christology
  or logos theology *or*
  logos Christology
systematics *or* systematic
  theology
theological hermeneutics

677 DEITY

NOUNS **1 deity, divinity,** divineness, supernatural
being, immortal; **godliness,** godlikeness; **godhood,**
godhead, godship, Fatherhood; heavenliness;
divine essence; **transcendence;** god, goddess

2 God; Lord, Maker, Creator, Supreme Being,
Almighty, King of Kings, Lord of Lords; Jehovah;
Yahweh, Adonai, Elohim <all Heb>; **Allah;** the
Great Spirit, Manitou, Prime Mover

3 <Hinduism> **Brahma,** the Supreme Soul, the
Essence of the Universe; **Atman,** the Universal Ego
or Self; **Vishnu,** the Preserver; **Siva,** the Destroyer,
the Regenerator

4 <Buddhism> **Buddha,** the Blessed One, the
Teacher, **the Lord Buddha,** bodhisattva, bodhi

5 <Zoroastrianism> **Ahura Mazda,** Ormazd,
Mazda, the Lord of Wisdom, the Wise Lord, the
Wise One, the King of Light, the Guardian of
Mankind

6 <Christian Science> **Mind, Divine Mind,** Spirit,
Soul Principle, Life, Truth, Love

7 world spirit *or* **soul,** *anima mundi* <L>, universal life force, world principle, **world-self,** universal ego *or* self, infinite spirit, supreme soul *or* principle, **oversoul, nous, Logos,** World Reason

8 **Nature, Mother Nature,** Dame Nature, Natura, Great Mother

9 **Godhead, Trinity;** Trimurti, Hindu trinity *or* triad

10 **Christ,** Jesus Christ, Son of God, Emmanuel, Redeemer, Messiah; the Way, the Truth, and the Life; Light of the World

11 **the Word, Logos,** the Word Made Flesh, **the Incarnation,** God Incarnate, the Hypostatic Union

12 God the Holy Ghost, **the Holy Ghost, the Holy Spirit,** the Spirit of God, the Spirit of Truth, the Paraclete, the Comforter, the Intercessor, the Dove

13 <divine functions> creation, preservation, dispensation; **providence, divine providence,** dealings *or* dispensations *or* visitations of providence

14 <functions of Christ> salvation, redemption; atonement, propitiation; mediation, intercession; judgment

15 <functions of the Holy Ghost> inspiration, unction, regeneration, sanctification, comfort, consolation, grace, witness

ADJS 16 **divine,** heavenly, celestial, empyrean; **godly, godlike** 692.9; **transcendent,** superhuman, supernatural; self-existent; Christly, Christlike, redemptive, salvational, propitiative, propitiatory, mediative, mediatory, intercessive, intercessional; incarnate, incarnated, made flesh; messianic

17 **almighty, omnipotent,** all-powerful; creating, creative, making, shaping; **omniscient,** providential, all-wise, all-knowing, all-seeing; **infinite,** boundless, limitless, unbounded, unlimited, undefined, omnipresent, ubiquitous; perfect, sublime; eternal, everlasting, timeless, perpetual, immortal, permanent; one; immutable, unchanging, changeless, eternally the same; supreme, sovereign, highest; holy, hallowed, sacred, numinous; glorious, radiant, luminous; majestic; good, just, loving, merciful; triune, tripersonal, three-personed, three-in-one

678 MYTHICAL AND POLYTHEISTIC GODS AND SPIRITS

NOUNS 1 **the gods,** the immortals; the major deities, the greater gods, *di majores* <L>; the minor deities, the lesser gods, *di minores* <L>; pantheon; theogony; **spirits,** animistic spirit *or* powers, manitou, huaca, nagual, mana, pokunt, tamanoas, wakan, zemi

2 **god,** *deus* <L>; **deity, divinity,** immortal, heathen god, pagan deity *or* divinity; **goddess,** *dea* <L>; deva, devi, the shining ones; **idol,** false god, devil-god

3 godling, godlet, godkin; **demigod,** half-god, hero; cult figure; demigoddess, heroine

4 **god, goddesses; Greek and Roman deities** <see list>; **Norse and Germanic deities** <see list>; **Celtic deities** <see list>; **Hindu deities** <see list>; **avatars of Vishnu; Egyptian deities** <see list>; **Semitic deities; Chinese deities; Japanese deities; specialized** *or* **tutelary deities** <see list>

5 **spirit,** intelligence, supernatural being; **genius,** daemon, demon; atua; **specter** 988; **evil spirits** 680

6 **elemental,** elemental spirit; sylph, spirit of the air; gnome, spirit of the earth, earth-spirit; salamander, fire-spirit; undine, water spirit, water-sprite

7 **fairyfolk,** elfenfolk, shee *or* sidhe <Ir>, **the little people** *or* **men,** the good folk *or* people, denizens of the air; **fairyland,** faerie

8 **fairy, sprite, fay,** fairy man *or* woman; **elf, brownie, pixie, gremlin,** ouphe, hob, cluricaune, puca *or* pooka *or* pwca, kobold, nisse, peri; **imp, goblin** 680.8; **gnome,** dwarf; **sylph,** sylphid; **banshee; leprechaun;** fairy queen; Ariel, Mab, Oberon, Puck, Titania, Béfind, Corrigan, Finnbeara; little green men

9 **nymph;** nymphet, nymphlin; **dryad,** hamadryad, wood nymph; vila *or* willi; tree nymph; oread, mountain nymph; limoniad, meadow *or* flower nymph; Napaea, glen nymph; Hyades; Pleiades, Atlantides

10 **water god, water spirit** *or* **sprite** *or* **nymph;** undine, nix, nixie, kelpie; **naiad,** limniad, fresh-water nymph; Oceanid, Nereid, sea nymph, ocean nymph, **mermaid,** sea-maid, sea-maiden, siren; Thetis; **merman,** man fish; **Neptune,** "the old man of the sea"—Homer; Oceanus, Poseidon, Triton; Davy Jones, Davy

11 **forest god, sylvan deity,** vegetation spirit *or* daemon, field spirit, fertility god, corn spirit, **faun, satyr,** silenus, panisc, paniscus, panisca; **Pan,** Faunus; Cailleac; Priapus; Vitharr *or* Vidar, the goat god; Jack-in-the-green, Green Man, little green man

12 **familiar spirit,** familiar; **genius, good genius,** daemon, demon, *numen* <L>, totem; **guardian, guardian spirit, guardian angel,** angel, good angel, ministering angel, **fairy godmother;** guide, control, attendant godling *or* spirit, invisible helper, special providence; **tutelary** *or* **tutelar god** *or* **genius** *or* **spirit;** *genius tutelae, genius loci, genius domus, genius familiae* <all L>; **household gods;** *lares familiaris, lares praestites, lares compitales, lares viales, lares permarini* <all L>; penates, lares and penates; ancestral spirits; manes, pitris

13 **Santa Claus,** Santa, Saint Nicholas, Saint Nick, Kriss Kringle, Father Christmas

14 mythology, mythicism; **legend, lore, folklore,** mythical lore; fairy lore, fairyism; mythologist; urban legend *or* myth

ADJS 15 mythic, mythical, mythological; fabulous, legendary; folkloric

16 divine, godlike

17 fairy, faery, **fairylike,** fairyish, fay; sylphine, sylphish, sylphy, sylphidine, sylphlike; **elfin,** elfish, elflike; gnomish, gnomelike; pixieish

18 nymphic, nymphal, nymphean, nymphlike

19 Greek and Roman deities

Aeolus	Momus
Apollo *or* Apollon *or*	Neptune *or* Poseidon <Gk>
Phoebus *or* Phoebus	Nike
Apollo	Nyx
Athena *or* Athena *or*	Olympic gods *or* Olympians
Minerva <Rom>	Persephone <Gk> *or*
Bacchus *or* Dionysus	Proserpina *or* Proserpine
Chaos	Pluto <Rom> *or* Hades *or*
Cupid *or* Amor *or* Eros <Gk>	Dis *or* Orcus
Demeter *or* Ceres <Rom>	Rhea *or* Ops
Diana *or* Artemis <Gk>	Saturn *or* Kronus <Gk>
Erebus	Venus *or* Aphrodite <Gk>
Ge *or* Gaea *or* Gaia *or*	Vesta *or* Hestia <Gk>
Tellus <Rom>	Vulcan *or* Hephaestus
Helios *or* Hyperion *or*	<Gk>
Phaëthon	Zeus <Gk> *or* Jupiter
Hymen	<Rom> *or* Jove *or* Jupiter
Juno *or* Hera <Gk>	Fulgur *or* Fulminator *or*
Lares and Penates	Jupiter Tonans *or* Jupiter
Mars *or* Ares <Gk>	Pluvius *or* Jupiter
Mercury *or* Hermes <Gk>	Optimus Maximus *or*
Mithras	Jupiter Fidius

20 Norse and Germanic deities

Aesir	Nanna
Asgard	Nerthus *or* Hertha
Balder	Njorth *or* Njord
Bor	Odin *or* Woden *or* Wotan
Bori	Reimthursen
Bragi	Sif
Forseti	Sigyn
Frey *or* Freyr	Thor *or* Donar
Freya *or* Freyja	Tyr *or* Tiu
Frigg *or* Frigga	Ull *or* Ullr
Heimdall	Vali
Hel	Vanir
Hermoder	Vitharr *or* Vidar
Höder *or* Hödr	Völund
Hoenir	Wayland
Ing	Weland
Ithunn *or* Idun	Wyrd
Loki	Ymir

21 Celtic deities

Aine	Blodenwedd
Amaethon	Bóann
Angus Og	Bodb
Arawn	Bran
Arianrhod	Brigit

Cernunnos	Llew Llaw Gyffes
Dagda	*or* Lleu
Danu	Lug *or* Lugh
Dewi	Macha
Dôn	Morrigan
Dylan	Neman
Epona	Ogma
Fomorians	Ogmios
Goibniu	Rhiannon
Gwydion	Shannon
Lir	Teutates

22 Hindu deities

Aditi	Jaganmati
Agni	Ka
Abhijit	Kala
Ardra	Kali
Aryaman	Kama
Asapurna	Kamsa
Asvins	Karttikeya
Avalokita *or* Avalokitesvara	Kaumudi
Bhaga	Krishna
Bhairava	Lakshmi
Bhairavi	Malhal Mata
Brahma	Manasa
Bhudevi	Marut
Brahma	Mitra
Brihaspati	Narada
Candika	Parjanya
Candra	Parvati
Chandi	Pushan *or* Pusan
Chitragupta	Rahu
Daksha	Rhibhus
Devaki	Rudra
Devi	Sarasvati
Dhara	Savitar
Dharma	Siddhi
Dhatar	Sita
Dharti Mai	Siva *or* Shiva
Didi Thakrun	Soma
Dipti	Surya
Durga	Uma
Dyaus	Ushas
Ganesa *or* Ganesh *or*	Vaja
Ganesha *or* Ganapati	Varuna
Garuda	Varuni
Gauri	Vayu
Hanuman	Vibhu
Hardaul	Vijaya
Himavat	Vishnu
Hiranyagarbha	Vivasvan
Hotra	Vrta
Indra *or* Indrani	Yama

23 Egyptian deities

Amon	Bes
Ammut	Buto
Anubis	Geb
Aten	Hapi
Bast	Horus
Bastet	Imhotep

Isis
Khem
Khensu
Ma'at
Min
Mut
Neph
Nephthys
Nut
Osiris

Ptah
Qebehsenuef
Ra or Amen-Ra
   or Re
Satet
Sekhmet
Selket
Seth or Set
Tefnut
Thoth

24 specialized or tutelary deities

agricultural deities 1069.4
goddesses of fertility 890.5
personifications of justice
   649.4
deities of the household
   228.30
deities of the nether world
   682.5
earth goddesses
Fates 964.3
forest god 678.11
goddesses of discord 456.1
gods of commerce
gods of evil 680.5

gods of lightning 1025.17
gods of marriage 563.13
love deities 104.7
moon goddesses 1072.12
Muses 986.2
music Muses 710.22
poetry Muses 720.10
rain gods 316.6
sea gods 240.3
sun gods 1072.14
thunder gods 56.5
war gods 458.12
water gods 678.10
wind gods 318.2

679 ANGEL, SAINT

NOUNS **1 angel,** celestial, celestial or heavenly being;
messenger of God; **seraph,** seraphim <pl>, angel of
love; **cherub, cherubim** <pl>, angel of light;
principality, archangel; recording angel; **saint,**
beatified soul, canonized mortal; patron saint;
martyr; redeemed or saved soul, soul in glory;
guardian angel, divine messenger

2 heavenly host, host of heaven, choir invisible,
angelic host, heavenly hierarchy, Sons of God,
ministering spirits; Amesha Spentas

3 <celestial hierarchy> seraphim, cherubim,
thrones; dominations or dominions, virtues,
powers; principalities, archangels, angels;
angelology

4 Azrael, angel of death, death's bright angel;
Abdiel, Chamuel, Gabriel, Jophiel, Michael,
Raphael, Uriel, Zadkiel

5 the Madonna; the Immaculate Conception;
Mariology, Mariolatry

ADJS **6 angelic,** angelical, **seraphic, cherubic;**
heavenly, celestial; archangelic; **saintly, sainted,**
full of grace, beatified, canonized; martyred;
saved, redeemed, glorified, in glory

680 EVIL SPIRITS

NOUNS **1 evil spirits, demons, demonkind,** powers
of darkness, spirits of the air, host of hell, hellish

host, hellspawn, denizens of hell, inhabitants of
Pandemonium, souls in hell, damned spirits, lost
souls, the lost, the damned

2 devil, diable <Fr>, diablo <Sp>, diabolus <L>, deil
<Scot>, Teufel <Ger>, diavolo <Ital>

3 Satan <see list>, Satanas

4 Beelzebub, Belial, Eblis, Azazel, Ahriman or
Angra Mainyu; Mephistopheles, Mephisto;
Shaitan, Sammael, Asmodeus; Abaddon, Apollyon;
Lilith; Aeshma, Pisacha, Putana, Ravana

5 <gods of evil> Set, Typhon, Loki; Nemesis; gods of
the nether world; Namtar, Azazel, Asmodeus,
Baba Yaga

6 demon, fiend, fiend from hell, **devil,** Satan, daeva,
rakshasa, dybbuk, shedu, gyre <Scot>, bad or evil
or unclean spirit; **hellion** <nf>, hellhound, hellkite
<old>, she-devil; cacodemon, incubus, succubus;
jinni, genie, genius, jinniyeh, afreet or afrit; evil
genius; barghest; **ghoul,** lamia, Lilith, yogini,
Baba Yaga, **vampire,** the undead

7 imp, pixie, sprite, elf, puck, kobold, diablotin
<Fr>, tokoloshe, poltergeist, **gremlin,** Dingbelle,
Fifinella, **bad fairy,** bad peri; little or young devil,
devilkin, deviling; erlking; Puck, Robin
Goodfellow, Hob, Hobgoblin

8 goblin, hobgoblin, hob, ouphe

9 bugbear, bugaboo, bogey, bogle, boggart; **booger,**
bugger, bug <old>, **booger-man, bogeyman,**
boogeyman; bête noire, fee-faw-fum, Mumbo
Jumbo

10 Fury, avenging spirit; the Furies, the Erinyes, the
Eumenides, the Dirae; Alecto, Megaera, Tisiphone

11 changeling, elf child; shape-shifter

12 werefolk, were-animals; werewolf, lycanthrope,
loup-garou <Fr>; werejaguar, jaguar-man,
uturuncu; wereass, werebear, werecalf, werefox,
werehyena, wereleopard, weretiger, werelion,
wereboar, werecrocodile, werecat, werehare

13 devilishness, demonishness, **fiendishness;**
devilship, devildom; horns, the cloven hoof, the
Devil's pitchfork

14 Satanism, diabolism, devil-worship, **demonism,**
devilry, diablerie, demonry; demonomy,
demonianism; black magic; Black Mass; sorcery
690; demonolatry, demon or devil or chthonian
worship, demonomancy, demonology, diabolology
or diabology, demonography, devil lore

15 Satanist, Satan-worshiper, diabolist, devil-
worshiper, demonist; **demonomist,** demoniast;
demonologist, demonologer; demonolater,
chthonian, demon worshiper; sorcerer 690.5

VERBS **16 demonize, devilize,** diabolize; possess,
obsess; bewitch, bedevil

ADJS **17 demoniac** or **demoniacal,** demonic or
demonical, demonish, demonlike; **devilish,**

devil-like; **satanic, diabolic, diabolical; hellish**
682.8; **fiendish,** fiendlike; ghoulish, ogreish; foul,
unclean, damned; inhuman

18 impish, puckish, elfish, elvish; mischievous 322.6

19 designations of Satan

Adversary	Mastema
Angel of the bottomless pit	Old Bendy <nf>
Angel *or* Prince of darkness	Old Enemy
Antichrist	Old Gentleman <nf>
Archfiend	Old Gooseberry <nf>
Apollyon	Old Harry <nf>
Author *or* Father of Evil	Old Ned <nf>
Beelzebub	Old Nick <nf>
Common Enemy	Old *or* Auld Clootie
Demon	<Scot nf>
Deuce <nf>	Old Poker <nf>
Devil Incarnate	Old Scratch <nf>
Dickens <nf>	Old Serpent
Eblis	O-Yama
Evil One	Prince of Darkness
Evil Spirit	Prince of the Devils
Father of Lies	Prince of the power of the
Fiend	air
Foul Fiend	Prince of this world
Haborym	Shaitan
His Satanic Majesty	Tempter
Lord of the Flies	Typhon
Lucifer	Wicked One

681 HEAVEN

<abode of the deity and blessed dead>

NOUNS **1 Heaven** <see list>; "my Father's house"—
Bible, "the great world of light, that lies behind all
human destinies"—Longfellow

2 the hereafter, the afterworld, immortal life, life to
come, immortality, eternal life, the afterlife 839.2,
life after death

3 Holy City, **Zion,** New Jerusalem, Heavenly *or*
Celestial City, Kingdom of God, City Celestial,
Heavenly City of God, City of God, *Civitas Dei*
<L>, "heaven's high city"—Francis Quarles

4 heaven of heavens, seventh heaven, the empyrean,
throne of God, God's throne, celestial throne, the
great white throne

5 <Christian Science> bliss, harmony, spirituality,
the reign of Spirit, the atmosphere of Soul

6 <Mormon> celestial kingdom, terrestrial
kingdom, telestial kingdom

7 <Muslim> Alfardaws, Assama *or* Assuma; Falak al
Aflak

8 <Hindu, Buddhist, and Theosophical> nirvana;
Buddha-field; devaloka, land of the gods;
kamavachara, kamaloka; devachan; samadhi

9 <mythological> Olympus, Mount Olympus;
Elysium, Elysian fields; fields of Aalu; Islands *or*

Isles of the Blessed, Happy Isles, Fortunate Isles
or Islands; Avalon; garden *or* abode of the Gods,
garden of the Hesperides, Bower of Bliss; Tir-na-
n'Og, Annwfn

10 <Norse> Valhalla, Asgard, Fensalir, Glathsheim,
Vingolf, Valaskjalf, Hlithskjalf, Thruthvang *or*
Thruthheim, Bilskirnir, Ydalir, Sökkvabekk,
Breithablik, Folkvang, Sessrymnir, Noatun,
Thrymheim, Glitnir, Himinbjorg, Vithi

11 <removal to heaven> **apotheosis, resurrection,
translation,** gathering, **ascension,** the Ascension;
assumption, the Assumption; removal to
Abraham's bosom

ADJS **12 heavenly,** heavenish; **paradisal, paradisaic,
paradisaical,** paradisiac, paradisiacal, paradisic,
paradisical; **celestial,** supernal, ethereal;
empyrean, empyreal; **unearthly,** unworldly;
otherworldly, extraterrestrial, extramundane,
transmundane, transcendental; Elysian,
Olympian; blessed, beatified, beatific *or* beatifical,
glorified, in glory; from on high

ADVS **13 celestially,** paradisally, supernally,
ethereally; in heaven, in Abraham's bosom, *in sinu
Abraham* <L>, on high, among the blest, in glory

14 designations of Heaven

a better place	Land o' the Leal <Scot>
abode of the blessed	my Father's house
Abraham's bosom	Olympus
better world	Paradise
Beulah	Svarga *or* Swarga *or*
Beulah Land	Swerga
eternal home	the happy land
eternity	the heavenly kingdom
Fiddler's Green	the kingdom of glory
firmament	the kingdom of God
glory	the kingdom of
God's kingdom	heaven
God's presence	the otherworld
happy hunting ground	the place up there
heaven above	the presence of God
high heaven	the Promised Land
inheritance of the saints in	the realm of light
light	the world above
kingdom come <nf>	Zion

682 HELL

NOUNS **1 hell, Hades,** Sheol, Gehenna, Tophet,
Abaddon, Naraka, jahannan, avichi, **perdition,**
Pandemonium, **inferno,** the pit, **the bottomless
pit,** the abyss, "a vast, unbottom'd, boundless
pit"—Robert Burns, **nether world,** lower world,
underworld, infernal regions, abode *or* world of
the dead, abode of the damned, eternal
damnation, place of torment, the grave, shades
below; **purgatory; limbo,** bardo

2 hellfire, fire and brimstone, lake of fire and brimstone, everlasting fire *or* torment, "the fire that never shall be quenched"—Bible

3 <mythological> **Hades,** Orcus, Tartarus, Avernus, Acheron, pit of Acheron; Amenti, Aralu; Hel, Niflhel, Niflheim, Naströnd

4 <rivers of Hades> Styx, Stygian creek; Acheron, River of Woe; Cocytus, River of Wailing; Phlegethon, Pyriphlegethon, River of Fire; Lethe, River of Forgetfulness

5 <deities of the nether world> Pluto, Orcus, Hades *or* Aides *or* Aidoneus, Dis *or* Dis pater, Rhadamanthus, Erebus, Charon, Cerberus, Minos; Osiris; Persephone, Proserpine, Proserpina, Persephassa, Despoina, Kore *or* Cora; Hel, Loki; Satan 680.3

VERBS **6 damn,** doom, send *or* consign to hell, cast into hell, doom to perdition, condemn to hell *or* eternal punishment

7 go to hell *or* to the devil, be damned, go the other way *or* to the other place <nf>

ADJS **8 hellish, infernal,** sulfurous, brimstone, fire-and-brimstone; chthonic, chthonian; pandemonic, pandemoniac; devilish; Plutonic, Plutonian; Tartarean; Stygian; Lethean; Acherontic; purgatorial, hellborn

ADVS **9 hellishly, infernally,** in hell, in hellfire, below, in torment

683 SCRIPTURE

NOUNS **1 scripture, scriptures, sacred writings** *or* **texts, bible;** canonical writings *or* books, sacred canon

2 Bible, Holy Bible, Scripture, the Scriptures, Holy Scripture, Holy Writ, the Book, the Good Book, the Book of Books, the Word, the Word of God; Vulgate, Septuagint, Douay Bible, Authorized *or* King James Version, Revised Version, American Revised Version; Revised Standard Version; Jerusalem Bible; Testament; canon

3 Old Testament, Tenach; Hexateuch, Octateuch; Pentateuch, Chumash, Five Books of Moses, **Torah,** the Law, the Jewish *or* Mosaic Law, Law of Moses; the Prophets, Nebiim, Major *or* Minor Prophets; the Writings, Hagiographa, Ketubim; Apocrypha, noncanonical writings

4 New Testament; Gospels, Evangels, the Gospel, Good News, Good *or* Glad Tidings; Synoptic Gospels, Epistles, Pauline Epistles, Catholic Epistles, Johannine Epistles; Acts, Acts of the Apostles; Apocalypse, Revelation

5 <Jewish> Torah, **Talmud,** Targum, Mishnah, Gemara; Masorah, Bahir, Midrash

6 <Islamic> **Koran,** Qur'an, Hadith, Sunna

7 <other texts> sacred text, scripture, sacred writings, canonical writings, canon; Avesta, **Zend-Avesta;** Granth, Adigranth; Tao Té Ching; Analects of Confucius; the Eddas; Arcana Caelestia; **Book of Mormon;** Science and Health with Key to the Scriptures

8 <Hindu> **the Vedas, Veda,** Rig-Veda, Yajur-Veda, Sama-Veda, Atharva-Veda, sruti; Brahmana, Upanishad, Aranyaka; Samhita; shastra, Smriti, Purana, Tantra, Agama; Bhagavad-Gita

9 <Buddhist> Tripitaka; Vinaya Pitaka, Sutta Pitaka, Abhidamma Pitaka; Dhammapada, Jataka; The Diamond Sutra, The Heart Sutra, The Lotus Sutra, Prajnaparamita Sutra

10 revelation, divine revelation; inspiration, afflatus, divine inspiration; theopneusty, theopneustia; theophany, theophania, epiphany; **mysticism,** direct *or* immediate intuition *or* communication, mystical experience, mystical intuition, contemplation, ecstasy; **prophecy,** prophetic revelation, apocalypse

ADJS **11 scriptural, Biblical,** Old-Testament, New-Testament, Gospel, Mosaic, Yahwist, Yahwistic, Elohist; **revealed, revelational;** prophetic, apocalyptic, apocalyptical; **inspired,** theopneustic; evangelic, evangelical, evangelistic, gospel; apostolic, apostolical; textual, textuary; canonical; Bible-thumping <nf>

12 Talmudic, Mishnaic, Gemaric, Masoretic; rabbinic

13 epiphanic, mystic, mystical

14 Koranic; Avestan; Eddic; Mormon

15 Vedic; tantrist

684 PROPHETS, RELIGIOUS FOUNDERS

NOUNS **1 prophet** 962.4, *vates sacer* <L>; Old Testament prophets <see list>; minor prophets

2 <Christian founders> **evangelist, apostle, disciple,** saint; Matthew, Mark, Luke, John; Paul; Peter; **the Fathers, fathers of the church**

3 Martin Luther, John Calvin, John Wycliffe, Jan Hus, John Wesley, John Knox, George Fox <Protestant reformers>; Emanuel Swedenborg <Church of the New Jerusalem>; Mary Baker Eddy <Christian Science>; Joseph Smith <Church of Jesus Christ of Latter-day Saints>

4 Buddha, Gautama Buddha <Buddhism>; Mahavira *or* Vardhamana *or* Jina <Jainism>; Mirza Ali Muhammad of Shiraz *or* the Bab <Babism>; Muhammad *or* Mohammed <Islam>; Confucius <Confucianism>; Lao-tzu <Taoism>; Zoroaster *or* Zarathustra <Zoroastrianism>; Nanak <Sikhism>

5 Old Testament prophets

Abraham	Jonah
Amos	Joseph
Daniel	Joshua
Ezekiel	Malachi
Habakkuk	Micah
Haggai	Moses
Hosea	Nahum
Isaac	Obadiah
Isaiah	Samuel
Jacob	Zechariah
Jeremiah	Zephaniah
Joel	

685 SANCTITY
<sacred quality>

NOUNS **1 sanctity,** sanctitude; **sacredness, holiness,** hallowedness, numinousness; sacrosanctness, sacrosanctity; heavenliness, transcendence, divinity, divineness 677.1; venerableness, **venerability, blessedness;** awesomeness, awfulness; inviolableness, **inviolability;** ineffability, unutterability, unspeakability, inexpressibility, inenarrableness; godliness 692.2; odor of sanctity

2 the sacred, the holy, the holy of holies, the numinous, the ineffable, the unutterable, the unspeakable, the inexpressible, the inenarrable, the transcendent

3 sanctification, hallowing; purification; beatitude, blessing; **glorification,** exaltation, enskying; **consecration,** dedication, devotion, setting apart; sainting, canonization, enshrinement; **sainthood, beatification; blessedness; grace,** state of grace; justification, justification by faith, justification by works

4 redemption, redeemedness, **salvation,** conversion, regeneration, new life, reformation, adoption; **rebirth, new birth, second birth, reincarnation,** spiritual rebirth; circumcision, spiritual purification *or* cleansing; spiritual awakening, metanoia

VERBS **5 sanctify, hallow; purify,** cleanse, wash one's sins away; **bless,** beatify; **glorify,** exalt, ensky; **consecrate,** dedicate, devote, set apart; **beatify, saint, canonize;** enshrine

6 redeem, regenerate, reform, convert, save, give salvation

ADJS **7 sacred, holy,** numinous, **sacrosanct, religious, spiritual,** heavenly, divine; faith-based; **venerable,** awesome, awful; inviolable, **inviolate,** untouchable; **ineffable,** unutterable, unspeakable, inexpressible, inenarrable

8 sanctified, hallowed; blessed, consecrated, devoted, dedicated, set apart; **glorified, exalted,** enskied; **saintly,** sainted, beatified, canonized

9 redeemed, saved, converted, regenerated, regenerate, justified, reborn, born-again, renewed; circumcised, spiritually purified *or* cleansed

WORD ELEMENTS **10** sacr-, sacro-, hier-, hiero-, hagi-, hagio-

686 UNSANCTITY

NOUNS **1 unsanctity,** unsanctitude; **unsacredness, unholiness,** unhallowedness, unblessedness; profanity, profaneness; unregenerateness, reprobation; **worldliness,** secularity, secularism; secular humanism

2 the profane, the unholy; the temporal, the secular, **the worldly,** the fleshly, the mundane; the world, the flesh, and the devil

ADJS **3 unsacred,** nonsacred, **unholy,** unhallowed, unsanctified, unblessed; profane, **secular, temporal, worldly,** fleshly, mundane; unsaved, unredeemed, unregenerate, reprobate

687 ORTHODOXY

NOUNS **1 orthodoxy,** orthodoxness, orthodoxism; **soundness,** soundness of doctrine, rightness, right belief *or* doctrine; **authoritativeness,** authenticity, canonicalness, canonicity; traditionalism; the truth, religious truth, gospel truth

2 the faith, true faith, apostolic faith, primitive faith; old-time religion, faith of our fathers

3 the Church, the true church, Holy Church, Church of Christ, the Bride of the Lamb, body of Christ, temple of the Holy Ghost, body of Christians, members in Christ, disciples *or* followers of Christ; apostolic church; universal church, the church universal; church visible, church invisible; church militant, church triumphant

4 true believer, orthodox Christian; Sunni Muslim; Orthodox Jew; orthodox, orthodoxian, orthodoxist; textualist, textuary; canonist; fundamentalist; the orthodox

5 strictness, strict interpretation, scripturalism, evangelicalism; hyperorthodoxy, puritanism, puritanicalness, purism; staunchness; straitlacedness, stiff-neckedness, hideboundness; hard line <nf>; **bigotry** 980.1; **dogmatism** 970.6; **fundamentalism,** literalism, precisianism; bibliolatry; Sabbatarianism; sabbatism

6 bigot 980.5; **dogmatist** 970.7

ADJS **7 orthodox,** orthodoxical; of the faith, of the true faith; **sound,** firm, faithful, true, true-blue, right-thinking; Christian; **evangelical; scriptural,** canonical; traditional, traditionalistic; literal, textual; standard, customary, conventional; **authoritative,** authentic, accepted, received, approved; correct, right, proper

8 **strict,** scripturalistic, evangelical; hyperorthodox, puritanical, purist *or* puristic, straitlaced; staunch; hidebound, hardline <nf>, creedbound; **bigoted** 980.10; **dogmatic** 970.22; **fundamentalist,** precisianist *or* precisianistic, literalist *or* literalistic; Sabbatarian

688 UNORTHODOXY

NOUNS 1 **unorthodoxy, heterodoxy;** unorthodoxness, **unsoundness,** un-Scripturality; **unauthoritativeness,** unauthenticity, uncanonicalness, uncanonicity; **nonconformity** 868

2 **heresy,** false doctrine, **misbelief; fallacy, error** 975

3 **infidelity,** infidelism; unchristianity; gentilism; **atheism, unbelief** 695.5

4 **paganism, heathenism;** paganry, heathenry; pagandom, heathendom; pagano-Christianism; allotheism; animism, animatism; idolatry 697

5 **heretic, misbeliever;** heresiarch; nonconformist 868.3; antinomian, Albigensian, Arian, Donatist, etc

6 **gentile;** non-Christian; **non-Jew,** goy, goyim, non-Jewish man *or shegets* <Yiddish>, non-Jewish woman *or shiksa* <Yiddish>; non-Muslim, non-Moslem, non-Muhammadan, non-Mohammedan, *giaour* <Turk>, kaffir; zendik, zendician, zendikite; non-Mormon; infidel; unbeliever 695.11

7 **pagan, heathen;** allotheist; animist; idolater 697.4

VERBS 8 **misbelieve, err,** stray, deviate, wander, go astray, stray from the path, step out of line <nf>, go wrong, fall into error; be wrong, be mistaken, be in error; serve Mammon

ADJS 9 **unorthodox,** nonorthodox, **heterodox, heretical; unsound; unscriptural,** uncanonical, apocryphal; **unauthoritative,** unauthentic, unaccepted, unreceived, unapproved; **fallacious,** erroneous 975.16; antinomian, Albigensian, Arian, Donatist, etc

10 **infidel,** infidelic, misbelieving; **atheistic,** unbelieving 695.19; **unchristian,** non-Christian; gentile, non-Jewish, goyish, uncircumcised; non-Muslim, non-Muham-madan, non-Mohammedan, non-Moslem, non-Islamic; non-Mormon

11 **pagan, paganish,** paganistic; **heathen, heathenish;** pagano-Christian; allotheistic; animist, animistic; idolatrous 697.7

689 OCCULTISM

NOUNS 1 **occultism, esoterics,** esotericism, esoterica, esoterism, esotery; cabalism, cabala *or* kabala *or* kabballa; yoga, yogism, yogeeism; **theosophy,** anthroposophy; symbolics, symbolism; anagogics; anagoge; hermetics; shamanism, spiritism, animism; mystery, mystification; hocus-pocus, mumbo jumbo; mysticism 683.10

2 **supernaturalism,** supranaturalism, preternaturalism, **transcendentalism; the supernatural,** the supersensible, the paranormal

3 **metaphysics,** hyperphysics, transphysical science, the first philosophy *or* theology

4 **psychics,** psychism, psychicism; **parapsychology, psychical** *or* **psychic research;** metapsychics, metapsychism, metapsychology; psychosophy; panpsychism; psychic monism

5 **spiritualism,** spiritism; mediumism; necromancy; séance, sitting; spirit 988.1

6 psychic *or* psychical phenomena, spirit manifestation; materialization; spirit rapping, table tipping *or* turning; poltergeistism, poltergeist; telekinesis, psychokinesis, power of mind over matter, telesthesia, teleportation; levitation; trance speaking, glossolalia; psychorrhagy; hallucination, déjà vu; séance; automatism, psychography, automatic *or* trance *or* spirit writing; Ouija board, Ouija; planchette; out-of-body experience; cosmic vibration, synchronicity; UFO sighting, alien encounter

7 **ectoplasm,** exteriorized protoplasm; aura, emanation, effluvium; ectoplasy; bioplasma

8 **extrasensory perception** *or* **ESP; clairvoyance,** lucidity, second sight, insight, sixth sense, inner sense, third eye, the force <nf>; intuition 934; foresight 961; premonition 133.1; clairsentience, clairaudience, crystal vision, psychometry, metapsychosis, feyness

9 **telepathy, mental telepathy, mind reading,** thought transference, telepathic transmission; telergy, telesthesia; telepathic dream, telepathic hallucination, cosmic consciousness

10 **divination** 962.2; **sorcery** 690

11 **occultist,** esoteric, mystic, mystagogue, cabalist, supernaturalist, transcendentalist; adept, mahatma; yogi, yogin, yogist; theosophist, anthroposophist; fork bender, unspeller

12 **parapsychologist;** psychist, psychicist; **metapsychist;** panpsychist; **metaphysician,** metaphysicist

13 **psychic; spiritualist,** spiritist, **medium,** ecstatic, spirit rapper, automatist, psychographist; necromancer

14 **clairvoyant;** clairaudient, clairsentient; seer, prophet; psychometer, psychometrist

15 **telepathist, mental telepathist, mind reader,** thought reader

16 **diviner** 962.4; **sorcerer** 690.5

17 **astral body,** astral, linga sharira, design body, subtle body, vital body, etheric body, bliss body, Buddhic body, spiritual body, soul body; kamarupa, desire *or* kamic body; causal body; mental *or* mind body

18 <seven principles of man, theosophy> spirit, atman; mind, manas; soul, buddhi; life principle, vital force, prana; astral body, linga sharira; physical *or* dense *or* gross body, sthula sharira; principle of desire, kama

19 **spiritualization,** etherealization, idealization; **dematerialization,** immaterialization, unsubstantialization; **disembodiment,** disincarnation

VERBS 20 **spiritualize,** spiritize; etherealize; idealize; **dematerialize,** immaterialize, unsubstantialize; **disembody,** disincarnate; teleport

21 practice spiritualism, hold a séance *or* sitting; call up spirits 690.11

22 **telepathize, read one's mind**

ADJS 23 **occult, esoteric, esoterical, mysterious,** mystic, mystical, recondite, obscure, arcane; anagogic, anagogical; metaphysic, metaphysical; cabalic, cabalistic; **paranormal, supernatural** 870.15; theosophical, theosophist, anthroposophical

24 **psychic, psychical, spiritual; spiritualistic,** spiritistic; mediumistic; **clairvoyant,** second-sighted, clairaudient, clairsentient; **telepathic; extrasensory,** psychosensory; supersensible, supersensual, pretersensual; telekinetic, psychokinetic; automatist; unconscious, subconscious; transphysical

690 SORCERY

NOUNS 1 **sorcery, necromancy, magic,** sortilege, **wizardry,** theurgy, gramarye <old>, rune, glamour; **witchcraft,** spellcraft, spellbinding, spellcasting; **witchery,** witchwork, bewitchery, enchantment; possession; **voodooism, voodoo,** hoodoo, wanga, juju, jujuism, obeah, obeahism; shamanism; magism, magianism; fetishism; totemism; vampirism; thaumaturgy, thaumaturgia, thaumaturgics, thaumaturgism; theurgy; alchemy; white *or* natural magic; sympathetic magic, chaos magic; **divination** 962.2; spell, charm 691

2 **black magic,** the black art; **diabolism, demonism,** diablerie, demonology, Satanism

3 <practices> magic circle; ghost dance; Sabbath, coven, witches' Sabbath *or* Sabbat; ordeal, ordeal by battle *or* fire *or* water *or* lots; Halloween, Walpurgis Night, witching hour, black mass

4 **conjuration,** conjurement, evocation, invocation; **exorcism,** exorcisation; exsufflation; **incantation** 691.4

5 **sorcerer, necromancer, wizard, wonder-worker,** warlock, theurgist; warlock, male witch; thaumaturge, thaumaturgist; miracle- *or* wonder-worker; alchemist; **conjurer; diviner** 962.4; dowser, water witch *or* diviner; diabolist; Faust, Comus

6 **magician,** mage, magus; Merlin; prestidigitator, illusionist 357.2

7 **shaman,** shamanist; **voodoo,** voodooist, wangateur, **witch doctor,** obeah doctor, **medicine man,** mundunugu, isangoma; witch-hunter, witch-finder; exorcist, exorciser; unspeller

8 **sorceress,** shamaness; **witch,** witchwoman <nf>, witchwife <Scot>, **hex, hag,** lamia; witch of Endor; coven, witches' coven, Weird Sisters <Shakespeare>

9 **bewitcher, enchanter, charmer, spellbinder; enchantress, siren,** vampire; Circe; Medusa, Medea, Gorgon, Stheno, Euryale

VERBS 10 sorcerize, shamanize; make *or* work magic, wave a wand, rub the ring *or* lamp; ride a broomstick; alchemize

11 **conjure, conjure up,** evoke, invoke, raise, summon, call up; **call up spirits,** conjure *or* conjure up spirits, summon spirits, raise ghosts, evoke from the dead

12 **exorcise,** lay; lay ghosts, **cast out devils;** unspell

13 cast a spell, wave a wand, bewitch 691.9

ADJS 14 sorcerous, necromantic, **magic, magical,** magian, numinous, thaumaturgic, thaumaturgical, miraculous, wizardlike, wizardly; alchemical, alchemistic, alchemistical; shaman, shamanic, shamanist *or* shamanistic; witchlike, witchy, witch; necromantic; voodoo, hoodoo <nf>, voodooistic; incantatory, incantational, spellbinding, hypnotic, autohypnotic; talismanic, fetishistic

691 SPELL, CHARM

NOUNS 1 **spell,** magic spell, **charm,** glamour, weird *or* cantrip <Scot>, wanga; hand of glory; evil eye, *malocchio* <Ital>, whammy <nf>; **hex, jinx, curse; exorcism**

2 **bewitchment, witchery, bewitchery; enchantment, entrancement,** fascination, captivation; illusion, maya; bedevilment; **possession, obsession**

3 **trance, ecstasy,** ecstasis, transport, mystic transport, seance; meditation, contemplation; **rapture;** yoga trance, dharana, dhyana, samadhi; hypnosis 22.7

4 **incantation, conjuration,** magic words *or* formula, invocation, evocation, chant; hocus-pocus, abracadabra, mumbo jumbo; open sesame, abraxas, paternoster

5 **charm, amulet, talisman, fetish,** periapt, phylactery; **voodoo, hoodoo,** juju, obeah, mumbo jumbo; **good-luck charm,** good-luck piece, **lucky piece** *or* **charm,** rabbit's-foot, lucky bean, four-leaf clover, whammy <nf>; mascot; madstone; love charm, philter; scarab, scarabaeus, scarabee; veronica, sudarium; swastika, fylfot, gammadion; potion; bell, book, and candle

6 **wish-bringer,** wish-giver; **wand, magic wand,** Aaron's rod; Aladdin's lamp, magic ring, magic belt, magic spectacles, magic carpet, seven-league boots; wishing well, wishing stone, wishing cap, Fortunatus's cap; cap of darkness, Tarnkappe, Tarnhelm; fern seed; **wishbone,** wishing bone, merrythought <Brit>

VERBS 7 **cast a spell,** spell, **spellbind; entrance,** trance, put in a trance; **hypnotize, mesmerize**

8 **charm,** becharm, **enchant, fascinate,** captivate, glamour

9 **bewitch,** witch, **hex, jinx;** voodoo, hoodoo; **possess, obsess;** bedevil, diabolize, demonize; hagride; overlook, look on with the evil eye, cast the evil eye

10 **put a curse on,** put a hex on, put a juju on, put obeah on, give the evil eye, give the *malocchio,* give a whammy <nf>

ADJS 11 **bewitching, witching;** illusory, illusive, illusionary; **charming, enchanting, entrancing, spellbinding, fascinating,** glamorous, Circean

12 **enchanted, charmed,** becharmed, charmstruck, charm-bound; **spellbound,** spell-struck, spell-caught; **fascinated,** captivated; **hypnotized, mesmerized;** under a spell, in a trance

13 **bewitched,** witched, witch-charmed, witch-held, witch-struck; hag-ridden; **possessed,** taken over, obsessed

692 PIETY

NOUNS 1 **piety, piousness,** pietism; **religion, faith; religiousness, religiosity,** religionism, religious-mindedness; theism; love of God, adoration; **devoutness,** devotion, devotedness, worship 696, worshipfulness, prayerfulness, cultism; faithfulness, dutifulness, observance, churchgoing, conformity 867; sanctimony; **reverence,** veneration; discipleship, followership;

daily communion; deism, mysticism, spirituality

2 **godliness,** godlikeness; fear of God; **sanctity,** sanctitude; odor of sanctity, beauty of holiness; **righteousness, holiness,** goodness; **spirituality,** spiritual-mindedness, holy-mindedness, heavenly-mindedness, godly-mindedness; **purity,** pureness, pure-heartedness, pureness of heart; **saintliness,** saintlikeness; saintship; sainthood; angelicalness, seraphicalness; heavenliness; **unworldliness,** unearthliness, other-worldliness

3 **zeal,** zealousness, zealotry, zealotism; unction; **evangelism, revival,** evangelicalism, revivalism; pentecostalism, charismatic movement; charismatic renewal, baptism in the spirit; charismatic gift, gift of tongues, glossolalia; **overreligiousness, religiosity,** overpiousness, overrighteousness, **overzealousness,** overdevoutness; bibliolatry; fundamentalism, militance, **fanaticism** 926.11; **sanctimony** 693

4 **believer,** truster, accepter, receiver; God-fearing man, pietist, religionist, saint, theist; **devotee,** devotionalist, votary; **zealot,** zealotist, fundamentalist, militant; **churchgoer,** churchman, churchite; pillar of the church; communicant, daily communicant; **convert,** proselyte, neophyte, catechumen; **disciple,** follower, servant, faithful servant; **fanatic**

5 **the believing, the faithful,** the righteous, the good; the elect, the chosen, the saved; the children of God, the children of light; Christendom, the Church 687.3

VERBS 6 **be pious, be religious; have faith,** trust in God, love God, fear God; witness, bear witness, affirm, **believe** 953.10; keep the faith, fight the good fight, let one's light shine, praise and glorify God, walk humbly with one's God; be observant, follow righteousness

7 **be converted, get religion** <nf>, receive *or* accept Christ, stand up for Jesus, be washed in the blood of the Lamb; be born again, see the light, meet God, enter the church

ADJS 8 **pious,** pietistic; **religious,** religious-minded; theistic; **devout,** devoted, devotional, dedicated, worshipful, prayerful, cultish, cultist, cultistic; **reverent,** reverential, venerative, venerational, adoring, solemn; faithful, dutiful, worshipful; orthodox; affirming, witnessing, believing 953.21; keeping the faith; **observant, practicing**

9 **godly, godlike; God-fearing; righteous, holy,** good; **spiritual,** spiritual-minded, holy-minded, godly-minded, heavenly-minded; **pure,** purehearted, pure in heart; **saintly,** saintlike; **angelic, angelical,** seraphic, seraphical; heavenly; **unworldly,** unearthly, otherwordly, not of the earth, not of this world

10 regenerate, regenerated, **converted, redeemed, saved,** God-fearing, theopathic, humble, prostrate; reborn, **born-again;** sanctified 685.8

11 zealous, zealotical; ardent, unctuous; **overreligious,** ultrareligious, overpious, overrighteous, **overzealous,** overdevout; holier-than-thou; crusading, missionary, Bible-thumping; **fanatical** 926.32; sanctimonious 693.5

693 SANCTIMONY

NOUNS **1 sanctimony, sanctimoniousness; pietism,** piety, **piousness,** pietisticalness, false piety; religionism, religiosity; **self-righteousness;** goodiness *and* goody-goodiness <nf>; pharisaism, pharisaicalness; Tartuffery, Tartuffism; **falseness, insincerity, hypocrisy** 354.6; affectation 500; **cant,** mummery, snivel, snuffle; unction, unctuousness, oiliness, smarm *and* smarminesss <nf>, mealymouthedness

2 lip service, mouth honor, mouthing, lip homage *or* worship *or* devotion *or* praise *or* reverence; formalism, solemn mockery; BOMFOG *or* brotherhood of man and fatherhood of God

3 pietist, religionist, **hypocrite,** religious hypocrite, canting hypocrite, pious fraud, religious *or* spiritual humbug, whited sepulcher, **pharisee,** Holy Willie <Robert Burns>, "a saint abroad and a devil at home"—Bunyan; bleeding heart <nf>; **canter,** ranter, snuffler, sniveler; dissembler, dissimulator; affecter, poser 500.8; **lip server,** lip worshiper, formalist; Pharisee, scribes and Pharisees; Tartuffe, Pecksniff, Mawworm, Joseph Surface

VERBS **4** be sanctimonious, be hypocritical; cant, snuffle, snivel; give mouth honor, render *or* pay lip service

ADJS **5 sanctimonious,** sanctified, **pious, pietistic, pietistical,** self-righteous, pharisaic, pharisaical, **holier-than-thou,** holier-than-the-pope <nf>; goody *and* goody-goody *and* goo-goo <nf>; **false, insincere, hypocritical** 354.33; affected 500.15; Tartuffish, Tartuffian; canting, sniveling, unctuous, mealymouthed, smarmy <nf>

694 IMPIETY

NOUNS **1 impiety, impiousness;** ungodliness, godlessness; **irreverence,** undutifulness; desertion, renegadism, apostasy, recreancy; backsliding, recidivism, lapse, fall *or* lapse from grace; **atheism, irreligion; unsanctity** 686

2 sacrilege, blasphemy, blaspheming, impiety; **profanity,** profaneness; sacrilegiousness,

blasphemousness; **desecration, profanation;** tainting, pollution, contamination

3 sacrilegist, **blasphemer,** Sabbath-breaker; deserter, renegade, apostate, recreant; backslider, recidivist; **atheist,** unbeliever 695.11

VERBS **4 desecrate, profane,** dishonor, unhallow, commit sacrilege

5 blaspheme; vilify, abuse 513.7; curse, swear 513.6; take in vain; taint, pollute, contaminate

ADJS **6 impious, irreverent,** undutiful; **profane,** profanatory; **sacrilegious, blasphemous;** renegade, apostate, recreant, backsliding, recidivist *or* recidivistic, lapsed, fallen, lapsed *or* fallen from grace; atheistic, **irreligious** 695.17; **unsacred** 686.3

695 NONRELIGIOUSNESS

NOUNS **1 nonreligiousness, unreligiousness; undeavoutness;** indevoutness, indevotion, undutifulness, nonobservance; adiaphorism, indifferentism, Laodiceanism, lukewarm piety; indifference 102; **laicism,** unconsecration; **deconsecration, secularization,** laicization, desacralization

2 secularism, worldliness, earthliness, earthiness, mundaneness; **unspirituality,** carnality; worldly-mindedness, earthly-mindedness, carnal-mindedness; materialism, Philistinism

3 ungodliness, godlessness, **unrighteousness, irreligion, unholiness,** unsaintliness, unangelicalness; unchristianliness, un-Christliness; impiety 694; **wickedness, sinfulness** 654.4

4 unregeneracy, unredeemedness, **reprobacy,** gracelessness, shriftlessness

5 unbelief, disbelief 955.1; infidelity, infidelism, faithlessness; **atheism;** nullifidianism, minimifidianism

6 agnosticism; skepticism, doubt, incredulity, Pyrrhonism, Humism; scoffing 508.1

7 freethinking, free thought, **latitudinarianism; humanism,** secular humanism; areligious

8 antireligion; antichristianism, antichristianity; antiscripturism

9 iconoclasm, iconoclasticism, image breaking

10 irreligionist; worldling, earthling; **materialist;** iconoclast, idoloclast; anti-Christian, antichrist

11 unbeliever, disbeliever, nonbeliever; **atheist, infidel, pagan, heathen,** heretic; nullifidian, minimifidian; secularist; **gentile** 688.6

12 agnostic; skeptic, doubter, dubitante, **doubting Thomas,** scoffer, Pyrrhonist, Humist

13 freethinker, latitudinarian, *esprit fort* <Fr>; humanist, secular humanist

VERBS **14 disbelieve,** doubt 955.6; scoff 508.9; **laicize,**
deconsecrate, **secularize,** desacralize

ADJS **15 nonreligious, unreligious,** having no
religious preference; **undevout,** indevout,
indevotional, undutiful, nonobservant,
nonpracticing; adiamorphic, indifferentist *or*
indifferentistic, Laodicean, lukewarm, indifferent
102.6; unconsecrated, **deconsecrated, secularized,**
laicized, desacralized

16 secularist, secularistic, worldly, earthly, earthy,
terrestrial, **mundane,** temporal; **unspiritual,
profane,** carnal, **secular;** humanistic, secular-
humanistic; worldly minded, earthly minded,
carnal-minded; **materialistic,** material, Philistine

17 ungodly, godless, **irreligious, unrighteous, unholy,**
unsaintly, unangelic, unangelical; impious 694.6;
wicked, sinful 654.16

18 unregenerate, unredeemed, **unconverted,** godless,
reprobate, graceless, shriftless, **lost, damned;**
lapsed, fallen, recidivist, recidivistic

19 unbelieving, disbelieving, faithless; infidel,
infidelic; **pagan, heathen; atheistic,** atheist;
nullifidian, minimifidian

**20 agnostic; skeptic, skeptical, doubtful, dubious,
incredulous,** Humean, Pyrrhonic; Cartesian

21 freethinking, latitudinarian

22 antireligious; antichristian; antiscriptural;
iconoclastic

696 WORSHIP

NOUNS **1 worship,** worshiping, **adoration, devotion,
homage, veneration, reverence,** honor; adulation,
esteem; cult, cultus, cultism; latria, dulia,
hyperdulia; falling down and worshiping,
prostration; co-worship; idolatry 697

2 glorification, glory, **praise,** extolment, laudation,
laud, exaltation, magnification, dignification

3 paean, laud; hosanna, hallelujah, alleluia; **hymn,**
hymn of praise, **doxology, psalm, anthem,** motet,
canticle, chorale; **chant,** versicle; mantra, Vedic
hymn *or* chant; plainsong, carol, gospel song;
Introit, Miserere; Gloria, Gloria in Excelsis, Gloria
Patri; Te Deum, Agnus Dei, Benedicite,
Magnificat, Nunc Dimittis; response, responsory,
report, answer; Trisagion; antiphon, antiphony;
offertory, offertory sentence *or* hymn; hymnody,
hymnology, hymnography, psalmody; hymnal

4 prayer, praying, **supplication, invocation,**
imploration, impetration, entreaty, beseechment,
appeal, petition, suit, aid prayer, bid *or* bidding
prayer, request, petitionary prayer, act of
contrition, penitential prayer, orison, obsecration,
obtestation, confession, rogation, **devotions;**
genuflection, prostration; silent prayer,

meditation, contemplation, communion;
intercession *or* intercessory prayer, suffrage;
grace, thanks, thanksgiving; litany; breviary,
canonical prayers; collect, collect of the Mass,
collect of the Communion; Angelus; Paternoster,
the Lord's Prayer; Hail Mary, Ave, Ave Maria;
Kyrie Eleison; Pax; chaplet; rosary, beads,
beadroll; Kaddish, Mourner's Kaddish; prayer
wheel *or* machine

5 benediction, blessing, benison, invocation,
benedicite; sign of the cross; laying on of hands

6 propitiation, appeasement 465.1; atonement 658

7 oblation, offering, sacrifice, immolation, incense;
libation, drink offering; burnt offering, holocaust;
thank offering, votive *or* ex voto offering; heave
offering, peace offering, sacramental offering, sin
or piacular offering, whole offering; human
sacrifice, mactation, infanticide, hecatomb;
self-sacrifice, self-immolation; sutteeism;
scapegoat, suttee; offertory, collection; penitence

8 divine service, **service,** public worship, **liturgy**
701.3, office, duty, exercises, **devotions;** meeting;
church service, church, celebration; **revival,**
revival meeting, camp meeting, tent meeting,
praise meeting; watch meeting, watch-night
service, watch night; **prayer meeting,** prayers,
prayer, call to prayer; morning devotions *or*
services *or* prayers, matins, lauds; prime, prime
song; tierce, undersong; sext; none, nones; novena;
evening devotions *or* services *or* prayers, vesper,
vespers, vigils, evensong; compline, night song *or*
prayer; bedtime prayer; Mass; pilgrimage, hajj

9 worshiper, adorer, venerator, votary, adulator,
communicant, daily communicant, celebrant,
churchgoer, chapelgoer, parishioner, follower;
prayer, suppliant, supplicant, supplicator,
petitioner; orans, orant; beadsman; revivalist,
evangelist; congregation; **idolater** 697.4; flock,
sheep, congregation, concourse, minyan <Heb>

10 <sacred object> cross, crucifix, chalice, relic,
incense, holy water, thurible, censer, chrism,
rosary beads, votive candle, vigil light; phylactery,
tefillin, mezuzah, menorah; totem, talisman,
charm, amulet

VERBS **11 worship, adore, reverence, venerate,
revere, honor,** respect, adulate, do *or* pay homage
to, pay divine honors to, do service, lift up the
heart, bow down and worship, humble oneself
before, prostrate, genuflect; **idolize** 697.5

12 glorify, praise, laud, exalt, extol, magnify, bless,
celebrate; praise God, praise *or* glorify the Lord,
bless the Lord, praise God from whom all
blessings flow; praise Father, Son, and Holy Ghost;
give thanks; sing praises, sing the praises of,
sound *or* resound the praises of; doxologize, hymn

13 **pray, supplicate,** invoke, petition, make
supplication, *daven* <Yiddish>; **implore, beseech**
440.11, obtest; offer a prayer, send up a prayer,
commune with God; **say one's prayers;** tell one's
beads, recite the rosary; **say grace, give** *or* **return
thanks;** pray over

14 **bless, give one's blessing,** give benediction, confer
a blessing upon, invoke benefits upon; cross, make
the sign of the cross over *or* upon; lay hands on

15 **propitiate,** make propitiation; appease 465.7; **offer
sacrifice,** sacrifice, make sacrifice to, immolate
before, offer up an oblation

ADJS 16 **worshipful,** worshiping; **adoring,** adorant;
devout, devotional; pious; **reverent,** reverential,
dedicated; **venerative,** venerational; solemn; at the
feet of; **prayerful,** praying, penitent, **supplicatory,**
supplicant, suppliant; precatory, precative,
imploring, honoring, on one's knees, on bended
knee; prone *or* prostrate before, in the dust;
blessing, benedictory, benedictional; propitiatory;
anthemic

INTERJS 17 **hallelujah!,** alleluia!, **hosanna!, praise
God!,** praise the Lord!, praise ye the Lord!, amen!,
Heaven be praised!, glory to God!, glory be to
God!, glory be to God in the highest!, bless the
Lord!, "hallowed be Thy Name!"—Bible, praise
God from whom all blessings flow; thanks be to
God!, *Deo gratias!* <L>; sursum corda! <Hindu>;
om!, om mani padme hum!

18 O Lord!, our Father which art in heaven!; God
grant!, pray God that!; God bless!, God save!, God
forbid!

697 IDOLATRY

NOUNS 1 **idolatry,** idolatrousness, idolism,
idolodulia, **idol worship;** heathenism, paganism;
image worship, iconolatry, iconoduly; cult,
cultism; totemism; **fetishism** *or* fetichism;
demonism, demonolatry, demon *or* devil worship,
Satanism; animal worship, snake worship, fire
worship, pyrolatry, Parsiism, Zoroastrianism; sun
worship, star worship, Sabaism; tree worship,
plant worship, Druidism, nature worship; phallic
worship, phallicism; hero worship; idolomancy

2 **idolization,** fetishization; **deification,** apotheosis

3 **idol; fetish,** totem, joss; **graven image, golden calf,**
effigy; devil-god; Baal, Jaganatha *or* Juggernaut;
sacred cow

4 **idolater,** idolatress, idolizer, idolatrizer, iconolater,
cultist, idolist, idol worshiper, image-worshiper;
fetishist, totemist; demon *or* devil worshiper,
demonolater, chthonian; animal worshiper,
zoolater, theriolater, therolater, snake worshiper,
ophiolater; fire worshiper, pyrolater, Parsi,

Zoroastrian; sun worshiper, heliolater; star
worshiper, Sabaist; tree worshiper, arborolater,
dendrolater, plant worshiper, Druid, nature
worshiper; phallic worshiper; anthropolater,
archaeolater, etc; groupie, hero-worshiper

VERBS 5 **idolatrize,** idolize, idolify, idol; fetishize,
fetish, totemize; **make an idol of, deify,**
apotheosize; idealize, lionize, hero-worship, look
up to

6 **worship idols,** worship the golden calf, *adorer le
veau d'or* <Fr>

ADJS 7 **idolatrous,** idolatric *or* idolatrical, **idol
worshiping;** idolistic, idolizing, iconolatrous,
cultish, fetishistic, totemistic; heathen, pagan;
demonolatrous, chthonian; heliolatrous;
bibliolatrous; zoolatrous; hero-worshiping,
lionizing

698 THE MINISTRY

NOUNS 1 **the ministry, pastorate,** pastorage, pastoral
care, cure *or* care of souls, **the Church,** the cloth,
the pulpit, the desk; **priesthood,** priestship;
apostleship; call, vocation, sacred calling; holy
orders; rabbinate

2 ecclesiasticalism, ecclesiology, priestcraft

3 **clericalism,** sacerdotalism; priesthood; priestism;
episcopalianism; ultramontanism

4 **monasticism,** monachism, monkery, **monkhood,**
friarhood; celibacy 565

5 ecclesiastical office <see list>, church office,
dignity

6 **papacy,** papality, **pontificate,** popedom, the
Vatican, Apostolic See, See of Rome, the Church

7 hierarchy, hierocracy; theocracy

8 **diocese, see,** archdiocese, bishopric,
archbishopric; province; synod, conference;
parish

9 **benefice,** living, **incumbency,** glebe, advowson;
curacy, cure, charge, cure *or* care of souls; prelacy,
rectory, vicarage

10 **holy orders, orders** 699.4, major orders, apostolic
orders, minor orders; calling, election,
nomination, appointment, preferment, induction,
institution, installation, investiture; conferment,
presentation; **ordination,** ordainment,
consecration, canonization, reading in <Brit>

VERBS 11 **be ordained, take holy orders,** take
orders, take vows, read oneself in <Brit>; **take the
veil,** wear the cloth

12 **ordain,** frock, **canonize, consecrate;** saint

ADJS 13 **ecclesiastic, ecclesiastical, churchly;
ministerial, clerical,** sacerdotal, **pastoral; priestly,**
priestish; prelatic, prelatical, prelatial; episcopal,
episcopalian; archiepiscopal; primatal, primatial,

primatical; canonical; capitular, capitulary; abbatical, abbatial; ultramontane; **evangelistic;** rabbinic, rabbinical; priest-ridden; parochial

14 **monastic,** monachal, **monasterial, monkish;** conventual

15 **papal, pontific, pontifical,** apostolic, apostolical; **popish** or papist or papistic or papistical or papish <nf>

16 **hierarchical,** hierarchal, hieratic; hierocratic; theocratic, theocratist

17 **ordained;** in orders, in holy orders, of the cloth

18 **ecclesiastical offices**

abbacy	pastorate or pastorship or
archbishopric or	pastorage
archiepiscopate or	pontificate or papacy or
archiepiscopacy	popedom
archdeaconry	prebend or prebendaryship
bishopric or bishopdom	or prebendal stall
canonry or canonicate	prelacy or prelature or
cardinalate or cardinalship	prelateship or
chaplaincy or chaplainship	prelatehood
curacy	presbytery or presbyterate
deaconry or deaconship	primacy or primateship
deanery or deanship	rabbinate
episcopate or episcopacy	rectorate or rectorship
ministry	vicariate or vicarship

699 THE CLERGY

NOUNS 1 **clergy, ministry,** the cloth; clerical order, clericals; **priesthood;** priestery; presbytery; prelacy; Sacred College; rabbinate; hierocracy, pastorage; clerical venue

2 **clergyman,** clergywoman, clergyperson, man or woman of the cloth, **divine, ecclesiastic, churchman, cleric,** clerical; clerk, clerk or person in holy orders, tonsured cleric; **minister, minister of the Gospel, parson, pastor,** abbé and curé <Fr>, **rector,** curate, vicar, man or woman of God, servant of God, shepherd, sky pilot and Holy Joe <nf>, reverend <nf>; supply minister or preacher, supply clergy; **chaplain;** military chaplain, padre <nf>; the Reverend, the Very or Right Reverend; Doctor of Divinity or DD; elder

3 **preacher,** sermoner, sermonizer, sermonist, homilist; pulpiter, pulpiteer; predicant, predikant; preaching friar; circuit rider; television or TV preacher, telepreacher <nf>

4 holy orders, major orders, priest or presbyter, deacon or diaconus, subdeacon or subdiaconus; minor orders, acolyte or acolytus, exorcist or exorcista, reader or lector, doorkeeper or ostiarius; ordinand, candidate for holy orders

5 **priest,** gallach <Heb>, **father,** father in Christ, **padre,** cassock, presbyter; curé, parish priest; confessor, father confessor, spiritual father or director or leader, holy father; penitentiary

6 **evangelist,** revivalist, evangel, evangelicalist; **missionary,** missioner; missionary apostolic, missionary rector, colporteur; television or TV evangelist, televangelist <nf>

7 benefice-holder, beneficiary, **incumbent;** resident, residentiary

8 church dignitary, ecclesiarch, ecclesiast, hierarch; minor or lay officer

9 <Catholic> pope, pontiff; cardinal, dean, archbishop, bishop, provost, high priest, ecclesiarch, canon, monsignor

10 <Mormon> deacon, teacher, priest, elder, Seventy, high priest, bishop, patriarch, apostle; Aaronic priesthood, Melchizedek priesthood

11 <Jewish> **rabbi,** rebbe, rabbin; chief rabbi; baal kore <Yiddish>; cantor; priest, kohen <Heb>, high priest; maggid; Levite; scribe

12 <Muslim> imam, qadi, sheikh, mullah, murshid, mufti, hajji, muezzin, dervish, abdal, fakir, santon, ayatollah

13 <Hindu> Brahman, pujari, purohit, pundit, guru, bashara, vairagi or bairagi, Ramwat, Ramanandi; sannyasi; yogi, yogin; bhikshu, bhikhari

14 <Buddhist> bonze, bhikku, poonghie, talapoin, bodhisattva, guru, lama; Grand Lama, Dalai Lama, Panchen Lama

15 <pagan> Druid, Druidess; flamen; hierophant, hierodule, hieros, daduchus, mystes, epopt

16 **religious,** religieux <Fr>; **monk,** monastic, lama, bhikkhu; brother, lay brother; cenobite, conventual; caloyer, hieromonach; **mendicant, friar;** pilgrim, palmer; stylite, pillarist, pillar saint; beadsman; prior, claustral or conventual prior, grand prior, general prior; abbot; lay abbot, abbacomes; hermit 584.5; ascetic 667.2; celibate 565.2

17 **nun,** sister, religieuse <Fr>, clergywoman, conventual; abbess, prioress; **mother superior,** lady superior, superioress, the reverend mother, holy mother; canoness, regular or secular canoness; novice, postulant

18 **religious orders**

Augustinian or Austin	Carmelite or White Friars
Friars	Carthusian
Augustinian Hermit	Cistercian
Barnabite	Cluniac
Benedictine or Black	Conventual
Monks	Crosier
Bernardine	Crutched Friars or Crossed
Bonhomme	Friars
Brigittine	Discalced Carmelite
Capuchin	Dominican or Black Friars

Franciscan *or* Gray Friars	Observant
Friars Minor	Oratorian
Friars Preacher	Pallottine Fathers and
Gilbertine	Brothers
Holy Cross	preaching Friars *or*
Hospitaler	brothers
Jesuit *or* Loyolite	Premonstratensian
Lorettine	Recollect *or* Recollet
Marist	Redemptorist
Maryknoll	Salesian
Maturine	Templar
Minorite	Trappist

700 THE LAITY

NOUNS **1 the laity, lay persons,** laymen, laywomen, nonclerics, nonordained persons, seculars, temporalty; brothers, sisters, brethren, sistren <nf>, people; flock, fold, sheep; **congregation,** parishioners, churchgoers, assembly; *minyan* <Heb>; **parish,** society; class

2 layman, layperson, laic, secular, churchman, **parishioner,** church member; brother, sister, lay brother, lay sister; laywoman, churchwoman; catchumen; communicant

ADJS **3 lay,** laic *or* laical; **nonecclesiastical,** nonclerical, nonministerial, nonpastoral, nonordained; nonreligious; **secular,** secularist; secularistic; temporal, popular, civil; congregational

701 RELIGIOUS RITES

NOUNS **1 ritualism,** rituality, ritualization, **ceremonialism, formalism,** liturgism; symbolism, symbolics; **cult,** cultus, cultism; sacramentalism, sacramentarianism; sabbatism, Sabbatarianism; ritualization, **solemnization,** solemn observance, **celebration;** liturgics, liturgiology

2 ritualist, ceremonialist, celebrant, liturgist, **formalist,** formulist, formularist; sacramentalist, sacramentarian; sabbatist, Sabbatarian; High-Churchman, High-Churchist; crucifer, thurifer, acolyte

3 rite <see list>, **ritual,** rituality, **liturgy,** holy rite; service, order of worship; **ceremony, ceremonial; observance,** ritual observance; **formality,** solemnity; **form,** formula, formulary, form of worship *or* service, mode of worship; prescribed form; service, function, duty, office, practice; **sacrament,** sacramental, mystery; ordinance; institution

4 seven sacraments, mysteries: baptism, confirmation, the Eucharist, penance, extreme unction, holy orders, matrimony

5 unction, sacred unction, sacramental anointment, chrism *or* chrisom, chrismation, chrismatory; **extreme unction, last rites,** viaticum; ointment; chrismal

6 baptism, baptizement; **christening; immersion,** total immersion; **sprinkling,** aspersion, aspergation; affusion, infusion; baptism for the dead; baptismal regeneration; baptismal gown *or* dress *or* robe, chrismal; baptistery, baptistry, **font; confirmation,** bar *or* bas mitzvah <Jewish>

7 Eucharist, Lord's Supper, Last Supper, Communion, Holy Communion, **the Sacrament,** the Holy Sacrament; intinction; consubstantiation, impanation, subpanation, transubstantiation; real presence; elements, consecrated elements, bread and wine, body and blood of Christ; Host, wafer, loaf, bread, altar bread, consecrated bread; Sacrament Sunday

8 Mass, *Missa* <L>, Eucharistic rites; **the Liturgy,** the Divine Liturgy; **parts of the Mass,** High Mass, Low Mass

9 <non-Christian rites> initiation, rite of passage; circumcision; bar mitzvah *and* bas mitzvah <Jewish>; Kaddish, shivah; female circumcision; ritual cleaning, ritual bathing; fertility rite; sun dance, rain dance, war dance, ghost dance, potlatch; witches' Sabbath, black mass; hara-kiri

10 sacred object *or* **article; ritualistic manual,** Book of Common Prayer, breviary, canon, haggadah <Jewish>, missal *or* Mass book, book of hours, lectionary, prayer book; siddur *and* mahzor <Jewish>

11 psalter, psalmbook; Psalm Book, Book of Common Order; the Psalms, Book of Psalms, the Psalter, the Psaltery

12 holy day, hallowday <nf>, holytide, holiday; feast, fast, fast day; Sabbath; Sunday, Lord's day; saint's day; church calendar, ecclesiastical calendar

13 Christian holy days <see list>; Jewish holy days <see list>

14 <Muslim holy days> Ramadan <month>, Bairam, Muharram

VERBS **15 celebrate, observe, keep, solemnize;** ritualize; celebrate Mass; communicate, administer Communion; attend Communion, receive the Sacrament, partake of the Lord's Supper; attend Mass

16 minister, officiate, do duty, **perform a rite,** perform service *or* divine service; administer a sacrament, administer the Eucharist, etc; anoint, chrism, bless; confirm, impose, lay hands on; make the sign of the cross

17 baptize, christen; dip, immerse; sprinkle, asperge; circumcise

18 confess, make confession, receive absolution;

shrive, hear confession; **absolve,** administer absolution; administer extreme unction

ADJS **19 ritualistic, ritual; ceremonial, ceremonious; formal,** formular, formulaic, formulary; liturgic, liturgical, **liturgistic, liturgical;** solemn, consecrated; High-Church; **sacramental,** sacramentarian; eucharistic, eucharistical, baptismal; paschal; Passover; matrimonial, nuptial; funereal

20 religious rites

ablution	litany
absolution	love feast *or* agape
anointing of the sick	lustration
aspersion *or* asperges	offertory
celebration	pax *or* kiss of peace
cleansing *or* purification	penitence *or* act of
confession *or* auricular	contrition
confession *or* the	processional
confessional *or* the	reciting the rosary *or*
confessionary	telling one's beads
confirmation	sign of the cross *or*
greater *or* lesser litany	signum crucis <L> *or*
high celebration	signing *or* crossing
imposition *or* laying on of	oneself
hands	sprinkling
invocation	Stations of the Cross
invocation of saints	thurification *or* censing
last rites	viaticum

21 Western Christian holy days

Advent <pre-Christmas>	Good Friday <Fri before
All Saints' Day *or*	Easter>
Allhallows <Nov 1>	Hallowmas *or* Allhallow-
all Souls' Day <Nov 2>	mas *or* Allhallowtide *or*
Annunciation *or* Lady Day	Halloween *or* Allhallows
<Mar 25>	*or* All Saints' Day *or* All
Ascension Day *or* Holy	Souls' Day <Oct 31>
Thursday <40 days after	Holy Thursday *or* Maundy
Easter>	Thursday <before Easter>
Ash Wednesday <start of	Holy Week *or* Passion
Lent>	Week <before Easter>
Assumption <Aug 15>	Lammas *or* Lammas Day *or*
Candlemas *or* Candlemas	Lammastide *or* Feast of
Day *or* Presentation	St Peter's Chains <Aug 1>
<Feb 2>	Lent *or* Lententide <40
Christmas <Dec 25>	days before Easter>
Circumcision *or* Holy	Martinmas <Nov 11>
Name Day <Jan 1>	Michaelmas *or* Michael-
Corpus Christi <Thurs	mas Day *or* Michaelmas-
after Trinity Sun>	tide <Sept 29>
Easter *or* Eastertide <1st	Palm Sunday <Sun before
Sunday after 1st full moon	Easter>
after vernal equinox>	Pentecost *or* Whitsuntide
Easter Even *or* Holy	*or* Whitsun *or* Whitsun-
Saturday	day <7th Sun after
Ember days <beginning of	Easter>
seasons>	Quadragesima *or*
Epiphany *or* Three Kings'	Quadragesima Sunday
Day <Jan 6>	Septuagesima

Shrove Tuesday *or* Mardi	Twelfth-tide *or* Twelfth-
Gras *or* Carnival *or*	night *or* Twelfth-day
Pancake Day <Tues	<night before Epiphany>
before Ash Wednesday>	Whitweek and
Solemnity of Mary <Jan 1>	Whitmonday and
Trinity Sunday <Sun after	Whit-Tuesday, etc <after
Pentecost>	Pentecost>

22 Jewish holy days

Fast of Av *or* Ninth of Av *or*	Rosh Hodesh *or* Rosh
Tishah b'Av	Chodesh
Hanukkah *or* Feast of the	Shabuoth *or* Shavuoth *or*
Dedication *or* Feast of	Pentecost *or* Feast of
Lights	Weeks
High Holy Days <between	Shemini Atzeres
Rosh Hashanah and	Simhath Torah *or*
Yom Kippur>	Rejoicing over the
Lag b'Omer	Law
Passover *or* Pesach	Sukkoth *or* Feast of
Purim	Tabernacles
Rosh Hashanah *or* New	Yom Kippur *or* Day of
Year	Atonement

702 ECCLESIASTICAL ATTIRE

NOUNS **1 canonicals,** clericals <nf>, robes, cloth; **vestments,** vesture; regalia; liturgical garments, ceremonial attire; pontificals, pontificalia, episcopal vestments; habit, veil

2 robe, frock, mantle, gown, cloak, surplice, scapular, cassock, cope, hood, clerical collar, etc

3 staff, pastoral staff, **crosier, cross,** cross-staff, crook, paterissa

ADJS **4 vestmental,** vestmentary

703 RELIGIOUS BUILDINGS

NOUNS **1 church,** kirk <Scot>, bethel, **meetinghouse,** church house, **house of God,** place of worship, house of worship *or* prayer; conventicle; **mission;** basilica, major *or* patriarchal basilica, minor basilica; **cathedral,** cathedral church, *duomo* <Ital>; collegiate church

2 temple, fane; **tabernacle; synagogue,** *shul* <Yiddish>; **mosque,** masjid; dewal, girja; pagoda; kiack; pantheon; wat, ziggurat, pantheon

3 chapel, chapel of ease, chapel royal, side chapel, school chapel, sacrament chapel, Lady chapel, oratory, oratorium; chantry; sacellum, sacrarium

4 shrine, holy place, dagoba, cella, naos; sacrarium, sanctum sanctorum, holy of holies, delubrum; tope, stupa; reliquary, *reliquaire* <Fr>

5 sanctuary, holy of holies, sanctum, sanctum sanctorum, adytum, sacrarium

6 cloister, monastery, house, abbey, friary; priory,

priorate; lamasery; **convent, nunnery;** ashram, hermitage, retreat

7 **parsonage, pastorage,** pastorate, manse, **church house,** clergy house; presbytery, **rectory,** vicarage, deanery; glebe; chapter house; deanery, manse

8 bishop's palace; **Vatican;** Lambeth, Lambeth Palace

9 <church interior> vestry, sacristy, sacrarium, sanctuary, diaconicon or diaconicum; baptistery; aisle, ambry, apse, blindstory, chancel, choir, choir screen, cloisters, confessional, confessionary <old>, crypt, Easter sepulcher, narthex, nave, porch, presbytery, rood loft, rood stair, rood tower or spire or steeple, transept, triforium; organ loft

10 <church furnishings> piscina; stoup, holy-water stoup or basin; baptismal font; patent; reredos; jube, rood screen, rood arch, chancel screen; altar cloth, cerecloth, chrismal; communion or sacrament cloth, corporal, fanon, oblation cloth; rood cloth; baldachin, *baldacchino* <Ital>; kneeling stool, *prie-dieu* <Fr>; prayer rug or carpet or mat

11 <vessels> cruet; chalice; ciborium, pyx; chrismal, chrismatory; monstrance, ostensorium; reliquary; font, holy-water font

12 **altar,** scrobis; bomos, eschara, hestia; **Lord's table,** holy table, **Communion table,** chancel table, table of the Lord, God's board; rood altar; altar desk, missal stand; credence, prothesis, table or altar of prothesis, predella; superaltar, retable, retablo, ancona, gradin; altarpiece, altar side, altar rail, altar carpet, altar stair; altar facing or front, frontal; altar slab, altar stone, mensal

13 **pulpit, rostrum,** ambo; **lectern,** desk, reading desk

14 <seats> **pew; stall;** mourners' bench, anxious bench or seat, penitent form; amen corner; sedilia

ADJS 15 **churchly,** churchish, **ecclesiastical;** churchlike, templelike; cathedral-like, cathedralesque; tabernacular; synagogical, synagogal; pantheonic

16 **claustral, cloistered; monastic,** monachal, **monasterial; coventual,** conventical

704 SHOW BUSINESS, THEATER

NOUNS 1 **show business,** show biz <nf>, the entertainment industry; **the theater, the footlights, the stage, the boards,** the bright lights, Broadway, the Great White Way, the scenes <old>, traffic of the stage; avant-garde theater, contemporary theater, experimental theater, total theater, epic theater, theater of the absurd, theater of cruelty, guerrilla theater, street theater; stagedom, theater world, stage world, stageland, playland; **drama,** legitimate stage or theater, legit

<nf>, off Broadway, off-off-Broadway; music or musical theater, fringe theater; café theater, dinner theater; regional theater; repertory drama or theater, stock; summer theater, summer stock, straw hat or straw hat circuit <nf>; **vaudeville,** variety; **burlesque; circus,** carnival; magic show; theatromania, theatrophobia

2 **dramatics;** dramatization, dramaticism, dramatism; **theatrics,** theatricism, **theatricalism,** theatricality, staginess; theatricals, amateur theatricals; **histrionics,** histrionism; dramatic or histrionic or Thespian art; dramatic stroke, *coup de théâtre* <Fr>; **melodramatics,** sensationalism; **dramaturgy,** dramatic structure, play construction, dramatic form; dramatic irony, tragic irony

3 **theatercraft, stagecraft,** stagery, scenecraft; **showmanship**

4 **stage show, show; play,** stage play, piece, vehicle, work; **hit** or hit show <nf>, gasser <nf>, success, critical success, audience success, word-of-mouth success, box-office hit, long run; short run, failure, **flop** and bomb and turkey <nf>

5 **tragedy,** tragic drama, melodrama; tragic flaw; buskin, cothurnus; tragic muse, Melpomene

6 **comedy;** comic relief; comic muse, Thalia; black comedy or humor, satire, farce; sock, coxcomb, cap and bells, motley, bladder, slapstick, burlesque; historic comedy

7 **act, scene, number, turn,** bit and shtick <nf>, routine <nf>; curtain raiser or lifter; introduction; expository scene; monologue, soliloquy; **prologue,** epilogue; **entr'acte,** intermezzo, intermission, interlude, *divertissement* <Fr>, *divertimento* <Ital>, climax; **finale,** afterpiece; exodus, exode; chaser <nf>; curtain call, curtain; encore, ovation; hokum or hoke act <nf>; song and dance; burlesque act; stand-up comedy act; sketch, skit

8 **acting, playing,** playacting, performing, **performance,** taking a role or part, role-playing; **representation, portrayal, characterization,** interpretation, projection, enactment; **impersonation,** personation, miming, mimicking, mimicry, mimesis; pantomiming, mummery; Method acting; improvisation; ham and hammy acting and hamming or hamming up <nf>, camping it up <nf>, overacting, histrionics; stage presence; stage directions, **business,** stage business, *jeu de théâtre* <Fr>, acting device; stunt and gag <nf>; hokum or hoke <nf>; buffoonery, slapstick; patter; stand-up comedy; crossover

9 **repertoire, repertory;** stock

10 **role, part,** piece <nf>; cue, **lines,** side; cast; **character,** person, personage; lead, starring or lead or leading role, fat part, leading man, leading

woman *or* lady, hero, heroine; antihero; title role, top billing, protagonist, principal character; supporting role, supporting character; ingenue, *jeune première* or *jeune premier* <Fr>, romantic lead; <Fr>; *soubrette* <Fr>; villain, heavy <nf>, bad guy <nf>, antagonist, deuteragonist; bit, bit part, minor role, speaking part; feed *or* feeder, straight part; walking part, walk-on, extra; double, stand-in, stunt person, stunt man *or* woman, understudy; top banana, second banana, chorus, Greek chorus; stock part *or* character; **actor** 707.2

11 **engagement,** playing engagement, booking; **run; stand,** one-night stand *or* one-nighter; **circuit,** barnstorming, vaudeville circuit, borscht circuit; **tour, bus-and-truck, production tour;** date, gig <nf>

12 theatrical performance, **performance, show, presentation,** presentment, **production,** entertainment, stage presentation *or* performance; bill; **exhibit, exhibition;** benefit performance, benefit; personal appearance; showcase, tryout, preview; premiere, premier performance, debut, opening night; farewell performance, swan song <nf>; command performance; matinee; sellout, full house

13 **production,** mounting, staging, putting on; stage management; **direction,** *mise-en-scène* <Fr>; blocking; **rehearsal,** dress rehearsal, walk-through, run-through, technical *or* tech rehearsal *or* run, final dress, gypsy rehearsal *or* run-through *or* run

14 **theater, playhouse, house,** theatron, odeum; **auditorium; opera house,** opera; **hall,** music hall, concert hall; **amphitheater;** circle theater, arena, stadium, theater-in-the-round; vaudeville theater; burlesque theater; **little theater,** community theater; open-air theater, outdoor theater; Greek theater; children's theater; Elizabethan theater, Globe Theatre; showboat; dinner theater; cabaret, nightclub, club, night spot, *boîte de nuit* <Fr>

15 **auditorium,** seating; parquet, orchestra, **pit** <Brit>; **orchestra circle,** parquet circle, parterre; **dress circle;** fauteuil *or* theatre stall *or* **stall** <Brit>; **box,** box seat, **loge,** *baignoire* <Fr>; stage box; proscenium boxes, parterre boxes; balcony, gallery, mezzanine; **peanut gallery** *and* paradise <nf>; standing room; box office

16 **stage,** the boards; acting area, playing *or* performing area; thrust stage, three-quarter-round stage, theater-in-the-round; apron, passerelle, apron stage, forestage; proscenium stage, proscenium arch, proscenium; bridge; revolving stage; orchestra, pit, orchestra pit; **bandstand,** shell, band shell; stage right, R; stage left, L; upstage, downstage, backstage, center stage; **wings,** coulisse; dressing room, greenroom;

flies, fly gallery, fly floor; gridiron, grid <nf>; board, lightboard, switchboard; dock; prompter's box; curtain, grand drape, safety curtain, asbestos curtain, fire curtain; stage door

17 <stage requisites> **property, prop;** practical piece *or* prop <nf>, handprop; costume 5.9; theatrical makeup, makeup, greasepaint, blackface, clown white; spirit gum

18 stage lighting, lights, instruments; **footlights,** foots <nf>, floats; floodlight, flood; bunch light; battens, houselights; **limelight,** follow spot, spotlight *or* spot <nf>, following spot <nf>, arc light, arc, klieg *or* kleig light; color filter, color wheel, medium, gelatin *or* gel; projector, stroboscope *or* strobe *or* strobe light; lightboard; dimmer; marquee; light plot

19 **setting, stage setting,** stage set, **set,** *mise-en-scène* <Fr>; location, locale

20 **scenery,** decor; **scene;** screen, **flat;** cyclorama *or* cyc; batten; side scene, **wing,** coulisse; border; tormentor, **teaser;** wingcut, woodcut; transformation, transformation scene; flipper; counterweight; **curtain,** rag <nf>, hanging; **drop,** drop scene, drop curtain, scrim, cloth; **backdrop,** back cloth <Brit>; act drop *or* curtain; tab, tableau curtain

21 **playbook, script,** text, **libretto;** promptbook; book, book of words; **score; scenario,** continuity, shooting script; scene plot; lines, actor's lines, cue, sides; stage direction; prompt book

22 **dramatist; playwright,** playwriter, dramaturge; doctor *and* play doctor *and* play fixer <nf>; dramatizer; **scriptwriter, scenario writer,** scenarist, **scenarioist, screenwriter; gagman,** gag writer, joke writer, jokesmith; **librettist;** tragedian, comedian; farcist, *farceur* and *farceuse* <Fr>, farcer; melodramatist; monodramatist; mimographer; **choreographer**

23 **theater man,** theatrician; **showman,** exhibitor, **producer, impresario; director,** auteur; stage director, **stage manager;** set designer, scenewright; costume designer, costumer, *costumier* and *costumière* <Fr>, wardrobe master *or* mistress; dresser; hair *or* wigmaker *or* designer; makeup artist, visagiste; propsmaster *or* propsmistress; prompter; callboy; playreader; master of ceremonies, MC *or* emcee <nf>; box-office staff; ticket collector; usher, usherer, usherette, doorkeeper; ringmaster, equestrian director; barker, ballyhoo man *and* spieler <nf>

24 **stage technician, stagehand,** stage crew, machinist <old>, sceneman, scene master, **sceneshifter;** flyman; carpenter; **electrician;** sound man; scene painter, scenic artist, scenewright

25 agent, actor's agent, playbroker, ten-percenter <nf>; **booking agent;** advance agent, advance man; press agent; publicity man *or* agent; business manager, publicity manager

26 patron, patroness; **backer, angel** <nf>, promoter; Dionysus

27 playgoer, theatergoer; attender 221.5, spectator 918, audience 48.6, house; moviegoer, **motion-picture fan** <nf>; first-nighter; standee, groundling <old>; *claqueur* <Fr>, hired applauder; pass holder, deadhead <nf>, stage-door Johnny; critic, reviewer, talent scout

VERBS **28 dramatize,** theatricalize; melodramatize; scenarize; **present, stage, produce, mount, put on,** put on the stage, adapt for the stage; **put on a show;** try out, preview; give a performance; premiere; **open,** open a show, open a show cold <nf>; set the stage; ring up the curtain, ring down the curtain; **star, feature** <nf>, bill, **headline,** give top billing to; succeed, make *or* be a hit *and* have legs <nf>, be a gas *or* gasser *and* run out of gas <nf>; fail, flop *and* bomb *and* bomb out <nf>; script

29 act, perform, play, playact, tread the boards, strut one's stuff <nf>; appear, **appear on the stage;** act like a trouper; register; emotionalize, emote <nf>; pantomime, mime; patter; sketch; troupe, barnstorm <nf>; improvise, ad-lib, wing it <nf>; steal the show, upstage, steal the spotlight; **debut,** make one's debut *or* bow, come out, take the stage, make an entrance; act as foil *or* feeder, stooge <nf>, be straight man for; **star,** play the lead, get top billing, have one's name in lights, costar, understudy

30 enact, act out; represent, depict, portray; act *or* play *or* perform a part *or* role, role-play, take a part, sustain a part, act *or* play the part of; create a role *or* character; **impersonate,** personate; play opposite, support

31 overact, overdramatize, chew up the scenery <nf>, act all over the stage; **ham** *and* ham it up <nf>, camp it up; play to the gallery; **mug** <nf>, grimace; spout, rant, roar, declaim, "out-herod Herod"— Shakespeare; milk a scene, milk it; **underact,** underplay, fluff, go blank, throw away <nf>

32 rehearse, practice, go through, walk *or* run through, go over; block; go through one's part, read one's lines; learn one's lines, memorize, con *or* study one's part; be a fast *or* slow study; interpret the part, get into character

ADJS **33 dramatic,** dramatical <old>, **dramaturgic, dramaturgical; theatric, theatrical, histrionic, thespian;** scenic; **stagy;** theaterlike, stagelike; rehearsed, staged, interpreted, improvised; **spectacular; melodramatic;** ham *or* hammy *or* campy <nf>; overacted, overplayed, milked <nf>; underacted, underplayed, thrown away; musical, choral; **operatic;** choreographic, terpsichorean; ballet, balletic; legitimate; stellar, all-star; stagestruck, starstruck; stageworthy, actor-proof

34 tragic, heavy; buskined, cothurned; tragicomic *or* tragicomical

35 comic, light; tragicomical, **farcical, slapstick;** camp *or* campy <nf>; burlesque

ADVS **36 on the stage** *or* boards, before an audience, before the footlights; **in the limelight** *or* spotlight; onstage; downstage, upstage; backstage, off stage, behind the scenes; down left *or* DL; down right *or* DR; up left *or* UL; up right *or* UR

705 DANCE

NOUNS **1 dancing** <see list>, terpsichore, dance; the light fantastic; **choreography;** dance drama, choreodrama; **hoofing** <nf>

2 dance, hop <nf>, dancing party, **shindig** *and* shindy <nf>; **ball,** *bal* <Fr>; masked ball, masque, mask, masquerade ball, masquerade, *bal masqué* <Fr>, *bal costumé* <Fr>, fancy-dress ball, cotillion *or* cotillon; promenade, **prom** <nf>, formal <nf>; country dance, square dance, barn dance, hoedown; mixer, stag dance; record hop; dinner-dance, tea dance, *thé dansant* <Fr>, dinner dance

3 dancer, danseur, terpsichorean, **hoofer** <nf>, step dancer, tap dancer, clog dancer, go-go dancer, foxtrotter, etc; **ballet dancer; ballerina,** danseur, danseuse, coryphée; *première danseuse* *and* *danseur noble* <Fr>, corps de ballet; twinkletoes <nf>; classical dancer; **modern dancer;** *corps de ballet* <Fr>; figurant, figurante; **chorus girl, chorine,** chorus boy *or* man; chorus line; geisha *or* geisha girl; nautch girl, bayadere; hula girl; taxi dancer; topless dancer; burlesque dancer, strip-teaser, stripper *and* bump-and-grinder <nf>; choreographer

4 ballroom, dance hall, dancery; dance palace; discotheque, disco; dance floor; nightclub, casino

VERBS **5 dance, trip the light fantastic,** go dancing, "trip it as we go, on the light fantastic toe"— Milton, trip, skip, hop, foot, prance <nf>, **hoof** *and* hoof it <nf>, clog, tap-dance, fold-dance, etc; shake, shimmy, shuffle; waltz, one-step, two-step, foxtrot, etc; choreograph

ADJS **6 dancing, dance, terpsichorean;** balletic; choreographic

7 kinds of dancing

aerobic dancing	break dancing
ballet	character dancing
ballroom dancing	choral dancing
belly dancing	classical ballet

clog dancing
comedy ballet
country dancing
dirty dancing
disco dancing
fan dancing
flamenco
folklorico
folk dancing
go-go dancing
interpretive dancing
jazz dancing
jazz tap
jitterbugging
lap dancing
line dancing

marathon dancing
modern ballet
modern dance
morris dancing
ritual dancing
round dancing
slam dancing
social dancing
soft-shoe dancing
solo dancing
square dancing
step dancing
sword dancing
tap dancing
taxi dancing
trance dancing

706 MOTION PICTURES

NOUNS **1 motion pictures, movies, the movies, the pictures,** moving pictures, films, the films, the cinema, the screen, the big screen, the silver screen, the flicks *and* the flickers <nf>, motion-picture industry, moviedom, filmdom, Hollywood; **motion picture, movie, picture, film,** flick *and* flicker <nf>, picture show, motion-picture show, moving-picture show, photoplay, photodrama; **sound film,** silent film *or* silent; cinéma vérité *or* direct cinema; vérité; magic realism; **documentary film** *or* **movie,** docudrama, docutainment; **feature,** feature film, feature-length film, main attraction; theatrical film, big-screen film; **motion-picture genre** *or* **type;** TV film *or* movie, made-for-television movie *or* film, cable movie, miniseries; **short,** short movie, short subject; preview, sneak preview; independent film, indie; **B-movie,** B-picture, Grade B movie, low-budget picture; **educational film** *or* **movie,** training film, promotional film, trigger film; **underground film** *or* **movie,** experimental film *or* movie, avant-garde film *or* movie, representational film, art film *or* movie, surrealistic film *or* movie; **cartoon,** animated cartoon, animation, cel animation, claymation, computer graphics; animatron, audioanimatron; video <nf>, rental movie, pay-per-view movie, video-on-demand, **rated movie** *or* **film,** rating system, rating, G *or* general audience, PG *or* parental guidance suggested, PG-**13** *or* parents strongly cautioned, R *or* restricted *or* children under **17** require accompanying parent or guardian, NC-**17** *or* X *or* no children under **17** admitted; filmmaking, cinema

2 <movie type> drama, comedy, musical, love story, mystery, thriller, adventure, actioner, romance, Western, shoot-em-up <nf>, historical film, epic film, futuristic film, science-fiction *or* sci-fi film, foreign *or* foreign-language film, film noir, cult movie, girl *or* chick flick; date movie; art movie, buddy film

3 script, screenplay, motion-picture play *or* script, shooting script, storyboard, scenario, treatment, original screenplay, screen adaptation; plot, subplot, story; **dialogue,** book, lines; **role,** lead, romantic lead, stock character, ingenue, soubrette, cameo, bit, silent bit

4 motion-picture studio, movie studio, film studio, dream factory <nf>, animation studio, lot, back lot, sound stage, location; **set, motion-picture set, film set,** *mise-en-scène* <Fr>, properties *or* props, set dressing; **motion-picture company, film company,** production company; **producer,** filmmaker, moviemaker, **director,** auteur, screenwriter *or* scriptwriter *or* scenarist, editor *or* film editor, **actor, actress, film actor, film actress,** player, cinemactor, cinemactress, star, starlet, character actor, featured player, supporting actor *or* actress, supporting player, bit player, extra; **crew,** film crew

5 motion-picture photography, photography, cinematography, camera work, cinematics, camera work, camera angle, camera position, **shot, take,** footage, retake; screen test; **special effects,** rear-screen projection, mechanical effects, optical effects, process photography, FX; **color photography,** Technicolor *and* CinemaScope <trademark>; black-and-white, color, colorization; **cameraman** *or* **camerawoman, motion-picture cameraman** *or* **camerawoman,** cinematographer, director of photography *or* DP, first cameraman, lighting cameraman

6 motion-picture editing, film editing, editing, cutting, arranging, synchronizing; **transition,** fade, fade-out/fade-in, dissolve, lap *or* overlap dissolve, out-focus-dissolve, match dissolve, cross-dissolve, mix; colorizing, colorization; freeze-frame; McGuffin

7 motion-picture theater, movie theater, picture theater *or* house, film theater, cinema <Brit>, movie house *or* palace, dream palace <nf>, circuit theater, drive-in theater *or* movie, grind house <nf>, fleapit <Brit>, Cineplex, multiplex; **screen,** movie screen, motion-picture screen, silver screen, aspect ratio *or* format, screen proportion, wide-screen, Cinerama *and* Cinemascope *and* VistaVision *and* Ultra-Panavision <trademarks>

VERBS **8 film, shoot,** cinematize, filmmake; colorize

ADJS **9 motion-picture, movie, film,** cinema, cinematic, filmistic, filmic; colorized; black-and-white; animated; animatronic, audioanimatronic

707 ENTERTAINER

NOUNS **1** **entertainer,** public entertainer, performer; artist, artiste; impersonator, female impersonator; **vaudevillian,** vaudevillist; dancer 705.3, hoofer <nf>; song and dance man; chorus girl, show girl, chorine <nf>; coryphée; chorus boy *or* man; burlesque queen <nf>, **stripteaser,** exotic dancer, ecdysiast; stripper *and* peeler *and* stripteuse *and* bump-and-grinder <nf>; dancing girl, nautch girl, belly dancer; go-go dancer; geisha, geisha girl; mountebank; **magician,** conjurer, prestidigitator, sleight-of-hand artist; circus performer, clown; mummer, guiser <Scot>, guisard; singer, musician 710; performance artist

2 **actor, actress, player,** stage player *or* performer, playactor, histrion, histrio, thespian, Roscius, theatrical <nf>, trouper; child actor; mummer, pantomime, pantomimist; monologist, diseur, diseuse, reciter; dramatizer; mime, mimer, mimic, strolling player, stroller; barnstormer <nf>; character actor *or* actress, character man *or* woman, character; **villain,** antagonist, **bad guy *or* heavy *or* black hat <nf>, villainess; juvenile, ingenue; *jeune premier* and *jeune première* <Fr>; soubrette; foil, feeder *and* stooge <nf>, straight man *or* person; utility man *or* person; protean actor; featured actor, leading man *or* lady, lead actor *or* actress; Method actor; matinee idol <nf>, star of stage and screen; romantic lead

3 circus artist *or* performer; trapeze artist, aerialist, flier <nf>; high-wire artist, tightrope walker, slack-roper artist, equilibrist; **acrobat,** tumbler; bareback rider; juggler; lion tamer, sword swallower; snake charmer; clown; ringmaster, equestrian director

4 **motion-picture actor,** movie actor; **movie star,** film star; starlet; day player, under-five player, contract player

5 ham *or* ham actor <nf>; grimacer

6 **lead,** leading man *or* lady, leading actor *or* actress, principal, **star,** superstar, megastar, headliner, headline *or* feature attraction; costar; **hero, heroine,** protagonist; juvenile lead, *jeune premier or jeune première* <Fr>; first tragedian, heavy lead <nf>; **prima donna,** diva, singer 710.13; première danseuse, prima ballerina, *danseur noble* <Fr>

7 **supporting actor *or* actress; support,** supporting cast; **supernumerary,** super *or* supe <nf>, spear-carrier <nf>, **extra;** bit player; walking gentleman *or* lady <nf>, walk-on, mute; figurant, figurante; **understudy, stand-in,** standby, substitute, swing

8 **tragedian,** tragedienne

9 **comedian,** comedienne, **comic, funnyman;** farcist, farcer, *farceur* and *farceuse* <Fr>; stand-up comic

or comedian <nf>, light comedian, genteel comedian, low comedian, slapstick comedian, hokum *or* hoke comic <nf>

10 **buffoon,** *buffo* <Ital>, **clown, fool, jester, zany, merry-andrew,** jack-pudding, pickle-herring, **motley fool,** motley, wearer of the cap and bells; harlequin; Pierrot; Pantaloon, Pantalone; Punch, Punchinello, Pulcinella, Polichinelle; Punch and Judy; Hanswurst; Columbine; Harlequin; Scaramouch

11 **cast,** cast of characters, characters, persons of the drama, *dramatis personae* <L>; supporting cast; **company,** acting company, outfit, **troupe;** repertory company, stock company, touring company; ensemble, chorus, *corps de ballet* <Fr>; circus troupe

708 MUSIC

NOUNS **1** **music** <see list>, harmonious sound, "the only universal tongue"—Samuel Rogers; music appreciation, music theory

2 **melody,** melodiousness, **tunefulness,** musicalness, musicality; **tune, tone,** musical sound, musical quality, tonality; sweetness, dulcetness, mellifluence, mellifluousness

3 **harmony, concord,** concordance, concert, consonance *or* consonancy, consort, accordance, **accord,** monochord, concentus, symphony, diapason; synchronism, synchronization; **attunement,** tune, attune; chime, chiming; unison, unisonance, homophony, monody; **euphony;** chime; light *or* heavy harmony; two-part *or* three-part harmony, etc; harmony *or* music of the spheres; harmonics 709

4 **air,** aria, **tune, melody,** line, melodic line, refrain, note, **song,** solo, solo part, soprano part, treble, lay, descant, lilt, **strain,** measure; canto, cantus

5 **piece,** opus, **composition,** production, work; **score; arrangement,** adaptation, orchestration, harmonization, setting; **form;** transcription, accompaniment

6 **classical music,** classic; concert music, serious music, longhair music <nf>, symphonic music, chamber music, operatic music; semiclassic, semiclassical music

7 **popular music,** pop music, pop, light music, popular song *or* air *or* tune, **ballad;** hit, song hit, hit tune; Tin Pan Alley; karaoke; hip hop, rap music, gangsta rap; ambient music, mood music; chartbuster

8 **dance music,** ballroom music, **dances;** syncopated music, **syncopation; ragtime *or* rag, doo-wop; modern dance music

9 **jazz;** hot jazz, Dixieland, Basin Street, New

Orleans, Chicago, traditional jazz *or* trad <Brit nf>; **swing,** jive <nf>; bebop, bop <nf>; mainstream jazz; avant-garde jazz, the new music <nf>, modern jazz, progressive jazz, third-stream jazz, cool jazz, acid jazz; boogie *or* boogie-woogie; rhythm-and-blues *or* R and B, blues; walking bass, stride *or* stride piano

10 **rock-and-roll, rock music,** rock-'n'-roll, rock, hard rock, soft rock, acid rock, folk rock, country rock, rockabilly, hard core, full-tilt boogie, heavy metal, punk rock, New Wave, fusion, grunge, alternative rock

11 **folk music,** folk songs, ethnic music, ethnomusicology; folk ballads, balladry; border ballads; country music, hillbilly music; country-and-western music, western swing; old-time country music *or* old-timey music; bluegrass; field holler; ethnic music, soul, reggae, ska

12 **march,** martial *or* military music; military march, quick *or* quickstep march; processional march, recessional march; funeral *or* dead march; wedding march

13 **vocal music, song; singing,** caroling, warbling, lyricism, vocalism, **vocalization;** operatic singing, bel canto, coloratura, bravura; choral singing; folk singing; croon, crooning; yodel, yodeling; scat, scat singing; intonation; hum, humming; solmization, tonic sol-fa, solfeggio, solfège, sol-fa, sol-fa exercise

14 **song,** lay, *Lied* <Ger>, *chanson* <Fr>, carol, **ditty,** canticle, lilt; **ballad,** ballade, *ballata* <Ital>; *canzone* <Ital>; canzonet, *canzonetta* <Ital>; aubade, serenade, lullaby, barcarole, glee, lay, chantey *or* chanty *or* shantey, chant, plainsong, canticle, chorale, carol, hymn, psalm, anthem

15 **solo;** karaoke; **aria;** operatic aria

16 <Italian terms for arias> arietta, arioso; aria buffa, aria da capo, aria d'agilità, aria da chiesa, aria d'imitazione, aria fugata, aria parlante; bravura, aria di bravura; coloratura, aria di coloratura; cantabile, aria cantabile; recitativo

17 **sacred music, church music,** liturgical music; **hymn,** hymn-tune, hymnody, hymnology; **psalm,** psalmody; **chorale,** choral fantasy, anthem; motet; **oratorio;** passion; **mass;** requiem mass, requiem, missa brevis, missa solemnis; offertory, offertory sentence *or* hymn, **cantata;** doxology, introit, canticle, paean, prosodion; recessional

18 **part music,** polyphonic music, part song, part singing, ensemble music, ensemble singing; **duet,** duo, *duettino* <Ital>; **trio,** terzet, *terzetto* <Ital>; **quartet; quintet; sextet,** sestet; **septet,** septuor; **octet;** cantata, lyric cantata; madrigal, *madrigaletto* <Ital>; **chorus** 710.16, chorale, glee club, choir; choral singing; four-part, soprano-alto-tenor-base *or* SATB; barbershop quartet

19 **round, rondo,** rondeau, **roundelay,** catch, troll; rondino, rondoletto; **fugue,** canon, fugato

20 **polyphony,** polyphonism; **counterpoint,** contrapunto; **plainsong,** Gregorian chant, Ambrosian chant; *faux-bourdon* <Fr>; musica ficta, false music

21 monody, monophony, homophony

22 **part,** melody *or* voice part, **voice** 709.5, **line;** descant, canto, cantus, cantus planus *or* firmus, plain song, plain chant; prick song, cantus figuratus; soprano, tenor, treble, alto, contralto, baritone, bass, bassus; undersong; drone; **accompaniment;** continuo, basso continuo, figured bass, thorough bass; ground bass, basso ostinato; drone, drone bass, bourdon, burden

23 **response,** responsory report, answer; echo; antiphon, antiphony, antiphonal chanting *or* singing

24 **passage, phrase,** musical phrase, strain, part, motive, motif, theme, subject, figure; leitmotiv; **movement;** introductory phrase, anacrusis; statement, exposition, development, variation; division; period, musical sentence; section; **measure;** figure; **verse, stanza;** burden, bourdon; **chorus, refrain,** response; folderol, **ornament** 709.18, cadence 709.23, harmonic close, resolution; **coda,** tailpiece; ritornello; intermezzo, interlude; bass passage; tutti, tutti passage; bridge, bridge passage

25 <fast, slow, etc passages> presto, prestissimo; allegro, allegretto; scherzo, scherzando; adagio, adagietto; andante, andantino; largo, larghetto, larghissimo; crescendo; diminuendo, decrescendo; rallentando, ritardando; ritenuto; piano, pianissimo; forte, fortissimo; staccato, marcato, marcando; pizzicato; spiccato; legato; stretto

26 **overture, prelude,** *Vorspiel* <Ger>, **introduction,** operatic overture, dramatic overture, concert overture, voluntary, descant, vamp; curtain raiser

27 **impromptu, extempore, improvisation, interpolation;** cadenza; **ornament** 709.18, flourish, ruffles and flourishes, grace note, appoggiatura, mordent, upper mordent, inverted mordent; **run,** melisma; vamp; lick, hot lick, riff

28 **score,** musical score *or* copy, **music,** notation, musical notation, written music, copy, draft, transcript, transcription, version, edition, text, arrangement; part; full *or* orchestral score, compressed *or* short score, piano score, vocal score, instrumental score; tablature, lute tablature; opera score, opera; **libretto;** sheet music; **songbook,** songster; hymnbook, hymnal; music paper; music roll

29 **staff,** stave <Brit>; line, ledger line; bar, bar line; space, degree; brace

30 **execution, performance; rendering,** rendition, music-making, **touch, expression;** fingering; pianism; intonation; repercussion; pizzicato, staccato, spiccato, parlando, legato, cantando, rubato, demilegato, mezzo staccato, slur; glissando

31 **musicianship;** musical talent *or* flair, musicality; virtuosity; pianism; musical ear, ear for music; musical sense, sense of rhythm; absolute *or* perfect pitch; relative pitch

32 musical occasion; choral service, service of lessons and carols, service of song, sing <nf>, singing, community singing *or* sing, singfest, songfest, sing-in; karaoke; folk-sing *and* hootenanny <nf>; **festival,** music festival; opera festival; folk-music festival, jazz festival, rock festival; *Sängerfest* <Ger>, *eisteddfod* <Welsh>; jam session <nf>

33 **performance,** musical performance, **program,** musical program, program of music; **concert,** symphony concert, chamber concert; philharmonic concert, philharmonic; popular concert, pops *and* pop concert <nf>; promenade concert, prom <nf>; band concert; **recital;** service of music; concert performance <of an opera>; **medley,** potpourri; swan song, farewell performance

34 **musical theater, music theater, lyric theater,** musical stage, lyric stage; **music drama,** lyric drama; song-play, *Singspiel* <Ger>; **opera,** grand opera, light opera, ballad opera; comic opera, *opéra bouffe* <Fr>, *opera buffa* <Ital>; **operetta; musical comedy; musical;** Broadway musical; musical drama; **ballet,** *opéra ballet* <Fr>, comedy ballet, *ballet d'action* <Fr>, *ballet divertissement* <Fr>; dance drama; chorus show; **song-and-dance act;** minstrel, minstrel show

VERBS **35** **harmonize,** be harmonious, be in tune *or* concert, chord, **accord,** symphonize, synchronize, **chime, blend,** blend in, symphonize, segue; tune, attune, atone, sound together, sound in tune; assonate; melodize, musicalize

36 **tune, tune up,** attune, atone, chord, **put in tune;** voice, string; tone up, tone down

37 **strike up,** strike up a tune, **strike up the band,** break into music, pipe up, pipe up a song, yerk out <nf>, **burst into song**

38 **sing, vocalize,** carol, descant, lilt, troll, line out *and* belt out *and* tear off <nf>; **warble,** trill, tremolo, quaver, shake; **chirp,** chirrup, twit <Brit nf>, **twitter;** pipe, whistle, tweedle, tweedledee; **chant; intone,** intonate; **croon; hum; yodel;** roulade; chorus, choir, sing in chorus; **hymn,** anthem, psalm, "make a joyful noise unto the Lord"—Bible; sing the praises of; minstrel; ballad; **serenade;** sol-fa, do-re-mi, solmizate

39 **play, perform, execute, render,** do; interpret; make music; concertize; symphonize; chord; accompany; play by ear; play at, pound out *and* saw away at <nf>

40 **strum, thrum, pluck,** plunk, **pick,** twang, sweep the strings

41 **fiddle** <nf>, play violin *or* the violin; scrape *and* saw <nf>

42 **blow a horn,** sound *or* wind the horn, sound, blow, wind, **toot,** tootle, pipe, tweedle; bugle, carillon, clarion, fife, flute, trumpet, whistle; bagpipe, doodle <Brit nf>; lip, tongue, double-tongue, triple-tongue

43 **syncopate,** play jazz, swing, jive <nf>, rag <nf>, jam <nf>, riff <nf>

44 **beat time,** keep time, tap, tap out the rhythm, keep tempo; count, count the beats; beat the drum, **drum** 55.4, play drum *or* the drums, thrum, beat, thump, pound; tomtom; ruffle; beat *or* sound a tattoo

45 **conduct, direct,** lead, wield the baton

46 **compose, write, arrange, score, set, set to music,** put to music; musicalize, melodize, **harmonize; orchestrate;** instrument, instrumentate; **adapt,** make an adaptation; transcribe, transpose

ADJS **47** **musical, musically inclined,** musicianly, with an ear for music; virtuoso, virtuose, virtuosic; **music-loving,** music-mad, musicophile, philharmonic; absolute, aleatory, aleatoric

48 **melodious,** melodic; **musical,** music-like; **tuneful,** tunable; fine-toned, tonal, **pleasant-sounding,** agreeable-sounding, pleasant, appealing, agreeable, catchy, singable; **euphonious** *or* euphonic, **lyric, lyrical,** melic; **lilting,** songful, songlike; **sweet, dulcet,** sweet-sounding, achingly sweet, sweet-flowing; honeyed, mellifluent, mellifluous, mellisonant, music-flowing; rich, mellow; sonorous, canorous; golden, golden-toned; silvery, silver-toned; sweet-voiced, golden-voiced, silver-voiced, silver-tongued, golden-tongued, music-tongued; ariose, arioso, cantabile

49 **harmonious,** harmonic, symphonious; harmonizing, **chiming,** blending, well-blended, blended; **concordant,** consonant, accordant, according, **in accord,** in concord, in concert; synchronous, synchronized, in sync <nf>, symphonic, **in tune,** tuned, attuned; in unison, in chorus; unisonous, unisonant; homophonic, monophonic, monodic; assonant, assonantal; rhythmic

50 **vocal,** singing; **choral,** choric; four-part; operatic; hymnal; psalmic, psalmodic, psalmodial; sacred, liturgical; treble, soprano, tenor, alto, falsetto; coloratura, lyric, bravura, dramatic, heroic; baritone; bass

51 instrumental, orchestral, symphonic, concert; dramatico-musical; jazz, syncopated, jazzy, rock, swing

52 polyphonic, contrapuntal

ADJS, ADVS **53** <directions, style> legato; staccato; spiccato; pizzicato; forte, fortissimo; piano, pianissimo; sordo; crescendo, accrescendo; decrescendo, diminuendo, morendo; dolce; amabile; affettuoso, con affetto; amoroso, con amore lamentabile; agitato, con agitazione; leggiero; agilmente, con agilità; capriccioso, a capriccio; scherzando, scherzoso; appassionato, appassionatamente; abbandono; brillante; parlando; a cappella; trillando, tremolando, tremoloso; sotto voce; stretto

54 <slowly> largo, larghetto, allargando; adagio, adagietto; andante, andantino, andante moderato; calando; a poco; lento; ritardando, rallentando; downtempo

55 <fast> presto, prestissimo; veloce; accelerando; vivace, vivacissimo; desto, con anima, con brio; allegro, allegretto; affrettando, moderato

56 varieties of music

absolute music	elevator music or Muzak
acid rock	<trademark>
Afro-beat	ensemble music
aleatory music	field music
art music	folk music
art rock	folk rock
atonal music or atonalism	funk
background music or	fusion
mood music	gospel music
ballet music	Gregorian chant
baroque music	grunge
beach music	hard rock
big band	heavy metal
bluegrass	heavy rock
bubblegum	hillbilly music
calypso	hiphop
cathedral music	house music or House
chamber music	inspirational music
church music	instrumental music
circus music	jazz music or jazz
classical music	jazz rock
country-and-western	Latin rock
music	light music
country music	loft jazz
country rock	martial or military music
dance hall	new age or new wave
dance music	operatic music
deca-rock or glitter rock	organ music
Delta blues	part music
disco	piped music
ear candy <nf>	plainsong
easy listening music	political rock
electronic or synthesized	pomp rock
music	polyphonic music

pop-rock	romantic music
popular or pop music	sacred music
program music	salon music
progressive rock	semiclassical music
progressive soul	ska
psychobilly	soul music
punkabilly	swing music or swing
punk rock	technopop
raga-rock	thirdstream music
ragtime music or ragtime	through-composed music
rap music	twelve-tone music or
reggae	serialism
rhythm and blues or R and	vocal music
B or the blues	wind music
rock music or rock'n'roll	Zopf music
rockabilly	zydeco
rococo music	

709 HARMONICS, MUSICAL ELEMENTS

NOUNS **1 harmonics,** harmony; melodics; rhythmics; musicality; music, **music theory,** theory; musicology; musicography

2 harmonization; orchestration, instrumentation; arrangement, setting, adaptation, transcription; accompaniment; harmonic progression, chordal progression; phrasing, modulation, intonation, preparation, suspension, solution, resolution; tone painting

3 tone, tonality 50.3

4 pitch, tuning, tune, **tone, key, note,** register, tonality; height, depth; pitch range, tessitura; classical pitch, high pitch, diapason or normal or French pitch, international or concert or new philharmonic pitch, standard pitch, low pitch, Stuttgart or Scheibler's pitch, philharmonic pitch, philosophical pitch; temperament, equal temperament; absolute pitch, perfect pitch

5 voice, voce <Ital>; voce di petto <Ital>, chest voice; voce di testa <Ital>, head voice; **soprano,** mezzo-soprano, dramatic soprano, soprano spinto, lyric soprano, coloratura soprano; boy soprano; male soprano, castrato; alto, contralto; tenor, lyric tenor, operatic tenor, heldentenor or heroic tenor or Wagnerian tenor; countertenor or male alto; baritone, light or lyric baritone; **bass,** basso, basso profundo, basso cantante or lyric bass, basso buffo or comic bass, treble, falsetto, castrato

6 scale, gamut, register, compass, range, diapason; diatonic scale, chromatic scale, modal scale, enharmonic scale, major scale, minor scale, natural or harmonic or melodic minor, whole-tone scale; great scale; octave scale, dodecuple scale, pentatonic scale; tetrachordal scale; twelve-tone or dodecuple scale, tone block, tone row, tone cluster

7 sol-fa, tonic sol-fa, do-re-mi; Guidonian syllables, ut, re, mi, fa, sol, la; sol-fa syllables, do, re, mi, fa, sol, la, ti *or* si, do; solmization, solfeggio; fixed-do system, movable-do system; solmization; bobization

8 <diatonic series> tetrachord, chromatic tetrachord, enharmonic tetrachord, Dorian tetrachord; hexachord, hard hexachord, natural hexachord, soft hexachord; pentachord

9 **octave,** *ottava* <Ital>, eighth; *ottava alta* <Ital>, *ottava bassa* <Ital>; small octave, great octave; contraoctave, subcontraoctave, double contraoctave; one-line octave, two-line octave, four-line octave, two-foot octave, four-foot octave; tenor octave

10 **mode,** octave species; major mode, minor mode; Greek mode, Ionian mode, Dorian mode, Phrygian mode, Lydian mode, mixolydian mode, Aeolian mode, Locrian mode; hypoionian mode, hypodorian mode, hypophrygian mode, hypolydian mode, hypoaeolian mode, hypomixolydian mode, hypolocrian mode; Gregorian *or* ecclesiastical *or* church *or* medieval mode; plagal mode, authentic mode; Indian *or* Hindu mode, raga

11 **form,** arrangement, pattern, model, design; song *or* lied form, primary form; **sonata form,** sonata allegro, ternary form, symphonic form, canon form, toccata form, fugue form, rondo form

12 **notation,** character, mark, symbol, signature, sign, *segno* <Ital>; proportional notation; chart *or* paper <nf>, dot; custos, direct; cancel; bar, measure; measure *or* time signature, key signature; tempo mark, metronome *or* metronomic mark; fermata, hold, pause; *presa* <Ital>, lead; slur, tie, ligature, vinculum, enharmonic tie; swell; accent, accent mark, expression mark; ledger, staff, stave, line, space, brace, rest, interval

13 **clef;** C clef, soprano clef, alto *or* viola clef, tenor clef; F *or* bass clef, G *or* treble clef

14 **note,** musical note, notes of a scale; **tone** 50.2; **sharp, flat, natural; accidental;** double whole note, breve; whole note, semibreve; half note, minim; quarter note, crotchet; eighth note, quaver; sixteenth note, semiquaver; thirty-second note, demisemiquaver; sixty-fourth note, hemidemisemiquaver; tercet, triplet; sustained note, dominant, dominant note; enharmonic, enharmonic note; separation, hammering, staccato, spiccato; connected, smooth, legato; responding note, report; shaped note, patent note

15 **key,** key signature, tonality, sharps and flats; **keynote,** tonic; tonic key; major, minor, major *or* minor key, tonic major or minor; supertonic, mediant, submediant, dominant, subdominant, subtonic; pedal point, organ point

16 **harmonic,** harmonic tone, overtone, upper partial tone; flageolet tone

17 **chord,** *concento* <Ital>, combination of tones *or* notes; major *or* minor chord, primary *or* secondary chord, tonic chord, dominant chord; tertiary chord, third, fourth, etc; interval, major *or* minor interval

18 **ornament,** grace, arabesque, embellishment, *fioritura* <Ital>; **flourish,** roulade, flight, run; passage, division 708.24; florid phrase *or* passage; coloratura; incidental, incidental note; grace note, appoggiatura, arpeggio, acciaccatura; rubato; mordent, single mordent, double *or* long mordent; inverted mordent, pralltriller; turn, back *or* inverted turn; cadence, cadenza

19 **trill,** trillo; trillet, *trilleto* <Ital>; **tremolo,** tremolant, tremolando; quaver, quiver, tremble, tremor, flutter, falter, shake; **vibrato,** *Bebung* <Ger>

20 **interval,** degree, **step,** note, tone; second, third, fourth, fifth, sixth, seventh, octave; prime *or* unison interval, major *or* minor interval, harmonic *or* melodic interval, enharmonic interval, diatonic interval; parallel *or* consecutive intervals, parallel fifths, parallel octaves; whole step, major second; half step, halftone, semitone, minor second; augmented interval; diminished interval; diatonic semitone, chromatic semitone, less semitone, quarter semitone, tempered *or* mean semitone; quarter step, enharmonic diesis; diatessaron, diapason; *tierce de Picardie* <Fr> *or* Picardy third; augmented fourth *or* tritone

21 **rest,** pause; whole rest, breve rest, semibreve rest, half rest, minim, quarter rest, eighth rest, sixteenth rest, thirty-second rest, sixty-fourth rest

22 **rhythm, beat, meter, measure,** number *or* numbers, movement, **lilt, swing;** prosody, metrics; rhythmic pattern *or* phrase

23 cadence *or* cadency, authentic cadence, plagal cadence, mixed cadence, perfect *or* imperfect cadence, half cadence, deceptive *or* false cadence, interrupted *or* suspended cadence

24 **tempo, time, beat,** time pattern, timing; time signature; simple time *or* measure, compound time *or* measure; two-part *or* duple time, three-part *or* triple time, triplet, four-part *or* quadruple time, five-part *or* quintuple time, six-part *or* sextuple time, seven-part *or* septuple time, nine-part *or* nonuple time; two-four time, six-eight time, etc; tempo rubato, rubato; mixed times; **syncopation,** syncope; **ragtime,** rag <nf>; waltz time, three-four *or* three-quarter time, andante tempo, march tempo, etc; largo, etc; presto, etc

25 **accent,** accentuation, rhythmical accent *or* accentuation, ictus, emphasis, stress arsis, thesis

26 beat, throb, pulse, pulsation; downbeat, upbeat, offbeat; bar beat

ADJS **27 tonal,** tonic; chromatic, enharmonic; semitonic

28 rhythmic, rhythmical, cadent, cadenced, **measured, metric, metrical;** in rhythm, in numbers; beating, throbbing, pulsing, pulsating, pulsative, pulsatory

29 syncopated; ragtime, ragtimey <nf>; **jazz;** jazzy *and* jazzed *and* jazzed up <nf>, hot, swingy <nf>

ADVS **30 in time,** in tempo 709.24, *a tempo* <Ital>

710 MUSICIAN

NOUNS **1 musician,** musico, **music maker,** professional musician; performer, executant, interpreter, tunester, artiste, artist, concert artist, player, **virtuoso,** virtuosa; maestro; recitalist; **soloist,** duettist; singer; street musician, busker <chiefly Brit>

2 popular *or* pop musician; ragtime musician; **jazz musician, jazzman;** swing musician; big-band musician; **rock** *or* **rock'n'roll musician**

3 player, instrumentalist, instrumental musician; bandman, bandsman; orchestral musician; symphonist; concertist; accompanist, accompanyist

4 wind player, wind-instrumentalist, horn player, French-horn player *or* hornist, horner, piper, tooter; bassoonist, bugler, clarinetist, cornettist, fifer, oboist, piccoloist, saxophonist, trombonist; trumpeter, trumpet major; fluegelhornist; flutist *or* flautist

5 string musician, strummer, picker <nf>, thrummer, twanger; banjoist, banjo-picker <nf>, citharist, guitarist, guitar-picker <nf>, classical guitarist, folk guitarist, lute player, lutenist, lutist, lyrist, mandolinist, theorbist; violinist, fiddler <nf>; bass violinist, bassist, bass player, contrabassist; violoncellist, cellist, celloist; violist; harpist, harper; zitherist, psalterer

6 xylophonist, marimbaist, vibist *or* vibraphonist

7 pianist, pianiste, pianofortist, piano player, ivory tickler *or* thumper <nf>; keyboard player *or* keyboardist; harpsichordist, clavichordist, monochordist; accordionist, concertinist

8 organist, organ player

9 organ-grinder, hurdy-gurdist, hurdy-gurdyist, hurdy-gurdy man

10 drummer, percussionist, tympanist *or* timpanist, kettle-drummer; taborer

11 cymbalist, cymbaler; bell-ringer, **carilloneur,** campanologist, campanist; triangle player

12 orchestra, band, ensemble, combo <nf>, group; strings, woodwind *or* woodwinds, brass *or* brasses, string *or* woodwind *or* brass section, string *or* woodwind *or* brass choir; desks; garage band

13 singer, vocalist, vocalizer, voice, songster, songbird, warbler, lead singer, backup vocalist, caroler, melodist, minstrel, cantor; songstress, singstress, cantatrice, chanteuse, song stylist, canary <nf>; chanter, chantress; aria singer, lieder singer, opera singer, diva, prima donna; improvisator; rap singer; blues singer, torch singer <nf>; crooner, rock *or* rock-and-roll singer; yodeler; country singer, folk singer *or* folkie <nf>; psalm singer, hymner; Meistersinger; **singing voice, voice** 709.5

14 minstrel, ballad singer, balladeer, **bard,** rhapsode, rhapsodist; wandering *or* strolling minstrel, **troubadour,** trovatore, trouvère, minnesinger, scop, gleeman, fili, jongleur; street singer, wait; serenader; **folk singer,** folk-rock singer; country-and-western singer

15 choral singer, choir member, chorister, chorus singer, choralist; choirman, **choirboy; chorus girl,** chorine <nf>

16 chorus, chorale, choir, choral group, choral society, oratorio society, chamber chorus *or* *Kammerchor* <Ger>, men's *or* women's chorus, male chorus *or* *Männerchor* <Ger>, mixed chorus, ensemble, voices; **glee club,** *Liedertafel* and *Liederkranz* <Ger>, singing club *or* society; *a cappella* choir; choral symphony

17 conductor, leader, maestro, symphonic conductor, **music director,** director, *Kapellmeister* <Ger>; **orchestra leader, band leader, bandmaster,** band major, drum major

18 choirmaster, choral director *or* conductor, chorus master, song leader, *Kapellmeister* <Ger> *or* *maestro di cappella* <Ital>; choir chaplain, minister of music, precentor, cantor, chorister

19 concertmaster, concertmeister, *Konzertmeister* <Ger>, first violinist; first chair

20 composer, scorer, arranger, musicographer; melodist, melodizer; harmonist, harmonizer; **orchestrator;** adapter; symphonist; tone poet; ballad maker *or* writer, balladeer, balladist, balladmonger; madrigalist; lyrist; hymnist, hymnographer, hymnologist; contrapuntist; song writer *or* songwriter, songsmith, tunesmith; lyricist, librettist; musicologist, ethnomusicologist; music teacher

21 music lover, philharmonic person, **music fan** *and* music buff <nf>, musicophile; musicmonger; concertgoer, operagoer, opera lover; tonalist

22 <patrons> the Muses, the Nine, sacred Nine, tuneful Nine, Pierides; Apollo, Apollo Musagetes; Orpheus; Erato, Euterpe, Polymnia *or* Polyhymnia, Terpsichore, St Cecilia

23 songbird, singing bird, **songster,** feathered songster, warbler; nightingale, Philomel; bulbul, canary, cuckoo, lark, mavis, mockingbird, oriole, ringdove, song sparrow, thrush

711 MUSICAL INSTRUMENTS

1 musical instrument, instrument of music; electronic instrument, synthesizer, Mellotron <trademark>, Moog synthesizer <trademark>

2 string or **stringed instrument,** chordophone; strings, string choir

3 harp, lyre

4 plucked stringed instrument <see list>

5 viol or violin family <see list>, chest of viols; Stradivarius, Stradivari, Strad <nf>; Amati, Cremona, Guarnerius; bow, fiddlestick, fiddlebow; bridge, sound hole, soundboard, fingerboard, tuning peg, scroll; string, G string, D string, A string, E string

6 wind instrument, wind; aerophone; **horn,** pipe, tooter; mouthpiece, embouchure, lip, chops <nf>; valve, bell, reed, double reed, key, slide

7 brass wind <see list> brass or brass-wind instrument; brasses, brass choir

8 woodwind <see list>, wood or woodwind instrument; woods, woodwind choir; reed instrument, **reed;** double-reed instrument, **double reed; single-reed instrument,** single reed

9 bagpipe or bagpipes, pipes, union pipes, war pipes, Irish pipes, doodlesack, *Dudelsack* <Ger>; cornemuse, musette; sordellina; chanter, drone; pipe bag

10 mouth organ, mouth harp, harp, French harp <nf>, **harmonica,** harmonicon; jaws or Jew's harp, mouth bow; kazoo

11 accordion, piano accordion; **concertina;** squeeze box <nf>; mellophone; bandonion

12 keyboard instrument <see list>, **piano, harpsichord, clavichord, player piano;** music roll, piano player roll

13 organ, keyboard wind instrument

14 hurdy-gurdy, vielle, **barrel organ,** hand organ, grind organ, street organ

15 music box, musical box; orchestrion, orchestrina

16 percussion instrument <see list>, percussion, **drum;** drumstick, jazz stick, tymp stick

17 keyboard, fingerboard; console, **keys,** manual, claviature; piano keys, ivories <nf>, eighty-eight <nf>, organ manual, great, swell, choir, solo, echo; pedals

18 carillon, chimes 711.18, chime of bells; electronic carillon

19 organ stop, stop rank, register

20 string, chord, steel string, wound string, nylon string; fiddlestring, catgut; horsehair; music wire, piano wire

21 plectrum, plectron, pick

22 <aids> metronome, rhythmometer; tone measurer, monochord, sonometer; tuning fork, tuning bar, diapason; pitch pipe, tuning pipe; mute; music stand, music lyre; baton, conductor's baton, stick <nf>; MIDI

23 plucked stringed instruments

acoustic guitar	F-hole guitar
angelica or angel lute	gittern
Appalachian dulcimer	harp
Autoharp <trademark>	Hawaiian guitar
archlute	lute
balalaika	lyre
bandore	mando-bass
bandurria <Sp>	mando-cello
banjo	mandolin or mandola
banjolin	mandolute
banjorine	mandore
banjo-ukulele or	oud
banjuke or banjulele	pandora
or banjo-uke	psaltery
banjo-zither	rhythm guitar
bass guitar	samisen
bouzouki	sitar
centerhole guitar	Spanish guitar
chitarra	steel guitar
cittern	tamboura or tambura
classical guitar	theorbo
colascione	troubadour fiddle
concert guitar	ukulele or uke <nf>
Dobro guitar <trademark>	vina
electric guitar	zither

24 viol or violin family

alto or tenor viol	rebab
baritone viol or viola	rebec
d'amore	treble viol
baryton	trumpet marine or tromba
basso da camera <Ital>	marina
bass viol or viola da gamba	vielle
contrabass	viol or viola da braccio
crowd <old>	viol or viola da spalla
crwth	viol or viola di bordone
descant viol	viol or viola di fagotto
double bass or violone or	viola or tenor
bass viol or bass or	viola alta
doghouse or bass fiddle	viola bastarda
or bull fiddle <nf>	viola d'amore
gusla or gusle	viola pomposa
kit	violette
kit violin	violin or fiddle <nf>
lira da braccio	violinette
lira da gamba	violino piccolo
lyra viol	violoncello or cello
nyckelharpa	violoncello piccolo
pocket or kit fiddle	violotta

25 brass wind instruments *and* brasses

alpenhorn *or* alphorn
althorn *or* alto horn
ballad horn
baritone horn
bass horn
bombardon
buccina
bugle *or* bugle horn
clarion
cornet *or* cornet-à-pistons
cornopean
double-bell euphonium
E-flat horn
euphonium
F horn
flugelhorn
French horn
helicon
horn
hunting horn *or* corno di
  caccia <Ital>
key trumpet
lituus
lur
mellophone
nyas taranga
oliphant
ophicleide
orchestral horn
pocket trumpet
post horn
sackbut
saxcornet
saxhorn
saxophone
saxtuba
serpent
slide trombone *or*
  sliphorn <nf>
sousaphone
tenor tuba
tromba
trombone
trumpet
tuba
valve trombone
valve trumpet

26 woodwinds

aulos
bagpipe
bass *or* basset oboe
bass clarinet
basset horn
bassoon
bombarde
bombardon
clarinet *or* licorice
  stick <nf>
contrabassoon *or*
  contrafagotto
double bassoon
English horn *or* cor anglais
  <Fr>
fife
fipple flute *or* pipe
flageolet
flute
heckclarina
heckelphone *or* bass oboe
hornpipe
krummhorn *or* cromorne
  or cromorna *or*
  crumhorn
musette
nose-flute
oaten reed
oboe *or* hautboy *or*
  hautbois
oboe d'amore <Ital>
oboe da caccia <Ital>
ocarina *or* sweet
  potato <nf>
Pandean pipe
panpipe
pibgorn *or* pibcorn
piccolo
pipe
pommer
recorder
saxophone *or* sax <nf>
shakuhachi
shawm
sonorophone
syrinx *or* shepherd's pipe
tabor pipe
tenoroon
tin whistle *or*
  penny-whistle
transverse flute
whistle

27 keyboard stringed instruments

baby grand
cembalo
clarichord
clavichord
clavicittern
clavicymbal *or* clavicembalo
clavicytherium
clavier
concert grand
console piano
cottage piano
couched harp
digital piano
dulcimer harpsichord
electronic keyboard
fortepiano
grand piano
hammer dulcimer
harmonichord
harpsichord
lyrichord
manichord
melodion
melopiano
monochord
pair of virginals
parlor grand
pianette
pianino
piano *or* pianoforte
piano-violin
Pianola <trademark>
player *or* mechanical
  piano
sostinente pianoforte
spinet
square piano
street piano
upright *or* upright
  piano
violin piano
virginal

28 percussion instruments *and* drums

anvil
bass drum
bells
bones
bongo drum
carillon
castanets
celesta
chimes
clappers
conga
cowbell
crash cymbal
cymbals *or* potlids <nf>
drumhead
drumskin
finger cymbals
gamelan
glockenspiel
gong
handbells
highhat cymbal <nf>
kazoo
kettledrum *or* timbal *or*
  timpani
lithophone
lyra
maraca
marimba
mbira *or* kalimba
membranophone
metallophone
mirliton
musical glasses *or* glass
  harmonica
musical saw
nagara <India>
naker
orchestral bells
rattle
rattlebones
ride cymbal
side drum
sizzler
snappers
snare drum
spoons
tabor
tambourine
tam-tam
tenor drum
thumb piano
timbale
timbrel
timpani *or* kettledrums
tintinnabula
tom-tom
tonitruone
triangle
troll-drum
tubular bells
vibraphone *or* vibraharp *or*
  vibes <nf>
war drum
xylophone
xylorimba

29 reed organs

accordion
concertina
harmonica
harmonium
melodeon
mouth organ
organ
reed organ

712 VISUAL ARTS

NOUNS **1 visual arts; art, artwork,** the arts; **fine arts,**
beaux arts <Fr>; arts of design, **design,** designing;

art form; abstract art, representative art; **graphic arts** 713; plastic art; **arts and crafts;** decorative arts; primitive art, cave art; folk art; calligraphy; commercial art, applied art, industrial art; modern art; sculpture 715; ceramics 742; photography 714; etching, engraving 713.2; decoration 498.1; artist 716

2 **craft, manual art,** industrial art, **handicraft,** arts and crafts, artisan work, craftwork, artisanship; industrial design; woodcraft, woodwork, carpentry, woodworking, metalcraft, stonecraft; ceramics, glassmaking

3 <act or art of painting> **painting,** coloring, "a noble and expressive language"—Ruskin; the brush

4 <art of drawing> **drawing, draftsmanship, sketching, delineation; black and white,** charcoal; mechanical drawing, drafting; freehand drawing, life drawing

5 scenography, ichnography, orthographic *or* orthogonal projection

6 **artistry, art, talent,** artistic skill, flair, artistic flair, artistic invention; artiness *and* arty-craftiness *and* artsy-craftsiness <nf>; artistic temperament, artistic taste; virtu, artistic quality

7 **style;** lines; genre; **school,** movement <see list>; the grand style

8 **treatment; technique,** draftsmanship, brushwork, painterliness; **composition, design,** arrangement; grouping, balance; **color,** values; atmosphere, tone; shadow, shading; **line;** perspective

9 **work of art, object of art,** objet d'art, art object, art work, artistic production *or* creation, piece, **work, study, design, composition;** creation, brainchild; virtu, article *or* object *or* piece of virtu; **masterpiece,** *chef d'œuvre* <Fr>, masterwork, master <old>, old master, classic; museum piece; grotesque; statue; mobile, stabile; nude, still life; pastiche, *pasticcio* <Ital>; artware, artwork; bric-a-brac; kitsch

10 **picture; image, likeness, representation,** tableau; "a poem without words"—Horace; photograph 714.3; **illustration,** illumination; miniature; copy, reproduction; print, color print; engraving 713.2, stencil, block print; daub; abstraction, abstract; mural, fresco, wall painting; cyclorama, panorama; montage, collage, assemblage; still life, study in still life; tapestry, mosaic, stained glass, stained glass window, **icon,** altarpiece, diptych, triptych

11 **scene, view, scape; landscape;** waterscape, riverscape, seascape, seapiece; airscape, skyscape, cloudscape; snowscape; cityscape, townscape; farmscape; pastoral; treescape; diorama; exterior, interior

12 **drawing; delineation;** line drawing; **sketch, draft; black and white,** chiaroscuro; **charcoal, crayon, pen-and-ink,** pencil drawing, charcoal drawing, pastel, pastel painting, crayon drawing; silhouette; vignette; doodle; rough draft *or* copy, rough outline, study, design; caricature; cartoon, sinopia, **study,** design; *brouillon* and *ébauche* and *esquisse* <Fr>; diagram, graph; mechanical drawing; silver-print drawing, tracing; doodle, graffito, scribble

13 **painting, canvas,** easel-picture, "silent poetry"—Simonides, "the intermediate somewhat between a thought and a thing"—Coleridge; **oil painting,** oil; **watercolor,** water, aquarelle, wash, wash drawing; acrylic; finger painting; tempera, egg tempera; *gouache* <Fr>; sand painting

14 **portrait, portraiture, portrayal;** head; profile; silhouette, shadow figure; nude; miniature

15 **cartoon, caricature; comic strip;** comic section, comics, funny paper *and* funnies <nf>; comic book; animated cartoon, animation

16 <visual arts> animation, architecture, basketry, body decoration, bookbinding, calligraphy, caricature, clothing *or* fashion design, decorative arts, crafts, drawing, enamelwork, floral decoration, furnishings design, furniture design, glass design, graphic arts, illustration, intaglio, interior design, jewelry design, lacquerwork, landscape design, lithography, metalwork, mixed media, mosaic, painting, photography, plastic art, pottery, printmaking, relief *or* engraving, screen printing, sculpture, serigraphy, tapestry, typography, woodcut

17 **studio,** *atelier* <Fr>; **gallery** 386.9

18 <art equipment> palette; easel; paintbox; art paper, drawing paper, watercolor paper, tracing paper; sketchbook, sketchpad; canvas, artists' canvas; canvas board; scratchboard; lay figure; camera obscura, camera lucida; maulstick; palette knife, spatula; brush, paintbrush; air brush, spray gun; pencil, drawing pencil; pen, ink, marker, highlighter; crayon, charcoal, chalk, pastel; stump; painter's cream; ground; pigments, medium; siccative, drier; fixative, varnish; **paint** 35.8

VERBS 19 **portray, picture,** picturize, **depict, limn,** draw *or* paint a picture; **paint** 35.14; brush, brush in; color, tint, colorize; spread *or* lay on a color; **daub** <nf>; scumble; **draw, sketch, delineate; draft;** pencil, chalk, crayon, charcoal; draw in, pencil in; dash off, scratch <nf>; doodle; design; diagram; cartoon; copy, trace; stencil; touch up; hatch, crosshatch, shade; doodle

ADJS 20 **artistic,** painterly; **arty** *or* arty-crafty *or* artsy-craftsy *or* artsy-fartsy <nf>; **art-minded,** art-conscious; imaginative, creative, stylized, aesthetic; tasteful; beautiful; decorative, ornamental 498.10; **well-composed,** well-grouped, well-arranged, well-varied; of consummate art; in the grand style

21 **pictorial,** pictural, **graphic, picturesque;** picturable; photographic 714.17; scenographic; painty, pastose; scumbled; monochrome, polychrome; freehand

22 **art schools, groups, movements**

abstract expressionism	Madrid
action painting	Mannerist
Aesthetic Movement	Milanese
American scene painting	Modenese
art deco	modern art
Art Nouveau	modernism
Arts and Crafts movement	Momentum
Ashcan school *or* the Eight	'N'
avant-garde	Neapolitan
Barbizon school	neoclassicism
baroque	Neonism
Bauhaus	New Objectivity
Biedermeier	New York
Bolognese	op art
British	Origine
classical abstraction	Paduan
Cobra	Parisian
cubism	Phases
Dada	plein-air *or* pleinairism
De Stijl	pointillism
Der Blaue Reiter	pre-Columbian
Die Brücke	Pre-Raphaelite
Dutch	Raphaelite
eclectic	realism
expressionism	Reflex
fauvism *or* Les Fauves	Restany
Flemish	Rocky Mountain
Florentine	rococo
Fontainebleau	Roman *or* Romanesque
French	romanticism
Glasgow	Scottish Colorists
Gothic	Sienese
Honfleur	Spur
Hudson River	Suprematism
impressionism	tachisme
International Gothic *or* International	tenebrists
	The Ten
Italian	Tuscan
Jugendstil	Umbrian
L'Age d'or	Unit One
letrist	Venetian
Lombard	Wanderers
Madinensor	Washington

23 **design specialties**

accessory design	clothing design *or* fashion design
appearance design	
architectural design	computer-aided design *or* computer-assisted design
automotive design	
book design	
costume design	jewelry design
ergonomics *or* human engineering *or* human factors engineering	landscape architecture
	lighting design
	package design
environmental design	pottery design
fashion design	process design
furniture design	product design
garden design	research design
graphic design	stage design
handbag design	systems design
industrial design	textile design
information design	typographic design
interior design	urban design

713 GRAPHIC ARTS

NOUNS **1** **graphic arts, graphics,** graphic design; **printmaking; painting; drawing; relief-carving; photography** 714; **printing** 548; computer graphics, digital art, graphic artist 716.8

2 **engraving** <see list>, engravement, graving, enchasing, **tooling,** chiseling, incising, incision, lining, scratching, slashing, scoring; **inscription,** inscript; type-cutting; **marking,** line, scratch, slash, score; hatching, cross-hatching; etch, etching; stipple, stippling; tint, demitint, half tint; burr; photoengraving 548.1

3 **lithography,** planography, autolithography, artist lithography; chromolithography; photolithography, offset lithography 548.1

4 stencil printing, stencil; silk-screen printing, serigraphy; monotype; glass printing, decal, decalcomania; cameography

5 **print,** numbered print, imprint, impression, first impression, impress; negative; color print; **etching; lithograph;** autolithograph; chromolithograph; lithotype; crayon engraving, graphotype; **block, block print,** linoleum-block print, rubber-block print, wood engraving, **woodprint,** xylograph, **cut, woodcut,** woodblock; vignette

6 **plate,** steel plate, copperplate, chalcograph; zincograph; stone, lithographic stone; printing plate 548.8

7 **proof,** artist's proof, proof before letter, open-letter proof, remarque proof

8 **engraving tool, graver,** burin, tint tool, style, point, etching point, needle, etching needle, etching ball; etching ground *or* varnish; scorper; rocker; **die,** punch, stamp, intaglio, seal

VERBS **9** **engrave, grave, tool, enchase, incise, sculpture, inscribe,** character, **mark,** line, crease, score, scratch, scrape, cut, carve, chisel; groove, furrow 290.3; stipple, cribble; hatch, crosshatch; lithograph, autolithograph; **be a printmaker** *or* graphic artist; make prints *or* graphics; print 548.14

10 etch, eat, eat out, corrode, bite, bite in

ADJS **11 engraved, graven,** graved, glypt-*or* glypto-; tooled, enchased, chased, inscribed, incised, marked, lined, creased, cut, carved, glyphic, **sculptured,** insculptured, "insculp'd upon"— Shakespeare; grooved, furrowed 290.4; **printed, imprinted, impressed, stamped,** numbered

12 glyptic, glyptical, glyptographic, lapidary, lapidarian; xylographic, wood-block; lithographic, autolithographic, chromolithographic; aquatint, aquatinta, mezzotint

13 kinds of engraving

acid-blast	linocut
aquatint	lithograph
black-line engraving	metal cut
cerography	metal engraving
chalcography	mezzotint
chalk engraving	photochemical engraving
chasing	*or* photoetching
copperplate engraving	photoengraving
crayon engraving	plate engraving
cribbling *or* manière	pyrography *or* pyrogravure
criblée <Fr>	*or* pokerwork
drypoint *or* draw-point	relief etching
engraving	relief method
eccentric engraving	soft-ground etching
electric engraving	steel engraving
etching	stipple engraving
gem engraving	woodburning *or* xylopy-
glass-cutting	rography
glyptics *or* glyptography	woodcut *or* wood engraving
intaglio	xylography
lignography	zinc etching
line cut	zincography or zinc
line engraving	engraving

714 PHOTOGRAPHY

NOUNS **1 photography** <see list>, picture-taking; **cinematography,** motion-picture photography; color photography, black-and-white photography; photochromy, heliochromy; **3-D,** three-dimensional photography; photofinishing; photogravure; radiography, X-ray photography; photogrammetry, phototopography; digital photography; point-and-click, point-and-shoot

2 photographer 716.5, shutter-bug <nf>, photojournalist, press photographer, paparazzo, lensman, shooter *and* photog <nf>; digital artist

3 photograph, photo <nf>, heliograph, **picture,** shot <nf>; **snapshot,** snap <nf>, image; black-and-white photograph; color photograph, color print, heliochrome; Polaroid <trademark>; slide, diapositive, transparency; candid photograph; take; still, still photograph; photomural; montage, photomontage; aerial photograph, photomap; facsimile *or* fax transmission; telephotograph,

Telephoto <trademark>, Wirephoto <trademark>; photomicrograph, microphotograph; metallograph; microradiograph; electron micrograph; photochronograph, chronophotograph; radiograph, X ray; **portrait,** closeup; action shot, action sequence; pinup <nf>, cheesecake *and* beefcake <nf>; police photograph, **mug** or mug shot <nf>; rogues' gallery; photobiography

4 tintype or ferrotype, ambrotype, **daguerreotype,** calotype *or* talbotype, collotype *or* albertype *or* artotype *or* heliotype, photocollotype, autotype, vitrotype

5 print, photoprint, positive; glossy, matte, semi-matte; **enlargement, blowup;** photocopy, Photostat <trademark>, photostatic copy, stat <nf>, Xerox <trademark>, Xerox copy; microfilm, microfiche, microphotocopy, microprint, microcopy; blueprint, cyanotype; **slide,** transparency, lantern slide; contact printing, projection printing; photogravure; hologram; double exposure

6 shadowgraph, shadowgram, skiagraph, skiagram; radiograph, radiogram, scotograph; **X ray,** X-ray photograph, roentgenograph, roentgenogram; photofluorogram; photogram

7 spectrograph, spectrogram; spectroheliogram

8 <motion pictures> **shot; take, retake;** close-up, long shot, medium shot, full shot, group shot, deuce shot, matte shot, process shot, boom shot, travel shot, trucking shot, follow-focus shot, pan shot *or* panoramic shot, rap shot, reverse *or* reverse-angle shot, wild shot, zoom shot; motion picture; kinescope

9 exposure, time exposure; shutter speed; f-stop, lens opening; film rating, **film speed,** film gauge, ASA number, **DIN** or *Deutsche Industrie Normen* number, DX code; exposure meter, light meter

10 film; negative; printing paper, photographic paper; **plate;** dry plate; vehicle; motion-picture film, panchromatic film, monochromatic film, orthochromatic film, black-and-white film, color film, color negative film, color reversal film, Polaroid film <trademark>; microfilm, bibliofilm; sound-on-film, sound film; sound track, soundstripe; Super-8, videotape, 35mm; roll, cartridge; pack, bipack, tripack; frame; emulsion, dope, backing

11 camera, Kodak *and* Polaroid <trademark>; digital camera, digicam; disposable camera; photo booth; video camera, camcorder; TV camera, motion-picture camera, cinematograph *or* kinematograph <Brit>; security camera; scanner

12 projector; motion-picture projector, cineprojector, cinematograph *or* kinematograph <Brit>, vitascope; **slide projector,** magic lantern, stereopticon; slide viewer

13 processing solution; developer, soup <nf>; fixer, fixing bath, sodium thiosulfate *or* sodium hyposulfite *or* hypo; acid stop, stop bath, short-stop, short-stop bath; emulsion

VERBS 14 photograph, shoot <nf>, **take a photograph,** take a picture, take one's picture; **snap,** snapshot, snapshoot; **film,** get *or* capture on film; **mug** <nf>; daguerreotype, talbotype, calotype; Photostat <trademark>; xerox; microfilm; photomap; pan; **X-ray,** radiograph, roentgenograph

15 process; develop; print; blueprint; **blow up, enlarge**

16 project, show, screen

ADJS 17 photographic, photo; **photogenic,** picturesome; photosensitive, photoactive; panchromatic; telephotographic, telephoto; tintype; three-dimensional, 3-D

18 types of photography

acoustical holography	motion-picture photography
aerophotography *or* aerial photography *or* air photography	phonophotography
	photoheliography
	photojournalism
animation photography	photomacrography
architectural photography	photomicrography
astrophotography	photoreproduction
available-light photography	phototopography
	portraiture
candid photography	pyrophotography
chronophotography	radiation-field *or* Kirlian photography
cinematography *or* motion-picture photography	radiography
	reprography
cinephotomicrography	schlieren photography
color photography	skiagraphy
digital photography	spectroheliography
documentary photography	spectrophotography
electrophotography	sports photography
fashion photography	stereophotography
flash photography	still-life photography
heliophotography	stroboscopic photography
holography	studio photography
infrared photography	telephotography
integral photography	thermography
landscape photography	time-lapse photography
laser photography	underwater photography
macrophotography	uranophotography
microfilming	wildlife photography
microphotography	xerography
miniature photography	X-ray photography

715 SCULPTURE

NOUNS 1 sculpture, sculpturing; plastic art, **modeling; statuary; stonecutting;** gem-cutting, masonry; **carving,** stone carving, bone-carving, cameo carving, scrimshaw, *taille directe* <Fr>, whittling, woodcarving *or* xyloglyphy; embossing, **engraving** 713.2, **chasing,** toreutics, founding, casting, molding, plaster casting, lost-wax process, *cire perdue* <Fr>; soft sculpture; ice sculpture; sculptor 716.6

2 <sculptured piece> sculpture; glyph; statue; marble, bronze, terra cotta, scrimshaw, woodcarving; mobile, stabile; cast 785.6; found object, *objet trouvé* <Fr>; collage, assemblage

3 relief, relievo; **embossment,** boss; half relief, *mezzo-rilievo* <Ital>; high relief, *alto-rilievo* <Ital>; low relief, bas-relief, *basso-rilievo* <Ital>, *rilievo stiacciato* <Ital>; sunk relief, *cavo-rilievo* <Ital>, coelanaglyphic sculpture, **intaglio,** *intaglio rilievo or intaglio rilevato* <Ital>; *repoussé* <Fr>; glyph, anaglyph; glyptograph; **mask;** plaquette; **medallion; medal; cameo,** cameo glass, sculptured glass; cut glass

4 <tools, materials> chisel, point, mallet, burin, modeling tool, spatula; cutting torch, welding torch, soldering iron; solder; modeling clay, Plasticine <trademark>, sculptor's wax; plaster

VERBS 5 sculpture, sculp *or* sculpt <nf>, insculpture <old>; **carve,** chisel, cut, grave, engrave, chase; weld, solder; assemble; **model, mold;** cast, found

ADJS 6 sculptural, sculpturesque, sculptitory; statuary; **statuesque,** statuelike; **monumental,** marmoreal; plastic

7 sculptured, sculpted; sculptile; **molded, modeled,** ceroplastic; **carved,** chiseled; **graven,** engraven, engraved, incised; in relief, in high *or* low relief; glyphic, glyptic, anaglyphic, anaglyptic; anastatic; embossed, chased, hammered, toreutic; *repoussé* <Fr>; tactile

716 ARTIST

NOUNS 1 artist, *artiste* <Fr>, "a dreamer consenting to dream of the actual world"—Santayana, creator, maker; master, **old master;** dauber, daubster; copyist; **craftsman, artisan** 726.6

2 limner, delineator, depicter, picturer, portrayer, imager; **illustrator;** illuminator; calligrapher; commercial artist; drawer, renderer, doodler, scribbler; pastelist

3 draftsman, draftswoman, **sketcher, delineator; graphic artist;** drawer, architectural draftsman; crayonist, charcoalist, pastelist; **cartoonist, caricaturist,** animator

4 painter, *artiste-peintre* <Fr>; **colorist;** luminist, luminarist; **oil painter,** oil-colorist; **watercolorist;** aquarellist; finger painter; monochromist, polychromist; genre painter, historical painter, landscape painter, landscapist, miniaturist, portrait painter, portraitist, marine painter, still-life painter, animal painter, religious painter; pavement artist; sign painter; scene painter, scenewright, scenographer

5 **photographer,** photographist, lensman, **cameraperson,** camerawoman, cameraman; **cinematographer;** snapshotter, snap shooter, shutterbug <nf>; daguerreotypist, calotypist, talbotypist; skiagrapher, shadowgraphist, radiographer, X-ray technician; digital artist

6 **sculptor,** sculptress, sculpturer; earth artist, environmental artist; statuary; figurer, figurist, *figuriste* <Fr>, **modeler,** molder, wax modeler, clay modeler; graver, chaser, carver; molder, caster; stonecutter, mason, monumental mason, wood carver, xyloglyphic artist, whittler; ivory carver, bone carver, shell carver; gem carver, glyptic *or* glyptographic artist; engraver, etcher; lapidary

7 **ceramist, ceramicist, potter;** china decorator *or* painter, tile painter, majolica painter; glassblower, glazer, glass decorator, pyroglazer, glass cutter; enamelist, enameler

8 **printmaker,** graphic artist; **engraver,** graver, burinist; inscriber, carver; **etcher;** line engraver; **lithographer,** autolithographer, chromolithographer; serigrapher, silk-screen artist; cerographer, cerographist; chalcographer; gem engraver, glyptographer, lapidary; wood engraver, xylographer; pyrographer, xylopyrographer; zincographer

9 **designer, stylist,** styler; costume designer, dress designer, *couturier* <Fr>, *couturière* <Fr fem>; furniture designer, rug designer, textile designer

10 **architect,** civil architect; landscape architect, landscape gardener; city *or* urban planner, urbanist; functionalist

11 **decorator,** expert in decor, ornamentist, ornamentalist; **interior decorator** *or* designer, house decorator, room decorator, floral decorator, table decorator; window decorator *or* dresser; confectionery decorator

717 ARCHITECTURE, DESIGN

NOUNS 1 **architecture,** architectural design, building design, the art and technique of building, "inhabited sculpture"—Brancusi, "music in space"—Schelling, "the art of significant forms in space"—Claude Bragdon; **architectural science,** architectural engineering, structural engineering, architectural technology, building science, building technology; architectonics, tectonics; **architectural style** <see list>; **architectural specialty;** landscape architecture, landscape gardening 1069.2

2 **architectural element; ornamentation, architectural ornamentation;** column order, Doric, Ionic, Corinthian, Composite; **type of construction,** building type

3 **architect,** architectress, building designer; landscape architect, landscape gardener 1069.6; architectural engineer; city *or* urban planner, urbanist, urbanologist

4 **design, styling,** patterning, planning, shaping, "the conscious effort to impose meaningful order"—Victor Papanek; **design specialty**

5 <design specialties> accessory design, appearance design, architectural design, automotive design, book design, clothing design, costume design, ergonomics *or* ergonomy *or* human engineering *or* human factors engineering, fashion design, furniture design, graphics design, industrial *or* product design, interior design, jewelry design, landscape architecture, lighting design, package design, pottery design, reverse engineering, stage design, textile design, typographic design

6 **designer, stylist,** styler

ADJS 7 **architectural,** architectonic, tectonic; **design, designer**

8 **architectural styles and types**

absolute	early Gothic
academic	early Renaissance
action	earthwork
additive	eclectic
American colonial	ecological
American Georgian	Edwardian
Anglo-Saxon	Egyptian
Art Deco *or* Art Moderne	Elizabethan
Art Nouveau	Empire
arts and crafts	endless
baroque	English decorated
Bauhaus	Gothic
Beaux Arts	English Georgian
brutalist	English Renaissance
Byzantine	flamboyant Gothic
Carolingian	formalist
Chicago School	Francois Premier
Chinese	French colonial
churrigueresque *or*	French Renaissance
churrigueresco	functionalist
cinquecento	Georgian
Cistercian	German Renaissance
classical	gingerbread
colonial	Gothic
conceptual *or* invisible *or*	Great West Road
imaginary *or* nowhere	Greco-Roman
Decorated	Greek
de Stijl	Greek Revival
directed *or* programmed	hard
duck	high Gothic
early American	high Renaissance
early English	hi-tech

indeterminate
international *or* international Gothic
Islamic
Italianate
Italian Gothic
Italian Mannerism
Italian Renaissance
Jacobean
Japanese
Jesuit
kinetic
Louis XIV
Louis XV
mannerism
medieval
Mesopotamian
Mestizo
mission
moderne *or* modernism
neo-Gothic
neoclassical
new brutalist
New England colonial
Norman
organicist

Palladian
perpendicular *or* rectilinear
Persian
pneumatic
postmodern
Prairie
Queen Anne
Regency
Renaissance
rococo
Roman
Romanesque
Romanesque Revival
Romantic
Shingle
Southern colonial
Spanish
Stuart
tensile
Tudor
Utopian *or* fantastic *or* visionary
vernacular
Victorian
Victorian Gothic

9 architectural specialties

church *or* religious *or* ecclesiastical architecture
civic architecture
college architecture
commercial architecture
domestic architecture
governmental architecture

industrial architecture
institutional architecture
landscape architecture
library architecture
military architecture
museum architecture
recreational architecture

718 LITERATURE

NOUNS **1 literature, letters, belles lettres,** polite literature, humane letters, *litterae humaniores* <L>, republic of letters; **work, literary work, text, literary text; works, complete works, oeuvre, canon, literary canon, author's canon;** serious literature; **classics,** ancient literature; medieval literature, Renaissance literature, etc; national literature, English literature, French literature, etc; ethnic literature, black *or* Afro-American literature, Latino literature, etc; contemporary literature; underground literature; pseudonymous literature; folk literature; travel literature; wisdom literature; erotic literature, erotica; pornographic literature, pornography, porn *and* hard porn *and* soft porn <nf>, obscene literature, scatological literature; popular literature, pop literature <nf>; chick lit; kitsch

2 authorship, writing, authorcraft, pencraft, wordsmanship, **composition,** the art of composition, inditing, inditement; one's pen;

creative writing, literary art, verbal art, literary composition, literary production, verse-writing, short-story writing, novel-writing, playwriting, drama-writing; essay-writing; **expository writing;** technical writing; journalism, newspaper writing, editorial-writing, feature-writing, rewriting; magazine writing; songwriting, lyric-writing, libretto-writing; artistry, literary power, literary artistry, literary talent *or* flair, skill with words *or* language, facility in writing, ready pen; **writer's itch,** graphomania, scribblemania, graphorrhea, *cacoëthes scribendi* <L>

3 writer, scribbler <nf>, **penman,** pen, penner; pen *or* pencil driver *or* pusher <nf>, word-slinger, **inkslinger** *and* ink spiller *and* inkstained wretch <nf>, knight of the plume *or* pen *or* quill <nf>

4 author, writer, scribe <nf>, composer, inditer, penman, wordsmith, compiler; authoress, penwoman; **creative writer,** *littérateur* <Fr>, literary artist, literary craftsman *or* artisan *or* journeyman, belletrist, man of letters, literary scholar; wordsmith, word painter; freelance, freelance writer; ghostwriter, ghost <nf>; collaborator, coauthor; prose writer, logographer; fiction writer, fictioneer <nf>; story writer, **short story writer;** storyteller, narrator; **novelist;** novelettist; diarist; chronicler, historian, historiographer; biographer; **newspaperman; annalist; poet** 720.13; **dramatist,** humorist 489.12; scriptwriter, scenario writer, scenarist; nonfiction writer; article writer, magazine writer; **essayist;** monographer; reviewer, critic, literary critic, music critic, art critic, drama critic, dance critic; cultural commentator; columnist; pamphleteer; technical writer; copywriter, advertising writer; compiler, encyclopedist, bibliographer

5 hack writer, hack, literary hack, Grub Street writer <Brit>, **penny-a-liner, scribbler** <nf>, **potboiler** <nf>

VERBS **6 write,** author, pen, **compose, indite,** formulate, produce, prepare; dash off, knock off *or* out <nf>, throw on paper, pound *or* crank *or* grind *or* churn out; freelance; compile; collaborate, coauthor; ghostwrite, ghost <nf>; novelize; scenarize; pamphleteer; editorialize

ADJS **7 literary,** belletristic, lettered; classical

8 auctorial, authorial

719 HISTORY

NOUNS **1 history,** the historical discipline, the investigation of the past, the record of the past, the story of mankind, study of the past; historical research; **annals, chronicles,** memorabilia, chronology; chronicle, record 549; historical method, historical approach, philosophy of history, **historiography;** cliometrics; documentation, recording; narrative history, **oral history,** oral record, survivors' or witnesses' accounts; **biography, memoir,** memorial, **life, story, life story,** adventures, fortunes, reminiscences, experiences; résumé, vita, curriculum vitae or CV; life and letters, track record <nf>; legend, saint's legend, hagiology, hagiography; **autobiography, memoirs,** memorials, archive; **journal, diary,** confessions; **profile, biographical sketch;** obituary, necrology, martyrology; photobiography; case history; historiography, theory of history; epigraphy, archaeology; Clio, Muse of history; **the past** 837; **record, recording** 549.1; herstory <nf>

2 <history> "a set of lies agreed upon"—Napoleon, "philosophy learned from examples"—Dionysius of Halicarnassus

3 **story, tale, yarn, account, narrative,** narration, chronicle, tradition, legend, folk tale, folk history; **anecdote,** anecdotage; **epic,** epos, **saga;** minutes, notes; file, dossier; etymology

4 **historian,** cliometrician, historiographer; **chronicler,** annalist, recorder, archivist; **biographer,** memorialist, Boswell; autobiographer, autobiographist; diarist, Pepys; epigrapher, archaeologist

VERBS 5 **chronicle,** write history, historify; historicize; biograph, biography, biographize; immortalize; compile; document, report **record** 549.15

6 **narrate, tell, relate, recount,** report, **recite,** rehearse, give an account of; commentate, voice over

ADJS 7 **historical, historic,** historied, historically accurate; fact-based; historicized; historiographical; cliometric; **chronicled;** chronologic, chronological; **traditional, legendary;** biographical, autobiographic, autobiographical; documentary, documented, archival; hagiographic, hagiographical, martyrologic, martyrological; necrologic, necrological; retro

8 **narrative,** narrational; **fictional**

ADVS 9 **historically,** historically speaking; as chronicled, as history tells us, according to or by all accounts; as the record shows; retrospectively

720 POETRY

NOUNS 1 **poetry,** poesy, **verse, song, rhyme;** "musical thought",—Carlyle, "painting with the gift of speech"—Simonides, "not the thing said but a way of saying it"—A E Housman, "the music of the soul, and above all of great and of feeling souls"—Voltaire

2 **poetics,** poetcraft, versecraft, versification, versemaking, ars poetica <L>; "my craft and sullen art"—Dylan Thomas; **poetic language,** poetic diction, poeticism; **poetic license, poetic justice**

3 **bad poetry,** doggerel, versemongering, poetastering, poetastery; poesy; crambo, crambo clink or jingle <Scot>, Hudibrastic verse; nonsense verse, amphigory; macaronics, macaronic verse; lame verses, limping meters, halting meters

4 **poem, verse, rhyme;** verselet, versicle; lyric poem, dramatic poem, narrative poem

5 **book of verse,** garland, **collection, anthology;** poetic works, poesy, epos

6 **metrics, prosody, versification; scansion,** scanning; metrical pattern or form, prosodic pattern or form, meter, numbers, measure; quantitative meter, syllabic meter, accentual meter, accentual-syllabic meter, duple meter, triple meter; free verse, vers libre <Fr>; alliterative meter, Stabreim <Ger>

7 **meter, measure,** numbers; **rhythm, cadence,** movement, lilt, jingle, swing; sprung rhythm; **accent,** accentuation, metrical accent, stress, emphasis, ictus, **beat;** arsis, thesis; quantity, mora; metrical unit; **foot, metrical foot** <see list>; triseme, tetraseme; metrical group, metron, colon, period; dipody, syzygy, tripody, tetrapody, pentapody, hexapody, heptapody; monometer, dimeter, trimeter, tetrameter, pentameter, hexameter, heptameter, octameter; **iambic pentameter, dactylic hexameter;** Alexandrine; Saturnian meter; elegiac, elegiac couplet or distich, elegiac pentameter; heroic couplet; sprung rhythm; counterpoint; caesura, diaeresis, masculine caesura, feminine caesura; catalexis; anacrusis

8 **rhyme;** clink, crambo; **consonance, assonance; alliteration;** eye rhyme; male or masculine or single rhyme, female or feminine or double rhyme; initial rhyme, end rhyme; tail rhyme, rhyme royal; broken rhyme, half rhyme, near rhyme, pararhyme, slant rhyme; internal rhyme; terza rima, ottava rima; rime riche, identical rhyme; rhyme scheme; rhyming dictionary; unrhymed poetry, blank verse

9 <poetic divisions> **measure, strain; syllable; line;** verse; stanza, stave; strophe, antistrophe, epode; **canto,** book; **refrain, chorus,** burden; envoi; monostich, distich, tristich, tetrastich, pentastich, hexastich, heptastich, octastich; **couplet;** triplet, tercet, terza rima <Ital>; **quatrain;** sextet, sestet; septet; octave, octet, ottava rima <Ital>; rhyme royal; Spenserian stanza

10 **Muse;** the Muses, Pierides, Camenae <L>; Apollo, Apollo Musagetes; Calliope, Polyhymnia, Erato, Euterpe; Helicon, Parnassus; Castilian Spring,

Pierian Spring, Hippocrene; Bragi; **poetic genius,**
poesy, afflatus, fire of genius, **creative imagination**
986.2, **inspiration** 920.8

11 **poet,** poetess, poetress <old>, maker <old>; "the
painter of the soul"—Disraeli, "all who love, who
feel great truths, and tell them"—Philip James
Bailey; ballad maker; **bard, minstrel,** scop, fili,
baird, skald, **jongleur, troubadour,** *trovatore* <Ital>,
trouveur, *trouvère* <Fr>, *Meistersinger* <Ger>,
minnesinger; minor poet, major poet, arch-poet;
laureate, **poet laureate;** occasional poet; **lyric poet;**
epic poet; pastoral poet, pastoralist, idyllist,
bucoliast <old>; rhapsodist, rhapsode; vers-librist,
vers libriste <Fr>; elegist, librettist; lyricist, lyrist;
odist; satirist; sonneteer; modernist, imagist,
symbolist; Parnassian; beat poet

12 **bad poet;** rhymester, rhymer; metrist; versemaker,
versesmith, versifier, verseman, versemonger;
poetling, **poetaster,** poeticule; balladmonger

VERBS 13 **poetize, versify,** verse, write *or* compose
poetry, build the stately rime, sing deathless
songs, make immortal verse; tune one's lyre, climb
Parnassus, mount Pegasus; **sing;** elegize; poeticize

14 **rhyme,** assonate, alliterate; **scan;** jingle; cap verses
or rhymes

ADJS 15 **poetic, poetical,** poetlike; **lyrical, narrative,**
dramatic, lyrico-dramatic; bardic; runic, skaldic;
epic, heroic; mock-heroic, Hudibrastic; pastoral,
bucolic, eclogic, idyllic, Theocritean; didactic;
elegiac, elegiacal; dithyrambic, rhapsodic,
rhapsodical, Alcaic, Anacreontic, Homeric,
Pindaric, sapphic; Castalian, Pierian; Parnassian,
Sapphic; poetico-mythological; poetico-mystical,
poetico-philosophic; comic, concrete, epic, erotic,
folk, metaphysical, nonsense, pattern, satirical,
tragic

16 **metric, metrical, prosodic, prosodical; rhythmic,
rhythmical, measured,** cadenced, scanning,
scanned; accentual; iambic, dactylic, spondaic,
pyrrhic, trochaic, anapestic, antispastic, etc

17 **rhyming; assonant,** assonantal; **alliterative,**
onomatopoeic; resonant; jingling; musical, lilting

ADVS 18 **poetically, lyrically; metrically,
rhythmically,** in measure; musically

19 **metrical feet**

amphibrach	iamb *or* iambus
amphimacer	*or* iambic
anapest	ionic
antispast	molossus
bacchius	paeon
choriambus *or* choriamb	proceleusmatic
cretic *or* amphimacer	pyrrhic *or* dibrach
dactyl	spondee
dochmiac	tribrach
epitrite	trochee

721 PROSE

NOUNS 1 **prose;** prose fiction, nonfiction prose,
expository prose; prose rhythm; prose style; poetic
prose, polyphonic prose, prose poetry

2 **prosaism, prosaicism, prosaicness,** prosiness,
pedestrianism, **unpoeticalness; matter-of-
factness,** unromanticism, unidealism;
unimaginativeness 987; **plainness,** commonness,
commonplaceness, unembellishedness;
insipidness, flatness, vapidity; **dullness** 117

VERBS 3 **prose,** write prose *or* in prose; pedestrianize

ADJS 4 **prose,** in prose; unversified, nonpoetic,
nonmetricalf

5 **prosaic, prosy, prosing;** unpoetical, poetryless;
plain, common, commonplace, ordinary,
unembellished, mundane; **matter-of-fact,
unromantic, unidealistic,** unimpassioned;
pedestrian, **unimaginative** 987.5; insipid, vapid,
flat; humdrum, tiresome, **dull** 117.6

722 FICTION

NOUNS 1 **fiction,** narrative, narrative literature,
imaginative narrative, prose fiction; **narration,**
relation, relating, recital, rehearsal, telling,
retelling, recounting, recountal, review, portrayal,
graphic narration, description, delineation,
presentation; **storytelling,** tale-telling, yarn-
spinning *and* yarning <nf>; narrative poetry;
operatic libretto; computer *or* interactive fiction;
pulp fiction

2 **narration, narrative, relation, recital,** rehearsal,
telling, retelling, recounting, recountal, review;
storytelling, tale-telling, yarn spinning *or* yarning
<nf>

3 **story** <see list>, **short story,** tale, narrative, yarn,
account, narration, chronicle, relation, version;
novel <see list>, *roman* <Fr>

4 <story elements> **plot,** fable, argument, story, line,
story line, subplot, secondary plot, mythos;
structure, plan, architecture, architectonics,
scheme, design; **subject, topic, theme,** motif;
thematic development, development, continuity;
action, movement; incident, episode;
complication; rising action, turning point, climax,
defining moment, falling action, *peripeteia* <Gk>,
switch <nf>; *anagnorisis* <Gk>, recognition;
denouement, catastrophe; *deus ex machina* <L>;
catharsis; device, contrivance, **gimmick** <nf>;
angle *and* slant *and* twist <nf>; **character,**
characterization; **speech,** dialogue; **tone,
atmosphere,** mood; **setting,** locale, world, milieu,
background, backstory, region, local color

5 narrator, relator, reciter, recounter, *raconteur* <Fr>; **anecdotist; storyteller,** storier, taleteller, teller of tales, spinner of yarns *and* yarn spinner <nf>; word painter; **persona,** central consciousness, the I of the story; point-of-view <see list>; **author, writer,** short-story writer, **novelist,** novelettist, fictionist; fabulist, fableist, fabler, mythmaker, mythopoet; romancer, romancist; sagaman

VERBS **6 narrate, tell, relate, recount,** report, **recite,** rehearse, give an account of; tell a story, unfold a tale, a tale unfold, fable, fabulize; storify, fictionalize; romance; novelize; mythicize, mythify, mythologize, allegorize; retell

ADJS **7 fictional,** fictionalized; **novelistic,** novelized, novelettish; mythical, mythological, **legendary, fabulous;** mythopoeic, mythopoetic *or* mythopoetical; **allegorical** *or* allegoric, parabolic *or* parabolical; **romantic,** romanticized; historical, historicized, fact-based

8 narrative, narrational; storied, storified; **anecdotal,** anecdotic; epic *or* epical

9 types of stories

adventure story	horror story *or* chiller *and*
allegory	chiller-diller <nf>
apologue	lai
beast fable	legend
bedtime story	love story
chivalric romance	Milesian tale
classical detective story	mystery *or* mystery story
conte <Fr>	myth *or* mythos
crime story	nursery tale
cyberpunk	parable
detective story *or* detective	romance
yarn *or* whodunit <nf>	romantic adventure
dime novel *or* penny dread-	saga
ful <nf>	saint's legend
epic *or* epos	science fiction story *or*
exemplum *or* didactic tale	sci-fi story <nf>
or moral tale	short short story *or*
fable	short-short
fabliau	short story
fairy tale *or* Märchen <Ger>	sketch
fantasy	spy story
folktale *or* folk story	supernatural tale
gest *or* geste	suspense story
ghost story	thriller *or* thriller-diller
hard-boiled detective story	<nf>
or tough-tec story <nf>	vignette
hero tale	Western *or* Western story
historical fiction	*or* cowboy story

10 types of novels

adventure novel	bodice ripper <nf>
antinovel *or* anti-roman *or*	cliffhanger
nouveau roman	collage novel
autobiographical novel	comic novel
Bildungsroman <Ger>	detective novel

dime novel	political novel
dystopia *or* cacotopia *or*	pornographic novel
dystopian	problem novel
entertainment	proletarian novel
epic novel	propaganda novel
epistolary novel	psychological novel
erotic novel	psychological thriller
experimental novel	realistic novel
fantasy novel	regional novel
fictional *or* fictionalized	roman à clef <Fr>
biography	roman-fleuve <Fr> *or* river
Gothic novel	novel
historical novel	romance novel
historical romance *or*	satirical novel
bodice-ripper <nf>	science-fiction *or* sci-fi
Kunstlerroman <Ger>	novel
lyrical novel	sentimental novel
naturalistic novel	social melodrama
nouveau roman	sociological novel
novel of character	stream-of-consciousness
novel of ideas	novel
novel of incident	surrealistic novel
novel of manners	techno-thriller
novel of sensibility *or* senti-	thesis novel
mental novel	thriller *or* psychological
novel of the soil	thriller
novelette	utopia *or* utopian
novella *or* nouvelle <Fr>	novel
penny dreadful <Brit>	Victorian novel
picaresque novel	Western

11 narrative points of view

documentary *or* camera-	omniscient observer
eye observer	stream of consciousness *or*
fallible observer	interior monologue
first-person past narrator	third-person past narrator
first-person present	third-person present
narrator	narrator

723 CRITICISM OF THE ARTS

NOUNS **1 criticism,** criticism of the arts, esthetic *or* artistic criticism, aesthetic *or* artistic evaluation, aesthetic *or* artistic analysis, aesthetic *or* artistic interpretation, critical commentary, critique, critical analysis, critical interpretation, critical evaluation, metacriticism, exegetics, hermeneutics; **art criticism,** formalist criticism, expressionist criticism, neoformalist criticism; music criticism; dramatic criticism; dance criticism; aesthetics

2 review, critical notice, commentary, *compte rendu critique* <Fr>, critical treatment *or* treatise

3 literary criticism, Lit-Crit <nf>, literary analysis *or* evaluation *or* interpretation *or* exegetics *or* hermeneutics, poetics; **critical approach** *or* **school; literary theory,** theory of literature, critical theory, theory of criticism

4 **critic,** interpreter, exegete, analyst, explicator, theoretician, aesthetician; reviewer

VERBS 5 **criticize,** critique, evaluate, interpret, explicate, analyze, judge; theorize

ADJS 6 **critical,** evaluative, interpretive, exegetical, analytical, explicative

724 OCCUPATION

NOUNS 1 **occupation, work, job, employment,** business, employ, **activity, function,** enterprise, undertaking, **affairs,** labor; thing *and* bag <nf>; **affair, matter, concern,** concernment, **interest,** lookout <nf>; what one is doing *or* about; **commerce** 731

2 **task, work, stint, job,** labor, toil, industry, piece of work, **chore,** chare, odd job; **assignment, charge,** project, errand, **mission,** commission, **duty,** service, exercise; things to do, matters in hand, irons in the fire, fish to fry; homework, take-home work; busywork, makework

3 **function, office, duty, job,** province, place, **role,** rôle <Fr>, part; **capacity,** character, **position**

4 <sphere of work or activity> **field, sphere,** profession, trade, province, bailiwick, turf <nf>, department, area, discipline, subdiscipline, orb, orbit, realm, arena, domain, walk; **specialty, niche,** speciality <Brit>, line of country <Brit nf>; beat, round; shop; corporate culture; bricks and mortar, bricks and clicks

5 **position, job,** employment, gainful employment, situation, **office, post, place,** station, berth, billet, **appointment,** engagement, gig <nf>; incumbency, tenure; opening, vacancy; second job, moonlighting <nf>

6 **vocation, occupation, business, work, line, line of work,** line of business *or* endeavor, number <nf>, walk, **walk of life, calling,** mission, **profession, practice, pursuit, specialty,** specialization, *métier* <Fr>, mystery <old>, **trade,** racket *and* game <nf>; **career,** lifework, life's work; career track, Mommy track <nf>; **craft,** art, handicraft; careerism, career building

7 **avocation, hobby,** hobbyhorse <old>, sideline, by-line, side interest, pastime, spare-time activity, outside interest; amateur pursuit, amateurism; unpaid work, volunteer work

8 **professionalism,** professional standing *or* status

9 **nonprofessionalism, amateurism,** amateur standing *or* status

VERBS 10 **occupy, engage, busy,** devote, spend, **employ,** occupy oneself, busy oneself, go about one's business, devote oneself; pass *or* employ *or* spend the time; occupy one's time, take up one's time; attend to business, attend to one's work;

mind one's business, mind the store <nf>, stick to one's last *or* knitting <nf>; telecommute

11 **busy oneself with, do,** occupy *or* engage oneself with, employ oneself in *or* upon, pass *or* employ *or* spend one's time in; **engage in, take up,** devote oneself to, apply oneself to, address oneself to, have one's hands in, turn one's hand to; concern oneself with, make it one's business; **be about, be doing,** be occupied with, be engaged *or* employed in, be at work on; practice, follow as an occupation

12 **work,** work at, work for, have a job, be employed, **ply one's trade,** labor in one's vocation, do one's number <nf>, follow a trade, practice a profession, carry on a business *or* trade, keep up; **do** *or* **transact business,** carry on *or* conduct business; set up shop, set up in business, hang out one's shingle <nf>; stay employed, hold down a job <nf>; moonlight <nf>, consult; labor, toil 725.13,14

13 **officiate, function, serve; perform as, act as,** act *or* play one's part, **do duty,** discharge *or* perform *or* exercise the office *or* duties *or* functions of, serve in the office *or* capacity of

14 **hold office,** fill an office, occupy a post

ADJS 15 **occupied, busy,** working; practical, realistic 987.6; banausic, moneymaking, breadwinning, utilitarian 387.18; materialistic 695.16; workaday, workday, prosaic 117.8; **commercial** 731.22

16 **occupational, vocational,** functional; **professional,** pro <nf>; official; technical, industrial; all in the day's work

17 **avocational,** hobby, amateur, nonprofessional

ADVS 18 **professionally,** vocationally; as a profession *or* vocation; in the course of business

725 EXERTION

NOUNS 1 **exertion, effort, energy,** elbow grease; **endeavor** 403; **trouble, pains;** great *or* mighty effort, might and main, muscle, one's back, nerve, and sinew, hard *or* strong *or* long pull

2 **strain,** straining, **stress,** stressfulness, **stress and strain,** taxing, **tension,** stretch, rack; tug, pull, haul, heave; overexertion, overstrain, overtaxing, overextension, overstress

3 **struggle, fight, battle, tussle, scuffle, wrestle,** hassle <nf>

4 **work, labor, employment, industry, toil,** moil, travail, toil and trouble, sweat of one's brow; **drudgery, sweat,** slavery, spadework, shitwork <nf>, rat race <nf>; treadmill, unskilled labor, hewing of wood *and* drawing of water; dirty work, grunt work *and* donkey work *and* shit-work *and* scut work <nf>, thankless task; **makework,** tedious *or* stupid *or* idiot *or* tiresome work,

humdrum toil, grind <nf>, fag <chiefly Brit>; rubber room work *or* job *or* assignment, no-work job; **manual labor,** handwork, handiwork; forced labor; hand's turn, stroke of work, stroke; lick *and* lick of work *and* stitch of work <nf>; man-hour; **workload,** work schedule; task 724.2; fatigue 21

5 **hard work** *or* **labor, backbreaking work,** moil, warm work, uphill work, long haul, hard *or* tough grind <nf>, the hard way; **hard job** 1013.2; labor of Hercules; **laboriousness, toilsomeness,** effortfulness, **strenuousness, arduousness,** operosity, operoseness; onerousness, oppressiveness, burdensomeness; troublesomeness

6 **exercise** 84, exercising; **practice, drill, workout,** preparation; yoga; constitutional <nf>, stretch; violent exercise; physical education

7 exerciser; horizontal bar, parallel bars, horse, side horse, long horse, rings; trapeze; trampoline; Indian club; medicine ball; punching bag; rowing machine; weight, dumbbell, barbell

VERBS 8 **exert, exercise, ply, employ, use, put forth,** put out *and* make with <nf>; practice

9 **exert oneself,** use some elbow grease <nf>, spread oneself, put forth one's strength, bend every effort, bend might and main, spare no effort, put on a full-court press <nf>, tax one's energies, break a sweat <nf>; put *or* lay oneself out <nf>, go all out <nf>; endeavor 403.4; **do one's best; apply oneself,** come to grips with; hump *and* hump it *and* hump oneself <nf>, **buckle** *or* **knuckle** *or* bear <nf>, lay to; lay to the oars, ply the oar

10 **strain, tense, stress, stretch, tax,** press, rack; **pull, tug,** haul, **heave;** strain the muscles, strain every nerve *or* every nerve and sinew; put one's back into it <nf>; sweat blood; overwork, work night and day, take on too much, spread oneself too thin, overexert, overstrain, overtax, overextend; drive *or* whip *or* flog oneself

11 **struggle, strive, contend, fight, battle,** buffet, scuffle, tussle, wrestle, hassle <nf>, work *or* fight one's way, agonize, huff and puff, grunt and sweat, sweat it <nf>, make heavy weather of it

12 **work, labor;** busy oneself 724.10,11; turn a hand, do a hand's turn, do a lick of work, earn one's keep; chore, do the chores, char *or* do chars, chare <Brit>

13 **work hard; scratch** *and* **hustle** *and* **sweat** <nf>, **slave, sweat and slave** <nf>, slave away, toil away, hammer at; **hit the ball** *and* bear down *and* pour it on <nf>; burn the candle at both ends; work one's head off <nf>, work one's fingers to the bone, break one's back, bust one's hump *or* ass <nf>; put one's heart and soul into it; beaver *or* beaver away <Brit nf>, work like a beaver, work like a horse *or* cart horse *or* dog, work like a slave *or* galley slave, work like a coal heaver, work like a Trojan; work

overtime, be a workaholic <nf>, overwork, do double duty, work double hours *or* tides, **work day and night,** work late, **burn the midnight oil;** persevere; lucubrate, elucubrate; overwork 993.10

14 **drudge, grind** *and* **dig** <nf>, fag <Brit>, **grub, toil,** moil, toil and moil, travail, **plod, slog, peg, plug** <nf>, hammer, peg away *or* along, plug away *or* along <nf>, hammer away, pound away, struggle along, struggle on, work away; **get** *or* **keep one's nose to the grindstone;** wade through

15 **set to work, get rolling, get busy, get down to business** *or* **work,** roll up one's sleeves, spit on one's hands, gird up one's loins; **fall to work, fall to, buckle** *or* **knuckle down to** <nf>, **turn to, set to** *or* **about,** put *or* set one's hand to, start in, set up shop, enter on *or* upon, launch into *or* upon; **get on the job** *and* get going <nf>; **go to it** *and* **get with it** *and* get cracking *and* have at it *and* get one's teeth into it <nf>; hop *or* jump to it <nf>; **attack,** set at, **tackle** <nf>; **plunge into,** dive into; **pitch in** *or* **into** <nf>; light into *and* wade into *and* tear into *and* sail into <nf>, put *or* lay one's shoulder to the wheel, put one's hand to the plow; take on, undertake 404.3

16 **task, work, busy,** keep busy, fag <Brit>, sweat <nf>, **drive, tax;** overtask, overtax, **overwork,** overdrive; burden, oppress 297.13

ADJS 17 **laboring, working; struggling, striving,** straining; **drudging, toiling,** slaving, sweating *and* grinding <nf>, grubbing, **plodding,** slogging, pegging, plugging <nf>, persevering; hardworking; busy, industrious, hard at it

18 **laborious, toilsome, arduous, strenuous,** painful, effortful, operose, troublesome, onerous, oppressive, burdensome; wearisome, tiring, exhausting; **heavy,** hefty <nf>, tough <nf>, uphill, **backbreaking,** grueling, punishing, crushing, killing, Herculean; uphill; **labored,** forced, strained; straining, tensive, painstaking, **intensive;** hard-fought, hard-won, hard-earned

ADVS 19 **laboriously, arduously, toilsomely, strenuously,** operosely; effortfully, with effort, **hard,** by the sweat of one's brow; the hard way; with all one's might, for all one is worth, with a will, **with might and main,** with a strong hand, manfully; **hammer and tongs, tooth and nail,** *bec et ongles* <Fr>, heart and soul; **industriously** 330.27

726 WORKER, DOER

NOUNS 1 **doer, agent,** actor **performer, worker, practitioner,** perpetrator; **producer, maker,** creator, fabricator, **author,** mover, prime mover; go-getter; architect; **agent,** medium; **executor,** executant, executrix; **operator,** operative, operant, hand; subject *and* agent <gram>; coworker, colleague

2 worker, laborer, toiler, moiler; member of the working class, proletarian, prole <Brit nf>, blue-collar *or* lunch-bucket worker, laboring man, stiff *and* working stiff <nf>; **workman, working man; workwoman, working woman,** workfolk, workpeople; working girl, workgirl; **factory worker,** industrial worker; autoworker, steelworker; construction worker; **commuter;** home worker, telecommuter; **office worker, white-collar worker;** career woman, career girl; **jobholder,** wageworker, **wage earner,** salaried worker; **breadwinner;** wage slave; employee, servant 577; **hand, workhand,** hourly worker; **laborer,** common laborer, **unskilled laborer,** navvy <Brit>, day laborer, roust-about; casual, casual laborer; **agricultural worker** 1069.5; migrant worker, migrant; menial, flunky; piece-worker, jobber; factotum, jack-of-all-trades; full-time worker, part-time worker; temporary employee, temporary, office temporary, temp <nf>; freelance worker, freelance, freelancer, self-employed person, independent contractor, consultant; volunteer; domestic worker, clerical worker, sales worker, service worker, repair worker, artistic worker, technical worker; **labor force, work force,** crew, shop floor <Brit>, factory floor; personnel; labor market

3 drudge, grub, hack, fag, plodder, slave, galley slave, **workhorse,** beast of burden, slogger; grind *and* greasy grind <nf>, swot <Brit nf>; slave labor, sweatshop labor; busy bee *and* beaver *and* ant <nf>

4 professional, member of a learned profession, professional practitioner; businessman, businesswoman, career woman; executive; pro *and* old pro <nf>, seasoned professional; gownsman; doctor, lawyer, member of the clergy, teacher, accountant; social worker; health-care professional, military professional; law-enforcement professional, etc

5 amateur, nonprofessional, layman, member of the laity, laic

6 skilled worker, skilled laborer, **journeyman,** mechanic; **craftsman, handicraftsman;** craftswoman; craftsperson; craftspeople; **artisan,** artificer, artist; **maker,** *fabbro* <Ital>; **wright; technician;** apprentice, prentice <nf>; **master,** master craftsman, master workman, master carpenter, etc

7 engineer, professional engineer; **technician,** technical worker, techie <nf>; engineering, technology

8 smith; farrier <Brit>, forger, forgeman, metalworker; Vulcan, Hephaestus, Wayland *or* Völund

727 UNIONISM, LABOR UNION

NOUNS **1 unionism,** trade unionism, trades unionism <Brit>, labor unionism; **unionization; collective bargaining; arbitration,** nonbinding arbitration; industrial relations, labor relations, work relations; employee rights, employer rights; salary negotiations, labor negotiations, negotiated *or* negotiation points, employee demands, management demands

2 labor union, trade union, trades union <Brit>; organized labor; collective bargaining; **craft union,** guild, horizontal union; **industrial union,** vertical union; **local,** union local, local union; company union

3 union shop, preferential shop, **closed shop;** open shop; nonunion shop; **labor contract, union contract,** sweetheart contract, yellow-dog contract; maintenance of membership

4 unionist, labor unionist, trade unionist, union member, trades unionist <Brit>, organized *or* unionized worker, cardholder; shop steward, bargainer, negotiator; business agent; union officer; union *or* labor organizer, organizer, labor union official; union contractor

5 strike, walkout *or* tie-up <nf>, industrial action <Brit>, **job action;** slowdown, rulebook slowdown, sick-in *and* sickout *and* blue flu <nf>; work stoppage, sit-down strike, sit-down, wildcat strike, out-law strike, called strike, organized strike; sympathy strike; **slowdown,** work-to-rule, rule-book slowdown; general strike; **boycott,** boy-cottage, picketing, picket; buyer's *or* consumer's strike; **lock-out;** revolt 327.4

6 striker, picket; sitdown striker; holdout <nf>

7 <strike enforcer> **picket; goon** <nf>, strong-arm man; flying squadron *or* squad, goon squad <nf>

8 strikebreaker, scab *and* **rat** *and* **fink** *and* scissorbill <nf>, goon, **blackleg** <Brit>

VERBS **9 organize, unionize;** bargain, bargain collectively; arbitrate; submit to arbitration

10 strike, go on strike, go out, walk, walk out; hit the bricks <nf>, shut it down; slow down; sit down; **boycott;** picket; hold out <nf>; **lock out;** revolt 327.7

11 break a strike; scab *and* **rat** *and* **fink** <nf>, **blackleg** <Brit>

728 MONEY

NOUNS **1 money, currency, legal tender, medium of exchange,** circulating medium, sterling <Brit>,

cash, hard cash, cold cash; specie, coinage, mintage, coin of the realm, gold; **silver;** dollars; pounds, shillings, and pence; **the wherewithal,** the wherewith; lucre, **filthy lucre** <nf>, the almighty dollar, pelf, root of all evil, mammon; **hard currency,** soft currency; fractional currency; managed currency; necessity money, scrip, emergency money; monetary unit, monetary denomination

2 <nf terms> **dough, bread, jack, kale,** bucks, scratch, change, mazuma, mopus, gelt, gilt, coin, spondulicks, oof, ooftish, wampum, possibles, moolah, boodle, blunt, dinero, do-re-mi, **sugar,** brass, tin, rocks, simoleons, shekels, berries, chips, **bucks,** green, green stuff, the needful, grease, ointment, palm oil, gravy, cabbage, lettuce, whip-out, the necessary, loot

3 **wampum,** wampumpeag, peag, sewan, roanoke, shell money; cowrie

4 **specie,** hard money; coinage; coin, piece, piece of money, piece of silver or gold; roll of coins, rouleau; **gold piece;** ten-dollar gold piece, eagle; five-dollar gold piece, half eagle; twenty-dollar gold piece, double eagle; guinea, sovereign, pound sovereign, crown, half crown; doubloon; ducat; napoleon, louis d'or; moidore

5 **paper money; cash; bill,** dollar bill, etc; **note,** negotiable note or instrument, legal-tender note; **bank note,** bill of exchange, Federal Reserve note; national bank note; government note, treasury note; silver certificate; gold certificate; scrip; fractional note, shinplaster <nf>; fiat money, assignat

6 <nf terms> **folding money, green stuff,** the long green, folding green, lean green, mint leaves, lettuce, greenbacks, frogskins, skins

7 <US denominations> mill; cent, penny, copper, red cent <nf>; five cents, nickel; ten cents, dime; twenty-five cents, quarter, two bits <nf>; fifty cents, half-dollar, four bits <nf>; dollar, dollar bill; buck and smacker and frogskin and fish and skin <nf>; silver dollar, beau dollar <old>, cartwheel and iron man <nf>; two-dollar bill, two-spot <nf>; five-dollar bill; fiver and five-spot and fin <nf>; ten-dollar bill; tenner and ten-spot and sawbuck <nf>; twenty-dollar bill, double sawbuck <nf>; fifty-dollar bill, half a C <nf>; hundred-dollar bill; C and C-note and century and bill <nf>; five hundred dollars, half grand <nf>, five-hundred-dollar bill, half G <nf>; thousand dollars, G and grand <nf>, thousand-dollar bill, G-note and yard and big one <nf>

8 <British denominations> mite; farthing; halfpenny or ha'penny, bawbee <nf>, mag or meg <nf>; penny; pence, p; new pence, np; two-pence

or tuppence; threepence or thrippence, threepenny bit or piece; fourpence, fourpenny, groat; sixpence, tanner <nf>; teston; shilling, bob <nf>; florin; half crown, half-dollar <nf>; crown, dollar <nf>; pound, quid <nf>; guinea; fiver <£5>, tenner <£10>, pony <£25>, monkey <£500>, plum <£100,000>, marigold <£1,000,000> <nf>

9 **foreign money,** foreign denominations; **convertibility, foreign exchange;** rate of exchange or exchange rate; parity of exchange; agio

10 **counterfeit,** counterfeit money, funny or phony or bogus money <nf>, false or bad money, queer <nf>, base coin, green goods <nf>; **forgery,** bad check, rubber check and bounced check and kite <nf>

11 **negotiable instrument** or **paper,** commercial paper, paper, bill; **bill of exchange,** bill of draft; certificate, certificate of deposit or CD; **check,** cheque <Brit>; blank check; bank check, teller's check; treasury check; cashier's check, certified check; traveler's check or banker's check; letter of credit, commercial letter of credit; **money order** or MO; postal order or postoffice order <Brit>; draft, warrant, voucher, debenture; **promissory note, note, IOU;** note of hand; credit note; acceptance, acceptance bill, bank acceptance, trade acceptance; due bill; demand bill, sight bill, demand draft, sight draft; time bill, time draft; exchequer bill or treasury bill <Brit>; checkbook

12 **token, counter,** slug; **scrip, coupon; check, ticket,** tag; hat check, baggage check

13 **sum,** amount of money; round sum, lump sum

14 **funds, finances, moneys,** exchequer, purse, budget, pocket; treasury, treasure, substance, **assets,** resources, total assets, worth, net worth, **pecuniary resources, means,** available means or resources or funds, cash flow, wherewithal, command of money; balance; pool, **fund, kitty** <nf>, petty cash; war chest; checking account, bank account; Swiss bank account, unnumbered or unregistered bank account; reserves, cash reserves; savings, savings account, nest egg <nf>; life savings; bottom dollar <nf>; automated teller machine or ATM

15 **capital, fund;** moneyed capital; principal, corpus; circulating capital, floating capital; fixed capital, working capital, equity capital, **risk** or **venture capital;** capital structure; capital gains distribution; capitalization

16 **money market,** supply of short-term funds; tight money, cheap money; **borrowing** 621; **lending** 620; discounting, note discounting, note shaving, dealing in commercial paper

17 **bankroll;** roll or wad <nf>

18 **cash, ready money** or **cash,** the ready <nf>,

available funds, money in hand, cash in hand, balance in hand, immediate resources, **liquid assets,** cash supply, **cash flow;** treasury

19 **petty cash, pocket money, pin money,** spending money, mad money, cheddar <nf>, **change,** small change, pocket change; nickels and dimes *and* chicken feed *and* peanuts <nf>, pittance

20 precious metals; **gold,** yellow stuff <nf>; nugget, gold nugget; **silver, copper, nickel,** coin gold *or* silver; bullion, ingot, bar

21 standard of value, gold standard, silver standard; monometallism, bimetallism; money of account

22 <science of coins> **numismatics,** numismatology; numismatist, numismatologist

23 monetization; issuance, circulation; remonetization; demonetization; revaluation, devaluation

24 coining, coinage, mintage, striking, stamping; **counterfeiting, forgery;** coin-clipping

25 coiner, minter, mintmaster, moneyer; **counterfeiter, forger;** coin-clipper

VERBS 26 monetize; **issue,** utter, **circulate;** remonetize, reissue; demonetize; revalue, devalue, devaluate

27 discount, discount notes, deal in commercial paper, shave; borrow, lend 620.5

28 coin, mint; print, stamp; **counterfeit, forge;** utter, pass *or* shove the queer <nf>; pass a bad check, kite a check

29 **cash,** cash in <nf>, liquidate, convert into cash, realize

ADJS 30 **monetary, pecuniary,** nummary, nummular, **financial,** fiduciary; capital; fiscal; sumptuary; numismatic; sterling

31 convertible, liquid, negotiable

729 FINANCE, INVESTMENT

NOUNS 1 **finance, finances, money matters;** world of finance, financial world, financial industry, **high finance,** investment banking, international banking, Wall Street banking, Lombard Street; the gnomes of Zurich; economics 731; purse strings

2 **financing, funding, backing,** financial backing, **sponsorship, patronization,** support, financial support; **stake** *and* **grubstake** <nf>; subsidy 478.8; **capitalizing,** capitalization, provision of capital; deficit financing

3 personal finance; bank account, savings account, checking account; telebanking; budget; pension, 401K, Individual Retirement Account *or* IRA, Keogh plan

4 **investment, venture, risk,** plunge <nf>, speculation; prime investment; ethical *or*

conscience investment; money market, mutual fund, stock market, bond market; **divestment,** disinvestment

5 **banking,** money dealing, money changing; investment banking; banking industry

6 **financial condition,** state of the exchequer; **credit rating,** Dun & Bradstreet rating

7 **solvency,** soundness, solidity; credit standing, creditworthiness; unindebtedness

8 **crisis,** financial crisis; dollar crisis, dollar gap

9 **financier,** moneyman, **capitalist,** finance capitalist; Wall Streeter; investor; financial expert, economist, authority on money and banking; international banker

10 **financer, backer,** funder, **sponsor, patron, supporter,** angel <nf>, Maecenas; cash cow *and* staker *and* grubstaker <nf>, money-maker, money-spinner, meal ticket <nf>; **fundraiser**

11 **banker, money dealer,** moneymonger; money broker; discounter, note broker, bill broker <Brit>; moneylender 620.3; money changer, cambist; investment banker; bank president, bank manager, bank officer, loan officer, trust officer, banking executive; bank clerk, cashier, teller

12 **treasurer,** financial officer, bursar, purser, purse bearer, **cashier,** cashkeeper; accountant, auditor, controller *or* comptroller, bookkeeper; chamberlain, curator, steward, trustee; depositary, depository; receiver, liquidator; **paymaster;** Secretary of the Treasury, Chancellor of the Exchequer

13 **treasury,** treasure-house; subtreasury; **depository,** repository; storehouse 386.6; gold depository, Fort Knox; **strongbox, safe,** money chest, **coffer, locker, chest;** piggy bank, penny bank, bank; **vault,** strong room; safe-deposit *or* safety-deposit box *or* vault; cashbox, coin box, cash register, **till;** bursary; exchequer, fisc; **public treasury,** public funds, taxpayer funds *or* money, pork barrel, public crib *or* trough *or* till <nf>

14 **bank,** banking house, lending institution, savings institution; automated teller machine *or* ATM, cash machine; **central bank,** Bank of England *or* the Old Lady of Threadneedle Street, Bank of France; Federal Reserve Bank *or* System; World Bank, International Monetary Fund; clearing house

15 **purse, wallet, pocketbook, bag, handbag,** clutch, shoulder bag, porte-monnaie, **billfold,** money belt, money clip, poke <nf>, **pocket;** fanny pack; moneybag, purse strings

VERBS 16 **finance, back, fund, sponsor, patronize, support,** provide for, capitalize, provide capital *or* money for, pay for, bankroll <nf>, angel <nf>, put up the money, hold the purse strings; **stake** *or* grubstake <nf>; subsidize 478.19; set up, set up in business; refinance

17 **invest,** place, put, sink; **risk, venture;** make an investment, lay out money, place out *or* put out at interest; reinvest, roll over, plow back into <nf>; **invest in, put money in,** sink money in, pour money into, tie up one's money in; buy in *or* into, buy a piece *or* share of; financier; plunge <nf>, speculate 737.23; play the big board, play the stock exchange

ADJS 18 **solvent, sound,** substantial, solid, good, sound as a dollar, creditworthy; **able to pay,** good for, unindebted 624.23, out of the hole *or* the red

19 **insolvent,** unsound, indebted 623.8

20 financial, monetary, fiscal, pecuniary, economic; bull, bear

730 BUSINESSMAN, MERCHANT

NOUNS 1 **businessman,** businesswoman, businessperson, businesspeople; enterpriser, entrepreneur, man of commerce; small *or* little businessman; big businessman, magnate, tycoon <nf>, baron, king, top executive, business leader; director, manager 574.1; big boss; **industrialist,** captain of industry; banker, financier; robber baron; intrapreneur

2 **merchant,** merchandiser, marketer, **trader,** trafficker, **dealer,** monger, chandler; **tradesman,** tradeswoman; **storekeeper, shopkeeper;** regrater; **wholesaler,** jobber, middleman; importer, exporter; **distributor; retailer,** retail merchant, retail dealer *or* seller; **dealership, distributorship;** franchise; concession

3 **salesman,** seller, salesperson, salesclerk; **saleswoman,** saleslady, salesgirl; **clerk,** shop clerk, store clerk, shop assistant; floorwalker; **agent, sales agent,** selling agent; sales engineer; sales manager; salespeople, sales force, sales personnel; scalper *and* ticket scalper <nf>

4 **traveling salesman, traveler, commercial traveler,** traveling agent, traveling man *or* woman, road warrior, knight of the road, bagman <Brit>, drummer <old>; detail man; door-to-door salesman, canvasser

5 **vendor, peddler, huckster, hawker,** butcher <old>, higgler, cadger <Scot>, colporteur, chapman <Brit>; cheap-jack *and* cheap-john <nf>; coster *or* costermonger <Brit>; sidewalk salesman

6 **solicitor,** canvasser

7 <nf terms> tout, touter, **pitch-man** *or* **-woman** *or* person, barker, spieler, ballyhooer, **ballyhoo man**

8 **auctioneer,** auction agent

9 **broker,** note broker, bill broker <Brit>, discount broker, cotton broker, hotel broker, insurance broker, mortgage broker, diamond broker, furniture broker, ship broker, grain broker; stockbroker 737.10; pawnbroker 620.3; money broker, money changer, cambist; land broker, real estate broker, realtor, real estate agent, estate agent <Brit>

10 **ragman,** old-clothesman, rag-and-bone man <Brit>; **junkman,** junk dealer

11 **tradesmen, tradespeople,** tradesfolk, **merchantry**

ADJS 12 **business, commercial,** mercantile; entrepreneurial; auctionary

731 COMMERCE, ECONOMICS

NOUNS 1 **commerce, trade, traffic,** truck, intercourse, **dealing, dealings; business,** business dealings *or* affairs *or* relations, commercial affairs *or* relations; the business world, the world of trade *or* commerce, the marketplace, marketspace; merchantry, mercantile business; **market,** marketing, state of the market, buyers' market, sellers' market; **industry** 725.4; big business, small business; fair trade, free trade, reciprocal trade, unilateral trade, multilateral trade; most favored nation; balance of trade; restraint of trade; market leader; market indicator

2 **trade, trading, doing business, trafficking;** barter, bartering, **exchange,** interchange, swapping <nf>; give-and-take, horse trading <nf>, **dealing, deal-making,** wheeling and dealing <nf>; **buying and selling; wholesaling,** jobbing, brokerage, agency; **retailing,** merchandising 734.2; commercial trade, export and import

3 **negotiation, bargaining, haggling,** higgling, **dickering, chaffering,** chaffer, haggle; hacking out *or* working out *or* hammering out a deal, coming to terms; horse trading; collective bargaining, package bargaining, pattern bargaining

4 **transaction,** business *or* commercial transaction, **deal,** business deal, negotiation <old>, operation, turn; package deal

5 **bargain, deal** <nf>, dicker; agreement, contract; **trade, swap** <nf>; horse trade <nf>; trade-in; blind bargain, pig in a poke; hard bargain

6 **custom,** customers, clientele, patronage, patrons, trade; **goodwill,** repute, good name

7 **economy, economic system, market,** capitalist *or* capitalistic economy, free-enterprise *or* free-trade *or* private-enterprise economy, market economy, free-market economy, socialist *or* socialistic economy, collectivized economy; hot *or* overheated economy; healthy *or* sound economy, weak economy; **gross national product** *or* **GNP;** economic sector, public sector, private sector; economic self-sufficiency, autarky; economic

policy, fiscal policy, monetary policy; microeconomics, macroeconomics; privatization, nationalization, denationalization, supply-side economics; economic theory; open market

8 standard of living, standard of life, standard of comfort; real wages, take-home pay *or* take-home; **cost of living;** cost-of-living index, consumer price index

9 economic indicator, econometrics; gross national product *or* GNP, price index, consumer price index, retail price index, cost-of-living index; unemployment rate, national debt, budget deficit

10 business cycle, economic cycle, business fluctuations; peak, peaking; low, bottoming out <nf>; prosperity, boom <nf>; boomlet *or* miniboom; crisis, **recession, depression,** slow-down, cooling off, slump *and* bust <nf>, downturn, downtick <nf>; upturn, uptick <nf>, expanding economy, recovery; **growth,** economic growth, business growth, high growth rate, expansion, market expansion, **economic expansion; trade cycle;** trade deficit, trade gap, balance of payments; **monetary cycle; inflation,** deflation, stagflation

11 economics, eco *or* econ <nf>, economic science, the dismal science; political economy; dynamic economics; theoretical economics, plutology; classical economics, Keynesian economics, Keynesianism; supply side economics; econometrics; economism, economic determinism

12 economist, economic expert *or* authority; political economist

13 commercialism, mercantilism; industrialism; mass marketing, guerrilla marketing

14 commercialization; industrialization

VERBS **15 trade, deal, traffic, truck, buy and sell, do business; barter; exchange,** change, interchange, give in exchange, take in exchange, **swap** <nf>, switch; swap horses *and* horse-trade <nf>; trade off; trade in; trade sight unseen, make a blind bargain, sell a pig in a poke; marketize; **ply one's trade** 724.12

16 deal in, trade in, traffic in, handle, carry, be in; market, merchandise, **sell,** retail, wholesale, job

17 trade with, deal with, traffic with, traffic in, do business with, have dealings with, have truck with, transact business with; frequent as a customer, shop at, trade at, **patronize,** take one's business *or* trade to; open an account with, have an account with; export, import; market, merchandise

18 bargain, drive a bargain, negotiate, haggle, higgle, chaffer, huckster, **deal, dicker,** barter, make a deal, do a deal <Brit>, hack out *or* work out *or* hammer out a deal, do a deal; **bid,** bid for,

cheapen, beat down; underbid, outbid; drive a hard bargain; hold out for

19 strike a bargain, make a bargain, make a dicker, **make a deal,** get oneself a deal, put through a deal, shake hands, shake on it <nf>; bargain for, agree to; **come to terms** 332.10; be a bargain, be a go *and* be a deal <nf>, be on <nf>; network

20 put on a business basis *or* footing, make businesslike; commercialize; industrialize

21 <adjust the economy> cool *or* cool off the economy; heat *or* heat up the economy

ADJS **22 commercial, business, trade,** trading, **mercantile,** merchant; commercialistic, mercantilistic; industrial; wholesale, retail

22 economic, fiscal, monetary, pecuniary, financial, budgetary; inflationary, deflationary; socio-economic, politico-economic *or* -economical

732 ILLICIT BUSINESS

NOUNS **1** illicit business, illegitimate business, illegal operations, illegal commerce *or* traffic, shady dealings, **racket** <nf>; **the rackets** <nf>, the syndicate, **organized crime, Mafia,** Cosa Nostra; **black market,** gray market; **drug** *or* **narcotics traffic;** narcoterrorism; **prostitution,** streetwalking; **pimping,** traffic in women, white slavery; usury 623.3, loan-sharking *and* shylocking <nf>; protection racket; bootlegging, moon-shining <nf>; gambling 759.1; spam, computer virus *or* worm

2 smuggling, contrabandage, contraband; narcotics smuggling, dope smuggling <nf>, jewel smuggling, cigarette smuggling; gunrunning, rumrunning

3 contraband, smuggled goods; narcotics, drugs, dope <nf>, jewels, cigarettes; bootleg liquor; stolen goods *or* property, hot goods *or* items <nf>

4 racketeer; Mafioso; **black marketeer,** gray marketeer; bootlegger, moonshiner <nf>; pusher *and* dealer <nf>, narcotics *or* dope *or* drug pusher <nf>; **drug lord;** Medellin cartel

5 smuggler, contrabandist, runner; drug smuggler, mule <nf>; gunrunner, rumrunner

6 fence, receiver, **receiver of stolen goods,** swagman *and* swagsman <nf>, bagman, bagwoman

VERBS **7** <deal in illicit goods> push *and* shove <nf>; **sell under the counter; black-market,** black-marketeer; bootleg, moonshine <nf>; fence <nf>; spam

8 smuggle, run, sneak

733 PURCHASE

NOUNS **1 purchase, buying, purchasing,** acquisition; **shopping, marketing;** shopping around, comparison shopping; window-shopping; impulse buying; shopping spree, retail therapy; repurchase, rebuying; mail-order buying, catalog shopping; teleshopping, home shopping, online shopping; installment buying, hire purchase <Brit>; layaway purchase; **buying up,** cornering, coemption <old>; **buying** or **purchasing power; consumerism;** consumer society, consumer sovereignty, consumer power, acquisitive society; retail or consumer price index; wholesale price index; shopping list

2 **option,** first option, **first refusal,** refusal, preemption, right of preemption, prior right of purchase

3 **market,** public, purchasing public, target audience; urban market, rural market, youth market, suburban market, etc; **clientele, customers,** clientage, **patronage, custom,** trade; carriage trade; demand, consumer demand

4 **customer, client; patron,** patronizer <nf>, regular customer or buyer, regular; clientele; **prospect;** mark or sucker <nf>

5 **buyer,** purchaser, emptor, **consumer,** vendee; **shopper,** marketer; shopaholic; bargain-hunter; bidder; window-shopper, browser; purchasing agent, customer agent, personal shopper

6 by-bidder, decoy, come-on man and shill <nf>

VERBS 7 **purchase, buy,** procure, make or complete a purchase, make a buy, make a deal for, blow oneself to <nf>; **buy up,** regrate, **corner,** monopolize, engross, hoard; buy out; buy in, buy into, buy a piece of; repurchase, rebuy, buy back; buy on credit, buy on the installment plan, charge; buy sight unseen or blind; trade up

8 **shop, market, go shopping,** go marketing; **shop around;** window-shop, comparison-shop, **browse,** graze; impulse-buy; shop till one drops and hit the shops <nf>

9 **bid,** make a bid, offer, offer to buy, make an offer; give the asking price; by-bid, shill <nf>; bid up; bid in

ADJS 10 **purchasing, buying,** in the market; cliental

11 **bought,** store-bought, boughten or store-boughten <nf>, purchased

734 SALE

NOUNS 1 **sale; wholesale, retail; market, demand,** outlet; buyers' market, sellers' market; mass market; conditional sale; tie-in sale, tie-in; turnover; bill of sale; cash sale, cash-and-carry

2 **selling, merchandising, marketing; wholesaling,** jobbing; **retailing;** direct selling; sell-through; telemarketing; mail-order selling, direct-mail selling, catalog selling, direct marketing; viral marketing; television or video selling; online selling, e-commerce; **vending, peddling, hawking, huckstering;** hucksterism; market or marketing research, consumer research, consumer preference study, consumer survey, data warehousing; sales campaign, promotion, sales promotion; **salesmanship,** high-pressure salesmanship, hard sell <nf>, low-pressure salesmanship, soft sell <nf>; cold call; sellout; branding

3 **sale,** sellout, closing-out sale, going-out-of-business sale, inventory-clearance sale, distress sale, fire sale; bazaar; rummage sale, white elephant sale, garage sale, tag sale, yard sale, flea market; tax sale

4 **auction,** auction sale, vendue, outcry, sale at or by auction, sale to the highest bidder; Dutch auction; **auction block, block**

5 **sales talk, sales pitch,** patter; **pitch** or spiel or ballyhoo <nf>

6 **sales resistance,** consumer or buyer resistance

7 **salability,** salableness, commerciality, merchandisability, **marketability,** vendibility

VERBS 8 **sell, merchandise, market,** move, turn over, sell off, make or effect a sale; convert into cash, turn into money; **sell out,** close out; sell up <Brit>; **retail,** sell retail, sell over the counter; **wholesale,** sell wholesale, job, be jobber or wholesaler for; dump, unload, flood the market with, get rid of; sacrifice, sell at a sacrifice or loss; sell off, remainder; resell, sell over; undersell, undercut, cut under; sell short; sell on consignment; telemarket

9 **vend,** dispense, **peddle, hawk, huckster;** tout

10 **put up for sale,** put up, ask bids or offers for, offer for sale, offer at a bargain

11 **auction, auction off, auctioneer,** sell at auction, sell by auction, put up for auction, **put on the block,** bring under the hammer; knock down, sell to the highest bidder

12 **be sold, sell,** bring, realize, sell for; change hands; sell like hotcakes, be in demand

ADJS 13 **sales,** selling, market, **marketing, merchandising, retail,** retailing, wholesale, wholesaling; vending

14 **salable, marketable,** retailable, merchandisable, merchantable, commercial, vendible; in demand

15 **unsalable,** nonsalable, **unmarketable;** on one's hands, on the shelves, not moving, not turning over, unbought, unsold

ADVS 16 **for sale,** to sell, up for sale, in or on the market, in the marts of trade; at a bargain, marked down

17 **at auction,** at outcry, at public auction or outcry, by auction, **on the block,** under the hammer

735 MERCHANDISE

NOUNS **1 merchandise, commodities, wares, goods,** effects, vendibles; **items,** oddments; **consumer goods,** consumer items, retail goods, goods for sale; **stock, stock-in-trade;** staples; **inventory; line,** line of goods; sideline; job lot; mail-order goods, catalog goods; **luxury goods,** high-ticket *or* big-ticket *or* upscale items

2 commodity, ware, vendible, **product, article, item,** article of commerce *or* merchandise; staple, staple item, standard article; special, feature, leader, lead item, loss leader; seconds; drug, drug on the market

3 dry goods, soft goods; textiles; yard goods, white goods, linens, napery; men's wear, ladies' wear, children's wear, infants' wear; sportswear, sporting goods; leatherware, leather goods

4 hard goods, durables, durable goods; fixtures, white goods, **appliances** 385.4; tools and machinery 1040; **hardware,** ironmongery <Brit>; sporting goods, **housewares,** home furnishings, kitchenware; tableware, dinnerware; flatware, hollow ware; metalware, brassware, copperware, silverware, ironware, tinware; woodenware; glassware; chinaware, earthenware, clayware, stoneware, graniteware; enamelware; ovenware

5 furniture 229, furnishings, home furnishings

6 notions, sundries, novelties, knickknacks, odds and ends; toilet goods, toiletries; cosmetics; giftware

7 groceries, grocery <Brit>, food items, edibles, victuals, baked goods, packaged goods, canned goods, tinned goods <Brit>; green goods, **produce,** truck

736 MARKET

<place of trade>

NOUNS **1 market, mart, store, shop,** salon, boutique, wareroom, emporium, house, establishment, *magasin* <Fr>; **retail store; wholesale house, discount store, discount house, outlet store;** warehouse, megastore; mail-order house; **general store,** country store; **department store;** warehouse store, superstore, megastore; **co-op** <nf>, cooperative; **variety store,** variety shop, **dime store; ten-cent store** *or* five-and-ten *or* five-and-dime <nf>, thrift store *or* shop; convenience store, corner store, mom-and-pop store; chain store; concession; **trading post,** post; **supermarket,** grocery store; factory outlet, outlet store

2 marketplace, mart, market, open market, markct overt, agora; **shopping center, shopping plaza** *or* **mall,** plaza, mall, arcade, shopping *or* shop *or* commercial complex; factory outlet center;

warehouse; emporium, rialto; staple; **bazaar, fair,** trade fair, show, auto show, boat show, etc, exposition; flea market, flea fair, street market, farmers' market, fish market, meat market, *marché aux puces* <Fr>; trading post; home shopping, e-commerce *or* electronic commerce

3 booth, stall, stand; newsstand, kiosk, news kiosk; pushcart; roadside stand

4 vending machine, vendor, coin machine, coin-operated machine, slot machine, **automat;** redeemer *or* reverse vending machine

5 salesroom, wareroom; showroom; auction room

6 counter, shopboard <old>; notions counter; showcase; peddler's cart, pushcart

737 STOCK MARKET

NOUNS **1 stock market, the market, Wall Street;** securities market, commodity market; ticker market; open market, competitive market; steady market, strong market, hard *or* stiff market; unsteady market, spotty market; weak market; long market; top-heavy market; market index, stock price index, Dow-Jones Industrial Average

2 active market, brisk market, lively market

3 inactive market, slow market, stagnant market, flat market, tired market, sick market; investors on the sidelines

4 rising market, booming market, buoyant market; **bull market,** bullish market, bullishness

5 declining market, sagging market, retreating market, off market, soft market; **bear market,** bearish market, bearishness; **slump,** sag; break, break in the market; profit-taking, selloff; **crash,** smash

6 rigged market, manipulated market, pegged market, put-up market; **insider trading**

7 stock exchange, exchange, Wall Street, change <Brit>, **stock market,** bourse, **board;** the Exchange, New York Stock Exchange, the Big Board; American Stock Exchange, Amex, curb, curb market, curb exchange; over-the-counter market, telephone market, outside market; third market; exchange floor; commodity exchange, pit, corn pit, wheat pit, etc; quotation board; **ticker,** stock ticker; ticker tape

8 financial district, Wall Street, the Street; Lombard Street

9 stockbrokerage, brokerage, brokerage house, brokerage office; wire house; bucket shop *and* boiler room <nf>

10 stockbroker, sharcbrokcr <Brit>, **brokcr,** jobber, stockjobber, dealer, stock dealer; Wall Streeter; stock-exchange broker, *agent de bourse* <Fr>; floor broker, floor trader, floorman, specialist, market maker; pit man; curb broker; odd-lot dealer; two-dollar broker; day trader, night trader; broker's agent, customer's broker *or* customer's man, registered representative; bond crowd

11 **speculator,** adventurer, operator; big operator, smart operator; **plunger,** gunslinger; scalper; stag <Brit>; lame duck; margin purchaser; **arbitrager** *or* arbitrageur *or* arb <nf>; inside trader

12 **bear,** short, short seller; shorts, short interest, short side; short account, bear account

13 **bull,** long, longs, long interest, long side; long account, bull account

14 **stockholder,** stockowner, **shareholder, shareowner;** bondholder, coupon-clipper <nf>; stockholder of record

15 **stock company,** joint-stock company; issuing company; stock insurance company

16 **trust,** investment company; investment trust, holding company; closed-end investment company, closed-end fund; open-end fund, mutual fund, money-market fund; unit trust <Brit>; load fund, no-load fund, low-load fund, back-end fund; growth fund, income fund, dual purpose fund; trust fund; blind trust

17 **pool,** bear pool, bull pool, blind pool

18 **stockbroking,** brokerage, stockbrokerage, jobbing, stockjobbing, stockjobbery, stock dealing; bucketing, legal bucketing

19 **trading,** stock-market trading, market-trading; computer *or* programmed selling; playing the market <nf>; **speculation,** stockjobbing, stockjobbery; **venture,** flutter; flier, plunge; scalping; liquidation, profit taking; **arbitrage,** arbitraging; buying in, covering shorts; short sale; spot sale; round trade *or* transaction, turn; risk *or* venture capital, equity capital; money-market trading, foreign-exchange trading, agiotage; **buyout, takeover,** hostile takeover, takeover bid; leveraged buyout; greenmail; **leverage**

20 **manipulation, rigging; raid,** bear raid, bull raid; **corner,** corner in, corner on the market, monopoly; washing, washed *or* wash sale

21 **option,** stock option, right, **put, call,** put and call, right of put and call; straddle, spread; strip; strap

22 **panic,** bear panic, rich man's panic

VERBS 23 **trade, speculate,** venture, operate, **play the market,** buy *or* sell *or* deal in futures; **arbitrage; plunge,** take a flier <nf>; scalp; bucket, bucketshop; stag *or* stag the market <Brit>; trade on margin; pyramid; be long, go long, be long of the market, be on the long side of the market; be short, be short of the market, be on the short side of the market; margin up, apply *or* deposit margin; wait out the market, hold on; be caught short, miss the market, overstay the market; scoop

the market, make a scoop *or* killing *or* bundle *or* pile <nf>

24 **sell,** convert, liquidate; throw on the market, dump, unload; **sell short,** go short, make a short sale; cover one's short, fulfill a short sale; make delivery, clear the trade; close out, sell out, terminate the account

25 manipulate the market, **rig the market;** bear, **bear the market;** bull, **bull the market;** raid the market; hold *or* peg the market; whipsaw; wash sales

26 corner, get a corner on, **corner the market;** monopolize, engross; buy up, absorb

738 SECURITIES

NOUNS 1 **securities** <see list>, stocks and bonds, investment securities; arbitrage, program trading

2 **stock** <see list>, shares <Brit>, equity, equity security, corporate stock; stock split, split; reverse split; stock list; stock ledger, share ledger <Brit>; **holdings, portfolio,** investment portfolio

3 **share, lot;** preference share; dummy share; holding, holdings, stockholding, stockholdings; block; round lot, full lot, even lot, board lot; odd lot, fractional lot

4 **stock certificate,** certificate of stock; street certificate; interim certificate; **coupon**

5 **bond** <see list>; nominal rate, coupon rate, current yield, yield to maturity

6 **issue,** issuance; **flotation;** stock issue, secondary issue; bond issue; poison pill <nf>

7 **dividend;** regular dividend; extra dividend, special dividend, plum *and* melon <nf>; payout ratio; cumulative dividend, accumulated dividends, accrued dividends; interim dividend; cash dividend; stock dividend; optional dividend; scrip dividend; liquidating dividend; phony dividend; **interest** 623.3; **return, yield,** return on investment, payout, payback

8 **assessment,** Irish dividend

9 **price, quotation;** bid-and-asked prices, bid price, asked *or* asking *or* offering price; actual *or* delivery *or* settling price, put price, call price; opening price, closing price; high, low; market price, quoted price, flash price; issue price; fixed price; parity; **par,** issue par; par value, nominal value, face value; stated value; book value; market value; bearish prices, bullish prices; swings, fluctuations; flurry, flutter; rally, decline

10 **margin;** thin margin, shoestring margin; exhaust price

11 <commodities> spots, spot grain, etc; futures, future grain, etc

VERBS 12 **issue, float,** put on the market; issue stock, go public <nf>; float a bond issue

13 **declare a dividend,** cut a melon <nf>

ADVS **14** dividend off, ex dividend; dividend on, cum
dividend; coupon off, ex coupon; coupon on, cum
coupon; warrants off, ex warrants; warrants on,
cum warrants; when issued

15 kinds of securities

active securities
American Depository
   Receipts *or* ADRs
banker's acceptance
callable securities
certificate of accrual on
   treasury securities *or*
   CATS
certificate of deposit *or* CD
convertible securities *or*
   convertibles *or* CVs
corporation securities
debenture *or* certificate of
   indebtedness
digested securities
fixed-income securities
foreign securities
futures contract
gilt-edged securities
government securities
international securities
junior securities
legal securities
liquid yield option notes *or*
   LYONs
listed securities
margined securities
marketable securities
money-market certificate
mortgage-based securities
municipal securities

negotiable securities *or*
   negotiables
noncallable securities
note
obsolete securities
outside securities
outstanding securities
over-the-counter securities
pass-throughs *or* participation certificate
program trading
registered securities
senior securities
separate trading of
   registered interest *and*
   principal securities *or*
   STRIPS
short-term note
speculative securities *or*
   cats and dogs <nf>
stamped securities
treasury bill
treasury bond
treasury certificate
treasury investment
   growth receipts *or* TIGRs
treasury note
undigested securities
unlisted securities
unregistered securities
warrant

16 kinds of stock

active stock
assessable stock
authorized capital stock
blue chip stock *or* blue chip
borrowed stock
capital stock
common stock *or* ordinary
   shares <Brit>
convertible preferred stock
cumulative convertible
   preferred stock
cumulative preferred
   stock
cyclical stock
debenture stock
defensive stock
deferred stock
eighth stock
floating stock
growth stock
guaranteed stock
high-grade stock

hypothecated stock
inactive stock
income stock
industrials *or* rails *or*
   utilities, etc
initial public offering
issued capital stock
letter stock
loaned stock
long stock
new issue
no-par stock
nonassessable stock
nonvoting stock
over-the-counter stock
pale blue chip
participating preferred
   stock
penny stock
preferred stock *or*
   preference stock
   <Brit>

protective stock
quality stock
quarter stock
seasoned stock
short stock
small cap stock
special situation stock
specialty stock

speculative stock
standard stock
ten-share unit stock
treasury stock
unissued capital stock
voting stock
voting-right certificate
watered stock

17 kinds of bond

adjustment bond
annuity bond
appreciation bond
assented bond
asset-backed bond
assumed bond
baby bond
bearer bond
bearer certificate
bond anticipation note
callable bond
collateral trust bond
consolidated annuities *or*
   consols *or* bank
   annuities <Brit>
consolidated stock
convertible bond
convertible debenture
corporate bond
corporation stock <Brit>
coupon bond
current income bond
deep-discount bond
defense bond
deferred bond
definitive bond
discount bond
equipment bond
equipment note
equipment trust
equipment trust bond
equipment trust certificate
extended bond
Fannie Mae bond
Federal Agency bond
FICO bond
first mortgage bond *or* first
foreign bond
Freddie Mac bond
general mortgage bond
general obligation bond
gilt-edged bond
Ginnie Mae bond
government bond
guaranteed bond
high-grade bond
high-yield bond *or* junk
   bond <nf>
income bond
indenture

installment bond
interchangeable bond
interim bond
joint bond
junk bond
Liberty bond
long-term bond
mortgage-backed bond
municipal bond
negotiable bond
noncallable bond
nonnegotiable bond
optional bond
par bond
participating bond
perpetual bond
premium bond
purchase money bond
redeemable bond
refunding bond
registered bond
registered certificate
revenue bond
savings bond
second mortgage bond *or*
   second
secured bond
serial bond
Series EE bond
Series HH bond
short-term bond
sinking-fund bond
small bond
state bond
subordinated bond
tax anticipation note
tax-exempt bond
tax-free bond
treasury bill
treasury bond
treasury note
trust indenture
trustee mortgage bond
turnpike bond
unsecured bond
voting bond
war bond
Z-bond *or* accrual bond *or*
   accretion bond
zero coupon bond

18 kinds of mutual fund

aggressive growth mutual fund
assest management mutual fund
balanced mutual fund
bond mutual fund
capital appreciation mutual fund
closed-end mutual fund
corporate bond mutual fund
double tax-exempt bond mutual fund
equity mutual fund
equity-income mutual fund
federal municipal bond mutual fund
federal municipal money market mutual fund
fixed-income mutual fund
global bond mutual fund
global mutual fund
government bond mutual fund
growth and Income mutual fund
growth mutual fund
index mutual fund
international mutual fund
large-cap mutual fund
load mutual fund
mid-cap mutual fund
money market mutual fund
mutual funds of mutual fund
no-load mutual fund
small-cap mutual fund
speciality or Sector mutual fund
state municipal bond mutual fund
state municipal money market mutual fund
state tax-exempt income mutual fund
stock mutual fund
tax-exempt income mutual fund
tax-exempt money market fund
triple tax-exempt bond mutual fund
U.S. Government money market fund

739 WORKPLACE

NOUNS **1 workplace,** worksite, **workshop, shop;** shop floor, workspace, working space, work area, loft; **bench,** workbench, worktable; counter, worktop; **work station; desk,** desktop; **workroom; studio,** *atelier* <Fr>, library; parlor, beauty parlor, funeral parlor, etc; **establishment, facility,** installation; **company,** institution, house, firm, concern, agency, organization, **corporation; financial institution, stock exchange** 737.7, **bank** 729.14; **market, store** 736.1, mall, shopping mall, megamall, retail park; **restaurant, eating place** 8.17; hotel, motel; gas station; construction site, building site; dockyard, shipyard; farm, ranch, nursery; power station; government office; office park, science park; virtual company

2 hive, hive of industry, beehive; factory *or* mill *or* manufacturing town; hub of industry, center of manufacture, industrial town

3 plant, factory, works, manufactory <old>, manufacturing plant, installation, shop floor, job site, *usine* <Fr>; main plant, assembly plant, subassembly plant, feeder plant; foreign-owned plant, transplant; push-button plant, automated *or* cybernated *or* automatic *or* robot factory; assembly *or* production line; defense plant, munitions plant, armory, arsenal; **power plant** 1032.19; atomic energy plant; **machine shop; mill,** sawmill, flour mill, etc; **yard,** yards, railroad yard, brickyard, shipyard, dockyard, boatyard; rope-walk; mint; refinery, oil refinery, sugar refinery, etc; distillery, brewery, winery; boilery; bindery, bookbindery; packinghouse; cannery; dairy, creamery; pottery; tannery; sweatshop; **factory district,** industrial zone *or* area, industrial park, industrial estate <Brit>; factory belt, manufacturing quarter; enterprise zone

4 foundry, works, metalworks; steelworks, steelyard, steel mill; refinery, forge, furnace, bloomery; smelter; smithy, smithery, stithy, blacksmith shop *or* blacksmith's shop; brickworks; quarry, mine, colliery, coal mine; mint

5 repair shop, fix-it shop <nf>; **garage;** roundhouse; hangar

6 laboratory, lab <nf>; research laboratory, research installation *or* facility *or* center *or* park

7 office, shop <nf>; home *or* head *or* main office, headquarters, executive office, corporate *or* company headquarters; office suite, executive suite; chambers <chiefly Brit>; cubicle, closet, cabinet <old>, **study,** den, carrell; **embassy,** consulate, legation, chancery, chancellery; box office, booking office, ticket office; branch, branch office, local office, subsidiary office, bureau, business house; office *or* executive park; virtual office

8 <home workplace> **home office,** office, den, study; kitchen, laundry room, sewing room, workbench

740 WEAVING

NOUNS **1 weaving,** weave, warpage, weftage, warp and woof *or* weft, texture, tissue; **fabric, web,** webbing; **interweaving,** interweavement, intertexture; **interlacing,** interlacement, interlacery; crisscross; **intertwining,** intertwinement; intertieing, interknitting, interthreading, intertwisting; **lacing,** enlacement; **twining,** entwining, entwinement; wreathing, knitting, twisting; **braiding,** plaiting, plashing

2 braid, plait, pigtail, **wreath,** wreathwork

3 warp; woof, weft, filling; shoot, pick

4 weaver, interlacer, webster <old>, knitter, spinner; weaverbird, weaver finch, whirligig beetle

5 loom, weaver; hand loom; Navajo loom; knitting machine; spinning wheel; shuttle, distaff

VERBS **6 weave,** loom, tissue; **interweave, interlace, intertwine,** interknit, interthread, intertissue, intertie, intertwist; inweave, intort; web, net; **lace,** enlace; **twine,** entwine; **braid,** plait, pleach, **wreathe,** raddle, **knit,** twist, mat, wattle;

crisscross; twill, loop, noose; splice; felt, mat, brush, nap; interconnect

ADJS **7 woven,** loomed, textile; **interwoven, interlaced,** interthreaded, **intertwined,** interknit, intertissued, intertied, intertwisted; handwoven; **laced,** enlaced; **wreathed,** fretted, raddled, knit, knitted; **twined,** entwined; **braided,** plaited, platted, pleached; hooked; webbed; loomed

8 weaving, twining, entwining; **intertwining, interlacing,** interweaving, crosswise, crossways

741 SEWING

NOUNS **1 sewing, needlework,** stitchery, stitching; mending, basting, darning, hemming, quilting, embroidery, cross-stitching, needlepoint; **fancywork;** tailoring, garment making 5.32; suture

2 sewer, needleworker, seamstress, sempstress, needlewoman; seamster, sempster, **tailor,** needleman <old>, needler <Brit>; embroiderer, embroideress; knitter; garmentmaker 5.34

3 sewing machine, sewer, embroidery hoop

VERBS **4 sew, stitch,** needle; mend, baste; stitch up, sew up; **tailor**

742 CERAMICS

NOUNS **1 ceramics** <see list>, **pottery;** potting

2 ceramic ware, ceramics; pottery, crockery; china, porcelain; enamelware; refractory, cement; bisque, biscuit; pot, crock, vase, urn, jug, bowl; tile, tiling; brick, firebrick, refractory brick, adobe; glass 1029.2; industrial ceramics; ceramist, ceramicist, potter

3 <materials> **clay;** potter's clay or earth, fireclay, refractory clay; argil, adobe, terra cotta; porcelain clay, kaolin, china clay, china stone, marl, feldspar, petuntze or petuntse; flux; slip; glaze, overglaze, underglaze; crackle

4 potter's wheel, wheel; kick wheel, pedal wheel, hand-turned wheel, power wheel

5 kiln, oven, stove, furnace; acid kiln, brick kiln, cement kiln, enamel kiln, muffle kiln, limekiln, bottle kiln, beehive kiln, reverberatory, reverberatory kiln; pyrometer, pyrometric cone, Seger cone

VERBS **6** pot, shape, **throw,** throw or turn a pot; cast, mold; **fire,** bake; glaze

ADJS **7 ceramic,** earthen, clay, enamel, china, porcelain; fired, baked, glazed; refractory; hand-turned, hand-painted, thrown; industrial

8 ceramics

agateware	Allervale pottery
Albion ware	Aretine ware

Arita ware
Arretine ware or terra sigillata
basalt or basaltes or basaltware
Belleek ware
Berlin ware
biscuit or bisque ware
blackware
.blue and white ware
bone china
Castleford ware
Castor ware
champlevé or champlevé enamel
Chelsea porcelain
china or chinaware
Ch'ing porcelain
clayware
cloisonné or cloisonné enamel
Coalport
cottage china
crackle or crackleware
creamware
crockery
crouch ware
Crown Derby ware
Dedham pottery
delft or delftware
Derby porcelain
Doulton ware
Dresden china
earthenware
eggshell porcelain
enamel or enamelware
faience
glassware
glazed ware
gombroon
hard-paste porcelain
Hirado ware
Hizen porcelain
Imari ware
industrial ceramics
ironstone or ironstone china
istoriato ware
Jackfield ware
jasper or jasperware
Kakiemon ware
Kinkozan ware
lambrequin
Leeds pottery

Limoges or Limoges ware
Lowestoft ware
lusterware or luster pottery
majolica
Meissen ware
mezza-majolica
Nabeshima ware
Nanking ware
Old Worcester ware
ovenware
Palissy ware
Parian ware
Pennsylvania Dutch or German ware
porcelain
porcelain enamel
queensware
redware
refractory ware
Rockingham ware
Royal Copenhagen porcelain
Royal Doulton porcelain
Royal Worcester porcelain
salt-glazed ware
Samian ware
sanda ware
Satsuma ware
semiporcelain
Sèvres or Sèvres ware
Seto ware
slipware
soft-paste porcelain
Spode
spongeware
Staffordshire or Staffordshire ware
stoneware
Sung ware
T'ang ware
terra cotta
terra sigillata or Arretine ware
Tiffany glass
ting ware or ting yao
Toft ware
tulip ware
Wedgwood or Wedgwood ware
whiteware or white pottery
willowware
Worcester ware
yi-hsing ware or yi-hsing yao

743 AMUSEMENT

NOUNS **1 amusement, entertainment, diversion,** solace, divertisement, *divertissement* <Fr>, recreation, relaxation, regalement; **pastime,** *passe-temps* <Fr>; **mirth** 109.5; **pleasure, enjoyment** 95.1; clubbing

2 fun, action <nf>; funmaking, fun and games, **play, sport,** game; **good time,** lovely time, pleasant time; big time *and* **high time** *and* high old time <nf>, picnic *and* laughs *and* lots of laughs *and* ball <nf>, great fun, time of one's life; a short life and a merry one; wild oats

3 festivity, merrymaking, merriment, gaiety, jollity, jollification <nf>, **joviality, conviviality,** whoopee *and* hoopla <nf>; larking <nf>, cavorting, skylarking, racketing, mafficking <Brit nf>, holiday-making; **revelry,** revelment, reveling, revels; nightlife

4 festival, festivity, festive occasion, *fiesta* <Sp>, **fete,** gala, **gala affair, blowout** <nf>, **jamboree** <nf>; **high jinks,** do, great doings <nf>; *fête champêtre* <Fr>; **feast, banquet** 8.9; picnic 8.6; party 582.11; waygoose <Brit nf>, wayzgoose; fair, carnival; kermis; Oktoberfest <Ger>; Mardi Gras; Saturnalia; harvest festival, harvest home <Brit>; **field day;** gala day, feria

5 frolic, play, romp, rollick, frisk, gambol, caper, dido <nf>

6 revel, lark, escapade, ploy; **celebration** 487; **party** 582.11; **spree, bout, fling,** wingding *and* randan <nf>, randy <Scot>; **carouse, drinking bout** 88.5

7 round of pleasure, mad round, **whirl,** merry-go-round, the rounds, the dizzy rounds

8 sports 744; **athletics,** agonistics; athleticism

9 game; card game; board game; parlor game; role-playing game; children's game; computer game, video game; gambling game; table game; word game, Scrabble <tm>; indoor game, outdoor game; **play; contest** 457.3; race 457.12; **event, meet; bout, match,** go <nf>; gambling 759

10 tournament, tourney, gymkhana, **field day;** rally; **regatta**

11 playground, playscape; field, athletic field, playing field; football field, gridiron; baseball field, diamond; infield, outfield; soccer field; archery ground, cricket ground, polo ground, croquet ground *or* lawn, bowling green; bowling alley; links, golf links, golf course; fairway, putting green; **gymnasium,** gym <nf>; **court,** badminton court, basketball court, tennis court, racket court, squash court; billiard parlor, poolroom, pool hall; racecourse, track, course turf, oval; stretch; rink, glaciarium, ice rink, skating rink; skateboard park; **playroom** 197.12

12 swimming pool, pool, swimming bath <Brit>, plunge, plunge bath, natatorium; swimming hole; wading pool, kiddy pool; lap pool; wave pool; infinity pool

13 entertainment; entertainment industry, show business, show biz <nf>; **theater;** dinner theatre; **cabaret, tavern, roadhouse;** café dansant, chantant; big dance <nf>; nightclub, night spot *or* nitery *and* hot spot <nf>, *boîte* and *boîte de nuit* <Fr>; juke joint <nf>, discothèque or disco <nf>; dance hall, dancing pavilion, ballroom, dance floor; casino; **resort** 228.27

14 park, public park, pleasure garden *or* ground, pleasance, paradise, common, commons, playground; **amusement park,** Tivoli, fun fair, carnival; fairground; **theme park,** safari park

15 ride, merry-go-round, carousel, roundabout, ride, whirligig, whip, flying horses; Ferris wheel; seesaw, teeter-totter; slide; swing; roller coaster; chutes, chute-the-chute; funhouse, arcade, video arcade; -drome

16 toy, plaything, sport; bauble, knickknack, gimcrack, gewgaw, kickshaw, whim-wham, trinket; **doll,** action figure, paper doll, golliwog, rag doll, stuffed animal, teddy bear, puppet, glove puppet, marionette, toy soldier, tin soldier; dollhouse, doll carriage; hobbyhorse, cockhorse, rocking horse; hoop, hula hoop; top, spinning top, teetotum; pinwheel; jack-in-the-box; jacks, jackstones; jackstraws, pick-up sticks; blocks; checkerboard, chessboard; marble, mig, agate, steelie, taw; pop-gun, BB gun, air gun; slingshot, catapult <Brit>; ball; blocks, building blocks

17 chessman, man, piece; **bishop, knight, king, queen, pawn, rook** or castle

18 player, frolicker, frisker, **funmaker,** funster, gamboler; **pleasure-seeker,** pleasurer, pleasurist, **playboy** <nf>; **reveler, celebrant, merrymaker,** rollicker, skylarker, **carouser,** cutup <nf>; contestant 452.2

19 athlete, jock <nf>, **player,** sportsman, sportswoman, contender, amateur athlete, professional athlete, competitor, sportsman; letter man

20 master of ceremonies, MC *or* **emcee** <nf>, compère <Brit>, marshal; **toastmaster;** host, master of the revels, revel master; Lord of Misrule, Abbot of Unreason <Scot>; social director

VERBS **21 amuse, entertain, divert,** regale, beguile, solace, recreate, refresh, enliven, exhilarate, put in good humor; **relax,** loosen up; **delight, tickle, titillate,** tickle pink *or* to death <nf>, tickle the fancy; **make one laugh, strike one as funny,** raise a smile *or* laugh, convulse, set the table on a roar, be the death of; wow *and* slay *and* knock dead *and* kill *and* break one up *and* crack one up *and* fracture one <nf>; have them rolling in the aisles; keep them in stitches

22 amuse oneself, pleasure oneself, take one's pleasure, give oneself over to pleasure; get one's kicks *or* jollies <nf>; **relax,** let oneself go, loosen up; **have fun, have a good time,** have a ball *and* have lots of laughs <nf>, live it up *and* laugh it up <nf>; drown care, drive dull care away; beguile the time, kill time, while away the time; get away from it all

23 play, sport, disport; frolic, rollick, gambol, frisk, romp, caper, cut capers <nf>, lark about <Brit nf>, antic, curvet, cavort, caracole, flounce, trip, skip, dance; **cut up** <nf>, cut a dido <nf>, horse around <nf>, fool around, futz around <nf>, carry on <nf>

24 make merry, revel, roister, jolly, lark <nf>, skylark, **make whoopee** <nf>, let oneself go, **blow** *or* **let off steam;** cut loose, let loose, let go, let one's hair down <nf>, whoop it up, **kick up one's heels;** hell around *and* raise hell *and* blow off the lid <nf>; step out <nf>, go places and do things, go on the town, see life, **paint the town red** <nf>; go the dizzy rounds, go on the merry-go-round <nf>; **celebrate** 487.2; spree, **go on a spree,** go on a bust *or* toot *or* bender *or* binge *or* rip *or* tear <nf>; carouse, jollify <nf>, wanton, debauch, pub-crawl <chiefly Brit>, club-hop; **sow one's wild oats, have one's fling**

25 "eat, drink, and be merry"—Bible, feast, banquet

ADJS **26 amused,** entertained; diverted, **delighted,** tickled, tickled pink *or* to death <nf>, titillated

27 amusing, entertaining, diverting, beguiling; **fun,** funsome *and* more fun than a barrel of monkeys <nf>; recreative, recreational; **delightful,** titillative, titillating; humorous 488.4

28 festive, festal; merry, gay, jolly, jovial, joyous, joyful, gladsome, convivial, gala, hilarious; merrymaking, on the loose <nf>; on the town, out on the town

29 playful, sportive, sportful; **frolicsome,** gamesome, rompish, larkish, capersome; waggish 322.6

30 sporting, sports; **athletic,** agonistic; **gymnastic,** palaestral; **acrobatic**

ADVS **31 in fun,** for amusement, for fun, for the fun of it; for kicks *and* for laughs <nf>, for the devil *or* heck *or* hell of it <nf>; just to be doing

744 SPORTS

NOUNS **1 sport, sports, athletics,** athletic competition, game, sports activity, play, contest, match; round, set, tournament; aeronautical *or* air sport <see list>; animal sport <see list>; water *or* aquatic sport <see list>; **ball game; track and field** 755; **gymnastics** <see list>; indoor sport; **outdoor sport** <see list>; **winter sport** <see list>; contact sport; **combat sport,** martial art <see list>; **decathlon; triathlon,** biathlon; **bicycling,** bicycle touring, cross-country cycling, cyclo-cross,

bicycle moto-cross, road racing, off-road racing, track racing; **motor sport,** automobile racing 756, go-carting, jet-skiing, water skiing, motorcycling, moto-cross, dirt-biking, snowmobiling, soapbox racing; **in-line skating** *or* blading *or* Roller-blading <trademark>, roller skating, roller hockey, skateboarding; **target sport,** archery, field archery, darts, marksmanship, target shooting, skeet shooting, trap shooting; **throwing sport** <see list>; **weightlifting, bodybuilding,** iron-pumping <nf>, Olympic lifting, powerlifting, weight training; blood sport; extreme sport

VERBS **2 play, compete;** practice, train, work out; try out, go out for; follow

3 aeronautical *or* **air sports**

aerial skiing	helicopter flying
aerobatics	hydroplane racing
aeromodeling	kiting
aerotow	microlighting
ballooning	parachuting
bungee jumping	paragliding
flying	parasailing
freefalling	sky-diving
gliding	soaring
hang gliding	sports parachuting

4 animal sports

barrel racing	horseback riding
bronc riding *and* bronco busting	horsemanship
	horse racing
bullfighting	pack riding
bull riding	pigeon racing
calf roping	point-to-point
camel racing	polo
carriage driving	rodeo
cockfighting	show jumping
cross-country riding	steeplechase
dog racing	steer roping
dogsled racing	steer wrestling
dressage	team penning
driving	team roping
endurance riding	three-day event
equestrian sport	trail riding
falconry	trotting
greyhound racing	vaulting
harness racing 757.1	Western riding

5 aquatic *or* **water sports**

birling	jet skiing
boating	kayaking
body surfing	lifesaving
canoeing	motorboat racing
canoe polo	offshore yacht racing
canoe slalom	powerboat racing
distance swimming	rafting
diving	rowing
dragon boat racing	sailing
fin swimming	sailplaning
fishing	scuba diving
inner tube water polo	sculling

skin diving
snorkeling
surfing *or* surfboarding
swimming
synchronized swimming
underwater diving
underwater hockey
underwaterball

water polo
water skiing
whitewater canoeing
whitewater rafting
windsurfing *or*
   boardsailing *or*
   sailboarding
yachting

6 gymnastics

balance beam
floor exercises
horizontal bar
mini-trampolining
parallel bars
pommel horse
rings

rhythmic gymnastics
rings
trampolining
tumbling
uneven parallel
   bars
vaulting

7 outdoor sports

backpacking
camping
Frisbee <trademark>
hiking
ice climbing
mountaineering *or*
   alpinism

orienteering
rock climbing
speleology *or* spelunking
   <nf>
superalpinism *or* Alpine
   climbing
wilderness survival

8 winter sports

Alpine combined event
Alpine skiing
Alpine touring
bandy
biathlon
bobsledding
broomball
cross-country skiing *or*
   Nordic skiing *or* langlauf
curling
downhill skiing
figure skating
freestyle skiing *or*
   hotdogging <nf>
giant slalom
heli-skiing
hockey
ice boating *or* sailing
ice dancing
ice sailing
luge

mogul skiing
Nordic combined event
off-piste skiing
short-track speed skating
skating
skibob racing
skiing
skijoring
ski jumping
skiing
ski mountaineering
slalom
skiing
sledding
snowboarding
snowmobiling
snowshoeing
snow tubing
speed skating
super giant slalom
tobogganing

9 combat sports, martial arts

aikido *or* aiki-jutsu
arm *and* wrist wrestling
arnis
bando
bersilat
bojutsu
boxing
capoeira
Cornish wrestling
dumog
escrima
fencing

freestyle wrestling
glimae
go-ti
Greco-Roman wrestling
Greek boxing
haphido
hwarang-do
Iaido
Iaijutsu
Icelandic wrestling
jeet kune do
jobajutsu

jojutsu
jousting
judo
jujitsu *or* jujutsu
jukendo
kalari payat
karate
kendo
kenipo
kenjutsu
kiaijutsu
kick boxing
kobu-jutsu
kung-fu
kyujutsu
laido
lua
main tindju
mud wrestling

naginata-jutsu
ninjutsu
pankation
pentjak-silat
pukulan
quigong
sambo wrestling
savate
self-defence
stick fighting
sumo wrestling
tae kwon do
t'ai chi
tang soo do
tegumi
Thai kick boxing
wrestling
wu shu *or*
   wushu

10 throwing sports

boomeranging
discus throw
Frisbee <trademark>
hammer throw
horseshoe pitching
javelin throw

shot put
ultimate Frisbee <trade-
   mark> *or* ultimate *or*
   airborne soccer
ultimate skate Frisbee
   <trademark>

11 target sports

archery
boccie *or* bocci
bowling
Canadian 5-pin bowling
candlepins
carom billiards
clay pigeon shooting
croquet
curling
darts
duckpins
golf

green bowling
horseshoe pitching
pistol shooting
pool
rifle shooting
skittles <Brit>
sharpshooting
skeet *or* skeet
   shooting
snooker
tenpins
trapshooting

12 team games

arena football
Australian rules football
bandy
baseball
basketball
Canadian football
cricket
curling
field hockey
football
Gaelic football
hurling

ice hockey
lacrosse
netball
roller hockey
rounders <Brit>
rugby
soccer *or* association
   football <Brit>
softball
speedball
team handball
volleyball

13 court sports

badminton
court tennis
handball
jai alai *or*
   pelota

racquetball
squash
table tennis *or* Ping-Pong
   <trademark>
tennis

745 BASEBALL

NOUNS 1 baseball, ball, the national pastime, hardball; **organized baseball, league,** loop, circuit, **major league,** big league, the majors *and* the big time *and* the bigs <nf>, professional baseball, the National League *or* Senior Circuit, the American League *or* Junior Circuit; **minor league,** triple-A, the minors *and* bush leagues *and* the bushes <nf>, college baseball; Little League baseball; division championship, playoff, League Championship Series, league championship *or* pennant, World Series, All-Star Game; fantasy baseball; **farm team,** farm club, farm, farm system; rotisserie league; **ball park, ball field,** field, park; **stands, grandstand,** boxes, lower deck, upper deck, outfield stands, bleachers; **diamond;** dugout; **home plate, the plate,** platter *and* dish <nf>; **base line, line,** base path; **base, bag,** sack, **first,** first base, **second,** second base, keystone *and* keystone sack <nf>, **third,** third base, hot corner <nf>; **infield,** infield grass *or* turf; **outfield,** warning track, fences; foul line, foul pole; **mound,** pitcher's mound, hill; **equipment** <see list>, gear

2 baseball team, team, nine, roster, squad, the boys of summer, **club,** ball club, personnel, crew; **starting lineup, lineup batting order; starter, regular;** substitute, sub, utility player, benchwarmer *and* bench jockey <nf>, the bench; **pitcher,** hurler <nf>, motion, pitching motion, herky-jerky motion <nf>, **right-hander,** right-hand pitcher, righty <nf>, **left-hander, left-hand pitcher, lefty** *and* **southpaw** *and* portsider <nf>; **starting pitcher, starter,** fifth starter, spot starter; starting rotation, rotation, pitching rotation; **relief pitcher, reliever,** fireman *and* closer *and* stopper <nf>, long reliever, middle *or* inner reliever, short reliever, the bull pen; **battery; catcher,** backstop *and* receiver <nf>; **fielder,** glove man, outfielder, infielder, cover man, cut-off man, relay man; **first baseman,** first bagger *and* first sacker <nf>; **second baseman,** second bagger *and* second sacker *and* keystone bagger *and* keystone sacker <nf>; **third baseman,** third bagger *and* third sacker *and* hot-corner man <nf>; shortstop; **outfielder,** left fielder, center fielder, right fielder; pinch hitter; designated hitter *or* DH *or* desi; **batter, hitter,** man at the plate, man in the box *or* batter's box, **stance,** batting stance, pull hitter, power hitter, long ball hitter, slugger <nf>, spray hitter, contact hitter, banjo hitter <nf>, switch hitter, leadoff hitter, cleanup hitter, closer; base runner, runner, designated runner; **manager, pilot, coach,** batting coach, pitching coach, bench

coach, bullpen coach, first-base coach, third-base coach; official scorer; scout, talent scout

3 game, ball game, play, strategy; **umpire,** home-plate umpire, plate umpire, umpire in chief, umpire crew, first-base umpire, second-base umpire, third-base umpire; **pitch** <see list>, set, windup, kick, delivery, stuff, offering; **strike zone,** wheelhouse *and* kitchen <nf>; **throwing arm,** arm, cannon *and* soupbone <nf>; **balk; count,** balls and strikes, full count; **hit, base hit,** tater *and* bingle *and* dinger <nf>, opposite-field hit; hard-hit ball, shot *and* bullet *and* scorcher <nf>; **single,** seeing-eye hit *and* excuse-me hit *and* banjo hit <nf>; **double,** two-base hit, two-base shot, two-bagger; **triple,** three-base hit *or* three-base shot, three-bagger; **home run, homer,** four-bagger, long ball, tater *and* round trip *and* round tripper *and* circuit clout *and* big salami *and* dinger <nf>, one you can hang the wash on <nf>, grand-slam home run, grand-slammer, cheap homer *and* Chinese homer <nf>; **fly,** pop fly, pop-up, can of corn *and* looper *and* blooper *and* bloop *and* Texas Leaguer *and* banjo hit <nf>, sacrifice fly *or* sac fly <nf>; **line drive, liner,** line shot, rope *and* clothesline <nf>; **ground ball,** grounder, wormburner <nf>, slow roller, roller, bunt, drag bunt, bleeder *and* squibbler *and* nubber *and* dying quail <nf>, come-backer, chopper; **foul ball, foul; base on balls, walk,** intentional pass, free ticket *and* free ride <nf>; error, passed ball, unearned run, earned run; **out,** strikeout *or* K *or* punchout, put-out, foul-out, force-out, double play, DP, double killing *and* twin killing <nf>, triple play, triple killing <nf>, assist; **catch,** shoestring catch, basket catch, circus catch; squeeze play, hit-and-run play, pickoff play, pickoff, pitch-out; **base runner,** baseburner <nf>, pinch-runner; **run;** complete game; **inning,** frame, top of the inning, bottom of the inning, extra innings

4 statistics, averages, stats and numbers <nf>, percentages; batting average, earned-run average *or* ERA, slugging average *or* slugging percentage, fielding average, run batted in *or* RBI, ribby <nf>; **the record book,** the book

VERBS 5 play, play ball, take the field; **umpire,** call balls and strikes, officiate; **pitch, throw,** deliver, fire, offer, offer up, bring it *and* burn it *and* throw smoke *and* blow it by *and* throw seeds <nf>; throw a bean ball, dust the batter off, back the batter off; **relieve,** put out the fire <nf>; **bat, be up,** step up to the plate, be in the batter's box; **hit,** belt *and* clout *and* connect <nf>, golf, chop, tomahawk; **fly,** hit a fly, sky it *and* pop *and* pop up <nf>; **ground,** bounce, lay it down, lay down a bunt; sacrifice, hit a sacrifice fly; **hit,** get a base hit, put on one's hitting shoes <nf>; **connect,** blast it *and* cream it *and* tear the cover off *and* hit it right on the screws *and* hit it right on the button *and* hit with the good wood *and* get good wood on it <nf>; **hit a home run, homer,** hit it out; **single, double, triple;** get aboard, be a base runner; **walk, get a free ride** *or* free pass <nf>; **strike out,** go down *or* out on strikes, go down swinging, fan *and* whiff <nf>, be called out on strikes, be caught looking <nf>; ground out, fly out, pop out; catch, haul in, grab *and* glove *and* flag down <nf>; misplay, make an error, bobble *and* boot <nf>; take a trip to the showers <nf>

6 baseball equipment

bar mask	birdcage mask
base	catcher's mask
baseball *or* ball; pill *or* apple <nf>	chest protector
	cleats
bat; lumber *or* Louisville slugger <nf>	glove
	pine-tar rag
batting cage	rosin bag
batting glove	shin pads *or* shin
batting helmet	guards

7 baseball pitches

back door	floater
beanball *or* beaner	forkball
bender	gopher ball
breaking ball *or* breaker	intentional walk *or* pass
brush-off *or* brushing *or* dust-off	knuckleball *or* knuckler
	knucklecurve
Captain Hook	off-speed pitch
change-up *or* change-of-pace ball	palmball
	reverse curve
curve ball *or* curve *or* breaking ball *or* bender *or* Captain Hook *or* slurve	roundhouse curve
	sailing fastball
	screwball
	screwgy <nf>
cut fastball	sinker
dime	slider
duster	slow ball
eefus ball	spitball *or* spitter
fadeaway	split-finger fastball
fast ball *or* smoke *or* bullet *or* heater *or* hummer	splitter
	Uncle Charlie
	wild pitch

746 FOOTBALL

NOUNS **1 football, ball,** American football; **organized football, college football,** NCAA football, conference, league; conference championship, post-season game, bowl invitation, Cotton Bowl, Gator Bowl, Orange Bowl, Rose Bowl, Sugar Bowl, Fiesta Bowl, national championship *or* mythical national championship; **professional football,** pro football <nf>, National Football League *or* NFL; division championship, playoff, Super Bowl, Super Bowl championship, Pro Bowl; high school football; Pop Warner football, Pee Wee football; **stadium,** bowl, domed stadium, dome; **field, gridiron; line,** sideline, end line, end zone, goal line, goalpost, crossbar, yard line, midfield stripe, inbounds marker *or* hash mark; **equipment** <see list>, gear, armament; official, sideline crew, chain gang <nf>, zebra <nf>; fantasy football; arena football

2 football team, eleven, team, squad, roster, personnel; first team, regulars, starting lineup, offensive team *or* platoon, defensive team *or* platoon, special team, kicking team; substitute *or* sub, benchwarmer; **ball,** football, pigskin *and* oblate spheroid <nf>; **line, linemen, forward wall,** offensive linemen, front four, **end, tackle, nose tackle, guard, noseguard, center,** flanker, **tight end; backfield,** back, **quarterback,** signal-caller *or* field general <nf>, passer; **halfback, fullback,** kicker, punter, tailback, plunging back, slotback, flanker back, running back, wingback, blocking back, linebacker, defensive back, cornerback, safety, free safety, strong safety, weak safety; **pass receiver, receiver,** wide receiver *or* wide out, primary receiver

3 game, strategy, game plan, ball control; **official** <see list>, zebra <nf>; **kickoff,** kick, coin-toss *or* -flip, place kick, squib kick, free kick, onside kick, runback, kickoff return; **play** <see list>, down, first down, second down, third down, fourth down; **line,** line of scrimmage *or* scrimmage line, flat; **lineup, formation** <see list>; **pass from center, snap,** hand-to-hand snap; live ball, ball in play, ball out of play, dead ball, play stopped, ball whistled dead; **running play, passing play, kick; ball-carrier,** ball-handling, tuck, feint, hand-off, pocket, straightarm; **block,** blocking, body block, brush block, chop block, cross block, lead block, screen block, shoulder block; **tackle,** neck tackle, shirt tackle, face-mask tackle, sack; **yardage,** gain, loss, long yardage, short yardage; **forward pass, pass,** pass pattern <see list>, pitchout, screen pass, quick release, bomb <nf>, incomplete pass, completed pass, pass completion; **pass rush,** blitz; **possession,** loss of possession, turnover, fumble, pass interception, interception, turnover; in bounds, out of bounds; **penalty** <see list>, infraction, foul, flag on the play; **punt, kick,** quick kick, squib kick *or* knuckler; punt return, fair catch; **touchdown,** conversion, field goal, safety; **period, quarter, half,** halftime, intermission, two-minute warning, thirty-second clock, sudden-death overtime; **gun,** final gun

4 statistics, averages, stats *and* numbers <nf>, average running yardage, average passing yardage, average punting yardage, average punt-return yardage

VERBS **5 play,** kick, kick off, run, scramble, pass, punt; complete a pass, catch a pass; **block, tackle,** double-team, blindside, sack, blitz, red-dog; **lose possession,** fumble, bobble <nf>, give up the ball; **score,** get on the scoreboard; **officiate,** blow the whistle, whistle the ball dead, drop a flag, call a penalty

6 football equipment

cleats	mouth guard
face mask	numbers
football	pads
helmet	pants
hip pads	shirt *or* jersey
jersey	shoes
kicking tee	shoulder pads
kneepads	thigh pads

7 football officials

back judge	referee
chain gang <nf>	side judge
field judge	umpire
head linesman	zebra <nf>
line judge	

8 football plays and calls

automatic *or* audible	naked bootleg
blitz *or* red dog	naked reverse
bomb	off-tackle slant
bootleg	option
buck lateral	pass
conversion	pitchout
counter	play-action pass
cutback	plunge
draw	power sweep
end around	quarterback
end run	sneak
fair catch	quick kick
flare pass	reverse
flea-flicker	rollout
hail-Mary	scramble
hand-off	screen pass
inside run	slant
keeper	Statue of Liberty
lateral pass *or* lateral	sweep
man in motion	trap
mousetrap	two-point conversion

9 football formations

3–4 defense	man-to-man defense
4 3 2 2	nickel defense
4–3 defense	Notre Dame box
6 2 2 1	option
7 diamond	overshift
dime defense	power I
double coverage	prevent defense
double wing *or* wingback	pro set
flexbone *or* flex defense	run-and-shoot offense
huddle	shotgun offense
I	short punt formation

single coverage	undershift
single wing *or* wingback	veer
slot	weak side
split end	wedge *or* flying wedge
split T	
straight T	wing T
strong side	wishbone T
T formation	zone blocking
tight end	zone defense

10 football pass patterns

buttonhook	post pattern
circle	screen pass
crossing pattern	sideline pass
curl	slant-in pattern
down and out	spot pass
flag pattern	square-in
flare *or* swing pass	square-out
flood	streak pattern
fly	up the middle *or* the gut
hook pattern	zig in
look-in pass	zig out
option pass	Z pattern

11 football penalties

5-yard penalty	illegal use of hands
10-yard penalty	ineligible receiver
15-yard penalty	intentional grounding
clipping	kick-catching interference
crackback block	late hit <nf>
dead-ball foul	more than 11 players on
delay of game	the field
encroachment	offside
excessive timeouts	out-of-bounds kickoff
false start	pass interference
grabbing the face mask *or* facemask	personal foul
	piling on
holding	roughing the kicker
illegal blocking below the waist	roughing the passer
	running into the kicker
illegal formation	tackling by the facemask
illegal motion	tripping
illegal position	unnecessary roughness
illegal procedure	unsportsmanlike
illegal shift	conduct

747 BASKETBALL

NOUNS **1 basketball,** hoop, hoop sport, ball, b-ball, hoops; **organized basketball, college basketball,** NCAA *or* National Collegiate Athletic Association; **professional basketball,** pro basketball <nf>, National Basketball Association *or* NBA; **tournament,** competition, championship, Olympic Games, NCAA *or* National Collegiate Athletic Association Tournament, March Madness, Sweet 16, Final Four; NIT *or* National Invitational Tournament, NAIA *or* National Association of Intercollegiate Athletics Tournament; **basketball court, court,** hardwood *and* pine <nf>, forecourt, midcourt, backcourt, end line *or* base line, sideline, basket *or* hoop, iron <nf>, backboard, glass <nf>, defensive board, offensive board, free throw line, charity line <nf>, free throw lane *or* foul lane, key *and* keyhole <nf>, foul line *or* the line

2 basketball team, five, team, roster, squad, personnel; **basketball player,** hoopster, cager, hoopster *or* hooper, center, right forward, left forward, corner man, right guard, left guard, point guard, shooting guard, point player *or* playmaker, swingman, trailer, backcourt man, disher-upper, gunner, sixth man

3 basketball game, game, play, strategy, defense <see list>, offense <see list>; **official, referee,** umpire, official scorekeeper, timer; **foul,** violation <see list>, infraction; **play, strategy,** running game, fast break, passing game, draw and kick game; **jump,** center jump, jump ball, live ball; **pass,** passing, pass ball, assist, bounce pass, dish *and* feed <nf>; rebound; **tactics, action,** dribble, fake, hand-off, ball control, ball-handling, boxing out, sky shot *or* air ball, clear-out *or* outlet pass, basket hanging, freelancing, pivot *or* post, high post, low post, one-on-one, screening, pick, pick and roll, trap, turnover, steal *or* burn, out-of-bounds, dead ball, throw-in, corner throw, buzzer play; **restrictions,** three-second rule, five-second rule, ten-second rule, twenty-four-second rule, thirty-second rule; **shot** <see list>, **score, basket** *or* **field goal,** bucket <nf>, three-point play *or* three-pointer, free throw *or* foul shot; **quarter,** half, overtime period *or* overtime

VERBS **4 play,** play basketball, play ball, ride the pine <nf>, **dribble,** fake, pass, dish <nf>, work the ball around, take it coast to coast, give and go, sky it, clear the ball, hand off, **guard,** play tight, play loose, double-team, hand-check, block, screen, pick, press, set a pick, steal, burn, freelance, shoot, score, sink one *and* can *and* swish <nf>, finger-roll, tip it in, use the backboard, dunk, slam dunk, make a free throw, shoot a brick <nf>, rebound, clear the board, freeze the ball, kill the clock; **foul,** commit a foul *or* violation, foul out

5 basketball defensive strategies

box-and-one defense	sagging *or* collapsing
combination defense	defense
man-to-man defense	set pattern
matchup defense	slough
multiple defense	stack defense
pressure *or* pressing	zone defense *or*
defense	zone

6 basketball offensive strategies

ball-control offense	delay offense
clear out one side	fast-break offense

flip-flop offense	press
full-court press	pressure offense
full-court zone press	rotation offense
gap offense	run and gun
give and go offense	offense
half-court press	running offense
high post	shuffle offense
low post	stack offense
motion offense	stall offense

7 basketball fouls

blocking	palming
charging	personal foul *or* personal
disqualifying foul	pushing off
double dribble	stepping over the line <free
double foul	throw, throw-in>
force-out	technical foul *or* technical
goaltending	ten-second backcourt
hacking	violation
held ball	three-second lane
intentional foul	violation
kicking the ball	traveling *or* walking *or*
multiple foul	running with the ball
offensive foul	tripping

8 basketball shots

bank shot	jump shot *or* jumper
brick <nf>	lay-up
bunny <nf>	one-and-one
charity toss *and* charity	one-hand shot
throw *and* charity shot	pivot shot
<nf>	penalty free throw
cripple <nf>	scoop shot
dunk <nf>	set shot
finger-roll	slam dunk <nf>
free throw *or* foul shot *or*	swish <nf>
penalty shot	tip-in
hook shot *or* hook	two-hand shot

748 TENNIS

NOUNS **1 tennis,** lawn tennis, indoor tennis, outdoor tennis, singles, doubles, mixed doubles, Canadian doubles, team tennis; court *or* real *or* royal tennis; table tennis, Ping-Pong <trademark>; **organized tennis,** International Tennis Federation *or* ITF, United States Tennis Association *or* USTA; **tournament,** tennis competition, championship, crown, match, trophy; **tennis ball, ball, tennis racket, racket,** aluminum racket, Fiberglas racket, graphite racket, wooden racket, bat <nf>, sweet spot; **tennis court, court,** sideline, alley, doubles sideline, baseline, center mark, service line, half court line, backcourt, forecourt, midcourt, net, band; **surface,** slow surface, fast surface, grass surface *or* grass *or* grass court, hard court, clay court, competition court, all-weather court; squash, squash racquets, squash tennis, badminton

2 game, strategy, serve-and-volley, power game; **official, umpire,** baseline umpires *or* linesmen, line umpires *or* linesmen, service-line umpire *or* linesman, net-court judge; **play,** coin-toss, racket-flip, grip, Eastern grip, Continental grip, Western grip, two-handed grip, **stroke** <see list>, **shot,** service *or* serve, return, spin, top-spin, let ball *or* let, net-cord ball, rally, fault, double fault, foot fault; error, unforced error; **score, point,** service ace *or* ace, love, deuce, advantage *or* ad, game point, service break, break point, set point, match point, tiebreaker, lingering death <nf>, game, set, match; Van Alen Streamlined Scoring System *or* VASSS

VERBS **3 play tennis, play,** serve, return, drive, volley, smash, lob, place the ball, serve and volley, play serve-and-volley tennis, fault, foot-fault, double-fault, make an unforced error; **score** *or* **make a point,** score, ace one's opponent, break service, break back

4 tennis strokes

approach shot	lob volley
backhand	overhead
backhand drive	passing shot
chop	reverse twist service
drive	service *or* serve
drop shot	slice
forehand	smash *or* overhead
forehand drive	smash
ground drive	topspin
ground stroke	twist service
half-volley	two-handed backhand
lob	volley

749 HOCKEY

NOUNS **1 hockey,** ice hockey, Canadian national sport; **professional hockey,** National Hockey League *or* NHL, Clarence Campbell Conference, Smythe Division, Norris Division, Prince of Wales Conference, Patrick Division, Adams Division; **amateur hockey,** bantam hockey, midget hockey, pee-wee hockey, junior hockey, Canadian Amateur Hockey Association, Amateur Hockey Association of the United States, International Ice Hockey Federation; **competition,** series, championship, cup, Olympic Games, Stanley Cup, All-Star Game; **rink,** ice rink, hockey rink, boards, end zone, defending *or* defensive zone, attacking *or* offensive zone, neutral zone *or* center ice, blue line, red line, goal line, crease, goal *and* net *and* cage, face-off spot, face-off circle, penalty box, penalty bench, players' bench; **equipment,** gear <see list>; floor hockey

2 hockey team, team, skaters, squad, bench; line, forward line, center, forward, winger, right wingman, left wingman, linesman; **defense,** defender, right defenseman, left defenseman, goaltender *or* goalie, goalkeeper, goalminder; specialized player, playmaker, penalty killer, point *or* point man, enforcer <nf>

3 game, match; **referee,** linesman, goal judge, timekeepers, scorer; **foul,** penalty <see list>, infraction, offside, icing *or* icing the puck; **play,** skating, stick *or* puck handling, ragging, deking, checking, backchecking, forechecking, passing, shooting; **pass,** blind pass, drop pass, through-pass; **check** <see list>; **offense,** breakout, Montreal offense, headmanning, Toronto offense, play-off hockey, give-and-go, breakaway, peel-off, screening; **shot,** slap shot, wrist shot, backhand shot, flip, sweep shot; **power play; score,** point, finish off a play, feed, assist, hat trick; **period,** overtime *or* overtime period, sudden death overtime, shoot-out

4 field hockey, banty *or* bandy, hurley *or* hurling, shinty *or* shinny; International Hockey Board, *Fédération Internationale de Hockey* <Can>, International Federation of Women's Hockey Associations, United States Field Hockey Association, Field Hockey Association of America; **hockey field,** field, pitch, goal line, center line, center mark, bully circle, sideline, 7-yard line, alley, 25-yard line, striking *or* shooting circle, goalpost, goal, goal mouth; **equipment,** gear, stick, ball, shin pads

5 team, attack, outside left, inside left, center forward, inside right, outside right, defense, left halfback, center halfback, right halfback, left fullback, wing half, right fullback, goalkeeper

6 game, match; **umpire,** timekeeper; **foul,** infraction, advancing, obstructing, sticks, undercutting, **penalty,** free hit, corner hit, defense hit, penalty bully, penalty shot; **play, bully, bully-off,** pass-back, stroke <see list>, marking, pass, tackle, circular tackle, out-of-bounds, roll-in *or* push-in, hit-in; **goal,** point, score; **period,** half

VERBS **7 play, skate,** pass, check, block, stick-handle *or* puck-handle, face off, rag, deke, give-and-go, headman, break out, shoot, score, clear, dig, freeze the puck, center, ice *or* ice the puck; tackle, mark; make a hat trick

8 hockey equipment

abdominal protector	hip pads
catching glove	knee pads
chest protector	left-handed stick
elbow pads	leg pads
face mask	neutral stick
gloves	puck
goaltender's stick	right-handed stick
helmet	shin guards

shoulder pads	stick
skates	stick glove

9 hockey fouls and penalties

bench minor penalty	icing
board-checking *or*	interference
boarding	kneeing
body-checking	match penalty
butt-ending	major *or* five-minute
charging	penalty
clipping	minor *or* two-minute
crosschecking	penalty
ejection	misconduct penalty
elbowing	offsides
falling on the puck	penalty shot
fighting	poke checking
handling the puck	roughing
high-sticking	slashing
holding	spearing
hooking	tripping

750 BOWLING

NOUNS **1 bowling,** kegling *or* kegeling <nf>, tenpin bowling *or* tenpins, candlepin bowling *or* candlepins, duckpin bowling *or* duckpins, fivepin bowling, rubberband duckpin bowling, ninepins, skittles <Brit>; **bowling organization,** league, American Bowling Congress *or* ABC, Women's International Bowling Congress *or* WIBC, American Junior Bowling Congress; amateur bowling, league bowling; **professional bowling,** pro bowling <nf>, tour, Professional Bowlers Association *or* PBA, Professional Women's Bowling Association; **tournament,** competition, match-play tournament, round-robin tournament; **alley, lane,** gutter, foul line, rear cushion, bed, spot, pin spot, 1-3-strike pocket; **equipment, pin,** candlepin, duckpin, fivepin, rubberband duckpin, tenpin; automatic pinsetter; **ball,** two-hole ball, three-hole ball, bowling shoes; bowling bag

2 game *or* string, frame; **delivery,** grip, two-finger grip, three-finger grip, conventional grip, semi-fingertip grip, full-fingertip grip, **approach,** three-step approach *or* delivery, four-step approach, five-step approach, push-away, downswing, backswing, timing step, release, follow-through, straight ball, curve ball, backup, hook ball, gutter ball; **pocket,** Brooklyn side, Brooklyn hit *or* Jersey hit *or* crossover, **strike** *or* ten-strike, mark, double, turkey, foundation; **spare,** mark, leave, spare leave, split <see list>, railroad, open frame; **score,** pinfall, miss, perfect game *or* 300 game, Dutch

3 lawn bowling, green bowling, lawn bowls, bowling on the green, bowls; American Lawn Bowling Association; **bowling green,** green, crown green,

level green, rink, ditch; **ball,** bowl, jack *or* kitty, mat *or* footer; **team,** side, rink, lead *or* leader, second player, third player, skip

4 spare leaves and splits

baby split	fence
bed posts *or* fenceposts *or*	fit-in split
goal posts	Golden Gate
bucket	left fence
Christmas tree	mother-in-law
Cincinnati	right fence
converted split	washout
double pinochle	Woolworth
double wood *or* tandem	

751 GOLF

NOUNS **1** golf, the royal and ancient; **professional golf,** pro golf <nf>, tour, Professional Golfers Association of America *or* PGA, Ladies' Professional Golfers' Association *or* LPGA; **amateur golf,** club, United States Golf Association *or* USGA; **tournament** <see list>, championship, title, cup; **golf course,** course, links, 9-hole course, 18-hole course, penal course, strategic course, green, tee, teeing ground, back *or* championship marker, middle *or* men's marker, front *or* womens' marker, hole, par-3 hole, par-4 hole, par-5 hole, front nine *or* side, back nine *or* side, water hole, fairway, dogleg, obstruction, rub of the green, casual water, rough, hazard, water hazard, bunker, sand hazard, sand trap, beach <nf>, collar, apron, fringe, putting green, grass green, sand green, out of bounds, pin, flagstick, flag, lip, cup; **equipment** <see list>; nineteenth hole; miniature golf, putt-putt

2 golfer, player, scratch golfer *or* player, handicapped golfer, dub *and* duffer *and* hacker <nf>, linksman, putter; **team,** twosome, threesome, foursome; caddie

3 round, 9 holes, 18 holes, 72 holes, match, stroke play, match play, medal play, four-ball match, three-ball match, best ball, mixed foursome, Scotch foursome; **official,** referee, official observer, marker; **play,** golfing grip, overlapping *or* Vardon grip, reverse overlap, interlocking grip, full-finger grip, address, stance, closed stance, square stance, open stance, waggle, swing, backswing, downswing, follow-through, pivot, body pivot, tee-off; **stroke, shot** <see list>, backspin, bite, distance, carry, run, lie, plugged lie, blind, stymie; **score,** scoring, strokes, eagle, double eagle, birdie, par, bogey, double bogey, penalty, hole-in-one *and* ace, halved hole, gross, handicap, net

VERBS **4 play, shoot,** tee up, tee off, drive, hit, sclaff, draw, fade, pull, push, hook, slice, top, sky, loft, dunk, putt, can <nf>, borrow, hole out, sink, shoot par, eagle, double eagle, birdie, par, bogey, double bogey, make a hole in one, ace; play through; concede, default

INTERJ **5 fore!**

6 golf equipment

1 iron *or* driving iron	middle iron
2 iron *or* midiron	number 1 wood *or* driver
3 iron *or* mid mashie	number 2 wood *or* brassie
4 iron *or* mashie iron	number 3 wood *or* spoon
5 iron *or* mashie	number 4 wood *or* cleek *or* short spoon
6 iron *or* spade mashie	
7 iron *or* mashie niblick	number 5 wood *or* baffy
8 iron *or* pitching niblick	
9 iron *or* niblick	pitching wedge
ball *or* pill <nf>	putter
chipping iron club	sand iron
club cover	sand wedge
driver	short iron
golf bag	tee
golf cart	Texas wedge
golf glove	track iron
iron	utility iron
lofter *or* lofting iron	wedge
long iron	wood

7 golf shots

approach shot *or* approach	lob
blast	lofted shot
bunker shot	long iron shot
chip shot *or* chip	Mulligan *or* Shapiro
chip-and-run	pitch
cut shot	pitch-and-run
draw	pull
drive	punch
dubbed shot	putt
duck hook	recovery shot
fade	run-up
fairway wood shot	sand shot
full shot	sclaff
gimme <nf>	slice
hole in one	snake
hole out	tee shot
hook	water shot
lag	

752 SOCCER

NOUNS **1 soccer,** football, association football <Brit>, soccer football; **league,** college soccer, Intercollegiate Soccer Football Association of America, NCAA *or* National Collegiate Athletic Association, Federation of International Football Associations *or* FIFA; **tournament,** competition, championship, cup; **professional soccer,** pro soccer, North American Soccer League *or* NASL; **soccer field,** field, soccer pitch, pitch, goal line,

touch line, halfway line, penalty area, penalty spot *or* penalty-kick mark, goal area, goal, goalpost, crossbar, 6-yard box, 18-yard box, corner area, corner flag, center mark, center circle; **equipment,** gear, ball, suit, uniform, shirt, shorts, knee socks, shin guards, soccer shoes

2 team, squad, side, footballer <Brit>, forward, striker, outside right, inside right, center forward, lineman, midfielder, inside left, outside left, right half, center half, left half, defender, back, center back, right back, left back, winger, back four, sweeper, stopper, goalkeeper *or* goaltender *or* goalie

3 game, match; official, referee, linesman; **play,** coin-toss *or* -flip, 3-3-4 offense, 5-2 offense, man-to-man offense, kickoff, kick <see list>, throw-in, goal kick, corner kick *or* corner, offside, ball-control, pass, back-heel pass, outside-of-the-foot pass, push pass, back pass, tackle, sliding tackle, sliding block tackle, trap, chest trap, thigh trap, breakaway, header *or* head, shot, save; **rule,** law; **foul** <see list>; **penalty,** caution, red card, free kick, direct free kick, indirect free kick, caution, penalty kick, yellow card; **goal,** score, point, tie-breaker, series of penalty kicks, shootout, bonus point; **period,** quarter, overtime period

VERBS **4 play,** kick, kick off, trap, pass, dribble, screen, head, center, clear, mark, tackle, save

5 soccer kicks

banana kick	instep *or* inside-of-the-foot kick
bicycle kick	
chip	lofted kick
corner kick	long pass
direct free kick	low drive
flick kick	overhead volley
free kick	penalty kick
goal kick	punt
half-volley	scissors kick
	volley *or* volley kick

6 soccer fouls

charging dangerously	jumping at an opponent
charging from behind	kicking an opponent
charging the goalkeeper	obstruction
continual breaking of rules	offside
dangerous play	onside
dissenting from referee's decision	pushing an opponent
	spitting at an opponent
foul *or* abusive language	striking an opponent
handling the ball	tripping an opponent
holding an opponent	ungentlemanly conduct

753 SKIING

NOUNS **1** skiing, snow-skiing, Alpine skiing, downhill skiing, **Nordic skiing,** cross-country skiing *or* langlauf, snowboarding, ski-jumping, jumping, freestyle skiing *or* hotdog skiing *or* hotdogging, ballet skiing, mogul skiing, skijoring, helicopter skiing or heli-skiing, off-trail skiing, mountain skiing, grass-skiing, ski mountaineering; **organized skiing,** competitive skiing, *Fédération Internationale de Ski* <Fr> or FIS, International Freestyle Skiers Association, World Hot Dog Ski Association; **competition, championship,** cup, race; **slope,** ski slope, ski run, nursery or beginner's slope, expert's slope, intermediate slope, expert's trail, marked trail, moguled trail, course, trail, mogul; **ski lift, lift,** ski tow, rope tow, J-bar, chairlift, T-bar, poma; **race course,** downhill course, slalom course, giant slalom course, super giant slalom course, parallel or dual slalom course; starting gate, fall line, drop or vertical drop, control gate, obligatory gate, flagstick, open gate, closed or blind gate, hairpin, flush, H, men's course, women's course, **ski-jump,** ramp, inrun, outrun, hill rating, 60-point hill, normal hill, big hill, cross-country course; equipment, gear <see list>

2 skier, snow-skier, cross-country skier, ski-jumper, racer, downhill racer, slalom racer, giant slalom racer, mogul racer, snowboarder, freestyle skier, touring skier, forerunner, forejumper, skimeister

3 race, downhill race, slalom, giant slalom, super giant slalom or super G, slalom pole, rapid slalom pole, parallel or dual slalom, Alpine race, cross-country race, biathlon; **technique,** style, Arlberg technique, Lilienfeld technique, wedeln, **position,** tuck and egg, Vorlage, sitting position, inrun position, fish position, flight position; **maneuver, turn** <see list>

VERBS **4 ski,** run, schuss, traverse, turn, check; hot dog, ski freestyle; snowboard

5 skiing equipment

aluminum alloy pole	laminated wood ski
Alpine boots	metal ski
Arlberg or safety strap	molded boot
basket or snow basket	plastic ski
bent pole	pole or stick
cross-country binding	racing ski
cross-country pole	release binding
cross-country ski	short ski
double boot	ski boots
downhill pole	ski wax
downhill ski	slalom ski
fiberglass pole	snowboard
giant slalom ski	step-in binding
jumping ski	toe clamp

6 skiing maneuvers and turns

carved turn	double-pole stride
check	double-poling
Christiania or christie	edging
climb	Geländesprung
diagonal stride	herringbone
hockey stop	snowplow or double stem or wedge
jet turn	
jump turn	snowplow turn
kick turn	stem turn
parallel christie	stem christie
parallel swing	step acceleration
parallel turn	step turn
pole plant	Telemark
rotation turn	tempo
schuss	traverse
short swing	tuck
sideslip	unweighting
sidestep	uphill christie
snap	wedeln

754 BOXING

NOUNS **1 boxing, prizefighting,** fighting, pugilism, noble or manly art of self-defense, the noble or sweet science, fisticuffs, the fistic sport, the fights and the fight game <nf>, the ring; **amateur boxing,** Olympic Games, International Amateur Boxing Association or IABA, Amateur Athletic Union or AAU, Gold or Golden Gloves; **professional boxing,** International Boxing Federation, World Boxing Council or WBC, World Boxing Association or WBA, European Boxing Union, club boxing or fighting; Queensbury rules, Marquess of Queensbury rules; shadowboxing; **boxing ring, ring,** prize ring, square circle or ring, canvas, corner, ropes, bell; **equipment, gloves,** mitts and mittens <nf>, boxing shorts, tape, bandages, sparring helmet, mouthpiece; boxing purse

2 boxer, fighter, pugilist, prizefighter, pug and palooka <nf>, slugger, mauler; **weight** <see list>; division; **manager; trainer; handler,** second, sparring partner

3 fight, match, bout, prizefight, battle, duel, slugfest or haymaker <nf>; **official, referee,** ref <nf>, judge, timekeeper; **strategy, fight-plan, style,** stance, footwork, **offense, punch** <see list>, blow, belt and biff and sock <nf>, sparring, jabbing, socking, pummeling; **defense,** blocking, ducking, parrying, slipping, feint, clinching; **foul** <see list>; **win, knockout or KO,** technical knockout or TKO, decision, unanimous decision, split decision, win on points; **round,** canto and stanza <nf>

VERBS **4 fight, box,** punch, spar, mix it up <nf>, prizefight, jab, sock, clinch, break, block, catch, slip a punch, duck, feint, parry, heel, thumb, knock down, knock out, slug, maul, land a rabbit punch, hit below the belt; go down, go down for the count, hit the canvas <nf>, shadow-box

5 boxing weight divisions

light flyweight	welterweight
flyweight	light middleweight
bantamweight	middleweight
super bantamweight	light heavyweight
featherweight	cruiserweight
junior lightweight	heavyweight
lightweight	super-heavyweight
light welterweight	

6 boxing punches

backhand or backhander	Long Melford
backstroke	mishit or mislick
body blow or body slam	rabbit punch
bolo punch	right or right-hander
chop	round-arm blow
combination	roundhouse
corkscrew punch	short-arm blow
counter-punch	sideswipe
cross	sidewinder
flanker	sneak punch or sucker
follow-up	punch
haymaker	solar-plexus punch
hook	straight punch
jab	swing
knockdown punch	swipe
knockout punch	the one-two or the old
left or left-hander or	one-two
portsider	uppercut

755 TRACK AND FIELD

NOUNS **1 track, track and field,** athletics <Brit>,
light athletics <Ger>; governing organization,
International Athletic Federation or IAAF,
Amateur Athletic Union of the US or AAU,
Amateur Athletic Federation of Canada, Amateur
Athletic Union of Canada, National Federation of
State High School Athletic Associations; **games,**
competition, cup; **stadium, arena,** oval, armory,
field house; **track,** oval, lane, start line, starting
block, finish line, **infield;** lap, lap of honor, victory
lap

2 track meet, meet, games, program; **running event**,
race, run or running, heat, sprint racing, middle-
distance running, long-distance running, relay
racing, hurdles, cross-country racing; **field event**
<see list>; **all-around event,** decathlon <see list>,
heptathlon <see list>, pentathlon <see list>;
triathlon <see list>, biathlon <see list>; **walking,**
race walking, the walk, heel-and-toe racing

3 field events

discus throw	multi-event
hammer throw	contest
high jump	pole vault
javelin throw	shot put
long jump or broad jump	triple jump

4 heptathlon

100-meter hurdles	javelin
200-meter run	long jump
800-meter run	shot put
high jump	

5 decathlon

100-meter run	high jump
110-meter hurdles	javelin
400-meter run	long jump
1500-meter run	pole vault
discus	shot put

6 pentathlon

100-meter hurdles	javelin
200-meter run	long jump
high jump	

7 triathlon

100-meter dash	shot put
high jump	

8 biathlon

cross-country skiing	rifle shooting

756 AUTOMOBILE RACING

NOUNS **1 automobile racing, auto racing, car racing,**
motor sport; Indy car racing, stock-car racing,
drag racing, Formula car racing, midget-car
racing, hot-rod racing, autocross, go-karting;
racing association; race, competition,
championship; **track,** speedway, Indianapolis
Motor Speedway or the Brickyard <nf>, closed
course, road course or circuit, dirt track,
grasstrack, super speedway; **car, racing car** <see
list>, racer; **racing engine; supercharger,**
turbocharger, blower and windmill <nf>; **tires,**
racing tires, shoes <nf>, slicks; **body,** body work,
spoiler, sidepod, roll bar, roll cage; **wheel,** wire
wheel or wire, magnesium wheel or mag; **fuel,**
racing fuel, methanol, nitromethane or nitro,
blend, pop and juice <nf>

2 race driving, racing driver, driver, fast driver or
leadfoot <nf>, slow driver or balloon foot, novice
driver or yellowtail; off-roading

3 race, driving, start, Le Mans start, flying start,
paced start, grid start; **position,** qualifying,
qualifying heat, starting grid, inside position, pole
or pole position, bubble; **track,** turn, curve,
hairpin, switchback, banked turn, corner,
chicane, groove, shut-off, drift, straightaway or
chute, pit, pit area; **signal,** black flag, white flag,
checkered flag; **lap,** pace lap, victory lap or lane

VERBS **4 drive, race,** start, jump, rev, accelerate, put
the hammer down <nf>, slow down, back off,
stroke it, draft, fishtail, nerf, shut the gate

ADVS **5 at top speed,** flat-out, full-bore, ten-tenths
ride the rail, spin, spin out, crash, t-bone

6 racing cars

championship car	hobby car
compact sprint car	Indy car
dirt car	late-model sportsman
dragster	midget car
experimental car *or* X-car	modified stock car
Formula A	production car
formula car	prototype
Formula F	quarter-midget car
Formula One	Formula SCCA
Formula Super Vee	sportsman
Formula Vee	sports car
fuel dragster *or* slingshot *or* rail job	sprint car *or* big car
	stock car
fueler	supercharger
funny car	touring car
gas dragster	turbine car
grand touring car *or* GT	turbocharger

757 HORSE RACING

NOUNS **1 horse racing, the turf,** the sport of kings, the turf sport, the racing world *or* establishment; **flat racing; harness racing,** trotting, pacing; steeplechase, hurdle race, point-to-point race; **Jockey Club,** Trotting Horse Club, Thoroughbred Racing Association *or* TRA, Thoroughbred Racing Protective Bureau *or* TRPB, state racing commission; **General Stud Book, American Stud Book,** Wallace's Trotting Register; **Triple Crown,** Kentucky Derby, Preakness Stakes, Belmont Stakes; Grand National, Derby, 2000 Guineas, Sty Leger, Gold Cup Race, Oaks; **racetrack, track,** racecourse, turf, oval, course, strip; rail, inside rail, infield, paddock, post; turf track, steeplejack course; gate *and* barrier; **track locations** <see list> *and* **calls; track conditions,** footing; racing equipment, tack

2 jockey, jock, rider, race rider, pilot, bug boy <nf>, money rider; apprentice jockey, bug <nf>; breeder, owner; trainer; steward, racing secretary; **railbird** and race bird <nf>, turf-man; **racehorse, pony,** thoroughbred, standardbred, mount, flyer, running horse, trotter, pacer, quarter horse, bangtail *and* daisy-cutter and filly *and* gee-gee <nf>; **sire, dam,** stallion, stud, stud horse, racing stud, mare, brood mare, gelding, ridgeling *or* rigling; **horse,** aged horse, three-year-old, sophomore, two-year-old, juvenile, colt, racing colt, filly, baby, foal, tenderfoot, bug, maiden *or* maiden horse, yearling, weanling; **favorite,** chalk, choice, odds-on favorite, public choice, top horse; runner, front-runner, pacesetter; strong horse, router, stayer; winner *or* win horse, place horse, show horse, also-ran; **nag** and race-nag *and* beagle *and* beetle *and* hayburner *and* nine of hearts *and*

palooka *and* pelter *and* pig *and* plater *and* selling plater <nf>; **rogue,** bad actor, cooler

3 horse race, race; race meeting, race card, scratch sheet; **starters,** field, weigh-in *or* weighing-in, post parade, post time, post position *or* PP; **start, break,** off; easy race, romp, shoo-in, armchair ride, hand ride; **finish,** dead heat, blanket finish, photo finish, Garison finish; **dishonest race,** boat race *and* fixed race <nf>

4 statistics, records, condition book, chart, **form, racing form,** daily racing form, past performance, **track record,** dope *or* tip *or* tout sheet <nf>, par time, parallel-time chart; **betting;** pari-mutuel 759.4; horse-racing bets

VERBS **5 race, run; start, break, be off;** air *and* breeze; make a move, drive, extend, straighten out; fade, come back; screw in *or* through; ride out, run wide; **win,** romp *or* breeze in; **place, show,** be in the money; be out of the money

ADJS **6 winning, in the money;** losing, out of the money; on the chinstrap; out in front, on the Bill Daley

7 horse track locations *or* calls

backstretch	post
clubhouse turn	quarter pole *or* post
eighth pole *or* post	sixteenth pole *or* post
far turn	straightaway *or* home
five-eighths pole *or* post	stretch *or* home
half-mile pole *or* post	straight
mile pole *or* post	winner's circle

758 CARDPLAYING

NOUNS **1 cardplaying** *or* card playing, shuffling, cutting, cut, dealing, deal; **card game,** game; gambling 759, gambling games

2 card, playing card, board, pasteboard; **deck, pack; suit,** hearts, diamonds, spades, clubs, puppy-feet <nf>; hand; **face card,** blaze, coat card, coat, count card, court card, paint, paint-skin, picture card, redskin; **king,** figure, cowboy *and* sergeant from K Company <nf>, one-eyed king, king of hearts *or* suicide king; queen, bitch *and* hen *and* lady *and* mop-squeezer *and* whore <nf>, queen of spades, Black Maria *and* Maria *and* slippery Anne <nf>; **jack,** knave, boy *and* fishhook *and* j-bird *and* j-boy *and* john <nf>, one-eyed jack, jack of trumps *or* right bower, left bower; **joker,** bower, best bower; spot card, rank card, plain card; **ace,** bull *and* bullet *and* seed *and* spike <nf>, ace of diamonds *or* pig's eye <nf>, ace of clubs *or* puppyfoot <nf>; **two, deuce,** two-spot, duck <nf>, two of spades *or* curse of Mexico <nf>; **three, trey,** three-spot; **four,** four-spot, four of clubs *or* devil's bedposts <nf>; **five,** five-spot, fever <nf>; **six,** six-spot; **seven,** seven-spot, fishhook <nf>; **eight,**

eight-spot; **nine,** nine-spot, nine of diamonds *or* curse of Scotland <nf>; **ten,** ten-spot; wild card

3 **bridge,** auction bridge, contract bridge, rubber bridge, duplicate *or* tournament bridge; **bridge player,** partner, dummy, North and South, East and West, left hand opponent *or* LHO, bidder, responder, declarer, senior, dummy; **suit,** major suit, minor suit, trump suit *or* trumps, lay suit *or* plain suit *or* side suit; **call, bid** <see list>; pass; **hand** <see list>; **play,** lead, opening lead, **trick,** quick trick *or* honor trick, high-card trick, overtrick, odd trick, finesse, ruff, crossruff; **score,** adjusted score, grand slam, little slam *or* small slam, game, rubber, premium, honors *or* honors cards, yarborough, set *or* setback

4 **poker,** draw poker, stud poker, five-card stud, six-card stud, seven-card stud, eight-card stud, strip poker; poker hand, five of a kind, straight flush, royal flush, four of a kind, full house, full boat, flush, straight, three of a kind, two pairs, one pair; pot, jackpot, pool, ante, chip, stake, call, checking, raise

VERBS 5 **shuffle,** make up, make up the pack, fan *and* wash <nf>; cut; **deal,** serve, pitch <nf>

6 **bridge bids**

asking bid	overbid *or* overcall
bidding convention	pass
borderline bid	rebid
business double	redouble
demand bid	renege
double	response
forcing bid	sacrifice bid
forcing pass	score bid
free bid	shut-out bid
insufficient bid	sign-off
jump bid	skip bid
no-trump bid	suit bid
opening bid	takeout double
original bid	underbid

7 **bridge hands**

balanced hand	piano hand
doubleton	pianola hand
exposed hand	side strength
long trump	singleton
long suit	short suit
major tenace	tenace
minor tenace	unbalanced hand
offensive strength	void
perfect tenace	yarborough

759 GAMBLING

NOUNS 1 **gambling, playing, betting, action,** wagering, punting, hazarding, risking, staking, gaming, laying, taking *or* giving *or* laying odds, sporting <old>; **speculation, play;** drawing *or* casting lots, tossing *or* flipping a coin, sortition

2 **gamble, chance, risk, risky thing, hazard; gambling** *or* **gambler's chance,** betting proposition, bet, matter of chance, sporting chance, **luck of the draw,** hazard of the die, roll *or* cast *or* throw of the dice, turn *or* roll of the wheel, turn of the table, turn of the cards, fall of the cards, flip *or* toss of a coin, toss-up, toss; heads or tails, touch and go; blind bargain, pig in a poke; leap in the dark, shot in the dark; potshot, random shot, potluck; **speculation, venture,** flier *and* plunge <nf>; calculated risk; uncertainty 971; fortune, luck 972.1

3 **bet, wager, stake,** hazard, lay, play *and* chunk *and* shot <nf>; cinch bet *or* sure thing, mortal cinch *and* mortal lock *and* nuts <nf>; long shot; **ante;** parlay, double or nothing; **dice bet, craps bet,** golf bet, **horse-racing bet, poker bet,** roulette bet, telebet

4 **betting system; pari-mutuel,** off-track betting *or* OTB; perfecta, exacta, win, place, show, all-way bet, daily double

5 **pot, jackpot, pool, stakes, kitty; bank;** office pool

6 **gambling odds, odds,** price; **even** *or* **square odds,** even break; **short odds, long odds,** long shot; even chance, good chance, small chance, no chance 972.10; **handicapper,** odds maker, pricemaker

7 **gambling game** <see list>, game of chance, game, friendly game; card games

8 **dice, bones** *and* rolling bones *and* ivories *and* babies *and* cubes *and* devil's bones *or* teeth *and* galloping dominoes *and* golf balls *and* marbles and Memphis dominoes and Mississippi marbles and Missouri marbles <nf>, **craps,** crap shooting, crap game, bank craps *or* casino craps, muscle craps, African dominoes *and* African golf *and* alley craps *and* army craps *and* blanket craps *and* army marbles *and* Harlem tennis *and* poor man's roulette <nf> floating crap game, floating game, sawdust game; poker dice; **false** *or* crooked *or* loaded dice

9 <throw of dice> **throw, cast, rattle, roll, shot,** hazard of the die; dice points and rolls <see list>

10 **poker,** draw poker *or* draw *or* five-card draw *or* open poker, stud poker *or* stud *or* closed poker, five-card stud *or* seven-card stud, up card *or* open card, down card *or* closed card; common *or* community *or* communal card; highball, high-low, lowball; **straight** *or* **natural poker,** wild-card poker; **poker hand,** duke *and* mitt <nf>, good hand *or* cards, lock *or* cinch *or* cinch hand *or* ironclad hand *or* iron duke *or* mortal cinch *or* nut hand *or* nuts *or* immortals; bad hand *or* cards, trash *and* rags <nf>; **openers,** progressive openers,

bet, raise *or* kick *or* bump *or* pump *or* push, showdown

11 **blackjack** *or* **twenty-one** *or* vingt-et-un; deal, card count, stiff, hard seventeen, hard eighteen, soft count, soft hand, soft eighteen, hit, blackjack *or* natural *or* snap *or* snapper, California blackjack; cut card *or* indicator card *or* sweat card; card-counting *or* ace-count *or* number count

12 **roulette,** American roulette, European roulette; **wheel,** American wheel, European wheel, wheel well, canoe, fret; **layout,** column, damnation alley, outside; zero, double zero, knotholes *or* house numbers

13 **cheating,** cheating scheme, cheating method, angle, con *and* grift *and* move *and* racket *and* scam *and* sting <nf>; deception 356

14 **lottery,** drawing, sweepstakes *or* sweepstake *or* sweep; draft lottery; **raffle; state lottery,** Lotto, Pick Six, Pick Four; tombola <Brit>; number lottery, numbers pool, **numbers game** *or* **policy,** Chinese lottery <nf>; interest lottery, Dutch *or* class lottery; tontine; grab bag *or* barrel *or* box

15 **bingo,** slow death <nf>, beano, keno, lotto; bingo card, banker, counter

16 <gambling device> gambling wheel, wheel of fortune, big six wheel, Fortune's wheel, raffle wheel *or* paddle wheel; roulette wheel, American wheel, European wheel; raffle wheel; cage, birdcage; goose *or* shaker, gooseneck; pinball machine; slot machine, slot, the slots, one-armed bandit <nf>; **layout** *or* green cloth, gambling table, craps table, Philadelphia layout, roulette table; **cheating device,** gaff *and* gimmick *and* tool <nf>

17 pari-mutuel, pari-mutuel machine; totalizator, totalizer, tote *and* tote board <nf>, odds board

18 **chip, check, counter** bean *and* fish <nf>

19 **casino, gambling house, house,** store *and* shop <nf>, gaming house, betting house, betting parlor, gambling den, gambling hall, sporting house <old>, gambling hell <nf>; luxurious casino, carpet joint *and* rug joint <nf>; honest gambling house, right joint <nf>; disreputable gambling house, crib *and* dive *and* joint *and* sawdust joint *and* store *and* toilet <nf>; illegal gambling house, cheating gambling house, brace house *and* bust-out joint *and* clip joint *and* deadfall *and* flat joint *and* flat store *and* hell *and* juice joint *and* low den *and* nick joint *and* peek store *and* skinning house *and* snap house *and* sneak joint *and* steer joint *and* wire joint *and* wolf trap <nf>; **handbook, book,** sports book, bookie joint <nf>, racebook, horse parlor, horse room, off-track betting parlor, OTB

20 **bookmaker, bookie** <nf>, turf accountant; **tout,** turf consultant; numbers runner; bagman

21 **gambler, player,** gamester, sportsman *or* sporting man <old>, sport, hazarder <old>; **speculator,** venturer, adventurer; **bettor,** wagerer, punter; high-stakes gambler, money player, high roller, plunger; petty gambler, low roller, piker *and* tinhorn *and* tinhorn gambler <nf>; professional gambler, pro *and* nutman <nf>; skillful gambler, sharp, shark, sharper, dean *and* professor *and* river gambler *and* dice gospeller *and* sharpie <nf>; cardsharp *or* cardshark, cardsharper; card counter, counter, caser, matrix player; crap shooter *and* boneshaker <nf>; compulsive gambler; spectator, kibitzer, lumber *and* sweater *and* wood <nf>

22 **cheater,** cheat, air bandit *and* bilk *and* bunco artist *and* dildock *and* grec *and* greek *and* grifter *and* hustler *and* mechanic *and* mover *and* rook *and* worker <nf>; deceiver 357; **dupe, victim,** coll *and* flat *and* john *and* lamb *and* lobster *and* mark *and* monkey *and* patsy *and* **sucker** <nf>

VERBS **23** **gamble,** game, sport <old>, play, **try one's luck** *or* **fortune; speculate; run** *or* **bank a game;** draw lots, draw straws, lot, cut lots, **cast lots;** cut the cards *or* deck; match coins, toss, flip a coin, call, call heads or tails; shoot craps, play at dice, roll the bones <nf>; play the ponies <nf>; raffle off

24 **chance, risk, hazard,** set at hazard, **venture,** wager, take a flier <nf>; **gamble on,** take a gamble on; **take a chance,** take one's chance, take the chances of, try the chance, **chance it; take** *or* **run the risk,** run a chance; **take chances,** tempt fortune; **leave** *or* **trust to chance** *or* **luck,** rely on fortune, take a leap in the dark; buy a pig in a poke; take potluck; raise the stakes, up the ante

25 **bet, wager, gamble, hazard, stake,** punt, lay, lay down, put up, **make a bet, lay a wager,** give *or* take *or* lay odds, make book, get a piece of the action <nf>; plunge <nf>; **bet on** *or* **upon, back;** bet *or* play against; play *or* follow the ponies <nf>; parlay; **ante, ante up; cover, call,** match *or* meet a bet, see, fade; **check, sandbag** <nf>, **pass,** stand pat *or* stand stiff; betcha

26 **cheat, pluck** *and* skin *and* rook <nf>; load the dice, mark the cards

ADJS **27** **speculative, uncertain** 971.16; **hazardous, risky** 1006.10, dicey <nf>; **lucky,** winning, hot *and* red hot *and* on a roll <nf>; **unlucky,** losing, cold <nf>

28 **gambling games**

all fours	bridge
auction bridge	canasta
baccarat	casino
bezique	crazy eights
bingo	chemin de fer
blind poker	chuck-a-luck *or* birdcage

contract bridge or contract
craps
cribbage
draw poker
écarté
euchre
fan tan
faro
fish or go fish
gin
gin rummy
hazard
hearts
high, low, jack and the
  game
keno
loo
lottery
lotto
lowball poker
monte
numbers or policy
old maid
ombre

paddle wheel or raffle
  wheel
penny ante
picquet
pinball
pinochle
pitch and toss
poker
poker dice
quinze
rouge et noir
roulette
rum
rummy
seven-up
stud poker
three-card monte
trente-et-quarante
twenty-one or blackjack or
  vingt-et-un
war
wheel of fortune or big six
  wheel
whist

29 dice points and rolls

blanket roll or soft-pad
  roll
boxes or hard eight
craps
doublet
drop shot
dump over shot
eight or eighter from
  Decatur or Ada from
  Decatur or Ada Ross or
  Ada Ross the stable hoss
English or ass English or
  body English or Jonah
even roll
fimps or hard ten
five or fee-bee or fever or
  phoebe or little Phoebe
four or little Dick Fisher or
  little Dick or little joe or
  little joe from Baltimore
  or little joe from Chicago
  or little joe from
  Kokomo

greek shot
little natural or slow crap
nine or carolina or
  carolina nina or nina
  from caroliner or nina
  from carolina
number or point
puppy feet
seven or natural or little
  natural or pass or craps
  or skinny Dugan
six or captain hicks or
  sister hicks or Jimmy
  Hicks or sixie from dixie
  or sixty days or sice
ten or big dick or big Joe
  from Boston or slow
  crap
three or cock-eyes
twelve or boxcars or high
  noon or Gary Cooper
two or snake eyes or Dolly
  Parton

760 OTHER SPORTS

NOUNS **1 billiards**, pool, pocket billiards, snooker;
  billiard table, pool table, pocket, cue ball, cue
  stick, chalk; pool hall, billiards club
 2 boating, sailing, canoeing, rowing, sculling,
  windsurfing, sailboarding, surfing, rafting,
  whitewater rafting; yachting, competitive sailing,
  day sailing; sailboat, canoe, catamaran,
  rowboat, kayak; regatta, America's Cup; sailor,

yachtsman, yachtswoman, canoeist, rower,
  oarsman or oar, sculler, windsurfer, surfer,
  sailboarder; mariner, boater
 3 martial arts; judo, the way of gentleness; karate,
  the way of the empty hand, sport karate,
  recreational karate; tae kwon do, the way of the
  foot and fist; aikido, the way of harmony of the
  spirit, competition aikido; belt, grade, dan grade;
  dojo
 4 fencing; foil fencing, épée fencing, saber fencing,
  escrime <Fr>; en garde, parry, riposte, thrust,
  feint, lunge
 5 gymnastics; floor exercise, tumbling, vaulting,
  trampolining, balance beam, horizontal bar,
  uneven parallel bars, pommel or side horse,
  stationary rings
 6 mountain climbing, mountaineering, rock
  climbing, bouldering, free climbing, clean
  climbing, aid climbing, big wall climbing,
  snow climbing, ice climbing, Alpine-style
  climbing, alpinism; climbing expedition, base
  camp, advance camp; rock face
 7 ice skating, figure skating, free skating, pairs
  skating, ice dancing, speed skating; Olympic
  skating, professional skating; compulsory figure,
  loop, salchow, jump, axel jump, double axel, triple
  axel, toe jump, spin, camel spin, lay-back spin, sit
  spin
 8 swimming, natation; synchronized swimming,
  diving, scuba, snorkeling, skinny-dipping <nf>,
  dog-paddling, Olympic swimming; crawl or
  American crawl or Australian crawl, back crawl,
  backstroke, breaststroke, butterfly stroke; flutter
  kick, scissors kick, back kick, wedge kick, frog
  kick, whip kick; lifeguarding, lifesaving;
  swimming pool, natatorium

761 EXISTENCE

NOUNS **1 existence, being;** subsistence, entity,
  essence, esse, isness, absolute or transcendental
  essence, *l'être* <Fr>, pure being, *Ding-an-sich*
  <Ger, thing-in-itself>, noumenon; **occurrence,**
  presence, monadism; **materiality** 1052,
  substantiality 763; **life** 306
 2 reality, actuality, factuality, empirical or
  demonstrable or objective existence, the here and
  now; historicity; necessity; the real thing, the
  genuine article; facticity; **truth** 973; **authenticity;**
  sober or grim reality, hardball and the nitty-gritty
  <nf>, not a dream, more truth than poetry; thing,
  something, ens, entity, being, object, substance,
  phenomenon
 3 fact, the case, fact or truth of the matter, not
  opinion, not guesswork, what's what *and* where it's

at <nf>; **matter of fact; bare fact,** naked fact, bald fact, **simple fact,** sober fact, simple *or* sober truth; **cold fact,** hard fact, **stubborn fact, brutal fact,** painful fact, the nitty-gritty *and* the bottom line <nf>; **actual fact,** positive fact, absolute fact; **self-evident fact,** axiom, postulate, premise, accomplished fact, *fait accompli* <Fr>; **accepted fact,** conceded fact, admitted fact, fact of experience, well-known fact, established fact, inescapable fact, irreducible fact, indisputable fact, undeniable fact; **demonstrable fact,** provable fact; empirical fact; protocol, protocol statement *or* sentence *or* proposition; given fact, given, donné datum, **circumstance** 766; **salient fact,** significant fact; factlet, factoid, fact bite

 4 **the facts,** information 551, the particulars, the details, the specifics, **the data;** the dope *and* the scoop *and* the score *and* the skinny *and* the inside skinny <nf>; the picture <nf>, the gen <Brit nf>, what's what <nf>; the fact *or* facts *or* truth of the matter, the facts of the case, the whole story <nf>; essentials, basic *or* essential facts, brass tacks *or* nitty-gritty <nf>; fact sheet

 5 **self-existence,** uncreated being, noncontingent existence, aseity, innascibility

 6 **mere existence,** simple existence, **vegetable existence, vegetation,** mere tropism; couch potato

 7 (philosophy of being) ontology, metaphysics, existentialism

VERBS 8 exist, be, be in existence, be extant, have being; breathe, **live** 306.8; subsist, stand, obtain, hold, prevail, be the case; **occur,** be present, be there, be found, be true, be met with, happen to be

 9 **live on,** continue to exist, persist, last, stand the test of time, abide, endure 827.6

10 **vegetate,** merely exist, just be, pass the time

11 **exist in, consist in,** subsist in, lie in, rest in, repose in, reside in, abide in, inhabit, dwell in, **inhere in,** be present in, be a quality of, be comprised in, be contained in, be constituted by, be coextensive with

12 **become,** come to be, go, get, get to be, turn out to be, materialize; be converted into, turn into 858.17; grow 861.5; be changed

ADJS 13 existent, existing, in existence, de facto; **subsistent,** subsisting; **being,** in being; **living** 306.12; **present, extant, prevalent, current,** in force *or* effect, afoot, on foot, under the sun, on the face of the earth

14 **self-existent,** self-existing, innascible; uncreated, increate

15 **real, actual,** factual, veritable, for real <nf>, de facto, simple, sober, **hard; absolute, positive; self-evident,** axiomatic; accepted, conceded, stipulated, given; admitted, well-known, **established, inescapable, indisputable,**

undeniable; **demonstrable,** provable; empirical, **objective,** historical; **true** 973.13; honest-to-God <nf>, genuine, card-carrying <nf>, **authentic; substantial** 763.6

ADVS 16 really, actually; factually; genuinely, veritably, basically, **truly; in reality,** in actuality, in effect, in fact, de facto, in point of fact, as a matter of fact; positively, absolutely; no buts about it <nf>; no ifs, ands, or buts <nf>; obviously, manifestly 348.14

WORD ELEMENTS 17 onto-

762 NONEXISTENCE

NOUNS 1 nonexistence, nonsubsistence; **nonbeing,** unbeing, not-being, nonentity; **nothingness,** nothing, nullity, nihility, invalidity; vacancy, deprivation, emptiness, inanity, vacuity 222.2; vacuum, void 222.3; nix <nf>; negativeness, negation, negativity; nonoccurrence, nonhappening; **unreality,** nonreality, unactuality; nonpresence, absence 222

 2 **nothing, nil,** *nihil* <L>, *nichts* <Ger>, *nada* <Sp>, **naught, aught;** zero, 0, cipher; nothing whatever, nothing at all, nothing on earth *or* under the sun, no such thing; thing of naught 764.2

 3 <nf terms> **zilch, zip,** zippo, nix, goose egg, Billy be damn, diddly, shit, diddly shit, squat, diddly squat, Sweet Fanny Adams <Brit>, bubkes, beans, a hill of beans, a hoot, **a fart,** a fuck, fuck all *and* bugger all <Brit>, jack-shit, a rat's ass, chopped liver

 4 **none,** not any, none at all, not a one, not a blessed one <nf>, never a one, ne'er a one, nary one <nf>; **not a bit,** not a whit, not a hint, not a smitch *or* smidgen <nf>, not a speck, not a mite, not a particle, not an iota, not a jot, not a one, not a sausage <Brit>, not a scrap, not a trace, not a lick *or* a whiff <nf>, not a shadow, not a suspicion, not a shadow of a suspicion, neither hide nor hair

VERBS 5 not exist, not be in existence, not be met with, not occur, not be found, found nowhere, be absent *or* lacking *or* wanting, be null and void

 6 **cease to exist** *or* **be, be annihilated,** be destroyed, **be wiped out,** be extirpated, be eradicated; **go, vanish,** be no more, leave no trace; **vanish, disappear** 34.2, evaporate, fade, fade away *or* out, fly, flee, dissolve, melt away, die out *or* away, pass, pass away, pass out of the picture <nf>, turn to nothing *or* naught, peter out <nf>, come to an end, wind down, tail off *and* trail off <nf>, reach an all-time low; **perish, expire,** pass away, **die** 307.18

 7 **annihilate** 395.13, **exterminate** 395.14, eradicate, extirpate, **eliminate,** liquidate, **wipe out, stamp out,** waste *and* take out *and* nuke *and* zap <nf>, put an end to 395.12

ADJS **8 nonexistent,** unexistent, inexistent, nonsubsistent, unexisting, without being, nowhere to be found; **minus, missing,** lacking, wanting; **null, void,** devoid, empty, inane, vacuous; **negative,** less than nothing; absent

9 unreal, unrealistic, unactual, not real; merely nominal; **immaterial** 1053.7; **unsubstantial** 764.5; **imaginary, imagined,** make believe, **fantastic, fanciful, fancied** 986.19–22; illusory

10 uncreated, unmade, unborn, unbegotten, unconceived, unproduced

11 no more, extinct, defunct, dead 307.29, expired, passed away; vanished, gone glimmering; perished, obsolete, annihilated; gone, all gone; all over with, had it <nf>, finished *and* phut *and* pffft *and* kaput <nf>, down the tube *and* down the drain *and* up the spout <nf>, done for *and* dead and done for <nf>

ADVS **12 none, no,** not at all, in no way, to no extent

WORD ELEMENTS **13** nulli-

763 SUBSTANTIALITY

NOUNS **1 substantiality,** substantialness; materiality 1052; **substance, body,** mass; **solidity,** density, concreteness, **tangibility,** palpability, ponderability; **sturdiness, stability,** soundness, firmness, steadiness, stoutness, toughness, **strength,** durability

2 substance, stuff, fabric, material, matter 1052.2, medium, the tangible; **elements,** constituent elements, constituents, ingredients, components, atoms, building blocks, parts

3 something, thing, an existence; **being, entity,** unit, individual, entelechy, monad; **person,** persona, personality, body, soul; **creature,** created being, contingent being; **organism,** life form, living thing, life; **object** 1052.4

4 embodiment, incarnation, materialization, substantiation, concretization, hypostasis, reification

VERBS **5 embody,** incarnate, **materialize,** concretize, body forth, lend substance to, reify, entify, hypostatize

ADJS **6 substantial,** substantive; **solid, concrete; tangible,** sensible, appreciable, palpable, ponderable; **material** 1052.10; **real** 761.15; **created,** creatural, organismic *or* organismal, contingent

7 sturdy, stable, **solid,** sound, firm, steady, tough, stout, **strong,** rugged; **durable,** lasting, enduring; **hard, dense,** unyielding, steely, adamantine; **well-made,** well-constructed, well-built, well-knit; **well-founded,** well-established, well-grounded; **massive,** bulky, heavy, chunky

ADVS **8 substantially,** essentially, materially

WORD ELEMENTS **9** stere-, ont-

764 UNSUBSTANTIALITY

NOUNS **1 unsubstantiality,** insubstantiality, unsubstantialness; **immateriality** 1053; bodilessness, incorporeality, unsolidity, unconcreteness; **intangibility,** impalpability, imponderability; **thinness, tenuousness,** attenuation, tenuity, evanescence, subtlety, subtility, fineness, airiness, mistiness, vagueness, ethereality; **fragility, frailness; flimsiness** 16.2; **transience** 828, **ephemerality,** ephemeralness, fleetingness, fugitiveness

2 thing of naught, nullity, zero; **nonentity, nobody** *and* nonstarter *and* nebbish <nf>, nonperson, unperson, cipher, man of straw, jackstraw <old>, lay figure, puppet, dummy, hollow man; flash in the pan, dud <nf>; **trifle** 998.5; *nugae* <L>; nothing 762.2

3 spirit, air, **thin air,** breath, mere breath, smoke, vapor, mist, ether, **bubble,** "such stuff as dreams are made on"—Shakespeare, **shadow,** mere shadow; illusion 976; phantom 988.1

VERBS **4 spiritualize, disembody,** dematerialize; etherealize, **attenuate,** subtilize, rarefy, fine, refine; **weaken,** enervate, sap

ADJS **5 unsubstantial,** insubstantial, nonsubstantial, unsubstanced; intangible, impalpable, imponderable; **immaterial** 1053.7; **bodiless,** incorporeal, unsolid, unconcrete; weightless 298.10; **transient** 828.7, ephemeral, fleeting, fugitive

6 thin, tenuous, subtile, subtle, evanescent, fine, overfine, refined, rarefied; **ethereal,** airy, windy, spirituous, vaporous, gaseous; air-built, cloud-built; **chimerical,** gossamer, gossamery, gauzy, shadowy, phantomlike 988.7; dreamlike, **illusory, unreal;** fatuous, fatuitous, inane; **imaginary,** fanciful 986.20

7 fragile, frail 1050.4; **flimsy,** shaky, weak, papery, paper-thin, **unsound,** infirm 16.15

8 baseless, groundless, ungrounded, **without foundation,** unfounded, not well-founded, built on sand, "writ on water"—Keats

WORD ELEMENTS **9** pseudo-

765 STATE

NOUNS **1 state,** mode, modality; **status, situation,** status quo *or* status in quo, position, standing, footing, location, bearings, spot, walk of life; **rank,** estate, station, place, place on the ladder, **standing; condition,** circumstance 766; **case, lot;**

predicament, plight, pass, pickle *and* picklement *and* fix *and* jam *and* spot *and* bind <nf>

2 **the state of affairs,** the nature *or* shape of things, the way it shapes up <nf>, the way of the world, how things stack up <nf>, **how things stand,** how things are, the way of things, the way it is, like it is, where it's at <nf>, **the way things are,** the way of it, the way things go, how it goes, the way the cookie crumbles, **how it is,** the status quo *or* status in quo, the size of it <nf>; how the land lies, the lay of the land; shape, phase, state of the art; state of mind

3 **good condition, bad condition;** adjustment, fettle, form, order, repair, **shape** <nf>, trim

4 **mode, manner, way,** tenor, vein, fashion, style, lifestyle, way of life, preference, thing and bag <nf>; **form,** shape, guise, complexion, make-up; **role,** capacity, character, part; modus vivendi, modus operandi

VERBS 5 **be in** *or* **have** a certain state, be such *or* so *or* thus, **fare,** go on *or* along; **enjoy** *or* **occupy** a certain position; **get on** *or* **along,** come on *or* along <nf>; **manage** <nf>, **contrive, make out** <nf>, come through, get by; **turn out,** come out, stack up <nf>, shape up <nf>

ADJS 6 conditional, modal, formal, situational, statal

7 **in condition** *or* **order** *or* repair *or* shape; **out of order,** out of commission *and* **out of kilter** *or* kelter *and* out of whack <nf>

766 CIRCUMSTANCE

NOUNS 1 **circumstance, occurrence, occasion, event** 831, **incident;** juncture, conjuncture, contingency, eventuality; **condition** 765.1

2 **circumstances,** total situation, existing conditions *or* situation, set of conditions, terms of reference, **environment** 209, environing circumstances, context, frame, setting, surround, surrounding conditions, parameters, status quo *or* status in quo, setup; state of affairs; **the picture,** the whole picture, full particulars, ins and outs, ball game <nf>, the score <nf>, how things stand, the way the cookie crumbles, the whole nine yards, lay of the land, layout, play-by-play description, blow-by-blow account

3 **particular, instance, item, detail,** point, count, case, fact, matter, article, datum, element, part, ingredient, factor, facet, aspect, thing; **respect, regard,** angle; minutia, minutiae <pl>, trifle, petty *or* trivial matter; incidental, minor detail

4 **circumstantiality,** particularity, specificity, thoroughness, minuteness of detail; accuracy

5 **circumstantiation,** itemization, particularization, specification, spelling-out, detailing, anatomization, atomization, analysis 801

VERBS 6 **itemize, specify,** circumstantiate, particularize, **spell out, detail,** go *or* enter into detail, descend to particulars, give full particulars, put in context, atomize, anatomize; **analyze** 801.6; **cite,** instance, adduce, document, give *or* quote chapter and verse; **substantiate**

ADJS 7 **circumstantial,** conditional, provisional; **incidental,** occasional, contingent, adventitious, **accidental, chance,** fortuitous, casual, aleatory, aleatoric, unessential *or* inessential *or* nonessential; background

8 environmental, environing, surrounding, conjunctive, conjoined, contextual, attending, attendant, limiting, determining, parametric; grounded, based

9 **detailed, minute, full, particular,** meticulous, fussy, finicky *or* finicking *or* finical, persnickety, picayune, picky <nf>, nice <old>, precise, exact, specific, special

ADVS 10 **thus, thusly,** <nf>, in such wise, thuswise, this way, this-a-way <nf>, thus and thus, thus and so, **so,** just so, like so *and* yea <nf>, like this, like that, just like that; similarly 784.18, precisely

11 **accordingly, in that case, in that event, at that rate,** that being the case, such being the case, that being so, **under the circumstances,** the condition being such, as it is, as matters stand, as the matter stands, **therefore** 888.7, **consequently; as the case may be,** as it may be, according to circumstances; as it may happen *or* turn out, as things may fall; **by the same token,** equally

12 **circumstantially,** conditionally, provisionally; provided 959.12

13 **fully, in full, in detail,** minutely, specifically, particularly, in particular, wholly 792.13, *in toto* <L>, completely 794.14, **at length,** *in extenso* <L>, *ad nauseam* <L>

767 INTRINSICALITY

NOUNS 1 **intrinsicality,** internality, innerness, **inwardness; inbeing,** indwelling, immanence; **innateness, inherence,** indigenousness; essentiality, fundamentality; **subjectivity,** internal reality, nonobjectivity

2 **essence, substance,** stuff, very stuff, inner essence, essential nature, quiddity, esse; **quintessence, epitome,** embodiment, incarnation, model, pattern, purest type, typification, perfect example *or* exemplar, elixir, flower; **essential,** principle, essential principle, fundamental, hypostasis, postulate, axiom; **gist,** gravamen, **nub** <nf>, nucleus, center, focus, kernel, **core, pith,** meat; **heart,** soul, heart and soul, spirit, sap, lifeblood, marrow, entelechy

3 <nf terms> meat and potatoes, **nuts and bolts**, the nitty-gritty, the guts, the name of the game, the bottom line, where it's at, what it's all about, the ball game, the payoff, the score, where the rubber meets the road; back to basics; mother of all

4 **nature, character, quality,** suchness; **constitution,** crasis <old>, composition, **characteristics,** makeup, constituents, building blocks; physique 262.4, physio; **build,** body-build, somatotype, frame, constitution, genetic make-up, system; complexion <old>, humor *and* humors <old>; **temperament,** temper, fiber, **disposition,** spirit, ethos, genius, dharma; **way, habit,** tenor, cast, hue, tone, grain, vein, streak, stripe, mold, brand, stamp; **kind** 809.3, **sort, type,** ilk; **property, characteristic** 865.4; **tendency** 896; the way of it, the nature of the beast <nf>

5 **inner nature,** inside, insides <nf>, internal *or* inner *or* esoteric *or* intrinsic reality, iniety, true being, essential nature, what makes one tick <nf>, center of life, vital principle, nerve center; **spirit, indwelling spirit, soul, heart, heart and soul, breast, bosom, inner person,** heart of hearts, insight, secret heart, inmost heart *or* soul, secret *or* innermost recesses of the heart, heart's core, bottom *or* cockles of the heart; vitals, the quick, depths of one's being, guts *and* kishkes <nf>, where one lives <nf>; **vital principle,** archeus, life force, *élan vital* <Fr>

VERBS 6 **inhere,** indwell, belong to *or* permeate by nature, makes one tick <nf>; run in the blood, run in the family, inherit, be born so, have it in the genes, be made that way, be built that way <nf>, be part and parcel of

ADJS 7 **intrinsic,** internal, **inner,** inward; **inherent,** resident, implicit, immanent, indwelling; inalienable, unalienable, uninfringeable, unquestionable, unchallengeable, irreducible, qualitative; **ingrained,** in the very grain; infixed, implanted, inwrought, deep-seated; **subjective,** esoteric, private, secret

8 **innate, inborn,** born, congenital; **native, natural,** natural to, connatural, native to, indigenous; **constitutional,** bodily, physical, temperamental, organic; **inbred, genetic, hereditary,** inherited, bred in the bone, in the blood, running in the blood *or* race *or* strain, radical, rooted; connate, connatal, coeval; **instinctive,** instinctual, atavistic, primal

9 **essential,** of the essence, **fundamental; primary,** primitive, primal, elementary, elemental, simple, bare bones *and* no-frills *and* bread-and-butter <nf>, original, *ab ovo* <L>, **basic, gut** <nf>, basal, underlying; **substantive,** substantial, material; constitutive, constituent; mandatory, compulsory; must-have

ADVS 10 **intrinsically, inherently,** innately; internally, inwardly, immanently; originally, primally, primitively; **naturally, congenitally,** genetically, **by birth, by nature**

11 **essentially, fundamentally, primarily, basically; at bottom,** *au fond* <Fr>, at heart; in essence, at the core, in substance, in the main; substantially, materially, most of all; per se, of *or* in itself, as such, qua

WORD ELEMENTS 12 physi-, physic-

768 EXTRINSICALITY

NOUNS 1 **extrinsicality,** externality, outwardness, extraneousness, otherness, discreteness; foreignness; **objectivity,** nonsubjectivity, impersonality

2 **nonessential,** inessential *or* unessential, nonvitalness, carrying coals to Newcastle, gilding the lily; **accessory, extra,** collateral; the other, not-self; **appendage,** appurtenance, auxiliary, supernumerary; **supplement,** addition, addendum, superaddition, adjunct 254; **subsidiary,** subordinate, secondary; **contingency,** contingent, incidental, accidental, accident, happenstance, mere chance; **superfluity,** superfluousness; fifth wheel *and* tits on a boar <nf>; triviality

ADJS 3 **extrinsic, external,** outward, outside, outlying; **extraneous,** foreign; **objective,** nonsubjective, impersonal, extraorganismic *or* extraorganismal; not of this world

4 **unessential,** inessential *or* nonessential, unnecessary, nonvital, superfluous; **accessory, extra,** collateral, auxiliary, supernumerary; adventitious, appurtenant, adscititious; **additional, supplementary,** supplemental, superadded, supervenient, make-weight; **secondary,** subsidiary, subordinate; **incidental,** circumstantial, contingent; trivial, throwaway; **accidental, chance,** fortuitous, casual, aleatory, aleatoric; **indeterminate, unpredictable,** capricious

769 ACCOMPANIMENT

NOUNS 1 **accompaniment,** concomitance *or* concomitancy, withness and togetherness <nf>; synchronism, **simultaneity** 836, simultaneousness; coincidence, co-occurrence, concurrence, concurrency, coexistence, symbiosis; parallelism; coagency

2 **company, association,** consociation, **society,** community; **companionship, fellowship,** consortship, partnership; cohabitation

3 **attendant,** concomitant, corollary, **accessory,** appendage; **adjunct** 254

4 **accompanier, accompanist; attendant, companion, fellow, mate,** comate, consort, **partner;** companion piece

5 **escort, conductor, usher,** shepherd; **guide,** tourist guide, cicerone; **squire,** esquire, swain, cavalier; **chaperon,** duenna; **bodyguard,** guard, **convoy,** muscle <nf>; companion, sidekick <nf>, fellow traveler, travel companion, satellite, outrider; third wheel

6 **attendance, following, cortege, retinue, entourage,** suite, followers, followership, rout, train, body of retainers; **court,** cohort; parasite 138.5

VERBS **7** **accompany,** bear *or* keep one company, **keep company with,** companion, go *or* travel *or* run with, go together, go along for the ride <nf>, **go along with, attend,** wait on *or* upon; **associate with,** assort with, sort with, **consort with,** couple with, hang around with *and* hang out with *and* hang with <nf>, go hand in hand with; **combine** 805.3, **associate,** consociate, confederate, flock *or* band *or* herd together

8 **escort, conduct,** have in tow <nf>, marshal, **usher,** shepherd, **guide, lead; convoy,** guard; **squire,** esquire, **attend,** wait on *or* upon, **take out** <nf>; **chaperon;** attend, dance attendance on

ADJS **9** **accompanying, attending, attendant, concomitant,** accessory, collateral; **combined** 805.5, **associated,** coupled, paired; **fellow, twin, joint, joined** 800.13, conjoint, hand-in-hand, hand-in-glove, mutual; **simultaneous, concurrent,** coincident, synchronic, synchronized; correlative; parallel; complementary, accessory

ADVS **10** **hand in hand** *or* glove, arm in arm, side by side, cheek by jowl, shoulder to shoulder; therewith, therewithal, herewith

11 **together, collectively, mutually,** jointly, unitedly, in conjunction, conjointly, *en masse* <Fr>, communally, corporately, **in a body,** all at once, *ensemble* <Fr>, in association, in company; simultaneously, coincidentally, concurrently, at once

PREPS **12** **with, in company with, along with, together with,** in association with, coupled *or* paired *or* partnered with, in conjunction with

WORD ELEMENTS **13** co-, con-, col-, com-, cor-, meta-, syn-, sym-

770 ASSEMBLAGE

NOUNS **1** **assemblage, assembly, collection, gathering,** ingathering, forgathering, **congregation,** assembling; concourse, concurrence, conflux, confluence, convergence; collocation, juxtaposition, junction 800.1; combination 805; mobilization, call-up, muster, *attroupement* <Fr>; roundup, rodeo, corralling, shepherding, marshaling; **comparison** 943; canvass, census, data-gathering, survey, inventory

2 **assembly** <of persons>, *assemblée* <Fr>, **gathering, forgathering, congregation,** congress, conference, convocation, concourse, **meeting,** meet, **get-together** *and* turnout <nf>; convention, conventicle, synod, council, diet, **conclave,** levee; caucus; mass meeting, **rally,** sit-in, demonstration, demo <nf>; **session,** séance, sitting, sit-down <nf>; **panel,** forum, symposium, colloquium; committee, commission; *eisteddfod* <Welsh>; plenum, quorum; **party, festivity** 743.4, fete, at home, housewarming, soiree, reception, **dance,** ball, prom, do <chiefly Brit>, shindig *and* brawl <nf>; rendezvous, date, assignation

3 **company, group,** grouping, groupment, network, **party, band, knot, gang, crew,** complement, cast, outfit, pack, cohort, troop, troupe, tribe, **body,** corps, stable, bunch and mob and crowd <nf>; squad, platoon, battalion, regiment, brigade, division, fleet; **team,** squad, string; covey, bevy; posse, detachment, contingent, detail, *posse comitatus* <L>; phalanx; **party, faction,** movement, wing, persuasion; in-group, old-boy network, out-group, peer group, age group; coterie, salon, clique, **set;** junta, cabal

4 **throng, multitude, horde,** host, heap <nf>, army, panoply, legion; flock, cluster, galaxy; **crowd,** press, crush, flood, spate, deluge, mass, surge, storm, squeeze; **mob,** mass, rabble, rout, ruck, jam, *cohue* <Fr>, everybody and his uncle *or* his brother <nf>, all and them some

5 <animals> **flock, bunch, pack,** colony, host, troop, army, **herd, drove,** drive, drift, trip; pride <of lions>, sloth <of bears>, skulk <of foxes>, gang <of elk>, kennel <of dogs>, clowder <of cats>, pod <of seals>, gam <of whales>, **school** *or* shoal <of fish>, etc; <animal young> **litter**

6 <birds, insects> **flock,** flight, **swarm,** cloud; covey <of partridges>, bevy <of quail>, skein <of geese in flight>, gaggle <of geese on water>, watch <of nightingales>, charm <of finches>, murmuration <of starlings>, spring <of teal>; hive <of bees>, plague <of locusts>

7 **bunch, group,** grouping, groupment, crop, **cluster, clump,** knot, wad; grove, copse, thicket; **batch, lot,** slew <nf>, **mess** <nf>; tuft, wisp; tussock, hassock; shock, stook; arrangement, nosegay, posy, spray

8 **bundle,** bindle <nf>, **pack, package,** packet, deck, budget, **parcel,** fardel <nf>, sack, bag, poke <nf>, rag-bag <nf>, bale, truss, **roll,** rouleau, bolt; fagot, fascine, fasces; quiver, sheaf; bouquet, nosegay, posy

9 accumulation, cumulation, gathering, **amassment,** congeries, acervation, collection, collecting, grouping; agglomeration, conglomeration, glomeration, conglomerate, agglomerate; **aggregation,** aggregate; conglobation; **mass, lump,** gob <nf>, chunk *and* hunk <nf>, wad; snowball; stockpile, stockpiling

10 pile, heap, stack, mass; **mound, hill;** molehill, anthill; bank, embankment, dune; haystack, hayrick, haymow, haycock, cock, mow, rick; drift, snowdrift; pyramid

11 collection, collector's items, collectibles *or* collectables; **holdings,** fund, treasure, hoard; corpus, corpora, **body,** data, raw data; compilation, collectanea; ana; anthology, florilegium, treasury, store, stockpile; *Festschrift* <Ger>; chrestomathy; **museum, library,** zoo, menagerie, aquarium

12 set, suit, suite, series, outfit *and* kit <nf>

13 miscellany, miscellanea, collectanea; **assortment, medley, variety, mixture** 797; mixed bag, hodgepodge, conglomerate, **conglomeration,** omnium-gatherum <nf>, potpourri, smorgasbord; **sundries,** oddments, **odds and ends,** bits and pieces

14 <a putting together> **assembly,** assemblage; assembly line, production line; assembly-line production

15 collector, gatherer, accumulator, connoisseur, fancier, enthusiast, pack rat *and* magpie <nf>, hoarder; beachcomber; collection agent, bill collector, dunner; tax collector, tax man, exciseman <Brit>, customs agent, *douanier* <Fr>; **miser** 484.4

VERBS **16 come together, assemble, congregate, collect,** come from far and wide, come *or* arrive in a body; league 805.4, ally; **unite** 800.5; muster, **meet, gather, forgather,** gang up <nf>, mass, amass; **merge,** converge, flow together, fuse; group, flock, flock together; herd together; **throng, crowd,** swarm, teem, hive, surge, seethe, mill, stream, horde; **be crowded,** be mobbed, burst at the seams, be full to overflowing; **cluster,** bunch, bunch up, clot; gather around, gang around <nf>; rally, rally around; **huddle,** go into a huddle, close ranks; rendezvous, date; **couple,** copulate, link, link up

17 convene, meet, hold a meeting *or* session, sit; **convoke,** summon, call together

18 <bring *or* gather together> **assemble, gather;** drum up, muster, rally, **mobilize; collect,** collect up, fund-raise, take up a collection, raise, take up; **accumulate,** cumulate, **amass,** mass, bulk, batch; agglomerate, conglomerate, aggregate; **combine** 805.3, **network, join** 800.5, **bring together,** get

together, **gather together,** draw *or* lump *or* batch *or* bunch together, pack, pack in, cram, cram in; **bunch,** bunch up; **cluster,** clump; **group,** aggroup; **gather in,** get *or* whip in; scrape *or* scratch together, scrape up, together, rake *or* dredge *or* dig up; round up, corral, drive together; **put together,** make up, compile, colligate; collocate, **juxtapose,** pair, match, partner; hold up together, **compare** 943.4

19 pile, pile on, heap, stack, heap *or* pile *or* stack up; mound, hill, bank, bank up; rick; pyramid; drift; stockpile, build up

20 bundle, bundle up, **package,** parcel, parcel up, **pack,** bag, sack, truss, truss up; bale; wrap, **wrap up,** do *or* tie *or* bind up; roll up

ADJS **21 assembled, collected, gathered;** congregate, congregated; meeting, in session; **combined** 805.5; **joined** 800.13; joint, leagued 805.6; **accumulated,** cumulate, massed, **amassed;** heaped, stacked, piled; glomerate, agglomerate, conglomerate, aggregate; **clustered,** bunched, lumped, clumped, knotted; bundled, packaged, wrapped up; fascicled, fasciculated; herded, shepherded, rounded up

22 crowded, packed, crammed; bumper-to-bumper <nf>, jam-packed, packed *or* crammed like sardines <nf>, chockablock; **compact,** firm, solid, dense, close, serried; **teeming, swarming, crawling,** seething, bristling, populous, milling, **full** 794.11

23 cumulative, accumulative, total, overall

771 DISPERSION

NOUNS **1 dispersion** *or* **dispersal, scattering,** scatter, scatteration, diffraction; ripple effect; **distribution, spreading,** strewing, sowing, broadcasting, **broadcast, spread,** narrowcast, publication 352, **dissemination,** propagation, dispensation; **radiation,** divergence 171; expansion, splay; **diffusion,** circumfusion; **dilution,** attenuation, thinning, thinning-out, watering, watering-down, weakening; **evaporation,** volatilization, dissipation; fragmentation, shattering, pulverization; sprinkling, spattering; peppering, buckshot *or* shotgun pattern; deployment; diaspora

2 decentralization, deconcentration

3 disbandment, dispersion *or* dispersal, diaspora, separation, parting; breakup, split-up <nf>; **demobilization,** deactivation, **release,** detachment; dismissal 909.5; dissolution, disorganization, disintegration 806; population drift, urban sprawl, sprawl

VERBS **4 disperse, scatter,** diffract; **distribute, broadcast, sow,** narrowcast, disseminate, propagate, pass around *or* out, publish 352.10; **diffuse, spread,** dispread, circumfuse, strew, bestrew, dot; **radiate,** diverge 171.5; expand, splay, branch *or* fan *or* spread out; **issue, deal out,** dole out, retail, utter, dispense; sow broadcast, scatter to the winds; overscatter, overspread, oversow; sunder, hive off <nf>

5 **dissipate, dispel,** dissolve, attenuate, dilute, thin, thin out, water, water down, weaken; **evaporate,** volatilize; drive away, clear away, cast forth, blow off

6 **sprinkle,** besprinkle, asperge, **spatter,** splatter, splash; **dot,** spot, speck, speckle, freckle, stud; **pepper,** powder, dust; flour, crumb, bread, dredge

7 **decentralize,** deconcentrate

8 **disband, disperse, scatter, separate, part,** break up, split up; part company, go separate ways, bug out <nf>; **demobilize,** demob <nf>, deactivate, muster out, debrief, **release,** detach, discharge, let go; dismiss 909.18; **dissolve,** disorganize, disintegrate 806.3

ADJS 9 **dispersed, scattered, distributed,** dissipated, disseminated, strown, strewn, broadcast, **spread,** dispread; **widespread,** diffuse, discrete, sparse; **diluted,** thinned, thinned-out, watered, watered-down, weakened; **sporadic;** straggling, straggly; all over the lot *or* place <nf>, few and far between, from hell to breakfast <nf>

10 **sprinkled,** spattered, splattered, asperged, splashed, **peppered,** spotted, dotted, powdered, dusted, specked, speckled, **studded,** freckled

11 dispersive, **scattering, spreading,** diffractive *or* diffractional, **distributive,** disseminative, diffusive, dissipative, attenuative

ADVS 12 **scatteringly, dispersedly,** diffusely, sparsely, **sporadically,** *passim* <L>, **here and there;** in places, **in spots** <nf>; at large, everywhere, throughout, wherever you look *or* turn <nf>, in all quarters

772 INCLUSION

NOUNS 1 **inclusion, comprisal, comprehension,** coverage, envisagement, embracement, encompassment, incorporation, embodiment, assimilation, reception; **membership,** participation, admission, admissibility, eligibility, legitimation, legitimization; **power-sharing,** enablement, enfranchisement; **completeness** 794, **inclusiveness, comprehensiveness,** exhaustiveness; **whole** 792; openness, toleration *or* tolerance; universality, generality; inclusivism

2 **entailment, involvement, implication;** assumption, presumption, presupposition, subsumption

VERBS 3 **include, comprise, contain, comprehend,** hold, **take in; cover,** cover a lot of ground <nf>, occupy, take up, fill; fill in *or* out, build into, **complete** 794.6; **embrace,** encompass, enclose, encircle, incorporate, assimilate, embody, constitute, admit, receive, envisage; **legitimize,** legitimatize; **share power,** enable, enfranchise, cut in *and* deal in *and* give a piece of the action <nf>; among, count in, work in; **number among,** take into account *or* consideration

4 <include as a necessary circumstance *or* consequence> **entail, involve, implicate,** imply, assume, presume, presuppose, subsume, affect, take in, contain, comprise, **call for, require,** take, bring, lead to

ADJS 5 **included, comprised,** comprehended, envisaged, embraced, encompassed, added-in, covered, subsumed; bound up with, forming *or* making a part of, built-in, tucked-in, integrated; **involved** 898.4

6 **inclusive, including, containing, comprising, covering, embracing,** encompassing, enclosing, encircling, assimilating, incorporating, envisaging; counting, numbering; broad-brush *and* ballpark <nf>, all-in

7 **comprehensive, sweeping, complete** 794.9; whole 792.9; **all-comprehensive,** all-inclusive 864.14, non-exclusive; without omission *or* exception, **overall,** universal, global, wall-to-wall <nf>, around-the-world, **total,** blanket, omnibus, umbrella, across-the-board; encyclopedic, compendious; synoptic; bird's-eye, panoramic

773 EXCLUSION

NOUNS 1 **exclusion, barring,** debarring, debarment, preclusion, exception, omission, nonadmission, cutting-out, leaving-out, omission; **restriction, circumscription,** narrowing, demarcation; **rejection,** repudiation; **ban,** bar, taboo, injunction; relegation; prohibition, embargo, blockade; boycott, lockout; inadmissibility, excludability, exclusivity

2 **elimination, riddance,** culling, culling out, winnowing-out, shakeout, eviction, chasing, bum's rush <nf>; **severance** 802.2; withdrawal, **removal,** detachment, disjunction 802.1; discard, eradication, clearance, **ejection,** expulsion, suspension; **deportation, exile,** expatriation, ostracism, outlawing *or* outlawry; disposal, disposition; **liquidation, purge;** obliteration

3 **exclusiveness, narrowness,** tightness; **insularity,** snobbishness, parochialism, ethnocentrism, ethnicity, xenophobia, know-nothingism; special case, exemption; **segregation, separation,**

separationism, division; **isolation,** insulation, seclusion; quarantine; racial segregation, apartheid, color bar, Jim Crow, race hatred; **out-group; outsider,** non-member, stranger, the other, they; **foreigner, alien** 774.3, outcast 586.4, outlaw; *persona non grata* <L>; blacklist, blackball; monopoly; sexual discrimination

VERBS **4 exclude, bar,** debar, bar out, lock out, **shut out, keep out,** count out <nf>, close the door on, close out, cut out, cut off, preclude; **reject, repudiate,** blackball *and* turn thumbs down on <nf>, read *or* drum out, ease *or* freeze out *and* leave *or* keep out in the cold <nf>, cold-shoulder, send to Coventry <Brit>, ostracize, wave off *or* aside; **ignore,** turn a blind eye, turn a deaf ear, filter out, tune out; **ban,** prohibit, proscribe, taboo, **leave out,** omit, pass over, ignore; relegate; **blockade,** embargo; **tariff,** trade barrier

5 eliminate, get rid of, rid oneself of, **get quit of,** get shut of <nf>, **dispose of, remove,** abstract, eject, expel, give the bum's rush <nf>, kick downstairs, cast off *or* out, chuck <nf>, throw over *or* overboard <nf>; **deport, exile,** outlaw, expatriate; clear, clear out, clear away, clear the decks; **weed out,** pick out, **cut out,** strike off *or* out, elide, censor; eradicate, root up *or* out; **purge, liquidate**

6 segregate, separate, separate out *or* off, divide, cordon, cordon off; **isolate,** insulate, seclude; **set apart,** keep apart; **quarantine,** put in isolation; put beyond the pale, ghettoize; **set aside,** lay aside, put aside, keep aside, box off, wall off, fence off; **sort** *or* **pick out,** cull out, sift, screen, sieve, bolt, riddle, winnow, winnow out; thresh, thrash, gin

ADJS **7 excluded, barred,** debarred, precluded, kept-out, **shut-out, left-out,** left out in the cold <nf>, passed-over; not included, not in it, not in the picture <nf>; excepted, excused; **ignored;** cold-shouldered; relegated; **banned,** prohibited, proscribed, tabooed; **expelled,** ejected, **purged,** liquidated; deported, exiled; **blockaded,** embargoed

8 segregated, separated, cordoned-off, divided; isolated, insulated, secluded; **set apart,** sequestered; **quarantined; ghettoized,** beyond the pale; peripheral

9 exclusive, excluding, exclusory; seclusive, preclusive, exceptional, inadmissible, prohibitive, preventive, prescriptive, restrictive; separative, segregative, closed-door; select, selective; narrow, insular, parochial, ethnocentric, xenophobic, snobbish; racist, sexist

PREP **10 excluding, barring,** bar, exclusive of, precluding, omitting, without, absent, **leaving out; excepting, except, except for,** with the exception of, outside of <nf>, **save,** saving, save and except, let alone; **besides,** beside, **aside from**

774 EXTRANEOUSNESS

NOUNS **1 extraneousness, foreignness;** otherness, alienism, alienage, alienation; **extrinsicality** 768; **exteriority** 206; nonassimilation, nonconformity; intrusion

2 intruder, foreign body *or* element, foreign intruder *or* intrusion, interloper, encroacher; **impurity,** blemish 1004; speck 258.7, spot, macula, blot; mote, splinter *or* sliver, **weed,** misfit 789.4; oddball 870.4; black sheep

3 alien, stranger, foreigner, outsider, non-member, not one of us, not our sort, not the right sort, the other, outlander, *Uitlander* <Afrikaans>, tramontane, ultramontane, barbarian, foreign devil <China>, *gringo* <Sp>; **exile,** outcast, outlaw, wanderer, refugee, émigré, displaced person *or* DP, *déraciné* <Fr>; the Wandering Jew

4 newcomer, new arrival, *novus homo* <L>; *arriviste* <Fr>, Johnny-come-lately <nf>, new boy *or* man, new kid; **tenderfoot,** greenhorn; settler, emigrant, immigrant; recruit, rookie <nf>; **intruder, squatter,** gate-crasher, stowaway

ADJS **5 extraneous, foreign, alien,** strange, exotic, foreign-looking; unearthly, extraterrestrial 1072.26; exterior, **external;** extrinsic 768.3; ulterior, outside, outland, outlandish; barbarian, barbarous, barbaric; foreign-born; intrusive

ADVS **6** abroad, in foreign parts; oversea, **overseas,** beyond seas; on one's travels

WORD ELEMENTS **7** ep-, epi-, eph-, ex-, exo-, ef-, xen-, xeno-

775 RELATION

NOUNS **1 relation, relationship, connection;** relatedness, connectedness, **association** 617, **affiliation,** filiation, bond, union, alliance, **tie,** tie-in <nf>, link, linkage, linking, linkup, liaison; **addition** 253, adjunct 254, junction 800.1, **combination** 805, assemblage 770; deduction 255.1, disjunction 802.1, **contrariety** 779, **disagreement** 789, negative *or* bad relation; **positive** *or* **good relation, affinity, rapport,** mutual attraction, sympathy, accord 455; **closeness,** propinquity, **proximity,** approximation, contiguity, nearness 223, intimacy; **relations, dealings,** affairs, business, transactions, doings *and* truck <nf>, intercourse; **similarity** 784, homology

2 relativity, dependence, contingency; **relativism,** indeterminacy, uncertainty, variability, variance; **interrelation, correlation** 777

3 **kinship,** common source *or* stock *or* descent *or* ancestry, consanguinity, agnation, cognation, enation, relationship by blood 559; family relationship, affinity 564.1

4 **relevance, pertinence,** pertinency, cogency, relatedness, materiality, **appositeness,** germaneness; application, applicability, effect, appropriateness; **connection,** reference, **bearing,** concern, concernment, interest, respect, regard

VERBS 5 **relate to,** refer to, **apply to, bear on** *or* **upon,** respect, regard, **concern, involve,** touch, affect, interest; **pertain, pertain to,** appertain, appertain to, belong to, fit; **agree, agree with,** answer to, correspond to, chime with; **have to do with,** have connection with, link with *or* link up with, connect, reconnect, put in context, tie in with <nf>, liaise with <nf>, deal with, treat of, touch upon

6 **relate, associate, connect,** interconnect, ally, link, link up, wed, marry, marry up, weld, bind, tie, couple, bracket, equate, identify; bring into relation with, bring to bear upon, apply; **parallel,** parallelize, draw a parallel; symmetrize; **interrelate,** relativize, **correlate** 777.4

ADJS 7 **relative, comparative** relational; **relativistic,** indeterminate, uncertain, variable; **connective, linking,** associative; **relating,** pertaining, appertaining, pertinent, referring, referable

8 **approximate,** approximating, approximative, proximate; **near, close** 223.14; **comparable,** relatable, commensurable; **proportional,** proportionate, proportionable; correlative; **like,** homologous, **similar** 784.10

9 **related, connected; linked,** tied, coupled, knotted, twinned, wedded, wed, married *or* married up, welded, conjugate, bracketed, bound, yoked, spliced, conjoined, conjoint, conjunct, joined 800.13; **associated, affiliated,** filiated, **allied,** associate, affiliate; interlocked, **interrelated,** interlinked, involved, implicated, overlapping, interpenetrating, relevant, **correlated;** in the same category, of that kind *or* sort *or* ilk, corresponding; parallel, collateral; **congenial, en rapport** <Fr>, sympathetic, compatible, affinitive

10 **kindred, akin, related,** of common source *or* stock *or* descent *or* ancestry, agnate, cognate, enate, connate, connatural, congeneric *or* congenerous, consanguine *or* consanguineous, genetically related, by blood 559.6, affinal 564.4

11 **relevant, pertinent,** appertaining, **germane, apposite,** cogent, material, admissible, applicable, applying, pertaining, belonging, involving, appropriate, **apropos,** *à propos* <Fr>, to the purpose, **to the point,** in point, *ad rem* <L>

ADVS 12 **relatively,** comparatively, proportionately, not absolutely, to a degree, to an extent, to some extent; **relevantly,** pertinently, appositely, germanely

PREPS 13 **with** *or* **in relation to,** with *or* in reference to, **with** *or* **in regard to,** with respect to, in respect to *or* of, in what concerns, relative to, **relating** *or* **pertaining to,** pertinent to, appertaining to, referring to, in relation with, **in connection with,** apropos of, speaking of; **as to,** as for, as respects, as regards; in the matter of, on the subject of, in point of, on the score of; re, *in re* <L>; **about,** anent, of, on, upon, **concerning,** touching, respecting, **regarding**

776 UNRELATEDNESS

NOUNS 1 **unrelatedness,** irrelativeness, irrelation; **irrelevance,** irrelevancy, impertinence, inappositeness, uncogency, ungermaneness, immateriality, inapplicability; inconnection *or* disconnection, disconnect <nf>, inconsequence, independence; **unconnectedness,** separateness, delinkage, discreteness, dissociation, disassociation, disjuncture, disjunction 802.1

2 **misconnection,** misrelation, wrong *or* invalid linking, **mismatch,** mismatching, misalliance, *mésalliance* <Fr>; misapplication, misapplicability, misreference

3 **an irrelevance** *or* irrelevancy, quite another thing, something else again *and* a whole nother thing *and* a whole different story *and* a whole different ball game <nf>

VERBS 4 **not concern,** not involve, not imply, not implicate, not entail, not relate to, not connect with, have nothing to do with, have no business with, cut no ice *and* make no never mind <nf>, have no bearing

5 **foist,** drag in 213.6; **impose on** 643.7

ADJS 6 **unrelated,** irrelative, unrelatable, unrelational, **unconnected,** unallied, unlinked, **unassociated,** unaffiliated *or* disaffiliated; disrelated, disconnected, dissociated, detached, discrete, disjunct, removed, **separated,** segregated, apart, other, independent, marked off, bracketed; **isolated,** insular; **foreign, alien,** strange, exotic, outlandish; incommensurable, incomparable; inconsistent, inconsonant; extraneous 768.3

7 **irrelevant,** irrelative; **impertinent, inapposite,** ungermane, uncogent, inconsequent, inapplicable, immaterial, inappropriate, inadmissible; wide of *or* away from the point, *nihil ad rem* <L>, **beside the point,** beside the mark, wide of the mark, **beside the question,** off the subject, off-topic, not to the purpose, **nothing to do with the case,** not at issue, out-of-the-way; **unessential,** nonessential,

extraneous, extrinsic 768.3; incidental, parenthetical

8 farfetched, remote, distant, out-of-the-way, strained, forced, dragged in, neither here nor there, brought in from nowhere; **imaginary** 986.19; improbable 969.3

ADVS **9 irrelevantly,** irrelatively, impertinently, inappositely, ungermanely, uncogently, amiss; without connection, without reference *or* regard

777 CORRELATION
<reciprocal or mutual relation>

NOUNS **1 correlation,** corelation; correlativity, correlativism; **reciprocation,** reciprocity, reciprocality, two-edged sword, relativity 775.2; **mutuality,** communion, community, commutuality, common ground; **common denominator,** common factor; proportionality, direct *or* inverse relationship, direct *or* inverse ratio, direct *or* inverse proportion, covariation; **equilibrium, balance,** symmetry 264; **correspondence, equivalence,** equipollence, coequality

2 interrelation, interrelationship; **interconnection,** interlocking, interdigitation, intercoupling, interlinking, interlinkage, interalliance, interassociation, interaffiliation, interdependence, interdependency, codependency; dovetail

3 interaction, interworking, intercourse, intercommunication, **interplay;** alternation, seesaw; **meshing,** intermeshing, mesh, engagement; **complementation,** complementary relation, complementary distribution; **interweaving,** interlacing, intertwining 740.1; **interchange** 863, tit for tat, trade-off, *quid pro quo* <L>; **concurrence** 899, coaction, **cooperation** 450, compromise; codependency

4 correlate, correlative; **correspondent,** analogue, counterpart; reciprocator, reciprocatist; each other, one another

VERBS **5 correlate,** corelate; **interrelate, interconnect,** interassociate, interlink, intercouple, interlock, interdigitate, interally, intertie, interjoin, interdepend; interface; find common ground; dovetail

6 interact, interwork, **interplay,** mesh, intermesh, engage, fit, fit like a glove, dovetail, mortise; **interweave,** interlace, intertwine; **interchange;** coact, **cooperate;** codepend

7 reciprocate, correspond, correspond to, respond to, answer, answer to, go tit-for-tat; **complement,** coequal; **cut both ways,** cut two ways; counteract

ADJS **8 correlative,** corelative, correlational, corelational; **correlated,** corelated; **interrelated, interconnected,** internetworked, interassociated,

interallied, interaffiliated, interlinked, interlocked, intercoupled, intertied, interdependent; interchanged, converse

9 interacting, interactive, interworking, interplaying; in gear, in mesh; dovetailed, mortised; cooperative, **cooperating** 450.5

10 reciprocal, reciprocative, tit-for-tat, seesaw, seesawing; **corresponding,** correspondent, answering, analogous, homologous, equipollent, tantamount, equivalent, coequal; **complementary,** complemental

11 mutual, commutual, **common, joint, communal,** shared, sharing, conjoint; respective, two-way, cooperative

ADVS **12 reciprocally,** back and forth, backward and forward, backwards and forwards, alternately, seesaw, to and fro; vice versa,

13 mutually, commonly, communally, **jointly;** respectively, each to each; *entre nous* <Fr>, *inter se* <L>

WORD ELEMENTS **14** equi-

778 SAMENESS

NOUNS **1 sameness, identity,** identicalness, selfsameness, indistinguishability, undifferentiation, nondifferentiation, two peas in a pod; **coincidence,** correspondence, agreement, congruence; **equivalence, equality** 790, coequality; **synonymousness,** synonymity, synonymy; **oneness, unity,** homogeneity, consubstantiality; isogeny; homogeny

2 identification, likening, unification, coalescence, combination, union, fusion, merger, blending, melding, synthesis

3 the same, selfsame, very same, one and the same, identical same, no other, none other, very *or* actual thing, a distinction without a difference, the same difference <nf>; **equivalent** 784.3; **synonym;** homonym, homograph, homophone; ditto <nf>, *idem* <L>, *ipsissima verba* <L, the very words>; **duplicate,** double, clone *and* cookie-cutter copy <nf>, *Doppelgänger* <Ger>, twin, very image, look-alike, dead ringer <nf>, the image of, the picture of, spitting image *and* spit and image <nf>, **exact counterpart, copy** 785.1,3–5, replica, facsimile, carbon copy

VERBS **4 coincide, correspond,** agree, chime with, match, tally, go hand in glove with, twin; complement

5 identify, make one, **unify,** unite, join, combine, coalesce, synthesize, merge, blend, meld, fuse 804.3

6 reproduce, copy, reduplicate, **duplicate,** ditto <nf>, clone

ADJS **7 identical,** identic; **same, selfsame,** one, **one and the same,** all the same, all one, of the same kidney; **indistinguishable,** without distinction, without difference, undifferent, undifferentiated; **alike, all alike, like** 784.10, just alike, exactly alike, like two peas in a pod; **duplicate,** reduplicated, copied, twin; **homogeneous,** consubstantial; redundant, tautological

8 coinciding, coincident, coincidental; **corresponding,** correspondent, congruent; complementary; **synonymous, equivalent,** six of one and half a dozen of the other <nf>; **equal** 790.7, coequal, coextensive, coterminous; in or at parity

ADVS **9 identically,** synonymously, **alike;** coincidentally, correspondently, correspondingly, congruently; **equally** 790.11, coequally, coextensively, coterminously; on the same footing, on all fours with; **likewise,** the same way, just the same, as is, ditto, same here <nf>; *ibid* and *ibidem* <L>

779 CONTRARIETY

NOUNS **1 contrariety, oppositeness, opposition** 451; **antithesis, contrast,** contraposition 215, counterposition, contradiction, contraindication, contradistinction; **antagonism,** repugnance, oppugnance, oppugnancy, **hostility,** perversity, nay-saying, negativeness, orneriness <nf>, inimicalness, **antipathy,** scunner <nf>; **confrontation,** showdown, standoff, Mexican standoff <nf>, clashing, collision, cross-purposes 456.2, conflict; polarity; discrepancy, inconsistency, **disagreement** 789; antonymy

2 the opposite, the contrary, the antithesis, the reverse, the other way round or around, the inverse, the converse, the obverse, the counter; **the other side,** the mirror or reverse image, the other side of the coin, the flip or B side <nf>; the direct or polar opposite, the other or opposite extreme, other end of the spectrum; antipode, antipodes; countercheck or counterbalance or counterpoise, offset, setoff; **opposite pole,** antipole, counterpole, counterpoint; opposite number <nf>, vis-à-vis; **antonym,** opposite, opposite term, counterterm

3 (contrarieties when joined or coexisting) self-contradiction, **paradox** 789.2, antinomy, oxymoron, ambivalence, **irony,** enantiosis, equivocation, **ambiguity**

VERBS **4 go contrary to, run counter to,** counter, contradict, contravene, controvert, fly in the face of, be or play at cross-purposes, go against; **oppose,** be opposed to, go or run in opposition to, run counter to, side against; **conflict with,** come in conflict with, oppugn, conflict, clash; contrast with, **offset,** set off, countercheck or counterbalance, countervail; **counteract,** counterwork; counterpose or contrapose, counterpoise, juxtapose in opposition

5 reverse, invert, obvert, transpose 205.5, flip <nf>

ADJS **6 contrary;** contrarious, perverse, **opposite,** antithetic, antithetical, **contradictory,** counter, contrapositive, contrasted; **converse, reverse,** obverse, inverse; **adverse,** adversative or adversive, adversarial, **opposing, opposed,** oppositive, oppositional; anti <nf>, dead against; **antagonistic,** repugnant, oppugnant, perverse, contrarious, ornery <nf>, nay-saying, negative, hostile, combative, bellicose, belligerent, inimical, antipathetic, antipathetical, discordant; inconsistent, discrepant, conflicting, clashing, at cross-purposes, confronting, **confrontational,** confrontive, squared off <nf>, face to face, vis-à-vis, eyeball to eyeball and toe-to-toe <nf>, at loggerheads; contradistinct; antonymous; countervailing, counterpoised, balancing, counterbalancing, compensating

7 diametric, diametrical, diametrically opposite, diametrically opposed, at opposite poles, in polar opposition, antipodal or antipodean; retrograde; opposite as black and white or light and darkness or day and night or fire and water or the poles, etc, "Hyperion to a satyr"—Shakespeare

8 self-contradictory, **paradoxical,** antinomic, oxymoronic, ambivalent, **ironic;** equivocal, **ambiguous**

ADVS **9** contrarily, contrariwise, counter, conversely, inversely, **vice versa,** topsy-turvy, upside down, arsy-varsy <nf>, **on the other hand,** *per contra* <L>, **on** or **to the contrary,** *tout au contraire* <Fr>, at loggerheads, in flat opposition; rather, nay rather, quite the contrary, otherwise 780.11, just the other way, just the other way around, **oppositely,** just the opposite or reverse; by contraries, by way of opposition; against the grain, *à rebours* <Fr>; contrariously, perversely, ornerily <nf>

PREPS **10 opposite,** over against, contra, in contrast with, contrary to, vis-à-vis

WORD ELEMENTS **11** con-, contra-, counter-

780 DIFFERENCE

NOUNS **1 difference,** otherness, separateness, discreteness, distinctness, **distinction;** unlikeness, **dissimilarity** 787; **variation,** variance, variegation, variety, **mixture** 797, heterogeneity, **diversity; deviation,** divergence or divergency, departure; **disparity,** gap, inequality 791, odds; **discrepancy,** inconsistency, inconsonance, incongruity, discongruity, unconformity *or* nonconformity, disconformity, **strangeness** 870.1, unorthodoxy 688, incompatibility, irreconcilability; culture gap; **disagreement, dissent** 333, disaccord *or* disaccordance, inaccordance, discordance, dissonance, inharmoniousness, inharmony; **contrast,** opposition, **contrariety** 779; a far cry, a whale of a difference <nf>; difference of opinion; biodiversity

2 **margin,** wide *or* narrow margin, **differential;** differentia, distinction, point of difference; **nicety, subtlety,** refinement, delicacy, nice *or* fine *or* delicate *or* **subtle distinction,** fine point; shade *or* particle of difference, **nuance,** hairline; **seeming difference,** distinction without a difference

3 **a different thing,** a different story <nf>, **something else,** something else again <nf>, *tertium quid* <L, a third something>, *autre chose* <Fr>, another kettle of fish <nf>, another tune, different breed of cat <nf>, another can of worms, horse of a different color, bird of another feather; **nothing of the kind,** no such thing, **quite another thing; other, another,** tother *and* whole nother thing *and* different ball game *and* whole different ball game <nf>, special case, exception to the rule

4 **differentiation,** differencing, **discrimination,** distinguishing, **distinction;** demarcation, limiting, drawing the line; **separation, separateness,** discreteness 802.1, division, atomization, anatomization, analysis, disjunction, segregation, severance, severalization; **modification, alteration, change** 852, tweak, variation, diversification, disequalization; **particularization,** specification, individualization, individuation, personalization, specialization

VERBS 5 **differ, vary,** diverge, stand apart, be distinguished *or* distinct; **deviate from,** diverge from, divaricate from, depart from; **disagree with,** disaccord with, conflict with, contrast with, stand over against, clash with, jar with; not be like, bear no resemblance to 787.2, not square with, not accord with, not go on all fours with; ring the changes

6 **differentiate,** difference; **distinguish, make a distinction, discriminate, secern; separate,** sever, severalize, segregate, divide; **demarcate,** mark, mark out *or* off, set off, set apart, draw a line, set limits; **modify,** vary, diversify, disequalize, **change** 852.6,7; **particularize,** individualize, individuate, personalize, specify, specialize; atomize, analyze, anatomize, disjoin; split hairs, sharpen *or* refine a distinction, chop logic

ADJS 7 **different,** differing; unlike, not like, **dissimilar** 787.4; **distinct,** distinguished,

differentiated, discriminated, discrete, separated, separate, disjoined 802.21, widely apart; **various,** variant, varying, varied, heterogeneous, multifarious, motley, assorted, variegated, diverse, divers, **diversified** 783.4; **several,** many; **divergent,** deviative, diverging, deviating, departing; **disparate,** unequal 791.4; **discrepant,** inconsistent, inconsonant, incongruous, incongruent, unconformable, incompatible, irreconcilable; **disagreeing,** in disagreement; **at odds,** at variance, clashing, inaccordant, disaccordant, discordant, dissonant, inharmonious, out of tune; **contrasting,** contrasted, poles apart, poles asunder, worlds apart; **contrary** 779.6; **discriminable,** separable, severable

8 **other, another,** whole nother <nf>, else, otherwise, other than *or* from; not the same, not the type <nf>, not that sort, of another sort, of a sort *and* of sorts <nf>; **unique,** one of a kind, rare, **special,** peculiar, *sui generis* <L, of its own kind>, in a class by itself

9 **differentiative,** differentiating, diacritic, diacritical, differential; **distinguishing,** discriminating, discriminative, discriminatory, characterizing, individualizing, individuating, personalizing, differencing, separative; diagnostic; **distinctive,** contrastive, characteristic, peculiar, idiosyncratic

ADVS 10 **differently,** diversely, variously; in a different manner, in another way, with a difference; differentiatingly, distinguishingly

11 **otherwise,** in other ways, **in other respects;** elsewise, else, or else; than; other than; **on the other hand;** contrarily 779.9; alias

WORD ELEMENTS 12 all-, de-, dis-, heter-, xen-

781 UNIFORMITY

NOUNS 1 **uniformity, evenness,** equability; **steadiness,** stability 855, steadfastness, firmness, unbrokenness, seamlessness, constancy, unwaveringness, undeviatingness, persistence, perseverance, continuity, **consistency;** consonance, correspondence, accordance; unity, **homogeneity,** consubstantiality, monolithism; **equanimity,** equilibrium, unruffledness, serenity, tranquility, calm, calmness, cool <nf>

2 **regularity, constancy,** invariability, unvariation, undeviation, even tenor *or* pace, smoothness, clockwork regularity; **sameness** 778, **monotony,** monotonousness, undifferentiation, the same old thing <nf>, the daily round *or* routine, the treadmill; monotone, drone, dingdong, singsong, monologue

VERBS **3 persist, prevail,** persevere, run true to form *or* type, continue the same; drag on *or* along; hum, drone

4 make uniform, uniformize; **regulate,** regularize, normalize, stabilize, damp; **even, equalize,** symmetrize, harmonize, balance, balance up, equilibrize; **level,** level out *or* off, smooth, smooth out, even, even out, flatten; **homogenize, assimilate,** standardize, stereotype; clone <nf>

ADJS **5 uniform, equable,** equal, **even; level,** flat, smooth; **regular, constant,** steadfast, persistent, continuous; **unvaried,** unruffled, unbroken, seamless, undiversified, undifferentiated, unchanged; invariable, unchangeable, immutable; **unvarying,** undeviating, unchanging, steady, stable; cloned *or* clonish *and* cookie-cutter <nf>; **ordered,** balanced, measured; **orderly,** methodical, systematic, mechanical, faceless, robotlike, automatic; **consistent,** consonant, correspondent, accordant, homogeneous, **alike,** all alike, all of a piece, of a piece, consubstantial, monolithic; nonsexist, inclusive, nondiscriminatory

6 same, wall-to-wall, back-to-back; **monotonous, humdrum,** unrelieved, repetitive, drab, gray, ho-hum <nf>, samey <Brit nf>, usual, as usual; tedious, boring

ADVS **7 uniformly,** equably, **evenly;** monotonously, in a rut *or* groove, dully, tediously, routinely, unrelievedly

8 regularly; constantly, steadily, continually; **invariably,** without exception, at every turn, every time one turns around, all the time, all year round, week in week out, year in year out, day in day out, never otherwise; methodically, orderly, systematically; **always** 829.11; like clockwork

WORD ELEMENTS **9** equi-, hol-, hom-, is-, mon-

782 NONUNIFORMITY

NOUNS **1 nonuniformity, unevenness, irregularity,** raggedness, crazy-quilt, choppiness, jerkiness, **disorder** 810; **difference** 780; inequality; **inconstancy, inconsistency,** variability, changeability, changeableness, mutability, capriciousness, mercuriality, wavering, **instability, unsteadiness; variation, deviation,** deviance, divergence, differentiation, divarication, ramification; versatility, **diversity,** diversification, nonformalization; **nonconformity,** nonconformism, unconformity, unconformism, **unorthodoxy; pluralism,** variegation, variety, variousness, motleyness, dappleness; multiculturalism, multiculturism

VERBS **2 diversify, vary,** variegate 47.7, chop and change, waver, mutate; **differentiate,** divaricate,

diverge, ramify; **differ** 780.5; dissent 333.4; **disunify,** break up, break down, fragment, partition, **analyze** 801.6

ADJS **3 nonuniform,** ununiform, **uneven, irregular,** ragged, erose, choppy, jerky, jagged, rough, disorderly, unsystematic; **different** 780.7, unequal, unequable; **inconstant, inconsistent, variable,** varying, **changeable,** changing, mutable, capricious, impulsive, mercurial, erratic, spasmodic, sporadic, wavery, wavering, **unstable, unsteady;** deviating, deviative, deviatory, divergent, divaricate, ramified; **diversified,** variform, diversiform, nonformal; **nonconformist,** unorthodox; **pluralistic,** variegated, various, motley 47.9,12; multicultural, multiracial

ADVS **4 nonuniformly,** ununiformly, unequally, **unevenly, irregularly,** inconstantly, **inconsistently,** unsteadily, erratically, spasmodically, by fits and starts, capriciously, impulsively, sporadically; unsystematically, chaotically, helter-skelter, higgledy-piggledy; in all manner of ways, every which way <nf>, all over the shop *and* all over the ball park <nf>; here there and everywhere

WORD ELEMENTS **5** diversi-, vari-, heter-

783 MULTIFORMITY

NOUNS **1 multiformity,** multifariousness, **variety,** nonuniformity 782, **diversity,** diversification, variation, variegation 47, variability, versatility, proteanism, manifoldness, multiplicity, heterogeneity; omniformity, omnifariousness; pluralism, multiculturalism; everything but the kitchen sink <nf>, all colors of the rainbow, polymorphism, heteromorphism; allotropy *or* allotropism <chemistry>; Proteus, shapeshifting, shapeshifter; "her infinite variety"—Shakespeare

VERBS **2 diversify, vary,** change form, change shape, shift shape, ring changes, cover the spectrum, **variegate** 47.7; branch out, spread one's wings; have many irons in the fire

ADJS **3 multiform,** diversiform, variable, versatile; **protean,** proteiform; **manifold,** multifold, multiplex, multiple, multifarious, multiphase; polymorphous, polymorphic, heteromorphous, heteromorphic, metamorphic; omniform, omniformal, omnifarious, omnigenous; allotropic *or* allotropical <chemistry>

4 diversified, varied, assorted, heterogeneous, nonuniform; **various,** many and various, divers <old>, diverse, sundry, **several, many;** of all sorts *or* conditions *or* kinds *or* shapes *or* descriptions *or* types; multiethnic, multicultural; multifunctional

ADVS **5 variously, severally,** sundrily, multifariously, diversely, manifoldly

WORD ELEMENTS **6** allo-, diversi-, heter-, multi-, omni-, parti-, party-, poecil- *or* poikil-, poly-, vari-

784 SIMILARITY

NOUNS **1 similarity, likeness,** alikeness, **sameness,** similitude; **resemblance,** semblance; **analogy, correspondence,** conformity, accordance, agreement, comparability, commensurability, comparison, **parallelism, parity,** community, alliance, consimilarity; **approximation,** approach, closeness, nearness; assimilation, likening, **simile, metaphor,** parable, allegory; **simulation, imitation,** copying, aping, mimicking, taking-off, takeoff, burlesque, pastiche, *pasticcio* <Ital>; identity 778.1; equivalence; synonymy

2 kinship, affinity, connection, family resemblance *or* likeness, family favor, generic *or* genetic resemblance; connaturality *or* connaturalness, connature, connateness, congeneracy; compatibility

3 likeness, like, the like of *or* **the likes of** <nf>, point of likeness, point in common; suchlike, such; **analogue, parallel;** cognate, congener; **counterpart, complement, correspondent,** pendant, similitude, tally; **approximation,** rough idea, sketch; coordinate, reciprocal, obverse, equivalent; correlate, correlative; **close imitation** *or* reproduction *or* copy *or* facsimile *or* replica, near duplicate, simulacrum; **close match, match-up, fellow, mate;** soul mate, kindred spirit *or* soul, **companion, twin,** brother, sister, brother *or* sister under the skin; *mon semblable* <Fr>, second self, alter ego; a chip off the old block; **look-alike,** the image of, the picture of, shadow, another edition; related form

4 close *or* **striking resemblance,** startling *or* marked *or* decided resemblance; close *or* near likeness; **faint** *or* **remote resemblance,** mere hint *or* shadow

5 set, group, matching pair *or* set, his and hers <nf>, couple, pair, twins, look-alikes, two of a kind, birds of a feather, peas in a pod

6 (of words or sounds) assonance, alliteration, rhyme, slant rhyme, near rhyme, jingle, clink; pun, paronamasia

VERBS **7 resemble,** be like, bear resemblance; put one in mind of <nf>, remind one of, bring to mind, be reminiscent of, suggest, evoke, call up, call to mind; **look like,** favor <nf>, mirror; **take after,** favor, partake of, follow, appear *or* seem like, sound like; savor *or* smack of, be redolent of; **have all the earmarks of,** have every appearance of, have all the features of, have all the signs of,

have every sign *or* indication of; **approximate,** approach, near, come near, come close; **compare with,** stack up with <nf>; **correspond, match, parallel,** connect, relate; not tell apart, not tell one from the other; **imitate** 336.5, **simulate,** copy, ape, mimic, take off, counterfeit; nearly reproduce *or* duplicate *or* reduplicate

8 similarize, approximate, assimilate, bring near; connaturalize

9 assonate, alliterate, rhyme, chime; pun

ADJS **10 similar, like, alike,** something like, not unlike; **resembling,** resemblant, following, favoring <nf>, savoring *or* smacking of, suggestive of, **on the order of;** consimilar; **simulated, imitated,** imitation, copied, aped, mimicked, taken off, fake *or* phony <nf>, counterfeit, **mock,** synthetic, ersatz; nearly reproduced *or* duplicated *or* reduplicated; uniform with, homogeneous, identical 778.7

11 analogous, comparable; **corresponding,** correspondent, equivalent; **parallel,** paralleling; **matching,** cast in the same mold, of a kind, of a size, of a piece; duplicate, twin, of the same hue *or* stripe; mix-and-match

12 such as, suchlike, so

13 akin, affinitive, related; connatural, connate, cognate, agnate, enate, conspecific, correlative; congenerous, congeneric, congenerical; brothers *or* sisters under the skin

14 approximating, approximative, approximate, approximable; **near, close;** much of a muchness <Brit nf>, much the same, much at one, nearly the same, same but different; quasi, pseudo

15 very like, mighty like, powerful like <nf>, uncommonly like, remarkably like, extraordinarily like, strikingly like, **ridiculously like, for all the world like,** as like as can be; a lot alike, pretty much the same, the same difference *and* damned little difference <nf>; near-equal; as like as two peas in a pod, *comme deux gouttes d'eau* <Fr, like two drops of water>; faintly *or* remotely like

16 lifelike, speaking, faithful, living, breathing, to the life, **true to life** *or* nature; **realistic, natural**

17 (of words or sounds) assonant, assonantal, alliterative, alliteral; **rhyming,** jingling, chiming, punning

ADVS **18 similarly,** correspondingly, **like, likewise,** either; in the same manner, **in like manner,** in kind; in that way, like that, like this; **thus** 766.10; so; by the same token, by the same sign; identically 778.9

19 so to speak, in a manner of speaking, **as it were,** in a manner, in a way; kind of *and* sort of <nf>

785 COPY

NOUNS 1 copy, representation, facsimile, image, likeness 784.3, resemblance, semblance, similitude, picture, portrait, life mask, death mask, icon, simulacrum, twin; ectype; pastiche, *pasticcio* <Ital>; fair copy, faithful copy; certified copy; **imitation** 336.3, **counterfeit** 354.13, forgery, fake *and* phony <nf>

2 reproduction, duplication, reduplication; reprography; transcription; tracing, rubbing; mimeography, xerography, hectography

3 **duplicate, duplication,** dupe *and* ditto <nf>; **double,** cookie-cutter copy, clone; representation, **reproduction, replica,** repro <nf>, carbon copy, reduplication, facsimile, model, **counterpart;** a chip off the old block; triplicate, quadruplicate, etc; repetition 849

4 **transcript, transcription,** apograph, tenor <law>; **transfer,** tracing, rubbing, **carbon copy,** carbon; manifold <old>; microcopy, microform; microfiche, fiche; recording

5 **print,** offprint; **impression,** impress; **reprint,** proof, reproduction proof, repro proof *and* repro <nf>, second edition; photostatic copy, Photostat <trademark>, stat <nf>; mimeograph copy, Ditto copy <trademark>, hectograph copy, xerographic copy, Xerox copy <trademark> *or* Xerox <trademark>, carbon copy; **facsimile,** fax <nf>; **photograph,** positive, negative, print, enlargement, contact print, photocopy

6 **cast,** casting; mold, **molding,** die, stamp, seal

7 **reflection,** reflex; **shadow,** silhouette, outline 211.2; **echo**

VERBS 8 copy, reproduce, replicate, **duplicate,** dupe <nf>; clone; reduplicate; **transcribe;** trace; double; triplicate, quadruplicate, etc; manifold <old>, multigraph, mimeograph, mimeo, Photostat <trademark>, stat <nf>, facsimile, fax <nf>, hectograph, ditto, Xerox <trademark>, carbon-copy; microcopy, microfilm

ADVS 9 in duplicate, in triplicate, etc

786 MODEL
<thing copied>

NOUNS 1 model, pattern, standard, criterion, classic example, rule, mirror, paradigm; showpiece, showplace; **original,** urtext, *locus classicus* <L>; **type, prototype,** antetype, **archetype,** genotype, biotype, type specimen, type species; **precedent**

2 **example,** exemplar; **representative,** type, symbol, emblem, exponent; **exemplification,** illustration, demonstration, explanation; **instance,** relevant instance, **case,** typical example *or* case, case in point, object lesson

3 **sample, specimen;** piece, taste, swatch; instance, for-instance <nf>

4 **ideal,** *beau ideal,* ego ideal, ideal type, acme, highest *or* perfect *or* best type; cynosure, apotheosis, idol; **shining example,** role-model, **hero, superhero; model,** the very model, mirror, paragon, epitome; cult figure

5 artist's model, dressmaker's model, photographer's model, mannequin; dummy, lay figure; clay model, wood model, pilot model, mock-up

6 **mold, form** 262, cast, template, matrix, negative; **die,** punch, stamp, intaglio, seal, mint; last, shoe last

VERBS 7 set an example, set the pace, lead the way; **exemplify,** epitomize, fit the pattern; **emulate,** follow, hold up as a model, model oneself on

ADJS 8 model, exemplary, precedential, typical, paradigmatic, representative, standard, normative, classic; ideal

9 **prototypal,** prototypic, prototypical, archetypal, archetypic, archetypical, antitypic, antitypical

787 DISSIMILARITY

NOUNS 1 dissimilarity, unsimilarity; **dissimilitude,** dissemblance, **unresemblance; unlikeness,** unsameness; **disparity,** diversity, divergence, gap, **contrast, difference** 780; nonuniformity 782; uncomparability, uncomparableness, incomparability, incomparableness, uncommensurableness, uncommensurability, incommensurableness, incommensurability, no resemblance, no common ground; culture gap; **disguise,** dissimilation, camouflage, masking; cosmetics; poor imitation, bad likeness *or* copy, botched copy, mere caricature *or* counterfeit

VERBS 2 not resemble, bear no resemblance, not look like, **not compare with; differ** 780.5; have little *or* nothing in common; diverge, deviate

3 disguise, dissimilate, camouflage; do a cosmetic job on; vary 852.6

ADJS 4 dissimilar, unsimilar, unresembling, unresemblant; **unlike, unalike,** unidentical; **disparate,** diverse, divergent, **contrasting, different** 780.7; nonuniform 782.3; scarcely like, hardly like, a bit *or* mite different; **off,** a bit on the off side, offbeat <nf>; unmatched, odd, counter, out

5 **nothing like,** not a bit alike, not a bit of it, **nothing of the sort,** nothing of the kind, something else, something else again <nf>, different as night from day, quite another thing, cast in a different mold, not the same thing at all; not so you could tell it

and not that you would know it and **far from it**
and far other <nf>; way off, away off, a mile off,
way out, no such thing, no such a thing <nf>; "no
more like than an apple to an oyster"—Sir
Thomas More

6 **uncomparable,** not comparable, not to be
compared, incomparable; incommensurable,
uncommensurable, uncommensurate,
incommensurate; unrelated, extraneous

ADVS 7 **dissimilarly, differently** 780.10, with a
difference, disparately, contrastingly

788 AGREEMENT

NOUNS 1 **agreement, accord** 455, accordance;
concord, concordance; **harmony, cooperation** 450,
peace 464, *rapport* <Fr>, concert, consort,
consonance, unisonance, **unison,** union, chorus,
oneness; **correspondence,** coincidence,
intersection, overlap, parallelism, symmetry, tally,
equivalence 778.1; congeniality, compatibility,
affinity; **conformity,** conformance, conformation,
uniformity 781; congruity, congruence, congruency;
consistency, self-consistency, coherence;
synchronism, sync <nf>, timing; **assent** 332

2 **understanding,** entente; mutual *or* cordial
understanding, consortium, *entente cordiale* <Fr>;
compact 437

3 <general agreement> consensus, consentaneity,
consentaneousness, *consensus omnium* <L,
consent of all> *and consensus gentium* <L, consent
of the people>, sense, **unanimity** 332.5;
likemindedness, meeting *or* intersection *or*
confluence of minds, sense of the meeting; family
feeling; good vibrations <nf>

4 **adjustment, adaptation,** mutual adjustment,
compromise, coaptation, arbitration, arbitrament;
regulation, attunement, harmonization,
coordination, accommodation, squaring,
integration, assimilation; reconciliation,
reconcilement, synchronization; consensus-
building *or* -seeking

5 **fitness** *or* fittedness, **suitability, appropriateness,**
propriety, admissibility; **aptness,** aptitude,
qualification; **relevance** 775.4, felicity,
appositeness, applicability

VERBS 6 **agree, accord** 455.2, **harmonize, concur**
332.9, have no problem with, go along with <nf>,
cooperate 450.3, **correspond, conform,** coincide,
parallel, intersect, overlap, **match,** tally, hit,
register, lock, interlock, check <nf>, square,
dovetail, jibe <nf>; **be consistent,** cohere, stand *or*
hold *or* hang together, fall in together, fit together,
chime, chime with, chime in with; **assent** 332.8,

come to an agreement 332.10, be of one *or* the same
or like mind, subscribe to, see eye to eye, sing in
chorus, have a meeting of the minds, climb on the
bandwagon; **go together,** go with, conform with,
be uniform with, square with, sort *or* assort with,
go on all fours with, consist with, register with,
answer *or* respond to

7 <make agree> **harmonize,** coordinate, bring into
line, accord, make uniform 781.4, equalize 790.6,
similarize, assimilate, homologize; pull together;
adjust, set, regulate, **accommodate, reconcile,**
synchronize, sync <nf>; adapt, fit, tailor, measure,
proportion, adjust to, trim to, cut to, gear to, key
to; fix, **rectify,** true, true up, right, set right, make
plumb; **tune,** attune, put in tune

8 **suit,** fit, suit *or* fit to a tee, fit like a glove, **qualify,
do,** serve, answer, be OK <nf>, do the job *and* do
the trick *and* fill the bill *and* cut the mustard <nf>

ADJS 9 **agreeing, in agreement; in accord,
concurring,** positive, affirmative, in rapport, *en
rapport* <Fr>, **in harmony,** in accordance, in sync
<nf>, **at one,** on all fours, of one *or* the same *or*
like mind, **like-minded,** consentient,
consentaneous, **unanimous** 332.15, unisonous *or*
unisonant; **harmonious,** accordant, **concordant,**
consonant; **consistent,** self-consistent; uniform,
coherent, conformable, of a piece, equivalent,
coinciding 778.8, coincident, corresponding
or correspondent; answerable, reconcilable;
commensurate, proportionate; **congruous,**
congruent; **agreeable,** congenial, compatible,
cooperating *or* cooperative 450.5, coexisting *or*
coexistent, symbiotic; **synchronized,** synchronous,
synchronic; empathetic

10 **apt, apposite, appropriate, suitable;** applicable,
relevant, pertinent, likely, sortable, seasonable,
opportune; **fitting,** befitting, **suiting,** becoming;
fit, fitted, qualified, **suited,** adapted, geared,
tailored, dovetailing, meshing; **right,** just right,
well-chosen, **pat,** happy, felicitous, just what the
doctor ordered <nf>; to the point, to the purpose,
ad rem <L>, *à propos* <Fr>, **apropos,** on the button
and on the money <nf>, spot-on <Brit nf>

ADVS 11 **in step,** in concert, **in unison,** in chorus, **in
line, in conformity, in keeping,** hand in glove, just
right; with it <nf>; **unanimously, as one, with one
voice, harmoniously,** concordantly, consonantly,
in synchronization, in sync <nf>, **by consensus;**
agreeably, congenially, compatibly; fittingly

PREPS 12 in agreement with, together with, with,
right with, in there with, right along there with; in
line with, in keeping with; together on

PHRS 13 that's it, that's the thing, that's just the
thing, that's the very thing, that's the idea *and*
that's the ticket <nf>; right on <nf>; touché

789 DISAGREEMENT

NOUNS **1 disagreement, discord,** discordance *or* discordancy; **disaccord** 456, disaccordance, inaccordance; disunity, disunion; **disharmony,** unharmoniousness; dissonance, dissidence; **jarring,** clashing; **difference** 780, **variance,** divergence, diversity; **disparity,** discrepancy, inequality; antagonism, **opposition** 451, **conflict,** controversy, faction, oppugnancy, repugnance, dissension 456.3, argumentation 935.4; **dissent** 333, negation 335, contradiction; parting of the ways

2 inconsistency, incongruity, asymmetry, inconsonance, incoherence; **incompatibility,** irreconcilability, incommensurability; disproportion, disproportionateness, nonconformity *or* unconformity, nonconformability *or* unconformability, heterogeneity, heterodoxy, unorthodoxy, heresy; self-contradiction, paradox, antinomy, oxymoron, **ambiguity** 539.2, ambivalence, equivocality, equivocalness, mixed message *or* signal

3 unfitness, inappropriateness, unsuitability, impropriety; **inaptness,** inaptitude, **inappositeness, irrelevance** *or* irrelevancy, infelicity, uncongeniality, inapplicability, inadmissibility; abnormality, anomaly; **maladjustment,** misjoining, misjoinder; mismatch, mismatchment; misalliance, *mésalliance* <Fr>

4 misfit, nonconformist, individualist, inner-directed person, oddball <nf>; **freak,** sport, anomaly; naysayer, crosspatch, dissenter; a fish out of water, a square peg in a round hole <nf>

VERBS **5 disagree, differ** 780.5, vary, not see eye-to-eye, be at cross-purposes, tangle assholes <nf>, **disaccord** 456.8, **conflict,** clash, **jar,** jangle, jostle, collide, square off, cross swords, break, break off; **mismatch,** mismate, mismarry, misally; part company, split up; **dissent** 333.4, agree to disagree, object, **negate** 335.3, **contradict,** counter; be *or* march out of step, "hear a different drummer"—Thoreau

ADJS **6 disagreeing, differing** 780.7, **discordant** 456.15, disaccordant; dissonant, dissident; **inharmonious,** unharmonious, disharmonious; discrepant, disproportionate; divergent, variant; at variance, **at odds,** at war, at daggers drawn, at opposite poles, at loggerheads, at cross-purposes; **hostile,** antipathetic, antagonistic, repugnant; inaccordant, out of accord, out of whack <nf>; **jarring,** clashing, grating, jangling; **contradictory, contrary; disagreeable,** cross, cranky, disputatious, ornery <nf>, negative, uncongenial, incompatible; immiscible <chem>

7 inappropriate, inapt, unapt, inapposite, misplaced, **irrelevant,** malapropos, *mal à propos* <Fr>; **unsuited,** ill-suited; **unfitted,** ill-fitted; **maladjusted,** unadapted, ill-adapted; ill-sorted, ill-assorted, ill-chosen; ill-matched, ill-mated, mismatched, mismated, mismarried, misallied; **unfit,** inept, unqualified; unfitting, unbefitting; **unsuitable,** improper, **unbecoming,** unseemly; infelicitous, inapplicable, inadmissible; **unseasonable, untimely,** ill-timed; **out of place,** out of line, out of keeping, out of character, out of proportion, out of joint, out of tune, out of time, out of season, out of its element

8 inconsistent, incongruous, inconsonant, inconsequent, incoherent, **incompatible,** irreconcilable; incommensurable, incommensurate; disproportionate, out of proportion, self-contradictory, paradoxical, oxymoronic, **absurd; abnormal,** anomalous; misfiting; ambivalent, ambiguous

9 nonconformist, individualistic, inner-directed, perverse; **unorthodox,** heterodox, heretical

PREPS **10 in disagreement with, against,** agin <nf>, counter to, clean counter to, **contrary to,** in defiance of, in contempt of, in opposition to; out of line with, not in keeping with

WORD ELEMENTS **11** contra-, counter-, dis-, ill-, mal-, mis-

790 EQUALITY

NOUNS **1 equality, parity,** par, equation, **identity** 778.1; equivalence *or* equivalency, convertibility, **correspondence,** parallelism, equipollence, coequality; **likeness,** levelness, evenness, coextension; **balance,** poise, equipoise, **equilibrium,** equiponderance; symmetry, proportion; level playing field; **justice** 649, equity, equal rights

2 equating, equation; equalizing, equilibration, evening, evening up; coordination, integration, accommodation, adjustment; **even break** *and* fair shake <nf>, affirmative action, equal opportunity

3 the same 778.3; **tie, draw, standoff** *and* Mexican standoff *and* wash *and* dead heat <nf>, stalemate, deadlock, impasse, neck-and-neck race, photo finish, even money; tied *or* knotted score, deuce; a distinction without a difference, six of one and half a dozen of the other, Tweedledum and Tweedledee

4 equal, match, mate, twin, fellow, **like, equivalent,** opposite number, counterpart, answer <nf>, vis à vis, equipollent, coequal, parallel, ditto <nf>; synonym; **peer,** compeer, colleague, peer group

VERBS **5 equal, match, rival, correspond, be even-steven,** be tantmount to, be equal to; **keep pace with, keep step with, run abreast; amount to,** come to, come down to, run to, reach, touch; **measure up to,** come up to, stack up with <nf>, match up with; lie on a level with, **balance, parallel,** ditto <nf>; break even <nf>; **tie, draw,** knot; go shares, go halves, go Dutch

6 equalize; equate; even, equal out, equal, even up, even off, square, level, level out, level off, make both ends meet, synchronize; **balance,** strike a balance, poise, balance out, balance the accounts, balance the books; **compensate,** make up for, counterpoise; countervail, counterbalance, cancel; coordinate, integrate, proportion; fit, accommodate, adjust

ADJS **7 equal, equalized,** like, **alike, even,** level, par, **on a par,** at par, at parity, au pair, commensurate, proportionate, flush; on the same level, on the same plane, on the same *or* equal footing; on terms of equality, **on even** *or* **equal terms,** on even ground; on a level, on a level playing field, on a footing, in the same boat; **square,** quits, zero-sum, even-steven <nf>; half-and-half, **fifty-fifty;** nip and tuck, **drawn, tied,** neck-and-neck <nf>, abreast, too close to call, deadlocked, stalemated, knotted

8 equivalent, tantamount, equiparant, equipollent, coequal, coordinate; **identical** 778.7; corresponding *or* correspondent; convertible, much the same, as broad as long, neither more nor less, **all one,** all the same, neither here nor there

9 balanced, poised, apoise, **on an even keel;** equibalanced, equiponderant *or* equiponderous

10 equisized, equidimensional, equiproportional, equispaced; equiangular, isogonic, isometric; equilateral, equisided; coextensive

ADVS **11 equally, correspondingly, proportionately,** equivalently, **evenly; identically** 778.9; without distinction, indifferently; to the same degree, *ad eundem* <L>; as, **so;** as well; to all intents and purposes, other things being equal, *ceteris paribus* <L>; as much as to say

12 to a standoff <nf>, to a tie *or* draw

WORD ELEMENTS **13** co-, equi-, aequi-, homal-, is-, pari-

791 INEQUALITY

NOUNS **1 inequality, disparity, unevenness, contrariety** 779, **difference** 780; **irregularity,** nonuniformity 782, heterogeneity; **disproportion,** asymmetry; **unbalance,** imbalance, disequilibrium, overbalance, inclination of the balance, overcompensation, tippiness; **inadequacy,** insufficiency, shortcoming; **odds,**

handicap; **injustice,** inequity, tilting of the scales, unfair discrimination, second-class citizenship, untouchability; unfair advantage, loaded dice

VERBS **2 unequalize,** disproportion

3 unbalance, disbalance, disequilibrate, overbalance, overcompensate, **throw off balance,** upset, skew, destabilize

ADJS **4 unequal,** disparate, **uneven; irregular** 782.3; disproportionate, **out of proportion,** skew, skewed, asymmetric *or* asymmetrical; mismatched *or* ill-matched, ill-sorted; **inadequate,** insufficient; at a disadvantage

5 unbalanced, ill-balanced, overbalanced, off-balance, tippy, listing, heeling, leaning, canting, top-heavy, off-center; **lopsided,** slaunchways *and* cockeyed *and* skewgee *and* skygodlin <nf>, skew-whiff <Brit nf>; **unstable,** unsteady, tender <nautical>

ADVS **6 unequally,** disparately, disproportionately, variously, **unevenly;** nonuniformly 782.4

792 WHOLE

NOUNS **1 whole, totality, entirety,** collectivity; complex; integration, embodiment; **unity, integrity, wholeness;** organic unity, oneness; integer

2 total, sum, sum total, sum and substance, **the amount,** whole *or* gross amount, grand total; entity

3 all, the whole, the entirety, everything, all the above *or* all of the above <nf>, the aggregate, the assemblage, one and all, all and sundry, each and every <nf>, complete works; **package,** set, complement, package deal; **the lot,** the corpus, all she wrote <nf>, **the ensemble; be-all,** be-all and end-all, beginning and end, "alpha and omega"— Bible, A to Z, A to izzard, the whole range *or* spectrum, length and breadth, sum and substance; everything from soup to nuts *and* everything but the kitchen sink <nf>; grand design, world view, big picture

4 <nf terms> **whole bunch, whole mess, whole caboodle, the kit and caboodle, whole kit and caboodle,** whole kit and boodle, whole bit *or* shtick, whole megillah, **whole shooting match,** whole hog, whole animal <old>, **whole deal,** whole schmear, **whole shebang,** whole works, the works, the full monty <Brit nf>, whole ball of wax, whole show, whole nine yards

5 wholeness, totality, completeness 794, **unity, fullness,** inclusiveness, exhaustiveness, comprehensiveness; holism, holistic *or* total approach; universality

6 major part, best part, better part, **most; majority,** generality, plurality; **bulk, mass,** body, main body;

lion's share; substance, gist, meat, essence, thrust, gravamen

VERBS **7 form** *or* **make a whole,** constitute a whole; **integrate,** unite, form a unity

8 total, amount to, come to, run to *or* **into,** mount up to, add up to, tot *or* tot up to <nf>, tote *or* tote up to <nf>, reckon up to <nf>, aggregate to; aggregate, unitize; **number, comprise,** contain, encompass

ADJS **9** <not partial> **whole, total, entire,** aggregate, gross, all; integral, integrated; **one,** one and indivisible; **inclusive,** all-inclusive, **exhaustive,** comprehensive, omnibus, all-embracing, across-the-board, global; holistic; universal

10 intact, untouched, undamaged 1002.8, all in one piece <nf>, unimpaired, virgin, pristine, unspoiled, pure

11 undivided, uncut, unsevered, unclipped, uncropped, unshorn; **undiminished,** unreduced, complete

12 unabridged, uncondensed, unexpurgated

ADVS **13** <not partially> **wholly, entirely,** all; **totally,** *in toto* <L>, from start to finish, from soup to nuts <nf>, from A to Z, from A to izzard, across the board; **altogether, all put together,** in its entirety, *tout ensemble* <Fr>; **in all,** on all counts, in all respects, at large; **as a whole, in the aggregate,** in the lump, in the gross, in bulk, in the mass, *en masse* <Fr>, *en bloc* <Fr>; **collectively, corporately,** bodily, in a body, as a body; lock, stock, and barrel; hook, line, and sinker

14 on the whole, in the long run, over the long haul, all in all, to all intents and purposes, on balance, **by and large, in the main, mainly, mostly, chiefly,** substantially, essentially, effectually, **for the most part,** almost entirely, for all practical purposes, **virtually;** approximately, nearly, all but

WORD ELEMENTS **15** pan-, pant-, panta-, coen-

793 PART

NOUNS **1 part, portion, fraction;** percentage; **division** 802.1; **share,** parcel, dole, quota, piece *or* piece of the action <nf>; cut *and* slice *and* vigorish <nf>; **section,** sector, **segment;** quarter, quadrant; **item,** detail, particular; installment; **subdivision,** subset, subgroup, subspecies; detachment, contingent; focus group; **cross section,** sample, random sample, sampling; **component** 796.2, module, constituent, ingredient; **adjunct** 254; **remainder** 256; minority

2 <part of writing> section, front *or* back matter, prologue, epilogue, foreword, preface, introduction, afterword, text, chapter, verse, article; sentence, clause, phrase, segment, string,

constituent, paragraph, passage; number, book, fascicle; sheet, folio, page, signature, gathering

3 piece, particle, bit, scrap 248.3, bite, **fragment, morsel, crumb,** shard, potsherd, snatch, snack, appetizer; **cut,** cutting, clip, clipping, paring, shaving, rasher, snip, snippet, chip, slice, collop, dollop, scoop; **tatter, shred,** stitch; **splinter,** sliver; **shiver, smithereen** <nf>; **lump,** gob <nf>, gobbet, **hunk, chunk; stump,** butt, end, butt-end, fag-end, tail-end; modicum 248.2, moiety; bits and pieces, odds and ends; sound bite, outtake

4 member, organ; appendage; **limb; branch,** imp, bough, twig, sprig, spray, switch; runner, tendril; **off-shoot,** ramification, scion, spur; **arm** 906.5, **leg,** tail; hand 474.4; **wing,** pinion; lobe, lobule, hemisphere; facet, feature, integrant, integral part

5 dose, portion; slug *and* shot *and* nip *and* snort *and* dram <nf>; helping

VERBS **6 separate,** apportion, share, share out, distribute, cut, cut up, slice, slice up, divide 802.18; **analyze** 801.6

ADJS **7 partial,** part; **fractional,** sectional, componential, partitive; segmentary, segmental, modular; **fragmentary;** incomplete 795.4, open-ended

ADVS **8 partly, partially,** part, **in part**

9 piece by piece, bit by bit, part by part, **little by little,** inch by inch, foot by foot, drop by drop; **piecemeal,** piecewise, bitwise, inchmeal, by inchmeal; **by degrees,** by inches; **by** *or* **in snatches,** by *or* in installments, in lots, in small doses, in driblets, in dribs and drabs; in detail

WORD ELEMENTS **10** organo-; chir-; ali-, pter-, pterus-, pteryg-

794 COMPLETENESS

NOUNS **1 completeness, totality; wholeness** 792.5, **entireness, entirety; unity,** integrity, integrality, undividedness, intactness, untouchedness, unbrokenness; solidity, solidarity; **thoroughness,** exhaustiveness, unstintedness, inclusiveness, comprehensiveness, universality; pervasiveness, ubiquity, omnipresence; **universe,** cosmos, plenum

2 fullness, full; **amplitude, plenitude;** impletion, **repletion,** plethora; saturation, saturation point, satiety, congestion

3 full measure, fill, full house; max <nf>; **load, capacity, complement,** lading, **charge;** the whole bit <nf>; bumper, brimmer; bellyful *and* snootful <nf>, skinful *or* mouthful <nf>; **crush,** cram <nf>, jam-up <nf>

4 completion, fulfillment, consummation, culmination, perfection, realization, actualization, fruition, **accomplishment** 407, topping-off, closure

5 limit, end 820, **extremity,** extreme, **acme,** apogee, climax, **maximum,** max <nf>, ceiling, **peak,** summit, **pinnacle,** crown, top; **utmost,** uttermost, utmost extent, highest degree, nth degree *or* power, *ne plus ultra* <L>; **all, the whole** 792.3, the whole hog <nf>

VERBS **6** <make whole> **complete,** bring to completion *or* fruition, mature; **fill in, fill out,** piece out, top off, eke *or* eke out, round out; **make up,** make good, replenish, refill; **accomplish** 407.4, fulfill

7 fill, charge, load, lade, freight, weight; **stuff, wad,** pad, **pack,** crowd, **cram,** jam, jam-pack, ram in, chock; **fill up,** fill to the brim, brim, top up *or* top off, fill to overflowing, fill the measure of; supercharge, saturate, satiate, congest; overfill 993.15, make burst at the seams, surfeit

8 <be thorough> **go to all lengths, go all out, go the limit** <nf>, go the whole way, **go the whole hog** <nf>, cover a lot of ground, make a federal case of *and* make a big deal of *and* do up brown *and* do with a vengeance <nf>, **see it through** <nf>, follow out *or* up, follow *or* prosecute to a conclusion; leave nothing undone, not overlook a bet *and* use every trick in the book <nf>; **move heaven and earth, leave no stone unturned;** put the finishing touches to

ADJS **9 complete, whole, total,** global, **entire,** intact, solid; **full, full-fledged,** full-dress, **full-scale;** full-grown, mature, matured, ripe, developed; **uncut,** unabbreviated, undiminished, unexpurgated

10 thorough, thoroughgoing, thorough-paced, exhaustive, intensive, broad-based, wall-to-wall <nf>, house-to-house *and* door-to-door <nf>, A-to-Z, comprehensive, all-embracing, all-encompassing, omnibus, radical, sweeping; **pervasive,** all-pervading, ubiquitous, omnipresent, **universal; unmitigated, unqualified, unconditional,** unrestricted, unreserved, **all-out,** balls-out <Br>, wholesale, whole-hog <nf>; **out-and-out, through-and-through,** outright, downright, straight; congenital, born, **consummate,** unmitigated, unalloyed, perfect, veritable, egregious, deep-dyed, dyed-in-the-wool; **utter, absolute, total; sheer,** clear, clean, **pure,** plumb <nf>, **plain,** regular <nf>

11 full, filled, **replete,** plenary, capacity, flush, round; **brimful,** brimming; **chock-full,** chock-a-block, chuck-full, **cram-full,** topful, no room to spar; **jam-full, jam-packed, overcrowded;** stuffed, overstuffed, **packed, crammed,** *farci* <Fr>; **swollen** 259.13, bulging, bursting, bursting at the seams, ready to burst, full to bursting, fit to bust <nf>; as full as a tick, packed like sardines *or* herrings;

standing room only *or* SRO; **saturated,** satiated, soaked; fully laden, coming out of one's ears; congested; overfull 993.20, surfeited

12 fraught, freighted, **laden, loaded, charged,** burdened; heavy-laden; full-laden, full-fraught, full-charged, super-charged

13 completing, fulfilling, filling; completive *or* completory, consummative *or* consummatory, culminative, perfective; **complementary,** complemental

ADVS **14 completely, totally,** globally, **entirely, wholly, fully,** integrally, roundly, **altogether,** hundred percent, **exhaustively,** inclusively, comprehensively, bag and baggage *and* lock, stock, and barrel <nf>; **unconditionally,** unrestrictedly, unreservedly, with no strings attached, no ifs, ands, or buts; **one and all;** outright, *tout à fait* <Fr>; **thoroughly,** inside out <nf>; in full, in full measure; to the hilt

15 absolutely, perfectly, quite, right, stark, clean, sheer, plumb <nf>, plain; irretrievably, unrelievedly, irrevocably

16 utterly, to the utmost, all the way, **all out,** flat out <Brit>, *à outrance* <Fr>, *à toute outrance* <Fr>, hammer and tongs *and* tooth and nail <nf>, **to the full, to the limit,** to the max <nf>, mondo <nf>, to the backbone, to the marrow, to the nth degree *or* power, to the sky *or* skies, to the top of one's bent, **to a fare-thee-well,** to a fare-you-well *or* fare-ye-well, to beat the band *or* the Dutch *and* nine ways to Sunday <nf>, with a vengeance, all hollow <nf>

17 throughout, all over, overall, **inside and out, through and through;** through thick and thin, down to the ground <nf>, **from the ground up,** from the word 'go' *and* from the git-go <nf>; **to the end *or* bitter end,** to the death; **at full length,** *in extenso* <L>, *ad infinitum* <L>; every inch, every whit, every bit; root and branch, head and shoulders, heart and soul; to the brim, to the hilt, neck deep, up to the ears, up to the eyes; **in every respect,** in all respects, you name it <nf>; **on all counts,** at all points, for good and all

18 from beginning to end, from start to finish, from end to end, **from first to last, from A to Z,** from A to izzard, from soup to nuts *and* from hell to breakfast <nf>, from cover to cover; **from top to bottom,** *de fond en comble* <Fr>; from top to toe, **from head to foot,** *a capite ad calcem* <L>, cap-a-pie; **from stem to stern,** from clew to earing, fore and aft, from soup to nuts <nf>, *ab ovo usque ad mala*—<L, from eggs to apples>— Horace

WORD ELEMENTS **19** hol-, integri-, pan-, per-, tel-, teleut-

795 INCOMPLETENESS

NOUNS **1 incompleteness,** incompletion; **deficiency,** defectiveness, imperfection, **inadequacy;** underdevelopment, hypoplasia, **immaturity,** callowness, arrestment; **sketchiness,** scrappiness, patchiness; short measure *or* weight; lick and a promise

2 <part lacking> **deficiency,** want, **lack, need, deficit,** defect, **shortage,** shortfall, underage; wantage, outage, ullage, slippage; defalcation, arrearage, default; **omission,** gap, hiatus, hole, vacuum, break, lacuna, discontinuity, interval

VERBS **3** lack 992.7, want, want for; fall short 911.2; be arrested, underdevelop, undergrow

ADJS **4 incomplete, uncompleted, deficient,** defective, unfinished, imperfect, unperfected, **inadequate; undeveloped,** underdeveloped, undergrown, stunted, hypoplastic, **immature,** callow, infant, arrested, embryonic, **wanting, lacking,** needing, missing, **partial,** part, failing; in default, in arrear *or* arrears; **in short supply,** scanty; **short,** scant, shy <nf>; **sketchy,** patchy, scrappy; left hanging

5 mutilated, garbled, hashed, **mangled, butchered,** docked, hacked, lopped, truncated, castrated, cut short; abridged

ADVS **6 incompletely, partially,** by halves, by *or* in half measures, in installments, in *or* by bits and pieces; **deficiently,** imperfectly, inadequately

WORD ELEMENTS **7** semi-, parti-

796 COMPOSITION
<manner of being composed>

NOUNS **1 composition, constitution, construction,** formation, fabrication, fashioning, shaping, organization; **embodiment,** incorporation, incarnation; **make, makeup,** getup *or* setup <nf>; **building,** buildup, structure, structuring, shaping-up, compiling; **assembly,** assemblage, putting *or* piecing together; synthesis, syneresis; **combination** 805; **compound** 797.5; **junction** 800.1; **mixture** 797

2 component, constituent, ingredient, integrant, makings and fixings <nf>, **element, factor, part** 793, player, module, part and parcel; appurtenance, adjunct 254; **feature,** aspect, specialty, circumstance, detail, item

VERBS **3 compose, constitute,** construct, fabricate; **incorporate,** embody, incarnate; **form, organize,** structure, shape, shape up; **enter into,** go into, go to make up; **make, make up, build,** build up, assemble, put *or* piece together, compile; **consist of,** be a feature of, form a part of, combine *or*

unite in, merge in; **consist,** be made up of, be constituted of, contain; **synthesize; combine** 805.3; join 800.5; **mix**

ADJS **4 composed of,** formed of, **made of,** made up of, made out of, compact of, consisting of; composing, comprising, constituting, including, inclusive of, containing, incarnating, embodying, subsuming; contained in, embodied in

5 component, constituent, modular, integrant, integral; **formative,** elementary

797 MIXTURE

NOUNS **1** mixture, mixing, blending; **admixture,** composition, commixture, immixture, intermixture, **mingling,** minglement, commingling *or* comminglement, intermingling *or* interminglement, interlarding *or* interlardment; **eclecticism,** syncretism; **pluralism,** melting pot, multiculturism *or* multiculturalism, ethnic *or* racial *or* cultural diversity; **fusion,** interfusion, conflation; amalgamation, **integration,** alloyage, coalescence; **merger, combination** 805

2 imbuement, impregnation, infusion, suffusion, decoction, infiltration, instillment, instillation, permeation, pervasion, interpenetration, penetration; saturation, steeping, soaking, marination

3 adulteration, corruption, contamination, denaturalization, **pollution, doctoring** <nf>; fortifying, lacing, spiking <nf>; **dilution,** cutting <nf>, watering, watering down; debasement, bastardizing

4 crossbreeding, crossing, **interbreeding,** miscegenation; **hybridism,** hybridization, mongrelism, mongrelization; intermarriage

5 compound, mixture, admixture, intermixture, immixture, commixture, **composite, blend,** meld, composition, confection, concoction, **combination,** combo <nf>, ensemble, marriage; amalgam, alloy; paste, magma; cocktail

6 hodgepodge, hotchpotch, hotchpot; **medley, miscellany,** mélange, pastiche, *pasticcio* <Ital>, **conglomeration, assortment,** assemblage, mixed bag, ragbag, grab bag, olio, *olla podrida* <Sp>, **scramble, jumble,** mingle-mangle, **mix,** mishmash, **mess,** can of worms <nf>, dog's breakfast <Can nf>, mare's nest, rat's nest, hurrah's nest <nautical nf>, hash, patchwork, salad, gallimaufry, salmagundi, sundries, **potpourri,** stew, gumbo, sauce, slurry, omnium-gatherum, Noah's ark, **odds and ends,** oddments, all sorts, everything but the kitchen sink <nf>, all colors of the rainbow, broad spectrum, what you will

7 <slight admixture> **tinge, tincture, touch, dash, smack,** taint, tinct, tint, **trace,** vestige, hint, inkling, intimation, soupçon, suspicion, suggestion, whiff, modicum, thought, shade, tempering; sprinkling, seasoning, sauce, spice, infusion

8 hybrid, crossbreed, cross, mixed-blood, mixblood, **half-breed,** half-bred, half blood, half-caste; **mongrel,** cur; *ladino* <Sp>; mustee *or* mestee, *mestizo* <Sp>, *mestiza* <Sp fem>, *métis* <Fr>, *métisse* <Fr fem>; Eurasian; **mulatto,** high yellow <nf>, quadroon, quintroon, octoroon; sambo, zambo, *cafuso* <Pg>, Cape Colored <S Africa>, griqua <S Africa>; griffe; zebrule, zebrass, cattalo, mule, hinny, liger, tigon; tangelo, citrange, plumcot; alley cat

9 mixer, blender, beater, agitator, food processor, shaker; cement mixer, eggbeater, churn; homogenizer, colloid mill, emulsifier; crucible, melting pot

VERBS **10 mix,** admix, commix, immix, **intermix, mingle,** bemingle, commingle, immingle, **intermingle,** interlace, interweave, intertwine, interlard, intersperse, interleave; syncretize; **blend,** interblend, stir in; **amalgamate, integrate,** alloy, coalesce, **fuse, merge,** meld, compound, compose, conflate, concoct; **combine** 805.3; mix up, hash, stir up, **scramble,** conglomerate, shuffle, **jumble,** jumble up, mingle-mangle, throw *or* toss together, entangle; knead, work; homogenize, emulsify

11 imbue, imbrue, **infuse,** suffuse, transfuse, breathe, **instill,** infiltrate, **impregnate, permeate,** pervade, penetrate, leaven; **tinge, tincture,** entincture, temper, color, dye, flavor, season, dredge, besprinkle; **saturate,** steep, decoct, brew

12 adulterate, corrupt, contaminate, **debase,** infect, denaturalize, pollute, denature, bastardize, **tamper with, doctor** *and* doctor up <nf>; **fortify,** spike <nf>, pep up <nf>, lace; **dilute,** cut <nf>, water, water down <nf>

13 hybridize, crossbreed, cross, interbreed, miscegenate, mongrelize

ADJS **14 mixed, mingled,** blended, compounded, amalgamated; **combined** 805.5; **composite,** compound, **complex,** many-sided, multifaceted, intricate; **conglomerate,** pluralistic, multiracial, multicultural, multiethnic, multinational, heterogeneous, varied, **miscellaneous,** medley, motley, dappled, patchy, sundry, divers; promiscuous, indiscriminate, **scrambled, jumbled,** thrown together; half-and-half, fifty-fifty <nf>; amphibious; equivocal, **ambiguous,** ambivalent, ironic, syncretic, eclectic

15 hybrid, mongrel, interbred, **crossbred,** crossed, cross; **half-breed,** half-bred, half-blooded, half-caste

16 miscible, mixable, assimilable, integrable

PREPS **17 among,** amongst, 'mongst; **amid,** mid, amidst, midst, **in the midst of, in the thick of; with,** together with

798 SIMPLICITY

<freedom from mixture or complexity>

NOUNS **1 simplicity, purity,** simpleness, **plainness,** no frills, starkness, severity; unmixedness, monism; **unadulteration,** unsophistication, unspoiledness, intactness, fundamentality, elementarity, primitiveness *or* primitivity, primariness, naturalness; **singleness,** oneness, unity, integrity, homogeneity, uniformity 781; homeyness, unpretentiousness; unadornment; rusticity

2 simplification, streamlining, refinement, purification, distillation; **disentanglement,** disinvolvement; uncluttering, unscrambling, unsnarling, unknotting; stripping, stripping away *or* down, paring down, narrowing, confining, bracketing; **analysis** 801; deconstruction

3 oversimplification, oversimplicity, oversimplifying; **simplism,** reductivism; intellectual childishness *or* immaturity, conceptual crudity

VERBS **4 simplify,** streamline, **reduce,** reduce to elements *or* essentials, factorize; purify, refine, distill; strip, strip down; narrow, confine, bracket, zero in <nf>; streamline; oversimplify; **analyze** 801.6

5 disinvolve, disintricate, unmix, disembroil, **disentangle,** untangle, **unscramble, unsnarl,** unknot, untwist, unbraid, unweave, untwine, unwind, uncoil, unthread, **unravel,** ravel; **unclutter,** clarify, clear up, disambiguate, sort out, get to the core *or* nub *or* essence

ADJS **6 simple, plain,** bare, bare-bones and no-frills <nf>, mere; **single,** uniform, homogeneous, of a piece; **pure,** simon-pure, pure and simple; **essential,** elementary, indivisible, **primary,** primal, primitive, prime, pristine, **irreducible, fundamental,** basic, rustic; undifferentiable *or* undifferentiated, undifferenced, monolithic; **austere,** chaste, unadorned, uncluttered, spare, stark, severe; homely, homespun, grass-roots, back-to-nature, bread-and-butter, down-home *and* vanilla *or* plain-vanilla *and* white-bread <nf>; beginning, entry-level; common *or* garden, everyday; unpretentious; unadorned, natural

7 unmixed, unmingled, unblended, **uncombined,** uncompounded; unleavened; **unadulterated,** unspoiled, untouched, intact, virgin, uncorrupted, unsophisticated, unalloyed, untinged, undiluted, unfortified; **clear,** clarified, purified, refined, **distilled,** rectified; **neat, straight,** absolute, sheer, naked, bare

8 **uncomplicated, uninvolved,** incomplex, straightforward

9 **simplified,** streamlined, stripped down

10 **oversimplified, oversimple; simplistic,** reductive; intellectually childish *or* immature, conceptually crude

ADVS 11 **simply, plainly, purely;** merely, barely; **singly, solely,** only, **alone,** exclusively, just, simply and solely

WORD ELEMENTS 12 hapl-

799 COMPLEXITY

NOUNS 1 **complexity, complication, involvement,** complexness, involution, convolution, tortuousness, Byzantinism, *chinoiserie* <Fr>, tanglement, **entanglement,** perplexity, **intricacy,** intricateness, ramification, crabbedness, technicality, subtlety

2 **complex,** perplex <nf>, tangle, tangled skein, **mess** *and* snafu *and* fuck-up <nf>, ravel, snarl, snarl-up; knot, Gordian knot; **maze,** meander, Chinese puzzle, **labyrinth;** webwork, mesh; **wilderness, jungle,** morass, quagmire; Rube Goldberg contraption, Heath Robinson device <Brit>, wheels within wheels; mare's nest, rat's nest, hurrah's nest <nautical nf>, can of worms <nf>, snake pit; hard nut to crack, riddle of the Sphinx, squaring the circle

VERBS 3 **complicate, involve, perplex,** ramify; **confound, confuse,** muddle, **mix up,** mess up *and* ball up *and* bollix up *and* screw up *and* foul up *and* fuck up *and* snafu *and* muck up *and* louse up <nf>, implicate; **tangle,** entangle, embrangle, **snarl, snarl up,** ravel, knot, tie in knots

ADJS 4 **complex, complicated,** many-faceted, multifarious, ramified, perplexed, **confused,** confounded, **involved,** implicated, crabbed, **intricate,** elaborate, involuted, convoluted, multilayered, multilevel; **mixed up,** balled up *and* bollixed up *and* screwed up *and* loused up *and* fouled up *and* fucked up *and* snafued *and* mucked up *and* messed up *and* FUBAR <nf>; **tangled,** entangled, tangly, embrangled, **snarled,** knotted, matted, twisted, raveled; mazy, daedal, **labyrinthine,** labyrinthian, meandering; **devious,** roundabout, deep-laid, Byzantine, subtle

5 **inextricable,** irreducible, unknottable, unsolvable

800 JOINING

NOUNS 1 **joining, junction,** joinder, jointure, **connection, union,** unification, bond, bonding, connectedness *or* connectivity, conjunction, conjoining, conjugation, liaison, marriage, hookup <nf>, splice, tie, tie-up *and* tie-in <nf>, knotting, entanglement, commerce; merger, merging; symbiosis; **combination** 805; conglomeration, **aggregation,** agglomeration, congeries; **coupling,** copulation, accouplement, coupledness, **bracketing,** yoking, pairing, splicing, wedding; **linking,** linkup, linkage, bridging, **concatenation,** chaining, articulation, agglutination; **meeting,** meeting place *or* point, confluence, convergence, concurrence, concourse, gathering, massing, clustering; communication, intercommunication, intercourse

2 **interconnection,** interface, interjoinder, **interlinking,** interlocking, interdigitation; **interassociation,** interaffiliation

3 **fastening, attachment, affixation,** annexation; ligature, ligation, ligating; **binding,** bonding, gluing, sticking, tying, lashing, splicing, knotting, linking, trussing, girding, hooking, clasping, zipping, buckling, buttoning; knot <see list>; adhesive 803.4; splice, bond, fastener, Velcro

4 **joint,** join, joining, **juncture, union, connection,** link, connecting link, **coupling, accouplement;** clinch, embrace; articulation <anatomy and botany>, symphysis <anatomy>; **pivot, hinge; knee; elbow; wrist; ankle; knuckle; hip; shoulder; neck,** cervix; ball-and-socket joint, pivot joint, hinged joint, gliding joint; toggle joint; connecting rod, tie rod; seam, suture, stitch, closure, mortise and tenon, miter, butt, scarf, dovetail, rabbet, weld; boundary, interface

VERBS 5 **put together, join,** conjoin, **unite,** unify, bond, **connect,** associate, league, band, merge, **assemble,** accumulate; **join up,** become a part of, associate oneself, enter into, come aboard <nf>; **gather,** mobilize, marshal, mass, amass, **collect,** conglobulate; **combine** 805.3; **couple,** pair, accouple, copulate, conjugate, marry, wed, tie the knot <nf>, **link,** link up, build bridges, yoke, knot, splice, tie, chain, bracket, ligate; **concatenate,** articulate, agglutinate; glue, tape, cement, solder, weld; **put together,** fix together, lay together, piece together, clap together, tack together, stick together, lump together, roll into one; bridge over *or* between, span; **include,** encompass, take in, cover, embrace, comprise

6 **interconnect, interjoin,** interface, mesh, intertie, interassociate, interaffiliate, **interlink,** interlock, interdigitate

7 **fasten, fix, attach, affix,** annex, put to, set to; graft, engraft; **secure,** anchor, moor; cement, knit, set, grapple, belay, **make fast;** clinch, clamp, cramp; tighten, trim, trice up, screw up; cinch *or* cinch up

8 hook, hitch; **clasp,** hasp, clip, snap; **button,** buckle, zipper; lock, latch; **pin,** skewer, peg, nail, nail up, tack, staple, toggle, screw, bolt, rivet; **sew,** stitch; **wedge,** jam, stick; rabbet, butt, scarf, mortise, miter, dovetail; batten, batten down; cleat; **hinge,** joint, articulate

9 bind, tie, brace, truss, **lash,** leash, rope, strap, lace, wire, chain; handcuff; **splice,** bend; **gird,** girt, belt, girth, girdle, band, cinch; **tie up,** bind up, do up, batten; **wrap,** wrap up, bundle; shrink-wrap; **bandage,** bandage up, swathe, swaddle

10 yoke, hitch up, hook up; harness, harness up; halter, bridle; saddle; tether, fetter

11 <be joined> **join, connect, unite, meet,** meet up, link up, merge, converge, **come together;** communicate, intercommunicate, network, interface; knit, grow together; cohere, adhere, hang *or* hold together, clinch, embrace

ADJS **12 joint, combined,** joined, **conjoint,** conjunct, conjugate, corporate, compact, cooperative, cooperating; concurrent, coincident; inclusive, comprehensive; coherent

13 joined, united, connected, copulate, **coupled,** linked, knit, bridged, tight-knit, knitted, bracketed, associated, conjoined, incorporated, integrated, **merged,** gathered, assembled, accumulated, **collected; associated,** joined up, on board; **allied,** leagued, banded together; hand-in-hand, hand-in-glove, intimate, liaising; unseparated, undivided; **wedded,** matched, married, paired, yoked, mated; **tied, bound,** knotted, spliced, lashed; yogic

14 fast, fastened, fixed, secure, firm, close, tight, set, zipped up; **bonded,** glued, cemented, taped; **jammed,** wedged, stuck, frozen, seized, seized up

15 inseparable, impartible, **indivisible,** undividable, indissoluble, inalienable, inseverable, bound up in *or* with

16 joining, connecting, meeting; **communicating,** intercommunicating; **connective,** connectional; conjunctive, combinative, combinatorial, copulative, linking, bridging, binding; yogic

17 jointed, articulate

ADVS **18 jointly,** conjointly, corporately, **together; in common,** in partnership, mutually, in concord; **all together,** as one, in unison, in agreement, in harmony; concurrently, at once, at *or* in one fell swoop

19 securely, firmly, fast, tight; **inseparably,** indissolubly

20 knots

anchor knot	bow
barrel knot *or* blood knot	bowknot
becket knot	bowline
Blackwall hitch	bowline knot

builder's knot	midshipman's hitch
butcher's knot	monkey's fist
carrick bend	netting knot
cat's-paw	open hand knot
clinch	outside clinch
clove hitch	overhand knot
constrictor knot	prolonge knot
crossing knot	reef knot
crown knot	reeving-line bend
cuckold's neck	ring hitch *or* lark's head
diamond knot	ring knot
double hitch	rolling hitch
Englishman's tie	rope-yarn knot
eye splice	round seizing
figure-eight knot	round turn *and* half hitch
figure-of-eight bend	running bowline
fisherman's bend	running knot
fisherman's knot	sennit knot
flat knot	sheepshank
Flemish knot	Shelby knot
French shroud knot	short splice
German knot	shroud knot
granny knot	single knot
half crown	slide knot
half hitch	slipknot *or* nooseknot
half-Windsor knot	square knot
hangman's knot	star knot
harness hitch	stevedore's knot
hawser bend	stopper's knot
hawser fastening	studding-sail halyard bend
heaving-line bend	stunner hitch
inside clinch	surgeon's knot
lanyard knot	sword knot
long splice	tack bend
loop knot	timber knot *or* hitch
magnus hitch	truckman's knot
manrope knot	truelove knot
marlinespike hitch	Turk's-head
marling hitch	wall knot
masthead knot	weaver's knot *or* hitch
Matthew Walker knot	Windsor knot
mesh knot	

801 ANALYSIS

NOUNS **1 analysis,** analyzation, **breakdown,** breaking down, breakup, breaking up; anatomy, anatomizing, dissection; separation, **division, subdivision,** segmentation, reduction to elements *or* parts; chemical analysis, **assay *or*** assaying, resolution, titration, docimasy <old>, qualitative analysis, quantitative analysis, volumetric analysis, gravimetric analysis; ultimate analysis, proximate analysis; microanalysis, semimicroanalysis; profiling; racial profiling

2 itemization, enumeration, detailing, breakout, isolation; outlining, schematization, blocking, blocking out; resolution; scansion, parsing

3 **classification, categorization, sorting,** taxonomy, sorting out, sifting, sifting out, grouping, factoring, winnowing, shakeout, pigeonholing, categorizing; **weighing, evaluation,** gauging, assessment, appraisal, position statement *or* paper, **judgment** 946; impact statement

4 **outline,** structural outline, **plan,** scheme, schema, chart, flow chart, graph; table, table of contents, index; **diagram,** block diagram, exploded view, **blueprint; catalog,** *catalogue raisonné* <Fr>

5 **analyst, analyzer, examiner** 938.16; taxonomist

VERBS 6 **analyze, break down,** break up, anatomize, dissect, atomize, unitize; **divide, subdivide,** segment; assay, titrate; separate, make discrete, isolate, reduce, reduce to elements, resolve

7 **itemize,** enumerate, factorize, number, detail, break out; **outline,** schematize, block out, diagram, graph, chart; resolve; scan, parse

8 **classify,** class, **categorize,** catalog, sort, sort out, sift, group, factor, winnow, thrash out; weigh, weigh up, **evaluate, judge,** gauge 946.9, assess, appraise 946.9

ADJS 9 **analytical,** analytic; segmental; classificatory, enumerative; schematic

ADVS 10 **analytically,** by parts *or* divisions *or* sections; by categories *or* types

802 SEPARATION

NOUNS 1 **separation, disjunction,** severalty, disjointure, disjointing, split-up, splitting-up, demerger, delinkage, disarticulation, **disconnection,** disconnectedness, discontinuity, incoherence, disengagement, disunion, nonunion, disassociation, segregation; **parting,** alienation, estrangement, **removal,** withdrawal, isolation, detachment, sequestration, abstraction; **subtraction** 255; divorce, divorcement; **division,** subdivision, partition, compartmentalization, segmentation, marking off; districting, zoning; **dislocation,** luxation; separability, partibility, dividableness, divisibility; separatism; **separateness,** discreteness, singleness, monism, unitariness

2 **severance,** disseverment *or* disseverance, **sunderance,** scission, fission, cleavage, dichotomy, parting; **cutting, slitting,** slashing, **splitting,** slicing; **rending, tearing,** ripping, laceration, hacking, chopping, butchering, mutilation; section, resection; **surgery**

3 **disruption, dissolution,** abruption, cataclasm; revolution 860; **disintegration** 806, breakup, crack-up, shattering, splintering, fragmentizing, fragmentation; **bursting,** dissilience *or* dissiliency; **scattering,** dispersal, diffusion; **stripping,** scaling, exfoliation

4 **break,** breakage, **breach,** burst, **rupture, fracture; crack,** cleft, **fissure, cut, split,** slit; slash, slice; **gap, rift,** rent, rip, tear; chip, splinter, scale; dividing line, caesura, solidus

5 **dissection, analysis** 801, vivisection, resolution, breakdown, diaeresis; anatomy

6 **disassembly, dismantlement,** taking down *or* apart, dismemberment, dismounting; undoing, unbuilding; **stripping,** stripping away *or* down, divestiture, divestment, defoliation, deprivation; disrobing, unclothing, doffing

7 **separator,** sieve, centrifuge, ultracentrifuge; creamer, cream separator; breaker, stripper, mincer; slicer, cutter, microtome; analyzer

VERBS 8 **separate, divide, disjoin, disunite,** draw apart, dissociate, disassociate, grow apart, **disjoint,** disengage, disarticulate, **disconnect;** uncouple, unyoke; **part,** cut the knot, **divorce,** estrange; **alienate, segregate,** separate off, factor out, sequester, isolate, curtain off, shut off, set apart *or* aside, split off, cut off *or* out *or* loose *or* adrift; **withdraw, leave, depart,** take one's leave, cut out *and* split <nf>; pull out *or* away *or* back, stand apart *or* aside *or* aloof, step aside; subtract 255.9; delete 255.12; **expel,** eject, throw off *or* out, cast off *or* out

9 **come apart,** spring apart, fly apart, come unstuck, come unglued, come undone, come apart at the seams, **come** *or* **drop** *or* fall to pieces, **disintegrate, come to pieces,** go to pieces, fall apart, fall apart at the seams, fall to pieces, atomize, unitize, fragmentize, pulverize, break up, bust up <nf>, unravel; come *or* fall off, peel off, carry away; get loose, give way, start

10 **detach, remove,** disengage, take *or* lift off, doff; **unfasten, undo,** unattach, unfix; **free, release,** liberate, loose, unloose, unleash, unfetter; **unloosen,** loosen; cast off, weigh anchor; **unhook,** unhitch, unclasp, unclinch, unbuckle, unbutton, unsnap, unscrew, unpin, unbolt; **untie,** unbind, unknit, unbandage, unlace, unzip, unstrap, unchain; unstick, unglue

11 **sever, dissever,** cut off *or* away *or* loose, shear off, hack through, hack off, ax, amputate; **cleave, split,** fissure; sunder, cut in two, dichotomize, halve, bisect; **cut,** incise, carve, **slice,** pare, prune, trim, trim away, resect, excise 255.10; slit, snip, lance, scissor; **chop, hew,** hack, **slash;** gash, whittle, butcher; saw, jigsaw; **tear, rend,** rive, rend asunder

12 **break, burst,** bust <nf>, breach; **fracture, rupture; crack,** split, check, craze, fissure; snap; chip, scale, exfoliate

13 **shatter, splinter,** shiver, break to *or* into pieces, fragmentize, break to *or* into smithereens <nf>; **smash,** crush, crunch, squash, squish <nf>;

disrupt, demolish, break up, smash up; **scatter,** disperse, diffuse; **fragment,** fission, atomize; **pulverize** 1051.9, grind, cut to pieces, mince, make mincemeat of, make hamburger of <nf>

14 **tear** *or* **rip apart,** take *or* pull apart, **pick** *or* **rip** *or* **tear to pieces,** tear to rags *or* tatters, **shred,** rip to shreds; **dismember,** tear limb from limb, draw and quarter; **mangle,** lacerate, mutilate, maim; skin, flay, strip, peel, denude; defoliate

15 **disassemble,** take apart *or* down, tear down; **dismantle, demolish,** dismount, unrig <nautical>

16 **disjoint,** unjoint, **unhinge,** disarticulate, **dislocate,** luxate, throw out of joint, unseat

17 **dissect, analyze** 801.6, vivisect, anatomize, break down

18 **apportion, portion,** section, partition, compartmentalize, segment; **divide,** divide up, divvy *and* divvy up <nf>, **parcel,** parcel up *or* out, **split,** split up, cut up, subdivide; district, zone

19 **part company, part, separate,** split up, dispel, disband, scatter, **disperse,** break up, break it up <nf>, **go separate ways,** diverge

ADJS 20 **separate, distinct, discrete; unjoined, unconnected, unattached,** unaccompanied, unattended, unassociated; **apart,** asunder, **in two;** discontinuous, noncontiguous, divergent; **isolated,** insular, detached, detachable, free-standing, free-floating, autonomous; **independent,** self-contained, stand-alone <nf>; noncohesive, noncohering, incoherent 804.4; bipartite, dichotomous, multipartite, multisegmental; **subdivided,** partitioned, curtained-off, marked-off, compartmentalized

21 **separated,** disjoined, disjoint, disjointed, disjunct, **disconnected,** disengaged, detached, **disunited, divided,** removed, divorced, **alienated,** estranged, distanced, **segregated,** sequestered, isolated, cloistered, shut off; **scattered,** dispersed, helter-skelter; disarticulated, dislocated, luxated, out of joint

22 **unfastened, unbound,** uncaught, unfixed, **undone, loose, free,** loosened, unloosened, clear; **untied, unbound,** unknit, unleashed, unfettered, unchained, unlaced, unbandaged, unhitched; unstuck, unglued; unclasped, unclinched, unbuckled, unbuttoned, unzipped, unsnapped; unscrewed, unpinned, unbolted; **unanchored,** adrift, afloat, floating, free, free-floating

23 **severed, cut,** cleaved, cleft, cloven, riven, hewn, sheared; **splintered,** shivered, cracked, **split,** slit, reft; **rent, torn;** tattered, shredded, in shreds; quartered, **dismembered,** in pieces

24 **broken,** busted <nf>, **burst, ruptured,** dissilient; sprung; **shattered,** broken up, broken to pieces *or* bits, fragmentized, fragmentary, fragmented, in shards, in smithereens <nf>

25 **separating, dividing,** parting, distancing; separative, disjunctive

26 **separable,** severable, **divisible,** alienable, cleavable, partible; **fissionable,** fissile, scissile; dissoluble, dissolvable

ADVS 27 **separately,** severally, piecemeal, one by one; **apart,** adrift, asunder, **in two,** in twain; apart from, away from, aside from; abstractly, in the abstract, objectively, impersonally

28 **disjointedly,** unconnectedly, sporadically, spasmodically, discontinuously, by bits and pieces, by fits and starts

29 **to pieces,** all to pieces, **to bits, to smithereens** <nf>, to splinters, to shards, to tatters, to shreds

803 COHESION

NOUNS 1 **cohesion,** cohesiveness, **coherence, adherence, adhesion, sticking,** sticking together, cling, clinging, binding, colligation, inseparability; cementation, conglutination, agglutination; concretion, condensation, accretion, solidification, set, congelation, congealment, clotting, coagulation, curdling; **conglomeration,** conglobation, compaction, agglomeration, consolidation; inspissation, incrassation; **clustering,** massing, bunching, nodality; colloidality, emulsification

2 **consistency** 788.1, **connection, connectedness; junction** 800.1; **continuity, seriality, sequence** 815, **sequentialness, consecutiveness** 812.1, **orderliness**

3 **tenacity,** tenaciousness, **adhesiveness,** cohesiveness, retention, adherence; **tightness,** snugness; stickiness, **tackiness,** gluiness, gumminess, **viscidity,** consistency, viscosity, glutinosity, mucilaginousness; gelatinousness, jellylikeness, gelatinity; pulpiness; persistence *or* persistency, **stick-to-itiveness** <nf>, toughness, **stubbornness, obstinacy** 361, bulldoggedness *or* bulldoggishness, bullheadedness

4 <something adhesive or tenacious> **adhesive,** adherent, adherer; **bulldog,** barnacle, leech, limpet, remora; burr, cocklebur, clotbur, bramble, brier, prickle, thorn; sticker, bumper sticker, decalcomania, decal <nf>; **glue, cement,** gluten, mucilage, epoxy resin, paste, stickum *and* gunk <nf>; gum; resin, tar; **plaster,** adhesive plaster, court plaster; putty, size; syrup, molasses, honey; mucus; thickener; pulper; fixative; tape, Scotch tape <trademark>, masking tape; Velcro <trademark>; Band-Aid <trademark>

5 **conglomeration,** consolidation, **conglomerate,** breccia <geology>, agglomerate, agglomeration,

aggregate, congeries, cluster, bunch, mass, clot; concrete, concretion; compaction

VERBS **6 cohere, adhere, stick, cling,** cleave, hold; **persist,** stay, stay put <nf>; cling to, freeze to <nf>; hang on, hold on; take hold of, clasp, grasp, hug, embrace, clinch; **stick together, hang** or **hold together;** grow to, grow together; **solidify, set,** conglomerate, agglomerate, conglobate; **congeal,** coagulate, clabber <nf>, **clot; cluster,** mass, bunch

7 be consistent 788.6, **connect,** connect with, follow; **join** 800.11, link up

8 hold fast, stick close, stick like glue, stick like a wet shirt or wet T-shirt or second skin, hug or mold to the figure; stick closer than a brother, stick like a barnacle or limpet or leech, cling like ivy or a burr, hold on like a bulldog

9 stick together, cement, bind, colligate, paste, glue, agglutinate, conglutinate, gum; **weld,** fuse, **solder,** braze; gum up <nf>

ADJS **10 cohesive,** cohering, coherent; adhering, **sticking, clinging,** inseparable, cleaving, holding together; **cemented,** stuck, agglutinative, agglutinated, agglutinate, conglutinate, conglutinated; **concrete, condensed, solidified, set, congealed,** clotted, coagulated; conglomerated, conglobate, **compacted, consolidated,** agglomerated; **clustered,** massed, bunched, nodal

11 consistent 788.9, **connected;** continuous 812.8, **serial,** uninterrupted, contiguous, sequential, sequent, **consecutive** 812.9; orderly, tight; **joined** 800.13

12 adhesive, adherent, stickable, self-adhesive, retentive; **tenacious,** clingy; **sticky, tacky,** gluey, gummy, gummous, glutenous, **viscid,** viscous, viscose, glutinous; inspissate, incrassate; colloidal; gooey and gunky <nf>; **persistent,** tough, **stubborn, obstinate** 361.8, bulldoggish or bulldogged or bulldoggy, bullheaded; stick–to–it-ive <nf>

804 NONCOHESION

NOUNS **1 noncohesion,** uncohesiveness, incoherence, inconsistency, discontinuity 813, nonadhesion, unadhesiveness, unadherence, untenacity, immiscibility; **separateness,** discreteness, aloofness, standoffishness <nf>; **disjunction** 802.1, unknitting, unraveling, dismemberment; **dislocation; dissolution, chaos** 810.2, anarchy, **disorder** 810, confusion, entropy; **scattering,** dispersion or dispersal; diffusion

2 looseness, slackness, bagginess, **laxness,** laxity, relaxation, floppiness; sloppiness, shakiness, ricketiness

VERBS **3 loosen, slacken, relax;** slack, slack off; ease, ease off, let up; **loose, free,** let go, unleash; **disjoin,** unknit, unravel, dismember, undo, unfasten, unpin; **sow confusion,** open Pandora's box; unstick, unglue; **scatter,** disperse, diffuse

ADJS **4 incoherent,** uncoherent, noncoherent, **inconsistent, uncohesive, unadhesive,** nonadhesive, noncohesive, nonadherent, like grains of sand, **untenacious, unconsolidated,** tenuous; unjoined 802.20, disconnected, unconnected, unraveled, dismembered, gapped, open; **disordered** 810.12, chaotic, anarchic, anomic, confused; **discontinuous** 813.4, broken, detached, discrete, aloof, standoffish <nf>

5 loose, slack, lax, relaxed, easy, sloppy; shaky, rickety; flapping, streaming; loose-fitting, hanging, drooping, dangling; bagging, baggy

805 COMBINATION

NOUNS **1 combination,** combine, combo <nf>, composition, compounding; **union, unification,** marriage, wedding, coupling, accouplement, linking, linkage, yoking; **incorporation,** aggregation, agglomeration, conglomeration, congeries; **amalgamation, consolidation,** assimilation, **integration,** solidification, **encompassment,** inclusion, ecumenism; **junction** 800.1; conjunction, conjugation; **alliance,** affiliation, reaffiliation, **association** 617, **merger,** league, hookup <nf>, tie-up <nf>; **taking** 480, buyout, takeover, leveraged buyout; **federation, confederation,** confederacy; collaboration; federalization, centralization, cartel; **fusion,** blend, blending, meld, melding; coalescence, coalition; **synthesis,** syncretism, syneresis, syncrasy; syndication; **conspiracy,** cabal, junta; enosis <Gk>, Anschluss <Ger>; package, package deal; collection; **agreement** 788; **addition** 253

2 mixture 797, **compound** 797.5

VERBS **3 combine, unite, unify,** marry, wed, couple, link, yoke, yoke together; **incorporate, amalgamate, consolidate,** assimilate, **integrate,** solidify, coalesce, compound, put or lump together, roll into one, come together, make one, unitize; **connect, join** 800.5; **mix; add** 253.4; **merge,** meld, **blend,** stir in, merge or blend or meld or shade into, **fuse,** flux, melt into one, conflate; interfuse, interblend; **encompass,** include, comprise; **take,** take over, buy out; **synthesize,** syncretize; syndicate; reembody

4 league, ally, affiliate, associate, consociate; unionize, organize, cement a union; **federate, confederate,** federalize, centralize; **join forces,**

join *or* unite with, join *or* come together, join up
with <nf>, hook up with <nf>, tie up *or* in with
<nf>, **throw in with** <nf>, stand up with, go *or* be
in cahoots <nf>, **pool one's interests, join fortunes
with,** stand together, close ranks, make common
cause with; **marry, wed, couple, yoke,** yoke
together, link; **band together,** club together,
bunch, bunch up <nf>, gang up <nf>, gang, club;
team with, **team up with** <nf>, couple, pair,
double up, buddy up <nf>, pair off, partner; go in
partnership, go in partners <nf>; **conspire,** cabal,
put heads together

ADJS **5 combined, united, amalgamated,
incorporated, consolidated, integrated,**
assimilated, one, unitary, unitive, unitized, **joined**
800.13, joint 800.12, conjoint; conjunctive,
combinative *or* combinatory, connective,
conjugate; **merged,** blended, fused; **mixed;
synthesized,** syncretized, syncretistic, eclectic

6 leagued, enleagued, **allied, affiliated,** affiliate,
associated, associate, corporate; federated,
confederated, federate, confederate; **in league,** in
cahoots <nf>, in with; **conspiratorial,** cabalistic;
partners with, in partnership; teamed, coupled,
paired, married, wed, wedded, yoked, yoked
together, linked, linked up

7 combining, uniting, unitive, unitizing,
incorporating; merging, blending, fusing;
combinative, combinatory; associative; federative,
federal; corporative, incorporative, corporational;
coalescent, symphystic

806 DISINTEGRATION

NOUNS **1 disintegration, decomposition, dissolution,
decay,** coming-apart, resolution, disorganization,
degradation, breakup, breakdown, fragmentation,
atomization; corruption; ruin, **ruination,
destruction** 395; **erosion,** corrosion, crumbling,
dilapidation, wear, wear and tear, waste, wasting,
wasting away, ablation, ravagement, ravages of
time; **disjunction** 802.1; **incoherence** 804.1;
impairment 393

2 dissociation; electrolysis, catalysis, dialysis,
hydrolysis, proteolysis, thermolysis, photolysis
<all chemistry>, catabolism; catalyst, hydrolyst
<chemistry>; hydrolyte <chemistry>; **decay,**
fission <physics>, splitting, atom smashing

VERBS **3 disintegrate, decompose, decay,**
biodegrade, dissolve, come apart, disorganize,
break up 395.22, go to rack and ruin 395.24, crack
up, disjoin, unknit, split, fission, atomize, **come** *or*
fall to pieces; erode, corrode, ablate, consume,
wear *or* waste away, molder, molder away,
crumble, crumble into dust

4 <chemical terms> dissociate; catalyze, dialyze,
hydrolyze, electrolyze, photolyze; split, fission,
atomize

ADJS **5 disintegrative,** decomposing, disintegrating,
disruptive, disjunctive; **destructive, ruinous**
395.26; chaotic; **erosive,** corrosive, ablative;
resolvent, solvent, separative; **dilapidated,**
disintegrated, ruinous, shacky, worn-out, worn,
clapped-out <Brit nf>, moldering, ravaged,
wrecked, totaled <nf>; disintegrable,
decomposable, degradable, biodegradable

6 <chemical terms> dissociative; catalytic, dialytic,
hydrolytic, proteolytic, thermolytic, electrolytic,
photolytic; catabolic

WORD ELEMENTS **7** -lysis, lyso-, lysi-, -lyte

807 ORDER

NOUNS **1 order, arrangement** 808; **organization**
808.2; **disposition,** disposal, deployment,
marshaling; prioritization, putting in order;
formation, structure, configuration, array,
makeup, lineup, setup, layout; system, scheme,
schedule; routine, even tenor, standard operating
procedure; **peace,** quiet, quietude, **tranquillity;
regularity,** uniformity 781; symmetry, proportion,
concord, **harmony,** order, the music of the
spheres, Tao *or* Dào; chronological order

2 continuity, logical order, serial order, reverse
order, ascending *or* descending order, alphabetical
order, numerical order; **degree** 245; **hierarchy,**
pecking order, **gradation,** subordination,
superordination, rank, place, position, status;
progression; **sequence** 815; category, class

3 orderliness, trimness, tidiness, neatness; good
shape <nf>, good condition, fine fettle, good trim,
apple-pie order <nf>, a place for everything and
everything in its place; **discipline,** method,
methodology, methodicalness, system,
systematicness; anality, compulsiveness,
compulsive neatness

VERBS **4 order, arrange** 808.8, get it together <nf>,
organize, regulate; dispose, deploy, marshal;
form, form up, configure, structure, array, pull it
together, get *or* put one's ducks in a row <nf>,
straighten it out, get *or* put one's house in order,
run a tight ship, line up, set up, lay out; **pacify,**
quiet, cool off *or* down <nf>, **tranquilize;
regularize,** harmonize; **systematize,** methodize,
normalize, standardize, routinize; hierarchize,
categorize, classify, grade, rank, prioritize

5 form, take form, take order, **take shape,**
crystallize, **shape up;** arrange *or* range itself, place
itself, take its place, fall in, **fall** *or* **drop into place,**
fall into line *or* order *or* series, fall into rank, take

rank; come together, draw up, gather around, rally round; put to rights, whip into shape

ADJS 6 orderly, ordered, **regular, well-regulated, well-ordered, methodical, formal,** regular as clockwork, punctilious, uniform 781.5, **systematic,** symmetrical, **harmonious;** businesslike, routine, steady, normal, habitual, usual, en règle, in hand; **arranged** 808.14; scientific, businesslike

7 in order, in trim, to rights *and* in apple-pie order <nf>; **in condition,** in good condition, in kilter *or* kelter <nf>, in shape, in good shape <nf>, in perfect order, in good form, in fine fettle, in good trim, in the pink <nf>, in the pink of condition; **in repair,** in commission, in adjustment, in working order, fixed; up to scratch *or* snuff <nf>

8 tidy, trim, natty, neat, spruce, sleek, slick *and* slick as a whistle <nf>, smart, trig, dinky <Brit nf>, snug, tight, **shipshape,** shipshape and Bristol fashion; **well-kept,** well-kempt, well-cared-for, well-groomed; neat as a button *or* pin <nf>, not a hair out of place

ADVS 9 methodically, systematically, regularly, through channels, uniformly, harmoniously, like clockwork

10 in order, in turn, in sequence, in succession, hierarchically, in series, seriatim <L>; step by step, by stages

808 ARRANGEMENT
<putting in order>

NOUNS 1 arrangement, ordering, structuring, shaping, forming, configurating, configuration, constitution; **disposition, disposal, deployment,** placement, marshaling, **arraying; distribution,** collation, collocation, allocation, allotment, apportionment; **formation,** formulation, **configuration,** form, array; regimentation; syntax; **order** 807

2 organization, methodization, ordering, planning, charting, codification, regulation, regularization, routinization, normalization, rationalization; **adjustment,** harmonization, tuning, fine-tuning, tune-up, tinkering; **systematization,** ordination, coordination

3 grouping, classification 809, categorization, taxonomy; **gradation,** subordination, superordination, **ranking,** placement; **sorting,** sorting out, assortment, sifting, screening, triage, culling, selection, shakeout

4 table, code, digest, **index, inventory,** census; table of organization

5 arranger, organizer, coordinator, personal organizer; spreadsheet; **sorter,** sifter, **sieve,** riddle, **screen,** bolter, colander, grate, grating

6 <act of making neat> **cleanup,** red-up <nf>; tidy-up, trim-up, police-up <nf>

7 rearrangement, reorganization, reconstitution, **reordering, restructuring,** *perestroika* <Russ>, shake-up <nf>; **redeployment,** redisposition, realignment

VERBS 8 arrange, order 807.4, reduce to order, **put** *or* **get** *or* **set in order,** right, prioritize, put first things first, get one's ducks in a row <nf>; **put** *or* **set to rights, get it together** <nf>, **pull it together,** put in *or* into shape, whip into shape <nf>, sort out <chiefly Brit>, unsnarl, make sense out of <nf>

9 dispose, distribute, fix, place, set out, collocate, allocate, **compose,** space, **marshal,** rally, array; align, line, **line up,** form up, range; regiment; **allot, apportion,** parcel out, deal, **deal out**

10 organize, methodize, **systematize,** rationalize, regularize, get *or* put one's house in order; **harmonize,** synchronize, **tune,** tune up; **regularize,** routinize, normalize, standardize; **regulate,** adjust, coordinate, fix, settle; **plan,** chart, codify

11 classify 809.6, **group,** categorize; grade, gradate, rank, subordinate; **sort,** sort out <chiefly Brit>, assort; **separate,** divide; collate; **sift,** size, sieve, **screen,** bolt, riddle

12 tidy, **tidy up,** neaten, trim, **put in trim,** trim up, trig up <chiefly Brit>, **straighten up,** fix up <nf>, **clean up,** police *and* police up <nf>, groom, spruce *and* spruce up <nf>, **clear up,** clear the decks

13 rearrange, reorganize, reconstitute, **reorder, restructure,** reshuffle, rejigger <nf>, tinker *or* tinker with, tune, tune up, fine-tune; **shake up,** shake out; redispose, redistribute, reallocate, realign

ADJS 14 arranged, ordered, disposed, configured, composed, constituted, fixed, placed, aligned, ranged, arrayed, marshaled, grouped, ranked, **graded;** organized, methodized, **regularized,** routinized, normalized, standardized, **systematized;** regulated, harmonized, synchronized; **classified** 809.8, categorized, **sorted,** assorted; **orderly** 807.6

15 organizational, formational, structural

WORD ELEMENTS 16 tax-, taxi-, -taxia, -taxis

809 CLASSIFICATION

NOUNS 1 classification, categorization, classing, placement, ranging, **pigeonholing,** compartmentalizing, **sorting, grouping; grading,** stratification, ranking, rating, classing; division, subdivision; **cataloging,** codification, tabulation, rationalization, indexing, filing; **taxonomy,** typology; hierarchy; analysis 801, **arrangement** 808

2 **class, category, head, order, division,** branch, set, **group,** grouping, bracket, pigeonhole; **section,** heading, rubric, **label,** title; **grade,** rank, rating, status, estate, stratum, level, station, position; **caste,** clan, race, strain, blood, kin, sept; **subdivision,** subgroup, suborder, subclass, subcategory, subset; hyponym, hypernym, superordinate, subordinate

3 **kind, sort, ilk, type,** breed of cat <nf>, lot <nf>, **variety, species, genus,** *genre* <Fr>, phylum, denomination, designation, description, style, strain, manner, **nature, character,** persuasion, the like *or* likes of <nf>; **stamp, brand,** feather, color, stripe, line, grain, kidney; **make,** mark, label, shape, cast, form, mold, model; tribe, clan, race, strain, blood, kin, breed; league, realm, domain, sphere

4 **hierarchy,** class structure, power structure, pyramid, establishment, pecking order; natural hierarchy, order *or* chain of being, domain, realm, **kingdom,** animal kingdom, vegetable kingdom, mineral kingdom; the order of things

5 <botanical and zoological classifications, in descending order> **kingdom;** subkingdom, **phylum** <zoology>, branch <botany>; superclass, **class,** subclass, superorder, **order,** suborder, superfamily, **family,** subfamily, tribe, subtribe, **genus,** subgenus, series, section, superspecies, **species;** subspecies, **variety,** subvariety, scion; biotype, genotype

VERBS 6 **classify,** class, assign, designate; **categorize,** type, put down as, **pigeonhole,** place, **group, arrange** 808.8, range; **order** 807.4, put in order, rank, rate, **grade; sort,** assort; distribute; **divide, analyze** 801.6, subdivide, break down; **catalog,** list, file, tabulate, rationalize, **index,** alphabetize, digest, codify

ADJS 7 **classificational,** classificatory; **categorical,** **taxonomic** *or* **taxonomical,** typologic *or* typological; ordinal; divisional, divisionary, subdivisional; **typical,** typal; **special,** specific, characteristic, particular, peculiar, denominative, differential, distinctive, defining, varietal

8 **classified,** classed, **cataloged, pigeonholed,** indexed, ordered, sorted, assorted, **graded, grouped,** ranked, rated, stratified, hierarchic, hierarchical, pyramidal; placed; filed, on file; tabular, indexical

ADVS 9 **any kind** *or* sort, **of any description, at all,** whatever, soever, whatsoever

WORD ELEMENTS 10 speci-, specie-, gen-

810 DISORDER

NOUNS 1 **disorder, disorderliness, disarrangement,** derangement, disarticulation, disjunction 802.1, **disorganization;** discomposure, **dishevelment, disarray,** upset, disturbance, discomfiture, disconcertedness; **irregularity,** randomness, turbulence, perturbation, ununiformity *or* nonuniformity, unsymmetry *or* nonsymmetry, no rhyme or reason, **disproportion, disharmony;** indiscriminateness, promiscuity, promiscuousness, haphazardness; butterfly effect; **randomness,** randomicity, vagueness, trendlessness; entropy; **disruption** 802.3, destabilization; **incoherence** 804.1, unintelligibility; untogetherness <nf>; disintegration 806; "inharmonious harmony"— Horace

2 **confusion, chaos,** anarchy, misrule, license, madhouse; **Babel,** cognitive dissonance; **muddle,** morass, **mix-up** *and* foul-up *and* fuck-up *and* snafu *and* screw-up <nf>, ball-up <nf>, balls-up <Brit nf>, hoo-ha *and* fine how-de-do <nf>, pretty kettle of fish, pretty piece of business, nice piece of work; kafuffle, kerfuffle

3 **jumble, scramble, tumble, snarl-up, mess,** bloody *or* holy *or* unholy *or* god-awful mess <nf>, pickle <nf>, shemozzle <Brit>, **turmoil,** welter, mishmash, hash, helter-skelter, farrago, crazy-quilt, higgledy-piggledy; shambles, tohubohu; **clutter, litter, hodgepodge** 797.6, rat's nest, mare's nest, hurrah's nest <nautical>; topsy-turviness *or* topsy-turvydom, arsy-varsiness, hysteron proteron

4 **commotion, hubbub, Babel, tumult,** turmoil, **uproar, racket,** riot, **disturbance, rumpus** <nf>, ruckus *and* ruction <nf>, disruption, **fracas, hassle,** shemozzle <Brit nf>, shindy <nf>, hullabaloo, rampage; **ado,** to-do <nf>, trouble, bother, pother, dustup <Brit nf>, stir <nf>, **fuss,** brouhaha, foofaraw <nf>, aggro <Brit, Austral>; **row** *and* hassle <nf>, **brawl,** free-for-all <nf>, donnybrook *or* donnybrook fair, broil, embroilment, melee, scramble; helter-skelter, pell-mell, **roughhouse, rough-and-tumble**

5 **pandemonium, hell, bedlam,** witches' Sabbath, Babel, confusion of tongues, **cacophony,** din, noise, static, racket

6 slovenliness, **slipshodness,** carelessness, negligence; **untidiness,** uneatness, looseness, **messiness** <nf>, **sloppiness,** dowdiness, seediness, **shabbiness,** tawdriness, chintziness <nf>, shoddiness, tackiness <nf>, grubbiness <nf>, frowziness, blowziness; **slatternliness,** frumpishness <nf>, sluttishness; **squalor,** squalidness, sordidness; derangement

7 **slob** <nf>, **slattern, sloven,** frump <nf>, sloppy Joe, schlep, schlump; drab, **slut, trollop; pig, swine; litterbug**

VERBS **8** lapse into disorder, fall into confusion, come apart, come apart at the seams, dissolve into chaos, slacken 804.3, come unstuck *or* unglued <nf>, disintegrate 806.3, degenerate, detune, untune

9 **disorder, disarrange** 811.2, **disorganize,** dishevel; **confuse** 811.3, sow confusion, open Pandora's box, **muddle,** jumble, jumble up, mix up; **discompose** 811.4, **upset,** destabilize, unsettle, **disturb,** perturb

10 **riot, roister,** roil, carouse; **create a disturbance, make a commotion,** make trouble, cause a stir *or* commotion, **make an ado** *or* **to-do,** create a riot, **cut loose, run wild, run riot,** run amok, go on a rampage, go berserk

11 <nf terms> **kick up a row,** kick up a shindy *or* a fuss *or* a storm, piss up a storm, **raise the devil,** raise the deuce *or* dickens, raise a rumpus *or* a storm, raise a ruckus, raise Cain, **raise hell,** raise sand, raise the roof, whoop it up, hell around, horse around *or* about; **carry on,** go on, maffick <Brit>; **cut up,** cut up rough, roughhouse

ADJS **12** **unordered, orderless, disordered, unorganized, random, entropic, unarranged,** ungraded, unsorted, unclassified; untogether <nf>; **unmethodical,** immethodical; **unsystematic,** systemless, nonsystematic; disjunct, unjoined 802.20; disarticulated, **incoherent** 804.4; discontinuous; **formless,** amorphous, inchoate, shapeless; ununiform *or* nonuniform, unsymmetrical *or* nonsymmetrical, disproportionate, misshapen; **irregular, haphazard,** desultory, **erratic,** sporadic, spasmodic, fitful, promiscuous, indiscriminate, casual, frivolous, capricious, random, hit-or-miss, vague, dispersed, wandering, planless, undirected, **aimless,** straggling, straggly; senseless, meaningless, gratuitous

13 **disorderly, in disorder,** disordered, **disorganized, disarranged, discomposed,** dislocated, deranged, convulsed; **upset, disturbed,** perturbed, unsettled, discomfited, disconcerted; **turbulent,** turbid, roily; out of order, **out of place,** misplaced, shuffled; **out of kilter** *or* **kelter** <nf>, **out of whack** <nf>, out of gear, out of joint, out of tune, on the fritz <nf>, haywire; **cockeyed** *and* skewgee *and* slaunchways *and* skygodlin <nf>, skew-whiff <Brit <nf>, awry, amiss, askew, on the blink and haywire <nf>

14 **disheveled, mussed up** <nf>, messed up <nf>, slobby <nf>, **rumpled,** tumbled, ruffled, snarled, snaggy; **tousled,** tously; uncombed, shaggy, matted; windblown

15 **slovenly, slipshod, careless, loose, slack,** nonformal, negligent; **untidy, unsightly,** unneat, slobby *and* scuzzy <nf>, **unkempt; messy** <nf>, mussy <nf>, **sloppy** <nf>, scraggly, poky, seedy <nf>, **shabby,** shoddy, schlocky <nf>, lumpen, chintzy, grubby <nf>, **frowzy, blowzy,** tacky <nf>; **slatternly, sluttish, frumpish,** frumpy, draggletailed, drabbletailed, draggled, bedraggled; down at the heel, out at the heels, out at the elbows, in rags, ragged, raggedy-ass *or* ragged-ass <nf>, raggedy, tattered; **squalid,** sordid; dilapidated, ruinous, **beat-up** *and* shacky <nf>

16 **confused, chaotic,** anarchic, **muddled, jumbled,** scattered, scatterbrained, helter-skelter <nf>, higgledy-piggledy, hugger-mugger, skimble-skamble, in a mess; **topsy-turvy,** arsy-varsy, upside-down, ass-backwards <nf>; **mixed up, balled** *or* **bollixed up** <nf>, **screwed up** <nf>, mucked up <nf>, **fouled up** *and* fucked up *and* snafu <nf>; discomposed, discombobulated

ADVS **17** **in disorder, in disarray, in confusion,** Katy bar the door <nf>, in a jumble, in a tumble, in a muddle, in a mess; higgledy-piggledy, helter-skelter <nf>, hugger-mugger, skimble-skamble, harum-scarum <nf>, willy-nilly <nf>, all over, all over hell <nf>, **all over the place, all over the shop** <nf>

18 **haphazardly, unsystematically,** unmethodically, irregularly, desultorily, **erratically,** capriciously, promiscuously, indiscriminately, **sloppily** <nf>, **carelessly,** randomly, **fitfully;** by *or* at intervals, sporadically, spasmodically, by fits, **by fits and starts,** by *or* in snatches, in spots <nf>; every now and then *and* every once in a while <nf>; **at random,** at haphazard, **by chance, hit** *or* **miss**

19 **chaotically, anarchically,** turbulently, **riotously; confusedly,** dispersedly, vaguely, wanderingly, **aimlessly,** planlessly, senselessly

811 DISARRANGEMENT
<bringing into disorder>

NOUNS **1** **disarrangement, derangement,** misarrangement, convulsion, dislocation; **disorganization,** shuffling; **discomposure,** disturbance, perturbation, disconcertedness; **disorder** 810; insanity 926

VERBS **2** **disarrange, derange,** misarrange; **disorder,** disorganize, disorient, throw out of order, put out of gear, dislocate, upset the apple-cart, **disarray; dishevel,** rumple, ruffle; tousle <nf>, muss *and* **muss up** <nf>, mess *and* **mess up** <nf>; **litter, clutter,** scatter

3 **confuse, muddle, jumble,** confound, garble, tumble, scramble, snarl, tie in knots, fumble, pi; **shuffle,** riffle; **mix up,** snarl up, **ball** *or* **bollix up**

<nf>, **foul up** *and* fuck up *and* **screw up** *and* muck up *and* snafu <nf>; make a hash *or* mess of <nf>, play hob with <nf>; disrupt

4 **discompose,** throw into confusion, **upset, unsettle, disturb,** trip up, perturb, trouble, distract, throw <nf>, throw into a tizzy *or* snit *or* stew <nf>, agitate, convulse, embroil; **psych** *and* spook *and* bug <nf>; put out, inconvenience

ADJS 5 **disarranged** 810.13, **confused** 810.16, **disordered** 810.12

812 CONTINUITY
<uninterrupted sequence>

NOUNS 1 **continuity, uninterruption,** uninterruptedness, uninterrupted course, featurelessness, unrelievedness, monotony, unintermittedness, unbrokenness, **uniformity** 781, undifferentiation; fullness, plenitude; seamlessness, jointlessness, gaplessness, smoothness; **consecutiveness,** successiveness; continuousness, **endlessness, ceaselessness, incessancy; constancy** 847.2, continualness, constant flow; steadiness, steady state, equilibrium, stability 855

2 **series, succession,** run, **sequence,** consecution, progression, course, gradation; one thing after another; **continuum,** plenum; lineage, descent, filiation; **connection, concatenation,** catenation, catena, **chain,** chaining, linkup, articulation, reticulation, nexus; chain reaction, powder train; **train,** range, rank, **file, line, string,** thread, queue, **row,** bank, tier; windrow, swath; single file, Indian file; array; **round, cycle,** rotation, routine, the daily grind <nf>, recurrence, periodicity, flywheel effect, pendulum; endless belt *or* chain, M–bius band *or* strip, *la ronde* <Fr>, endless round; gamut, spectrum, scale; drone, monotone, hum, buzz

3 **procession, train, column, line, string, cortège;** stream, steady stream; cavalcade, caravan, motorcade; **parade,** pomp; dress parade; promenade, review, march-past, flyover, flypast <Brit>, funeral; skimmington <Brit>; chain gang, coffel; mule train, pack train; queue, crocodile <Brit>

VERBS 4 **continue,** be **continuous,** not stop, **connect, connect up, concatenate,** continuate, catenate, join 800.5, link *or* link up, **string together,** string, thread, chain *or* chain up, follow in *or* form a series, run on, maintain continuity

5 **align, line, line up,** string out, rank, array, range, arrange, get *or* put in a row

6 **line up, get in** *or* **get on line,** queue *or* queue up <Brit>, enqueue, make *or* form a line, get in

formation, get in line, **fall in,** fall in *or* into line, fall into rank, take rank, take one's place

7 **file,** defile, file off; **parade,** go on parade, promenade, march past, fly over, fly past <Brit>

ADJS 8 **continuous,** continued, **continual,** continuing; **uninterrupted, unintermittent,** unintermitted, featureless, unrelieved, monotonous; **connected, joined** 800.13, linked, chained, concatenated, catenated, articulated; **unbroken,** serried, **uniform** 781.5, homogeneous, homogenized, cloned *or* clonish *and* cookie-cutter <nf>, undifferentiated, wall-to-wall *and* back-to-back <nf>, seamless, jointless, gapless, smooth, unstopped; unintermitting, unremitting; **incessant, constant,** steady, stable, **ceaseless,** unceasing, **endless,** unending, never-ending, **interminable,** perpetual, perennial; **cyclical,** repetitive, **recurrent,** periodic; straight, running, **nonstop; round-the-clock,** twenty-four-hour, all-hours; immediate, direct

9 **consecutive, successive,** successional, back-to-back <nf>, in order, running; progressive; **serial,** ordinal, seriate, catenary; sequent, **sequential;** linear, lineal, in-line; chronological

ADVS 10 **continuously, continually; uninterruptedly, unintermittently; without cease,** without stopping, with every other breath, without a break, back-to-back *and* wall-to-wall <nf>, unbrokenly, gaplessly, seamlessly, jointlessly, **connectedly,** together, cumulatively, on end; unceasingly, **endlessly,** *ad infinitum* <L>, perennially, **interminably,** again and again, repeatedly, time after time, time and again, time and time again, repetitively, cyclically, monotonously, unrelievedly, week in week out, year in year out, year-round, on and on, at *or* on a stretch; round the clock, all day long, all the livelong day, 24-7 *or* 24/7

11 **consecutively, progressively,** sequentially, successively, **in succession,** one after the other, back-to-back <nf>, **in turn,** turn about, turn and turn about; step by step; running, hand running <nf>; **serially,** in a series, *seriatim* <L>; **in a line,** in a row, in column, in file, in a chain, in single file, in Indian file

813 DISCONTINUITY
<interrupted sequence>

NOUNS 1 **discontinuity,** discontinuousness, discontinuation, discontinuance, noncontinuance; **incoherence** 804.1, **disconnectedness,** disconnection, delinkage, decoupling, discreteness, **disjunction** 802.1; **nonuniformity** 782; irregularity, **intermittence,** fitfulness 851.1;

brokenness; nonseriality, nonlinearity, non sequitur; incompleteness 795; episode, parenthesis; time lag, time warp; broken thread, missing link; digression, non sequitur, parenthesis

2 interruption, suspension, break, fissure, breach, gap, hiatus, lacuna, caesura, crevasse; **interval, pause,** interim 826, lull, cessation, letup <nf>, **intermission**

VERBS **3 discontinue, interrupt** 857.10, **break,** break off, **disjoin,** disconnect; **disarrange** 811.2; intermit 851.2; pause; digress

ADJS **4 discontinuous,** noncontinuous, unsuccessive, **incoherent** 804.4, nonserial, nonlinear, nonsequential, discontinued, **disconnected,** unconnected, unjoined 802.20, delinked, decoupled, *décousu* <Fr>, **broken;** nonuniform 782.3, irregular; broken, broken off, fragmentary, **interrupted,** suspended; disjunctive, discrete, discretive; **intermittent, fitful** 851.3, stop-and-go, on-again off-again; scrappy, snatchy, spotty, patchy, jagged; choppy, chopped-off, herky-jerky <nf>, jerky, spasmodic; episodic, parenthetic

ADVS **5 discontinuously, disconnectedly,** brokenly, fragmentarily; at intervals; **haphazardly** 810.18, randomly, occasionally, infrequently, now and then, now and again, intermittently, fitfully, **by fits and starts,** by fits, by snatches, by catches, by jerks, spasmodically, episodically, by skips, skippingly, *per saltum* <L>; willy-nilly, **here and there,** in spots, sporadically, patchily

814 PRECEDENCE
<in order>

NOUNS **1 precedence** or precedency, antecedence or antecedency, anteposition, anteriority, precession; the lead, front position, front seat, pole position, first chair; **priority,** preference, urgency; top priority, taking precedence, preemption; prefixation, prothesis; **superiority** 249; **dominion** 417.6; **precursor** 816; prelude 816.2; preliminaries, run-up and walk-up <nf>; preceding 165.1

VERBS **2 precede,** antecede, **come first,** come or go before, **go ahead of, go in advance,** stand first, stand at the head, **head,** head up <nf>, front, **lead** 165.2, take precedence, have priority, preempt; lead off, kick off, usher in; pilot, lead the way, blaze a trail, spearhead; head the table or board, sit on the dais; rank, outrank, rate; anticipate, foreshadow

3 <place before> **prefix, preface,** premise, prelude, prologize, preamble, introduce

ADJS **4 preceding,** precedent, **prior,** antecedent, anterior, precessional, **leading** 165.3; preemptive; **preliminary,** precursory, prevenient, prefatory, exordial, prelusive, preludial, proemial,

preparatory, initiatory, propaedeutic, inaugural; **first, foremost,** headmost, **chief** 249.14

5 former, foregoing, erstwhile, one-time, late, previous; aforesaid, aforementioned, beforementioned, above-mentioned, aforenamed, forenamed, forementioned, said, named, same

ADVS **6 before** 216.12; above, hereinbefore, hereinabove, *supra* <L>, *ante* <L>

815 SEQUENCE

NOUNS **1 sequence,** logical sequence, **succession,** successiveness, consecution, **consecutiveness,** following, coming after, accession; descent, lineage, line, family tree; **series** 812.2, serialization; **order,** order of succession; **priority; progression,** procession, rotation; **continuity** 812; **continuation;** prolongation, extension, posteriority; suffixation, subjunction, postposition; subsequence, sequel; cycle, process

VERBS **2 succeed, follow, ensue,** come or go after, **come next; inherit,** take the mantle of, step into the shoes or place of, take over; segue; tailgate, follow on the heels of, tail <nf>

3 <place after> suffix, append, subjoin

ADJS **4 succeeding, successive, following, ensuing,** sequent, sequential, sequacious, posterior, **subsequent,** consequent; proximate, **next;** appendant, suffixed, postpositive, postpositional; serial; progressive; tailgating

816 PRECURSOR

NOUNS **1 precursor, forerunner,** foregoer, *voorlooper* <Dutch>, vaunt-courier, avant-courier, front- or lead-runner; pioneer, voortrekker <Dutch>, frontiersman, bushwhacker; scout, pathfinder, explorer, point, point man, trailblazer or trailbreaker, guide; **leader** 574.6, leadoff man or woman, bellwether, fugleman; **herald,** announcer, *buccinator* <L>, messenger, harbinger, stormy petrel; **predecessor,** forebear, precedent, antecedent, **ancestor; vanguard, avant-garde,** avant-gardist, innovator, groundbreaker; prequel

2 curtain raiser, countdown, run-up and walk-up <nf>, lead-in, warm-up, kickoff, opening gun or shot; **opening episode,** first episode, prequel; **prelude, preamble, preface,** prologue, foreword, introduction, *avant-propos* <Fr>, protasis, proem, proemium, prolegomenon or prolegomena, exordium; **prefix,** prefixture; frontispiece; **preliminary,** front matter; overture, voluntary, verse; premise, presupposition, postulate, prolepsis; **innovation, breakthrough** <nf>, leap

VERBS **3 go before, pioneer,** blaze or break the trail,

break new ground, be in the van *or* vanguard; guide; **lead** 165.2, lead *or* show the way; **precede** 814.2; herald, count down, run up, lead in, forerun, usher in, introduce

ADJS **4 preceding** 814.4; preliminary, exploratory, pioneering, trailblazing, door-opening, kickoff, inaugural; **advanced,** avant-garde, original 337.5

817 SEQUEL

NOUNS **1 sequel,** sequela *or* sequelae, sequelant, sequent, sequitur, **consequence** 887.1; **continuation,** continuance, **follow-up** *or* **follow-through** <nf>, perseverance; caboose; **supplement,** addendum, appendix, back matter; postfix, suffix; postscript *or* PS, subscript, postface; postlude, **epilogue,** conclusion, peroration, codicil; refrain, chorus, coda; envoi, colophon, tag; afterthought, second thought, double take <nf>, *arrière-pensée* <Fr>, *esprit d'escalier* <Fr>; parting *or* Parthian shot; last words, swan song, dying words, famous last words

2 afterpart, afterpiece; **wake,** trail, train, queue; **tail,** tailpiece, rear, rear end; tab, tag, trailer

3 aftermath, afterclap, afterglow, afterimage, aftereffect, side effect, by-product, spin-off, aftertaste; **aftergrowth,** aftercrop; **afterbirth,** placenta, secundines; afterpain

4 successor, replacement, backup, backup man *or* woman, substitute, stand-in; **descendant,** posterity, **heir,** inheritor

VERBS **5 succeed,** follow, come next, come after, come on the heels of; **follow through,** carry through, take the next step, drop the other shoe

818 BEGINNING

NOUNS **1 beginning, commencement, start,** running *or* flying start, starting point, square one <nf>, **outset,** outbreak, **onset,** oncoming, get-go; dawn; **creation, foundation, establishment, establishing, institution, origin,** origination, setting-up, setting in motion; **launching,** launch, launch *or* launching pad; alpha, A; **opening,** rising of the curtain; day one; first crack out of the box <nf>, leadoff, kickoff *and* jump-off *and* send-off *and* start-off *and* take-off *and* blast-off *and* git-go <nf>, the word 'go' <nf>; fresh start, new departure; **opening wedge,** leading edge, cutting edge, thin end of the wedge; entry level, bottom rung, bottom of the ladder, low place on the totem pole; daybreak

2 beginner, neophyte, tyro; newcomer 774.4, new arrival, Johnny-come-lately <nf>; entry-level employee, low man on the totem pole; entrant, **novice,** novitiate, probationer, catechumen; **recruit,**

raw recruit, rookie <nf>; **apprentice,** trainee, learner, student; baby, infant, newborn; nestling, fledging; freshman 572.6; tenderfoot, greenhorn, greeny <nf>, initiate; debutant, deb <nf>; starter

3 first, first ever, prime, primal, primary, **initial,** alpha; **initiation,** initialization, first move, opening move, gambit, **first step,** baby step, *le premier pas* <Fr>, openers, starters, first lap, first round, first inning, first stage, first leg; breaking-in, warming-up; first blush, first glance, first sight, first impression; early days

4 origin, origination, **genesis, inception,** incipience *or* incipiency, inchoation; **divine creation,** creationism, creation science; **birth,** birthing, bearing, parturition, pregnancy, nascency *or* nascence, nativity; **infancy,** babyhood, childhood, youth; freshman year; incunabula, beginnings, cradle; fountainhead, wellspring, source

5 inauguration, installation *or* installment, induction, **introduction,** initiation; inception; setting in motion; embarkation *or* embarkment, **launching,** floating, flotation, unveiling; debut, first appearance, coming out <nf>; opener <nf>, preliminary, curtain raiser *or* lifter; maiden speech, inaugural address

6 basics, essentials, rudiments, elements, nuts and bolts <nf>; **principles,** principia, first principles, first steps, **outlines, primer,** hornbook, first reader, grammar, alphabet, **ABC's,** abecedarium; introduction, induction; groundwork, spacework

VERBS **7 begin, commence, start; start up, kick** *or* **click in** <nf>; **start in, start off, start out, set out,** set sail, set in, set to *or* about, go *or* swing into action, get to *or* down to, **turn to,** fall to, pitch in <nf>, dive in <nf>, plunge into, head into <nf>, **go ahead,** let her rip <nf>, fire *or* blast away <nf>, take *or* jump *or* kick *or* tee *or* blast *or* send off <nf>, get the show on the road <nf>, get *or* set *or* start the ball rolling <nf>, roll it *and* let it roll <nf>

8 make a beginning, make a move <nf>, **start up,** get going <nf>, get off, set forth, set out, launch forth, get off the ground <nf>, **get under way,** set up shop, get in there <nf>; set a course, **get squared away** <nf>; make an auspicious beginning, **get off to a good start,** make a dent; get in on the ground floor <nf>; **break in, warm up,** get one's feet wet <nf>, cut one's teeth

9 enter, enter on *or* **upon** *or* **into, embark in** *or* **on** *or* **upon,** take up, go into, have a go at <chiefly Brit>, take a crack *or* whack *or* shot at <nf>; **debut,** make one's debut

10 initiate, originate, create, invent; **precede** 814.2, **take the initiative, take the first step,** take the lead, pioneer 816.3; **lead,** lead off, lead the way; **ahead,** head up <nf>, stand at the head, stand first; **break the ice,** take the plunge, break ground, cut the first turf, lay the first stone, get one's feet wet

11 **inaugurate,** institute, **found, establish,** set up <nf>; **install,** initiate, induct; **introduce,** broach, bring up, lift up, raise; **launch,** float; christen <nf>; **usher in,** ring in <nf>; **set on foot,** set abroach, set agoing, turn on, kick-start *and* jump-start <nf>, start up, start going, start the ball rolling <nf>, get cracking <nf>

12 **open,** open up, breach, open the door to, cut the ribbon; open fire

13 **originate, take** *or* **have origin,** be born, take birth, get started, come into the world, **become,** come to be, get to be <nf>, see the light of day, rise, **arise,** take rise, take its rise, **come forth, issue,** issue forth, come out, spring *or* crop up; burst forth, break out, erupt, irrupt; debut

14 **engender, beget, procreate** 78.8; **give birth to, bear,** birth, bring to birth, bring into the world; father, mother, sire

ADJS 15 **beginning, initial,** initiatory *or* initiative; incipient, inceptive, **introductory,** inchoative, inchoate; inaugural *or* inauguratory; **prime,** primal, **primary,** primitive, primeval; **original, first,** first ever, first of all; aboriginal, autochthonous; **elementary,** elemental, **fundamental,** foundational; **rudimentary,** rudimental, abecedarian; **ancestral,** primogenital *or* primogenitary; **formative, creative,** procreative, inventive; embryonic, in embryo, in the bud, budding, fetal, gestatory, parturient, pregnant, in its infancy, formative; infant, infantile, incunabular; **natal,** nascent, prenatal, antenatal, neonatal; early; pregame

16 **preliminary, prefatory,** preludial, proemial, precursory, preparatory; entry-level, door-opening; prepositive, prefixed

17 **first, foremost,** front, frontal, up-front <nf>, **head, chief, principal,** premier, **leading, main,** flagship, foremost; maiden

ADVS 18 **first,** firstly, **at first,** first off, first thing, for openers *or* starters <nf>, as a gambit, up front <nf>, **in the first place,** first and foremost, before everything, *primo* <L>; **principally,** mainly, chiefly, most of all; **primarily,** initially; **originally, in the beginning,** *in limine* <L>, **at the start,** at first glance *or* first blush, at the outset, at the first go-off <nf>; from the ground up, from the foundations, from the beginning, **from scratch** <nf>, from the first, **from the word 'go'** *and* from the get-go <nf>, *ab origine* <L>, *ab initio* <L>; *ab ovo* <L>

WORD ELEMENTS 19 acro-, arche-, eo-, ne-, neo-, proto-; *Ur-* <Ger>

819 MIDDLE

NOUNS 1 **middle,** median, midmost, **midst;** thick, thick of things; **center** 208.2, inside; **heart, core,** nucleus, kernel, heart of the matter; **mean** 246, midpoint; interior 207.2; midriff, diaphragm; **waist,** waistline, zone, girth, tummy *and* belly girt <nf>; equator; diameter; midday, midnight

2 **mid-distance,** middle distance; **equidistance; half,** moiety; **middle ground,** middle of the road, centrism; halfway point *or* place, midway, midcourse, midstream, halfway house; bisection; neutral ground, gray area, happy medium; middle way

VERBS 3 seek the middle, bisect, split down the middle; center, focus; average 246.2; double, fold, middle <nautical>; straddle, compromise

ADJS 4 **middle, medial,** median, mesial, middling, mediocre, average, **medium** 246.3, mezzo <music>, **mean,** mid; **midmost,** middlemost; **central** 208.11, core, nuclear; focal, pivotal; interior, inside, internal; **intermediate,** intermediary; equidistant, halfway, midway, equatorial, diametral, midfield, midcourse, midstream; midland, mediterranean; midships, amidships; centrist, moderate, middle-of-the-road; center-seeking, centripetal

ADVS 5 **midway, halfway, in the middle,** betwixt and between <nf>, halfway in the middle <nf>; plump *or* smack *or* slap- *or* smack-dab in the middle <nf>; half-and-half, neither here nor there, *mezzo-mezzo* <Ital>; medially, mediumly; in the mean; *in medias res* <L>; **in the midst of,** in the thick of; midships, amidships

WORD ELEMENTS 6 mid-, medi-, medio-, mes-, meso-, mesio-; intermedi-, intermedio-

820 END

NOUNS 1 **end,** end point, ending, perfection, be-all and end-all, **termination, terminus, terminal,** terminating, term, period, **expiration,** expiry, phaseout, phasedown, discontinuation, closeout, **cessation** 857, ceasing, consummation, culmination, close, **conclusion, finish, finis, finale,** the end, finishing, finalizing *or* finalization, a wrap <nf>, quietus, stoppage, windup *and* payoff <nf>, curtain, curtains <nf>, all she wrote <nf>, fall of the curtain, end of the road *or* line <nf>; decease, taps, **death** 307; **last,** demise, "latter end"—Bible, last gasp *or* breath, final twitch, last throe, last legs, last hurrah <nf>; omega, Ω, izzard, Z; **goal,** destination, stopping place, resting place, finish line, tape *and* wire <nf>, journey's end, last stop; denouement, catastrophe, apocalypse, final solution, resolution; last *or* final words, peroration, swan song, dying words, envoi, coda, epilogue; **fate, destiny,** last things, eschatology, last trumpet, Gabriel's trumpet, crack of doom, doom; **effect 887; happy ending,** Hollywood ending, walking into the sunset

2 **extremity, extreme; limit** 794.5, ultimacy, definitiveness, **boundary,** farthest bound, jumping-off place, Thule, *Ultima Thule* <L>, **pole; tip,** point, nib; tail, **tail end,** butt end, tag, tag end, fag end; bitter end; stub, stump, butt; bottom dollar <nf>, bottom of the barrel <nf>

3 **close,** closing, cessation; decline, lapse; **homestretch, last lap** or **round** or **inning** <nf>, ninth inning, last stage; beginning of the end; deadline, closing time

4 **finishing stroke,** ender, **end-all,** quietus, stopper, **deathblow,** death stroke, *coup de grâce* <Fr>, kiss of death, mortal blow; **finisher,** clincher, equalizer, crusher, **settler;** knockout *and* knockout blow <nf>; sockdolager, KO *or* kayo *and* kayo punch <nf>; final stroke, finishing *or* perfecting *or* crowning touch, last dab *or* lick <nf>, last straw <nf>

VERBS 5 **end, terminate,** determine, close, close out, close the books on, phase out *or* down, **finish, conclude,** finish with, resolve, finish *or* wind up <nf>; **put an end to,** put a period to, put paid to <Brit>, put *or* lay to rest, **make an end of,** bring to an end, bring to a close *or* halt, end up; **get it over,** get over with *or* through with <nf>, be done with; bring down *or* drop the curtain; put the lid on <nf>, fold up <nf>, wrap *and* wrap up <nf>, sew up <nf>; call off <nf>, call all bets off <nf>; **dispose of,** polish off <nf>; kibosh *and* put the kibosh on <nf>, put the skids under <nf>; **stop, cease** 857.6; perorate; abort; scrap *and* scratch <nf>; **kill** 308.13, extinguish, scrag *and* waste *and* take out *and* zap <nf>, **give the quietus,** put the finisher *or* settler on <nf>, knock on *or* in the head, knock out <nf>, kayo *or* KO <nf>, shoot down *and* shoot down in flames <nf>, stop dead in one's tracks, wipe out <nf>; **cancel, delete,** expunge, censor, censor out, blank out, erase

6 **come to an end, draw to a close, expire, die** 307.18, come to rest, end up, land up; lapse, become void *or* extinct *or* defunct, run out, run its course, have its time *and* have it <nf>, pass, **pass away,** die away, wear off *or* away, go out, blow over, be all over, be no more; peter out, fizzle out

7 **complete** 794.6, perfect, finish, finish off, finish up, polish of, put the last *or* final *or* finishing touches on, finalize <nf>

ADJS 8 **ended, at an end, terminated, concluded, finished, complete** 794.9, perfected, settled, decided, set at rest; **over, all over,** all up <nf>; all

off <nf>, all bets off <nf>; **done,** done with, over with, over and done with, through *and* through with <nf>; wound up <nf>, washed up <nf>; all over but the shouting <nf>; **dead 307.29, defunct,** extinct; **finished,** defeated, out of action, disabled, *hors de combat* <Fr>; **canceled, deleted,** expunged, censored *or* censored out, blanked *or* blanked out, bleeped *or* bleeped out; scrapped

9 <nf terms> **belly-up, dead meat,** kaput, shot, done for, SOL *or* shit out of luck, scragged, shot down, shot down in flames, down in flames, wasted, zapped, pffft *or* phut, wiped out, washed up, down and out, down the tubes, totaled

10 **ending, closing, concluding, finishing,** culminating *or* culminative, consummative *or* consummatory, **ultimate,** definitive, perfecting *or* perfective, terminating, crowning, capping, conclusive

11 **final, terminal,** terminating *or* terminative, determinative, definitive, **conclusive; last,** last-ditch <nf>, last but not least, eventual, farthest, extreme, boundary, border, limbic, limiting, polar, endmost, ultimate; caudal, tail, tail-end

ADVS 12 **finally,** in fine; **ultimately, eventually, as a matter of course; lastly,** last, **at last,** at the last *or* end *or* conclusion, at length, at long last; **in conclusion, in sum;** conclusively, once and for all

13 **to the end, to the bitter end, all the way,** to the last gasp, the last extremity, **to a finish,** *à outrance* <Fr>, till hell freezes over <nf>, "to the edge of doom, "to the last syllable of recorded time"—both Shakespeare

PHRS 14 **that's all for, that's final, that's that,** that's all she wrote *and* that buttons it up <nf>, that's the end of the matter, so much for that, nuf said *and* enough said <nf>; the subject is closed, the matter is ended, the deal is off <nf>; "the rest is silence"—Shakespeare

WORD ELEMENTS 15 acr-, acro-, tel-, telo-, tele-

15 **conclusions and complimentary closes**

affectionately	respectfully
always	respectfully yours
best	sincerely
best regards	sincerely yours
best wishes	with all good
cheers	wishes
cordially	with all my love
cordially yours	with love
ever	with peace
ever yours	with regards
faithfully	yours affectionately
faithfully yours	yours faithfully
lovingly	yours most sincerely
most sincerely	yours respectfully
namaste	yours sincerely
regards	yours truly

821 TIME

NOUNS 1 time, duration, *durée* <Fr>, lastingness, continuity 812, term, while, tide, space; real time; psychological time; biological time; tense 530.12; **period** 824, time frame, timespan; time warp; cosmic time; kairotic time; quality time; space-time 158.6; the past 837, the present 838, the future 839; timebinding; **chronology** 832.1, chronometry, chronography, horology; tempo; time travel

2 Time, **Father Time,** Cronus, Kronos; "a sandpile we run our fingers in"—Sandburg

3 tract of time, corridors of time, whirligig of time, glass *or* hourglass of time, sands of time, ravages of time, noiseless foot of Time, scythe of Time, time's winged chariot

4 passage of time, course of time, lapse of time, progress of time, process of time, succession of time, time-flow, flow *or* flowing *or* flux of time, sweep of time, stream *or* current *or* tide of time, time and tide, march *or* step of time, flight of time, time's caravan, "Time's revolving wheels"—Petrarch; timeframe

VERBS 5 elapse, lapse, **pass, expire,** run its course, run out, go *or* pass by; **flow,** tick away *or* by *or* on, run, proceed, advance, roll *or* press on, roll by, flit, fly, slip, slide, glide; drag by *or* on; **continue** 812.4, last, **endure,** go *or* run *or* flow on

6 spend time, pass time, put in time, employ *or* use time, fill *or* occupy time, kill time <nf>, consume time, take time, take up time, while away the time; find *or* look for time; race with *or* against time, buy time, work against time, run out of time, make time stand still; weekend, winter, summer; keep time, mark time, measure time

ADJS 7 temporal, chronological, timewise; chronometric, chronographic; durational, durative; lasting, continuous 812.8; temporary, pending

ADVS 8 when, at which time, what time *and* whenas <old>, at which moment *or* instant, on which occasion, **upon which, whereupon,** at which, in which time, at what time, in what period, on what occasion, whenever

9 at that time, on that occasion, at the same time as, at the same time *or* moment that, then, concurrently, simultaneously, contemporaneously

10 in the meantime, meanwhile 826.5; during the time; for the duration; at a stretch

11 then, thereat, thereupon, **at that time,** at that moment *or* instant, in that case *or* instance, on that occasion; **again,** at another time, at some other time, anon

12 whenever, whene'er, whensoever, whensoe'er, **at whatever time,** at any time, anytime, no matter when; if ever, once

13 in the year of our Lord, *anno Domini* <L>, AD, in the Common *or* Christian Era, CE; *ante Christum* <L>, AC, before Christ, BC, before the Common *or* Christian era, BCE; *anno urbis conditae* <L>, AUC; *anno regni* <L>, AR

PREPS 14 during, pending, durante <law>; **in the course of,** in the process of, in the middle of; **in the time of,** at the time of, in the age *or* era of; over, through, **throughout,** throughout the course of, **for the period of;** until the conclusion of

15 until, till, to, unto, **up to,** up to the time of

16 CONJS when, while, whilst <chiefly Brit>, the while; **during the time that,** at the time that, at the same time that, at *or* during which time; **whereas, as long as,** as far as

17 PHRS time flies, *tempus fugit* <L>, time runs out, time marches on, "Time and tide stayeth for no man"—Richard Braithwaite

WORD ELEMENTS 18 chron-, chrono-, -chronous

822 TIMELESSNESS

NOUNS 1 timelessness, neverness, datelessness, eternity 829.1,2; no time, no time at all, running out of time; time out of time, stopping time; everlasting moment; immortality

2 <a time that will never come> Greek calends *or* kalends, when hell freezes over, the thirtieth of February

ADJS 3 timeless, dateless

ADVS 4 never, ne'er, **not ever,** at no time, on no occasion, not at all; **nevermore;** never in the world, never on earth; not in donkey's years <Brit>, never in all one's born days <nf>, never in my life, *jamais de la vie* <Fr>

5 without date, *sine die* <L>, open, openended

823 INFINITY

NOUNS 1 infinity, infiniteness, infinitude, the all, the be-all and end-all; **boundlessness, limitlessness, endlessness;** illimitability, interminability, termlessness; **immeasurability,** unmeasurability, immensity, incalculability, innumerability, incomprehensibility; measurelessness, countlessness, unreckonability, numberlessness; exhaustlessness, inexhaustibility; universality, "world without end"—Bible; **all-inclusiveness,** all-comprehensiveness; **eternity** 829.1,2, **perpetuity** 829, forever; eons; vastness; bottomless pit

VERBS 2 have no limit *or* **bounds** *or* **end,** know no limit *or* bounds *or* end, be without end, **go on and**

on, go on forever, never cease *or* end; last forever, perpetuate

ADJS **3 infinite, boundless, endless, limitless,** termless, shoreless; unbounded, uncircumscribed, **unlimited,** illimited, infinitely continuous *or* extended, stretching *or* extending everywhere, without bound, without limit *or* end, no end of *or* to, bottomless; illimitable, **interminable,** interminate; **immeasurable,** incalculable, unreckonable, innumerable, incomprehensible, beyond comprehension, unfathomable; measureless, countless, sumless; **unmeasured,** unmeasurable, immense, unplumbed, untold, unnumbered, without measure *or* number *or* term; exhaustless, inexhaustible; **all-inclusive,** all-comprehensive 864.14, **universal** 864.14; **perpetual, eternal** 829.7; "as boundless as the sea"—Shakespeare; mind-boggling <nf>

ADVS **4 infinitely, illimitably,** boundlessly, limitlessly, **interminably; immeasurably,** measurelessly, immensely, incalculably, innumerably, incomprehensibly; **endlessly,** without end *or* limit; *ad infinitum* <L>, to infinity; **forever, eternally** 829.10, in perpetuity, "to the last syllable of recorded time"—Shakespeare

824 PERIOD
<portion or point of time>

NOUNS **1 period, point, juncture,** stage; **interval,** lapse of time, time frame, space, span, timespan, stretch, time-lag, time-gap; **time,** while, **moment,** minute, instant, hour, day, **season;** psychological moment; pregnant *or* fateful moment, fated moment, kairos, moment of truth; **spell** 825

2 <periods> **moment, second,** millisecond, microsecond, nanosecond; **minute,** New York minute <nf>; hour, man-hour; **day,** sun; weekday; **week;** fortnight; **month,** moon, lunation; calendar month, lunar month; **quarter; semester,** trimester, term, session, academic year; **year,** annum, sun, twelvemonth; common year, regular year, intercalary year, leap year, bissextile year, defective year, perfect *or* abundant year; solar year, lunar year, sidereal year; fiscal year; calendar year; quinquennium, lustrum, luster; **decade,** decennium, decennary; **century; millennium**

3 term, time, duration, **tenure;** spell 825

4 age, generation, time, day, date, cycle; eon *or* aeon; Platonic year, great year, *annus magnus or annus mirabilis* <L>

5 era, epoch, age; Golden Age, Silver Age; Ice Age, glacial epoch; Stone Age, Bronze Age, Iron Age, steel Age; Middle Ages, Dark Ages; Era of Good

Feeling; Jacksonian Age; Reconstruction Era *and* Gilded Age <1870s and 1880s>; Gay Nineties *and* Naughty Nineties *and* Mauve Decade *and* Golden Age *and* Gilded Age <1890s>; Roaring Twenties *and* Golden Twenties *and* Mad Decade *and* Age of the Red-Hot Mamas *and* Jazz Age *and* Flapper Era <1920s>; Depression Era; New Deal Era; Prohibition Era

6 <modern age> Technological Age, Automobile Age, Air Age, Jet Age, Supersonic Age, Atomic Age, Electronic Age, Computer Age, Space Age, Age of Anxiety, Age of Aquarius

7 calendars

Abyssinian	Islamic *or* Moslem *or*
Aztec	Mohammedan
Babylonian	Jewish
Buddhist	Julian
Chinese	lunar
church *or* ecclesiastical	lunisolar
Egyptian	Mayan
Episcopalian liturgical	Mexican
French Revolutionary *or*	Newgate
Revolutionary	Orthodox Christian
Greek	perpetual
Greek Orthodox	Roman
Gregorian	Roman Catholic
Hebrew	Runic
Hindu *or* Hinduist	Sikhist *or* Sikh
Inca	solar
Indian	Western

8 geological time periods

Algonkian	Mississippian
Archean	Oligocene
Archeozoic	Ordovician
Cambrian	Paleocene
Carboniferous	Paleozoic
Cenozoic	Pennsylvanian
Comanchean	Permian
Cretaceous	Pleistocene
Devonian	Pliocene
Eocene	Precambrian
Glacial	Proterozoic
Holocene *or* Recent Epoch	Quaternary
Jurassic	Silurian
Lower Cretaceous	Tertiary
Lower Tertiary	Triassic
Mesozoic	Upper Cretaceous
Miocene	Upper Tertiary

825 SPELL
<period of duty, etc>

NOUNS **1 spell,** fit, stretch, go <nf>

2 turn, bout, round, inning, innings <Brit>, time, time at bat, place, say, whack *and* go <nf>; opportunity, chance; **relief, spell;** one's turn, one's move <nf>, one's say

3 shift, work shift, **tour,** tour of duty, stint, bit, **watch, trick,** time, **turn,** relay, spell *or* turn of work; day shift, night shift, swing shift, graveyard shift <nf>, dogwatch, anchor watch; lobster trick *or* tour, sunrise watch; split shift, split schedule; flextime *or* flexitime; halftime, part-time, full-time; **overtime**

4 term, time; **tenure,** continuous tenure, tenure in *or* of office; **enlistment, hitch** <nf>, tour; prison term, stretch <nf>; fiscal year; biorhythm, circadian rhythm, biological clock

VERBS **5 take one's turn,** have a go <nf>; **take turns,** alternate, turn and turn about; **time off, spell** *and* **spell off** <nf>, **relieve,** cover, **fill in for,** take over for; put in one's time, work one's shift; **stand one's watch** *or* **trick,** keep a watch; have one's innings <Brit>; do a stint; hold office, have tenure *or* tenure of appointment; **enlist,** sign up; reenlist, re-up <nf>; do a hitch <nf>, do a tour *or* tour of duty; serve *or* do time

826 INTERIM

<intermediate period>

NOUNS **1 interim, interval, interlude, intermission,** pause, break, **time-out,** recess, coffee break, halftime *or* halftime intermission, interruption; **lull,** quiet spell, resting point, point of repose, plateau, letup, relief, vacation, holiday, time off, off-time; downtime; **respite** 20.2; **intermission,** interval <Brit>, entr'acte; *intermezzo* <Ital>; interregnum

2 meantime, meanwhile, while, the while

VERBS **3 intervene,** interlude, interval; **pause,** break, **recess,** declare a recess; call a halt *or* break *or* intermission; **call time** *or* time-out; take five *and* ten, etc *and* take a break <nf>

ADJS **4 interim, temporary,** tentative, provisional, provisory

ADVS **5 meanwhile, meantime, in the meanwhile** *or* **meantime,** in the interim, *ad interim* <L>; between acts *or* halves *or* periods, betweenwhiles, betweentimes, between now and then; till *or* until then; *en attendant* <Fr>, in the intervening time, during the interval, at the same time, for the nonce, for a time *or* season; *pendente lite* <L>

827 DURATION

NOUNS **1 durability, endurance,** duration, durableness, **lastingness,** *longueur* <Fr>, perenniality, abidingness, long-lastingness, perdurability; **continuance,** perseverance, maintenance, **steadfastness,** constancy, **stability** 855, **persistence, permanence** 853, standing, long standing; **longevity,** long-livedness; **antiquity, age; survival,** survivability, viability, defiance *or* defeat of time; **service life,** serviceable life, useful life, shelf life, mean life; **perpetuity** 829

2 protraction, prolongation, continuation, extension, lengthening, drawing- *or* stretching- *or* dragging- *or* spinning-out, lingering; perpetuation; procrastination 846.5

3 length of time, distance of time, vista *or* stretch *or* desert of time; corridor *or* tunnel of time

4 long time, long while, long; **age** and **ages** <nf>, aeon, century, eternity, years, **years on end,** time immemorial, coon's age <nf>, donkey's years <Brit nf>, month of Sundays <nf>, right smart spell <nf>

5 lifetime, life, life's duration, life expectancy, lifespan, expectation of life, period of existence, all the days of one's life; **generation, age;** all one's born days *or* natural life <nf>

VERBS **6 endure, last** *or* **last out,** bide, **abide,** dwell, perdure, **continue,** run, extend, **go on,** carry on, hold on, keep on, stay on, run on, stay the course, go the distance, go through with, grind *or* slog on, grind *or* plug away; live, **live on,** continue to be, subsist, exist, tarry; get *or* keep one's head above water; **persist,** persevere; hang in *and* hang in there *and* hang tough <nf>; maintain, sustain, **remain, stay,** keep, hold, stand, prevail, last long, hold out; **survive,** defy *or* defeat time; live to fight another day; perennate; live on, live through; wear, wear well; stand the test of time

7 linger on, linger, tarry, go on, **go on and on, wear on,** crawl, creep, drag, **drag on,** drag along, drag its slow length along, drag a lengthening chain

8 outlast, outstay, last out, outwear, **outlive, survive**

9 protract, prolong, continue, **extend, lengthen,** lengthen out, **draw out, spin out,** drag *or* stretch out; linger on, dwell on; dawdle, procrastinate, temporize, drag one's feet

ADJS **10 durable,** perdurable, **lasting, enduring,** perduring, **abiding, continuing,** remaining, staying, **stable** 855.12, persisting, **persistent,** perennial; inveterate, agelong; **steadfast, constant,** intransient, immutable, unfading, evergreen, sempervirent, **permanent** 853.7, perennial, **long-lasting,** long-standing, of long duration *or* standing, diuturnal; long-term; **long-lived,** tough, hardy, vital, longevous *or* longeval; **ancient,** aged, antique; macrobiotic; chronic; **perpetual** 829.7

11 protracted, prolonged, extended, lengthened; **long,** overlong, time-consuming, interminable, marathon, lasting, **lingering,** languishing; long-continued, long-continuing, long-pending; drawn- *or* stretched- *or* dragged- *or* spun-out, long-drawn, **long-drawn-out;** long-winded, prolix, verbose 538.12

12 daylong, nightlong, weeklong, monthlong, yearlong

13 **lifelong,** livelong, lifetime, for life

ADVS **14** **for a long time, long, for long, interminably,** unendingly, undyingly, persistently, protractedly, enduringly; for ever so long <nf>, for many a long day, for life *or* a lifetime, for an age *or* ages, for a coon's *or* dog's age <nf>, for a month of Sundays <nf>, for donkey's years <Brit nf>, **forever and a day, forever and ever, for years on end, for days on end,** etc; all the year round, all the day long, the livelong day, as the day is long; morning, noon, and night; hour after hour, day after day, month after month, year after year; day in day out, month in month out, year in year out; till hell freezes over <nf>, till you're blue in the face <nf>, till the cows come home <nf>, till shrimps learn to whistle <nf>, till doomsday, from now till doomsday, from here to eternity, till the end of time; since time began, from way back, long ago, long since, time out of mind, time immemorial

828 TRANSIENCE
<short duration>

NOUNS **1** **transience** *or* transiency, transientness, **impermanence** *or* impermanency, transitoriness, changeableness 854, rootlessness, **mutability, instability, temporariness,** fleetingness, **momentariness;** finitude; **ephemerality,** ephemeralness, short duration; evanescence, volatility, fugacity, **short-livedness; mortality,** death, perishability, corruptibility, caducity; **expedience** 995, ad hoc, ad hockery *or* ad hocism, adhocracy; fugacity, fugaciousness; one-hit wonder

2 **brevity, briefness,** shortness; swiftness 174, fleetness

3 **short time, little while,** little, **instant, moment** 830.3, mo <nf>, small space, span, spurt, **short spell;** no time, less than no time; bit *or* **little bit,** a breath, the wink of an eye, pair of winks <nf>; **two shakes** *and* two shakes of a lamb's tail <nf>, half a mo <nf>; just a second

4 **transient,** transient guest *or* boarder, temporary lodger; **sojourner;** passer, passerby; **wanderer; vagabond,** drifter, derelict, homeless person, bag person, tramp, hobo, bum <nf>; caller, guest, visitor

5 **ephemeron,** ephemera, ephemeral; ephemerid, ephemeris, ephemerides <pl>; mayfly; bubble, smoke; nine days' wonder, flash in the pan, passing fancy; snows of yesteryear, *neiges d'antan* <Fr>; shooting star, meteor; ship that passes in the night

VERBS **6** <be transient> **flit, fly,** fleet; **pass, pass away, vanish, evaporate,** dissolve, evanesce, disappear, fade, melt, sink; fade like a shadow *or* dream, vanish like a dream, vanish into thin air, burst like a bubble, **go up in smoke,** melt like snow

ADJS **7** **transient, transitory,** transitive; **temporary,** temporal; **impermanent,** unenduring, undurable, nondurable, nonpermanent; frail, brittle, fragile, insubstantial; changeable 854.6, **mutable, unstable,** inconstant 854.7; capricious, fickle, impulsive, impetuous; **short-lived, ephemeral,** fly-by-night, evanescent, volatile, **momentary;** deciduous; **passing,** fleeting, flitting, flying, fading, dying; fugitive, fugacious; perishable, mortal, corruptible; here today and gone tomorrow; **expedient** 995.5, ad-hoc

8 **brief, short,** short-time, quick, brisk, swift, fleet, speedy, "short and sweet"—Thomas Lodge; meteoric, cometary, flashing, flickering; short-term, short-termed

ADVS **9** **temporarily,** for the moment, for the time, *pro tempore* <L>, pro tem, for the nonce, **for the time being,** for a time, awhile

10 **transiently,** impermanently, evanescently, transitorily, changeably, mutably, ephemerally, fleetingly, flittingly, flickeringly, **briefly, shortly,** swiftly, quickly, **for a little while,** for a short time; **momentarily,** for a moment; **in an instant** 830.7

829 PERPETUITY
<endless duration>

NOUNS **1** **perpetuity,** perpetualness; **eternity,** eternalness, sempiternity, infinite duration; everness, foreverness, **everlastingness, permanence** 853, ever-duringness, duration 827, perdurability, indestructibility; **constancy,** stability, immutability, continuance, perseverance, continualness, perennialness *or* perenniality, **ceaselessness,** unceasingness, incessancy; timelessness 822; **endlessness,** never-endingness, **interminability; infinity** 823; coeternity

2 **forever, an eternity,** endless time, **time without end**

3 **immortality,** eternal life, **deathlessness,** imperishability, undyingness, incorruptibility *or* incorruption, athanasy *or* athanasia, life everlasting; eternal youth, fountain of youth

4 **perpetuation,** preservation, eternalization, immortalization; eternal re-creation, eternal return *or* recurrence; steady-state universe

VERBS **5** **perpetuate, preserve,** preserve from oblivion, keep fresh *or* alive, perennialize, eternalize, eternize, **immortalize;** monumentalize; freeze, embalm

6 last *or* endure forever, **go on forever,** go on and on, live forever, **have no end,** have no limits *or* bounds *or* term, never cease *or* end *or* die *or* pass

ADJS 7 **perpetual, everlasting,** everliving, ever-being, ever-abiding, ever-during, ever-durable, permanent 853.7, perdurable, indestructible; **eternal,** sempiternal, eterne <old>, **infinite** 823.3, aeonian *or* eonian; dateless, ageless, timeless, immemorial; **endless,** unending, never-ending, without end, **interminable,** nonterminous, nonterminating; **continual,** continuous, steady, **constant, ceaseless,** nonstop, unceasing, never-ceasing, **incessant,** unremitting, unintermitting, uninterrupted; coeternal

8 **perennial,** indeciduous, **evergreen,** sempervirent, ever-new, ever-young; ever-blooming, ever-bearing

9 **immortal,** everlasting, **deathless,** undying, never-dying, **imperishable,** incorruptible, amaranthine; fadeless, **unfading,** never-fading, ever-fresh; frozen, embalmed

ADVS 10 **perpetually,** in perpetuity, **everlastingly, eternally, permanently** 853.9, perennially, perdurably, indestructibly, **constantly,** continually, steadily, **ceaselessly,** unceasingly, never-ceasingly, **incessantly,** never-endingly, **endlessly,** unendingly, **interminably,** without end, world without end, time without end, "from everlasting to everlasting"—Bible; **infinitely,** ad infinitum <L> 823.4

11 **always, all along,** all the time, all the while, at all times, *semper et ubique* <L, always and everywhere>; ever and always, **invariably,** without exception, never otherwise, *semper eadem* <L, ever the same; Elizabeth I>

12 **forever, forevermore, for ever and ever,** forever and aye; forever and a day <nf>, now and forever, *ora e sempre* <Ital>, "yesterday and today and forever"—Bible; **ever, evermore,** ever and anon, ever and again; aye, for aye; **for good,** for keeps <nf>, for good and all, for all time; throughout the ages, from age to age, in all ages; **to the end of time,** till time stops *or* runs out, "to the last syllable of recorded time"—Shakespeare, to the crack of doom, to the last trumpet, till doomsday; till you're blue in the face <nf>, till hell freezes over <nf>, till the cows come home <nf>

13 **for life,** for all one's natural life, for the term of one's days, while life endures, while one draws breath, in all one's born days <nf>; from the cradle to the grave, from the womb to the tomb; **till death,** till death do us part

830 INSTANTANEOUSNESS
<imperceptible duration>

NOUNS 1 **instantaneousness** *or* **instantaneity,** momentariness, **momentaneousness** <old>, **immediateness** *or* immediacy, near-simultaneity *or* -simultaneousness; instant gratification; simultaneity 836

2 **suddenness, abruptness, precipitateness,** precipitance *or* precipitancy; **unexpectedness,** unanticipation, inexpectation 131

3 **instant, moment, second,** sec <nf>, split second, millisecond, microsecond, nanosecond, half a second, half a mo <Brit nf>, minute, **trice,** twinkle, **twinkling, twinkling** *or* **twinkle of an eye,** twink, **wink,** bat of an eye <nf>, **flash,** crack, tick, stroke, coup, breath, twitch; two shakes of a lamb's tail *and* two shakes *and* shake *and* half a shake *and* **jiffy** *and* jiff *and* half a jiffy <nf>

ADJS 4 **instantaneous,** instant, momentary, momentaneous <old>, **immediate,** presto, quick as thought *or* lightning; lightning-like, lightning-swift; nearly simultaneous; simultaneous; split-second; urgent, on-the-spot; fast-food, convenience-food; ready-to-wear, off-the-rack

5 **sudden, abrupt,** precipitant, **precipitate, precipitous; hasty,** headlong, impulsive, impetuous; speedy, swift, quick; **unexpected** 131.10, unanticipated, unpredicted, unforeseen, unlooked-for; **surprising** 131.11, startling, electrifying, shocking, nerve-shattering

ADVS 6 **instantly,** instanter, momentaneously <old>, momentarily, momently, **instantaneously, immediately, right off the bat** <nf>; on the instant, on the dot <nf>, on the nail

7 **quickly, in an instant, in a trice, in a second,** in a moment, in a mo *or* half a mo <Brit nf>, in a bit *or* little bit, in a jiff *or* jiffy *or* half a jiffy <nf>, in a flash, in a wink <nf>, in a twink, **in a twinkling, in the twinkling of an eye, as quick as a wink,** as quick as greased lightning <nf>, in two shakes *or* a shake *or* half a shake <nf>, in two shakes of a lamb's tail <nf>, before you can say 'Jack Robinson' <nf>; **in no time,** in less than no time, in nothing flat <nf>, in short order; at the drop of a hat *or* handkerchief, like a shot, like a shot out of hell <nf>; with the speed of light

8 **at once,** at once and on the spot, **then and there, now, right now, right away, right off,** straightway, straightaway, forthwith, this minute, this very minute, **without delay,** without the least delay, in a hurry <nf>, *pronto* <Sp>, *subito* <Ital>; **simultaneously,** at the same instant, in the same breath; **all at once,** all together, at one time, at a stroke, at one stroke, at a blow, at one blow, at one

swoop, "at one fell swoop"—Shakespeare; at one jump, *per saltum* <L>, *uno saltu* <L>

9 **suddenly,** sudden, of a sudden, on a sudden, **all of a sudden, all at once: abruptly,** sharp; **precipitously** or precipitately, precipitantly, impulsively, impetuously, hastily; dash; smack, bang, slap, plop, plunk, plump, pop; **unexpectedly** 131.14, out of a clear blue sky, when least expected, before you know it; on short notice, without notice or warning, without further ado, unawares, **surprisingly** 131.15, startlingly, like a thunderbolt or thunderclap, like a flash, like a bolt from the blue

10 PHRS no sooner said than done

831 EVENT

NOUNS 1 **event, eventuality,** eventuation, effect 887, issue, outcome, result, aftermath, consequence; **realization,** materialization, coming to be or pass, incidence; contingency, contingent; accident 972.6

2 event, **occurrence, incident, episode, experience, adventure,** hap, **happening,** happenstance, **phenomenon,** fact, matter of fact, reality, particular, circumstance, **occasion,** turn of events; **nonevent,** pseudo-event, media event or happening, photo opportunity; what's happening

3 **affair, concern, matter,** thing, concernment, interest, **business,** job <nf>, **transaction,** proceeding, doing; current affairs or events; cause célèbre, matter of moment

4 **affairs, concerns, matters,** circumstances, relations, **dealings, proceedings,** doings, goings-on <nf>; course or run of events, run of things, the way of things, the way things go, what happens, current of events, march of events; the world, life, the times; order of the day; **conditions, state of affairs,** environing or ambient phenomena, state or condition of things

VERBS 5 **occur, happen** 972.11, hap, eventuate, **take place,** come or go down <nf>, go on, **transpire,** be realized, come, **come off** <nf>, **come about,** come true, **come to pass,** pass, pass off, go off, fall, **befall,** betide; **be found,** be met with

6 **turn up, show up** <nf>, **come along,** come one's way, cross one's path, come into being or existence, chance, **crop up,** spring up, pop up <nf>, arise, come forth, come or draw on, appear, approach, materialize, present itself, be destined for one

7 **turn out, result** 887.4

8 **experience, have, know, feel,** taste; **encounter, meet,** meet with, meet up with <nf>, run up against <nf>; **undergo, go through,** pass through,

be subjected to, be exposed to, stand under, labor under, **endure, suffer,** sustain, pay, spend

ADJS 9 **happening, occurring, current, actual,** passing, taking place, on, **going on,** ongoing <nf>, **prevalent, prevailing,** that is, that applies, in the wind, afloat, afoot, under way, in hand, **on foot,** ado, doing; incidental, circumstantial, accompanying; accidental; occasional; resultant; eventuating

10 **eventful, momentous, stirring,** bustling, full of incident; phenomenal

11 **eventual, coming, final,** last, **ultimate; contingent,** collateral, secondary, indirect

ADVS 12 **eventually, ultimately, finally, in the end, after all is said and done, in the long run, over the long haul;** in the course of things, in the natural way of things, as things go, as times go, as the world goes, as the tree falls, the way the cookie crumbles <nf>, as things turn out, as it may be or happen or turn out, as luck or fate or destiny wills

CONJS 13 **in the event that, if, in case,** if it should happen that, just in case, in any case, in either case, in the contingency that, in case that; provided 959.12

832 MEASUREMENT OF TIME

NOUNS 1 **chronology,** timekeeping, timing, clocking, horology, **chronometry,** horometry, chronoscopy, chronography; watch- or clock-making; scheduling, calendar-making; **dating,** carbon-14 dating, radiocarbon dating, dendrochronology

2 **time of day, time** 821, **the time,** the exact time; time of night; **hour,** minute; stroke of the hour, time signal, bell

3 standard time, civil time, zone time, slow time <nf>; mean time, solar time, mean solar time, sidereal time, apparent time, local time; military time, 24-hour clock, 12-hour clock; universal time or Greenwich time or Greenwich mean time or GMT, Eastern time, Central time, Mountain time, Pacific time; Atlantic time; Alaska time, Yukon time; daylight-saving time; fast time <nf>, summer time <Brit>; **time zone**

4 **date,** point of time, time, day; postdate, antedate; datemark; date line, International Date Line; calends, nones, ides; name day, saint's day; red-letter day, anniversary

5 epact, annual epact, monthly or menstrual epact

6 **timepiece,** timekeeper, **timer, chronometer, ship's** watch; horologe, horologium; **clock,** Big Ben, ticker <nf>, **watch,** turnip <nf>; hourglass, sundial; watch or clock movement, clockworks, watchworks

7 **almanac,** The Old Farmer's Almanac, Nautical Almanac, Poor Richard's Almanac, World Almanac

8 **calendar,** calends; calendar stone, chronogram; almanac *or* astronomical calendar, ephemeris; perpetual calendar; Chinese calendar, church *or* ecclesiastical calendar, Cotsworth calendar, Gregorian calendar, Hebrew *or* Jewish calendar, Hindu calendar, international fixed calendar, Julian calendar, Muslim calendar, Republican *or* Revolutionary calendar, Roman calendar, ordo calendar

9 **chronicle, chronology, register,** registry, record; **annals,** journal, diary; time sheet, time book, **log,** daybook; timecard, time ticket, clock card, check sheet; datebook; date slip; **timetable,** schedule, timeline, time schedule, time chart, schedule; time scale; time study, motion study, time and motion study

10 **chronologist,** chronologer, chronographer, horologist, horologer; watchmaker *or* clockmaker; timekeeper, timer; chronicler, annalist, diarist, historian, historiographer; calendar maker, calendarist

VERBS 11 **time, fix** *or* **set the time,** mark the time; **keep time,** mark time, measure time, beat time; **clock** <nf>; watch the clock; set the alarm; synchronize

12 **punch the clock** and punch in and punch out and **time in** and **time out** <nf>; ring in, ring out; clock in, clock out; check in, check out; check off

13 **date,** be dated, date at *or* from, date back, bear a date of, bear the date of, carry a date; fix *or* set the date, make a date; **predate,** backdate, antedate; **postdate; update,** bring up to date; datemark; date-stamp; dateline

14 chronologize, chronicle, calendar, intercalate

ADJS 15 **chronologic<al>,** temporal, timekeeping; **chronometric<al>,** chronoscopic, chronographic *or* chronographical, chronogrammatic *or* chronogrammatical, horologic *or* horological, horometric *or* horometrical, metronomic *or* metronomical, calendric *or* calendrical, intercalary *or* intercalated; dated; annalistic, diaristic; calendarial

ADVS 16 **o'clock,** of the clock, by the clock; half past, half *or* half after <Brit>; a quarter of *or* to, a quarter past *or* after

833 ANACHRONISM
<false estimation or knowledge of time>

NOUNS 1 **anachronism,** chronological *or* historical error, **mistiming, misdating,** misdate, postdating, antedating; parachronism, metachronism,

prochronism; prolepsis, anticipation; earliness, lateness, tardiness, unpunctuality

VERBS 2 **mistime, misdate;** antedate, foredate, postdate; lag

ADJS 3 **anachronous** *or* anachronistical *or* **anachronistic,** parachronistic, metachronistic, prochronistic, unhistorical, unchronological; **mistimed, misdated;** antedated, foredated, postdated; ahead of time, **beforehand, early;** behind time, **behindhand, late,** unpunctual, tardy; **overdue,** past due; unseasonable, out of season; **dated,** out-of-date

834 PREVIOUSNESS

NOUNS 1 **previousness,** earliness 845, antecedence *or* antecedency, priority, **anteriority, precedence** or precedency 814, precession; *status quo ante* <L>, previous *or* prior state, earlier state; preexistence; **anticipation,** predating, antedating; antedate; **past time** 837.1

2 antecedent, precedent, premise; forerunner, **precursor** 816, ancestor

VERBS 3 **be prior,** be before *or* early *or* earlier, come on the scene *or* appear earlier, **precede, antecede, forerun,** come *or* go before, set a precedent; **herald,** usher in, proclaim, announce; **anticipate,** antedate, predate; **preexist**

ADJS 4 **previous, prior, early** 845.7, **earlier,** *ci-devant* or *ci-dessus* <Fr>, **former,** fore, prime, first, **preceding** 165.3, foregoing, above, anterior, **anticipatory,** antecedent; **preexistent;** older, elder, senior

5 prewar, ante-bellum, before the war; prerevolutionary; premundane *or* antemundane; prelapsarian, before the Fall; antediluvian, before the Flood; protohistoric, prehistoric 837.10; precultural; pre-Aryan; pre-Christian; premillenarian, premillennial; anteclassical, preclassical, pre-Roman, pre-Renaissance, pre-Romantic, pre-Victorian, etc

ADVS 6 **previously,** priorly, **hitherto, heretofore,** thitherto, theretofore; **before, early** 845.11, **earlier,** ere, erenow, ere then, *or* ever; already, yet; before all; **formerly** 837.13

PREPS 7 **prior to, previous to, before,** in advance of, in anticipation of, in preparation for

WORD ELEMENTS 8 ante-, anti-, fore-, pre-, pro-, prot-, proto-, proter-, protero-, supra-

835 SUBSEQUENCE
<later time>

NOUNS 1 **subsequence,** posteriority, **succession, ensuing, following** 166, sequence, coming after, supervenience, supervention; lateness 846; afterlife, next life; remainder 256, hangover <nf>; postdating; postdate; future time 839.1

2 sequel 817, **follow-up,** sequelae, **aftermath; consequence, effect** 887; **posterity,** offspring, descendant, heir, inheritor; **successor;** replacement, line, **lineage,** dynasty, family

VERBS **3 come** or **follow** or **go after, follow, follow on** or **upon, succeed,** replace, take the place of, displace, overtake, supervene; **ensue,** issue, emanate, attend, **result;** follow up, trail, track, come close on or tread on the heels of, "follow hard upon"—Shakespeare, dog the footsteps of; **step into** or **fill the shoes of,** don the mantle of, assume the robe of

ADJS **4 subsequent, after, later,** after-the-fact, *post factum* and *ex post facto* <L>, posterior, **following, succeeding,** successive, sequent, lineal, consecutive, ensuing, attendant; **junior,** cadet, puisne <law>, younger

5 posthumous, afterdeath; **postprandial,** postcibal, postcenal, after-dinner; **post-war,** *postbellum* <L>, after the war; **postdiluvian,** postdiluvial, after the flood, postlapsarian, after the Fall, post-industrial, post-modern, post-millenial, etc

ADVS **6 subsequently, after, afterwards,** after that, after all, **later, next,** since; **thereafter,** thereon, thereupon, therewith, **then;** in the process or course of time, as things worked out, in the sequel; at a subsequent or later time, in the aftermath; *ex post facto* <L>; hard on the heels or on the heels

7 after which, on or **upon which, whereupon,** whereon, whereat, whereto, whereunto, wherewith, wherefore, on, upon; hereinafter

PREPS **8 after, following, subsequent to,** later than, past, beyond, behind; below, farther down or along

WORD ELEMENTS **9** ante-, anti-, fore-, pre-, pro-, prot-, proto-, proter-, protero-, supra-; epi-, eph-, infra-, meta-, post-

836 SIMULTANEITY

NOUNS **1 simultaneity** or **simultaneousness,** coincidence, co-occurrence, concurrence or concurrency, concomitance or concomitancy; **coexistence; contemporaneousness** or contemporaneity, coetaneousness or coetaneity, coevalness or coevalneity; unison; **synchronism,** synchronization, sync <nf>, isochronism; accompaniment 769, agreement 788

2 contemporary, coeval, concomitant, compeer; age group, peer group

3 tie, dead heat, draw, wash <nf>

VERBS **4 coincide,** co-occur, concur; **coexist;** coextend; **synchronize,** isochronize, put or be in phase, be in time, keep time, time; contemporize; **accompany** 769.7, **agree** 788.6, match, go along with, go hand in hand, keep pace with, keep in step; sync <nf>

ADJS **5 simultaneous, concurrent,** co-occurring, coinstantaneous, concomitant; **tied,** neck-and-neck; coexistent, coexisting; **contemporaneous,** contemporary, coetaneous, coeval; coterminous, conterminous; unison, unisonous; photo-finish; isochronous, isochronal; coeternal; accompanying 769.9, collateral; agreeing 788.9

6 synchronous, synchronized, synchronic or synchronal, in sync <nf>, isochronal, isochronous; **in time,** in step, in tempo, in phase, with or on the beat, in sync <nf>

ADVS **7 simultaneously, concurrently,** coinstantaneously; **together,** all together, **at the same time,** at one and the same time, as one, as one man, in concert with, in chorus, with one voice, in unison, in a chorus, in the same breath; at one time, at a clip <nf>; synchronously, **synchronically,** isochronously, in phase, **in sync** <nf>, with or on the beat, on the downbeat

837 THE PAST

NOUNS **1 the past,** past, foretime, former times, past times, times past, water under the bridge, **days** or **times gone by, bygone times** or **days,** bygones, **yesterday, yesteryear;** recent past, just or only yesterday; history, past **history;** dead past, dead hand of the past; the years that are past, "the days that are no more"—Tennyson, "the irrevocable Past"—Longfellow

2 old or **olden times,** early times, **old** or **olden days,** the olden time, times of old, **days of old, days** or **times of yore,** yore, yoretime, foretime, eld <old>, good old times or days, the way it was, glory days, lang syne or auld lang syne <Scot>, **the long ago,** time out of mind, days beyond recall; the old story, the same old story

3 antiquity, ancient times, time immemorial, ancient history, prehistory, protohistory, remote age or time, remote or far or dim or **distant past,** distance of time, past age, way back when; geological past, ice age; ancientness 842.1

4 memory 989, **remembrance, recollection, reminiscence, fond remembrance, retrospection,** retrospective, musing on the past, looking back, reprise; "the remembrance of things past"—Shakespeare, "la recherche du temps perdu"—Proust; **reliving,** reexperiencing; revival 396.3; youth 301

5 <grammatical terms> past tense, preterit, perfect tense, past perfect tense, pluperfect, historical present tense, past progressive tense, past participle; aorist; perfective aspect; preterition

VERBS **6 pass,** be past, **be a thing of the past,** be history, elapse, lapse, slip by *or* away, be gone, fade, fade away, be dead and gone, be all over, have run its course, have run out, have had its day; pass into history; **disappear** 34.2; **die** 307.18

ADJS **7 past, gone,** by, **gone-by, bygone,** gone glimmering, bypast, ago, **over,** departed, passed, passed away, elapsed, lapsed, vanished, faded, no more, lost forever, long gone, irrecoverable, never to return, not coming back; **dead** 307.29, dead as a dodo, expired, extinct, dead and buried, defunct, deceased; run out, blown over, finished, forgotten, wound up; **passé, obsolete,** has-been, dated, antique, **antiquated**

8 reminiscent 989.21, **retrospective, remembered** 989.22, **recollected; relived, reexperienced; restored, revived**; retro; diachronic

9 <grammatical terms> past, preterit *or* preteritive, pluperfect, past perfect; aorist, aoristic; perfective

10 former, past, fore, **previous,** late, recent, **once, onetime,** sometime, **erstwhile,** then, quondam; obsolescent; retired, emeritus, superannuated; **prior** 834.4; **ancient, immemorial,** early, primitive, primeval, prehistoric; **old,** olden

11 foregoing, aforegoing, **preceding** 814.4; last, latter

12 back, backward, into the past; early; retrospective, retro, retroactive, *ex post facto* <L>, *a priori* <L>

ADVS **13 formerly, previously, priorly** 834.6; **earlier, before,** before now, erenow, erst, whilom, erewhile, **hitherto, heretofore,** thitherto, aforetime, beforetime, **in the past,** in times past; then; **yesterday,** only yesterday, recently; **historically,** prehistorically, in historic *or* prehistoric times

14 once, once upon a time, one day, one fine morning, time was

15 ago, since, gone by; back, back when; backward, to *or* into the past; **retrospectively,** reminiscently, retroactively

16 long ago, long since, **a long while** *or* **time ago,** some time ago *or* since, some time back, a way *or* away back <nf>, ages ago, **years ago,** donkey's years ago <Brit nf>; **in times past,** in times gone by, in the old days, in the good old days; **anciently, of old, of yore,** in ancient times, in olden times, in the olden times, **in days of yore,** early, in the memory of man, time out of mind

17 since, ever since, until now; **since long ago, long since,** from away back <nf>, since days of yore, ages ago, **from time immemorial,** from time out of mind, aeons ago, since the world was made, since the world was young, since time began, since the year one, since Hector was a pup and since God knows when <nf>

WORD ELEMENTS **18** archae-, archaeo-, archeo-; pale-, paleo-, praeter-, preter-, retro-; -ed, y- <old>

838 THE PRESENT

NOUNS **1 the present,** presentness, present time, the here and now; **now,** the present juncture *or* occasion, the present moment, the present hour *or* minute, this instant *or* second *or* moment, **the present day** *or* **time** etc; **the present age; today,** this day, **this day and age; this point,** this stage, this hour, **now,** nowadays, the now, the way things are, the nonce, **the time being; the times,** our times, these days, modern times; **contemporaneousness** *or* contemporaneity, nowness, actuality, topicality; **newness** 841, modernity; the Now Generation, the me generation; historical present *and* present tense <gram>, present participle

ADJS **2 present, immediate,** latest, current, running, extant, **existent,** existing, actual, topical, being, that is, as is, that be; **present-day,** present-time, present-age, **modern** 841.13, modern-day; **contemporary,** contemporaneous; up-to-date, up-to-the-minute, fresh, with it <nf>, **new** 841.7

ADVS **3 now, at present, at this point,** at this juncture, at this stage *or* at this stage of the game, on the present occasion, **at this time,** at this moment *or* instant, at the present time; **today,** this day, in these days, **in this day and age,** in our time, **nowadays;** this night, **tonight;** here, hereat, **here and now,** *hic et nunc* <L>, even now, but now, **just now,** as of now, as things are; on the spot; for the nonce, for the time being; for this occasion; in the moment

4 until now, hitherto, till now, thitherto, **hereunto,** heretofore, until this time, by this time, **up to now,** up to the present, up to this time, to this day, to the present moment, to this very instant, **so far,** thus far, **as yet, to date,** yet, already, still, now *or* then as previously

WORD ELEMENTS **5** ne-, neo-, nov-, novo-; cen-, ceno-, caen-, caeno-, -cene

839 THE FUTURE

NOUNS **1 the future,** future, futurity, what is to come, imminence 840, subsequence 835, eventuality 831.1, **hereafter,** aftertime, afteryears, **time to come,** years to come, etc; **futurism,** futuristics; **tomorrow,** the morrow, the morning after, *mañana* <Sp>; **immediate** *or* **near future,** time just ahead, immediate prospect, offing, next period; **distant future,** remote *or* deep *or* far future, long run, long term; **by-and-by,** the sweet by-and-by <nf>; time ahead, course ahead, **prospect,** outlook, anticipation, expectation, project, probability, prediction, extrapolation, forward look, foresight, prevision, prevenience, envisionment, envisagement, prophecy, divination, clairvoyance, crystal ball; what is to be *or* come; determinism; future tense, future perfect; futurism; the womb of time

2 **destiny** 964.2, **fate,** doom, karma, kismet, what bodes *or* looms, what is fated *or* destined *or* doomed, what is written, what is in the books, "whatever limits us"—Emerson; the Fates, the *Parcae or Parcae* Fates, Lachesis, Clotho, Atropos, Moira, Moirai, **the hereafter,** the great hereafter, a better place, Paradise, Heaven, Elysian Fields, Happy Isles, the Land of Youth *or* Tir na n'Og, Valhalla; Hades, the Underworld, Hell, Gehenna; **the afterworld,** the otherworld, **the next world,** the world to come, life *or* world beyond the grave, **the beyond,** the great beyond, the unknown, the great unknown, **the grave,** home *or* abode *or* world of the dead, eternal home; "the great world of light, that lies behind all human destinies"— Longfellow; a**fterlife, postexistence,** future state, **life to come,** life after death

3 **doomsday,** doom, day of doom, day of reckoning, crack of doom, trumpet *or* trump of doom; **Judgment Day,** Day of Judgment, the Judgment; eschatology, last things, **last days**

4 **futurity;** ultimateness, eventuality, finality

5 **advent, coming, approach of time,** time drawing on

VERBS 6 **come,** come on, **approach,** near, **draw on** *or* **near;** be to be *or* come; be fated *or* destined *or* doomed, be in the books, be in the cards; **loom,** threaten, await, stare one in the face, be imminent 840.2; lie ahead *or* in one's course, lie just around the corner; **predict,** foresee, envision, envisage, see ahead, previse, foretell, prophesy; **anticipate, expect,** hope, hope for, look for, look forward to, **project,** plot, plan, scheme, think ahead, extrapolate, take the long view

7 **live on,** postexist, survive, get by *or* through, make it <nf>

ADJS 8 **future, later,** hereafter; **coming, forthcoming, imminent** 840.3, approaching, nearing, close at hand, waiting in the wings, nigh, **prospective; eventual** 831.11, ultimate, to-be, **to come; projected,** plotted, planned, looked- *or* hoped-for, desired, emergent, **predicted,** prophesied, foreseen, anticipated, anticipatory, previsional, prevenient, envisioned, envisaged, probable,

extrapolated; determined, fatal, fatidic, fated, destinal, destined, doomed; eschatological; futuristic

ADVS 9 **in the future,** in aftertime, **afterward** *or* afterwards, **later,** at a later time, after a time *or* while, anon; **by and by,** in the sweet by-and-by <nf>; **tomorrow,** *mañana* <Sp>, the day after tomorrow; *proximo* <L>, prox, **in the near** *or* **immediate future,** just around the corner, **imminently** 840.4, **soon, before long;** probably, predictably, hopefully; fatally, by destiny *or* necessity

10 in future, **hereafter,** hereinafter, thereafter, **henceforth, henceforward** *or* henceforwards, thence, **thenceforth,** thenceforward *or* thenceforwards, over the long haul *or* short haul <nf>, from this time forward, from this day on *or* forward, from this point, from this *or* that time, from then on, **from here** *or* **now on, from now on in** <nf>, from here in *or* out <nf>, from this moment on

11 **in time, in due time,** in due season *or* course, all in good time, **in the fullness of time,** in God's good time, in the course *or* process of time, **eventually** 831.12, **ultimately,** in the long run

12 **sometime, someday, some of these days,** one of these days, some fine day *or* morning, one fine day *or* morning, some sweet day, sometime *or* other, somewhen, **sooner** *or* **later,** when all is said and done

PREPS 13 **about to,** at *or* **on the point of,** on the eve of, on the brink *or* edge *or* verge of, near to, close upon, in the act of

840 IMMINENCE
<future event>

NOUNS 1 **imminence** *or* **imminency,** impendence *or* impendency, forthcomingness; **forthcoming,** coming, **approach, loom;** immediate *or* near future; futurity 839.1

VERBS 2 **be imminent, impend, overhang,** hang *or* lie over, **loom,** hang over one's head, hover, **threaten, menace,** lower; brew, gather; **come** *or* **draw on,** draw near *or* nigh, rush up on one, forthcome, **approach, loom up, near,** be on the horizon, be in the offing, be just around the corner, await, face, **confront, loom,** stare one in the face, be in store, breathe down one's neck, be about to be borning

ADJS 3 **imminent, impending,** impendent, **overhanging,** hanging over one's head, waiting, lurking, **threatening, looming,** lowering, **menacing,** lying in ambush; **brewing,** gathering, preparing; **coming, forthcoming, upcoming, to**

come, about to be, about *or* going to happen, **approaching, nearing,** looming, looming up, looming in the distance *or* future; **near, close,** immediate, instant, soon to be, **at hand,** near at hand, close at hand; **in the offing,** on the horizon, **in prospect,** already in sight, just around the corner, in view, in one's eye, in store, in reserve, **in the wind,** in the womb of time; on the knees *or* lap of the gods, in the cards <nf>; that will be, that is to be; future 839.8

ADVS **4 imminently,** impendingly; **any time,** any time now, any moment, any second, any minute, any hour, any day; **to be expected,** as may be expected, as may be

CONJS **5 on the point of, on the verge of,** on the eve of

841 NEWNESS

NOUNS **1 newness,** freshness, maidenhood, dewiness, pristineness, mint condition, new-mintedness, newbornness, virginity, intactness, greenness, immaturity, rawness, callowness, brand-newness; presentness, nowness; **recentness,** recency, lateness; **novelty,** gloss of novelty, newfangledness *or* newfangleness; originality 337.1; **uncommonness,** unusualness, strangeness, unfamiliarity

2 novelty, innovation, neology, neologism, newfangled device *or* contraption <nf>, neoism, neonism, **new *or* latest wrinkle** <nf>, **the last word *or* the latest thing** <nf>, *dernier cri* <Fr>; what's happening *and* what's in *and* the in thing *and* where it's at <nf>; new ball game; new look, latest fashion *or* fad; advance guard, vanguard, **avant-garde;** neophilia, neophiliac; start-up

3 modernity, modernness; modernism; modernization, updating, *aggiornamento* <Ital>; state of the art; postmodernism, space age

4 modern, modern man; modernist; modernizer; neologist, neoterist, neology, neologism, neoterism, neoteric; modern *or* rising *or* new generation; neonate, fledgling, stripling, neophyte, *novus homo* <L>, new man, upstart, *arriviste* <Fr>, *nouveau riche* <Fr>, parvenu; Young Turk, bright young man, comer <nf>; trendsetter; new kid on the block <nf>

VERBS **5 innovate, invent,** make from scratch *or* from the ground up, coin, new-mint, mint, inaugurate, neologize, neoterize; **renew,** renovate 396.17; give a new lease on life

6 modernize, streamline; update, **bring up to date,** keep *or* stay current, move with the times

ADJS **7 new,** young, **fresh,** fresh as a daisy, fresh as the morning dew; **unused, firsthand, original;**

untried, untouched, unhandled, unhandseled, untrodden, unbeaten; virgin, virginal, intact, maiden, maidenly; green, vernal; dewy, pristine, ever-new, sempervirent, evergreen; **immature,** undeveloped, raw, callow, fledgling, unfledged, nestling; neological, neologistic, neophytic

8 fresh, additional, further, other, another; **renewed**

9 new-made, new-built, new-wrought, new-shaped, new-mown, new-minted, new-coined, uncirculated, in mint condition, mint, new-begotten, new-grown, new-laid; **newfound;** newborn, neonatal, new-fledged; **new-model,** late-model, like new, factory-new, factory-fresh, oven-fresh, in its original carton

10 <nf terms> **brand-new,** fire-new, **brand-spanking new,** spanking, **spanking new; just out; hot,** hottest, hot off the fire *or* griddle *or* spit, hot off the press; newfangled *or* newfangle

11 novel, original, unique, different; strange, unusual, uncommon; unfamiliar, unheard-of; **first, first ever** 818.15

12 recent, late, newly come, of yesterday; latter, later

13 modern, contemporary, present-day, present-time, twentieth-century, latter-day, space-age, neoteric, now <nf>, topical, **newfashioned,** fashionable, modish, mod, *à la mode* <Fr>, **up-to-date,** up-to-datish, **up-to-the-minute, in,** abreast of the times; **advanced,** progressive, forward-looking, modernizing, **avant-garde;** ultramodern, ultra-ultra, ahead of its time, far out, way out, modernistic, modernized, streamlined; postmodern, trendy, faddish

14 state-of-the-art, newest, latest, the very latest, up-to-the-minute, last, most recent, newest of the new, farthest out

ADVS **15 newly,** freshly, new, **anew,** once more, from the ground up, from scratch <nf>, *ab ovo* <L>, *de novo* <L>, **afresh, again;** as new

16 now, recently, lately, latterly, **of late,** not long ago, a short time ago, the other day, only yesterday; just now, right now <nf>; neoterically

842 OLDNESS

NOUNS **1 oldness, age,** eld <old>, hoary eld; elderliness, seniority, senior citizenship, senility, **old age** 303.5; **ancientness, antiquity,** dust of ages, rust *or* cobwebs of antiquity; venerableness, eldership, primogeniture, great *or* hoary age, "the ancient and honourable"—Bible; old order, old style, *ancien régime* <Fr>; **primitiveness,** primordialism *or* primordiality, aboriginality; atavism

2 tradition, custom, immemorial usage, immemorial wisdom; Sunna <Muslim>; Talmud *and* Mishnah <Jewish>, ancient wisdom, ways of the fathers; traditionalism *or* traditionality; oral tradition; myth, mythology, legend, lore, folklore, folktale, folk motif, folk history; racial memory, archetypal myth *or* image *or* pattern, archetype; collective unconscious; hive mind; "Spiritus Mundi"—Yeats

3 **antiquation, superannuation,** staleness, disuse; **old-fashionedness,** unfashionableness, out-of-dateness; **old-fogyishness,** fogyishness, stuffiness, stodginess, fuddy-duddiness

4 **antiquarianism;** classicism, medievalism, Pre-Raphaelitism, longing *or* yearning *or* nostalgia for the past; **archaeology;** Greek archaeology, Roman archaeology, etc, Assyriology, Egyptology, Sumerology; crisis archeology, industrial archeology, underwater *or* marine archeology, paleology, epigraphy, paleontology, human paleontology, paleethnology, paleonanthropology, paleoethnography; paleozoology, paleornithology, prehistoric anthropology

5 **antiquarian,** antiquary, *laudator temporis* acti <L>; dryasdust, the Rev Dr Dryasdust, Jonathan Oldbuck, Herr Teufelsdr–ckh; **archaeologist;** classicist, medievalist, Miniver Cheevy, Pre-Raphaelite; antique dealer, antique collector, antique-car collector; archaist

6 **antiquity, antique,** archaism; **relic,** relic of the past; **remains,** survival, vestige, ruin *or* ruins; old thing, oldie and golden oldie <nf>; monument; **fossil,** index fossil, zone fossil, trace fossil, fossil record; petrification, petrified wood, petrified forest; **artifact,** artefact, eolith, mezzolith, microlith, neolith, paleolith, plateaulith; cave painting, petroglyph; ancient manuscript 547.11; museum piece

7 **ancient,** man *or* woman *or* person of old, old Homo, **prehistoric mankind** <see list>; preadamite, antediluvian; anthropoid, humanoid; primate, fossil man, protohuman, prehuman, missing link, apeman, hominid; **primitive, aboriginal,** aborigine, bushman, autochthon; **caveman,** cave dweller, troglodyte; bog man, bog body, Lindow man; Stone Age man, Bronze Age man, Iron Age man

8 <antiquated person> back number <nf>; pop *and* pops *and* dad <nf>, dodo *and* old dodo <nf>; fossil *and* antique *and* relic <nf>; **mossback** <nf>, longhair *and* square <nf>, **mid-Victorian,** antediluvian; old liner, old believer, conservative, hard-shell, traditionalist, reactionary; has-been, **fogy, old fogy,** regular old fogy, old poop *or* crock <nf>, **fud** and **fuddy-duddy** <nf>, eld <nf>; granny <nf>, **old woman,** matriarch; **old man,** patriarch, elder, *starets* <Russ>, old-timer <nf>, Methuselah

VERBS 9 **age,** grow old 303.10, grow *or* have whiskers; **antiquate,** fossilize, date, **superannuate,** outdate; obsolesce, go out of use *or* style, molder, fust, rust, fade, perish; lose currency *or* novelty; become obsolete *or* extinct; belong to the past, be a thing of the past; deteriorate, crumble

ADJS 10 **old, age-old,** auld <Scot>, olden <old>, old-time, old-timey <nf>; **ancient,** antique, archaic, venerable, hoary; of old, of yore; dateless, timeless, ageless; **immemorial,** old as Methuselah *or* Adam, old as God, old as history, old as time, old as the hills, out of the Ark; **elderly** 303.16

11 **primitive,** prime, primeval, primogenial, primordial, pristine; atavistic; **aboriginal,** autochthonous; ancestral, patriarchal; **prehistoric,** protohistoric, preglacial, preadamite, antepatriarchal; prehuman, protohuman, humanoid; archetypal

12 **traditional;** mythological, heroic; **legendary,** unwritten, oral, handed down; true-blue, tried and true; **prescriptive, customary,** conventional, understood, admitted, recognized, acknowledged, received; **hallowed, time-honored,** immemorial; **venerable,** hoary, worshipful; **long-standing, of long standing,** long-established, established, fixed, inveterate, rooted; folk, of the folk, folkloric, legendary

13 **antiquated,** grown old, **superannuated, antique, old,** age-encrusted, of other times, old-world; Victorian, mid-Victorian; historic, classical, medieval, Gothic; antediluvian; **fossil,** fossilized, petrified

14 **stale, fusty, musty,** rusty, dusty, moldy, mildewed; **worn, timeworn,** time-scarred; **moth-eaten,** moss-grown, crumbling, moldering, gone to seed, dilapidated, ruined, ruinous

15 **obsolete, passé, extinct,** gone out, gone-by, dead, past, run out, **outworn**

16 **old-fashioned,** old-fangled, old-timey <nf>, **dated, out, out-of-date, outdated, outmoded,** out of style *or* fashion, out of use, disused, out of season, **unfashionable,** styleless, **behind the times,** of the old school, old hat *and* back-number *and* has-been <nf>

17 **old-fogyish,** fogyish, old-fogy; fuddy-duddy, square *and* corny *and* cornball <nf>; **stuffy, stodgy; aged** 303.16, senile, bent *or* wracked *or* ravaged with age

18 **secondhand, used,** worn, previously owned, **unnew,** not new, pawed-over; hand-me-down and reach-me-down <nf>

19 **older,** senior, 3r, major, elder, dean, **oldest,** eldest, first-born, firstling, primogenitary; former 837.10

20 **archaeological,** paleological; antiquarian; archaic; paleolithic, eolithic, neolithic, mezzolithic

ADVS 21 anciently 837.16

22 Stone Age cultures

Acheulean
Aurignacian
Azilian
Capsian
Chellean
Combe-Capelle
Cro-Magnon
Dabban
Eolithic
Goodwin
Magdalenian
Middle Awash
Mousterian
Neolithic
Oldowan
Olduvai
Paleolithic
Pre-Chellean
Solutrean

23 prehistoric men and manlike primates

Aurignacian man
Australanthropus
Australopithecus
Australopithecus afarensis
Australopithecus africanus
Australopithecus boisei
Australopithecus robustus
Bronze Age man
Brünn race
caveman or cave dweller
Cro-Magnon man
Dawn man <the Piltdown hoax>
eolithic man
Florisbad man
Furfooz or Grenelle man
Galley Hill man
Gigantopithecus
Grimaldi man
Heidelberg man
hominid
Homo erectus
Homo habilis
Iron Age man
Java man
Lucy
Meganthropus
Neanderthal man
neolithic man
Oreopithecus
paleolithic man
Paranthropus
Peking man
Piltdown man <hoax>
Pithecanthropus
Plesianthropus
protohuman
Rhodesian man
Sinanthropus
Stone Age man
Swanscombe man
Zinjanthropus

24 prehistoric animals

allosaurus
ammonite
anatosaurus
ankylosaurus
apatosaurus
archaeohippus
archaeopteryx
archaeornis
archaeotherium
archelon
archosaur
arthrodiran
atlantosaurus
aurochs
baryonyx Walker
basilosaurus
bothriolepis
brachiosaurus
brontops
brontosaurus
brontothere
camarasaurus
cantius trigonodus
ceratopsid
ceratosaurus
cetiosaurus
coccostean
coelacanth
coelodont
compsognathus
coryphodon
cotylosaur
creodont
crossopterygian
cynodictis
cynodont
deinonychus
denversaurus
diacodexis
diatryma
dimetrodon
dinichthyid
dinosaur
dinothere
diplodocus
dipnoan
diprotodon
dodo
duck-billed dinosaur
edaphosaurid

elasmosaurus
eohippus
eryopsid
eurypterid
eurypterus remipes
giant sloth
glyptodont
gorgosaurus
hadrosaurus
hesperornis
hoplophoneus
hyaenodon
hyracodont
hyracothere
ichthyornis
ichthyosaurus
iguanodon
imperial mammoth or elephant
labyrinthodont
machairodont
mamenchisaurus
mammoth
mastodon
megalosaurus
megathere
merodus
merychippus
merycoidodon
merycopotamus
mesohippus
mesosaur
miacis
mosasaurus
nummulite
ornithomimid
ornithopod
ostracoderm
palaeodictyopteron
palaeomastodon
palaeoniscid
palaeophis
palaeosaur
palaeospondylus
pelycosaur
phytosaur
pinchosaurus
plesiosaurus
pliosaur
protoceratops
protohippus
protylopus
pteranodon
pteraspid
pterichthys
pterodactyl
pterosaur
quetzalcoatlus northropii
raptor
rhamphorhynchus
saber-toothed cat or tiger
sauropod
scelidosaurus
smilodon
stegocephalian
stegodon
stegosaurus
struthiomimus
teleoceras
therapsid
theriodont
theropod
thrinaxodon liorhinus
titanosaurus
titanothere
trachodon
triceratops
trilobite
tyrannosaurus or tyrannosaurus rex
uintathere
urus
woolly or northern mammoth

843 TIMELINESS

NOUNS 1 **timeliness, seasonableness, opportuneness,** convenience; **expedience** or **expediency,** meetness, fittingness, fitness, appropriateness, rightness, propriety, suitability; **favorableness, propitiousness,** auspiciousness, felicitousness; **ripeness,** pregnancy, cruciality, criticality, criticalness, expectancy, loadedness, chargedness

2 **opportunity, chance, time, occasion; opening,** room, scope, space, place, liberty; clear stage, fair field, level playing field, fair game, fair shake and even break <nf>; **opportunism;** equal opportunity, nondiscrimination, affirmative action, positive

discrimination <Brit>; trump card; a leg up, stepping-stone, rung of the ladder; time's forelock; window of opportunity

3 **good opportunity, good chance,** favorable opportunity, golden opportunity, well-timed opportunity, the chance of a lifetime, a once-in-a-lifetime chance, happy coincidence, lucky break; suitable occasion, proper occasion, suitable *or* proper time, **good time,** high time, due season; propitious *or* well-chosen moment; window of opportunity

4 **crisis, critical point,** crunch, crucial period, climax, climacteric; **turning point,** hinge, turn, turn of the tide, cusp, nexus; **emergency, exigency,** juncture *or* conjuncture *or* convergence of events, critical juncture, crossroads; **pinch,** clutch <nf>, rub, push, pass, strait, extremity, spot <nf>; **emergency,** state of emergency, red alert, race against time

5 **crucial moment,** critical moment, loaded *or* charged moment, decisive moment, kairotic moment, kairos, pregnant moment, defining moment, turning point, climax, **moment of truth,** crunch *and* when push comes to shove <nf>, when the balloon goes up <Brit nf>, point of no return; **psychological moment,** right moment; nick of time, eleventh hour; **zero hour,** H-hour, D-day, A-day, target date, deadline; crisis management

VERBS 6 **be timely,** suit *or* befit the time *or* season *or* occasion, come *or* fall just right

7 **take** *or* **seize the opportunity,** use the occasion, take the chance; take the bit in the teeth, leap into the breach, take the bull by the horns, bite the bullet, **make one's move,** cross the Rubicon, *prendre la balle au bond* <Fr, take the ball on the rebound>; **commit oneself,** make an opening, drive an entering wedge

8 **improve the occasion,** turn to account *or* good account, avail oneself of, **take advantage of,** put to advantage, profit by, **cash in** *or* **capitalize on;** take time by the forelock, seize the opportunity, seize the present hour, *carpe diem* <L, seize the day>, make hay while the sun shines; strike while the iron is hot; not be caught flatfooted, not be behindhand, not be caught looking <nf>, don't let the chance slip by, get going *and* get off the dime <nf>

ADJS 9 **timely, well-timed, seasonable, opportune,** *in loco* <L>, convenient; **expedient,** meet, fit, fitting, befitting, suitable, sortable, appropriate; **favorable, propitious,** ripe, auspicious, lucky, providential, heaven-sent, fortunate, happy, felicitous; heaven-sent

10 **critical, crucial,** pivotal, climactic, climacteric *or* climacterical, decisive; pregnant, kairotic, loaded, charged; exigent, emergent; eleventh-hour

11 **incidental, occasional, casual,** accidental; parenthetical, by-the-way

ADVS 12 **opportunely, seasonably, propitiously,** auspiciously, in proper time *or* season, in due time *or* course *or* season, in the fullness of time, **in good time,** all in good time; in the nick of time, just in time, at the eleventh hour; now *or* never

13 **incidentally, by the way, by the by; while on the subject,** speaking of, *à propos* <Fr>, apropos *or* apropos of; **in passing,** *en passant* <Fr>; parenthetically, by way of parenthesis, *par parenthése* <Fr>; for example, *par exemple* <Fr>

14 a bird in the hand is worth two in the bush, better late than never, every minute *or* moment counts; live for the moment, you can't take it with you

844 UNTIMELINESS

NOUNS 1 **untimeliness, unseasonableness,** inopportuneness, inopportunity, unripeness, inconvenience; **inexpedience,** irrelevance *or* irrelevancy; **awkwardness,** inappropriateness, impropriety, unfitness, unfittingness, wrongness, unsuitability; **unfavorableness,** unfortunateness, inauspiciousness, unpropitiousness, infelicity; **intrusion,** interruption; **prematurity** 845.2; **lateness** 846, afterthought, thinking too late, *l'esprit de l'escalier* <Fr>; anachronism; staircase wit

2 **wrong time, bad time,** wrong *or* bad *or* poor timing, unsuitable time, unfortunate time; evil hour, unlucky day *or* hour, off-year, *contretemps* <Fr>; inopportune moment

VERBS 3 **ill-time, mistime,** miss the time; **lack the time,** not have time, have other *or* better things to do, be otherwise occupied, be engaged, be preoccupied, have other fish to fry <nf>

4 **talk out of turn,** speak inopportunely, interrupt, **put one's foot in one's mouth** <nf>, intrude, butt in *and* stick one's nose in <nf>, **go off half-cocked** <nf>, open one's big mouth *or* big fat mouth <nf>; blow it <nf>, speak too late *or* too soon

5 **miss an opportunity, miss the chance, miss out, miss the boat,** miss one's turn, lose the opportunity, ignore opportunity's knock, lose the chance, blow the chance <nf>, throw away *or* waste *or* neglect the opportunity, allow the occasion to go by, let slip through one's fingers, be left at the starting gate *or* post, be caught looking <nf>, oversleep, lock the barn door after the horse is stolen

ADJS 6 **untimely, unseasonable, inopportune, ill-timed,** ill-seasoned, mistimed, unripe, unready, ill-considered, too late *or* soon, out of phase *or* time *or* sync; ill-starred; **inconvenient,** unhandy, discommodious; **inappropriate,** irrelevant, improper, unfit, wrong, out of line, off-base, unsuitable, **inexpedient,** unfitting, unbefitting, untoward, malapropos, *mal à propos* <Fr>, intrusive; **unfavorable,** unfortunate, infelicitous, inauspicious, **unpropitious,** unhappy, unlucky, misfortuned; **premature** 845.8; not in time, **late** 846.16

ADVS **7 inopportunely, unseasonably,** inconveniently, inexpediently; **unpropitiously,** inauspiciously, unfortunately, in an evil hour, at just the wrong time

845 EARLINESS

NOUNS **1 earliness,** early hour, time to spare; **head start,** running start, ground floor, first crack, early start, beginnings, first *or* early stage, very beginning, preliminaries; **anticipation, foresight,** prevision, prevenience; advance notice, lead time, a stitch in time, readiness, preparedness, preparation; first light

2 prematurity, prematureness; **untimeliness** 844; precocity, **precociousness,** forwardness; precipitation, precipitancy, haste, hastiness, **overhastiness,** rush, impulse, impulsivity, impulsiveness

3 promptness, promptitude, punctuality, punctualness, readiness; instantaneousness 830, immediateness *or* immediacy, summariness, decisiveness, **alacrity, quickness** 174.1, speediness, swiftness, rapidity, expeditiousness, expedition, dispatch

4 early bird <nf>, early riser, early *or* first comer, first arrival, first on the scene; Johnny-on-the-spot <nf>; **precursor** 816

VERBS **5 be early,** be ahead of time, take time by the forelock, be up and stirring, be beforehand *or* betimes, be ready and waiting, be off and running; gain time, draw on futurity *or* on the future; get there first; get a wiggle on *or* hop to it <nf>

6 anticipate, foresee, foreglimpse, previse, see the handwriting on the wall, foretaste, pave the way for, prevent <old>; **forestall,** forerun, go before, **get ahead of,** win the start, break out ahead, get a head start, steal a march on, beat someone to the punch *or* the draw <nf>; **jump the gun,** beat the gun, go off half-cocked <nf>; preempt; take the words out of one's mouth

ADJS **7 early,** bright and early and with the birds <nf>, **beforetime,** in good time *or* season; **forehand,** forehanded; foresighted, **anticipative** *or* **anticipatory,** prevenient, previsional

8 premature, too early, too soon, oversoon; previous and a bit previous <nf>, prevenient; **untimely;**

precipitate, hasty 830.5, **overhasty,** too soon off the mark, too quick on the draw *or* trigger *or* uptake <nf>; **unprepared,** unripe, impulsive, rushed, unmatured; unpremeditated, unmeditated, ill-considered, **half-cocked** and **half-baked** <nf>, unjelled, uncrystallized, not firm; **precocious, forward, advanced,** far ahead, born before one's time

9 prompt, punctual, immediate, instant, instantaneous 830.4, **quick** 174.15, speedy, swift, expeditious, summary, decisive, apt, alert, **ready,** alacritous, Johnny-on-the-spot <nf>; as soon as possible *or* ASAP

10 earlier, previous 834.4

ADVS **11 early, bright and early, beforehand, beforetime,** early on, betimes, precociously, **ahead of time,** foresightedly, in advance, in anticipation, ahead, before, **with time to spare**

12 in time, in good time, soon enough, time enough, early enough; just in time, **in the nick of time,** with no time to spare, just under the wire, without a minute to spare

13 prematurely, too soon, oversoon, untimely, too early, before its *or* one's time; **precipitately,** impulsively, in a rush, hastily, **overhastily;** at half cock <nf>

14 punctually, precisely, exactly, sharp; **on time,** on the minute *or* instant, to the minute *or* second, **on the dot** <nf>, spot on *and* bang on <Brit nf>, at the gun

15 promptly, without delay, without further delay *or* ado, directly, **immediately,** immediately if not sooner <nf>, **instantly** 830.6, instanter, on the instant, on the spot, **at once,** right off, **right away, straightway,** straightaway, **forthwith,** *pronto* <Sp>, *subito* <Ital>, PDQ *or* pretty damned quick <nf>, **quickly,** swiftly, speedily, with all speed, **summarily,** decisively, smartly, expeditiously, apace, in no time, in less than no time; no sooner said than done

16 soon, presently, directly, shortly, in a short time *or* while, **before long,** ere long, in no long time, in a while, **in a little while, after a while, by and by,** anon, betimes, *bientôt* <Fr>, in due time, in due course, at the first opportunity; in a moment *or* minute, *tout à l'heure* <Fr>

PHRS **17** the early bird gets the worm

846 LATENESS

NOUNS **1 lateness, tardiness, belatedness, unpunctuality;** late hour, small hours; eleventh hour, last minute, high time; unreadiness, unpreparedness; untimeliness 844

2 delay, stoppage, jam *and* logjam <nf>, obstruction, tie-up *and* bind <nf>, **block,** blockage, **hang-up**

<nf>; delayed reaction, double take, afterthought; **retardation** *or* retardance, slow development, slowdown *and* slow-up <nf>, slowness, lag, time lag, lagging, dragging, dragging one's feet *and* foot-dragging <nf>, pigeonholing; **detention, suspension, holdup** <nf>, **obstruction, hindrance;** delaying action, delaying tactics; **wait, halt, stay, stop,** down-time, break, pause, interim 826, respite; reprieve, stay of execution; moratorium; **red tape,** red-tapery, red-tapeism, bureaucratic delay, *paperasserie* <Fr>; delay of game

3 waiting, cooling one's heels <nf>, **tarrying,** tarriance <old>; **lingering, dawdling,** dalliance, dallying, dillydallying; back burner

4 postponement, deferment *or* **deferral,** prorogation, putting-off, tabling, holding up, holding in suspension, carrying over; **prolongation,** protraction, continuation, extension of time; **adjournment** *or* adjournal, adjournment sine die

5 procrastination, "the thief of time"—Edward Young, cunctation, hesitation 362.3; **temporization, a play for time, stall** *and* tap-dancing <nf>; Micawberism, Fabian policy; **dilatoriness,** slowness, backwardness, remissness, slackness, laxness

6 latecomer, late arrival, Johnny-come-lately; slow starter, dawdler, dallier, dillydallier; late bloomer *or* developer; retardee; late riser, slug-abed; ten o'clock scholar

VERBS **7 be late, not be on time,** be overdue, be behindhand, show up late, miss the boat; keep everyone waiting; **stay late,** stay up late *or* into the small hours, burn the midnight oil, keep late hours; get up late, keep banker's hours; oversleep

8 delay, retard, detain, make late, slacken, lag, drag, drag one's feet *and* stonewall <nf>, dilly-dally, slow down, **hold up** <nf>, hold *or* keep back, check, **stay, stop,** arrest, impede, **block,** hinder, obstruct, throw a monkey wrench in the works <nf>, confine; tie up with red tape

9 postpone, delay, defer, put off, give one a rain check <nf>, shift off, hold off *or* up <nf>, prorogue, put on hold *or* ice *or* the back burner <nf>, reserve, waive, **suspend,** hang up, stay, hang fire; protract, drag *or* stretch out <nf>, **prolong, extend,** spin *or* string out, **continue, adjourn,** recess, take a recess, prorogue; **hold over,** lay over, stand over, let the matter stand, **put aside,** lay *or* set *or* push aside, lay *or* set by, **table,** lay on the table, pigeonhole, **shelve,** put on the shelf, put on ice <nf>; consult one's pillow about, sleep on

10 be left behind, be outrun *or* outdistanced, make a slow start, be slow *or* late *or* last off the mark, be left at the post *or* starting gate; bloom *or* develop late

11 procrastinate, be dilatory, hesitate, let something slide, hang, hang back, hang fire; **temporize,** gain *or* make time, **play for time,** drag one's feet <nf>, hold off <nf>; **stall,** stall off, **stall for time,** stall *or* stooge around *and* tap-dance <nf>; talk against time, filibuster

12 wait, delay, stay, bide, abide, **bide** *or* **abide one's time,** take one's time, take time, mark time; **tarry, linger, loiter,** dawdle, dally, dillydally; hang around *or* about *or* out <nf>, stick around <nf>; **hold on** <nf>, sit tight <nf>, hold one's breath; wait a minute *or* second, wait up; hold everything *and* hold your horses *and* hold your water *and* keep your shirt on <nf>; wait *or* stay up, sit up; **wait and see,** bide the issue, see which way the cat jumps, see how the cookie crumbles *or* the ball bounces <nf>, let sleeping dogs lie; wait for something to turn up; **await** 130.8

13 wait impatiently, tear one's hair *and* sweat it out *and* champ *or* chomp at the bit <nf>

14 be kept waiting, be stood up <nf>, be left; **cool one's heels** <nf>

15 overstay, overtarry

ADJS **16 late, belated, tardy,** slow, slow on the draw *or* uptake *or* trigger <nf>, **behindhand,** never on time, backward, back, **overdue, long-awaited, untimely; unpunctual,** unready; latish; **delayed,** detained, **held up** <nf>, **retarded, arrested,** blocked, **hung up** *and* in a bind <nf>, obstructed, stopped, jammed, congested; weather-bound; **postponed, in abeyance,** held up, put off, **on hold** *or* put on hold <nf>, on the back burner *or* put on the back burner <nf>; delayed-action; moratory

17 dilatory, delaying, Micawberish; slow *or* late *or* last off the mark; **procrastinating,** procrastinative *or* procrastinatory, go-slow; **obstructive,** obstructionist *or* obstructionistic, bloody-minded <Brit nf>; **lingering,** loitering, lagging, dallying, dillydallying, **slow,** sluggish, laggard, foot-dragging, shuffling, backward; easygoing, **lazy, lackadaisical; remiss,** slack, work-shy, lax

18 later 835.4; last-minute, eleventh-hour, deathbed

ADVS **19 late, behind, behindhand, belatedly,** backward, slow, **behind time,** after time; far on, deep into; late in the day, at the last minute, at the eleventh hour, none too soon, in the nick of time, under the wire

20 tardily, slow, slowly, deliberately, dilatorily, sluggishly, lackadaisically, leisurely, at one's leisure, lingeringly; until all hours, into the night

847 FREQUENCY

NOUNS **1 frequency,** frequence, **oftenness; commonness,** usualness, prevalence, **common** occurrence, routineness, habitualness; **incidence,** relative incidence; radio frequency

2 constancy, continualness, steadiness, sustainment, **regularity,** noninterruption *or* uninterruption, nonintermission *or* unintermission, incessancy, ceaselessness, constant flow, continuity 812; perpetuity 829; repetition 849; **rapidity** 174.1; rapid recurrence *or* succession, rapid *or* quick fire, tattoo, **staccato,** chattering, stuttering; **vibration,** shuddering, juddering <Brit>, pulsation, **oscillation** 916

VERBS **3** be frequent, occur often, have a high incidence, continue 812.4, recur 850.5; shudder, judder <Brit>, vibrate, oscillate 916.10; frequent, hang out at <nf>

ADJS **4 frequent,** oftentime, many, many times, **recurrent,** recurring, **oft-repeated,** thick-coming; **common,** of common occurrence, not rare, thick on the ground <Brit>, **prevalent,** usual, routine, habitual, ordinary, everyday; frequentative <gram>

5 constant, continual 812.8, **perennial; steady,** sustained, **regular;** periodic; **incessant, ceaseless, unceasing,** unintermitting, unintermittent *or* unintermitted, unremitting, relentless, unrelenting, unchanging, unvarying, uninterrupted, unstopped, unbroken; **perpetual** 829.7; repeated 849.12; **rapid, staccato,** stuttering, chattering, machine gun; pulsating, juddering <Brit>, vibrating, **oscillating** 916.15

ADVS **6 frequently, commonly,** usually, ordinarily, routinely, habitually; **often,** oft, **oftentimes,** oft times; **repeatedly** 849.16, **again and again, time after time; most often** *or* frequently, in many instances, **many times,** many a time, full many a time, many a time and oft, as often as can be, as often as not, more often than not; **in quick** *or* **rapid succession;** often enough, not infrequently, not seldom, unseldom; as often as you wish *or* like, whenever you wish *or* like

7 constantly, continually 812.10, **steadily,** sustainedly, **regularly,** as regular as clockwork, with every other breath, every time one turns around, right along <nf>, unvaryingly, uninterruptedly, unintermittently, **incessantly,** unceasingly, **ceaselessly,** without cease *or* ceasing, perennially, all the time, at all times, ever, ever and anon, on and on, without letup *or* break *or* intermission, without stopping; **perpetually, always** 829.11; **rapidly;** all year round, every day, every hour, every moment; daily, hourly, daily and hourly; **night and day,** day and night; **morning, noon, and night;** hour after hour, day after day, month after month, year after year; **day in day out,** month in month out, year in year out

848 INFREQUENCY

NOUNS **1 infrequency,** infrequence, unfrequentness, seldomness; occasionalness; **rarity, scarcity, scarceness,** rareness, **uncommonness,** uniqueness, unusualness; **sparsity** 885.1; **slowness** 175; one-time offer

ADJS **2 infrequent,** unfrequent, **rare,** scarce, scarce as hens' teeth, scarcer than hens' teeth, **uncommon,** unique, unusual, almost unheard-of, seldom met with, seldom seen, few and far between, **sparse** 885.5; one-time, one-shot, once in a lifetime; **slow** 175.10; like snow in August; unprecedented

3 occasional, casual, incidental; odd, sometime, extra, side, off, off-and-on, out-of-the-way, spare, sparetime, **part-time**

ADVS **4 infrequently,** unfrequently, **seldom, rarely, uncommonly,** scarcely, hardly, **scarcely** *or* **hardly ever,** very seldom, not often, only now and then, at infrequent intervals, unoften, off-and-on; **sparsely** 885.8

5 occasionally, on occasion, **sometimes, at times,** at odd times, every so often <nf>, at various times, on divers occasions, **now and then,** every now and then <nf>, now and again, **once in a while,** every once in a while <nf>, every now and then, every now and again, once and again, once *or* twice, betweentimes, betweenwhiles, at intervals, **from time to time;** only occasionally, only when the spirit moves, only when necessary, only now and then, at infrequent intervals, once in a blue moon *and* once in a coon's age <nf>; irregularly, sporadically

6 once, one-time, on one occasion, just *or* only once, just this once, once and no more, once for all, once and for all *or* always

849 REPETITION

NOUNS **1 repetition, reproduction,** duplication 874, reduplication, doubling, redoubling; **recurrence,** reoccurrence, cyclicality, return, reincarnation, rebirth, reappearance, renewal, resumption; resurfacing, reentry; echo, reecho, parroting; ditto; do-over; regurgitation, rehearsal, rote recitation; **quotation; imitation** 336; plagiarism 621.2; reexamination, second *or* another look

2 iteration, reiteration, recapitulation, recap and wrapup <nf>, retelling, recounting, recountal, **recital, rehearsal, restatement,** rehash <nf>; reissue, reprint; review, summary, précis, résumé, summing up, peroration; going over *or* through, practicing; reassertion, reaffirmation; elaboration, dwelling upon; **copy** 785

3 **redundancy, tautology,** tautologism, pleonasm, macrology, battology; stammering, stuttering; padding, filling, filler, expletive

4 **repetitiousness,** repetitiveness, stale *or* unnecessary repetition; harping; **monotony,** monotone, drone; **tedium** 118, daily round *or* grind, same old story; **humdrum,** dingdong, singsong, chime, jingle, jingle-jangle, trot, pitter-patter; **rhyme, alliteration,** assonance, slant *or* near rhyme; hamster wheel, treadmill; echolalia, **repeated sounds** 55

5 **repeat,** repetend, bis, ditto <nf>, echo; **refrain,** burden, chant, undersong, chorus, bob; bob wheel, bob and wheel; ritornel, *ritornello* <Ital>; rerun; rehash; reprint, reissue; remake; second helping

6 **encore,** repeat performance, repeat, **reprise;** replay, replaying, return match; repeat order

VERBS 7 **repeat, redo,** do again, do over, do a repeat, **reproduce, duplicate** 874.3, reduplicate, double, redouble, ditto <nf>, **echo, parrot,** reecho; **rattle off,** reel off, regurgitate; renew, reincarnate, revive; come again *and* run it by again <nf>, say again, repeat oneself, **quote,** repeat word for word *or* verbatim, repeat like a broken record; **copy, imitate** 336.5; plagiarize 621.4, 336.5; **reexamine,** take *or* have a second look, take *or* have another look

8 **iterate, reiterate, rehearse, recapitulate, recount,** rehash <nf>, **recite, retell,** retail, **restate,** reword, review, run over, sum up, summarize, précis, resume, encapsulate; reissue, reprint; do *or* say over again, **go over** *or* **through,** practice, say over, go over the same ground, give an encore, quote oneself, go the same round, fight one's battles over again; **tautologize,** battologize, pad, fill; **reaffirm,** reassert

9 **dwell on** *or* **upon,** insist upon, **harp on,** beat a dead horse, have on the brain, constantly recur *or* revert to, labor, belabor, hammer away at, always trot out, sing the same old song *or* tune, play the same old record, plug the same theme, never hear the last of; **thrash** *or* **thresh over,** cover the same ground, go over again and again, go over and over

10 **din, ding;** drum 55.4, beat, hammer, pound; **din in the ear,** din into, drum into, say over and over

11 <be repeated> **repeat, recur,** reoccur, **come again,** come round again, go round again, come up again, resurface, reenter, **return, reappear, resume;** resound, reverberate, echo; revert, turn *or* go back; keep coming, come again and again, happen over and over, run through like King Charles's head

ADJS 12 **repeated,** reproduced, doubled, redoubled; **duplicated,** reduplicated; regurgitated, recited by rote; **echoed,** reechoed, parroted; **quoted,**

plagiarized; **iterated, reiterated,** reiterate; retold, **twice-told;** warmed up *or* over, *réchauffé* <Fr>

13 **recurrent,** recurring, **returning,** reappearing, revenant, ubiquitous, ever-recurring, cyclical, periodic, yearly, monthly, weekly, daily, circadian, thick-coming, frequent, incessant, continuous 812.8, year-to-year, month-to-month, week-to-week, etc; haunting, thematic

14 **repetitious,** repetitive, repetitional *or* repetitionary, repeating, recursive; **duplicative,** reduplicative; **imitative** 336.9, parrotlike; echoing, reechoing, echoic; **iterative, reiterative,** reiterant; recapitulative, recapitulatory; battological, **tautological** *or* **tautologous, redundant;** hamster-wheel

15 **monotonous,** monotone; **tedious;** harping, labored, belabored, cliché-ridden; **humdrum,** singsong, chiming, chanting, dingdong <nf>, jog-trot, jingle-jangle; **rhymed, rhyming, alliterative,** alliterating, assonant

ADVS 16 **repeatedly, often, frequently, recurrently, every time one turns around,** with every other breath, like a tolling bell, **again and again, over and over,** over and over again, many times over, time and again, **time after time,** times without number, **ad nauseam;** year in year out, week in week out, etc, year after year, day after day, day by day, "tomorrow and tomorrow and tomorrow"— Shakespeare; **many times,** several times, a number of times, many a time, many a time and oft, full many a time and oft; every now and then, every once in a while; recursively

17 **again,** over, over again, **once more,** *encore* and *bis* <Fr>, two times, twice over, ditto; **anew,** *de novo* <L>, afresh; from the beginning, *da capo* <Ital>

INTERJS 18 **encore!,** *bis!* <Fr>, once more!, again!

850 REGULARITY OF RECURRENCE

NOUNS 1 **regularity,** regularness, clockwork regularity, predictability, punctuality, smoothness, **steadiness, evenness, unvariableness, methodicalness,** systematicalness; **repetition** 849; **uniformity** 781; **constancy** 847.2; usual suspects

2 **periodicity,** periodicalness; cyclical motion, piston motion, pendulum motion, regular wave motion, undulation, **pulsation; intermittence** *or* intermittency, alternation; rhythm 709.22, meter, beat; **oscillation** 916; **recurrence,** go-round, reoccurrence, reappearance, return, the eternal return, **cyclicalness,** cyclicality, seasonality; resurfacing, reentry

3 **round, revolution, rotation, cycle,** circle, wheel, **circuit; beat,** upbeat, downbeat, thesis, arsis,

pulse; systole, diastole; course, series, **bout, turn,** rota <Brit>, spell 825

4 **anniversary, commemoration;** immovable feast, annual holiday; biennial, triennial, quadrennial, quinquennial, sextennial, septennial, octennial, nonennial, decennial, tricennial, jubilee, silver jubilee, golden jubilee, diamond jubilee; centennial, centenary; quasquicentennial; sesquicentennial; bicentennial, bicentenary; tercentennial, tercentenary, tricentenary; quincentennial, quincentenary; **wedding anniversary,** silver wedding anniversary, golden wedding anniversary; **birthday,** birthdate, natal day, b-day <nf>; saint's day, name day; leap year, bissextile day; annual holiday, government holiday, bank holiday; **religious holiday,** holy day

VERBS 5 <occur periodically> **recur, reoccur, return, repeat** 849.7, reappear, **come again,** come up again, be here again, resurface, reenter, **come round** or **around,** come round again, come in its turn; **rotate, revolve,** turn, circle, wheel, cycle, **roll around,** roll about, wheel around, go around, go round; **intermit,** alternate, **come and go,** ebb and flow; undulate 916.11; **oscillate** 916.10, **pulse, pulsate** 916.12; commute, shuttle

ADJS 6 **regular, systematic** or systematical, methodical, ordered, orderly, regular as clockwork; everyday; **uniform** 781.5; **constant** 847.5

7 **periodic** or periodical, seasonal, epochal, **cyclic** or cyclical, serial, isochronal, metronomic; measured, steady, even, **rhythmic** or rhythmical 709.28; **recurrent,** recurring, reoccurring; **intermittent,** reciprocal, alternate, every other; circling, wheeling, rotary, rotational, wavelike, undulant, undulatory, oscillatory 916.15, pulsing, beating 916.18

8 **momentary,** momently, **hourly; daily,** diurnal, quotidian, circadian, nightly, tertian; biorhythmic; **weekly,** tertian, hebdomadal, hebdomadary; biweekly, semiweekly; fortnightly; **monthly,** menstrual, catamenial, estrous; bimonthly, semimonthly; quarterly; biannual, semiannual, semiyearly, half-yearly, semestral; **yearly, annual;** perennial; biennial, triennial, decennial, etc; centennial, centenary; bissextile; secular

ADVS 9 **regularly, systematically, methodically,** like clockwork, at regular intervals, punctually, steadily; at stated times, at fixed or established periods; intermittently, every so often, every now and then; **uniformly** 781.7; **constantly** 847.7

10 **periodically, recurrently, seasonally,** cyclically, epochally; rhythmically, on the beat, in time, synchronously, **hourly, daily,** etc; every hour, every day, etc; hour by hour, day by day, etc; from hour to hour, from day to day, *de die in diem* <L>

11 **alternately, by turns, in turns, in rotation,** turn about, **turn and turn about,** reciprocally, every other, one after the other; to and fro, up and down, from side to side; off and on, make and break, round and round

PHRS 12 **what goes around comes around,** *plus ça change plus c'est la même chose* <Fr>

851 IRREGULARITY OF RECURRENCE

NOUNS 1 **irregularity,** unmethodicalness, unsystematicness; **inconstancy, unevenness, unsteadiness,** uncertainty, desultoriness; **variability,** capriciousness, unpredictability, whimsicality, eccentricity; stagger, wobble, weaving, erraticness; roughness; **fitfulness, sporadicity** or sporadicalness, spasticity, jerkiness, fits and starts, patchiness, spottiness, choppiness, brokenness, disconnectedness, discontinuity 813; **intermittence, fluctuation; nonuniformity** 782; arrhythmia *and* fibrillation <medical>; assymetry; unusualness

VERBS 2 **intermit, fluctuate,** vary, lack regularity, go by fits and starts; break, disconnect

ADJS 3 **irregular,** unregular, unsystematic, unmethodical or immethodical; **inconstant, unsteady, uneven, unrhythmical,** unmetrical, rough, unequal, uncertain, unsettled; **variable,** deviative, heteroclite; **capricious, erratic,** off-again-on-again, eccentric; wobbly, wobbling, weaving, staggering, lurching, careening; **fitful, spasmodic** or spasmodical, spastic, spasmic, **jerky,** herky-jerky <nf>, halting; **sporadic,** patchy, spotty, scrappy, snatchy, catchy, choppy, halting, **broken, disconnected, discontinuous** 813.4; **nonuniform** 782.3; **intermittent,** intermitting, **desultory, fluctuating, wavering,** wandering, rambling, veering; flickering, guttering; haphazard, disorderly

ADVS 4 **irregularly,** unsystematically, unmethodically; **inconstantly, unsteadily, unevenly,** unrhythmically, roughly, uncertainly; **variably,** capriciously, unpredictably, whimsically, eccentrically, wobblingly, lurchingly, erratically; **intermittently, disconnectedly, discontinuously** 813.5; **nonuniformly** 782.4; **brokenly, desultorily,** patchily, spottily, in spots, in snatches; **by fits and starts,** by fits, by jerks, by snatches, by catches; **fitfully, sporadically, jerkily, spasmodically,** haltingly; **off and on,** at irregular intervals, sometimes and sometimes not; when the mood strikes, when the spirit moves, at random

852 CHANGE

NOUNS 1 change, alteration, modification; variation, variety, difference, diversity, diversification; **deviation,** diversion, aberrance *or* aberrancy, **divergence; switch, switchover, changeover, turn,** change of course, turnabout, about-face, U-turn, **reversal,** flip-flop <nf>; apostasy, defection, change of heart, change of mind; **shift,** transition, **modulation,** qualification; **conversion, renewal,** revival, revivification, retro; remaking, reshaping, re-creation, redesign, restructuring, *perestroika* <Russ>; role reversal; realignment, **adaptation, adjustment,** accommodation, fitting, tweaking, tweak; **reform,** reformation, **improvement,** amelioration, melioration, mitigation, constructive change, **betterment,** change for the better; **take** *and* **new take** <nf>; **social mobility,** vertical mobility, horizontal mobility, upward *or* downward mobility; gradual change, progressive change, **continuity** 812; **degeneration, deterioration,** worsening, degenerative change, change for the worse, disorder 810, entropy; changeableness 854; rolling stone

2 revolution, revolt, **break,** break with the past, sudden change, radical *or* revolutionary *or* violent *or* total change, catastrophic change, **upheaval,** overthrow, **quantum jump** *or* **leap,** sea change; **discontinuity** 813

3 transformation, transmogrification; **translation;** metamorphosis, metamorphism; makeover; **mutation,** transmutation, permutation, vicissitude; **mutant,** mutated form, sport; **transfiguration** *or* transfigurement; metathesis, transposition, translocation, **displacement,** metastasis, heterotopia; **transubstantiation,** consubstantiation; transanimation, transmigration, reincarnation, metempsychosis avatar; metasomatism, metasomatosis; catalysis; metabolism, anabolism, catabolism; metagenesis; transformism; redecoration

4 innovation, introduction, discovery, invention, launching; neologism, neoterism, coinage; **breakthrough,** leap, quantum jump *or* leap, new phase; **novelty** 841.2

5 transformer, transmogrifier, innovator, innovationist, introducer; precursor 816; **alterant,** alterer, alterative, **agent,** catalytic agent, catalyst; the wind *or* winds of change; **leaven,** yeast, ferment; **modifier,** modificator; magician

VERBS 6 be changed, change, undergo a change, go through a change, sing *or* dance to a different tune <nf>, be converted into, turn into 858.17; **alter,** mutate, modulate; transmutate; **vary,** checker, diversify; **deviate, diverge,** turn, take a turn, take a new turn, turn aside, turn the corner, **shift,** veer, jibe, tack, come about, come round *or* around, haul around, chop, chop and change, swerve, warp; change sides, change horses in midstream; **revive,** be renewed, feel like a new person; **improve,** ameliorate, meliorate, mitigate, turn the corner; **degenerate, deteriorate, worsen;** hit bottom, bottom out <nf>, reach the nadir, flop <nf>

7 change, work *or* **make a change, alter,** change someone's tune; **mutate; modify;** adapt; modulate, accommodate, adjust, fine-tune, fit, **qualify; vary, diversify; convert, renew, recast, revamp** <nf>, change over, exchange, **revive;** remake, reshape, re-create, redesign, **rebuild,** reconstruct, restructure; realign; refit; **reform, improve,** better, ameliorate, meliorate, mitigate; **revolutionize,** turn upside down, subvert, overthrow, break up; worsen, deform, denature; ring the changes; give a turn to, give a twist to, turn the tide, turn the tables, turn the scale *or* balance; shift the scene; shuffle the cards; turn over a new leaf; **about-face,** do an about-face, do a 180 <nf>, change direction, reverse oneself, turn one's coat, sing *or* dance to a different tune, flip-flop <nf>, make a U-turn, change one's mind

8 transform, transfigure, transmute, transmogrify; **translate;** transubstantiate, metamorphose; metabolize; perform magic, conjure

9 innovate, make innovations, invent, discover, make a breakthrough, make a quantum jump *or* leap, **pioneer** 816.3, **revolutionize, introduce,** introduce new blood; neologize, neoterize, coin

ADJS 10 changed, altered, modified, qualified, **transformed,** transmuted, **metamorphosed;** translated, metastasized; deviant, aberrant, mutant; divergent; **converted, renewed,** revived, **rebuilt,** remodeled; **reformed,** improved, **better,** ameliorative, ameliatory; before-and-after; **degenerate, worse,** unmitigated; subversive, **revolutionary;** changeable 854.6,7

11 innovational, innovative, ameliorative

12 metamorphic, metabolic, anabolic, catabolic; metastatic, **catalytic**

13 presto, presto chango, hey presto <Brit>

PHRS 14 the shoe is on the other foot

853 PERMANENCE

NOUNS 1 permanence *or* permanency, **immutability, changelessness,** unchangingness, invariableness *or* invariability; **unchangeableness,** unchangeability, unchangingness, inalterability *or* inalterableness, inconvertibility *or* inconvertibleness; **fixedness, constancy,** steadfastness, firmness, solidity, immovableness *or* immovability, persistence *or* persistency, establishment, faithfulness, **lastingness, abidingness, endurance,** duration, continuance, perseverance, continuity, standing, long standing, inveteracy; durableness, durability 827.1; **perpetualness** 829.1; **stability** 855; **unchangeability** 855.4; **immobility,** stasis, frozenness, hardening, **rigidity; quiescence,** torpor, coma

  2 **maintenance, preservation** 397, **conservation**

  3 **conservatism, conservativeness,** opposition *or* resistance to change, unprogressiveness, fogyism, fuddy-duddyism, backwardness, old-fashionedness, standpattism <nf>; ultraconservatism, arch-conservatism; misocainea, misoneism; political conservatism, rightism 611.1; laissez-faireism 329.1; old school tie <Brit>; "adherence to the old and tried, against the new and untried"—Lincoln

  4 **conservative,** conservatist; conservationist; ultraconservative, arch-conservative, knee-jerk conservative <nf>, **diehard,** standpat *and* standpatter <nf>, **old fogy,** fogy, stick-in-the-mud <nf>, mossback <nf>, *laudator temporis acti* <L>, rightist, right-winger 611.9; old school

VERBS 5 **remain, endure** 827.6, last, stay, persist, bide, abide, stand, hold, subsist; be ever the same; take root, be here to stay; cast in stone

  6 **be conservative,** save, preserve, oppose change, stand on ancient ways; stand pat *and* stand still <nf>; **let things take their course,** leave things as they are, let be, let *or* leave alone, stick with it *and* let it ride <nf>, follow a hands-off policy, let well enough alone, do nothing; stop *or* turn back the clock

ADJS 7 **permanent, changeless, unchanging, immutable,** unvarying, unshifting; unchanged, unchangeable, unvaried, **unaltered,** inalterable, inviolate, undestroyed, intact; **constant, persistent,** sustained, fixed, firm, solid, steadfast, like the Rock of Gibraltar, faithful; unchecked, unfailing, unfading; **lasting, enduring,** abiding, remaining, staying, continuing; **durable** 827.10, entrenched; **perpetual** 829.7; **stable** 855.12; **unchangeable** 855.17; **immobile, static,** stationary, frozen, **rigid,** rocklike; **quiescent,** torpid, comatose, vegetable

  8 **conservative, preservative,** old-line, **diehard,** standpat <nf>, opposed to change; backward, backward-looking, old-fashioned, **unprogressive,** nonprogressive, unreconstructed, status-quo, stuck-in-the-mud; ultraconservative, misoneistic, fogyish, **old-fogyish; right-wing** 611.17; *laissez-faire* <Fr>, hands-off; noninvasive, noninterventionist

ADVS 9 **permanently,** abidingly, lastingly, steadfastly, unwaveringly, changelessly, unchangingly;

enduringly, **perpetually,** invariably, **forever, always** 829.11; statically, rigidly, inflexibly

 10 *in status quo* <L>, as things are, **as is, as usual,** as per usual <nf>; at a stand *or* standstill, without a shadow of turning

PHRS 11 *plus ça change, plus c'est la même chose* <Fr, the more it changes, the more it's the same thing>; if it isn't broken don't fix it, let sleeping dogs lie

854 CHANGEABLENESS

NOUNS 1 **changeableness,** changefulness, **changeability, alterability,** convertibility, modifiability; **mutability,** permutability, impermanence, **transience,** transitoriness; mobility, motility, movability; plasticity, malleability, workability, rubberiness, fluidity; **resilience, adaptability,** adjustability, **flexibility,** suppleness; **nonuniformity** 782

  2 **inconstancy, instability,** changefulness, unstableness, **unsteadiness,** unsteadfastness, unfixedness, unsettledness, rootlessness; **uncertainty,** undependability, inconsistency, shiftiness, unreliability; **variability,** variation, variety, restlessness, deviability; unpredictability, irregularity 851.1; **desultoriness,** waywardness, wantonness; **erraticism, eccentricity;** freakishness, freakery; flightiness, impulsiveness *or* impulsivity, mercuriality, moodiness, whimsicality, **capriciousness,** caprice, **fickleness** 364.3

  3 **changing, fluctuation,** vicissitude, **variation, shiftingness;** alternation, oscillation, **vacillation,** pendulation; **mood swings; wavering,** shifting, shuffling, teetering, tottering, seesawing, teeter-tottering; **exchange,** trading, musical chairs; bobbing and weaving

  4 <comparisons> rollercoaster, Proteus, kaleidoscope, chameleon, shifting sands, rolling stone, April showers, cloud shapes, feather in the wind; water; wheel of fortune; whirligig; mercury, quicksilver; the weather, weathercock, weather vane; moon, phases of the moon; iridescence

VERBS 5 **change, fluctuate, vary; shift; alternate, vacillate,** tergiversate, oscillate, pendulate, waffle <Brit nf>, blow hot and cold <nf>; ebb and flow, wax and wane; go through phases, waver, shuffle, swing, sway, wobble, wobble about, flounder, stagger, teeter, totter, **seesaw, teeter-totter;** back and fill, turn, blow hot and cold, ring the changes, have as many phases as the moon; **exchange,** trade, play musical chairs; metamorphose

ADJS 6 **changeable, alterable,** alterative, modifiable; mutable, permutable, impermanent, transient, **transitory,** rollercoaster; **variable,** checkered, ever-changing, many-sided, kaleidoscopic, variegated; **movable,** mobile, motile; plastic, malleable, rubbery, fluid; **resilient, adaptable,** adjustable, **flexible,** supple, able to adapt, able to roll with the punches *or* bend without breaking; protean, proteiform; metamorphic; **nonuniform** 782.3

7 **inconstant, changeable, changeful, changing, shifting,** uncertain, inconsistent, in a state of flux; **shifty,** unreliable, undependable; **unstable, unfixed,** infirm, restless, **unsettled,** unstaid, **unsteady,** wishy-washy, spineless, shapeless, amorphous, indecisive, irresolute, waffling <Brit nf>, blowing hot and cold <nf>, like a feather in the wind, unsteadfast, unstable as water; **variable,** deviable, dodgy <nf>; unaccountable, unpredictable; vicissitudinous *or* vicissitudinary; whimsical, **capricious, fickle** 364.6, off-again-on-again; **erratic, eccentric,** freakish; volatile, giddy, dizzy, ditzy <nf>, scatterbrained, mercurial, moody, flighty, impulsive, impetuous; **fluctuating,** alternating, **vacillating, wavering,** wavery, wavy, mazy, flitting, flickering, guttering, fitful, shifting, shuffling; irregular, spasmodic 851.3; **desultory,** rambling, roving, vagrant, homeless, wanton, wayward, wandering, afloat, adrift; **unrestrained, undisciplined,** irresponsible, uncontrolled, fast and loose

ADVS 8 **changeably, variably, inconstantly,** shiftingly, shiftily, uncertainly, **unsteadily,** unsteadfastly, whimsically, capriciously, desultorily, erratically, waveringly; **impulsively, impetuously,** precipitately; back and forth, to and fro, in and out, off and on, on and off, round and round

855 STABILITY

NOUNS 1 **stability, firmness, soundness, substantiality, solidity; security,** secureness, securement; **rootedness,** fastness; reliability 970.4; **steadiness,** steadfastness; constancy 847.2, invariability, undeflectability; **imperturbability,** unflappability <nf>, nerve, steady *or* unshakable nerves, nerves of steel, unshakableness, unsusceptibility, unimpressionability, stolidness *or* stolidity, stoicism, **cool** <nf>, *sang-froid* <Fr>; iron will; **equilibrium, balance,** stable state, stable equilibrium, homeostasis; steady state; emotional stability, balanced personality; aplomb; **uniformity** 781

2 **fixity,** fixedness, fixture, fixation; infixion, implantation, embedment; **establishment, stabilization,** confirmation, entrenchment; inveteracy, deep-rootedness, **deep-seatedness**

3 **immobility,** immovability, unmovability, immovableness, irremovability, immotility; inextricability; **firmness,** solidity, unyieldingness, rigidity, **inflexibility** 1046.3; inertia, *vis inertiae* <L>, inertness; immobilization

4 **unchangeableness, unchangeability,** unalterability, inalterability, unmodifiability, **immutability,** incommutability, inconvertibility; nontransferability; lastingness, **permanence** 853; irrevocability, indefeasibility, **irreversibility;** irretrievability, unreturnableness, unrestorableness; intransmutability

5 **indestructibility, imperishability,** incorruptibility, inextinguishability, immortality, **deathlessness;** invulnerability, invincibility, inexpugnability, impregnability; ineradicability, indelibility, ineffaceability, inerasableness

6 <comparisons> rock, Rock of Gibraltar, bedrock, pillar *or* tower of strength, foundation; leopard's spots

VERBS 7 **stabilize,** stabilitate *or* stabilify <old>; **firm, firm up** <nf>; **steady, balance,** counterbalance, ballast; **immobilize,** freeze, keep, retain; **transfix,** stick, hold, pin *or* nail down <nf>; set *or* cast *or* write in stone

8 **secure,** make sure *or* secure, firm up, tie, tie off *or* up, chain, tether; cleat, belay; **wedge, jam, seize; make fast, fasten,** fasten down; **anchor,** moor; batten *and* batten down; "build one's house upon a rock"—Bible; **confirm,** ratify

9 **fix, define,** set, **settle; establish,** found, ground, lodge, seat, **entrench; root;** infix, ingrain, set in, plant, implant, engraft, bed, embed; **print,** imprint, **stamp,** inscribe, **etch,** engrave, impress; deep-dye, **dye in the wool;** stereotype

10 <become firmly fixed> **root, take root,** strike root, settle down; **stick,** stick fast; seize, seize up, freeze; **catch, jam,** lodge, foul

11 **stand fast,** stand *or* remain firm, **stand pat** <nf>, stay put <nf>, hold fast, not budge, not budge an inch, **stand** *or* **hold one's ground,** persist, persevere, hold one's own, dig in one's heels, take one's stand, **stick to one's guns,** put one's foot down <nf>; **hold out,** stick *or* gut *or* tough it out and hang tough <nf>, stay the course; **hold up; weather,** weather the storm, ride it out, get home free <nf>; be imperturbable, be unflappable *and* not bat an eye *or* eyelash *and* keep one's cool <nf>

ADJS 12 **stable, substantial, firm, solid, sound,** stabile; firm as Gibraltar, solid as a rock, rock-like, built on bedrock, **fast, secure; steady, unwavering,** steadfast; **balanced,** in equilibrium, in a stable state; **well-balanced; imperturbable,** unflappable <nf>, unshakable, **cool** <nf>, unimpressionable, unsusceptible, impassive, stolid, stoic; without nerves, without a nerve in one's body, unflinching, iron-willed; **reliable** 970.17, predictable; fiducial

13 **established,** stabilized, **entrenched,** vested, firmly established; **well-established,** well-founded, **well-grounded,** on a rock, in or on bedrock, aground; old-line, long-established; **confirmed, inveterate; settled, set;** well-settled, well-set, in place, entrenched; **rooted,** well-rooted; **deep-rooted, deep-seated,** deep-set, deep-settled, deep-fixed, deep-dyed, deep-engraven, deep-grounded, deep-laid; **infixed, ingrained,** implanted, engrafted, embedded, ingrown, inwrought; impressed, indelibly impressed, imprinted; engraved, etched, graven, embossed; **dyed-in-the-wool**

14 **fixed,** fastened, anchored, riveted; **set, settled, stated;** staple

15 **immovable,** unmovable, **immobile,** immotile, unmoving, **irremovable, stationary,** frozen, not to be moved, at a standstill, on dead center; **firm, unyielding,** adamant, adamantine, rigid, **inflexible** 1046.12; pat, standpat <nf>; at anchor

16 **stuck, fast,** stuck fast, **fixed, transfixed, caught,** fastened, tied, chained, tethered, anchored, moored, held, inextricable; **jammed,** impacted, congested, packed, wedged; seized, seized up, frozen; aground, grounded, stranded, high and dry

17 **unchangeable,** not to be changed, changeless, unchanged, unchanging, unvarying, unvariable, **unalterable,** unaltered, unalterative, **immutable,** incommutable, inconvertible, unmodifiable; insusceptible of change; **constant, invariable,** undeviating, undeflectable; lasting, unremitting, **permanent** 853.7; irrevocable, indefeasible, **irreversible,** nonreversible, reverseless; irretrievable, unrestorable, unreturnable, nonreturnable; intransmutable, inert, noble <chemistry>

18 **indestructible,** undestroyable, **imperishable,** nonperishable, incorruptible; **deathless,** immortal, undying; **invulnerable, invincible,** inexpugnable, impregnable, indivisible; **ineradicable,** indelible, ineffaceable, inerasable; **inextinguishable,** unquenchable, quenchless, undampable

PHRS 19 **stet, let it stand; what's done is done**

856 CONTINUANCE

<continuance in action>

NOUNS 1 **continuance, continuation, ceaselessness,** unceasingness, uninterruptedness, unremittingness, **continualness** 812.1; **prolongation, extension, protraction, perpetuation,** lengthening, spinning or stringing out; **survival** 827.1, holding out, hanging on or in; **maintenance,** sustenance, sustained action or activity; pursuance; run, way, straight or uninterrupted course; **progress,** progression; **persistence, perseverance** 360; **endurance** 827.1, **stamina,** staying power; **continuity** 812; **repetition** 849

2 **resumption, recommencement,** rebeginning, reestablishment, revival, recrudescence, resuscitation, **renewal,** reopening, reentrance, reappearance; **fresh start,** new beginning; another try, another shot or crack or go <nf>

VERBS 3 **continue** 812.4, keep or stay with it, keep or stay at it, carry on; **remain,** bide, **abide, stay,** tarry, linger; **go on,** go along, **keep on,** keep on keeping on, keep going, carry on, see it through, stay on, hold on, hold one's way or course or path, hold steady, run on, jog on, drag on, bash ahead or on <nf>, slog on, soldier on, plug away <nf>, grind away or on, stagger on, put one foot in front of the other; never cease, cease not; **endure** 827.6

4 **sustain, protract, prolong, extend,** perpetuate, lengthen, spin or string out; **maintain,** keep, hold, retain, preserve; **keep up,** keep going, keep alive, **survive** 827.6

5 **persist, persevere,** keep at it 360.2, stick it out, stick to it, stick with it, never say die, see it through, hang in and hang tough and not know when one is licked <nf>; survive, make out, manage, get along, get on, eke out an existence, keep the even tenor of one's way; go on, go on with, go on with the show <nf>, press on; perseverate, iterate, reiterate, **harp,** go on about, chew one's ear off and run off at the mouth <nf>, beat a dead horse

6 **resume, recommence,** rebegin, **renew,** reestablish; **revive,** resuscitate, recrudesce; reenter, reopen, **return to,** go back to, begin again, take up again, make a new beginning, make a fresh start, start all over, have another try, have another shot or crack or go <nf>

ADJS 7 **continuing, abiding** 827.10; staying, remaining, sticking; **continuous** 812.8, **ceaseless, unceasing,** unending, endless, incessant, unremitting, steady, sustained, protracted, undying, indefatigable, **persistent; repetitious, repetitive** 849.14; **resumed,** recommenced, rebegun, renewed, reopened

857 CESSATION

NOUNS 1 **cessation, discontinuance,** discontinuation, phaseout, phasedown, scratching and scrubbing and breakoff <nf>; **desistance,** desinence, cease, surcease, **ceasing,** ending, halting, stopping, termination; **close,** closing, shutdown; sign-off; log-off; **relinquishment,** renunciation, abandonment, breakup

2 **stop,** stoppage, **halt, stay, arrest,** check, cutoff <nf>; stand, **standstill;** full stop, dead stop, screaming *or* grinding *or* shuddering *or* squealing halt; **strike** 727.5, walkout, work stoppage, sit-down strike, lockout; sick-out and blue flu <nf>; **end,** ending, endgame, final whistle, gun, bell, checkmate; **tie,** stalemate, deadlock, wash *and* toss-up <nf>, standoff *and* Mexican standoff <nf>; **terminal,** end of the line, rest stop, stopping place, terminus; closure

3 **pause, rest, break,** caesura, fermata, **recess, intermission,** interim 826, intermittence, interval, interlude, *intermezzo* <Ital>; **respite,** letup <nf>; **interruption, suspension,** time-out, break in the action, breathing spell *or* space, cooling-off period; **postponement** 846.4, rain-out; **remission;** abeyance, stay, drop, lull, lapse; truce, cease-fire, stand-down; **vacation, holiday,** time off, day off, recess, playtime, leisure

4 <grammatical terms> pause, juncture, boundary, caesura; <punctuation> stop *or* point *or* period, comma, serial comma, Oxford comma, colon, semicolon

5 <legislatures> **cloture,** clôture <Fr>; cloture by compartment, kangaroo cloture; guillotine <Brit>; closure of debate

VERBS 6 **cease, discontinue, end, stop, halt,** end-stop, terminate, close the books on, close the books, put paid to <Brit>, abort, cancel, scratch *and* scrub <nf>, hold, **quit,** stay, belay <nf>; **desist, refrain,** leave off, lay off <nf>, give over, **have done with;** cut it out *and* drop it *and* knock it off <nf>, relinquish, renounce, abandon; **come to an end** 820.6, draw to a close; hang up, ring off <nf>

7 **stop, come to a stop** *or* **halt,** halt, stop in one's tracks, skid to a stop, stop dead, **stall; bring up, pull up,** pull in, head in, draw up, **fetch up; stop short,** come up short, bring up short, come to a screaming *or* squealing *or* grinding *or* shuddering halt, stop on a dime <nf>, come to a full stop, put on the brake, come to a standstill, grind to a halt, fetch up all standing; **stick,** jam, hang fire, seize, seize up, freeze; **cease fire,** stand down; run into a brick wall

8 <stop work> **lay off, knock off** <nf>, call it a day <nf>, call it quits <nf>; lay down one's tools, **shut up shop,** close shop, shut down, lock up, close down, secure <nautical nf>; **strike,** walk out, call a strike, go *or* go out on strike, stand down; work to rule

9 **pause, rest,** let up *and* take it easy <nf>, **relax,** rest on one's oars; **recess,** take *or* call a recess; call

time-out; **take a break,** break, take five *or* ten; hang fire; catch one's breath, take a breather

10 **interrupt, suspend,** intermit, **break, break off,** take a break <nf>, cut off, break *or* snap the thread

11 **put a stop to, call a halt to,** get it over with, blow the whistle on <nf>, **put an end to** 820.5, put paid to <Brit nf>, call off the dogs <nf>; **stop, stay, halt, arrest, check,** flag down, wave down; block, brake, dam, stem, stem the tide *or* current; pull up, draw rein, put on the brakes, hit the brake pedal; **bring to a stand** *or* **standstill,** bring to a close *or* halt, freeze, bring to, bring up short, **stop dead** *or* dead in one's tracks, set one back on his heels, stop cold, stop short, cut short, check in full career; checkmate, stalemate, deadlock; thwart; do in <nf>

12 **turn off, shut off,** shut, shut down, close; **phase out,** phase down, taper off, wind up *or* down; **kill, cut,** cut off short, switch off

INTERJS 13 **cease!, stop!, halt!,** *halte!* <Fr>, hold!, freeze!, stay!, desist!, quit it!; **let up!,** easy!, take it easy!, relax!, get off it!, **leave off!,** *arrêtez!* <Fr>, stop it!, forget it!, no more!, have done!, *tenez!* <Fr>, **hold everything!, hold it!,** hold to!, hold on!, whoa!, that's it!, that's enough!, that will do!, enough!, enough is enough!, genug!, all right already!, *basta!* <Ital>

14 <nf terms> **cut it out!,** cool it!, bag it!, chill out!, call it quits!, can it!, turn it off!, chuck it!, stow it!, drop it!, lay off!, all right already!, come off it!, **knock it off!,** break it off!, break it up!

858 CONVERSION
<change to something different>

NOUNS 1 **conversion,** reconversion, **change-over,** turning into, becoming; convertibility; **change** 852, sea change, **transformation,** transubstantiation, transmutation, metamorphosis; **transition,** transit, **switch** *and* **switchover** <nf>, passage, **shift; reversal,** about-face *and* flip-flop <nf>, role reversal, *volte-face* <Fr>; makeover, do-over, complete change, 360-degree change, 360 <nf>; **relapse,** lapse, descent; **breakthrough, growth,** progress, development; transcendence; **resolution** 940.1; reduction, simplification; **assimilation,** naturalization, adoption, assumption; processing; alchemy

2 **new start, new beginning,** fresh start, clean slate, square one <nf>; **reformation, reform, regeneration, revival, reclamation,** redemption, amendment, improvement 392, renewal, recrudescence, **rebirth,** renascence, new birth,

change of heart; change of mind *or* commitment *or* allegiance *or* loyalty *or* conviction

3 apostasy, renunciation, **defection, desertion,** treason, crossing-over, abandonment; degeneration 393.3

4 **rehabilitation,** reconditioning, recovery, readjustment, reclamation, restoration; **reeducation, reinstruction; repatriation**

5 **indoctrination,** reindoctrination, counterindoctrination; **brainwashing,** menticide; subversion, alienation, corruption

6 **conversion,** proselytization, proselytism, evangelization, persuasion 375.3; indoctrination; spiritual rebirth

7 **convert, proselyte,** neophyte, catechumen, disciple, new man *or* woman, born-again person

8 **apostate, defector,** turncoat, traitor, deserter, **renegade**

9 **converter, proselyter,** proselytizer, **missionary, apostle, evangelist,** televangelist; reformer, rehabilitator

10 <instruments> philosopher's stone, melting pot, crucible, alembic, test tube, caldron, retort, mortar; potter's wheel, anvil, lathe; converter, transformer, transducer, engine, motor, machine 1040.3

VERBS 11 **convert,** reconvert; **change over,** switch *and* switch over <nf>, **shift,** slide into; **do over,** re-do, make over, rejigger <nf>; **change, transform** 852.5,8, transmute, metamorphose; **change into, turn into, become,** resolve into, assimilate to, bring to, reduce to, naturalize; **make,** render; **reverse,** do an about-face; change one's tune, sing a different tune, dance to another tune; turn back 859.5

12 **re-form,** remodel, reshape, refashion, recast; regroup, redeploy, rearrange 808.13; **renew,** new-model; be reborn, be born again, be a new person, feel like a new person; get it together *and* get one's act *or* shit together *and* get one's ducks in a row <nf>; **regenerate, reclaim,** redeem, amend, set straight; **reform, rehabilitate,** set on the straight and narrow, make a new man of, restore self-respect; mend *or* change one's ways, **turn over a new leaf,** put on the new man, undergo a personality change

13 **defect,** renege, wimp *or* chicken *or* cop out <nf>, turn one's coat, desert, apostatize, change one's colors, turn against, turn traitor; leave *or* desert a sinking ship; lapse, relapse; degenerate

14 **rehabilitate,** recondition, reclaim, recover, restore, readjust; **reeducate, reinstruct; repatriate**

15 **indoctrinate, brainwash,** reindoctrinate, counterindoctrinate; subvert, alienate, win away, corrupt

16 **convince, persuade,** wean, bring over, sweep off one's feet <nf>, **win over;** proselyte, **proselytize,** evangelize

17 be converted into, **turn into** *or* **to, become** 761.12, **change into,** alter into, run *or* fall *or* pass into, slide *or* glide into, **grow into,** ripen into, **develop** *or* **evolve into,** merge *or* blend *or* melt into, shift into, lapse into, open into, resolve itself *or* settle into, come round to

ADJS 18 **convertible,** changeable, resolvable, transmutable, **transformable, transitional, modifiable;** reformable, reclaimable, renewable

19 **converted, changed, transformed;** naturalized, assimilated; **reformed,** regenerated, renewed, redeemed, reborn, born-again; liquidated; brainwashed

20 **apostate, treasonable, traitorous,** degenerate, **renegade**

859 REVERSION

<change to a former state>

NOUNS 1 **reversion,** reverting, retroversion, retrogradation, **retrogression,** retrocession, regress, **relapse** 394, **regression, backsliding,** lapse, slipping back, backing, recidivism, recidivation; reconversion; **reverse, reversal,** turnabout, about-face, right about-face, 180-degree shift *or* change, flip-flop <nf>, **turn; return,** returning, retreat; disenchantment; **reclamation, rehabilitation,** redemption, return to the fold; **reinstatement,** restitution, restoration; retroaction; turn of the tide

2 **throwback,** atavism

3 **returnee, repeater;** prodigal son, lost lamb; reversioner, reversionist; recidivist, habitual criminal *or* offender, two-time loser <nf>; backslider

VERBS 4 **revert,** retrovert, **regress, retrogress,** retrograde, retrocede, **reverse, return,** return to the fold; backslide, slip back, recidivate, lapse, lapse back, relapse 394.4

5 **turn back, change back, go back, hark back,** cry back, break back, **turn,** turn around *or* about; make a round trip; do an about-face *and* flip-flop *and* do a flip-flop *and* hang a 180 <nf>, ricochet; undo, turn back the clock, put the genie back into the bottle, put the toothpaste back into the tube; go back to go *or* to square one *or* to the drawing board <nf>

6 **revert to, return to,** recur to, go back to; hark *or* cry back to

ADJS 7 **reversionary,** reversional, **regressive,** recessive, **retrogressive, retrograde;** reactionary; recidivist *or* recidivistic, recidivous, lapsarian;

retroverse, retrorse; retroactive; atavistic;
revertible, returnable, reversible, recoverable
WORD ELEMENTS 8 retro-

860 REVOLUTION
<sudden or radical change>

NOUNS 1 **revolution, radical** *or* **total change, violent change,** striking alteration, sweeping change, clean sweep, clean slate, square one <nf>, tabula rasa; transilience, quantum leap *or* jump; **overthrow,** overturn, upset, *bouleversement* <Fr>, convulsion, spasm, subversion, coup d'état; breakup, breakdown; **cataclysm, catastrophe,** debacle, *débâcle* <Fr>; **revolution,** revolutionary war, war of national liberation; bloodless revolution, palace revolution; technological revolution, electronic *or* communications *or* computer *or* information revolution; green revolution; counterrevolution; **revolt** 327.4, reign of terror

2 **revolutionism,** revolutionariness, anarchism, syndicalism, terrorism; Bolshevism *or* Bolshevikism <Russia>, Carbonarism <Italy>, Sinn Feinism <Ireland>, Jacobinism <France>; sans-culottism <France>, *sans-culotterie* <Fr>, Castroism <Cuba>, Maoism <China>, Shining Path <Peru>, Sandinistism <Nicaragua>

3 **revolutionist, revolutionary,** revolutionizer; **rebel** 327.5; anarchist, anarch, syndicalist, criminal syndicalist, terrorist 671.9; subversive; red; Red Republican <France>, *bonnet rouge* <Fr>; Jacobin <France>, sans-culotte, sans-culottist; Yankee *or* Yankee Doodle *or* Continental <US>; Puritan *or* Roundhead <Brit>; Bolshevik *or* Bolshevist *or* Bolshie <Rus>, Marxist, Leninist, Communist, Commie <nf>, Red, Trotskyite *or* Trotskyist, Castroist *or* Castroite <Cuba>, Guevarist, Maoist; Vietcong *or* VC *and* Cong *and* Charley <Vietnam>; *Carbonaro* <Ital>, Carbonarist <Ital>; Sinn Feiner, Fenian <Ir>; revolutionary junta

VERBS 4 **revolutionize, make a radical change,** make a clean sweep, break with the past; **overthrow, overturn,** throw the rascals out *and* let heads roll <nf> *boulverse* <Fr>, upset; revolt 327.7

ADJS 5 **revolutionary;** revulsive, revulsionary; transilient; subversive, insurgent; cataclysmic, catastrophic; **radical,** sweeping 794.10; **insurrectionary** 327.11

6 **revolutionist, revolutionary,** anarchic *or* anarchical, syndicalist, terrorist *or* terroristic, agin the government <nf>; Bolshevistic, Bolshevik; sans-culottic, sans-culottish; Jacobinic *or* Jacobinical, Carbonarist, Fenian, Marxist, Leninist, Communist, Trotskyist *or* Trotskyite,

Guevarist, Castroist *or* Castroite, Maoist, Vietcong, Mau-Mau

861 EVOLUTION

NOUNS 1 **evolution, evolving,** evolvement; evolutionary change, gradual change, step-by-step change, peaceful *or* nonviolent change; **development, growth,** rise, incremental change, developmental change, natural growth *or* development; flowering, blossoming; ripening, coming of age, maturation 303.6; accomplishment 407; **advance,** advancement, furtherance; **progress,** progression; **elaboration,** enlargement, amplification; **expansion;** devolution, degeneration 393.3

2 **unfolding,** unfoldment, unrolling, unfurling, unwinding; revelation, gradual revelation

3 <biological terms> **genesis;** phylogeny, phylogenesis; ontogeny, ontogenesis; physiogeny, physiogenesis; **biological evolution,** speciation, convergent evolution, parallel evolution; natural selection, adaptation; horotely, bradytely, tachytely; gradualism; microevolution, macroevolution; polygenesis, polygeny

4 **evolutionism,** theory of evolution; **Darwinism,** Darwinianism, punctuated equilibrium, Neo-Darwinism, organic evolution, survival of the fittest; Haeckelism, Lamarckism *or* Lamarckianism, Neo-Lamarckism, Lysenkoism, Weismannism, Spencerianism; social Darwinism, social evolution

VERBS 5 **evolve; develop, grow,** wax, change gradually *or* step-by-step; **progress, advance,** come a long way; accomplish 407.4; ripen, mellow, mature 303.9, maturate; flower, bloom, blossom, bear fruit; degenerate

6 **elaborate, develop, work out,** enlarge, enlarge on *or* upon, amplify, **expand,** expand on *or* upon, detail, go *or* enter into detail, go into, flesh out, **pursue,** spell out <nf>; complete 407.6

7 unfold, unroll, unfurl, unwind, unreel, uncoil, reveal, reveal *or* expose gradually

ADJS 8 **evolutionary,** evolutional, evolutionist *or* evolutionistic; **evolving, developing, unfolding; maturing,** maturational, maturative; **progressing, advancing;** devolutionary, degenerative; genetic, phylogenetic, ontogenetic, physiogenetic; horotelic, bradytelic, tachytelic

862 SUBSTITUTION
<change of one thing for another>

NOUNS 1 **substitution, exchange, change,** switch, switcheroo <nf>, swap, commutation, subrogation; **surrogacy;** vicariousness, **representation,** deputation, **delegation;** deputyship, **agency, power of attorney; supplanting,** supplantation, succession; **replacement,** displacement, shuffle; provision, provisionalness *or* provisionality, adhocracy, ad hockery *or* ad hocery, ad hocism; superseding, supersession *or* supersedure; tit for tat, *quid pro quo* <L>; job sharing; novation

2 **substitute, sub** <nf>, **substitution, replacement,** backup, second *or* third string <nf>, secondary, utility player, succedaneum; **change, exchange; ersatz,** phony *and* fake <nf>, counterfeit, imitation 336, copy 785; surrogate; reserves, bench <nf>, backup, backup personnel, spares; **alternate,** alternative, next best thing, lesser of two evils; **successor,** supplanter, superseder, capper <nf>; **proxy,** dummy, ghost; vicar, agent, representative; **deputy** 576; locum tenens, vice, vice-president, vice-regent, etc; **relief,** fill-in, **stand-in, understudy, pinch hitter** *or* runner <nf>; double; **equivalent,** equal; ringer <nf>; ghostwriter; **analogy,** comparison; **metaphor,** metonymy, euphemism, synecdoche <all grammar>; **symbol, sign,** token, icon; makeshift 995.2

3 **scapegoat, goat** <nf>, fall guy *and* can-carrier *and* patsy *and* catch dog <nf>, whipping boy, lamb to the slaughter

VERBS 4 **substitute, exchange, change,** take *or* ask *or* offer in exchange, switch, swap, ring in <nf>, **put in the place of,** change for, make way for, give place to; commute, redeem, compound for; **pass off,** pawn *or* foist *or* palm *or* fob off; rob Peter to pay Paul; dub in; make do with, shift with, put up with; shuffle

5 **substitute for,** sub for <nf>, subrogate; **act for,** double for *or* as, stand *or* sit in for, understudy for, fill in for, serve as proxy, don the mantle of, change places with, swap places with <nf>, stand in the stead of, step into *or* fill the shoes of, pinch-hit *and* pinch-run <nf>; deputize; relieve, spell *and* spell off <nf>, cover for; ghost, ghostwrite; **represent** 576.14; **supplant, supersede,** succeed, **replace,** displace, **take the place of,** crowd out, cut out <nf>

6 <nf terms> **cover up for,** front for; **take the rap for** *and* take the fall for <nf>, carry the can *and* be the goat *or* patsy *or* fall guy <nf>

7 **delegate, deputize,** depute, **commission,** give the nod to <nf>, designate an agent *or* a proxy

ADJS 8 **substitute, alternate, alternative,** other, tother <nf>, equivalent, token, dummy, pinch, utility, backup, secondary; ad hoc, provisional; **vicarious,** ersatz, mock, phony *and* fake *and* bogus <nf>, counterfeit, imitation 336.8; **proxy,** deputy;

makeshift, reserve, **spare,** stopgap, temporary, provisional, tentative

9 **substitutional,** substitutionary, substitutive, provisional, supersessive; **substituted,** substituent

10 **replaceable,** substitutable, supersedable, expendable

ADVS 11 **instead, rather,** *faute de mieux* <Fr>; in its stead *or* place; in one's stead, in one's behalf, in one's place, in one's shoes; by proxy; as an alternative; *in loco parentis* <L>

PREPS 12 **instead of,** in the stead of, rather than, sooner than, **in place of,** in the place of, **in** *or* **on behalf of, in lieu of; for,** as proxy for, as a substitute for, as representing, in preference to, as an alternative to; **replacing,** as a replacement for, vice

WORD ELEMENTS 13 pro-, vice-, quasi-, pseudo-

863 INTERCHANGE
<double or mutual change>

NOUNS 1 **interchange, exchange,** counterchange; **transposition,** transposal; mutual transfer *or* replacement; mutual admiration, mutual support; **cooperation** 450; commutation, permutation, intermutation; alternation; **interplay, tradeoff, compromise, reciprocation** 777.1, reciprocality, reciprocity, mutuality, two-way traffic, alternation; *give-and-take,* something for something, *quid pro quo* <L>, measure for measure, tit for tat, an eye for an eye, "an eye for an eye and a tooth for a tooth"—Bible; retaliation, *lex talionis* <L>; cross fire; battledore and shuttlecock; repartee

2 **trading, swapping** <nf>; trade, swap <nf>, even trade, even-steven trade, **switch;** barter 731.2; logrolling, back scratching, pork barrel; pawning, castling <chess>

3 **interchangeability,** exchangeability, changeability, standardization; convertibility, commutability, permutability

VERBS 4 **interchange, exchange,** change, counterchange; alternate; **transpose;** convert, commute, permute; **trade, swap** <nf>, **switch;** bandy, bandy about, play at battledore and shuttlecock; **reciprocate, trade off,** compromise, settle, settle for, respond, keep a balance; **give and take,** give tit for tat, give as much as one takes, give as good as one gets, return the compliment *or* favor, pay back, compensate, **requite,** return; **retaliate,** get back at, get even with, be quits with; logroll, scratch each other's back, **cooperate** 450.3

ADJS 5 **interchangeable, exchangeable,** changeable, standard; equivalent; **even,** equal; returnable,

convertible, commutable, permutable; commutative; retaliatory, equalizing; **reciprocative** *or* **reciprocating, reciprocatory, reciprocal, traded-off,** two-way**; mutual,** give-and-take**; exchanged, transposed,** switched, **swapped** <nf>, traded, **interchanged;** requited, reciprocated

ADVS **6 interchangeably, exchangeably; in exchange, in return; even, evenly,** *au pair* <Fr>**; reciprocally,** mutually; **in turn,** each in its turn, every one in his turn, by turns, turn about, turn and turn about

PHRS **7** one good turn deserves another; you scratch my back I scratch yours

864 GENERALITY

NOUNS **1 generality, universality,** cosmicality, inclusiveness 772.1; worldwideness, globality *or* globalism, ecumenicity *or* ecumenicalism; catholicity; **internationalism,** cosmopolitanism; **generalization,** universalization, globalization, ecumenization, internationalization; **labeling,** stereotyping

2 prevalence, commonness, commonality, usualness, **currency,** occurrence; **extensiveness,** widespreadness, pervasiveness, sweepingness, rifeness, rampantness; **normality,** normalness, averageness, ordinariness, routineness, habitualness, standardness

3 average, ruck, **run,** general *or* common *or* average *or* ordinary run, **run of the mill;** any Tom, Dick, or Harry; Everyman; common *or* average man, the man in the street, John Q Public, John *or* Jane Doe, ordinary Joe, Joe Six-pack, Joe Blow, lowest common denominator; girl next door; everyman, everywoman; *homme moyen sensuel* <Fr>

4 all, everyone, everybody, each and every one, one and all, all comers *and* all hands *and* every man Jack *and* every mother's son <nf>, every living soul, **all the world,** everyone and his brother, *tout le monde* <Fr>, the devil and all <nf>, **whole, totality** 792.1; **everything,** all kinds *or* all manner of things; you name it *and* what have you *and* all the above <nf>; Anytown

5 any, anything, any one, aught, either; **anybody, anyone**

6 whatever, whate'er, **whatsoever,** whatsoe'er, **what, whichever,** anything soever which, no matter what *or* which, what have you, what you will

7 whoever, whoso, **whosoever, whomever,** whomso, **whomsoever,** anyone, no matter who, anybody

8 <Idea *or* expression> **generalization,** general idea, **abstraction,** generalized proposition; glittering generality, sweeping statement, vague generalization; **truism, platitude, conventional wisdom,** commonplace, *lieu commun* <Fr>, *locus communis* <L>; **cliché,** tired cliché, bromide, trite *or* hackneyed expression; labeling, stereotyping

VERBS **9 generalize, universalize,** catholicize, ecumenicize, globalize, internationalize; **broaden, widen, expand,** extend, spread; make a generalization, deal in generalities *or* abstractions; **label,** stereotype

10 prevail, predominate, obtain, dominate, reign, rule; be in force *or* effect; be the rule *or* fashion, be the rage *or* thing <nf>, have currency, be in <nf>

ADJS **11 general, generalized, nonspecific,** generic, **indefinite,** indeterminate, vague, abstract, nebulous, unspecified, undifferentiated, featureless, uncharacterized, bland, neutral

12 prevalent, prevailing, common, popular, **current,** running; regnant, reigning, **ruling, predominant,** predominating, **dominant; rife, rampant,** pandemic, epidemic, besetting; **ordinary, normal, average, usual,** routine, standard, par for the course <nf>, stereotyped, stereotypical; public, communal

13 extensive, broad, wide, liberal, diffuse, large-scale, broad-scale, broad-scope, broadly-based, wide-scale, **sweeping; cross-disciplinary,** interdisciplinary; widespread, far-spread, far-stretched, **far-reaching,** far-going, far-embracing, far-extending, far-spreading, far-flying, far-ranging, **far-flung,** wide-flung, wide-reaching, wide-extending, wide-extended, wide-ranging, wide-stretching; **wholesale, indiscriminate;** rife; panoramic, bird's-eye

14 universal, cosmic *or* cosmical, heaven-wide, galactic, planetary, world-wide, transnational, planet-wide, **global; total,** allover, holistic; catholic, **all-inclusive,** all-including, **all-embracing,** all-encompassing, all-comprehensive, all-comprehending, all-filling, all-pervading, all-covering, encyclopedic; nonsectarian, nondenominational, ecumenic *or* ecumenical; omnipresent, ubiquitous; **cosmopolitan,** international; **national,** nation-wide, country-wide, state-wide

15 every, all, any, whichever, whichsoever; **each,** each one; every one, each and every, each and all, **one and all, all and sundry,** all and some

16 trite, commonplace, hackneyed, platitudinous, truistic, overworked, quotidian; common *or* garden

ADVS **17 generally, in general; generally speaking,** speaking generally, **broadly,** broadly speaking, **roughly,** roughly speaking, as an approximation; **usually, as a rule, ordinarily, commonly, normally,** routinely, as a matter of course, in the usual course; **by and large,** at large, altogether, overall, over the long haul <nf>, **all things considered,** taking one thing with another, taking all things together, on balance, **all in all,** taking all in all, taking it for all in all, **on the whole,** as a whole, **in the long run,** for the most part, for better *or* for worse; **prevailingly, predominantly, mostly,** chiefly, mainly

18 **universally,** galactically, cosmically; **everywhere, all over,** the world over, all over the world, internationally; in every instance, without exception, **invariably, always,** never otherwise

WORD ELEMENTS 19 glob-, globo-, omn-, omni-, pan-, pano-, pant-, panto-, panta-

865 PARTICULARITY

NOUNS 1 **particularity, individuality, singularity, differentiation,** differentness, distinctiveness, uniqueness; identity, individual *or* separate *or* concrete identity; **personality,** personship, personal identity; soul; **selfness,** selfhood, ipseity, **egohood,** self-identity; oneness 872.1, wholeness, integrity; personal equation, human factor; **nonconformity** 868; **individualism,** particularism; nominalism

2 **speciality, specialness,** specialty, specificality, **specificness,** definiteness; special case; specialty of the house, soup du jour, flavor of the month, today's specials

3 **the specific,** the special, **the particular,** the concrete, the individual, the unique

4 **characteristic, peculiarity, singularity,** particularity, specialty, individualism, **character,** property, nature, **trait,** quirk, point of character, bad point, good point, saving grace, redeeming feature, mannerism, keynote, trick, **feature,** distinctive feature, lineament; claim to fame, expertise, métier, forte; **mark,** marking, **earmark,** hallmark, index, signature; badge, token; **brand,** cast, stamp, cachet, seal, mold, cut, figure, shape, configuration; impress, impression; differential, differentia; **idiosyncrasy,** idiocrasy, eccentricity, peculiarity; **quality, property, attribute;** savor, flavor, taste, gust, aroma, odor, smack, tang, taint

5 **self, ego; oneself, I,** myself, me, my humble self, number one <nf>, yours truly <nf>; yourself, himself, herself, itself; ourselves, yourselves; themselves; you; he, she; him, her; they, them; it; inner self, inner man; subliminal *or* subconscious self; superego, better self, ethical self; other self, alter ego, alter, *alterum* <L>; inner child, child within

6 **specification, designation, stipulation,** specifying, designating, stipulating, singling-out, featuring, highlighting, focusing on, denomination; **allocation,** attribution, fixing, selection, assignment, pinning down; specifications, particulars, minutiae, fine print

7 **particularization, specialization;** individualization, peculiarization, personalization; localization; itemization 766.5; special interest, pursuit, vocation, field

8 **characterization,** distinction, **differentiation;** definition, description

VERBS 9 **particularize, specialize; individualize,** peculiarize, personalize; **descend to particulars,** go into detail, get precise, get down to brass tacks *or* to cases <nf>, get down to the nitty-gritty <nf>, come to the point, lay it on the line <nf>, spell out; **itemize** 766.6, detail, spell out

10 **characterize, distinguish, differentiate, define, describe; mark, earmark,** mark off, mark out, demarcate, **set apart,** make special *or* unique; keynote <nf>, sound the keynote, set the tone *or* mood, set the pace; be characteristic, **be a feature *or* trait of**

11 **specify,** specialize, **designate, stipulate,** determine, single out, feature, highlight, focus on, mention, select, pick out, **fix,** set, assign, pin down; **name,** denominate, name names, state, mark, check, check off, **indicate, signify,** point out, put *or* lay one's finger on; mention, cite, quote, attribute

ADJS 12 **particular, special, especial, specific, express,** precise, **concrete; singular, individual,** individualist *or* individualistic, unique; **personal,** private, intimate, inner, solipsistic, esoteric; respective, several; **fixed, definite, defined,** distinct, different, different as night and day, determinate, certain, absolute; **distinguished,** noteworthy, **exceptional, extraordinary;** minute, detailed

13 **characteristic, peculiar, singular,** single, quintessential, intrinsic, unique, qualitative, **distinctive,** marked, distinguished, notable, nameable; appropriate, proper; idiosyncratic, idiocratic, **in character, true to form,** typical

14 **this,** this and no other, this one, this single; **these; that,** that one; those

ADVS 15 **particularly, specially, especially, specifically, expressly,** concretely, exactly, precisely, **in particular,** to be specific; **definitely, distinctly; minutely,** in detail, item by item, singly, separately

16 **personally,** privately, idiosyncratically, **individually; in person,** in the flesh, *in propria persona* <L>; as for me, for all of me, **for my part, as far as I am concerned**

17 **characteristically, peculiarly,** singularly, intrinsically, **uniquely,** markedly, **distinctively,** in its own way, like no other

18 namely, nominally, **that is to say,** *videlicet* <L>, viz, *scilicet* <L>, scil, sc, **to wit**

19 each, apiece; severally, respectively, one by one, each to each; *per annum* or *per diem* or *per capita* <L>

PREPS **20 per, for each**

WORD ELEMENTS **21** -ness, -hood, -dom; aut-, auto-, idio-, self-; -acean, -aceous, -ey, -y, -ious, -ous, -ish, -ist, -istic, -istical, -itious, -itic, -ose, -some

866 SPECIALTY

<object of special attention or preference>

NOUNS **1 specialty,** speciality, **line, pursuit, pet subject, business, line of business, line of country** <Brit>, **field,** area, main interest; **vocation** 724.6; **forte, métier, strong point,** long suit; specialism, specialization; technicality; **way,** manner, **style,** type; **lifestyle,** way of life, preferences; cup of tea *and* bag *and* thing *and* thang *and* weakness <nf>

2 special, feature, main feature; **leader,** lead item, leading card

3 specialist, specializer, **expert, authority,** savant, scholar, connoisseur, maven <nf>; technical expert, technician, techie <nf>, nerd <nf>; pundit, critic; amateur, dilettante; fan, buff, freak *and* nut <nf>, aficionado

VERBS **4 specialize, feature; narrow, restrict,** limit, confine; specialize in, **go in for,** be into <nf>, have a weakness *or* taste for, be strong in, follow, pursue, **make one's business;** major in, minor in; do one's thing <nf>

ADJS **5 specialized,** specialist, specialistic; down one's alley <nf>, cut out for one, fits one like a glove; technical; **restricted, limited,** confined; **featured,** feature; **expert, authoritative,** knowledgeable

867 CONFORMITY

NOUNS **1 conformity; conformance,** conformation, other-directedness; **compliance,** acquiescence, goose step, lockstep, obedience, observance, subordination, traditionalism, **orthodoxy;** strictness; **accordance,** accord, **correspondence,** harmony, agreement, **uniformity** 781, **consistency,** congruity; **accommodation,** adaptation, adaption, pliancy, malleability, flexibility, adjustment; reconciliation, reconcilement; **conventionality** 579.1

2 conformist, conformer, sheep, trimmer, parrot, yes-man, organization man, company man, lackey; **conventionalist,** Mrs Grundy, Babbitt, Philistine, middle-class type, button-down *or* white-bread type <nf>, **bourgeois,** burgher,

Middle American, plastic person *and* clone *and* square <nf>, three-piecer *and* yuppie <nf>, Barbie Doll <trademark nf>; model child; teenybopper <nf>; **formalist,** methodologist, perfectionist, precisianist *or* precisian, stick-in-the-mud; anal character, compulsive character; pedant

VERBS **3 conform, comply, correspond,** accord, harmonize; **adapt,** adjust, **accommodate,** bend, meet, suit, fit, shape; **comply with,** agree with, tally with, chime *or* fall in with, go by, be guided *or* regulated by, observe, follow, bend, yield, take the shape of; **adapt to,** adjust to, gear to, assimilate to, **accommodate to** *or* **with; reconcile,** settle, compose; rub off corners; **make conform,** shape, lick into shape, mold, force into a mold; straighten, rectify, correct, **discipline**

4 follow the rule, toe the mark, do it according to Hoyle *or* by the book <nf>, play the game <nf>; go through channels; **fit in, follow the crowd,** go with the crowd, follow the fashion, swim *or* go with the stream *or* tide *or* current, get on the bandwagon, trim one's sails to the breeze, follow the beaten path, **do as others do, get** *or* **stay in line,** fall in *or* into line, fall in with; run true to form; **keep in step,** goose-step, walk in lockstep; keep up to standard, pass muster, come up to scratch <nf>

ADJS **5 conformable, adaptable,** adaptive, adjustable; **compliant,** pliant, complaisant, malleable, flexible, plastic, acquiescent, unmurmuring, other-directed, submissive, tractable, obedient

6 conformist, conventional 579.5, bourgeois, plastic *and* square *and* straight *and* white-bread *and* white-bready *and* button-down *and* buttoned-down <nf>, cloned *and* clonish *and* cookie-cutter <nf>; **orthodox,** traditionalist *or* traditionalistic; kosher; **formalistic,** legalistic, precisianistic, anal, compulsive; pedantic, stuffy *and* hidebound <nf>, strait-laced, uptight <nf>; in accord, in keeping, in line, in step, in lockstep; **corresponding,** accordant, concordant, harmonious

ADVS **7** conformably, conformingly, in conformity, **obediently, pliantly,** flexibly, malleably, complaisantly, yieldingly, **compliantly,** submissively; **conventionally,** traditionally; anally, **compulsively;** pedantically

8 according to rule, *en regle* <Fr>, according to regulations; **according to Hoyle** *and* **by the book** *and* by the numbers <nf>

PREPS **9 conformable to, in conformity with,** in compliance with; **according to, in accordance with, consistent with, in harmony with,** in agreement with, in correspondence to; adapted to, adjusted to, accommodated to; proper to, suitable for, agreeable to, agreeably to; answerable to, in obedience to; congruent with, uniform with, in uniformity with; **in line with,** in step with, in lock-step with, **in keeping with; after, by, per, as per**

PHRS **10 don't rock the boat, don't make waves,** get in line, shape up, shape up *or* ship out <nf>; when in Rome do as the Romans do

868 NONCONFORMITY

NOUNS **1 nonconformity,** unconformity, nonconformism, **inconsistency,** incongruity; **inaccordance,** disaccord, disaccordance; originality 337.1; **nonconformance,** disconformity; **nonobservance, noncompliance,** nonconcurrence, **dissent** 333, **protest** 333.2, rebellion, disagreement, contrariety, recalcitrance, refractoriness, recusance *or* recusancy; **deviation** 870.1, deviationism

2 unconventionality, unorthodoxy 688, revisionism, heterodoxy, heresy, originality, Bohemianism, beatnikism, hippiedom, counterculture, iconoclasm; eccentricity; alternative lifestyle *or* society *or* medicine

3 nonconformist, unconformist, **original,** eccentric, gonzo <nf>, deviant, deviationist, maverick <nf>, rebel, dropout, Bohemian, beatnik, free spirit, freethinker, independent, hippie, hipster, freak <nf>, flower child, New-Age Traveler; **misfit,** square peg in a round hole, fish out of water; *enfant terrible* <Fr>; **dissenter** 333.3; **heretic** 688.5; sectary, sectarian; nonjuror

VERBS **4 not conform,** nonconform, not comply; **get out of line** *and* **rock the boat** *and* make waves <nf>, **leave the beaten path, go out of bounds,** upset the apple cart, break step, break bounds; drop out, opt out; **dissent** 333.4, swim against the current *or* against the tide *or* upstream, **protest** 333.5; "hear a different drummer"—Thoreau

ADJS **5 nonconforming,** unconforming, nonconformable, unadaptable, unadjustable; **uncompliant,** unsubmissive; **nonobservant;** contrary, recalcitrant, refractory, recusant; **deviant,** deviationist, atypic *or* atypical, unusual; **dissenting** 333.6, **dissident;** antisocial

6 unconventional, unorthodox, eccentric, gonzo <nf>, heterodox, heretical; unfashionable, not done, not kosher, not cricket <Brit nf>; offbeat <nf>, way out *and* far out *and* kinky *and* out in left field <nf>, fringy, breakaway, **out-of-the-way; original,** maverick, Bohemian, beat, hippie, counterculture; **nonformal,** free and easy <nf>; outside the box

7 out of line, out of keeping, out of order *or* place, misplaced, **out of step,** out of turn <nf>, out of tune

869 NORMALITY

NOUNS **1** normality, normalness, typicality, normalcy, naturalness; health, wholesomeness, propriety, regularity; naturalism, naturism, realism; order 807

2 usualness, ordinariness, commonness, commonplaceness, averageness, mediocrity; generality 864, prevalence, currency

3 the normal, the usual, the ordinary, the common, the commonplace, the day-to-day, the way things are, the normal order of things; common *or* garden variety, the run of the mine *or* the mill

4 rule, law, principle, standard, criterion, canon, code, code of practice, maxim, prescription, guideline, rulebook, the book <nf>, regulation, reg *or* regs <nf>; norm, model, rule of behavior, ideal, ideal type, specimen type, exemplar; rule *or* law *or* order of nature, natural *or* universal law; form, formula, formulary, formality, prescribed *or* set form; standing order, standard operating procedure; hard-and-fast rule, Procrustean law

5 normalization, standardization, regularization; codification, formalization

VERBS **6** normalize, standardize, regularize; codify, formalize

7 do the usual thing, make a practice of, carry on, carry on as usual, do business as usual

ADJS **8** normal, natural; general 864.11; typical, unexceptional; normative, prescribed, model, ideal, desired, white-bread *or* white-bready <nf>; naturalistic, naturistic, realistic; orderly 807.6

9 usual, regular; customary, habitual, accustomed, wonted, normative, prescriptive, standard, regulation, conventional; common, commonplace, ordinary, average, everyday, mediocre, familiar, household, vernacular, stock; prevailing, predominating, current, popular; universal 864.14

ADVS **10** normally, naturally; normatively, prescriptively, regularly; typically, usually, commonly, ordinarily, customarily, habitually, generally; mostly, chiefly, mainly, for the most part, most often *or* frequently; as a rule, as a matter of course; as usual, as per usual <nf>; as may be expected, to be expected, as things go

WORD ELEMENTS **11** norm-, normo-

870 ABNORMALITY

NOUNS **1 abnormality,** abnormity; **unnaturalness,** unnaturalism, strangeness; **anomaly,** anomalousness, anomalism; **aberration,** aberrance *or* aberrancy; **atypicality,** atypicalness; **irregularity, deviation,** divergence, **difference** 780; **eccentricity,** erraticism, unpredictability, unpredictableness, randomness, chaos; **monstrosity,** teratism <see list>, amorphism, heteromorphism; **subnormality; inferiority** 250; **superiority** 249; **derangement** 811.1

2 **unusualness, uncommonness,** unordinariness, unwontedness, exceptionalness, exceptionality, extraordinariness; **rarity,** rareness, **uniqueness; prodigiousness,** marvelousness, wondrousness, fabulousness, mythicalness, remarkableness, stupendousness; **incredibility** 955.3, incredibility, inconceivability, **impossibility** 967

3 **oddity, queerness,** curiousness, quaintness, **peculiarity, absurdity** 967.1, singularity; **strangeness,** outlandishness; bizarreness, *bizarrerie* <Fr>; fantasticality, anticness; **freakishness, grotesqueness,** grotesquerie, strangeness, weirdness, gonzo <nf>, monstrousness, monstrosity, malformation, deformity, teratism

4 <odd person> oddity, **character** <nf>, type, **case** <nf>, natural, original, odd fellow, queer specimen; **oddball** *and* **weirdo** <nf>, odd *or* queer fish, queer duck, rum one <Brit nf>; **rare bird,** *rara avis* <L>; flake, eccentric 927.3; *meshuggenah* <Yiddish>; **freak** *and* **screwball** *and* **crackpot** *and* **kook** *and* **nut** *and* bird *and* gonzo <nf>; **fanatic, crank,** zealot; **outsider, alien,** foreigner; **alien,** extraterrestrial, Martian, little green man, visitor from another planet; pariah, loner, lone wolf, solitary, hermit; hobo, tramp; maverick; **outcast,** outlaw, scapegoat; **nonconformist** 868.3

5 <odd thing> **oddity, curiosity, wonder,** funny *or* peculiar *or* strange thing; **abnormality, anomaly; rarity,** improbability, exception, one in a thousand *or* million; **prodigy,** prodigiosity; curio, conversation piece; museum piece

6 **monstrosity, monster** <see list>, miscreation, abortion, teratism, abnormal *or* defective birth, abnormal *or* defective fetus; **freak,** freak of nature, *lusus naturae* <L>

7 **supernaturalism,** supernaturalness, supernaturality, supranaturalism, supernormalness, **preternaturalism,** supersensibleness, superphysicalness, superhumanity; **the paranormal;** numinousness; **unearthliness,** unworldliness, **otherworldliness,** eeriness; transcendentalism; New Age; the supernatural, **the occult,** the supersensible; **paranormality;** supernature, supranature; **mystery,** mysteriousness, miraculousness, strangeness; faerie, witchery, elfdom

8 **miracle, sign, signs and portents, prodigy, wonder,** wonderwork, ferlie <Scot>; thaumatology, thaumaturgy; fantasy, enchantment

ADJS 9 **abnormal, unnatural; anomalous,** anomalistic; **irregular,** eccentric, erratic, deviative, divergent, **different** 780.7; **aberrant,** stray, straying, wandering; heteroclite, heteromorphic; formless, shapeless, amorphous; **subnormal**

10 **unusual,** unordinary, **uncustomary,** unwonted, **uncommon, unfamiliar,** atypic *or* atypical, unheard-of, *recherché* <Fr>; **rare, unique,** *sui generis* <L, of its own kind>; **out of the ordinary,** out of this world, out-of-the-way, out of the common, out of the pale, **off the beaten track,** offbeat, breakaway; unexpected, not to be expected, unthought-of, undreamed-of

11 **odd, queer, peculiar, absurd** 967.7, **singular, curious, oddball** <nf>, weird *and* kooky *and* freaky *and* freaked-out <nf>, quaint, **eccentric,** gonzo <nf>, funny, rum <Brit nf>; **strange, outlandish, off-the-wall** <nf>, surreal, not for real <nf>, passing strange, "wondrous strange"— Shakespeare; **weird,** unearthly; off, out

12 **fantastic,** fantastical, fanciful, antic, **unbelievable** 955.10, **impossible, incredible,** logic-defying, incomprehensible, unimaginable, unexpected, unaccountable, inconceivable

13 **freakish,** freak *or* freaky <nf>; **monstrous, deformed,** malformed, misshapen, **misbegotten,** teratogenic, teratoid; **grotesque, bizarre,** bizarre <nf>, baroque, rococo

14 **extraordinary, exceptional, remarkable,** noteworthy, **wonderful, marvelous,** fabulous, mythical, legendary; **stupendous,** stupefying, prodigious, portentous, phenomenal; unprecedented, unexampled, unparalleled, not within the memory of man; indescribable, unspeakable, ineffable

15 **supernatural,** supranatural, **preternatural; supernormal,** hypernormal, preternormal, **paranormal; superphysical,** hyperphysical; numinous; supersensible, **supersensual,** pretersensual; **superhuman,** preterhuman, unhuman, nonhuman; **supramundane,** extramundane, transmundane, extraterrestrial; **unearthly, unworldly, otherworldly, eerie;** fey; psychical, **spiritual, occult; transcendental; mysterious,** arcane, esoteric

16 **miraculous, wondrous,** wonder-working, thaumaturgic *or* thaumaturgical, necromantic, **prodigious; magical,** enchanted, bewitched

ADVS 17 **unusually, uncommonly, incredibly, unnaturally,** abnormally, unordinarily, **uncustomarily,** unexpectedly; **rarely, seldom,** seldom if ever, once in a thousand years, hardly, hardly ever

18 **extraordinarily, exceptionally, remarkably, wonderfully, marvelously,** prodigiously,

fabulously, unspeakably, ineffably, phenomenally, stupendously

19 oddly, queerly, peculiarly, singularly, curiously, quaintly, **strangely,** outlandishly, **fantastically,** fancifully; **grotesquely, monstrously; eerily, mysteriously,** supernaturally

WORD ELEMENTS **20** terat-, terato-; medus-, medusi-, -pagus, anom-, anomo-, anomal-, anomalo-, anomali-, dys-, dis-, mal-, ne-, neo-, par-, para-, poly-, pseud-, pseudo-

21 mythical and imaginary monsters

abominable snowman *or* yeti	Loch Ness monster
Argus	manticore
basilisk	Medusa
Bigfoot *or* Sasquatch	mermaid
Briareus	merman
bucentur	Midgard serpent
Cacus	Minotaur
Caliban	Mylodont
centaur	nixie
Cerberus	ogre
Ceto	ogress
Charybdis	opinicus
chimera	Orthos *or* Orthros
cockatrice	Pegasus
Cyclops	Pongo
dipsas	Python
dragon	roc
drake <old>	Sagittary
Echidna	salamander
Erebus	Sarsquatch
Frankenstein	satyr
Geryon	Scylla
Gigantes	sea horse
Gorgon	sea serpent
green-eyed monster	simurgh *or* simurg
Grendel	siren
griffin	Sphinx
Harpy	Talos
hippocampus	troll
hippocentaur	Typhoeus
hippocerf	Typhon
hippogriff	unicorn
hircocervus	vampire
Hydra	werewolf
Jabberwock	windigo
Kraken	wivern *or* wyvern
Ladon	xiphopagus
Lamia	yowie
Leviathan	zombie

871 LIST

NOUNS **1 list, enumeration, itemization,** listing, shopping *or* grocery list; laundry list; want list *and* wish list; hit list *and* shit list *and* drop-dead list *and* enemies list <nf>; blacklist; to-do list; items,

schedule, agenda; register, registry, inventory, repertory, tally; database *and* data base; **spreadsheet,** electronic spreadsheet; **checklist;** tally sheet; active list, civil list <Brit>, retired list, sick list; waiting list; blacklist; short list; reading list; syllabus; A-list, B-list, etc

2 table, contents, table of contents; computer listing, menu; chart

3 catalog; classified catalog, *catalogue raisonné* <Fr>; **card catalog, bibliography,** finding list, handlist, reference list; filmography, discography; publisher's catalog *or* list; **file,** filing system, letter file, pigeonholes

4 dictionary, word list, **lexicon, glossary, thesaurus, Roget's, vocabulary,** terminology, nomenclator; promptorium, gradus; **gazetteer; almanac;** telephone directory, address book; book of lists

5 bill, statement, account, itemized account, invoice; ledger, books; **bill of fare, menu,** carte, wine list, dessert menu; **bill of lading,** manifest, waybill, docket

6 roll, roster, scroll, rota; **roll call,** muster, **census,** nose *or* head count <nf>, **poll,** questionnaire, returns, census report *or* returns; property roll, tax roll, cadastre; muster roll; checkroll, checklist; jury list *or* panel; calendar, docket, **agenda,** order of business; daybook, journal, agenda book, diary; **program,** dramatis personae, credits, lineup; honor roll, dean's list; timetable, schedule, itinerary, prospectus

7 index, listing, tabulation; **cataloging, itemization,** filing, card file, card index, Rolodex <trademark>, thumb index, indexing; **registration,** registry, enrollment

VERBS **8 list, enumerate, itemize, tabulate, catalog,** tally; **register,** post, enter, **enroll, book;** impanel; **file,** pigeonhole, classify; **index;** inventory; calendar; score, keep score; **schedule,** program, put on the agenda; diarize; short-list

ADJS **9 listed, enumerated, entered, itemized, cataloged,** tallied, inventoried; filed, **indexed, tabulated; scheduled,** programmed; put on the agenda; inventorial, glossarial, cadastral, classificatory, taxonomic; registered, recorded, noted

872 ONENESS
<state of being one>

NOUNS **1 oneness, unity, singleness,** singularity, **individuality,** identity, selfsameness; **particularity** 865; **uniqueness;** intactness, inviolability, purity, simplicity 798, irreducibility, **integrity,** integrality; **unification,** uniting, integration, fusion, combination 805; **solidification,** solidity, solidarity,

indivisibility, undividedness, **wholeness** 792.5;
univocity, organic unity; uniformity 781

2 **aloneness,** loneness, **loneliness, lonesomeness,**
soleness, singleness; **privacy,** solitariness, **solitude;**
separateness, aloofness, detachment, seclusion,
sequestration, **withdrawal, alienation,** standing *or*
moving *or* keeping apart, **isolation,** "splendid
isolation"—Sir William Goschen; celibacy, single
blessedness

3 **one, I, 1, unit,** ace, atom; monad; one and only,
none else, no other, nothing else, nought beside

4 **individual,** single, unit, **integer, entity,** singleton,
item, article, point, module; person, wight <old>,
persona, soul, body, warm body <nf>; **individuality,**
personhood; isolated case, single instance

VERBS 5 **unify,** reduce to unity, unitize, make one;
integrate, unite 805.3

6 **stand alone,** stand *or* move *or* keep apart, keep
oneself to oneself, withdraw, alienate *or* seclude *or*
sequester *or* isolate oneself, feel out of place;
individuate, become an individual; go solo, paddle
one's own canoe, do one's own thing <nf>

ADJS 7 **one, single, singular, individual, sole,**
unique, a certain, **solitary, lone;** exclusive;
integral, indivisible, irreducible, monadic,
monistic, unanalyzable, noncompound, atomic,
unitary, unitive, unary, undivided, solid, whole-
cloth, seamless, uniform 781.5, simple 798.6, whole
792.9; an, any, any one, either

8 alone, solitary, solo, *solus* <L>; isolated, insular,
apart, separate, separated, alienated, withdrawn,
aloof, standoffish, detached, removed; **lone, lonely,**
lonesome, lonely-hearts; **private,** reserved,
reticent, reclusive, shy, nonpublic, ungregarious;
friendless, kithless, homeless, rootless,
companionless, **unaccompanied,** unescorted,
unattended; **unaided,** unassisted, unabetted,
unsupported, unseconded; **single-handed,** solo,
one-man, one-woman, one-person

9 **sole, unique,** singular, absolute, unrepeated,
alone, lone, **only,** only-begotten, **one and only,** first
and last; odd, impair, unpaired, azygous; celibate

10 **unitary, integrated,** integral, integrant; **unified,**
united, rolled into one, composite

11 **unipartite,** unipart, **one-piece;** monadic *or*
monadal; **unilateral, one-sided;** unilateralist,
uniangulate, unibivalent, unibranchiate,
unicameral, unicellular, unicuspid, unidentate,
unidigitate; **unidimensional, unidirectional;**
uniflorous, unifoliate, unifoliolate, unigenital,
uniglobular, unilinear, uniliteral, unilobed,
unilobular, unilocular, unimodular, unimolecular,
uninuclear, uniocular, unisexual, unisex; unipolar,
univalent, univocal; one-size; monolingual,
monochromatic

12 **unifying, uniting,** unific; **combining,** combinative
805.5,7, combinatory; connective, connecting,
connectional; conjunctive 800.16, conjunctival;
coalescing, coalescent

ADVS 13 **singly, individually,** particularly, severally,
one by one, one at a time; **singularly,** in the
singular; **alone,** by itself, *per se* <L>; **by oneself,** by
one's lonesome <nf>, on one's own, under one's
own steam, **single-handedly, solo,** unaided;
separately, apart; **once** 848.6

14 **solely, exclusively, only,** merely, **purely,** simply;
entirely, wholly, totally; **integrally, indivisibly,**
irreducibly, unanalyzably, undividedly

873 DOUBLENESS

NOUNS 1 **doubleness, duality,** dualism, duplexity,
twoness; twofoldness, biformity; polarity;
conjugation, pairing, coupling, yoking; **doubling,**
duplication 874, twinning, bifurcation; **dichotomy,**
bisection 875, halving, splitting down the middle
or fifty-fifty; **duplicity,** two-facedness, double-
think, hypocrisy, Dr. Jekyll and Mr. Hyde; **irony,**
enantiosis, ambiguity, equivocation, equivocality,
ambivalence; Janus

2 **two,** 2, II, twain <old>; **couple, pair, matching**
pair, twosome, set of two, duo, duet, brace, team,
span, yoke, double harness; match, matchup,
mates; **couplet,** distich, double, doublet; duad,
dyad; the two, **both;** Darby and Joan; tandem

3 **deuce;** pair, doubleton; **craps** *and* **snake eyes**
<gambling>

4 **twins,** pair of twins <nf>, identical twins,
fraternal twins, exact mates, look-alikes, dead
ringers <nf>, mirror image, carbon copy,
Doppelganger, spit and image *or* spitting image;
Tweedledum and Tweedledee, Siamese twins;
Twin stars, Castor and Pollux, Gemini

VERBS 5 **double,** duplicate, replicate, dualize, twin;
halve, split down the middle *or* fifty fifty <nf>,
bifurcate, dichotomize, bisect, transect; team,
yoke, yoke together, span, double-team, double-
harness; **mate, match,** couple, conjugate; **pair,** pair
off, pair up, couple up, team up, match up, buddy
up <nf>; talk out of both sides of one's mouth at
once; square; copy, mirror, echo

ADJS 6 **two,** twain <old>; **dual, double,** duple, duplex,
doubled, twinned, duplicated, replicated,
dualized; **dualistic;** dyadic; duadic; biform;
bipartite, bipartisan, bilateral, either-or, two-
sided, double sided, binary; dichotomous;
bifurcated, bisected, dichotomized, split down the
middle *or* fifty fifty <nf>; twin, identical, matched,
twinned, duplicated; **two-faced,** duplicitous,
hypocritical, double-faced, Janus-like; second,

secondary; two-way, two-ply, dual-purpose,
two-dimensional

7 both, the two, the pair; for two, tête-à-tête,
à deux <Fr>

8 coupled, paired, yoked, yoked together, matched,
matched up, mated, paired off, paired up, teamed
up, buddied up <nf>; **bracketed;** conjugate,
conjugated; biconjugate, bigeminate; bijugate

PHRS **9** it takes two to tango *and* it's not a one-way
street <nf>

WORD ELEMENTS **10** ambi-, amph-, amphi-, bi-,
bin-, bis-, deut-, deuto-, deuter-, deutero-, di-, dis-,
didym-, didymo-, duo-, dyo-, gem-, twi-, zyg-,
zygo-

11 Scrabble words, acceptable two-letter

AA	IN
AB	IS
AD	IT
AE	JO
AG	KA
AH	KI
AI	LA
AL	LI
AM	LO
AN	MA
AR	ME
AS	MI
AT	MM
AW	MO
AX	MU
AY	MY
BA	NA
BE	NE
BI	NO
BO	NU
BY	OD
DE	OE
DO	OF
ED	OH
EF	OI
EH	OM
EL	ON
EM	OP
EN	OR
ER	OS
ES	OW
ET	OX
EX	OY
FA	PA
FE	PE
GO	PI
HA	QI
HE	RE
HI	SH
HM	SI
HO	SO
ID	TA
IF	TI

TO	WO
UH	XI
UM	XU
UN	YA
UP	YE
US	YO
UT	ZA
WE	

874 DUPLICATION

NOUNS **1 duplication, reduplication,** replication,
conduplication; **reproduction, repro** <nf>,
doubling; twinning, gemination, ingemination;
repetition 849, iteration, reiteration, echoing;
imitation 336, parroting; **copying** 336.1; **duplicate**
785.3

2 repeat, encore, repeat performance; echo; do-over,
retry

VERBS **3 duplicate,** dupe <nf>, ditto <nf>; **double,**
double up; multiply by two; twin, geminate,
ingeminate; **reduplicate, reproduce,** replicate,
redouble; **repeat** 849.7; **copy,** carbon-copy

ADJS **4 double, doubled, duplicate,** duplicated,
reproduced, replicated, cloned, twinned,
geminate, geminated, dualized

ADVS **5 doubly; twofold,** as much again, twice as
much; twice, two times

6 secondly, second, secondarily, **in the second place**
or instance

7 again, another time, **once more,** once again, over
again, yet again, *encore and bis* <Fr>; **anew,**
afresh, new, freshly, newly

WORD ELEMENTS **8** bi-, bis-, deuter-, deutero-, di-,
dis-, diphy-, diphyo-, dipl-, diplo-, diss-, disso-,
twi-

875 BISECTION

NOUNS **1 bisection,** halving, bipartition, bifidity;
dichotomy, halving, division, in half *or* **by two,**
splitting *or* dividing *or* cutting in two, splitting *or*
dividing fifty-fifty <nf>; subdivision; bifurcation,
forking, ramification, branching

2 half, moiety; hemisphere, semisphere, semicircle,
fifty percent; half-and-half *and* fifty-fifty <nf>

3 bisector, diameter, equator, halfway mark,
divider, partition 213.5, line of demarcation,
boundary 211.3

VERBS **4 bisect, halve, divide, in half** *or* **by two,**
transect, subdivide; cleave, fission, **divide** *or* split
or **cut in two,** share and share alike, go halfers *or*
go Dutch <nf>, **dichotomize;** bifurcate, fork,
ramify, branch

ADJS **5 half, part, partly, partial,** halfway

6 halved, bisected, divided; dichotomous; bifurcated, forked *or* forking, ramified, branched, branching; riven, **split,** cloven, cleft

7 bipartite, bifid, biform, bicuspid, biaxial, bicameral, binocular, binomial, binominal, biped, bipetalous, bipinnate, bisexual, bivalent, unibivalent

ADVS **8 in half,** in halves, **in two,** in twain, by two, down the middle; half-and-half *and* fifty-fifty <nf>; apart, asunder

WORD ELEMENTS **9** bi-, demi-, dich-, dicho-, hemi-, semi-, sesqui-

876 THREE

NOUNS **1 three, 3,** III, **trio,** trey, **threesome,** trialogue, set of three, tierce <cards>, leash, troika; **triad,** trilogy, trine, **trinity,** triunity, ternary, ternion; **triplet,** tercet, terzetto; trefoil, shamrock, clover; tripod, trivet; **triangle,** tricorn, trihedron, trident, trisul, triennium, trimester, trinomial, trionym, triphthong, triptych, triplopy, trireme, triseme, triskelion, triumvirate; triple crown, triple threat; trey *and* threespot <cards>, deuce-ace <dice>; triple-decker; menage a trois; hat trick

2 threeness, triplicity, triality, tripleness, trebleness, threefoldness; triunity, trinity

ADJS **3 three, triple,** triplex, trinal, trine, trial; triadic *or* triadical; triune, three-in-one, *tria juncta in uno* <L>; triform; treble; triangular, deltoid, fan-shaped; triannual; trifold

WORD ELEMENTS **4** tri-, ter-, ternati-

877 TRIPLICATION

NOUNS **1 triplication,** triplicity, trebleness, **threefoldness;** triplicate

VERBS **2 triplicate, triple, treble, multiply by three,** threefold; cube

ADJS **3 triple,** triplicate, **treble, threefold,** trifold, triplex, trinal, trine, tern, ternary, ternal, ternate; three-ply; trilogic *or* trilocial

4 third, tertiary

ADVS **5 triply, trebly,** trinely; **threefold; thrice,** three times, again and yet again

6 thirdly, in the third place

WORD ELEMENTS **7** cub-, cubo-, cubi-; ter-; tert-, trit-, trito-

878 TRISECTION

NOUNS **1 trisection,** tripartition, trichotomy, trifurcation

2 third, tierce, third part, one-third; *tertium quid* <L, a third something>

VERBS **3 trisect, divide in thirds** *or* **three,** third, trichotomize; trifurcate

ADJS **4 tripartite,** trisected, triparted, **three-parted,** trichotomous; three-sided, trihedral, trilateral; **three-dimensional;** three-forked, three-pronged, trifurcate; trident, tridental, tridentate, trifid; tricuspid; three-footed, tripodic, tripedal; trifoliate, trifloral, triflorate, triflorous, tripetalous, triadelphous, triarch; trimerous, 3-merous; three-cornered, tricornered, tricorn; trigonal, trigonoid; triquetrous, triquetral; trigrammatic, triliteral; *triangular,* triangulate, deltoid

879 FOUR

NOUNS **1 four, 4,** IV, tetrad, quatern, quaternion, quaternary, quaternity, **quartet, quadruplet, foursome;** quatre; Little Joe *and* Little Joe from Kokomo *and* Little Dick Fisher <gambling>; quadrennium; tetralogy; tetrapody; tetraphony, four-part diaphony; quadrille, square dance; quatrefoil *or* quadrifoil, four-leaf clover; tetragram, tetragrammaton; quadrangle, quad <nf>, rectangle; tetrahedron; tetragon, square; biquadrate; quadrinomial; quadrature, squaring; quadrilateral

2 fourness, quaternity, quadruplicity, fourfoldness

VERBS **3 square, quadrate,** form *or* make four; form fours *or* squares; **cube, dice**

ADJS **4 four;** foursquare; quaternary, quartile, quartic, quadric, quadratic; tetrad, tetradic; quadrinomial, biquadratic; tetractinal, four-rayed, **quadruped,** four-legged; quadrivalent, tetravalent; quadrilateral 278.9

WORD ELEMENTS **5** quadr-, quadri-, quadru-, tetr-, tetra-, tessar-, tessara-, tri-, trip-, tripl-, triplo-, tris-

880 QUADRUPLICATION

NOUNS **1 quadruplication,** quadruplicature, quadruplicity, fourfoldness

VERBS **2 quadruple, quadruplicate,** fourfold, form *or* make four, multiply by four; quadrate, biquadrate, quadruplex

ADJS **3 quadruplicate, quadruple,** quadraple, **quadruplex, fourfold,** four-ply, four-part, tetraploid, quadrigeminal, biquadratic

WORD ELEMENTS **4** quadr-, quadri, quadru-, quater-, tetr-, tetra-, tetrakis-

881 QUADRISECTION

NOUNS **1 quadrisection,** quadripartition, **quartering**

2 fourth, one-fourth, **quarter,** one-quarter, fourth part, twenty-five percent, twenty-five cents, two bits <old nf>; quartern; quart; farthing; quarto *or* 4to *or* 4°

VERBS **3 divide by four** *or* **into four; quadrisect, quarter**

ADJS **4 quadrisected, quartered,** quarter-cut; quadripartite, quadrifid, quadriform; quadrifoliate, quadrigeminal, quadripinnate, quadriplanar, quadriserial, quadrivial, quadrifurcate, quadrumanal *or* quadrumanous

5 fourth, quarter

ADVS **6 fourthly,** in the fourth place; quarterly, by quarters

882 FIVE AND OVER

NOUNS **1 five,** V, cinque <cards and dice>, Phoebe *and* Little Phoebe *and* fever <gambling>; quintet, fivesome, quintuplets, quints <nf>, cinquain, quincunx, pentad; fifth; **five dollars,** fiver *and* fin *and* finniff *and* five bucks <nf>; pentagon, pentahedron, pentagram; pentapody, pentameter, pentastich; pentarchy; Pentateuch; pentachord; pentathlon; five-pointed star, pentacle, pentalpha, mullet <heraldry>; five-spot <nf>; quinquennium

2 six, VI, sixie from Dixie *and* sister Hicks *and* Jimmy Hicks *and* Captain Hicks <gambling>, **half a dozen, sextet,** sestet, sextuplets, hexad; hexagon, hexahedron, hexagram, six-pointed star, estoile <heraldry>, Jewish star, star of David, *Magen David* <Heb>; hexameter, hexapody, hexastich; hexapod; hexarchy; Hexateuch; hexastyle; hexachord; six-shooter; sixth sense; six-pack

3 seven, VII, heptad, little natural <crapshooting>; septet, heptad; heptagon, heptahedron; heptameter, heptastich; septemvir, heptarchy; Septuagint, Heptateuch; heptachord; **week;** seven deadly sins; seven seas; Seven Wonders of the World

4 eight, VIII, ogdoad, eighter *or* Ada from Decatur <crapshooting>, Ada Ross *and* Ada Ross the stable hoss <gambling>; octad, octonary; octagon, octahedron; octastylos *or* oktostylos; octave, octavo *or* 8vo; octachord; octet *or* octal, octameter; Octateuch; piece of eight; Eightfold Path

5 nine, IX, niner <radio communication>, Nina from Carolina *and* Nina Ross the stable hoss *and* Nina Nina ocean liner <gambling>; ennead; nonagon *or* enneagon, enneahedron; novena; enneastylos; nine days' wonder

6 ten, X, Big Dick *and* Big Dick from Battle Creek <gambling>; decade; decagon, decahedron; decagram, decigram, decaliter, deciliter, decare, decameter, decimeter, decastere; decapod;

decastylos; decasyllable; decemvir, decemvirate, decurion; decennium, decennary; Ten Commandments *or* Decalogue; tithe; decathlon

7 <eleven to ninety> **eleven; twelve, dozen,** boxcar *and* boxcars <gambling>, duodecimo *or* twelvemo *or* 12mo, **teens; thirteen,** long dozen, baker's dozen; **fourteen,** two weeks, fortnight; **fifteen,** quindecima, quindene, quindecim, quindecennial; **sixteen,** sixteenmo *or* 16mo; **twenty, score; twenty-four,** four and twenty, two dozen, twenty-fourmo *or* 24mo; **twenty-five,** five and twenty, quarter of a hundred *or* century; thirty-two, thirty-twomo *or* 32mo; **forty,** twoscore, quadragenarian; **fifty,** L, half a hundred; **sixty,** sexagenary; Sexagesima; sexagenarian, threescore; **sixty-four,** sixty-fourmo *or* 64mo *or* sexagesimo-quarto; **seventy,** septuagenarian, threescore and ten; **eighty,** octogenarian, fourscore; **ninety,** nonagenarian, four-score and ten

8 hundred, century, C, one C <nf>; centennium, centennial, centenary; centenarian; cental, centigram, centiliter, centimeter, centare, centistere; hundredweight *or* cwt; hecatomb; centipede; centumvir, centumvirate, centurion; <120> great *or* long hundred; <144> gross; <150> sesquicentennial, sesquicentenary; <200> bicentenary, bicentennial; <300> tercentenary, tercentennial, etc

9 five hundred, D, five centuries; five C's <nf>

10 thousand, M, chiliad; **millennium;** G *and* grand *and* thou *and* yard <nf>; chiliagon, chiliahedron *or* chiliaüdron; chiliarchia *or* chiliarch; millepede; milligram, milliliter, millimeter, kilogram *or* kilo; kiloliter, kilometer; kilocycle, kilohertz; kilobyte; gigabyte; **ten thousand,** myriad; **one hundred thousand,** lakh <India>

11 million; ten million, crore <India>

12 billion, thousand million, milliard

13 trillion, quadrillion, quintillion, sextillion, septillion, octillion, nonillion, decillion, undecillion, duodecillion, tredecillion, quattuordecillion, quindecillion, sexdecillion, septendecillion, octodecillion, novemdecillion, vigintillion; googol, googolplex; zillion *and* jillion <nf>

14 <division into five *or* more parts> quinquesection, quinquepartition, sextipartition, etc; decimation, decimalization; fifth, sixth, etc; **tenth, tithe,** decima

VERBS **15** <divide by five, etc> quinquesect; decimalize

16 <multiply by five, etc> fivefold, sixfold, etc; quintuple, quintuplicate; sextuple, sextuplicate; centuple, centuplicate

ADJS **17 fifth,** quinary; **fivefold, quintuple,**
quintuplicate; quinquennial; quinquepartite,
pentadic, quinquefid; quincuncial, pentastyle;
pentad, pentavalent, quinquevalent; pentagonal

18 sixth, senary; **sixfold, sextuple;** sexpartite,
hexadic, sextipartite, hexapartite; hexagonal,
hexahedral, hexangular; hexad, hexavalent;
sextuplex, hexastyle; sexennial; hexatonic

19 seventh, septimal; **sevenfold, septuple,** septenary;
septempartite, heptadic, septemfid; heptagonal,
heptahedral, heptangular; heptamerous;
hebdomal

20 eighth, octonary; **eightfold, octuple;** octadic;
octal, octofid, octaploid; octagonal, octahedral,
octan, octangular; octosyllabic; octastyle

21 ninth, novenary, nonary; **ninefold, nonuple,**
enneadic; enneahedral, enneastyle, nonagonal

22 tenth, denary, **decimal,** tithe; **tenfold, decuple;**
decagonal, decahedral; decasyllabic; decennial

23 eleventh, undecennial, undecennary

24 twelfth, duodenary, duodenal; duodecimal

25 thirteenth, fourteenth, etc; eleventeenth,
umpteenth <nf>; in one's teens

26 twentieth, vicenary, vicennial, vigesimal,
vicesimal

27 sixtieth, sexagesimal, sexagenary

28 seventieth, septuagesimal, septuagenary

29 hundredth, centesimal, **centennial,** centenary,
centurial; **hundredfold, centuple,** centuplicate;
secular; centigrado

30 thousandth, millenary, **millennial; thousandfold**

31 millionth; billionth, quadrillionth, quintillionth,
etc

WORD ELEMENTS **32** pent-, penta-, pen-, quinqu-,
quinque-, quintquinti-; hex-, hexa-, sex-, sexi-,
sexti-; hept-, hepta-, sept-, septi-; oct-, octa-, octo-;
non-, nona-, ennea-; deca-, deka-, deci-; undec-,
hendec-, hendeca-; dodec-, dodeca-; icos-, icosa-,
icosi-, eicos-, eicosa-; cent-, centi-, hect-, hecto-,
hecato-, hecaton; kilo-, milli-; meg-, mega-,
micro-; giga-, nano-; pico-

883 PLURALITY

<more than one>

NOUNS **1 plurality,** pluralness; a greater number, a
certain number; **several,** some, a few 885.2, more;
plural number, the plural; compositeness,
nonsingleness, nonuniqueness; **pluralism** 782.1,
variety; numerousness 884

2 majority, plurality, more than half, the greater
number, the greatest number, **most,**
preponderance *or* preponderancy, greater *or*
better part, **bulk, mass;** lion's share

3 pluralization, plurification <old>

4 multiplication, multiplying, proliferation,
increase 251; duplication 874; multiple, multiplier,
multiplicand, product, factor; factorization,
exponentiation; multiplication table; lowest *or*
least common multiple, greatest common divisor,
highest *or* greatest common factor; prime factor,
submultiple, power, square, cube, fourth power,
exponent, index, square root, cube root, surd, root
mean square, factorial

VERBS **5 pluralize,** plurify <old>; raise to *or* make
more than one

6 multiply, proliferate, **increase** 251.4,6, duplicate
874.3

ADJS **7 plural,** pluralized, more than one, more,
several, severalfold; **some,** certain; not singular,
composite, nonsingle, nonunique; plurative
<logic>; **pluralistic** 782.3, various; many, beaucoup
<nf>, numerous 884.6

8 multiple, multiplied, multifold, **manifold** 884.6;
increased 251.7; multinomial *and* polynomial
<mathematics>

9 majority, most, the greatest number

ADVS **10 in the majority;** and others, et al, et cetera
253.14; plurally

WORD ELEMENTS **11** multi-; -fold

884 NUMEROUSNESS

NOUNS **1 numerousness, multiplicity, manyness,**
manifoldness, multifoldness, multitudinousness,
multifariousness, teemingness, swarmingness,
rifeness, profuseness, profusion; **plenty,**
abundance 991.2; **countlessness,** innumerability,
infinitude, infinity

2 <indefinite number> **a number,** a certain number,
one or two, two or three, **a few, several,** parcel,
passel <nf>; eleventeen *and* umpteen <nf>; lots

3 <large number> **multitude, throng** 770.4; a many,
numbers, quantities, lots 247.4, flocks, **scores,**
scads, oodles; an abundance of, all kinds *or* sorts
of, no end of, quite a few, tidy sum; muchness, any
number of, **large amount; host, army,** more than
one can shake a stick at, fistful *and* slew *and*
shitload *and* shithouse full <nf>, legion, rout,
ruck, mob, jam, clutter; **swarm, flock** 770.5, flight,
cloud, hail, bevy, covey, shoal, hive, nest, pack,
litter, bunch 770.7; a world of, a mass of, worlds of,
masses of; small fortune

4 <immense number> **a myriad,** a thousand, **a**
thousand and one, *a lakh* <India>, *a crore* <India>,
a million, a billion, a quadrillion, a nonillion, etc
882.13; umpteen, a zillion *or* jillion *or* gazillion *or*
bazillion <nf>; googol, googolplex

VERBS **5 teem with,** overflow with, **abound with,**
burst with, bristle with, pullulate with, **swarm**

with, throng with, creep with, **crawl with, be alive with, have coming out of one's ears** *and* **have up the gazoo** *and* **kazoo** <nf>; clutter, crowd, jam, pack, overwhelm, overflow; multiply 883.6; outnumber; overcrowd

ADJS **6 numerous, many, manifold,** not a few, no few; **very many,** full many, **ever so many,** considerable *and* quite some <nf>, quite a few; **multitudinous,** multitudinal, multifarious, multifold, multiple, **myriad,** thousand, million, billion; zillion *and* jillion <nf>; heaped-up; numerous as the stars, numerous as the sands, numerous as the hairs on the head

7 several, divers, **sundry,** various; fivish, sixish, etc; some five *or* six, etc; upwards of

8 abundant, copious, ample, plenteous, **plentiful** 991.7, thick on the ground <Brit>

9 teeming, swarming, crowding, thronging, overflowing, overcrowded, overwhelming, bursting, **crawling, alive with,** lousy with <nf>, populous, prolific, proliferating, crowded, packed, jammed, bumper-to-bumper <nf>, jam-packed, like sardines in a can <nf>, thronged, studded, bristling, rife, lavish, prodigal, superabundant, **profuse,** in profusion, thick, **thick with,** thick-coming, thick as hail *or* flies

10 innumerable, numberless, unnumbered, countless, uncounted, **uncountable,** unquantifiable, unreckonable, untold, incalculable, immeasurable, unmeasured, measureless, inexhaustible, endless, infinite, without end *or* limit, more than one can tell, more than you can shake a stick at <nf>, no end of *or* to; countless as the stars *or* sands; **astronomical,** galactic; millionfold, trillionfold, etc

11 and many more, *cum multis aliis* <L>, and what not, and heaven knows what

ADVS **12 numerously,** multitudinously, **profusely,** swarmingly, teemingly, thickly, copiously, **abundantly, prodigally; innumerably,** countlessly, infinitely, incalculably, inexhaustibly, immeasurably; in throngs, in crowds, in swarms, in heaps, *acervatim* <L>; **no end** <nf>

WORD ELEMENTS **13** multi-, myri-, myrio-, pluri-, poly-

885 FEWNESS

NOUNS **1 fewness,** infrequency, **sparsity,** sparseness, **scarcity, paucity, scantiness, meagerness,** miserliness, niggardliness, tightness, thinness, stringency, restrictedness; chintziness *and* chinchiness *and* stinginess <nf>; scrimpiness *and* skimpiness <nf>; **rarity,** exiguity; smallness 258.1; unsubstantiality *or* insubstantiality; skeleton staff

2 a few, too few, mere *or* piddling *or* piddly few, only a few, **small number,** limited *or* piddling *or* piddly number, not enough to count *or* matter, not enough to shake a stick at, **handful, scattering,** corporal's guard, sprinkling, trickle; low *or* poor turnout, too few to mention

3 minority, least; the minority, the few; minority group; "we happy few"—Shakespeare; minimum; less, least

ADJS **4 few, not many;** hardly *or* scarcely any, precious little *or* few, of small number, to be counted on one's fingers, too few

5 sparse, scant, **scanty,** exiguous, **infrequent,** sporadic, scarce, scarce as hen's teeth <nf>, poor, piddling, piddly, thin, slim, **meager,** not much; miserly, niggardly, cheeseparing, tight; chintzy *and* chinchy *and* stingy <nf>, scrimpy *and* skimpy <nf>, skimping *and* scrimping <nf>; **scattered,** sprinkled, spotty, **few and far between; rare,** seldom met with, seldom seen, not thick on the ground <Brit>

6 fewer, less, smaller, not so much *or* many, reduced, minimal

7 minority, least

ADVS **8 sparsely,** *sparsim* <L>, **scantily, meagerly,** exiguously, piddlingly; stingily *and* scrimpily *and* skimpily <nf>, thinly; **scarcely,** rarely, infrequently; **scatteringly,** scatterdly, spottily, in dribs and drabs *and* in bits and pieces <nf>, here and there, in places, in spots

886 CAUSE

NOUNS **1 cause, occasion,** antecedents, **grounds,** ground, background, backstory, stimulus, base, **basis,** element, principle, factor; **determinant,** determinative; causation, causality, cause and effect, karma; etiology

2 reason, reason why, rationale, reason for *or* behind, underlying reason, rational ground, **explanation,** answer, **the why,** the wherefore, the whatfor *or* whyfor <nf>, **the why and wherefore,** the idea <nf>, the big idea <nf>; stated cause, pretext, pretense, excuse

3 immediate cause, proximate cause, trigger, spark; **domino effect,** causal sequence, chain *or* nexus of cause and effect, ripple effect, slippery slope, contagion effect, knock-on *or* knock-on effect <chiefly Brit>; transient cause, occasional cause; formal cause; efficient cause; ultimate cause, immanent cause, remote cause, causing cause, *causa causans* <L>, first cause; **final cause,** *causa finalis* <L>, **end,** end in view, teleology; provocation, **last straw,** straw that broke the camel's back, match in the powder barrel;

butterfly effect *or* strange attraction *or* sensitive dependence on initial conditions; planetary influence, astrological influence

4 author, agent, **originator,** generator, begetter, engenderer, producer, maker, beginner, **creator,** mover, inventor; **parent, mother, father,** sire; **prime mover,** *primum mobile* <L>; causer, effector; inspirer, instigator, catalyst, mobilizer; motivator, inspiration

5 source, origin, genesis, original, origination, **derivation, rise, beginning,** conception, inception, commencement, **head;** provenance, provenience, background; **root,** radix, radical, taproot, grass roots; stem, stock; etymology

6 fountainhead, headwater, headstream, riverhead, springhead, headspring, **mainspring,** wellspring, wellhead, well, **spring, fountain,** fount, font, *fons et origo* <L>; mine, quarry

7 vital force *or* **principle,** *élan vital* <Fr>, reproductive urge, a gleam in one's father's eye <nf>; **egg,** ovum 305.12, **germ,** germen <old>, spermatozoon 305.11, nucleus 305.7, **seed; embryo** 305.14; bud 310.23; loins; **womb,** matrix, uterus

8 birthplace, breeding place, breeding ground, birthsite, rookery, hatchery; **hotbed,** forcing bed; incubator, brooder; **nest,** nidus; **cradle,** nursery

9 <a principle *or* **movement> cause, principle,** interest, issue, burning issue, commitment, faith, great cause, lifework; reason for being, *raison d'être* <Fr>; **movement,** mass movement, activity; **drive, campaign, crusade;** zeal, passion, fanaticism

VERBS **10 cause,** be the cause of, lie at the root of; **bring about, bring to pass,** effectuate, **effect,** bring to effect, realize; **impact,** impact on, influence; **occasion, make, create, engender,** generate, **produce,** breed, work, do; **originate,** give origin to, give occasion to, **give rise to,** spark, spark off, set off, trigger, trigger off; **give birth to, beget,** bear, bring forth, labor *or* travail and bring forth, author, **father,** sire, sow the seeds of; gestate, **conceive,** have the idea, have a bright idea <nf>; set up, set afloat, **set on foot;** found, establish, inaugurate, institute; engineer

11 induce, lead, procure, get, obtain, contrive, **effect,** bring, **bring on,** draw on, **call forth, elicit, evoke, provoke,** inspire, influence, instigate, egg on, **motivate;** draw down, open the door to; suborn; superinduce; incite, kindle

12 determine, decide, turn the scale, have the last word, tip the scale; **necessitate,** entail, require; contribute to, have a hand in, lead to, conduce to; **advance, forward,** influence, subserve; **spin off,** hive off <Brit>

ADJS **13 causal,** causative; chicken-and-egg <nf>; occasional; originative, institutive, constitutive;

at the bottom of, behind the scenes; **formative,** determinative, effectual, decisive, pivotal; etiological

14 original, primary, primal, primitive, pristine, primo <nf>, primeval, aboriginal, **elementary,** elemental, **basic,** basal, **rudimentary,** crucial, central, radical, **fundamental;** embryonic, in embryo, *in ovo* <L>, germinal, seminal, pregnant; **generative,** genetic, protogenic; effectual

WORD ELEMENTS **15** uter-, utero-, metr-, metro-, -metrium, venter; etio-, aetio-, prot-, proto-; -facient, -factive, -fic, -ic, -ical, -etic

887 EFFECT

NOUNS **1 effect, result,** resultant, **consequence,** consequent, sequent, sequence, sequel, sequela, sequelae; event, eventuality, eventuation, **upshot, outcome,** logical outcome, possible outcome, scenario; **outgrowth,** spin-off, offshoot, offspring, issue, aftermath, legacy; side effect; **product** 893, precipitate, distillate, **fruit,** first fruits, crop, harvest, payoff; development, corollary; derivative, derivation, by-product; net result, end result; karma

2 impact, force, **repercussion,** reaction; backwash, backlash, reflex, recoil, response; mark, print, imprint, impress, impression; significance, import, meaning

3 aftereffect, aftermath, aftergrowth, aftercrop, **afterclap,** aftershock, afterimage, afterglow, aftertaste; wake, trail, track; domino effect

VERBS **4 result, ensue, issue, follow,** attend, accompany; **turn out, come out,** fall out, redound, **work out,** pan out <nf>, fare; have a happy result, turn out well, come up roses <nf>; turn out to be, prove, prove to be; **become of,** come of, come about; **develop,** unfold; **eventuate,** terminate, end; **end up,** land up <Brit>, come out, wind up

5 result from, be the effect of, be due to, originate in *or* from, **come from,** come out of, grow from, **grow out of,** follow from *or* on, proceed from, descend from, emerge from, issue from, ensue from, emanate from, flow from, **derive from,** accrue from, rise *or* arise from, take its rise from, **spring from, stem from,** sprout from, bud from, germinate from; **spin off; depend on,** hinge *or* pivot *or* turn on, hang on, be contingent on; pay off, bear fruit

ADJS **6 resultant, resulting, following, ensuing; consequent,** consequential, following, sequent, sequential, sequacious; necessitated, entailed, required; **final;** derivative, derivational

ADVS **7 consequently, as a result,** as a consequence, in consequence, in the event, naturally, *naturellement* <Fr>, necessarily, of necessity, inevitably, of course, as a matter of course, and so, it follows that; **therefore; accordingly** 766.11; **finally**

CONJS **8 resulting from,** coming from, arising from, deriving *or* derivable from, consequent to, in consequence of; **owing to, due to;** attributed *or* attributable to, dependent *or* contingent on; **caused by,** occasioned by, **at the bottom of;** required by, entailed by, following from, following strictly from

PHRS **9** one thing leads to another, *post hoc, ergo propter hoc* <L>, what goes up must come down <nf>, what goes around comes around <nf>

888 ATTRIBUTION
<assignment of cause>

NOUNS **1 attribution, assignment,** assignation, **ascription, imputation,** arrogation, placement, application, attachment, saddling, **charge, blame; indictment; responsibility,** answerability; **credit,** honor; accounting for, reference to, derivation from, connection with; guilt by association; etiology

2 acknowledgment, citation, tribute; confession; **reference;** trademark, signature; **by-line,** credit line

VERBS **3 attribute, assign, ascribe, impute,** give, place, put, apply, attach, refer

4 attribute to, ascribe to, impute to, assign to, **lay to,** put *or* set down to, apply to, refer to, point to; **pin on,** pinpoint <nf>, fix on *or* upon, attach to, accrete to, connect with, fasten upon, hang on <nf>, **saddle on *or* upon,** place upon, **father upon,** settle upon, saddle with; blame, **blame for,** blame on *or* upon, charge on *or* upon, place *or* put the blame on, place the blame *or* responsibility for, indict, **fix the responsibility for,** point to one, put the finger on *and* finger <nf>, fix the burden of, **charge to,** lay to one's charge, place to one's account, set to the account of, account for, lay at the door of, bring home to; acknowledge, confess; **credit *or* accredit with;** put words in one's mouth

5 trace to, follow the trail to; **derive from,** trace the origin *or* derivation of; affiliate to, filiate to, father, fix the paternity of

ADJS **6 attributable, assignable, ascribable, imputable,** traceable, referable, accountable, explicable; owing, **due,** assigned *or* referred to, derivable from, derivative, derivational; **charged,** alleged, imputed, putative; **credited, attributed**

ADVS **7 hence, therefore,** therefor, **wherefore,** wherefrom, whence, then, thence, *ergo* <L>, for

which reason; **consequently** 887.7; **accordingly** 766.11; **because of that,** for that, by reason of that, for that reason, for the reason that, in consideration of something, from *or* for that cause, **on that account,** on that ground, thereat; **because of this, on this account,** for this cause, on account of this, *propter hoc* <L>, for this reason, hereat; thus, thusly <nf>, thuswise; on someone's head, on *or* at someone's doorstep

8 why, whyever, whyfor *and* for why <nf>, how come <nf>, how is it that, **wherefore, what for,** for which, **on what account,** on account of what *or* which, for what *or* whatever reason, from what cause, *pourquoi* <Fr>

PREPS **9 because of,** by reason of, **as a result of,** by *or* in virtue of, **on account of,** on the score of, for the sake of, **owing to, due to,** thanks to; **considering,** in consideration of, **in view of;** after

CONJS **10 because,** *parce que* <Fr>, **since,** as, for, **whereas, inasmuch as, forasmuch as, insofar as, insomuch as,** as things go; in that, for the cause that, for the reason that, in view of the fact that, taking into account that, **seeing that,** seeing as how <nf>, being as how <nf>; **resulting from** 887.8

889 OPERATION

NOUNS **1 operation, functioning, action, performance,** performing, **working, work,** workings, exercise, practice; agency; implementation; operations; **management** 573, **direction, conduct, running, carrying-on** *or* **-out,** execution, seeing to, overseeing, oversight; **handling,** manipulation; responsibility 641.2; **occupation** 724; joint operation

2 process, procedure, proceeding, course; what makes it tick; **act,** step, measure, initiative, *démarche* <Fr>, move, maneuver, motion

3 workability, operability, operativeness, performability, negotiability <nf>, manageability, compassability, manipulatability, maneuverability; **practicability, feasibility,** viability

4 operator, operative, operant; **handler,** manipulator; **manager** 574.1, **executive** 574.3; functionary, agent; driver

VERBS **5 operate, function, run, work; manage, direct** 573.8, **conduct; carry on** *or* **out** *or* **through,** make go *or* work, carry the ball <nf>, perform; **handle,** manipulate, maneuver; deal with, see to, take care of; occupy oneself 724.10; be responsible for 641.6

6 operate on, **act on** or **upon, work on, affect, influence,** bear on, impact, impact on; have to do with, treat, focus or concentrate on; bring to bear on

7 <be operative> **operate, function, work, act, perform, go, run,** be in action or operation or commission; percolate and perk and tick <nf>; be effective, go into effect, have effect, take effect, militate; be in force; have play, have free play

8 **function as,** work as, **act as,** act or play the part of, have the function or role or job or mission of; do one's thing <nf>

ADJS **9** **operative, operational,** go <nf>, **functional, practical,** in working order; **effective,** effectual, efficient, efficacious; relevant, significant

10 **workable, operable,** operatable, **performable,** actable, **doable,** manageable, compassable, negotiable, manipulatable, maneuverable; **practicable, feasible,** practical, viable, useful

11 **operating, operational, working, functioning,** operant, functional, acting, active, running, **going,** going on, ongoing; **in operation,** in action, **in practice, in force,** in play, in exercise, at work, on foot; **in process,** in the works, on the fire, in the pipe or pipeline <nf>, in hand, up and going

12 operational, functional; **managerial** 573.12; agential, agentive or agentival; manipulational

WORD ELEMENTS **13** -age, -al, -ance, -ence, -ation, -ing, -ion, -ism, -ization, -isation, -ment, -osis, -sis, -th, -ure

890 PRODUCTIVENESS

NOUNS **1** **productiveness, productivity,** productive capacity; **fruitfulness,** fructification, procreativeness, progenitiveness, **fertility,** fecundity, fecundation, prolificness, prolificity, prolificacy; **pregnancy; luxuriance, exuberance,** generousness, bountifulness, plentifulness, plenteousness, richness, lushness, **abundance** 991.2, superabundance, copiousness, teemingness, swarmingness, uberty; teeming womb or loins

2 proliferation, multiplication, fructification, pullulation, teeming; **reproduction** 78, **production** 892

3 **fertilization, enrichment,** fecundation; propagation, pollination; insemination; impregnation 78.3

4 **fertilizer,** dressing, top dressing, enricher, richener, procreator, propagator; organic fertilizer, manure, muck, mulch, night soil, dung, guano, compost, leaf litter, leaf mold, humus, peat moss, castor-bean meal, bone meal, fish meal; commercial fertilizer, inorganic fertilizer, chemical fertilizer, phosphate,

superphosphate, ammonia, nitrogen, nitrate, potash, ammonium salts, sulfate, lime, marl

5 <goddesses of fertility> Demeter, Ceres, Isis, Astarte or Ashtoreth, Venus of Willenburg; <gods> Frey, Priapus, Dionysus, Pan, Baal; fertility cult

6 <comparisons> rabbit, Hydra, warren, seed plot, hotbed, rich soil, land flowing with milk and honey

VERBS **7** **produce, be productive, proliferate,** pullulate, fructify, be fruitful, **multiply,** procreate, propagate, generate, multiply, mushroom, spin off, hive off <Brit>, engender, beget, teem; **reproduce** 78.7,8

8 **fertilize, enrich,** make fertile, richen, fatten, feed; fructify, fecundate, fecundify, prolificate; inseminate, impregnate 78.10; pollinate, germinate, seed; cross-fertilize, cross-pollinate; dress, top-dress; manure, compost, feed, mulch, marl

ADJS **9** **productive, fruitful,** fructiferous, fecund; **fertile, pregnant,** seminal, **rich,** flourishing, thriving, blooming; **prolific,** proliferous, uberous, **teeming,** swarming, bursting, bursting out, plenteous, **plentiful,** copious, generous, bountiful, **abundant** 991.7, **luxuriant, exuberant, lush,** superabundant; creative

10 **bearing, yielding, producing;** fruitbearing, fructiferous

11 **fertilizing, enriching,** richening, fattening, fecundatory, fructificative, **seminal,** germinal

891 UNPRODUCTIVENESS

NOUNS **1** **unproductiveness,** unproductivity, ineffectualness 19.3; **unfruitfulness,** fruitlessness, **barrenness,** nonfruition, dryness, aridity, dearth, famine; sterileness, **sterility,** unfertileness, **infertility,** infecundity; wasted or withered loins, dry womb; **birth control, contraception,** family planning, planned parenthood; abortion; impotence 19, incapacity

2 **wasteland, waste,** desolation, barren or **barrens,** barren land; heath; **desert,** Sahara, sands, desert sands, karroo <Africa>, badlands, dust bowl, salt flat, Death Valley, Arabia Deserta, lunar waste or landscape; desert island; wilderness, howling wilderness, **wild, wilds;** treeless plain; bush, brush, outback <Austral>; fallowness, aridness; desertification, desertization

VERBS **3** be unproductive, **come to nothing,** come to naught, prove infertile, hang fire <nf>, flash in the pan, fizzle or peter out <nf>; **lie fallow;** stagnate, run to seed

ADJS **4** **unproductive,** nonproductive or nonproducing; **infertile, sterile,** unfertile or nonfertile, **unfruitful,** unfructuous, acarpous <botany>, infecund, unprolific or nonprolific; **impotent,** gelded 19.19; **ineffectual** 19.15; **barren, desert, arid,** dry, dried-up, sere, exhausted, drained, leached, sucked dry, wasted, gaunt, **waste, desolate,** jejune; **childless,** issueless, without issue, *sine prole* <L>; fallow, unplowed, unsown, untilled, uncultivated, unfecundated; celibate; virgin; menopausal

5 **uncreative,** noncreative, nonseminal, nongerminal, unfructified, unpregnant; uninventive, unoriginal, derivative

892 PRODUCTION

NOUNS 1 **production, creation, making, origination, invention, conception,** innovation, originating, engenderment, engendering, genesis, beginning; **devising,** hatching, fabrication, **concoction,** coinage, mintage, **contriving,** contrivance; **authorship;** creative effort, **generation** 78.6; improvisation, making do; **gross national product** or **GNP,** net national product or NNP, national production of goods and services

2 **production, manufacture** or **manufacturing, making, producing,** devising, design, fashioning, framing, forming, formation, formulation; engineering, tooling-up; processing, conversion; casting, **shaping,** molding; machining, milling, finishing; **assembly,** composition, elaboration; **workmanship, craftsmanship, skill** 413; **construction, building,** erection, architecture; **fabrication,** prefabrication; handiwork, handwork, handicraft, crafting; **mining,** extraction, smelting, **refining; growing,** cultivation, **raising,** harvesting

3 **industrial production, industry, mass production,** volume production, **assembly-line production;** production line, assembly line; modular production or assembly, standardization; division of labor, industrialization; heavy industry; light industry; **cottage industry;** piecework, farmed-out work

4 **establishment, foundation,** constitution, institution, installation, formation, **organization,** inauguration, **inception, setting-up,** realization, materialization, effectuation; spinning-off, hiving-off <Brit>

5 **performance, execution, doing, accomplishment, achievement,** productive effort or effect, realization, bringing to fruition, fructification, effectuation, operation 889; overproduction, glut; underproduction, scarcity; **productiveness** 890, fructuousness

6 **bearing, yielding, birthing; fruition,** fruiting, fructification

7 **producer, maker,** craftsman, wright, smith; **manufacturer,** industrialist; **creator,** begetter, engenderer, **author,** mother, **father,** sire; **ancestors** 560.7; **precursor** 816; **originator,** initiator, establisher, inaugurator, introducer, institutor, beginner, mover, prime mover, motive force, instigator; **founder,** organizer, founding father, founding or founder member, founding partner, cofounder; **inventor,** discoverer, deviser; developer; engineer; **builder,** constructor, artificer, **architect,** planner, **conceiver,** designer, **shaper,** master or leading spirit; executor, executrix; facilitator, animator; **grower,** raiser, cultivator; effector, realizer; **apprentice, journeyman, master,** master craftsman or workman, artist, past master

VERBS 8 **produce, create, make, manufacture, form,** formulate, evolve, mature, elaborate, fashion, **fabricate,** prefabricate, cast, shape, configure, carve out, mold, extrude, frame; **construct, build,** erect, put up, set up, run up, raise, rear; make up, get up, prepare, compose, write, indite, devise, design, concoct, compound, churn out and crank out and pound out and hammer out and grind out and rustle up and gin up <nf>; **put together, assemble,** piece together, patch together, whomp up and fudge together and slap up or together <nf>, improvise 365.8; **make to order,** custom-make, custom-build, purpose-build <Brit>

9 **process,** convert 858.11; mill, machine; carve, chisel; **mine,** extract, pump, smelt, **refine; raise,** rear, **grow,** cultivate, harvest

10 **establish, found,** constitute, institute, install, form, **set up, organize,** equip, endow, inaugurate, realize, materialize, effect, effectuate

11 **perform, do,** work, act, execute, **accomplish, achieve** 407.4, **deliver,** come through with, realize, engineer, effectuate, **bring about,** bring to fruition or into being, cause; mass-produce, volume-produce, industrialize; overproduce; underproduce; **be productive** 890.7

12 **originate, invent, conceive,** discover, **make up, devise, contrive,** concoct, fabricate, coin, mint, frame, hatch, hatch or cook up, strike out; improvise, make do with; think up, think out, dream up, **design,** plan, formulate, set one's wits to work; **generate, develop,** mature, **evolve;** breed, engender, beget, spawn, hatch; bring forth, give rise to, give being to, bring or call into being; procreate 78.8

13 **bear, yield, produce,** furnish; **bring forth,** usher into the world; fruit, **bear fruit,** fructify; spawn

ADJS 14 **productional, creational,** formational;

executional; **manufacturing,** manufactural, fabricational, **industrial,** smokestack

15 **constructional, structural,** building, housing, edificial; **architectural,** architectonic

16 **creative, originative,** causative, **productive** 890.9, **constructive,** formative, fabricative, demiurgic; inventive; generative 78.16

17 **produced, made, caused, brought about;** effectuated, executed, performed, done; grown, raised

18 **made,** man-made; **manufactured,** created, crafted, formed, shaped, molded, cast, forged, machined, milled, fashioned, **built, constructed,** fabricated; **mass-produced,** volume-produced, assembly-line; **well-made,** well-built, well-constructed; **homemade,** homestyle, homespun, **handmade,** handcrafted, handicrafted, self-made, DIY *or* do it yourself; machine-made; **processed; assembled,** put together; **custom-made,** custom-built, purpose-built <Brit>, custom, made to order, bespoke; **ready-made,** ready-formed, ready-prepared, ready-to-wear, ready-for-wear, off-the-shelf, off-the-rack; prefabricated, prefab <nf>; **mined,** extracted, smelted, **refined; grown, raised,** harvested, gathered

19 **invented,** originated, **conceived,** discovered, newfound; fabricated, coined, minted, new-minted; **made-up,** made out of whole cloth

20 **manufacturable, producible,** productible

ADVS 21 **in production;** in the works, in hand, on foot; under construction; in the pipeline; on-line

893 PRODUCT

NOUNS 1 **product,** end product, production, manufacture, wares; **work,** œuvre <Fr>, **handiwork, artifact; creation;** creature; **offspring,** child, fruit, fruit of one's loins; **result, effect** 887, issue, outgrowth, outcome; **invention,** origination, coinage, mintage *or* new mintage, brainchild; **concoction,** composition; opus, opuscule; apprentice work; journeyman work; **masterwork, masterpiece,** chef d'œuvre <Fr>, *Meisterstück* <Ger>, work of an artist *or* a master *or* a past master, crowning achievement; piece of work; gross national product 892.1

2 **production,** produce, proceeds, net, **yield, output,** throughput; **crop,** harvest, take <nf>, return, bang <nf>

3 **extract, distillation,** essence; **by-product,** secondary *or* incidental product, spin-off, outgrowth, offshoot; **residue,** leavings, waste, waste product, industrial waste, solid waste, lees, dregs, ash, slag

4 <amount made> make, making; batch, lot, run, boiling

894 INFLUENCE

NOUNS 1 **influence,** influentiality; **power** 18, force, clout <nf>, potency, pressure, effect, indirect *or* incidental power, **say,** the final say, the last word, say-so *and* a lot to do with *or* to say about <nf>, veto power; **prestige,** favor, good feeling, credit, esteem, repute, personality, leadership, charisma, magnetism, charm, enchantment; **weight,** moment, consequence, importance, eminence; **authority** 417, control, domination, hold; **sway** 612.1, reign, rule; **mastery,** ascendancy, supremacy, dominance, predominance, preponderance; upper hand, whip hand, trump card; leverage, purchase; **persuasion** 375.3, suasion, suggestion, subtle influence, insinuation

2 **favor,** special favor, **interest; pull** *and* drag *and* suction <nf>; **connections,** the right people, inside track <nf>; amicus curiae

3 **backstairs influence,** intrigues, deals, schemes, **games,** Machiavellian *or* Byzantine intrigues, ploys, sway; **wires** *and* **strings** *and* ropes <nf>; **wire-pulling** <nf>; **influence peddling;** lobby, lobbying, lobbyism; Big Brother

4 **sphere of influence,** orbit, ambit; bailiwick, vantage, stamping ground, footing, **territory,** turf, home turf, constituency, **power base,** niche

5 **influenceability,** swayableness, movability; **persuadability,** persuadableness, persuasibility, suasibility, openness, open-mindedness, get-at-ableness <Brit nf>, perviousness, accessibility, receptiveness, responsiveness, amenableness; **suggestibility, susceptibility,** impressionability, malleability; weakness 16; putty in one's hands

6 <influential person *or* thing> **influence,** good influence; bad influence, sinister influence; **person** *or* **woman** *or* **man of influence,** an influential, an affluential, a presence, a palpable presence, a mover and shaker <nf>, a person to be reckoned with, a player *or* player on the scene, major player; heavyweight, big wheel *and* biggie *and* heavy *or* big *or* long-ball hitter *and* piledriver *and* big fish in a small pond <nf>, very important person *or* VIP <nf>, big shot *or* bigwig *or* big cheese *or* big kahuna <nf>; wheeler-dealer <nf>, influencer, **wire-puller** <nf>; **powerbroker; power behind the throne,** gray eminence, éminence grise <Fr>, hidden hand, manipulator, friend at *or* in court, kingmaker; **influence peddler,** five-percenter, lobbyist; Svengali, Rasputin; **pressure group,** special-interest group, special interests, single-issue group, PAC *or* political action committee;

lobby; the Establishment, big government; ingroup, court, powers that be 575.15, superpower, lords of creation; **key,** key to the city, access, open sesame

VERBS **7 influence,** make oneself felt, **affect,** weigh with, **sway,** bias, bend, incline, dispose, predispose, **move,** prompt, lead; color, tinge, tone, slant, impart spin; **induce, persuade** 375.23, jawbone *and* twist one's arm *and* hold one's feet to the fire <nf>, work, work *or* bend to one's will; lead by the nose <nf>, wear down, soften up; win friends and influence people, ingratiate oneself

8 <exercise influence over> **govern** 612.11, **rule, control** 612.12, order, **regulate,** direct, guide; **determine,** decide, dispose; have the say *or* say-so, have veto power over, have the last word, call the shots *and* be in the driver's seat *and* wear the pants <nf>; charismatize

9 exercise *or* **exert influence, use one's influence, bring pressure to bear upon,** lean on <nf>, act on, **work on,** bear upon, throw one's weight around *or* into the scale, say a few words to the right person *or* in the right quarter; charismatize; draw, draw on, lead on, magnetize; **approach,** go up to with hat in hand, make advances *or* overtures, make up to *or* get cozy with <nf>; get at *or* get the ear of <nf>; **pull strings** *or* **wires** *or* **ropes,** wire-pull <nf>; lobby, lobby through; wheel and deal <nf>

10 have influence, be influential, carry weight, weigh, tell, count, cut ice, throw a lot of weight <nf>, have a lot to do with *or* say about <nf>; be the decisive factor *or* the one that counts, have pull *or* suction *or* drag *or* leverage <nf>; have a way with one, have personality *or* magnetism *or* charisma, charm the birds out of the trees, charm the pants off one <nf>, be persuasive; have an in <nf>, have the inside track <nf>; have full play; have friends in high places

11 have influence *or* power *or* a hold over, have pull *or* clout with <nf>; **lead by the nose, twist** *or* **turn** *or* **wind around one's little finger,** have in one's pocket, keep under one's thumb, make sit up and beg *or* lie down and roll over; hypnotize, mesmerize, **dominate** 612.14

12 gain influence, **get in with** <nf>, ingratiate oneself with, get cozy with <nf>; make peace, **mend fences;** gain a footing, take hold, move in, take root, strike root in, make a dent in; gain a hearing, make one's voice heard, make one sit up and take notice, be listened to, be recognized; get the mastery *or* control of, get the inside track <nf>, gain a hold upon; change the preponderance, turn the scale *or* balance, turn the tables

ADJS **13 influential, powerful** 18.12, affluential, potent, strong, to be reckoned with; **effective,** effectual, efficacious, telling; **weighty,** momentous, important, consequential, substantial, earth-shattering, **prestigious,** estimable, authoritative, reputable; **persuasive,** suasive, personable, **winning,** magnetic, charming, enchanting, charismatic

14 <in a position of influence> **well-connected,** favorably situated, near the seat of power; **dominant** 612.17, **predominant,** preponderant, prepotent, prepollent, regnant, ruling, swaying, prevailing, prevalent, on the throne, in the driver's seat <nf>; **ascendant,** in the ascendant, in ascendancy

15 influenceable, swayable, movable; persuadable, persuasible, suasible, open, open-minded, pervious, accessible, receptive, responsive, amenable; **under one's thumb,** in one's pocket, on one's payroll; coercible, bribable, compellable, vulnerable; **plastic, pliant,** pliable, malleable; **suggestible, susceptible, impressionable,** weak 16.12

895 ABSENCE OF INFLUENCE

NOUNS **1 lack of influence** *or* **power** *or* **force,** uninfluentiality, **unauthoritativeness,** powerlessness, forcelessness, impotence 19, impotency; **ineffectiveness,** inefficaciousness, inefficacy, ineffectuality; **no say,** no say-so, nothing to do with *or* say about <nf>; unpersuasiveness, lack of personality *or* charm, lack of magnetism *or* charisma; **weakness** 16, wimpiness *or* wimpishness <nf>

2 uninfluenceability, unswayableness, unmovability; **unpersuadability,** impersuadability, impersuasibility, unreceptiveness, imperviousness, unresponsiveness; unsuggestibility, **unsusceptibility,** unimpressionability; invulnerability; **obstinacy** 361

ADJS **3 uninfluential, powerless,** forceless, impotent 19.13; **weak** 16.12, wimpy *or* wimpish <nf>; unauthoritative; **ineffective,** ineffectual, inefficacious; **of no account,** no-account, without any weight, featherweight, lightweight

4 uninfluenceable, unswayable, unmovable; unpliable, unyielding, inflexible; **unpersuadable** 361.13, impersuadable, impersuasible, unreceptive, unresponsive, unamenable; impervious, closed to; **unsuggestible, unsusceptible,** unimpressionable; invulnerable; **obstinate** 361.8

5 uninfluenced, unmoved, unaffected, unswayed

896 TENDENCY

NOUNS **1 tendency, inclination, leaning,** penchant, proneness, conatus, weakness, susceptibility; liability 897, readiness, willingness, eagerness, aptness, aptitude, **disposition, proclivity, propensity,** predisposition, **predilection,** a thing for <nf>, affinity, prejudice, **liking,** delight, soft spot, penchant; **yen,** lech <nf>, hunger, thirst; instinct *or* feeling for, sensitivity to; **bent, turn, bias,** slant, tilt, spin <nf>, cast, warp, twist, leaning; probability 968; diathesis <medicine>, tropism <biology>

2 trend, drift, course, current, *Tendenz* <Ger>, flow, stream, mainstream, main current, movement, glacial movement, motion, run, **tenor,** tone, **set,** set of the current, swing, bearing, line, direction, the general tendency *or* drift, the main course, the course of events, the way the wind blows, **the way things go,** sign of the times, spirit of the age *or* time, time spirit, *Zeitgeist* <Ger>; climate; the way it looks

VERBS **3 tend,** have a tendency, **incline,** be disposed, **lean, trend,** have a penchant, set, **go,** head, lead, point, verge, turn, warp, tilt, bias, bend to, work *or* gravitate *or* set toward; show a tendency *or* trend *or* set *or* direction, swing toward, point to, look to; **conduce,** contribute, serve, redound to; bode well

ADJS **4 tending;** tendentious *or* tendential; **leaning, inclining,** inclinatory, inclinational; **mainstream,** main-current, mainline

PREPS **5 tending to, conducive to,** leading to, inclined toward, inclining toward, heading *or* moving *or* swinging *or* working toward, pointing to

6 inclined to, leaning to, prone to, disposed to, drawn to, predisposed to, given to; **apt to, likely to, liable to** 897.6, calculated to, minded to, ready to, in a fair way to

897 LIABILITY

NOUNS **1 liability, likelihood** *or* **likeliness; probability** 968, contingency, chance 972, eventuality 831.1; weakness, **proneness** 896.1; **possibility** 966, **responsibility** 641.2, legal responsibility; **indebtedness** 623.1, financial commitment *or* obligation, pecuniary obligation

2 susceptibility, liability, susceptivity, liableness, **openness, exposure; vulnerability** 1006.4

VERBS **3 be liable; be subjected** *or* **subjected to,** be a pawn *or* plaything of, be the prey of, lie under; **expose oneself to, lay** *or* **leave oneself open to,** open the door to; **gamble,** stand to lose *or* gain, stand a chance, **run the chance** *or* **risk,** let down

one's guard *or* defenses; **admit of,** open the possibility of, be in the way of, bid *or* stand fair to; **owe,** be in debt *or* indebted for

4 incur, contract, invite, welcome, run, **bring on, bring down,** bring upon *or* down upon, bring upon *or* down upon oneself; **be responsible for** 641.6; fall into, fall in with; get, gain, acquire

ADJS **5 liable, likely, prone; probable; responsible,** legally responsible, answerable; **in debt, indebted,** financially burdened, heavily committed, overextended; **exposed, susceptible, at risk,** overexposed, open, like a sitting duck, **vulnerable**

6 liable to, subject to, standing to, in a position to, incident to, dependent on; **susceptible** *or* **prone to,** susceptive to, **open** *or* vulnerable *or* **exposed to,** naked to, in danger of, within range of, at the mercy of; **capable of,** ready for; **likely to, apt to** 896.6; obliged to, responsible *or* answerable for

CONJS **7 lest,** that, **for fear that**

898 INVOLVEMENT

NOUNS **1 involvement,** involution, **implication, entanglement,** enmeshment, engagement, involuntary presence *or* cooperation, embarrassment; relation 775; **inclusion** 772; **absorption** 983.3

VERBS **2 involve, implicate,** tangle, **entangle,** embarrass, enmesh, engage, **draw in,** drag *or* hook *or* suck into, catch up in, **make a party to;** interest, concern; **absorb** 983.13

3 be involved, be into <nf>, partake, participate, take an interest, interest oneself, have a role *or* part

ADJS **4 involved, implicated;** interested, concerned, a party to; **included** 772.5

5 involved in, implicated in, tangled *or* entangled in, enmeshed in, **caught up in,** tied up in, wrapped up in, all wound up in, dragged *or* hooked *or* sucked into; in deep, deeply involved, **up to one's neck** *or* **ears in,** up to one's elbows *or* ass in, head over heels in, **absorbed in** 983.17, immersed *or* submerged in, far-gone

899 CONCURRENCE

NOUNS **1 concurrence, collaboration,** coaction, **co-working,** collectivity, combined effort *or* operation, united *or* concerted action, concert, synergy; **cooperation** 450; **agreement** 788; metooism; **coincidence,** simultaneity 836, synchronism; concomitance, accompaniment 769; **union,** junction 800.1, **conjunction,** combination

805, association, alliance, consociation; conspiracy, collusion, cahoots <nf>; concourse, confluence; **accordance** 455.1, concordance, correspondence, consilience; symbiosis, parasitism; saprophytism; meeting of the minds

VERBS **2 concur, collaborate,** coact, **co-work,** synergize; **cooperate** 450.3; conspire, collude, connive, be in cahoots <nf>, go in together; **combine** 805.3, **unite, associate** 805.4, coadunate, join, conjoin; harmonize; **coincide,** synchronize, happen together; **accord** 455.2, correspond, **agree** 788.6

3 go with, **go along with, go hand in hand with,** be hand in glove with, team or join up with, buddy up with <nf>; keep pace with, run parallel to

ADJS **4 concurrent,** concurring; **coacting,** coactive, **collaborative,** collective, **co-working,** cooperant, synergetic or synergic or synergistic; **cooperative** 450.5; conspiratorial, collusive; **united, joint,** conjoint, **combined, concerted,** associated, associate, coadunate; **coincident,** synchronous, synchronic, in sync, coordinate; concomitant, accompanying 769.9; meeting, uniting, combining; **accordant, agreeing** 788.9, concordant, harmonious, consilient, at one with; symbiotic, parasitic, saprophytic

ADVS **5 concurrently,** coactively, **jointly, conjointly, concertedly,** in concert, in harmony or unison with, synchronously, **together; with one accord,** with one voice, as one, as one man; hand in hand, hand in glove, shoulder to shoulder, cheek by jowl

900 COUNTERACTION

NOUNS **1 counteraction, counterworking; opposition** 451, opposure, counterposition or contraposition, confutation, **contradiction; antagonism,** repugnance, oppugnance or oppugnancy, **antipathy, conflict, friction,** interference, clashing, collision; reaction, repercussion, **backlash, recoil,** kick, backfire, boomerang effect; resistance, recalcitrance, dissent 333, revolt 327.4, perverseness, nonconformity 868, crankiness, crotchetiness, orneriness <nf>, renitency; going against the current or against the tide, swimming upstream; **contrariety** 779

2 neutralization, nullification, annulment, cancellation, voiding, invalidation, vitiation, frustration, thwarting, undoing; **offsetting,** counterbalancing, countervailing, balancing; negation; equilibrium

3 counteractant, counteractive, **counteragent;** counterirritant; **antidote,** remedy, preventive or preventative, prophylactic, contraceptive; **neutralizer,** nullifier, offset; antacid, buffer

4 counterforce, countervailing force, counterinfluence, counterpressure; countercheck; counterpoise, counterbalance, counterweight; countercurrent, crosscurrent, undercurrent; counterblast; headwind, foul wind, crosswind; friction, drag

5 countermeasure, counterattack, counterstep; **counterblow** or counterstroke or countercoup or counterblast, counterfire; counterrevolution, counterinsurgency; counterterrorism; counterculture; **retort,** comeback <nf>; defense 460

VERBS **6 counteract,** counter, counterwork, counterattack, countervail; counterpose or contrapose, **oppose,** antagonize, **go in opposition to, go** or **run counter to, go** or **work against,** go clean counter to, go or fly in the face of, run against, beat against, militate against; **resist,** fight back, bite back, lift a hand against, defend oneself; **dissent,** dissent from; **cross,** confute, **contradict,** contravene, oppugn, **conflict,** be antipathetic or hostile or inimical, interfere or conflict with, come in conflict with, **clash,** collide, meet head-on, lock horns; rub or go against the grain; swim upstream or against the tide or against the current; boomerang; countercheck

7 neutralize, nullify, annul, cancel, cancel out, negate, negative, negativate, invalidate, vitiate, void, frustrate, stultify, thwart, come or bring to nothing, undo; **offset, counterbalance** 338.5; buffer

ADJS **8** counteractive or counteractant, **counteracting, counterworking, counterproductive,** countervailing; **opposing,** oppositional; contradicting, contradictory; **antagonistic,** hostile, antipathetic, inimical, oppugnant, repugnant, **conflicting, clashing;** reactionary; resistant, recalcitrant, dissentient, dissident, revolutionary, breakaway, nonconformist, perverse, cranky, crotchety, ornery <nf>, renitent

9 neutralizing, nullifying, stultifying, annulling, canceling, negating, invalidating, vitiating, voiding; equalizing; **balanced,** counterbalanced, poised, in poise, offset, **zero-sum; offsetting,** counterbalancing, countervailing; antacid, buffering; antidotal

ADVS **10 counteractively,** antagonistically, **opposingly, in opposition to, counter to**

WORD ELEMENTS **11** ant-, anti-, anth-, contra-, counter-

901 SUPPORT

NOUNS **1 support, backing, aid** 449; **upholding,
upkeep,** carrying, carriage, maintenance,
sustaining, sustainment, sustenance, sustentation;
reinforcement, backup; subsidy, subvention;
support services, infrastructure; moral support;
emotional *or* psychological support, security
blanket <nf>; reassurance; **power base,
constituency, party;** supportive relationship,
supportive therapy; strokes <nf>; **approval** 509;
assent, concurrence 332.1; **reliance** 953.1; life-
support, life-sustainment

2 supporter, support; upholder, bearer, carrier,
sustainer, maintainer; staff 273.2, stave, cane,
stick, walking stick, alpenstock, crook, crutch;
advocate 616.9; **stay, prop,** fulcrum, **bracket,
brace,** bracer, guy, guywire *or* guyline, shroud,
rigging, standing rigging; ballast; bulwark,
anchor; buttress, shoulder, arm, good right arm;
mast, sprit, yard, yardarm; **mainstay,** backbone,
spine, neck, cervix; athletic supporter, jock and
jockstrap <nf>, G-string <nf>; brassiere, bra <nf>,
bandeau, corset, girdle, foundation garment;
reinforcement, reinforce, reinforcing, reinforcer,
strengthener, stiffener; back, backing; rest, resting
place

3 <mythology> Atlas, Hercules, Telamon, Chukwa
or The Tortoise which Supports the Earth

4 buttress, buttressing; abutment, shoulder;
bulwark, rampart; **embankment,** bank, retaining
wall, bulkhead, bulkheading, plank buttress,
piling; **breakwater,** seawall, mole, **jetty,** jutty,
groin; **pier,** pier buttress, buttress pier; flying
buttress, *arc-boutant* <Fr>, arch buttress; hanging
buttress; **beam**

5 footing, foothold, toehold, hold, perch, **purchase**
906.2; **standing,** stand, stance, standing place, pou
sto, *point d'appui* <Fr>, *locus standi* <L>; footrest,
footplate, footrail

6 foundation, *fond* <Fr>, firm foundation, **base,
basis, footing,** basement, pavement, **ground,**
grounds, **groundwork, seat,** sill, floor *or*
flooring, fundament; bed, bedding; **substructure,**
substruction, substratum; infrastructure;
understructure, understruction, underbuilding,
undergirding, undercarriage, underpinning,
bearing wall; stereobate, stylobate; firm *or*
solid ground, *terra firma* <L>; solid rock *or*
bottom, rock bottom, bedrock; hardpan;
riprap; **fundamental** 997.6, **principle, premise**
957.1; grounds, precedent; root, radical;
rudiment

7 foundation stone, footstone; **cornerstone,
keystone,** headstone, first stone, quoin; roadbed

8 base, pedestal; stand, standard; **shaft** 273,
upright, column, pillar, post, jack, pole, staff,
stanchion, pier, pile *or* piling, king-post, queen-
post, pilaster, newel-post, banister, baluster,
balustrade, colonnade, caryatid; dado, die; plinth,
subbase; surbase; socle; **trunk,** stem, **stalk,**
pedicel, peduncle, footstalk

9 sill, groundsel; mudsill; window sill; doorsill,
threshold; doorstone

10 frame, underframe, infrastructure, chassis,
skeleton; armature; **mounting,** mount, **backing,
setting;** surround

11 handle, hold, grip, grasp, haft, helve

12 scaffold, scaffolding, *échafaudage* <Fr>; stage,
staging

13 platform; stage, estrade, dais, floor; **rostrum,
podium, pulpit,** speaker's platform *or* stand,
soapbox <nf>; hustings, **stump;** tribune, tribunal;
emplacement; catafalque; landing stage, landing;
heliport, landing pad; launching pad; **terrace,** step
terrace, deck; **balcony, gallery**

14 shelf, ledge, shoulder, corbel, beam-end; mantel,
mantelshelf, mantelpiece; retable, superaltar,
gradin, *gradino* <Ital>, predella; hob

15 table, board, **stand; bench,** workbench; **counter,**
bar, buffet; **desk,** writing table, **secretary,**
secrétaire <Fr>, escritoire; **lectern,** reading stand,
ambo, reading desk

16 trestle, horse; sawhorse, buck *or* sawbuck;
clotheshorse; trestle board *or* table, trestle and
table; trestlework, trestling; A-frame

17 seat, chair; saddle, howdah

18 <saddle parts> **pommel,** horn; jockey; girth, girt,
surcingle, bellyband; cinch, stirrup

19 sofa, **bed; couch;** the sack *and* the hay *and* kip *and*
doss <nf>; futon; bedstead; **litter, stretcher,**
gurney

20 bedding, underbed, underbedding; **mattress,**
paillasse, pallet; air mattress, foam-rubber
mattress, innerspring mattress; sleeping bag; pad,
mat, rug; litter, bedstraw; **pillow,** cushion, bolster;
springs, bedsprings, box springs; futon

VERBS **21 support, bear,** carry, **hold, sustain,
maintain, bolster, reinforce,** back, back up,
shoulder, give *or* furnish *or* afford *or* supply *or*
lend support; go to bat for <nf>; **hold up, bear up,**
bolster up, keep up, buoy up, keep afloat, back up;
uphold, upbear, upkeep; **brace, prop,** crutch,
buttress; shore, **shore up;** stay, mainstay;
underbrace, undergird, underprop, underpin,
underset; **underlie,** be at the bottom of, form the
foundation of; cradle; cushion, pillow; **subsidize;**
subvene; assent 332.8; concur 332.9; **approve** 509.9

22 rest on, stand on, lie on, recline on, repose on,
bear on, **lean on,** abut on; **sit on,** perch, ride,

piggyback on; **straddle,** bestraddle, stride, bestride; be based on, rely on

ADJS **23 supporting, supportive, bearing,** carrying, burdened; **holding,** upholding, maintaining, sustaining, sustentative, suspensory; bracing, propping, shoring, bolstering, buttressing; life-sustaining; collaborative, corroborative, cooperative

24 supported, borne, upborne, held, buoyed-up, **upheld, sustained,** maintained; **braced,** guyed, stayed, propped, shored or shored up, bolstered, buttressed; based or founded or grounded on

ADVS **25 on, across, astride, astraddle,** straddle, straddle-legged, straddleback, on the back of; horseback, on horseback; pickaback or piggyback

902 IMPULSE, IMPACT
<driving and striking force>

NOUNS **1 impulse,** impulsion, impelling force, impellent; **drive,** driving force or power; **motive power, power** 18; **force,** irresistible force; clout <nf>; **impetus; momentum;** moment, moment of force; propulsion 904.1; incitement 375.4, incentive 375.7, compulsion 424

2 thrust, push, shove, boost <nf>; **pressure; stress;** press; **prod, poke, punch, jab,** dig, nudge; **bump,** jog, joggle, jolt; **jostle,** hustle; **butt,** bunt; head <of water, steam, etc>

3 impact, collision, clash, appulse, **encounter,** meeting, impingement, **bump, crash,** crump, whomp; **carom,** carambole, cannon; sideswipe <nf>; smash and crunch <nf>; **shock, brunt; concussion,** percussion; **thrusting, ramming,** bulling, **bulldozing,** shouldering, muscling, steamrollering, railroading; hammering, smashing, mauling, sledgehammering; onslaught 459.1

4 hit, blow, stroke, knock, rap, pound, slam, bang, crack, **whack, smack, thwack,** smash, dash, swipe, swing, **punch, poke, jab,** dig, drub, thump, pelt, cut, chop, dint, slog; drubbing, drumming, tattoo, fusillade; beating 604.4

5 <nf terms> **sock,** bang, bash, bat, belt, bonk, bust, clip, clout, duke, swat, yerk, plunk, larrup, paste, lick, biff, clump, clunk, clonk, wallop, whop, slam, slug, whomp, swack

6 punch, boxing punch, blow, belt, sock

7 tap, rap, pat, dab, chuck, touch, tip; love-tap; **snap, flick, flip,** fillip, flirt, whisk, brush; **peck,** pick

8 slap, smack, flap; **box, cuff,** buffet; **spank;** whip, **lash,** cut, stripe

9 kick, boot; punt, drop kick, place kick, kicking, calcitration <old>

10 stamp, stomp <nf>, drub, clump, clop

VERBS **11** impel, give an impetus, **set going or**

 agoing, put or set in motion, give momentum; **drive, move,** animate, actuate, forward; **thrust,** power; drive or whip on; goad; **propel;** motivate, incite 375.17; compel 424.4

12 thrust, push, shove, boost <nf>; press, stress, **bear,** bear upon, bring pressure to bear upon; **ram,** ram down, tamp, pile drive, jam, crowd, cram; bull, bulldoze, muscle, steamroller, railroad; **drive, force,** run; **prod, goad, poke, punch, jab,** dig, nudge; **bump,** jog, joggle, jolt, shake, rattle; **jostle,** hustle, hurtle; elbow, shoulder; **butt,** bunt, buck <nf>, run or bump or butt against, bump up against, knock or run one's head against; assault

13 collide, come into collision, be on a collision course, **clash,** meet, encounter, confront each other, impinge; percuss, concuss; **bump, hit, strike, knock, bang;** run into, bump into, bang into, slam into, smack into, **crash into, impact,** smash into, dash into, carom into, cannon into <Brit>; rear-end; **hit against,** strike against, knock against; foul, fall or run foul or afoul of; hurtle, hurt; **carom,** cannon <chiefly Brit>; **sideswipe** <nf>; **crash,** smash, crump, whomp; smash up or crack up or crunch <nf>

14 hit, strike, knock, knock down or out, smite; land a blow, draw blood; **poke, punch, jab,** thwack, **smack,** clap, crack, swipe, **whack;** deal, fetch, swipe at, take a punch at, throw one at <nf>, deal or fetch a blow, hit a clip <nf>, let have it; **thump,** snap; strike at 459.16

15 <nf terms> **belt,** bat, clout, bang, slam, bash, biff, paste, wham, whop, clump, bonk, wallop, clip, cut, plunk, swat, soak, sock, slog, slug, yerk <old>, clunk, clonk

16 pound, beat, hammer, maul, sledgehammer, **knock, rap, bang,** thump, **drub,** buffet, **batter,** pulverize, paste <nf>, patter, pommel, pummel, pelt, baste, lambaste; thresh, thrash; flail; spank, flap; whip

17 <nf terms> **clobber,** knock for a loop, marmelize <Brit>, knock cold, dust off, bash up, punch out, rough up, slap down, smack down, sandbag, work over, deck, coldcock, wallop, larrup

18 tap, rap, pat, dab, chuck, touch, tip; **snap, flick, flip,** fillip, tickle, flirt, whisk, **graze,** brush; bunt; **peck,** pick, beak

19 slap, smack, flap; **box, cuff,** buffet; **spank;** whip

20 club, cudgel, blackjack, sandbag, cosh <Brit>

21 kick, boot, kick about or around, calcitrate <old>; kick downstairs <old>; kick out; knee

22 stamp, stomp <nf>, trample, tread, drub, clump, clop

ADJS **23 impelling,** impellent; impulsive, pulsive,

moving, motive, animating, actuating, **driving;** thrusting

24 concussive, percussive, crashing, smashing

903 REACTION

NOUNS 1 **reaction, response,** respondence, feedback; reply, answer 939.1, **rise** <nf>; **reflex,** reflection, **reflex action;** echo, bounce back, reverberation, resonance, sympathetic vibration; return; reflux, refluence; action and reaction; opposite response, negative response, retroaction, revulsion; predictable response, automatic *or* autonomic reaction, knee-jerk *and* knee-jerk response <nf>, spontaneous *or* unthinking response, spur-of-the-moment response; conditioned reflex

2 **recoil, rebound,** resilience, repercussion, *contrecoup* <Fr>; **bounce, bound, spring,** bounce-back; **repulse, rebuff; backlash,** backlashing, kickback, **kick,** a kick like a mule <nf>, recalcitration <old>; **backfire, boomerang;** ricochet, carom, cannon <Brit>

3 <a drawing back *or* aside> **retreat,** recoil, fallback, pullout, pullback, contingency plan, backup plan; evasion, avoidance, sidestepping; **flinch,** wince, cringe; **side step,** shy; **dodge, duck** <nf>

4 **reactionary,** reactionist, recalcitrant

VERBS 5 **react, respond,** reply, answer, riposte, snap back, come back at <nf>; rise to the fly, take the bait; go off half-cocked *or* at half cock

6 **recoil, rebound,** resile; **bounce, bound, spring; spring** *or* **fly back,** bounce *or* bound back, snap back; repercuss, have repercussions; **kick,** kick back, kick like a mule <nf>, recalcitrate <old>; **backfire, boomerang;** backlash, lash back; ricochet, carom, cannon *and* cannon off <Brit>

7 **pull** *or* **draw back,** retreat, recoil, fade, **fall back,** reel back, hang back, start back, shrink back, give ground; **shrink, flinch, wince, cringe,** blink, blench, quail; **shy,** shy away, start *or* turn aside, evade, avoid, sidestep, weasel, weasel out, cop out <nf>; **dodge, duck** <nf>; jib, swerve, sheer off, give a wide berth

8 get a reaction, get a response, evoke a response, ring a bell, strike a responsive chord, strike fire, strike *or* hit home, hit a nerve, get a rise out of <nf>

ADJS 9 **reactive,** reacting, merely reactive; **responsive,** respondent, responding, antiphonal; **quick on the draw** *or* trigger *or* uptake; **reactionary,** retroactionary, retroactive, revulsive, **reflex,** reflexive, knee-jerk <nf>; refluent

10 recoiling, rebounding, **resilient; bouncing,** bouncy, bounding, springing, springy; repercussive; recalcitrant

ADVS 11 **on the rebound,** on the return, on the bounce; on the spur of the moment, off the top of the head

904 PUSHING, THROWING

NOUNS 1 **pushing, propulsion, propelling; shoving,** butting; **drive, thrust,** motive power, driving force, means of propulsion; **push, shove;** butt, bunt; shunt, impulsion 902.1

2 **throwing, projection,** jaculation, ejaculation, trajection, flinging, slinging, **pitching, tossing,** casting, hurling, lobbing, chucking, chunking <nf>, heaving, firing *and* burning *and* pegging <nf>; bowling, rolling; **shooting,** firing, gunnery, gunning, musketry; trap-shooting, skeet *or* skeet shooting; archery

3 **throw, toss, fling, sling, cast, hurl,** chuck, chunk <nf>, lob, **heave,** shy, **pitch,** peg <nf>; **flip;** put, shot-put; <football> pass, forward pass, lateral pass, lateral; <tennis> serve, service; bowl; <baseball> pitch

4 **shot,** discharge; ejection 909; detonation 56.3; gunfire; gun, cannon; bullet; **salvo, volley,** fusillade, tattoo, spray; bowshot, gunshot, stoneshot, potshot

5 **projectile;** ejecta, ejectamenta; **missile;** ball; discus, quoit

6 **propeller,** prop <nf>, airscrew, prop-fan; propellant, propulsor, driver; screw, wheel, screw propeller, twin screws; bow thruster; paddle wheel; turbine; fan, impeller, rotor; piston

7 **thrower, pitcher,** hurler, bowler <cricket>, chucker, chunker <nf>, **heaver, tosser,** flinger, slinger, caster, jaculator, ejaculator; bowler; shot-putter; javelin thrower; discus thrower, discobolus

8 **shooter,** shot; **gunner,** gun, **gunman; rifleman,** musketeer, carabineer, pistoleer; cannoneer, artilleryman; Nimrod, hunter 382.5; trapshooter; archer, bowman, toxophilite; **marksman, markswoman,** targetshooter, **sharpshooter,** sniper; good shot, dead shot, deadeye, **crack shot**

VERBS 9 **push, propel,** impel, **shove,** thrust 902.11; **drive, move,** forward, advance, traject; sweep, sweep along; butt, bunt; shunt; pole, row; pedal, treadle; **roll,** troll, bowl, trundle

10 **throw, fling, sling, pitch, toss, cast, hurl, heave, chuck,** chunk *and* peg <nf>, lob, shy, fire, burn, pepper <nf>, launch, dash, let fly, let go, let rip, let loose; catapult; **flip,** snap, jerk; bowl; pass; serve; put, put the shot; bung <Brit nf>, dart, lance, tilt, fork, pitchfork; pelt 459.27

11 **project,** jaculate, ejaculate

12 **shoot, fire,** fire off, let off, let fly, **discharge,** eject 909.13; detonate 56.8; gun <nf>, pistol; sharpshoot;

shoot at 459.22, gun for <nf>; strike, hit, plug <nf>; shoot down, fell, drop, stop in one's tracks; **riddle, pepper,** pelt, pump full of lead <nf>; snipe, pick off; torpedo; pot; potshoot, potshot, take a potshot; load, prime, charge; cock

13 start, start off, start up, give a start, crank up, give a push *or* shove <nf>, jump-start, kick-start, **put** *or* **set in motion, set on foot,** set going *or* agoing, start going; **kick off** *and* **start the ball rolling** <nf>; get off the ground *or* off the mark, **launch,** launch forth *or* out, float, set afloat; send, send off *or* forth; bundle off

ADJS **14 propulsive,** propulsory, **propellant,** propelling; **motive; driving, pushing, shoving**

15 projectile, trajectile, jaculatory, ejaculatory; **ballistic,** missile; ejective

16 jet-propelled, rocket-propelled, steam-propelled, gasoline-propelled, gas-propelled, diesel-propelled, wind-propelled, self-propelled, etc

17 <means of propulsion> battery, diesel, diesel-electric, electric, gas *or* gasoline, gravity, jet, plasma-jet, prop-fan, pulse-jet, ram-jet, reaction, resojet, rocket, spring, steam, turbofan, turbojet, turbopropeller *or* turboprop, wind

905 PULLING

NOUNS **1 pulling, traction, drawing,** draft, dragging, heaving, tugging, towing; pulling *or* tractive power, **pull;** tug-of-war; towing, towage; towrope, towbar, towing cable *or* hawser; tow car, wrecker; **hauling,** haulage, drayage; man-hauling, man-haulage; attraction 907; extraction 192

2 pull, draw, heave, haul, tug, tow, lug, a long pull *and* a strong pull, strain, drag

3 jerk, yank <nf>, quick *or* sudden pull; **twitch,** tweak, pluck, hitch, wrench, snatch, start, bob; **flip,** flick, flirt, flounce; jig, **jiggle;** jog, joggle

VERBS **4 pull, draw, heave, haul,** hale, lug, **tug, tow,** take in tow; trail, train; **drag,** man-haul, draggle, snake <nf>; troll, trawl

5 jerk, yerk <nf>, **yank** <nf>; **twitch,** tweak, pluck, snatch, hitch, wrench, snake <nf>; **flip,** flick, flirt, flounce; **jiggle,** jig, jigget, jigger; jog, joggle

ADJS **6 pulling, drawing,** tractional, tractive, hauling, tugging, towing, towage; man-hauled

906 LEVERAGE

<mechanical advantage applied to moving or raising>

NOUNS **1 leverage,** fulcrumage; **pry,** prize <nf>

2 purchase, hold, advantage; **foothold,** toehold, footing; differential purchase; collier's purchase; traction

3 fulcrum, axis, pivot, bearing, rest, resting point, *point d'appui* <Fr>; thole, tholepin, rowlock, oarlock

4 lever; pry, prize <nf>; **bar,** pinch bar, crowbar, crow, pinchbar, iron crow, wrecking bar, ripping bar, claw bar; cant hook, peavey; **jimmy;** handspike, marlinespike; boom, spar, beam, outrigger; pedal, treadle, crank; limb

5 arm; forearm; wrist; elbow; upper arm, biceps

6 tackle, purchase

7 *windlass; capstan* <nautical>; **winch,** crab; reel; Chinese windlass, Spanish windlass

VERBS **8** get a purchase, get leverage, get a foothold; **pry,** prize, **lever,** wedge; pry *or* prize out; **jimmy,** crowbar, pinchbar

9 reel in, wind in, bring in, draw in, pull in, crank in, trim, tighten, tauten, draw taut, take the strain; windlass, winch, crank, reel; tackle

907 ATTRACTION

<a drawing toward>

NOUNS **1 attraction,** traction 905.1, attractiveness, attractivity; mutual attraction *or* magnetism; pulling power, **pull,** drag, draw, tug; magnetism 1032.7; gravity, gravitation; centripetal force; capillarity, capillary attraction; adduction; **affinity, sympathy; allurement** 377; come-on

2 attractor, attractant, attrahent; adductor; cynosure, focus, center, center of attraction *or* attention; crowd-pleaser *or* drawer, charismatic figure; drawing card; side show; freak show; **lure** 377.3

3 magnet, artificial magnet, field magnet, bar magnet, horseshoe magnet, electromagnet, solenoid, paramagnet, permanent magnet, keeper, superconducting magnet, electromagnetic lifting magnet, magnetic needle; lodestone, magnetite; magnetic pole, magnetic north; lodestar, polestar; siderite

VERBS **4 attract, pull, draw,** drag, tug, pull *or* draw towards, have an attraction; **magnetize,** magnet, be magnetic; **lure;** adduct

ADJS **5** attracting, drawing, pulling, dragging, tugging; eye-catching; **attractive, magnetic;** charismatic; magnetized, attrahent; sympathetic; **alluring;** adductive, adducent; associative

ADVS **6** attractionally, attractively; magnetically; charismatically

908 REPULSION

<a thrusting away>

NOUNS **1 repulsion,** repellence *or* repellency, **repelling;** mutual repulsion, polarization;

disaffinity; centrifugal force; magnetic repulsion, diamagnetism; antigravity; repulsive force; ejection 909

2 repulse, rebuff; dismissal, cold shoulder, snub, spurning, brush-off, cut; kiss-off <nf>; turn-off <nf>; rejection; refusal; discharge 909.5

VERBS **3 repulse, repel, rebuff, turn back,** put back, beat back, force *or* drive *or* push **or** thrust back; drive away, chase, chase off *or* away; send off *or* away, send about one's business, **send packing,** pack off, dismiss; snub, cut, brush off, drop; kiss off <nf>, show someone the door; spurn, refuse; **ward off,** hold off, keep off, fend off, fight off, drive off, push off, keep at arm's length; slap *or* smack down <nf>; eject 909.13, discharge 909.19

ADJS **4 repulsive,** repellent, **repelling;** diamagnetic, of opposite polarity, centrifugal, abducent, abductive; off-putting

ADVS **5** repulsively, repellently

909 EJECTION

NOUNS **1 ejection,** ejectment, throwing out, **expulsion, discharge,** extrusion, obtrusion, detrusion, **ousting, ouster,** removal, kicking *or* booting *or* chucking out <nf>; throwing *or* kicking downstairs; the boot *and* the bounce *and* the bum's rush *and* the old heave-ho <nf>, the chuck *or* the push <Brit nf>; defenestration; **rejection** 372; jettison

2 eviction, ousting, dislodgment, dispossession, expropriation; **ouster,** throwing overboard

3 depopulation, dispeoplement, unpeopling; devastation, desolation

4 banishment, relegation, exclusion 773; **excommunication,** disfellowship; **disbarment,** unfrocking, defrocking; proscription; **expatriation, exile,** exilement; outlawing *or* outlawry, fugitation <Scot>; **ostracism,** ostracization, thumbs-down, thumbing-down, *pollice verso* <L>, blackballing, silent treatment, sending to Coventry, cold shoulder; **deportation,** transportation, **extradition;** rustication; degradation, **demotion** 447, stripping, depluming, displuming; deprivation

5 dismissal, discharge, forced separation, *congé* <Fr>; outplacement; **firing** *and* canning <nf>, **cashiering,** drumming out, dishonorable discharge, rogue's march; disemployment, **layoff,** removal, surplusing, displacing, furloughing; suspension; **retirement;** marching orders, the elbow, the bounce, **the sack** *and* the chuck <Brit nf>, heave-ho <nf>; the boot *and* the gate *and* the ax *and* the sack <nf>; walking

papers *or* ticket <nf>, pink slip <nf>; deposal 447

6 evacuation, voidance, voiding; **elimination,** removal; **clearance, clearing,** clearage; unfouling, freeing; scouring *or* cleaning out, unclogging; exhaustion, exhausting, venting, emptying, depletion; **unloading,** off-loading, discharging cargo *or* freight; draining, drainage; egress 190.2; **excretion,** defecation 12.2,4

7 disgorgement, disemboguement, expulsion, ejaculation, **discharge,** emission; **eruption,** eructation, extravasation, **blowout, outburst;** outpour, jet, spout, squirt, spurt

8 vomiting, vomition, **disgorgement, regurgitation,** egestion, emesis, the pukes *and* the heaves <nf>; **retching,** heaving, gagging; nausea; vomit, vomitus, puke *and* puking *and* barf *and* barfing <nf>, spew, egesta; the dry heaves <nf>; vomiturition

9 belch, burp <nf>, belching, wind, gas, eructation; **hiccup**

10 fart <nf>, **flatulence** *or* flatulency, flatuosity, flatus, breaking wind, passing gas, gas, wind

11 ejector, expeller, -fuge; **ouster,** evictor; **bouncer** *and* chucker <nf>, chucker-out <Brit nf>

12 dischargee, expellee; ejectee; evictee

VERBS **13 eject, expel, discharge,** extrude, obtrude, detrude, exclude, **reject,** cast, remove; **oust, bounce** *and* give the hook <nf>, **put out, turn out,** thrust out; **throw out,** run out <nf>, cast out, chuck out, give the chuck to <Brit nf>, toss out, heave out, throw *or* kick downstairs; kick *or* boot out <nf>; give the bum's rush *or* give the old heave-ho *or* throw out on one's ear <nf>; defenestrate; jettison, throw overboard, discard, junk, throw away; **be rid of,** be shut of, see the last of

14 drive out, run out, chase out, chase away, run off, **rout out;** drum out, read out; freeze out <nf>, push out, force out, send packing, send about one's business; **hunt out,** harry out; **smoke out,** drive into the open; run out of town, ride on a rail

15 evict, oust, dislodge, dispossess, put out, turn out, **turn out of doors,** turn out of house and home, turn *or* put out bag and baggage, throw into the street; unhouse, unkennel

16 depopulate, dispeople, unpeople; devastate, desolate

17 banish, expel, cast out, thrust out, relegate, **ostracize,** disfellowship, exclude, send down, **blackball,** spurn, thumb down, turn thumbs down on, snub, cut, give the cold shoulder, send to Coventry, give the silent treatment; **excommunicate; exile, expatriate, deport,** transport, send away, **extradite; deport; outlaw,** fugitate <Scot>, ban, proscribe; rusticate

18 dismiss, send off *or* **away, turn off** *or* **away,** bundle, bundle off *or* out, hustle out, pack off, **send packing,** send about one's business, send to the showers <nf>; bow out, **show the door,** show the gate; **give the gate** *or* the air <nf>

19 dismiss, discharge, expel, cashier, drum out, disemploy, outplace, separate forcibly *or* involuntarily, **lay off,** suspend, surplus, furlough, turn off, make redundant, riff <nf>, turn out, release, let go, let out, remove, displace, replace, strike off the rolls, give the pink slip ; unfrock, defrock; degrade, demote, strip, deplume, displume, deprive; depose, disbar 447.4; break, bust <nf>; **retire,** put on the retired list; pension off, superannuate, put out to pasture; read out of; kick upstairs

20 <nf terms> **fire, can, sack, bump,** bounce, kick, boot, give the ax, give the gate, give one the sack *or* the ax *or* the boot *or* the gate *or* the air *or* one's walking papers, send one to the showers, show one the door *or* gate

21 do away with, exterminate, annihilate; purge, liquidate; **shake off,** shoo, dispel; **throw off,** fling off, cast off; **eliminate, get rid of** 773.5; throw away 390.7

22 evacuate, void; eliminate, remove; **empty,** empty out, deplete, **exhaust,** vent, drain; **clear, purge,** clean *or* scour out, clear off *or* away, clear, unfoul, unclog, flush out, blow, blow out, sweep out, make a clean sweep, clear the decks; defecate 12.13

23 unload, off-load, unlade, unpack, disburden, unburden, **discharge, dump;** unship, break bulk; pump out

24 let out, give vent to, give out *or* off, throw off, blow off, **emit, exhaust,** evacuate, let go; **exhale,** expire, breathe out, let one's breath out, blow, puff; fume, steam, vapor, smoke, reek; open the sluices *or* floodgates, turn on the tap

25 disgorge, debouch, disembogue, **discharge, exhaust, expel,** ejaculate, throw out, **cast forth,** send out *or* forth; **erupt,** eruct, **blow out,** extravasate; **pour out** *or* **forth,** pour, outpour, decant; spew, jet, spout, squirt, **spurt;** cough up

26 vomit, spew, **disgorge, regurgitate,** egest, **throw up,** bring up, be sick <Brit>, sick up <Brit nf>, cast *or* heave the gorge; **retch,** keck, **heave, gag;** reject; be seasick, feed the fish

27 <nf terms> **puke,** upchuck, chuck up, urp, oops, oops up, shoot *or* blow *or* toss one's cookies *or* lunch, barf, ralph, ralph up, blow grits, cough up

28 belch, burp <nf>, eruct, eructate; **hiccup**

29 <nf terms> **fart,** let *or* lay *or* cut a fart <nf>, let *or* break wind, cut the cheese

ADJS **30 ejective, expulsive,** ejaculatory, emissive, extrusive; eliminant; vomitive, vomitory; eructative; flatulent, flatuous; **rejected** 372.3, rejective

INTERJS **31 go away!,** begone!, get you gone!, go along!, get along!, **run along!, get along with you!,** away!, away with you!, **off with you!,** off you go!, on your way!, go about your business!, be off!, **get out of here!,** get out!, clear out!, leave!, get a life!, get out of town!, *allez!* <Fr>, *allez-vous-en!* <Fr>, *va-t'-en!* <Fr>, *raus mit dir!* <Ger>, *heraus!* <Ger>, *váyase!* <Sp>, *via!* *or* *va' via!* <Ital>, shoo!, scat!, git! <nf>, "go and hang yourself"—Plautus

32 <nf terms> **beat it!, scram!,** buzz off!, bug off!, shoo!, skiddoo!, skedaddle!, vamoose!, cheese it!, make yourself scarce!, **get lost!,** take a walk!, take a hike!, go chase yourself!, go play in the traffic!, get the hell out!, push off!, shove off!, take a powder!, blow!

910 OVERRUNNING

NOUNS **1 overrunning, overgoing, overpassing;** overrun, overpass; **overspreading,** overgrowth; inundation, whelming, overwhelming; burying, burial; seizure, taking 480; overflowing 238.6; exaggeration 355; surplus, excess 993; superiority 249

2 infestation, infestment; **invasion,** swarming, swarm, teeming, ravage, plague; **overrunning, overswarming,** overspreading; lousiness, pediculosis

3 overstepping, transgression, trespass, inroad, usurpation, incursion, intrusion, **encroachment,** infraction, **infringement**

VERBS **4 overrun, overgo, overpass,** overreach, go beyond; overstep, overstride, overstep the mark *or* bounds; overleap, overjump; **overshoot,** overshoot the mark, overshoot the field; exaggerate 355.3; superabound, exceed, **overdo** 993.10

5 overspread, bespread, spread over, spill over; **overgrow,** grow over, run riot, cover, swarm over, teem over

6 infest, beset, invade, swarm, ravage, plague; **overrun, overswarm,** overspread; **creep with, crawl with,** swarm with; seize 480.14

7 run over, overrun; **ride over,** override, **run down,** ride down; **trample, trample on** *or* **upon,** trample down, tread upon, step on, walk on *or* over, trample underfoot, **ride roughshod over;** hit-and-run; **inundate, whelm, overwhelm;** overflow 238.17; shout down

8 pass, go *or* **pass by,** get *or* shoot ahead of; bypass; **pass over, cross,** go across, ford; step over, overstride, bestride, straddle

9 overstep, transgress, trespass, intrude, break

bounds, overstep the bounds, go too far, know no bounds, **encroach, infringe,** invade, breach, irrupt, make an inroad *or* incursion *or* intrusion, advance upon; usurp

ADJS **10 overrun, overspread,** overpassed, bespread; overgrown; inundated, whelmed, overwhelmed; buried

11 infested, beset, ravaged, teeming, lagued; lousy, pediculous, pedicular; wormy, grubby; ratty

911 SHORTCOMING
<motion or action short of>

NOUNS **1 shortcoming,** falling short, not measuring up, coming up short, **shortfall; shortage,** short measure, underage, deficit, limitation; **inadequacy** 795.1; insufficiency 992; delinquency; **default,** defalcation; arrear, **arrears,** arrearage; decline, slump; defectiveness, imperfection 1003; **inferiority** 250; **undercommitment; failure** 410

VERBS **2 fall short, come short, run short,** stop short, not make the course, not reach; not measure up, not hack it *and* not make the grade *and* not make the cut <nf>, not make it, not make out; want, want for, lack, not have it <nf>, **be found wanting,** not answer, not fill the bill, not suffice; not reach to, not stretch; decline, lag, lose ground, slump, collapse, fall away, run out of gas *or* steam; **lose out, fail** 410.9

3 fall through, fall down, **fall to the ground,** fall flat, **collapse,** break down; get bogged down, get mired, get mired down, get hung up, come to nothing, come to naught, end up *or* go up in smoke; **fizzle** *or* peter *or* poop out <nf>; not make it; fall *or* drop by the wayside, end "not with a bang but a whimper"—T S Eliot

4 miss, miscarry, go amiss, go astray, **miss the mark,** miss by a mile <nf>; misfire; **miss out,** miss the boat *or* bus; miss stays, miss one's mooring

ADJS **5 short of,** short, fresh *or* clean out of <nf>, not all *or* what it is cracked up to be; **deficient, inadequate** 795.4; **insufficient** 992.9; undercommitted; **inferior** 250.6; **lacking,** wanting, minus; unreached

ADVS **6 behind, behindhand, in arrears** *or* arrear

7 amiss, astray, beside the mark, below the mark, beside the point, far from it, to no purpose, in vain, vainly, fruitlessly, bootlessly

912 ELEVATION
<act of raising>

NOUNS **1 elevation, raising, lifting,** upping, boosting *and* hiking <nf>; **rearing,** escalation, **erection;** uprearing, uplifting; upbuoying; **uplift,** upheaval,

upthrow, upcast, upthrust; **exaltation;** apotheosis, deification; beatification, canonization; enshrinement, assumption; *sursum corda* <L>; height 272; ascent 193; increase 251; antigravity; orogeny

2 lift, boost *and* **hike** <nf>, hoist, heave; a leg up; promotion

3 lifter, erector; crane, derrick, gantry crane, crab; **jack,** jackscrew; **hoist,** lift, hydraulic lift; forklift; hydraulic tailgate; lever 906.4; windlass 906.7; tackle; yeast, leaven

4 elevator, *ascenseur* <Fr>, **lift** <Brit>; escalator, moving staircase *or* stairway, ski lift, chair lift; dumbwaiter

VERBS **5 elevate, raise, rear,** escalate, up, boost *and* hike <nf>; **erect, heighten, lift,** levitate, boost <nf>, **hoist,** heist <nf>, heft, heave; raise up, rear up, lift up, hold up, set up; stick up, cock up, perk up; buoy up, upbuoy; **upraise, uplift,** uphold, uprear, uphoist; upheave, upthrow, upcast; throw up, cast up; jerk up, hike <nf>; knock up, lob, loft; sky <nf>

6 exalt, elevate, ensky; deify, apotheosize; beatify, canonize; enshrine; put on a pedestal

7 give a lift, give a boost, give a leg up <nf>, **help up,** put on; mount, horse; enhance, upgrade

8 pick up, take up, pluck up, **gather up;** draw up, fish up, haul up, drag up; dredge, dredge up

ADJS **9 raised, lifted, elevated;** upraised, **uplifted,** upcast; **reared,** upreared; rearing, rampant; upthrown, upflung; **exalted, lofty;** deified, apotheosized; canonized, sainted, beatified; enshrined, sublime; antigravitational; stilted, on stilts; erect, upright 200.11; high 272.14

10 elevating, elevatory, escalatory; **lifting; uplifting;** erective, erectile; levitative

913 DEPRESSION
<act of lowering>

NOUNS **1 depression, lowering; sinking;** ducking, submergence, pushing *or* thrusting under, down-thrust, down-thrusting, detrusion, pushing *or* pulling *or* hauling down; reduction, de-escalation, diminution; demotion 447, debasement, degradation; concavity, hollowness 284.1; descent 194; decrease 252; deflation; sinkhole, crater

2 downthrow, downcast; **overthrow,** overturn 205.2; **precipitation,** fall, downfall; downpour, downpouring

3 crouch, stoop, bend, squat; **bow,** genuflection, kneeling, kowtow, kowtowing, salaam, reverence, obeisance, **curtsy;** bob, duck, nod; prostration, supination; crawling, groveling; abasement, self-abasement

VERBS **4 depress, lower,** let *or* take down, debase, de-escalate, **sink,** bring low, deflate, reduce, couch; pull *or* haul down, take down a peg <nf>; bear down, downbear, squash; thrust *or* press *or* push down, detrude; indent 284.14

5 fell, drop, bring down, fetch down, down <nf>, take down, take down a peg, lay low, reduce to the ranks; **raze,** rase, raze to the ground; **level,** lay level; pull down, pull about one's ears; **cut down,** chop down, hew down, whack down <nf>, mow down; **knock down,** dash down, send headlong, **floor,** deck *and* lay out <nf>, lay by the heels, ground, **bowl down** *or* **over** <nf>; trip, trip up, topple, tumble; **prostrate,** supinate; throw, **throw** *or* fling *or* cast down, **precipitate;** bulldog; spread-eagle <nf>, pin, pin down; blow over *or* down

6 overthrow, overturn 205.6; depose 447.4; demote 447.3

7 drop, let go of, let drop *or* fall

8 crouch, duck, cringe, **cower; stoop, bend, stoop down, squat,** squat down, get down, hunker *and* hunker down *and* get down on one's hunkers <nf>; hunch, hunch down, hunch over, scrooch *or* scrouch down <nf>

9 bow, bend, kneel, genuflect, bend the knee, **curtsy,** make a low bow, make a leg, make a reverence *or* an obeisance, salaam, bob, duck; **kowtow,** prostrate oneself; crawl, grovel; wallow, welter

10 sit down, seat oneself, park oneself <nf>, **be seated** 173.10

11 lie down, couch, drape oneself, **recline** 201.5; prostrate, supinate, prone <nf>; flatten oneself, prostrate oneself; hit the ground *or* the dirt <nf>

ADJS **12 depressed, lowered,** debased, reduced, **fallen,** deflated; sunk, **sunken,** submerged; downcast, downthrown; prostrated, prostrate 201.8; low, at a low ebb; falling, precititous

914 CIRCUITOUSNESS

NOUNS **1 circuitousness,** circuity, circuition <old>; **roundaboutness,** indirection, ambagiousness <old>, meandering, deviance *or* deviancy, **deviation** 164; deviousness, **digression,** circumlocution 538.5; **excursion,** excursus; **circling, wheeling,** circulation, rounding, orbit, **orbiting; spiraling,** spiral, gyring, gyre; circumambulation, circumambience *or* circumambiency, circumflexion, circumnavigation, circummigration; turning, **turn** 164.1; circularity 280; convolution 281

2 circuit, round, revolution, **circle,** full circle, go-round, **cycle,** orbit, ambit; pass; round trip, *aller-retour* <Fr>; **beat,** rounds, **walk,** tour, turn, lap, loop; round robin; traffic circle, roundabout, rotary

3 detour, bypass, roundabout way, roundabout, ambages <old>, circuit, circumbendibus <nf>, the long way around, digression, deviation, excursion

VERBS **4 go roundabout,** meander, deviate, go around Robin Hood's barn, take *or* go the long way around, twist and turn; **detour,** make a detour, **go around,** go round about, go out of one's way, **bypass;** deviate 164.3; digress 538.9; **talk in circles,** say in a roundabout way; equivocate 936.9, shilly-shally; dodge 368.8

5 circle, circuit, describe a circle, make a circuit, move in a circle, **circulate; go round** *or* **around,** go about; **wheel,** orbit, go into orbit, round; make a pass; come full circle, close the circle, make a round trip, return to the starting point; cycle; spiral, gyre; go around in circles, chase one's tail, go round and round; revolve 915.9; **compass,** encompass, encircle, surround; skirt, flank; go the round, make the round of, make one's rounds, circuiteer <old>; lap; circumambulate, circummigrate; circumnavigate, girdle, girdle the globe

6 turn, go around, round, turn *or* round a corner, corner, round a bend, double *or* round a point

ADJS **7 circuitous, roundabout, out-of-the-way, devious, oblique, indirect,** ambagious <old>, meandering, backhanded; **deviative** 164.7, **deviating,** digressive, discursive, excursive; equivocatory 936.14; evasive 368.15; vacillating 362.10; **circular** 280.11, **round,** wheel-shaped, O-shaped; spiral, helical; orbital; rotary 915.15

8 circumambient, circumambulatory, circumforaneous, circumfluent, circumvolant, circumnavigatory, circumnavigable

ADVS **9 circuitously, deviously, obliquely,** ambagiously <old> **indirectly, round about,** about it *and* about, round Robin Hood's barn, in a roundabout way, by a side door, by a side wind; circlewise, wheelwise

915 ROTATION

NOUNS **1 rotation, revolution,** roll, **gyration, spin,** circulation; axial motion, rotational motion, angular motion, angular momentum, angular velocity; circumrotation, circumgyration, circumvolution, full circle; **turning, whirling,** swirling, **spinning,** wheeling, reeling, whir; **spiraling,** twisting upward *or* downward, gyring, volution, turbination; centrifugation; swiveling, pivoting, swinging; **rolling,** trolling, trundling, bowling, volutation <old>

2 **whirl,** wheel, reel, **spin, turn,** round; spiral, helix, helicoid, gyre; pirouette; **swirl,** twirl, **eddy,** gurge, surge; vortex, **whirlpool,** maelstrom, Charybdis; dizzy round, rat race; tourbillion, **whirlwind** 318.13, twister; rotary, roundabout, traffic circle

3 revolutions, **revs** <nf>; revolutions per minute *or* rpm

4 **rotator, rotor; roller,** rundle; **whirler,** whirligig, **top,** whirlabout; **merry-go-round,** carousel, roundabout; **wheel,** disk; Ixion's wheel; rolling stone; revolving door; spit, rotisserie; whirling dervish

5 **axle, axis; pivot,** gudgeon, trunnion, **swivel, spindle,** arbor, pole, radiant; fulcrum 901.2; pin, pintle; **hub,** nave; axle shaft, axle spindle, axle bar, axle-tree; distaff; mandrel; gimbal; **hinge,** hingle <nf>; rowlock, oarlock

6 **axle box,** journal, journal box; hotbox; universal joint

7 **bearing,** ball bearing, journal bearing, saw bearing, tumbler bearing, main bearing, needle bearing, roller bearing, thrust bearing, bevel bearing, bushing; jewel; headstock

8 <science of rotation> trochilics, gyrostatics

VERBS 9 **rotate, revolve, spin, turn,** round, **go round** *or* **around,** turn round *or* around; **spiral, gyrate,** gyre, whirl like a dervish; circumrotate, circumvolute; circle, circulate; **swivel, pivot, wheel,** swing; pirouette, turn a pirouette; wind, twist, screw, crank; wamble

10 **roll,** trundle, troll, **bowl;** roll up, **furl**

11 **whirl,** whirligig, twirl, **wheel, reel, spin,** spin like a top *or* teetotum, whirl like a dervish; centrifuge, centrifugate; **swirl,** gurge, surge, **eddy,** whirlpool

12 <move around in confusion> **seethe, mill,** mill around *or* about, stir, roil, moil, be turbulent

13 <roll about in> **wallow, welter,** grovel, roll, flounder, tumble

ADJS 14 **rotating, revolving, turning,** gyrating; **whirling, swirling,** twirling, **spinning,** wheeling, **reeling; rolling,** trolling, bowling

15 **rotary, rotational,** rotatory, rotative; trochilic, vertiginous; circumrotatory, circumvolutory, circumgyratory; spiral, spiralling, helical, gyral, gyratory, gyrational, gyroscopic, gyrostatic; whirly, swirly, gulfy; whirlabout, whirligig; vortical, cyclonic, tornadic, whirlwindy, whirlwindish

ADVS 16 **round, around,** round about, **in a circle; round and round,** in circles, like a horse in a mill; in a whirl, in a spin; head over heels, heels over head; clockwise, counterclockwise, anticlockwise, widdershins

916 OSCILLATION

<motion to and fro>

NOUNS 1 **oscillation, vibration,** vibrancy; to-and-fro motion; harmonic motion, simple harmonic motion; libration, nutation; pendulation; **fluctuation,** vacillation, wavering 362.2; electrical oscillation, mechanical oscillation, oscillating current; libration of the moon, libration in latitude *or* longitude; vibratility; **frequency,** frequency band *or* spectrum; resonance, resonant *or* resonance frequency; **periodicity** 850.2

2 **waving,** wave motion, **undulation,** undulancy; **brandishing, flourishing,** flaunting, shaking, swaying; brandish, flaunt, flourish; wave 238.14

3 **pulsation, pulse, beat, throb;** beating, throbbing; systole, diastole; rat-a-tat, staccato, rataplan, drumming 55.1; **rhythm, tempo** 709.24; **palpitation,** flutter, arrhythmia, pitter-patter, pit-a-pat; fibrillation, ventricular fibrillation, tachycardia, ventricular tachycardia <all medicine>; **heartbeat,** heartthrob

4 **wave,** wave motion, ray; transverse wave, longitudinal wave; electromagnetic wave, electromagnetic radiation; **light** 1025; **radio wave** 1034.11; mechanical wave; acoustic wave, **sound wave** 50.1; transverse wave; seismic wave, **shock wave;** de Broglie wave; diffracted wave, guided wave; one- *or* two- *or* three-dimensional wave; periodic wave; standing wave, node, antinode; sea wave, surface wave, **tidal wave,** tsunami, seismic sea wave; traveling wave; surge, storm surge; amplitude, crest, trough; scend; **surf,** roller, curler, comber, whitecap, white horse; tube; wavelength; frequency, frequency band *or* spectrum; resonance, resonant *or* resonance frequency; period; wave number; diffraction; reinforcement, interference; in phase, out of phase; wave equation, Schrödinger equation; Huygens' principle

5 **alternation, reciprocation;** regular *or* rhythmic play, **coming and going,** to-and-fro, back-and-forth, ebb and flow, *va-et-vien* <Fr>, flux and reflux, systole and diastole, ups and downs, wax and wane, systole and diastole; sine wave, Lissajous figure *or* curve; **seesawing, teetering,** tottering, **teeter-tottering;** seesaw, teeter, teeter-totter, wigwag; zig-zag, zig-zagging, zig, zag

6 **swing,** swinging, **sway,** swag; **rock, lurch, roll, reel,** careen; wag, waggle; wave, waver; swing of the pendulum

7 seismicity, seismism; seismology, seismography, seismometry

8 <instruments> oscilloscope, oscillograph, oscillometer; wavemeter; harmonograph;

vibroscope, vibrograph; kymograph; seismoscope, seismograph, seismometer; wave gauge

9 **oscillator, vibrator;** pendulum, pendulum wheel; metronome; swing; seesaw, teeter, teeter-totter, teeterboard, teetery-bender; rocker, rocking chair, cradle; rocking stone, logan stone, shuttle; shuttlecock

VERBS 10 **oscillate, vibrate,** librate, nutate; pendulate; **fluctuate,** vacillate, waver, wave; resonate; **swing, sway,** swag, dangle, **reel, rock, lurch, roll,** careen, toss, pitch; **wag,** waggle; **wobble,** coggle <Scot>, wamble; **bob,** bobble; squeg; shake, flutter 916.11

11 **wave, undulate; brandish, flourish,** flaunt, shake, swing, wield; float, fly; **flap, flutter;** wag, wigwag

12 **pulsate, pulse, beat, throb,** not miss a beat; **palpitate,** go pit-a-pat; miss a beat; beat time, beat out, tick, ticktock; drum 55.4

13 **alternate,** reciprocate, swing, **go to and fro,** to-and-fro, **come and go,** pass and re-pass, ebb and flow, wax and wane, ride and tie, hitch and hike, back and fill; **seesaw,** teeter, **teeter-totter;** shuttle, shuttlecock, battledore and shuttlecock; **wigwag,** wibble-wabble; zigzag

14 <move up and down> **pump, shake,** bounce

ADJS 15 **oscillating,** oscillatory; **vibrating,** vibratory, harmonic; vibratile; librational, libratory; nutational; **periodic,** pendular, pendulous; **fluctuating,** fluctuational, fluctuant; wavering; vacillating, vacillatory; resonant

16 **waving, undulating,** undulatory, undulant; seismic

17 **swinging, swaying,** dangling, **reeling, rocking, lurching,** careening, **rolling,** tossing, pitching

18 pulsative, pulsatory, pulsatile; **pulsating, pulsing, beating, throbbing, palpitating,** palpitant, pit-a-pat, staccato; rhythmic 709.28

19 **alternate, reciprocal,** reciprocative; sine-wave; **back-and-forth, to-and-fro,** up-and-down, seesaw

20 seismatical, seismological, seismographic, seismometric; successive, successory, sussultatory

ADVS 21 **to and fro, back and forth,** backward and forward, backwards and forwards, **in and out, up and down,** seesaw, shuttlewise, from side to side, from pillar to post, off and on, ride and tie, hitch and hike, round and round, like buckets in a well

917 AGITATION
<irregular motion>

NOUNS 1 **agitation, perturbation,** hecticness, conturbation <old>; **frenzy, excitement** 105; **trepidation** 127.5, trepidity, fidgets *and* jitters *and* ants in the pants <nf>, antsiness *and* jitteriness <nf>, heebie-jeebies <nf>, jumpiness, nervousness, yips <nf>, nerviness <Brit>, nervosity, twitter, upset; **unrest, malaise, unease,** restlessness; fever, feverishness, febrility; **disquiet,** disquietude, inquietude, discomposure, hand-wringing; **stir, churn, ferment,** fermentation, foment; seethe, seething, ebullition, boil, boiling; embroilment, roil, turbidity, fume; **disturbance, commotion,** moil, **turmoil, turbulence** 671.2, **swirl, tumult,** tumultuation, hubbub, shemozzle <Brit nf>, rout, fuss, row, to-do, bluster, fluster, flurry, flutteration, hoo-ha *and* flap <nf>, bustle, brouhaha, bobbery, hurly-burly; maelstrom; **disorder** 810

2 **shaking, quaking,** palsy, **quivering, quavering, shivering, trembling,** tremulousness, **shuddering, vibration;** juddering <Brit>, succussion; jerkiness, fits and starts, spasms; jactation, jactitation; joltiness, bumpiness, the shakes *and* the shivers *and* the cold shivers <nf>, ague, chattering; chorea, rigor, St Vitus's dance; delirium tremens *or* the DT's

3 **shake, quake, quiver, quaver,** falter, **tremor, tremble, shiver, shudder,** twitter, didder, dither; **wobble; bob,** bobble; **jog,** joggle; **shock, jolt,** jar, jostle; **bounce,** bump; **jerk, twitch,** tic, grimace, rictus, vellication; jig, jiggle; the shakes <nf>

4 **flutter,** flitter, flit, **flicker, waver,** dance; shake, quiver 917.3; **sputter, splutter; flap,** flop <nf>; **beat,** beating; **palpitation,** throb, pit-a-pat, pitter-patter

5 **twitching, jerking,** vellication; **fidgets,** fidgetiness; itchiness, formication, pruritus

6 **spasm, convulsion,** cramp, **paroxysm,** throes; **orgasm,** sexual climax; epitasis, eclampsia; **seizure,** grip, attack, **fit,** access, ictus; epilepsy, falling sickness; stroke, apoplexy

7 **wiggle, wriggle;** wag, waggle; writhe, **squirm**

8 **flounder,** flounce, stagger, totter, stumble, falter; wallow, welter; **roll, rock, reel, lurch,** careen, **swing, sway; toss, tumble,** pitch, plunge

9 <instruments> **agitator,** shaker, jiggler, vibrator; beater, stirrer, paddle, whisk, eggbeater; churn; blender

VERBS 10 **agitate, shake, disturb, perturb,** shake up, perturbate, **disquiet, discompose, upset, trouble, unsettle, stir,** swirl, flurry, flutter, flutter the dovecot, fret, roughen, ruffle, rumple, ripple, ferment, convulse; **churn,** whip, whisk, beat, paddle; **excite** 105.12; **stir up,** cause a stir *or* commotion, muddy the waters, shake up a hornet's nest <nf>; work up, shake up, churn up, whip up, beat up; roil, rile <nf>; disarrange 811.2

11 **shake, quake, vibrate,** jactitate; **tremble, quiver, quaver,** falter, **shudder, shiver,** twitter, didder, chatter; shake in one's boots *or* shoes, quake *or* shake *or* tremble like an aspen leaf, have the jitters

or the shakes <nf>, have ants in one's pants <nf>; have an ague; **wobble; bob,** bobble; jiggle, **jog,** joggle; **shock, jolt,** jar, jostle, hustle, jounce, **bounce,** jump, bump

12 **flutter,** flitter, flit, flick, **flicker,** gutter, bicker, wave, **waver,** dance; **sputter, splutter; flap,** flop <nf>, flip, beat, slat; **palpitate,** pulse, throb, pitter-patter, go pit-a-pat

13 **twitch, jerk,** vellicate; itch; **jig, jiggle,** jigger *or* jigget <nf>; **fidget,** have the fidgets

14 **wiggle, wriggle;** wag, waggle; **writhe, squirm,** twist and turn; have ants in one's pants <nf>

15 **flounder,** flounce, **stagger,** totter, stumble, falter, blunder, wallop; **struggle,** labor; **wallow, welter; roll, rock, reel, lurch,** career, career, **swing, sway; toss, tumble,** thrash about, **pitch, plunge,** pitch and plunge, toss and tumble, toss and turn, be the sport of winds and waves; **seethe**

ADJS 16 **agitated, disturbed, perturbed, disquieted, discomposed, troubled, upset, ruffled,** flurried, flustered, unsettled; stirred up, shaken, shaken up, all worked up, all shook up <nf>; troublous, feverish, fidgety *and* jittery *and* antsy <nf>, jumpy, nervous, nervy <Brit>, restless, uneasy, unquiet, unpeaceful; all of a twitter <nf>, all of a flutter, giddy, in a spin; turbulent; excited 105.18,20,22

17 **shaking, vibrating,** chattering; **quivering, quavering, quaking, shivering, shuddering, trembling, tremulous,** palsied, aspen; successive, successatory; **shaky,** quivery, quavery, shivery, trembly; wobbly; juddering

18 **fluttering, flickering, wavering,** guttering, dancing; sputtering, spluttering, sputtery; fluttery, flickery, bickering, flicky, wavery, unsteady, desultory

19 **jerky,** herky-jerky <nf>, twitchy *or* twitchety, jerking, **twitching, fidgety, jumpy,** jiggety <nf>, vellicative; **spastic, spasmodic,** eclamptic, orgasmic, convulsive; fitful, saltatory

20 **jolting,** jolty, **joggling,** joggly, jogglety, jouncy, **bouncy, bumpy,** choppy, rough; **jarring,** bone-bruising

21 **wriggly,** wriggling, crawly, creepy-crawly <nf>; **wiggly,** wiggling; squirmy, squirming; writhy, writhing, antsy <nf>

ADVS 22 **agitatedly, troublously, restlessly,** uneasily, unquietly, unpeacefully, nervously, feverishly; **excitedly**

23 **shakily,** quiveringly, quaveringly, quakingly, **tremblingly,** shudderingly, tremulously; flutteringly, waveringly, unsteadily, desultorily; **jerkily,** spasmodically, fitfully, by jerks, by snatches, saltatorily, by fits and starts, "with many a flirt and flutter"—Pope

918 SPECTATOR

NOUNS 1 **spectator, observer; looker, onlooker,** looker-on, **watcher,** gazer, gazer-on, gaper, goggler, eyer, **viewer,** seer, beholder, perceiver, percipient; spectatress, spectatrix; **witness, eyewitness; bystander,** passerby; innocent bystander; sidewalk superintendent; kibitzer; girl-watcher, ogler, drugstore cowboy <nf>; bird-watcher; **viewer,** television-viewer, televiewer, video-gazer, TV-viewer, couch potato <nf>, armchair quarterback; peeping tom

2 **attender** 221.5, attendee; theatergoer; **audience** 48.6, house, crowd, gate, fans

3 **sightseer,** excursionist, **tourist,** rubberneck *or* **rubbernecker** <nf>; slummer; tour group

4 **sightseeing,** rubbernecking <nf>, lionism <Brit nf>; **tour,** walking tour, bus tour, sightseeing tour *or* excursion, **rubberneck tour** <nf>; grand tour, globetrotting; spectator sport

VERBS 5 **spectate** <nf>, witness, **see** 27.12, look on, eye, **ogle, gape;** take in, **look at, watch;** attend 221.8

6 **sightsee,** see the sights, take in the sights, lionize *or* see the lions <Brit nf>; **rubberneck** <nf>; go slumming; go on a tour, join a tour; take the grand tour, globe-trot

ADJS 7 spectating, spectatorial; onlooking; sight-seeing, rubberneck <nf>; passing by, caught in the cross-fire *or* in the middle

919 INTELLECT
<mental faculty>

NOUNS 1 **intellect, mind,** *mens* <L>; mental *or* intellectual faculty, nous, **reason, rationality,** rational *or* reasoning faculty, power of reason, *Vernunft* <Ger>, *esprit* <Fr>, *raison* <Fr>, ratio, discursive reason, **intelligence,** mentality, mental capacity, **understanding,** reasoning, intellection, conception; cognition, perception; **brain, brains,** brainpower, smarts *and* gray matter <nf>; **thought** 931; head, headpiece

2 **wits, senses, faculties,** parts, capacities, intellectual gifts *or* talents, mother wit; intellectuals <old>; consciousness 928.2

3 **inmost mind,** inner recesses of the mind, mind's core, deepest mind, center of the mind; inner man; subconscious, subconscious mind; inmost heart

4 **psyche, spirit,** spiritus, **soul,** geist, *âme* <Fr>, **heart, mind,** inner mind, inner being, anima, *anima humana* <L>, animus; tabula rasa; shade, shadow, manes; breath, pneuma, breath of life, divine breath; *atman* and *purusha* and *buddhi* and

jiva and *jivatma* <all Skt>; *ba* and *khu* <Egyptian myth>; *ruach* and *nephesh* <Hebrew>; spiritual being, inner man; **ego,** the self, the I

5 **life principle,** vital principle, vital spirit *or* soul, *élan vital* <Fr>, **vital force,** *prana* <Hindu>; essence *or* substance of life, individual essence, *ousia* <Gk>; divine spark, vital spark *or* flame; chi *or* qi, tao, ahimsa

6 **brain** 2.15, seat *or* organ of thought; sensory, sensorium; encephalon; gray matter, head, cerebrum, pate *and* sconce *and* noddle <nf>; noodle *or* noggin *or* bean *or* upper story <nf>; sensation 24

ADJS 7 **mental, intellectual, rational, reasoning, thinking,** noetic, conceptive, conceptual, phrenic; intelligent 920.12; noological; endopsychic, psychic, psychical, psychologic, psychological, spiritual; cerebral; subjective, internal

920 INTELLIGENCE, WISDOM
<mental capacity>

NOUNS 1 **intelligence, understanding,** *Verstand* <Ger>, **comprehension,** apprehension, mental *or* intellectual grasp, prehensility of mind, intellectual power, brainpower, thinking power, power of mind *or* thought; ideation, conception; integrative power, esemplastic power; rationality, reasoning *or* deductive power, ratiocination; **sense, wit,** mother wit, natural *or* native wit; **intellect** 919; **intellectuality,** intellectualism; capacity, mental capacity, **mentality,** caliber, reach *or* compass *or* scope of mind; **IQ** *or* intelligence quotient, mental ratio, mental age; sanity 925; knowledge 928

2 **smartness, braininess,** smarts *and* savvy <nf>, **brightness, brilliance, cleverness,** aptness, aptitude, native cleverness, mental alertness, nous, **sharpness, keenness,** acuity, acuteness; high IQ, **mental ability** *or* **capability,** gift, gifts, giftedness, **talent, flair, genius;** quickness, nimbleness, quickness *or* nimbleness of wit, adroitness, dexterity; sharp-wittedness, keen-wittedness, quick-wittedness, nimble-wittedness; nimble mind, mercurial mind, quick parts, clear *or* quick thinking; ready wit, quick wit, sprightly wit, *esprit* <Fr>

3 **shrewdness, artfulness, cunning,** cunningness, canniness, **craft, craftiness,** wiliness, guilefulness, slickness <nf>, **slyness,** pawkiness <Brit>, foxiness <nf>, peasant *or* animal cunning, low cunning; subtility, subtilty, **subtlety;** insinuation, insidiousness, deviousness

4 **sagacity,** sagaciousness, **astuteness, acumen,** longheadedness; **foresight,** foresightedness, providence; **farsightedness,** farseeingness, longsightedness; **discernment, insight,** intuition, penetration, acuteness, acuity; perspicacity, perspicaciousness, perspicuity, perspicuousness; incisiveness, trenchancy, cogency; **percipience** *or* percipiency, **perception,** apperception; **sensibility** 24.2

5 **wisdom,** ripe wisdom, seasoned understanding, mellow wisdom, wiseness, sageness, sagacity, sapience, good *or* sound understanding; Sophia <female personification of wisdom>; erudition 928.5; **profundity,** profoundness, depth; broadmindedness 979; **conventional wisdom,** received wisdom, prudential judgment

6 **sensibleness, reasonableness,** reason, rationality, sanity, saneness, **soundness; practicality,** practical wisdom, practical mind; **sense,** good *or* common *or* plain sense, **horse sense** <nf>; due sense of; level head, cool head, **levelheadedness,** balance, coolheadedness, coolness; soberness, sobriety, **sober-mindedness;** savvy, smarts

7 **judiciousness, judgment,** good *or* sound judgment, cool judgment, soundness of judgment, discernment; **prudence,** prudentialism, providence, policy, polity; weighing, consideration, circumspection, circumspectness, reflection, reflectiveness, **thoughtfulness; discretion,** discreetness; **discrimination**

8 **genius,** *Geist* <Ger>, spirit, soul; daimonion, demon, daemon; **inspiration,** afflatus, divine afflatus; Muse; fire of genius; **creativity;** talent 413.4; creative thought 986.2

9 <intelligent being> **intelligence, intellect,** head, brain, mentality, consciousness; wise man 921; intellectual, thinker, academic, savant, scholar, walking encyclopedia; adept, maven

VERBS 10 **have all one's wits about one,** have all one's marbles *and* have smarts *or* savvy <nf>, have a head on one's shoulders **and** have one's head screwed on right <nf>; have method in one's madness; use one's head *or* wits, get *or* keep one's wits about one; know what's what, know the score <nf>, be wise as a serpent *or* an owl; be reasonable, listen to reason; be realistic, get real

11 be brilliant, **scintillate,** sparkle, coruscate

ADJS 12 **intelligent,** intellectual <old>; ideational, conceptual, conceptive, discursive; sophic, noetic, phrenic; **knowing, understanding, reasonable, rational, sensible, bright;** sane 925.4; not so dumb <nf>, strong-minded

13 **clear-witted,** clearheaded, clear-eyed, clearsighted; no-nonsense; awake, **wide-awake,** alive, **alert,** on the ball <nf>

14 **smart, brainy** <nf>, **bright, brilliant,** scintillating; **clever,** apt, **gifted,** talented; **sharp,** keen; **quick,**

nimble, adroit, astute, dexterous; **sharp-witted,** keen-witted, needle-witted, **quick-witted,** quick-thinking, steel-trap, nimble-witted, quick on the trigger *or* uptake <nf>; smart as a whip, sharp as a tack <nf>; nobody's fool *and* no dumbbell *and* not born yesterday <nf>, all there <nf>; nerdy, nerdish, nerdlike

15 **shrewd, artful, cunning, knowing, crafty, wily,** guileful, canny, slick, sly, pawky <Brit>, smart as a fox, foxy *and* crazy like a fox <nf>; **subtle,** subtile; insinuating, insidious, devious, Byzantine, calculating

16 **sagacious, astute,** longheaded, argute; **understanding, discerning,** penetrating, incisive, acute, trenchant, cogent, piercing; **foresighted,** foreseeing; forethoughted, forethoughtful, provident; **farsighted,** farseeing, longsighted; **perspicacious,** perspicuous; **perceptive, percipient,** apperceptive, appercipient

17 **wise, sage,** sapient, seasoned, **knowing,** knowledgeable; **learned** 928.21; **profound,** deep; wise as an owl *or* a serpent, wise as Solomon; wise beyond one's years, in advance of one's age, wise in one's generation; broad-minded 979.8

18 **sensible, reasonable,** reasoning, **rational, logical; practical,** pragmatic; philosophical; commonsense, commonsensical <nf>; **levelheaded,** balanced, coolheaded, cool, clearheaded, **sound, sane,** sober, **sober-minded,** well-balanced, lucid; realistic, ratiocinative; well thought-out; profound

19 **judicious,** judicial, judgmatic, judgmatical, **prudent,** prudential, politic, careful, provident, **considerate,** circumspect, sapient, **thoughtful,** reflective, reflecting; **discreet;** discriminative, discriminating; **well-advised,** well-judged, enlightened

ADVS 20 **intelligently, understandingly,** knowingly, discerningly; **reasonably,** rationally, sensibly; **smartly, cleverly; shrewdly,** artfully, cunningly; **wisely,** sagaciously, astutely; **judiciously, prudently,** discreetly, providently, considerately, circumspectly, thoughtfully

921 WISE PERSON

NOUNS 1 **wise man, wise woman, sage,** sapient, man *or* woman of wisdom; **master, mistress,** authority, mastermind, master spirit of the age, oracle; **philosopher,** thinker, lover of wisdom; rabbi; doctor; great soul, mahatma, guru, rishi; *starets* <Russ>, elder, wise old man, elder statesman; philosopher king; illuminate; seer; mentor; intellect, man of intellect; mandarin, **intellectual** 929; savant, **scholar** 929.3; logician,

dialectician, sophist, syllogist, metaphysician; adept

2 Solomon, Socrates, Plato, Mentor, Nestor, Confucius, Buddha, Gandhi, Albert Schweitzer, Martin Luther King Jr

3 **the wise,** the intelligent, the sensible, the prudent, the knowing, the understanding

4 Seven Wise Men of Greece, Seven Sages, Seven Wise Masters; Solon, Chilon, Pittacus, Bias, Periander, Epimenides, Cleobulus, Thales

5 Magi, Three Wise Men, Wise Men of the East, Three Kings; Three Kings of Cologne; Gaspar *or* Caspar, Melchior, Balthasar

6 **wiseacre,** wisehead, wiseling, **witling,** wisenheimer <nf>, wise guy, smart ass <nf>; wise fool; Gothamite, wise man of Gotham, wise man of Chelm

922 UNINTELLIGENCE

NOUNS 1 **unintelligence,** unintellectuality <old>, unwisdom, unwiseness, intellectual *or* mental weakness; **senselessness, witlessness, mindlessness,** brainlessness, primal stupidity, *Urdummheit* <Ger>, reasonlessness, lackwittedness, lackbrainedness, slackwittedness, slackmindedness; **irrationality; ignorance** 930; **foolishness** 923; incapacity, ineptitude; low IQ, low mental age

2 **unperceptiveness,** imperceptiveness, insensibility, impercipience *or* impercipiency, undiscerningness, unapprehendingness, **incomprehension,** nonunderstanding; **blindness,** mindblindness, purblindness; **unawareness,** lack of awareness, unconsciousness, lack of consciousness; **shortsightedness,** nearsightedness, dim-sightedness

3 **stupidity,** stupidness, *bêtise* <Fr>, **dumbness** <nf>, **doltishness,** boobishness, duncery <old>, dullardism, blockishness, cloddishness, lumpishness, sottishness, **asininity,** ninnyism, simplemindedness, simpletonianism; oafishness, oafdom, yokelism, loutishness; **density,** denseness, opacity; grossness, crassness, crudeness, boorishness; **dullness,** dopiness <nf>, **obtuseness,** sluggishness, bovinity, cowishness, slowness, lethargy, stolidity, hebetude; **dim-wittedness,** dimness, **dull-wittedness,** slow-wittedness, beef-wittedness, dull-headedness, **thick-wittedness,** thick-headedness, unteachability, ineducability; wrongheadedness

4 <nf terms> **blockheadedness,** woodenheadedness, klutziness, dunderheadedness, goofiness, jolterheadedness *or* joltheadedness <Brit>, chowderheadedness, chuckleheadedness,

beetleheadedness, chumpiness, numskulledness *or* numskullery, cabbageheadedness, sapheadedness, muttonheadedness, meatheadedness, fatheadedness, boneheadedness, knuckleheadedness, blunderheadedness

5 **muddleheadedness,** addleheadedness, addlepatedness, puzzleheadedness

6 **empty-headedness,** empty-mindedness, absence of mind, airheadedness *and* bubbleheadedness <nf>; **vacuity,** vacuousness, vacancy, vacuum, emptiness, mental void, blankness, hollowness, inanity, vapidity, jejunity

7 **superficiality, shallowness, unprofundity,** lack of depth, unprofoundness, thinness; shallow-wittedness, shallow-mindedness; **frivolousness,** flightiness, lightness, fluffiness, frothiness, volatility, dizziness *and* ditziness <nf>

8 **feeblemindedness,** weak-mindedness; infirmity, weakness, feebleness, softness, mushiness <nf>

9 **mental deficiency,** mental retardation, amentia, mental handicap, subnormality, mental defectiveness; brain damage; **arrested development,** infantilism, retardation, retardment, backwardness; **simplemindedness,** simple-wittedness, simpleness, simplicity; **idiocy,** idiotism <old>, profound idiocy, **imbecility, half-wittedness,** blithering idiocy; moronity, moronism, **cretinism;** mongolism, mongolianism, mongoloid idiocy, Down's syndrome; insanity 926

10 **senility,** senilism, senile weakness, senile debility, caducity, decrepitude, senectitude, decline; **childishness, second childhood, dotage, dotardism;** anility; senile dementia, senile psychosis, Alzheimer's disease

11 **puerility,** puerilism, immaturity, **childishness; infantilism,** babyishness

VERBS 12 **be stupid,** show ignorance, not have all one's marbles; drool, slobber, drivel, dither, blither, blather, maunder, dote, burble; not see an inch beyond one's nose, not have enough sense to come in out of the rain, not find one's way to first base; lose one's mind *or* marbles; not be all there; have a low IQ

ADJS 13 **unintelligent,** unintellectual <old>, **unthinking, unreasoning, irrational,** unwise, inept, **not bright;** ungifted, untalented; **senseless,** insensate; **mindless, witless, reasonless, brainless,** pin-brained, pea-brained, of little brain, headless, empty-headed; **lackwitted,** lackbrained, slackwitted, slackminded, lean-minded, lean-witted, short-witted; **foolish** 923.8; **ignorant** 930.11

14 **undiscerning, unperceptive,** imperceptive, impercipient, insensible, unapprehending, uncomprehending, nonunderstanding; **shortsighted,** myopic, nearsighted, dim-sighted; **blind,** purblind, mind-blind, blind as a bat; blinded, blindfold, blindfolded

15 **stupid, dumb,** dullard, **doltish,** blockish, klutzy *and* klutzish <nf>, duncish, duncical, cloddish, clottish <Brit>, chumpish <nf>, lumpish, **oafish,** boobish, sottish, **asinine,** lamebrained, Boeotian; **dense,** thick <nf>, opaque, gross, crass, fat; bovine, cowish, beef-witted, beef-brained, beefheaded; unteachable, ineducable; wrongheaded

16 **dull,** dull of mind, **dopey** <nf>, **obtuse,** blunt, dim, wooden, heavy, sluggish, slow, **slow-witted,** hebetudinous, **dim-witted, dull-witted,** blunt-witted, dull-brained, dull-headed, dull-pated, **thick-witted,** thick-headed, thick-pated, thick-skulled, thick-brained, fat-witted, gross-witted, gross-headed

17 <nf terms> **blockheaded,** woodenheaded, stupidheaded, dumbheaded, dunderheaded, blunderheaded, clueless *or* jolterheaded *or* joltheaded *or* jingle-brained <Brit>, chowderheaded, chuckleheaded, beetleheaded, nitwitted, numskulled, cabbageheaded, pumpkin-headed, sapheaded, lunkheaded, muttonheaded, meatheaded, fatheaded, boneheaded, knuckleheaded, clodpated; dead from the neck up, dead above *or* between the ears, muscle-bound between the ears; featherheaded, airheaded, bubbleheaded, out to lunch, lunchy, dufus, dufus-assed, spastic, spazzy, three bricks shy of a load, without brain one, not playing with a full deck, not sixteen ounces to the pound, not all there, soft in the head

18 **muddleheaded, fuddlebrained** *and* scramblebrained <nf>, mixed-up, muddled, addled, addleheaded, **addlepated,** addlebrained, muddybrained, puzzleheaded, blear-witted; dizzy <nf>, muzzy, foggy

19 **empty-headed,** empty-minded, empty-noddled, empty-pated, empty-skulled; **vacuous,** vacant, empty, hollow, inane, vapid, jejune, blank, airheaded *and* bubbleheaded <nf>; **rattlebrained,** rattleheaded; scatterbrained 985.16

20 **superficial, shallow, unprofound;** shallow-witted, shallow-minded, shallow-brained, shallow-headed, shallow-pated; **frivolous,** dizzy *and* ditzy <nf>, flighty, light, volatile, frothy, fluffy, **featherbrained, birdwitted, birdbrained**

21 **feebleminded, weak-minded,** weak, feeble,

infirm, soft, soft in the head, weak in the upper story <nf>

22 **mentally deficient,** mentally defective, mentally handicapped, retarded, **mentally retarded,** backward, arrested, subnormal, not right in the head, **not all there** <nf>; **simpleminded,** simplewitted, simple, simpletonian; **half-witted,** half-baked <nf>; **idiotic, moronic, imbecile,** imbecilic, cretinous, cretinistic, mongoloid, spastic <nf>; crackbrained, cracked, crazy; babbling, driveling, slobbering, drooling, blithering, dithering, maundering, burbling; brain-damaged

23 **senile,** decrepit, doddering, doddery; **childish,** childlike, in one's second childhood, **doting**

24 **puerile,** immature, **childish;** childlike; **infantile,** infantine; **babyish,** babish

ADVS 25 **unintelligently, stupidly;** insensately, foolishly

923 FOOLISHNESS

NOUNS 1 **foolishness, folly,** foolery, foolheadedness, **stupidity, asininity,** niaiserie <Fr>; bêtise <Fr>; **inanity, fatuity,** fatuousness; ineptitude; **silliness; frivolousness,** frivolity, giddiness; triviality, triflingness, nugacity, desipience; **nonsense,** tomfoolery, poppycock; **senselessness, insensateness, witlessness, thoughtlessness,** brainlessness, mindlessness; **idiocy, imbecility; craziness, madness,** lunacy, **insanity,** daftness; **eccentricity, queerness,** crankiness, crackpottedness; weirdness; screwiness and nuttiness and wackiness and goofiness and daffiness and battiness and sappiness <nf>; zaniness, zanyism, **clownishness, buffoonery,** clowning, fooling or horsing or dicking around <nf>

2 **unwiseness,** unwisdom, **injudiciousness, imprudence;** indiscreetness, **indiscretion,** inconsideration, thoughtlessness, witlessness, inattention, unthoughtfulness, lack of sensitivity; **unreasonableness, unsoundness, unsensibleness,** senselessness, reasonlessness, **irrationality, unreason,** inadvisability; recklessness; childishness, immaturity, puerility, callowness; gullibility, bamboozlability <nf>; inexpedience 996; unintelligence 922; pompousness, stuffiness

3 **absurdity,** absurdness, **ridiculousness;** ludicrousness 488.1; **nonsense,** nonsensicality, stuff and nonsense, codswallop <Brit nf>, horseshit and bullshit <nf>; **preposterousness,** fantasticalness, monstrousness, wildness, **outrageousness**

4 <foolish act> **folly, stupidity,** act of folly, absurdity, sottise <Fr>, foolish or stupid thing, dumb thing to do <nf>; fool or fool's trick, dumb trick <nf>; **imprudence, indiscretion,** imprudent or unwise step; blunder 975.5, blooper <nf>, gaffe

5 stultification; infatuation; trivialization

VERBS 6 **be foolish;** be stupid 922.12; **act** or **play the fool;** get funny, do the crazy act or bit or shtick <nf>; **fool, tomfool** <nf>, **trifle,** frivol; **fool** or **horse around** <nf>, dick around <nf>, clown, clown around; **make a fool of oneself,** make a monkey of oneself <nf>, stultify oneself, invite ridicule, put oneself out of court, play the buffoon; **lose one's head, take leave of one's senses,** go haywire; pass from the sublime to the ridiculous; strain at a gnat and swallow a camel; tilt at windmills; tempt fate, never learn

7 stultify, infatuate, turn one's head, befool; gull, dupe; **make a fool of,** make a monkey of and play for a sucker and put on <nf>

ADJS 8 **foolish,** fool <nf>, foolheaded <nf>, **stupid, dumb** <nf>, clueless <Brit nf>, **asinine,** wet <Brit>; buffoonish; **silly,** apish, dizzy <nf>; **fatuous,** fatuitous, inept, **inane;** futile; **senseless, witless, thoughtless,** insensate, brainless; **idiotic,** moronic, imbecile, imbecilic, spastic <nf>; **crazy, mad,** daft, **insane;** infatuated, besotted, credulous, gulled, befooled, beguiled, fond, doting, gaga; sentimental, maudlin; dazed, fuddled

9 <nf terms> **screwy, nutty,** cockeyed, wacky, goofy, daffy, loony, batty, sappy, kooky, flaky, damn-fool, out of it, out to lunch, lunchy, dorky, dippy, bird-brained, spaced-out, doodle-brained, lame, ditzy, dizzy, loony-tune, dopey, fluffheaded, loopy, scatty, zerking

10 **unwise,** injudicious, **imprudent,** unpolitic, impolitic, contraindicated, **counterproductive;** indiscreet; inconsiderate, thoughtless, mindless, witless, unthoughtful, unthinking, unreflecting, unreflective; **unreasonable, unsound, unsensible,** senseless, insensate, reasonless, **irrational,** reckless, inadvisable; inexpedient 996.5; **ill-advised, ill-considered,** ill-gauged, ill-judged, ill-imagined, ill contrived, ill devised, on the wrong track, unconsidered; unadvised, misadvised, misguided; undiscerning; unforseeing, unseeing, shortsighted, myopic; suicidal, self-defeating

11 **absurd, nonsensical,** insensate, ridiculous, laughable, ludicrous 488.4; **foolish, crazy;** preposterous, cockamamie <nf>, fantastic, fantastical, grotesque, monstrous, wild, weird,

outrageous, incredible, beyond belief, outré <Fr>, extravagant, **bizarre;** high-flown

12 foolable, befoolable, gullible, bamboozlable <nf>; naive, artless, guileless, inexperienced, impressionable; malleable, like putty; persuasible, biddable

ADVS **13 foolishly, stupidly,** sillily, idiotically; **unwisely,** injudiciously, imprudently, indiscreetly, inconsiderately; myopically, blindly, senselessly, unreasonably, thoughtlessly, witlessly, imsensately, unthinkingly; absurdly, ridiculously

924 FOOL

NOUNS **1 fool, damn fool,** tomfool, perfect fool, born fool; *schmuck* <Yiddish>; **ass,** jackass, stupid ass, egregious ass; zany, **clown, buffoon,** doodle; sop, milksop; mome <old>, mooncalf, softhead; figure of fun; **lunatic** 926.15; **ignoramus** 930.7

2 **stupid person, dolt, dunce,** clod, Boeotian, **dullard,** *niais* <Fr>, donkey, yahoo, thickwit, **dope, nitwit,** dimwit, lackwit, half-wit, lamebrain, putz, lightweight, witling

3 <nf terms> **chump, boob,** booby, sap, prize sap, klutz, basket case, dingbat, dingdong, ding-a-ling, **ninny,** ninnyhammer, **nincompoop,** looby, noddy, saphead, mutt, jerk, jerk-off, asshole, goof, schlemiel, sawney <Brit>, galoot, gonzo, dumbo, dweeb, dropshop, dipshit, nerd, twerp, yo-yo

4 <nf terms> **blockhead, airhead,** bubblehead, fluffhead, featherhead, woodenhead, dolthead, dumbhead, dummy, dum-dum, dumbo, dumb cluck, dodo head, doodoohead, dumbbell, dumb bunny, stupidhead, dullhead, bufflehead, bonehead, jughead, thickhead, thickskull, numskull, putz, lunkhead, chucklehead, knucklehead, chowderhead, headbanger *and* jolterhead <Brit>, muttonhead, beefhead, meathead, noodle, noodlehead, thimblewit, pinhead, pinbrain, peabrain, cabbagehead, pumpkin head, fathead, blubberhead, muddlehead, puzzlehead, addlebrain, addlehead, addlepate, tottyhead <old>, puddinghead, stupe, mushhead, blunderhead, dunderhead, dunderpate, clodpate, clodhead, clodpoll, jobbernowl *and* gaby *and* gowk <Brit>, vegetable, dim-bulb, twit, sucker

5 **oaf, lout,** boor, lubber, oik <Brit>, **gawk,** gawky, **lummox,** yokel, rube, hick, hayseed, bumpkin, clod, clodhopper

6 **silly,** silly Billy <nf>, **silly ass, goose**

7 **scatterbrain,** scatterbrains *and* shatterbrain *or* shatterplate <old>, ditz <nf>, **rattlebrain,** rattlehead, rattlepate, **harebrain,** featherbrain, shallowbrain, shallowpate <old>, featherhead, giddybrain, giddyhead, giddypate, **flibbertigibbet**

8 **idiot,** driveling *or* blithering *or* adenoidal *or* congenital idiot; **imbecile, moron, half-wit,** natural, natural idiot, born fool, natural-born fool, mental defective, defective; cretin, mongolian *or* mongoloid idiot, basket case *and* spastic *and* spaz <nf>; simpleton, simp <nf>, juggins *and* jiggins <nf>, clot *and* berk <Brit nf>, golem

9 **dotard,** senile; fogy, **old fogy,** fuddy-duddy, old fart *or* fud

925 SANITY

NOUNS **1 sanity, saneness,** sanemindedness, soundness, **soundness of mind,** soundmindedness, sound mind, healthy mind, right mind <nf>, senses, reason, **rationality,** reasonableness, intelligibility, lucidity, coherence, stability, balance, wholesomeness; normalness, normality, normalcy; **mental health;** mental hygiene; mental balance *or* poise *or* equilibrium; sobriety, sober senses; a sound mind in a sound body, a healthy mind in a healthy body; contact with reality; lucid interval; knowing right from wrong; good sense, common sense, wits

VERBS **2 come to one's senses,** sober down *or* up, recover one's sanity *or* balance *or* equilibrium, get things into proportion; see in perspective; have all one's marbles <nf>; have a good head on one's shoulder; have one's wits about one

3 **bring to one's senses,** bring to reason

ADJS **4 sane,** sane-minded, not mad, **rational,** reasonable, sensible, **lucid,** normal, wholesome, clearheaded, clearminded, sober, balanced, **sound,** mentally sound, of sound mind, *compos mentis* <L>, sound-minded, healthy-minded, right, right in the head, **in one's right mind,** in possession of one's faculties *or* senses, together *and* all there <nf>; in touch with reality; with both oars in the water *and* playing with a full deck <nf>

926 INSANITY, MANIA

NOUNS **1 insanity,** insaneness, unsaneness, **lunacy, madness,** *folie* <Fr>, **craziness, daftness,** oddness, strangeness, queerness, abnormality; loss of touch *or* contact with reality, loss of mind *or* reason; dementedness, dementia, athymia, brainsickness, mindsickness, mental sickness, sickness; **criminal insanity,** homicidal mania, hemothymia; **mental illness, mental disease;** brain damage; rabidness, **mania,** furor; alienation, aberration, mental disturbance, **derangement,** distraction, disorientation, mental derangement *or* disorder, unbalance, mental instability, unsoundness, **unsoundness of mind;** unbalanced mind, diseased *or* unsound mind, **sick mind,** disturbed *or* troubled *or* clouded mind, shattered mind, mind overthrown *or* unhinged, darkened mind, disordered mind *or* reason; senselessness, witlessness, reasonlessness, irrationality; possession, pixilation; mental deficiency 922.9

2 <nf terms> **nuttiness,** craziness, daffiness, battiness, screwiness, goofiness, kookiness, wackiness, dottiness, pottiness, *mishegas* <Yiddish>, looniness, lunchiness, balminess; bats in the belfry, a screw loose, one wheel in the sand, one sandwich short of a picnic; lame brains

3 **psychosis,** psychopathy, psychopathology, psychopathic condition; certifiability; **neurosis;** psychopathia sexualis, sexology 75.18; pathological drunkenness *or* intoxication, dipsomania; pharmacopsychosis, drug addiction 87.1; moral insanity, psychopathic personality, *folie du doute* and *folie à deux* <Fr>, abulia 362.4

4 **schizophrenia, dementia praecox,** mental dissociation, dissociation of personality; catatonic schizophrenia, catatonia, residual schizophrenia, hebephrenia, hebephrenic schizophrenia; schizothymia; schizophasia; thought disorder; schizoid personality, split personality, schizotypal personality; **paranoia,** paraphrenia, paranoiac *or* paranoid psychosis; paranoid schizophrenia; schizoaffective disorder

5 **depression, melancholia,** depressive psychosis, dysthymia, barythymia, lypothymia; melancholia hypochrondriaca; involutional melancholia *or* psychosis; stuporous melancholia, melancholia attonita; flatuous melancholia; melancholia religiosa; postpartum depression; **manic-depressive disorder, manic-depression, bipolar disorder;** cyclothymia, poikilothymia, mood swings

6 **rabies, hydrophobia,** lyssa, canine madness; dumb *or* sullen rabies, paralytic rabies; furious rabies

7 **frenzy, furor,** fury, maniacal excitement, fever, **rage; seizure,** attack, acute episode, episode, **fit,** paroxysm, spasm, **convulsion; snit,** *crise* <Fr>; amok, murderous insanity *or* frenzy, homicidal mania, hemothymia; psychokinesia; furor epilepticus

8 **delirium,** deliriousness, brainstorm; calenture of the brain, afebrile delirium, lingual delirium, delirium mussitans; incoherence, wandering, raving, ranting; exhaustion delirium *or* infection, exhaustion psychosis

9 **delirium tremens,** mania *or* dementia a potu, delirium alcoholicum *or* ebriositatis

10 <nf terms> **the DT's,** the horrors, the shakes, the heebie-jeebies, the jimjams, the screaming meemies; blue Johnnies, blue devils, pink elephants, pink spiders, snakes, snakes in the boots, wigout

11 **fanaticism,** fanaticalness, **rabidness, overzealousness,** overenthusiasm, ultrazealousness, zealotry, zealotism, bigotry, perfervidness; extremism, extremeness, extravagance, excessiveness, overreaction; overreligiousness 692.3

12 **mania** <see lists>, **craze, infatuation, enthusiasm,** passion, fascination, crazy fancy, bug <nf>, rage, furor; manic psychosis; megalomania

13 **obsession,** prepossession, preoccupation, **hang-up** <nf>, **fixation,** tic, complex, fascination; hypercathexis; **compulsion,** morbid drive, obsessive compulsion, irresistible impulse; **monomania,** ruling passion, fixed idea, *idée fixe* <Fr>, one-track mind; **possession**

14 **insane asylum,** asylum, lunatic asylum, **madhouse,** mental institution, mental home, bedlam; **bughouse** and nuthouse and laughing academy and **loony bin** and **booby hatch** and funny farm <nf>; mental hospital, psychopathic hospital *or* ward, psychiatric hospital *or* ward; padded cell, rubber room

15 **lunatic, madman, madwoman,** dement, phrenetic *and* fanatic <old>, *fou* and *aliéné* <Fr>, non compos, *bacayaro* <Japanese>; bedlamite, Tom o' Bedlam; demoniac, energumen; mental case, **maniac,** raving lunatic; homicidal maniac, psychopathic killer, berserk *or* berserker; borderline case; mental defective, idiot 923.8; hypochondriac; melancholic, depressive; neurotic; headcase

16 <nf terms> **nut,** nutso, nutter, nutball, nutbar, nutcase, loon, loony, loony tune, headcase <Brit>, crazy, psycho, crackpot, screwball, weirdie, weirdo, kook, flake, crackbrain, *meshugana* <Yiddish>, fruitcake, schizo, wack, wacko, wigger, sickie, sicko, space cadet

17 **psychotic,** psycho <nf>, mental, mental case, certifiable case, **psychopath,** psychopathic case; psychopathic personality; paranoiac, paranoid; schizophrenic, schizophrene, schizoid; schiz *and* schizy *and* schizo <nf>; catatoniac; hebephreniac; manic-depressive; megalomaniac

18 **fanatic,** infatuate, **bug** <nf>, **nut** <nf>, **buff** *and* **fan** <nf>, freak <nf>, *fanatico* and *aficionado* <Sp>, devotee, **zealot, enthusiast,** energumen; monomaniac, crank <nf>; lunatic fringe

19 psychiatry, alienism, psychiatric care, psychotherapy; psychiatrist, alienist, psychotherapist

VERBS **20 be insane, be out of one's mind,** not be in one's right mind, not be right in the head, **not be all there** <nf>, have a demon *or* devil; have bats in the belfry *and* have a screw loose, not have all one's buttons *or* marbles <nf>, not play with a full deck *and* not have both oars in the water <nf>; **wander, ramble; rave,** rage, **rant,** have a fit; dote, babble; drivel, drool, slobber, slaver; froth *or* foam at the mouth, run mad, run amok, go berserk

21 go mad, take leave of one's senses, lose one's mind *or* senses *or* reason *or* wits, **crack up,** go off one's head <nf>

22 <nf terms> **go crazy, go bats,** go cuckoo, go bughouse, go nuts, go nutso, go out of one's gourd *or* skull *or* tree, go off one's nut *or* rocker, go off the track *or* trolley, go off the deep end, blow one's top *or* stack, pop one's cork, flip one's lid *or* wig, wig out, go ape *or* apeshit, schiz out, go bananas, go crackers *and* go bonkers <Brit>, go bonzo, blow one's mind, freak out, flip out, go hog wild, go round the bend <Brit>, have a screw loose, have bats in one's belfry, have rocks in one's head, lose one's marbles

23 addle the wits, **affect one's mind, go to one's head**

24 madden, dement, **craze,** mad <old>, make mad, send mad, **unbalance,** unhinge, undermine one's reason, **derange,** distract, frenzy, shatter, **drive insane** *or* mad *or* **crazy,** put *or* send out of one's mind, overthrow one's mind *or* reason, drive up the wall <nf>

25 obsess, possess, beset, infatuate, **preoccupy,** be uppermost in one's thoughts, have a thing about <nf>; grip, hold, get a hold on, not let go; **fixate; drive,** compel, impel

ADJS **26 insane,** unsane, **mad,** stark-mad, mad as a hatter, mad as a march hare, **stark-staring mad,** maddened, **sick,** crazed, **lunatic,** moonstruck, **daft, non compos mentis,** non compos, *baca* <Japanese>, **unsound,** of unsound mind, **demented, deranged,** deluded, disoriented, unhinged, **unbalanced,** unsettled, distraught, wandering, mazed, crackbrained, brainsick, sick *or* soft in the head, not right, not in one's right mind, **touched,** touched in the head, **out of one's mind,** out of one's senses *or* wits, bereft of reason, reasonless, irrational, deprived of reason, senseless, witless; hallucinated; manic; queer, queer in the head, odd, strange, off, flighty <old>; abnormal 870.9, mentally deficient 922.22

27 <nf terms> **crazy, nutty,** daffy, dotty, dippy, crazy as a bedbug *or* coot *or* loon, loony, loony-tune, goofy, wacky, balmy *or* barmy, flaky, kooky, potty, batty, ape, apeshit, wiggy, lunchy, out to lunch, bonzo, bats, nuts, nutso, nutty as a fruitcake, fruity, fruitcakey, screwy, screwball, screwballs, crackers <Brit>, bananas, bonkers <Brit>, loopy, beany, buggy, bughouse, bugs, cuckoo, slaphappy, flipped, freaked-out, off-the-wall, gaga, haywire, off in the upper story, off one's nut *or* rocker, off the track *or* trolley, off the hinges, round the bend <Brit>, minus some buttons, nobody home, with bats in the belfry, just plain nuts, loco, mental <Brit>, psycho, cracked, not right in the head, tetched, off one's head, out of one's head, out of one's gourd *or* skull, out of one's tree, not all there, *meshuga* *or* *meshugga* <Yiddish>, not tightly wrapped, three bricks shy of a load, rowing with one oar in the water, up the wall, off the wall, schizzy, schizoid, schizo

28 psychotic, psychopathic, psychoneurotic, mentally ill, mentally sick, certifiable; sociopathic; traumatized, deluded, disturbed, neurotic; schizophrenic, schizoid, schiz *or* schizy <nf>; hypochondriacal; dissociated, disconnected; depressed, depressive; manic; manic-depressive; maniacal; paranoiac, **paranoid;** catatonic; brain-damaged, brain-injured

29 possessed, possessed with a demon *or* devil, **pixilated, bedeviled,** demonized, devil-ridden, demonic, demonical, demoniacal

30 rabid, maniac *or* **maniacal,** manic, raving mad, stark-raving mad, **frenzied, frantic,** frenetic; **mad,** madding, **wild, furious, violent;** desperate; hysterical, **beside oneself,** like one possessed, uncontrollable; **raving, raging,** ranting; frothing *or* foaming at the mouth; **amok, berserk,** running wild; maenadic, corybantic, bacchic, Dionysiac

31 delirious, out of one's head <nf>, off one's head <nf>, off, deluded; **giddy,** dizzy, lightheaded; hallucinating, **wandering, rambling, raving, ranting,** babbling, incoherent

32 fanatic, fanatical, rabid; overzealous, ultrazealous, **overenthusiastic,** zealotic, bigoted, perfervid; **extreme,** extremist, extravagant, inordinate; **unreasonable, irrational; wild-eyed,** wild-looking, haggard; overreligious

33 obsessed, possessed, prepossessed, infatuated, preoccupied, fixated, **hung up** <nf>, besotted, gripped, held, fussy; monomaniac *or* monomaniacal; anal-retentive

34 obsessive, obsessional; **obsessing, possessing, preoccupying,** gripping, holding; driving, impelling, **compulsive, compelling;** anal-retentive

ADVS **35** madly, insanely, crazily; deliriously; fanatically, rabidly, etc

36 manias by subject

\<activity> ergasiomania
\<acute mania> hyperma-
  nia
\<alcohol> alcoholomania
\<alcoholic beverages>
  dipsomania
\<animals> zoomania
\<ablutomania> bathing
\<Beatles> Beatlemania
\<becoming larger>
  macromania
\<becoming smaller>
  micromania
\<bed rest> clinomania
\<bees> apimania
\<being in vehicles>
  amaxomania
\<birds> ornithomania
\<blushing> erythromania
\<book theft> bibliokleptomania
\<books> bibliomania
\<bullets> ballistomania
\<buying> oniomania
\<cats> ailuromania
\<China> Chinamania
\<cliffs> cremnomania
\<complaints> paramania
\<counting> arithmomania
\<crossing bridges>
  gephyromania
\<crowds> demomania *or*
  ochlomania
\<dancing> choreomania
\<Dante> Dantomania
\<death; the dead>
  necromania
\<death> thanatomania
\<deep melancholy>
  lypemania
\<delirium tremens>
  tromomania
\<demonic possession>
  cacodemonomania
\<dogs> cynomania
\<drinking water>
  hydrodipsomania
\<drinking> potomania
\<England> Anglomania
\<erotica> eroticomania
\<erotic literature>
  erotographomania
\<falsities> pseudomania
\<female lust> nympho-
  mania
\<fires> pyromania
\<fish> ichthyomania
\<flowers> anthomania

\<food; eating> phago-
  mania
\<food> sitomania
\<foreigners> xenomania
\<foul speech> coprolalo-
  mania
\<France> Francomania *or*
  Gallomania
\<freedom> eleuthromania
\<fur> doramania
\<gaiety> cheromania
\<genitals> edeomania
\<Germany> Germanoma-
  nia *or* Teutonomania
\<God> theomania
\<great wealth> cresomania
  or plutomania
\<Greece> Grecomania
\<grinding one's teeth>
  bruxomania
\<hair> trichomania
\<home> oikomania
\<homesickness> philopat-
  ridomania
\<horses> hippomania
\<hypnosis> mesmeromania
\<icons> iconomania
\<idols> idolomania
\<imagined disease>
  nosomania
\<incurable insanity>
  acromania
\<information> infomania
\<insects> entomomania
\<Italy> Italomania
\<lies; exaggerations>
  mythomania
\<light> photomania
\<lycanthropy> lycomania
\<male lust> satyromania
\<marriage> gamomania
\<medicines> pharmaco-
  mania
\<melancholia> tristimania
\<men> andromania
\<mice> musomania
\<mild mania> hypomania
  or submania
\<money> chrematomania
\<moral insanity>
  pathomania
\<movement> kinesomania
\<murder> homicidomania
\<music> melomania *or*
  musicomania
\<nakedness> gymnomania
\<narcotics> letheomania
\<night> noctimania

\<noise> phonomania
\<novelty> kainomania
\<nudity> nudomania
\<nymphomania> hystero-
  mania *or* oestromania *or*
  uteromania
\<one's own wisdom>
  sophomania
\<one's self> egomania
\<one subject> monomania
\<open spaces> agoramania
\<opium> opiomania
\<own importance>
  megalomania
\<penis> mentulomania
\<picking at growths>
  phaneromania
\<pinching off one's hair>
  trichorrhexomania
\<plants> florimania
\<pleasing delusions>
  amenomania
\<pleasure> hedonomania
\<politics> politicomania
\<pornography> pornogra-
  phomania
\<postage stamps>
  timbromania
\<priests> hieromania
\<public employment>
  empleomania
\<railroad travel> siderodromomania
\<religion> entheomania
\<reptiles> ophidiomania
\<return home> nostomania
\<running away> drapeto-
  mania
\<Russia> Russomania
\<satyriasis> gynecomania
\<sea> thalassomania
\<second coming of Christ>
  parousiamania
\<several subjects>
  oligomania
\<sexual pleasure>

37 manias by name

ablutomania \<washing,
  bathing>
acromania \<incurable
  insanity>
agoramania \<open spaces>
agromania \<living alone>
agyiomania \<streets>
ailuromania \<cats>
alcoholomania \<alcohol>
amaxomania \<being in
  vehicles>
amenomania \<pleasing

aphrodisiomania *or*
  erotomania
\<sin> hamartomania
\<sitting> kathisomania
\<sleep> hypnomania
\<snow> chionomania
\<solitude> automania
\<speech> lalomania
\<spending> squander-
  mania
\<stealing> kleptomania
\<stillness> eremiomania
\<suicide> autophono-
  mania
\<sun> heliomania
\<surgery> tomomania
\<symmetry> symmetro-
  mania
\<talking> logomania
\<testicles> orchidomania
\<theater> theatromania
\<thinking> phronemo-
  mania
\<travel> hodomania
\<traveling> dromomania
\<tuberculosis> phthisio-
  mania
\<United States> America-
  mania
\<wandering> ecdemio-
  mania
\<wanderlust> poriomania
\<washing, bathing>
  ablutomania
\<water> hydromania
\<wine> enomania *or*
  oinomania
\<woods> hylomania
\<words> verbomania
\<work> ergomania
\<writing for publication>
  typomania
\<writing verse> metromania
\<writing> graphomania *or*
  scribblemania *or*
  scribomania

delusions>
Americamania \<United
  States>
andromania \<men>
Anglomania \<England>
anthomania \<flowers>
aphrodisiomania *or*
  erotomania \<sexual
  pleasure>
apimania \<bees>
arithmomania \<counting>
automania \<solitude>

autophonomania <suicide>
ballistomania <bullets>
Beatlemania <the Beatles>
bibliomania <books>
bibliokleptomania <book theft>
bruxomania <grinding one's teeth>
cacodemonomania <demonic possession>
cheromania <gaiety>
Chinamania <China>
chionomania <snow>
choreomania <dancing>
chrematomania <money>
cleptomania <stealing>
clinomania <bed rest>
coprolalomania <foul speech>
cremnomania <cliffs>
cresomania <great wealth>
cynomania <dogs>
Dantomania <Dante>
demomania <crowds>
dipsomania <alcoholic beverages>
doramania <fur>
drapetomania <running away>
dromomania <traveling>
ecdemiomania <wandering>
edeomania <genitals>
egomania <one's self>
eleuthromania <freedom>
empleomania <public employment>
enomania <wine>
entheomania <religion>
entomomania <insects>
eremiomania <stillness>
ergasiomania <activity>
ergomania <work>
eroticomania <erotica>
erotographomania <erotic literature>
erotomania <sexual desire>
erythromania <blushing>
etheromania <ether>
ethnomania <ethnic or racial autonomy>
florimania <plants>
Francomania <France>
Gallomania <France>
gamomania <marriage>
gephyromania <crossing bridges>
glazomania <list making>

Germanomania <Germany>
Gorbymania <Mikhail S Gorbachev>
graphomania <writing>
Grecomania <Greece>
gymnomania <nakedness>
gynecomania <male lust>
hamartomania <sin>
hedonomania <pleasure>
heliomania <sun>
hieromania <priests>
hippomania <horses>
hodomania <travel>
homicidomania <murder>
hydrodipsomania <drinking water>
hydromania <water>
hylomania <woods>
hypermania <acute mania>
hypnomania <sleep>
hypomania <mild mania>
hysteromania <female lust>
ichthyomania <fish>
iconomania <icons>
idolomania <idols>
infomania <information>
Italomania <Italy>
kainomania <novelty>
kathisomania <sitting>
kinesomania <movement>
kleptomania <stealing>
lalomania <speech>
letheomania <narcotics>
litigiomania <legal disputes>
logomania <talking>
lycomania <lycanthropy>
lypemania <deep melancholy>
macromania <becoming larger>
megalomania <self-importance>
melomania <music>
mentulomania <penis>
mesmeromania <hypnosis>
metromania <writing>
micromania <becoming smaller>
monomania <one idea or subject>
musicomania <music>
musomania <mice>
mythomania <lying, exaggerations>

necromania <death; the dead>
nesomania <islands>
noctimania <night>
nosomania <imagined disease>
nostomania <homesickness>
nudomania <nudity>
nymphomania <female lust>
ochlomania <crowds>
oestromania <female lust>
oikomania <home>
oinomania <wine>
oligomania <several subjects>
oniomania <buying>
onomatomania <words, names>
ophidiomania <reptiles>
orchidomania <testicles>
ornithomania <birds>
paramania <complaints>
parousiamania <second coming of Christ>
pathomania <moral insanity>
phagomania <food; eating>
phaneromania <growths on one's body>
pharmacomania <medicines>
philopatridomania <homesickness>
phonomania <noise>
photomania <light>
phronemomania <thinking>
phthisiomania <tuberculosis>
plutomania <great wealth>

politicomania <politics>
poriomania <wanderlust>
pornographomania <pornography>
potomania <drinking; delirium tremens>
pseudomania <falsities>
pyromania <fire>
Russomania <Russia>
satyromania <male lust>
scribblemania <writing>
scribomania <writing>
siderodromomania <railroad travel>
sitomania <food>
sophomania <wisdom>
squandermania <spending>
submania <mild mania>
symmetromania <symmetry>
Teutonomania <Germany>
thalassomania <sea>
thanatomania <death>
theatromania <theater>
theomania <God>
timbromania <postage stamps>
tomomania <surgery>
trichomania <hair>
trichotillomania <pulling out one's hair>
tristimania <melancholia>
tromomania <delirium tremens>
Turkomania <Turkey>
typomania <writing for publication>
uteromania <female lust>
verbomania <words>
xenomania <foreigners>
zoomania <animals>

927 ECCENTRICITY

NOUNS **1** eccentricity, idiosyncrasy, idiocrasy, erraticism, erraticness, queerness, oddity, peculiarity, strangeness, singularity, freakishness, freakiness, quirkiness, crotchetiness, dottiness, crankiness, crankism, crackpotism; whimsy, whimsicality; abnormality, anomaly, unnaturalness, irregularity, deviation, deviancy, differentness, divergence, aberration; nonconformity, unconventionality 868.2

2 quirk, idiosyncrasy, twist, kink, crank, quip, trick, mannerism, crotchet, conceit, whim, maggot, maggot in the brain, bee in one's bonnet *or* head <nf>

3 eccentric, erratic, character; odd person 870.4; nonconformist 868.3, recluse 584.5

4 freak, character, crackpot, nut, screwball, weirdie, weirdo, kook, queer potato, oddball, flake, strange duck, odd fellow, crank, bird, goofus, wack, wacko

ADJS **5** eccentric, erratic, idiocratic, idiocratical, idiosyncratic, idiosyncratical, queer, queer in the head, odd, peculiar, strange, fey, singular, anomalous, freakish, funny; unnatural, abnormal, irregular, divergent, deviative, deviant, different, exceptional; unconventional 868.6; crotchety, quirky, dotty, maggoty <Brit>, cranky, crank, crankish, whimsical, twisted; solitary, reclusive, antisocial

6 <nf terms> kooky, goofy, birdy, funny, kinky, loopy, goofus, haywire, squirrely, screwy, screwball, nutty, wacky, flaky, oddball, wacko, lunch, out to lunch, nobody home, weird

928 KNOWLEDGE

NOUNS **1** **knowledge,** knowing, knowingness, ken; **command,** reach; **acquaintance, familiarity,** intimacy; private knowledge, privity; **information,** data, database, datum, items, facts, factual base, corpus; **certainty, sure** *or* **certain knowledge** 970.1; protocol, protocol statement *or* sentence *or* proposition; intelligence; practical knowledge, **experience, know-how, expertise,** métier; technic, technics, technique; self-knowledge; *ratio cognoscendi* <L>

2 **cognizance;** cognition, noesis; **recognition, realization; perception,** insight, apperception, sudden insight, illumination, dawning, aha reaction, flashing <nf>; **consciousness, awareness,** mindfulness, note, notice; altered state of consciousness *or* ASC; **sense,** sensibility; appreciation, appreciativeness

3 **understanding, comprehension, apprehension,** intellection, prehension; conception, conceptualization, ideation; hipness *and* savvy <nf>; **grasp,** mental grasp, grip, **command,** mastery; precognition, familiarity, foreknowledge 961.3, clairvoyance 689.8; intelligence, wisdom 920; savoir-faire, *Aufklarung* <Ger>, 101 <nf>

4 **learning, enlightenment, education, schooling, instruction,** edification, illumination; acquirements, acquisitions, attainments, accomplishments, skills; sophistication; store of knowledge; liberal education; acquisition of knowledge 570.1

5 **scholarship, erudition,** eruditeness, **learnedness,** reading, letters; **intellectuality,** intellectualism; **literacy;** computer literacy, computeracy, numeracy; **culture, literary culture, high culture,** book learning, booklore; **bookishness,** bookiness, **pedantry,** pedantism, donnishness <Brit>; bluestockingism; bibliomania, book madness, bibliolatry, bibliophilism; classicism, classical scholarship, humanism, humanistic scholarship

6 **profound knowledge,** deep knowledge, total command *or* mastery; specialism, specialized *or* special knowledge; expertise, proficiency 413.1; wide *or* vast *or* extensive knowledge, generalism, general knowledge, interdisciplinary *or* cross-disciplinary knowledge; **encyclopedic knowledge,** polymathy, polyhistory, pansophy; **omniscience,** all-knowingness

7 slight knowledge 930.5

8 tree of knowledge, tree of knowledge of good and evil; forbidden fruit; bo *or* bodhi tree

9 **lore, body of knowledge,** corpus, body of learning, store of knowledge, system of knowledge, treasury of information; common knowledge; **canon;** literature, literature of the field, publications, materials; bibliography; encyclopedia, cyclopedia

10 **science,** ology <see list>, **art, study, discipline; field,** field of inquiry, concern, province, domain, area, arena, sphere, branch *or* field of study, branch *or* department of knowledge, specialty, academic specialty, academic discipline; **technology, technics,** technicology, high technology, high-tech *or* hi-tech <nf>; social science, natural science; applied science, pure science, experimental science; Big Science

11 **scientist,** man of science; **technologist;** practical scientist, experimental scientist; boffin <Brit>; savant, **scholar** 929.3; authority, expert, maven <nf>; technocrat; intellectual; egghead <nf>

VERBS **12** **know, perceive, apprehend,** prehend, cognize, recognize, discern, see, make out; conceive, conceptualize; **realize, appreciate, understand, comprehend,** fathom; dig *and* savvy <nf>; wot *or* wot of <Brit nf>, ken <Scot>, have, possess, **grasp,** seize, have hold of; have knowledge of, be informed, be apprised of, command, master, have a good command of, have information about, be acquainted with, be conversant with, be cognizant of, be conscious *or* aware of; know something by heart *or* by rote *or* from memory

13 **know well, know full well,** know damn well *or* darn well <nf>, have a good *or* thorough knowledge of, be well-informed, be learned in, be proficient in, **be up on** <nf>, be master of, command, be thoroughly grounded in, retain, **have down pat** or **cold** <nf>, have it taped <Brit nf>, have at one's fingers' ends or fingertips, have in one's head, **know by heart** or rote, **know like a book,** know like the back of one's hand, **know backwards,** know backwards and forwards, **know inside out,** know down to the ground <nf>, **know one's stuff** and know one's onions <nf>, know a thing or two, know one's way around; be expert in; **know the ropes,** know all the ins and outs, know the score <nf>, know all the answers <nf>; know what's what

14 learn 570.6; come to one's knowledge 551.15

ADJS 15 **knowing,** knowledgeable, informed; **cognizant, conscious, aware, mindful, sensible;** intelligent 920.12; **understanding, comprehending,** apprehensive, apprehending; **perceptive,** insightful, apperceptive, percipient, perspicacious, apperceptive, prehensile; shrewd, sagacious, wise 920.17; omniscient, all-knowing

16 **cognizant of, aware of, conscious of, mindful of, sensible to** or **of, appreciative of,** appreciatory of, no stranger to, seized of <Brit>; privy to, in the secret, let into, in the know <nf>, behind the scenes or curtain; alive to, awake to; **wise to** <nf>, hep to and on to <nf>; streetwise, street-smart; apprised of, informed of; undeceived, undeluded

17 <nf terms> **hep, hip,** on the beam, go-go, **with it,** into, really into, groovy; chic, clued-up, clued in, in the know, trendy

18 **informed, enlightened, instructed,** versed, well-versed, educated, schooled, **taught;** posted, briefed, primed, trained; **up on,** up-to-date, abreast of, au courant <Fr>, au fait <Fr>, in the picture, wise to <nf>

19 **versed in, informed in,** read or well-read in, up on, strong in, at home in, master of, expert or authoritative in, proficient in, **familiar with,** at home with, **conversant with, acquainted with,** intimate with

20 **well-informed,** well-posted, well-educated, **well-grounded, well-versed, well-read,** widely read

21 **learned, erudite, educated, cultured,** cultivated, lettered, literate, civilized, **scholarly,** scholastic, studious; wise 920.17; **profound,** deep, abstruse; **encyclopedic,** pansophic, polymath or polymathic, polyhistoric

22 **book-learned,** book-read, **literary,** book-taught, book-fed, book-wise, book-smart, **bookish,** booky, book-minded; book-loving, bibliophilic, bibliophagic; **pedantic,** donnish <Brit>, scholastic, inkhorn; **bluestocking**

23 **intellectual,** intellectualistic; **highbrow** and highbrowed and highbrowish <nf>; elitist

24 **self-educated,** self-taught, autodidactic

25 **knowable,** cognizable, recognizable, **understandable, comprehensible,** apprehendable, apprehensible, prehensible, graspable, seizable, discernible, conceivable, appreciable, perceptible, distinguishable, ascertainable, discoverable

26 **known, recognized,** ascertained, conceived, grasped, apprehended, prehended, seized, perceived, discerned, appreciated, **understood, comprehended,** realized; pat and **down pat** <nf>

27 **well-known,** well-understood, well-recognized, **widely known,** commonly known, universally recognized, generally or universally admitted; **familiar,** familiar as household words, household, **common, current; proverbial;** public, notorious; known by every schoolboy; talked-of, talked-about, in everyone's mouth, **on everyone's tongue** or **lips;** commonplace, trite 117.9, hackneyed, platitudinous, truistic

28 **scientific; technical, technological,** technicological; high-tech or hi-tech <nf>; **scholarly;** disciplinary

ADVS 29 **knowingly, consciously, wittingly,** with forethought, understandingly, intelligently, studiously, learnedly, eruditely, as every schoolboy knows

30 **to one's knowledge, to the best of one's knowledge,** as far as one can see or tell, as far as one knows, as well as can be said

31 **-ologies by name**

abiology <inanimate things>	<ancient or historical artifacts>
acarology <lice and ticks>	archology <government>
acrology <initial sounds or signs>	areology <Mars>
adenology <glands>	argyrology <money boxes>
aesthology <sensory organs>	aristology <dining>
agrology <soil>	arthrology <joints>
alethology <truth>	asthenology <diseases of debility>
algology or phycology <algae, seaweeds>	astrolithology <meteorites>
ambrology <amber>	astrology <stellar and planetary influence>
anatripsology <friction>	atmology <water vapor>
andrology <male diseases>	audiology <hearing disorders>
angiology <blood vessels>	auxology <growth>
anorganology <inorganic things>	axiology <values, ethics>
anthropology <mankind>	azoology <inanimate things>
apiology or melittology <bees>	bacteriology <bacteria>
arachnology or araneology <spiders>	balneology <therapeutic baths>
archeology or archaeology	barology <weight>
	batology <brambles>
	bibliology <books>

bioecology <biological interrelationships>
biology <life, living things>
biometeorology <organic-atmospheric interrelationships>
bromatology <food>
brontology <thunder>
bryology or muscology <mosses>
Buddhhology <Buddha, Buddhahood>
caliology <bird nests>
campanology <bells; bell-ringing>
carcinology <crustaceans>
cardiology <heart>
carpology or pomology <fruits>
cartology <maps>
cephalology <the head>
cetology <whales, dolphins>
chollology or choledology <bile>
choreology <dance notation>
chorology <geographical boundaries>
chrondrology <cartilage>
chronology <dates, time>
climatology <climate>
coleopterology <beetles>
conchology <shells>
cosmology <universe>
craniology <skull>
criminology <criminal behavior>
crustaceology <crustaceans>
cryology <snow and ice>
cryptology <codes and ciphers>
curiology <picture writing>
cyesiology <pregnancy>
cytology <cells>
cytopathology <cell pathology>
dactylology <fingers>
deltiology <picture postcards>
demology <human activities>
dendrochronology <tree-ring dating>
dendrology <trees, shrubs>
deontology <ethics>
dermatology <skin>

desmology <ligaments>
diabiology <the devil, devils>
dipteriology <flies>
dittology <double interpretation>
docimology <metal assaying>
dolorology <pain>
dosiology <dosage>
dysteleology <purposelessness>
ecclesiology <churches; church history>
ecology <environment>
edaphology <soils>
Egyptology <ancient Egypt>
eidology <mental imagery>
electrology <electricity>
embryology <embryos>
endocrinology <endocrine glands>
enterology <internal organs>
entomology <insects>
epiphuytology <plant diseases>
epistemology <human knowledge>
eremology <deserts>
ergology <work and its effects>
eschatology <last things, esp final judgment>
ethnology <races and ethnic groups>
ethology <animal behavior>
etiology <causes, esp of disease>
etymology <derivation and history of words>
exobiology <life on other planets>
faunology <animal distribution>
fetology <fetus>
fluviology <watercourses, rivers>
garbology or garbageology <garbage, refuse>
gastrology <stomach>
gemology <gemstones>
geology <Earth's crust>
geomorphology <origin of geological features>
geratology <approaching extinction>

gerontology <old age>
glaciology <glaciers>
glossology <linguistics>
gnotobiology <germ-free biology>
grammatology <systems of writing>
graphology <handwriting>
gynecology <women's health>
hagiology <saints>
hamartiology <sin>
hedonology <pleasure>
helcology <ulcers>
heliology <Sun>
helminthology <worms, esp parasitic worms>
hematology <blood>
heortology <religious festivals>
hepatology <liver>
heresiology <heresies>
herpetology <reptiles>
hierology <sacred things>
hippology <horses>
hippopathology <diseases of the horse>
histology or histiology <tissues and organs>
historology <history>
horology <time, clocks>
hydrology <water>
hyetology <rainfall>
hygiology <health and hygiene>
hygrology <humidity>
hymenology <membranes>
hymenopterology <wasps, bees, ants>
hypnology <sleep; hypnotism>
hysterology <uterus>
iatrology <healing, medicine>
ichnolithology or ichnology <fossil footprints>
ichthyology or piscology <fish>
immunology <immunity to diseases>
irenology <peace>
journology <newspapers>
kalology <beauty>
kinesiology <bodily movement>
lalopathology <speech therapy>
laryngology <larynx>

lexicology <word forms and meanings>
lepidopterology <butterflies, moths>
limnology <lakes and ponds>
lithology or lithoidology <rock, stone>
loimology <infectious diseases>
malacology <mollusks>
malacostracology <crustaceology>
mantology <divination>
mastology <mammals>
meteorology <atmosphere and weather>
metrology <weights and measures>
microbiology <microorganisms>
micrology <tiny things>
microseismology <earthquake tremors>
morphology <form, shape>
muscology <mosses>
musicology <music>
mycology <fungi>
myology <muscles>
myrmecology <ants>
naology <church buildings>
nasology or rhinology <nose>
neonatology <newborns>
nephology <clouds>
nephrology <kidneys>
neurology <nervous system>
neuropathology <nervous system pathology>
neurypnology <hypnotism>
nomology <law>
noology <intuition>
nosology <classification of diseases>
nostology <old age, geriatrics>
numerology <numbers>
numismatology <coins>
odontology <the teeth>
oenology or enology <wine>
olfactology <smells>
ombrology <rain>
oncology <tumors>
oneirology <dreams>
onomasiology or onomatology <names, naming>

ontology <being, meta-
physics>
oology <eggs, esp birds'>
ophiology <snakes>
ophthalmology <eyes>
organology <body organs>
orismology <terminology>
ornithology <birds>
orology or oreology
<mountains>
ornithology <birds>
oryctology <fossils>
osmology <odors>
osteology <bones>
otolaryngology <ear, nose,
throat>
otology <ear>
paleobiology <fossil life>
paleoethnology <prehis-
toric mankind>
paleoichtyology <fossil
fishes>
paleontology <early history
of life>
paleoornithology <fossil
birds>
paleopedology <early
soils>
paleoetiology <explanation
of past phenomena>
paleozoology or zoogeolol-
ogy <fossil animals>
palynology <pollen,
spores>
parapsychology <beyond
psychology>
parasitology <parasites>
paroemiology <proverbs>
pathology <diseases>
pedology <soil science>
penology <punishment>
petrology or stromatology
<rocks>
pharmacology <drugs>
phenology <natural
cycles>
philology <languages>
phitology <political
economy>
phlebology <blood vessels>
phonology <vocal sounds>
photology <light and
optics>
phrenology <skull shape>
phycology <algae>
physicotheology <natural
theology>
physiology <living body>
phytology <plants>

phytopathology <plant
diseases>
phytophysiology <plant
physiology>
phytoserology <plant
viruses>
piscatology <fishing>
pistology <religious faith>
planetology <planets>
pleology <running water>
pneumatology <spirit>
pomology <fruits>
ponerology <evil>
posology <drug adminis-
potamology <rivers>
proctology <anus, rectum>
promorphology <funda-
mental shapes and
forms>
psephology <election
statistics>
psychology <the mind>
psychonosology <mental
diseases>
psychopathology <insanity>
psychophysiology <body
and mind>
pteridology <ferns>
pterology <insect wings>
pterylology <feathers>
ptochology <pauperism,
unemployment>
pyretology <fever>
pyrgology <towers>
pyrology <fire and heat>
radiology or R–ntgenology
<X-rays>
reflexology <reflexes and
behavior>
rheology <flow and
deformation of matter>
rhinology <nose>
roentgenology <medical
X-rays>
runology <runes>
satanology <devil worship>
scatology <feces>
seismology <earthquakes>
selenology <the Moon>
semasiology <word
meanings>
sematology or semeiology
<symptoms>
semiology <signs,
symbols>
serology <serums>
silphology <larval forms>
sinology <China>

siphonapterology <fleas>
sitology <diet, dietetics>
sociobiology <biology and
behavior>
sociology <society>
somatology <organic
bodies>
sophiology <ideas>
soteriology <salvation>
speciology <species>
spectrology <ghosts,
phantoms>
speleology <caves>
spermatology <sperm>
sphygmoology <the pulse>
splanchnology <the
viscera>
splenology <the spleen>
stereology <2-, 3-dimen-
sional figures>
stoichiology <fundamental
laws>
stomatology <mouth>
storiology <folklore>
suicidology <suicide>
symbology <symbols>
synchronology <compara-
tive chronology>
synecology <plant, animal
communities>
systematology <ordered
arrangements>
taxology <scientific
classification>
technology <mechanical
and manufacturing arts>
tectology <structural
morphology>
teleology <aims, deter-
mined ends>
teratology <tall tales;
monsters>
terminology <system of
names or terms>

thanatology <death>
thaumatology <miracles>
theology <divinity>
thermology or thermatol-
ogy <heat>
therology <mammals>
thremmatology <plant or
animal breeding>
threpsology <nutrition>
tidology <tides>
timbrology <stamps,
stamp-collecting>
timology <values>
tocology <obstetrics>
tonology <tones,
speech>
toxicology <poisons>
traumatology <wounds;
shock>
tribology <friction;
interacting surfaces>
trichology <hair>
typhology <blindness>
ufology <UFOs>
uranology <astronomy>
urbanology <cities>
urology <urogenital organs
and diseases>
venereology <veneral
disease>
vermiology <worms>
vexillology <flags>
victimology <victims>
virology <viruses>
vulcanology <volcanoes>
xyloology <the structure of
wood>
zoology <animal life>
zoonosology <animal
diseases>
zoophysiology <animal
physiology>
zymology or zymotechnol-
ogy <fermentation>

32 -ologies by subject

<aims, determined ends>
teleology
<ancient or historical
artifacts> archeology
<animal behavior>
ethology
<animal diseases>
zoonosology
<animal distribution>
faunology
<animal life> zoology
<animal physiology>
zoophysiology

<ants> myrmecology
<anus, rectum> proctology
<astronomy> uranology
<atmosphere and weather>
meteorology
<beauty> kalology
<bees> apiology or
melittology
<beetles> coleopterology
<being, metaphysics>
ontology
<bells; bell-ringing>
campanology

<bile> cholology *or* choledology

<biological interrelationships> bioecology

<bird nests> caliology

<birds> ornithology

<blindness> typhology

<blood vessels> angiology *or* phlebology

<blood> hematology

<body and mind> psychophysiology

<body organs> organology

<bones> osteology

<books> bibliology

<cartilage> chrondrology

<causes of disease> etiology

<caves> speleology

<cell pathology> cytopathology

<cells> cytology

<China> sinology

<church buildings> naology

<churches; church history> ecclesiology

<cities> urbanology

<classification of diseases> nosology

<clouds> nephology

<codes and ciphers> cryptology

<coins> numismatology

<comparative chronology> synchronology

<crustaceans> carcinology *or* crustaceology

<crustaceology> malacostracology

<dance notation> choreology

<dates, dating> chronology

<death> thanatology

<derivation and history of words> etymology

<deserts> eremology

<devil worship> satanology

<didactic literature> gnomology

<diet> sitology

<dining> aristology

<diseases of debility> asthenology

<diseases> pathology

<divination> mantology

<divinity> theology

<dosage> dosiology *or* dosology *or* posology

<double interpretation> dittology

<dreams> oneirology

<drugs> pharmacology

<ear> otology

<early history of life> paleontology

<early soils> paleopedology

<Earth's crust> geology

<earthquake tremors> microseismology

<earthquakes> seismology

<eggs> oology

<election statistics> psephology

<electricity> electrology

<embryos> embryology

<endocrine glands> endocrinology

<environment> ecology *or* environmentology

<evil> ponerology

<explanation of past phenomena> paleoetiology

<extinction> geratology

<eyes> ophthalmology

<feathers> pterylology

<female health and disease> gynecology

<fermentation> zymology *or* zymotechnology

<ferns> pteridology

<fetus> fetology

<fever> pyretology

<fingers> dactylology

<fire and heat> pyrology

<fish> ichthyology *or* piscology

<fishing> piscatology

<flags> vexillology

<fleas> siphonapterology

<flies> dipteriology

<flow and deformation of matter> rheology

<folklore> storiology

<food> bromatology

<form, shape> morphology

<fossil animals> paleozoology *or* zoogeolology

<fossil birds> paleoornithology

<fossil excrement> scatology

<fossil fishes> paleoichtyology

<fossil footprints> ichnolithology *or* ichnology

<fossil life> paleobiology

<fossils> oryctology

<friction> anatripsology

<fruits> carpology *or* pomology

<fundamental laws> stoichiology

<fundamental shapes and forms> promorphology

<fungi> mycology

<garbage, refuse> garbology *or* garbageology

<geographical boundaries> chorology

<germ-free biology> gnotobiology

<glands> adenology

<government> archology

<growth> auxology

<hair> trichology

graphology

<head> cephalology

<healing, medicine> iatrology

<health and hygiene> hygiology

<hearing disorders> audiology

<heart> cardiology

<heat> thermology *or* thermatology

<heresies> heresiology

<history> historology

<horses> hippology

<human activities> demology

<human knowledge> epistemology

<humidity> hygrology

<hypnotism> neurypnolohy

<ideas> sophiology

<immunity to diseases> immunology

<inanimate things> abiology *or* azoology

<infectious diseases> loimology

<initial sounds *or* signs> acrology

<inorganic things> anorganology

<insanity> psychopathology

<insect wings> pterology

<insects> entomology

<interacting surfaces> tribology

<internal organs> enterology

<intuition> noology

<joints> arthrology

<lakes and ponds> limnology

<language meaning> semasiology

<languages> philology

<larval forms> silphology

<larynx> laryngology

<last things, esp final judgment> eschatology

<law> nomology

<lice and ticks> acarology

<life on other planets> exobiology

<life, living things> biology

<ligaments> desmology

<light and optics> photology

<linguistics> glossology

<liver> hepatology

<living body> physiology

<male diseases> andrology

<mammals> mastology *or* therology

<mankind> anthropology

<maps> cartology

<Mars> areology

<mechanical and manufacturing arts> technology

<membranes> hymenology

<mental diseases> psychonosology

<mental imagery> eidology

<metal assaying> docimology

<meteorites> astrolithology

<microorganisms> microbiology

<miracles> thaumatology

<mollusks> mallacology

<monsters> teratology

<moral obligation> deontology

<mosses> bryology *or* muscology

<mountains> orology *or* oreology

<mouth diseases> stomatology

<muscles> myology

<names, naming> onomasiology *or* onomatology
<natural cycles> phenology
<natural theology> physicotheology
<nervous system> neurology
<newspapers> journology
<nose> nasology *or* rhinology
<nutrition> threpsology
<obstetrics> tocology
<odors> osmology
<old age, geriatrics> nostology
<old age> gerontology
<ordered arrangements> systematology
<organic bodies> somatology
<organic-atmospheric interrelationships> biometeorology
<pain> dolorology
<pathology of the nervous system> neuropathology
<peace> irenology
<physiology of the nervous system> neurophysology
<picture postcards> deltiology
<picture writing> curiology
<plant diseases> epiphuytology *or* phytopathology
<plant *or* animal breeding> thremmatology
<plant physiology> phytophysiology
<plant viruses> phytoserology
<plants> phytology
<poisons> toxicology
<political economy> phitology
<pollen> palynology
<pregnancy> cyesiology
<prehistoric mankind> paleoethnology
<proverbs> paroemiology
<punishment of crime> penology
<purposelessness> dysteleology
<races and peoples> ethnology
<rain> ombrology

<rainfall> hyetology
<religious faith> pistology
<religious festivals> heortology
<reptiles> herpetology
<rivers> potamology
<rock, stone> lithology *or* lithoidology
<rocks> petrology *or* stromatology
<runes> runology
<running water> pleology
<sacred things> hierology
<saints> hagiology
<salvation> soteriology
<scientific classification> taxology
<seaweeds> algology *or* phycology
<sensory organs> aesthology
<serums> serology
<shells> conchology
<sin> hamartiology
<skin> dermatology
<skull shape> phrenology
<skull> craniology
<sleep> hypnology
<smells> olfactology
<snakes> ophiology
<society> sociology
<soils> edaphology *or* pedology
<species> speciology
<spectroscopic analysis> spectrology
<sperm> spermatology
<spiders> arachnology *or* araneology
<spirit> pneumatology
<spleen> splenology
<stamps, stamp-collecting> timbrology
<stellar and planetary influence> astrology
<stomach> gastrology
<structural morphology> tectology
<structure of wood> xyloology
<suicide> suicidology
<Sun> heliology
<symptoms> sematology *or* semeiology
<system of names *or* terms> terminology
<teeth> odontology
<terminology> orismology

<the devil, devils> diabiology
<the mind> psychology
<the Moon> selenology
<the pulse> sphygmoology
<therapeutic agents> acology
<therapeutic baths> balneology
<thunder> brontology
<tides> tidology
<time, clocks> horology
<tiny things> micrology
<tissues and organs> histology *or* histiology
<towers> pyrgology
<tree-ring dating> dendrochronology
<trees> dendrology
<truth> alethology
<tumors> oncology
<ulcers> helcology
<universe> cosmology
<urogenital organs and diseases> urology
<uterus> hysterology
<values> timology

33 social sciences

anthropology
anthropometry
applied psychology
archaeology *or* archeology
cartography
cultural anthropology
domestic science
economics
ethnography
ethnology
experimental psychology
genetics and growth studies
geography
history

<victims> victimology
<viscera> splanchnology
<vocal sounds> phonology
<volcanoes> vulcanology
<wasps, bees, ants> hymenopterology
<water vapor> atmology
<water> hydrology
<weight> barology
<weights and measures> metrology
<whales and dolphins> cetology
<wine> oenology *or* enology
<words and meanings> lexicology
<work and its effects> ergology
<worms, esp parasitic worms> helminthology
<worms> vermiology
<wounds, shock> traumatology
<X-rays> radiology *or* Roentgenology

human evolution
human geography
linguistic anthropology
linguistics
paleoanthropology
physical anthropology
physical geography
political science
primatology
psychology
social anthropology
social geography
social psychology
social statistics
sociology

929 INTELLECTUAL

NOUNS **1 intellectual, intellect,** intellectualist, literate, member of the intelligentsia, white-collar intellectual; "someone whose mind watches itself"—Camus; brainworker, thinker; brain *and* rocket scientist *and* brain surgeon <nf>; **pundit, Brahmin, mandarin,** egghead *and* pointy-head <nf>; **highbrow** <nf>; wise man 921.1

2 intelligentsia, literati, illuminati; intellectual elite; clerisy; literati

3 scholar, scholastic <old>, clerk *or* learned clerk <old>; a gentleman and a scholar; student 572;

learned man, man of learning, giant of learning, colossus of knowledge, mastermind, **savant,** pundit; genius 413.12; polymath, polyhistor *or* polyhistorian, **mine of information,** walking encyclopedia; literary man, *littérateur* <Fr> *or* litterateur, **man of letters;** philologist, philologue; philomath, lover of learning; philosopher, philosophe; bookman; **academician,** academic, schoolman; classicist, classicalist, Latinist, humanist; Renaissance man *or* woman

4 **bookworm,** bibliophage; **grind** *and* greasy grind <nf>; **booklover, bibliophile,** bibliophilist, philobiblist, bibliolater, bibliolatrist; bibliomaniac, bibliomane

5 **pedant; formalist, precisionist,** precisian, purist, *précieux* <Fr>, **bluestocking,** *bas bleu* <Fr>, *précieuse* <Fr fem>; Dr Pangloss <Voltaire>, Dryasdust <Rev Dr Carlyle>

6 **dilettante, half scholar,** sciolist, **dabbler,** dabster, amateur, trifler, smatterer; grammaticaster, philologaster, criticaster, philosophaster, Latinitaster

930 IGNORANCE

NOUNS 1 **ignorance,** ignorantness, **unknowingness,** unknowing, nescience; lack of information, knowledge-gap, hiatus of learning; empty-headedness, blankmindedness, vacuousness, vacuity, inanity; tabula rasa; **unintelligence** 922; **unacquaintance, unfamiliarity; greenness,** greenhornism, rawness, callowness, unripeness, green in the eye, **inexperience** 414.2; innocence, ingenuousness, simpleness, simplicity; crass *or* gross *or* primal *or* pristine ignorance; ignorantism, know-nothingism, obscurantism; agnosticism; *tamas* <Hindu>

2 **incognizance, unawareness, unconsciousness, insensibility,** unwittingness, nonrecognition; deniability; nonrealization, incomprehension; **unmindfulness;** mindlessness; blindness 30, deafness 49

3 **unenlightenment, benightedness,** benightment, dark, darkness; savagery, barbarism, paganism, heathenism, Gothicism; age of ignorance, dark age; rural idiocy

4 **unlearnedness, inerudition,** ineducation, unschooledness, unletteredness; **unscholarliness,** unstudiousness; **illiteracy,** illiterateness, functional illiteracy, semiliteracy; **unintellectuality,** unintellectualism, Philistinism, bold ignorance

5 **slight knowledge,** vague notion, imperfect knowledge, a little learning, glimmering, glimpse <old>, smattering, **smattering of knowledge,** smattering of ignorance, **half-learning,** semi-learning, semi-ignorance, sciolism; **superficiality,** shallowness, surface-scratching; **dilettantism,** dilettantship, amateurism

6 **the unknown,** the unknowable, the strange, the unfamiliar, the incalculable; **matter of ignorance,** sealed book, riddle, enigma, mystery, puzzle 971.3; *terra incognita* <L>, unexplored ground *or* territory; frontier, frontiers of knowledge, **unknown quantity,** x, y, z, n; dark horse; guesswork, anybody's guess; complete blank; closed *or* sealed book; all Greek <nf>

7 **ignoramus, know-nothing;** no scholar, puddinghead, dunce, fool 924; simpleton; **illiterate;** aliterate; **lowbrow** <nf>; unintelligentsia, illiterati; **greenhorn,** greeny <nf>, beginner, tenderfoot, neophyte, novice, duffer <nf>; **dilettante,** dabbler 929.6; layperson; **middlebrow** <nf>

VERBS 8 **be ignorant,** be green, have everything to learn, **know nothing,** know from nothing <nf>; wallow in ignorance; not know any better; **not know what's what,** not know what it is all about, not know the score <nf>, not be with it <nf>, not know any of the answers; not know the time of day *or* what o'clock it is, not know beans, not know the first thing about, not know one's ass from one's elbow <nf>, not know the way home, not know enough to come in out of the rain, not know chalk from cheese, **not know up from down,** not know which way is up

9 **be in the dark,** be blind, labor in darkness, walk in darkness, be benighted, grope in the dark, have nothing to go on, have a lot to learn

10 **not know,** not rightly know <nf>, know not, know not what, know nothing of, wot not of <Brit nf>, be innocent of, have no idea *or* notion *or* conception, **not have the first idea, not have the least** *or* **remotest idea,** be clueless *and* not have a clue <nf> not have idea one, not have the foggiest <nf>, **not pretend to say,** not take upon oneself to say; be stumped; not know the half of it; not know from Adam, not know from the man in the moon; wonder, wonder whether; half-know, have a little learning, scratch the surface, know a little, smatter, dabble, toy with, coquet with; pass, give up

ADJS 11 **ignorant,** nescient, **unknowing,** uncomprehending, **know-nothing;** simple, **dumb** <nf>, empty, empty-headed, blank, blankminded, vacuous, inane, **unintelligent** 922.13; **ill-informed, uninformed, unenlightened,** unilluminated, unapprized, unposted <nf>, clueless <nf>, pig-ignorant <Brit nf>; **unacquainted, unconversant,** unversed, uninitiated, **unfamiliar,** strange to; **inexperienced** 414.17; **green,** callow, innocent, ingenuous, gauche, awkward, naive, unripe, raw; groping, tentative, unsure

12 **unaware, unconscious, insensible, unknowing, incognizant;** mindless, witless; unprehensive, unrealizing, nonconceiving, **unmindful,** unwitting, unsuspecting; unperceiving, impercipient, unhearing, unseeing, uninsightful; unaware of, in ignorance of, unconscious of, unmindful of, insensible to, out of it <nf>, not with it <nf>; **blind to, deaf to,** dead to, a stranger to; asleep, napping, **off one's guard,** caught napping, caught tripping, tamasic, indifferent

13 **unlearned, inerudite,** unerudite, **uneducated,** unschooled, uninstructed, untutored, unbriefed, untaught, unedified, unguided; ill-educated, misinstructed, misinformed, mistaught, led astray; hoodwinked, deceived; **illiterate,** functionally illiterate, unlettered, grammarless; **unscholarly,** unscholastic, unstudious; **unliterary, unread,** unbookish, unbook-learned, bookless <old>, unbooked; **uncultured,** uncultivated, unrefined, rude, Philistine; barbarous, pagan, heathen; Gothic; nonintellectual, **unintellectual; lowbrow** and lowbrowed and lowbrowish <nf>; lesser-known

14 **half-learned,** half-baked <nf>, half-cocked and half-assed <nf>, sciolistic; semiskilled; **shallow, superficial;** immature, sophomoric, sophomorical; **dilettante,** dilettantish, smattering, dabbling, amateur, amateurish, inexperienced; **wise in one's own conceit**

15 **benighted, dark,** in darkness, in the dark

16 **unknown,** unbeknown <nf>, unheard <old>, **unheard-of,** unapprehended, unapparent, unperceived, unsuspected; unexplained, unascertained; uninvestigated, unexplored; unidentified, unclassified, uncharted, unfathomed, unplumbed, virgin, untouched; undisclosed, unrevealed, undivulged; undiscovered, unexposed, sealed; **unfamiliar,** strange; incalculable, **unknowable,** incognizable, undiscoverable; enigmatic 522.17, mysterious, puzzling

ADVS 17 **ignorantly, unknowingly,** unmindfully, unwittingly, witlessly, unsuspectingly, **unawares;** unconsciously, insensibly; for anything or aught one knows, not that one knows

INTERJS 18 **God knows!,** God only knows! Lord knows!, Heaven knows!, nobody knows!, damned if I know!, search me!, **beats me!,** beats the hell or heck or shit out of me!, your guess is as good as mine!, it has me guessing!, it's Greek to me!; **search me!,** you've got me!, I give up!, I pass!, **who knows?,** how should I know?, I don't know what!

931 THOUGHT
<exercise of the intellect>

NOUNS 1 **thought, thinking, cogitation,** cerebration, ideation, noesis, mentation, intellection, intellectualization, ratiocination; using one's head or noodle <nf>; workings of the mind; **reasoning** 935; **brainwork, headwork,** mental labor or effort, mental act or process, act of thought, mental or intellectual exercise; deep-think <nf>; **way of thinking,** logic, habit of thought or mind, thought-pattern; heavy thinking, straight thinking; conception, conceit <old>, conceptualization; abstract thought, imageless thought; excogitation, thinking out or through; thinking aloud; **idea** 932; creative thought 986.2

2 **consideration, contemplation, reflection, speculation, meditation, musing, rumination, deliberation,** lucubration, brooding, study, **pondering,** weighing, revolving, turning over in the mind, looking at from all angles, noodling or noodling around <nf>; lateral thought or thinking; advisement, counsel

3 **thoughtfulness,** contemplativeness, speculativeness, reflectiveness; **pensiveness,** wistfulness, reverie, musing, melancholy; **preoccupation, absorption, engrossment,** abstraction, brown study, intense or deep or profound thought; **concentration,** study, close study; deep thinking

4 **thoughts,** burden of one's mind, mind's content; inmost or innermost thoughts or mind, secret thoughts, mind's core, one's heart of hearts; **train of thought,** current or flow of thought or ideas, succession or sequence or chain of thought or ideas; **stream of consciousness; association,** association of ideas

5 **mature thought,** developed thought, ripe idea; **afterthought,** *arrière-pensée* <Fr>, *esprit d'escalier* <Fr>, second thought or thoughts; **reconsideration,** reappraisal, revaluation, rethinking, re-examination, review, thinking over

6 **introspection,** self-communion, self-counsel, self-consultation, subjective inspection or speculation, head trip <nf>; meditation

7 subject for thought, food for thought, something to chew on, something to get one's teeth into

VERBS 8 **think, cogitate,** cerebrate, put on one's thinking or considering cap <nf>, intellectualize, ideate, conceive, conceptualize, form ideas, entertain ideas; **reason** 935.15; **use one's head** *or* brain, use one's noodle *or* noggin <nf>, use *or* exercise the mind, set the brain *or* wits to work, bethink oneself, have something on one's mind, have a lot on one's mind

9 **think hard,** think one's head off, **rack** *or* **ransack one's brains,** crack one's brains <nf>, **beat** *or* **cudgel one's brains,** work one's head to the bone, do some heavy thinking, bend *or* apply the mind, knit one's brow; sweat *or* stew over <nf>, hammer *or* hammer away at; puzzle, **puzzle over**

10 **concentrate,** concentrate the mind *or* thoughts, concentrate on *or* upon, attend closely to, brood on, **focus on** *or* **upon,** give *or* devote the mind to, glue the mind to, cleave to the thought of, fix the mind *or* thoughts upon, bend the mind upon, bring the mind to bear upon; get to the point; gather *or* collect one's thoughts, pull one's wits together, focus *or* fix one's thoughts, marshal *or* arrange one's thoughts *or* ideas

11 **think about,** cogitate, **give** *or* **apply the mind to,** put one's mind to, apply oneself to, bend *or* turn the mind *or* thoughts to, direct the mind upon, **give thought to, trouble one's head about,** occupy the mind *or* thoughts with; think through *or* out, puzzle out, sort out, reason out, excogitate, ratiocinate, work out, take stock of

12 **consider, contemplate, speculate, reflect, wonder, study, ponder,** perpend, **weigh, deliberate, debate, meditate, muse, brood, ruminate,** chew the cud <nf>, digest; introspect, be abstracted; wrinkle one's brow; fall into a brown study, retreat into one's mind *or* thoughts; **toy with, play with,** play around with, flirt *or* coquet with the idea

13 **think over, ponder over, brood over, muse over, mull over, reflect over,** con over, **deliberate over,** run over, **meditate over,** ruminate over, chew over, digest, turn over, **revolve,** revolve *or* turn over in the mind, deliberate upon, meditate upon, muse on *or* upon, bestow thought *or* consideration upon, noodle *or* noodle around <nf>

14 **take under consideration,** entertain, take under advisement, take under active consideration, inquire into, **think it over,** have a look at *and* see about <nf>; **sleep upon,** consult with *or* advise with *or* take counsel of one's pillow

15 **reconsider, re-examine,** review; revise one's thoughts, reappraise, revaluate, rethink; view in a new light, have second thoughts, think better of

16 **think of,** bethink oneself of, seize on, flash on <nf>; tumble to <nf>; **entertain the idea of,** entertain thoughts of; conceive of; have an idea of, have thoughts about; **have in mind, contemplate,**

consider, have under consideration; take it into one's head; **bear in mind, keep in mind,** hold the thought; harbor an idea, keep *or* hold an idea, cherish *or* foster *or* nurse *or* nurture an idea; ideate, premise, theorize, invent

17 <look upon mentally> **contemplate, look upon, view, regard,** see, view with the mind's eye, **envisage,** envision, **visualize** 986.15, imagine, image; meditate

18 **occur to,** occur to one's mind, occur, **come to mind,** rise to mind, rise in the mind, come into one's head, impinge on one's consciousness, claim one's mind *or* thoughts, pass through one's head *or* mind, dawn upon one, **enter one's mind,** pass in the mind *or* thoughts, cross one's mind, race *or* tumble through the mind, flash on *or* across the mind; **strike,** strike one, strike the mind, grab one <nf>, **suggest itself,** present itself, offer itself, present itself to the mind *or* thoughts, give one pause

19 **impress, make an impression, strike,** grab <nf>, hit; catch the thoughts, arrest the thoughts, seize one's mind, sink *or* penetrate into the mind, embed itself in the mind, lodge in the mind, **sink in** <nf>

20 **occupy the mind** *or* **thoughts,** engage the thoughts, monopolize the thoughts, fasten itself on the mind, seize the mind, fill the mind, take up one's thoughts; **preoccupy,** occupy, **absorb, engross,** absorb *or* enwrap *or* engross the thoughts, obsess the mind, run in the head; foster in the mind; come uppermost, be uppermost in the mind; have in *or* on one's mind, **have on the brain** <nf>, have constantly in one's thoughts

ADJS 21 **cognitive,** prehensive, **thought,** conceptive, conceptual, conceptualized, ideative, ideational, noetic, **mental,** cerebral; **rational** 935.18, logical, ratiocinative; **thoughtful,** cogitative, **contemplative, reflective, speculative, deliberative, meditative, ruminative,** ruminant, in a brown study, museful <old>; **pensive,** wistful, musing; introspective; thinking, reflecting, contemplating, pondering, deliberating, excogitating, excogitative, meditating, ruminating, musing, reasoned, cogitative, studious, studying, sober, serious, deepthinking; concentrating, focused, on task, concentrative, concentrated, attentive

22 absorbed *or* engrossed in thought, **absorbed, engrossed,** introspective, rapt, **wrapped in thought, lost in thought,** pensive, abstracted, immersed in thought, buried in thought, engaged in thought, occupied, **preoccupied**

ADVS **23 thoughtfully,** contemplatively, reflectively, meditatively, ruminatively, musefully <old>, cogitatively, introspectively; **pensively,** wistfully; on reconsideration, on second thought

24 on one's mind, on the brain *and* on one's chest <nf>, in the thoughts; in the heart, *in petto* <Ital>, in one's inmost *or* innermost thoughts

932 IDEA

NOUNS **1 idea; thought,** mental *or* intellectual object, **notion, concept,** conception, conceit, fancy; **perception, sense, impression,** mental impression, image, **mental image,** picture in the mind, mental picture, representation, recept, visualization; imago, ideatum, noumenon, essence; memory trace; **sentiment,** apprehension; reflection, observation; **opinion** 953.6; viewpoint, point of view; supposition, **theory** 951; plan, scheme

2 <philosophy> ideatum, ideate; noumenon; universal, universal concept *or* conception; idée-force; Platonic idea *or* form, archetype, prototype, subsistent form, eternal object, transcendent universal, eternal universal, pattern, model, exemplar, ideal, transcendent idea *or* essence, universal essence, innate idea; Aristotelian form, form-giving cause, formal cause; complex idea, simple idea; percept; construct of memory and association; Kantian idea, supreme principle of pure reason, regulative first principle, highest unitary principle of thought, transcendent nonempirical concept; Hegelian idea, highest category, the Absolute, the Absolute Idea, the Self-determined, the realized ideal; logical form *or* category; noosphere <Teilhard de Chardin>; history of ideas, *Geistesgeschichte* <Ger>; **idealism** 1053.3

3 abstract idea, abstraction, general idea, generality, abstract

4 main idea, intellectual *or* philosophical basis, leading *or* principal idea, fundamental *or* basic idea, *idée-maitresse* <Fr>, guiding principle, crowning principle, **big idea** <nf>, precept, premise

5 novel idea, intellectual *or* conceptual breakthrough, new *or* **latest wrinkle** <nf>, new slant *or* twist *or* take <nf>

6 good idea, great idea, not a bad idea; **bright thought,** bright *or* brilliant idea, **insight; brainchild** *and* **brainstorm** <nf>, brain wave <nf>, **inspiration;** quantum leap

7 absurd idea, crazy idea, fool notion *and* brainstorm <nf>

8 ideology, system of ideas, body of ideas, system of theories; world view, *Weltanschauung* <Ger>; philosophy; **ethos**

ADJS **9** ideational, ideal, **conceptual, conceptive,** notional, fanciful, imaginative; **intellectual; theoretical** 951.13; **ideological**

10 ideaed, notioned, thoughted

933 ABSENCE OF THOUGHT

NOUNS **1 thoughtlessness,** thoughtfreeness; **vacuity,** vacancy, **emptiness of mind, empty-headedness,** blankness, mental blankness, blankmindedness; fatuity, inanity, foolishness 923; tranquillity, calm of mind, meditation; **nirvana,** ataraxia, calm *or* tranquillity of mind; **oblivion,** forgetfulness, lack *or* loss of memory, amnesia; mental block; quietism, passivity, apathy; blank mind, fallow mind, tabula rasa; unintelligence 922; ignorance; head in the clouds

VERBS **2 not think, make the mind a blank,** let the mind lie fallow; **not think of,** not consider, be unmindful of; **not enter one's mind** *or* **head,** be far from one's mind *or* head *or* thoughts; pay no attention *or* mind

3 get it off one's mind, get it off one's chest <nf>, clear the mind, relieve one's mind; **put it out of one's thoughts,** dismiss from the mind *or* thoughts, push from one's thoughts, put away thought

ADJS **4 thoughtless, thoughtfree,** incogitant, **unthinking,** unreasoning; unideaed; unintellectual; **vacuous,** vacant, blank, blankminded, relaxed, empty, **empty-headed,** fallow, fatuous, inane 922.19; unoccupied; calm, tranquil; nirvanic; oblivious, ignorant; quietistic, passive

5 unthought-of, undreamed-of, unconsidered, unconceived, unconceptualized; unimagined, unimaged; imageless

934 INTUITION, INSTINCT

NOUNS **1 intuition, intuitiveness, sixth sense;** intuitive reason *or* knowledge, direct perception *or* apprehension, immediate apprehension *or* perception, unmediated perception *or* apprehension, subconscious perception, unconscious *or* subconscious knowledge, immediate cognition, knowledge without thought *or* reason, flash of insight; intuitive understanding, tact, spontaneous sense; **revelation,** epiphany, moment of illumination; **insight,** inspiration, aperçu; precognition, anticipation, a priori knowledge; *satori* <Japanese>, *buddhi* <Skt>; woman's intuition; second sight, second-sightedness, precognition 961.3, clairvoyance 689.8, extrasensory perception, presentiment; intuitionism, intuitivism; noology

2 **instinct,** natural instinct, unlearned capacity, innate *or* inborn proclivity, native *or* natural tendency, **impulse,** blind *or* unreasoning impulse, vital impulse; **libido, id,** primitive self; archetype, archetypal pattern *or* idea; unconscious *or* subconscious urge *or* drive; collective unconscious, race memory; **reflex,** spontaneous reaction, unthinking response, knee-jerk, Pavlovian response, gut reaction <nf>

3 **hunch** <nf>, sense, **presentiment, premonition,** preapprehension, intimation, foreboding; suspicion, **impression,** intuition, intuitive impression, **feeling,** forefeeling, vague feeling *or* idea, funny feeling <nf>, feeling in one's bones, gut feeling <nf>, flash

VERBS 4 **intuit, sense, feel,** feel intuitively, **feel** *or* **know in one's bones** <nf>, **have a feeling,** have a funny feeling <nf>, **get** *or* **have the impression, have a hunch** <nf>, just know, know instinctively; grok <nf>; perceive, divine

ADJS 5 **intuitive,** intuitional, sensing, sensitive, perceptive, feeling; second-sighted, precognitive 961.7, telepathic, clairvoyant

6 **instinctive,** natural, **inherent, innate,** unlearned; unconscious, subliminal; **involuntary, automatic,** spontaneous, impulsive, reflex, knee-jerk <nf>; **instinctual,** libidinal

ADVS 7 **intuitively,** by intuition; **instinctively,** automatically, spontaneously, on *or* by instinct, **instinctually**

935 REASONING

NOUNS 1 **reasoning, reason,** logical thought, discursive reason, rationalizing, rationalization, ratiocination; the divine faculty, "a harmony among irrational impulses"—Santayana; **rationalism, rationality,** discourse *or* discourse of reason <old>; sweet reason, reasonableness; demonstration, proof 957; specious reasoning, sophistry 936; philosophy 952

2 **logic,** logics; **dialectics,** dialectic, dialecticism; art of reason, science of discursive thought; formal logic, material logic; doctrine of terms, doctrine of the judgment, doctrine of inference, traditional *or* Aristotelian logic, Ramist *or* Ramistic logic, modern *or* epistemological logic,

pragmatic *or* instrumental *or* experimental logic; psychological logic, psychologism; symbolic *or* mathematical logic, logistic; propositional calculus, calculus of individuals, functional calculus, combinatory logic, algebra of relations, algebra of classes, set theory, Boolean algebra; mereology

3 <methods> a priori reasoning, a fortiori reasoning, a posteriori reasoning; discursive reasoning; **deduction, deductive reasoning,** syllogism, syllogistic reasoning; hypothetico-deductive method; **induction, inductive reasoning,** epagoge; philosophical induction, inductive *or* Baconian method; **inference; generalization,** particularization; synthesis, analysis; hypothesis and verification

4 **argumentation, argument, controversy, dispute, disagreement, disputation, polemic, debate,** disceptation <old>, eristic, art of dispute; **contention, wrangling, bickering,** hubbub 53.3, quibble, bicker, setto <nf>, rhubarb *and* hassle <nf>, passage of arms; war of words, verbal engagement *or* contest, logomachy, flyting; paper war, *guerre de plume* <Fr>; adversarial procedure, confrontational occasion; academic disputation, defense of a thesis; defense, apology, apologia, apologetics; dialectics, dialecticism; pilpul, casuistry; polemics; litigation; examination, cross-examination

5 **argument,** *argumentum* <L>; **case, plea,** pleading, *plaidoyer* <Fr>, brief; special pleading; **reason, consideration; refutation,** elenchus, ignoratio elenchi; stance, position; grounds, evidence; pros, cons, **pros and cons;** talking point; **dialogue,** reasoning together, dialectic; formal argument; rationale, pretext, premise

6 **syllogism;** prosyllogism; mode; figure; mood; pseudosyllogism, paralogism; sorites, progressive *or* Aristotelian sorites, regressive *or* Goclenian sorites; categorical syllogism; enthymeme; dilemma; **rule,** rule of deduction, transformation rule; modus ponens, modus tollens

7 **premise, proposition, position,** assumed position, sumption, **assumption,** supposal, presupposition, **hypothesis, thesis, theorem,** lemma, **statement,** affirmation, categorical proposition, premise, assertion, basis, ground, foundation; **postulate, axiom, postulation,** postulatum; data; major premise, minor premise; first principles; a priori principle, apriorism; philosophical proposition, philosopheme; hypothesis ad hoc, sentential *or* propositional function, truth-function, truth table, truth-value

8 **conclusion** 946.4

9 **reasonableness,** reasonability, **logicalness,** logicality, **rationality, sensibleness, soundness,** justness, justifiability, admissibility, cogency; sense, common **sense,** sound sense, sweet reason, **logic, reason;** plausibility 968.3

10 **good reasoning, right thinking,** sound reasoning, ironclad reasoning, irrefutable logic; cogent argument, **cogency;** strong argument, knockdown argument; good case, good reason, sound evidence, strong point

11 **reasoner,** ratiocinator, **thinker; rationalist;** rationalizer; synthesizer; **logician,** logistician; logicaster; dialectician; syllogist, syllogizer; sophist 936.6; philosopher 952.8

12 **arguer, controversialist, disputant, plaintiff, defendant, debater,** eristic, argufier <nf>, advocate, wrangler, proponent, litigator, mooter, lawyer, jurist, Philadelphia lawyer <nf>, guardhouse or latrine or forecastle lawyer <nf>, disceptator <old>, pilpulist, casuist; polemic, polemist, polemicist; logomacher, logomachist; apologist

13 **contentiousness,** litigiousness, **quarrelsomeness,** argumentativeness, disputatiousness, testiness, feistiness <nf>, combativeness; ill humor 110

14 **side,** interest; **the affirmative,** pro, yes, aye, yea; **the negative,** con, no, nay

VERBS 15 **reason;** logicalize, logicize; rationalize, provide a rationale; intellectualize; bring reason to bear, apply or use reason, put two and two together; construe, **deduce, infer, generalize; synthesize, analyze, work out; theorize,** hypothesize; premise; philosophize; syllogize; ratiocinate

16 **argue,** argufy <nf>, **dispute,** discept <old>, dissent, disagree, logomachize, polemize, polemicize, moot, **bandy words, chop logic, plead,** pettifog <nf>, join issue, give and take, cut and thrust, try conclusions, cross swords, lock horns, **contend, contest,** spar, **bicker, wrangle,** hassle <nf>, have it out, have words; thrash out; take one's stand upon, **put up an argument** <nf>; take sides, take up a side; argue to no purpose; **quibble, squabble, cavil** 936.9; litigate

17 **be reasonable, be logical, make sense,** figure <nf>, **stand to reason,** be demonstrable, be irrefutable; hold good, hold water <nf>; have a leg to stand on; show wisdom

ADJS 18 **reasoning, rational,** ratiocinative or ratiocinatory; analytic, analytical; conceptive, conceptual; cerebral, noetic, phrenic

19 **argumentative, argumental, dialectic, dialectical, controversial, disputatious, contentious, quarrelsome,** dissenting, disputing, litigious, combative, factious, testy, feisty <nf>, petulant, ill-humored 110.18, eristic, eristical, polemic, polemical, logomachic, logomachical, pilpulistic, pro and con; diectic, apodeictic, aporetic; at cross-purposes, at odds

20 **logical, reasonable, rational, cogent, sensible, sane, wise, sound,** well-thought-out, legitimate, just, justifiable, admissible; credible 953.24; plausible 968.7; as it should be, as it ought to be; well-argued, **well-founded, well-grounded**

21 **reasoned, advised, considered, calculated,** meditated, contemplated, deliberated, studied, weighed, thought-out, well-reasoned

22 dialectic, dialectical, maieutic; syllogistic, syllogistical, enthymematic, enthymematical, soritical, epagogic, inductive, deductive, inferential, synthetic, synthetical, analytic, analytical, discursive, heuristic; a priori, a fortiori, a posteriori; categorical, hypothetical, propositional, postulated, conditional

23 **deducible, derivable, inferable;** sequential, following

ADVS 24 **reasonably, logically, rationally,** by the rules of logic, **sensibly,** sanely, soundly; syllogistically, analytically; realistically, pragmatically, plausibly; **in reason,** in all reason, within reason, within the bounds or limits of reason, within reasonable limitations, **within bounds,** within the bounds of possibility, as far as possible, in all conscience

936 SOPHISTRY
   <specious reasoning>

NOUNS 1 **sophistry,** sophistication, sophism, philosophism, **casuistry,** Jesuitry, Jesuitism, subtlety, oversubtlety; **false or specious reasoning, rationalization,** evasive reasoning, vicious reasoning, sophistical reasoning, special pleading; **fallacy,** fallaciousness; **speciousness,** speciosity, superficial or apparent soundness, plausibleness, plausibility; **insincerity, disingenuousness; equivocation,** equivocalness; fudging and waffling <nf>, fudge and mudge <Brit nf>; perversion, distortion, misapplication; vicious circle, circularity; mystification, obfuscation, obscurantism; reduction, trivialization

2 **illogicalness,** illogic, illogicality, **unreasonableness, irrationality, reasonlessness, senselessness, unsoundness,** unscientificness, invalidity, untenableness, inconclusiveness; **inconsistency,** incongruity, antilogy; invalidity

3 <specious argument> **sophism,** sophistry, insincere argument, mere rhetoric, philosophism, solecism; paralogism,

pseudosyllogism; claptrap, moonshine, empty words, doubletalk, doublespeak, "sound and fury, signifying nothing"—Shakespeare; bad case, weak point, flawed argument, circular argument; **fallacy,** logical fallacy, formal fallacy, material fallacy, verbal fallacy; *argumentum ad hominem, argumentum ad baculum, argumentum ad captandum, argumentum ad captandum vulgus* <all L>, crowd-pleasing argument, argument by analogy, *tu quoque* <L>, argument, *petitio principii* <L>, begging the question, **circular argument,** undistributed middle, *non sequitur* <L>, *hysteron proteron* <Gk>, *post hoc* and *ergo propter hoc* <L>, paradox; contradition in terms

4 **quibble,** quiddity, quodlibet, quillet <old>, Jesuitism, **cavil;** quip, quirk, shuffle, dodge

5 **quibbling, caviling,** boggling, captiousness, nit-picking, **bickering; logic-chopping,** choplogic, **hairsplitting,** trichoschistism; subterfuge, chicane, chicanery, pettifoggery; **equivocation,** tergiversation, prevarication, **evasion, hedging, pussyfooting** <nf>, **sidestepping,** dodging, shifting, shuffling, fencing, parrying, boggling, paltering, beating around the bush

6 **sophist,** sophister, philosophist <old>, **casuist,** Jesuit; choplogic <old>, logic-chopper; paralogist

7 **quibbler, caviler,** pettifogger, hairsplitter, captious *or* picayune critic, nitpicker; **equivocator,** Jesuit, mystifier, mystificator, obscurantist, prevaricator, palterer, tergiversator, shuffler, mudger <Brit nf>; **hedger;** pussyfoot *or* **pussyfooter** <nf>, waffler <nf>

VERBS 8 reason speciously, reason ill, paralogize, reason in a circle, argue insincerely, pervert, distort, misapply; explain away, rationalize; prove that black is white and white black; not have a leg to stand on

9 **quibble, cavil, bicker,** boggle, chop logic, **split hairs,** nitpick, pick nits; Jesuitize; **equivocate,** mystify, obscure, prevaricate, tergiversate, doubletalk, doublespeak, tap-dance <nf>, misrepresent, misinform, fudge, palter, fence, parry, shift, shuffle, **dodge,** shy, **evade,** sidestep, hedge, skate around <Brit nf>, pussyfoot <nf>, evade the issue; twist, slant; **beat about** *or* **around the bush,** avoid the issue, not come to the point, **beg the question;** pick holes in, pick to pieces; blow hot and cold; strain at a gnat and swallow a camel

ADJS 10 **sophistical,** sophistic, philosophistic, philosophistical <old>, casuistic, casuistical, Jesuitic, Jesuitical, **fallacious, specious,** colorable, plausible, hollow, superficially *or* apparently sound; deceptive, illusive, empty; overrefined, oversubtle, **insincere, disingenuous**

11 **illogical, unreasonable, irrational, reasonless,** contrary to reason, **senseless,** without reason, **without rhyme** *or* **reason; unscientific,** nonscientific, unphilosophical; **invalid,** inauthentic, unauthentic, faulty, flawed, paralogical, fallacious; inconclusive, inconsequent, inconsequential, not following; **inconsistent,** incongruous, absonant <old>, loose, unconnected; contradictory, **self-contradictory,** self-annulling, self-refuting, oxymoronic

12 **unsound, unsubstantial,** insubstantial, weak, feeble, poor, flimsy, unrigorous, inconclusive, unproved, unsustained, poorly argued

13 **baseless, groundless,** ungrounded, **unfounded,** ill-founded, unbased, **unsupported,** unsustained, invalid, **without foundation,** without basis *or* sound basis; **untenable, unsupportable,** unsustainable; **unwarranted,** idle, empty, vain

14 **quibbling, caviling, equivocatory,** equivocal, captious, nitpicky *and* nit-picking <nf>, bickering; picayune, petty, trivial, trifling; paltering, shuffling, hedging, pussyfooting <nf>, **evasive; hairsplitting,** trichoschistic, logic-chopping, choplogic *or* choplogical <old>

ADVS 15 **illogically, unreasonably, irrationally, reasonlessly, senselessly;** baselessly, groundlessly; untenably, unsupportably, unsustainably; out of all reason, out of all bounds

937 TOPIC

NOUNS 1 **topic, subject,** subject of thought, **matter, subject matter,** what it is about, **concern,** focus of interest *or* attention, discrete matter, category; field, branch, discipline; **theme,** burden, **text,** motif, motive, angle, business at hand, **case,** matter in hand, **question, problem, issue,** bone of contention; **point,** point at issue, point in question, topic for discussion, main point, gist 997.6; plot; item on the agenda; head, heading, chapter, rubric, category; contents, substance, meat, essence, material part, basis; living issue, topic of the day; thesis

2 **caption, title, heading, head,** superscription, rubric; **headline;** overline; banner, banner head *or* line, streamer; searchead, screamer; spread, spreadhead; drop head, dropline, hanger; running head *or* title, jump head; **subhead, subheading,** subtitle; legend, motto, epigraph; title page

VERBS 3 focus on, have regard to, distinguish, lift up, set forth, specify, zero in on <nf>, center on, be concerned with; include; caption, title, head, head up <nf>; **headline;** subtitle, subhead

ADJS 4 **topical, thematic**

938 INQUIRY

NOUNS **1 inquiry,** inquiring, probing, **inquest** 307.17, inquirendo; inquisition; interpellation; inquiring mind; analysis 801

2 examination, school examination, examen, **exam** <nf>, **test, quiz;** oral examination, oral, doctor's oral, master's oral, viva voce examination, viva <nf>; catechesis, catchization; **audition, hearing;** multiple-choice test, multiple-guess test <nf>; written examination, written <nf>, blue book <nf>, test paper; course examination, midterm, midyear, midsemester; qualifying examination, preliminary examination, prelim <nf>; take-home examination; unannounced examination, pop or shotgun or surprise quiz <nf>; final examination, **final** <nf>, comprehensive examination, comps <nf>, great go <old> or greats <Oxford>; honors <Brit>, tripos <Cambridge>

3 examination, inspection, scrutiny; survey, review, perusal, look-over, once over and look-see <nf>, perlustration, **study,** look-through, scan, run-through; visitation; overhaul, overhauling; quality control; confirmation, cross-check

4 investigation, indagation <old>, **research,** legwork <nf>, inquiry into; data-gathering, gathering or amassing evidence; perscrutation, **probe,** searching investigation, close inquiry, exhaustive study; police inquiry or investigation, criminal investigation, detective work, detection, sleuthing; investigative bureau or agency, bureau or department of investigation; legislative investigation, Congressional investigation, hearing; witch-hunt, fishing expedition, Inquisition

5 preliminary or tentative examination; quick or cursory inspection, glance, quick look, first look, once-over-lightly <nf>

6 checkup, check; spot check; physical examination, **physical,** physical checkup, health examination; self-examination; exploratory examination; testing, drug testing, alcohol testing, random testing; bench test

7 re-examination, reinquiry, recheck, **review,** reappraisal, revaluation, rethinking, revision, rebeholding, second or further look

8 reconnaissance; recce and recco and recon <nf>; **reconnoitering,** reconnoiter, exploration, **scouting;** exploratory survey

9 surveillance, shadowing, following, trailing, tailing <nf>, 24-hour surveillance, observation, stakeout <nf>; **spying, espionage,** espial, **intelligence,** military intelligence, intelligence work, cloak-and-dagger work <nf>; intelligence agency, secret service, secret police; counterespionage, counterintelligence; wiretap, wiretapping, bugging <nf>, electronic surveillance; tagging

10 question, query, inquiry, demand <old>, **interrogation,** interrogatory; interrogative; frequently asked question or FAQ; **problem, issue, topic** 937, case or point in question, bone of contention, controversial point, question before the house, debating point, controversy, question or point at issue, **moot point** or case, question mark, *quodlibet* <L>; difficult question, vexed or knotty question, burning question; sixty-four-thousand-dollar question; leader, leading question; feeler, trial balloon, fishing question; trick question, poser, stumper, tough nut to crack, conundrum, enigma, mind-boggler <nf>; trivia question; cross-question, rhetorical question; cross-interrogatory; catechism, catechizing; easy question

11 interview, press conference, press opportunity, photo opportunity, photo op <nf>

12 questioning, interrogation, querying, asking, seeking, pumping, probing, inquiring; **quiz,** quizzing, **examination;** challenge, dispute; interpellation, bringing into question; catechizing, catechization; catechetical method, Socratic method or induction

13 grilling, the grill <nf>, inquisition, pumping; police interrogation; **the third-degree** <nf>; direct examination, redirect examination, **cross-examination,** cross-interrogation, **cross-questioning**

14 canvass, survey, inquiry, questionnaire, questionary; exit poll; **poll, public-opinion poll,** opinion poll or survey, statistical survey, opinion sampling, voter-preference survey; consumer-preference survey, market-research survey; consumer research, market research

15 search, searching, **quest, hunt,** hunting, stalk, stalking, still hunt, dragnet, posse, search party; search warrant; search-and-destroy operation or mission; **rummage, ransacking,** turning over or upside down; **forage;** house-search, perquisition, domiciliary visit; exploration, probe; **body search,** frisk and toss and shake and shakedown and skin-search and body-shake and pat-down search <nf>; all-points bulletin

16 inquirer, asker, prober, querier, querist, **questioner,** questionist, interrogator; interviewer; interrogatrix; interpellator; **quizzer,** examiner, catechist; inquisitor, inquisitionist; cross-questioner, cross-interrogator, **cross-examiner;** interlocutor; **pollster,** poller, sampler, canvasser, opinion sampler; **interviewer; detective** 576.10; **secret agent** 576.9; quiz-master

17 **examiner,** examinant, **tester; inspector,** scrutinizer, scrutator, scrutineer, quality-control inspector; **monitor,** reviewer; fact-checker; check-out pilot; observer; visitor, visitator; **investigator,** indagator <old>; editor, copy editor, proofreader

18 seeker, hunter, searcher, perquisitor; rummager, ransacker; digger, delver; zetetic; **researcher, fact finder,** researchist, research worker, market researcher, consumer researcher; surveyor

19 **examinee,** examinant, examinate, questionee, quizzee; interviewee; informant, subject, interviewee; witness; candidate; defendant, plaintiff, suspect

VERBS 20 **inquire, ask, question, query; make inquiry,** take up *or* institute *or* pursue *or* follow up *or* conduct *or* carry on an inquiry, ask after, inquire after, ask about, ask questions, put queries; inquire of, require an answer, ask a question, put a question to, pose *or* set *or* propose *or* propound a question; bring into question, interpellate; **demand** <old>, **want to know;** introspect

21 **interrogate, question, query, quiz, test, examine;** catechize; **pump,** pump for information, shoot questions at, pick the brains of, worm out of; interview; draw one out

22 **grill,** put on the grill <nf>, inquisition, pump, make inquisition; roast <nf>, put the pressure on *and* put the screws to *and* go over <nf>; **cross-examine, cross-question,** cross-interrogate, cross <nf>; third-degree <nf>, give *or* put through the third degree <nf>; put to the question; extract information, pry *or* prize out; run *or* put through the mill <nf>

23 **investigate,** indagate <old>, sift, **explore, look into,** peer into, **search into, go into, delve into,** dig into, poke into, pry into; fact-find; **probe, sound, plumb, fathom; check into, check on, check out,** nose into, see into; poke about, root around *or* about, scratch around *or* about, cast about *or* around

24 **examine, inspect, scrutinize, survey,** canvass, **look at,** peer at, eyeball <nf>, **observe, scan, peruse, study; look over,** give the once-over <nf>, run the eye over, cast *or* pass the eyes over, scope out <nf>; go over, run over, pass over, pore over; overlook, overhaul; **monitor, review,** pass under review; set an examination, give an examination; **take stock of,** size *or* **size up,** take the measure <nf>; **check, check out, check over** *or* **through; check up on;** autopsy, postmortem 307.17; soul-search

25 **make a close study of, research, scrutinize,** examine thoroughly, vet <Brit>, **go deep into,** look closely at, probe; examine point by point, go over with a fine-tooth comb, go over step by step, subject to close scrutiny, view *or* try in all its phases, get down to nuts and bolts <nf>; perscrutate, perlustrate

26 **examine cursorily,** take a cursory view of, give a quick *or* cursory look, give a once-over-lightly <nf>, give a dekko <Brit nf>, **scan, skim, skim over** *or* **through,** slur, slur over, slip *or* skip over *or* through, **glance at,** give the once-over <nf>, pass over lightly, zip through, **dip into, touch upon,** touch upon lightly *or* in passing, **hit the high spots; thumb through,** flip through the pages, turn over the leaves, leaf *or* page *or* flick through

27 **re-examine,** recheck, reinquire, **reconsider,** reappraise, revaluate, rethink, **review,** revise, rebehold, take another *or* a second *or* a further look; retrace, retrace one's steps, go back over; rejig *or* rejigger <nf>; take back to the old drawing board

28 **reconnoiter,** make a reconnaissance, case <nf>, scout, **scout out,** spy, **spy out,** play the spy, peep; **watch,** put under surveillance, stake out <nf>; bug <nf>; check up on, check up

29 **canvass, survey,** make a survey; **poll,** conduct a poll, sample, **questionnaire** <nf>

30 **seek, hunt,** look <old>, **quest, pursue,** go in pursuit of, follow, go in search of, prowl after, see to, try to find; **look up, hunt up; look for,** look around *or* about for, look for high and low, look high and low, search out, **search for,** seek for, **hunt for,** cast *or* beat about for; shop around for; **fish for, angle for,** bob for, dig for, delve for, go on a fishing expedition; **ask for,** inquire for; **gun for,** go gunning for; still-hunt <nf>

31 **search, hunt, explore;** research; read up on; **hunt through, search through, look through, go through;** dig, delve, burrow, root, pick over, poke, pry; look round *or* around, poke around, nose around, smell around; beat the bushes; forage; frisk <nf>

32 **grope,** grope for, **feel for,** fumble, grabble, scrabble, feel around, poke around, pry around, beat about, grope in the dark; **feel** *or* **pick one's way**

33 **ransack, rummage, rake, scour, comb;** rifle; **look everywhere,** look into every hole and corner, **look high and low,** look upstairs and downstairs, **look all over,** look all over hell <nf>, search high heaven, turn upside down, turn inside out, **leave no stone unturned;** shake down *and* shake *and* toss <nf>

34 search out, hunt out, spy out, scout out, **ferret out,** fish out, pry out, winkle out <Brit nf>, dig out, root out, grub up

35 trace, stalk, track, trail; follow, follow up, shadow, tail <nf>, dog the footsteps of, have *or* keep an eye on; nose, nose out, **smell** *or* **sniff out,** follow the trail *or* scent *or* spoor of; follow a clue; **trace down, hunt down, track down, run down, run to earth**

ADJS **36 inquiring, questioning, querying,** quizzing; **quizzical, curious; interrogatory,** interrogative, interrogational; inquisitorial, inquisitional; visitatorial, visitorial; catechistic, catechistical, catechetic, catechetical

37 examining, examinational; scrutatorial, examinatorial; **testing,** trying, **tentative;** groping, feeling; inspectional; **inspectorial;** interpellant; **investigative,** indagative <old>; zetetic; heuristic, investigatory, investigational; **exploratory,** explorative, explorational; fact-finding; analytic, analytical; curious

38 searching, probing, prying, nosy <nf>; poking, digging, fishing, delving; in search *or* quest of, looking for, **out for,** on the lookout for, **in the market for,** loaded *or* out for bear <nf>; all-searching; fact-finding, knowledge-seeking

ADVS **39 in question, at issue,** in debate *or* dispute, **under consideration,** under active consideration, **under advisement,** *subjudice* <L>, under examination, under investigation, under surveillance, up *or* open for discussion; **before the house, on the docket, on the agenda, on the table, on the floor**

939 ANSWER

NOUNS **1 answer, reply, response,** responsion, replication; answering, respondence; riposte, **uptake** <nf>, **retort, rejoinder,** reaction 903, return, **comeback** *and* **take** <nf>, back answer, short answer, back talk, backchat <nf>; **repartee,** backchat, clever *or* ready *or* witty reply *or* retort, snappy comeback <nf>, witty repartee; yes-and-no answer, evasive reply; **acknowledgment,** receipt, confirmation; rescript, rescription; antiphon; **echo,** reverberation 54.2

2 rebuttal, counterstatement, counterreply, counterclaim, counterblast, counteraccusation, countercharge, *tu quoque* <L, you too>, defense, contraremonstrance; **rejoinder,** replication, defense, rebutter, surrebutter *or* surrebuttal, surrejoinder; confutation, refutation; last word, parting shot

3 answerer, replier, responder, **respondent,** responser; defendant

VERBS **4 answer,** make *or* give answer, return answer, return for answer, offer, proffer, **reply, respond,** say, say in reply; **retort,** riposte, **rejoin,** return, throw back, flash back; come back *and* come back at *and* come right back at <nf>, answer back *and* talk back *and* shoot back <nf>, **react; acknowledge,** make *or* give acknowledgement; echo, reecho, reverberate 54.7

5 rebut, make a rebuttal; **rejoin,** surrebut, surrejoin; counterclaim, countercharge; confute, refute; have the last word, have the final say; fire the parting shot; lip off <nf>

ADJS **6 answering, replying, responsive,** respondent, responding; rejoining, returning; antiphonal; echoing, echoic, reechoing 54.10; confutative, refutative; acknowledging, confirming

ADVS **7 in answer,** in reply, in response, in return, in rebuttal

940 SOLUTION

<answer to a problem>

NOUNS **1 solution,** resolution, **answer, reason, explanation** 341.4; **finding,** conclusion, determination, ascertainment, verdict, judgment; **outcome, upshot,** denouement, **result,** issue, end 820, end result; accomplishment 407; **solving,** working, **working-out,** finding-out, resolving, **clearing up,** cracking; **unriddling,** riddling, unscrambling, unraveling, sorting out, untwisting, unspinning, unweaving, untangling, disentanglement; **decipherment, deciphering, decoding,** decryption; interpretation 341; **happy ending** *or* outcome, the answer to one's prayers, the light at the end of the tunnel; possible solution, **scenario**

VERBS **2 solve, resolve,** find the solution *or* answer, problem-solve, **clear up,** get, get right, do, work, **work out, find out, figure out,** dope *and* dope out <nf>; **straighten out, iron out,** sort out, puzzle out; debug; psych *and* psych out <nf>; **unriddle,** riddle, unscramble, undo, untangle, disentangle, untwist, unspin, unweave, **unravel,** ravel, ravel out; **decipher, decode,** decrypt, crack, do the math; **make out,** interpret 341.9; **answer, explain** 341.10; unlock, pick *or* open the lock; find the key of, find a clue to; **get to the bottom** *or* **heart of, fathom,** plumb, bottom; have it, hit it, hit upon a solution, hit the nail on the head, hit it on the nose <nf>; guess, divine, guess right; end happily, work out right *and* come up roses <nf>

ADJS **3 solvable, soluble, resolvable,** open to solution, capable of solution, workable, doable, answerable;

explainable, explicable, determinable, ascertainable; **decipherable,** decodable

941 DISCOVERY

NOUNS **1 discovery, finding, detection,** spotting, catching, catching sight of, sighting, espial; recognition, determination, distinguishment; locating, **location; disclosure, exposure, revelation, uncovering, unearthing,** digging up, exhumation, excavation, bringing to light *or* view; **find,** trove, treasure trove, *trouvaille* <Fr>, strike, lucky strike; accidental *or* chance discovery, happening *or* stumbling upon, tripping over, casual discovery; serendipity; **learning, finding out,** determining, becoming conscious *or* cognizant of, becoming aware of; self-discovery; realization, enlightenment; rediscovery; invention; archaeology

VERBS **2 discover, find,** get; strike, hit; put *or* lay one's hands on, lay one's fingers on, **locate** 159.10; **hunt down,** search out, trace down, track down, **run down, run** *or* **bring to earth;** trace; **learn, find out,** determine, become cognizant *or* conscious of, become aware of, get it <nf>; discover *or* find out the hard way, discover to one's cost; discover *or* find oneself; rediscover; invent

3 come across, run across, meet with, meet up with <nf>, fall in with, **encounter, run into,** bump into <nf>, come *or* run up against <nf>, **come on** *or* **upon, hit on** *or* **upon,** strike on, light on *or* upon, alight on *or* upon, fall on, tumble on *or* upon; **chance on** *or* **upon,** happen on *or* upon *or* across, **stumble on** *or* **upon,** *or* **across** *or* **into,** stub one's toe on *or* upon, trip over, bump up against, blunder upon, discover serendipitously

4 uncover, unearth, dig up, disinter, exhume, excavate; **disclose, expose, reveal,** blow the lid off, crack wide open, **bring to light,** lay bare; **turn up,** root up, rootle up <Brit>, fish up; worm out, ferret out, winkle out <Brit>, pry out

5 detect, spot, <nf>, **see, lay eyes on,** catch sight of, catch a glimpse of, perceive, **spy,** espy, descry, sense, pick up, notice, discern, **perceive, make out, recognize,** distinguish, identify

6 scent, catch the scent of, sniff, smell, get a whiff of <nf>, **get wind of;** sniff *or* scent *or* smell out, nose out; be on the right scent, be near the truth, be warm <nf>, burn <nf>, have a fix on, place

7 catch, catch out; catch off side, catch off base; catch tripping, **catch napping, catch off-guard,** catch asleep at the switch; **catch at,** catch in the act, **catch red-handed,** catch in *flagrante delicto*, **catch with one's pants down** <nf>, catch flat-footed, have the goods on <nf>, ensnare

8 <detect the hidden nature of> **see through, penetrate,** see as it really is, see in its true colors, see the inside of, read between the lines, see the cloven hoof; open the eyes to, tumble to, catch on to, wise up to <nf>; **be on to, be wise to, be hep to** <nf>, have one's measure, **have one's number,** have dead to rights <nf>, read someone like a book

9 turn up, show up, be found; discover itself, expose *or* betray itself; hang out <nf>; materialize, **come to light,** come out; come along, come to hand; show one's true colors

ADJS **10** on the right scent, **on the right track,** on the trail of; **hot** *and* **warm** <nf>; **discoverable,** determinable, findable, **detectable,** spottable, disclosable, exposable, locatable, **discernible;** exploratory

INTERJS **11 eureka!,** I have it!, at last!, at long last!, finally!, *thalassa!* or *thalatta!* <Gk>; ah hah!

942 EXPERIMENT

NOUNS **1 experiment, experimentation;** experimental method; testing, trying, trying-out, **trial;** research and development *or* R and D; running it up the flagpole <nf>, trying it on *or* out <nf>, exploration, bench test; **trial and error,** hit and miss, cut and try <nf>; empiricism, experimentalism, pragmatism, instrumentalism; **rule of thumb;** tentativeness, tentative method; control experiment, controlled experiment, **control;** experimental design; experimental proof *or* verification; noble experiment; single-blind experiment, double-blind experiment; guesswork

2 test, trial, try; essay; check; docimasy <old>, assay; determination, blank determination; **proof,** verification; touchstone, standard, criterion 300.2; crucial test; acid test, litmus *or* litmus-paper test; ordeal, crucible; probation; **feeling out, sounding out;** test case; first *or* rough draft, rough sketch, mock-up; stab *and* crack *and* whack <nf>; *brouillon* <Fr>; trial balloon

3 tryout, workout, **rehearsal,** practice; pilot plan *or* program; **dry run,** dummy run, practice run; *Gedankenexperiment* <Ger>; road test; **trial run,** practical test; shakedown, shakedown cruise; bench test; flight test, test flight *or* run; audition, hearing

4 feeler, probe, sound, sounder; **trial balloon,** *ballon d'essai* <Fr>, pilot balloon, barometer; weather vane, weathercock; straw to show the wind, straw vote; sample, random sample, experimental sample

5 laboratory, lab <nf>, research laboratory, research center *or* establishment *or* facility *or* institute, experiment station, field station, research and development *or* R and D establishment; **proving ground;** think tank <nf>, workshop

6 experimenter, experimentist, experimentalist, empiricist, bench scientist, **researcher,** research worker, R and D worker; experimental engineer; **tester,** tryer-out, test driver, test pilot; essayer; assayer; analyst, analyzer, investigator

7 subject, experimental subject, experimentee, testee, patient, sample; laboratory animal, experimental *or* test animal, **guinea pig,** lab rat

VERBS **8 experiment,** experimentalize, **research,** make an experiment, **run an experiment,** run a sample *or* specimen; **test, try,** essay, cut and try <nf>, **test** *or* **try out,** have a dry run *or* dummy run *or* rehearsal *or* test run, rehearse; run it up the flagpole and see who salutes <nf>; put to the test, **put to the proof, prove, verify,** validate, substantiate, confirm, put to trial, bring to test, make a trial of, give a trial to; **give a try,** have a go, give it a go <nf>, have *or* take a stab *or* crack *or* whack at <nf>; sample, taste; assay; play around *or* fool around with <nf>; try out under controlled conditions; give a tryout *or* workout <nf>, **road-test,** shake down; try one out, put one through his paces; experiment *or* practice upon; try it on; try on, try it for size <nf>; try one's strength, see what one can do; send up a trial balloon

9 sound out, check out, feel out, sound, get a sounding *or* reading *or* sense, probe, **feel the pulse,** read; **put** *or* **throw out a feeler,** put out feelers, send up a trial balloon, fly a kite; **see which way the wind blows,** see how the land lies, test out, test the waters; take a straw vote, take a random sample, use an experimental sample

10 stand the test, stand up, hold up, hold up in the wash, pass, **pass muster,** get by <nf>, make it *and* hack it *and* cut the mustard <nf>, meet *or* satisfy requirements

ADJS **11 experimental, test, trial;** pilot; testing, proving, trying; probative, probatory, verificatory; probationary; **tentative,** provisional; empirical; trial-and-error, hit-or-miss, cut-and-try; heuristic

12 tried, well-tried, tested, proved, verified, confirmed, tried and true

ADVS **13 experimentally,** by rule of thumb, by trial and error, by hit and miss, hit *or* miss, by guess and by God

14 on trial, under examination, **on** *or* **under probation,** under suspicion, **on approval**

943 COMPARISON

NOUNS **1 comparison,** compare, examining side by side, matching, matchup, holding up together, proportion <old>, comparative judgment *or* estimate; **likening,** comparing, **analogy;** parallelism; comparative relation; weighing, balancing; opposing, opposition, **contrast;** contrastiveness, distinctiveness, distinction 944.3; confrontment, confrontation; **relation** 775, relating, relativism; correlation 777; simile, similitude, metaphor, allegory, figure *or* trope of comparison; comparative degree; comparative method; comparative linguistics, comparative grammar, comparative literature, comparative anatomy, etc

2 collation, comparative scrutiny, point-by-point comparison; **verification, confirmation, checking;** check, cross-check

3 comparability, comparableness, comparativeness; analogousness, equivalence, **commensurability;** proportionateness *or* proportionability <old>; ratio, proportion, balance; **similarity** 784

VERBS **4 compare, liken,** assimilate, similize, liken to, compare with; **make** *or* **draw a comparison,** run a comparison, do a comparative study, bring into comparison; **analogize,** bring into analogy; relate 775.6; metaphorize; **draw a parallel,** parallel; **match,** match up; examine side by side, view together, hold up together; weigh *or* measure against; confront, bring into confrontation, **contrast, oppose,** set in opposition, set off against, set in contrast, **put** *or* **set over against,** set *or* place against, counterpose; compare and contrast, note similarities and differences; **weigh,** balance

5 collate, scrutinize comparatively, compare point by point, painstakingly match; **verify, confirm, check, cross-check**

6 compare notes, exchange views *or* observations, match data *or* findings, put heads together <nf>

7 be comparable, compare, compare to *or* **with,** not compare with 787.2, admit of comparison, be commensurable, be of the same order *or* class, be worthy of comparison, be fit to be compared; **measure up to, come up to,** match up with, stack up with <nf>, hold a candle to <nf>; **match, parallel;** vie, vie with, rival; **resemble** 784.7

ADJS **8 comparative, relative** 775.7, **comparable,** commensurate, commensurable, parallel, matchable, **analogous;** analogical; collatable; **correlative;** much at one, much of a muchness <nf>; **similar** 784.10; something of the sort *or* to that effect

9 incomparable, incommensurable, not to be compared, of different orders; apples and oranges; **unlike, dissimilar** 7876.4

ADVS **10 comparatively, relatively;** comparably; dollar for dollar, pound for pound, ounce for ounce, etc; on the one hand, on the other hand

PREPS **11 compared to, compared with,** as compared with, by comparison with, **in comparison with, beside,** over against, taken with; than

944 DISCRIMINATION

NOUNS **1 discrimination,** discriminateness, discriminatingness, discriminativeness; seeing *or* making distinctions, appreciation of differences; analytic power *or* faculty; **criticalness; finesse,** refinement, delicacy; niceness of distinction, nicety, subtlety, refined discrimination, critical niceness; **tact, tactfulness,** feel, feeling, sense, **sensitivity** 24.3, **sensibility** 24.2; intuition, instinct 934; appreciation, appreciativeness; judiciousness 920.7; taste, discriminating taste, aesthetic *or* artistic judgment; palate, fine *or* refined palate; ear, good ear, educated ear; eye, good eye; connoisseurship, savvy <nf>, selectiveness, fastidiousness 495

2 discernment, critical discernment, penetration, **perception,** perceptiveness, **insight,** perspicacity; **flair; judgment,** acumen 920.4; analysis 801

3 distinction, contradistinction, distinctiveness <old>; **distinguishment, differentiation** 780.4, winnowing, shakeout, separation, separationism, division, segregation, segregationism, demarcation; nice *or* subtle *or* fine distinction, **nuance,** shade of difference, microscopic distinction; hairsplitting, trichoschistism

VERBS **4 discriminate, distinguish,** draw *or* make distinctions, contradistinguish, compare and contrast, pick and choose, secern, distinguish in thought, **separate,** separate out, divide, analyze 801.6, subdivide, **segregate,** sever, severalize, **differentiate,** demark, demarcate, mark the interface, set off, **set apart,** grade, graduate, sift, sift out, sieve, sieve out, winnow, screen, screen out, sort, classify, sort out; **pick out, select** 371.14; separate the sheep from the goats, separate the men from the boys, separate the wheat from the tares *or* chaff, winnow the chaff from the wheat; **draw the line,** fix *or* set a limit; **split hairs,** draw *or* make a fine *or* overfine *or* nice *or* subtle distinction, subtilize

5 be discriminating, discriminate, exercise discrimination, tell which is which; **be tactful,** show *or* exercise tact; be tasteful, use one's palate; shop around, pick and choose; use advisedly

6 distinguish between, make *or* **draw a distinction,** appreciate differences, see nuances *or* shades of difference, see the difference, tell apart, tell one thing from another, know which is which, know what's what <nf>, not confound *or* mix up; "know a hawk from a handsaw"—Shakespeare, know one's ass from one's elbow <nf>

ADJS **7 discriminating, discriminate,** discriminative, selective; discriminatory; **tactful, sensitive;** appreciative, appreciatory; **critical;** distinctive <old>, **distinguishing;** differential; precise, accurate, exact; nice, fine, delicate, subtle, subtile, refined; fastidious 495.9; distinctive, contrastive

8 discerning, perceptive, perspicacious, insightful; **astute, judicious** 920.19; perfectionist, choosy

9 discriminable, distinguishable, separable, differentiable, contrastable, opposable

ADVS **10 discriminatingly,** discriminatively, discriminately; with finesse; **tactfully; tastefully**

945 INDISCRIMINATION

NOUNS **1 indiscrimination,** indiscriminateness, undiscriminatingness, undiscriminativeness, unselectiveness, **uncriticalness, unparticularness;** syncretism; unfastidiousness; lack of refinement, coarseness *or* crudeness *or* crudity of intellect; **casualness,** promiscuousness, **promiscuity; indiscretion,** indiscreetness, **imprudence** 923.2; **untactfulness,** tactlessness, lack of feeling, insensitivity, **insensibility** 25, unmeticulousness, unpreciseness 340.4, inexactitude; **generality** 864, catholicity, catholic tastes; indifference; color blindness, tone-deafness; impartiality

2 indistinction, indistinctness, vagueness 32.2; **indefiniteness** 971.4; uniformity 781; facelessness, impersonality; indistinguishableness, **undistinguishableness,** indiscernibility; a distinction without a difference; randomness, generality, universality

VERBS **3 confound, confuse,** mix, mix up, muddle, tumble, jumble, jumble together, **blur,** blur distinctions, overlook distinctions; lump together, take as one, roll into one

4 use loosely, use unadvisedly

ADJS **5 undiscriminating, indiscriminate,** indiscriminative, undiscriminative, undifferentiating, unselective; wholesale, **general** 864.11, **blanket; uncritical,** uncriticizing, undemanding, nonjudgmental; **unparticular,** unfastidious; unsubtle; **casual, promiscuous;** undiscerning; unexacting, unmeticulous 340.13;

indiscreet, undiscreet, **imprudent; untactful,** tactless, insensitive; catholic; indifferent; color-blind

6 **indistinguishable,** undistinguishable, undistinguished, indiscernible, **indistinct,** indistinctive, **without distinction,** not to be distinguished, undiscriminated, nondiscriminatory, inclusive, unindividual, unindividualized, undifferentiated, **alike,** six of one and half a dozen of the other <nf>; desultory; undefined, **indefinite;** faceless, impersonal; standard, interchangeable, stereotyped, uniform 781.5; random; miscellaneous, motley

946 JUDGMENT

NOUNS 1 **judgment,** judging, adjudgment, adjudication, judicature, deeming <old>; judgment call <nf>; arbitrament, arbitration 466.2; **resolution** 359; good judgment 920.7; **choice** 371; **discrimination** 944

2 **criticism; censure** 510.3; **approval** 509; **critique,** review, notice, critical notice, report, comment; book review, critical review, thumbnail review; literary criticism, art criticism, music criticism, etc, critical journal, critical bibliography

3 **estimate, estimation; view, opinion** 953.6; **assessment,** assessing, **appraisal,** appraisement, appraising, appreciation, reckoning, **stocktaking,** valuation, valuing, **evaluation,** evaluating, value judgment, evaluative criticism, analyzing, weighing, weighing up, gauging, ranking, rank-ordering, **rating;** measurement 300; comparison 943; second opinion; public opinion

4 **conclusion, deduction, inference,** consequence, consequent, corollary; derivation, illation; induction; judgment day

5 **verdict, decision,** resolution <old>, **determination, finding,** holding; diagnosis, prognosis; **decree, ruling,** consideration, order, **pronouncement,** deliverance; **award,** action, **sentence; condemnation,** doom; dictum; precedent; edict, decree; execution of judgment

6 **judge,** judger, adjudicator, justice; arbiter 596.1; referee, umpire

7 **critic,** criticizer; connoisseur, cognoscente <Ital>; literary critic, man of letters; textual critic; editor; social critic, muckraker; captious critic, smellfungus, caviler, carper, faultfinder; criticaster, criticule, critickin; **censor,** censurer; **reviewer, commentator,** commenter; scholiast, annotator

VERBS 8 **judge,** exercise judgment or the judgment; make a judgment call <nf>; adjudge, adjudicate; be judicious or judgmental; **consider, regard,** hold, **deem, esteem, count, account,** think of; allow

<nf>, **suppose, presume** 951.10, opine, form an opinion, give or pass or express an opinion, weigh in and put in one's two cents' worth <nf>

9 **estimate,** form an estimate, make an estimation; **reckon,** call, guess, figure <nf>; **assess, appraise,** give an appreciation, **gauge, rate, rank,** rank-order, put in rank order, class, mark, **value,** deem, **evaluate,** valuate, place or set a value on, weigh, weigh up, prize, appreciate; size up or take one's measure <nf>, **measure** 300.10

10 **conclude,** draw a conclusion, be forced to conclude, **come to or arrive at a conclusion, come up with a conclusion** and **end up** <nf>; find, hold; deduce, derive, take as proved or demonstrated, extract, **gather,** collect, glean, fetch; **infer,** draw an inference; induce; **reason,** reason that; put two and two together

11 **decide, determine; find,** hold, ascertain; **resolve** 359.7, **settle,** fix; make a decision, come to a decision, **make up one's mind,** settle one's mind, come down <nf>, settle the matter

12 **sit in judgment,** hold the scales, hold court; **hear,** give a hearing to; **try** 598.18; **referee, umpire,** officiate; arbitrate 466.6

13 **pass judgment, pronounce judgment,** utter a judgment, deliver judgment; agree on a verdict, return a verdict, hand down a verdict, **bring in a verdict, find,** find for or against; pronounce on, act on, **pronounce,** report, **rule,** decree, order; **sentence,** pass sentence, hand down a sentence, doom, condemn; charge the jury

14 **criticize,** critique; **censure** 510.13, pick holes in, pick to pieces; **approve** 509.9; **review;** comment upon, annotate; moralize upon; pontificate; vet <nf>

15 **rank, rate,** count, be regarded, be thought of, be in one's estimation

ADJS 16 **judicial, judiciary,** judicative, judgmental; juridic, juridical, juristic, juristical; **judicious** 920.19; **evaluative; critical; approbatory** 509.16

ADVS 17 **all things considered, on the whole, taking one thing with another,** on balance, taking everything into consideration or account; everything being equal, other things being equal, *ceteris paribus* <L>, taking into account, considering, after all, this being so; therefore, wherefore; on the one hand, on the other hand, having said that; *sub judice* <L>, in court, before the bench or bar or court

947 PREJUDGMENT

NOUNS 1 **prejudgment,** prejudication, forejudgment; **preconception, presumption, supposition, presupposition,** presupposal, presurmise, preapprehension, prenotion, **prepossession; predilection,** predisposition; preconsideration, **predetermination,** predecision, preconclusion, premature judgment; ulterior motive, hidden agenda, *parti pris* <Fr>, an ax to grind, **prejudice** 980.3

VERBS **2 prejudge,** forejudge; **preconceive, presuppose, presume,** presurmise; **be predisposed;** predecide, predetermine, preconclude, judge beforehand *or* prematurely, judge before the evidence is in, have one's mind made up; **jump to a conclusion,** go off half-cocked *or* at half cock *and* beat the gun *and* jump the gun *and* shoot from the hip <nf>

ADJS **3 prejudged,** forejudged, **preconceived,** preconceptual, **presumed, presupposed,** presurmised; predetermined, predecided, preconcluded, judged beforehand *or* prematurely; **predisposed,** predispositional; prejudicial, prejudging, prejudicative

948 MISJUDGMENT

NOUNS **1 misjudgment,** poor judgment, error in judgment, warped *or* flawed *or* skewed judgment; **miscalculation,** miscomputation, **misreckoning, misestimation,** misappreciation, misperception, misevaluation, misvaluation, misconjecture, wrong impression; **misreading,** wrong construction, misconstruction, **misinterpretation** 342; **inaccuracy, error** 975; unmeticulousness 340.4; injudiciousness 923.2; wrong end of the stick

VERBS **2 misjudge,** judge amiss, **miscalculate, misestimate, misreckon,** misappreciate, misperceive, get a wrong impression, misevaluate, misvalue, miscompute, misdeem, misesteem, misthink, misconjecture; **misread,** misconstrue, put the wrong construction on things, get wrong, misread the situation *or* case; **misinterpret** 342.2; err 975.9; fly in the face of facts; get hold of the wrong end of the stick <nf>

949 OVERESTIMATION

NOUNS **1 overestimation,** overestimate, **overreckoning,** overcalculation, **overrating,** overassessment, overvaluation, overappraisal; overreaction; **overstatement, exaggeration** 355, hype <nf>

VERBS **2 overestimate, overreckon,** overcalculate, overcount, overmeasure, see more than is there; **overrate,** overassess, overappraise, overesteem, **overvalue,** overprize, overprice, think *or* make too much of, put on a pedestal, idealize, see only the

good points of; overreact to; **overstate, exaggerate** 355.3; pump up *and* jump up *and* make a big deal *or* Federal case <nf>; hype <nf>

ADJS **3 overestimated, overrated,** puffed up, pumped up <nf>, overvalued, on the high side; **exaggerated** 355.4

950 UNDERESTIMATION

NOUNS **1 underestimation,** misestimation, underestimate, **underrating,** underreckoning, undervaluation, misprizing, misprizal, misprision; **belittlement, depreciation,** deprecation, **minimization,** disparagement 512; conservative estimate; negative outlook, pessimism

VERBS **2 underestimate,** misestimate, **underrate,** underreckon, **undervalue,** underprize, **misprize,** underprice; **make little of,** set at little, set at naught, set little by, attach little importance to, not do justice to, sell short, think little of, make *or* think nothing of, see less than is there, miss on the low side, set no store by, make light of, shrug off, soft-pedal <nf>; **depreciate, deprecate,** minimize, belittle, bad-mouth *and* poor-mouth *and* put down *and* run down <nf>, take someone for an idiot *or* a fool; disparage 512.8; play down, understate

ADJS **3 underestimated, underrated,** undervalued, on the low side; unvalued, unprized, misprized; underpriced, cheap

951 THEORY, SUPPOSITION

NOUNS **1 theory,** theorization, *theoria* <Gk>; theoretics, theoretic, theoric <old>; **hypothesis,** hypothecation, hypothesizing; **speculation,** mere theory; doctrinairism, doctrinality, doctrinarity; analysis, **explanation,** abstraction; theoretical basis *or* justification; body of theory, theoretical structure *or* construct; unified theory

2 theory, explanation, proposed *or* tentative explanation, rationalization, proposal, proposition, statement covering the facts *or* evidence; **hypothesis,** working hypothesis

3 supposition, supposal, supposing; **presupposition,** presupposal; **assumption, presumption, conjecture, inference, surmise, guesswork; postulate,** postulation, *postulatum* <L>, set of postulates; **proposition, thesis, concept, premise** 935.7; **axiom** 974.2

4 guess, conjecture, unverified supposition, perhaps, speculation, guesswork, surmise, educated guess; guesstimate *and* hunch *and* shot *and* stab <nf>; rough guess, wild guess, blind guess, bold conjecture, shot in the dark <nf>, crude estimate

5 <vague supposition> **suggestion,** bare suggestion, **suspicion, inkling, hint, clue, sense, feeling, feeling in one's bones, intuition** 934, **intimation, impression, notion,** mere notion, hunch *and* sneaking suspicion <nf>, instinct, trace of an idea, half an idea, vague idea, hazy idea, **idea** 932

6 supposititiousness, presumptiveness, presumableness, theoreticalness, hypotheticalness, conjecturableness, speculativeness

7 **theorist, theorizer,** theoretic, **theoretician,** notionalist <old>; **speculator;** hypothesist, hypothesizer; doctrinaire, doctrinarian; inquirer; synthesizer; armchair authority *or* philosopher; thinker; researcher, experimenter

8 **supposer,** assumer, surmiser, **conjecturer, guesser,** guessworker, speculator, gambler

VERBS 9 **theorize, hypothesize, hypothecate,** form a hypothesis, **speculate,** postulate, have *or* entertain a theory, espouse a theory, generalize

10 **suppose, assume, presume, surmise,** expect, **suspect, infer, understand, gather, conclude, deduce, consider,** reckon, reason, derive, divine, imagine, **fancy,** dream, conceive, **believe, deem,** repute, feel, **think,** be inclined to think, opine, say, daresay, be afraid <nf>; take, take it, take it into one's head, take for, take to be, take for granted, take as a precondition, **presuppose, presurmise,** prefigure; provisionally accept *or* admit *or* agree to, take one up on <nf>, grant, stipulate, take it as given, let, let be, say *or* assume for argument's sake, say for the hell of it <nf>; draw a mental picture

11 **conjecture, guess,** guesstimate <nf>, give a guess, talk off the top of one's head <nf>, hazard a conjecture, venture a guess, risk assuming *or* stating, tentatively suggest, go out on a limb <nf>

12 **postulate, predicate, posit,** set forth, lay down, put forth, assert; pose, advance, **propose, propound** 439.5

ADJS 13 **theoretical, hypothetical,** hypothetic; postulatory, notional; **speculative, conjectural,** blue-sky; impressionistic, intuitive 934.5; general, generalized, abstract, ideal; unverified, merely theoretical, academic, moot; impractical, armchair, thought-provoking

14 **supposed, suppositive, assumed, presumed, conjectured, inferred,** understood, deemed, **reputed,** reputative, putative, alleged, accounted as; suppositional, suppositious, assumptive, **presumptive;** guessed; given, granted, taken as *or* for granted, agreed, stipulated; **postulated,**

postulational, premised; granted for the sake of argument

15 **supposable, presumable,** assumable, conjecturable, surmisable, imaginable, premissable

ADVS 16 **theoretically, hypothetically,** *ex hypothesi* <L>, notionally, conceptually, ideally; **in theory,** in idea, in the ideal, in the abstract, on paper, in Never-Neverland <nf>

17 **supposedly,** supposably, **presumably,** presumedly, assumably, assumedly, presumptively, assumptively, reputedly, presumingly; suppositionally, suppositiously; **seemingly,** in seeming, quasi; as it were; on the assumption that

18 conjecturably, **conjecturally;** to guess, to make a guess, **as a guess,** as a rough guess *or* an approximation, speculatively

CONJS 19 **supposing,** supposing that, **assuming that,** allowing that, if we assume that, let's say that, granting *or* granted that, given that, on the assumption *or* supposition that; if, as if, as though, by way of hypothesis

952 PHILOSOPHY

NOUNS 1 **philosophy**; philosophical inquiry *or* investigation, philosophical speculation; inquiry *or* investigation into first causes; branch of philosophy <see list>, department *or* division of philosophy; school of philosophy <see list>, philosophic system, school of thought; philosophic doctrine, philosophic theory; theory of knowledge; philosophastry, philosophastering; sophistry 936

2 **viewpoint,** point of view, outlook, attitude, opinion; feeling, sentiment, idea, thought, notion; tenet, dogma, doctrine, canon, principle; assertion, proposition, premise, assumption, precept, thesis, postulate, hypothesis, concept; supposition, presupposition, conjecture, speculation; maxim, axiom; rationalization, justification; conclusion, judgment; philosophical system, belief system, value system, set of beliefs *or* values, ethics, morals, school of thought, moral code, code of conduct, value judgment, standards, principles, ideology

3 Platonic philosophy, Platonism, philosophy of the Academy; Aristotelian philosophy, Aristotelianism, philosophy of the Lyceum, Peripateticism, Peripatetic school; Stoic philosophy, Stoicism, philosophy of the Porch *or* Stoa; Epicureanism, philosophy of the Garden

4 **materialism; idealism** 1053.3

5 monism, philosophical unitarianism, mind-stuff theory; pantheism, cosmotheism; hylozoism

6 pluralism; dualism, mind-matter theory

7 <political and economic philosophy> anarchism, capitalism, collectivism, communism, internationalism, isolationism, Marxism, monetarism, nationalism, socialism, utilitarianism, utopianism

8 philosopher, philosophizer, philosophe; philosophaster; **thinker,** speculator; casuist; metaphysician, cosmologist, logician, dialectician, syllogist; sophist 936.6; idealist, idealogue, visionary, dreamer

VERBS **9 philosophize,** reason 935.15, probe

ADJS **10 philosophical,** philosophic, sophistical 936.10; philosophicohistorical, philosophicolegal, philosophicojuristic, philosophicopsychological, philosophicoreligious, philosophicotheological; notional, abstract, esoteric, ideological, ideational, hypothetical, theoretical

11 absurdist, acosmistic, aesthetic, African, agnostic, Alexandrian, analytic, animalistic, animist *or* animistic, atomistic, etc <see list of schools and doctrines>

12 Aristotelian, Peripatetic; Augustinian, Averroist *or* Averroistic, Bergsonian, Berkeleian, Cartesian, Comtian, Hegelian, Neo-Hegelian, Heideggerian, Heraclitean, Humean, Husserlian, Kantian, Leibnizian, Parmenidean, Platonic, Neoplatonic, pre-Socratic, Pyrrhonic, Pyrrhonian, Pythagorean, Neo-Pythagorean, Sartrian, Schellingian, Schopenhauerian, Scotist, Socratic, Spencerian, Thomist *or* Thomistic, Viconian, Wittgensteinian

13 branches *or* departments of philosophy

aesthetics *or* theory of beauty *or* philosophy of art
analytic philosophy
axiology *or* value theory
casuistry
commonsense *or* naïve realism
cosmology
deontology
ethics *or* moral philosophy
logic *or* theory of argument
metaphysics *or* first philosophy *or* theory of existence
ontology *or* science of being
phenomenology
philosophy of biology
philosophy of education
philosophy of history
philosophy of language *or* semantics
philosophy of law
philosophy of logic
philosophy of nature
philosophy of physics
philosophy of religion
philosophy of science
philosophy of signs *or* semiotics
political philosophy
sentential *or* propositional calculus
teleology
theology
theory of knowledge *or* epistemology *or* gnosiology

14 schools and doctrines of philosophy

Augustinianism
Aristotelianism
Atomism
Augustinianism
Averroism
Baconism

Bergsonism
Berkeleianism
Bonaventurism
Bradleianism
Brahmanism
Buddhism
Cartesianism
Comtism
Confucianism
cosmotheism
criticism *or* critical philosophy
Cynicism
Cyrenaic hedonism *or* Cyrenaicism
deconstructionism
deism
dialectical materialism
dualism
eclecticism
egoism
egoistic hedonism
Eleaticism *or* the Elean school
empiricism
Epicureanism
Eretrian school
eristic school
essentialism
ethicism
ethics
eudaemonism
existentialism *or* existential philosophy
Fabianism
Fichteanism
Gnosticism
hedonism
Hegelianism
Heideggerianism
Heracliteanism
Herbartianism
Hinduism
Hobbism
humanism
Humism
hylomorphism
hylotheism
hylozoism
idealism
immaterialism
individualism
instrumentalism
intuitionism
Ionian school
Jainism
Juddaism
Kantianism
Leibnizianism

linguistic and analytic philosophy
logical empiricism *or* logical positivism
Manichaeism
Marxism
materialism
mechanism
Megarianism
mentalism
Mimamsa
Mithraism
monism
mysticism
naturalism
Neo-Hegelianism
Neo-Platonism
Neo-Pythagoreanism
Neo-Scholasticism
neocriticism
Neoplatonism
new ethical movement
nominalism
noumenalism
Nyaya
ontologism
ontology
optimism
ordinary language philosophy
organic mechanism
organicism
panlogism
panpneumatism
panpsychism
pantheism
panthelism
Parmenidean school
patristic philosophy
patristicism
Peripateticism
pessimism
phenomenalism
phenomenology
philosophy of organism
philosophy of signs
philosophy of the ante-Nicene Fathers
philosophy of the post-Nicene Fathers
physicalism
physicism
Platonism
pluralism
positivism
pragmatism *or* pragmaticism
probabilism
Protestantism

psychism
psychological hedonism
Puritanism
Purva Mimamsa
Pyrrhonism
Pythagoreanism
rationalism
realism
Sankhya
Sartrianism
Satyagraha
Schellingism
Scholasticism
Schopenhauerism
Scotism
secular humanism
semiotic *or* semiotics *or*
   semi-idiotics <nf>
sensationalism
sensism
Shintoism
Sikhism

skepticism
Socratism *or* Socratic
   philosophy
solipsism
Sophism *or* Sophistry
Spencerianism
Spinozism
Stoicism
substantialism
syncretism
Taoism
theism
Thomism
transcendentalism
universalistic
   hedonism
utilitarianism
Uttara Mimamsa
Valsheshika
vitalism
voluntarism
zetetic philosophy

953 BELIEF

NOUNS **1 belief,** credence, credit, believing, faith,
trust; hope; **confidence,** assuredness,
convincedness, persuadedness, **assurance;**
sureness, surety, **certainty** 970; **reliance,
dependence,** reliance on *or* in, dependence on,
stock *and* store <nf>; acceptation, acception,
acceptance; reception, acquiescence; blind faith,
full faith and credit; suspension of disbelief;
fideism; **credulity** 954

2 a belief, tenet, dogma, precept, **principle,
principle** *or* **article of faith,** premise, canon,
maxim, axiom; **doctrine,** teaching

3 system of belief; religion, faith 675.1, belief-
system; **school, cult, ism,** philosophy, **ideology,**
Weltanschauung <Ger>, world view; political faith
or belief *or* philosophy; **creed, credo,** credenda,
dogma, canon; articles of religion, articles of
faith, creedal *or* doctrinal statement, formulated
or stated belief; gospel; catechism

4 statement of belief *or* **principles, manifesto,**
position paper; solemn declaration; deposition,
affidavit, sworn statement

5 conviction, persuasion, certainty; firm belief,
moral certainty, implicit *or* staunch belief, settled
judgment, mature judgment *or* belief, fixed
opinion, unshaken confidence, steadfast faith,
rooted *or* deep-rooted belief

6 opinion, sentiment, feeling, sense, impression,
reaction, **notion, idea, thought,** mind, thinking,
way of thinking, attitude, stance, posture,
position, mindset, **view,** viewpoint, eye, sight,
lights, observation, **conception,** concept, conceit,

estimation, estimate, consideration, angle, **theory**
951, conjecture, supposition, assumption,
presumption, **conclusion, judgment** 946, personal
judgment; **point of view** 978.2; public opinion,
public belief, general belief, prevailing belief *or*
sentiment, *consensus gentium* <L>, common belief,
community sentiment, popular belief,
conventional wisdom, vox pop, *vox populi* <L>,
climate of opinion; ethos; mystique; anecdotal
evidence

7 profession, confession, declaration, **profession** *or*
confession *or* **declaration of faith**

8 believability, persuasiveness, believableness,
convincingness, **credibility, credit,
trustworthiness, plausibility,** tenability,
acceptability, conceivability; **reliability** 970.4

9 believer, truster; religious believer; true believer;
the assured, the faithful, the believing; fideist;
ideologist, ideologue; conformist; innocent, naÔf

VERBS **10 believe, credit, trust, accept,** receive, buy
<nf>; give credit *or* credence to, give faith to, put
faith in, take stock in *or* set store by <nf>, take to
heart, attach weight to; be led to believe; accept
implicitly, believe without reservation, rest
assured, take for granted, take *or* accept for
gospel, take as gospel truth <nf>, take *or* accept
on faith, take on trust *or* credit, pin one's faith on;
take at face value; **take one's word for,** trust one's
word, take at one's word; fall for; **buy** *and* **buy into**
<nf>, **swallow** 954.6; **be certain** 970.9

**11 think, opine, be of the opinion, be persuaded, be
convinced;** be afraid <nf>, **have the idea,** have an
idea, **suppose, assume, presume, judge** 946.8,
guess, surmise, suspect, have a hunch <nf>, have
an inkling, expect <nf>, have an impression, be
under the impression, have a sense *or* the sense,
conceive, ween *and* trow <old>, **imagine, fancy,**
daresay; **deem, esteem, hold, regard, consider,
maintain,** reckon, estimate; hold as, account as,
set down as *or* for, view as, look upon as, take for,
take, take it, get it into one's head

12 state, assert, swear, swear to God <nf>, declare,
affirm, vow, avow, avouch, warrant, asseverate,
confess, be under the impression, profess, express
the belief, swear to a belief; depose, make an
affidavit *or* a sworn statement

13 hold the belief, have the opinion, entertain a
belief *or* an opinion, adopt *or* embrace a belief,
take as an article of faith; foster *or* nurture *or*
cherish a belief, be wedded to *or* espouse a belief;
get hold of an idea, get it into one's head, form a
conviction

14 be confident, have confidence, **be satisfied, be
convinced, be certain,** be easy in one's mind
about, be secure in the belief, **feel sure, rest**

assured, rest in confidence; doubt not, **have no doubt,** have no misgivings *or* diffidence *or* qualms, have no reservations, have no second thoughts

15 **believe in, have faith in,** pin one's faith to, confide in, **have confidence in,** place *or* repose confidence in, place reliance in, put onself in the hands of, **trust in,** put trust in, have simple *or* childlike faith in, rest in, repose in *or* hope in <old>; give *or* get the benefit of the doubt

16 **rely on** *or* **upon, depend on** *or* **upon,** place reliance on, rest on *or* upon, repose on, lean on, **count on,** calculate on, reckon on, **bank on** *or* **upon** <nf>; **trust to** *or* **unto, swear by,** take one's oath upon; **bet on** *and* gamble on *and* lay money on *and* bet one's bottom dollar on *and* make book on <nf>; take one's word for

17 **trust, confide in, rely on, depend on,** repose, place trust *or* confidence in, have confidence in, **trust in** 953.15, trust utterly *or* implicitly, deem trustworthy, think reliable *or* dependable, take one's word, take at one's word

18 **convince; convert, win over,** lead one to believe, bring over, bring round, take in, talk over, talk around, bring to reason, bring to one's senses, **persuade, lead to believe, give to understand; satisfy, assure;** put one's mind at rest on; sell *and* sell one on <nf>; make *or* carry one's point, bring *or* drive home to; cram down one's throat *and* beat into one's head <nf>; be convincing, carry conviction; inspire belief *or* confidence; evangelize, proselytize, propagandize

19 **convince oneself, persuade oneself,** sell oneself <nf>, make oneself easy about, make oneself easy on that score, satisfy oneself on that point, make sure of, make up one's mind

20 **find credence, be believed,** be accepted, be received; be swallowed *and* go down *and* pass current <nf>; produce *or* carry conviction; have the ear of, gain the confidence of

ADJS 21 **believing,** of belief, preceptive, principled; attitudinal; **believing, undoubting, undoubtful,** doubtless <old>; faithful <old>, God-fearing, pious, pietistic, observant, **devout;** under the impression, impressed with; **convinced, confident,** positive, dogmatic, secure, **persuaded,** sold on, **satisfied, assured;** born again; **sure, certain** 970.13; fideistic

22 **trusting, trustful,** trusty <old>, **confiding, unsuspecting, unsuspicious,** without suspicion; childlike, innocent, guileless, naive 416.5; **knee-jerk, credulous** 954.8; relying, depending, reliant, dependent; gullible, naive

23 **believed, credited, held, trusted, accepted;** received, of belief, authoritative, maintained; **undoubted,** unsuspected, **unquestioned,** undisputed, uncontested

24 **believable, credible,** creditable; **tenable,** conceivable, **plausible,** colorable, realistic; worthy of faith, trustworthy, trusty; fiduciary; reliable 970.17; unimpeachable, unexceptionable, **unquestionable** 970.15

25 fiducial, fiduciary; convictional

26 **convincing,** convictional, well-founded, **persuasive,** assuring, impressive, satisfying, satisfactory, confidence-building; decisive, absolute, conclusive, determinative; authoritative

27 **doctrinal, creedal,** preceptive, canonical, dogmatic, confessional, mandatory, of faith

ADVS 28 **believingly, undoubtingly,** undoubtfully, without doubt *or* question *or* quibble, unquestioningly; **trustingly,** trustfully, unsuspectingly, unsuspiciously; piously, devoutly; with faith; **with confidence,** on *or* upon trust, on faith, on one's say-so

29 **in one's opinion, to one's mind,** in one's thinking, **to one's way of thinking,** the way one thinks, **in one's estimation,** according to one's lights, **as one sees it, to the best of one's belief;** in the opinion of, in the eyes of

954 CREDULITY

NOUNS 1 **credulity, credulousness,** inclination *or* disposition to believe, ease of belief, will *or* willingness to believe, wishful belief *or* thinking; **blind faith,** unquestioning belief, knee-jerk response *or* agreement <nf>; uncritical acceptance, premature *or* unripe acceptation, hasty *or* rash conviction; **trustfulness, trustingness, unsuspiciousness,** unsuspectingness; uncriticalness, unskepticalness; overcredulity, overcredulousness, overtrustfulness, overopenness to conviction *or* persuasion, gross credulity; infatuation, fondness, dotage; one's blind side

2 **gullibility, dupability,** bamboozlability <nf>, cullibility <old>, **deceivability,** seduceability, persuadability, hoaxability; biddability; easiness <nf>, softness, weakness; **simpleness,** simplicity, **ingenuousness, unsophistication; greenness,** naïveness, **naïveté,** naivety

3 **superstition,** superstitiousness; popular belief, **old wives' tale;** tradition, lore, folklore; charm, spell 691

4 trusting soul; **dupe** 358; sucker *and* patsy *and* easy mark *and* pushover<nf>

VERBS 5 **be credulous,** accept unquestioningly; not boggle at anything, **believe anything,** be easy of belief *or* persuasion, be uncritical, believe at the drop of a hat, be a dupe, think the moon is made of green cheese, buy a pig in a poke

6 <nf or nf terms> kid oneself, fall for, swallow, swallow anything, swallow whole, not choke or gag on; swallow hook, line, and sinker; eat up, lap up, devour, gulp down, gobble up or down, buy, buy into, bite, nibble, rise to the fly, take the bait, swing at, go for, tumble for, be taken in, be suckered, be a sucker or a patsy or an easy mark

7 **be superstitious;** knock on wood, keep one's fingers crossed

ADJS 8 **credulous, knee-jerk** <nf>, easy of belief, ready or inclined to believe, easily taken in; **undoubting** 953.21; **trustful, trusting; unsuspicious, unsuspecting;** unthinking, uncritical, unskeptical; overcredulous, overtrustful, overtrusting, overconfiding; fond, infatuated, doting; **superstitious**

9 **gullible, dupable,** bamboozlable <nf>, cullible <old>, **deceivable, foolable, deludable, exploitable,** victimizable, seduceable, persuadable, hoaxable, humbugable, hoodwinkable; biddable; soft, easy <nf>, **simple; ingenuous, unsophisticated, green, naive** 416.5

955 UNBELIEF

NOUNS 1 **unbelief, disbelief,** nonbelief, unbelievingness, discredit; refusal or inability to believe; **incredulity** 956; **unpersuadedness,** unconvincedness, lack of conviction; **denial** 335.2, **rejection** 372; misbelief, heresy 688.2; infidelity, atheism, **agnosticism** 695.6; minimifidianism, nullifidianism

2 **doubt, doubtfulness, dubiousness,** dubiety; half-belief; **reservation, question,** question in one's mind; **skepticism,** skepticalness; total skepticism, Pyrrhonism; **suspicion,** suspiciousness, wariness, leeriness, **distrust, mistrust, misdoubt,** distrustfulness, mistrustfulness; **misgiving,** self-doubt, diffidence; qualm; scruple and scrupulousness <old>; hesitation; apprehension 127.4; **uncertainty** 971; shadow of doubt, credibility gap

3 **unbelievability,** unbelievableness, **incredibility, implausibility,** impossibility, improbability, inconceivability, untenableness, untenability; unpersuasiveness, unconvincingness; **doubtfulness, questionableness;** credibility gap; unreliability 971.6

4 doubter, doubting Thomas; scoffer, skeptic, cynic, pooh-pooher, nay-sayer, disbeliever, nonbeliever, unbeliever 695.11

VERBS 5 **disbelieve,** unbelieve, misbelieve, **not believe,** find hard to believe, not admit, refuse to admit, not buy <nf>, take no stock in and set no store by <nf>; **discredit,** refuse to credit, refuse to

give credence to, give no credit or credence to; gag on, **not swallow** 956.3; negate, **deny** 335.4, nay-say, say nay; scoff at, pooh-pooh; **reject** 372.2

6 **doubt, be doubtful, be dubious, be skeptical,** doubt the truth of, beg leave to doubt, **have one's doubts,** have or harbor or entertain doubts or suspicions, half believe, have reservations, **take with a grain of salt,** be from Missouri <nf>, scruple <old>, **distrust, mistrust,** misgive, cross one's fingers; **be uncertain** 971.9; **suspect,** smell a rat and see something funny <nf>; **question,** query, **challenge, contest, dispute,** cast doubt on, greet with skepticism, keep one's eye on, treat with reserve, bring or call into question, raise a question, throw doubt upon, awake a doubt or suspicion; **doubt one's word,** give one the lie; doubt oneself, be diffident

7 **be unbelievable,** be incredible, be hard to swallow, defy belief, pass belief, be hard to believe, strain one's credulity, **stagger belief;** shake one's faith, undermine one's faith; perplex, boggle the mind, stagger, fill with doubt

ADJS 8 **unbelieving, disbelieving,** nonbelieving; faithless, without faith; unconfident, unconvinced, unconverted; nullifidian, minimifidian, creedless; **incredulous** 956.4; repudiative; **heretical** 688.9; **irreligious** 695.17

9 **doubting, doubtful, in doubt, dubious; questioning; skeptical,** Pyrrhonic, from Missouri <nf>; **distrustful, mistrustful, untrustful,** mistrusting, untrusting; **suspicious,** suspecting, scrupulous <old>, shy, wary, leery; **agnostic; uncertain**

10 **unbelievable, incredible,** unthinkable, **implausible,** unimaginable, inconceivable, not to be believed, **hard to believe,** hard of belief, beyond belief, unworthy of belief, not meriting or not deserving belief, tall <nf>; **defying belief,** staggering belief, passing belief; **mind-boggling,** preposterous, absurd, ridiculous, unearthly, ungodly; **doubtful, dubious,** doubtable, dubitable, **questionable,** problematic, problematical, **unconvincing,** open to doubt or suspicion; **suspicious,** suspect, funny; so-called, self-styled; thin and a bit thin <nf>; thick and a bit thick and a little too thick <nf>

11 under a cloud, unreliable

12 **doubted, questioned,** disputed, contested, moot; **distrusted,** mistrusted; **suspect,** suspected, **under suspicion,** under a cloud; **discredited,** exploded, rejected, **disbelieved**

ADVS 13 **unbelievingly,** doubtingly, **doubtfully, dubiously,** questioningly, **skeptically,** suspiciously; **with a grain of salt,** with reservations, with some allowance, with caution

14 **unbelievably, incredibly,** unthinkably, implausibly, inconceivably, unimaginably, staggeringly

956 INCREDULITY

NOUNS **1 incredulity, incredulousness,** uncredulousness, refusal *or* disinclination to believe, resistance *or* resistiveness to belief, tough-mindedness, hardheadedness, **inconvincibility,** unconvincibility, unpersuadability, unpersuasibility; **suspiciousness,** suspicion, wariness, leeriness, guardedness, cautiousness, caution; **skepticism** 955.2

2 ungullibility, uncullibility <old>, **undupability, undeceivability,** unhoaxability, unseduceability; **sophistication**

VERBS **3 refuse to believe,** resist believing, **not allow oneself to believe,** be slow to believe *or* accept; not kid oneself <nf>; **disbelieve** 955.5; **be skeptical** 955.6; **not swallow,** not be able to swallow *or* down <nf>, not go for *and* **not fall for** <nf>, not be taken in by; **not accept, not buy** *or* **buy into** <nf>, **reject** 372.2

ADJS **4 incredulous,** uncredulous, **hard of belief,** shy of belief, disposed to doubt, indisposed *or* disinclined to believe, unwilling to accept; impervious to persuasion, **inconvincible,** unconvincible, unpersuadable, unpersuasible; **suspicious, suspecting,** wary, leery, cautious, guarded; **skeptical** 955.9

5 ungullible, uncullible <old>, **undupable, undeceivable, unfoolable, undeludable,** unhoaxable, unseduceable, hoaxproof; **sophisticated, wise, hardheaded,** practical, realistic, tough-minded; nobody's fool, not born yesterday, nobody's sucker *or* patsy <nf>

957 EVIDENCE, PROOF

NOUNS **1 evidence, proof; reason to believe,** reason, grounds for belief; **ground, grounds,** material grounds, **facts, data,** information, record, premises, basis for belief; piece *or* item of evidence, **fact,** datum, relevant fact; **indication, manifestation, sign, symptom,** mark, token, mute witness; body of evidence, documentation; muniments, title deeds and papers; chain of evidence; **clue; exhibit; intelligence; lowdown** <nf>

2 testimony, attestation, attest <old>, **witness;** testimonial, testimonium <old>; **statement, declaration, assertion,** asseveration, affirmation 334, avouchment, avowal, averment, allegation, admission, **disclosure** 351, profession, word; confession; **deposition,** legal evidence, sworn evidence *or* testimony; *procès-verbal* <Fr>; compurgation; affidavit, sworn statement; instrument in proof, *pièce justificative* <Fr>

3 proof, demonstration, ironclad proof, incontrovertible proof, proof positive, conclusive proof; **determination, establishment, settlement; conclusive evidence,** indisputable evidence, incontrovertible evidence, damning evidence, unmistakable sign, sure sign, absolute indication, smoking gun <nf>; open-and-shut case; burden of proof, onus, *onus probandi* <L>; the proof of the pudding

4 confirmation, substantiation, proof, proving, proving out, bearing out, affirmation, attestation, **authentication, validation, certification,** ratification, **verification; corroboration, support,** supporting evidence, corroboratory evidence, fortification, buttressing, bolstering, backing, backing up, reinforcement, undergirding, strengthening, circumstantiation, fact sheet; **documentation;** proof of purchase

5 citation, cite <nf>, **reference,** quotation; **exemplification,** instance, example, case, case in point, particular, item, illustration, demonstration; cross reference

6 witness, eyewitness, spectator, earwitness; **bystander,** passerby; **deponent, testifier,** attestant, attester, attestator, voucher, swearer; **informant,** informer; character witness; cojuror, compurgator

7 provability, demonstrability, determinability; confirmability, supportability, verifiability

VERBS **8 evidence, evince,** furnish evidence, **show, go to show, mean,** tend to show, witness to, testify to; **demonstrate, illustrate,** exhibit, manifest, display, express, set forth; approve; **attest; indicate, signify,** signalize, symptomatize, mark, **denote, betoken, point to,** give indication of, show signs of, bear on, touch on; **connote, imply, suggest,** involve; argue, breathe, tell, bespeak; **speak for itself,** speak volumes

9 testify, attest, give evidence, witness, witness to, **give** *or* **bear witness; disclose** 351.4; vouch, state one's case, **depose,** depone, **warrant, swear,** take one's oath, acknowledge, avow, **affirm,** avouch, aver, allege, asseverate, **certify, give one's word;** turn state's evidence, rat *and* squeal *and* sing <nf>; grass <Brit nf>

10 prove, demonstrate, show, afford proof of, prove to be, prove true; **establish, fix, determine, ascertain,** make out, remove all doubt; **settle,** settle the matter; **set at rest;** clinch *and* cinch *and* nail down <nf>; **prove one's point,** make one's case, bring home to, make good, have *or* make out a case; hold good, hold water; follow, follow from, follow as a matter of course

11 confirm, affirm, **attest,** warrant, uphold <Brit nf>, **substantiate, authenticate, validate, certify,** ratify, **verify;** circumstantiate, **corroborate, bear out,**

support, buttress, **sustain,** fortify, bolster, back, back up, reinforce, undergird, strengthen; **document;** probate, prove; double-check

12 **adduce,** produce, **advance, present,** bring to bear, **offer,** proffer, invoke, obtest, allege <old>, plead, **bring forward,** bring on; rally, marshal, deploy, array; call to witness, call to *or* put in the witness box

13 **cite, name,** call to mind; **instance,** cite a particular *or* particulars, cite cases *or* a case in point, itemize, particularize, produce an instance, give a for-instance <nf>; **exemplify,** example <old>, **illustrate,** demonstrate; **document; quote,** quote chapter and verse

14 **refer to,** direct attention to, **appeal to,** invoke; make reference to; cross-refer, make a cross-reference; reference, cross-reference

15 **have evidence** *or* **proof,** have a case, possess incriminating evidence, **have something on** <nf>; **have the goods on** *and* have dead to rights *or* bang to rights <nf>

ADJS 16 **evidential,** evidentiary, **factual,** symptomatic, **significant, relevant, indicative,** attestative, attestive, probative; founded on, grounded on, based on; implicit, suggestive; material, telling, convincing, weighty; overwhelming, damning; **conclusive,** determinative, **decisive,** final, incontrovertible, irresistible, indisputable, irrefutable, sure, certain, absolute; documented, documentary; **valid, admissible;** adducible; firsthand, authentic, reliable 970.17, empirical, eyewitness; hearsay, circumstantial, presumptive, nuncupative, cumulative, ex parte

17 **demonstrative,** demonstrating, demonstrational, telltale; evincive, apodictic

18 **confirming,** confirmatory, confirmative, certificatory; substantiating, **verifying,** verificative; **corroborating,** corroboratory, **corroborative,** supportive, **supporting**

19 **provable, demonstrable,** demonstratable, apodictic, evincible, attestable, **confirmable,** checkable, **substantiatable, establishable,** supportable, sustainable, **verifiable,** validatable, authenticatable

20 **proved, proven, demonstrated,** shown; **established,** fixed, **settled, determined,** nailed down <nf>, ascertained; evident, self-evident; **confirmed, substantiated,** attested **authenticated, certified, validated, verified;** circumstantiated, **corroborated,** borne out; cross-checked, double-checked; collated; ostensible

21 **unrefuted,** unconfuted, unanswered, uncontroverted, uncontradicted, **undenied; unrefutable** 970.15

ADVS 22 **evidentially,** according to the evidence, on the evidence, as attested by, judging by; **in confirmation, in corroboration of, in support of;** at first hand, at second hand; dead to rights *or* bang to rights *and* with a smoking gun *and* with one's pants down <nf>

23 **to illustrate,** to prove the point, as an example, as a case in point, to name an instance, by way of example, **for example, for instance,** to cite an instance, as an instance, e.g., *exempli gratia* <L>; as, **thus**

24 **which see, q.v.,** *quod vide* <L>; *loco citato* <L>, loc cit; *opere citato* <L>, op cit

PHRS 25 **it is proven,** *probatum est* <L>, there is nothing more to be said, it must follow; QED, *quod erat demonstrandum* <L>

958 DISPROOF

NOUNS 1 **disproof,** disproving, disproval, **invalidation,** disconfirmation, explosion, negation, redargution <old>; exposure, exposé; *reductio ad absurdum* <L>; circumstantial evidence, hearsay evidence, inadmissible evidence, incriminating evidence

2 **refutation, confutation,** confounding, refutal, **rebuttal, answer,** complete answer, crushing *or* effective rejoinder, squelch, comeback; discrediting; **overthrow,** overthrowal, upset, upsetting, subversion, undermining, demolition; renunciation; contention; **contradiction,** controversion, **denial** 335.2

3 **conclusive argument, elenchus, knockdown argument, floorer,** sockdolager <nf>; **clincher** *or* crusher *or* **settler** *and* finisher *and* squelcher <nf>

VERBS 4 **disprove, invalidate,** disconfirm, discredit, prove the contrary, belie, give the lie to, redargue <old>; **negate,** negative; **expose, show up;** explode, blow up, blow sky-high, **puncture,** deflate, **shoot** *or* **poke full of holes, cut to pieces, cut the ground from under; knock the bottom out of** <nf>, knock the props *or* chocks out from under, knock down, take the ground from under, undercut, cut the ground from under one's feet, not leave a leg to stand on, have the last word, leave nothing to say, put *or* lay to rest

5 **refute, confute, confound, rebut,** parry, answer, **answer conclusively,** dismiss, dispose of; **overthrow,** overturn, overwhelm, upset, subvert, defeat, demolish, undermine; argue down, argue into a corner; show what's what; floor *and* finish *and* settle *and* squash *and* squelch <nf>, crush, smash all opposition; silence, put *or* reduce to silence, shut up, stop the mouth of; nonplus, take the wind out of one's sails;

contradict, controvert, counter, run counter, **deny** 335.4

ADJS **6 refuting, confuting,** confounding, confutative, refutative, refutatory, discomfirmatory; contradictory, contrary 335.5

7 disproved, disconfirmed, **invalidated,** negated, negatived, discredited, belied; **exposed,** shown up; **punctured,** deflated, **exploded; refuted,** confuted, confounded; **upset, overthrown,** overturned; **contradicted,** disputed, denied, impugned; dismissed, discarded, rejected 372.3

8 unproved, not proved, unproven, **undemonstrated,** unshown, not shown; **untried,** untested; **unestablished,** unfixed, **unsettled, undetermined,** unascertained; **unconfirmed, unsubstantiated,** unattested, **unauthenticated,** unvalidated, uncertified, **unverified; uncorroborated,** unsustained, **unsupported,** unsupported by evidence, **groundless,** without grounds *or* basis, **unfounded** 936.13; **inconclusive,** indecisive; **moot,** sub judice; not following

9 unprovable, controvertible, **undemonstrable,** undemonstratable, unattestable, unsubstantiatable, **unsupportable,** unconfirmable, unsustainable, unverifiable

10 refutable, confutable, **disprovable,** defeasible

959 QUALIFICATION

NOUNS **1 qualification, limitation, limiting, restriction,** circumscription, **modification,** hedge, hedging; setting conditions, conditionality, provisionality, circumstantiality; specification; **allowance, concession,** cession, grant; grain of salt; **reservation, exception,** waiver, exemption; **exclusion,** ruling out, including out <nf>; specialness, special circumstance, special case, special treatment; **mental reservation,** salvo <old>, *arrière-pensée* <Fr>, crossing one's fingers; extenuating circumstances

2 condition, provision, proviso, stipulation, whereas; definition; frame of reference; **specification,** parameter, given, *donnée* <Fr>; **limitation,** limiting condition, boundary condition; **contingency, circumstance** 766; **catch** *and* joker *and* kicker *and* string *and* a string to it <nf>; **requisite, prerequisite,** obligation; *sine qua non* <L>, *conditio sine qua non* <L>; clause, escape clause, escapeway, escape hatch, saving clause; escalator clause; **terms,** provisions; grounds; small *or* fine print *and* fine print at the bottom <nf>; ultimatum

VERBS **3 qualify, limit,** condition <old>, hedge, hedge about, **modify, restrict,** restrain, circumscribe, delimit, set limits *or* conditions, box

in <nf>, narrow, set criteria; adjust to, regulate by; alter 852.6; **temper, season,** leaven, soften, modulate, moderate, assuage, **mitigate,** palliate, abate, reduce, diminish

4 make conditional, make contingent, **condition;** make it a condition, attach a condition *or* proviso, **stipulate;** insist upon, make a point of; **have a catch** *and* have a joker *or* kicker *and* have a joker in the deck *and* have a string attached <nf>; cross one's fingers behind one's back

5 allow for, make allowance for, make room for, provide for, open the door to, take account of, **take into account** *or* **consideration, consider,** consider the circumstances; allow, **grant, concede,** admit, admit exceptions, see the special circumstances; **relax,** relax the condition, **waive, set aside,** ease, lift temporarily, pull one's punches <nf>; disregard, **discount,** leave out of account; consider the source, take with a grain of salt

6 depend, hang, rest, hinge; **depend on** *or* **upon, hang on** *or* **upon, rest on** *or* **upon,** rest with, repose upon, lie on, lie with, stand on *or* upon, be based on, be bounded *or* limited by, be dependent on, be predicated on, **be contingent** *or* **conditional on; hinge on** *or* **upon, turn on** *or* **upon, revolve on** *or* **upon,** have as a fulcrum

ADJS **7 qualifying,** qualificative, qualificatory, **modifying,** modificatory, altering; **limiting, limitational, restricting,** limitative, restrictive, bounding; circumstantial, contingent; **extenuating,** extenuatory, **mitigating,** mitigative, mitigatory, modulatory, palliative, assuasive, lenitive, softening

8 conditional, provisional, provisory, stipulatory; parametric; specificative; **specified, stipulated,** defined, fixed, stated, given; **temporary,** expedient

9 contingent, dependent, depending; contingent on, **dependent on, depending on,** predicated on, based on, hanging *or* hinging on, turning on, revolving on; depending on circumstances; circumscribed by, hedged *or* hedged about by; boxed in <nf>; **subject to,** incidental to, incident to

10 qualified, modified, conditioned, limited, restricted, delimited, hedged, hedged about; **tempered, seasoned,** leavened, palliative, softened, moderated, **mitigated,** modulated

ADVS **11 conditionally, provisionally, with qualifications,** with a string *or* catch *or* joker *or* kicker to it <nf>; with a reservation *or* an exception, with a grain of salt; **temporarily,** for the time being

CONJS **12 provided,** provided that, provided always, **providing,** with this proviso, it being provided; **on condition,** on condition that, **with the stipulation,** with the understanding, according as, subject to

13 **granting, admitting, allowing,** admitting that, allowing that, seeing that; exempting, waiving

14 if, an *or* an' <old>, if and when, only if, if and only if, if it be so, if it be true that, if it so happens *or* turns out

15 **so,** just so, so that <old>, **so as, so long as, as long as**

16 **unless,** unless that, **if not, were it not,** were it not that; **except, excepting,** except that, with the exception that, save, **but; without,** absent

960 NO QUALIFICATIONS

NOUNS 1 **unqualifiedness,** unlimitedness, **unconditionality,** unrestrictedness, **unreservedness,** uncircumscribedness; categoricalness; **absoluteness,** definiteness, **explicitness;** decisiveness

ADJS 2 **unqualified, unconditional,** unconditioned, **unrestricted,** unhampered, **unlimited,** uncircumscribed, unmitigated, **categorical,** straight, **unreserved,** without reserve; unaltered, unadulterated, intact; **implicit,** unquestioning, undoubting, unhesitating; **explicit, express, unequivocal,** clear, unmistakable; **peremptory,** indisputable, inappealable; **without exception,** admitting no exception, unwaivable; **positive, absolute, flat,** definite, definitive, determinate, decided, decisive, fixed, final, conclusive; **complete, entire, whole, total,** global; **utter,** perfect, downright, outright, out-and-out, straight-out <nf>, all-out, flat-out <nf>

ADVS 3 <nf terms> **no ifs, ands,** *or* **buts; no strings attached,** no holds barred, no catch *or* joker *or* kicker, no joker in the deck, no small print *or* fine print, no fine print at the bottom; downright, that's that, what you see is what you get

961 FORESIGHT

NOUNS 1 **foresight,** foreseeing, looking ahead, **prevision,** divination 962.2, forecast; **prediction** 962; **foreglimpse,** foreglance, foregleam; preview, prepublication; **prospect,** prospection; **anticipation,** contemplation, envisionment, envisagement; **foresightedness; farsightedness,** longsightedness, farseeingness; sagacity, providence, discretion, preparation, provision, forehandedness, readiness, consideration, prudence 920.7

2 **forethought, premeditation,** predeliberation, preconsideration 380.3; caution 494; lead time, advance notice; run-up; plan, long-range plan, contingency plan; prospectus

3 **foreknowledge,** foreknowing, forewisdom, **precognition,** prescience, presage, presentiment, foreboding; clairvoyance 689.8; foreseeability 962.8; insight; premonition, expectation

4 **foretaste,** antepast <old>, prelibation

VERBS 5 **foresee,** see beforehand *or* ahead, foreglimpse, foretaste, **anticipate,** contemplate, envision, envisage, **look forward to,** look ahead, look beyond, look *or* pry *or* peep into the future; **predict** 962.9; think ahead *or* beforehand; have an eye to the future

6 **foreknow,** know beforehand, precognize, know in advance, have prior knowledge; smell in the wind, scent from afar; **have a presentiment, have a premonition** 133.10; see the handwriting on the wall, have a hunch *or* feel in one's bones <nf>, just know, intuit 934.4

ADJS 7 **foreseeing, foresighted; foreknowing, precognizant,** precognitive, prescient; divinatory 962.11; **forethoughted,** forethoughtful; anticipant, anticipatory, expectant; **farseeing, farsighted,** longsighted; sagacious, provident, providential, forehanded, prepared, ready, prudent 920.19; intuitive 934.5; clairvoyant, telepathic

8 foreseeable 962.13; foreseen 962.14; predictable; intuitable

ADVS 9 **foreseeingly, foreknowingly,** with foresight; against the time when, for a rainy day

962 PREDICTION

NOUNS 1 **prediction, foretelling,** foreshowing, forecasting, **prognosis,** prognostication, presage <old>, presaging; **prophecy,** prophesying, vaticination; **soothsaying,** soothsay; prefiguration, prefigurement, prefiguring; preshowing, presignifying, presigning <old>; **forecast, promise;** apocalypse; prospectus; foresight 961; presentiment, foreboding; omen 133.3,6; **guesswork,** speculation, guestimation <nf>, hunch, feeling; **probability** 968, statistical prediction, actuarial prediction; improbability 969

2 **divination** <see list>, divining; **augury,** haruspication, haruspicy, pythonism, mantic, mantology <old>; **fortunetelling,** crystal gazing, palm-reading, palmistry, tea-leaf reading, tarot reading, I Ching; crystal ball; astrology, horoscopy, astrology 1072.20; sorcery 690; clairvoyance 689.8, telepathy

3 dowsing, witching, water witching; **divining rod** *or* stick, wand, witch *or* witching stick, dowsing rod, doodlebug; water diviner, dowser, water witch *or* witcher; hydromancy

4 predictor, foreteller, prognosticator, seer, foreseer, forecaster, foreknower, presager <old>, prefigurer; **forecaster;** prophet, prophesier, soothsayer, *vates* <L>; **diviner,** divinator; augur; psychic 689.13; clairvoyant; prophetess, seeress, divineress, pythoness; Druid; **fortuneteller;** crystal gazer; palmist; geomancer; haruspex *or* aruspex, astrologer 1072.23; weather prophet 317.6; prophet of doom, calamity howler, Cassandra; prophets 684; speculator

5 <nf terms> **dopester, tipster, tout** *or* touter

6 sibyl; Pythia, Pythian, Delphic sibyl; Babylonian *or* Persian sibyl, Cimmerian sibyl, Cumaean sibyl, Erythraean sibyl, Hellespontine *or* Trojan sibyl, Libyan sibyl, Phrygian sibyl, Samian sibyl, Tiburtine sibyl

7 oracle; Delphic *or* Delphian oracle, Python, Pythian oracle; Delphic tripod, tripod of the Pythia; Dodona, oracle *or* oak of Dodona; sage

8 predictability, divinability, foretellableness, **calculability, foreseeability,** foreknowableness

VERBS **9 predict,** make a prediction, **foretell, soothsay,** prefigure, **forecast, prophesy, prognosticate,** call <nf>, make a prophecy *or* prognosis, vaticinate, forebode, presage, see ahead, see *or* tell the future, read the future, see in the crystal ball; **foresee** 961.5; dope *and* dope out <nf>; call the turn *and* call one's shot <nf>; **divine;** witch *or* dowse for water; **tell fortunes,** fortune-tell, cast one's fortune; read one's hand, read palms, read tea leaves, cast a horoscope *or* nativity; **guess,** speculate, guesstimate <nf>, make an educated guess; **bet, bet on, gamble**

10 portend, foretoken 133.11, foreshow, foreshadow

ADJS **11 predictive,** predictory, predictional; **foretelling,** forewarning, forecasting; prefiguring, prefigurative, presignifying, presignificative; **prophetic,** prophetical, fatidic, fatidical, apocalyptic, apocalyptical; vatic, vaticinatory, vaticinal, mantic, sibyllic, sibylline, fatidic, fatidical; **divinatory, oracular,** auguring, augural; haruspical; **foreseeing** 961.7; presageful, presaging; **prognostic,** prognosticative, prognosticatory; fortunetelling; weather-wise

12 ominous, premonitory, foreboding 133.16, unfavorable, adverse

13 predictable, divinable, foretellable, calculable, anticipatable; **foreseeable, foreknowable,** precognizable; **probable** 968.6; improbable 969.3

14 predicted, prophesied, presaged, **foretold, forecast,** foreshown; foreseen, foreglimpsed, **foreknown**

15 fortune-telling methods

aptitude test	lithomancy
astrology *or* horoscope	Magic 8-Ball ™
belomancy	mantology
cartomancy	metopomancy
Chinese astrology	myomancy
chirography	necromancy
chirology	numerology
chiromancy	ololygmancy
clairvoyance	oracle consultation
crystal ball gazing	palmistry *or* palm
divination sticks	reading
dream interpretation	pegomancy
fortune cards	personality test
fortune cookie	phrenology
geloscopy	retromancy
graphology	runes
gyromancy	séance
I Ching *or* I-Ching	soothsaying
ichthyomancy	stercomancy
intelligence quotient test *or*	stone-casting
IQ test	Tarot card reading
knissomancy	tea-leaf reading
lecanomancy	xenomancy

963 NECESSITY

NOUNS **1 necessity,** necessariness, necessitude <old>, necessitation, entailment; mandatoriness, mandatedness, obligatoriness, **obligation,** obligement; compulsoriness, **compulsion, duress** 424.3

2 requirement, requisite, requisition; **necessity, need, want,** occasion; need for, **call for, demand,** demand for; desideratum, desideration; **prerequisite,** prerequirement; **must,** must item; sine qua non; **essential,** indispensable, must-have; the necessary, the needful; necessities, necessaries, essentials, bare necessities, fundamentals

3 needfulness, requisiteness; **essentiality,** essentialness, vitalness; **indispensability,** indispensableness; irreplaceability; irreducibleness, irreducibility

4 urgent need, dire necessity; exigency *or* exigence, **urgency,** imperative, imperativeness, immediacy, pressingness, pressure; "necessity's sharp pinch"—Shakespeare; matter of necessity, case of need *or* emergency, **matter of life and death; predicament** 1013.4

5 involuntariness, unwilledness, **instinctiveness;** compulsiveness; reflex action, Pavlovian reaction, conditioning, automatism; echolalia, echopraxia; automatic writing; **instinct,** impulse 365; blind impulse *or* instinct, knee-jerk reaction, sheer chemistry

6 choicelessness, no choice, no alternative, lack of choice, **Hobson's choice,** only choice, zero option, coercion; Catch-22; that *or* nothing; not a pin to choose, six of one and half a dozen of the other, distinction without a difference; indiscrimination 945

7 inevitability, inevitableness, **unavoidableness,** necessity, inescapableness, inevasibleness, unpreventability, undeflectability, ineluctability; irrevocability, indefeasibility; uncontrollability; relentlessness, inexorability, unyieldingness, inflexibility; fatedness, fatefulness, **certainty,** sureness; *force majeure* <Fr>, vis major, act of God, inevitable accident, unavoidable casualty; **predetermination;** God's will, will of Allah; doom, karma, one's lot, **fate** 964.2

VERBS **8 necessitate, oblige,** dictate, **constrain;** coerce, impel, force, mandate; insist upon, **compel** 424.4

9 require, need, want, lack, must have, feel the want of, have occasion for, be in need of, be hurting for <nf>, stand in need of, not be able to dispense with, not be able to do without; **call for,** cry for, cry out for, clamor for; **demand,** ask, claim, exact; prerequire <old>; need *or* want doing, take doing <nf>, be indicated

10 be necessary, lie under a necessity, be one's fate; be a must <nf>; can't be avoided, can't be helped; be under the necessity of, be in for; be obliged, **must,** need *or* needs must <old>, **have to,** have got to <nf>, should, need, **need to,** have need to; not able to keep from, not able to help, **cannot help but,** cannot do otherwise; be forced *or* driven

11 have no choice *or* **alternative,** have one's options reduced *or* closed *or* eliminated, have no option but, cannot choose but, be robbed *or* relieved of choice; be pushed to the wall, be driven into a corner; take it *or* leave it *and* like it *or* lump it <nf>, have that *or* nothing

ADJS **12 necessary, obligatory, compulsory,** entailed, mandatory, fundamental; **exigent, urgent,** necessitous, importunate, **imperative;** choiceless, without choice, out of one's hands *or* control

13 requisite, needful, required, needed, necessary, **wanted, called for,** indicated, imperative; **essential, vital, indispensable,** unforgoable, irreplaceable; irreducible, irreductible; prerequisite

14 involuntary, instinctive, automatic, mechanical, reflex, reflexive, knee-jerk <nf>, autonomic, conditioned; **unconscious,** unthinking, blind; **unwitting,** unintentional, independent of one's will, unwilling, unwilled, against one's will, collateral; compulsory, **compulsive;** forced; **impulsive** 365.9

15 inevitable, unavoidable, necessary, **inescapable,** inevasible, unpreventable, undeflectable, ineluctable, irrevocable, indefeasible; uncontrollable, unstoppable; relentless, inexorable, unyielding, inflexible; irresistible, resistless; **certain,** fateful, **sure,** sure as fate, sure as death, sure as death and taxes; preordained, predestined, **destined, fated** 964.9; necessitarian, deterministic

ADVS **16 necessarily, needfully,** requisitely; **of necessity,** from necessity, need *or* needs <old>, perforce; without choice; **willy-nilly,** *nolens volens* <L>, willing *or* unwilling, *bon gré mal gré* <Fr>, whether one will *or* not; come what may; compulsorily

17 if necessary, if need be, if worst comes to worst; for lack of something better, *faute de mieux* <Fr>

18 involuntarily, instinctively, automatically, mechanically, by reflex, reflexively; blindly, **unconsciously,** unthinkingly, without premeditation; **unwittingly,** unintentionally; **compulsively; unwillingly** 325.8

19 inevitably, unavoidably, necessarily, **inescapably,** come hell *or* high water <nf>, inevasibly, unpreventably, ineluctably; irrevocably, indefeasibly; uncontrollably; relentlessly, inexorably, unyieldingly, inflexibly; fatefully, **certainly, surely**

PHRS **20 it is necessary, it must be,** if need be, it needs must be *or* it must needs be <old>, it will be, there's no two ways about it, it must have its way; it cannot be helped, there is no helping it *or* help for it, that's the way the cookie crumbles *or* the ball bounces <nf>, what will be will be, it's God's will; the die is cast; it is fated 964.11

964 PREDETERMINATION

NOUNS **1 predetermination, predestination,** foredestiny, **preordination,** foreordination, foreordainment; decree; foregone conclusion, par for the course <nf>, preconceived notion *or* opinion; **necessity** 963; foreknowledge, prescience 961.3

2 fate, fatality, **fortune, lot,** cup, portion, appointed lot, **karma,** kismet, weird, *moira* <Gk>, future 839; **destiny,** destination, **end,** final lot; **doom,** foredoom <old>, God's will, will of Heaven; **inevitability** 963.7; the handwriting on the wall; book of fate; Fortune's wheel, wheel of fortune *or* chance; astral influences, stars, planets, constellation, astrology 1072.20; unlucky day, ides of March, Friday, Friday the thirteenth, *dies funestis* <L>

3 Fates, *Fata* <L>, Parcae, *Moirai* <Gk>, Clotho, Lachesis, Atropos; Nona, Decuma, Morta; Weird

Sisters, Weirds; Norns; Urdur, Verthandi, Skuld;
Fortuna, Lady or Dame Fortune, *Tyche* <Gk>;
Providence, Heaven

4 **determinism, fatalism,** necessitarianism,
necessarianism, predeterminism;
predestinarianism, Calvinism, election

5 **determinist, fatalist,** necessitarian, necessarian;
predestinationist, predestinarian, Calvinist

VERBS 6 **predetermine, predecide,** preestablish,
preset; **predestine,** predestinate, **preordain,**
foreordain; agree beforehand, preconcert

7 **destine, predestine,** necessitate 963.8, destinate
<old>, **ordain,** fate, mark, appoint, decree, intend;
come with the territory <nf>; have in store for;
doom, foredoom

ADJS 8 **determined, predetermined, predecided,**
preestablished, **predestined,** predestinate,
preordained, foreordained; foregone; open-and-
shut; arranged

9 **destined, fated,** fateful, fatal <old>, ordained,
written, in the cards, marked, appointed <old>, in
store, cut-and-dried; **doomed,** foredoomed,
devoted; inevitable 963.15

10 **deterministic, fatalistic,** necessitarian,
necessarian

PHRS 11 **it is fated, it is written,** it's in the cards;
what will be will be, *che sarà sarà* <Ital>, *que será
será* <Sp>; *c'est la vie* and *c'est la guerre* <Fr>

965 PREARRANGEMENT

NOUNS 1 **prearrangement,** preordering,
preconcertedness; premeditation, plotting,
planning, scheming; directed verdict; **reservation,**
booking; overbooking

2 <nf terms> **put-up job,** packed or rigged game or
jury, packed deal, stacked deck, cold deck, boat
race, tank job; **frame-up,** frame, setup

3 **schedule, program,** programma, **bill,** card,
calendar, docket, slate; playbill; batting order,
lineup, roster, rota <chiefly Brit>; blueprint,
budget; **prospectus;** schedule or program of
operation, **order of the day,** things to be done,
agenda, list of agenda; protocol; laundry list and
wish list <nf>; **bill of fare, menu,** *carte du jour* <Fr>

VERBS 4 **prearrange,** precontrive, predesign <old>,
preorder, preconcert; premeditate, plot, plan,
scheme; **reserve,** book, overbook

5 <nf terms> **fix, rig,** pack, cook, cook up; **stack the
cards,** cold-deck, pack the deal; put in the bag,
sew up; frame, frame-up, set up; **throw,** tank, go
in the tank, hold a boat race

6 **schedule, line up** <nf>, **slate, book,** book in, bill,
program, calendar, docket, budget, put on the
agenda

ADJS 7 **prearranged,** precontrived, predesigned
<old>, preordered, preconcerted, cut out;
premeditated, plotted, planned, schemed; cut-and-
dried, cut-and-dry

8 <nf terms> **fixed, rigged, put-up,** packed, stacked,
cooked, cooked-up; **in the bag,** on ice, iced,
cinched, sewed up; **framed, framed-up,** set-up

9 **scheduled, slated,** booked, billed, booked-in, to
come

966 POSSIBILITY

NOUNS 1 **possibility,** possibleness, **the realm of
possibility,** the domain of the possible,
conceivableness, **conceivability,** thinkability,
thinkableness, imaginability; **probability,
likelihood** 968.1; what may be, what might be,
what is possible, what one can do, what can be
done, the possible, the attainable, the feasible;
potential, potentiality, virtuality; contingency,
eventuality; **chance, prospect, odds; outside
chance** <nf>, off chance, remote possibility, ghost
of a chance; hope, outside hope, small hope, slim
odds; **good possibility, good chance,** safe bet, even
chance 972.7; bare possibility 972.9

2 **practicability, practicality, feasibility; workability,**
operability, actability, performability,
realizability, negotiability; **viability,** viableness;
achievability, doability, compassability,
attainability; surmountability, superability; realm
of possibility

3 **accessibility,** access, **approachability, openness,**
reachableness, come-at-ableness *and* get-at-
ableness <nf>; **penetrability,** perviousness;
obtainability, obtainableness, **availability,
donability, procurability,** procurableness,
securableness, getableness, acquirability

VERBS 4 **be possible,** could be, might be, **have or
stand a chance or good chance, bid fair to**

5 **make possible, enable,** permit, permit of, clear the
road or path for, smooth the way for, open the way
for, open the door to, open up the possibility of,
give a chance to

ADJS 6 **possible,** within the bounds or realm or
range or domain of possibility, in one's power, in
one's hands, humanly possible; **probable, likely**
968.6; **conceivable,** conceivably possible,
imaginable, thinkable, cogitable; plausible 968.7;
potential, virtual; contingent; able, apt

7 **practicable, practical, feasible; workable,** actable,
performable, effectible <old>, realizable,
compassable, operable, negotiable, doable,
swingable, bridgeable; **viable; achievable,
attainable;** surmountable, superable,
overcomable

8 **accessible, approachable,** come-at-able *and* get-at-able <nf>, **reachable,** within reach; **open,** open to; **penetrable,** get-in-able <nf>, pervious; **obtainable, attainable, available,** procurable, securable, findable, easy to come by, getable, to be had, donable

ADVS 9 **possibly, conceivably,** imaginably, feasibly; within the realm of possibility; **perhaps,** perchance, haply; maybe, it may be, for all *or* aught one knows

10 **by any possibility, by any chance,** by any means, **by any manner of means;** in any way, in any possible way, **at any cost, at all,** if at all, ever; on the bare possibility, on the off chance, by merest chance

11 **if possible,** if humanly possible, **God willing,** *Deo volente* <L>, wind and weather permitting, Lord willing and the creek don't rise

967 IMPOSSIBILITY

NOUNS 1 **impossibility,** impossibleness, the realm *or* domain of the impossible, **inconceivability,** unthinkability, unimaginability, what cannot be, what can never be, what cannot happen, hopelessness, Chinaman's chance *and* a snowball's chance in hell *and* no way in hell <nf>, **no chance** 972.10; **self-contradiction,** unreality, absurdity, paradox, oxymoron, logical impossibility; impossible, the impossible, impossibilism; no-no <nf>

2 **impracticability,** unpracticability, **impracticality, unfeasibility; unworkability,** inoperability, unperformability; **unachievability, unattainability;** unrealizability, uncompassability; insurmountability, **insuperability**

3 **inaccessibility,** unaccessibility; **unapproachability,** un-come-at-ableness <nf>, unreachableness; **impenetrability,** imperviousness; **unobtainability,** unobtainableness, **unattainability, unavailability,** unprocurableness, unsecurableness, ungettableness <nf>, unacquirability; undiscoverability, unascertainableness

VERBS 4 **be impossible,** be an impossibility, **not have a chance,** be a waste of time; **contradict itself,** be a logical impossibility, be a paradox; fly in the face of reason

5 **attempt the impossible,** try for a miracle, look for a needle in a haystack *or* in a bottle of hay, try to be in two places at once, try to fetch water in a sieve *or* catch the wind in a net *or* weave a rope of sand *or* get figs from thistles *or* gather grapes from thorns *or* make bricks from straw *or* make cheese of chalk *or* make a silk purse out of a sow's

ear *or* change the leopard's spots *or* get blood from a turnip; ask the impossible, cry for the moon; turn back time; walk on water

6 **make impossible, rule out,** disenable, disqualify, close out, **bar,** prohibit, put out of reach, leave no chance, make things difficult

ADJS 7 **impossible, not possible,** beyond the bounds of possibility *or* reason, contrary to reason, at variance with the facts; **inconceivable, unimaginable, unthinkable, not to be thought of, out of the question;** hopeless; **absurd,** ridiculous, preposterous; **self-contradictory,** paradoxical, oxymoronic, logically impossible; **ruled-out,** excluded, closed-out, **barred,** prohibited, forbidden; self-contradictory, self-defeating

8 **impracticable, impractical, unpragmatic, unfeasible; unworkable,** unviable, unperformable, inoperable, undoable, unnegotiable, unbridgeable; **unachievable, unattainable,** uneffectible <old>; unrealizable, uncompassable; insurmountable, unsurmountable, **insuperable,** unovercomable; **beyond one,** beyond one's power, beyond one's control, out of one's depth, too much for

9 **inaccessible,** unaccessible; **unapproachable,** un-come-at-able <nf>; **unreachable,** beyond reach, out of reach; **impenetrable,** impervious; closed to, denied to, lost to, closed forever to; **unobtainable, unattainable, unavailable,** unprocurable, unsecurable, ungettable <nf>, unacquirable; not to be had, **not to be had for love *or* money;** undiscoverable, unascertainable; back-ordered

ADVS 10 **impossibly, inconceivably,** unimaginably, unthinkably; not at any price

PHRS 11 no can do, no way, no way José <nf>, yeah right <nf>

968 PROBABILITY

NOUNS 1 **probability, likelihood,** likeliness, liability, aptitude, verisimilitude; **chance, odds; expectation, outlook,** prospect; favorable prospect, well-grounded hope, some *or* reasonable hope, fair expectation; **good chance** 972.8; presumption, presumptive evidence; tendency; probable cause, reasonable ground *or* presumption; leaning; probabilism; possibility 966

2 **mathematical probability,** statistical probability, statistics, **predictability;** probability theory, game theory, theory of games; operations research; probable error, standard deviation; stochastic *or* statistical independence, stochastic variable; probability curve, frequency curve, frequency polygon, frequency distribution, probability function, probability density function, probability distribution, cumulative distribution function;

statistical mechanics, quantum mechanics, uncertainty *or* indeterminancy principle, Maxwell-Boltzmann distribution law, Bose-Einstein statistics, Fermi-Dirac statistics; **mortality table,** actuarial table, life table, combined experience table, Commissioners Standard Ordinary table; blip, hiccup

3 **plausibility; reasonability** 935.9; **credibility** 953.8; verisimilitude

VERBS 4 **be probable, seem likely,** could be, offer a good prospect, offer the expectation, have *or* run a good chance, be in the running, come as no surprise; **promise,** be promising, make fair promise, **bid fair to,** stand fair to, show a tendency, be in the cards, have the makings of, have favorable odds, lead one to expect; **make probable,** probabilize, make more likely, smooth the way for; increase the chances

5 **think likely, daresay,** venture to say; anticipate; **presume,** suppose 951.10

ADJS 6 **probable, likely, liable, apt,** verisimilar, in the cards, odds-on; **promising, hopeful,** fair, in a fair way; foreseeable, **predictable; presumable,** presumptive; **statistical,** actuarial; mathematically *or* statistically probable, predictable within limits; prone, apt

7 **plausible,** colorable, apparent <old>; **reasonable** 935.20; credible 953.24; **conceivable** 966.6

ADVS 8 **probably, in all probability** *or* **likelihood,** likely, **most likely, very likely;** as likely as not, very like *and* like enough *and* like as not <nf>; **doubtlessly,** doubtless, **no doubt,** indubitably; **presumably,** presumptively; by all odds, ten to one, a hundred to one, dollars to doughnuts

PHRS 9 **there is reason to believe,** I am led to believe, it can be supposed, it would appear, it stands to reason, it might be thought, one can assume, appearances are in favor of, the chances *or* odds are, you can bank on it, you can make book on it, you can bet on it, you can bet your bottom dollar, you can just bet, you can't go wrong; I daresay, I venture to say

969 IMPROBABILITY

NOUNS 1 **improbability, unlikelihood,** unlikeliness; **doubtfulness,** dubiousness, **questionableness; implausibility,** incredibility 955.3; little expectation, low order of probability, poor possibility, bare possibility, faint likelihood, poor prospect, poor outlook, a ghost of a chance, fat chance <nf>, chance in a million; long shot; **small chance** 972.9; Hollywood ending

VERBS 2 **be improbable, not be likely,** be a stretch of the imagination, strain one's credulity, go beyond

reason, go beyond belief, go far afield, go beyond the bounds of reason *or* probability, be far-fetched *or* fetched from afar, be a long shot

ADJS 3 **improbable, unlikely,** unpromising, hardly possible, logic-defying, scarcely to be expected *or* anticipated; statistically improbable; **doubtful,** dubious, **questionable,** doubtable, dubitable, more than doubtful; far-fetched, **implausible,** incredible 955.10; unlooked-for, unexpected, unpredictable; back-ordered

PHRS 4 **not likely!,** no fear!, never fear!, I ask you!, you should live so long! <nf>, don't hold your breath!, don't bet *or* make book on it <nf>

970 CERTAINTY

NOUNS 1 **certainty, certitude,** certainness, **sureness,** surety, **assurance, assuredness,** certain knowledge; **positiveness, absoluteness, definiteness,** dead *or* moral *or* absolute certainty; unequivocalness, unmistakableness, unambiguity, nonambiguity, univocity, univocality; **infallibility,** infallibilism, inerrability, inerrancy; **necessity,** determinacy, determinateness, noncontingency, Hobson's choice, ineluctability, predetermination, predestination, **inevitability** 963.7; **truth** 973; **proved fact,** probatum

2 <nf terms> **sure thing,** dead certainty, dead cert <Brit nf>, dead-sure thing, sure bet, sure card, aces wired, cinch, lead-pipe cinch, dead cinch, lock, mortal lock, shoo-in, open-and-shut case

3 **unquestionability, undeniability,** indubitability, indubitableness, **indisputability,** incontestability, incontrovertibility, **irrefutability,** unrefutability, unconfutability, irrefragability, unimpeachability; **doubtlessness, questionlessness; demonstrability,** provability, verifiability, confirmability; factuality, **reality,** actuality 761.2

4 **reliability, dependability, dependableness, validity, trustworthiness,** faithworthiness; unerringness; predictability, calculability; stability, substantiality, firmness, **soundness,** solidity, staunchness, steadiness, **steadfastness;** secureness, **security;** invincibility 15.4; **authoritativeness, authenticity**

5 **confidence,** confidentness, conviction, belief 953, fixed *or* settled belief, **sureness, assurance, assuredness,** surety, security, certitude; **faith,** subjective certainty; trust 953.1; **positiveness, cocksureness; self-confidence, self-assurance, self-reliance;** poise 106.3; courage 492; **overconfidence, oversureness,** overweening <old>, overweeningness, hubris; pride 136, arrogance 141, pomposity 501.7, self-importance 140.1

6 dogmatism, dogmaticalness, pontification, **positiveness,** positivism, peremptoriness, **opinionatedness,** self-opinionatedness; bigotry; infallibilism

7 dogmatist, dogmatizer, opinionist, doctrinaire, bigot; positivist; infallibilist

8 ensuring, assurance; reassurance, reassurement; **certification;** ascertainment, **determination,** establishment; **verification, corroboration,** substantiation, validation, collation, check, cross-check, double-check, checking; independent *or* objective witness; **confirmation**

VERBS **9 be certain, be confident,** feel sure, rest assured, have sewed up <nf>, **have no doubt,** doubt not; know, just know, know for certain; **bet on** *and* gamble on *and* bet one's bottom dollar on *and* bet the ranch on <nf>; admit of no doubt; **go without saying,** *aller sans dire* <Fr>, be axiomatic *or* apodictic, bet one's life <nf>

10 dogmatize, lay down the law, pontificate, oracle, oraculate, proclaim, assert oneself

11 make sure, make certain, make sure of, make no doubt, make no mistake; remove *or* dismiss *or* expunge *or* erase all doubt; **assure, ensure,** insure, **certify; ascertain, get a fix** *or* **lock on** <nf>; **find out,** get at, see to it, see that; **determine,** decide, **establish,** settle, fix, lock in *and* nail down *and* clinch *and* cinch <nf>, pin down, clear up, sort out, set at rest; assure *or* satisfy oneself, make oneself easy about *or* on that score; **reassure**

12 verify, confirm, test, prove, audit, **collate,** validate, check, check up *or* on *or* out <nf>, check over *or* through, **double-check,** triple-check, cross-check, recheck, check and doublecheck, check up and down, check over and through, check in and out, measure twice cut once

ADJS **13 certain, sure,** sure-enough <nf>; well-founded; bound; **positive, absolute, definite,** perfectly sure, apodictic; decisive, conclusive; clear, clear as day, clear and distinct, unequivocal, unmistakable, unambiguous, nonambiguous, univocal; **necessary,** determinate, ineluctable, predetermined, predestined, **inevitable** 963.15; true 973.13

14 <nf terms> dead sure, sure as death, sure as death and taxes, sure as fate, sure as can be, sure as shooting, sure as God made little green apples, sure as hell *or* the devil, shit-sure, as sure as I live and breathe

15 obvious, patent, unquestionable, unexceptionable, undeniable, self-evident, axiomatic; indubitable, unarguable, indisputable, incontestable, **irrefutable,** unrefutable, unconfutable, incontrovertible, irrefragable, unanswerable, inappealable, unimpeachable, absolute; admitting no question *or* dispute *or* doubt *or* denial; **demonstrable,** demonstratable, provable, verifiable, testable, confirmable; well-founded, well-established, well-grounded; factual, **real,** historical, actual 761.15

16 undoubted, not to be doubted, indubious, **unquestioned, undisputed, uncontested,** uncontradicted, unchallenged, uncontroverted, uncontroversial; **doubtless, questionless,** beyond a shade *or* shadow of doubt, past dispute, beyond question

17 reliable, dependable, sure, surefire <nf>, **trustworthy, trusty,** faithworthy, **to be depended** *or* **relied upon,** to be counted *or* reckoned on; predictable, calculable; **secure, solid, sound, firm,** fast, **stable, substantial,** staunch, steady, **steadfast, faithful, unfailing;** true to one's word; invincible

18 authoritative, authentic, magisterial, **official;** cathedral, ex cathedra; standard, approved, accepted, received, pontific; from *or* straight from the horse's mouth

19 infallible, inerrable, inerrant, unerring

20 assured, made sure; **determined, decided, ascertained; settled, established,** fixed, cinched *and* iced *and* sewed up *and* taped <nf>, set, stated, determinate, secure; **certified,** attested, guaranteed, warranted, tested, tried, proved; wired *and* cinched *and* open-and-shut *and* nailed down *and* in the bag *and* on ice <nf>

21 confident, sure, secure, **assured,** reassured, decided, determined; **convinced,** persuaded, positive, **cocksure; unhesitating,** unfaltering, unwavering; **undoubting** 953.21; **self-confident, self-assured, self-reliant,** sure of oneself; poised 106.13; unafraid; **overconfident, oversure,** overweening, hubristic; proud 136.8, arrogant 141.9, pompous 501.22, self-important 140.8

22 dogmatic, dogmatical, dogmatizing, pronunciative, didactic, **positive,** positivistic, peremptory, pontifical, oracular; **opinionated,** opinioned, opinionative, conceited 140.11; **self-opinionated,** self-opinioned; doctrinarian, doctrinaire; bigoted

ADVS **23 certainly, surely, assuredly, positively, absolutely, definitely,** decidedly; without batting an eye <nf>; decisively, distinctly, clearly, unequivocally, unmistakably; **for certain,** for sure *and* for a fact <nf>, in truth, certes *or* forsooth <old>, and no mistake <nf>; **for a certainty,** to a certainty, *à coup sûr* <Fr>; **most certainly,** most assuredly; **indeed,** indeedy <nf>; truly; **of course,** as a matter of course; **by all means,** by all manner of means; at any rate, at all events; nothing else

but <nf>, no two ways about it, no buts about it
<nf>; no ifs, ands, *or* buts

24 **surely, sure, to be sure,** sure enough, for sure
<nf>; sure thing *and* surest thing you know <nf>

25 **unquestionably, without question, undoubtedly,
beyond the shadow of a doubt, beyond a reasonable
doubt, indubitably, admittedly, undeniably,**
unarguably, indisputably, incontestably,
incontrovertibly, irrefutably, irrefragably;
doubtlessly, doubtless, **no doubt, without doubt,**
beyond doubt *or* question, out of question

26 **without fail,** unfailingly, whatever may happen,
come what may, come hell *or* high water <nf>;
cost what it may, *coûte que coûte* <Fr>; rain *or*
shine, live *or* die, sink *or* swim

PHRS 27 **it is certain,** there is no question, there is
not a shadow of doubt, that's for sure <nf>; that
goes without saying, *cela va sans dire* <Fr>;
that is evident, that leaps to the eye, *cela saute
aux yeux* <Fr>

971 UNCERTAINTY

NOUNS 1 **uncertainty, incertitude, unsureness,**
uncertainness; indemonstrability, unverifiability,
unprovability, unconfirmability; **unpredictability,**
unforeseeableness, incalculability,
unaccountability; **indetermination,**
indeterminacy, indeterminism; **relativity,**
relativism, contingency, conditionality;
randomness, chance, chanciness, hit-or-missness,
luck; entropy; **indecision,** indecisiveness,
undecidedness, undeterminedness; **hesitation,
hesitancy; suspense,** suspensefulness, agony *or*
state of suspense; **fickleness, capriciousness,**
whimsicality, **erraticness,** erraticism,
changeableness 854; **vacillation, irresolution** 362;
trendlessness; Heisenberg *or* indeterminacy *or*
uncertainty principle; question mark; back order;
mixed blessing

2 **doubtfulness, dubiousness, doubt,** dubiety,
dubitancy, dubitation <old>; **questionableness,
disputability,** contestability, controvertibility,
refutability, confutability, deniability; disbelief
955.1

3 **bewilderment,** disconcertion, disconcertedness,
disconcert, disconcertment, **embarrassment,
confoundment,** discomposure, unassuredness,
confusion, cognitive dissonance; **perplexity,
puzzlement,** baffle, **bafflement,** predicament,
plight, **quandary, dilemma,** horns of a dilemma,
nonplus; **puzzle,** problem, riddle, conundrum,
mystery, enigma; fix *and* jam *and* pickle *and*
scrape *and* stew <nf>; perturbation, **disturbance,
upset, bother,** pother

4 **vagueness, indefiniteness, indecisiveness,**
indeterminateness, indeterminableness,
indefinableness, **unclearness, indistinctness,**
haziness, fogginess, mistiness, murkiness,
blurriness, fuzziness; **obscurity,** obscuration;
looseness, laxity, inexactness, inaccuracy,
imprecision; **broadness, generality,** sweepingness;
ill-definedness, amorphousness, shapelessness,
blobbiness; inchoateness, disorder, incoherence

5 **equivocalness,** equivocality, polysemousness,
ambiguity 539

6 **unreliability, undependability,
untrustworthiness,** unfaithworthiness,
treacherousness, treachery; **unsureness,
insecurity, unsoundness, infirmity,** insolidity,
unsolidity, **instability,** insubstantiality,
unsubstantiality, **unsteadfastness,** unsteadiness,
desultoriness, shakiness; **precariousness,** hazard,
danger, risk, riskiness, diceyness *and* dodginess
<Brit nf>, knife-edge, moment of truth, tightrope
walking, peril, perilousness, ticklishness,
slipperiness, shiftiness, shiftingness;
speculativeness; **unauthoritativeness,**
unauthenticity

7 **fallibility,** errability, errancy, liability to error

8 <an uncertainty> **gamble, guess,** piece of
guesswork, question mark, estimate, guesstimate
and ball-park figure <nf>; **chance, wager; toss-up**
and **coin-toss** <nf>, **touch and go;** contingency,
double contingency, possibility upon a possibility;
question, open question; undecided issue, loose
end; wild guess; **gray area,** twilight zone,
borderline case; blind bargain, pig in a poke,
sight-unseen transaction; leap in the dark; enigma

VERBS 9 **be uncertain, feel unsure; doubt,** have
one's doubts, **question,** puzzle over, agonize over;
wonder, wonder whether, wrinkle one's brow; not
know what to make of, not be able to make head
or tail of; be at sea, float in a sea of doubt; be at
one's wit's end, **not know which way to turn,** be of
two minds, be at sixes and sevens, not know where
one stands, have mixed feelings, not know
whether one stands on one's head *or* one's heels,
be in a dilemma *or* quandary, flounder, grope,
beat about, thrash about, not know whether one is
coming *or* going, go around in circles; go off in all
directions at once

10 **hang in doubt,** hang over one's head, stop to
consider, think twice; **falter,** dither, **hesitate,
vacillate** 362.8

11 **depend,** all depend, be contingent *or* conditional
on, hang on *or* upon; **hang, hang in the balance,**
be touch and go, tremble in the balance, **hang in
suspense; hang by a thread,** cliffhang, hang by a
hair, hang by the eyelids

12 **bewilder, disconcert,** discompose, **upset,** perturb, **disturb, dismay,** tie one in knots; abash, **embarrass, put out,** pother, **bother,** moider <Brit nf>, flummox <nf>, keep one on tenterhooks

13 **perplex, baffle, confound,** daze, amaze <old>, maze, addle, fuddle, muddle, **mystify, puzzle,** nonplus, put to one's wit's end; keep one guessing, keep in suspense

14 <nf terms> **stump,** boggle <Brit>, buffalo, bamboozle, stick, floor, throw, get, beat, beat the shit out of, lick

15 **make uncertain, obscure, muddle, muddy,** fuzz, fog, **confuse** 985.7

ADJS **16** **uncertain, unsure; doubting, agnostic, skeptical,** unconvinced, unpersuaded; chancy, dicey <Brit>, touch-and-go; **unpredictable,** unforeseeable, incalculable, uncountable, unreckonable, unaccountable, undivinable; indemonstrable, unverifiable, unprovable, unconfirmable; **equivocal,** polysemous, inexplicit, imprecise, ambiguous; **fickle, capricious,** whimsical, **erratic,** variable, wavering, irresponsible, changeable 854.6; **hesitant,** hesitating; **indecisive, irresolute** 362.9

17 **doubtful,** iffy <nf>; **in doubt,** *in dubio* <L>; dubitable, doubtable, **dubious, questionable, problematic, problematical, speculative,** conjectural, suppositional; debatable, moot, arguable, **disputable,** contestable, controvertible, **controversial,** refutable, confutable, deniable; mistakable; **suspicious,** suspect; open to question *or* doubt; in question, in dispute, at issue

18 **undecided, undetermined, unsettled,** unfixed, unestablished; untold, uncounted; pendent, dependent, **pending,** depending, contingent, conditional, conditioned; **open,** in question, at issue, **in the balance, up in the air,** up for grabs <nf>, in limbo, **in suspense,** in a state of suspense, suspenseful

19 **vague, indefinite, indecisive, indeterminate,** indeterminable, **undetermined,** unpredetermined, undestined; **random,** stochastic, entropic, **chance,** chancy <nf>, dicey *and* dodgy <Brit nf>, aleatory *or* aleatoric, hit-or-miss; indefinable, undefined, ill-defined, unclear, unplain, **indistinct,** fuzzy, **obscure, confused, hazy,** shadowy, shadowed forth, misty, foggy, fog-bound, murky, blurred, blurry, veiled; **loose, lax, inexact, inaccurate,** imprecise; nonspecific, unspecified; **broad, general,** sweeping; amorphous, shapeless, blobby; inchoate, disordered, orderless, chaotic, incoherent

20 **unreliable, undependable, untrustworthy,** unfaithworthy, treacherous, unsure, not to be depended *or* relied on; **insecure, unsound, infirm,**

unsolid, **unstable,** unsubstantial, insubstantial, **unsteadfast,** unsteady, desultory, shaky; **precarious,** hazardous, dangerous, perilous, risky, ticklish; shifty, shifting, slippery, slippery as an eel; provisional, tentative, temporary

21 **unauthoritative, unauthentic, unofficial,** nonofficial, apocryphal; **uncertified, unverified,** unchecked, unconfirmed, uncorroborated, unauthenticated, unvalidated, unattested, unwarranted; **undemonstrated, unproved**

22 **fallible, errable,** errant, liable *or* open to error, error-prone

23 **unconfident, unsure, unassured, insecure,** unsure of oneself; unselfconfident, unselfassured, unselfreliant

24 **bewildered, dismayed,** distracted, distraught, abashed, **disconcerted, embarrassed,** discomposed, **put-out, disturbed, upset,** perturbed, **bothered,** all hot and bothered <nf>; **confused** 985.12; clueless, without a clue, guessing, mazed, in a maze; turned around, going around in circles, like a chicken with its head cut off <nf>; in a fix *or* stew *or* pickle *or* jam *or* scrape <nf>; **lost,** astray, abroad, adrift, **at sea,** off the track, out of one's reckoning, out of one's bearings, disoriented

25 **in a dilemma,** on the horns of a dilemma; **perplexed, confounded, mystified, puzzled, nonplussed, baffled,** bamboozled <nf>, buffaloed <nf>; **at a loss, at one's wit's end,** fuddled, addled, muddled, dazed; **on tenterhooks,** in suspense; with bated breath

26 <nf terms> **beat,** licked, stuck, floored, stumped, thrown, buffaloed, boggled <Brit>

27 **bewildering, confusing, distracting, disconcerting,** discomposing, **dismaying, embarrassing,** disturbing, **upsetting,** perturbing, bothering; **perplexing, baffling, mystifying, mysterious, puzzling,** funny, funny peculiar, confounding; **problematic** *or* problematical; intricate 799.4; **enigmatic** 522.17

ADVS **28** **uncertainly,** in an uncertain state, **unsurely; doubtfully, dubiously;** in suspense, at sea, on the horns of a dilemma, at sixes and sevens; perplexedly, disconcertedly, confusedly, dazedly, mazedly, in a daze, in a maze, around in circles

29 **vaguely, indefinitely,** indeterminably, indefinably, **indistinctly,** indecisively, **obscurely; broadly, generally,** in broad *or* general terms

972 CHANCE
<absence of assignable cause>

NOUNS **1** **chance,** happenstance, hap; **luck;** good luck *or* fortune, serendipity, happy chance, dumb luck <nf>, rotten *and* tough luck <nf>; **fortune, fate, destiny,** whatever comes, *moira* <Gk>, lot 964.2; **fortuity, randomness,** randomicity, fortuitousness, adventitiousness, indeterminateness *or* indeterminacy, problematicness, uncertainty 971, flukiness <nf>, casualness, flip of a coin, crazy quilt, patternlessness, trendlessness, accidentality; break <nf>, the breaks <nf>, run of luck, the luck of the draw, the rub of the green, run *or* turn of the cards, fall *or* throw of the dice, the way things fall, the way the cards fall, how they fall, the way the cookie crumbles *or* the ball bounces <nf>; uncertainty principle, principle of indeterminacy, Heisenberg's principle; **probability** 968, stochastics, theory of probability, law of averages, statistical probability, actuarial calculation; random sample, **risk, risk-taking, chancing, gamble** 759.2; **opportunity** 843.2

2 Chance, Fortune, Lady *or* Dame Fortune, wheel of fortune, Fortuna, the fickle finger of fate <nf>; Luck, Lady Luck; "a nickname of Providence"—de Chamfort, "blind Chance"—Lucan

3 **purposelessness, causelessness,** randomness, dysteleology, **unpredictability** 971.1, designlessness, **aimlessness;** lack of motive, no attributable cause, nonintention

4 **haphazard,** chance-medley <law>, **random;** random shot; potluck; spin of the wheel

5 **vicissitudes,** vicissitudes of fortune, ins and outs, **ups and downs,** ups and downs of life, chapter of accidents, feast and famine; **chain of circumstances,** concatenation of events, chain reaction, vicious circle, causal nexus, **domino effect**

6 <chance event> **happening,** hap, happenstance; **fortuity, accident,** casualty, adventure, hazard; contingent, contingency; **fluke** <nf>, freak, freak occurrence *or* accident, coincidence; chance hit, lucky shot, long shot, one in a million, long odds

7 **even chance,** even break *and* fair shake <nf>, even *or* square odds, level playing field, touch and go, odds; **half a chance,** fifty-fifty; toss, **toss-up,** standoff <nf>

8 **good chance, sporting chance,** good opportunity, good possibility; odds-on, odds-on chance, **likelihood, possibility** 966, probability 968, favorable prospect, well-grounded hope; **sure bet,** sure thing *and* dollars to doughnuts <nf>; **best bet,** main chance, winning chance

9 **small chance,** little chance, dark horse, **poor prospect** *or* prognosis, poor lookout <nf>, little opportunity, poor possibility, **unlikelihood, improbability** 969, hardly a chance, not half a chance; **off chance, outside chance** <nf>, remote

possibility, bare possibility, a ghost of a chance, slim chance, gambling chance, **fighting chance** <nf>; poor bet, long odds, long shot <nf>, hundred-to-one shot <nf>, one chance in a million

10 **no chance,** not a Chinaman's chance *and* not a snowball's chance in hell <nf>, Buckley's chance <Austral nf>, not a prayer; **impossibility** 967, hopelessness

VERBS 11 **chance,** bechance <old>, betide, come *or* happen by chance, hap, hazard, **happen** 831.5, happen *or* fall on, come, come *or* happen along, bump into <nf>, **turn up,** pop up <nf>, **befall;** fall to one's lot, be one's fate

12 **risk,** take a chance, run a risk, push *or* press one's luck, lay one's ass on the line *and* put one's money where one's mouth is <nf>, **gamble, bet** 759.25; risk one's neck *and* shoot the works *and* go for broke <nf>; **predict** 962.9, prognosticate, make book <nf>; call someone's bluff

13 have a chance *or* an opportunity, **stand a chance, run a good chance, bid** *or* **stand fair to,** admit of; be in it *or* in the running <nf>; have *or* take a chance at, have a fling *or* shot at <nf>; have a small *or* slight chance, be a dark horse, barely have a chance

14 **not have** *or* **stand a chance,** have no chance *or* opportunity, not have a prayer, not have a Chinaman's chance <nf>, not stand a snowball's chance in hell <nf>; not be in it <nf>, be out of it <nf>, **be out of the running**

ADJS 15 **chance;** chancy <nf>, dicey <Brit nf>, **risky** <nf>; **fortuitous, accidental,** aleatory *or* aleatoric; **lucky,** fortunate, blessed by fortune, serendipitous; **casual,** adventitious, incidental, contingent, iffy <nf>; **causeless,** uncaused; indeterminate, undetermined; **unexpected** 131.10, **unpredictable,** unforeseeable, unlooked-for, **unforeseen; fluky** <nf>; fatal, fatidic, destinal

16 **purposeless, causeless,** designless, **aimless,** driftless, undirected, objectless, unmotivated, mindless; **haphazard, random,** dysteleological, stochastic, stray, inexplicable, unaccountable, promiscuous, indiscriminate, casual, leaving much to chance

17 **unintentional,** unintended, **unmeant, unplanned,** undesigned, unpurposed, unthought-of; **unpremeditated,** unmeditated, unprompted, unguided, unguarded; **unwitting, unthinking,** unconscious, involuntary; collateral

18 impossible 967.7; **improbable** 969.3; certain 970.13; **probable** 968.6

ADVS 19 **by chance,** perchance, **by accident, accidentally, casually,** incidentally, by coincidence, **unpredictably, fortuitously, out of a clear blue sky;** by a piece of luck, by a fluke <nf>, by good fortune; **as it chanced, as luck would have it,** by hazard, as it may happen, as it may be, as the case may be, as it may chance, as it may turn up *or* out; somehow, in some way, in some way *or* other, somehow *or* other, for some reason

20 **purposelessly, aimlessly; haphazardly, randomly,** dysteleologically, stochastically, inexplicably, unaccountably, promiscuously, indiscriminately, casually, **at haphazard, at random,** at hazard

21 **unintentionally, without design, unwittingly,** unthinkingly, unexpectedly, unconsciously, involuntarily

INTERJS 22 break a leg!, best of luck! good luck!

PHR 23 it's a crapshoot

973 TRUTH

<conformity to fact or reality>

NOUNS 1 **truth, trueness, verity,** veridicality, conformity to fact *or* reality *or* the evidence *or* the data, simple *or* unadorned truth, very truth, sooth *or* good sooth <old>; more truth than poetry; **unerroneousness, unfalseness,** unfallaciousness; historical truth, **objective truth, actuality,** historicity, impersonality; **fact, actuality, reality** 761.2, the real world, things as they are; the true, ultimate truth; eternal verities; truthfulness, veracity 644.3

2 **a truth, a self-evident truth, an axiomatic truth, an axiom;** a premise, a given, a donnée *or* donné, an accomplished fact *or fait accompli* <Fr>

3 **the truth,** the truth of the matter, the case; the home truth, the unvarnished truth, the simple truth, the basic truth, indisputable truth, the unadorned truth, the naked truth, the plain truth, the unqualified truth, the honest truth, the sober truth, the exact truth, the straight truth; the absolute truth, the intrinsic truth, the unalloyed truth, the cast-iron truth, the hard truth, the stern truth, gospel, gospel truth, Bible truth, revealed truth; the whole truth and nothing but the truth

4 <nf terms> **what's what,** how it is, how things are, like it is, where it's at, dinkum oil <Austral>, the straight of it, the straight goods *or* skinny *or* scoop, the honest-to-God truth, God's truth, the real thing, the very model, the genuine article, the very thing, it, the article, the goods, the McCoy, the real McCoy, no imitation, chapter and verse, the gospel, the gospel truth, the lowdown, the skinny

5 **accuracy, correctness,** care for truth, attention to fact, right, subservience to the facts *or* the data, **rightness, trueness, rigor, rigorousness, exactness, exactitude; preciseness, precision;** mathematical precision, pinpoint accuracy *or* precision, scientific exactness *or* exactitude;

factualness, factualism; **faultlessness,** perfection, absoluteness, flawlessness, impeccability, unimpeachability; **faithfulness, fidelity;** literalness, literality, literalism, textualism, the letter, literal truth; strictness, severity, rigidity; niceness, nicety, delicacy, subtlety, fineness, refinement; **meticulousness** 339.3; attention to detail; pinpoint accuracy, mathematical precision, clockwork precision

6 **validity, soundness,** solidity, substantiality, **justness;** authority, **authoritativeness; cogency,** weight, force, persuasiveness

7 **genuineness, authenticity,** bona fides, bona fideness, **legitimacy; realness, realism,** photographic realism, absolute realism, realistic representation, **naturalism,** naturalness, truth to nature, **lifelikeness,** truth to life, slice of life, *tranche de vie* <Fr>, kitchen sink, true-to-lifeness, verisimilitude, *vraisemblance* <Fr>, faithful rendering, verism, verismo, faithfulness; absolute likeness, **literalness,** literality, literalism, truth to the letter; socialist realism; inartificiality, unsyntheticness; **unspuriousness,** unspeciousness, unfictitiousness, artlessness, unaffectedness; **honesty, sincerity;** unadulteration 798.1

VERBS 8 **be true,** be the case; conform to fact, square *or* chime with the facts *or* evidence; **prove true,** prove to be, **prove out,** be so in fact; **hold true, hold good, hold water** <nf>, hold *or* stick together <nf>, **hold up, hold up in the wash** <nf>, wash <nf>, **stand up,** stand the test, be consistent *or* self-consistent, **hold,** remain valid; **be truthful**

9 seem true, ring true, sound true, **carry conviction,** convince, persuade, win over, hold *or* have the ring of truth

10 **be right, be correct,** be just right, get it straight; be OK <nf>, add up; **hit the nail on the head,** hit it on the nose *or* on the money *and* say a mouthful <nf>, hit the bull's-eye, score a bull's-eye

11 **be accurate, dot one's i's and cross one's t's,** draw *or* cut it fine <nf>, be precise; make precise, precise, particularize; stick to the letter, go by the book

12 **come true, come about,** attain fulfillment, **turn out, come to pass *or* to be,** happen as expected, become a reality

ADJS 13 **true, truthful; unerroneous,** not in error, in conformity with the facts *or* the evidence *or* reality, on the up-and-up *or* strictly on the up-and-up <nf>; gospel, **hard,** cast-iron; unfalse, unfallacious, unmistaken; **real, veritable,** veracious, sure-enough <nf>, objective, true to the facts, in conformity with the facts *or* the evidence *or* the data *or* reality, **factual, actual** 761.15, effectual, **historical,** documentary; objectively true; **certain,** undoubted, unquestionable 970.15; unrefuted, unconfuted, undenied; **ascertained, proved, proven, verified,** validated, **certified,** demonstrated, confirmed, determined, established, attested, substantiated, **authenticated,** corroborated; true as gospel; substantially true, categorically true; **veracious** 644.16

14 **valid, sound, well-grounded, well-founded,** conforming to the facts *or* the data *or* the evidence *or* reality, hard, solid, substantial; consistent, self-consistent, logical; **good, just,** sufficient; **cogent, weighty, authoritative; legal, lawful,** legitimate, **binding**

15 **genuine, authentic,** veridic, veridical, **real, natural, realistic, naturalistic,** true to reality, **true to nature, lifelike,** true to life, verisimilar, veristic; **literal,** following the letter, letter-perfect, *au pied de la lettre* <Fr>, true to the letter; verbatim, verbal, word-perfect, **word-for-word;** true to the spirit; **legitimate,** rightful, lawful; **bona fide,** card-carrying <nf>, **good,** sure-enough <nf>, **sincere, honest;** candid, honest-to-God <nf>, dinkum <Austral nf>; **inartificial, unsynthetic;** unspurious, unspecious, unsimulated, unfaked, unfeigned, **undisguised, uncounterfeited, unpretended, unaffected, unassumed; unassuming, simple,** unpretending, unfeigning, undisguising; **unfictitious,** unfanciful, unfabricated, unconcocted, uninvented, unimagined; unromantic; **original,** unimitated, uncopied; unexaggerated, undistorted; unflattering, unvarnished, uncolored, unqualified; **unadulterated** 798.7, honest-to-goodness; **pure,** simon-pure; **sterling,** twenty-four carat, all wool *and* a yard wide <nf>

16 **accurate, correct, right,** proper, just; all right *or* OK *or* okay <nf>, just right as rain, right, dead right, on target *and* on the money *and* on the nose *and* on the button <nf>, bang on <Brit nf>, straight, straight-up-and-down; **faultless,** flawless, impeccable, unimpeachable, unexceptionable; **absolute, perfect,** letter-perfect; **meticulous** 339.12; factual, literal

17 **exact, precise,** express; even, square; absolutely *or* definitely *or* positively right; **faithful;** direct; **unerring, undeviating, constant; infallible, inerrant, inerrable; strict,** close, severe, **rigorous,** rigid; mathematically exact, mathematical; mechanically *or* micrometrically precise; scientifically exact, scientific; religiously exact, religious; **nice,** delicate, subtle, **fine,** refined; pinpoint, microscopic

ADVS 18 **truly, really,** really-truly <nf>, **verily,** veritably, forsooth *or* in very sooth <old>, **in truth,** in good *or* very truth, **actually,** historically, objectively, impersonally, rigorously, strictly, strictly speaking, unquestionably, without question, **in reality, in fact,** factually, technically, in point of fact, as a matter of fact, for that matter, for the matter of that, to tell the truth, if you want to know the truth, to state the fact *or* truth, of a truth, with truth; **indeed,** indeedy <nf>; **certainly; indubitably, undoubtedly** 970.25; no buts about it <nf>, nothing else but

19 **genuinely, authentically, really,** naturally, **legitimately, honestly,** veridically; warts and all; unaffectedly, unassumedly, from the heart, in one's heart of hearts, with all one's heart and soul

20 **accurately, correctly,** rightly, properly, straight; **perfectly, faultlessly,** flawlessly, impeccably, unimpeachably, unexceptionably; **just right,** just so; **so,** sic

21 **exactly, precisely,** to a T, expressly; **just, dead,** right, straight, even, square, **plumb,** directly, squarely, point-blank; unerringly, undeviatingly; verbatim, **literally,** *literatim* <L>, verbally, word-perfectly, word for word, word by word, word for word and letter for letter, *verbatim et litteratim* <L>, in the same words, *ipsissimis verbis* <L>, to the letter, according to the letter, *au pied de la lettre* <Fr>; **faithfully, strictly, rigorously,** rigidly; **definitely, positively, absolutely; in every respect,** in all respects, for all the world, neither more nor less

22 **to be exact, to be precise, strictly, technically, strictly speaking,** not to mince the matter, by the book

23 **to a nicety,** to a T *or* tittle, to a turn, to a hair, to *or* within an inch

PHRS 24 **right!, that's right, that is so,** amen!, that's it, that's just it, just so, it is that, *c'est ça* <Fr>; **you are right,** right you are, right as rain, it is for a fact, you speak truly, as you say, **right;** believe it *or* not; touché!

25 <nf terms> **right on!,** you better believe it!, you've got something there, I'll say, I'll tell the world, I'll drink to that, righto, quite, rather!, you got it!, you said it, you said a mouthful, now you're talking, you can say that again, you're not kidding, that's for sure, ain't it the truth?, you're damn tootin', don't I know it?, you're telling me?, you're not just whistling Dixie, bet your ass *or* sweet ass *or* bippy *or* boots *or* life *or* you bet the rent, fucking ay, fucking ay right

974 WISE SAYING

NOUNS 1 **maxim, aphorism,** apothegm *or* apophthegm, **epigram, dictum, adage, proverb,** gnome, words of wisdom, **saw, saying,** witticism, sentence, expression, phrase, catchword, catchphrase, word, byword, mot, motto, moral; **precept,** prescript, teaching, text, verse, sutra, distich, sloka; golden saying, proverbial saying; common *or* current saying, stock saying, pithy saying, wise saying *or* expression, oracle, sententious expression *or* saying; **conventional wisdom, common knowledge; ana, analects, proverbs, wisdom, wisdom literature, collected sayings**

2 **axiom, truth,** a priori truth, postulate, truism, self-evident truth, general *or* universal truth, home truth, obvious truth, intrinsic truth; elephant in the room; theorem; **proposition;** brocard, **principle,** *principium* <L>, settled principle; **formula; rule, law,** dictate <old>, **dictum;** golden rule

3 **platitude, cliché, saw, old saw, commonplace, banality,** bromide, **chestnut** <nf>, corn <nf>, triticism <old>, tired phrase, trite saying, hackneyed *or* stereotyped saying, stock phrase, commonplace expression, *lieu commun* <Fr>, *locus communis* <L>, **familiar tune** *or* **story, old song** *or* **story,** old song and dance <nf>, twice-told tale, retold story; reiteration 849.2; prosaicism, prosaism; prose; old joke 489.9

4 **motto, slogan,** watchword, catchword, catchphrase, tag line *or* tag, byword; **device;** epithet; inscription, epigraph

VERBS 5 aphorize, apothegmatize, epigrammatize, coin a phrase; proverb

ADJS 6 **aphoristic, proverbial,** epigrammatic, epigrammatical, **axiomatical; sententious, pithy,** gnomic, pungent, succinct, enigmatic, pointed; formulistic, formulaic; **cliché** *or* clichéd, banal, tired, stock, trite, tritical <old>, **platitudinous** 117.9

ADVS 7 **proverbially,** to coin a phrase, in a nutshell, **as the saying is** *or* **goes,** as they say, as the fellow says <nf>, as it has been said, as it was said of old

975 ERROR

NOUNS 1 **error, erroneousness; untrueness,** untruthfulness, **untruth; wrongness, wrong; falseness, falsity; fallacy, fallaciousness,** self-contradiction; fault, **faultiness,** defectiveness; **sin** 655.1, sinfulness, peccancy, flaw, flawedness, *hamartia* <Gk>; misdoing, misfeasance; errancy, aberrancy, aberration, **deviancy,** wrongdoing; **heresy,** unorthodoxy, heterodoxy; perversion, **distortion; mistaking,** misconstruction, misapplication, misprision <old>; **delusion, illusion** 976; misjudgment 948; **misinterpretation**

342; faulty reasoning, flawed logic; fallibility, human error

2 **inaccuracy,** inaccurateness, **incorrectness, uncorrectness, inexactness,** unfactualness, inexactitude, **unpreciseness,** imprecision, unspecificity, looseness, laxity, unrigorousness; tolerance, allowance; negligence; approximation; **deviation,** standard deviation, probable error, predictable error, range of error; uncertainty 971

3 **mistake, error,** *erratum* <L>, *corrigendum* <L>; **fault,** *faute* <Fr>; gross error, bevue; human error; **misconception, misapprehension, misunderstanding;** misstatement, misquotation; misreport; **misprint, typographical error,** typo <nf>, printer's error, typist's error; clerical error; misidentification; **misjudgment, miscalculation** 948.1; misplay; misdeal; miscount; misuse; failure, miss, miscarriage

4 **slip,** slipup *and* miscue <nf>; **lapse,** *lapsus* <L>, **oversight,** omission, balk <old>, inadvertence *or* inadvertency, loose thread; **misstep,** trip, stumble, false *or* wrong step, wrong *or* bad *or* false move; false note; **slip of the tongue,** *sus linguae and lapsus linguae* <L>; **slip of the pen,** *lapsus calami* <L>; Freudian slip

5 **blunder, faux pas,** gaffe, solecism; stupidity, indiscretion 923.4; **botch, bungle** 414.5

6 <nf terms> **goof, boo-boo,** muff, flub, foozle, bloomer, bloop, blooper, boot, bobble, boner, bonehead play *or* trick, dumb trick, boob stunt, fool mistake; howler, clanger <Brit>, screamer; fuck-up, screw-up, foul-up, snafu, muck-up, balls-up <Brit>, louse-up; pratfall, whoops

7 **grammatical error, solecism,** anacoluthon, anacoluthia, misusage, faulty syntax, missaying, mispronunciation; **bull, Irish bull,** fluff, **malapropism,** malaprop, Mrs Malaprop <R B Sheridan>; Pickwickian sense; spoonerism, marrow-sky; hypercorrection, hyperform; folk etymology; catachresis; misspelling

VERBS 8 **not hold water** *and* not hold together <nf>, not stand up, not square, not figure <nf>, not add up, **not hold up, not hold up in the wash** *and* not wash <nf>

9 **err,** fall into error, **go wrong, go amiss,** go astray, go *or* get out of line, go awry, stray, get off-base <nf>, **deviate,** wander, transgress, sin; **lapse, slip, slip up,** trip, stumble; **miscalculate** 948.2

10 **be wrong, mistake oneself, be mistaken, be in error, be at fault,** be out of line, be off the track, be in the wrong, miss the truth, miss the point, miss by a mile <nf>, have another think coming <nf>; take wrong, receive a false impression, take the shadow for the substance, misconstrue, misinterpret, be misled, be misguided; deceive

oneself, be deceived, delude oneself; labor under a false impression, get it wrong

11 bark up the wrong tree, back the wrong horse, count one's chickens before they are hatched

12 misdo, do amiss; misuse, misemploy, misapply; misconduct, mismanage; miscall, miscount, miscalculate, misdeal, misplay, misfield; misprint, miscite, misquote, misread, misreport, misspell

13 mistake, make a mistake; miscue *and* make a miscue <nf>; **misidentify; misunderstand,** misapprehend, misconceive, **misinterpret** 342.2; **confuse** 811.3, mix up, not distinguish

14 blunder, make a blunder, make a faux pas, blot one's copy book, make a colossal blunder, make a false *or* wrong step, make a misstep; **misspeak,** misspeak oneself, trip over one's tongue; embarrass oneself, have egg on one's face <nf>; blunder into; **botch, bungle** 414.11

15 <nf terms> **make** *or* **pull a boner** *or* boo-boo *or* blooper; drop a brick <Brit>, goof, fluff, duff <Brit>, foozle, boot, bobble, blow, blow it, drop the ball; fuck up, screw up, foul up, muck up, louse up; put *or* stick one's foot in it *or* in one's mouth; muff one's cue, muff *or* blow *or* fluff one's lines, fall flat on one's face *or* ass, step on one's dick, trip up

ADJS **16 erroneous, untrue,** not true, **not right;** unfactual, **wrong,** all wrong; peccant, perverse, corrupt; **false, fallacious,** self-contradictory; **illogical** 936.11; **unproved** 958.8; **faulty,** faultful, flawed, defective, **at fault;** out, off, all off, off the track *or* rails; wide <old>, wide of the mark, beside the mark; amiss, awry, askew, deviant, deviative, deviational; erring, errant, **aberrant;** straying, astray, adrift; **heretical,** unorthodox, heterodox; abroad, all abroad; perverted, **distorted; delusive,** deceptive, **illusory**

17 inaccurate, incorrect, inexact, unfactual, **unprecise,** imprecise, unspecific, loose, lax, unrigorous; negligent; **vague;** approximate, approximative; out of line, out of plumb, out of true, out of square; off-base <nf>

18 mistaken, in error, erring, under an error, **wrong, all wet** <nf>, full of bull *or* shit *or* hot air *or* it *or* prunes *or* crap *or* beans <nf>; off *or* out in one's reckoning; in the wrong box, in the right church but the wrong pew

19 unauthentic *or* **inauthentic, unauthoritative, unreliable** 971.20; **misstated,** misreported, miscited, misquoted, **garbled;** unfounded 936.13; spurious

ADVS **20 erroneously, falsely,** by mistake, fallaciously; faultily, faultfully; **untrue** <old>, untruly; **wrong,** wrongly; **mistakenly;** amiss, astray, on the wrong track

21 inaccurately, incorrectly, inexactly, unprecisely, by guess and by God *or* by golly <nf>

INTERJS **22** whoops! *and* sorry about that <nf>

PHRS **23 you are wrong, you are mistaken,** you're all wet *or* you're way off *or* you have another guess coming *or* don't kid yourself <nf>

976 ILLUSION

NOUNS **1 illusion, delusion,** deluded belief; **deception** 356, **trick;** self-deception, self-deceit, self-delusion; dereism, autism; **misconception, misbelief,** false belief, wrong impression, warped *or* distorted conception; **bubble, chimera,** vapor; wishful thinking, *ignis fatuus* <L>, will-o'-the-wisp; **dream,** dream vision; dreamworld, dreamland, dreamscape; **daydream;** pipe dream *and* trip <nf>; fool's paradise, castle in the air, fond illusion, dreamscape; maya, confabulation

2 illusoriness, illusiveness, delusiveness; **falseness,** fallaciousness; **unreality,** unactuality; unsubstantiality, airiness, immateriality; **idealization** 986.7; **seeming,** semblance, simulacrum, **appearance,** false *or* specious appearance, show, false show, false light; **magic, sorcery** 690, illusionism, sleight of hand, prestidigitation, magic show, magic act; magician, **sorcerer** 690.5, illusionist, Prospero <Shakespeare>; Mahamaya <Hindu>, magus, wizard, conjuror

3 fancy, phantasy, imagination 986

4 phantom, phantasm, phantasma, wraith, specter; shadow, shade; phantasmagoria; **fantasy,** wildest dream; **figment of the imagination** 986.5, phantom of the mind; **apparition, appearance; vision,** waking dream, image <old>; shape, form, figure, presence; eidolon, idolum; "such stuff as dreams are made on"—Shakespeare

5 optical illusion, trick of eyesight; afterimage, spectrum, ocular spectrum

6 mirage, fata morgana, will-o'-the-wisp, looming

7 hallucination; hallucinosis; tripping <nf>, mind-expansion; consciousness-expansion; delirium tremens 926.9; dream 986.9

VERBS **8 go on a trip** *and* **blow one's mind** <nf>, freak out <nf>; **hallucinate;** expand one's consciousness; make magic, prestidigitate

ADJS **9 illusory,** illusive; illusional, illusionary; Barmecide *or* Barmecidal; **delusory,** delusive; delusional, delusionary, deluding; dereistic, autistic; **dreamy, dreamlike; visionary; imaginary** 986.19; **erroneous** 975.16; **deceptive;** self-deceptive, self-deluding; **chimeric, chimerical, fantastic; unreal,** unactual, unsubstantial 764.5, airy; unfounded 936.13; **false,** fallacious, misleading;

specious, seeming, apparent, ostensible, supposititious, all in the mind; spectral, apparitional, phantom, phantasmal; phantasmagoric, surreal
10 **hallucinatory,** hallucinative, hallucinational; hallucinogenic, psychedelic, consciousness-expanding, mind-expanding, mind-blowing <nf>

977 DISILLUSIONMENT

NOUNS 1 **disillusionment,** disillusion, **disenchantment,** undeception, unspelling, return to reality, loss of one's illusions, loss of innocence, cold light of reality, enlightenment, bursting of the bubble; awakening, rude awakening, bringing back to earth; disappointment 132; debunking <nf>
VERBS 2 **disillusion,** disillude, disillusionize; **disenchant,** unspell, uncharm, break the spell *or* charm; **disabuse, undeceive;** correct, **set right** *or* **straight,** put straight, tell the truth, enlighten, let in on, put one wise <nf>; clear the mind of; open one's eyes, awaken, wake up, unblindfold; disappoint 132.2; dispel *or* dissipate one's illusions, rob *or* strip one of one's illusions; bring one back to earth, let down easy <nf>; **burst** *or* **prick the bubble,** puncture one's balloon <nf>; let the air out of, take the wind out of; knock the props out from under, take the ground from under; debunk <nf>; expose, show up 351.4
3 be disillusioned, be disenchanted, get back to earth, get one's feet on the ground, have one's eyes opened, return to *or* embrace reality; charge to experience; have another thing *or* guess coming <nf>
ADJS 4 **disillusioning,** disillusive, disillusionary, **disenchanting,** disabusing, undeceiving, enlightening
5 disillusioned, disenchanted, unspelled, uncharmed, disabused, undeceived, stripped *or* robbed of illusion, enlightened, set right, put straight; with one's eyes open, sophisticated, **blasé;** disappointed 132.5

978 MENTAL ATTITUDE

NOUNS 1 **attitude,** mental attitude; psychology; **position, posture,** stance; **way of thinking; feeling, sentiment,** the way one feels; feeling tone, affect, affectivity, emotion, emotivity; opinion 953.6
2 **outlook,** mental outlook; *Anschauung* <Ger>, **point of view, viewpoint, standpoint, perspective,** *optique* <Fr>; position, stand, place, situation; side; footing, basis; where one is *or* sits *or* stands; **view,** sight, light, eye; respect, regard; angle, angle of vision, slant, way of looking at things, slant on things, where one is coming from <nf>; **frame of**

reference, intellectual *or* ideational frame of reference, framework, arena, world, universe, world *or* universe of discourse, system, reference system; phenomenology
3 **disposition, character, nature, temper, temperament,** mettle, constitution, complexion *and* humor <old>, makeup, stamp, type, stripe, kidney, make, mold; **turn of mind, inclination,** mind, **tendency,** grain, vein, set, mental set, mindset, **leaning,** animus, propensity, proclivity, predilection, preference, predisposition; **bent, turn, bias,** slant, cast, warp, twist; idiosyncrasy, eccentricity, individualism; diathesis, aptitude; strain, streak
4 **mood, humor, feeling, feelings, temper, frame of mind, state of mind, mental state, mindset, morale,** cue *or* frame <old>, tone, note, **vein; mind,** heart, spirit *or* **spirits**
5 <pervading attitudes> **climate,** mental *or* intellectual climate, spiritual climate, moral climate, mores, norms, climate of opinion, **ethos,** ideology, *Weltanschauung* <Ger>, world view; *Zeitgeist* <Ger>, spirit of the time *or* the age
VERBS 6 **take the attitude,** feel about it, look at it, **view,** look at in the light of; **be disposed to,** tend *or* incline toward, prefer, lean toward, be bent on
ADJS 7 **attitudinal; temperamental, dispositional,** inclinational, constitutional; emotional, affective; mental, intellectual, ideational, ideological; spiritual; characteristic 865.13; innate
8 **disposed,** dispositioned, **predisposed, prone, inclined, given,** bent, bent on, apt, likely, **minded, in the mood** *or* **humor**
ADVS 9 **attitudinally; temperamentally, dispositionally,** constitutionally; emotionally; mentally, intellectually, ideationally, ideologically; morally, spiritually; **by temperament** *or* **disposition,** by virtue of mind-set, by the logic of character *or* temperament; from one's standpoint *or* viewpoint *or* angle, from where one stands *or* sits, from where one is; within the frame of reference *or* framework *or* reference system *or* universe of discourse

979 BROAD-MINDEDNESS

NOUNS 1 **broad-mindedness,** wide-mindedness, large-mindedness; **breadth,** broadness, broad gauge, latitude; **unbigotedness,** unhideboundness, unprovincialism, noninsularity, unparochialism, cosmopolitanism; ecumenicity, ecumenicism, ecumenicalism, ecumenism; broad mind, spacious mind
2 **liberalness, liberality,** catholicity, **liberalmindedness;** liberalism, libertarianism,

latitudinarianism; freethinking, free
thought

3 open-mindedness, openness, receptiveness,
receptivity; persuadableness, persuadability,
persuasibility; open mind

4 tolerance, toleration; **indulgence,** lenience or
leniency 427, condonation, lenity; **forbearance,
patience,** long-suffering; easiness, **permissiveness;
charitableness,** charity, **generousness,
magnanimity** 652.2; **compassion** 427.1, sympathy;
sensitivity

5 unprejudicedness, unbiasedness; impartiality
649.3, evenhandedness, equitability, **justice** 649,
fairness 649.2, justness, **objectivity, detachment,
dispassionateness, disinterestedness,**
impersonality; indifference, neutrality;
unopinionatedness

6 liberal, liberalist; libertarian; freethinker,
latitudinarian, ecumenist, ecumenicist; big
person, broad-gauge person; bleeding heart,
bleeding-heart liberal

VERBS **7 keep an open mind,** be big <nf>, judge not,
not write off, suspend judgment, listen to reason,
open one's mind to, see both sides, judge on the
merits; **live and let live;** lean over backwards,
tolerate 134.5; **accept,** be easy with, **view with
indulgence, condone,** brook, abide with, be
content with; **live with** <nf>; shut one's eyes to,
look the other way, wink at, blink at, **overlook,
disregard, ignore**

ADJS **8 broad-minded,** wide-minded, large-minded,
broad, wide, wide-ranging, broad-gauged,
catholic, spacious of mind; **unbigoted,**
unfanatical, **unhidebound,** unprovincial,
cosmopolitan, noninsular, unparochial;
ecumenistic, ecumenical

9 liberal, liberal-minded, liberalistic;
libertarian; freethinking, latitudinarian;
bleeding-heart

10 open-minded, open, receptive, rational,
admissive; **persuadable,** persuasible;
unopinionated, **unopinioned,** unwedded to an
opinion; **unpositive, undogmatic;** uninfatuated,
unbesotted, unfanatical

11 tolerant 134.9, tolerating; **indulgent, lenient** 427.7,
condoning, forbearing, forbearant <old>, **patient,**
**long-suffering; charitable, generous,
magnanimous** 652.6; compassionate 427.7,
sympathetic, sensitive

**12 unprejudiced, unbiased, unprepossessed,
unjaundiced; impartial,** evenhanded, **fair, just**
649.7, equitable, **objective, dispassionate,
impersonal, detached, disinterested;** indifferent,
neutral; **unswayed, uninfluenced,** undazzled;
non-sexist, inclusive

13 liberalizing, liberating, broadening,
enlightening

980 NARROW-MINDEDNESS

NOUNS **1 narrow-mindedness,** narrowness,
illiberality, uncatholicity; little-mindedness,
**small-mindedness, smallness, littleness,
meanness, pettiness;** close-mindedness; **bigotry,**
bigotedness, fanaticism, *odium theologicum* <L>;
insularity, insularism, provincialism,
parochialism; **hideboundness,** straitlacedness,
stuffiness <nf>; authoritarianism;
shortsightedness, nearsightedness, purblindness;
blind side, blind spot, tunnel vision, blinders;
closed mind, mean mind, petty mind, shut mind;
narrow views *or* sympathies, cramped ideas; *parti
pris* <Fr>, an ax to grind

2 intolerance, intoleration; **uncharitableness,**
ungenerousness; unforbearance; noncompassion,
insensitivity

3 prejudice, prejudgment, forejudgment,
predilection, prepossession, preconception; **bias,**
bent, leaning, inclination, twist; **jaundice,**
jaundiced eye; **partiality,** partialism, partisanship,
favoritism, onesidedness, undispassionateness,
undetachment

4 discrimination, social discrimination, minority
prejudice; xenophobia, know-nothingism;
chauvinism, ultranationalism, superpatriotism;
fascism; **class consciousness,** class prejudice, class
distinction, class hatred, class war; anti-Semitism;
redbaiting <nf>; **racism,** racialism, race hatred,
race prejudice, race snobbery, racial
discrimination; white *or* black supremacy, white *or*
black power; **color line,** color bar; **social barrier,**
Jim Crow, Jim Crow law; **segregation,** apartheid;
sex discrimination, sexism, manism, masculism,
male chauvinism, feminism, womanism; ageism,
age discrimination; class prejudice, class hatred,
social prejudice; glass ceiling

5 bigot, intolerant, illiberal, little person, Archie
Bunker <nf>; **racist,** racialist, racial supremacist,
white *or* black supremacist, pig <nf>; **chauvinist,**
ultranationalist, jingo, superpatriot; **sexist,** male
chauvinist, male chauvinist pig *or* MCP <nf>,
manist, masculist, feminist, female chauvinist,
womanist, **dogmatist, doctrinaire** 970.7; fanatic

VERBS **6 close one's mind,** shut the eyes of one's
mind, take narrow views, put on blinders, blind
oneself, have a blind side *or* spot, have tunnel
vision, constrict one's views; not see beyond one's
nose *or* an inch beyond one's nose; **view with a
jaundiced eye,** see but one side of the question,
look only at one side of the shield

7 prejudge, forejudge, judge beforehand, precondemn, prejudicate <old>, take one's opinions ready-made, accede to prejudice

8 discriminate against, draw the line, draw the color line; bait, **bash;** red-bait

9 prejudice, prejudice against, prejudice the issue, prepossess, **jaundice, influence, sway, bias,** bias one's judgment; warp, twist, bend, distort

ADJS **10 narrow-minded,** narrow, narrow-gauged, closed, closed-minded, cramped, constricted, po-faced <Brit>, *borné* <Fr>, little-minded, small-minded, mean-minded, petty-minded, narrow-hearted, narrow-souled, narrow-spirited, mean-spirited, small-souled; **small, little, mean, petty;** uncharitable, ungenerous; bigot, **bigoted,** fanatical; **illiberal,** unliberal, uncatholic; provincial, insular, parochial; **hidebound,** creedbound, **straitlaced,** stuffy <nf>; authoritarian; **shortsighted,** nearsighted, purblind; deaf, deaf-minded, deaf to reason

11 intolerant, untolerating; **unindulgent,** uncondoning, unforbearing

12 discriminatory; prejudiced, prepossessed, **biased, jaundiced,** colored; **partial,** one-sided, partisan; influenced, swayed, warped, twisted; interested, nonobjective, **undetached,** undispassionate; xenophobic, know-nothing; **chauvinistic,** ultranationalist, superpatriotic; **racist,** racialist, anti-Negro, antiblack, antiwhite; anti-Semitic; sexist; dogmatic, doctrinaire, **opinionated** 970.22

981 CURIOSITY

NOUNS **1 curiosity,** curiousness, **inquisitiveness; interest,** interestedness, lively interest; thirst *or* desire *or* lust *or* itch for knowledge, mental acquisitiveness, inquiring *or* curious mind; **attention** 983; **alertness, watchfulness,** vigilance; **nosiness** *and* snoopiness <nf>, prying, snooping <nf>; eavesdropping; officiousness, meddlesomeness 214.2; **morbid curiosity, ghoulishness;** voyeurism, scopophilia, prurience, prurient interest; rubbernecking <nf>

2 inquisitive person, quidnunc; **inquirer,** questioner, querier, querist, inquisitor, inquisitress; detective; **busybody,** gossip, *yenta* <Yiddish>, **pry,** Paul Pry, **snoop,** snooper, nosy Parker <nf>; eavesdropper; sightseer; rubbernecker *or* rubberneck <nf>; watcher, Peeping Tom, voyeur, scopophiliac; Lot's wife; explorer

VERBS **3 be curious, want to know, take an interest in,** take a lively interest, burn with curiosity; be alert, alert oneself, watch, be watchful, be vigilant; prick up one's ears, keep one's ear to the ground; eavesdrop; interrogate, quiz, question, inquire,

query; keep one's eyes open, keep one's eye on, stare, gape, peer, gawk, rubber *and* rubberneck <nf>; seek, dig up, dig around for, nose out, nose around for; investigate

4 pry, snoop, peep, peek, spy, nose, nose into, have a long *or* big nose, poke *or* stick one's nose in; meddle 214.7

ADJS **5 curious, inquisitive,** inquisitorial, inquiring, interested, quizzical; **alert,** keen, tuned in <nf>, **attentive** 983.15; burning with curiosity, eaten up *or* consumed with curiosity, curious as a cat; agape, agog, all agog, openmouthed, open-eyed; gossipy; overcurious, supercurious; morbidly curious, **morbid, ghoulish; prurient,** itchy, voyeuristic, scopophiliac; rubbernecking <nf>

6 prying, snooping, **nosy** *and* **snoopy** <nf>; meddlesome 214.9

982 INCURIOSITY

NOUNS **1 incuriosity,** incuriousness, **uninquisitiveness;** boredom; **inattention** 984; **uninterestedness,** disinterest, disinterestedness, **unconcern,** uninvolvement, detachment, **indifference** 102, indifferentness, indifferentism, uncaring, **apathy,** passivity, passiveness, impassivity, impassiveness, listlessness, stolidity, **lack of interest;** carelessness, heedlessness, regardlessness, insouciance, unmindfulness; unperturbability; aloofness, detachment, withdrawal, reclusiveness; intellectual inertia; catatonia, autism; gullibility, credulity, blind faith; objectivity

VERBS **2 take no interest in, not care;** mind one's own business, pursue the even tenor of one's way, glance neither to the right nor to the left, keep one's nose out, keep an open mind; be indifferent, not care less <nf>, lack emotion; disregard; take it *or* leave it; take on trust; live and let live

ADJS **3 incurious, uninquisitive,** uninquiring; bored; **inattentive** 984.6; **uninterested,** unconcerned, disinterested, uninvolved, nonaligned, detached, **indifferent,** impersonal, **apathetic,** passive, impassive, stolid, phlegmatic, imperturbable, listless; careless, heedless, regardless, insouciant, mindless, unmindful; aloof, detached, distant, withdrawn, reclusive, sequestered, eremitic; catatonic, autistic; apathetic, not bothered; lackadaisical; unbiased, objective

983 ATTENTION

NOUNS **1 attention, attentiveness,** mindfulness, regardfulness, heedfulness; **attention span; heed,** ear; consideration, thought, mind; **awareness, consciousness, alertness** 339.5; **observation,** observance, advertence, advertency, **note, notice,** remark, put one's finger on, **regard,** respect; **intentness,** intentiveness, concentration; diligence, assiduity, assiduousness, earnestness; **care** 339.1; **curiosity** 981

2 interest, concern, concernment; **curiosity** 981; **enthusiasm,** passion, ardor, zeal; cathexis; matter of interest, special interest; solicitude

3 engrossment, absorption, intentness, single-mindedness, **concentration, application,** study, studiousness, **preoccupation,** engagement, **involvement, immersion,** submersion; obsession, monomania; rapt attention, absorbed attention *or* interest; deep study, deep *or* profound thought, contemplation, meditation

4 close attention, close study, scrutiny, fixed regard, rapt *or* fascinated attention, whole *or* total *or* undivided attention; minute *or* meticulous attention, attention to detail, microscopic *or* microscopical scrutiny, finicalness, finickiness; constant *or* unrelenting attention, close observance, harping, strict attention; special consideration

VERBS **5 attend to,** look to, **see to,** advert to, be aware of; **pay attention to,** pay regard to, give mind to, pay mind to <nf>, not forget, spare a thought for, **give heed to;** bethink, bethink oneself; have a look at; **turn to,** give thought to, trouble one's head about; give one's mind to, direct one's attention to, turn *or* bend *or* set the mind *or* attention to; **devote oneself to,** devote the mind *or* thoughts to, fix *or* rivet *or* focus the mind *or* thoughts on, set one's thoughts on, apply the mind *or* attention to, apply oneself to, **occupy oneself with, concern oneself with,** give oneself up to, be absorbed *or* engrossed in, be into <nf>; sink one's teeth, take an interest in, take hold of; **have a lot on one's mind** *or* **plate;** be preoccupied with; **lose oneself in; hang on one's words,** hang on the lips; **drink in,** drink in with rapt attention; be solicitous, suck up to <nf>, brown-nose <nf>

6 heed, attend, be heedful, tend, **mind, watch, observe, regard,** look, see, view, mark, remark, animadvert <old>, **note, notice,** take note *or* notice, get a load of <nf>

7 hearken to, hark, **listen, hear,** give ear to, lend an ear to, incline *or* bend an ear to, prick up the ears, strain one's ears, **keep one's ears open,** unstopper one's ears, have *or* keep an ear to the ground, listen with both ears, **be all ears**

8 pay attention *or* **heed, take heed,** give heed, **look out, watch out** <nf>, **take care** 339.7; look lively *or* alive, **look sharp,** stay *or* be alert, sit up and take notice; be on the ball *or* keep one's eye on the ball *or* not miss a trick *or* not overlook a bet <nf>, keep

a weather eye out *or* on; miss nothing; get after, seize on, keep one's eyes open 339.8; attend to business, mind one's business; pay close *or* strict attention, strain one's attention, not relax one's concern, give one's undivided attention, give special attention to, dance attendance on; keep in the center of one's attention, keep uppermost in one's thought; **concentrate on,** focus *or* fix on; **study,** scrutinize, survey; be obsessed with; cathect

9 take cognizance of, take note *or* **notice of,** take heed of, **take account of, take into consideration** *or* **account, bear in mind,** keep *or* hold in mind, reckon with, keep in sight *or* view, not lose sight of, have in one's eye, have an eye to, have regard for

10 call attention to, direct attention to, **bring under** *or* **to one's notice,** hold up to notice, bring to attention, **mention,** mention in passing, touch on; **single out,** pick out, lift up, focus on, call *or* bring to notice, direct to the attention, **feature,** highlight, brightline; **direct to,** address to; **mention,** specify, mention in passing, touch on, cite, **refer to,** allude to; **alert one,** call to one's attention, put one wise *and* put one on <nf>; **point out, point to,** point at, put *or* lay one's finger on; **excite** *or* **stimulate attention,** drum up attention

11 meet with attention, fall under one's notice; **catch the attention,** strike one, impress one, draw *or* hold *or* focus the attention, take *or* catch *or* meet *or* strike the eye, get *or* catch one's ear, attract notice *or* attention, arrest *or* engage attention, fix *or* rivet one's attention, arrest the thoughts, awaken the mind *or* thoughts, **excite notice,** arouse notice, arrest one's notice, invite *or* solicit attention, claim *or* demand attention, act as a magnet

12 interest, concern, involve in *or* with, affect the interest, give pause; **pique, titillate,** tantalize, tickle, tickle one's fancy, **attract,** invite, **fascinate, provoke, stimulate, arouse, excite,** pique one's interest, excite interest, excite *or* whet one's interest, arouse one's passion *or* enthusiasm, turn one on <nf>

13 engross, absorb, immerse, **occupy, preoccupy, engage,** involve, monopolize, exercise, take up; **obsess; grip, hold, arrest, hold the interest, fascinate, enthrall,** spellbind, **hold spellbound,** grab <nf>, charm, enchant, mesmerize, hypnotize, catch; absorb the attention, claim one's thoughts, engross the mind *or* thoughts, engage the attention, involve the interest, occupy the attention, monopolize one's attention, engage the mind *or* thoughts

14 come to attention, stand at attention

ADJS **15 attentive, heedful, mindful, regardful, advertent;** intent, intentive, on top of <nf>, diligent, assiduous, intense, earnest, concentrated; **careful** 339.10, on guard, vigilant; **observing,** observant; watchful, aware, conscious, alert 339.14; **curious** 981.5; agog, openmouthed; open-eared, open-eyed, **all eyes, all ears,** all eyes and ears; on the job <nf>, on the ball *and* Johnny-on-the-spot <nf>; **meticulous** 339.12, sedulous, nice, finical, finicky, finicking, niggling

16 **interested,** concerned; **alert to, sensitive to, on the watch; curious** 981.5; tantalized, piqued, titillated, tickled, **attracted,** fascinated, excited, turned-on <nf>; keen on *or* about, enthusiastic, passionate; fixating, cathectic

17 **engrossed, absorbed,** totally absorbed, single-minded, **occupied, preoccupied, engaged,** devoted, devoted to, intent, intent on, monopolized, obsessed, monomaniacal, swept up, taken up with, **involved, caught up in,** wrapped in, **wrapped up in,** engrossed in, **absorbed in** *or* with *or* by, **lost in, immersed in,** submerged in, buried in; over head and ears in, head over heels in <nf>, up to one's elbows in, up to one's ears in; contemplating, contemplative, studying, studious, meditative, meditating; solicitous, indulgent

18 **gripped, held, fascinated, enthralled, rapt, spellbound,** charmed, enchanted, mesmerized, **hypnotized,** fixed, caught, riveted, **arrested,** switched on <nf>

19 **interesting, stimulating, provocative,** provoking, thought-provoking, thought-challenging, thought-inspiring; **titillating,** tickling, **tantalizing, inviting, exciting; piquant,** lively, racy, juicy, succulent, spicy, rich; readable

20 **engrossing, absorbing,** consuming, **gripping,** riveting, holding, **arresting,** engaging, attractive, **fascinating, enthralling, spellbinding,** enchanting, magnetic, hypnotic, mesmerizing, mesmeric; obsessive, obsessing

ADVS 21 **attentively,** with attention; **heedfully,** mindfully, regardfully, advertently; observingly, observantly; **interestedly,** with interest; **raptly,** with rapt attention; engrossedly, absorbedly, preoccupiedly; devotedly, **intently,** without distraction, **with undivided attention**

INTERJS 22 **attention!, look!,** see!, look you!, look here!, looky! <nf>, witness!; tah-dah! <nf>, presto!, hey presto! <Brit>, voilà!; lo!, behold!, lo and behold!; **hark!,** listen!, listen up! <nf>, hark ye!, hear ye!, oyez!; *nota bene* <L, note well>, NB; mark my words

23 **hey!, hail!, ahoy!, hello!,** hollo!, hallo!, halloo!, halloa!, ho!, heigh!, hi!, hist!; hello there!, ahoy there!, yo!

984 INATTENTION

NOUNS 1 **inattention,** inattentiveness, **heedlessness, unheedfulness, unmindfulness, thoughtlessness,** inconsideration; **incuriosity** 982, **indifference** 102; inadvertence *or* inadvertency; unintentness, unintentiveness; disregard, disregardfulness, regardlessness, apathy; **flightiness** 985.5, giddiness 985.4, lightmindedness, dizziness *and* ditziness <nf>, scattiness <Brit nf>; levity, frivolousness, flippancy; shallowness, superficiality; **inobservance,** unobservance, nonobservance; **unalertness,** unwariness, unwatchfulness; **obliviousness,** unconsciousness, unawareness; **carelessness,** negligence 340.1, oversight; distraction, **absentmindedness, woolgathering, daydreaming** 985.2, head in the clouds; attention deficit disorder *or* ADD, attention deficit hyperactivity disorder *or* ADHD

VERBS 2 **be inattentive, pay no attention,** pay no mind <nf>, not attend, not notice, **take no note** *or* **notice of,** take no thought *or* account of, miss, not heed, give no heed, pay no regard to, not listen, hear nothing, not hear a word; **disregard, overlook, ignore,** pass over *or* by, have no time for, let pass *or* get by *or* get past; think little of, think nothing of, **slight,** make light of; **close** *or* **shut one's eyes to,** see nothing, be blind to, turn a blind eye, **look the other way, blink at, wink at,** connive at; stick *or* bury *or* hide one's head in the sand; **turn a deaf ear to,** stop one's ears, let come in one ear and go out the other, tune out <nf>; let well enough alone; not trouble oneself with, not trouble one's head with *or* about; **be unwary,** be off one's guard, be caught out

3 **wander, stray,** divagate, wander from the subject, ramble; have no attention span, have a short attention span, let one's attention wander, allow one's mind to wander, get off the track <nf>; **fall asleep at the switch** <nf>, woolgather, **daydream** 985.9

4 **dismiss,** dismiss *or* drive from one's thoughts; **put out of mind,** put out of one's head *or* thoughts, wean *or* force one's thoughts from, **think no more of, forget, forget it,** forget about it, **let it go** <nf>, let slip, not give it another *or* a second thought, **drop the subject,** give it no more thought, obliviate; turn one's back upon, turn away from, turn one's attention from, walk away, abandon, leave out in the cold <nf>; put *or* set *or* lay aside, push *or* thrust aside *or* to one side, wave aside; put on the back burner *or* on hold <nf>; **turn up one's nose at,** sneeze at; **shrug off, brush off** *or* **aside** *or* **away,** blow off *and* laugh off *or* away <nf>, dismiss with a laugh; slight 157.6, kiss off *and* slap *or* smack down <nf>

5 escape notice *or* **attention,** escape one, get by, be missed, pass one by, not enter one's head, never occur to one, fall on deaf ears, not register, go over one's head

ADJS **6 inattentive, unmindful,** inadvertent, thoughtless, **incurious** 982.3, **indifferent** 102.6; **heedless,** unheeding, unheedful, regardless, *distrait* <Fr>, **disregardful,** disregardant; **unobserving,** inobservant, unobservant, unnoticing, unnoting, unremarking, unmarking; **distracted** 985.10; **careless, negligent** 340.10; **scatterbrained, giddy** 985.16, ditzy <nf>, scatty <Brit nf>, flighty; absent-minded, out to lunch <nf>

7 oblivious, unconscious, insensible, dead to the world, out of it *and* not with it <nf>; blind, deaf; **preoccupied** 985.11; in a world of one's own

8 unalert, unwary, unwatchful, unvigilant, uncautious, incautious; **unprepared,** unready; unguarded, **off one's guard,** off-guard; **asleep,** sleeping, nodding, napping; **asleep at the switch** *and* asleep on the job *and* **not on the job** *and* goofing off *and* looking out the window <nf>; daydreaming, woolgathering

985 DISTRACTION, CONFUSION

NOUNS **1 distraction,** distractedness, **diversion,** separation *or* withdrawal of attention, divided attention, competing stimuli; too much on one's mind *or* on one's plate, cognitive dissonance, sensory overload; **inattention** 984

2 abstractedness, abstraction, preoccupation, absorption, engrossment, depth of thought, fit of abstraction; **absentmindedness, absence of mind; bemusement,** musing, musefulness <old>; **woolgathering,** mooning <nf>, moonraking <old>, stargazing, **dreaming, daydreaming,** fantasying, pipe-dreaming <nf>, castle-building; **brown study,** study, reverie, muse, dreamy abstraction, quiet *or* muted ecstasy, trance; dream, **daydream,** fantasy, pipe dream <nf>; daydreamer, Walter Mitty

3 confusion, fluster, flummox <nf>, **flutter,** flurry, ruffle; disorientation, **muddle, muddlement,** fuddle *and* fuddlement <nf>, befuddlement, muddleheadedness, daze, maze <nf>; unsettlement, disorganization, **disorder,** chaos, **mess** *and* mix-up *and* snafu <nf>, balls-up *and* shemozzle <Brit nf>, shuffle, jumble, **discomfiture, discomposure, disconcertion,** discombobulation <nf>, **bewilderment, embarrassment, disturbance,** perturbation, **upset,** frenzy, pother, bother, botheration *and* stew <nf>, pucker <old>; tizzy *and* swivet *and* sweat <nf>; haze, fog, mist, cloud; maze; **perplexity** 971.3

4 dizziness, vertigo, vertiginousness, spinning head, swimming, swimming of the head, **giddiness,** wooziness <nf>, **lightheadedness;** tiddliness <Brit nf>, **drunkenness** 88.1,3

5 flightiness, giddiness, volatility, mercuriality; **thoughtlessness,** witlessness, brainlessness, empty-headedness, frivolity, frivolousness, dizziness *and* ditziness <nf>, scattiness <Brit nf>, foolishness 923; **scatterbrain, flibbertigibbet** 924.7

VERBS **6 distract, divert,** detract, distract the attention, divert *or* detract attention, divert the mind *or* thoughts, draw off the attention, call away, take the mind off of, relieve the mind of, cause the mind to stray *or* wander, put off the track, derail, throw off the scent, lead the mind astray, beguile; throw off one's guard, catch off balance, put off one's stride, trip up

7 confuse, throw into confusion *or* chaos, entangle, **mix up, fluster;** flummox <nf>, **flutter,** put into a flutter, **flurry, rattle, ruffle,** moider <Brit nf>; **muddle,** fuddle <nf>, **befuddle, addle,** addle the wits, **daze, maze, dazzle,** bedazzle; **upset, unsettle,** raise hell, disorganize; throw into a tizzy *or* swivet; **disconcert, discomfit, discompose,** discombobulate <nf>, disorient, disorientate, **bewilder, embarrass, put out, disturb, perturb, bother,** pother, bug <nf>; fog, mist, cloud, becloud; **perplex** 971.13

8 dizzy, make one's head swim, cause vertigo, send one spinning, whirl the mind, swirl the senses, make one's head reel *or* whirl *or* spin *or* revolve, go to one's head; **intoxicate** 88.22

9 muse, moon <nf>, **dream, daydream,** pipe-dream <nf>, fantasy; abstract oneself, be lost in thought, let one's attention wander, let one's mind run on other things, dream of *or* muse on other things; **wander, stray, ramble,** divagate, let one's thoughts *or* mind wander, give oneself up to reverie, **woolgather, go woolgathering,** let one's wits go bird's nesting, **be in a brown study,** be absent, be somewhere else, stargaze, be out of it *and* be not with it <nf>

ADJS **10 distracted, distraught,** *distrait* <Fr>; **wandering, rambling; wild, frantic, beside oneself**

11 abstracted, bemused, museful <old>, **musing, preoccupied, absorbed, engrossed,** taken up; **absentminded, absent,** faraway, elsewhere, somewhere else, not there; pensive, meditative; lost, **lost in thought,** wrapped in thought; rapt, transported, ecstatic; dead to the world, **unconscious, oblivious; dreaming, dreamy,** drowsing, dozing, nodding, half-awake, betwixt sleep and waking, napping; **daydreaming,** daydreamy, pipe-dreaming <nf>; **woolgathering,** mooning *and* moony <nf>, moonraking <old>, castle-building, in the clouds, off in the clouds, stargazing, in a reverie

12 **confused, mixed-up,** crazy mixed-up <nf>; **flustered,** fluttered, **ruffled, rattled,** fussed <nf>; **upset, unsettled,** off-balance, off one's stride; **disorganized, disordered,** disoriented, disorientated, chaotic, jumbled, in a jumble, shuffled; shaken, shook <nf>, **disconcerted, discomposed,** discombobulated <nf>, **embarrassed, put-out, disturbed, perturbed,** bothered, all hot and bothered <nf>; in a stew *or* botheration <nf>; in a pucker <old>; in a tizzy *or* swivet *or* sweat <nf>, in a pother; **perplexed**

13 **muddled,** in a muddle; fuddled <nf>, **befuddled;** muddleheaded, fuddlebrained <nf>; puzzleheaded, puzzlepated; **addled,** addleheaded, addlepated, addlebrained; adrift, at sea, foggy, fogged, in a fog, hazy, muzzy <nf>, misted, misty, cloudy, beclouded

14 **dazed,** mazed, **dazzled,** bedazzled, in a daze; **silly,** knocked silly, cockeyed <nf>; **groggy** <nf>, **dopey** <nf>, woozy <nf>; **punch-drunk** *and* punchy *and* **slap-happy** <nf>

15 **dizzy, giddy,** vertiginous, spinning, swimming, turned around, going around in circles; lightheaded, tiddly <Brit nf>, **drunk, drunken** 88.31

16 scatterbrained, shatterbrained *or* shatterpated <old>, rattlebrained, rattleheaded, rattlepated, scramblebrained, harebrain, harebrained, **giddy, dizzy** *and* ditzy *and* gaga <nf>, scatty <Brit nf>, giddy-brained, giddy-headed, giddy-pated, giddy-witted, giddy as a goose, fluttery, frivolous, featherbrained, featherheaded; **thoughtless, witless, brainless, empty-headed** 922.19

17 **flighty,** volatile, mercurial

986 IMAGINATION

NOUNS 1 **imagination,** imagining, imaginativeness, **fancy, fantasy,** conceit <old>; mind's eye; flight of fancy, fumes of fancy; fantasticism

2 **creative thought,** conception; lateral thinking, association of ideas; productive *or* constructive *or* creative imagination, creative power *or* ability, esemplastic imagination *or* power, shaping imagination, poetic imagination, artistic imagination, blue-sky thinking; mythopoeia, *mythopoesis* <Gk>; mythification, mythicization; inspiration, stimulus, muse; Muses: Calliope <epic poetry>, Clio <history>, Erato <lyric and love poetry>, Euterpe <music>, Melpomene <tragedy>, Polyhymnia <sacred song>, Terpsichore <dancing and choral song>, Thalia <comedy>, Urania <astronomy>; genius 920.8; afflatus, divine afflatus; frenzy, ecstasy

3 **invention, inventiveness, originality, creativity, fabrication,** creativeness, **ingenuity;** productivity, prolificacy, **fertility,** fecundity; rich *or* teeming imagination, fertile *or* pregnant imagination, seminal *or* germinal imagination, fertile mind; imagineering; **fiction,** fictionalization

4 **lively imagination,** active fancy, **vivid imagination,** colorful *or* highly colored *or* lurid imagination, warm *or* ardent imagination, fiery *or* heated imagination, excited imagination, bold *or* daring *or* wild *or* fervent imagination; verve, vivacity of imagination

5 **figment of the imagination,** creature of the imagination, creation *or* coinage of the brain, fiction of the mind, maggot <old>, whim, whimsy, figment, imagination, invention; caprice, vagary; brainchild; **imagining,** fancy, idle fancy, vapor, imagery; **fantasy, make-believe;** fabrication; phantom, vision, apparition, insubstantial image, eidolon, **phantasm** 976.4; **fiction,** myth, romance; wildest dreams, stretch of the imagination; **chimera, bubble, illusion** 976; hallucination, delirium, sick fancy; trip *or* drug trip <nf>

6 **visualization, envisioning,** envisaging, picturing, objectification, imaging, calling to *or* before the mind's eye, figuring *or* portraying *or* representing in the mind; depicting *or* delineating in the imagination; conceptualization; **picture, vision, image,** mental image, mental picture, visual image, visualization, vivid *or* lifelike image, eidetic image, concept, **conception,** mental representation *or* presentation, *Vorstellung* <Ger>; image-building, **imagery,** word-painting; poetic image, poetic imagery; imagery study; imagism, imagistic poetry

7 **idealism, idealization; ideal,** ideality; rose-colored glasses; visionariness, **utopianism;** flight of fancy, play of fancy, imaginative exercise; **romanticism,** romanticizing, romance; **quixotism,** quixotry; dreamery; **impracticality,** unpracticalness, **unrealism,** unreality; **wishful thinking,** wish fulfillment, wish-fulfillment fantasy, dream come true; autistic thinking, dereistic thinking, autism, dereism, autistic distortion

8 **dreaminess,** dreamfulness, musefulness, pensiveness; dreamlikeness; **dreaming, musing; daydreaming,** pipe-dreaming <nf>, dreamery, fantasying, castlebuilding

9 **dream; reverie, daydream, pipe dream** <nf>, wishful thinking; **brown study** 985.2; **vision; nightmare,** incubus, bad dream

10 **air castle, castle in the air,** castle in the sky *or* skies, castle in Spain; Xanadu *and* pleasure dome of Kubla Khan, pie in the sky, end of the rainbow

11 **utopia** *or* Utopia <Sir Thomas More>, **paradise, heaven** 681, **heaven on earth;** millennium, kingdom come; dreamland, dream world, lotus land, land of dreams, land of enchantment, land of heart's desire, wonderland, cloudland, fairyland, land of faerie, faerie; Eden, Garden of Eden; the Promised Land, land of promise, land of plenty, land of milk and honey, Canaan, Goshen; Shangri-la, Atlantis, Arcadia, Agapemone, Camelot, Avalon, Happy Valley, land of Prester John, El Dorado, Emerald City, Treasure Island, Wonderland, Seven Cities of Cibola, Quivira; Laputa; Cockaigne, Big Rock-Candy Mountain, Fiddler's Green, never-never land, Neverland, Cloudcuckooland *or* Nephelococcygia, Erewhon, Land of Youth, Fountain of Youth, Tir-na-n'Og <Ir>; dystopia *or* kakotopia; Pandemonium; Middle Earth

12 **imaginer, fancier,** fantast; fantasist; mythmaker, mythopoet; mythifier, mythicizer; **inventor; creative artist,** composer, poet, creative writer; imagineer

13 **visionary, idealist;** prophet, **seer; dreamer, daydreamer,** dreamer of dreams, castle-builder, lotus-eater, **wishful thinker; romantic,** romanticist, romancer; Quixote, Don Quixote; utopian, utopianist, utopianizer; escapist, ostrich; enthusiast, rhapsodist

VERBS 14 **imagine, fancy, conceive,** conceit <old>, conceptualize, ideate, figure to oneself; **invent, create, originate, make,** think up, dream up, shape, mold, coin, hatch, concoct, fabricate, produce; **suppose** 951.10; **fantasize;** fictionalize; use one's imagination; give free rein to the imagination, let one's imagination riot *or* run riot *or* run wild, allow one's imagination to run away with one; experience imaginatively *or* vicariously

15 **visualize,** vision, **envision, envisage, picture, image,** objectify; picture in one's mind, picture to oneself, **view with the mind's eye,** contemplate in the imagination, form a mental picture of, represent, **see,** just see, have a picture of; call up, summon up, conjure up, **call to mind,** realize; have an inspiration

16 **idealize,** utopianize, quixotize, rhapsodize; **romanticize,** romance; paint pretty pictures of, paint in bright colors; see through rose-colored glasses; **build castles in the air** *or* **Spain;** live in a dream world

17 **dream;** dream of, dream on; **daydream,** pipe-dream <nf>, get *or* have stars in one's eyes, have one's head in the clouds, indulge in wish fulfillment; fantasy, conjure up a vision; blow one's mind *and* go on a trip *and* trip *and* freak out <nf>

ADJS 18 **imaginative,** conceptual, conceptive, ideational, ideative, notional; perceptive; **inventive, original,** innovative, originative, esemplastic, shaping, **creative, ingenious, resourceful; productive, fertile,** fecund, prolific, seminal, germinal, teeming, pregnant; **inspired,** visioned

19 **imaginary,** imaginational, notional; **imagined, fancied; unreal,** unrealistic, airy-fairy <Brit>, unactual, nonexistent, never-never; visional, supposititious, **all in the mind; illusory;** not of this world

20 **fanciful, notional,** notiony <nf>, whimsical, maggoty <Brit>; airy-fairy <nf>; brain-born; fancy-bred, fancy-born, fancy-built, fancy-framed, fancy-woven, fancy-wrought; dream-born, dream-built, dream-created; **fantastic, fantastical,** fantasque, extravagant, preposterous, outlandish, wild, baroque, rococo, florid; Alice-in-Wonderland, bizarre, grotesque, Gothic

21 **fictitious, make-believe, figmental,** fictional, fictive, fabricated, fictionalized; nonhistorical, nonfactual, nonactual, nonrealistic; **fabulous, mythic, mythical,** mythological, legendary; mythified, mythicized

22 **chimeric, chimerical, aerial, ethereal,** phantasmal; vaporous, vapory; gossamer; air-built, cloud-built, cloud-born, cloud-woven

23 **ideal, idealized;** utopian, Arcadian, Edenic, paradisal; pie in the sky <nf>; heavenly, celestial; millennial

24 **visionary, idealistic, quixotic; romantic, romanticized,** romancing, romanticizing; poetic *or* poetical; storybook; **impractical, unpractical, unrealistic;** wish-fulfilling, autistic, dereistic; starry-eyed, dewy-eyed; in the clouds, with one's head in the clouds; airy, **otherworldly,** transmundane, transcendental

25 **dreamy, dreamful; dreamy-eyed,** dreamy-minded, dreamy-souled; dreamlike; day-dreamy, **dreaming, daydreaming,** pipe-dreaming <nf>, castle-building; **entranced,** tranced, in a trance, dream-stricken, enchanted, spellbound, spelled, charmed

26 **imaginable, fanciable, conceivable, thinkable,** cogitable; **supposable** 951.15

987 UNIMAGINATIVENESS

NOUNS 1 **unimaginativeness,** unfancifulness; **prosaicness,** prosiness, prosaism, prosaicism, unpoeticalness; **staidness, stuffiness** <nf>; stolidity; **dullness, dryness;** aridness, aridity, barrenness, infertility, infecundity; **unoriginality,** uncreativeness, uninventiveness, dearth of ideas

2 <practical attitude> **realism,** realisticness, **practicalness, practicality, practical-mindedness,**

sober-mindedness, sobersidedness,
hardheadedness, matter-of-factness; down-to-earthness, earthiness, worldliness, secularism; real world, the here and now; nuts and bolts, no nonsense, no frills; **pragmatism,** pragmaticism, positivism, scientism; unidealism, unromanticalness, unsentimentality; sensibleness, saneness, reasonableness, rationality; freedom from illusion, lack of sentimentality; lack of feeling 94

3 **realist,** pragmatist, positivist, practical person, hardhead

VERBS 4 **keep both feet on the ground,** stick to the facts, call a spade a spade; **come down to earth,** come down out of the clouds, know when the honeymoon is over.

ADJS 5 **unimaginative, unfanciful;** unidealized, unromanticized; **prosaic,** prosy, prosing, unpoetic, unpoetical; **literal,** literal-minded; earthbound, mundane; **staid, stuffy** <nf>; stolid; **dull, dry;** arid, barren, infertile, infecund; **unoriginal,** uninspired; hedged, undaring, unaspiring, **uninventive** 891.5

6 **realistic,** realist, **practical;** pragmatic, pragmatical, scientific, scientistic, positivistic; **unidealistic,** unideal, **unromantic, unsentimental, practical-minded,** sober-minded, sobersided, **hardheaded,** straight-thinking, **matter-of-fact, down-to-earth, with both feet on the ground;** worldly, earthy, secular; sensible, sane, reasonable, rational, sound, sound-thinking; **reductive, simplistic**

988 SPECTER

NOUNS 1 **specter, ghost,** spectral ghost, **spook** <nf>, **phantom,** phantasm, phantasma, **wraith, shade,** shadow, fetch, **apparition,** appearance, presence, shape, form, eidolon, idolum, revenant, larva; **spirit;** sprite, shrouded spirit, disembodied spirit, departed spirit, restless *or* wandering spirit *or* soul, soul of the dead, dybbuk; oni; Masan; astral spirit, astral; unsubstantiality, immateriality, incorporeal, incorporeity, incorporeal being *or* entity; walking dead man, zombie; jinn *or* dijn, genie; duppy; vision, theophany; materialization; haunt *or* hant <nf>; banshee; poltergeist; control, guide; manes, lemures; grateful dead

2 White Lady, White Lady of Avenel, White Ladies of Normandy; Brocken specter; Wild Hunt; Flying Dutchman

3 **double,** etheric double *or* self, co-walker, *Doppelgänger* <Ger>, doubleganger, fetch, wraith

4 **eeriness, ghostliness, weirdness, uncanniness, spookiness** <nf>

5 **possession,** spirit control; obsession,

VERBS 6 **haunt,** hant <nf>, spook <nf>; **possess,** control; obsess

ADJS 7 **spectral,** specterlike; **ghostly,** ghostish, ghosty, ghostlike; **spiritual, psychic,** psychical; **phantomlike,** phantom, phantomic *or* phantomical, phantasmal, phantasmic, **wraithlike,** wraithy, shadowy; etheric, ectoplasmic, astral, ethereal 764.6; incorporeal 1053.7; **occult, supernatural** 870.15

8 **disembodied,** bodiless, immaterial 1053.7, discarnate, decarnate, decarnated

9 **weird, eerie,** eldritch, **uncanny,** unearthly, macabre; **spooky** *and* spookish *and* hairy <nf>

10 **haunted,** spooked *and* spooky <nf>, spirit-haunted, ghost-haunted, specter-haunted; **possessed,** ghost-ridden; obsessed

989 MEMORY

NOUNS 1 **memory, remembrance, recollection,** mind, *souvenir* <Fr>; memory trace, engram; mind's eye, eye of the mind, mirror of the mind, tablets of the memory; corner *or* recess of the memory, inmost recesses of the memory; Mnemosyne, mother of the Muses; short-term memory, long-term memory, anterograde memory; computer memory, information storage; group memory, collective memory, mneme, racial memory; atavism; cover *or* screen memory, affect memory; eye *or* visual memory, kinesthetic memory; skill, verbal response, emotional response

2 **retention, retentiveness,** retentivity, memory span; good memory, retentive memory *or* mind; total memory, eidetic memory *or* imagery, photographic memory, total recall; camera-eye

3 **remembering, remembrance, recollection,** recollecting, exercise of memory, **recall,** recalling; reflection, reconsideration; **retrospect,** retrospection, hindsight, looking back, harking back; flashback, **reminiscence,** review, contemplation of the past, review of things past, nostalgia; **memoir; memorization,** memorizing, **rote,** rote memory, rote learning, learning by heart, commitment to memory; déjà vu

4 **recognition, identification, reidentification,** distinguishment; realization 928.2

5 **reminder, remembrance,** remembrancer; **prompt,** prompter, tickler; prompting, cue, hint; jogger <nf>, flapper; *aide-mémoire* <Fr>, **memorandum** 549.4

6 **memento, remembrance, token, trophy, souvenir, keepsake, relic,** favor, token of remembrance; commemoration, memorial 549.12; *memento*

mori <L>; **memories, memorabilia,** memorials; history, memoirs

7 memorability, rememberability

8 mnemonics, memory training, mnemotechny, mnemotechnics, mnemonization; mnemonic, mnemonic device, *aide-mémoire* <Fr>

VERBS **9 remember, recall, recollect,** flash on *and* mind <nf>; have a good *or* ready memory, remember clearly, remember as if it were yesterday; have total recall, remember everything; reflect; **think of,** bethink oneself <old>; **call** *or* **bring to mind,** recall to mind, call up, summon up, conjure up, evoke, reevoke, revive, recapture, call back, bring back; **think back,** go back, **look back,** cast the eyes back, carry one's thoughts back, look back upon things past, use hindsight, retrospect, **see in retrospect,** go back over, hark back, retrace, reconstruct, review, hark back, turn back time; review, review in retrospect; write one's memoirs

10 reminisce, rake *or* dig up the past

11 recognize, know, tell, distinguish, make out; identify, place, have; spot *and* nail *and* peg *and* cotton on <nf>, **reidentify,** know again, recover *or* recall knowledge of, know by sight; realize 928.12

12 keep in memory, bear in mind, keep *or* hold in mind, hold *or* retain the memory of, **keep in view,** have in mind, hold *or* carry *or* retain in one's thoughts, store in the mind, **retain, keep;** tax *or* burden the memory, **treasure, cherish,** treasure up in the memory, enshrine *or* embalm in the memory, cherish the memory of; keep up the memory of, keep the memory alive, keep alive in one's thoughts; brood over, dwell on *or* upon, fan the embers, let fester in the mind, let rankle in the breast

13 be remembered, sink in, penetrate, make an impression; live *or* dwell in one's memory, be easy to recall, remain in one's memory, be green *or* fresh in one's memory, stick in the mind, remain indelibly impressed on the memory, be stamped on one's memory, **never be forgotten; haunt one's thoughts,** obsess, run in the head, be in one's thoughts, be on one's mind; be burnt into one's memory, plague one; be like King Charles's head; **rankle,** rankle in the breast, fester in the mind

14 recur, recur to the mind, return to mind, come back, resurface, reenter

15 come to mind, pop into one's head, come to me, come into one's head, flash on the mind, pass in review

16 memorize, commit to memory, con; study; **learn by heart,** get by heart, learn *or* get by rote, get word-perfect *or* letter-perfect, learn word for word, learn verbatim; know by heart *or* from memory, have by heart *or* rote, have at one's

fingers' ends *or* tips; repeat by heart *or* rote, give word for word, recite, repeat, parrot, repeat like a parrot, say one's lesson, rattle *or* reel off; be a quick study; retain

17 fix in the mind *or* memory, instill, infix, inculcate, impress, imprint, stamp, inscribe, etch, grave, engrave; **impress on the mind, get into one's head,** drive *or* hammer into one's head, get across, get into one's thick head *or* skull <nf>; **burden the mind with,** task the mind with, load *or* stuff *or* cram the mind with; inscribe *or* stamp *or* rivet in the memory, set in the tablets of memory, etch indelibly in the mind

18 refresh the memory, review, restudy, **brush up, rub up,** polish up *and* bone up <nf>, get up on; **cram** <nf>, swot up <Brit nf>

19 remind, put in mind, remember, put in remembrance, bring back, bring to recollection, refresh the memory of; **remind one of, recall,** suggest, **put one in mind of; take one back,** carry back, carry back in recollection; **jog the memory,** awaken *or* arouse the memory, flap the memory, give a hint *or* suggestion, refresh one's memory; **prompt,** prompt the mind, give the cue, hold the promptbook; nudge, pull by the sleeve, nag; brush up; make a note

20 try to recall, think hard, rack *or* ransack one's brains, **cudgel one's brains,** crack one's brains <nf>; have on the tip of one's tongue, have on the edge of one's memory *or* consciousness

ADJS **21 recollective, memoried;** mnemonic; retentive; **retrospective,** in retrospect; **reminiscent,** nostalgic, **mindful, remindful, suggestive,** redolent, evocative

22 remembered, recollected, recalled; retained, pent-up in the memory, kept in remembrance, enduring, lasting, **unforgotten;** present to the mind, lodged in one's mind, stamped on the memory; vivid, eidetic, fresh, green, alive

23 remembering, mindful, keeping *or* bearing in mind, holding in remembrance; unable to forget, haunted, plagued, obsessed, nagged, rankled

24 memorable, rememberable, recollectable; notable

25 unforgettable, never to be forgotten, never to be erased from the mind, **indelible,** indelibly impressed on the mind, fixed in the mind; haunting, persistent, recurrent, nagging, plaguing, rankling, festering; obsessing, obsessive

26 memorial, commemorative

ADVS **27 by heart,** *par cœur* <Fr>, **by rote, by** *or* **from memory,** without book; **memorably;** rememberingly

28 in memory of, to the memory of, in remembrance *or* commemoration, *in memoriam* <L>; *memoria in aeterna* <L>, in perpetual remembrance

990 FORGETFULNESS

NOUNS **1 forgetfulness,** unmindfulness, absentmindedness, **memorylessness;** short memory, short memory span, little retentivity or recall, mind or memory like a sieve; loose memory, vague or fuzzy memory, dim or hazy recollection; **lapse of memory,** decay of memory; **obliviousness, oblivion,** nirvana; obliteration; Lethe, Lethe water, waters of Lethe or oblivion; river of oblivion; insensibility; trance; nepenthe; **forgetting;** heedlessness 340.2; forgiveness 148; senior moment, memory lapse

2 loss of memory, memory loss, amnesia, failure, blackout; **memory gap,** blackout <nf>; fugue; agnosia, unrecognition, body-image agnosia, ideational agnosia, astereognosis or astereocognosy; paramnesia, retrospective falsification, false memory, misremembrance; amnesiac

3 block, blocking, **mental block,** memory obstruction; repression, suppression, defense mechanism, conversion, sublimation, symbolization

VERBS **4 be forgetful,** suffer memory loss, be absentminded, have a short memory, have a mind or memory like a sieve, have a short memory span, be unable to retain, have little recall, forget one's own name, be oblivious; misremember

5 forget, clean forget <nf>; **not remember,** disremember and disrecollect <nf>, fail to remember, forget to remember, **have no remembrance or recollection of,** be unable to recollect or recall, draw a blank <nf>; lose, lose sight of, lose one's train of thought, lose track of what one was saying; have on the tip of the tongue; blow or go up in or fluff one's lines, forget one's lines, dry up; misremember, misrecollect

6 efface or erase from the memory, consign to oblivion, unlearn, obliterate, **dismiss from one's thoughts** 984.4; **forgive** 148.3,5

7 be forgotten, escape one, miss, **slip one's mind,** fade or die away from the memory, slip or escape the memory, drop from one's thoughts; fall or sink into oblivion, go in one ear and out the other

ADJS **8 forgotten,** clean forgotten <nf>, **unremembered,** disremembered and disrecollected <nf>, **unrecollected, unretained, unrecalled,** past recollection or recall, out of the mind, lost, erased, effaced, obliterated, gone out of one's head or recollection, beyond recall, consigned to oblivion, buried or sunk in oblivion; out of sight out of mind; misremembered, misrecollected; half-remembered; on the tip of one's tongue

9 forgetful, forgetting, inclined to forget, **memoryless, unremembering, unmindful,** absentminded, **oblivious,** insensible to the past, with a mind or memory like a sieve; blank, vacant, vacuous, empty-headed, absent-minded; suffering from or stricken with amnesia, amnesic, amnestic; blocked, repressed, suppressed, sublimated, converted; heedless 340.11; Lethean; in a trance, preoccupied, spaced-out <nf>, out to lunch <nf>

10 forgettable, unrememberable, unrecollectable; effaceable, eradicable, erasable

ADVS **11 forgetfully,** forgettingly, unmindfully, absentmindedly, **obliviously**

991 SUFFICIENCY

NOUNS **1 sufficiency,** sufficientness, **adequacy,** adequateness, **enough,** a competence or competency; satisfactoriness, satisfaction, satisfactory amount, enough to go around; good or adequate supply; exact measure, right amount, no more and no less; bare sufficiency, minimum, bare minimum, just enough, enough to get by on, enough to live on; self-sufficiency

2 plenty, plenitude, plentifulness, plenteousness, muchness <old>; myriad, myriads, numerousness 884; **amplitude,** ampleness; substantiality, substantialness; **abundance, copiousness;** exuberance, riotousness; **bountifulness,** bounteousness, liberalness, **liberality,** generousness, **generosity; lavishness, extravagance, prodigality;** luxuriance, fertility, teemingness, productiveness 890; **wealth, opulence** or opulency, richness, affluence; more than enough; maximum; **fullness,** full measure, repletion, repleteness; **overflow, outpouring,** flood, inundation, flow, shower, spate, stream, gush, avalanche; landslide; **prevalence,** profuseness, **profusion,** riot; **superabundance** 993.2; **overkill;** no end of, great abundance, great plenty, quantities, much, as much as one could wish, one's fill, more than one can shake a stick at, lots, a fistful <nf>, **scads** 247.4; bumper crop, rich harvest, foison <old>; rich vein, bonanza, oodles and luau <nf>; an ample sufficiency, enough and to spare, enough and then some; fat of the land

3 cornucopia, horn of plenty, horn of Amalthea, endless supply, bottomless well or pit

VERBS **4 suffice, do,** just do, serve, **answer,** quench; work, be equal to, **avail;** answer or serve the purpose, do the trick <nf>, **suit;** qualify, meet, fulfill, **satisfy,** meet requirements; **pass muster,** make the grade or the cut and hack it and cut the mustard *and* **fill the bill** <nf>, measure up to, prove acceptable; get by *and* scrape by <nf>, do it, do'er <nf>, do in a pinch, **pass,** pass in the dark <nf>; hold, stand, stand up, take it, bear; stretch <nf>, reach, go around; rise to the occasion

5 **abound,** be plentiful, exuberate <old>, teem, **teem with,** creep with, crawl with, swarm with, be lousy with <nf>, bristle with; proliferate 890.7; **overflow,** run over, flood; flow, stream, rain, **pour,** shower, gush; flow with milk and honey, rain cats and dogs *and* stink of *and* roll in <nf>

ADJS 6 **sufficient,** sufficing; **enough, ample,** substantial, **plenty, satisfactory, adequate,** decent, due; competent, up to the mark, up to snuff; commensurate, proportionate, corresponding 788.9; suitable, fit 788.10; good, **good enough,** plenty good enough <nf>; sufficient for *or* to *or* unto, up to, equal to; barely sufficient, minimal, minimum; hand-to-mouth

7 **plentiful,** plenty, **plenteous,** plenitudinous; **galore** *and* a gogo *and* up the gazoo *or* kazoo *and* up to the ass in <nf>, in plenty, in quantity *or* quantities, aplenty <nf>; numerous 884.6; beaucoup <nf>, much, many 247.8; **ample,** all-sufficing; wholesale; well-stocked, well-provided, well-furnished, well-found; abundant, abounding, **copious,** exuberant, riotous; flush; **bountiful,** bounteous, **lavish, generous, liberal, extravagant, prodigal; luxuriant,** fertile, productive 890.9, **rich,** fat, **wealthy, opulent, affluent;** maximal; **full,** replete, well-filled, running over, overflowing; inexhaustible, exhaustless, bottomless; **profuse,** profusive, effuse, diffuse; **prevalent,** prevailing, rife, rampant, epidemic; lousy with <nf>, teeming 884.9; **superabundant** 993.19; a dime a dozen

ADVS 8 **sufficiently, amply,** substantially, **satisfactorily, enough;** competently, **adequately;** minimally

9 **plentifully,** plenteously, **aplenty** <nf>, **in plenty,** in quantity *or* quantities, in good supply; **abundantly,** in abundance, copiously, no end <nf>; **superabundantly** 993.24; **bountifully,** bounteously, **lavishly, generously, liberally, extravagantly, prodigally;** maximally; **fully,** in full measure, to the full, overflowingly; inexhaustibly, exhaustlessly, bottomlessly; exuberantly, luxuriantly, riotously; richly, opulently, affluently; **profusely,** diffusely, effusely; beyond one's wildest dreams, beyond the dreams of avarice

992 INSUFFICIENCY

NOUNS 1 **insufficiency, inadequacy,** insufficientness, inadequateness; short supply, seller's market; none to spare; unsatisfactoriness, nonsatisfaction, nonfulfillment, coming *or* falling short *or* shy, slippage, shortfall; **undercommitment;** disappointment, too little too late; a band-aid <nf>, a drop in the bucket *or* the ocean, a lick and a promise, a cosmetic measure; **incompetence,** incompetency, unqualification, unsuitability 789.3

2 **meagerness,** exiguousness, exiguity, scrimpiness, skimpiness, scantiness, spareness; meanness, miserliness, niggardliness, narrowness <nf>, stinginess, parsimony; smallness, slightness, puniness, paltriness; thinness, leanness, slimness, slim pickings <nf>, slenderness, scrawniness; jejuneness, jejunity; austerity; skeleton crew, corporal's guard

3 **scarcity,** scarceness; **sparsity,** sparseness; **scantiness,** scant sufficiency; **dearth, paucity,** poverty; **rarity,** rareness, uncommonness

4 **want, lack, need, deficiency, deficit, shortage, shortfall,** wantage, **incompleteness,** defectiveness, shortcoming 911, imperfection; **absence** 222, omission; **destitution,** impoverishment, beggary, deprivation; starvation, famine, drought, drying-up

5 **pittance,** dole, scrimption <nf>; drop in the bucket *or* the ocean; **mite,** bit 248.2; short allowance, short commons, half rations, cheeseparings and candle ends; mere subsistence, starvation wages; widow's mite

6 **dietary deficiency,** vitamin deficiency; undernourishment, undernutrition, **malnutrition,** malnourishment, starvation diet, half rations, bread and water; Lenten fare, Spartan fare

VERBS 7 **want, lack, need, require;** miss, feel the want of, be sent away empty-handed; run short of

8 **be insufficient,** not qualify, be found wanting, leave a lot to be desired, kick the beam, not make it *and* not hack it *and* not make the cut *and* not cut it *and* not cut the mustard <nf>, be beyond one's depth *or* ken, be in over one's head, **fall short,** fall shy, come short, not come up to; run short; want, want for, lack, fail, fail of *or* in; cramp one's style <nf>

ADJS 9 **insufficient,** unsufficing, **inadequate;** found wanting, defective, incomplete, imperfect, deficient, lacking, failing, wanting; **too few,** undersupplied, low on, light on; **too little,** not enough, precious little, a trickle *or* mere trickle; **unsatisfactory,** unsatisfying; cosmetic, merely cosmetic, surface, superficial, symptomatic, merely symptomatic; **incompetent,** unequal to, unqualified, not up to it, not up to snuff, beyond one's depth *or* over one's head, outmatched; short-staffed, understaffed, short-handed

10 **meager, slight,** scrimpy, skimp, skimpy, exiguous; scant, **scanty,** spare; miserly, niggardly, stingy,

narrow <nf>, parsimonious, mean; hard to find, out of stock; austere, Lenten, Spartan, abstemious, ascetic; stinted, frugal, sparing; poor, impoverished; small, puny, paltry; thin, lean, slim, slender, scrawny; dwarfish, dwarfed, stunted, undergrown; straitened, limited; jejune, watered, watery, unnourishing, unnutritious; subsistence, starvation

11 **scarce, sparse, scanty; in short supply,** at a premium; **rare,** uncommon, infrequent; scarcer than hen's teeth <nf>; not to be had, not to be had for love *or* money, not to be had at any price; out of print, out of stock *or* season, nonexistent; few and far between

12 **ill-provided,** ill-furnished, ill-equipped, ill-found, ill off; **unprovided,** unsupplied, unreplenished; bare-handed; unfed, underfed, undernourished; shorthanded, undermanned; **empty-handed, poor,** pauperized, impoverished, beggarly; hungry, starved, half-starved, on short commons, starving, starveling, famished, anorectic

13 **wanting, lacking, needing, missing, in want of;** for want of, in default of, in the absence of; short, **short of,** scant of; shy, **shy of** *or* **on; out of,** clean *or* fresh out of <nf>, destitute of, bare of, void of, empty of, devoid of, forlorn of, bereft of, deprived of, denuded of, unpossessed of, unblessed with, bankrupt in; out of pocket; at the end of one's rope *or* tether

ADVS 14 **insufficiently; inadequately,** unsubstantially, incompletely

15 **meagerly, slightly,** sparely, punily, scantily, poorly, frugally, sparingly

16 **scarcely, sparsely, scantily,** skimpily, scrimpily; **rarely,** uncommonly

PREPS 17 **without,** minus, less, sans, absent

WORD ELEMENTS 18 hyp-, hypo-, under-, mal-, ill-, sub-

993 EXCESS

NOUNS 1 **excess, excessiveness, inordinance,** inordinateness, nimiety, **immoderateness,** immoderacy, immoderation, **extravagance** *or* extravagancy, intemperateness, incontinence, overindulgence, **intemperance** 669; unrestrainedness, abandon; gluttony 672; **extreme,** extremity, **extremes; boundlessness** 823.1; overlargeness, overgreatness, monstrousness, enormousness 247.1; overgrowth, overdevelopment, hypertrophy, gigantism, giantism, elephantiasis; **overmuch,** overmuchness, too much, too-muchness; **exorbitance** *or* exorbitancy, undueness, **outrageousness,** unconscionableness, **unreasonableness;** radicalism, extremism 611.4;

egregiousness; fabulousness, hyperbole, **exaggeration** 355

2 **superabundance,** overabundance, superflux, **plethora,** redundancy, overprofusion, too many, too much, too much of a good thing, **overplentifulness,** overplenteousness, overplenty, **oversupply,** overstock, overaccumulation, **oversufficiency,** overmuchness, overcopiousness, overlavishness, overluxuriance, overbounteousness, overnumerousness; lavishness, **extravagance** *or* extravagancy, **prodigality; plenty** 991.2; **more than enough, enough and to spare,** enough in all conscience; **overdose,** overmeasure, one too many; too much of a good thing, egg in one's beer <nf>; more than one knows what to do with, drug on the market; spate, avalanche, landslide, deluge, flood, inundation; *embarras de richesses* <Fr>, embarrassment of riches, money to burn <nf>; overpopulation; spare tire, fifth wheel; lagniappe

3 **overfullness,** plethora, **surfeit, glut;** satiety 994; engorgement, repletion, congestion; hyperemia; **saturation,** supersaturation; **overload,** overburden, overcharge, surcharge, overfreight, overweight; **overflow,** overbrimming, overspill; **insatiability,** insatiableness; all the market can bear

4 **superfluity,** superfluousness, fat; **redundancy,** redundance; unnecessariness, needlessness; fifth wheel *and* tits on a boar <nf>; featherbedding, payroll padding; duplication, duplication of effort, overlap; **luxury,** extravagance, frill *and* **frills** *and* bells and whistles *and* gimcrackery <nf>; frippery, froufrou, overadornment, bedizenment, gingerbread; **ornamentation, embellishment** 498.1; expletive, **padding, filling;** pleonasm, tautology; verbosity, prolixity 538.2; more than one really wants to know

5 **surplus,** surplusage, leftovers, plus, **overplus,** overstock, **overage,** overset, overrun, **overmeasure, oversupply;** margin; **remainder, balance, leftover, extra, spare,** something extra *or* to spare; bonus, dividend; lagniappe <nf>; gratuity, tip, *pourboire* <Fr>

6 **overdoing,** overcarrying, **overreaching,** supererogation; **overkill;** piling on <nf>, overimportance, overemphasis; overuse; overreaction; **overwork, overexertion,** overexercise, overexpenditure, overtaxing, overstrain, tax, strain; too much on one's plate, too many irons in the fire, too much at once; **overachievement,** overachieving

7 **overextension, overdrawing,** drawing *or* spreading too thin, **overstretching,** overstrain, overstraining, stretching, straining, stretch, strain, tension, extreme tension, snapping *or* breaking point;

overexpansion; inflation, distension, overdistension, edema, turgidity, swelling, bloat, bloating 259.2

VERBS **8 superabound,** overabound, **know no bounds, swarm,** pullulate, run riot, luxuriate, **teem;** overflow, flood, overbrim, overspill, spill over, overrun, overspread, overswarm, overgrow, fill, saturate; meet one at every turn; hang heavy on one's hands, remain on one's hands; burst at the seams

9 exceed, surpass, pass, top, transcend, go beyond; overpass, overstep, overrun, **overreach,** overshoot, overshoot the mark

10 overdo, go too far, do twice over, do it to death <nf>, pass all bounds, know no bounds, overact, **carry too far,** overcarry, go to an extreme, **go to extremes,** go overboard, go *or* jump off the deep end; **run *or* drive into the ground; make a big deal of** *and* **make a Federal case of** <nf>; overemphasize, overstress; max out; overplay, overplay one's hand <nf>; **overreact,** protest too much; overreach oneself; **overtax,** overtask, overexert, overexercise, overstrain, overdrive, overspend, exhaust, overexpend, overuse; overtrain; **overwork,** overlabor; overelaborate, overdevelop, tell more than one wants to know; overstudy; burn the candle at both ends; **spread oneself too thin, take on too much,** have too much on one's plate, have too many irons in the fire, do too many things at once; **exaggerate** 355.3; **overindulge** 669.5

11 pile it on, lay it on, **lay it on thick,** lay it on with a trowel <nf>, talk too much, exaggerate

12 carry coals to Newcastle, teach fishes to swim, teach one's grandmother to suck eggs, kill the slain, beat *or* flog a dead horse, labor the obvious, butter one's bread on both sides, preach to the converted, paint *or* gild the lily, "to gild refined gold, to paint the lily, to throw a perfume on the violet"—Shakespeare

13 overextend, overdraw, overstretch, overstrain, stretch, strain; reach the breaking *or* snapping point; **overexpand,** overdistend, overdevelop, inflate, swell 259.4

14 oversupply, overprovide, overlavish, overfurnish, overequip; **overstock;** overprovision, overprovender; overdose; flood the market, oversell; **flood, deluge,** inundate, engulf, swamp, whelm, overwhelm; lavish with, be prodigal with

15 overload, overlade, **overburden,** overweight, **overcharge,** surcharge; **overfill,** stuff, crowd, cram, jam, pack, jam-pack, **congest,** choke; **overstuff,** overfeed; gluttonize 672.4; **surfeit, glut, gorge,** satiate 994.4; **saturate,** soak, drench, supersaturate, supercharge

ADJS **16 excessive, inordinate, immoderate,** overweening, hubristic, **intemperate, extravagant,** incontinent; unrestrained, unbridled, abandoned; gluttonous 672.6; **extreme; overlarge, overgreat,** overbig, larger than life, monstrous, enormous, jumbo, elephantine, gigantic 247.7; overgrown, overdeveloped, hypertrophied; **overmuch,** too much, a bit much, de trop; **exorbitant, undue, outrageous,** unconscionable, **unreasonable;** fancy *and* high *and* stiff *and* steep <nf>; **out of bounds** *or* **all bounds,** out of sight *and* out of this world <nf>, **boundless** 823.3; egregious; fabulous, hyperbolic, hyperbolical, **exaggerated** 355.4

17 superfluous, redundant; excess, in excess, duplicative; unnecessary, unessential, nonessential, **needless,** otiose, expendable, dispensable, needless, unneeded, gratuitous, uncalled-for; expletive; pleonastic, tautologous, tautological; verbose, prolix 538.12; *de trop* <Fr>, supererogatory, supererogative; spare, to spare; on one's hands

18 surplus, overplus; **remaining,** unused, **leftover;** over, **over and above; extra, spare,** supernumerary, for lagniappe <nf>, as a bonus

19 superabundant, overabundant, plethoric, **overplentiful,** overplenteous, overplenty, **oversufficient, overmuch; lavish, prodigal,** overlavish, overbounteous, overgenerous, overliberal; overcopious, overluxuriant, riotous, overexuberant; overprolific, overnumerous; **swarming,** pullulating, **teeming,** overpopulated, overpopulous; plentiful 991.7

20 overfull, overloaded, overladen, overburdened, overfreighted, overfraught, overweighted, **overcharged,** surcharged, **saturated,** drenched, soaked, supersaturated, supercharged; **surfeited, glutted,** gorged, overfed, bloated, replete, swollen, satiated 994.6, **stuffed,** overstuffed, **crowded, overcrowded, crammed,** jammed, packed, jam-packed, like sardines in a can *or* tin, bumper-to-bumper <nf>; choked, **congested,** stuffed up; **overstocked, oversupplied; overflowing,** in spate, running over, filled to overflowing; plethoric, hyperemic; **bursting,** ready to burst, bursting at the seams, at the bursting point, overblown, distended, **swollen, bloated** 259.13

21 overdone, overwrought; overdrawn, overstretched, overstrained; overwritten, overplayed, overacted

ADVS **22 excessively, inordinately, immoderately, intemperately,** overweeningly, hubristically, **overly,** over, **overmuch,** too much; **too,** too-too <nf>; **exorbitantly, unduly, unreasonably,** unconscionably, **outrageously**

23 in *or* **to excess, to extremes,** to the extreme, all out *and* to the max <nf>, flat out <Brit nf>, to a fault, too far, out of all proportion

24 superabundantly, overabundantly, **lavishly, prodigally, extravagantly;** more than enough, plentifully 991.9; without measure, out of measure, beyond measure

25 superfluously, redundantly, supererogatorily; tautologously; unnecessarily, needlessly, beyond need, beyond reason, to a fare-thee-well <nf>

PREPS **26 in excess of,** over, beyond, past, above, **over and above,** above and beyond

WORD ELEMENTS **27** arch-, hyper-, over-, super-, sur-, ultra-, extra-

994 SATIETY

NOUNS **1 satiety, satiation, satisfaction, fullness, surfeit, glut,** repletion, engorgement; contentment; **fill, bellyful** and skinful <nf>; **saturation,** oversaturation, saturatedness, supersaturation; saturation point; more than enough, enough in all conscience, all one can stand or take; too much of a good thing, much of a muchness <nf>

2 satedness, surfeitedness, cloyedness, jadedness; overfullness, fed-upness <nf>

3 cloyer, surfeiter, sickener; **overdose;** a diet of cake; warmed-over cabbage

VERBS **4 satiate, sate, satisfy,** slake, allay; **surfeit, glut, gorge,** engorge; **cloy,** jade, pall; **fill,** fill up; saturate, oversaturate, supersaturate; **stuff,** overstuff, cram; **overfill,** overgorge, overdose, overfeed

5 have enough, have about enough of, have quite enough, **have one's fill;** have too much, have too much of a good thing, **have a bellyful** or skinful <nf>, have an overdose, **be fed up** <nf>, have all one can take or stand, have it up to here and up the gazoo or kazoo <nf>, have had it

ADJS **6 satiated, sated, satisfied,** slaked, allayed; **surfeited, gorged,** replete, engorged, **glutted; cloyed,** jaded; **full,** full of, with one's fill of, **overfull,** saturated, oversaturated, supersaturated; **stuffed,** overstuffed, crammed, overgorged, overfed; **fed up** and fed to the gills or fed to the teeth and stuffed to the gills <nf>; **with a bellyful** or skinful <nf>, with enough of; disgusted, **sick of,** tired of, sick and tired of

7 satiating, sating, satisfying, filling; surfeiting, overfilling; jading, **cloying,** cloysome

INTERJS **8** enough!, basta <Ital>, genug! and genug shayn! <Yiddish>, all right already! enough already!

995 EXPEDIENCE

NOUNS **1 expedience** or **expediency, advisability,** politicness, **desirability,** recommendability;

fitness, **fittingness, appropriateness,** propriety, decency <old>, seemliness, **suitability,** rightness, feasibility, **convenience;** seasonableness, timeliness, **opportuneness; usefulness** 387.3; **advantage, advantageousness,** beneficialness, **profit,** profitability, percentage and mileage <nf>, worthwhileness, fruitfulness; wisdom, prudence 920.7; **temporariness, provisionality**

2 expedient, means, means to an end, **provision, measure, step, action,** effort, **stroke,** stroke of policy, coup, **move,** countermove, **maneuver,** demarche, course of action; tactic, **device,** contrivance, artifice, stratagem, **shift; gimmick** and dodge and trick <nf>; **resort,** resource; answer, solution; quick-and-dirty solution <nf>; working proposition, working hypothesis; **temporary expedient, improvisation,** ad hoc measure, ad hoc or ad hockery or ad hocism; **fix** and **quick fix** <nf>, jury-rigged expedient, **makeshift,** stopgap, shake-up, jury-rig; last expedient, **last resort** or resource, pis aller <Fr>, last shift, trump

VERBS **3 expedite one's affair,** work to one's advantage, not come amiss, come in handy, be just the thing, be just what the doctor ordered <nf>, fit to a T or like a glove or like a second skin; forward, advance, promote, profit, advantage, benefit; **work, serve,** answer, answer or serve one's purpose, fill the bill and do the trick <nf>; suit the occasion, **be fitting,** fit, befit, be right

4 make shift, make do, make out <nf>, rub along <Brit>, cope, manage, manage with, get along on, get by on, do with; do as well as or the best one can; use a last resort, scrape the bottom of the barrel

ADJS **5 expedient, desirable,** to be desired, much to be desired, **advisable, politic,** recommendable; **appropriate, meet, fit, fitting,** befitting, **right, proper,** good, decent <old>, **becoming,** seemly, likely, congruous, **suitable,** sortable, feasible, doable, swingable <nf>, **convenient,** happy, heaven-sent, felicitous; timely, seasonable, opportune, well-timed, in the nick of time; **useful** 387.18; **advantageous,** favorable; **profitable,** fructuous, worthwhile, worth one's while; **wise** 920.17

6 practical, practicable, pragmatic or pragmatical, banausic; feasible, workable, operable, realizable; **efficient,** effective, **effectual**

7 makeshift, makeshifty, **stopgap,** band-aid <nf>, improvised, improvisational, **jury-rigged; last-ditch; ad hoc;** quick and dirty <nf>; temporary, provisional, tentative

ADVS **8 expediently, fittingly,** fitly, **appropriately, suitably,** sortably, congruously, rightly, properly, decently <old>, feasibly, conveniently; practically;

seasonably, opportunely; desirably, advisably; advantageously, to advantage, all to the good; as a last resort

PHRS **9** there's more than one way to skin a cat, where there's a will there's a way

996 INEXPEDIENCE

NOUNS **1** **inexpedience** or inexpediency, **undesirability, inadvisability,** impoliticness or impoliticalness; **unwiseness** 923.2; **unfitness, unfittingness, inappropriateness, unaptness, unsuitability,** incongruity, **unmeetness,** wrongness, unseemliness; **inconvenience** or inconveniency, awkwardness; ineptitude, inaptitude; unseasonableness, untimeliness, inopportuneness; unfortunateness, infelicity; disadvantageousness, unprofitableness, unprofitability, worthlessness, futility, uselessness 391

2 **disadvantage, drawback, liability; detriment,** impairment, prejudice, loss, damage, hurt, harm, mischief, injury; **a step back** or **backward,** a loss of ground; **handicap** 1012.6, disability; drag, millstone around one's neck

3 **inconvenience,** discommodity, incommodity, disaccommodation <old>, **trouble, bother;** inconvenientness, inconveniency, **unhandiness,** awkwardness, clumsiness, unwieldiness, troublesomeness, clunkiness <nf>; gaucheness, gaucherie

VERBS **4** **inconvenience,** put to inconvenience, **put out, discommode,** incommode, disaccommodate <old>, disoblige, **burden, embarrass; trouble, bother,** put to trouble, put to the trouble of, **impose upon;** harm, disadvantage 1000.6

ADJS **5** **inexpedient, undesirable, inadvisable, counterproductive,** impolitic, impolitical, unpolitic, not to be recommended, contraindicated; **impractical, impracticable,** dysfunctional, unworkable; **ill-advised, ill-considered, unwise; unfit, unfitting,** unbefitting, **inappropriate, unsuitable,** unmeet, inapt, inept, unseemly, **improper, wrong,** bad, out of place, out of order, incongruous, ill-suited; malapropos, *mal à propos* <Fr>, inopportune, untimely, ill-timed, badly timed, unseasonable; infelicitous, unfortunate, unhappy; unprofitable 391.12; futile 391.13

6 **disadvantageous,** unadvantageous, **unfavorable;** unprofitable, profitless, unrewarding, worthless, useless 391.9; **detrimental,** deleterious, injurious, harmful, prejudicial, disserviceable

7 **inconvenient, incommodious,** discommodious; **unhandy, awkward,** clumsy, unwieldy, troublesome, onerous; gauche

ADVS **8** **inexpediently, inadvisably,** impoliticly or impolitically, **undesirably; unfittingly, inappropriately, unsuitably,** ineptly, inaptly, incongruously; inopportunely, unseasonably; infelicitously, unfortunately, unhappily

9 **disadvantageously,** unadvantageously, unprofitably, unrewardingly; uselessly 391.15; **inconveniently,** unhandily, with difficulty, ill

997 IMPORTANCE

NOUNS **1** **importance, significance, consequence,** consideration, **import,** note, mark, **moment, weight, gravity;** materiality; concern, concernment, interest; **first order,** high order, high rank; **priority,** primacy, precedence, preeminence, paramountcy, superiority, **supremacy;** value, worth, merit, excellence 999.1; self-importance 140.1; emphasis, oomph <nf>; front burner

2 **notability, noteworthiness,** remarkableness, salience, memorability; **prominence, eminence, greatness,** distinction, magnitude; prestige, esteem, repute, reputation, honor, glory, renown, dignity, **fame** 662.1; **stardom,** celebrity, celebrity-hood, superstardom; semicelebrity

3 **gravity, graveness, seriousness,** solemnity, weightiness; *gravitas* <L>, grave affair; no joke, no laughing matter, nothing to sneeze at <nf>, hardball <nf>, matter of life and death, heavy scene <nf>

4 **urgency,** imperativeness, exigence or exigency; **momentousness, crucialness, cruciality;** consequentiality, consequentialness; **press,** pressure, high pressure, **stress,** tension, **pinch;** clutch and crunch <nf>; **crisis, emergency;** moment of truth, turning point, climax, defining moment; crunch

5 **matter of importance** or **consequence,** thing of interest, point of interest; matter of concern, object of note, one for the book and something to write home about <nf>, something special, no tea party, no picnic; not chicken feed <nf>; vital concern or interest; notabilia, memorabilia, great doings

6 **salient point,** cardinal point, high point, great point, key point; important thing, chief thing, **the point, main point,** main thing, essential matter, **essence,** the name of the game and the bottom line and what it's all about and where it's at <nf>, substance, gravamen, *sine qua non* <L>, issue, real issue, front-burner issue <nf>, prime issue; **essential,** fundamental, substantive point, material point; **gist, nub** <nf>, **heart,** meat, pith, kernel, **core; crux,** crucial or pivotal or critical point, pivot; turning point, **climax, cusp, crisis;** keystone, cornerstone; landmark, milestone, bench mark; linchpin; secret weapon, trump card

7 **feature, highlight,** high spot, main attraction, centerpiece, pièce de résistance; outstanding feature; best part, cream

8 **personage, important person,** person of importance *or* consequence, **great man** *or* **woman,** man *or* woman of mark *or* note, **somebody, notable,** notability, figure; **celebrity,** famous person, person of renown, personality; name, big name, megastar, nabob, **mogul,** captain of industry, panjandrum, person to be reckoned with, very important person, heavyweight; sachem; mover and shaker, lord of creation; **worthy,** pillar of society, salt of the earth, elder, father; **dignitary,** dignity; **magnate;** tycoon <nf>, baron; power; power elite, Establishment; interests; brass, top brass; top people, the great; ruling circle, lords of creation; the top, the summit

9 <nf terms> **big shot,** wheel, **big wheel,** big boy, big cat, big fish, biggie, big cheese, big noise, big-timer, big-time operator, **bigwig,** big man, big gun, **high-muck-a-muck** *or* high-muckety-muck, kingpin, lion, something, **VIP,** brass hat, high man on the totem pole, suit; sacred cow, little tin god, tin god; big man on campus *or* BMOC; 800-pound gorilla; queen bee, heavy momma; first fiddle; mega-

10 **chief, principal,** chief executive, chief executive officer *or* CEO, paramount, lord of the manor, overlord, **king,** queen, monarch, electronics king, etc; leading light, luminary, master spirit, **star,** superstar, superman, superwoman, prima donna, lead 707.6

11 <nf terms> **boss, honcho,** big enchilada, biggest frog in the pond, big man, top *or* high man on the totem pole, top dog, Mr Big, head cheese, his nibs, himself, man upstairs

VERBS 12 **matter,** import <old>, signify, **count, tell, weigh, carry weight,** cut ice *and* cut some ice <nf>, be prominent, stand out, mean much; be something, be somebody, amount to something; have a key to the executive washroom; be featured, star, get top billing, take the limelight

13 **value, esteem, treasure, prize,** appreciate, respect, **rate highly,** think highly of, think well of, **think much of,** set store by; give *or* attach *or* ascribe importance to; make much of, make a fuss *or* stir about, make an ado *or* much ado about; hold up as an example

14 **emphasize, stress,** lay emphasis *or* stress upon, feature, highlight, brightline, place emphasis on, give emphasis to, **accent, accentuate, punctuate,**

point up, bring to the fore, put in the foreground, put in bright lights; prioritize; **highlight,** spotlight; **star, underline, underscore,** italicize; overemphasize, overstress, overaccentuate, hammer home, rub in; harp on; dwell on, belabor; attach too much importance to, make a big deal *or* Federal case of <nf>, make a mountain out of a molehill; pull no punches <nf>

15 **feature,** headline <nf>; **star,** give top billing to

16 **dramatize, play up** <nf>, splash, make a production of; put on the map

ADJS 17 **important, major, consequential, momentous, significant, considerable,** substantial, material, **great,** grand, big; superior, world-shaking, earthshaking; big-time *and* big-league *and* major-league *and* heavyweight <nf>; high-powered <nf>, double-barreled <nf>; bigwig *and* bigwigged <nf>; name *and* big-name <nf>, self-important 140.8; mega; A-1 <nf>

18 **of importance, of significance, of consequence,** of note, of moment, of weight; of concern, of concernment, of interest, not to be overlooked *or* despised, not hay *and* not chopped liver *and* not to be sneezed at <nf>; viable

19 **notable, noteworthy, celebrated, remarkable, marked, standout** <nf>, of mark, signal; **memorable,** rememberable, unforgettable, classic, historic, never to be forgotten; striking, telling, salient; **eminent, prominent,** conspicuous, noble, **outstanding, distinguished;** prestigious, esteemed, estimable, elevated, sublime, reputable 662.15; **extraordinary,** *extraordinaire* <Fr>, out of the ordinary, **exceptional, special,** rare; top-ten

20 **weighty,** heavy, **grave,** sober, sobering, **solemn, serious,** earnest; portentous, fateful, fatal; formidable, awe-inspiring, imposing, larger than life; world-shaking, earth-shattering

21 **emphatic, decided, positive, forceful,** forcible; **emphasized, stressed,** accented, accentuated, punctuated, pointed; underlined, underscored, starred, italicized, highlighted; red-letter, in red letters, in letters of fire

22 **urgent, imperative,** imperious, **compelling, pressing,** high-priority, high-pressure, crying, clamorous, insistent, instant, exigent; crucial, critical, pivotal, acute; fateful

23 **vital, all-important,** crucial, of vital importance, life-and-death *or* life-or-death; earth-shattering, epoch-making; **essential,** fundamental, indispensable, basic, substantive, bedrock, material; **central,** focal; bottom-line *and* meat-and-potatoes *and* gut <nf>; grass-roots

24 **paramount, principal, leading, foremost, main, chief,** number one <nf>, premier, **prime, primary,** preeminent, **supreme,** capital <old>, cardinal;

highest, uppermost, topmost, toprank, ranking, of the first rank, world-class, **dominant,** predominant, master, controlling, **overruling,** overriding, all-absorbing

ADVS **25 importantly, significantly,** consequentially, materially, momentously, greatly, grandly; eminently, prominently, conspicuously, outstandingly, saliently, signally, notably, markedly, remarkably

26 at the decisive moment, in the clutch *and* when the chips are down *and* when push comes to shove <nf>

998 UNIMPORTANCE

NOUNS **1 unimportance, insignificance,** inconsequence, inconsequentiality, indifference, **immateriality;** inessentiality; ineffectuality; unnoteworthiness, unimpressiveness; inferiority, secondariness, low order of importance, low priority, dispensability, expendability, marginality; lack of substance; **smallness,** littleness, slightness, inconsiderableness, negligibility; irrelevancy, meaninglessness; **pettiness,** puniness, pokiness, picayune, picayunishness; marginalization; irrelevance 776.1

2 paltriness, poorness, **meanness,** sorriness, sadness, pitifulness, contemptibleness, pitiableness, despicableness, miserableness, wretchedness, vileness, crumminess <nf>, shabbiness, shoddiness, cheapness, cheesiness, beggarliness, worthlessness, uselessness, unworthiness, meritlessness; tawdriness, meretriciousness, gaudiness 501.3

3 triviality, trivialness, triflingness, nugacity, nugaciousness; **superficiality,** shallowness; slightness, slenderness, slimness, flimsiness; **frivolity,** frivolousness, lightness, levity; **foolishness,** silliness, inanity, emptiness, vacuity; triteness, vapidity, vanity, idleness, futility; **much ado about nothing,** tempest *or* storm in a teacup *or* teapot, much cry and little wool, piss *and* wind *and* big deal <nf>; pettiness; snap of the fingers

4 trivia, triviata, **trifles; trumpery,** *nugae* <L>, gimcrackery, knickknackery, bric-a-brac; **rubbish,** trash, chaff; peanuts *and* chicken feed *and* chickenshit *and* Mickey Mouse <nf>, small change; small beer; froth, "trifles light as air"— Shakespeare; minutiae, details, minor details; inessential, nonessential

5 trifle, triviality, oddment, bagatelle, fribble, **gimcrack, gewgaw,** frippery, froth, **trinket,** bibelot, curio, **bauble,** gaud, toy, **knickknack,** knickknackery, kickshaw, minikin <old>, whim-

wham, folderol; pin, button, hair, straw, rush, feather, fig, bean, hill of beans <nf>, molehill, row of pins *or* buttons <nf>, sneeshing <Brit nf>, pinch of snuff; bit, snap; a curse, a continental, a hoot *and* a damn *and* a darn *and* a shit <nf>, a tinker's damn; picayune, rap, sou, halfpenny, farthing, brass farthing, cent, red cent, two cents, twopence *or* tuppence <Brit>, penny, dime, plugged nickel; peppercorn; drop in the ocean *or* the bucket; fleabite, pinprick; joke, jest, farce, mockery, child's play; small potatoes

6 an insignificancy, an inessential, a marginal matter *or* affair, a trivial *or* paltry affair, a small *or* trifling *or* minor matter, **no great matter;** a little thing, *peu de chose* <Fr>, hardly *or* scarcely anything, matter of no importance *or* consequence, matter of indifference; **a nothing, a big nothing, a naught,** a mere nothing, nothing in particular, nothing to signify, nothing to speak *or* worth speaking of, nothing to think twice about, nothing to boast of, nothing to write home about, thing of naught, *rien du tout* <Fr>, nullity, nihility; **technicality,** mere technicality; red herring

7 a nobody, insignificance, hollow man, jackstraw <old>, **nonentity,** nonperson, empty suit *and* nebbish <nf>, an obscurity, a nothing, cipher, little man, nobody one knows; lightweight, mediocrity; whippersnapper *and* whiffet *and* pip-squeak *and* squirt *and* shrimp *and* scrub *and* runt <nf>; squit <Brit nf>, punk <nf>; small potato, small potatoes; **the little fellow,** the little guy <nf>, **the man in the street;** common man 864.3; man of straw, dummy, figurehead; **small fry,** Mr and Mrs Nobody, John Doe and Richard Roe *or* Mary Roe; Tom, Dick, and Harry; Brown, Jones, and Robinson

8 trifling, dallying, **dalliance,** flirtation, flirtiness, coquetry; toying, fiddling, playing, fooling, **puttering,** tinkering, pottering, piddling; dabbling, smattering; loitering, idling 331.4

9 <nf terms> **monkeying, monkeying around,** buggering around, diddling around, fiddling around, frigging *or* fricking around, horsing around, fooling around, kidding around, messing around, pissing around, playing around, screwing around, mucking around, farting around; jerking off

10 trifler, dallier, fribble; **putterer,** potterer, piddler, tinkerer, smatterer, dabbler; amateur, dilettante, Sunday painter; **flirt, coquet**

VERBS **11 be unimportant,** be of no importance, not signify, **not matter,** not count, signify nothing, matter little, **not make any difference; cut no ice, not amount to anything,** make no never mind *and* not amount to a hill of beans *or* a damn <nf>; have no clout *or* pull

12 attach little importance to, give little weight to; make little of, underplay, de-emphasize, downplay, play down, **minimize,** marginalize, disregard, **make light of,** think little of, throw away, **make** *or* **think nothing of,** take no account of, set little by, set no store by, set at naught; snap one's fingers at; not care a straw about; not give a shit *or* a hoot *or* two hoots for <nf>, not give a damn about, not give a dime a dozen for; bad-mouth <nf>, deprecate, depreciate 512.8; **trivialize**

13 make much ado about nothing, make mountains out of molehills, have a storm *or* tempest in a teacup *or* teapot

14 trifle, dally; flirt, coquet; toy, fribble, **play, fool,** play at, **putter, potter,** tinker, **piddle; dabble,** smatter; toy with, fiddle with, fool with, play with; idle, loiter 331.12,13; nibble, niggle, nickel-and-dime <nf>

15 <nf terms> **monkey, monkey around,** fiddle, fiddle around, fiddle-faddle, frivol, horse around, fool around, play around, mess around, kid around, **screw around,** muck around, muck about <Brit>, fart around, piss around, bugger around, diddle around, frig around; jerk off

ADJS **16 unimportant, of no importance,** of little *or* small importance, of no great importance, **of no account,** of no significance, of no concern, of no matter, of little *or* no consequence, no great shakes <nf>; no skin off one's nose *or* elbow *or* ass <nf>; inferior, secondary, of a low order of importance, low-priority, expendable; marginal; one-dimensional, two-dimensional; not apropos, not related, irrelevant

17 insignificant 248.6, **inconsequential, immaterial,** of no consequence, insubstantial; nonessential, unessential, inessential, **not vital,** back-burner <nf>, dispensable; unnoteworthy, unimpressive; **inconsiderable,** inappreciable, negligible; **small, little,** minute, footling, petit <old>, minor, inferior; technical

18 <nf terms> **measly, small-time, two-bit,** Mickey Mouse, chickenshit, nickel-and-dime, low-rent, piddly, pissy-ass, dinky, poky <Brit>, tinhorn, punk; not worth a dime *or* a red cent *or* beans *or* a hill of beans *or* bubkes *or* shit, not worth a second thought; **one-horse, two-by-four,** jerkwater

19 trivial, trifling; fribble, fribbling, nugacious, nugatory; catchpenny; **slight,** slender, flimsy; **superficial, shallow; frivolous, light,** windy, airy, frothy; idle, futile, vain, otiose; **foolish,** fatuous, asinine, **silly; inane,** empty, vacuous; trite, vapid; unworthy of serious consideration

20 petty, puny, piddling, piffling, niggling, pettifogging, technical, picayune, picayunish; small-beer

21 paltry, poor, common, **mean, sorry, sad,** pitiful, pitiable, pathetic, **despicable, contemptible,** beneath contempt, **miserable, wretched,** beggarly, vile, **shabby,** scrubby, scruffy, shoddy, scurvy, scuzzy <nf>, scummy, **crummy** *and* cheesy <nf>, **trashy,** rubbishy, garbagey <nf>, trumpery, gimcracky <nf>; tinpot <nf>; **cheap,** worthless, valueless, twopenny *or* twopenny-halfpenny <Brit>, two-for-a-cent *or* -penny, dime-a-dozen; tawdry, meretricious, gaudy 501.20; mickey mouse *or* rinky-dink <nf>

22 unworthy, worthless, meritless, unworthy of regard *or* consideration, beneath notice; no great shakes <nf>

ADVS **23 unimportantly, insignificantly, inconsequentially,** immaterially, unessentially; **pettily,** paltrily; **trivially,** triflingly; superficially, shallowly; frivolously, lightly, idly

PHRS **24 it does not matter,** it matters not, it does not signify, mox nix <nf>, **it is of no consequence** *or* **importance, it makes no difference,** it makes no never mind <nf>, it cannot be helped, it is all the same; *n'importe* and *de rien* and *ça ne fait rien* <Fr>; it will all come out in the wash <nf>, it will be all the same a hundred years from now

25 no matter, never mind, think no more of it, do not give it another *or* a second thought, don't lose any sleep over it, let it pass, let it go <nf>, ignore it, forget it <nf>, skip it *and* drop it <nf>; fiddle-dee-dee

26 what does it matter?, what matter?, what's the difference?, what's the diff? <nf>, what do I care?, what of it?, what boots it?, what's the odds?, so what?, what else is new?; for aught one cares, big deal <nf>

999 GOODNESS
<good quality or effect>

NOUNS **1 goodness, excellence, quality,** class <nf>; **virtue,** grace; **merit,** desert; **value, worth; fineness,** goodliness, fairness, niceness; **superiority,** first-rateness, **skillfulness** 413.1, proficiency; wholeness, **soundness,** healthiness 81.1; **virtuousness** 653.1; **kindness, benevolence,** benignity 143.1; beneficialness, helpfulness 449.10; favorableness, auspiciousness 133.8; expedience, advantageousness 995.1; **usefulness** 387.3; pleasantness, agreeableness 97.1; cogency, validity; profitableness, rewardingness 472.4

2 superexcellence, supereminence, preeminence, supremacy, primacy, paramountcy, peerlessness, unsurpassedness, matchlessness, superfineness; **superbness,** exquisiteness, **magnificence,** splendidness, splendiferousness, marvelousness, distinction

3 tolerableness, tolerability, goodishness, passableness, fairishness, **adequateness, satisfactoriness,** acceptability, admissibility; sufficiency 991

4 good, welfare, well-being, **benefit;** public weal, common good; **interest, advantage; behalf,** behoof, edification; blessing, benison, boon; **profit,** avail <old>, gain, betterment; world of good; favor, advantage; use, usefulness

5 good thing, a thing to be desired, "a consummation devoutly to be wish'd"— Shakespeare; **treasure,** gem, jewel, diamond, pearl; boast, pride, **pride and joy;** prize, trophy, plum; winner *and* no slouch *and* nothing to sneeze at <nf>; catch, find <nf>, *trouvaille* <Fr>; godsend, windfall; tour de force, chef-d'oeuvre, masterpiece; bestseller; collector's item; hit

6 first-rater, topnotcher, world-beater; wonder, prodigy, genius, virtuoso, **star, superstar;** luminary, leading light, one in a thousand *or* a million; hard *or* tough act to follow <nf>; good egg

7 <nf terms> **dandy, jim dandy, dilly, humdinger, pip,** pippin, **peach,** ace, beaut, **lulu, daisy,** darb, doozy, honey, sweetheart, dream, lollapalooza, bitch, hot shit *or* poo, pisser, pistol, corker, whiz, blinger, **crackerjack,** knockout, something else, something else again, barn-burner, killer, killer-diller, smash, smash hit, the nuts, the cat's pajamas *or* balls *or* meow, bitch-kitty, whiz, whizbang, wow, wowser

8 the best, the very best, the best ever, the top of the heap *or* the line <nf>, head of the class, tops; **quintessence,** essence, prime, optimum, superlative; **choice, pick, select, elect, elite,** *corps d'élite* <Fr>, chosen; **cream, flower,** fat; cream *or* pick of the crop, *crème de la crème* <Fr>, grade A, salt of the earth; *pièce de résistance* <Fr>; prize, champion, queen; nonesuch, paragon, nonpareil; gem of the first water

9 harmlessness, hurtlessness, uninjuriousness, **innocuousness,** benignity, benignancy; unobnoxiousness, inoffensiveness; innocence; heart of gold, kindness of heart, milk of human kindness

VERBS **10 do good, profit,** avail; do a world of good; **benefit, help, serve,** be of service, advance, advantage, favor 449.11,14,17,19; be the making of, make a man *or* woman of; do no harm, break no bones

11 excel, surpass, outdo, pass, do *or* go one better, transcend; do up brown *or* in spades <nf>, do with a vengeance; be as good as, equal, emulate, rival, vie, vie with, challenge comparison, go one-on-one with <nf>; **make the most of, optimize,** exploit; cream off <Brit>, skim off the cream

ADJS **12 good, excellent,** *bueno* <Sp>, *bon* <Fr>, bonny <Brit>, **fine, nice,** goodly, fair; **splendid, capital, grand,** elegant <nf>, braw <Scot>, famous <nf>, noble; royal, regal, fit for a king; very good, *très bon* <Fr>; boo-yah <nf>; commendable, laudable, estimable 509.20; skillful 413.22; **sound,** healthy 81.5; virtuous; kind, benevolent 143.15; beneficial, helpful 449.21; profitable; favorable, auspicious 133.17; expedient, advantageous 995.5; useful 387.18; pleasant 97.6; cogent, valid 973.14

13 <nf terms> **great,** swell, dandy, bitchin', jim dandy, neat, neato, cool, super, super-duper, bully <old>, tough, mean, gnarly, heavy, bad, groovy, out of sight, fab, fantabulous, marvy, gear, something else, ducky, dynamite, keen, killer, hot, nifty, sexy, spiffy, spiffing, ripping, nobby, peachy, peachy-keen, delicious, scrumptious, not too shabby, tits, out of this world, hunky-dory, crackerjack, boss, stunning, corking, smashing, solid, all wool and a yard wide; rum *or* wizard <Brit>, bonzer <Austral>; bang-up, jam-up, slap-up, ace-high, fine and dandy, just dandy, but good, OK, okay, A-OK; copacetic, peachy keen; phat

14 superior, above par, head and shoulders above, **crack** <nf>; **high-grade, high-class,** high-quality, high-caliber, high-test, **world-class,** grade A; impressive

15 superb, super <nf>, **superexcellent, supereminent,** superfine, **exquisite; magnificent,** splendid, splendiferous, tremendous, immense, **marvelous, wonderful,** glorious, divine, heavenly, terrific, sensational; sterling, golden; gilt-edged *and* gilt-edge, blue-chip; of the highest type, of the best sort, of the first water, as good as good can be, as good as they come, as good as they make 'em *and* out of this world <nf>

16 best, very best, greatest *and* top-of-the-line <nf>, **prime,** optimum, optimal; **choice, select, elect,** elite, **picked,** handpicked; **prize, champion; supreme,** paramount, **unsurpassed,** surpassing, unparalleled, unmatched, unmatchable, matchless, makeless <old>, **peerless;** quintessential; for the best, all for the best

17 first-rate, first-class, in a class by itself; of the first *or* highest degree; unmatched, matchless; champion, record-breaking

18 <nf terms> **A-1, A number one,** primo, first-chop, tip-top, top-notch, topflight, top-drawer, tops; topping *or* top-hole <Brit>

19 up to par; up to standard, **up to snuff** <nf>; **up to the mark,** up to the notch *and* **up to scratch** <nf>

20 tolerable, goodish, fair, fairish, moderate, tidy <nf>, **decent,** respectable, presentable, good enough, **pretty good, not bad,** not amiss, not half bad, not so bad, **adequate, satisfactory, all right,**

OK *or* okay <nf>; better than nothing; **acceptable,** admissible, **passable,** unobjectionable, unexceptionable; workmanlike; sufficient 991.6

21 **harmless,** hurtless, unhurtful; well-meaning, well-meant; **uninjurious,** undamaging, **innocuous,** innoxious, innocent; unobnoxious, inoffensive; nonmalignant, **benign;** nonpoisonous, nontoxic, nonvirulent, nonvenomous

ADVS 22 **excellently, nicely,** finely, **capitally, splendidly, famously,** royally; **well,** very well, **fine** <nf>, right, aright; one's best, at one's best, at the top of one's bent

23 **superbly,** exquisitely, **magnificently,** tremendously, immensely, terrifically, **marvelously, wonderfully,** gloriously, divinely

24 **tolerably, fairly,** fairishly, moderately, respectably, **adequately, satisfactorily,** passably, **acceptably,** unexceptionably, presentably, decently; fairly well, well enough, pretty well; **rather, pretty**

1000 BADNESS

<bad quality or effect>

NOUNS 1 **badness, evil,** evilness, viciousness, damnability, reprehensibility; moral badness, dereliction, peccancy, iniquity, sinfulness, wickedness 654.4; unwholesomeness, unhealthiness 82.1; inferiority 1005.3; unskillfulness 414.1; unkindness, malevolence 144; inauspiciousness, unfavorableness 133.7; inexpedience 996; unpleasantness 98; invalidity 19.3; inaccuracy 975.2; improperness 638.1; deviltry

2 **terribleness, dreadfulness,** direness, **awfulness** <nf>, horribleness; **atrociousness, outrageousness,** heinousness, nefariousness; **notoriousness, egregiousness,** scandalousness, shamefulness, **infamousness; abominableness,** odiousness, **loathsomeness, detestableness,** despicableness, contemptibleness, hatefulness; **offensiveness,** grossness, obnoxiousness; squalor, squalidness, sordidness, **wretchedness,** filth, **vileness,** fulsomeness, **nastiness,** rankness, **foulness,** noisomeness; disgustingness, repulsiveness; uncleanness 80; beastliness, bestiality, brutality; **rottenness** *and* lousiness <nf>; the pits <nf>; shoddiness, shabbiness; scurviness, **baseness** 661.3; **worthlessness** 998.2

3 **evil, bad, wrong, ill; harm, hurt, injury, damage, detriment; destruction** 395; despoliation; mischief, havoc; outrage, atrocity; crime, foul play; abomination, grievance, vexation, woe, crying evil; poison 1001.3; blight, venom, toxin, **bane** 1001; **corruption,** pollution, infection, befoulment, defilement; environmental pollution, fly in the ointment, worm in the apple *or* rose; skeleton in the closet; snake in the grass, Pandora's Box; "something rotten in the state of Denmark"— Shakespeare; ills the flesh is heir to; the worst; *annus horribilis* <L>

4 **bad influence,** malevolent influence, evil star, **ill wind;** evil genius, **hoodoo** *and* **jinx** <nf>, **Jonah; curse,** enchantment, whammy *and* double *or* triple whammy <nf>, spell, hex, voodoo; **evil eye,** *malocchio* <Ital>; malediction; collateral damage

5 **harmfulness, hurtfulness,** injuriousness, banefulness, balefulness, detrimentalness, deleteriousness, perniciousness, mischievousness, noxiousness, venomousness, poisonousness, toxicity, virulence, noisomeness, **malignance** *or* **malignancy, malignity, viciousness;** unhealthiness 82.1; disease 85; deadliness, lethality 308.9; ominousness 133.6

VERBS 6 work evil, do ill; **harm, hurt; injure,** scathe, wound, **damage; destroy** 395.10; despoil, prejudice, disadvantage, impair, disserve, distress; **wrong,** do wrong, do wrong by, aggrieve, do evil, do a mischief, do an ill office to; **molest,** afflict; lay a hand on; get into trouble; **abuse,** bash <nf>, batter, outrage, violate, maltreat, mistreat 389.5; torment, **harass,** hassle <nf>, persecute, savage, crucify, torture 96.18; play mischief *or* havoc with, wreak havoc on, play hob with <nf>; **corrupt,** deprave, taint, pollute, infect, befoul, defile; poison, envenom, blight; **curse,** put a whammy on <nf>, give the evil eye, hex, jinx, bewitch; spell *or* mean trouble, threaten, menace 514.2; doom; condemn 602.3

ADJS 7 **bad, evil, ill,** untoward, black, sinister; **wicked, wrong,** peccant, iniquitous, **vicious; sinful** 654.16; criminal; unhealthy 82.5; **inferior** 1005.9; unskillful 414.15; unkind, malevolent 144.19; inauspicious, unfavorable 133.16; inexpedient 996.5; unpleasant 98.17; invalid 19.15; inaccurate 975.17; improper 638.3

8 <nf terms> **lousy,** punk, bum, badass, shitty, crappy, cruddy, cheesy, dog-ass, gnarly, gross, raunchy, piss-poor, rat-ass, **crummy,** grim, low-rent, low-ride, putrid, icky, skanky, yecchy, vomity, barfy, stinking, stinky, creepy, hairy, god-awful, gosh-awful

9 **terrible, dreadful,** awful <nf>, dire, horrible, horrid; atrocious, outrageous, heinous, villainous, nefarious; enormous, monstrous; **deplorable,** lamentable, regrettable, pitiful, pitiable, woeful, woesome <old>, grievous, sad 98.20; flagrant, **scandalous,** shameful, **shocking,** infamous, **notorious,** arrant, **egregious;** unclean 80.20; shoddy, schlocky <nf>, shabby, scurvy, **base** 661.12; **odious, obnoxious,** offensive, gross,

disgusting, repulsive, loathsome, **abominable, detestable, despicable, contemptible,** beneath contempt, hateful; blameworthy, **reprehensible;** rank, fetid, foul, filthy, vile, fulsome, noisome, **nasty,** squalid, sordid, **wretched;** beastly, brutal; as bad as they come, as bad as they make 'em <nf>, as bad as bad can be; worst; too bad; below par, subpar, not up to scratch or snuff or the mark, poor-quality, **worthless**

10 **execrable, damnable;** damned, accursed, cursed 513.9; infernal, hellish, devilish, fiendish, satanic, ghoulish, demoniac, demonic, demonical, diabolic, diabolical, unholy, ungodly

11 evil-fashioned, ill-fashioned, evil-shaped, ill-shaped, evil-qualitied, evil-looking, ill-looking, evil-favored, ill-favored, evil-hued, evil-faced, evil-minded, evil-eyed, ill-affected <old>, evil-gotten, ill-gotten, ill-conceived

12 **harmful, hurtful,** scatheful, **baneful,** baleful, distressing, **injurious, damaging, detrimental,** deleterious, counterproductive, **pernicious,** mischievous; noxious, mephitic, venomous, venenate, poisonous, venenous, veneniferous, toxic, virulent, noisome; malignant, malign, malevolent, malefic, vicious; prejudicial, disadvantageous, disserviceable; corruptive, corrupting, corrosive, corroding; deadly, lethal; ominous 133.16

ADVS 13 **badly,** bad <nf>, ill, evil, evilly, wrong, wrongly, amiss; to one's cost

14 **terribly, dreadfully,** dreadful <nf>, **horribly,** horridly, **awfully** <nf>, **atrociously, outrageously;** flagrantly, scandalously, shamefully, shockingly, infamously, notoriously, egregiously, grossly, offensively, nauseatingly, fulsomely, odiously, **vilely,** obnoxiously, **disgustingly,** loathsomely; wretchedly, sordidly, shabbily, basely, abominably, detestably, despicably, contemptibly, foully, nastily; brutally, bestially, savagely, viciously; something fierce or terrible <nf>

15 **harmfully, hurtfully, banefully,** balefully, **injuriously, damagingly, detrimentally,** deleteriously, counterproductively, **perniciously,** mischievously; noxiously, venomously, poisonously, toxically, virulently, noisomely; **malignantly,** malignly, malevolently, malefically, **viciously;** prejudicially, disadvantageously, disserviceably; corrosively, corrodingly

1001 BANE

NOUNS 1 **bane, curse, affliction,** infliction, visitation, **plague, pestilence,** pest, calamity, **scourge,** torment, open wound, running sore, grievance, woe, burden, crushing burden; disease 85; death 307; evil, harm 1000.3; destruction 395; vexation 96.2; thorn, thorn in the flesh or side, pea in the shoe; bugbear, **bête noire,** bogy, bogeymen, nemesis, arch-nemesis

2 **blight,** blast; canker, cancer; mold, fungus, mildew, smut, must, rust; rot, dry rot; **pest;** worm, worm in the apple or rose; moth <old>

3 **poison, venom,** venin, virus <old>, toxic, toxin, toxicant; eradicant, **pesticide; insecticide,** insect powder, bug bomb <nf>; roach powder, roach paste; stomach poison, contact poison, systemic insecticide or systemic, fumigant, chemosterilant; chlorinated hydrocarbon insecticide, organic chlorine; organic phosphate insecticide; carbamate insecticide, sheepdip; termiticide, miticide, acaricide, vermicide, anthelminthic; rodenticide, ratsbane, rat poison; **herbicide,** defoliant, Agent Orange, paraquat, **weed killer;** fungicide; microbicide, germicide, antiseptic, disinfectant, antibiotic; **toxicology;** toxic waste, **environmental pollutant;** hemlock, arsenic, cyanide; carcinogen

4 **miasma, mephitis,** malaria <old>; effluvium, exhaust, exhaust gas; coal gas, chokedamp, blackdamp, firedamp; air or atmospheric pollution, smoke, smog, exhaust fumes, carbon monoxide; secondhand smoke; acid rain

5 sting, stinger, dart; **fang,** tang <nf>; beesting, snakebite

6 **poisonous plants**

aconite	horsetail
amanita	jack-in-the-pulpit
angel's trumpet	jimsonweed
banewort	laburnum
bearded darnel	larkspur
belladonna	locoweed
black henbane	marijuana
black nightshade	mayapple
bleeding heart	mescal bean
castor-oil plant	monkshood
chinaberry	nightshade
corn cackle	nux vomica
cowbane	opium poppy
datura	poinsettia
deadly nightshade	poison bean
death camas	poisonberry
death cup or angel	poison bush
devil's trumpet	poison hemlock or parsley
elderberry	poison ivy
ergot	poison oak
fiddleneck	poison rye grass
foxglove	poison sumac
gastrolobium	poison tobacco
hairy vetch	poisonweed
hellebore	pokeweed
hemlock	sheep laurel
henbane	thornapple

tobacco
upas
water hemlock

white snakeroot
wisteria
wolfsbane

1002 PERFECTION

NOUNS 1 perfection, faultlessness, flawlessness, defectlessness, indefectibility, impeccability, absoluteness; infallibility; spotlessness, stainlessness, taintlessness, purity, immaculateness; sinlessness; chastity 664

2 soundness, integrity, intactness, wholeness, entireness, completeness; **fullness,** plenitude; finish; mint condition

3 acme of perfection, pink, pink of perfection, culmination, perfection, height, top, acme, ultimate, summit, pinnacle, peak, highest pitch, climax, consummation, *ne plus ultra* <L>, **the last word,** a dream come true

4 pattern *or* standard *or* mold *or* norm of perfection, very model, quintessence; archetype, prototype, exemplar, mirror, **epitome;** *ne plus ultra* <L>, perfect specimen, highest type; **classic,** masterwork, masterpiece, *chef d'œuvre* <Fr>, crowning achievement, showpiece; **ideal** 786.4; role model; **paragon** 659.4; a 10 <nf>

VERBS 5 perfect, develop, flesh out, ripen, mature; improve 392.7; crown, culminate, put on the finishing touch; lick *or* whip into shape, fine-tune; complete 407.6; do to perfection 407.7

ADJS 6 perfect, ideal, faultless, flawless, unflawed, defectless, not to be improved, picture-perfect, **impeccable,** absolute; **just right,** just so; spotless, stainless, taintless, unblemished, untainted, unspotted, immaculate, **pure,** uncontaminated, unadulterated, unmixed; sinless; chaste 664.4; indefective <old>, indefectible, trouble-free; infallible; beyond all praise, irreproachable, unfaultable, *sans peur et sans reproche* <Fr>, **matchless, peerless** 249.15; A-1, world-class, number-one

7 sound, intact, whole, entire, complete, integral; **full;** total, utter, unqualified 960.2

8 undamaged, unharmed, unhurt, uninjured, unscathed, **unspoiled,** virgin, inviolate, **unimpaired;** harmless, scatheless; **unmarred,** unmarked, unscarred, unscratched, undefaced, unbruised; **unbroken,** unshattered, untorn; undemolished, undestroyed; undeformed, unmutilated, unmangled, unmaimed; unfaded, unworn, unwithered, bright, fresh, untouched, pristine, mint; none the worse for wear, right as rain

9 perfected, finished, polished, refined; done to a T *or* to a turn; **classic, classical,** masterly, masterful,

expert, proficient; ripened, ripe, matured, mature; developed, fully developed; thorough-going, thorough-paced; **consummate,** quintessential, archetypical, exemplary, model

ADVS 10 perfectly, ideally; **faultlessly, flawlessly, impeccably; just right;** spotlessly; immaculately, purely; infallibly; **wholly, entirely, completely, fully,** thoroughly, totally, absolutely 794.15

11 to perfection, to a turn, to a T, to a finish, to a nicety; to a fare-thee-well *or* fare-you-well *or* fare-ye-well <nf>; to beat the band <nf>

1003 IMPERFECTION

NOUNS 1 imperfection, imperfectness, room for improvement; **unperfectedness; faultiness, defectiveness,** defectibility; **shortcoming, deficiency,** lack, want, shortage, **inadequacy,** inadequateness; erroneousness, **fallibility;** inaccuracy, inexactness, inexactitude 975.2; **unsoundness,** incompleteness, patchiness, sketchiness, unevenness; **impairment** 393; **mediocrity** 1005; immaturity, undevelopment 406.4; impurity, adulteration 797.3

2 fault, *faute* <Fr>, **defect, deficiency, inadequacy,** imperfection, kink, defection <old>, hangup; **flaw,** hole, bug <nf>; something missing; catch <nf>, fly in the ointment, problem, little problem, curate's egg <Brit>, snag, drawback; **crack,** rift; **weakness,** frailty, infirmity, failure, **failing, foible, shortcoming;** weak point, Achilles' heel, vulnerable place, chink in one's armor, weak link, soft spot, underbelly; **blemish,** taint 1004.3; **malfunction,** glitch <nf>

VERBS 3 fall short, come short, miss, miss out, miss the mark, miss by a mile <nf>, not qualify, fall down <nf>, **not measure up,** not come up to par, not come up to the mark, not come up to scratch *or* to snuff <nf>, not pass muster, not bear inspection, not hack it *and* not make it *and* not cut it *and* not make the cut <nf>; not make the grade; fail

ADJS 4 imperfect, not perfect, less than perfect; good in parts; unperfected; **defective, faulty, inadequate, deficient,** short, not all it's cracked up to be <nf>, lacking, wanting, found wanting; off; erroneous, **fallible;** inaccurate, inexact, imprecise 975.17; **unsound, incomplete,** unfinished, partial, patchy, sketchy, uneven, unthorough; makeshift 995.7; **damaged, impaired** 393.27; mediocre 1005.7; **blemished** 1004.8; half-baked <nf>, immature, undeveloped 406.12; impure, adulterated, mixed

ADVS 5 imperfectly, inadequately, deficiently; **incompletely,** partially; **faultily, defectively**

1004 BLEMISH

NOUNS 1 blemish, disfigurement, disfiguration, **defacement;** scar, keloid, cicatrix; needle scar, track *or* crater <nf>; scratch; scab; blister, vesicle, bulla, bleb; weal, wale, welt, wen, sebaceous cyst; port-wine stain *or* mark, hemangioma, strawberry mark, macula; pock, pustule; pockmark, pit; nevus, birthmark, mole; freckle, lentigo; milium, whitehead, blackhead, comedo, pimple, zit <nf>, hickey <nf>, sty; crud; wart, verruca; **crack,** craze, check, rift, split; **deformity,** deformation, warp, twist, kink, **distortion; flaw, defect, fault** 1003.2

2 discoloration, discolorment, discolor <old>; bruise; foxing

3 stain, taint, tarnish; mark, brand, **stigma;** maculation, macule, macula; **spot, blot,** blur, **blotch,** patch, speck, speckle, fleck, flick, flyspeck; daub, dab; **smirch, smudge,** smutch *or* smouch, smut, **smear;** splotch, splash, splatter, spatter; bloodstain; eyesore; caste mark, tattoo, brand

VERBS 4 blemish, disfigure, deface, **flaw, mar;** scab; scar, cicatrize, scarify; **crack,** craze, check, split; **deform,** warp, twist, kink, **distort**

5 spot, bespot, **blot, blotch, speck, speckle,** bespeckle, maculate <old>; freckle; flyspeck; **spatter, splatter,** splash, splotch

6 stain, bestain, **discolor,** smirch, besmirch, **taint,** attaint, **tarnish; mark, stigmatize,** brand; smear, besmear, daub, bedaub, slubber <Brit nf>; blur, slur <nf>; **darken, blacken;** smoke, besmoke; scorch, singe, sear; dirty, **soil** 80.16

7 bloodstain, bloody, ensanguine

ADJS 8 blemished, disfigured, defaced, **marred,** scarred, keloidal, cicatrized, scarified, stigmatized, scabbed, scabby; pimpled, pimply; cracked, crazed, checked, split; deformed, warped, twisted, kinked, distorted; **faulty, flawed, defective** 1003.4

9 spotted, spotty, maculate, maculated, macular, blotched, **blotchy,** splotched, splotchy; **speckled,** speckly, bespeckled; freckled, freckly, freckle-faced; spattered, splattered, splashed

10 stained, discolored, foxed, foxy, **tainted, tarnished,** smirched, besmirched; stigmatized, stigmatic, stigmatiferous; darkened, blackened; murky, smoky, inky; polluted, **soiled** 80.21

11 bloodstained, blood-spattered, **bloody,** sanguinary, **gory,** ensanguined

1005 MEDIOCRITY

NOUNS 1 mediocrity, mediocreness, fairishness, modestness, modesty, moderateness, middlingness, **indifference;** respectability, passableness, **tolerableness** 999.3; **dullness,** lackluster, tediousness 117.1

2 ordinariness, averageness, normalness, normality, **commonness, commonplaceness;** unexceptionality, unremarkableness, unnoteworthiness; conventionality

3 inferiority, inferiorness, **poorness,** lowliness, humbleness, **baseness, meanness, commonness,** coarseness, tackiness, tack; **second-rateness,** third-rateness, fourth-rateness

4 low grade, low class, low quality, poor quality; second best, next best

5 mediocrity, second-rater, third-rater, fourth-rater, nothing *or* nobody special, no great shakes <nf>, no prize, no prize package, no brain surgeon, no rocket scientist, not much of a bargain, small potatoes *and* small beer <nf>; tinhorn <nf>; **nobody, nonentity** 998.7; middle class, bourgeoisie, burgherdom; suburbia, the burbs <nf>; Middle America, silent majority

6 irregular, second, third; schlock <nf>

ADJS 7 mediocre, middling, indifferent, fair, fairish, fair to middling <nf>, moderate, modest, medium, betwixt and between; respectable, passable, tolerable; so-so, *comme ci comme ça* <Fr>; of a kind, of a sort, of sorts <nf>; nothing to brag about, not much to boast of, nothing to write home about; bush-league; dull, lackluster, tedious 117.6; insipid, vapid, wishy-washy, namby-pamby

8 ordinary, average, normal, **common, commonplace,** garden *and* garden-variety <nf>, run-of-mine *or* -mill, run-of-the-mine *or* -mill, vanilla <nf>; **unexceptional, unremarkable, unnoteworthy,** unspectacular, nothing *or* nobody special *and* no great shakes <nf>, no prize, no prize package, no brain surgeon, no rocket scientist; conventional; middle-class, bourgeois, plastic <nf>; suburban; usual, regular

9 inferior, poor, punk <nf>, **base, mean, common,** coarse, cheesy *and* tacky <nf>, tinny; shabby, seedy; cheap, Mickey Mouse <nf>, paltry; irregular; second-best; **second-rate,** third-rate, fourth-rate; **second-class,** third-class, fourth-class, etc; **low-grade, low-class,** low-quality, low-test, low-rent *and* low-ride <nf>

10 below par, below standard, **below the mark** <nf>, substandard, **not up to scratch** *or* snuff *or* the mark <nf>, not up to sample *or* standard *or* specification, off

ADVS 11 mediocrely, middlingly, fairly, fairishly, middling well, fair to middling <nf>, moderately, modestly, **indifferently, so-so;** passably, **tolerably**

12 inferiorly, poorly, basely, meanly, commonly

1006 DANGER

NOUNS **1 danger, peril, endangerment, imperilment, jeopardy, hazard, risk,** cause for alarm, **menace, threat** 514; **crisis, emergency,** hot spot, nasty *or* tricky spot, pass, pinch, strait, plight, predicament 1013.4; powder keg, time bomb; dangerous *or* unpredictable *or* uncontrollable person, loose cannon <nf>; rocks *or* breakers *or* white water ahead, gathering clouds, storm clouds; dangerous ground, yawning *or* gaping chasm, quicksand, thin ice; hornet's nest; house of cards, cardhouse; hardball <nf>, no tea party, no picnic; desperate situation; hazardous materials

2 dangerousness, hazardousness, riskiness, treachery, precariousness 971.6, chanciness, dodginess <chiefly Brit nf>, diceyness <nf>, **perilousness; unsafeness,** unhealthiness <nf>; criticalness; **ticklishness,** slipperiness, touchiness, delicacy, ticklish business *and* shaky ground <nf>; **insecurity,** unsoundness, instability, unsteadiness, shakiness, totteriness, wonkiness <Brit nf>; sword of Damocles; **unreliability,** undependability, untrustworthiness 971.6; **unsureness,** unpredictability, **uncertainty,** doubtfulness, dubiousness 971.2

3 exposure, openness, liability, nonimmunity, susceptibility; **unprotectedness, defenselessness,** nakedness, helplessness; lamb, sitting duck; roadkill <nf>; naiveté

4 vulnerability, pregnability, penetrability, assailability, vincibility; weakness 16; vulnerable point, **weak link, weak point, soft spot,** heel of Achilles, chink, chink in one's armor, "the soft underbelly"—Sir Winston Churchill; tragic flaw, fatal flaw

5 <hidden danger> snags, rocks, reefs, ledges; coral heads; shallows, shoals; sandbank, sandbar, sands; quicksands; crevasses; rockbound *or* ironbound coast, lee shore; undertow, undercurrent; **pitfall;** snake in the grass; trap, booby trap, springe, snare, tripwire, pitfall; snarling dog, ticking package; cloud on the horizon

VERBS **6 endanger, imperil,** peril; **risk, hazard, gamble, gamble with; jeopardize,** jeopard, jeopardy, compromise, put in danger, **put in jeopardy,** put on the spot *and* lay on the line <nf>; **expose,** lay open; incur danger, run into *or* encounter danger

7 take chances, take a chance, chance, risk, stake, gamble, hazard, press *or* push one's luck, **run the chance** *or* **risk** *or* **hazard;** risk one's neck, run a risk, go out on a limb, stick one's neck out<nf>, **expose oneself,** bare one's breast, lower one's guard, **lay oneself open to,** leave oneself wide open, open the door to, let oneself in for; drive recklessly; **tempt Providence** *or* **fate,** forget the odds, **defy danger,** skate on thin ice, court destruction, dance on the razor's edge, go in harm's way, hang by a hair *or* a thread, stand *or* sleep on a volcano, sit on a barrel of gunpowder, build a house of cards, put one's head in the lion's mouth, "beard the lion in his den"—Sir Walter Scott, march up to the cannon's mouth, play with fire, go through fire and water, go out of one's depth, go to sea in a sieve, carry too much sail, sail too near the wind; risk one's life, throw caution to the wind, **take one's life in one's hand, dare, face up to, brave** 492.10

8 be in danger, be in peril, be *in extremis,* be in a desperate case, have one's name on the danger list, have the chances *or* odds against one, have one's back to the wall, have something hanging over one's head; be despaired of; hang by a thread; tremble on the verge, totter on the brink, teeter on the edge; feel the ground sliding from under one; have to run for it; race against time *or* the clock; be threatened, be on the spot *or* in a bind <nf>

ADJS **9 dangerous,** dangersome <nf>, **perilous,** periculous, parlous, jeopardous, bad, ugly, serious, critical, explosive, attended *or* beset *or* fraught with danger; alarming, too close for comfort *or* words, **menacing, threatening** 514.3

10 hazardous, risky, chancy, dodgy <chiefly Brit nf>, dicey <nf>, hairy <nf>, aleatory, aleatoric, riskful, full of risk; **adventurous,** venturous, venturesome; **speculative,** wildcat

11 unsafe, unhealthy <nf>; **unreliable, undependable, untrustworthy,** treacherous, **insecure, unsound,** unstable, unsteady, shaky, tottery, wonky <Brit nf>, rocky; **unsure, uncertain,** unpredictable, doubtful, dubious; on the brink *or* verge

12 precarious, ticklish, touchy, touch-and-go, **critical, delicate;** slippery, slippy; on thin ice, on slippery ground; hanging by a thread, trembling in the balance; nerve-racking

13 in danger, in jeopardy, in peril, at risk, in a bad way; **endangered, imperiled, jeopardized,** *in periculo* <L>, at the last extremity, *in extremis* <L>, in deadly peril, *in periculo mortis* <L>, in desperate case; threatened, up against it, in a bad way, on the spot *and* on *or* in the hot seat <nf>; sitting on a powder keg; between the hammer and the anvil, between Scylla and Charybdis, between two fires, between the devil and the deep blue sea, between a rock and a hard place <nf>; in a predicament 1013.21; cornered

14 unprotected, unshielded, unsheltered, uncovered, unscreened, **unguarded, undefended,** unattended, unwatched, unfortified; armorless, unarmored, **unarmed,** bare-handed, weaponless; guardless, ungarrisoned, insecure, **defenseless, helpless;** unwarned, unsuspecting

15 exposed, open, out in the open, naked, bare; out on a limb <nf>; liable, susceptible, nonimmune

16 vulnerable, naïve, **pregnable,** penetrable, expugnable; assailable, attackable, surmountable; conquerable, beatable <nf>, vincible; weak 16.12–14

ADVS **17 dangerously, perilously, hazardously, riskily,** critically, unsafely; **precariously,** ticklishly; at gun point

1007 SAFETY

NOUNS **1 safety,** safeness, **security,** surety <old>, assurance; risklessness, immunity, clear sailing; **protection,** safeguard 1008.3; harmlessness 999.9; airworthiness, crashworthiness, roadworthiness, seaworthiness; invulnerability 15.4; safety in numbers; wide berth, safe distance; safekeeping

VERBS **2 be safe, be on the safe side; keep safe, come through;** weather, ride out, weather the storm; keep one's head above water, tide over; keep a safe distance; land on one's feet; save one's bacon <nf>, save one's neck; lead a charmed life, have nine lives

3 play safe <nf>, **keep on the safe side,** give danger a wide berth, watch oneself, watch out, take precautions 494.6, demand assurances; assure oneself, make sure, keep an eye or a weather eye out, look before one leaps; **save, protect** 1008.18

ADJS **4 safe, secure, safe and sound,** not at risk; immune, immunized; insured; **protected** 1008.21; on the safe side; unthreatened, unmolested; unhurt, unharmed, unscathed, intact, untouched, with a whole skin, undamaged, whole

5 unhazardous, undangerous, unperilous, unrisky, riskless, **unprecarious;** fail-safe, trouble-free; recession-proof; guaranteed, warranteed; dependable, reliable, trustworthy, sound, stable, steady, firm 970.17; "founded upon a rock"—Bible; as safe as houses; harmless; invulnerable; -proof

6 in safety, out of danger, past danger, out of the meshes or toils, in, home, out of the woods and over the hump or home free <nf>, free and dry <Brit nf>, **in the clear, out of harm's reach or way;** under cover, under lock and key; in shelter, in harbor or port, at anchor or haven, in the shadow of a rock; on sure or solid ground, on *terra firma,* high and dry, above water; in safe keeping

7 snug, cozy, home free; crashworthy, roadworthy, airworthy, seaworthy, seakindly

ADVS **8 safely, securely,** reliably, dependably; with safety, **with impunity**

INTERJS **9 all's well!,** all clear!, all serene!, A-OK!; ally-ally out'n free!

PHRS **10** the danger is past, the storm has blown over, the coast is clear

1008 PROTECTION

NOUNS **1 protection, guard, shielding, safekeeping; policing, law enforcement; patrol, patroling,** community policing, professional or bureaucratic policing; eye, protectiveness, watchfulness, vigilance, watchful eye, shepherding; house-sitting <nf>; protective custody; **safeguarding, security,** security industry, public safety, safety 1007; **shelter, cover,** shade, shadow <old>, windbreak, lee; **refuge** 1009; preservation 397; **defense** 460; protective coating, Teflon coating <trademark>

2 protectorship, guardianship, stewardship, custodianship; **care, charge, keeping, nurture, nurturing, nurturance, custody, fostering, fosterage,** cocooning, fatherly or motherly eye; **hands,** safe hands, wing; **auspices, patronage, tutelage, guidance; ward,** wardship, wardenship, watch and ward; cure, pastorship, pastorage, pastorate; **oversight,** jurisdiction, management, ministry, administration, government, governance; **child care,** infant care, daycare, family service, aftercare; baby-sitting, baby-minding <Brit>

3 safeguard, palladium, **guard,** preventive measure, precautionary steps, **precaution; shield, screen,** aegis; umbrella, protective umbrella; patent, copyright; **bulwark** 460.4; backstop; fender, mudguard, **bumper, buffer, cushion,** pad, padding; seat or safety belt; protective clothing; shin guard, knuckle guard, knee guard, nose guard, hand guard, arm guard, ear guard, finger guard, foot guard; goggles, mask, face mask, welder's mask, fencer's mask; safety shoes; helmet, hard hat <nf>, crash helmet, sun helmet; cowcatcher, pilot; dashboard; windshield, windscreen <Brit>; dodger and cockpit dodger <Brit>; life preserver 397.6; lifeline, safety rail, guardrail, handrail; governor; safety, safety switch, interlock; safety valve, safety plug; fuse, circuit breaker; insulation; safety glass, laminated glass; lightning rod, lightning conductor; **anchor,** bower, sea anchor, sheet anchor, drogue; **parachute; safety net;** prophylactic, preventive 86.20; contraceptive 86.23

4 insurance, assurance <Brit>; **annuity,** variable annuity; **social security** 611.7; nest egg, savings account, provision; **insurance company,** stock company, mutual company; **insurance policy,** policy, certificate of insurance; deductible; insurance man, underwriter, insurance broker, insurance agent, insurance adjuster, actuary; lemon law

5 **protector, keeper,** protectress, safekeeper, minder; patron, patroness; tower, pillar, strong arm, tower of strength, rock; champion; **defender** 460.7

6 **guardian, warden,** governor; **custodian,** steward, **keeper, caretaker,** warder <Brit>, attendant; caregiver; next friend, prochein ami, guardian *ad litem;* **curator,** conservator; janitor; castellan; **shepherd,** herd, cowherd; **game warden,** gamekeeper; **ranger,** forest ranger, forester; lifeguard, lifesaver <Brit>; air warden; guardian angel

7 **chaperon,** duenna; **governess;** escort

8 **nurse, nursemaid,** nurserymaid, nanny <chiefly Brit>, amah, ayah, mammy <nf>; dry nurse, wet nurse; **baby-sitter,** baby-minder <Brit>, sitter <nf>

9 **guard,** guarder, guardsman <old>, warder; **outguard, outpost; picket,** outlying picket, inlying picket, outrider; advance guard, **vanguard,** van; **rear guard;** coast guard; armed guard, security guard; jailer 429.10; bank guard; railway *or* train guard; goalkeeper, goaltender, goalie <nf>; garrison; cordon, *cordon sanitaire* <Fr>

10 **watchman, watch,** watcher; watchkeeper; **lookout,** lookout man, **sentinel,** picket, **sentry; scout,** vedette; **point,** forward observer, spotter; **patrol, patrolman,** patroller, roundsman; night watchman, Charley <nf>; fireguard, fire patrolman, fire warden; airplane spotter; Argus

11 **watchdog,** bandog, guard dog, attack dog; sheep dog; Cerberus

12 **doorkeeper, doorman, gatekeeper,** Cerberus, warden, **porter, janitor,** commissionaire <Brit>, *concierge* <Fr>, ostiary, usher; receptionist

13 **picket, picketer,** demonstrator, picket line; counterdemonstrator

14 **bodyguard,** safeguard; **convoy, escort;** guards, praetorian guard; guardsman; yeoman *or* yeoman of the guard *or* beefeater, gentleman-at-arms, Life Guardsman <all England>

15 **policeman, policewoman, constable, officer,** police officer, *flic* <Fr nf>, *gendarme* <Fr>, *carabiniere* <Ital>; peace officer, law enforcer, law enforcement agent, arm of the law; military policeman *or* MP; detective 576.10; police matron; patrolman, police constable <Brit>; trooper, mounted policeman, state police, state trooper; reeve, portreeve; **sheriff, marshal;** deputy sheriff, deputy, bound bailiff, catchpole, beagle <nf>, bombailiff <Brit nf>; sergeant, police sergeant;

roundsman; lieutenant, police lieutenant; captain, police captain; inspector, police inspector; superintendent, chief of police; commissioner, police commissioner; government man, federal, fed *and* G-man <nf>; narc <nf>; **bailiff,** tipstaff, tipstaves <pl>; mace-bearer, lictor, sergeant at arms; beadle; traffic officer, meter maid; dective

16 <nf terms> cop, copper, John Law, bluecoat, bull, flatfoot, gumshoe, gendarme, shamus, dick, pig, flattie, bizzy *and* bobby *and* peeler <Brit>, Dogberry; the cops, the law, the fuzz, feds, heat; New York's finest; tec, op

17 **police, police force,** law enforcement agency; the force, forces of law and order, long arm of the law; **constabulary;** state police, troopers *or* state troopers, highway patrol, county police, provincial police; security force; special police; tactical police, riot police; SWAT *or* special weapons and tactics, SWAT team, **posse,** *posse comitatus* <L>; **vigilantes,** vigilance committee; secret police, political police; Federal Bureau of Investigation *or* FBI; military police *or* MP; shore patrol *or* SP; Scotland Yard <Brit>; *Sûreté* <France>; Cheka, NKVD, MVD, OGPU <Russ>; Gestapo <Ger>; Royal Canadian Mounted Police *or* RCMP *and* Mounties <Can>; Interpol, International Criminal Police Commission; neighborhood watch

VERBS 18 **protect, guard, safeguard, secure, keep,** bless, make safe, **police, enforce the law;** keep from harm; **insure,** underwrite; ensure, guarantee 438.9; patent, copyright, register; **cushion;** champion, go to bat for <nf>; ride shotgun <nf>, fend, defend 460.8; **shelter, shield, screen, cover,** cloak, shroud <old>, temper the wind to the shorn lamb; **harbor, haven;** nestle; compass about, fence; arm, armor; put in a safe place, keep under cover

19 **care for, take care of;** preserve, conserve; provide for, support; take charge of, **take under one's wing,** make one a protégé; **look after,** see after, **attend to, minister to,** look *or* see to, look *or* watch out for <nf>, have *or* keep an eye on *or* upon, keep a sharp eye on *or* upon, **watch over,** keep watch over, **watch, mind, tend;** keep tab *or* tabs on <nf>; **shepherd,** ride herd on <nf>; **chaperon,** matronize; baby-sit <nf>; **foster, nurture, cherish, nurse; mother,** be a mother *or* father to

20 **watch, keep watch, keep guard,** keep watch over, keep vigil, keep watch and ward; stand guard, stand sentinel; be on the lookout 339.8; mount guard; **police,** patrol, pound a beat <nf>, go on one's beat

ADJS 21 **protected, guarded,** safeguarded, defended; safe 1007.4–6; patented, copyrighted; **sheltered, shielded,** screened, covered, cloaked; policed; armed 460.14; invulnerable

22 under the protection of, under the shield of, under the auspices of, under the aegis of, **under one's wing,** under the wing of, under the shadow of one's wing

23 protective, custodial, guardian, tutelary; curatorial; vigilant, watchful, on the watch, on top of; prophylactic, preventive; immunizing; protecting, guarding, safeguarding, sheltering, **shielding,** screening, covering; fostering, parental; defensive 460.11; Teflon-coated <trademark>

1009 REFUGE

NOUNS **1 refuge, sanctuary,** safehold, **asylum, haven, port,** harborage, **harbor;** harbor of refuge, port in a storm, snug harbor, safe haven; game sanctuary, bird sanctuary, preserve, forest preserve, game preserve; stronghold 460.6; **political asylum;** Rock of Gibraltar

2 recourse, resource, resort; last resort or resource, *dernier ressort* and *pis aller* <Fr>; **hope; expedient** 995.2

3 shelter, cover, covert, coverture; concealment 346; *abri* <Fr>, dugout, cave, earth, funk hole <Brit nf>, foxhole; **bunker;** trench; storm cellar, storm cave, cyclone cellar; air-raid shelter, bomb shelter, bombproof, fallout shelter, safety zone or isle or island; stockade, fort

4 asylum, home, retreat; **poorhouse,** almshouse, workhouse <Brit>, poor farm; **orphanage; hospice,** hospitium; old folks' home, rest home, nursing home, old soldiers' home, sailors' snug harbor; foster home; safe house; halfway house; retirement home or village or community, life-care home, continuing-care retirement community or CCRC

5 retreat, recess, hiding place, **hideaway,** hideout, hidey-hole <nf>, priest hole; **sanctum, inner sanctum, sanctum sanctorum,** holy ground, holy of holies, adytum; private place, privacy <old>, secret place; **den,** lair, mew; safe house; **cloister,** hermitage, ashram, cell; **ivory tower;** study, library

6 harbor, haven, port, seaport, port of call, free port, treaty port, home port; hoverport; harborage, **anchorage,** anchorage ground, protected anchorage, moorage, moorings; **roadstead,** road, roads; berth, slip; **dock,** dockage, marina, basin; dry dock; shipyard, dockyard; **wharf, pier,** quay; harborside, dockside, pierside, quayside, landing, landing place or stage, jetty, jutty <old>; breakwater, mole, groin; seawall, embankment, bulkhead

VERBS **7 take refuge, take shelter,** seek refuge, **claim sanctuary,** claim refugee status, ask for political asylum, seek asylum; run into port; fly to, throw oneself into the arms of; bar the gate, lock or bolt the door, raise the drawbridge, let the portcullis down; take cover 346.8

8 find refuge or sanctuary, make port, reach safety; seclude or sequester oneself, dwell or live in an ivory tower; make port

1010 PROSPERITY

NOUNS **1 prosperity,** prosperousness, thriving or flourishing condition; **success** 409; **welfare, well-being,** weal, happiness, felicity; quality of life; comfortable or easy circumstances, **comfort, ease,** security; **life of ease,** life of Riley <nf>, **the good life; clover** and **velvet** <nf>, **bed of roses, luxury,** lap of luxury, Easy Street and Fat City and hog heaven <nf>; the affluent life, gracious life, gracious living; fat of the land; fleshpots, fleshpots of Egypt; milk and honey, loaves and fishes; a chicken in every pot, a car in every garage; purple and fine linen; high standard of living; upward mobility; **affluence, wealth** 618

2 good fortune or **luck,** happy fortune, **fortune, luck,** the breaks <nf>; **fortunateness, luckiness,** felicity <old>; blessing, smiles of fortune, fortune's favor

3 stroke of luck, piece of good luck; blessing; **fluke** and lucky strike and scratch hit and **break** <nf>, **good** or **lucky break** <nf>; **run** or **streak of luck** <nf>; bonanza; Midas touch

4 good times, piping times, bright or palmy or halcyon days, days of wine and roses, rosy era; heyday; prosperity, era of prosperity; fair weather, sunshine; golden era, **golden age,** golden time, golden days, Saturnian age, reign of Saturn, *Saturnia regna* <L>; honeymoon; holiday; prime, youth; age of Aquarius, millennium; **utopia** 986.11; **heaven** 681

5 roaring trade, land-office business <nf>, bullishness, bull or bullish market, seller's market; **boom,** booming economy, expanding economy

6 lucky dog <nf>, lucky devil, fortune's favorite, favorite of the gods, fortune's child, destiny's darling

VERBS **7 prosper,** enjoy prosperity, **fare well,** get on well, do well, have it made or hacked <nf>, have a good thing going, have everything going one's way, get on swimmingly, go great guns <nf>; **turn out well, go well,** take a favorable turn; **succeed;** come on or along <nf>, come a long way, get on <nf>; **advance,** progress, make progress, make headway, get ahead <nf>, move up in the world, pull oneself up by one's own boot-straps

8 thrive, flourish, boom; blossom, bloom, flower; batten, fatten, grow fat; be fat, dumb, and happy <nf>

9 be prosperous, make good, make one's mark, rise *or* get on in the world, make a noise in the world <nf>, do all right by oneself <nf>, **make one's fortune;** grow rich; drive a roaring trade, do a land-office business <nf>, rejoice in a seller's market

10 live well, live in clover *or* on velvet <nf>, **live a life of ease,** live *or* lead the life of Riley, **live high, live high on the hog** <nf>, live on *or* off the fat of the land, ride the gravy train *and* piss on ice <nf>, roll in the lap of luxury; bask in the sunshine, have one's place in the sun; have a good *or* fine time of it

11 be fortunate, be lucky, be in luck, luck out <nf>, have all the luck, have one's moments <nf>, **lead** *or* **have a charmed life;** fall into the shithouse *and* come up with a five-dollar gold piece <nf>; **get a break** *and* get the breaks <nf>; hold aces *and* turn up trumps *or* roses <nf>; have a run of luck *and* hit a streak of luck <nf>; have it break good for one <nf>, have a stroke of luck; strike it lucky *and* make a lucky strike *and* strike oil <nf>, **strike it rich** <nf>, hit it big <nf>, strike a rich vein, come into money, drop into a good thing

ADJS **12 prosperous,** in good case; **successful,** rags-to-riches; **well-paid, high-income,** higher-income, well-heeled *and* upscale <nf>; **affluent, wealthy; comfortable,** comfortably situated, **easy;** on Easy Street *and* in Fat City *and* in hog heaven <nf>, **in clover** *and* **on velvet** <nf>, on a bed of roses, in luxury, high on the hog <nf>; up in the world, on top of the heap <nf>

13 thriving, flourishing, prospering, booming <nf>; vigorous, exuberant; in full swing, going strong <nf>; halcyon, palmy, balmy, rosy, piping, clear, fair; blooming, blossoming, flowering, fruiting; fat, sleek, in good case; fat, dumb, and happy <nf>

14 fortunate, lucky, providential; in luck; blessed, blessed with luck, favored; born under a lucky star, born with a silver spoon in one's mouth, born on the sunny side of the hedge; out of the woods, over the hump; **auspicious**

ADVS **15 prosperously, thrivingly, flourishingly,** boomingly, swimmingly <nf>

16 fortunately, luckily, providentially

1011 ADVERSITY

NOUNS **1 adversity,** adverse circumstances, difficulties, hard knocks *and* rough going <nf>, **hardship, trouble,** troubles, "sea of troubles"— Shakespeare, **rigor,** vicissitude, care, stress, pressure, stress of life; hard case *or* plight, **hard life,** dog's life, vale of tears; wretched *or* miserable *or* hard *or* unhappy lot, tough *or* hard row to hoe <nf>, ups and downs of life, things going against one; bitter cup, bitter pill; bummer *and* downer <nf>; the bad part, the downside <nf>; annoyance, irritation, aggravation; **difficulty** 1013; **trial,** tribulation, cross, bane, curse, blight, **affliction** 96.8; plight, predicament 1013.4; the pits <nf>, raw deal <nf>; turkey shoot <nf>

2 misfortune, mishap, ill hap, **misadventure, mischance,** *contretemps* <Fr>, grief; **disaster, calamity, catastrophe,** meltdown, cataclysm, **tragedy;** missed chance; **shock, blow,** hard *or* nasty *or* staggering blow; **accident,** casualty, collision, crash, plane *or* car crash; **wreck,** shipwreck; smash *and* smashup *and* crack-up *and* pileup <nf>; bad news <nf>

3 reverse, reversal, reversal of fortune, **setback,** check, severe check, backset *and* throwback <nf>; **comedown,** descent, down

4 unfortunateness, unluckiness, lucklessness, ill success; unprosperousness; starcrossed *or* ill-fated life; "the slings and arrows of outrageous fortune"—Shakespeare; inauspiciousness 133.7

5 bad luck, ill luck, **hard luck,** hard lines <Brit>, **tough** *or* **rotten luck** <nf>, raw deal <nf>, bad *or* tough *or* rotten break <nf>, bad patch, devil's own luck; **ill fortune,** bad fortune, evil fortune, evil star, ill wind, evil dispensation; frowns of fortune

6 hard times, bad times, sad times; evil day, ill day; rainy day; hard *or* stormy *or* heavy weather, storm clouds; **depression, recession, slump,** economic stagnation, **bust** <nf>; rough patch, bad spell; winter of discontent

7 unfortunate, poor unfortunate, the plaything *or* toy *or* sport of fortune, fortune's fool; **loser** *and* sure loser *and* non-starter <nf>, born loser; hard case *and* sad sack *and* hard-luck guy <nf>; *schlemiel* or *schlimazel* <Yiddish>; odd man out; the underclass, the dispossessed, the homeless, the wretched of the earth; victim 96.11, victim of fate; martyr

VERBS **8 go hard with,** go ill with; run one hard; **oppress, weigh on** *or* **upon,** weigh heavy on, weigh down, **burden,** overburden, load, overload, bear hard upon, lie on, lie hard *or* heavy upon; try one, put one out

9 have trouble; be born to trouble, be born under an evil star; **have a hard time of it,** be up against it <nf>, make heavy weather of it, meet adversity, have a bad time, lead *or* live a dog's life, have a tough *or* hard row to hoe; bear the brunt, bear more than one's share; be put to one's wit's end, not know which way to turn; **be unlucky, have bad**

or **rotten luck,** be misfortuned, get the short *or* shitty end of the stick <nf>, hit the skids <nf>

10 **come to grief,** have a mishap, suffer a misfortune, fall, be stricken, be staggered, be shattered, be poleaxed, be felled, come a cropper <Brit nf>, be clobbered <nf>; run aground, go on the rocks *or* shoals, split upon a rock; sink, drown; **founder**

11 **fall on evil days, go** *or* **come down in the world,** go downhill, slip, be on the skids <nf>, come down, have a comedown, fall from one's high estate; deteriorate, **degenerate,** run *or* go to seed, sink, decline; **go to pot** <nf>, go to the dogs, go belly up <nf>; reach the depths, touch bottom, hit rock bottom; have seen better days

12 bring bad luck; hoodoo *and* hex *and* jinx *and* Jonah *and* put the jinx on <nf>; put the evil eye on, whammy <nf>, put the *or* a double whammy on <nf>

ADJS 13 **adverse, untoward, detrimental, unfavorable;** sinister; hostile, antagonistic, inimical; contrary, counter, counteractive, conflicting, opposing, opposed, opposite, in opposition; **difficult, troublesome, troublous, hard,** trying, rigorous, stressful; wretched, miserable 96.26; **not easy;** harmful 1000.12

14 **unfortunate, unlucky, unprovidential,** unblessed, **unprosperous,** sad, unhappy, hapless, fortuneless, misfortuned, luckless, donsie <Brit nf>; **out of luck,** short of luck; **down on one's luck** <nf>, badly *or* ill off, down in the world, in adverse circumstances; underprivileged, depressed; ill-starred, evil-starred, born under a bad sign, born under an evil star, planet-stricken, planet-struck, star-crossed; fatal, dire, doomful, funest <old>, **ominous, inauspicious** 133.16; **in a jam** *and* in a pickle *or* pretty pickle *and* in a tight spot *and* between a rock *and* a hard place <nf>, between the devil and the deep blue sea, caught in the crossfire *or* middle; up a tree *and* up the creek *or* up shit creek without a paddle *and* up to one's ass in alligators <nf>

15 **disastrous, calamitous, catastrophic, cataclysmic,** cataclysmal, **tragic,** ruinous, wreckful <old>, fatal, dire, black, woeful, sore, baneful, grievous; destructive 395.26; **life-threatening, terminal**

ADVS 16 **adversely, untowardly,** detrimentally, **unfavorably;** contrarily, conflictingly, opposingly, oppositely

17 **unfortunately, unluckily,** unprovidentially, sadly, unhappily, **as ill luck would have it;** by ill luck, by ill hap; in adverse circumstances, if worse comes to worse

18 **disastrously,** calamitously, catastrophically, cataclysmically, grievously, woefully, sorely, banefully, tragically, crushingly, shatteringly

INTERJS 19 **tough luck!,** tough tiddy! *and* tough shit! *and* tough darts! <nf>

1012 HINDRANCE

NOUNS 1 **hindrance,** hindering, **hampering,** let, let *or* hindrance; **check, arrest,** arrestment, arrestation; fixation; **impediment,** holdback; **resistance, opposition** 451; suppression, **repression, restriction, restraint** 428; **obstruction,** blocking, blockage, clogging, occlusion; **bottleneck,** traffic jam, gridlock; speed bump, sleeping policeman <Brit>; **interruption,** interference; **retardation,** retardment, **detention,** detainment, **delay,** holdup, setback; **inhibition;** constriction, squeeze, stricture, cramp, stranglehold; **closure,** closing up *or* off; obstructionism, bloody-mindedness <Brit>, negativism, foot-dragging <nf>; nuisance value

2 **prevention, stop, stoppage, stopping,** arrestation, estoppel; stay, staying, halt, halting **prohibition,** forbiddance; debarment; **determent,** deterrence, **discouragement; forestalling, preclusion, obviation,** foreclosure

3 **frustration, thwarting, balking, foiling; discomfiture, disconcertion,** bafflement, confounding; **defeat,** upset; check, checkmate, balk, foil <old>; derailing, derailment; vicious circle

4 **obstacle, obstruction,** obstructer; **hang-up** <nf>; **block,** blockade, cordon, curtain; **difficulty,** hurdle, hazard, bed of nails; **deterrent,** determent; **drawback,** objection; **stumbling block,** stumbling stone, stone in one's path; fly in the ointment, one small difficulty, **hitch,** hang-up <nf>, **catch,** joker <nf>, a "but," a "however"; bureaucracy, red tape, regulations

5 **barrier, bar;** gate, portcullis; **fence, wall,** stone wall, brick wall, impenetrable wall; seawall, jetty, groin, mole, breakwater; **bulwark, rampart,** defense, buffer, bulkhead, parapet, breastwork, work, earthwork, mound; bank, embankment, levee, dike; ditch, moat; dam, weir, leaping weir, barrage, milldam, beaver dam, cofferdam, wicket dam, shutter dam, bear-trap dam, hydraulic-fill dam, rock-fill dam, arch dam, arch-gravity dam, gravity dam; boom, jam, logjam; roadblock; speed bump; backstop; iron curtain, bamboo curtain; glass ceiling

6 **impediment,** embarrassment, hamper; encumbrance, cumbrance; **trouble,** difficulty 1013; **handicap,** disadvantage, inconvenience, penalty; white elephant; **burden,** burthen <old>, imposition, onus, cross, weight, deadweight, ball and chain, millstone around one's neck; **load,** pack, cargo, freight, charge; impedimenta,

lumber; technical difficulty, flat tire, gremlin, glitch, bug <nf>, hiccup <nf>

7 curb, check, countercheck, arrest, **stay, stop,** damper, holdback; **brake,** clog, drag, drogue, remora; chock, scotch, spoke, spoke in one's wheel; doorstop; check-rein, bearing rein, martingale; bit, snaffle, pelham, curb bit; shackle, chain, fetter, trammel 428.4; sea anchor, drift anchor, drift sail, drag sail *or* sheet; boot *or* Denver boot

8 hinderer, impeder, **marplot,** obstructer; frustrater, thwarter; obstructionist, negativist; filibuster, filibusterer

9 spoilsport, wet blanket, **killjoy,** grouch, grinch *and* sourpuss <nf>, malcontent, **dog in the manger** <nf>, party pooper <nf>

VERBS **10 hinder, impede, inhibit, arrest, check,** countercheck, scotch, **curb,** snub; **resist, oppose** 451.3; stonewall <nf>, stall, stall off; **suppress, repress** 428.8; **interrupt,** intercept <old>; intervene, interfere, intermeddle, meddle 214.7; damp, dampen, pour *or* dash *or* throw cold water; **retard,** slacken, **delay,** detain, **hold back, keep back,** set back, hold up <nf>; **restrain** 428.7; keep *or* hold in check, bottle up, dam up

11 hamper, impede, cramp, embarrass; trammel, entrammel, enmesh, entangle, ensnarl, entrap, entwine, involve, entoil, toil, net, lime, tangle, snarl; fetter, shackle; **handcuff,** tie one's hands; **encumber,** cumber, **burden,** lumber, **saddle with,** weigh *or* weight down, press down; hang like a millstone round one's neck; **handicap,** put at a disadvantage; lame, cripple, hobble, hamstring; cramp one's style, crab one's deal; gum up *or* gum up the works <nf>

12 obstruct, get *or* **stand in the way;** dog, block, block the way, put up a roadblock, blockade, block up, occlude; **jam,** crowd, pack; **bar,** barricade, bolt, lock; **debar,** shut out; shut off, **close,** close off *or* up, close tight, shut tight; constrict, squeeze, squeeze shut, **strangle,** strangulate, **stifle,** suffocate, **choke,** choke off, chock; stop up 293.7

13 stop, stay, halt, bring to a stop, put a stop *or* end to, bring to a shuddering *or* screeching halt <nf>; **brake,** slow down, put on the brakes, hit the brakes <nf>; **block, stall, stymie,** deadlock; nip in the bud

14 prevent, prohibit, forbid; bar, estop; save, help, **keep from; deter, discourage,** dishearten; **avert, parry, keep off, ward off, stave off, fend off,** fend, repel, deflect, turn aside; **forestall,** foreclose, **preclude,** exclude, debar, **obviate,** anticipate; rule out

15 thwart, frustrate, foil, cross, balk; spike, scotch, checkmate; **counter,** contravene, counteract,

countermand, counterwork; stand in the way of, confront, brave, defy, challenge; **defeat** 412.6; **discomfit,** upset, **disrupt, confound,** flummox <nf>, discountenance, put out of countenance, **disconcert, baffle,** nonplus, perplex, stump <nf>; throw on one's beam ends, trip one up, throw one for a loss <nf>; **circumvent,** elude; sabotage, **spoil, ruin,** dish <nf>, dash, blast; **destroy** 395.10; throw a wrench in the machinery, **throw a monkey wrench** *or* **spanner** <Brit> **into the works** <nf>; put a spoke in one's wheel, scotch one's wheel, spike one's guns, put one's nose out of joint <nf>, upset one's applecart; **derail;** take the wind out of one's sails, steal one's thunder, cut the ground from under one, knock the chocks *or* props from under one, knock the bottom out of <nf>; tie one's hands, clip one's wings

16 <nf terms> **queer, crab, foul up, louse up,** snafu, bollix *or* bollix up, gum, **gum up,** gum up the works; crimp, cramp, **put a crimp in,** cramp one's style; cook one's goose, cut one down to size; give one a hard time

ADJS **17 hindering,** troublesome; **inhibitive,** inhibiting, suppressive, repressive; constrictive, strangling, stifling, choking; restrictive 428.12; **obstructive,** obstructing, occlusive, obstruent <old>; cantankerous <nf>, bloody-minded <Brit>, contrary, crosswise; interruptive, interrupting; in the way

18 hampering, impeding, counterproductive, impedimental, impeditive; onerous, oppressive, burdensome, cumbersome, cumbrous, encumbering

19 preventive, preventative, avertive, prophylactic; **prohibitive, forbidding; deterrent,** deterring, **discouraging;** preclusive, forestalling; foot-dragging

20 frustrating, confounding, disconcerting, baffling, defeating

ADVS **21** under handicap, at a disadvantage, on the hip <old>, with everything against one

1013 DIFFICULTY

NOUNS **1 difficulty,** difficultness; **hardness, toughness** <nf>, strain, the hard way <nf>, **rigor,** rigorousness, ruggedness; **arduousness,** laboriousness, strenuousness, toilsomeness, severity; **troublesomeness,** bothersomeness; onerousness, oppressiveness, burdensomeness; formidability, hairiness <nf>; complication, intricacy, **complexity** 799; abstruseness 522.2

2 tough proposition *and* tough one *and* toughie <nf>, large *or* tall order <nf>; **hard job, tough job**

and heavy lift <nf>, big undertaking, backbreaker, ballbuster <nf>, **chore,** man-sized job; brutal task, Herculean task, Augean task; uphill work *or* going, rough go <nf>, **heavy sledding,** hard pull <nf>, dead lift <old>; tough lineup to buck <nf>, hard road to travel; hard *or* tough nut to crack *and* hard *or* tough row to hoe *and* hard row of stumps <nf>; bitch <nf>; **handful** <nf>, all one can manage, no easy task

3 **trouble, the matter;** headache <nf>, problem, besetment, **inconvenience,** disadvantage; the bad part, the downside <nf>; **ado,** great ado; peck of troubles, "sea of troubles"—Shakespeare; hornet's nest, Pandora's box, can of worms <nf>; **evil** 1000.3; **bother, annoyance** 98.7; **anxiety, worry** 126.2

4 **predicament, plight,** spot of trouble, **strait,** straits, parlous straits, tightrope, knife-edge, thin edge; **pinch, bind,** pass, clutch, situation, emergency; pretty pass, nice *or* pretty predicament, pretty *or* fine state of affairs, **sorry plight;** slough, quagmire, morass, swamp, quicksand; **embarrassment,** embarrassing position *or* situation; **complication,** imbroglio; the devil to pay

5 <nf terms> **pickle,** crunch, hobble, pretty pickle, fine kettle of fish, how-do-you-do, fine how-do-you-do; **spot, tight spot; squeeze, tight squeeze,** ticklish *or* tricky spot, hot spot, hot seat, sticky wicket <Brit>; **scrape, jam, hot water,** tail in a gate, tit in the wringer; **mess,** holy *or* unholy mess, mix, stew; hell to pay; no-win situation

6 **impasse, corner** *and* **box** *and* **hole** <nf>, cleft stick; **cul-de-sac, blind alley, dead end,** dead-end street, blank wall; **extremity, end of one's rope** *or* **tether,** wit's end, nowhere to turn; **stalemate,** deadlock; stand, standoff, standstill, logjam, halt, stop

7 **dilemma,** horns of a dilemma, double bind, damned-if-you-do-and-damned-if-you-don't, no-win situation, **quandary,** nonplus, conundrum; **vexed question,** thorny problem, knotty point, knot, crux, node, nodus, Gordian knot, hard nut to crack, can of worms, headache, poser, teaser, perplexity, puzzle, enigma 522.8; paradox, oxymoron; asses' bridge, *pons asinorum* <L>; bad hair day; trilemma, tetralemma

8 **crux, hitch, pinch, rub,** snag, hurdle, catch, joker <nf>, where the shoe pinches, complication

9 **unwieldiness, unmanageability; unhandiness,** inconvenience, impracticality; **awkwardness, clumsiness; cumbersomeness,** ponderousness, bulkiness, hulkiness; ham-handedness

VERBS 10 **be difficult, present difficulties, pose problems, take some doing** <nf>

11 **have difficulty, have trouble,** have a rough time <nf>, hit a snag, have a hard time of it, have one's hands full, have one's work cut out, get off to a bad start *or* on the wrong foot; be hard put, have much ado with; labor under difficulties, labor under a disadvantage, have the cards stacked against one *and* have two strikes against one <nf>; struggle, **flounder,** beat about, make heavy weather of it; have one's back to the wall, not know where to turn, come to a dead end *or* standstill, not know whether one is coming *or* going, go around in circles, swim against the current; walk a tightrope, walk on eggshells *or* hot coals, dance on a hot griddle

12 **get into trouble,** plunge into difficulties; **let oneself in for, put one's foot in it** <nf>; **get in a jam** *or* **hot water** *or* **the soup** <nf>, **get into a scrape** <nf>, **get in a mess** *or* **hole** *or* **box** *or* **bind** <nf>; paint oneself into a corner <nf>, get one's ass in a bind *and* put oneself in a spot <nf>, put one's foot in one's mouth, strike a bad patch, be up a tree; have a tiger by the tail; burn one's fingers; get all tangled *or* snarled *or* wound up, get all balled *or* bollixed up <nf>

13 **trouble,** beset; **bother,** pother, get one down, <nf>, **disturb, perturb,** irk, plague, **torment,** drive one up the wall <nf>, give one gray hair, make one lose sleep; **harass, vex, distress** 96.16; inconvenience, **put out,** put out of the way, discommode 996.4; **concern, worry** 126.5; **puzzle, perplex** 971.13; put to it, give one trouble, complicate matters; give one a hard time *and* give one a bad time *and* make it tough for <nf>; be too much for; ail, be the matter; tree <nf>

14 **cause trouble,** bring trouble; ask for trouble, ask for it <nf>, bring down upon one, bring down upon one's head, bring down around one's ears; **stir up a hornet's nest,** kick up *or* piss up a fuss *or* storm *or* row <nf>; stir up a hornet's nest, open Pandora's box, open a can of worms <nf>, put fire to tow; **raise hob** *or* **hell** <nf>; raise merry hell *and* play hob *and* play hell <nf>, play the deuce *or* devil <nf>

15 **put in a hole** <nf>, put in a spot <nf>; **embarrass; involve,** enmesh, entangle

16 **corner,** run *and* drive into a corner <nf>, **tree** <nf>, chase up a tree *or* stump <nf>, drive *or* force to the wall, push one to the wall, put one's back to the wall, have one on the ropes <nf>

ADJS 17 **difficult,** difficile; **not easy,** no picnic, hairy; **hard, tough** *and* **rough** *and* **rugged** <nf>, rigorous, brutal, severe; wicked *and* mean *and* hairy <nf>, **formidable; arduous, strenuous, toilsome, laborious,** operose, Herculean; steep, uphill; hard-fought; hard-earned; jawbreaking; knotty, knotted; thorny, spiny, set with thorns; delicate, ticklish, tricky, sticky <nf>, critical, easier said than done, like pulling teeth; exacting, demanding; intricate, complex 799.4; abstruse 522.16; hard-ass <nf>

18 **troublesome,** besetting; **bothersome,** irksome, vexatious, painful, plaguey <nf>, problematic, annoying 98.22; **burdensome,** oppressive, onerous, heavy *and* hefty <nf>, crushing, backbreaking; **trying,** grueling

19 **unwieldy, unmanageable, unhandy;** inconvenient, impractical; **awkward, clumsy, cumbersome,** unmaneuverable; contrary, perverse, crosswise; ponderous, bulky, hulky, hulking, ungainly

20 **troubled,** trouble-plagued, beset, sore beset; **bothered, vexed,** irked, annoyed 96.21; plagued, **harassed** 96.24; distressed, perturbed 96.22; inconvenienced, embarrassed; put to it *and* hard put to it <nf>; **worried, anxious** 126.6,7; puzzled

21 **in trouble, in deep trouble, in a predicament, in a sorry plight,** in a pretty pass; in deep water, out of one's depth

22 <nf terms> **in deep shit** *or* doo-doo, in a jam, in a pickle, in a pretty pickle, in a spot, in a tight spot, in a fix, in a hole, in a bind, in a box; in a mess, in a scrape, in hot water, in the soup; up a tree, up to one's ass in alligators, up the creek, up shit creek without a paddle, in Dutch, on the spot, behind the eight ball, on Queer Street, out on a limb, on the hot seat

23 **in a dilemma,** dilemmatic, on the horns of a dilemma, **in a quandary;** between two stools; between Scylla and Charybdis, between the devil and the deep blue sea, between a rock and a hard place <nf>

24 **at an impasse, at one's wit's end, at a loss,** at a stand *or* standstill, deadlocked; **nonplussed,** at a nonplus; **baffled, perplexed, bewildered,** mystified, stuck *and* stumped <nf>, stymied

25 **cornered,** in a corner, with one's back to the wall; **treed** *and* **up a tree** *and* up a stump <nf>; **at bay,** *aux abois* <Fr>

26 **straitened,** reduced to dire straits, in desperate straits, **pinched,** sore *or* sorely pressed, **hard-pressed, hard up** <nf>, **up against it** <nf>; driven from pillar to post; **desperate, in extremities,** *in extremis* <L>, **at the end of one's rope** *or* **tether**

27 **stranded, grounded,** aground, **on the rocks,** high and dry; **stuck,** stuck *or* set fast; foundered, swamped; castaway, marooned, wrecked, shipwrecked

ADVS 28 **with difficulty,** difficultly, with much ado; hardly, painfully; the hard way, **arduously, strenuously, laboriously,** toilsomely

29 **unwieldily, unmanageably, unhandily,** inconveniently; **awkwardly, clumsily, cumbersomely;** ponderously

1014 FACILITY

NOUNS 1 **facility, ease, easiness,** facileness, effortlessness; lack of hindrance, **smoothness,** freedom; clear coast, clear road *or* course; smooth road, royal road, highroad; easy going, plain sailing, smooth *or* straight sailing; clarity, intelligibility 521; uncomplexity, uncomplicatedness, **simplicity** 798

2 **handiness, wieldiness,** wieldableness, handleability, manageability, **manageableness,** maneuverability; **convenience,** practicality, practicableness, untroublesomeness; **flexibility,** pliancy, **pliability,** ductility, malleability; adaptability, feasibility

3 **easy thing,** mere child's play, simple matter, mere twist of the wrist; easy target, sitting duck <nf>; sinecure; open road

4 <nf terms> **cinch, snap,** pushover, breeze, waltz, duck soup, velvet, picnic, pie, cherry pie, apple pie, cakewalk, piece of cake <Brit>, kid stuff, turkey shoot, no-brainer, setup, high road, walkover, no sweat

5 **facilitation, facilitating, easing,** smoothing, smoothing out, smoothing the way; **speeding,** expediting, expedition, quickening, hastening; streamlining; lubricating, greasing, oiling

6 **disembarrassment, disentanglement, disencumbrance,** disinvolvement, uncluttering, uncomplicating, unscrambling, unsnarling, disburdening, unburdening, unhampering; **extrication,** disengagement, **freeing,** clearing; deregulation; **simplification** 798.2

VERBS 7 **facilitate, ease; grease the wheels** <nf>; **smooth, smooth** *or* **pave the way,** ease the way, grease *or* soap the ways <nf>, prepare the way, **clear the way,** make all clear for, make way for; run interference for <nf>, open the way, open the door to; not stand in the way of; **open up, unclog,** unblock, unjam, unbar, loose 431.6; **lubricate,** make frictionless *or* dissipationless, remove friction, grease, oil; **speed, expedite,** quicken, hasten; **help along,** help on its way; **aid** 449.11; **explain,** make clear 521.6; **simplify** 798.4

8 **do easily,** make short work of, do with one's hands tied behind one's back, do with both eyes shut, do standing on one's head, do hands down, sail *or* dance *or* waltz through, wing it <nf>, take to like a duck to water

9 **disembarrass, disencumber, unload,** relieve, disburden, unhamper, get out from under;

disentangle, disembroil, disinvolve, unclutter, unscramble, unsnarl; **extricate,** disengage, **free,** free up, clear; liberate 431.4

10 **go easily, run smoothly,** work well, work like a machine, go like clockwork *or* a sewing machine; present no difficulties, give no trouble, be painless, be effortless; flow, roll, glide, slide, coast, sweep, sail

11 **have it easy, have it soft** <nf>, have it all one's own way, have the game in one's hands, have it in the bag; win easily; breeze in <nf>, walk over the course <nf>, win in a walk *or* in a canter *or* hands down <nf>

12 **take it easy** *and* **go easy** <nf>, swim with the stream, drift with the current, go with the tide; cool it *and* not sweat it <nf>; take the line of least resistance; take it in one's stride, make little *or* light of, think nothing of

ADJS 13 **easy, facile, effortless,** smooth, painless; soft <nf>, cushy <nf>; plain, uncomplicated, straightforward, **simple** 798.6, Mickey Mouse <nf>, simple as ABC <nf>, easy as pie *and* easy as falling off a log <nf>, downhill all the way, like shooting fish in a barrel, like taking candy from a baby, no sooner said than done; **clear;** glib; **light,** unburdensome; nothing to it; casual, throwaway <nf>

14 **smooth-running,** frictionless, dissipationless, easy-running, easy-flowing; well-lubricated, well-oiled, well-greased

15 **handy, wieldy,** wieldable, handleable; tractable; flexible, pliant, yielding, malleable, ductile, pliable, **manageable,** maneuverable; **convenient,** foolproof, goofproof <nf>, practical, untroublesome, user-friendly; adaptable, feasible

ADVS 16 **easily,** facilely, **effortlessly, readily, simply,** lightly, swimmingly <nf>, without difficulty; no sweat *and* like nothing *and* slick as a whistle <nf>; hands down <nf>, with one hand tied behind one's back, with both eyes closed, standing on one's head; like a duck takes to water; **smoothly,** frictionlessly, like clockwork; on easy terms

1015 UGLINESS

NOUNS 1 **ugliness, unsightliness, unattractiveness,** uncomeliness, unhandsomeness, unbeautifulness, unprettiness, unloveliness, unaestheticness, unpleasingness 98.1; unprepossessingness, ill-favoredness, inelegance; **homeliness,** plainness; unshapeliness, shapelessness; ungracefulness, gracelessness, clumsiness, ungainliness 414.3; **uglification, uglifying, disfigurement,** defacement; dysphemism; cacophony

2 **hideousness,** horridness, horribleness, frightfulness, dreadfulness, terribleness, awfulness <nf>; **repulsiveness** 98.2, repugnance, repugnancy, repellence, repellency, offensiveness, forbiddingness, loathsomeness; ghastliness, gruesomeness, grisliness; **deformity,** misshapenness

3 forbidding countenance, vinegar aspect, wry face, face that would stop a clock

4 **eyesore,** blot, blot on the landscape, blemish, **sight** <nf>, **fright, horror, mess,** no beauty, no beauty queen, ugly duckling; baboon; **scarecrow,** gargoyle, monster, **monstrosity,** teratism; witch, bag *and* dog <nf>, **hag,** harridan; something the cat dragged in, back end of a bus

VERBS 5 **offend,** offend the eye, offend one's aesthetic sensibilities, **look bad;** look something terrible *and* look like hell *and* look like the devil *and* look a sight *or* a fright *or* a mess *or* like something the cat dragged in <nf>; **uglify, disfigure,** deface, blot, blemish, mar, scar, spoil; dysphemize

ADJS 6 **ugly, unsightly, unattractive, unhandsome, unpretty, unlovely,** uncomely, **inelegant; unbeautiful,** unbeauteous, beautiless, unaesthetic, unpleasing 98.17; **homely, plain;** not much to look at, not much for looks, short on looks <nf>, hard on the eyes <nf>; ugly as sin, ugly as the wrath of God, ugly as hell, homely as a mud fence, homely enough to sour milk, homely enough to stop a clock, not fit to be seen, grotty <nf>; **uglified, disfigured,** defaced, blotted, blemished, marred, spoiled; dysphemized, dysphemistic; cacophonous, cacophonic

7 **unprepossessing, ill-favored,** hard-favored, evil-favored, ill-featured; ill-looking, evil-looking; hard-featured, hard-visaged; grim, grim-faced, grim-visaged; hatchet-faced, horse-faced

8 **unshapely,** shapeless, **ill-shaped,** ill-made, ill-proportioned; **deformed,** misshapen, misproportioned, malformed, misbegotten; grotesque, scarecrowish, gargoylish; monstrous, teratic, cacogenic

9 **ungraceful,** ungraced, graceless; clumsy, clunky <nf>, **ungainly** 414.20

10 **inartistic,** unartistic, **unaesthetic; unornamental, undecorative**

11 **hideous, horrid, horrible, frightful, dreadful, terrible, awful** <nf>; **repulsive** 98.18, repellent, repelling, rebarbative, **repugnant,** offensive, foul, forbidding, loathsome, loathly <old>, revolting; **ghastly,** gruesome, grisly

ADVS 12 **uglily,** homelily, uncomelily, **unattractively, unhandsomely, unbeautifully, unprettily**

13 **hideously, horridly, horribly, frightfully, dreadfully, terribly, awfully** <nf>; **repulsively, repugnantly,** offensively, forbiddingly, loathsomely, revoltingly; gruesomely, ghastly

1016 BEAUTY

NOUNS **1 beauty, beautifulness,** beauteousness, **prettiness, handsomeness, attractiveness** 97.2, **loveliness, pulchritude, charm,** grace, elegance, exquisiteness; bloom, glow; the beautiful; source of aesthetic pleasure *or* delight; beauty unadorned

2 comeliness, fairness, sightliness, personableness, becomingness, pleasingness 97.1, goodliness, bonniness, agreeability, agreeableness; charisma

3 good looks, good appearance, good effect; good proportions, aesthetic proportions; **shapeliness,** good figure, good shape, *belle tournure* <Fr>, nice body, lovely build, physical *or* bodily charm, curvaceousness, curves <nf>, pneumaticness, sexy body, sexiness; good bone structure; 10 <nf>; bodily grace, **gracefulness,** gracility; good points, **beauties, charms, delights,** perfections, good features, delicate features

4 daintiness, delicacy, delicateness; **cuteness** *or* cunningness <nf>

5 gorgeousness, ravishingness; **gloriousness,** heavenliness, sublimity; **splendor,** splendidness, splendiferousness, splendorousness *or* splendrousness, sublimeness, resplendence; **brilliance,** brightness, radiance, luster; **glamour** 377.1

6 thing of beauty, vision, picture <nf>, poem, eyeful <nf>, **sight for sore eyes** <nf>, cynosure; masterpiece

7 beauty, charmer, *charmeuse* <Fr>; beauty queen, beauty contest winner, beauty pageant winner, Miss America, Miss USA, Miss World, Miss Universe, bathing beauty; **glamour girl,** cover girl, model, arm candy <nf>; sex goddess; **belle,** reigning beauty, great beauty, lady fair; beau ideal, paragon; enchantress; "the face that launch'd a thousand ships"—Marlowe

8 <nf terms> **doll, dish, cutie,** angel, angelface, babyface, beaut, honey, dream, looker, good-looker, stunner, dazzler; dreamboat, hunk; fetcher, bird *and* crumpet <Brit>, peach, knockout, raving beauty, centerfold, pinup girl, pinup, bunny, cutie *or* cutesy pie, cute *or* slick chick, pussycat, sex kitten, ten; treasure; hottie, it girl, babe

9 <famous beauties> Venus, Venus de Milo; Aphrodite; Adonis, Hyperion, Narcissus; Astarte; Freya; Helen of Troy, Cleopatra; the Graces, houri, peri

10 beautification, prettification, cutification <nf>, **adornment;** decoration 498.1; **beauty care,** beauty treatment, cosmetology; facial <nf>; manicure; hairdressing; cosmetic surgery, plastic surgery

11 makeup, cosmetics, beauty products, beauty-care products; war paint *and* drugstore complexion <nf>; pancake makeup; powder, talcum, talcum powder; foundation, base; rouge, blush *or* blusher, paint; lip rouge, **lipstick,** lip color; **nail polish;** greasepaint, clown white; eye makeup, eyeliner, mascara, eye shadow, kohl; cold cream, hand cream *or* lotion, vanishing cream, foundation cream; mudpack; eyebrow pencil; puff, powder puff; makeup brush; compact, vanity case; toiletries, shampoo, soap, deodorant, perfume

12 beautician, beautifier, cosmetologist, makeup artist, cosmetician; hairdresser, *coiffeur* and *coiffeuse* <Fr>, hairstylist; barber; manicurist, pedicurist

13 beauty parlor *or* salon *or* shop, *salon de beauté* <Fr>, hairdressing salon, hair salon; barbershop, barber

14 hairdressing, hair styling, hair coloring, barbering; shave, depilation, tweezing, electrolysis, waxing; hair replacement; hairstyle, hairdo; haircut, trim, permanent, perm; crop, bob, cut, ponytail, plait, cornrows, braids, pigtails, bangs, chignon, bun, beehive, pompadour, pageboy, dreadlocks, sideburns, crewcut, number one buzz, number three buzz, flattop, ducktail, DA, Mohawk, Afro

VERBS **15 beautify, prettify,** cutify <nf>, pretty up *or* gussy up *or* doll up <nf>, grace, **adorn; decorate** 498.8; set off, set off to advantage *or* good advantage, become one; **glamorize; make up,** paint *and* put on one's face <nf>, titivate, cosmetize, cosmeticize; primp

16 look good; look like a million *and* look fit to kill *and* knock dead *and* knock one's eyes out <nf>; take the breath away, beggar description; shine, beam, **bloom, glow**

ADJS **17 beautiful, beauteous,** endowed with beauty; **pretty, handsome, attractive** 97.7, pulchritudinous, **lovely, graceful,** gracile; elegant; esthetic, aesthetically appealing; **cute;** pretty as a picture; tall dark and handsome; picturesque, scenic

18 comely, fair, good-looking, nice-looking, well-favored, **personable,** presentable, agreeable, becoming, pleasing 97.6, goodly, bonny, likely <nf>, **sightly;** pleasing to the eye, lovely to behold; **shapely,** well-built, built, well-shaped, well-proportioned, well-made, well-formed, stacked *or* well-stacked <nf>, shapely, curvaceous, curvy <nf>, pneumatic, amply endowed, built for comfort *or* built like a brick shithouse <nf>, buxom, callipygian, callipygous; Junoesque, statuesque, goddess-like; slender 270.16; Adonis-like, hunky <nf>

19 fine, exquisite, flowerlike, **dainty, delicate;** *mignon* <Fr>

20 **gorgeous, ravishing; glorious,** heavenly, divine, sublime; **resplendent,** splendorous *or* splendrous, splendiferous, **splendid; brilliant,** bright, radiant, shining, beaming, glowing, blooming, abloom, sparkling, **dazzling; glamorous;** babelicious <nf>

21 <nf terms> **eye-filling, easy on the eyes,** not hard to look at, drop-dead gorgeous, long on looks, looking fit to kill, dishy <chiefly Brit>; cutesy, cutesy-poo; raving, devastating, **stunning,** killing

22 **beautifying,** cosmetic; decorative 498.10; cosmetized, cosmeticized, beautified, made-up, mascaraed, titivated

ADVS **23** **beautifully,** beauteously, **prettily, handsomely, attractively, becomingly,** comelily; elegantly, exquisitely; charmingly, enchantingly

24 **daintily, delicately; cutely**

25 **gorgeously, ravishingly;** ravingly *and* devastatingly *and* stunningly <nf>; **gloriously,** divinely, sublimely; **resplendently,** splendidly, splendorously, splendrously; **brilliantly,** brightly, radiantly, glowingly, **dazzlingly**

WORD ELEMENTS **26** cal-, calo-, callo-, cali-, calli-

1017 MATHEMATICS

NOUNS **1** **mathematics** <see list>, math <US nf>, maths <Brit nf>, mathematic, **numbers, figures;** pure mathematics, abstract mathematics, applied mathematics, higher mathematics, elementary mathematics, classical mathematics, metamathematics, new mathematics; algorithm, logarithm; mathematical element <see list>

2 <mathematical operations> notation, **addition** 253, **subtraction** 255, **multiplication, division,** numeracy, calculation, computation, reckoning, proportion, practice, equation, extraction of roots, inversion, reduction, involution, evolution, approximation, interpolation, extrapolation, transformation, differentiation, integration; arithmetic operation, algebraic operation, logical operation, associative operation, distributive operation

3 **number** <see list>, **numeral,** *numero* <Sp and Ital>, no *or* n, digit, binary digit *or* bit, **cipher,** character, symbol, sign, notation, figure, base; decimal

4 <number systems> **Arabic numerals,** algorism *or* algorithm, Roman numerals; **decimal system,** binary system, octal system, duodecimal system, hexadecimal system; place-value notation, positional notation, fixed-point notation, floating-point notation

5 large number, astronomical number, boxcar number <nf>, zillion *and* jillion <nf>; googol,

googolplex; infinity, infinite number, transfinite number, infinitude 823.1; billion, trillion, etc 882.12-13

6 **sum,** summation, difference, product, **number, count,** x number, n number; account, cast, **score, reckoning, tally,** tale, the story *and* whole story *and* all she wrote <nf>, the bottom line <nf>, **aggregate, amount,** quantity 244; **whole** 792, **total** 792.2, running total; box score <nf>

7 **ratio, rate, proportion; quota,** quotum; **percentage,** percent; **fraction,** proper fraction, improper fraction, compound fraction, continued fraction, decimal fraction; common *or* vulgar fraction; geometric ratio *or* proportion, arithmetical proportion, harmonic proportion; rule of three; numerator, denominator; body mass index

8 **series, progression;** arithmetical progression, geometrical progression, harmonic progression; Fibonacci numbers

9 **numeration, enumeration, numbering, counting,** count, accounting, census, inventorying, telling, tally, tallying, scoring; page numbering, pagination, foliation; counting on the fingers, dactylonomy; **measurement** 300; quantification, quantifying, quantization

10 **calculation, computation, estimation, reckoning,** figuring, number work, mental arithmetic, calculus; adding, footing, casting, ciphering, totaling, toting *or* totting <nf>; rounding up, rounding down, rounding off

11 **summation, summary, summing, summing up, recount,** recounting, rehearsal, capitulation, **recapitulation,** recap *and* rehash <nf>, statement, **reckoning, count,** bean-counting <nf>, repertory, census, inventory, head count, nose count, body count; account, accounts; **table,** reckoner, ready reckoner

12 **division;** long division, short division, divisibility; quotient, ratio, proportion, percentage, fraction; reciprocal, inverse, dividend, divisor, aliquot part, remainder, residue; numerator, denominator, common denominator

13 **account of, count of,** a reckoning of, **tab** *or* **tabs of** <nf>, tally of, check of, track of

14 **figures, statistics,** indexes *or* indices; vital statistics

15 **calculator** <see list>, **computer** 1042.2; estimator, figurer, reckoner, abacist, pollster; statistician, actuary; number-cruncher <nf>; accountant, bookkeeper 628.7

16 **mathematician, arithmetician;** geometer, geometrician; algebraist, trigonometrician, statistician, geodesist, mathematical physicist, topologist; analyst

VERBS 17 number, numerate, number off, **enumerate, count, tell, tally,** give a figure to, put a figure on, call off, name, call over, run over; **count noses** or **heads** <nf>, call the roll; census, poll; page, paginate, foliate; **measure** 300.10; **round,** round out or off or down; quantify, quantitate, quantize

18 calculate, compute, estimate, reckon, figure, solve, reckon at, put at, cipher, cast, tally, score; **figure out,** do the math, work out, dope out <nf>, determine; take account of, figure in and figure on <nf>; arithmetize; **add,** add up, sum, **subtract,** take away, **multiply, divide,** multiply out, cross-multiply, times, algebraize, extract roots, raise to the power of, cube, square, decimalize; factor, factor out, factorize; **measure** 300.10

19 sum up, sum, summate, say it all <nf>; aggregate, **figure up,** cipher up, reckon up, **count up, add up,** foot up, cast up, score up, **tally up; total,** total up, tote or tot up <nf>; **summarize, recapitulate,** recap and rehash <nf>, **recount,** rehearse, recite, relate; detail, itemize, inventory; round up, round down, round off

20 keep account of, keep count of, **keep track of, keep tab** or **tabs** <nf>, keep tally, keep a check on or of

21 check, verify 970.12, double-check, check on or out; **prove,** demonstrate; balance, balance the books; **audit,** overhaul; take stock, inventory

ADJS 22 mathematical, numeric or numerical, numerary, arithmetic or arithmetical, algebraic or algebraical, geometric or geometrical, trigonometric or trigonometrical, analytic or analytical, combinatorial, topological, statistical

23 numeric or **numerical,** numeral, numerary, numerative; **odd,** impair, **even,** pair; arithmetical, algorismic or algorithmic; **cardinal, ordinal;** figural, **figurate,** figurative, **digital;** aliquot, submultiple, **reciprocal,** prime, fractional, decimal, exponential, **logarithmic,** logometric, differential, integral; positive, negative; rational, irrational, transcendental; surd, radical; real, imaginary; possible, impossible, finite, infinite, transfinite; integral, whole; decenary, binary, ternary; signed, unsigned, nonnegative

24 numerative, enumerative; calculative, computative, estimative; **calculating,** computing, computational, estimating; statistical; quantifying, quantizing

25 calculable, computable, **reckonable,** estimable, countable, numberable, enumerable, numerable; **measurable,** mensurable, quantifiable; addable, subtractive, multipliable, dividable

26 branches and kinds of mathematics

addition algebra	Lagrangian function
affine geometry	Laplace's equation
algebra	linear algebra
algebraic geometry	line geometry
algebraic topology	mathematical biology
analysis	mathematical biophysics
analytic geometry	mathematical computing
applied mathematics	mathematical ecology
arithmetic	mathematical geography
associative algebra	mathematical logic
binary arithmetic	mathematical physics
Boolean algebra	matrix algebra
calculus	measure theory
calculus of differences	metageometry
category theory	modular arithmetic
circle geometry	multiple algebra
combinatorial mathematics or combinatorics	natural geometry
	nilpotent algebra
combinatorial topology	noncommutative algebra
commutative algebra	non-Euclidean geometry
complex or double algebra	n-tuple linear algebra
control theory	number theory
denumerative geometry	numerical analysis
descriptive geometry	operational calculus
differential calculus	operations research
differential geometry	plane geometry
division algebra	plane trigonometry
elementary arithmetic	point-set topology
elementary or ordinary algebra	political arithmetic
	potential theory
equivalent algebras	probability theory
Euclidean geometry	projective geometry
Fourier analysis	proper subalgebra
functional analysis	quadratics
game theory	quaternian algebra
geodesic geometry	reducible algebra
geodesy	Riemannian geometry
geometry	semisimple algebra
G–del's proof	set theory
graph theory	simple algebra
graphic algebra	solid geometry
group theory	speculative geometry
harmonic analysis	sphere geometry
higher algebra	spherical trigonometry
higher arithmetic	statistics
homological algebra	subalgebra
hyperalgebra	systems analysis or theory
hyperbolic geometry	topology
infinitesimal calculus	trigonometry or trig <nf>
integral calculus	universal algebra
intuitional geometry	universal geometry
invariant subalgebra	vector algebra
inverse geometry	zero algebra

27 mathematical elements

addend	argument
algorithm	auxiliary equation
aliquot	base
antilogarithm	Bessel function

binomial
characteristic
characteristic equation
characteristic function
characteristic polynomial
characteristic root or
  characteristic value
  or eigenvalue or latent
  root or proper
  value
characteristic
  vector
coefficient
combination
common divisor or
  measure
complement
congruence
coordinate
constant
cosecant
cosine
cotangent
cube
cube root
decimal
denominator
derivative
determinant
difference or
  remainder
differential
discriminate
dividend
division sign
divisor
e
elliptical function
empty set or
  null set
equal sign
equation
exponent
exponential
expression
factor
factorial
formula
fraction
function
greatest common divisor
  or GCD
haversine
hyperbolic
i
increment
index
integral
Laplace transform

least common denomina-
  tor or LCD
least common multiple or
  LCM
logarithm or log
mantissa
matrix
minuend
minus sign
mixed decimal
modulus
monomial
multinomial
multiple
multiplicand
multiplicator
multiplier
norm
numerator
parameter
part
permutation
pi
plus sign
polynomial
power
quadratic equation
quaternion
quotient
radical
radix
reciprocal
repeating or circulating
  decimal
root
secant
sequence
series
set
simultaneous
  equations
sine
solution
square root
submultiple
subtrahend
summand
tangent
tensor
topological
  group
topological space
variable
vector
vector product
vector sum
versed sine or
  versine
vulgar fraction

28 kinds of numbers

abundant number
algebraic number
Avogadro's
binary number
cardinal number or
  cardinal
complex or Gaussian
  integer
complex number
composite or rectangular
  number
deficient or defective
  number
directed number
even number or pair
Fermat number
figurate number
finite number
fraction
imaginary number or pure
  imaginary
infinity
integer or whole number
irrational number or

irrational
Mersenne number
mixed number
natural number
negative number
nonnegative number
odd number or impair
ordinal number or ordinal
perfect number
polygonal number
positive number
prime or rectilinear
  number or prime
pyramidal number
random number
rational number or rational
real number or real
round or rounded number
serial number
signed number
surd or surd quantity
transcendental number
transfinite number
whole number

29 calculators

abacus
adding machine
analog computer
arithmograph
arithmometer
calculating machine
cash register
compass
computer
counter
difference engine
digital computer
Napier's bones or rods
number-cruncher <nf>

online calculator
pari-mutuel machine
pocket calculator
programmable calculator
quipu
rule
scientific calculator
score card
slide rule or sliding scale
suan pan
tabulator
tally or tally stick
totalizator
Turing machine

1018 PHYSICS

NOUNS **1 physics;** natural or physical science;
philosophy or second philosophy or natural
philosophy or physic <old>; **branch of physics** <see
list>; physical theory, quantum theory, relativity
theory, special relativity theory, general relativity
theory, unified field theory, grand unified theory
or GUT, superunified theory or theory of
everything or TOE, eightfold way, string theory,
superstring theory, kinetic theory, wave theory,
electromagnetic theory

  2 physicist, aerophysicist, astrophysicist,
  biophysicist, etc

ADJS **3 physical;** aerophysical, astrophysical,
  biophysical, etc

4 branches of physics

acoustics	iatrophysics
aerodynamics	kinematics
aerophysics	macrophysics
applied physics	magnetism
astrophysics	mathematical physics
basic conductor physics	mechanics
biophysics	medicophysics
chaos theory *or* chaos	microphysics
dynamics *or* chaology	molecular physics
chemical physics *or*	morphophysics
chemicophysics	myophysics
classical physics *or*	Newtonian mechanics
Newtonian physics	nuclear physics
condensed-matter physics	optics
cryogenics	organismic physics
crystallography	physical chemistry *or*
cytophysics	physicochemistry
dynamics	physical optics
electricity	physicomathematics
electrodynamics	plasma physics
electromagnetism	psychophysics
electron optics	quantum physics
electronics *or* electron	radiation physics
physics	radionics
electrophysics	solar physics
fluid dynamics	solid-state physics
fluid mechanics	statics
geometric optics	stereophysics
geophysics	theoretical physics
high-energy physics	thermodynamics
hyperphysics	X-ray crystallography
hypophysics	zoophysics

1019 HEAT

NOUNS **1 heat, hotness,** heatedness; superheat, superheatedness; calidity *or* caloric <old>; **warmth,** warmness; incalescence; radiant heat, thermal radiation, induction heat, convector *or* convected heat, coal heat, gas heat, oil heat, hot-air heat, steam heat, electric heat, solar heat, dielectric heat, ultraviolet heat, atomic heat, molecular heat; latent heat, specific heat; animal heat, body heat, blood heat, hypothermia; fever heat, fever, pyrexia, feverishness, flush, calescence; heating, burning 1020.5; smoke detector

2 <metaphors> **ardor,** ardency, **fervor,** fervency, fervidness, fervidity; eagerness 101; excitement 105; **anger** 152.5,8,9; **sexual desire** 75.5; love 104

3 temperature, temp <nf>; room temperature, comfortable temperature; comfort index, temperature-humidity index *or* THI; flash point; boiling point; melting point, freezing point; dew point; recalescence point; zero, absolute zero; thermometry, pyrometry

4 lukewarmness, tepidness, tepidity; tepidarium

5 torridness, torridity; extreme heat, intense heat, torrid heat, red heat, white heat, tropical heat, sweltering heat, African heat, Indian heat, Bengal heat, summer heat, oppressive heat; **hot wind** 318.6; incandescence, flash point

6 sultriness, stuffiness, closeness, oppressiveness; humidity, humidness, mugginess, stickiness <nf>, swelter, fug; tropical heat; overheating

7 hot weather, sunny *or* sunshiny weather; sultry weather, stuffy weather, humid weather, muggy weather, sticky weather <nf>, HHH <nf>; summer, midsummer, high summer; Indian Summer, **dog days,** canicular days, canicule; **heat wave,** hot wave, hot spell, warm front, heat haze; broiling sun, midday sun; vertical rays; warm weather, fair weather; global warming, greenhouse effect

8 hot day, summer day; **scorcher** *and* **roaster** *and* broiler *and* sizzler *and* swelterer <nf>

9 hot air, superheated air; thermal; firestorm

10 hot water, boiling water; **steam,** vapor; volcanic water; hot *or* warm *or* thermal spring, thermae; geyser, Old Faithful; steaminess; boiling point

11 <hot place> **oven, furnace,** fiery furnace, inferno, hell; heater, warmer, burner; steam bath, sauna, solarium; **tropics,** subtropics, Torrid Zone, Sahara, Dearth Valley; equator; melting point

12 glow, incandescence, fieriness; **flush, blush, bloom,** redness 41, rubicundity, rosiness; whiteness 37; thermochromism; hectic, hectic flush; sunburn

13 fire; blaze, flame, ingle, devouring element; **combustion, ignition,** ignition temperature *or* point, flash *or* flashing point; **conflagration;** flicker 1025.8, wavering *or* flickering flame, "lambent flame"—Dryden; smoldering fire, sleeping fire; marshfire, fen fire, ignis fatuus, will-o'-the-wisp; fox fire; witch fire, St Elmo's fire, corposant; **cheerful fire,** cozy fire, crackling fire; **roaring fire,** blazing fire; **raging fire,** sheet of fire, sea of flames; bonfire, balefire; beacon fire, beacon, signal beacon, watch fire; towering inferno; alarm fire, two-alarm fire, three-alarm fire, etc; wildfire, prairie fire, forest fire; backfire; brushfire; open fire; campfire; smudge fire; death fire, pyre, funeral pyre, crematory; burning ghat; fireball; first-degree burn, second-degree burn, third-degree burn

14 flare, flare-up, **flash,** flash fire, **blaze,** burst, outburst; deflagration

15 spark, sparkle; **scintillation,** scintilla; ignescence

16 coal, live coal, brand, firebrand, **ember,** burning ember; **cinder**

17 fireworks <see list>, **pyrotechnics** *or* pyrotechny

18 <perviousness to heat> transcalency; adiathermancy, athermancy

19 **thermal unit;** British thermal unit *or* BTU; Board of Trade unit *or* BOT; centigrade thermal unit; centigrade *or* Celsius scale, Fahrenheit scale; **calorie,** mean calorie, centuple *or* rational calorie, small calorie, large *or* great calorie, kilocalorie, kilogram-calorie; therm; joule

20 **thermometer,** thermal detector; mercury, glass; thermostat; calorimeter; thermograph, thermostat

21 <science of heat> thermochemistry, thermology, thermotics, thermodynamics; volcanology; pyrology, pyrognostics; pyrotechnics *or* pyrotechny, ebulliometry; calorimetry

VERBS 22 <be hot> **burn** 1020.24, **scorch,** parch, scald, **swelter, roast,** toast, cook, bake, fry, broil, sizzle, boil, seethe, simmer, stew; **be in heat;** shimmer with heat, give off waves of heat, radiate heat; **blaze,** combust, spark, **catch fire, flame** 1020.23, flame up, **flare,** flare up; **flicker** 1025.26; **glow,** incandesce, flush, blush, bloom; smolder; steam; sweat 12.16; gasp, pant; **suffocate, stifle,** smother, choke; keep warm; run a temperature; sunbathe

23 **smoke, fume,** reek, smolder; smudge; carbonize

ADJS 24 **warm,** calid <old>, **thermal,** thermic; **toasty** <nf>, warm as toast; **sunny,** sunshiny, sunbaked; fair, mild, genial; summery, aestival; **temperate,** warmish; balmy, **tropical,** equatorial, subtropical; semitropical; **tepid, lukewarm,** luke; room-temperature; blood-warm, blood-hot; unfrozen

25 **hot, heated, torrid,** thermal, thermic; **sweltering,** sweltry, canicular; **burning,** parching, scorching, searing, scalding, blistering, baking, roasting, toasting, broiling, grilling, simmering, sizzling; **boiling,** seething, ebullient; **piping hot,** scalding hot, burning hot, roasting hot, scorching hot, sizzling hot, smoking hot; **red-hot,** white-hot; ardent; flushed, sweating, sweaty, sudorific; overwarm, overhot, overheated; hot as fire, hot as a three-dollar pistol <nf>, hot as hell *or* blazes, hot as the hinges of hell, hot enough to roast an ox, hot enough to fry an egg on, so hot you can fry eggs on the sidewalk <nf>, like a furnace *or* an oven; feverish; hot and humid, HHH <nf>

26 **fiery,** igneous, firelike, pyric; combustive, conflagrative

27 **burning, ignited,** kindled, enkindled, **blazing,** ablaze, ardent, flaring, flaming, aflame, inflamed, alight, **afire, on fire,** in flames, in a blaze, flagrant <old>; conflagrant, comburent; live, living; molten; **glowing,** aglow, in a glow, incandescent, candescent, candent; sparking, scintillating, scintillant, ignescent; **flickering,** aflicker,

guttering; unquenched, unextinguished; slow-burning; **smoldering; smoking,** fuming, reeking

28 **sultry, stifling, suffocating, stuffy, close,** oppressive, steamy; **humid, sticky** <nf>, **muggy**

29 warm-blooded, hot-blooded

30 isothermal, isothermic; centigrade, Fahrenheit

31 diathermic, diathermal, transcalent; adiathermic, adiathermal, athermanous

32 pyrological, pyrognostic, pyrotechnic *or* pyrotechnical; pyrogenic *or* pyrogenous *or* pyrogenetic; thermochemical; thermodynamic, thermodynamical

WORD ELEMENTS 33 igni-, pyr-, pyro-; therm-, thermo-, -thermous

34 **fireworks**

Bengali-light	pastille
bomb	peeoy
candlebomb	petard
cannon cracker	pinwheel
cap	rocket
Catherine wheel	Roman candle
chaser	serpent
cherry bomb	six-inch salute
colored fire	skyrocket
cracker	snake
cracker bonbon	sparkler
firecracker	squib
fizgig *or* fisgig	tantrum
fizzer	throwdown
flare	torpedo
flowerpot	tourbillion
fountain	Vesuvius fountain
girandole	volcano
ladyfinger	wheel
mandarin cracker	whiz-bang
maroon	

1020 HEATING

NOUNS 1 **heating, warming,** calefaction, torrefaction, increase *or* raising of temperature; superheating; pyrogenesis; decalescence, recalescence; preheating; **heating system** <see list>, heating method; solar radiation, insolation; dielectric heating; induction heating; heat exchange; cooking 11

2 **boiling,** seething, **stewing,** ebullition, ebullience *or* ebulliency, coction; decoction; **simmering;** boil; simmer

3 **melting, fusion,** liquefaction, liquefying, liquescence, running; **thawing,** thaw; liquation; fusibility; thermoplasticity

4 **ignition, lighting,** lighting up *or* off, **kindling,** firing; reaching flash point *or* flashing point

5 **burning, combustion,** blazing, flaming; **scorching,** parching, singeing; **searing,** branding; **blistering,**

vesication; **cauterization,** cautery; **incineration; cremation;** suttee, self-cremation, self-immolation; the stake, burning at the stake, *auto da fé* <Pg>; scorification; carbonization; oxidation, oxidization; calcination; cupellation; deflagration; distilling, distillation; refining, smelting; pyrolysis; cracking, thermal cracking, destructive distillation; **spontaneous combustion,** thermogenesis

6 **burn,** scald, scorch, singe; sear; brand; sunburn, sunscald; windburn; mat burn; first- *or* second- *or* third-degree burn

7 **incendiarism, arson,** torch job <nf>, fire-raising <Brit>; **pyromania;** pyrophilia; pyrolatry, fire worship

8 **incendiary, arsonist,** torcher <nf>; pyromaniac, firebug <nf>; pyrophile, fire buff <nf>; pyrolater, fire worshiper

9 **flammability, inflammability,** combustibility; spontaneous combustion

10 **heater, warmer; stove, oven, furnace; cooker,** cookery; firebox; tuyere, tewel <old>; burner, jet, gas jet, pilot light *or* burner, element, heating element, Bunsen burner; heat lamp; heating pipe, steam pipe, hot-water pipe; heating duct, caliduct

11 **fireplace, hearth,** ingle; **fireside,** hearthside, ingleside, inglenook, ingle cheek <Scot>, chimney corner; hearthstone; hob, hub; fireguard, fireboard, fire screen, fender; chimney, chimney piece, chimney-breast, chimney-pot, chimney-stack, flue, grate; smokehole; brazier, kiln, smelter, forge; pyre

12 **fire iron; andiron,** firedog; tongs, pair of tongs, fire tongs, coal tongs; poker, stove poker, salamander, fire hook; lifter, stove lifter; pothook, crook, crane, chain; trivet, tripod; spit, turnspit; grate, grating; gridiron, grid, griddle, grill, griller; damper

13 **incinerator,** cinerator, burner; solid-waste incinerator, garbage incinerator; **crematory,** cremator, crematorium, burning ghat; calcinatory

14 **blowtorch,** blowlamp <Brit>, blast lamp, torch, alcohol torch, butane torch; soldering torch; blowpipe; **burner; welder;** acetylene torch *or* welder, cutting torch *or* blowpipe, oxyacetylene blowpipe *or* torch, welding blowpipe *or* torch

15 cauterant, cauterizer, cauter, cautery; thermocautery, actual cautery; hot iron, **branding iron,** brand iron, brand; moxa; electrocautery; **caustic, corrosive,** mordant, escharotic, potential cautery; acid; lunar caustic; radium

16 <products of combustion> scoria, sullage, slag, dross; **ashes,** ash; **cinder,** clinker, coal; coke, charcoal, brand, lava, carbon, calx; **soot,** smut, coom <Brit nf>; **smoke,** smudge, fume, reek

VERBS 17 **heat,** raise *or* increase the temperature, heat up, hot *or* hot up <Brit>, **warm,** fire, fire up, stoke up; chafe; take the chill off; tepefy; gas-heat, oil-heat, hot-air-heat, hot-water-heat, steam-heat, electric-heat, solar-heat; superheat; overheat; preheat; **reheat,** recook, warm over *or* up; mull; steam; foment; cook 11.5; glow; cook, roast, toast, bake, braise, broil, fry

18 <metaphors> **excite, inflame;** incite, **kindle, arouse** 375.17,19; anger, **enrage**

19 insolate, sun-dry; **sun,** bask, bask in the sun, sun oneself, sunbathe, suntan, get a tan, tan

20 **boil, stew, simmer, seethe;** distill; scald, parboil, steam

21 **melt,** melt down, liquefy; **run,** colliquate, **fuse,** flux; refine, smelt; render; **thaw,** thaw out, unfreeze; defrost, de-ice

22 **ignite, set fire to, fire, set on fire, set alight, kindle,** enkindle, inflame, **light,** light up, strike a light, put a match *or* torch to, torch <nf>, touch off, **burn,** conflagrate; **build a fire;** rekindle, relight, relume; feed, feed the fire, **stoke,** stoke the fire, add fuel to the flame; bank; poke *or* stir the fire, blow up the fire, fan the flame; open the draft; reduce to ashes

23 **catch fire,** catch on fire, catch, take fire, **burn, flame,** combust, blaze, **blaze up, burst into flames,** go up in flames

24 **burn,** torrefy, **scorch, parch, sear; singe,** swinge; **blister,** vesicate; **cauterize,** brand, burn in; char, coal, carbonize; scorify; calcine; pyrolyze, crack; solder, weld, fuse, lag; vulcanize; cast, found; oxidize, oxidate; deflagrate; cupel; burn off; blaze, flame 1019.22

25 **burn up,** incendiarize, **incinerate, cremate,** consume, burn *or* reduce to ashes, **burn to a crisp,** burn to a cinder; **burn down,** burn to the ground, **go up in smoke;** burn at the stake

ADJS 26 **heating, warming,** chafing, calorific; calefactory, calefactive, calefacient, calorifacient, calorigenic; fiery, burning 1019.25,27; cauterant, cauterizing; calcinatory

27 **inflammatory,** inflammative, **inflaming, kindling,** enkindling, lighting; **incendiary,** incendive; arsonous

28 **flammable, inflammable, combustible,** burnable

29 **heated,** het *or* het up <nf>, hotted up <Brit>, **warmed,** warmed up, centrally heated, gas-heated, oil-heated, kerosene-heated, hot-water-heated, hot-air-heated, steam-heated, solar-heated, electric-heated, baseboard-heated; superheated; overheated; preheated; **reheated,** recooked, **warmed-over,** *réchauffé* <Fr>; hot 1019.25

30 **burned, burnt,** burned to the ground, incendiarized, torched <nf>, burned-out *or* -down,

gutted; **scorched, blistered, parched, singed, seared, charred,** pyrographic, adust; sunburned; **burnt-up,** incinerated, cremated, consumed, consumed by fire; ashen, ashy, carbonized, pyrolyzed, pyrolytic

31 **molten, melted,** fused, liquefied; liquated; meltable, fusible; thermoplastic

32 **heating systems**

baseboard heating	hypocaust
central heating	kerosene heating
convection heating	oil heating
electric heating	panel heating
furnace heating	radiant heating
gas heating	solar heating
heat pump	space heating
hot-air heating	steam heating
hot-water heating	stove heating

1021 FUEL

NOUNS 1 **fuel** <see list>, energy source; heat source, firing, combustible *or* inflammable *or* flammable material, burnable, combustible, inflammable, flammable; fossil fuel, nonrenewable energy *or* fuel source; alternate *or* alternative energy source *or* alternate energy, renewable energy *or* fuel source; solar energy, solar radiation, insolation; wind energy; geothermal energy, geothermal heat, geothermal gradient; synthetic fuels *or* synfuels; solid fuel; fuel starter; fuel additive, dope, fuel dope; propellant; **oil** 1056; gas 1067

2 slack, coal dust, coom *or* comb <Brit nf>, culm

3 **firewood,** stovewood, wood; woodpile; kindling, **kindlings,** kindling wood; brush, brushwood; fagot, bavin <Brit>; log, backlog, yule log *or* yule clog <old>

4 **lighter,** light, igniter, sparker; pocket lighter, cigar *or* cigarette lighter, butane lighter; **torch,** flambeau, taper, spill; brand, **firebrand;** portfire; **flint,** flint *and* steel; **detonator,** fuse, spark plug, ignition system

5 **match,** matchstick, lucifer; friction match, locofoco *and* vesuvian *and* vesta *and* fusee *and* Congreve *or* Congreve match <old>; safety match; matchbook

6 **tinder,** touchwood; **punk,** spunk, German tinder, amadou; tinder fungus; pyrotechnic sponge; tinderbox

7 renewable energy, soft energy; solar power, solar energy, alternate energy; photovoltaic cell, solar cell; wind power; geothermal energy; water power, hydroelectric power; wave power, tidal power; biomass

VERBS 8 **fuel,** fuel up; fill up, top off; refuel; coal, oil; **stoke, feed,** add fuel to the flame; detonate, explode

ADJS 9 **fuel,** energy, heat; fossil-fuel; alternate- *or* alternative-energy; oil-fired, coal-fired, etc; gas-powered, oil-powered, wind-powered, etc; water-driven, hydroelectric, etc; wood-burning; coaly, carbonaceous, carboniferous; anthracite; clean-burning; bituminous; high-sulfur; lignitic; peaty; gas-guzzling

10 **fuels**

alcohol	leaded gasoline
alternative fuel	lignite *or* brown coal
anthracite *or* hard coal	liquid oxygen
aviation fuel *or* gas	lump coal
benzine	methane
bituminous *or* soft coal	methanol
blind coal	motor fuel
briquette *or* briquet	mustard-seed coal
broken coal	naphtha
buckwheat coal	natural gas
butane	nuclear power *and* nuclear
cannel *or* cannel coal	energy
carbon	nut coal
charcoal	octane
chestnut coal	oil *or* petroleum
coal	pea coal
coal gas	peat *or* turf
coke	pentane
crude oil	petrol <Brit>
diesel fuel *or* diesel *or*	premium *or* high-test
diesel oil *or* derv <Brit>	gasoline
egg coal	producer *or* air gas
electricity	propane
ethane	propellant
ethanol	regular gasoline
ethyl gasoline	renewable energy
flaxseed coal	rocket fuel
gas carbon	sea coal
gasohol	solar power
gasoline *or* gas	steamboat coal
glance coal	stove coal
grate coal	unleaded *or* lead-free
heptane	gasoline
hexane	water power
high-octane gasoline	white gasoline
isooctane	wind power
jet fuel	wood
kerosene *or* paraffin <Brit>	

1022 INCOMBUSTIBILITY

NOUNS 1 **incombustibility, uninflammability,** noninflammability, **nonflammability;** unburnableness; fire resistance

2 **extinguishing,** extinguishment, extinction, **quenching,** dousing <nf>, **snuffing,** putting out; **choking, damping, stifling, smothering,** smotheration; controlling; fire fighting; going out, dying, burning out, flame-out, burnout

3 **extinguisher, fire extinguisher;** fire apparatus, fire engine, hook-and-ladder, ladder truck; ladder pipe, snorkel, deluge set, deck gun; pumper, superpumper; **foam,** carbon-dioxide foam, Foamite <trademark>, foam extinguisher; drypowder extinguisher; carbon tetrachloride, carbon tet; water, soda, acid, wet blanket; sprinkler, automatic sprinkler, sprinkler system, sprinkler head; hydrant, fire hydrant, fireplug; fire hose

4 **fire fighter, fireman,** fire-eater <nf>; pumpman; forest fire fighter, fire warden, fire-chaser, smokechaser, smokejumper; volunteer fireman, vamp <nf>; fire department, fire brigade <chiefly Brit>

5 **fireproofing;** fire resistance; fireproof *or* fire-resistant *or* fire-resisting *or* fire-resistive *or* fire-retardant material, fire retardant; asbestos; amianthus, earth flax, mountain flax; asbestos curtain, fire wall; fire break, fire line

VERBS 6 **fireproof,** flameproof

7 **fight fire; extinguish, put out, quench,** out, douse <nf>, **snuff,** snuff out, blow out, stamp out; stub out, dinch <nf>; **choke, damp, smother, stifle,** slack; bring under control, contain

8 **burn out, go out, die,** die out *or* down *or* away; fizzle *and* **fizzle out** <nf>; flame out

ADJS 9 **incombustible, noncombustible, uninflammable,** noninflammable, noncombustive, **nonflammable,** unburnable; asbestine, asbestous, asbestoid, asbestoidal; amianthine

10 **fireproof, flameproof,** fireproofed, fire-retarded, fire-resisting *or* -resistant *or* -resistive, fire-retardant

11 **extinguished,** quenched, snuffed, **out;** contained, under control

1023 COLD

NOUNS 1 **cold, coldness; coolness,** coolth, freshness; low temperature, arctic temperature, drop *or* decrease in temperature, lack of heat; **chilliness,** nippiness, freshness, crispness, briskness, sharpness, bite; **chill, nip,** sharp air; **frigidity, iciness,** frostiness, extreme *or* intense cold, gelidity, algidity, algidness; **rawness,** bleakness, keenness, sharpness, bitterness, severity, inclemency, rigor; freezing point; cryology; cryonics; cryogenics; absolute zero

2 <sensation of cold> **chill,** chilliness, chilling; shivering, chills, **shivers,** cold shivers, shakes, didders <Brit nf>, dithers, chattering of the teeth; creeps, **cold creeps** <nf>; **gooseflesh, goose pimples,** goose *or* duck bumps <nf>, horripilation; **frostbite, chilblains,** kibe, cryopathy; ache, aching; ice-cream headache

3 **cold weather,** bleak weather, raw weather, bitter weather, wintry weather, arctic weather, **freezing weather,** zero weather, subzero weather; **cold wave,** snap, **cold snap,** cold spell, cold front; **freeze,** frost, hard frost, deep freeze, arctic frost, big freeze, hard freeze; winter, wintriness, depths of winter, hard winter, arctic conditions; wintry wind 318.7; coolness, chill, nip in the air, chilliness, nippiness; chill factor, wind-chill factor; ice age

4 <cold place> Siberia, Hell, Novaya Zemlya, Alaska, Iceland, the Hebrides, Greenland, the Yukon, Tierra del Fuego, Lower Slobbovia <Al Capp>; North Pole, South Pole; Frigid Zones; the Arctic, Arctic Circle *or* Zone; Antarctica, the Antarctic; Antarctic Circle *or* Zone; tundra; the freezer, the deep-freeze, igloo

5 **ice,** frozen water; ice needle *or* crystal; **icicle,** iceshockle <Brit nf>; cryosphere; ice sheet, ice field, ice barrier, ice front; **floe, ice floe,** sea ice, ice island, ice raft, ice pack; ice foot, ice belt; shelf ice, sheet ice, pack ice, bay ice, berg ice, field ice; **iceberg,** berg, growler; calf; snowberg; **icecap,** *jokul* <Iceland>; ice pinnacle, serac, nieve penitente; **glacier,** glacieret, glaciation, ice dike; piedmont glacier; icefall; ice banner; ice cave; **sleet,** glaze, glazed frost, verglas; snow ice; névé, black ice, granular snow, firn; ground ice, anchor ice, frazil; lolly; sludge, slob *or* slob ice <chiefly Can>; ice cubes; crushed ice; Dry Ice <trademark>, solid carbon dioxide; icequake; ice storm, freezing rain

6 **hail,** hailstone; soft hail, graupel, snow pellets, tapioca snow; **hailstorm**

7 **frost,** Jack Frost; **hoarfrost,** hoar, rime, rime frost, white frost; black frost; hard frost, sharp frost; killing frost; frost smoke; frost line; permafrost; silver frost; glaze frost; ground frost

8 **snow;** granular snow, corn snow, spring corn, spring snow, powder snow, wet snow, tapioca snow; **snowfall; snowstorm,** snow blast, snow squall, snow flurry, flurry, snow shower, blizzard, whiteout; **snowflake,** snow-crystal, flake, crystal; snow dust; **snowdrift,** snowbank, snow cover, snowscape, snow blanket, snow mantle, snow wreath <Brit nf>, driven snow, drifting snow; snowcap; snow banner; snow blanket; snow bed, snowpack, snowfield, mantle of snow; snowscape; snowland; snowshed; snow line; snowball, snowman; snowslide, snowslip, avalanche; snow slush, **slush,** slosh, snowmelt, melt, meltwater; snowbridge; snow fence; snowhouse, igloo; mogul

VERBS 9 freeze, be cold, grow cold, lose heat; **shiver, quiver,** shiver to death, quake, shake, tremble, shudder, didder <Brit nf>, dither; **chatter; chill,** have a chill, have the cold shivers; **freeze,** freeze to death, freeze one's balls off <nf>, die *or* perish with the cold, horripilate, have goose pimples, have goose *or* duck bumps <nf>; have chilblains; get frostbite

10 <make cold> **freeze, chill,** chill to the bone *or* marrow, make one shiver, make one's teeth chatter; **nip,** bite, cut, **pierce,** penetrate, penetrate to the bone, go through *or* right through; freshen; air-condition; glaciate; freeze-dry; **freeze** 1024.11; frost, frostbite; numb, benumb; **refrigerate** 1024.10

11 **hail, sleet, snow;** snow in; snow under; **frost,** ice, ice up, ice over, glaze, glaze over, freeze over

ADJS 12 **cool,** coolish, temperate; chill, **chilly,** parky <Brit nf>; **fresh,** brisk, crisp, bracing, sharpish, **invigorating,** stimulating

13 **unheated,** unwarmed; unmelted, unthawed

14 **cold, freezing,** freezing cold, **crisp, brisk,** nipping, **nippy, snappy** <nf>, **raw, bleak, keen, sharp,** bitter, biting, pinching, cutting, **piercing,** penetrating, perishing; inclement, severe, rigorous; snowcold; sleety; slushy; **icy,** icelike, **ice-cold,** glacial, ice-encrusted; cryospheric; supercooled; **frigid,** bitter *or* bitterly cold, gelid, algid; below zero, subzero; numbing; **wintry,** wintery, winterlike, winterbound, hiemal, brumal, hibernal; **arctic,** Siberian, boreal, hyperborean; stone-cold, cold as death, cold as ice, cold as marble, cold as charity

15 <nf terms> **cold as hell,** cold as a welldigger's ass, cold as a witch's tit *or* kiss, cold enough to freeze the tail *or* balls off a brass monkey, cold as a bastard *or* a bitch, colder than hell *or* the deuce *or* the devil

16 <feeling cold> **cold, freezing; cool, chilly,** nippy; **shivering,** shivery, shaky, dithery; algid, aguish, aguey; chattering, with chattering teeth; **frozen** 1024.14, half-frozen, frozen to death, chilled to the bone, blue with cold, *figé de froid* <Fr>, so cold one could spit ice cubes

17 **frosty,** frostlike; **frosted,** frosted-over, frost-beaded, frost-covered, frost-chequered, rimed, **hoary,** hoar-frosted, rime-frosted; frost-riven, frost-rent; frosty-faced, frosty-whiskered; frostbound, frost fettered

18 **snowy,** snowlike, niveous, nival; snow-blown, snow-drifted, snow-driven; **snow-covered,** snow-clad, snow-mantled, snow-robed, snow-blanketed, snow-sprinkled, snow-lined, snow-encircled, snow-laden, snow-loaded, snow-hung; **snow-capped,** snow-peaked, snow-crested, snow-crowned, snow-tipped, snow-topped; snow-bearded; snow-feathered; snow-still

19 frozen out *or* in, **snowbound,** snowed-in, **icebound**

20 **cold-blooded,** hypothermic, heterothermic, poikilothermic; cryogenic; cryological

WORD ELEMENTS 21 cryo- *or* kryo-, frigo-, psychro-; glacio-; chio-, chion-

1024 REFRIGERATION
<reduction of temperature>

NOUNS 1 **refrigeration,** infrigidation, reduction of temperature; **cooling, chilling; freezing,** glacification, glaciation, congelation, congealment; refreezing, regelation; mechanical refrigeration, electric refrigeration, electronic refrigeration, gas refrigeration; food freezing, quick freezing, deep freezing, sharp freezing, blast freezing, dehydrofreezing; adiabatic expansion, adiabatic absorption, adiabatic demagnetization; cryogenics; super-cooling; air conditioning, **air cooling,** *climatisation* <Fr>; climate control

2 refrigeration anesthesia, crymoanesthesia, hypothermia *or* hypothermy; crymotherapy, cryo-aerotherapy; cold cautery, cryocautery; cryopathy

3 **cooler,** chiller; water cooler, air cooler, air conditioner; ventilator; fan; surface cooler; ice cube, ice pail *or* bucket, wine cooler; ice bag, ice pack, cold pack

4 **refrigerator,** refrigeratory, **icebox,** ice chest; Frigidaire <trademark>, fridge <nf>, electric refrigerator, electronic refrigerator, gas refrigerator, refrigerator-freezer; refrigerator car, refrigerator truck, reefer <nf>; freezer ship; ice house

5 **freezer, deep freeze,** deep-freezer, quick-freezer, sharp-freezer; ice-cream freezer; ice machine, ice-cube machine, freezing machine, refrigerating machine *or* engine; **ice plant,** icehouse, refrigerating plant

6 **cold storage; frozen-food locker,** locker, freezer locker, locker plant; coolhouse; coolerman; frigidarium; cooling tower

7 <cooling agent> **coolant; refrigerant;** cryogen; ice, Dry Ice <trademark>, ice cubes; freezing mixture, liquid air, ammonia, carbon dioxide, Freon <trademark>, ether; ethyl chloride; liquid air, liquid oxygen *or* lox, liquid nitrogen, liquid helium, etc

8 **antifreeze,** coolant, radiator coolant, alcohol, ethylene glycol

9 refrigerating engineering, refrigerating engineer

VERBS 10 **refrigerate; cool, chill;** refresh, freshen; ice, ice-cool; water-cool, air-cool, **air-condition;** ventilate

11 **freeze** 1023.9,10, ice, glaciate, congeal; **deep-freeze,** quick-freeze, sharp-freeze, blast-freeze;

freeze solid; freeze-dry; **nip,** blight, blast; refreeze, regelate

ADJS **12 refrigerative,** refrigeratory, refrigerant, frigorific, algific; **cooling, chilling; freezing,** congealing; quick-freezing, deep-freezing, sharp-freezing, blast-freezing; freezable, glaciable

13 cooled, chilled; air-conditioned; iced, ice-cooled; air-cooled, water-cooled; super-cooled

14 frozen, frozen solid, glacial, gelid, congealed; icy, ice-cold, icy-cold, ice, icelike; deep-frozen, quick-frozen, sharp-frozen, blast-frozen; frostbitten, frostnipped

15 antifreeze, antifreezing

1025 LIGHT

NOUNS **1 light,** radiant or luminous energy, visible radiation, radiation in the visible spectrum, **illumination,** illuminance, **radiation, radiance** or radiancy, irradiance or irradiancy, irradiation, emanation; "God's first creature"—Francis Bacon, "the first of painters"—Emerson; light wave; highlight; sidelight; photosensitivity; light source 1026; **invisible light,** black light, infrared light, ultraviolet light

2 shine, shininess, **luster, sheen, gloss,** glint, glister; **glow, gleam,** flush, sunset glow; light emission; lambency; **incandescence,** candescence; shining light; afterglow; skylight, air glow, night glow, day glow, twilight glow

3 lightness, luminousness, lightedness, luminosity, luminance; **lucidity,** lucence or lucency, translucence or translucency; backlight

4 brightness, brilliance or brilliancy, **splendor,** radiant splendor, **glory, radiance** or radiancy, resplendence or resplendency, **vividness,** luminance, contrast, flamboyance or flamboyancy; effulgence, refulgence or refulgency, fulgentness, fulgidity, fulgor; **glare,** blare, blaze; bright light, brilliant light, blazing light, glaring light, dazzling light, blinding light; TV lights, Klieg light, footlights, house lights; streaming light, flood of light, burst of light

5 ray, radiation 1037, **beam, gleam,** leam <Scot>, **stream, streak, pencil, patch,** ray of light, beam of light; ribbon, ribbon of light, streamer, stream of light; electromagnetic radiation; violet ray, ultraviolet ray, infrared ray, X ray, gamma ray, invisible radiation; actinic ray or light, actinism; atomic beam, atomic ray; laser beam; solar rays; photon; visible spectrum

6 flash, blaze, flare, flame, gleam, glint, glance; blaze or flash or gleam of light; green flash; solar flare, solar prominence, facula; Bailey's beads

7 glitter, glimmer, shimmer, twinkle, blink; sparkle, spark; **scintillation,** scintilla; coruscation; **glisten,** glister, spangle, tinsel, glittering, glimmering, shimmering, twinkling; stroboscopic or strobe light <nf>; blinking; firefly, glowworm

8 flicker, flutter, dance, quiver; flickering, fluttering, bickering, guttering, dancing, quivering, lambency; wavering or flickering light, play, play of light, dancing or glancing light; light show; "the lambent easy light"—Dryden

9 reflection; reflected or incident light; reflectance, albedo; blink, iceblink, ice sky, snowblink, waterblink, water sky

10 daylight, dayshine, day glow, light of day; day, daytime, daytide; **natural light; sunlight, sunshine,** shine; noonlight, white light, midday sun, noonday or noontide light, "the blaze of noon"—Milton; broad day or daylight, full sun; bright time; dusk, twilight 315.3; the break or crack of dawn, cockcrow, dawn 314.3; sunburst, sunbreak; **sunbeam,** sun spark, ray of sunshine; green flash; solar energy; ambient light

11 moonlight, moonshine, moonglow; **moonbeam,** moonrise

12 starlight, starshine; earthshine

13 luminescence; luciferin, luciferase; phosphor, luminophor; **ignis fatuus, will-o'-the-wisp,** will-with-the-wisp, wisp, jack-o'-lantern, marshfire; friar's lantern; fata morgana; fox fire; St Elmo's light or fire, corona discharge, wild fire, witch fire, corposant; double corposant; bioluminescence, thermoluminescence, fluorescence, phosphorescence, radioluminescence

14 halo, nimbus, aura, **aureole,** circle, ring, glory; **rainbow,** solar halo, lunar halo, ring around the sun or moon; white rainbow or fogbow; **corona,** solar corona, lunar corona; parhelion, parhelic circle or ring, mock sun, sun dog; anthelion, antisun, countersun; paraselene, mock moon, moon dog

15 <nebulous light> nebula 1072.7; zodiacal light, gegenschein, counterglow, streamers

16 polar lights, **aurora; northern lights, aurora borealis,** merry dancers; southern lights, **aurora australis;** aurora polaris; aurora glory; streamer or curtain or arch aurora; polar ray

17 lightning, flash or **stroke of lightning,** fulguration, fulmination, bolt, lightning strike, **bolt of lightning,** streak, bolt from the blue, **thunderbolt,** thunderstroke, thunderball, fireball, firebolt, levin bolt or brand; fork or forked lightning, chain lightning, globular or ball lightning, summer or heat lightning, sheet lightning, dark lightning; Jupiter Fulgur or Fulminator; Thor

18 **iridescence,** opalescence, nacreousness, pearliness; **rainbow;** nacre, mother-of-pearl; nacreous *or* mother-of-pearl cloud

19 **lighting, illumination,** artificial light *or* lighting; lamp light, arc light, calcium light, candlelight, electric light, fluorescent light, gaslight, incandescent light, mercury-vapor light, neon light, sodium light, strobe light, torchlight, streetlight, floodlight, spotlight; Christmas tree lights, safety light; tonality; light and shade, black and white, chiaroscuro, clairobscure, contrast, highlights; photoemission, light-emitting diode *or* LED, liquid-crystal display *or* LCD, light pen

20 **illuminant,** luminant; electricity; gas, illuminating gas; oil, petroleum, benzine; gasoline, petrol <Brit>; kerosene, paraffin <Brit>, coal oil; light source 1026; fire, lantern

21 <measurement of light> **candle power,** luminous intensity, luminous power, luminous flux, flux, intensity, light; quantum, **light quantum, photon;** unit of light <see list>, unit of flux; lux, candle-meter, lumen meter, lumeter, lumen, candle lumen; **exposure meter,** light meter, ASA scale, Scheiner scale

22 <science of light> photics, photology, photometry; **optics,** geometrical optics, physical optics; dioptrics, catoptrics, fiber optics; actinology, actinometry; heliology, heliometry, heliography

23 <light units> *bougie décimale* <Fr>, British candle, candle, candle-foot, candle-hour, decimal candle, foot-candle, Hefner candle, international candle, lamp-hour, lumen-hour

VERBS 24 **shine,** shine forth, **burn, give light,** incandesce; glow, beam, gleam, glint, luster, glance; **flash, flare, blaze, flame,** fulgurate; **radiate,** shoot, shoot out rays, send out rays; spread *or* diffuse light; be bright, shine brightly, beacon; **glare;** daze, blind, dazzle, bedazzle

25 **glitter, glimmer, shimmer, twinkle, blink,** spangle, tinsel, coruscate; **sparkle,** spark, **scintillate; glisten,** glister, glisk <Scot>

26 **flicker,** bicker, gutter, **flutter, waver, dance,** play, quiver

27 **luminesce,** phosphoresce, fluoresce; iridesce, opalesce

28 **grow light,** grow bright, light, **lighten,** brighten; dawn, break

29 **illuminate,** illumine, illume, luminate, **light, light up, lighten,** enlighten, brighten, brighten up, irradiate; bathe *or* flood with light; relumine, relume; **shed light upon,** cast *or* throw light upon, shed luster on, shine upon, overshine; spotlight, highlight; floodlight; beacon

30 **strike a light,** light, **turn** *or* **switch on the light,** open the light <nf>, make a light, shine a light

ADJS 31 **luminous,** luminant, luminative, luminificent, luminiferous, luciferous *or* lucific <old>, luciform, illuminant; **incandescent,** candescent; **lustrous,** orient; **radiant,** irradiative; **shining,** shiny, burning, lamping, streaming; **beaming,** beamy; **gleaming,** gleamy, glinting; **glowing,** aglow, suffused, blushing, flushing; rutilant, rutilous; **sunny, sunshiny,** bright and sunny, light as day; starry, starlike, starbright

32 **light,** lightish, lightsome; **lucid,** lucent, luculent, relucent; translucent, translucid, pellucid, diaphanous, transparent; **clear,** serene; **cloudless,** unclouded, unobscured

33 **bright, brilliant, vivid, splendid,** splendorous, splendent, **resplendent,** bright and shining; fulgid <old>, fulgent, effulgent, refulgent; **flamboyant,** flaming; **glaring,** glary, garish; **dazzling,** bedazzling, blinding, pitiless; shadowless, shadeless

34 **shiny,** shining, **lustrous, glossy,** glassy, *glacé* <Fr>, bright as a new penny, **sheeny, polished,** burnished, shined

35 **flashing,** flashy, **blazing, flaming, flaring, burning,** fulgurant, fulgurating; aflame, ablaze; meteoric

36 **glittering, glimmering, shimmering, twinkling, blinking, glistening,** glistering; glittery, glimmery, glimmerous, shimmery, twinkly, blinky, spangly, tinsely; **sparkling, scintillating,** scintillant, scintillescent, coruscating, coruscant

37 **flickering,** bickering, **fluttering, wavering, dancing,** playing, quivering, lambent; flickery, flicky <nf>, aflicker, fluttery, wavery, quivery; blinking, flashing, stroboscopic

38 **iridescent,** opalescent, nacreous, pearly, pearl-like; rainbowlike

39 **luminescent,** photogenic; autoluminescent, bioluminescent

40 **illuminated,** luminous, **lightened,** enlightened, brightened, **lighted,** lit, **lit up,** well-lit, flooded *or* bathed with light, floodlit; irradiated, irradiate; **alight, glowing,** aglow, lambent, suffused with light; ablaze, blazing, in a blaze, fiery; lamplit, lanternlit, candlelit, torchlit, gaslit, firelit; sunlit, moonlit, starlit; spangled, bespangled, tinseled, studded; starry, starbright, star-spangled, star-studded

41 **illuminating,** illumining, **lighting, lightening,** brightening

42 **luminary,** photic; photologic *or* photological; photometric *or* photometrical; heliological, heliographic; actinic, photoactinic; catoptric *or* catoptrical; luminal

43 photosensitive; photophobic; phototropic

WORD ELEMENTS 44 phot-, photo-, lumin-, lumino-, lumini-; fluoro- *or* fluori-; irido-; actino-, actini-

1026 LIGHT SOURCE

NOUNS **1 light source,** source of light, **luminary,**
illuminator, luminant, illuminant, incandescent
body *or* point, **light,** glim; **lamp,** light bulb, electric
light bulb, lantern, candle, taper, torch, flame;
match; **fluorescent light, fluorescent tube,**
fluorescent lamp; starter, ballast; "a lamp unto my
feet, and a light unto my path"—Bible; fire 1019.13;
sun, moon, stars 1072.4

2 candle, taper; dip, farthing dip, tallow dip; tallow
candle; wax candle, bougie; soy candle; rush
candle, rushlight; corpse candle; votary candle

3 torch, flaming torch, flambeau, cresset, link <old>;
flare, signal flare, fusee; beacon

4 traffic light *or* light, stop-and-go light; stop *or* red
light, go *or* green light, caution *or* amber light,
pedestrian light

5 firefly, lightning bug, lampyrid, **glowworm,**
fireworm; fire beetle; lantern fly, candle fly;
luciferin, luciferase; phosphor, luminophor

6 chandelier, gasolier, electrolier, hanging *or* ceiling
fixture, luster; corona, corona lucis, crown, circlet;
light holder, light fixture, candlestick; torchiere

7 wick, taper; candlewick, lampwick

1027 DARKNESS, DIMNESS

NOUNS **1 darkness, dark, lightlessness; obscurity,**
obscure, tenebrosity, tenebrousness, leadenness;
night 315.4, dead of night, deep night; sunlessness,
moonlessness, starlessness; **pitch-darkness,**
pitch-blackness, utter *or* thick *or* total darkness,
intense darkness, velvet darkness, Cimmerian *or*
Stygian *or* Egyptian darkness, Stygian gloom,
Erebus; **blackness,** swarthiness 38.2; darkest hour

2 darkishness, darksomeness, **duskiness,** duskness;
murkiness, murk; dimness, dim, dimming;
semidarkness, semidark, partial darkness, bad
light, dim light, half-light, *demi-jour* <Fr>;
gloaming, crepuscular light, **dusk,** twilight
314.4/315.3; romantic lighting, dimmed lights

3 shadow, shade, shadiness; umbra, umbrage,
umbrageousness; thick *or* dark shade, gloom;
mere shadow; penumbra; silhouette; skiagram,
skiagraph

4 gloom, gloominess, somberness, sombrousness,
somber; lowering, lower

5 dullness, flatness, lifelessness, **drabness,**
deadness, somberness, **lackluster, lusterlessness,**
lack of sparkle *or* sheen; matte, matte finish

6 darkening, dimming, bedimming; obscuration,
obscurement, obumbration, obfuscation;
eclipsing, occulting, blocking the light;
shadowing, shading, overshadowing, overshading,
overshadowment, **clouding,** overclouding,
obnubilation, gathering of the clouds, overcast;
blackening 38.5; extinguishment 1022.2; hatching,
cross-hatching

7 blackout, dimout, brownout; fadeout

8 eclipse, occultation; total eclipse, partial eclipse,
central eclipse, annular eclipse; solar eclipse,
lunar eclipse

VERBS **9 darken,** bedarken; **obscure,** obfuscate,
obumbrate; **eclipse,** occult, occultate, block the
light; **black out,** brown out; black, brown; blot out;
overcast, darken over; **shadow, shade,** cast a
shadow, spread a shadow *or* shade over, encompass
with shadow, overshadow; **cloud,** becloud, encloud,
cloud over, overcloud, obnubilate; gloom, begloom,
somber, cast a gloom over, murk; **dim, bedim,** dim
out; mattify; blacken 38.7

10 dull, mat, deaden; **tone down**

11 turn *or* switch off the light, close the light <nf>;
extinguish 1022.7

12 grow dark, darken, darkle, lower *or* lour; gloom
<old>, gloam <Scot>; dusk; **dim, grow dim;** go out

ADJS **13 dark, black,** darksome, darkling; **lightless,**
beamless, rayless, unlighted, **unilluminated,** unlit;
obscure, caliginous, **obscured,** obfuscated,
eclipsed, occulted, clothed *or* shrouded *or* veiled
or cloaked *or* mantled in darkness; tenebrous,
tenebrific, tenebrious, tenebrose; Cimmerian,
Stygian; **pitch-dark,** pitch-black, pitchy, dark as
pitch, dark as the inside of a black cat; ebon,
ebony; night-dark, night-black, dark *or* black as
night; night-clad, night-cloaked, night-
enshrouded, night-mantled, night-veiled, night-
hid, night-filled; sunless, moonless, starless

14 gloomy, gloomful <old>, glooming, dark and
gloomy, Acheronian, Acherontic, **somber,**
sombrous; lowering; **funereal;** stormy, cloudy,
clouded, overcast; ill-lighted, ill-lit

15 darkish, darksome, **semidark; dusky,** dusk;
fuscous, subfuscous, subfusc; **murky,** murksome,
murk <old>; **dim,** dimmed, bedimmed, dimmish,
dimpsy <Brit nf>, half-lit, semidark; dark-colored
38.9

16 shadowy, shady, shadowed, shaded, casting a
shadow, tenebrous, darkling, umbral,
umbrageous; overshadowed, overshaded,
obumbrate, obumbrated; penumbral

17 lackluster, lusterless; dull, dead, deadened,
lifeless, somber, **drab,** wan, **flat,** mat, murky

18 obscuring, obscurant

ADVS **19 in the dark,** darkling, in darkness; in the
night, in the dark of night, in the dead of night, at
or by night; dimly, wanly

1028 SHADE

<a thing that shades>

NOUNS **1 shade,** shader, **screen, light shield, curtain,** drape, drapery, blind *or* blinds, veil; **awning,** sunblind <Brit>; **sunshade,** parasol, **umbrella,** beach umbrella; cover 295.2; shadow 1027.3; partial eclipse

2 eyeshade, eyeshield, visor, bill; goggles, colored spectacles, smoked glasses, dark glasses, **sunglasses,** shades <nf>

3 lamp shade; moonshade; globe, light globe

4 light filter, filter, diffusing screen; smoked glass, frosted glass, ground glass; stained glass; butterfly; gelatin filter, celluloid filter; frosted lens; lens hood; sunscreen; sun roof

VERBS **5 shade, screen,** veil, curtain, shutter, draw the curtains, put up *or* close the shutters; cover 295.19; **shadow** 1027.9; cast a shadow

ADJS **6 shading, screening,** veiling, curtaining; shadowing; covering

7 shaded, screened, veiled, curtained; sunproof; visored; shadowed, shady 1027.16

1029 TRANSPARENCY

NOUNS **1 transparency,** transparence, transpicuousness, show-through, transmission *or* admission of light; **lucidity,** pellucidity, **clearness, clarity,** limpidity; nonopacity, uncloudedness; **crystallinity,** crystal-clearness; **glassiness,** glasslikeness, vitreousness, vitrescence; vitreosity, hyalescence; **diaphanousness,** diaphaneity, sheerness, thinness, **gossameriness,** filminess, gauziness; colorlessness

2 transparent substance, diaphane; **glass** <see list>, glassware, glasswork; vitrics; stemware; window, pane, windowpane, light, windowlight, shopwindow; vitrine; showcase, display case; watch crystal *or* glass; water, air

VERBS **3** be transparent, show through; pass *or* transmit light; vitrify; reveal; crystallize

ADJS **4 transparent,** transpicuous, light-pervious; show-through, see-through, peekaboo, revealing; **lucid,** lucent, pellucid, **clear,** limpid; nonopaque, colorless, unclouded, **crystalline,** crystal, **crystal-clear,** clear as crystal; **diaphanous,** diaphane <old>, sheer, thin; **gossamer,** gossamery, filmy, flimsy, gauzy, open-textured; insubstantial

5 glass, glassy, glasslike, clear as glass, vitric, vitreous, vitriform, hyaline, hyalescent; hyalinocrystalline

WORD ELEMENTS **6** vitri-

7 glass

agate glass	lead glass
antimony glass	milk glass
arsenic glass	mirror
Baccarat glass	obsidian
basalt glass	opal glass
Bilbao glass	opaline
borax glass	optical glass
blown glass	ornamental glass
bone glass	Orrefors glass
bottle glass	photosensitive glass
bulletproof glass	plastic glass
camphor glass	plate glass
carnival glass	porcelain glass
Chevalier glass	pressed glass
coralene	prism glass
cranberry glass	Pyrex <trademark>
crown glass	quartz glass
cryolite glass	reinforced glass
crystal *or* crystal glass	rhinestone
custard glass	rock crystal
cut glass	ruby glass
etched glass	safety glass
Fiberglas <trademark>	Sandwich glass
flashed glass	satin glass
flat glass	sheet glass
flint glass	show glass
float glass	Silex glass <trademark>
Fostoria <trademark>	stained glass
frosted glass	Steuben glass
fused quartz	Swedish glass
glass bead	Syracuse watch glass
glass brick	tempered glass *or*
glass wool	tempered safety glass
ground glass	uranium glass
hobnail glass	uviol glass
ice glass	Venetian glass
lace glass	Vitaglass <trademark>
Lalique glass	vitreous silica
laminated glass *or*	Waterford glass
laminated safety glass	window glass
lead crystal	wire *or* wired glass

1030 SEMITRANSPARENCY

NOUNS **1 semitransparency,** semipellucidity, semidiaphaneity; semiopacity

2 translucence, translucency, lucence, lucency, translucidity, pellucidity, lucidity; transmission *or* admission of light; milkiness, pearliness, opalescence

VERBS **3 frost,** frost over

ADJS **4 semitransparent,** semipellucid, semidiaphanous, semiopaque; frosty, frosted; milky, pearly, opalescent, opaline

5 translucent, lucent, translucid, lucid, pellucid; semitranslucent, semipellucid

1031 OPAQUENESS

NOUNS **1 opaqueness,** opacity, intransparency, nontranslucency, imperviousness to light, adiaphanousness; roil, roiledness, turbidity, turbidness; cloudiness; blackness; **darkness, obscurity,** inscrutability, **dimness** 1027

VERBS **2** opaque, **darken, obscure** 1027.9; **cloud,** becloud; devitrify

ADJS **3 opaque,** intransparent, nontransparent, nontranslucent, adiaphanous, impervious to light, impenetrable; **dark,** black, **obscure** 1027.13, lightproof; **cloudy,** roiled, roily, grumly <Scot>, turbid; covered; semiopaque

1032 ELECTRICITY, MAGNETISM

NOUNS **1 electricity; electrical science** <see list>; **electrical** or **electric unit,** unit of measurement

2 current, electric current <see list>, current flow, amperage, electric stream or flow, juice <nf>; power source, power supply

3 electric or **electrical field,** static field, electrostatic field, field of electrical force; tube of electric force, electrostatic tube of force; **magnetic field,** magnetic field of currents; **electromagnetic field;** variable field; static electricity

4 circuit, electrical circuit, path

5 charge, electric or **electrical charge,** positive charge, negative charge; live wire

6 discharge, arc, electric discharge; **shock,** electroshock, galvanic shock

7 magnetism, magnetic attraction; **electromagnetism;** magnetization; diamagnetism, paramagnetism, ferromagnetism; residual magnetism, magnetic remanence; magnetic memory, magnetic retentiveness; magnetic elements; magnetic dip or inclination, magnetic variation or declination; hysteresis, magnetic hysteresis, hysteresis curve, magnetic friction, magnetic lag or retardation, magnetic creeping; permeability, magnetic permeability, magnetic conductivity; magnetic circuit, magnetic curves, magnetic figures; magnetic flux, gilbert, weber, maxwell; magnetic moment; magnetic potential; magnetic viscosity; magnetics

8 polarity, polarization; **pole, positive pole, anode, negative pole, cathode,** magnetic pole, magnetic axis; north pole, N pole; south pole, S pole

9 magnetic force or **intensity,** magnetic flux density, gauss, oersted; magnetomotive force; magnetomotivity; magnetic tube of force; line of force; **magnetic field, electromagnetic field**

10 electromagnetic radiation, light, radio wave, microwave, infrared radiation, visible radiation, ultraviolent radiation or UV, UVA, UVB, X-rays, gamma rays; radar; electromagnetic spectrum, visible spectrum, radio spectrum

11 electroaffinity, electric attraction; electric repulsion

12 voltage, volt, **electromotive force** or EMF, electromotivity, potential difference; **potential, electric potential;** tension, high tension, low tension

13 resistance, ohm, ohms, ohmage, ohmic resistance, electric resistance; surface resistance, skin effect, volume resistance; insulation resistance; reluctance, magnetic **reluctance** or resistance; specific reluctance, reluctivity; **reactance,** inductive reactance, capacitive reactance; **impedance**

14 conduction, electric conduction; **conductance,** conductivity, mho; superconductivity; gas conduction, ionic conduction, metallic conduction, liquid conduction, photoconduction; **conductor,** semiconductor, superconductor; **nonconductor,** dielectric, insulator

15 induction; electrostatic induction, magnetic induction, electromagnetic induction, electromagnetic induction of currents; self-induction, mutual induction; **inductance,** inductivity, henry

16 capacitance, capacity, farad; collector junction capacitance, emitter junction capacitance, resistance capacitance

17 gain, available gain, current gain, operational gain

18 electric power, wattage, watts; electric horsepower; hydroelectric power, hydroelectricity; power load

19 powerhouse, power station, power plant, central station; oil-fired power plant, coal-fired power plant; hydroelectric plant; nuclear or atomic power plant; power grid, distribution system

20 blackout, power failure, power cut, power loss; **brownout,** voltage drop, voltage loss

21 electrical device, electrical appliance; **battery** <see list>, accumulator, storage battery, storage device; **electric meter,** meter; **wire, cable,** electric wire, electric cord, cord, power cord, power cable

22 electrician, electrotechnician; radio technician 1034.24; **wireman; lineman,** linesman; rigger; groundman; power worker

23 electrotechnologist, electrobiologist, electrochemist, electrometallurgist, electrophysicist, electrophysiologist, **electrical engineer**

24 electrification, electrifying, supplying electricity

25 electrolysis; ionization; galvanization, electrogalvanization; electrocoating, electroplating, electrogilding, electrograving, electroetching; ion, cation, anion; electrolyte, ionogen; nonelectrolyte

VERBS **26 electrify, galvanize,** energize, **charge;** wire, wire up; shock; **generate,** step up, amplify, stiffen; step down; plug in, loop in; switch on *or* off, turn on *or* off, turn on *or* off the juice <nf>, power down, power up; short-circuit, short

27 magnetize; electromagnetize; demagnetize, degauss

28 electrolyze; ionize; galvanize, electrogalvanize; electroplate, electrogild

29 insulate, isolate; **ground**

ADJS **30 electric, electrical, electrifying;** galvanic, voltaic; dynamoelectric, hydroelectric, photoelectric, piezoelectric, etc; electrothermal, electrochemical, electromechanical, electropneumatic, electrodynamic, static, electrostatic; electromotive; electrokinetic; electroscopic, galvanoscopic; electrometric, galvanometric, voltametric; **electrified,** electric-powered, battery-powered, cordless; solar-powered

31 magnetic, electromagnetic; diamagnetic, paramagnetic, ferromagnetic; **polar**

32 electrolytic; hydrolytic; ionic, anionic, cationic; ionogenic

33 electrotechnical; electroballistic, electrobiological, electrochemical, electrometallurgical, electrophysiological

34 charged, electrified, live, hot; high-tension, low-tension

35 positive, plus, electropositive; **negative,** minus, electronegative

36 nonconducting, nonconductive, insulating, dielectric

WORD ELEMENTS **37** electr-, electro-; rheo-; magnet-, magneto-

38 electrical sciences

electrical engineering	electrophysiology
electroacoustics	electrostatics
electroballistics	electrotechnology *or*
electrobiology	electrotechnics
electrochemistry	electrotherapeutics *or*
electrodynamics	electrotherapy
electrokinematics	electrothermics
electrokinetics	galvanism
electromagnetics	hydroelectricity
electromechanics	magnetics
electrometallurgy	magnetometry
electrometry	photoelectricity
electronics	pyroelectricity
electro-optics	thermionics
electrophotomicrography	thermoelectricity
electrophysics	voltaism

39 electric currents

absorption current	low-frequency current
active current	magnetizing current
alternating current *or* AC	multiphase current
conduction current	oscillating current
convection current	pulsating direct current
delta current	reactive current
dielectric displacement	rotary current
current	single-phase alternating
direct current *or* DC	current
displacement current	stray current
eddy current	supercurrent
emission current	thermionic current
exciting current	thermoelectric current
free alternating current	three-phase alternating
galvanic current	current
high-frequency current	transient current
induced current	voltaic current
induction current	watt current
ionization current	wattless *or* idle current
juice <nf>	

40 batteries

A battery	Leyden battery
AA battery	Leyden jar
AAA battery	mercury cell
acid cell	nickel-cadmium battery
accumulator	nine-volt battery
air cell	primary battery
alkaline battery *or* cell	primary cell
atomic battery	secondary battery
B battery	secondary cell
C battery	solar battery
cell	solar cell
D battery	storage battery
dry battery	storage cell
dry cell	voltaic battery
electronic battery	voltaic cell
fuel cell	voltaic pile
lead-acid battery	wet cell

1033 ELECTRONICS

NOUNS **1 electronics,** radionics, radioelectronics; electron physics, electrophysics, electron dynamics; electron optics; semiconductor physics, transistor physics; photoelectronics, photoelectricity; microelectronics; electronic engineering; avionics; electron microscopy; nuclear physics 1038; radio 1034; television 1035; radar 1036; automation 1041

2 <electron theory> electron theory of atoms, electron theory of electricity, electron theory of solids, free electron theory of metals, band theory of solids

3 electron <see list>, negatron, cathode particle, beta particle; thermion; electron capture, electron transfer; electron spin; electron state, energy level;

ground state, excited state; electron pair, lone pair, shared pair, electron-positron pair, duplet, octet; electron cloud; shells, electron layers, electron shells, valence shell, valence electrons, subvalent electrons; electron affinity, relative electron affinity

4 **electronic effect;** Edison effect, thermionic effect, photoelectric effect

5 **electron emission; thermionic emission;** photoelectric emission, photoemission; collision emission, bombardment emission, secondary emission; field emission; grid emission, thermionic grid emission; electron ray, electron beam, cathode ray, anode ray, positive ray, canal ray; glow discharge, cathode glow, cathodoluminescence, cathodofluorescence; electron diffraction

6 electron flow, electron stream, electron *or* **electronic current;** electric current 1032.2; electron gas, electron cloud, space charge

7 **electron volt;** ionization potential; input voltage, output voltage; base signal voltage, collector signal voltage, emitter signal voltage; battery supply voltage; screen-grid voltage; inverse peak voltage; voltage saturation

8 **electronic circuit,** transistor circuit, semiconductor circuit; vacuum-tube circuit, thermionic tube circuit; **printed circuit, microcircuit; chip, silicon chip,** microchip; **circuitry**

9 **conductance,** electronic conductance; **resistance,** electronic resistance

10 **electron tube, vacuum tube,** tube, valve <Brit>, thermionic tube; radio tube, television tube; **special-purpose tube; vacuum tube component**

11 **photoelectric tube** *or* **cell, phototube,** photocell; electron-ray tube, **electric eye;** photosensitivity, **photosensitive devices**

12 **transistor,** semiconductor *or* solid-state device

13 **electronic device, electronic meter,** electronic measuring device; **electronic tester,** electronic testing device

14 **electronics engineer,** electronics physicist

ADJS 15 **electronic;** photoelectronic, **photoelectric;** autoelectronic; microelectronic; thermoelectronic; thermionic; anodic, cathodic; transistorized

16 **electrons**

beta particle	f-electron
bonding electron	free electron
bound electron	nuclear electron
conduction electron	orbital electron
d-electron	p-electron
delta ray	peripheral electron
excess electron	photoelectron
extranuclear electron	planetary electron

positive electron	spinning electron
primary electron	surface-bound
recoil electron	electron
secondary electron	valence electron
s-electron	wandering electron

1034 RADIO

NOUNS 1 **radio, wireless** <Brit>; radiotelephony, radiotelegraphy; radio communications, telecommunication 347.1

2 radiotechnology, radio engineering, communication engineering; radio electronics, radioacoustics; radiogoniometry

3 **radio, radio receiver** <see list>; radio telescope; **radio set, receiver,** receiving set, **wireless** *and* wireless set <Brit>, set; cabinet, console, housing; chassis; receiver part

4 **radio transmitter** <see list>, **transmitter;** transmitter part; microphone 50.9, radiomicrophone; **antenna,** aerial

5 radiomobile, mobile transmitter, remote-pickup unit

6 **radio station,** transmitting station, **studio,** studio plant; AM station, FM station, shortwave station, ultrahigh-frequency station, clear-channel station; direction-finder station, RDF station; relay station, radio relay station, microwave relay station; amateur station, ham station <nf>, ham shack <nf>; pirate radio station, offshore station; Internet radio; satellite radio

7 **control room,** mixing room, monitor room, monitoring booth; **control desk,** console, master control desk, instrument panel, control panel *or* board, jack field, mixer <nf>

8 **network,** net, radio links, **hookup,** communications net, circuit, network stations, network affiliations, affiliated stations; coaxial network, circuit network, coast-to-coast hookup, satellite network

9 **radio circuit,** radio-frequency circuit, audio-frequency circuit, superheterodyne circuit, amplifying circuit; electronic circuit 1033.8

10 **radio signal,** radio-frequency *or* RF signal, direct signal, shortwave signal, AM signal, FM signal; reflected signal, bounce; unidirectional signal, beam; signal-noise ratio; **radio-frequency** *or* **RF amplifier,** radio-frequency *or* RF stage; radio silence

11 **radio wave,** electric wave, electromagnetic wave, hertzian wave; shortwave, long wave, microwave, high-frequency wave, low-frequency wave, medium wave; ground wave, sky wave; carrier, carrier wave; **wavelength**

12 frequency; radio frequency *or* RF, intermediate frequency *or* IF, audio frequency *or* AF; high frequency *or* HF; very high frequency *or* VHF; ultrahigh frequency *or* UHF; superhigh frequency *or* SHF; extremely high frequency *or* EHF; medium frequency *or* MF; low frequency *or* LF; very low frequency *or* VLF; upper frequencies, lower frequencies; **carrier frequency;** spark frequency; spectrum, frequency spectrum; cycles, CPS, hertz, Hz, **kilohertz, kilocycles; megahertz, megacycles**

13 band, frequency band, standard band, broadcast band, amateur band, citizens band, police band, shortwave band, FM band; **channel,** radio channel, broadcast channel

14 modulation; amplitude modulation *or* AM; frequency modulation *or* FM; phase modulation *or* PM; sideband, side frequency, single sideband, double sideband

15 amplification, radio-frequency *or* RF amplification, audio-frequency *or* AF amplification, intermediate-frequency *or* IF amplification, high-frequency amplification

16 radio broadcasting, broadcasting, the air waves, radiocasting; **airplay, airtime;** commercial radio, public radio, college radio, satellite radio, Citizens Band *or* CB, amateur radio, ham radio; AM broadcasting, FM broadcasting, shortwave broadcasting, public broadcasting; **transmission, radio transmission;** direction *or* beam transmission, asymmetric *or* vestigial transmission; multipath transmission, multiplex transmission; mixing, volume control, sound *or* tone control, fade-in, fade-out; broadcasting regulation, Federal Communications Commission *or* FCC

17 pickup, outside pickup, **remote pickup,** spot pickup

18 radiobroadcast, broadcast, radiocast, **radio program;** rebroadcast, rerun; simulcast; electronic *or* broadcast journalism, broadcast news, newscast, newsbreak, newsflash; all-news radio *or* format; sportscast; **talk radio;** talk show, audience-participation show, call-in *or* phone-in show, interview show; network show; commercial program, commercial; sustaining program, sustainer; serial, soap opera <nf>; taped program, canned show <nf>, electrical transcription; sound effects

19 signature, station identification, call letters, call sign; theme song; **station break,** pause for station identification

20 commercial, commercial announcement, commercial message, message, **spot announcement,** spot *and* plug <nf>

21 reception; fading, fade-out; **drift,** creeping, crawling; **interference,** noise interference, station interference; **static,** atmospherics, noise; blasting, blaring; blind spot; **jamming,** deliberate interference

22 radio listener, listener-in *and* tuner-inner <nf>; radio audience, listeners, **listenership**

23 broadcaster, radiobroadcaster, radiocaster; newscaster, sportscaster; commentator, news commentator; anchor, news anchor, anchorman *or* anchorwoman; host, talk-show host, talk jockey <nf>; veejay *or* VJ; announcer, voiceover; disk jockey *or* DJ *or* deejay <nf>; shock jock <nf>; master of ceremonies, MC *or* emcee <nf>; program director, programmer; sound-effects man, sound man

24 radioman, radio technician, radio engineer; radiotrician, radio electrician, radio repairman; **radio operator;** control engineer, volume engineer; mixer; **amateur radio operator, ham** *and* ham operator <nf>, radio amateur; Amateur Radio Relay League *or* ARRL; monitor; radiotelegrapher 347.16

VERBS **25 broadcast,** radiobroadcast, radiocast, simulcast, **radio, wireless** <Brit>, radiate, **transmit,** send; narrowcast; shortwave; beam; newscast, sportscast, put *or* go on the air, sign on; go off the air, sign off

26 monitor, check

27 listen in, tune in; tune up, tune down, tune out, tune off

ADJS **28 radio, wireless** <Brit>; radiosonic; neutrodyne; heterodyne; superheterodyne; shortwave; radio-frequency, audio-frequency; high-frequency, low-frequency, etc; radiogenic

29 radio receivers

all-wave receiver	ghetto blaster *or* box *or*
AM receiver	beat box *or* box
AM tuner	headband receiver
AM-FM receiver	loudspeaker
AM-FM tuner	mobile radio
antenna	multiplex receiver
aviation radio	pager *or* beeper
battery radio	pocket radio
boom box <nf>	portable radio
car radio	radar receiver
citizens band *or* CB radio	radio direction finder *or*
or CB	RDF
clock radio	radio-phonograph
communications	radio-record player
receiver	radiophone
crystal set	railroad radio
direction finder	receiver
facsimile receiver *or* fax	rechargeable-battery radio
FM receiver	regenerative receiver
FM tuner	relay receiver

scanner
ship-to-shore radio
shortwave receiver
single-signal receiver
six-band receiver
stereo receiver
superheterodyne
telephone receiver
three-way or three-power
  receiver
transceiver

30 radio transmitters

AM transmitter
amateur or ham transmit-
  ter or rig <nf>
arc or spark transmitter
continuous-wave or CW
  transmitter
Dictograph <trademark>
facsimile transmitter or
  fax
fan marker
FM transmitter
link transmitter
microphone
picture transmitter
portable transmitter
pulse transmitter
radio beacon
radio marker
radio range beacon

transistor radio
transmit-receiver
transponder
tuner
two-way radio
universal receiver
VHF-FM receiver
walkie-talkie
Walkman <trademark>
weather radio
wireless

radiometeorograph
radiosonde
radiotelephone transmitter
relay transmitter
RT transmitter
shortwave transmitter
spark transmitter
standby transmitter
tape transmitter
teleprinter
television transmitter
Telex
transceiver
transmitter receiver or
  transceiver
vacuum-tube transmitter
VHF-FM transmitter
walkie-talkie

1035 TELEVISION

NOUNS **1 television, TV, video,** telly <Brit nf>; the small screen or the tube <nf>, the boob tube <nf>; **network television,** free television, local television; the dream factory; subscription television, pay TV; cable television, cable TV, cable-television system or cable system, cable; closed-circuit television or closed circuit TV; public-access television or public-access TV; public broadcasting; satellite broadcasting, satellite television; digital television; high-definition television, HDTV

2 television broadcast, telecast, TV show; direct broadcast, live show <nf>; taped show, canned show <nf>; prime time, prime-time show or attraction; syndicated program; television drama or play, teleplay, made-for-television or –TV movie; telefilm; series, dramatic series, miniseries; situation comedy or sitcom <nf>; variety show; game show; **serial,** daytime serial, soap opera or soap <nf>; reality television; quiz show; giveaway show; panel show; talk show; electronic or broadcast journalism, broadcast news, newscast, news show; documentary, docudrama; telethon; public service announcement; edutainment,

infotainment; film pickup; colorcast; simulcast; childrens' television, kidvid <nf>; television or TV performer, television or TV personality; news anchor, anchor, anchor man, anchor woman, anchor person; ratings, Nielsen rating, sweeps; people meter

3 televising, telecasting; facsimile broadcasting; monitoring, mixing, shading, blanking, switching; scanning, parallel-line scanning, interlaced scanning

4 <transmission> photoemission, audioemission; television channel, TV band; video or picture channel, audio or sound channel, video frequency; picture carrier, sound carrier; beam, scanning beam, return beam; triggering pulse, voltage pulse, output pulse, timing pulse, equalizing pulse; synchronizing pulse, vertical synchronizing pulse, horizontal synchronizing pulse; video signal, audio signal; IF video signal, IF audio signal; synchronizing signal, blanking signal

5 <reception> **picture, image; color television,** dot-sequential or field-sequential or line-sequential color television; **black-and-white television;** HDTV or high-definition television; definition, blacker than black synchronizing; shading, black spot, hard shadow; test pattern, scanning pattern, grid; vertical interference, rain; granulation, scintillation, snow, snowstorm; flare, bloom, woomp; picture shifts, blooping, rolling; double image, multiple image, ghost; video static, noise, picture noise; signal-to-noise ratio; fringe area

6 television studio, TV station

7 mobile unit, TV mobile; video truck, audio truck, transmitter truck

8 transmitter, televisor; audio transmitter, video transmitter; transmitter part, adder, encoder; television mast, television tower; satellite transmitter

9 relay links, boosters, booster amplifiers, relay transmitters, **booster** or **relay stations;** microwave link; aeronautical relay, stratovision; communication satellite, satellite relay; Telstar, Intelsat, Syncom; Comsat

10 television camera, telecamera, pickup camera, pickup; **camera tube,** iconoscope, orthicon, vidicon; video camera, camcorder; mobile camera

11 television receiver, television or **TV set,** TV, telly <Brit nf>, televisor, boob tube and idiot box <nf>; **picture tube,** cathode-ray tube, kinescope, monoscope, projection tube; receiver part, amplifier, detector, convertor, electron tube, deflector, synchronizer, limiter, mixer; portable television or TV set; digital television; **screen,** telescreen, videoscreen; raster; **video-cassette**

recorder *or* **VCR,** videorecorder, video-tape recorder; video tape, video-cassette; videophone, Picturephone <trademark>; satellite dish, dish <nf>; television recording, videocassette, videocassette recorder *or* VCR, videotape

12 **televiewer, viewer;** television *or* viewing audience; viewership

13 **television technician,** TV man *or* woman, television *or* TV repairman *or* repairwoman, television engineer; monitor, sound *or* audio monitor, picture *or* video monitor; pickup unit man, cameraman, camerawoman, sound man, sound woman; media personality, host, newscaster, newsreader, commentator, announcer

VERBS 14 **televise, telecast;** colorcast; simulcast

15 **teleview,** watch television *or* TV; telerecord, record, tape; channel-surf, graze <nf>; zap <nf>

ADJS 16 **televisional,** televisual, televisionary, **video;** telegenic, videogenic; in synchronization, in sync <nf>, locked in

WORD ELEMENTS 17 tele-, video-, TV-

1036 RADAR, RADIOLOCATORS

NOUNS 1 **radar,** radio detection *and* ranging; **radar set,** radiolocator <Brit>; radar part; oscilloscope, radarscope; radar antenna; radar reflector

2 airborne radar, aviation radar; **navar,** navigation *and* ranging; **teleran,** television radar air navigation; radar bombsight, K-1 bombsight; radar dome, radome

3 **loran,** long range aid to navigation; **shoran,** short range aid to navigation; GEE navigation, consolan

4 **radiolocator;** direction finder, radio direction finder *or* RDF; radiogoniometer, high-frequency direction finder *or* HFDF, huff-duff <nf>; radio compass, wireless compass <Brit>

5 **radar speed meter,** electronic cop <nf>; radar highway patrol; radar detector, Fuzzbuster <trademark>

6 **radar station,** control station; Combat Information Center *or* CIC; Air Route Traffic Control Center *or* ARTCC; beacon station, display station; fixed station, home station; portable field unit, mobile trailer unit; tracking station; direction-finder station, radio compass station; triangulation stations

7 **radar beacon, racon;** transponder; radar beacon buoy, marker buoy, radar marked beacon, ramark

8 <radar operations> data transmission, scanning, scan conversion, flector tuning, signal modulation, triggering signals; phase adjustment, locking signals; triangulation, three-pointing; mapping; range finding; tracking, automatic tracking, locking on; precision focusing,

pinpointing; radar-telephone relay; radar navigation

9 <applications> detection, interception, ranging, ground control of aircraft, air-traffic control, blind flying, blind landing, storm tracking, hurricane tracking; radar fence *or* screen; radar astronomy

10 **pulse,** radio-frequency *or* RF pulse, high-frequency *or* HF pulse, intermediate-frequency *or* IF pulse, trigger pulse, echo pulse

11 **signal,** radar signal; transmitter signal, output signal; return signal, echo signal, video signal, reflection, picture, target image, display, signal display, trace, reading, return, **echo, bounces, blips, pips;** spot, CRT spot; three-dimensional *or* 3-D display, double-dot display; deflection-modulated *or* DM display, intensity-modulated *or* IM display; radio-frequency *or* RF echoes, intermediate-frequency *or* IF signal; beat signal, Doppler signal, local oscillator signal; beam, beavertail beam

12 **radar interference,** deflection, refraction, superrefraction; atmospheric attenuation, signal fades, blind spots, false echoes; clutter, ground clutter, sea clutter

13 <radar countermeasure> **jamming, radar jamming;** tinfoil, aluminum foil, chaff, window <Brit>

14 **radar technician,** radar engineer, radarman; air-traffic controller; jammer

VERBS 15 **transmit, send,** radiate, beam; **jam**

16 **reflect,** return, echo, bounce back

17 **receive, tune in,** pick up, spot, home on; pinpoint; identify, trigger; lock on; sweep, scan; map

1037 RADIATION, RADIOACTIVITY

NOUNS 1 **radiation,** radiant energy; ionizing radiation; **radioactivity,** activity, radioactive radiation *or* emanation, atomic *or* nuclear radiation; natural radioactivity, artificial radioactivity; curiage; specific activity, high-specific activity; actinic radiation, ultra-violet *or* violet radiation; radiotransparency, radiolucence *or* radiolucency; radiopacity; radiosensitivity, radiosensibility; half-life; radiocarbon dating; contamination, decontamination; saturation point; radiac *or* radioactivity detection identification *and* computation; fallout 1038.16; China syndrome, nuclear winter

2 **radioluminescence, autoluminescence;** cathode luminescence; Cerenkov radiation, synchrotron radiation

3 **ray, radiation** <see list>, cosmic ray bombardment, electron shower; electron emission 1033.5

4 radioactive particle; alpha particle, beta particle; heavy particle; high-energy particle; meson, mesotron; cosmic particle, solar particle, aurora particle, V-particle

5 <radioactive substance> radiator; alpha radiator, beta radiator, gamma radiator; fluorescent paint, radium paint; radium; fission products; radiocarbon, radiocopper, radioiodine, radiothorium, etc; mesothorium; **radioactive element** <see list>, radioelement; radioisotope; tracer, tracer element, tracer atom; radioactive waste

6 <units of radioactivity> curie, dose equivalent, gray, half-life, megacurie, microcurie, millicurie, multicurie, rad, roentgen

7 counter, radioscope, radiodetector, **atom-tagger;** ionization chamber; ionizing event; X-ray spectrograph, X-ray spectrometer

8 radiation physics, radiological physics; radiobiology, radiochemistry, radiometallography, radiography, roentgenography, roentgenology, radiometry, spectroradiometry, radiotechnology, radiopathology; radiology; radiotherapy; radioscopy, curiescopy, roentgenoscopy, radiostereoscopy, fluoroscopy, photofluorography, orthodiagraphy; X-ray photometry, X-ray spectrometry; tracer investigation, atom-tagging; **unit of radioactivity** <see list>; exposure, dose, absorbed dose

9 radiation physicist; radiobiologist, radiometallographer, radiochemist, etc; radiologist

VERBS **10 radioactivate,** activate, **irradiate,** charge; radiumize; **contaminate,** poison, infect

ADJS **11 radioactive,** activated, radioactivated, irradiated, charged, **hot; contaminated,** infected, poisoned; exposed; radiferous; radioluminescent, autoluminescent

12 radiable; radiotransparent, radioparent, radiolucent; radiopaque, radium-proof; radiosensitive

13 rays, radiation

actinic ray	extraordinary ray
alpha ray *or* radiation	gamma ray *or* radiation
anode ray	Grenz ray
Becquerel ray	infraroentgen ray
beta ray *or* radiation	Leonard ray
canal ray	nuclear radiation
cathode ray	ordinary ray
cosmic ray *or* radiation	positive ray
crepuscular ray	Roentgen ray
delta ray	X ray *or* radiation

14 radioactive elements

actinium	berkelium
americium	californium
astatine	curium
einsteinium	polonium
fermium	promethium
francium	protactinium
hahnium	radium
lawrencium	radon *or* radium
mendelevium	emanation
neptunium	technetium
nobelium	thorium
plutonium	uranium

1038 NUCLEAR PHYSICS

NOUNS **1 nuclear physics,** particle physics, nucleonics, atomics, atomistics, atomology, atomic science; quantum mechanics, wave mechanics; molecular physics; thermionics; mass spectrometry, mass spectrography; radiology 1037.8

2 <atomic theory> quantum theory, Bohr theory, Dirac theory, Rutherford theory, Schrödinger theory, Lewis-Langmuir *or* octet theory, Thomson's hypothesis; law of conservation of mass, law of definite proportions, law of multiple proportions, law of Dulong and Petit, law of parity, correspondence principle; Standard Model; supersymmetry theory, unified field theory; atomism; quark model

3 atomic scientist, nuclear physicist, particle physicist; radiologist 1037.9

4 atom <see lists>; tracer, tracer atom, tagger atom; atomic model, nuclear atom; nuclide; **ion; shell,** subshell, planetary shell, valence shell; **atomic unit;** atomic constant; atomic mass, atomic weight, atomic number, proton number, mass number, nucleon number, neutron number

5 isotope; protium, deuterium *or* heavy hydrogen *and* tritium <of hydrogen>; radioactive isotope, **radioisotope;** carbon 14, strontium 90, uranium 235; artificial isotope; isotone; isobar, isomer, nuclear isomer

6 elementary particle, fundamental particle, atomic particle, **subatomic particle** <see list>, subnuclear particle, ultraelementary particle; **atomic nucleus, nucleus,** *Kern* <Ger>; **nuclear particle,** nucleon; proton, neutron <see list>; deuteron *or* deuterium nucleus, triton *or* tritium nucleus, alpha particle *or* helium nucleus; **nuclear force,** weak force *or* weak nuclear force, strong force *or* strong nuclear force; weak interaction, strong interaction; fifth force; nucleosynthesis; nuclear resonance, Mössbauer effect, nuclear magnetic resonance *or* NMR; strangeness; charm

7 atomic cluster, molecule; radical, simple radical, compound radical, chain, straight chain, branched chain, side chain; ring, closed chain, cycle; homocycle, heterocycle; benzene ring *or* nucleus, Kekulé formula; lattice, space-lattice

8 **fission, nuclear fission,** fission reaction; **atom-smashing,** atom-chipping, **splitting the atom;** atomic reaction; atomic disintegration *or* decay, alpha decay, beta decay, gamma decay; stimulation, dissociation, photodisintegration, ionization, nucleization, cleavage; neutron reaction, proton reaction, etc; reversible reaction, nonreversible reaction; thermonuclear reaction; **chain reaction;** exchange reaction; breeding; disintegration series; bombardment, atomization; bullet, target; proton gun

9 **fusion, nuclear fusion,** fusion reaction, thermonuclear reaction, thermonuclear fusion, laser-induced fusion, cold fusion

10 **fissionable material,** nuclear fuel; fertile material; **critical mass,** noncritical mass; parent element, daughter element; end product

11 **accelerator** <see list>, **particle accelerator,** atomic accelerator, atom smasher, atomic cannon

12 mass spectrometer, mass spectrograph

13 **reactor** <see list>, **nuclear reactor, pile,** atomic pile, reactor pile, chain-reacting pile, chain reactor, **furnace,** atomic *or* nuclear furnace, neutron factory; fast pile, intermediate pile, slow pile; lattice; bricks; rods; radioactive waste

14 atomic engine, **atomic** *or* **nuclear power plant,** reactor engine

15 **atomic energy, nuclear energy** *or* **power,** thermonuclear power; activation energy, binding energy, mass energy; energy level; atomic research, atomic project; Atomic Energy Commission *or* AEC

16 **atomic explosion, atom blast, A-blast; thermonuclear explosion,** hydrogen blast, **H-blast;** ground zero; blast wave, Mach stem; Mach front; mushroom cloud; **fallout,** airborne radioactivity, fission particles, dust cloud, radioactive dust; flash burn; **atom bomb** *or* **atomic bomb** *or* **A-bomb, hydrogen bomb,** thermonuclear bomb, nuke <nf>; A-bomb shelter, fallout shelter

VERBS 17 **atomize,** nucleize; activate, accelerate; bombard, cross-bombard; cleave, fission, **split** *or* **smash the atom**

ADJS 18 **atomic;** atomistic; atomiferous; monatomic, diatomic, triatomic, tetratomic, pentatomic, hexatomic, heptatomic; heteratomic, heteroatomic; subatomic, subnuclear, ultraelementary; dibasic, tribasic; cyclic, isocyclic, homocyclic, heterocyclic; isotopic, isobaric, isoteric

19 **nuclear, thermonuclear,** isonuclear, homonuclear, heteronuclear, extranuclear

20 **fissionable,** fissile, scissile

21 **atoms**

acceptor atom	isobar
anion	isotere
antiatom	isotopic isobar
asymmetric carbon atom	labeled atom
Bohr atom	neutral atom
cation	normal atom
diradical *or* biradical	nuclear isomer
discrete atom	nuclide
excited atom	radiation
free radical	atom
hot atom	recoil atom
impurity atom	stripped atom

22 **subatomic or elementary particles**

alpha particle	omega *or* omega-zero *or*
antibaryon	omega nought particle
antielectron	phi-meson
antilepton	photino
antimeson	photon
antineutrino	pion *or* pi-meson
antineutron	positron *or* positive
antiparticle	electron
antiproton	proton
antiquark	quark
b *or* bottom quark	quark color
baryon	quark flavor
beta particle	quarkonium
B meson *or* B particle	rho particle
boson	s *or* strange quark
cascade particle	sigma particle
D meson *or* D particle	slepton
deuteron	squark
electron	strange particle
energy particle	subnuclear particle
fermion	superstring
flavor	tachyon
gauge boson	tardyon
gluino	tau *or* tauon *or* tau lepton
gravitino	tau meson
graviton	tau neutrino *or* tauonic
hadron	neutrino
Higgs boson	technifermion
hyperon	t *or* top quark
intermediate-vector boson	triton
J/psi *or* J *or* psi particle	u *or* up quark
kaon *or* K meson *or* K	upsilon
particle	virtual particle
lambda particle	weakon
lepton	WIMP *or* weakly
magnetic monopole	interactive massive
matter particle	particle
meson *or* mesotron	W particle
muon *or* mu-meson	xi-particle
neucleon	zino
neutrino	Z particle
neutron	Z-zero particle

23 **neutrons**

delayed neutron	monoenergetic
fast neutron	neutron

photoneutron
resonance neutron

slow neutron
thermal neutron

24 accelerators

atom smasher
betatron
bevatron
cascade transformer
charge-exchange
  accelerator
Cockcroft-Walton voltage
  multiplier
colliding-beam machine *or*
  collider
cosmotron
cyclotron
electron accelerator
electrostatic generator

induction accelerator
linear accelerator
microwave linear
  accelerator
particle accelerator
positive-ion accelerator
superconducting supercol-
  lider *or* SSC
synchrocyclotron
synchrotron
tevatron
tokamak
Van de Graaff generator
wake-field accelerator

25 reactors

boiling water reactor
breeder reactor
CANDU *or* Canada
  deuterium oxide-ura-
  nium reactor
gas-cooled reactor
fast-breeder reactor
fusion reactor
heterogeneous reactor

homogeneous reactor
nuclear reactor
plutonium reactor
power-breeder reactor
power reactor
pressurized-water
  reactor
stellarator
uranium reactor

1039 MECHANICS

NOUNS **1 mechanics** <see list>; leverage 906; **tools and machinery** 1040

2 statics <see list>

3 dynamics <see list>, **kinetics,** energetics

4 hydraulics, fluid dynamics, hydromechanics, hydrokinetics, fluidics, hydrodynamics, hydrostatics; hydrology, hydrography, hydrometry, fluviology

5 pneumatics, pneumatostatics; aeromechanics, aerophysics, aerology, aerometry, aerography, aerotechnics, aerodynamics, aerostatics

6 engineering, mechanical engineering, jet engineering, etc; engineers

ADJS **7 mechanical,** mechanistic, mechanized; locomotive, locomotor; motorized, power-driven; hydraulic, electronic; labor-saving; zoomechanical, biomechanical, aeromechanical, hydromechanical, etc; souped-up

8 static; biostatic, electrostatic, geostatic, etc

9 dynamic, dynamical, kinetic, kinetical, kinematic, kinematical; geodynamic, radiodynamic, electrodynamic, etc

10 pneumatic, pneumatological; aeromechanical, aerophysical, aerologic, aerological, aerotechnical, aerodynamic, aerostatic, aerographic, aerographical

11 hydrologic, hydrometric, hydrometrical, hydromechanic, hydromechanical, hydrodynamic, hydrostatic, hydraulic

12 kinds and branches of mechanics

aerodynamics
aeromechanics
animal mechanics
applied mechanics
atomechanics
auto mechanics
biomechanics
celestial mechanics
classical mechanics
dynamics
electromechanics
fluid mechanics
hydromechanics *or*
  hydrodynamics
kinematics
kinetics
magnetohydrodynamics *or*
  MHD

matrix mechanics
mechanical arts
Newtonian mechanics
micromechanics
practical mechanics
pure *or* abstract
  mechanics
quantum mechanics
rational mechanics
servomechanics
statistical
  mechanics
telemechanics
theoretical *or* analytical
  mechanics
wave mechanics
zoomechanics *or*
  biomechanics

13 kinds and branches of statics

aerostatics
biostatics
electrostatics
geostatics
gnathostatics
graphostatics
gyrostatics
hemastatics *or*
  hematostatics

hydrostatics
hygrostatics
magnetostatics
rheostatics
social statics
stereostatics
thermostatics

14 kinds and branches of dynamics

aerodynamics
astrodynamics
barodynamics
biodynamics
cardiodynamics
chromodynamics
electrodynamics
fluid
  dynamics
geodynamics
gnathodynamics
hemadynamics *or*
  hematodynamics
hydrodynamics
kinesiology

magnetohydrodynamics *or*
  magnetofluid dynamics
megadynamics
myodynamics
pharmacodynamics
photodynamics
phytodynamics
pneodynamics *or*
  pneumatics
pneumodynamics
quantum chromodynamics
radiodynamics
thermodynamics
trophodynamics
zoodynamics

1040 TOOLS, MACHINERY

NOUNS **1 tool, instrument, implement, utensil; apparatus, device,** mechanical device, contrivance, contraption <nf>, gadget, gizmo, gimcrack, gimmick <nf>, means, mechanical means; gadgetry; **hand tool; power tool;** machine tool; speed tool; precision tool *or* instrument; garden tool, agricultural tool; **mechanization,** mechanizing; motorizing

2 cutlery, edge tool; **knife, ax,** dagger, sword, blade, cutter, whittle; steel, cold steel, naked steel; shiv *and* pigsticker *and* toad stabber *and* toad sticker <nf>; perforator, piercer, puncturer, point; sharpener; **saw;** trowel; shovel; plane; drill; valve 239.10

3 machinery, enginery; **machine, mechanism,** mechanical device; heavy machinery, earthmoving machinery, earthmover; farm machinery; mill; welder; pump; **engine,** motor; engine part; power plant, **power source,** drive, motive power, prime mover; **appliance,** convenience, facility, utility, home appliance, mechanical aid; fixture; labor-saving device

4 mechanism, machinery, **movement,** movements, **action, motion, works,** workings, inner workings, what makes it work, innards, nuts and bolts, what makes it tick; drive train, power train; wheelwork, **wheelworks,** wheels, gear, wheels within wheels, epicyclic train; clockworks, watchworks, servomechanism 1041.13; robot, automaton

5 simple machine; lever, wheel and axle, pulley, inclined plane; machine part, gear, gearwheel, shaft, crank, rod, hub, cam, coupling, bearing, ball bearing, roller bearing, journal, bush, differential

6 machine tool; drill, press drill, borer, lathe, mill, broaching machine, facing machine, threading machine, tapping machine, grinder, planer, shaper, saw

7 hand tool; hammer, screwdriver, drill, punch, awl, wrench, pliers, clamp, vise, chisel, wedge, ax, knife, saw, lever, crowbar, jack, pulley, wheel

8 garden tool; spade, shovel, trowel, fork, rake, hoe, tiller, plow, hedge trimmer, shears, lawn mower

9 gear, gearing, gear train; gearwheel, cogwheel, rack; **gearshift;** low, intermediate, high, neutral, reverse; differential, differential gear *or* gearing; **transmission,** gearbox; automatic transmission; selective transmission; standard transmission, stick shift, manual transmission, five-speed, five on the floor; synchronized shifting, synchromesh; spur gear, rack and pinion, helical gear, bevel gear, skew gear, worm gear, internal gear, external gear; gear tooth

10 clutch, cone clutch, plate clutch, dog clutch, disk clutch, multiple-disk clutch, rim clutch, friction clutch, cone friction clutch, slip friction clutch, spline clutch, rolling-key clutch

11 tooling, tooling up; **retooling;** instrumentation, industrial instrumentation; servo instrumentation

12 mechanic, mechanician; grease monkey <nf>; artisan, artificer; machinist, machiner; auto mechanic, aeromechanic, etc

VERBS **13 tool,** tool up, instrument; retool; **machine,** mill; **mechanize,** motorize; sharpen

ADJS **14 mechanical;** machinelike; power, powered, power-driven, motor-driven, motorized; **mechanized,** mechanistic; electronic; labor-saving

15 agricultural, gardening tools

baler	pick
billhook	pickax
binder	pitchfork
blower	plow
brush cutter	pruner
cant hook	pruning saw
chisel plow	rake
colter	reaper
combine	roller
crop duster	rototiller
cultivator	scuffle hoe
dibble or dibber	scythe
draw hoe	shears
edger	shovel
flail	shredder
grub hoe	sickle
harvester	spade
hayfork	spading fork
hay rake	sprinkler
hedge clipper	tiller
hoe	tractor
lawn mower	trowel
loy	weed trimmer
mattock	wheelbarrow
maul	

16 blacksmithing tools

anvil	hoof tester
ball peen hammer	hot chisel
blower	mandrel
chisel	nipper
clinch cutter	post drill
clincher	post vise
clipping hammer	power hammer
cold chisel	pritchel
creaser	puncher
cross peen hammer	rasp
dipper	set hammer
drift	sledge hammer
drill	straight peen hammer
fileflatter	swage
floor mandrel	swage block
forge	swedge
fuller	swedge block
hammer	tongs
hardie	treadle hammer
hoof gauger	vise

17 cutting, pointed, edged tools

adz	carving knife
awl	chisel
ax	cleaver
bill	clipper
blade	cold chisel
bodkin	drove or boaster
bolster chisel	firmer chisel
burin	gouge
butcher knife	graver

hardy
hatchet
hook
jackknife
knife
machete
masonry chisel
paring chisel
pick
pinking shears
pipe cutter

punch
razor
router
scissors
scorper
scraper
scythe
shears
sickle
square-end chisel
wire cutter

18 drills

auger
bench drill
bit
bore
bow drill
breast drill
broach
cordless drill
corkscrew
countersink
diamond drill
drill press
eggbeater drill

electric drill
gimlet
hand drill
portable drill
power drill
push drill
reamer
rose reamer
seed drill
twist drill
wimble
woodborer

19 fastening, gripping tools

adjustable bar clamp
band clamp
bar clamp
bench dog
bench vise
bent-nose pliers
brace
C-clamp
channel-type pliers
chuck
clamp
claw
clip
corner clamp
cutting pliers
diagonal-cutting pliers
electric riveter
forceps
glue gun
grip
hand vise
holddown clamp
joint fastener
lineman's pliers
locking pliers

long-nose pliers
nail puller
needlenose pliers
pincers
pinchcock
pipe clamp
plate joiner
pliers
power nailer
pucellas
puller
riveter
screw clamp
slip-joint pliers
snap ring pliers
spring clamp
staple gun
stapler
toggle clamp
tongs
tweezers
vise
vise grip
web clamp

20 hammers, mallets

ball peen hammer
beetle
blacksmith's hammer
brick hammer
bushhammer
chipping hammer
claw hammer

cross peen hammer
demolition hammer
double-claw hammer
drywall hammer
electric hammer
engineer's hammer
framing hammer

fuller
joiner's mallet
long-handled hammer
machinist's hammer
maul
peen hammer
pile hammer
rip hammer
rubber mallet
scutch
shingler's hammer

shoemaker's hammer
sledgehammer
small anvil
soft-faced hammer
soft-faced mallet
stonemason's hammer
tack hammer
tilt hammer
triphammer
Warington hammer
wooden mallet

21 measuring, marking tools

bevel
butt gauge
caliper
carpenter's level
carpenter's pencil
carpenter's square
center punch
chalk liner
combination square
compass
depth gauge
dividers
electronic level
feeler gauge
folding rule
framing square
gauge
level
line level
marking gauge
mason's level
micrometer

miter box
miter square
mortise gage
plumb bob
plumb rule
protractor
rafter square
rule
ruler
scale
scratch awl
scriber
slide caliper
square
steel rule
straight edge
studfinder
tape measure
torpedo level
T square
turning caliper
wing divider

22 saws

backsaw
band saw
bench saw
bucksaw
butcher's saw
buzz saw
chain saw
circular saw
compass saw
coping saw
crosscut saw
crown saw
cutoff saw
diamond saw
dovetail saw
dry-wall saw
electric saw
flooring saw
flush cut saw
folding saw
frame saw
fretsaw
hacksaw
hand saw

jeweler's saw
jigsaw
keyhole saw
log saw
lumberman's saw
meat saw
one-man crosscut
 saw
pad saw
panel saw
pit saw
plumber's saw
portable circular saw
power saw
radial arm saw
reciprocating saw
ripsaw
saber saw
scroll saw
stationary circular
 saw
table saw
tree saw
two-handed saw

two-man crosscut
saw

utility saw
vertical saw

23 screwdrivers

auger screwdriver
cabinet-pattern screw-
   driver
clutch-head tip screwdriver
cordless screwdriver
electric screwdriver
flat-head screwdriver
impact driver

magnetic screwdriver
offset screwdriver
Phillips screwdriver
ratcheting screwdriver
screw gun
spiral ratchet screwdriver
stubby screwdriver
Yankee screwdriver

24 shaping, smoothing tools

adz
anvil
beading plane
belt sander
bench plane
block plane
brick trowel
buffer
bullnose plane
chamfering plane
circular file
corner trowel
die
disk sander
double cut file
drum sander
electric sander
emery wheel
file
finishing sander
flat file
flatter
float
fore plane
grinder
grinding wheel
grindstone
grooving plane
half-round file
hand sander
hone
jack plane

lathe
machine tool
multiplane
oilstone
plane
planer
power sander
putty knife
rasp
round file
router
router plane
sander
sandpaper
scraper
shaper
sharpener
shavehook
single cut file
slipstone
smoothing plane
spokeshave
stone
swage
swage block
tamper
thickness planer
trimming plane
trowel
trying plane
waterstone
whetstone

25 shovels, diggers

bail
bar spade
bull tongue
coal shovel
cultivator
ditch spade
draw hoe
fire shovel
fork
garden spade
garden trowel
grub hoe
hoe
irrigating shovel

loy
mattock
peat spade
pitchfork
plow
posthole digger
power shovel
rake
scoop
scooper
spade
spatula
spud
trowel

26 wrenches

adjustable wrench
Allen wrench
alligator wrench
bicycle wrench
box wrench
box-end wrench
box or open-end
   wrench
crescent Wrench
crowfoot wrench
flare-nut wrench
gooseneck wrench
hexagonal wrench
lug wrench

monkey wrench
obstruction wrench
open-end wrench
pin wrench
pipe-gripping wrench
pipe wrench
ratcheting box-end
   wrench
socket wrench
spanner
spark plug wrench
Stillson wrench
torque wrench
valve wrench

1041 AUTOMATION

NOUNS 1 **automation,** automatic control; robotization, cybernation; **self-action,** self-activity; self-movement, self-motion, **self-propulsion;** self-direction, self-determination, self-government, automatism, self-regulation; automaticity, automatization; servo instrumentation; computerization

2 autonetics, automatic or automation technology, automatic electronics, automatic engineering, automatic control engineering, servo engineering, **servomechanics,** system engineering, systems analysis, feedback system engineering; **cybernetics;** telemechanics; radiodynamics, radio control; systems planning, systems design; circuit analysis; bionics; communication or communications theory, information theory

3 **automatic control,** cybernation, servo control, robot control, robotization; cybernetic control; electronic control, electronic-mechanical control; feedback control, digital feedback control, analog feedback control; cascade control, piggyback control <nf>; supervisory control; action, control action; derivative or rate action, reset action; control agent; control means

4 semiautomatic control; **remote control,** push-button control, remote handling, tele-action; radio control; telemechanics; telemechanism; telemetry, telemeter, telemetering; transponder; bioinstrument, bioinstrumentation

5 control system, **automatic control system,** servo system, robot system; closed-loop system; open-sequence system; linear system, nonlinear system; carrier-current system; integrated system, complex control system; data system, data-handling system, data-reduction system, data-input system, data-interpreting system, digital data reducing system; process-control system, annunciator system, flow-control system,

motor-speed control system; automanual system; automatic telephone system; electrostatic spraying system; automated factory, automatic *or* robot factory, push-button plant; servo laboratory, servolab; electronic banking; electronic cottage

6 **feedback,** closed sequence, feedback loop, closed loop; multiple-feed closed loop; process loop, quality loop; feedback circuit, current-control circuit, direct-current circuit, alternating-current circuit, calibrating circuit, switching circuit, flip-flop circuit, peaking circuit; multiplier channels; open sequence, linear operation; positive feedback, negative feedback; reversed feedback, degeneration

7 <functions> accounting, analysis, automatic electronic navigation, automatic guidance, braking, comparison of variables, computation, coordination, corrective action, fact distribution, forecasts, impedance matching, inspection, linear *or* nonlinear calibrations, manipulation, measurement of variables, missile guidance, output measurement, processing, rate determination, record keeping, statistical communication, steering, system stabilization, ultrasonic *or* supersonic flow detection

8 **process control,** bit-weight control, color control, density control, dimension control, diverse control, end-point control, flavor control, flow control, fragrance control, hold control, humidity control, light-intensity control, limit control, liquid-level control, load control, pressure control, precision-production control, proportional control, quality control, quantity control, revolution control, temperature control, time control, weight control

9 variable, process variable; simple variable, complex variable; manipulated variable; steady state, transient state

10 values, target values; set point; differential gap; proportional band; dead band, dead zone; neutral zone

11 time constants; time lead, gain; time delay, dead time; lag, process lag, hysteresis, holdup, output lag; throughput

12 automatic device, automatic; semi-automatic; self-actor, self-mover; **robot, automation,** mechanical man; cyborg; bionic man, bionic woman

13 **servomechanism,** servo; cybernion, automatic machine; **servomotor;** synchro, selsyn, autosyn; synchronous motor, synchronous machine

14 **system component; control mechanism; regulator, control,** controller, **governor;**

servo control, servo regulator; control element

15 **automatic detector;** automatic analyzer; automatic indicator

16 **control panel,** console; coordinated panel, graphic panel; panelboard, set-up board

17 **computer, computer science** 1042, electronic computer, electronic brain; electronic organizer; information machine, thinking machine; computer unit, hardware, computer hardware

18 <automatic devices> automatic pilot *or* autopilot, automaton, guided missile, robot, self-starter, speedometer

19 **control engineer,** servo engineer, system engineer, systems analyst, automatic control system engineer, feedback system engineer, automatic technician, robot specialist; computer engineer, computer technologist, computer technician, **computer programmer;** cybernetic technologist, cyberneticist

VERBS 20 **automate,** automatize, robotize; robot-control, servo-control; program; computerize

21 **self-govern,** self-control, **self-regulate,** selfdirect

ADJS 22 **automated,** cybernated, robotized; **automatic,** automatous, **spontaneous; self-acting,** self-active; **self-operating,** self-operative, self-working; **self-regulating,** self-regulative, self-governing, self-directing; **self-regulated, self-controlled,** self-governed, self-directed, self-steered; self-adjusting, self-closing, self-cocking, self-cooking, self-dumping, self-emptying, self-lighting, self-loading, self-opening, self-priming, self-rising, self-sealing, self-starting, self-winding, automanual; semiautomatic; computerized, computer-controlled

23 **self-propelled,** self-moved, horseless; **self-propelling,** self-moving, self-propellent; self-driven, self-drive; **automotive,** automobile, automechanical; **locomotive,** locomobile

24 **servomechanical,** servo-controlled; **cybernetic;** isotronic

25 **remote-control,** remote-controlled, telemechanic; telemetered, telemetric; by remote control

WORD ELEMENTS 26 aut-, auto-, automat-, automato-, self-

1042 COMPUTER SCIENCE

NOUNS 1 **computer science** <see list>, computer systems *and* applications, computer hardware *and* software, computers, digital computers, computing, machine computation, number-crunching <nf>; **computerization,** digitization; **data processing,** electronic data processing *or* EDP, data storage and retrieval; data bank;

information science, information processing, informatics; computer security; computer crime *or* fraud, computer virus *or* worm; hacking

2 **computer,** electronic data processor, information processor, electronic brain, digital computer, general purpose computer, analog computer, hybrid computer, machine, **hardware,** computer hardware, microelectronics device; **processor,** central processing unit *or* CPU, multiprocessor, microprocessor, coprocessor, mainframe computer *or* mainframe, dataflow computer, hybrid computer, work station, minicomputer, microcomputer, personal computer *or* PC, home computer, desktop computer, laptop computer, notebook computer, briefcase computer, graphics tablet, pocket computer, handheld computer, personal organizer, personal digital assistant *or* PDA, minisupercomputer, superminicomputer, supermicrocomputer, supercomputer, graphoscope, array processor, neurocomputer, neural computer; multimedia computer; neural net *or* network, semantic net *or* network; management information system *or* MIS; clone; abacus, calculator

3 **circuitry,** circuit, integrated circuit, logic circuit, **chip,** silicon chip, gallium arsenide chip, semiconductor chip, hybrid chip, wafer chip, superchip, microchip, neural network chip, transputer, **board,** printed circuit board *or* PCB, card, motherboard; **peripheral,** peripheral device *or* unit, input device, output device; expansion slot; **port,** channel interface, serial interface, serial port, parallel port; **read-write head;** vacuum tube, transistor, bus, LED, network adapter, small computer systems interface *or* SCSI, register

4 **input device,** keyboard, keypad; reader, tape reader, card punch, scanner, optical scanner, optical character reader, optical character recognition *or* OCR device, data tablet *or* tablet, touchscreen, light pen, mouse, joystick, trackball, wand

5 **drive, disk drive,** floppy disk drive, hard disk drive *or* Winchester drive *or* hard drive, tape drive, removable drive, flash drive, external hard drive

6 **disk, magnetic disk, floppy disk** *or* floppy <nf> *or* diskette, minifloppy, microfloppy, hard *or* fixed *or* Winchester disk, removable disk, optical disk, disk pack; magnetic tape *or* mag tape <nf>, magnetic tape unit, magnetic drum; CD-ROM, compact-disk read-only memory, magneto-optical disk

7 **memory, storage,** memory bank, memory chip, firmware; **main memory,** main storage *or* store, cache memory *or* cache, random-access memory *or* RAM, read-only memory *or* ROM, programmable read-only memory *or* PROM,

semiconductor memory, magnetic core memory, core, core storage *or* store, solid-state memory, auxiliary *or* secondary memory, disk pack, magnetic disk, primary storage, backing store, read/write memory, optical disk memory, bubble memory; read-only memory *or* ROM, programmable read-only memory *or* PROM

8 **retrieval, access,** random access, sequential access, direct access, data capture, capture

9 **output device,** peripheral, terminal, workstation, video terminal, video display terminal *or* VDT, video display unit *or* VDU, visual display unit *or* VDU, graphics terminal, **monitor,** screen, display, cathode ray tube *or* CRT, monochrome monitor, color monitor, RGB monitor, active matrix display, window; **printer,** color printer, **serial printer,** character printer, impact printer, dot-matrix printer, daisy-wheel *or* printwheel printer, drum printer, **line printer,** line dot-matrix printer, chain printer, **page printer,** nonimpact printer, laser printer, electronic printer, graphics printer, color graphics printer, ink-jet printer, thermal printer, bubble-jet printer, electrostatic printer; plotter; **modem** *or* modulator-demodulator

10 **forms, computer forms, computer paper,** continuous stationery

11 **software, program,** computer program, source program, object program, binary file, binary program; program suite, suite of applications; bundle; software package, courseware, groupware, routine, subroutine, intelligent agent *or* agent, autonomous agent; application software; applet; authoring software; shareware, freeware

12 **systems program, operating system** *or* **OS,** disk operating system *or* DOS, system software; Microsoft <trademark> disk operating system *or* MS-DOS <trademark>; UNIX; control program monitor *or* CPM; **word processor,** text editor, editor, print formatter, WYSIWYG *or* what-you-see-is-what-you-get word processor, post-formatted word processor; spreadsheet, electronic spreadsheet, desktop publishing program, database management system *or* DBMS, authoring tool, utility program, screen saver, computer game, **computer application** <see list>, applications program, application software, bootloader *or* bootstrap loader

13 **language** <see list>, assembler *or* assemblage language, programming language, machine language, machine-readable language, conventional programming language, computer language, high-level language, fourth generation language, macro language, preprocessor language, compiler, interpreter, low-level

language, application development language, assembly language, assembly code, object code, job-control language *or* JCL, procedural language, problem-oriented language, query language; **computer** *or* **electronic virus,** computer worm, phantom bug, Trojan horse, logic bomb; source code, machine code; loader, parser, debugger; Java, HTML, SGML

14 **bit, binary digit,** infobit, kilobit, megabit, gigabit, terbit; **byte,** kilobyte, megabyte

15 **data, information,** database, data capture, database management, data warehousing, file, record, data bank, input, input-output *or* I/O; **file,** data set, record, data record, data file, text file

16 **network, computer network,** communications network, local area network *or* LAN, workgroup computing, mesh; neural network, neural net; **on-line system,** interactive system, on-line service; intranet; Internet

17 **programmer, liveware,** wetware; software engineer, computer engineer, computer scientist; systems programmer, system software specialist, application programmer, systems analyst, systems engineer, system operator *or* sysop; computer designer, computer architect, operator, technician, key puncher, keyboarder; techie; hacker <nf>; spammer

18 <computer terms> access, archive, authoring, backup, bandwidth, batch processing, baud rate, benchmark, beta test, binary tree, bit, bitmap, block, bookmark, boot, bootstrap, bug, byte, cgi, click, clickthrough, clock rate, command, compatibility, computerate, computer-friendly, computer-literate, controller, crash, cursor, desktop, diagnostic, diff, digital, direct access, directory, display, domain name, dot-com, download, downtime, drag and drop, emulator, escape key, field, file, file folder, file format, file sharing, footprint, FTP, function key, gigabyte, gopher, graphics, grep, hacking, helpdesk, home page, hot key, icon, input, interactive, interface, job, key, kilobyte, login, logon, logoff, megabyte, menu, message board, millennium bug, morphing, mouse potato, multimedia, multitasking, mouse potato <nf>, output, parity, password, plug-and-play, portal site, power user, pulldown, queue, random access, real time, record, save, scrollable, search engine, search engine optimization, sector, sequential access, signature, sleep mode, smiley, spell-checker, task bar, toolbar, toolkit, turnkey operation, upload, URL, username, virus, WYSIWYG *or* what you see is what you get

19 <computer communications> Internet, the Net <nf>, World Wide Web *or* Web *or* WWW, cyberspace, information superhighway; Internet service provider *or* ISP, electronic mail *or* e-mail *or* email, mailbox, website, communications protocol; compression, encryption; intranet; Usenet; local area network *or* LAN, wide area network *or* WAN, file server, client-server; browser; gateway; search engine; bulletin board service *or* BBS, chat room, newsgroup, workgroup; netizen, surfer; spam; wiki; Weblog *or* blog; DSL, cable modem

20 artificial intelligence, knowledge engineering, knowledge representation, intelligent retrieval, natural language processing, expert systems, speech synthesis, robotics, hypertext, hypermedia, intelligent agent

VERBS **21** **computerize,** digitize; **program,** boot, boot up, initialize, log in, log out, run, load, download, upload, **compute,** crunch numbers <nf>; capture; **keyboard,** key in, input; browse, surf; search, google; cut and paste; export, import; bookmark

ADJS **22** **computerized;** wired; machine-usable, computer-usable; computer-aided, computer-assisted; computer-driven, computer-guided, computer-controlled, computer-governed; computer-literate, computerate

23 **branches of computer science**

artificial intelligence *or* AI	information retrieval *or* IR
automata theory	information storage and
combinatorial processes	retrieval
compiler design	information technology *or*
computer-aided design *or*	IT
CAD	language processing
computer-aided *or*	logical design
computer-assisted	machine organization
learning *or* CAL	management information
computer-aided manufac-	system *or* MIS
turing *or* CAM	natural language process-
computer-aided molecular	ing
design *or* CAMD	neural networks
computer-aided testing *or*	nonnumerical applications
CAT	numerical analysis
computer applications	numerical applications
computer architecture	office automation
computer-based learning	operating systems
computer graphics	optimization
computer-integrated	programming
manufacture *or* CIM	programming languages
computer-managed	robotics
instruction *or* CMI	simulation
computer systems	switching theory
cybernetics	symbol manipulation
data entry	systems analysis
data processing	theory of computation
desktop publishing	theory of formal languages
electronic data processing	utility programs

24 computer applications

authoring tool	desktop publishing *or* DTP
batch processing	electronic publishing
communications software	Internet access *or* Internet
computer art	service provider
computer bulletin boards	software
computer conferencing	musical instrument digital
computer games	interface program *or*
computer graphics	MIDI
computer typesetting	office automation
computer-aided design	program
computer-aided	presentation software
engineering	screen saver
computer-aided manufac-	simulation software
turing	spell checking
computer-assisted	spreadsheet program
instruction	time-sharing
database management	Web design software
system	word processing

25 computer languages

ADA	FORTRAN *or* formula
ALGOL *or* algorithmic-	translator
oriented language	GPSS
APL *or* a programming	HTML
language	IPL-V
APT *or* automatic	Java
programmed	JOSS
tools	JOVIAL
awk *or* Aho Weinberger	Lex
and Kernighan	LISP *or* list-processing
BAL *or* basic assembly	Logo
language	MUMPS
BASIC *or* beginners	OCCAM
all-purpose symbolic	PASCAL
instruction code	Perl
BCPL	pic
C	PILOT *or* programmed
C++	inquiry learning *or*
COBOL *or* common	teaching
business-oriented	PL/1 *or* programming
language	language 1
COMIT	Ratfor
COMPACT II	RPG II
CPL	SNOBOL *or* sno *or*
efl	string-oriented symbolic
eqn	language
FLOWMATIC	SOL
FORMAC	yacc or yet another
FORTH	computer compiler

1043 ENGINEERING

NOUNS **1 engineering**, mechanical engineering, civil engineering, chemical engineering, electrical engineering, mining and metallurgy, industrial engineering; automotive engineering, aerospace engineering, aeronautical engineering, astronautical engineering, marine engineering, agricultural engineering; structural engineering, transportation engineering, hydraulic engineering, geotechnical engineering, construction engineering; material engineering, biochemical engineering, environmental engineering

2 engineer, registered engineer; mechanical engineer, civil engineer, chemical engineer, electrical engineer, mining engineer, metallurgical engineer, industrial engineer; automotive engineer, aerospace engineer, aeronautical engineer, astronautical engineer, marine engineer, agricultural engineer; structural engineer, transportation engineer, hydraulic engineer, construction engineer; material engineer, biochemical engineer, biomedical engineer, environmental engineer; electronics engineer; mechanic, technician

3 <engine types> internal-combustion, external-combustion; Wankel, reciprocating, steam, gasoline, diesel, jet, turboprop, turbojet, rocket, Stirling, locomotive; automotive, aircraft, marine, railroad

VERBS **4** engineer, construct, build, erect, survey, map, excavate, dig, grade, dredge, drill, tunnel, blast, pave; process, manufacture, measure; reverse-engineer

1044 FRICTION

NOUNS **1 friction, rubbing,** rub, frottage; frication *and* confrication *and* perfrication <old>; **drag,** skin friction; **resistance,** frictional resistance; static friction, rolling friction, internal friction, sliding friction, slip friction

2 abrasion, attrition, erosion, wearing away, wear, detrition, ablation; rubbing against *or* together; ruboff; corrosion; erasure, erasing, rubbing away *or* off *or* out, obliteration; **grinding, filing,** rasping, limation; fretting; galling; **chafing, chafe;** levigation; **scraping,** grazing, scratching, scuffing; scrape, scratch, **scuff;** scrubbing, scrub; scouring, scour; **polishing,** burnishing, sanding, smoothing, dressing, buffing, shining; sandblasting; abrasive; brass-rubbing, heelball rubbing, graphite rubbing

3 massage, massaging, stroking, kneading; **rubdown;** backrub; massotherapy, massage therapy; whirlpool bath, Jacuzzi <trademark>; vibrator; facial massage, facial

4 massager, **masseur, masseuse,** massage therapist; massotherapist

5 <mechanics> force of friction; force of viscosity; coefficient of friction; friction head; friction clutch, friction drive, friction gearing, friction pile, friction saw, friction welding

VERBS **6 rub,** frictionize; **massage,** knead, rub down; caress, pet, stroke 73.8; pulverize; smooth, iron

7 abrade, abrase, gnaw, gnaw away; **erode,** erode away, ablate, wear, wear away, corrode; erase, rub away *or* off *or* out, rub against; **grind, rasp, file, grate; chafe,** fret, gall; **scrape,** scratch, **graze,** raze <old>, **scuff,** bark, skin; **fray,** frazzle; **scrub, scour**

8 buff, burnish, polish, rub up, sandpaper, **sand,** smooth, dress, shine, furbish, sandblast; brush, curry

ADJS **9 frictional,** friction; fricative; **rubbing**

10 abrasive, abradant, attritive, gnawing, erosive, ablative; scraping; **grinding, rasping;** chafing, fretting, galling

1045 DENSITY

NOUNS **1 density,** denseness, **solidity, solidness,** firmness, **compactness, closeness,** spissitude <old>; **congestion,** congestedness, crowdedness, jammedness; **impenetrability,** impermeability, imporosity; hardness 1046; incompressibility; specific gravity, relative density; **consistency,** consistence, thick consistency, thickness; viscidity, viscosity, **viscousness, thickness,** gluiness, ropiness

2 indivisibility, inseparability, impartibility, infrangibility, indiscerptibility; indissolubility; cohesion, coherence 803; unity 792.1; insolubility, infusibility

3 densification, condensation, compression, concentration, inspissation, concretion, consolidation, conglobulation; hardening, **solidification** 1046.5; agglutination, clumping, clustering

4 thickening, inspissation; congelation, **congealment, coagulation,** clotting, **setting,** concretion; gelatinization, gelatination, jellification, jellying, **jelling,** gelling; **curdling,** clabbering; **distillation**

5 precipitation, deposit, sedimentation; precipitate

6 solid, solid body, body, mass, bulk; lump, clump, cluster; block, cake; node, knot; concrete, concretion; conglomerate, conglomeration

7 clot, coagulum, coagulate; blood clot, grume, embolus, crassamentum; **coagulant,** coagulator, clotting factor, coagulase, coagulose, thromboplastin *or* coagulin; casein, caseinogen, paracasein, legumin; **curd,** clabber, loppered milk *and* bonnyclabber <nf>, clotted cream, Devonshire cream

8 <instruments> densimeter, densitometer; aerometer, hydrometer, lactometer, urinometer, pycnometer

VERBS **9 densify,** inspissate, densen; **condense, compress,** compact, **consolidate, concentrate,** come to a head; **congest; squeeze, press, crowd,** cram, jam, pack, ram down; steeve; pack *or* jam in; **solidify** 1046.8

10 thicken, thick <old>; inspissate, incrassate; **congeal, coagulate, clot,** set, concrete; gelatinize, gelatinate, jelly, jellify, **jell,** gel; **curdle,** curd, clabber, lopper <nf>; cake, lump, clump, cluster, knot

11 precipitate, deposit, sediment, sedimentate

ADJS **12 dense, compact, close;** close-textured, close-knit, close-woven, tight-knit; serried, **thick, heavy,** massy, thickset, thick-packed, thick-growing, thick-spread, thick-spreading; **condensed, compressed,** compacted, concrete, consolidated, concentrated; **crowded, jammed,** packed, jam-packed, packed *or* jammed in, packed *or* jammed in like sardines; **congested,** crammed, crammed full; **solid,** firm, substantial, massive; impenetrable, impermeable, imporous, nonporous; hard 1046.10; incompressible; viscid, viscous, ropy, gluey; thick enough to be cut with a knife <nf>

13 indivisible, nondivisible, undividable, **inseparable,** impartible, infrangible, indiscerptible, indissoluble; cohesive, coherent 803.10; unified; insoluble, indissolvable, infusible

14 thickened, inspissate *or* inspissated, incrassate; **congealed, coagulated, clotted,** grumous; **curdled,** curded, clabbered; **jellied,** jelled *or* gelled, gelatinized; lumpy, lumpish; caked, cakey; coagulant, coagulating

ADVS **15 densely,** compactly, **close,** closely, **thick,** thickly, heavily; solidly, firmly

1046 HARDNESS, RIGIDITY

NOUNS **1 hardness,** durity <old>, induration; **callousness,** callosity; stoniness, rock-hardness, flintiness, steeliness; **strength, toughness** 1049; solidity, impenetrability, density 1045; restiveness, resistance 453; obduracy 361.1; hardness of heart 94.3

2 rigidity, rigidness, rigor <old>; **firmness,** renitence *or* renitency, incompressibility; nonresilience *or* nonresiliency, inelasticity; **tension,** tensity, **tenseness,** tautness, tightness

3 stiffness, inflexibility, unpliability, unmalleability, intractability, unbendingness, unlimberness, starchiness; **stubbornness,** unyieldingness 361.2; **unalterability,** immutability; immovability 855.3; inelasticity, irresilience *or* irresiliency; inextensibility *or* unextensibility, unextendibility, inductility

4 temper, tempering; chisel temper, die temper, razor temper, saw file temper, set temper, spindle temper, tool temper; precipitation hardening, heat treating; hardness test, Brinell test; hardness scale, Brinell number *or* Brinell hardness number *or* Bhn; indenter; hardener, hardening, hardening agent

5 hardening, toughening, induration, firming; **strengthening; tempering,** case hardening, steeling; seasoning; **stiffening,** rigidification, starching; **solidification, setting,** curing, caking, concretion; crystallization, granulation; callusing; sclerosis, arteriosclerosis, atherosclerosis, hardening of the arteries; lithification; lapidification <old>; **petrification,** fossilization, ossification; glaciation; cornification, hornification; calcification; vitrification, vitrifaction

6 <comparisons> stone, rock 1059, adamant, granite, flint, marble, diamond; steel, iron, nails; concrete, cement; brick; oak, heart of oak; bone; Mohs' scale

VERBS **7 harden,** indurate, firm, **toughen** 1046.7; **callous; temper,** anneal, oil-temper, heat-temper, **case-harden,** steel; season; **petrify,** lapidify <old>, fossilize; lithify; vitrify; calcify; ossify; cornify, hornify

8 solidify, concrete, **set,** take a set, cure, cake; condense, thicken 1045.10; **crystallize,** granulate, candy; hard-boil; anneal; freeze

9 stiffen, rigidify, starch; **strengthen, toughen** 1046.7; back, brace, reinforce, shore up; **tense, tighten,** tense up, tension; trice up, screw up

ADJS **10 hard, solid,** dure <old>, lacking give, **tough** 1049.4; resistive, resistant, steely, steellike, iron-hard, ironlike; **stony,** rocky, stonelike, rock-hard, rocklike, lapideous, lapidific, lapidifical, lithoid *or* lithoidal; diamondlike, adamant, adamantine; flinty, flintlike; marble, marblelike; granitic, granitelike; gritty; concrete, cement, cemental; horny; bony, osseous, ossific; petrifactive; vitreous; hard-boiled; hard as nails *or* a rock, etc 1046.6; dense 1045.12; obdurate 361.10; hard-hearted 94.12

11 rigid, stiff, firm, renitent, incompressible; **tense, taut, tight,** unrelaxed; nonresilient, inelastic; **rodlike,** virgate; ramrod-stiff, ramrodlike, pokerlike; stiff as a poker *or* rod *or* board, stiff as buckram; starched, starchy

12 inflexible, unflexible, **unpliable, unpliant, unmalleable, intractable,** untractable, intractile, **unbending,** unlimber, **unyielding** 361.9, ungiving, **stubborn, unalterable,** immutable; **immovable** 855.15; **adamant,** adamantine; **inelastic,** nonelastic, irresilient; inextensile, inextensible,

unextensible, inextensional, unextendible, nonstretchable, inductile; intransigent

13 hardened, toughened, steeled, indurate, indurated, fortified; **callous,** calloused; **solidified,** set; crystallized, granulated; petrified, lapidified <old>, fossilized; vitrified; sclerotic; ossified; cornified, hornified; calcified; crusted, crusty, incrusted; **stiffened, strengthened,** rigidified, backed, reinforced; frozen solid

14 hardening, toughening, indurative; petrifying, petrifactive

15 tempered, case-hardened, heat-treated, **annealed,** oil-tempered, heat-tempered, tempered in fire; seasoned; indurate, indurated

1047 SOFTNESS, PLIANCY

NOUNS **1 softness,** give, nonresistiveness, insolidity, unsolidity, nonrigidity; **gentleness,** easiness, delicacy, tenderness; *morbidezza* <Ital>; lenity, leniency 427; mellowness; fluffiness, flossiness, downiness, featheriness; velvetiness, plushiness, satininess, silkiness; sponginess, pulpiness

2 pliancy, pliability, plasticity, flexibility, flexility, flexuousness, bendability, ductility, ductibility <old>, tensileness, tensility, tractility, **tractability,** amenability, adaptability, facility, give, **suppleness,** willowiness, **litheness, limberness; elasticity** 1048, **resilience,** springiness, resiliency, rubberiness; sponginess, pulpiness, doughiness, compressibility; malleability, moldability, fictility, sequacity <old>; **impressionability,** susceptibility, responsiveness, receptiveness, sensibility, sensitiveness; formability, formativeness; extensibility, extendibility; agreeability 324.1; submissiveness 433.3

3 flaccidity, flaccidness, **flabbiness, limpness,** rubberiness, floppiness; **looseness,** laxness, laxity, laxation, relaxedness, relaxation

4 <comparisons> putty, clay, dough, blubber, rubber, wax, butter, soap, pudding; velvet, plush, satin, silk; wool, fleece; pillow, cushion; kapok; baby's bottom; puff; fluff, floss, flue; down, feathers, feather bed, eiderdown, swansdown, thistledown; breeze, zephyr; foam; snow

5 softening, softening-up, **easing,** padding, cushioning; mollifying, mollification; **relaxation,** laxation; mellowing; tenderizing

VERBS **6 soften,** soften up; unsteel; **ease,** cushion; gentle, mollify, milden; **subdue,** tone *or* tune down; mellow; tenderize; **relax,** laxate, loosen; limber, limber up, supple; massage, knead, plump, plump up, fluff, fluff up, shake up; **mash,** whip, **smash,** squash, pulp, pulverize; masticate, macerate; thaw, liquefy

7 **yield, give,** relent, relax, bend, unbend, give way; comply; mellow, loosen up, chill out <nf>; submit 433.6,9

ADJS 8 **soft,** nonresistive, nonrigid; mild, **gentle, easy, delicate, tender;** complaisant 427.8; mellow, mellowy <old>; **softened,** mollified; whisper-soft, soft as putty or clay or dough, etc 1047.4, soft as a kiss or a sigh or a whisper or a baby's bottom

9 **pliant, pliable, flexible,** flexile, flexuous, **plastic, elastic** 1048.7, **ductile,** sequacious or facile <old>, tractile, **tractable, yielding,** giving, bending; adaptable, **malleable,** moldable, shapable, fabricable, fictile; compliant 324.5, submissive 433.12; **impressionable,** impressible, susceptible, responsive, receptive, sensitive; **formable,** formative; **bendable; supple,** willowy, **limber; lithe,** lithesome, lissome, double-jointed, loose-limbed, whippy; **elastic,** resilient, springy; extensile, extensible, extendible; putty, waxy, doughy, pasty, puttylike

10 **flaccid, flabby, limp,** rubbery, flimsy, floppy; **loose,** lax, relaxed, slack, unstrung

11 **spongy,** pulpy, pithy, medullary; edematous; foamy; juicy

12 **pasty, doughy;** loamy, clayey, argillaceous

13 **squashy,** squishy, squushy, squelchy, mooshy

14 **fluffy,** flossy, **downy,** pubescent, feathery; fleecy, flocculent, woolly, lanate; furry

15 **velvety,** velvetlike, velutinous; plushy, plush; **satiny,** satinlike; cottony; **silky,** silken, silklike, sericeous, soft as silk

16 **softening, easing;** subduing, mollifying, emollient; demulcent; **relaxing,** loosening

ADVS 17 **softly, gently,** easily, delicately, tenderly; compliantly 324.9, submissively 433.17

1048 ELASTICITY

NOUNS 1 **elasticity, resilience** or resiliency, **give;** snap, **bounce,** bounciness; **stretch, stretchiness,** stretchability; extensibility; tone, tonus, tonicity; **spring, springiness;** rebound 903.2; **flexibility** 1047.2; **adaptability,** responsiveness; **buoyancy** or buoyance; **liveliness** 330.2

2 **stretching;** extension; distension 259.2; **stretch, tension, strain**

3 **elastic;** elastomer; **rubber,** gum elastic; stretch fabric, latex, spandex; gum, chewing gum 1062.6; whalebone, baleen; rubber band, rubber ball, handball, tennis ball; sponge rubber, crepe rubber; spring; springboard; trampoline; racket, battledore; gutta-percha; neoprene; spring, shock absorber

VERBS 4 **stretch;** extend; distend 259.4; flex

5 **give,** yield 1047.7; bounce, spring, snap back, recoil, rebound, spring back 903.6

6 **elasticize;** rubberize, rubber; vulcanize, plasticize

ADJS 7 **elastic, resilient, springy,** bouncy; **stretchable, stretchy,** stretch; extensile; **flexible** 1047.9; flexile; **adaptable,** adaptive, responsive; buoyant; lively 330.17; tensile

8 rubber, **rubbery,** rubberlike; rubberized

1049 TOUGHNESS

NOUNS 1 **toughness, resistance, ruggedness; strength, hardiness, vitality, stamina** 15.1, sturdiness; stubbornness, stiffness; **unbreakableness** or **unbreakability,** infrangibility; cohesiveness, tenacity, viscidity 803.3; durability, lastingness 827.1; **hardness** 1046; **leatheriness,** leatherlikeness; stringiness; staying power

2 <comparisons> leather; gristle, cartilage

VERBS 3 **toughen,** harden, stiffen, work-harden, **temper,** strengthen; season; be tough; **endure, hang tough** <nf>

ADJS 4 **tough, resistant;** shockproof, shock-resistant, impactproof, impact-resistant; stubborn, stiff; **heavy-duty;** hard or tough as nails; **strong, hardy,** vigorous; cohesive, **tenacious,** viscid; **durable,** lasting 827.10; untiring; **hard** 1046.10; chewy <nf>; leathery, leatherlike, coriaceous, tough as leather; sinewy, wiry; gristly, cartilaginous; stringy, fibrous; long-lasting

5 **unbreakable,** nonbreakable, infrangible, unshatterable, shatterproof, chip-proof, fractureproof; bulletproof, bombproof, fireproof; indestructible

6 **toughened,** hardened, tempered, annealed; seasoned; casehardened; vulcanized

1050 BRITTLENESS, FRAGILITY

NOUNS 1 **brittleness, crispness,** crispiness; **fragility, frailty,** damageability, delicacy 16.2, flimsiness, **breakability,** breakableness, frangibility, fracturableness, crackability, crackableness, crunchability, crushability, crushableness; lacerability; fissility; friability, friableness, crumbliness 1051, flakiness; vulnerableness, **vulnerability** 1006.4; inelasticity

2 <comparisons> eggshell, old bone, piecrust, peanut brittle; matchwood, balsa, old paper, parchment, rice paper, dead leaf; glass, glass jaw, china, ice, icicle, glass house; house of cards; lamina, shale, slate, pottery

VERBS 3 **break, shatter,** fragment, fragmentize, fragmentate, fall to pieces, shard, fracture, chip off, flake, shiver, **disintegrate** 806.3

ADJS 4 **brittle, crisp,** crispy; **fragile, frail,** delicate 16.14, flimsy, **breakable,** frangible, crushable, crackable, crunchable, fracturable; lacerable; **shatterable,** shattery, shivery, splintery; friable, crumbly 1051.13, flaky; fissile, scissile; brittle as glass; **vulnerable** 1006.16; wafer-thin, papery; inelastic

1051 POWDERINESS, CRUMBLINESS

NOUNS 1 **powderiness,** pulverulence, dustiness; chalkiness; **mealiness,** flouriness, branniness; efflorescence, bloom

2 **granularity, graininess,** granulation; **sandiness, grittiness,** gravelliness, sabulosity, sandiness

3 **friability,** pulverableness, crispness, crumbliness, flakiness; brittleness 1050

4 **pulverization,** comminution, trituration, attrition, detrition; levigation; reduction to powder *or* dust, pestling; fragmentation, sharding; brecciation; atomization, micronization; **powdering, crumbling,** flaking; abrasion 1044.2; **grinding,** milling, grating, shredding; granulation, granulization; **beating, pounding, shattering,** flailing, mashing, smashing, crushing; disintegration 806, decomposition

5 **powder, dust,** chalk; dust ball *or* kitten *or* bunny, slut's wool <Brit nf>, lint; efflorescence; **crumb,** crumble; **meal,** bran, flour, farina, grist; grits, groats; filings, raspings, sawdust; soot, smut; **particle, particulate,** particulates, airborne particles, air pollution; fallout; cosmic dust; dust cloud, dust devil; spore, pollen

6 **grain,** granule, granulet; **grit, sand; gravel,** shingle; detritus, debris; breccia, collapse breccia; speck, mote, particle

7 **pulverizer,** comminutor, triturator, levigator; **crusher; mill; grinder;** granulator, pepper grinder, pepper mill; **grater,** cheese grater, nutmeg grater; **shredder;** pestle, **mortar and pestle; masher;** pounder; grindstone, millstone, quern, quernstone, muller; roller, steamroller; hammer; abrasive

8 koniology; konimeter

VERBS 9 **pulverize, powder,** comminute, triturate, contriturate, levigate, bray, pestle, disintegrate, reduce to powder *or* dust, grind to powder *or* dust, grind up; **fragment,** shard, shatter; brecciate; atomize, micronize; **crumble,** crumb, chip, flake; **granulate,** granulize, grain; **grind, grate, shred,** abrade 1044.7; **mill,** flour; **beat, pound, mash, smash, crush,** crunch, flail, squash, scrunch <nf>; grate, shred, mince, kibble

10 <be reduced to powder> **powder,** come *or* fall to dust, **crumble,** crumble to *or* into dust, **disintegrate** 806.3, fall to pieces, break up; effloresce; granulate, grain

ADJS 11 **powdery, dusty,** powder, pulverulent, pulverous, lutose; **pulverized,** pulverant, powdered, disintegrated, comminute, gone to dust, reduced to powder, dust-covered; **particulate; ground, grated,** pestled, milled, stone-ground, comminuted, triturated, levigated; sharded, **crushed; fragmented; shredded;** sifted; **fine,** impalpable; **chalky,** chalklike; **mealy,** floury, farinaceous; branny; furfuraceous, scaly, scurfy; flaky 296.7; detrited, detrital; scobiform, scobicular; efflorescent

12 **granular, grainy,** granulate, **granulated; sandy, gritty,** sabulous, arenarious, arenaceous, arenose; shingly, shingled, pebbled, pebbly; **gravelly;** breccial, brecciated

13 **pulverable, pulverizable,** pulverulent, triturable; **friable,** crimp <old>, crisp, **crumbly**

1052 MATERIALITY

NOUNS 1 **materiality,** materialness; **corporeity,** corporality, corporeality, corporealness, bodiliness, embodiment, existence; **substantiality** 763, concreteness 763.1; **physicalness,** physicality; tangibility; palpability

2 **matter, material,** materiality, **substance** 763.2, **stuff,** hyle; raw material, organic matter; **primal matter,** initial substance, xylem; brute matter; **element;** chemical element 1060.2; the four elements; earth, air, fire, water; elementary particle, fundamental particle; elementary unit, building block, unit of being, monad; constituent, component; **atom** 1038.4; atomic particle 1038.6; **molecule;** material world, physical world, real world, nature, natural world; hypostasis, substratum; plenum; antimatter

3 **body,** physical body, material body, corpus <nf>, anatomy <nf>, person, **figure, form,** frame, **physique,** carcass <nf>, bones, flesh, clay, clod, hulk; soma; **torso, trunk;** warm body <nf>

4 **object, article, thing,** material thing, affair, something, entity; whatsit <nf>, what's-its-name 528.2; something *or* other, *etwas* <Ger>, *eppes* <Yiddish>, *quelque chose* <Fr>; artifact; inanimate object; animate being

5 <nf terms> **gadget** 1040.1; thingum, **thingamabob,** thingumadad, thingy, thingumadoodle, **thingamajig** *or* thingumajig, thingumajigger, thingumaree, thingummy, **doodad,** dofunny, **dojigger,** dojiggy, domajig, domajigger, **dohickey** *or* doohickey, dowhacky, flumadiddle, gigamaree, **gimmick, gizmo,** dingus, hickey, jigger, hootmalalie, hootenanny, whatchy, widget, whatsis *or* whatsit, gismo *or* gizmo, deely-bobber

6 materialism, physicism, epiphenomenalism, identity theory of mind, atomism, mechanism; physicalism, behaviorism, instrumentalism, pragmatism, pragmaticism; historical materialism, dialectical materialism, Marxism; **positivism,** logical positivism, positive philosophy, empiricism, **naturalism;** realism, natural realism, commonsense realism, commonsense philosophy, naïve realism, new realism, critical realism, representative realism, epistemological realism; substantialism; hylomorphism; hylotheism; hylozoism; worldliness, earthliness, animalism, secularism, temporality

7 materialist, physicist, atomist; historical *or* dialectical materialist, Marxist; **naturalist;** realist, natural realist, commonsense realist, commonsense philosopher, epistemological realist; humanist, positivist; physical scientist

8 materialization, corporealization; substantialization, substantiation; **embodiment, incorporation,** personification, **incarnation,** manifestation; **reincarnation,** reembodiment, transmigration, metempsychosis

VERBS **9 materialize** 763.5, corporalize; substantialize, substantify, substantiate; **embody** 763.5, body, **incorporate,** corporify, personify, **incarnate; reincarnate,** reembody, transmigrate; externalize

ADJS **10 material,** materiate, hylic, **substantial** 763.6, tangible; **corporeal,** corporeous, corporal, **bodily; physical,** somatic, somatical, somatous; **fleshly;** worldly, earthly, here-and-now, **secular,** temporal, **unspiritual,** nonspiritual; empirical, spatiotemporal; objective, clinical

11 embodied, bodied, **incorporated, incarnate**

12 materialist *or* **materialistic,** atomistic, mechanist, mechanistic; Marxian, Marxist; **naturalist, naturalistic, positivist, positivistic;** commonsense, **realist,** realistic; hylotheistic; hylomorphous; hylozoic, hylozoistic

1053 IMMATERIALITY

NOUNS **1 immateriality,** immaterialness; incorporeity, incorporeality, incorporealness, **bodilessness; unsubstantiality** 764, unsubstantialness; **intangibility,** impalpability, imponderability; inextension, nonextension; nonexteriority, nonexternality; **unearthliness, unworldliness,** ethereality, unreality; **supernaturalism** 689.2; **spirituality,** spiritualness, spirituousness <old>, otherworldliness, ghostliness, shadowiness; occultism 689, the occult, occult phenomena; ghost-raising, ghost-hunting, ghostbusting <nf>; psychism, psychics,

psychic *or* psychical research, psychicism; spirit world, astral plane

2 incorporeal, incorporeity, immateriality, unsubstantiality 764

3 immaterialism, idealism, philosophical idealism, metaphysical idealism; objective idealism; absolute idealism; epistemological idealism; monistic idealism, pluralistic idealism; critical idealism; transcendental idealism; subjectivism; solipsism; subjective idealism; **spiritualism;** personalism; panpsychism, psychism, animism, hylozoism, animatism; Platonism, Platonic realism, Berkeleianism, Cambridge Platonism, Kantianism, Hegelianism, New England Transcendentalism; Neoplatonism; Platonic idea *or* ideal *or* form, pure form, form, universal; transcendental object; transcendental

4 immaterialist, **idealist;** Berkeleian, Platonist, Hegelian, Kantian; Neoplatonist; **spiritualist;** psychist, panpsychist, animist; **occultist** 689.11; medium; ghost-raiser, ghost-hunter, ghostbuster <nf>

5 dematerialization; **disembodiment,** disincarnation; **spiritualization**

VERBS **6** dematerialize, immaterialize, unsubstantialize, insubstantialize, desubstantialize, **disembody,** disincarnate; **spiritualize,** spiritize; meditate

ADJS **7 immaterial,** nonmaterial; **unsubstantial** 764.5, insubstantial, **intangible,** impalpable, imponderable; unextended, extensionless; **incorporeal,** incorporate, incorporeous; **bodiless,** unembodied, without body, asomatous; **disembodied,** disbodied, discarnate, decarnate, decarnated; metaphysical; **unphysical,** nonphysical; **unfleshly;** airy, ghostly, spectral, phantom, shadowy, ethereal; **spiritual,** astral, psychic *or* psychical; **unearthly, unworldly, otherworldly,** extramundane, transmundane; supernatural; **occult;** parapsychological

8 idealist, idealistic, immaterialist, immaterialistic; solipsistic; spiritualist, spiritualistic; panpsychist, panpsychistic; animist, animistic; Platonic, Platonistic, Berkeleian, Hegelian, Kantian; Neoplatonic, Neoplatonistic

1054 MATERIALS

NOUNS **1 materials,** substances, stuff, matter; **raw material, staple, stock,** grist, basic material; material resources *or* means; store, supply 386; strategic materials; matériel; natural resource

2 <building materials> sticks and stones, lath and plaster, bricks and mortar, wattle and daub; **roofing,** roofage, tiles, shingles; walling, siding;

flooring, pavement, paving material, paving, paving stone; masonry, stonework, flag, flagstone, ashlar, stone 1059.1; covering materials; mortar, plasters; **cement, concrete,** cyclopean concrete, ferroconcrete, prestressed concrete, reinforced concrete, slag concrete, cinder concrete; brick, firebrick; cinder block, concrete block; clinker, adobe, clay; **tile,** tiling; glass, steel, slate, cobble, tar, asphalt, gravel

3 **wood** <see list>, **lumber, timber,** forest-product; hardwood, softwood; stick, stick of wood, stave; billet; log, pole, post, beam 273.3, **board,** plank; deal; two-by-four, three-by-four, etc; slab, puncheon; slat, splat, lath; boarding, timbering, timberwork, planking; lathing, lathwork; sheeting; paneling, panelboard, panelwork; plywood, plyboard; sheathing, sheathing board; siding, sideboard; weatherboard, clapboard; shingle, shake; log; driftwood; firewood, kindling, stovewood; cordwood; cord, cordage; brushwood; dead wood; pulpwood, sapwood, alburnum, heartwood, duramen; early wood, late wood, springwood, summerwood

4 cane, bamboo, rattan

5 **paper,** paper stock, stock; sheet, leaf, page; quire, ream, stationery; cardboard

6 **plastic** <see list>; thermoplastic; thermosetting plastic; resin plastic; cellulose plastic; protein plastic; cast plastic, molded plastic, extruded plastic; molding compounds; laminate; adhesive; plasticizer; polymer; **synthetic;** synthetic fabric *or* textile *or* cloth; synthetic rubber

VERBS 7 gather *or* procure materials; **store, stock,** stock up 386.11, lay in, restock; **process,** utilize

8 woods

acacia	coconut
alder	cork
applewood	cottonwood
ash	cypress
aspen	dogwood
balsa	ebony
balsam	elder
banyan	elm *or* elmwood
bass *or* basswood	eucalyptus
beech *or* beechwood	fig
betel palm	fir
birch	fruit wood
boxwood	gum *or* gumwood
brierwood	hawthorn
burl	hazel *or* hazelwood
buttonwood	hemlock
cacao	hickory
cedar *or* cedarwood	ironwood
cherry	juniper
chestnut	knotty pine
citrus	lancewood

larch	redwood
laurel	rosewood
lignum vitae	rubber
linden	sandalwood
loblolly pine	satinwood
locust	sequoia
logwood	sisal
magnolia	sour gum
mahogany	spruce
maple	sugar maple
mesquite	sumac
monkeypod	sycamore
myrtle	teak *or* teakwood
oak	tulipwood
olive	tupelo
palm	walnut
pear	willow
pecan	yew
pine	zebrawood
poplar	

9 plastics

acetate	neoprene
acetate nitrate	nitrate
acrylic	nylon
alkyd	phenolic
aminoplast	phenolic urea
Bakelite <trademark>	Plexiglas <trademark>
casein plastic	polyester
cellophane	polyethylene
celluloid	polymeric amide
cellulose acetate	polypropylene
cellulose ether	polystyrene
cellulose nitrate	polyurethane
cellulosic	polyvinyl chloride *or* PVC
coumarone-indene	polyvinyl-formaldehyde
epoxy	resinoid
fluorocarbon plastic	silicone resin
Formica <trademark>	Styrofoam <trademark>
furane	Teflon <trademark>
laminate	terpene
lignin	tetrafluoroethylene
Lucite <trademark>	urea
melamine	urea formaldehyde
multiresin	vinyl
Mylar <trademark>	Vinylite <trademark>

10 polymers

addition polymer	plasticizer
atactic polymer	Plexiglas <trademark>
chloroprene rubber	polycarbonate
condensation polymer	polyester
copolymer	polyethylene *or* polyethene
epoxide resin	*or* polythene
homopolymer	polypropylene *or* polypro-
isoprene rubber	pene
isotactic polymer	polystyrene
macromolecule	polyurethane
monomer	polyvinyl chloride *or*
nylon	PVC

resin
stereoregular polymer
syndiotactic polymer

Teflon <trademark>
thermosetting plastic
vulcanite

11 paper

bond paper
carbon paper
cardboard
computer paper
crepe paper
fiberboard
foolscap
glossy paper
laminated paper
newsprint
onionskin
paper towel

posterboard
rag paper
rice paper
stationery
tissue paper
toilet paper
tracing paper
typing paper
watermarked paper
wax paper
wrapping paper
writing paper

1055 INORGANIC MATTER

NOUNS **1 inorganic matter,** nonorganic matter; inanimate or lifeless or nonliving matter, inorganized or unorganized matter, inert matter, dead matter, **brute matter;** mineral kingdom or world; matter, mere matter

2 inanimateness, inanimation, **lifelessness,** inertness; **insensibility,** insentience, insensateness, senselessness, unconsciousness, unfeelingness

3 inorganic chemistry; chemicals 1060

ADJS **4 inorganic,** unorganic, nonorganic; **mineral,** nonbiological; nonbiodegradable; unorganized, inorganized; material 1052.10

5 inanimate, inanimated, unanimated, exanimate, azoic, nonliving, dead, **lifeless,** soulless; inert; insentient, unconscious, nonconscious, **insensible,** insensate, senseless, unfeeling; dumb, mute

1056 OILS, LUBRICANTS

NOUNS **1 oil,** *oleum* <L>; **fat,** lipid, **grease;** sebum, tallow, vegetable oil, animal oil; **ester,** glyceryl ester; fixed oil, fatty oil, nonvolatile oil, volatile oil, essential oil; saturated fat, hydrogenated fat, unsaturated fat, polyunsaturated fat; drying oil, semidrying oil, nondrying oil; glycerol, wax

2 lubricant, lubricator, lubricating oil, lubricating agent, antifriction; graphite, plumbago, black lead; silicone; glycerin or glycerine; silicone; wax, cerate; mucilage, mucus, synovia; spit, spittle, saliva; Vaseline <trademark>, petroleum jelly, K-Y <trademark>; soap, lather

3 ointment, balm, salve, lotion, cream, unguent, unguentum, inunction, inunctum, unction, chrism or chrisom; soothing syrup, lenitive, embrocation, demulcent, emollient, liniment; spikenard, nard; balsam; **pomade,** pomatum, brilliantine; styling mousse, styling gel; cold

cream, hand lotion, face cream, lanolin; eyewash, collyrium; sun-block, sun-tan lotion, tanning cream

4 petroleum, rock oil, fossil oil, shale oil, coal oil; **fuel;** fuel oil; mineral oil; crude oil, crude; motor oil; gasoline or gas; kerosene, paraffin

5 oiliness, greasiness, unctuousness, unctiousness, unctuosity; **fattiness,** fatness, pinguidity; richness; sebaceousness; adiposis, adiposity; **soapiness,** saponacity or saponaceousness; smoothness, slickness, sleekness, **slipperiness,** lubricity; waxiness; creaminess; soapiness, saponaceousness

6 lubrication, lubricating, **oiling, greasing,** lubrification <old>; nonfriction; lubricity, lube <nf>, grease or lube job <nf>; **anointment,** unction, inunction; chrismatory, chrismation

7 lubritorium, lubritory; grease rack, grease pit; lubricator, oilcan, grease gun

VERBS **8 oil,** grease; **lubricate,** lubrify <old>; **anoint,** salve, unguent, embrocate, dress, pour oil or balm upon; smear, daub; slick, slick on <nf>; pomade; lard; glycerolate, glycerinate, glycerinize; wax, beeswax; smooth the way and soap the way and grease the wheels <nf>; soap, lather

ADJS **9 oily, greasy; unctuous,** unctional; unguinous; **oleaginous,** oleic; unguentary, **unguent,** unguentous; chrismal, chrismatory; **fat, fatty,** adipose; pinguid, pinguedinous, pinguescent; rich; sebaceous; blubbery, tallowy, suety; lardy, lardaceous; buttery, butyraceous; soapy, saponaceous; paraffinic; mucoid; smooth, slick, sleek, **slippery;** sebaceous; creamy; waxy, waxen, cereous, cerated

10 lubricant, lubricating, **lubricative,** lubricatory, lubricational; lenitive, unguentary, emollient, soothing, moisturizing

WORD ELEMENTS **11** ole-, oleo-, oli-; lip-, lipo-, lipar-, liparo-; cer-, cero-; sebo-, sebi-; steat-, steato-; petr-, petro-, petri-

1057 RESINS, GUMS

NOUNS **1 resin; gum,** gum resin; oleoresin; hard or varnish resin, vegetable resin; synthetic resin, plastic, resinoid; resene; **rosin,** colophony, colophonium, colophonone, resinate

VERBS **2** resin, resinize, resinate; rosin

ADJS **3 resinous,** resinic, resiny; resinoid; rosiny; **gummy,** gummous, gumlike; pitchy

1058 MINERALS, METALS

NOUNS **1 mineral** <see list>; inorganic substance, lifeless matter found in nature; extracted matter *or* material; **mineral world** *or* **kingdom;** mineral resources; mineraloid, gel mineral, mineral aggregate; mineralization; crystalline element *or* compound; inorganic mineral, natural mineral, silicate, carbonate, oxide, sulfide, sulfate etc

2 **ore** <see list>, mineral; mineral-bearing material; unrefined *or* untreated mineral; natural *or* native mineral

3 **metal,** elementary metal <see list>; metallics; native metals, alkali metals, earth metals, alkaline-earth metals, noble metals, precious metals, base metals, rare metals, rare-earth metals *or* elements; metalloid, semimetal, nonmetal; gold *or* silver bullion; gold dust; leaf metal, metal leaf, metal foil; metalwork, metalware; metallicity, metalleity

4 **alloy,** alloyage, fusion, compound; **amalgam**

5 **cast, casting; ingot, bullion;** pig, sow; sheet metal; button, gate, regulus

6 **mine,** pit, **quarry; diggings, workings;** open cut, opencast; bank; shaft; coal mine, colliery; strip mine; gold mine, silver mine, etc

7 **deposit,** mineral deposit, pay dirt; **vein, lode,** seam, dike, ore bed; shoot *or* chute, ore shoot *or* chute; chimney; stock; placer, placer deposit, placer gravel; country rock; lodestuff, gangue, matrix, veinstone

8 **mining;** coal mining, gold mining, etc; long-wall mining; room-and-pillar mining; strip mining; placer mining; hydraulic mining; prospecting; mining claim, lode claim, placer claim; gold fever; gold rush

9 **miner,** mineworker, pitman; coal miner, collier <Brit>; gold miner, gold digger; gold panner; placer miner; quarry miner; **prospector,** desert rat <nf>, sourdough; wildcatter; **forty-niner;** hand miner, rockman, powderman, driller, draw man; butty

10 **mineralogy;** mineralogical chemistry; crystallography; **petrology,** petrography, micropetrography; **geology;** mining geology, mining engineering

11 **metallurgy;** metallography, metallurgical chemistry, metallurgical engineering, physical metallurgy, powder metallurgy, electrometallurgy, hydrometallurgy, pyrometallurgy, production metallurgy, extractive metallurgy

12 **mineralogist; metallurgist,** electrometallurgist, metallurgical engineer; **petrologist,** petrographer; **geologist;** mining engineer

VERBS 13 mineralize; petrify 1046.7

14 **mine;** quarry; pan, pan for gold; prospect; hit pay dirt; mine out

ADJS 15 **mineral;** inorganic 1055.4; mineralized, petrified; asbestine, carbonous, graphitic, micaceous, alabastrine, quartzose, silicic; sulfurous, sulfuric; ore-bearing, ore-forming

16 **metal, metallic,** metallike, metalline, metalloid *or* metalloidal, metalliform; semimetallic; nonmetallic; metallo-organic *or* metallorganic, organometallic; bimetallic, trimetallic; metalliferous, metalbearing

17 brass, brassy, brazen; bronze, bronzy; copper, coppery, cuprous, cupreous; gold, golden, gilt, aureate; nickel, nickelic, nickelous, nickeline; silver, silvery; iron, ironlike, ferric, ferrous, ferruginous; steel, steely; tin, tinny; lead, leaden; pewter, pewtery; mercurial, mercurous, quicksilver; gold-filled, gold-plated, silver-plated, etc

18 **mineralogical, metallurgical,** petrological, crystallographic

19 **minerals**

alabaster	fluorite
amphibole	fluorspar
anhydrite	fool's gold
antimony	garnet
apatite	glauconite
argillite	graphite
arsenic	gypsum
asbestos	holosiderite
asphalt	hornblende
augite	ilmenite
azurite	iolite
barite	iron pyrites
bauxite	jet
bitumen	kaolinite
boron	kyanite
brimstone	lazurite
bromine	lignite
brookite	lime
brucite	magnesite
calcite	malachite
carbon	maltha
carnelian	marcasite
chalcedony	marl
chert	meerschaum
chlorite	mica
chromite	microlite
clay	microlith
coal	mineral charcoal
coke	mineral coal
corundum	mineral oil
cryolite	mineral salt
diamond	mineral tallow
diatomite	mineral tar
dolomite	mineral wax
elaterite	molybdenite
emery	monazite
epidote	moonstone
epsomite	obsidian
feldspar	olivine
flint	orthoclase

ozokerite
peat
peridot
perlite
phosphate rock
phosphorus
pitchblende
pumice
pumicite
pyrite
pyroxene
quartz
realgar
red clay
rhodonite
rock salt
serpentine
siderite

silica
silicate
silicon
sodalite
spar
spinel
sulfur
talc
tellurium
topaz
tourmaline
tripoli
umber
vermiculite
wollastonite
wulfenite
zeolite
zircon

20 ores

amblygonite
argentite
arsenopyrite *or*
   mispickel
azurite
barite
bauxite
beryl
bornite
calaverite
carnotite
cassiterite
celestite
cerussite
chalcocite
chalcopyrite
chromite
cinnabar
cuprite
galena
garnierite
goethite
hematite
hemimorphite
hydrozincite

ilmenite
iron ore
ironstone
limonite
lodestone
magnetite
malachite
molybdenite
monazite
niobite
pitchblende
pyrargyrite
pyrite
scheelite
siderite
smithsonite
sphalerite
stibnite
sylvanite
tetrahedrite
tinstone
turgite
uranitite
wolframite
zincite

21 metallic elements

actinium
aluminum
americium
antimony
barium
beryllium
bismuth
cadmium
cerium
cesium
chromium
cobalt
copper
dysprosium

erbium
europium
gadolinium
gallium
germanium
gold
hafnium
holmium
indium
iridium
iron
lanthanum
lawrencium
lead

lithium
lutetium
magnesium
manganese
mercury
molybdenum
neodymium
nickel
niobium
osmium
palladium
phosphorus
platinum
polonium
potassium
praseodymium
promethium
protactinium
quicksilver
radium
rhenium
rhodium

rubidium
ruthenium
samarium
scandium
silver
sodium
strontium
tantalum
technetium
terbium
thallium
thorium
thulium
tin
titanium
tungsten
uranium
vanadium
ytterbium
yttrium
zinc
zirconium

1059 ROCK

NOUNS **1 rock, stone** <see list>; living rock, rock formation; **igneous rock,** plutonic *or* abyssal rock, hypabyssal rock, magmatic rock, acid rock, mafic rock, felsic rock, ultrabasic rock, ultramafic rock; volcanic rock, extrusive *or* effusive rock, scoria; magma, intrusive rock; granite, basalt, porphyry, **lava,** aa *and* pahoehoe <Hawaiian>; **sedimentary rock,** lithified sediment, stratified rock, clastic rock, nonclastic rock; limestone, sandstone; **metamorphic rock,** schist, gneiss; conglomerate, pudding stone, breccia, rubble, rubblestone, scree, talus, tuff, tufa, brash; sarsen, sarsen stone, druid stone; monolith; crag, craig <Scot>; bedrock; mantlerock, regolith; saprolite, geest, laterite; building stone

2 sand; grain of sand; sands of the sea; sand pile, sand dune, sand hill; sand reef, sandbar

3 gravel, shingle, chesil <Brit>

4 pebble, pebblestone, gravelstone; jackstone *and* checkstone <nf>; fingerstone; slingstone; drakestone; spall

5 boulder, river boulder, shore boulder, glacial boulder

6 geological sediment, organic sediment, inorganic sediment, oceanic sediment, alluvial deposit, lake sediment, glacial deposit, eolian deposit; mud, sand, silt, clay, loess; rock, boulder, stone, gravel, granule, pebble

7 precious stone, gem, gemstone <see list>; stone: crystal, crystal lattice, crystal system;

semiprecious stone; gem of the first water;
birthstone

8 petrification, petrifaction, lithification,
crystallization; rock cycle, sedimentation,
deposition, consolidation, cementation,
compaction, magmatism, metamorphosis,
recrystallization, foliation

9 geology, geoscience, petrology, crystallography;
petrochemistry; petrogenesis

VERBS 10 petrify, lithify, crystallize, turn to stone;
harden 1046.7

ADJS 11 **stone, rock,** lithic; petrified; petrogenic,
petrescent; adamant, adamantine; flinty, flintlike;
marbly, marblelike; granitic, granitelike; slaty,
slatelike

12 **stony, rocky,** lapideous; stonelike, rocklike, lithoid
or lithoidal; sandy, gritty 1051.12; gravelly, shingly,
shingled; pebbly, pebbled; porphyritic, trachytic;
crystal, crystalline; bouldery, rock- or boulder-
strewn, rock-studded, rock-ribbed; craggy;
monolithic

WORD ELEMENTS 13 petr-, petro-, petri-, saxi-,
lith-, litho-, -lith; grano-; blast-, blasto-, -blast,
orth-, ortho-, par-; para-; -clast; -lithic, litic;
-clastic; crystall-, crystallo-

14 **stones**

anthraconite	greenstone
aplite	grit
basalt	gritrock or gritstone
beetlestone	hairstone
boulder	hoarstone
brimstone	ironstone
brownstone	lava
buhr or buhrstone	limestone
cairngorm	lodestone
chalk	Lydian stone
clinkstone	marble
dendrite	megalith
diabase	menhir
diorite	milkstone
dolerite	monolith
dolmen	mudstone
dolomite	obsidian
dripstone	omphalos
eaglestone	pitchstone
emery	porphyry
fieldstone	pumice
flag or flagstone	quarrystone
flint	quartz
floatstone	quartzite
freestone	rance
geode	rottenstone
gneiss	sandstone
goldstone	serpentine
granite	shale
granulite	slab
graywacke	slate

stone	steatite
slate	stinkstone
smokestone	tinstone
snakestone	touchstone
soapstone	trap or traprock
stalactite	tufa
stalagmite	wacke
starstone	whitestone

15 **gemstones**

achroite	jade or jadestone
agate	jargoon
alexandrite	jasper
amethyst	kunzite
aquamarine	lapis lazuli
beryl	moonstone
black opal	morganite
bloodstone	onyx
brilliant	opal
carbuncle	pearl
carnelian	peridot
cat's-eye	plasma
chalcedony	rhodolite
chrysoberyl	rose quartz
chrysolite	ruby
chrysoprase	sapphire
citrine	sard
coral	sardonyx
demantoid or Uralian	siberite
emerald	spinel or spinel ruby
diamond	sunstone
emerald	tanzanite
fire opal	tiger's eye
garnet	topaz
girasol	tourmaline
harlequin opal	turquoise
heliotrope	water sapphire
hyacinth	white sapphire
jacinth	zircon

1060 CHEMISTRY, CHEMICALS

NOUNS 1 **chemistry,** chemical science, science of
substances, science of matter; branch of
chemistry <see list>

2 **element** <see list>, chemical element; table of
elements, periodic table, periodic table of
elements; **radical group;** free radical, diradical;
ion, anion, cation; atom 1038.4; **molecule,**
macromolecule; trace element, microelement,
micronutrient, minor element; **chemical, chemical
compound;** organic chemical, biochemical,
inorganic chemical; fine chemicals, heavy
chemicals; agent, **reagent;** metal, nonmetal,
semimetal, metalloid, heavy metal, alkali metal,
noble metal; alkaline-earth element, transition
element, noble gas, rare-earth element,
lanthanide, actinide, transuranic element,

supertransuranic element, superheavy element; inert gas, rare gas; period, short period, long period; family, group; s-block, p-block, d-block, f-block; chemical equation

3 **acid;** hydracid, oxyacid, sulfacid; acidity; **base, alkali,** nonacid; pH; neutralizer, antacid; alkalinity

4 **valence,** valency <Brit>, positive valence, negative valence; monovalence, univalence, bivalence, trivalence, tervalence, quadrivalence, tetravalence, etc, multivalence, polyvalence; covalence, electrovalence

5 **atomic weight,** atomic mass, atomic volume, mass number; **molecular weight,** molecular mass, molecular volume; atomic number, valence number

6 **chemicalization,** chemical process <see list>, chemical action, chemism; **chemical apparatus,** beaker, Bunsen burner, burette, centrifuge, condenser, crucible, graduated cylinder or graduate, pipette, test tube

7 chemist, chemical scientist; agricultural chemist, analytical chemist, astrochemist, biochemist, inorganic chemist, organic chemist, physical chemist, physiochemist, theoretical chemist, etc

VERBS **8** **chemicalize,** chemical; alkalize, alkalinize, alkalify; acidify, acidulate, acetify; borate, carbonate, chlorinate, hydrate, hydrogenate, hydroxylate, nitrate, oxidize, reduce, pepsinate, peroxidize, phosphatize, sulfate, sulfatize, sulfonate; calcify, carburize, deuterate, esterify, fluorinate, fluoridate, halogenate, tritrate; isomerize, metamerize, polymerize, copolymerize, homopolymerize; ferment, work; catalyze 806.4; electrolyze; bond, intercalate, invert, neutralize, ionize

ADJS **9** **chemical;** astrochemical, biochemical, chemicobiologic; physicochemical, physiochemical, chemicophysical, chemicobiological, chemicophysiologic or chemicophysiological, chemicodynamic, chemicoengineering, chemicomechanical, chemicomineralogical, chemicopharmaceutical, chemurgic, electrochemical, iatrochemical, chemotherapeutic or chemotherapeutical, chemophysiologic or chemophysiological, macrochemical, microchemical, physicochemical, phytochemical, photochemical, radiochemical, thermochemical, zoochemical; organic, inorganic; elemental, elementary; acid; alkaline, alkali, nonacid, basic; isomeric, isomerous, metameric, metamerous, heteromerous, polymeric, polymerous, copolymeric, copolymerous, monomeric, monomerous, dimeric, dimerous, etc

10 valent; univalent, monovalent, monatomic, bivalent, trivalent, tervalent, quadrivalent, tetravalent, etc, multivalent, polyvalent; covalent, electrovalent

WORD ELEMENTS **11** chem-, chemo-, chemi-, chemic-, chemico-; -mer, -merous, -meric; -valent

12 **branches of chemistry**

actinochemistry	metallurgy
agricultural chemistry	microchemistry
alchemy or alchemistry	mineralogical chemistry
analytical chemistry	natural product chemistry
applied chemistry	neurochemistry
astrochemistry	nuclear chemistry
atomic chemistry	organic chemistry
biochemistry	pathological chemistry or
biogeochemistry	pathochemistry
business chemistry	petrochemistry
capillary chemistry	pharmaceutical chemistry
catalysis	phonochemistry
chemiatry	photochemistry
chemical dynamics	physical chemistry or phys-
chemical engineering	iochemistry
chemical physics	physiological chemistry or
chemicobiology	physiochemistry
chemicoengineering	phytochemistry
chemophysiology	piezochemistry
chemurgy <old>	pneumatochemistry
colloid chemistry	polymer chemistry
colorimetry or colorimet-	psychobiochemistry or
ric analysis	psychochemistry
crystallography	pure chemistry
cytochemistry	quantum chemistry
electrochemistry	radiochemistry
engineering chemistry	soil chemistry
galactochemistry	spectrochemistry
galvanochemistry	stereochemistry
geochemistry	structural chemistry
histochemistry	surface chemistry
hydrochemistry	synthetic chemistry
iatrochemistry	technochemistry
immunochemistry	theoretical chemistry
industrial chemistry	thermochemistry
inorganic chemistry	topochemistry
lithochemistry	ultramicrochemistry
macrochemistry	zoochemistry or
magnetochemistry	zoochemy
metachemistry	zyochemistry or zymurgy

13 **chemical elements**

actinium or Ac	boron or B
aluminum or Al	bromine or Br
americium or Am	cadmium or Cd
antimony or Sb	calcium or Ca
argon or Ar or A	californium or Cf
arsenic or As	carbon or C
astatine or At	cerium or Ce
barium or Ba	cesium or Cs
berkelium or Bk	chlorine or Cl
beryllium or Be	chromium or Cr
bismuth or Bi	cobalt or Co

copper *or* Cu
curium *or* Cm
dysprosium *or* Dy
einsteinium *or* Es *or* E
erbium *or* Er
europium *or* Eu
fermium *or* Fm
fluorine *or* F
francium *or* Fr
gadolinium *or* Gd
gallium *or* Ga
germanium *or* Ge
gold *or* Au
hafnium *or* Hf
helium *or* He
holmium *or* Ho
hydrogen *or* H
indium *or* In
iodine *or* I
iridium *or* Ir
iron *or* Fe
krypton *or* Kr
lanthanum *or* La
lawrencium *or* Lw
lead *or* Pb
lithium *or* Li
lutetium *or* Lu
magnesium *or* Mg
manganese *or* Mn
mendelevium *or* Md *or* Mv
mercury *or* Hg
molybdenum *or* Mo
neodymium *or* Nd
neon *or* Ne
neptunium *or* Np
nickel *or* Ni
niobium *or* Nb
nitrogen *or* N
nobelium *or* No
osmium *or* Os
oxygen *or* O
palladium *or* Pd
phosphorus *or* P

platinum *or* Pt
plutonium *or* Pu
polonium *or* Po
potassium *or* K
praseodymium *or* Pr
promethium *or* Pm
protactinium *or* Pa
radium *or* Ra
radon *or* Rn
rhenium *or* Re
rhodium *or* Rh
rubidium *or* Rb
ruthenium *or* Ru
samarium *or* Sm
scandium *or* Sc
selenium *or* Se
silicon *or* Si
silver *or* Ag
sodium *or* Na
strontium *or* Sr
sulfur *or* S
tantalum *or* Ta
technetium *or* Tc
tellurium *or* Te
terbium *or* Tb
thallium *or* Tl
thorium *or* Th
thulium *or* Tm
tin *or* Sn
titanium *or* Ti
tungsten *or* wolfram *or* W
unnihexium *or* Unh
unnilpentium *or* Unp *or* hahnium
unnilquadrium *or* Unq *or* rutherfordium
uranium *or* U
vanadium *or* V
xenon *or* Xe
ytterbium *or* Yb
yttrium *or* Y
zinc *or* Zn
zirconium *or* Zr

14 chemical processes
acetification
acidification *or* acidulation
alkalization *or* alkalinization
aromatization
carbonation
catalysis
chain reaction
chlorination
condensation
copolymerization
cyclization
electrolysis
electrophilic reaction
fermentation *or* ferment

geometric isomerization
heterolysis
heterolytic fission
homolysis
homolytic fission
homopolymerization
hydration
hydrogenation
hydroxylation
ionization
isomerization
isotope effect
metamerization
neutralization
nitration

nucleophilic reaction
optical isomerization
oxidation
oxidization
phosphatization
photochemical reaction
polymerization
position isomerization
pyrolysis

radiochemical reaction
reduction
ring opening
saturation
sulfation
sulfatization
sulfonation
synthesis
tautoisomerization

1061 LIQUIDITY

NOUNS **1 liquidity, fluidity,** fluidness, liquidness, liquefaction 1064; wateriness; rheuminess, runniness; **juiciness,** sappiness, succulence; milkiness, lactescence; lactation; chylifaction, chylification; serosity; suppuration; **moisture, wetness** 1065.1; **fluency,** flow, flowage, flux, fluxion, fluxility <old>; **circulation;** turbulence, turbidity, turbulent flow; streamline flow; hemorrhage; suppuration, secretion; liquid state; solubleness; fluid mechanics, hydrology

2 fluid, liquid; liquor 10.49, drink, beverage; liquid extract, fluid extract, condensation; **juice, sap,** latex, extract; milk, whey, buttermilk, ghee; water 1065.3; **body fluid, blood;** stock, meat juice, gravy, sauce, soup; semiliquid 1062.5; fluid mechanics, hydraulics, etc 1039.4; solvent, liquefier, liquefacient; solution, infusion, decoction

3 flowmeter, fluidmeter, hydrometer, sphygmomanometer

ADJS **4 fluid,** fluidal, fluidic, **fluent, flowing,** flexible *or* fluxile <old>, fluxional, fluxionary, runny; circulatory, **circulation,** turbid; **liquid,** liquidy; watery 1065.16; **juicy,** sappy, succulent, moist; **wet** 1065.15; uncongealed, unclotted; rheumy; bloody; liquefied, liquefying, liquefiable

5 milky, lacteal, lacteous, **lactic;** lactescent, lactiferous; milk, milch

1062 SEMILIQUIDITY

NOUNS **1 semiliquidity,** semifluidity; butteriness, creaminess; pulpiness 1063

2 viscosity, viscidity, viscousness, slabbiness, lentor <old>; thickness, spissitude <old>, heaviness, stodginess; **stickiness, tackiness,** glutinousness, glutinosity, toughness, tenaciousness, tenacity, **adhesiveness,** clinginess, clingingness, **gumminess,** gauminess <nf>, gumlikeness; **ropiness, stringiness;** clamminess, sliminess, mucilaginousness; gooeyness *and* gunkiness <nf>; **gluiness,** gluelikeness; syrupiness, treacliness <Brit>; gelatinousness, jellylikeness, gelatinity, gelation; colloidality; doughiness, pastiness;

thickening, curdling, clotting, coagulation, incrassation, inspissation, clabbering *and* loppering *or* lobbering <nf>, jellification

3 **mucosity,** mucidness, mucousness, pituitousness <old>, snottiness <nf>; **sliminess**

4 **muddiness,** muckiness, miriness, **slushiness,** sloshiness, sludginess, **sloppiness,** slobbiness, slabbiness <old>, squashiness, squelchiness, **ooziness; turbidity,** turbidness, dirtiness

5 **semiliquid,** semifluid; **goo** *and* goop *and* gook *and* gunk *and* glop <nf>, sticky mess, gaum <nf>; **paste,** pap, pudding, putty, **butter,** cream; **pulp** 1063.2; **jelly,** gelatin *or* gelatine, jell, gel, jam, agar, isinglass; **glue;** size; **gluten;** mucilage; mucus; **dough,** batter; mousse, pudding; **syrup,** molasses, treacle <Brit>, honey; egg white, albumen, glair; starch, cornstarch; **curd,** clabber, bonnyclabber; gruel, porridge, loblolly <nf>; soup, gumbo, gravy, purée, pulp; yogurt

6 **gum** 1057.1, chewing gum, bubble gum; chicle, chicle gum

7 **emulsion,** emulsoid; emulsification; emulsifier; **colloid,** colloider

8 **mud, muck, mire, slush, slosh,** sludge, slob <Ir>, squash, swill, **slime; slop, ooze, mire;** clay, slip; gumbo; gook *or* gunk *or* gook *or* glop *or* guck <nf>

9 **mud puddle, puddle,** loblolly <nf>, slop; **mudhole,** slough, muckhole, chuckhole, chughole <nf>; hog wallow

VERBS 10 **emulsify,** emulsionize; colloid, colloidize; cream; churn, whip, beat up; **thicken,** inspissate, incrassate, curdle, clot, coagulate, congeal, clabber *and* lopper <nf>; jell, jelly, jellify, gel

ADJS 11 **semiliquid,** semifluid, semifluidic; buttery; creamy; emulsive, colloidal; **pulpy** 1063.6; half-frozen, half-melted

12 **viscous, viscid,** viscose, slabby; **thick,** heavy, stodgy, soupy, thickened, inspissated, incrassated; curdled, clotted, grumous, coagulated, clabbered *and* loppered <nf>; **sticky, tacky,** tenacious, adhesive, clingy, clinging, tough; gluey, gluelike, glutinous, glutenous, glutinose; gumbo, gumbolike; **gummy,** gaumy <nf>, gummous, gumlike, **syrupy;** treacly <Brit>; ropy, stringy; mucilaginous, clammy, slimy, slithery; gooey *and* gunky *and* gloppy *and* goopy *and* gooky <nf>; **gelatinous,** jellylike, jellied, jelled; tremelloid *or* tremellose; glairy; **doughy, pasty;** starchy, amylaceous; pulpy, soft, mushy

13 **mucous,** muculent, mucoid, mucinous, pituitous <old>, phlegmy, snotty <nf>; mucific, muciferous

14 **slimy; muddy,** miry, mucky, **slushy, sloshy,** sludgy, sloppy, slobby, slabby <old>, splashy, **squashy,** squishy, **squelchy, oozy,** sloughy, plashy, sposhy <nf>; **turbid, dirty**

1063 PULPINESS

NOUNS 1 **pulpiness,** pulpousness; softness 1047; flabbiness; **mushiness,** mashiness, squashiness, creaminess; **pastiness,** doughiness; **sponginess,** pithiness; fleshiness, overripeness, succulence

2 **pulp, paste, mash, mush,** smash, squash, crush; tomato paste *or* pulp; pudding, porridge, sponge; sauce, butter; poultice, cataplasm, plaster; pith; paper pulp, wood pulp, sulfate pulp, sulfite pulp, rag pulp; pulpwood; pulp lead, white lead; dental *or* tooth pulp

3 **pulping,** pulpification, pulpefaction; blending, steeping; digestion; **maceration,** mastication

4 **pulper,** pulpifier, macerator, pulp machine *or* engine, digester; **masher,** smasher, potato masher, ricer, beetle; blender, food processor, food mill

VERBS 5 **pulp,** pulpify; **macerate,** masticate, chew; regurgitate; **mash,** smash, squash, crush

ADJS 6 **pulpy,** pulpous, pulpal, pulpar, pulplike, pulped; **pasty,** doughy; pultaceous; **mushy;** macerated, masticated, chewed; regurgitated; **squashy,** squelchy, squishy; soft, flabby; fleshy, succulent; **spongy,** pithy

1064 LIQUEFACTION

NOUNS 1 **liquefaction,** liquefying, liquidizing, liquidization, fluidification, fluidization; liquescence *or* liquescency, deliquescence, deliquiation *and* deliquium <old>; **solution,** dissolution, dissolving; **infusion,** soaking, steeping, brewing; **melting,** thawing, running, fusing, fusion; decoagulation, unclotting; solubilization; colliquation; lixiviation, percolation, leaching

2 **solubility,** solubleness, dissolvability, dissolvableness, dissolubility, dissolubleness; meltability, fusibility

3 **solution;** decoction, infusion, mixture; chemical solution; lixivium, leach, leachate; **suspension,** colloidal suspension; **emulsion,** gel, aerosol

4 **solvent** <see list>, dissolvent, dissolver, dissolving agent, resolvent, resolutive, **thinner,** diluent; anticoagulant; liquefier, liquefacient; menstruum; universal solvent, alkahest; flux

VERBS 5 **liquefy,** liquidize, liquesce, fluidify, fluidize; **melt, run,** thaw, colliquate; melt down; fuse, flux; deliquesce; **dissolve,** solve; thin, cut; solubilize; hold in solution; unclot, decoagulate; leach, lixiviate, percolate; **infuse,** decoct, steep, soak, brew

ADJS 6 **liquefied, melted, molten,** thawed; unclotted, decoagulated; in solution, in suspension, liquescent, deliquescent; colloidal

7 **liquefying,** liquefactive; colliquative, melting, fusing, thawing; **dissolving,** dissolutive, dissolutional

8 **solvent,** dissolvent, resolvent, resolutive, thinning, cutting, diluent; alkahestic

9 liquefiable; **meltable,** fusible, thawable; **soluble, dissolvable,** dissoluble; water-soluble

10 **solvents**

acetone	furfural
alcohol	gasoline
alkahest	glycerol
amyl alcohol	glycol
benzene	kerosene
benzine *or* benzol	methyl alcohol
carbolic acid	naphtha
carbon disulfide	pentane
carbon tetrachloride *or*	phenol
carbon tet <nf>	propylene glycol
chloroform	pyridine
denatured alcohol	toluene
ether	turpentine
ethyl acetate	urethane
ethyl chloride	xylene *or* xylol

1065 MOISTURE

NOUNS 1 **moisture,** damp, wet; **dampness, moistness,** moistiness, **wetness,** wettedness, wettishness, **wateriness,** humor *or* humectation <old>; soddenness, soppiness, soppingness, sogginess; swampiness, bogginess, marshiness; dewiness; mistiness, fogginess 319.4; raininess, pluviosity, showeriness; rainfall; exudation 190.6; secretion 13

2 **humidity,** humidness, **dankness,** dankishness, **mugginess,** closeness, stickiness, sweatiness; absolute humidity, relative humidity; dew point, saturation, saturation point; humidification

3 **water,** *aqua* <L>, *agua* <Sp>, *eau* <Fr>; Adam's ale *or* wine, H_2O; hydrol; hard water, soft water; heavy water; water supply, water system, waterworks; drinking water, tap water; rain water, rain 316; snowmelt, melt water; **groundwater,** underground water, subsurface water, subterranean water; water table, aquifer, artesian basin, artesian spring, sinkhole; spring water, well water; seawater, salt water; limewater; fresh water; standing water; mineral water *or* waters; soda water, carbonated water; steam, water vapor; hydrosphere; hydrometeor; head, hydrostatic head; hydrothermal water; distilled water; wetting agent, wetting-out agent, liquidizer, moisturizer; humidifier; bottled water, commercially bottled water, designer water <nf>; water cycle, hydrological cycle, evaporation, transpiration, precipitation, runoff, percolation

4 **dew, dewdrops,** dawn *or* morning dew, night dew, evening damp; fog drip, false dew; guttation; haze, mist, fog, cloud

5 **sprinkle, spray,** sparge, shower; spindrift, spume, froth, foam; **splash,** plash, swash, slosh; **splatter,** spatter

6 **wetting, moistening, dampening,** damping; humidification; dewing, bedewing; **watering, irrigation;** hosing, wetting *or* hosing down; **sprinkling, spraying,** spritzing <nf>, sparging, aspersion, aspergation; **splashing,** swashing, splattering, spattering; affusion, baptism; bath, bathing, rinsing, laving; **flooding,** drowning, inundation, deluge; **immersion, submersion** 367.2

7 **soaking,** soakage, soaking through, sopping, **drenching,** imbruement, sousing; ducking, dunking <nf>; soak, drench, souse; **saturation,** permeation; waterlogging; **steeping,** maceration, seething, infusion, brewing, imbuement; injection, impregnation; infiltration, percolation, leaching, lixiviation; pulping 1063.3

8 **sprinkler,** sparger, sparge, sprayer, speed sprayer, concentrate sprayer, mist concentrate sprayer, spray, spray can, atomizer, aerosol; nozzle; aspergil, aspergillum; **shower,** shower bath, shower head, needle bath; syringe, fountain syringe, douche, enema, clyster; sprinkling *or* watering can; water pistol *or* gun, squirt gun; lawn sprinkler; sprinkling system, sprinkler head; hydrant, irrigator

9 <sciences> hygrology, hygrometry, psychrometry, hydrography, hydrology; hydraulics; hydrotherapy, hydrotherapeutics, taking the waters

10 <instruments> hygrometer, hair hygrometer, hygrograph, hygrodeik, hygroscope, hygrothermograph; psychrometer, sling psychrometer; hydrostat; rain gauge *or* pluviometer; hydrograph; humidor; hygrostat

VERBS 11 be damp, not have a dry thread; **drip,** weep; **seep, ooze,** percolate; exude 190.15; sweat; secrete 13.5

12 **moisten, dampen,** moisturize, damp, **wet,** wet down; humidify, humect *or* humectate <old>; **water, irrigate;** dew, bedew; **sprinkle,** besprinkle, **spray,** spritz <nf>, sparge, asperge; bepiss; **splash,** dash, **swash, slosh, splatter, spatter,** bespatter; dabble, paddle; slop, slobber; hose, hose down; syringe, douche; sponge; dilute, adulterate

13 **soak, drench,** imbrue, **souse, sop,** sodden; **saturate,** permeate; **bathe,** lave, wash, rinse, douche, flush; water soak, waterlog; **steep,** seethe, macerate, infuse, imbue, brew, impregnate, inject, injest; infiltrate, percolate, leach, lixiviate

14 **flood,** float, **inundate, deluge,** turn to a lake *or* sea, swamp, whelm, overwhelm, drown; duck, dip,

dunk <nf>; **submerge** 367.7; sluice, pour on, flow on; rain 316.10

ADJS **15 moist,** moisty; **damp,** dampish; **wet,** wettish; undried, tacky; **humid, dank, muggy, sticky;** dewy, bedewed, roric *and* roriferous <old>; rainy 316.11; marshy, swampy, fenny, boggy

16 watery, waterish, **aqueous, aquatic;** liquid; **splashy,** plashy, sloppy, swashy <Brit>; hydrous, hydrated; hydraulic; moist; hydrodynamic, hydraulic

17 soaked, drenched, soused, bathed, steeped, macerated; **saturated,** permeated; **watersoaked, waterlogged; soaking, sopping; wringing wet,** soaking wet, sopping wet, wet to the skin, like a drowned rat; **sodden,** soppy, **soggy,** soaky; dripping, **dripping wet;** dribbling, seeping, weeping, oozing; flooded, overflowed, whelmed, swamped, engulfed, inundated, deluged, drowned, submerged, submersed, immersed, dipped, dunked <nf>; awash, weltering

18 wetting, dampening, moistening, watering, humectant; **drenching, soaking,** sopping; **irrigational,** irriguous <old>

19 hygric, hygrometric, hygroscopic, hygrophilous, hygrothermal

WORD ELEMENTS **20** hydr-, hydro-, hydrat-, hydrato-, aqui-, aqua-; hygr-, hygro-

1066 DRYNESS

NOUNS **1 dryness, aridness,** aridity, waterlessness, siccity; **drought;** juicelessness, saplessness; **thirst,** thirstiness, dehydration, xerostomia; corkiness; watertightness, watertight integrity; parchedness

2 <comparisons> desert, dust, bone, parchment, stick, mummy, biscuit, cracker

3 drying, desiccation, drying up, exsiccation; **dehydration,** anhydration; evaporation; air-drying; blow-drying; freeze-drying; insolation, sunning; drainage; withering, mummification; dehumidification; blotting

4 drier, desiccator, desiccative, siccative, exsiccative, exsiccator, **dehydrator,** dehydrant; dehumidifier; evaporator; hair-drier, blow-dryer; clothes dryer; tumbler-dryer; absorbent; clothesline

VERBS **5** thirst; drink up, soak up, sponge up; parch

6 dry, desiccate, exsiccate, dry up, **dehydrate,** anhydrate; evaporate; dehumidify; air-dry; drip-dry; dry off; insolate, sun, sun-dry; hang out to dry, air; spin-dry, tumbler-dry; blow-dry; freeze-dry; smoke, smoke-dry; cure; torrefy, burn, fire, kiln, **bake, parch,** scorch, sear; **wither, shrivel;** wizen, weazen; mummify; sponge, blot, soak up; **wipe,** rub, swab, brush; towel; drain 192.12; evaporate

ADJS **7 dry, arid; waterless,** unwatered, undamped, anhydrous; **bone-dry,** dry as dust, dry as a bone; like parchment, parched; droughty; juiceless, sapless; moistureless; **thirsty,** thirsting, athirst; high and dry; sandy, dusty; desert, Saharan

8 rainless, fine, fair, bright and fair, pleasant

9 dried, dehydrated, desiccated, dried-up, exsiccated; evaporated; squeezed dry; **parched, baked,** sunbaked, burnt, scorched, **seared,** sere, sun-dried, adust; wind-dried, air-dried; drip-dried; blow-dried; freeze-dried; **withered, shriveled,** wizened, weazened; corky; mummified

10 drying, dehydrating, desiccative, desiccant, exsiccative, exsiccant, siccative, siccant; evaporative

11 watertight, waterproof, moistureproof, dampproof, leakproof, seepproof, dripproof, stormproof, stormtight, rainproof, raintight, showerproof, floodproof; dry-shod

1067 VAPOR, GAS

NOUNS **1 vapor,** volatile; **fume, reek,** exhalation, breath, effluvium, expiration; fluid; **miasma,** mephitis, malaria <old>, fetid air, fumes; **smoke,** smudge; smog; wisp *or* plume *or* puff of smoke; **damp,** chokedamp, blackdamp, firedamp, afterdamp; **steam,** water vapor; **cloud** 319

2 gas <see list>; rare *or* noble *or* inert gas, halogen gas; fluid, compressible fluid; **atmosphere, air** 317; pneumatics, aerodynamics 1039.5

3 vaporousness, vaporiness; vapor pressure *or* tension; **aeriness; ethereality,** etherialism; **gaseousness,** gaseous state, gassiness, gaseity; **gas,** stomach gas, gassiness, flatulence, flatus, wind, windiness, farting <nf>, flatuosity <old>; burping; fluidity

4 volatility, vaporability, vaporizability, evaporability

5 vaporization, evaporation, volatilization, gasification; sublimation; distillation, fractionation; etherification; aeration, aerification; fluidization; atomization; exhalation; fumigation; smoking; steaming; etherealization; exhalation

6 vaporizer, evaporator; atomizer, aerosol, spray; propellant; condenser; still, retort

7 vaporimeter, manometer, pressure gauge; gas meter, gasometer; pneumatometer, spirometer; aerometer, airometer; eudiometer

VERBS **8 vaporize, evaporate,** volatilize, **gasify;** sublimate, sublime; distill, fractionate; etherify; **aerate,** aerify; carbonate, oxygenate, hydrogenate, chlorinate, halogenate, etc; atomize, spray; fluidize; **reek, fume;** exhale, give off, emit, send out, exhale; **smoke; steam;** fumigate, perfume; **etherize**

ADJS **9 vaporous,** vaporish, vapory, vaporlike; **airy, aerial, ethereal,** atmospheric; **gaseous,** in the gaseous state, gasified, gassy, gaslike, gasiform, fizzy, carbonated; vaporing; **reeking,** reeky; miasmic *or* miasmal *or* miasmatic, mephitic, fetid, effluvial; **fuming,** fumy; smoky, smoking, smoggy; steamy, steaming; ozonic; oxygenous; oxyacetylene; pneumatic, aerostatic, aerodynamic

10 volatile, volatilizable; **vaporable,** vaporizable, vaporescent, vaporific; **evaporative,** evaporable

WORD ELEMENTS **11** vapo-, vapori-, atm-, atmo-; aer-, aero-, mano-, pneum-, pneumo-, pneumat-, pneumato-

12 gases

acetylene *or* ethyne	ketene
air *or* producer gas	krypton
ammonia	lewisite
argon	liquid oxygen
avgas	marsh *or* swamp gas
biogas	mephitis
blister gas	methane
bottled gas	mustard gas
butane	natural gas
carbon dioxide	neon
carbon monoxide	nerve gas
carbonic-acid gas	nitric oxide
carbureted-hydrogen gas	nitrogen
chlorine	nitrogen dioxide
chlorofluorocarbon	nitrous oxide *or*
coal gas	laughing gas
damp	noble gas
ethane	oil gas
ether *or* ethyl ether	oxygen
ethyl chloride	ozone
ethylene *or* ethene *or*	phosgene *or* carbon
olefiant gas	oxychloride
ethylene oxide	phosphine
fluorocarbon	Pintsch gas
fluorine	poison gas
formaldehyde	propane
Freon <trademark>	propylene
helium	radon
hydrogen	refrigerator gas
hydrogen bromide	sewer gas
hydrogen chloride	sneeze gas
hydrogen cyanide	synthesis gas
hydrogen fluoride	tear gas *or* lachrymatory
hydrogen iodide	gas
hydrogen sulfide	vesicatory gas
ideal *or* perfect gas	vinyl chloride
illuminating gas	water *or* blue gas
inert gas	xenon

1068 BIOLOGY

NOUNS **1 biology** <see list>, biological science, life science, the science of life, the study of living things; **botany** <see list>, plant biology, phytobiology, phytology, plant science; **plant kingdom,** vegetable kingdom; **plants 310,** flora, plantlife; **zoology** <see list>, animal biology, animal science; **animal kingdom,** kingdom Animalia, phylum, class, order, family, genus, species; **animals 311,** fauna, animal life

2 biologist, naturalist, life scientist; **botanist,** plant scientist, plant biologist, phytobiologist, phytologist; **zoologist,** animal biologist, animal scientist <for other agent NOUNS add -ist *or* -er to names of branches listed>

3 life science; natural history, biological science; anatomy, biochemistry, biology, biophysics, botany, cell biology, embryology, ethnobiology, microbiology, paleontology, pathology, physiology, zoology; taxonomy, systematics; nanoscience

ADJS **4 biological,** biologic, microbiological; **botanical,** botanic, plant, phytological, phytologic, phytobiological; **zoological,** zoologic, faunal <for other ADJS add -ic *or* -ical to the names of branches listed>

5 branches of biology

aerobiology	electrophysiology
agrobiology	embryology
anatomy	enzymology
aquatic biology	ethnobiology
aquatic microbiology	eugenics
autoecology	evolution
bacteriology	exobiology *or* astrobiology
biobehavioral science	*or* bioastronautics *or*
biochemical genetics	space biology *or* space
biochemistry	bioscience *or* xenobiol-
biodynamics	ogy
bioecology	genetics
biogeography	gnotobiosis
biometry *or* biometrics *or*	histology
biostatistics	human ecology
bionics	hydrobiology
biophysics	hydrology *or* hydrogeology
biostatistics	*or* geohydrology
biotechnology *or* biotech	limnology
<nf>	marine biology
biothermodynamics	mathematical biology
biophysics	medicine
botany	microbiology
cell biology	molecular biology
cell physiology	morphology
chronobiology	natural classification
cryobiochemistry	natural history
cryobiology	neurobiology
cytogenetics	neurochemistry
cytology	neuroendocrinology
cytotaxonomy	neurogenetics
ecology *or* bioecology *or*	neuroscience
bionomics	organology
electrobiology	paleontology

palynology
parasitology
phylogenetic classification
   or phyletic classification
   or phyletics
physiology
population biology
population genetics
proteomics

radiobiology
sociobiology
somatology
synecology
taxonomy *or* systematics
virology
zoogeography *or* animal
   geography
zoology

6 branches of botany

agriculture
agrobiology
agronomy
algology
applied botany
aquiculture
bacteriology
botanical histochemistry
bryology
dendrology
economic botany
ethnobotany
evolution
floriculture
forestry
fungology
genetics
geobotany
gnotobiology
histology
horticulture
hydroponics
mycology
olericulture
paleobotany
palynology
phycology
physiology
phytobiology

phytochemistry
phytoecology
phytography
phytology
phytosociology
plant anatomy *or* phytot-
   omy
plant biochemistry *or*
   phytochemistry
plant breeding
plant cytology
plant ecology *or* phytoecology
plant geography *or*
   phytogeography
plant morphology
plant pathology *or*
   phytopathology *or*
   vegetable pathology
plant physiology *or*
   vegetable physiology
plant taxonomy
pomology
pteridology
research botany
seed biology
silviculture
systematic botany *or*
   taxonomy

7 branches of zoology

anatomy
animal behavior
animal chemistry *or*
   zoochemistry
animal pathology *or*
   zoopathology
animal physiology *or*
   zoonomy
animal psychology
apiculture
applied zoology
arachnology
behavioral ecology
biochemistry
biometrics
biophysics
comparative anatomy *or*
   zootomy
comparative embryology

comparative psychology
conchology
cytogenetics
cytology
ecology
embryology
endocrinology
entomology
ethology
evolution
genetics
helminthology
herpetology
histology
ichthyology
invertebrate zoology
malacology
mammalogy
marine biology

morphology
ophiology
ornithology
paleontology
parasitology
physiological chemistry
physiology
protozoology
research zoology

sociobiology
systematic zoology *or*
   systematics *or*
   taxonomy
vertebrate zoology
veterinary medicine
wildlife management
zoogeography
zoography

1069 AGRICULTURE

NOUNS 1 agriculture, farming <see list>, husbandry;
cultivation, culture, geoponics, tillage, tilth; green
revolution; agrology, agronomy, agronomics,
agrotechnology, agricultural science, agroscience,
agriscience; thremmatology; agroecosystem;
agrogeology, agricultural geology; agrochemistry;
agricultural engineering; agricultural economics;
rural economy *or* economics, farm economy *or*
economics, agrarian economy *or* economics,
agrarianism, agrarian society; agribusiness *or*
agrobusiness, agribiz <nf>, agroindustry;
sharecropping; intensive farming, factory
farming, mixed farming, crop farming, organic
farming, subsistence farming

2 horticulture, gardening; landscape gardening,
landscape architecture, groundskeeping; truck
gardening, market gardening, olericulture; flower
gardening, flower-growing, floriculture;
viniculture, viticulture; orcharding, fruit-growing,
pomiculture, citriculture; arboriculture,
silviculture; indoor gardening

3 forestry, arboriculture, tree farming, silviculture,
forest management; Christmas tree farming;
forestation, afforestation, reforestation;
lumbering, logging; deforestation; woodcraft

4 <agricultural deities> vegetation spirit *or* daemon,
fertility god *or* spirit, year-daemon, forest god *or*
spirit, green man, corn god, Ceres, Demeter, Gaea,
Triptolemus, Dionysus, Persephone, Kore, Flora,
Aristaeus, Pomona, Frey

5 agriculturist, agriculturalist; agrologist,
agronomist; **farmer,** granger, husbandman,
yeoman, cultivator, tiller, sodbuster, **tiller of the
soil;** rural economist, agrotechnician; boutique
farmer, contour farmer, crop-farmer, dirt farmer
<nf>, truck farmer, etc; gentleman-farmer;
peasant, *campesino* <Sp>, *Bauer* <Ger>,
countryman, rustic, **grower,** raiser; **planter,**
tea-planter, coffee-planter, etc; peasant holder *or*
proprietor, *kulak* and *muzhik* <Russ>; tenant
farmer, crofter <Brit>, peasant farmer;
sharecropper, cropper, collective farm worker,
kolkhoznik <Russ>, *kibbutznik* <Yiddish>;

agricultural worker, farm worker, farmhand, farm laborer, migrant *or* migratory worker *or* laborer, bracero, picker; plowman, plowboy; farmboy, farmgirl; planter, sower; reaper, harvester, harvestman; haymaker

6 **horticulturist, nurseryman, gardener,** grower, green thumb, propagator; landscape gardener, landscapist, landscape architect; truck gardener, market gardener, olericulturist; **florist,** floriculturist; vinegrower, viniculturist, viticulturist, vintager; *vigneron* <Fr>; vinedresser; orchardist, orchardman, fruitgrower

7 **forester;** arboriculturist, arborist, silviculturist, dendrologist, verderer, tree farmer, topiarist; conservationist; **ranger,** forest ranger, forest manager; woodsman, woodman <Brit>, woodcraftsman, woodlander; **logger, lumberman,** timberman, lumberjack, lumberer; woodcutter, wood chopper; tapper; tree surgeon

8 **farm,** farmplace, farmstead, farmhold <old>, farmery <Brit>, farmlet; **grange,** location <Austral>, pen <Jamaica>; boutique farm, crop farm, dirt farm, tree farm, etc; **plantation,** cotton plantation, etc, *hacienda* <Sp>; croft, homecroft <Brit>; **homestead,** steading; toft <Brit>; mains <Brit nf>; demesne, homefarm, demesne farm, manor farm; **barnyard,** farmyard, barton <Brit nf>; collective farm, *kolkhoz* <Russ>, *kibbutz* <Heb>; farmland, cropland, arable land, plowland, fallow; grassland, pasture 310.8

9 **field, tract,** plat, **plot, patch,** piece *or* parcel of land; cultivated land; clearing; hayfield, corn field, wheat field, etc; paddy, paddy field, rice paddy

10 **garden** <see list>, *jardin* <Fr>; bed, **flower bed,** border, ornamental border; paradise; garden spot; **vineyard,** vinery, grapery, grape ranch; herbarium; botanical garden; compost pile *or* heap, seed tray

11 **nursery; conservatory, greenhouse,** glasshouse <Brit>, forcing house, summerhouse, lathhouse, **hothouse,** coolhouse; potting shed; force *or* forcing bed, forcing pit, **hotbed,** cold frame; seedbed; cloche; pinery, orangery

12 **growing, raising,** rearing, cultivation; **green thumb**

13 **cultivation,** cultivating, culture, **tilling, dressing,** working; harrowing, plowing, contour plowing, furrowing, listing, fallowing, weeding, hoeing, pruning, thinning; overcropping, overcultivation; irrigation, overirrigation

14 **planting,** setting; **sowing, seeding,** semination, insemination; breeding, hydridizing; **dissemination,** broadcast, broadcasting; transplantation, resetting; retimbering, reforestation

15 **harvest,** harvesting, **reaping, gleaning,** gathering, cutting; nutting; cash crop, root crop, **crop** 472.5

VERBS 16 **farm, ranch,** work the land; **grow, raise,** rear; crop; dryfarm; sharecrop; **garden; have a green thumb**

17 **cultivate,** culture, **dress, work, till,** till the soil, dig, delve, spade; mulch; **plow,** plow in, plow under, plow up, list, fallow, backset <W US>, double-dig, rototill, fork; take cuttings, graft; irrigate; **harrow,** rake; **weed,** weed out, hoe, cut, prune, thin, thin out; force; overcrop, overcultivate; slash and burn; top-dress, compost, fertilize 890.8

18 **plant,** implant <old>, **set,** put in; **sow, seed,** seed down, seminate, inseminate; **disseminate,** broadcast, sow broadcast, scatter seed; drill; bed; dibble; transplant, reset, pot, **transplant;** vernalize; **forest,** afforest; deforest; retimber, reforest

19 **harvest, reap,** crop, **glean, gather,** gather in, bring in, get in the harvest, reap and carry; **pick,** pluck; dig, grabble <S US>; mow, cut; hay; nut; crop herbs

ADJS 20 **agricultural, agrarian,** agro-, geoponic, geoponical, agronomic, agronomical; farm, **farming;** arable; rustic, bucolic **rural** 233.6

21 **horticultural;** olericultural; vinicultural, viticultural; arboricultural, silvicultural

22 **types of farming**

boutique farming	livestock farming
contour farming	mixed farming
crop farming	organic farming
dirt farming <nf>	sharecropping
dry farming	share farming
dryland farming	slash-and-burn
factory farming	strip farming
fruit farming	stubble-mulch farming *or*
grain farming	trash farming
hydroponics *or* tank	subsistence farming
farming	tree farming
intensive farming	truck farming

23 **garden types**

allotment	flower bed
alpine garden	flower garden
antique garden	formal garden
apiary	fragrance garden
arboretum	French formal garden
beer garden	greenhouse
border garden	hanging garden
botanical garden *or*	heirloom garden
botanic garden	herb garden
bottle garden	herbarium
conservatory	home garden
cottage garden	hotbed
cutting garden	hothouse
dish garden	hydroponics
dry garden	indoor garden

Italian garden	roof garden
Japanese garden	rose garden
kitchen garden	sunken garden
knot garden	tea garden
market garden	terraced garden
maze garden	terrarium
nursery	truck garden
orchard	vegetable garden
organic garden	victory garden
ornamental garden	walled garden
physic garden	water garden
potager	winter garden
rock garden *or*	xeriscape
rockery	Zen garden

1070 ANIMAL HUSBANDRY

NOUNS **1 animal husbandry,** animal rearing *or* raising *or* culture, stock raising, **ranching;** zooculture, zootechnics, zootechny; thremmatology; gnotobiotics; herding, grazing, keeping flocks and herds, running livestock, livestock farming; transhumance; breeding, stockbreeding, stirpiculture; horse training, dressage, manÈge; horsemanship; pisciculture, fish culture; apiculture, bee culture, beekeeping; cattle raising; sheepherding; stock farming, fur farming; factory farming; pig-keeping; dairy-farming, chicken-farming, pig-farming, etc; cattle-ranching, mink-ranching, etc

2 stockman, stock raiser, stockkeeper <Austral>; breeder, stockbreeder; sheepman; cattleman, cow keeper, cowman, grazier <Brit>; **rancher,** ranchman, ranchero; ranchhand; dairyman, dairy farmer; milkmaid; **stableman,** stableboy, **groom,** hostler, equerry; trainer, breaker, tamer; broncobuster *and* buckaroo <nf>; **blacksmith,** horseshoer, farrier

3 herder, drover, herdsman, herdboy; **shepherd,** shepherdess, **sheepherder,** sheepman; goatherd; swineherd, pigman, pigherd, hogherd; gooseherd, gooseboy, goosegirl; swanherd; **cowherd,** neatherd <Brit>; cowboy, cowgirl, cowhand, puncher *and* **cowpuncher** *and* cowpoke <nf>, waddy <W US>, cowman, cattleman, vaquero <Sp>, gaucho; horseherd, **wrangler,** horse wrangler

4 apiarist, apiculturist, **beekeeper,** beeherd

5 farm, stock farm, animal farm; **ranch,** rancho, rancheria; station <Austral>; horse farm, stable, stud farm; **cattle ranch;** dude ranch; pig farm, piggery; chicken farm *or* ranch, turkey farm, duck farm, poultry farm; sheep farm *or* ranch; fur farm *or* ranch, mink farm *or* ranch; **dairy farm;** factory farm; animal enclosure

VERBS **6 raise, breed,** rear, grow, hatch, feed, nurture, fatten; keep, run; ranch, farm; culture; back-breed

7 tend; groom, rub down, brush, curry, currycomb; water, drench, feed, fodder; bed, bed down, litter; milk; harness, saddle, hitch, bridle, yoke; gentle, handle, manage; tame, train, break

8 drive, herd, drove <Brit>, herd up, punch cattle, **shepherd,** ride herd on; spur, goad, prick, lash, whip; wrangle, round up; corral, cage

1071 EARTH SCIENCE

NOUNS **1 earth science, earth sciences** <see list>; geoscience; geography, geology, rock hunting *and* rock hounding <nf>, geological science, oceanography, oceanographic science, meteorology, atmospheric science, planetary science, space science

2 earth scientist, geoscientist; **geologist,** rock hound *and* rock hunter <nf>, **geographer, oceanographer, astronomer,** star-gazer <nf>, **meteorologist,** weather man <for other agent NOUNS, add -ist *or* -er to names of branches listed below>

3 earth sciences

aerology	invertebrate paleontology
aeronomy	hydrology *or*
astrogeology	geohydrology *or*
bathymetry	hydrogeology
biogeography	lithostratigraphy
biostratigraphy	magnetostratigraphy
chronostratigraphy	marine geology
climatology	metamorphic petrology
crystallography	meteorology
economic geology	micropaleontology
engineering geology	mineralogy
environmental geology	mining geology
geoarchaeology *or*	oceanography
archaeological geology	oceanology
geobotanical prospecting	paleobiogeography
geobotany	paleobotany
geochemistry	paleoclimatology
geochronology	paleogeography
geochronometry	paleogeophysics
geocosmogony	paleolimnology
geodesy	paleomagnetism
geodynamics	paleontology
geography	paleopedology
geological cartography	palynology
geology	pedology *or* soil
geomagnetism	science
geomorphology	petrochemistry
geophysics	petrogenesis
geopolitics	petrography
geoscience	petroleum geology
glacial geology	petrology *or* lithology
glaciology	physical climatology
gravimetry	physical geography *or*
historical geology	physiography
hydrography	physical geology
igneous petrology	physical oceanography

planetology
plate *or* global tectonics
radiometric dating
sedimentary petrology
sedimentology
seismography
seismology
stratigraphy
structural geology
submarine geology

tectonic *or* geotectonic *or*
   structural geology
tectonics
tectonophysics
thalassography
topography
urban geology
vertebrate paleontology
volcanology *or*
   vulcanology

1072 THE UNIVERSE, ASTRONOMY

NOUNS **1 universe, world, cosmos,** cosmological model; creation, created universe, created nature, all, **all creation,** all tarnation <nf>, all *or* everything that is, all being, totality, totality of being, sum of things; omneity, allness; nature, system; wide world, whole wide world, "world without end"—Bible; plenum; **macrocosm,** macrocosmos, megacosm; metagalaxy; open universe, closed universe, inflationary universe, flat universe, oscillating universe, steady-state universe, expanding universe, pulsating universe; Einsteinian universe, Newtonian universe, Friedmann universe; Ptolemaic universe, Copernican universe; sidereal universe

2 the heavens, heaven, **sky, firmament;** empyrean, welkin, *caelum* <L>, lift *or* lifts <nf>; **the blue,** blue sky, azure, cerulean, the blue serene; **ether, air,** hyaline; vault, cope, canopy, vault *or* canopy of heaven, "that inverted bowl they call the sky"— Omar Khayyám, starry sphere, celestial sphere, starry heaven *or* heavens; Caelus

3 space, outer space, cosmic space, deep space, empty space, ether space, pressureless space, celestial spaces, interplanetary *or* interstellar *or* intergalactic *or* intercosmic space, metagalactic space, **the void,** the void above, ocean of emptiness; chaos; outermost reaches of space; astronomical unit, light-year, parsec; interstellar medium; close encounter

4 stars, fixed stars, starry host; music *or* harmony of the spheres; orb, sphere; **heavenly body,** celestial body *or* sphere; **comet; comet cloud; morning star,** daystar, Lucifer, Phosphor, Phosphorus; **evening star,** Vesper, Hesper, Hesperus, Venus; **North Star,** polestar, polar star, lodestar, Polaris; Dog Star, Sirius, Canicula; Bull's Eye, Aldebaran

5 constellation <see list>, **configuration,** asterism, stellar group, stellar population; zodiacal constellation; cluster, **star cluster,** galactic cluster, open cluster, globular cluster, stellar association, supercluster; Magellanic clouds

6 galaxy, island universe, galactic nebula; spiral galaxy *or* nebula, spiral; barred spiral galaxy *or* nebula, barred spiral; elliptical *or* spheroidal galaxy; disk galaxy; irregular galaxy; radio galaxy; lenticular galaxy; active galaxy; Seyfert galaxy, starburst galaxy; **the Local Group; the Galaxy, the Milky Way,** the galactic circle, *Via Lactea* <L>; galactic cluster, supergalaxy; great attractor; chaotic attractor; continent of galaxies, great wall *or* sheet of galaxies; galactic coordinates, galactic pole, galactic latitude, galactic longitude; galactic noise, cosmic noise; galactic nucleus, active galactic nucleus; cosmic string; Hubble classification

7 nebula, nebulosity; gaseous nebula; hydrogen cloud; dark nebula; dust cloud; dark matter; interstellar cloud; planetary nebula; whirlpool nebula; cirro-nebula; ring nebula; diffuse nebula; emission nebula; reflection nebula; absorption nebula; galactic nebula; anagalactic nebula; bright diffuse nebula; dark nebula, dark cloud, coalsack; Nebula of Lyra *or* Orion, Crab Nebula, the Coalsack, Black Magellanic Cloud; nebulous stars; nebular hypothesis

8 star <see list>; **quasar,** quasi-stellar radio source; **pulsar,** pulsating star, eclipsing binary X-ray pulsar; luminary; Nemesis, the Death Star; Hawking radiation; magnitude, stellar magnitude, visual magnitude; relative magnitude, absolute magnitude, apparent nebula; star *or* stellar populations; mass-luminosity law; spectrum-luminosity diagram, Hertzsprung-Russell diagram; star catalog, star atlas, star chart, sky atlas, sky survey, Messier catalog, Dreyer's New General Catalog *or* NGC; star cloud, star cluster, globular cluster, open cluster; Pleiades *or* Seven Sisters, Hyades, Beehive; stellar evolution, stellar birth, protostar, molecular cloud, main sequence, gravitational collapse, dying star, red giant, white dwarf; nova, supernova, supernova remnant, neutron star, pulsar, **black hole,** giant black hole, mini-black hole, starving black hole, supermassive black hole, frozen black hole, event horizon, singularity, white hole, active galactic nucleus

9 planet, wanderer, wandering star, terrestrial planet, inferior planet, superior planet, secondary planet, major planet; minor planet, planetoid, asteroid; asteroid belt; Earth; Jupiter; Mars, the Red Planet; Mercury; Neptune; Pluto; Saturn; Uranus; Venus; solar system; syzygy

10 Earth, planet Earth, third planet, the world, *terra* <L>; **globe,** terrestrial globe, Spaceship Earth, the blue planet; geosphere, biosphere, magnetosphere; vale, vale of tears; Mother Earth, Ge *or* Gaea *or* Gaia, Tellus *or* Terra; whole wide world, four corners of the earth, the length and breadth of the land

11 **moon, satellite,** natural satellite; orb of night, queen of heaven, queen of night; silvery moon; **new moon,** wet moon; **crescent moon,** crescent, increscent moon, increscent, waxing moon, waxing crescent moon, first quarter, last quarter; decrescent moon, decrescent, waning moon, waning crescent moon; gibbous moon; **half-moon,** demilune; **full moon, harvest moon,** hunter's moon; horned moon; **eclipse,** lunar eclipse, eclipse of the moon; artificial satellite 1075.6,14

12 <moon goddess, the moon personified> Diana, Phoebe, Cynthia, Artemis, Hecate, Selene, Luna, Astarte, Ashtoreth; man in the moon

13 **sun;** orb of day, daystar; sunshine, solar radiation, sunlight; solar disk; photosphere, chromosphere, corona; sunspot; sunspot cycle; solar flare, solar prominence; solar wind; **eclipse,** eclipse of the sun, solar eclipse, total eclipse, partial eclipse, central eclipse, annular eclipse; corona, solar corona, Baily's beads

14 <sun god *or* goddess, the sun personified> Sol, Helios, Hyperion, Titan, Phaëthon, Phoebus, Phoebus Apollo, Apollo, Ra *or* Amen-Ra, Shamash, Surya, Savitar, Amaterasu

15 **meteor;** falling *or* shooting star, meteoroid, fireball, bolide; **meteorite,** meteorolite; micrometeoroid, micrometeorite; aerolite; chondrite; siderite; siderolite; tektite; meteor dust, cosmic dust; meteor trail, meteor train; meteor swarm; meteor *or* meteoric shower; radiant, radiant point; meteor crater

16 **orbit, circle, trajectory;** circle of the sphere, great circle, small circle; **ecliptic; zodiac;** zone; meridian, celestial meridian; colures, equinoctial colure, solstitial colure; equator, celestial equator, equinoctial, equinoctial circle *or* line; equinox, vernal equinox, autumnal equinox; longitude, celestial longitude, geocentric longitude, heliocentric longitude, galactic longitude, astronomical longitude, geographic *or* geodetic longitude; apogee, perigee; aphelion, perihelion; period; revolution, eccentric inclination, rotation, rotational axis, rotational period; parabolic orbit, hyperbolic orbit

17 **observatory,** astronomical observatory; radio observatory, orbiting astronomical observatory *or* OAO, orbiting solar observatory *or* OSO; ground-based observatory, optical observatory, infrared observatory; **planetarium;** orrery; **telescope,** astronomical telescope; planisphere, astrolabe, flux collector; reflector, refractor, Newtonian telescope, Cassegrainian telescope; **radio telescope,** radar telescope; **spectroscope,** spectrograph; spectrohelioscope, spectroheliograph; coronagraph; heliostat, coelostat; **observation;** seeing, bright time, dark time

18 **cosmology,** cosmography, **cosmogony;** stellar cosmogeny, astrogony; cosmism, cosmic philosophy, cosmic evolution; nebular hypothesis; **big bang** *or* expanding universe theory, oscillating *or* pulsating universe theory, steady state *or* continuous creation theory, plasma theory; creationism, creation science

19 **astronomy, stargazing,** uranology, starwatching, astrognosy, astrography, uranography, uranometry; astrophotography, stellar photometry; spectrography, spectroscopy, radio astronomy, radar astronomy, X-ray astronomy; **astrophysics,** solar physics; celestial mechanics, gravitational astronomy; astrolithology; meteoritics; astrogeology; stellar statistics; astrochemistry, cosmochemistry; optical astronomy, observational astronomy; infrared astronomy, ultraviolet astronomy; exobiology, astrobotany

20 **astrology,** astromancy, **horoscopy;** astrodiagnosis; natural astrology; judicial *or* mundane astrology; genethliacism, genethlialogy, genethliacs, genethliac astrology; **horoscope,** nativity; zodiac, **signs of the zodiac; house,** mansion; house of life, mundane house, planetary house *or* mansion; aspect

21 **cosmologist;** cosmogenist, cosmogener; cosmographer, cosmographist; cosmic philosopher, cosmist

22 **astronomer,** stargazer, observer, uranologist, uranometrist, uranographer, uranographist, astrographer, astrophotographer; radio astronomer, radar astronomer; **astrophysicist,** solar physicist; astrogeologist; cosmochemist

23 **astrologer,** astrologian, astromancer, stargazer, Chaldean, astroalchemist, horoscoper, horoscopist, genethliac <old>

ADJS **24** **cosmic,** cosmical, **universal;** cosmologic *or* cosmological, cosmogonal, cosmogonic *or* cosmogonical; cosmographic, cosmographical

25 **celestial, heavenly, empyrean,** empyreal; uranic; **astral, starry, stellar,** stellary, sphery; star-spangled, star-studded; cometary; galactic, intergalactic, extragalactic; side-real; zodiacal; equinoctial; **astronomic** *or* **astronomical,** astrophysical, astrologic *or* astrological, astrologistic, astrologous; **planetary,** planetarian, planetal, circumplanetary; planetoidal, planetesimal, asteroidal; **solar,** heliacal; terrestrial; **lunar,** lunular, lunate, lunulate, lunary, cislunar, translunar, Cynthian; semilunar; meteoric, meteoritic; extragalactic, anagalactic; galactic; nebular, nebulous, nebulose; interstellar, intersidereal; interplanetary; intercosmic

26 extraterrestrial, exterrestrial, extraterrene, extramundane, alien, space; **transmundane, otherworldly,** transcendental; extrasolar

ADVS **27 universally,** everywhere

28 star types

A star
alpha
astral body
B star
beta
binary star
black dwarf
blaze star
blue-white giant
brown dwarf
C star *or* carbon star
Cepheid *or* Cepheid variable
circumpolar star
close binary star
comparison star
dark star
delta
double star
dwarf star
early-type star
eclipsing binary
eclipsing variable
eruptive variable
evening star
F star
fixed star
flare star
gamma
giant star
gravity star
Greenwich star
G star
hydrogen star
intrinsic variable
irregular star
K star

late-type star
long-period variable
M star
main sequence star
morning star
multiple star
N star
nautical star
nebulous star
neutron star
nova
O-type star
quasar
quasi-stellar radio source
R star
radio star
red dwarf
red giant
red supergiant
RR Lyrae star
runaway star
semiregular variable
silicon star
solar *or* sun star
spectroscopic binary
standard star
supermassive star
supernova
variable star
visible *or* visual binary
white dwarf
x-ray binary star
x-ray star
yellow dwarf
yellow giant
zenith star

29 constellations

Air Pump *or* Pump
Andromeda *or* the Chained Lady
Antlia *or* Antlia Pneumatica *or* the Air Pump
Apus *or* the Bird of Paradise
Aquarius *or* the Water Bearer
Aquila *or* the Eagle
Ara *or* the Altar
Argo *or* Argo Navis *or* the Ship Argo
Aries *or* the Ram
Auriga *or* the Charioteer

Big Dipper *or* Ursa Major *or* Charles' Wain
Bootes *or* the Herdsman
Caelum *or* Caela Sculptoris *or* the Sculptor's Tool *or* Chisel
Camelopardalis *or* Camelopardus *or* the Giraffe
Cancer *or* the Crab
Canes Venatici *or* the Hunting Dogs
Canis Major the Larger Dog *or* Orion's Hound
Canis Minor *or* the Lesser Dog
Capricorn *or* the Goat

Carina *or* the Keel
Cassiopeia *or* the Lady in the Chair
Centaurus *or* the Centaur
Cepheus *or* the Monarch
Cetus *or* the Whale
Chamaeleon *or* the Chameleon
Circinus *or* the Compasses
Columba *or* Columba Noae *or* Noah's Dove
Coma Berenices *or* Berenice's Hair
Corona Australis *or* the Wreath *or* the Southern Crown
Corona Borealis *or* the Northern Crown
Corvus *or* the Crow
Crater *or* the Cup
Crux *or* the Southern Cross
Cygnus *or* the Swan
Delphinus *or* the Dolphin
Dorado *or* Swordfish
Draco *or* the Dragon
Equuleus *or* the Foal
Eridanus *or* the River
Fornax *or* the Furnace
Gemini *or* the Twins
Grus *or* the Crane
Hercules
Horologium *or* the Clock
Hydra *or* the Sea Serpent
Hydrus *or* the Water Snake
Indus *or* the Indian
Lacerta *or* the Lizard
Leo *or* the Lion
Leo Minor *or* the Lesser Lion
Lepus *or* the Hare
Libra *or* the Balance
Little Dipper *or* Ursa Minor
Lupus *or* the Wolf
Lynx *or* the Lynx
Lyra *or* the Lyre
Malus *or* the Mast
Mensa *or* the Table
Microscopium *or* the Microscope
Monoceros *or* the Unicorn

Musca *or* the Fly
Norma *or* the Rule
Northern Cross
Octans *or* the Octant
Ophiuchus *or* the Serpent Bearer
Orion *or* the Giant Hunter
Orion's Belt
Orion's Sword
Pavo *or* the Peacock
Pegasus *or* the Winged Horse
Perseus
Phoenix
Pictor *or* the Painter
Pisces *or* the Fishes
Piscis Australis *or* the Southern Fish
Puppis *or* the Stern
Pyxis *or* Mariner's Compass
Reticulum *or* the Net
Sagitta *or* the Arrow
Sagittarius *or* the Archer
Scorpio *or* Scorpius *or* the Scorpion
Sculptor
Scutum *or* the Shield
Serpens *or* the Serpent
Sextans *or* the Sextant
Southern Cross
Taurus *or* the Bull
Telescopium *or* the Telescope
Triangulum *or* the Triangle
Triangulum Australe *or* the Southern Triangle
Tucana *or* the Toucan
Ursa Major *or* the Great Bear *or* the Big Dipper
Ursa Minor *or* the Lesser Bear *or* the Little Dipper
Vela *or* the Sails
Virgo *or* the Virgin *or* Maiden
Volans *or* Piscis Volans *or* the Flying Fish
Vulpecula *or* the Little Fox

30 signs of the zodiac

Capricorn the Goat <Dec 23–Jan 19>
Aquarius the Water Carrier <Jan 20–Feb 19>
Pisces the Fishes <Feb 20–Mar 21>
Aries the Ram <Mar 22–Apr 20>

Taurus the Bull <Apr 21–May 21>
Gemini the Twins <May 22–June 22>
Cancer the Crab <June 23–July 23>
Leo the Lion <July 24–Aug 23>

Virgo the Virgin <Aug 24–Sept 23>

Libra the Scales or the Balance <Sept 24–Oct 23>

Scorpio the Scorpion <Oct 24–Nov 22>

Sagittarius the Archer <Nov 23–Dec22>

1073 THE ENVIRONMENT

NOUNS **1 the environment,** the natural world, the ecology, global ecology, ecosystem, global ecosystem, the biosphere, the ecosphere, the balance of nature, macroecology, microecology; **ecology,** bioregion; **environmental protection,** environmental policy; **environmental control,** environmental management; environmental assessment, environmental auditing, environmental monitoring, environmental impact analysis; emission control; **environmental science** <see list>, environmentology

2 environmental destruction, ecocide, ecocatastrophe; environmental pollution, pollution, contamination; **air pollution,** atmospheric pollution, air quality; **water pollution,** stream pollution, lake pollution, ocean pollution, groundwater pollution, pollution of the aquifer; **environmental pollutant** <see list>; eutrophication; **biodegradation,** biodeterioration, microbial degradation

3 environmentalist, conservationist, preservationist, nature-lover, environmental activist, doomwatcher <Brit>, duck-squeezer *and* ecofreak *and* tree-hugger *and* eagle freak <nf>; Green Panther

4 environmental sciences

autecology	environmental
bioecology *or* bionomics	horticulture
ecology	environmental
environmental archaeology	management
environmental biology	environmental toxicology
environmental chemistry	human ecology
environmental design	land management
environmental engineering	synecology
environmental geology	wildlife management
environmental health	zoo-ecology

5 environmental pollutants

acid rain	carbon tetrachloride
aerosol sprays	carcinogens
aircraft noise	chemical waste
asbestos	chlordane
automobile exhaust	chlorine
azo compounds	chlorobenzenes
benzene	chloroethanes
beryllium	chlorofluorocarbons *or*
calcium carbonates	CFCs
carbon dioxide	chlorohydrocarbons
carbon monoxide	chloromethane

chlorophenol	leaded gasoline
chloropropanones	leptophos
chlorpropham	malathion
chromium	mercury
coal smoke	metalaxyl
dibromochloropropane *or*	methyl ethyl ketone
DBCP	methyl parathion
dichlorides	mining waste
dichloroacetate	mirex
dichlorobenzenes	nabam
dichlorodiphenyltrichloro-	naphthalene
ethane *or* DDT	nitro compounds
dichloroethanes	nitrogen oxides
dichlorophenol	nitroso compounds
dichloropropane	noise
dioxins	nuclear waste
endosulfan	paraquat dichloride
endrin	parathion
ethanes	pentachloraphenol *or* PCP
ethylene	pesticides
ethylene dibromide *or* EDB	phosphate
ethylene glycol	polybrominated biphenyls
ethylene oxide	*or* PBBs
exhaust fumes	polychlorinated biphenyls
fenoxaprop ethyl	*or* PCBs
fluorenes	radon
fluorocarbons	radionuclides
fluorohydrocarbons	secondhand smoke
formaldehyde	sewage
fungicides	smog
gasoline	smoke
halon	solid waste
heptachlor	sulfur oxides
herbicides	sulfuric acid
hexachlorethane	tobacco smoke
hexone	toxaphene
hydrocarbons	toxic waste
hydrochlorofluorocarbon	trichloroacetic acid
or HCFC	trichlorobenzene
industrial particulate	trichloroethylene *or* TCE
matter	trimethylbenzenes
isocyanuric acid	triphenyltin hydroxide *or*
kepone	DuTer <trademark>
lead	ultraviolet radiation
lead paint	vinyl chloride

1074 ROCKETRY, MISSILERY

NOUNS **1 rocketry,** rocket science *or* engineering *or* research *or* technology; **missilery,** missile science *or* engineering *or* research *or* technology; rocket *or* missile testing; ground test, firing test, static firing; rocket *or* missile project *or* program; instrumentation; telemetry

2 rocket, rocket engine *or* **motor,** reaction engine *or* motor; rocket thruster, thruster; retrorocket; rocket exhaust; plasma jet, plasma engine; ion engine; jetavator

3 **rocket, missile** <see list>, **ballistic missile, guided missile; torpedo;** projectile rocket, ordnance rocket, combat *or* military *or* war rocket; bird <nf>; **payload; warhead,** nuclear *or* thermonuclear warhead, atomic warhead; multiple *or* multiple-missile warhead

4 **rocket bomb,** flying bomb *or* torpedo, cruising missile; **robot bomb,** robomb, *Vergeltungswaffe* <Ger>, V-weapon, P-plane; **buzzbomb,** bumblebomb, doodle-bug

5 **multistage rocket, step rocket;** two- *or* three-stage rocket, two- *or* three-step rocket; single-stage rocket, single-step rocket, one-step rocket; **booster,** booster unit, booster rocket, takeoff booster *or* rocket; piggyback rocket

6 **test rocket,** research rocket, high-altitude research rocket, registering rocket, instrument rocket, instrument carrier, test instrument vehicle, rocket laboratory; probe

7 **proving ground,** testing ground; firing area; impact area; control center, mission control, bunker; radar tracking station, tracking station, visual tracking station; meteorological tower

8 **rocket propulsion,** reaction propulsion, jet propulsion, blast propulsion; **fuel, propellant,** solid fuel, liquid fuel, hydrazine, liquid oxygen *or* lox; charge, propelling *or* propulsion charge, powder charge *or* grain, high-explosive charge; **thrust,** constant thrust; **exhaust,** jet blast, backflash

9 **rocket launching** *or* **firing,** ignition, launch, shot, shoot; countdown; **lift-off,** blast-off; guided *or* automatic control, programming; flight, trajectory; **burn; burnout,** end of burning; velocity peak, *Brennschluss* <Ger>; altitude peak, ceiling; descent; airburst; impact

10 **rocket launcher,** projector; **launching** *or* **launch pad,** launching platform *or* rack, firing table; **silo;** takeoff ramp; tower projector, launching tower; launching mortar, launching tube, projector tube, firing tube; rocket gun, bazooka, antitank rocket, *Panzerfaust* <Ger>; superbazooka; multiple projector, calliope, Stalin organ, Katusha; antisubmarine projector, Mark 10, hedgehog <nf>; Minnie Mouse launcher, mousetrap <nf>; Meilewagen

11 rocket scientist *or* technician, rocketeer *or* rocketer, rocket *or* missile man, rocket *or* missile engineer

VERBS **12** **rocket, skyrocket**

13 launch, project, **shoot, fire,** blast off; abort

14 **rockets, missiles**

AAM *or* air-to-air missile
AA target rocket
ABM *or* antiballistic missile
airborne rocket
anchor rocket
antiaircraft rocket
antimine rocket
antimissile
antiradar rocket
antisubmarine *or* antisub rocket
antitank rocket
ASM *or* air-to-surface missile
ATA missile *or* air-to-air
ATG rocket *or* air-to-ground
atom-rocket
ATS *or* air-to-ship
AUM *or* air-to-underwater missile
barrage rocket
bat bomb
bazooka rocket
bombardment rocket
booster
chemical rocket
combat high-explosive rocket
Congreve rocket
countermissile
demolition rocket
fin-stabilized rocket
fireworks rocket
flare rocket
flying tank
GAPA *or* ground-to-air pilotless aircraft
glide bomb
GTA rocket *or* ground-to-air
GTG rocket *or* ground-to-ground
guided missile
harpoon rocket
high-altitude rocket
homing rocket
HVAR *or* high velocity aircraft rocket
ICBM *or* intercontinental ballistic missile
incendiary antiaircraft rocket
incendiary rocket
ion rocket
IRBM *or* intermediate range ballistic missile
launch vehicle *or* launcher
line-throwing rocket
liquid-fuel rocket
long-range rocket
MIRV *or* multiple independently targetable re-entry vehicle
MRV *or* multiple re-entry vehicle
multistage rocket
ram rocket
retro-float light
retrorocket
rockoon
SAM *or* surface-to-air missile
scud
signal rocket
skyrocket
smart rocket
smokeless powder rocket
smoke rocket
snake *or* antimine
solid-fuel rocket
solid rocket booster *or* SRB
space rocket
spinner
spin-stabilized rocket
SSM *or* surface-to-surface missile
STS rocket *or* ship-to-shore
submarine killer
supersonic rocket
target missile
torpedo rocket
training rocket *or* missile
trajectory missile
transoceanic rocket
ullage rocket
vernier *or* vernier rocket
window rocket *or* antiradar
winged rocket
XAAM *or* experimental air-to-air missile
XASM *or* experimental air-to-surface missile
XAUM *or* experimental air-to-underwater missile
XSAM *or* experimental surface-to-air missile
XSSM *or* experimental surface-to-surface missile

1075 SPACE TRAVEL

NOUNS **1 space travel, astronautics,** cosmonautics, **space flight,** navigation of empty space; interplanetary travel, space exploration; manned flight; space walk; space navigation, astrogation; **space science,** space technology *or* engineering; **aerospace science,** aerospace technology *or* engineering; space *or* aerospace research; space *or* aerospace medicine, bioastronautics; astrionics; escape velocity; rocketry 1074; multistage flight, step flight, shuttle flights; trip to the moon, trip to Mars, grand tour; space terminal, target planet; space age; space tourism, astrotourism

2 spacecraft <see list>, **spaceship, space rocket,** rocket ship, manned rocket, interplanetary rocket; rocket 1074.2; orbiter; **shuttle,** space shuttle; **capsule, space capsule,** ballistic capsule; **nose cone, heat shield,** heat barrier, thermal barrier; module, command module, lunar excursion module *or* LEM, lunar module *or* LM; moon ship, Mars ship, etc; deep-space ship; exploratory ship, reconnaissance rocket; ferry rocket, tender rocket, tanker ship, fuel ship; **multistage rocket** 1074.5, shuttle rocket, retrorocket, rocket thruster *or* thruster, attitude-control rocket, main rocket; **burn;** space docking, docking, docking maneuver; **orbit,** parking orbit, geostationary orbit; earth orbit, apogee, perigee; lunar *or* moon orbit, apolune, perilune, apocynthion, pericynthion; **guidance system,** terrestrial guidance; soft landing, hard landing; injection, insertion, lunar insertion, Earth insertion; **reentry, splashdown**

3 flying saucer, unidentified flying object *or* UFO; foo fighter

4 rocket engine 1074.2; atomic power plant; solar battery; power cell

5 space station, astro station, **space island,** island base, cosmic stepping-stone, halfway station, advance base; manned station; inner station, outer station, transit station, space airport, **spaceport,** spaceport station, space platform, space dock, launching base, research station, space laboratory, space observatory; tracking station, radar tracking station; radar station, radio station; radio relay station, radio mirror; space mirror, solar mirror; moon station, moon base, lunar base, lunar city, observatory on the moon

6 artificial satellite <see list>, **satellite,** space satellite, robot satellite, unmanned satellite, sputnik; communications satellite, active communications satellite, communications relay satellite, weather satellite, earth satellite, astronomical satellite, meteorological satellite, geostationary satellite, geosynchronous satellite, spy satellite, orbiting observatory, space observatory, geophysical satellite, navigational satellite, geodetic satellite, research satellite, interplanetary monitoring satellite, automated satellite; **probe, space probe,** geo probe, interplanetary explorer, planetary probe; orbiter, lander

7 <satellite telemetered recorders> micro-instrumentation; aurora particle counter, cosmic ray counter, gamma ray counter, heavy particle counter, impulse recorder, magnetometer, solar ultraviolet detector, solar X-ray detector, telecamera

8 astronaut, astronavigator, cosmonaut, **spaceman, spacewoman,** space crew member, shuttle crew member, space traveler, rocketeer, rocket pilot; space doctor; space crew; planetary colony, lunar colony; extraterrestrial visitor, alien, saucerman, man from Mars, Martian, little green man; close encounter

9 rocketry, rocket propulsion; burn, thrust, escape velocity, orbit, parking orbit, transfer orbit, insertion, injection, trajectory, flyby, rendezvous, docking, reentry, splashdown, soft landing, hard landing; launch vehicle, multistage rocket, payload, retrorocket, solid rocket booster, engine, booster, propellant, liquid fuel, solid fuel; **rocket society,** American Rocket Society, American Interplanetary Society, British Interplanetary Society

10 <space hazards> cosmic particles, intergalactic matter, aurora particles, radiation, cosmic ray bombardment; rocket *or* satellite debris, space junk <nf>; meteors, meteorites; asteroids; meteor dust impacts, meteoric particles, space bullets; extreme temperatures; the bends, blackout, weightlessness

11 space suit, pressure suit, G suit, anti-G suit; space helmet

VERBS **12** travel in space, go into outer space; launch, lift off, blast off, enter orbit, orbit the earth, go into orbit, orbit the moon, etc; navigate in space, astrogate; escape earth, break free, leave the atmosphere, shoot into space; rocket to the moon, park in space, hang *or* float in space, space-walk

ADJS **13 astronautical,** cosmonautical, spacetraveling, spacefaring; astrogational; rocketborne, spaceborne; extravehicular

14 spacecraft, artificial satellites, space probes

A-1
Alouette
Anik
Anna
Apollo
Ariane
Ariel
Astro
ATDA
Atlas-Score
ATS
Aurora 7 <Mercury>
Biosatellite
Cassini
communications satellites
 or comsats
Comsat
Copernicus
cosmic background
 explorer or COBE
Cosmos
Courier
D1-C
D2-D
Deep Space
Diapason
Discoverer
Early Bird
Echo

Einstein
Elektron
ERS
ESSA or environmental
 survey satellite
Explorer
Explorer 760
Faith 7 <Mercury>
FR-1
Freedom 7 <Mercury>
Friendship 7 <Mercury>
Galileo
GATV
Gemini
Geostationary Operational
 Environmental Satellite
 or GOES
Greb
Hubble Space Telescope
Injun
Intelsat
killersat
Lageos or laser geody-
 namic satellite
Lani Bird
Liberty Bell 7 <Mercury>
Lofti
Luna
Lunar Orbiter

Lunar Prospector
Lunik
Mariner
Mars Global Surveyor
Mars Pathfinder
Mars Sojourner
Mars Surveyor
Mercury
Midas
MIR
Molniya
Nimbus
OAO or orbiting astronom-
 ical observatory
OGO or orbiting geophysi-
 cal observatory
orbiter
OSO or orbiting solar
 observatory
OV1
OV3
Pageos
Pegasus
Pioneer
Polyot
probe
Proton
Ranger
Relay
ROSAT

Samos
San Marco
Secor
Sigma 7 <Mercury>
Skylab
Solar Max
Soyuz
Spacelab
space shuttle or
 shuttle
space station
Spartan
Sputnik
Stardust
Surveyor
Syncom
Tardis
Telstar
TIROS or television and
 infrared observation
 satellite
Transit
Ulysses
Vanguard
Venera
Viking
Voskhod
Vostok
WRESAT
Zondd

Index

How to Use This Index

Numbers after index entries refer to categories and paragraphs in the front section of this book, not to page numbers. The part of the number before the decimal point refers to the category in which you will find synonyms and related words for the word you are looking up. The part of the number after the decimal point refers to the paragraph or paragraphs within the category. Look at the index entry for **abdomen** on the next page:

abdomen 2.18

This entry listing tells you that you can find words related to **abdomen** in paragraph 18 of category 2.

Words, of course, frequently have more than one meaning. Each of those meanings may have synonyms or associated related words. Look at the entry for **abhor**:

abhor dislike 99.3
hate 103.5

This tells you that you will find synonyms for **abhor** in the sense meaning "dislike" in category 99, paragraph 3. It also tells you that you will find synonyms for **abhor**, meaning "hate," in category 103, paragraph 5.

In many cases, words are spelled the same as nouns, verbs, adjectives, etc. Look at the entry for **abandon** and notice that here you are directed to **abandon** when it is used as a noun and when it is used as a verb in a variety of meanings. Here, as in the examples above, you are referred to the category and paragraph number.

Not all words in the main part of the book are included in the index. Many adverbs ending with **-ly** have been left out of the index, but you will find the common adverbs ending in **-ly** here, such as **lightly** or **easily**. If you can't find the adverb ending in -**ly** that you are looking for, look up the word in its adjective form and go to that category. Frequently, you can use the words in the adjective paragraphs you find and convert them into the adverb you are looking for by simply adding **-ly** to the adjective.

To make it easier to find phrases, they are indexed according to the first word of the phrase, unless that first word is an article such as **a**, **the**, or **an**. You do not have to guess what the main word of the phrase is to find it in the index. Simply look up the first word in the phrase. For example, **hot air** will be found in the Hs, **fat cat** in the Fs, and **let go** in the Ls.

A-1 important 997.17
  perfect 1002.6
abaft aft 182.69
  after 217.14
abandon
  n zeal 101.2
  fury 105.8
  carelessness 340.2
  unrestraint 430.3
  turpitude 654.5
  excess 993.1
  v quit 188.9
  leave undone 340.7
  desert 370.5
  break the habit 374.3
  discard 390.7
  surrender 433.8
  disregard 435.3
  relinquish 475.3
  swear off 668.8
  cease 857.6
  dismiss 984.4
abandoned
  zealous 101.9
  frenzied 105.25
  available 222.15
  neglected 340.14
  forsaken 370.8
  disused 390.10
  unrestrained 430.24
  relinquished 475.5
  forlorn 584.12
  outcast 586.10
  corrupt 654.14
  profligate 665.25
  excessive 993.16
abase debase 137.5
  demote 447.3
abashed
  distressed 96.22
  humiliated 137.14
  bewildered 971.24
abate weaken 16.10
  relieve 120.5
  decrease 252.6
  bate 252.8
  subtract 255.9
  discount 631.2
  moderate 670.6
  relax 670.9
  qualify 959.3
abatement
  weakening 16.5
  relief 120.1
  decrease 252.1
  discount 631.1
  modulation 670.2
abattoir 308.12
abbé 699.2
abbess
  mistress 575.2
  nun 699.17
abbey 703.6
abbot 699.16
abbreviate
  delete 255.12
  contract 260.7
  shorten 268.6
  be brief 537.5
abbreviated
  short 268.8

shortened 268.9
  concise 537.6
abbreviation
  deletion 255.5
  contraction 260.1
  shortening 268.3
  shortening 537.4
  abridgment 557.1
ABC's
  writing system 546.3
  elementary education 568.5
  basics 818.6
abdicate give up 370.7
  cease to use 390.4
  resign 448.2
abdication 475.1
abdomen 2.18
abdominal 2.31
abduct seize 480.14
  abduce 482.20
abduction
  seizure 480.2
  kidnapping 482.9
abductor 483.10
abeam 218.11
abed 20.11
Abélard and Héloïse 104.17
aberrant
  deviative 164.7
  wrong 638.3
  changed 852.10
  abnormal 870.9
  erroneous 975.16
aberration
  deviation 164.1
  divergence 171.1
  obliquity 204.1
  abnormality 870.1
  insanity 926.1
  eccentricity 927.1
  error 975.1
abet advance 162.5
  encourage 375.21
  aid 449.11
  encourage 449.14
abettor
  prompter 375.10
  accomplice 616.3
  supporter 616.9
abeyance
  inertness 173.4
  discontinuance 390.2
  pause 857.3
abhor dislike 99.3
  hate 103.5
abhorrent
  offensive 98.18
  unlikable 99.7
  hating 103.7
abide await 130.8
  endure 134.5
  inhabit 225.7
  live on 761.9
  endure 827.6
  wait 846.12
  remain 853.5
  continue 856.3
abide by
  assent 332.8
  observe 434.2
  execute 437.9

abide in 761.11
abiding
  n habitation 225.1
  adj resident 225.13
  durable 827.10
  permanent 853.7
  continuing 856.7
ability
  capability 18.2
  means 384.2
  preparedness 405.4
  skill 413.1
  talent 413.4
abject penitent 113.9
  humblehearted 137.11
  obsequious 138.14
  submissive 433.12
  base 661.12
abjure
  n recant 363.8
  v deny 335.4
  give up 370.7
  reject 372.2
  cease to use 390.4
  relinquish 475.3
ablate decrease 252.6
  consume 388.3
  wear 393.20
  waste 473.5
  disintegrate 806.3
  abrade 1044.7
ablaze fervent 93.18
  burning 1019.27
  flashing 1025.35
  illuminated 1025.40
able
  capable 18.14
  fitted 405.17
  competent 413.24
  possible 966.6
able-bodied 15.16
abloom floral 310.38
  ripe 407.13
  gorgeous 1016.20
ablution 79.5
ably capably 18.16
  skillfully 413.31
abnormal wrong 638.3
  inconsistent 789.8
  unnatural 870.9
  insane 926.26
  eccentric 927.5
abnormality
  disease 85.1
  wrong 638.1
  unfitness 789.3
  unnaturalness 870.1
  fluke 870.1
  oddity 870.5
  insanity 926.1
  eccentricity 927.1
aboard here 159.23
  on board 182.62
abode location 159.1
  habitation 225.1
  dwelling 228
  living place 228.1
abolish nullify 395.13
  repeal 445.2
abolition
  extinction 395.6

repeal 445.1
A-bomb 1038.16
abominable
  offensive 98.18
  wrong 638.3
  wicked 654.16
  base 661.12
  terrible 1000.9
abominate 103.5
abomination
  defilement 80.4
  hostility 99.2
  hate 103.1
  hated thing 103.3
  horror 638.2
  iniquity 654.3
  evil 1000.3
aborigine native 227.3
  ancient 842.7
abort miscarry 410.15
  end 820.5
  cease 857.6
  launch 1074.13
abortion
  miscarriage 410.5
  monstrosity 870.6
  unproductiveness 891.1
abortive
  fruitless 391.12
  unsuccessful 410.18
abound
  teem with 884.5
  exuberate 991.5
about
  adv around 209.12
  near 223.20
  approximately 244.6
  prep around 223.26
  in relation to 775.13
about-face
  n reverse 163.3
  denial 335.2
  switch 363.1
  change 852.1
  conversion 858.1
  reversion 859.1
  v regress 163.10
  change 852.7
about to
  adj prepared 405.16
  prep at the point of 839.13
above
  adj superior 249.12
  higher 272.19
  previous 834.4
  adv additionally 253.11
  on high 272.21
  before 814.6
  prep on 295.37
  beyond 522.26
  in excess of 993.26
above all 249.17
above all that 141.12
above and beyond 993.26
aboveboard
  adj straight 644.14
  adv openly 348.15
above it all 94.13
above suspicion 657.8
above water
  unindebted 624.23

in safety 1007.6
ab ovo
  adj essential 767.9
  adv first 818.18
  newly 841.15
abracadabra 691.4
abrade subtract 255.9
  grind 287.8
  injure 393.13
  wear 393.20
  abrase 1044.7
  pulverize 1051.9
abrasion trauma 85.38
  subtraction 255.1
  roughness 288.1
  attrition 1044.2
  pulverization 1051.4
abrasive
  n cleanser 79.17
  smoother 287.4
  abrasion 1044.2
  pulverizer 1051.7
  adj unpleasant 98.17
  out of humor 110.17
  rugged 288.7
  abradant 1044.10
abreast
  in parallel 203.7
  beside 218.11
  informed 928.18
abridge reduce 252.7
  delete 255.12
  abbreviate 268.6
  take from 480.21
  shorten 557.5
abridged
  shortened 268.9
  concise 537.6
  condensed 557.6
  mutilated 795.5
abridgment
  decrease 252.1
  deletion 255.5
  shortening 268.3
  deprivation 480.6
  aphorism 537.3
  compendium 557.1
abroad
  adj nonresident 222.12
  bewildered 971.24
  erroneous 975.16
  adv extensively 158.12
  outdoors 206.11
  far and wide 261.16
  wide 261.19
  in foreign parts 774.6
abrogate
  abolish 395.13
  repeal 445.2
abrupt steep 204.18
  blunt 286.3
  precipitate 401.10
  commanding 420.13
  gruff 505.7
  sudden 830.5
abruptly short 268.13
  precipitately 401.15
  gruffly 505.9
abscess
  symptom 85.9
  sore 85.37

abscissa 300.5
abscond quit 188.9
  flee 368.10
absconded 222.11
absconder 368.5
absence
  nonpresence 222.1
  nonattendance 222.4
  nonexistence 762.1
  want 992.4
absent
  adj not present 222.11
  abstracted 985.11
  prep lacking 222.19
  excluding 773.10
  without 992.17
  conj unless 959.16
absentee 222.5
absentee ballot vote 371.6
  ballot 609.19
absentminded
  abstracted 985.11
  forgetful 990.9
absolute
  omnipotent 18.13
  downright 247.12
  affirmative 334.8
  authoritative 417.15
  imperious 417.16
  mandatory 420.12
  unrestricted 430.27
  governmental 612.16
  musical 708.47
  real 761.15
  thorough 794.10
  unmixed 798.7
  particular 865.12
  sole 872.9
  convincing 953.26
  evidential 957.16
  unqualified 960.2
  certain 970.13
  obvious 970.15
  accurate 973.16
  perfect 1002.6
absolutely
  adv extremely 247.22
  affirmatively 334.10
  really 761.16
  fully 794.15
  certainly 970.23
  exactly 973.21
  perfectly 1002.10
  interj yes 332.18
absolute monarch 575.8
absoluteness 1002.1
absolve
  forgive 148.3
  exempt 430.14
  acquit 601.4
  declare a moratorium 625.9
  confess 701.18
absorb digest 7.18
  adsorb 187.13
  consume 388.3
  understand 521.7
  acquire 570.7
  corner 737.26
  involve 898.2
  occupy the thoughts 931.20
  engross 983.13

absorbed
  engrossed in thought 931.22
  occupied 983.17
  abstracted 985.11
absorbent
  n sorption 187.6
  drier 1066.4
  adj sorbent 187.17
absorbing
  deep-felt 93.24
  engrossing 983.20
absorption
  body function 2.17
  digestion 7.8
  sorption 187.6
  permeation 221.3
  consumption 388.1
  ingestion 570.2
  involvement 898.1
  thoughtfulness 931.3
  engrossment 983.3
  abstractedness 985.2
absquatulation
  absence 222.4
  flight 368.4
abstain refrain 329.3
  not use 390.5
  remain neutral 467.5
  deny oneself 667.3
  abstain from 668.7
abstainer ascetic 667.2
  abstinent 668.4
abstemious
  continent 664.6
  abstinent 668.10
  meager 992.10
abstention disuse 390.1
  neutrality 467.1
  abstinence 668.2
abstinence disuse 390.1
  fasting 515.1
  continence 664.3
  asceticism 667.1
  refraining 668.2
  moderation 670.1
abstract
  n shortening 268.3
  abridgment 557.1
  picture 712.10
  abstract idea 932.3
  v subtract 255.9
  shorten 268.6
  steal 482.13
  eliminate 773.5
  adj recondite 522.16
  general 864.11
  theoretical 951.13
abstracted shortened 268.9
  absorbed in thought 931.22
  bemused 985.11
abstraction subtraction 255.1
  theft 482.1
  picture 712.10
  separation 802.1
  generalization 864.8
  thoughtfulness 931.3
  abstract idea 932.3
  theory 951.1
  abstractedness 985.2
abstruse
  concealed 346.11

absorbed
  recondite 522.16
  learned 928.21
  difficult 1013.17
absurd vain 391.13
  humorous 488.4
  nonsensical 520.7
  inconsistent 789.8
  odd 870.11
  foolish 923.11
  unbelievable 955.10
  impossible 967.7
abulia weak will 362.4
  psychosis 926.3
abundance
  quantity 247.3
  store 386.1
  wordiness 538.2
  numerousness 884.1
  productiveness 890.1
  plenty 991.2
abundant much 247.8
  diffuse 538.11
  copious 884.8
  productive 890.9
  plentiful 991.7
abuse
  n misuse 389.1
  mistreatment 389.2
  berating 510.7
  vilification 513.2
  seduction 665.6
  v exploit 387.16
  misuse 389.4
  mistreat 389.5
  berate 510.19
  vilify 513.7
  seduce 665.20
  blaspheme 694.5
  work evil 1000.6
abusive caustic 144.23
  insulting 156.8
  condemnatory 510.22
  disparaging 512.13
  cursing 513.8
  threatening 514.3
abut adjoin 223.9
  juxtapose 223.13
  rest on 901.22
abysmal huge 257.20
  abyssal 275.11
abyss crack 224.2
  something deep 275.2
  ocean depths 275.4
  pit 284.4
  hell 682.1
academese 545.3
academia 567.5
academic
  n teacher 571.1
  adj learning 567.13
  scholastic 568.19
  studious 570.17
  pedagogic 571.11
  theoretical 951.13
academician 929.3
academic journal 555.1
academy school 567.1
  secondary school 567.4
accede assent 332.8
  submit 433.6
  consent 441.2

account
n recounting 349.3
record 549.1
report 549.7
information 551.1
credit account 622.2
fee 624.5
reckoning 628.2
statement 628.3
worth 630.2
esteem 662.3
story 719.3
tale 722.3
bill 871.5
sum 1017.6
summary 1017.11
v judge 946.8
accountability 130.4
accountable
interpretable 341.17
responsible 641.17
attributable 888.6
accountant
recorder 550.1
bookkeeper 628.7
professional 726.4
treasurer 729.12
calculator 1017.15
accountant general 628.7
account for
explain 341.10
justify 600.9
attribute to 888.4
accounting
n report 549.7
accountancy 628.6
numeration 1017.9
automation 1041.7
adj bookkeeping 628.12
accredit ratify 332.12
authorize 443.11
commission 615.10
attribute to 888.4
accredited
authorized 443.17
commissioned 615.19
accretion 472.2
accrue grow 251.6
be received 479.8
mature 623.7
result from 887.5
acculturate
naturalize 226.4
accustom 373.9
make better 392.9
accumulate grow 251.6
store up 386.11
collect 472.11
assemble 770.18
put together 800.5
accumulation
increase 251.1
store 386.1
collection 472.2
cumulation 770.9
accuracy
meticulousness 339.3
circumstantiality 766.4
correctness 973.5
accurate
meticulous 339.12

discriminating 944.7
correct 973.16
accurately
meticulously 339.16
correctly 973.20
accursed cursed 513.9
execrable 1000.10
accusation charge 599.1
accusal 599.1
accusatory 599.13
accuse
bring accusation 599.7
censure 510.13
accused
n defendant 599.6
adj charged 599.15
accuser 599.5
accustomed
wont 373.15
usual 869.9
ace military pilot 185.3
short distance 223.2
modicum 248.2
superior 249.4
skillful person 413.14
friend 588.4
game 748.2
round 751.4
card 758.2
one 872.3
first-rate 999.7
acedia apathy 94.4
wretchedness 96.6
unconcern 102.2
dejection 112.3
despair 125.2
languor 331.6
ace in the hole
advantage 249.2
reserve 386.3
aceldama
place of killing 308.12
battlefield 463.2
acerbic bitter 64.6
sour 67.5
pungent 68.6
caustic 144.23
resentful 152.26
acetaminophen 86.12
acetify sour 67.4
chemicalize 1060.8
acharya 571.1
ache
n aching 26.5
pain 96.5
cold 1023.2
v suffer 26.8
discomfort 96.19
grieve 112.17
ache for 100.16
achievable 966.7
achieve arrive 186.6
do 328.6
accomplish 407.4
succeed with 409.11
perform 892.11
achievement
arrival 186.1
production 328.2
act 328.3
accomplishment 407.1

exploit 492.6
heraldry 647.2
performance 892.5
Achilles' heel
weak point 16.4
fault 1003.2
aching
n ache 26.5
pain 96.5
yearning 100.5
cold 1023.2
adj achy 26.12
pained 96.23
desirous of 100.22
achromatic 36.7
acid
n sour 67.2
LSD 87.10
bitterness 152.3
cauterant 1020.15
extinguisher 1022.3
hydracid 1060.3
adj acrimonious 17.14
acidulous 67.6
pungent 68.6
out of humor 110.17
caustic 144.23
resentful 152.26
vigorous 544.11
chemical 1060.9
acidhead 87.21
acidic
caustic 144.23
resentful 152.26
acidify sour 67.4
chemicalize 1060.8
acidity acrimony 17.5
sourness 67.1
pungency 68.1
causticity 144.8
bitterness 152.3
acid 1060.3
acid rain 1001.4
acid reflux
ache 26.5
gastrointestinal disease
85.29
acid rock 708.10
acid test 942.2
acidulous
acrimonious 17.14
acid 67.6
caustic 144.23
resentful 152.26
acknowledge
thank 150.4
admit 332.11
confess 351.7
reply 553.11
pay for 624.18
attribute to 888.4
answer 939.4
testify 957.9
acknowledged
accepted 332.14
conventional 579.5
traditional 842.12
acknowledge the corn 332.11
acknowledgment
thanks 150.2
recognition 332.3

confession 351.3
commendation 509.3
letter 553.2
receipt 627.2
due 639.2
apology 658.2
citation 888.2
answer 939.1
acme
summit 198.2
supremacy 249.3
height 272.2
ideal 786.4
limit 794.5
culmination 1002.3
acne 85.35
acolyte assistant 616.6
holy orders 699.4
acoustic
n sound 50.1
adj auditory 48.13
sonic 50.17
phonetic 524.30
acoustics 50.5
acoustic theory 50.5
acquaint inform 551.8
introduce 587.14
acquaintance
information 551.1
acquaintedness 587.4
friend 588.1
knowledge 928.1
acquaintanceship 587.4
acquiesce
be willing 324.3
assent 332.8
submit 433.6
comply 441.3
acquiescent
resigned 134.10
willing 324.5
obedient 326.3
assenting 332.13
submissive 433.12
consenting 441.4
conformable 867.5
acquire get 472.8
receive 479.6
take 480.13
absorb 570.7
receive 627.3
incur 897.4
**acquired immune deficiency
syndrome or AIDS**
deficiency diseases 85.11
venereal disease or VD 85.18
acquisition
acquirement 472.1
gaining 472.1
receiving 479.1
taking 480.1
purchase 733.1
acquisitive
greedy 100.27
acquiring 472.15
selfish 651.5
acquit
bring in a verdict 598.20
clear 601.4
acquitment
acquittal 601.1

additional
additive 253.8
supplementary 253.10
unessential 768.4
fresh 841.8
additive
n adjunct 254.1
adj additional 253.8
addle intoxicate 88.22
perplex 971.13
confuse 985.7
addled
intoxicated 88.31
muddleheaded 922.18
in a dilemma 971.25
befuddled 985.13
add on 253.4
address
n abode 228.1
behavior 321.1
skill 413.1
request 440.1
remark 524.3
speech 543.2
name and address 553.9
greeting 585.4
round 751.3
v solicit 440.14
speak to 524.26
make a speech 543.9
direct 553.13
court 562.21
greet 585.10
address book 871.4
addressee
inhabitant 227.2
recipient 479.3
correspondent 553.8
address oneself to
practice 328.8
undertake 404.3
busy oneself with 724.11
add to increase 251.4
augment 253.5
enlarge 259.4
adduction 907.1
add up compute 253.6
be right 973.10
sum up 1017.19
adenoidal 525.12
adept
n expert 413.11
occultist 689.11
adj skillful 413.22
adequacy ability 18.2
satisfactoriness 107.3
mean 246.1
sufficiency 991.1
adequate able 18.14
satisfactory 107.11
sufficient 991.6
tolerable 999.20
adfiliation 450.2
adhere join 800.11
cohere 803.6
adherent
n hanger-on 138.6
associate 166.2
commender 509.8
follower 616.8
adhesive 803.4

adj adhesive 803.12
adhere to
observe 434.2
execute 437.9
hold 474.6
adhesion retention 474.1
fidelity 644.7
cohesion 803.1
adhesive
n fastening 800.3
adherent 803.4
plastic 1054.6
adj adherent 803.12
viscous 1062.12
adhesive bandage 86.33
ad hoc
n transience 828.1
expedient 995.2
adj extemporaneous 365.12
unprepared 406.8
transient 828.7
substitute 862.8
makeshift 995.7
ad hominem attack 512.2
adieu
n leave-taking 188.4
interj farewell! 188.22
ad infinitum
lengthily 267.10
throughout 794.17
continuously 812.10
infinitely 823.4
perpetually 829.10
adios! 188.22
adipose
corpulent 257.18
oily 1056.9
adiposity
corpulence 257.8
oiliness 1056.5
adit
entrance 189.5
channel 239.1
adjacent 223.16
adjective 530.3
adjoin
border 211.10
join 223.9
juxtapose 223.13
add 253.4
adjoining 223.16
adjourn 846.9
adjournment 846.4
adjudicate 946.8
adjunct
n thing added 253.1
addition 254.1
expansion 259.1
associate 616.1
nonessential 768.2
attendant 769.3
relation 775.1
part 793.1
component 796.2
adj added 253.9
adjure
administer an oath 334.7
entreat 440.11
adjust
orient 161.11
size 257.15

accustom 373.9
fit 405.8
arrange 437.8
reconcile 465.8
settle 466.7
compromise 468.2
make agree 788.7
equalize 790.6
organize 808.10
change 852.7
conform 867.3
adjustable
versatile 413.25
changeable 854.6
conformable 867.5
adjusted
accustomed 373.15
fitted 405.17
adjustment
rehabilitation 92.27
orientation 161.4
habituation 373.7
fitting 405.2
compact 437.1
accommodation 465.4
compromise 468.1
good condition 765.3
adaptation 788.4
equating 790.2
organization 808.2
change 852.1
conformity 867.1
adjutant 616.6
adjuvant
n adjunct 254.1
adj remedial 86.39
helping 449.20
ad lib
n improvisation 365.5
unpreparedness 406.1
adv at will 323.5
extemporaneously 365.15
ad-lib
v improvise 365.8
be unprepared 406.6
adj extemporaneous 365.12
unprepared 406.8
administer
execute 437.9
parcel out 477.8
give 478.12
administrate 573.11
administer justice 594.5
govern 612.11
give 643.6
administer to 577.13
administration
performance 328.2
governance 417.5
distribution 477.2
principal 571.8
executive function 573.3
government 612.1
giving 643.2
protectorship 1008.2
administrative authoritative
417.15
governmental 612.16
administrative assistant 577.3
administrator
principal 571.8

director 574.1
admirable
endearing 104.24
praiseworthy 509.20
admiral 575.20
admire
cherish 104.20
respect 155.4
approve 509.9
admirer
enthusiast 101.4
lover 104.11
supporter 616.9
admissible
acceptable 107.12
receptive 187.16
eligible 371.24
permissible 443.15
justifiable 600.14
relevant 775.11
logical 935.20
evidential 957.16
tolerable 999.20
admission
admittance 187.2
entrance 189.1
naturalization 226.3
acknowledgment
332.3
confession 351.3
permission 443.1
receiving 479.1
fee 630.6
inclusion 772.1
testimony 957.2
admit receive 187.10
enter 189.7
naturalize 226.4
acknowledge 332.11
confess 351.7
permit 443.9
take in 479.6
welcome 585.7
include 772.3
allow for 959.5
admit of
be liable 897.3
have a chance 972.13
admitted
accepted 332.14
disclosive 351.10
permitted 443.16
received 479.10
approved 509.19
conventional 579.5
real 761.15
traditional 842.12
admixture
addition 253.1
mixture 797.1
compound 797.5
admonish
dissuade 379.3
warn 399.5
exhort 422.6
reprove 510.17
admonition
dissuasion 379.1
warning 399.1
advice 422.1
reproof 510.5

ad nauseam
 lengthily 267.10
 at length 538.16
 fully 766.13
 repeatedly 849.16
ado
 n agitation 105.4
 bustle 330.4
 commotion 810.4
 trouble 1013.3
 adj happening 831.9
adobe
 n ceramic ware 742.2
 building material 1054.2
 adj earthy 234.5
adolescence 303.1
adolescent
 n youngster 302.1
 adj grown 14.3
 pubescent 301.13
 immature 406.11
Adonis 1016.9
adopt naturalize 226.4
 approve 371.15
 use 384.5
 appropriate 480.19
 borrow 621.4
 usurp 640.8
adopted child 561.3
adoptive parent 560.8
adorable
 desirable 100.30
 endearing 104.24
adore enjoy 95.13
 cherish 104.20
 respect 155.4
 worship 696.11
adorn ornament 498.8
 make grandiloquent 545.7
 honor 662.12
 beautify 1016.15
adrenaline rush 17.3
adrift
 adj afloat 182.61
 unfastened 802.22
 inconstant 854.7
 bewildered 971.24
 erroneous 975.16
 muddled 985.13
 adv separately 802.27
adroit skillful 413.22
 smart 920.14
adsorb 187.13
adsorption 187.6
adulation praise 509.5
 flattery 511.1
adult
 n grownup 304.1
 adj grown 14.3
 mature 303.12
 lascivious 665.29
 obscene 666.9
adult education 567.5
adulterate dilute 16.11
 rarefy 299.3
 tamper with 354.17
 weaken 393.12
 corrupt 797.12
adulterated
 diluted 16.19
 rare 299.4

imperfect 1003.4
adulterer 665.13
adulterous 665.27
adultery
 copulation 75.7
 love affair 104.5
 illicit sex 665.7
adulthood 303.1
adumbrate
 foreshow 133.9
 image 349.11
 hint 551.10
advance
 n progression 162.1
 approach 167.1
 course 172.2
 increase 251.1
 improvement 392.1
 offer 439.1
 promotion 446.1
 furtherance 449.5
 lending 620.1
 loan 620.2
 evolution 861.1
 v progress 162.2
 further 162.5
 approach 167.3
 move 172.5
 grow 251.6
 be instrumental 384.7
 improve 392.7
 make better 392.9
 make good 409.10
 propose 439.5
 promote 446.2
 be useful 449.17
 lend 620.5
 elapse 821.5
 evolve 861.5
 determine 886.12
 push 904.9
 postulate 951.12
 adduce 957.12
 expedite one's affair 995.3
 do good 999.10
 prosper 1010.7
advance! 459.32
advanced front 216.10
 aged 303.16
 improved 392.13
 preceding 816.4
 modern 841.13
 premature 845.8
advancement
 progression 162.1
 improvement 392.1
 promotion 446.1
 furtherance 449.5
 lending 620.1
 evolution 861.1
advantage
 n vantage 249.2
 benefit 387.4
 facility 449.9
 game 748.2
 purchase 906.2
 expedience 995.1
 good 999.4
 v avail 387.17
 be useful 449.17
 expedite one's affair 995.3

do good 999.10
advantageous
 useful 387.18
 gainful 472.16
 expedient 995.5
 good 999.12
advent approach 167.1
 arrival 186.1
 coming 839.5
adventitious
 circumstantial 766.7
 unessential 768.4
 chance 972.15
adventure act 328.3
 emprise 404.2
 exploit 492.6
 event 831.2
 happening 972.6
adventure athlete 178.1
adventurer
 traveler 178.1
 mercenary 461.17
 daredevil 493.4
 upstart 606.7
 speculator 737.11
 gambler 759.21
adventure traveler 178.1
adventurous
 dynamic 330.23
 enterprising 404.8
 daring 492.21
 foolhardy 493.9
 hazardous 1006.10
adverb 530.3
adverbial 530.3
adversarial
 contrapositive 215.5
 oppositional 451.8
 contrary 779.6
adversarial procedure 935.4
adversary
 n opponent 452.1
 enemy 589.6
 adj oppositional 451.8
adverse
 oppositional 451.8
 contrary 779.6
 untoward 1011.13
adversity 1011
advertent 983.15
advertise
 publish 352.10
 publicize 352.15
 flaunt 501.17
 inform 551.8
advertisement 352.6
advertising 352.5
advice counsel 422
 tip 551.3
 news 552.1
 message 552.4
advisable 995.5
advise warn 399.5
 counsel 422.5
 inform 551.8
advised
 intentional 380.8
 reasoned 935.21
advisement advice 422.1
adviser counsel 422.3
 informant 551.5

advisor 422.3
advisory
 recommendatory 422.8
 conciliar 423.5
 informative 551.18
advocacy
 promotion 352.5
 advice 422.1
 patronage 449.4
 recommendation 509.4
advocate
 n defender 460.7
 deputy 576.1
 friend 588.1
 lawyer 597.1
 justifier 600.8
 associate 616.9
 supporter 901.2
 arguer 935.12
 v urge 375.14
 advise 422.5
 abet 449.14
 defend 460.8
 commend 509.11
 defend 600.10
aegis patronage 449.4
 safeguard 1008.3
aeon age 824.4
 long time 827.4
aerate air 317.11
 foam 320.5
 vaporize 1067.8
aerial
 n radio transmitter 1034.4
 adj aviation 184.49
 high 272.14
 airy 317.12
 chimeric 986.22
 vaporous 1067.9
aerialist 707.3
aerial ladder 193.4
aerification 1067.5
aerify 317.11
aerobe 85.42
aerobics 84.2
aerodynamic
 aviation 184.49
 pneumatic 1039.10
 vaporous 1067.9
aerodynamics
 pneumatics 1039.5
 gas 1067.2
aerography
 meteorology 317.5
 pneumatics 1039.5
aerology
 meteorology 317.5
 pneumatics 1039.5
aerometer
 density 1045.8
 vaporimeter 1067.7
aerometry 1039.5
aeronaut aviator 185.1
 balloonist 185.7
aeronautical 184.49
aeronautical engineering
 1043.1
aeronautics 184.1
aeroplane
 n aircraft 181.1
 v fly 184.36

aerosol
solution 1064.3
sprinkler 1065.8
vaporizer 1067.6
aerospace
n atmosphere 184.32
adj aviation 184.49
aerospace engineering 1043.1
aerospace technology 1075.1
aerostatic
aviation 184.49
pneumatic 1039.10
vaporous 1067.9
aerostatics 1039.5
aerotechnics 1039.5
aery 317.12
aesthete 496.5
aesthetic
tasteful 496.7
artistic 712.19
absurdist 952.11
aesthetician 723.4
aesthetics
artistic taste 496.4
criticism 723.1
aestival green 44.4
seasonal 313.9
warm 1019.24
aestivate
hibernate 22.15
lie idle 331.16
AF tone 50.2
frequency 1034.12
afar 261.15
afeared 127.22
affable pleasant 97.6
good-natured 143.14
indulgent 427.8
courteous 504.14
informal 581.3
sociable 582.22
cordial 587.16
affair
love affair 104.5
undertaking 404.1
social gathering 582.10
occupation 724.1
concern 831.3
object 1052.4
affaire d'honneur 457.7
affairs action 328.1
occupation 724.1
relation 775.1
concerns 831.4
affect
n feeling 93.1
attitude 978.1
v wear 5.44
touch 93.14
impress 93.15
move 145.5
imitate 336.5
manifest 348.5
sham 354.21
assume 500.12
entail 772.4
relate to 775.5
operate on 889.6
influence 894.7
affectation
behavior 321.1

sham 354.3
pretension 500.1
airs 500.1
style 532.2
elegance 533.3
grandiloquence 545.1
sanctimony 693.1
affecting
touching 93.22
distressing 98.20
pitiful 145.8
affection
disease 85.1
feeling 93.1
liking 100.2
love 104.1
amorousness 104.2
friendship 587.1
affectionate
loving 104.26
kind 143.13
affective
emotional 93.17
attitudinal 978.7
affectless
insensible 25.6
unfeeling 94.9
affiance
n betrothal 436.3
v be engaged 436.6
affianced
n fiancé 104.16
adj promised 436.8
affidavit
deposition 334.3
certificate 549.6
declaration 598.7
statement of principles 953.4
testimony 957.2
affiliate
n branch 617.10
member 617.11
v naturalize 226.4
adopt 371.15
cooperate 450.3
join 617.14
league 805.4
adj related 775.9
leagued 805.6
affiliates 617.12
affiliation
naturalization 226.3
adoption 371.4
alliance 450.2
blood relationship 559.1
lineage 560.4
association 582.6
sect 675.3
relation 775.1
combination 805.1
affinity
inclination 100.3
preference 371.5
accord 455.1
marriage relationship 564.1
familiarity 587.5
relation 775.1
kinship 775.3
similarity 784.2
agreement 788.1
tendency 896.1

attraction 907.1
affirm
ratify 332.12
assert 334.5
announce 352.12
say 524.23
be pious 692.6
state 953.12
testify 957.9
confirm 957.11
affirmation
ratification 332.4
assertion 334.1
declaration 334.1
deposition 334.3
consent 441.1
remark 524.3
premise 935.7
testimony 957.2
confirmation 957.4
affirmative
n yes 332.2
consent 441.1
adj affirming 334.8
consenting 441.4
agreeing 788.9
affix
n added to writing 254.2
morphology 526.3
v add 253.4
fasten 800.7
afflatus
inspiration 375.9
revelation 683.10
Muse 720.10
genius 920.8
afflict pain 26.7
disorder 85.50
distress 96.16
aggrieve 112.19
work evil 1000.6
affliction
disease 85.1
infliction 96.8
bane 1001.1
adversity 1011.1
affluent
n tributary 238.3
adj flowing 238.24
wealthy 618.14
plentiful 991.7
prosperous 1010.12
afflux approach 167.1
influx 189.2
flow 238.4
afford provide 385.7
give 478.12
furnish 478.15
have money 618.11
well afford 626.7
yield 627.4
affordable 633.7
afforestation
woodland 310.13
forestry 1069.3
affray 457.4
affright
n fear 127.1
v frighten 127.15
affront
n provocation 152.11

indignity 156.2
v offend 152.21
disrespect 156.5
confront 216.8
oppose 451.5
defy 454.3
brave 492.10
affusion baptism 701.6
wetting 1065.6
afghan 295.10
aficionado
enthusiast 101.4
attender 221.5
supporter 616.9
specialist 866.3
fanatic 926.18
afield 261.19
afire fervent 93.18
zealous 101.9
inspired 375.31
burning 1019.27
afloat
adj floating 182.60
adrift 182.61
flooded 238.25
afoot 405.23
reported 552.15
unfastened 802.22
happening 831.9
inconstant 854.7
adv on board 182.62
at sea 240.9
aflush 139.13
aflutter 105.3
afoot
adj astir 330.19
on foot 405.23
existent 761.13
happening 831.9
adv walking 177.43
aforementioned 814.5
aforethought
n intentionality 380.3
adj premeditated 380.9
afoul of sail into 182.41
collide 902.13
afraid scared 127.22
weak-willed 362.12
cowardly 491.10
afresh newly 841.15
repeated 849.17
again 874.7
African-American 312.3
aft
adj rear 217.9
adv abaft 182.69
after 217.14
after
adj rear 217.9
subsequent 835.4
adv behind 166.6
aft 217.14
like 336.12
in pursuit of 382.12
subsequently 835.6
following 835.8
conformable to 867.9
because of 888.9
after a fashion
limited 248.10
somehow 384.11

after all
  notwithstanding 338.8
  subsequently 835.6
  all things considered 946.17
after all is said and done, in
    spite of
  notwithstanding 338.8
  eventually 831.12
aftercare 1008.2
afterglow
  remainder 256.1
  aftermath 817.3
  aftereffect 887.3
  shine 1025.2
afterimage
  remainder 256.1
  aftermath 817.3
  aftereffect 887.3
  optical illusion 976.5
afterlife 681.2
aftermath yield 472.5
  afterclap 817.3
  event 831.1
  sequel 835.2
  result 887.1
  aftereffect 887.3
afternoon
  n post meridiem 315.1
  adj post meridian 315.7
afterparty
  treat 95.3
  celebration 487.1
aftertaste taste 62.1
  aftermath 817.3
  aftereffect 887.3
afterthought
  change of mind 363.1
  sequel 817.1
  untimeliness 844.1
  delay 846.2
  mature thought 931.5
afterwards
  subsequently 835.6
  in the future 839.9
afterword 254.2
afterworld
  the hereafter 681.2
  destiny 839.2
aftmost 217.9
again
  adv additionally 253.11
  notwithstanding 338.8
  then 821.11
  newly 841.15
  over 849.17
  another time 874.7
  interj encore! 849.18
again and again
  continuously 812.10
  frequently 847.6
  repeatedly 849.16
against
  adj disapproving 510.21
  prep toward 161.26
  contraposed 215.7
  up against 223.25
  in preparation for 405.24
  opposed to 451.10
  in disagreement with 789.10
against the grain
  adj unlikable 99.7

  adv backwards 163.13
  crosswise 170.13
  cross-grained 288.12
  in opposition 451.9
  contrarily 779.9
agape love 104.1
  benevolence 143.4
  accord 455.1
agape
  wondering 122.9
  expectant 130.11
  gaping 292.18
  curious 981.5
agasp 21.12
age
  n time of life 303.1
  years 303.1
  generation 824.4
  era 824.5
  durability 827.1
  long time 827.5
  duration 827.5
  oldness 842.1
  v ripen 303.10
  grow old 842.9
aged ripe 303.13
  elderly 303.16
  mature 304.7
  durable 827.10
  old-fogyish 842.17
agee 204.14
ageism class 607.1
  discrimination 980.4
ageless perpetual 829.7
  old 842.10
agency
  instrumentality 384.3
  commission 615.1
  trade 731.2
  workplace 739.1
  substitution 862.1
  operation 889.1
agenda
  record book 549.11
  roll 871.6
  schedule 965.3
agent
  intermediary 213.4
  instrument 384.4
  mediator 466.3
  director 574.1
  representative 576.1
  deputy 576.3
  lawyer 597.1
  assignee 615.9
  assistant 616.6
  advance man 704.25
  doer 726.1
  salesman 730.3
  transformer 852.5
  substitute 862.2
  author 886.4
  operator 889.4
  element 1060.2
agent provocateur
  shill 357.5
  instigator 375.11
Age of Enlightenment 392.3
Age of Reason 392.3
age-old 842.10
ages 827.4

age spot 2.4
agglomeration
  accumulation 770.9
  joining 800.1
  cohesion 803.1
  conglomeration 803.5
  combination 805.1
agglutination
  addition 253.1
  joining 800.1
  cohesion 803.1
  densification 1045.3
agglutinative 803.10
aggrandize
  increase 251.4
  enlarge 259.4
  exaggerate 355.3
  promote 446.2
  glorify 662.13
aggravate annoy 96.13
  irritate 96.14
  vex 98.15
  worsen 119.2
  provoke 152.24
  intensify 251.5
  impair 393.9
  sow dissension 456.14
  antagonize 589.7
aggravated battery 459.1
aggravating
  annoying 98.22
  exasperating 119.5
aggravation annoyance 96.2
  irritation 96.3
  vexatiousness 98.7
  excitation 105.11
  worsening 119.1
  increase 119.1
  resentment 152.1
  intensification 251.2
  adversity 1011.1
aggregate
  n accumulation 770.9
  sum 1017.6
  v math term 253.2
  assemble 770.18
  total 792.8
  adj assembled 770.21
  whole 792.9
aggregation
  accumulation 770.9
  joining 800.1
  combination 805.1
aggression
  enterprise 330.7
  warlikeness 458.10
  attack 459.1
aggressive energetic 17.13
  enterprising 330.23
  partisan 456.17
  warlike 458.20
  offensive 459.30
  gruff 505.7
aggressor 459.12
aggrieve pain 96.17
  oppress 112.19
  offend 152.21
  work evil 1000.6
aghast
  wondering 122.9
  terrified 127.26

agile fast 174.15
  quick 330.18
  alert 339.14
  nimble 413.23
agility quickness 330.3
  alertness 339.5
  nimbleness 413.2
aging
  n maturation 303.6
  adj growing old 303.17
agita
  sore spot 24.4
  ache 26.5
  gastrointestinal disease
    85.29
  agitation 105.4
agitated
  distressed 96.22
  perturbed 105.23
  anxious 126.7
  jittery 128.12
  bustling 330.20
  disturbed 917.16
agitation
  perturbation 105.4
  excitation 105.11
  anxiety 126.1
  trepidation 127.5
  nervousness 128.1
  bustle 330.4
  incitement 375.4
  turbulence 671.2
  violence 917
  stimulation 917.1
agitator rebel 327.5
  instigator 375.11
  troublemaker 593.2
  mixer 797.9
  shaker 917.9
agitprop
  instigator 375.11
  propaganda 569.2
aglow burning 1019.27
  luminous 1025.31
  illuminated 1025.40
agnate
  n kinfolk 559.2
  lineage 560.4
  adj related 559.6
  lineal 560.18
  kindred 775.10
  akin 784.13
agnostic
  n skeptic 695.12
  adj skeptic 695.20
  absurdist 952.11
  doubting 955.9
  uncertain 971.16
ago
  adj past 837.7
  adv since 837.15
agog eager 101.8
  excited 105.20
  wondering 122.9
  expectant 130.11
  curious 981.5
  attentive 983.15
agonize pain 26.7
  suffer 26.8
  torture 96.18
  cause unpleasantness 96.19

region 231.1
plot 231.4
air strike 459.4
airstrip 184.23
airtight resistant 15.20
close 293.12
air-traffic control 184.1
air-traffic controller
aviation 184.1
radar technician 1036.14
airward 272.21
airway air lane 184.33
air passage 239.13
airworthy
aviation 184.49
snug 1007.7
airy
lighthearted 109.12
thin 270.16
high 272.14
light 298.10
rare 299.4
atmospheric 317.12
windy 318.21
careless 340.11
unsubstantial 764.6
illusory 976.9
visionary 986.24
trivial 998.19
immaterial 1053.7
vaporous 1067.9
aisle passageway 383.3
church interior 703.9
aisleway 383.3
ait 235.2
ajar clashing 61.5
gaping 292.18
akimbo 278.6
akin in accord 455.3
related 559.6
kindred 775.10
affinitive 784.13
alabaster
n whiteness 37.2
smoothness 287.3
adj whitish 37.8
à la carte 8.11
alack 98.31
alacrity
eagerness 101.1
willingness 324.1
quickness 330.3
hastiness 401.2
promptness 845.3
Aladdin's lamp 691.6
à la mode
stylish 578.12
fashionably 578.17
modern 841.13
alarm
n fear 127.1
warning 399.1
danger signal 400.1
red light 400.1
signal 517.15
call 517.16
v frighten 127.15
alert 400.3
alarm clock 400.1
alarming
frightening 127.28

dangerous 1006.9
alarmist 127.8
alas 98.31
albeit 338.8
albinism
faulty eyesight 28.1
whiteness 37.1
albino
n whiteness 37.1
adj albinic 37.10
album
record book 549.11
compilation 554.7
albumen egg 305.15
semiliquid 1062.5
albuminous 305.23
alchemist 690.5
alchemy sorcery 690.1
conversion 858.1
alcohol sedative 86.12
spirits 88.13
antifreeze 1024.8
alcohol flush syndrome 41.3
alcoholic
n addict 87.21
drinker 88.11
adj spirituous 88.37
alcoholism
substance abuse 87.1
dipsomania 88.3
alcopop 10.49
alcove nook 197.3
summerhouse 228.12
recess 284.7
alderman
public official 575.17
legislator 610.3
alderperson
public officials 575.17
legislator 610.3
aleatoric
musical 708.47
circumstantial 766.7
unessential 768.4
vague 971.19
chance 972.15
hazardous 1066.10
aleatory
musical 708.47
circumstantial 766.7
unessential 768.4
vague 971.19
chance 972.15
hazardous 1006.10
alee leeward 182.68
downwind 218.9
alehouse 88.20
alert
n warning sign 399.3
alarm 400.1
v warn 399.5
alarm 400.3
tip off 551.11
adj awake 23.8
wary 339.14
prepared 405.16
prompt 845.9
clear-witted 920.13
curious 981.5
attentive 983.15
Alfredo 10.12

alfresco
outdoor 206.8
exterior 206.11
airy 317.12
algae 310.4
algebraic 1017.22
algebraic operation 1017.2
algesia 26.4
algid
cold 1023.14
frigid 1023.16
algorithm
mathematics 1017.1
Arabic numerals 1017.4
alias
n pseudonym 527.8
adj nominal 527.15
adv otherwise 780.11
alibi
n pretext 376.1
justification 600.4
v excuse 600.11
alien
n exclusiveness 773.3
stranger 774.3
oddity 870.4
astronaut 1075.8
v transfer 629.3
adj extraterritorial 206.9
oppositional 451.8
extraneous 774.5
unrelated 776.6
extraterrestrial 1072.26
alienate
sow dissension 456.14
antagonize 589.7
transfer 629.3
separate 802.8
indoctrinate 858.15
alienation
defense mechanism 92.23
dissent 333.1
falling-out 456.4
disaccord 589.2
transfer 629.1
extraneousness 774.1
separation 802.1
indoctrination 858.5
aloneness 872.2
insanity 926.1
alight
v land 184.43
arrive 186.8
light upon 194.7
adj burning 1019.27
illuminated 1025.40
alight upon
light upon 194.10
meet 223.11
come across 941.3
align level 201.6
parallelize 203.5
dispose 808.9
line 812.5
alignment
orientation 161.4
parallelism 203.1
affiliation 450.2
align oneself with
back 449.13
side with 450.4

alike identical 778.7
congruent 778.9
uniform 781.5
similar 784.10
equal 790.7
indistinguishable 945.6
alimentary 7.21
alimentation
nutrition 7.1
food 10.3
alimony 478.8
aliquot 1017.23
A-list 871.1
alive living 306.12
active 330.17
alert 339.14
clear-witted 920.13
remembered 989.22
alive and kicking
healthy 83.9
living 306.12
alive to sensible 24.11
cognizant of 928.16
alkali
n acid 1060.3
adj chemical 1060.9
alkali metal 1060.1
alkaline-earth element
1060.1
alkalinity 1060.3
alkalizer 86.25
all
n the whole 792.3
limit 794.5
everyone 864.4
universe 1072.1
adj whole 792.9
every 864.15
adv wholly 792.13
the all 823.1
all aboard 182.62
all-absorbing 997.24
Allah 677.2
all along 829.11
all and sundry
n all 792.3
adj every 864.15
all around
handy 387.20
versatile 413.25
all-around event 755.2
all at once
together 769.11
abruptly 830.8
suddenly 830.9
allay gratify 95.8
relieve 120.5
pacify 465.7
moderate 670.6
satiate 994.4
all but nearly 223.22
on the whole 792.14
all clear
n alarm 400.1
adj unindebted 624.23
interj all's well! 1007.9
all-consuming 395.27
all creation 1072.1
all ears listening 48.14
vigilant 339.13
attentive 983.15

figurative 536.3
allusory 519.6
alluvious 234.6
alluvium deposit 176.9
  land 234.1
  overflow 238.6
  dregs 256.2
all wet 975.18
ally
  n country 232.1
  associate 616.1
  v cooperate 450.3
  come together 770.16
  relate 775.6
  league 805.4
alma mater 567.5
almanac reference book 554.9
  The Old Farmer's Almanac
    832.7
  calendar 832.8
  dictionary 871.4
almighty
  adj powerful 18.13
  omnipotent 677.17
  adv very 247.18
almost 223.22
alms act of kindness 143.7
  donation 478.6
almsgiver
  philanthropist 143.8
  giver 478.11
almshouse 1009.4
almsman
  beneficiary 479.4
  poor man 619.4
aloft on board 182.62
  on high 272.21
aloha
  n leave-taking 188.4
  interj farewell! 188.22
  greetings! 585.15
alone
  adj secluded 584.11
  solitary 872.8
  sole 872.9
  adv independently 430.33
  simply 798.11
  singly 872.13
along
  v walk 177.27
  adv forward 162.8
  lengthwise 267.11
alongside
  adj side 218.6
  adv board and board 182.70
  in parallel 203.7
  aside 218.10
  prep beside 218.11
along with also 253.13
  with 769.12
aloof
  adj apathetic 94.13
  unsociable 141.12
  reticent 344.10
  standoffish 583.6
  Incoherent 804.4
  alone 872.8
  incurious 982.3
  adv at a distance 261.14
  on high 272.21
aloofness 261.1

aloud audibly 50.18
  loudly 53.14
alp 237.6
alpen 272.18
alpha beginning 818.1
  first 818.3
alphabet
  n representation 349.1
  symbols 546.3
  writing 547.1
  letter 547.9
  basics 818.6
  v letter 546.6
alphabetic
  literal 546.8
  ideographic 547.26
alphabetical order 807.2
alphabetize letter 546.6
  classify 809.6
alphabet soup 10.10
alpha female 249.4
alpha male 249.4
alpine highland 237.8
  hilly 272.18
alpinist traveler 178.1
  climber 193.6
already
  previously 834.6
  until now 838.4
alright 107.12
also
  adv additionally 253.11
  conj and 253.13
also known as 527.15
also-ran failure 410.8
  loser 412.5
  candidate 610.9
  jockey 757.2
altar 703.12
altarpiece altar 703.12
  picture 712.10
alter
  n self 865.5
  v castrate 255.11
  be changed 852.6
  change 852.7
  qualify 959.3
alterable 854.6
alteration
  differentiation 780.4
  change 852.1
altercation
  quarrel 456.5
  contention 457.1
alter ego deputy 576.1
  friend 588.1
  right-hand man 616.7
  likeness 784.3
  self 865.5
alterer 852.5
alternate
  n deputy 576.1
  substitute 862.2
  v vacillate 362.8
  take one's turn 825.5
  recur 850.5
  change 854.5
  interchange 863.4
  reciprocate 916.13
  adj periodic 850.7
  substitute 862.8

reciprocal 916.19
alternate energy
  fuel 1021.1
  renewable energy 1021.7
alternate energy source 1021.1
alternating 854.7
alternation
  interaction 777.3
  periodicity 850.2
  changing 854.3
  interchange 863.1
  reciprocation 916.5
alternative
  n loophole 369.4
  option 371.2
  substitute 862.2
  adj elective 371.22
  substitute 862.8
alternative energy 17.1
alternative energy source
  1021.1
alternative lifestyle
  sexual preference 75.10
  nonconformity 868.2
alternative medicine
  practice of medicine 90.13
  unconventionality 868.2
alternative rock 708.10
although 338.8
altimeter 272.9
altitude
  height 272.1
  coordinates 300.5
alto
  n high voice 58.6
  part 708.22
  harmonics 709.5
  adj high 58.13
  vocal 708.50
altogether
  additionally 253.11
  wholly 792.13
  completely 794.14
  generally 864.17
the altogether 6.3
alto-rilievo
  protuberance 283.2
  relief 715.3
altruism
  benevolence 143.4
  public spirit 591.1
  unselfishness 652.1
altruist 143.8
altruistic
  benevolent 143.15
  unselfish 652.5
alum 260.6
alumna 572.8
alumnus 572.8
alveolar
  indented 284.17
  phonetic 524.30
alveolus
  cavity 284.2
  indentation 284.6
  speech organ 524.18
always regularly 781.8
  all along 829.11
  constantly 847.7
  permanently 853.9
  universally 864.18

Alzheimer's disease 85.25
AM morning 314.1
  modulation 1034.14
amalgam
  compound 797.5
  alloy 1058.4
amalgamate
  cooperate 450.3
  mix 797.10
  combine 805.3
amalgamation
  affiliation 450.2
  mixture 797.1
  combination 805.1
amanuensis
  writer 547.13
  recorder 550.1
  agent 576.3
amass store up 386.11
  collect 472.11
  assemble 770.18
  put together 800.5
amassed stored 386.14
  assembled 770.21
amateur
  n enthusiast 101.4
  connoisseur 496.6
  nonprofessional 726.5
  specialist 866.3
  dilettante 929.6
  trifler 998.10
  adj avocational 724.17
  half-learned 930.14
amateurish
  unskilled 414.16
  half-learned 930.14
amateurism
  inexperience 414.2
  avocation 724.7
  nonprofessionalism 724.9
  slight knowledge 930.5
amatory
  amorous 104.25
  lovemaking 562.23
amaze
  n wonder 122.1
  v astonish 122.6
  perplex 971.13
amazement
  wonder 122.1
  marvel 122.2
amazing 122.12
amazon
  mannish female 76.9
  giantess 257.13
Amazon 461.6
ambages
  convolution 281.1
  circumlocution 538.5
  detour 914.3
ambassador 576.6
ambergris 70.2
ambidextrous
  ambidextral 219.6
  falsehearted 354.31
  versatile 413.25
  treacherous 645.21
ambience
  environment 209.1
  milieu 209.3
ambient light 1025.10

ambient music 708.7
ambient temperature 317.4
ambiguity
 unintelligibility 522.1
 complexity of meaning 539.1
 gray area 539.1
 equivoque 539.2
 self-contradiction 779.3
 inconsistency 789.2
 doubleness 873.1
 equivocalness 971.5
ambiguous
 unintelligible 522.13
 equivocal 539.4
 self-contradictory 779.8
 mixed 797.14
 uncertain 971.16
ambition
 ambitiousness 100.10
 desire 100.11
 motive 375.1
 intention 380.1
ambitious
 aspiring 100.28
 agressive 330.23
 enterprising 404.8
 ostentatious 501.18
ambivalence
 psychological stress 92.17
 irresolution 362.1
 self-contradiction 779.3
 inconsistency 789.2
 doubleness 873.1
ambivalent
 irresolute 362.9
 self-contradictory 779.8
 mixed 797.14
amble
 n walk 177.10
 gait 177.12
 v go slowly 175.6
 stride 177.28
 go on horseback 177.34
amblyopia 28.2
ambrosia
 delicacy 10.8
 sweetening 66.2
 perfumery 70.2
ambulance chaser 597.3
ambulate 177.27
ambulatory
 n passageway 383.3
 adj traveling 177.36
ambulatory care 83.5
ambush
 n trap 346.3
 v surprise 131.7
 ambuscade 346.10
 attack 459.14
âme 919.4
ameliorate
 improve 392.7
 make better 392.9
 be changed 852.6
 change 852.7
ameliorating 120.9
amelioration
 improvement 392.1
 change 852.1
amen
 n affirmative 332.2

v ratify 332.12
 adv right! 973.24
 interj yes 332.18
 so be it 332.20
amenable
 resigned 134.10
 willing 324.5
 consenting 441.4
 responsible 641.17
 influenceable 894.15
amend improve 392.7
 make better 392.9
 revise 392.12
 remedy 396.13
 re-form 858.12
amende 600.3
amendment
 improvement 392.1
 revision 392.4
 new start 858.2
amends
 compensation 338.1
 reparation 396.6
 restitution 481.2
 recompense 624.3
 atonement 658.1
amenities
 creature comforts 121.3
 courtesies 504.7
 etiquette 580.3
amenity
 pleasantness 97.1
 facility 449.9
 polite act 504.1
 courtesy 504.6
amentia 922.9
America
 world region 231.6
 United States 232.3
American dream
 ambition 100.10
 airy hope 124.3
American eagle 647.6
American Indian 312.3
Americanism
 language 523.8
 patriotism 591.2
Americanize 226.4
American Sign Language
 523.12
amiable pleasant 97.6
 good-natured 143.14
 indulgent 427.8
 sociable 582.22
 hospitable 585.11
 friendly 587.15
amicable pleasant 97.6
 favorable 449.22
 in accord 455.3
 friendly 587.15
amicus curiae
 deputy 576.1
 lawyer 597.1
 favor 894.2
amid between 213.12
 among 797.17
amidships
 adj middle 819.4
 adv midway 819.5
amidst between 213.12
 among 797.17

amigo 588.3
amino acid 7.6
amiss
 adj disorderly 810.13
 erroneous 975.16
 adv irrelevantly 776.9
 astray 911.7
 erroneously 975.20
 badly 1000.13
amity accord 455.1
 friendship 587.1
ammonia
 fertilizer 890.4
 coolant 1024.7
ammunition 462.13
amnesia trance 92.19
 thoughtlessness 933.1
 loss of memory 990.2
amnesty
 n pardon 148.2
 peace treaty 464.7
 peace offer 465.2
 exemption 601.2
 v forgive 148.3
 acquit 601.4
amobarbital and secobarbital
 86.12
amoeba 85.42
amoebic 258.15
amok
 n frenzy 926.7
 adj frenzied 105.25
 rabid 926.30
among
 v include 772.3
 prep at 159.27
 between 213.12
 amongst 797.17
amor 104.8
Amor love god 104.1
 deity 104.7
amoral
 dishonest 645.16
 vice-prone 654.11
amorality
 unmorality 636.4
 vice 654.1
amore 104.1
amorous sexual 75.25
 amatory 104.25
amorphic
 formless 263.4
 obscure 522.15
amorphous
 formless 263.4
 obscure 522.15
 unordered 810.12
 inconstant 854.7
 abnormal 870.9
 vague 971.19
amortization
 payment 624.1
 transfer 629.1
amount count 244.1
 quantity 244.2
 degree 245.1
 price 630.1
 sum 1017.6
amount to cost 630.13
 equal 790.5
 total 792.8

amour 104.5
amour-propre 104.1
amouse-bouche 8.2
amperage power 18.1
 current 1032.2
amphibian
 n seaplane 181.8
 plant 310.3
 creature 311.3
 batrachian 311.26
 adj reptile 311.47
amphibious
 versatile 413.25
 mixed 797.14
amphibious aircraft 181.8
amphitheater
 hall 197.4
 arena 463.1
 schoolroom 567.11
 theater 704.14
ample
 satisfactory 107.11
 spacious 158.11
 much 247.8
 voluminous 257.17
 broad 269.6
 abundant 884.8
 sufficient 991.6
 plentiful 991.7
amplification
 aggravation 119.1
 increase 251.1
 expansion 259.1
 translation 341.3
 exaggeration 355.1
 expatiation 538.6
 evolution 861.1
 radio-frequency
  amplification 1034.15
amplifier
 listening device 48.8
 audio 50.10
amplify
 aggravate 119.2
 increase 251.4
 enlarge 259.4
 exaggerate 355.3
 expatiate 538.7
 elaborate 861.6
 electrify 1032.26
amplitude sound 50.1
 loudness 53.1
 spaciousness 158.5
 quantity 244.1
 greatness 247.1
 size 257.1
 breadth 269.1
 wordiness 538.2
 fullness 794.2
 wave 916.4
 plenty 991.2
amputate
 excise 255.10
 sever 802.11
amputation 255.3
amputee 85.45
amscray 188.7
amulet 691.5
amuse-gueule 10.8
amusement
 pleasure 95.1

merriment 109.5
diversion 743.1
entertainment 743.1
amusing
humorous 488.4
witty 489.15
entertaining 743.27
ana archives 549.2
compilation 554.7
excerpts 557.4
collection 770.11
maxim 974.1
anabolism
body function 2.20
metabolism 7.12
transformation 852.3
anachronism
false estimation of time 833
chronological error 833.1
anachronistic 833.3
anaerobe 85.42
anaerobic respiration 2.21
anagram
wordplay 489.8
riddle 522.9
anal retentive 474.8
overfastidious 495.12
conformist 867.6
analects
compilation 554.7
excerpts 557.4
maxim 974.1
analeptic
n remedy 86.1
tonic 86.8
adj refreshing 9.3
remedial 86.39
tonic 86.44
restorative 396.22
analgesic
n anesthetic 25.3
sedative 86.12
adj deadening 25.9
sedative 86.45
relieving 120.9
analogy
parallelism 203.1
similarity 784.1
substitute 862.2
comparison 943.1
anal-retentive
obsessed 926.33
obsessive 926.34
analysis
psychoanalysis 92.6
discussion 541.6
commentary 556.2
circumstantiation 766.5
differentiation 780.4
simplification 798.2
breaking down 801.1
analyzation 801.1
dissection 802.5
classification 809.1
reasoning 935.3
inquiry 938.1
discernment 944.2
theory 951.1
automation 1041.7
analyst
psychologist 92.10

critic 723.4
analyzer 801.5
experimenter 942.6
analytic
schematic 801.9
reasoning 935.18
dialectic 935.22
examining 938.37
absurdist 952.11
mathematical 1017.22
analyze
grammaticize 530.16
discuss 541.11
criticize 723.5
itemize 766.6
differentiate 780.6
diversify 782.2
separate 793.6
simplify 798.4
break down 801.6
dissect 802.17
classify 809.6
reason 935.15
discriminate 944.4
anaphylactic 24.12
anaphylaxis 24.3
anarchic
formless 263.4
lawless 418.6
turbulent 671.18
unruly 671.19
illegal 674.6
incoherent 804.4
confused 810.16
revolutionist 860.6
anarchist
law-breaker 418.3
radical 611.12
revolutionist 860.3
anarchy
formlessness 263.1
lawlessness 418.2
illegality 674.1
noncohesion 804.1
confusion 810.2
anathema
hated thing 103.3
censure 510.3
curse 513.1
anathematize
censure 510.13
curse 513.5
condemn 602.3
anatomical 266.6
anatomize
itemize 766.6
differentiate 780.6
analyze 801.6
dissect 802.17
anatomy body 2.1
human form 262.4
structure 266.1
anthropology 312.10
analysis 801.1
dissection 802.5
physical being 1052.3
ancestor parent 560.8
precursor 816.1
antecedent 834.2
ancestral
parental 560.17

beginning 818.15
primitive 842.11
ancestry blood relationship
559.1
kinfolk 559.2
progenitorship 560.1
genealogy 560.5
nobility 608.2
anchor
n mooring 180.16
safeguard 1008.3
broadcaster 1034.23
television broadcast 1035.2
v settle 159.17
moor 182.15
land 186.8
bind 428.10
fasten 800.7
secure 855.8
anchorage
establishment 159.7
ship 180.16
destination 186.5
fee 630.6
harbor 1009.6
anchorite
recluse 584.5
ascetic 667.2
anchorman or anchorwoman
1034.23
ancient
n man of old 842.7
adj aged 303.16
durable 827.10
former 837.10
old 842.10
ancient history 837.3
ancillary
additional 253.10
helping 449.20
and 253.13
andante
n slow motion 175.2
music 708.25
adj music 708.54
andiron 1020.12
and/or 371.29
andric 76.12
androgynous 75.31
androgyny
intersexuality 75.12
effeminacy 77.2
and so forth 253.14
anecdotal 722.8
anecdotal evidence 953.6
anecdote 719.3
anemia weakness 16.1
paleness 36.2
symptom 85.9
anemic weak 16.12
colorless 36.7
chlorotic 85.61
anemometer
speedometer 174.7
weather vane 318.16
anent 775.13
anesthesia
insensibility 25.1
unfeeling 94.1
numb 94.2
relief 120.1

anesthesiologist 90.4
anesthetic
n sleep-inducer 22.10
general anesthetic 25.3
drug 86.15
adj deadening 25.9
remedy 86.47
relieving 120.9
anesthetist 90.11
anesthetize
put to sleep 22.20
deaden 25.4
numb 94.8
relieve 120.5
anew newly 841.15
repeated 849.17
again 874.7
angel
n ladylove 104.14
angel defender 460.7
giver 478.11
endearment term 562.6
benefactor 592.1
supporter 616.9
innocent 657.4
holy man 659.6
familiar spirit 678.12
celestial being 679.1
heaven figure 679.1
patron 704.26
financer 729.10
beauty 1016.8
v subsidize 478.19
finance 729.16
angelic
endearing 104.24
virtuous 653.5
innocent 657.6
seraphic 679.6
godly 692.9
anger
n darkness 38.2
ill humor 110.1
vexation 152.1
wrath 152.5
violence 671.1
heat metaphor 1019.2
v lose one's temper
152.17
make angry 152.22
heat 1020.18
angina 26.5
angioplasty 85.19
angle
n viewpoint 27.7
aspect 33.3
station 159.2
point 278.2
partiality 650.3
plot 722.4
cheating 759.13
particular 766.3
outlook 978.2
v deviate 164.3
oblique 204.9
go sideways 218.5
crook 278.5
plot 381.9
fish 382.10
maneuver 415.10
favor 650.8

anonymous
private 345.13
anon 528.3
anorexia 7.13
anorexia nervosa 270.6
fasting 515.1
another
n a different thing 780.3
adj additional 253.10
other 780.8
fresh 841.8
answer
n communication 343.1
remark 524.3
letter 553.2
defense 600.2
paean 696.3
response 708.23
equal 790.4
reaction 903.1
retort 939.1
reply 939.1
solution 940.1
refutation 958.2
expedient 995.2
v communicate with 343.8
avail 387.17
reply 553.11
defend 600.10
reciprocate 777.7
suit 788.8
react 903.5
make answer 939.4
solve 940.2
refute 958.5
suffice 991.4
expedite one's affair 995.3
answerable
responsible 641.17
agreeing 788.9
liable 897.5
solvable 940.3
answer for
go for 349.10
commit 436.5
represent 576.14
be responsible for 641.6
take the responsibility 641.9
answering machine 549.1
ant 311.33
antacid
n gastric antacid 86.25
counteractant 900.3
acid 1060.3
adj antidotal 86.41
neutralizing 900.9
antagonism
hostility 99.2
opposition 451.2
warlikeness 458.10
enmity 589.3
contrariety 779.1
disagreement 789.1
counteraction 900.1
antagonist
opponent 452.1
enemy 589.6
role 704.10
actor 707.2
antagonize repel 99.6
aggravate 119.2

contend against 451.4
set against 589.7
counteract 900.6
ante
n bet 759.3
v pay over 624.15
bet 759.25
ante-bellum 834.5
antecede
precede 814.2
be prior 834.3
antecedent
n precursor 816.1
precedent 834.2
adj leading 165.3
preceding 814.4
previous 834.4
antecedents
ancestors 560.7
cause 886.1
antechamber 197.20
antedate
n date 832.4
previousness 834.1
v date 832.13
mistime 833.2
be prior 834.3
antediluvian
n ancient 842.7
back number 842.8
adj prewar 834.5
antiquated 842.13
antelope
swiftness 174.6
hoofed animal 311.5
antemeridian 314.6
antenna whiskers 3.10
feeler 73.4
radio transmitter 1034.4
anterior front 216.10
preceding 814.4
previous 834.4
anteroom 197.20
anthem
n paean 696.3
sacred music 708.17
v sing 708.38
anthemic 696.16
anthill hill 237.4
pile 770.10
anthology
compilation 554.7
excerpts 557.4
book of verse 720.5
collection 770.11
anthrax 85.41
anthropocentric 312.13
anthropoid
n ancient 842.7
adj manlike 312.14
anthropological 312.13
anthropology 312.10
anthropomorphic
animal 311.39
manlike 312.14
religious 675.25
anti oppositional 451.8
contrary 779.6
antibacterial cleansing 79.28
antibiotic
n panacea 86.3

miracle drug 86.29
poison 1001.3
adj antidotal 86.41
antibody blood 2.25
immunity 83.4
antitoxin 86.27
antic
n prank 489.10
v play 743.23
adj gay 109.14
fantastic 870.12
antichrist 695.10
anticipate expect 130.5
be prior 834.3
come 839.6
foresee 845.6
predict 961.5
prevent 1012.14
anticipating
pregnant 78.18
expectant 130.11
anticipation
expectation 130.1
carefulness 339.1
anachronism 833.1
previousness 834.1
the future 839.1
earliness 845.1
intuition 934.1
foresight 961.1
anticipatory
expectant 130.11
previous 834.4
future 839.8
early 845.7
foreseeing 961.7
anticlimax 488.3
anticoagulant 1064.4
antidepressant
n drug 87.3
adj psychochemical 86.46
antidotal 900.9
antidote
counterpoison 86.26
counteractant 900.3
antiestablishment 333.6
antifreeze
n coolant 1024.8
adj antifreezing 1024.15
antigen blood 2.25
immunity 83.4
antitoxin 86.27
antihero 704.10
anti-inflammatory agent
86.12
anti-inflammatory drug 86.12
antinomian
n anarchist 418.3
heretic 688.5
adj anarchic 418.6
unorthodox 688.9
antinomy
self-contradiction 779.3
inconsistency 789.2
antipasto 10.9
antipathetic
oppositional 451.8
hostile 589.10
contrary 779.6
disagreeing 789.6
counteractive 900.8

antipathy
dislike 99.2
loathing 103.1
hated thing 103.3
refusal 325.1
hostility 451.2
enmity 589.3
contrariety 779.1
counteraction 900.1
antiphon paean 696.3
response 708.23
answer 939.1
antipodes
opposites 215.2
remote region 261.4
poles 779.2
Antipodes 231.6
antipyretic
n febrifuge 86.14
adj antidotal 86.41
antiquarian
n antiquary 842.5
adj archaeological 842.20
antiquated
disused 390.10
past 837.7
grown old 842.13
antique
n relic 842.6
back number 842.8
adj disused 390.10
durable 827.10
past 837.7
old 842.10
antiquated 842.13
antiquity
durability 827.1
ancient times 837.3
oldness 842.1
antique 842.6
antireligious 695.22
anti-Semitism
hate 103.1
discrimination 980.4
antiseptic
n disinfectant 86.21
poison 1001.3
adj sanitary 79.27
disinfectant 86.43
antisocial
misanthropic 590.3
eccentric 927.5
antithesis
contraposition 215.1
contrariety 779.1
antithetical
contrapositive 215.5
oppositional 451.8
contrary 779.6
antitoxin
antitoxic serum 86.27
inoculation 91.16
antler 285.4
antonym word 526.1
the opposite 779.2
antonyms 215.2
antrum 284.2
antsy
excited 105.23
restless 105.27
apprehensive 127.24

impatient 135.6
agitated 917.16
wriggly 917.21
anus
digestive system 2.18
asshole 292.5
anvil ear 2.10
instrument of conversion
858.10
anxiety
unpleasure 96.1
eagerness 101.1
apprehensiveness 126.1
anxiousness 126.1
fear 127.4
suspense 130.3
impatience 135.1
trouble 1013.3
anxious
pleasureless 96.20
eager 101.8
concerned 126.7
apprehensive 127.24
in suspense 130.12
impatient 135.6
troubled 1013.20
any
n some 244.3
anything 864.5
adj quantitative 244.5
every 864.15
one 872.7
anybody 864.5
anyhow
carelessly 340.18
anyway 384.10
any kind 809.9
anyone any 864.5
whoever 864.7
any one
n any 864.5
adj one 872.7
anyplace 159.22
anything some 244.3
any 864.5
anytime
whenever 821.12
imminently 840.4
Anytown 864.4
anyway 384.10
anywhere
adj addicted 87.25
adv wherever 159.22
aorta 2.23
apace swiftly 174.17
hastily 401.12
promptly 845.15
apart
adj distant 261.8
secluded 584.8
unrelated 776.6
separate 802.20
alone 872.8
adv away 261.17
privately 345.19
separately 802.27
singly 872.13
in half 875.8
apartheid
seclusion 584.1
exclusiveness 773.3

discrimination 980.4
apartment 228.13
apathetic insensible 25.6
incurious 982.3
apathy
insensibility 25.1
lack of feeling 94.4
unconcern 102.2
despair 125.2
inertness 173.4
languor 331.6
indifference 467.2
thoughtlessness 933.1
incuriosity 982.1
ape
n strong man 15.7
wild animal 311.22
imitator 336.4
ruffian 593.4
violent person 671.10
v mimic 336.6
impersonate 349.12
gesture 517.21
resemble 784.7
adj crazy 926.27
aperçu
treatise 556.1
abridgment 557.1
intuition 934.1
apéritif appetizer 10.9
drink 88.9
aperture
opening 292.1
passageway 383.3
apex summit 198.2
height 272.2
angle 278.2
speech organ 524.18
aphasia muteness 51.2
loss of speech 525.6
aphorism
witticism 489.7
epigram 537.3
maxim 974.1
aphoristic 537.6
aphrodisiac
love potion 75.6
aphroditous 75.26
Aphrodite Love 104.7
beauty 1016.9
apical 198.10
apiece 865.19
apish imitative 336.9
representational 349.13
foolish 923.8
aplenty
adj sufficient 991.7
adv plentifully 991.9
aplomb
equanimity 106.3
verticalness 200.1
self-control 359.5
stability 855.1
apnea 85.9
apocalypse
disclosure 351.1
revelation 683.10
prediction 962.1
Apocalypse 683.4
apocalyptic
ominous 133.16

scriptural 683.11
predictive 962.11
apocryphal
spurious 354.26
unorthodox 688.9
unauthoritative 971.21
apogee summit 198.2
boundary 211.3
long way 261.2
limit 794.5
orbit 1072.16
spacecraft 1075.2
Apollo music 710.22
Muse 720.10
sun 1072.14
apologetic
n apology 600.3
justifier 600.8
adj penitent 113.9
justifying 600.13
atoning 658.7
apologia apology 600.3
argumentation 935.4
apologist
defender 460.7
justifier 600.8
supporter 616.9
arguer 935.12
apologize
repent 113.7
beg pardon 658.5
apology
penitence 113.4
pretext 376.1
apologia 600.3
excuse 658.2
argumentation 935.4
apophthegm 974.1
apoplectic
n sick person 85.43
adj anemic 85.61
apoplexy seizure 85.6
paralysis 85.27
upheaval 671.5
spasm 917.6
apostasy dissent 333.1
denial 335.2
recreancy 363.2
desertion 370.2
backsliding 394.2
nonobservance 435.1
Protestantism 675.10
impiety 694.1
change 852.1
renunciation 858.3
apostate
n dissenter 333.3
turncoat 363.5
backslider 394.3
Protestant 675.20
sacrilegist 694.3
defector 858.8
adj recreant 363.11
relapsing 394.5
Protestant 675.28
impious 694.6
treasonable 858.20
apostle disciple 572.2
religion 684.2
clergy 699.10
converter 858.9

apostolic
abstinent 668.10
scriptural 683.11
papal 698.15
apostrophe
remark 524.3
soliloquy 542.1
apothecary 86.35
apothegm
witticism 489.7
maxim 974.1
apotheosis
respect 155.1
praise 509.5
glorification 662.8
removal to heaven 681.11
idolization 697.2
ideal 786.4
elevation 912.1
appall offend 98.11
terrify 127.17
dismay 127.19
appalling horrid 98.19
terrible 127.30
remarkable 247.10
appanage 471.5
apparatus
equipment 385.4
impedimenta 471.3
tool 1040.1
apparel
n clothing 5.1
v outfit 5.39
apparent visible 31.6
appearing 33.11
exterior 206.7
manifest 348.8
specious 354.27
plausible 968.7
illusory 976.9
apparently visibly 31.8
seemingly 33.12
externally 206.10
manifestly 348.14
falsely 354.35
apparition ghost 33.1
appearance 33.5
phantom 976.4
figment of the imagination
986.5
specter 988.1
apparitor 133.4
appeal
n delightfulness 97.2
desirability 100.13
loveableness 104.6
allurement 377.1
entreaty 440.2
appeal motion 598.10
prayer 696.4
v attract 377.6
entreat 440.11
appealing
delightful 97.7
alluring 377.8
imploring 440.17
melodious 708.48
appeal to
entreat 440.11
address 524.26
refer to 957.14

relevant 775.11
apt 788.10
timely 843.9
characteristic 865.13
expedient 995.5
appropriation
allotment 477.3
taking over 480.4
theft 482.1
plagiarism 482.8
adoption 621.2
usurpation 640.3
approval
respect 155.1
ratification 332.4
consent 441.1
high marks 509.5
approbation 509.1
esteem 662.3
support 901.1
criticism 946.2
approve
ratify 332.12
adopt 371.15
consent 441.2
accept 509.9
support 901.21
criticize 946.14
evidence 957.8
approved
accepted 332.14
chosen 371.26
received 479.10
favored 509.19
conventional 579.5
orthodox 687.7
authoritative 970.18
approximate
v be around 223.8
imitate 336.5
resemble 784.7
similarize 784.8
adj approaching
167.4
near 223.14
approximating 775.8
similar 784.14
inaccurate 975.17
v approach 167.3
approximately
also 223.23
nearly 244.6
on the whole 792.14
approximation
approach 167.1
nearness 223.1
measurement 300.1
reproduction 336.3
relation 775.1
similarity 784.1
likeness 784.3
inaccuracy 975.2
notation 1017.2
appurtenance
adjunct 254.1
equipment 385.4
facility 449.9
belongings 471.2
prerogative 642.1
nonessential 768.2
component 796.2

apron clothing 5.17
runway 184.23
stage 704.16
golf 751.1
apropos
relevant 775.11
apt 788.10
incidentally 843.13
apse arch 279.4
church 703.9
apt skillful 413.22
appropriate 533.7
teachable 570.18
apposite 788.10
prompt 845.9
smart 920.14
probable 968.6
disposed 978.8
aptitude
innate skill 413.5
teachableness 570.5
fitness 788.5
tendency 896.1
smartness 920.2
probability 968.1
disposition 978.3
apt to
adj liable to 897.6
prep inclined to 896.6
aquacize
n aquatics 182.11
v swim 182.56
aquaerobics 84.2
aquarium
vivarium 228.24
collection 770.11
aquascape 241.1
aquatic
n creatures 311.3
adj water-dwelling 182.58
watery 1065.16
aquatics 182.11
aqueduct
watercourse 239.2
trench 290.2
aqueous 1065.16
aquiline hooked 279.8
birdlike 311.48
aquiver 105.20
Arab 178.4
arabesque
n network 170.3
detailed design 498.2
ornament 709.18
adj ornate 498.12
Arabesque 554.15
Arabic numerals 1017.4
arable 1069.20
arachnid 311.32
arbiter
arbitrator 466.4
connoisseur 496.6
referee 596.1
judge 946.6
arbitrage
n stocks 737.19
v trade 737.23
arbitrary
voluntary 324.7
capricious 364.5
unthinking 365.10

imperious 417.16
arbitration
arbitrament 466.2
unionism 727.1
adjustment 788.4
judgment 946.1
arbitrator arbiter 466.4
go-between 576.4
judge 596.1
arbor
summerhouse 228.12
axle 915.5
arboreal forked 171.10
arborical 310.39
arboretum 397.7
Arborio rice 10.36
arc
n curve 279.2
lights 704.18
discharge 1032.6
v curve 279.6
arcade corridor 197.18
fence 212.4
pillar 273.5
arch 279.4
passageway 383.3
Arcadian rustic 233.6
natural 416.6
ideal 986.23
arcane secret 345.11
implied 519.7
recondite 522.16
supernatural 870.15
arch
n foot 199.5
span 279.4
monument 549.12
v curve 279.6
adj chief 249.14
mischievous 322.6
cunning 415.12
archaeological 842.20
archaeologist 842.5
archaeology
history 719.1
antiquarianism 842.4
discovery 941.1
archaic language 523.2
archaism
archaicism 526.12
antiquity 842.6
archangel 679.1
archbishop 699.9
archdiocese
region 231.5
diocese 698.8
arched bowed 279.10
convex 283.13
archenemy
opponent 452.1
enemy 589.6
archer 904.8
archery ballistics 462.3
sport 744.1
throwing 904.2
archetypal 842.11
archetype
engram 92.29
form 262.1
original 337.2
model 786.1

philosophy 932.2
instinct 934.2
standard of perfection
1002.4
archetypical
unimitated 337.6
prototypal 786.9
perfected 1002.9
Archie Bunker 980.5
archipelago 235.2
architect planner 381.6
draftsman 716.10
landscape planner 717.3
doer 726.1
producer 892.7
architectonics 717.1
architectress 717.3
architectural
structural 266.6
design 717.7
constructional 892.15
architecture
structure 266.1
design 717.4
construction 717.1
plot 722.4
production 892.2
archives
storehouse 386.6
preserve 397.7
public records 549.2
registry 549.3
archivist 550.1
archway 279.4
arctic unfeeling 94.9
northern 161.14
seasonal 313.9
cold 1023.14
ardent alcoholic 88.37
fervent 93.18
zealous 101.9
amorous 104.25
willing 324.5
industrious 330.22
vehement 544.13
cordial 587.16
fiery 671.22
hot 1019.25
burning 1019.27
ardor animation 17.4
passion 93.2
desire 100.1
zeal 101.2
love 104.1
willingness 324.1
industry 330.6
vehemence 544.5
interest 983.2
heat 1019.2
arduous
laborious 725.18
difficult 1013.17
area space 158.1
location 159.1
region 231.1
size 257.1
study 568.8
occupation 724.4
specialty 866.1
science 928.10
Area 51 345.1

arear 163.13
areligious 695.7
arena space 158.1
  hall 197.4
  setting 209.2
  enclosed place 212.3
  sphere 231.2
  sports venue 463.1
  scene of action 463.1
  occupation 724.4
  track 755.1
  science 928.10
  outlook 978.2
arena football 746.1
argosy ship 180.1
  fleet 180.10
  navy 461.27
argot
  Greek 522.7
  jargon 523.9
arguable 971.17
argue
  affirm 334.5
  signify 517.17
  mean 518.8
  support 600.10
  reason 935.16
  evidence 957.8
argument
  quarrel 456.5
  contention 457.1
  pleadings 598.6
  testimony 598.8
  defense 600.2
  plot 722.4
  reason 935.4
  case 935.5
  specious argument
    936.3
aria
  air 708.4
  solo 708.15
arid
  dull 117.6
  unproductive 891.4
  unimaginative 987.5
  dry 1066.7
aright 999.22
arise
  get up 23.6
  appear 33.8
  emerge 190.11
  ascend 193.8
  rise 200.8
  revolt 327.7
  originate 818.13
  turn up 831.6
arise from 887.5
aristocracy
  the best 249.5
  mastership 417.7
  upper class 607.2
  social status 607.3
  noble rank 608
  nobility 608.1
  aristocracy 608.1
  blue blood 608.2
  government 612.4
aristocrat
  patrician 607.4
  nobleman 608.4

aristocratic
  dignified 136.12
  lordly 141.11
  imperious 417.16
  upper-class 607.10
  noble 608.10
  governmental 612.16
arithmetic 1017.22
arithmetical 1017.22
arithmetic operation 1017.2
arithmetize 1017.18
arm
  n appendage 2.7
  inlet 242.1
  branch 617.10
  game 745.3
  member 793.4
  supporter 901.2
  forearm 906.5
  v empower 18.10
  equip 385.8
  fortify 460.9
  protect 1008.18
armada 461.27
armament
  provision 385.1
  equipment 385.4
  arms 462.1
  football 746.1
arm candy 1016.6
armchair 951.13
armchair quarterback
  arbitrator 466.4
  spectator 918.1
armed provided 385.13
  prepared 405.16
  embattled 458.22
  heeled 460.14
  protected 1008.21
armed forces 461.20
arm in arm
  adj near 223.14
  adv sociably 582.25
  amicably 587.22
  hand in hand 769.10
armistice 465.5
armor
  n callousness 94.3
  shell 295.15
  armature 460.3
  v fortify 460.9
  protect 1008.18
armory
  storehouse 386.6
  arsenal 462.2
  insignia 647.1
  heraldry 647.2
  plant 739.3
  track 755.1
arms
  military science 458.5
  matériel 462.1
  weapons 462.1
  heraldry 647.2
arms control peace treaty
    464.7
  disarmament 465.6
arms race 458.9
arm-twisting
  inducement 375.3
  coercion 424.3

  threat 514.1
army branch 461.21
  military units 461.22
  forces 461.23
  throng 770.4
  group of animals 770.5
  multitude 884.3
aroma odor 69.1
  fragrance 70.1
  characteristic 865.4
aromatherapy odorousness
    69.2
  fragrance 70.1
aromatic
  n perfumery 70.2
  adj odorous 69.9
  fragrant 70.9
around
  adv in every direction 161.25
  round 209.12
  near 223.20
  rotating 915.16
  prep through 161.27
  about 223.26
arousal
  awakening 23.2
  stimulation 105.1
  excitation 105.11
  elicitation 192.5
  incitement 375.4
arouse energize 17.10
  wake someone up 23.5
  excite 105.12
  provoke 152.24
  elicit 192.14
  incite 375.17
  rouse 375.19
  alarm 400.3
  interest 983.12
  heat 1020.18
arousing
  n excitation 105.11
  adj aphrodisiac 75.26
  extractive 192.17
arraignment
  censure 510.3
  indictment 598.3
  accusation 599.1
arrange plan 381.8
  prepare 405.6
  settle 437.8
  mediate 466.7
  compose 708.46
  order 807.4
  align 808.8
  classify 809.6
arranged
  planned 381.12
  contracted 437.11
  orderly 807.6
  composed 808.14
arrangement
  form 262.1
  structure 266.1
  plan 381.1
  preparation 405.1
  compact 437.1
  adjustment 465.4
  compromise 468.1
  ornamentation 498.1
  appointment 582.8

  piece 708.5
  score 708.28
  harmonization 709.2
  music 709.11
  treatment 712.8
  order 807.1
  configuration 808.1
  organization 808.1
  classification 809.1
arrant
  downright 247.12
  conspicuous 348.12
  wicked 654.16
  base 661.12
  terrible 1000.9
array
  n clothing 5.1
  army 461.23
  order 807.1
  arrangement 808.1
  series 812.2
  v clothe 5.39
  ornament 498.8
  order 807.4
  dispose 808.9
  align 812.5
  adduce 957.12
arrayed clothing 5.45
  embattled 458.22
  arranged 808.14
arrears debt 623.2
  shortcoming 911.1
arrest
  n seizure 85.6
  slowing 175.4
  restraint 428.1
  arrestment 429.6
  confinement 480.2
  stop 857.2
  hindrance 1012.1
  curb 1012.7
  v slow 175.9
  restrain 428.7
  confine 429.15
  capture 480.18
  delay 846.8
  put a stop to 857.11
  engross 983.13
  hinder 1012.10
arrested
  retarded 175.12
  undeveloped 406.12
  restrained 428.13
  incomplete 795.4
  late 846.16
  mentally deficient 922.22
  gripped 983.18
arrested development
  fixation 92.21
  mental deficiency 922.9
arrival
  landing 184.18
  entrant 186.1
  incomer 189.4
arrive
  appear 33.8
  arrive at 186.6
  make good 409.10
arrivederci! 188.22
arriving
  adj approaching 186.9

harsh 144.24
contractive 260.11
strict 425.6
astrologer
predictor 962.4
astrologian 1072.23
astrological 1072.25
astrology
divination 962.2
fate 964.2
astrology 1072.20
astronaut
traveler 178.1
aviator 185.1
astronavigator 1075.8
astronautical engineering
1043.1
astronomer
earth scientist 1071.2
stargazer 1072.22
astronomical
large 247.7
huge 257.20
innumerable 884.10
the universe 1072.25
astronomy
cosmos 1072.1
stargazing 1072.19
astrophysical
physical 1018.3
celestial 1072.25
astrophysics 1072.19
astrotourism 1075.1
astute cunning 415.12
sagacious 920.16
discerning 944.8
asunder
adj distant 261.8
separate 802.20
adv separately 802.27
in half 875.8
as usual
adj same 781.6
adv in status quo 853.10
normally 869.10
as well
additionally 253.11
equally 790.11
as yet 838.4
asylum
hiding place 346.4
infirmary 926.14
refuge 1009.1
home 1009.4
asymmetric
distorted 265.10
unequal 791.4
asymmetry
distortion 265.1
inconsistency 789.2
inequality 791.1
asymptotic 169.3
at by 159.27
in 207.13
at all anyhow 384.10
any kind 809.9
by any possibility 966.10
at all costs 338.9
at a loss
adj in a dilemma 971.25
at an impasse 1013.24

adv unprofitably 473.9
at any rate
limited 248.10
notwithstanding
338.8
anyhow 384.10
certainly 970.23
ataraxy apathy 94.4
unconcern 102.2
inexcitability 106.1
quiescence 173.1
at arm's length 261.14
at a standstill
adj motionless 173.13
inactive 331.17
immovable 855.15
at an impasse 1013.24
adv at a halt 329.7
in status quo 853.10
at a stretch
continuously 812.10
in the meantime 821.10
atavism
inversion 205.1
relapse 394.1
oldness 842.1
throwback 859.2
memory 989.1
atavistic
inverted 205.7
innate 767.8
primitive 842.11
reversionary 859.7
at bay
adj cornered 1013.25
adv defensively 460.16
at best 248.10
at bottom deep 275.16
essentially 767.11
at cost 633.10
at cross-purposes
adj at odds 456.16
at outs 589.12
contrary 779.6
disagreeing 789.6
adv in opposition 451.9
at ease
adj content 107.7
comfortable 121.12
adv at rest 20.11
atelier library 197.6
studio 712.16
workplace 739.1
at fault
blameworthy 510.25
guilty 656.3
erroneous 975.16
at first sight
vision 27.22
apparently 33.12
at hand
adj present 221.12
handy 387.20
imminent 840.3
adv near 223.20
at heart 767.11
atheism
infidelity 688.3
impiety 694.1
unorthodoxy 695.5
unbelief 955.1

atheist
n sacrilegist 694.3
impious person 695.11
adj unbelieving 695.19
atherosclerosis 1046.5
athlete 743.19
athletic able-bodied 15.16
sporting 743.30
athletics sports 743.8
gymnastics 744.1
track 755.1
athletic shoes 5.27
at home
n social gathering 582.10
assembly 770.2
adj at ease 121.12
adv in the bosom of one's
family 225.16
at home with
used to 373.16
friends with 587.17
versed in 928.19
athwart
adj transverse 170.9
oblique 204.19
adv crosswise 170.13
transversely 204.24
in opposition 451.9
prep opposed to 451.10
atilt
adj inclining 204.15
adv slantingly 204.23
at issue
adj doubtful 971.17
undecided 971.18
adv in opposition 451.9
in question 938.39
at it 330.21
Atlantis 986.11
at large
adj escaped 369.11
free 430.21
adv at length 538.16
scatteringly 771.12
wholly 792.13
generally 864.17
atlas pillar 273.5
reference book 554.9
Atlas strong man 15.6
support 901.3
at last
adv finally 820.12
interj eureka! 941.11
at least 248.10
at length
lengthily 267.10
lengthwise 267.11
ad nauseam 538.16
fully 766.13
finally 820.12
at liberty idle 331.18
free 430.21
at loose ends
idle 331.18
irresolute 362.9
atmosphere
milieu 209.3
aerosphere 317.2
treatment 712.8
plot 722.4
gas 1067.2

atmospheric 317.12
at most 248.10
at odds
adj unwilling 325.5
oppositional 451.8
at variance 456.16
at outs 589.12
different 780.7
disagreeing 789.6
adv in opposition 451.9
atoll 235.2
atom modicum 248.2
particle 258.8
one 872.3
tracer 1038.4
matter 1052.2
element 1060.2
atom bomb
n atomic explosion 1038.16
v bomb 459.23
atomic
infinitesimal 258.14
one 872.7
atomistic 1038.18
atomic energy 1038.15
atomic nucleus 1038.6
atomic number 1060.5
atomic scientist 1038.3
atomic war 458.1
atomic weight
unit of measure 297.5
weight 297.8
chemistry 1060.5
atomize
demolish 395.17
itemize 766.6
differentiate 780.6
analyze 801.6
come apart 802.9
shatter 802.13
disintegrate 806.3
nucleize 1038.17
pulverize 1051.9
vaporize 1067.8
atomizer perfume 70.6
sprinkler 1065.8
vaporizer 1067.6
atom smasher 1038.11
atonal 61.4
atonality 61.1
at once hastily 401.12
together 769.11
jointly 800.18
at once 830.8
promptly 845.15
atone
compensate 338.4
make restitution 481.5
repay 624.11
make amends 658.4
harmonize 708.35
tune 708.36
at one
unanimous 332.15
in accord 455.3
agreeing 788.9
atonement
compensation 338.1
peace offer 465.2
restitution 481.2
recompense 624.3

alluring 377.8
attracting 907.5
engrossing 983.20
beautiful 1016.17
attributable
adj due 639.10
assignable 888.6
conj resulting from 887.8
attribute
n syntax 530.2
insignia 647.1
characteristic 865.4
v assign 888.3
attribution
specification 865.6
assignment of cause 888
designation 888.1
attributive noun 530.5
attrition
weakening 16.5
regret 113.1
decrement 252.3
reduction 255.2
consumption 388.1
abrasion 1044.2
pulverization 1051.4
attune
n harmony 708.3
v fit 405.8
harmonize 708.35
tune 708.36
make agree 788.7
attuned in accord 455.3
harmonious 708.49
at variance
adj at odds 456.16
at outs 589.12
different 780.7
disagreeing 789.6
adv in opposition 451.9
at war
adj at odds 456.16
disagreeing 789.6
adv up in arms 458.23
at which 821.8
atwitter 105.20
at worst 248.10
atypical
nonconforming 868.5
unusual 870.10
auburn
reddish-brown 40.4
redheaded 41.10
au courant 928.18
auction
n sale 734.4
v sell 734.11
auctionary 730.12
auctioneer
n auction agent 730.8
v sell 734.11
audacious
insolent 142.9
defiant 454.7
daring 492.21
foolhardy 493.9
audacity
insolence 142.1
defiance 454.1
daring 492.4
foolhardiness 493.3

audible auditory 48.13
hearable 50.16
audience audition 48.2
auditory 48.6
attender 221.5
recipient 479.3
conference 541.5
playgoer 704.27
spectator 918.2
audio 48.13
audio frequency
n tone 50.2
frequency 1034.12
adj radio 1034.28
audiologist 90.11
audiometry 48.9
audio-visual 48.13
audit
n accounting 628.6
v be taught 570.11
take account of 628.9
verify 970.12
check 1017.21
audition recital 48.1
hearing 48.2
examination 938.2
tryout 942.3
auditor listener 48.5
recipient 479.3
student 572.1
superintendent 574.2
accountant 628.7
treasurer 729.12
auditorial 48.13
auditorium hall 197.4
arena 463.1
schoolroom 567.11
theater 704.14
parquet 704.15
auditory
n audience 48.6
adj audio 48.13
auditory sensation 48.1
auf Wiedersehen! 188.22
auger
n point 285.3
v perforate 292.15
aught some 244.3
nothing 762.2
any 864.5
augment
aggravate 119.2
increase 251.4
add to 253.5
enlarge 259.4
augur
n predictor 962.4
v hint 133.11
augur well 124.9
augury omen 133.3
divination 962.2
august dignified 136.12
venerable 155.12
eminent 247.9
au naturel 11.6
aunt 559.3
au pair girl 577.8
aura milieu 209.3
illustriousness 662.6
ectoplasm 689.7
halo 1025.14

aural eye 2.28
auditory 48.13
aureole radiation 171.2
circle 280.2
halo 1025.14
au revoir! 188.22
auricle
the hearing sense 2.10
ear 310.29
auricular
auditory 48.13
confidential 345.14
aurora dawn 314.3
foredawn 314.4
polar lights 1025.16
Aurora 314.2
auscultate 48.10
auspices
patronage 449.4
supervision 573.2
protectorship 1008.2
auspicious
promising 124.12
of good omen 133.17
timely 843.9
good 999.12
fortunate 1010.14
austere harsh 144.24
strict 425.6
inornate 499.9
plain-speaking 535.3
ascetic 667.4
simple 798.6
meager 992.10
austerity
harshness 144.9
strictness 425.1
inornateness 499.4
plain speech 535.1
thrift 635.1
asceticism 667.1
meagerness 992.2
autarchy
independence 430.5
government 612.4
absolutism 612.8
auteur
theater man 704.23
motion-picture studio 706.4
authentic
original 337.5
straight 644.14
orthodox 687.7
real 761.15
evidential 957.16
authoritative 970.18
genuine 973.15
authenticate
ratify 332.12
confirm 957.11
authenticated
accepted 332.14
proved 957.20
true 973.13
authenticity
nonimitation 337.1
candor 644.4
orthodoxy 687.1
reality 761.2
reliability 970.4
genuineness 973.7

author
n writer 547.15
discourser 556.3
literary person 718.4
narrator 722.5
doer 726.1
agent 886.4
producer 892.7
v write 547.21
pen 718.6
cause 886.10
authoring software 1042.11
authoritarian
authoritative 417.15
imperious 417.16
strict 425.6
governmental 612.16
narrow-minded 980.10
authoritative
powerful 18.12
skillful 413.22
vested with authority 417.15
imperious 417.16
preceptive 419.4
commanding 420.13
orthodox 687.7
specialized 866.5
influential 894.13
convincing 953.26
authentic 970.18
valid 973.14
the authorities
the powers that be 575.15
the government 612.3
authority
power 18.1
supremacy 249.3
expert 413.11
sanction 417.12
prerogative 417.1
authoritativeness 417.2
prestige 417.4
governance 417.5
command 420.1
authorization 443.3
connoisseur 496.6
certificate 549.6
informant 551.5
direction 573.1
commission 615.1
prerogative 642.1
specialist 866.3
influence 894.1
wise man 921.1
scientist 928.11
validity 973.6
authorize
empower 18.10
ratify 332.12
prescribe 420.9
sanction 443.11
commission 615.10
legalize 673.9
authorized
authoritative 417.15
empowered 443.17
commissioned 615.19
legal 673.11
authorship
creation 547.2
writing 718.2

bad turn 144.13
bad vibes 93.7
bad word oath 513.4
  barbarism 526.6
baffle
  n silencer 51.4
  bewilderment 971.3
  v muffle 51.9
  disappoint 132.2
  be incomprehensible 522.10
  perplex 971.13
  thwart 1012.15
baffled
  disappointed 132.5
  in a dilemma 971.25
  at an impasse 1013.24
bafflement
  disappointment 132.1
  discomfiture 412.2
  bewilderment 971.3
  frustration 1012.3
baffling
  bewildering 971.27
  frustrating 1012.20
bag
  n genitals 2.13
  contraceptive 86.23
  dose 87.20
  sack 195.2
  hang 202.2
  quantity 247.3
  breast 283.6
  old woman 304.3
  preference 371.5
  take 480.10
  occupation 724.1
  purse 729.15
  baseball 745.1
  mode 765.4
  bundle 770.8
  specialty 866.1
  eyesore 1015.4
  v load 159.15
  hang 202.6
  package 212.9
  bulge 283.11
  acquire 472.9
  catch 480.17
  rob 482.16
  bundle 770.20
bag and baggage
  n impedimenta 471.3
  adv free and clear 469.12
  completely 794.14
bagatelle
  hardly anything 248.5
  trifle 998.5
baggage
  freight 176.6
  container 195.1
  impedimenta 471.3
  strumpet 665.14
baggy
  drooping 202.10
  formless 263.4
  bulging 283.15
  loose 804.5
bag lady 619.4
bagman
  traveling salesman 730.4
  fence 732.6

bookmaker 759.20
bag of bones 2.2
bag of tricks 384.2
bag person displaced person
  160.4
  vagabond 178.3
  transient 828.4
baignoire 704.15
bail
  n pledge 438.2
  arraignment 598.3
  v ladle 176.17
bailiff steward 574.4
  policeman 1008.15
bailiwick area 231.2
  region 231.5
  arena 463.1
  bureau 594.4
  occupation 724.4
  sphere of influence 894.4
bail out
  n rescue 398.1
  aid 449.1
  v parachute 184.47
  emerge 190.11
  escape 369.6
  pledge 438.10
  aid 449.11
bait
  n snare 356.13
  incentive 375.7
  lure 377.3
  v annoy 96.13
  lure 377.5
  discriminate against 980.8
baited 96.24
bake cook 11.5
  pot 742.6
  be hot 1019.22
  dry 1066.6
baker 11.3
baker's dozen
  extra 254.4
  gratuity 478.5
  thirteen 882.7
bakery food preparation 11.4
  sweetness 66.1
baking
  n cooking 11.2
  adj hot 1019.25
balance
  n equanimity 106.3
  mean 246.1
  difference 255.8
  remainder 256.1
  symmetry 264.1
  offset 338.2
  supply 386.2
  harmony 533.2
  account 628.2
  justice 649.1
  moderation 670.1
  treatment 712.8
  funds 728.14
  correlation 777.1
  equality 790.1
  stability 855.1
  sensibleness 920.6
  sanity 925.1
  comparability 943.3
  surplus 993.5

v symmetrize 264.3
  weigh 297.10
  offset 338.5
  hesitate 362.7
  keep accounts 628.8
  make uniform 781.4
  equal 790.5
  make the same 790.6
  stabilize 855.7
  compare 943.4
  check 1017.21
balanced
  composed 106.13
  symmetric 264.4
  harmonious 533.8
  just 649.7
  uniform 781.5
  poised 790.9
  stable 855.12
  neutralizing 900.9
  sensible 920.18
  sane 925.4
balance sheet 628.4
balance the books
  keep accounts 628.8
  equalize 790.6
  check 1017.21
balcony
  gallery 197.22
  auditorium 704.15
  platform 901.13
bald hairless 6.17
  uncovered 292.17
  open 348.10
  unadorned 499.8
  plain-speaking 535.3
balderdash
  nonsense 520.2
  bombast 545.2
bale
  n wretchedness 96.6
  burden 297.7
  bundle 770.8
  v bundle 770.20
balk
  n disappointment 132.1
  discomfiture 412.2
  game 745.3
  slip 975.4
  frustration 1012.3
  v disappoint 132.2
  refuse 325.3
  stickle 361.7
  thwart 1012.15
balky
  reluctant 325.6
  obstinate 361.8
ball
  n sphere 282.2
  shot 462.19
  dance 705.2
  fun 743.2
  baseball 745.1
  prolate spheroid 746.1
  football team 746.2
  basketball 747.1
  tennis 748.1
  field hockey 749.4
  bowling 750.1
  bocci 750.3
  soccer 752.1

assembly 770.2
  projectile 904.5
  v copulate 75.21
  snowball 282.7
  have a party 582.21
ballad
  n popular music 708.7
  song 708.14
  v sing 708.38
balladeer
  minstrel 710.14
  composer 710.20
balladry 708.11
ball and chain
  wife 563.8
  impediment 1012.6
ballast
  n counterbalance 297.4
  offset 338.2
  light source 1026.1
  v trim ship 182.49
  weight 297.12
  stabilize 855.7
ball bearing 915.7
ball-breaker 77.6
ball dress 5.11
balled up 799.4
ballerina 705.3
ballet
  n musical theater 708.34
  adj dramatic 704.33
balletic
  dramatic 704.33
  dancing 705.6
ball game 766.2
ballistic 904.15
ballistics 462.3
ballocks 2.13
ball of fire
  energizer 17.6
  man of action 330.8
balloon
  n aerostat 181.11
  bag 195.2
  sphere 282.2
  bubble 320.1
  v grow 14.2
  fly 184.36
  increase 251.6
  enlarge 259.5
  ball 282.7
  bulge 283.11
ballooning
  n aviation 184.1
  increase 251.1
  adj drooping 202.10
  bulging 283.15
balloonist 185.7
ballot
  n vote 371.6
  slate 609.19
  v vote 371.18
ballpark figure
  measurement 300.1
  gamble 971.8
ballroom hall 197.4
  dance emporium 705.4
  entertainment 743.13
balls genitals 2.13
  pep 17.3
  tits 283.7

balls 492.2
fearlessness 492.3
bullshit 520.3
dandy 999.7
balls-out 794.10
ballsy 492.18
ball up
    n confusion 810.2
    v spoil 393.11
    complicate 799.3
    confuse 811.3
ball-up
    bungle 414.5
    confusion 810.2
ballyhoo
    n publicity 352.4
    exaggeration 355.1
    sales talk 734.5
    v publicize 352.15
    exaggerate 355.3
ballyhooed 355.4
balm anesthetic 25.3
    perfumery 70.2
    remedy 86.1
    medicine 86.4
    lotion 86.11
    condolence 147.1
    moderator 670.3
    ointment 1056.3
balmy fragrant 70.9
    palliative 86.40
    bright 97.11
    relieving 120.9
    crazy 926.27
    thriving 1010.13
balneal 79.28
baloney
    humbug 354.14
    bullshit 520.3
balsa 180.11
balsam perfumery 70.2
    remedy 86.1
    medicine 86.4
    balm 86.11
    ointment 1056.3
balsamic
    palliative 86.40
    relieving 120.9
balustrade fence 212.4
    post 273.4
    base 901.8
Bambi 572.9
bambino 302.9
bamboo grass 310.5
    cane 1054.4
bamboo curtain
    frontier 211.5
    veil of secrecy 345.3
    barrier 1012.5
bamboozle
    deceive 356.14
    stump 971.14
ban
    n prohibition 444.1
    disapproval 510.1
    curse 513.1
    ostracism 586.3
    exclusion 773.1
    v excise 255.10
    prohibit 444.3
    disapprove 510.10

ostracize 586.6
exclude 773.4
banish 909.17
banal trite 117.9
    medium 246.3
    aphoristic 974.6
banality triteness 117.3
    platitude 974.3
bananas 926.27
band
    n stripe 47.5
    dressing 86.33
    strip 271.4
    circle 280.3
    layer 296.1
    jewel 498.6
    line 517.6
    association 617.1
    orchestra 710.12
    tennis 748.1
    company 770.3
    frequency 1034.13
    v variegate 47.7
    encircle 209.7
    cooperate 450.3
    put together 800.5
    bind 800.9
bandage
    n dressing 86.33
    strip 271.4
    wrapper 295.18
    v blind 30.7
    treat 91.24
    bind 800.9
Band-Aid 86.33
band-aid
    n pretext 376.1
    adj makeshift 995.7
B and B 228.15
bandeau brassiere 5.24
    heraldry 647.2
    supporter 901.2
banded 47.15
bandha 283.3
bandied about 552.15
bandit
    military aircraft 181.9
    brigand 483.4
banditry theft 482.3
    plundering 482.6
bandmaster 710.17
bandstand 704.16
band together
    cooperate 450.3
    accompany 769.7
    league 805.4
the bandwagon 578.5
bandwidth 1042.18
bandy
    n field hockey 749.4
    v interchange 863.4
    adj deformed 265.12
    bowed 279.10
bandy about
    publish 352.10
    interchange 863.4
bandy-legged 265.12
bane death 307.1
    killing 308.1
    end 395.2
    destroyer 395.8

enemy 589.6
evil 1000.3
affliction 1001.1
curse 1001.1
baneful
    unhealthful 82.5
    horrid 98.19
    ominous 133.16
    deadly 308.23
    harmful 1000.12
    disastrous 1011.15
bang
    n tuft 3.6
    energy 17.3
    power 18.1
    noise 53.3
    report 56.1
    detonation 56.3
    dose 87.20
    excitement 105.3
    gunfire 459.8
    explosion 671.7
    production 893.2
    hit 902.4
    blow 902.5
    v din 53.7
    crack 56.6
    blast 56.8
    close 293.6
    collide 902.13
    strike 902.15
    pound 902.16
    adv suddenly 830.9
    interj boom! 56.13
banging crashing 56.11
    large 257.21
bangle 498.6
bang one's head against a brick wall
    be impotent 19.7
    be useless 391.8
bangs 3.6
banish
    ostracize 586.6
    expel 909.17
banishment
    ostracism 586.3
    relegation 909.4
banister
    post 273.4
    base 901.8
banjo hit 745.3
bank
    n incline 204.4
    border 211.4
    side 218.1
    shore 234.2
    slope 237.2
    shoal 276.2
    storehouse 386.6
    preserve 397.7
    lending institution 620.4
    treasury 729.13
    banking house 729.14
    workplace 739.1
    pot 759.5
    pile 770.10
    series 812.2
    buttress 901.4
    barrier 1012.5
    mine 1058.6

v maneuver 184.40
    incline 204.10
    store 386.10
    fortify 460.9
    pile 770.19
    ignite 1020.22
bankable useful 387.18
    valuable 387.22
    gainful 472.16
    paying 624.21
bank account
    account 622.2
    funds 728.14
bankbook 628.4
banker
    lender 620.3
    money dealer 729.11
    businessman 730.1
    bingo 759.15
banker's hours 268.1
bank holiday 20.4
banking
    maneuvers 184.13
    money dealing 729.5
bank note 728.5
bank on
    hope 124.6
    plan 380.6
    rely upon 953.16
bankroll
    n means 384.2
    roll 728.17
    v subsidize 478.19
    finance 729.16
bankrupt
    n failure 410.7
    poor man 619.4
    insolvent 625.4
    v impoverish 619.6
    ruin 625.8
    adj ruined 395.28
    destitute 619.9
    insolvent 625.11
bankruptcy
    impairment 393.1
    failure 410.1
    insolvency 625.3
bank statement 627.2
bank upon
    rely on 953.16
    plan 380.6
banned
    prohibited 444.7
    excluded 773.7
banner
    n poster 352.7
    rallying device 458.11
    sign 517.1
    trophy 646.3
    flag 647.7
    caption 937.2
    adj chief 249.14
banner ad 352.6
banns
    betrothal 436.3
    wedding 563.3
banquet
    n feast 8.9
    festival 743.4
    v feast 8.24

dull 117.6
vacant 222.14
fruitless 391.12
unproductive 891.4
unimaginative 987.5
barrens 891.2
barricade fortify 460.9
obstruct 1012.12
barrier boundary 211.3
fence 212.4
partition 213.5
obstruction 293.3
lock 428.5
fortification 460.4
horse racing 757.1
bar 1012.5
barring
n exclusion 773.1
prep off 255.14
excluding 773.10
barrio 230.6
barrister 597.1
barroom 88.20
barrow hill 237.4
tomb 309.16
swine 311.9
monument 549.12
bartender
liquor dealer 88.19
waiter 577.7
barter
n transfer 629.1
commerce 731.2
trading 863.2
v transfer 629.3
trade 731.15
basal basic 199.8
essential 767.9
original 886.14
basalt 1059.1
base
n station 159.2
point of departure 188.5
basement 199.2
headquarters 208.6
bottom 274.4
baseball 745.1
cause 886.1
foundation 901.6
pedestal 901.8
makeup 1016.11
acid 1060.3
v establish 159.16
adj offensive 98.18
servile 138.13
inadequate 250.7
dastardly 491.12
vulgar 497.15
populational 606.8
knavish 645.17
wicked 654.16
low 661.12
terrible 1000.9
inferior 1005.9
baseboard 199.2
baseborn
populational 606.8
illegitimate 674.7
base camp 760.6
based on
supported 901.24

evidential 957.16
contingent 959.9
base hospital 91.21
base jump 181.3
base-jump 184.47
baseless
unsubstantiated 764.8
groundless 936.13
baseline
point of departure 188.5
baseball 745.1
basketball 747.1
tennis 748.1
basement latrine 12.10
cellar 197.17
base 199.2
storehouse 386.6
foundation 901.6
base metals 1058.3
baseness 497.1
base pay 624.4
bash
n attempt 403.3
party 582.12
blow 902.5
v injure 393.13
censure 510.13
strike 902.15
discriminate against 980.8
work evil 1000.6
bashert 104.10
bashful fearful 127.23
shy 139.12
demurring 325.7
unsociable 583.5
reticent 344.10
bashing
persecution 389.3
censure 510.3
basic basal 199.8
essential 767.9
simple 798.6
original 886.14
vital 997.23
chemical 1060.9
basics
elementary education
    568.5
essentials 818.6
basic training
preparation 405.1
training 568.3
basilar 199.8
basilica 703.1
basin washbasin 79.12
container 195.1
bed 199.4
plain 236.1
valley 237.7
cavity 284.2
harbor 1009.6
basis
point of departure 188.5
motive 375.1
warrant 600.6
cause 886.1
foundation 901.6
premise 935.7
topic 937.1
outlook 978.2
bask 1020.19

basket
n genitals 2.13
container 195.1
basketball 747.1
score 747.3
v package 212.9
basket case
fool 924.3
idiot 924.8
basketwork 170.3
bask in 95.13
bas-relief
protuberance 283.2
relief 715.3
bass
n part 708.22
voice 709.5
adj deep 54.11
vocal 708.50
bassist 710.5
basso 709.5
basso continuo 708.22
bastard
n man 76.5
illegitimate 561.5
bad person 660.5
adj spurious 354.26
illegitimate 674.7
bastardize 797.12
baste cook 11.5
whip 604.13
pound 902.16
bastille 429.8
bastion 460.6
bat
n the blind 30.4
drinking spree 88.6
tennis 748.1
blow 902.5
v play 745.5
strike 902.15
batch
n amount 244.2
lot 247.4
lump 257.10
bunch 770.7
product 893.4
v assemble 770.18
bate decrease 252.6
abate 252.8
subtract 255.9
blunt 286.2
discount 631.2
relax 670.9
bated muffled 52.17
reduced 252.10
bath
n bathe 79.8
dip 79.9
shower 79.10
washbasin 79.12
wetting 1065.6
v wash 79.19
bathe
n bath 79.8
aquatics 182.11
v wash 79.19
treat 91.24
swim 182.56
soak 1065.13
bather 182.12

bathetic 93.21
bathhouse 79.10
bathing
balneation 79.7
aquatics 182.11
wetting 1065.6
bathing suit 5.29
bathos
sentimentality 93.8
sadness 112.1
anticlimax 488.3
bathrobe 5.21
bathroom
latrine 12.10
bathing place 79.10
lavatory 197.26
baths
bathing place 79.10
health resort 91.23
spa 228.27
bathtub 79.12
bathysphere 367.5
bat of an eye 830.3
baton staff 273.2
scepter 417.9
insignia 647.1
heraldry 647.2
stigma 661.6
illegitimacy 674.2
music 711.22
batrachian
n amphibian 311.26
adj reptile 311.47
bats 926.27
battalion
military unit 461.22
company 770.3
batten
n strip 271.4
scenery 704.20
v close 293.6
gluttonize 672.4
hook 800.8
secure 855.8
thrive 1010.8
batter
n baseball team 745.2
semiliquid 1062.5
v mistreat 389.5
injure 393.13
thrash soundly 604.14
rage 671.11
pound 902.16
work evil 1000.6
battered 393.33
battering trauma 85.38
unruliness 671.3
battery
military unit 461.22
artillery 462.11
corporal punishment 604.4
baseball team 745.2
electrical device 1032.21
battle
n contention 457.4
war 458.1
operation 458.4
struggle 725.3
fight 754.3
v oppose 451.4
quarrel 456.11

suffer 443.10
bear witness
be pious 692.6
testify 957.9
beastly hoggish 80.24
offensive 98.18
horrid 98.19
cruel 144.26
animal 311.39
gruff 505.7
carnal 663.6
terrible 1000.9
beast of burden
pack animal 176.8
drudge 726.3
beat
n staccato 55.1
parasite 138.5
sphere 231.2
routine 373.5
route 383.1
accent 524.10
news item 552.3
rhythm 709.22
tempo 709.24
throb 709.26
meter 720.7
occupation 724.4
periodicity 850.2
round 850.3
circuit 914.2
pulsation 916.3
flutter 917.4
v get tired 21.6
drum 55.4
sail near the wind 182.25
change course 182.30
best 249.7
foam 320.5
deceive 356.19
hunt 382.9
injure 393.13
vanquish 411.5
defeat 412.9
whip 604.13
time 708.44
din 849.10
pound 902.16
pulsate 916.12
agitate 917.10
flutter 917.12
stump 971.14
pulverize 1051.9
adj tired 21.8
defeated 412.15
without money 619.10
unconventional 868.6
licked 971.26
beat about
change course 182.30
grope 938.32
be uncertain 971.9
have difficulty 1013.11
beat a dead horse
be useless 391.8
dwell on 849.9
persist 856.5
carry coals to Newcastle 993.12
beat around the bush
dodge 368.8

circumlocute 538.10
quibble 936.9
beat back 908.3
beat down
sadden 112.18
raze 395.19
subdue 432.9
domineer 612.15
cheapen 633.6
bargain 731.18
beaten burnt-out 21.10
bubbly 320.6
habitual 373.14
defeated 412.14
beaten path
routine 373.5
path 383.2
beater hunter 382.5
mixer 797.9
agitator 917.9
beatific happy 95.16
blissful 97.9
heavenly 681.12
beatified happy 95.16
eminent 662.18
angelic 679.6
heavenly 681.12
sanctified 685.8
raised 912.9
beatify gladden 95.9
glorify 662.13
sanctify 685.5
exalt 912.6
beating
n staccato 55.1
defeat 412.1
corporal punishment 604.4
hit 902.4
pulsation 916.3
flutter 917.4
pulverization 1051.4
adj staccato 55.7
rhythmic 709.28
periodic 850.7
pulsative 916.18
beat into one's head
inculcate 568.12
convince 953.18
beat it
v depart 188.7
leave 222.10
flee 368.11
interj go away! 909.31
beatitude
happiness 95.2
sanctification 685.3
beatnik 868.3
beat one's brains 931.9
beat one's breast 115.11
beat out best 249.7
pulsate 916.12
beat someone to the punch 845.6
beat the drum for
publicize 352.15
espouse 509.13
beat the rap
get off 369.7
go free 431.9
beat the system 409.13

beat time
keep rhythm 708.44
time 832.11
pulsate 916.12
beat up
v punish 604.15
agitate 917.10
emulsify 1062.10
adj tired 21.8
spoiled 393.29
dilapidated 393.33
slovenly 810.15
beau
n inamorato 104.12
dandy 500.9
v court 562.21
Beau Brummel
dandy 500.9
person of fashion 578.7
beaucoup
adj much 247.8
plural 883.7
plentiful 991.7
adv greatly 247.15
beau monde noble 608.1
the rich 618.6
beaut
first-rate 999.7
beauty 1016.8
beautician 1016.12
beautification
development 392.2
prettification 1016.10
beautified
improved 392.13
beautifying 1016.22
beautiful
adj artistic 712.19
beauteous 1016.17
interj bravo! 509.22
beautiful people 578.6
beautify
develop 392.10
ornament 498.8
prettify 1016.15
beauty harmony 533.2
attractiveness 1016.1
beautifulness 1016.1
charmer 1016.7
beauty pageant winner 1016.6
beauty parlor
workplace 739.1
salon de beauté 1016.13
beauty queen 1016.7
beauty sleep 22.2
beaux arts 712.1
beaver
n beard 3.8
man of action 330.8
v work hard 725.13
bebop 708.9
be buddies 587.9
becalm 173.11
becalmed 173.17
because 888.10
bechance 972.11
be chapfallen 132.4
becharm
delight 95.10
enamor 104.22
fascinate 377.7

charm 691.8
beck and call 420.5
beckon
n gesture 517.14
v attract 377.6
gesture 517.21
becloud fog 319.7
conceal 346.6
confuse 985.7
darken 1027.9
opaque 1031.2
become behoove 641.4
come to be 761.12
originate 818.13
convert 858.11
change into 858.17
become of 887.4
become one
get married 563.15
beautify 1016.15
becoming
n conversion 858.1
adj decorous 496.9
rightful 639.8
decent 664.5
apt 788.10
expedient 995.5
comely 1016.18
be crestfallen 132.4
bed
n bottom 199.1
floor 199.4
furniture 229.1
watercourse 239.2
layer 296.1
accommodations 385.3
presswork 548.9
marriage 563.1
bowling 750.1
foundation 901.6
sofa 901.19
garden 1069.10
v rest 20.6
retire 22.17
put to bed 22.19
inset 191.5
house 225.10
fix 855.9
plant 1069.18
tend 1070.7
bed and board 385.3
bed and breakfast 228.15
bedarken blacken 38.7
darken 1027.9
bedaub soil 80.16
coat 295.24
stain 1004.6
bedazzle blind 30.7
astonish 122.6
confuse 985.7
shine 1025.24
bedazzled
blinded 30.10
dazed 985.14
bedbug 311.37
bedchamber 197.7
bedding blanket 295.10
layer 296.1
foundation 901.6
underbed 901.20

bedecked clothing 5.45
  ornamented 498.11
bedevil annoy 96.13
  demonize 680.16
  bewitch 691.9
bedeviled
  tormented 96.24
  possessed 926.29
bedew 1065.12
bedfast 85.59
bedfellow companion 588.3
  associate 616.1
bedim 1027.9
bedimming
  inconspicuousness 32.2
  decoloration 36.3
  darkening 1027.6
be disenchanted 132.4
bedizen dress up 5.42
  color 35.14
  ornament 498.8
bedizened
  ornamented 498.11
  grandiloquent 545.8
bedlam
  noise 53.3
  pandemonium 810.5
  insane asylum 926.14
bed of nails
  unpleasure 96.2
  obstacle 1012.4
bed of roses
  comfort 121.1
  prosperity 1010.1
Bedouin 178.4
bedpan 12.11
bedraggled
  soiled 80.21
  slovenly 810.15
bedrape 5.39
bedridden 85.59
bedrock
  n bottom 199.1
  base 274.4
  stability 855.6
  foundation 901.6
  rock 1059.1
  adj bottom 199.7
  deepest 275.15
  vital 997.23
bedroom
  n boudoir 197.7
  v restrict 428.9
bedroom community
  environment 209.1
  town 230.1
bedsheet 295.10
bedsore 85.37
bedspread 295.10
bedsprings 901.20
bedstead 901.19
bedtime sleep 22.2
  night 315.4
bedwarf 252.9
bee honeybee 311.34
  quilting bee 582.14
beef
  n food 10.14
  muscularity 15.2
  power 18.1
  complaint 115.5

weight 297.1
  cattle 311.6
  objection 333.2
  bone of contention 456.7
  v be discontented 108.6
  complain 115.16
  object 333.5
beefcake sex object 75.4
  real man 75.6
  photograph 714.3
beefeater 1008.14
beefheaded 922.15
beefing
  n complaint 115.5
  adj discontented 108.8
  complaining 115.20
beefsteak 10.18
beef up
  strengthen 15.13
  intensify 251.5
  add to 253.5
beefy strong 15.15
  corpulent 257.18
beehive nest 228.25
  hive 739.2
bee in one's bonnet 927.2
beekeeper 1070.4
beekeeping 1070.1
beeline
  shortcut 268.5
  straight line 277.2
Beelzebub 680.4
beep
  n noise 53.5
  v blare 53.10
beeper
  telephone 347.4
  alarm 400.1
beer 88.16
beer and skittles 95.1
beerbelly 2.19
beer garden 88.20
beery
  intoxicated 88.31
  sentimental 93.21
beeswax 1056.8
beetle
  n insect 311.32
  jockey 757.2
  pulper 1063.4
  v overhang 202.7
  adj overhanging 202.11
beetle-browed
  sullen 110.24
  overhanging 202.11
be exasperated 135.5
befall occur 831.5
  chance 972.11
befit behoove 641.4
  expedite one's affair 995.3
befitting apt 788.10
  timely 843.9
  expedient 995.5
befog cover 295.19
  cloud 319.7
  conceal 346.6
befool fool 356.15
  stultify 923.7
before
  adv in front 165.4
  ahead 216.12

preferably 371.29
  above 814.6
  previously 834.6
  formerly 837.13
  early 845.11
  prep in the presence of 221.18
  prior to 834.7
beforehand
  adj anachronistic 833.3
  adv early 845.11
before long in the future 839.9
  soon 845.16
beforementioned 814.5
before one's eyes
  adj visible 31.6
  adv before 216.12
  openly 348.15
before the bar
  adv all things considered 946.17
  phrs in litigation 598.22
before the house 938.38
beforetime
  adj early 845.7
  adv formerly 837.13
  early 845.11
befoul defile 80.17
  misuse 389.4
  work evil 1000.6
befouling 393.2
befriend aid 449.11
  make friends with 587.10
  benefit 592.3
befrilled
  ornamented 498.11
  ornate 545.11
befringed 211.12
befuddle
  intoxicate 88.22
  confuse 985.7
befuddled 985.13
beg
  n governor 575.13
  v evade 368.7
  find means 384.6
  entreat 440.11
  scrounge 440.15
beget procreate 78.8
  engender 818.14
  cause 886.10
  produce 890.7
  originate 892.12
begetter parent 560.8
  author 886.4
  producer 892.7
beggar
  n vagabond 178.3
  bum 331.9
  nonworker 331.11
  mendicant 440.8
  poor man 619.4
  wretch 660.2
  v strip 480.24
  impoverish 619.6
beggar description
  stagger belief 122.8
  look good 1016.16
beggarly
  obsequious 138.14
  low 497.15
  indigent 619.8

base 661.12
  ill-provided 992.12
  paltry 998.21
begild color 35.14
  yellow 43.3
begin 818.7
begin again 856.6
beginner novice 572.9
  neophyte 818.2
  author 886.4
  producer 892.7
beginner's slope 753.1
beginning
  n start 818
  commencement 818.1
  source 886.5
  production 892.1
  adj simple 798.6
  initial 818.15
beginnings
  origin 818.4
  earliness 845.1
beg off abandon 370.5
  refuse 442.3
begone
  v depart 188.6
  interj go away! 909.31
beg pardon
  repent 113.7
  apologize 658.5
begrime 80.15
begrudge envy 154.2
  refuse 325.3
  deny 442.4
  stint 484.5
beg the question
  dodge 368.8
  quibble 936.9
beg to differ 333.4
beguile
  deceive 356.14
  fascinate 377.7
  amuse 743.21
  distract 985.6
beguiled
  wondering 122.9
  foolish 923.8
beguiling
  n allurement 377.1
  adj wonderful 122.10
  deceptive 356.21
  alluring 377.8
  amusing 743.27
be had 632.8
behalf benefit 387.4
  good 999.4
behave act 321.4
  conduct oneself 321.5
  be good 328.4
behavior
  conditioning 92.26
  tendency 321
  conduct 321.1
  action 328.1
behavioral
  behaviorist 321.7
  acting 328.10
behaviorism
  behavioral science 321.3
  materialism 1052.6
behaviorist 321.7

bespoke tailored 5.48
  made 892.18
best
  v excel 249.6
  beat 249.7
  vanquish 411.5
  defeat 412.6
  adj superlative 249.13
  reduced 633.9
  the tops 999.16
  n creature comforts 121.3
  the top of the line 249.5
  choice 999.8
best behavior
  n obedience 326.1
  v behave oneself 321.5
  obey 326.2
best bet 972.8
best case
  n hope 124.1
  adj promising 124.12
bestial cruel 144.26
  animal 311.39
  unrefined 497.12
  carnal 663.6
  savage 671.21
bestiality
  perversion 75.11
  cruelty 144.11
  sadism 144.12
  unrefinement 497.3
  carnality 663.2
  terribleness 1000.2
be still 51.14
bestir oneself
  stir 330.11
  make haste 401.5
best man
  wedding party 563.4
  assistant 616.6
bestow spend 387.13
  give 478.12
  administer 643.6
bestraddle
  mount 193.12
  rise above 272.11
  overlie 295.30
  rest on 901.22
bestride mount 193.12
  rise above 272.11
  overlie 295.30
  dominate 612.14
  rest on 901.22
  pass 910.8
best seat in the house 33.6
best seller
  great success 409.3
  book 554.1
best wishes
  congratulation 149.1
  regards 504.8
  greetings 585.3
bet
  n gamble 759.2
  wager 759.3
  poker 759.10
  v ante 759.25
  predict 962.9
  risk 972.12
be taken down a rung 137.9
betake oneself 177.18

beta particle
  electron 1033.3
  radioactive particle 1037.4
beta test 1042.18
betcha 759.25
bête noire
  frightener 127.9
  enemy 589.6
  bugbear 680.9
  bane 1001.1
be that as it may 338.8
be the bane of one's existence 98.16
bethink oneself
  think 931.8
  attend to 983.5
  remember 989.9
betide occur 831.5
  chance 972.11
betimes early 845.11
  soon 845.16
bétise stupidity 922.3
  foolishness 923.1
betoken augur 133.11
  manifest 348.5
  signify 517.17
  mean 518.8
  evidence 957.8
bet on bet 759.25
  rely on 953.16
  predict 962.9
  be certain 970.9
betray inform 351.6
  deceive 356.14
  defect 370.6
  rat on 551.12
  double-cross 645.14
  seduce 665.20
betrayal
  divulgence 351.2
  apostasy 363.2
  desertion 370.2
  betrayment 645.8
  seduction 665.6
betrayed 132.5
betrothal love affair 104.5
  promise 436.3
betrothed
  n fiancé 104.16
  adj promised 436.8
better
  v excel 249.6
  improve 392.9
  change 852.7
  adj superior 249.12
  preferable 371.25
  augmented 392.14
  changed 852.10
better half
  spouse 563.6
  wife 563.8
betterment
  improvement 392.1
  change 852.1
better self
  compunction 113.2
  self 865.5
betting parlor 759.19
bettor 759.21
between 213.12

between the devil and the deep blue sea
  in danger 1006.13
  unfortunate 1011.14
  in a dilemma 1013.23
between the lines 519.5
betweentimes
  meanwhile 826.5
  occasionally 848.5
betwixt 213.12
betwixt and between
  adj ambiguous 539.4
  mediocre 1005.7
  adv midway 819.5
  prep between 213.12
bet your life 973.25
be unable 19.8
bevel
  n incline 204.4
  instrument 278.4
  type 548.6
  adj inclining 204.15
beveled 204.15
beverage liquid 8.4
  drink 10.49
  spirits 88.13
  fluid 1061.2
beverage types 10.56
bevy company 770.3
  assemblage 770.6
  multitude 884.3
bewail regret 113.6
  lament 115.10
beware 494.7
bewhiskered
  bearded 3.25
  trite 117.9
bewilder
  astonish 122.6
  disconcert 971.12
  confuse 985.7
bewildered
  wondering 122.9
  dismayed 971.24
  at an impasse 1013.24
bewildering
  wonderful 122.10
  confusing 971.27
bewitch
  delight 95.10
  enamor 104.22
  fascinate 377.7
  demonize 680.16
  cast a spell 690.13
  witch 691.9
  work evil 1000.6
bewitched
  enamored 104.27
  wondering 122.9
  witched 691.13
  miraculous 870.16
bewitching
  delightful 97.7
  alluring 377.8
  witching 691.11
bey
  ruler 575.9
  governor 575.13
beyond
  adv additionally 253.11
  prep distant 261.21

  past 522.26
  after 835.8
  in excess of 993.26
the beyond 839.2
beyond a shadow of doubt 970.16
beyond belief
  absurd 923.11
  unbelievable 955.10
beyond compare
  adj peerless 249.15
  adv extremely 247.22
beyond measure
  extremely 247.22
  superabundantly 993.24
beyond one
  adj hard to understand 522.14
  impracticable 967.8
  adv unrealistic 19.20
beyond question
  adj undoubted 970.16
  adv unquestionably 970.25
beyond recall 125.15
beyond the call of duty 492.1
beyond the pale
  prohibited 444.7
  unpraiseworthy 510.24
  segregated 773.8
beyond words 98.19
bhikkhu
  celibate 565.2
  religious 699.16
biannual 850.8
bias
  n inclination 100.3
  deviation 164.1
  bend 204.3
  diagonal 204.7
  preference 371.5
  partiality 650.3
  tendency 896.1
  disposition 978.3
  prejudice 980.3
  v deflect 164.5
  oblique 204.9
  pervert 265.6
  influence 894.7
  tend 896.3
  prejudice 980.9
  adj inclining 204.15
  transverse 204.19
  adv diagonally 204.25
biaxial 875.7
bib
  n apron 5.17
  v drink 8.29
  tipple 88.24
bibacious 88.35
bibelot trinket 498.4
  trifle 998.5
Bible scripture 683.1
  Holy Bible 683.2
Biblical 683.11
bibliographer
  writer 547.15
  author 718.4
bibliography
  makeup 554.12
  bibliology 554.19

Modern Language
Association Bibliography
558.4
directory 574.10
catalog 871.3
lore 928.9
bibliolatry
strictness 687.5
zeal 692.3
scholarship 928.5
bibliophile
booklover 554.18
bookworm 929.4
bibliophilic 928.22
bibulous
bibacious 88.35
sorbent 187.17
intemperate 669.7
bicameral
legislative 613.11
bipartite 875.7
bicentenary 850.4
bicentennial
anniversary 850.4
hundred 882.8
biceps member 2.7
arm 906.5
bicker
n quarrel 456.5
argumentation 935.4
v quarrel 456.11
flutter 917.12
argue 935.16
quibble 936.9
flicker 1025.26
bickerer 461.1
bicoastal 207.8
bicolored 47.9
bicorn 279.11
bicuspid
n teeth 2.8
adj bipartite 875.7
bicycle
n cycle 179.8
v exercise 84.4
ride 177.33
bicycling
riding 177.6
sport 744.1
bicyclist 178.11
bid
n attempt 403.2
offer 439.1
entreaty 440.2
invitation 440.4
bridge 758.3
v command 420.8
offer 439.6
bargain 731.18
bet 733.9
bid come
summon 420.11
invite 440.13
bidding
command 420.1
summons 420.5
invitation 440.4
bidding war 360.1
biddy woman 77.6
female animal 77.9
poultry 311.28

maid 577.8
bide expect 130.8
endure 134.5
be still 173.7
sit through 827.6
wait 846.12
remain 853.5
continue 856.3
bide one's time
expect 130.8
be still 173.7
do nothing 329.2
wait 846.12
bidet washbasin 79.12
hunter 311.13
bid fair to
be liable 897.3
be possible 966.4
be probable 968.4
have a chance 972.13
biennial
n plant 310.3
anniversary 850.4
adj momentary 850.8
bier 309.13
biff
n energy 17.3
fight 754.3
blow 902.5
v strike 902.15
bifid 875.7
bifocals 29.3
bifurcated
forked 171.10
two 873.6
halved 875.6
bifurcation
forking 171.3
angle 278.2
doubleness 873.1
bisection 875.1
big enthusiastic 101.10
arrogant 141.9
large 257.16
adult 303.12
inflated 502.12
magnanimous 652.6
eminent 662.18
important 997.17
bigamist 563.11
bigamous 563.19
big-ball hitter 894.6
the Big Board 737.7
big-box store 386.6
Big Brother 894.3
big bucks 618.3
big business 731.1
big cheese
top dog 575.4
influential person 894.6
big shot 997.9
big dance 743.13
big deal
n triviality 998.3
phrs what does it matter?
998.26
big-eyed 100.27
big fish in a small pond 894.6
big game
animal life 311.1
quarry 382.7

biggety conceited 140.11
impudent 142.10
biggie influential person 894.6
big shot 997.9
big government 894.6
big gun 997.9
big hand 509.2
bighearted
benevolent 143.15
liberal 485.4
magnanimous 652.6
bight inlet 242.1
angle 278.2
big kahuna 894.6
big league
n baseball 745.1
adj important 997.17
big mouth
braggart 502.5
talkativeness 540.1
big-mouthed
talkative 540.9
boastful 502.10
big name
n celebrity 662.9
personage 997.8
adj important 997.17
big one
debacle 395.4
US denominations 728.7
bigot
n hater 103.4
obstinate person 361.6
prejudiced person 687.6
dogmatist 970.7
intolerant 980.5
adj narrow-minded 980.10
bigotry hate 103.1
obstinacy 361.1
strictness 687.5
fanaticism 926.11
dogmatism 970.6
narrow-mindedness 980.1
the big picture 381.1
big pond 240.1
big shot superior 249.4
top dog 575.4
politics 610.7
influential person 894.6
big shot 997.9
big sleep 307.1
big talk
exaggeration 355.1
boasting 502.2
grandiloquence 545.1
big talker 540.4
big ticket
n high price 632.3
adj expensive 632.11
big time
n fun 743.2
adj important 997.17
big wheel
influence 894.6
important person 997.9
bigwig
n top dog 575.4
influential person 894.6
big shot 997.9
adj important 997.17
bijou 498.6

bike
n cycle 179.8
v ride 177.33
biker 178.11
bikini 5.29
bilateral sided 218.7
two 873.6
bile digestion 2.17
body function 7.8
secretion 13.2
ill humor 110.1
bitterness 152.3
bilge
n offal 80.9
receptacle of filth 80.12
bulge 283.3
bullshit 520.3
v bulge 283.11
bilgewater offal 80.9
refuse 391.4
bilingual 523.16
bilious anemic 85.61
sour 110.23
bilk
n cheater 759.22
v disappoint 132.2
cheat 356.18
bill
n nose 283.8
point of land 283.9
poster 352.7
advertising matter 352.8
declaration 598.7
omnibus bill 613.9
debt 623.1
fee 624.5
account 628.3
law 673.3
theatrical performance
704.12
paper money 728.5
legal tender 728.7
negotiable instrument 728.11
statement 871.5
schedule 965.3
eyeshade 1028.2
v publicize 352.15
send a statement 628.11
dramatize 704.28
schedule 965.6
bill and coo 562.14
billboard 352.7
bill collector
creditor 622.4
collector 770.15
billed hooked 279.8
scheduled 965.9
billet
n letter 553.2
heraldry 647.2
position 724.5
wood 1054.3
v house 225.10
billfold 729.15
Bill Gates 618.8
billiards 760.1
billion
n thousand million 882.12
large number 1017.5
adj numerous 884.6
billionaire 618.7

billionth 882.31
bill of attainder 602.2
bill of fare menu 8.14
  bill 871.5
  schedule 965.3
bill of goods 356.9
bill of health
  pass 443.7
  certificate 549.6
bill of particulars 599.1
Bill of Rights
  right 430.2
  constitution 673.6
bill of sale 734.1
billow
  n wave 238.14
  v surge 238.22
  bulge 283.11
billowy curved 279.7
  wavy 281.10
  bulging 283.15
billy goat
  male animal 76.8
  goat 311.8
bimbo
  roughneck 593.4
  strumpet 665.14
  violent person 671.10
bimonthly
  n periodical 555.1
  adj momentary 850.8
bin 386.6
binary digit
  number 1017.3
  bit 1042.14
bind
  n state 765.1
  delay 846.2
  predicament 1013.4
  v border 211.10
  stop 293.7
  compel 424.4
  restrain 428.10
  commit 436.5
  indenture 615.18
  obligate 641.12
  relate 775.6
  tie 800.9
  stick together 803.9
binder
  dressing 86.33
  wrapper 295.18
  payment 624.1
binding
  n edging 211.7
  wrapper 295.18
  bookbinding 554.14
  fastening 800.3
  cohesion 803.1
  adj preceptive 419.4
  mandatory 420.12
  compulsory 424.11
  obligatory 641.15
  joining 800.16
  valid 973.14
bind up
  bundle 770.20
  bind 800.9
binge
  n celebration 487.1
  v stuff 8.25

drink 88.6
  celebrate 487.2
  overindulge 669.5
bingo 759.15
binocs 29.4
binocular optic 29.9
  bipartite 875.7
binoculars 29.4
binomial
  terminological 527.17
  bipartite 875.7
biochemical
  n element 1060.2
  adj chemical 1060.9
biochemistry 1068.3
biodegradable
  degradable 393.47
  disintegrative 806.5
bioethics 636.1
biographer 719.4
biographical 719.7
biography
  n history 719.1
  v chronicle 719.5
biohazard 85.32
biological
  organic 305.17
  related 559.6
  botanical 1068.4
biological clock 306.2
biological urge 75.5
biological war 458.1
biological weapon 462.1
biologist 1068.2
biology
  organic matter 305.1
  animal life 311.1
  the study of living things
    1068.1
  biological science 1068.1
bioluminescence 1025.13
biomechanical 1039.7
bionics 1041.2
biophysicist 1018.2
biopsy 91.12
biorhythm life force 306.2
  term 825.4
biosphere
  organic matter 305.1
  ecosphere 306.7
  atmosphere 317.2
  Earth 1072.10
biotaxy 305.3
bioterror 459.1
bioterrorism 127.7
biotic 305.17
biowarfare 459.1
bipartisan
  partisan 609.44
  two 873.6
bipartisanship 450.1
bipartite
  separate 802.20
  two 873.6
  bifid 875.7
biped
  n creature 311.3
  adj bipartite 875.7
birch
  n rod 605.2
  v whip 604.13

bird poultry 10.22
  man 76.5
  woman 77.6
  fowl 311.27
  oddity 870.4
  freak 927.4
  beauty 1016.8
  rocket 1074.3
birdbrained 922.20
birdcage gambling wheel 759.16
  birdhouse 228.23
birdcall
  animal noise 60.1
  call 517.16
birdhouse 228.23
bird in hand 469.1
bird of passage
  wanderer 178.2
  bird 311.27
bird of prey
  hunter 311.27
  extortionist 480.12
bird sanctuary
  preserve 397.7
  refuge 1009.1
birds and the bees 75.2
bird's-eye 864.13
bird's-eye view
  viewpoint 27.7
  appearance 33.6
  abridgment 557.1
birds of a feather 784.5
bird song 60.1
bird-watcher 918.1
birth
  n genesis 1.1
  beginning 1.1
  generation 78.6
  life 306.1
  lineage 560.4
  heredity 560.6
  aristocracy 607.3
  nobility 608.2
  origin 818.4
  v engender 818.14
  adj related 559.6
birth control 891.1
birth control device 86.23
birthday 850.4
**birthday flowers and
    birthstones** 487.6
birthday suit 6.3
birth defect 85.1
birthing center 91.21
birthmark mark 517.5
  blemish 1004.1
birth parent 560.8
birthplace
  fatherland 232.2
  breeding place 886.8
birthright
  inheritance 479.2
  prerogative 642.1
birthstone 1059.7
biscotti
  biscuit 10.30
  cookie 10.43
biscotto 10.30
biscuit sinker 10.30
  cookie 10.43
  ceramic ware 742.2

dryness 1066.2
bisect sever 802.11
  seek the middle 819.3
  double 873.5
  halve 875.4
bisector 875.3
bisexual
  n homosexual 75.14
  adj homosexual 75.30
  bipartite 875.7
bisexuality
  sexuality 75.2
  sexual preference 75.10
bishop clergy 699.10
  chessman 743.17
bishopric region 231.5
  mastership 417.7
  diocese 698.8
bison 311.6
bisque 742.2
bistro restaurant 8.17
  bar 88.20
bit short distance 223.2
  modicum 248.2
  point 285.3
  portion 477.5
  information theory 551.7
  act 704.7
  role 704.10
  script 706.3
  piece 793.3
  shift 825.3
  short time 828.3
  pittance 992.5
  trifle 998.5
  curb 1012.7
  binary digit 1042.14
a bit to a degree 245.7
  scarcely 248.9
bit by bit
  by degrees 245.6
  piece by piece 793.9
bitch
  n woman 77.6
  female animal 77.9
  shrew 110.12
  complaint 115.5
  dog 311.16
  objection 333.2
  strumpet 665.14
  card 758.2
  first-rate 999.7
  tough proposition 1013.2
  v be discontented 108.6
  sulk 110.14
  complain 115.16
  object 333.5
  bungle 414.12
bitch-slap
  mortify 98.13
  humiliate 137.4
  offend 156.5
bitchy irascible 110.20
  malicious 144.20
  spiteful 144.21
  disparaging 512.13
bite
  n morsel 8.2
  light meal 8.7
  acrimony 17.5
  pang 26.2

blank
n absence 222.1
void 222.3
document 549.5
adj dull 117.6
vacant 222.14
closed 293.9
reticent 344.10
unadorned 499.8
inexpressive 522.20
empty-headed 922.19
thoughtless 933.4
blank check
latitude 430.4
carte blanche 443.4
privilege 642.2
negotiable paper 728.11
blanket
n coverlet 295.10
coating 295.12
v cover 295.19
conceal 346.6
adj comprehensive 772.7
undiscriminating 945.5
blankie 295.10
blankminded
ignorant 930.11
thoughtless 933.4
blank out 820.5
blank slate 222.3
blank verse 720.8
blank wall 293.3
blare
n blast 53.5
rasp 58.3
brightness 1025.4
v blast 53.10
sound harshly 58.9
cry 60.2
proclaim 352.13
speak 524.25
blaring
n reception 1034.21
adj noisy 53.13
blarney
n flattery 511.1
bullshit 520.3
style 532.2
v flatter 511.6
blasé apathetic 94.13
nonchalant 106.15
weary 118.11
languid 331.20
sophistication 413.9
experienced 413.28
disillusioned 977.5
blaspheme
curse 513.5
vilify 694.5
blasphemous
cursing 513.8
impious 694.6
blasphemy
curse 513.1
sacrilege 694.2
blast
n noise 53.3
blare 53.5
detonation 56.3
excitement 105.3
gust 318.5

success 409.4
charge 462.16
party 582.12
explosion 671.7
blight 1001.2
v din 53.7
blare 53.10
detonate 56.8
use 87.22
kill 308.14
blow 318.19
blow up 395.18
pull the trigger 459.22
curse 513.5
explode 671.14
thwart 1012.15
freeze 1024.11
interj damn! 513.12
blasted high 87.24
disappointed 132.5
blighted 393.42
ruined 395.28
curse 513.10
blast off
v begin 818.7
launch 1074.13
n beginning 818.1
rocket launching 1074.9
blat
n blare 53.5
rasp 58.3
v blare 53.10
sound harshly 58.9
cry 60.2
speak 524.25
blatant
noisy 53.13
vociferous 59.10
howling 60.6
conspicuous 348.12
gaudy 501.20
blatantly
distressingly 247.21
conspicuously 348.16
gaudily 501.27
blather
n nonsense 520.2
chatter 540.3
v talk nonsense 520.5
chatter 540.5
be stupid 922.12
blaze
n outburst 105.9
notch 289.1
pointer 517.4
mark 517.5
card 758.2
fire 1019.13
flare 1019.14
brightness 1025.4
flash 1025.6
v notch 289.4
proclaim 352.13
mark 517.19
be hot 1019.22
catch fire 1020.23
burn 1020.24
shine 1025.24
blaze up
flare up 152.19
catch fire 1020.23

blazon
n display 501.4
heraldry 647.2
v proclaim 352.13
ornament 498.8
bleach
n decoloration 36.3
bleacher 36.4
v decolor 36.5
pale 36.6
whiten 37.5
clean 79.18
bleached
decolored 36.8
clean 79.25
vacant 222.14
weatherworn 393.34
bleachers
observation post 27.8
baseball 745.1
bleak distressing 98.20
gloomy 112.24
hopeless 125.12
windblown 318.23
cold 1023.14
bleakness
distressfulness 98.5
gloom 112.7
vacancy 222.2
cold 1023.1
bleary-eyed 28.13
bleat 60.2
bleb sore 85.37
bulge 283.3
bubble 320.1
blemish 1004.1
bleed
hemorrhage 12.17
let blood 91.27
suffer 96.19
grieve 112.17
pity 145.3
exude 190.15
draw off 192.12
exploit 387.16
take from 480.21
strip 480.24
overprice 632.7
bleeding
n hemorrhage 12.8
decoloration 36.3
symptom 85.9
bloodletting 91.20
drawing 192.3
adj bloody 12.23
pained 96.23
pitying 145.7
bleeding edge 165.1
bleeding heart
n sentimentality 93.8
wretchedness 96.6
heartache 112.9
philanthropist 143.8
compassionateness 145.2
pietist 693.3
liberal 979.6
adj liberal 611.19
pious 979.9
bleed white
exploit 387.16
consume 388.3

strip 480.24
overprice 632.7
bleep out excise 255.10
suppress 428.8
blemish
n mark 517.5
intruder 774.2
fault 1003.2
disfigurement 1004.1
blot 1004.1
eyesore 1015.4
v deform 265.7
mark 517.19
disfigure 1004.4
offend 1015.5
injure 393.13
blemished
deformed 265.12
unvirtuous 654.12
imperfect 1003.4
disfigured 1004.8
ugly 1015.6
blench flinch 127.13
demur 325.4
pull back 903.7
blend
n hybrid word 526.11
automobile racing 756.1
compound 797.5
combination 805.1
v harmonize 708.35
identify 778.5
mix 797.10
combine 805.3
blender mixer 797.9
agitator 917.9
blend in with 455.2
bless gladden 95.9
congratulate 149.2
thank 150.4
approve 509.9
praise 509.12
sanctify 685.5
glorify 696.12
give one's blessing 696.14
protect 1008.18
blessed happy 95.16
curse 513.10
heavenly 681.12
sanctified 685.8
fortunate 1010.14
blessed event 1.1
blessed-out 95.17
blessed with 469.9
blessing
n act of kindness 143.7
congratulation 149.1
consent 441.1
godsend 472.7
benefit 478.7
approval 509.1
sanctification 685.3
benediction 696.5
good 999.4
good fortune 1010.2
stroke of luck 1010.3
adj worshipful 696.16
blight
n disease 85.1
evil 1000.3
blast 1001.2

adversity 1011.1
v spoil 393.10
work evil 1000.6
freeze 1024.11
blighted
disappointed 132.5
spoiled 393.28
blasted 393.42
ruined 395.28
blighter 660.2
blimey! 122.21
blimp aerostat 181.11
heavyweight 257.12
stuffed shirt 501.9
blind
n rage 152.10
aviation 184.1
ambush 346.3
trick 356.6
pretext 376.1
stratagem 415.3
round 751.3
shade 1028.1
v cover the eyes 30.7
conceal 346.6
hoodwink 356.17
shine 1025.24
adj insensible 25.6
poor-sighted 28.11
sightless 30.9
high 87.24
fuddled 88.33
pitiless 146.3
closed 293.9
concealed 346.11
unpersuadable 361.13
obscure 522.15
undiscerning 922.14
involuntary 963.14
oblivious 984.7
blind alley
n obstruction 293.3
impasse 1013.6
adj closed 293.9
blind date
appointment 582.8
rendezvous 582.9
blinders blindfold 30.5
narrow-mindedness 980.1
blind faith 954.1
blindfold
n eye patch 30.5
v blind 30.7
hoodwink 356.17
adj blinded 30.10
undiscerning 922.14
blinding
n blindness 30.1
adj obscuring 30.11
garish 35.20
rainy 316.11
bright 1025.33
blindness
insensibility 25.1
faulty eyesight 28.1
sightlessness 30.1
total darkness 30.1
carelessness 340.2
unpersuadableness 361.5
unperceptiveness 922.2
incognizance 930.2

blinds
the blind 30.4
shade 1028.1
blindsided 131.12
blind spot
blindness 30.1
narrow-mindedness 980.1
reception 1034.21
blind to
insensible 94.10
unaware 930.12
bling 498.5
bling-bling 498.5
blink
n glance 27.4
glitter 1025.7
reflection 1025.9
v wink 28.10
flinch 127.13
slight 340.8
pull back 903.7
glitter 1025.25
blink at
be blind 30.8
condone 148.4
suffer 443.10
keep an open mind 979.7
be inattentive 984.2
blinkers
spectacles 29.3
blindfold 30.5
signals 517.15
blinking
n winking 28.7
glitter 1025.7
adj poor-sighted 28.11
glittering 1025.36
flickering 1025.37
blintz 10.45
blips 1036.11
bliss happiness 95.2
pleasantness 97.1
heaven 681.5
blissful happy 95.16
pleasant 97.6
beatific 97.9
B-list
n inferior 250.2
list 871.1
adj inferior 250.6
blister
n sore 85.37
bulge 283.3
bubble 320.1
blemish 1004.1
v criticize 510.20
burn 1020.24
blistering
n burning 1020.5
adj bubbly 320.6
hot 1019.25
blithe 109.11
blithering 922.22
blitz
n attack 459.1
game 746.3
v blow up 395.18
attack 459.14
pull the trigger 459.22
play 746.5
blitzkrieg 459.1

blizzard
windstorm 318.11
snow 1023.8
bloat
n oversize 257.5
distension 259.2
overextension 993.7
v grow 251.6
enlarge 259.4
expand 259.5
bloated
puffed up 136.10
increased 251.7
corpulent 257.18
distended 259.13
deformed 265.12
bulging 283.15
pompous 501.22
overfull 993.20
blob sphere 282.2
bulge 283.3
blobby formless
263.4
vague 971.19
bloc 617.1
block
n suppression 92.24
boundary 211.3
city block 230.7
plot 231.4
lump 257.10
obstruction 293.3
execution 605.5
print 713.5
auction 734.4
share 738.3
game 746.3
delay 846.2
mental state 990.3
obstacle 1012.4
solid 1045.6
v stop 293.7
cover 295.19
fend off 460.10
play 746.5
pick 747.4
check 749.7
fight 754.4
delay 846.8
cease 857.11
obstruct 1012.12
hinder 1012.13
blockade
n enclosure 212.1
closure 293.1
obstruction 293.3
siege 459.5
exclusion 773.1
obstacle 1012.4
v enclose 212.5
stop 293.7
besiege 459.19
fortify 460.9
exclude 773.4
obstruct 1012.12
blockage seizure 85.6
suppression 92.24
obstruction 293.3
delay 846.2
hindrance 1012.1
blockbuster 131.2

blockhead
bungler 414.8
fool 924.4
blockhouse 460.6
blockish 922.15
block out form 262.7
outline 381.11
itemize 801.7
blocks 743.16
blocky 268.10
blog
n written matter 547.10
literature 547.12
record books 549.11
computer communications
1042.19
v be published 352.16
write 547.21
blogger
author 547.15
hack writer 547.16
recorder 549.13
blogging
publication 352.1
authorship 547.2
bloke 76.5
blond
n hair color 35.9
adj flaxen-haired 37.9
yellow-haired 43.5
blood
n whole blood 2.25
life force 306.2
killing 308.1
dandy 500.9
relationship 559.1
kinfolk 559.2
race 559.4
lineage 560.4
offspring 561.1
nobility 608.2
class 809.2
kind 809.3
fluid 1061.2
adj circulatory 2.33
blood and thunder
n emotionalism 93.9
adj sensational 105.32
blood bank
transfusion 91.18
hospital room 197.25
bloodbath carnage 308.4
destruction 395.1
blood-borne 12.23
blood brother 559.3
bloodcurdling 127.29
bloodied 96.25
bloodless weak 16.12
colorless 36.7
dull 117.6
pacific 464.9
bloodletting
bleeding 91.20
drawing 192.3
killing 308.1
bloodline lineage 560.4
offspring 561.1
bloodlust
cruelty 144.11
violence 671.1
bloodmobile 91.18

blood money
recompense 624.3
fee 624.5

blood relationship
bond 559.2
kinship 775.3

bloodshed killing 308.1
war 458.1

bloodshot 28.13

blood-sport 382.2

bloodstained 1004.11

bloodstream 2.25

bloodsucker
parasite 311.37
extortionist 480.12

bloodthirsty
cruel 144.26
murderous 308.24
warlike 458.20

blood types 2.34

blood vessel 2.23

bloody
v bleed 12.17
torture 96.18
injure 393.13
bloodstain 1004.7
adj circulatory 2.33
bleeding 12.23
sanguine 41.7
cruel 144.26
murderous 308.24
warlike 458.20
cursed 513.9
savage 671.21
bloodstained 1004.11

bloody hands 656.1

bloom
n reddening 41.3
health 83.1
youth 301.1
flower 310.24
budding 310.26
beauty 1016.1
glow 1019.12
television reception 1035.5
v enjoy good health 83.6
mature 303.9
flower 310.35
ripen 407.8
evolve 861.5
thrive 1010.8
look good 1016.16
be hot 1019.22

bloop 745.3

blooper game 745.3
goof 975.6

blossom
n plant 310.24
flowering 310.26
v grow 14.2
expand 259.7
mature 303.9
flower 310.35
ripen 407.8
evolve 861.5
thrive 1010.8

blot
n soil 80.5
obliteration 395.7
stigma 661.6
intruder 774.2

stain 1004.3
eyesore 1015.4
v blacken 38.7
absorb 187.13
obliterate 395.16
stigmatize 661.9
spot 1004.5
offend 1015.5
dry 1066.6

blotch
n spottiness 47.3
soil 80.5
mark 517.5
stain 1004.3
v blacken 38.7
variegate 47.7
mark 517.19
spot 1004.5

blotchy dingy 38.11
blemished 47.13
spotted 1004.9

blot out delete 255.12
kill 308.14
obliterate 395.16
darken 1027.9

blotter LSD 87.10
sorption 187.6
record book 549.11

blotto 88.33

blouse 5.15

blow
n feast 8.9
cocaine 87.7
pain 96.5
surprise 131.2
disappointment 132.1
plant 310.24
flowering 310.26
gust 318.5
windstorm 318.11
act 328.3
slap 604.3
fight 754.3
hit 902.4
punch 902.6
misfortune 1011.2
v burn out 21.5
blare 53.10
use 87.22
leave 222.10
flower 310.35
waft 318.19
flee 368.11
spoil 393.11
ripen 407.8
bungle 414.12
squander 486.3
boast 502.7
talk big 545.6
blow a horn 708.42
evacuate 909.22
let out 909.24
make a boner 975.15
interj go away! 909.31

blow about 352.16

blow a gasket
get excited 105.17
fly into a rage 152.20

blow-by-blow description 349.3

blow down raze 395.19
fell 913.5

blower ventilator 317.10
bellows 318.17
fan 318.18
braggart 502.5
automobile racing 756.1

blow for blow 506.3

blowhard
n braggart 502.5
v boast 502.7

blowhole outlet 190.9
air passage 239.13

blow hot and cold
vacillate 362.8
keep off and on 364.4
change 854.5
quibble 936.9

blow-in
insert 191.2
advertising matter 352.8

blown
windblown 318.23
tainted 393.41
blighted 393.42

blow off steam 743.24

blow one's cool 105.17

blow one's cover 351.8

blow one's mind
use 87.22
lose self-control 128.8
go mad 926.22
freak out 976.8
dream 986.17

blow one's top
get excited 105.17
fly into a rage 152.20
go mad 926.22

blowout feast 8.9
party 582.12
explosion 671.7
festival 743.4
disgorgement 909.7

blow out
run out 190.13
erupt 671.13
explode 671.14
evacuate 909.22
disgorge 909.25
fight fire 1022.7

blow out the cobwebs 9.2

blow over
die down 318.19
come to an end 820.6
fell 913.5

blowpipe
blower 318.17
blowtorch 1020.14

blow the lid off
disclose 351.4
uncover 941.4

blow the whistle
have no patience with 135.5
inform on 551.13
play 746.5

blow to 624.19

blowtorch
jet plane 181.3
blowlamp 1020.14

blowup outburst 152.9
intensification 251.2
explosion 671.7
print 714.5

blow up excite 105.12
get pumped 105.17
fly into a rage 152.20
intensify 251.5
enlarge 259.4
strike dead 308.18
blow 318.19
misrepresent 350.3
blast 395.18
come to nothing 410.13
praise 509.12
explode 671.14
process 714.15
disprove 958.4

blowy 318.21

blowzy
red-complexioned 41.9
corpulent 257.18
slovenly 810.15

blubber
n softness 1047.4
v weep 115.12
bubble 320.4
speak 524.25
mumble 525.9

blubbery 1056.9

bludgeon
intimidate 127.20
coerce 424.7
threaten 514.2

blue
n blueness 45.1
proof 548.5
the heavens 1072.2
v azure 45.2
adj bluish 45.3
melancholy 112.23
deathly 307.28
obscene 666.9

blue blood
aristocracy 607.3
upper class 607.4
nobility 608.2
nobleman 608.4

blue-blooded
upper-class 607.10
wellborn 608.11

blue book
official document 549.8
register 549.9
information 551.1
examination 938.2

blue-chip 999.15

blue-collar worker 726.2

bluegrass 708.11

blue in the face 105.25

bluejacket
mariner 183.1
navy man 183.4

blue language 513.3

bluenose 500.11

blue-pencil
delete 255.12
revise 392.12
obliterate 395.16

blue-plate special 8.6

blueprint
n representation 349.1
plan 381.1
diagram 381.3
proof 548.5

bogart 503.3

bog down 243.2

bogey
n frightener 127.9
military aircraft 181.9
bugbear 680.9
round 751.3
v play 751.4

bogeyman
frightener 127.9
bugbear 680.9

bogeymen 1001.1

boggle
n demur 325.2
bungle 414.5
v astonish 122.6
start 127.12
demur 325.4
object 333.5
not know one's own mind 362.6
bungle 414.11
lose one's nerve 491.8
quibble 936.9
stump 971.14

boggle the mind
astonish 122.6
be unbelievable 955.7

boggy marshy 243.3
moist 1065.15

bogus
spurious 354.26
substitute 862.8

Bohemian
n nomad 178.4
nonconformist 868.3
adj informal 581.3
unconventional 868.6

boil
n dish 10.7
sore 85.37
swelling 283.4
turbulence 671.2
agitation 917.1
heating 1020.2
v cook 11.5
sanitize 79.24
be angry 152.15
bubble 320.4
seethe 671.12
be hot 1019.22
stew 1020.20

boil down 268.6

boiler room
noisemaker 53.6
confidence game 356.10
stockbrokerage 737.9

boiling over
fervent 93.18
heated 105.22

boiling point 1019.1

boisterous noisy 53.13
turbulent 105.24
blustering 503.4
rampageous 671.20

bold insolent 142.9
brazen 142.11
seaworthy 180.18
steep 204.18
protruding 283.14
in relief 283.18

conspicuous 348.12
defiant 454.7
courageous 492.16
foolhardy 493.9
immodest 666.6

boldfaced
brazen 142.11
typographic 548.20

bole cylinder 282.4
stem 310.21

boll sphere 282.2
seed vessel 310.30

bollixed up 799.4

bollix up spoil 393.11
bungle 414.12
complicate 799.3
confuse 811.3
hinder 1012.16

Bolshevik
n radical 611.12
Communist 611.13
revolutionist 860.3
adj Communist 611.21
revolutionist 860.6

bolster
n bedding 901.20
v comfort 121.6
aid 449.12
encourage 492.15
support 901.21
confirm 957.11

bolt
n a length 267.2
apostasy 363.2
change one's mind 363.7
flight 368.4
desertion 370.2
lock 428.5
arrow 462.6
missile 462.18
bundle 770.8
lightning 1025.17
v gobble 8.23
refine 79.22
speed 174.8
close 293.6
flee 368.10
defect 370.6
gluttonize 672.4
segregate 773.6
hook 800.8
classify 808.11
obstruct 1012.12

bolt-hole
hiding place 346.4
secret passage 346.5
means of escape 369.3

bolt out of the blue 131.2

bolt upright
vertical 200.11
straight 200.13

bolus bite 8.2
pill 86.7
sphere 282.2

bomb
n marijuana 87.11
surprise 131.2
failure 410.2
bombshell 462.20
stage show 704.4
game 746.3

v fall flat 117.4
blow up 395.18
fail 410.10
attack 459.23
dramatize 704.28

bombardier crew 185.4
artilleryman 461.11

bombardment
bombing 459.7
fission 1038.8

bombast
n boasting 502.1
nonsense 520.2
bombastry 545.2
v talk big 545.6

bombastic
pompous 501.22
inflated 502.12
stiff 534.3
fustian 545.9

bombed out 87.24

bomber alarmist 127.8
destroyer 395.8
artilleryman 461.11
violent person 671.9

bombshell
surprise 131.2
bomb 462.20

bomb shelter 346.4

bomb threat 514.1

bona fide
adj straight 644.14
genuine 973.15
adv faithfully 644.25

bonanza
source of supply 386.4
rich source 618.4
plenty 991.2

bon appetit! 8.35

bond
n shackle 428.4
compact 437.1
security 438.1
pledge 438.2
fidelity 644.7
nominal rate 738.5
relation 775.1
joining 800.1
fastening 800.3
v secure 438.9
pledge 438.10
put together 800.5
adj subjugated 432.14

bondage 432.1

bondholder 737.14

bond rating 630.3

bondsman
subject 432.7
guarantor 438.6

bone
n the skeleton 2.2
whiteness 37.2
hardness 1046.6
dryness 1066.2
v study 570.12
adj skeleton 2.26

bonehead
bungler 414.9
fool 924.4

bone of contention
apple of discord 456.7

question 938.10

boner bungle 414.5
goof 975.6

bones heart 93.3
corpse 307.15
refuse 391.4
dice 759.8
body 1052.3

bone to pick
bone of contention 456.7
grudge 589.5

bone up
study up 570.14
refresh the memory 989.18

bonfire 1019.13

bonhomie
good nature 143.2
hospitality 585.1
cordiality 587.6

bon jour! 585.15

bonkers 926.27

bon mot 489.7

bonne bouche 10.8

bonnet cloak 5.40
top 295.21

bonny good 999.12
comely 1016.18

bon ton custom 373.1
fashion 578.1
chic 578.2
upper class 607.2

bonus extra 254.4
find 472.6
gratuity 478.5
premium 624.6
surplus 993.5

bon vivant
eater 8.16
connoisseur 496.6
sociable person 582.16
boon companion 588.5
sensualist 663.3

bon voyage! 188.22

bony
skeleton 2.26
lean 270.17
hard 1046.10

boo
n marijuana 87.11
booing 508.3
v hiss 508.10
interj bah! 157.10

boob dupe 358.2
fool 924.3

boo-boo
n bungle 414.5
goof 975.6
v make *or* pull a boner 975.15

boobs 283.7

boob tube 1035.11

booby loser 412.5
fool 924.3

booby hatch 926.14

booby prize 646.2

booby trap
ambush 346.3
deception 356.12
hidden danger 1006.5

boodle bribe 378.2
booty 482.11
spoils of office 609.35

money 728.2
boogie-woogie 708.9
boo-hoo 115.12
book
  n publication 352.1
  volume 554.1
  edition 554.1
  printed product 554.3
  part 554.13
  periodical 555.1
  playbook 704.21
  script 706.3
  poetry 720.9
  casino 759.19
  part of writing 793.2
  v depose 334.6
  flee 368.11
  curse 513.5
  record 549.15
  accuse 599.7
  employ 615.14
  keep accounts 628.8
  list 871.8
  prearrange 965.4
  schedule 965.6
bookbinding 554.14
bookcase
  storehouse 386.6
  bookbinding 554.14
  bookholder 554.17
bookdealer 554.2
book end 554.17
bookie 759.20
booking
  registration 549.14
  engagement 615.4
  show 704.11
  prearrangement 965.1
bookish learned 570.17
  studentlike 572.12
  book-smart 928.22
bookkeeper
  recorder 550.1
  accountant 628.7
  treasurer 729.12
  calculator 1017.15
bookkeeping
  n accounting 628.6
  adj recording 628.12
book learning 928.5
booklet 554.11
booklover
  philobiblist 554.18
  bookworm 929.4
bookmaker 759.20
bookmark 517.10
book packager 554.2
book report 549.7
book review 946.2
book reviewer 556.4
books
  account book 628.4
  bill 871.5
bookseller 554.2
bookshelf 554.17
bookstore 554.16
book value 738.9
bookworm
  booklover 554.18
  nerd 572.10
  bibliophage 929.4

boom
  n noise 53.3
  reverberation 54.2
  volume 56.4
  float 180.11
  intensification 251.2
  explosion 671.7
  business cycle 731.10
  lever 906.4
  roaring trade 1010.5
  barrier 1012.5
  v hum 52.13
  din 53.7
  reverberate 54.7
  thunder 56.9
  speed 174.9
  ship activity 182.48
  grow 251.6
  speak 524.25
  thrive 1010.8
  interj bang! 56.13
boom box 50.11
boomerang
  n missile 462.18
  retaliation 506.1
  recoil 903.2
  v return 903.6
booming
  n hum 52.7
  reverberation 54.2
  explosion 56.4
  adj humming 52.20
  loud 53.11
  reverberating 54.12
  thundering 56.12
  thriving 1010.13
boon
  n godsend 472.7
  benefit 478.7
  good 999.4
  adj convivial 582.23
boondocks
  open space 158.4
  hinterland 233.2
  remote region 261.4
  woodland 310.13
boor bungler 414.8
  vulgarian 497.6
  peasant 606.6
  oaf 924.5
boorish insensible 25.6
  countrified 233.7
  bungling 414.20
  churlish 497.13
  ill-bred 505.6
boost
  n increase 251.1
  improvement 392.1
  promotion 446.1
  assist 449.2
  theft 482.4
  commendation 509.3
  thrust 902.2
  lift 912.2
  v cheer 109.7
  increase 251.4
  publicize 352.15
  make better 392.9
  promote 446.2
  be useful 449.17
  rob 482.16

commend 509.11
  thrust 902.12
  elevate 912.5
booster dose 86.6
  inoculation 91.16
  enthusiast 101.5
  publicist 352.9
  thief 483.1
  commender 509.8
  multistage rocket 1074.5
boot
  n excitement 105.3
  navy man 183.4
  recruit 461.18
  novice 572.9
  torture 605.4
  kick 902.9
  goof 975.6
  v cloak 5.40
  play 745.5
  kick 902.21
  dismiss 909.20
  make a boner 975.15
  computerize 1042.21
bootblack 577.5
boot camp 461.6
booth
  compartment 197.2
  hut 228.9
  stall 736.3
bootleg
  v distill 88.30
  illicit goods 732.7
  adj illegal 674.6
bootlegger
  liquor dealer 88.19
  racketeer 732.4
bootless
  ineffective 19.15
  fruitless 391.12
  unsuccessful 410.18
bootlicker
  flatterer 138.4
  assenter 332.6
bootlicking
  n obsequiousness 138.2
  adj obsequious 138.14
bootmaker 5.38
boot out 909.13
booty gain 472.3
  take 480.10
  spoil 482.11
boo-yah 999.12
booze
  n spirits 88.13
  v imbibe 8.29
  use 87.22
  drink 88.25
bop 708.9
bordello
  disapproved place 228.28
  brothel 665.9
border
  n exterior 206.2
  limbus 211.4
  frontier 211.5
  partition 213.5
  side 218.1
  sphere 231.2
  size 257.1
  scenery 704.20

garden 1069.10
  v edge 211.10
  side 218.4
  adjoin 223.9
  adj final 820.11
bordering
  n edging 211.7
  adj environing 209.8
  fringing 211.11
  adjacent 223.16
borderland
  frontier 211.5
  sphere 231.2
  hinterland 233.2
borderline 211.11
borderline case
  lunatic 926.15
  gamble 971.8
bore
  n annoyance 96.2
  crashing bore 118.4
  wave 238.14
  diameter 269.3
  hole 292.3
  v give no pleasure 96.12
  leave one cold 118.7
  excavate 284.15
  perforate 292.15
boreal
  northern 161.14
  seasonal 313.9
  windy 318.21
  cold 1023.14
boredom
  unpleasure 96.1
  weariness 118.3
  languor 331.6
  incuriosity 982.1
borehole 292.3
borer 285.3
boring
  n hole 292.3
  adj irritating 26.13
  wearying 118.10
  same 781.6
born
  given birth 1.4
  innate 767.8
  thorough 794.10
born-again
  redeemed 685.9
  regenerate 692.10
  converted 858.19
borne 901.24
borne out 957.20
born for 413.29
born yesterday 416.5
borough town 230.1
  region 231.5
  election district 609.16
borrow
  imitate 336.5
  rob 482.16
  plagiarize 482.19
  take a loan of 621.3
  go in debt 623.6
  discount 728.27
  play 751.4
borrowing
  plagiarism 482.8
  loan word 526.7

appropriation 621.2
money-raising 621.1
debt 623.1
money market 728.16
borscht circuit 704.11
borstal
prison 429.8
reform school 567.9
bosh humbug 354.14
bullshit 520.3
bos'n 183.7
bosom
n heart 93.3
interior 207.2
breast 283.6
inner nature 767.5
v keep secret 345.7
conceal 346.7
hold 474.7
embrace 562.18
bosom buddy 588.4
bosomy
corpulent 257.18
bulging 283.15
pectoral 283.19
boss
n superior 249.4
bulge 283.3
print 517.7
superintendent 574.2
master 575.1
politics 610.7
important person 997.11
v emboss 283.12
roughen 288.4
direct 573.8
supervise 573.10
adj supervising 573.13
governing 612.17
excellent 999.13
bossism
authoritativeness 417.3
politics 609.1
bossy
n female animal 77.9
cattle 311.6
adj in relief 283.18
imperious 417.16
botanical
vegetable 310.36
biological 1068.4
botanical garden 1069.10
botany biology 1068.1
plants 310.1
botch
n slipshodness 340.3
bad likeness 350.2
fiasco 410.6
bungle 414.5
blunder 975.5
v do carelessly 340.9
misdraw 350.4
spoil 393.10
miss 410.14
bungle 414.11
blunder 975.14
both
n two 873.2
adj the two 873.7
bother
n annoyance 96.2

dither 105.6
bustle 330.4
imposition 643.1
commotion 810.4
bewilderment 971.3
confusion 985.3
inconvenience 996.3
trouble 1013.3
v annoy 96.13
distress 96.16
vex 98.15
concern 126.4
presume upon 640.7
bewilder 971.12
confuse 985.7
inconvenience 996.4
trouble 1013.13
bothered
annoyed 96.21
distressed 96.22
anxious 126.7
bewildered 971.24
confused 985.12
troubled 1013.20
bothersome
annoying 98.22
troublesome 126.10
difficult 1013.18
bottle
n container 195.1
v package 212.9
put up 397.11
bottleneck
convergence 169.1
contraction 260.1
narrow place 270.3
obstruction 293.3
hindrance 1012.1
bottle up enclose 212.6
secrete 346.7
suppress 428.8
confine 429.12
retain 474.5
hinder 1012.10
bottom
n ship 180.1
under side 199.1
bed 199.4
buttocks 217.4
marsh 243.1
base 274.4
valley 284.9
pluck 359.3
fortitude 492.5
v base on 199.6
solve 940.2
adj bottommost 199.7
reduced 633.9
bottom dollar
funds 728.14
extremity 820.2
bottom-dwelling 645.16
bottom feeder 607.7
bottoming out 731.10
bottomless
greedy 100.27
abysmal 275.11
plentiful 991.7
bottomless pit
depths 275.3
infinity 823.1

cornucopia 991.3
bottomless well 991.3
the bottom line
essential content 196.5
fact 761.3
essence 767.3
salient point 997.6
sum 1017.6
bottom of the barrel 820.2
bottom out
base on 199.6
be changed 852.6
boudoir 197.7
bouffant 259.13
bough branch 310.20
member 793.4
bought 733.11
bougie 1026.2
bouillabaisse 10.11
bouillon 10.14
boulder 1059.5
bounce
n lightheartedness 109.3
leap 366.1
swagger 501.8
recoil 903.2
shake 917.3
radio signal 1034.10
elasticity 1048.1
v leap 366.5
caper 366.6
bluster 503.3
play 745.5
recoil 903.6
eject 909.13
dismiss 909.20
alternate 916.14
shake 917.11
give 1048.5
bounce a check 625.6
bounce back
n reaction 903.1
v reverberate 54.7
recover 396.19
recoil 903.6
reflect 1036.16
bouncer 909.11
bouncing
n leaping 366.3
adj strong 15.15
hale 83.12
active 330.17
leaping 366.7
recoiling 903.10
bound
n boundary 211.3
leap 366.1
recoil 903.2
v speed 174.8
circumscribe 210.4
limit 210.5
separate 211.8
border 211.10
enclose 212.5
leap 366.5
recoil 903.6
adj limited 210.7
enclosed 212.10
stopped 293.11
resolute 359.11
tied 428.16

promised 436.8
obliged 641.16
related 775.9
joined 800.13
certain 970.13
boundary
n limitation 210.2
bound 211.3
border 211.3
fence 212.4
size 257.1
joint 800.4
extremity 820.2
grammar 857.4
bisector 875.3
adj bordering 211.11
final 820.11
bounder
vulgarian 497.6
cad 660.7
bound for 161.26
boundless large 247.7
almighty 677.17
infinite 823.3
excessive 993.16
bound over 615.21
bountiful liberal 485.4
productive 890.9
plentiful 991.7
bounty gratuity 478.5
subsidy 478.8
liberality 485.1
bonus 624.6
bouquet fragrance 70.1
nosegay 310.25
compliment 509.6
bundle 770.8
bourgeois
n townsman 227.6
vulgarian 497.6
member of the middle class 607.6
conformist 867.2
adj common 497.14
upper-class 607.10
capitalist 611.23
conformist 867.6
ordinary 1005.8
bourgeoisie
middle class 607.5
mediocrity 1005.5
bout spree 88.5
contest 457.3
boxing 457.9
revel 743.6
game 743.9
fight 754.3
turn 825.2
round 850.3
boutique 736.1
boutique hotel 228.15
boutonniere 310.25
bovine
n cattle 311.6
adj unconcerned 102.7
inexcitable 106.10
complacent 107.10
ungulate 311.45
stupid 922.15
bow curve 279.2
bend 279.3

bulge 283.3
longbow 462.7
violin family 711.5
bow
n obeisance 155.2
prow 216.3
greeting 585.4
crouch 913.3
v fawn 138.7
make obeisance 155.6
curve 279.6
lose 412.12
submit 433.10
bend 913.9
bowdlerize
clean 79.18
delete 255.12
shorten 268.6
bowel movement
defecation 12.2
feces 12.4
bowels
digestive system 2.18
insides 207.4
depths 275.3
bower
summerhouse 228.12
card 758.2
safeguard 1008.3
Bowery 230.6
bowie knife 462.5
bowl
n tableware 8.12
cavity 284.2
arena 463.1
ceramic ware 742.2
football 746.1
lawn bowling 750.3
throw 904.3
v be concave 284.12
hollow 284.13
push 904.9
throw 904.10
roll 915.10
bowl down
astonish 122.6
startle 131.8
fell 913.5
bowlegged 265.12
bowlegs 265.3
bowl over
astonish 122.6
surprise 131.7
startle 131.8
fell 913.5
bow out quit 188.9
exit 190.12
absent oneself 222.8
die 307.19
dismiss 909.18
box
n container 195.1
compartment 197.2
cottage 228.8
coffin 309.11
storehouse 386.6
gift 478.4
slap 604.3
auditorium 704.15
slap 902.8
impasse 1013.6

v package 212.9
wrap 295.20
restrict 428.9
contend 457.13
hit 604.12
fight 754.4
slap 902.19
box cutter 462.5
boxed packed 212.12
covered 295.31
boxer pugilist 461.2
fighter 754.2
box in enclose 212.5
confine 212.6
restrict 428.9
qualify 959.3
boxing packaging 212.2
fighting 457.9
sports 754
prizefighting 754.1
box office
attendance 221.4
receipts 627.1
office 739.7
box score 1017.6
boy
n heroin 87.9
lad 302.5
man 577.4
card 758.2
interj goody! 95.21
boycott
n objection 333.2
ostracism 586.3
strike 727.5
exclusion 773.1
v object 333.5
ostracize 586.6
strike 727.10
boyfriend admirer 104.12
friend 588.1
boyhood
childhood 301.2
young people 302.2
boyish thin 270.16
childish 301.11
immature 406.11
boy toy 104.11
boy wonder 413.12
bra brassiere 5.24
supporter 901.2
brace
n dressing 86.33
verticalness 200.1
staff 708.29
two 873.2
supporter 901.2
v refresh 9.2
strengthen 15.13
stand 200.7
bind 800.9
support 901.21
stiffen 1046.9
bracelet circle 280.3
jewel 498.6
brace oneself
be determined 359.8
prepare oneself 405.13
bracer refreshment 9.1
tonic 86.8
drink 88.8

supporter 901.2
brace up refresh 9.2
strengthen 15.13
cheer up 109.9
recuperate 396.19
take courage 492.13
encourage 492.15
bracing
n refreshment 9.1
adj refreshing 9.3
energizing 17.15
healthful 81.5
tonic 86.44
supporting 901.23
cool 1023.12
bracket
n boundary 211.3
class 809.2
supporter 901.2
v parenthesize 212.8
grammaticize
530.16
relate 775.6
simplify 798.4
put together 800.5
bracket creep 632.3
brackets 211.3
brackish nasty 64.7
salty 68.9
bract 310.28
brag
n boasting 502.1
braggart 502.5
v boast 502.6
bluster 503.3
praise 509.12
braggart
n egotist 140.5
boaster 502.5
blusterer 503.2
adj boastful 502.10
bragging rights 502.2
Brahman cattle 311.6
nobleman 608.4
clergy 699.13
Brahmin snob 141.7
aristocrat 607.4
intellectual 929.1
braid
n hair 3.7
cord 271.2
plait 740.2
v spin 271.6
weave 740.6
Braille 30.6
brain
n encephalon 2.15
sensory area 919.1
seat of thought 919.6
intelligence 920.9
intellectual 929.1
v strike dead 308.18
adj nerve 2.30
brainchild
writing 547.10
work of art 712.9
product 893.1
good idea 932.6
figment of the imagination
986.5
brain-damaged 926.28

brain death
fatal disease 85.2
death 307.1
brainless
unintelligent 922.13
foolish 923.8
scatterbrained 985.16
brainstorm
caprice 364.1
impulse 365.1
delirium 926.8
good idea 932.6
absurd idea 932.7
brainteaser 522.9
brain trust 423.1
brain twister 522.8
brainwash
inculcate 568.12
propagandize 569.4
indoctrinate 858.15
brainy 920.14
braise cook 11.5
brown 40.2
brake
n thicket 310.15
curb 1012.7
v slow 175.9
put a stop to 857.11
halt 1012.13
bramble
thorn 285.5
shrubbery 310.9
adhesive 803.4
brambly 285.10
bran feed 10.4
hull 295.16
powder 1051.5
branch
n divergence 171.4
stream 238.1
tributary 238.3
fork 310.20
part of the service 461.21
lineage 560.4
offshoot 561.4
organ 617.10
sect 675.3
office 739.7
member 793.4
class 809.2
arm 809.5
v fork 171.7
spread 259.6
angle 278.5
bisect 875.4
branching
n forking 171.3
bisection 875.1
adj forked 171.10
leafy 310.41
halved 875.6
branch off deviate 164.3
fork 171.7
branch of knowledge 568.8
branch out fork 171.7
spread 259.6
disperse 771.4
brand
n mark 517.5
label 517.13
stigma 661.6

nature 767.4
kind 809.3
characteristic 865.4
stain 1004.3
coal 1019.16
burn 1020.6
cauterant 1020.15
combustion product 1020.16
lighter 1021.4
v mark 517.19
label 517.20
stigmatize 661.9
stain 1004.6
burn 1020.24
brandish
  n waving 916.2
  v manifest 348.5
  flaunt 501.17
  wave 916.11
brand loyalty 326.1
brand-new 841.10
brandy 88.15
brash
  n rainstorm 316.2
  rock 1059.1
  adj impudent 142.10
  defiant 454.7
  rash 493.7
  gruff 505.7
brass
  n impudence 142.3
  rashness 493.1
  monument 549.12
  orchestra 710.12
  money 728.2
  personage 997.8
  adj brazen 1058.17
the brass the best 249.5
  directorate 574.11
  commissioned officer 575.18
brassiere bra 5.24
  supporter 901.2
brass knuckles 462.4
brass tacks 761.4
brass wind instrument 711.7
brassy noisy 53.13
  raucous 58.15
  brazen 142.11
  defiant 454.7
  immodest 666.6
  brass 1058.17
brat urchin 302.4
bravado defiance 454.1
  daring 492.4
  boasting 502.1
  bluster 503.1
brave
  n military man 461.6
  brave person 492.7
  v endure 134.5
  confront 216.8
  defy 454.3
  face 492.10
  take chances 1006.7
  thwart 1012.15
  adj courageous 492.16
  showy 501.19
bravery courage 492.1
  finery 498.3
bravo
  n killer 308.11

combatant 461.1
blusterer 503.2
ruffian 593.3
interj congratulations! 149.4
bravissimo! 509.22
bravura
  n skill 413.1
  daring 492.4
  display 501.4
  vocal music 708.13
  aria 708.16
  adj skillful 413.22
  showy 501.19
  vocal 708.50
brawl
  n noise 53.3
  quarrel 456.5
  free-for-all 457.5
  party 582.12
  turbulence 671.2
  assembly 770.2
  commotion 810.4
  v be noisy 53.9
  quarrel 456.11
  contend 457.13
brawler rebel 327.5
  oppositionist 452.3
  combatant 461.1
brawling noisy 53.13
  vociferous 59.10
brawn
  muscularity 15.2
  organic matter 305.1
brawny
  able-bodied 15.16
  corpulent 257.18
bray
  n blare 53.5
  rasp 58.3
  v blare 53.10
  sound harshly 58.9
  cry 60.2
  speak 524.25
  pulverize 1051.9
brazen
  v brave 492.10
  adj reddish-brown 40.4
  noisy 53.13
  raucous 58.15
  insolent 142.11
  defiant 454.7
  gaudy 501.20
  hardened 654.17
  immodest 666.6
  brass 1058.17
  rash 493.7
brazen it out 360.4
breach
  n crack 224.2
  violation 435.2
  falling-out 456.4
  misdeed 655.2
  break 802.4
  interruption 813.2
  v cleave 224.4
  rupture 292.14
  violate 435.4
  break 802.12
  open 818.12
breach of confidence 645.5
breach of faith 645.6

bread
  n food 10.1
  pain 10.28
  support 449.3
  Eucharist 701.7
  money 728.2
  v feed 8.18
  sprinkle 771.6
breadth space 158.1
  size 257.1
  width 269.1
  expanse 269.1
  extent 300.3
  broad-mindedness
    979.1
breadwinner 726.2
break
  n respite 20.2
  trauma 85.38
  act of kindness 143.7
  start 188.2
  boundary 211.3
  crack 224.2
  escape 369.1
  falling-out 456.4
  cheapening 633.4
  declining market 737.5
  horse race 757.3
  deficiency 795.2
  breakage 802.4
  interruption 813.2
  interim 826.1
  delay 846.2
  revolution 852.2
  pause 857.3
  chance 972.1
  stroke of luck 1010.3
  v weaken 16.9
  take a rest 20.8
  change course 182.30
  set out 188.8
  cleave 224.4
  billow 238.22
  be published 352.16
  accustom 373.9
  injure 393.13
  crack up 393.23
  conquer 412.10
  subdue 432.9
  domesticate 432.11
  violate 435.4
  depose 447.4
  train 568.13
  domineer 612.15
  go bankrupt 625.7
  ruin 625.8
  cheapen 633.6
  fight 754.4
  race 757.5
  disagree 789.5
  burst 802.12
  discontinue 813.3
  intervene 826.3
  pause 857.9
  interrupt 857.10
  dismiss 909.19
  grow light 1025.28
  shatter 1050.3
  tend 1070.7
breakable frail 16.14
  brittle 1050.4

breakaway
  n apostasy 363.2
  desertion 370.2
  scoring chance 749.3
  game 752.3
  adj rebellious 327.11
  dissenting 333.6
  repudiative 363.12
  unconventional 868.6
  unusual 870.10
  counteractive 900.8
break away
  n apostacize 363.7
  v revolt 327.7
  escape 369.6
  defect 370.6
break bread with 8.21
breakdown
  exhaustion 21.2
  collapse 85.8
  impairment 393.1
  debacle 395.4
  failure 410.3
  analysis 801.1
  dissection 802.5
  disintegration 806.1
  revolution 860.1
break down
  burn out 21.5
  aggrieve 112.19
  weep 115.12
  founder 393.24
  be impaired 393.26
  raze 395.19
  subdue 432.9
  diversify 782.2
  analyze 801.6
  dissect 802.17
  classify 809.6
  fall through 911.3
breakers wave 238.14
  foam 320.2
break even 790.5
breakfast
  n meal 8.6
  v dine 8.21
break for 161.9
break forth
  burst forth 33.9
  emerge 190.11
  be revealed 351.8
break ground
  weigh anchor 182.18
  initiate 818.10
break in
  n burglary 482.5
  v enter 189.7
  intrude 214.5
  interrupt 214.6
  breach 292.14
  accustom 373.9
  domesticate 432.11
  train 568.13
  make a beginning 818.8
breaking news 351.1
breaking point 993.7
breaking story 552.3
break loose
  escape 369.6
  extricate 431.7
breakneck fast 174.15

steep 204.18
precipitate 401.10
reckless 493.8
break off
n cessation 857.1
v disaccustom 374.2
disagree 789.5
discontinue 813.3
interrupt 857.10
break one's heart 112.19
break one's neck
be active 330.14
make haste 401.5
do one's best 403.14
break one up
make laugh 116.9
amuse 743.21
breakout escape 369.1
game 749.3
itemization 801.2
break out take ill 85.47
find vent 369.10
extricate 431.7
free oneself from 431.8
erupt 671.13
play 749.7
itemize 801.7
originate 818.13
break the ice
prepare the way 405.12
cultivate 587.12
initiate 818.10
break the news
divulge 351.5
report 552.11
breakthrough
improvement 392.1
attack 459.1
curtain-raiser 816.2
innovation 852.4
conversion 858.1
break through
breach 292.14
find vent 369.10
make good 409.10
breakup decay 393.6
destruction 395.1
debacle 395.4
disbandment 771.3
analysis 801.1
disruption 802.3
disintegration 806.1
revolution 860.1
break up laugh 116.8
decay 393.22
break 393.23
be destroyed 395.22
disband 771.8
diversify 782.2
analyze 801.6
come apart 802.9
shatter 802.13
part company 802.19
disintegrate 806.3
change 852.7
powder 1051.10
breakwater
point of land 283.9
buttress 901.4
harbor 1009.6
barrier 1012.5

break water
submarines 182.47
shoot up 193.9
break wind 909.29
break with 456.10
breast
n fowl part 10.23
heart 93.3
bosom 283.6
inner nature 767.5
v confront 216.8
contend against 451.4
breast-beating 658.2
breast-feed 8.19
breastwork 1012.5
breath breathing 2.21
respite 20.2
murmur 52.4
odor 69.1
touch 73.1
life 306.1
vitality 306.2
puff 318.3
spirit 764.3
instant 830.3
psyche 919.4
vapor 1067.1
breathe take a rest 20.8
murmur 52.10
have an odor 69.6
smell 69.8
live 306.8
tell confidentially
345.9
manifest 348.5
divulge 351.5
mean 518.8
say 524.22
speak 524.25
tip off 551.11
exist 761.8
imbue 797.11
evidence 957.8
breathe easy 120.8
breather 402.1
breathing
n respiration 2.21
adj respiratory 2.32
living 306.12
lifelike 784.16
breathing room
leisure 402.1
latitude 430.4
breathing space
respite 20.2
room 158.3
latitude 430.4
breathing spell
respite 20.2
truce 465.5
pause 857.3
breathless
winded 21.12
mute 51.12
fervent 93.18
eager 101.8
wondering 122.9
impatient 135.6
stuffy 173.16
dead 307.29
precipitate 401.10

breathtaking
exciting 105.30
astonishing 122.12
breathy 525.12
breech
n bottom 199.1
rear 217.1
v cloak 5.40
breeches 5.18
breed
n race 559.4
lineage 560.4
offspring 561.1
kind 809.3
v procreate 78.8
be pregnant 78.12
grow 251.6
train 568.13
cause 886.10
originate 892.12
raise 1070.6
breeding
n procreation 78.2
good breeding 504.4
training 568.3
fission 1038.8
planting 1069.14
animal husbandry 1070.1
adj pregnant 78.18
breeding ground 886.8
breeze
n light wind 318.4
easy 1014.4
softness 1047.4
v speed 174.9
blow 318.19
race 757.5
breezeway 197.18
breezy
lighthearted 109.12
airy 317.12
windy 318.21
active 330.17
brethren brother 559.3
the laity 700.1
brevet decree 420.4
grant 443.5
commission 615.1
brevity shortness 268.1
taciturnity 344.2
conciseness 537.1
briefness 828.2
brew
n spirits 88.13
beer 88.16
concoction 405.3
v cook 11.5
grow 14.2
distill 88.30
expand 259.7
blow 318.19
plot 381.9
make up 405.7
imbue 797.11
be imminent 840.2
liquefy 1064.5
soak 1065.13
brewer 88.19
brewery
distillery 88.21
plant 739.3

brew pub 8.17
brewski 10.49
bribable
corruptible 378.4
improbity 645.23
influenceable 894.15
bribe
n incentive 375.7
bribe money 378.2
gratuity 478.5
v throw a sop to 378.3
bribery
graft 378.1
bribing 378.1
bric-a-brac
trinket 498.4
work of art 712.9
trivia 998.4
brick
n pavement 383.6
good person 659.2
ceramic ware 742.2
hardness 1046.6
building material 1054.2
v face 295.23
brickbat
n indignity 156.2
disrespect 156.3
missile 462.18
v pelt 459.27
bricks and clicks 724.4
brick wall 1012.5
brickyard 739.3
bridal
n wedding 563.3
adj matrimonial 563.18
bride 563.5
bridegroom 563.5
bridesmaid 563.4
bridge
n observation post 27.8
railway 383.7
span 383.9
stage 704.16
passage 708.24
violin family 711.5
auction bridge 758.3
v overlie 295.30
bridged 800.13
bridgehead
vanguard 216.2
stronghold 460.6
bridging
n joining 800.1
adj overlying 295.36
joining 800.16
bridle
n shackle 428.4
v give oneself airs 141.8
anger 152.17
restrain 428.7
bind 428.10
mince 500.14
yoke 800.10
tend 1070.7
brief
n airmanship 184.3
brief 184.48
report 549.7
abridgment 557.1
argument 935.5

adj published 352.17
dispersed 771.9
broadcasting 343.5
broaden
increase 251.4
grow 251.6
enlarge 259.4
expand 259.5
widen 269.4
generalize 864.9
broadening
n increase 251.1
expansion 259.1
adj liberalizing 979.13
broad humor 489.1
broadly
extensively 158.12
far and wide 261.16
humorously 488.7
candidly 644.23
generally 864.17
vaguely 971.29
broad-minded
nonrestrictive 430.25
wise 920.17
wide-minded 979.8
broadsheet 352.8
broad-shouldered
able-bodied 15.16
virile 76.13
broadside
n side 218.1
announcement 352.2
advertising matter 352.8
volley 459.9
information 551.1
adv laterally 218.8
breadthwise 269.9
Broadway 704.1
brochure advertising matter
352.8
booklet 554.11
brogue 524.8
broil
n dish 10.7
cooking 11.2
quarrel 456.5
free-for-all 457.5
turbulence 671.2
commotion 810.4
v cook 11.5
quarrel 456.11
contend 457.13
be hot 1019.22
broke bereft 473.8
without money 619.10
insolvent 625.11
broken
domesticated 228.34
rough 288.6
impaired 393.27
in disrepair 393.37
ruined 395.28
conquered 412.17
subdued 432.15
meek 433.15
insolvent 625.11
busted 802.24
incoherent 804.4
discontinuous 813.4
irregular 851.3

broken-down
overcome 112.29
dilapidated 393.33
brokenhearted 112.29
broken-in 373.15
broken record 118.5
broker
intermediary 213.4
go-between 576.4
businessman 730.9
stockbroker 737.10
brokerage fee 630.6
trade 731.2
commerce 737.9
stockbroking 737.18
bromide
generalization 864.8
platitude 974.3
bronchial 2.32
bronco 311.10
broncobuster
rider 178.8
stockman 1070.2
Bronx cheer
cry 59.1
dissent 333.1
boo 508.3
boo 508.10
reproving look 510.8
bronze
n sculpture 715.2
v brown 40.2
adj reddish-brown 40.4
brass 1058.17
brooch 498.6
brood
n race 559.4
family 559.5
offspring 561.1
v be pregnant 78.12
consider 931.12
brooder
sourpuss 112.13
coop 228.22
poultry 311.28
birthplace 886.8
brood over
grieve 112.17
harbor revenge 507.5
think over 931.13
keep in memory 989.12
brook
n stream 238.1
v endure 134.5
submit 433.6
suffer 443.10
keep an open mind 979.7
broom 79.23
broomstick 270.8
broth 10.10
brothel
disapproved place 228.28
sewer 654.7
house of prostitution 665.9
brother buddy 559.3
friend 588.1
associate 616.1
member 617.11
religious 699.16
layman 700.2
likeness 784.3

brotherhood
kindness 143.1
blood relationship 559.1
fellowship 587.2
association 617.3
brotherly love
love 104.1
benevolence 143.4
accord 455.1
brouhaha noise 53.3
outcry 59.4
excitement 105.4
turbulence 671.2
commotion 810.4
agitation 917.1
brow eyelashes 3.12
looks 33.4
summit 198.2
head 198.6
border 211.4
forehead 216.5
browbeat
intimidate 127.20
domineer 612.15
browbeaten 432.16
brown
n brownness 40.1
heroin 87.9
v cook 11.5
embrown 40.2
darken 1027.9
adj brownish 40.3
brown-bag 8.21
brownie flatterer 138.4
dwarf 258.5
fairy 678.8
Brownie points 662.3
brown-nose
n flatterer 138.4
assenter 332.6
v fawn 138.7
brown-nosing
n obsequiousness 138.2
adj obsequious 138.14
brownout
n darkness 1027.7
blackout 1032.20
v darken 1027.9
brown study
thoughtfulness 931.3
abstractedness 985.2
dream 986.9
browse feed on 8.28
scan 570.13
shop 733.8
browser 1042.19
bruise
n trauma 85.38
discoloration 1004.2
v pain 96.17
mistreat 389.5
injure 393.13
thrash soundly 604.14
bruiser ruffian 593.4
violent person 671.10
bruit
n report 552.6
v publish 352.10
bruit about 352.10
brumal seasonal 313.9
cold 1023.14

brunch 8.6
brunet
n hair color 35.9
adj black-haired 38.13
brown 40.3
brown-haired 40.5
brunt 902.3
brush
n plant beard 3.9
touch 73.1
tail 217.6
contact 223.5
hinterland 233.2
scrub 310.16
fight 457.4
art equipment 712.17
wasteland 891.2
tap 902.7
firewood 1021.3
v touch lightly 73.7
sweep 79.23
speed 174.9
contact 223.10
portray 712.18
tap 902.18
dry 1066.6
tend 1070.7
brush aside
dismiss 984.4
reject 372.2
brush away 372.2
brush off
n rejection 372.1
repulse 908.2
v sweep 79.23
repulse 908.3
dismiss 984.4
brush up groom 79.20
perfect 392.11
study up 570.14
refresh the memory 989.18
brusque taciturn 344.9
gruff 505.7
concise 537.6
candid 644.17
brutal cruel 144.26
deadly 308.23
animal 311.39
unrefined 497.12
carnal 663.6
savage 671.21
terrible 1000.9
difficult 1013.17
brutality
cruelty 144.11
unkindness 144.12
unrefinement 497.3
carnality 663.2
violence 671.1
terribleness 1000.2
brutalize callous 94.6
bear malice 144.15
rage 671.11
brute
n beast 144.14
animal 311.2
barbarian 497.7
savage 593.5
violent person 671.9
adj cruel 144.26
animal 311.39

carnal 663.6
brute force
  power 18.1
  force 424.2
bub boy 302.5
  brother 559.3
bubble
  n airy hope 124.4
  structure 266.2
  sphere 282.2
  bulge 283.3
  lightness 298.2
  globule 320
  bleb 320.1
  race 756.3
  spirit 764.3
  ephemeron 828.5
  illusion 976.1
  figment of the imagination
    986.5
  fragility 1050.2
  v ripple 52.11
  foam up 320.4
bubble over
  be enthusiastic 101.7
  carbonate 320.4
bubbly light 298.10
  burbly 320.6
  active 330.17
buccaneer
  n mariner 183.1
  hijacker 483.7
  v pirate 482.18
buck
  n male animal 76.8
  boy 302.5
  hoofed animal 311.5
  goat 311.8
  hare 311.23
  leap 366.1
  money 728.7
  trestle 901.16
  v leap 366.5
  contend against 451.4
  thrust 902.12
buckaroo
  rider 178.8
  stockman 1070.2
bucket
  n ship 180.1
  basketball game 747.3
  v ladle 176.17
  trade 737.23
buckets
  v rain 316.10
  adv to and fro 916.21
buck for 375.14
buckle
  n distortion 265.1
  v distort 265.5
  exert oneself 725.9
  hook 800.8
buckled 265.10
buckle down to
  undertake 404.3
  set to work 725.15
buck naked 6.14
buck-passing 415.5
bucks 728.2
buckskin 311.11
bucktooth 2.8

buck up
  refresh 9.2
  cheer up 109.9
  take courage 492.13
  encourage 492.15
buck up! 109.20
bucolic rustic 233.6
  natural 416.6
  poetic 720.15
bud
  n boy 302.5
  burgeon 310.23
  brother 559.3
  friend 588.4
  vital force 886.7
  v graft 191.6
  vegetate 310.34
Buddha Deity 677.4
  religious founder 684.4
  Solomon 921.2
Buddha nature 106.2
Buddhism 675.14
budding
  n bodily 14.1
  growth 259.3
  vegetation 310.32
  adj grown 14.3
  expanding 259.12
  immature 301.10
  beginning 818.15
buddy boy 302.5
  brother 559.3
  friend 588.4
  henchman 610.8
  partner 616.2
  co-worker 616.5
buddy-buddy 587.20
buddy film 706.2
budge 172.5
budget
  n amount 244.2
  store 386.1
  portion 477.5
  expenses 626.3
  accounts 628.1
  funds 728.14
  bundle 770.8
  schedule 965.3
  v ration 477.10
  spend 626.5
  schedule 965.6
  adj accounting 628.12
  cheap 633.7
budget crunch 619.1
buenos días! 585.15
buff
  n enthusiast 101.5
  follower 166.2
  attender 221.5
  commender 509.8
  supporter 616.9
  specialist 866.3
  fanatic 926.18
  v polish 287.7
  burnish 1044.8
  adj yellow 43.4
the buff nudity 6.3
  skin 295.3
buffalo
  n cattle 311.6
  v stump 971.14

buffer
  n partition 213.5
  counteractant 900.3
  safeguard 1008.3
  barrier 1012.5
  v neutralize 900.7
buffer state 223.6
buffer zone 465.5
buffet feast 8.9
  restaurant 8.17
  table 901.15
buffet
  n disappointment 132.1
  knock 604.3
  slap 902.8
  v mistreat 389.5
  injure 393.13
  contend against 451.4
  slap 604.12
  whip 604.13
  struggle 725.11
  pound 902.16
  knock 902.19
buffoon
  mischief-maker 322.3
  buffo 707.10
  fool 924.1
buffoonery
  clownishness 489.5
  acting 704.8
  foolishness 923.1
bug
  n microphone 50.9
  germ 85.42
  enthusiast 101.5
  insect 311.32
  bugbear 680.9
  jockey 757.2
  mania 926.12
  fanatic 926.18
  fault 1003.2
  v listen 48.10
  annoy 96.13
  bulge 283.11
  importune 440.12
  nag 510.16
  discompose 811.4
  reconnoiter 938.28
  confuse 985.7
bugbear
  frightener 127.9
  false alarm 400.2
  bugaboo 680.9
  bane 1001.1
bug-eyed
  cross-eyed 28.12
  bulged 283.16
bugger
  n sexual pervert 75.16
  man 76.5
  mischief-maker 322.3
  bad person 660.5
  bugbear 680.9
  v disable 19.9
  masturbate 75.22
  spoil 393.11
  bungle 414.12
buggy
  n car 179.10
  adj insectile 311.51
  crazy 926.27

bugle
  n nose 283.8
  v blare 53.10
  blow a horn 708.42
bugle call
  call to arms 458.7
  signal 517.16
bug off! 909.32
build
  n muscularity 15.2
  frame 262.1
  human form 262.4
  structure 266.1
  nature 767.4
  v establish 159.16
  increase 251.4
  enlarge 259.4
  construct 266.5
  compose 796.3
  produce 892.8
building
  n house 228.5
  structure 266.1
  edifice 266.2
  composition 796.1
  production 892.2
  adj constructional 892.15
building blocks
  essential content 196.5
  substance 763.2
build on 199.6
buildout 259.1
buildup
  increase 251.1
  promotion 352.5
  commendation 509.3
  composition 796.1
build up
  aggravate 119.2
  increase 251.4
  enlarge 259.4
  publicize 352.15
  exaggerate 355.3
  prepare oneself 405.13
  compose 796.3
built made 892.18
  comely 1016.18
built-in 772.5
bulb sphere 282.2
  bulge 283.3
  root 310.22
bulb and stalk 310.66
bulbous
  spherical 282.9
  bulging 283.15
  vegetable 310.36
bulge
  n goozle 2.19
  advantage 249.2
  bilge 283.3
  v bilge 283.11
bulging
  n convexity 283.1
  protuberance 283.2
  adj rotund 282.8
  spherical 282.9
  swelling 283.15
  full 794.11
bulimia 672.1
bulk
  n quantity 244.1

greatness 247.1
size 257.1
bulkiness 257.9
thickness 269.2
major part 792.6
majority 883.2
v loom 247.5
size 257.15
enlarge 259.4
expand 259.5
assemble 770.18
bulkhead
partition 213.5
buttress 901.4
harbor 1009.6
barrier 1012.5
bulky large 247.7
hulky 257.19
thick 269.8
sturdy 763.7
unwieldy 1013.19
bull
n male animal 76.8
cattle 311.6
humbug 354.14
decree 420.4
jailer 429.10
bullshit 520.3
long 737.13
card 758.2
grammatical error 975.7
police 1008.16
v talk nonsense 520.5
manipulate the market
  737.25
thrust 902.12
adj masculine 76.12
bulldog
n brave person 492.7
adhesive 803.4
v fell 913.5
bulldoze
intimidate 127.20
raze 395.19
defeat 412.9
coerce 424.8
threaten 514.2
domineer 612.15
thrust 902.12
bulldozer
n strong man 15.6
tractor 179.18
adj coercive 424.12
bullet swiftness 174.6
round 462.19
game 745.3
card 758.2
shot 904.4
fission 1038.8
bulletin
n press release 352.3
report 549.7
information 551.1
news report 552.5
v publicize 352.15
bulletin board 352.7
bullet point 47.3
bullet points 551.1
bulletproof 15.20
bullfight 457.4
bullfighter 461.4

bullfrogs 316.10
bullheaded
obstinate 361.8
adhesive 803.12
bullion
precious metals 728.20
cast 1058.5
bullish 124.11
bull market
rising market 737.4
roaring trade 1010.5
bull session 541.2
bull's-eye center 208.2
objective 380.2
score 409.5
bullshit
n humbug 354.14
boasting 502.2
shit 520.3
absurdity 923.3
v boast 502.7
talk nonsense 520.5
bullwhack 605.1
bullwhacker 178.9
bully
n beef 10.14
strong man 15.7
tormentor 96.10
combatant 461.1
blusterer 503.2
ruffian 593.3
game 749.6
v intimidate 127.20
coerce 424.7
bluster 503.3
domineer 612.15
adj excellent 999.13
bulwark
n fortification 460.4
buttress 901.4
safeguard 1008.3
barrier 1012.5
v fortify 460.9
bum
n drunk 88.12
vagabond 178.3
buttocks 217.5
stiff 331.9
failure 410.8
beggar 440.8
wretch 660.2
transient 828.4
v hum 52.13
wander 177.23
beg 440.15
adj bad 1000.8
the bum's rush 909.1
bum around 331.12
bumble 414.11
bumbledom 612.10
bumbler 414.8
bummer
substance abuse 87.1
vagabond 178.3
nonworker 331.11
beggar 440.8
wretch 660.2
adversity 1011.1
bump
n thud 52.3
report 56.1

atmosphere 184.32
bulge 283.3
swelling 283.4
talent 413.4
demotion 447.1
print 517.7
poker 759.10
thrust 902.2
impact 902.3
shake 917.3
v crack 56.6
demote 447.3
thrust 902.12
collide 902.13
dismiss 909.20
shake 917.11
bumper
n drink 8.4
partition 213.5
full measure 794.3
safeguard 1008.3
adj large 257.16
bump into meet 223.11
collide 902.13
come across 941.3
bumpkin peasant 606.6
oaf 924.5
bump off
n homicide 308.2
v kill 308.14
bumptious
conceited 140.11
insolent 142.9
defiant 454.7
immodest 666.6
bump up 251.4
bumpy bulging 283.15
rough 288.6
nappy 294.7
jolting 917.20
bum's rush 372.1
bum steer 356.2
bun braid 3.7
roll 10.31
bunch
n amount 244.2
bulge 283.3
clique 617.6
company 770.3
group of animals 770.5
assemblage 770.7
conglomeration 803.5
multitude 884.3
v come together 770.16
assemble 770.18
cohere 803.6
league 805.4
bunchy 283.15
bunco
n fraud 356.8
cheater 357.4
v cheat 356.18
bundle
n gain 472.3
wealth 618.3
bindle 770.8
v snuggle 121.10
way of walking 177.28
package 212.9
hasten 401.4
move quickly 401.5

cuddle 562.17
swaddle 770.20
bind 800.9
dismiss 909.18
bundle off start 904.13
dismiss 909.18
bundle up clothe 5.39
bundle 770.20
bung
n anus 292.5
stopper 293.4
v stop 293.7
injure 393.13
bungalow 228.8
bungee-jumping 366.3
bungle
n fiasco 410.6
blunder 414.5
error 975.5
v do carelessly 340.9
miss 410.14
blunder 414.11
fail 975.14
bunion sore 85.37
swelling 283.4
bunk
n humbug 354.14
boasting 502.2
bullshit 520.3
v inhabit 225.7
house 225.10
bunker
n basement 197.17
cave 284.5
storehouse 386.6
entrenchment 460.5
stronghold 460.6
golf 751.1
shelter 1009.3
proving ground 1074.7
v provision 385.9
bunkum
humbug 354.14
boasting 502.2
flattery 511.1
bullshit 520.3
political jargon 609.37
bunny hare 311.23
beauty 1016.8
bunt
n game 745.3
thrust 902.2
pushing 904.1
v thrust 902.12
tap 902.18
push 904.9
bunting 647.7
buoy
n float 180.11
life preserver 397.6
marker 517.10
v lighten up 298.8
buoyant
lighthearted 109.12
floaty 298.14
recuperative 396.23
elastic 1048.7
buoy up cheer 109.7
buoy 298.8
support 901.21
elevate 912.5

burble
  n flow 184.29
  v ripple 52.11
  bubble 320.4
  be stupid 922.12
burden
  n affliction 96.8
  load 196.2
  capacity 257.2
  burthen 297.7
  duty 641.1
  charge 643.3
  guilt 656.1
  part 708.22
  passage 708.24
  poetry 720.9
  repeat 849.5
  topic 937.1
  bane 1001.1
  impediment 1012.6
  v distress 96.16
  oppress 98.16
  load 159.15
  add 253.4
  burthen 297.13
  task 725.16
  inconvenience 996.4
  go hard with 1011.8
  hamper 1012.11
burdened
  weighted 297.18
  fraught 794.12
  supporting 901.23
burden of proof 957.3
burdensome
  oppressive 98.24
  onerous 297.17
  laborious 725.18
  hampering 1012.18
  troublesome 1013.18
bureau 594.4
bureaucracy
  routine 373.5
  the authorities 575.15
  officialism 612.10
bureaucratic
  governmental 612.16
  executive 612.18
burg 230.1
burgeon
  n branch 310.20
  bud 310.23
  v grow 14.2
  expand 259.7
  vegetate 310.34
burgher
  townsman 227.6
  respectable citizen 659.3
  conformist 867.2
burglar 483.3
burglary 482.5
burgoo 10.11
burial interment 309.1
  funeral 309.5
  tomb 309.16
  concealment 346.1
  submergence 367.2
  overrunning 910.1
buried
  underground 275.12
  underwater 275.13

concealed 346.11
overrun 910.10
engrossed 983.17
burl 283.3
burlesque
  n imitation 336.1
  reproduction 336.3
  bad likeness 350.2
  exaggeration 355.1
  wit 489.1
  lampoon 508.6
  disparagement 512.5
  show business 704.1
  similarity 784.1
  v misrepresent 350.3
  exaggerate 355.3
  ridicule 508.11
  lampoon 512.12
  adj comical 488.6
  farcical 508.14
burly
  able-bodied 15.16
  corpulent 257.18
burn
  n smart 26.3
  trauma 85.38
  stream 238.1
  deception 356.9
  theft 482.4
  basketball game 747.3
  scald 1020.6
  rocket launching 1074.9
  spacecraft 1075.2
  v pain 26.7
  brown 40.2
  be angry 152.15
  cremate 309.20
  deceive 356.19
  injure 393.13
  rob 482.16
  execute 604.17
  rage 671.11
  play 747.4
  throw 904.10
  scent 941.6
  be hot 1019.22
  ignite 1020.22
  catch fire 1020.23
  torrefy 1020.24
  shine 1025.24
  dry 1066.6
burner destroyer 395.8
  heater 1020.10
  incinerator 1020.13
  blowtorch 1020.14
burn in effigy 661.9
burning
  n smart 26.3
  cremation 309.2
  discard 390.3
  capital punishment 604.7
  throwing 904.2
  heat 1019.1
  combustion 1020.5
  adj sore 26.11
  colorful 35.19
  zestful 68.7
  in heat 75.28
  feverish 85.58
  fervent 93.18
  zealous 101.9

excited 105.22
resentful 152.26
seething 152.29
near 223.14
vehement 544.13
hot 1019.25
ignited 1019.27
heating 1020.26
luminous 1025.31
flashing 1025.35
burnish
  n polish 287.2
  smoother 287.4
  v polish 287.7
  buff 1044.8
burn one's bridges
  leave home 188.17
  be determined 359.8
burnout fatigue 21.1
  apathy 94.4
  extinguishing 1022.2
  rocket launching 1074.9
burn out fatigue 21.4
  get tired 21.5
  go out 1022.8
burnt
  red-complexioned 41.9
  burned 1020.30
  dried 1066.9
burn the candle at both ends
  squander 486.3
  dissipate 669.6
  overdo 993.10
burn the midnight oil
  study 570.12
  work hard 725.13
  be late 846.7
burn up annoy 96.13
  consume 388.3
  incendiarize 1020.25
burp
  n belch 909.9
  v expel 909.28
burr
  n rasp 58.3
  thorn 285.5
  seed vessel 310.30
  accent 524.8
  engraving 713.2
  adhesive 803.4
  v hum 52.13
  sound harshly 58.9
burro 311.15
burrow
  n lair 228.26
  cave 284.5
  v settle 159.17
  excavate 284.15
  hide 346.8
  search 938.31
bursar payer 624.9
  treasurer 729.12
burst
  n report 56.1
  detonation 56.3
  outburst 105.9
  resentment 152.9
  run 174.3
  bustle 330.4
  volley 459.9
  violence 671.6

explosion 671.7
separate 802.4
flare 1019.14
v blast 56.8
break 393.23
explode 671.14
break 802.12
adj impaired 393.27
broken 802.24
burst forth
  break forth 33.9
  emerge 190.11
  vegetate 310.34
  erupt 671.13
  originate 818.13
burst in enter 189.7
  intrude 214.5
  breach 292.14
bursting
  n disruption 802.3
  adj banging 56.11
  excited 105.20
  explosive 671.24
  full 794.11
  teeming 884.9
  productive 890.9
  brimming 993.20
burst one's bubble
  sadden 112.18
  shatter one's hopes 125.11
burst out erupt 671.13
  exclaim 59.7
  laugh 116.8
bury inter 309.19
  secrete 346.7
  submerge 367.7
bury oneself in 570.12
bury the hatchet
  forget 148.5
  make peace 465.9
bus
  n car 179.10
  public vehicle 179.13
  v haul 176.13
  ride 177.33
busboy 577.7
bush
  marijuana 87.11
  lining 196.3
  hinterland 233.2
  shrubbery 310.9
  woodland 310.13
  brush 310.16
  wasteland 891.2
bushed 21.8
bush-league 1005.7
bushwhack
  surprise 131.7
  kill 308.14
  attack 459.15
bushwhacker
  irregular 461.16
  precursor 816.1
bushy hairy 3.24
  arboreal 310.39
  sylvan 310.40
business
  n action 328.1
  activity 330.1
  undertaking 404.1
  company 617.9

duty 641.1
acting 704.8
occupation 724.1
vocation 724.6
commerce 731.1
relation 775.1
affair 831.3
specialty 866.1
adj occupational 730.12
commercial 731.22
the business 356.9
business casual 5.20
businesslike 807.6
businessman
businessperson 730.1
businesswoman 730.1
business manager 704.25
busman's holiday 20.3
buss
n kiss 562.4
v kiss 562.19
bust
n drinking spree 88.6
breast 283.6
figure 349.6
failure 410.2
washout 410.8
arrest 429.6
demotion 447.1
monument 549.12
insolvency 625.3
business cycle 731.10
blow 902.5
hard times 1011.6
v flunk 410.17
arrest 429.16
domesticate 432.11
demote 447.3
depose 447.4
go under 625.7
bankrupt 625.8
explode 671.14
break 802.12
dismiss 909.19
busted
impaired 393.27
without money 619.10
insolvent 625.11
broken 802.24
bust in enter 189.7
breach 292.14
bustle
n excitement 105.4
fuss 330.4
haste 401.1
bluster 503.1
agitation 917.1
v fuss 330.12
hasten 401.4
move quickly 401.5
bustling
fussing 330.20
eventful 831.10
bust out 431.8
busty
corpulent 257.18
pectoral 283.19
busy
v occupy 724.10
task 725.16
adj meddlesome 214.9

full of business 330.21
ornate 498.12
occupied 724.15
busybody
n meddler 214.4
newsmonger 552.9
inquisitive person 981.2
v meddle 214.7
adj meddlesome 214.9
busywork 724.2
but
notwithstanding 338.8
unless 959.16
butch
n mannish female 76.9
adj homosexual 75.30
butcher
n killer 308.11
vendor 730.5
v slaughter 308.17
misdraw 350.4
bungle 414.11
rage 671.11
sever 802.11
butchered
botched 414.21
mutilated 795.5
butler steward 574.4
man 577.4
major-domo 577.10
butt
n cigarette 89.5
buttocks 217.5
remainder 256.1
objective 380.2
laughingstock 508.7
piece 793.3
joint 800.4
extremity 820.2
thrust 902.2
pushing 904.1
v adjoin 223.9
hook 800.8
thrust 902.12
push 904.9
butte plateau 237.3
hill 237.4
butter
n suavity 504.5
softness 1047.4
semiliquid 1062.5
pulp 1063.2
v coat 295.24
flatter 511.6
butterfingers 414.9
butterflies 128.2
butterfly effect
disorder 810.1
immediate cause 886.3
buttery
n storehouse 386.6
larder 386.8
adj slippery 287.12
suave 504.18
flattering 511.8
oily 1056.9
semiliquid 1062.11
butt heads 451.3
butt in intrude 214.5
interrupt 214.6
mediate 466.6

talk out of turn 844.4
buttinsky 422.3
buttocks bottom 199.1
rump 217.4
button
n chin 216.6
runt 258.4
bulge 283.3
insignia 647.1
trifle 998.5
cast 1058.5
v close 293.6
hook 800.8
buttoned-down 867.6
buttonhole
n bouquet 310.25
v bore 118.7
importune 440.12
address 524.26
button up
be silent 51.6
close 293.6
complete 407.6
butt out
v not interfere 430.17
phrs none of your business
214.10
buttress
n supporter 901.2
buttressing 901.4
v strengthen 15.13
help 449.12
support 901.21
confirm 957.11
buxom
merry 109.15
corpulent 257.18
comely 1016.18
buy
n bargain 633.3
v assent 332.8
bribe 378.3
take advice 422.7
purchase 733.7
believe 953.10
kid oneself 954.6
buyer 733.5
buyers' market
low price 633.2
cheapening 633.4
commerce 731.1
sale 734.1
buyer's remorse 113.1
buy into
take advice 422.7
invest 729.17
purchase 733.7
believe 953.10
kid oneself 954.6
buyout
n trading 737.19
combination 805.1
v purchase 733.7
combine 805.3
buzz
n sibilation 57.1
rasp 58.3
tingle 74.1
substance abuse 87.1
telephone call 347.13
report 552.6

series 812.2
v hum 52.13
sibilate 57.2
sound harshly 58.9
flathat 184.42
telephone 347.19
publish 352.10
speak 524.25
tip off 551.11
buzzer 400.1
buzzing
n hum 52.7
flathatting 184.17
adj humming 52.20
buzz off
v depart 188.7
interj go away! 909.31
buzzworthy 100.30
BVD 5.22
by
adj past 837.7
adv in reserve 386.17
prep at 159.27
through 161.27
beside 218.11
by means of 384.13
conformable to 867.9
by all means
adv certainly 970.23
interj yes 332.18
by all odds
by far 247.17
probably 968.8
by and by
in the future 839.9
soon 845.16
by and large
approximately 244.6
on the whole 792.14
generally 864.17
by any means
anyhow 384.10
by any possibility 966.10
by bits and pieces
incompletely 795.6
disjointedly 802.28
by chance
haphazardly 810.18
perchance 972.19
by degrees
degreewise 245.6
piece by piece 793.9
by design 380.10
by dint of
adv usefully 387.26
prep by virtue of 18.18
by means of 384.13
by ear 365.15
bye-bye 22.2
by express mail 401.13
by far 247.17
by fits and starts
nonuniformly 782.4
disjointedly 802.28
haphazardly 810.18
discontinuously 813.5
irregularly 851.4
shakily 917.23
bygone 837.7
by hand 176.19
by heart 989.27

campground 463.3
campus arena 463.1
  schoolhouse 567.10
can
  n latrine 12.10
  toilet 12.11
  battleship 180.7
  container 195.1
  ass 217.5
  jail 429.9
  marker 517.10
  v be able 18.11
  package 212.9
  put up 397.11
  may 443.13
  sink 747.4
  play 751.4
  dismiss 909.20
Canadian provinces and
  territories 231.12
canal
  n duct 2.23
  channel 239.1
  watercourse 239.2
  inlet 242.1
  narrow place 270.3
  trench 290.2
  v furrow 290.3
canape 62.4
canard
  fabrication 354.10
  report 552.6
canary
  n singer 710.13
  songbird 710.23
  adj yellow 43.4
cancel
  n obliteration 395.7
  repeal 445.1
  notation 709.12
  v excise 255.10
  delete 255.12
  abolish 395.13
  obliterate 395.16
  repeal 445.2
  declare a moratorium 625.9
  equalize 790.6
  end 820.5
  cease 857.6
  neutralize 900.7
canceled forgiven 148.7
  ended 820.8
cancellate 170.11
cancer growth 85.39
  blight 1001.2
cancerous 85.61
candescent
  burning 1019.27
  luminous 1025.31
candid
  v talkative 540.9
  adj communicative 343.10
  artless 416.5
  free-acting 430.23
  natural 499.7
  plain-speaking 535.3
  frank 644.17
  genuine 973.15
candidacy 609.10
candidate
  desirer 100.12

petitioner 440.7
  aspirant 610.9
  assignee 615.9
candle
  light source 1026.1
  taper 1026.2
candlelit 1025.40
can do
  v be able 18.11
  adj energetic 17.13
  active 330.17
candor
  communicativeness
    343.3
  artlessness 416.1
  plain speech 535.1
  talkativeness 540.1
  candidness 644.4
  fairness 649.2
candy
  n sweets 10.40
  amyl nitrate 87.5
  v sweeten 66.3
  solidify 1046.8
candy store 66.1
candy-stripe
  n stripe 47.5
  adj striped 47.15
cane
  n blind 30.6
  staff 273.2
  grass 310.5
  stem 310.21
  rod 605.2
  supporter 901.2
  bamboo 1054.4
  v whip 604.13
canicular
  seasonal 313.9
  hot 1019.25
canine
  n teeth 2.8
  creature 311.3
  dog 311.16
  adj doggish 311.41
canker
  n sore 85.37
  blight 1001.2
  v corrupt 393.12
  corrode 393.21
  decay 393.22
cankered
  diseased 85.60
  irascible 110.19
  decayed 393.40
cannibal
  n eater 8.16
  killer 308.11
  creature 311.3
  savage 593.5
  adj eating 8.31
cannibalize 365.8
cannon
  n artillery 462.11
  game 745.3
  impact 902.3
  recoil 903.2
  shot 904.4
  v pull the trigger 459.22
  collide 902.13
  recoil 903.6

cannonade
  n boom 56.4
  volley 459.9
  v pull the trigger 459.22
cannonball
  swiftness 174.6
  plunge 367.1
  shot 462.19
cannot 19.8
canny cunning 415.12
  cautious 494.8
  economical 635.6
  shrewd 920.15
canoe
  n roulette 759.12
  v navigate 182.13
can of corn 745.3
can of worms
  hodgepodge 797.6
  complex 799.2
  trouble 1013.3
canon music 280.9
  measure 300.2
  precept 419.2
  literature 547.12
  compilation 554.7
  law 673.3
  Bible 683.2
  round 708.19
  scripture 718.1
  rule 869.4
  lore 928.9
  a belief 953.2
canonical
  preceptive 419.4
  theological 676.4
  scriptural 683.11
  orthodox 687.7
  ecclesiastic 698.13
  doctrinal 953.27
canonize
  glorify 662.13
  sanctify 685.5
  ordain 698.12
  exalt 912.6
canopy
  n the heavens 1072.2
  v cover 295.19
cant
  n inclination 204.2
  angle 278.2
  hypocrisy 354.6
  Greek 522.7
  jargon 523.9
  sanctimony 693.1
  v change course 182.30
  careen 182.43
  incline 204.10
  be hypocritical 354.23
  speak 523.18
  be sanctimonious 693.4
cantankerous
  irascible 110.20
  perverse 361.11
  hindering 1012.17
cantata
  sacred music 708.17
  part music 708.18
canteen 8.17
canter
  n run 174.3

hypocrite 357.8
  pietist 693.3
  v speed 174.8
  go on horseback 177.34
canticle paean 696.3
  song 708.14
  sacred music 708.17
cantilever 202.3
cantina 8.17
canto air 708.4
  part 708.22
  poetry 720.9
  fight 754.3
canton region 231.5
  heraldry 647.2
cantor clergy 699.11
  singer 710.13
  choirmaster 710.18
canvas sail 180.14
  tent 295.8
  arena 463.1
  painting 712.13
  art equipment 712.17
  boxing 754.1
canvass
  n vote 371.6
  solicitation 440.5
  campaign 609.13
  assemblage 770.1
  survey 938.14
  v vote 371.18
  solicit 440.14
  discuss 541.11
  electioneer 609.40
  examine 938.24
  survey 938.29
canvasser
  traveling salesman 730.4
  solicitor 730.6
canyon 237.7
cap
  n headdress 5.25
  LSD 87.10
  summit 198.2
  top part 198.4
  architectural topping 198.5
  cover 295.5
  fuse 462.15
  type 548.6
  v cloak 5.40
  top 198.9
  excel 249.6
  cover 295.21
  complete 407.6
  give in kind 506.6
capability ability 18.2
  preparedness 405.4
  skill 413.1
  talent 413.4
capable able 18.14
  fitted 405.17
  competent 413.24
  liable to 897.6
capacious
  spacious 158.11
  voluminous 257.17
capacitate 405.8
capacities 919.2
capacity
  n ability 18.2
  spaciousness 158.5

case
  n sick person 85.43
  infatuation 104.3
  container 195.1
  frame 266.4
  blanket 295.10
  hull 295.16
  casing 295.17
  grammar 530.9
  type 548.6
  bookbinding 554.14
  lawsuit 598.1
  state 765.1
  particular 766.3
  example 786.2
  oddity 870.4
  argument 935.5
  topic 937.1
  citation 957.5
  v package 212.9
  wrap 295.20
  reconnoiter 938.28
the case fact 761.3
  the truth 973.3
casebook
  reference book 554.9
  text 554.10
case-hardened
  callous 94.12
  obstinate 361.8
  accustomed 373.15
  hardened 654.17
  tempered 1046.15
case history
  medical history 91.10
  record 719.1
casement frame 266.4
  window 292.7
case the joint 482.16
caseworker 143.8
cash
  n payment 624.1
  dollars 728.1
  ready money 728.18
  v pay 624.17
  transact 728.29
  adv cash on the barrelhead
    624.25
cashbook
  record book 549.11
  account book 628.4
cashbox 729.13
cash crunch 619.1
cashier
  n payer 624.9
  banker 729.11
  treasurer 729.12
  v depose 447.4
  dismiss 909.19
cash in die 307.19
  cash 728.29
cash in on
  take advantage of 387.15
  profit 472.12
  improve the occasion 843.8
casing frame 266.4
  case 295.17
casino
  haunt 228.27
  ballroom 705.4
  entertainment 743.13

gambling house 759.19
casita 228.8
cask
  n container 195.1
  cylinder 282.4
  v package 212.9
casket
  n coffin 309.11
  v confine 212.6
Cassandra
  pessimist 125.7
  warner 399.4
  predictor 962.4
casserole 10.7
cassette 50.12
cassette tape 549.1
cassock 699.5
cast
  n slough 2.5
  glance 27.4
  strabismus 28.5
  looks 33.4
  color 35.1
  dressing 86.33
  hint 248.4
  form 262.1
  team 617.7
  role 704.10
  cast of characters 707.11
  sculpture 715.2
  throw 759.9
  nature 767.4
  company 770.3
  copy 785.6
  mold 786.6
  kind 809.3
  characteristic 865.4
  tendency 896.1
  throw 904.3
  disposition 978.3
  sum 1017.6
  casting 1058.5
  v give birth 1.3
  shed 6.10
  put violently 159.13
  change course 182.30
  form 262.7
  plan 381.8
  discard 390.7
  sculpture 715.5
  produce 892.8
  throw 904.10
  eject 909.13
  calculate 1017.18
  burn 1020.24
  adj born 1.4
  formative 262.9
  made 892.18
cast about
  change course 182.30
  investigate 938.23
cast aside
  put away 390.6
  discard 390.7
castaway
  n derelict 370.4
  discard 390.3
  outcast 586.4
  adj abandoned 370.8
  discarded 390.11
  outcast 586.10

stranded 1013.27
cast down
  v chagrin 96.15
  sadden 112.18
  disappoint 132.2
  raze 395.19
  fell 913.5
  adj distressed 96.22
  dejected 112.22
caste rank 245.2
  social status 607.1
  community 617.2
  class 809.2
cast forth
  dissipate 771.5
  disgorge 909.25
castigate
  criticize 510.20
  punish 604.10
casting sculpture 715.1
  copy 785.6
  production 892.2
  throwing 904.2
  calculation 1017.10
  cast 1058.5
cast-iron strong 15.15
  unyielding 361.9
  true 973.13
castle estate 228.7
  stronghold 460.6
  chessman 743.17
castle-building
  n abstractedness 985.2
  dreaminess 986.8
  adj abstracted 985.11
  dreamy 986.25
cast lots 759.23
castoff derelict 370.4
  discard 390.3
cast off take off 6.6
  weigh anchor 182.18
  discard 390.7
  waste 473.5
  eliminate 773.5
  separate 802.8
  detach 802.10
  do away with 909.21
cast-off adrift 182.61
  discarded 390.11
  outcast 586.10
castoff clothes 5.5
cast out
  eliminate 773.5
  separate 802.8
  eject 909.13
  banish 909.17
castrate unman 19.12
  feminize 77.12
  geld 255.11
  cripple 393.14
  domineer 612.15
castrated
  unmanned 19.19
  unsexual 75.29
  crippled 393.30
  mutilated 795.5
cast the first stone
  censure 510.13
  incriminate 599.10
cast up erect 200.9
  elevate 912.5

sum up 1017.19
casual
  n irregular 461.16
  poor man 619.4
  worker 726.2
  adj in dishabille 5.47
  unconcerned 102.7
  nonchalant 106.15
  careless 340.11
  unpremeditated 365.11
  informal 581.3
  circumstantial 766.7
  unessential 768.4
  unordered 810.12
  incidental 843.11
  occasional 848.3
  undiscriminating 945.5
  chance 972.15
  purposeless 972.16
  easy 1014.13
casualty fatality 308.8
  chance event 972.6
  misfortune 1011.2
casuistry
  insincerity 354.5
  ethical philosophy 636.2
  argumentation 935.4
  sophistry 936.1
cat sharp vision 27.11
  man 76.5
  bitch 110.12
  feline 311.20
  whip 605.1
catabolism
  the body 2.20
  metabolism 7.12
  transformation 852.3
cataclasm 802.3
cataclysm
  overflow 238.6
  debacle 395.4
  upheaval 671.5
  revolution 860.1
  misfortune 1011.2
catacombs 309.16
catalepsy
  stupor 22.6
  unconsciousness 25.2
  paralysis 85.27
  trance 92.19
  inertness 173.4
catalog
  n description 349.2
  record 549.1
  book 549.11
  reference 554.9
  directory 574.10
  account book 628.4
  outline 801.4
  classified list 871.3
  v record 549.15
  classify 801.8
  represent 809.6
  list 871.8
catalysis
  dissociation 806.2
  transformation 852.3
catalyst
  instigator 375.11
  dissociation 806.2
  transformer 852.5

author 886.4
catamaran 760.2
cataphor 22.5
cataplexy
paralysis 85.27
trance 92.19
catapult
n takeoff 184.8
sling 462.9
toy 743.16
v throw 904.10
cataract
n blindness 30.1
descent 194.1
waterfall 238.11
v descend 194.5
overflow 238.17
catastrophe
debacle 395.4
upheaval 671.5
plot 722.4
end 820.1
revolution 860.1
misfortune 1011.2
catatonic
unconscious 25.8
unfeeling 94.9
inert 173.14
unsociable 583.5
psychotic 926.28
incurious 982.3
catcall
n noisemaker 53.6
boo 508.3
v boo 508.10
catch
n desire 100.11
lover 104.11
surprise 131.2
trick 356.6
proviso 421.3
lock 428.5
seizure 480.2
take 480.10
round 708.19
game 745.3
good thing 999.5
fault 1003.2
obstacle 1012.4
crux 1013.8
v hear 48.11
take sick 85.47
jump at 101.6
row 182.53
attend 221.8
trap 356.20
acquire 472.8
hook 472.9
take 480.17
understand 521.7
play 745.5
fight 754.4
fix 855.10
discover 941.7
engross 983.13
flame up 1020.23
catch at straws
be hopeful 124.7
be rash 493.5
find fault 510.15

catcher taker 480.11
baseball team 745.2
catch fire
be excitable 105.16
succeed 409.7
catch on 578.8
be hot 1019.22
heat up 1020.23
catching
n seizure 480.2
discovery 941.1
adj poisonous 82.7
contagious 85.62
alluring 377.8
taking 480.25
catch it 604.20
catch on succeed 409.7
understand 521.7
become popular 578.8
catch one's breath
take a rest 20.8
recuperate 396.19
catch short 131.7
catch the eye show 31.4
appear 33.8
meet with attention 983.11
catch up
overtake 174.13
seize 480.14
catchword
call to arms 458.7
clue 517.9
phrase 526.9
makeup 554.12
maxim 974.1
motto 974.4
catchy
deceptive 356.21
melodious 708.48
irregular 851.3
catechism
doctrine 676.2
question 938.10
system of belief 953.3
catechize teach 568.10
inculcate 568.12
interrogate 938.21
catechumen
novice 572.9
believer 692.4
beginner 818.2
convert 858.7
categorical
classificational 809.7
dialectic 935.22
unqualified 960.2
categorize
analyze 801.8
arrange 808.11
classify 809.6
category class 809.2
topic 937.1
catenary
n sinkage 194.2
curve 279.2
adj consecutive 812.9
cater 385.9
catercorner
v cut 204.11
adj transverse 204.19
adv diagonally 204.25

caterer 11.3
catering cooking 11.1
provision 385.1
caterpillar larva 302.12
insect 311.32
cater to toady to 138.8
indulge 427.6
serve 449.18
caterwaul
n screech 58.4
cry 59.1
animal noise 60.1
v screech 58.8
cry 59.6
wail 60.2
catharsis
defecation 12.2
cleansing 79.2
purgation 92.25
release 120.2
cathartic
n cleanser 79.17
laxative 86.17
adj cleansing 79.28
laxative 86.48
relieving 120.9
cathedral
n church 703.1
adj authoritative 970.18
catheter 239.6
cathexis
cathection 92.34
feeling 93.1
interest 983.2
cathode 1032.8
cathode ray 1033.5
catholic
universal 864.14
broad-minded 979.8
Catholic
n Roman Catholic 675.19
adj religious denomination 675.29
cathouse
disapproved place 228.28
brothel 665.9
cation
electrolysis 1032.25
element 1060.2
cat man 483.3
catnap
n nap 22.3
v sleep 22.13
cat-o'-nine-tails 605.1
cat's-paw
sycophant 138.3
breeze 318.4
dupe 358.1
instrument 384.4
deputy 576.1
agent 576.3
follower 616.8
cattle
animal life 311.1
kine 311.6
rabble 606.3
cattleman
stockman 1070.2
herder 1070.3
cattle rustler 483.8

catty peevish 110.22
spiteful 144.21
feline 311.42
disparaging 512.13
cattycorner
adj transverse 204.19
adv diagonally 204.25
catwalk 383.2
Caucasian race 312.2
white man 312.3
caucus
n legislative gathering 609.9
election 609.15
party 617.4
assembly 770.2
v politick 609.38
caudal tail 217.11
final 820.11
caught stuck 855.16
gripped 983.18
caught short
surprised 131.12
unprepared 406.8
caught up in
involved in 898.5
engrossed 983.17
caulk 293.7
cause
n motive 375.1
lawsuit 598.1
warrant 600.6
reason 886.2
occasion 886.1
principle 886.9
v prompt 375.13
compel 424.4
reason 886.10
perform 892.11
cause célèbre
report 552.6
affair 831.3
caused by 887.8
causeless
chance 972.15
purposeless 972.16
causerie chat 541.3
treatise 556.1
causeway 295.22
caustic
n curve 279.2
cauterant 1020.15
adj acrimonious 17.14
bitter 64.6
pungent 68.6
penetrating 105.31
out of humor 110.17
mordant 144.23
resentful 152.26
satiric 508.13
hostile 589.10
cauterant
n cauterizer 1020.15
adj heating 1020.26
cauterize 1020.24
caution
n wariness 339.1
hesitation 362.3
dissuasion 379.1
warning 399.1
advice 422.1
collateral 438.3

carefulness 494.1
cautiousness 494.1
tip-off 551.3
game 752.3
incredulity 956.1
forethought 961.2
v dissuade 379.3
warn 399.5
admonish 422.6
cautious slow 175.10
careful 339.10
hesitant 362.11
wary 494.8
incredulous 956.4
cavalcade 812.3
cavalier
n beau 104.12
rider 178.8
gallant 504.9
knight 608.5
escort 769.5
adj disdainful 141.13
gruff 505.7
cave
n lair 228.26
cavern 284.5
debacle 395.4
shelter 1009.3
v sink 194.6
collapse 260.10
hollow 284.13
caveat dissuasion 379.1
warning 399.1
advice 422.1
caveat emptor 419.2
cave in weaken 16.9
sink 194.6
collapse 260.10
hollow 284.13
breach 292.14
break down 393.24
yield 433.7
cave-in collapse 260.4
debacle 395.4
caveman real man 76.6
ancient 842.7
cavern 284.5
cavernous
abysmal 275.11
concave 284.16
cavil
n criticism 510.4
quibble 936.4
v find fault 510.15
argue 935.16
quibble 936.9
cavity
compartment 197.2
crack 224.2
pit 275.2
concavity 284.2
opening 292.1
cavort
n caper 366.2
v caper 366.6
play 743.23
caw
n rasp 58.3
v sound harshly 58.9
bird sound 60.5
cay 235.2

cease
n cessation 857.1
v disappear 34.2
quiet 173.8
close shop 293.8
give up 370.7
perish 395.23
end 820.5
discontinue 857.6
interj stop! 857.13
cease-fire truce 465.5
pause 857.3
ceaseless nonstop 812.8
perpetual 829.7
constant 847.5
continuing 856.7
cede give up 370.7
yield 433.7
surrender 433.8
relinquish 475.3
transfer 629.3
ceiling
distinctness 31.2
atmosphere 184.32
boundary 211.3
height 272.1
roof 295.6
price index 630.4
limit 794.5
rocket launching 1074.9
celebrate party 487.2
praise 509.12
formalize 580.5
glorify 696.12
observe 701.15
make merry 743.24
celebrated
distinguished 662.16
notable 997.19
celebration
spree 88.5
treat 95.3
rejoicing 116.1
observance 487.1
ceremony 580.4
ritualism 701.1
revel 743.6
celebrity glory 247.2
publicity 352.4
repute 662.1
man of mark 662.9
notability 997.2
personage 997.8
celebutante 662.9
celerity velocity 174.1
quickness 330.3
celestial
n angel 679.1
adj divine 677.16
angelic 679.6
heavenly 681.12
ideal 986.23
the universe 1072.25
celibate
n abstainer 565.2
religious 699.16
adj monastic 565.6
continent 664.6
abstinent 668.10
sole 872.9
unproductive 891.4

cell
compartment 197.2
bioplast 305.4
prison 429.8
refuge 584.6
clique 617.6
retreat 1009.5
cellar basement 197.17
storehouse 386.6
cell biology 1068.3
cellist 710.5
cell phone number 347.12
cellular 305.19
cellulose 305.6
Celsius scale 1019.19
cement
n pavement 383.6
ceramic ware 742.2
adhesive 803.4
hardness 1046.6
building material
1054.2
v floor 295.22
plaster 295.25
put together 800.5
fasten 800.7
stick together 803.9
adj hard 1046.10
cemetery 309.15
cenotaph tomb 309.16
monument 549.12
censer 70.6
censor
n restrictionist 428.6
faultfinder 510.9
conscience 636.5
critic 946.7
v delete 255.12
cover up 345.8
suppress 428.8
end 820.5
censorious averse 99.8
fastidious 495.9
prudish 500.19
disapproving 510.22
condemnatory 602.5
censorship
suppression 92.24
deletion 255.5
veil of secrecy 345.3
restraint 428.2
censure
n reprehension 510.3
incrimination 599.2
condemnation 602.1
stigma 661.6
criticism 946.2
v reprehend 510.13
incriminate 599.10
condemn 602.3
stigmatize 661.9
criticize 946.14
census
n contents 196.1
population 227.1
assemblage 770.1
table 808.4
roll 871.6
numeration 1017.9
summation 1017.11
v number 1017.17

cent money 728.7
trifle 998.5
centenarian
old man 304.2
hundred 882.8
centennial
n anniversary 850.4
hundred 882.8
adj momentary 850.8
hundredth 882.29
center
n interior 207.2
centrum 208.2
mean 246.1
middle course 467.3
moderatism 611.2
core 611.10
football team 746.2
basketball team 747.2
hockey team 749.2
essence 767.2
median 819.1
attractor 907.2
v converge 169.2
centralize 208.9
play 749.7
position 752.4
centerpiece
focus 208.4
feature 997.7
center stage 704.16
centigrade scale 1019.19
centipede
insect 311.32
hundred 882.8
central
n exchange 347.7
telephone operator 347.9
adj interior 207.6
centric 208.11
medium 246.3
chief 249.14
phonetic 524.30
middle 819.4
original 886.14
vital 997.23
central air conditioning 317.9
Central Intelligence Agency
576.12
centralize
converge 169.2
center 208.9
league 805.4
centrifugal 171.8
centrifugal force
centripetal force 18.6
repulsion 908.1
centrifuge
n separator 802.7
v whirl 915.11
centripetal
converging 169.3
focal 208.13
middle 819.4
centripetal force
centrifugal force 18.6
attraction 907.1
centrist
n nonpartisan 609.28
political follower 611.10
moderate 670.4

adj neutral 467.7
  moderate 611.18
  middle 819.4
centurion
  Army noncommissioned
    officer 575.19
  hundred 882.8
century money 728.7
  moment 824.2
  long time 827.4
  eleven 882.7
  hundred 882.8
cephalic 198.14
ceramic 742.7
ceramics
  visual arts 712.1
  pottery 742.1
  earthenware 742.1
  ceramic ware 742.2
cereal
  n breakfast food 10.34
  grass 310.5
  adj vegetable 310.36
cereal bar 10.43
cereal grain 10.4
cereal grasses 310.52
cerebellum 2.15
cerebral nerve 2.30
  mental 919.7
cerebral matter 2.15
cerebrate 931.8
cerebrum brain part 2.15
  mental capacity 919.6
ceremonial
  n formality 580.1
  ceremony 580.4
  rite 701.3
  adj solemn 580.8
  ritualistic 701.19
ceremonious
  respectful 155.8
  gallant 504.15
  solemn 580.8
  ritualistic 701.19
ceremony
  celebration 487.1
  formality 580.1
  function 580.4
  rite 701.3
cerise 41.6
certain
  expectant 130.11
  quantitative 244.5
  secured 438.11
  particular 865.12
  plural 883.7
  evidential 957.16
  inevitable 963.15
  sure 970.13
  impossible 972.18
  true 973.13
  belief 953.21
certainly 332.18
certainty
  expectation 130.1
  knowledge 928.1
  belief 953.1
  conviction 953.5
  inevitability 963.7
  sureness 970.1
  certitude 970.1

certifiable 926.28
certificate
  n certification 549.6
  negotiable instrument 728.11
  v authorize 443.11
certification
  ratification 332.4
  deposition 334.3
  authorization 443.3
  credential 549.6
  confirmation 957.4
  ensuring 970.8
certified
  accepted 332.14
  affirmed 334.9
  secured 438.11
  proved 957.20
  assured 970.20
  true 973.13
certify ratify 332.12
  depose 334.6
  secure 438.9
  authorize 443.11
  testify 957.9
  confirm 957.11
  make sure 970.11
cerulean
  n the heavens 1072.2
  adj blue 45.3
cervix genitals 2.13
  contraction 260.1
  joint 800.4
  supporter 901.2
cessation
  standstill 173.3
  abandonment 370.1
  disuse 390.2
  interruption 813.2
  end 820.1
  close 820.3
  stop 857.2
  discontinuance 857.1
cession
  abandonment 370.3
  surrender 433.2
  relinquishment 475.1
  transfer 629.1
  qualification 959.1
cesspool 80.12
cgi 1042.18
chafe
  n trauma 85.38
  irritation 96.3
  abrasion 1044.2
  v pain 26.7
  irritate 96.14
  feel anxious 126.6
  be impatient 135.4
  be angry 152.15
  provoke 152.24
  injure 393.13
  heat 1020.17
  abrade 1044.7
chaff
  n remainder 256.1
  hull 295.16
  lightness 298.2
  refuse 391.4
  rabble 606.3
  trivia 998.4
  radar 1036.13

v banter 490.5
  scoff 508.9
chagrin
  n distress 96.4
  humiliation 137.2
  v embarrass 96.15
chain
  n mountain 237.6
  jewel 498.6
  insignia 647.1
  series 812.2
  curb 1012.7
  fire iron 1020.12
  atomic cluster 1038.7
  v bind 428.10
  put together 800.5
  join 800.9
  continue 812.4
  secure 855.8
chain ball 563.6
chain gang
  prisoner 429.11
  procession 812.3
chain reaction
  series 812.2
  vicissitudes 972.5
  fission 1038.8
chain restaurant 8.17
chains 428.4
chain-smoke
  n smoking 89.10
  v use 87.22
  smoke 89.14
chair
  n furniture 229.1
  mastership 417.7
  authority 417.10
  instructorship 571.10
  chairman 574.5
  seat 901.17
  v administer 573.11
  govern 612.11
  install 615.12
the chair
  capital punishment 604.7
  execution 605.5
chairmanship
  mastership 417.7
  directorship 573.4
chairperson 574.5
chaise 179.4
chalet 228.8
chalice 703.11
chalk
  n whiteness 37.2
  art equipment 712.17
  jockey 757.2
  v whiten 37.5
  mark 517.19
  record 549.15
  portray 712.18
chalky white 37.7
  powdery 1051.11
challenge
  n objection 333.2
  opposition 451.1
  resistance 453.1
  dare 454.2
  declaration of war 458.6
  questioning 938.12
  v confront 216.8

object 333.5
  demand 421.5
  claim 421.6
  contradict 451.6
  offer resistance 453.3
  defy 454.3
  compete 457.18
  make war on 458.14
  doubt 955.6
  thwart 1012.15
challenging
  provocative 375.27
  defiant 454.7
chamber
  n toilet 12.11
  room 197.1
  compartment 197.2
  bedroom 197.7
  council 423.1
  v enclose 212.5
chamberlain
  major-domo 577.10
  treasurer 729.12
chambermaid 577.8
chamber music 708.6
chamber of commerce 617.9
chamber pot 12.11
chambers
  apartment 228.13
  office 739.7
chameleon
  variegation 47.6
  timeserver 363.4
  changeableness 854.4
champ
  n bite 8.2
  victor 411.2
  champion 413.15
  v chew 8.27
champ at the bit
  have energy 17.11
  be impatient 135.4
  wait impatiently 846.13
champion
  n superior 249.4
  victor 411.2
  champ 413.15
  defender 460.7
  deputy 576.1
  justifier 600.8
  supporter 616.9
  the best 999.8
  protector 1008.5
  v back 449.13
  defend 460.8
  justify 600.10
  protect 1008.18
  adj peerless 249.15
  best 999.16
  first-rate 999.17
chance
  n gamble 759.2
  turn 825.2
  opportunity 843.2
  liability 897.1
  possibility 966.1
  probability 968.1
  uncertainty 971.1
  lottery 971.8
  absence of assignable cause
    972

tolerant 979.11
charity love 104.1
 benevolence 143.4
 patronage 449.4
 accord 455.1
 almsgiving 478.3
 donation 478.6
 cardinal virtues 653.3
 tolerance 979.4
charity case 619.4
charity event 478.9
charlatan
 n impostor 357.6
 adj quack 354.28
charlatanism 354.7
charley horse 26.2
charm
 n delightfulness 97.2
 loveableness 104.6
 allurement 377.1
 lure 377.3
 jewel 498.6
 sorcery 690.1
 magic spell 691.1
 spell 691.1
 amulet 691.5
 assemblage 770.6
 influence 894.1
 superstition 954.3
 beauty 1016.1
 elementary particle 1038.6
 v delight 95.10
 enamor 104.22
 persuade 375.23
 fascinate 377.7
 becharm 691.8
 engross 983.13
charmer deceiver 357.1
 tempter 377.4
 slyboots 415.6
 bewitcher 690.9
 beauty 1016.7
charming
 delightful 97.7
 endearing 104.24
 alluring 377.8
 bewitching 691.11
 influential 894.13
charm offensive 97.2
charnel house
 mortuary 309.9
 tomb 309.16
chart
 n map 159.5
 representation 349.1
 diagram 381.3
 statistics 757.4
 outline 801.4
 v locate 159.11
 represent 349.8
 plot 381.10
 itemize 801.7
 organize 808.10
chartbuster 708.7
charter
 n exemption 430.8
 permission 443.1
 grant 443.5
 rental 615.6
 v authorize 443.11
 commission 615.10

hire 615.15
 rent out 615.16
charter flight 184.9
charter school 567.4
chartreuse 44.4
chary wary 494.9
 economical 635.6
chase
 n furrow 290.1
 woodland 310.13
 pursuit 382.1
 hunting 382.2
 v follow 166.3
 emboss 283.12
 pursue 382.8
 hunt 382.9
 make haste 401.5
 court 562.21
 sculpture 715.5
 repulse 908.3
chase away
 repulse 908.3
 drive out 909.14
chaser drink 88.9
 pursuer 382.4
 act 704.7
 sculptor 716.6
chasm crack 224.2
 pit 275.2
 concavity 284.4
 opening 292.1
chassis base 199.2
 structure 266.4
 frame 901.10
 radio 1034.3
chaste tasteful 496.7
 celibate 499.6
 elegant 533.6
 immaculate 653.6
 virtuous 664.4
 abstinent 668.10
 simple 798.6
 perfect 1002.6
chasten
 simplify 499.5
 punish 604.10
 moderate 670.6
chastened meek 433.15
 restrained 670.11
chastise reprove 510.17
 punish 604.10
chastity elegance 533.1
 purity 653.2
 celibacy 664.3
 virtue 664.1
 abstinence 668.2
 perfection 1002.1
chat
 n talk 540.3
 cozy chat 541.3
 v chatter 540.5
 visit 541.9
château 228.7
chatelaine jewel 498.6
 mistress 575.2
 governor 575.6
chattel subject 432.7
 property 471.1
chatter
 n rattle 55.3
 speech 524.1

jabber 540.3
 v rattle 55.6
 bird sound 60.5
 speak 524.19
 protract 538.8
 talk 540.5
 shake 917.11
 freeze 1023.9
chatty
 v talkative 540.9
 adj conversational 541.12
 intimate 582.24
chauffeur
 n driver 178.10
 man 577.4
 v ride 177.33
chauvinist
 n militarist 461.5
 misanthrope 590.2
 patriot 591.3
 bigot 980.5
 adj militaristic 458.21
 public-spirited 591.4
cheap
 adj worthless 391.11
 stingy 484.9
 inexpensive 633.7
 disgraceful 661.11
 paltry 998.21
 inferior 1005.9
 adv cheaply 633.10
cheapen corrupt 393.12
 depreciate 633.6
 bargain 731.18
cheat
 n fake 354.13
 fraud 356.8
 cheater 357.3
 deceiver 759.22
 v victimize 356.18
 be dishonest 645.11
 be promiscuous 665.19
 rook 759.26
cheat sheet 482.8
check
 n plaid 47.4
 trauma 85.38
 slowing 175.4
 crack 224.2
 opening 292.1
 measure 300.2
 discomfiture 412.2
 restraint 428.1
 confinement 429.1
 mark 517.5
 label 517.13
 speech sound 524.12
 statement 628.3
 negotiable instrument 728.11
 token 728.12
 game 749.3
 chip 759.18
 stop 857.2
 checkup 938.6
 collation 943.2
 ensuring 970.8
 blemish 1004.1
 reverse 1011.3
 hindrance 1012.1
 frustration 1012.3
 curb 1012.7

v look 27.13
 variegate 47.7
 slow 175.9
 cleave 224.4
 injure 393.13
 thwart 412.11
 restrain 428.7
 confine 429.12
 fend off 460.10
 mark 517.19
 play 749.7
 ski 753.4
 bet 759.25
 agree 788.6
 break 802.12
 delay 846.8
 put a stop to 857.11
 specify 865.11
 examine 938.24
 collate 943.5
 verify 970.12
 blemish 1004.4
 hinder 1012.10
 recalculate 1017.21
 monitor 1034.26
 adj checked 47.14
checkered
 checked 47.14
 changeable 854.6
check in arrive 186.6
 die 307.19
 record 549.15
 punch the clock 832.12
checking account
 finances 622.2
 funds 728.14
checklist
 directory 574.10
 list 871.1
 roll 871.6
checkmate
 n discomfiture 412.2
 stop 857.2
 frustration 1012.3
 v defeat 412.11
 put a stop to 857.11
 thwart 1012.15
checkout 188.1
check out look 27.13
 depart 188.7
 clock out 188.13
 die 307.19
 qualify 405.15
 punch out 832.12
 investigate 938.23
 examine 938.24
 verify 970.12
 check 1017.21
checks and balances 246.1
cheddar 728.19
cheek impudence 142.3
 side 218.1
 rashness 493.1
cheek by jowl
 adj near 223.14
 adv hand in glove 769.10
 concurrently 899.5
 phrs side by side 218.12
cheeky
 impudent 142.10
 defiant 454.7

cheer
    n food 10.1
    cry 59.1
    happiness 95.2
    cheerfulness 109.1
    hurrah 116.2
    applause 509.2
    conviviality 582.3
    v refresh 9.2
    cry 59.6
    please 95.9
    gladden 109.7
    rejoice 116.6
    comfort 121.6
    give hope 124.9
    assent 332.8
    encourage 492.15
    applaud 509.10
cheerful happy 95.16
    pleasant 97.6
    glad 109.11
    cheering 109.16
    optimistic 124.11
    homelike 228.33
cheerless
    pleasureless 96.20
    distressing 98.20
    unhappy 112.21
    hopeless 125.12
cheese 10.48
cheesecake 714.3
cheesed-off 96.21
cheeseparing
    n parsimony 484.1
    economizing 635.2
    adj parsimonious 484.7
    economical 635.6
    sparse 885.5
cheesy base 661.12
    paltry 998.21
    bad 1000.8
    inferior 1005.9
chef 11.3
chef d'oeuvre
    masterpiece 413.10
    work of art 712.9
    product 893.1
    standard of perfection
        1002.4
chemical
    n element 1060.2
    v chemicalize 1060.8
    adj biochemical 1060.9
chemical engineering
    1043.1
chemical equation 1060.2
chemist
    pharmacist 86.35
    drugstore 86.36
chemistry
    sexual desire 75.5
    bad feeling 93.7
    science 1060.1
cheque 728.11
cherish
    hold dear 104.20
    foster 449.16
    retain 474.7
    keep in memory 989.12
    care for 1008.19
cherry bomb 53.6

cherub child 302.3
    endearment term 562.6
    angel 679.1
chessboard check 47.4
    toy 743.16
chess master 417.7
chest
    n breast 283.6
    storehouse 386.6
    treasury 729.13
    adj pectoral 283.19
chestnut
    n horse 311.11
    old joke 489.9
    platitude 974.3
    adj reddish-brown 40.4
    redheaded 41.10
chesty conceited 140.11
    corpulent 257.18
    pectoral 283.19
chevalier rider 178.8
    gallant 504.9
    knight 608.5
chevron zigzag 204.8
    angle 278.2
    heraldry 647.2
    military insignia 647.5
chew
    n bite 8.2
    chewing tobacco 89.7
    v masticate 8.27
    smoke 89.14
    disapprove 510.18
    pulp 1063.5
chewed-up 393.27
chewing gum
    elastic 1048.3
    gum 1062.6
chew out 510.18
chew the fat 541.8
chewy delightful 97.8
    tough 1049.4
chi 919.5
chiaroscuro
    drawing 712.12
    lighting 1025.19
chic
    n smartness 578.3
    adj dressed up 5.46
    smart 578.13
    knowledgeable 928.17
chicanery
    quackery 354.7
    chicane 356.4
    trick 356.6
    stratagem 415.3
    knavery 645.2
    quibbling 936.5
chichi ornate 498.12
    showy 501.19
    ultrafashionable 578.14
chick woman 77.6
    gal 302.7
    fledgling 302.10
    bird 311.27
    poultry 311.28
    endearment term 562.6
chicken
    n poultry 10.22
    weakling 16.6
    homosexual 75.14

    effeminate male 77.10
    poultry 311.28
    dupe 358.2
    coward 491.5
    military insignia 647.5
    v lose one's nerve 491.8
    adj weak 16.12
    effeminate 77.14
    irresolute 362.12
    cowardly 491.10
chicken feed
    feed 10.4
    petty cash 728.19
    trivia 998.4
chicken out
    hesitate 362.7
    compromise 468.2
    lose one's nerve 491.8
    defect 858.13
chicken-pecked 326.5
chick flick 706.2
chicklet 311.27
chick lit 718.1
chide 510.17
chief
    n superior 249.4
    superintendent 574.2
    master 575.1
    head 575.3
    potentate 575.8
    heraldry 647.2
    principal 997.10
    adj leading 165.3
    top 198.10
    front 216.10
    main 249.14
    directing 573.12
    governing 612.17
    preceding 814.4
    first 818.17
    paramount 997.24
chief cook and bottle washer
    574.2
chiefly
    mainly 249.17
    on the whole 792.14
    first 818.18
    generally 864.17
    normally 869.10
chieftain 575.8
chiffon
    n finery 498.3
    adj bubbly 320.6
chigger 311.36
chignon braid 3.7
    false hair 3.13
chilblain sore 85.37
    cold 1023.2
child one 302.3
    person 312.5
    simple soul 416.3
    descendant 561.3
    innocent 657.4
    product 893.1
child's play 998.5
childbearing 1.1
childhood
    preteens 301.2
    origin 818.4
childishness
    childlikeness 301.4

    senility 922.10
    puerility 922.11
    unwiseness 923.2
childless 891.4
childlike
    childish 301.11
    artless 416.5
    innocent 657.6
    senile 922.23
    puerile 922.24
    trusting 953.22
children
    young people 302.2
    family 559.5
    offspring 561.1
child support 624.8
child within 865.5
chill
    n symptom 85.9
    unfeeling 94.1
    indifference 102.1
    dejection 112.3
    deterrent 379.2
    aloofness 583.2
    enmity 589.1
    cold 1023.1
    frost 1023.2
    v disincline 379.4
    freeze 1023.9
    frost 1023.10
    refrigerate 1024.10
    adj unfeeling 94.9
    unfriendly 589.9
    cool 1023.12
chilling
    n cold 1023.2
    refrigeration 1024.1
    adj frightening 127.28
    refrigerative 1024.12
chill out 1047.7
chilly unfeeling 94.9
    aloof 141.12
    reticent 344.10
    unsociable 583.6
    unfriendly 589.9
    cool 1023.12
    feeling cold 1023.16
chime
    n ringing 54.3
    harmony 708.3
    repetitiousness 849.4
    v ring 54.8
    interrupt 214.6
    say 524.22
    harmonize 708.35
    assonate 784.9
    agree 788.6
chimera
    airy hope 124.4
    illusion 976.1
    figment of the imagination
        986.5
chimerical
    thin 764.6
    illusory 976.9
    imaginary 986.22
chimney valley 237.7
    flue 239.14
    fireplace 1020.11
    deposit 1058.7
chimpanzee 311.22

the believing 692.5
Christian
  n respectable citizen 659.3
  Nazarene 675.17
  adj kind 143.13
  honest 644.13
  orthodox 687.7
Christianity 675.7
Christian name 527.4
Christian Scientist 675.24
Christlike
  humblehearted 137.11
  kind 143.13
  divine 677.16
Christmas
  n Yuletide 313.6
  v vacation 20.9
chromatic
  colorational 35.16
  tonal 709.27
chromatics 35.10
chromatography 35.10
chromosome
  allosome 305.8
  heredity 560.6
chronic
  confirmed 373.18
  durable 827.10
chronicle
  n record 549.1
  history 719.1
  annals 719.3
  story 722.3
  chronology 832.9
  v record 549.15
  write history 719.5
  chronologize 832.14
chronicler annalist 550.2
  historian 719.4
  chronologist 832.10
chronography time 821.1
  chronology 832.1
chronological
  historical 719.7
  temporal 821.7
chronological order 807.1
chronology
  history 719.1
  time 821.1
  timekeeping 832.1
  chronicle 832.9
chronometer
  navigation 182.2
  timepiece 832.6
chrysalis 302.12
chthonian
  n Satanist 680.15
  idolater 697.4
  adj hellish 682.8
  idolatrous 697.7
chubby
  corpulent 257.18
  stubby 268.10
chub out 259.8
chuck
  n food 10.2
  tap 902.7
  throw 904.3
  v bird sound 60.5
  put violently 159.13
  reject 372.2

discard 390.7
  eliminate 773.5
  tap 902.18
  throw 904.10
chuckhole
  pothole 284.3
  mud puddle 1062.9
chuckle
  n ripple 52.5
  laughter 116.4
  v laugh 116.8
chuck up 909.27
chug-a-lug 88.25
Chukwa 901.3
chum
  n friend 588.4
  v associate with 582.18
chummy 587.20
chump dupe 358.2
  fool 924.3
chunder 99.4
chunk
  n amount 244.2
  lump 257.10
  portion 477.5
  bet 759.3
  accumulation 770.9
  piece 793.3
  throw 904.3
  v throw 904.10
chunky
  corpulent 257.18
  stubby 268.10
  sturdy 763.7
church school 617.5
  sect 675.3
  divine service 696.8
  church 703.1
  calendar 832.8
the Church
  the true church
    687.3
  the believing 692.5
  the ministry 698.1
  papacy 698.6
churchgoer
  attender 221.5
  believer 692.4
  worshiper 696.9
  the laity 700.1
churchly
  ecclesiastic 698.13
  churchish 703.15
churchman
  believer 692.4
  clergyman 699.2
  layman 700.2
Church of England 675.11
churchyard 309.15
churlish
  irascible 110.19
  countrified 233.7
  boorish 497.13
  gruff 505.7
churn
  n mixer 797.9
  blend 917.1
  agitator 917.9
  v seethe 671.12
  agitate 917.10
  emulsify 1062.10

churn out write 547.21
  pen 718.6
  produce 892.8
chute parachute 181.13
  outlet 190.9
  incline 204.4
  rapids 238.10
  gutter 239.3
  race 756.3
  deposit 1058.7
chutzpah
  impudence 142.3
  rashness 493.1
  fearlessness 492.3
CIA 576.12
CIA man 576.9
ciao! 188.22
cicatrix mark 517.5
  blemish 1004.1
cicerone
  traveler 178.1
  interpreter 341.7
  guide 574.7
  escort 769.5
cigar 89.4
cigarette 89.5
cilia
  eyelashes 3.12
  organelle 305.5
cinch
  n dupe 358.2
  sure success 409.2
  poker 759.10
  saddle parts 901.18
  certainty 970.2
  easy 1014.4
  v fasten 800.7
  bind 800.9
  prove 957.10
  make sure 970.11
cincture
  n surrounding 209.5
  enclosed place 212.3
  circle 280.3
  v encircle 209.7
cinder dregs 256.2
  coal 1019.16
  combustion product 1020.16
cinder block 1054.2
cinema
  n motion-picture theater
    706.7
  adj motion-picture 706.9
cinematic 706.9
cinematographer
  motion-picture photography
    706.5
  photographer 716.5
Cineplex 706.7
cinerary 309.22
cinereous colorless 36.7
  gray 39.4
cipher
  n discord 61.1
  cryptography 345.6
  symbol 517.2
  Greek 522.7
  signature 527.10
  letter 546.1
  nothing 762.2
  thing of naught 764.2

a nobody 998.7
  number 1017.3
  v code 345.10
  calculate 1017.18
circa
  adv approximately 244.6
  prep about 223.26
circadian
  recurrent 849.13
  momentary 850.8
circle
  n environment 209.1
  region 230.9
  sphere 231.2
  curve 279.2
  circus 280.2
  jewel 498.6
  clique 617.6
  round 850.3
  circuit 914.2
  halo 1025.14
  orbit 1072.16
  v move 172.5
  encircle 209.7
  round 280.10
  recur 850.5
  circuit 914.5
  rotate 915.9
circuit
  n journey 177.5
  environment 209.1
  sphere 231.2
  circle 280.2
  route 383.1
  engagement 704.11
  baseball 745.1
  routine 850.3
  round 914.2
  detour 914.3
  electrical circuit 1032.4
  network 1034.8
  circuitry 1042.3
  v circle 914.5
circuitous
  deviative 164.7
  oblique 204.13
  convolutional 281.6
  circumlocutory 538.14
  roundabout 914.7
circuitry
  electronic circuit 1033.8
  computer parts 1042.3
circular
  n announcement 352.2
  advertising matter 352.8
  booklet 554.11
  adj round 280.11
  circuitous 914.7
circularity
  curvature 279.1
  roundness 280.1
  orbit 280.1
  circuitousness 914.1
  sophistry 936.1
circulate
  distribute 352.10
  be published 352.16
  deliver 478.13
  monetize 728.26
  circle 914.5
  rotate 915.9

circulation
n blood 2.25
publication 352.1
monetization 728.23
circuitousness 914.1
rotation 915.1
liquidity 1061.1
adj fluid 1061.4

circumcise 701.17

circumcision 685.4

circumference
exterior 206.2
bounds 211.1
circle 280.2

circumferential
environing 209.8
outlining 211.14

circumlocution
convolution 281.1
roundaboutness 538.5
circuitousness 914.1

circumnavigate
navigate 182.13
circle 914.5

circumscribe
bound 210.4
limit 211.8
contract 260.7
restrict 428.9
qualify 959.3

circumscription
restriction 210.2
limiting 210.1
confines 211.1
boundary 211.3
enclosure 212.1
contraction 260.1
restraint 428.3
exclusion 773.1
qualification 959.1

circumspect
slow 175.10
careful 339.10
cautious 494.8
judicious 920.19

circumstance
pomp 501.6
fact 761.3
state 765.1
existing conditions 766.2
occurrence 766.1
component 796.2
event 831.2
qualification 959.2

circumstances
environment 209.1
assets 471.7
total situation 766.2
affairs 831.4

circumstantial
conditional 766.7
unessential 768.4
happening 831.9
evidential 957.16
qualifying 959.7

circumstantiate
itemize 766.6
confirm 957.11

circumvent
deceive 356.14
avoid 368.6

evade 368.7
outwit 415.11
thwart 1012.15

circus town 230.9
circle 280.2
arena 463.1
show business 704.1

cirrous
threadlike 271.7
cloudy 319.8

cirrus filament 271.1
coil 281.2

cist 309.16

cistern 241.1

citadel 460.6

citation
incrimination 599.2
eulogy 646.4
acknowledgment 888.2
reference 957.5

Citation 311.15

cite summon 420.11
accuse 599.7
honor 646.8
itemize 766.6
name 957.13
call attention to 983.10

citified 230.11

citizen national 227.4
freeman 430.11
noncombatant 464.5

citizen journalism 547.2

citizenry
population 227.1
the people 606.1

citizens band 1034.13

citizenship
native-born citizenship
226.2
public spirit 591.1

citrus fruit 10.38

city
n metropolis 230
town 230.1
region 231.5
adj urban 230.11

city dweller 227.6

city father
public official 575.17
legislator 610.3

city hall
town hall 230.5
political party 609.24
capitol 613.4

city planner
artist 716.10
architect 717.3

city planning 230.10

city slicker
townsman 227.6
sophisticate 413.17

city-state 232.1

civic urban 230.11
public 312.16
public-spirited 591.4
political 609.43
governmental 612.16

civic duty 641.1

civics 609.2

civil public 312.16
decorous 496.9

courteous 504.14
sociable 582.22
governmental 612.16
lay 700.3

Civil Air Patrol 184.7

civil ceremony 563.3

civil code 673.5

civil death 602.2

civil disobedience 327.1

civil disorder 327.4

civil engineering 1043.1

civilian dress 5.8

civilian life 465.6

clvility
cultivation 392.3
decorousness 496.2
courtesy 504.1
manners 504.6
amenities 504.7
social convention 579.1
etiquette 580.3
sociability 582.1

civilization
culture 373.2
cultivation 392.3
courtesy 504.1

civilize
humanize 312.12
make better 392.9
teach 568.10

civilized
improved 392.13
elegant 496.8
learned 928.21

civil law 673.5

civil liberties
freedom 430.2
human rights 642.3

civil rights
freedom 430.2
human rights 642.3

civil servant 575.16

civil union 563.1

civil war 458.1

civvies 5.8

clabber
n clot 1045.7
semiliquid 1062.5
v cohere 803.6
thicken 1045.10
emulsify 1062.10

clack
n noisemaker 53.6
rattle 55.3
snap 56.2
chatter 540.3
v rattle 55.6
snap 56.7
bird sound 60.5
chatter 540.5

clad 5.45

cladding exterior 206.2
plating 295.13
lamina 296.2

claim
n extortion 192.6
profession 376.2
demand 421.1
possession 469.1
estate 471.4
declaration 598.7

prerogative 642.1
v extort 192.15
pretext 376.3
demand 421.5
pretend to 421.6
possess 469.4
take 480.13
require 963.9

claimant
petitioner 440.7
accuser 599.5

clairvoyance ESP 689.8
the future 839.1
understanding 928.3
intuition 934.1
foreknowledge 961.3
divination 962.2

clairvoyant 962.4

clam
n discord 61.1
marine animal 311.29
man of few words
344.5
v fish 382.10

clambake meal 8.6
party 582.12
electioneering 609.12

clamber
n ascent 193.1
v climb 193.11

clammy sweaty 12.22
viscous 1062.12

clamor
n noise 53.3
outcry 59.4
clash 61.2
entreaty 440.2
v be noisy 53.9
vociferate 59.8
complain 115.15

clamor for
wish for 100.16
demand 421.5
entreat 440.11
require 963.9

clamorous noisy 53.13
vociferous 59.10
turbulent 105.24
demanding 421.9
urgent 997.22

clamp
n contractor 260.6
hold 474.2
v squeeze 260.8
fasten 800.7

clampdown 428.1

clamp down on
restrain 428.7
suppress 428.8
domineer 612.15

clam up
v be silent 51.6
keep to oneself 344.6
keep secret 345.7
interj silence! 51.14

clan race 559.4
community 617.2
clique 617.6
class 809.2
kind 809.3

clandestine 345.12

clangor
n noise 53.3
ringing 54.3
rasp 58.3
v be noisy 53.9
ring 54.8
sound harshly 58.9

clank
n ringing 54.3
rasp 58.3
v ring 54.8
sound harshly 58.9
speak poorly 525.7

clannish
contemptuous 157.8
exclusive 495.13
racial 559.7
cliquish 617.18

clansman 559.2

clap
n noise 53.3
report 56.1
applause 509.2
v crack 56.6
put violently 159.13
close 293.6
applaud 509.10
hit 902.14

clapboard
n wood 1054.3
v face 295.23

clapper
noisemaker 53.6
bell 54.4

claptrap
humbug 354.14
nonsense 520.2
bull 520.3
specious argument 936.3

claque 509.8

clarification
refinement 79.4
explanation 341.4

clarify refine 79.22
explain 341.10
make clear 521.6
disinvolve 798.5

clarinetist 710.4

clarion call 458.7

clarity
distinctness 31.2
clearness 521.2
elegance 533.1
facility 1014.1
transparency 1029.1

clash
n report 56.1
rasp 58.3
jangle 61.2
disaccord 456.1
fight 457.4
hostility 589.3
impact 902.3
v conflict 35.15
crack 56.6
sound harshly 58.9
strike a sour note 61.3
disagree 456.8
contend 457.13
go contrary to 779.4
fight 789.5

counteract 900.6
collide 902.13

clasp
n hold 474.2
embrace 562.3
v stay near 223.12
hold 474.6
seize 480.14
embrace 562.18
hook 800.8
cohere 803.6

class
n rank 245.2
nomenclature 527.1
race 559.4
form 572.11
social class 607.1
community 617.2
school 617.5
the laity 700.1
category 809.2
classifications 809.5
goodness 999.1
biology 1068.1
v analyze 801.8
classify 809.6
estimate 946.9

class envy 154.1

classic
n book 554.1
classical music 708.6
work of art 712.9
standard of perfection 1002.4
adj simple 499.6
elegant 533.6
model 786.8
perfected 1002.9

classical
downright 247.12
tasteful 496.7
simple 499.6
elegant 533.6
literary 547.24
artistic 718.7
antiquated 842.13
perfected 1002.9

classicist purist 533.4
antiquarian 842.5
scholar 929.3

classification
veil of secrecy 345.3
nomenclature 527.1
analysis 801.3
grouping 808.3
categorization 809.1
listing 809.1

classify
keep secret 345.7
analyze 801.8
group 808.11
class 809.6
discriminate 944.4

classmate
schoolchild 572.3
companion 588.3

classroom
n schoolroom 567.11
adj scholastic 567.13

classy
ostentatious 501.18

chic 578.13

clatter
n noise 53.3
rattle 55.3
chatter 540.3
v rattle 55.6
chatter 540.5
gossip 552.12

clause phrase 529.1
part 554.13
bill 613.9
part of writing 793.2
condition 959.2

clavichord 711.12

claw torture 96.18
injure 393.13
seize 480.14

clawed tortured 96.25
pedal 199.9
prehensile 474.9

claws governance 417.5
clutches 474.4
control 612.2

clay
n pipe 89.6
land 234.1
corpse 307.15
humankind 312.1
person 312.5
ceramics 742.3
softness 1047.4
body 1052.3
mud 1062.8
adj ceramic 742.7

clayey earthy 234.5
pasty 1047.12

clean
v cleanse 79.18
adj pure 79.25
shapely 264.5
skillful 413.22
honest 644.13
virtuous 653.6
spotless 657.7
chaste 664.4
thorough 794.10
adv cleanly 79.29
absolutely 794.15

clean bill of health
healthiness 83.2
pass 443.7
certificate 549.6

clean-cut distinct 31.7
shapely 264.5
clear 521.11

clean-limbed 264.5

cleanliness
purity 79.1
innocence 657.1
chastity 664.1

clean out clean 79.18
strip 480.24
evacuate 909.22

cleanse clean 79.18
release 120.6
sanctify 685.5

cleanser
sweeper 79.16
cleaner 79.17

clean-shaven 6.17

cleansing
n cleaning 79.2
release 120.2
adj cleaning 79.28
relieving 120.9
atoning 658.7

clean slate void 222.3
innocence 657.1
new start 858.2
revolution 860.1

cleanup gain 472.3
red-up 808.6

clean up clean 79.18
complete 407.6
triumph 411.3
profit 472.12
tidy 808.12

clear
n clarity 521.2
v refine 79.22
take off 184.38
rise above 272.11
unclose 292.12
leap 366.5
manage 409.12
extricate 431.7
profit 472.12
justify 600.9
acquit 601.4
pay in full 624.13
pass 749.7
play 752.4
eliminate 773.5
evacuate 909.22
disembarrass 1014.9
adj distinct 31.7
audible 50.16
vacant 222.14
open 292.17
manifest 348.8
free 430.21
unhampered 430.26
quit 430.31
crystal-clear 521.11
legible 521.12
elegant 533.6
unindebted 624.23
innocent 657.6
thorough 794.10
unmixed 798.7
unfastened 802.22
unqualified 960.2
certain 970.13
thriving 1010.13
easy 1014.13
light 1025.32
transparent 1029.4
adv wide 261.19

clearance room 158.3
open space 158.4
altitude 184.35
interval 224.1
distance 261.1
latitude 430.4
authorization 443.3
pass 443.7
justification 600.1
acquittal 601.1
payment 624.1
elimination 773.2
evacuation 909.6

clear-cut
distinct 31.7
lost 473.7
clear 521.11
clearheaded
sober 516.3
clear-witted 920.13
sane 925.4
clearing opening 292.1
extrication 431.3
justification 600.1
acquittal 601.1
evacuation 909.6
disembarrassment 1014.6
field 1069.9
clearing house 729.14
clearly visibly 31.8
audibly 50.18
positively 247.19
manifestly 348.14
intelligibly 521.13
certainly 970.23
clear out
v disappear 34.2
clean 79.18
depart 188.7
flee 368.11
eliminate 773.5
evacuate 909.22
interj go away! 909.31
clear sailing 1007.1
clear-sighted
clear-eyed 27.21
clear-witted 920.13
clear the air
explain 341.10
pacify 465.7
moderate 670.6
clear the decks
trim ship 182.49
prepare 405.6
take precautions 494.6
eliminate 773.5
tidy 808.12
evacuate 909.22
clear the way
prepare the way 405.12
facilitate 1014.7
clear up explain 341.10
disinvolve 798.5
tidy 808.12
solve 940.2
make sure 970.11
cleavage
falling-out 456.4
severance 802.2
fission 1038.8
cleave crack 224.4
open 292.11
demolish 395.17
sever 802.11
cohere 803.6
bisect 875.4
atomize 1038.17
cleft
n crack 224.2
notch 289.1
opening 292.1
falling-out 456.4
break 802.4
adj cut 224.7

severed 802.23
halved 875.6
cleft palate 265.3
clemency pity 145.1
leniency 427.1
clench
n hold 474.2
v hold 474.6
seize 480.14
clerestory floor 197.23
top 198.1
clergy priesthood 699.1
ministry 699.1
clergyperson 699.2
clerical
n clergyman 699.2
adj secretarial 547.28
ecclesiastic 698.13
clerical worker 726.2
clerk writer 547.13
recorder 550.1
agent 576.3
accountant 628.7
clergyman 699.2
salesman 730.3
scholar 929.3
clever skillful 413.22
well-laid 413.30
cunning 415.12
witty 489.15
teachable 570.18
smart 920.14
cliché
n triteness 117.3
catchword 526.9
generalization 864.8
platitude 974.3
adj aphoristic 974.6
click
n thud 52.3
snap 56.2
v thud 52.15
snap 56.7
succeed 409.7
befriend 587.11
clicking
n ticking 55.2
adj staccato 55.7
click language 523.7
clickthrough 1042.18
client
n advisee 422.4
dependent 432.6
customer 733.4
adj subject 432.13
clientele 733.3
cliff precipice 200.3
slope 237.2
climacteric
n change of life 303.7
crisis 843.4
adj critical 843.10
climactic top 198.10
critical 843.10
climate
milieu 209.3
zone 231.3
weather 317.3
mental climate 978.5
climate change 317.4
climatic 317.13

climatology 317.5
climax
n copulation 75.7
summit 198.2
finishing touch 407.3
upheaval 671.5
plot 722.4
limit 794.5
crisis 843.4
crucial moment 843.5
urgency 997.4
salient point 997.6
acme of perfection 1002.3
v come 75.24
top 198.9
complete 407.6
climb
n ascent 193.1
acclivity 204.6
v move 172.5
ascend 184.39
clamber 193.11
incline 204.10
climb down
n recant 363.8
v humble oneself 137.7
get down 194.7
climber
traveler 178.1
ascender 193.6
plant 310.4
upstart 606.7
clime zone 231.3
weather 317.3
clinch
n hold 474.2
joint 800.4
v hold 474.6
seize 480.14
fight 754.4
fasten 800.7
join 800.11
cohere 803.6
prove 957.10
make sure 970.11
clincher
finishing stroke 820.4
conclusive argument 958.3
cling
n hold 474.2
cohesion 803.1
v stay near 223.12
hold 474.6
retain 474.7
cohere 803.6
clinic facility 91.21
hospital room 197.25
clinical 90.15
clink
n thud 52.3
ringing 54.3
jail 429.9
rhyme 720.8
assonance 784.6
v thud 52.15
ring 54.8
clinker
discord 61.1
dregs 256.2
combustion product 1020.16
building material 1054.2

clip
n velocity 172.4
excerpt 557.3
piece 793.3
blow 902.5
v speed 174.9
excise 255.10
shorten 268.6
deceive 356.19
hold 474.6
retain 474.7
rob 482.16
abridge 557.5
overprice 632.7
hook 800.8
strike 902.15
clipper 181.8
clippings 557.4
clique
n social set 582.5
coterie 617.6
company 770.3
v associate with 582.18
cliquish
contemptuous 157.8
exclusive 495.13
clannish 617.18
C-list
n inferior 250.2
adj inferior 250.6
clitoris 2.13
cloak
n overgarment 5.12
cover 295.2
pretext 376.1
robe 702.2
v mantle 5.40
cover 295.19
conceal 346.6
protect 1008.18
cloak-and-dagger
sensational 105.32
covert 345.12
cloakroom 197.15
clobber
best 249.7
defeat 412.9
punish 604.15
beat 902.17
clock
n furniture 229.1
timepiece 832.6
v check out 188.13
time 832.11
clock in
arrive 186.6
punch the clock 832.12
clock off 188.7
clock watcher
idler 331.8
shirker 368.3
clockwise
adj right 219.4
adv rightward 161.24
round 915.16
clod land 234.1
lump 257.10
bungler 414.8
peasant 606.6
stupid person 924.2
oaf 924.5

body 1052.3
cloddish
  countrified 233.7
  boorish 497.13
  stupid 922.15
clog
  n obstruction 293.3
  curb 1012.7
  v stop 293.7
  dance 705.5
clogs 5.27
cloister
  n corridor 197.18
  enclosed place 212.3
  passageway 383.3
  monastery 703.6
  retreat 1009.5
  v enclose 212.6
  confine 429.12
cloistered
  quiescent 173.12
  walled off 212.10
  enclosing 212.11
  confined 429.19
  recluse 584.10
  claustral 703.16
  separated 802.21
clone
  n the same 778.3
  duplicate 785.3
  conformist 867.2
  v reproduce 778.6
  make uniform 781.4
  copy 785.8
clop-clop 55.1
close
  n completion 407.2
  closing 820.3
  cessation 857.1
  v approach 167.3
  converge 169.2
  surround 209.6
  shut 293.6
  arrange 437.8
  contend 457.13
  end 820.5
  turn off 857.12
  obstruct 1012.12
close
  n enclosed place 212.3
  plot 231.4
  adj stuffy 173.16
  near 223.14
  narrow 270.14
  tight 293.12
  meticulous 339.12
  taciturn 344.9
  secret 345.11
  secretive 345.15
  concealed 346.11
  stingy 484.9
  phonetic 524.30
  concise 537.6
  unsociable 583.5
  familiar 587.19
  crowded 770.22
  approximate 775.8
  approximating 784.14
  fast 800.14
  imminent 840.3
  exact 928.17

sultry 1019.28
  dense 1045.12
  adv around 209.12
  nigh 223.20
  nearly 223.22
  densely 1045.15
close call 369.2
closed shut 293.9
  secret 345.11
  inhospitable 586.7
  narrow-minded 980.10
closed-minded
  unpersuadable 361.13
  narrow-minded 980.10
close down
  close shop 293.8
  suppress 428.8
  stop work 857.8
close encounter
  space 1072.3
  astronaut 1075.8
closefisted 484.9
close in approach 167.3
  converge 169.2
  enclose 212.5
close-mindedness 980.1
closemouthed
  taciturn 344.9
  secretive 345.15
close one's eyes to
  be blind 30.8
  condone 148.4
  be inattentive 984.2
close out
  n end 820.1
  v reject 372.2
  complete 407.6
  keep accounts 628.8
  deal 734.8
  sell 737.24
  exclude 773.4
  end 820.5
  make impossible 967.6
close shave 369.2
closet
  n latrine 12.10
  sanctum 197.8
  clothes room 197.15
  bathroom 197.26
  storehouse 386.6
  office 739.7
  v confine 212.6
  adj secret 345.11
close up
  n motion picture 714.8
  v converge 169.2
  shut 293.6
  close shop 293.8
  heal 396.21
  complete 407.6
  obstruct 1012.12
closing arguments 598.8
closure shutting 293.1
  closing 293.1
  completion 794.4
  joint 800.4
  hindrance 1012.1
clot
  n bungler 414.8
  conglomeration 803.5
  idiot 924.8

coagulum 1045.7
  v come together 770.16
  cohere 803.6
  thicken 1045.10
  emulsify 1062.10
cloth material 4.1
  sail 180.14
  canonicals 702.1
  scenery 704.20
clothe enclothe 5.39
  empower 18.10
  cover 295.19
  equip 385.8
clothes apparel 5.1
  blanket 295.10
clothes-conscious 578.13
clotheshorse
  dandy 500.9
  person of fashion 578.7
  trestle 901.16
clothier 5.33
clothing
  n apparel 5.1
  wear 5.1
  adj dress 5.45
clothing design 717.5
cloture
  legislative procedure 613.6
  cessation 857.5
cloud
  high fog 319.1
  assemblage 770.6
  multitude 884.3
  confusion 985.3
  vapor 1067.1
  v cover 295.19
  becloud 319.7
  conceal 346.6
  confuse 985.7
  darken 1027.9
  opaque 1031.2
cloud base 319.1
cloudburst 316.2
cloudless 1025.32
cloud nine
  happiness 95.2
  summit 198.2
cloudy stormy 318.22
  nebulous 319.8
  obscure 522.15
  muddled 985.13
  gloomy 1027.14
  opaque 1031.3
clout
  n power 18.1
  authoritativeness 417.2
  vigor 544.3
  influence 894.1
  impulse 902.1
  blow 902.5
  v play 745.5
  strike 902.15
cloven cleft 224.7
  severed 802.23
  halved 875.6
clover feed 10.4
  comfort 121.1
  three 876.1
  prosperity 1010.1
cloverleaf 170.2

clown
  n bungler 414.8
  humorist 489.12
  vulgarian 497.6
  peasant 606.6
  circus performer 707.3
  buffoon 707.10
  fool 924.1
  v be foolish 923.6
cloying nasty 64.7
  oversweet 66.5
  sentimental 93.21
  satiating 994.7
club
  n haunt 228.27
  fist 462.4
  rod 605.2
  fellowship 617.3
  theater 704.14
  baseball team 745.2
  golf 751.1
  v whip 604.13
  league 805.4
  cudgel 902.20
clubby 582.22
clubfoot
  foot 199.5
  deformity 265.3
club-hop
  go on a spree 88.28
  make merry 743.24
clubhouse 228.27
clubwoman
  person of fashion 578.7
  sociable person 582.16
  member 617.11
cluck 60.5
clue cue 517.9
  tip-off 551.3
  hint 551.4
  evidence 957.1
clueful 351.10
clue one in 351.4
clump
  n thud 52.3
  lump 257.10
  bulge 283.3
  growth 310.2
  bunch 770.7
  blow 902.5
  stamp 902.10
  solid 1045.6
  v thud 52.15
  way of walking 177.28
  assemble 770.18
  strike 902.15
  stamp 902.22
  thicken 1045.10
clumsy
  n bungler 414.9
  adj bulky 257.19
  slipshod 340.12
  bungling 414.20
  inelegant 534.2
  inconvenient 996.7
  unwieldy 1013.19
  ungraceful 1015.9
clunk
  n thud 52.3
  blow 902.5
  v thud 52.15

strike 902.15
cluster
  n throng 770.4
  bunch 770.7
  conglomeration 803.5
  solid 1045.6
  v come together 770.16
  assemble 770.18
  cohere 803.6
  thicken 1045.10
clutch
  n amount 244.2
  hold 474.2
  offspring 561.2
  crisis 843.4
  urgency 997.4
  predicament 1013.4
  cone clutch 1040.10
  v hold 474.6
  seize 480.14
clutch at straws 124.7
clutches
  governance 417.5
  claws 474.4
  control 612.2
clutter
  n jumble 810.3
  multitude 884.3
  radar interference 1036.12
  v disarrange 811.2
  teem with 884.5
coach
  n preparer 405.5
  tutor 571.5
  trainer 571.6
  baseball team 745.2
  v advise 422.5
  tutor 568.11
coach-and-four 179.5
coachman driver 178.9
  man 577.4
coact cooperate 450.3
  interact 777.6
  concur 899.2
coactive
  compulsory 424.10
  cooperative 450.5
  concurrent 899.4
coadjutant
  n assistant 616.6
  adj cooperative 450.5
coagulate
  n clot 1045.7
  v cohere 803.6
  thicken 1045.10
  emulsify 1062.10
coagulation
  thickening 1045.4
  viscosity 1062.2
coal
  n blackness 38.4
  live coal 1019.16
  combustion product 1020.16
  v provision 385.9
  burn 1020.24
  fuel 1021.8
coal black 38.8
coalesce
  cooperate 450.3
  identify 778.5
  mix 797.10

combine 805.3
coalescent 872.12
coalition
  affiliation 450.2
  front 609.33
  association 617.1
  combination 805.1
coarse raucous 58.15
  bitter 64.6
  offensive 98.18
  thick 269.8
  rough 288.6
  textured 294.6
  undeveloped 406.12
  gross 497.11
  ill-bred 505.6
  inelegant 534.2
  populational 606.8
  carnal 663.6
  vulgar 666.8
  inferior 1005.9
coarsened 94.12
coast
  n slide 194.4
  border 211.4
  side 218.1
  shore 234.2
  v be still 173.7
  glide 177.35
  navigate 182.13
  sail coast-wise
    182.39
  slide 194.9
  do nothing 329.2
  take it easy 331.15
  go easily 1014.10
coastal
  bordering 211.11
  littoral 234.7
coast guard
  rescuer 398.2
  branch 461.21
  navy 461.27
  guard 1008.9
coastguardsman 183.4
coat
  n hair 3.2
  outerwear 5.13
  color 35.8
  cover 295.2
  blanket 295.12
  lamina 296.2
  card 758.2
  v cloak 5.40
  color 35.14
  spread on 295.24
coating
  n color 35.8
  painting 35.12
  covering 295.1
  blanket 295.12
  lamina 296.2
  adj covering 295.35
coat of arms 647.2
coattails 449.4
coauthor
  n writer 547.15
  collaborator 616.4
  author 718.4
  v write 547.21
  publish 718.6

coax
  n prompter 375.10
  v urge 375.14
  lure 377.5
  importune 440.12
coaxial 208.14
coaxial cable 347.17
cob ear 310.29
  race horse 311.14
cobalt 91.8
cobbler
  shoemaker 5.38
  mender 396.10
cobblestone
  n pavement 383.6
  v floor 295.22
Cobb salad 10.37
cobelligerent 232.1
cobweb filament 271.1
  lightness 298.2
  snare 356.13
coccus 85.42
co-chairman 574.5
cochlear 281.8
cochleated 279.18
cock
  n male animal 76.8
  valve 239.10
  stopper 293.4
  poultry 311.28
  weather vane 318.16
  pile 770.10
  v regress 163.5
  prime 405.9
  shoot 904.12
cock-a-doodle-doo 60.5
cockamamie 923.11
cock-and-bull story 354.11
cockatrice
  traitor 357.10
  heraldry 647.2
cockeyed
  cross-eyed 28.12
  drunk 88.33
  askew 204.14
  distorted 265.10
  unbalanced 791.5
  disorderly 810.13
  foolish 923.9
  dazed 985.14
cockle
  n wrinkle 291.3
  marine animal 311.29
  v wrinkle 291.6
cockles of the heart
  heart 93.3
  inner nature 767.5
Cockney 523.7
cockpit 463.1
cockroach 311.36
cocksure 970.21
cocktail 88.9
cocktail hour 315.2
cocktail lounge 88.20
cocky conceited 140.11
  impudent 142.10
  defiant 454.7
cocoa 40.3
coconspirator
  schemer 381.7
  accomplice 616.3

cocoon 302.12
coction 1020.2
coda adjunct 254.1
  added to writing 254.2
  passage 708.24
  sequel 817.1
  end 820.1
coddle cook 11.5
  indulge 427.6
  foster 449.16
  caress 562.16
code
  n cryptography 345.6
  telegraph 347.2
  precept 419.2
  Greek 522.7
  ethics 636.1
  digest 673.5
  table 808.4
  rule 869.4
  v encode 345.10
code of honor 641.2
codependency 777.3
code red 399.1
codetalker 576.9
code word
  cryptography 345.6
  implication 519.2
  catchword 526.9
codex
  manuscript 547.11
  rare book 554.6
codger 304.2
codicil
  added to writing 254.2
  bequest 478.10
  sequel 817.1
codification 673.6
codify digest 673.10
  organize 808.10
  classify 809.6
  normalize 869.6
co-ed 572.5
coeducational 568.18
coequal
  n equal 790.4
  v reciprocate 777.7
  adj symmetric 264.4
  reciprocal 777.10
  coinciding 778.8
  equivalent 790.8
coerce
  use violence 424.7
  domineer 612.15
coercion 424.3
coercive 424.12
coeternal
  perpetual 829.7
  simultaneous 836.5
coeval
  n contemporary 836.2
  adj innate 767.8
  simultaneous 836.5
coexistence
  foreign policy 609.5
  simultaneity 836.1
coexisting
  agreeing 788.9
  simultaneous 836.5
coextend parallel 203.4
  coincide 836.4

coextensive
parallel 203.6
coinciding 778.8
coffee 40.3
coffee break meal 8.7
respite 20.2
interim 826.1
coffee shop 8.17
coffer
n treasury 729.13
v store 386.10
coffin
n casket 309.11
v confine 212.6
inter 309.19
cofounder 892.7
cog
n inferior 250.2
projection 285.4
v cheat 356.18
cogent powerful 18.12
relevant 775.11
sagacious 920.16
logical 935.20
valid 973.14
good 999.12
cogitate
ruminate 931.8
think about 931.11
cognate
n root 526.2
kinfolk 559.2
lineage 560.4
likeness 784.3
adj related 559.6
lineal 560.18
kindred 775.10
akin 784.13
cognition 928.2
cognitive 931.21
cognitive therapy 92.5
cognizance
thanks 150.2
due 639.2
cognition 928.2
cognizant
sensible 24.11
knowing 928.15
cognomen name 527.3
surname 527.5
nomenclature 527.6
nickname 527.7
cognoscente
connoisseur 496.6
critic 946.7
cogwheel 1040.9
cohabit copulate 75.21
inhabit 225.7
live together 563.17
cohabitation 769.2
cohere agree 788.6
join 800.11
adhere 803.6
coherent clear 521.11
agreeing 788.9
clinging 803.10
indivisible 1045.13
cohesion adhesion
803.1
sticking 803.1
indivisibility 1045.2

cohesive
cohering 803.10
indivisible 1045.13
tough 1049.4
cohort hanger-on 138.6
military unit 461.22
henchman 610.8
associate 616.1
accomplice 616.3
attendance 769.6
company 770.3
coif
n hairdo 3.15
v cut the hair 3.22
cloak 5.40
top 295.21
coiffure
n hairdo 3.15
v cut the hair 3.22
coil
n braid 3.7
a length 267.2
whorl 281.2
v curl 281.5
coin
n angle 278.2
money 728.2
specie 728.4
v mint 728.28
innovate 841.5
change 852.9
originate 892.12
imagine 986.14
coinage
neologism 526.8
money 728.1
coining 728.24
innovation 852.4
production 892.1
result 893.1
coin a phrase 974.5
coincide assent 332.9
correspond 778.4
agree 788.6
co-occur 836.4
concur 899.2
coincidence
accompaniment 769.1
sameness 778.1
agreement 788.1
simultaneity 836.1
concurrence 899.1
coincidental 778.8
coital 75.25
coitus 75.7
coke cocaine 87.7
combustion product 1020.16
col ridge 237.5
valley 237.7
colander refinery 79.13
porousness 292.8
arranger 808.5
cold
n low temperature 1023.1
chilliness 1023.1
adj unconscious 25.8
chromatic 35.16
unsexual 75.29
unfeeling 94.9
indifferent 102.6
dull 117.6

insolent 142.9
heartless 144.25
stone-dead 307.30
reticent 344.10
aloof 583.6
unfriendly 589.9
speculative 759.27
freezing 1023.14
chilly 1023.16
cold blood 94.1
cold-blooded
unfeeling 94.9
heartless 144.25
hypothermic 1023.20
cold comfort 108.1
cold cream
cleanser 79.17
makeup 1016.11
ointment 1056.3
cold feet 491.4
coldhearted
unfeeling 94.9
heartless 144.25
cold shoulder
n aloofness 583.2
repulse 908.2
banishment 909.4
v snub 157.5
slight 340.8
cold sore allergy 85.34
sore 85.37
cold spell 1023.3
cold storage
storage 386.5
discontinuance 390.2
frozen-food locker 1024.6
cold sweat sweat 12.7
hostility 99.2
trepidation 127.5
nervousness 128.2
cold turkey 87.1
cold water 379.2
coleslaw 10.37
colic ache 26.5
symptom 85.9
colicky aching 26.12
anemic 85.61
coliseum 463.1
collaborate
be willing 324.3
cooperate 450.3
write 547.21
act the traitor 645.15
co-author 718.6
concur 899.2
collaboration 805.1
collaborator
subversive 357.11
apostate 363.5
author 547.15
cooperator 616.4
author 718.4
collage 712.10
collapse
n weakness 16.1
exhaustion 21.2
breakdown 85.8
descent 194.1
decline 252.2
prostration 260.4
impairment 393.1

debacle 395.4
crash 410.3
defeat 412.1
insolvency 625.3
v weaken 16.9
burn out 21.5
take sick 85.47
descend 194.5
cave 260.10
break down 393.24
fail 410.12
go bankrupt 625.7
fall short 911.2
fall through 911.3
collapsed 194.12
collapsible 260.11
collar
n circle 280.3
foam 320.2
shackle 428.4
arrest 429.6
insignia 647.1
golf 751.1
v arrest 429.16
acquire 472.9
capture 480.18
collate classify 808.11
scrutinize comparatively 943.5
verify 970.12
collateral
n security 438.3
kinfolk 559.2
nonessential 768.2
adj parallel 203.6
additional 253.10
related 559.6
unessential 768.4
accompanying 769.9
related 775.9
eventual 831.11
simultaneous 836.5
collateral damage
impairment 393.1
loss 473.1
bad influence 1000.4
collation
light meal 8.7
arrangement 808.1
comparative scrutiny 943.2
ensuring 970.8
colleague
companion 588.3
associate 616.1
equal 790.4
collect
n prayer 696.4
v store up 386.11
gather 472.11
come together 770.16
assemble 770.18
put together 800.5
conclude 946.10
collected
composed 106.13
stored 386.14
assembled 770.21
joined 800.13
collection
store 386.1
gathering 472.2

condolence 147.1
blanket 295.10
aid 449.1
function of Holy Ghost
677.15
prosperity 1010.1
v console 121.6
condole with 147.2
aid 449.11
abet 449.14
comfortable
vacational 20.10
pleased 95.15
content 107.7
comfy 121.11
homelike 228.33
wealthy 618.14
prosperous 1010.12
comforter
consoler 121.5
blanket 295.10
moderator 670.3
comfort station
latrine 12.10
bathroom 197.26
comfort zone
rest 20.1
pleasure 95.1
comic
n humorist 489.12
comedian 707.9
adj farcical 488.6
witty 489.15
light 704.35
comics 712.15
comic strip 489.1
coming
n appearance 33.1
approach 167.1
arrival 186.1
advent 839.5
imminence 840.1
adj approaching 167.4
arriving 186.9
emerging 190.18
superior 249.12
successful 409.14
due 639.7
eventual 831.11
future 839.8
imminent 840.3
coming out
emergence 190.1
debut 582.15
inauguration 818.5
comity courtesy 504.1
etiquette 580.3
comma 857.4
command
n field of view 31.3
supremacy 249.3
will 323.1
skill 413.1
governance 417.5
precept 419.1
order 420.1
commandment 420.1
compulsion 424.1
direction 573.1
control 612.2
knowledge 928.1

understanding 928.3
v rule 249.11
rise above 272.11
will 323.2
order 420.8
possess 469.4
direct 573.8
govern 612.11
know well 928.13
command performance 704.12
commandant
jailer 429.10
governor 575.6
commissioned officer 575.18
commandeer
attach 480.20
enlist 615.17
commander ship's officer 183.7
superior 249.4
governor 575.6
commissioned officer 575.18
naval officer 575.20
commanding
authoritative 417.15
imperious 420.13
directing 573.12
governing 612.17
commandment
rule 419.2
command 420.1
commandos 461.15
command post 208.6
commatism 537.2
commemoration
celebration 487.1
anniversary 850.4
memento 989.6
commemorative
celebrative 487.3
memorial 989.26
commence 818.7
commencement
ceremony 580.4
beginning 818.1
source 886.5
commend
commit 478.16
speak highly of 509.11
commendable
praiseworthy 509.20
good 999.12
commensal eating 8.31
cooperative 450.5
commensurable
approximate 775.8
comparative 943.8
commensurate
satisfactory 107.11
agreeing 788.9
equal 790.7
comparative 943.8
sufficient 991.6
comment
n word of explanation 341.5
commentary 556.2
criticism 946.2
v remark 524.24
commentary
added to writing 254.2
comment 341.5
treatise 556.2

review 723.2
commentator
interpreter 341.7
reviewer 556.4
critic 946.7
broadcaster 1034.23
commerce
copulation 75.7
communication 343.1
social life 582.4
occupation 724.1
trade 731.1
business 731.1
commercial
n advertisement 352.6
radiobroadcast 1034.18
announcement 1034.20
adj occupied 724.15
business 730.12
trade 731.22
salable 734.14
commercialism 731.13
commercialize
profit 472.12
put on a business footing
731.20
commingle 797.10
comminute
v pulverize 1051.9
adj powdery 1051.11
commiserate pity 145.3
condole with 147.2
commissar
tyrant 575.14
public official 575.17
delegate 576.2
commissary
provisions 10.5
provider 385.6
store 386.1
delegate 576.2
commission
n performance 328.2
precept 419.1
injunction 420.2
portion 477.5
deputy 576.13
legislature 613.1
delegation 615.1
assignment 615.1
dividend 624.7
task 724.2
assembly 770.2
v repair 396.14
command 420.8
represent 576.14
authorize 615.10
delegate 862.7
commissioner
public official 575.17
delegate 576.2
policeman 1008.15
commit do 328.6
confine 429.17
engage 436.5
agree 436.5
contract 437.5
dedicate 477.11
consign 478.16
commission 615.10
obligate 641.12

commitment
zeal 101.2
resolution 359.1
undertaking 404.1
committal 404.2
obligation 436.2
dedication 477.4
consignment 478.2
devotion 587.7
commission 615.1
duty 641.1
unselfishness 652.1
cause 886.9
commitment ceremony 563.3
commit oneself
be determined 359.8
undertake 404.3
take the responsibility 641.9
seize the opportunity 843.7
commit suicide 308.22
committed
zealous 101.9
resolute 359.11
promised 436.8
devoted 587.21
obliged 641.16
unselfish 652.5
committee
subcommittee 423.2
delegation 576.13
assembly 770.2
commixture
mixture 797.1
compound 797.5
commodious
comfortable 121.11
spacious 158.11
useful 387.18
commodity 735.2
commodity market 737.1
commodore 575.20
common
n green 310.7
estate 471.4
park 743.14
the normal 869.3
adj trite 117.9
medium 246.3
inferior 250.6
public 312.16
cooperative 450.5
communal 476.9
commonplace 497.14
simple 499.6
vernacular 523.20
plain-speaking 535.3
populational 606.8
prosaic 721.5
mutual 777.11
frequent 847.4
prevalent 864.12
usual 869.9
well-known 928.27
paltry 998.21
ordinary 1005.8
inferior 1005.9
common denominator 777.1
commoner
student 572.7
common man 606.5
common good 999.4

obsessive 926.34
urgent 997.22
compendious
short 268.8
concise 537.6
abridged 557.6
comprehensive 772.7
compendium 557.1
compensate
symmetrize 264.3
make compensation
338.4
remedy 396.13
make restitution 481.5
requite 506.5
pay 624.10
atone 658.4
equalize 790.6
interchange 863.4
compensated 624.22
compensation
defense mechanism 92.23
symmetrization 264.2
repayment 338.1
recompense 338.1
reparation 396.6
reimbursement 481.2
reprisal 506.2
penalty 603.1
damages 624.3
pay 624.4
atonement 658.1
compete
contend 457.18
play 744.2
competence
power 18.1
ability 18.2
preparedness 405.4
skill 413.1
authority 417.1
competent able 18.14
fitted 405.17
capable 413.24
authoritative 417.15
legal 673.11
sufficient 991.6
competitive
oppositional 451.8
competitory 457.23
competitor
contestant 452.2
combatant 461.1
athlete 743.19
compilation
omnibus 554.7
code 673.5
collection 770.11
compile codify 673.10
assemble 770.18
compiler 1042.13
compiling 796.1
complacent
bovine 107.10
vain 140.8
complain
dissatisfy 108.5
groan 115.15
object 333.5
offer resistance 453.3
accuse 599.7

complainer
malcontent 108.3
lamenter 115.8
faultfinder 510.9
complaint disease 85.1
grievance 115.4
objection 333.2
resistance 453.1
disapproval 510.1
arraignment 598.3
declaration 598.7
accusation 599.1
complaisant
pleasant 97.6
considerate 143.16
indulgent 427.8
submissive 433.12
courteous 504.14
conformable 867.5
soft 1047.8
complement
n hand 183.6
adjunct 254.1
syntax 530.2
team 617.7
company 770.3
likeness 784.3
all 792.3
full measure 794.3
v reciprocate 777.7
complementary
reciprocal 777.10
completing 794.13
complete
v perform 328.9
perfect 407.6
execute 437.9
include 772.3
bring to fruition 794.6
end 820.7
elaborate 861.6
develop 1002.5
adj downright 247.12
perfect 407.12
comprehensive 772.7
undivided 792.11
whole 794.9
ended 820.8
unqualified 960.2
sound 1002.7
complete change 858.1
complete game 745.3
completely 766.13
completion
performance 328.2
completing 407.2
execution 437.4
fulfillment 794.4
complex
n inferiority complex 92.22
culture 373.2
whole 792.1
perplex 799.2
obsession 926.13
adj hard to understand
522.14
mixed 797.14
complicated 799.4
difficult 1013.17
complexion
n looks 33.4

color 35.1
personality 92.11
mode 765.4
nature 767.4
disposition 978.3
v color 35.14
complexity
convolution 281.1
abstruseness 522.2
complication 799.1
difficulty 1013.1
compliance
resignation 134.2
willingness 324.1
obedience 326.1
assent 332.1
complaisance 427.2
submission 433.1
observance 434.1
consent 441.1
conformity 867.1
complicate
intensify 251.5
add 253.4
make unintelligible 522.12
involve 799.3
complication
disease 85.1
abstruseness 522.2
plot 722.4
complexity 799.1
difficulty 1013.1
predicament 1013.4
complicit 450.5
complicity
intrigue 381.5
cooperation 450.1
participation 476.1
guilt 656.1
compliment
n congratulation 149.1
regards 504.8
polite commendation 509.6
flattery 511.1
v congratulate 149.2
pay a compliment 509.14
flatter 511.5
complimentary
congratulatory 149.3
approbatory 509.16
flattering 511.8
gratuitous 634.5
comply obey 326.2
assent 332.8
submit 433.6
acquiesce 441.3
conform 867.3
component
n part 793.1
constituent 796.2
matter 1052.2
adj constituent 796.5
components
contents 196.1
substance 763.2
comportment 321.1
compose
make up 405.7
arrange 437.8
reconcile 465.8
settle 466.7

compromise 468.2
pen 547.21
set 548.16
calm 670.7
write 708.46
author 718.6
constitute 796.3
mix 797.10
dispose 808.9
conform 867.3
produce 892.8
composed
collected 106.13
content 107.7
unastonished 123.3
arranged 808.14
composed salad 10.37
composer
songwriter 547.15
scorer 710.20
author 718.4
composite
n compound 797.5
adj mixed 797.14
unitary 872.10
plural 883.7
composition
contents 196.1
form 262.1
structure 266.1
concoction 405.3
compromise 468.1
diction 532.1
written piece 547.2
writing 547.10
typesetting 548.2
atonement 658.1
piece 708.5
treatment 712.8
work of art 712.9
authorship 718.2
nature 767.4
construction 796.1
constitution 796.1
mixture 797.1
compound 797.5
combination 805.1
production 892.2
product 893.1
compositor 554.2
compost 890.4
compost heap 391.7
composure
countenance 106.2
contentment 107.1
unastonishment 123.1
quiescence 173.1
self-control 359.5
compound
n word form 526.4
composition 796.1
mixture 797.5
combination 805.2
alloy 1058.4
v make up 405.7
compromise 468.2
mix 797.10
combine 805.3
produce 892.8
adj mixed 797.14
Compounding 805.1

compound noun
  phrase 529.1
  noun 530.5
comprehend
  understand 521.7
  include 772.3
  know 928.12
comprehension
  inclusion 772.1
  intelligence 920.1
  understanding 928.3
comprehensive
  great 247.6
  voluminous 257.17
  broad 269.6
  sweeping 772.7
  whole 792.9
  thorough 794.10
  joint 800.12
compress
  n dressing 86.33
  v reduce 252.7
  contract 260.7
  squeeze 260.8
  shorten 268.6
  densify 1045.9
compressed
  contracted 260.12
  shortened 268.9
  concise 537.6
  dense 1045.12
compression bandage
  86.33
comprise
  internalize 207.5
  include 772.3
  entail 772.4
  total 792.8
  put together 800.5
  combine 805.3
compromise
  n adjustment 465.4
  middle course 467.3
  mutual concession 468
  composition 468.1
  foreign policy 609.5
  atonement 658.1
  agreement 788.4
  interchange 863.1
  v reconcile 465.8
  reach an agreement 468.2
  interchange 863.4
  endanger 1006.6
compromise oneself 661.7
comptroller
  superintendent 574.2
  accountant 628.7
  treasurer 729.12
compulsion power 18.1
  urge 375.6
  obligation 424.1
  duty 424.1
  impulse 902.1
  obsession 926.13
  necessity 963.1
compulsive
  driving 424.10
  overfastidious 495.12
  conformist 867.6
  obsessive 926.34
  involuntary 963.14

compulsory
  mandatory 420.12
  driving 424.10
  obligatory 424.11
  necessary 963.12
compunction
  qualm 113.2
  demur 325.2
  objection 333.2
computation
  adding 253.3
  measurement 300.1
  calculation 1017.10
  automation 1041.7
compute
  add up 253.6
  measure 300.10
  calculate 1017.18
  computerize 1042.21
computer
  calculator 1017.15
  computer science 1041.17
  electronic data processor
    1042.2
computer engineer 1042.17
computer-friendly 1042.18
computer game program
    1042.12
  game 743.9
computerized
  automated 1041.22
  machine-usable 1042.22
computer language 523.12
computer-literate 1042.18
computer networking 347.18
computer program 1042.11
computer scientist 1042.17
comrade
  companion 588.3
  associate 616.1
  member 617.11
comradeship
  affiliation 450.2
  camaraderie 582.2
  fellowship 587.2
con
  n prisoner 429.11
  cheating 759.13
  side 935.14
  v cheat 356.18
  persuade 375.23
  study 570.12
  memorize 989.16
  adj oppositional 451.8
  disapproving 510.21
  prep opposed to 451.10
con artist 357.4
concatenation
  association 92.33
  joining 800.1
  series 812.2
concave
  n cavity 284.2
  v hollow 284.13
  adj bowed 279.10
  concaved 284.16
concavity
  compartment 197.2
  crack 224.2
  curvature 279.1
  hollowness 284.1

  imprint 284.1
  cavity 284.2
  print 517.7
  depression 913.1
conceal
  keep secret 345.7
  hide 346.6
concealment
  invisibility 32.1
  secrecy 345.1
  hiding 346.1
  veil 346.1
  hiding place 346.4
  shelter 1009.3
concede
  acknowledge 332.11
  confess 351.7
  play 751.4
  allow for 959.5
conceit
  n pride 136.1
  conceitedness 140.4
  caprice 364.1
  witticism 489.7
  foppery 500.4
  boasting 502.1
  quirk 927.2
  thought 931.1
  idea 932.1
  opinion 953.6
  imagination 986.1
  v flatter 511.5
  imagine 986.14
conceited
  vain 136.9
  self-proud 140.11
  contemptuous 157.8
  foppish 500.17
  boastful 502.10
  dogmatic 970.22
conceivable
  knowable 928.25
  believable 953.24
  possible 966.6
  plausible 968.7
  imaginable 986.26
conceive
  get in the family way 78.11
  vivify 306.10
  understand 521.7
  phrase 532.4
  cause 886.10
  originate 892.12
  know 928.12
  think 931.8
  suppose 951.10
  believe 953.11
  imagine 986.14
concentrate
  n extract 192.8
  v converge 169.2
  extraction 192.16
  focus 208.10
  intensify 251.5
  contract 260.7
  narrow thoughts 931.10
  densify 1045.9
concentration
  convergence 169.1
  extract 192.7
  formula 192.8

  centralization 208.8
  intensification 251.2
  contraction 260.1
  industry 330.6
  firmness 359.2
  perseverance 360.1
  thoughtfulness 931.3
  attention 983.1
  engrossment 983.3
  densification 1045.3
concentration camp
  camp 228.29
  place of killing 308.12
  prison 429.8
concentric 208.14
concept
  idea 932.1
  opinion 953.6
  visualization 986.6
conception
  conceiving 78.4
  plan 381.1
  source 886.5
  production 892.1
  intellect 919.1
  intelligence 920.1
  understanding 928.3
  thought 931.1
  idea 932.1
  opinion 953.6
  creative thought 986.2
  visualization 986.6
conceptual
  mental 919.7
  intelligent 920.12
  cognitive 931.21
  ideational 932.9
  imaginative 986.18
conceptualize
  know 928.12
  think 931.8
  imagine 986.14
conceptual model 349.1
concern
  n sensitivity 24.3
  sympathy 93.5
  anxiety 126.1
  considerateness 143.3
  carefulness 339.1
  undertaking 404.1
  company 617.9
  occupation 724.1
  workplace 739.1
  relevance 775.4
  affair 831.3
  science 928.10
  topic 937.1
  interest 983.2
  importance 997.1
  v give anxiety 126.4
  relate to 775.5
  involve 898.2
  interest 983.12
  trouble 1013.13
concerning 775.13
concert
  n unanimity 332.5
  cooperation 450.1
  harmony 708.3
  performance 708.33
  agreement 788.1

concurrence 899.1
  v plan 381.8
  cooperate 450.3
  adj instrumental 708.51
concerted
  cooperative 450.5
  concurrent 899.4
concert hall hall 197.4
  theater 704.14
concession
  acknowledgment 332.3
  confession 351.3
  grant 443.5
  compromise 468.1
  giving 478.1
  discount 631.1
  merchant 730.2
  market 736.1
  qualification 959.1
concessory 426.5
conchoidal 279.18
concierge 1008.12
conciliate 465.7
conciliatory
  forgiving 148.6
  unbelligerent 464.10
  pacificatory 465.12
concise short 268.8
  taciturn 344.9
  brief 537.6
conclave council 423.1
  ecclesiastical council 423.4
  conference 541.5
  political convention 609.8
  assembly 770.2
conclude resolve 359.7
  complete 407.6
  arrange 437.8
  end 820.5
  draw a conclusion 946.10
  suppose 951.10
conclusion
  affirmation 334.1
  completion 407.2
  signing 437.3
  sequel 817.1
  end 820.1
  reasonableness 935.8
  solution 940.1
  deduction 946.4
  opinion 953.6
conclusions and
    complimentary closes
    820.15
conclusive
  completing 407.9
  mandatory 420.12
  final 820.11
  convincing 953.26
  evidential 957.16
  unqualified 960.2
  certain 970.13
conclusive proof 957.3
concoct
  fabricate 354.18
  plot 381.9
  make up 405.7
  mix 797.10
  produce 892.8
  originate 892.12
  imagine 986.14

concoction
  fabrication 354.10
  decoction 405.3
  compound 797.5
  production 892.1
  product 893.1
concomitant
  n adjunct 254.1
  attendant 769.3
  contemporary 836.2
  adj accompanying 769.9
  simultaneous 836.5
  concurrent 899.4
concord
  n unanimity 332.5
  treaty 437.2
  cooperation 450.1
  accord 455.1
  harmony 708.3
  agreement 788.1
  order 807.1
  v cooperate 450.3
concordance
  unanimity 332.5
  cooperation 450.1
  accord 455.1
  reference book 554.9
  harmony 708.3
  agreement 788.1
  concurrence 899.1
concordant
  unanimous 332.15
  cooperative 450.5
  in accord 455.3
  pacific 464.9
  harmonious 708.49
  agreeing 788.9
  conformist 867.6
  concurrent 899.4
concourse
  convergence 169.1
  flow 238.4
  assemblage 770.1
  assembly 770.2
  joining 800.1
  concurrence 899.1
concrete
  n ground covering 199.3
  pavement 383.6
  conglomeration 803.5
  solid 1045.6
  hardness 1046.6
  building material
    1054.2
  v floor 295.22
  plaster 295.25
  thicken 1045.10
  solidify 1046.8
  adj substantial 763.6
  cohesive 803.10
  particular 865.12
  dense 1045.12
  hard 1046.10
concubine
  subject 432.7
  wife 563.8
  mistress 665.17
concupiscence
  sexual desire 75.5
  desire 100.1
  lasciviousness 665.5

concur accord 332.9
  cooperate 450.3
  agree 788.6
  coincide 836.4
  collaborate 899.2
  support 901.21
concurrence
  convergence 169.1
  parallelism 203.1
  assent 332.1
  unanimity 332.5
  cooperation 450.1
  accompaniment 769.1
  assemblage 770.1
  interaction 777.3
  joining 800.1
  simultaneity 836.1
  collaboration 899.1
  agreement 899.1
  support 901.1
concussion
  trauma 85.38
  shock 671.8
  impact 902.3
condemn
  destroy 395.10
  censure 510.13
  damn 602.3
  pass judgment 946.13
  work evil 1000.6
condemnation
  censure 510.3
  judgment 598.9
  conviction 602.1
  damnation 602.1
  verdict 946.5
condemnatory
  censorious 510.22
  accusing 599.13
  damnatory 602.5
condensation 1061.2
condense trickle 238.18
  intensify 251.5
  contract 260.7
  shorten 268.6
  be brief 537.5
  abridge 557.5
  densify 1045.9
  solidify 1046.8
condescend deign 137.8
  give oneself airs 141.8
  consent 441.2
condescending 141.9
condescension
  humility 137.3
  arrogance 141.1
condign right 637.3
  due 639.8
condiment
  cooking 11.1
  flavoring 63.3
condition
  n fitness 84.1
  disease 85.1
  rank 245.2
  preparedness 405.4
  stipulation 421.2
  state 765.1
  circumstance 766.1
  provision 959.2
  v limit 210.5

  accustom 373.9
  repair 396.14
  fit 405.8
  inculcate 568.12
  train 568.13
  qualify 959.3
  make conditional 959.4
conditional
  n mood 530.11
  adj modal 765.6
  circumstantial 766.7
  dialectic 935.22
  provisional 959.8
  undecided 971.18
conditioning
  n classical conditioning
    92.26
  habituation 373.7
  fitting 405.2
  inculcation 568.2
  training 568.3
  involuntariness 963.5
  adj healthful 81.5
condolence
  comfort 121.4
  pity 145.1
  consolation 147
  reassurance 147.1
condom 86.23
condominium
  apartment house 228.14
  participation 476.1
condone accept 134.7
  overlook 148.4
  suffer 443.10
  keep an open mind 979.7
conducive
  adj modal 384.8
  helpful 449.21
  prep tending to 896.5
conduct
  n behavior 321.1
  performance 328.2
  direction 573.1
  operation 889.1
  v transport 176.12
  channel 239.15
  practice 328.8
  perform 328.9
  direct 573.8
  lead an orchestra 708.45
  escort 769.8
  operate 889.5
conduction
  transferal 176.1
  electric conduction 1032.14
conductor
  trainman 178.13
  director 574.1
  leader 574.6
  musician 710.17
  escort 769.5
  conduction 1032.14
conduit
  channel 239.1
  passageway 383.3
cone
  n loudspeaker 50.8
  conoid 282.5
  plant 310.27
  v round 282.6

reticence 344.3
self-control 359.5
urge 375.6
compulsion 424.1
restraint 428.1
confinement 429.1
temperance 668.1
moderation 670.1

constrict
contract 260.7
narrow 270.11
close 293.6
obstruct 1012.12

constricted
contracted 260.12
narrow 270.14
closed 293.9
narrow-minded 980.10

construct
n structure 266.2
v build 266.5
compose 796.3
produce 892.8

construction
structure 266.1
frame 266.2
interpretation 341.1
explanation 518.3
word form 526.4
phrase 529.1
composition 796.1
production 892.2

constructive
interpretative 341.14
helpful 449.21
creative 892.16

construe
interpret 341.9
translate 341.12

consular 576.17

consulate house 228.5
mastership 417.7
office 739.7

consult 541.10

consultant
expert 413.11
adviser 422.3

consultation
advice 422.1
conference 541.5

consultive 422.8

consume devour 8.22
decrease 252.6
shrink 260.9
use 387.13
spend 388.3
impair 393.19
destroy 395.10
lose 473.5
waste 486.4
expend 626.5
disintegrate 806.3
burn up 1020.25

consumer
eater 8.16
user 387.9
buyer 733.5

consuming
n consumption 388.1
adj agonizing 98.23
destructive 395.26

engrossing 983.20

consummate
v top 198.9
accomplish 407.4
adj top 198.10
downright 247.12
complete 407.12
thorough 794.10
perfected 1002.9

consumption
eating 8.1
tuberculosis 85.17
decrement 252.3
shrinking 260.3
use 387.1
using up 388.1
consuming 388.1
impairment 393.4
destruction 395.1
waste 473.2
expenditure 626.1

contact
n touch 73.1
addict 87.21
nearness 223.5
communication 343.1
go-between 576.4
v be heard 48.12
come near 223.10
communicate with 343.8

contact sport 744.1

contagious
poisonous 82.7
infectious 85.62
transferable 176.18
communicable 343.11

contain
internalize 207.5
limit 210.5
enclose 212.5
close 293.6
restrain 428.7
include 772.3
entail 772.4
total 792.8
compose 796.3
fight fire 1022.7

container
receptacle 195.1
can 195.1
enclosed place 212.3
cavity 284.2

containment
surrounding 209.5
enclosure 212.1
foreign policy 609.5

contaminate
defile 80.17
infect 85.51
corrupt 393.12
blaspheme 694.5
adulterate 797.12
radioactivate 1037.10

contamination
defilement 80.4
unhealthfulness 82.1
infection 85.4
corruption 393.2
hybrid word 526.11
sacrilege 694.2
adulteration 797.3

radiation 1037.1
environmental destruction
1073.2

contemn disdain 157.3
reject 372.2

contemplate
scrutinize 27.14
expect 130.5
meditate 380.5
study 570.12
consider 931.12
think of 931.16
mull over 931.17
foresee 961.5

contemplation
scrutiny 27.6
expectation 130.1
quiescence 173.1
inaction 329.1
study 570.3
revelation 683.10
trance 691.3
prayer 696.4
consideration 931.2
foresight 961.1
engrossment 983.3

contemporary
n coeval 836.2
adj simultaneous 836.5
present 838.2
modern 841.13

contempt hate 103.1
insolence 142.1
indignity 156.2
disdain 157.1
disrespect 157.1
rejection 372.1
defiance 454.1
deprecation 510.2
disparagement 512.1

contemptible
offensive 98.18
base 661.12
paltry 998.21
terrible 1000.9
hateful 103.8

contemptuous
hating 103.7
arrogant 141.13
insolent 142.9
insulting 156.8
disdainful 157.8
rejective 372.4
defiant 454.7
condemnatory 510.22
disparaging 512.13

contend
contrapose 215.4
affirm 334.5
insist 421.8
contest 457.13
compete 457.18
struggle 725.11
argue 935.16

contender
competitor 452.2
combatant 461.1

contend for
try for 403.9
strive for 457.20
defend 600.10

contend with
treat 387.12
offer resistance 453.3
engage with 457.17

content
components 196.1
n material within 196.1
stuffing 196.1
capacity 257.2
makeup 554.12
table 871.2

content
n pleasure 95.1
contentment 107.1
v satisfy 107.4
adj pleased 95.15
contented 107.7
willing 324.5
assenting 332.13
consenting 441.4

content creation 547.2

contention
contraposition 215.1
opposition 451.1
disaccord 456.1
quarrel 456.5
contest 457.1
fight 457.1
hostility 589.3
argumentation 935.4

contentious
quarrelsome 110.26
aggravating 119.5
warlike 458.20
argumentative 935.19

contest
n contention 457.1
engagement 457.3
game 743.9
sport 744.1
v deny 335.4
contend against 451.4
contradict 451.6
oppose 457.13
dispute 457.21
argue 935.16
doubt 955.6

contestant
n competitor 452.2
combatant 461.1
player 743.18
adj contending 457.22

context
environment 209.1
circumstances 766.2

context clue 523.14

contiguity
juxtaposition 223.3
relation 775.1

contiguous
adjacent 223.16
consistent 803.11

continence
limitation 210.2
celibacy 565.1
abstemiousness 664.3
abstinence 668.2
moderation 670.1

continent
n world region 231.6
mainland 235.1

adj abstemious 664.6
abstinent 668.10
contingency
  circumstance 766.1
  nonessential 768.2
  relativity 775.2
  event 831.1
  liability 897.1
  condition 959.2
  possibility 966.1
  uncertainty 971.1
  gamble 971.8
  chance event 972.6
contingency plan 961.2
contingent
  n portion 477.5
  nonessential 768.2
  company 770.3
  part 793.1
  event 831.1
  chance event 972.6
  adj in contact 223.17
  substantial 763.6
  circumstantial 766.7
  unessential 768.4
  eventual 831.11
  qualifying 959.7
  dependent 959.9
  possible 966.6
  undecided 971.18
  chance 972.15
contingent on 887.8
continual
  continuous 812.8
  perpetual 829.7
  constant 847.5
continuation
  adjunct 254.1
  payment 624.1
  sequence 815.1
  sequel 817.1
  protraction 827.2
  postponement 846.4
  continuance 856.1
continue lengthen 267.6
  persevere 360.2
  be continuous 812.4
  elapse 821.5
  endure 827.6
  protract 827.9
  postpone 846.9
  be frequent 847.3
  stay with it 856.3
continuing
  persevering 360.8
  continuous 812.8
  durable 827.10
  permanent 853.7
  abiding 856.7
continuity
  playbook 704.21
  plot 722.4
  uniformity 781.1
  consistency 803.2
  logical order 807.2
  uninterruption 812.1
  cohesion 812.1
  sequence 815.1
  time 821.1
  constancy 847.2
  change 852.1

continuance 856.1
continuous
  omnipresent 221.13
  uniform 781.5
  consistent 803.11
  continued 812.8
  temporal 821.7
  perpetual 829.7
  recurrent 849.13
  continuing 856.7
continuum space 158.1
  omnipresence 221.2
  series 812.2
contort deflect 164.5
  distort 265.5
  convolve 281.4
  misinterpret 342.2
contortion
  n deflection 164.2
  distortion 265.1
  adj torsional 265.9
contour
  n outline 211.2
  tournure 262.2
  v outline 211.9
contra
  n oppositionist 452.3
  adj negative 335.5
  oppositional 451.8
  adv in opposition 451.9
  prep opposed to 451.10
  opposite 779.10
contraband
  n prohibition 444.1
  smuggling 732.2
  illicit goods 732.3
  adj prohibited 444.7
  illegal 674.6
contraceptive
  birth control device 86.23
  safeguard 1008.3
contract
  n make small 258.9
  undertaking 404.1
  obligation 436.2
  compact 437.1
  v take sick 85.47
  compress 260.7
  shorten 268.6
  narrow 270.11
  close 293.6
  commit 436.5
  be engaged 436.6
  compact 437.5
  acquire 472.8
  incur 897.4
contraction
  decrease 252.1
  compression 260.1
  narrowing 270.2
  abbreviation 537.4
  stenography 547.8
contractive
  decreasing 252.11
  compressible 260.11
contractual 437.10
contradict deny 335.4
  reject 372.2
  cross 451.6
  go contrary to 779.4
  disagree 789.5

counteract 900.6
  refute 958.5
contradiction
  denial 335.2
  rejection 372.1
  refusal 442.1
  opposition 451.1
  ambiguity 539.1
  contrariety 779.1
  disagreement 789.1
  counteraction 900.1
  refutation 958.2
contradictory
  negative 335.5
  oppositional 451.8
  contrary 779.6
  disagreeing 789.6
  counteractive 900.8
  illogical 936.11
  refuting 958.6
contradistinction
  contrariety 779.1
  distinction 944.3
contraindicated
  prohibited 444.7
  unwise 923.10
  inexpedient 996.5
contraindication 379.1
contralto
  n part 708.22
  voice 709.5
  adj deep 54.11
contraposition
  opposition 215.1
  anteposition 215.1
  contrast 451.1
  contrariety 779.1
  counteraction 900.1
contraption
  novelty 841.2
  tool 1040.1
contrariety
  offensiveness 98.2
  contraposition 215.1
  hostility 451.2
  relation 775.1
  oppositeness 779.1
  difference 780.1
  inequality 791.1
  nonconformity 868.1
  counteraction 900.1
contrary
  adj negative 335.5
  perverse 361.11
  oppositional 451.8
  contrarious 779.6
  different 780.7
  disagreeing 789.6
  nonconforming 868.5
  refuting 958.6
  adverse 1011.13
  hindering 1012.17
  unwieldy 1013.19
  adv opposite 215.6
contrast
  n contraposition 215.1
  contrariety 779.1
  difference 780.1
  dissimilarity 787.1
  comparison 943.1
  lighting 1025.19

v contrapose 215.4
  compare 943.4
contravene deny 335.4
  violate 435.4
  contradict 451.6
  break the law 674.5
  go contrary to 779.4
  counteract 900.6
  thwart 1012.15
contretemps
  wrong time 844.2
  misfortune 1011.2
contribute
  provide 385.7
  participate 476.5
  subscribe 478.14
  tend 896.3
contribute to
  advance 162.5
  be useful 449.17
  subscribe 478.14
  determine 886.12
contribution
  demand 421.1
  participation 476.1
  giving 478.1
  donation 478.6
  treatise 556.1
  tax 630.9
contributor 478.11
contributory
  additional 253.10
  helpful 449.21
  donative 478.25
contrite 113.9
contrition regret 113.1
  apology 658.2
contrivance
  plan 381.1
  intrigue 381.5
  instrument 384.4
  stratagem 415.3
  plot 722.4
  production 892.1
  expedient 995.2
  tool 1040.1
contrive plan 381.8
  manage 409.12
  maneuver 415.10
  fare 765.5
  induce 886.11
  originate 892.12
control
  n supremacy 249.3
  self-control 359.5
  skill 413.1
  governance 417.5
  restraint 428.1
  subjection 432.1
  direction 573.1
  mastery 612.2
  moderation 670.1
  familiar spirit 678.12
  influence 894.1
  experiment 942.1
  specter 988.1
  system component 1041.14
  v pilot 184.37
  possess authority 417.13
  restrain 428.7
  direct 573.8

hold in hand 612.12
moderate 670.6
exercise influence 894.8
haunt 988.6
control freak 359.1
controlled force 462.22
controller
superintendent 574.2
accountant 628.7
treasurer 729.12
system component 1041.14
controlling
n extinguishing 1022.2
adj authoritative 417.15
restraining 428.11
directing 573.12
governing 612.17
paramount 997.24
control oneself
compose oneself 106.7
restrain oneself 668.6
controversial
contentious 110.26
argumentative 935.19
doubtful 971.17
controversy
quarrel 456.5
contention 457.1
disagreement 789.1
argumentation 935.4
controvert deny 335.4
contradict 451.6
discuss 541.11
go contrary to 779.4
refute 958.5
controvertible
unprovable 958.9
doubtful 971.17
contumacious
defiant 327.10
ungovernable 361.12
contumely
insolence 142.1
indignity 156.2
contempt 157.1
berating 510.7
vilification 513.2
contusion 85.38
conundrum
riddle 522.9
bewilderment 971.3
convalescence 396.8
convalescent 396.23
convalescent home 91.21
convection 176.1
convene
summon 420.11
meet 770.17
convenience
latrine 12.10
comfortableness 121.2
benefit 387.4
leisure 402.1
facility 449.9
timeliness 843.1
expedience 995.1
handiness 1014.2
machinery 1040.3
convenience store 736.1
convenient
comfortable 121.11

nearby 223.15
handy 387.20
timely 843.9
expedient 995.5
convent 703.6
convention
custom 373.1
rule 419.2
ecclesiastical council 423.4
compact 437.1
treaty 437.2
conference 541.5
fashion 578.1
social rule 579.1
etiquette 580.3
political convention 609.8
assembly 770.2
conventional
customary 373.13
preceptive 419.4
contractual 437.10
decorous 579.5
ceremonious 580.8
orthodox 687.7
traditional 842.12
conformist 867.6
usual 869.9
ordinary 1005.8
conventional medicine 90.13
converge
come together 169.2
focus 208.10
near 223.7
assemble 770.16
join 800.11
convergence
coming together 169
meeting 169.1
centralization 208.8
nearness 223.1
assemblage 770.1
joining 800.1
conversance 587.5
conversant with
used to 373.16
versed in 928.19
conversation
communication 343.1
speech 524.1
interchange of speech 541.1
converse 541.1
social life 582.4
conversational
v talkative 540.9
adj communicational
343.9
vernacular 523.20
colloquial 541.12
conversation piece 870.5
converse
v communicate 343.6
speak 524.19
talk together 541.8
converse
n inverse 205.4
opposite side 215.3
communication 343.1
conversation 541.1
social life 582.4
adj contrapositive 215.5
contrary 779.6

convert
n apostate 363.5
disciple 572.2
believer 692.4
proselyte 858.7
v invert 205.5
misuse 389.4
redeem 685.6
sell 737.24
change 852.7
reconvert 858.11
interchange 863.4
process 892.9
convince 953.18
converted
improved 392.13
redeemed 685.9
regenerate 692.10
altered 852.10
changed 858.19
forgetful 990.9
convertible
liquid 728.31
equivalent 790.8
changeable 858.18
interchangeable 863.5
convertor 1035.11
convex
n bulge 283.3
adj bowed 279.10
rotund 282.8
convexed 283.13
convey
transport 176.12
channel 239.15
communicate 343.7
say 524.22
transfer 629.3
conveyability
transferability 176.2
communicability 343.4
conveyable
transferable 176.18
communicable 343.11
moveable 629.5
conveyance
transportation 176.3
vehicle 179.1
informing 343.2
theft 482.1
transfer 629.1
conveyor 176.7
convict
n prisoner 429.11
criminal 660.9
v bring in a verdict 598.20
condemn 602.3
convicted 602.6
conviction hope 124.1
condemnation 602.1
persuasion 953.5
confidence 970.5
convince
persuade 375.23
cause to believe 858.16
convert 953.18
seem true 973.9
convinced belief 953.21
confident 970.21
convincing
convictional 953.26

evidential 957.16
conviviality
joviality 582.3
festivity 743.3
convocation
summons 420.5
ecclesiastical council 423.4
ceremony 580.4
assembly 770.2
convolution
curvature 279.1
involution 281.1
grandiloquence 545.1
complexity 799.1
circuitousness 914.1
convoy
n escort 769.5
bodyguard 1008.14
v maneuver 182.46
escort 769.8
convulse pain 26.7
torture 96.18
amuse 743.21
discompose 811.4
agitate 917.10
convulsion seizure 85.6
symptom 85.9
outburst 105.9
laughter 116.4
fit 152.8
fall 395.3
upheaval 671.5
disarrangement 811.1
revolution 860.1
spasm 917.6
frenzy 926.7
coo murmur 52.10
bird sound 60.5
speak 524.25
co-occurrence 836.1
cook
n chef 11.3
maid 577.8
v prepare food 11.5
tamper with 354.17
spoil 393.11
do for 395.11
prearrange 965.5
be hot 1019.22
heat 1020.17
cookbook 11.4
cookery
cooking 11.1
kitchen 11.4
heater 1020.10
cookie biscuit 10.43
man 76.5
cooking area 11.4
cookout 8.6
Cook's tour 20.3
cook up cook 11.5
fabricate 354.17
improvise 365.8
plot 381.9
originate 892.12
prearrange 965.5
cool
n composure 106.2
unastonishment 123.1
moderation 670.1
uniformity 781.1

v monopolize 469.6
purchase 733.7
get a corner on 737.26
turn 914.6
run into a corner 1013.16
cornerstone
foundation 901.7
salient point 997.6
corn-fed 257.18
cornice 198.5
cornified pointed 285.9
hardened 1046.13
cornrow 3.7
cornucopia store 386.1
source of supply 386.4
horn of plenty 991.3
corny trite 117.9
old-fogyish 842.17
corollary adjunct 254.1
attendant 769.3
effect 887.1
conclusion 946.4
corona
n cigar 89.4
radiation 171.2
circle 280.2
flower 310.28
halo 1025.14
chandelier 1026.6
sun 1072.13
adj circular 280.11
coronation
authority 417.12
installation 615.3
coroner doctor 90.4
autopsy 307.17
coronet circle 280.2
jewel 498.6
heraldry 647.2
royal insignia 647.3
corporal
n Army noncommissioned
officer 575.19
naval officer 575.20
church 703.10
adj material 1052.10
corporate
associated 617.16
joint 800.12
leagued 805.6
corporate culture 724.4
corporation goozle 2.19
workplace 739.1
corporeal 1052.10
corps branch 461.21
military unit 461.22
association 617.1
company 770.3
corpse slim 270.8
dead body 307.15
corpse pose 201.1
corpulent stout 257.18
thick 269.8
corpus capital 728.15
collection 770.11
knowledge 928.1
lore 928.9
body 1052.3
corpuscle blood 2.25
cell 305.4
corpus delicti 307.15

corral enclose 212.5
acquire 472.9
assemble 770.18
drive 1070.8
correct
v revise 392.12
remedy 396.13
reprove 510.17
punish 604.10
conform 867.3
disillusion 977.2
adj meticulous 339.12
mannerly 504.16
grammatical 530.17
appropriate 533.7
conventional 579.5
right 637.3
orthodox 687.7
accurate 973.16
correction
measurement 300.1
revision 392.4
reparation 396.6
reproof 510.5
punishment 604.1
corrective
n remedy 86.1
adj remedial 86.39
emendatory 392.16
punishing 604.23
correlation
relativity 775.2
reciprocal relation 777
mutuality 777.1
comparison 943.1
correlative
n correspondent 777.4
likeness 784.3
adj accompanying
769.9
approximate 775.8
correlative 777.8
akin 784.13
comparative 943.8
correspondence
symmetry 264.1
communication 343.1
accord 455.1
record 549.1
written communication
553.1
letter writing 553.1
correlation 777.1
sameness 778.1
uniformity 781.1
similarity 784.1
agreement 788.1
equality 790.1
conformity 867.1
concurrence 899.1
correspondent
n letter writer 553.8
journalist 555.4
correlate 777.4
likeness 784.3
adj reciprocal 777.10
coinciding 778.8
uniform 781.5
analogous 784.11
agreeing 788.9
equivalent 790.8

corridor airway 184.33
entrance 189.5
hall 197.18
region 231.1
passageway 383.3
corrigible
improvable 392.17
remediable 396.25
manageable 433.14
corroborate 957.11
corrode
decrease 252.6
erode 393.21
etch 713.10
disintegrate 806.3
corrosion
decrement 252.3
decay 393.6
disintegration 806.1
corrosive
n cauterant 1020.15
adj acid 110.17
caustic 144.23
corrupting 393.44
vigorous 544.11
disintegrative 806.5
harmful 1000.12
corrugated rough 288.6
rugged 288.7
furrowed 290.4
wrinkled 291.8
corrupt
v defile 80.17
bribe 378.3
debase 393.12
decay 393.22
misteach 569.3
sully 654.10
adulterate 797.12
indoctrinate 858.15
work evil 1000.6
adj bribable 378.4
decayed 393.40
dishonest 645.16
corrupted 654.14
erroneous 975.16
corruptible
bribable 378.4
venal 645.23
transient 828.7
corruption filth 80.7
perversion 265.2
bribery 378.1
pollution 393.2
decay 393.6
wordplay 489.8
mispronunciation
525.5
barbarism 526.6
solecism 531.2
misteaching 569.1
improbity 645.1
turpitude 654.4
adulteration 797.3
indoctrination 858.5
evil 1000.3
corsage shirt 5.15
bouquet 310.25
corsair 483.7
corset stays 5.23
supporter 901.2

cortege funeral 309.5
attendance 769.6
procession 812.3
cortex exterior 206.2
skin 295.3
shell 295.15
armor 460.3
cosignage 438.3
cosmetic
exterior 206.7
shallow 276.5
hasty 401.9
insufficient 992.9
beautifying 1016.22
cosmetics
appearance 33.2
exteriority 206.1
pretext 376.1
notions 735.6
dissimilarity 787.1
makeup 1016.11
cosmetic surgery 90.2
cosmic large 247.7
universal 864.14
cosmologic 1072.24
cosmology 1072.18
cosmonaut 1075.8
cosmopolitan
n citizen 227.4
sophisticate 413.17
adj traveled 177.40
public 312.16
experienced 413.28
chic 578.13
universal 864.14
broad-minded 979.8
cosmos
completeness 794.1
universe 1072.1
cossack 461.12
cosset
n favorite 104.15
v indulge 427.6
foster 449.16
caress 562.16
cost
n loss 473.1
expenses 626.3
value 630.1
high price 632.3
v spend 626.5
sell for 630.13
cost-effective 635.6
costive 293.11
costly 632.11
cost of living
expenses 626.3
standard of living
731.8
costume
n clothing 5.1
suit 5.6
costumery 5.9
theater 704.17
v outfit 5.41
costume design 717.5
cot 228.8
coterie
social set 582.5
clique 617.6
company 770.3

coterminous
adjacent 223.16
coinciding 778.8
simultaneous 836.5
cottage
cot 228.8
Aldine 554.15
cottager 227.1
cotton 86.33
cotton-picking 661.12
cotton to
fall in love 104.21
get along 455.2
be friends 587.9
couch
n lair 228.26
sofa 901.19
v rest 20.6
lie low 274.5
lurk 346.9
say 524.22
phrase 532.4
depress 913.4
lie down 913.11
the couch 92.6
couchant
recumbent 201.8
low 274.7
couch potato
idler 331.8
spectator 918.1
cougar 311.21
cough 2.21
cough drops 86.16
coughing 85.9
cough up 624.16
council
n advice 422.1
committee 423.2
conclave 423.1
conference 541.5
directorate 574.11
tribunal 595.1
cabinet 613.3
association 617.1
assembly 770.2
adj conciliar 423.5
councilman
public official 575.17
legislator 610.3
counsel
n advice 422.1
adviser 422.3
lawyer 597.1
legal representation 597.4
consideration 931.2
v advise 422.5
confer 541.10
counseling 92.6
counselor
psychologist 92.10
adviser 422.3
lawyer 597.1
count
n amount 244.2
accusation 599.1
nobleman 608.4
returns 609.21
game 745.3
particular 766.3
total 1017.6

summation 1017.11
v quantify 244.4
beat time 708.44
have influence 894.10
judge 946.8
rank 946.15
matter 997.12
number 1017.17
countdown
rocket launching 1074.9
curtain-raiser 816.2
countenance
n looks 33.4
composure 106.2
face 216.4
authorization 443.3
patronage 449.4
approval 509.1
v accept 134.7
encourage 375.21
suffer 443.10
abet 449.14
approve 509.9
counter
n stern 217.7
retaliation 506.1
type 548.6
token 728.12
shopboard 736.6
workplace 739.1
bingo 759.15
gambler 759.21
table 901.15
radioscope 1037.7
v deny 335.4
oppose 451.3
contend against 451.4
fend off 460.10
retaliate 506.4
defend 600.10
go contrary to 779.4
disagree 789.5
counteract 900.6
refute 958.5
thwart 1012.15
adj backward 163.12
oppositional 451.8
contrary 779.6
dissimilar 787.4
adverse 1011.13
adv opposite 215.6
in opposition 451.9
contrarily 779.9
counteract
contrapose 215.4
offset 338.5
oppose 451.3
go contrary to 779.4
counter 900.6
thwart 1012.15
counterattack
n attack 459.1
countermeasure 900.5
v launch an attack 459.17
counteract 900.6
counterbalance
n makeweight 297.4
offset 338.2
the opposite 779.2
counterforce 900.4
v weigh 297.10

offset 338.5
go contrary to 779.4
equalize 790.6
stabilize 855.7
neutralize 900.7
countercharge
n recrimination 599.3
rebuttal 939.2
v recriminate 599.11
rebut 939.5
counterclockwise
adj left 220.4
adv clockwise 161.24
backwards 163.13
round 915.16
counterculture
n dissent 333.1
unconventionality 868.2
countermeasure 900.5
adj dissenting 333.6
unconventional 868.6
counterespionage 938.9
counterfeit
n fake 354.13
phony money 728.10
copy 785.1
substitute 862.2
v imitate 336.5
fabricate 354.18
sham 354.21
affect 500.12
coin 728.28
resemble 784.7
adj imitation 336.8
spurious 354.26
similar 784.10
substitute 862.8
counterforce 900.4
counterinsurgency
900.5
counterintelligence
secret service 576.12
surveillance 938.9
counterirritant 900.3
countermand
n take back 445.1
v repeal 445.2
thwart 1012.15
countermeasure 900.5
countermine
n entrenchment 460.5
v plot 381.9
countermove 995.2
counteroffensive 459.1
counterorder
n countermand 445.1
v repeal 445.2
counterpane 295.10
counterpart
correlate 777.4
likeness 784.3
duplicate 785.3
equal 790.4
counterpoint
polyphony 708.20
meter 720.7
the opposite 779.2
counterpose
go contrary to 779.4
counteract 900.6
compare 943.4

counterproductive
ineffective 19.15
counteractive 900.8
unwise 923.10
inexpedient 996.5
harmful 1000.12
hampering 1012.18
counterrevolution
revolution 860.1
countermeasure 900.5
countersign
n identification 517.11
password 517.12
signature 527.10
v ratify 332.12
promise 436.4
counterspy 576.9
counterstatement
defense 600.2
rebuttal 939.2
counter to
counteractively 900.10
opposed to 451.10
in disagreement with 789.10
countervailing
n neutralization 900.2
adj compensating 338.6
contrary 779.6
counteractive 900.8
neutralizing 900.9
counterweight
offset 338.2
scenery 704.20
counterforce 900.4
countess 608.6
counting
n numeration 1017.9
adj inclusive 772.6
countless much 247.8
infinite 823.3
innumerable 884.10
count on hope 124.6
look forward to 130.6
plan 380.6
rely on 953.16
count out 773.4
countrified 233.7
country
n region 231.1
nation 232.1
land 232.1
jury 596.6
adj rustic 233.6
country bumpkin 606.6
country house 228.5
countryman
fellow citizen 227.5
peasant 606.6
agriculturist 1069.5
country music 708.11
countryside 233.1
count sheep 23.3
count up 1017.19
county region 231.5
country 232.1
county line 211.3
county seat 230.4
coup act 328.3
attempt 403.2
stratagem 415.3
seizure 480.2

instant 830.3
expedient 995.2
coup de foudre 104.2
coup d'état revolt 327.4
seizure 480.2
revolution 860.1
couple
n set 784.5
two 873.2
v copulate 75.21
wed 563.14
get married 563.15
come together 770.16
relate 775.6
put together 800.5
combine 805.3
league 805.4
double 873.5
couplet poetry 720.9
two 873.2
coupon token 728.12
stock certificate 738.4
courage pluck 359.3
fortitude 492.5
bravery 492.1
confidence 970.5
courageous
resolute 359.14
plucky 492.16
courier
messenger 353.1
guide 574.7
course
n serving 8.10
dish 10.7
direction 161.1
progression 162.1
career 172.2
travel 177.1
journey 177.5
voyage 182.6
heading 184.34
flow 238.4
channel 239.1
layer 296.1
policy 381.4
route 383.1
manner 384.1
arena 463.1
track 517.8
study 568.8
golf 751.1
skiing 753.1
horse racing 757.1
series 812.2
round 850.3
process 889.2
trend 896.2
v travel 177.18
traverse 177.20
flow 238.16
hunt 382.9
adv under way 182.63
course of action 995.2
courser swiftness 174.6
horse 311.10
hunter 382.5
war-horse 461.30
court
n enclosed place 212.3
estate 228.7

council 423.1
courtship 562.7
judiciary 594.2
law court 595.2
courthouse 595.6
legislature 613.1
playground 743.11
basketball 747.1
tennis 748.1
attendance 769.6
influence 894.6
v curry favor 138.9
solicit 440.14
woo 562.21
cultivate 587.12
adj tribunal 595.7
courteous
sensitive 24.12
respectful 155.8
polite 504.14
sociable 582.22
courtesan 665.15
courtesy
sensitivity 24.3
act of kindness 143.7
respect 155.1
good behavior 321.2
politeness 504.1
courteousness 504.1
civility 504.6
sociability 582.1
courthouse
town hall 230.5
court 595.6
capitol 613.4
courtier
sycophant 138.3
follower 166.2
flatterer 511.4
court jester 489.12
courtliness
proud bearing
136.2
gallantry 504.2
courtesy 504.6
etiquette 580.3
courtly
dignified 136.12
gallant 504.15
flattering 511.8
court-martial
military court 595.4
trial 598.5
courtroom 595.6
courtship 562.7
court sports 744.13
courtyard 212.3
couscous 10.36
cousin 559.3
couturier
dressmaker 5.36
designer 716.9
cove man 76.5
nook 197.3
inlet 242.1
arch 279.4
cave 284.5
recess 284.7
coven 690.8
covenant
n compact 437.1

v come to an agreement
332.10
contract 437.5
cover
n serving 8.10
food service 8.11
dish 10.7
Air Force mission 184.11
ground covering 199.3
covering 295.2
lid 295.5
blanket 295.10
concealment 346.1
veil 346.2
hiding place 346.4
disguise 356.11
pretext 376.1
anonymity 528.1
bookbinding 554.14
protection 1008.1
shelter 1009.3
shade 1028.1
v color 35.14
copulate 75.21
be pregnant 78.12
extend 158.9
traverse 177.20
close 293.6
stop 293.7
cover up 295.19
compensate 338.4
explain 341.10
conceal 346.6
hide under 376.4
bet 759.25
include 772.3
put together 800.5
take one's turn 825.5
overspread 910.5
protect 1008.18
shade 1028.5
coverage size 257.1
scope 295.1
protection 295.2
news 552.1
inclusion 772.1
cover charge
food service 8.11
fee 630.6
covered stadium 462.1
cover for 862.5
cover girl 1016.7
cover one's ass
save face 136.7
defend 460.8
covert
n plumage 3.18
lair 228.26
cover 295.2
thicket 310.15
hiding place 346.4
shelter 1009.3
adj covered 295.31
clandestine 345.12
concealed 346.11
latent 519.5
cover-up
veil of secrecy 345.3
pretext 376.1
covet crave 100.18
envy 154.2

covey company 770.3
assemblage 770.6
multitude 884.3
cow
n female animal 77.9
cattle 311.6
v intimidate 127.20
domineer 612.15
cowabunga 116.2
coward
n jellyfish 491.5
adj cowardly 491.10
cowardice frailty 16.2
fear 127.1
weak will 362.4
submission 433.1
spinelessness 491.2
cowardliness 491.1
cowardly weak 16.12
fearful 127.23
weak-willed 362.12
coward 491.10
cowardship 491.1
cowboy rider 178.8
violent person 671.10
card 758.2
herder 1070.3
cower be weak 16.8
fawn 138.7
quail 491.9
crouch 913.8
cowl
n cover 295.2
v hood 295.19
cowlick 3.6
cow town
frontier 211.5
hinterland 233.2
co-worker 616.5
coxcomb dandy 500.9
comedy 704.6
coxswain
n steersman 183.8
guide 574.7
v pilot 182.14
coy shy 139.12
amatory 562.23
coyote 311.19
cozen 356.18
cozy pleased 95.15
comfortable 121.11
homelike 228.33
conversational 541.12
intimate 582.24
snug 1007.7
crab
n malcontent 108.4
complainer 115.9
marine animal 311.29
vermin 311.36
windlass 906.7
lifter 912.3
v be discontented 108.6
complain 115.16
maneuver 184.40
hinder 1012.16
adj sour 67.5
crabbed sour 67.5
irascible 110.19
stricken in years 303.18
hard to understand 522.14

stiff 534.3
complex 799.4
crack
n stripe 47.5
report 56.1
snap 56.2
detonation 56.3
trauma 85.38
cocaine 87.7
cleft 224.2
furrow 290.1
opening 292.1
attempt 403.3
witticism 489.7
remark 524.3
break 802.4
instant 830.3
hit 902.4
fault 1003.2
blemish 1004.1
v clap 56.6
snap 56.7
blast 56.8
lose self-control
    128.8
cleave 224.4
furrow 290.3
open 292.11
unclose 292.12
explain 341.10
injure 393.13
break 393.23
separate 802.12
hit 902.14
solve 940.2
blemish 1004.4
burn 1020.24
adj skillful 413.22
superior 999.14
crack down on
restrain 428.7
suppress 428.8
attack 459.15
cracked raucous 58.15
dissonant 61.4
cleft 224.7
gaping 292.16
impaired 393.27
severed 802.23
mentally deficient 922.22
crazy 926.27
blemished 1004.8
cracker
biscuit 10.30
noisemaker 53.6
wilderness settler 227.10
dryness 1066.2
crackerjack
n skillful person 413.14
good person 659.2
first-rate 999.7
adj skillful 413.22
excellent 999.13
crackle
n snap 56.2
trauma 85.38
v pop 56.7
crackpot oddity 870.4
lunatic 926.16
freak 927.4
crack the whip 573.1

crack up
n exhaustion 21.2
collapse 85.8
mental disorder 92.14
frayed nerves 128.4
crash 184.20
impairment 393.1
debacle 395.4
disruption 802.3
misfortune 1011.2
v burn out 21.5
laugh 116.8
lose self-control 128.8
crash 184.44
disintegrate 806.3
collide 902.13
go mad 926.21
cradle
n refinery 79.13
fatherland 232.2
infancy 301.5
origin 818.4
birthplace 886.8
v put to bed 22.19
foster 449.16
calm 670.7
support 901.21
craft ship 180.1
deceit 356.3
skill 413.1
art 413.7
cunning 415.1
stratagem 415.3
manual work 712.2
vocation 724.6
shrewdness 920.3
crafted 892.18
crafts 712.15
craftsman
expert 413.11
artist 716.1
skilled worker 726.6
producer 892.7
crafty
falsehearted 354.31
deceitful 356.22
cunning 415.12
cautious 494.8
sly 645.18
shrewd 920.15
crag
precipice 200.3
mountain 237.6
projection 285.4
rock 1059.1
craggy rugged 288.7
stony 1059.12
cram
n study 570.3
full measure 794.3
v stuff 8.25
tutor 568.11
study up 570.14
gluttonize 672.4
assemble 770.18
fill 794.7
thrust 902.12
refresh the memory 989.18
overload 993.15
satiate 994.4
densify 1045.9

cramp
n pang 26.2
seizure 85.6
pain 96.5
restriction 428.3
spasm 917.6
hindrance 1012.1
v weaken 16.10
confine 212.6
contract 260.7
squeeze 260.8
restrict 428.9
fasten 800.7
hamper 1012.11
hinder 1012.16
adj narrow 270.14
hard to understand 522.14
cramped limited 210.7
enclosed 212.10
little 258.10
contracted 260.12
constricted 270.14
restricted 428.15
stiff 534.3
narrow-minded 980.10
cramp one's style 1012.16
cramps 85.29
crane
n lifter 912.3
fire iron 1020.12
v gaze 27.15
be long 267.5
demur 325.4
cranium 198.7
crank
n amphetamines 87.4
malcontent 108.4
sorehead 110.11
complainer 115.9
angle 278.2
caprice 364.1
punishment 605.3
oddity 870.4
lever 906.4
fanatic 926.18
quirk 927.2
freak 927.4
v zigzag 204.12
angle 278.5
reel in 906.9
rotate 915.9
adj eccentric 927.5
cranked up 251.7
crank up
increase 251.4
start 904.13
cranky
discontented 108.8
irascible 110.19
complaining 115.20
capricious 364.5
disagreeing 789.6
counteractive 900.8
eccentric 927.5
cranny nook 197.3
crack 224.2
furrow 290.1
hiding place 346.4
crap
n defecation 12.2
feces 12.4

heroin 87.9
humbug 354.14
bull 520.3
v defecate 12.13
crape 115.7
crapper
latrine 12.10
toilet 12.11
craps dice 759.8
deuce 873.3
crapulent
intoxicated 88.31
intemperate 669.7
gluttonous 672.6
crash
n noise 53.3
report 56.1
substance abuse 87.1
crack-up 184.20
descent 194.1
decline 252.2
impairment 393.1
debacle 395.4
collapse 410.3
defeat 412.1
insolvency 625.3
declining market 737.5
impact 902.3
misfortune 1011.2
v sleep 22.14
go to bed 22.18
din 53.7
boom 56.6
use 87.22
crack up 184.44
penetrate 189.8
descend 194.5
intrude 214.5
inhabit 225.7
billow 238.22
break down 393.24
fall 410.12
go bankrupt 625.7
cheapen 633.6
collide 902.13
adv at top speed 756.5
crash course 568.8
crash diet fast 515.2
diet 7.13
crass downright 247.12
thick 269.8
coarse 497.11
ill-bred 505.6
stupid 922.15
crate
n car 179.10
storehouse 386.6
v package 212.9
wrap 295.20
crater valley 237.7
pit 275.2
cavity 284.2
blemish 1004.1
crave covet 100.18
request 440.9
entreat 440.11
craven
n dastard 491.6
adj cowardly 491.12
craving
n coveting 100.6

adj desiring 100.24

craw
digestive system 2.18
narrow place 270.3

crawfish
retreat 163.6
marine animal 311.28

crawfish out
retreat 163.6
recant 363.8

crawl
n slow motion 175.2
creeping 177.17
aquatics 182.11
v feel creepy 74.7
fawn 138.7
go slow 175.6
creep 177.26
lie 201.5
get low 274.5
linger on 827.7
bow 913.9

crawl with
pervade 221.7
teem with 884.5
infest 910.6
abound 991.5

crayon
n drawing 712.12
art equipment 712.17
v portray 712.18

craze
n stripe 47.5
trauma 85.38
greed 100.8
eagerness 101.1
fury 105.8
crack 224.2
caprice 364.1
fad 578.5
mania 926.12
blemish 1004.1
v cleave 224.4
injure 393.13
break 802.12
madden 926.24
blemish 1004.4

crazy
n lunatic 926.16
adj variegated 47.9
distorted 265.10
mentally deficient 922.22
foolish 923.8
absurd 923.11
nutty 926.27
adv swiftly 174.18

crazy about
enthusiastic 101.11
nuts about 104.30

creak
n screech 58.4
insect sound 58.5
v stridulate 58.7
screech 58.8

cream
n whiteness 37.2
cleanser 79.17
superior 249.5
upper class 607.2
the best 999.8
ointment 1056.3

semiliquid 1062.5
v foam 320.5
defeat 412.9
emulsify 1062.10
adj whitish 37.8
yellow 43.4

cream of the crop 578.6

crease
n fold 291.1
wrinkle 291.3
hockey 749.1
v fold 291.5
wrinkle 291.6
engrave 713.9

create form 262.7
originate 337.4
initiate 818.10
cause 886.10
produce 892.8
imagine 986.14

creation
forming 262.5
structure 266.1
divine function 677.13
work of art 712.9
beginning 818.1
production 892.1
work 893.1
universe 1072.1

creative
nonimitative 337.5
falsehearted 354.31
wrong 638.3
dishonest 645.16
illegal 674.6
almighty 677.17
beginning 818.15
productive 890.9
originative 892.16
imaginative 986.18

creative writer 986.12

creativity
nonimitation 337.1
genius 920.8
invention 986.3

creator artist 716.1
doer 726.1
author 886.4
producer 892.7

creature
sycophant 138.3
inferior 250.2
organism 305.2
animal 311.2
person 312.5
assenter 332.6
instrument 384.4
dependent 432.6
figurehead 575.5
deputy 576.1
retainer 577.1
follower 616.8
something 763.3
product 893.1

credence altar 703.12
belief 953.1

credential
preparedness 405.4
recommendation 509.4
identification 517.11
certificate 549.6

credibility
honesty 644.3
believability 953.8
plausibility 968.3

credibility gap
untruthfulness 354.8
deceitfulness 645.3
unbelievability 955.3

credible logical 935.20
believable 953.24
plausible 968.7

credit
n thanks 150.2
difference 255.8
trust 622.1
receipts 627.1
entry 628.5
due 639.2
honor 646.1
esteem 662.3
attribution 888.1
influence 894.1
belief 953.1
credible 953.8
v thank 150.4
pay 622.5
keep accounts 628.8
believe 953.10

creditable
praiseworthy 509.20
honest 644.13
reputable 662.15

credit crunch 619.1

creditor 622.4

credit union
association 617.1
lending institution 620.4
credit 622.1

credo religion 675.1
doctrine 676.2
system of belief 953.3

credulous foolish 923.8
trusting 953.22
knee-jerk 954.8

creed affirmation 334.1
policy 381.4
religion 675.1
doctrine 676.2
system of belief 953.3

creedbound strict 687.8
narrow-minded 980.10

creek stream 238.1
inlet 242.1

creep
n slow motion 175.2
crawling 177.17
bad person 660.5
v feel creepy 74.7
fawn 138.7
go slow 175.6
crawl 177.26
lurk 346.9
linger on 827.7

creep in enter 189.7
intrude 214.5
join 617.14

creeps
creeping of the flesh 74.4
trepidation 127.5
nervousness 128.2
cold 1023.2

creep with
pervade 221.7
teem with 884.5
infest 910.6
abound 991.5

creepy crawly 74.11
spooky 127.31
bad 1000.8

cremation
incineration 309.2
burning 1020.5

crematorium
mortuary 309.9
incinerator 1020.13

crenellated
notched 289.5
fortified 460.12

creole 523.11

crêpe 10.45

crepitant 56.10

crepuscular 315.8

crepuscule
foredawn 314.4
dusk 315.3

crescendo
n loudness 53.1
increase 251.1
expansion 259.1
music 708.25
v din 53.7
grow 251.6
enlarge 259.4
increase 259.5
adj music 708.53

crescent
n circle 230.9
curve 279.5
semicircle 280.8
heraldry 647.2
moon 1072.11
adj grown 14.3
increasing 251.8
expanding 259.12
curving 279.11

crest
n feather 3.16
summit 198.2
top part 198.4
mountain 237.6
notching 289.2
heraldry 647.2
wave 916.4
v top 198.9

crestfallen glum 112.25
disappointed 132.5
humiliated 137.14

cretin 924.8

cretinism 922.9

crevasse
n valley 237.7
pit 275.2
v open 292.11

crevice 224.2

crew aircrew 185.4
staff 577.11
clique 617.6
team 617.7
motion-picture studio 706.4
baseball team 745.2
company 770.3

crewcut 1016.14

crib
n compartment 197.2
quarters 228.4
hut 228.9
translation 341.3
storehouse 386.6
garner 386.7
plagiarism 482.8
brothel 665.9
casino 759.19
v confine 212.6
imitate 336.5
cheat 356.18
confine 429.12
rob 482.16
plagiarize 482.19
adopt 621.4
adj infant 301.12
crick
n pang 26.2
insect sound 58.5
stream 238.1
v stridulate 58.7
cricket
noisemaker 53.6
locust 311.35
propriety 637.2
fairness 649.2
crier 353.3
crime
wrongdoing 655.1
misdeed 655.2
offense 674.4
crime fighting 604.1
criminal
n evildoer 593.1
perpetrator 645.10
felon 660.9
adj wrong 638.3
dishonest 645.16
wicked 654.16
evil 655.5
guilty 656.3
illegal 674.6
bad 1000.7
criminal contempt 505.2
criminalize prohibit 444.3
ostracize 586.6
criminal law 673.5
criminology 673.7
crimp
n lock 3.5
trench 290.2
fold 291.1
wrinkle 291.3
cheat 357.3
abductor 483.10
v curl 281.5
notch 289.4
furrow 290.3
fold 291.5
wrinkle 291.6
abduct 482.20
hinder 1012.16
adj pulverable 1051.13
crimson
v color 41.4
redden 41.5
change color 105.19
blush 139.8
adj red 41.6

cringe
n retreat 903.3
v be weak 16.8
flinch 127.13
fawn 138.7
retract 168.3
cower 491.9
pull back 903.7
crouch 913.8
crinkle
n convolution 281.1
wrinkle 291.3
v rustle 52.12
convolve 281.4
ruffle 288.5
wrinkle 291.6
cripple
n defective 85.45
v weaken 16.10
disable 19.9
lame 393.14
hamper 1012.11
crisis
financial trouble 729.8
business cycle 731.10
critical point 843.4
urgency 997.4
salient point 997.6
danger 1006.1
crisis management 843.5
crisp
v curl 281.5
fold 291.5
adj refreshing 9.3
curly 281.9
clear 521.11
concise 537.6
aphoristic 974.6
cool 1023.12
cold 1023.14
brittle 1050.4
pulverable 1051.13
crisscross
v cross 170.6
adj cross 170.8
adv crosswise 170.13
criterion
measure 300.2
model 786.1
rule 869.4
test 942.2
critic
opinion maker 341.7
connoisseur 496.6
faultfinder 510.9
columnist 547.15
commentator 556.4
judge 596.1
author 718.4
interpreter 723.4
specialist 866.3
criticizer 946.7
critical
meticulous 339.12
explanatory 341.15
fastidious 495.9
faultfinding 510.23
dissertational 556.6
evaluative 723.6
crucial 843.10
discriminating 944.7

judicial 946.16
urgent 997.22
dangerous 1006.9
precarious 1006.12
difficult 1013.17
critical care 197.25
criticism
exegetics 341.8
adverse reaction 510.4
commentary 556.2
review of the arts 723.1
censure 946.2
criticize pan 510.14
write upon 556.5
critique 723.5
judge 946.14
critter animal 311.2
cattle 311.6
horse 311.10
croak
n rasp 58.3
speech defect 525.1
v sound harshly 58.9
bird sound 60.5
complain 115.15
forebode 133.10
die 307.19
kill 308.14
speak poorly 525.7
crock
n horse 311.12
ceramic ware 742.2
v intoxicate 88.23
crocodile 311.24
Croesus 618.8
croft 231.4
cromulent 100.30
Cronus 821.2
crony
companion 588.3
associate 616.1
cronyism 609.35
crook
n deviation 164.1
bias 204.3
shaft 273.2
angle 278.2
curve 279.2
cheater 357.4
scepter 417.9
thief 483.1
evildoer 593.1
ecclesiastical insignia 647.4
criminal 660.9
staff 702.3
supporter 901.2
fire iron 1020.12
v deflect 164.5
oblique 204.9
distort 265.5
angle 278.5
curve 279.6
crooked askew 204.14
zigzag 204.20
distorted 265.10
fake 265.11
angular 278.6
hooked 279.8
falsehearted 354.31
dishonest 645.16
crooner 710.13

crop
n digestive system 2.18
head of hair 3.4
breast 283.6
growth 310.2
yield 472.5
whip 605.1
bunch 770.7
effect 887.1
production 893.2
harvest 1069.15
v feed on 8.28
excise 255.10
shorten 268.6
farm 1069.16
harvest 1069.19
crop circle 310.8
crop out
be exposed 31.5
appear 33.8
crop up
originate 818.13
turn up 831.6
crosier shaft 273.2
scepter 417.9
ecclesiastical insignia 647.4
staff 702.3
cross
n affliction 96.8
crux 170.4
staff 273.2
signature 527.10
monument 549.12
execution 605.5
insignia 647.1
heraldry 647.2
rood 702.3
hybrid 797.8
adversity 1011.1
impediment 1012.6
v disappoint 132.2
converge 169.2
crisscross 170.6
traverse 177.20
navigate 182.13
deny 335.4
oppose 451.3
contradict 451.6
bless 696.14
hybridize 797.13
counteract 900.6
pass 910.8
thwart 1012.15
adj irascible 110.19
angry 152.28
crossing 170.8
transverse 170.9
cruciform 170.10
oppositional 451.8
disagreeing 789.6
hybrid 797.15
adv crosswise 170.13
in opposition 451.9
crossbow 462.7
crossbreed
n hybrid 797.8
v procreate 78.8
hybridize 797.13
cross-check
n examination 938.3
collation 943.2

ensuring 970.8
v collate 943.5
verify 970.12
cross-country racing 755.2
crosscurrent flow 238.4
wind 318.1
opposition 451.1
counterforce 900.4
crossed
disappointed 132.5
cross 170.8
cruciform 170.10
hybrid 797.15
cross-examination
trial 598.5
argumentation 935.4
grilling 938.13
cross-eyed 28.12
cross-fertilization 78.3
cross-fertilize
reproduce 78.10
fertilize 890.8
cross fire 863.1
crossgrained
adj irascible 110.19
rough 288.6
coarse 294.6
negative 335.5
perverse 361.11
adv crosswise 170.13
against the grain 288.12
cross-hatching
network 170.3
line 517.6
engraving 713.2
crossing-over 858.3
cross-interrogation 938.13
cross one's fingers
be hopeful 124.7
await 130.8
doubt 955.6
cross one's heart
depose 334.6
promise 436.4
cross one's mind 931.18
cross out delete 255.12
obliterate 395.16
crosspatch
sorehead 110.11
misfit 789.4
crosspiece 170.5
cross purposes
hostility 451.2
disagreement 456.2
contrariety 779.1
crossroads
convergence 169.1
village 230.2
crisis 843.4
cross section
crossing 170.1
representative 349.7
part 793.1
cross-sex friendship 587.8
crosswind airflow 318.1
counterforce 900.4
crosswise
adj transverse 170.9
oblique 204.19
hindering 1012.17
unwieldy 1013.19

adv decussatively 170.13
transversely 204.24
crossword
enigma 522.8
riddle 522.9
crotch genitals 2.13
fork 171.4
crotchet angle 278.2
caprice 364.1
note 709.14
quirk 927.2
crotchety
capricious 364.5
counteractive 900.8
eccentric 927.5
crouch
n stoop 913.3
v fawn 138.7
lie low 274.5
bow down 433.10
cower 491.9
duck 913.8
crow
n blackness 38.4
laughter 116.4
speech defect 525.1
lever 906.4
v bird sound 60.5
laugh 116.8
put up a bold front 454.5
exult 502.9
speak 524.25
crow's-feet 291.3
crowbar
n extractor 192.9
lever 906.4
v get a purchase 906.8
crowd
n audience 48.6
social circle 582.5
the masses 606.2
clique 617.6
company 770.3
throng 770.4
attender 918.2
v make one's way 162.4
hurry 401.4
make haste 401.5
come together 770.16
fill 794.7
teem with 884.5
thrust 902.12
overload 993.15
obstruct 1012.12
densify 1045.9
crowd in enter 189.7
thrust in 191.7
intrude 214.5
crown
n summit 198.2
top part 198.4
architectural topping 198.5
head 198.6
supremacy 249.3
circle 280.2
finishing touch 407.3
victory 411.1
jewel 498.6
volume 554.4
trophy 646.3
heraldry 647.2

royal insignia 647.3
specie 728.4
money 728.8
tennis 748.1
limit 794.5
chandelier 1026.6
v top 198.9
cover 295.21
complete 407.6
take command 417.14
install 615.12
honor 646.8
glorify 662.13
perfect 1002.5
the Crown
sovereignty 417.8
the government 612.3
crowning
topping 198.11
chief 249.14
completing 407.9
ending 820.10
crowning achievement 1002.4
crown of thorns 96.8
crown roast 10.16
crucial critical 843.10
original 886.14
urgent 997.22
vital 997.23
crucible mixer 797.9
instrument of conversion
858.10
test 942.2
crucifix 170.4
crucifixion
agony 26.6
torment 96.7
capital punishment 604.7
crucify pain 26.7
torture 96.18
execute 604.17
stigmatize 661.9
work evil 1000.6
crude
n raw material 406.5
petroleum 1056.4
adj garish 35.20
offensive 98.18
raw 406.10
undeveloped 406.12
coarse 497.11
gaudy 501.20
ill-bred 505.6
inelegant 534.2
base 661.12
crudity
undevelopment 406.4
coarseness 497.2
baseness 661.3
cruel painful 26.10
cruel-hearted 144.26
pitiless 146.3
murderous 308.24
savage 671.21
cruelty
cruelness 144.11
unkindness 144.12
pitilessness 146.1
cruise
n journey 177.5
voyage 182.6

v journey 177.21
navigate 182.13
fly 184.36
make good 409.10
cruiser traveler 178.1
police car 179.11
motorboat 180.4
battleship 180.7
cruller 10.44
crumb
n scrap 248.3
minute 258.7
piece 793.3
powder 1051.5
v sprinkle 771.6
pulverize 1051.9
crumble
n powder 1051.5
v weaken 16.9
decrease 252.6
decay 393.22
be destroyed 395.22
disintegrate 806.3
pulverize 1051.9
powder 1051.10
crumbly frail 16.14
brittle 1050.4
pulverable 1051.13
crummy base 661.12
paltry 998.21
bad 1000.8
crumple
n wrinkle 291.3
v distort 265.5
ruffle 288.5
wrinkle 291.6
crunch
n rasp 58.3
poverty 619.1
concussion 671.8
crisis 843.4
crucial moment 843.5
impact 902.3
urgency 997.4
predicament 1013.5
v grate 58.10
shatter 802.13
collide 902.13
pulverize 1051.9
crunched 265.10
crusade
n campaign 458.3
cause 886.9
v espouse 509.13
crush
n liking 100.2
infatuation 104.3
squeezing 260.2
throng 770.4
full measure 794.3
pulp 1063.2
v sadden 112.18
aggrieve 112.19
unnerve 128.10
abase 137.5
squeeze 260.8
conquer 412.10
suppress 428.8
subdue 432.9
shatter 802.13
refute 958.5

pulverize 1051.9
pulp 1063.5
crushing
  n wretchedness 96.6
  suppression 428.2
  subdual 432.4
  pulverization 1051.4
  adj mortifying 98.21
  oppressive 98.24
  humiliating 137.15
  laborious 725.18
  troublesome 1013.18
crust
  n bread 10.28
  impudence 142.3
  exterior 206.2
  land 234.1
  incrustation 295.14
  upper class 607.2
  v incrust 295.27
crustacean
  n marine animal 311.29
  invertebrate 311.31
  adj invertebrate 311.50
crusty
  irascible 110.20
  impudent 142.10
  gruff 505.7
  hardened 1046.13
crutch
  n genitals 2.13
  fork 171.4
  staff 273.2
  aid 901.2
  v support 449.12
  help 901.21
crux cross 170.4
  enigma 522.8
  salient point 997.6
  dilemma 1013.7
  hitch 1013.8
cry
  n yell 59.1
  call 59.1
  animal noise 60.1
  weeping 115.2
  lament 115.3
  cheer 116.2
  publicity 352.4
  entreaty 440.2
  catchword 526.9
  report 552.6
  v call 59.6
  yelp 60.2
  weep 115.12
  wail 115.13
  cheer 116.6
  proclaim 352.13
crybaby 16.6
cry for wish for 100.16
  demand 421.5
  entreat 440.11
  require 963.9
cry havoc warn 399.5
  alarm 400.3
crying
  n weeping 115.2
  adj vociferous 59.10
  howling 60.6
  tearful 115.21
  demanding 421.9

urgent 997.22
cryogenics cold 1023.1
  refrigeration 1024.1
crypt compartment 197.2
  understructure 266.3
  cavity 284.2
  tomb 309.16
  church 703.9
cryptic secret 345.11
  latent 519.5
  implied 519.7
  enigmatic 522.17
cryptography
  exegetics 341.8
  cryptoanalysis 345.6
  writing 547.1
crystal
  n amphetamines 87.4
  snow 1023.8
  adj transparent 1029.4
  stony 1059.12
crystal ball
  the future 839.1
  divination 962.2
crystallize form 807.5
  solidify 1046.8
  petrify 1059.10
crystallography
  mineralogy 1058.10
  geology 1059.9
cry uncle weaken 16.9
  flinch 127.13
cry wolf 400.3
cub
  n boy 302.5
  fledgling 302.10
  adj unaccustomed 374.4
  immature 406.11
cubbyhole nook 197.3
  small space 258.3
  hiding place 346.4
cube triplicate 877.2
  square 879.3
cube farm 197.6
cubes 759.8
cubic spatial 158.10
  quadrangular 278.9
cubicle nook 197.3
  bedroom 197.7
cuckold 665.22
cuckoldry
  love affair 104.5
  illicit sex 665.7
cuckoo
  n imitator 336.4
  songbird 710.23
  v bird sound 60.5
  adj crazy 926.27
cud bite 8.2
  chewing tobacco 89.7
cuddle comfort 121.10
  snuggle 562.17
cuddly 104.24
cudgel whip 604.13
  club 902.20
cue braid 3.7
  tail 217.6
  clue 517.9
  tip 551.3
  hint 551.4
  role 704.10

playbook 704.21
  mood 978.4
  reminder 989.5
cuff
  n slap 604.3
  punishment 902.8
  v slap 604.12
  hit 902.19
cuffs 428.4
cuisine food 10.1
  cooking 11.1
  kitchen 11.4
cul-de-sac
  obstruction 293.3
  impasse 1013.6
culinary 11.6
cull excise 255.10
  select 371.14
  collect 472.11
culling
  elimination 773.2
  grouping 808.3
culmination
  summit 198.2
  completion 407.2
  accomplishment 794.4
  end 820.1
  acme of perfection 1002.3
culpable
  blameworthy 510.25
  guilty 656.3
culprit 660.8
cult ism 675.2
  worship 696.1
  ritualism 701.1
  system of belief 953.3
cultist
  n religionist 675.15
  adj pious 692.8
cultivate
  sensitize 24.7
  develop 392.10
  foster 449.16
  train 568.13
  nurture 587.12
  process 892.9
  culture 1069.17
cultivated
  improved 392.13
  elegant 496.8
  well-bred 504.17
  learned 928.21
cultural 568.18
cultural layer 296.1
cultural literacy 570.1
cultural studies 312.10
culture
  n humankind 312.1
  society 373.2
  cultivation 392.3
  taste 496.1
  good breeding 504.4
  scholarship 928.5
  agriculture 1069.1
  cultivation 1069.13
  v growth 1069.17
  raise 1070.6
cultured
  improved 392.13
  elegant 496.8
  well-bred 504.17

learned 928.21
culvert 239.2
cumbersome
  bulky 257.19
  onerous 297.17
  bungling 414.20
  hampering 1012.18
  unwieldy 1013.19
cumbrous
  bulky 257.19
  onerous 297.17
  stiff 534.3
  hampering 1012.18
cum laude 646.11
cumulate
  v store up 386.11
  assemble 770.18
  adj assembled 770.21
cumulative
  additive 253.8
  accumulative 770.23
  evidential 957.16
cunctation 846.5
cuneiform
  n phonetic symbol 546.2
  adj triangular 278.8
cunning
  n falseheartedness 354.4
  deceit 356.3
  skill 413.1
  craftiness 415.1
  artfulness 415.1
  shrewdness 920.3
  adj falsehearted 354.31
  deceitful 356.22
  skillful 413.22
  well-laid 413.30
  crafty 415.12
  shrewd 920.15
cup
  n container 195.1
  cupful 196.4
  cavity 284.2
  victory 411.1
  monument 549.12
  trophy 646.3
  hockey 749.1
  golf 751.1
  soccer 752.1
  skiing 753.1
  track 755.1
  fate 964.2
  v bleed 91.27
  ladle 176.17
  be concave 284.12
  hollow 284.13
cupboard
  container 195.1
  storehouse 386.6
cupholder meal 8.6
Cupid symbol 104.8
  Love 104.7
cupidity 100.8
cupola tower 272.6
  arch 279.4
  roof 295.6
cupping
  bloodletting 91.20
  drawing 192.3
cur mongrel 311.18
  beast 660.6

curable 396.25
curate 699.2
curative
  remedial 86.39
  tonic 396.22
curator steward 574.4
  treasurer 729.12
  guardian 1008.6
curb
  n kerb 211.6
  pavement 383.6
  restraint 428.1
  stock exchange 737.7
  check 1012.7
  v slow 175.9
  restrain 428.7
  hinder 1012.10
curd
  n clot 1045.7
  semiliquid 1062.5
  v thicken 1045.10
curdle thicken 1045.10
  emulsify 1062.10
cure
  n remedy 86.1
  treatment 91.14
  curing 396.7
  commission 615.1
  benefice 698.9
  protectorship 1008.2
  v remedy 86.38
  treat 91.24
  disaccustom 374.2
  restore 396.15
  preserve 397.9
  prepare 405.6
  solidify 1046.8
  dry 1066.6
curé 699.5
cure-all 86.3
curfew 315.5
curie 1037.6
curio oddity 870.5
  trifle 998.5
curiosity desire 100.1
  marvel 122.2
  oddity 870.5
  inquisitiveness 981
  alertness 981.1
  attention 983.1
  interest 983.2
curious careful 339.10
  odd 870.11
  inquiring 938.36
  inquisitive 981.5
  attentive 983.15
  interested 983.16
curl
  n lock 3.5
  exercise 84.2
  curve 279.2
  coil 281.2
  v curve 279.6
  coil 281.5
curler
  curling iron 281.3
  wave 916.4
curlicue 281.2
curl up rest 20.6
  snuggle 121.10
curly 281.9

curmudgeon
  sorehead 110.11
  niggard 484.4
currency
  publicity 352.4
  fashionableness 578.2
  money 728.1
  prevalence 864.2
  usualness 869.2
current
  n direction 161.1
  course 172.2
  flow 238.4
  wind 318.1
  trend 896.2
  thoughts 931.4
  electricity 1032.2
  v follow the rule 867.4
  adj published 352.17
  customary 373.13
  reported 552.15
  fashionable 578.11
  existent 761.13
  happening 831.9
  present 838.2
  prevalent 864.12
  usual 869.9
  well-known 928.27
current affairs 552.1
current events 551.1
curriculum 568.8
curried cooked 11.7
  zestful 68.7
curry
  n stew 10.11
  v cook 11.5
  comb 79.21
  tend 1070.7
curry favor 138.9
curse
  n affliction 96.8
  malediction 513
  hex 513.1
  oath 513.4
  spell 691.1
  bad influence 1000.4
  bane 1001.1
  adversity 1011.1
  v accurse 513.5
  swear 513.6
  blaspheme 694.5
  work evil 1000.6
cursed
  accursed 513.9
  execrable 1000.10
cursive 547.22
cursory
  insignificant 248.6
  shallow 276.5
  unwilling 325.5
  careless 340.11
  hasty 401.9
curt short 268.8
  taciturn 344.9
  gruff 505.7
  concise 537.6
curtail reduce 252.7
  subtract 255.9
  contract 260.7
  shorten 268.6
  restrain 428.7

  take from 480.21
curtain
  n cover 295.2
  partition 345.3
  veil 346.2
  act 704.7
  stage 704.16
  scenery 704.20
  end 820.1
  obstacle 1012.4
  shade 1028.1
  v cover 295.19
  conceal 346.6
  shade 1028.5
curtain call 704.7
curtain raiser act 704.7
  overture 708.26
  countdown 816.2
  inauguration 818.5
curtains death 307.1
  end 820.1
curtsy
  n obeisance 155.2
  greeting 585.4
  crouch 913.3
  v bow 155.6
  show respect 433.10
  greet 585.10
  be polite 913.9
curvaceous
  curved 279.7
  comely 1016.18
curvature curving 279.1
  turn 279.1
curve
  n deviation 164.1
  angle 278.2
  sinus 279.2
  trick 356.6
  race 756.3
  v deviate 164.3
  deflect 164.5
  angle 278.5
  turn 279.6
  adj curved 279.7
curvy crooked 204.20
  wavy 279.7
  comely 1016.18
cushion
  n silencer 51.4
  partition 213.5
  moderator 670.3
  bedding 901.20
  safeguard 1008.3
  softness 1047.4
  v muffle 51.9
  relieve 120.5
  absorb the shock 670.8
  support 901.21
  protect 1008.18
  soften 1047.6
cushioned 121.11
cushy
  comfortable 121.11
  easy 1014.13
cusp point 285.3
  crisis 843.4
  salience 997.6
cuss
  n oath 513.4
  v curse 513.6

cussedness
  ill humor 110.3
  malice 144.5
  perversity 361.3
custodian cleaner 79.14
  hospital staff 90.11
  jailer 429.10
  steward 574.4
  guardian 1008.6
custodianship
  vigilance 339.4
  usage 387.2
  preservation 397.1
  custody 429.5
  thrift 635.1
  protectorship 1008.2
custody vigilance 339.4
  storage 386.5
  preservation 397.1
  custodianship 429.5
  directorship 573.4
  protectorship 1008.2
custom
  n behavior 321.1
  convention 373.1
  rite 373.1
  habit 373.3
  fashion 578.1
  social more 579.1
  patronage 731.6
  market 733.3
  tradition 842.2
  adj made 892.18
customary
  wonted 373.13
  conventional 579.5
  orthodox 687.7
  traditional 842.12
  usual 869.9
customer man 76.5
  client 733.4
customize 405.8
customized 405.17
custom-made
  tailored 5.48
  made 892.18
customs 630.10
cut
  n trauma 85.38
  pain 96.5
  indignity 156.2
  snub 157.2
  absence 222.4
  crack 224.2
  degree 245.1
  gains 251.3
  curtailment 252.4
  reduction 255.2
  form 262.1
  shortcut 268.5
  notch 289.1
  furrow 290.1
  trench 290.2
  lamina 296.2
  attempt 403.3
  thrust 459.3
  portion 477.5
  gibe 508.2
  mark 517.5
  dividend 624.7
  discount 631.1

sadden 112.18
cloud 319.7
stain 1004.6
bedarken 1027.9
grow dark 1027.12
opaque 1031.2
dark horse
candidate 610.9
the unknown 930.6
small chance 972.9
dark humor 489.1
darkness
blindness 30.1
inconspicuousness 32.2
blackness 38.1
duskiness 38.2
gloom 112.7
night 315.4
obscurity 522.3
unenlightenment 930.3
lightlessness 1027.1
opaqueness 1031.1
dark-skinned 38.10
darling
n sweetheart 104.9
favorite 104.15
child 302.3
endearment term 562.6
adj beloved 104.23
darn
v repair 396.14
curse 513.5
interj damn! 513.12
a darn 998.5
dart
n swiftness 174.6
arrow 462.6
sting 1001.5
v speed 174.8
throw 904.10
Darwinism 861.4
dash
n vim 17.2
disappointment 132.1
run 174.3
hint 248.4
haste 401.1
showiness 501.3
display 501.4
line 517.6
spirit 544.4
admixture 797.7
hit 902.4
v sadden 112.18
unnerve 128.10
disappoint 132.2
speed 174.8
billow 238.22
make haste 401.5
defeat 412.11
mark 517.19
throw 904.10
thwart 1012.15
moisten 1065.12
adv suddenly 830.9
interj damn! 513.12
dashboard meal 8.6
dashing
fast 174.15
showy 501.19
chic 578.13

dash off
hasten off 188.10
do carelessly 340.9
improvise 365.8
make haste 401.5
write 547.21
portray 712.18
transcribe 718.6
dash one's hope
shatter 125.11
disappoint 132.2
dastardly 491.12
data records 551.1
the facts 761.4
collection 770.11
knowledge 928.1
premise 935.7
evidence 957.1
information 1042.15
database 871.1
data point 552.3
data processing 1042.1
data transmission 347.2
date
n lover 104.11
appointment 582.8
engagement 704.11
assembly 770.2
age 824.4
point of time 832.4
v come together 770.16
be dated 832.13
age 842.9
datebook 549.11
dated chronologic 832.15
anachronous 833.3
past 837.7
old-fashioned 842.16
dateless timeless 822.3
perpetual 829.7
old 842.10
date movie 706.2
date rape
perversion 75.11
sexual possession 480.3
datum particular 766.3
knowledge 928.1
evidence 957.1
daub
n bad likeness 350.2
picture 712.10
stain 1004.3
v color 35.14
soil 80.16
coat 295.24
misdraw 350.4
portray 712.18
stain 1004.6
oil 1056.8
daughter
brother 559.3
descendant 561.3
daunt deter 127.18
dissuade 379.3
domineer 612.15
daunting 127.28
dauntless
plucky 359.14
unafraid 492.19
dawdle
n slowpoke 175.5

idler 331.8
v lag 166.4
linger 175.8
dally 331.14
protract 827.9
wait 846.12
dawn
n morning 314.3
beginning 818.1
daylight 1025.10
v grow light 1025.28
adj morning 314.6
dawn on 521.5
dawn upon one 931.18
day period 824.1
moment 824.2
age 824.4
date 832.4
daylight 1025.10
day after day
for a long time 827.14
constantly 847.7
repeatedly 849.16
daybook
record book 549.11
periodical 555.1
account book 628.4
chronicle 832.9
daybreak 314.3
daycare 1008.1
day-care center 567.2
daydream
n wistfulness 100.4
illusion 976.1
abstractedness 985.2
dream 986.9
v wander 984.3
muse 985.9
dream 986.17
day in day out
regularly 781.8
for a long time 827.14
constantly 847.7
daylight dawn 314.3
publicity 352.4
dayshine 1025.10
daylong 827.12
day off vacation 20.3
holiday 20.4
absence 222.4
pause 857.3
day of reckoning 839.3
day of rest 20.5
daytime 1025.10
day trip 20.3
daze
n trance 92.19
confusion 985.3
v blind 30.7
astonish 122.6
perplex 971.13
confuse 985.7
shine 1025.24
dazed stupefied 25.7
blinded 30.10
foolish 923.8
in a dilemma 971.25
mazed 985.14
dazzle
n showiness 501.3
v blind 30.7

astonish 122.6
cut a dash 501.13
confuse 985.7
shine 1025.24
dazzling
blinding 30.11
gorgeous 1016.20
bright 1025.33
db 50.7
D-day zero hour 459.13
crucial moment
843.5
deacon
holy orders 699.4
clergy 699.10
deactivate
disarm 465.11
disband 771.8
dead
n silence 51.1
corpse 307.15
the majority 307.16
adj tired 21.8
asleep 22.22
insensible 25.6
unconscious 25.8
colorless 36.7
muffled 52.17
insipid 65.2
dull 117.6
inert 173.14
closed 293.9
lifeless 307.29
languid 331.20
no more 762.11
ended 820.8
past 837.7
obsolete 842.15
lackluster 1027.17
inanimate 1055.5
adv directly 161.23
extremely 247.22
exactly 973.21
deadbeat 138.5
dead duck 125.8
deaden weaken 16.10
desensitize 25.4
muffle 51.9
numb 94.8
relieve 120.5
moderate 670.6
cushion 670.8
dull 1027.10
dead end
n obstruction 293.3
impasse 1013.6
adj closed 293.9
deadening
n weakening 16.5
relief 120.1
modulation 670.2
adj numbing 25.9
anesthetic 86.47
relieving 120.9
mitigating 670.14
deadeye 904.8
dead giveaway 351.2
deadhead
freeloader 634.3
playgoer 704.27
dead letter 520.1

decapitate 604.17
decathlon sport 744.1
  track meet 755.2
decay
  n filth 80.7
  decomposition 393.6
  rot 393.7
  disintegration 806.1
  dissociation 806.2
  v decompose 393.22
  disintegrate 806.3
decease
  n death 307.1
  end 820.1
  v die 307.18
deceased
  n corpse 307.15
  adj dead 307.29
  past 837.7
deceit
  falseness 356.3
  stratagem 415.3
deceitful
  falsehearted 354.31
  false 356.22
  cunning 415.12
  improper 645.18
deceive lie 354.19
  beguile 356.14
  live by one's wits 415.9
  outwit 415.11
  impose on 643.7
  be dishonest 645.11
  seduce 665.20
deceiver imitator 336.4
  misleader 357.1
  deluder 357.1
  evildoer 593.1
  con man 645.10
  criminal 660.9
  seducer 665.12
  cheater 759.22
deceleration
  slowing 175.4
  decline 252.2
  restraint 428.1
decent kind 143.13
  indulgent 427.8
  decorous 496.9
  conventional 579.5
  right 637.3
  honest 644.13
  modest 664.5
  sufficient 991.6
  expedient 995.5
  tolerable 999.20
decentralization
  divergence 171.1
  deconcentration 771.2
deception
  concealment 346.1
  sham 354.3
  falseness 356.3
  calculated lie 356.1
  hoax 356.7
  cheating 759.13
  illusion 976.1
deceptive
  deceiving 356.21
  sophistical 936.10
  erroneous 975.16

illusory 976.9
decibel 50.7
decide
  resolve 359.7
  induce 375.22
  determine 886.12
  exercise influence 894.8
  judge 946.11
  make sure 970.11
  will 323.2
decide against 444.5
decided
  downright 247.12
  affirmative 334.8
  resolute 359.11
  ended 820.8
  unqualified 960.2
  assured 970.20
  confident 970.21
  emphatic 997.21
decide upon 371.16
deciduous
  descending 194.11
  arboreal 310.39
  perennial 310.44
  transient 828.7
decimal tenth 882.22
  numeric 1017.23
decimate
  slaughter 308.17
  destroy 395.10
decipher
  explain 341.10
  make clear 521.6
  solve 940.2
decipherable
  intelligible 521.10
  legible 521.12
  solvable 940.3
decision will 323.1
  resolution 359.1
  choice 371.1
  judgment 598.9
  fight 754.3
  verdict 946.5
decisive
  resolute 359.11
  mandatory 420.12
  critical 843.10
  prompt 845.9
  causal 886.13
  convincing 953.26
  evidential 957.16
  unqualified 960.2
  certain 970.13
deck
  n dose 87.20
  ground covering 199.3
  layer 296.1
  card 758.2
  bundle 770.8
  platform 901.13
  v clothe 5.39
  overcome 412.7
  ornament 498.8
  beat 902.17
  fell 913.5
deckhand 183.6
declaim
  proclaim 352.13
  speak 524.19

hold forth 543.10
  overact 704.31
declamatory
  elocutionary 543.12
  grandiloquent 545.8
declaration
  acknowledgment 332.3
  affirmation 334.1
  announcement 352.2
  decree 420.4
  remark 524.3
  statement 598.7
  profession 953.7
  testimony 957.2
declare affirm 334.5
  announce 352.12
  command 420.8
  speak 524.23
  state 953.12
declare war
  contend 457.13
  make war on 458.14
déclassé
  n outcast 586.4
  adj upper-class 607.10
decline
  n sinkage 194.2
  declivity 204.5
  declension 252.2
  deterioration 393.3
  cheapening 633.4
  price 738.9
  close 820.3
  shortcoming 911.1
  senility 922.10
  v weaken 16.9
  fail 85.48
  recede 168.2
  sink 194.6
  slope 204.10
  decrease 252.6
  age 303.10
  reject 372.2
  sink 393.17
  refuse 442.3
  grammaticize 530.16
  cheapen 633.6
  fall short 911.2
  fall on evil days 1011.11
declivity descent 204.5
  slope 237.2
decoction extract 192.7
  product 192.8
  concoction 405.3
  imbuement 797.2
  boiling 1020.2
  solution 1064.3
decode
  make clear 521.6
  solve 940.2
decoding
  translation 341.3
  explanation 341.4
  information theory
    551.7
  solution 940.1
décolleté
  n nudity 6.3
  adj unclad 6.13
decoloration 36.3
decommission 465.11

decompose
  decay 393.22
  disintegrate 806.3
decompression
  rest 20.1
  composure 106.2
  relief 120.1
  rarefaction 299.2
deconcentrate 771.7
deconsecrate
  depose 447.4
  disbelieve 695.14
decontamination
  sanitation 79.3
  extenuation 600.5
  radiation 1037.1
decontrolled 430.27
decor furniture 229.1
  ornamentation 498.1
  scenery 704.20
decorate add 253.4
  trim 498.8
  ornament 545.7
  honor 646.8
  beautify 1016.15
decoration extra 254.4
  ornamentation 498.1
  honor 646.5
  insignia 647.1
  visual arts 712.1
  beautification 1016.10
decorative
  ornamental 498.10
  artistic 712.19
  beautifying 1016.22
decorative arts 712.1
decorator 716.11
decorous solemn 111.3
  tasteful 496.9
  conventional 579.5
  ceremonious 580.8
  right 637.3
  decent 664.5
decorum
  decorousness 496.2
  social convention 579.1
  etiquette 580.3
  propriety 637.2
  decency 664.2
decoy
  n trap 356.12
  shill 357.5
  lure 377.3
  by-bidder 733.6
  v trap 356.20
  lure 377.5
decrease
  n descent 194.1
  lessening 252.1
  decrescence 252.1
  reduction 255.2
  contraction 260.1
  deterioration 393.3
  waste 473.2
  depression 913.1
  v quantify 244.4
  graduate 245.4
  diminish 252.6
  reduce 252.7
  subtract 255.9
  contract 260.7

waste 473.5
decree
  n command 420.4
  law 673.3
  verdict 946.5
  predetermination 964.1
  v will 323.2
  command 420.8
  legislate 613.10
  legalize 673.9
  pass judgment 946.13
decrepit unsound 16.15
  stricken in years 303.18
  dilapidated 393.33
  senile 922.23
decrescendo
  n faintness 52.1
  decline 252.2
  music 708.25
  adj faint 52.16
  decreasing 252.11
  music 708.53
  adv decreasingly 252.12
decriminalize
  authorize 443.11
  legalize 673.9
decry
  censure 510.13
  disparage 512.8
dedicate
  commit 477.11
  sanctify 685.5
dedicated
  zealous 101.9
  resolute 359.11
  devoted 587.21
  unselfish 652.5
  sanctified 685.8
dedicate oneself to
  be determined 359.8
  espouse 509.13
dedication
  zeal 101.2
  resolution 359.1
  commitment 477.4
  makeup 554.12
  devotion 587.7
  duty 641.1
  unselfishness 652.1
  sanctification 685.3
deduce elicit 192.14
  reason 935.15
  conclude 946.10
  suppose 951.10
deduct reduce 252.7
  subtract 255.9
  discount 631.2
deductible
  n insurance 1008.4
  adj tax-free 630.16
deduction
  decrease 252.1
  subtraction 255.1
  decrement 255.7
  tax 630.9
  discount 631.1
  relation 775.1
  reasoning 935.3
  conclusion 946.4
deductive
  subtractive 255.13

dialectic 935.22
deed
  n act 328.3
  exploit 492.6
  v transfer 629.3
deedholder 470.2
deejay 1034.23
deely-bobber 1052.5
deem judge 946.8
  suppose 951.10
  think 953.11
de-emphasize
  minimize 252.9
  moderate 670.6
  attach little importance to 998.12
deep
  n pit 275.2
  secret 345.5
  adj colored 35.17
  resonant 54.11
  heart-felt 93.24
  spacious 158.11
  interior 207.6
  great 247.6
  broad 269.6
  profound 275.10
  cunning 415.12
  recondite 522.16
  wise 920.17
  learned 928.21
  adv beyond one's depth 275.16
the deep sea 240.1
  ocean depths 275.4
deep blue 45.3
deep-dyed
  fast-dyed 35.18
  confirmed 373.18
  thorough 794.10
  established 855.13
deepen aggravate 119.2
  intensify 251.5
  broaden 269.4
  lower 275.8
deep-felt 93.24
deep-freezer 1024.5
deep-fry 11.5
deep-rooted deep 275.10
  confirmed 373.18
  established 855.13
deep-sea
  aquatic 182.58
  oceanic 240.8
  deep-water 275.14
deep-seated
  deep 275.10
  confirmed 373.18
  intrinsic 767.7
  established 855.13
deep-set deep 275.10
  confirmed 373.18
  established 855.13
deep-six abandon 370.5
  discard 390.7
deep sleep 22.5
the Deep South 231.7
deep thought
  thoughtfulness 931.3
  engrossment 983.3
deep throat 551.5

deer 311.5
de-escalation
  decrease 252.1
  modulation 670.2
  depression 913.1
deface deform 265.7
  blemish 1004.4
  offend 1015.5
de facto
  adj existent 761.13
  real 761.15
  adv really 761.16
defame malign 512.9
  stigmatize 661.9
default
  n absence 222.4
  disobedience 327.1
  neglect 340.1
  nonobservance 435.1
  arrears 623.2
  nonpayment 625.1
  shortcoming 911.1
  v be absent 222.7
  neglect 340.6
  lose 473.4
  not pay 625.6
  play 751.4
defeat
  n disappointment 132.1
  failure 410.1
  beating 412.1
  frustration 1012.3
  v disappoint 132.2
  best 249.7
  do for 395.11
  triumph over 411.5
  worst 412.6
  overcome 412.7
  refute 958.5
  thwart 1012.15
defeatism negation 335.1
  uncourageousness 491.2
defeatist
  n pessimist 125.7
  adj pessimistic 125.16
defecate
  have a bowel movement 12.13
  evacuate 909.22
defect
  n disease 85.1
  apostatize 363.7
  deficiency 795.2
  fault 1003.2
  blemish 1004.1
  v leave home 188.17
  emigrate 190.16
  deny 335.4
  secede 370.6
  disregard 435.3
  renege 858.13
defection
  departure 188.1
  emigration 190.7
  denial 335.2
  apostasy 363.2
  desertion 370.2
  nonpayment 625.1
  change 852.1
  conversion 858.3
  fault 1003.2

defective
  n cripple 85.45
  idiot 924.8
  adj incomplete 795.4
  erroneous 975.16
  insufficient 992.9
  imperfect 1003.4
  blemished 1004.8
defend guard 460.8
  offer in defense 600.10
  protect 1008.18
defendant
  oppositionist 452.3
  litigant 598.11
  accused 599.6
defender
  champion 460.7
  justifier 600.8
  supporter 616.9
  team 752.2
  protector 1008.5
defense protection 460
  front 460.1
  pleadings 598.6
  plea 600.2
  basketball game 747.3
  hockey strategy 749.2
  team 749.5
  fight 754.3
  countermeasure 900.5
  argumentation 935.4
  rebuttal 939.2
  wall 1008.1
  barrier 1012.5
defense lawyer 597.1
defenseless
  helpless 19.18
  forlorn 584.12
  unprotected 1006.14
defense mechanism
  reaction 92.23
  avoidance 368.1
  instinct 460.1
  block 990.3
defensive
  defending 460.11
  protective 1008.23
defer retreat 163.6
  retract 168.3
  postpone 846.9
deference respect 155.1
  obedience 326.1
  submission 433.1
  observance 434.1
  courtesy 504.1
  duty 641.1
deferential
  respectful 155.8
  obedient 326.3
  obeisant 433.16
  courteous 504.14
  dutiful 641.13
defer to respect 155.4
  obey 326.2
  submit to 433.9
  observe 434.2
defiance
  impenitence 114.2
  refractoriness 327.2
  ungovernability 361.4
  resistance 453.1

defying 454
disobedience 454.1
declaration of war 458.6
defiant
impenitent 114.5
disobedient 327.8
refractory 327.10
ungovernable 361.12
defying 454.7
deficiency
inadequacy 250.3
incompleteness 795.1
want 795.2
lack 992.4
imperfection 1003.1
fault 1003.2
deficient
inadequate 250.7
slipshod 340.12
incomplete 795.4
short of 911.5
insufficient 992.9
imperfect 1003.4
deficit difference 255.8
debt 623.1
arrears 623.2
deficiency 795.2
shortcoming 911.1
want 992.4
defile
n valley 237.7
narrow place 270.3
passageway 383.3
v foul 80.17
march 177.30
misuse 389.4
corrupt 393.12
vilify 512.10
impair 654.10
stigmatize 661.9
seduce 665.20
file 812.7
work evil 1000.6
define
circumscribe 210.4
interpret 341.9
mark 517.19
name 527.11
fix 855.9
characterize 865.10
defined distinct 31.7
circumscribed 210.6
clear 521.11
particular 865.12
defining
limiting 210.9
classificational 809.7
definite distinct 31.7
audible 50.16
circumscribed 210.6
resolute 359.11
clear 521.11
particular 865.12
unqualified 960.2
certain 970.13
definite article 530.6
definition
distinctness 31.2
circumscription 210.1
interpretation 341.1
explanation 518.3

clearness 521.2
naming 527.2
characterization 865.8
television reception 1035.5
definitive
limiting 210.9
downright 247.12
ending 820.10
final 820.11
unqualified 960.2
deflate disable 19.10
humiliate 137.4
reduce 252.7
collapse 260.10
cheapen 633.6
disprove 958.4
deflation
humiliation 137.2
decrease 252.1
contraction 260.4
collapse 410.3
cheapening 633.4
business cycle 731.10
deflect deviate 164.5
oblique 204.9
curve 279.6
disincline 379.4
prevent 1012.14
deflection
bending 164.2
obliquity 204.1
angle 278.2
curve 279.3
radar interference 1036.12
deflector 1035.11
deflower
corrupt 393.12
possess sexually 480.15
seduce 665.20
defluxion outflow 190.4
descent 194.1
stream 238.4
defoliant 1001.3
defoliate 802.14
deforestation 1069.3
deform distort 263.3
misshape 265.7
change 852.7
blemish 1004.4
deformation
disfigurement 265.3
misrepresentation 350.1
deterioration 393.3
blemish 1004.1
deformed
malformed 265.12
freakish 870.13
blemished 1004.8
unshapely 1015.8
deformity disease 85.1
cripple 85.45
deformation 265.3
oddity 870.3
blemish 1004.1
hideousness 1015.2
defraud cheat 356.18
steal 482.13
defray 624.18
defrock depose 447.4
disgrace 661.8
dismiss 909.19

defrost 1020.21
deft 413.22
defunct dead 307.29
no more 762.11
ended 820.8
past 837.7
defuse relieve 120.5
keep the peace 464.8
pacify 465.7
moderate 670.6
defy
n challenge 454.2
v confront 216.8
disobey 327.6
violate 435.4
bid defiance 454.3
dare 492.9
resist 453.2
make war on 458.14
thwart 1012.15
dégagé
nonchalant 106.15
careless 340.11
informal 581.3
degenerate
n reprobate 660.4
v corrupt 393.12
deteriorate 393.16
go wrong 654.9
lapse into disorder 810.8
be changed 852.6
defect 858.13
evolve 861.5
fall on evil days 1011.11
adj deteriorating 393.45
corrupt 654.14
changed 852.10
apostate 858.20
degradable
biodegradable 393.47
disintegrative 806.5
degradation
deterioration 393.3
decay 393.6
demotion 447.1
knavery 645.2
turpitude 654.5
baseness 661.3
infamy 661.4
disintegration 806.1
banishment 909.4
depression 913.1
degrade abase 137.5
corrupt 393.12
demote 447.3
disparage 512.8
disgrace 661.8
dismiss 909.19
degree grade 245.1
rank 245.1
measure 300.2
extent 300.3
class 607.1
academic honor 648.6
staff 708.29
interval 709.20
continuity 807.2
degrees
points of the compass 161.3
graduate 572.8
dehortation 379.1

dehumanize 144.15
dehumidify 1066.6
dehydrate
preserve 397.9
dry 1066.6
dehydration 1066.1
deice 1020.21
deification
respect 155.1
praise 509.5
glorification 662.8
idolization 697.2
elevation 912.1
deify respect 155.4
praise 509.12
glorify 662.13
idolatrize 697.5
exalt 912.6
deign condescend 137.8
give oneself airs 141.8
consent 441.2
deism 675.5
deist 675.16
deity divinity 677.1
spirit 677.1
god 678.2
déjà vu 689.6
remembering 989.3
deject 112.18
dejected sullen 110.24
depressed 112.22
dejection
defecation 12.2
excrement 12.3
sullenness 110.8
depression 112.3
de jure 673.13
delay
n slowing 175.4
stoppage 846.2
hindrance 1012.1
v dawdle 175.8
slow 175.9
do nothing 329.2
put away 390.6
retard 846.8
postpone 846.9
wait 846.12
hinder 1012.10
delectable tasty 63.8
delicious 97.10
delectation 95.2
delegate
n legate 576.2
v commit 478.16
commission 615.10
deputize 862.7
delegation
authority 417.12
commitment 478.2
deputation 576.13
commission 615.1
substitution 862.1
delete erase 255.12
obliterate 395.16
separate 802.8
end 820.5
deleted absent 222.11
ended 820.8
deleterious
disadvantageous 996.6

harmful 1000.12
deliberate
  v hesitate 362.7
  confer 541.10
  discuss 541.11
  consider 931.12
  adj slow 175.10
  intentional 380.8
  leisurely 402.6
  cautious 494.8
deliberated
  intentional 380.8
  reasoned 935.21
deliberation
  slowness 175.1
  intentionality 380.3
  leisureliness 402.2
  caution 494.1
  discussion 541.6
  legislative procedure 613.6
  consideration 931.2
deliberative
  conciliar 423.5
  legislative 613.11
  cognitive 931.21
delicacy tidbit 10.8
  frailty 16.2
  sensitivity 24.3
  unhealthiness 85.3
  sensibility 93.4
  tenderness 93.6
  considerateness 143.3
  insignificance 248.1
  thinness 270.4
  smoothness 294.3
  lightness 298.1
  meticulousness 339.3
  nicety 495.3
  taste 496.1
  decency 664.2
  margin 780.2
  discrimination 944.1
  accuracy 973.5
  dangerousness 1006.2
  daintiness 1016.4
  softness 1047.1
  brittleness 1050.1
delicate frail 16.14
  sensitive 24.12
  soft-colored 35.22
  tasty 63.8
  feeling 93.20
  considerate 143.16
  dainty 248.7
  thin 270.16
  smooth 294.8
  light 298.12
  meticulous 339.12
  nice 495.11
  elegant 496.8
  decent 664.5
  discriminating 944.7
  exact 973.17
  precarious 1006.12
  difficult 1013.17
  fine 1016.19
  soft 1047.8
  brittle 1050.4
delicatessen 8.17
delicious edible 8.33
  tasty 63.8

delightful 97.7
delectable 97.10
excellent 999.13
delight
  n happiness 95.2
  tendency 896.1
  v delectate 95.10
  be pleased 95.12
  rejoice 116.5
  exult 502.9
  amuse 743.21
delighted pleased 95.15
  amused 743.26
delightful tasty 63.8
  exquisite 97.7
  amusing 743.27
Delilah 665.15
delimit
  circumscribe 210.4
  mark 517.19
delimitation
  circumscription 210.1
  boundary 211.3
delineate outline 211.9
  represent 349.8
  describe 349.9
  plan 381.11
  portray 712.18
delineation
  outline 211.2
  representation 349.1
  description 349.2
  diagram 381.3
  line 517.6
  drawing 712.4
  sketch 712.12
  fiction 722.1
delineator limner 716.2
  draftsman 716.3
delinquency
  misbehavior 322.1
  disobedience 327.1
  nonobservance 435.1
  nonpayment 625.1
  wrong 638.1
  vice 654.1
  misdeed 655.2
  lawbreaking 674.3
  shortcoming 911.1
delinquent
  n evildoer 593.1
  defaulter 625.5
  wrongdoer 660.8
  adj defaulting 625.10
  wrong 638.3
deliquescent
  decreasing 252.11
  liquefied 1064.6
delirious feverish 85.58
  fervent 93.18
  overzealous 101.12
  frenzied 105.25
  out of one's head 926.31
delirium fever 85.7
  fury 105.8
  deliriousness 926.8
  figment of the imagination
  986.5
delirium tremens
  alcoholism 88.3
  shaking 917.2

mania 926.9
hallucination 976.7
deliver release 120.6
  transfer 176.10
  do 328.6
  rescue 398.3
  accomplish 407.4
  succeed 409.7
  liberate 431.4
  hand 478.13
  say 524.22
  send 629.3
  play 745.5
  perform 892.11
deliverance
  release 120.2
  escape 369.1
  rescue 398.1
  liberation 431.1
  giving 478.1
  transfer 629.1
  verdict 946.5
deliverer
  preserver 397.5
  savior 592.2
delivery birth 1.1
  transportation 176.3
  escape 369.1
  rescue 398.1
  liberation 431.1
  giving 478.1
  articulation 524.5
  transfer 629.1
  pitch 745.3
  game 750.2
dell highland 237.7
  valley 284.9
delocalize 176.11
delouse 79.24
Delphic oracle 962.7
delta fork 171.4
  plain 236.1
  point of land 283.9
deltoid
  diverging 171.8
  spread 259.11
  triangular 278.8
  three 876.3
  tripartite 878.4
delude deceive 356.10
  be mistaken 975.10
deluded 926.26
deluge
  n torrent 238.5
  overflow 238.6
  rainstorm 316.2
  throng 770.4
  superabundance 993.2
  wetting 1065.6
  v overflow 238.17
  submerge 367.7
  oversupply 993.14
  flood 1065.14
delusion sham 354.3
  deception 356.1
  error 975.1
  illusion 976.1
delusional 356.21
deluxe 501.21
delve
  excavate 284.15

search 938.31
cultivate 1069.17
demagnetize 1032.27
demagogue
  n instigator 375.11
  speaker 543.4
  v declaim 543.10
demand
  n extortion 192.6
  stipulation 421.2
  claim 421.1
  request 440.1
  fee 630.6
  prerogative 642.1
  imposition 643.1
  sale 734.1
  question 938.10
  requirement 963.2
  v extort 192.15
  prescribe 420.9
  summon 420.11
  ask 421.5
  oblige 424.5
  request 440.9
  charge 630.12
  impose 643.4
  inquire 938.20
  require 963.9
demanding
  meticulous 339.12
  exacting 421.9
  strict 425.6
  importunate 440.18
  difficult 1013.17
demand-pull inflation 632.33
demarcate
  circumscribe 210.4
  mark 517.19
  differentiate 780.6
  characterize 865.10
  discriminate 944.4
demarcation
  circumscription 210.1
  exclusion 773.1
  differentiation 780.4
  distinction 944.3
demasculinize
  unman 19.12
  feminize 77.12
demean 137.5
demeaning
  inferior 250.6
  disgraceful 661.11
demeanor looks 33.4
  behavior 321.1
demented
  turbulent 671.18
  insane 926.26
dementia 926.1
demesne
  sphere 231.2
  real estate 471.6
  farm 1069.8
Demeter
  fertility 890.5
  agricultural deity 1069.4
demigod
  brave person 492.7
  hero 659.5
  godling 678.3
demilitarize 465.11

dependability
trustworthiness 644.6
reliability 970.4
dependable
trustworthy 644.19
reliable 970.17
unhazardous 1007.5
dependence
substance abuse 87.1
hope 124.1
pendency 202.1
dependence 432.3
supporter 616.9
relativity 775.2
belief 953.1
dependency
pendency 202.1
dependence 432.3
dependent 432.6
possession 469.1
dependent
n hanger-on 138.6
follower 166.2
charge 432.6
retainer 577.1
adj pendent 202.9
subject 432.13
trusting 953.22
contingent 959.9
undecided 971.18
depend on
be at the mercy of 432.12
result from 887.5
rely on 953.16
trust 953.17
depend 959.6
depersonalization 92.20
depict
represent 349.8
describe 349.9
enact 704.30
portray 712.18
depiction
representation 349.1
description 349.2
depilation 1016.14
depilatory 6.4
deplane 186.8
deplete consume 388.3
waste 473.5
evacuate 909.22
depletion
decrement 252.3
reduction 255.2
consumption 388.1
waste 473.2
evacuation 909.6
deplorable
distressing 98.20
regrettable 113.10
disgraceful 661.11
terrible 1000.9
deplore
regret 113.6
lament 115.10
deploy locate 159.11
diverge 171.5
spread 259.6
prepare 405.6
order 807.4
adduce 957.12

deployment
placement 159.6
divergence 171.1
expansion 259.1
battle array 458.2
order 807.1
arrangement 808.1
deplume
demote 447.3
strip 480.24
disgrace 661.8
dismiss 909.19
depopulate
slaughter 308.17
dispeople 909.16
deport transfer 176.10
emigrate 190.16
eliminate 773.5
banish 909.17
deportment 321.1
depose dislodge 160.6
depone 334.6
remove from office
447.4
dismiss 909.19
overthrow 913.6
state 953.12
testify 957.9
deposit
n placement 159.6
sediment 176.9
collateral 438.3
payment 624.1
precipitation 1045.5
mineral deposit 1058.7
v lay 78.9
repose 159.14
secrete 346.7
store 386.10
pledge 438.10
precipitate 1045.11
deposition
placement 159.6
dregs 256.2
sworn statement 334.3
deposal 447.2
certificate 549.6
declaration 598.7
statement of belief 953.4
testimony 957.2
depository
storehouse 386.6
trustee 470.5
treasurer 729.12
treasury 729.13
depot 386.6
deprave
corrupt 393.12
work evil 1000.6
depravity
turpitude 654.5
baseness 661.3
deprecate
discommend 510.12
underestimate 950.2
attach little importance to
998.12
deprecatory
self-effacing 139.10
condemnatory 510.22
disparaging 512.13

depreciate
reduce 252.7
subtract 255.9
waste 473.5
deprecate 510.12
disparage 512.8
discount 631.2
cheapen 633.6
underestimate 950.2
attach little importance to
998.12
depreciation
decrease 252.1
reduction 255.2
deterioration 393.3
waste 473.2
deprecation 510.2
disparagement 512.1
discount 631.1
cheapening 633.4
underestimation 950.1
depredate
destroy 395.10
plunder 482.17
depress
sadden 112.18
reduce 252.7
lower 274.6
deepen 275.8
indent 284.14
press down 913.4
depressant
n sedative 86.12
drug 87.3
adj sedative 86.45
depressing 112.30
depressed
pleasureless 96.20
dejected 112.22
low 274.7
indented 284.17
lowered 913.12
unfortunate 1011.14
depression
mental disorder
92.14
wretchedness 96.6
distressfulness 98.5
dejection 112.3
decrease 252.1
lowness 274.1
deepening 275.7
concavity 284.1
cavity 284.2
notch 289.1
business cycle 731.10
lowering 913.1
melancholia 926.5
hard times 1011.6
Depression Era 824.5
deprivation
absence 222.1
refusal 442.1
deposal 447.2
loss 473.1
divestment 480.6
indigence 619.2
nonexistence 762.1
disassembly 802.6
banishment 909.4
want 992.4

deprive
take from 480.21
dismiss 909.19
deprived limited 210.7
bereaved 307.34
indigent 619.8
deprived of
bereft 473.8
wanting 992.13
depth space 158.1
interiority 207.1
size 257.1
thickness 269.2
deepness 275.1
pit 275.2
pitch 709.4
wisdom 920.5
deputation
authority 417.12
delegation 576.13
commission 615.1
substitution 862.1
deputize
empower 18.10
represent 576.14
commission 615.10
delegate 862.7
deputy
n mediator 466.3
director 574.1
representative 576.1
proxy 576.1
lawyer 597.1
assignee 615.9
assistant 616.6
substitute 862.2
policeman 1008.15
adj deputative 576.16
deracinate
dislodge 160.6
extract 192.10
exterminate 395.14
derail miscarry 410.15
distract 985.6
thwart 1012.15
derange afflict 85.50
disarrange 811.2
madden 926.24
derangement
disorder 810.1
disarrangement 811.1
abnormality 870.1
insanity 926.1
derby contest 457.3
race 457.12
Derby 757.1
deregulate
not interfere 430.16
politicize 611.16
deregulation
noninterference 430.9
disembarrassment 1014.6
derelict
n bum 331.9
castoff 370.4
outcast 586.4
wretch 660.2
transient 828.4
adj negligent 340.10
abandoned 370.8
dilapidated 393.33

eager 101.8
amorous 104.25
desirous of
keen on 100.22
envious 154.3
desist
v cease to use 390.4
cease 857.6
interj cease! 857.13
desk furniture 229.1
pulpit 703.13
workplace 739.1
table 901.15
desktop computer 1042.2
desktop publishing program
1042.12
desolate
v agonize 98.12
aggrieve 112.19
destroy 395.10
depopulate 909.16
adj wretched 96.26
distressing 98.20
disconsolate 112.28
forlorn 584.12
unproductive 891.4
desolation
wretchedness 96.6
harshness 98.4
disconsolateness 112.12
destruction 395.1
forlornness 584.4
wasteland 891.2
depopulation 909.3
despair
n wretchedness 96.6
dejection 112.3
desperation 125.2
v lose heart 112.16
despair of 125.10
desperado
killer 308.11
ruffian 593.3
criminal 660.9
desperate
hopeless 125.12
reckless 493.8
rabid 926.30
straitened 1013.26
desperation 125.2
despicable
offensive 98.18
base 661.12
paltry 998.21
terrible 1000.9
despise hate 103.5
disdain 157.3
reject 372.2
flout 454.4
deprecate 510.12
despite
n hate 103.1
spite 144.6
indignity 156.2
contempt 157.1
defiance 454.1
adv in spite of 338.9
despoil
corrupt 393.12
destroy 395.10
strip 480.24

plunder 482.17
seduce 665.20
work evil 1000.6
despoliation
destruction 395.1
loss 473.1
plundering 482.6
evil 1000.3
despondency
n wretchedness 96.6
dejection 112.3
despair 125.2
v lose heart 112.16
despondent
dejected 112.22
hopeless 125.12
despot 575.14
despotic
imperious 417.16
governmental 612.16
despotism
absolutism 612.8
tyranny 612.9
dessert serving 8.10
delicacy 10.8
desserts 604.1
destabilize 810.9
destigmatize
justify 600.9
acquit 601.4
destination goal 186.5
objective 380.2
address 553.9
end 820.1
fate 964.2
destined future 839.8
inevitable 963.15
fated 964.9
destiny portion 477.5
end 820.1
predestiny 839.2
fate 964.2
chance 972.1
destitute bereft 473.8
down-and-out 619.9
insolvent 625.11
destitution
indigence 619.2
want 992.4
de-stress 120.5
destroy excise 255.10
kill 308.13
spoil 393.10
deal destruction 395.10
defeat 412.6
rage 671.11
work evil 1000.6
thwart 1012.15
destroyer
battleship 180.7
ruiner 395.8
savage 593.5
destructible 16.14
destruction
excision 255.3
killing 308.1
impairment 393.1
ruin 395.1
defeat 412.1
loss 473.1
violence 671.1

disintegration 806.1
evil 1000.3
bane 1001.1
destructive
poisonous 82.7
deadly 308.23
destroying 395.26
violent 671.16
disintegrative 806.5
disastrous 1011.15
desuetude
abandonment 370.1
disuse 390.1
desultory
deviative 164.7
discursive 538.13
unordered 810.12
irregular 851.3
inconstant 854.7
fluttering 917.18
unreliable 971.20
detach
commission 615.10
enlist 615.17
disband 771.8
remove 802.10
detached
apathetic 94.13
reticent 344.10
free 430.21
aloof 583.6
secluded 584.8
impartial 649.9
unrelated 776.6
distinct 802.20
separated 802.21
incoherent 804.4
alone 872.8
unprejudiced 979.12
incurious 982.3
detachment
apathy 94.4
unconcern 102.2
reticence 344.3
military unit 461.22
aloofness 583.2
seclusion 584.1
impartiality 649.3
company 770.3
disbandment 771.3
elimination 773.2
part 793.1
separation 802.1
aloneness 872.2
unprejudicedness 979.5
incuriosity 982.1
detail
n meticulousness 339.3
military unit 461.22
motif 498.7
particular 766.3
company 770.3
part 793.1
component 796.2
v allot 477.9
amplify 538.7
commission 615.10
itemize 766.6
analyze 801.7
elaborate 861.6
particularize 865.9

sum up 1017.19
details
description 349.2
trivia 998.4
detain
slow 175.9
confine 429.12
delay 846.8
hinder 1012.10
detangle 431.7
detect 941.5
detectable
visible 31.6
discoverable 941.10
detection
investigation 938.4
discovery 941.1
radar 1036.9
detective
operative 576.10
inquirer 938.16
policeman 1008.15
détente
pacification 465.1
foreign policy 609.5
detention
slowing 175.4
imprisonment 429.3
delay 846.2
hindrance 1012.1
deter daunt 127.18
disincline 379.4
prevent 1012.14
detergent 79.17
deteriorate
aggravate 119.2
impair 393.9
sicken 393.16
be changed 852.6
degenerate 1011.11
determinant
n boundary 211.3
heredity 560.6
cause 886.1
adj bordering 211.11
determinate
circumscribed 210.6
particular 865.12
unqualified 960.2
certain 970.13
assured 970.20
determination
circumscription 210.1
measurement 300.1
will 323.1
resolution 359.1
obstinacy 361.1
intention 380.1
endeavor 403.1
solution 940.1
discovery 941.1
test 942.2
verdict 946.5
proof 957.3
ensuring 970.8
determine
direct 161.5
circumscribe 210.4
will 323.2
resolve 359.7
induce 375.22

intend 380.4
learn 570.6
end 820.5
specify 865.11
decide 886.12
exercise influence 894.8
discover 941.2
decide 946.11
prove 957.10
make sure 970.11
determined
circumscribed 210.6
resolute 359.11
trial 403.16
future 839.8
proved 957.20
predetermined 964.8
assured 970.20
confident 970.21
true 973.13
determinism
the future 839.1
fatalism 964.4
deterrent
n determent 379.2
obstacle 1012.4
adj frightening 127.28
dissuasive 379.5
warning 399.7
preventive 1012.19
detest dislike 99.3
hate 103.5
detestable
offensive 98.18
hateful 103.8
terrible 1000.9
dethrone 447.4
detonate blast 56.8
explode 671.14
shoot 904.12
fuel 1021.8
detour
n deviation 164.1
byway 383.4
bypass 914.3
v deviate 164.3
go roundabout 914.4
detoxification 87.1
detoxify 516.2
detract subtract 255.9
distract 985.6
detraction
minimization 252.5
reduction 255.2
disparagement 512.1
detrain 186.8
detriment
impairment 393.1
loss 473.1
disadvantage 996.2
evil 1000.3
detrimental
disadvantageous 996.6
harmful 1000.12
adverse 1011.13
detritus deposit 176.9
remainder 256.1
grain 1051.6
de trop
excessive 993.16
superfluous 993.17

deuce game 748.2
card 758.2
pair 873.3
deuced 513.10
deus ex machina 722.4
devaluate
cheapen 633.6
monetize 728.26
devalue corrupt 393.12
monetize 728.26
devastate
destroy 395.10
depopulate 909.16
devastation
destruction 395.1
depopulation 909.3
develop
age 14.2
grow 251.6
enlarge 259.4
become larger 259.5
expand 259.7
mature 303.9
manifest 348.5
disclose 351.4
improve 392.7
elaborate 392.10
amplify 538.7
train 568.13
process 714.15
turn into 858.17
evolve 861.5
get better 861.6
result 887.4
originate 892.12
perfect 1002.5
developer
planner 381.6
processing solution 714.13
producer 892.7
developing world
free agent 430.12
the poor 619.3
development
bodily development 14.1
birth 78.6
increase 251.1
growth 259.3
maturation 303.6
refinement 392.2
amplification 538.6
training 568.3
passage 708.24
plot 722.4
conversion 858.1
evolution 861.1
effect 887.1
deviance
deviation 164.1
obliquity 204.1
wrong 638.1
nonuniformity 782.1
circuitousness 914.1
deviant
n sexual pervert 75.16
nonconformist 868.3
adj homosexual 75.30
deviative 164.7
oblique 204.13
wrong 638.3
changed 852.10

nonconforming 868.5
eccentric 927.5
erroneous 975.16
deviate
n sexual pervert 75.16
v depart from 164.3
deflect 164.5
oblique 204.9
digress 538.9
go wrong 654.9
misbelieve 688.8
be changed 852.6
go roundabout 914.4
err 975.9
deviation
orientation 161.4
divergence 164.1
deviance 164.1
divergency 171.1
obliquity 204.1
distortion 265.1
digression 538.4
difference 780.1
nonuniformity 782.1
change 852.1
nonconformity 868.1
abnormality 870.1
circuitousness 914.1
detour 914.3
eccentricity 927.1
inaccuracy 975.2
device
surgery 91.19
trick 356.6
pretext 376.1
plan 381.1
instrumentality 384.3
instrument 384.4
stratagem 415.3
sign 517.1
signature 527.10
figure of speech 536.1
letter 546.1
heraldry 647.2
plot 722.4
motto 974.4
expedient 995.2
tool 1040.1
devil
n beast 144.14
dust storm 318.12
mischief-maker 322.3
daredevil 493.4
printer 548.12
enemy 589.6
ruffian 593.3
monster 593.6
wretch 660.2
rascal 660.3
violent person
671.9
diable 680.2
demon 680.6
v cook 11.5
annoy 96.13
devilish cruel 144.26
mischievous 322.6
diabolic 654.13
demoniac 680.17
hellish 682.8
execrable 1000.10

devil-may-care
unconcerned 102.7
nonchalant 106.15
reckless 493.8
deviltry 1000.1
devil worship
Satanism 680.14
idolatry 697.1
devious
deviative 164.7
oblique 204.13
dishonest 645.16
complex 799.4
circuitous 914.7
shrewd 920.15
devise
n bequest 478.10
v plan 381.8
bequeath 478.18
produce 892.8
originate 892.12
devitalize
weaken 16.10
unman 19.12
afflict 85.50
devoid
vacant 222.14
nonexistent 762.8
devoid of 992.13
devoir 641.1
devolve
relapse 394.4
commission 615.10
change hands 629.4
devote
spend 387.13
dedicate 477.11
sanctify 685.5
occupy 724.10
devoted
zealous 101.9
loving 104.26
obedient 326.3
resolute 359.11
observant 434.4
dedicated 587.21
faithful 644.20
unselfish 652.5
sanctified 685.8
pious 692.8
destined 964.9
engrossed 983.17
devotee
desirer 100.12
enthusiast 101.4
lover 104.11
believer 692.4
fanatic 926.18
devote oneself to
practice 328.8
be determined 359.8
undertake 404.3
espouse 509.13
busy oneself with 724.11
attend to 983.5
devotion
zeal 101.2
love 104.1
resolution 359.1
dedication 477.4
commitment 587.7

duty 641.1
fidelity 644.7
unselfishness 652.1
sanctification 685.3
piety 692.1
worship 696.1
devour
swallow 8.22
enjoy 95.13
ingest 187.11
destroy 395.10
gluttonize 672.4
kid oneself 954.6
devouring
n eating 8.1
adj greedy 100.27
devout
zealous 101.9
observant 434.4
pious 692.8
worshipful 696.16
belief 953.21
dew
n dewdrops 1065.4
v moisten 1065.12
dew point
temperature 1019.3
humidity 1065.2
dewy
young 301.9
immature 301.10
new 841.7
moist 1065.15
dewy-eyed 986.24
dexterity
rightness 219.2
skill 413.1
smartness 920.2
dexterous
right-handed 219.5
skillful 413.22
smart 920.14
diabetic 85.61
diabolic cruel 144.26
diabolical 654.13
demoniac 680.17
execrable 1000.10
diabolism
Satanism 680.14
black magic 690.2
diacritical mark
punctuation 530.15
letter 546.1
diadem circle 280.2
jewel 498.6
royal insignia 647.3
diaeresis meter 720.7
dissection 802.5
diagnosis
examination 91.12
interpretation 341.1
verdict 946.5
diagnostic
interpretative 341.14
indicative 517.23
differentiative 780.9
diagonal
crosspiece 170.5
oblique 204.7
straight line 277.2
line 517.6

diagram
n representation 349.1
plot 381.3
drawing 712.12
outline 801.4
v represent 349.8
plot 381.10
grammaticize 530.16
portray 712.18
itemize 801.7
diagrammatic 517.23
dial 216.4
dialect language 523.1
idiom 523.7
diction 532.1
dialectic
n discussion 541.6
logic 935.2
argument 935.5
adj argumentative
935.19
dialectical 935.22
dialogue talk 541.2
script 706.3
plot 722.4
argument 935.5
diameter size 257.1
bore 269.3
straight line 277.2
middle 819.1
bisector 875.3
diametric 779.7
diamond
n good person 659.1
playground 743.11
baseball 745.1
good thing 999.5
hardness 1046.6
v figure 498.9
The Diamond Sutra 683.9
Diana 1072.12
diapason range 158.2
harmony 708.3
scale 709.6
interval 709.20
music 711.22
diaper 5.19
diaphanous
dainty 248.7
thin 270.16
light 1025.32
transparent 1029.4
diaphragm
digestive system 2.18
loudspeaker 50.8
contraceptive 86.23
partition 213.5
middle 819.1
diarist writer 547.15
author 718.4
historian 719.4
chronologist 832.10
diarrhea
defecation 12.2
symptom 85.9
diary
record book 549.11
periodical 555.1
history 719.1
chronicle 832.9
diaspora 771.3

diastole
distension 259.2
round 850.3
pulsation 916.3
diatonic scale 709.6
diatribe berating 510.7
speech 543.2
dice
n gambling device 759.8
v square 879.3
dicey
speculative 759.27
uncertain 971.16
vague 971.19
chance 972.15
hazardous 1006.10
dichaeologia 600.5
dichotomy
severance 802.2
doubleness 873.1
bisection 875.1
dichromatic
chromatic 35.16
variegated 47.9
dick detective 576.10
gumshoe 576.11
police 1008.16
dick around 923.6
dicker
n compact 437.1
bargain 731.5
v bargain 731.18
Dick Turpin 483.11
dictate
n precept 419.1
command 420.1
law 673.3
axiom 974.2
v command 420.8
prescribe 420.9
oblige 424.5
dominate 612.14
necessitate 963.8
dictator 575.14
dictatorial
lordly 141.11
imperious 417.16
governmental 612.16
dictatorship
mastership 417.7
directorship 573.4
government 612.4
absolutism 612.8
diction phrasing 529.2
word-usage 532
words 532.1
dictionary
reference book 554.9
word list 871.4
dictum
affirmation 334.1
rule 419.2
decree 420.4
remark 524.3
verdict 946.5
maxim 974.1
axiom 974.2
didactic
preceptive 419.4
advisory 422.8
educational 568.18

poetic 720.15
dogmatic 970.22
didactive 419.4
diddle
n deception 356.9
v copulate 75.21
waste time 331.13
dally 331.14
deceive 356.14
fake 356.19
die
n engraving tool 713.8
cast 785.6
mold 786.6
base 901.8
v disappear 34.2
decease 307.18
decline 393.17
perish 395.23
stall 410.16
cease to exist 762.6
come to an end 820.6
pass 837.6
burn out 1022.8
die away
disappear 34.2
recede 168.2
decrease 252.6
cease to exist 762.6
come to an end 820.6
burn out 1022.8
die down quiet 173.8
decrease 252.6
burn out 1022.8
die for 100.14
diehard
n obstinate person
361.6
rightwinger 611.9
conservative 853.4
adj conservative 853.8
the die is cast 963.20
die laughing 116.8
die out disappear 34.2
be dying 307.25
cease to exist 762.6
burn out 1022.8
diesel means of propulsion
904.17
engine type 1043.3
diet
n dieting 7.13
council 423.1
legislature 613.1
assembly 770.2
v go on a diet 7.19
eat 8.20
slenderize 270.13
dietary
n diet 7.13
adj dietetic 7.23
dietitian
nutritionist 7.15
hospital staff 90.11
diff 1042.18
differ dissent 333.4
argue 456.8
vary 780.5
diversify 782.2
not resemble 787.2
disagree 789.5

difference
  n remainder 255.8
  dissent 333.1
  disagreement 456.2
  heraldry 647.2
  dissimilarity 780.1
  otherness 780.1
  nonuniformity 782.1
  argument 789.1
  inequality 791.1
  change 852.1
  abnormality 870.1
  sum 1017.6
  v differentiate 780.6
different
  differing 780.7
  nonuniform 782.3
  dissimilar 787.4
  novel 841.11
  particular 865.12
  abnormal 870.9
  eccentric 927.5
differential
  n margin 780.2
  characteristic 865.4
  gear 1040.9
  adj differentiative 780.9
  classificational 809.7
  discriminating 944.7
  numeric 1017.23
differentiate
  signify 517.17
  difference 780.6
  diversify 782.2
  characterize 865.10
  discriminate 944.4
differentiation
  indication 517.3
  differencing 780.4
  nonuniformity 782.1
  particularity 865.1
  characterization 865.8
  distinction 944.3
  notation 1017.2
difficult perverse 361.11
  finical 495.10
  hard to understand
    522.14
  adverse 1011.13
  difficile 1013.17
difficulties
  poverty 619.1
  adversity 1011.1
difficulty
  annoyance 96.2
  disagreement 456.2
  abstruseness 522.2
  adversity 1011.1
  obstacle 1012.4
  impediment 1012.6
  difficultness 1013.1
diffidence
  fearfulness 127.3
  self-effacement 139.2
  demur 325.2
  hesitation 362.3
  doubt 955.2
diffraction
  deflection 164.2
  dispersion 771.1
  wave 916.4

diffuse
  v deflect 164.5
  radiate 171.6
  transfer 176.10
  pervade 221.7
  rarefy 299.3
  publish 352.10
  disperse 771.4
  shatter 802.13
  loosen 804.3
  adj deflective 164.8
  rare 299.4
  formless 538.11
  dispersed 771.9
  extensive 864.13
  plentiful 991.7
diffusion
  deflection 164.2
  radiation 171.2
  transferal 176.1
  permeation 221.3
  rarefaction 299.2
  publication 352.1
  waste 473.2
  diffuseness 538.1
  dispersion 771.1
  disruption 802.3
  noncohesion 804.1
diffusive
  formless 538.11
  dispersive 771.11
dig
  n disrespect 156.3
  pit 284.4
  thrust 902.2
  hit 902.4
  v respond 93.11
  deepen 275.8
  excavate 284.15
  read one loud and clear
    521.8
  study 570.12
  drudge 725.14
  play 749.7
  thrust 902.12
  know 928.12
  search 938.31
  cultivate 1069.17
  harvest 1069.19
digest
  n abridgment 557.1
  code 673.5
  table 808.4
  v assimilate 7.18
  take 134.8
  absorb 187.13
  consume 388.3
  understand 521.7
  learn 570.7
  codify 673.10
  classify 809.6
  consider 931.12
  think over 931.13
digestion
  ingestion 2.17
  assimilation 7.8
  sorption 187.6
  consumption 388.1
  absorption 570.2
  pulping 1063.3
digicam 714.11

dig in
  remain firm 359.9
  fortify 460.9
digit finger 73.5
  foot 199.5
  number 1017.3
digital prehensile 474.9
  numeric 1017.23
  computer term 1042.18
digital art 713.1
digital artist
  photographer 714.2
  photographer 716.5
digital camera 714.11
digital photography 714.1
digital television
  television 1035.1
  television receiver 1035.11
dignified solemn 111.3
  stately 136.12
  lofty 544.14
dignify formalize 580.5
  honor 662.12
dignitary 997.8
dignity solemnity 111.1
  proud bearing 136.2
  elegance 533.1
  loftiness 544.6
  formality 580.1
  prestige 662.4
  ecclesiastical office
    698.5
  notability 997.2
  personage 997.8
digression
  deviation 164.1
  obliquity 204.1
  departure 538.4
  circuitousness 914.1
  detour 914.3
digs 228.4
dig up
  extract 192.10
  disinter 192.11
  acquire 472.9
  assemble 770.18
  uncover 941.4
  be curious 981.3
dike
  n crack 224.2
  lake 241.1
  trench 290.2
  barrier 1012.5
  deposit 1058.7
  v excavate 284.15
  furrow 290.3
dilapidated
  unsteady 16.16
  ramshackle 393.33
  disintegrative 806.5
  slovenly 810.15
  stale 842.14
dilate enlarge 259.4
  make larger 259.5
  bulge 283.11
  amplify 538.7
dilation
  distension 259.2
  swelling 283.4
  exaggeration 355.1
  amplification 538.6

dilatory
  dawdling 175.11
  reluctant 325.6
  indolent 331.19
  delaying 846.17
dilemma
  no choice 371.3
  syllogism 935.6
  bewilderment 971.3
  horns of a dilemma 1013.7
dilemmatic 1013.23
dilettante
  enthusiast 101.4
  connoisseur 496.6
  specialist 866.3
  half scholar 929.6
  ignoramus 930.7
  trifler 998.10
diligence
  industry 330.6
  painstakingness 339.2
  perseverance 360.1
  studiousness 570.4
  attention 983.1
diligent
  industrious 330.22
  painstaking 339.11
  persevering 360.8
  studious 570.17
  attentive 983.15
dillydally dawdle 175.8
  dally 331.14
  wait 846.12
dilogical 539.4
dilute
  v cut 16.11
  abate 252.8
  thin 270.12
  rarefy 299.3
  dissipate 771.5
  adulterate 797.12
  adj insipid 65.2
  rare 299.4
diluvium deposit 176.9
  dregs 256.2
dim
  n darkishness 1027.2
  v blind 30.7
  blur 32.4
  decolor 36.5
  darken 1027.9
  grow dark 1027.12
  adj dim-sighted 28.13
  inconspicuous 32.6
  colorless 36.7
  faint 52.16
  obscure 522.15
  dull 922.16
  darkish 1027.15
dime
  n money 728.7
  v inform on 551.13
dime-a-dozen
  dirt cheap 633.8
  plentiful 991.7
  common 998.21
dimension space 158.1
  size 257.1
dime store 736.1
diminish relieve 120.5
  abase 137.5

recede 168.2
decrease 252.6
reduce 252.7
subtract 255.9
narrow 270.11
languish 393.18
extenuate 600.12
moderate 670.6
qualify 959.3
diminution relief 120.1
decrease 252.1
reduction 255.2
modulation 670.2
depression 913.1
diminutive
n runt 258.4
nickname 527.7
adj miniature 258.12
nominal 527.15
dimple
n indentation 284.6
v indent 284.14
dim view 510.1
dimwit 924.2
din
n noise 53.3
pandemonium 810.5
v boom 53.7
ding 849.10
dine feed 8.18
dinner 8.21
diner meal 8.6
eater 8.16
restaurant 8.17
dining room 197.11
ding
n ringing 54.3
disrespect 156.3
v ring 54.8
din 849.10
ding-a-ling
ringing 54.3
fool 924.3
dingdong
n ringing 54.3
regularity 781.2
repetitiousness 849.4
fool 924.3
v ring 54.8
adj monotonous 849.15
dingy colorless 36.7
grimy 38.11
gray 39.4
dirty 80.22
dining room
restaurant 8.17
cafeteria 197.11
dinky inferior 250.6
little 258.10
tidy 807.8
insignificant 998.18
dinner
n meal 8.6
v dine 8.21
dinner party 8.9
dinnerware 735.4
dinosaur
behemoth 257.14
reptile 311.24
dint
n power 18.1

indentation 284.6
print 517.7
hit 902.4
v indent 284.14
diocese region 231.5
see 698.8
Dionysus
bibulousness 88.2
patron 704.26
fertility 890.5
agricultural deity 1069.4
diorama spectacle 33.7
scene 712.11
dip
n bath 79.9
declivity 204.5
cavity 284.2
submergence 367.2
pickpocket 483.2
candle 1026.2
v color 35.14
ladle 176.17
maneuver 184.40
incline 204.10
submerge 367.7
signal 517.22
baptize 701.17
flood 1065.14
diphthong 524.12
diploma grant 443.5
certificate 549.6
diplomacy skill 413.1
Machiavellianism 415.2
foreign policy 609.5
diplomat expert 413.11
Machiavellian 415.8
diplomatist 576.6
diplomatic
n diplomat 576.6
foreign policy 609.5
adj skillful 413.22
cunning 415.12
ambassadorial 576.17
political 609.43
diplomatic agent 576.6
diplomatic doctrine 609.5
dipsomania
substance abuse 87.1
alcoholism 88.3
psychosis 926.3
diptych
record book 549.11
picture 712.10
dire horrid 98.19
terrible 127.30
ominous 133.16
bad 1000.9
unfortunate 1011.14
disastrous 1011.15
dire straits 619.1
direct
v exercise influence 894.8
adj directional 161.12
straight 277.6
artless 416.5
free-acting 430.23
natural 499.7
clear 521.11
elegant 533.6
plain-speaking 535.3
lineal 560.18

candid 644.17
continuous 812.8
exact 973.17
adv directly 161.23
direction bearing 161.1
directionality 161.1
motivation 375.2
precept 419.1
directive 420.3
advice 422.1
pointer 517.4
address 553.9
teaching 568.1
supervision 573.2
management 573.1
government 612.1
production 704.13
operation 889.1
trend 896.2
directive
n direction 420.3
adj directable 161.13
motivating 375.25
commanding 420.13
advisory 422.8
directing 573.12
direct marketing
telephone call 347.13
selling 734.2
director librarian 558.3
person in charge 574.1
directeur 574.1
governor 575.6
theater man 704.23
motion-picture studio 706.4
conductor 710.17
businessman 730.1
directorship 417.1
directory
n council 423.1
register 549.9
information 551.1
reference book 554.9
guidebook 574.10
directorate 574.11
adj directing 573.12
dirge
n funeral song 115.6
last offices 309.4
funeral 309.5
v lament 115.10
dirigible
n aerostat 181.11
adj directable 161.13
dirt
n grime 80.6
land 234.1
scandal 552.8
obscenity 666.4
v dirty 80.15
dirt cheap 633.8
dirt poor 619.10
dirty
v dirty up 80.15
stain 1004.6
adj dingy 38.11
grimy 80.22
stormy 318.22
cloudy 319.8
cursing 513.8
unfair 650.10

evil-minded 654.15
base 661.12
lascivious 665.29
obscene 666.9
slimy 1062.14
dirty blond 35.9
dirty look 27.5
dirty pool
juggling 356.5
smear campaign 609.14
treachery 645.6
unfairness 650.2
dirty trick trick 356.6
treachery 645.6
dirty word oath 513.4
barbarism 526.6
disability
inability 19.2
disease 85.1
handicap 603.2
disadvantage 996.2
disable
disenable 19.9
afflict 85.50
cripple 393.14
disabled
weakened 16.18
incapacitated 19.16
crippled 393.30
ended 820.8
disabled person 85.45
disabuse 977.2
disaccord
n dissent 333.1
hostility 451.2
unharmonious relationship 456
discord 456.1
ruffled feelings 589.2
difference 780.1
disagreement 789.1
nonconformity 868.1
v discord 456.8
disagree 789.5
disaccustomed 374.4
disadvantage
n handicap 603.2
drawback 996.2
impediment 1012.6
trouble 1013.3
v inconvenience 996.4
work evil 1000.6
disadvantaged
inferior 250.6
indigent 619.8
the disadvantaged
the underprivileged 606.4
the poor 619.3
disaffected
averse 99.8
alienated 589.11
unfaithful 645.20
disaffirm 335.4
disagree dissent 333.4
refuse 442.3
differ 456.8
dispute 789.5
disagreeable
unsavory 64.5
unpleasant 98.17
irascible 110.19

unkind 144.16
disagreeing 789.6
disagreement
dissent 325.1
dissidence 333.1
refusal 442.1
difficulty 456.2
disapproval 510.1
relation 775.1
contrariety 779.1
difference 780.1
disaccord 789
discord 789.1
nonconformity 868.1
disagree with
not be good for 82.4
dissent 333.4
differ 780.5
disallow deny 335.4
refuse 442.3
prohibit 444.3
disapprove 510.10
not pay 625.6
disappear
be invisible 32.3
vanish 34.2
quit 188.9
absent oneself 222.8
hide 346.8
perish 395.23
cease to exist 762.6
flit 828.6
pass 837.6
disappearance
invisibility 32.1
vanishing 34.1
disappearing 34.1
absence 222.4
flight 368.4
disappoint
dissatisfy 108.5
shatter one's hopes 125.11
defeat expectation 132.2
disillusion 977.2
disappointed
discontented 108.7
bitterly disappointed 132.5
unaccomplished 408.3
disapproving 510.21
disillusioned 977.5
disappointment 992.1
disapprobation
dislike 99.1
resentment 152.1
dissent 333.1
disapproval 510.1
disrepute 661.1
disapproval
dislike 99.1
resentment 152.1
dissent 333.1
rejection 372.1
disapprobation 510.1
disparagement 512.1
disapprove reject 372.2
disfavor 510.10
stigmatize 661.9
disarm disable 19.9
lay down one's arms 465.11
disarmament 465.6
disarming 504.18

disarrange
dislocate 160.5
disorder 810.9
derange 811.2
discontinue 813.3
agitate 917.10
disarray
n disorder 810.1
v undress 6.7
disarrange 811.2
disassemble
demolish 395.17
take apart 802.15
disassociation
unrelatedness 776.1
separation 802.1
disaster
fatality 308.8
debacle 395.4
upheaval 671.5
misfortune 1011.2
disastrous
destructive 395.26
convulsive 671.23
calamitous 1011.15
disavow
n recant 363.8
v deny 335.4
disavowal denial 335.2
recantation 363.3
rejection 372.1
disband disarm 465.11
disperse 771.8
part company 802.19
disbar depose 447.4
dismiss 909.19
disbelief
nonreligious 695.5
unbelief 955.1
doubtfulness 971.2
disbelieve doubt 695.14
unbelieve 955.5
refuse to believe 956.3
disburden ease 120.7
lighten 298.6
confess 351.7
unload 909.23
disembarrass 1014.9
disburse
parcel out 477.8
spend 626.5
disc record 50.12
recording media
549.10
discard
n derelict 370.4
rejection 372.1
discarding 390.3
elimination 773.2
v abandon 370.5
reject 372.2
eliminate 390.7
eject 909.13
discern see 27.12
perceive 521.9
know 928.12
detect 941.5
discernible visible 31.6
manifest 348.8
knowable 928.25
on the right scent 941.10

discerning
sagacious 920.16
perceptive 944.8
discharge
n humor 2.24
excretion 12.1
excrement 12.3
detonation 56.3
release 120.2
emergence 190.1
outflow 190.4
performance 328.2
accomplishment 407.1
exemption 430.8
freedom 431.2
observance 434.1
execution 437.4
acquittal 601.1
payment 624.1
acknowledgment 627.2
explosion 671.7
shot 904.4
repulse 908.2
ejection 909.1
dismissal 909.5
disgorgement 909.7
arc 1032.6
v excrete 12.12
blast 56.8
exude 190.15
perform 328.9
accomplish 407.4
exempt 430.14
release 431.5
perform 434.3
execute 437.9
acquit 601.4
pay in full 624.13
erupt 671.13
explode 671.14
disband 771.8
shoot 904.12
repulse 908.3
eject 909.13
dismiss 909.19
unload 909.23
disgorge 909.25
disciple
enthusiast 101.4
follower 166.2
protégé 572.2
associate 616.8
religion 684.2
believer 692.4
convert 858.7
disciplinarian 575.14
discipline
n limitation 210.2
self-control 359.5
strictness 425.1
training 568.3
study 568.8
punishment 604.1
government 612.1
temperance 668.1
occupation 724.4
orderliness 807.3
science 928.10
v limit 210.5
hold a tight hand upon 425.4
train 568.13

punish 604.10
govern 612.11
conform 867.3
disclaim
n recant 363.8
v deny 335.4
reject 372.2
refuse 442.3
disclose unclose 292.12
manifest 348.5
reveal 351.4
signify 517.17
say 524.22
inform 551.8
uncover 941.4
testify 957.9
disclosure
appearance 33.1
opening 292.1
informing 343.2
manifestation 348.1
revelation 351.1
publicizing 351.1
indication 517.3
discovery 941.1
testimony 957.2
disco 743.13
discolor
n discoloration 1004.2
v decolor 36.5
mark 517.19
stain 1004.6
discombobulate
agitate 105.14
confuse 985.7
discomfit chagrin 96.15
dismay 127.19
overwhelm 412.8
confuse 985.7
thwart 1012.15
discomfiture
chagrin 96.4
disappointment 132.1
rout 412.2
disorder 810.1
confusion 985.3
frustration 1012.3
discomfort
n pain 26.1
unpleasure 96.1
distressfulness 98.5
v chagrin 96.16
distress 98.14
disconcert
n bewilderment 971.3
v chagrin 96.15
mortify 98.13
agitate 105.14
dismay 127.19
bewilder 971.12
confuse 985.7
thwart 1012.15
disconnect 802.8
disconnected
unrelated 776.6
separated 802.21
incoherent 804.4
discontinuous 813.4
irregular 851.3
disconsolate
wretched 96.26

dish
n serving 8.10
tableware 8.12
culinary preparation 10.7
cooking 11.1
baseball 745.1
basketball game 747.3
beauty 1016.8
v ladle 176.17
be concave 284.12
hollow 284.13
do for 395.11
play 747.4
thwart 1012.15
dishabille 5.20
disharmony
discord 61.1
disaccord 456.1
disagreement 789.1
disorder 810.1
dishearten
dissatisfy 108.5
sadden 112.18
daunt 127.18
prevent 1012.14
dishevel
disorder 810.9
disarrange 811.2
dishonest
falsehearted 354.31
insincere 354.32
untruthful 354.34
dishonorable 645.16
dishonesty
falseheartedness 354.4
untruthfulness 354.8
fraud 356.8
improbity 645.1
dishonor
n disrespect 156.1
nonpayment 625.1
improbity 645.1
disrepute 661.1
v offend 156.5
not pay 625.6
disgrace 661.8
desecrate 694.4
dish out
ladle 176.17
parcel out 477.8
give 478.12
administer 643.6
dishpan 79.12
dish up
ladle 176.17
provide 385.7
offer 439.4
propose 439.5
dishwasher
washbasin 79.12
washer 79.15
dishwater
symbol of weakness 16.7
offal 80.9
refuse 391.4
dishy delightful 97.8
desirable 100.30
alluring 377.8
beautiful 1016.21
disillusion
n disapproval 510.1

disillusionment 977.1
v disappoint 132.2
disillude 977.2
disincentive 379.2
disinclination
dislike 99.1
refusal 325.1
disinfect 79.24
disinfectant
n cure 86.21
poison 1001.3
adj antiseptic 86.43
disingenuous
insincere 354.32
deceitful 645.18
sophistical 936.10
disinherit 480.23
disintegrate
weaken 16.9
strike dead 308.18
decay 393.22
break 393.23
demolish 395.17
be destroyed 395.22
disband 771.8
come apart 802.9
decompose 806.3
lapse into disorder 810.8
be brittle 1050.3
pulverize 1051.9
powder 1051.10
disintegration
frailty 16.2
decay 393.6
destruction 395.1
disbandment 771.3
disruption 802.3
coming-apart 806.1
decomposition 806.1
disorder 810.1
pulverization 1051.4
disinterest
n apathy 94.4
unconcern 102.2
impartiality 649.3
unselfishness 652.1
incuriosity 982.1
v disincline 379.4
disinterested
apathetic 94.13
unconcerned 102.7
impartial 649.9
unselfish 652.5
unprejudiced 979.12
incurious 982.3
disinvolve
extricate 431.7
disintricate 798.5
disembarrass 1014.9
disjoin
differentiate 780.6
separate 802.8
loosen 804.3
disintegrate 806.3
discontinue 813.3
disjointed
dislocated 160.9
separated 802.21
disjunction
elimination 773.2
relation 775.1

unrelatedness 776.1
differentiation 780.4
separation 802.1
noncohesion 804.1
disintegration 806.1
disorder 810.1
discontinuity 813.1
disk circle 280.2
lamina 296.2
recording media 549.10
rotator 915.4
magnetic disk 1042.6
diskette
recording media 549.10
disk 1042.6
disk jockey 1034.23
dislike
n unpleasure 96.1
distaste 99.1
hate 103.1
v mislike 99.3
have it in for 103.6
dislocate
displace 160.5
disjoint 802.16
disarrange 811.2
dislocation
displacement 160.1
separation 802.1
noncohesion 804.1
disarrangement 811.1
dislodge
unplace 160.6
remove 176.11
extricate 431.7
evict 909.15
disloyal
apostate 363.11
unfaithful 645.20
dismal gray 39.4
distressing 98.20
gloomy 112.24
dull 117.6
hopeless 125.12
pessimistic 125.16
funereal 309.22
dismantle
demolish 395.17
disassemble 802.15
dismay
n fear 127.1
v distress 98.14
disconcert 127.19
bewilder 971.12
dismayed
frightened 127.25
cowardly 491.10
bewildered 971.24
dismember
torture 604.16
tear apart 802.14
loosen 804.3
dismiss slight 157.6
reject 372.2
release 431.5
depose 447.4
acquit 601.4
disband 771.8
repulse 908.3
send off 909.18
discharge 909.19

refute 958.5
dismiss from one's thoughts 984.4
dismissal snub 157.2
rejection 372.1
release 431.2
deposal 447.2
acquittal 601.1
disbandment 771.3
repulse 908.2
discharge 909.5
dismount
dislodge 160.6
get down 194.7
disassemble 802.15
disobedience
refusal 325.1
noncompliance 327.1
nonobedience 327.1
lawlessness 418.1
refusal 442.1
disoblige offend 156.5
inconvenience 996.4
disorder
n disease 85.1
formlessness 263.1
misbehavior 322.1
anarchy 418.2
nonuniformity 782.1
noncohesion 804.1
disarrangement 810.1
disorderliness 810.1
change 852.1
agitation 917.1
vagueness 971.4
confusion 985.3
v afflict 85.50
deform 263.3
disorganize 810.9
disarrange 811.2
disorganization
decay 393.6
destruction 395.1
anarchy 418.2
disbandment 771.3
disintegration 806.1
disorder 810.1
disarrangement 811.1
confusion 985.3
disorientation
orientation 161.4
insanity 926.1
confusion 985.3
disoriented
insane 926.26
bewildered 971.24
confused 985.12
disown
n recant 363.8
v deny 335.4
reject 372.2
dispossess 480.23
disparage
disrespect 156.4
disdain 157.3
subtract 255.9
deprecate 510.12
depreciate 512.8
stigmatize 661.9
underestimate 950.2

disparaging
disrespectful 156.7
condemnatory 510.22
derogatory 512.13
disparate
different 780.7
dissimilar 787.4
unequal 791.4
disparity dissent 333.1
lack of agreement
456.2
difference 780.1
dissimilarity 787.1
disagreement 789.1
inequality 791.1
dispassion
unfeeling 94.1
apathy 94.4
unconcern 102.2
inexcitability 106.1
impartiality 649.3
moderation 670.1
dispatch
n velocity 174.1
killing 308.1
performance 328.2
quickness 330.3
accomplishment 407.1
information 551.1
message 552.4
letter 553.2
promptness 845.3
v devour 8.22
send 176.15
kill 308.13
perform 328.9
hasten 401.4
accomplish 407.4
mail 553.12
dispel disappear 34.2
dissipate 771.5
part company 802.19
do away with 909.21
dispensable
apportioned 477.12
justifiable 600.14
superfluous 993.17
insignificant 998.17
dispensary
drugstore 86.36
hospital room 197.25
dispensation
permission 443.1
relinquishment 475.1
distribution 477.2
administration 573.3
government 612.1
privilege 642.2
divine function 677.13
dispersion 771.1
dispense
exempt 430.14
permit 443.9
parcel out 477.8
give 478.12
vend 734.9
disperse 771.4
dispense with
not use 390.5
exempt 430.14
relinquish 475.3

disperse
disappear 34.2
deflect 164.5
radiate 171.6
spread 259.6
rarefy 299.3
parcel out 477.8
scatter 771.4
disband 771.8
shatter 802.13
part company 802.19
loosen 804.3
dispersion
deflection 164.2
radiation 171.2
expansion 259.1
rarefaction 299.2
distribution 477.2
scattering 771.1
disbandment 771.3
noncohesion 804.1
dispirited
dejected 112.22
weary 118.11
displace
dislocate 160.5
remove 176.11
depose 447.4
come after 835.3
substitute for 862.5
dismiss 909.19
displaced person
stateless person 160.4
migrant 178.5
fugitive 368.5
outcast 586.4
display
n appearance 33.2
spectacle 33.7
externalization 206.4
front 216.1
demonstration 348.2
publication 352.1
show 501.4
signal 1036.11
v externalize 206.5
manifest 348.5
make public 352.11
flaunt 501.17
signify 517.17
evidence 957.8
displeased averse 99.8
discontented 108.7
disapproving 510.21
displeasing
unsavory 64.5
unpleasant 98.17
unlikable 99.7
unsatisfactory 108.9
displeasure
unpleasure 96.1
unpleasantness 98.1
dislike 99.1
unhappiness 112.2
resentment 152.1
disapproval 510.1
displosion 56.3
disposal
placement 159.6
discard 390.3
relinquishment 475.1

distribution 477.2
administration 573.3
transfer 629.1
elimination 773.2
order 807.1
arrangement 808.1
dispose locate 159.11
take direction 161.7
induce 375.22
parcel out 477.8
order 807.4
distribute 808.9
influence 894.7
exercise influence
894.8
disposed
adj willing 324.5
arranged 808.14
dispositioned 978.8
prep inclined to 896.6
dispose of devour 8.22
kill 308.13
perform 328.9
discard 390.7
put an end to 395.12
accomplish 407.4
relinquish 475.3
give away 478.21
eliminate 773.5
end 820.5
refute 958.5
disposition
placement 159.6
will 323.1
plan 381.1
governance 417.5
battle array 458.2
relinquishment 475.1
distribution 477.2
administration 573.3
government 612.1
transfer 629.1
nature 767.4
elimination 773.2
order 807.1
arrangement 808.1
tendency 896.1
character 978.3
dispossess
foreclose 480.23
evict 909.15
dispossession
loss 473.1
reclaiming 480.7
eviction 909.2
disproportion
n distortion 265.1
inconsistency 789.2
inequality 791.1
disorder 810.1
v deform 265.7
unequalize 791.2
disproportionate
exaggerated 355.4
disagreeing 789.6
inconsistent 789.8
unequal 791.4
unordered 810.12
disprove deny 335.4
invalidate 958.4
disputable 971.17

disputatious
contentious 110.26
resistant 453.5
partisan 456.17
argumentative 935.19
dispute
n resistance 453.1
quarrel 456.5
contention 457.1
argumentation 935.4
questioning 938.12
v object 333.5
deny 335.4
offer resistance 453.3
quarrel 456.11
contest 457.21
argue 935.16
doubt 955.6
disqualification
inability 19.2
unpreparedness 406.1
disqualify
invalidate 19.11
make impossible 967.6
disquiet
n unpleasure 96.1
trepidation 105.5
anxiety 126.1
fearfulness 127.5
nervousness 128.1
impatience 135.1
agitation 917.1
v give no pleasure 96.12
distress 96.16
excite 105.14
concern 126.4
frighten 127.15
agitate 917.10
disquisition
treatise 556.1
lesson 568.7
disregard
n unconcern 102.2
forgiveness 148.1
snub 157.2
neglect 340.1
rejection 372.1
nonobservance 435.1
defiance 454.1
inattention 984.1
v take 134.8
condone 148.4
slight 157.6
disobey 327.6
neglect 340.6
reject 372.2
lose sight of 435.3
flout 454.4
allow for 959.5
keep an open mind 979.7
be inattentive 984.2
disrepair
uselessness 391.1
impairment 393.1
disreputable
n bad person 660.1
adj discreditable 661.10
disrepute 661.1
disrespect
n impudence 142.2
irreverence 156.1

low esteem 156.1
disobedience 327.1
discourteousness 505.2
disapproval 510.1
v not respect 156.4
disrobe 6.7
disrupt shatter 802.13
thwart 1012.15
disruption
misbehavior 322.1
destruction 395.1
anarchy 418.2
falling-out 456.4
dissolution 802.3
disorder 810.1
dissatisfaction
unpleasure 96.1
discontent 108.1
disappointment 132.1
resentment 152.1
dissent 333.1
disapproval 510.1
dissatisfied
discontented 108.7
disappointed 132.5
disapproving 510.21
dissect analyze 801.6
separate 802.17
dissemblance sham 354.3
dissimilarity 787.1
dissemble conceal 346.6
sham 354.21
dissembler
imitator 336.4
deceiver 357.1
pietist 693.3
disseminate
transfer 176.10
communicate 343.7
publish 352.10
disperse 771.4
plant 1069.18
dissension
dissent 333.1
hostility 451.2
dissent 456.3
disagreement 789.1
dissent
n complaint 115.4
dissension 325.1
dissidence 333.1
refusal 442.1
resistance 453.1
dissension 456.3
disapproval 510.1
Protestantism 675.10
difference 780.1
disagreement 789.1
nonconformity 868.1
counteraction 900.1
v dissent from 333.4
refuse 442.3
offer resistance 453.3
diversify 782.2
disagree 789.5
not conform 868.4
counteract 900.6
dissertation 556.1
disservice
bad deed 144.13
injustice 650.4

dissident
n dissenter 333.3
oppositionist 452.3
adj dissenting 333.6
disaccordant 456.15
disagreeing 789.6
nonconforming 868.5
counteractive 900.8
dissimilar
different 780.7
unsimilar 787.4
incomparable 943.9
dissimilitude 787.1
dissimulate 354.20
dissimulator
imitator 336.4
deceiver 357.1
pietist 693.3
dissipate
disappear 34.2
spend 387.13
waste 473.5
go to waste 473.6
squander 486.3
be promiscuous 665.19
plunge into dissipation 669.6
dispel 771.5
dissociate
separate 802.8
chemical terms 806.4
dissociated 776.6
dissociate oneself from 510.10
dissoluble
separable 802.26
liquefiable 1064.9
dissolute
corrupt 654.14
profligate 665.25
licentious 669.8
dissolution
disappearance 34.1
decrement 252.3
death 307.1
decay 393.6
destruction 395.1
disbandment 771.3
disruption 802.3
noncohesion 804.1
disintegration 806.1
liquefaction 1064.1
dissolvable
separable 802.26
liquefiable 1064.9
dissolve
n motion-picture editing 706.6
v disappear 34.2
destroy 395.10
cease to exist 762.6
dissipate 771.5
disband 771.8
disintegrate 806.3
flit 828.6
liquefy 1064.5
dissonant
discordant 61.4
different 780.7
disagreeing 789.6
dissuade 379.3
distaff
n woman 77.5

axle 915.5
adj feminine 77.13
distance
n station 159.2
setting 209.2
farness 261.1
remoteness 261.1
length 267.1
extent 300.3
reticence 344.3
aloofness 583.2
round 751.3
v outdistance 249.10
distance education
college 567.5
teaching 568.1
distance learning 567.5
distant faint 52.16
aloof 141.12
distal 261.8
reticent 344.10
aloof 583.6
farfetched 776.8
incurious 982.3
distaste dislike 99.1
refusal 325.1
disapproval 510.1
distasteful
unsavory 64.5
unpleasant 98.17
unlikable 99.7
distemper
n color 35.8
illness 85.1
disease 85.41
v color 35.14
annoy 96.13
distended
corpulent 257.18
dilated 259.13
bulging 283.15
overfull 993.20
distension
expanding 259.2
swelling 283.4
overextension 993.7
stretching 1048.2
distich poetry 720.9
two 873.2
maxim 974.1
distill refine 79.22
brew 88.30
leak 190.14
extraction 192.16
trickle 238.18
simplify 798.4
boil 1020.20
vaporize 1067.8
distillation
refinement 79.4
leakage 190.5
take out 192.7
extract 192.8
essential content 196.5
trickle 238.7
simplification 798.2
product 893.3
burning 1020.5
thickening 1045.4
vaporization 1067.5

distinct plain 31.7
audible 50.16
manifest 348.8
clear 521.11
different 780.7
separate 802.20
particular 865.12
distinction glory 247.2
elegance 533.1
nobility 608.2
honor 646.1
mark 662.5
difference 780.1
margin 780.2
differentiation 780.4
characterization 865.8
comparison 943.1
contradistinction 944.3
notability 997.2
distinctive
audible 50.16
typical 349.15
differentiative 780.9
classificational 809.7
characteristic 865.13
discriminating 944.7
distinguish see 27.12
honor 662.12
differentiate 780.6
characterize 865.10
focus on 937.3
detect 941.5
discriminate 944.4
recognize 989.11
distinguished
eminent 247.9
superior 249.12
honored 646.9
distingué 662.16
different 780.7
particular 865.12
characteristic 865.13
notable 997.19
distort deflect 164.5
deform 263.3
contort 265.5
misinterpret 342.2
misrepresent 350.3
falsify 354.16
corrupt 393.12
reason speciously 936.8
prejudice 980.9
blemish 1004.4
distortion
audio distortion 50.13
deflection 164.2
twistedness 265
torsion 265.1
misinterpretation 342.1
misrepresentation 350.1
bad likeness 350.2
deliberate falsehood 354.9
sophistry 936.1
error 975.1
blemish 1004.1
distract
disincline 379.4
discompose 811.4
madden 926.24
divert 985.6

doll woman 77.6
　ladylove 104.14
　miniature 258.6
　gal 302.7
　figure 349.6
　endearment term 562.6
　good person 659.2
　toy 743.16
　beauty 1016.8
dollar currency 728.7
　money 728.8
dollars to doughnuts
　n good chance 972.8
　adv probably 968.8
dollhouse
　small space 258.3
　toy 743.16
dollop 793.3
doll up dress up 5.42
　ornament 498.8
　beautify 1016.15
dolorous
　distressing 98.20
　sorrowful 112.26
dolphin 311.29
dolt bungler 414.8
　stupid person 924.2
domain sphere 231.2
　country 232.1
　real estate 471.6
　occupation 724.4
　hierarchy 809.4
　science 928.10
domain name 1042.18
dome
　n hall 197.4
　head 198.6
　highlands 237.1
　mountain 237.6
　tower 272.6
　arch 279.4
　football 746.1
　v curve 279.6
　top 295.21
domestic
　n servant 577.2
　adj residential 228.32
　recluse 584.10
domesticate
　settle 159.17
　accustom 373.9
　tame 432.11
domicile
　n abode 228.1
　v inhabit 225.7
　house 225.10
dominance
　dominion 417.6
　influence 894.1
dominant
　n note 709.14
　key 709.15
　adj chief 249.14
　victorious 411.7
　authoritative 417.15
　governing 612.17
　prevalent 864.12
　influential 894.14
　paramount 997.24
dominate show 31.4
　rise above 272.11

　subjugate 432.8
　predominate 612.14
　prevail 864.10
　have influence over 894.11
domineering
　n arrogance 141.1
　authoritativeness 417.3
　despotism 612.9
　adj arrogant 141.9
　imperious 417.16
dominion
　sphere 231.2
　country 232.1
　supremacy 249.3
　governance 417.5
　dominance 417.6
　ownership 469.2
　control 612.2
　precedence 814.1
domino effect
　immediate cause 886.3
　aftereffect 887.3
　vicissitudes 972.5
don
　n man 76.7
　teacher 571.1
　v put on 5.43
donate provide 385.7
　give 478.12
done
　adj well-done 11.8
　tired 21.8
　worn-out 393.36
　completed 407.11
　ended 820.8
　produced 892.17
　interj so be it 332.20
done deal act 328.3
　accomplishment 407.1
done for dead 307.29
　dying 307.32
　spoiled 393.29
　ruined 395.29
　defeated 412.14
　no more 762.11
　ended 820.9
done with
　disused 390.10
　completed 407.11
　ended 820.8
Don Juan
　beau 104.12
　deceiver 357.1
　tempter 377.4
　philanderer 562.12
　libertine 665.10
donkey ass 311.15
　obstinate person 361.6
　stupid person 924.2
donnybrook noise 53.4
　quarrel 456.5
　commotion 810.4
donor provider 385.6
　giver 478.11
do-nothing
　passive 329.6
　indolent 331.19
Don Quixote
　knight 608.5
　visionary 986.13
don't ask don't tell 458.19

donut 10.44
doodad 498.4
doodle
　n drawing 712.12
　fool 924.1
　v waste time 331.13
　dally 331.14
　scribble 547.20
　blow a horn 708.42
　portray 712.18
doohickey 1052.5
doom
　n death 307.1
　destruction 395.2
　condemnation 602.1
　end 820.1
　destiny 839.2
　doomsday 839.3
　verdict 946.5
　fate 964.2
　v condemn 602.3
　damn 682.6
　pass judgment 946.13
　destine 964.7
　work evil 1000.6
do one's bit
　lay down one's life for one's
　　country 307.24
　be willing 324.3
　do one's duty 641.10
do one's duty feast 8.24
　perform 434.3
　perform one's duty 641.10
do one's heart good
　please 95.6
　gratify 95.8
　make proud 136.6
do one's own thing disregard
　　435.3
　stand alone 872.6
　function as 889.8
do one's part
　be willing 324.3
　do 328.6
　share 476.6
　do one's duty 641.10
door entrance 189.5
　porch 189.6
　outlet 190.9
　doorway 292.6
doormat wig 3.14
　weakling 16.6
　dupe 358.2
doorstep 193.5
doorway porch 189.6
　door 292.6
do out of cheat 356.18
　take from 480.21
do over
　reproduce 78.7
　repeat 849.7
　convert 858.11
do-over
　repetition 849.1
　conversion 858.1
　repeat 874.2
dope
　n anesthetic 25.3
　drug 87.3
　film 714.10
　contraband 732.3

　stupid person 924.2
　fuel 1021.1
　v put to sleep 22.20
　deaden 25.4
　medicate 91.25
　relieve 120.5
　solve 940.2
　predict 962.9
the dope
　information 551.1
　the facts 761.4
dopey inert 173.14
　languid 331.20
　dull 922.16
　foolish 923.9
　dazed 985.14
Doppelgänger
　the same 778.3
　double 988.3
do right by 143.9
dormant
　asleep 22.22
　inert 173.14
　passive 329.6
　languid 331.20
　latent 519.5
dormition 22.1
dormitory
　bedroom 197.7
　inn 228.15
dorsal 217.10
DOS 1042.12
dose
　n venereal disease
　　85.18
　draft 86.6
　hit 87.20
　amount 244.2
　portion 793.5
　radiation physics 1037.8
　v medicate 91.25
　administer 643.6
a dose of one's own medicine
　　506.2
dossier 549.5
dot
　n spottiness 47.3
　modicum 248.2
　minute 258.7
　endowment 478.9
　mark 517.5
　notation 709.12
　v variegate 47.7
　interspace 224.3
　mark 517.19
　disperse 771.4
　sprinkle 771.6
dotage old age 303.5
　senility 922.10
　credulity 954.1
dot-com 1042.18
dote on 104.18
do the honors
　extend courtesy 504.12
　entertain 585.8
　introduce 587.14
do the math
　plan 380.6
　learn 570.6
　solve 940.2
　calculate 1017.18

do the right thing
  behave oneself 321.5
  do one's duty 641.10
  be good 653.4
do the right thing by
  observe 434.2
  be just 649.5
do the trick do 328.6
  avail 387.17
  accomplish 407.4
  succeed with 409.11
  suit 788.8
  suffice 991.4
  expedite one's affair 995.3
do time
  be imprisoned 429.18
  take one's turn 825.5
dotty
  spotted 47.13
  crazy 926.27
  eccentric 927.5
double
  n deviation 164.1
  fold 291.1
  image 349.5
  game 745.3
  string 750.2
  the same 778.3
  duplicate 785.3
  substitute 862.2
  etheric double 988.3
  v turn back 163.8
  intensify 251.5
  fold 291.5
  play 745.5
  copy 785.8
  seek the middle 819.3
  repeat 849.7
  double 873.5
  duplicate 874.3
  adj falsehearted 354.31
  treacherous 645.21
  two 873.6
  doubled 874.4
double agent
  traitor 357.10
  secret agent 576.9
double-charge 632.7
double-check
  n ensuring 970.8
  v verify 970.12
  check 1017.21
double-cross
  deceive 356.14
  betray 645.14
double-dealing
  n falseheartedness 354.4
  treachery 645.6
  adj falsehearted 354.31
  treacherous 645.21
double-edged
  acrimonious 17.14
  sharp 285.8
double entendre
  joke 489.6
  ambiguity 539.1
  equivocation 539.2
double exposure 714.5
double meaning 539.1
double or nothing 759.3
doubles 748.1

double standard 354.4
doublet root 526.2
  two 873.2
double take
  sequel 817.1
  delay 846.2
double-talk
  n nonsense 520.2
  speech sound 524.12
  specious argument 936.3
  v quibble 936.9
double vision 28.1
doubt
  n apprehension 127.4
  suspiciousness 153.2
  agnosticism 695.6
  doubtfulness 955.2
  uncertainty 971.2
  v suffer pangs of jealousy
    153.3
  disbelieve 695.14
  be doubtful 955.6
  be uncertain 971.9
doubtful
  dishonest 645.16
  agnostic 695.20
  doubting 955.9
  unbelievable 955.10
  improbable 969.3
  iffy 971.17
  unsafe 1006.11
doubting Thomas
  agnostic 695.12
  doubter 955.4
doubtless
  adj belief 953.21
  undoubted 970.16
  adv probably 968.8
  unquestionably 970.25
douche
  n washing 79.5
  bath 79.8
  sprinkler 1065.8
  v wash 79.19
  moisten 1065.12
  soak 1065.13
dough soldier 461.7
  money 728.2
  softness 1047.4
  semiliquid 1062.5
doughboy 461.7
doughnut 10.44
doughnut hole
  cake 10.42
  doughnut 10.44
doughty strong 15.15
  courageous 492.16
doughy pasty 1047.12
  viscous 1062.12
  pulpy 1063.6
dour sullen 110.24
  harsh 144.24
  unyielding 361.9
  strict 425.6
  firm 425.7
douse take off 6.6
  submerge 367.7
  fight fire 1022.7
dove bird 311.27
  simple soul 416.3
  pacifist 464.6

  innocent 657.4
dovecote 228.23
dovetail
  n joint 800.4
  v interact 777.6
  agree 788.6
  hook 800.8
dowager woman 77.5
  old woman 304.3
  widow 566.4
  mistress 575.2
  aristocrat 607.4
dowdiness 810.6
dowdy
  n pastry 10.41
  adj shabby 393.32
dowel 283.3
do well 1010.7
dower
  n talent 413.4
  endowment 478.9
  v endow 478.17
  adj endowed 478.26
do without
  not use 390.5
  relinquish 475.3
  abstain 668.7
Dow-Jones Industrial Average
    737.1
down
  n beard 3.8
  fluff 3.19
  descent 194.1
  plain 236.1
  hill 237.4
  smoothness 294.3
  lightness 298.2
  game 746.3
  reverse 1011.3
  softness 1047.4
  v devour 8.22
  tipple 88.24
  take 134.8
  descend 194.5
  thin 270.12
  change 852.7
  fell 913.5
  adj ill 85.56
  laid up 85.59
  dejected 112.22
  motionless 173.13
  descending 194.11
  lower 274.8
  defeated 412.14
  recorded 549.17
  adv downward 194.13
  cash 624.25
Down's syndrome 922.9
down-and-out
  n poor man 619.4
  adj ruined 395.28
  destitute 619.9
  ended 820.9
down-at-the-heel
  shabby 393.32
  indigent 619.8
  slovenly 810.15
downbeat
  n beat 709.26
  round 850.3
  adj depressing 112.30

  pessimistic 125.16
downcast
  n downthrow 913.2
  adj dejected 112.22
  downturned 194.12
  depressed 913.12
downer
  n annoyance 96.2
  dejection 112.3
  despair 125.2
  sinkage 194.2
  adversity 1011.1
  adj depressing 112.30
downers 87.5
downfall descent 194.1
  rainstorm 316.2
  fall 395.3
  collapse 410.3
  defeat 412.1
  downthrow 913.2
downgrade
  n descent 194.1
  declivity 204.5
  v reduce 252.7
  demote 447.3
  adj sloping downward
    204.16
  adv down 194.13
  slantingly 204.23
downhearted 112.22
downhill
  n declivity 204.5
  adj descending 194.11
  sloping downward 204.16
  adv down 194.13
  slantingly 204.23
down-home
  comfortable 121.11
  informal 581.3
  simple 798.6
down in the dumps 112.22
download 1042.18
down-low 345.1
down on averse 99.8
  disapproving 510.21
down on one's luck 1011.14
down pat 928.26
down payment 624.1
downplay
  minimize 252.9
  moderate 670.6
  attach little importance to
    998.12
downpour
  descent 194.1
  flow 238.4
  rainstorm 316.2
  downthrow 913.2
downright
  adj vertical 200.11
  outright 247.12
  candid 644.17
  thorough 794.10
  unqualified 960.2
  adv down 194.13
  extremely 247.22
  no ifs, ands, or buts 960.3
the downside
  adversity 1011.1
  trouble 1013.3
downsize 252.7

downstage
n stage 704.16
adv on the stage 704.36
downstairs
down 194.13
below 274.10
downtempo 708.54
down the drain
lost 473.7
wasted 486.9
no more 762.11
down the hatch! 88.38
down-the-line 407.14
down the tube
ruined 395.29
lost 473.7
no more 762.11
downtime respite 20.2
leisure 402.1
interim 826.1
delay 846.2
down-to-earth 987.6
downtown
n city district 230.6
adj urban 230.11
adv down 194.13
downtrodden 432.16
downturn
descent 194.1
decline 252.2
deterioration 393.3
business cycle 731.10
down under 231.6
downward
adj flowing 172.8
descending 194.11
adv down 194.13
downward mobility
deterioration 393.3
class 607.1
change 852.1
"the downward slope" 303.5
downy feathery 3.27
smooth 287.10
smooth-textured 294.8
light 298.10
fluffy 1047.14
do wonders 409.7
dowry
n talent 413.4
endowment 478.9
adj endowed 478.26
doxology paean 696.3
sacred music 708.17
doyen senior 304.5
chief 575.3
doze
n sleep 22.2
v sleep 22.13
dozen 882.7
drab
n strumpet 665.14
slob 810.7
adj brown 40.3
same 781.6
lackluster 1027.17
Draconian 144.26
Dracula 127.9
draft
n beverage 8.4
dose 86.6

drink 88.7
submergence 275.6
wind 318.1
diagram 381.3
demand 421.1
recruit 461.18
writing 547.10
abridgment 557.1
enlistment 615.7
score 708.28
drawing 712.12
negotiable instrument 728.11
pulling 905.1
v draw off 192.12
outline 381.11
write 547.19
enlist 615.17
portray 712.18
drive 756.4
drag
n substance abuse 87.1
smoking 89.10
annoyance 96.2
killjoy 112.14
tedious person 118.5
slowing 175.4
gait 177.12
resistance 184.27
burden 297.7
favor 894.2
pull 905.2
attraction 907.1
disadvantage 996.2
curb 1012.7
friction 1044.1
v use 87.22
smoke 89.14
lag 166.4
go slow 175.6
dawdle 175.8
way of walking 177.28
hang 202.6
smooth 287.5
linger on 827.7
delay 846.8
pull 905.4
attract 907.4
drag and drop 1042.18
drag in
interpose 213.6
foist 776.5
drag into 898.2
dragnet
snare 356.13
seizure 480.2
search 938.15
dragon
sorehead 110.11
violent person 671.9
drag on
be tedious 118.6
persist 781.3
linger on 827.7
continue 856.3
drag one's feet
go slow 175.6
hesitate 362.7
protract 827.9
delay 846.8
procrastinate 846.11

dragoon
n cavalryman 461.12
v intimidate 127.20
compel 424.4
coerce 424.7
drag out go slow 175.6
elicit 192.14
lengthen 267.6
diffuse 538.8
protract 827.9
postpone 846.9
drag queen 75.15
drag racing 756.1
drain
n receptacle of filth 80.12
outflow 190.4
sough 239.5
consumption 388.1
demand 421.1
waste 473.2
v disable 19.9
decolor 36.5
run out 190.13
draw off 192.12
subtract 255.9
exploit 387.16
consume 388.3
waste 473.5
take from 480.21
strip 480.24
evacuate 909.22
dry 1066.6
drake
male animal 76.8
poultry 311.28
dram
n beverage 8.4
drink 88.7
modicum 248.2
dose 793.5
v tipple 88.24
drama
show business 704.1
representation 349.1
drama queen 93.1
dramatic
emotionalistic 93.19
theatrical 501.24
thespian 704.33
vocal 708.50
poetic 720.15
dramatic poem 720.4
dramatist
author 547.15
playwright 704.22
writer 718.4
dramatize
manifest 348.5
affect 500.12
theatricalize 704.28
play up 997.16
drape
n pendant 202.4
cover 295.2
shade 1028.1
v clothe 5.39
hang 202.6
drastic 671.16
drat! 513.12
draw
n attendance 221.4

valley 237.7
lure 377.3
poker 759.10
the same 790.3
tie 836.3
pull 905.2
attraction 907.1
v smoke 89.14
extract 192.10
draw off 192.12
contract 260.7
lengthen 267.6
represent 349.8
describe 349.9
lure 377.5
acquire 472.8
receive 479.6
portray 712.18
play 751.4
equal 790.5
exercise influence 894.9
pull 905.4
attract 907.4
draw a blank
fail 410.10
forget 990.5
draw and quarter
torture 604.16
tear apart 802.14
draw apart
antagonize 589.7
separate 802.8
drawback
discount 631.1
disadvantage 996.2
fault 1003.2
obstacle 1012.4
drawer lure 377.3
storehouse 386.6
draftsman 716.3
draw in retract 168.3
suck 187.12
contract 260.7
narrow 270.11
lure 377.5
portray 712.18
involve 898.2
reel in 906.9
drawing
n extraction 192.1
drafting 192.3
representation 349.1
diagram 381.3
draftsmanship 712.4
delineation 712.12
graphic arts 713.1
lottery 759.14
pulling 905.1
adj pulling 905.6
attracting 907.5
drawing card 377.3
drawing room
parlor 197.5
room on train 197.10
society 578.6
drawl
n slowness 175.1
accent 524.8
v speak 524.25
speak poorly 525.7
draw lots 759.23

drawn
  tired-looking 21.9
  lengthened 267.8
  equal 790.7
draw out
  extract 192.10
  elicit 192.14
  lengthen 267.6
  diffuse 538.8
  protract 827.9
draw the line at 325.3
draw up
  write 547.19
  form 807.5
  stop 857.7
  pick up 912.8
dray 179.2
dread
  n unpleasure 96.1
  anxiety 126.1
  fear 127.1
  suspense 130.3
  v fear 127.10
  expect 130.5
  adj terrible 127.30
dreadful
  adj horrid 98.19
  terrible 127.30
  venerable 155.12
  remarkable 247.11
  bad 1000.9
  hideous 1015.11
  adv terribly 1000.14
dreadlock 3.7
dream
  n aspiration 100.9
  airy hope 124.4
  illusion 976.1
  hallucination 976.7
  abstractedness 985.2
  reverie 986.9
  first-rate 999.7
  beauty 1016.8
  v suppose 951.10
  muse 985.9
  dream of 986.17
dreamland sleep 22.2
  illusion 976.1
  utopia 986.11
dream up
  originate 892.12
  imagine 986.14
dreamy sleepy 22.21
  tranquilizing 670.15
  illusory 976.9
  abstracted 985.11
  dreamful 986.25
dreary gray 39.4
  distressing 98.20
  gloomy 112.24
  dull 117.6
  tedious 118.9
  ominous 133.16
dredge
  n excavator 284.10
  v extract 192.10
  excavate 284.15
  sprinkle 771.6
  imbue 797.11
  pick up 912.8

dredge up
  extract 192.10
  assemble 770.18
  pick up 912.8
dregs grounds 256.2
  refuse 391.4
  rabble 606.3
  extract 893.3
drench
  n inhibition 8.4
  drink 88.7
  soaking 1065.7
  v overload 993.15
  soak 1065.13
  tend 1070.7
dress
  n clothing 5.1
  suit 5.6
  gown 5.16
  insignia 647.1
  v clothe 5.39
  groom 79.20
  smooth 287.5
  equip 385.8
  prepare 405.6
  ornament 498.8
  fertilize 890.8
  buff 1044.8
  oil 1056.8
  cultivate 1069.17
  adj clothing 5.45
dressage 1070.1
dress down
  dress up 5.42
  disapprove 510.18
  punish 604.15
dress-down
  dishabille 5.20
  in dishabille 5.47
dressed to kill
  dressed up 5.46
  chic 578.13
dressing clothing 5.1
  stuffing 10.27
  application 86.33
  disapproval 510.6
  fertilizer 890.4
  abrasion 1044.2
  cultivation 1069.13
dressing room
  closet 197.15
  stage 704.16
dress rehearsal 704.13
dress-up clothes 5.10
dried-up shrunk 260.13
  wasted 393.35
  unproductive 891.4
  dried 1066.9
drift
  n direction 161.1
  deviation 164.1
  course 172.2
  deposit 176.9
  drift angle 184.28
  flow 238.4
  meaning 518.1
  race 756.3
  group of animals 770.5
  pile 770.10
  trend 896.2
  reception 1034.21

  v stray 164.4
  wander 177.23
  drift off course 182.29
  float 182.54
  fly 184.36
  do nothing 329.2
  take it easy 331.15
  pile 770.19
drifter
  displaced person 160.4
  wanderer 178.2
  bum 331.9
  fisher 382.6
  wretch 660.2
  transient 828.4
drift off 22.16
driftwood 1054.3
drill
  n exercise 84.2
  point 285.3
  action 328.1
  rule 373.4
  training 568.3
  study 570.3
  exercise 725.6
  cutlery 1040.2
  v deepen 275.8
  excavate 284.15
  perforate 292.15
  train 568.13
  study 570.12
  plant 1069.18
drink
  n potation 8.4
  beverage 10.49
  dram 88.7
  cocktail 88.9
  spirits 88.13
  ocean 240.1
  fluid 1061.2
  v drink in 8.29
  use 87.22
  tipple 88.24
  ingest 187.11
  absorb 187.13
drink in drink 8.29
  absorb 187.13
  learn 570.7
  attend to 983.5
drinking habit 87.1
drink to drink 8.29
  toast 88.29
drink up drink 8.29
  tipple 88.24
  absorb 187.13
  thirst 1066.5
drip
  n tedious person 118.5
  leakage 190.5
  trickle 238.7
  v leak 190.14
  trickle 238.18
  be damp 1065.11
drive
  n vim 17.2
  power 18.1
  desire 100.1
  acceleration 174.4
  ride 177.7
  enterprise 330.7
  motive 365.1

  urge 375.6
  haste 401.1
  campaign 458.3
  attack 459.1
  vigor 544.3
  group of animals 770.5
  cause 886.9
  impulse 902.1
  pushing 904.1
  machinery enginery 1040.3
  disk drive 1042.5
  v set in motion 172.6
  ride 177.33
  drift off course 182.29
  pilot 184.37
  excavate 284.15
  hustle 330.13
  hunt 382.9
  compel 424.4
  launch an attack 459.17
  guide 573.9
  task 725.16
  play tennis 748.3
  play 751.4
  race 756.4
  ride 757.5
  impel 902.11
  thrust 902.12
  push 904.9
  obsess 926.25
  herd 1070.8
drive a bargain 731.18
drive at 380.4
drive away
  dissipate 771.5
  repulse 908.3
drive back 908.3
drive crazy 926.24
drive home to 953.18
drive-in movie 706.7
drive insane 926.24
drive-in theater 706.7
drivel
  n saliva 13.3
  nonsense 520.2
  v salivate 13.6
  talk nonsense 520.5
  be incomprehensible 522.10
  be stupid 922.12
  be insane 926.20
drive off 908.3
drive on
  make one's way 162.4
  hustle 330.13
  urge on 375.16
  hasten 401.4
  impel 902.11
driver reinsman 178.9
  motorist 178.10
  tyrant 575.14
  man 577.4
  race driving 756.2
  operator 889.4
  propeller 904.6
driver's license 443.6
driver's seat 417.10
drive-through 8.11
drive-through meal 8.6
drive up the wall
  annoy 96.13
  madden 926.24

dry 1066.6
interj silence! 51.14
DSL 1042.19
dual
　n number 530.8
　adj two 873.6
dual citizen 227.4
dualism theism 675.5
　doubleness 873.1
　pluralism 952.6
dualist 675.16
dub
　n bungler 414.9
　golfer 751.2
　v smooth 287.5
　name 527.11
dub in 862.4
dubious
　deceptive 356.21
　irresolute 362.9
　dishonest 645.16
　agnostic 695.20
　doubting 955.9
　unbelievable 955.10
　improbable 969.3
　doubtful 971.17
　unsafe 1006.11
ducal 608.10
ducat 728.4
duchess 608.6
duchy region 231.5
　country 232.1
duck
　n man 76.5
　poultry 311.28
　submergence 367.2
　avoidance 368.1
　loser 412.5
　endearment term 562.6
　card 758.2
　retreat 903.3
　crouch 913.3
　v avoid 164.6
　retract 168.3
　prevaricate 344.7
　submerge 367.7
　dodge 368.8
　shirk 368.9
　fight 754.4
　pull back 903.7
　crouch 913.8
　bow 913.9
　flood 1065.14
duck out
　absent oneself 222.8
　flee 368.11
　slip away 368.12
duck soup 1014.4
ducky
　n ladylove 104.14
　adj excellent 999.13
duct vessel 2.23
　channel 239.1
ductile docile 433.13
　handy 1014.15
　pliant 1047.9
dud
　n impotent 19.6
　false alarm 400.2
　failure 410.2
　abortion 410.5

flop 410.8
candidate 610.9
thing of naught 764.2
v clothe 5.39
dude man 76.5
　dandy 500.9
dudette 77.6
dudgeon 152.7
duds clothing 5.1
　garment 5.3
due
　n debt 623.1
　one's due 639.2
　prerogative 642.1
　adj expected 130.13
　owed 623.10
　right 637.3
　payable 639.7
　entitled to 639.10
　just 649.7
　attributable 888.6
　sufficient 991.6
　adv directly 161.23
duel
　n single combat 457.7
　fight 754.3
　v contend 457.13
duelist 461.1
dues debt 623.1
　fee 630.6
　deserts 639.3
duet cooperation 450.1
　part music 708.18
　two 873.2
due to
　conj resulting from 887.8
　prep because of 888.9
duffel equipment 385.4
　impedimenta 471.3
duffer
　incompetent 414.7
　bungler 414.9
　golfer 751.2
dugout cave 284.5
　hiding place 346.4
　entrenchment 460.5
　baseball 745.1
　shelter 1009.3
dugs 283.6
duke nobleman 608.4
　poker 759.10
　blow 902.5
duke it out 457.17
dulce de leche 10.40
dulcet pleasant 97.6
　melodious 708.48
dulcify sweeten 66.3
　pacify 465.7
　calm 670.7
dull
　v weaken 16.10
　deaden 25.4
　decolor 36.5
　muffle 51.9
　blunt 94.7
　relieve 120.5
　blunt 286.2
　moderate 670.6
　mat 1027.10
　adj weak 16.12
　insensible 25.6

colorless 36.7
gray 39.4
muffled 52.17
unfeeling 94.9
apathetic 94.13
inexcitable 106.10
dry 117.6
tedious 118.9
inert 173.14
blunt 286.3
languid 331.20
plain-speaking 535.3
prosaic 721.5
dull of mind 922.16
unimaginative 987.5
mediocre 1005.7
lackluster 1027.17
dullard 924.2
dull roar 51.1
duly noted 549.17
dumb
　adj mute 51.12
　animal 311.39
　taciturn 344.9
　stammering 525.13
　stupid 922.15
　foolish 923.8
　ignorant 930.11
　inanimate 1055.5
dumbbell
　exerciser 725.7
　fool 924.4
dumbfound
　silence 51.8
　astonish 122.6
dumbstruck
　mute 51.12
　wondering 122.9
dumbwaiter 912.4
dummy
　n mute 51.3
　reproduction 336.3
　figure 349.6
　fake 354.13
　instrument 384.4
　composition 548.2
　figurehead 575.5
　deputy 576.1
　follower 616.8
　bridge 758.3
　thing of naught 764.2
　artist's model 786.5
　substitute 862.2
　fool 924.4
　a nobody 998.7
　adj spurious 354.26
　substitute 862.8
dump
　n sty 80.11
　receptacle of filth 80.12
　humiliation 137.2
　disrespect 156.3
　hovel 228.11
　disapproved place 228.28
　derelict 370.4
　store 386.1
　storehouse 386.6
　trash pile 391.6
　armory 462.2
　v abase 137.5
　place 159.12

load 159.15
discard 390.7
relinquish 475.3
sell 734.8
divest 737.24
unload 909.23
dumpling 10.33
dump on
　abase 137.5
　be disrespectful 156.6
　disdain 157.3
dumps
　sulks 110.10
　blues 112.6
dumpy
　corpulent 257.18
　dwarf 258.13
　stubby 268.10
dun
　n horse 311.11
　creditor 622.4
　statement 628.3
　v importune 440.12
　bill 628.11
　adj brown 40.3
dunce
　stupid person 924.2
　ignoramus 930.7
dunderhead 924.2
dune hill 237.4
　pile 770.10
dung
　n feces 12.4
　fertilizer 890.4
　v defecate 12.13
dungeon 429.8
dunghill
　n manure pile 80.10
　adj dastardly 491.12
dunk
　submerge 367.7
　play 751.4
　flood 1065.14
duo
　part music 708.18
　two 873.2
duodecimal system 1017.4
duodenal 882.24
dupe
　n sycophant 138.3
　dupable person 358
　gull 358.1
　instrument 384.4
　simple soul 416.3
　laughingstock 508.7
　agent 576.3
　cheater 759.22
　duplicate 785.3
　trusting soul 954.4
　v deceive 356.14
　copy 785.8
　duplicate 874.3
　stultify 923.7
duplex
　n apartment house 228.14
　adj two 873.6
duplicate
　n image 349.5
　the same 778.3
　replica 785.3
　duplication 874.1

adj terrestrial 234.4
Earth planet 1072.9
  the world 1072.10
earthborn human
  312.13
  populational 606.8
earthbound
  terrestrial 234.4
  unimaginative 987.5
earthen earthy 234.5
  ceramic 742.7
earthling person 312.5
  irreligionist 695.10
earthly
  terrestrial 234.4
  secularist 695.16
  material 1052.10
earthquake 671.5
earthshaking
  loud 53.11
  important 997.17
earthworm 311.38
earthy earthen 234.5
  human 312.13
  coarse 497.11
  populational 606.8
  carnal 663.6
  vulgar 666.8
  secularist 695.16
  realistic 987.6
ear worm 422.2
ease
  n rest 20.1
  pleasure 95.1
  contentment 107.1
  relief 120.1
  comfort 121.1
  leisure 402.1
  aid 449.1
  elegance 533.1
  fluency 544.2
  informality 581.1
  prosperity 1010.1
  facility 1014.1
  v relax 20.7
  relieve 120.5
  release 120.6
  comfort 121.6
  abate 252.8
  lighten 298.6
  liberalize 430.13
  aid 449.11
  extenuate 600.12
  calm 670.7
  relax 670.9
  loosen 804.3
  allow for 959.5
  facilitate 1014.7
  soften 1047.6
ease in 191.3
easel 712.17
ease off
  let up 20.7
  avoid 164.6
  slow 175.9
  relax 670.9
  loosen 804.3
ease out 773.4
ease up relax 20.7
  slow 175.9
  relax 670.9

ease up on
  have pity 145.4
  be easy on 427.5
east
  n points of the compass
   161.3
  adj northern 161.14
  adv E 161.17
East 231.6
East Coast 231.7
easter
  n north wind 318.8
  v go west 161.8
eastward
  n points of the compass
   161.3
  adv east 161.17
easy
  adj pleased 95.15
  nonchalant 106.15
  content 107.7
  comfortable 121.11
  at ease 121.12
  good-natured 143.14
  slow 175.10
  light 298.12
  indolent 331.19
  leisurely 402.6
  unstrict 426.5
  lenient 427.7
  elegant 533.6
  fluent 544.9
  informal 581.3
  cheap 633.7
  wanton 665.26
  loose 804.5
  gullible 954.9
  prosperous 1010.12
  facile 1014.13
  soft 1047.8
  adv cautiously 494.12
  interj careful! 494.14
  cease! 857.13
easy come 486.8
easy does it
  interj take it easy! 402.8
  careful! 494.14
  phrs take it easy 175.15
easygoing
  unconcerned 102.7
  nonchalant 106.15
  content 107.7
  careless 340.11
  unstrict 426.5
  lenient 427.7
  free 430.21
  informal 581.3
  dilatory 846.17
easy mark dupe 358.2
  trusting soul 954.4
easy money 472.6
easy on the eyes 1016.21
easy pickings 358.2
Easy Street 1010.1
easy target 1014.3
eat feed 8.20
  take 134.8
  ingest 187.11
  consume 388.3
  corrode 393.21
  etch 713.10

eat away
  subtract 255.9
  corrode 393.21
eat crow
  n recant 363.8
  v humble oneself 137.7
  eat dirt 433.11
eat humble pie
  n recant 363.8
  v humble oneself 137.7
  eat dirt 433.11
eating disorder mental
  disorder 92.14
  gluttony 672.1
eat one's words
  n recant 363.8
  v humble oneself 137.7
eat up
  v devour 8.22
  feast 8.24
  enjoy 95.13
  consume 388.3
  kid oneself 954.6
  interj chow down! 8.35
eau de Cologne 70.3
eau de parfum 70.2
eaves 295.6
eavesdrop
  listen 48.10
  be curious 981.3
eaves trough 239.3
ebb
  n standstill 173.3
  tide 238.13
  decline 252.2
  deterioration 393.3
  v recede 168.2
  move 172.5
  quiet 173.8
  flow 238.16
  decrease 252.6
  decline 393.17
ebb and flow
  n tide 238.13
  alternation 916.5
  v billow 238.22
  change 854.5
  alternate 916.13
ebony
  n blackness 38.1
  darkness 38.4
  adj black 38.8
  dark 1027.13
e-book 554.3
ebullient
  excited 105.20
  bubbly 320.6
  active 330.17
  hot 1019.25
eccentric
  n nonconformist 868.3
  oddity 870.4
  erratic 927.3
  adj off-center 160.12
  humorous 488.4
  irregular 851.3
  inconstant 854.7
  unconventional 868.6
  abnormal 870.9
  odd 870.11
  erratic 927.5

eccentricity
  humorousness 488.1
  irregularity 851.1
  inconstancy 854.2
  abnormality 870.1
  foolishness 923.1
  idiosyncrasy 927.1
  disposition 978.3
ecclesiastic
  n clergyman 699.2
  adj ministerial 698.13
ecclesiastical
  ecclesiastic 698.13
  churchly 703.15
  mode 709.10
ecdysiast
  nudity 6.3
  entertainer 707.1
ECG 91.9
echelon
  flight formation 184.12
  rank 245.2
  battle array 458.2
echo
  n reverberation 54.2
  sympathy 93.5
  imitator 336.4
  response 708.23
  keyboard 711.17
  reflection 785.7
  repetition 849.1
  repeat 849.5
  duplicate 874.2
  reaction 903.1
  answer 939.1
  signal 1036.11
  v reverberate 54.7
  respond 93.11
  concur 332.9
  imitate 336.5
  repeat 849.7
  recurrence 849.11
  answer 939.4
  reflect 1036.16
éclat publicity 352.4
  display 501.4
  applause 509.2
  repute 662.1
eclectic
  selective 371.23
  mixed 797.14
  combined 805.5
eclecticism
  selectivity 371.10
  sectarianism 675.4
  mixture 797.1
eclipse
  n disappearance 34.1
  covering 295.1
  occultation 1027.8
  moon 1072.11
  sun 1072.13
  v blind 30.7
  overshadow 249.8
  cover 295.19
  conceal 346.6
  darken 1027.9
eco-friendly 397.12
ecological 209.9
ecology 1073.1
e-commerce 736.2

economic cheap 633.7
　thrifty 635.6
　socio-economic 731.23
economic indicator 731.9
economics
　finance 729.1
　trade 731.1
　eco 731.11
economist
　economizer 635.3
　financier 729.9
　economic expert 731.12
economy
　n parsimony 484.1
　thrift 635.1
　economic system 731.7
　adj cheap 633.7
ecosphere
　organic matter 305.1
　biosphere 306.7
　atmosphere 317.2
　the environment 1073.1
ecosystem 1073.1
ecru brown 40.3
　yellow 43.4
ecstasy
　amphetamines 87.4
　passion 93.2
　happiness 95.2
　amorousness 104.2
　fury 105.8
　revelation 683.10
　trance 691.3
ecstatic
　n psychic 689.13
　adj overjoyed 95.17
　frenzied 105.25
　abstracted 985.11
ectomorph 92.12
ectoplasm cell 305.4
　exteriorized protoplasm
　　689.7
ecumenical
　cooperative 450.5
　universal 864.14
　broad-minded 979.8
ecumenism
　cooperation 450.1
　moderation 670.1
　combination 805.1
　broad-mindedness 979.1
eczema 85.34
eddy
　n agitation 105.4
　back stream 238.12
　whirl 915.2
　v gurge 238.21
　whirl 915.11
edema symptom 85.9
　increase 251.1
　distension 259.2
　swelling 283.4
　overextension 993.7
Eden 986.11
edge
　n acrimony 17.5
　pungency 68.1
　summit 198.2
　border 211.4
　advantage 249.2
　straight line 277.2

　sharpness 285.1
　sharp edge 285.2
　v border 211.10
　side 218.4
　go sideways 218.5
　sharpen 285.7
edge in enter 189.7
　interpose 213.6
　intrude 214.5
edge out outdo 249.9
　triumph 411.3
　defeat 412.6
edgy
　excitable 105.28
　nervous 128.11
　impatient 135.6
edible 8.33
edict
　announcement 352.2
　decree 420.4
　law 673.3
edification
　teaching 568.1
　learning 928.4
edifice house 228.5
　structure 266.2
edify
　make better 392.9
　teach 568.10
edit delete 255.12
　comment upon 341.11
　revise 392.12
　write 547.19
edition rendering 341.2
　issue 554.5
　score 708.28
editor interpreter 341.7
　publisher 554.2
　journalist 555.4
　commentator 556.4
　motion-picture studio 706.4
　examiner 938.17
　critic 946.7
　systems program 1042.12
editorial
　n commentary 556.2
　adj explanatory 341.15
　journalistic 555.5
educate
　make better 392.9
　teach 568.10
educated
　improved 392.13
　learned 570.16
　informed 928.18
　scholarly 928.21
educated guess 951.4
education
　cultivation 392.3
　teaching 568.1
　learning 570.1
　erudition 928.4
educational 551.18
educe 192.14
EEG 91.9
eel 10.24
eerie awesome 122.11
　creepy 127.31
　deathly 307.28
　supernatural 870.15
　weird 988.9

efface 395.16
effect
　n power 18.1
　aspect 33.3
　intention 380.1
　meaning 518.1
　relevance 775.4
　end 820.1
　event 831.1
　sequel 835.2
　consequence 887.1
　result 887.1
　product 893.1
　influence 894.1
　v do 328.6
　use 384.5
　accomplish 407.4
　execute 437.9
　cause 886.10
　induce 886.11
　establish 892.10
effective
　powerful 18.12
　able 18.14
　effectual 387.21
　vigorous 544.11
　operative 889.9
　influential 894.13
　practical 995.6
effects
　equipment 385.4
　property 471.1
　merchandise 735.1
effectual able 18.14
　effective 387.21
　causal 886.13
　operative 889.9
　influential 894.13
　true 973.13
　practical 995.6
effeminate
　n mama's boy 77.10
　v feminize 77.12
　adj frail 16.14
　homosexual 75.30
　womanish 77.14
effervescence
　sibilation 57.1
　agitation 105.4
　bubbling 320.3
　liveliness 330.2
effervescent
　sibilant 57.3
　excited 105.20
　bubbly 320.6
　active 330.17
effete weak 16.12
　weakened 16.18
　ineffective 19.15
　dull 117.6
　used up 388.5
　worn-out 393.36
　deteriorating 393.45
efficacious able 18.14
　effectual 387.21
　operative 889.9
　influential 894.13
efficiency
　ability 18.2
　utility 387.3
　skill 413.1

efficient able 18.14
　effectual 387.21
　competent 413.24
　economical 635.6
　operative 889.9
　practical 995.6
effigy 349.5
efflorescence
　skin eruption 85.36
　flowering 310.26
　powderiness 1051.1
　powder 1051.5
effluent
　n excrement 12.3
　tributary 238.3
　refuse 391.4
　adj outgoing 190.19
effluvium odor 69.1
　ectoplasm 689.7
　miasma 1001.4
　vapor 1067.1
effluxion 190.4
effort act 328.3
　endeavor 403.1
　attempt 403.2
　undertaking 404.1
　exertion 725.1
　expedient 995.2
effortless 1014.13
effrontery 142.1
effulgence 1025.4
effuse
　v excrete 12.12
　emerge 190.11
　exude 190.15
　adj plentiful 991.7
effusive
　v talkative 540.9
　adj outgoing 190.19
　communicative 343.10
　diffuse 538.11
egalitarianism 612.4
egest excrete 12.12
　vomit 909.26
egestion excretion 12.1
　vomiting 909.8
egg
　n ovum 305.12
　ovule 305.15
　race 753.3
　vital force 886.7
　v pelt 459.27
eggement 375.4
egghead
　snob 141.7
　nerd 572.10
　scientist 928.11
　intellectual 929.1
egg on urge on 375.16
　induce 886.11
egg on one's face
　chagrin 96.4
　mortification 98.6
　humiliation 137.2
eggshell
　n egg 305.15
　fragility 1050.2
　adj soft-colored 35.22
　whitish 37.8
ego psyche 92.28
　egotism 140.3

self 865.5
psyche 919.4
egocentric
n egotist 140.5
adj unfeeling 94.9
egotistic 140.10
egoist
proudling 136.3
egotist 140.5
egomaniac 140.1
egotism egoism 140.3
selfishness 651.1
egotist egoist 140.5
self-seeker 651.3
egotistical
self-centered 140.10
selfish 651.5
ego trip vanity 140.1
selfishness 651.1
egregious
remarkable 247.10
downright 247.12
thorough 794.10
excessive 993.16
terrible 1000.9
egress
n departure 188.1
exit 190.2
outlet 190.9
channel 239.1
evacuation 909.6
v exit 190.12
eiderdown
down 3.19
blanket 295.10
softness 1047.4
eidetic 989.22
eidolon aspect 33.3
phantom 976.4
figment of the imagination
986.5
specter 988.1
eight team 617.7
card 758.2
number 882.4
eighth
n octave 709.9
adj octonary 882.20
eighty-six 390.7
Einstein theory 158.6
either
n any 864.5
adj one 872.7
adv similarly 784.18
either-or
ambiguous 539.4
two 873.6
ejaculate exclaim 59.7
climax 75.24
project 904.11
disgorge 909.25
eject erupt 671.13
eliminate 773.5
separate 802.8
shoot 904.12
repulse 908.3
expel 909.13
ejection
excretion 12.1
excrement 12.3
outburst 190.3

elimination 773.2
shot 904.4
repulsion 908.1
discharge 909.1
ejectment 909.1
eke out
support oneself 385.12
be poor 619.5
complete 794.6
EKG 91.9
el 179.14
elaborate
v develop 392.10
amplify 538.7
ornament 545.7
develop 861.6
produce 892.8
adj painstaking 339.11
ornate 498.12
grandiose 501.21
complex 799.4
elaborated 533.9
elaboration
development 392.2
ornamentation 498.1
amplification 538.6
iteration 849.2
evolution 861.1
production 892.2
élan animation 17.4
eagerness 101.1
gaiety 109.4
elapse lapse 821.5
pass 837.6
elastic
n elastomer 1048.3
adj expansive 259.9
recuperative 396.23
pliant 1047.9
resilient 1048.7
elate
v exalt 109.8
make proud 136.6
adj overjoyed 95.17
rejoicing 116.10
crowing 502.13
elbow
n member 2.7
angle 278.2
joint 800.4
arm 906.5
v angle 278.5
thrust 902.12
elbow bender 88.12
elbow grease 725.1
elbowroom room 158.3
latitude 430.4
elder
n old man 304.2
senior 304.5
master 575.1
public official 575.17
clergy 699.10
back number 842.8
wise man 921.1
personage 997.8
adj previous 834.4
older 842.19
elder statesman
expert 413.11
statesman 610.2

wise man 921.1
El Dorado 986.11
e-learning 567.5
elect
n elite 371.12
upper class 607.2
aristocracy 608.1
the best 999.8
v choose 371.13
vote in 371.20
support 609.41
adj chosen 371.26
exclusive 495.13
best 999.16
the elect 692.5
election
choice 371.1
appointment 371.9
authority 417.12
general election 609.15
holy orders 698.10
determinism 964.4
electioneer
n campaigner 610.10
v campaign 609.40
elective
voluntary 324.7
volitional 371.22
selective 371.23
electorate
population 227.1
region 231.5
selector 371.7
electors 609.22
Electra complex 92.22
electric
n streetcar 179.17
adj exciting 105.30
provocative 375.27
galvanic 1032.30
electrical engineering
1043.1
electric blanket 295.10
electric chair 605.5
electric current
current 1032.2
electron flow 1033.6
electric field 1032.3
electrician
stage technician 704.24
electrotechnician 1032.22
electricity
swiftness 174.6
telegraph 347.2
illuminant 1025.20
electrical science 1032.1
electric power
manpower 18.4
wattage 1032.18
electrify energize 17.10
agitate 105.14
startle 131.8
galvanize 1032.26
electrolysis 1032.25
electromagnetic field
electric field 1032.3
magnetic force 1032.9
electron atom 258.8
negatron 1033.3
electronic book 554.3
electronic device 1033.13

electronic mail computer
networking 347.18
delivery 353.5
correspondence 553.1
mail 553.4
postal service 553.7
computer communications
1042.19
electronic media 551.5
electronics radio 347.3
electron physics 1033.1
radionics 1033.1
electron theory of atoms
1033.2
electrostatic
electric 1032.30
static 1039.8
eleemosynary
benevolent 143.15
philanthropic 478.22
gratuitous 634.5
elegance
parsimony 484.1
taste 496.1
ornateness 498.2
overniceness 500.5
grandeur 501.5
good breeding 504.4
refinement 533.1
grace 533.1
fluency 544.2
smartness 578.3
etiquette 580.3
decency 664.2
beauty 1016.1
elegant graceful 496.8
ornate 498.12
overnice 500.18
grandiose 501.21
tasteful 533.6
fluent 544.9
chic 578.13
decent 664.5
good 999.12
beautiful 1016.17
elegiac
n meter 720.7
adj dirgelike 115.22
poetic 720.15
elegy 115.6
element
natural environment 209.4
particular 766.3
component 796.2
cause 886.1
heater 1020.10
matter 1052.2
chemical element 1060.2
elemental
n elemental spirit 678.6
adj basic 199.8
climatal 317.13
essential 767.9
beginning 818.15
original 886.14
chemical 1060.9
elementary basic 199.8
essential 767.9
component 796.5
simple 798.6
beginning 818.15

original 886.14
chemical 1060.9
elementary school 567.3
elements
contents 196.1
elementary education 568.5
Eucharist 701.7
substance 763.2
basics 818.6
the elements 317.3
elephant drugs 87.18
beast of burden 176.8
behemoth 257.14
pachyderm 311.4
elephantine dull 117.6
bulky 257.19
huge 257.20
elephantlike 311.46
stiff 534.3
excessive 993.16
elephant in the room 974.2
elevate elate 109.8
erect 200.9
heighten 272.13
make better 392.9
promote 446.2
glorify 662.13
raise 912.5
exalt 912.6
elevated
n train 179.14
adj drunk 88.33
lofty 136.11
eminent 247.9
increased 251.7
high 272.14
lofty 544.14
grandiloquent 545.8
magnanimous 652.6
eminent 662.18
raised 912.9
elevation ascent 193.1
erection 200.4
increase 251.1
height 272.1
steep 272.2
diagram 381.3
promotion 446.1
loftiness 544.6
magnanimity 652.2
distinction 662.5
glorification 662.8
raising 912.1
elevator
people mover 176.5
garner 386.7
ascenseur 912.4
eleven team 617.7
football team 746.2
twelve 882.7
eleventh hour
curfew 315.5
crucial moment 843.5
lateness 846.1
elf dwarf 258.5
brat 302.4
mischief-maker 322.3
fairy 678.8
imp 680.7
elfish
mischievous 322.6

fairy 678.17
impish 680.18
elicit educe 192.14
prompt 375.13
induce 886.11
elide shorten 268.6
eliminate 773.5
eligibility
qualification 371.11
inclusion 772.1
eligible
n eligibility 371.11
adj qualified 371.24
eliminate excrete 12.12
excise 255.10
murder 308.16
discard 390.7
exterminate 395.14
annihilate 762.7
get rid of 773.5
do away with 909.21
evacuate 909.22
elimination
excretion 12.1
disappearance 34.1
excision 255.3
homicide 308.2
discard 390.3
extinction 395.6
riddance 773.2
evacuation 909.6
elision
shortening 268.3
abbreviation 537.4
elite
n superior 249.5
elect 371.12
society 578.6
upper class 607.2
aristocracy 608.1
clique 617.6
the best 999.8
adj exclusive 495.13
socially prominent 578.16
best 999.16
elixir panacea 86.3
medicine 86.4
extract 192.8
essential content 196.5
essence 767.2
elk 311.5
ell adjunct 254.3
angle 278.2
ellipse curve 279.2
oval 280.6
ellipsis
shortening 268.3
abbreviation 537.4
ellipsoid
n sphere 282.2
adj parabolic 279.13
spherical 282.9
elliptical
oblong 267.9
shortened 268.9
parabolic 279.13
elliptical trainer 84.1
elocution speech 524.1
public speaking 543.1
elongated
lengthened 267.8

oblong 267.9
elope 368.10
elopement
flight 368.4
wedding 563.3
eloquence
articulateness 524.4
public speaking 543.1
rhetoric 544.1
else
adj other 780.8
adv additionally 253.11
otherwise 780.11
elsewhere
adj abstracted 985.11
adv away 222.18
elucidate
explain 341.10
make clear 521.6
elude evade 368.7
outwit 415.11
thwart 1012.15
elvish
mischievous 322.6
impish 680.18
Elysian blissful 97.9
heavenly 681.12
Elysian Fields
mythological 681.9
destiny 839.2
emaciate
v shrink 260.9
thin 270.12
waste 393.19
adj haggard 270.20
emaciation
symptom 85.9
shrinking 260.3
emaceration 270.6
waste 393.4
e-mail address 553.9
emanate radiate 171.6
emerge 190.11
come after 835.3
emanation odor 69.1
radiation 171.2
emergence 190.1
ectoplasm 689.7
light 1025.1
emancipated
free 430.21
liberated 431.10
emasculate
v unman 19.12
feminize 77.12
castrate 255.11
cripple 393.14
adj unmanned 19.19
embalm perfume 70.8
lay out 309.21
mummify 397.10
perpetuate 829.5
embankment
shore 234.2
railway 383.7
pile 770.10
buttress 901.4
harbor 1009.6
barrier 1012.5
embargo
n closure 293.1

prohibition 444.1
exclusion 773.1
v stop 293.7
prohibit 444.3
exclude 773.4
embark send 176.15
get under way 182.19
go aboard 188.15
embark on 818.9
embarrass
chagrin 96.15
mortify 98.13
humiliate 137.4
involve 898.2
bewilder 971.12
confuse 985.7
inconvenience 996.4
hamper 1012.11
put in a hole 1013.15
embarrassed
distressed 96.22
humiliated 137.14
blushing 139.13
indebted 623.8
bewildered 971.24
confused 985.12
troubled 1013.20
embarrassment
chagrin 96.4
mortification 98.6
humiliation 137.2
shyness 139.4
involvement 898.1
bewilderment 971.3
confusion 985.3
impediment 1012.6
predicament 1013.4
embarrassment of riches 993.2
embassy house 228.5
message 552.4
foreign office 576.7
commission 615.1
office 739.7
embattled
battled 458.22
fortified 460.12
embed inset 191.5
internalize 207.5
fix 855.9
embellish falsify 354.16
develop 392.10
ornament 498.8
bombast 545.7
embellishment
development 392.2
ornamentation 498.1
ornateness 545.4
ornament 709.18
superfluity 993.4
ember dregs 256.2
coal 1019.16
embezzle misuse 389.4
steal 482.13
embitter sour 110.16
aggrieve 112.19
aggravate 119.2
provoke 152.24
impair 393.9
antagonize 589.7
embittered sour 110.23
aggravated 119.4

resentful 152.26
impaired 393.27
emblazon color 35.14
ornament 498.8
flaunt 501.17
praise 509.12
emblem symbol 517.2
insignia 647.1
example 786.2
embodiment
manifestation 348.1
impersonation 349.4
representative 349.7
incarnation 763.4
essence 767.2
inclusion 772.1
whole 792.1
composition 796.1
materiality 1052.1
materialization 1052.8
embody manifest 348.5
image 349.11
incarnate 763.5
include 772.3
compose 796.3
materialize 1052.9
embolden
encourage 375.21
abet 449.14
motivate 492.15
embolism 293.3
embossed
in relief 283.18
sculptured 715.7
established 855.13
embouchure
mouth 292.4
wind instrument 711.6
embrace
n hold 474.2
hug 562.3
welcome 585.2
greeting 585.4
joint 800.4
v surround 209.6
wrap 295.20
adopt 371.15
hold 474.6
retain 474.7
seize 480.14
hug 562.18
welcome 585.9
include 772.3
put together 800.5
join 800.11
cohere 803.6
embroider
falsify 354.16
ornament 498.8
grandiloquent 545.7
embroidery exaggeration 355.1
sewing 741.1
embroilment
agitation 105.4
quarrel 456.5
fight 457.4
turbulence 671.2
commotion 810.4
agitation 917.1
embryo
zygote 305.14

vital force 886.7
embryology 1068.3
embryonic
infinitesimal 258.14
germinal 305.22
undeveloped 406.12
incomplete 795.4
beginning 818.15
original 886.14
emcee steward 574.4
theater man 704.23
master of ceremonies 743.20
broadcaster 1034.23
emend
make better 392.9
revise 392.12
remedy 396.13
emendation
explanation 341.4
revision 392.4
emended 392.13
emerald 44.4
Emerald City 986.11
emerge
show 31.4
appear 33.8
come out 190.11
find vent 369.10
emergency
hospital room 197.25
crisis 843.4
urgency 997.4
danger 1006.1
predicament 1013.4
emergency preparedness
405.4
emergent
emerging 190.18
future 839.8
critical 843.10
emeritus
n academic rank 571.3
adj retired 448.3
emery 287.8
emetic
n nastiness 64.3
cleanser 79.17
vomitive 86.18
adj cleansing 79.28
vomitive 86.49
emigrant
migrant 178.5
goer 190.10
newcomer 774.4
emigrate
migrate 177.22
leave home 188.17
out-migrate 190.16
eminence hill 237.4
glory 247.2
height 272.1
steep 272.2
protuberance 283.2
prestige 417.4
distinction 662.5
influence 894.1
notability 997.2
éminence grise
Machiavellian 415.8
politics 610.6
influence 894.6

eminent
prominent 247.9
superior 249.12
high up 272.14
protruding 283.14
authoritative 417.15
high 662.18
notable 997.19
eminent domain 417.1
emir
Muslim ruler 575.10
prince 608.7
Sir 648.3
emissary
messenger 353.1
delegate 576.2
diplomat 576.6
emit excrete 12.12
exude 190.15
issue 352.14
say 524.22
let out 909.24
vaporize 1067.8
emollient
n balm 86.11
ointment 1056.3
adj palliative 86.40
relieving 120.9
softening 1047.16
lubricant 1056.10
emote
emotionalize 93.13
affect 500.12
act 704.29
emotion feeling 93.1
excitement 105.1
attitude 978.1
emotional
affective 93.17
excitable 105.28
attitudinal 978.7
emotional intelligence 93.1
emotive
feeling 93.17
emotionalistic 93.19
affecting 93.22
empathic
sensitive 24.12
condoling 147.3
in accord 455.3
empathize with
respond 93.11
condole with 147.2
empathy
sensitivity 24.3
sympathy 93.5
accord 455.1
emperor 575.8
emphasis
impressiveness 524.10
accent 709.25
meter 720.7
emphasize 997.14
emphatic
affirmative 334.8
vehement 544.13
decided 997.21
empire country 232.1
dominion 417.5
sovereignty 417.8
government 612.1

empirical
real 761.15
experimental 942.11
empiricism
ethical philosophy 636.2
experiment 942.1
materialism 1052.6
emplacement
location 159.1
placement 159.6
platform 901.13
emplane 188.15
employ
n use 387.1
service 577.12
occupation 724.1
v practice 328.8
use 387.10
spend 387.13
hire 615.14
occupy 724.10
exert 725.8
employee
subordinate 432.5
hireling 577.3
pensioner 577.3
assistant 616.6
worker 726.2
emporium
market 736.1
marketplace 736.2
empower
enable 18.10
authorize 443.11
commission 615.10
empty
v run out 190.13
draw off 192.12
evacuate 909.22
adj ineffective 19.15
hungry 100.25
dull 117.6
vacant 222.14
concave 284.16
insincere 354.32
vain 391.13
meaningless 520.6
inexpressive 522.20
nonexistent 762.8
empty-headed 922.19
ignorant 930.11
thoughtless 933.4
sophistical 936.10
baseless 936.13
trivial 998.19
empty-headed
empty-minded 922.19
ignorant 930.11
thoughtless 933.4
scatterbrained 985.16
empty-nester 560.8
empurpled 46.3
emulate follow 336.7
compete 457.18
set an example 786.7
excel 999.11
emulsify mix 797.10
emulsionize 1062.10
emulsion film 714.10
emulsoid 1062.7
solution 1064.3

enable
empower 18.10
fit 405.8
authorize 443.11
include 772.3
make possible 966.5
enact perform 328.9
manifest 348.5
impersonate 349.12
accomplish 407.4
legislate 613.10
legalize 673.9
act out 704.30
enamel
n blanket 295.12
v color 35.14
coat 295.24
adj ceramic 742.7
enamelwork 712.15
enamored 104.27
enate
n kinfolk 559.2
lineage 560.4
adj related 559.6
lineal 560.18
kindred 775.10
akin 784.13
encampment
camping 225.4
camp 228.29
campground 463.3
encapsulate
shorten 268.6
wrap 295.20
abridge 557.5
iterate 849.8
encase confine 212.6
package 212.9
wrap 295.20
enchant
delight 95.10
fascinate 377.7
charm 691.8
engross 983.13
enchanted
overjoyed 95.17
enamored 104.27
wondering 122.9
charmed 691.12
miraculous 870.16
gripped 983.18
dreamy 986.25
encipher 345.10
encircle
surround 209.7
enclose 212.5
circle 280.10
besiege 459.19
include 772.3
enclose 914.5
enclave
enclosed place 212.3
plot 231.4
enclitic
added to writing 254.2
morphology 526.3
enclose
internalize 207.5
surround 209.6
circumscribe 210.4
bound 211.8

close in 212.5
confine 429.12
include 772.3
enclosure
the enclosed 196.6
surrounding 209.5
confinement 212.1
enclosed place 212.3
place of confinement 429.7
fortification 460.4
encode 345.10
encomiastic 509.16
encompass
extend 158.9
surround 209.6
enclose 212.5
circle 280.10
wrap 295.20
besiege 459.19
include 772.3
total 792.8
put together 800.5
combine 805.3
encircle 914.5
encore
n repeat performance 849.6
repeat 874.2
v applaud 509.10
adv recurrently 849.17
again 874.7
interj bravo! 509.22
bis! 849.18
encounter
n meeting 223.4
contest 457.3
impact 902.3
v approach 167.3
confront 216.8
meet 223.11
oppose 451.5
come up against 457.15
experience 831.8
collide 902.13
come across 941.3
encourage cheer 109.7
comfort 121.6
hearten 375.21
admonish 422.6
abet 449.14
be useful 449.17
hearten 492.15
encouraging
cheering 109.16
comforting 121.13
promising 124.12
provocative 375.27
encroach intrude 214.5
usurp 640.8
overstep 910.9
encroachment
intrusion 214.1
impairment 393.1
usurpation 640.3
overstepping 910.3
encrust 295.27
encumber add 253.4
burden 297.13
hamper 1012.11
encumbered
weighted 297.18
indebted 623.8

encyclical 352.2
encyclopedia
reference book 554.9
lore 928.9
encyclopedic
comprehensive 772.7
learned 928.21
end
n boundary 211.3
remainder 256.1
death 307.1
motive 375.1
objective 380.2
fatality 395.2
completion 407.2
gain 472.3
portion 477.5
football team 746.2
piece 793.3
limit 794.5
end point 820.1
stop 857.2
immediate cause 886.3
solution 940.1
fate 964.2
v kill 308.13
put an end to 395.12
perish 395.23
complete 407.6
terminate 820.5
cease 857.6
result 887.4
endanger 1006.6
endearing
delightful 97.7
lovable 104.24
endeavor
n act 328.3
effort 403.1
attempt 403.2
exertion 725.1
v strive 403.5
undertake 404.3
exert oneself 725.9
endemic
contagious 85.62
native 226.5
endless wordy 538.12
continuous 812.8
infinite 823.3
perpetual 829.7
continuing 856.7
innumerable 884.10
endocrine
n digestive secretion 13.2
adj glandular 13.8
endomorph 92.12
endorse ratify 332.12
adopt 371.15
secure 438.9
consent 441.2
abet 449.14
approve 509.9
support 609.41
endow empower 18.10
provide 385.7
invest 478.17
establish 892.10
endowed
provided 385.13

talented 413.29
dowered 478.26
end up arrive 186.6
end 820.5
come to an end 820.6
result 887.4
conclude 946.10
endurance
strength 15.1
patience 134.1
perseverance 360.1
durability 827.1
permanence 853.1
continuance 856.1
endure bear 134.5
condone 148.4
keep alive 306.11
persevere 360.2
suffer 443.10
resist 453.2
afford 626.7
live on 761.9
elapse 821.5
last 827.6
experience 831.8
remain 853.5
continue 856.3
toughen 1049.3
end user 387.9
enema washing 79.5
cleanser 79.17
clyster 86.19
sprinkler 1065.8
enemies list 871.1
enemy
n opponent 452.1
foe 589.6
adj oppositional 451.8
warlike 458.20
energetic
vigorous 17.13
powerful 18.12
active 330.17
industrious 330.22
energize
dynamize 17.10
vivify 306.10
motivate 375.12
electrify 1032.26
energy
n strength 15.1
vigor 17.1
power 18.1
liveliness 330.2
industry 330.6
exertion 725.1
adj fuel 1021.9
energy bar 10.43
enervate weaken 16.10
unman 19.12
fatigue 21.4
afflict 85.50
spiritualize 764.4
enervation
weakening 16.5
helplessness 19.4
fatigue 21.1
unhealthiness 85.3
languor 331.6
enfant terrible
brat 302.4

mischief-maker 322.3
spoiled child 427.4
enfeeble weaken 16.10
disable 19.9
afflict 85.50
enfeebled
weakened 16.18
tired 21.7
enflame 375.18
enfold
internalize 207.5
surround 209.6
fold 291.5
wrap 295.20
embrace 562.18
enforce apply 387.11
compel 424.4
execute 437.9
legalize 673.9
enfranchise
liberate 431.4
authorize 443.11
include 772.3
enfranchisement
empowerment 18.8
vote 371.6
liberation 431.1
authorization 443.3
inclusion 772.1
engage induce 375.22
attract 377.6
attempt 403.6
commit 436.5
contract 437.5
take on 457.16
employ 615.14
occupy 724.10
interact 777.6
involve 898.2
engross 983.13
engage in
practice 328.8
undertake 404.3
busy oneself with 724.11
engagement
inducement 375.3
undertaking 404.1
obligation 436.2
betrothal 436.3
contest 457.3
participation 476.1
proposal 562.8
appointment 582.8
employment 615.4
playing engagement
704.11
position 724.5
interaction 777.3
involvement 898.1
engrossment 983.3
engaging
delightful 97.7
alluring 377.8
engrossing 983.20
en garde 760.4
engender
procreate 78.8
beget 818.14
cause 886.10
produce 890.7
originate 892.12

engine
instrument of conversion
858.10
machinery enginery 1040.3
engineer
n engineman 178.12
planner 381.6
combat engineer 461.14
professional engineer 726.7
producer 892.7
v plot 381.9
manage 409.12
maneuver 415.10
direct 573.8
perform 892.11
engineering 1043.1
English 341.12
English Channel 239.1
English-speaking 524.31
engorge stuff 8.25
ingest 187.11
destroy 395.10
gluttonize 672.4
satiate 994.4
engrail 47.7
engrave
impress upon 93.16
indent 284.14
furrow 290.3
figure 498.9
mark 517.19
print 548.14
record 549.15
grave 713.9
sculpture 715.5
fix 855.9
fix in the mind 989.17
engraving
excavation 284.11
mark 517.5
visual arts 712.15
engross
absorb 187.13
fatten 259.8
monopolize 469.6
write 547.19
purchase 733.7
corner 737.26
occupy the mind
931.20
take in 983.13
engrossed in 983.17
engulf ingest 187.11
overflow 238.17
submerge 367.7
overwhelm 395.21
oversupply 993.14
enhance
aggravate 119.2
intensify 251.5
make better 392.9
enhancement
aggravation 119.1
intensification 251.2
exaggeration 355.1
improvement 392.1
enigma secret 345.5
mystery 522.8
the unknown 930.6
bewilderment 971.3
dilemma 1013.7

enigmatic
wonderful 122.10
secret 345.11
cryptic 522.17
unknown 930.16
bewildering 971.27
ambiguous 539.4
enjoin command 420.8
admonish 422.6
restrain 428.7
prohibit 444.3
impose 643.4
enjoy savor 63.5
pleasure in 95.13
possess 469.4
enjoyment
pleasure 95.1
amusement 743.1
enkindle
excite 105.12
kindle 375.18
ignite 1020.22
enlace 740.6
enlarge
aggravate 119.2
increase 251.4
size 257.15
expand 259.4
grow 259.5
amplify 538.7
process 714.15
elaborate 861.6
enlargement
aggravation 119.1
increase 251.1
expansion 259.1
exaggeration 355.1
amplification 538.6
print 714.5
photoprint 785.5
evolution 861.1
enlighten
explain 341.10
make better 392.9
inform 551.8
teach 568.10
disillusion 977.2
illuminate 1025.29
enlightening
explanatory 341.15
informative 551.18
educational 568.18
disillusioning 977.4
liberalizing 979.13
enlightenment
explanation 341.4
cultivation 392.3
information 551.1
teaching 568.1
learning 928.4
disillusionment 977.1
enlist install 191.4
induce 375.22
participate 476.5
list 615.17
join 617.14
take one's turn 825.5
enlistee recruit 461.18
member 617.11
enliven refresh 9.2
energize 17.10

stimulate 105.13
cheer 109.7
inspire 375.20
amuse 743.21
en masse
cooperatively 450.6
together 769.11
wholly 792.13
enmesh trap 356.20
catch 480.17
involve 898.2
hamper 1012.11
put in a hole 1013.15
enmity hostility 99.2
bitterness 103.2
hatefulness 451.2
disaccord 456.1
contention 457.1
unfriendliness 589.1
ennoble promote 446.2
glorify 662.13
ennui unpleasure 96.1
weariness 118.3
languor 331.6
enormity
indignity 156.2
greatness 247.1
hugeness 257.7
misdeed 655.2
baseness 661.3
enormous large 247.7
huge 257.20
excessive 993.16
terrible 1000.9
enough
n sufficiency 991.1
adj satisfactory 107.11
sufficient 991.6
sated 994.6
adv satisfactorily 107.15
sufficiently 991.8
interj cease! 857.13
en passant
on the way 176.20
incidentally 843.13
enplane 188.15
en plein air 206.11
enqueue 812.6
enrage excite 105.12
infuriate 152.25
heat 1020.18
enraptured
overjoyed 95.17
enamored 104.27
frenzied 105.25
wondering 122.9
en règle 867.8
enrich
vitaminize 7.20
make better 392.9
ornament 498.8
ornament 545.7
richen 618.9
fertilize 890.8
enrobe 5.39
enroll install 191.4
record 549.15
be taught 570.11
enlist 615.17
join 617.14
list 871.8

en route
on the way 176.20
on the move 177.42
ensconce settle 159.17
conceal 346.6
ensemble
n furniture 229.1
cast 707.11
orchestra 710.12
chorus 710.16
compound 797.5
adv together 769.11
enshrine
enclose 212.5
inter 309.19
glorify 662.13
sanctify 685.5
exalt 912.6
enshroud clothe 5.39
wrap 295.20
conceal 346.6
ensign
Navy officer 575.20
insignia 647.1
flag 647.7
enslave
subjugate 432.8
appropriate 480.19
domineer 612.15
ensnare trap 356.20
lure 377.5
catch 480.17
ensue succeed 815.2
come after 835.3
result 887.4
ensure secure 438.9
make sure 970.11
protect 1008.18
entail
n inheritance 479.2
v bequeath 478.18
signify 517.17
imply 519.4
transfer 629.3
involve 772.4
determine 886.12
entangle trap 356.20
catch 480.17
complicate 799.3
involve 898.2
confuse 985.7
hamper 1012.11
put in a hole 1013.15
entente treaty 437.2
understanding 788.2
enter appear 33.8
go in 189.7
insert 191.3
record 549.15
join 617.14
keep accounts 628.8
enter on 818.9
list 871.8
enter into
participate 476.5
compose 796.3
put together 800.5
enter 818.9
enterprise vim 17.2
act 328.3
enterprisingness 330.7

plan 381.1
endeavor 403.1
undertaking 404.1
daring 492.4
exploit 492.6
company 617.9
occupation 724.1
entertain hold 474.7
have a party 582.20
entertain guests 585.8
amuse 743.21
take under consideration
931.14
entertainment meal 8.5
pleasure 95.1
party 582.11
theatrical performance 704.12
amusement 743.1
entertainment industry 743.13
enter upon
undertake 404.3
set to work 725.15
enter 818.9
enthrall delight 95.10
fascinate 377.7
subjugate 432.8
engross 983.13
enthrone
install 615.12
glorify 662.13
enthusiasm
animation 17.4
eagerness 101.1
willingness 324.1
vehemence 544.5
mania 926.12
interest 983.2
enthusiastic
energetic 17.13
fervent 93.18
enthused and big 101.10
willing 324.5
vehement 544.13
interested 983.16
entice 377.5
entire
n male animal 76.8
horse 311.10
adj whole 792.9
complete 794.9
unqualified 960.2
sound 1002.7
entitle
authorize 443.11
name 527.11
entitled
authorized 443.17
warranted 639.9
entitlement generation 651.1
entity existence 761.1
something 763.3
individual 872.4
entomb confine 212.6
inter 309.19
entourage
follower 166.2
environment 209.1
attendance 769.6
entrails
digestive system 2.18
insides 207.4

entrance
put to sleep 22.20
delight 95.10
fascinate 377.7
cast a spell 691.7
entrance entrée 187.3
access 189.1
entry 189.1
opening 189.5
insertion 191.1
vestibule 197.19
intrusion 214.1
channel 239.1
door 292.6
entranced
overjoyed 95.17
wondering 122.9
dreamy 986.25
entrant incomer 189.4
competitor 452.2
novice 572.9
beginner 818.2
entrap trap 356.20
catch 480.17
hamper 1012.11
entreaty appeal 440.2
prayer 696.4
entrée serving 8.10
dish 10.7
entrée 187.3
entrance 189.1
entrench
intrude 214.5
fortify 460.9
fix 855.9
entre nous
confidentially 345.20
mutually 777.13
entrep(tm)t 386.6
entrepreneuer 381.6
entrepreneur 730.1
entropy
inertness 173.4
formlessness 263.1
information theory 551.7
noncohesion 804.1
disorder 810.1
change 852.1
uncertainty 971.1
entrust commit 478.16
commission 615.10
give credit 622.6
entry entrée 187.3
entrance 189.1
opening 189.5
vestibule 197.19
door 292.6
memorandum 549.4
registration 549.14
item 628.5
entry fee 630.6
entwine weave 740.6
hamper 1012.11
enumerate
quantify 244.4
itemize 801.7
list 871.8
number 1017.17
enunciate affirm 334.5
announce 352.12
say 524.22

envelop clothe 5.39
surround 209.6
wrap 295.20
conceal 346.6
envelope
n exterior 206.2
wrapper 295.18
illustriousness 662.6
v besiege 459.19
enviable 100.30
envious
discontented 108.7
jealous 153.5
envying 154.3
environment
neighborhood 209.1
natural environment 209.4
surrounding 209.5
circumstances 766.2
the natural world 1073.1
environmental engineering
1043.1
environment-friendly 397.12
environs
environment 209.1
nearness 223.1
region 231.1
envision expect 130.5
contemplate 380.5
come 839.6
think of 931.17
foresee 961.5
visualize 986.15
envoy delegate 576.2
diplomat 576.6
envoy extraordinary 576.6
envy
n discontent 108.1
jealousy 153.1
resentfulness 154.1
enviousness 154.1
v be envious of 154.2
enwrap clothe 5.39
surround 209.6
package 212.9
wrap 295.20
enzyme 7.9
eon 824.4
eons 823.1
epaulet 647.5
ephemeral
n plant 310.3
ephemeron 828.5
adj mortal 307.33
perennial 310.44
unsubstantial 764.5
transient 828.7
epic
n story 719.3
adj huge 257.20
poetic 720.15
narrative 722.8
epicedium 115.6
epicenter control center 208.5
upheaval 671.5
epicureanism
gastronomy 8.15
pleasure-loving 95.4
aesthetic taste 496.4
sensuality 663.1
epicurism 672.2

epidemic
  n plague 85.5
  adj contagious 85.62
  prevalent 864.12
  plentiful 991.7
epidermic
  epidermal 2.27
  exterior 206.7
  cutaneous 295.32
epigram
  witticism 489.7
  aphorism 537.3
  maxim 974.1
epigrammatic
  concise 537.6
  aphoristic 974.6
epigraph
  lettering 546.5
  caption 937.2
  motto 974.4
epigraphy 341.8
epilepsy seizure 85.6
  spasm 917.6
epilogue
  added to writing 254.2
  act 704.7
  part of writing 793.2
  sequel 817.1
  end 820.1
epiphany visibility 31.1
  appearance 33.1
  manifestation 348.1
  revelation 683.10
  intuition 934.1
episcopal 698.13
episode
  interjection 213.2
  digression 538.4
  plot 722.4
  discontinuity 813.1
  event 831.2
  frenzy 926.7
episteme 413.9
epistle 553.2
epitaph 309.18
epithalamium 563.3
epithet
  n oath 513.4
  name 527.3
  nickname 527.7
  motto 974.4
  v vilify 513.7
epitome
  shortening 268.3
  abridgment 557.1
  paragon 659.4
  essence 767.2
  ideal 786.4
  pattern of perfection 1002.1
epitomize
  shorten 268.6
  set an example 786.7
epoch 824.5
epode 720.9
eponym root 526.2
  name 527.3
equal
  n match 790.4
  substitute 862.2
  v parallel 203.4
  match 790.5

excel 999.11
  adj parallel 203.6
  symmetric 264.4
  proportionate 477.13
  coinciding 778.8
  uniform 781.5
  equalized 790.7
  interchangeable 863.5
equality
  symmetry 264.1
  justice 649.1
  sameness 778.1
  parity 790.1
equalize level 201.6
  symmetrize 264.3
  smooth 287.5
  make uniform 781.4
  make agree 788.7
  equate 790.6
equal opportunity
  equating 790.2
  opportunity 843.2
equal rights 790.1
equanimity
  equilibrium 106.3
  uniformity 781.1
equate
  parallelize 203.5
  relate 775.6
  equalize 790.6
equator zone 231.3
  circle 280.3
  middle 819.1
  bisector 875.3
  hot place 1019.11
  orbit 1072.16
equestrian
  n rider 178.8
  adj ungulate 311.45
equidistant
  parallel 203.6
  central 208.11
  middle 819.4
equilibrium
  equanimity 106.3
  symmetry 264.1
  inaction 329.1
  harmony 533.2
  moderation 670.1
  correlation 777.1
  uniformity 781.1
  equality 790.1
  continuity 812.1
  stability 855.1
equine
  n horse 311.10
  adj ungulate 311.45
equinox
  vernal equinox 313.7
  orbit 1072.16
equip outfit 5.41
  furnish 385.8
  fit 405.8
  establish 892.10
equipment
  supplies 385.2
  provision 385.1
  matériel 385.4
  preparation 405.1
  fitting 405.2
  talent 413.4

baseball 745.1
  football 746.1
  hockey 749.1
  field hockey 749.4
  bowling 750.1
  golf 751.1
  soccer 752.1
  skiing 753.1
  boxing 754.1
equitable just 649.7
  impartial 649.9
  unprejudiced 979.12
equity estate 471.4
  justice 649.1
  stock 738.2
  equality 790.1
equivalence
  correlation 777.1
  sameness 778.1
  agreement 788.1
  equality 790.1
  comparability 943.3
equivalent
  n offset 338.2
  the same 778.3
  likeness 784.3
  equal 790.4
  substitute 862.2
  adj reciprocal 777.10
  coinciding 778.8
  analogous 784.11
  agreeing 788.9
  tantamount 790.8
  substitute 862.8
  interchangeable 863.5
equivocal
  n ambiguity 539.2
  adj prevaricating 344.11
  untruthful 354.34
  ambiguous 539.4
  self-contradictory 779.8
  mixed 797.14
  uncertain 971.16
equivocate
  prevaricate 344.7
  lie 354.19
  vacillate 362.8
  dodge 368.8
  weasel 539.3
  go roundabout 914.4
  quibble 936.9
era 824.5
eradicate
  extract 192.10
  excise 255.10
  exterminate 395.14
  annihilate 762.7
  eliminate 773.5
erase delete 255.12
  kill 308.14
  obliterate 395.16
  end 820.5
  abrade 1044.7
Erato music 710.22
  Muse 720.10
  creative thought 986.2
Erebus
  nether world deity 682.5
  darkness 1027.1
erect
  v elevate 200.9

produce 892.8
  elevate 912.5
  adj proud 136.8
  vertical 200.11
  honest 644.13
  raised 912.9
erection
  sexual desire 75.5
  erecting 200.4
  house 228.5
  structure 266.2
  production 892.2
  elevation 912.1
eremite 584.5
erg 17.7
ergo 888.7
ergonomics 717.5
eristic
  n argumentation 935.4
  arguer 935.12
  adj partisan 456.17
  argumentative 935.19
ermine heraldry 647.2
  royal insignia 647.3
erode disappear 34.2
  recede 168.2
  decrease 252.6
  subtract 255.9
  consume 388.3
  wear 393.20
  corrode 393.21
  waste 473.5
  disintegrate 806.3
  abrade 1044.7
erogenous 75.25
Eros god 104.1
  Love 104.7
erose notched 289.5
  nonuniform 782.3
erosion
  decrement 252.3
  subtraction 255.1
  consumption 388.1
  wear 393.5
  waste 473.2
  disintegration 806.1
  abrasion 1044.2
erotic sexual 75.25
  amorous 104.25
  lascivious 665.29
erotica
  literature 547.12
  pornographic literature 718.1
err stray 164.4
  miss 410.14
  go wrong 654.9
  do wrong 655.4
  misbelieve 688.8
  misjudge 948.2
  fall into error 975.9
errand
  commission 615.1
  task 724.2
errant
  deviative 164.7
  wandering 177.37
  fallible 971.22
  erroneous 975.16
errata 554.12
erratic
  n eccentric 927.3

honest 644.13
ethics principles 636.1
  duty 641.1
ethnic
  n person 312.5
  adj racial 559.7
ethnic cleansing 308.4
ethnicity
  humankind 312.1
  race 559.4
  exclusiveness 773.3
ethology 321.3
ethos culture 373.2
  ethics 636.1
  nature 767.4
  ideology 932.8
  opinion 953.6
  climate 978.5
etiology cause 886.1
  attribution 888.1
etiquette
  good behavior 321.2
  custom 373.1
  mannerliness 504.3
  social convention 579.1
  social code 580.3
etymologist 523.15
etymology 526.15
eudaimonia 95.2
eugenics
  improvement 392.1
  heredity 560.6
euhemeristic 341.15
eulogy dirge 115.6
  last offices 309.4
  praise 509.5
  speech 543.2
  citation 646.4
eunuch impotent 19.6
  sexlessness 75.9
eupathy 107.1
euphemism
  overniceness 500.5
  catchword 526.9
  affectation 533.3
euphonious
  harmonious 533.8
  melodious 708.48
euphoric pleased 95.15
  content 107.7
  cheerful 109.11
euphuistic
  overnice 500.18
  affected 533.9
  grandiloquent 545.8
eureka! 941.11
Europe
  world region 231.6
  continent 235.1
Eurotrash 250.2
eurythmic 264.4
Euterpe music 710.22
  Muse 720.10
  creative thought 986.2
euthanasia
  natural death 307.6
  killing 308.1
evacuate defecate 12.13
  quit 188.9
  abandon 370.5
  void 909.22

let out 909.24
evade avoid 164.6
  prevaricate 344.7
  elude 368.7
  escape 369.6
  outwit 415.11
  remain neutral 467.5
  be dishonest 645.11
  pull back 903.7
  quibble 936.9
evaluate
  measure 300.10
  price 630.11
  criticize 723.5
  classify 801.8
  estimate 946.9
evanescence
  disappearance 34.1
  recession 168.1
  infinitesimalness 258.2
  unsubstantiality 764.1
  transience 828.1
evanescent
  infinitesimal 258.14
  thin 764.6
  transient 828.7
evangelical
  scriptural 683.11
  orthodox 687.7
  strict 687.8
evangelist herald 353.2
  lecturer 543.5
  religion 684.2
  worshiper 696.9
  revivalist 699.6
  converter 858.9
evangelistic
  scriptural 683.11
  ecclesiastic 698.13
evaporate
  disappear 34.2
  preserve 397.9
  cease to exist 762.6
  dissipate 771.5
  flit 828.6
  dry 1066.6
  vaporize 1067.8
evasion
  prevarication 344.4
  secrecy 345.1
  avoidance 368.1
  escape 369.1
  circumvention 415.5
  neutrality 467.1
  retreat 903.3
  quibbling 936.5
Eve 77.5
even
  n evening 315.2
  v level 201.6
  symmetrize 264.3
  smooth 287.5
  make uniform 781.4
  equalize 790.6
  adj horizontal 201.7
  parallel 203.6
  symmetric 264.4
  straight 277.6
  smooth 287.10
  neutral 467.7
  just 649.7

equable 670.13
  uniform 781.5
  equal 790.7
  periodic 850.7
  interchangeable 863.5
  exact 973.17
  numeric 1017.23
  adv chiefly 249.17
  notwithstanding 338.8
  interchangeably 863.6
  exactly 973.21
even break
  gambling odds 759.6
  equating 790.2
  opportunity 843.2
  even chance 972.7
evenhanded
  just 649.7
  impartial 649.9
  unprejudiced 979.12
evening
  symmetrization 264.2
  equating 790.2
evening
  n post meridiem 315
  eve 315.2
  adj evensong 315.8
event game 743.9
  circumstance 766.1
  eventuality 831.1
  occurrence 831.2
  effect 887.1
even-tempered
  inexcitable 106.10
  equable 670.13
event horizon 1072.8
eventuality
  circumstance 766.1
  event 831.1
  the future 839.1
  futurity 839.4
  effect 887.1
  liability 897.1
  possibility 966.1
ever forever 829.12
  constantly 847.7
  by any possibility 966.10
everglade 243.1
evergreen
  n plant 310.3
  tree 310.10
  adj arboreal 310.39
  perennial 310.44
  durable 827.10
  perennial 829.8
  new 841.7
everlasting
  tedious 118.9
  almighty 677.17
  perpetual 829.7
  immortal 829.9
ever so greatly 247.15
  chiefly 249.17
ever so little 248.9
every 864.15
everybody
  the people 606.1
  all 864.4
everyday
  customary 373.13
  simple 499.6

vernacular 523.20
  frequent 847.4
  usual 869.9
everyman 864.3
every now and then
  haphazardly 810.18
  occasionally 848.5
  repeatedly 849.16
  regularly 850.9
everyone
  the people 606.1
  all 864.4
every so often
  occasionally 848.5
  regularly 850.9
everything all 792.3
  all 864.4
everywhere
  adj omnipresent 221.13
  adv everywheres 158.13
  from everywhere 158.14
  in every direction 161.25
  scatteringly 771.12
  generally 864.18
  universally 1072.27
evict dislodge 160.6
  dispossess 480.23
  oust 909.15
eviction
  dislocation 160.1
  dispossession 480.7
  elimination 773.2
  ousting 909.2
evidence
  n distinctness 31.2
  appearance 348.1
  manifestness 348.3
  clue 517.9
  information 551.1
  testimony 598.8
  grounds for belief 957.1
  proof 957.1
  v manifest 348.5
  evince 957.8
evil
  n vice 654.1
  iniquity 654.3
  misdeed 655.2
  badness 1000.1
  ill 1000.3
  bane 1001.1
  trouble 1013.3
  adj ominous 133.16
  wrong 638.3
  wicked 654.16
  bad 1000.7
  adv badly 1000.13
evil eye gaze 27.5
  malevolence 144.4
  curse 513.1
  spell 691.1
  bad influence 1000.4
evince manifest 348.5
  evidence 957.8
eviscerate
  weaken 16.10
  disembowel 192.13
evocation
  elicitation 192.5
  description 349.2
  summons 420.5

banishment 909.4
qualification 959.1
exclusive
　n news item 552.3
　adj contemptuous 157.8
　limiting 210.9
　closed 293.9
　selective 371.23
　prohibitive 444.6
　selective 495.13
　aloof 583.6
　cliquish 617.18
　excluding 773.9
　one 872.7
exclusive right 642.1
exclusivity
　contempt 157.1
　selectness 495.5
　seclusiveness 583.3
　partisanism 617.13
　exclusion 773.1
excogitate 931.11
excommunicated 372.3
excommunication
　deposal 447.2
　curse 513.1
　condemnation 602.1
　banishment 909.4
excoriation
　unclothing 6.1
　torment 96.7
　censure 510.3
excrement
　dejection 12.3
　filth 80.7
excretion discharge 12
　egestion 12.1
　secretion 13.1
　exuding 190.6
　evacuation 909.6
excruciating
　sensitive 24.13
　painful 26.10
　agonizing 98.23
exculpate
　forgive 148.3
　justify 600.9
　acquit 601.4
excursion
　deviation 164.1
　journey 177.5
　obliquity 204.1
　digression 538.4
　circuitousness 914.1
　detour 914.3
excursus
　deviation 164.1
　digression 538.4
　treatise 556.1
　circuitousness 914.1
excuse
　n pardon 148.2
　pretext 376.1
　cop-out 600.4
　acquittal 601.1
　apology 658.2
　reason 886.2
　v forgive 148.3
　exempt 430.14
　alibi 600.11
　acquit 601.4

execrable
　offensive 98.18
　cursed 513.9
　wicked 654.16
　base 661.12
　damnable 1000.10
execration hate 103.1
　hated thing 103.3
　berating 510.7
　curse 513.1
execute kill 308.13
　perform 328.9
　accomplish 407.4
　perform 434.3
　complete 437.9
　put to death 604.17
　play 708.39
　produce 892.11
execution
　killing 308.1
　action 328.2
　accomplishment 407.1
　observance 434.1
　completion 437.4
　attachment 480.5
　capital punishment 604.7
　performance 708.30
　operation 889.1
　performance 892.5
executive
　n officer 574.3
　governor 575.6
　operator 889.4
　adj grandiose 501.21
　officiating 573.14
　administrative 612.18
　expensive 632.11
the executive 574.11
executor doer 726.1
　producer 892.7
exegesis
　explanation 341.4
　comment 341.5
exegetic
　interpretative 341.14
　explanatory 341.15
exemplar
　representative 349.7
　paragon 659.4
　example 786.2
　rule 869.4
　philosophy 932.2
　pattern of perfection 1002.4
exemplary
　typical 349.15
　warning 399.7
　praiseworthy 509.20
　model 786.8
　perfected 1002.9
exemplify
　explain 341.10
　image 349.11
　set an example 786.7
　cite 957.13
exempt
　v free 430.14
　acquit 601.4
　adj immune 430.30
exemption
　pardon 148.2
　exception 430.8

immunity 601.2
qualification 959.1
exercise
　n physical conditioning
　　84.1
　motion 84.2
　action 328.1
　use 387.1
　training 568.3
　lesson 568.7
　study 570.3
　ceremony 580.4
　task 724.2
　exercising 725.6
　operation 889.1
　v work out 84.4
　annoy 96.13
　practice 328.8
　use 387.1
　train 568.13
　exert 725.8
　engross 983.13
exert use 387.10
　exercise 725.8
exertion use 387.1
　endeavor 403.1
　effort 725.1
exfoliate scale 6.11
　layer 296.5
　break 802.12
exfoliation
　unclothing 6.1
　stratification 296.4
　disruption 802.3
exhalation
　breathing 2.21
　murmur 52.4
　odor 69.1
　outflow 190.4
　cloud 1067.1
　vaporization 1067.5
exhaust
　n wash 184.30
　outflow 190.4
　outlet 190.9
　miasma 1001.4
　rocket propulsion 1074.8
　v weaken 16.10
　unman 19.12
　fatigue 21.4
　oppress 98.16
　run out 190.13
　draw off 192.12
　spend 387.13
　consume 388.3
　strip 480.24
　waste 486.4
　evacuate 909.22
　let out 909.24
　disgorge 909.25
　overdo 993.10
exhaustion
　weakness 16.1
　debilitation 16.5
　draining 21.2
　unhealthiness 85.3
　collapse 85.8
　decrement 252.3
　consumption 388.1
　waste 473.2
　evacuation 909.6

exhaustive great 247.6
　broad 269.6
　complete 407.12
　whole 792.9
　thorough 794.10
exhibit
　n display 348.2
　theatrical performance
　　704.12
　evidence 957.1
　v externalize 206.5
　manifest 348.5
　flaunt 501.17
　evidence 957.8
exhibition
　spectacle 33.7
　demonstration 348.2
　display 501.4
　theatrical performance
　　704.12
exhibitionism
　unclothing 6.1
　perversion 75.11
　display 501.4
　immodesty 666.2
exhilarate refresh 9.2
　energize 17.10
　stimulate 105.13
　cheer 109.7
　inspire 375.20
　amuse 743.21
exhilaration
　refreshment 9.1
　energizing 17.8
　happiness 95.2
　excitement 105.1
　excitation 105.11
　good humor 109.2
　inspiration 375.9
exhortation
　inducement 375.3
　advice 422.1
　call to arms 458.7
　speech 543.2
exhumation
　disinterment 192.2
　discovery 941.1
exigency
　insistence 421.4
　crisis 843.4
　urgent need 963.4
　urgency 997.4
exigent
　meticulous 339.12
　demanding 421.9
　strict 425.6
　critical 843.10
　necessary 963.12
　urgent 997.22
exiguous little 258.10
　sparse 885.5
　meager 992.10
exile
　n displaced person 160.4
　migrant 178.5
　emigration 190.7
　outcast 586.4
　elimination 773.2
　alien 774.3
　banishment 909.4
　v emigrate 190.16

ostracize 586.6
eliminate 773.5
banish 909.17
exist be present 221.6
live 306.8
be 761.8
endure 827.6
existence
presence 221.1
life 306.1
being 761.1
existentialism 761.7
exit
n departure 188.1
egress 190.2
outlet 190.9
channel 239.1
death 307.1
flight 368.4
passageway 383.3
v disappear 34.2
depart 188.6
make an exit 190.12
absent oneself 222.8
find vent 369.10
exit strategy 192.1
exodus departure 188.1
egress 190.2
act 704.7
exonerate 601.4
exonerative 148.6
exorbitant
exaggerated 355.4
demanding 421.9
overpriced 632.12
violent 671.16
excessive 993.16
exorcism
conjuration 690.4
spell 691.1
exorcist shaman 690.7
holy orders 699.4
exoskeleton 206.2
exotic
n plant 310.3
adj colorful 35.19
distant 261.8
alluring 377.8
extraneous 774.5
unrelated 776.6
expand increase 251.4
grow 259.4
enlarge 259.5
spread 259.6
broaden 269.4
rarefy 299.3
amplify 538.7
disperse 771.4
elaborate 861.6
generalize 864.9
expand on
amplify 538.7
elaborate 861.6
expanse space 158.1
spaciousness 158.5
greatness 247.1
size 257.1
breadth 269.1
expansion
space 158.1
increase 251.1

size 257.1
increase in size 259
extension 259.1
exaggeration 355.1
amplification 538.6
business cycle 731.10
dispersion 771.1
evolution 861.1
expansive
spacious 158.11
voluminous 257.17
extensive 259.9
broad 269.6
communicative 343.10
talkative 540.9
expatriate
n migrant 178.5
outcast 586.4
v migrate 177.22
leave home 188.17
emigrate 190.16
eliminate 773.5
banish 909.17
expect hope 124.6
be expectant 130.5
come 839.6
suppose 951.10
think 953.11
expectation
unastonishment 123.1
hope 124.1
anticipation 130.1
expectance 130.1
dueness 639.1
the future 839.1
probability 968.1
expecting
pregnant 78.18
unastonished 123.3
expectant 130.11
expectorate 13.6
expedience
transience 828.1
timeliness 843.1
advisability 995.1
goodness 999.1
expediency
propriety 637.2
timeliness 843.1
expedience 995.1
expedient
n instrumentality 384.3
stratagem 415.3
means 995.2
recourse 1009.2
adj useful 387.18
transient 828.7
timely 843.9
conditional 959.8
desirable 995.5
good 999.12
expedite
advance 162.5
send 176.15
hasten 401.4
be useful 449.17
facilitate 1014.7
expedition
velocity 174.1
journey 177.5
quickness 330.3

adventure 404.2
furtherance 449.5
campaign 458.3
promptness 845.3
facilitation 1014.5
expeditious fast 174.15
quick 330.18
hasty 401.9
prompt 845.9
expel
transfer 176.10
depose 447.4
eliminate 773.5
separate 802.8
eject 909.13
banish 909.17
dismiss 909.19
disgorge 909.25
expend
spend 387.13
consume 388.3
waste 486.4
pay out 624.14
spend 626.5
expendable
consumable 388.6
replaceable 862.10
superfluous 993.17
unimportant 998.16
expenditure use 387.1
consumption 388.1
waste 473.2
spending 626.1
price 630.1
expense loss 473.1
expenditure 626.1
charges 626.3
price 630.1
expensive 632.11
experience
n sensation 24.1
practice 413.9
event 831.2
knowledge 928.1
v sense 24.6
feel 93.10
have 831.8
experienced
accustomed 373.15
practiced 413.28
experiment
n attempt 403.2
testing 942.1
trial 942.1
v see what one can do 403.10
experimentalize 942.8
expert
n adept 413.11
adviser 422.3
connoisseur 496.6
specialist 866.3
scientist 928.11
adj skillful 413.22
specialized 866.5
perfected 1002.9
expertise skill 413.1
aesthetic taste 496.4
knowledge 928.1
profound knowledge 928.6
expert's slope 753.1
expert systems 1042.2

adventure 404.2

expiate
compensate 338.4
atone 658.4
expiration
breathing 2.21
death 307.1
end 820.1
expire die 307.18
perish 395.23
cease to exist 762.6
come to an end 820.6
elapse 821.5
let out 909.24
explain
explicate 341.10
make clear 521.6
expound 568.16
justify 600.9
excuse 600.11
solve 940.2
facilitate 1014.7
explain away
explain 341.10
extenuate 600.12
reason speciously 936.8
explainer 341.7
explain oneself 341.10
explanation
explication 341.4
definition 518.3
justification 600.1
example 786.2
reason 886.2
solution 940.1
theory 951.1
theorization 951.2
expletive
n exclamation 59.2
oath 513.4
redundancy 849.3
superfluity 993.4
adj superfluous 993.17
explicable
interpretable 341.17
attributable 888.6
solvable 940.3
explicate
explain 341.10
make clear 521.6
amplify 538.7
criticize 723.5
explicit manifest 348.8
clear 521.11
candid 644.17
unqualified 960.2
explode blast 56.8
be excitable 105.16
fly into a rage 152.20
grow 251.6
destruct 395.18
come to nothing 410.13
blow up 671.14
disprove 958.4
fuel 1021.8
exploit
n act 328.3
feat 492.6
v take advantage of 387.15
use 387.16
overprice 632.7

exploration
adventure 404.2
reconnaissance 938.8
search 938.15
exploratory
preceding 816.4
examining 938.37
exploratory survey 938.8
explore
investigate 938.23
search 938.31
explosion
detonation 56.3
outbreak 105.9
outburst 152.9
intensification 251.2
discharge 671.7
disproof 958.1
explosive
n high explosive 462.14
speech sound 524.12
adj banging 56.11
excitable 105.28
hot-tempered 110.25
bursting 671.24
dangerous 1006.9
exponent
interpreter 341.7
representative 349.7
deputy 576.1
supporter 616.9
example 786.2
exponential growth 251.1
export
n transferal 176.1
exporting 190.8
v transfer 176.10
send 176.15
send abroad 190.17
expose
divest 6.5
unclose 292.12
disclose 351.4
stigmatize 661.9
uncover 941.4
disprove 958.4
disillusion 977.2
endanger 1006.6
exposé
disclosure 351.1
disproof 958.1
expose oneself to 897.3
exposition
spectacle 33.7
explanation 341.4
display 348.2
disclosure 351.1
treatise 556.1
lesson 568.7
passage 708.24
marketplace 736.2
expository
explanatory 341.15
manifesting 348.9
dissertational 556.6
expostulate
object 333.5
dissuade 379.3
admonish 422.6
exposure
unclothing 6.1

visibility 31.1
distinctness 31.2
appearance 33.1
navigation 159.3
display 348.2
disclosure 351.1
publicity 352.4
repute 662.1
time exposure 714.9
susceptibility 897.2
discovery 941.1
disproof 958.1
openness 1006.3
radiation physics 1037.8
expound
explain 341.10
exposit 568.16
express
n carrier 176.7
train 179.14
messenger 353.1
message 552.4
v send 176.15
extraction 192.16
affirm 334.5
manifest 348.5
describe 349.9
signify 517.17
say 524.22
phrase 532.4
evidence 957.8
adj fast 174.15
manifest 348.8
clear 521.11
particular 865.12
unqualified 960.2
exact 973.17
adv posthaste 401.13
expression
extraction 192.1
extract 192.7
manifestation 348.1
indication 517.3
remark 524.3
word 526.1
phrase 529.1
diction 532.1
eloquence 544.1
execution 708.30
maxim 974.1
expressive
manifesting 348.9
descriptive 349.14
indicative 517.23
meaningful 518.10
graphic 544.10
express lane 401.1
express mail 553.4
expropriate
attach 480.20
dispossess 480.23
expulsion
transferal 176.1
deposal 447.2
elimination 773.2
ejection 909.1
disgorgement 909.7
expunge
delete 255.12
obliterate 395.16
end 820.5

expurgate clean 79.18
delete 255.12
exquisite
n dandy 500.9
adj sensitive 24.13
painful 26.10
tasty 63.8
delightful 97.7
meticulous 339.12
nice 495.11
overnice 500.18
chic 578.13
superb 999.15
fine 1016.19
exsanguineous 36.7
exsiccated 1066.9
extant remaining 256.7
existent 761.13
present 838.2
extemporaneous
extemporary 365.12
unprepared 406.8
extemporize
improvise 365.8
be unprepared 406.6
extend reach 158.9
increase 251.4
enlarge 259.4
grow 259.5
spread 259.6
reach out 261.5
be long 267.5
lengthen 267.6
broaden 269.4
straighten 277.5
offer 439.4
give 478.12
diffuse 538.8
race 757.5
endure 827.6
protract 827.9
postpone 846.9
sustain 856.4
generalize 864.9
stretch 1048.4
extension
space 158.1
increase 251.1
adjunct 254.1
addition 254.3
size 257.1
expansion 259.1
length 267.1
lengthening 267.4
telephone 347.4
meaning 518.1
sequence 815.1
protraction 827.2
continuance 856.1
stretching 1048.2
extensive
spacious 158.11
large 247.7
voluminous 257.17
expansive 259.9
long 267.7
broad 269.6
general 864.13
extensive knowledge 928.6
extent space 158.1
spaciousness 158.5

quantity 244.1
degree 245.1
size 257.1
distance 261.1
length 267.1
breadth 269.1
measure 300.3
extenuate
weaken 16.10
abate 252.8
mitigate 600.12
moderate 670.6
extenuating
justifying 600.13
qualifying 959.7
exterior
n appearance 33.2
external 206.2
scene 712.11
adj external 206.7
extraneous 774.5
exterminate kill 308.13
eliminate 395.14
annihilate 762.7
do away with 909.21
extermination
killing 308.1
extinction 395.6
external
n exterior 206.2
adj exterior 206.7
extrinsic 768.3
extraneous 774.5
external hard drive 1042.5
exterrestrial
extraterritorial 206.9
space 1072.26
exterritorial 206.9
extinct gone 34.4
no more 762.11
ended 820.8
past 837.7
obsolete 842.15
extinction
disappearance 34.1
excision 255.3
death 307.1
extermination 395.6
extinguishing 1022.2
extinguish
overshadow 249.8
excise 255.10
quench 395.15
suppress 428.8
end 820.5
fight fire 1022.7
turn off the light 1027.11
extirpate
excise 255.10
exterminate 395.14
annihilate 762.7
extol praise 509.12
glorify 696.12
extort exact 192.15
demand 421.5
wrest 480.22
steal 482.13
extortionate
extractive 192.17
demanding 421.9
rapacious 480.26

overpriced 632.12

extra
n bonus 254.4
newspaper 555.2
motion-picture studio 706.4
supporting actor 707.7
nonessential 768.2
surplus 993.5
adj additional 253.10
unused 390.12
unessential 768.4
occasional 848.3
surplus 993.18
adv additionally 253.11

extract
n perfumery 70.2
extraction 192.8
excerpt 557.3
distillation 893.3
v refine 79.22
take out 192.10
subtract 255.9
select 371.14
rescue 398.3
process 892.9
conclude 946.10

extracting 192.1

extraction
refinement 79.4
egress 190.2
taking out 192
withdrawal 192.1
extract 192.8
reduction 255.2
excerpt 557.3
lineage 560.4
production 892.2
pulling 905.1

extracurricular 568.20

extradite
transfer 176.10
restore 481.4
banish 909.17

extra large size 257.4

extramarital 665.27

extramural
extraterritorial 206.9
scholastic 567.13

extraneous
extrinsic 768.3
foreign 774.5
unrelated 776.6
irrelevant 776.7

extraordinary
wonderful 122.10
unexpected 131.10
remarkable 247.10
particular 865.12
exceptional 870.14
notable 997.19

extrapolate 839.6

extrapolation
adjunct 254.1
the future 839.1
notation 1017.2

extrasensory 689.24

extrasensory perception
intuition 934.1
mental state 22.5

extraterrestrial
n oddity 870.4

adj extraterritorial 206.9
heavenly 681.12
extraneous 774.5
supernatural 870.15
otherworldly 1072.26

extravagant
exaggerated 355.4
prodigal 486.8
gaudy 501.20
grandiose 501.21
inflated 502.12
diffuse 538.11
overpriced 632.12
intemperate 669.7
violent 671.16
absurd 923.11
fanatic 926.32
fanciful 986.20
plentiful 991.7
excessive 993.16

extravaganza 354.10

extravagation 501.3

extravehicular 1075.13

extreme
n exaggeration 355.1
limit 794.5
extremity 820.2
excess 993.1
adj sensitive 24.13
bordering 211.11
great 247.13
farthest 261.12
rebellious 327.11
exaggerated 355.4
radical 611.20
intemperate 669.7
violent 671.16
final 820.11
fanatic 926.32
excessive 993.16

extremes 993.1

extremism
rebelliousness 327.3
reform 392.5
radicalism 611.4
fanaticism 926.11
excess 993.1

extremist
n rebel 327.5
reformer 392.6
radical 611.12
adj radical 611.20
fanatic 926.32

extremity
wretchedness 96.6
summit 198.2
foot 199.5
boundary 211.3
moribundity 307.8
violence 671.1
limit 794.5
extreme 820.2
crisis 843.4
excess 993.1
impasse 1013.6

extricate extract 192.10
rescue 398.3
free 431.7
disembarrass 1014.9

extrication
extraction 192.1

escape 369.1
rescue 398.1
freeing 431.3
disembarrassment 1014.6

extrinsic
exterior 206.7
formal 580.7
external 768.3
extraneous 774.5
irrelevant 776.7

extrovert
n personality type 92.12
adj extroverted 92.41

extroverted
out-going 92.41
communicative 343.10

extrude
emerge 190.11
protrude 283.10
produce 892.8
eject 909.13

exuberance
happiness 95.2
gaiety 109.4
unrestraint 430.3
wordiness 538.2
productiveness 890.1
plenty 991.2

exuberant
fervent 93.18
gay 109.14
luxuriant 310.43
unrestrained 430.24
diffuse 538.11
productive 890.9
plentiful 991.7
thriving 1010.13

exude excrete 12.12
sweat 12.16
exudate 190.15
be damp 1065.11

exult rejoice 116.5
triumph 502.9

exultant
overjoyed 95.17
rejoicing 116.10
crowing 502.13

exultation
rejoicing 116.1
crowing 502.4

exurbanite 227.6

exuvial 6.18

eye
n visual organ 2.9
vision 27.1
look 27.3
eyeball 27.9
circlet 280.5
supervision 573.2
detective 576.11
discrimination 944.1
opinion 953.6
outlook 978.2
protection 1008.1
v look 27.13
scrutinize 27.14
gaze 27.15
flirt 562.20
spectate 918.5
adj optic 2.28
visual 27.20

the eye 27.3

eyeball
n eye 2.9
visual organ 27.9
v look 27.13
examine 938.24
adj visual 27.20

eyeball to eyeball
contrapositive 215.5
opposite 215.6
front 216.10
in opposition 451.9
contrary 779.6

eyebrows 3.12

eye-catching
alluring 377.8
attracting 907.5

an eye for 413.5

an eye for an eye
tit for tat 506.3
interchange 863.1

eyeglasses 29.3

eyelashes 3.12

eyelet 280.5

eyelid eye 2.9
visual organ 27.9

eye of the storm
center 208.2
storm 671.4

eye-opening
astonishing 122.12
surprising 131.11
disclosive 351.10

eyer 918.1

eyesight vision 27.1
field of view 31.3

eyesore stain 1004.3
blot 1015.4

eyewitness
spectator 918.1
witness 957.6

eyrie 228.23

Fabianism
reform 392.5
socialism 611.6

fable
n fabrication 354.10
plot 722.4
v narrate 722.6

fabled 662.16

fabric material 4.1
essential content
196.5
house 228.5
structure 266.1
building 266.2
frame 266.4
weaving 740.1
substance 763.2

fabricate invent 354.18
compose 796.3
produce 892.8
originate 892.12
imagine 986.14

fabrication
structure 266.1
falsehood 354.10
composition 796.1
production 892.1
manufacture 892.2
invention 986.3

false alarm
cry of wolf 400.2
failure 410.8
false eyelashes 3.13
falsehood
falseness 354.1
untruthfulness 354.8
lie 354.11
false image 350.2
false negative 354.1
false positive
falseness 354.1
false alarm 400.2
falsetto
n high voice 58.6
speech defect 525.1
voice 709.5
adj high 58.13
vocal 708.50
falsify
pervert 265.6
belie 354.16
lie 354.19
be dishonest 645.11
misrepresent 350.3
falter
n demur 325.2
hesitation 362.3
trill 709.19
shake 917.3
flounder 917.8
v despair 125.10
dawdle 175.8
demur 325.4
hesitate 362.7
lose one's nerve 491.8
stammer 525.8
shake 917.11
flounder 917.15
hang in doubt 971.10
fam 559.5
fame glory 247.2
publicity 352.4
repute 662.1
notability 997.2
familiar
n friend 588.1
familiar spirit 678.12
adj trite 117.9
insolent 142.9
customary 373.13
vernacular 523.20
informal 581.3
intimate 582.24
friendly 587.19
usual 869.9
well-known 928.27
familiarity
informality 581.1
sociability 582.1
intimacy 587.5
presumption 640.2
knowledge 928.1
familiarize
accustom 373.9
inform 551.8
familiar with
used to 373.16
versed in 928.19
family
n nomenclature 527.1

kinfolk 559.2
race 559.4
brood 559.5
lineage 560.4
offspring 561.1
community 617.2
classifications 809.5
sequel 835.2
biology 1068.1
adj racial 559.7
lineal 560.18
family jewels 2.13
family tree 560.5
famine
unproductiveness 891.1
want 992.4
famine price 632.3
famished
hungry 100.25
ill-provided 992.12
famous eminent 247.9
distinguished 662.16
good 999.12
fan
n enthusiast 101.5
follower 166.2
fork 171.4
attender 221.5
ventilator 317.10
flabellum 318.18
commender 509.8
supporter 616.9
specialist 866.3
propeller 904.6
fanatic 926.18
cooler 1024.3
v excite 105.12
spread 259.6
air 317.11
incite 375.17
fail 410.10
play 745.5
shuffle 758.5
fanatic
n enthusiast 101.4
obstinate person 361.6
believer 692.4
oddity 870.4
lunatic 926.15
infatuate 926.18
bigot 980.5
adj obstinate 361.8
fiery 671.22
fanatical 926.32
fanaticism
overzealousness 101.3
obstinacy 361.1
turbulence 671.2
zeal 692.3
cause 886.9
rabidness 926.11
narrow-mindedness 980.1
fanciful
capricious 364.5
unreal 762.9
thin 764.6
fantastic 870.12
ideational 932.9
notional 986.20
fan club 509.8

fancy
n desire 100.1
inclination 100.3
love 104.1
will 323.1
caprice 364.1
impulse 365.1
preference 371.5
idea 932.1
phantasy 976.3
imagination 986.1
figment of the imagination 986.5
v desire 100.14
love 104.18
suppose 951.10
think 953.11
imagine 986.14
adj edible 8.33
skillful 413.22
ornate 498.12
ostentatious 501.18
grandiose 501.21
grand 545.11
expensive 632.11
overpriced 632.12
excessive 993.16
interj imagine! 122.22
fancy-free 565.7
fancy that! 122.22
fandangle 520.2
fanfare blare 53.5
celebration 487.1
Aldine 554.15
fang teeth 2.8
sting 1001.5
fanged toothlike 285.14
prehensile 474.9
fangs 474.4
fan mail 553.4
fanny 217.5
fan out diverge 171.5
spread 259.6
disperse 771.4
fantasize
fabricate 354.18
imagine 986.14
fantastic
wonderful 122.10
remarkable 247.10
fabricated 354.29
capricious 364.5
unreal 762.9
unbelievable 870.12
absurd 923.11
illusory 976.9
fanciful 986.20
fantasy
n defense mechanism 92.23
desire 100.1
caprice 364.1
miracle 870.8
phantom 976.4
abstractedness 985.2
imagination 986.1
figment of the imagination 986.5
v muse 985.9
dream 986.17
fantasy baseball 745.1

fan the flame
excite 105.12
incite 375.17
sow dissension 456.14
ignite 1020.22
far
adj distant 261.8
adv by far 247.17
far off 261.15
far and away
by far 247.17
superlatively 249.16
farce stuffing 10.27
wit 489.1
burlesque 508.6
trifle 998.5
farcical comic 488.6
witty 489.15
burlesque 508.14
comic 704.35
fare
n food 10.1
traveler 178.1
fee 630.6
v eat 8.20
travel 177.18
journey 177.21
be in a certain state 765.5
result 887.4
farewell
n leave-taking 188.4
v take leave 188.16
adj departing 188.18
interj good-bye! 188.22
fare well succeed 409.7
prosper 1010.7
farfetched 776.8
far-flung long 267.7
extensive 864.13
far from it
adj nothing like 787.5
adv amiss 911.7
interj no 335.8
by no means 335.9
far gone
ill 85.56
intoxicated 87.23
far-gone
intoxicated 88.31
worn-out 393.36
involved in 898.5
farm
n house 228.5
baseball 745.1
farmplace 1069.8
stock farm 1070.5
v ruralize 233.5
die 307.19
rent out 615.16
ranch 1069.16
raise 1070.6
adj rustic 233.6
agricultural 1069.20
farmer
peasant 606.6
tax collector 630.10
agriculturist 1069.5
farmlet 1069.8
farm out 615.16
farmers' market 736.2

far out
 extreme 247.13
 modern 841.13
 unconventional 868.6
farrow
 n offspring 561.2
 v give birth 1.3
farsighted
 clear-sighted 27.21
 poor-sighted 28.11
 sagacious 920.16
 foreseeing 961.7
fart
 n stinker 71.3
 bad person 660.5
 zilch 762.3
 flatulence 909.10
 v let a fart 909.29
farther
 adj additional 253.10
 thither 261.10
 adv additionally 253.11
farthing
 modicum 248.2
 money 728.8
 fourth 881.2
 trifle 998.5
fasces scepter 417.9
 insignia 647.1
 bundle 770.8
fascinate
 delight 95.10
 enamor 104.22
 thrill 105.15
 captivate 377.7
 charm 691.8
 interest 983.12
 engross 983.13
fascinating
 delightful 97.7
 wonderful 122.10
 alluring 377.8
 bewitching 691.11
 engrossing 983.20
fascination
 delightfulness 97.2
 inclination 100.3
 eagerness 101.1
 amazement 122.1
 wonderfulness 122.3
 allurement 377.1
 bewitchment 691.2
 mania 926.12
 obsession 926.13
fascism
 government 612.4
 despotism 612.7
 discrimination 980.4
fashion
 n aspect 33.3
 form 262.1
 structure 266.1
 custom 373.1
 manner 384.1
 mode 532.2
 style 578.1
 mode 765.4
 v form 262.7
 produce 892.8
fashion design
 garment making 5.32

 visual arts 712.15
 design specialties 717.5
fast
 n lack of food 515.2
 abstinence 668.2
 holy day 701.12
 v not eat 515.4
 adj deep-dyed 35.18
 swift 174.15
 close 293.12
 confirmed 373.18
 devoted 587.21
 profligate 665.25
 fastened 800.14
 stable 855.12
 stuck 855.16
 reliable 970.17
 adv swiftly 174.17
 securely 800.19
fasten close 293.6
 bind 428.10
 fix 800.7
 secure 855.8
fasten upon
 seize on 480.16
 blame 599.8
 impose 643.4
 attribute to 888.4
fast food 10.1
fast-food restaurant 8.17
fast-forward
 run 174.3
 hastening 401.3
fastidious
 clean 79.25
 particular 495.9
 elegant 496.8
 conscientious 644.15
 discriminating 944.7
fasting
 n abstinence from food 515.1
 penance 658.3
 asceticism 667.1
 adj hungry 100.25
 uneating 515.5
fast lane dissipation 669.2
 aspiring 100.28
fast track 174.3
fat
 n glyceride 7.7
 superfluity 993.4
 the best 999.8
 oil 1056.1
 v fatten 259.8
 adj corpulent 257.18
 distended 259.13
 stubby 268.10
 thick 269.8
 heavy 297.16
 gainful 472.16
 wealthy 618.14
 stupid 922.15
 plentiful 991.7
 thriving 1010.13
 oily 1056.9
fatal
 deadly 308.23
 destructive 395.26
 future 839.8
 destined 964.9
 chance 972.15

 weighty 997.20
 unfortunate 1011.14
 disastrous 1011.15
fatal flaw 1006.4
fatalism
 composure 106.2
 resignation 134.2
 determinism 964.4
fatality
 ominousness 133.6
 inauspiciousness 133.7
 fatal accident 308.8
 deadliness 308.9
 fate 964.2
fat cat 618.7
fat chance
 n improbability 969.1
 interj nope 335.10
fate
 n doom 395.2
 portion 477.5
 end 820.1
 destiny 839.2
 inevitability 963.7
 fatality 964.2
 chance 972.1
 v allot 477.9
 destine 964.7
fateful
 ominous 133.16
 destructive 395.26
 inevitable 963.15
 destined 964.9
 weighty 997.20
fathead 924.4
father
 n senior 304.5
 brother 559.3
 sire 560.9
 priest 699.5
 author 886.4
 producer 892.7
 personage 997.8
 v procreate 78.8
 engender 818.14
 cause 886.10
 trace to 888.5
fatherland 232.2
fathom
 sound 275.9
 measure 300.10
 understand 521.7
 know 928.12
 investigate 938.23
 solve 940.2
fatigue
 n weakness 16.1
 weakening 16.5
 tiredness 21.1
 symptoms 85.9
 languor 331.6
 work 725.4
 v tire 21.4
 burn out 21.5
 be tedious 118.6
fatten nourish 8.19
 increase 251.4
 size 257.15
 fat 259.8
 thicken 269.5
 make better 392.9

 fertilize 890.8
 thrive 1010.8
 raise 1070.6
fatuous
 ineffective 19.15
 vain 391.13
 thin 764.6
 foolish 923.8
 thoughtless 933.4
 trivial 998.19
faucet valve 239.10
 stopper 293.4
fault
 n crack 224.2
 vice 654.2
 misdeed 655.2
 game 748.2
 error 975.1
 mistake 975.3
 defect 1003.2
 blemish 1004.1
 v complain 115.15
 deprecate 510.12
 play tennis 748.3
faultfinding
 n complaint 115.4
 critisism 510.4
 disparagement 512.1
 adj discontented 108.7
 plaintive 115.19
 critical 510.23
faultless
 innocent 657.6
 accurate 973.16
 perfect 1002.6
faulty
 ungrammatic 531.4
 guilty 656.3
 illogical 936.11
 erroneous 975.16
 imperfect 1003.4
 blemished 1004.8
fauna
 animal life 311.1
 biology 1068.1
Faust 690.5
faux 336.8
faux pas 975.5
favor
 n looks 33.4
 inclination 100.3
 act of kindness 143.7
 pity 145.1
 respect 155.1
 face 216.4
 superiority 249.1
 preference 371.5
 patronage 449.4
 benefit 478.7
 approval 509.1
 letter 553.2
 good terms 587.3
 privilege 642.2
 esteem 662.3
 influence 894.1
 special favor 894.2
 memento 989.6
 v desire 100.14
 be kind 143.9
 respect 155.4
 choose 371.17

fight 754.3
v lash out at 459.16
fight 754.4
feisty
  hot-tempered 110.25
  defiant 327.10
  plucky 359.14
  perverse 361.11
  partisan 456.17
  argumentative 935.19
felicitation 149.1
felicitous pleasant 97.6
  decorous 496.9
  appropriate 533.7
  eloquent 544.8
  apt 788.10
  timely 843.9
  expedient 995.5
felicity happiness 95.2
  aptitude 413.5
  decorousness 496.2
  elegance 533.1
  eloquence 544.1
  fitness 788.5
  prosperity 1010.1
  good fortune 1010.2
feline
  n creature 311.3
  cat 311.20
  adj felid 311.42
  covert 345.12
  cunning 415.12
fell
  n fur 4.2
  plain 236.1
  plateau 237.3
  hill 237.4
  skin 295.3
  v level 201.6
  strike dead 308.18
  raze 395.19
  conquer 412.10
  shoot 904.12
  drop 913.5
  adj terrible 127.30
  cruel 144.26
fellatio 75.7
fellow
  n man 76.5
  doctor 90.4
  beau 104.12
  boy 302.5
  person 312.5
  image 349.5
  teacher 571.1
  friend 588.1
  companion 588.3
  associate 616.1
  member 617.11
  accompanier 769.4
  likeness 784.3
  equal 790.4
  adj cooperative 450.5
  accompanying 769.9
fellow feeling 104.1
fellowship
  n cooperation 450.1
  affiliation 450.2
  accord 455.1
  subsidy 478.8
  instructorship 571.10

camaraderie 582.2
social life 582.4
association 582.6
companionship 587.2
sodality 617.3
scholarship 646.7
sect 675.3
company 769.2
v associate with 582.17
felon sore 85.37
  evildoer 593.1
  criminal 660.9
felony
  misdeed 655.2
  offense 674.4
felt 4.1
female
  n female being 77.4
  adj feminine 77.13
feminine
  n gender 530.10
  adj female 77.13
feminine caesura 720.7
femininity
  femaleness 77.1
  feminality 77.1
  womankind 77.3
  maturity 303.2
feminism
  effeminacy 77.2
  women's rights 642.4
  discrimination 980.4
femme fatale
  tempter 377.4
  demimonde 665.15
fen 243.1
fence
  n wall 212.4
  fortification 460.4
  receiver 732.6
  barrier 1012.5
  v wall 212.7
  dodge 368.8
  contend 457.13
  fortify 460.9
  illicit goods 732.7
  quibble 936.9
  protect 1008.18
fence in enclose 212.5
  fence 212.7
  confine 429.12
fencer 461.1
fence-sitting
  n irresolution 362.1
  neutrality 467.1
  adj irresolute 362.9
  repudiative 363.12
fend fend off 460.10
  protect 1008.18
  prevent 1012.14
fender partition 213.5
  safeguard 1008.3
  fireplace 1020.11
fend off
  ward off 460.10
  repulse 908.3
  prevent 1012.14
feng shui 498.1
feral frenzied 105.25
  cruel 144.26
  deadly 308.23

funereal 309.22
animal 311.39
savage 671.21
ferment
  n bread 10.28
  agitation 105.4
  dudgeon 152.7
  leavening 298.4
  bubbling 320.3
  bustle 330.4
  turbulence 671.2
  transformer 852.5
  agitation 917.1
  v sour 67.4
  leaven 298.7
  bubble 320.4
  incite 375.17
  seethe 671.12
  agitate 917.10
  chemicalize 1060.8
fermentation
  souring 67.3
  commotion 105.4
  leavening 298.4
  bubbling 320.3
  agitation 917.1
fern 310.4
ferocious
  frenzied 105.25
  cruel 144.26
  warlike 458.20
  savage 671.21
ferret
  sharp vision 27.11
  wild animal 311.22
ferret out
  search out 938.34
  uncover 941.4
Ferris wheel 743.15
ferrous 1058.17
ferry
  n passageway 383.3
  v haul 176.13
  fly 184.36
fertile productive 890.9
  imaginative 986.18
  plentiful 991.7
fertility
  wordiness 538.2
  productiveness 890.1
  invention 986.3
  plenty 991.2
fertility rite 701.9
fertilize fructify 78.10
  enrich 890.8
  cultivate 1069.17
fervent fervid 93.18
  zealous 101.9
  heated 105.22
  industrious 330.22
  vehement 544.13
fervid craving 100.24
  zealous 101.9
  heated 105.22
fervor zeal 101.2
  love 104.1
  industry 330.6
  vehemence 544.5
  heat metaphor 1019.2
festal vacational 20.10
  festive 743.28

festering
  n pus 12.6
  soreness 26.4
  sore 85.37
  corruption 393.2
  adj suppurative 12.21
  sore 26.11
  decayed 393.40
  unforgettable 989.25
festination 401.3
festival
  musical occasion 708.32
  festivity 743.4
festive
  convivial 582.23
  festal 743.28
festivity treat 95.3
  rejoicing 116.1
  celebration 487.1
  conviviality 582.3
  merrymaking 743.3
  festival 743.4
  assembly 770.2
festoon
  n curve 279.2
  bouquet 310.25
  v ornament 545.7
Festschrift
  compilation 554.7
  collection 770.11
fetal embryonic 305.22
  undeveloped 406.12
  beginning 818.15
fetch
  n range 158.2
  trick 356.6
  stratagem 415.3
  specter 988.1
  double 988.3
  v bring 176.16
  travel 177.18
  sail for 182.35
  arrive 186.6
  attract 377.6
  cost 630.13
  hit 902.14
  conclude 946.10
fetching delightful 97.7
  alluring 377.8
fete festival 743.4
  assembly 770.2
fetid
  malodorous 71.5
  filthy 80.23
  offensive 98.18
  terrible 1000.9
fetish
  n charm 691.5
  idol 697.3
  v idolatrize 697.5
fetishism
  perversion 75.11
  animism 675.6
  sorcery 690.1
  idolatry 697.1
fetlock tuft 3.6
  foot 199.5
fetter
  n shackle 428.4
  curb 1012.7
  v bind 428.10

yoke 800.10
hamper 1012.11
fettle
  n fitness 84.1
  good condition 765.3
  v groom 79.20
fettuccine 10.33
fetus 305.14
feud
  n quarrel 456.5
  possession 469.1
  revenge 507.1
  animosity 589.4
  v quarrel 456.11
  contend 457.13
feudal
  imperious 417.16
  subject 432.13
  real 471.9
fever
  n feverishness 85.7
  symptom 85.9
  fever of excitement 105.7
  card 758.2
  five 882.1
  agitation 917.1
  frenzy 926.7
  heat 1019.1
  v take sick 85.47
few insignificant 248.6
  least 250.8
  not many 885.4
a few plurality 883.1
  a number 884.2
  too few 885.2
the few 885.3
few and far between
  infrequent 848.2
  sparse 885.5
fey
  supernatural 870.15
  eccentric 927.5
fiancé 104.16
fiasco
  disappointment 132.1
  botch 410.6
fiat decree 420.4
  authorization 443.3
fib
  n lie 354.11
  v lie 354.19
fiber nutrient 7.3
  filament 271.1
  organic matter 305.1
  nature 767.4
fiberglass 295.23
fiber optics optics 29.7
  light 1025.23
fibrillation
  symptom 85.9
  irregularity 851.1
  pulsation 916.3
fibrous
  threadlike 271.7
  tough 1049.4
fickle irresolute 362.9
  flighty 364.6
  unfaithful 645.20
  transient 828.7
  inconstant 854.7
  uncertain 971.16

fiction
  fabrication 354.10
  lie 354.11
  writing 547.10
  story 722
  narrative 722.1
  invention 986.3
  figment of the imagination
    986.5
fictional
  fabricated 354.29
  narrative 719.8
  fictionalized 722.7
  fictitious 986.21
fictitious
  spurious 354.26
  fabricated 354.29
  make-believe 986.21
fiddle
  n deception 356.9
  v repair 396.14
  play violin 708.41
  trifle 998.15
fidelity
  perseverance 360.1
  observance 434.1
  faithfulness 644.7
  accuracy 973.5
fidget be excited 105.18
  have the fidgets 128.6
  twitch 917.13
fidgety jittery 128.12
  bustling 330.20
  agitated 917.16
  jerky 917.19
fiduciary
  n trustee 470.5
  adj in trust 438.13
  believable 953.24
  fiducial 953.25
fiefdom 469.1
field space 158.1
  airport 184.22
  setting 209.2
  enclosed place 212.3
  sphere 231.2
  plot 231.4
  latitude 430.4
  arena 463.1
  battlefield 463.2
  study 568.8
  heraldry 647.2
  occupation 724.4
  playground 743.11
  baseball 745.1
  football 746.1
  field hockey 749.4
  soccer 752.1
  horse race 757.3
  specialty 866.1
  science 928.10
  tract 1069.9
the field 452.2
field goal game 746.3
  basketball game 747.3
field hockey 749.4
field of vision
  vision 27.1
  field of view 31.3
fiend enthusiast 101.5
  monster 593.6

  violent person 671.9
  demon 680.6
fierce frenzied 105.25
  passionate 105.29
  cruel 144.26
  infuriated 152.32
  warlike 458.20
  violent 671.16
  savage 671.21
fiery red 41.6
  feverish 85.58
  fervent 93.18
  zealous 101.9
  heated 105.22
  passionate 105.29
  hot-tempered 110.25
  vehement 544.13
  hotheaded 671.22
  igneous 1019.26
  heating 1020.26
  illuminated 1025.40
fiesta treat 95.3
  festival 743.4
fife 708.42
fifteen minutes of fame
  glory 247.2
  illustriousness 666.2
fifth
  n interval 709.20
  quinquesection 882.14
  adj quinary 882.17
fifth column 357.11
fifth-column 645.22
fifth wheel
  nonessential 768.2
  superfluity 993.4
fifty-fifty
  n half 875.2
  even chance 972.7
  adj symmetric 264.4
  neutral 467.7
  proportionate 477.13
  equal 790.7
  mixed 797.14
  in half 875.8
fig clothing 5.1
  trifle 998.5
fight
  n quarrel 456.5
  contest 457.3
  battle 457.4
  warlikeness 458.10
  struggle 725.3
  match 754.3
  v clash 35.15
  contend against 451.4
  quarrel 456.11
  contend 457.13
  war 458.13
  struggle 725.11
  box 754.4
fighter
  combatant 461.1
  boxer 754.2
fighting
  n contention 457.1
  quarreling 457.9
  war 458.1
  boxing 754.1
  adj contending 457.22
  warlike 458.20

fight off fend off 460.10
  repulse 908.3
fight the good fight
  contend 457.13
  be good 653.4
  be pious 692.6
figment
  fabrication 354.10
  figment of the imagination
    986.5
figurative
  representational 349.13
  indicative 517.23
  meaningful 518.10
  symbolic 519.10
  tropologic 536.3
  ornate 545.11
  numeric 1017.23
figurative language 536.1
figure
  n aspect 33.3
  apparition 33.5
  gestalt 92.32
  outline 211.2
  form 262.1
  human form 262.4
  figurine 349.6
  diagram 381.3
  motif 498.7
  display 501.4
  figure of speech 536.1
  ornateness 545.4
  price 630.1
  repute 662.1
  celebrity 662.9
  passage 708.24
  card 758.2
  characteristic 865.4
  syllogism 935.6
  phantom 976.4
  personage 997.8
  body 1052.3
  v form 262.7
  image 349.11
  plan 381.8
  filigree 498.9
  designate 517.18
  metaphorize 536.2
  be somebody 662.10
  be reasonable 935.17
  estimate 946.9
  calculate 1017.18
figurehead prow 216.3
  figure 349.6
  nominal head 575.5
  deputy 576.1
  follower 616.8
  insignia 647.1
  a nobody 998.7
figure in
  participate 476.5
  calculate 1017.18
figure of speech
  turn of expression 536
  figure 536.1
  ornateness 545.4
figure on plan 380.6
  calculate 1017.18
figure out plan 380.6
  solve 940.2
  calculate 1017.18

fitful unordered 810.12
 discontinuous 813.4
 irregular 851.3
 inconstant 854.7
 jerky 917.19
fit in have place 159.9
 implant 191.8
 follow the rule 867.4
fit like a glove
 interact 777.6
 suit 788.8
 expedite one's affair 995.3
fitness ability 18.2
 health 83.1
 physical conditioning 84.1
 physical fitness 84.1
 eligibility 371.11
 preparedness 405.4
 decorousness 496.2
 propriety 637.2
 suitability 788.5
 timeliness 843.1
 expedience 995.1
fit out outfit 5.41
 equip 385.8
fitted eligible 371.24
 provided 385.13
 adapted 405.17
 competent 413.24
 apt 788.10
fitting
 n checking the fit 405.2
 change 852.1
 adj useful 387.18
 decorous 496.9
 appropriate 533.7
 right 637.3
 apt 788.10
 timely 843.9
 expedient 995.5
fit to be tied 152.30
five
 basketball team 747.2
 card 758.2
 V 882.1
five 617.7
five-alarm 15.22
five-and-dime 736.1
five-card stud 759.10
five second rule 600.5
fix
 n navigation 159.3
 circumnavigation 182.2
 state 765.1
 bewilderment 971.3
 expedient 995.2
 v locate 159.11
 establish 159.16
 direct 161.5
 circumscribe 210.4
 quantify 244.4
 castrate 255.11
 form 262.7
 perforate 292.15
 kill 308.14
 resolve 359.7
 accustom 373.9
 bribe 378.3
 perfect 392.11
 do for 395.11
 repair 396.14

 prepare 405.6
 defeat 412.9
 prescribe 420.9
 arrange 437.8
 get even with 506.7
 punish 604.11
 make agree 788.7
 fasten 800.7
 dispose 808.9
 organize 808.10
 define 855.9
 specify 865.11
 decide 946.11
 prove 957.10
 prearrange 965.5
 make sure 970.11
fix and toke 87.20
fixate
 psychologize 92.36
 obsess 926.25
fixation
 libido fixation 92.21
 establishment 159.7
 motionlessness 173.2
 fixity 855.2
 obsession 926.13
 hindrance 1012.1
fixative perfumery 70.2
 art equipment 712.17
fixer mender 396.10
 lawyer 597.3
 wire-puller 609.30
 processing solution 714.13
fixings 796.2
fixing to
 adj prepared 405.16
 prep in preparation for 405.24
fixity motionlessness 173.2
 fixedness 855.2
fixity of purpose 359.4
fix on direct 161.5
 attribute to 888.4
 pay attention 983.8
fixture adjunct 254.1
 fixity 855.2
 machinery 1040.3
fixtures equipment 385.4
 hard goods 735.4
fix-up 582.8
fix up equip 385.8
 repair 396.14
 cure 396.15
 prepare 405.6
 make up 405.7
 reconcile 465.8
 ornament 498.8
 tidy 808.12
fizz
 n sibilation 57.1
 bubbling 320.3
 v sibilate 57.2
 bubble 320.4
fizzle
 n sibilation 57.1
 disappointment 132.1
 bubbling 320.3
 failure 410.2
 v sibilate 57.2
 be disappointing 132.3
 bubble 320.4

 come to nothing 410.13
 burn out 1022.8
fizzle out weaken 16.9
 be disappointing 132.3
 come to nothing 410.13
 be unproductive 891.3
 fall through 911.3
 burn out 1022.8
fjord 242.1
flabbergast 122.6
flabby weak 16.12
 impotent 19.13
 flaccid 1047.10
 pulpy 1063.6
flaccid weak 16.12
 flabby 1047.10
flack appearance 33.2
 promotion 352.5
 publicist 352.9
flag
 n leaf 310.19
 pavement 383.6
 trophy 646.3
 banner 647.7
 golf 751.1
 building material 1054.2
 v weaken 16.9
 fatigue 21.4
 burn out 21.5
 fail 85.48
 dawdle 175.8
 floor 295.22
 languish 393.18
 figure 498.9
 signal 517.22
flag down signal 517.22
 play 745.5
 put a stop to 857.11
flagellate oneself
 regret 113.6
 do penance 658.6
 deny oneself 667.3
flagellation
 corporal punishment 604.4
 penance 658.3
 asceticism 667.1
flagging
 n slowing 175.4
 pavement 383.6
 adj languishing 16.21
 tired 21.7
 slow 175.10
 deteriorating 393.45
flagrant
 downright 247.12
 conspicuous 348.12
 gaudy 501.20
 wicked 654.16
 base 661.12
 immodest 666.6
 terrible 1000.9
 burning 1019.27
flagship 818.17
flagstaff 273.1
flagstone
 pavement 383.6
 building material 1054.2
flail whip 604.13
 pound 902.16
 pulverize 1051.9
flail at 459.16

flair ability 18.2
 talent 413.4
 aptitude 413.5
 display 501.4
 artistry 712.6
 smartness 920.2
 discernment 944.2
flak
 dissension 456.3
 artillery 462.11
 criticism 510.4
flake
 n cocaine 87.7
 flock 296.3
 lunatic 926.16
 freak 927.4
 snow 1023.8
 v scale 6.11
 variegate 47.7
 layer 296.5
flaked-out 22.22
flake off scale 6.11
 depart 188.7
flake out 22.14
flaky
 n addict 87.21
 adj flocculent 296.7
 capricious 364.5
 foolish 923.9
 crazy 926.27
 eccentric 927.6
 powdery 1051.11
flamboyance
 ornateness 498.2
 showiness 501.3
 brightness 1025.4
flamboyant
 ornate 498.12
 grandiloquent 545.8
 bright 1025.33
flame
 n love 104.1
 beau 104.12
 fire 1019.13
 flash 1025.6
 light source 1026.1
 v redden 41.5
 be hot 1019.22
 catch fire 1020.23
 burn 1020.24
 shine 1025.24
flameproof
 v fireproof 1022.6
 adj resistant 15.20
 fireproof 1022.10
flaming
 n burning 1020.5
 adj red 41.6
 fervent 93.18
 zealous 101.9
 heated 105.22
 grandiloquent 545.8
 fiery 671.22
 burning 1019.27
 bright 1025.33
 flashing 1025.35
flammable
 n fuel 1021.1
 adj inflammable 1020.28
flange border 211.4
 bulge 283.3

flank
n side 218.1
v side 218.4
launch an attack 459.17
defend 460.8
circle 914.5
flank attack 459.1
flannels 5.22
flap
n noise 53.4
report 56.1
dither 105.6
bulge 283.3
overlayer 295.4
lamina 296.2
bustle 330.4
turbulence 671.2
slap 902.8
agitation 917.1
flutter 917.4
v crack 56.6
hang 202.6
pound 902.16
slap 902.19
wave 916.11
flutter 917.12
flare
n expansion 259.1
alarm 400.1
signal 517.15
explosion 671.7
flare-up 1019.14
flash 1025.6
torch 1026.3
television reception 1035.5
v spread 259.6
be hot 1019.22
shine 1025.24
flare-up outbreak 105.9
outburst 152.9
explosion 671.7
flare 1019.14
flash
n glance 27.4
excitement 105.3
swiftness 174.6
impulse 365.1
skillful person 413.14
bulletin 552.5
explosion 671.7
instant 830.3
flare 1019.14
blaze 1025.6
v burst forth 33.9
telegraph 347.20
flaunt 501.17
signal 517.22
shine 1025.24
flashback 989.3
flash drive 1042.5
flash-frying 11.2
flashing
n unclothing 6.1
cognizance 928.2
adj showy 501.19
brief 828.8
flashy 1025.35
flickering 1025.37
flash in the pan
n impotent 19.6
false alarm 400.2

great success 409.3
abortion 410.5
failure 410.7
thing of naught 764.2
ephemeron 828.5
v come to nothing 410.13
be unproductive 891.3
flash on think of 931.16
remember 989.9
flash point 1019.5
flashy garish 35.20
showy 501.19
grandiloquent 545.8
flashing 1025.35
flat
n floor 197.23
horizontal 201.3
apartment 228.13
plain 236.1
shoal 276.2
smoothness 287.3
scenery 704.20
note 709.14
game 746.3
cheater 759.22
adj soft-colored 35.22
colorless 36.7
muffled 52.17
dissonant 61.4
insipid 65.2
dull 117.6
spatial 158.10
inert 173.14
horizontal 201.7
recumbent 201.8
champaign 236.2
deflated 260.14
lean 270.17
low 274.7
straight 277.6
smooth 287.10
phonetic 524.30
without money 619.10
prosaic 721.5
uniform 781.5
unqualified 960.2
lackluster 1027.17
adv horizontally 201.9
flatfoot
deformity 265.3
detective 576.11
police 1008.16
flatland
horizontal 201.3
plain 236.1
flatline 307.2
flat out
at full speed 174.20
extremely 247.22
at top speed 756.5
utterly 794.16
unqualified 960.2
in excess 993.23
flatten level 201.6
straighten 277.5
smooth 287.5
raze 395.19
conquer 412.10
make uniform 781.4
flatter fawn 138.7
congratulate 149.2

importune 440.12
praise 509.12
adulate 511.5
flatterer 509.8
flattering
obsequious 138.14
congratulatory 149.3
importunate 440.18
approbatory 509.16
adulatory 511.8
flattery
congratulation 149.1
praise 509.5
laudation 511
adulation 511.1
flatulence
distension 259.2
grandiloquence 545.1
fart 909.10
vaporousness 1067.3
flatulent
distended 259.13
pompous 501.22
bombastic 545.9
ejective 909.30
flatware tableware 8.12
hard goods 735.4
flaunt
n display 501.4
waving 916.2
v manifest 348.5
vaunt 501.17
wave 916.11
flaunting
n display 501.4
waving 916.2
adj garish 35.20
showy 501.19
gaudy 501.20
grandiloquent 545.8
flautist 710.4
flavor
n taste 62.1
flavoring 63.3
odor 69.1
characteristic 865.4
v savor 63.7
imbue 797.11
flavor control 1041.8
flavorless 65.2
flavorsome
flavorful 63.9
delectable 97.10
flaw
n crack 224.2
gust 318.5
vice 654.2
error 975.1
fault 1003.2
blemish 1004.1
v blemish 1004.4
flawed
unvirtuous 654.12
illegal 674.6
illogical 936.11
erroneous 975.16
blemished 1004.8
flawless
accurate 973.16
perfect 1002.6
flaxen 43.4

flay peel 6.8
strip 480.24
criticize 510.20
tear apart 802.14
flea vermin 311.36
jumper 366.4
fleabag 228.15
flea-bitten 47.13
flea in one's ear 399.1
a flea in one's ear
rejection 372.1
repulse 442.2
reproof 510.5
flea market sale 734.3
marketplace 736.2
fleck
n tuft 3.6
spottiness 47.3
modicum 248.2
minute 258.7
mark 517.5
stain 1004.3
v variegate 47.7
mark 517.19
fledgling
n youngster 302.1
boy 302.5
birdling 302.10
bird 311.27
novice 572.9
modern 841.4
adj immature 406.11
new 841.7
flee disappear 34.2
run off 188.12
fly 368.10
escape 369.6
cease to exist 762.6
fleece
n hair 3.2
head of hair 3.4
fur 4.2
whiteness 37.2
skin 295.3
softness 1047.4
v divest 6.5
cheat 356.18
strip 480.24
plunder 482.17
overprice 632.7
fleet
n ships 180.10
navy 461.27
company 770.3
v speed 174.8
flit 828.6
adj fast 174.15
agile 413.23
brief 828.8
fleet-footed 174.15
fleeting
vanishing 34.3
receding 168.5
unsubstantial 764.5
transient 828.7
flesh meat 10.13
sexuality 75.2
skin 295.3
organic matter 305.1
humankind 312.1
kinfolk 559.2

carnality 663.2
body 1052.3
the flesh 663.2
flesh out amplify 538.7
  elaborate 861.6
  perfect 1002.5
flesh pink 41.8
fleshpots
  disapproved place 228.28
  sewer 654.7
  prosperity 1010.1
fleshy corpulent 257.18
  pulpy 1063.6
fleur-de-lis
  insignia 647.1
  heraldry 647.2 ·
flex
  n bend 279.3
  v curve 279.6
flexible folded 291.7
  versatile 413.25
  unstrict 426.5
  docile 433.13
  changeable 854.6
  conformable 867.5
  handy 1014.15
  pliant 1047.9
  elastic 1048.7
flibbertigibbet
  scatterbrain 924.7
  flightiness 985.5
flick
  n thud 52.3
  touch 73.1
  mark 517.5
  motion pictures 706.1
  tap 902.7
  jerk 905.3
  stain 1004.4
  v touch 73.6
  tap 902.18
  jerk 905.5
  flutter 917.12
flickering
  n flicker 1025.8
  adj brief 828.8
  irregular 851.3
  inconstant 854.7
  fluttering 917.18
  burning 1019.27
  bickering 1025.37
flier speeder 174.5
  train 179.14
  aviator 185.1
  advertising matter 352.8
  circus artist 707.3
  trading 737.19
  gamble 759.2
flight
  defense mechanism 92.23
  course 172.2
  velocity 174.1
  migration 177.4
  aviation 184.1
  trip 184.9
  departure 188.1
  fugitation 368.4
  escape 369.1
  air force 461.29
  arrow 462.6
  ornament 709.18

assemblage 770.6
multitude 884.3
rocket launching 1074.9
flight attendant
  crew 185.4
  attendant 577.5
flight of fancy
  imagination 986.1
  idealism 986.7
flight path
  airway 184.33
  route 383.1
flighty fickle 364.6
  inconstant 854.7
  superficial 922.20
  insane 926.26
  inattentive 984.6
  volatile 985.17
flimflam
  n lie 354.11
  humbug 354.14
  deception 356.1
  caprice 364.1
  v deceive 356.19
flimsy
  n writing 547.10
  adj frail 16.14
  thin 270.16
  rare 299.4
  fragile 764.7
  unsound 936.12
  trivial 998.19
  flaccid 1047.10
  brittle 1050.4
flinch
  n retreat 903.3
  v shrink 127.13
  be startled 131.5
  retract 168.3
  demur 325.4
  hesitate 362.7
  pull back 903.7
fling
  n attempt 403.3
  revel 743.6
  throw 904.3
  v put violently 159.13
  speed 174.8
  throw 904.10
fling off
  flounce out 188.11
  say 524.22
  do away with 909.21
fling oneself at
  make advances 439.7
  court 562.21
flint lighter 1021.4
  hardness 1046.6
flinty callous 94.12
  pitiless 146.3
  firm 359.12
  unyielding 361.9
  hard 1046.10
  stone 1059.11
flip
  n reverse 363.1
  game 749.3
  tap 902.7
  throw 904.3
  jerk 905.3
  v get excited 105.17

lose self-control 128.8
talkative 540.9
reverse 779.5
tap 902.18
throw 904.10
jerk 905.5
flutter 917.12
adj impudent 142.10
flip-flop
  n reverse 363.1
  change 852.1
  conversion 858.1
  reversion 859.1
  v change 852.7
  turn back 859.5
flip-flopped 205.7
flip-flopper 362.5
flip of a coin
  gamble 759.2
  chance 972.1
flip out
  get excited 105.17
  get angry 152.18
  go mad 926.22
flippant
  impudent 142.10
  careless 340.11
  ridiculing 508.12
flipped 926.27
flipper aquatics 182.11
  scenery 704.20
flip phone 347.4
flip side 215.3
the flip side
  inverse 205.4
  the opposite 779.2
flirt
  n lover 104.11
  tempter 377.4
  coquette 562.11
  tap 902.7
  jerk 905.3
  trifler 998.10
  v lure 377.5
  coquet 562.20
  tap 902.18
  jerk 905.5
  trifle 998.14
flirtation
  love affair 104.5
  allurement 377.1
  flirtiness 562.9
  trifling 998.8
flit
  n homosexual 75.15
  velocity 174.1
  flutter 917.4
  v speed 174.8
  travel 177.18
  migrate 177.22
  wander 177.23
  glide 177.35
  elapse 821.5
  fly 828.6
  flutter 917.12
flitter
  n flutter 917.4
  v flutter 917.12
flitting
  n wandering 177.3
  adj wandering 177.37

transient 828.7
inconstant 854.7
float
  n raft 180.11
  v haul 176.13
  ride 182.54
  swim 182.56
  take off 193.10
  buoy 298.8
  levitate 298.9
  issue 738.12
  inaugurate 818.11
  start 904.13
  wave 916.11
  flood 1065.14
float a loan
  lend 620.5
  borrow 621.3
floater wanderer 178.2
  voter 609.23
floating
  n aquatics 182.11
  voting 609.18
  inauguration 818.5
  adj wandering 177.37
  afloat 182.60
  buoyant 298.14
  unfastened 802.22
flocculent hairy 3.24
  flaky 296.7
flock tuft 3.6
  flake 296.3
  the laity 700.1
  throng 770.4
  group of animals 770.5
  assemblage 770.6
  multitude 884.3
flock to 450.4
flock together
  associate with 582.17
  accompany 769.7
  come together 770.16
floe 1023.5
flog urge 375.14
  whip 604.13
flood
  n torrent 238.5
  overflow 238.6
  tide 238.13
  quantity 247.3
  increase 251.1
  high tide 272.8
  rainstorm 316.2
  lights 704.18
  throng 770.4
  plenty 991.2
  superabundance
    993.2
  v flow 238.16
  overflow 238.17
  abound 991.5
  superabound 993.8
  oversupply 993.14
  float 1065.14
floodgate outlet 190.9
  flood-hatch 239.11
floodlight
  n lights 704.18
  v illuminate 1025.29
flood tide tide 238.13
  high tide 272.8

v transport 176.14
flummery 520.2
flummox
  n confusion 985.3
  v fail 410.10
  bewilder 971.12
  confuse 985.7
  thwart 1012.15
flunk
  n abortion 410.5
  v fail 410.9
  disappoint 410.17
flunky sycophant 138.3
  pursuer 166.2
  inferior 250.2
  subordinate 432.5
  retainer 577.1
  lackey 577.6
  follower 616.8
  worker 726.2
fluorescent light 1026.1
flurry
  n agitation 105.4
  velocity 174.1
  rain 316.1
  gust 318.5
  bustle 330.4
  haste 401.1
  bluster 503.1
  price 738.9
  agitation 917.1
  confusion 985.3
  snow 1023.8
  v excite 105.14
  agitate 917.10
  confuse 985.7
flush
  n warmth 35.2
  reddening 41.3
  washing 79.5
  health 83.1
  fever 85.7
  thrill 105.2
  blushing 139.5
  jet 238.9
  skiing 753.1
  glow 1019.12
  shine 1025.2
  v redden 41.5
  wash 79.19
  change color 105.19
  elate 109.8
  make proud 136.6
  blush 139.8
  show resentment 152.14
  level 201.6
  flow 238.16
  hunt 382.9
  be hot 1019.22
  soak 1065.13
  adj red-complexioned 41.9
  hale 83.12
  fresh 83.13
  horizontal 201.7
  wealthy 618.14
  full 794.11
  plentiful 991.7
  adv horizontally 201.9
flushed
  red-complexioned 41.9
  fresh 83.13

feverish 85.58
fervent 93.18
overjoyed 95.17
heated 105.22
cheerful 109.11
rejoicing 116.10
puffed up 136.10
blushing 139.13
crowing 502.13
hot 1019.25
flush it 410.17
flush syndrome 41.3
fluster
  n dither 105.6
  bustle 330.4
  bluster 503.1
  agitation 917.1
  confusion 985.3
  v agitate 105.14
  confuse 985.7
flute
  n furrow 290.1
  v furrow 290.3
  fold 291.5
  speak 524.25
  blow a horn 708.42
flutist 710.4
flutter
  n audio distortion 50.13
  staccato 55.1
  trepidation 105.5
  dither 105.6
  bustle 330.4
  haste 401.1
  trill 709.19
  trading 737.19
  price 738.9
  pulsation 916.3
  flitter 917.4
  confusion 985.3
  flicker 1025.8
  v drum 55.4
  excite 105.14
  be excited 105.18
  oscillate 916.10
  wave 916.11
  agitate 917.10
  flitter 917.12
  confuse 985.7
  flicker 1025.26
fluvial 238.23
flux
  n excretion 12.1
  defecation 12.2
  symptom 85.9
  course 172.2
  flow 238.4
  tide 238.13
  ceramics 742.3
  measurement of light 1025.22
  liquidity 1061.1
  solvent 1064.4
  v treat 91.24
  combine 805.3
  melt 1020.21
  liquefy 1064.5
fly
  n overlayer 295.4
  insect 311.32
  snare 356.13

game 745.3
v disappear 34.2
speed 174.8
transport 176.12
glide 177.35
be airborne 184.36
pilot 184.37
run off 188.12
take off 193.10
flee 368.10
play 745.5
cease to exist 762.6
elapse 821.5
flit 828.6
wave 916.11
fly at 459.18
flyblown filthy 80.23
  blighted 393.42
fly-by-night
  untrustworthy 645.19
  transient 828.7
flying
  n aviation 184.1
  adj vanishing 34.3
  high 87.24
  flowing 172.8
  fast 174.15
  airborne 184.50
  hasty 401.9
  transient 828.7
flying buttress 901.4
flying colors
  great success 409.3
  victory 411.1
Flying Dutchman
  wanderer 178.2
  mariner 183.1
  White Lady 988.2
fly in the face of
  disobey 327.6
  deny 335.4
  oppose 451.3
  offer resistance 453.3
  flout 454.4
  go contrary to 779.4
  counteract 900.6
fly in the ointment
  evil 1000.3
  fault 1003.2
  obstacle 1012.4
flyleaf 554.12
fly off at a tangent
  fly into a rage 152.20
  avoid 164.6
  diverge 171.5
fly off the handle
  get excited 105.17
  fly into a rage 152.20
fly on the wall
  viewpoint 27.7
  listener 48.5
flytrap 356.12
FM signal 1034.10
foal
  n fledgling 302.10
  horse 311.10
  jockey 757.2
  v give birth 1.3
foam
  n saliva 13.3
  whiteness 37.2

lightness 298.2
froth 320.2
extinguisher 1022.3
softness 1047.4
sprinkle 1065.5
v bubble 320.4
froth 320.5
seethe 671.12
foam at the mouth
  be angry 152.15
  be insane 926.20
foamy light 298.10
  foam-flecked 320.7
fob
  n bag 195.2
  jewel 498.6
  v cheat 356.18
fob off on 643.7
focal converging 169.3
  confocal 208.13
  chief 249.14
  vital 997.23
focus
  n convergence 169.1
  focal point 208.4
  centralization 208.8
  essence 767.2
  attractor 907.2
  v focalize 208.10
focus group 793.1
focus on
  specify 865.11
  operate on 889.6
  concentrate 931.10
  have regard to 937.3
  pay attention 983.8
  call attention to 983.10
fodder
  n feed 10.4
  v feed 8.18
  tend 1070.7
foe
  opponent 452.1
  enemy 589.6
fog
  n atmosphere 184.32
  grass 310.5
  pea soup 319.3
  obscurity 522.3
  confusion 985.3
  v blur 32.4
  cover 295.19
  cloud 319.7
  make uncertain 971.15
  confuse 985.7
foggy
  inconspicuous 32.6
  soupy 319.10
  obscure 522.15
  muddleheaded 922.18
  vague 971.19
  muddled 985.13
foghorn
  warning sign 399.3
  alarm 400.1
  signal 517.15
fogy
  old-timer 842.8
  conservative 853.4
  dotard 924.9

foible
vice 654.2
fault 1003.2
foil
n lamina 296.2
discomfiture 412.2
motif 498.7
actor 707.2
frustration 1012.3
v disappoint 132.2
outwit 415.11
thwart 1012.15
foist 776.5
foist oneself upon 214.5
fold
n enclosed place 212.3
cavity 284.2
crease 291.1
double 291.1
lamina 296.2
the laity 700.1
v collapse 260.10
fold on itself 291.5
close shop 293.8
fail 410.10
embrace 562.18
go bankrupt 625.7
seek the middle 819.3
folder
advertising matter 352.8
booklet 554.11
bookholder 554.17
folderol finery 498.3
nonsense 520.2
passage 708.24
trifle 998.5
fold in 291.5
folding
n mountain 237.6
creasing 291.4
bookbinding 554.14
adj folded 291.7
fold up
collapse 260.10
fold 291.5
close shop 293.8
fail 410.10
go bankrupt 625.7
end 820.5
foliage 310.18
foliation
stratification 296.4
foliage 310.18
numeration 1017.9
folio volume 554.4
makeup 554.12
bookholder 554.17
part of writing 793.2
folk
n population 227.1
race 559.4
family 559.5
the people 606.1
adj traditional 842.12
folk history story 719.3
tradition 842.2
folklore
mythology 678.14
tradition 842.2
superstition 954.3
folk music 708.11

folks
kinfolk 559.2
family 559.5
the people 606.1
folk singer
singer 710.13
minstrel 710.14
folk singing 708.13
folksy 581.3
folktale 842.2
follicle 310.30
follow
n pursuit 382.1
v look 27.13
attach oneself to 138.11
go after 166.3
parallelize 203.5
be behind 217.8
be inferior 250.4
practice 328.8
emulate 336.7
pursue 382.8
take advice 422.7
observe 434.2
understand 521.7
court 562.21
play 744.2
resemble 784.7
set an example 786.7
be consistent 803.7
come next 815.2
succeed 817.5
come after 835.3
specialize 866.4
conform 867.3
result 887.4
seek 938.30
trace 938.35
prove 957.10
follower
enthusiast 101.4
lover 104.11
hanger-on 138.6
successor 166.2
inferior 250.4
pursuer 382.4
apostle 572.2
retainer 577.1
disciple 616.8
believer 692.4
follow from
result from 887.5
prove 957.10
following
n going behind 166
heeling 166.1
follower 166.2
imitation 336.1
pursuit 382.1
attendance 769.6
sequence 815.1
subsequence 835.1
surveillance 938.9
adj trailing 166.5
pursuing 382.11
similar 784.10
succeeding 815.4
subsequent 835.4
resultant 887.6
deducible 935.23
prep after 835.8

follow-through
game 750.2
round 751.3
sequel 817.1
follow up
prosecute to a conclusion 360.5
pursue 382.8
be thorough 794.8
come after 835.3
trace 938.35
follow-up
case history 91.10
pursuit 382.1
news item 552.3
sequel 817.1
subsequence 835.2
folly
foolishness 923.1
foolish act 923.4
foment
n agitation 917.1
v excite 105.12
relieve 120.5
incite 375.17
heat 1020.17
fond
n foundation 901.6
adj loving 104.26
hopeful 124.10
foolish 923.8
credulous 954.8
fondle stroke 73.8
foster 449.16
hold 474.7
caress 562.16
fond of
desirous of 100.22
enamored of 104.29
font jet 238.9
source of supply 386.4
type 548.6
baptism 701.6
church vessels 703.11
fountainhead 886.6
food nutrient 7.3
sustenance 10.1
foodstuff 10.1
food additive preservative 397.4
vitaminization 7.14
food coloring 35.8
food for thought 931.7
food preparer 11.3
food processor 1063.4
foofaraw dither 105.6
bustle 330.4
finery 498.3
turbulence 671.2
commotion 810.4
foo fighter 1075.3
foofooraw
noise 53.4
quarrel 456.6
fool
n dupe 358.1
laughingstock 508.7
buffoon 707.10
stupid person 924.2
damn fool 924.1
ignoramus 930.7

v befool 356.15
be foolish 923.6
trifle 998.14
adj foolish 923.8
fool around
banter 490.6
play 743.23
be foolish 923.6
trifle 998.15
fool around with
meddle 214.7
experiment 942.8
foolery
buffoonery 489.5
gibe 508.2
foolishness 923.1
foolhardy
daring 492.21
harebrained 493.9
fool-hasty 401.11
fooling
n deception 356.1
buffoonery 489.5
banter 490.1
bantering 490.2
ridicule 508.1
trifling 998.8
adj bantering 490.7
ridiculing 508.12
foolish
mischievous 322.6
nonsensical 520.7
unintelligent 922.13
fool 923.8
absurd 923.11
trivial 998.19
foolproof
resistant 15.20
handy 1014.15
fool with meddle 214.7
trifle 998.14
foot
n member 2.7
sail 180.14
base 199.2
extremity 199.5
meter 720.7
v speed 174.8
walk 177.27
way of walking 177.28
make way 182.21
float 182.54
dance 705.5
footage length 267.1
motion-picture photography 706.5
football sport 746.1
football team 746.2
soccer 752.1
foot-dragging
n slowness 175.1
refusal 325.1
delay 846.2
hindrance 1012.1
adj slow 175.10
dilatory 846.17
foothills
the country 233.1
highlands 237.1
foothold hold 474.2
footing 901.5

formula rule 419.2
  form 419.3
  law 673.3
  rite 701.3
  rule 869.4
  axiom 974.2
formulary
  n formula 419.3
  law 673.3
  rite 701.3
  norm 869.4
  adj preceptive 419.4
  formal 580.7
  ritualistic 701.19
formulate say 524.22
  phrase 532.4
  write 547.21
  legalize 673.9
  compose 718.6
  produce 892.8
fornicate
  copulate 75.21
  be promiscuous 665.19
for real
  adj real 761.15
  adv positively 247.19
forsake abandon 370.5
  be unfaithful 645.12
forsaken unloved 99.10
  available 222.15
  abandoned 370.8
  forlorn 584.12
  outcast 586.10
forsooth
  certainly 970.23
  truly 973.18
forswear
  n recant 363.8
  v deny 335.4
  give up 370.7
  reject 372.2
  relinquish 475.3
  swear off 668.8
forsworn
  untruthful 354.34
  apostate 363.11
  rejected 372.3
  relinquished 475.5
  deceitful 645.18
fort 460.6
forte
  n talent 413.4
  music 708.25
  specialty 866.1
  adj loud 53.11
  music 708.53
  adv loudly 53.14
forth
  adv forward 162.8
  hence 188.20
  out 190.21
  prep out of 190.22
forthcoming
  n appearance 33.1
  approach 167.1
  imminence 840.1
  adj approaching 167.4
  emerging 190.18
  future 839.8
  imminent 840.3
  in preparation 405.22

for the birds 98.25
for the hell of it
  for fun 95.20
  in fun 743.31
for the most part
  chiefly 249.17
  on the whole 792.14
  generally 864.17
  normally 869.10
for the nonce
  meanwhile 826.5
  temporarily 828.9
  now 838.3
for the period of 821.14
for the sake of
  on behalf of 380.11
  in order to 449.26
  because of 888.9
for the time being
  temporarily 828.9
  now 838.3
  conditionally 959.11
forthright
  adj candid 644.17
  adv directly 161.23
forthwith at once 830.8
  promptly 845.15
fortification
  vitaminization 7.14
  strengthening 15.5
  work 460.4
  confirmation 957.4
fortify vitaminize 7.20
  refresh 9.2
  strengthen 15.13
  add to 253.5
  embattle 460.9
  adulterate 797.12
  confirm 957.11
a fortiori
  adj dialectic 935.22
  adv chiefly 249.17
fortitude strength 15.1
  patience 134.1
  willpower 359.4
  hardihood 492.5
  cardinal virtues 653.3
Fort Knox 729.13
fortnight
  moment 824.2
  eleven 882.7
fortress 460.6
fortuitous
  circumstantial 766.7
  unessential 768.4
  chance 972.15
fortuity chance 972.1
  chance event 972.6
fortunate
  auspicious 133.17
  successful 409.14
  timely 843.9
  chance 972.15
  lucky 1010.14
fortune wealth 618.1
  gamble 759.2
  fate 964.2
  chance 972.1
  good fortune 1010.2
fortune cookie 10.43
fortune hunter 651.3

fortuneteller 962.4
fortune-telling methods
  962.15
forty plot 231.4
  eleven 882.7
forty-niner
  traveler 178.1
  miner 1058.9
forty winks 22.3
forum square 230.8
  conference 423.3
  arena 463.1
  discussion 541.6
  tribunal 595.1
  assembly 770.2
forward
  n team 752.2
  v advance 162.5
  send 176.15
  be instrumental 384.7
  make better 392.9
  hasten 401.4
  be useful 449.17
  deliver 478.13
  determine 886.12
  impel 902.11
  push 904.9
  expedite one's affair
    995.3
  adj eager 101.8
  insolent 142.9
  progressive 162.6
  meddlesome 214.9
  front 216.10
  willing 324.5
  strong-willed 359.15
  foolhardy 493.9
  immodest 666.6
  premature 845.8
  adv forwards 162.8
  frontward 216.13
forward-looking
  progressive 162.6
  modern 841.13
fosse trench 290.2
  entrenchment 460.5
fossil
  n remainder 256.1
  antiquity 842.6
  back number 842.8
  adj antiquated 842.13
fossilized
  stricken in years 303.18
  antiquated 842.13
  hardened 1046.13
foster
  v nourish 8.19
  advance 162.5
  look after 339.9
  motivate 375.12
  encourage 375.21
  make better 392.9
  nurture 449.16
  hold 474.7
  train 568.13
  care for 1008.19
  adj related 559.6
foster-care 449.3
foster child
  dependent 432.6
  descendant 561.3

fostering
  n accommodations 385.3
  support 449.3
  training 568.3
  protectorship 1008.2
  adj helping 449.20
  protective 1008.23
foul
  n unfairness 650.2
  baseball game 745.3
  football game 746.3
  basketball game 747.3
  hockey game 749.3
  game 749.6
  match 752.3
  fight 754.3
  v defile 80.17
  stop 293.7
  misuse 389.4
  catch 480.17
  play 747.4
  fix 855.10
  collide 902.13
  adj nasty 64.7
  malodorous 71.5
  filthy 80.23
  unhealthful 82.5
  offensive 98.18
  inert 173.14
  stopped 293.11
  stormy 318.22
  decayed 393.40
  cursing 513.8
  unfair 650.10
  wicked 654.16
  base 661.12
  vulgar 666.8
  obscene 666.9
  demoniac 680.17
  terrible 1000.9
  hideous 1015.11
  adv afoul 182.72
fouled up 799.4
foulmouthed
  caustic 144.23
  cursing 513.8
  obscene 666.9
foul play
  homicide 308.2
  chicanery 356.4
  treachery 645.6
  unfairness 650.2
foul-smelling 71.5
foul up spoil 393.11
  complicate 799.3
  confuse 811.3
  make a boner 975.15
  hinder 1012.16
foul-up
  bungle 414.5
  bungler 414.9
  goof 414.9
  confusion 810.2
  goof 975.6
found
  establish 159.16
  form 262.7
  sculpture 715.5
  inaugurate 818.11
  fix 855.9
  cause 886.10

misfit 789.4
specialist 866.3
nonconformist 868.3
oddity 870.4
monstrosity 870.6
fanatic 926.18
character 927.4
chance event 972.6
adj bizarre 870.13
freaked out 105.25
freakish
capricious 364.5
inconstant 854.7
freak 870.13
eccentric 927.5
freak out delight 95.11
lose self-control 128.8
go mad 926.22
go on a trip 976.8
dream 986.17
freak show 907.2
freak someone out 128.10
freckle
n spottiness 47.3
mark 517.5
blemish 1004.1
v variegate 47.7
mark 517.19
spot 1004.5
free
v release 120.6
unclose 292.12
rescue 398.3
liberalize 430.13
exempt 430.14
liberate 431.4
extricate 431.7
acquit 601.4
detach 802.10
loosen 804.3
disembarrass 1014.9
adj available 222.15
open 292.17
voluntary 324.7
idle 331.18
communicative 343.10
escaped 369.11
leisure 402.5
at liberty 430.21
quit 430.31
liberated 431.10
liberal 485.4
gratuitous 634.5
candid 644.17
profligate 665.25
unfastened 802.22
adv freely 430.32
as a gift 478.27
gratuitously 634.6
free and easy
nonchalant 106.15
lighthearted 109.12
careless 340.11
free 430.21
informal 581.3
convivial 582.23
unconventional 868.6
free association 92.33
freebie
n gift 478.4
costlessness 634.1

adj gratuitous 634.5
freedom
leisure 402.1
liberty 430.1
liberality 485.1
privilege 642.2
candor 644.4
facility 1014.1
free enterprise
noninterference 430.9
policy 609.4
capitalism 611.8
free-for-all noise 53.4
knock-down-and-drag-out
457.5
commotion 810.4
freehand
free-acting 430.23
pictorial 712.20
free hand
latitude 430.4
carte blanche 443.4
liberality 485.1
freeholder
householder 227.7
landowner 470.3
legislator 610.3
freeing
n release 120.2
escape 369.1
rescue 398.1
liberation 431.1
freedom 431.2
extrication 431.3
evacuation 909.6
disembarrassment
1014.6
adj benefiting 592.4
free lance
free agent 430.12
mercenary 461.17
writer 547.15
author 718.4
worker 726.2
free-lance
stand on one's own two feet
430.20
author 547.21
write 718.6
freeloader
parasite 138.5
nonworker 331.11
guest 585.6
free rider 634.3
free love
sexology 75.18
love 104.1
illicit sex 665.7
free man 566.2
freemasonry
affiliation 450.2
fellowship 587.2
free of
adj quit 430.31
prep absent 222.19
free-range 430.26
free ride
costlessness 634.1
game 745.3
free rider 634.3
free spirit 868.3

free-standing
independent 430.22
separate 802.20
freestyle 182.11
freestyle skiing 753.1
free swimming 182.11
freethinking
n liberalism 430.10
free thought 695.7
liberalness 979.2
adj nonrestrictive 430.25
latitudinarian 695.21
liberal 979.9
free thought
liberalism 430.10
freethinking 695.7
liberalness 979.2
free throw 747.3
free time 402.1
free trade
noninterference 430.9
policy 609.4
commerce 731.1
free up 1014.9
freewheeling 430.22
free will will 323.1
voluntariness 324.2
choice 371.1
free choice 430.6
free with one's money 485.4
free woman 566.2
freeze
n cold weather 1023.3
v deaden 25.4
numb 94.8
take fright 127.11
terrify 127.17
be still 173.7
preserve 397.9
speak poorly 525.7
perpetuate 829.5
stabilize 855.7
fix 855.10
stop 857.7
put a stop to 857.11
be cold 1023.9
freeze 1023.9
chill 1023.10
ice up 1023.10
ice 1024.11
interj cease! 857.13
the freeze 589.1
freeze-dry
preserve 397.9
freeze 1024.11
dry 1066.6
freeze out
exclude 773.4
drive out 909.14
freezing
n food preservation 397.2
refrigeration 1024.1
adj cold 1023.14
feeling cold 1023.16
refrigerative 1024.12
freight
n transportation 176.3
freightage 176.6
train 179.14
load 196.2
burden 297.7

haulage 630.7
charge 643.3
impediment 1012.6
v load 159.15
transport 176.12
send 176.15
burden 297.13
fill 794.7
freighter carrier 176.7
train 179.14
French hours 268.1
frenetic
overzealous 101.12
overactive 330.24
rabid 926.30
frenzied
overzealous 101.12
frantic 105.25
overactive 330.24
turbulent 671.18
rabid 926.30
frenzy
n seizure 85.6
overzealousness 101.3
fury 105.8
turbulence 671.2
agitation 917.1
furor 926.7
confusion 985.3
v excite 105.12
enrage 152.25
madden 926.24
frequency
oftenness 847.1
routineness 847.1
oscillation 916.1
wave 916.4
radio frequency 1034.12
frequent
v haunt 221.10
adj habitual 373.14
oftentime 847.4
recurrent 849.13
frequent flier 184.10
fresco
n painting 35.12
picture 712.10
v color 35.14
fresh
n stream 238.1
torrent 238.5
adj refreshing 9.3
clean 79.25
green 83.13
impudent 142.10
additional 253.10
windy 318.21
original 337.5
unused 390.12
inexperienced 414.17
present 838.2
new 841.7
additional 841.8
remembered 989.22
undamaged 1002.8
cool 1023.12
freshen refresh 9.2
clean 79.18
air 317.11
blow 318.19
perfect 392.11

refrigerate 1024.10
freshet stream 238.1
  torrent 238.5
fresh-faced fresh 83.13
  young 301.9
freshman
  undergraduate 572.6
  novice 572.9
  beginner 818.2
fret
  n ache 26.5
  irritation 96.3
  dither 105.6
  dudgeon 152.7
  network 170.3
  heraldry 647.2
  roulette 759.12
  v pain 26.7
  irritate 96.14
  sulk 110.14
  grieve 112.17
  complain 115.15
  make anxious 126.5
  feel anxious 126.6
  be impatient 135.4
  be angry 152.15
  provoke 152.24
  injure 393.13
  wear 393.20
  agitate 917.10
  abrade 1044.7
fretful
  peevish 110.22
  plaintive 115.19
  impatient 135.6
  bustling 330.20
fretting
  n worry 126.2
  impatience 135.1
  abrasion 1044.2
  adj irritating 26.13
  troublesome 126.10
  impatient 135.6
  abrasive 1044.10
friable
  brittle 1050.4
  pulverable 1051.13
friar 699.16
fricassee
  n stew 10.11
  v cook 11.5
fricking around 998.9
friction
  n touching 73.2
  opposition 451.2
  disaccord 456.1
  hostility 589.3
  counteraction 900.1
  rubbing 1044.1
  adj frictional 1044.9
Friday abstinence 668.2
  fate 964.2
Friday the thirteenth 964.2
fridge 1024.4
fried cooked 11.7
  high 87.24
  drunk 88.33
friend 588.1
friendless
  helpless 19.18
  forlorn 584.12

alone 872.8
friendly
  comfortable 121.11
  homelike 228.33
  favorable 449.22
  sociable 582.22
  hospitable 585.11
  friendlike 587.15
friendship
  comradeship 587
  friendliness 587.1
frigging around 998.9
fright
  n fear 127.1
  eyesore 1015.4
  v frighten 127.15
frighten fright 127.15
  startle 131.8
  alarm 400.3
frightening
  n intimidation 127.6
  adj frightful 127.28
frighten off
  scare away 127.21
  dissuade 379.3
frightful
  frightening 127.28
  remarkable 247.11
  hideous 1015.11
frigid unsexual 75.29
  unfeeling 94.9
  reticent 344.10
  aloof 583.6
  cold 1023.14
frill
  n edging 211.7
  extra 254.4
  fold 291.1
  finery 498.3
  ornateness 545.4
  superfluity 993.4
  v fold 291.5
frilly ornate 498.12
  showy 501.19
fringe
  n tuft 3.6
  exterior 206.2
  border 211.4
  edging 211.7
  golf 751.1
  adj exterior 206.7
fringe benefits 624.6
frippery finery 5.10
  frills 498.3
  superfluity 993.4
  trifle 998.5
frisk
  n caper 366.2
  frolic 743.5
  search 938.15
  v rejoice 116.5
  go on horseback 177.34
  caper 366.6
  play 743.23
  search 938.31
frisky gay 109.14
  active 330.17
fritter away 486.5
frivolity
  merriment 109.5
  lightness 298.1

waggishness 489.4
  foolishness 923.1
  flightiness 985.5
  triviality 998.3
frivolous
  merry 109.15
  litigious 598.21
  unordered 810.12
  superficial 922.20
  scatterbrained 985.16
  trivial 998.19
frizz
  n lock 3.5
  v cook 11.5
frizzy 281.9
fro 163.13
frock
  n garment 5.3
  suit 5.6
  dress 5.16
  robe 702.2
  v cloak 5.40
  ordain 698.12
frog
  derogatory names 232.7
  amphibian 311.26
  jumper 366.4
frogman
  swimmer 182.12
  navy man 183.4
  diver 367.4
frolic
  n prank 489.10
  play 743.5
  v exude cheerfulness 109.6
  rejoice 116.5
  play 743.23
from at 159.27
  away from 188.21
  out of 190.22
  off 255.14
from A to Z
  wholly 792.13
  from beginning to end
   794.18
from bad to worse 119.6
from scratch
  first 818.18
  newly 841.15
from soup to nuts
  wholly 792.13
  from beginning to end
   794.18
from the word 'go' and from
  the get-go 818.18
from time to time 848.5
frond leaf 310.19
  branch 310.20
front
  n appearance 33.2
  leading 165.1
  atmosphere 184.32
  exteriority 206.1
  facade 206.2
  forepart 216.1
  fore 216.1
  vanguard 216.2
  weather map 317.4
  sham 354.3
  pretext 376.1
  mediator 466.3

affectation 500.1
  figurehead 575.5
  movement 609.33
  v contrapose 215.4
  be in front 216.7
  confront 216.8
  oppose 451.5
  offer resistance 453.3
  defy 454.3
  brave 492.10
  precede 814.2
  adj frontal 216.10
  phonetic 524.30
  first 818.17
the front 463.2
frontage
  navigation 159.3
  front 216.1
frontal
  n fore 216.1
  altar 703.12
  adj anterior 216.10
front burner
  front 216.1
  importance 997.1
front for
  be in front 216.7
  represent 576.14
  take the place of
   862.6
frontier
  n boundary 211.3
  border 211.5
  front 216.1
  hinterland 233.2
  remote region 261.4
  the unknown 930.6
  adj bordering 211.11
frontispiece
  front 216.1
  curtain-raiser 816.2
front man front 216.1
  mediator 466.3
  figurehead 575.5
front marker 751.1
front matter
  front 216.1
  added to writing 254.2
  makeup 554.12
  part of writing 793.2
  curtain-raiser 816.2
front page 216.1
front-page 552.13
front-runner
  vanguard 216.2
  jockey 757.2
  precursor 816.1
front yard 216.1
frost
  n failure 410.2
  enmity 589.1
  cold weather 1023.3
  Jack Frost 1023.7
  v whiten 37.5
  top 198.9
  freeze 1023.10
  hail 1023.11
  frost over 1030.3
frostbite
  n cold 1023.2
  v freeze 1023.10

frosted
n beverage 10.49
adj white 37.7
unfeeling 94.9
frosty 1023.17
semitransparent 1030.4
frosting
sweets 10.40
whitening 37.3
topping 198.3
frosty white 37.7
unfeeling 94.9
reticent 344.10
aloof 583.6
unfriendly 589.9
frostlike 1023.17
semitransparent 1030.4
froth
n saliva 13.3
dregs 256.2
lightness 298.2
foam 320.2
trivia 998.4
sprinkle 1065.5
v bubble 320.4
foam 320.5
froth at the mouth 926.20
frothy light 298.10
foamy 320.7
showy 501.19
superficial 922.20
trivial 998.19
froward
disobedient 327.8
perverse 361.11
frown
n scowl 110.9
offense 152.2
reproving look 510.8
v look sullen 110.15
show resentment 152.14
frozen unfeeling 94.9
terrified 127.26
fast 800.14
immortal 829.9
permanent 853.7
immovable 855.15
stuck 855.16
feeling cold 1023.16
frozen solid 1024.14
fructification
productiveness 890.1
proliferation 890.2
performance 892.5
bearing 892.6
fructuous 995.5
frugal
parsimonious 484.7
cheap 633.7
economical 635.6
temperate 668.9
meager 992.10
frugality
parsimony 484.1
thrift 635.1
temperance 668.1
fruit
n produce 10.38
homosexual 75.15
seed 310.31
yield 472.5

offspring 561.1
effect 887.1
product 893.1
v bear 892.13
fruitbearing 890.10
fruitcake
homosexual 75.15
lunatic 926.16
fruitful 890.9
fruition pleasure 95.1
accomplishment 407.1
bearing 892.6
fruitless
ineffective 19.15
gainless 391.12
unsuccessful 410.18
fruits gain 472.3
receipts 627.1
fruits de mer 10.24
fruity
flavorful 63.9
fragrant 70.9
vegetable 310.36
crazy 926.27
frump
old woman 304.3
slob 810.7
frustaneous 391.9
frustrate
disappoint 132.2
thwart 412.11
outwit 415.11
neutralize 900.7
hinder 1012.15
frustrated
unsexual 75.29
disappointed 132.5
frustration
psychological stress 92.17
disappointment 132.1
discomfiture 412.2
circumvention 415.5
neutralization 900.2
thwarting 1012.3
fry
n dish 10.7
marine animal 311.29
offspring 561.2
v cook 11.5
brown 40.2
execute 604.17
be hot 1019.22
FUBAR 799.4
fuck copulate 75.21
deceive 356.19
mistreat 389.6
a fuck 762.3
fucked up 810.16
fucked-up
botched 414.22
complex 799.4
fuck off depart 188.7
leave 222.10
idle 331.12
fuck-off 331.8
fuck over 389.6
fuck up spoil 393.11
bungle 414.12
complicate 799.3
confuse 811.3
make a boner 975.15

fuck-up fiasco 410.6
bungle 414.5
goof 414.9
bungler 414.9
complex 799.2
confusion 810.2
goof 975.6
fuddle
n intoxication 88.1
confusion 985.3
v intoxicate 88.23
perplex 971.13
confuse 985.7
fuddy-duddy
n fussbudget 495.7
back number 842.8
dotard 924.9
adj old-fogyish 842.17
fudge
n nonsense 520.2
v slight 340.8
falsify 354.16
fabricate 354.18
cheat 356.18
fuel
n automobile racing 756.1
energy source 1021.1
petroleum 1056.4
rocket propulsion 1074.8
v provision 385.9
fuel up 1021.8
adj energy 1021.9
fugaciousness 828.1
fugitive
n fleer 368.5
escapee 369.5
criminal 660.9
adj vanishing 34.3
receding 168.5
wandering 177.37
runaway 368.16
escaped 369.11
unsubstantial 764.5
transient 828.7
fugue trance 92.19
round 708.19
loss of memory 990.2
führer leader 574.6
tyrant 575.14
fulcrum
supporter 901.2
axis 906.3
axle 915.5
fulfill
carry out 328.7
accomplish 407.4
observe 434.2
execute 437.9
complete 794.6
suffice 991.4
fulfillment
adjustment 92.27
contentment 107.1
accomplishment 407.1
observance 434.1
execution 437.4
completion 794.4
fuliginous 38.11
full
n fullness 794.2
adj colored 35.17

loud 53.11
resonant 54.10
intoxicated 88.31
great 247.6
corpulent 257.18
broad 269.6
thick 269.8
stopped 293.11
unrestricted 430.27
detailed 766.9
crowded 770.22
complete 794.9
filled 794.11
plentiful 991.7
satiated 994.6
sound 1002.7
full-blooded
strong 15.15
red-complexioned 41.9
upper-class 607.10
wellborn 608.11
full bloom
maturity 303.2
flowering 310.26
full-blown
full-sized 257.22
mature 303.13
full boat 758.4
full-bodied
flavorful 63.9
thick 269.8
full circle circuit 914.2
rotation 915.1
full-figured 257.18
full-fledged
developed 14.3
full-sized 257.22
grown 259.12
mature 303.13
complete 794.9
full frontal
nudity 6.3
front 216.1
full-grown
developed 14.3
full-sized 257.22
grown 259.12
mature 303.13
ripe 407.13
complete 794.9
full measure fill 794.3
plenty 991.2
full of beans
healthy 83.9
gay 109.14
full of holes 393.32
full of hope 124.10
full of hot air 975.18
full of it 975.18
full of oneself 140.12
full of piss and vinegar
energetic 17.13
healthy 83.9
gay 109.14
vigorous 544.11
full-on
adj energetic 17.3
adverb extremely 247.22
full-scale
full-sized 257.22
complete 794.9

furtherance
  progression 162.1
  improvement 392.1
  helping along 449.5
  evolution 861.1
furthermore 253.11
further oneself 162.2
furthest
  extreme 247.13
  farthest 261.12
furtive covert 345.12
  in hiding 346.14
  deceitful 356.22
fury
  n passion 93.2
  overzealousness 101.3
  furor 105.8
  sorehead 110.11
  bitch 110.12
  rage 152.10
  witch 593.7
  turbulence 671.2
  violent person 671.9
  frenzy 926.7
  adv swiftly 174.18
fuse
  n detonator 462.15
  safeguard 1008.3
  v cooperate 450.3
  come together 770.16
  identify 778.5
  mix 797.10
  stick together 803.9
  combine 805.3
  melt 1020.21
  liquefy 1064.5
fusillade
  n detonation 56.3
  volley 459.9
  capital punishment 604.7
  hit 902.4
  shot 904.4
  v pull the trigger 459.22
fusilli 10.33
fusion affiliation 450.2
  identification 778.2
  mixture 797.1
  combination 805.1
  oneness 872.1
  melting 1020.3
  nuclear fusion 1038.9
  alloy 1058.4
  liquefaction 1064.1
fuss
  n dither 105.6
  bustle 330.4
  quarrel 456.5
  fussbudget 495.7
  finery 498.3
  bluster 503.1
  turbulence 671.2
  commotion 810.4
  agitation 917.1
  v agitate 105.14
  complain 115.15
  feel anxious 126.6
  be impatient 135.4
  bustle 330.12
  be hard to please 495.8
fuss at 510.16
fussbudget 495.7

fussy restless 105.27
  bustling 330.20
  meticulous 339.12
  finical 495.10
  ornate 498.12
  detailed 766.9
fustian
  n nonsense 520.2
  bombast 545.2
  adj bombastic 545.9
fusty malodorous 71.5
  trite 117.9
  blighted 393.42
  stale 842.14
futile ineffective 19.15
  vain 125.13
  useless 391.13
  unsuccessful 410.18
  foolish 923.8
  inexpedient 996.5
  trivial 998.19
futility
  ineffectiveness 19.3
  hopelessness 125.1
  vanity 391.2
  failure 410.1
  meaninglessness 520.1
  inexpedience 996.1
  triviality 998.3
future
  n fiancé 104.16
  tense 530.12
  the future 839.1
  fate 964.2
  adj later 839.8
  imminent 840.3
the future 821.1
futures 738.11
futz around 743.23
fuzz
  n down 3.19
  smoothness 294.3
  lightness 298.2
  v cover 295.19
  make uncertain 971.15
the fuzz 1008.16
Fuzzbuster 1036.5
F-word 513.4
gab
  n speech 524.1
  chatter 540.3
  v speak 524.19
  babble 524.20
  chatter 540.5
Gabriel herald 353.2
  Azrael 679.4
gad about
  journey 177.21
  wander 177.23
gadfly goad 375.8
  prompter 375.10
gadget tool 1040.1
  thing 1052.5
gadzooks 122.21
Gaea
  agricultural deity 1069.4
  Earth 1072.10
gaffe 975.5
gag
  n silencer 51.4
  shackle 428.4

joke 489.6
  acting 704.8
  v disable 19.10
  silence 51.8
  feel disgust 99.4
  vomit 909.26
gaga 923.8
gage marijuana 87.11
  pledge 438.2
  challenge 454.2
gaggle
  n assemblage 770.6
  v bird sound 60.5
gag order 444.1
gaiety colorfulness 35.4
  happiness 95.2
  gayness 109.4
  finery 498.3
  showiness 501.3
  conviviality 582.3
  festivity 743.3
gain
  n increase 251.1
  profit 472.3
  game 746.3
  good 999.4
  available gain 1032.17
  time constants 1041.11
  v arrive 186.6
  grow 251.6
  persuade 375.23
  improve 392.7
  triumph 411.3
  acquire 472.8
  receive 479.6
  incur 897.4
gainful valuable 387.22
  productive 472.16
gain ground
  progress 162.2
  accelerate 174.10
  improve 392.7
gain on 174.13
gains winnings 251.3
  profit 472.3
  receipts 627.1
gainsay deny 335.4
  contradict 451.6
gait velocity 172.4
  pace 177.12
gal woman 77.6
  dame 302.7
  person 312.5
gala
  n festival 743.4
  adj festive 743.28
galactic spatial 158.10
  large 247.7
  universal 864.14
  innumerable 884.10
  celestial 1072.25
galaxy celebrity 662.9
  throng 770.4
  island universe 1072.6
the Galaxy 1072.6
gale outburst 105.9
  breeze 318.4
  windstorm 318.11
galeated 279.20
gall
  n digestive secretion 13.2

acridness 64.2
  trauma 85.38
  irritation 96.3
  affliction 96.8
  ill humor 110.1
  impudence 142.3
  rancor 144.7
  bitterness 152.3
  bulge 283.3
  rashness 493.1
  v pain 26.7
  irritate 96.14
  injure 393.13
  abrade 1044.7
gallant
  n beau 104.12
  brave person 492.7
  dandy 500.9
  cavalier 504.9
  libertine 665.10
  adj courageous 492.16
  showy 501.19
  chivalrous 504.15
  profligate 665.25
gallantry
  courage 492.1
  gallantness 504.2
  courtship 562.7
  profligacy 665.3
gallbladder 2.16
gallery
  observation post 27.8
  audience 48.6
  hall 197.4
  corridor 197.18
  porch 197.21
  balcony 197.22
  showroom 197.24
  layer 296.1
  passageway 383.3
  museum 386.9
  entrenchment 460.5
  auditorium 704.15
  studio 712.16
  platform 901.13
galley kitchen 11.4
  sailboat 180.3
  proof 548.5
galley slave
  boatman 183.5
  subject 432.7
  drudge 726.3
Gallicism 523.8
gallivant
  wander 177.23
  flirt 562.20
gallop
  n run 174.3
  gait 177.12
  v speed 174.8
  go on horseback 177.34
gallows 605.5
the gallows 604.7
galore
  adj plentiful 991.7
  adv greatly 247.15
galvanize
  energize 17.10
  stimulate 105.13
  plate 295.26
  motivate 375.12

electrify 1032.26
electrolyze 1032.28
gambit trick 356.6
attempt 403.2
stratagem 415.3
first 818.3
gamble
n bet 759.2
guess 971.8
chance 972.1
v game 759.23
bet 759.25
be liable 897.3
predict 962.9
risk 972.12
endanger 1006.6
take chances 1006.7
gamble on
chance 759.24
rely on 953.16
be certain 970.9
gambling
illicit business 732.1
game 743.9
cardplaying 758.1
betting 759
playing 759.1
gambling game 743.9
gambol
n caper 366.2
frolic 743.5
v exude cheerfulness 109.6
rejoice 116.5
caper 366.6
play 743.23
game
n meat 10.13
desire 100.11
sweetheart 104.9
animal life 311.1
objective 380.2
plan 381.1
intrigue 381.5
quarry 382.7
stratagem 415.3
contest 457.3
laughingstock 508.7
vocation 724.6
fun 743.2
card game 743.9
sport 744.1
ball game 745.3
artifice 746.3
basketball game 747.3
strategy 748.2
match 749.3
contest 749.6
frame 750.2
meet 752.3
cardplaying 758.1
bridge 758.3
gambling game 759.7
v gamble 759.23
adj willing 324.5
plucky 359.14
crippled 393.30
resolute 492.17
game face 467.4
gamekeeper
guardian 1008.6
hunter 382.5

game over 410.2
game plan
plan 381.1
project 381.2
game 746.3
game preserve
preserve 397.7
refuge 1009.1
game reserve 397.7
game room 197.12
game-show 1035.2
gamete 305.10
game warden
preserver 397.5
guardian 1008.6
gamin
vagabond 178.3
brat 302.4
gaming license 443.6
gamut range 158.2
scale 709.6
series 812.2
gamy strong 68.8
malodorous 71.5
tainted 393.41
gander
male animal 76.8
poultry 311.28
a gander 27.3
Gandhi 921.2
gang
n staff 577.11
association 617.1
company 770.3
group of animals 770.5
v league 805.4
gang bang
copulation 75.7
sexual possession 480.3
ganglord 660.10
gangly lean 270.17
giant 272.16
gangplank 189.5
gangrene
n filth 80.7
mortification 85.40
v decay 393.22
gangsta rap 708.7
gangster bandit 483.4
evildoer 593.1
criminal 660.9
the underworld 660.10
gang up on 459.14
gang up with 582.18
gangway
n entrance 189.5
interj open up! 292.23
the gantlet 604.2
Ganymede
homosexual 75.14
carrier 176.7
attendant 577.5
gap
n interval 224.1
crack 224.2
ridge 237.5
valley 284.9
opening 292.1
difference 780.1
dissimilarity 787.1
deficiency 795.2

break 802.4
interruption 813.2
v cleave 224.4
gape 292.16
gape
n gaze 27.5
crack 224.2
opening 292.1
gaping 292.2
v gaze 27.15
wonder 122.5
gap 292.16
spectate 918.5
be curious 981.3
gaping
n yawning 292.2
adj wondering 122.9
expectant 130.11
cleft 224.7
spread 259.11
abysmal 275.11
yawning 292.18
gapless 812.8
garage band 710.12
garage carport 197.27
repair shop 739.5
garb
n clothing 5.1
looks 33.4
v clothe 5.39
garbage offal 80.9
heroin 87.9
refuse 391.4
bull 520.3
Greek 522.7
garbage dump
receptacle of filth 80.12
derelict 370.4
trash pile 391.6
garble
n Greek 522.7
v pervert 265.6
misinterpret 342.2
misrepresent 350.3
falsify 354.16
make unintelligible 522.12
confuse 811.3
garbology 391.6
garçon boy 302.5
man 577.4
garden
n compilation 554.7
horticulture 1069.10
v farm 1069.16
adj floral 310.38
simple 499.6
ordinary 1005.8
gardener man 577.4
horticulturist 1069.6
garden flower 310.24
gardening
flower 310.24
horticulture 1069.2
Garden of Eden 986.11
garden tool garden tool 1040.8
garden types 1069.23
garden variety 869.3
garden-variety
simple 499.6
ordinary 1005.8

Gargantuan large 247.7
huge 257.20
gargle
n dentifrice 86.22
drink 88.7
v wash 79.19
tipple 88.24
gargoyle spout 239.8
eyesore 1015.4
garish lurid 35.20
gaudy 501.20
grandiloquent 545.8
bright 1025.33
garland
n circle 280.2
bouquet 310.25
compilation 554.7
trophy 646.3
heraldry 647.2
book of verse 720.5
v figure 498.9
garment
n vestment 5.3
v clothe 5.39
garner
n granary 386.7
v store up 386.11
garnish
n ornamentation 498.1
v attach 480.20
ornament 498.8
garniture 498.1
garret 197.16
garrison
n stronghold 460.6
military unit 461.22
guard 1008.9
v fortify 460.9
garrote
n suffocation 308.6
capital punishment 604.7
v strangle 308.19
execute 604.17
garrulous 540.9
garter 646.5
gas
n success 409.4
boasting 502.2
poppycock 520.3
chatter 540.3
belch 909.9
fart 909.10
fuel 1021.1
illuminant 1025.20
volatile 1067.1
rare gas 1067.2
vaporousness 1067.3
v provision 385.9
talk nonsense 520.5
chatter 540.5
gas chamber
place of killing 308.12
execution 605.5
the gas chamber 604.7
gasconade
n boasting 502.1
v boast 502.6
bluster 503.3
gaseous rare 299.4
thin 764.6
vaporous 1067.9

gash
  n trauma 85.38
  crack 224.2
  notch 289.1
  furrow 290.1
  refuse 391.4
  mark 517.5
  v cleave 224.4
  notch 289.4
  furrow 290.3
  injure 393.13
  mark 517.19
  sever 802.11
gasket 293.5
gaslit 1025.40
gasoline 1025.20
gasp
  n breathing 2.21
  v burn out 21.5
  speak 524.25
  be hot 1019.22
gassiness
  distension 259.2
  talkativeness 540.1
  vaporousness 1067.3
gas station 739.1
gassy
  v talkative 540.9
  adj distended 259.13
  pompous 501.22
  inflated 502.12
  bombastic 545.9
  vaporous 1067.9
gastric 2.31
gastronome 8.16
gastronomy
  epicurism 8.15
  aesthetic taste 496.4
  gourmandise 672.2
gastropod 311.3
gastropub 8.17
gat opening 292.1
  gun 462.10
gate entrance 189.5
  porch 189.6
  channel 239.4
  valve 239.10
  floodgate 239.11
  receipts 627.1
  horse racing 757.1
  attender 918.2
  barrier 1012.5
  cast 1058.5
the gate 909.5
gâteau 10.42
gate-crasher
  intruder 214.3
  guest 585.6
  newcomer 774.4
gatehouse 228.9
gatekeeper 1008.12
gather
  n fold 291.1
  v grow 14.2
  expand 259.7
  fold 291.5
  blow 318.19
  collect 472.11
  come together 770.16
  assemble 770.18
  put together 800.5

  be imminent 840.2
  conclude 946.10
  suppose 951.10
  harvest 1069.19
gathering
  n sore 85.37
  collection 472.2
  bookbinding 554.14
  social gathering 582.10
  removal to heaven 681.11
  assemblage 770.1
  assembly 770.2
  accumulation 770.9
  part of writing 793.2
  joining 800.1
  harvest 1069.15
  adj imminent 840.3
Gatsbyesque 501.18
gauche
  bungling 414.20
  ignorant 930.11
  inconvenient 996.7
gaucho rider 178.8
  herder 1070.3
gaudy garish 35.20
  coarse 497.11
  tawdry 501.20
  grandiloquent 545.8
  paltry 998.21
gauge
  n size 257.1
  measure 300.2
  v size 257.15
  measure 300.10
  classify 801.8
  estimate 946.9
gaunt lean 270.17
  unproductive 891.4
gauntlet 454.2
gauze
  dressing 86.33
  fog 319.3
gauzy thin 270.16
  smooth 294.8
  unsubstantial 764.6
  transparent 1029.4
gavel 417.9
gawk
  n bungler 414.8
  oaf 924.5
  v gaze 27.15
  wonder 122.5
  be curious 981.3
gawky
  n oaf 924.5
  adj lean 270.17
  bungling 414.20
gay colorful 35.19
  homosexual 75.30
  intoxicated 88.31
  happy 95.16
  gay as a lark 109.14
  showy 501.19
  convivial 582.23
  profligate 665.25
  festive 743.28
gay-friendly 75.30
gay marriage 563.1
gay pride 75.14
gaze
  n stare 27.5

  v gloat 27.15
  wonder 122.5
gazebo
  observation post 27.8
  summerhouse 228.12
gazelle
  swiftness 174.6
  hoofed animal 311.5
  jumper 366.4
gazette
  official document 549.8
  periodical 555.1
  newspaper 555.2
a gazillion 884.4
gear
  n clothing 5.1
  rigging 180.12
  cordage 271.3
  equipment 385.4
  impedimenta 471.3
  baseball 745.1
  football 746.1
  hockey 749.1
  field hockey 749.4
  golf 751.1
  soccer 752.1
  skiing 753.1
  mechanism 1040.4
  gearing 1040.9
  v equip 385.8
  adj excellent 999.13
geared high 87.24
  apt 788.10
gee
  v avoid 164.6
  interj my! 122.21
gee whillikers 513.12
gee whiz 513.12
geisha dancer 705.3
  entertainer 707.1
Geist 920.8
gel
  n lights 704.18
  semiliquid 1062.5
  solution 1064.3
  v thicken 1045.10
gelatin
  sweets 10.40
  lights 704.18
  semiliquid 1062.5
geld feminize 77.12
  castrate 255.11
gelded
  unmanned 19.19
  unproductive 891.4
gelding
  impotent 19.6
  sexlessness 75.9
  castration 255.4
  horse 311.10
  jockey 757.2
gelid cold 1023.14
  frozen 1024.14
gem
  n jewel 498.6
  good person 659.1
  good thing 999.5
  precious stone 1059.7
  v figure 498.9
geminate
  v duplicate 874.3

  adj double 874.4
Gemini 873.4
Gemütlichkeit
  pleasantness 97.1
  sociability 582.1
gendarme
  officer 1008.15
  police 1008.16
gender sex 75.1
  masculine 530.10
gene
  genetic material 305.9
  heredity 560.6
genealogy
  register 549.9
  pedigree 560.5
general
  n commissioned officer
    575.18
  adj public 312.16
  communal 476.9
  common 497.14
  governing 612.17
  generalized 864.11
  normal 869.8
  undiscriminating 945.5
  theoretical 951.13
  vague 971.19
general delivery 553.4
general hospital 91.21
generality mean 246.1
  major part 792.6
  universality 864.1
  usualness 869.2
  abstract idea 932.3
  indiscrimination 945.1
  vagueness 971.4
generalization
  custom 373.1
  generality 864.1
  general idea 864.8
  reasoning 935.3
generally
  approximately 223.23
  on the average 246.5
  in general 864.17
  normally 869.10
  vaguely 971.29
general store 736.1
general strike
  revolt 327.4
  strike 727.5
generate procreate
    78.8
  cause 886.10
  originate 892.12
  electrify 1032.26
generation
  procreation 78.2
  birth 78.6
  age 824.4
  lifetime 827.5
  production 892.1
generation gap 456.1
Generation Y 302.2
generator 886.4
generic 864.11
generosity
  benevolence 143.4
  liberality 485.1
  hospitality 585.1

getaway
acceleration 174.4
departure 188.1
start 188.2
escape 369.1

get away depart 188.6
set out 188.8
escape 369.6

get away from it all
vacation 20.9
amuse oneself 743.22

get away with
devour 8.22
get off 369.7
put over 409.11

get back at
retaliate 506.4
interchange 863.4

get behind
regress 163.5
lag 166.4
be behind 217.8
back 449.13

get better 396.19

get bigger 14.2

get by get off 369.7
support oneself 385.12
succeed with 409.11
manage 409.12
be in a certain state 765.5
live on 839.7
stand the test 942.10
escape notice 984.5
suffice 991.4

get cracking
v hurry 401.6
set to work 725.15
interj make haste! 401.17

get down devour 8.22
use 87.22
alight 194.7
crouch 913.8

get even with
even the score 506.7
revenge 507.4
settle with 624.12
interchange 863.4

get-go 818.1

get going
v depart 188.7
make haste 401.6
undertake 404.3
set to work 725.15
make a beginning 818.8
improve the occasion 843.8
interj make haste! 401.17

get high on
enjoy 95.13
be excited 105.18

get hold of
communicate with 343.8
acquire 472.9
seize 480.14
understand 521.7
learn 570.6

get in
arrive 186.6
enter 189.7
mount 193.12
intrude 214.5
collect 472.11

assemble 770.18

get into don 5.43
penetrate 189.8
join 617.14

get it
read one loud and clear 521.11
be punished 604.20

get it over with
complete 407.6
put a stop to 857.11

get it straight 973.10

get it together
focus 208.10
make better 392.9
order 807.4
arrange 808.8
re-form 858.12

get lost
v depart 188.7
not interfere 430.17
interj go away! 909.31

get next to
ingratiate oneself 138.10
befriend 587.11
get on good terms with 587.13

get nowhere 410.13

get off climax 75.24
use 87.22
depart 188.6
set out 188.8
get down 194.7
escape 369.7
go free 431.9
make a beginning 818.8

get off it 857.12

get on don 5.43
use 87.22
annoy 96.13
depart 188.6
mount 193.12
age 303.10
make good 409.10
manage 409.12
be in a certain state 765.5
persist 856.5
prosper 1010.7

get one down
annoy 96.13
sadden 112.18
trouble 1013.13

get one's back up
anger 152.17
make angry 152.23
provoke 152.24

get one's dues 639.6

get one's feet wet 818.1

get one's goat
annoy 96.13
make angry 152.23

get one's hands on
acquire 472.9
seize 480.14

get one's way 323.3

get on one's nerves
grate on 58.11
irritate 96.14
jangle the nerves 128.9

get on the ball 401.17

get on the bandwagon
attach oneself to 138.11
concur 332.9
follow the fashion 578.10
support 609.41
follow the rule 867.4

get out
v depart 188.7
exit 190.12
extract 192.10
be revealed 351.8
issue 352.14
escape 369.6
extricate 431.7
print 548.14
interj go away! 909.31

get out from under
be relieved 120.8
disembarrass 1014.9

get out of
elicit 192.14
evade 368.7
shirk 368.9
escape 369.6
free oneself from 431.8
go free 431.9

get out of town! 909.31

get over move 172.5
communicate 343.7
rally 392.8
recover 396.20
come through 521.5
make clear 521.6

get real 920.10

get rid of
murder 308.16
discard 390.7
put an end to 395.12
free oneself from 431.8
relinquish 475.3
eliminate 773.5
do away with 909.21

get rolling
depart 188.7
set to work 725.15

get taller 14.2

get the better of
win 411.5
defeat 412.6
outwit 415.11

get the drift 521.8

get the hang of
understand 521.7
master 570.9

get the lead out
v speed 174.9
be active 330.14
make haste 401.6
interj make haste! 401.17

get the picture
take action 328.5
read one loud and clear 521.11

get through
penetrate 189.8
carry out 328.7
bring about 407.5
complete 407.6
live on 839.7

get through to
be heard 48.12

communicate with 343.8

get to be heard 48.12
make anxious 126.5
arrive 186.6
extend to 261.6
communicate with 343.8
bribe 378.3
begin 818.7

get together
come to an agreement 332.10
cooperate 450.3
collect 472.11
assemble 770.18

get-together
social gathering 582.10
assembly 770.2

get tough
exert strength 15.12
remain firm 359.9

get under one's skin
affect 93.14
annoy 96.13

get under way
shove off 182.19
depart 188.6
undertake 404.3
make a beginning 818.8

getup wardrobe 5.2
costume 5.9
structure 266.1
enterprise 330.7
composition 796.1

get up dress up 5.42
awake 23.4
get out of bed 23.6
rise 200.8
make up 405.7
study up 570.14
produce 892.8

get-up-and-go
energy 17.3
enterprise 330.7

get up on
master 570.9
study up 570.14
refresh the memory 989.18

get wind of
hear 48.11
know 551.15
scent 941.6

get with it
v take action 328.5
set to work 725.15
interj make haste! 401.17

get word
hear 48.11
learn 551.14

geyser jet 238.9
hot water 1019.10

ghastly
colorless 36.7
terrible 127.30
deathly 307.28
hideous 1015.11

ghetto
n the inner city 80.11
city district 230.6
adj urban 230.11

ghettoized
indigent 619.8
segregated 773.8

ghost
n frightener 127.9
writer 547.15
author 718.4
substitute 862.2
specter 988.1
television reception 1035.5
v float 182.54
author 547.21
write 718.6
substitute for 862.5
ghostlike
deathly 307.28
spectral 988.7
ghostly
deathly 307.28
spectral 988.7
immaterial 1053.7
ghost story 354.11
ghost town 230.1
ghostwriter
writer 547.15
author 718.4
substitute 862.2
ghoul
frightener 127.9
thief 483.1
monster 593.6
demon 680.6
ghoulish
terrible 127.30
demoniac 680.17
curious 981.5
execrable 1000.10
GI 461.7
giant
n strong man 15.6
amazon 257.13
longlegs 272.7
adj huge 257.20
gigantic 272.16
gibberish
nonsense 520.2
Greek 522.7
jargon 523.9
gibe
n indignity 156.2
witticism 489.7
scoff 508.2
v scoff 508.9
giblets viscera 2.16
food 10.20
fowl part 10.23
insides 207.4
Gibraltar 15.8
giddy intoxicated 88.31
inconstant 854.7
delirious 926.31
inattentive 984.6
dizzy 985.15
scatterbrained 985.16
gift
n talent 413.4
present 478.4
costlessness 634.1
smartness 920.2
v give 478.12
contribute 478.14
gifted
talented 413.29
studentlike 572.12

smart 920.14
gift horse 478.4
gift of the gab
style 532.2
eloquence 544.1
gig
n position 724.5
v fish 382.10
gigantic
herculean 15.17
large 247.7
huge 257.20
giant 272.16
excessive 993.16
gigantism
greatness 247.1
oversize 257.5
hugeness 257.7
excess 993.1
giggle
n laughter 116.4
v laugh 116.8
gigolo beau 104.12
procurer 665.18
gild color 35.14
yellow 43.3
make pleasant 97.5
coat 295.24
falsify 354.16
ornament 545.7
Gilded Age 824.5
gild the lily
make pleasant 97.5
ornament 545.7
carry coals to Newcastle
993.12
gilt
n swine 311.9
sham 354.3
finery 498.3
money 728.2
adj yellow 43.4
brass 1058.17
gimmick trick 356.6
lure 377.3
stratagem 415.3
plot 722.4
gambling wheel 759.16
expedient 995.2
tool 1040.1
thing 1052.5
gimmickry
deception 356.1
machination 415.4
finery 498.3
showiness 501.3
gimmicky
deceitful 356.22
cunning 415.12
showy 501.19
gin
n trap 356.12
v trap 356.20
segregate 773.6
ginchy 75.25
ginger energy 17.3
zest 68.2
gingerbread
n finery 498.3
superfluity 993.4
adj ornate 498.12

gingerbread man 349.6
gingerly
adj cautious 494.8
adv cautiously 494.12
ginormous 247.7
giraffe 311.5
gird strengthen 15.13
encircle 209.7
bind 800.9
girdle
n corset 5.23
strip 271.4
circle 280.3
supporter 901.2
v encircle 209.7
surround 280.10
bind 800.9
circle 914.5
gird up one's loins
strengthen 15.13
prepare oneself 405.13
militarize 458.19
set to work 725.15
girl woman 77.5
basuco 87.7
cocaine 87.7
doll 104.13
ladylove 104.14
girlie 302.6
old woman 304.3
maid 577.8
drama 706.2
girl Friday 577.3
girlfriend
ladylove 104.14
companion 588.3
girlhood
childhood 301.2
young people 302.2
girlish feminine 77.13
thin 270.16
childish 301.11
immature 406.11
a girl thing 77.1
girly man 77.2
girt
n circle 280.3
saddle parts 901.18
v bind 800.9
adj encircled 209.11
girth
n size 257.1
circle 280.3
middle 819.1
saddle parts 901.18
v bind 800.9
gismo or **gizmo** 1052.5
gist
essential content 196.5
meaning 518.1
summary 557.2
essence 767.2
major part 792.6
topic 937.1
salient point 997.6
give
n softness 1047.1
pliancy 1047.2
elasticity 1048.1
v communicate 343.7
provide 385.7

donate 478.12
say 524.22
present 634.4
administer 643.6
attribute 888.3
soften 1047.7
yield 1048.5
transfer 629.3
give and take
compensate 338.4
contend 457.13
compromise 468.2
retaliate 506.4
be just 649.5
interchange 863.4
argue 935.16
give-and-take
n offset 338.2
compromise 468.1
banter 490.1
retaliation 506.1
conversation 541.1
justice 649.1
trade 731.2
interchange 863.1
adj interchangeable 863.5
give a pink slip 447.4
giveaway
n divulgence 351.2
adj reduced 633.9
give away betray 351.6
discard 390.7
break 393.23
relinquish 475.3
dispose of 478.21
join in marriage 563.14
give back
restore 396.11
restitute 481.4
give birth bear 1.3
reproductive 78.13
vivify 306.10
give in bow to 250.5
yield 433.7
deliver 478.13
given
n fact 761.3
condition 959.2
a truth 973.2
adj allowed 478.24
gratuitous 634.5
real 761.15
supposed 951.14
conditional 959.8
disposed 978.8
give notice
herald 133.13
announce 352.12
warn 399.5
inform 551.8
given that 951.19
given to 896.6
give off excrete 12.12
exude 190.15
let out 909.24
vaporize 1067.8
give one a bellyful 118.6
give one a pain in the ass
118.6
give oneself airs
be stuck on oneself 140.6

go around
move 172.5
surround 209.6
recur 850.5
go roundabout 914.4
circle 914.5
turn 914.6
rotate 915.9
suffice 991.4
go astray
stray 164.4
miscarry 410.15
digress 538.9
go wrong 654.9
misbelieve 688.8
miss 911.4
err 975.9
goat
he-goat 311.8
jumper 366.4
laughingstock 508.7
lecher 665.11
scapegoat 862.3
go at travel 177.19
undertake 404.3
attack 459.14
challenge 459.15
goatee 3.8
go away
v disappear 34.2
recede 168.2
diverge 171.5
depart 188.6
interj begone! 909.31
gob bite 8.2
navy man 183.4
amount 244.2
lump 257.10
sphere 282.2
mouth 292.4
accumulation 770.9
piece 793.3
go back on
abandon 370.5
repeal 445.2
be unfaithful 645.12
gobble gulp 8.23
bird sound 60.5
ingest 187.11
consume 388.3
destroy 395.10
gluttonize 672.4
gobbledygook
nonsense 520.2
Greek 522.7
jargon 523.9
bombast 545.2
political jargon 609.37
gobbler
male animal 76.8
poultry 311.28
glutton 672.3
gobble up
consume 388.3
destroy 395.10
monopolize 469.6
kid oneself 954.6
go between
interpose 213.6
be instrumental 384.7
mediate 466.6

go-between
intermediary 213.4
interpreter 341.7
messenger 353.1
instrument 384.4
mediator 466.3
middleman 576.4
goblin fairy 678.8
hobgoblin 680.8
gobs lot 247.4
wealth 618.3
gobsmacked 122.9
go by be called 527.13
elapse 821.5
conform 867.3
pass 910.8
god hero 659.5
deus 678.2
goddesses 678.4
God 677.2
god-awful 1000.8
God bless! 696.18
God bless me! 122.21
God bless you! 188.22
goddam it! 513.11
goddess hero 659.5
deity 678.2
god 678.4
god-fearing 155.9
God-fearing
godly 692.9
belief 953.21
God forbid
by no means 335.9
Heaven forbid! 510.27
O Lord! 696.18
godforsaken
available 222.15
out-of-the-way 261.9
forlorn 584.12
God knows! 930.18
godless ungodly 695.17
unregenerate 695.18
godlike great 247.9
eminent 662.18
superhuman 677.16
divine 678.16
godly 692.9
godliness
virtue 653.1
deity 677.1
sanctity 685.1
godlikeness 692.2
godly virtuous 653.5
divine 677.16
godlike 692.9
godown 386.6
go down
capsize 182.44
descend 194.5
sink 194.6
plunge 367.8
decline 393.17
fail 410.11
lose 412.12
play 745.5
fight 754.4
occur 831.5
find credence 953.20
go downhill
weaken 16.9

descend 194.5
incline 204.10
decline 393.17
sink 410.11
fall on evil days 1011.11
go down the tubes regress
163.5
go to waste 473.6
godparent 438.6
god's acre 309.15
godsend boon 472.7
good thing 999.5
God's gift 140.1
Godspeed
n leave-taking 188.4
interj farewell! 188.22
go Dutch
pay for 624.18
bisect 875.4
God willing 966.11
go easy
v swim with the stream
1014.12
interj careful! 494.14
phrs easy does it 175.15
go easy on take pity on 145.4
indulge 427.5
gofer
subordinate 432.5
attendant 577.5
go for love 104.19
head for 161.9
fetch 176.16
pass for 349.10
intend 380.4
abet 449.14
attack 459.15
kid oneself 954.6
go for broke
n call to arms 458.7
v be determined 359.8
persevere 360.7
do one's best 403.14
do to perfection 407.7
court danger 493.6
risk 972.12
go for it
attempt 403.7
do one's best 403.14
go gangbusters 330.14
go-getter
enterprise 330.7
doer 726.1
go-getting 330.7
goggle
n gaze 27.5
v gaze 27.15
squint 28.9
bulge 283.11
adj bulged 283.16
goggles spectacles 29.3
safeguard 1008.3
eyeshade 1028.2
go halvsies 624.18
go in for practice 328.8
adopt 371.15
undertake 404.3
study to be 570.15
specialize 866.4
going-over
apostasy 363.2

iteration 849.2
disapproval 510.6
going rate 630.2
goings-on
behavior 321.1
activity 330.1
affairs 831.4
going steady 104.5
go into enter 189.7
undertake 404.3
participate 476.5
discuss 541.11
write upon 556.5
join 617.14
compose 796.3
embark on 818.9
elaborate 861.6
investigate 938.23
go in together 899.2
gold
n yellowness 43.1
wealth 618.1
money 728.1
precious metals 728.20
adj yellow 43.4
brass 1058.17
goldbrick
n slowpoke 175.5
idler 331.8
neglecter 340.5
confidence game 356.10
shirker 368.3
v leave undone 340.7
shirk 368.9
golden yellow 43.4
auspicious 133.17
precious 632.10
melodious 708.48
superb 999.15
brass 1058.17
Golden Age 824.5
golden days 1010.4
golden mean
mean 246.1
middle course 467.3
temperance 668.1
moderation 670.1
golden parachute 624.4
golden rule
rule 419.2
ethical philosophy 636.2
axiom 974.2
golden shower 12.5
gold medal 646.2
gold mine
source of supply 386.4
rich source 618.4
mine 1058.6
gold-plated
plated 295.33
expensive 632.11
brass 1058.17
gold rush 1058.8
golf
n sports 751
the royal and ancient 751.1
v play 745.5
golf course
green 310.7
playground 743.11
golf 751.1

circle 914.5
rotate 915.9
go-round
periodicity 850.2
circuit 914.2
gory
circulatory 2.33
sanguine 41.7
murderous 308.24
bloodstained 1004.11
gosh! 513.12
gosling
fledgling 302.10
poultry 311.28
gospel
n good news 552.2
system of belief 953.3
the truth 973.3
the real thing 973.4
adj scriptural 683.11
true 973.13
the Gospel 683.4
gossamer
n filament 271.1
lightness 298.2
adj dainty 248.7
thin 270.16
threadlike 271.7
smooth 294.8
unsubstantial 764.6
chimeric 986.22
transparent 1029.4
gossip
n chatter 540.3
talk 552.7
newsmonger 552.9
companion 588.3
inquisitive person 981.2
v chatter 540.5
chat 541.9
talk over the back fence
552.12
Gothic
unrefined 497.12
antiquated 842.13
unlearned 930.13
fanciful 986.20
go through
penetrate 189.8
carry out 328.7
squander 486.3
spend 626.5
rehearse 704.32
experience 831.8
iterate 849.8
search 938.31
freeze 1023.10
go through with
take action 328.5
carry through 360.5
endure 827.6
go together 788.6
go-to guy 577.3
go to hell
go to ruin 395.24
be damned 682.7
go to it 725.15
go to one's head
intoxicate 88.22
puff up 140.7
addle the wits 926.23

dizzy 985.8
go to pieces
weaken 16.9
lose self-control 128.7
decay 393.22
be destroyed 395.22
come apart 802.9
go to pot
go to ruin 395.24
go to waste 473.6
go bankrupt 625.7
fall on evil days 1011.11
go to press 548.18
go to the dogs
go to ruin 395.24
go bankrupt 625.7
fall on evil days 1011.11
go to the wall
die 307.19
go to ruin 395.24
fail 410.9
go bankrupt 625.7
gouge
n indentation 284.6
furrow 290.1
v blind 30.7
excavate 284.15
furrow 290.3
deceive 356.19
overprice 632.7
gouge out
extract 192.10
excavate 284.15
perforate 292.15
goulash 10.11
go under
go to ruin 395.24
sink 410.11
lose 412.12
go bankrupt 625.7
go up against
encounter 457.15
engage 457.16
go up in smoke
disappear 34.2
come to nothing 410.13
go to waste 473.6
flit 828.6
fall through 911.3
burn up 1020.25
gourmand eater 8.16
connoisseur 496.6
sensualist 663.3
glutton 672.3
gourmet
n eater 8.16
connoisseur 496.6
sensualist 663.3
adj edible 8.33
tasty 63.8
gourmet food 10.8
gout 85.22
goût taste 62.1
savor 63.2
govern
restrain 428.7
direct 573.8
regulate 612.11
exercise influence 894.8
governance
authority 417.5

direction 573.1
government 612.1
protectorship 1008.2
governess
teacher 571.2
mistress 575.2
chaperon 1008.7
government
region 231.5
authority 417.5
direction 573.1
political science 609.2
administration 612.1
governance 612.1
protectorship 1008.2
government issue 385.4
governor
jailer 429.10
father 560.9
director 574.1
ruler 575.6
administrator 575.13
safeguard 1008.3
guardian 1008.6
system component 1041.14
governor-general 575.13
governorship
mastership 417.7
directorship 573.4
go wild 330.14
go with
stay near 223.12
take action 328.5
concur 332.9
choose 371.13
undertake 404.3
accompany 769.7
agree 788.6
go along with 899.3
go without 668.7
go with the flow
be content 107.5
take it easy 331.15
follow the fashion 578.10
gown
n garment 5.3
dress 5.16
robe 702.2
v cloak 5.40
go wrong
be disappointing 132.3
get out of order 393.25
go to ruin 395.24
miscarry 410.15
stray 654.9
misbelieve 688.8
err 975.9
goy 688.6
GPS 159.8
grab
n seizure 480.2
v jump at 101.6
acquire 472.9
seize 480.14
capture 480.18
usurp 640.8
play 745.5
impress 931.19
engross 983.13
grab bag lottery 759.14
hodgepodge 797.6

grace
n delightfulness 97.2
benevolence 143.4
act of kindness 143.7
pity 145.1
pardon 148.2
thanks 150.2
skill 413.1
benefit 478.7
taste 496.1
elegance 533.1
fluency 544.2
reprieve 601.3
conscience 636.5
function of Holy Ghost 677.15
sanctification 685.3
prayer 696.4
ornament 709.18
goodness 999.1
beauty 1016.1
v ornament 498.8
honor 662.12
beautify 1016.15
graceful skillful 413.22
agile 413.23
tasteful 496.8
courteous 504.14
elegant 533.6
fluent 544.9
beautiful 1016.17
graceless
bungling 414.20
inelegant 534.2
irreclaimable 654.18
unregenerate 695.18
ungraceful 1015.9
the Graces 1016.9
grace with 478.17
gracile thin 270.16
tasteful 496.8
elegant 533.6
beautiful 1016.17
gracious
adj pleasant 97.6
kind 143.13
indulgent 427.8
liberal 485.4
elegant 496.8
courteous 504.14
informal 581.3
hospitable 585.11
interj my! 122.21
gradation
graduation 245.3
phonetics 524.13
class 607.1
continuity 807.2
grouping 808.3
series 812.2
grade
n incline 204.4
degree 245.1
student 572.11
class 607.1
category 809.2
v level 201.6
incline 204.10
graduate 245.4
size 257.15
smooth 287.5
order 807.4

group 808.11
classify 809.6
grade school 567.3
gradient rising 200.5
 incline 204.4
gradual slow 175.10
 gradational 245.5
graduate
 n expert 413.11
 alumnus 572.8
 v grade 245.4
 size 257.15
 measure 300.10
 improve 392.7
 succeed 409.7
 promote 446.2
 adj scholastic 568.19
 studentlike 572.12
graduated cylinder
 goniometer 278.4
 chemicalization 1060.6
graduation
 gradation 245.3
 promotion 446.1
 ceremony 580.4
graffito inscription 546.5
 drawing 712.12
graft
 n insertion 191.1
 inlay 191.2
 fraud 356.8
 bribery 378.1
 theft 482.1
 booty 482.11
 politics 609.34
 spoils of office 609.35
 v engraft 191.6
 fasten 800.7
grain
 n feed 10.4
 modicum 248.2
 minute 258.7
 texture 294.1
 grass 310.5
 seed 310.31
 nature 767.4
 kind 809.3
 disposition 978.3
 granule 1051.6
 v color 35.14
 coarsen 294.4
 pulverize 1051.9
 powder 1051.10
grain of salt 959.1
grammar
 rules of language 530.1
 diction 532.1
 textbook 554.10
 basics 818.6
grammarian 523.15
grammar school
 elementary school 567.3
 secondary school 567.4
grammatical
 linguistic 523.19
 syntactical 530.17
gramps old man 304.2
 grandfather 560.14
granary 386.7
grand
 n money 728.7

thousand 882.10
 adj dignified 136.12
 great 247.6
 large 257.16
 grandiose 501.21
 lofty 544.14
 eminent 662.18
 important 997.17
 good 999.12
grandeur
 proud bearing 136.2
 greatness 247.1
 sizableness 257.6
 grandness 501.5
 loftiness 544.6
 distinction 662.5
grandfather
 n old man 304.2
 grandsire 560.13
 v exempt 430.14
grandfather clause 430.8
grandiloquence
 exaggeration 355.1
 pompousness 501.7
 long word 526.10
 style 532.2
 grandiosity 545
 magniloquence 545.1
grandiose grand 501.21
 grandiloquent 545.8
grandiosity
 sizableness 257.6
 grandeur 501.5
 grandiloquence 545.1
grand-juror 596.7
grandmother
 old woman 304.3
 grandam 560.15
grand slam score 409.5
 victory 411.1
 bridge 758.3
grandstand
 n observation post 27.8
 baseball 745.1
 v exercise skill 413.20
 show off 501.16
grange farmstead 228.6
 farm 1069.8
granite
 hardness 1046.6
 rock 1059.1
granny
 old woman 304.3
 fussbudget 495.7
 grandmother 560.16
 back number 842.8
grant
 n concession 443.5
 giving 478.1
 subsidy 478.8
 privilege 642.2
 qualification 959.1
 v acknowledge 332.11
 confess 351.7
 consent 441.2
 permit 443.9
 give 478.12
 suppose 951.10
 allow for 959.5
granular
 infinitesimal 258.14

rough 294.6
 grainy 1051.12
granulated
 unsmooth 288.6
 rough 294.6
 hardened 1046.13
 granular 1051.12
granulation
 unsmoothness 288.1
 roughness 294.2
 television reception 1035.5
 hardening 1046.5
 granularity 1051.2
 pulverization 1051.4
granule
 modicum 248.2
 grain 1051.6
grapevine plant 310.4
 gossip 551.5
 report 552.6
 news channel 552.10
graph
 n diagram 381.3
 letter 546.1
 drawing 712.12
 outline 801.4
 v plot 381.10
 itemize 801.7
graphic
 representational 349.13
 descriptive 349.14
 expressive 544.10
 written 547.22
 pictorial 712.20
graphic arts
 printing 548.1
 visual arts 712.1
 graphics 713.1
graphic design 713.1
graphics tablet 1042.2
graphite 1056.2
graph paper 47.6
grapple
 n hold 474.2
 v contend 457.13
 hold 474.6
 seize 480.14
 fasten 800.7
grapple with
 contest 451.4
 contend 457.13
 engage with 457.17
 brave 492.10
grasp
 n hold 474.2
 control 612.2
 handle 901.11
 understanding 928.3
 v hold 474.6
 seize 480.14
 understand 521.7
 cohere 803.6
 know 928.12
grasping
 n greed 100.8
 adj greedy 100.27
 demanding 421.9
 acquisitive 472.15
 retentive 474.8
 rapacious 480.26
 selfish 651.5

graspy greedy 100.27
 acquisitive 472.15
 rapacious 480.26
 selfish 651.5
grass
 n marijuana 87.11
 gramineous plant 310.5
 grassland 310.8
 tennis 748.1
 v feed 8.18
grasshopper
 n locust 311.35
 jumper 366.4
 adj improvident 406.15
grassland
 the country 233.1
 land 234.1
 plain 236.1
 grass 310.8
 farm 1069.8
grass roots
 bottom 199.1
 the country 233.1
 source 886.5
grass-roots basic 199.8
 populational 606.8
 simple 798.6
grassy green 44.4
 verdant 310.42
grate
 n network 170.3
 arranger 808.5
 fire iron 1020.12
 v pain 26.7
 rasp 58.10
 sound a sour note 61.3
 irritate 96.14
 net 170.7
 abrade 1044.7
 pulverize 1051.9
grateful pleasant 97.6
 thankful 150.5
 welcome 585.12
grate on jar on 58.11
 irritate 96.14
 get on one's nerves 128.9
gratify feed 8.18
 satisfy 95.8
 content 107.4
 make proud 136.6
 indulge 427.6
gratifying
 pleasant 97.6
 welcome 585.12
grating
 n network 170.3
 arranger 808.5
 fire iron 1020.12
 pulverization 1051.4
 adj irritating 26.13
 jarring 58.16
 dissonant 61.4
 unnerving 128.15
 disagreeing 789.6
gratis
 adj gratuitous 634.5
 adv as a gift 478.27
 gratuitously 634.6
gratitude
 thankfulness 150
 gratefulness 150.1

gratuitous
impudent 142.10
voluntary 324.7
given 478.24
gratis 634.5
unordered 810.12
superfluous 993.17
gratuity bribe 378.2
largess 478.5
costlessness 634.1
surplus 993.5
grave
n death 307.1
tomb 309.16
monument 549.12
v record 549.15
engrave 713.9
sculpture 715.5
fix in the mind 989.17
adj painful 26.10
dark 38.9
deep 54.11
sedate 106.14
solemn 111.3
gloomy 112.24
dignified 136.12
great 247.6
heavy 297.16
lofty 544.14
ceremonious 580.8
base 661.12
weighty 997.20
the grave
hell 682.1
destiny 839.2
gravedigger 309.8
gravel
n pavement 383.6
grain 1051.6
shingle 1059.3
v irritate 96.14
graven
engraved 713.11
sculptured 715.7
established 855.13
graveness
darkness 38.2
gravity 997.3
graveyard 309.15
gravidity 78.5
gravitate
descend 194.5
drop 297.15
lean 896.3
gravitation
descent 194.1
weight 297.5
attraction 907.1
gravity
sedateness 106.4
solemnity 111.1
gloom 112.7
proud bearing 136.2
weight 297.5
loftiness 544.6
formality 580.1
attraction 907.1
importance 997.1
graveness 997.3
weight 297.1

gravy find 472.6
gratuity 478.5
bonus 624.6
gray
n brunet 35.9
grayness 39.1
horse 311.11
units of radioactivity 1037.6
v gray 39.3
grizzle 39.3
adj colorless 36.7
ashen 39.4
gray 39.4
gloomy 112.24
aged 303.16
same 781.6
gray area
middle course 467.3
ambiguity 539.1
gamble 971.8
graybeard
silver-haired person 39.2
old man 304.2
gray color varieties 39.6
gray-haired
gray-headed 39.5
aged 303.16
gray literature 547.10
gray matter
intellect 919.1
brain 919.6
graze
n touch 73.1
contact 223.5
v feed 8.18
feed on 8.28
touch lightly 73.7
contact 223.10
tap 902.18
abrade 1044.7
grazing
n eating 8.1
touch 73.1
grassland 310.8
abrasion 1044.2
animal husbandry 1070.1
adj in contact 223.17
grease
n gratuity 478.5
flattery 511.1
money 728.2
oil 1056.1
v smooth 287.5
bribe 378.3
facilitate 1014.7
oil 1056.8
grease monkey
aircraftsman 185.6
mechanic 1040.12
greasepaint
theater 704.17
makeup 1016.11
greaser 232.7
grease the palm
bribe 375.23
pay off 378.3
pay 624.16
grease the wheels
facilitate 1014.7
oil 1056.8

greasy
slippery 287.12
oily 1056.9
greasy grind
nerd 572.10
drudge 726.3
bookworm 929.4
greasy spoon 8.17
great
n skillful person 413.14
keyboard 711.17
adj pregnant 78.18
grand 247.6
chief 249.14
large 257.16
authoritative 417.15
magnanimous 652.6
eminent 662.18
important 997.17
excellent 999.13
interj bravo! 509.22
the great 997.8
great-coat 5.13
Great Divide
middle of nowhere 261.4
watershed 272.5
the greatest 249.4
greathearted
benevolent 143.15
liberal 485.4
courageous 492.16
magnanimous 652.6
great house 228.7
greed
greediness 100.8
selfishness 651.1
gluttony 672.1
greedy
avaricious 100.27
acquisitive 472.15
selfish 651.5
gluttonous 672.6
Greek gibberish 522.7
member 617.11
green
n greenness 44.1
verdigris 44.3
lawn 310.7
money 728.2
lawn bowling 750.3
golf 751.1
adj virid 44.4
sour 67.5
fresh 83.13
jealous 153.5
young 301.10
immature 406.11
inexperienced 414.17
new 841.7
ignorant 930.11
gullible 954.9
remembered 989.22
greenbacks 728.6
Green Berets 461.15
green color varieties 44.6
greener pastures 124.1
greenery 310.1
"green-eyed monster" 163.1
greenhorn
n dupe 358.1
incompetent 414.7

novice 572.9
newcomer 774.4
beginner 818.2
ignoramus 930.7
adj unaccustomed 374.4
greenhouse
summerhouse 228.12
nursery 1069.11
greenish blue 44.4
Greenland
continent 235.1
remote region 261.4
cold place 1023.4
green light
permission 443.1
signal 517.15
traffic light 1026.4
the green light
start 188.2
ratification 332.4
green plant 310.3
greenroom
anteroom 197.20
stage 704.16
greens
vegetables 10.35
salad 10.37
plants 310.1
green thumb 1069.12
green with jealousy 153.5
greet
n weeping 115.2
v weep 115.12
address 524.26
hail 585.10
greeter 585.5
greeting remark 524.3
salutation 585.4
greetings
n welcome 186.4
regards 504.8
salutations 585.3
interj salutations! 585.15
greetings and farewells 585.17
gregarious
talkative 540.9
sociable 582.22
Gregorian chant 708.20
greige
n grayness 39.1
adj. gray 39.4
gremlin
fairy 678.8
imp 680.7
grenadier
longlegs 272.7
infantryman 461.9
grep 1042.18
greyhound 174.6
grid
n network 170.3
stage 704.16
fire iron 1020.12
television reception 1035.5
v net 170.7
griddle
n fire iron 1020.12
v cook 11.5
griddlecake 10.45
gridiron
network 170.3

stage 704.16
playground 743.11
football 746.1
fire iron 1020.12
gridlock
obstruction 293.3
hindrance 1012.1
grief pain 96.5
wretchedness 96.6
distressfulness 98.5
sorrow 112.10
regret 113.1
misfortune 1011.2
grievance
affliction 96.8
complaint 115.4
objection 333.2
injustice 650.4
evil 1000.3
bane 1001.1
grieve
pain 96.17
distress 98.14
sorrow 112.17
aggrieve 112.19
lament 115.10
move 145.5
offend 152.21
grieving
n lamentation 115.1
adj lamenting 115.18
grievous
distressing 98.20
sorrowful 112.26
pitiful 145.8
terrible 1000.9
disastrous 1011.15
griffin 647.2
grift fraud 356.8
stratagem 415.3
cheating 759.13
grill
n restaurant 8.17
dish 10.7
inquisition 938.13
fire iron 1020.12
v cook 11.5
torture 604.16
put on the grill 938.22
grille 170.3
grilling
n cooking 11.2
the grill 938.13
adj hot 1019.25
grim
pleasureless 96.20
horrid 98.19
sullen 110.24
solemn 111.3
unhappy 112.21
gloomy 112.24
hopeless 125.12
terrible 127.30
harsh 144.24
unyielding 361.9
strict 425.6
bad 1000.8
unprepossessing 1015.7
grimace
n scowl 110.9
wry face 265.4

shake 917.3
v suffer 26.8
shudder at 99.5
look sullen 110.15
make a face 265.8
overact 704.31
grime
n dirt 80.6
v dirty 80.15
Grim Reaper 307.2
grimy dingy 38.11
dirty 80.22
grin
n smile 116.3
v smile 116.7
grin and bear it
be of good cheer 109.10
accept 134.7
submit 433.6
grinch
killjoy 112.14
spoilsport 1012.9
grind
n rasp 58.3
tedium 118.1
routine 373.5
study 570.3
nerd 572.10
swotter 572.10
work 725.4
hard work 725.5
drudge 726.3
repetitiousness 849.4
bookworm 929.4
v chew 8.27
pain 26.7
grate 58.10
sharpen 285.7
file 287.8
grind 287.8
write 547.21
train 568.13
study 570.12
dominate 612.14
domineer 612.15
write 718.6
drudge 725.14
shatter 802.13
endure 827.6
abrade 1044.7
pulverize 1051.9
grind in
urge 375.14
inculcate 568.12
grinding
n study 570.3
abrasion 1044.2
pulverization 1051.4
adj irritating 26.13
grating 58.16
oppressive 98.24
imperious 417.16
laboring 725.17
abrasive 1044.10
grind one's teeth 152.14
gringo 774.3
grip
n acrimony 17.5
skill 413.1
governance 417.5
hold 474.2

control 612.2
game 748.2
game or string 750.2
handle 901.11
spasm 917.6
understanding 928.3
v hold 474.6
seize 480.14
obsess 926.25
engross 983.13
gripe
n ache 26.5
complaint 115.5
control 612.2
indigence 619.2
v pain 26.7
annoy 96.13
be discontented 108.6
complain 115.16
seize 480.14
gripped
obsessed 926.33
held 983.18
gripping
retentive 474.8
obsessive 926.34
engrossing 983.20
grisly
terrible 127.30
deathly 307.28
hideous 1015.11
grist 386.2
gristle 1049.2
grit
n pluck 359.3
fortitude 492.5
grain 1051.6
v irritate 96.14
grit one's teeth 359.8
grits food 10.2
powder 1051.5
gritty rough 294.6
plucky 359.14
fearless 492.18
hard 1046.10
granular 1051.12
stony 1059.12
grizzled white 37.7
gray 39.4
grizzly bear 110.11
groan
n rasp 58.3
lament 115.3
complaint 115.4
v sound harshly 58.9
wail 115.13
complain 115.15
sigh 318.20
groaning board 8.9
groceries
food 10.2
provisions 10.5
grocery 735.7
grocery list 871.1
grocery store 736.1
grog
n spirits 88.13
v tipple 88.24
groggy
unsteady 16.16
inert 173.14

dazed 985.14
groin fork 171.4
buttress 901.4
harbor 1009.6
barrier 1012.5
groom
n newlywed 563.5
stockman 1070.2
v dress 79.20
train 568.13
tidy 808.12
tend 1070.7
groomed 405.16
groomsman
wedding party 563.4
assistant 616.6
groove
n crack 224.2
furrow 290.1
routine 373.5
path 383.2
type 548.6
race 756.3
v cleave 224.4
excavate 284.15
furrow 290.3
engrave 713.9
groove on 95.13
groovy
adj knowledgeable
928.17
excellent 999.13
interj goody! 95.21
grope contact 223.10
feel one's way 938.32
be uncertain 971.9
gross
n gain 472.3
receipts 627.1
round 751.3
v profit 472.12
yield 627.4
adj nasty 64.7
filthy 80.23
offensive 98.18
downright 247.12
corpulent 257.18
thick 269.8
rough 294.6
luxuriant 310.43
coarse 497.11
ill-bred 505.6
inelegant 534.2
base 661.12
carnal 663.6
vulgar 666.8
whole 792.9
stupid 922.15
bad 1000.8
terrible 1000.9
gross out offend 98.11
repel 99.6
gross profit margin 627.1
grotesque
n work of art 712.9
adj deformed 265.12
freakish 870.13
absurd 923.11
fanciful 986.20
unshapely 1015.8
grotto 284.5

grouch
  n malcontent 108.4
  sorehead 110.11
  complainer 115.9
  spoilsport 1012.9
  v be discontented 108.6
  sulk 110.14
  complain 115.16
grouchy
  discontented 108.8
  irascible 110.20
  complaining 115.20
ground
  n color 35.8
  station 159.2
  ground covering 199.3
  bed 199.4
  horizontal 201.3
  setting 209.2
  enclosed place (enclosure)
    212.3
  region 231.1
  land 234.1
  ocean depths 275.4
  motive 375.1
  arena 463.1
  warrant 600.6
  art equipment 712.17
  cause 886.1
  foundation 901.6
  premise 935.7
  evidence 957.1
  v establish 159.16
  shipwreck 182.42
  limit 210.5
  restrict 428.9
  confine 429.12
  teach 568.10
  play 745.5
  fix 855.9
  fell 913.5
  insulate 1032.29
  adj bottom 199.7
  powdery 1051.11
ground-breaking 404.8
grounder 745.3
ground floor
  floor 197.23
  earliness 845.1
groundhog
  black clouds 133.5
  excavator 284.10
  wild animal 311.22
grounding
  preparation 405.1
  elementary education 568.5
groundless
  unsubstantial 764.8
  baseless 936.13
  unproved 958.8
grounds nearness 223.1
  dregs 256.2
  green 310.7
  real estate 471.6
  warrant 600.6
  cause 886.1
  foundation 901.6
  evidence 957.1
  condition 959.2
group
  n amount 244.2

  association 617.1
  clique 617.6
  sect 675.3
  orchestra 710.12
  company 770.3
  bunch 770.7
  set 784.5
  class 809.2
  v size 257.15
  assemble 770.18
  analyze 801.8
  arrange 808.11
  classify 809.6
groupie fan 101.5
  idolater 697.4
grouping
  association 617.1
  treatment 712.8
  company 770.3
  bunch 770.7
  analysis 801.3
  arrangement 808.3
  classification 809.1
  class 809.2
grouse
  n complaint 115.5
  v be discontented 108.6
  complain 115.16
grouser
  malcontent 108.4
  complainer 115.9
grout 295.25
grove
  valley 284.9
  woodlet 310.14
  bunch 770.7
grovel fawn 138.7
  creep 177.26
  lie 201.5
  lie low 274.5
  bow down 433.10
  be promiscuous 665.19
  bow 913.9
  wallow 915.13
grow develop 14.2
  increase 251.6
  expand 259.7
  grow up 272.12
  mature 303.9
  vegetate 310.34
  become 761.12
  evolve 861.5
  process 892.9
  farm 1069.16
  raise 1070.6
growl
  n reverberation 54.2
  boom 56.4
  rasp 58.3
  v boom 56.9
  sound harshly 58.9
  snarl 60.4
  complain 115.15
  show resentment 152.14
  sigh 318.20
  speak 524.25
growling
  n reverberation 54.2
  adj reverberating 54.12
  discontented 108.7
  irascible 110.19

grown mature 14.3
  full-grown 259.12
  adult 303.12
  produced 892.17
  made 892.18
grownup 304.1
grown-up
  mature 14.3
  grown 259.12
  adult 303.12
grow on one
  enamor 104.22
  become a habit 373.10
grow out of
  overdevelop 14.2
  expand 259.7
  result from 887.5
growth
  bodily development 14.1
  symptom 85.9
  neoplasm 85.39
  gain 251.1
  increase in size 259
  development 259.3
  maturation 303.6
  stand 310.2
  vegetation 310.32
  business cycle 731.10
  conversion 858.1
  evolution 861.1
grow up mature 14.2
  ascend 193.8
  expand 259.7
  grow 272.12
  age 303.9
  ripen 407.8
grub
  n food 10.2
  larva 302.12
  drudge 726.3
  v excavate 284.15
  drudge 725.14
grubby dirty 80.22
  slovenly 810.15
  infested 910.11
grudge
  n hostility 99.2
  spite 589.5
  v envy 154.2
  refuse 325.3
  deny 442.4
  stint 484.5
grudge match 451.1
grudging
  n envy 154.1
  adj envious 154.3
  reluctant 325.6
  niggardly 484.8
gruel
  n symbol of weakness 16.7
  thinness 270.7
  semiliquid 1062.5
  v weaken 16.10
grueling
  weakening 16.20
  fatiguing 21.13
  punishing 604.23
  laborious 725.18
  troublesome 1013.18
gruesome
  terrible 127.30

  deathly 307.28
  hideous 1015.11
gruff
  raucous 58.15
  irascible 110.19
  brusque 505.7
grumble
  n reverberation 54.2
  thunder 56.4
  rasp 58.3
  v boom 56.9
  sound harshly 58.9
  growl 60.4
  complain 115.15
grumbling
  n reverberation 54.2
  complaint 115.4
  adj discontented 108.7
  irascible 110.19
grump
  n malcontent 108.4
  sorehead 110.11
  v be discontented 108.6
  sulk 110.14
  complain 115.16
Grundyism 579.1
grungy dirty 80.22
  filthy 80.23
  offensive 98.18
grunt
  n animal noise 60.1
  dogface 461.10
  v snort 60.3
  complain 115.15
  speak 524.25
grunt worker 607.9
G-spot 75.5
G string 711.5
G-string
  waistband 5.19
  supporter 901.2
guacamole 10.9
guano feces 12.4
  fertilizer 890.4
guarantee
  n oath 334.4
  promise 436.1
  security 438.1
  guarantor 438.6
  v depose 334.6
  promise 436.4
  secure 438.9
  protect 1008.18
guarantor
  endorser 332.7
  warrantor 438.6
guaranty
  n security 438.1
  guarantor 438.6
  v secure 438.9
guard
  n trainman 178.13
  vigilance 339.4
  jailer 429.10
  defense 460.1
  defender 460.7
  football team 746.2
  escort 769.5
  protection 1008.1
  safeguard 1008.3
  guarder 1008.9

v preserve 397.8
restrain 428.7
defend 460.8
play 747.4
escort 769.8
protect 1008.18
guard against
defend 460.8
take precautions 494.6
guarded
vigilant 339.13
reticent 344.10
restrained 428.13
cautious 494.8
incredulous 956.4
protected 1008.21
guardian
n jailer 429.10
steward 574.4
familiar spirit 678.12
warden 1008.6
adj protective 1008.23
guardian angel
penitence 113.4
defender 460.7
conscience 636.5
familiar spirit 678.12
custodian 1008.6
gubernatorial 612.16
guerrilla
irregular 461.16
violent person 671.9
guerrilla marketing 731.13
guerrilla warfare 458.1
guess
n conjecture 951.4
gamble 971.8
v solve 940.2
estimate 946.9
conjecture 951.11
think 953.11
predict 962.9
guesstimate 962.9
guesswork
supposition 951.3
guess 951.4
prediction 962.1
guest
n visitor 585.6
v entertain 585.8
guest house 228.15
guest list 585.6
guest room 197.7
guff bull 520.3
chatter 540.3
guffaw
n laughter 116.4
v laugh 116.8
guidance
navigation 159.3
advice 422.1
patronage 449.4
teaching 568.1
direction 573.1
protectorship 1008.2
guidance counselor 466.5
guide
n gutter 239.3
interpreter 341.7
adviser 422.3
pointer 517.4

teacher 571.1
guider 574.7
familiar spirit 678.12
escort 769.5
precursor 816.1
specter 988.1
v lead 165.2
pilot 182.14
advise 422.5
teach 568.10
steer 573.9
escort 769.8
go before 816.3
exercise influence
894.8
guidebook
information 551.1
handbook 554.8
directory 574.10
guided imagery 90.13
guide dog blind 30.6
dog 311.16
guideline plan 381.1
law 419.2
rule 869.4
guidepost pointer 517.4
guide 574.7
guiding light
inspiration 375.9
motive 375.1
guiding star 574.8
guild 617.3
guile deceit 356.3
cunning 415.1
guileful deceitful 356.22
cunning 415.12
shrewd 920.15
guileless
undeceptive 644.18
foolable 923.12
trusting 953.22
guillotine
n capital punishment 604.7
execution 605.5
legislative procedure 613.6
cloture 857.5
v execute 604.17
guilt culpability 656
guiltiness 656.1
guilt by association 888.1
guiltless chaste 653.6
innocent 657.6
guilt someone 656.2
guilty
adj at fault 656.3
adv shamefacedly 656.5
guinea pig
wild animal 311.22
subject 942.7
guise clothing 5.1
aspect 33.3
looks 33.4
cover 295.2
behavior 321.1
pretext 376.1
manner 384.1
mode 765.4
guitarist 710.5
gulag 429.8
gulch valley 237.7
watercourse 239.2

gulf crack 224.2
eddy 238.12
ocean 240.2
cove 242
inlet 242.1
hole 275.2
pit 284.4
opening 292.1
gull
n dupe 358.1
v deceive 356.14
cheat 356.18
stultify 923.7
gullible foolable
923.12
dupable 954.9
gullible person 358.1
Gulliver 178.2
gully
n valley 237.7
watercourse 239.2
v furrow 290.3
gulp
n breathing 2.21
drink 8.4
drink 8.29
ingestion 187.4
v gobble 8.23
ingest 187.11
gluttonize 672.4
gum
n elastic 1048.3
resin 1057.1
chewing gum 1062.6
v chew 8.27
stick together 803.9
hinder 1012.16
gumbo
n semiliquid 1062.5
mud 1062.8
adj earthy 234.5
viscous 1062.12
gummy
adhesive 803.12
resinous 1057.3
viscous 1062.12
gumption 330.7
gumshoe
n detective 576.11
police 1008.16
v creep 177.26
lurk 346.9
gum up disable 19.9
spoil 393.11
bungle 414.12
hinder 1012.16
gun
n killer 308.11
artilleryman 461.11
mercenary 461.17
firearm 462.10
ruffian 593.4
game 746.3
stop 857.2
shot 904.4
shooter 904.8
v hunt 382.9
shoot 904.12
gun down
kill 308.14
strike dead 308.18

gunfire fire 459.8
shot 904.4
gung ho
n call to arms 458.7
adj energetic 17.13
enthusiastic 101.10
gunk slime 80.8
adhesive 803.4
semiliquid 1062.5
gunky filthy 80.23
viscous 1062.12
gunman killer 308.11
mercenary 461.17
ruffian 593.3
shooter 904.8
gunner hand 183.6
crew 185.4
artilleryman 461.11
basketball team 747.2
shooter 904.8
gunrunning 732.2
gunshot
detonation 56.3
short distance 223.2
shot 904.4
gun-shy fearful 127.23
jittery 128.12
gunslinger 737.11
gurgle ripple 52.11
trickle 238.18
bubble 320.4
gurney 901.19
guru teacher 571.1
master 575.1
holy man 659.6
clergy 699.13
wise man 921.1
gush
n outflow 190.4
ascent 193.1
flow 238.4
jet 238.9
increase 251.1
unction 511.2
wordiness 538.2
outburst 671.6
plenty 991.2
v emotionalize 93.13
be enthusiastic 101.7
run out 190.13
shoot up 193.9
flow 238.16
jet 238.20
chatter 540.5
abound 991.5
gushiness 540.1
gushing
n wordiness 538.2
adj sentimental 93.21
flowing 238.24
flattering 511.8
diffuse 538.11
gushy
v talkative 540.9
adj diffuse 538.11
gusset 191.2
gussy up dress up 5.42
ornament 498.8
beautify 1016.15
gust taste 62.1
liking 100.2

eagerness 101.1
outburst 105.9
wind gust 318.5
characteristic 865.4
gusto vim 17.2
animation 17.4
savor 63.2
passion 93.2
pleasure 95.1
liking 100.2
eagerness 101.1
gaiety 109.4
gusty tasty 63.8
windy 318.21
gut
n goozle 2.19
heart 93.3
inlet 242.1
v eviscerate 192.13
destroy 395.10
plunder 482.17
adj emotional 93.17
interior 207.6
unpremeditated 365.11
essential 767.9
vital 997.23
gut feeling 934.3
gutless weak 16.12
wishy-washy 16.17
uncourageous 491.11
gut reaction
feeling 93.1
impulse 365.1
guts viscera 2.16
goozle 2.19
strength 15.1
zest 68.2
heart 93.3
contents 196.1
insides 207.4
pluck 359.3
fearlessness 492.3
nut and bolts 767.3
inner nature 767.5
gut sensation 93.1
gutsy strong 15.15
plucky 359.14
fearless 492.18
gutter
n trough 239.3
drain 239.5
trench 290.2
pavement 383.6
sewer 654.7
bowling 750.1
v flutter 917.12
flicker 1025.26
adj disgraceful 661.11
vulgar 666.8
guttermouth 497.6
guttersnipe
vagabond 178.3
vulgarian 497.6
guttural raucous 58.15
inarticulate 525.12
gut-wrenching 105.30
guy man 76.5
supporter 901.2
a guy thing 76.1
guzzle
n goozle 2.19

drink 8.4
drinking spree 88.6
swig 88.7
v drink 8.29
tipple 88.24
gluttonize 672.4
gym fitness 84.1
arena 463.1
playground 743.11
gymnasium
fitness 84.1
playroom 197.12
arena 463.1
playground 743.11
gymnastics
exercise 84.2
physical education 568.9
sport 744.1
gyp
n female animal 77.9
dog 311.16
deception 356.9
cheater 357.4
v deceive 356.19
gypsy 178.4
gypsy cab 179.13
gyrate move 172.5
rotate 915.9
ha'penny 728.8
haberdasher 5.33
habit
n clothing 5.1
suit 5.6
substance abuse 87.1
convention 373
habitude 373.3
mannerism 500.2
nature 767.4
v outfit 5.41
habitat
environment 209.1
habitation 225.1
dwelling 228.1
home 228.18
habitation
occupancy 225.1
inhabiting 225.1
abode 228.1
habitual regular 373.14
orderly 807.6
frequent 847.4
usual 869.9
habitué
n attender 221.5
guest 585.6
adj habituated 373.17
hacienda
farmstead 228.6
farm 1069.8
hack
n breathing 2.21
driver 178.9
coachman 178.10
public vehicle 179.13
notch 289.1
horse 311.12
hunter 311.13
attempt 403.3
mark 517.5
hack writer 547.16
politician 610.4

scribbler 718.5
drudge 726.3
v go on horseback 177.34
accomplish 407.4
sever 802.11
hacker
incompetent 414.7
golfer 751.2
liveware 1042.17
hack it
be able 18.11
do 328.6
achieve one's purpose
 409.8
manage 409.12
stand the test 942.10
suffice 991.4
hackneyed
trite 117.9
habitual 373.14
hackneyed expression 526.9
hack writer
writing 547.16
hack 718.5
Hades hell 682.1
nether world 682.3
nether world deity 682.5
destiny 839.2
hag old woman 304.3
witch 593.7
sorceress 690.8
eyesore 1015.4
haggard
tired-looking 21.9
colorless 36.7
frenzied 105.25
dejected 112.22
poor 270.20
deathly 307.28
fanatic 926.32
haggle
n negotiation 731.3
v bargain 731.18
hagiography 719.1
ha-ha
n laughter 116.4
trench 290.2
v laugh 116.8
hail
n greeting 585.4
multitude 884.3
hailstone 1023.6
v cry 59.6
assent 332.8
applaud 509.10
signal 517.22
address 524.26
greet 585.10
sleet 1023.11
interj all hail! 509.23
greetings! 585.15
hey! 983.23
hair
pile 3.2
short distance 223.2
modicum 248.2
narrowness 270.1
filament 271.1
skin 295.3
theater man 704.23
trifle 998.5

haircut 3.15
hairdo 3.15
hairdresser 1016.12
hairdressing 1016.10
hair-drier 1066.4
hairless 6.17
hairpiece 3.14
hairpin
n deviation 164.1
zigzag 204.8
skiing 753.1
race 756.3
v deflect 164.5
adj crooked 204.20
hair-raiser 127.9
hair salon beauty parlor or
 salon or shop 1016.13
hair shirt
self-reproach 113.3
penance 658.3
hairsplitter 936.7
hairsplitting
n overfastidiousness 495.4
criticism 510.4
quibbling 936.5
distinction 944.3
adj overfastidious 495.12
critical 510.23
quibbling 936.14
hairstyle 3.15
hair weave 3.14
hairy hirsute 3.24
threadlike 271.7
bristly 288.9
nappy 294.7
cutaneous 295.32
weird 988.9
bad 1000.8
difficult 1013.17
the hairy eyeball 27.5
hajj 177.5
halcyon bright 97.11
quiescent 173.12
pacific 464.9
thriving 1010.13
hale
v pull 905.4
adj strong 15.15
hearty 83.12
half
n portion 477.5
football game 746.3
basketball game 747.3
game 749.6
mid-distance 819.2
moiety 875.2
adj proportionate 477.13
part 875.5
adv o'clock 832.16
half a mind 323.1
half-assed
slipshod 340.12
unskillful 414.15
botched 414.22
half-learned 930.14
half-baked
immature 406.11
premature 845.8
mentally deficient 922.22
half-learned 930.14
imperfect 1003.4

half-breed
n hybrid 797.8
adj hybrid 797.15
half-cocked
immature 406.11
premature 845.8
half-learned 930.14
half-heard 52.16
halfhearted
wishy-washy 16.17
indifferent 102.6
half-life 1037.6
half-mast 517.22
half-moon
crescent 279.5
heavenly body 1072.11
half nelson 474.3
half note 709.14
halftime game 746.3
shift 825.3
interim 826.1
halftone
color system 35.7
interval 709.20
half-truth 354.11
halfway
adj middle 819.4
half 875.5
adv midway 819.5
halfway house
mid-distance 819.2
asylum 1009.4
half-wit
stupid person 924.2
idiot 924.8
halitosis 71.1
hall entrance 189.5
assembly hall 197.4
corridor 197.18
house 228.5
arena 463.1
schoolhouse 567.10
theater 704.14
hallelujah
n cheer 116.2
paean 696.3
interj alleluia! 696.17
hallmark
n sign 517.1
label 517.13
characteristic 865.4
v label 517.20
hall of famer 413.15
halloo
n cry 59.1
v cry 59.6
address 524.26
interj oh! 122.20
hey! 983.23
hallow celebrate 487.2
sanctify 685.5
hallucinate 976.8
hallucination
deception 356.1
hallucinosis 976.7
figment of the imagination 986.5
hallucinogen
psychoactive drug 86.13
drug 87.3

hallway
entrance 189.5
corridor 197.18
halo radiation 171.2
circle 280.2
illustriousness 662.6
nimbus 1025.14
halt
n respite 20.2
standstill 173.3
delay 846.2
stop 857.2
prevention 1012.2
impasse 1013.6
v be weak 16.8
quiet 173.8
dawdle 175.8
way of walking 177.28
stammer 525.8
cease 857.6
stop 857.7
put a stop to 857.11
hinder 1012.13
adj crippled 393.30
interj cease! 857.13
halter
n shackle 428.4
execution 605.5
v yoke 800.10
halting
n cessation 857.1
prevention 1012.2
adj slow 175.10
crippled 393.30
stammering 525.13
stiff 534.3
irregular 851.3
halve share 476.6
sever 802.11
double 873.5
bisect 875.4
ham
n member 2.7
leg 177.14
village 230.2
acting 704.8
grimacer 707.5
radioman 1034.24
v affect 500.12
overact 704.31
adj dramatic 704.33
ham-and-egger 606.5
hamburger 10.14
hamburger joint 8.17
ham-fisted
bungling 414.20
inelegant 534.2
ham it up
emotionalize 93.13
affect 500.12
overact 704.31
hamlet village 230.2
region 231.5
Hamlet 542.2
hammer
n ear 2.10
tool 1040.1
v rage 671.11
drudge 725.14
din 849.10
pound 902.16

think hard 931.9
hammer away at
dwell on 849.9
think hard 931.9
hammer out
form 262.7
do carelessly 340.9
discuss 541.10
produce 892.8
ham operator 1034.24
hamper
n shackle 428.4
impediment 1012.6
v package 212.9
burden 297.13
bind 428.10
impede 1012.11
hamster wheel
routine 373.5
repetitiousness 849.4
hamster-wheel 849.14
hamstring disable 19.9
render powerless 19.10
cripple 393.14
hamper 1012.11
hand
n member 2.7
deckhand 183.6
side 218.1
person 312.5
act 328.3
skill 413.1
governance 417.5
assist 449.2
applause 509.2
pointer 517.4
signature 527.10
handwriting 547.3
control 612.2
worker 726.2
bridge 758.3
member 793.4
v deliver 478.13
transfer 629.3
handbag bag 195.2
money holder 729.15
handbags at dawn 456.6
handbag situation 456.6
handball 1048.3
handbill 352.8
handbook
manual 554.8
directory 574.10
casino 759.19
handcrafted 892.18
handcuff
disable 19.10
bind 428.10
hamper 1012.11
hand down
bequeath 478.18
transfer 629.3
handful
modicum 248.2
a few 885.2
tough proposition 1013.2
handheld computer 1042.2
handicap
n disease 85.1
burden 297.7

disability 603.2
round 751.3
inequality 791.1
disadvantage 996.2
impediment 1012.6
v burden 297.13
penalize 603.4
hamper 1012.11
handicraft craft 712.2
vocation 724.6
production 892.2
hand in glove
cooperative 450.5
cooperatively 450.6
sociably 582.25
familiar 587.19
amicably 587.22
accompanying 769.9
arm in arm 769.10
in step 788.11
joined 800.13
concurrently 899.5
hand in hand
near 223.14
cooperatively 450.6
sociably 582.25
familiar 587.19
amicably 587.22
accompanying 769.9
arm in arm 769.10
joined 800.13
concurrently 899.5
hand it to bow to 250.5
compliment 509.14
handiwork act 328.3
work 725.4
production 892.2
product 893.1
handkerchief 5.25
handle
n bulge 283.3
pretext 376.1
name 527.3
title 648.1
hold 901.11
v touch 73.6
pilot 182.14
behave 321.6
perform 328.9
use 387.10
treat 387.12
discuss 541.11
write upon 556.5
direct 573.8
deal in 731.16
operate 889.5
tend 1070.7
handle with kid gloves
be careful 339.7
be easy on 427.5
handling touching 73.2
performance 328.2
usage 387.2
utilization 387.8
treatise 556.1
direction 573.1
operation 889.1
handmade 892.18
handmaiden
instrument 384.4
maid 577.8

hardball reality 761.2
　gravity 997.3
　danger 1006.1
hardbody 15.6
hard-boiled
　firm 15.18
　obdurate 361.10
　hard 1046.10
hard copy 547.10
hard-core
　unyielding 361.9
　fiery 671.22
hardcover 554.3
hard disk
　recording media 549.10
　disk 1042.6
hard disk drive 1042.5
hard-drinking 88.35
hard drive 1042.5
hard drug 87.3
hard-earned
　laborious 725.18
　difficult 1013.17
harden
　strengthen 15.13
　callous 94.6
　accustom 373.9
　indurate 1046.7
　toughen 1049.3
　petrify 1059.10
hardened callous 94.12
　impenitent 114.5
　heartless 144.25
　accustomed 373.15
　hard 654.17
　toughened 1046.13
　tough 1049.6
hard feelings
　bad feeling 93.7
　bitterness 152.3
　animosity 589.4
hard hat patriot 591.3
　conservative 611.9
　safeguard 1008.3
hardheaded
　obstinate 361.8
　ungullible 956.5
　realistic 987.6
hard-hearted
　callous 94.12
　heartless 144.25
　hardened 654.17
　hard 1046.10
hard knocks 1011.1
hard labor
　punishment 604.2
　backbreaking work
　　725.5
hard line
　unyieldingness 361.2
　strictness 425.1
　warlikeness 458.10
　orthodoxy 687.5
hard-line
　unyielding 361.9
　strict 425.6
　militaristic 458.21
　fiery 671.22
hard liquor 88.13
hard news 552.1
hard-nosed 361.10

hard nut to crack
　enigma 522.8
　tough proposition 1013.2
hard-of-hearing 49.6
hard on 223.24
hard-on 75.5
hard-pressed
　straitened 1013.26
　hurried 401.11
hard rock 708.10
hard sell
　inducement 375.3
　importunity 440.3
　selling 734.2
hard up poor 619.7
　straitened 1013.26
hardware
　hard goods 735.4
　computer hardware 1041.17
　central processing unit 1042.2
the hard way
　n difficulty 1013.1
　adv laboriously 725.19
　with difficulty 1013.28
hardwood
　n basketball 747.1
　wood 1054.3
　adj arboreal 310.39
hardwoods 310.49
hardworking
　industrious 330.22
　laboring 725.17
hardy strong 15.15
　hale 83.12
　insolent 142.9
　perennial 310.44
　courageous 492.16
　durable 827.10
　tough 1049.4
hare
　swiftness 174.6
　leveret 311.23
harebrained
　capricious 364.5
　foolhardy 493.9
　scatterbrained 985.16
harem 563.10
hark
　v listen 48.10
　hearken to 983.7
　interj hark ye! 48.16
　attention! 983.22
hark back
　turn back 859.5
　remember 989.9
harlequin
　n check 47.4
　variegation 47.6
　buffoon 707.10
　v variegate 47.7
　adj variegated 47.9
harlot
　n prostitute 665.16
　adj prostitute 665.28
harm
　n impairment 393.1
　disadvantage 996.2
　evil 1000.3
　bane 1001.1
　v impair 393.9
　inconvenience 996.4

　work evil 1000.6
harmful
　unhealthful 82.5
　malicious 144.20
　disadvantageous 996.6
　hurtful 1000.12
　adverse 1011.13
harmless
　hurtless 999.21
　undamaged 1002.8
　unhazardous 1007.5
harmonic
　n tone 50.2
　harmonic tone 709.16
　adj harmonious 708.49
　oscillating 916.15
harmonica 711.10
harmonious
　chromatic 35.16
　pleasant 97.6
　symmetric 264.4
　cooperative 450.5
　in accord 455.3
　balanced 533.8
　friendly 587.15
　harmonic 708.49
　agreeing 788.9
　orderly 807.6
　conformist 867.6
　concurrent 899.4
harmonize
　symmetrize 264.3
　cooperate 450.3
　get along 455.2
　reconcile 465.8
　be harmonious 708.35
　compose 708.46
　make uniform 781.4
　agree 788.6
　make agree 788.7
　order 807.4
　organize 808.10
　conform 867.3
　concur 899.2
harmony
　symmetry 264.1
　unanimity 332.5
　cooperation 450.1
　accord 455.1
　peace 464.1
　proportion 533.2
　good terms 587.3
　heaven 681.5
　concord 708.3
　harmonics 709.1
　agreement 788.1
　order 807.1
　conformity 867.1
harness
　n wardrobe 5.2
　parachute 181.13
　caparison 385.5
　armor 460.3
　v yoke 800.10
　tend 1070.7
harp
　n lyre 711.3
　mouth organ 711.10
　v persist 856.5
harp on dwell on 118.8
　belabor 849.9

　emphasize 997.14
harpoon 480.17
harpsichord 711.12
harpy
　extortionist 480.12
　monster 593.6
harridan
　strumpet 665.14
　eyesore 1015.4
harried
　tormented 96.24
　worried 126.8
harrow
　n projection 285.4
　v pain 26.7
　torture 96.18
　smooth 287.5
　cultivate 1069.17
harrowing
　n cultivation 1069.13
　adj painful 26.10
　agonizing 98.23
harry annoy 96.13
　make anxious 126.5
　persecute 389.7
　attack 459.14
　besiege 459.19
harsh
　acrimonious 17.14
　painful 26.10
　off-color 35.21
　raucous 58.15
　dissonant 61.4
　clashing 61.5
　bitter 64.6
　pungent 68.6
　distressing 98.20
　oppressive 98.24
　rough 144.24
　pitiless 146.3
　rugged 288.7
　strict 425.6
　gruff 505.7
　inarticulate 525.12
　inelegant 534.2
hart male animal 76.8
　hoofed animal 311.5
harum-scarum
　adj reckless 493.8
　boisterous 671.20
　adv in disorder 810.17
harvest
　n autumn 313.4
　yield 472.5
　effect 887.1
　production 893.2
　harvesting 1069.15
　v acquire 472.8
　process 892.9
　reap 1069.19
has-been
　n back number 842.8
　adj past 837.7
　old-fashioned 842.16
hash
　n meat 10.13
　hashish 87.8
　fiasco 410.6
　bungle 414.5
　hodgepodge 797.6
　jumble 810.3

v mix 797.10
hash house 8.17
hash over 541.11
Hasidic 675.30
hasp 800.8
hassle
  n quarrel 456.6
  struggle 725.3
  commotion 810.4
  argumentation 935.4
  v vex 98.15
  quarrel 456.12
  nag 510.16
  struggle 725.11
  argue 935.16
  work evil 1000.6
haste
  n impatience 135.1
  velocity 174.1
  impulsiveness 365.2
  hurry 401.1
  recklessness 493.2
  prematurity 845.2
  v speed 174.8
  hasten 401.4
hasten
  be impatient 135.4
  advance 162.5
  speed 174.8
  accelerate 174.10
  haste 401.4
  make haste 401.5
  be useful 449.17
  facilitate 1014.7
hasty
  hot-tempered 110.25
  impatient 135.6
  fast 174.15
  impulsive 365.9
  hurried 401.9
  unprepared 406.8
  reckless 493.8
  sudden 830.5
  premature 845.8
hat
  n headdress 5.25
  v cloak 5.40
  top 295.21
hatch
  n porch 189.6
  offspring 561.2
  v be born 1.2
  be pregnant 78.12
  fabricate 354.18
  plot 381.9
  mark 517.19
  portray 712.18
  engrave 713.9
  originate 892.12
  imagine 986.14
  raise 1070.6
hatchet job demolition 395.5
  aspersion 512.4
hatchet man
  killer 308.11
  combatant 461.1
  disparager 512.6
  ruffian 593.4
  henchman 610.8
hate
  n hostility 99.2

aversion 103
malice 103.1
hated thing 103.3
antagonism 589.3
v have deep feelings 93.12
dislike 99.3
detest 103.5
bear ill will 589.8
hate crime 103.1
hateful
  offensive 98.18
  loathsome 103.8
  malicious 144.20
  hostile 589.10
  terrible 1000.9
hatred hostility 99.2
  abhorrence 103.1
  antagonism 589.3
haughty vain 136.9
  arrogant 141.9
  contemptuous 157.8
  high 272.14
haul
  n distance 261.1
  take 480.10
  booty 482.11
  strain 725.2
  pull 905.2
  v cart 176.13
  sail against the wind 182.24
  ship activity 182.48
  strain 725.10
  pull 905.4
haunch 218.1
haunt
  n haunt 228.27
  specter 988.1
  v oppress 98.16
  make anxious 126.5
  frequent 221.10
  hant 988.6
haunted worried 126.8
  spooked 988.10
  remembering 989.23
haunting
  recurrent 849.13
  unforgettable 989.25
haute couture 5.32
haute cuisine 11.1
hauteur arrogance 141.1
  contempt 157.1
  height 272.1
have give birth 1.3
  affirm 334.5
  deceive 356.19
  compel 424.4
  suffer 443.10
  possess 469.4
  hold 474.7
  receive 479.6
  understand 521.7
  experience 831.8
  know 928.12
  doubt 955.6
  recognize 989.11
have breakfast 8.21
have dinner 8.20
have it in for
  dislike 99.3
  loathe 103.6
  bear ill will 589.8

have it made
  make good 409.10
  prosper 1010.7
have it out
  contend with 457.17
  argue 935.16
have lunch 8.21
haven
  n destination 186.5
  refuge 1009.1
  harbor 1009.6
  v protect 1008.18
have no remorse 114.3
have the creeps 74.7
have the heebie-jeebies 74.7
have to
  be compelled 424.9
  be necessary 963.10
having a field day 20.12
havoc
  n evil 1000.3
  v destroy 395.10
haw avoid 164.6
  stammer 525.8
hawk
  n sharp vision 27.11
  bird 311.27
  militarist 461.5
  patriot 591.3
  v salivate 13.6
  hunt 382.9
  vend 734.9
the hawk 318.7
hawk-eyed
  clear-sighted 27.21
  vigilant 339.13
hay
  n feed 10.4
  marijuana 87.11
  v harvest 1069.19
the hay 901.19
haystack 770.10
haywire
  impaired 393.38
  disorderly 810.13
  crazy 926.27
  eccentric 927.6
hazard
  n golf 751.1
  gamble 759.2
  bet 759.3
  unreliability 971.6
  chance event 972.6
  danger 1006.1
  obstacle 1012.4
  v presume 640.6
  risk 759.24
  bet 759.25
  chance 972.11
  endanger 1006.6
  take chances 1006.7
hazardous materials
  refuse 391.4
  danger 1006.1
haze
  n LSD 87.10
  fog 319.3
  confusion 985.3
  v cloud 319.7
  banter 490.5
hazel 40.3

hazy
  inconspicuous 32.6
  formless 263.4
  foggy 319.10
  obscure 522.15
  vague 971.19
  muddled 985.13
HDTV
  television 1035.1
  reception 1035.5
he male 76.4
  self 865.5
head
  n member 2.7
  head of hair 3.4
  latrine 12.10
  addict 87.21
  enthusiast 101.5
  fan 101.5
  have or take a direction 161.7
  sail 180.14
  top part 198.4
  architectural topping 198.5
  headpiece 198.6
  front 216.1
  headwaters 238.2
  superior 249.4
  point of land 283.9
  plant 310.27
  types of inflorescence 310.27
  person 312.5
  foam 320.2
  makeup 554.12
  abridgment 557.1
  superintendent 574.2
  portrait 712.14
  office 739.7
  game 752.3
  class 809.2
  source 886.5
  thrust 902.2
  intellect 919.1
  brain 919.6
  intelligence 920.9
  intelligent being 920.9
  topic 937.1
  caption 937.2
  water 1065.3
  v take direction 161.7
  lead 165.2
  sail 180.14
  top 198.9
  be in front 216.7
  gravitate 297.15
  direct 573.8
  govern 612.11
  play 752.4
  precede 814.2
  tend 896.3
  focus on 937.3
  adj top 198.10
  front 216.10
  directing 573.12
  governing 612.17
  first 818.17
headache ache 26.5
  annoyance 96.2
  tedious person 118.5
  trouble 1013.3
head and shoulders above
  superlative 249.13

superior 999.14
headband 554.14
head count
population 227.1
roll 871.6
summation 1017.11
headdress
hairdo 3.15
headgear 5.25
headfirst
precipitately 401.15
recklessly 493.11
headhunter
executive search agency 615.5
killer 308.11
heading
n direction 161.1
leading 165.1
course 184.34
top part 198.4
front 216.1
supervision 573.2
class 809.2
topic 937.1
caption 937.2
adj leading 165.3
topping 198.11
headline
n caption 937.2
v dramatize 704.28
focus on 937.3
feature 997.15
headlong
adj fast 174.15
steep 204.18
impulsive 365.9
precipitate 401.10
reckless 493.8
sudden 830.5
adv precipitately 401.15
recklessly 493.11
impulsively 365.13
headmaster 571.8
head off 164.6
head office 739.7
head-on
adj front 216.10
adv afoul 182.72
in opposition 451.9
head over heels
inversely 205.8
precipitately 401.15
recklessly 493.11
round 915.16
inverted 205.7
headphone
loudspeaker 50.8
radiophone 347.5
headpiece
headdress 5.25
top part 198.4
head 198.6
intellect 919.1
headquarters
central station 208.6
office 739.7
headroom 224.1
heads 215.3
heads or tails 759.2
head start
advantage 249.2

earliness 845.1
headstone 901.7
headstrong
obstinate 361.8
lawless 418.5
heads up! 292.23
head up
be in front 216.7
direct 573.8
precede 814.2
initiate 818.10
focus on 937.3
headway
progression 162.1
way 182.9
improvement 392.1
headwear 5.25
headwind
atmosphere 184.32
wind 318.1
nautical 318.10
opposition 451.1
counterforce 900.4
heady
intoxicating 88.36
exciting 105.30
foamy 320.7
lawless 418.5
heal treat 91.24
cure 396.15
heal over 396.21
health
n well-being 83.1
normality 869.1
adj medical 90.15
health care
health protection 83.5
medical care 90.1
medicine 90.1
health center 91.21
health club
health care 83.5
fitness 84.1
health food
nutrient 7.3
food 10.1
health insurance
health care 83.5
medicine 90.1
welfarism 611.7
health spa 84.1
healthy
wellness 81.5
healthful 83.8
large 257.16
good 999.12
heap
n car 179.10
amount 244.2
lot 247.4
store 386.1
throng 770.4
pile 770.10
v load 159.15
give 478.12
pile 770.19
heap up load 159.15
store up 386.11
collect 472.11
pile 770.19

heap upon
furnish 478.15
give freely 485.3
hear
v sense 24.6
listen 48.10
catch 48.11
know 551.15
try 598.18
sit in judgment 946.12
hearken to 983.7
interj hark! 48.16
bravo! 509.22
hear a different drummer
disobey 327.6
dissent 333.4
hearing
n senses 24.5
auditory sense 48.1
audition 48.1
aural sense 48.2
earshot 48.4
trial 598.5
examination 938.2
investigation 938.4
tryout 942.3
adj auditory 48.13
hearken 48.10
hearken to obey 326.2
hark 983.7
hearsay
n report 552.6
adj evidential 957.16
hearse
n funeral car 309.10
v inter 309.19
heart
n viscera 2.16
food 10.20
passion 93.2
soul 93.3
love 104.1
essential content 196.5
interior 207.2
center 208.2
life force 306.2
fortitude 492.5
essence 767.2
inner nature 767.5
middle 819.1
psyche 919.4
mood 978.4
salient point 997.6
v confess 351.7
heartache
wretchedness 96.6
aching heart 112.9
heartbeat
life force 306.2
pulsation 916.3
heartbreak
harshness 98.4
heartache 112.9
heartbreaker 562.12
heartburn ache 26.5
jealousy 153.1
hear tell of hear 48.11
know 551.15
hearten energize 17.10
cheer 109.7
comfort 121.6

motivate 375.21
abet 449.14
encourage 492.15
heartening
n encouragement 492.8
adj cheering 109.16
comforting 121.13
heartfelt 93.24
hearth home 228.2
family 559.5
fireplace 1020.11
heartland inland 207.3
region 231.1
middle America 231.7
heartless unfeeling 94.9
apathetic 94.13
dejected 112.22
unkind 144.25
pitiless 146.3
uncourageous 491.11
hardened 654.17
heartrending
agonizing 98.23
pitiful 145.8
hearts
amphetamines 87.4
card 758.2
heartsick
wretched 96.26
disconsolate 112.28
heartstrings 93.3
Heart Sutra 683.9
heartthrob
loved one 104.10
pulsation 916.3
heart-to-heart
n chat 541.3
adj candid 644.17
heartwarming
delightful 97.7
pleasant 97.6
cheering 109.16
hearty
n mariner 183.1
boon companion 588.5
adj strong 15.15
energetic 17.13
hale 83.12
fervent 93.18
zealous 101.9
gay 109.14
convivial 582.23
hospitable 585.11
cordial 587.16
hear ye
hark! 48.16
attention! 983.22
heat
n sexual desire 75.5
fever 85.7
passion 93.2
zeal 101.2
fever of excitement 105.7
anger 152.5
race 457.12
hotness 1019.1
v cook 11.5
excite 105.12
incite 375.17
raise the temperature 1020.17
adj fuel 1021.9

heated
cooked 11.7
fervent 93.18
zealous 101.9
passionate 105.22
fiery 671.22
hot 1019.25
het 1020.29
heater gun 462.10
warmer 1020.10
heath
plain 236.1
wasteland 891.2
heat haze 1019.17
heathen
n pagan 688.7
unbeliever 695.11
adj pagan 688.11
unbelieving 695.19
idolatrous 697.7
unlearned 930.13
heat up
aggravate 119.2
intensify 251.5
incite 375.17
antagonize 589.7
heat wave
weather 317.3
hot weather 1019.7
heave
n wave 238.14
strain 725.2
throw 904.3
pull 905.2
lift 912.2
v feel disgust 99.4
be excited 105.18
ship activity 182.48
pitch 182.55
billow 238.22
strain 725.10
throw 904.10
pull 905.4
vomit 909.26
elevate 912.5
heaven
happiness 95.2
summit 198.2
height 272.2
utopia 986.11
good times 1010.4
the heavens 1072.2
Heaven
abode of the deity and
blessed dead 681
destiny 839.2
Fates 964.3
Heaven forbid! 510.27
Heaven knows! 930.18
heavenly
blissful 97.9
divine 677.16
angelic 679.6
otherworldly 681.12
sacred 685.7
godly 692.9
ideal 986.23
superb 999.15
gorgeous 1016.20
celestial 1072.25
heavenly body 1072.4

heavens
summit 198.1
height 272.2
the heavens 1072.2
heaven-sent
timely 843.9
expedient 995.5
heave to
sail against the wind
182.24
come to a stop 182.33
heaving
n trepidation 105.5
throwing 904.2
pulling 905.1
vomiting 909.8
adj respiratory 2.32
heavy
n heavyweight 257.12
role 704.10
actor 707.2
adj sleepy 22.21
deep 54.11
pregnant 78.18
oppressive 98.24
sad 112.20
dull 117.6
inert 173.14
great 247.6
thick 269.8
ponderous 297.16
luxuriant 310.43
cloudy 319.8
languid 331.20
phonetic 524.30
stiff 534.3
tragic 704.34
laborious 725.18
sturdy 763.7
unintelligent 922.16
weighty 997.20
excellent 999.13
troublesome 1013.18
dense 1045.12
viscous 1062.12
adv heavily 297.21
heavy-duty 1049.4
heavy hand
firm hand 425.3
despotism 612.9
heavy-handed
insensible 25.6
bungling 414.20
inelegant 534.2
heavy heart
wretchedness 96.6
sadness 112.1
heavy hitter 894.6
heavy industry 892.3
heavyset
corpulent 257.18
thick 269.8
heavyweight
n pig 257.12
weight 297.3
influence 894.6
adj heavy 297.16
important 997.17
hebetude apathy 94.4
languor 331.6
stupidity 922.3

Hebrew
n Jew 675.21
adj Jewish 675.30
hecatomb
butchery 308.3
destruction 395.1
oblation 696.7
hundred 882.8
heck! 513.12
heckle comb 79.21
annoy 96.13
heckling 59.1
hectic
n reddening 41.3
glow 1019.12
adj red-complexioned 41.9
feverish 85.58
overzealous 101.12
heated 105.22
overactive 330.24
hector
n braggart 502.5
blusterer 503.2
v annoy 96.13
intimidate 127.20
bluster 503.3
hedge
n boundary 211.3
caution 494.1
qualification 959.1
v limit 210.5
fence 212.7
dodge 368.8
take precautions 494.6
quibble 936.9
qualify 959.3
hedgehog
wild animal 311.22
launcher 462.21
rocket launcher 1074.10
hedge in
circumscribe 210.4
enclose 212.5
fence 212.7
hedge one's bets 494.6
hedging
n limitation 210.2
caution 494.1
quibbling 936.5
qualification 959.1
adj demurring 325.7
quibbling 936.14
hedonic treadmill
pleasure-loving 95.4
routine 373.5
hedonism
pleasure-loving 95.4
ethical philosophy 636.2
selfishness 651.1
sensuality 663.1
hedonistic
pleasure-loving 95.18
selfish 651.5
sensual 663.5
heebie-jeebies 917.1
heed
n carefulness 339.1
observance 434.1
caution 494.1
attention 983.1
v listen 48.10

obey 326.2
care 339.6
observe 434.2
attend 983.6
heedful
considerate 143.16
careful 339.10
cautious 494.8
attentive 983.15
heedless
unconcerned 102.7
inconsiderate 144.18
careless 340.11
unthinking 365.10
improvident 406.15
incurious 982.3
inattentive 984.6
forgetful 990.9
heel
n foot 199.5
rear 217.1
stern 217.7
bad person 660.5
v turn round 163.9
deviate 164.3
follow 166.3
careen 182.43
equip 385.8
fight 754.4
heeled addicted 87.25
provided 385.13
armed 460.14
heel of Achilles 1006.4
heft
n weight 297.1
v weigh 297.10
elevate 912.5
hefty strong 15.15
corpulent 257.18
heavy 297.16
laborious 725.18
troublesome 1013.18
Hegelian
n immaterialist 1053.4
adj Aristotelian 952.12
idealist 1053.8
hegemony
superiority 249.1
supremacy 249.3
dominance 417.6
mastership 417.7
hegira
departure 188.1
flight 368.4
heifer
female animal 77.9
gal 302.7
cattle 311.6
height
degree 245.1
supremacy 249.3
size 257.1
tallness 272
heighth 272.1
rise 272.2
pitch 709.4
elevation 912.1
acme of perfection 1002.3
heighten
increase 272.13
elevate 912.5

until now 838.4
herewith
 therewith 384.12
 hand in hand 769.10
heritage
 inheritance 479.2
 heredity 560.6
hermaphrodite
 n intersex 75.17
 adj androgynal 75.31
hermeneutics
 exegetics 341.8
 criticism 723.1
Hermes 353.1
hermetically sealed 293.12
hermetics 345.5
hermit recluse 584.5
 ascetic 667.2
 religious 699.16
 oddity 870.4
hero victor 411.2
 brave person 492.7
 god 659.5
 celebrity 662.9
 godling 678.3
 role 704.10
 lead 707.6
 ideal 786.4
heroic eminent 247.9
 huge 257.20
 courageous 492.16
 magnanimous 652.6
 vocal 708.50
 poetic 720.15
 traditional 842.12
heroics
 rashness 493.1
 boasting 502.1
heroine
 brave person 492.7
 hero 659.5
 celebrity 662.9
 godling 678.3
 role 704.10
 lead 707.6
heroism
 glory 247.2
 courage 492.1
 magnanimity 652.2
hero's welcome 186.4
hero worship
 love 104.1
 respect 155.1
 praise 509.5
 idolatry 697.1
hero-worship
 respect 155.4
 praise 509.12
Herr 76.7
hesitancy demur 325.2
 hesitation 362.3
 caution 494.1
 uncertainty 971.1
hesitant
 demurring 325.7
 tentative 362.11
 cautious 494.8
 uncertain 971.16
hesitate demur 325.4
 pause 362.7
 stammer 525.8

procrastinate 846.11
 hang in doubt 971.10
hesitation demur 325.2
 hesitance 362.3
 caution 494.1
 stammering 525.3
 procrastination 846.5
 uncertainty 971.1
heterodoxy
 unorthodoxy 688.1
 inconsistency 789.2
 unconventionality 868.2
 error 975.1
heterogeneity
 difference 780.1
 multiformity 783.1
 inconsistency 789.2
 inequality 791.1
heterogeneous
 different 780.7
 diversified 783.4
 mixed 797.14
heterosexual 75.13
het up
 excited 105.22
 angry 152.30
 heated 1020.29
heuristic
 examining 938.37
 experimental 942.11
hew form 262.7
 sever 802.11
hex
 n curse 513.1
 sorceress 690.8
 spell 691.1
 bad influence 1000.4
 v curse 513.5
 bewitch 691.9
 work evil 1000.6
 bring bad luck 1011.12
hexagonal
 pentagonal 278.10
 sixth 882.18
hey oh! 122.20
 greetings! 585.15
 howdy! 585.16
 hail! 983.23
HHH
 hot weather 1018.7
 hot 1019.25
hi greetings! 585.15
 hey! 983.23
hiatus interval 224.1
 opening 292.1
 deficiency 795.2
 interruption 813.2
hibernate
 aestivate 22.15
 do nothing 329.2
 lie idle 331.16
 be latent 519.3
hibernation sleep 22.2
 inactivity 331.1
hiccup
 n breathing 2.21
 belch 909.9
 v belch 909.28
hick
 n bungler 414.9
 simple soul 416.3

peasant 606.6
 oaf 924.5
 adj not urbane 233.8
hickey sore 85.37
 blemish 1004.1
 thing 1052.5
hicklike 233.8
hidden invisible 32.5
 secret 345.11
 concealed 346.11
 latent 519.5
 implied 519.7
 recondite 522.16
hidden agenda 375.1
hide
 n fur 4.2
 lamina 296.2
 v disappear 34.2
 conceal 346.6
 conceal oneself 346.8
 store up 386.11
 defeat 412.9
 punish 604.15
hideaway
 hiding place 346.4
 sanctum 584.6
 retreat 1009.5
hideous horrid 98.19
 terrible 127.30
 ugly 1015.11
hideout
 hiding place 346.4
 retreat 1009.5
hide out 346.8
hiding
 n covering 295.1
 concealment 346.1
 hiding place 346.4
 defeat 412.1
 punishment 604.5
 adj concealing 346.15
hiding place
 hideaway 346.4
 retreat 1009.5
hie speed 174.8
 travel 177.18
hiemal seasonal 313.9
 cold 1023.14
hierarchy
 rank 245.2
 mastership 417.7
 the authorities 575.15
 class 607.1
 government 612.4
 hierocracy 698.7
 continuity 807.2
 class structure 809.4
hieroglyphic
 representation 349.1
 phonetic symbol 546.2
higgledy-piggledy
 n jumble 810.3
 adj confused 810.16
 adv nonuniformly 782.4
 in disorder 810.17
high
 n stupor 22.6
 substance abuse 87.1
 intoxication 88.1
 excitement 105.1
 weather map 317.4

secondary school 567.4
 price 738.9
 gear 1040.9
 adj high-pitched 58.13
 nasty 64.7
 strong 68.8
 malodorous 71.5
 bent 87.24
 drunk 88.33
 overjoyed 95.17
 excited 105.20
 cheerful 109.11
 lofty 136.11
 spacious 158.11
 great 247.9
 high-reaching 272.14
 tainted 393.41
 phonetic 524.30
 noble 608.10
 expensive 632.11
 magnanimous 652.6
 eminent 662.18
 raised 912.9
 excessive 993.16
 adv on high 272.21
 intemperately 669.10
high and dry
 stuck 855.16
 in safety 1007.6
 stranded 1013.27
 dry 1066.7
high and low 158.13
high-and-mighty
 lordly 141.11
 eminent 662.18
highball
 n drink 88.9
 poker 759.10
 v speed 174.9
highborn
 upper-class 607.10
 wellborn 608.11
highbrow
 snob 141.7
 intellectual 929.1
high-class 999.14
high-definition television
 television 1035.1
 reception 1035.5
high dudgeon 152.7
higher-up
 superior 249.4
 politics 610.7
highest
 n supremacy 249.3
 adj top 198.10
 superlative 249.13
 higher 272.19
 almighty 677.17
 paramount 997.24
highfalutin
 n boasting 502.2
 bombast 545.2
 adj lofty 136.11
 arrogant 141.9
 ostentatious 501.18
 inflated 502.12
 grandiloquent 545.8
high-flown
 lofty 136.11
 arrogant 141.9

exaggerated 355.4
ostentatious 501.18
inflated 502.12
grandiloquent 545.8
absurd 923.11
high-flying
aspiring 100.28
ostentatious 501.18
grandiloquent 545.8
high frequency 1034.12
high-frequency 1034.28
high-handed 417.16
High Holy Day 20.4
high hopes 124.1
high horse 141.1
high jinks 743.4
highland
n highlands 237.1
uplands 272.3
adj rustic 233.6
upland 272.17
highlands
the country 233.1
high country 237
uplands 237.1
highland 272.3
high life
society 578.6
upper class 607.2
aristocracy 608.1
highlight
n feature 997.7
light 1025.1
v manifest 348.5
signify 517.17
specify 865.11
call attention to 983.10
emphasize 997.14
illuminate 1025.29
high-living 669.8
highly 247.15
high-maintenance 339.12
high-minded
lofty 136.11
honest 644.13
magnanimous 652.6
Highness 648.2
high on the hog
intemperately 669.10
prosperous 1010.12
high-pitched
strident 58.13
high 272.14
high point 997.6
high-powered
powerful 18.12
important 997.17
high pressure
inducement 375.3
coercion 424.3
importunity 440.3
urgency 997.4
high-pressure
v urge 375.14
coerce 424.8
adj powerful 18.12
climatal 317.13
urgent 997.22
high priest top dog 575.4
religious figure 699.9
high profile 31.2

high-profile 31.7
high-quality 999.14
high-rise 272.14
high school 567.4
high society
society 578.6
upper class 607.2
aristocracy 608.1
high-society
socially prominent 578.16
upper-class 607.10
high-spirited
excitable 105.28
mischievous 322.6
high standing 247.2
high-strung
excitable 105.28
touchy 110.21
nervous 128.11
hightail speed 174.9
run off 188.12
high tech 928.10
high-tech 928.28
high time fun 743.2
good opportunity 843.3
lateness 846.1
highway 383.5
highway interchange 170.2
highwayman 483.5
highway robbery
theft 482.3
overcharge 632.5
hijack coerce 424.7
rob 482.16
hike
n walk 177.10
go for a walk 177.29
increase 251.1
make larger 259.4
lift 912.2
v march 177.30
increase 251.4
enlarge 259.4
elevate 912.5
hike up
increase 251.4
make larger 259.4
hilarious merry 109.15
humorous 488.4
festive 743.28
hilarity
merriment 109.5
laughter 116.4
humorousness 488.1
hill
n down 237.4
plateau 272.4
bulge 283.3
baseball 745.1
pile 770.10
v pile 770.19
hillbilly
n wilderness settler 227.10
peasant 606.6
adj not urbane 233.8
hill of beans
zilch 762.3
trifle 998.5
hilly
rolling 237.8
knobby 272.18

hind
n female animal 77.9
hoofed animal 311.5
peasant 606.6
adj rear 217.9
hind end 217.1
hinder
v restrain 428.7
fend off 460.10
delay 846.8
impede 1012.10
adj rear 217.9
hindquarter 217.3
hindrance
restraint 428.1
delay 846.2
impediment 1012
hindering 1012.1
hindsight 989.3
Hindu
Christian Scientist 675.24
life principle 919.5
hinge
n joint 800.4
crisis 843.4
axle 915.5
v hook 800.8
depend 959.6
hinky 645.16
hint
n tinge 62.3
soupçon 248.4
remainder 256.1
warning 399.1
piece of advice 422.2
indication 517.3
clue 517.9
implication 519.2
gentle hint 551.4
admixture 797.7
suggestion 951.5
memory 989.5
v augur 133.11
promise 133.12
signify 517.17
imply 519.4
intimate 551.10
hinterland
n inland 207.3
setting 209.2
region 231.1
back country 233.2
adj inland 207.7
back 233.9
hip
n side 218.1
joint 800.4
adj fashionable 578.11
knowledgeable 928.17
hip hop 708.7
hippie
n nonconformist 868.3
adj unconventional 868.6
hippo
heavyweight 257.12
behemoth 257.14
pachyderm 311.4
Hippocratic oath 334.4
hippopotamus
behemoth 257.14
pachyderm 311.4

hire
n rental 615.6
pay 624.4
fee 630.6
v employ 615.14
rent 615.15
rent out 615.16
hireling
n mercenary 461.17
employee 577.3
adj employed 615.20
corruptible 645.23
hirsute hairy 3.24
feathery 3.27
bristly 288.9
nappy 294.7
his nibs 997.11
hiss
n sibilation 57.1
boo 508.3
speech defect 525.1
v sibilate 57.2
growl 60.4
bubble 320.4
boo 508.10
speak 524.25
hissing
n audio distortion 50.13
sibilation 57.1
ridicule 508.1
boo 508.3
adj sibilant 57.3
ridiculing 508.12
hist hark! 48.16
hey! 983.23
historian
annalist 550.2
cliometrician 719.4
historical
historic 719.7
fictional 722.7
real 761.15
obvious 970.15
true 973.13
historicity
reality 761.2
truth 973.1
historiography 719.1
history
n record 549.1
the investigation of the past
719
the historical discipline 719.1
the past 837.1
adj ruined 395.29
histrionic
emotionalistic 93.19
affected 500.15
theatrical 501.24
dramatic 704.33
hit
n dose 87.20
excitement 105.3
homicide 308.2
success 409.4
score 409.5
criticism 510.4
stage show 704.4
popular music 708.7
game 745.3
blackjack 759.11

blow 902.4
v impress 93.15
travel 177.19
arrive 186.6
contact 223.10
kill 308.14
beg 440.15
attack 459.14
criticize 510.14
swing 745.5
play 751.4
agree 788.6
collide 902.13
strike 902.14
shoot 904.12
impress 931.19
discover 941.2
hit and miss
n experiment 942.1
adj slipshod 340.12
carelessly 340.18
hit-and-run
v run over 910.7
adj dastardly 491.12
hit below the belt
n unfairness 650.2
v do wrong 650.6
hit bottom
base on 199.6
decline 393.17
be changed 852.6
hitch
n pang 26.2
gait 177.12
term 825.4
jerk 905.3
obstacle 1012.4
crux 1013.8
v way of walking 177.28
beat one's way 177.31
join in marriage 563.14
hook 800.8
jerk 905.5
tend 1070.7
hitchhike 177.31
hitchhiker 178.6
hitherto
previously 834.6
formerly 837.13
hit home 903.8
hit it big 1010.11
hit it off 587.9
hit list 871.1
hit man
killer 308.11
violent person 671.9
hit on
make advances 439.8
burlesque 508.11
come across 941.3
hit or miss
slipshod 340.12
carelessly 340.18
unordered 810.12
haphazardly 810.18
experimental 942.11
experimentally 942.13
vague 971.19
hitter 745.2
hit the books 570.12
hit the jackpot 409.9

hit the nail on the head
solve 940.2
be right 973.10
hit the road
wander 177.23
depart 188.7
hit the sack 22.18
hit the spot 95.7
hit up beg 440.15
borrow 621.3
hit upon arrive at 186.7
light upon 194.10
come across 941.3
**HIV or human
   immunodeficiency virus**
85.42
hive
n nest 228.25
hive of industry 739.2
assemblage 770.6
multitude 884.3
v settle 159.17
come together 770.16
hive mind
psyche 92.28
tradition 842.2
hives allergy 85.34
skin eruption 85.36
HIV-positive 85.61
hoar
n frost 1023.7
adj white 37.7
gray 39.4
gray-haired 39.5
aged 303.16
hoard
n store 386.1
gain 472.3
v store up 386.11
not use 390.5
hoarfrost 1023.7
hoarse raucous 58.15
inarticulate 525.12
hoary white 37.7
gray 39.4
gray-haired 39.5
aged 303.16
old 842.10
traditional 842.12
frosty 1023.17
hoax
n fake 354.13
deception 356.7
v deceive 356.14
hobble
n slow motion 175.2
gait 177.12
shackle 428.4
predicament 1013.5
v disable 19.10
go slow 175.6
way of walking 177.28
cripple 393.14
bind 428.10
hamper 1012.11
hobby
n avocation 724.7
adj avocational 724.17
hobbyhorse
n avocation 724.7
toy 743.16

v pitch 182.55
hobgoblin
frightener 127.9
goblin 680.8
Hobgoblin 680.7
hobnob with
associate with
   582.17
be friends 587.9
hobo
n vagabond 178.3
bum 331.9
beggar 440.8
wretch 660.2
transient 828.4
oddity 870.4
v wander 177.23
Hobson's choice
dilemma 371.3
restriction 428.3
choicelessness 963.6
certainty 970.1
hock
n leg 177.14
pledge 438.2
v pledge 438.10
hockey sports 749
ice hockey 749.1
hocus-pocus
n juggling 356.5
trick 356.6
nonsense 520.2
occultism 689.1
incantation 691.4
v deceive 356.14
trick 356.19
hodgepodge
miscellany 770.13
mix 797.6
jumble 810.3
hoe 1069.17
hog
n pig 80.13
drugs 87.18
swine 311.9
self-seeker 651.3
glutton 672.3
v monopolize 469.6
appropriate 480.19
hoggish
piggish 80.24
greedy 100.27
ungulate 311.45
monopolistic 469.11
gluttonous 672.6
hogpen 80.11
hogwash
humbug 354.14
refuse 391.4
bull 520.3
hog-wild 105.25
ho-hum dull 117.6
tedious 118.15
same 781.6
hoi polloi
inferior 250.2
the masses 606.2
hoist
n lift 912.2
lifter 912.3
v elevate 912.5

hoity-toity
n arrogance 141.1
adj arrogant 141.9
upper-class 607.10
interj my! 122.21
hokey
trite 117.9
imitation 336.8
hokum
humbug 354.14
bull 520.3
acting 704.8
hold
n basement197.17
storehouse 386.6
custody 429.5
stronghold 460.6
possession 469.1
purchase 474.2
seizure 480.2
control 612.2
notation 709.12
influence 894.1
footing 901.5
handle 901.11
purchase 906.2
v use 87.22
extend 158.9
refrain 329.3
affirm 334.5
store up 386.11
restrain 428.7
confine 429.12
possess 469.4
grip 474.6
keep 474.7
exist 761.8
include 772.3
cohere 803.6
endure 827.6
remain 853.5
stabilize 855.7
sustain 856.4
cease 857.6
support 901.21
obsess 926.25
judge 946.8
conclude 946.10
decide 946.11
think 953.11
be true 973.8
engross 983.13
suffice 991.4
hold a candle to
943.7
hold a grudge 152.12
hold back
suppress 106.8
slow 175.9
reserve 386.12
not use 390.5
restrain 428.7
deny 442.4
withhold 484.6
restrain oneself 668.6
abstain 668.7
delay 846.8
hinder 1012.10
hold down
suppress 428.8
subjugate 432.8

holder container 195.1
  possessor 470.1
  recipient 479.3
hold fast
  remain firm 359.9
  stay with it 360.4
  restrain 428.7
  hold 474.6
  stick close 803.8
  stand fast 855.11
hold forth offer 439.4
  declaim 543.10
  expound 568.16
hold in restrain 428.7
  retain 474.5
holding
  n possession 469.1
  estate 471.4
  retention 474.1
  share 738.3
  verdict 946.5
  adj addicted 87.25
  possessing 469.9
  retentive 474.8
  supporting 901.23
  obsessive 926.34
  engrossing 983.20
holdings
  supply 386.2
  property 471.1
  stock 738.2
  share 738.3
  collection 770.11
hold it! 857.13
hold off demur 325.4
  not use 390.5
  fend off 460.10
  postpone 846.9
  procrastinate 846.11
  repulse 908.3
hold office
  hold a post 609.42
  fill an office 724.14
  take one's turn 825.5
hold on
  v direct 161.5
  stay with it 360.4
  hold 474.6
  trade 737.23
  cohere 803.6
  endure 827.6
  wait 846.12
  continue 856.3
  interj cease! 857.13
hold out
  not weaken 15.10
  remain firm 359.9
  stay with it 360.4
  balk 361.7
  offer 439.4
  resist 453.2
  stand fast 453.4
  strike 727.10
  endure 827.6
  stand fast 855.11
holdover
  remainder 256.1
  officeholder 610.11
hold together
  cooperate 450.3
  agree 788.6

join 800.11
  cohere 803.6
  be true 973.8
holdup slowing 175.4
  theft 482.3
  overcharge 632.5
  delay 846.2
  hindrance 1012.1
  time constants 1041.11
hold up
  not weaken 15.10
  slow 175.9
  buoy 298.8
  stay with it 360.4
  restrain 428.7
  help 449.12
  resist 453.2
  rob 482.14
  flaunt 501.17
  overprice 632.7
  delay 846.8
  postpone 846.9
  stand fast 855.11
  support 901.21
  elevate 912.5
  stand the test 942.10
  be true 973.8
  hinder 1012.10
hole
  n sty 80.11
  atmosphere 184.32
  compartment 197.2
  basement 197.17
  crack 224.2
  hovel 228.11
  lair 228.26
  disapproved place 228.28
  small space 258.3
  pit 275.2
  cavity 284.2
  cave 284.5
  opening 292.1
  perforation 292.3
  hiding place 346.4
  score 409.5
  sewer 654.7
  golf 751.1
  deficiency 795.2
  fault 1003.2
  impasse 1013.6
  v perforate 292.15
the hole 429.8
hole in one
  score 409.5
  round 751.3
hole-in-the-wall
  nook 197.3
  hut 228.9
  small space 258.3
holiday
  n vacation 20.3
  day off 20.4
  absence 222.4
  celebration 487.1
  interim 826.1
  pause 857.3
  v vacation 20.9
  adj vacational 20.10
holier-than-thou
  hypocritical 354.33
  sanctimonious 693.5

holistic whole 792.9
  universal 864.14
holler
  n cry 59.1
  complaint 115.5
  valley 237.7
  v cry 59.6
  complain 115.16
  object 333.5
hollow
  n compartment 197.2
  valley 237.7
  pit 275.2
  cavity 284.2
  opening 292.1
  v be concave 284.12
  hollow out 284.13
  adj deep 54.11
  dull 117.6
  vacant 222.14
  concave 284.16
  insincere 354.32
  vain 391.13
  empty-headed 922.19
  sophistical 936.10
holly 44.4
holocaust
  torment 96.7
  slaughter 308.1
  butchery 308.3
  destruction 395.1
  oblation 696.7
the Holocaust 308.4
holograph
  n autograph 337.3
  handwriting 547.3
  writing 547.10
  document 549.5
  adj written 547.22
holy almighty 677.17
  sacred 685.7
  godly 692.9
holy cow 122.19
holy orders
  the ministry 698.1
  calling 698.10
  major orders 699.4
  seven sacraments 701.4
holy table 703.12
holy terror
  frightener 127.9
  brat 302.4
  ruffian 593.4
  violent person 671.10
homage respect 155.1
  obeisance 155.2
  obedience 326.1
  submission 433.1
  praise 509.5
  duty 641.1
  fidelity 644.7
  worship 696.1
home
  n home sweet home 228.2
  habitat 228.18
  fatherland 232.2
  asylum 1009.4
  adj residential 228.32
  in safety 1007.6
home economics
  cooking 11.1

domestic management 573.6
home free 1007.6
the home front 232.2
homeland 232.2
homeless
  n poor man 619.4
  adj unplaced 160.10
  forlorn 584.12
  destitute 619.9
  alone 872.8
the homeless
  the underprivileged 606.4
  the poor 619.3
  unfortunate 1011.7
homely
  comfortable 121.11
  humble 137.10
  homelike 228.33
  common 497.14
  plain 499.6
  plain-speaking 535.3
  informal 581.3
  populational 606.8
  simple 798.6
  ugly 1015.6
homemade 892.18
homemaker 575.2
home office room 197.6
  home workplace 739.8
homeopathic 90.15
homeopathy 90.13
homeowner 227.7
home plate 745.1
homer
  n mail carrier 353.6
  score 409.5
  game 745.3
  v play 745.5
Homeric huge 257.20
  poetic 720.15
homeroom 208.6
home run score 409.5
  game 745.3
home schooling elementary
    school 567.3
  teaching 568.1
  elementary education 568.5
home shopping purchase 733.1
  marketplace 736.2
homesick
  wistful 100.23
  melancholy 112.23
homespun
  n plain speech 535.1
  adj rough 288.6
  natural 416.6
  common 497.14
  plain 499.6
  plain-speaking 535.3
  simple 798.6
  made 892.18
homestead home 228.2
  farm 1069.8
homesteader
  settler 227.9
  tenant 470.4
homestretch 820.3
homestyle 892.18
homeward
  adj arriving 186.9
  adv clockwise 161.24

horde
  n the masses 606.2
  throng 770.4
  v come together 770.16
horizon vision 27.1
  field of view 31.3
  skyline 201.4
  the distance 261.3
horizontal
  n plane 201.3
  adj level 201.7
  straight 277.6
hormone 13.2
horn
  n loudspeaker 50.8
  noisemaker 53.6
  mountain 237.6
  projection 285.4
  telephone 347.4
  alarm 400.1
  wind instrument 711.6
  saddle parts 901.18
  v gore 459.26
horndog 75.16
horned
  crescent-shaped 279.11
  pointed 285.9
hornet 311.34
hornet's nest
  nest 228.25
  danger 1006.1
  trouble 1013.3
horn in 214.5
horns of a dilemma
  n bewilderment 971.3
  dilemma 1013.7
  adv uncertainly 971.28
hornswoggler 358.2
horny lustful 75.27
  pointed 285.9
  lascivious 665.29
  hard 1046.10
horology 832.1
horoscope 1072.20
horrendous
  horrid 98.19
  terrible 127.30
horrible
  horrid 98.19
  terrible 127.30
  remarkable 247.11
  bad 1000.9
  hideous 1015.11
horrid horrible 98.19
  terrible 127.30
  bad 1000.9
  hideous 1015.11
horrific horrid 98.19
  terrible 127.30
horrified 127.26
horrify offend 98.11
  terrify 127.17
horrifying horrid 98.19
  terrible 127.30
horripilation
  trepidation 127.5
  roughness 288.2
  cold 1023.2
horror
  torment 96.7
  hostility 99.2

  fear 127.1
  frighteningness 127.2
  frightener 127.9
  abomination 638.2
  eyesore 1015.4
horror-stricken 127.26
hors d'oeuvre bite 8.2
  appetizer 10.9
  sample 62.4
horse
  n symbol of strength 15.8
  heroin 87.9
  beast of burden 176.8
  horseflesh 311.10
  exerciser 725.7
  jockey 757.2
  trestle 901.16
  v give a lift 912.7
horse around
  misbehave 322.4
  play 743.23
  create disorder 810.11
  be foolish 923.6
  trifle 998.15
horseback
  n ridge 237.5
  adv on horseback 177.44
  astride 901.25
horseback riding 177.6
horse-drawn 177.44
horsehair
  hair 3.2
  string 711.20
horseman 178.8
horsemanship
  riding 177.6
  skill 413.1
  animal husbandry 1070.1
horse of a different color 780.3
horseplay
  misbehavior 322.1
  buffoonery 489.5
horsepower 18.4
horse race
  contest 457.3
  challenge 457.12
  election 609.15
  race 757.3
horse-race 457.19
horse racing
  the sport of kings 757
  the turf 757.1
horse sense 920.6
horseshoe 279.5
horse whisperer 90.7
hortatory
  persuasive 375.29
  advisory 422.8
  educational 568.18
horticultural
  floral 310.38
  olericultural 1069.21
horticulture
  flower 310.24
  gardening 1069.2
hosanna
  n cheer 116.2
  paean 696.3
  interj hallelujah! 696.17
hose
  n hosiery 5.28

  tube 239.6
  v deceive 356.19
  moisten 1065.12
hosiery 5.28
hosing deception 356.9
  wetting 1065.6
hospice inn 228.15
  asylum 1009.4
hospitable
  comforting 121.13
  receptive 187.16
  liberal 485.4
  sociable 582.22
  welcoming 585.11
  cordial 587.16
hospital 91.21
hospitality
  comfortableness 121.2
  receptivity 187.9
  housing 225.3
  liberality 485.1
  sociability 582.1
  cordiality 585.1
  hospitableness 585.1
  congeniality 587.6
hospitalize 85.50
host
  n army 461.23
  receptionist 585.5
  master of ceremonies 743.20
  throng 770.4
  group of animals 770.5
  multitude 884.3
  broadcaster 1034.23
  v entertain 585.8
Host 701.7
hostage 438.2
hostel 228.15
hostess crew 185.4
  attendant 577.5
  waiter 577.7
  host 585.5
hostile dark 38.9
  unpleasant 98.17
  oppositional 451.8
  warlike 458.20
  antagonistic 589.10
  contrary 779.6
  disagreeing 789.6
  counteractive 900.8
  adverse 1011.13
  dislike 99.8
hostility darkness 38.2
  bad feeling 93.7
  unpleasantness 98.1
  malice 99.2
  contraposition 215.1
  antagonism 451.2
  contention 457.1
  warlikeness 458.10
  hate 589.3
  contrariety 779.1
hot
  v heat 1020.17
  adj red 41.6
  zestful 68.7
  lustful 75.27
  in heat 75.28
  feverish 85.58
  fervent 93.18
  zealous 101.9

  passionate 105.22
  hot-tempered 110.25
  angry 152.30
  near 223.14
  fugitive 368.16
  stolen 482.23
  distinguished 662.16
  lascivious 665.29
  fiery 671.22
  syncopated 709.29
  speculative 759.27
  brand-new 841.10
  on the right scent 941.10
  excellent 999.13
  torrid 1019.25
  heated 1020.29
  charged 1032.34
  radioactive 1037.11
hot air boasting 502.2
  bull 520.3
  chatter 540.3
  bombast 545.2
  superheated air 1019.9
hot-air balloon 181.11
hot-air balloonist 185.7
hot and humid 1019.25
hotbed birthplace 886.8
  productiveness 890.6
  nursery 1069.11
hot-blooded
  lustful 75.27
  zealous 101.9
  warm-blooded 1019.29
hot dirt 551.2
hot dog
  n show-off 501.11
  v grandstand 413.20
  showboat 501.16
  interj oh boy ! 95.21
hotel 228.15
hotfooting 401.3
hotheaded
  passionate 105.29
  hot-tempered 110.25
  reckless 493.8
  fiery 671.22
hothouse 1069.11
hot key 1042.18
hot line
  telephone call 347.13
  line 347.17
hot poop 551.2
hot pot 10.11
hot seat
  capital punishment 604.7
  execution 605.5
  predicament 1013.5
hot spot
  entertainment 743.13
  danger 1006.1
  predicament 1013.5
hot spring
  health resort 91.23
  hot water 1019.10
hottie
  sex object 75.4
  doll 1016.7
hot tip 551.2
hot tub bath 79.8
  fitness 84.1

hot under the collar
  heated 105.22
  angry 152.30
hot water
  predicament 1013.5
  boiling water 1019.10
hound
  n enthusiast 101.5
  beast 660.6
  v annoy 96.13
  make anxious 126.5
  follow 166.3
  pursue 382.8
  hunt 382.9
  persecute 389.7
hour period 824.1
  moment 824.2
  time of day 832.2
  the present 838.1
hourglass 260.1
hourglass figure 260.1
house
  n audience 48.6
  cabin 197.9
  dwelling 228.5
  structure 266.2
  council 423.1
  race 559.4
  family 559.5
  lineage 560.4
  company 617.9
  cloister 703.6
  theater 704.14
  market 736.1
  workplace 739.1
  casino 759.19
  attender 918.2
  astrology 1072.20
  v domicile 225.10
  accommodate 385.10
house arrest arrest 429.6
  form of punishment 604.2
houseboat 228.5
housebound 331.18
housebreak
  accustom 373.9
  domesticate 432.11
  train 568.13
housebreaker 483.3
housebreaking
  habituation 373.7
  burglary 482.5
  training 568.3
housebroken
  accustomed 373.15
  subdued 432.15
  meek 433.15
  mannerly 504.16
household
  n home 228.2
  family 559.5
  adj residential 228.32
  simple 499.6
  usual 869.9
  well-known 928.27
household effects
  furniture 229.1
  property 471.1
householder
  homeowner 227.7
  proprietor 470.2

housekeeper
  steward 574.4
  major-domo 577.10
housekeeping
  domesticity 228.3
  domestic management
    573.6
house of cards
  weakness 16.1
  danger 1006.1
  fragility 1050.2
houseplant 310.3
house-poor 619.7
housewares 735.4
housewarming 770.2
housewife 575.2
housing
  n hangar 184.24
  domiciliation 225.3
  abode 228.1
  quarters 228.4
  cover 295.2
  horsecloth 295.11
  radio 1034.3
  adj constructional 892.15
hovel sty 80.11
  dump 228.11
hover fly 184.36
  take off 193.10
  levitate 298.9
  hesitate 362.7
  be imminent 840.2
Hovercraft
  hovercar 179.22
  flying platform 181.7
how 384.9
how come 888.8
howdah 901.17
how do you do? 585.15
how-do-you-do
  greeting 585.4
  predicament 1013.5
however
  notwithstanding 338.8
  anyhow 384.10
howl
  n noise 53.3
  screech 58.4
  cry 59.1
  animal noise 60.1
  lament 115.3
  complaint 115.5
  objection 333.2
  v screech 58.8
  cry 59.6
  grunt 60.2
  wail 115.13
  complain 115.16
  sigh 318.20
  object 333.5
howler joke 489.6
  goof 975.6
howling
  n audio distortion 50.13
  animal noise 60.1
  lamentation 115.1
  adj shrill 58.14
  yowling 60.6
  frenzied 105.25
  plaintive 115.19
  remarkable 247.11

hoyden
  n mannish female 76.9
  schoolgirl 302.8
  adj mannish 76.14
hub convergence 169.1
  center 208.2
  axle 915.5
  fireplace 1020.11
hubba hubba! 95.21
hubbub noise 53.3
  outcry 59.4
  bustle 330.4
  turbulence 671.2
  commotion 810.4
  agitation 917.1
  argumentation 935.4
hubris
  presumptuousness 141.2
  insolence 142.1
  rashness 493.1
  presumption 640.2
  confidence 970.5
hubristic lordly 141.11
  insolent 142.9
  rash 493.7
  presumptuous 640.11
  confident 970.21
  excessive 993.16
huckster
  n publicist 352.9
  vendor 730.5
  v bargain 731.18
  vend 734.9
huddle
  n conference 541.5
  v stay near 223.12
  come together 770.16
hue
  n color 35.1
  color quality 35.6
  nature 767.4
  v color 35.14
hue and cry noise 53.3
  outcry 59.4
  publicity 352.4
  pursuit 382.1
  alarm 400.1
huff
  n dudgeon 152.7
  v intimidate 127.20
  provoke 152.24
  enlarge 259.4
  blow 318.19
huffing 2.32
huffy irascible 110.20
  provoked 152.27
hug
  n hold 474.2
  embrace 562.3
  welcome 585.2
  greeting 585.4
  v stay near 223.12
  hold 474.6
  harbor 474.7
  seize 480.14
  embrace 562.18
  welcome 585.9
  cohere 803.6
huge
  herculean 15.17
  large 247.7

  immense 257.20
hula hoop 743.16
hulk ship 180.1
  largeness 257.11
  wreck 393.8
  body 1052.3
hulking bulky 257.19
  bungling 414.20
  unwieldy 1013.19
hull
  n ship 180.1
  shell 295.16
  seed vessel 310.30
  v husk 6.9
hullabaloo noise
    53.4
  outcry 59.4
  bustle 330.4
hullo! 585.15
hum
  n audio distortion 50.13
  humming 52.7
  vocal music 708.13
  series 812.2
  v thrum 52.13
  stammer 525.8
  sing 708.38
  persist 781.3
human
  n person 312.5
  adj kind 143.13
  pitying 145.7
  hominal 312.13
human behavior 321.3
human being 312.5
hum and haw
  prevaricate 344.7
  hesitate 362.7
  stammer 525.8
humane kind 143.13
  pitying 145.7
  lenient 427.7
human engineering 717.5
human error 975.1
human factors engineering
    717.5
humanism
  naturalistic humanism
    312.11
  freethinking 695.7
  scholarship 928.5
humanist
  freethinker 695.13
  scholar 929.3
humanitarian
  n philanthropist 143.8
  adj benevolent 143.15
humanity
  kindness 143.1
  pity 145.1
  humankind 312.1
  human nature 312.6
  humanness 312.8
  leniency 427.1
humankind
  human race 312.1
  mankind 312.1
human nature
  humanity 312.6
  humanness 312.8
human race 312.1

humble
v humiliate 137.4
conquer 412.10
subdue 432.9
demote 447.3
adj penitent 113.9
resigned 134.10
lowly 137.10
modest 139.9
inferior 250.6
meek 433.15
populational 606.8
unselfish 652.5

humbled
penitent 113.9
reduced 137.13
humiliated 137.14
conquered 412.17
subdued 432.15

humbug
n sham 354.3
quackery 354.7
humbuggery 354.14
hoax 356.7
impostor 357.6
nonsense 520.2
v deceive 356.14

humdinger 999.7

humdrum
n tedium 118.1
repetitiousness 849.4
adj tedious 118.9
prosaic 721.5
same 781.6
monotonous 849.15

humectant 1065.18

humid sultry 1019.28
moist 1065.15

humidifier 1065.3

humidify 1065.12

humidity
sultriness 1019.6
humidness 1065.2

humiliate
mortify 98.13
humble 137.4
offend 156.5
subdue 432.9
demote 447.3
disgrace 661.8

humiliating
mortifying 98.21
humiliative 137.15
insulting 156.8
disgraceful 661.11

humiliation
chagrin 96.4
mortification 98.6
embarrassment 137.2
indignity 156.2
snub 157.2
subdual 432.4
demotion 447.1
disgrace 661.5

humility
resignation 134.2
humbleness 137.1
selflessness 137.1
modesty 139.1
inferiority 250.1
meekness 433.5

unselfishness 652.1

hummock 237.4

hummocky 283.15

humongous
remarkable 247.10
huge 257.20

humor
n lymph 2.24
blood 2.25
personality tendency 92.11
caprice 364.1
pleasantry 489.1
wit 489.1
nature 767.4
disposition 978.3
mood 978.4
moisture 1065.1
v indulge 427.6

humorist wit 489.12
writer 547.15
author 718.4

humorless 112.21

humorous funny 488.4
witty 489.15
amusing 743.27

hump
n mountain 237.6
bulge 283.3
v speed 174.9
curve 279.6
be active 330.14
make haste 401.6
exert oneself 725.9

humpbacked
hunchbacked 265.13
bowed 279.10

hun 395.8

hunch
n feeling 93.1
premonition 133.1
bulge 283.3
forewarning 399.2
sense 934.3
guess 951.4
suggestion 951.5
v curve 279.6
crouch 913.8

hunchbacked 265.13

hunch over 913.8

hundred region 231.5
century 882.8

hung 202.9

hunger
n eating 8.1
craving 100.6
appetite 100.7
tendency 896.1
v eat 8.20
hunger for 100.19

hung jury 596.6

hungry
craving 100.24
hungering 100.25

hungry ghost 100.6

hung up
distressed 96.22
late 846.16
obsessed 926.33

hunk strong man 15.6
hulk 15.7
real man 76.6

amount 244.2
lump 257.10
accumulation 770.9
piece 793.3

hunker down 913.8

hunky strong 15.15
virile 76.13
comely 1016.18

hunky-dory 999.13

hunt
n hunting 382.2
search 938.15
v pursue 382.8
go hunting 382.9
persecute 389.7
seek 938.30
search 938.30

hunter
stalking-horse 311.13
sporting dog 311.17
pursuer 382.4
huntsman 382.5
shooter 904.8
seeker 938.18

hunt for 938.29

hunting
n pursuit 382.1
gunning 382.2
search 938.15
adj pursuing 382.11

hurdle
n leap 366.1
obstacle 1012.4
v leap 366.5

hurdy-gurdy 711.14

hurl
n throw 904.3
v feel disgust 99.4
put violently 159.13
throw 904.10

hurler
baseball team 745.2
thrower 904.7

hurling
field hockey 749.4
throwing 904.2

hurly-burly
excitement 105.4
agitation 917.1

hurrah
n cry 59.1
cheer 116.2
v cheer 116.6
interj bravo! 509.22

hurricane
outburst 105.9
windstorm 318.11
storm 671.4

hurried
hasty 401.9
rushed 401.11
reckless 493.8

hurry
n agitation 105.4
velocity 174.1
haste 401.1
v move 172.5
speed 174.8
hasten 401.4
make haste 401.5

hurry up
v accelerate 174.10
hasten 401.4
make haste 401.5
interj make haste! 401.16

hurt
n pain 26.1
discomfort 96.5
impairment 393.1
disadvantage 996.2
evil 1000.3
v pain 26.7
anguish 26.8
afflict 96.17
suffer 96.19
offend 152.21
impair 393.9
injure 393.13
collide 902.13
work evil 1000.6
adj pained 26.9
in pain 26.23
impaired 393.27

hurting
n pain 26.1
impairment 393.1
adj pained 26.9
painful 26.10

hurtle
speed 174.8
thrust 902.12
collide 902.13

hurt one's feelings
pain 96.17
offend 152.21

husband
n married man 563.7
master 575.1
v reserve 386.12
economize 635.4

husband and wife 563.9

husbandry
direction 573.1
domestic management 573.6
thrift 635.1
agriculture 1069.1

hush
n silence 51.1
sibilation 57.1
v fall silent 51.7
silence 51.8
sibilate 57.2
cover up 345.8
calm 670.7
interj silence! 51.14

hushed
silent 51.10
quiescent 173.12
secret 345.11
restrained 670.11

hush-hush
v silence 51.8
cover up 345.8
adj secret 345.11

hush money
bribe 378.2
fee 624.5

husk
n hull 295.16
seed vessel 310.30
v hull 6.9

husky
n beast of burden 176.8
adj strong 15.15
raucous 58.15

hussy
impudent person 142.5
strumpet 665.14

hustle
n enterprise 330.7
haste 401.1
thrust 902.2
v drive 330.13
deceive 356.19
hasten 401.4
make haste 401.5
work hard 725.13
thrust 902.12
shake 917.11

hustler speeder 174.5
man of action 330.8
cheater 357.4
prostitute 665.16
gambler 759.22

hut 228.9

hutch
n hut 228.9
storehouse 386.6
v store 386.10

Hyades nymph 678.9
star 1072.8

hyaline
n the heavens 1072.2
adj glass 1029.5

hybrid
n hybrid word 526.11
crossbreed 797.8
adj mongrel 797.15

hydrant
fire hydrant 239.12
extinguisher 1022.3

hydrate 1060.8

hydraulic
hydrologic 1039.11
watery 1065.16

hydraulics
fluid dynamics 1039.4
liquid 1061.2

hydrodynamics
flow 238.4
hydraulics 1039.4

hydroelectric 1032.30

hydroelectric power
energy 17.1
manpower 18.4
renewable energy 1021.7
electric power 1032.18

hydrogenate
chemicalize 1060.8
vaporize 1067.8

hydrogen bomb 1038.16

hydrologic 1039.11

hydrology 1039.4

hydrolysis 806.2

hydrolytic
chemical terms 806.6
electrolytic 1032.32

hydromechanic 1039.11

hydrometer
density 1045.8
flowmeter 1061.3

hydrometric 1039.11

hydrophobia
disease 85.41
rabies 926.6

hydroplane
n seaplane 181.8
v fly 184.36

hydrops 85.9

hydrosphere
ocean 240.1
water 1065.3

hydrostatic 1039.11

hydrous 1065.16

hyena fox 311.19
savage 593.5
beast 660.6

hygiene
sanitation 79.3
hygienics 81.2

hygienic
sanitary 79.27
healthful 81.5

hygienist 81.3

hygrology 1065.9

hygrometer
weather instrument 317.8
moisture 1065.10

hygroscopic 1065.19

hymen membrane 2.6
wedding 563.3

hymn
n thanks 150.2
paean 696.3
sacred music 708.17
v glorify 696.12
sing 708.38

hymnal
n score 708.28
adj vocal 708.50

hymnist 710.20

hype
n commendation 509.3
v urge 375.14
commend 509.11

hyper
overwrought 105.26
overactive 330.24

hyperactive 330.24

hyperbola 279.2

hyperbole
misrepresentation 350.1
exaggeration 355.1
excess 993.1

hyperborean
northern 161.14
out-of-the-way 261.9
cold 1023.14

hypercritical
overfastidious 495.12
critical 510.23

Hyperion
beauty 1016.9
sun 1072.14

hyperkinetic 330.24

hypersensitive
sensitive 24.12
touchy 110.21
overfastidious 495.12

hypersensitivity
sensitivity 24.3
touchiness 110.5
overfastidiousness 495.4

hypertension
symptom 85.9
cardiovascular disease 85.19

hypertext 1042.2

hyperthermia 85.7

hypertrophy
n oversize 257.5
excess 993.1
v grow 14.2
expand 259.7

hyphenate
grammaticize 530.16

hypnosis
mesmeric sleep 22.7
trance 691.3

hypnotherapy 92.6

hypnotic
n sleep-inducer 22.10
adj sleep-inducing 22.23
hypnoid 22.24
sedative 86.45
alluring 377.8
engrossing 983.20

hypnotism 22.8

hypnotist 22.9

hypnotize
put to sleep 22.20
fascinate 377.7
cast a spell 691.7
have influence 894.11
engross 983.13

hypnotized
wondering 122.9
enchanted 691.12
gripped 983.18

hypochondria
unhealthiness 85.3
hypochondriasis 112.4

hypochondriac
neurotic 92.39
dejected 112.22

hypocrisy
hypocriticalness 354.6
deceit 356.3
affectation 500.1
sanctimony 693.1
doubleness 873.1

hypocrite
imitator 336.4
phony 357.8
pietist 693.3

hypocritical
canting 354.33
pretexted 376.5
assumed 500.16
two 873.6
sanctimonious 693.5

hypodermic
n inoculation 91.16
needle 285.3
adj cutaneous 2.27

hypodermis 2.4

hypostasis
noun 530.5
embodiment 763.4
essence 767.2
matter 1052.2

hypostatize 763.5

hypotension 85.9

hypothecate
pledge 438.10

theorize 951.9

hypothermia
heat 1019.1
refrigeration anesthesia 1024.2

hypothesis
premise 935.7
theory 951.1
supposition 951.2

hypothesize
reason 935.15
theorize 951.9

hypothetical
dialectic 935.22
theoretical 951.13

hysteresis
magnetism 1032.7
time constants 1041.11

hysteria 105.8

hysteric neurotic 92.39
emotionalistic 93.19
overzealous 101.12

hysterical
emotionalistic 93.19
overzealous 101.12
frenzied 105.25
humorous 488.5

hysteron proteron
jumble 810.3
specious argument 936.3

I self 865.5
one 872.3

iambic 720.16

ibid 778.9

ice
n glace 10.47
amphetamines 87.4
smoothness 287.3
jewelry 498.5
frozen water 1023.5
coolant 1024.7
fragility 1050.2
v top 198.9
kill 308.14
play 749.7
hail 1023.11
refrigerate 1024.10
freeze 1024.11
adj frozen 1024.14

iceberg 1023.5

icebox 1024.4

icebox cookie 10.43

icebreaker 180.6

ice cloud 319.2

ice-cold cold 1023.14
frozen 1024.14

ice cream 10.47

ice-cream float 10.47

ice cubes ice 1023.5
coolant 1024.7

iced prearranged 965.8
assured 970.20
cooled 1024.13

ice hockey 749.1

ice pack ice 1023.5
cooler 1024.3

ice rink 749.1

ice sculpture 715.1

ice-skate 177.35

ice skates 179.21

I Ching 962.2

imbibe
drink 8.29
tipple 88.24
ingest 187.11
receive 187.13
absorb 570.7
imbricate
v overlie 295.30
adj overlying 295.36
imbroglio
quarrel 456.5
predicament 1013.4
imbrue
imbue 797.11
soak 1065.13
imbue color 35.14
pervade 221.7
inspire 375.20
inculcate 568.12
imbrue 797.11
soak 1065.13
imbuement
permeation 221.3
inculcation 568.2
impregnation 797.2
soaking 1065.7
imitate
copy 336.5
adopt 621.4
resemble 784.7
repeat 849.7
imitation
n reproduction 78.1
copying 336
simulation 336.1
re-creation 336.3
impersonation 349.4
fake 354.13
burlesque 508.6
adoption 621.2
similarity 784.1
copy 785.1
repetition 849.1
substitute 862.2
duplication 874.1
adj mock 336.8
spurious 354.26
similar 784.10
substitute 862.8
immaculate
clean 79.25
honest 644.13
virtuous 653.6
spotless 657.7
chaste 664.4
perfect 1002.6
immanence
presence 221.1
intrinsicality 767.1
immanent
present 221.12
intrinsic 767.7
immaterial
unreal 762.9
unsubstantial 764.5
irrelevant 776.7
disembodied 988.8
insignificant 998.17
nonmaterial 1053.7
immateriality
invisibility 32.1

rarity 299.1
unsubstantiality 764.1
unrelatedness 776.1
illusoriness 976.2
specter 988.1
unimportance 998.1
incorporealness 1053.1
immaterialness 1053.1
incorporeal 1053.2
immaterialize
spiritualize 689.20
dematerialize 1053.6
immature
unadult 301.10
unripe 406.11
inexperienced 414.17
incomplete 795.4
new 841.7
puerile 922.24
half-learned 930.14
imperfect 1003.4
immaturity
youthfulness 301.3
undevelopment 406.4
inexperience 414.2
incompleteness 795.1
newness 841.1
puerility 922.11
unwiseness 923.2
imperfection 1003.1
immeasurable
large 247.7
infinite 823.3
innumerable 884.10
immediacy
presence 221.1
nearness 223.1
instantaneousness 830.1
promptness 845.3
urgent need 963.4
immediate
adj present 221.12
adjacent 223.16
nearest 223.19
hasty 401.9
continuous 812.8
instantaneous 830.4
the present 838.2
imminent 840.3
prompt 845.9
interj make haste!
　401.16
immediate family 559.2
immemorial
perpetual 829.7
former 837.10
old 842.10
traditional 842.12
immense large 247.7
huge 257.20
infinite 823.3
superb 999.15
immensity
greatness 247.1
hugeness 257.7
infinity 823.1
immerge 367.7
immerse
submerge 367.7
baptize 701.17
engross 983.13

immersed
underwater 275.13
soaked 1065.17
immersion
submergence 367.2
baptism 701.6
engrossment 983.3
wetting 1065.6
immersive 367.9
immigrant
migrant 178.5
incomer 189.4
citizen 227.4
settler 227.9
newcomer 774.4
immigrate
migrate 177.22
in-migrate 189.11
immigration
migration 177.4
in-migration 189.3
imminence
expectation 130.1
approach 167.1
threat 514.1
the future 839.1
forthcomingness
　840.1
impendence 840.1
imminent
expected 130.13
approaching 167.4
threatening 514.3
future 839.8
impending 840.3
immobile
motionless 173.13
passive 329.6
permanent 853.7
immovable 855.15
immobility
motionlessness 173.2
inaction 329.1
inactivity 331.1
permanence 853.1
immovability 855.3
immoderate
unrestrained 430.24
overpriced 632.12
intemperate 669.7
violent 671.16
excessive 993.16
immodest
conceited 140.11
unmodest 666.6
immolate 308.13
immolation
killing 308.1
oblation 696.7
immoral
dishonest 645.16
vice-prone 654.11
immorality 654.1
immortal
n celebrity 662.9
god 678.2
adj peerless 249.15
eminent 662.18
almighty 677.17
everlasting 829.9
indestructible 855.18

immortality
life 306.1
posthumous fame 662.7
eternal life 829.3
indestructibility 855.5
immortalize
glorify 662.13
chronicle 719.5
perpetuate 829.5
immovable
unfeeling 94.9
firm 359.12
unyielding 361.9
unmovable 855.15
inflexible 1046.12
immune
resistant 83.14
exempt 430.30
safe 1007.4
immunity
resistance 83.4
immunization 91.15
pardon 148.2
freedom 430.8
exemption 601.2
privilege 642.2
safety 1007.1
immunization
immunity 83.4
immunization therapy 91.15
immunize 91.28
immunology 91.15
immure
enclose 212.6
confine 429.12
imprison 429.14
immured
enclosed 212.10
jailed 429.21
immutable
persevering 360.8
unyielding 361.9
almighty 677.17
uniform 781.5
durable 827.10
permanent 853.7
unchangeable 855.17
inflexible 1046.12
imp
n brat 302.4
mischief-maker 322.3
fairy 678.8
pixie 680.7
member 793.4
v graft 191.6
impact
n power 18.1
meaning 518.1
concussion 671.8
force 887.2
striking force 902
collision 902.3
rocket launching 1074.9
v thrust in 191.7
cause 886.10
operate on 889.6
collide 902.13
impacted 855.16
impair
v subtract 255.9
damage 393.9

work evil 1000.6
adj sole 872.9
numeric 1017.23

impaired
damaged 393.27
imperfect 1003.4

impaired hearing 49.1

impaired vision 28.1

impairment
reduction 255.2
damage 393.1
flaw 393.1
disintegration 806.1
disadvantage 996.2
imperfection 1003.1

impale torture 96.18
perforate 292.15
stab 459.25
punish 604.16
stigmatize 661.9

impalpable
infinitesimal 258.14
unsubstantial 764.5
powdery 1051.11
immaterial 1053.7

impanel
record 549.15
select a jury 598.16
list 871.8

impanelment
registration 549.14
jury selection 598.4

impart transfer 176.10
communicate 343.7
disclose 351.4
give 478.12
say 524.22

impartable
transferable 176.18
communicable 343.11
giveable 478.23

impartial
neutral 467.7
impersonal 649.9
unprejudiced 979.12

impartiality
neutrality 467.1
detachment 649.3
moderation 670.1
unprejudicedness 979.5

imparting 343.2

impasse
obstruction 293.3
the same 790.3
corner 1013.6

impassion
excite 105.12
incite 375.17

impassioned
fervent 93.18
zealous 101.9
amorous 104.25
excited 105.20
vehement 544.13

impassive
unfeeling 94.9
inexcitable 106.10
quiescent 173.12
reticent 344.10
inexpressive 522.20
stable 855.12

incurious 982.3

impatience
eagerness 101.1
restlessness 135.1
anxiety 135.1
impulsiveness 365.2

impatient
eager 101.8
anxious 135.6
impulsive 365.9

impeach
censure 510.13
arraign 598.15
accuse 599.7

impeachable
blameworthy 510.25
guilty 656.3

impeachment
deposal 447.2
censure 510.3
arraignment 598.3
accusation 599.1

impeccable
spotless 657.7
accurate 973.16
perfect 1002.6

impecunious 619.7

impedance 1032.13

impede
slow 175.9
delay 846.8
hinder 1012.10
hamper 1012.11

impediment
obstruction 293.3
hindrance 1012.1
embarrassment 1012.6

impedimenta
freight 176.6
equipment 385.4
luggage 471.3
impediment 1012.6

impel
set in motion 172.6
motivate 375.12
compel 424.4
give an impetus 902.11
push 904.9
obsess 926.25

impelling
moving 172.7
motivating 375.25
impellent 902.23
obsessive 926.34

impend
be as expected 130.10
overhang 202.7
be imminent 840.2

impending
overhanging 202.11
imminent 840.3

impenetrable
impregnable 15.19
impervious 293.13
luxuriant 310.43
unintelligible 522.13
inaccesible 967.9
dense 1045.12

impenitent 114.5

imperative
n rule 419.2

command 420.1
mood 530.11
duty 641.1
urgent need 963.4
adj authoritative 417.15
imperious 417.16
mandatory 420.12
commanding 420.13
compulsory 424.10
binding 424.11
vigorous 544.11
obligatory 641.15
necessary 963.12
urgent 997.22

imperceptible
invisible 32.5
infinitesimal 258.14

imperceptive
insensible 25.6
undiscerning 922.14

imperfect
n tense 530.12
adj inadequate 250.7
impaired 393.27
incomplete 795.4
insufficient 992.9
not perfect 1003.4

imperfection
inadequacy 250.3
vice 654.2
incompleteness 795.1
shortcoming 911.1
want 992.4
defectiveness 1003.1
imperfectness 1003.1
fault 1003.2

imperial
n beard 3.8
volume 554.4
adj imperious 417.16
sovereign 417.17

imperialism
sovereignty 417.8
foreign policy 609.5
government 612.7

imperialist 611.9

imperil 1006.6

imperiled 1006.13

imperious
lordly 141.11
imperial 417.16
sovereign 417.17
commanding 420.13
compulsory 424.10
obligatory 641.15
urgent 997.22

imperishable
immortal 829.9
indestructible 855.18

impermanence
transience 828.1
changeableness 854.1

impermanent
transient 828.7
changeable 854.6

impermeable
impervious 293.13
dense 1045.12

impersonal
reticent 344.10
formal 580.7

impartial 649.9
extrinsic 768.3
indistinguishable
945.6
unprejudiced 979.12

impersonate
mimic 336.6
image 349.11
personate 349.12
pose as 354.22
enact 704.30

impersonation
imitation 336.1
personation 349.4
acting 704.8

impersonator
imitator 336.4
impostor 357.6
masquerader 357.7
entertainer 707.1

impersuadable 895.4

impertinence
impudence 142.2
meddling 214.2
defiance 454.1
unrelatedness 776.1

impertinent
impudent 142.10
meddlesome 214.9
defiant 454.7
irrelevant 776.7

imperturbable
inexcitable 106.10
stable 855.12

impervious
resistant 15.20
callous 94.12
impenetrable 293.13
uninfluenceable 895.4
inaccessible 967.9

impetration
request 440.1
entreaty 440.2
prayer 696.4

impetuous
energetic 17.13
passionate 105.29
impatient 135.6
impulsive 365.9
precipitate 401.10
reckless 493.8
transient 828.7
sudden 830.5
inconstant 854.7

impetus
animation 17.4
acceleration 174.4
impulse 902.1

impiety
irreverence 694.1
impiousness 694.1
sacrilege 694.2
ungodliness 695.3

impinge
intrude 214.5
contact 223.10
collide 902.13

impingement
intrusion 214.1
contact 223.5
impact 902.3

impious
irreverent 694.6
ungodly 695.17
impish
mischievous 322.6
puckish 680.18
implacable
unyielding 361.9
revengeful 507.7
implant graft 191.6
transplant 191.8
inculcate 568.12
fix 855.9
plant 1069.18
implantation
insertion 191.1
inculcation 568.2
fixity 855.2
implanted
confirmed 373.18
intrinsic 767.7
established 855.13
implausible
unbelievable 955.10
improbable 969.3
implement
n instrument 384.4
agent 576.3
tool 1040.1
v carry out 328.7
bring about 407.5
execute 437.9
implementation
performance 328.2
accomplishment
407.1
impliable
unyielding 361.9
firm 425.7
implicate
imply 519.4
incriminate 599.10
entail 772.4
complicate 799.3
involve 898.2
implicated
participating 476.8
implied 519.7
accused 599.15
guilty 656.3
related 775.9
complex 799.4
involved 898.4
implication
meaning 518.1
connotation 519.2
hint 551.4
accusation 599.1
incrimination 599.2
guilt 656.1
entailment 772.2
involvement 898.1
implicative
indicative 517.23
suggestive 519.6
implicit
unspoken 51.11
tacit 519.8
intrinsic 767.7
evidential 957.16
unqualified 960.2

implied meant 518.11
implicated 519.7
tacit 519.8
implode 260.10
implore
admonish 422.6
entreat 440.11
pray 696.13
imploring
n entreaty 440.2
adj entreating 440.17
worshipful 696.16
implosion 260.4
imply
promise 133.12
mean 518.8
implicate 519.4
hint 551.10
accuse 599.7
entail 772.4
evidence 957.8
impolite
unrefined 497.12
discourteous 505.4
impolitic
botched 414.21
unwise 923.10
inexpedient 996.5
imponderable
infinitesimal 258.14
unweighable 298.18
unsubstantial 764.5
immaterial 1053.7
import
n transferal 176.1
bringing in 187.7
entrance 189.1
meaning 518.1
implication 519.2
importance 997.1
v transfer 176.10
bring in 187.14
mean 518.8
imply 519.4
matter 997.12
importance
prestige 417.4
distinction 662.5
influence 894.1
significance 997.1
repute 997.1
important
authoritative 417.15
prominent 662.17
influential 894.13
major 997.17
important person
chief 575.3
celebrity 662.9
personage 997.8
importation
transferal 176.1
bringing in 187.7
entrance 189.1
importunate
annoying 98.22
strong-willed
359.15
demanding 421.9
teasing 440.18
necessary 963.12

importune
v motivate 375.14
make advances 439.7
urge 440.12
adj annoying 98.22
importunity
insistence 421.4
importunateness 440.3
impose
intrude 214.5
prescribe 420.9
demand 421.5
oblige 424.5
compose 548.16
charge 630.12
impose on 643.4
minister 701.16
imposed
mandatory 420.12
inflicted 643.8
impose upon
intrude 214.5
exploit 387.16
presume on 640.7
impose 643.4
take advantage of 643.7
inconvenience 996.4
imposing
dignified 136.12
corpulent 257.18
grandiose 501.21
weighty 997.20
imposition
intrusion 214.1
fraud 356.8
demand 421.1
composition 548.2
tax 630.9
presumption 640.2
inconsiderateness 643.1
infliction 643.1
injustice 650.4
impediment 1012.6
impossibility
hopelessness 125.1
unusualness 870.2
the realm of the impossible
967.1
inconceivability 967.1
no chance 972.10
impossible
n impossibility 967.1
adj unacceptable 108.10
out of the question 125.14
fantastic 870.12
not possible 967.7
improbable 972.18
numeric 1017.23
phrs I refuse 442.7
impost
demand 421.1
tax 630.9
impostor
imitator 336.4
fake 354.13
ringer 357.6
imposture
imitation 336.1
sham 354.3
quackery 354.7
fraud 356.8

impotence
weakness 16.1
powerlessness 19.1
feebleness 19.1
sexuality 75.2
sexlessness 75.9
futility 391.2
laxness 426.1
unproductiveness 891.1
lack of influence 895.1
impotent
n weakling 19.6
adj weak 16.12
powerless 19.13
unsexual 75.29
useless 391.9
lax 426.4
unproductive 891.4
uninfluential 895.3
impound
enclose 212.5
confine 429.12
attach 480.20
impoverish
consume 388.3
strip 480.24
reduce 619.6
bankrupt 625.8
impoverished
used up 388.5
indigent 619.8
meager 992.10
ill-provided 992.12
impractical
theoretical 951.13
impracticable 967.8
visionary 986.24
inexpedient 996.5
unwieldy 1013.19
impracticality
impracticability 967.2
idealism 986.7
unwieldiness 1013.9
imprecation
entreaty 440.2
curse 513.1
imprecise lax 426.4
ungrammatic 531.4
uncertain 971.16
vague 971.19
inaccurate 975.17
imperfect 1003.4
imprecision
unmeticulousness 340.4
laxness 426.1
vagueness 971.4
inaccuracy 975.2
impregnable
impenetrable 15.19
indestructible 855.18
impregnate
reproduce 78.10
inculcate 568.12
imbue 797.11
fertilize 890.8
soak 1065.13
impregnation
reproduction 78.3
inculcation 568.2
imbuement 797.2
fertilization 890.3

soaking 1065.7
impresario
director 574.1
theater man 704.23
impress
n indentation 284.6
character 517.7
etching 548.3
print 713.5
reprint 785.5
characteristic 865.4
impact 887.2
v affect 93.15
indent 284.14
attract 377.6
avail oneself of 387.14
attach 480.20
abduct 482.20
mark 517.19
print 548.14
inculcate 568.12
enlist 615.17
be somebody 662.10
fix 855.9
make an impression 931.19
fix in the mind 989.17
impressed
affected 93.23
engraved 713.11
established 855.13
impression aspect 33.3
feeling 93.1
form 262.1
concavity 284.1
indentation 284.6
imitation 336.1
description 349.2
character 517.7
etching 548.3
edition 554.5
inculcation 568.2
print 713.5
reprint 785.5
characteristic 865.4
impact 887.2
idea 932.1
hunch 934.3
suggestion 951.5
opinion 953.6
impressionable
sensible 24.11
sensitive 93.20
teachable 570.18
influenceable 894.15
foolable 923.12
pliant 1047.9
impressive
sensible 24.11
exciting 105.30
grandiose 501.21
vigorous 544.11
convincing 953.26
impress upon 93.16
imprimatur
ratification 332.4
permit 443.6
imprint
n indentation 284.6
character 517.7
label 517.13
etching 548.3

makeup 554.12
print 713.5
impact 887.2
v indent 284.14
mark 517.19
print 548.14
fix 855.9
fix in the mind 989.17
imprinted
engraved 713.11
established 855.13
imprison enclose 212.5
incarcerate 429.14
imprisoned
enclosed 212.10
jailed 429.21
imprisonment
enclosure 212.1
jailing 429.3
punishment 604.2
improbability
inexpectation 131.1
oddity 870.5
prediction 962.1
unlikelihood 969.1
small chance 972.9
improbable
unexpected 131.10
farfetched 776.8
predictable 962.13
unlikely 969.3
impossible 972.18
improbity
falseheartedness 354.4
dishonesty 645.1
impromptu
n improvisation 365.5
extempore 708.27
adj extemporaneous 365.12
unprepared 406.8
adv extemporaneously
365.15
improper
misbehaving 322.5
vulgar 497.10
ungrammatic 531.4
inelegant 534.2
wrong 638.3
inapt 640.10
wicked 654.16
indecent 666.5
inappropriate 789.7
untimely 844.6
inexpedient 996.5
bad 1000.7
impropriety
misbehavior 322.1
vulgarity 497.1
barbarism 526.6
inelegance 534.1
wrong 638.1
undueness 640.1
injustice 650.1
misdeed 655.2
indecency 666.1
unfitness 789.3
untimeliness 844.1
improve
take advantage of 387.15
grow better 392.7
recuperate 396.19

train 568.13
be changed 852.6
change 852.7
perfect 1002.5
improved
bettered 392.13
changed 852.10
improvement
progression 162.1
betterment 392.1
restoration 396.1
training 568.3
change 852.1
new start 858.2
improvidence
thriftlessness 406.2
rashness 493.1
improvident
prodigal 406.15
rash 493.7
improvisation
extemporization 365.5
unpreparedness 406.1
impromptu 708.27
production 892.1
expedient 995.2
improvise
extemporize 365.8
be unprepared 406.6
produce 892.8
originate 892.12
improvised
extemporaneous
365.12
unprepared 406.8
makeshift 995.7
imprudence
rashness 493.1
unwiseness 923.2
foolish act 923.4
indiscrimination 945.1
imprudent rash 493.7
unwise 923.10
undiscriminating 945.5
impudence
impertinence 142.2
disrespect 156.1
defiance 454.1
rashness 493.1
impudent
impertinent 142.10
disrespectful 156.7
defiant 454.7
rash 493.7
impugn deny 335.4
censure 510.13
incriminate 599.10
impugned
accused 599.15
disproved 958.7
impulse
manpower 18.4
sudden thought 365.1
natural impulse 365.1
urge 375.6
prematurity 845.2
driving force 902
impulsion 902.1
instinct 934.2
involuntariness 963.5
impulse buy 365.1

impulsive fickle 364.6
impetuous 365.9
motivating 375.25
precipitate 401.10
nonuniform 782.3
transient 828.7
sudden 830.5
premature 845.8
inconstant 854.7
impelling 902.23
instinctive 934.6
involuntary 963.14
impunity 601.2
impure
unclean 80.20
inelegant 534.2
unvirtuous 654.12
unchaste 665.23
obscene 666.9
imperfect 1003.4
impurity
uncleanness 80.1
inelegance 534.1
vice 654.1
unchastity 665.1
intruder 774.2
imperfection 1003.1
imputable
blameworthy 510.25
attributable 888.6
imputation
criticism 510.4
aspersion 512.4
accusation 599.1
stigma 661.6
attribution 888.1
impute accuse 599.7
attribute 888.3
in
n entrée 187.3
entrance 189.5
adj entering 189.12
participating 476.8
on good terms 587.18
modern 841.13
in safety 1007.6
adv inward 189.13
inside 207.10
by authority of 417.20
prep at 159.27
into 189.14
interior 207.13
in a bad way ill 85.56
worn-out 393.36
in danger 1006.13
inability
incapability 19.2
unskillfulness 414.1
in a bind late 846.16
in trouble 1013.22
inaccessible
out-of-the-way 261.9
reticent 344.10
aloof 583.6
inaccordance
difference 780.1
disagreement 789.1
nonconformity 868.1
inaccordant
different 780.7
disagreeing 789.6

inaccuracy
  unmeticulousness 340.4
  misrepresentation 350.1
  misjudgment 948.1
  vagueness 971.4
  inaccurateness 975.2
  badness 1000.1
  imperfection 1003.1
inaccurate
  unmeticulous 340.13
  vague 971.19
  incorrect 975.17
  bad 1000.7
  imperfect 1003.4
in a class by itself
  peerless 249.15
  other 780.8
  first-rate 999.17
inaction
  motionlessness 173.2
  passivity 329.1
  passiveness 329.1
  inactivity 331.1
in action acting 328.10
  operating 889.11
inactivate 19.9
inactive inert 173.14
  passive 329.6
  unactive 331.17
  leisurely 402.6
inactivity rest 20.1
  motionlessness 173.2
  passivity 329.1
  inaction 331.1
  leisureliness 402.2
in addition 253.11
inadequacy
  inability 19.2
  unsatisfactoriness
    108.2
  mediocrity 250.3
  unskillfulness 414.1
  inequality 791.1
  incompleteness 795.1
  shortcoming 911.1
  insufficiency 992.1
  imperfection 1003.1
  fault 1003.2
inadequate
  ineffective 19.15
  unsatisfactory 108.9
  mediocre 250.7
  incompetent 414.19
  unequal 791.4
  incomplete 795.4
  short of 911.5
  insufficient 992.9
  imperfect 1003.4
inadmissible
  unacceptable 108.10
  exclusive 773.9
  irrelevant 776.7
  inappropriate 789.7
in advance ahead 165.4
  before 216.12
  on loan 620.7
  early 845.11
inadvertence
  neglect 340.1
  slip 975.4
  inattention 984.1

inadvertent
  negligent 340.10
  unthinking 365.10
  unpremeditated 365.11
  inattentive 984.6
inadvisable
  unwise 923.10
  inexpedient 996.5
in a fog
  concealed 346.11
  muddled 985.13
in agreement
  adj unanimous 332.15
  cooperative 450.5
  agreeing 788.9
  adv jointly 800.18
  prep together with
    788.12
  conformable to 867.9
in a jam
  bewildered 971.24
  unfortunate 1011.14
  in trouble 1013.22
in a jiffy
  in short order 174.19
  hastily 401.12
  quickly 830.7
inalienable
  intrinsic 767.7
  inseparable 800.15
in all conscience
  positively 247.19
  rightly 637.4
  candidly 644.23
  in justice 649.11
  reasonably 935.24
in all fairness 649.11
in all likelihood 968.8
in all respects
  wholly 792.13
  throughout 794.17
  exactly 973.21
in all seriousness
  resolutely 359.17
  candidly 644.23
inalterable
  persevering 360.8
  permanent 853.7
in a manner of speaking
  limited 248.10
  figuratively 536.4
  so to speak 784.19
in a mess
  adj confused 810.16
  in trouble 1013.22
  adv in disorder 810.17
inamorato 104.12
inane
  ineffective 19.15
  insipid 65.2
  dull 117.6
  vacant 222.14
  vain 391.13
  meaningless 520.6
  nonexistent 762.8
  thin 764.6
  empty-headed 922.19
  foolish 923.8
  ignorant 930.11
  thoughtless 933.4
  trivial 998.19

inanimate
  n gender 530.10
  adj dead 307.29
  languid 331.20
  inanimated 1055.5
inanity
  ineffectiveness 19.3
  insipidness 65.1
  dullness 117.1
  void 222.3
  futility 391.2
  meaninglessness 520.1
  nonexistence 762.1
  empty-headedness 922.6
  foolishness 923.1
  ignorance 930.1
  thoughtlessness 933.1
  triviality 998.3
in anticipation
  adj expectant 130.11
  in readiness 405.21
  adv early 845.11
in a nutshell
  small 258.16
  shortly 268.12
  concisely 537.8
  in brief 557.7
in any event
  notwithstanding 338.8
  anyhow 384.10
in A-1 condition 83.8
inappetence
  apathy 94.4
  undesirousness 102.3
inapplicable
  unserviceable 391.14
  irrelevant 776.7
  inappropriate 789.7
inapposite
  irrelevant 776.7
  inappropriate 789.7
inappreciable
  infinitesimal 258.14
  insignificant 998.17
inapprehensible 522.13
inappropriate
  vulgar 497.10
  wrong 638.3
  improper 640.10
  indecent 666.5
  irrelevant 776.7
  inapt 789.7
  untimely 844.6
  inexpedient 996.5
inapt
  unskillful 414.15
  inappropriate 789.7
  inexpedient 996.5
inaptitude
  unskillfulness 414.1
  unfitness 789.3
  inexpedience 996.1
in arrears
  adj due 623.10
  defaulting 625.10
  incomplete 795.4
  adv behind 911.6
inarticulate
  mute 51.12
  shy 139.12
  unintelligible 522.13

  indistinct 525.12
inartificial
  natural 406.13
  artless 416.6
  plain 499.7
  genuine 973.15
inartistic 1015.10
in a rut
  adj habituated 373.17
  adv uniformly 781.7
inasmuch as 888.10
in a stew
  adj in a dither 105.21
  anxious 126.7
  impatient 135.6
  in a temper 152.31
  bewildered 971.24
  confused 985.12
  adv excitedly 105.33
in a sweat
  adj sweaty 12.22
  in a dither 105.21
  impatient 135.6
  confused 985.12
  adv excitedly 105.33
in a tizzy
  adj in a dither 105.21
  confused 985.12
  adv excitedly 105.33
inattention
  unconcern 102.2
  neglect 340.1
  nonobservance 435.1
  unwiseness 923.2
  incuriosity 982.1
  inattentiveness 984.1
  distraction 985.1
inattentive
  unconcerned 102.7
  negligent 340.10
  unskillful 414.15
  nonobservant 435.5
  incurious 982.3
  unmindful 984.6
inaudible 51.10
inaugural
  n speech 543.2
  ceremony 580.4
  adj preceding 814.4
  prior 816.4
  beginning 818.15
inaugurate insert 191.4
  install 615.12
  institute 818.11
  innovate 841.5
  cause 886.10
  establish 892.10
inauguration
  location 159.7
  admission 187.2
  ceremony 580.4
  installation 615.3
  installment 818.5
  establishment 892.4
inauspicious
  ominous 133.16
  untimely 844.6
  bad 1000.7
  unfortunate 1011.14
inauthentic
  illogical 936.11

unauthoritative 975.19
in a way
  to a degree 245.7
  limited 248.10
  so to speak 784.19
in awe
  adj wondering 122.9
  reverent 155.9
  adv in wonder 122.18
  in fear 127.33
in bad taste
  vulgar 497.10
  inelegant 534.2
in behalf of
  adv by proxy 576.18
  prep for 449.26
  instead of 862.12
in black and white 547.22
inborn 767.8
inbound arriving 186.9
  entering 189.12
inbred bred 78.17
  innate 767.8
inbreed 78.8
in brief
  in short 537.8
  in summary 557.7
in cahoots
  adj leagued 805.6
  adv in cooperation 450.7
incalculable
  infinite 823.3
  innumerable 884.10
  unknown 930.16
  uncertain 971.16
incalescence 1019.1
incandesce
  be hot 1019.22
  shine 1025.24
incandescence
  glow 1019.12
  shine 1025.2
incandescent
  burning 1019.27
  luminous 1025.31
incantation
  conjuration 690.4
  spell 691.4
incapable
  n cripple 85.45
  incompetent 414.7
  adj unable 19.14
  unfitted 406.9
  incompetent 414.19
incapacitate
  disable 19.9
  afflict 85.50
  cripple 393.14
incapacitated
  weakened 16.18
  disabled 19.16
  crippled 393.30
incapacity
  infirmity 16.3
  inability 19.2
  unskillfulness 414.1
  unproductiveness 891.1
  unintelligence 922.1
incarcerate
  enclose 212.5
  imprison 429.14

incarcerated
  enclosed 212.10
  jailed 429.21
incarceration
  enclosure 212.1
  imprisonment 429.3
  punishment 604.2
incarnate
  v manifest 348.5
  image 349.11
  embody 763.5
  compose 796.3
  materialize 1052.9
  adj divine 677.16
  embodied 1052.11
incarnation
  appearance 33.1
  manifestation 348.1
  impersonation 349.4
  embodiment 763.4
  essence 767.2
  composition 796.1
  materialization 1052.8
in case 831.13
incautious rash 493.7
  unalert 984.8
incendiarism 1020.7
incendiary
  n instigator 375.11
  violent person 671.9
  arsonist 1020.8
  adj incitive 375.28
  inflammatory 1020.27
incense
  n fragrance 70.1
  joss stick 70.4
  suavity 504.5
  flattery 511.1
  oblation 696.7
  v perfume 70.8
  excite 105.12
  provoke 152.24
  incite 375.17
incensory 70.6
incentive
  n inducement 375.7
  impulse 902.1
  adj incitive 375.28
inception origin 818.4
  source 886.5
  establishment 892.4
incertitude 971.1
incessancy
  continuity 812.1
  perpetuity 829.1
  constancy 847.2
incessant
  continuous 812.8
  perpetual 829.2
  constant 847.5
  recurrent 849.13
  continuing 856.7
incest perversion 75.11
  illicit sex 665.7
inch go slow 175.6
  creep 177.26
in character
  to be expected 130.14
  characteristic 865.13
in charge
  adj under arrest 429.22

  supervising 573.13
  governing 612.17
  adv in authority 417.21
inchmeal
  by degrees 245.6
  piece by piece 793.9
inchoate formless 263.4
  unordered 810.12
  vague 971.19
inchoative
  n aspect 530.13
  adj beginning 818.15
in chorus
  adj harmonious 708.49
  adv unanimously 332.17
  cooperatively 450.6
  in step 788.11
  simultaneously 836.7
incidence event 831.1
  frequency 847.1
incident
  plot 722.4
  circumstance 766.1
  event 831.2
incidental
  n ornament 709.18
  particular 766.3
  nonessential 768.2
  adj circumstantial 766.7
  unessential 768.4
  irrelevant 776.7
  happening 831.9
  occasional 843.11
  infrequent 848.3
  chance 972.15
incinerate
  strike dead 308.18
  cremate 309.20
  destroy 395.10
  burn up 1020.25
incineration
  cremation 309.2
  discard 390.3
  burning 1020.5
incinerator 1020.13
incipience 818.4
incipient 818.15
incise cleave 224.4
  notch 289.4
  furrow 290.3
  open 292.11
  injure 393.13
  record 549.15
  engrave 713.9
  sever 802.11
incised notched 289.5
  furrowed 290.4
  engraved 713.11
incision trauma 85.38
  crack 224.2
  notch 289.1
  furrow 290.1
  engraving 713.2
incisive energetic 17.13
  acrimonious 17.14
  caustic 144.23
  vigorous 544.11
  sagacious 920.16
incisor 2.8
incite excite 105.12
  instigate 375.17

  admonish 422.6
  impel 902.11
  heat 1020.18
incitement
  excitation 105.11
  incitation 375.4
  incentive 375.7
  impulse 902.1
incivility
  unrefinement 497.3
  discourtesy 505.1
inclemency
  harshness 144.9
  pitilessness 146.1
  violence 671.1
  cold 1023.1
inclement harsh 144.24
  pitiless 146.3
  cold 1023.14
inclination
  penchant 100.3
  obeisance 155.2
  direction 161.1
  descent 194.1
  leaning 204.2
  incline 204.4
  will 323.1
  preference 371.5
  aptitude 413.5
  partiality 650.3
  tendency 896.1
  disposition 978.3
  prejudice 980.3
incline
  n stairs 193.3
  inclination 204.4
  slope 237.2
  v take direction 161.7
  lean 204.10
  gravitate 297.15
  be willing 324.3
  induce 375.22
  influence 894.7
  tend 896.3
inclined
  inclining 204.15
  willing 324.5
  moved 375.30
  disposed 978.8
inclining
  inclined 204.15
  tending 896.4
in clover
  adj pleased 95.15
  prosperous 1010.12
  adv in comfort 121.15
include
  internalize 207.5
  enclose 212.5
  comprise 772.3
  put together 800.5
  combine 805.3
included
  comprised 772.5
  involved 898.4
including
  adj inclusive 772.6
  composed of 796.4
  prep with 253.12
inclusion
  surrounding 209.5

enclosure 212.1
affiliation 450.2
incorporation 772.1
comprisal 772.1
combination 805.1
involvement 898.1
inclusive
including 772.6
whole 792.9
joint 800.12
inclusivism 772.1
incognito
n privacy 345.2
cover 356.11
masquerader 357.7
anonymity 528.1
adj private 345.13
disguised 346.13
anonymous 528.3
incognizance 930.2
incoherence
dislocation 160.1
unintelligibility 522.1
inconsistency 789.2
separation 802.1
noncohesion 804.1
disintegration 806.1
disorder 810.1
discontinuity 813.1
delirium 926.8
vagueness 971.4
incoherent
unintelligible 522.13
inconsistent 789.8
separate 802.20
uncohesive 804.4
unordered 810.12
discontinuous 813.4
delirious 926.31
vague 971.19
in cold blood
unfeelingly 94.14
heartlessly 144.34
intentionally 380.10
incombustible 1022.9
income entrance 189.1
gain 472.3
pay 624.4
receipts 627.1
incoming
n entrance 189.1
adj arriving 186.9
entering 189.12
incommensurable
unrelated 776.6
uncomparable 787.6
inconsistent 789.8
unlike 943.9
incommensurate
unsatisfactory 108.9
uncomparable 787.6
inconsistent 789.8
incommodious
narrow 270.14
inconvenient 996.7
incommunicable 122.13
incommunicado 346.11
incommutable 855.17
incomparable
peerless 249.15
unrelated 776.6

uncomparable 787.6
incommensurable 943.9
incompatible
unsociable 583.5
unfriendly 589.9
different 780.7
disagreeing 789.6
inconsistent 789.8
incompetence
inability 19.2
inadequacy 250.3
unpreparedness 406.1
unskillfulness 414.1
insufficiency 992.1
incompetent
n impotent 19.6
incapable 414.7
adj unable 19.14
inadequate 250.7
unfitted 406.9
incapable 414.19
insufficient 992.9
incomplete
partial 793.7
uncompleted 795.4
insufficient 992.9
imperfect 1003.4
in compliance with
adv obediently 326.6
prep conformable to 867.9
incomprehensible
wonderful 122.10
unintelligible 522.13
infinite 823.3
fantastic 870.12
incomprehension
unperceptiveness 922.2
incognizance 930.2
incompressible
dense 1045.12
rigid 1046.11
inconceivable
wonderful 122.10
fantastic 870.12
unbelievable 955.10
impossible 967.7
in concert
adj cooperative 450.5
in accord 455.3
harmonious 708.49
adv unanimously 332.17
in step 788.11
concurrently 899.5
inconclusive
illogical 936.11
unsound 936.12
unproved 958.8
in condition
healthy 83.8
hale 83.12
out of order 765.7
in order 807.7
in conformity
adj obedient 326.3
adv in step 788.11
conformably 867.7
incongruency 456.1
incongruity
humorousness 488.1
difference 780.1
inconsistency 789.2

nonconformity 868.1
illogicalness 936.2
inexpedience 996.1
incongruous
off-color 35.21
humorous 488.4
different 780.7
inconsistent 789.8
illogical 936.11
inexpedient 996.5
in conjunction with
additionally 253.12
with 769.12
inconsequence
unrelatedness 776.1
unimportance 998.1
inconsequent
irrelevant 776.7
inconsistent 789.8
illogical 936.11
inconsequential
insignificant 248.6
illogical 936.11
unimportant 998.17
inconsiderable
insignificant 248.6
unimportant 998.17
inconsiderate
unthoughtful 144.18
careless 340.11
unthinking 365.10
ill-bred 505.6
unwise 923.10
inconsistency
contrariety 779.1
difference 780.1
nonuniformity 782.1
incongruity 789.2
noncohesion 804.1
inconstancy 854.2
nonconformity 868.1
illogicalness 936.2
inconsistent
contrary 779.6
different 780.7
nonuniform 782.3
incongruous 789.8
incoherent 804.4
inconstant 854.7
illogical 936.11
inconsolable
sorrowful 112.26
disconsolate 112.28
inconsonant
different 780.7
inconsistent 789.8
inconspicuous 32.6
inconstancy
irresolution 362.1
fickleness 364.3
infidelity 645.5
nonuniformity 782.1
irregularity 851.1
instability 854.2
inconstant
fickle 364.6
nonobservant 435.5
unfaithful 645.20
nonuniform 782.3
transient 828.7
irregular 851.3

changeable 854.7
incontestable
impregnable 15.19
obvious 970.15
incontinence
greed 100.8
unrestraint 430.3
prodigality 486.1
uncontinence 665.2
intemperance 669.1
excess 993.1
incontinent
unrestrained 430.24
prodigal 486.8
uncontinent 665.24
intemperate 669.7
excessive 993.16
incontrovertible
evidential 957.16
obvious 970.15
inconvenience
n imposition 643.1
untimeliness 844.1
inexpedience 996.1
discommodity 996.3
impediment 1012.6
trouble 1013.3
unwieldiness 1013.9
v presume on 640.7
put to inconvenience 996.4
trouble 1013.13
inconvenient
untimely 844.6
incommodious 996.7
unwieldy 1013.19
inconvertible
unpayable 625.13
unchangeable 855.17
inconvincible 956.4
incorporate
include 772.3
compose 796.3
combine 805.3
materialize 1052.9
incorporated
associated 617.16
joined 800.13
combined 805.5
embodied 1052.11
incorporation
affiliation 450.2
inclusion 772.1
composition 796.1
combination 805.1
materialization 1052.8
incorporeal
n specter 988.1
incorporeity 1053.2
adj unsubstantial 764.5
spectral 988.7
immaterial 1053.7
incorrect
ungrammatic 531.4
inelegant 534.2
wrong 638.3
inaccurate 975.17
incorrigible
past hope 125.15
ungovernable 361.12
confirmed 373.18
irreclaimable 654.18

incorrupt
unsinful 653.7
innocent 657.6
incorruptible
trustworthy 644.19
immortal 829.9
indestructible 855.18
incrassate
v thicken 269.5
congeal 1045.10
emulsify 1062.10
adj distended 259.13
thickened 1045.14
increase
n aggravation 119.1
ascent 193.1
gain 251.1
addition 253.1
adjunct 254.1
expansion 259.1
improvement 392.1
multiplication 883.4
elevation 912.1
v develop 14.2
aggravate 119.2
quantify 244.4
graduate 245.4
enlarge 251.4
increase 251.6
add to 253.5
expand 259.4
develop 259.5
grow 259.7
multiply 883.6
increased
aggravated 119.4
heightened 251.7
expanded 259.10
multiple 883.8
incredible
wonderful 122.10
remarkable 247.10
fantastic 870.12
absurd 923.11
unbelievable 955.10
improbable 969.3
incredulity
agnosticism 695.6
unbelief 955.1
ungullibility 956.2
incredulousness 956.1
incredulous
agnostic 695.20
unbelieving 955.8
uncredulous 956.4
increment
increase 251.1
adjunct 254.1
incriminate 599.10
incrimination 599.2
incrustation
covering 295.1
crust 295.14
incubate 78.12
incubation 78.5
incubator 886.8
incubus
frightener 127.9
burden 297.7
demon 680.6
dream 986.9

inculcate
indoctrinate 568.12
fix in the mind 989.17
inculcated 373.18
inculcation 568.2
inculpable 657.8
inculpate 599.10
inculpated
accused 599.15
guilty 656.3
incumbency
burden 297.7
responsibility 641.2
benefice 698.9
position 724.5
incumbent
n inhabitant 227.2
tenant 470.4
officeholder 610.11
benefice-holder 699.7
adj overhanging 202.11
overlying 295.36
onerous 297.17
incur 897.4
incurable
n sick person 85.43
adj past hope 125.15
incuriosity
unconcern 102.2
uninquisitiveness 982.1
incuriousness 982.1
inattention 984.1
incurious
unconcerned 102.7
uninquisitive 982.3
inattentive 984.6
incursion influx 189.2
intrusion 214.1
raid 459.4
overstepping 910.3
incurve curve 279.6
be concave 284.12
incurved
curved 279.7
concave 284.16
indebted grateful 150.5
in debt 623.8
obliged 641.16
insolvent 729.19
liable 897.5
indecency
sexual desire 75.5
vulgarity 497.1
unchastity 665.1
immodesty 666.2
indelicacy 666.1
indecent vulgar 497.10
unchaste 665.23
indelicate 666.5
indecipherable 522.19
indecision
irresolution 362.1
uncertainty 971.1
indecisive
wishy-washy 16.17
formless 263.4
irresolute 362.9
inconstant 854.7
unproved 958.8
uncertain 971.16
vague 971.19

indecorous
vulgar 497.10
inelegant 534.2
wrong 638.3
indecent 666.5
indecorum
vulgarity 497.1
wrong 638.1
indecency 666.1
indeed
adv positively 247.19
chiefly 249.17
certainly 970.23
truly 973.18
interj astonishment 122.19
yes! 332.18
indefatigable
industrious 330.22
persevering 360.8
continuing 856.7
indefeasible
unchangeable 855.17
inevitable 963.15
indefensible
unacceptable 108.10
unjustifiable 650.12
indefinable
indescribable 122.13
inexplicable 522.18
vague 971.19
indefinite
inconspicuous 32.6
formless 263.4
general 864.11
indistinguishable 945.6
vague 971.19
indeliberate 365.11
indelible
deep-dyed 35.18
deep-felt 93.24
indestructible 855.18
unforgettable 989.25
indelicacy
vulgarity 497.1
indecency 666.1
in demand
desired 100.29
salable 734.14
indemnification
compensation 338.1
reparation 481.2
recompense 624.3
atonement 658.1
indemnify
compensate 338.4
make restitution 481.5
requite 506.5
pay 624.10
indemnity
pardon 148.2
compensation 338.1
security 438.1
exemption 601.2
recompense 624.3
atonement 658.1
indemonstrable 971.16
indent
n indentation 284.6
summons 420.5
demand 421.1
request 440.1

appropriation 480.4
print 517.7
v dent 284.14
notch 289.4
summon 420.11
demand 421.5
request 440.9
appropriate 480.19
depress 913.4
indentation
indent 284.6
excavation 284.11
notch 289.1
texture 294.1
print 517.7
indented dented 284.17
notched 289.5
indenture
n indentation 284.6
binding over 615.8
v article 615.18
indentured servant
432.7
independence
pride 136.1
nationhood 232.6
voluntariness 324.2
self-control 359.5
self-determination 430.5
self-help 449.6
rallying device 458.11
neutrality 467.1
nonpartisanism 609.26
wealth 618.1
unrelatedness 776.1
independent
n free agent 430.12
neutral 467.4
nonpartisan 609.28
moderate 611.10
adj proud 136.8
voluntary 324.7
strong-willed 359.15
self-dependent 430.22
self-helpful 449.23
neutral 467.7
nonpartisan 609.45
moderate 611.18
wealthy 618.14
unrelated 776.6
separate 802.20
indescribable
ineffable 122.13
extraordinary 870.14
indestructible
perpetual 829.7
undestroyable 855.18
in detail
meticulously 339.16
at length 538.16
fully 766.13
piece by piece 793.9
particularly 865.15
indeterminate
formless 263.4
obscure 522.15
unessential 768.4
relative 775.7
general 864.11
vague 971.19
chance 972.15

inexplicit
ambiguous 539.4
uncertain 971.16
inexpressible
indescribable 122.13
sacred 685.7
inexpressive 522.20
inexpugnable
impregnable 15.19
indestructible 855.18
inextensible 1046.12
inextinguishable 855.18
in extremis
dying 307.32
in danger 1006.13
straitened 1013.26
inextricable
inexplicable 522.18
irreducible 799.5
stuck 855.16
in fact really 761.16
truly 973.18
infallibility
certainty 970.1
perfection 1002.1
infallible
inerrable 970.19
exact 973.17
perfect 1002.6
infamous wrong 638.3
knavish 645.17
wicked 654.16
disreputable 661.10
terrible 1000.9
infamy
abomination 638.2
iniquity 654.3
infamousness 661.4
infancy inability 19.2
immaturity 301.3
babyhood 301.5
origin 818.4
infant
n youngster 302.1
baby 302.9
simple soul 416.3
schoolchild 572.3
innocent 657.4
beginner 818.2
adj infantile 301.12
incomplete 795.4
beginning 818.15
infantile
infant 301.12
beginning 818.15
puerile 922.24
infantilism
mental deficiency 922.9
puerility 922.11
infantryman
pedestrian 178.6
foot soldier 461.9
infarction 293.3
infatuate
n enthusiast 101.4
lover 104.11
fanatic 926.18
v enamor 104.22
fascinate 377.7
stultify 923.7
obsess 926.25

adj enamored 104.27
infatuated
overzealous 101.12
enamored 104.27
foolish 923.8
obsessed 926.33
credulous 954.8
infatuation liking 100.2
overzealousness 101.3
infatuatedness 104.3
stultification 923.5
mania 926.12
credulity 954.1
in favor of
adj approving 509.17
prep for 449.26
approving of 509.21
infect defile 80.17
disease 85.51
inspire 375.20
corrupt 393.12
work evil 1000.6
radioactivate 1037.10
infected unclean 80.20
diseased 85.60
radioactive 1037.11
infection
defilement 80.4
contagion 85.4
infectious disease 85.13
inspiration 375.9
corruption 393.2
evil 1000.3
infectious
poisonous 82.7
contagious 85.62
infectious disease 85.13
infecund
unproductive 891.4
unimaginative 987.5
infelicitous
ungrammatic 531.4
inelegant 534.2
inappropriate 789.7
untimely 844.6
inexpedient 996.5
infelicity
wretchedness 96.6
unhappiness 112.2
solecism 531.2
inelegance 534.1
unfitness 789.3
untimeliness 844.1
inexpedience 996.1
infer imply 519.4
reason 935.15
conclude 946.10
suppose 951.10
inference
implication 519.2
reasoning 935.3
conclusion 946.4
supposition 951.3
inferential
suggestive 519.6
dialectic 935.22
inferior
n underling 250.2
subordinate 432.5
retainer 577.1
adj unable 19.14

subordinate 250.6
lower 274.8
subject 432.13
short of 911.5
unimportant 998.16
insignificant 998.17
bad 1000.7
poor 1005.9
inferiority
inability 19.2
subordinacy 250.1
subservience 432.2
abnormality 870.1
shortcoming 911.1
unimportance 998.1
badness 1000.1
inferiorness 1005.3
inferiority complex
complex 92.22
self-effacement 139.2
infernal cruel 144.26
diabolic 654.13
hellish 682.8
execrable 1000.10
inferno hell 682.1
hot place 1019.11
inferred implied 519.7
supposed 951.14
infertile
unproductive 891.4
unimaginative 987.5
infertility
unproductiveness 891.1
unimaginativeness 987.1
infest 910.6
infestation 910.2
infidel
n gentile 688.6
unbeliever 695.11
adj infidelic 688.10
unbelieving 695.19
infidelity
love affair 104.5
unfaithfulness 645.5
infidelism 688.3
atheism 695.5
unbelief 955.1
infield playground 743.11
baseball 745.1
track 755.1
horse racing 757.1
infighting
dissension 456.3
contention 457.1
boxing 457.9
infiltrate absorb 187.13
filter in 189.10
intrude 214.5
launch an attack 459.17
imbue 797.11
soak 1065.13
infiltration
sorption 187.6
entrance 189.1
intrusion 214.1
attack 459.1
imbuement 797.2
soaking 1065.7
infiltrator 214.3
infinite
spacious 158.11

omnipresent 221.13
large 247.7
huge 257.20
almighty 677.17
boundless 823.3
perpetual 829.7
innumerable 884.10
numeric 1017.23
infinitesimal 258.14
infinity
omnipresence 221.2
greatness 247.1
distance 261.1
length 267.1
limitlessness 823
infiniteness 823.1
perpetuity 829.1
large number 1017.5
infinity pool 743.12
infirm
unsound 16.15
unhealthy 85.54
stricken in years 303.18
weak-willed 362.12
unvirtuous 654.12
fragile 764.7
inconstant 854.7
feebleminded 922.21
unreliable 971.20
infirmity
unsoundness 16.3
disease 85.1
unhealthiness 85.3
old age 303.5
weak will 362.4
vice 654.2
feeblemindedness 922.8
unreliability 971.6
fault 1003.2
infix
n interjection 213.2
added to writing 254.2
morphology 526.3
v implant 191.8
add 253.4
inculcate 568.12
fix 855.9
fix in the mind 989.17
infixed
confirmed 373.18
intrinsic 767.7
established 855.13
inflame energize 17.10
pain 26.7
make red 41.4
excite 105.12
provoke 152.24
incite 375.17
heat 1020.18
ignite 1020.22
inflamed sore 26.11
red 41.6
feverish 85.58
diseased 85.60
excited 105.20
fiery 671.22
burning 1019.27
inflammable
n fuel 1021.1
adj excitable 105.28
flammable 1020.28

inflammation
soreness 26.4
symptom 85.9
inflammatory disease 85.10
excitation 105.11
incitement 375.4
inflammatory
exciting 105.30
incitive 375.28
inflammative 1020.27
inflate puff up 140.7
increase 251.4
enlarge 259.4
exaggerate 355.3
talk big 545.6
heat the economy 632.9
overextend 993.13
inflated
increased 251.7
distended 259.13
exaggerated 355.4
pompous 501.22
swollen 502.12
bombastic 545.9
inflation increase 251.1
distension 259.2
exaggeration 355.1
pompousness 501.7
style 532.2
grandiloquence 545.1
price index 630.4
high price 632.3
business cycle 731.10
overextension 993.7
inflationary
expansive 259.9
overpriced 632.12
inflect curve 279.6
modulate 524.28
grammaticize 530.16
inflection angle 278.2
bend 279.3
intonation 524.6
morphology 526.3
inflexible firm 359.12
unyielding 361.9
strict 425.7
immovable 855.15
uninfluenceable 895.4
inevitable 963.15
intractable 1046.12
inflict do 328.6
wreak 643.5
infliction affliction 96.8
punishment 604.1
imposition 643.1
bane 1001.1
in flight
adj fugitive 368.16
adv on the wing 184.51
inflorescence 310.26
inflorescent 310.38
inflow influx 189.2
flow 238.4
wind 318.1
influence
n power 18.1
supremacy 249.3
motivation 375.2
machination 415.4
prestige 417.4

influentiality 894.1
good influence 894.6
v motivate 375.22
cause 886.10
induce 886.11
determine 886.12
operate on 889.6
make oneself felt 894.7
prejudice 980.9
influence peddler
Machiavellian 415.8
wire-puller 609.30
politician 610.5
influence 894.6
influential
authoritative 417.15
powerful 894.13
influx inflow 189.2
intrusion 214.1
in focus 31.7
infomercial 352.6
infopreneur 551.5
in force powerful 18.12
in use 387.25
existent 761.13
operating 889.11
inform
v pervade 221.7
betray 351.6
inspire 375.20
tell 551.8
report 552.11
teach 568.10
adj formless 263.4
informality
unceremoniousness 581.1
informalness 581.1
informal language 523.5
informal vote 371.6
informant
informer 551.5
examinee 938.19
witness 957.6
information
communication 343.1
facts 551.1
info 551.1
news 552.1
teaching 568.1
arraignment 598.3
accusation 599.1
knowledge 928.1
data 1042.15
information overload 551.1
information retrieval 551.7
information technology 551.7
information theory
communications 343.5
electronic communications
347.1
data storage 551.1
autonetics 1041.2
informative
informing 551.18
educational 568.18
informed
prepared 405.16
clued-in 551.17
knowing 928.15
cognizant of 928.16
enlightened 928.18

up on 928.19
informer
traitor 357.10
informant 551.5
betrayer 551.6
accuser 599.5
witness 957.6
inform on
disclose 351.6
inform 551.12
accuse 599.7
betray 645.14
infra 274.10
infraction
disobedience 327.1
violation 435.2
wrong 638.1
lawbreaking 674.3
foul 746.3
basketball game 747.3
game 749.3
hockey game 749.6
overstepping 910.3
infrangible
firm 15.18
indivisible 1045.13
unbreakable 1049.5
infrared 41.6
infrastructure
inferior 250.2
understructure 266.3
directorate 574.11
support 901.1
foundation 901.6
frame 901.10
infrequency
seldomness 848
rarity 848.1
fewness 885.1
infrequent
rare 848.2
sparse 885.5
infringe
intrude 214.5
violate 435.4
adopt 621.4
usurp 640.8
break the law 674.5
overstep 910.9
infringement
intrusion 214.1
disobedience 327.1
impairment 393.1
violation 435.2
adoption 621.2
usurpation 640.3
lawbreaking 674.3
overstepping 910.3
in front
adj front 216.10
adv ahead 165.4
before 216.12
prep facing 215.7
in full at length 538.16
fully 766.13
completely 794.14
in full bloom 303.13
in full swing
adj unweakened 15.21
astir 330.19
thriving 1010.13

adv actively 330.25
in fun
mischievously 322.7
in sport 489.19
for amusement 743.31
infundibular
conical 282.12
concave 284.16
infuriate
v excite 105.12
enrage 152.25
antagonize 589.7
adj infuriated 152.32
turbulent 671.18
infuriated 152.32
infuse insert 191.3
extraction 192.16
inspire 375.20
inculcate 568.12
imbue 797.11
liquefy 1064.5
soak 1065.13
infusion
insertion 191.1
extract 192.7
distillation 192.8
inspiration 375.9
inculcation 568.2
baptism 701.6
imbuement 797.2
admixture 797.7
liquefaction 1064.1
solution 1064.3
soaking 1065.7
in general 864.17
ingenious
skillful 413.22
cunning 415.12
imaginative 986.18
ingenue
simple soul 416.3
role 704.10
script 706.3
actor 707.2
ingenuity
skill 413.1
invention 986.3
ingenuous
immature 301.10
artless 416.5
candid 644.17
ignorant 930.11
gullible 954.9
ingest devour 8.22
eat 187.11
consume 388.3
absorb 570.7
ingesta 10.1
ingestion
body function 2.17
digestion 7.8
eating 8.1
reception 187.4
consumption 388.1
absorption 570.2
ingle home 228.2
fire 1019.13
fireplace 1020.11
inglenook home 228.2
recess 284.7
fireplace 1020.11

ingleside home 228.2
　fireplace 1020.11
inglorious
　humble 137.10
　disreputable 661.10
　unrenowned 661.14
ingoing
　n entrance 189.1
　adj introverted 92.40
　entering 189.12
in good shape
　healthy 83.8
　in order 807.7
ingot
　precious metals
　　728.20
　cast 1058.5
ingrain color 35.14
　fix 855.9
ingrained
　deep-dyed 35.18
　confirmed 373.18
　intrinsic 767.7
　established 855.13
ingrate 151.2
ingratiate oneself
　insinuate oneself 138.10
　influence 894.7
　gain influence 894.12
ingratiating
　obsequious 138.14
　suave 504.18
ingratitude
　unthankfulness 151.1
　ungratefulness 151.1
ingredient
　particular 766.3
　part 793.1
　component 796.2
ingress
　entrance 189.1
　inlet 189.5
　channel 239.1
ingroup clique 617.6
　influence 894.6
ingrown 855.13
inhabit settle 159.17
　occupy 225.7
　people 225.9
　exist in 761.11
inhabitant dweller 227
　population 227.1
　inhabiter 227.2
inhalant medicine 86.4
　drug 87.3
inhalation
　breathing 2.21
　drawing in 187.5
inhale smell 69.8
　smoke 89.14
　draw in 187.12
in hand unused 390.12
　undertaken 404.7
　in preparation 405.22
　possessed 469.8
　under control 612.19
　restrained 670.11
　orderly 807.6
　happening 831.9
　operating 889.11
　in production 892.21

inharmonious
　off-color 35.21
　dissonant 61.4
　disaccordant 456.15
　different 780.7
　disagreeing 789.6
in harmony
　in accord 455.3
　agreeing 788.9
　jointly 800.18
in heat 75.28
inherence
　presence 221.1
　intrinsicality 767.1
inherent present 221.12
　intrinsic 767.7
　instinctive 934.6
inherit be heir to 479.7
　inhere 767.6
　succeed 815.2
inheritable
　heritable 560.20
　transferable 629.5
inheritance
　property 471.1
　bequest 478.10
　heritance 479.2
　heredity 560.6
inherited
　hereditary 560.19
　innate 767.8
inheritor heir 479.5
　successor 817.4
　sequel 835.2
inhibit suppress 106.8
　restrain 428.7
　confine 429.12
　prohibit 444.3
　retain 474.5
　hinder 1012.10
inhibiting
　restraining 428.11
　hindering 1012.17
inhibition
　suppression 92.24
　restraint 428.1
　prohibition 444.1
　retention 474.1
　hindrance 1012.1
inhibitive
　restraining 428.11
　prohibitive 444.6
　hindering 1012.17
in honor of 487.4
inhospitable
　unkind 144.16
　unhospitable 586.7
　unfriendly 589.9
inhospitality
　unkindness 144.1
　uncordialness 586.1
　inhospitableness 586.1
　enmity 589.1
inhuman
　cruel 144.26
　savage 671.21
　demoniac 680.17
inhumane 144.26
inhumanity
　cruelty 144.11
　act of cruelty 144.12

　violence 671.1
inhume 309.19
inimical
　oppositional 451.8
　warlike 458.20
　unfriendly 589.9
　contrary 779.6
　counteractive 900.8
　adverse 1011.13
inimitable 249.15
in installments
　on credit 622.10
　piece by piece 793.9
　incompletely 795.6
iniquitous
　malicious 144.20
　unjust 650.9
　wicked 654.16
　wrongdoing 655.5
　bad 1000.7
iniquity
　injustice 650.1
　evil 654.3
　misdeed 655.2
　badness 1000.1
initial
　n first 818.3
　v ratify 332.12
　letter 546.6
　adj beginning 818.15
initials
　identification 517.11
　signature 527.10
Initial Teaching Alphabet
　546.3
initiate
　n novice 572.9
　member 617.11
　v install 191.4
　preinstruct 568.14
　originate 818.10
　inaugurate 818.11
　adj skilled 413.26
initiation
　establishment 159.7
　admission 187.2
　elementary education
　　568.5
　ceremony 580.4
　first 818.3
　inauguration 818.5
initiative
　n vim 17.2
　act 328.3
　enterprise 330.7
　undertaking 404.1
　referendum 613.8
　process 889.2
　adj introductory 187.18
　beginning 818.15
inject use 87.22
　insert 191.3
　inspire 375.20
　soak 1065.13
injection remedy 86.6
　narcotic shot 87.20
　inoculation 91.16
　entrance 189.1
　insertion 191.1
　interjection 213.2
　intrusion 214.1

　soaking 1065.7
　spacecraft 1075.2
injudicious
　rash 493.7
　unwise 923.10
injunction
　precept 419.1
　charge 420.2
　court order 420.6
　restraint 428.1
　prohibition 444.1
　exclusion 773.1
injure mistreat 389.5
　impair 393.9
　hurt 393.13
　work evil 1000.6
injured pained 96.23
　impaired 393.27
injurious
　unhealthful 82.5
　impaired 393.27
　corrupting 393.44
　disadvantageous 996.6
　harmful 1000.12
injury pain 96.5
　indignity 156.2
　mistreatment 389.2
　impairment 393.1
　loss 473.1
　injustice 650.4
　misdeed 655.2
　disadvantage 996.2
　evil 1000.3
injustice
　misrepresentation 350.1
　presumption 640.2
　unjustness 650.1
　wrong 650.4
　misdeed 655.2
　inequality 791.1
ink
　n blackness 38.4
　v blacken 38.7
ink black 38.8
in keeping with
　in agreement with 788.12
　conformable to 867.9
inkling hint 551.4
　admixture 797.7
　suggestion 951.5
inky black 38.8
　stained 1004.10
inland
　n inlands 207.3
　adj interior 207.7
　adv inward 207.11
in-laws 564.2
inlay
　n insert 191.2
　lining 196.3
　v inset 191.5
　implant 191.8
　fill 196.7
in league in cooperation 450.7
　leagued 805.6
inlet entrance 189.5
　cove 242.1
　opening 292.1
　passageway 383.3
in lieu of 862.12
in limbo 971.18

in line in step 788.11
  conformist 867.6
in line with
  adv directly 161.23
  prep in agreement with 788.12
  conformable to 867.9
in love 104.28
inmate 227.2
in memoriam 989.28
in memory of
  in honor of 487.4
  to the memory of 989.28
in-migrate
  migrate 177.22
  enter 189.11
inmost interior 207.6
  private 345.13
in motion
  moving 172.7
  under way 172.9
inn 228.15
in name only
  pretexted 376.5
  nominal 527.15
innards viscera 2.16
  contents 196.1
  insides 207.4
  mechanism 1040.4
innate
  hereditary 560.19
  inborn 767.8
  instinctive 934.6
  attitudinal 978.7
inner
  n interior 207.2
  adj interior 207.6
  intrinsic 767.7
  particular 865.12
inner child 865.5
inner circle
  council 423.1
  clique 617.6
inner city 230.6
inner-directed
  introverted 92.40
  moved 375.30
  independent 430.22
  nonconformist 789.9
inner light 636.5
inner man
  interior 207.2
  self 865.5
  inmost mind 919.3
  psyche 919.4
innermost
  interior 207.6
  private 345.13
inner nature
  interior 207.2
  inside 767.5
inner workings 1040.4
inning game 745.3
  turn 825.2
innocence
  artlessness 416.1
  naturalness 499.2
  purity 653.2
  guiltlessness 657.1
  innocency 657.1
  chastity 664.1
  ignorance 930.1

  harmlessness 999.9
innocent
  n child 302.3
  dupe 358.1
  simple soul 416.3
  baby 657.4
  adj immature 301.10
  artless 416.5
  natural 499.7
  chaste 653.6
  unfallen 657.6
  chaste 664.4
  ignorant 930.11
  trusting 953.22
  harmless 999.21
innocuous
  humble 137.10
  justifiable 600.14
  harmless 999.21
innominable 122.13
innominate 528.3
in no time
  in short order 174.19
  quickly 830.7
  promptly 845.15
innovate
  originate 337.4
  invent 841.5
  make innovations 852.9
innovation
  nonimitation 337.1
  original 337.2
  curtain-raiser 816.2
  novelty 841.2
  introduction 852.4
innovator
  precursor 816.1
  transformer 852.5
innoxious 999.21
innuendo
  sarcasm 508.5
  aspersion 512.4
  implication 519.2
  hint 551.4
  accusation 599.1
innumerable
  infinite 823.3
  numberless 884.10
inobservance
  nonobservance 435.1
  inattention 984.1
inobservant
  nonobservant 435.5
  inattentive 984.6
inoculate
  immunize 91.28
  insert 191.3
  inspire 375.20
  inculcate 568.12
inoculation
  vaccination 86.28
  injection 91.16
  insertion 191.1
  inculcation 568.2
inoffensive
  odorless 72.5
  justifiable 600.14
  harmless 999.21
in on 476.8
in one's power
  under control 612.19

  possible 966.6
inoperable
  past hope 125.15
  unserviceable 391.14
  impracticable 967.8
in operation in use 387.25
  operating 889.11
inoperative
  ineffective 19.15
  unserviceable 391.14
  in disrepair 393.37
inopportune
  untimely 844.6
  inexpedient 996.5
in opposition to
  adv counteractively 900.10
  prep opposite to 215.7
  opposed to 451.10
  in disagreement with
    789.10
in order in trim 807.7
  in turn 807.10
in order to 405.24
inordinance 993.1
inordinate
  exaggerated 355.4
  overpriced 632.12
  intemperate 669.7
  fanatic 926.32
  excessive 993.16
inorganic
  unorganic 1055.4
  mineral 1058.15
inornate 499.9
in other words 341.18
in particular
  fully 766.13
  particularly 865.15
in passing
  on the way 176.20
  hastily 401.12
  incidentally 843.13
inpatient
  sick person 85.43
  inhabitant 227.2
in person
  presence 221.17
  personally 865.16
in place located 159.18
  in position 159.20
  present 221.12
  provided 385.13
  established 855.13
in place of 862.12
in plain sight
  visible 31.6
  openly 348.15
inpouring 189.12
in power
  powerful 18.12
  in authority 417.21
in practice
  in use 387.25
  operating 889.11
in process 889.11
in production
  in preparation 405.22
  in the works 892.21
in progress
  in mid-progress 162.7
  undertaken 404.7

  in preparation 405.22
in public openly 348.15
  publicly 352.19
in pursuit of 382.12
input
  n entrance 189.1
  data 1042.15
  v computerize 1042.21
inquest autopsy 307.17
  jury 596.6
  trial 598.5
  inquiry 938.1
in question
  at issue 938.39
  doubtful 971.17
  undecided 971.18
inquietude
  unpleasure 96.1
  excitement 105.5
  anxiety 126.1
  trepidation 127.5
  agitation 917.1
inquire ask 938.20
  be curious 981.3
inquirer student 572.1
  asker 938.16
  inquisitive person 981.2
inquiring
  n inquiry 938.1
  questioning 938.12
  adj questioning 938.36
  curious 981.5
inquiry trial 598.5
  examination 938.2
  inquiring 938.1
  question 938.10
  canvass 938.14
inquisition
  n tribunal 595.1
  trial 598.5
  inquiry 938.1
  grilling 938.13
  v grill 938.22
Inquisition 938.4
inquisitive
  meddlesome 214.9
  curious 981.5
inquisitor ·
  inquirer 938.16
  inquisitive person 981.2
in rags shabby 393.32
  indigent 619.8
  slovenly 810.15
in reality
  really 761.16
  truly 973.18
in regard to 775.13
in repair
  out of order 765.7
  in order 807.7
in reserve back 386.17
  in readiness 405.21
  imminent 840.3
in return
  in compensation 338.7
  in retaliation 506.9
  interchangeably 863.6
  in answer 939.7
inroad
  n intrusion 214.1
  impairment 393.1

immaterial 1053.7
insubstantiality
thinness 270.4
rarity 299.1
immateriality 764.1
unreliability 971.6
in succession
in order 807.10
continuously 812.11
insufferable 98.25
insufficiency
inability 19.2
unsatisfactoriness 108.2
insignificance 248.1
inferiority 250.3
shallowness 276.1
inequality 791.1
shortcoming 911.1
inadequacy 992.1
insufficient
unsatisfactory 108.9
inadequate 250.7
unequal 791.4
short of 911.5
unsufficing 992.9
insular
n islander 235.4
adj local 231.9
insulated 235.7
secluded 584.8
exclusive 773.9
unrelated 776.6
separate 802.20
alone 872.8
narrow-minded 980.10
insularity island 235.2
exclusiveness 773.3
narrow-mindedness 980.1
insulate proof 15.14
isolate 235.5
segregate 773.6
nonconduct 1032.29
insulated insular 235.7
segregated 773.8
insulation
exclusiveness 773.3
safeguard 1008.3
insult
n indignity 156.2
contempt 157.1
gibe 508.2
v offend 156.5
disdain 157.3
ridicule 508.8
insulting
insolent 142.9
disrespectful 156.8
insuperable
impregnable 15.19
impracticable 967.8
insupportable 98.25
insuppressible 361.12
insurance
security 438.1
precaution 494.3
assurance 1008.4
insurance company 1008.4
insurance policy 1008.4
insure secure 438.9
make sure 970.11
protect 1008.18

insured
secured 438.11
safe 1007.4
insurer
endorser 332.7
guarantor 438.6
insurgence 327.4
insurgent
n rebel 327.5
adj rebellious 327.11
insurmountable 967.8
insurrection 327.4
insurrectionary
n rebel 327.5
adj rebellious 327.11
revolutionary 860.5
insusceptible 94.9
in suspense
on tenterhooks 130.12
inert 173.14
undecided 971.18
in a dilemma 971.25
uncertainly 971.28
in sync
harmonious 708.49
agreeing 788.9
in step 788.11
synchronous 836.6
simultaneously 836.7
concurrent 899.4
televisional 1035.16
intact
unpierced 293.10
immature 301.10
preserved 397.13
continent 664.6
untouched 792.10
complete 794.9
unmixed 798.7
new 841.7
permanent 853.7
unqualified 960.2
sound 1002.7
safe 1007.4
intaglio
engraving tool 713.8
relief 715.3
mold 786.6
intake entrance 189.1
inlet 189.5
receipts 627.1
intangibility
infinitesimalness 258.2
unsubstantiality 764.1
immateriality 1053.1
intangible
infinitesimal 258.14
unsubstantial 764.5
immaterial 1053.7
intangibles 471 7
integer whole 792.1
individual 872.4
integral whole 792.9
component 796.5
one 872.7
unitary 872.10
sound 1002.7
numeric 1017.23
integrate
symmetrize 264.3
equalize 790.6

form a whole 792.7
mix 797.10
combine 805.3
unify 872.5
integrated
whole 792.9
joined 800.13
combined 805.5
unitary 872.10
integration
symmetrization 264.2
affiliation 450.2
adjustment 788.4
equating 790.2
whole 792.1
mixture 797.1
combination 805.1
oneness 872.1
notation 1017.2
integrity
artlessness 416.1
probity 644.1
wholeness 792.1
completeness 794.1
simplicity 798.1
particularity 865.1
oneness 872.1
soundness 1002.2
integument
exterior 206.2
skin 295.3
intel 551.1
intellect
intellectual faculty 919.1
mind 919.1
intelligence 920.1
knowledge 920.9
wise man 921.1
intellectual 929.1
intellectual
n wise man 921.1
scientist 928.11
learned person 929.3
intellect 929.1
adj mental 919.7
intelligent 920.12
knowledgeable 928.23
ideational 932.9
attitudinal 978.7
intellectuality
intelligence 920.1
scholarship 928.5
intellectualize
think 931.8
reason 935.15
intelligence
information 551.1
news 552.1
teachableness 570.5
secret service 576.12
spirit 678.5
intellect 919.1
mental grasp 920.1
understanding 920.1
mental capacity 920.9
knowledge 928.1
brains 928.3
surveillance 938.9
intelligence agent 576.9
intelligence quotient 920.1
intelligence service 576.12

intelligence testing 92.8
intelligence work 938.9
intelligent
teachable 570.18
mental 919.7
intellectual 920.12
knowing 928.15
intelligent agent computer
1042.2
software 1042.11
intelligentsia 929.2
intelligibility
meaningfulness 518.5
comprehensibility 521.1
facility 1014.1
intelligible
meaningful 518.10
comprehensible 521.10
intemperance
bibulousness 88.2
unrestraint 430.3
prodigality 486.1
incontinence 665.2
indulgence 669.1
intemperateness 669.1
gluttony 672.1
excess 993.1
intemperate
unrestrained 430.24
prodigal 486.8
incontinent 665.24
indulgent 669.7
violent 671.16
gluttonous 672.6
excessive 993.16
intend purpose 380.4
plan 381.8
have in mind 518.9
intended
n fiancé 104.16
adj intentional 380.8
promised 436.8
meant 518.11
intense
penetrating 15.22
energetic 17.13
sensitive 24.13
colorful 35.19
fervent 93.18
zealous 101.9
great 247.6
violent 671.16
attentive 983.15
intensified
aggravated 119.4
increased 251.7
intensify pain 26.7
aggravate 119.2
heighten 251.5
grow 251.6
intensity energy 17.1
colorfulness 35.4
loudness 53.1
zeal 101.2
greatness 247.1
violence 671.1
measurement of light
1025.22
intensive
laborious 725.18
thorough 794.10

intent
  n intention 380.1
  meaning 518.2
  adj zealous 101.9
  attentive 983.15
  engrossed 983.17
intention will 323.1
  motive 375.1
  aim 380
  intent 380.1
  plan 381.1
  meaning 518.2
inter 309.19
interact 777.6
interacting
  communicational 343.9
  interactive 777.9
interaction
  communication 343.1
  interworking 777.3
inter alia 253.11
interassociation
  interrelation 777.2
  interconnection 800.2
interbreed 797.13
interbreeding 797.4
intercalate
  interpose 213.6
  chronologize 832.14
intercede 466.6
intercept
  listen 48.10
  hinder 1012.10
interception
  game 746.3
  radar 1036.9
intercession
  mediation 466.1
  function of Christ
    677.14
  prayer 696.4
intercessional
  mediatory 466.8
  divine 677.16
intercessor
  mediator 466.3
  lawyer 597.1
interchange
  n crossing 170.2
  transferal 176.1
  communication 343.1
  passageway 383.3
  retaliation 506.1
  trade 731.2
  interaction 777.3
  mutual transfer 863
  exchange 863.1
  v communicate 343.6
  get along 455.2
  trade 731.15
  interact 777.6
  exchange 863.4
interchangeable
  transferable 176.18
  exchangeable 863.5
  indistinguishable 945.6
intercollegiate 567.13
intercom
  sound reproduction system
    50.11
  Interphone 347.6

intercommunicate
  communicate 343.6
  join 800.11
intercommunication
  communication 343.1
  social life 582.4
  interaction 777.3
  joining 800.1
intercommunicational 343.9
interconnect
  relate 775.6
  correlate 777.5
  interjoin 800.6
interconnection
  interrelation 777.2
  interjoinder 800.2
intercosmic 1072.25
intercourse
  copulation 75.7
  communication 343.1
  conversation 541.1
  social life 582.4
  commerce 731.1
  relation 775.1
  interaction 777.3
  joining 800.1
interdenominational 675.27
interdependency 777.2
interdependent 777.8
interdict
  n restraint 428.1
  prohibition 444.1
  v prohibit 444.3
interdigitation
  interrelation 777.2
  interconnection 800.2
interdisciplinary
  scholastic 568.19
  extensive 864.13
interest
  n incentive 375.7
  allurement 377.1
  benefit 387.4
  undertaking 404.1
  patronage 449.4
  estate 471.4
  gain 472.3
  portion 477.5
  party 617.4
  lending 620.1
  premium 623.3
  prerogative 642.1
  partiality 650.3
  selfishness 651.1
  occupation 724.1
  dividend 738.7
  relevance 775.4
  affair 831.3
  cause 886.9
  favor 894.2
  side 935.14
  curiosity 981.1
  concern 983.2
  importance 997.1
  good 999.4
  v attract 377.6
  relate to 775.5
  involve 898.2
  concern 983.12
interested
  partisan 617.19

partial 650.11
  involved 898.4
  discriminatory 980.12
  curious 981.5
  concerned 983.16
interest group
  pressure group 609.31
  party 617.4
interesting
  alluring 377.8
  stimulating 983.19
interest rate
  lending 620.1
  interest 623.3
interface
  boundary 211.3
  middle course 467.3
  joint 800.4
interfere
  intrude 214.5
  hinder 1012.10
interference
  intrusion 214.1
  counteraction 900.1
  wave 916.4
  hindrance 1012.1
  reception 1034.21
interfering 214.8
interfuse
  intersperse 213.7
  combine 805.3
interfusion
  interspersion 213.3
  mixture 797.1
intergalactic 1072.25
interim
  n interval 224.1
  interruption 813.2
  intermediate period 826
  meantime 826.1
  delay 846.2
  pause 857.3
  adj temporary 826.4
interior
  n inside 207.2
  inland 207.3
  scene 712.11
  middle 819.1
  adj internal 207.6
  inland 207.7
  private 345.13
  middle 819.4
interior decorating 498.1
interiority
  inwardness 207.1
  internalness 207.1
  depth 275.1
interjacent 213.10
interject
  insert 191.3
  interpose 213.6
  remark 524.24
interjection
  insertion 191.1
  interpolation 213.2
  intrusion 214.1
  remark 524.3
  part of speech 530.3
interjoin
  correlate 777.5
  interconnect 800.6

interlace weave 740.6
  interact 777.6
  mix 797.10
interlaced
  webbed 170.12
  woven 740.7
interlacing
  n weaving 740.1
  interaction 777.3
  adj weaving 740.8
interlard
  intersperse 213.7
  mix 797.10
interlibrary loan 558.1
interlining 196.3
interlink
  correlate 777.5
  interconnect 800.6
interlinked
  related 775.9
  correlative 777.8
interlock
  n safeguard 1008.3
  v correlate 777.5
  agree 788.6
  interconnect 800.6
interlocked
  related 775.9
  correlative 777.8
interlocking
  interrelation 777.2
  interconnection 800.2
interlocutory
  mediatory 466.8
  conversational 541.12
interlope 214.5
interloper
  intruder 214.3
  outsider 774.2
interloping 214.1
interlude
  n respite 20.2
  act 704.7
  passage 708.24
  interim 826.1
  pause 857.3
  v intervene 826.3
intermarriage 563.1
intermarry 563.15
intermeddle
  meddle 214.7
  hinder 1012.10
intermediary
  n intermedium 213.4
  instrument 384.4
  mediator 466.3
  go-between 576.4
  adj intervening 213.10
  medium 246.3
  modal 384.8
  mediatory 466.8
  middle 819.4
intermediate
  n instrument 384.4
  mediator 466.3
  go-between 576.4
  gear 1040.9
  v mediate 466.6
  adj intervening 213.10
  medium 246.3
  mediatory 466.8

living 306.12
personally 865.16
in the gutter
poorly 250.9
destitute 619.6
corrupt 654.14
in the hole 623.8
in the know
informed 551.17
cognizant of 928.16
knowledgeable 928.17
in the limelight
publicly 352.19
prominent 662.17
on the stage 704.36
in the long run
on the average 246.5
on the whole 792.14
eventually 831.12
in time 839.11
generally 864.17
in the market for
adj searching 938.38
prep after 382.12
in the midst of
adv midway 819.5
prep at 159.27
between 213.12
among 797.17
in the moment 838.3
in the mood
willing 324.5
disposed 978.8
in the neighborhood of
adv near 223.20
at a price 630.17
prep about 223.26
in the nick of time
opportunely 843.12
in time 845.12
expedient 995.5
in the pink
healthy 83.9
in order 807.7
in the red
at a loss 473.9
destitute 619.9
indebted 623.8
in the same boat 790.7
in the same breath
at once 830.8
simultaneously 836.7
in the swim 578.11
in the thick of
adv midway 819.5
prep between 213.12
among 797.17
in the wind
against the wind 182.65
happening 831.9
imminent 840.3
in the works
adj planned 381.12
undertaken 404.7
in preparation 405.22
operating 889.11
adv in production 892.21
intimacy
copulation 75.7
nearness 223.1
sociability 582.1

familiarity 587.5
relation 775.1
knowledge 928.1
intimate
n friend 588.1
v advise 422.5
imply 519.4
hint 551.10
adj interior 207.6
near 223.14
homelike 228.33
private 345.13
familiar 582.24
friendly 587.19
joined 800.13
particular 865.12
intimate apparel 5.22
intimation
hint 248.4
piece of advice 422.2
sign 517.9
implication 519.2
clue 551.4
admixture 797.7
hunch 934.3
suggestion 951.5
in time
in tempo 709.30
synchronous 836.6
in due time 839.11
in good time 845.12
periodically 850.10
intimidate cow 127.20
dissuade 379.3
coerce 424.7
bluster 503.3
threaten 514.2
domineer 612.15
intimidated
terrified 127.26
cowardly 491.10
intimidating
dissuasive 379.5
threatening 514.3
intimidation
frightening 127.6
dissuasion 379.1
coercion 424.3
bluster 503.1
threat 514.1
into
adj knowledgeable 928.17
prep in 189.14
inside 207.13
intolerable
insufferable 98.25
unlikable 99.7
unacceptable 108.10
downright 247.12
intolerance
intoleration 135.2
obstinacy 361.1
narrow-mindedness 980.2
intolerant
n bigot 980.5
adj unforbearing 135.7
obstinate 361.8
untolerating 980.11
intonate
inflect 524.28
sing 708.38

intonation tone 50.2
inflection 524.6
vocal music 708.13
execution 708.30
harmonization 709.2
intone 708.38
in toto fully 766.13
wholly 792.13
intoxicate
inebriate 88.22
thrill 105.15
dizzy 985.8
intoxicated
under the influence 87.23
inebriated 88.31
fervent 93.18
frenzied 105.25
intoxicating
intoxicative 88.36
exciting 105.30
intoxication
poisoning 85.31
inebriation 88.1
happiness 95.2
fury 105.8
intractable
insubordinate 327.9
ungovernable 361.12
inflexible 1046.12
intramural
intramarginal 207.8
scholastic 567.13
intransient 827.10
intransigence 361.2
intransigent
n obstinate person 361.6
oppositionist 452.3
adj unyielding 361.9
in transit
on the way 176.20
on the move 177.42
intransitive
n verb 530.4
adj grammatical 530.17
intransmutable 855.17
intraterritorial 207.8
intravenous 91.17
intrepid 492.16
intricacy
abstruseness 522.2
complexity 799.1
difficulty 1013.1
intricate
hard to understand 522.14
mixed 797.14
complex 799.4
bewildering 971.27
difficult 1013.17
intrigue
n love affair 104.5
web of intrigue 381.5
stratagem 415.3
deceitfulness 645.3
v fascinate 377.7
plot 381.9
maneuver 415.10
intrigued 95.15
intriguing
delightful 97.7
alluring 377.8
scheming 381.13

intrinsic
interior 207.6
internal 767.7
characteristic 865.13
introduce
bring in 187.14
insert 191.3
propose 439.5
preinstruct 568.14
present 587.14
prefix 814.3
go before 816.3
inaugurate 818.11
innovate 852.9
introducer
transformer 852.5
producer 892.7
introduction
bringing in 187.7
entrance 189.1
insertion 191.1
interjection 213.2
makeup 554.12
elementary education 568.5
acquaintance 587.4
legislative procedure 613.6
act 704.7
overture 708.26
part of writing 793.2
curtain-raiser 816.2
inauguration 818.5
basics 818.6
innovation 852.4
introductory
introductive 187.18
educational 568.18
beginning 818.15
introit 708.17
Introit 696.3
intromission
admission 187.2
insertion 191.1
intromit receive 187.10
insert 191.3
introspect 931.12
introspection 931.6
introspective
cognitive 931.21
absorbed in thought 931.22
introversion
personality tendency 92.11
inversion 205.1
interiority 207.1
reticence 344.3
introvert
n personality type 92.12
v invert 205.5
adj introverted 92.40
introverted
introvert 92.40
inverted 205.7
reticent 344.10
intrude enter 189.7
interpose 213.6
obtrude 214.5
talk out of turn 844.4
overstep 910.9
intruder incomer 189.4
interloper 214.3
foreign body 774.2
newcomer 774.4

intrusion
entrance 189.1
interposition 213.1
interference 214.1
obtrusion 214.1
extraneousness 774.1
intruder 774.2
untimeliness 844.1
overstepping 910.3
intrusive
entering 189.12
obtrusive 214.8
overactive 330.24
extraneous 774.5
untimely 844.6
intuit sense 934.4
foreknow 961.6
intuition
extrasensory perception 689.8
intuitiveness 934.1
hunch 934.3
discrimination 944.1
suggestion 951.5
intuitive
premonitory 133.15
intuitional 934.5
theoretical 951.13
foreseeing 961.7
intumescence
growth 85.39
distension 259.2
swelling 283.4
in tune in accord 455.3
harmonious 708.49
in turn in order 807.10
consecutively 812.11
interchangeably 863.6
inundate
aggrieve 112.19
overflow 238.17
submerge 367.7
overwhelm 395.21
raid 459.20
run over 910.7
oversupply 993.14
flood 1065.14
inundated
overcome 112.29
flooded 238.25
underwater 275.13
overrun 910.10
soaked 1065.17
inundation
overflow 238.6
submergence 367.2
wordiness 538.2
overrunning 910.1
plenty 991.2
superabundance 993.2
wetting 1065.6
in unison
unanimously 332.17
cooperatively 450.6
harmonious 708.49
in step 788.11
jointly 800.18
simultaneously 836.7
inure callous 94.6
accustom 373.9
inured callous 94.12
accustomed 373.15

hardened 654.17
inusitation 390.1
invade intrude 214.5
raid 459.20
usurp 640.8
infest 910.6
overstep 910.9
invader intruder 214.3
assailant 459.12
in vain
unsuccessfully 410.19
amiss 911.7
invalid
n impotent 19.6
sick person 85.43
recluse 584.5
v afflict 85.50
adj ineffective 19.15
unhealthy 85.54
repealed 445.3
illogical 936.11
bad 1000.7
invalidate
disqualify 19.11
abolish 395.13
repeal 445.2
neutralize 900.7
disprove 958.4
invalidated
disabled 19.16
disproved 958.7
invalidation
repeal 445.1
neutralization 900.2
disproof 958.1
invalidity
ineffectiveness 19.3
unhealthiness 85.3
illogicalness 936.2
badness 1000.1
invaluable 632.10
invariable
tedious 118.9
uniform 781.5
unchangeable 855.17
invasion
intrusion 214.1
raid 459.4
usurpation 640.3
infestation 910.2
invasive
entering 189.12
intrusive 214.8
attacking 459.29
invective
n sarcasm 508.5
berating 510.7
vilification 513.2
speech 543.2
adj condemnatory 510.22
inveigh against 510.13
inveigle trap 356.20
lure 377.5
inveiglement 377.1
invent originate 337.4
fabricate 354.18
initiate 818.10
innovate 841.5
change 852.9
produce 892.12
discover 941.2

imagine 986.14
invented
fabricated 354.29
originated 892.19
invention
fabrication 354.10
innovation 852.4
production 892.1
product 893.1
discovery 941.1
inventiveness 986.3
figment of the imagination 986.5
inventive
cunning 415.12
beginning 818.15
creative 892.16
imaginative 986.18
inventor
producer 892.7
imaginer 986.12
inventory
n contents 196.1
store 386.1
record 549.1
account book 628.4
merchandise 735.1
assemblage 770.1
table 808.4
list 871.1
summation 1017.11
v take account of 628.9
list 871.8
sum up 1017.19
check 1017.21
inverse
n reverse 205.4
opposite side 215.3
v invert 205.5
adj contrapositive 215.5
contrary 779.6
inversion
turning over 205
inverting 205.1
notation 1017.2
invert
n homosexual 75.14
v inverse 205.5
invertebrate
n weakling 16.6
creature 311.3
coward 491.5
adj invertebral 311.50
weak-willed 362.12
invest clothe 5.39
empower 18.10
establish 159.16
insert 191.4
surround 209.6
wrap 295.20
provide 385.7
besiege 459.19
endow 478.17
commission 615.10
install 615.12
spend 626.5
place 729.17
invested
clothing 5.45
provided 385.13
endowed 478.26

investigate
discuss 541.11
indagate 938.23
investigation
discussion 541.6
indagation 938.4
investigative journalism 552.1
investigator
detective 576.10
examiner 938.17
investiture clothing 5.1
establishment 159.7
admission 187.2
giving 478.1
commission 615.1
installation 615.3
holy orders 698.10
investment clothing 5.1
empowerment 18.8
provision 385.1
siege 459.5
endowment 478.9
commission 615.1
money matters 729
venture 729.4
investment manager 628.7
investor 729.9
inveteracy
customariness 373.6
permanence 853.1
fixity 855.2
inveterate
confirmed 373.18
durable 827.10
traditional 842.12
established 855.13
invidious
malicious 144.20
jealous 153.5
envious 154.3
in view visible 31.6
expected 130.13
present 221.12
imminent 840.3
in view of 888.9
invigorate refresh 9.2
strengthen 15.13
energize 17.10
stimulate 105.13
cheer 109.7
invigorating
refreshing 9.3
energizing 17.15
healthful 81.5
tonic 86.44
cheering 109.16
cool 1023.12
invincible
impregnable 15.19
peerless 249.15
persevering 360.8
indestructible 855.18
reliable 970.17
inviolable
impregnable 15.19
trustworthy 644.19
sacred 685.7
inviolate honest 644.13
sacred 685.7
permanent 853.7
undamaged 1002.8

invisible
imperceptible 32.5
infinitesimal 258.14
unrevealed 346.12
invitation
incentive 375.7
allurement 377.1
offer 439.1
invite 440.4
invite
n invitation 440.4
v encourage 375.21
attract 377.6
ask 440.13
incur 897.4
interest 983.12
inviting delightful 97.7
receptive 187.16
provocative 375.27
alluring 377.8
invitational 440.19
interesting 983.19
invocation
summons 420.5
entreaty 440.2
conjuration 690.4
prayer 696.4
benediction 696.5
in vogue 578.11
invoice
n statement 628.3
bill 871.5
v bill 628.11
invoke summon 420.11
entreat 440.11
address 524.26
conjure 690.11
pray 696.13
adduce 957.12
refer to 957.14
involuntary
unwilling 325.5
unpremeditated 365.11
obligatory 424.11
intuitive 934.6
instinctive 963.14
unintentional 972.17
involuted
convolutional 281.6
complex 799.4
involution
convolution 281.1
deterioration 393.3
complexity 799.1
involvement 898.1
notation 1017.2
involve surround 209.6
signify 517.17
imply 519.4
ornament 545.7
incriminate 599.10
entail 772.4
relate to 775.5
complicate 799.3
implicate 898.2
evidence 957.8
engross 983.13
hamper 1012.11
put in a hole 1013.15
involved
participating 476.8

implied 519.7
accused 599.15
indebted 623.8
partial 650.11
guilty 656.3
included 772.5
related 775.9
complex 799.4
implicated 898.4
engrossed 983.17
involvement
sympathy 93.5
surrounding 209.5
mediation 466.1
participation 476.1
incrimination 599.2
partiality 650.3
guilt 656.1
entailment 772.2
complexity 799.1
involuntary cooperation
898.1
involution 898.1
engrossment 983.3
invulnerable
impregnable 15.19
indestructible 855.18
uninfluenceable 895.4
unhazardous 1007.5
protected 1008.21
inward
n interior 207.2
adj entering 189.12
in 189.13
interior 207.6
inside 207.11
private 345.13
intrinsic 767.7
inwards
n viscera 2.16
insides 207.4
adv in 189.13
inside 207.11
in with
on good terms 587.18
leagued 805.6
in writing 547.22
in your dreams
adv. in no degree 248.11
interjs. by no means 335.9
ion atom 258.8
electrolysis 1032.25
atom 1038.4
element 1060.2
ionic 1032.32
Ionic 717.2
ionization
electrolysis 1032.25
fission 1038.8
ionize 1032.28
iota modicum 248.2
minute 258.7
IOU 728.11
iPod 50.11
ipse dixit
affirmation 334.1
decree 420.4
ipseity 865.1
IQ 920.1
irascibility
excitability 105.10

irritability 110.2
perversity 361.3
dissension 456.3
irascible
excitable 105.28
irritable 110.19
perverse 361.11
partisan 456.17
irate 152.28
ire 152.5
irenic
unbelligerent 464.10
pacificatory 465.12
iridesce opalesce 47.8
luminesce 1025.27
iridescence
rainbow 47.2
opalescence 1025.18
iridescent
soft-colored 35.22
rainbowlike 47.10
opalescent 1025.38
iridiated 47.10
iris eye 2.9
sight 27.9
variegation 47.6
Iris 353.1
irk
n tedium 118.1
v annoy 96.13
vex 98.15
be tedious 118.6
trouble 1013.13
irked annoyed 96.21
weary 118.11
troubled 1013.20
irksome
annoying 98.22
wearying 118.10
troublesome 1013.18
iron
n symbol of strength 15.8
cycle 179.8
basketball 747.1
hardness 1046.6
v press 287.6
adj unyielding 361.9
firm 425.7
brass 1058.17
Iron Age 824.5
ironbound
rugged 288.7
firm 425.7
bound 428.16
ironclad firm 425.7
armored 460.13
iron curtain
frontier 211.5
veil of secrecy 345.3
communism 611.5
barrier 1012.5
iron grip 474.2
iron hand
governance 417.5
firm hand 425.3
control 612.2
despotism 612.9
ironic witty 489.15
satiric 508.13
suggestive 519.6
ambiguous 539.4

self-contradictory 779.8
mixed 797.14
iron out reconcile 465.8
solve 940.2
irons 428.4
iron will 359.4
irony wit 489.1
sarcasm 508.5
ambiguity 539.1
self-contradiction 779.3
doubleness 873.1
irradiate
v radiumize 91.26
preserve 397.9
illuminate 1025.29
radioactivate 1037.10
adj illuminated 1025.40
irradiated
illuminated 1025.40
radioactive 1037.11
irradiation
food preservation 397.2
light 1025.1
irrational
unintelligent 922.13
unwise 923.10
insane 926.26
illogical 936.11
numeric 1017.23
irrationality
unintelligence 922.1
unwiseness 923.2
insanity 926.1
illogicalness 936.2
irreclaimable
past hope 125.15
irredeemable 654.18
irreconcilable
n oppositionist 452.3
adj unyielding 361.9
vengeful 507.7
alienated 589.11
different 780.7
inconsistent 789.8
irrecoverable
past hope 125.15
past 837.7
irredeemable
past hope 125.15
unpayable 625.13
irreclaimable 654.18
irreducible
intrinsic 767.7
simple 798.6
inextricable 799.5
one 872.7
requisite 963.13
irreformable
past hope 125.15
irreclaimable 654.18
irrefutable
evidential 957.16
obvious 970.15
irregular
n casual 461.16
second 1005.6
adj distorted 265.10
rough 288.6
informal 581.3
illegal 674.6
nonuniform 782.3

unequal 791.4
unordered 810.12
discontinuous 813.4
unregular 851.3
inconstant 854.7
abnormal 870.9
eccentric 927.5
inferior 1005.9
irregularity
distortion 265.1
roughness 288.1
unsmoothness 294.2
informality 581.1
nonuniformity 782.1
inequality 791.1
disorder 810.1
discontinuity 813.1
unmethodicalness 851.1
inconstancy 854.2
abnormality 870.1
eccentricity 927.1
irregular verb 530.4
irrelevance
unrelatedness 776.1
unfitness 789.3
untimeliness 844.1
unimportance 998.1
irrelevant
unrelated 776.7
inappropriate 789.7
untimely 844.6
insignificant 998.17
irreligion
impiety 694.1
ungodliness 695.3
irreligious
impious 694.6
ungodly 695.17
unbelieving 955.8
irremediable
past hope 125.15
ruined 395.28
irremovable 855.15
irreparable 125.15
irreplaceable
used up 388.5
requisite 963.13
irreprehensible 657.8
irrepressible
cheerful 109.11
ungovernable 361.12
unrestrained 430.24
irreproachable
honest 644.13
inculpable 657.8
perfect 1002.6
irresistible
impregnable 15.19
powerful 18.12
delightful 97.7
great 247.6
alluring 377.8
overpowering 412.18
compulsory 424.10
evidential 957.16
inevitable 963.15
irresolute
wishy-washy 16.17
irresolved 362.9
inconstant 854.7
uncertain 971.16

irresolution
frailty 16.2
indecision 362.1
uncertainty 971.1
irrespective of 338.9
irresponsible
lawless 418.5
exempt 430.30
untrustworthy 645.19
inconstant 854.7
irretrievable
past hope 125.15
lost 473.7
unchangeable 855.17
irreverence
disrespect 156.1
impiety 694.1
irreverent
disrespectful 156.7
impious 694.6
irreversible
past hope 125.15
directional 161.12
confirmed 373.18
unchangeable 855.17
irrevocable
past hope 125.15
mandatory 420.12
unchangeable 855.17
inevitable 963.15
irrigate dilute 16.11
wash 79.19
moisten 1065.12
irrigation washing 79.5
wetting 1065.6
cultivation 1069.13
irritability
sensitivity 24.3
excitability 105.10
irascibility 110.2
dissension 456.3
irritable sensitive 24.12
excitable 105.28
irascible 110.19
nervous 128.11
partisan 456.17
irritant
n irritation 96.3
adj irritating 26.13
irritate pain 26.7
displease 96.14
aggravate 119.2
get on one's nerves 128.9
provoke 152.24
impair 393.9
sow dissension 456.14
irritated sore 26.11
annoyed 96.21
aggravated 119.4
provoked 152.27
impaired 393.27
irritating painful 26.13
pungent 68.6
annoying 98.22
aggravating 119.5
irritation
soreness 26.4
annoyance 96.3
excitation 105.11
aggravation 119.1
resentment 152.1

incitement 375.4
adversity 1011.1
irrupt burst forth 33.9
enter 189.7
intrude 214.5
originate 818.13
overstep 910.9
irruption
outburst 105.9
intrusion 214.1
raid 459.4
irruptive
entering 189.12
attacking 459.29
Isis 890.5
Islam 675.13
Islamic 675.31
island
n airport 184.22
isle 235.2
v insulate 235.5
adj insular 235.7
islander 235.4
island-hop 235.5
isle 235.2
ism school 617.5
cult 675.2
system of belief 953.3
isobar
weather map 317.4
isotope 1038.5
isogeny 778.1
isolate
insulate 235.5
excise 255.10
quarantine 429.13
segregate 773.6
analyze 801.6
separate 802.8
nonconduct 1032.29
isolated
quiescent 173.12
insular 235.7
private 345.13
quarantined 429.20
secluded 584.8
segregated 773.8
unrelated 776.6
separate 802.20
separated 802.21
alone 872.8
isolation
defense mechanism
92.23
privacy 345.2
quarantine 429.2
seclusion 584.1
exclusiveness 773.3
itemization 801.2
separation 802.1
aloneness 872.2
isolationism
noninterference 430.9
seclusion 584.1
foreign policy 609.5
isolationist
free agent 430.12
recluse 584.5
isomer 1038.5
isometric
n weather map 317.4

adj climatal 317.13
equisized 790.10
isometrics 84.2
isotherm 317.4
isothermal 1019.30
isothermic 1019.30
isotope 1038.5
Israelite
n Jew 675.21
adj Jewish 675.30
issue
n emergence 190.1
amount 244.2
publication 352.1
escape 369.1
edition 554.5
family 559.5
offspring 561.1
platform 609.7
issuance 738.6
event 831.1
cause 886.9
effect 887.1
product 893.1
topic 937.1
question 938.10
solution 940.1
salient point 997.6
v be born 1.2
appear 33.8
set out 188.8
emerge 190.11
flow 238.16
quantify 244.4
bring out 352.14
be published 352.16
find vent 369.10
parcel out 477.8
give 478.12
print 548.14
monetize 728.26
float 738.12
disperse 771.4
originate 818.13
come after 835.3
result 887.4
issueless 891.4
issue price 738.9
issuing
n appearance 33.1
emergence 190.1
adj emerging 190.18
isthmus
contraction 260.1
narrow place 270.3
it self 865.5
what's what 973.4
italic
n type 548.6
adj written 547.22
italicize 997.14
italicized
written 547.22
emphatic 997.21
it beats me 522.27
itch
n itching 74.3
sexual desire 75.5
craving 100.6
v tingle 74.5
twitch 917.13

itch for lust 75.20
 wish for 100.16
itching
 n itch 74.3
 symptom 85.9
 craving 100.6
 adj itchy 74.10
 lustful 75.27
 craving 100.24
 lascivious 665.29
itchy sensitive 24.12
 itching 74.10
 lascivious 665.29
 curious 981.5
item
 n memorandum 549.4
 entry 628.5
 commodity 735.2
 particular 766.3
 part 793.1
 component 796.2
 individual 872.4
 citation 957.5
 adv additionally 253.11
itemization
 description 349.2
 circumstantiation 766.5
 enumeration 801.2
 particularization 865.7
 list 871.1
 index 871.7
itemize specify 766.6
 enumerate 801.7
 particularize 865.9
 list 871.8
 cite 957.13
 sum up 1017.19
items contents 196.1
 merchandise 735.1
 list 871.1
 knowledge 928.1
iterate
 reiterate 849.8
 persist 856.5
iteration
 wordiness 538.2
 reiteration 849.2
 duplication 874.1
iterative
 n aspect 530.13
 adj diffuse 538.11
 repetitious 849.14
it girl 1016.7
itinerant
 n wanderer 178.2
 adj traveling 177.36
itinerary
 n route 383.1
 directory 574.10
 adj traveling 177.36
itself 865.5
itsy-bitsy 258.11
IUD 86.23
ivied halls 567.5
ivories teeth 2.8
 keyboard 711.17
 dice 759.8
ivory
 n whiteness 37.2
 smoothness 287.3
 adj whitish 37.8

ivory tower
 seclusion 584.1
 retreat 584.6
 refuge 1009.5
ivy
 n plant 310.4
 adj green 44.4
Ivy League 746.1
izzard 820.1
jab
 n attack 459.3
 thrust 902.2
 hit 902.4
 v use 87.22
 scoff 508.9
 thrust 902.12
 hit 902.14
jabber
 n nonsense 520.2
 mumbling 525.4
 chatter 540.3
 v talk nonsense 520.5
 mumble 525.9
 chatter 540.5
jabberer 540.4
jack
 n mariner 183.1
 ass 311.15
 flag 647.7
 money 728.2
 lawn bowling 750.3
 card 758.2
 base 901.8
 lifter 912.3
 v hunt 382.9
jackal fox 311.19
 follower 616.8
jackass ass 311.15
 fool 924.1
jacket
 n outerwear 5.13
 skin 295.3
 hull 295.16
 wrapper 295.18
 bookbinding 554.14
 v cloak 5.40
jackknife 367.1
jack-of-all-trades 413.11
jackpot award 646.2
 pot 759.5
jackrabbit hare 311.23
 jumper 366.4
jacks 743.16
jack squat 248.11
jack up increase 251.4
 call down 510.18
jactitation
 boasting 502.1
 shaking 917.2
Jacuzzi bath 79.8
 fitness 84.1
 massage 1044.3
jade
 n horse 311.12
 strumpet 665.14
 v fatigue 21.4
 burn out 21.5
 be tedious 118.6
 satiate 994.4
jaded tired 21.7
 weary 118.11

 languid 331.20
 worn-out 393.36
 satiated 994.6
jag
 n drinking spree 88.6
 projection 285.4
 notch 289.1
 v notch 289.4
jagged angular 278.6
 rugged 288.7
 notched 289.5
 nonuniform 782.3
 discontinuous 813.4
jaguar variegation 47.6
 wild cat 311.21
jail
 n prison 429.8
 v enclose 212.5
 imprison 429.14
jailbird
 prisoner 429.11
 criminal 660.9
jailbreak 369.1
jailed
 enclosed 212.10
 jugged 429.21
jailer gaoler 429.10
 penologist 604.9
 guard 1008.9
Jainist 675.24
jalopy 179.10
jam
 n sweets 10.40
 obstruction 293.3
 state 765.1
 throng 770.4
 delay 846.2
 multitude 884.3
 bewilderment 971.3
 barrier 1012.5
 predicament 1013.5
 semiliquid 1062.5
 v drown out 53.8
 stop 293.7
 have a party 582.21
 fill 794.7
 hook 800.8
 secure 855.8
 fix 855.10
 stop 857.7
 teem with 884.5
 thrust 902.12
 overload 993.15
 obstruct 1012.12
 transmit 1036.15
 densify 1045.9
jamb leg 177.14
 post 273.4
jamboree 743.4
jam in enter 189.7
 thrust in 191.7
jammed
 stopped 293.11
 fast 800.14
 late 846.16
 stuck 855.16
 teeming 884.9
 overfull 993.20
 dense 1045.12
jamming
 reception 1034.21

 radar 1036.13
jam-packed
 stopped 293.11
 crowded 770.22
 full 794.11
 teeming 884.9
 overfull 993.20
 dense 1045.12
jam session 708.32
Jane Doe alias 527.8
 common woman 606.5
 average 864.3
jangle
 n noise 53.3
 ringing 54.3
 rasp 58.3
 clash 61.2
 disaccord 456.1
 v ring 54.8
 sound harshly 58.9
 grate on 58.11
 sound a sour note 61.3
 differ 456.8
 disagree 789.5
jangling
 grating 58.16
 clashing 61.5
 disagreeing 789.6
janitor
 cleaner 79.14
 guardian 1008.6
 doorkeeper 1008.12
Janus 873.1
japanning 35.12
jape
 n joke 489.6
 gibe 508.2
 v joke 489.13
 banter 490.5
 scoff 508.9
jar
 n rasp 58.3
 clash 61.2
 start 131.3
 disaccord 456.1
 shake 917.3
 v sound harshly 58.9
 sound a sour note 61.3
 agitate 105.14
 startle 131.8
 package 212.9
 put up 397.11
 differ 456.8
 disagree 789.5
 shake 917.11
jargon
 n nonsense 520.2
 Greek 522.7
 lingo 523.9
 argot 523.11
 technical term 526.5
 v speak 523.18
jarring
 n disaccord 456.1
 disagreement 789.1
 adj grating 58.16
 clashing 61.5
 exciting 105.30
 unnerving 128.15
 surprising 131.11
 disagreeing 789.6

jolting 917.20
jaundice
  n yellow skin 43.2
  symptom 85.9
  jealousy 153.1
  prejudice 980.3
  v yellow 43.3
  prejudice 980.9
jaundiced
  yellow-faced 43.6
  sour 110.23
  jealous 153.5
  discriminatory 980.12
jaunt
  n journey 177.5
  walk 177.10
  v journey 177.21
  wander 177.23
jaunty
  lighthearted 109.12
  showy 501.19
  chic 578.13
javelin 462.8
jaw
  n mouth 292.4
  v berate 510.19
  speak 524.20
  chatter 540.5
jawbreaker
  long word 526.10
  high-sounding words 545.3
jawbreaking
  sesquipedalian 545.10
  difficult 1013.17
jaw-dropping 122.12
jaws 474.4
jaywalk 177.27
jaywalker 178.6
jazz
  n energy 17.3
  hot jazz 708.9
  adj instrumental 708.51
  syncopated 709.29
Jazz Age 824.5
jazz musician 710.2
jazz up energize 17.10
  stimulate 105.13
  intensify 251.5
jazzy showy 501.19
  instrumental 708.51
  syncopated 709.29
JD 302.4
jealous jaundiced 153.5
  envious 154.3
jealousy
  jealousness 153.1
  resentment 153.1
  envy 154.1
jeans 5.18
jeepers 513.12
jeer
  n indignity 156.2
  gibe 508.2
  v scoff 508.9
jeering
  n indignity 156.2
  ridicule 508.1
  adj ridiculing 508.12
jejune insipid 65.2
  dull 117.6
  haggard 270.20

shallow 276.5
unproductive 891.4
empty-headed 922.19
meager 992.10
jell
  n semiliquid 1062.5
  v thicken 1045.10
  emulsify 1062.10
jellied
  thickened 1045.14
  viscous 1062.12
jelling 1045.4
jelly
  n sweets 10.40
  semiliquid 1062.5
  v thicken 1045.10
  emulsify 1062.10
jellyfish weakling 16.6
  vacillator 362.5
  coward 491.5
jenny
  female animal 77.9
  spinner 271.5
  ass 311.15
jeopardize 1006.6
jeopardy
  n danger 1006.1
  v endanger 1006.6
Jeremiah 399.4
jerk
  n bad person 660.5
  yank 905.3
  shake 917.3
  fool 924.3
  v be excited 105.18
  preserve 397.9
  throw 904.10
  yerk 905.5
  twitch 917.13
jerking
  n food preservation
    397.2
  twitching 917.5
  adj jerky 917.19
jerkwater 998.18
jerky
  n meat 10.13
  beef 10.14
  adj convulsive 671.23
  nonuniform 782.3
  discontinuous 813.4
  irregular 851.3
  herky-jerky 917.19
jerry-built 16.14
jest
  n joke 489.6
  gibe 508.2
  laughingstock 508.7
  trifle 998.5
  v joke 489.13
  banter 490.5
jester humorist 489.12
  buffoon 707.10
jesting
  n bantering 490.2
  adj witty 489.15
Jesuit sophist 936.6
  quibbler 936.7
jesuitic
  insincere 354.32
  sophistical 936.10

jet
  n blackness 38.4
  jet plane 181.3
  ascent 193.1
  spout 238.9
  outburst 671.6
  disgorgement 909.7
  heater 1020.10
  v fly 184.36
  run out 190.13
  shoot up 193.9
  spout 238.20
  disgorge 909.25
Jet Age 824.6
jet-black 38.8
jeté 366.1
jet flight 184.1
jet lag 21.1
jet plane
  swiftness 174.6
  jet 181.3
jet power
  manpower 18.4
  propulsion 184.25
jet-propelled
  flying 184.50
  rocket-propelled 904.16
jet propulsion
  propulsion 184.25
  rocket propulsion 1074.8
jetsam 370.4
jet set traveler 178.1
  society 578.6
jet-setter 178.1
jetstream 184.32
jettison
  n abandonment 370.1
  discard 390.3
  ejection 909.1
  v abandon 370.5
  discard 390.7
  eject 909.13
jetty
  n buttress 901.4
  harbor 1009.6
  barrier 1012.5
  adj black 38.8
jeu d'esprit 489.7
Jew 675.21
jewel
  n favorite 104.15
  bijou 498.6
  good person 659.1
  bearing 915.7
  good thing 999.5
  v figure 498.9
jewelry 498.5
Jewish 675.30
Jezebel
  witch 593.7
  strumpet 665.14
  demimonde 665.15
jib start 127.12
  avoid 164.6
  hesitate 362.7
  pull back 903.7
jibe
  change course 182.30
  agree 788.6
  be changed 852.6
jiffy 830.3

jig
  n snare 356.13
  leap 366.1
  jerk 905.3
  shake 917.3
  v jerk 905.5
  twitch 917.13
jigger
  n drink 88.7
  vermin 311.36
  fisher 382.6
  thing 1052.5
  v jerk 905.5
  twitch 917.13
jiggle
  n jerk 905.3
  shake 917.3
  v jerk 905.5
  twitch 917.13
jillion
  n trillion 882.13
  large number 1017.5
  adj numerous 884.6
jilt
  n deceiver 357.1
  v abandon 370.5
  discard 390.7
jilted 99.10
jilter 357.1
jilting 370.1
Jim Crow
  seclusion 584.1
  exclusiveness 773.3
  discrimination 980.4
jim-dandy 999.13
jiminy! 122.21
jimjams
  trepidation 127.5
  nervousness 128.2
jimmy
  n lever 906.4
  v get a purchase 906.8
jingle
  n ringing 54.3
  meter 720.7
  assonance 784.6
  repetitiousness 849.4
  v ring 54.8
  rhyme 720.14
jingling
  n ringing 54.3
  adj ringing 54.13
  rhyming 720.17
  assonant 784.17
jingo
  n militarist 461.5
  patriot 591.3
  bigot 980.5
  adj militaristic 458.21
jingoism
  warlikeness 458.10
  patriotism 591.2
jingoistic
  militaristic 458.21
  public-spirited 591.4
jinni 680.6
jinx
  n spell 691.1
  bad influence 1000.4
  v bewitch 691.9
  work evil 1000.6

bring bad luck 1011.12
jitney 179.13
jitters
  nervousness 128.2
  agitation 917.1
jittery
  jumpy 128.12
  agitated 917.16
jive
  n bull 520.3
  jazz 708.9
  v banter 490.6
  syncopate 708.43
job
  n act 328.3
  theft 482.4
  occupation 724.1
  task 724.2
  function 724.3
  position 724.5
  affair 831.3
  v rent 615.15
  hire out 615.16
  deal in 731.16
  sell 734.8
Job 134.3
job action 727.5
jobber
  intermediary 213.4
  worker 726.2
  merchant 730.2
  stockbroker 737.10
jobbing
  Machiavellianism 415.2
  trade 731.2
  selling 734.2
  stockbroking 737.18
jobholder 726.2
jobless 331.18
job lot 735.1
job site 739.3
jock real man 76.6
  soldier 461.7
  athlete 743.19
  jockey 757.2
  supporter 901.2
jockey
  n speeder 174.5
  rider 178.8
  jock 757.2
  saddle parts 901.18
  v maneuver 415.10
  compete 457.18
jocose 489.15
jocularity
  merriment 109.5
  wittiness 489.2
Joe Schmo 606.1
Joe Sixpack
  the people 606.1
  common man 606.5
jog
  n slow motion 175.2
  gait 177.12
  bulge 283.3
  notch 289.1
  thrust 902.2
  jerk 905.3
  shake 917.3
  v exercise 84.4
  plod 175.7

walk 177.27
trot 177.28
thrust 902.12
jerk 905.5
shake 917.11
jogger 989.5
joggle
  n bulge 283.3
  notch 289.1
  thrust 902.2
  jerk 905.3
  shake 917.3
  v thrust 902.12
  jerk 905.5
  shake 917.11
jog on march on 162.3
  continue 856.3
jog the memory 989.19
jog trot run 174.3
  slow motion 175.2
  routine 373.5
jog-trot tedious 118.9
  monotonous 849.15
john latrine 12.10
  toilet 12.11
  bathroom 197.26
  card 758.2
  cheater 759.22
John Bull country 232.5
  the government 612.3
John Doe alias 527.8
  the people 606.1
  common man 606.5
  average 864.3
John Hancock
  ratification 332.4
  signature 527.10
johnny latrine 12.10
  toilet 12.11
  guy 76.5
Johnny 461.7
johnnycake 10.29
Johnny-come-lately
  newcomer 774.4
  beginner 818.2
  latecomer 846.6
Johnny-on-the-spot
  n benefactor 592.1
  adj prompt 845.9
  attentive 983.15
John Q Public
  the people 606.1
  the man in the street 864.3
Johnsonian 545.8
joie de vivre
  animation 17.4
  pleasure 95.1
join
  n joint 800.4
  v adjoin 223.9
  juxtapose 223.13
  flow 238.16
  cooperate 450.3
  side with 450.4
  participate 476.5
  join in marriage 563.14
  associate with 582.17
  enlist 615.17
  join up 617.14
  assemble 770.18
  identify 778.5

compose 796.3
put together 800.5
connect 800.11
be consistent 803.7
combine 805.3
continue 812.4
concur 899.2
join battle 457.16
joined
  adjacent 223.16
  accompanying 769.9
  assembled 770.21
  related 775.9
  joint 800.12
  united 800.13
  consistent 803.11
  combined 805.5
  continuous 812.8
joiner
  sociable person 582.16
  member 617.11
join forces 805.4
joining
  n meeting 223.4
  addition 253.1
  connection 800.1
  junction 800.1
  joint 800.4
  adj connecting 800.16
joint
  n meat 10.13
  marijuana cigarette 87.12
  crack 224.2
  disapproved place 228.28
  jail 429.9
  sewer 654.7
  brothel 665.9
  casino 759.19
  join 800.4
  v hook 800.8
  adj cooperative 450.5
  communal 476.9
  accompanying 769.9
  assembled 770.21
  mutual 777.11
  connected 800.12
  combined 805.5
  concurrent 899.4
joint effort 450.1
joint operation 450.1
joint ownership 476.1
jointure
  endowment 478.9
  joining 800.1
joke
  n jest 489.6
  laughingstock 508.7
  trifle 998.5
  v jest 489.13
  banter 490.5
joker man 76.5
  surprise 131.2
  mischief-maker 322.3
  trick 356.6
  deceiver 357.1
  proviso 421.3
  humorist 489.12
  bill 613.9
  card 758.2
  condition 959.2
  obstacle 1012.4

crux 1013.8
jokester
  mischief-maker 322.3
  deceiver 357.1
  humorist 489.12
joking
  n wittiness 489.2
  bantering 490.2
  adj witty 489.15
jollies
  excitement 105.3
  marines 461.28
jollity merriment 109.5
  conviviality 582.3
  festivity 743.3
jolly
  n navy man 183.4
  v banter 490.6
  flatter 511.6
  make merry 743.24
  adj intoxicated 88.31
  merry 109.15
  convivial 582.23
  festive 743.28
jollying
  n bantering 490.3
  adj bantering 490.7
Jolly Roger 647.7
jolly well 247.15
jolt
  n drink 88.7
  excitement 105.3
  start 131.3
  thrust 902.2
  shake 917.3
  v agitate 105.14
  startle 131.8
  way of walking 177.28
  thrust 902.12
  shake 917.11
jolting exciting 105.30
  surprising 131.11
  jolty 917.20
Jonah
  n bad influence 1000.4
  v bring bad luck 1011.12
jongleur
  minstrel 710.14
  poet 720.11
josh joke 489.13
  banter 490.6
joshing
  n wittiness 489.2
  bantering 490.3
  ridicule 508.1
  adj witty 489.15
  ridiculing 508.12
joss 697.3
joss stick 70.4
jostle
  n thrust 902.2
  shake 917.3
  v sound a sour note 61.3
  differ 456.8
  contend 457.13
  rob 482.14
  disagree 789.5
  thrust 902.12
  shake 917.11
jostling
  n theft 482.3

adj clashing 61.5
jot modicum 248.2
  minute 258.7
  mark 517.5
jounce 917.11
journal
  record book 549.11
  periodical 555.1
  account book 628.4
  history 719.1
  chronicle 832.9
  axle box 915.6
journalese
  n jargon 523.10
  adj journalistic
    555.5
journalism
  authorship 547.2
  news 552.1
  the press 555.3
  literature 718.2
journalist 555.4
journey
  n trip 177.5
  v travel 177.21
journeying
  n travel 177.1
  adj traveling 177.36
journeyman
  n expert 413.11
  skilled worker 726.6
  producer 892.7
  adj competent 413.24
joust
  n contest 457.3
  v contend 457.13
jovial merry 109.15
  convivial 582.23
  festive 743.28
joviality
  merriment 109.5
  conviviality 582.3
  festivity 743.3
jowl 218.1
joy
  n happiness 95.2
  merriment 109.5
  v be pleased 95.12
  rejoice 116.5
  exult 502.9
joyful happy 95.16
  merry 109.15
  cheering 109.16
  festive 743.28
joyless
  pleasureless 96.20
  distressing 98.20
  unhappy 112.21
joyous happy 95.16
  merry 109.15
  festive 743.28
joyride
  n ride 177.7
  v ride 177.33
joy stick 87.12
JP 596.1
Jr 301.15
jubilant
  overjoyed 95.17
  rejoicing 116.10
  crowing 502.13

jubilate rejoice 116.5
  celebrate 487.2
  exult 502.9
jubilation treat 95.3
  rejoicing 116.1
  crowing 502.4
jubilee rejoicing 116.1
  celebration 487.1
  anniversary 850.4
Judaic 675.30
Judaism 675.12
Judas
  traitor 357.10
  criminal 660.9
judge
  n arbitrator 466.4
  connoisseur 496.6
  adjudicator 596.1
  magistrate 596.1
  fight 754.3
  judger 946.6
  v mediate 466.6
  administer justice 594.5
  try 598.18
  criticize 723.5
  classify 801.8
  exercise judgment 946.8
  think 953.11
judgeship 594.3
judgment
  judiciary 594.2
  decision 598.9
  condemnation 602.1
  punishment 604.1
  function of Christ 677.14
  classification 801.3
  judiciousness 920.7
  solution 940.1
  discernment 944.2
  assessment 946.3
  judging 946.1
  opinion 953.6
judgmental
  averse 99.8
  fastidious 495.9
  condemnatory 510.22
  judicial 946.16
Judgment Day 839.3
judicature
  judiciary 594.2
  tribunal 595.1
  court 595.2
  judgment 946.1
judicial
  jurisdictional 594.6
  tribunal 595.7
  legal 673.11
  judicious 920.19
  judiciary 946.16
judicial process
  judiciary 594.2
  lawsuit 598.1
judicial system 594.2
judiciary
  n judicial system 594.2
  tribunal 595.1
  adj jurisdictional 594.6
  tribunal 595.7
  judicial 946.16
judicious
  cautious 494.8

moderate 670.10
  intelligent 920.19
  discerning 944.8
  judicial 946.16
jug
  n jail 429.9
  ceramic ware 742.2
  v imprison 429.14
Juggernaut 697.3
juggle
  n trick 356.6
  v tamper with 354.17
  deceive 356.14
juggler trickster 357.2
  cheat 357.3
  circus artist 707.3
juggling 356.5
jughead horse 311.12
  fool 924.4
juice liquor 88.14
  automobile racing 756.1
  current 1032.2
  fluid 1061.2
juiceless 1066.7
juicy tasty 63.8
  delectable 97.10
  immature 301.10
  interesting 983.19
  fluid 1061.4
juju
  bad feeling 93.7
  animism 675.6
  sorcery 690.1
  charm 691.5
jukebox 50.11
juke joint 743.13
jumble
  n Greek 522.7
  hodgepodge 797.6
  scramble 810.3
  confusion 985.3
  v deform 263.3
  make unintelligible 522.12
  mix 797.10
  disorder 810.9
  confuse 811.3
  confound 945.3
jumbled
  hard to understand 522.14
  mixed 797.14
  chaotic 810.16
  confused 985.12
jumbo
  n largeness 257.11
  behemoth 257.14
  adj huge 257.20
  excessive 993.16
Jumbo 311.4
jumbo jet 181.3
jumbo mortgage 438.4
jump
  n progression 162.1
  step 177.11
  flight 184.9
  ascent 193.1
  interval 224.1
  advantage 249.2
  increase 251.1
  leap 366.1
  promotion 446.1
  basketball game 747.3

v start 127.12
  be startled 131.5
  way of walking 177.28
  parachute 184.47
  leave undone 340.7
  leap 366.5
  flee 368.10
  escape 369.6
  promote 446.2
  lift one's hand against
    457.14
  attack 459.15
  seize on 480.16
  drive 756.4
  shake 917.11
jump down someone's throat
  152.2
jumper leaper 366.4
  diver 367.4
jump in enter 189.7
  mount 193.12
  interrupt 214.6
jumping
  n leaping 366.3
  skiing 753.1
  adj leaping 366.7
jumping-off place
  small town 230.3
  remote region 261.4
  extremity 820.2
jump on
  suppress 428.8
  disapprove 510.18
jump out of one's skin 127.11
jump ship quit 188.9
  play truant 222.9
jump the gun
  be impatient 135.4
  anticipate 845.6
  prejudge 947.2
jump to a conclusion 947.2
jump to it 725.15
jump up
  shoot up 193.9
  rise 200.8
  increase 251.4
  overestimate 949.2
jumpy fearful 127.23
  jittery 128.12
  bustling 330.20
  agitated 917.16
  jerky 917.19
junction
  juxtaposition 223.3
  addition 253.1
  passageway 383.3
  railway 383.7
  assemblage 770.1
  relation 775.1
  composition 796.1
  joining 800.1
  consistency 803.2
  combination 805.1
  concurrence 899.1
juncture
  pause 524.9
  circumstance 766.1
  joint 800.4
  period 824.1
  grammar 857.4
jungle 799.2

keep a stiff upper lip
  keep cool 106.9
  be of good cheer 109.10
  keep up one's courage
    492.14
keep a straight face 111.2
keep at it
  keep going 330.15
  persevere 360.2
  continue 856.3
  persist 856.5
keep away from
  keep one's distance 261.7
  avoid 368.6
keep back slow 175.9
  keep secret 345.7
  reserve 386.12
  not use 390.5
  restrain 428.7
  delay 846.8
  hinder 1012.10
keep books 628.8
keep busy
  keep going 330.15
  task 725.16
keep down
  suppress 428.8
  subjugate 432.8
  domineer 612.15
keeper preserver 397.5
  jailer 429.10
  possessor 470.1
  protector 1008.5
  guardian 1008.6
keep faith 644.9
keep from refrain 329.3
  keep secret 345.7
  avoid 368.6
  restrain 428.7
  abstain 668.7
  prevent 1012.14
keep going
  keep on 330.15
  persevere 360.2
  continue 856.3
  sustain 856.4
keep house
  settle 159.17
  housekeep 228.31
keep in restrain 428.7
  confine 429.12
  retain 474.5
keeping
  n symmetry 264.1
  preservation 397.1
  custody 429.5
  observance 434.1
  retention 474.1
  protectorship 1008.2
  adj preservative 397.12
  retentive 474.8
keep in mind
  think of 931.16
  take cognizance of 983.9
  keep in memory 989.12
keep in sight look 27.13
  be vigilant 339.8
  take cognizance of 983.9
keep in touch! 188.22
keep off
  fend off 460.10

repulse 908.3
  prevent 1012.14
keep on
  keep going 330.15
  persevere 360.2
  endure 827.6
  continue 856.3
keep one's cool
  be cool 106.6
  keep calm 106.9
  accept 123.2
  be moderate 670.5
  stand fast 855.11
keep one's distance
  efface oneself 139.7
  avoid 157.7
  distance oneself 261.7
  keep to oneself 344.6
  shun 368.6
  remain aloof 583.4
keep one's ears open
  listen 48.10
  hearken to 983.7
keep one's eyes open
  keep awake 23.3
  look 27.13
  be vigilant 339.8
  beware 494.7
  be curious 981.3
  pay attention 983.8
keep one's fingers crossed
  be hopeful 124.7
  be superstitious 954.7
keep one's head above water
  support oneself 385.12
  win through 409.13
  endure 827.6
  be safe 1007.2
keep one's nose to the
    grindstone
  keep going 330.15
  keep doggedly at 360.3
  drudge 725.14
keep one's shirt on
  keep cool 106.9
  be patient 134.4
keep one's word 644.9
keep on ice 397.9
keep out 773.4
keep posted 551.16
keep quiet 173.7
keepsake 989.6
keep score 871.8
keep secret 345.7
keep still 51.5
keep tabs on
  keep informed 551.16
  care for 1008.19
keep the faith
  be hopeful 124.7
  observe 434.2
  be pious 692.6
keep the peace
  remain at peace 464.8
  be moderate 670.5
  calm 670.7
keep time
  beat time 708.44
  spend time 821.6
  time 832.11
  coincide 836.4

keep to oneself
  be silent 51.5
  remain aloof 344.6
  keep secret 345.7
  retain 474.5
  keep oneself to oneself 583.4
keep track of
  keep informed 551.16
  keep account of 1017.20
keep under wraps 346.6
keep up
  not weaken 15.10
  persevere 360.2
  preserve 397.8
  follow the fashion 578.10
  work 724.12
  sustain 856.4
  support 901.21
keif 22.1
keister 217.5
kelp 310.4
kelpie 678.10
ken
  n vision 27.1
  field of view 31.3
  knowledge 928.1
  v see 27.12
  understand 521.7
  know 928.12
kennel
  n doghouse 228.21
  drain 239.5
  trench 290.2
  dog 311.16
  pavement 383.6
  group of animals 770.5
  v enclose 212.5
keno 759.15
kept reserved 386.15
  preserved 397.13
kept woman 665.17
kerchief 5.25
kerfuffle 810.2
kernel nut 10.39
  essential content 196.5
  center 208.2
  seed 310.31
  essence 767.2
  middle 819.1
  salient point 997.6
kerosene 1025.20
key
  n color 35.1
  island 235.2
  opener 292.10
  translation 341.3
  telegraph 347.2
  clue 517.9
  pitch 709.4
  key signature 709.15
  wind instrument 711.6
  basketball 747.1
  influence 894.6
  computer terms 1042.18
  v close 293.6
  adj central 208.11
keyboard
  n fingerboard 711.17
  input device 1042.4
  v autotype 548.15
  computerize 1042.21

keyed up 105.20
keyhole 747.1
key in
  n type 548.6
  v computerize 1042.21
keynote
  n sign 517.1
  key 709.15
  characteristic 865.4
  v characterize 865.10
keynoter 610.7
keynote speaker 543.4
keys ecclesiastical insignia
  647.4
  keyboard 711.17
key signature
  notation 709.12
  key 709.15
keystone arch 279.4
  baseball 745.1
  foundation stone 901.7
  salient point 997.6
key up excite 105.12
  intensify 251.5
khaki 40.3
khakis 5.18
khan ruler 575.9
  Muslim ruler 575.10
  prince 608.7
  Sir 648.3
kibbutz
  communion 476.2
  farm 1069.8
kibitz meddle 214.7
  advise 422.5
kibitzer meddler 214.4
  adviser 422.3
  gambler 759.21
  spectator 918.1
kibosh disable 19.9
  end 820.5
kick
  n energy 17.3
  zest 68.2
  excitement 105.3
  complaint 115.5
  objection 333.2
  signal 517.15
  hint 551.4
  baseball 745.3
  football 746.3
  soccer 752.3
  poker 759.10
  counteraction 900.1
  boot 902.9
  recoil 903.2
  v use 87.22
  be discontented 108.6
  complain 115.16
  object 333.5
  break the habit 374.3
  signal 517.22
  swear off 668.8
  football 746.5
  soccer 752.4
  boot 902.21
  recoil 903.6
  dismiss 909.20
kick around
  subdue 432.9
  discuss 541.11

domineer 612.15
kick 902.21
kick-ass 18.12
kick back relax 20.7
  compose oneself 106.7
  do nothing 329.2
  repay 624.11
  discount 631.2
  recoil 903.6
kicker
  malcontent 108.4
  complainer 115.9
  surprise 131.2
  proviso 421.3
  football team 746.2
  condition 959.2
kick in die 307.19
  provide 385.7
  contribute 478.14
  pay 624.16
  begin 818.7
kick in the teeth 442.2
kickoff
  n football 746.3
  soccer 752.3
  curtain-raiser 816.2
  beginning 818.1
  adj preceding 816.4
kick off die 307.19
  propose 439.5
  football 746.5
  soccer 752.4
  precede 814.2
  begin 818.7
  start 904.13
kick out kick 902.21
  eject 909.13
kick pleat 291.2
kickshaw delicacy 10.8
  trinket 498.4
  toy 743.16
  trifle 998.5
kick the bucket 307.19
kick the habit
  use 87.22
  overcome 412.7
  swear off 668.8
kick up a storm
  complain 115.16
  fly into a rage 152.20
  create disorder 810.11
kick upstairs
  promote 446.2
  depose 447.4
  dismiss 909.19
kid
  n child 302.3
  fledgling 302.10
  goat 311.8
  v fool 356.15
  joke 489.13
  banter 490.6
  trifle 998.15
kidder
  deceiver 357.1
  banterer 490.4
kidding
  n deception 356.1
  banter 490.1
  bantering 490.3
  adj bantering 490.7

ridiculing 508.12
kiddy pool 743.12
kid gloves 427.1
kidnap seize 480.14
  abduct 482.20
kidnapper 483.10
kidnapping
  seizure 480.2
  abduction 482.9
kidney viscera 2.16
  kind 809.3
  disposition 978.3
kill
  n stream 238.1
  killing 308.1
  quarry 382.7
  v make laugh 116.9
  excise 255.10
  delete 255.12
  slay 308.13
  cover up 345.8
  put an end to 395.12
  obliterate 395.16
  suppress 428.8
  veto 444.5
  legislate 613.10
  amuse 743.21
  end 820.5
  turn off 857.12
killer
  n slayer 308.11
  ruffian 593.3
  violent person 671.9
  first-rate 999.7
  adj excellent 999.13
killing
  n violent death 307.5
  slaying 308.1
  gain 472.3
  unruliness 671.3
  adj fatiguing 21.13
  deadly 308.23
  laborious 725.18
  beautiful 1016.21
killjoy
  spoilsport 112.14
  pessimist 125.7
  hinderer 1012.9
kill oneself 308.22
kill time
  waste time 331.13
  amuse oneself 743.22
  spend time 821.6
kiln
  n oven 742.5
  v dry 1066.6
kilo 882.10
kilocycle 882.10
kilogram 882.10
kilometer 882.10
kilowatt-hour 17.7
kin kinfolk 559.2
  class 809.2
  kind 809.3
kind
  n race 559.4
  nature 767.4
  sort 809.3
  adj kindly 143.13
  forgiving 148.6
  indulgent 427.8

favorable 449.22
  friendly 587.15
  good 999.12
kindergarten 567.2
kindergartner 572.3
kindhearted 143.13
kindle energize 17.10
  excite 105.12
  flare up 152.19
  enkindle 375.18
  heat 1020.18
  ignite 1020.22
kindling
  n ignition 1020.4
  firewood 1021.3
  adj inflammatory 1020.27
kind of
  to a degree 245.7
  so to speak 784.19
kindred
  n blood relationship 559.1
  kinfolk 559.2
  adj related 559.6
  akin 775.10
kindred soul 784.3
kine 311.6
kinematograph
  camera 714.11
  projector 714.12
kinescope 714.8
kinesic 517.25
kinesis 172.1
kinetic energetic 17.13
  dynamic 1039.9
kinfolk 559.2
king potentate 575.8
  prince 608.7
  businessman 730.1
  chessman 743.17
  card 758.2
  chief 997.10
kingdom country 232.1
  biological classification 305.3
  nomenclature 527.1
  hierarchy 809.4
  classifications 809.5
kingfish 575.4
kingmaker
  Machiavellian 415.8
  politics 610.6
  influence 894.6
kingpin 575.4
kingship
  supremacy 249.3
  sovereignty 417.8
  aristocracy 608.9
king-size great 247.7
  large 257.16
  huge 257.20
  oversize 257.23
kink
  n pang 26.2
  coil 281.2
  caprice 364.1
  quirk 927.2
  fault 1003.2
  blemish 1004.1
  v curl 281.5
  blemish 1004.4
kinked curly 281.9
  blemished 1004.8

kinky curly 281.9
  capricious 364.5
  unconventional 868.6
  eccentric 927.6
kinship
  accord 455.1
  blood relationship 559.1
  common source 775.3
  affinity 784.2
kinsmen 559.2
kiosk hut 228.9
  summerhouse 228.12
  booth 736.3
kipper
  n fish 10.24
  marine animal 311.29
  v preserve 397.9
kirk 703.1
kishkes viscera 2.16
  insides 207.4
  inner nature 767.5
kismet destiny 839.2
  fate 964.2
kiss
  n touch 73.1
  contact 223.5
  buss 562.4
  greeting 585.4
  v touch lightly 73.7
  contact 223.10
  osculate 562.19
  greet 585.10
kissable 104.24
kiss and make up 465.10
kiss and tell 351.6
kiss ass
  bow down 433.10
  flatter 511.5
kiss-ass 138.14
kiss good-bye 473.4
kiss off
  relinquish 475.3
  repulse 908.3
  dismiss 984.4
kit
  fledgling 302.10
  cat 311.20
  equipment 385.4
  impedimenta 471.3
  set 770.12
kitchen
  n restaurant 8.17
  cookroom 11.4
  storeroom 197.14
  baseball 745.3
  adj cooking 11.6
kitchen cabinet
  council 423.1
  cabinet 613.3
kitchen sink
  washbasin 79.12
  genuineness 973.7
kite
  n aircraft 181.1
  box kite 181.14
  counterfeit 728.10
  v take off 193.10
kith and kin 559.2
kitsch vulgarity 497.1
  writing 547.12
  work of art 712.9

literature 718.1
kitten
n child 302.3
fledgling 302.10
cat 311.20
v give birth 1.3
kittenish
feminine 77.13
gay 109.14
infant 301.12
feline 311.42
kitty cat 311.20
funds 728.14
lawn bowling 750.3
pot 759.5
kittycorner
adj transverse 204.19
adv diagonally 204.25
klutz bungler 414.9
fool 924.3
klutzy
inelegant 534.2
stupid 922.15
knack art 413.6
trinket 498.4
knave
mischief-maker 322.3
rascal 660.3
card 758.2
knavery
stratagem 415.3
roguery 645.2
iniquity 654.3
knavish
mischievous 322.6
roguish 645.17
wicked 654.16
knead stroke 73.8
form 262.7
mix 797.10
rub 1044.6
soften 1047.6
knee
n member 2.7
leg 177.14
angle 278.2
joint 800.4
v kick 902.21
knee-deep deep
275.10
shallow 276.5
knee-high
little 258.10
low 274.7
kneel fawn 138.7
bow 155.6
bend 913.9
kneeling
obeisance 155.2
submission 433.1
crouch 913.3
kneel to
bow down 433.10
entreat 440.11
knell
n ringing 54.3
dirge 115.6
death 307.1
passing bell 309.6
v ring 54.8
lament 115.10

knickknack
trinket 498.4
toy 743.16
trifle 998.5
knife
n sword 462.5
cutlery 1040.2
v stab 459.25
knife-edge
sharp edge 285.2
unreliability 971.6
predicament 1013.4
knight
n rider 178.8
combatant 461.1
gallant 504.9
cavalier 608.5
chessman 743.17
v promote 446.2
knight-errantry 652.2
knighthood
military science 458.5
aristocracy 608.9
knightly
adj courageous 492.16
gallant 504.15
noble 608.10
magnanimous 652.6
adv courageously 492.22
courteously 504.19
magnanimously 652.8
knit
v contract 260.7
wrinkle 291.6
heal 396.21
weave 740.6
fasten 800.7
join 800.11
adj woven 740.7
joined 800.13
knitted
contracted 260.12
wrinkled 291.8
joined 800.13
knitting
contraction 260.1
weaving 740.1
knob
n hill 237.4
sphere 282.2
bulge 283.3
v roughen 288.4
knobbed
studded 283.17
nappy 294.7
knobbliness 288.1
knobby
hilly 272.18
studded 283.17
knock
n report 56.1
criticism 510.4
hit 902.4
v crack 56.6
criticize 510.14
collide 902.13
hit 902.14
pound 902.16
knock about
wander 177.23
mistreat 389.5

knock around
wander 177.23
discuss 541.11
knock dead
delight 95.11
amuse 743.21
look good 1016.16
knock down
sadden 112.18
unnerve 128.10
raze 395.19
acquire 472.9
disparage 512.8
auction 734.11
fight 754.4
hit 902.14
fell 913.5
knock-down-and-drag-out
n quarrel 456.6
free-for-all 457.5
adj boisterous 671.20
knocker 512.6
knock for a loop
delight 95.11
beat 902.17
knock heads together
coerce 424.8
hold a tight hand upon 425.4
punish 604.15
knockoff 336.3
knock off
take a rest 20.8
excise 255.10
die 307.19
kill 308.14
do carelessly 340.9
improvise 365.8
accomplish 407.4
defeat 412.9
rob 482.16
write 547.21
compose 718.6
stop work 857.8
knock one's socks off
delight 95.11
astonish 122.6
fascinate 377.7
knock on wood
be hopeful 124.7
be superstitious 954.7
knockout
unconsciousness 25.2
victory 411.1
fight 754.3
finishing stroke 820.4
first-rate 999.7
beauty 1016.8
knock out
disable 19.10
get tired 21.6
deaden 25.4
delight 95.11
form 262.7
do carelessly 340.9
do for 395.11
write 547.21
compose 718.6
fight 754.4
end 820.5
hit 902.14
knock over 395.19

knoll 237.4
knot
n braid 3.7
distortion 265.1
sphere 282.2
bulge 283.3
enigma 522.8
company 770.3
bunch 770.7
complex 799.2
fastening 800.3
dilemma 1013.7
solid 1045.6
v distort 265.5
equal 790.5
complicate 799.3
put together 800.5
thicken 1045.10
knotted studded 283.17
gnarled 288.8
wrinkled 291.8
assembled 770.21
related 775.9
equal 790.7
complex 799.4
joined 800.13
difficult 1013.17
knotty studded 283.17
gnarled 288.8
hard to understand 522.14
difficult 1013.17
know understand 521.7
be informed 551.15
be friends 587.9
experience 831.8
perceive 928.12
be certain 970.9
recognize 989.11
know all the answers
know backwards and
forwards 413.19
know well 928.13
**know backwards and
forwards**
know all the answers
413.19
know well 928.13
know-how skill 413.1
knowledge 928.1
knowing
n knowledge 928.1
adj intentional 380.8
experienced 413.28
cunning 415.12
intelligent 920.12
shrewd 920.15
wise 920.17
knowledgeable 928.15
know it all 140.6
know-it-all
n egotist 140.5
adj conceited 140.11
knowledge
information 551.1
learning 570.1
intelligence 920.1
cognizance 928.2
knowing 928.1
knowledgeable
specialized 866.5
knowing 928.15

knowledge engineering 1042.2

known as 527.14

know no bounds
overstep 910.9
superabound 993.8
overdo 993.10

know nothing 930.8

know-nothing
n ignoramus 930.7
adj ignorant 930.11
discriminatory 980.12

know well know 551.15
master 570.9
know full well 928.13

know what's what
know backwards and
forwards 413.19
have all one's wits about one
920.10
know well 928.13
distinguish between 944.6

knub 294.1

knuckle
n joint 800.4
v exert oneself 725.9

knuckle down to
undertake 404.3
submit 433.6
set to work 725.15

knucklehead 924.4

knuckleheaded 922.17

knuckles 462.4

knurl
n bulge 283.3
v notch 289.4

knurled
studded 283.17
gnarled 288.8

KO
n unconsciousness 25.2
victory 411.1
fight 754.3
finishing stroke 820.4
v deaden 25.4
do for 395.11
end 820.5

Kodak 714.11

kohl 1016.11

kook oddity 870.4
lunatic 926.16
freak 927.4

kooky odd 870.11
foolish 923.9
crazy 926.27
eccentric 927.6

Koran 683.6

Kore
nether world deity 682.5
agricultural deity 1069.4

kosher edible 8.33
clean 79.25
right 637.3
legal 673.11
conformist 867.6

kowtow
n obeisance 155.2
crouch 913.3
v fawn 138.7
kneel 155.6
lie 201.5

bow down 433.10
bend 913.9

Kraut vegetables 10.35
derogatory names 232.7
soldier 461.7

kudos praise 509.5
citation 646.4
repute 662.1

kvetch
n malcontent 108.4
complaint 115.5
complainer 115.9
faultfinder 510.9
v be discontented
108.6
complain 115.16

L LSD 87.10
adjunct 254.3
angle 278.2
stage 704.16
eleven 882.7

lab workplace 739.6
laboratory 942.5

label
n tag 517.13
name 527.3
heraldry 647.2
class 809.2
kind 809.3
v tag 517.20
name 527.11
generalize 864.9

labia 2.13

labial 211.13

labor
n birth 1.1
occupation 724.1
task 724.2
work 725.4
v give birth 1.3
be busy 330.10
endeavor 403.5
work 724.12
exert oneself 725.12
dwell on 849.9
flounder 917.15

laboratory
hospital room 197.25
workplace 739.6
lab 942.5

laboratory test 91.12

labor camp 429.8

labored ornate 498.12
stiff 534.3
laborious 725.18
monotonous 849.15

laborer subject 432.7
commoner 607.9
worker 726.2

laboring
n interpretation 341.1
amplification 538.6
adj working 725.17

labor in vain
n labor lost 391.3
v be useless 391.8
fail 410.9

laborious
industrious 330.22
toilsome 725.18
difficult 1013.17

labor of love
act of kindness 143.7
costlessness 634.1

labor organizer 727.4

labor-saving 635.6

labor under ail 85.46
experience 831.8

labor under a disadvantage
1013.11

labor union
association 617.1
trade unionism 727.1
trade union 727.2

labor unionist 727.4

labyrinth 799.2

labyrinthine
deviative 164.7
distorted 265.10
curved 279.7
convolutional 281.6
grandiloquent 545.8
complex 799.4

lace
n material 4.1
network 170.3
strip 271.4
v whip 604.13
weave 740.6
adulterate 797.12
bind 800.9

laced netlike 170.11
woven 740.7

lacerate
v pain 26.7
torture 96.18
injure 393.13
tear apart 802.14
adj notched 289.5

lacerated
pained 26.9
tortured 96.25
notched 289.5
impaired 393.27

laceration
trauma 85.38
torment 96.7
severance 802.2

lachrymal
circulatory 2.33
secretory 13.7
tearful 115.21

lachrymose
secretory 13.7
tearful 115.21

lacing
network 170.3
corporal punishment
604.4
weaving 740.1
adulteration 797.3

lack
n absence 222.1
indigence 619.2
deficiency 795.2
want 992.4
imperfection 1003.1
v be poor 619.5
be incomplete 795.3
fall short 911.2
want 992.7
be insufficient 992.8

lackadaisical
unconcerned 102.7
nonchalant 106.15
languid 331.20
dilatory 846.17

lackey
n retainer 577.1
flunky 577.6
follower 616.8
v serve 577.13

lacking
adj absent 222.11
bereft 473.8
nonexistent 762.8
incomplete 795.4
short of 911.5
insufficient 992.9
wanting 992.13
imperfect 1003.4
prep absent 222.19

lackluster
n colorlessness 36.1
mediocrity 1005.1
dullness 1027.5
adj colorless 36.7
mediocre 1005.7
lusterless 1027.17

lack of feeling
unfeeling 94.1
unconcern 102.2
indiscrimination 945.1

lackwitted 922.13

laconic
n man of few words 344.5
adj taciturn 344.9
concise 537.6

lacquer
n blanket 295.12
v color 35.14
coat 295.24

lacquered 287.11

lacquerwork 712.15

lactate nourish 8.19
secrete 13.5

lactation humor 2.24
secretion 13.1
liquidity 1061.1

lacteal secretory 13.7
milky 1061.5

lactose intolerance 85.22

lacuna interval 224.1
cavity 284.2
opening 292.1
deficiency 795.2
interruption 813.2

lacustrian
n lake dweller 241.2
adj lakish 241.5

lacy netlike 170.11
thin 270.16

lad man 76.5
boy 302.5

ladder 193.4

lade load 159.15
burden 297.13
fill 794.7

laden weighted 297.18
fraught 794.12

la-di-da 500.15

ladies' man
beau 104.12

languid weak 16.12
  tired 21.7
  sleepy 22.21
  apathetic 94.13
  inert 173.14
  slow 175.10
  languorous 331.20
languish weaken 16.9
  fail 85.48
  lose heart 112.16
  decrease 252.6
  pine 393.18
languishing
  n unhealthiness 85.3
  yearning 100.5
  adj drooping 16.21
  unhealthy 85.54
  wistful 100.23
  loving 104.26
  dejected 112.22
  decreasing 252.11
  deteriorating 393.45
  protracted 827.11
languor weakness 16.1
  fatigue 21.1
  sleepiness 22.1
  apathy 94.4
  inertness 173.4
  slowness 175.1
  languidness 331.6
languorous weak 16.12
  inert 173.14
  slow 175.10
  languid 331.20
lanky
  n slim 270.8
  adj lean 270.17
  tall 272.16
lanolin 1056.3
lantern tower 272.6
  roof 295.6
  light source 1026.1
lantern jaws 270.5
lap
  n drink 8.4
  touch 73.1
  front 216.1
  swash 238.8
  overlayer 295.4
  lamina 296.2
  race 457.12
  track 755.1
  car race 756.3
  circuit 914.2
  v clothe 5.39
  lap up 8.30
  ripple 52.11
  lick 73.9
  tipple 88.24
  lead 165.2
  overtake 174.13
  surround 209.6
  border 211.10
  overflow 238.17
  plash 238.19
  fold 291.5
  wrap 295.20
  overlie 295.30
  cuddle 562.17
  circle 914.5
lap dancer 6.3

lap dog favorite 104.15
  sycophant 138.3
  dog 311.16
lapel 291.1
lapidary
  n printmaker 716.8
  adj elegant 533.6
  glyptic 713.12
lapin 311.23
lap of luxury 1010.1
lappet pendant 202.4
  fold 291.1
lapping
  n drinking 8.3
  lap 238.8
  adj rippling 52.19
  overlying 295.36
lap pool 743.12
lapse
  n regression 163.1
  sinkage 194.2
  decline 252.2
  neglect 340.1
  deterioration 393.3
  relapse 394.1
  misdeed 655.2
  impiety 694.1
  close 820.3
  pause 857.3
  conversion 858.1
  reversion 859.1
  slip 975.4
  v regress 163.5
  sink 194.6
  invert 205.5
  neglect 340.6
  decline 393.17
  relapse 394.4
  go wrong 654.9
  come to an end 820.6
  elapse 821.5
  pass 837.6
  defect 858.13
  revert 859.4
  err 975.9
lapsed inverted 205.7
  nonobservant 435.5
  unvirtuous 654.12
  carnal 663.6
  impious 694.6
  unregenerate 695.18
  past 837.7
lapse of memory 990.1
lapse of time
  passage of time 821.4
  period 824.1
laptop computer 1042.2
lap up
  sponge up 8.30
  tipple 88.24
  kid oneself 954.6
larboard
  n left side 220.1
  adj left 220.4
  adv leftward 220.6
larcenous 482.21
larceny 482.2
lard make better 392.9
  oil 1056.8
larder
  provisions 10.5

  store 386.1
  pantry 386.8
lares and penates
  household deity 228.30
  property 471.1
  familiar spirit 678.12
large immense 247.7
  sizable 257.16
  liberal 485.4
largehearted
  benevolent 143.15
  liberal 485.4
  magnanimous 652.6
large-minded 979.8
larger than life
  large 257.16
  huge 257.20
  full-sized 257.22
  excessive 993.16
  weighty 997.20
large-scale
  large 257.16
  extensive 864.13
largess
  act of kindness 143.7
  gratuity 478.5
  liberality 485.1
largesse 485.1
largo
  n slow motion 175.2
  music 708.25
  tempo 709.24
  adj music 708.54
lariat 356.13
lark
  n ascent 193.7
  songbird 710.23
  revel 743.6
  v make merry 743.24
larrup punish 604.15
  beat 902.17
larva chrysalis 302.12
  embryo 305.14
  insect 311.32
  specter 988.1
larval 305.22
larynx 524.18
lascivious
  lustful 75.27
  desirous 100.21
  amorous 104.25
  lecherous 665.29
laser surgery 91.19
lash
  n goad 375.8
  whip 605.1
  slap 902.8
  v anchor 182.15
  goad 375.15
  bind 428.10
  criticize 510.20
  whip 604.13
  join 800.9
  drive 1070.8
lashing
  corporal punishment
    604.4
  fastening 800.3
lass woman 77.5
  ladylove 104.13
  girl 302.6

lassitude
  weakness 16.1
  fatigue 21.1
  languor 331.6
lasso
  n circle 280.2
  snare 356.13
  v catch 480.17
last
  n mold 786.6
  end 820.1
  v keep alive 306.11
  persevere 360.2
  stay with it 360.4
  live on 761.9
  elapse 821.5
  endure 827.6
  outlast 827.8
  remain 853.5
  adj departing 188.18
  completing 407.9
  final 820.11
  eventual 831.11
  foregoing 837.11
  state-of-the-art 841.14
  adv finally 820.12
last-ditch
  final 820.11
  makeshift 995.7
lasting
  persevering 360.8
  sturdy 763.7
  temporal 821.7
  durable 827.10
  protracted 827.11
  permanent 853.7
  unchangeable 855.17
  remembered 989.22
  tough 1049.4
last minute 846.1
last-minute hasty 401.9
  later 846.18
last name 527.5
last resort
  expedient 995.2
  recourse 1009.2
last rites
  last offices 309.4
  unction 701.5
last straw 886.3
Last Supper 701.7
last word
  supremacy 249.3
  ultimatum 439.3
  meaning 518.1
  administration 573.3
the last word
  the rage 578.4
  novelty 841.2
  influence 894.1
  acme of perfection 1002.3
latch close 293.6
  hook 800.8
late
  adj retarded 175.12
  dead 307.29
  anachronous 833.3
  former 837.10
  recent 841.12
  untimely 844.6
  belated 846.16

football 746.1
bowling 750.1
soccer 752.1
combination 805.1
v cooperate 450.3
come together 770.16
put together 800.5
ally 805.4
leagued
assembled 770.21
joined 800.13
enleagued 805.6
League of Nations
supranational government
    12.7
United Nations 614.1
leak
n leakage 190.5
opening 292.1
divulgence 351.2
escape 369.1
v leak out 190.14
communicate 343.7
disclose 351.4
betray 351.6
go to waste 473.6
hint 551.10
leakage entrance 189.1
leaking 190.5
escape 369.1
waste 473.2
leak in 189.10
leak out leak 190.14
be revealed 351.8
find vent 369.10
leakproof
resistant 15.20
watertight 1066.11
leaky exudative 190.20
apertured 292.19
lean
n inclination 204.2
v incline 204.10
gravitate 297.15
be willing 324.3
tend 896.3
adj thin 270.17
plain-speaking 535.3
meager 992.10
leaning
n desire 100.3
inclination 204.2
preference 371.5
aptitude 413.5
partiality 650.3
tendency 896.1
disposition 978.3
prejudice 980.3
adj inclining 204.15
unbalanced 791.5
tending 896.4
lean on
coerce 424.8
threaten 514.2
exercise influence 894.9
rest on 901.22
rely on 953.16
lean-to 228.9
lean toward
desire 100.14
prefer 371.17

take the attitude 978.6
leap
n progression 162.1
ascent 193.1
interval 224.1
degree 245.1
increase 251.1
jump 366.1
curtain-raiser 816.2
innovation 852.4
v speed 174.8
jump 366.5
make haste 401.5
leap before one looks 401.7
leapfrog
n leap 366.1
v leap 366.5
leaping
n jumping 366.3
adj happy 95.16
ascending 193.14
jumping 366.7
leap year
moment 824.2
anniversary 850.4
learn
understand 521.7
come to know 551.14
get 570.6
master 570.9
come to one's knowledge
    928.14
discover 941.2
learn by heart 989.16
learned
educated 570.16
studentlike 572.12
wise 920.17
erudite 928.21
learner
student 572.1
beginner 818.2
learning
intellectual acquirement 570.1
enlightenment 928.4
discovery 941.1
lease
n possession 469.1
rental 615.6
v inhabit 225.7
rent 615.15
rent out 615.16
leasehold
n possession 469.1
adj freehold 471.10
leaseholder 470.4
lease-lend
rent out 615.16
lend 620.5
leash
n shackle 428.4
three 876.1
v bind 428.10
join 800.9
least
n minority 885.3
adj humble 137.10
smallest 250.8
minority 885.7
leather
n fur 4.2

hide 4.3
toughness 1049.2
v punish 604.15
leatherneck 183.4
leave
n vacation 20.3
leave-taking 188.4
absence 222.4
consent 441.1
permission 443.1
game 750.2
v depart 188.6
leave over 256.6
bereave 307.27
vegetate 310.34
leave undone 340.7
abandon 370.5
permit 443.9
resign 448.2
bequeath 478.18
separate 802.8
interj go away! 909.31
leave alone
let alone 329.4
not interfere 430.16
give permission 443.12
be conservative 853.6
leave behind
overtake 174.13
outdistance 249.10
leave 256.6
bereave 307.27
abandon 370.5
leaved
green 44.4
leafy 310.41
leaven
n bread 10.28
leavening 298.4
transformer 852.5
v pervade 221.7
raise 298.7
imbue 797.11
qualify 959.3
leavening
n bread 10.28
fermentation 298.4
adj raising 298.17
leave no stone unturned
prosecute to a conclusion
    360.5
make every effort 403.15
take precautions 494.6
be thorough 794.8
ransack 938.33
leave of absence
vacation 20.3
absence 222.4
leave off
v give up 370.7
break the habit 374.3
cease to use 390.4
cease 857.6
interj cease! 857.13
leave one cold
not be affected by
    94.5
fall flat 117.4
bore 118.7
leave out 773.4
leave-taking 188.4

leave undone
leave 340.7
slight 340.8
neglect 408.2
leave word
communicate 343.7
inform 551.8
leaving
n departure 188.1
absence 222.4
abandonment 370.1
adj departing 188.18
leaving out off 255.14
excluding 773.10
leaving-out 773.1
leavings
remainder 256.1
refuse 391.4
extract 893.3
lecher
philanderer 562.12
reprobate 660.4
satyr 665.11
lechery
philandering 562.10
lasciviousness 665.5
lectern pulpit 703.13
table 901.15
lection 341.2
lector lecturer 571.7
holy orders 699.4
lecture
n reproof 510.5
prelection 543.3
lesson 568.7
v reprove 510.17
prelect 543.11
expound 568.16
lecturer
praelector 543.5
academic rank 571.3
lector 571.7
lecturing
n public speaking 543.1
adj educational 568.18
ledge
horizontal 201.3
border 211.4
layer 296.1
shelf 901.14
ledger
record book 549.11
account book 628.4
bill 871.5
lee
n lee side 218.2
protection 1008.1
adj side 218.6
leech
n doctor 90.4
parasite 138.5
sail 180.14
bloodsucker 311.37
extortionist 480.12
adhesive 803.4
v bleed 91.27
leeching 91.20
leer
n look 27.3
scornful laugh 508.4
signal 517.15

v scrutinize 27.14
signal 517.22
leering
n ridicule 508.1
adj ridiculing 508.12
leery wary 494.9
doubting 955.9
incredulous 956.4
lees dregs 256.2
refuse 391.4
extract 893.3
leeward
n lee side 218.2
adj side 218.6
adv clockwise 161.24
to leeward 182.68
downwind 218.9
leeway room 158.3
way 182.9
drift 184.28
interval 224.1
distance 261.1
latitude 430.4
left
n left side 220.1
liberalism 611.3
liberal 611.11
adj departed 188.19
left-hand 220.4
remaining 256.7
abandoned 370.8
adv leftward 220.6
left-handed
insulting 156.8
oblique 204.13
sinistromanual 220.5
bungling 414.20
left-hander
southpaw 220.3
baseball team 745.2
leftist
n liberal 611.11
adj liberal 611.19
left-out 773.7
leftover
n surplus 993.5
adj remaining 256.7
surplus 993.18
leftward
clockwise 161.24
to the left 220.6
left wing left side 220.1
liberalism 611.3
left-wing left 220.4
liberal 611.19
left-wing conspiracy 609.24
left-winger
left side 220.1
liberal 611.11
lefty
n left-hander 220.3
baseball team 745.2
adj left-handed 220.5
leg
n body part 2.7
fowl part 10.23
limb 177.14
voyage 182.6
shank 273.6
member 793.4
v walk 177.27

legacy bequest 478.10
inheritance 479.2
effect 887.1
legal
permissible 443.15
recorded 549.17
just 649.7
legitimate 673.11
valid 973.14
legal age 303.2
legal counselor 597.1
legalistic formal 580.7
jurisprudent 673.12
conformist 867.6
legality
permissibility 443.8
justice 649.1
lawfulness 673.1
legitimacy 673.1
legalization
authorization 443.3
legitimation 673.2
legalize
authorize 443.11
legitimize 673.9
legal system
judiciary 594.2
law 673.4
legal tender 728.1
legate delegate 576.2
diplomat 576.6
legatee 479.4
legation
foreign office 576.7
commission 615.1
office 739.7
legato
n music 708.25
execution 708.30
note 709.14
adj music 708.53
legend map 159.5
posthumous fame 662.7
mythology 678.14
history 719.1
tradition 842.2
caption 937.2
legendary
fabricated 354.29
distinguished 662.16
mythic 678.15
historical 719.7
fictional 722.7
traditional 842.12
extraordinary 870.14
fictitious 986.21
legible 521.12
legion
military unit 461.22
throng 770.4
multitude 884.3
legionary 461.6
legislate
make laws 613.10
legalize 673.9
legislation
lawmaking 613.5
legalization 673.2
law 673.3
legislative
legislatorial 613.11

legal 673.11
legislator
public official 575.17
lawmaker 610.3
legislature
council 423.1
legislative body 613.1
legislation 613.5
legit
n show business 704.1
adj legal 673.11
legitimacy
authority 417.1
permissibility 443.8
justifiability 600.7
legality 673.1
genuineness 973.7
legitimate
v authorize 443.11
legalize 673.9
adj permissible 443.15
justifiable 600.14
legal 673.11
dramatic 704.33
logical 935.20
valid 973.14
genuine 973.15
leg man 555.4
legume plant 310.4
seed vessel 310.30
legwork 938.4
lei 310.25
leisure
n idleness 331.2
ease 402.1
pause 857.3
adj idle 331.18
leisured 402.5
leisure class 331.11
leisured
idle 331.18
leisure 402.5
leitmotiv 708.24
lemon
n sour 67.2
failure 410.2
adj yellow 43.4
lend loan 620.5
discount 728.27
lend a hand 449.11
lend an ear 48.10
lender 620.3
lending loaning 620.1
money market 728.16
lend-lease
n rental 615.6
lending 620.1
v rent out 615.16
lend 620.5
length size 257.1
distance 261.1
longness 267.1
extent 300.3
lengthen increase 251.4
prolong 267.6
protract 827.9
sustain 856.4
lengthened
prolonged 267.8
protracted 827.11

lengthening
n prolongation 267.4
protraction 827.2
continuance 856.1
adj increasing 251.8
lengthy long 267.7
giant 272.16
wordy 538.12
leniency patience 134.1
considerateness 143.3
pity 145.1
unstrictness 426.2
mercifulness 427
lenientness 427.1
modulation 670.2
tolerance 979.4
softness 1047.1
lenient patient 134.9
considerate 143.16
pitying 145.7
unstrict 426.5
mild 427.7
permissive 443.14
tolerant 979.11
lenitive
n palliative 86.10
moderator 670.3
ointment 1056.3
adj palliative 86.40
relieving 120.9
moderating 670.16
qualifying 959.7
lubricant 1056.10
lens eye 2.9
glass 29.2
Lent fast day 515.3
penance 658.3
Lenten
fasting 515.5
abstinent 668.10
meager 992.10
lentil 310.4
lento 708.54
lentoid 279.12
leonine 311.42
leopard
variegation 47.6
wild cat 311.21
leper 586.4
leprechaun 678.8
lesbian
n homosexual 75.14
mannish female 76.9
adj homosexual 75.30
lesion sore 85.37
trauma 85.38
pain 96.5
less
adj inferior 250.6
reduced 252.10
fewer 885.6
adv decreasingly 252.12
prep off 255.14
without 992.17
lessee lodger 227.8
tenant 470.4
lessen relieve 120.5
decrease 252.6
reduce 252.7
subtract 255.9
extenuate 600.12

moderate 670.6
lessening
 n relief 120.1
 decrease 252.1
 deterioration 393.3
 modulation 670.2
 adj decreasing 252.11
 mitigating 670.14
lesser inferior 250.6
 reduced 252.10
lesser-known
 anonymous 528.3
 unlearned 930.12
lesson warning 399.1
 reproof 510.5
 teaching 568.7
lest 897.7
let
 n rental 615.6
 game 748.2
 hindrance 1012.1
 v draw off 192.12
 permit 443.9
 rent 615.15
 rent out 615.16
 suppose 951.10
 adj employed 615.20
let alone
 v leave undone 340.7
 avoid 368.6
 not use 390.5
 abstain 668.7
 adv additionally 253.11
 prep with 253.12
 excluding 773.10
let be let alone 329.4
 leave undone 340.7
 not interfere 430.16
 be conservative 853.6
 suppose 951.10
letdown
 disappointment 132.1
 humiliation 137.2
 slowing 175.4
 collapse 410.3
 modulation 670.2
let down
 v rest 20.7
 disappoint 132.2
 slow 175.9
 deceive 356.14
 deteriorate 393.16
 betray 645.14
 relax 670.9
 depress 913.4
 adj discontented 108.7
 disappointed 132.5
let drop betray 351.6
 remark 524.24
 drop 913.7
let fly throw 904.10
 shoot 904.12
let go condone 148.4
 let pass 329.5
 neglect 340.6
 leave undone 340.7
 cease to use 390.4
 exempt 430.14
 let oneself go 430.19
 release 431.5
 relinquish 475.4

acquit 601.4
make merry 743.24
disband 771.8
loosen 804.3
throw 904.10
dismiss 909.19
let out 909.24
lethal deadly 308.23
 harmful 1000.12
lethality
 deadliness 308.9
 harmfulness 1000.5
lethargic sleepy 22.21
 apathetic 94.13
 languid 331.20
lethargy
 sleepiness 22.1
 stupor 22.6
 apathy 94.4
 languor 331.6
 stupidity 922.3
let in receive 187.10
 welcome 585.7
let in on divulge 351.5
 tip 551.11
 disillusion 977.2
let it all hang out
 lighten 120.7
 confess 351.7
 let oneself go 430.19
let it go
 v forget 148.5
 dismiss 984.4
 phrs no matter 998.25
let loose
 let oneself go 430.19
 release 431.5
 loose 431.6
 make merry 743.24
 throw 904.10
let off
 v exempt 430.14
 release 431.5
 acquit 601.4
 rent out 615.16
 explode 671.14
 shoot 904.12
 adj exempt 430.30
let on confess 351.7
 sham 354.21
let one's hair down
 lighten 120.7
 divulge 351.5
 let oneself go 430.19
 chat 541.9
 not stand on ceremony 581.2
 make merry 743.24
let one have it
 attack 459.15
 disapprove 510.18
 punish 604.11
let out
 draw off 192.12
 lengthen 267.6
 disclose 351.4
 divulge 351.5
 release 431.5
 say 524.22
 rent out 615.16
 dismiss 909.19
 give vent to 909.24

let pass accept 134.7
 let go 329.5
 be inattentive 984.2
let slip let go 329.5
 neglect 340.6
 betray 351.6
 lose 473.4
 dismiss 984.4
let something go 148.4
letter
 n representation 349.1
 symbol 546.1
 written character 547.9
 writing 547.10
 type 548.6
 message 552.4
 epistle 553.2
 v initial 546.6
 adj epistolary 553.14
letter carrier
 carrier 176.7
 postman 353.5
lettered literal 546.8
 learned 928.21
letterer 547.13
letterhead label 517.13
 address 553.9
lettering
 initialing 546.5
 writing 547.1
 handwriting style 547.4
letter of credit
 credit instrument 622.3
 negotiable instrument 728.11
letter of the law 673.1
letter-perfect 973.15
letterpress
 printing 548.1
 print 548.3
 printed matter 548.10
letters
 writing system 546.3
 literary work 547.12
 record 549.1
 literature 718.1
 scholarship 928.5
letter writer 553.8
letter writing 553.1
letting go 475.1
letting one in on 343.2
letup slowing 175.4
 decrease 252.1
 modulation 670.2
 interruption 813.2
 interim 826.1
 pause 857.3
let-up 120.1
let up
 v relax 20.7
 slow 175.9
 decrease 252.6
 ease up 670.9
 loosen 804.3
 pause 857.9
 interj cease! 857.13
let well enough alone
 be content 107.5
 be inattentive 984.2
leukocyte 2.25
levant
 flee 368.10

not pay 625.6
Levant 231.6
levanter
 north wind 318.8
 defaulter 625.5
levee
 social gathering 582.10
 assembly 770.2
 barrier 1012.5
level
 n floor 197.23
 horizontal 201.3
 plain 236.1
 degree 245.1
 smoothness 287.3
 layer 296.1
 class 607.1
 classification 809.2
 v flatten 201.6
 smooth 287.5
 raze 395.19
 make uniform 781.4
 equalize 790.6
 fell 913.5
 adj horizontal 201.7
 straight 277.6
 smooth 287.10
 just 649.7
 uniform 781.5
 equal 790.7
 adv horizontally 201.9
level at 459.22
level head
 equanimity 106.3
 sensibleness 920.6
levelheaded
 composed 106.13
 equable 670.13
 sensible 920.18
level off
 land 184.43
 make uniform 781.4
 equalize 790.6
lever
 n instrument 384.4
 leverage 906.4
 lifter 912.3
 v get a purchase 906.8
leverage
 trading 737.19
 influence 894.1
 fulcrumage 906.1
 mechanics 1039.1
leviathan ship 180.1
 behemoth 257.14
Leviathan 311.29
levitate
 ascend 193.8
 rise 298.9
 elevate 912.5
levitation
 ascent 193.1
 lightness 298.1
 psychic phenomena 689.6
levity
 lightheartedness 109.3
 merriment 109.5
 lightness 298.1
 fickleness 364.3
 waggishness 489.4
 ridicule 508.1

inattention 984.1
triviality 998.3
levy
  n demand 421.1
  call to arms 458.7
  recruit 461.18
  attachment 480.5
  enlistment 615.7
  tax 630.9
  v demand 421.5
  call to arms 458.18
  attach 480.20
  enlist 615.17
  charge 630.12
  impose 643.4
lewd lascivious 665.29
  obscene 666.9
lex 673.3
lexeme sign 518.6
  word 526.1
lexicographer
  interpreter 341.7
  linguist 523.15
lexicography
  exegetics 341.8
  lexicology 526.14
lexicologist 523.15
lexicology
  semantics 518.7
  lexicography 526.14
lexicon
  vocabulary 526.13
  reference book 554.9
  dictionary 871.4
lexigraphic
  lexical 526.19
  literal 546.8
lexis 526.13
liabilities
  expenses 626.3
  accounts 628.1
liability debt 623.1
  responsibility 641.2
  tendency 896.1
  indebtedness 897.2
  likelihood 897.1
  susceptibility 897.2
  probability 968.1
  disadvantage 996.2
  exposure 1006.3
liable chargeable 623.9
  responsible 641.17
  likely 897.5
  probable 968.6
  exposed 1006.15
liable to
  adj subject to 897.6
  prep inclined to 896.6
liaison love affair 104.5
  intermediary 213.4
  instrument 384.4
  relation 775.1
  joining 800.1
liar 357.9
libation drink 8.4
  alcohol 88.7
  oblation 696.7
libel
  n monstrous lie 354.12
  slander 512.3
  declaration 598.7

v slander 512.11
liberal
  n left side 220.1
  free agent 430.12
  left-winger 611.11
  liberalist 979.6
  adj left 220.4
  nonrestrictive 430.25
  philanthropic 478.22
  free 485.4
  hospitable 585.11
  liberalistic 611.19
  magnanimous 652.6
  extensive 864.13
  liberal-minded 979.9
  plentiful 991.7
liberal arts 568.3
liberalism
  noninterference 430.9
  libertarianism 430.10
  progressivism 611.3
  liberalness 979.2
Liberalism 609.25
liberality
  giving 478.1
  gratuity 478.5
  generosity 485.1
  liberalness 485.1
  hospitality 585.1
  magnanimity 652.2
  liberalness 979.2
  plenty 991.2
liberalize 430.13
liberate
  rescue 398.3
  liberalize 430.13
  free 431.4
  detach 802.10
  disembarrass 1014.9
liberated free 430.21
  freed 431.10
liberation escape 369.1
  rescue 398.1
  liberalism 430.10
  freeing 431.1
  theft 482.1
liberator 592.2
libertarian
  n free agent 430.12
  liberal 979.6
  adj nonrestrictive 430.25
  liberal 979.9
libertine
  n free agent 430.12
  philanderer 562.12
  swinger 665.10
  adj nonrestrictive 430.25
libertinism
  liberalism 430.10
  profligacy 665.3
liberty vacation 20.3
  freedom 430.1
  exemption 430.8
  permission 443.1
  grant 443.5
  privilege 642.2
  opportunity 843.2
libidinal
  sexual 75.25
  desirous 100.21
  instinctive 934.6

libidinous lustful 75.27
  desirous 100.21
  lascivious 665.29
libido sexuality 75.2
  psyche 92.28
  desire 100.1
  love 104.1
  amorousness 104.2
  instinct 934.2
librarian
  recorder 550.1
  professional librarian 558.3
  steward 574.4
library stacks 197.6
  storehouse 386.6
  preserve 397.7
  edition 554.5
  book depository 558.1
  collection 770.11
  retreat 1009.5
libration 916.1
librettist
  dramatist 704.22
  composer 710.20
  poet 720.11
libretto playbook 704.21
  score 708.28
license
  n lawlessness 418.1
  freedom 430.1
  exemption 430.8
  permission 443.1
  permit 443.6
  commission 615.1
  presumption 640.2
  privilege 642.2
  profligacy 665.3
  confusion 810.2
  v authorize 443.11
  commission 615.10
licensed exempt 430.30
  authorized 443.17
licensing agreement 437.1
licentious lawless 418.5
  unrestrained 430.24
  presumptuous 640.11
  profligate 665.25
  dissipated 669.8
lichen 310.4
licit permissible 443.15
  legal 673.11
lick
  n sip 62.2
  touch 73.1
  velocity 172.4
  hint 248.4
  attempt 403.3
  impromptu 708.27
  work 725.4
  blow 902.5
  v lap up 8.30
  taste 62.7
  touch 73.9
  best 249.7
  defeat 412.9
  punish 604.15
  stump 971.14
licked defeated 412.15
  beaten 971.26
lickerish lustful 75.27
  desirous 100.21

lascivious 665.29
lickety-split 174.17
licking eating 8.1
  defeat 412.1
  punishment 604.5
lid body part 2.9
  headdress 5.25
  eye 27.9
  stopper 293.4
  cover 295.5
lido 234.2
lie
  n navigation 159.3
  direction 161.1
  falsehood 354.11
  round 751.3
  v extend 158.9
  be located 159.10
  ride at anchor 182.16
  lie down 201.5
  be present 221.6
  tell a lie 354.19
  be dishonest 645.11
lie detector 92.8
lie down rest 20.6
  lie 201.5
  couch 913.11
lief 324.9
liege
  n subject 432.7
  master 575.1
  retainer 577.1
  adj subject 432.13
lie in give birth 1.3
  be located 159.10
  sail for 182.35
  exist in 761.11
lie in state 309.21
lie in wait 346.9
lie low squat 274.5
  do nothing 329.2
  hide 346.8
  beware 494.7
  be latent 519.3
lien mortgage 438.4
  general lien 438.5
  possession 469.1
lie on weigh on 297.11
  rest on 901.22
  depend 959.6
  go hard with 1011.8
lieu location 159.1
  place 159.4
lieutenant
  subordinate 432.5
  commissioned officer 575.18
  Navy officer 575.20
  deputy 576.1
  assistant 616.6
  policeman 1008.15
life
  n animation 17.4
  energizer 17.6
  eagerness 101.1
  gaiety 109.4
  vitality 306.1
  living 306.1
  person 312.5
  liveliness 330.2
  history 719.1
  existence 761.1

v savor 63.5
enjoy 95.13
desire 100.14
love 104.18
adj approximate 775.8
identical 778.7
similar 784.10
equal 790.7
adv how 384.9
similarly 784.18
prep in imitation of 336.12
like a bat out of hell 174.18
like a bump on a log
　adj passive 329.6
　adv inertly 173.20
like a fish out of water 160.11
like a hog on ice 361.12
like a thief in the night
　unexpectedly 131.14
　surreptitiously 345.18
　deceitfully 356.24
　dishonestly 645.24
like clockwork
　smoothly 287.13
　uniformly 781.8
　methodically 807.9
　regularly 850.9
　easily 1014.16
likelihood
　liability 897.1
　possibility 966.1
　probability 968.1
　good chance 972.8
likely
　adj apt 788.10
　liable 897.5
　possible 966.6
　probable 968.6
　disposed 978.8
　expedient 995.5
　comely 1016.18
　adv probably 968.8
likely story 600.4
likely to
　adj liable to 897.6
　prep inclined to 896.6
like mad swiftly 174.18
　excessively 247.23
　recklessly 493.11
　violently 671.25
like-minded
　unanimous 332.15
　in accord 455.3
　agreeing 788.9
liken 943.4
likeness
　aspect 33.3
　image 349.5
　picture 712.10
　similarity 784.1
　like 784.3
　copy 785.1
　equality 790.1
like white on rice 198.16
likewise
　adv additionally 253.11
　identically 778.9
　similarly 784.18
　interj yeah 332.19
liking desire 100.2
　love 104.1

will 323.1
tendency 896.1
Lilliputian
　n dwarf 258.5
　adj dwarf 258.13
lilt
　n air 708.4
　song 708.14
　rhythm 709.22
　meter 720.7
　v exude cheerfulness 109.6
　rejoice 116.5
　speak 524.25
　sing 708.38
lily whiteness 37.2
　effeminate male 77.10
lily-livered
　weak 16.12
　cowardly 491.10
limb member 2.7
　leg 177.14
　border 211.4
　branch 310.20
　body part 793.4
　lever 906.4
limber
　v soften 1047.6
　adj weak 16.12
　pliant 1047.9
limber up
　prepare oneself 405.13
　soften 1047.6
limbo
　place of confinement 429.7
　hell 682.1
lime
　n whiteness 37.2
　sour 67.2
　snare 356.13
　v trap 356.20
　hamper 1012.11
limelight
　publicity 352.4
　lights 704.18
limen
　sensibility 24.2
　boundary 211.3
limit
　n the last straw 135.3
　summit 198.2
　environment 209.1
　limitation 210.2
　bounds 211.1
　boundary 211.3
　capacity 257.2
　end 794.5
　extremity 820.2
　v restrict 210.5
　bound 211.8
　narrow 270.11
　restrain 428.9
　specialize 866.4
　qualify 959.3
　adj bordering 211.11
limitation
　limiting 210.2
　boundary 211.3
　narrowness 270.1
　restriction 428.3
　estate 471.4
　qualification 959.1

condition 959.2
limited
　n train 179.14
　adj circumscribed 210.7
　local 231.9
　little 258.10
　narrow 270.14
　restricted 428.15
　restrained 670.11
　specialized 866.5
　qualified 959.10
　meager 992.10
limited war 458.1
limiting
　n circumscription 210.1
　limitation 210.2
　differentiation 780.4
　qualification 959.1
　adj restricting 210.9
　bordering 211.11
　enclosing 212.11
　restrictive 428.12
　environmental 766.8
　final 820.11
　qualifying 959.7
limitless greedy 100.27
　unrestricted 430.27
　almighty 677.17
　infinite 823.3
limn outline 211.9
　represent 349.8
　describe 349.9
　portray 712.18
limner 716.2
limousine 179.13
limp
　n slow motion 175.2
　gait 177.12
　v be weak 16.8
　go slow 175.6
　way of walking 177.28
　adj weak 16.12
　drooping 202.10
　flaccid 1047.10
limpet 803.4
limpid clear 521.11
　elegant 533.6
　transparent 1029.4
limping slow 175.10
　crippled 393.30
line
　n direction 161.1
　ships 180.10
　boundary 211.3
　vanguard 216.2
　strip 267.3
　cord 271.2
　wire line 347.17
　policy 381.4
　route 383.1
　railway 383.7
　manner 384.1
　battlefield 463.2
　score 517.6
　track 517.8
　letter 553.2
　race 559.4
　lineage 560.4
　endearment 562.5
　policy 609.4
　air 708.4

part 708.22
staff 708.29
treatment 712.8
engraving 713.2
poetry 720.9
plot 722.4
vocation 724.6
merchandise 735.1
baseball 745.1
sideline 746.1
linemen 746.2
line of scrimmage 746.3
hockey team 749.2
kind 809.3
series 812.2
procession 812.3
sequence 815.1
sequel 835.2
specialty 866.1
trend 896.2
v fill 196.7
border 211.10
plaster 295.25
outline 381.11
mark 517.19
engrave 713.9
dispose 808.9
align 812.5
lineage race 559.4
　line 560.4
　offspring 561.1
　series 812.2
　sequence 815.1
　sequel 835.2
lineal straight 277.6
　racial 559.7
　family 560.18
　consecutive 812.9
　subsequent 835.4
lineaments aspect 33.3
　looks 33.4
　exterior 206.2
　outline 211.2
　face 216.4
　appearance 262.3
linear straight 277.6
　consecutive 812.9
linebacker 746.2
line in the sand 451.1
lineman
　trainman 178.13
　telephone man 347.10
　soccer team 752.2
　electrician 1032.22
linemen 746.2
linen clothing 5.1
　shirt 5.15
　underclothes 5.22
　blanket 295.10
liner ocean liner 180.5
　lining 196.3
　game 745.3
lines looks 33.4
　outline 211.2
　camp 228.29
　manner 384.1
　role 704.10
　playbook 704.21
　style 712.7
lineup plan 381.1
　game 746.3

order 807.1
roll 871.6
schedule 965.3
line up
make parallel 203.5
order 807.4
dispose 808.9
align 812.5
get in line 812.6
schedule 965.6
line up one's ducks 405.11
linger lag 166.4
dawdle 175.8
dally 331.14
linger on 827.7
wait 846.12
continue 856.3
lingerer
slowpoke 175.5
idler 331.8
lingerie 5.22
lingering
n dawdling 175.3
idling 331.4
protraction 827.2
waiting 846.3
adj reverberating 54.12
dawdling 175.11
protracted 827.11
dilatory 846.17
lingo language 523.1
jargon 523.9
lingua franca 523.11
lingual glossal 62.10
linguistic 523.19
speech 524.29
linguist
linguistic scientist 523.15
polyglot 523.16
linguistic
communicational 343.9
lingual 523.19
speech 524.29
linguistics 518.7
liniment 86.11
lining liner 196.3
bookbinding 554.14
engraving 713.2
link
n intermediary 213.4
relation 775.1
joint 800.4
torch 1026.3
v way of walking 177.28
come together 770.16
relate 775.6
put together 800.5
join 800.11
be consistent 803.7
combine 805.3
league 805.4
continue 812.4
linkage relation 775.1
joining 800.1
combination 805.1
linked related 775.9
joined 800.13
leagued 805.6
continuous 812.8
linking
n relation 775.1

joining 800.1
fastening 800.3
combination 805.1
adj grammatical 530.17
relative 775.7
joining 800.16
linotype 548.15
lint down 3.19
dressing 86.33
powder 1051.5
lintel 189.6
lion
symbol of strength 15.8
wild cat 311.21
brave person 492.7
heraldry 647.2
celebrity 662.9
important person 997.9
lionhearted 492.16
lionize
praise 509.12
glorify 662.13
sightsee 918.6
lion's share 257.11
lip
n back talk 142.4
border 211.4
bulge 283.3
lawyer 597.3
wind instrument 711.6
golf 751.1
v sass 142.8
say 524.22
blow a horn 708.42
lip-clap 73.1
lipid fat 7.7
oil 1056.1
lip reader 49.2
lips genitals 2.13
mouth 292.4
vocal organ 524.18
lip service
hypocrisy 354.6
mouth honor 693.2
lipstick
n makeup 1016.11
v make red 41.4
liquefaction
melting 1020.3
liquidity 1061.1
fluidification 1064
liquefying 1064.1
liquefied
molten 1020.31
melted 1064.6
liquefy melt 1020.21
liquidize 1064.5
liquefying
n melting 1020.3
liquefaction 1064.1
adj liquefactive 1064.7
liqueur 88.15
liquid
n beverage 10.49
speech sound 524.12
fluid 1061.2
adj phonetic 524.30
convertible 728.31
fluid 1061.4
watery 1065.16
liquid air 1024.7

liquid assets
assets 471.7
cash 728.18
liquidate excise 255.10
kill 308.13
murder 308.16
exterminate 395.14
depose 447.4
pay in full 624.13
cash 728.29
sell 737.24
annihilate 762.7
eliminate 773.5
do away with 909.21
liquidated paid 624.22
excluded 773.7
liquidation
homicide 308.2
extinction 395.6
deposal 447.2
payment 624.1
trading 737.19
elimination 773.2
liquidator payer 624.9
treasurer 729.12
liquid fuel 1075.9
liquid lunch 87.1
liquid oxygen
coolant 1024.7
rocket propulsion
1074.8
liquor
n beverage 10.49
sedative 86.12
spirits 88.13
fluid 1061.2
v drink 88.25
lisp
n sibilation 57.1
speech defect 525.1
v sibilate 57.2
speak poorly 525.7
lisping
n speech defect 525.1
adj inarticulate 525.12
lissome 1047.9
list
n stripe 47.5
contents 196.1
inclination 204.2
border 211.4
edging 211.7
enclosed place 212.3
record 549.1
itemization 871.1
enumeration 871.1
v careen 182.43
tumble 194.8
incline 204.10
border 211.10
record 549.15
enlist 615.17
classify 809.6
enumerate 871.8
cultivate 1069.17
interj hark! 48.16
listen
v hark 48.10
hearken to 983.7
interj hark! 48.16
attention! 983.22

listener hearer 48.5
recipient 479.3
listen in listen 48.10
telephone 347.19
tune in 1034.27
listening
n hearing 48.1
audition 48.2
adj attentive 48.14
listen to listen 48.10
obey 326.2
listing
n registration 549.14
list 871.1
index 871.7
cultivation 1069.13
adj inclining 204.15
unbalanced 791.5
listless weak 16.12
apathetic 94.13
unconcerned 102.7
weary 118.11
languid 331.20
incurious 982.3
listmaker 549.12
list-maker 547.15
listmaking 549.1
list price 630.1
lit drunk 88.33
illuminated 1025.40
litany 696.4
literacy 928.5
literal lettered 546.8
orthodox 687.7
genuine 973.15
unimaginative 987.5
literal meaning 518.1
literary
written 547.24
belletristic 718.7
book-learned 928.22
literary critic
author 547.15
critic 718.4
judge 946.7
literary lion 547.15
literate
n intellectual 929.1
adj learned 928.21
literature
advertising matter 352.8
writing 547.10
written word 547.12
letters 718.1
lore 928.9
lithe 1047.9
lithic 1059.11
lithograph
n print 713.5
v engrave 713.9
lithographer 716.8
lithography
coloring 35.11
printing 548.1
planography 713.3
litigant
n oppositionist 452.3
litigator 598.11
adj litigious 598.21
litigate sue 598.13
legalize 673.9

litigation
contention 457.1
lawsuit 598.1
argumentation 935.4
litigator 598.11
litigious
contentious 110.26
partisan 456.17
litigant 598.21
argumentative 935.19
litter
n fledgling 302.10
bier 309.13
rubbish 391.5
offspring 561.2
jumble 810.3
multitude 884.3
sofa 901.19
bedding 901.20
v give birth 1.3
disarrange 811.2
tend 1070.7
littérateur
writer 547.15
author 718.4
scholar 929.3
litterbug 810.7
littering 1.1
little
n modicum 248.2
short time 828.3
adj insignificant 248.6
inadequate 250.7
small 258.10
short 268.8
ungenerous 651.6
base 661.12
narrow-minded 980.10
insignificant 998.17
adv scarcely 248.9
small 258.16
a little
n short distance 223.2
adv by degrees 245.6
to a degree 245.7
scarcely 248.9
little by little
gradually 175.14
by degrees 245.6
piece by piece 793.9
little fellow child 302.3
common man 606.5
little known 661.14
little-minded 980.10
the little people 678.7
little plate 62.4
littoral
n shore 234.2
ocean zone 240.4
adj aquatic 182.58
bordering 211.11
coastal 234.7
liturgic
ceremonious 580.8
ritualistic 701.19
liturgy ceremony 580.4
divine service 696.8
rite 701.3
the Liturgy 701.8
live
v inhabit 225.7

be alive 306.8
be somebody 662.10
exist 761.8
endure 827.6
adj living 306.12
active 330.17
burning 1019.27
charged 1032.34
live and learn 570.10
live and let live
let alone 329.4
not interfere 430.16
keep an open mind 979.7
live by one's wits
cheat 356.18
play a deep game 415.9
be dishonest 645.11
lived-in 121.11
live down 658.4
live forever 829.6
live-in
interior 207.6
resident 225.13
live it up
enjoy oneself 95.14
have a party 582.21
amuse oneself 743.22
live large 95.14
livelihood 449.3
liveliness
animation 17.4
zest 68.2
passion 93.2
eagerness 101.1
gaiety 109.4
life 306.1
lively activity 330.2
spirit 544.4
elasticity 1048.1
lively
adj energetic 17.13
zestful 68.7
fervent 93.18
eager 101.8
gay 109.14
fast 174.15
active 330.17
spirited 544.12
interesting 983.19
elastic 1048.7
adv actively 330.25
liven energize 17.10
cheer 109.7
live off 138.12
live on feed on 8.28
continue to exist 761.9
endure 827.6
postexist 839.7
live or die
adv without fail 970.26
phrs come what may
359.20
liver viscera 2.16
organ 2.17
digestion 7.8
food 10.20
liver spot 2.4
livery wardrobe 5.2
uniform 5.7
insignia 647.1
livestock 311.1

live through
win through 409.13
endure 827.6
live up to observe 434.2
execute 437.9
live wire
man of action 330.8
charge 1032.5
live with endure 134.5
keep an open mind 979.7
livid colorless 36.7
black and blue 38.12
gray 39.4
blue 45.3
purple 46.3
angry 152.28
deathly 307.28
living
n habitation 225.1
life 306.1
support 449.3
benefice 698.9
adj energetic 17.13
resident 225.13
organic 305.17
alive 306.12
existent 761.13
lifelike 784.16
burning 1019.27
living being
organism 305.2
living being 306.3
animal 311.2
living floor 296.1
living large 95.18
living quarters
housing 225.3
quarters 228.4
living room 197.5
lizard 311.24
llama 176.8
llano plain 236.1
grassland 310.8
lo 122.20
load
n affliction 96.8
freight 176.6
lading 196.2
quantity 247.3
burden 297.7
charge 462.16
portion 477.5
wealth 618.3
tax 643.3
full measure 794.3
impediment 1012.6
v lade 159.15
fill 196.7
burden 297.13
tamper with 354.17
prime 405.9
fill 794.7
shoot 904.12
go hard with 1011.8
computerize 1042.21
loaded drunk 88.33
weighted 297.18
prepared 405.16
wealthy 618.15
fraught 794.12
critical 843.10

loader 183.9
loading
placement 159.6
burden 297.7
imposition 643.1
loaf
n lump 257.10
Eucharist 701.7
v idle 331.12
loafer vagabond 178.3
idler 331.8
beggar 440.8
loafers 5.27
loafing 331.4
loamy earthy 234.5
pasty 1047.12
loan
n the lend 620.2
v lend 620.5
lo and behold 122.20
loaner 620.3
loaning 620.1
loan shark 620.3
loan-shark 620.5
loan-sharking
lending 620.1
illicit business 732.1
loathe dislike 99.3
hate 103.5
loathing
n hostility 99.2
hate 103.1
adj hating 103.7
loathsome
offensive 98.18
terrible 1000.9
hideous 1015.11
lob
n throw 904.3
v play tennis 748.3
throw 904.10
elevate 912.5
lobar 202.12
lobby
n vestibule 197.19
bungler 414.8
legislative lobby 609.32
influence 894.6
v urge 375.14
exercise influence 894.9
lobbying
inducement 375.3
political influence 609.29
backstairs influence 894.3
lobbyist lobby 609.32
influence 894.6
lobe ear 2.10
pendant 202.4
member 793.4
lobo 311.19
lobster
n marine animal 311.29
cheater 759.22
v row 182.53
local
n bar 88.20
train 179.14
native 227.3
branch 617.10
labor union 727.2
adj localized 231.9

idiomatic 523.22
local color milieu 209.3
  plot 722.4
locale location 159.1
  area 209.2
  arena 463.1
  setting 704.19
  plot 722.4
localism dialect 523.7
  barbarism 526.6
  policy 609.4
locality location 159.1
  habitat 228.18
localize locate 159.11
  restrict 428.9
local yokel 227.3
locate situate 159.11
  settle 159.17
  discover 941.2
locating
  placement 159.6
  discovery 941.1
location place 159.1
  situation 159.1
  placement 159.6
  setting 704.19
  motion-picture studio 706.4
  state 765.1
  discovery 941.1
  farm 1069.8
loch lake 241.1
  inlet 242.1
Loch Ness monster 311.29
lock
  n tress 3.5
  standstill 173.3
  floodgate 239.11
  bolt 428.5
  wrestling 474.3
  poker 759.10
  sure thing 970.2
  v close 293.6
  agree 788.6
  hook 800.8
  obstruct 1012.12
lockbox 346.4
locker storehouse 386.6
  treasury 729.13
  cold storage 1024.6
locket 498.6
lock horns
  quarrel 456.12
  contend with 457.17
  counteract 900.6
  argue 935.16
lock in imprison 429.14
  retain 474.5
  make sure 970.11
lockjaw 85.6
lockout exclusion 773.1
  stop 857.2
lock out close 293.6
  strike 727.10
  exclude 773.4
lockup
  confinement 429.1
  prison 429.8
lock up enclose 212.5
  close 293.6
  secrete 346.7
  imprison 429.14

loco
  n disease 85.41
  adj crazy 926.27
locomotion
  mobility 172.3
  travel 177.1
locomotive
  traveling 177.36
  vehicular 179.23
  mechanical 1039.7
  self-propelled 1041.23
locus 159.1
locust 311.35
locution
  language 523.1
  utterance 524.2
  word 526.1
  phrase 529.1
  diction 532.1
lode
  source of supply 386.4
  rich source 618.4
  deposit 1058.7
lodestar focus 208.4
  motive 375.1
  guiding star 574.8
  stars 1072.4
lodestone desire 100.11
  magnet 907.3
lodge
  n house 228.5
  cottage 228.8
  lair 228.26
  branch 617.10
  v deposit 159.14
  inhabit 225.7
  house 225.10
  accommodate 385.10
  store 386.10
  fix 855.9
  repair 855.10
lodger roomer 227.8
  tenant 470.4
lodging
  n habitation 225.1
  housing 225.3
  abode 228.1
  quarters 228.4
  adj resident 225.13
loess deposit 176.9
  dregs 256.2
loft
  n library 197.6
  attic 197.16
  workplace 739.1
  v play 751.4
  elevate 912.5
lofty elevated 136.11
  arrogant 141.9
  eminent 247.9
  high 272.14
  ostentatious 501.18
  eloquent 544.14
  grandiloquent 545.8
  impartial 649.9
  magnanimous 652.6
  renowned 662.18
  raised 912.9
log
  n speedometer 174.7
  record book 549.11

accounts book 628.4
  chronicle 832.9
  firewood 1021.3
  wood 1054.3
  v ship activity 182.48
  record 549.15
  keep accounts 628.8
logarithmic 1017.23
log cabin 228.8
loge 704.15
logger 1069.7
loggia 197.18
logging
  registration 549.14
  forestry 1069.3
logic
  analytic reasoning 935.2
  reasonableness 935.9
logical sensible 920.18
  cognitive 931.21
  reasonable 935.20
  valid 973.14
logic-chopping
  n quibbling 936.5
  adj quibbling 936.14
logician 935.11
login 1042.18
logistics 385.1
logjam delay 846.2
  barrier 1012.5
logo patent 210.3
  symbol 517.2
  label 517.13
  insignia 647.1
logogram
  representation 349.1
  wordplay 489.8
  symbol 517.2
  phonetic symbol 546.2
logomachy
  quarrel 456.5
  contention 457.1
  argumentation 935.4
logomania 540.2
logorrhea
  wordiness 538.2
  logomania 540.2
logotype patent 210.3
  symbol 517.2
  label 517.13
  type 548.6
log out 1042.21
logroller
  wire-puller 609.30
  politics 610.6
logrolling
  political influence 609.29
  legislative procedure
    613.6
  trading 863.2
logy inert 173.14
  languid 331.20
log zs 22.14
loin 217.3
loincloth 5.19
loins 886.7
loiter lag 166.4
  dawdle 175.8
  dally 331.14
  wait 846.12
  trifle 998.14

loiterer slowpoke 175.5
  idler 331.8
loitering
  n dawdling 175.3
  idling 331.4
  trifling 998.8
  adj dawdling 175.11
  dilatory 846.17
Loki evil 680.5
  nether world deity 682.5
loll
  n recumbency 201.2
  v rest 20.6
  lie 201.5
lollapaloosa 999.7
lolling
  n idling 331.4
  adj recumbent 201.8
lollygag dawdle 175.8
  dally 331.14
  make love 562.15
lollygagger 175.5
lollygagging
  n love affair 104.5
  dawdling 175.3
  lovemaking 562.2
  adj dawdling 175.11
lone solitary 584.11
  one 872.7
  alone 872.8
  sole 872.9
loneliness
  solitude 584.3
  aloneness 872.2
lonely solitary 584.11
  alone 872.8
lonely hearts club 563.12
loner recluse 584.5
  self-seeker 651.3
  oddity 870.4
lonesomeness
  solitude 584.3
  aloneness 872.2
lone wolf
  self-seeker 651.3
  oddity 870.4
long
  n bull 737.13
  long time 827.4
  adj lengthy 267.7
  giant 272.16
  wordy 538.12
  protracted 827.11
  adv for a long time 827.14
long ago for a long time
    827.14
  long since 837.16
longanimity
  patience 134.1
  forgiveness 148.1
  submission 433.1
long ball 745.3
long-ball hitter 894.6
long distance
  telephone operator 347.9
  telephone call 347.13
long-distance 261.8
long-established
  confirmed 373.18
  traditional 842.12
  established 855.13

longevity haleness 83.3
  old age 303.5
  life 306.1
  durability 827.1
longhair 842.8
longhand 547.22
long haul 261.2
longing
  n yearning 100.5
  adj wistful 100.23
longitude map 159.5
  zone 231.3
  length 267.1
  coordinates 300.5
  orbit 1072.16
long-lasting 827.10
long-lived living 306.12
  durable 827.10
long-lost gone 34.4
  absent 222.11
  lost 473.7
long range 261.2
long-range 261.8
long shot
  motion picture 714.8
  bet 759.3
  gambling odds 759.6
  chance event 972.6
  small chance 972.9
longsighted
  poor-sighted 28.11
  sagacious 920.16
  foreseeing 961.7
long since
  for a long time 827.14
  long ago 837.16
  since 837.17
long-standing
  durable 827.10
  traditional 842.12
long-suffering
  n patience 134.1
  forgiveness 148.1
  submission 433.1
  tolerance 979.4
  adj patient 134.9
  forgiving 148.6
  submissive 433.12
  tolerant 979.11
long suit
  talent 413.4
  specialty 866.1
long-term 827.10
long time length 267.1
  long while 827.4
long-tongued 540.9
long way 261.2
long-winded
  tedious 118.9
  lengthened 267.8
  wordy 538.12
  protracted 827.11
long word
  hard word 526.10
  high-sounding words 545.3
loo 12.10
looby vulgarian 497.6
  peasant 606.6
  fool 924.3
look
  n sight 27.3

aspect 33.3
  looks 33.4
  hint 248.4
  information 551.4
  v peer 27.13
  gaze 27.15
  appear to be 33.10
  be vigilant 339.8
  seek 938.30
  heed 983.6
  interj attention! 983.22
look after look 27.13
  nurture 339.9
  serve 577.13
  care for 1008.19
look ahead 961.5
look-alikes set 784.5
  twins 873.4
look alive
  v be vigilant 339.8
  pay attention 983.8
  interj make haste! 401.16
look around 938.30
look at look 27.13
  spectate 918.5
  examine 938.24
look back 989.9
look down one's nose
  look askance 27.18
  shudder at 99.5
  give oneself airs 141.8
  be hard to please 495.8
look down upon
  disdain 157.3
  rise above 272.11
looked-for
  expected 130.13
  future 839.8
looker recipient 479.3
  spectator 918.1
  beauty 1016.8
look for hope 124.6
  look forward to 130.6
  solicit 440.14
  come 839.6
  seek 938.30
look for trouble
  defy 454.3
  pick a quarrel 456.13
look forward to
  reckon on 130.6
  come 839.6
  foresee 961.5
look in enter 189.7
  visit 582.19
looking glass 29.6
looking up
  promising 124.12
  improving 392.15
look like
  appear to be 33.10
  augur 133.11
  resemble 784.7
look on see 27.12
  look 27.13
  attend 221.8
  spectate 918.5
lookout
  observation 27.2
  observation post 27.8
  view 33.6

vigilance 339.4
  warner 399.4
  occupation 724.1
  watchman 1008.10
look out
  v be vigilant 339.8
  beware 494.7
  pay attention 983.8
  interj careful! 494.14
look over
  scrutinize 27.14
  front on 216.9
  examine 938.24
looks 33.4
look the other way
  be blind 30.8
  let alone 329.4
  keep an open mind 979.7
  be inattentive 984.2
look through 938.30
look-through 938.3
look to
  look forward to 130.6
  avail oneself of 387.14
  prepare for 405.11
  tend 896.3
  attend to 983.5
  care for 1008.19
look up improve 392.7
  seek 938.30
look up to 155.4
looky-loo 178.1
loom
  n weaver 740.5
  imminence 840.1
  v appear 33.8
  ascend 193.8
  bulk 247.5
  threaten 514.2
  weave 740.6
  come 839.6
  be imminent 840.2
looming
  n mirage 976.6
  adj ominous 133.16
  imminent 840.3
loon 926.16
loony
  n lunatic 926.16
  adj foolish 923.9
  crazy 926.27
loonybin 926.14
loop
  n spiral loop 184.16
  circle 280.2
  bulge 283.3
  baseball 745.1
  circuit 914.2
  v maneuver 184.40
  encircle 209.7
  curve 279.6
  weave 740.6
looper 745.3
loophole
  observation post 27.8
  outlet 190.9
  way out 369.4
loose
  n freedom 430.1
  v set free 431.6
  relax 670.9

detach 802.10
  loosen 804.3
  facilitate 1014.7
  adj adrift 182.61
  drooping 202.10
  negligent 340.10
  escaped 369.11
  lax 426.4
  free 430.21
  unrestrained 430.24
  ungrammatic 531.4
  discursive 538.13
  informal 581.3
  wanton 665.26
  unfastened 802.22
  slack 804.5
  slovenly 810.15
  illogical 936.11
  vague 971.19
  inaccurate 975.17
  flaccid 1047.10
loose ends
  slipshodness 340.3
  nonaccomplishment 408.1
loosen
  loose 431.6
  relax 670.9
  detach 802.10
  slacken 804.3
  soften 1047.6
loosening
  n laxness 426.1
  modulation 670.2
  adj softening 1047.16
loosen up
  amuse 743.21
  amuse oneself 743.22
loose woman 665.14
loot
  n booty 482.11
  money 728.2
  v seize 480.14
  plunder 482.17
  raze 671.11
looter 483.6
looting
  n rapacity 480.9
  plundering 482.6
  unruliness 671.3
  adj plunderous 482.22
lop
  n wave 238.14
  roughness 288.2
  v hang 202.6
  excise 255.10
  adj drooping 202.10
lope
  n run 174.3
  v speed 174.8
  go on horseback 177.34
lopped 795.5
loppy 202.10
lopsided
  distorted 265.10
  unbalanced 791.5
loquacity 540.1
loran
  ship navigation 182.2
  airplane navigation 184.6
  long-range navigation
    1036.3

lord proprietor 470.2
  master 575.1
  nobleman 608.4
Lord 648.2
lord it over 612.15
lordly dignified 136.12
  arrogant 141.11
  imperious 417.16
lordship
  supremacy 249.3
  mastership 417.7
  ownership 469.2
  aristocracy 608.9
Lordship 648.2
lore mythology 678.14
  tradition 842.2
  body of knowledge 928.9
  superstition 954.3
Lorelei 377.4
lorgnette 29.3
lorry 179.12
lose fail 410.9
  lose out 412.12
  incur loss 473.4
  waste 486.4
  forget 990.5
lose face
  bow to 250.5
  incur disgrace 661.7
lose ground
  regress 163.5
  slow 175.9
  fall short 911.2
lose heart
  despond 112.16
  despair 125.10
lose one's head 923.6
lose one's mind
  be stupid 922.12
  go mad 926.21
loser inferior 250.2
  failure 410.2
  disappointment 410.8
  defeatee 412.5
  loss 473.1
  insolvent 625.4
  unfortunate 1011.7
lose sight of
  neglect 340.6
  disregard 435.3
  forget 990.5
lose track of 340.6
lose weight 270.13
losing battle 125.1
losing streak 473.1
loss
  disappearance 34.1
  decrement 252.3
  impairment 393.1
  losing hold of 473
  losing 473.1
  game 746.3
  disadvantage 996.2
loss of memory
  thoughtlessness 933.1
  amnesia 990.2
loss of speech 525.6
lost vanished 34.4
  past hope 125.15
  unwon 412.13
  gone 473.7

wasted 486.9
  irreclaimable 654.18
  unregenerate 695.18
  bewildered 971.24
  abstracted 985.11
  forgotten 990.8
the lost 680.1
lost cause 125.8
lost in 983.17
lost in thought
  absorbed in thought 931.22
  abstracted 985.11
lost soul 660.4
lot
  n plot 231.4
  amount 244.2
  lots 247.4
  real estate 471.6
  portion 477.5
  motion-picture studio 706.4
  share 738.3
  state 765.1
  bunch 770.7
  kind 809.3
  amount made 893.4
  fate 964.2
  chance 972.1
  v allot 477.9
  gamble 759.23
the lot 792.3
Lothario beau 104.12
  libertine 665.10
lotion toilet water 70.3
  cleanser 79.17
  balm 86.11
  ointment 1056.3
lots lot 247.4
  real estate 471.6
  multitude 884.3
  plenty 991.2
lottery 759.14
lottery winner 409.6
lotus-eater idler 331.8
  visionary 986.13
The Lotus Sutra 683.9
loud
  adj intense 15.22
  garish 35.20
  loud-sounding 53.11
  demanding 421.9
  coarse 497.11
  gaudy 501.20
  adv loudly 53.14
loud and clear
  adj affirmative 334.8
  clear 521.11
  adv affirmatively 334.10
loudmouthed
  loud voiced 53.12
  vociferous 59.10
loudness
  garishness 35.5
  sound 50.1
  intensity 53.1
  coarseness 497.2
  showiness 501.3
lounge
  n anteroom 197.20
  v rest 20.6
  lie 201.5
  idle 331.12

lounger 331.8
lounging
  n recumbency 201.2
  idling 331.4
  adj recumbent 201.8
louring 319.8
louse vermin 311.36
  bad person 660.5
loused up 799.4
louse up spoil 393.11
  bungle 414.12
  complicate 799.3
  goof 975.6
  make a boner 975.15
  hinder 1012.16
lousy infested 910.11
  bad 1000.8
lout bungler 414.8
  simple soul 416.3
  vulgarian 497.6
  peasant 606.6
  oaf 924.5
loutish
  countrified 233.7
  bungling 414.20
  boorish 497.13
  ill-bred 505.6
louver 239.13
lovable
  desirable 100.30
  endearing 104.24
love
  n sexuality 75.2
  liking 100.2
  affection 104.1
  sweetheart 104.9
  benevolence 143.4
  accord 455.1
  regards 504.8
  endearment term 562.6
  friendship 587.1
  cardinal virtues 653.3
  game 748.2
  heat metaphor 1019.2
  v savor 63.5
  have deep feelings 93.12
  enjoy 95.13
  desire 100.14
  be fond of 104.18
Love Cupid 104.7
  Deity 677.6
love affair 104.5
love child 561.5
love-hate 215.5
loveless unloved 99.10
  undesirous 102.8
love letter 562.13
love-life 75.2
lovelock 3.5
lovelorn unloved 99.10
  loving 104.26
lovely delightful 97.7
  endearing 104.24
  beautiful 1016.17
lovemaking
  sexuality 75.2
  copulation 75.7
  love 104.1
  dalliance 562.1
love nest 582.9
love potion 75.6

lover desirer 100.12
  admirer 104.11
  endearment term 562.6
  friend 588.1
  supporter 616.9
lovesick 104.26
love story 706.2
loving lovesome 104.26
  kind 143.13
  careful 339.10
  almighty 677.17
lovingkindness 143.1
low
  n weather map 317.4
  business cycle 731.10
  price 738.9
  gear 1040.9
  v cry 60.2
  adj faint 52.16
  deep 54.11
  dejected 112.22
  humble 137.10
  insignificant 248.6
  inferior 250.6
  short 268.8
  unelevated 274.7
  dying 307.32
  base 497.15
  disapproving 510.21
  phonetic 524.30
  inelegant 534.2
  populational 606.8
  cheap 633.7
  wicked 654.16
  base 661.12
  vulgar 666.8
  depressed 913.12
  adv faintly 52.21
  near the ground 274.9
lowball 759.10
lowborn 606.8
lowbrow
  n ignoramus 930.7
  adj unlearned 930.13
Low Church 675.11
low class 1005.4
low-class 1005.9
low-cut 6.13
low density 299.1
the lowdown
  inside information 551.2
  what's what 973.4
low-down 661.12
the lowdown dope 551.2
lower
  n scowl 110.9
  gloom 1027.4
  v look sullen 110.15
  sadden 112.18
  forebode 133.10
  show resentment 152.14
  threaten 514.2
  be imminent 840.2
  grow dark 1027.12
lower
  v abase 137.5
  sink 194.6
  reduce 252.7
  debase 274.6
  deepen 275.8
  excavate 284.15

demote 447.3
cheapen 633.6
depress 913.4
adj inferior 250.6
reduced 252.10
debased 274.8
lower case 548.6
lower-case literal 546.8
typographic 548.20
lower class
n inferior 250.2
commoners 606.1
social status 607.7
adj the working class 607.10
lowered humbled 137.13
reduced 252.10
low 274.7
depressed 913.12
lower house 613.1
lower oneself
condescend 137.8
give oneself airs 141.8
incur disgrace 661.7
lowest humble 137.10
bottom 199.7
least 250.8
lower 274.8
reduced 633.9
lowest common denominator
clearness 521.2
average 864.3
lucky charm charm 691.5
low grade 1005.4
low-grade 1005.9
low key reserve 139.3
reticence 344.3
lowland
n the country 233.1
plain 236.1
lowlands 274.3
adj rustic 233.6
lowlife 660.2
low-maintenance
comfortable 121.11
unstrict 426.5
lowness faintness 52.1
resonance 54.1
dejection 112.3
insignificance 248.1
inadequacy 250.3
stubbiness 268.2
shortness 274.1
commonness 497.5
baseness 661.3
low opinion 510.1
low-pitched 54.11
low price 633.2
low priority 998.1
low profile
distinctness 31.2
inconspicuousness 32.2
reserve 139.3
reticence 344.3
low-profile 32.6
low-spirited
dejected 112.22
dull 117.6
low-test 1005.9
low tide tide 238.13
low water 274.2
low voice 52.4

lox fish 10.24
coolant 1024.7
rocket propulsion 1074.8
loyal
zealous 101.9
obedient 326.3
firm 359.12
persevering 360.8
observant 434.4
faithful 644.20
loyalist 609.27
loyal opposition 609.24
loyalty
zeal 101.2
obedience 326.1
firmness 359.2
perseverance 360.1
duty 641.1
fidelity 644.7
lozenge pill 86.7
heraldry 647.2
LPGA 751.1
luau
source of supply 386.4
rich source 618.4
plenty 991.2
lubber
mariner 183.2
idler 331.8
bungler 414.8
oaf 924.5
lubricant
n smoother 287.4
lubricator 1056.2
adj lubricating 1056.10
lubricate smooth 287.5
facilitate 1014.7
oil 1056.8
lubricated drunk 88.33
slippery 287.12
lubricating
n facilitation 1014.5
lubrication 1056.6
adj lubricant 1056.10
lubrication 1056.6
lubricious
slippery 287.12
lascivious 665.29
lubritorium 1056.7
lucid clear 521.11
elegant 533.6
sane 925.4
light 1025.32
transparent 1029.4
translucent 1030.5
lucid dreaming 22.5
lucidity
distinctness 31.2
clearness 521.2
elegance 533.1
extrasensory perception 689.8
sanity 925.1
lightness 1025.3
transparency 1029.1
translucence 1030.2
lucifer 1021.5
Lucifer 1072.4
luck gamble 759.2
uncertainty 971.1
chance 972.1

good fortune 1010.2
Luck 972.2
lucky
auspicious 133.17
speculative 759.27
timely 843.9
chance 972.15
fortunate 1010.14
lucky break 1010.3
lucky piece 691.5
lucrative
gainful 472.16
paying 624.21
lucre gain 472.3
wealth 618.1
money 728.1
lucubration
writing 547.10
treatise 556.1
study 570.3
consideration 931.2
ludicrous
humorous 488.4
absurd 923.11
lug
n body part 2.10
ear 48.7
v transport 176.12
pull 905.4
luggage
freight 176.6
container 195.1
impedimenta 471.3
lugubrious
sorrowful 112.26
pessimistic 125.16
lukewarm
unfeeling 94.9
indifferent 102.6
nonreligious 695.15
warm 1019.24
lull
n respite 20.2
silence 51.1
calm 173.5
inactivity 331.1
interruption 813.2
interim 826.1
pause 857.3
v relieve 120.5
quiet 173.8
calm 670.7
lullaby 22.10
lulling
n relief 120.1
modulation 670.2
adj tranquilizing 670.15
lulu 999.7
lumbago 85.9
lumbar region 217.3
lumber
n rubbish 391.5
gambler 759.21
impediment 1012.6
wood 1054.3
v plod 175.7
way of walking 177.28
bungle 414.11
hamper 1012.11
lumbering
n forestry 1069.3

adj slow 175.10
bulky 257.19
bungling 414.20
stiff 534.3
lumberjack 1069.7
lumberyard 386.6
lumen 1025.22
luminary
n celebrity 662.9
chief 997.10
first-rater 999.6
light source 1026.1
adj photic 1025.42
luminesce 1025.27
luminescence 1025.13
luminescent 1025.39
luminous clear 521.11
almighty 677.17
luminant 1025.31
illuminated 1025.40
lummox bungler 414.9
oaf 924.5
lump
n clump 257.10
bulge 283.3
swelling 283.4
bungler 414.9
print 517.7
accumulation 770.9
piece 793.3
solid 1045.6
v thicken 1045.10
lumpen
n the underprivileged 606.4
adj countrified 233.7
idle 331.18
base 661.12
slovenly 810.15
lumpish
countrified 233.7
bulky 257.19
formless 263.4
onerous 297.17
languid 331.20
bungling 414.20
boorish 497.13
stupid 922.15
thickened 1045.14
lump sum 728.13
lump together
assemble 770.18
put together 800.5
combine 805.3
lumpy bulky 257.19
formless 263.4
gnarled 288.8
nappy 294.7
thickened 1045.14
Luna 1072.12
lunacy
foolishness 923.1
insanity 926.1
lunar
crescent-shaped 279.11
celestial 1072.25
lunar eclipse
eclipse 1027.8
moon 1072.11
lunar module 1075.2
lunatic
n fool 924.1

madman 926.15
adj insane 926.26
lunatic fringe
radical 611.12
fanatic 926.18
lunch
n meal 8.6
v dine 8.21
adj eccentric 927.6
lunch counter 8.17
luncheon 8.6
lunchroom 8.17
lung
n viscera 2.16
adj respiratory 2.32
lunge
n thrust 459.3
v way of walking
177.28
lunkhead 924.4
lunkheaded 922.17
lupine
canine 311.41
rapacious 480.26
lurch
n gait 177.12
bias 204.3
swing 916.6
flounder 917.8
v way of walking 177.28
pitch 182.55
tumble 194.8
oscillate 916.10
flounder 917.15
lurching
irregular 851.3
swinging 916.17
lure
n snare 356.13
incentive 375.7
charm 377.3
attractor 907.2
v trap 356.20
induce 375.22
allure 377.5
attract 907.4
lurid garish 35.20
colorless 36.7
brown 40.3
red 41.6
sensational 105.32
deathly 307.28
gaudy 501.20
grandiloquent 545.8
obscene 666.9
lurk couch 346.9
be latent 519.3
lurking
in hiding 346.14
latent 519.5
imminent 840.3
luscious tasty 63.8
oversweet 66.5
delectable 97.10
lush
n drunk 88.12
v drink 88.25
adj tasty 63.8
luxuriant 310.43
ornate 545.11
productive 890.9

lust
n sexual desire 75.5
craving 100.6
greed 100.8
will 323.1
lasciviousness 665.5
v lust after 75.20
desire 100.14
crave 100.18
luster
n polish 287.2
illustriousness 662.6
moment 824.2
gorgeousness 1016.5
shine 1025.2
chandelier 1026.6
v polish 287.7
shine 1025.24
lusterless colorless 36.7
lackluster 1027.17
lustful prurient 75.27
desirous 100.21
lascivious 665.29
lustful leer 27.3
lustral cleansing 79.28
atoning 658.7
lustrous
illustrious 662.19
luminous 1025.31
shiny 1025.34
lusty strong 15.15
energetic 17.13
hale 83.12
corpulent 257.18
Lutheran 675.28
lux 1025.22
luxate dislocate 160.5
disjoint 802.16
luxuriant
flourishing 310.43
ornate 498.12
grandiloquent 545.11
productive 890.9
plentiful 991.7
luxuriate
vegetate 310.34
superabound 993.8
luxuriate in
enjoy 95.13
indulge 669.4
luxurious
delightful 97.7
comfortable 121.11
ornate 498.12
grandiose 501.21
wealthy 618.14
expensive 632.11
sensual 663.5
luxury pleasure 95.1
delightfulness 97.2
grandeur 501.5
sensuality 663.1
superfluity 993.4
prosperity 1010.1
lyceum hall 197.4
secondary school 567.4
lying
n recumbency 201.2
lowness 274.1
untruthfulness 354.8
adj recumbent 201.8

untruthful 354.34
lying-in 1.1
lymph 2.24
lymphatic
n duct 2.23
adj circulatory 2.33
secretory 13.7
languid 331.20
lynch kill 308.13
hang 604.18
lynching killing 308.1
capital punishment
604.7
lynch law 418.2
lynx
sharp vision 27.11
wild cat 311.21
lyre 711.3
lyric melodious 708.48
vocal 708.50
poetic 720.15
lyricist
composer 710.20
poet 720.11
lyric poem 720.4
lyric theater 708.34
lysis 395.1
ma 560.12
ma'am 77.8
Mab 678.8
macabre
terrible 127.30
deathly 307.28
weird 988.9
macadam
ground covering 199.3
pavement 383.6
macaroni
noodles 10.33
dandy 500.9
mace scepter 417.9
insignia 647.1
macerate
torture 96.18
shrink 260.9
pulp 1063.5
soak 1065.13
Mach 174.2
Machiavellian
n deceiver 357.1
schemer 381.7
Machiavel 415.8
politics 610.6
adj falsehearted 354.31
scheming 381.13
cunning 415.12
machinate plot 381.9
maneuver 415.10
machination
chicanery 356.4
intrigue 381.5
manipulation 415.4
machinator
traitor 357.10
schemer 381.7
strategist 415.7
politics 610.6
machine
n automobile 179.9
political party 609.24
association 617.1

instrument of conversion
858.10
machinery 1040.3
computer 1042.2
v process 892.9
tool 1040.13
machine gun 847.5
machine-made 892.18
machinery
instrumentality 384.3
equipment 385.4
instrument 1040.1
machine 1040.3
mechanism 1040.4
machine shop 739.3
machine tool 1040.6
machinist stage technician
704.24
mechanic 1040.12
machismo
male sex 76.2
courage 492.1
macho
virile 76.13
courageous 492.16
macro 257.20
macrobiotic 827.10
macrocosm 1072.1
macroeconomics 731.7
macroevolution 861.3
macrolevel 246.1
macronutrient 7.11
maculate
v variegate 47.7
spot 1004.5
adj spotted 47.13
unvirtuous 654.12
unchaste 665.23
spotted 1004.9
mad
n anger 152.5
v madden 926.24
adj frenzied 105.25
angry 152.30
reckless 493.8
turbulent 671.18
foolish 923.8
insane 926.26
rabid 926.30
mad about
enthusiastic 101.11
crazy about 104.30
madam woman 77.8
mistress 575.2
Mrs 648.4
procurer 665.18
madcap
n humorist 489.12
daredevil 493.4
adj foolhardy 493.9
madden excite 105.12
enrage 152.25
antagonize 589.7
dement 926.24
maddening 105.30
madder 41.4
mad dog ruffian 593.3
violent person 671.9
made formative 262.9
successful 409.14
produced 892.17

man-made 892.18
mademoiselle
　woman 77.8
　girl 302.6
made of 796.4
made-up
　fabricated 354.29
　invented 892.19
　beautified 1016.22
mad for 100.22
madhouse 926.14
madman 926.15
madness fury 105.8
　foolishness 923.1
　insanity 926.1
Madonna 679.5
madrigal 708.18
maelstrom eddy 238.12
　bustle 330.4
　whirl 915.2
　agitation 917.1
maestro
　teacher 571.1
　musician 710.1
Mae West 397.6
maffick be noisy 53.9
　celebrate 487.2
　create disorder 810.11
Mafia
　the underworld
　　660.10
　illicit business 732.1
Mafioso
　violent person 671.9
　racketeer 732.4
magazine
　storehouse 386.6
　armory 462.2
　periodical 555.1
magenta 46.3
maggot
　whiteness 37.2
　larva 302.12
　insect 311.32
　caprice 364.1
　quirk 927.2
　figment of the imagination
　　986.5
maggoty
　nasty 64.7
　filthy 80.23
　capricious 364.5
　blighted 393.42
　eccentric 927.5
　fanciful 986.20
Magi 921.5
magic
　n illustriousness 662.6
　sorcery 690.1
　illusoriness 976.2
　v summon 420.11
　adj illustrious 662.19
　sorcerous 690.14
magical
　illustrious 662.19
　sorcerous 690.14
　miraculous 870.16
magic bullet
　remedy 86.1
　antibiotic 86.29
magic carpet 691.6

magician
　trickster 357.2
　master 413.13
　mage 690.6
　entertainer 707.1
　illusoriness 976.2
magic lantern 714.12
magic show 976.2
magic wand 691.6
magisterial
　dignified 136.12
　lordly 141.11
　chief 249.14
　skillful 413.22
　imperious 417.16
　jurisdictional 594.6
　authoritative 970.18
magistracy
　region 231.5
　mastership 417.7
　magistrature 594.3
magistrate
　arbitrator 466.4
　executive 574.3
　public official 575.17
　judge 596.1
Magna Charta 430.2
magna cum laude 646.11
magnanimity
　ambition 100.10
　forgiveness 148.1
　glory 247.2
　liberality 485.1
　magnanimousness 652.2
　tolerance 979.4
magnanimous
　forgiving 148.6
　eminent 247.9
　liberal 485.4
　great-souled 652.6
　tolerant 979.11
magnate
　nobleman 608.4
　businessman 730.1
　personage 997.8
magnet
　n desire 100.11
　focus 208.4
　artificial magnet 907.3
　v attract 907.4
magnetic
　influential 894.13
　attracting 907.5
　engrossing 983.20
　electromagnetic 1032.31
magnetic field
　electric field 1032.3
　magnetic force 1032.9
magnetic force 1032.9
magnetic pole
　magnet 907.3
　polarity 1032.8
magnetic storage 549.1
magnetic tape
　recording media 549.10
　disk 1042.6
magnetism
　desirability 100.13
　allurement 377.1
　influence 894.1
　attraction 907.1

electrical science 1032
　magnetic attraction
　　1032.7
magnetize
　put to sleep 22.20
　exercise influence 894.9
　attract 907.4
　electromagnetize 1032.27
magnification
　aggravation 119.1
　intensification 251.2
　expansion 259.1
　exaggeration 355.1
　praise 509.5
　glorification 662.8
　adoration 696.2
magnificence
　grandeur 501.5
　superexcellence 999.2
magnificent
　eminent 247.9
　grandiose 501.21
　superb 999.15
magnified
　aggravated 119.4
　increased 251.7
　exaggerated 355.4
　eminent 662.18
magnifique 122.10
magnify
　aggravate 119.2
　intensify 251.5
　enlarge 259.4
　exaggerate 355.3
　praise 509.12
　glorify 662.13
　adore 696.12
magnitude
　quantity 244.1
　greatness 247.1
　size 257.1
　star 1072.8
magnum opus 413.1
magpie chatterer 540.4
　collector 770.15
magus 690.6
maharani
　sovereign queen 575.11
　princess 608.8
mahatma
　master 413.13
　holy man 659.6
　occultist 689.11
　wise man 921.1
mahogany
　n smoothness 287.3
　adj reddish-brown 40.4
maid
　n girl 302.6
　single woman 565.4
　maidservant 577.8
　v serve 577.13
maiden
　n girl 302.6
　single woman 565.4
　execution 605.5
　jockey 757.2
　adj childish 301.11
　unmarried 565.7
　first 818.17
　new 841.7

maidenhead
　membrane 2.6
　childhood 301.2
　celibacy 565.1
　continence 664.3
maiden lady 565.4
maiden name 527.5
maiden speech 818.5
mail
　n plumage 3.18
　shell 295.15
　armor 460.3
　post 553.4
　v send 176.15
　post 553.12
mailbox 553.6
mail carrier 353.5
mail coach 353.6
maillot 5.29
mailman
　postman 353.5
　postal service 553.7
mail-order 553.14
mail-order house 736.1
maim disable 19.9
　injure 393.13
　cripple 393.14
　tear apart 802.14
maiming
　emasculation 19.5
　impairment 393.1
main
　n continent 235.1
　water main 239.7
　ocean 240.1
　adj great 247.6
　chief 249.14
　first 818.17
　paramount 997.24
main dish 10.7
main idea 932.4
mainland
　n continent 235.1
　adj continental 235.6
mainlander 235.3
mainline
　v use 87.22
　adj tending 896.4
main office
　headquarters 208.6
　office 739.7
main point
　summary 557.2
　topic 937.1
　salient point 997.6
mainspring
　motive 375.1
　fountainhead 886.6
mainstay
　n supporter 616.9
　support 901.2
　v support 901.21
mainstream
　n trend 896.2
　adj tending 896.4
main street 230.6
maintain affirm 334.5
　provide 385.7
　preserve 397.8
　insist 421.8
　aid 449.12

retain 474.5
defend 600.10
treat 624.19
endure 827.6
sustain 856.4
support 901.21
think 953.11
maintenance
  reparation 396.6
  preservation 397.1
  aid 449.3
  retention 474.1
  treatment 624.8
  durability 827.1
  preservation 853.2
  continuance 856.1
  support 901.1
maintenance man 396.10
maître d'hôtel
  waiter 577.7
  major-domo 577.10
majestic
  dignified 136.12
  eminent 247.9
  sovereign 417.17
  grandiose 501.21
  lofty 544.14
  almighty 677.17
majesty
  proud bearing 136.2
  glory 247.2
  sovereignty 417.8
  grandeur 501.5
  loftiness 544.6
  potentate 575.8
Majesty 648.2
major
  n adult 304.1
  study 568.8
  commissioned officer 575.18
  key 709.15
  adj older 842.19
  important 997.17
majordomo
  steward 574.4
  butler 577.10
major in
  study to be 570.15
  specialize 866.4
majority
  n maturity 303.2
  race 312.2
  major part 792.6
  plurality 883.2
  adj most 883.9
the majority
  dead 307.16
  the masses 606.2
majority leader 610.3
major league 745.1
major player 894.6
make
  n form 262.1
  structure 266.1
  yield 472.5
  receipts 627.1
  composition 796.1
  kind 809.3
  amount made 893.4
  disposition 978.3
  v use 87.22

travel 177.19
sail for 182.35
arrive 186.6
flow 238.16
act 328.4
do 328.6
perform 328.9
make up 405.7
accomplish 407.4
compel 424.4
execute 437.9
acquire 472.8
compose 796.3
convert 858.11
cause 886.10
produce 892.8
imagine 986.14
make a beeline
  go directly 161.10
  take a short cut 268.7
  be straight 277.4
make a bid
  offer 439.6
  bid 733.9
make a clean sweep
  revolutionize 860.4
  evacuate 909.22
make a comfort stop 12.12
make a deal
  contract 437.5
  compromise 468.2
  bargain 731.18
  strike a bargain 731.19
make a dent in
  impress 93.15
  gain influence 894.12
make advances
  communicate with 343.8
  approach 439.7
  cultivate 587.12
  exercise influence 894.9
make a face
  shudder at 99.5
  grimace 265.8
make a Federal case 949.2
make a fool of
  fool 356.15
  outwit 415.11
  stultify 923.7
make a go of it
  succeed 409.7
  succeed with 409.11
make a killing
  score a success 409.9
  triumph 411.3
  profit 472.12
  trade 737.23
make allowance for
  extenuate 600.12
  allow for 959.5
make amends
  compensate 338.4
  make restitution 481.5
  requite 506.5
  repay 624.11
  atone 658.4
make an appearance
  appear 33.8
  arrive 186.6
  attend 221.8
  be manifest 348.7

make an example of 604.10
make an impression
  be heard 48.12
  affect emotionally 93.15
  impress 931.19
  be remembered 989.13
make a point of
  resolve 359.7
  contend for 457.20
  make conditional 959.4
make a scene 93.13
make a show of
  sham 354.21
  affect 500.12
make believe 354.20
make-believe
  n figment of the imagination
    986.5
  adj spurious 354.26
  fictitious 986.21
make clear
  explain 341.10
  manifest 348.5
  make understandable 521.6
  facilitate 1014.7
make do 995.4
make ends meet
  support oneself 385.12
  economize 635.4
make fun of
  joke 489.13
  ridicule 508.8
make good
  straighten 277.5
  compensate 338.4
  remedy 396.13
  come through 409.10
  observe 434.2
  make restitution 481.5
  grow rich 618.10
  repay 624.11
  meet an obligation 641.11
  keep faith 644.9
  atone 658.4
  complete 794.6
  prove 957.10
  be prosperous 1010.9
make haste
  v speed 174.8
  hasten 401.5
  interj make it quick! 401.16
make hay while the sun
  shines
  make the most of one's time
    330.16
  improve the occasion 843.8
make headway
  progress 162.2
  make way 182.21
  improve 392.7
  make good 409.10
  prosper 1010.7
make it
  be able 18.11
  arrive 186.6
  make good 409.10
  manage 409.12
  live on 839.7
  stand the test 942.10
make known
  communicate 343.7

divulge 351.5
make public 352.11
make light of
  underestimate 950.2
  be inattentive 984.2
  attach little importance to
    998.12
  take it easy 1014.12
make love
  copulate 75.21
  procreate 78.8
  bill and coo 562.14
make merry
  celebrate 487.2
  revel 743.24
make money
  profit 472.12
  grow rich 618.10
make no bones about 359.10
make nothing of
  not understand 522.11
  underestimate 950.2
  attach little importance to
    998.12
make one fed-up 118.6
make one's mark
  make good 409.10
  cut a dash 501.13
  be somebody 662.10
  be prosperous 1010.9
make one's way
  work one's way 162.4
  support oneself 385.12
  make better 392.9
  make good 409.10
make oneself at home 121.8
make out see 27.12
  copulate 75.21
  support oneself 385.12
  manage 409.12
  execute 437.9
  perceive 521.9
  write 547.19
  record 549.15
  make love 562.15
  be in a certain state
    765.5
  persist 856.5
  know 928.12
  solve 940.2
  detect 941.5
  prove 957.10
  recognize 989.11
  make shift 995.4
make-out artist 562.12
make over
  reproduce 78.7
  transfer 176.10
  transfer property 629.3
  convert 858.11
make peace
  cease hostilities 465.9
  settle 466.7
  gain influence 894.12
make plain
  explain 341.10
  manifest 348.5
make possible
  permit 443.9
  enable 966.5
make public 352.11

maker artist 716.1
  poet 720.11
  doer 726.1
  skilled worker 726.6
  author 886.4
  producer 892.7
make sense
  be understandable 521.4
  be reasonable 935.17
makeshift
  n improvisation 365.5
  substitute 862.2
  expedience 995.2
  adj extemporaneous 365.12
  unprepared 406.8
  substitute 862.8
  expedient 995.7
  imperfect 1003.4
make sure
  take precautions 494.6
  secure 855.8
  make certain 970.11
  play safe 1007.3
make the best of it
  be optimistic 124.8
  accept 134.7
  submit 433.6
make the grade
  be able 18.11
  manage 409.12
  suffice 991.4
make the most of
  take advantage of 387.15
  excel 999.11
make the scene
  appear 33.8
  go to 177.25
  arrive 186.6
  make good 409.10
  participate 476.5
make tracks
  speed 174.9
  run off 188.12
  leave 222.10
  flee 368.11
make trade-off 468.2
makeup
  form 262.1
  structure 266.1
  design 554.12
  theater 704.17
  nature 767.4
  composition 796.1
  order 807.1
  disposition 978.3
  cosmetics 1016.11
make up
  fabricate 354.18
  improvise 365.8
  get up 405.7
  arrange 437.8
  shake hands 465.10
  print 548.16
  shuffle 758.5
  assemble 770.18
  complete 794.6
  compose 796.3
  produce 892.8
  originate 892.12
  beautify 1016.15
makeup artist 1016.12

make up one's mind
  resolve 359.7
  choose 371.16
  persuade oneself 375.24
  decide 946.11
  convince oneself 953.19
make up to
  curry favor 138.9
  head for 161.9
  communicate with 343.8
  cultivate 587.12
  repay 624.11
  exercise influence 894.9
make waves
  agitate 105.14
  misbehave 322.4
  oppose 451.3
  offer resistance 453.3
  not conform 868.4
make way
  v gather way 182.21
  make an opening 292.13
  interj open up! 292.23
make whoopee 487.2
making
  n reproduction 78.1
  forming 262.5
  structure 266.1
  acquisition 472.1
  production 892.1
  manufacture 892.2
  amount made 893.4
  adj almighty 677.17
makings
  gain 472.3
  component 796.2
maladjusted
  incompetent 414.19
  wrong 638.3
  inappropriate 789.7
maladjustment
  mental disorder 92.14
  unskillfulness 414.1
  wrong 638.1
  unfitness 789.3
maladroit
  inadequate 250.7
  bungling 414.20
malady 85.1
malaise
  pain 26.1
  disease 85.1
  unpleasure 96.1
  discontent 108.1
  dejection 112.3
  anxiety 126.1
  nervousness 128.1
  agitation 917.1
malapropism
  wordplay 489.8
  solecism 531.2
  grammatical error
    975.7
malapropos
  inappropriate 789.7
  untimely 844.6
  inexpedient 996.5
malaria miasma 1001.4
  vapor 1067.1
malarial 85.61
malarkey 520.3

malcontent
  n maverick 108.3
  lamenter 115.8
  rebel 327.5
  spoilsport 1012.9
  adj discontented 108.7
mal de mer 85.30
male
  n male being 76.4
  adj masculine 76.12
male chauvinism
  misanthropy 590.1
  discrimination 980.4
male chauvinist
  misanthrope 590.2
  bigot 980.5
malediction 513.1
maledictory 513.8
malefactor
  evildoer 593.1
  wrongdoer 660.8
maleness sex 75.1
  masculinity 76.1
  maturity 303.2
male organs 2.13
male sex 76.2
malevolence
  hate 103.1
  inconsiderateness 144.3
  ill will 144.4
  hostility 589.3
  badness 1000.1
malevolent
  n evildoer 593.1
  adj ill-disposed 144.19
  hostile 589.10
  harmful 1000.12
  bad 1000.7
malevolent influence 1000.4
malfeasance
  misbehavior 322.1
  misuse 389.1
  mismanagement 414.6
  wrong 638.1
  wrongdoing 655.1
  misdeed 655.2
malformation
  deformity 265.3
  wrong 638.1
  oddity 870.3
malformed
  deformed 265.12
  freakish 870.13
  unshapely 1015.8
malfunction
  n impairment 393.1
  abortion 410.5
  wrong 638.1
  fault 1003.2
  v get out of order 393.25
malice hate 103.1
  maliciousness 144.5
  hostility 589.3
malicious
  maleficent 144.20
  hostile 589.10
malign
  v defame 512.9
  adj poisonous 82.7
  malicious 144.20
  deadly 308.23

  savage 671.21
  harmful 1000.12
malignancy
  poisonousness 82.3
  malice 144.5
  deadliness 308.9
  harmfulness 1000.5
malignant
  poisonous 82.7
  anemic 85.61
  malicious 144.20
  deadly 308.23
  hostile 589.10
  savage 671.21
  harmful 1000.12
malinger
  leave undone 340.7
  shirk 368.9
malingerer
  neglecter 340.5
  impostor 357.6
  shirker 368.3
malingering
  n shirking 368.2
  adj evasive 368.15
mall path 383.2
  marketplace 736.2
  workplace 739.1
malleable docile 433.13
  teachable 570.18
  changeable 854.6
  conformable 867.5
  influenceable 894.15
  foolable 923.12
  handy 1014.15
  pliant 1047.9
mallet 715.4
malnourishment 992.6
malnutrition 992.6
malocchio gaze 27.5
  malevolence 144.4
  curse 513.1
  spell 691.1
  bad influence 1000.4
malodorous nasty 64.7
  bad-smelling 69.9
  fetid 71.5
  filthy 80.23
  offensive 98.18
malposition 160.3
malpractice
  misuse 389.1
  mismanagement 414.6
  wrong 638.1
  wrongdoing 655.1
maltreat
  mistreat 389.5
  work evil 1000.6
maltreatment 389.2
mama 560.12
mama's boy
  weakling 16.6
  effeminate male 77.10
  spoiled child 427.4
mammal 311.3
mammalian
  pectoral 283.19
  vertebrate 311.40
mammary gland 283.6
mammon wealth 618.1
  money 728.1

mammoth
  n behemoth 257.14
  pachyderm 311.4
  adj large 247.7
  huge 257.20
mammy
  mother 560.12
  nurse 1008.8
man
  n mankind 76.3
  male 76.4
  beau 104.12
  hanger-on 138.6
  adult 304.1
  humankind 312.1
  person 312.5
  husband 563.7
  manservant 577.4
  follower 616.8
  chessman 743.17
  v equip 385.8
  fortify 460.9
  interj goody! 95.21
the Man
  Caucasian 312.3
  official 575.16
the man 417.1
mana power 18.1
  the gods 678.1
man-about-town
  sophisticate 413.17
  dandy 500.9
  person of fashion 578.7
  sociable person 582.16
manacle
  n shackle 428.4
  v disable 19.10
  bind 428.10
manacled 428.16
manage pilot 182.14
  perform 328.9
  support oneself 385.12
  use 387.10
  treat 387.12
  accomplish 407.4
  contrive 409.12
  direct 573.8
  govern 612.11
  economize 635.4
  be in a certain state 765.5
  persist 856.5
  operate 889.5
  make shift 995.4
  tend 1070.7
manageability
  governability 433.4
  workability 889.3
  handiness 1014.2
manageable
  governable 433.14
  cheap 633.7
  workable 889.10
  handy 1014.15
management
  supremacy 249.3
  performance 328.2
  usage 387.2
  utilization 387.8
  supervision 573
  direction 573.1
  executive 574.3

  directorate 574.11
  the authorities 575.15
  government 612.1
  thrift 635.1
  operation 889.1
  protectorship 1008.2
manager director 574.1
  governor 575.6
  businessman 730.1
  baseball team 745.2
  boxer 754.2
  operator 889.4
managerial
  directing 573.12
  operational 889.12
mañana
  n the future 839.1
  adv in the future 839.9
man and wife 563.9
man cave 197.17
manchild 302.5
mandarin
  n snob 141.7
  official 575.16
  wise man 921.1
  intellectual 929.1
  adj studious 570.17
mandate
  n country 232.1
  authority 417.1
  injunction 420.2
  possession 469.1
  referendum 613.8
  commission 615.1
  v command 420.8
mandated 420.12
mandatory
  n country 232.1
  adj preceptive 419.4
  mandated 420.12
  obligatory 424.11
  required 641.15
  doctrinal 953.27
  necessary 963.12
mandibles mouth 292.4
  clutches 474.4
mandrake 22.10
mane 3.2
man-eater eater 8.16
  marine animal 311.29
  savage 593.5
manège riding 177.6
  animal husbandry 1070.1
maneuver
  n exercise 84.2
  act 328.3
  stratagem 415.3
  operation 458.4
  race 753.3
  process 889.2
  expedient 995.2
  v execute a maneuver 182.46
  take action 328.5
  plot 381.9
  manipulate 415.10
  direct 573.8
  operate 889.5
maneuverable
  workable 889.10
  handy 1014.15

maneuvering
  intrigue 381.5
  machination 415.4
man Friday
  employee 577.3
  right-hand man 616.7
mange 85.41
manger 197.2
mangle press 287.6
  tear apart 802.14
mangled
  impaired 393.27
  mutilated 795.5
manhandle
  exert strength 15.12
  remove 176.11
  transport 176.12
  mistreat 389.5
man-hater hater 103.4
  misanthrope 590.2
man-hating
  n misanthropy 590.1
  adj misanthropic 590.3
manhood
  bodily development 14.1
  masculinity 76.1
  mankind 76.3
  maturity 303.2
  courage 492.1
man-hour work 725.4
  moment 824.2
mania craving 100.6
  overzealousness 101.3
  mental sickness 926.1
  insanity 926.1
  delirium tremens 926.9
  craze 926.12
maniac
  n lunatic 926.15
  adj frenzied 105.25
  rabid 926.30
maniacal
  frenzied 105.25
  rabid 926.30
manic excited 105.20
  insane 926.26
  psychotic 926.28
manic-depressive
  n psychotic 926.17
  adj psychotic 926.28
manic state 105.1
manicure
  n beautification 1016.10
  v groom 79.20
manicurist 1016.12
manifest
  n statement 628.3
  bill 871.5
  v unclose 292.12
  show 348.5
  disclose 351.4
  flaunt 501.17
  signify 517.17
  evidence 957.8
  adj visible 31.6
  apparent 348.8
manifestation
  visibility 31.1
  appearance 33.1
  expression 348.1
  disclosure 351.1

  display 501.4
  indication 517.3
  evidence 957.1
manifested 348.13
manifesting 348.9
manifesto
  n affirmation 334.1
  announcement 352.2
  statement of belief 953.4
  v affirm 334.5
manifold
  n transcript 785.4
  v copy 785.8
  adj multiform 783.3
  multiple 883.8
manikin dwarf 258.5
  figure 349.6
man in the street 606.5
manipulate touch 73.6
  pilot 184.37
  tamper with 354.17
  use 387.10
  exploit 387.16
  maneuver 415.10
  direct 573.8
  operate 889.5
manipulated 354.29
manipulation
  touching 73.2
  masturbation 75.8
  intrigue 381.5
  utilization 387.8
  machination 415.4
  direction 573.1
  rigging 737.20
  operation 889.1
  automation 1041.7
manipulative
  scheming 381.13
  using 387.19
  cunning 415.12
manipulator
  strategist 415.7
  operator 889.4
  influence 894.6
mankind man 76.3
  humankind 312.1
manlike
  masculine 76.12
  anthropoid 312.14
manly masculine 76.12
  courageous 492.16
  honest 644.13
man-made
  spurious 354.26
  made 892.18
manna delicacy 10.8
  support 449.3
  godsend 472.7
  benefit 478.7
manned
  provided 385.13
  armed 460.14
mannequin
  figure 349.6
  artist's model 786.5
manner aspect 33.3
  exteriority 206.1
  behavior 321.1
  custom 373.1
  mode 384

way 384.1
style 532.2
state 765.4
kind 809.3
specialty 866.1
mannered
behavioral 321.7
affected 500.15
elegant 533.9
figurative 536.3
mannerism sham 354.3
affectation 500.1
preciosity 500.2
style 532.2
elegance 533.3
characteristic 865.4
quirk 927.2
manner of preparation 11.2
manner of speaking
way of saying 524.7
phrase 529.1
style 532.2
figure of speech 536.1
manners
behavior 321.1
custom 373.1
mannerliness 504.3
etiquette 580.3
mannish
homosexual 75.30
masculine 76.12
mannified 76.14
man of action 330.8
man of the family 76.10
man of the house 575.1
man of the world
sophisticate 413.17
person of fashion 578.7
man-of-war 180.6
manor 471.6
manor house 228.5
manorial
residential 228.32
real 471.9
manpower 18.4
manqué 410.18
manse house 228.5
parsonage 703.7
mansion
estate 228.7
astrology 1072.20
manslaughter 308.2
mantel 901.14
mantilla 5.26
mantle
n cover 295.2
scepter 417.9
insignia 647.1
robe 702.2
v cloak 5.40
redden 41.5
change color 105.19
blush 139.8
show resentment 152.14
cover 295.19
foam 320.5
take command 417.14
mantled clothed 5.45
covered 295.31
man-to-man
plain-speaking 535.3

intimate 582.24
familiar 587.19
mantra 696.3
manual
handbook 554.8
textbook 554.10
keyboard 711.17
manual art 712.2
manual labor 725.4
manufacture
n structure 266.1
preparation 405.1
production 892.2
product 893.1
v fabricate 354.18
produce 892.8
manufactured
fabricated 354.29
made 892.18
manufacturer 892.7
manufacturing
n production 892.2
adj productional 892.14
manure
n feces 12.4
fertilizer 890.4
v fertilize 890.8
manure pile 80.10
manuscript
n handwriting 547.3
writing 547.10
copy 548.4
rare book 554.6
adj written 547.22
manustrupration 75.8
many much 247.8
different 780.7
diversified 783.4
frequent 847.4
plural 883.7
numerous 884.6
plentiful 991.7
many-sided sided 218.7
versatile 413.25
mixed 797.14
changeable 854.6
Maoism
communism 611.5
revolutionism 860.2
Maoist
n Communist 611.13
revolutionist 860.3
adj Communist 611.21
revolutionist 860.6
map
n chart 159.5
face 216.4
representation 349.1
diagram 381.3
v locate 159.11
represent 349.8
plot 381.10
receive 1036.17
mapmaker
charter 159.5
measurer 300.9
mapped 300.13
mar deform 265.7
spoil 393.10
bungle 414.11
blemish 1004.4

offend 1015.5
marathon 827.11
maraud 482.17
marauder 483.6
marauding
n plundering 482.6
adj plunderous 482.22
marble
n variegation 47.6
smoothness 287.3
sculpture 715.2
toy 743.16
hardness 1046.6
v variegate 47.7
adj white 37.7
hard 1046.10
marbled mottled 47.12
striped 47.15
marbleize 47.7
marbleized 47.15
marblelike
hard 1046.10
stone 1059.11
marcel
n hairdo 3.15
v cut the hair 3.22
march
n progression 162.1
walk 177.10
quick gait 177.13
boundary 211.3
frontier 211.5
sphere 231.2
objection 333.2
martial music 708.12
v mush 177.30
border 211.10
object 333.5
marcher 178.6
marching orders 909.5
March Madness 747.1
march to a different drummer
333.4
Mardi Gras treat 95.3
festival 743.4
mare
female animal 77.9
plain 236.1
horse 311.10
jockey 757.2
margin
n room 158.3
border 211.4
interval 224.1
distance 261.1
latitude 430.4
collateral 438.3
thin margin 738.10
wide margin 780.2
surplus 993.5
v border 211.10
marginal
bordering 211.11
unimportant 998.16
marginalia
addition 254.2
memorandum 549.4
margin of error 164.1
marina 1009.6
marinate 397.9
marination 797.2

marine
n navy man 183.4
navy 461.27
adj nautical 182.57
oceanic 240.8
marine animal 311.29
marine biology 240.6
marine engineering 1043.1
marine park 228.19
mariner traveler 178.1
seaman 183.1
marines
elite troops 461.15
sea soldiers 461.28
marionette figure 349.6
toy 743.16
marital 563.18
maritime
nautical 182.57
oceanic 240.8
mark
n boundary 211.3
degree 245.1
dupe 358.2
objective 380.2
sign 517.1
marking 517.5
marker 517.10
signature 527.10
distinction 662.5
notation 709.12
customer 733.4
game 750.2
cheater 759.22
kind 809.3
characteristic 865.4
impact 887.2
evidence 957.1
importance 997.1
stain 1004.3
v celebrate 487.2
signify 517.17
make a mark 517.19
grammaticize 530.16
letter 546.6
engrave 713.9
hockey 749.7
soccer 752.4
differentiate 780.6
characterize 865.10
specify 865.11
estimate 946.9
evidence 957.8
destine 964.7
heed 983.6
stain 1004.6
Mark 684.2
markdown 633.4
mark down
record 549.15
price 630.11
cheapen 633.6
marked
remarkable 247.10
superior 249.12
designated 517.24
distinguished 662.16
engraved 713.11
characteristic 865.13
destined 964.9
notable 997.19

marker mark 517.10
monument 549.12
recorder 550.1
round 751.3
market
n square 230.8
commerce 731.1
public 733.3
sale 734.1
place of trade 736
mart 736.1
marketplace 736.2
workplace 739.1
v deal in 731.16
shop 733.8
sell 734.8
adj sales 734.13
the market 737.1
marketable 734.14
market index 737.1
market indicator
731.1
marketing
n commerce 731.1
purchase 733.1
selling 734.2
adj sales 734.13
marketize 731.15
market leader 731.1
marketplace
square 230.8
arena 463.1
mart 736.2
market research
selling 734.2
canvass 938.14
market value
worth 630.2
price 738.9
marking mark 517.5
insignia 647.1
engraving 713.2
game 749.6
characteristic 865.4
mark my words 983.22
mark off
circumscribe 210.4
measure off 300.11
plot 381.10
allot 477.9
mark 517.19
differentiate 780.6
characterize 865.10
marksman
expert 413.11
infantryman 461.9
shooter 904.8
marksmanship
skill 413.1
sport 744.1
mark time await 130.8
be still 173.7
time 832.11
wait 846.12
marmalade 10.40
maroon
v abandon 370.5
adj red 41.6
marooned
abandoned 370.8
stranded 1013.27

marquee poster 352.7
lights 704.18
marquis 608.4
marred
deformed 265.12
spoiled 393.28
blemished 1004.8
ugly 1015.6
marriage
sexuality 75.2
matrimony 563.1
wedding 563.3
joining 800.1
combination 805.1
marriageable
grown 14.3
adolescent 301.13
adult 303.12
nubile 563.20
marriage broker 563.12
marriage license 443.6
marriage money 478.9
marriage vow 436.3
married
matrimonial 563.18
wedded 563.21
related 775.9
joined 800.13
leagued 805.6
marrow
food 10.20
essential content 196.5
center 208.2
essence 767.2
marry
join in marriage 563.14
get married 563.15
relate 775.6
put together 800.5
combine 805.3
league 805.4
Mars war-god 458.12
planet 1072.9
marsh
receptacle of filth 80.12
swamp 243.1
marshland 243.1
marshal
n commissioned officer
575.18
master of ceremonies 743.20
policeman 1008.15
v prepare 405.6
escort 769.8
put together 800.5
order 807.4
dispose 808.9
adduce 957.12
marshland 243.1
marshy swampy 243.3
moist 1065.15
mart square 230.8
market 736.1
marketplace 736.2
martial 458.20
martial arts 760.3
martial law
militarization 458.9
government 612.4
Martian oddity 870.4
astronaut 1075.8

martinet 575.14
martyr
n sufferer 96.11
angel 679.1
v pain 26.7
torture 96.18
kill 308.13
martyrdom agony 26.6
torment 96.7
killing 308.1
punishment 604.2
martyred pained 26.9
dead 307.29
angelic 679.6
marvel
n wonder 122.1
phenomenon 122.2
v wonder 122.5
marvelous
wonderful 122.10
remarkable 247.10
extraordinary 870.14
superb 999.15
Marxism
communism 611.5
socialism 611.6
materialism 1052.6
Marxist
n Communist 611.13
socialist 611.14
revolutionist 860.3
materialist 1052.7
adj Communist 611.21
revolutionist 860.6
materialist 1052.12
mascara 1016.11
mascot 691.5
masculine
n male 76.4
gender 530.10
adj male 76.12
masculinity sex 75.1
maleness 76
masculineness 76.1
maturity 303.2
mash
n meal 8.6
feed 10.4
infatuation 104.3
pulp 1063.2
v make advances 439.8
soften 1047.6
pulverize 1051.9
pulp 1063.5
masher dandy 500.9
philanderer 562.12
pulverizer 1051.7
pulper 1063.4
mask
n cover 295.2
reticence 344.3
disguise 356.11
pretext 376.1
dance 705.2
relief 715.3
safeguard 1008.3
v cover 295.19
conceal 346.6
falsify 354.16
masked
covered 295.31

disguised 346.13
masochism 75.11
masochist 75.16
mason 716.6
masonry
sculpture 715.1
building material 1054.2
masque cover 356.11
dance 705.2
masquerade
n costume 5.9
impersonation 349.4
sham 354.3
cover 356.11
dance 705.2
v hide 346.8
masquerader 357.7
mass
n amount 244.1
quantity 247.3
size 257.1
lump 257.10
thickness 269.2
weight 297.5
store 386.1
sacred music 708.17
substantiality 763.1
throng 770.4
accumulation 770.9
major part 792.6
conglomeration 803.5
majority 883.2
solid 1045.6
v load 159.15
come together 770.16
assemble 770.18
put together 800.5
cohere 803.6
adj gravitational 297.20
populational 606.8
adv heavily 297.22
Mass
divine service 696.8
Missa 701.8
massacre
n carnage 308.4
unruliness 671.3
v slaughter 308.17
defeat 412.9
massage
n massaging 1044.3
v stroke 73.8
treat 91.24
rub 1044.6
soften 1047.6
massage therapist 1044.4
massage therapy 1044.3
mass communications 343.5
masses lot 247.4
interior 250.2
the masses 606.2
masseuse 1044.4
massify 244.4
massive
large 247.7
bulky 257.19
thick 269.8
heavy 297.16
onerous 297.17
sturdy 763.7
dense 1045.12

quantity 244.1
motive 375.1
undertaking 404.1
writing 547.10
copy 548.4
occupation 724.1
substance 763.2
particular 766.3
affair 831.3
topic 937.1
material 1052.2
inorganic matter 1055.1
v fester 12.15
be important 997.12
matter of course 373.4
matter of fact
prosaicness 117.2
fact 761.3
event 831.2
matter-of-fact
prosaic 117.8
simple 499.6
plain-speaking 535.3
prosaic 721.5
realistic 987.6
matter of life and death
urgent need 963.4
point of interest 997.3
mattify 1027.9
mattress 901.20
maturation
bodily development 14.1
growth 259.3
adolescence 301.6
development 303.6
improvement 392.2
completion 407.2
evolution 861.1
mature
v grow 14.2
expand 259.7
grow up 303.9
grow old 304.6
develop 392.10
ripen 407.8
accrue 623.7
complete 794.6
evolve 861.5
produce 892.8
originate 892.12
perfect 1002.5
adj developed 14.3
grown 259.12
adult 303.12
grown old 303.13
middle-aged 304.7
prepared 405.16
ripe 407.13
experienced 413.28
due 623.10
complete 794.9
perfected 1002.9
matured
ripe 407.13
experienced 413.28
complete 794.9
perfected 1002.9
maturing
n bodily development 14.1
growth 259.3
adj evolutionary 861.8

maturity
adulthood 303.2
preparedness 405.4
completion 407.2
debt 623.1
maudlin
intoxicated 88.31
sentimental 93.21
foolish 923.8
maul mistreat 389.5
harm 393.13
injure 393.13
rage 671.11
fight 754.4
pound 902.16
mauled 96.23
mausoleum
tomb 309.16
monument 549.12
mauve 46.3
maven
expert 413.11
adviser 422.3
connoisseur 496.6
specialist 866.3
scientist 928.11
maverick
n cattle 311.6
rebel 327.5
obstinate person 361.6
nonconformist 868.3
oddity 870.4
adj unconventional 868.6
mavis 710.23
maw
digestive system 2.18
mouth 292.4
mawkish nasty 64.7
oversweet 66.5
sentimental 93.21
the max
n supremacy 249.3
adj extreme 247.13
maxed-out
burnt-out 21.10
used up 388.4
worn-out 393.36
maxim precept 419.2
rule 869.4
a belief 953.2
aphorism 974.1
maximal top 198.10
superlative 249.13
plentiful 991.7
maximize 251.4
maximum
n summit 198.2
supremacy 249.3
limit 794.5
plenty 991.2
adj top 198.10
great 247.6
superlative 249.13
may be able 18.11
can 443.13
maybe 966.9
Mayday 400.1
mayhem 393.1
mayor 575.17
mayoralty
mastership 417.7

magistracy 594.3
Mazda 677.5
maze
n complex 799.2
confusion 985.3
v perplex 971.13
confuse 985.7
mazel tov! 149.5
mazy deviative 164.7
flowing 238.24
curved 279.7
convolutional 281.6
complex 799.4
inconstant 854.7
MC steward 574.4
theater man 704.23
master of ceremonies 743.20
broadcaster 1034.23
McCarthyism 389.3
McGuffin 706.6
MD 90.4
me 865.5
mea culpa
penitence 113.4
apology 658.2
meadow marsh 243.1
grassland 310.8
meager
insignificant 248.6
dwarf 258.13
narrow 270.14
lean 270.17
sparse 885.5
slight 992.10
meal repast 8.5
feed 10.4
cereal 10.34
powder 1051.5
meal ticket
support 449.3
financer 729.10
mealy colorless 36.7
powdery 1051.11
mealymouth 138.3
mealymouthed
obsequious 138.14
flattering 511.8
sanctimonious 693.5
insincere 354.32
mean
n median 246.1
middle course 467.3
middle 819.1
v augur 133.11
manifest 348.5
intend 380.4
indicate 517.17
signify 518.8
imply 519.4
evidence 957.8
adj irascible 110.20
humble 137.10
servile 138.13
malicious 144.20
cruel 144.26
envious 154.3
intervening 213.10
medium 246.3
insignificant 248.6
inadequate 250.7
niggardly 484.8

low 497.15
populational 606.8
ungenerous 651.6
base 661.12
middle 819.4
narrow-minded 980.10
meager 992.10
paltry 998.21
excellent 999.13
inferior 1005.9
difficult 1013.17
mean business 359.8
meander
n bend 279.3
convolution 281.1
complex 799.2
v stray 164.4
wander 177.23
convolve 281.4
go roundabout 914.4
meandering
n convolution 281.1
discursiveness 538.3
circuitousness 914.1
adj deviative 164.7
wandering 177.37
flowing 238.24
curved 279.7
convolutional 281.6
complex 799.4
circuitous 914.7
meanie 660.5
meaning
n ominousness 133.6
interpretation 341.1
intention 380.1
indication 517.3
significance 518.1
implication 519.2
lexicology 526.14
adj meaningful 518.10
meaningful
premonitory 133.15
indicative 517.23
meaning 518.10
expressive 544.10
meaningless
uncommunicative 344.8
useless 391.9
unmeaning 520.6
unordered 810.12
meanness
ill humor 110.3
humility 137.1
servility 138.1
malice 144.5
envy 154.1
insignificance 248.1
inadequacy 250.3
niggardliness 484.2
vulgarity 497.1
commonness 497.5
ungenerousness 651.2
baseness 661.3
narrow-mindedness 980.1
meagerness 992.2
paltriness 998.2
inferiority 1005.3
means mode 384
manner 384.1
way 384.2

supply 386.2
assets 471.7
funds 728.14
expedient 995.2
tool 1040.1
means to an end
means 384.2
expedient 995.2
meant
intentional 380.8
signified 518.11
implied 519.7
meantime
n meanwhile 826.2
adv meanwhile 826.5
meanwhile
n meantime 826.2
adv in the meantime 821.10
meantime 826.5
measly anemic 85.61
base 661.12
insignificant 998.18
measurable
mensurable 300.14
calculable 1017.25
measure
n space 158.1
quantity 244.1
amount 244.2
degree 245.1
size 257.1
capacity 257.2
length 267.1
measurement 300.1
measuring instrument 300.2
act 328.3
portion 477.5
sign 517.1
harmony 533.2
law 673.3
air 708.4
passage 708.24
notation 709.12
rhythm 709.22
metrics 720.6
meter 720.7
poetry 720.9
process 889.2
expedient 995.2
v traverse 177.20
quantify 244.4
size 257.15
gauge 300.10
make agree 788.7
estimate 946.9
number 1017.17
calculate 1017.18
measured
quantitative 244.5
gauged 300.13
harmonious 533.8
temperate 668.9
rhythmic 709.28
metric 720.16
uniform 781.5
periodic 850.7
measure for measure
compensation 338.1
tit for tat 506.3
justice 649.1
interchange 863.1

measurement
quantity 244.1
size 257.1
quantification 300.1
measure 300.1
estimate 946.3
numeration 1017.9
measure out
measure off 300.11
parcel out 477.8
measure up to
equal 790.5
be comparable 943.7
measuring
n measurement 300.1
adj metric 300.12
meat
n genitals 2.13
diet 7.13
meal 8.5
food 10.1
flesh 10.13
nut 10.39
sex object 75.4
copulation 75.7
essential content 196.5
support 449.3
meaning 518.1
summary 557.2
essence 767.2
major part 792.6
topic 937.1
salient point 997.6
v feed 8.18
meat cuts and joints 10.54
meat-eater eater 8.16
strong man 15.7
violent person 671.10
meat-eating 8.31
meathead 924.4
meathooks 474.4
meaty
corpulent 257.18
meaningful 518.10
mechanic
aircraftsman 185.6
mender 396.10
worker 607.9
skilled worker 726.6
cheater 759.22
mechanician 1040.12
mechanical
uniform 781.5
involuntary 963.14
mechanistic 1039.7
machinelike 1040.14
mechanical engineering 1043.1
mechanics art 413.7
the physics of force and
  motion 1039
leverage 1039.1
mechanism
instrumentality 384.3
instrument 384.4
art 413.7
machinery 1040.3
works 1040.4
materialism 1052.6
mechanistic
mechanical 1039.7
materialist 1052.12

mechanize 1040.13
mechanized 1040.14
medal
military honor 646.6
insignia 647.1
relief 715.3
medalist 413.15
medallion
medal 646.6
relief 715.3
meddle
intermeddle 214.7
advise 422.5
pry 981.4
hinder 1012.10
meddler
intermeddler 214.4
adviser 422.3
meddlesome
meddling 214.9
prying 981.6
meddling
n intermeddling 214.2
adj meddlesome 214.9
media
communications 343.5
telecommunications 347.1
medial
intervening 213.10
medium 246.3
middle 819.4
median
n mean 246.1
middle 819.1
adj intervening 213.10
medium 246.3
middle 819.4
media player 50.11
mediary 213.4
media studies 343.1
mediate
interpose 213.6
be instrumental 384.7
reconcile 465.8
intermediate 466.6
mediating
n mediation 466.1
adj modal 384.8
mediatory 466.8
mediation
instrumentality 384.3
pacification 465.1
intermediation 466.1
mediating 466.1
function of Christ 677.14
mediator
intermediary 213.4
instrument 384.4
intermediator 466.3
go-between 576.4
moderator 670.3
mediatory
mediatorial 466.8
divine 677.16
mediatrix 466.3
Medicaid
health care 83.5
welfarism 611.7
medical doctor 90.4
medical examiner
doctor 90.4

autopsy 307.17
medical practice
medicine 90.1
practice of medicine 90.13
Medicare
health care 83.5
welfarism 611.7
medicate 91.25
medication
medicine 86.4
therapy 91.1
treatment 91.14
medicinal
n medicine 86.4
adj remedial 86.39
medicine
n medicament 86.4
liquor 88.14
medical practice 90.1
v medicate 91.25
medicine man 690.7
medico 90.4
medieval 842.13
medievalist 842.5
mediocre
medium 246.3
inadequate 250.7
unskillful 414.15
middle 819.4
usual 869.9
imperfect 1003.4
middling 1005.7
mediocrity mean 246.1
inadequacy 250.3
unskillfulness 414.1
incompetent 414.7
usualness 869.2
a nobody 998.7
imperfection 1003.1
ordinariness 1005.2
mediocreness 1005.1
second-rater 1005.5
meditate
contemplate 380.5
consider 931.12
meditation
inaction 329.1
trance 691.3
prayer 696.4
consideration 931.2
engrossment 983.3
meditation retreat 228.27
meditative
passive 329.6
cognitive 931.21
engrossed 983.17
abstracted 985.11
medium
n color 35.8
essential content 196.5
natural environment 209.4
intermediary 213.4
mean 246.1
instrument 384.4
mediator 466.3
middle course 467.3
volume 554.4
go-between 576.4
psychic 689.13
lights 704.18
art equipment 712.17

doer 726.1
substance 763.2
immaterialist 1053.4
adj done 11.8
intervening 213.10
mean 246.3
middle 819.4
mediocre 1005.7
medium of exchange 728.1
medley
n performance 708.33
miscellany 770.13
hodgepodge 797.6
adj chromatic 35.16
variegated 47.9
mixed 797.14
Medusa 690.9
meed portion 477.5
recompense 624.3
meek
resigned 134.10
humblehearted 137.11
modest 139.9
gentle 433.15
unbelligerent 464.10
meerschaum 89.6
meet
n contest 457.3
game 743.9
track meet 755.2
assembly 770.2
v converge 169.2
confront 216.8
encounter 223.11
concur 332.9
observe 434.2
oppose 451.5
compete 457.18
brave 492.10
come together 770.16
convene 770.17
join 800.11
experience 831.8
conform 867.3
collide 902.13
suffice 991.4
adj decorous 496.9
conventional 579.5
just 649.7
timely 843.9
expedient 995.5
approachable 167.5
meet halfway
make up 465.10
mediate 466.6
compromise 468.2
meet head-on
contrapose 215.4
meet 223.11
confront 451.5
offer resistance 453.3
brave 492.10
counteract 900.6
meeting
n convergence 169.1
meeting up 223.4
contest 457.3
conference 541.5
rendezvous 582.9
divine service 696.8
assembly 770.2

joining 800.1
impact 902.3
adj converging 169.3
in contact 223.17
assembled 770.21
joining 800.16
concurrent 899.4
meetinghouse
hall 197.4
church 703.1
meeting of minds
unanimity 332.5
consensus 788.3
meeting of the minds
n accord 455.1
concurrence 899.1
v agree 788.6
meet the eye show 31.4
appear 33.8
meet with attention
983.11
mega 257.20
megacycles 1034.12
megamall 739.1
megaphone 48.8
me generation
selfishness 651.1
the present 838.1
megrims
animal diseases 85.41
blues 112.6
melancholia
mental disorder 92.14
wretchedness 96.6
melancholy 112.5
depression 926.5
melancholic
n personality type 92.12
sourpuss 112.13
adj melancholy 112.23
weary 118.11
melancholy
n wretchedness 96.6
melancholia 112.5
weariness 118.3
thoughtfulness 931.3
adj sullen 110.24
melancholic 112.23
weary 118.11
n sullenness 110.8
mélange 797.6
melanism 38.1
meld
n compound 797.5
combination 805.1
v identify 778.5
mix 797.10
combine 805.3
melding
identification 778.2
combination 805.1
melee free-for-all 457.5
commotion 810.4
meliorate
improve 392.7
make better 392.9
be changed 852.6
change 852.7
mellifluous sweet 66.4
pleasant 97.6
melodious 708.48

mellow
v mature 303.9
ripen 407.8
evolve 861.5
soften 1047.6
adj soft-colored 35.22
resonant 54.10
intoxicated 88.31
pleasant 97.6
mature 303.13
ripe 407.13
melodious 708.48
soft 1047.8
mellowing
maturation 303.6
softening 1047.5
melodics 709.1
melodist singer 710.13
composer 710.20
melodrama 93.9
melodramatic
emotionalistic 93.19
sensational 105.32
dramatic 704.33
melodramatics
emotionalism 93.9
dramatics 704.2
melody
melodiousness 708.2
air 708.4
melon
political patronage 609.36
dividend 738.7
melt disappear 34.2
affect 93.14
have pity 145.4
move 145.5
flit 828.6
melt down 1020.21
liquefy 1064.5
meltable
molten 1020.31
liquefiable 1064.9
melt away
disappear 34.2
decrease 252.6
cease to exist 762.6
meltdown
outburst 671.6
misfortune 1011.2
melt down
extract 192.16
explode 671.14
melt 1020.21
liquefy 1064.5
melted
penitent 113.9
molten 1020.31
liquefied 1064.6
melting
n disappearance 34.1
fusion 1020.3
liquefaction 1064.1
adj vanishing 34.3
loving 104.26
pitying 145.7
liquefying 1064.7
melting point 1019.11
melting pot
mixture 797.1
mixer 797.9

instrument of conversion
858.10
the melting pot 232.3
member appendage 2.7
affiliate 617.11
organ 793.4
membership
association 582.6
members 617.12
inclusion 772.1
membrane
membrana 2.6
lamina 296.2
memento
monument 549.12
remembrance 989.6
memo 549.4
memoir
memorandum 549.4
treatise 556.1
history 719.1
remembering 989.3
memorabilia
archives 549.2
history 719.1
memento 989.6
matter of importance 997.5
memorable
rememberable 989.24
notable 997.19
memorandum
memo 549.4
reminder 989.5
memorandum book 549.11
memorial
n record 549.1
memorandum 549.4
monument 549.12
history 719.1
memento 989.6
adj celebrative 487.3
commemorative 989.26
memorialize
petition 440.10
celebrate 487.2
memorize
get by rote 570.8
commit to memory 989.16
memory
engram 92.29
celebration 487.1
recording media 549.10
posthumous fame 662.7
retrospection 837.4
recollection 989.1
remembrance 989.1
storage 1042.7
memory lapse 990.1
men work force 18.9
mankind 76.3
staff 577.11
menace
n threat 514.1
danger 1006.1
v forebode 133.10
threaten 514.2
be imminent 840.2
work evil 1000.6
menacing
ominous 133.16
threatening 514.3

imminent 840.3
ménage home 228.2
family 559.5
domestic management 573.6
menagerie
zoo 228.19
collection 770.11
mend
n improvement 392.1
v get well 83.7
improve 392.7
make better 392.9
repair 396.14
mendacity
untruthfulness 354.8
lie 354.11
Mendel's law 560.6
mender 396.10
mendicancy
beggary 440.6
indigence 619.2
mendicant
n nonworker 331.11
beggar 440.8
ascetic 667.2
religious 699.16
adj supplicatory 440.16
indigent 619.8
ascetic 667.4
mending
n improvement 392.1
reparation 396.6
adj improving 392.15
menfolk 76.3
menial
n servant 577.2
worker 726.2
adj servile 138.13
serving 577.14
meniscus 279.5
men marker 751.1
menopause 303.7
men's course 753.1
menses 12.9
menstrual
bleeding 12.24
regular 850.8
menstrual discharge 12.9
menstruate 12.18
menstruation 12.9
mensuration
measurement 300.1
science of measurement 300.8
menswear 5.1
mental
n psychotic 926.17
adj intellectual 919.7
crazy 926.27
cognitive 931.21
attitudinal 978.7
mental abuse 144.11
mental block 990.3
mental capacity 920.1
mental case 926.17
mental cruelty 144.11
mental deficiency 926.1
mental disorder
emotional disorder 92.14
insanity 926.1

mental health
health 83.1
sanity 925.1
mental hospital 926.14
mental illness
mental disorder 92.14
insanity 926.1
mentality
intellect 919.1
intelligence 920.1
intelligent being 920.9
mentally retarded 922.22
mental picture
idea 932.1
visualization 986.6
mental state 978.4
mental states 92.1
mental telepathy 689.9
mention
n remark 524.3
information 551.1
citation 646.4
v remark 524.24
specify 865.11
call attention to 983.10
mentor preparer 405.5
adviser 422.3
teacher 571.1
wise man 921.1
Mentor 921.2
mentorship 422.1
menu bill of fare 8.14
statement 871.5
schedule 965.3
menuboard 8.14
meow 60.2
Mephistopheles 680.4
mercantile
business 730.12
commercial 731.22
mercantilism 731.13
mercantilistic 731.22
Mercedes-Benz 249.4
mercenary
n hireling 461.17
employee 577.3
adj greedy 100.27
employed 615.20
corruptible 645.23
merchandise
n provisions 385.2
goods 735.1
commodities 735.1
v deal in 731.16
sell 734.8
merchandising
n trade 731.2
selling 734.2
adj sales 734.13
merchant
n provider 385.6
businessperson 730
merchandiser 730.2
adj commercial 731.22
merchant marine
ships 180.10
branch 461.21
navy 461.27
merci! 150.6
merciful
kind 143.13

pitying 145.7
lenient 427.7
almighty 677.17
merciless
pitiless 146.3
savage 671.21
mercurial fast 174.15
active 330.17
irresolute 362.9
fickle 364.6
nonuniform 782.3
inconstant 854.7
flighty 985.17
brass 1058.17
mercury
swiftness 174.6
guide 574.7
changeableness 854.4
thermometer 1019.20
Mercury
messenger 353.1
planet 1072.9
mercy kindness 143.1
act of kindness 143.7
pity 145.1
leniency 427.1
mercy killing 308.1
mere
n lake 241.1
marsh 243.1
adj sheer 248.8
simple 798.6
mere caricature 787.1
mere child
simple soul 416.3
innocent 657.4
mere child's play 1014.3
mere existence 761.6
mere facade 500.1
mere farce 489.1
merely adequate 246.3
a mere nothing 998.6
mereology 935.2
mere show 500.1
mere skin and bones 270.17
mere subsistence 992.5
mere suggestion 551.4
mere technicality 998.6
meretricious
specious 354.27
coarse 497.11
gaudy 501.20
grandiloquent 545.8
prostitute 665.28
paltry 998.21
a mere trickle 992.9
merge
converge 169.2
submerge 367.7
cooperate 450.3
come together 770.16
identify 778.5
mix 797.10
put together 800.5
join 800.11
combine 805.3
merger
convergence 169.1
affiliation 450.2
identification 778.2
mixture 797.1

joining 800.1
combination 805.1
merging
converging 169.3
combining 805.7
meridian
n map 159.5
summit 198.2
zone 231.3
noon 314.5
orbit 1072.16
adj top 198.10
noon 314.7
meringue sweets 10.40
foam 320.2
merit
n importance 997.1
goodness 999.1
v deserve 639.5
merited
warranted 639.9
just 649.7
meritless 998.22
meritorious
praiseworthy 509.20
due 639.10
reputable 662.15
merkin 3.14
Merlin 690.6
mermaid
swimmer 182.12
spirit of the sea 240.3
water god 678.10
merriment
merriness 109.5
rejoicing 116.1
waggishness 489.4
conviviality 582.3
festivity 743.3
merriness 109.5
merry
intoxicated 88.31
mirthful 109.15
festive 743.28
merry-go-round
round of pleasure 743.7
carousel 743.15
rotator 915.4
merrymaking
n treat 95.3
conviviality 582.3
festivity 743.3
adj festive 743.28
mesa plain 236.1
tableland 237.3
plateau 272.4
mesh
n network 170.3
interaction 367.7
complex 799.2
network 1042.16
v net 170.7
trap 356.20
catch 480.17
interact 777.6
meshes
network 170.3
snare 356.13
meshing
n interaction 777.3
adj apt 788.10

mesmeric
hypnotic 22.24
alluring 377.8
engrossing 983.20
mesmerism 22.8
mesmerize
hypnotize 22.20
fascinate 377.7
cast a spell 691.7
have influence over 894.11
engross 983.13
mesmerized
wondering 122.9
enchanted 691.12
gripped 983.18
mesmerizer
hypnotist 22.9
deceiver 357.1
mesomorph 92.12
mesomorphism 92.11
meson atom 258.8
radioactive particle 1037.4
mess
n meal 8.5
rations 10.6
filth 80.7
dining room 197.11
amount 244.2
lot 247.4
formlessness 263.1
fiasco 410.6
bungle 414.5
portion 477.5
bunch 770.7
hodgepodge 797.6
complex 799.2
jumble 810.3
confusion 985.3
predicament 1013.5
eyesore 1015.4
v feed 8.18
defile 80.17
disarrange 811.2
message
communication 343.1
advertisement 352.6
information 551.1
dispatch 552.4
letter 553.2
commercial 1034.20
message board 1042.18
mess around 998.15
messed up
spoiled 393.29
botched 414.22
complex 799.4
disheveled 810.14
messenger
n harbinger 133.4
message-bearer 353.1
delegate 576.2
precursor 816.1
v send 176.15
mess hall
restaurant 8.17
dining room 197.11
messiah 574.6
messiness
uncleanness 80.1
formlessness 263.1
slipshodness 340.3

slovenliness 810.6
messmate 588.3
mess up defile 80.17
deform 263.3
spoil 393.11
bungle 414.12
complicate 799.3
disarrange 811.2
messy dirty 80.22
slipshod 340.12
slovenly 810.15
mestizo 797.8
metabolic
digestive 2.31
plasmatic 262.10
metamorphic 852.12
metabolic rate 2.2
metabolism
metabolic process 2.20
basal metabolism 7.12
transformation 852.3
metabolize digest 7.18
transform 852.8
metal
n heraldry 647.2
elementary metal 1058.3
v floor 295.22
adj metallic 1058.16
metallic
raucous 58.15
metal 1058.16
metallurgist 1058.12
metallurgy 1058.11
metalworker 726.8
metalworks 739.4
metamorphic
multiform 783.3
metabolic 852.12
changeable 854.6
metamorphosis 852.3
metanoia 685.4
metaphor
similarity 784.1
substitute 862.2
comparison 943.1
metaphorical
indicative 517.23
meaningful 518.10
symbolic 519.10
figurative 536.3
metaphysician
parapsychologist 689.12
philosopher 952.8
metaphysics
hyperphysics 689.3
ontology 761.7
metastasis
transferal 176.1
grammar 205.3
transformation 852.3
mete
n boundary 211.3
v quantify 244.4
measure 300.10
parcel out 477.8
give 478.12
administer 643.6
meteor 1072.15
meteoric
increasing 251.8
brief 828.8

flashing 1025.35
celestial 1072.25
meteorological instrument
317.8
meteorologist
crew 185.4
weather scientist 317.6
earth scientist 1071.2
meteorology
weather science 317.5
earth science 1071.1
meter
n measure 300.2
measurer 300.9
rhythm 709.22
metrics 720.6
prosody 720.7
periodicity 850.2
electrical device 1032.21
v measure 300.10
method
behavior 321.1
plan 381.1
manner 384.1
means 384.2
art 413.7
orderliness 807.3
methodical
punctilious 580.10
uniform 781.5
orderly 807.6
regular 850.6
methodized
planned 381.12
arranged 808.14
methodologist 867.2
methodology
behavior 321.1
plan 381.1
manner 384.1
orderliness 807.3
Methuselah
old man 304.2
back number 842.8
meticulous
exacting 339.12
strict 425.6
observant 434.4
fastidious 495.9
punctilious 580.10
conscientious 644.15
detailed 766.9
accurate 973.16
attentive 983.15
métier talent 413.4
vocation 724.6
specialty 866.1
metric
measuring 300.12
rhythmic 709.28
metrical 720.16
metrics
accent 524.10
rhythm 709.22
prosody 720.6
metric system 300.1
métro 179.14
metronome
notation 709.12
music 711.22
oscillator 916.9

metronomic
chronologic 832.15
periodic 850.7
metropolis
capital 208.7
town 230.1
region 231.5
metta 143.1
mettle
animation 17.4
pluck 359.3
fortitude 492.5
disposition 978.3
mettlesome
energetic 17.13
excitable 105.28
plucky 359.14
resolute 492.17
mew
n lair 228.26
retreat 1009.5
v cry 60.2
enclose 212.5
confine 429.12
mewl 60.2
mews 228.20
mezzanine 197.23
mezzo 819.4
mezzo-soprano
n high voice 58.6
voice 709.5
adj high 58.13
miasma
stench 71.1
mephitis 1001.4
vapor 1067.1
miasmic
malodorous 71.5
poisonous 82.7
offensive 98.18
vaporous 1067.9
Mick 232.7
Mickey Finn
anesthetic 25.3
chloral hydrate 87.6
drink 88.9
Mickey Mouse
n finery 498.3
trivia 998.4
adj vulgar 497.10
insignificant 998.18
inferior 1005.9
easy 1014.13
Mickey-Mouse 248.6
micro 258.12
microbe germ 85.42
minute 258.7
organism 305.2
microbiology 1068.3
microcosm 258.6
microdot 549.10
microeconomics 731.7
microevolution 861.3
microfiche
recording media 549.10
transcript 785.4
microfilm
n recording media 549.10
film 714.10
v photograph 714.14
copy 785.8

micronutrient 7.11
microorganism
germ 85.42
minute 258.7
organism 305.2
microphone mike 50.9
radio transmitter 1034.4
microphonic 50.16
microscope 29.1
microscopic
telescopic 29.10
infinitesimal 258.14
exact 973.17
microscopy optics 29.7
littleness 258.18
microtome 802.7
microwave
n radio wave 1034.11
v cook 11.5
micturition 12.5
mid
adj phonetic 524.30
middle 819.4
prep between 213.12
among 797.17
Midas 618.8
midday
n noon 314.5
adj noon 314.7
midden dunghill 80.10
derelict 370.4
trash pile 391.6
middle
n center 208.2
mean 246.1
voice 530.14
midpoint 819.1
median 819.1
v centralize 208.9
seek the middle 819.3
adj central 208.11
intervening 213.10
mediatory 466.8
medial 819.4
middle age 303.4
middle-aged
mid-life 303.14
mature 304.7
Middle Ages 824.5
Middle America
inland 207.3
US region 231.7
the people 606.1
middle class 607.5
mediocrity 1005.5
Middle American
n conformist 867.2
adj inland 207.7
middlebrow 930.7
middle class
middle order 607.5
mediocrity 1005.5
middle-class
upper-class 607.10
ordinary 1005.8
the middle class 606.1
Middle Earth 986.11
Middle East 231.6
middle ground
mean 246.1
middle course 467.3

mid-distance 819.2
middleman
intermediary 213.4
mediator 466.3
go-between 576.4
merchant 730.2
middle marker 751.1
middlemost
central 208.11
middle 819.4
middle of the road
middle course 467.3
moderatism 611.2
mid-distance 819.2
mean 246.1
middle-of-the-road
medium 246.3
moderate 611.18
middle 819.4
middle-of-the-roader
centrist 611.10
moderate 670.4
middle-of-the-roadism 611.2
middleperson 213.4
middle school 567.4
middle way
temperance 668.1
moderation 670.1
mid-distance 819.2
middleweight 297.3
the Middle West 231.7
middling
medium 246.3
middle 819.4
mediocre 1005.7
middy 183.4
Mideast 231.6
midge dwarf 258.5
minute 258.7
midget
n dwarf 258.5
adj dwarf 258.13
midget hockey 749.1
midland
n inland 207.3
adj inland 207.7
middle 819.4
Midland 523.7
midlife crisis 303.4
midmost
n middle 819.1
adj central 208.11
middle 819.4
midnight
n dead of night 315.6
adj black 38.8
nocturnal 315.9
midnight blue 45.3
midriff
digestive system 2.18
partition 213.5
middle 819.1
midsection 213.5
midshipman
navy man 183.4
undergraduate 572.6
midst
n middle 819.1
prep between 213.12
among 797.17
midsun 314.5

midterm 938.2
midtown
n city district 230.6
adj urban 230.11
mid-Victorian
n prude 500.11
back number 842.8
adj prudish 500.19
antiquated 842.13
midway
n mid-distance 819.2
adj neutral 467.7
middle 819.4
adv mediumly 246.4
halfway 819.5
midwife
health care professional 90.8
instrument 384.4
mien looks 33.4
exteriority 206.1
behavior 321.1
miff
n dudgeon 152.7
v annoy 96.13
provoke 152.24
miffed annoyed 96.21
provoked 152.27
might strength 15.1
power 18.1
greatness 247.1
authoritativeness 417.2
might be 966.4
mighty
adj strong 15.15
powerful 18.12
great 247.6
huge 257.20
authoritative 417.15
eminent 662.18
adv very 247.18
migraine 26.5
migrant migrator 178.5
bird 311.27
worker 726.2
migrant worker
migrant 178.5
worker 726.2
agriculturist 1069.5
migrate 177.22
migration
transferal 176.1
transmigration 177.4
departure 188.1
mikado 575.9
mike 50.9
milady woman 77.5
title 648.2
milch 1061.5
milcher 311.6
mild insipid 65.2
bright 97.11
good-natured 143.14
lenient 427.7
meek 433.15
moderate 670.10
warm 1019.24
soft 1047.8
mildew
n fetidness 71.2
decay 393.6
blight 1001.2

v decay 393.22
mildewed
malodorous 71.5
blighted 393.42
stale 842.14
mileage
distance 261.1
length 267.1
benefit 387.4
fee 624.5
expedience 995.1
milepost post 273.4
pointer 517.4
marker 517.10
miles per hour 174.1
milestone
marker 517.10
salient point 997.6
milieu
environment 209.1
ambience 209.3
region 231.1
arena 463.1
plot 722.4
militancy
activity 330.1
warlikeness 458.10
militant
n man of action 330.8
combatant 461.1
believer 692.4
adj active 330.17
warlike 458.20
militarism
warlikeness 458.10
foreign policy 609.5
government 612.4
militarist 461.5
militarization 458.9
militarize 458.19
military 458.20
military court 595.4
military issue 385.4
military law 673.5
military officer 575.18
military operations
war 458.1
operation 458.4
military police 1008.17
military science 458.5
military tactics 458.5
military time 832.3
militate 889.7
militate against
contend against 451.4
counteract 900.6
militia 461.24
milk
n humor 2.24
whiteness 37.2
fluid 1061.2
v draw off 192.12
exploit 387.16
take from 480.21
strip 480.24
tend 1070.7
adj milky 1061.5
milk and honey 1010.1
milk and water 16.7
milker 311.6
milking 192.3

milk run 184.11
milksop weakling 16.6
  effeminate male 77.10
  coward 491.5
  fool 924.1
milk varieties 10.58
milky
  wishy-washy 16.17
  white 37.7
  lacteal 1061.5
the Milky Way 1072.6
mill
  n money 728.7
  plant 739.3
  machinery 1040.3
  pulverizer 1051.7
  v notch 289.4
  come together 770.16
  process 892.9
  seethe 915.12
  tool 1040.13
  pulverize 1051.9
milled made 892.18
  powdery 1051.11
millenarian
  n optimist 124.5
  adj optimistic 124.11
millennial
  thousandth 882.30
  ideal 986.23
millennium
  moment 824.2
  thousand 882.10
  utopia 986.11
  good times 1010.4
milliner 5.37
millinery
  headdress 5.25
  garment making 5.32
milling
  production 892.2
  pulverization 1051.4
million
  n ten million 882.11
  adj numerous 884.6
millionaire 618.7
millions 618.2
millstone burden 297.7
  pulverizer 1051.7
millstone around one's neck
  affliction 96.8
  disadvantage 996.2
  impediment 1012.6
millstream 238.1
mill town 739.2
milord 648.2
milquetoast
  n manageability 433.4
  coward 491.5
  adj henpecked 326.5
  manageable 433.14
Milquetoast
  weakling 16.6
  vacillator 362.5
mime
  n imitator 336.4
  impersonation 349.4
  actor 707.2
  v mimic 336.6
  impersonate 349.12
  gesture 517.21

act 704.29
mimeograph
  n printing 548.1
  v print 548.14
  copy 785.8
mimer imitator 336.4
  actor 707.2
mimetic
  imitative 336.9
  representational 349.13
mimic
  n imitator 336.4
  actor 707.2
  v imitate 336.6
  impersonate 349.12
  resemble 784.7
  adj imitative 336.9
mimicry
  mockery 336.2
  impersonation 349.4
  acting 704.8
miming
  impersonation 349.4
  acting 704.8
minaret 272.6
minatory 514.3
mince
  n meat 10.13
  gait 177.12
  v walk 177.28
  be affected 500.14
  speak poorly 525.7
  extenuate 600.12
  shatter 802.13
mind
  n psyche 92.28
  desire 100.1
  will 323.1
  intention 380.1
  theosophy 689.18
  intellect 919.1
  intelligence 919.4
  opinion 953.6
  disposition 978.3
  mood 978.4
  attention 983.1
  memory 989.1
  v take amiss 152.13
  refuse 325.3
  obey 326.2
  care 339.6
  beware 494.7
  heed 983.6
  remember 989.9
  care for 1008.19
Mind 677.6
mind-altering drug 87.3
mind-blowing
  exciting 105.30
  hallucinatory 976.10
mind-boggler 522.8
mind-boggling
  deadening 25.9
  astonishing 122.12
  frightening 127.28
  unbelievable 955.10
minded willing 324.5
  moved 375.30
  disposed 978.8
mind-expanding
  psychochemical 86.46

hallucinatory 976.10
mindful
  considerate 143.16
  careful 339.10
  observant 434.4
  cautious 494.8
  knowing 928.15
  attentive 983.15
  recollective 989.21
  remembering 989.23
mindless
  unconcerned 102.7
  inconsiderate 144.18
  cruel 144.26
  animal 311.39
  unrefined 497.12
  savage 671.21
  unintelligent 922.13
  unwise 923.10
  unaware 930.12
  purposeless 972.16
  incurious 982.3
mind map 349.1
mind-numbing 117.6
mind one's own business
  not interfere 430.16
  take no interest in 982.2
mind one's P's and Q's
  behave oneself 321.5
  be careful 339.7
  mind one's manners 504.11
mind reader 689.15
mind reading 689.9
mind your own business
  214.10
mine
  n pit 284.4
  trap 356.12
  source of supply 386.4
  entrenchment 460.5
  bomb 462.20
  rich source 618.4
  fountainhead 886.6
  quarry 1058.6
  v extract 192.10
  deepen 275.8
  excavate 284.15
  undermine 393.15
  blow up 395.18
  plant a mine 459.24
  fortify 460.9
  take from 480.21
  process 892.9
  quarry 1058.14
miner excavator 284.10
  mineworker 1058.9
mineral
  n inorganic substance 1058.1
  ore 1058.2
  adj inorganic 1055.4
  inanimate 1058.15
mineral kingdom
  mineral 1058.1
  hierarchy 809.4
  inorganic matter 1055.1
mineralogy 1058.10
mineral oil 1056.4
mineral spring 91.23
mineral water 1065.3
mineworker 1058.9
mingle 797.10

mingling 797.1
mingy niggardly 484.8
  ungenerous 651.6
mini
  n runt 258.4
  miniature 258.6
  adj miniature 258.12
miniature
  n mini 258.6
  image 349.5
  picture 712.10
  portrait 712.14
  adj insignificant 248.6
  diminutive 258.12
miniature golf 751.1
miniaturization 252.1
miniaturize 258.9
miniaturized
  reduced 252.10
  miniature 258.12
mini-break 20.4
minim
  n modicum 248.2
  minute 258.7
  note 709.14
  rest 709.21
  adj least 250.8
minimal least 250.8
  miniature 258.12
  sufficient 991.6
minimal force 462.22
minimalistic 250.8
minimization
  reduction 252.5
  underestimation 950.1
minimize
  reduce 252.9
  disparage 512.8
  underestimate 950.2
  attach little importance to
    998.12
minimum
  n modicum 248.2
  sufficiency 991.1
  adj least 250.8
  sufficient 991.6
minimum wage 624.4
mining
  extraction 192.1
  deepening 275.7
  excavation 284.11
  production 892.2
  coal mining 1058.8
mining engineer 1058.12
minion favorite 104.15
  sycophant 138.3
  instrument 384.4
  retainer 577.1
  follower 616.8
minister
  n public official 575.17
  delegate 576.2
  diplomat 576.6
  clergyman 699.2
  v officiate 701.16
ministerial
  modal 384.8
  helping 449.20
  administrative 573.14
  diplomatic 576.17
  executive 612.18

ecclesiastic 698.13
ministering
 modal 384.8
 helping 449.20
 serving 577.14
minister of state 575.17
minister to treat 91.24
 be instrumental 384.7
 aid 449.18
 serve 577.13
 care for 1008.19
ministration aid 449.1
 service 577.12
ministry aid 449.1
 the authorities 575.15
 service 577.12
 bureau 594.4
 cabinet 613.3
 clergy 699.1
 protectorship 1008.2
minor
 n youngster 302.1
 study 568.8
 key 709.15
 adj inferior 250.6
 immature 301.10
 insignificant 998.17
minority
 n inability 19.2
 inferiority 250.1
 immaturity 301.3
 race 312.2
 least 885.3
 adj least 885.7
minority group
 party 617.4
 minority 885.3
minority interests 609.31
minority leader 610.3
minority opinion 333.1
minor league 745.1
minor prophets 684.1
Minos
 Pontius Pilate 596.5
 justice 649.4
 nether world deity
  682.5
minstrel
 n musical theater 708.34
 singer 710.13
 ballad singer 710.14
 poet 720.11
 v sing 708.38
minstrel show 708.34
mint
 n lot 247.4
 gain 472.3
 wealth 618.3
 plant 739.3
 mold 786.6
 v form 262.7
 coin 728.28
 innovate 841.5
 originate 892.12
 adj unused 390.12
 new-made 841.9
 undamaged 1002.8
mintage money 728.1
 coining 728.24
 production 892.1
 product 893.1

mint condition
 healthiness 83.2
 newness 841.1
minted formative 262.9
 invented 892.19
minus
 n math terms 255.6
 deduction 255.7
 adj bereft 473.8
 nonexistent 762.8
 short of 911.5
 positive 1032.35
 prep off 255.14
 without 992.17
minuscule
 n type 548.6
 adj miniature 258.12
 literal 546.8
minute
 n entry 628.5
 period 824.1
 moment 824.2
 instant 830.3
 time of day 832.2
 the present 838.1
 v record 549.15
 keep accounts 628.8
 adj tiny 258.11
 meticulous 339.12
 detailed 766.9
 particular 865.12
 insignificant 998.17
minutemen 461.24
minutes
 memorandum 549.4
 report 549.7
minute steak 10.18
minutiae
 modicum 248.2
 detail 258.7
 particular 766.3
 trivia 998.4
minx woman 77.6
 impudent person 142.5
 brat 302.4
 mischief-maker 322.3
miracle marvel 122.2
 sign 870.8
miracle drug 86.29
miracle-worker 690.5
miraculous
 wonderful 122.10
 sorcerous 690.14
 wondrous 870.16
mirage apparition 33.5
 disappointment 132.1
 deception 356.1
 fata morgana 976.6
mire
 n slime 80.8
 receptacle of filth 80.12
 marsh 243.1
 mud 1062.8
 v dirty 80.15
 bemire 243.2
mirror
 n glass 29.6
 furniture 229.1
 paragon 659.4
 model 786.1
 ideal 786.4

pattern of perfection 1002.4
 v imitate 336.5
 image 349.11
 resemble 784.7
mirror image 779.2
mirror-image 264.4
mirroring
 imitation 336.1
 image 349.5
mirth merriment 109.5
 amusement 743.1
miry dirty 80.22
 marshy 243.3
 slimy 1062.14
misadventure 1011.2
misalliance
 marriage 563.1
 misconnection 776.2
 unfitness 789.3
misanthrope
 hater 103.4
 misanthropist 590.2
misanthropy
 hate 103.1
 people-hating 590
 misanthropism 590.1
misapplication
 misinterpretation 342.1
 misuse 389.1
 misconnection 776.2
 sophistry 936.1
 error 975.1
misapply
 misinterpret 342.2
 misuse 389.4
 reason speciously 936.8
 misdo 975.12
misapprehend
 misinterpret 342.2
 mistake 975.13
misapprehension
 misinterpretation 342.1
 mistake 975.3
misappropriate 389.4
misappropriation 389.1
misbegotten
 deformed 265.12
 illegitimate 674.7
 freakish 870.13
 unshapely 1015.8
misbehave
 behave 321.4
 misdemean 322.4
 transgress 654.8
 do wrong 655.4
misbehavior
 good behavior 321.2
 misconduct 322.1
 wrongdoing 655.1
misbelief
 heresy 688.2
 unbelief 955.1
 illusion 976.1
misbelieve err 688.8
 disbelieve 955.5
misbeliever 688.5
miscalculate
 misjudge 948.2
 err 975.9
miscalculation
 misjudgment 948.1

mistake 975.3
miscarriage
 abortion 410.5
 mistake 975.3
miscarriage of justice 650.4
miscarry
 abort 410.15
 miss 911.4
miscegenate
 get married 563.15
 hybridize 797.13
miscegenation
 marriage 563.1
 crossbreeding 797.4
miscellany
 compilation 554.7
 excerpts 557.4
 assortment 770.13
 hodgepodge 797.6
mischance 1011.2
mischief
 mischievousness 322.2
 mischief-maker 322.3
 impairment 393.1
 disaccord 456.1
 disadvantage 996.2
 evil 1000.3
mischief-maker
 mischief 322.3
 instigator 375.11
 troublemaker 593.2
mischievous
 mischief-loving 322.6
 impish 680.18
 harmful 1000.12
misconceive
 misinterpret 342.2
 mistake 975.13
misconception
 misinterpretation 342.1
 mistake 975.3
 illusion 976.1
misconduct
 n misbehavior 322.1
 misuse 389.1
 mismanagement 414.6
 wrongdoing 655.1
 v mismanage 414.13
 misdo 975.12
misconstruction
 perversion 265.2
 misinterpretation 342.1
 deliberate falsehood 354.9
 solecism 531.2
 misjudgment 948.1
 error 975.1
misconstrue
 pervert 265.6
 misinterpret 342.2
 misjudge 948.2
miscue
 n bungle 414.5
 slip 975.4
 v bungle 414.11
 err 975.13
misdate
 n anachronism 833.1
 v mistime 833.2
misdated 833.3
misdating 833.1
misdeed 655.2

misdemeanor
  misbehavior 322.1
  misdeed 655.2
  offense 674.4
misdirect pervert 265.6
  mislead 356.16
  mismanage 414.13
  misteach 569.3
misdirected
  botched 414.21
  mistaught 569.5
misdirection
  perversion 265.2
  misleading 356.2
  mismanagement 414.6
  misteaching 569.1
mise en place 381.1
mise-en-scène
  setting 209.2
  production 704.13
  stage setting 704.19
  motion-picture studio
    706.4
miser niggard 484.4
  collector 770.15
miserable
  wretched 96.26
  unhappy 112.21
  base 661.12
  paltry 998.21
  adverse 1011.13
Miserere 696.3
miserly greedy 100.27
  stingy 484.9
  sparse 885.5
  meager 992.10
misery pain 26.1
  wretchedness 96.6
  unhappiness 112.2
  sorrow 112.10
misfeasance
  misbehavior 322.1
  misuse 389.1
  mismanagement 414.6
  wrongdoing 655.1
  misdeed 655.2
  error 975.1
misfire
  n abortion 410.5
  v come to nothing 410.13
  miss 911.4
misfit
  intruder 774.2
  naysayer 789.4
  nonconformist 868.3
misfortune 1011.2
misgiving
  n anxiety 126.1
  apprehension 127.4
  nervousness 128.1
  foreboding 133.2
  doubt 955.2
  adj anxious 126.7
  apprehensive 127.24
misgovern 414.13
misguide
  mislead 356.16
  mismanage 414.13
  misteach 569.3
misguided
  botched 414.21

mistaught 569.5
  unwise 923.10
mishandle
  misuse 389.4
  mistreat 389.5
  mismanage 414.13
mishandling
  misuse 389.1
  mismanagement 414.6
mishap 1011.2
mishmash
  hodgepodge 797.6
  jumble 810.3
misidentify 975.13
misinform
  mislead 356.16
  misteach 569.3
misinformation
  misleading 356.2
  misteaching 569.1
misinformed
  mistaught 569.5
  unlearned 930.13
misinterpret
  pervert 265.6
  misunderstand 342.2
  misjudge 948.2
  mistake 975.13
misinterpretation
  perversion 265.2
  misunderstanding 342.1
  misjudgment 948.1
  error 975.1
misjudge
  misinterpret 342.2
  judge amiss 948.2
misjudgment
  misinterpretation 342.1
  error in judgment 948.1
  poor judgment 948.1
  error 975.1
  mistake 975.3
mislay misplace 160.7
  lose 473.4
mislaying 160.3
mislead lie 354.19
  misguide 356.16
  misteach 569.3
  betray 645.14
  seduce 665.20
misleading
  n misguidance 356.2
  misteaching 569.1
  adj deceptive 356.21
  misteaching 569.6
  illusory 976.9
mismanage
  misuse 389.4
  mishandle 414.13
  misdo 975.12
mismanagement
  misuse 389.1
  mishandling 414.6
mismatch
  n misconnection 776.2
  unfitness 789.3
  v disagree 789.5
mismatched
  inappropriate 789.7
  unequal 791.4
misname 527.12

misnomer
  n wrong name 527.9
  v misname 527.12
misogynist hater 103.4
  celibate 565.2
  misanthrope 590.2
misogyny hate 103.1
  celibacy 565.1
  misanthropy 590.1
misplace mislay 160.7
  lose 473.4
misplaced
  mislaid 160.11
  inappropriate 789.7
  disorderly 810.13
  out of line 868.7
misplay
  n mistake 975.3
  v play 745.5
  misdo 975.12
misprint
  n mistake 975.3
  v misdo 975.12
misprize disdain 157.3
  underestimate 950.2
misprized disliked 99.9
  underestimated 950.3
mispronounce 525.11
mispronunciation
  misspeaking 525.5
  grammatical error 975.7
misquote
  misinterpret 342.2
  misrepresent 350.3
  falsify 354.16
  misdo 975.12
misquoted
  falsified 265.11
  unauthentic 975.19
misread
  v misinterpret 342.2
  misjudge 948.2
  misdo 975.12
  adj misinterpreted 342.3
misreading
  misinterpretation 342.1
  misjudgment 948.1
misremember 990.5
misrender
  pervert 265.6
  misinterpret 342.2
misrendering 342.1
misrepresent
  pervert 265.6
  belie 350.3
  falsify 354.16
misrepresentation
  perversion 265.2
  distortion 350.1
  misinterpretation 350.1
  deliberate falsehood 354.9
misrepresented 265.11
misrule
  n mismanagement 414.6
  anarchy 418.2
  confusion 810.2
  v mismanage 414.13
miss
  n girl 302.6
  near-miss 410.4
  game 750.2

mistake 975.3
  v leave undone 340.7
  miss the mark 410.14
  lose 473.4
  miscarry 911.4
  be inattentive 984.2
  want 992.7
  fall short 1003.3
Miss 77.8
Miss America 1016.7
misshape
  n deformity 265.3
  v deform 263.3
  distort 265.7
misshapen
  deformed 265.12
  unordered 810.12
  freakish 870.13
  unshapely 1015.8
missile
  n weapon 462.18
  projectile 904.5
  rocket 1074.3
  adj projectile 904.15
missilery
  arms 462.1
  ballistics 462.3
  missile science 1074.1
  rocketry 1074.1
missing
  gone 34.4
  absent 222.11
  nonexistent 762.8
  incomplete 795.4
  wanting 992.13
missing link 842.7
missing person 222.5
mission
  n Air Force mission 184.11
  adventure 404.2
  operation 458.4
  delegation 576.13
  commission 615.1
  duty 641.1
  church 703.1
  task 724.2
  vocation 724.6
  v commission 615.10
missionary
  evangelist 699.6
  converter 858.9
mission kill 462.22
missive 553.2
misspeak
  mispronounce 525.11
  blunder 975.14
misspell 975.12
misspent 486.9
misstate
  misrepresent 350.3
  falsify 354.16
misstatement
  misrepresentation 350.1
  deliberate falsehood 354.9
  mistake 975.3
misstep misdeed 655.2
  slip 975.4
miss the boat
  miss an opportunity 844.5
  be late 846.7
  miss 911.4

mocking
  n adoption 621.2
  adj ridiculing 508.12
mockingbird
  imitator 336.4
  songbird 710.23
mock-up
  reproduction 336.3
  artist's model 786.5
mod 841.13
modal
  instrumental 384.8
  conditional 765.6
modality
  form 262.1
  manner 384.1
  instrumentality 384.3
  state 765.1
mode form 262.1
  manner 384.1
  mood 530.11
  style 532.2
  fashion 578.1
  octave species 709.10
  shape 765.1
  manner 765.4
  syllogism 935.6
model
  n form 262.1
  measure 300.2
  reproduction 336.3
  original 337.2
  image 349.5
  figure 349.6
  paragon 659.4
  celebrity 662.9
  arrangement 709.11
  essence 767.2
  duplicate 785.3
  thing copied 786
  pattern 786.1
  ideal 786.4
  rule 869.4
  philosophy 932.2
  beauty 1016.7
  v form 262.7
  sculpture 715.5
  adj praiseworthy 509.20
  exemplary 786.8
  normal 869.8
  perfected 1002.9
modeled
  formative 262.9
  sculptured 715.7
modeler 716.6
modeling
  forming 262.5
  imitation 336.1
  sculpture 715.1
moderate
  n centrist 611.10
  moderatist 670.4
  v slow 175.9
  limit 210.5
  mediate 466.6
  restrain 670.6
  qualify 959.3
  adj sedate 106.14
  slow 175.10
  medium 246.3
  lenient 427.7

neutral 467.7
  centrist 611.18
  cheap 633.7
  temperate 668.9
  moderating 670.10
  middle 819.4
  tolerable 999.20
  mediocre 1005.7
moderation
  sedateness 106.4
  limitation 210.2
  middle course 467.3
  temperance 668.1
  restraint 670.1
  moderateness 670.1
moderative 670.2
moderato 708.55
moderator
  arbitrator 466.4
  judge 596.1
  mitigator 670.3
modern
  n modern man 841.4
  adj fashionable 578.11
  present 838.2
  contemporary 841.13
modern art 712.1
modernist
  poet 720.11
  modern 841.4
modernization 841.3
modernize 841.6
modest
  humble 137.10
  meek 139.9
  inferior 250.6
  demurring 325.7
  reticent 344.10
  cheap 633.7
  unselfish 652.5
  decent 664.5
  mediocre 1005.7
modesty
  humility 137.1
  unpretentiousness 139.1
  meekness 139.1
  demur 325.2
  reticence 344.3
  unselfishness 652.1
  decency 664.2
  mediocrity 1005.1
modicum minim 248.2
  portion 477.5
  piece 793.3
modifiable
  changeable 854.6
  convertible 858.18
modification
  speech sound 524.12
  differentiation 780.4
  change 852.1
  qualification 959.1
modified
  changed 852.10
  qualified 959.10
modifier syntax 530.2
  transformer 852.5
modify
  differentiate 780.6
  change 852.7
  qualify 959.3

modish dressed up 5.46
  stylish 578.12
  modern 841.13
modiste 5.36
modular partial 793.7
  component 796.5
modulate inflect 524.28
  moderate 670.6
  be changed 852.6
  change 852.7
  qualify 959.3
modulation
  intonation 524.6
  abatement 670.2
  harmonization 709.2
  change 852.1
  amplitude modulation
    1034.14
modulator 670.3
module part 793.1
  component 796.2
  individual 872.4
  spacecraft 1075.2
modus operandi 384.1
modus vivendi
  behavior 321.1
  truce 465.5
mogul skiing 753.1
  personage 997.8
  snow 1023.8
Mogul 575.10
Mohammedan
  n Muslim 675.23
  adj Muslim 675.31
Mohs' scale 1046.6
moiety portion 477.5
  community 617.2
  piece 793.3
  mid-distance 819.2
  half 875.2
moil
  n work 725.4
  agitation 917.1
  v drudge 725.14
  seethe 915.12
moiré
  n variegation 47.6
  adj iridescent 47.10
moisten 1065.12
moistening
  n wetting 1065.6
  adj wetting 1065.18
moisture rain 316.1
  liquidity 1061.1
  dampness 1065.1
  damp 1065.1
moisture-proof 1066.11
moisturizer 1065.3
molar 2.8
molasses
  sweetening 66.2
  adhesive 803.4
  semiliquid 1062.5
mold
  n germ 85.42
  land 234.1
  form 262.1
  structure 266.1
  plant 310.4
  original 337.2
  decay 393.6

nature 767.4
  cast 785.6
  die 786.6
  kind 809.3
  characteristic 865.4
  disposition 978.3
  blight 1001.2
  v form 262.7
  decay 393.22
  sculpture 715.5
  pot 742.6
  conform 867.3
  produce 892.8
  imagine 986.14
moldable docile 433.13
  teachable 570.18
  pliant 1047.9
molded
  formative 262.9
  sculptured 715.7
  made 892.18
molder
  n sculptor 716.6
  v quiet 173.8
  decay 393.22
  disintegrate 806.3
  age 842.9
moldering
  quiescent 173.12
  blighted 393.42
  disintegrative 806.5
  stale 842.14
molding
  forming 262.5
  structure 266.1
  sculpture 715.1
  cast 785.6
  production 892.2
moldy
  malodorous 71.5
  blighted 393.42
  stale 842.14
mole the blind 30.4
  growth 85.39
  bulge 283.3
  mark 517.5
  buttress 901.4
  blemish 1004.1
  harbor 1009.6
  barrier 1012.5
molecular 258.14
molecular weight
  weight 297.5
  chemistry 297.8
  atomic weight 1060.5
molecule
  modicum 248.2
  atom 258.8
  atomic cluster 1038.7
  matter 1052.2
  element 1060.2
molehill hill 237.4
  pile 770.10
  trifle 998.5
Moleskine 549.11
molest annoy 96.13
  mistreat 389.5
  work evil 1000.6
mollify relieve 120.5
  pacify 465.7
  calm 670.7

soften 1047.6
mollifying
n softening 1047.5
adj pacificatory 465.12
tranquilizing 670.15
softening 1047.16
mollycoddle
n weakling 16.6
effeminate male 77.10
spoiled child 427.4
v indulge 427.6
molt shed 6.10
waste 473.5
molten melted 1020.31
liquefied 1064.6
mom 560.12
moment prestige 417.4
period 824.1
second 824.2
short time 828.3
instant 830.3
influence 894.1
impulse 902.1
importance 997.1
momentary
transient 828.7
instantaneous 830.4
momently 850.8
moment of truth
period 824.1
crucial moment 843.5
unreliability 971.6
urgency 997.4
momentous
authoritative 417.15
eventful 831.10
influential 894.13
important 997.17
momentum
motion 172.1
course 172.2
impulse 902.1
monad atom 258.8
something 763.3
one 872.3
matter 1052.2
monarch 575.8
monarchic
sovereign 417.17
governmental 612.16
monarchism
radicalism 611.4
government 612.7
monarchist 611.9
monarchy
government 612.4
absolutism 612.8
monasterial
monastic 698.14
claustral 703.16
monastery 703.6
monastic
n celibate 565.2
religious 699.16
adj celibate 565.6
monachal 698.14
claustral 703.16
monasticism
celibacy 565.1
asceticism 667.1
monachism 698.4

monaural system 50.11
monde 578.6
monetary unit 728.1
money wealth 618.1
currency 728.1
moneybags 618.7
money changer
banker 729.11
broker 730.9
money-hungry 100.27
money in hand 728.18
money in the bank 472.6
money-laundering 673.2
moneylender
lender 620.3
banker 729.11
money-mad 100.27
moneymaking
n acquisition 472.1
adj gainful 472.16
paying 624.21
occupied 724.15
moneyman 729.9
money manager 628.7
money market 728.16
money order 728.11
money-raising 621.1
money-saving 635.6
money-spinner 729.10
monger 730.2
mongolism 922.9
mongoloid 922.22
Mongoloid 312.2
mongoloid idiot 924.8
mongrel
n cur 311.18
beast 660.6
hybrid 797.8
adj hybrid 797.15
mongrelization 797.4
mongrelize 797.13
moniker 527.3
monition
dissuasion 379.1
warning 399.1
advice 422.1
tip 551.3
monitor
n warner 399.4
adviser 422.3
shackle 428.4
informant 551.5
teaching fellow 571.4
superintendent 574.2
examiner 938.17
radioman 1034.24
television technician 1035.13
output device 1042.9
v be taught 570.11
examine 938.24
check 1034.26
monitoring
vigilance 339.4
televising 1035.3
monitory
n advice 422.1
adj premonitory 133.15
dissuasive 379.5
warning 399.7
advisory 422.8
informative 551.18

monk
wild animal 311.22
celibate 565.2
religious 699.16
monkey
n temper 152.6
wild animal 311.22
imitator 336.4
dupe 358.1
laughingstock 508.7
cheater 759.22
v trifle 998.15
monkey business 356.5
monkeying 998.9
monkeyshines
buffoonery 489.5
prank 489.10
monkey with 214.7
monkhood 698.4
monkish
inornate 499.9
celibate 565.6
monastic 698.14
mono 50.11
monochrome
n color system 35.7
adj chromatic 35.16
pictorial 712.20
monocle 29.3
monocratic
authoritative 417.15
imperious 417.16
governmental 612.16
monody
dirge 115.6
harmony 708.3
monophony 708.21
monogamist 563.11
monogram
identification 517.11
signature 527.10
letter 546.1
monograph 556.1
monolith
monument 549.12
rock 1059.1
monolithic
uniform 781.5
simple 798.6
stony 1059.12
monologist 542.2
monologue
soliloquy 542.1
regularity 781.2
monomania
obsession 926.13
engrossment 983.3
monomaniac
n fanatic 926.18
adj obsessed 926.33
monopolist
n restrictionist 428.6
self-seeker 651.3
adj monopolistic 469.11
monopolize hog 469.6
appropriate 480.19
purchase 733.7
corner 737.26
engross 983.13
monopoly
restraint 428.1

monopolization 469.3
manipulation 737.20
monorail 179.14
monosyllable 526.1
monotheism 675.5
monotheist 675.16
monotheistic 675.25
monotone
n tone 50.2
regularity 781.2
series 812.2
repetitiousness 849.4
adj sounding 50.15
monotonous 849.15
monotonous
tedious 118.9
same 781.6
continuous 812.8
monotone 849.15
monotony tone 50.2
tedium 118.1
regularity 781.2
continuity 812.1
repetitiousness 849.4
monsieur 76.7
Monsignor 648.5
monsoon season 313.1
wet weather 316.4
monster
n frightener 127.9
beast 144.14
largeness 257.11
behemoth 257.14
fiend 593.6
violent person 671.9
monstrosity 870.6
eyesore 1015.4
adj large 247.7
huge 257.20
monstrosity
hugeness 257.7
deformity 265.3
abnormality 870.1
oddity 870.3
monster 870.6
eyesore 1015.4
monstrous
large 247.7
huge 257.20
deformed 265.12
wicked 654.16
base 661.12
savage 671.21
freakish 870.13
absurd 923.11
excessive 993.16
terrible 1000.9
unshapely 1015.8
montage picture 712.10
photograph 714.3
month 824.2
monthlies 12.9
monthlong 827.12
monthly
n periodical 555.1
adj recurrent 849.13
momentary 850.8
monument
tower 272.6
gravestone 309.17
figure 349.6

humiliation 137.2
penance 658.3
asceticism 667.1
mortified
diseased 85.60
distressed 96.22
humiliated 137.14
decayed 393.40
mortify chagrin 96.15
embarrass 98.13
humiliate 137.4
decay 393.22
mortifying
embarrassing 98.21
humiliating 137.15
mortise interact 777.6
hook 800.8
mortuary
n morgue 309.9
adj deathly 307.28
funereal 309.22
mosaic
n check 47.4
picture 712.10
adj checked 47.14
Mosaic 683.11
mosey 175.6
Moslem
n Muslim 675.23
adj Muslim 675.31
Moslemism 675.13
mosque 703.2
mosquito 311.37
moss marsh 243.1
plant 310.4
mossback
back number 842.8
conservative 853.4
mossbacked 303.18
mossy 310.42
most
n supremacy 249.3
major part 792.6
majority 883.2
adj extreme 247.13
superlative 249.13
majority 883.9
adv extremely 247.22
the most 249.16
most likely 968.8
mot witticism 489.7
maxim 974.1
mote modicum 248.2
minute 258.7
lightness 298.2
stronghold 460.6
intruder 774.2
motel 228.16
mothball 71.3
moth-eaten trite 117.9
stricken in years 303.18
blighted 393.42
stale 842.14
mother
n parent 559.3
genetrix 560.11
bad person 660.5
author 886.4
producer 892.7
v procreate 78.8
foster 449.16

engender 818.14
care for 1008.19
adj native 226.5
Mother 648.5
Mother Earth 1072.10
mother figure 92.31
motherhood
blood relationship 559.1
maternity 560.3
mothering 449.3
mother-in-law 564.2
motherland 232.2
motherless
helpless 19.18
bereaved 307.34
forlorn 584.12
mother lode 618.4
Mother Nature 677.8
mother of all
representative 349.7
meat 767.3
mother-of-pearl
n variegation 47.6
iridescence 1025.18
adj soft-colored 35.22
iridescent 47.10
mother superior
mistress 575.2
nun 699.17
mother tongue 523.3
motif edging 211.7
ornamental motif 498.7
passage 708.24
plot 722.4
topic 937.1
motile moving 172.7
changeable 854.6
motility
mobility 172.3
changeableness 854.1
motion
n exercise 84.2
movement 172.1
travel 177.1
activity 330.1
proposal 439.2
gesture 517.14
bill 613.9
baseball team 745.2
process 889.2
trend 896.2
mechanism 1040.4
v gesture 517.21
motion discomfort 85.30
**motion for summary
judgment** 598.12
motionless
unmoving 173.13
passive 329.6
inactive 331.17
motion picture
cinematography 706.1
pictures 714.8
motion sickness 85.30
motivate
set in motion 172.6
move 375.12
induce 886.11
impel 902.11
motivated
moved 375.30

teachable 570.18
motivating force 17.6
motivation
motion 172.1
reason 375.1
moving 375.2
teachableness 570.5
motivational
moving 172.7
motivating 375.25
motive
n reason 375.1
intention 380.1
passage 708.24
topic 937.1
adj moving 172.7
motivating 375.25
impelling 902.23
propulsive 904.14
motive power
energizer 17.6
mobility 172.3
impulse 902.1
pushing 904.1
machinery 1040.3
motivity 172.3
mot juste 533.1
motley
n costume 5.9
comedy 704.6
buffoon 707.10
v variegate 47.7
adj chromatic 35.16
variegated 47.9
mottled 47.12
different 780.7
mixed 797.14
nonuniform 782.3
motor
n automobile 179.9
instrument of conversion 858.10
machinery 1040.3
v ride 177.33
adj moving 172.7
motorboat
n powerboat 180.4
v navigate 182.13
motorcade 812.3
motorcar 179.9
motorcycle
n cycle 179.8
v ride 177.33
motorcyclist 178.11
motor-driven 1040.14
motoring 177.6
motor inn 228.16
motorist 178.10
motorize 1040.13
motor launch 180.4
motorman 178.12
motor oil 1056.4
motor vehicle 179.9
mottle
n spottiness 47.3
mark 517.5
v variegate 47.7
mark 517.19
mottled 47.12
motto heraldry 647.2
caption 937.2

maxim 974.1
slogan 974.4
moue scowl 110.9
grimace 265.4
mound
n hill 237.4
monument 549.12
baseball 745.1
pile 770.10
barrier 1012.5
v pile 770.19
mount
n ascent 193.1
mountain 237.6
horse 311.10
hunter 311.13
jockey 757.2
frame 901.10
v copulate 75.21
move 172.5
go on horseback 177.34
soar 184.39
ascend 193.8
climb 193.11
get on 193.12
rise 200.8
increase 251.6
tower 272.10
grow 272.12
dramatize 704.28
give a lift 912.7
mountain mount 237.6
quantity 247.3
plateau 272.4
bulge 283.3
mountain climber 193.6
mountain dew 88.18
mountaineer
traveler 178.1
climber 193.6
wilderness settler 227.10
mountain lion 311.21
mountain man 227.10
mountainous
hilly 237.8
large 247.7
huge 257.20
high 272.18
mountain range
mountain 237.6
plateau 272.4
mountaintop
summit 198.2
mountain 237.6
mountebank
impostor 357.6
entertainer 707.1
mountebankery 354.7
mounted policeman
rider 178.8
policeman 1008.15
Mounties 1008.17
mounting
n course 172.2
ascent 193.1
increase 251.1
production 704.13
frame 901.10
adj flowing 172.8
ascending 193.14
high 272.14

Mount Olympus 681.9
mount up to
 cost 630.13
 total 792.8
mourn distress 98.14
 grieve 112.17
 lament 115.10
mourner
 lamenter 115.8
 griever 309.7
mournful
 distressing 98.20
 sorrowful 112.26
 plaintive 115.19
 funereal 309.22
mourning
 n lamentation 115.1
 weeds 115.7
 adj lamenting 115.18
mouse woman 77.6
 trauma 85.38
 shrinking violet 139.6
 runt 258.4
 coward 491.5
 input device 1042.4
mouse-colored 39.4
mouser 311.20
mousetrap trap 356.12
 rocket launcher 1074.10
mousse sweets 10.40
 foam 320.2
mousy gray 39.4
 silent 51.10
 fearful 127.23
 shy 139.12
 rodent 311.44
 cowardly 491.10
mouth
 n digestive system 2.18
 eater 8.16
 inlet 242.1
 maw 292.4
 v chew 8.27
 lick 73.9
 grimace 265.8
 be hypocritical 354.23
 speak 524.19
 mumble 525.9
 declaim 543.10
mouthful bite 8.2
 high-sounding words 545.3
 full measure 794.3
mouthing
 hypocrisy 354.6
 mumbling 525.4
 lip service 693.2
mouth organ 711.10
mouthpiece
 telephone 347.4
 mediator 466.3
 informant 551.5
 spokesman 576.5
 lawyer 597.3
 wind instrument 711.6
 boxing 754.1
mouthwash
 cleanser 79.17
 dentifrice 86.22
mouth-watering
 n saliva 13.3
 adj appetizing 63.10

desirable 100.30
 alluring 377.8
mouthy 545.9
movable
 transferable 176.18
 changeable 854.6
 influenceable 894.15
movable feast 20.4
movables
 furniture 229.1
 belongings 471.2
move
 n act 328.3
 attempt 403.2
 stratagem 415.3
 cheating 759.13
 process 889.2
 expedient 995.2
 v affect 93.14
 excite 105.12
 touch 145.5
 settle 159.17
 progress 162.2
 budge 172.5
 set in motion 172.6
 remove 176.11
 travel 177.18
 behave 321.4
 act 328.4
 motivate 375.12
 admonish 422.6
 propose 439.5
 sell 734.8
 influence 894.7
 impel 902.11
 push 904.9
move away
 recede 168.2
 depart 188.6
move back 163.6
moved
 affected 93.23
 excited 105.20
 motivated 375.30
move in
 settle 159.17
 inhabit 225.7
 take possession 472.10
 gain influence 894.12
move into
 inhabit 225.7
 undertake 404.3
movement
 defecation 12.2
 feces 12.4
 exercise 84.2
 motion 172.1
 moving 176.4
 travel 177.1
 behavior 321.1
 act 328.3
 activity 330.1
 operation 458.4
 gesture 517.14
 front 609.33
 passage 708.24
 rhythm 709.22
 style 712.7
 meter 720.7
 plot 722.4
 company 770.3

cause 886.9
 trend 896.2
 mechanism 1040.4
move out 188.6
mover wanderer 178.2
 prompter 375.10
 doer 726.1
 cheater 759.22
 author 886.4
 producer 892.7
mover and shaker 375.1
move smoothly 287.9
movie
 n motion pictures 706.1
 adj motion-picture
  706.9
moviegoer
 playgoer 704.27
 attender 221.5
movie star 707.4
moving
 n motion 172.1
 removal 176.4
 travel 177.1
 motivation 375.2
 adj affecting 93.22
 distressing 98.20
 exciting 105.30
 pitiful 145.8
 progressive 162.6
 stirring 172.7
 traveling 177.36
 motivating 375.25
 lofty 544.14
 impelling 902.23
moving spirit
 inspiration 375.9
 prompter 375.10
moving staircase 912.4
mow
 n scowl 110.9
 grimace 265.4
 garner 386.7
 pile 770.10
 v grimace 265.8
 shorten 268.6
 smooth 287.5
 harvest 1069.19
mow down raze 395.19
 fell 913.5
moxie energy 17.3
 power 18.1
 liveliness 330.2
 pluck 359.3
 skill 413.1
 fearlessness 492.3
MP legislator 610.3
 policeman 1008.15
 police 1008.17
Mr common man 606.5
 man 76.7
Mr Nice Guy 143.8
Mrs 77.8
Mrs Grundy
 fussbudget 495.7
 social convention 579.1
 conventionalist 579.3
 conformist 867.2
Mr Universe 15.6
Ms 77.8
MS 547.10

much
 n quantity 247.3
 plenty 991.2
 adj many 247.8
 plentiful 991.7
 adv greatly 247.15
much ado about nothing
 overreaction 355.2
 triviality 998.3
mucho 247.15
mucilage
 adhesive 803.4
 lubricant 1056.2
 semiliquid 1062.5
muck
 n filth 80.7
 slime 80.8
 fertilizer 890.4
 mud 1062.8
 v dirty 80.15
muck around 998.15
mucked up
 spoiled 393.29
 complex 799.4
 confused 810.16
muckrake 512.10
muckraker
 disparager 512.6
 critic 946.7
muckraking
 defamation 512.2
 smear campaign 609.14
muck up dirty 80.15
 spoil 393.11
 complicate 799.3
 confuse 811.3
 make a boner 975.15
mucky filthy 80.23
 slimy 1062.14
mucous 1062.13
mucous membrane 2.6
mucus
 digestive secretion 13.2
 filth 80.7
 lubricant 1056.2
 semiliquid 1062.5
mud dirt 80.6
 marsh 243.1
 muck 1062.8
muddle
 n formlessness 263.1
 fiasco 410.6
 disorder 810.2
 confusion 985.3
 v deform 263.3
 bungle 414.11
 complicate 799.3
 disorder 810.9
 disarrange 811.3
 confound 945.3
 perplex 971.13
 make uncertain
  971.15
 confuse 985.7
muddled
 intoxicated 88.31
 confused 810.16
 muddleheaded 922.18
 in a dilemma 971.25
 in a muddle 985.13
muddlehead 924.4

muddleheaded
fuddlebrained 922.18
muddled 985.13
muddle through
make one's way 162.4
manage 409.12
muddy
v dirty 80.15
make uncertain 971.15
adj colorless 36.7
dingy 38.11
dirty 80.22
marshy 243.3
obscure 522.15
slimy 1062.14
mud flat 243.1
mudhole pothole 284.3
mud puddle 1062.9
mudlark 178.3
mudpack 1016.11
mud puddle 1062.9
mud room 197.13
mudslinger 512.6
mudslinging
defamation 512.2
smear campaign
609.14
muff
n bungle 414.5
bungler 414.9
goof 975.6
v bungle 414.11
muffin 10.31
muffle
n silencer 51.4
nose 283.8
v proof 15.14
silence 51.8
mute 51.9
cover 295.19
cover up 345.8
muffled muted 52.17
covered 295.31
latent 519.5
muffled tone 52.2
muffler 51.4
muffle up clothe 5.39
cover up 345.8
mufti civilian dress 5.8
disarmament 465.6
judge 596.3
clergy 699.12
mug
n face 216.4
mouth 292.4
dupe 358.2
laughingstock 508.7
ruffian 593.4
photograph 714.3
v grimace 265.8
attack 459.15
rob 482.16
rage 671.11
overact 704.31
photograph 714.14
mugger
assailant 459.12
robber 483.5
nerd 572.10
ruffian 593.4
violent person 671.9

mugging attack 459.1
theft 482.3
muggle
Brit terms 572.7
comman man 606.5
muggy sultry 1019.28
moist 1065.15
mug shot 714.3
mugwump
vacillator 362.5
timeserver 363.4
free agent 430.12
neutral 467.4
nonpartisan 609.28
mugwumpery
irresolution 362.1
neutrality 467.1
nonpartisanism 609.26
Muhammad 684.4
Muhammadan
n Muslim 675.23
adj Muslim 675.31
Muhammadanism 675.13
mulatto 797.8
mulch 1069.17
mulct
n fine 603.3
v cheat 356.18
fine 603.5
mule
beast of burden 176.8
spinner 271.5
ass 311.15
obstinate person 361.6
smuggler 732.5
hybrid 797.8
mulish ungulate 311.45
obstinate 361.8
mull
n point of land 283.9
v sweeten 66.3
heat 1020.17
mullion 273.4
mull over 931.13
multicolor
n variegation 47.1
adj variegated 47.9
multifaceted
sided 218.7
mixed 797.14
multifarious
different 780.7
multiform 783.3
complex 799.4
numerous 884.6
multifold
multiform 783.3
multiple 883.8
numerous 884.6
multiform 783.3
multiformity
diversity 783.1
multifariousness 783.1
multifunctional 783.4
multilateral
sided 218.7
multiangular 278.11
multilingual 523.16
multimedia 1042.18
multimillionaire 618.7
multinational 797.14

multiparous 78.15
multipartite 802.20
multiphase 783.3
multiple
n multiplication 883.4
adj multiform 783.3
multiplied 883.8
numerous 884.6
multiplication
procreation 78.2
multiplying 883.4
proliferation 890.2
notation 1017.2
multiplication table 883.4
multiplicity
multiformity 783.1
numerousness 884.1
multiplied
increased 251.7
multiple 883.8
multiplier 883.4
multiply procreate 78.8
grow 251.6
proliferate 883.6
teem with 884.5
produce 890.7
calculate 1017.18
multiplying
n multiplication 883.4
adj increasing 251.8
multiracial
nonuniform 782.3
mixed 797.14
multitude
quantity 247.3
assembly 770.4
throng 884.3
multitudinous
much 247.8
numerous 884.6
mum
n silence 51.1
adj mute 51.12
taciturn 344.9
interj silence! 51.14
mumble
n murmur 52.4
mumbling 525.4
v chew 8.27
murmur 52.10
speak 524.25
mutter 525.9
mumbling
n murmur 52.4
muttering 525.4
adj murmuring 52.18
mumbo jumbo
juggling 356.5
obscurity 522.3
jargon 523.9
occultism 689.1
incantation 691.4
charm 691.5
nonsense 520.2
Mumbo Jumbo 680.9
mummer
masquerader 357.7
entertainer 707.1
actor 707.2
mummery
hypocrisy 354.6

cover 356.11
ceremony 580.4
sanctimony 693.1
acting 704.8
mummification
corpse 307.15
embalmment 309.3
preserving 397.3
drying 1066.3
mummify
lay out 309.21
embalm 397.10
dry 1066.6
mummy corpse 307.15
mother 560.12
dryness 1066.2
mumps sulks 110.10
blues 112.6
munch
n bite 8.2
v chew 8.27
munching 8.1
mundane
unsacred 686.3
secularist 695.16
prosaic 721.5
unimaginative 987.5
municipal building 230.5
municipality
town 230.1
bureau 594.4
munificence 485.1
munificent 485.4
munition
n equipment 385.4
v equip 385.8
munitions
equipment 385.4
store 386.1
arms 462.1
mural
n picture 712.10
adj partitioned 213.11
murder
n homicide 308.2
v commit murder 308.16
bungle 414.11
murderer 308.11
murderous
cruel 144.26
slaughterous 308.24
savage 671.21
murderous insanity 926.7
murk
n gloom 112.7
obscurity 522.3
darkishness 1027.2
v blacken 38.7
darken 1027.9
adj darkish 1027.15
murky dingy 38.11
gloomy 112.24
obscure 522.15
vague 971.19
stained 1004.10
darkish 1027.15
murmur
n murmuring 52.4
lament 115.3
v mutter 52.10
complain 115.15

sigh 318.20
speak 524.25
mumble 525.9
murmurer 108.3
murmuring
  n murmur 52.4
  complaint 115.4
  mumbling 525.4
  adj murmurous 52.18
  discontented 108.7
muscle
  n the muscles 2.3
  muscularity 15.2
  exertion 725.1
  v exert strength 15.12
  thrust 902.12
  adj skeleton 2.26
muscle-bound
  firm 425.7
  able-bodied 15.16
muscle in 214.5
muscle man
  strong man 15.6
  hulk 15.7
  ruffian 593.4
  violent person 671.10
muscle-relaxant 86.45
muscular skeleton 2.26
  able-bodied 15.16
muscularity 15.2
musculature
  the muscles 2.3
  muscularity 15.2
muse
  n inspiration 375.9
  abstractedness 985.2
  creative thought 986.2
  v remark 524.24
  consider 931.12
  moon 985.9
Muse
  the Muses 720.10
  genius 920.8
Muses 986.2
museum gallery 386.9
  preserve 397.7
  collection 770.11
museum piece
  work of art 712.9
  oddity 870.5
mush
  n sentimentality 93.8
  face 216.4
  mouth 292.4
  pulp 1063.2
  v march 177.30
mushroom
  n drugs 87.19
  plant 310.4
  v grow 14.2
  expand 259.7
  grow round 282.7
mushy
  wishy-washy 16.17
  sentimental 93.21
  pulpy 1063.6
music
  harmonious sound
    708.1
  score 708.28
  harmonics 709.1

musical
  n musical theater 708.34
  adj musically inclined 708.47
  melodious 708.48
  rhyming 720.17
musical comedy 708.34
musicality
  melody 708.2
  musicianship 708.31
  harmonics 709.1
music appreciation 708.1
music box 711.15
music director 710.17
music festival 708.32
music hall hall 197.4
  theater 704.14
musician
  entertainer 707.1
  music maker 710.1
  musico 710.1
musicianship 708.31
music lover 710.21
music maker 710.1
musicologist 710.20
musicology 709.1
music roll score 708.28
  keyboard instrument
    711.12
music school 567.7
musing
  n consideration 931.2
  thoughtfulness 931.3
  abstractedness 985.2
  dreaminess 986.8
  adj cognitive 931.21
  abstracted 985.11
musk 70.2
musketeer
  infantryman 461.9
  shooter 904.8
musketry
  gunfire 459.8
  arms 462.1
  ballistics 462.3
  throwing 904.2
Muslim
  n Muhammadan 675.23
  adj Islamic 675.31
Muslimism 675.13
Muslim rulers 608.7
muss 811.2
mussed up 810.14
mussy 810.15
must
  n fetidness 71.2
  wine 88.17
  duty 641.1
  requirement 963.2
  blight 1001.2
  v be necessary 963.10
  adj in heat 75.28
  mandatory 420.12
  obligatory 641.15
mustache 3.11
mustachios 3.11
mustang 311.10
mustard plaster 86.33
muster
  n call to arms 458.7
  enlistment 615.7
  assemblage 770.1

roll 871.6
  v avail oneself of 387.14
  summon 420.11
  call to arms 458.18
  enlist 615.17
  come together 770.16
  assemble 770.18
mustering out 465.6
muster roll 871.6
muster up
  prompt 375.13
  summon 420.11
must have 963.9
must-have
  essential 767.9
  requirement 963.2
must-see 122.10
musty malodorous 71.5
  in heat 75.28
  trite 117.9
  blighted 393.42
  stale 842.14
mutability
  death rate 307.12
  nonuniformity 782.1
  transience 828.1
  changeableness 854.1
mutable mortal 307.33
  irresolute 362.9
  nonuniform 782.3
  transient 828.7
  changeable 854.6
mutant
  n violent person 671.9
  transformation 852.3
  adj savage 671.21
  changed 852.10
mutate diversify 782.2
  be changed 852.6
  change 852.7
mutation
  phonetics 524.13
  transformation 852.3
mute
  n dummy 51.3
  silencer 51.4
  mourner 309.7
  speech sound 524.12
  supporting actor 707.7
  music 711.22
  v muffle 51.9
  adj mum 51.12
  taciturn 344.9
  stammering 525.13
  inanimate 1055.5
muted muffled 52.17
  phonetic 524.30
mutilate excise 255.10
  deform 265.7
  injure 393.13
  tear apart 802.14
mutilated
  deformed 265.12
  impaired 393.27
  garbled 795.5
mutilation
  trauma 85.38
  excision 255.3
  deformity 265.3
  impairment 393.1
  severance 802.2

mutineer
  n rebel 327.5
  anarchist 418.3
  v revolt 327.7
mutinous
  unwilling 325.5
  rebellious 327.11
  lawless 418.5
mutiny
  n revolt 327.4
  lawlessness 418.1
  v revolt 327.7
mutter
  n murmur 52.4
  lament 115.3
  mumbling 525.4
  v murmur 52.10
  complain 115.15
  sigh 318.20
  speak 524.25
  mumble 525.9
mutterer 108.3
muttering
  n murmur 52.4
  mumbling 525.4
  adj murmuring 52.18
  discontented 108.7
mutton mouton 10.16
  sheep 311.7
muttonhead 924.4
muttonheaded 922.17
mutual
  cooperative 450.5
  communal 476.9
  accompanying 769.9
  correlative 777.11
  interchangeable 863.5
mutual attraction
  inclination 100.3
  relation 775.1
  attraction 907.1
mutual company 1008.4
mutual friend 588.1
mutual fund 737.16
mutuality
  cooperation 450.1
  accord 455.1
  correlation 777.1
  interchange 863.1
mutual understanding
  unanimity 332.5
  understanding 788.2
muzzle
  n silencer 51.4
  nose 283.8
  mouth 292.4
  shackle 428.4
  v disable 19.10
  silence 51.8
muzzy drunk 88.33
  inarticulate 525.12
  muddleheaded 922.18
  muddled 985.13
myopia 28.3
myopic
  poor-sighted 28.11
  undiscerning 922.14
  unwise 923.10
myriad
  n thousand 882.10
  plenty 991.2

adj numerous 884.6
myrmidon
  retainer 577.1
  employee 577.3
  follower 616.8
myrrh 70.2
myself 865.5
my stars 122.21
mysteries 701.4
mysterious
  awesome 122.11
  secret 345.11
  concealed 346.11
  inexplicable 522.18
  ambiguous 539.4
  occult 689.23
  supernatural 870.15
  unknown 930.16
  bewildering 971.27
mystery
  wonderfulness 122.3
  secret 345.5
  inexplicability 522.6
  enigma 522.8
  occultism 689.1
  rite 701.3
  vocation 724.6
  supernaturalism 870.7
  the unknown 930.6
  bewilderment 971.3
mystic
  n occultist 689.11
  adj latent 519.5
  inexplicable 522.18
  epiphanic 683.13
  occult 689.23
mystical
  inexplicable 522.18
  epiphanic 683.13
  occult 689.23
mysticism
  revelation 683.10
  occultism 689.1
mystification
  concealment 346.1
  obscurity 522.3
  misteaching 569.1
  occultism 689.1
  sophistry 936.1
mystified
  in a dilemma 971.25
  at an impasse 1013.24
mystify
  make unintelligible 522.12
  misteach 569.3
  quibble 936.9
  perplex 971.13
mystifying
  misteaching 569.6
  bewildering 971.27
mystique
  illustriousness 662.6
  cult 675.2
  opinion 953.6
myth
  fabrication 354.10
  posthumous fame 662.7
  mythology 678.14
  tradition 842.2
  figment of the imagination
    986.5

mythical
  fabricated 354.29
  distinguished 662.16
  mythic 678.15
  fictional 722.7
  extraordinary 870.14
  fictitious 986.21
mythical monsters
  127.9
mythicize 722.6
mythmaker
  narrator 722.5
  imaginer 986.12
mythological
  mythic 678.15
  fictional 722.7
  legendary 842.12
  fictitious 986.21
mythology
  mythicism 678.14
  tradition 842.2
mythomania 354.8
my word 122.19
NA 87.1
nab arrest 429.16
  acquire 472.9
  capture 480.18
nabbing 480.2
nabob governor 575.13
  rich man 618.7
  personage 997.8
nacre variegation 47.6
  iridescence 1025.18
nacré 47.10
nacreous
  soft-colored 35.22
  variegated 47.10
  iridescent 1025.38
nada 762.2
nadir bottom 199.1
  boundary 211.3
  base 274.4
nads
  genitals 2.13
  cheek 142.3
nag
  n tormentor 96.10
  horse 311.10
  oatburner 311.12
  jockey 757.2
  v annoy 96.13
  urge 375.14
  importune 440.12
  niggle 510.16
  remind 989.19
nagging
  n importunity 440.3
  criticism 510.4
  adj peevish 110.22
  importunate 440.18
  critical 510.23
  unforgettable 989.25
naiad 678.10
naïf dupe 358.1
  simple soul 416.3
nail acquire 472.9
  seize 480.14
  catch 480.17
  punish 604.15
  hook 800.8
  recognize 989.11

nail down
  stabilize 855.7
  prove 957.10
  make sure 970.11
naive immature 301.10
  artless 416.5
  natural 499.7
  foolable 923.12
  ignorant 930.11
  trusting 953.22
  gullible 954.9
naïveté
  artlessness 416.1
  naturalness 499.2
  gullibility 954.2
naked nude 6.14
  visible 31.6
  open 292.17
  manifest 348.10
  unadorned 499.8
  unmixed 798.7
  exposed 1006.15
naked eye organ 2.9
  eye 27.9
  field of view 31.3
namby-pamby
  n weakling 16.6
  sentimentality 93.8
  adj frail 16.14
  sentimental 93.21
  overnice 500.18
  mediocre 1005.7
name
  n appellation 527.3
  repute 662.1
  celebrity 662.9
  personage 997.8
  v nominate 371.19
  designate 517.18
  denominate 527.11
  appoint 615.11
  specify 865.11
  cite 957.13
  number 1017.17
  adj important 997.17
name-calling 512.2
named chosen 371.26
  called 527.14
  former 814.5
name-dropper
  snob 141.7
  upstart 606.7
  self-seeker 651.3
nameless
  anonymous 528.3
  unrenowned 661.14
name of the game 518.1
namesake 527.3
naming
  n nomination 371.8
  indication 517.3
  calling 527.2
  appointment 615.2
  adj indicative 517.23
nanny
  female animal 77.9
  goat 311.8
  nurse 1008.8
nanoscience 1068.3
nap
  n snooze 22.3

  texture 294.1
  v sleep 22.13
napery material 4.1
  dry goods 735.3
napkin 8.13
nappies 5.19
napping sleepy 22.21
  unaware 930.12
  unalert 984.8
  abstracted 985.11
nappy feathery 3.27
  intoxicated 88.31
  pily 294.7
narc detective 576.10
  policeman 1008.15
narcissism
  perversion 75.11
  vanity 140.1
  selfishness 651.1
narcissist
  sexual pervert 75.16
  egotist 140.5
  self-seeker 651.3
narcissistic vain 140.8
  egotistic 140.10
  selfish 651.5
Narcissus egotist 140.5
  beauty 1016.9
narcosis stupor 22.6
  insensibility 25.1
  deadness 94.2
  apathy 94.4
narcotic
  n anesthetic 25.3
  drug 87.3
  adj sleep-inducing 22.23
  deadening 25.9
  sedative 86.45
  palliative 670.16
narcotics addict 87.21
narcotics agent 576.10
narcotics pusher 732.4
narcotics traffic 732.1
narcotize
  put to sleep 22.20
  deaden 25.4
  numb 94.8
  relieve 120.5
  moderate 670.6
narcotized
  sleepy 22.21
  insensible 25.6
  unconscious 25.8
  intoxicated 87.23
  unfeeling 94.9
nares
  olfactory organ 69.5
  nose 283.8
narrate tell 719.6
  fabricate 722.6
narration
  description 349.2
  story 719.3
  fiction 722.1
  narrative 722.2
  fabrication 722.3
narrative
  n story 719.3
  fiction 722.1
  narration 722.2
  fabrication 722.3

adj narrational 719.8
poetic 720.15
fictional 722.8
narrative poem 720.4
narrator 722.5
narrow
  n inlet 242.1
  narrow place 270.3
  v limit 210.5
  contract 260.7
  constrict 270.11
  restrict 428.9
  simplify 798.4
  specialize 866.4
  qualify 959.3
  adj limited 210.7
  slender 270.14
  meticulous 339.12
  stingy 484.9
  prudish 500.19
  phonetic 524.30
  poor 619.7
  exclusive 773.9
  narrow-minded 980.10
  meager 992.10
narrow down 159.11
narrow escape 369.2
narrow-gauge 270.14
narrowing
  n contraction 260.1
  tapering 270.2
  exclusion 773.1
  simplification 798.2
  adj restrictive 428.12
narrow margin 780.2
narrow-mindedness
  small-mindedness 980.1
  narrowness 980.1
narrows inlet 242.1
  narrow place 270.3
narrow the gap
  approach 167.3
  converge 169.2
nasal
  n speech sound 524.12
  adj respiratory 2.32
  phonetic 524.30
  inarticulate 525.12
nasalization 525.1
nasalize 525.10
nascency birth 1.1
  origin 818.4
nascent 818.15
nasty
  v defile 80.17
  adj unpleasant 64.7
  filthy 80.23
  offensive 98.18
  malicious 144.20
  ill-bred 505.6
  obscene 666.9
  terrible 1000.9
nasty crack 489.7
nasty look 510.8
natal native 226.5
  beginning 818.15
nation population 227.1
  country 232.1
  humankind 312.1
  race 559.4
the nation 606.1

national
  n citizen 227.4
  adj public 312.16
  racial 559.7
  populational 606.8
  universal 864.14
national anthem 458.11
national assembly 613.1
national debt 623.1
national defense 460.2
national emergency 458.9
National Guard 461.24
nationalism
  nationhood 232.6
  patriotism 591.2
  foreign policy 609.5
nationalist 591.3
nationality
  nativeness 226.1
  country 232.1
  nationhood 232.6
  humankind 312.1
  patriotism 591.2
nationalization
  naturalization 226.3
  communization 476.3
  attachment 480.5
  socialism 611.6
nationalize
  communize 476.7
  attach 480.20
  politicize 611.16
national park 397.7
national security 438.1
native
  n dweller 227.2
  indigene 227.3
  adj indigenous 226.5
  undeveloped 406.13
  natural 416.6
  plain 499.7
  innate 767.8
Native American 312.3
native environment 228.18
native land 232.2
native language 523.3
nativity birth 1.1
  nativeness 226.1
  origin 818.4
  astrology 1072.20
NATO 437.2
natter
  n chatter 540.3
  v speak 524.20
  chatter 540.5
natty chic 578.13
  tidy 807.8
natural
  n sure success 409.2
  talented person 413.12
  note 709.14
  blackjack 759.11
  oddity 870.4
  idiot 924.8
  adj typical 349.15
  native 406.13
  artless 416.6
  plain 499.7
  elegant 533.6
  plain-speaking 535.3
  related 559.6

informal 581.3
  innate 767.8
  lifelike 784.16
  normal 869.8
  instinctive 934.6
  genuine 973.15
natural-born 226.5
natural history 1068.3
natural history museum 386.9
naturalism
  naturalness 416.2
  normality 869.1
  genuineness 973.7
  materialism 1052.6
naturalist
  n materialist 1052.7
  biologist 1068.2
  adj materialist 1052.12
naturalistic
  descriptive 349.14
  typical 349.15
  normal 869.8
  genuine 973.15
  materialist 1052.12
naturalization
  naturalized citizenship
    226.3
  habituation 373.7
  conversion 858.1
naturalize
  grant citizenship 226.4
  accustom 373.9
  convert 858.11
naturalized
  adopted 226.6
  accustomed 373.15
  converted 858.19
naturalized citizen 227.4
natural law 869.4
natural resource 1054.1
natural right 642.1
natural science
  science 928.10
  physics 1018.1
natural selection 861.3
natural state 406.3
natural world 1052.2
nature
  naturalness 406.3
  unaffectedness 416.2
  character 767.4
  kind 809.3
  characteristic 865.4
  disposition 978.3
  matter 1052.2
  universe 1072.1
Nature 677.8
nature preserve 310.13
naturist 6.3
naturistic naked 6.14
  normal 869.8
naught 762.2
naughty
  misbehaving 322.5
  disobedient 327.8
  wicked 654.16
naughty bits 2.13
naughty word 526.6
nausea symptom 85.9
  nauseation 85.30
  unpleasure 96.1

hostility 99.2
  vomiting 909.8
nauseant
  n nastiness 64.3
  cleanser 79.17
  emetic 86.18
  adj nasty 64.7
nauseate disgust 64.4
  offend 98.11
nauseated
  nauseous 85.57
  pleasureless 96.20
nauseating nasty 64.7
  filthy 80.23
  offensive 98.18
nauseous nasty 64.7
  nauseated 85.57
  pleasureless 96.20
nautical
  marine 182.57
  oceanic 240.8
naval 182.57
naval academy 567.6
naval cadet 183.4
naval officer
  ship's officer 183.7
  fleet admiral 575.20
naval vessel 180.6
navar navigation 184.6
  airborne radar
    1036.2
nave center 208.2
  church 703.9
  axle 915.5
navel 208.2
navigate locate 159.11
  journey 177.21
  sail 182.13
  pilot 182.14
  fly 184.36
navigation
  guidance 159.3
  topography 159.8
  direction 161.1
  water travel 182.1
  aviation 184.6
  bearing 573.1
navigational
  locational 159.19
  nautical 182.57
navigator
  mariner 183.1
  hand 183.6
  ship's officer 183.7
  crew 185.4
  guide 574.7
navvy
  excavator 284.10
  worker 726.2
navy
  chewing tobacco 89.7
  ships 180.10
  branch 461.21
  naval forces 461.27
navy man 183.4
nay
  n negation 335.1
  vote 371.6
  refusal 442.1
  side 935.14
  interj no 335.8

nay-sayer
  oppositionist 452.3
  misfit 789.4
  doubter 955.4
nay-saying
  n negation 335.1
  contrariety 779.1
  adj negative 335.5
  contrary 779.6
Nazarene 675.17
Nazism 612.7
NB 983.22
NCO 575.19
Neanderthal
  n barbarian 497.7
  adj unrefined 497.12
neap
  n tide 238.13
  low tide 274.2
  adj low 274.7
near
  v approach 167.3
  come near 223.7
  resemble 784.7
  come 839.6
  be imminent 840.2
  adj approaching 167.4
  left 220.4
  close 223.14
  narrow 270.14
  stingy 484.9
  familiar 587.19
  approximate 775.8
  approximating 784.14
  imminent 840.3
  adv nigh 223.20
  nearly 223.22
  prep at 159.27
  nigh 223.24
nearby
  adj handy 223.15
  adv aside 218.10
  near 223.20
near death 85.56
Near East 231.6
near-equal 784.15
nearer 223.18
nearest 223.19
nearing
  n approach 167.1
  adj approaching 167.4
  near 223.14
  future 839.8
  imminent 840.3
near-miss
  narrow escape 369.2
  crash 184.20
  meeting 223.4
  miss 410.4
nearsighted
  poor-sighted 28.11
  undiscerning 922.14
  narrow-minded 980.10
neat
  n cattle 311.6
  adj shipshape 180.20
  shapely 264.5
  skillful 413.22
  elegant 533.6
  plain-speaking 535.3
  chic 578.13

  unmixed 798.7
  tidy 807.8
  excellent 999.13
neaten 808.12
neat-fingered 413.23
neath 274.11
neb nose 283.8
  point 285.3
nebbish weakling 16.6
  thing of naught 764.2
  a nobody 998.7
nebula light 1025.15
  nebulosity 1072.7
nebulous cloudy 319.8
  obscure 522.15
  general 864.11
  celestial 1072.25
necessaries 963.2
necessary
  n latrine 12.10
  adj obligatory 424.11
  mandatory 641.15
  required 963.12
  requisite 963.13
  inevitable 963.15
  certain 970.13
necessitate
  require 424.5
  determine 886.12
  oblige 963.8
  destine 964.7
necessity
  compulsion 424.1
  indigence 619.2
  prerequisite 963.2
  necessariness 963.1
  requirement 963.2
  inevitability 963.7
  predetermination 964.1
  certainty 970.1
neck
  n fowl part 10.23
  contraction 260.1
  narrow place 270.3
  joint 800.4
  supporter 901.2
  v hang 604.18
neck-and-neck
  equal 790.7
  simultaneous 836.5
necking 562.2
necklace
  circle 280.3
  jewel 498.6
necktie 5.31
necrological
  funereal 309.22
  documentary 549.18
  historical 719.7
necrology
  obituary 307.13
  monument 549.12
  history 719.1
necromancer
  psychic 689.13
  sorcerer 690.5
necromancy
  spiritualism 689.5
  sorcery 690.1
necromantic
  sorcerous 690.14

  miraculous 870.16
necrophilia 75.11
necrophiliac 75.16
necrosis symptom 85.9
  gangrene 85.40
nectar delicacy 10.8
  sweetening 66.2
nectarize 66.3
nectarous tasty 63.8
  sweet 66.4
née 1.4
need
  n desire 100.1
  indigence 619.2
  deficiency 795.2
  requirement 963.2
  want 992.4
  v be poor 619.5
  require 963.9
  be necessary 963.10
  want 992.7
  adv necessarily 963.16
needing
  desirous 100.21
  incomplete 795.4
  wanting 992.13
needle
  n energizer 17.6
  sound reproduction system
    50.11
  mountain 237.6
  point 285.3
  thorn 285.5
  leaf 310.19
  pointer 517.4
  compass 574.9
  v annoy 96.13
  perforate 292.15
  goad 375.15
  banter 490.6
  sew 741.4
the needle 605.5
needlepoint 741.1
needless
  unnecessary 391.10
  superfluous 993.17
needlework 741.1
needleworker
  garmentmaker 5.34
  sewer 741.2
needling 375.5
need to 963.10
the needy 619.3
nefarious
  wicked 654.16
  base 661.12
  terrible 1000.9
negate abnegate 335.3
  abolish 395.13
  refuse 442.3
  contradict 451.6
  disagree 789.5
  neutralize 900.7
  disbelieve 955.5
  disprove 958.4
negating
  n negation 335.1
  adj neutralizing 900.9
negation
  disaffirmation 335.2
  negating 335.1

  extinction 395.6
  refusal 442.1
  opposition 451.1
  nonexistence 762.1
  disagreement 789.1
  disproof 958.1
negative
  n math terms 255.6
  negation 335.1
  refusal 442.1
  veto 444.2
  graphic arts 713.5
  film 714.10
  print 785.5
  mold 786.6
  v negate 335.3
  abolish 395.13
  refuse 442.3
  veto 444.5
  neutralize 900.7
  disprove 958.4
  adj pessimistic 125.16
  negatory 335.5
  unconsenting 442.6
  oppositional 451.8
  nonexistent 762.8
  contrary 779.6
  disagreeing 789.6
  numeric 1017.23
  electric 1032.35
  interj no 335.8
negativism
  defense mechanism 92.23
  pessimism 125.6
  negation 335.1
  resistance 453.1
  hindrance 1012.1
negativist
  pessimist 125.7
  oppositionist 452.3
  hinderer 1012.8
neglect
  n negligence 340.1
  neglectfulness 340.1
  nonaccomplishment 408.1
  mismanagement 414.6
  nonobservance 435.1
  v slight 157.6
  overlook 340.6
  leave undone 408.2
  disregard 435.3
neglected
  unthanked 151.5
  unattended to 340.14
  needless 391.10
  unaccomplished 408.3
neglecter 340.5
negligee 5.20
negligence
  unconcern 102.2
  neglect 340.1
  thoughtlessness 365.3
  improvidence 406.2
  mismanagement 414.6
  laxness 426.1
  nonobservance 435.1
  slovenliness 810.6
  inaccuracy 975.2
  inattention 984.1
negligent
  n neglecter 340.5

neutralizer
counteractant 900.3
acid 1060.3
neutron 1038.6
never
adv noway 248.11
ne'er 822.4
interj by no means 335.9
never-dying 829.9
never-ending
continuous 812.8
perpetual 829.7
never fear 969.4
Neverland 986.11
never mind
who cares? 102.11
no matter 998.25
nevermore 822.4
never-never land 986.11
never say die
not weaken 15.10
be hopeful 124.7
be determined 359.8
stay with it 360.4
stand fast 453.4
persist 856.5
nevertheless
notwithstanding 338.8
anyhow 384.10
nevus growth 85.39
bulge 283.3
mark 517.5
blemish 1004.1
new
adj additional 253.10
original 337.5
unaccustomed 374.4
unused 390.12
fashionable 578.11
present 838.2
young 841.7
adv newly 841.15
again 874.7
New Age 870.7
new arrival
newcomer 774.4
beginner 818.2
newbie 572.9
new birth revival 396.3
redemption 685.4
new start 858.2
newborn born 1.4
infant 301.12
new-made 841.9
new boy
incomer 189.4
novice 572.9
newcomer 774.4
newcomer
incomer 189.4
novice 572.9
new arrival 774.4
beginner 818.2
new driver 178.10
newel 273.4
newfangled 841.10
new-fashioned
fashionable 578.11
modern 841.13
new guard
border 211.4

vanguard 216.2
new kid
incomer 189.4
newcomer 774.4
new left 609.24
New Left 611.4
new life 685.4
new look 841.2
newlywed 563.5
newlyweds 563.9
new man
n newcomer 774.4
modern 841.4
convert 858.7
v re-form 858.12
new money 618.1
new moon 1072.11
new new thing 578.5
news information 552
tidings 552.1
newspaper 555.2
news brief 552.5
newscast
n radiobroadcast 1034.18
television broadcast 1035.2
v broadcast 1034.25
newscaster 1034.23
Newsfeed 552.5
new slant 932.5
newsletter 552.1
newsman 555.4
news media 552.1
newsmonger
informant 551.5
rumormonger 552.9
newspaper news 552.1
news medium 555.2
newspaperman
writer 547.15
newsmonger 552.9
journalist 555.4
author 718.4
newsperson 552.9
news report 552.5
newsserver 552.1
newsstand 736.3
newsworthy 552.13
newsy
v talkative 540.9
adj communicative 343.10
newsworthy 552.13
gossipy 552.14
New Testament 683.4
new to
unaccustomed 374.4
inexperienced 414.17
new twist 932.5
New World 231.6
next
adj adjacent 223.16
nearest 223.19
succeeding 815.4
adv subsequently 835.6
next big thing
caprice 364.1
great success 409.3
fad 578.5
next life 835.1
next of kin 559.2
next to
v learn 551.14

prep at 159.27
the next world 839.2
nexus 812.2
Niagara 238.11
nib nose 283.8
point 285.3
extremity 820.2
nibble
n bite 8.2
v feed 8.18
pick 8.26
chew 8.26
kid oneself 954.6
trifle 998.14
nibbling 8.1
niblet 8.2
nice tasty 63.8
pleasant 97.6
kind 143.13
meticulous 339.12
dainty 495.11
elegant 496.8
right 637.3
conscientious 644.15
detailed 766.9
discriminating 944.7
exact 973.17
attentive 983.15
good 999.12
nice guy 659.2
nicety
meticulousness 339.3
niceness 495.3
taste 496.1
margin 780.2
discrimination 944.1
accuracy 973.5
niche
nook 197.3
recess 284.7
hiding place 346.4
nick
n notch 289.1
jail 429.9
mark 517.5
type 548.6
v notch 289.4
rob 482.16
mark 517.19
nickel
n money 728.7
precious metals 728.20
adj brass 1058.17
nickel-and-dime
insignificant 248.6
measly 998.18
nickelodeon 50.11
nickname
n sobriquet 527.7
v name 527.11
nick of time 843.5
nicotine 89.9
nicotine addict 87.21
nicotine addiction
substance abuse 87.1
smoking 89.10
nicotinic 89.15
nictating 28.11
niece 559.3
nifty chic 578.13
excellent 999.13

niggard
n tightwad 484.4
adj niggardly 484.8
nigger 312.3
niggle
n criticism 510.4
v nag 510.16
trifle 998.14
niggling
n criticism 510.4
adj insignificant 248.6
critical 510.23
attentive 983.15
petty 998.20
nigh
v near 223.7
adj left 220.4
near 223.14
adv near 223.20
nearly 223.22
prep near 223.24
night
n blackness 38.4
close of day 315.2
nighttime 315.4
darkness 1027.1
adj nocturnal 315.9
night and day
n opposites 215.2
adv constantly 847.7
night black
black 38.8
dark 1027.13
night blindness 30.2
nightcap
sleep-inducer 22.10
drink 88.9
nightclothes 5.57
night clothes 5.21
nightclub bar 88.20
theater 704.14
entertainment 743.13
night crawler 311.38
nightdress 5.21
nightfall 315.2
nightgown 5.21
nightie 5.21
nightingale 710.23
night letter 347.14
nightlong
adj nocturnal 315.9
continuing 827.12
adv nightly 315.11
nightmare
torment 96.7
frightener 127.9
dream 986.9
night prayer 696.8
nights 315.11
night spot
theater 704.14
entertainment 743.13
nighttime
n night 315.4
adj nocturnal 315.9
nightwalk
creep 177.26
noctambulate 177.32
lurk 346.9
nightwalking
n noctambulation 177.9

noisy
noiseful 53.13
vociferous 59.10
blustering 503.4

nomad
n Bedouin 178.4
adj wandering 177.37

nomadic 177.37

nomadism 177.3

no-man's-land
prohibition 444.1
battlefield 463.2

no matter 998.25

no matter what
n whatever 864.6
interj by no means 335.9

nom de plume 527.8

nomen name 527.3
term 527.6

nomenclature
naming 527.2
terminology 527.1

nominal
n noun 530.5
adj cognominal 527.15
grammatical 530.17
formal 580.7
cheap 633.7

nominal charge 633.2

nominalism 865.1

nominate
choose 371.19
name 527.11
support 609.41
appoint 615.11

nomination
designation 371.8
caucus nomination 609.11
appointment 615.2
holy orders 698.10

nominative
n case 530.9
adj nominal 527.15
denominative 527.16

nominee 615.9

no more
adj gone 34.4
dead 307.29
extinct 762.11
past 837.7
interj stop! 857.13

nonacceptance
rejection 372.1
refusal 442.1

nonaccomplishment
nonachievement 408.1
failure 410.1

nonadherent
nonobservant 435.5
incoherent 804.4

nonadmission 773.1

nonage 301.3

nonagenarian
old man 304.2
ninety 882.7

nonaggression 464.4

nonaggressive
indolent 331.19
unbelligerent 464.10

nonalcoholic 516.4

nonalcoholic beverage 10.49

nonaligned
independent 430.22
neutral 467.7

nonaligned nation
country 232.1
free agent 430.12
neutral 467.4

nonalignment
neutrality 467.1
moderatism 611.2

nonattendance 222.4

nonattendant 222.11

nonbeliever 695.11

nonbelieving 955.8

nonbelligerent 464.5

nonbiodegradable 1055.4

nonbreakable 1049.5

the nonce 838.1

nonce word 526.8

nonchalance
apathy 94.4
unconcern 102.2
casualness 106.5

nonchalant
apathetic 94.13
unconcerned 102.7
blasé 106.15

noncohering 802.20

noncohesion
nonadhesion 804.1
uncohesiveness 804.1

noncohesive
separate 802.20
incoherent 804.4

noncom 575.19

noncombatant
n nonbelligerent 464.5
adj unbelligerent 464.10

noncommissioned officer
enlisted man 461.8
superintendent 574.2

noncommittal 494.8

noncommitted 467.7

noncommunicable 122.13

non-compete 210.9

noncompetitive 450.5

noncompletion 408.1

noncompliance
disobedience 327.1
nonobservance 435.1
refusal 442.1
nonconformity 868.1

non compos mentis 926.26

nonconducting 1032.36

nonconductive 1032.36

nonconductor 1032.14

nonconforming
disobedient 327.8
dissenting 333.6
nonobservant 435.5
unconforming 868.5

nonconformist
n rebel 327.5
dissenter 333.3
heretic 688.5
misfit 789.4
unconformist 868.3
oddity 870.4
eccentric 927.3
adj nonuniform 782.3
individualistic 789.9

counteractive 900.8

nonconformity
obliquity 204.1
disobedience 327.1
dissent 333.1
nonobservance 435.1
unorthodoxy 688.1
extraneousness 774.1
difference 780.1
nonuniformity 782.1
inconsistency 789.2
particularity 865.1
nonconformance 868.1
unconformity 868.1
counteraction 900.1
eccentricity 927.1

noncontiguous 802.20

nonconvergent 203.6

noncooperation
disobedience 327.1
opposition 451.1
hostility 451.2
resistance 453.1
disaccord 456.1

noncooperative
insubordinate 327.9
oppositional 451.8
resistant 453.5

noncreative 891.5

nondenominational
nonsectarian 675.27
universal 864.14

nondescript
formless 263.4
simple 499.6

nondutiable 630.16

none
n divine service 696.8
not any 762.4
adv no 762.12

nonelastic 1046.12

nonemotional 94.9

nonentity
weakling 16.6
nonexistence 762.1
thing of naught 764.2
a nobody 998.7
mediocrity 1005.5

none of your business 214.10

nonessential
n inessential 768.2
adj needless 391.10
circumstantial 766.7
unessential 768.4
irrelevant 776.7
superfluous 993.17
insignificant 998.17

nonesuch
marvel 122.2
the best 999.8

nonetheless
notwithstanding 338.8
anyhow 384.10

non-exclusive 772.7

nonexistence
absence 222.1
nonbeing 762.1
nonsubsistence 762.1

nonexistent gone 34.4
absent 222.11
unexistent 762.8

imaginary 986.19

nonexpectant 131.9

nonfactual 986.21

nonfeasance
disobedience 327.1
neglect 340.1
nonaccomplishment 408.1
mismanagement 414.6
nonobservance 435.1
misdeed 655.2

nonfertile 891.4

nonfiction 547.10

nonflammability 1022.1

nonflammable 1022.9

nonformal
n substandard language 523.6
jargon 523.9
adj in dishabille 5.47
vernacular 523.20
nonuniform 782.3
slovenly 810.15
unconventional 868.6

nonfulfillment
nonaccomplishment 408.1
nonobservance 435.1
insufficiency 992.1

nonfunctional 391.14

nonhuman 870.15

nonimitation 337.1

nonintellectual 930.13

noninterference
neglect 340.1
nonintervention 430.9
policy 609.4

noninterruption 847.2

nonintervention
avoidance 368.1
noninterference 430.9
policy 609.4

noninvolvement
inaction 329.1
avoidance 368.1
neutrality 467.1

non-Jew 688.6

non-lethal weapon 462.22

nonliving 1055.5

nonliving matter 1055.1

nonmalignant 999.21

nonmandatory 324.7

nonmedical therapist 90.9

nonmedical therapy 91.2

nonmetal 1058.3

nonmetallic 1058.16

nonmilitant 464.10

nonmusical 61.4

no-no prohibition 444.1
oath 513.4

nonobjective 980.12

nonobservance
nonadherence 435.1
inobservance 435.1
refusal 442.1
nonreligiousness 695.1
nonconformity 868.1
inattention 984.1

nonobservant
inobservant 435.5
nonreligious 695.15
nonconforming 868.5

nonoccupancy 222.2

nostrum 86.2
no sweat 1014.16
nosy
  meddlesome 214.9
  searching 938.38
  prying 981.6
not 335.8
nota bene 983.22
notability glory 247.2
  distinction 662.5
  celebrity 662.9
  noteworthiness 997.2
  personage 997.8
not a bit
  n none 762.4
  adv noway 248.11
  interj no 335.8
notable
  n celebrity 662.9
  personage 997.8
  adj remarkable 247.10
  conspicuous 348.12
  distinguished 662.16
  characteristic 865.13
  memorable 989.24
  noteworthy 997.19
not accept deny 335.4
  not permit 444.4
  refuse to believe 956.3
not admit deny 335.4
  disbelieve 955.5
not allow 444.4
not all there
  mentally deficient 922.22
  crazy 926.27
not a peep 51.1
notarize 332.12
notarized 332.14
notarized statement
  deposition 334.3
  certificate 549.6
notary endorser 332.7
  recorder 550.1
not a sound 51.1
not at all
  adv noway 248.11
  none 762.12
  never 822.4
  interj by no means 335.9
notate
  represent 349.8
  grammaticize 530.16
notation
  comment 341.5
  representation 349.1
  memorandum 549.4
  entry 628.5
  score 708.28
  character 709.12
  addition 1017.2
  number 1017.3
not bad
  adj tolerable 999.20
  interj bravo! 509.22
not believe 955.5
not budge
  do nothing 329.2
  balk 361.7
  stand fast 855.11
not buy refuse 442.3
  disbelieve 955.5

refuse to believe 956.3
not care
  not mind 102.4
  take no interest in 982.2
not care for
  dislike 99.3
  neglect 340.6
not care to 325.3
notch
  n crack 224.2
  ridge 237.5
  degree 245.1
  indentation 284.6
  cleft 289.1
  nick 289.1
  mark 517.5
  v indent 284.14
  nick 289.4
  mark 517.19
notched
  indented 284.17
  nicked 289.5
notching 289.2
not comparable
  inadequate 250.7
  uncomparable 787.6
not compare 250.4
not count 998.11
not counting 255.14
not cricket
  wrong 638.3
  unfair 650.10
  unconventional 868.6
not done
  underdone 11.9
  wrong 638.3
  unfair 650.10
  unconventional 868.6
note
  n observation 27.2
  animal noise 60.1
  milieu 209.3
  added to writing 254.2
  comment 341.5
  sign 517.1
  remark 524.3
  memorandum 549.4
  certificate 549.6
  letter 553.2
  treatise 556.1
  entry 628.5
  distinction 662.5
  air 708.4
  pitch 709.4
  musical note 709.14
  interval 709.20
  paper money 728.5
  negotiable instrument
    728.11
  cognizance 928.2
  mood 978.4
  attention 983.1
  importance 997.1
  v signify 517.17
  remark 524.24
  record 549.15
  keep accounts 628.8
  heed 983.6
not easy
  adverse 1011.13
  difficult 1013.17

notebook
  record book 549.11
  book 554.1
notebook computer 1042.2
not enough 992.9
not even 335.9
noteworthy
  remarkable 247.10
  particular 865.12
  extraordinary 870.14
  notable 997.19
not give a crap 102.4
not give a hoot 102.4
not give a shit 102.4
not have a chance
  be impossible 967.4
  have no chance 972.14
not hesitate 359.10
nothing void 222.3
  nil 762.2
  thing of naught 764.2
nothing doing
  interj nope 335.10
  God forbid! 510.27
  phrs I refuse 442.7
nothing like 787.5
nothingness
  unconsciousness 25.2
  space 158.1
  void 222.3
  nonexistence 762.1
nothing of the kind
  n a different thing 780.3
  adj nothing like 787.5
  interj no 335.8
nothing special
  n mediocrity 1005.5
  adj ordinary 1005.8
not hold up 975.8
notice
  n observation 27.2
  announcement 352.2
  press release 352.3
  publicity 352.4
  advertisement 352.6
  warning 399.1
  demand 421.1
  information 551.1
  commentary 556.2
  cognizance 928.2
  criticism 946.2
  attention 983.1
  v see 27.12
  detect 941.5
  heed 983.6
noticeable visible 31.6
  remarkable 247.10
  measurable 300.14
  manifest 348.8
  conspicuous 348.12
notification
  informing 343.2
  announcement 352.2
  warning 399.1
  information 551.1
notify herald 133.13
  warn 399.5
  inform 551.8
not in keeping with 789.10
not in the habit of 374.4
not in the mood 325.5

notion caprice 364.1
  impulse 365.1
  intention 380.1
  plan 381.1
  idea 932.1
  suggestion 951.5
  opinion 953.6
notional
  capricious 364.5
  ideational 932.9
  theoretical 951.13
  imaginative 986.18
  imaginary 986.19
  fanciful 986.20
notions 735.6
not know 930.10
not kosher
  dishonest 645.16
  unfair 650.10
  unconventional 868.6
not likely 442.7
not listen
  disobey 327.6
  be inattentive 984.2
not make sense
  be meaningless 520.4
  be incomprehensible
    522.10
not matter 998.11
not mind
  not care 102.4
  disobey 327.6
notoriety
  conspicuousness 348.4
  publicity 352.4
  disreputability 661.2
  repute 662.1
notorious
  conspicuous 348.12
  knavish 645.17
  disreputable 661.10
  distinguished 662.16
  immodest 666.6
  well-known 928.27
  terrible 1000.9
not permit 444.4
not remember 990.5
not right
  mentally deficient 922.22
  insane 926.26
  crazy 926.27
  erroneous 975.16
not see coming 131.4
not stand for
  not permit 444.4
  discountenance 510.11
not surprised 130.11
not swallow
  disbelieve 955.5
  refuse to believe 956.3
not there 985.11
not to be believed 955.10
not to be had
  inaccessible 967.9
  scarce 992.11
not tolerate
  not permit 444.4
  discountenance 510.11
not to mention
  adv additionally 253.11
  prep with 253.12

not touch
  avoid 368.6
  not use 390.5
  abstain 668.7
not true false 354.25
  erroneous 975.16
not understand 522.11
not wash 975.8
not with it
  unaware 930.12
  oblivious 984.7
notwithstanding 338.8
not work
  be impotent 19.7
  fail 410.9
noumenon 932.1
noun 530.5
nourish feed 7.17
  nurture 8.19
  encourage 375.21
  foster 449.16
nourishing
  n nutrition 7.1
  adj nutritious 7.21
  eating 8.31
nourishment
  nutrition 7.1
  nutriment 10.3
  support 449.3
nous world spirit 677.7
  intellect 919.1
  smartness 920.2
nouveau riche
  n vulgarian 497.6
  upstart 606.7
  modern 841.4
  adj populational 606.8
nouvelle cuisine food 10.1
  cooking 11.1
nova 10.24
novation 862.1
novel
  n book 554.1
  story 722.3
  adj original 337.5
  new 841.11
novelist writer 547.15
  author 718.4
  narrator 722.5
novelty
  nonimitation 337.1
  fad 578.5
  merchandise 735.6
  newness 841.1
  innovation 841.2
  alteration 852.4
novena
  divine service 696.8
  nine 882.5
novice novitiate 572.9
  nun 699.17
  beginner 818.2
  ignoramus 930.7
now
  n the present 838.1
  adj modern 841.13
  adv at once 830.8
  at present 838.3
  recently 841.16
  interj make haste!
    401.16

now and then
  discontinuously 813.5
  occasionally 848.5
noway
  adv noways 248.11
  interj by no means 335.9
no way
  n despair 125.2
  interj nope 335.10
  God forbid! 510.27
  phrs I refuse 442.7
  no can do 967.11
No way in hell 967.1
nowhere
  n remote region 261.4
  adv in no place 222.17
nowise 248.11
now or never 843.12
noxious nasty 64.7
  malodorous 71.5
  unhealthful 82.5
  poisonous 82.7
  offensive 98.18
  malicious 144.20
  harmful 1000.12
nozzle bib nozzle 239.9
  nose 283.8
  sprinkler 1065.8
NSAID 86.12
nth degree 794.5
nuance degree 245.1
  implication 519.2
  margin 780.2
  distinction 944.3
nub
  essential content 196.5
  center 208.2
  bulge 283.3
  texture 294.1
  essence 767.2
  salient point 997.6
nubbin runt 258.4
  bulge 283.3
nubby studded 283.17
  nappy 294.7
nubile grown 14.3
  adolescent 301.13
  adult 303.12
  marriageable 563.20
nuclear
  nucleate 208.12
  nucleal 305.21
  middle 819.4
  thermonuclear 1038.19
nuclear bomb 462.2
nuclear energy
  energy 17.1
  atomic energy 1038.15
nuclear fission 1038.8
nuclear fusion 1038.9
nuclear physicist 1038.3
nuclear physics
  electronics 1033.1
  atomic science 1038.1
  particle physics 1038.1
nuclear power
  atomic energy 1038.15
  manpower 18.4
nuclear reactor 1038.13
nuclear war 458.1
nuclear weapons 462.1

nucleus center 208.2
  cell nucleus 305.7
  essence 767.2
  middle 819.1
  vital force 886.7
  elementary particle 1038.6
nude
  n work of art 712.9
  adj naked 6.14
  unadorned 499.8
nudge
  n contact 223.5
  signal 517.15
  hint 551.4
  thrust 902.2
  v set in motion 172.6
  contact 223.10
  goad 375.15
  importune 440.12
  signal 517.22
  thrust 902.12
  remind 989.19
nudist
  n nudity 6.3
  adj naked 6.14
nudity nakedness 6.3
  unadornment 499.3
nudzh
  n tormentor 96.10
  v annoy 96.13
nugatory
  ineffective 19.15
  insignificant 248.6
  worthless 391.11
  trivial 998.19
nugget lump 257.10
  precious metals 728.20
nuisance
  annoyance 96.2
  tormentor 96.10
  bore 118.4
nuisance value 1012.1
null vacant 222.14
  meaningless 520.6
  nonexistent 762.8
null and void
  vacant 222.14
  repealed 445.3
nullification
  denial 335.2
  extinction 395.6
  repeal 445.1
  policy 609.4
  neutralization 900.2
nullify deny 335.4
  abolish 395.13
  repeal 445.2
  declare a moratorium 625.9
  neutralize 900.7
nullity
  meaninglessness 520.1
  nonexistence 762.1
  thing of naught 764.2
  an insignificancy 998.6
numb
  v deaden 25.4
  benumb 94.8
  relieve 120.5
  freeze 1023.10
  adj insensible 25.6
  apathetic 94.13

  unconcerned 102.7
  languid 331.20
number
  n amount 244.2
  deception 356.9
  singular 530.8
  edition 554.5
  act 704.7
  rhythm 709.22
  vocation 724.6
  part of writing 793.2
  numeral 1017.3
  sum 1017.6
  v quantify 244.4
  total 792.8
  itemize 801.7
  numerate 1017.17
number among 772.3
number-cruncher 1017.15
numbering
  n numeration 1017.9
  adj inclusive 772.6
numberless 884.10
number one
  n urine 12.5
  victor 411.2
  self 865.5
  v urinate 12.14
  adj governing 612.17
  paramount 997.24
number one buzz 1016.14
numbers
  quantity 244.1
  rhythm 709.22
  metrics 720.6
  meter 720.7
  statistics 746.4
  multitude 884.3
  mathematics 1017.1
numbers runner 759.20
Number 10 Downing Street
  228.5
number three buzz 1016.14
numbing
  n relief 120.1
  adj deadening 25.9
  anesthetic 86.47
  relieving 120.9
  cold 1023.14
numerable
  measurable 300.14
  calculable 1017.25
numeral
  n number 1017.3
  adj numeric 1017.23
numerate 1017.17
numeration 1017.9
numerative
  measuring 300.12
  numeric 1017.23
  enumerative 1017.24
numerator ratio 1017.7
  division 1017.12
numeric
  mathematical 1017.22
  numeral 1017.23
numerous
  much 247.8
  large 257.16
  plural 883.7
  many 884.6

plentiful 991.7
numinous
awesome 122.11
unintelligible 522.13
illustrious 662.19
almighty 677.17
sacred 685.7
sorcerous 690.14
supernatural 870.15
numismatic 728.30
numismatics 728.22
numskull 924.4
nun marker 517.10
celibate 565.2
sister 699.17
nuncio
messenger 353.1
diplomat 576.6
nunnery 703.6
nuptial
v join in marriage 563.14
adj sexual 75.25
matrimonial 563.18
nuptials 563.3
nurse
n health care professional
90.8
sister 90.10
nursemaid 1008.8
v nourish 8.19
treat 91.24
foster 449.16
hold 474.7
train 568.13
care for 1008.19
nursemaid maid 577.8
nurse 1008.8
nursery bedroom 197.7
hospital room 197.25
preschool 567.2
skiing 753.1
birthplace 886.8
conservatory 1069.11
nurseryman 1069.6
nursery school 567.2
nursing home 1009.4
nurture
n nutrition 7.1
nutriment 10.3
support 449.3
training 568.3
protectorship 1008.2
v nourish 7.17
feed 8.19
look after 339.9
encourage 375.21
make better 392.9
foster 449.16
hold 474.7
train 568.13
care for 1008.19
raise 1070.6
nut
n food 10.39
enthusiast 101.5
seed 310.31
specialist 866.3
oddity 870.4
lunatic 926.16
fanatic 926.18
freak 927.4

v harvest 1069.19
nuthouse 926.14
Nutrasweet 66.2
nutrient
n nutritive 7.3
adj nutritious 7.21
nutriment
nutrient 7.3
nourishment 10.3
nutrition
nourishment 7.1
eating 8.1
cooking 11.1
nutritionist 7.15
nutritious
nutritive 7.21
eating 8.31
nutritive value 7.1
nutriture 449.3
nuts
n genitals 2.13
bet 759.3
poker 759.10
adj crazy 926.27
nuts about
enthusiastic 101.11
crazy about 104.29
nuts and bolts 1040.4
nutshell
n modicum 248.2
adj shortened 268.9
abridged 557.6
nutty flavorful 63.9
foolish 923.9
crazy 926.27
eccentric 927.6
nuzzle stroke 73.8
cuddle 562.17
nymph larva 302.12
embryo 305.14
insect 311.32
deity 678.9
nymphet
schoolgirl 302.8
strumpet 665.14
nymph 678.9
nymphomania
sexual desire 75.5
lasciviousness 665.5
nymphomaniac
sexual pervert 75.16
strumpet 665.14
oaf bungler 414.8
simple soul 416.3
lout 924.5
oafish bungling 414.20
stupid 922.15
oak
symbol of strength 15.8
hardness 1046.6
oak leaf 647.5
oar paddle 180.15
boatman 183.5
oarsman 183.5
oath vow 334.4
promise 436.1
profane oath 513.4
oats 10.4
obcordate 279.15
obdurate
insensible 25.6

impenitent 114.5
heartless 144.25
tough 361.10
firm 425.7
hardened 654.17
hard 1046.10
obedience
resignation 134.2
compliance 326.1
submission 433.1
conformity 867.1
obedient
resigned 134.10
compliant 326.3
submissive 433.12
dutiful 641.13
conformable 867.5
obeisance
obsequiousness 138.2
reverence 155.2
submission 433.1
crouch 913.3
obeisant
obsequious 138.14
prostrate 155.10
deferential 433.16
obelisk tower 272.6
monument 549.12
Oberon 678.8
obese corpulent 257.18
oversize 257.23
obesity oversize 257.5
corpulence 257.8
obey accept 134.7
mind 326.2
submit 433.6
obfuscate deform 263.3
conceal 346.6
make unintelligible
522.12
misteach 569.3
darken 1027.9
obituary
n obit 307.13
monument 549.12
history 719.1
adj funereal 309.22
documentary 549.18
object
v protest 333.5
offer resistance 453.3
disapprove 510.10
disagree 789.5
object
n objective 380.2
intent 518.2
syntax 530.2
something 763.3
article 1052.4
objectify
externalize 206.5
visualize 986.15
objecting
protesting 333.7
resistant 453.5
objection demur 325.2
protest 333.2
resistance 453.1
disapproval 510.1
defense 600.2
obstacle 1012.4

objectionable
offensive 98.18
unacceptable 108.10
unpraiseworthy 510.24
objectional 98.18
objective
n will 323.1
object 380.2
adj unfeeling 94.9
impartial 649.9
real 761.15
extrinsic 768.3
true 973.13
unprejudiced 979.12
objectivity
unfeeling 94.1
extrinsicality 768.1
unprejudicedness 979.5
object lesson
warning 399.1
lesson 568.7
example 786.2
objector
dissenter 333.3
oppositionist 452.3
objet d'art 712.9
oblation gift 478.4
offering 696.7
obligate
v commit 436.5
oblige 641.12
adj obliged 641.16
obligated
promised 436.8
chargeable 623.9
obliged 641.16
obligation
act of kindness 143.7
gratitude 150.1
undertaking 404.1
compulsion 424.1
commitment 436.2
security 438.1
debt 623.1
duty 641.1
condition 959.2
necessity 963.1
obligative 530.11
obligatory
mandatory 420.12
compulsory 424.11
binding 641.15
necessary 963.12
oblige be kind 143.9
necessitate 424.5
indulge 427.6
accommodate 449.19
obligate 641.12
require 963.8
obliged grateful 150.5
obligated 641.16
obliging
n indulgence 427.3
adj considerate 143.16
indulgent 427.8
permissive 443.14
courteous 504.14
oblique
n diagonal 204.7
v deviate 204.9
adj transverse 170.9

devious 204.13
circumlocutory 538.14
circuitous 914.7
obliterate
expunge 395.16
declare a moratorium 625.9
efface from the memory
990.6
obliteration
erasure 395.7
moratorium 625.2
forgetfulness 990.1
obliviate 984.4
oblivion
unconsciousness 25.2
insensibility 94.2
carelessness 340.2
thoughtlessness 933.1
forgetfulness 990.1
oblivious asleep 22.22
unconscious 25.8
insensible 94.10
careless 340.11
thoughtless 933.4
inattentive 984.7
abstracted 985.11
forgetful 990.9
oblong
oblongated 267.9
quadrangular 278.9
obloquy criticism 510.4
vilification 513.2
infamy 661.4
obnoxious
offensive 98.18
base 661.12
terrible 1000.9
oboist 710.4
obscene offensive 98.18
cursing 513.8
lascivious 665.29
lewd 666.9
coarse 497.11
obscenity filth 80.7
offensiveness 98.2
coarseness 497.2
cursing 513.3
oath 513.4
lasciviousness 665.5
dirtiness 666.4
obscure
n darkness 1027.1
v blind 30.7
deform 263.3
cover 295.19
cloud 319.7
conceal 346.6
make unintelligible 522.12
misteach 569.3
quibble 936.9
make uncertain 971.15
darken 1027.9
opaque 1031.2
adj inconspicuous 32.6
formless 263.4
concealed 346.11
hard to understand 522.14
vague 522.15
ambiguous 539.4
unrenowned 661.14
uncertain 971.19

dark 1027.13
opaque 1031.3
obscured blinded 30.10
covered 295.31
concealed 346.11
latent 519.5
hard to understand
522.14
dark 1027.13
obscurity
inconspicuousness 32.2
formlessness 263.1
obscuration 522.3
diffuseness 538.1
vagueness 971.4
darkness 1027.1
opaqueness 1031.1
obsequies 309.4
obsequious
servile 138.14
obeisant 155.10
deferential 433.16
flattering 511.8
observable visible 31.6
manifest 348.8
observance regard 27.2
obedience 326.1
vigilance 339.4
custom 373.1
adherence 434.1
observation 434.1
execution 437.4
celebration 487.1
ceremony 580.4
piety 692.1
rite 701.3
conformity 867.1
attention 983.1
observant
vigilant 339.13
respectful 434.4
dutiful 641.13
pious 692.8
belief 953.21
attentive 983.15
observation
regard 27.2
observation post 27.8
observance 434.1
remark 524.3
idea 932.1
surveillance 938.9
opinion 953.6
attention 983.1
observatory 1072.17
observatory
observation post 27.8
astronomical observatory
1072.17
observe see 27.12
look 27.13
obey 326.2
keep 434.2
execute 437.9
celebrate 487.2
remark 524.24
formalize 580.5
perform a rite 701.15
conform 867.3
examine 938.24
heed 983.6

observer
military pilot 185.3
spectator 918.1
examiner 938.17
obsess oppress 98.16
demonize 680.16
bewitch 691.9
possess 926.25
engross 983.13
haunt 988.6
be remembered 989.13
obsessed affected 93.23
bewitched 691.13
possessed 926.33
engrossed 983.17
haunted 988.10
remembering 989.23
obsession
bewitchment 691.2
prepossession 926.13
engrossment 983.3
possession 988.5
obsessive
obsessional 926.34
engrossing 983.20
unforgettable 989.25
obsolesce
fall into disuse 390.9
age 842.9
obsolescence 390.1
obsolete
n archaism 526.12
adj out of action 19.17
disused 390.10
past 837.7
passé 842.15
obstacle
obstruction 293.3
hindrance 1012.4
obstetric 90.15
obstinacy
strength 15.1
refusal 325.1
defiance 327.2
resolution 359.1
perseverance 360.1
stubbornness 361.1
obstinateness 361.1
firmness 425.2
hostility 451.2
resistance 453.1
tenacity 803.3
uninfluenceability 895.2
obstinate strong 15.15
disobedient 327.8
resolute 359.11
persevering 360.8
stubborn 361.8
firm 425.7
oppositional 451.8
adhesive 803.12
uninfluenceable 895.4
obstreperous
noisy 53.13
vociferous 59.10
defiant 327.10
ungovernable 361.12
unruly 671.19
obstruct slow 175.9
stop 293.7
oppose 451.3

fend off 460.10
delay 846.8
get in the way 1012.12
obstructed
stopped 293.11
late 846.16
obstruction
slowing 175.4
clog 293.3
golf 751.1
delay 846.2
hindrance 1012.1
obstacle 1012.4
obstructionist
oppositionist 452.3
hinderer 1012.8
obstructive
n oppositionist 452.3
adj oppositional 451.8
resistant 453.5
dilatory 846.17
hindering 1012.17
obtain fetch 176.16
elicit 192.14
acquire 472.8
receive 479.6
exist 761.8
prevail 864.10
induce 886.11
obtainable
attainable 472.14
accessible 966.8
obtrude intrude 214.5
eject 909.13
obtrusive
conceited 140.11
insolent 142.9
intrusive 214.8
conspicuous 348.12
gaudy 501.20
obtuse insensible 25.6
unfeeling 94.9
blunt 286.3
negative 335.5
dull 922.16
obverse
n opposite side 215.3
front 216.1
likeness 784.3
adj contrapositive 215.5
contrary 779.6
obviate 1012.14
obvious distinct 31.7
manifest 348.8
patent 970.15
occasion
n pretext 376.1
circumstance 766.1
event 831.2
opportunity 843.2
cause 886.1
requirement 963.2
v be timely 843.6
cause 886.10
occasional
circumstantial 766.7
happening 831.9
incidental 843.11
casual 848.3
causal 886.13
occident 161.3

Occident 231.6
occidental 161.14
occipital 217.10
occlude close 293.6
  obstruct 1012.12
occlusion seizure 85.6
  closure 293.1
  hindrance 1012.1
occlusive
  n speech sound 524.12
  adj phonetic 524.30
  hindering 1012.17
occult
  v cover 295.19
  conceal 346.6
  darken 1027.9
  adj secret 345.11
  concealed 346.11
  latent 519.5
  recondite 522.16
  esoteric 689.23
  supernatural 870.15
  spectral 988.7
  immaterial 1053.7
the occult secret 345.5
  supernaturalism 870.7
  immateriality 1053.1
occultation
  disappearance 34.1
  covering 295.1
  concealment 346.1
  eclipse 1027.8
occultism
  supernaturalism 689.2
  esoterics 689.1
  immateriality 1053.1
occultist
  esoteric 689.11
  immaterialist 1053.4
occupancy
  habitation 225.1
  possession 469.1
occupant
  inhabitant 227.2
  tenant 470.4
occupation
  habitation 225.1
  action 328.1
  possession 469.1
  appropriation 480.4
  work 724.1
  vocation 724.6
  operation 889.1
occupational hazard 85.32
occupational medicine
  90.13
occupation layer 296.1
occupied
  inhabited 225.12
  busy 330.21
  engaged 724.15
  absorbed in thought 931.22
  engrossed 983.17
occupy pervade 221.7
  inhabit 225.7
  possess 469.4
  appropriate 480.19
  engage 724.10
  include 772.3
  occupy the mind 931.20
  engross 983.13

occur be present 221.6
  exist 761.8
  happen 831.5
  occur to 931.18
occurrence
  appearance 33.1
  presence 221.1
  existence 761.1
  circumstance 766.1
  event 831.2
  prevalence 864.2
ocean
  sea 240.1
  the deep 240.2
  quantity 247.3
ocean depths
  ocean 240.1
  the deep sea 275.4
ocean floor 240.4
oceanic
  nautical 182.57
  marine 240.8
ocean liner 180.5
oceanographer
  thalassographer 240.7
  measurer 300.9
  earth scientist 1071.2
oceanography
  thalassography 240.6
  sounding 275.5
  earth science 1071.1
Oceanus
  spirit of the sea 240.3
  water god 678.10
ocelot
  variegation 47.6
  wild cat 311.21
ocherous orange 42.2
  yellow 43.4
ochre 40.1
Ockham's razor 484.1
octagonal
  pentagonal 278.10
  eighth 882.20
octave harmonics 709.9
  interval 709.20
  poetry 720.9
  eight 882.4
octet cooperation 450.1
  part music 708.18
  poetry 720.9
  eight 882.4
  electron 1033.3
octogenarian
  old man 304.2
  eighty 882.7
ocular visual 27.20
  optic 29.9
oculist
  ophthalmologist 29.8
  doctor 90.4
OD
  n mariner 183.1
  ship's officer 183.7
  commissioned officer 575.18
  v take sick 85.47
  commit suicide 308.22
odalisque subject 432.7
  demimonde 665.15
odd remaining 256.7
  dissimilar 787.4

  occasional 848.3
  queer 870.11
  sole 872.9
  insane 926.26
  eccentric 927.5
  numeric 1017.23
oddball
  n intruder 774.2
  misfit 789.4
  oddity 870.4
  freak 927.4
  adj odd 870.11
  eccentric 927.6
oddity queerness 870.3
  character 870.4
  curiosity 870.5
  eccentricity 927.1
odd job 724.2
odds advantage 249.2
  gambling odds 759.6
  difference 780.1
  inequality 791.1
  probability 968.1
  even chance 972.7
odds and ends
  remainder 256.1
  notions 735.6
  miscellany 770.13
  hodgepodge 797.6
odiferous 69.9
Odin 458.12
odious filthy 80.23
  offensive 98.18
  unlikable 99.7
  base 661.12
  terrible 1000.9
odium hate 103.1
  infamy 661.4
odor smell 69.1
  fragrance 70.1
  characteristic 865.4
odorize scent 69.7
  perfume 70.8
odorizer 70.6
odorless 72.5
odorous
  odoriferous 69.9
  fragrant 70.9
  malodorous 71.5
odyssey 177.2
Oedipus complex 92.22
oenophile 496.5
oeuvre
  literature 547.12
  complete works 718.1
of 775.13
of age adult 303.12
  marriageable 563.20
of consequence 997.18
of course
  adv consequently 887.7
  certainly 970.23
  interj yes 332.18
off
  n horse race 757.3
  v kill 308.14
  put an end to 395.12
  adj dissonant 61.4
  right 219.4
  idle 331.18
  tainted 393.41

  dissimilar 787.4
  occasional 848.3
  odd 870.11
  insane 926.26
  delirious 926.31
  erroneous 975.16
  imperfect 1003.4
  below par 1005.10
  adv hence 188.20
  oceanward 240.11
  at a distance 261.14
  prep from 255.14
offal slough 80.9
  refuse 391.4
off and on
  adj occasional 848.3
  adv infrequently 848.4
  alternately 850.11
  irregularly 851.4
  changeably 854.8
  to and fro 916.21
off-balance
  eccentric 160.12
  unbalanced 791.5
  confused 985.12
off-base untimely 844.6
  misbehaving 322.5
  wrong 638.3
  inaccurate 975.17
offbeat
  n beat 709.26
  adj dissimilar 787.4
  unconventional 868.6
  unusual 870.10
off-center
  eccentric 160.12
  distorted 265.10
off chance
  possibility 966.1
  small chance 972.9
off-color off-tone 35.21
  ill 85.56
  wrong 638.3
  risqué 666.7
off-course 164.8
off duty
  on vacation 20.12
  idle 331.18
offend
  give offense 98.11
  provoke 152.21
  affront 156.5
  do wrong 655.4
  offend the eye 1015.5
offender 660.8
offense umbrage 152.2
  provocation 152.11
  indignity 156.2
  violation 435.2
  attack 459.1
  misdeed 655.2
  wrong 674.4
  basketball game 747.3
  hockey 749.3
  fight 754.3
offensive
  n attack 459.1
  adj nasty 64.7
  malodorous 71.5
  objectionable 98.18
  insulting 156.8

warlike 458.20
combative 459.30
vulgar 497.10
ill-bred 505.6
obscene 666.9
terrible 1000.9
hideous 1015.11
offer
n attempt 403.2
proffer 439.1
offering 439.1
giving 478.1
v put to choice 371.21
attempt 403.6
proffer 439.4
give 478.12
bid 733.9
play 745.5
answer 939.4
adduce 957.12
offered 324.7
offering offer 439.1
gift 478.4
donation 478.6
oblation 696.7
game 745.3
offertory
donation 478.6
paean 696.3
oblation 696.7
sacred music 708.17
offer up
provide 385.7
offer 439.4
play 745.5
off-guard
negligent 340.10
unalert 984.8
offhand
adj nonchalant 106.15
careless 340.11
unpremeditated 365.11
extemporaneous 365.12
informal 581.3
adv carelessly 340.18
extemporaneously 365.15
informally 581.4
off hours 331.2
office
n act of kindness 143.7
library 197.6
function 387.5
aid 449.1
ceremony 580.4
bureau 594.4
commission 615.1
divine service 696.8
rite 701.3
duty 724.3
position 724.5
shop 739.7
v direct 573.8
office boy
errand boy 353.4
attendant 577.5
officeholder
official 575.16
office-bearer 610.11
office park 739.1
officer
n executive 574.3

official 575.16
commissioned officer 575.18
policeman 1008.15
v govern 612.11
official
n executive 574.3
officer 575.16
agent 576.3
football 746.3
basketball 747.3
tennis 748.2
golf 751.3
soccer 752.3
boxing 754.3
adj authoritative 417.15
preceptive 419.4
recorded 549.17
governmental 612.16
executive 612.18
occupational 724.16
correct 970.18
officialdom 575.15
officialese
jargon 523.10
political jargon 609.37
officiate
administer 573.11
minister 701.16
function 724.13
baseball 745.5
football 746.5
sit in judgment 946.12
officious
meddlesome 214.9
overactive 330.24
offing
the distance 261.3
the future 839.1
offish arrogant 141.12
reticent 344.10
aloof 583.6
off-key 61.4
off-limits
restricted 210.8
prohibited 444.7
off-message 164.7
off-roading 756.2
off-road racing 744.1
offscourings offal 80.9
remainder 256.1
refuse 391.4
rabble 606.3
off-season
n season 313.1
adj seasonal 313.9
offset
n setoff 338.2
printing 548.1
print 548.3
offshoot 561.4
the opposite 779.2
counteractant 900.3
v set off 338.5
cushion 670.8
go contrary to 779.4
neutralize 900.7
adj neutralizing 900.9
offset printing 548.1
offsetting
n compensation 338.1
neutralization 900.2

adj compensating 338.6
neutralizing 900.9
offshoot fork 171.4
adjunct 254.1
sprig 310.20
offset 561.4
party 617.4
branch 617.10
sect 675.3
member 793.4
effect 887.1
extract 893.3
offshore 240.11
offspring child 302.3
family 559.5
posterity 561.1
descendant 561.3
sequel 835.2
effect 887.1
product 893.1
off the beaten track
secluded 584.8
unusual 870.10
off the cuff
adj extemporaneous 365.12
adv extemporaneously
365.15
off-the-peg clothes 5.54
off the record
adj confidential 345.14
adv confidentially 345.20
off-the-wall
unexpected 131.10
odd 870.11
crazy 926.27
off-topic 776.7
off year 844.2
often frequently 847.6
repeatedly 849.16
ogle
n gaze 27.5
flirtation 562.9
v scrutinize 27.14
gaze 27.15
flirt 562.20
spectate 918.5
ogre frightener 127.9
monster 593.6
oh O! 122.20
my! 122.21
oh boy 95.21
ohm 1032.13
oh my 122.21
oil
n balm 86.11
flattery 511.1
painting 712.13
fuel 1021.1
illuminant 1025.20
oleum 1056.1
v medicate 91.25
smooth 287.5
provision 385.9
flatter 511.6
facilitate 1014.7
fuel 1021.8
grease 1056.8
oiling
facilitation 1014.5
lubrication 1056.6
oil-painting 35.12

oily
slippery 287.12
insincere 354.32
suave 504.18
flattering 511.8
greasy 1056.9
oink out 8.25
ointment
anesthetic 25.3
balm 86.11
unction 701.5
money 728.2
lubricant 1056.3
okay
n consent 441.1
permission 443.1
v consent 441.2
permit 443.9
adj acceptable 107.12
accurate 973.16
excellent 999.13
tolerable 999.20
interj yeah 332.19
okey-dokey
yeah 332.19
consent 441.1
old aged 303.16
disused 390.10
experienced 413.28
former 837.10
age-old 842.10
antiquated 842.13
old age age 303.5
oldness 842.1
old ball 563.6
old codger 304.2
the old country
world region 231.6
fatherland 232.2
old days 837.2
older
n senior 304.5
adj mature 304.7
previous 834.4
senior 842.19
oldest
n senior 304.5
adj older 842.19
Old Faithful 1019.10
old-fashioned
disused 390.10
gallant 504.15
old-fangled 842.16
conservative 853.8
old fogy
back number 842.8
conservative 853.4
dotard 924.9
old hand 413.16
old hat trite 117.9
old-fashioned 842.16
old lady
ladylove 104.14
old woman 304.3
wife 563.8
old-line
conservative 611.17
unchanged 853.8
established 855.13
old maid
fussbudget 495.7

prude 500.11
spinster 565.4
old man beau 104.12
elder 304.2
father 560.9
forefather 560.10
grandfather 560.13
husband 563.7
commissioned officer 575.18
back number 842.8
the Old Man
ship's officer 183.7
commissioned officer 575.18
old master
work of art 712.9
artist 716.1
old money 618.1
old pro
veteran 413.16
professional 726.4
old salt mariner 183.3
veteran 413.16
old saw 974.3
old school 853.4
old story 974.3
Old Testament 683.3
old-timer
old man 304.2
veteran 413.16
back number 842.8
old times 837.2
old wives' tale 954.3
old woman
effeminate male 77.10
old lady 304.3
fussbudget 495.7
grandmother 560.16
wife 563.8
back number 842.8
Old World 231.6
old-world
gallant 504.15
antiquated 842.13
ole 509.22
olfactories 69.5
olfactory 69.12
olio stew 10.11
hodgepodge 797.6
olive 44.4
olive branch 465.2
ology 928.10
Olympian
apathetic 94.13
arrogant 141.12
high 272.14
reticent 344.10
aloof 583.6
impartial 649.9
heavenly 681.12
Olympics 457.3
Olympus 681.9
ombudsman 466.3
omega 820.1
omelet 10.26
omen
n portent 133.3
warning sign 399.3
prediction 962.1
v foreshow 133.9
ominous
portentous 133.16

threatening 514.3
premonitory 962.12
harmful 1000.12
unfortunate 1011.14
omission
deletion 255.5
neglect 340.1
nonaccomplishment 408.1
mismanagement 414.6
nonobservance 435.1
misdeed 655.2
exclusion 773.1
deficiency 795.2
slip 975.4
want 992.4
omit delete 255.12
leave undone 340.7
exclude 773.4
omitting 773.10
omnibus
n public vehicle 179.13
compilation 554.7
adj comprehensive 772.7
whole 792.9
thorough 794.10
omnifarious 783.3
omnipotence 18.3
omnipotent
powerful 18.13
almighty 677.17
omnipresence
all-presence 221.2
completeness 794.1
omnipresent
all-present 221.13
almighty 677.17
thorough 794.10
omniscience 928.6
omniscient
almighty 677.17
knowing 928.15
omnivorous eating 8.31
greedy 100.27
gluttonous 672.6
on
adj addicted 87.25
happening 831.9
adv forward 162.8
on foot 177.43
under way 182.63
after which 835.7
across 901.25
prep at 159.27
toward 161.26
atop 198.16
against 223.25
upon 295.37
with relation to 775.13
on account 622.10
on account of
for 449.26
because of 888.9
on and off 854.8
on and on
increasingly 251.9
continuously 812.10
constantly 847.7
on-again off-again 813.4
on a par 790.7
on approval
at choice 371.27

on trial 942.14
on a wing and a prayer 124.11
on behalf of for 449.26
instead of 862.12
on board here 159.23
on shipboard 182.62
present 221.12
joined 800.13
on call handy 387.20
on demand 421.12
cash 624.25
once
adj former 837.10
adv whenever 821.12
once upon a time 837.14
one time 848.6
singly 872.13
once in a while 848.5
once upon a time 837.14
oncoming
n approach 167.1
beginning 818.1
adj progressive 162.6
approaching 167.4
on condition 959.12
on demand
at demand 421.12
cash 624.25
on duty 330.21
one
n child 302.3
person 312.5
I 872.3
adj quantitative 244.5
married 563.21
almighty 677.17
identical 778.7
whole 792.9
combined 805.5
single 872.7
one and all
n entire 792.3
all 864.4
adj every 864.15
adv unanimously 332.17
completely 794.14
one and only
n one 872.3
adj sole 872.9
one-armed bandit 759.16
one at a time 872.13
one by one
separately 802.27
each 865.19
singly 872.13
on edge nervous 128.11
in suspense 130.12
impatient 135.6
one-hit wonder 828.1
one-horse
insignificant 248.6
inferior 250.6
little 258.10
unimportant 998.18
one-horse town 230.3
180-degree change 859.1
180-degree shift 859.1
101 928.3
one-man band
free agent 430.12
recluse 584.5

one mind 332.5
on end
vertically 200.13
continuously 812.10
oneness accord 455.1
sameness 778.1
agreement 788.1
whole 792.1
simplicity 798.1
particularity 865.1
singleness 872.1
unity 872.1
one-night stand
copulation 75.7
engagement 704.11
one-on-one
n basketball game 747.3
adj contrapositive 215.5
front 216.10
personal 312.15
in opposition 451.9
plain-speaking 535.3
familiar 587.19
one-pack-a-day habit 87.1
one-piece 872.11
onerous
oppressive 98.24
heavy 297.17
laborious 725.18
hampering 1012.18
troublesome 1013.18
oneself 865.5
one-sided sided 218.7
distorted 265.10
partial 650.11
unipartite 872.11
discriminatory 980.12
one-stop
nearby 223.15
handy 387.20
onetime 837.10
one time
adj infrequent 848.2
adv once 848.6
one-track mind 926.13
one-trick pony 413.12
one-upmanship
cunning 415.1
competition 457.2
one-way 161.12
ongoing
n progression 162.1
course 172.2
adj progressive 162.6
improving 392.15
happening 831.9
operating 889.11
on guard
adj vigilant 339.13
cautious 494.8
adv defensively 460.16
on hand present 221.12
in store 386.16
handy 387.20
possessed 469.8
on high
high up 272.21
celestially 681.13
on hold
neglected 340.14
late 846.16

open-eyed
wondering 122.9
vigilant 339.13
curious 981.5
attentive 983.15
open fire
n fire 1019.13
v pull the trigger 459.22
open 818.12
interj attack! 459.32
open forum
forum 423.3
arena 463.1
discussion 541.6
openhanded
liberal 485.4
magnanimous 652.6
openhearted
artless 416.5
liberal 485.4
hospitable 585.11
candid 644.17
opening
appearance 33.1
entree 187.3
entrance 189.5
outlet 190.9
vacancy 222.2
crack 224.2
aperture 292.1
display 348.2
passageway 383.3
position 724.5
beginning 818.1
opportunity 843.2
opening move 818.3
opening night 704.12
open market
marketplace 736.2
stock market 737.1
open mind 979.3
open-minded
nonrestrictive 430.25
influenceable 894.15
open 979.10
openmouthed
vociferous 59.10
wondering 122.9
gaping 292.18
curious 981.5
attentive 983.15
surprised 131.12
openness
approachability 167.2
receptivity 187.9
exteriority 206.1
communicativeness 343.3
manifestness 348.3
artlessness 416.1
plain speech 535.1
talkativeness 540.1
candor 644.4
inclusion 772.1
influenceability 894.5
susceptibility 897.2
accessibility 966.3
open-mindedness 979.3
exposure 1006.3
open question 971.8
open road
wandering 177.3

easy thing 1014.3
open season 313.1
open sesame
n opener 292.10
password 517.12
incantation 691.4
influence 894.6
interj open up! 292.23
open shop 727.3
open to liable to 897.6
accessible 966.8
open to question 971.17
open up
v spread 259.6
open 292.11
come out 348.6
disclose 351.4
confess 351.7
make public 352.11
let oneself go 430.19
propose 439.5
begin 818.12
facilitate 1014.7
interj open sesame! 292.23
open warfare 458.1
opera theater 704.14
score 708.28
musical theater 708.34
operable
usable 387.23
workable 889.10
practicable 966.7
practical 995.6
opera glasses 29.4
operagoer 710.21
opera house 704.14
operant
n doer 726.1
operator 889.4
adj operating 889.11
opera singer 710.13
operate
treat 91.24
pilot 182.14
act 328.4
plot 381.9
use 387.10
trade 737.23
function 889.5
be operative 889.7
operate on treat 91.24
act on 889.6
operatic
dramatic 704.33
vocal 708.50
operating
n motion 172.1
adj acting 328.10
operational 889.11
operating room 197.25
operation
surgery 90.2
surgical intervention 91.19
motion 172.1
action 328.1
act 328.3
function 387.5
utilization 387.8
undertaking 404.1
military operation 458.4
transaction 731.4

workings 889.1
functioning 889.1
performance 892.5
operational
acting 328.10
operative 889.9
operating 889.11
functional 889.12
operative
n secret agent 576.9
detective 576.10
doer 726.1
operator 889.4
adj powerful 18.12
acting 328.10
effectual 387.21
operational 889.9
operator surgeon 90.5
man of action 330.8
telephone operator 347.9
schemer 381.7
politics 610.6
doer 726.1
speculator 737.11
operative 889.4
liveware 1042.17
operetta 708.34
operose
painstaking 339.11
laborious 725.18
difficult 1013.17
ophthalmic eye 2.28
visual 27.20
optic 29.9
ophthalmologist 29.8
opiate
sleep-inducer 22.10
anesthetic 25.3
drug 87.3
opine remark 524.24
judge 946.8
suppose 951.10
think 953.11
opinion advice 422.1
idea 932.1
estimate 946.3
sentiment 953.6
attitude 978.1
opinionated
obstinate 361.8
dogmatic 970.22
opinion poll 938.14
opium 22.10
opossum 311.22
opponent
n adversary 452.1
adj oppositional 451.8
opportune apt 788.10
timely 843.9
expedient 995.5
opportunist
n timeserver 363.4
schemer 381.7
adj scheming 381.13
opportunity turn 825.2
probability 843.2
chance 972.1
oppose
contrapose 215.4
dissent 333.4
deny 335.4

counter 451.3
offer resistance 453.3
disapprove 510.10
go contrary to 779.4
counteract 900.6
compare 943.4
hinder 1012.10
oppose change 853.6
opposed
contrapositive 215.5
unwilling 325.5
oppositional 451.8
disapproving 510.21
contrary 779.6
adverse 1011.13
opposed to 451.10
opposed to change 853.8
opposer 452.3
opposing
n contraposition 215.1
opposition 451.1
resistance 453.1
comparison 943.1
adj contrapositive 215.5
dissenting 333.6
negative 335.5
oppositional 451.8
disapproving 510.21
contrary 779.6
opposing party 452.1
opposing side 452.1
opposite
n inverse 205.4
poles 215.2
contrary 779.2
adj contrapositive 215.5
fronting 216.11
oppositional 451.8
contrary 779.6
adverse 1011.13
adv poles apart 215.6
prep against 223.25
over against 779.10
opposite number
the opposite 779.2
equal 790.4
opposition
contraposition 215.1
refusal 325.1
dissent 333.1
opposing 451.1
resistance 453.1
disapproval 510.1
contrariety 779.1
difference 780.1
disagreement 789.1
counteraction 900.1
comparison 943.1
hindrance 1012.1
oppositional
opponent 451.8
contrary 779.6
counteractive 900.8
opposition party 609.24
oppress
burden 98.16
sadden 112.18
aggrieve 112.19
weight down 297.13
persecute 389.7
domineer 612.15

task 725.16
go hard with 1011.8
oppressed
  sad 112.20
  weighted 297.18
  subjugated 432.14
  downtrodden 432.16
oppression
  affliction 96.8
  dejection 112.3
  stuffiness 173.6
  burden 297.7
  persecution 389.3
  despotism 612.9
oppressive
  burdensome 98.24
  depressing 112.30
  stuffy 173.16
  onerous 297.17
  imperious 417.16
  laborious 725.18
  hampering 1012.18
  troublesome 1013.18
  sultry 1019.28
oppressor 575.14
opprobrium
  vilification 513.2
  infamy 661.4
oppugn
  contradict 451.6
  quarrel 456.11
  dispute 457.21
  go contrary to 779.4
  counteract 900.6
opsimath 572.1
opt 371.13
optic
  n eye 2.9
  vision 27.9
  adj eye 2.28
  visual 27.20
  optical 29.9
optical illusion 976.5
optical instrument 29.1
optician 29.8
optics
  optical physics 29.7
  light 1025.23
optimal 999.16
optimism
  cheerfulness 109.1
  optimisticalness 124.2
  sanguine expectation 130.2
optimist 124.5
optimistic
  cheerful 109.11
  upbeat 124.11
  expectant 130.11
optimum
  n the best 999.8
  adj best 999.16
option discretion 371.2
  free will 430.6
  first option 733.2
  stock option 737.21
optional
  voluntary 324.7
  elective 371.22
optometrist
  oculist 29.8
  doctor 90.4

optometry 29.7
opulence wealth 618.1
  plenty 991.2
opulent
  wealthy 618.14
  plentiful 991.7
opus writing 547.10
  book 554.1
  piece 708.5
  product 893.1
or
  n yellowness 43.1
  heraldry 647.2
  adj yellow 43.4
  conj either[bu8]or 371.29
OR 197.25
oracle
  n wise man 921.1
  Delphic oracle 962.7
  maxim 974.1
  v dogmatize 970.10
oracular
  predictive 962.11
  dogmatic 970.22
oral
  n examination 938.2
  adj mouthlike 292.22
  communicational 343.9
  speech 524.29
  traditional 842.12
oral agreement 332.1
oral history 547.12
orange
  n orangeness 42.1
  adj orangeish 42.2
  color varieties 42.3
orangery 1069.11
orate 543.10
oration 543.2
orator 543.6
oratorical 543.12
oratorio 708.17
oratory
  public speaking 543.1
  eloquence 544.1
  chapel 703.3
orb
  n eye 2.9
  vision 27.9
  region 231.2
  sphere 282.2
  royal insignia 647.3
  occupation 724.4
  stars 1072.4
  adj spherical 282.9
orbit
  n domain 231.2
  rank 245.2
  circle 280.2
  sphere 282.2
  route 383.1
  occupation 724.4
  sphere of influence 894.4
  circuitousness 914.1
  circuit 914.2
  circle 1072.16
  spacecraft 1075.2
  v encircle 280.10
  circle 914.5
orbiting 914.1
orchard 310.14

orchestra
  audience 48.6
  auditorium 704.15
  stage 704.16
  band 710.12
orchestrate 708.46
orchestration
  piece 708.5
  harmonization 709.2
orchestrator 710.20
ordain install 191.4
  command 420.8
  allot 477.9
  legislate 613.10
  appoint 615.11
  legalize 673.9
  frock 698.12
  destine 964.7
ordained
  in orders 698.17
  destined 964.9
ordeal trial 96.9
  occultism 690.3
  test 942.2
order
  n rank 245.2
  manner 384.1
  precept 419.1
  command 420.1
  demand 421.1
  peacefulness 464.2
  nomenclature 527.1
  harmony 533.2
  race 559.4
  caste 607.1
  community 617.2
  fellowship 617.3
  school 617.5
  decoration 646.5
  medal 646.6
  sect 675.3
  good condition 765.3
  arrangement 807.1
  taxonomy 807.1
  arrangement 808.1
  class 809.2
  classifications 809.5
  sequence 815.1
  normality 869.1
  verdict 946.5
  biology 1068.1
  v outfit 5.41
  command 420.8
  demand 421.5
  request 440.9
  direct 573.8
  organize 807.4
  arrange 808.8
  classify 809.6
  exercise influence 894.8
  pass judgment 946.13
ordered
  harmonious 533.8
  uniform 781.5
  orderly 807.6
  arranged 808.14
  regular 850.6
ordering
  direction 573.1
  class 607.1
  arrangement 808.1

organization 808.2
orderless
  formless 263.4
  unordered 810.12
  vague 971.19
orderly
  n hospital staff 90.11
  attendant 577.5
  adj pacific 464.9
  harmonious 533.8
  punctilious 580.10
  uniform 781.5
  consistent 803.11
  ordered 807.6
  arranged 808.14
  regular 850.6
  normal 869.8
  adv regularly 781.8
order of the day
  affairs 831.4
  schedule 965.3
the order of things 809.4
ordinal
  classificational 809.7
  consecutive 812.9
  numeric 1017.23
ordinance rule 419.2
  decree 420.4
  law 673.3
  rite 701.3
ordinary
  n food service 8.11
  heraldry 647.2
  the usual 869.3
  adj medium 246.3
  inferior 250.6
  customary 373.13
  common 497.14
  simple 499.6
  populational 606.8
  prosaic 721.5
  frequent 847.4
  prevalent 864.12
  usual 869.9
  average 1005.8
ordinate
  n coordinates 300.5
  v appoint 615.11
ordination
  admission 187.2
  appointment 615.2
  holy orders 698.10
  organization 808.2
ordnance arms 462.1
  artillery 462.11
ordure feces 12.4
  filth 80.7
ore raw material 406.5
  mineral 1058.2
or else 780.11
organ instrument 384.4
  periodical 555.1
  branch 617.10
  keyboard wind instrument
    711.13
  member 793.4
organ-grinder 710.9
organic
  structural 266.6
  organismic 305.17
  innate 767.8

organic farming 1069.1
organic matter
  living matter 305.1
  animate matter 305.1
organism body 2.1
  structure 266.1
  organization 305.2
  something 763.3
organist 710.8
organization
  contour 262.2
  structure 266.1
  organism 305.2
  plan 381.1
  military unit 461.22
  establishment 617.8
  sect 675.3
  workplace 739.1
  composition 796.1
  order 807.1
  methodization 808.2
  production 892.4
organizational
  associational 617.17
  formational 808.15
organize form 262.7
  construct 266.5
  plan 381.8
  unionize 727.9
  compose 796.3
  league 805.4
  order 807.4
  methodize 808.10
  establish 892.10
organized drunk 88.33
  organic 305.17
  planned 381.12
  arranged 808.14
organized crime
  the underworld 660.10
  illicit business 732.1
organized labor 727.2
organizer
  planner 381.6
  unionist 727.4
  arranger 808.5
  producer 892.7
organ player 710.8
organ stop 711.19
orgasm
  copulation 75.7
  fury 105.8
  spasm 917.6
orgasmic
  lustful 75.27
  frenzied 105.25
  turbulent 671.18
  convulsive 671.23
  jerky 917.19
orgiastic
  frenzied 105.25
  carnal 663.6
  incontinent 665.24
  saturnalian 669.9
orgy spree 88.5
  fury 105.8
  dissipation 669.2
oriel 197.3
orient
  n points of the compass
    161.3

v orientate 161.11
  accustom 373.9
  adj luminous 1025.31
Orient 231.6
oriental 161.14
Oriental 312.3
orientation
  navigation 159.3
  direction 161.1
  bearings 161.4
  habituation 373.7
orienteering 159.3
orienter 422.3
orifice 292.1
origami 291.4
origin
  etymology 526.15
  beginning 818.1
  origination 818.4
  source 886.5
original
  n real thing 337.2
  writing 547.10
  model 786.1
  nonconformist 868.3
  oddity 870.4
  source 886.5
  adj basic 199.8
  native 226.5
  actual 337.5
  unused 390.12
  essential 767.9
  preceding 816.4
  beginning 818.15
  new 841.7
  novel 841.11
  unconventional 868.6
  primary 886.14
  genuine 973.15
  imaginative 986.18
originality
  nonimitation 337.1
  newness 841.1
  nonconformity 868.1
  unconventionality 868.2
  invention 986.3
original sin 655.3
originate
  invent 337.4
  initiate 818.10
  take origin 818.13
  cause 886.10
  result from 887.5
  produce 892.12
  imagine 986.14
origination
  beginning 818.1
  origin 818.4
  source 886.5
  production 892.1
  product 893.1
originative
  causal 886.13
  creative 892.16
  imaginative 986.18
originator
  author 886.4
  producer 892.7
oriole 710.23
orison 696.4
Ormazd 677.5

ornament
  n extra 254.4
  ornamentation 498.1
  figure of speech 536.1
  ornateness 545.4
  honor 646.1
  decoration 646.5
  passage 708.24
  impromptu 708.27
  grace 709.18
  v add 253.4
  decorate 498.8
  make grandiloquent 545.7
ornamental
  decorative 498.10
  artistic 712.19
ornamentalist 716.11
ornamentation
  decoration 498.1
  ornament 498.1
  ornateness 545.4
  architectural element 717.2
  superfluity 993.4
ornamented
  adorned 498.11
  figurative 536.3
ornate elegant 498.12
  purple 545.11
ornery irascible 110.20
  malicious 144.20
  defiant 327.10
  negative 335.5
  perverse 361.11
  oppositional 451.8
  contrary 779.6
  disagreeing 789.6
  counteractive 900.8
orography 237.6
orotund 545.8
orphan
  n survivor 256.3
  derelict 370.4
  v bereave 307.27
  adj bereaved 307.34
orphanage 1009.4
orthodontic 90.15
orthodox
  n true believer 687.4
  adj firm 425.7
  conventional 579.5
  orthodoxical 687.7
  conformist 867.6
Orthodox 675.30
orthodoxy
  firmness 425.2
  religion 675.1
  soundness of doctrine 687
  orthodoxness 687.1
  conformity 867.1
Orthodoxy 675.9
orthogonal
  perpendicular 200.12
  right-angled 278.7
  quadrangular 278.9
orthography 546.4
orthopedic 90.15
orts remainder 256.1
  refuse 391.4
Oscar 646.2
oscillate
  vacillate 362.8

  be frequent 847.3
  recur 850.5
  change 854.5
  vibrate 916.10
oscillating
  vacillating 362.10
  constant 847.5
  oscillatory 916.15
oscillation
  vacillation 362.2
  constancy 847.2
  periodicity 850.2
  changing 854.3
  vibration 916.1
oscillator 916.9
oscillatory
  vacillating 362.10
  periodic 850.7
  oscillating 916.15
oscilloscope
  instrument 916.8
  radar 1036.1
osculate contact
    223.10
  kiss 562.19
Osiris 682.5
osmose 187.13
osmosis
  transferal 176.1
  sorption 187.6
ossified skeleton 2.26
  hardened 1046.13
ossify callous 94.6
  harden 1046.7
ossuary
  mortuary 309.9
  urn 309.12
  tomb 309.16
ostensible
  apparent 33.11
  conspicuous 348.12
  specious 354.27
  pretexted 376.5
  illusory 976.9
ostentation
  display 348.2
  conspicuousness 348.4
  sham 354.3
  ornateness 498.2
  pretension 501.1
  ostentatiousness 501.1
  grandiloquence 545.1
ostentatious
  pretentious 501.18
  grandiloquent 545.8
  ornate 498.12
osteopath 90.4
osteopathy 73.2
ostracism
  disapproval 510.1
  ostracization 586.3
  elimination 773.2
  banishment 909.4
ostracize
  disapprove 510.10
  turn thumbs down 586.6
  exclude 773.4
  banish 909.17
other
  n a different thing 780.3
  adj additional 253.10

unrelated 776.6
another 780.8
fresh 841.8
substitute 862.8
other-directed
  extroverted 92.41
  moved 375.30
  conformable 867.5
other half 563.6
others 256.3
other self
  friend 588.1
  self 865.5
other side 215.3
otherwise
  adj other 780.8
  adv contrarily 779.9
  in other ways 780.11
other woman
  lover 104.10
  mistress 665.17
otherworldly
  heavenly 681.12
  supernatural 870.15
  visionary 986.24
  immaterial 1053.7
  extraterrestrial 1072.26
otic ear 2.28
  auditory 48.13
otiose idle 331.18
  fruitless 391.12
  unserviceable 391.14
  trivial 998.19
otology 48.9
ought to 641.3
oui 332.18
Ouija 689.6
ounce
  modicum 248.2
  weight 297.8
oust depose 447.4
  eject 909.13
  evict 909.15
ouster
  ejection 909.1
  eviction 909.2
  ejector 909.11
out
  n outlet 190.9
  excuse 600.4
  game 745.3
  v be revealed 351.8
  fight fire 1022.7
  adj asleep 22.22
  unconscious 25.8
  dead-drunk 88.32
  dislocated 160.9
  exterior 206.7
  disused 390.10
  dissimilar 787.4
  old-fashioned 842.16
  odd 870.11
  erroneous 975.16
  extinguished 1022.11
  adv to the point of
    exhaustion 21.14
  audibly 50.18
  hence 188.20
  forth 190.21
  externally 206.10
  at a loss 473.9

prep from 188.21
out of 190.22
outage 795.2
out-and-out
  downright 247.12
  thorough 794.10
  unqualified 960.2
outback
  n open space 158.4
  hinterland 233.2
  remote region 261.4
  wasteland 891.2
  adj hinterland 233.9
  secluded 584.8
outbalance 297.14
outbrave 492.11
outbreak
  emotional outburst 105.9
  revolt 327.4
  outburst 671.6
  beginning 818.1
outbuilding 228.9
outburst
  exclamation 59.2
  emotional outburst 105.9
  outburst of anger 152.9
  ejection 190.3
  outbreak 671.6
  disgorgement 909.7
  flare 1019.14
outcast
  n recluse 584.5
  social outcast 586.4
  exclusiveness 773.3
  alien 774.3
  oddity 870.4
  adj unplaced 160.10
  forlorn 584.12
  cast-off 586.10
outclass outdo 249.9
  defeat 412.6
out cold asleep 22.22
  unconscious 25.8
  dead-drunk 88.32
outcome ending 190.9
  event 831.1
  effect 887.1
  product 893.1
  solution 940.1
outcrop
  n visibility 31.1
  v appear 33.8
outcry
  n noise 53.3
  vociferation 59.4
  lament 115.3
  auction 734.4
  v vociferate 59.8
outdate 842.9
outdated
  disused 390.10
  old-fashioned 842.16
outdistance
  distance 249.10
  reach out 261.5
outdo outrival 249.9
  defeat 412.6
  excel 999.11
outdoor 206.8
outdoors
  n outside 206.3

adv out of doors 206.11
outer 206.7
outermost 206.7
outer space
  the universe 158.1
  remote region 261.4
  depths 275.3
  space 1072.3
outface 492.11
outfield
  playground 743.11
  baseball 745.1
outfielder 745.2
outfit
  n wardrobe 5.2
  costume 5.9
  equipment 385.4
  military unit 461.22
  impedimenta 471.3
  clique 617.6
  team 617.7
  company 770.3
  set 770.12
  v costume 5.41
  equip 385.8
outflank 415.11
outflow
  n outflowing 190.4
  flow 238.4
  spendings 626.2
  v run out 190.13
outflowing
  n outflow 190.4
  adj outgoing 190.19
out for after 382.12
  out to 403.17
  searching 938.38
out for oneself
  v stand on one's own two
    feet 430.20
  adj pitiless 146.3
outgoer 190.10
outgoing
  n egress 190.2
  adj extroverted 92.41
  outbound 190.19
  communicative 343.10
out-group
  company 770.3
  exclusiveness 773.3
outgrow develop 14.2
  grow 259.7
outgrowth
  bodily development 14.1
  growth 85.39
  expansion 259.3
  effect 887.1
  product 893.1
  extract 893.3
outguess 415.11
outhouse latrine 12.10
  hut 228.9
outing journey 177.5
  disclosure 351.1
out in the open
  openly 348.15
  exposed 1006.15
outland
  n outdoors 206.3
  adj extraneous 774.5
outlander 774.3

outlandish
  wonderful 122.10
  extraterritorial 206.9
  unrefined 497.12
  inelegant 534.2
  extraneous 774.5
  unrelated 776.6
  odd 870.11
  fanciful 986.20
outlast outtalk 540.7
  outstay 827.8
outlaw
  n outcast 586.4
  evildoer 593.1
  criminal 660.9
  exclusiveness 773.3
  alien 774.3
  oddity 870.4
  v prohibit 444.3
  ostracize 586.6
  eliminate 773.5
  banish 909.17
  adj illegal 674.6
outlawed prohibited 444.7
  outcast 586.10
  illegal 674.6
outlawry
  illegality 674.1
  elimination 773.2
  banishment 909.4
outlay
  n spendings 626.2
  v spend 626.5
outlet catharsis 92.25
  egress 190.9
  opening 292.1
  escape 369.1
  passageway 383.3
  sale 734.1
outline
  n exterior 206.2
  boundary 211.2
  contour 262.2
  diagram 381.3
  treatise 556.1
  abridgment 557.1
  reflection 785.7
  structural outline 801.4
  v contour 211.9
  describe 349.9
  line 381.11
  abridge 557.5
  itemize 801.7
outlive 827.8
outlook
  n viewpoint 27.7
  observation post 27.8
  field of view 31.3
  view 33.6
  expectations 130.4
  dueness 639.1
  the future 839.1
  probability 968.1
  mental outlook 978.2
  v outbrave 492.11
out loud 50.18
outlying exterior 206.7
  extrinsic 768.3
outmaneuver
  outdo 249.9
  deceive 356.14

defeat 412.6
outwit 415.11
outmoded
disused 390.10
old-fashioned 842.16
outmost 206.7
outnumber 884.5
out of
v retreat 163.6
prep out of 190.22
out of from 188.21
ex 190.22
escaped 369.11
bereft 473.8
wanting 992.13
out of bounds
n game 746.3
adj restricted 210.8
prohibited 444.7
overpriced 632.12
excessive 993.16
out of character 789.7
out of commission
out of action 19.17
motionless 173.13
impaired 393.38
out of condition 765.7
out of contact 94.9
out of control 430.24
out of danger 1007.6
out-of-date
disused 390.10
anachronous 833.3
old-fashioned 842.16
out-of-doors 206.8
out of favor
disliked 99.9
in disrepute 661.13
out of focus 32.6
out of hand
ungovernable 361.12
extemporaneously 365.15
unrestrained 430.24
out of harm's way 1007.6
out of humor
discontented 108.7
out of temper 110.17
unhappy 112.21
out of it
out of action 19.17
sleepy 22.21
unconscious 25.8
inadequate 250.7
foolish 923.9
unaware 930.12
oblivious 984.7
out of joint
dislocated 160.9
in disrepair 393.37
inappropriate 789.7
separated 802.21
disorderly 810.13
out of keeping
inappropriate 789.7
out of line 868.7
out of kilter
impaired 393.38
out of condition 765.7
disorderly 810.13
out of line
misbehaving 322.5

wrong 638.3
inappropriate 789.7
untimely 844.6
out of keeping 868.7
inaccurate 975.17
out of luck 1011.14
out of one's mind 926.26
out of order
misbehaving 322.5
unserviceable 391.14
in disrepair 393.37
out of condition 765.7
disorderly 810.13
out of line 868.7
inexpedient 996.5
out of phase
n wave 916.4
adj untimely 844.6
out of place
misplaced 160.11
inappropriate 789.7
disorderly 810.13
out of line 868.7
inexpedient 996.5
out-of-pocket
bereft 473.8
at a loss 473.9
poor 619.7
wanting 992.13
out of practice 414.18
out of print 992.11
out of proportion
inappropriate 789.7
inconsistent 789.8
unequal 791.4
out of reach
out-of-the-way 261.9
beyond reach 261.18
inaccessible 967.9
out of season
unseasonal 313.9
inappropriate 789.7
anachronous 833.3
old-fashioned 842.16
scarce 992.11
out of shape
deformed 265.12
out of practice 414.18
out of sight
adj invisible 32.5
gone 34.4
blissful 97.9
absent 222.11
far 261.15
out of reach 261.18
overpriced 632.12
excessive 993.16
excellent 999.13
interj goody! 95.21
out of sorts
ill 85.56
out of humor 110.17
unhappy 112.21
out of step 868.7
out of style 842.16
out of the blue
unexpected 131.10
unexpectedly 131.14
out of the ordinary
unusual 870.10
notable 997.19

out of the question
adj hopeless 125.14
rejected 372.3
impossible 967.7
interj by no means 335.9
phrs I refuse 442.7
out of the running
out of action 19.17
disappointing 132.6
inadequate 250.7
out-of-the-way
unexpected 131.10
deviative 164.7
godforsaken 261.9
out of reach 261.18
secluded 584.8
irrelevant 776.7
farfetched 776.8
occasional 848.3
unconventional 868.6
unusual 870.10
circuitous 914.7
out of this world
blissful 97.9
extreme 247.13
unusual 870.10
excessive 993.16
excellent 999.13
superb 999.15
out of touch 94.9
out of tune
dissonant 61.4
in disrepair 393.37
disaccordant 456.15
different 780.7
inappropriate 789.7
disorderly 810.13
out of line 868.7
out of whack
unserviceable 391.14
impaired 393.38
out of condition 765.7
disagreeing 789.6
disorderly 810.13
out of work 331.18
out on a limb
exposed 1006.15
in trouble 1013.22
outpatient 85.43
outperform 249.9
outpost
frontier 211.5
vanguard 216.2
hinterland 233.2
remote region 261.4
guard 1008.9
outpouring
n outflow 190.4
plenty 991.2
adj outgoing 190.19
output yield 472.5
receipts 627.1
production 893.2
outrage
n indignity 156.2
mistreatment 389.2
injustice 650.4
misdeed 655.2
evil 1000.3
v offend 152.21
insult 156.5

mistreat 389.5
violate 435.4
work evil 1000.6
outrageous
insulting 156.8
overpriced 632.12
undue 640.9
disgraceful 661.11
violent 671.16
absurd 923.11
excessive 993.16
terrible 1000.9
outré 923.11
outreach
outdo 249.9
be long 267.5
deceive 356.14
outwit 415.11
outright
adj downright 247.12
thorough 794.10
unqualified 960.2
adv freely 430.32
free and clear 469.12
completely 794.14
outrun
n skiing 753.1
v overtake 174.13
outdo 249.9
defeat 412.6
outset
n beginning 818.1
v set out 188.8
outshine
outdo 249.9
defeat 412.6
outside
n appearance 33.2
exterior 206.2
outdoors 206.3
roulette 759.12
adj exterior 206.7
outdoor 206.8
extrinsic 768.3
extraneous 774.5
adv externally 206.10
outdoors 206.11
outside chance
possibility 966.1
small chance 972.9
outside interest 724.7
outside of 773.10
outsider
exclusiveness 773.3
alien 774.3
oddity 870.4
outside the box 868.6
outsize
n oversize 257.5
adj large 247.7
oversize 257.23
outskirts
environment 209.1
bounds 211.1
frontier 211.5
town 230.1
city district 230.6
remote region 261.4
outsmart
deceive 356.14
outwit 415.11

outspoken
  communicative 343.10
  artless 416.5
  free-acting 430.23
  speaking 524.31
  candid 644.17
outstanding
  exterior 206.7
  eminent 247.9
  remarkable 247.10
  superior 249.12
  superlative 249.13
  remaining 256.7
  protruding 283.14
  conspicuous 348.12
  due 623.10
  prominent 662.17
  notable 997.19
outstare 492.11
outstretched 259.11
outstrip lead 165.2
  overtake 174.13
  loom 247.5
  outdo 249.9
outtalk persuade 375.23
  outspeak 540.7
out to 403.17
outward
  adj apparent 33.11
  exterior 206.7
  formal 580.7
  extrinsic 768.3
  adv forth 190.21
outwear 827.8
outweigh excel 249.6
  overweigh 297.14
outwit outdo 249.9
  deceive 356.14
  outfox 415.11
outworn
  disused 390.10
  obsolete 842.15
oval
  n ovule 280.6
  playground 743.11
  track 755.1
  horse racing 757.1
  adj ovate 280.12
ovarian genital 2.29
  glandular 13.8
ovary 2.13
ovation
  celebration 487.1
  applause 509.2
oven kiln 742.5
  hot place 1019.11
over
  adj superior 249.12
  remaining 256.7
  higher 272.19
  ended 820.8
  past 837.7
  surplus 993.18
  adv inversely 205.8
  additionally 253.11
  on high 272.21
  again 849.17
  excessively 993.22
  prep all over 159.28
  through 161.27
  beyond 261.21

on 295.37
  during 821.14
  in excess of 993.26
overabundance 993.2
overabundant 993.19
overact affect 500.12
  overdramatize 704.31
  overdo 993.10
overacted
  affected 500.15
  dramatic 704.33
  overdone 993.21
overactive 330.24
overactivity 330.9
overage excess 256.4
  surplus 993.5
overall
  adj cumulative 770.23
  comprehensive 772.7
  adv throughout 794.17
  generally 864.17
overall length 267.1
overambitious 101.12
over and above
  adj surplus 993.18
  prep with 253.12
  in excess of 993.26
over and over 849.16
over-anxious
  overzealous 101.12
  anxious 126.7
overassess 949.2
overawe
  daunt 127.18
  domineer 612.15
overbearing
  n authoritativeness 417.3
  adj arrogant 141.9
  imperious 417.16
overblown
  past one's prime 303.15
  overfull 993.20
overboard 182.74
overburden
  n onerousness 297.2
  burden 297.7
  overfullness 993.3
  v burden 297.13
  overload 993.15
  go hard with 1011.8
overburdened
  careworn 126.9
  weighted 297.18
  overfull 993.20
overcareful 494.11
overcast
  n atmosphere 184.32
  cloudiness 319.4
  darkening 1027.6
  v cloud 319.7
  darken 1027.9
  adj cloudy 319.8
  gloomy 1027.14
overcautious 494.11
overcharge
  n cathexis 92.34
  surcharge 632.5
  overfullness 993.3
  v exaggerate 355.3
  ornament 545.7
  charge 630.12

overprice 632.7
  overload 993.15
overclouded 319.8
overcoat 5.13
overcome
  v unnerve 128.10
  excel 249.6
  defeat 411.5
  surmount 412.7
  adj dead-drunk 88.32
  overwrought 105.26
  crushed 112.29
  unnerved 128.14
  defeated 412.14
overcompensation
  defense mechanism 92.23
  inequality 791.1
overconfidence
  rashness 493.1
  confidence 970.5
overconfident
  rash 493.7
  confident 970.21
overconscientious
  overfastidious 495.12
  conscientious 644.15
overcooked 11.8
overcount 949.2
overcritical
  overfastidious 495.12
  critical 510.23
overcrossing 383.9
overcrowded
  full 794.11
  teeming 884.9
  overfull 993.20
overdeveloped
  grown 14.3
  oversize 257.23
  expanded 259.12
  excessive 993.16
overdo
  exaggerate 355.3
  overindulge 669.5
  overrun 910.4
  go too far 993.10
overdone done 11.8
  exaggerated 355.4
  affected 500.15
  grandiloquent 545.8
  overwrought 993.21
overdose
  n superabundance 993.2
  cloyer 994.3
  v take sick 85.47
  commit suicide 308.22
  oversupply 993.14
  satiate 994.4
overdraft arrears 623.2
  insolvency 625.3
overdraw
  misrepresent 350.3
  exaggerate 355.3
  overspend 486.7
  overextend 993.13
overdrawn
  exaggerated 355.4
  overdone 993.21
overdress 5.42
overdrive task 725.16
  overdo 993.10

overdue
  expected 130.13
  anachronous 833.3
  late 846.16
overeager
  overzealous 101.12
  reckless 493.8
over-easy 10.26
overeat 672.5
overelaborate
  v overdo 993.10
  adj ornate 498.12
  affected 533.9
  grandiloquent 545.8
overemotional
  emotionalistic 93.19
  excitable 105.28
overemphasis
  exaggeration 355.1
  overdoing 993.6
overemphasize
  overdo 993.10
  emphasize 997.14
overenthusiastic
  overzealous 101.12
  reckless 493.8
  fanatic 926.32
overestimate
  n overestimation 949.1
  v exaggerate 355.3
  overpraise 511.7
  overreckon 949.2
overestimated
  exaggerated 355.4
  overrated 949.3
overexcited 105.26
overexercise
  n overdoing 993.6
  v overdo 993.10
overexert strain 725.10
  overdo 993.10
overexpand 993.13
overexpansion 993.7
overextend
  strain 725.10
  overdraw 993.13
overextension
  overactivity 330.9
  strain 725.2
  overdrawing 993.7
overexuberant 993.19
overfed
  oversize 257.23
  overgorged 672.7
  overfull 993.20
  satiated 994.6
overfill fill 794.7
  overload 993.15
  satiate 994.4
overflow
  n spillage 238.6
  wordiness 538.2
  plenty 991.2
  overfullness 993.3
  v flow over 238.17
  teem with 884.5
  run over 910.7
  abound 991.5
  superabound 993.8
overflowing
  n overflow 238.6

oversimplification
undevelopment 406.4
oversimplicity 798.3
oversize
n outsize 257.5
adj oversized 257.23
oversleep sleep 22.13
miss an opportunity 844.5
be late 846.7
overspend
spend more than one has 486.7
overpay 632.8
overdo 993.10
overspread
v pervade 221.7
cover 295.19
disperse 771.4
bespread 910.5
infest 910.6
superabound 993.8
adj overrun 910.10
overstate
misrepresent 350.3
falsify 354.16
exaggerate 355.3
overestimate 949.2
overstay 846.15
overstep
presume on 640.7
overrun 910.4
transgress 910.9
exceed 993.9
overstrain
n fatigue 21.1
strain 725.2
overdoing 993.6
overextension 993.7
v fatigue 21.4
strain 725.10
overdo 993.10
overextend 993.13
overstuffed
upholstered 295.34
full 794.11
overfull 993.20
satiated 994.6
oversubtle
overfastidious 495.12
sophistical 936.10
oversupply
n superabundance 993.2
surplus 993.5
v overprovide 993.14
oversweet 66.5
overt 348.10
overt act 328.3
overtake
intoxicate 88.23
outstrip 174.13
come after 835.3
overtax
burden 297.13
overprice 632.7
strain 725.10
task 725.16
overdo 993.10
over-the-counter drug 86.4
over the hill
past one's prime 303.15
out of practice 414.18

overthrow
n overturn 205.2
fall 395.3
defeat 412.1
deposal 447.2
change 852.2
revolution 860.1
downthrow 913.2
refutation 958.2
v turn over 205.6
revolt 327.7
destroy 395.20
overcome 412.7
depose 447.4
change 852.7
revolutionize 860.4
overturn 913.6
refute 958.5
overthrown
ruined 395.28
defeated 412.14
disproved 958.7
overtime
basketball game 747.3
hockey 749.3
shift 825.3
overtire 21.4
overtired 21.11
overtone tone 50.2
milieu 209.3
meaning 518.1
implication 519.2
harmonics 709.16
overture
n offer 439.1
prelude 708.26
curtain-raiser 816.2
v make advances 439.7
overturn
n upset 205.2
fall 395.3
defeat 412.1
revolution 860.1
downthrow 913.2
v capsize 182.44
turn over 205.6
destroy 395.20
overcome 412.7
revolutionize 860.4
overthrow 913.6
refute 958.5
overvalue 949.2
overview
scrutiny 27.6
abridgment 557.1
overweening
n presumptuousness 141.2
insolence 142.1
confidence 970.5
adj vain 140.8
presumptuous 141.10
insolent 142.9
rash 493.7
confident 970.21
excessive 993.16
overweight
n oversize 257.5
weight 297.1
overfullness 993.3
v burden 297.13
outweigh 297.14

overload 993.15
adj corpulent 257.18
oversize 257.23
heavy 297.16
overwhelm
be strong 15.9
drown out 53.8
aggrieve 112.19
astonish 122.6
pervade 221.7
overflow 238.17
submerge 367.7
destroy 395.21
whelm 412.8
subdue 432.9
raid 459.20
teem with 884.5
run over 910.7
refute 958.5
oversupply 993.14
overwhelmed
overwrought 105.26
overcome 112.29
wondering 122.9
flooded 238.25
defeated 412.14
overrun 910.10
overwhelming
n permeation 221.3
overflow 238.6
overrunning 910.1
adj impregnable 15.19
exciting 105.30
astonishing 122.12
irresistible 412.18
teeming 884.9
evidential 957.16
overwork
n overdoing 993.6
v work hard 725.13
task 725.16
overdo 993.10
overworked
ornate 498.12
trite 864.16
overwrought
overexcited 105.26
exaggerated 355.4
ornate 498.12
grandiloquent 545.8
overdone 993.21
overzealous
ultrazealous 101.12
obstinate 361.8
reckless 493.8
zealous 692.11
fanatic 926.32
ovine 311.45
oviparous 305.23
ovipyriform 279.14
ovoid
n oval 280.6
adj oval 280.12
spherical 282.9
ovule
oval 280.6
ovum 305.12
egg 305.15
ovum egg 305.12
copulation 75.7
vital force 886.7

owe be indebted 623.5
be liable 897.3
owed payable 623.10
due 639.7
owing payable 623.10
due 639.7
attributable 888.6
owing to
conj resulting from 887.8
prep because of 888.9
owl bird of ill omen 133.5
bird 311.27
owlish 570.17
own
v acknowledge 332.11
confess 351.7
have title to 469.5
adj possessed 469.8
own accord 430.7
owner proprietor 470.2
jockey 757.2
ownership 469.2
own free will 430.7
owning
n confession 351.3
possession 469.1
adj possessing 469.9
ox
symbol of strength 15.8
beast of burden 176.8
cattle 311.6
bungler 414.8
oxcart 179.3
Oxford comma 857.4
Oxford gray 39.4
oxidation decay 393.6
burning 1020.5
oxidize corrode 393.21
burn 1020.24
chemicalize 1060.8
oxygenate air 317.11
vaporize 1067.8
oxymoron
ambiguity 539.1
self-contradiction 779.3
inconsistency 789.2
impossibility 967.1
dilemma 1013.7
oyez! hark! 48.16
attention! 983.22
oyster fowl part 10.23
marine animal 311.29
ozone 317.1
pa 560.10
PA
sound reproduction system 50.11
hospital staff 90.11
practice of medicine 90.13
pablum 65.1
pabulum 10.3
pace
n velocity 172.4
step 177.11
gait 177.12
v lead 165.2
walk 177.27
walk back and forth 177.28
go on horseback 177.34
row 182.53
measure 300.10

pair off average 246.2
  get married 563.15
  league 805.4
  double 873.5
paisano 227.5
pajamas 5.21
pal
  n friend 588.4
  v associate with 582.18
palace 228.7
palace revolution 860.1
paladin defender 460.7
  brave person 492.7
palaestra 463.1
palatable edible 8.33
  tasty 63.8
  desirable 100.30
palate taste 62.1
  taste bud 62.5
  vocal organ 524.18
  discrimination 944.1
palatial
  residential 228.32
  grandiose 501.21
palaver
  n flattery 511.1
  nonsense 520.2
  speech 524.1
  chatter 540.3
  talk 541.2
  conference 541.5
  v flatter 511.5
  chatter 540.5
  confer 541.10
palazzo 228.7
pale
  n bounds 211.1
  enclosed place 212.3
  sphere 231.2
  plot 231.4
  leg 273.6
  heraldry 647.2
  v blur 32.4
  decolor 36.5
  lose color 36.6
  change color 105.19
  take fright 127.11
  fence 212.7
  adj inconspicuous
    32.6
  soft-colored 35.22
  colorless 36.7
  whitish 37.8
  unhealthy 85.54
  dull 117.6
  deathly 307.28
pale blue 45.3
paleface 312.3
paleography
  exegetics 341.8
  linguistics 523.13
  writing system 546.3
  handwriting 547.3
paleolith 842.6
paleolithic 842.20
paleontology 1068.3
palette 712.17
palindrome
  grammar 205.3
  wordplay 489.8
palinode 363.3

palisade
  n precipice 200.3
  fence 212.4
  slope 237.2
  leg 273.6
  v fence 212.7
  fortify 460.9
pall
  n cover 295.2
  graveclothes 309.14
  veil of secrecy 345.3
  v be tedious 118.6
  satiate 994.4
palladium 1008.3
pallbearer 309.7
pallet 901.20
palliate relieve 120.5
  extenuate 600.12
  moderate 670.6
  qualify 959.3
palliative
  n alleviative 86.10
  extenuation 600.5
  moderator 670.3
  adj lenitive 86.40
  relieving 120.9
  justifying 600.13
  alleviative 670.16
  qualifying 959.7
palliative care 83.5
pallid colorless 36.7
  dull 117.6
  terrified 127.26
pallor color 35.1
  paleness 36.2
  dullness 117.1
  deathliness 307.11
palm
  n clutches 474.4
  trophy 646.3
  v touch 73.6
  take 480.13
  steal 482.13
palmate 171.8
palmistry 962.2
palm off on 643.7
palm oil
  incentive 375.7
  gratuity 478.5
palm reading 962.2
palmy 1010.13
palooka fighter 461.2
  boxer 754.2
  jockey 757.2
palp 73.4
palpable
  touchable 73.11
  weighable 297.19
  manifest 348.8
  substantial 763.6
palpate 73.6
palpitant staccato 55.7
  pulsative 916.18
palpitate drum 55.4
  be excited 105.18
  pulsate 916.12
  flutter 917.12
palpitating 916.18
palpitation
  staccato 55.1
  excitement 105.5

  trepidation 127.5
  pulsation 916.3
  flutter 917.4
palsied
  anemic 85.61
  stricken in years 303.18
  shaking 917.17
palsy
  n paralysis 85.27
  shaking 917.2
  v deaden 25.4
  adj chummy 587.20
palsy-walsy
  n friend 588.4
  v befriend 587.11
  adj chummy 587.20
palter
  prevaricate 344.7
  quibble 936.9
paltry
  ungenerous 651.6
  base 661.12
  meager 992.10
  poor 998.21
  inferior 1005.9
paludal 243.3
pampas plain 236.1
  grassland 310.8
pamper
  indulge 427.6
  foster 449.16
pampering 427.3
pamphlet 554.11
pan
  n container 195.1
  face 216.4
  v cook 11.5
  criticize 510.14
  photograph 714.14
  mine 1058.14
Pan
  forest god 678.11
  fertility 890.5
panacea 86.3
panache feather 3.16
  showiness 501.3
pancake
  n griddlecake 10.45
  v land 184.43
panchromatic 714.17
pancreas viscera 2.16
  digestive organ 2.17
  digestion 7.8
pancreatic 13.8
pandect
  treatise 556.1
  abridgment 557.1
  code 673.5
pandemic
  n epidemic 85.5
  adj contagious 85.62
  prevalent 864.12
pandemonium
  noise 53.3
  turbulence 671.2
Pandemonium
  hell 682.1
  utopia 986.11
pander
  n procurer 665.18
  v vulgarize 497.9

  prostitute oneself 665.21
pandering 665.8
pander to
  toady to 138.8
  aid 449.18
  serve 577.13
pandit 571.1
Pandora's box
  affliction 96.8
  trouble 1013.3
pandowdy 10.41
pane
  bread 10.28
  window 292.7
  lamina 296.2
  transparent substance
    1029.2
panegyric
  n praise 509.5
  adj approbatory 509.16
panel
  n partition 213.5
  lamina 296.2
  forum 423.3
  discussion 541.6
  jury 596.6
  litigant 598.11
  assembly 770.2
  v select a jury 598.16
paneling 1054.3
panelist 543.4
panel show 1035.2
panel truck 179.12
pang throe 26.2
  pain 96.5
  compunction 113.2
panhandle 440.15
panhandler
  nonworker 331.11
  beggar 440.8
panhandling 440.6
panic
  n fear 127.1
  nervousness 128.1
  joke 489.6
  bear panic 737.22
  v start 127.12
  put in fear 127.16
  overwhelm 412.8
panicked
  panicky 127.27
  defeated 412.14
panicky
  panic-prone 127.27
  nervous 128.11
  cowardly 491.10
panic room 197.17
panjandrum 502.5
panning
  n ridicule 508.1
  adj ridiculing 508.12
panoply armor 460.3
  throng 770.4
panorama view 33.6
  spectacle 33.7
  picture 712.10
panoramic 772.7
pan out 887.4
pan shot 714.8
pansy weakling 16.6
  homosexual 75.15

pant
n breathing 2.21
v burn out 21.5
be excited 105.18
speak 524.25
be hot 1019.22

Pantaloon
old man 304.2
buffoon 707.10

pantheism
religion 675.5
philosophy 952.5

pantheistic 675.25

pantheon
the gods 678.1
temple 703.2

panther 311.21

panting
n breathlessness 21.3
trepidation 105.5
adj respiratory 2.32
breathless 21.12
eager 101.8
precipitate 401.10

pantomime
n impersonation 349.4
gesture 517.14
actor 707.2
v impersonate 349.12
gesture 517.21
act 704.29

pantry closet 197.15
larder 386.8

pants 5.18

pantywaist
weakling 16.6
effeminate male 77.10

pap diet 7.13
nutriment 10.3
breast 283.6
father 560.10
semiliquid 1062.5

papa 560.10

papacy
mastership 417.7
papality 698.6

papal 698.15

Papal Court 595.3

papalism 675.8

paper
n whiteness 37.2
thinness 270.7
writing 547.10
document 549.5
newspaper 555.2
treatise 556.1
complimentary ticket 634.2
negotiable instrument 728.11
paper stock 1054.5
v face 295.23

paperback 554.3

paper cut 85.38

paper profits 472.3

papers
naturalization 226.3
archives 549.2

paper tiger 500.7

paperweight 297.6

papery frail 16.14
thin 270.16
wasted 393.35

fragile 764.7

papilla 283.6

papillary 283.19

papilloma 283.3

papist
n Catholic 675.19
adj Catholic 675.29
papal 698.15

papoose 302.9

pappose 3.25

pappy
n father 560.10
adj insipid 65.2

papyrus 547.11

par
n mean 246.1
price 738.9
round 751.3
equality 790.1
v golf 751.4
adj equal 790.7

parabola 279.2

parabolical
parabolic 279.13
fictional 722.7

parachute
n chute 181.13
life preserver 397.6
safeguard 1008.3
v bail out 184.47
descend 194.5
plunge 367.6

parachute jump
parachute 181.13
plunge 367.1

parachutist 185.8

parade
n spectacle 33.7
walk 177.10
path 383.2
display 501.4
procession 812.3
v go for a walk 177.29
march 177.30
manifest 348.5
flaunt 501.17
file 812.7

parade ground 463.1

paradiddle 55.1

paradigm
morphology 526.3
model 786.1

paradigm shift 363.1

paradisal
blissful 97.9
heavenly 681.12
ideal 986.23

paradise
observation 27.8
happiness 95.2
preserve 397.7
auditorium 704.15
park 743.14
utopia 986.11
garden 1069.10

Paradise 839.2

paradisiac blissful 97.9
heavenly 681.12

paradox
self-contradiction 779.3
inconsistency 789.2

impossibility 967.1
dilemma 1013.7

paradoxical
self-contradictory 779.8
inconsistent 789.8
impossible 967.7

paradoxical sleep 22.5

paraeducator 571.4

paraffin 1025.20

paragon superior 249.4
ideal 659.4
model 786.4
the best 999.8
pattern of perfection 1002.4
beauty 1016.7

paragraph
n phrase 529.1
part 554.13
treatise 556.1
part of writing 793.2
v diction 532.4

parallel
n map 159.5
paralleler 203.2
zone 231.3
entrenchment 460.5
likeness 784.3
equal 790.4
v be parallel 203.4
relate 775.6
resemble 784.7
agree 788.6
equal 790.5
compare 943.4
be comparable 943.7
adj paralleling 203.6
side 218.6
accompanying 769.9
related 775.9
analogous 784.11
comparative 943.8

parallel bars 725.7

paralleling
parallel 203.6
analogous 784.11

parallelism
alignment 203
coextension 203.1
side 218.1
symmetry 264.1
accompaniment 769.1
similarity 784.1
agreement 788.1
equality 790.1
comparison 943.1

paralogism
syllogism 935.6
specious argument 936.3

paralysis
symptom 85.9
paralyzation 85.27
inaction 329.1

paralytic
n cripple 85.45
adj anemic 85.61
passive 329.6

paralyze disable 19.10
deaden 25.4
numb 94.8
astonish 122.6
terrify 127.17

paralyzed
disabled 19.16
drunk 88.33
terrified 127.26
passive 329.6

paramedic
hospital staff 90.11
parachutist 185.8
diver 367.4

parameter
measure 300.2
condition 959.2

paramount
n master 575.1
potentate 575.8
chief 997.10
adj top 198.10
chief 249.14
governing 612.17
principal 997.24
best 999.16

paramountcy
supremacy 249.3
importance 997.1
superexcellence 999.2

paramour lover 104.11
mistress 665.17

paranoia
mental disorder 92.14
dissociation 92.20
schizophrenia 926.4

paranoid
n psychotic 926.17
adj psychotic 926.28

paranymph
wedding party 563.4
deputy 576.1
assistant 616.6

parapet 1012.5

paraphernalia
equipment 385.4
belongings 471.2

paraphilia 75.11

paraphrase
n reproduction 336.3
translation 341.3
v imitate 336.5
rephrase 341.13

paraplegia 85.27

paraplegic 85.45

paraprofessional
teaching fellow 571.4
assistant 616.6

parapsychology 689.4

parasite
barnacle 138.5
follower 166.2
plant 310.4
vermin 311.36
bloodsucker 311.37
nonworker 331.11
attendance 769.6

parasitic
obsequious 138.14
indolent 331.19
rapacious 480.26
concurrent 899.4

parasitism
obsequiousness 138.2
concurrence 899.1

parasol umbrella 295.7
  shade 1028.1
paratrooper
  parachutist 185.8
  diver 367.4
paratroops
  elite troops 461.15
  army 461.23
parboiled 11.7
Parcae 964.3
parcel
  n amount 244.2
  real estate 471.6
  bundle 770.8
  part 793.1
  a number 884.2
  v package 212.9
  quantify 244.4
  apportion 477.6
  portion out 477.8
  bundle 770.20
  separate 802.18
  dispose 808.9
parceled packed 212.12
  apportioned 477.12
parceling 477.1
parcel of land
  plot 231.4
  field 1069.9
parch shrink 260.9
  be hot 1019.22
  burn 1020.24
  dry 1066.6
parched thirsty 100.26
  shrunk 260.13
  burned 1020.30
  dried 1066.9
parchment
  writing 547.10
  manuscript 547.11
  document 549.5
  fragility 1050.2
  dryness 1066.2
pardner friend 588.4
  partner 616.2
pardon
  n pity 145.1
  excuse 148.2
  acquittal 601.1
  v have pity 145.4
  forgive 148.3
  acquit 601.4
pardonable 600.14
pare peel 6.8
  reduce 252.7
  excise 255.10
  cheapen 633.6
  sever 802.11
paregoric
  n sedative 86.12
  adj sedative 86.45
parent
  n progenitor 560.8
  author 886.4
  v foster 449.16
  adj ancestral 560.17
parentage 560.1
parental
  loving 104.26
  ancestral 560.17
  protective 1008.23

parental unit 559.1
parenthesis
  grammar 205.3
  interjection 213.2
  discontinuity 813.1
parenthesize
  bracket 212.8
  grammaticize 530.16
parenthetical
  interjectional 213.9
  irrelevant 776.7
  incidental 843.11
paresis 85.27
par excellence 249.16
parfait 10.47
par for the course
  n rule 373.4
  predetermination 964.1
  adj medium 246.3
  typical 349.15
  prevalent 864.12
parfum 70.2
parget
  color 35.14
  plaster 295.25
pariah
  recluse 584.5
  outcast 586.4
  oddity 870.4
parietal
  enclosing 212.11
  partitioned 213.11
parietes 213.5
pari-mutuel
  statistics 757.4
  betting system 759.4
  pari-mutuel machine 759.17
paring flake 296.3
  piece 793.3
parish region 231.5
  diocese 698.8
  the laity 700.1
parishioner 700.2
parity price 738.9
  similarity 784.1
  equality 790.1
park
  n enclosed place 212.3
  green 310.7
  grassland 310.8
  woodland 310.13
  preserve 397.7
  armory 462.2
  public park 743.14
  baseball 745.1
  v place 159.12
  settle 159.17
parlance
  language 523.1
  diction 532.1
parlay
  n bet 759.3
  v increase 251.4
  bet 759.25
parley
  n advice 422.1
  peace offer 465.2
  conference 541.5
  v confer 541.10
parliament 613.1
parliamentarianism 612.7

parliamentary
  n train 179.14
  adj governmental 612.16
  legislative 613.11
parlor
  living room 197.5
  workplace 739.1
parlor car 197.10
parlous 1006.9
parochial
  local 231.9
  exclusive 773.9
  narrow-minded 980.10
parochialism
  exclusiveness 773.3
  narrow-mindedness 980.1
parochial school 567.8
parody
  n imitation 336.1
  reproduction 336.3
  bad likeness 350.2
  wit 489.1
  burlesque 508.6
  v imitate 336.5
  misrepresent 350.3
  burlesque 508.11
  lampoon 512.12
parol
  n utterance 524.2
  adj speech 524.29
parole
  n release 431.2
  promise 436.1
  language 523.1
  utterance 524.2
  v release 431.5
parolee 429.11
paroxysm pang 26.2
  seizure 85.6
  outburst 105.9
  fit 152.8
  upheaval 671.5
  spasm 917.6
  frenzy 926.7
parquet check 47.4
  ground covering 199.3
  auditorium 704.15
parrot
  n tedium 118.1
  imitator 336.4
  conformist 867.2
  v mimic 336.6
  repeat 849.7
  memorize 989.16
parrotlike
  tedious 118.9
  imitative 336.9
  diffuse 538.11
  repetitious 849.14
parrotry 336.2
parry prevaricate 344.7
  dodge 368.8
  fend off 460.10
  fight 754.4
  quibble 936.9
  refute 958.5
  prevent 1012.14
parrying
  prevarication 344.4
  fight 754.3
  quibbling 936.5

parse
  grammaticize 530.16
  itemize 801.7
parsimonious
  sparing 484.7
  economical 635.6
  meager 992.10
parsimony
  frugality 484
  parsimoniousness 484.1
  thrift 635.1
  meagerness 992.2
parsing grammar 530.1
  itemization 801.2
parson 699.2
parsonage house 228.5
  pastorage 703.7
part
  n contents 196.1
  region 231.1
  amount 244.2
  a length 267.2
  function 387.5
  estate 471.4
  apportioning 477.5
  section 554.13
  role 704.10
  melody part 708.22
  passage 708.24
  score 708.28
  occupation 724.3
  mode 765.4
  particular 766.3
  portion 793.1
  component 796.2
  v interspace 224.3
  open 292.11
  die 307.18
  apportion 477.6
  divorce 566.5
  disband 771.8
  separate 802.8
  part company 802.19
  adj partial 793.7
  incomplete 795.4
  half 875.5
  partly 793.8
partake eat 8.20
  participate 476.5
  take 480.13
  be involved 898.3
partake in 476.6
partaking
  n participation 476.1
  association 582.6
  adj participating 476.8
part and parcel 796.2
parterre 704.15
parthenogenesis 78.6
parthenogenetic 78.16
Parthian shot
  leave-taking 188.4
  gibe 508.2
  remark 524.3
  sequel 817.1
partial
  n tone 50.2
  adj partisan 617.19
  interested 650.11
  part 793.7
  incomplete 795.4

half 875.5
discriminatory 980.12
imperfect 1003.4
partiality
inclination 100.3
love 104.1
preference 371.5
partisanism 617.13
one-sidedness 650.3
prejudice 980.3
partial to
desirous of 100.22
fond of 104.29
partible 802.26
participant
n participator 476.4
adj participating 476.8
participate
take part 476.5
be involved 898.3
participating 476.8
participation
partaking 476.1
association 582.6
inclusion 772.1
participator 476.4
participial 530.17
participle 530.3
particle
modicum 248.2
minute 258.7
part of speech 530.3
piece 793.3
powder 1051.5
parti-color
n variegation 47.1
v variegate 47.7
adj variegated 47.9
particular
n instance 766.3
part 793.1
event 831.2
citation 957.5
adj meticulous 339.12
selective 371.23
proportionate 477.13
fastidious 495.9
detailed 766.9
classificational 809.7
special 865.12
particularity
meticulousness 339.3
fastidiousness 495.1
circumstantiality 766.4
uniqueness 865
individuality 865.1
characteristic 865.4
oneness 872.1
particularization
description 349.2
circumstantiation 766.5
differentiation 780.4
specialization 865.7
reasoning 935.3
particularize
amplify 538.7
itemize 766.6
differentiate 780.6
specialize 865.9
cite 957.13
be accurate 973.11

parting
n departure 188.1
leave-taking 188.4
death 307.1
disbandment 771.3
separation 802.1
adj departing 188.18
separating 802.25
parting shot
leave-taking 188.4
gibe 508.2
sequel 817.1
partisan
n follower 166.2
irregular 461.16
friend 588.1
party member 609.27
supporter 616.9
adj polarizing 456.17
party 609.44
supporting 617.19
partial 650.11
discriminatory 980.12
partisanism
politics 609.1
partisanship 609.25
association 617.13
partiality 650.3
sectarianism 675.4
partisan politics 609.1
partition
n dividing wall 213.5
apportionment 477.1
separation 802.1
bisector 875.3
v set apart 213.8
apportion 477.6
diversify 782.2
separate 802.18
partitioned
walled 213.11
separate 802.20
part music 708.18
partner
n participator 476.4
spouse 563.6
companion 588.3
associate 616.2
bridge 758.3
accompanier 769.4
v cooperate 450.3
assemble 770.18
league 805.4
partner in crime
henchman 610.8
collaborator 616.4
partnership
affiliation 450.2
participation 476.1
bar 597.4
association 617.1
company 769.2
part of speech 530.3
parts talent 413.4
substance 763.2
wits 919.2
part time 825.3
part-time 848.3
parturient
pregnant 78.18
beginning 818.15

parturition birth 1.1
origin 818.4
part with discard 390.7
relinquish 475.3
give away 478.21
party
n man 76.5
endorser 332.7
telephoner 347.11
participator 476.4
entertainment 582.11
litigant 598.11
accuser 599.5
political party 609.24
interest 617.4
sect 675.3
festival 743.4
revel 743.6
assembly 770.2
company 770.3
support 901.1
v enjoy oneself 95.14
have a party 582.21
dissipate 669.6
adj partisan 609.44
associating 617.19
party animal 669.3
party down 487.2
party hack
partisan 609.27
politician 610.4
party-hearty 669.7
party line
line 347.17
policy 609.4
party pooper 1012.9
par value worth 630.2
price 738.9
parvenu
n vulgarian 497.6
upstart 606.7
rich man 618.7
modern 841.4
adj populational 606.8
pashadom
mastership 417.7
aristocracy 608.9
pass
n ridge 237.5
valley 237.7
narrow place 270.3
ravine 284.9
trick 356.6
passageway 383.3
proposal 439.2
passport 443.7
thrust 459.3
complimentary ticket 634.2
football 746.3
basketball game 747.3
hockey 749.3
hockey game 749.6
soccer 752.3
bridge 758.3
state 765.1
crisis 843.4
circuit 914.2
danger 1006.1
predicament 1013.4
v excrete 12.12
disappear 34.2

progress 162.2
overtake 174.13
transmit 176.10
travel 177.18
average 246.2
outdistance 249.10
die 307.18
ratify 332.12
communicate 343.7
adopt 371.15
spend 387.13
pass away 390.9
perish 395.23
succeed 409.7
promote 446.2
deliver 478.13
bequeath 478.18
not understand 522.11
legislate 613.10
transfer 629.3
change hands 629.4
football 746.5
basketball 747.4
hockey 749.7
soccer 752.4
bet 759.25
cease to exist 762.6
come to an end 820.6
elapse 821.5
flit 828.6
occur 831.5
be past 837.6
throw 904.10
go by 910.8
not know 930.10
stand the test 942.10
suffice 991.4
exceed 993.9
excel 999.11
passable
acceptable 107.12
tolerable 999.20
mediocre 1005.7
passage duct 2.23
progression 162.1
course 172.2
transferal 176.1
travel 177.1
migration 177.4
voyage 182.6
entrance 189.5
corridor 197.18
valley 237.7
channel 239.1
act 328.3
passageway 383.3
part 554.13
excerpt 557.3
legislation 613.5
phrase 708.24
ornament 709.18
part of writing 793.2
conversion 858.1
passageway
n entrance 189.5
corridor 197.18
channel 239.1
opening 292.1
pass 383.3
interj open up! 292.23
pass away 34.2

passbook 628.4
pass by slight 157.6
  reject 372.2
  be inattentive 984.2
passé past 837.7
  obsolete 842.15
passed chosen 371.26
  past 837.7
passenger 178.1
passerby traveler 178.1
  transient 828.4
  spectator 918.1
  witness 957.6
pass for go for 349.10
  impersonate 349.12
  pose as 354.22
passim
  here and there 159.25
  scatteringly 771.12
passing
  n disappearance 34.1
  departure 188.1
  death 307.1
  promotion 446.1
  legislation 613.5
  basketball game 747.3
  game 749.3
  adj vanishing 34.3
  moving 172.7
  flowing 172.8
  traveling 177.36
  medium 246.3
  hasty 401.9
  transient 828.7
  happening 831.9
  adv awesomely 122.15
passing by
  n rejection 372.1
  adj spectating 918.7
  prep through 161.27
passing fair 122.15
passing fancy
  infatuation 104.3
  caprice 364.1
passion
  sexual desire 75.5
  passionateness 93.2
  pain 96.5
  torment 96.7
  desire 100.1
  liking 100.2
  zeal 101.2
  love 104.1
  fury 105.8
  rage 152.10
  will 323.1
  vehemence 544.5
  turbulence 671.2
  sacred music 708.17
  cause 886.9
  mania 926.12
  interest 983.2
passionate lustful 75.27
  fervent 93.18
  zealous 101.9
  amorous 104.25
  heated 105.22
  fiery 105.29
  hot-tempered 110.25
  vehement 544.13
  turbulent 671.22

  interested 983.16
passionless
  unfeeling 94.9
  undesirous 102.8
passive
  n voice 530.14
  adj apathetic 94.13
  resigned 134.10
  inert 173.14
  inactive 329.6
  submissive 433.12
  neutral 467.7
  thoughtless 933.4
  incurious 982.3
passive resistance
  resignation 134.2
  disobedience 327.1
  inaction 329.1
  resistance 453.1
passivity apathy 94.4
  resignation 134.2
  quiescence 173.1
  inertness 173.4
  inaction 329.1
  languor 331.6
  submission 433.1
  thoughtlessness 933.1
  incuriosity 982.1
passkey 292.10
pass muster
  meet with approval 509.15
  follow the rule 867.4
  stand the test 942.10
  suffice 991.4
pass out faint 25.5
  disappear 34.2
  be drunk 88.27
  exit 190.12
  die 307.19
  issue 352.14
  deliver 478.13
  disperse 771.4
Passover 701.19
pass over
  condone 148.4
  consign 176.10
  traverse 177.20
  die 307.18
  neglect 340.6
  leave undone 340.7
  slight 340.8
  deliver 478.13
  transfer 629.3
  exclude 773.4
  pass 910.8
  examine 938.24
  be inattentive 984.2
passport 443.7
pass the buck
  transfer 176.10
  outwit 415.11
  impose on 643.7
  be unfaithful 645.12
pass the hat 440.15
pass the time
  waste time 331.13
  occupy 724.10
  vegetate 761.10
pass through
  traverse 177.20
  penetrate 189.8

  experience 831.8
pass up slight 157.6
  leave undone 340.7
  reject 372.2
  abstain 668.7
password 517.12
past
  n tense 530.12
  the past 837.1
  adj gone 837.7
  preterit 837.9
  former 837.10
  obsolete 842.15
  prep beyond 261.21
  unintelligible 522.26
  after 835.8
  in excess of 993.26
pasta 10.33
past due 833.3
paste
  n noodles 10.33
  fake 354.13
  finery 498.3
  jewelry 498.5
  compound 797.5
  adhesive 803.4
  blow 902.5
  semiliquid 1062.5
  pulp 1063.2
  v defeat 412.9
  stick together 803.9
  strike 902.15
  pound 902.16
pastel
  n softness 35.3
  drawing 712.12
  art equipment 712.17
  adj soft-colored 35.22
pasteurization 79.3
pasteurize 79.24
pasteurized 79.27
pastiche
  n imitation 336.1
  reproduction 336.3
  adoption 621.2
  work of art 712.9
  similarity 784.1
  copy 785.1
  hodgepodge 797.6
  v imitate 336.5
pastille 70.4
pastime
  avocation 724.7
  amusement 743.1
past master
  master 413.13
  producer 892.7
pastor 699.2
pastoral
  n scene 712.11
  adj rustic 233.6
  natural 416.6
  pacific 464.9
  ecclesiastic 698.13
  poetic 720.15
pastoral staff
  staff 273.2
  ecclesiastical insignia 647.4
  attire 702.3
pastorate
  the ministry 698.1

  parsonage 703.7
  protectorship 1008.2
pastrami 10.14
pastry 10.41
pasturage feed 10.4
  grassland 310.8
pasture
  n eating 8.1
  feed 10.4
  grassland 310.8
  farm 1069.8
  v feed 8.18
pasty colorless 36.7
  doughy 1047.12
  viscous 1062.12
  pulpy 1063.6
pat
  n thud 52.3
  lump 257.10
  endearment 562.5
  tap 902.7
  v thud 52.15
  caress 562.16
  tap 902.18
  adj apt 788.10
  immovable 855.15
  known 928.26
patch
  n spottiness 47.3
  plot 231.4
  scrap 248.3
  mark 517.5
  military insignia 647.5
  stain 1004.3
  ray 1025.5
  field 1069.9
  v do carelessly 340.9
  repair 396.14
patch test 91.15
patch up
  do carelessly 340.9
  remedy 396.13
  repair 396.14
  settle 466.7
patchwork check 47.4
  hodgepodge 797.6
patchy spotted 47.13
  shabby 393.32
  incomplete 795.4
  mixed 797.14
  discontinuous 813.4
  irregular 851.3
  imperfect 1003.4
pate head 198.6
  brain 919.6
pâté 10.21
patent
  n copyright 210.3
  exemption 430.8
  permission 443.1
  grant 443.5
  privilege 642.2
  church 703.10
  safeguard 1008.3
  v limit 210.5
  preserve 397.8
  authorize 443.11
  protect 1008.18
  adj distinct 31.7
  manifest 348.8
  obvious 970.15

patented limited 210.7
  authorized 443.17
  protected 1008.21
patent medicine
  nostrum 86.2
  medicine 86.4
pater father 560.9
  ancestor 560.10
paterfamilias
  father 560.9
  master 575.1
paternal loving 104.26
  ancestral 560.17
paternalism 612.8
paternity
  blood relationship 559.1
  fatherhood 560.2
Paternoster 696.4
path deviation 164.1
  airway 184.33
  way 383.1
  route 383.1
  trail 383.2
  track 517.8
  circuit 1032.4
pathetic affecting 93.22
  distressing 98.20
  pitiful 145.8
  paltry 998.21
pathfinder
  traveler 178.1
  preparer 405.5
  precursor 816.1
pathogen 85.42
pathogenic
  unhealthful 82.5
  disease-causing 85.53
pathological
  unwholesome 85.55
  diseased 85.60
pathology 85.1
pathos sympathy 93.5
  distressfulness 98.5
  sadness 112.1
  pity 145.1
pathway 383.2
patience
  inexcitability 106.1
  forbearance 134.1
  patientness 134.1
  forgiveness 148.1
  perseverance 360.1
  leniency 427.1
  tolerance 979.4
patient
  n sick person 85.43
  subject 942.7
  adj inexcitable 106.10
  armed with patience 134.9
  forgiving 148.6
  persevering 360.8
  lenient 427.7
  tolerant 979.11
patina verdigris 44.2
  polish 287.2
  lamina 296.2
patinate 44.3
patio 197.21
pâtisserie 10.41
pâtissier 11.3
patois dialect 523.7

jargon 523.9
pat on the back
  n congratulation 149.1
  encouragement 492.8
  v comfort 121.6
  motivate 375.21
  encourage 492.15
  compliment 509.14
patria 232.2
patriarch
  old man 304.2
  father 560.9
  master 575.1
  clergy 699.10
  back number 842.8
patriarchal
  aged 303.16
  ancestral 560.17
  governmental 612.16
  primitive 842.11
patrician
  n aristocrat 607.4
  nobleman 608.4
  adj upper-class 607.10
  noble 608.10
patrifocal 560.17
patrilineage 559.1
patrilineal 559.6
patrimony 479.2
patriot 591.3
patriotic 591.4
patriotism 591.2
patrol
  n protection 1008.1
  watchman 1008.10
  v traverse 177.20
  watch 1008.20
patrol car 179.11
patrolman
  watchman 1008.10
  policeman 1008.15
patron
  ship's officer 183.7
  attender 221.5
  provider 385.6
  giver 478.11
  master 575.1
  benefactor 592.1
  associate 616.9
  supporter 704.26
  financer 729.10
  customer 733.4
  protector 1008.5
patronage
  fosterage 449.4
  recommendation 509.4
  political patronage 609.36
  custom 731.6
  market 733.3
  protectorship 1008.2
patronize
  condescend 137.8
  give oneself airs 141.8
  sponsor 449.15
  finance 729.16
  trade with 731.17
patronizing
  n arrogance 141.1
  adj arrogant 141.9
patronym 527.5
patroon 575.1

patsy dupe 358.2
  cheater 759.22
  scapegoat 862.3
  trusting soul 954.4
patter
  n thud 52.3
  staccato 55.1
  rain 316.1
  jargon 523.9
  acting 704.8
  sales talk 734.5
  v thud 52.15
  drum 55.4
  rain 316.10
  speak 523.18
  talk 524.19
  chatter 540.5
  act 704.29
  pound 902.16
pattern gestalt 92.32
  form 262.1
  structure 266.1
  measure 300.2
  behavior 321.1
  original 337.2
  habit 373.3
  diagram 381.3
  motif 498.7
  paragon 659.4
  harmonics 709.11
  essence 767.2
  model 786.1
  philosophy 932.2
pattern baldness 6.4
patter of tiny feet 1.1
paucity fewness 885.1
  scarcity 992.3
Paul 684.2
paunch 2.18
paunchy 257.18
pauper 619.4
pauperism 619.2
pauperize 619.6
pauperized
  indigent 619.8
  ill-provided 992.12
pause
  n respite 20.2
  demur 325.2
  juncture 524.9
  hiatus 524.9
  notation 709.12
  rest 709.21
  interruption 813.2
  interim 826.1
  delay 846.2
  ceasing 857.3
  grammar 857.4
  v take a rest 20.8
  demur 325.4
  hesitate 362.7
  intervene 826.3
  cease 857.9
pave 295.22
paved 295.31
pavement
  ground covering 199.3
  rug 295.9
  paving 383.6
  foundation 901.6
  building material 1054.2

pave the way
  prepare the way 405.12
  facilitate 1014.7
pavilion 228.9
paw
  n member 2.7
  foot 199.5
  v touch 73.6
pawky cunning 415.12
  shrewd 920.15
pawn
  n inferior 250.2
  instrument 384.4
  pledge 438.2
  chessman 743.17
  v pledge 438.10
  borrow 621.3
pawnbroker
  lender 620.3
  lending institution 620.4
  broker 730.9
pawnshop 620.4
paw print 517.7
pax
  n peace 464.1
  interj silence! 51.14
pax vobiscum
  farewell! 188.22
  peace! 464.11
pay
  n punishment 604.1
  payment 624.4
  v do 328.6
  avail 387.17
  be profitable 472.13
  requite 506.5
  punish 604.11
  render 624.10
  spend 626.5
  yield 627.4
  overpay 632.8
  experience 831.8
payable owed 623.10
  due 639.7
pay as you go 624.17
pay attention
  listen 48.10
  care 339.6
  pay attention 983.8
pay a visit 582.19
pay back
  compensate 338.4
  make restitution 481.5
  requite 506.5
  repay 624.11
  interchange 863.4
payback time 338.1
pay COD 624.17
pay damages 481.5
payday 624.4
pay dearly 632.8
pay dirt 1058.7
payee 479.3
payer 624.9
pay heed 983.8
pay homage to
  show respect for 155.5
  worship 696.11
pay in full 624.13
pay in kind 624.11
pay lip service 693.4

payload freight 176.6
  load 196.2
  charge 462.16
  rocket 1074.3
paymaster payer 624.9
  treasurer 729.12
payment
  incentive 375.7
  punishment 604.1
  defrayal 624
  paying 624.1
  pay 624.4
  expenditure 626.1
pay no mind
  not think 933.2
  be inattentive 984.2
pay off
  bring off the wind 182.23
  drift off course 182.29
  bribe 378.3
  avail 387.17
  be profitable 472.13
  requite 506.5
  pay in full 624.13
  yield 627.4
payoff 767.3
payola 378.2
pay one's debt to society
  429.18
pay one's dues
  do one's duty 641.10
  atone 658.4
pay one's respects 504.12
pay out
  parcel out 477.8
  punish 604.11
  settle with 624.12
  fork out 624.14
  spend 626.5
pay phone 347.4
pay respect to 155.5
payroll 624.4
pay the bill
  pay in full 624.13
  pay for 624.18
  treat 624.19
pay the penalty 658.4
pay the piper
  take one's punishment 604.21
  pay for 624.18
pay through the nose 632.8
pay tribute
  praise 509.12
  honor 646.8
pay TV 1035.1
pay up
  contribute 478.14
  pay in full 624.13
  pay 624.16
PBX 347.8
PBX operator 347.9
PC 1042.2
PCP 87.18
PDQ
  in short order 174.19
  promptly 845.15
pea 310.4
peabrain 924.4
peace silence 51.1
  drugs 87.18
  comfortableness 121.2

quiescence 173.1
  accord 455.1
  peacefulness 464
  pax 464.1
  truce 465.5
  agreement 788.1
  order 807.1
peace and quiet 464.2
peace be with you!
  farewell! 188.22
  peace! 464.11
peaceful calm 106.12
  comfortable 121.11
  quiescent 173.12
  homelike 228.33
  in accord 455.3
  pacific 464.9
  moderate 670.10
peaceful coexistence
  peaceableness 464.4
  foreign policy 609.5
peacekeeper 466.5
peace-keeping force 465.1
peacekeeping mission
  truce 465.5
  mediation 466.1
peacemaker
  pacifist 464.6
  make-peace 466.5
  moderator 670.3
peace offering
  peace offer 465.2
  gift 478.4
  atonement 658.1
  oblation 696.7
peace officer 1008.15
peace of mind
  composure 106.2
  contentment 107.1
  peace of heart 464.3
peace pipe pipe 89.6
  peace offer 465.2
peace talks 148.1
peace treaty 464.7
peach
  n first-rate 999.7
  beauty 1016.8
  v betray 351.6
  inform on 551.13
  adj orange 42.2
peaches-and-cream 35.22
peach fuzz beard 3.8
  smoothness 294.3
peachy feathery 3.27
  excellent 999.13
peachy keen 999.13
peacock
  n variegation 47.6
  male animal 76.8
  bird 311.27
  strutter 501.10
  v pose 500.13
  strut 501.15
peacock blue 45.3
peak
  n summit 198.2
  highland 237.1
  mountain 237.6
  wave 238.14
  plateau 272.4
  projection 285.4

speech sound 524.12
  business cycle 731.10
  limit 794.5
  acme of perfection 1002.3
  v fail 85.48
  top 198.9
  billow 238.22
peaked unhealthy 85.54
  topped 198.12
  thin 270.20
peal
  n blare 53.5
  ringing 54.3
  boom 56.4
  v din 53.7
  blare 53.10
  ring 54.8
  boom 56.9
peanut 258.4
peanut gallery
  observation post 27.8
  auditorium 704.15
peanuts
  petty cash 728.19
  trivia 998.4
pearl
  n comparisons 37.2
  drop 282.3
  good person 659.1
  good thing 999.5
  adj whitish 37.8
  gray 39.4
pearl diver 367.4
pearl gray 39.4
Pearl Harbor 459.2
pearl white 37.8
pearly
  soft-colored 35.22
  whitish 37.8
  gray 39.4
  variegated 47.10
  iridescent 1025.38
pearly gates 87.10
pear-shaped 279.14
peasant
  vulgarian 497.6
  countryman 606.6
  agriculturist 1069.5
peasantry 233.3
peas in a pod 784.5
pea soup 319.3
peat bog 243.1
peat moss 890.4
pebble
  n modicum 248.2
  pebblestone 1059.4
  v floor 295.22
pebbled
  granular 1051.12
  stony 1059.12
peccadillo 655.2
peck
  n quantity 247.3
  lot 247.4
  tap 902.7
  v pick 8.26
  tap 902.18
pecking order 809.4
pectoral 283.19
peculiar
  personal 312.15

indicative 517.23
  other 780.8
  differentiative 780.9
  classificational 809.7
  characteristic 865.13
  odd 870.11
  eccentric 927.5
peculiarity habit 373.3
  mannerism 500.2
  sign 517.1
  characteristic 865.4
  oddity 870.3
  eccentricity 927.1
pecuniary 728.30
pedagogical
  scholastic 568.19
  pedagogic 571.11
pedagogy 568.1
pedal
  n lever 906.4
  v ride 177.33
  push 904.9
  adj plantar 199.9
peddle 734.9
peddler 730.5
peddling 734.2
pedestal 901.8
pedestrian
  n walker 178.6
  adj dull 117.6
  traveling 177.36
  unskillful 414.15
  prosaic 721.5
pediatric 90.15
pedigree register 549.9
  genealogy 560.5
pee
  n urine 12.5
  v urinate 12.14
peek
  n glance 27.4
  v look 27.13
  pry 981.4
peekaboo 1029.4
peel
  n skin 295.3
  lamina 296.2
  stronghold 460.6
  v pare 6.8
  excise 255.10
  tear apart 802.14
peel off pilot 184.37
  come apart 802.9
peel out leave 222.10
  flee 368.11
peep
  n glance 27.4
  v look 27.13
  bird sound 60.5
  reconnoiter 938.28
  pry 981.4
peeper eye 2.9
  sight organ 27.9
peepers 29.3
peephole 27.8
peeping 58.14
peeping tom 918.1
peer
  n nobleman 608.4
  equal 790.4
  v look 27.13

be curious 981.3
peer group
company 770.3
equal 790.4
peerless
matchless 249.15
best 999.16
perfect 1002.6
peeve
n hated thing 103.3
complaint 115.4
grudge 589.5
v annoy 96.13
provoke 152.24
peewee
n runt 258.4
adj tiny 258.11
peg
n tooth 2.8
drink 8.4
liquor 88.7
degree 245.1
leg 273.6
bulge 283.3
stopper 293.4
throw 904.3
v plod 175.7
walk 177.27
hustle 177.28
drudge 725.14
hook 800.8
throw 904.10
Pegasus 311.15
pejorative 512.13
pellet
n sphere 282.2
shot 462.19
v pelt 459.27
pell-mell
agitation 105.4
commotion 810.4
pelt
n hair 3.2
fur 4.2
skin 295.3
hit 902.4
v rain 316.10
stone 459.27
pound 902.16
throw 904.10
shoot 904.12
pelvis 2.13
pen
n enclosed place 212.3
place of confinement 429.7
prison 429.8
writing 547.1
writer 547.13
author 718.3
farm 1069.8
v enclose 212.5
confine 429.12
write 547.19
compose 718.6
penal code 673.5
penal colony 429.8
penal institution 429.8
penalize
bring in a verdict 598.20
condemn 602.3
put a penalty on 603.4

punish 604.10
penalty
judgment 598.9
penance 603.1
penalization 603.1
punishment 604.1
football 746.3
game 749.3
sports event 749.6
golf 751.3
soccer 752.3
impediment 1012.6
penalty box 749.1
penalty shot 749.6
penance
regret 113.4
penalty 603.1
penitence 658.3
seven sacraments 701.4
pen-and-ink
writing 547.1
drawing 712.12
penchant
inclination 100.3
preference 371.5
tendency 896.1
pencil
n art equipment 712.17
ray 1025.5
v mark 517.19
write 547.19
portray 712.18
pendant hanger 202.4
adjunct 254.1
likeness 784.3
pending
adj pendent 202.9
overhanging 202.11
undecided 971.18
prep during 821.14
pendulous
pendent 202.9
oscillating 916.15
pendulum series 812.2
oscillator 916.9
penetrate bite 68.5
affect 93.14
interpenetrate 189.8
insert 191.3
pervade 221.7
perforate 292.15
get across 521.5
perceive 521.9
imbue 797.11
see through 941.8
be remembered 989.13
freeze 1023.10
penetrating
intense 15.22
acrimonious 17.14
shrill 58.14
pungent 68.6
strong 69.10
deep-felt 93.24
piercing 105.31
caustic 144.23
vigorous 544.11
sagacious 920.16
cold 1023.14
penile 2.29

peninsula
continent 235.1
point of land 283.9
penis 2.13
penis envy 154.1
penitence
penitence 113.4
apology 658.2
penance 658.3
oblation 696.7
penitent
n confessor 113.5
adj repentant 113.9
penitential prayer 696.4
penitentiary
n prison 429.8
priest 699.5
adj penitent 113.9
penmanship 547.3
pen name 527.8
pennant flag 647.7
baseball 745.1
penne 10.33
penned enclosed 212.10
written 547.22
penniless bereft 473.8
destitute 619.9
Pennsylvania Dutch 523.7
penny money 728.7
cent 728.8
penny-ante
insignificant 248.6
inferior 250.6
worthless 391.11
penny loafers 5.27
penny pincher 484.4
penny-wise and pound-foolish
parsimonious 484.7
prodigal 486.8
penologist 604.9
penology 604.1
pen pal 553.8
pension
n subsidy 478.8
v depose 447.4
subsidize 478.19
pensioner
dependent 432.6
beneficiary 479.4
student 572.7
employee 577.3
pension off scrap 390.8
depose 447.4
resign 448.2
subsidize 478.19
dismiss 909.19
pensive
melancholy 112.23
cognitive 931.21
abstracted 985.11
pentagon 882.1
pentagram 882.1
pentameter
meter 720.7
five 882.1
pentathlon
contest 755.2
track meet 755.6
five 882.1
penthouse house 228.5
apartment 228.13

roof 295.6
pent-up
enclosed 212.10
confined 429.19
peon sycophant 138.3
subject 432.7
retainer 577.1
peasant 606.6
people
n population 227.1
kinfolk 559.2
race 559.4
family 559.5
the laity 700.1
v settle 159.17
inhabit 225.9
people's republic 232.1
the people
human race 312.1
humankind 312.4
the population 606.1
the populace 606.1
pep energy 17.3
liveliness 330.2
spirit 544.4
pepper
n energy 17.3
v variegate 47.7
flavor 63.7
pull the trigger 459.22
mark 517.19
sprinkle 771.6
throw 904.10
shoot 904.12
pepper-and-salt 47.12
pepper spray 462.22
peppery zestful 68.7
hot-tempered 110.25
pep pills 87.4
peppy energetic 17.13
active 330.17
spirited 544.12
pep rally 375.4
pep talk 543.2
peptic 7.22
peptide 7.6
per by means of 384.13
for each 865.20
conformable to 867.9
per annum 865.19
per capita
proportionate 477.13
each 865.19
perceive sense 24.6
see 27.12
feel 93.10
understand 521.9
know 928.12
detect 941.5
percent 1017.7
percentage
incentive 375.7
benefit 387.4
estate 471.4
gain 472.3
portion 477.5
discount 631.1
part 793.1
expedience 995.1
ratio 1017.7

perceptible visible 31.6
  measurable 300.14
  manifest 348.8
  knowable 928.25
perception
  sensation 24.1
  vision 27.1
  sagacity 920.4
  cognizance 928.2
  idea 932.1
  discernment 944.2
perceptive
  sensible 24.11
  sagacious 920.16
  knowing 928.15
  discerning 944.8
perch
  n birdhouse 228.23
  footing 901.5
  v settle 159.17
  sit 173.10
  get down 194.7
  inhabit 225.7
  rest on 901.22
percolate refine 79.22
  exude 190.15
  trickle 238.18
  be operative 889.7
  liquefy 1064.5
  be damp 1065.11
  soak 1065.13
percolator 79.13
percussion noise 53.3
  concussion 671.8
  percussion instrument
    711.16
  impact 902.3
percussionist 710.10
per diem 865.19
peregrine
  n wanderer 178.2
  adj traveling 177.36
perennial
  n plant 310.3
  adj ephemeral 310.44
  continuous 812.8
  durable 827.10
  indeciduous 829.8
  constant 847.5
perestroika
  reproduction 78.1
  reconstruction 396.5
  rearrangement 808.7
  change 852.1
perfect
  n tense 530.12
  v excel 249.6
  touch up 392.11
  accomplish 407.6
  complete 820.7
  develop 1002.5
  adj downright 247.12
  complete 407.12
  unrestricted 430.27
  thorough 794.10
  unqualified 960.2
  accurate 973.16
  ideal 1002.6
perfect binding 554.14
perfected
  improved 392.13

ended 820.8
  finished 1002.9
perfection
  development 392.2
  accomplishment 407.2
  completion 794.4
  end 820.1
  accuracy 973.5
  flawlessness 1002.1
  faultlessness 1002.1
  acme of perfection 1002.3
perfectionist
  n optimist 124.5
  precision 495.6
  conformist 867.2
  adj optimistic 124.11
perfect storm 96.9
perforate
  v pierce 292.15
  adj apertured 292.19
perform
  execute 328.9
  manifest 348.5
  impersonate 349.12
  accomplish 407.4
  practice 434.3
  act 704.29
  play 708.39
  operate 889.5
  be operative 889.7
  do 892.11
performance
  deed 328.2
  act 328.3
  display 348.2
  impersonation 349.4
  accomplishment 407.1
  observance 434.1
  ceremony 580.4
  acting 704.8
  theatrical performance
    704.12
  execution 708.30
  musical performance 708.33
  operation 889.1
  production 892.5
performance anxiety 126.1
performer
  phony 500.7
  entertainer 707.1
  musician 710.1
  doer 726.1
perform one's duty 641.10
perform surgery 90.14
perfume
  n fragrance 70.1
  perfumery 70.2
  v odorize 69.7
  scent 70.8
  vaporize 1067.8
perfunctory
  indifferent 102.6
  unwilling 325.5
  reluctant 325.6
  careless 340.11
perfuse
  bleed 91.27
  transfer 176.10
  filter in 189.10
  insert 191.3
  pervade 221.7

perhaps
  n guess 951.4
  adv possibly 966.9
perigee
  juxtaposition 223.3
  orbit 1072.16
  spacecraft 1075.2
peril
  n unreliability 971.6
  danger 1006.1
  v endanger 1006.6
perimenopausal 303.14
perimenopause
  middle age 303.4
  change of life 303.7
perimeter
  environment 209.1
  bounds 211.1
period
  menstruation 12.9
  degree 245.1
  season 313.1
  phrase 529.1
  passage 708.24
  meter 720.7
  football 746.3
  game 749.3
  hockey 749.6
  soccer 752.3
  end 820.1
  time 821.1
  portion of time 824
  point 824.1
  grammar 857.4
  wave 916.4
  orbit 1072.16
periodic
  continuous 812.8
  recurrent 849.13
  seasonal 850.7
  oscillating 916.15
periodical
  n publication 352.1
  magazine 555.1
  serial 555.1
  adj journalistic 555.5
  seasonal 850.7
periodic table 1060.2
peripatetic
  n wanderer 178.2
  pedestrian 178.6
  adj traveling 177.36
  discursive 538.13
peripheral
  n circuitry 1042.3
  adj exterior 206.7
  environing 209.8
  outlining 211.14
peripheral vision 27.1
periscope 367.5
perish
  disappear 34.2
  die 307.18
  expire 395.23
  cease to exist 762.6
  age 842.9
perishable
  mortal 307.33
  transient 828.7
perish the thought!
  510.27

perjury
  deliberate falsehood 354.9
  deceitfulness 645.3
perk
  n gain 472.3
  v be operative 889.7
  adj conceited 140.11
perk up refresh 9.2
  energize 17.10
  cheer up 109.9
  improve 392.7
  recuperate 396.19
  elevate 912.5
perky
  lighthearted 109.12
  conceited 140.11
  active 330.17
permanent
  n hairdo 3.15
  adj persevering 360.8
  almighty 677.17
  durable 827.10
  perpetual 829.7
  changeless 853.7
  unchangeable 855.17
permeable
  exudative 190.20
  pervious 292.21
permeate
  pervade 221.7
  imbue 797.11
  soak 1065.13
permission
  ratification 332.4
  exemption 430.8
  consent 441.1
  okay 443.1
  leave 443.1
permissive
  n mood 530.11
  adj negligent 340.10
  lawless 418.5
  unstrict 426.5
  indulgent 427.8
  nonrestrictive 430.25
  consenting 441.4
  admissive 443.14
permit
  n license 443.6
  v ratify 332.12
  consent 441.2
  allow 443.9
  make possible 966.5
permutation
  transformation 852.3
  interchange 863.1
peroxide 36.5
perpendicular
  n vertical 200.2
  straight line 277.2
  adj plumb 200.12
  right-angled 278.7
perpetrate 328.6
perpetrator
  evildoer 593.1
  criminal 645.10
  bad person 660.9
  doer 726.1
perpetual
  almighty 677.17
  infinite 823.3

durable 827.10
everlasting 829.7
constant 847.5
permanent 853.7
perpetual motion 172.2
perpetuate
preserve 829.5
sustain 856.4
perplex
n complex 799.2
v astonish 122.6
be incomprehensible 522.10
complicate 799.3
be unbelievable 955.7
baffle 971.13
confuse 985.7
thwart 1012.15
trouble 1013.13
perquisite gain 472.3
gratuity 478.5
booty 482.11
bonus 624.6
perquisited 385.13
per se
essentially 767.11
singly 872.13
persecute annoy 96.13
make anxious 126.5
oppress 389.7
work evil 1000.6
persecution complex 92.22
persevere endure 134.5
persist 360.2
balk 361.7
win through 409.13
carry on 781.3
continue 856.5
persist
keep alive 306.11
persevere 360.2
insist 421.8
live on 761.9
prevail 781.3
cohere 803.6
endure 827.6
remain 853.5
continue 856.5
persistent
reverberating 54.12
resolute 359.11
persevering 360.8
habitual 373.14
demanding 421.9
uniform 781.5
adhesive 803.12
durable 827.10
permanent 853.7
continuing 856.7
unforgettable 989.25
persistent vegetative state 22.6
person
human form 262.4
human 312.5
first person 530.7
role 704.10
someone 763.3
individual 872.4
body 1052.3
personable
influential 894.13
comely 1016.18

personal
n aspersion 512.4
adj individual 312.15
private 345.13
marked 517.24
particular 865.12
personal ad 352.6
personal appearance 704.12
personal computer 1042.2
personal day 20.3
personal digital assistant
appointment 582.8
computer 1042.2
personal effects
equipment 385.4
belongings 471.2
personal finance 729.3
personal guarantee 436.1
personal initiative 430.7
personality
psyche 92.28
person 312.5
aspersion 512.4
something 763.3
particularity 865.1
influence 894.1
personage 997.8
personal matter 345.5
personal property 471.2
personal responsibility 430.7
personal shopper 733.5
personal time 20.3
personal time off 20.3
persona non grata
outcast 586.4
bad person 660.1
exclusiveness 773.3
personify image 349.11
metaphorize 536.2
materialize 1052.9
personnel
work force 18.9
staff 577.11
baseball team 745.2
football team 746.2
basketball team 747.2
persons 606.1
person-to-person call 347.13
perspective
field of view 31.3
view 33.6
station 159.2
distance 261.1
treatment 712.8
outlook 978.2
perspiration
humor 2.24
sweat 12.7
perspire 12.16
persuade
prevail on 375.23
admonish 422.6
convert 858.16
influence 894.7
convince 953.18
seem true 973.9
persuasion
inducement 375.3
school 617.5
sect 675.3
company 770.3

kind 809.3
conversion 858.6
influence 894.1
conviction 953.5
persuasive
n incentive 375.7
adj suasive 375.29
influential 894.13
convincing 953.26
pert cheerful 109.13
conceited 140.11
impudent 142.10
active 330.17
defiant 454.7
immodest 666.6
pertain 775.5
pertinent relative 775.7
relevant 775.11
perturb distress 96.16
excite 105.14
disorder 810.9
discompose 811.4
agitate 917.10
bewilder 971.12
confuse 985.7
trouble 1013.13
peruke 3.14
peruse scrutinize 27.14
study 570.12
examine 938.24
pervade
permeate 221.7
imbue 797.11
pervasive
deep-felt 93.24
pervading 221.14
thorough 794.10
perve 75.16
perverse
irascible 110.19
negative 335.5
obstinant 361.11
oppositional 451.8
contrary 779.6
nonconformist 789.9
counteractive 900.8
erroneous 975.16
unwieldy 1013.19
pervert
n sexual pervert 75.16
reprobate 660.4
v distort 265.6
misinterpret 342.2
misrepresent 350.3
falsify 354.16
misuse 389.4
corrupt 393.12
misteach 569.3
reason speciously 936.8
pervious
exudative 190.20
permeable 292.21
influenceable 894.15
accessible 966.8
pescetarian 668.4
pesky
annoying 98.22
importunate 440.18
pessimism
dejection 112.3
cynicism 125.6

suspense 130.3
pessimist
n killjoy 112.14
cynic 125.7
adj pessimistic 125.16
pest epidemic 85.5
annoyance 96.2
tormentor 96.10
bore 118.4
bane 1001.1
blight 1001.2
pester annoy 96.13
importune 440.12
nag 510.16
pesthole sty 80.11
epidemic 85.5
pesticide killer 308.11
poison 1001.3
pestilence
epidemic 85.5
bane 1001.1
pestle
n pulverizer 1051.7
v pulverize 1051.9
pet
n ladylove 104.14
favorite 104.15
dudgeon 152.7
endearment term 562.6
v stroke 73.8
indulge 427.6
caress 562.16
rub 1044.6
adj beloved 104.23
petal leaf 310.19
flower 310.28
peter out weaken 16.9
get tired 21.6
be disappointing 132.3
be consumed 388.4
come to nothing 410.13
cease to exist 762.6
be unproductive 891.3
fall through 911.3
pet food 10.4
petit 998.17
petite 258.10
petition
n request 440.1
prayer 696.4
v present a petition 440.10
pray 696.13
pet name 527.7
pet peeve
hated thing 103.3
complaint 115.4
grudge 589.5
petrified
terrified 127.26
antiquated 842.13
hardened 1046.13
mineral 1058.15
stone 1059.11
petroleum
illuminant 1025.20
rock oil 1056.4
petroleum jelly 1056.2
pet subject 866.1
petticoat 77.13
petting touching 73.2
indulgence 427.3

lovemaking 562.2
petty
  insignificant 248.6
  inadequate 250.7
  ungenerous 651.6
  base 661.12
  quibbling 936.14
  narrow-minded 980.10
  puny 998.20
petty cash 728.19
petty larceny 482.2
petty officer first class 575.20
petulant
  discontented 108.7
  peevish 110.22
  plaintive 115.19
  capricious 364.5
pew
  compartment 197.2
  church 703.14
pewter 1058.17
pfc 461.8
PG 706.1
PGA 751.1
pH 1060.3
phalanx
  military unit 461.22
  company 770.3
phallic 2.29
phallic symbol 92.30
phantasm
  deception 356.1
  phantom 976.4
  figment of the imagination
    986.5
  specter 988.1
phantasmagoric 976.8
phantom
  n apparition 33.5
  whiteness 37.2
  frightener 127.9
  spirit 764.3
  phantasm 976.4
  figment of the imagination
    986.5
  specter 988.1
  adj illusory 976.9
  spectral 988.7
  immaterial 1053.7
pharaoh ruler 575.9
  tyrant 575.14
pharmaceutical 86.50
pharmacist 86.35
pharmacy
  pharmacology 86.34
  drugstore 86.36
  hospital room 197.25
pharynx
  digestive system 2.18
  vocal organ 524.18
phase 33.3
phase in 245.4
phase out
  graduate 245.4
  reduce 252.7
  cease to use 390.4
  end 820.5
  turn off 857.12
phases of the moon 854.4
phenom
  marvel 122.2

success 409.4
successful person 409.6
talented person 413.12
phenomenal
  wonderful 122.10
  eventful 831.10
  extraordinary 870.14
phenomenology 978.2
phenomenon
  apparition 33.5
  marvel 122.2
  event 831.2
phew!
  yuck 98.31
  oh! 122.20
philanderer
  beau 104.12
  lover 562.12
  libertine 665.10
philanthropic
  benevolent 143.15
  eleemosynary 478.22
philanthropist
  altruist 143.8
  giver 478.11
philharmonic
  n performance 708.33
  adj musical 708.47
Philistine
  n vulgarian 497.6
  conformist 867.2
  adj callous 94.12
  common 497.14
  secularist 695.16
  unlearned 930.13
philosopher
  wise man 921.1
  scholar 929.3
  reasoner 935.11
  philosophizer 952.8
philosopher king 921.1
philosophical
  calm 106.12
  patient 134.9
  sensible 920.18
  philosophic 952.10
philosophize
  reason 935.15
  be philosophic 952.9
philosophy
  composure 106.2
  ideology 932.8
  reasoning 935.1
  school of thought 952.1
  physics 1018.1
phlebotomy
  bloodletting 91.20
  drawing 192.3
phlegm
  humor 2.24
  apathy 94.4
  languor 331.6
phlegmatic
  n personality type 92.12
  adj apathetic 94.13
  inert 173.14
  languid 331.20
  incurious 982.3
phobia
  hated thing 103.3
  fear 127.1

phobic neurotic 92.39
  afraid 127.22
phoenix 659.5
phone
  n sound 50.1
  telephone 347.4
  speech sound 524.12
  v telephone 347.19
phone book
  telephone number 347.12
  reference book 554.9
  directory 574.10
phoneme 524.12
phone number 347.12
phonetic
  n phonetic symbol 546.2
  adj linguistic 523.19
  phonic 524.30
phonetic alphabet 546.3
phonetics hearing 48.9
  articulatory phonetics
    524.13
  spelling 546.4
phonetic spelling 546.4
phonic auditory 48.13
  acoustic 50.17
  phonetic 524.30
phonograph 50.11
phonograph record
  record 50.12
  recording media 549.10
phony
  n imitator 336.4
  fake 354.13
  impostor 357.6
  hypocrite 357.8
  affecter 500.7
  copy 785.1
  substitute 862.2
  adj imitation 336.8
  spurious 354.26
  assumed 500.16
  similar 784.10
  substitute 862.8
phooey 157.10
phosphate 890.4
phosphoresce 1025.27
photic 1025.42
photochemical 1060.9
photochemical process 548.1
photocomposition 548.2
photocopy 714.5
photoelectric
  electric 1032.30
  electronic 1033.15
photoengraving
  printing 548.1
  engraving 713.2
photo finish
  horse race 757.3
  the same 790.3
photogenic
  photographic 714.17
  luminescent 1025.39
photograph
  n description 349.2
  picture 712.10
  photo 714.3
  print 785.5
  v shoot 714.14
  n image 349.5

photograph album 554.7
photographer
  journalist 555.4
  shutter-bug 714.2
  artist 716.5
photographic
  pictorial 712.20
  photo 714.17
photographic memory 989.2
photographic reproduction
  548.1
photography
  optics 29.7
  printing 548.1
  motion-picture photography
    706.5
  visual arts 712.1
  graphic arts 713.1
  picture-taking 714.1
photometry 1025.23
photon
  energy unit 17.7
  ray 1025.5
  measurement of light
    1025.22
photo-offset 548.1
photo opportunity
  conference 541.5
  event 831.2
  interview 938.11
photoprint 714.5
photosensitive
  photographic 714.17
  photophobic 1025.43
photosphere 1072.13
photostatic copy
  print 714.5
  copy 785.5
phrase
  n sign 518.6
  remark 524.3
  expression 529.1
  part 554.13
  passage 708.24
  part of writing 793.2
  maxim 974.1
  v say 524.22
  express 532.4
  adj phrasal 529.4
phraseology
  language 523.1
  jargon 523.9
  vocabulary 526.13
phrasing diction 529.2
  harmonics 709.2
phylogenesis 861.3
phylum
  nomenclature 527.1
  lineage 560.4
  kind 809.3
  classifications 809.5
  biology 1068.1
physic
  n medicine 86.4
  laxative 86.17
  health care 90.1
  physics 1018.1
  v treat 91.24
physical
  n checkup 938.6
  adj carnal 663.6

piecrust crust 295.14
  fragility 1050.2
pied
  n foot 199.5
  adj mottled 47.12
pied-à-terre 228.8
piedmont 237.1
Pied Piper of Hamelin 377.4
pie-eyed 88.33
pie in the sky 986.23
pier pillar 273.5
  buttress 901.4
  base 901.8
  harbor 1009.6
pierce pain 26.7
  affect 93.14
  hurt 96.17
  penetrate 189.8
  perforate 292.15
  injure 393.13
  stab 459.25
  perceive 521.9
  freeze 1023.10
pierce the ears
  din 53.7
  grate on 58.11
piercing
  n hole 292.3
  stabbing 459.10
  adj intense 15.22
  acrimonious 17.14
  painful 26.10
  loud 53.11
  shrill 58.14
  pungent 68.6
  deep-felt 93.24
  penetrating 105.31
  caustic 144.23
  vigorous 544.11
  violent 671.16
  sagacious 920.16
  cold 1023.14
piety religiousness 692.1
  piousness 692.1
  sanctimony 693.1
piffle
  n bull 520.3
  v talk nonsense 520.5
pig eater 8.16
  pork 10.17
  filthy person 80.13
  cycle 179.8
  heavyweight 257.12
  swine 311.9
  beast 660.6
  glutton 672.3
  jockey 757.2
  slob 810.7
  bigot 980.5
  police 1008.16
  cast 1058.5
pig's eye 758.2
pigeon
  n bird 311.27
  dupe 358.2
  v deceive 356.14
  cheat 356.18
pigeonhole
  n small space 258.3
  hiding place 346.4
  class 809.2

  v put away 390.6
  legislate 613.10
  classify 809.6
  postpone 846.9
  list 871.8
pigeonholed
  neglected 340.14
  classified 809.8
pigeonholes 871.3
pigeon loft 228.23
pigeon-toed 265.12
pig farm 1070.5
piggish hoggish 80.24
  greedy 100.27
  ungulate 311.45
  gluttonous 672.6
piggy 311.9
piggyback 901.25
piggy bank 729.13
pighead 361.6
pig in a poke
  bargain 731.5
  gamble 759.2
piglet
  fledgling 302.10
  swine 311.9
pigment
  n color 35.8
  paint 712.17
  v color 35.14
pigmentation 35.11
pig out stuff 8.25
  overeat 672.5
pigpen sty 80.11
  hovel 228.11
pigskin 746.2
pigsty sty 80.11
  hovel 228.11
pigtail braid 3.7
  chewing tobacco 89.7
  tail 217.6
  coil 281.2
piker vagabond 178.3
  gambler 759.21
Pilates 84.2
pile
  n hair 3.2
  plant beard 3.9
  down 3.19
  lot 247.4
  structure 266.2
  leg 273.6
  texture 294.1
  leaf 310.19
  store 386.1
  gain 472.3
  wealth 618.3
  heap 770.10
  base 901.8
  reactor 1038.13
  v load 159.15
  pile on 770.19
piled on 643.8
piledriver
  strong man 15.6
  influence 894.6
pile in 193.12
pile into 459.15
pile it on
  exaggerate 355.3
  talk big 545.6

  lay it on 993.11
piles 85.37
pile up
  shipwreck 182.42
  store up 386.11
  pile 770.19
pilfer misuse 389.4
  steal 482.13
pilgrim
  n traveler 178.1
  religious 699.16
  v journey 177.21
pilgrimage
  n wandering 177.3
  journey 177.5
  adventure 404.2
  v journey 177.21
piling buttress 901.4
  base 901.8
piling on
  cruelty 144.11
  persecution 389.3
  overdoing 993.6
pill bolus 86.7
  tedious person 118.5
  sphere 282.2
  bad person 660.5
the pill 86.23
pillage
  n plundering 482.6
  v seize 480.14
  plunder 482.17
  rage 671.11
pillar tower 272.6
  column 273.5
  cylinder 282.4
  monument 549.12
  base 901.8
  protector 1008.5
pillar of society
  bourgeois 607.6
  good citizen 659.3
  personage 997.8
pillar of strength 855.6
pillbox 460.6
pillory
  n shackle 428.4
  punishment 605.3
  v ridicule 508.8
  punish 604.10
  disgrace 661.8
  stigmatize 661.9
pillow
  n bedding 901.20
  softness 1047.4
  v support 901.21
pillowcase 295.10
pill popper 87.21
pill pusher 86.35
pill roller 86.35
pilot
  n steersman 183.8
  aviator 185.1
  guide 574.7
  baseball team 745.2
  jockey 757.2
  safeguard 1008.3
  v steer 182.14
  control 184.37
  guide 573.9
  adj experimental 942.11

piloting 161.1
pilot light 1020.10
pilot program 942.3
pimp
  n reprobate 660.4
  procurer 665.18
  v prostitute oneself
    665.21
pimple
  n sore 85.37
  swelling 283.4
  print 517.7
  blemish 1004.1
  v roughen 288.4
pin
  n member 2.7
  stopper 293.4
  jewel 498.6
  insignia 647.1
  bowling 750.1
  golf 751.1
  axle 915.5
  trifle 998.5
  v hook 800.8
  fell 913.5
PIN 517.11
pin a medal on 646.8
pinball machine 759.16
pince-nez 29.3
pincer movement 459.5
pincers
  extractor 192.9
  clutches 474.4
pinch
  n pang 26.2
  modicum 248.2
  small space 258.3
  squeezing 260.2
  urge 375.6
  arrest 429.6
  indigence 619.2
  crisis 843.4
  urgency 997.4
  danger 1006.1
  predicament 1013.4
  crux 1013.8
  v pain 26.7
  converge 169.2
  sail near the wind 182.25
  squeeze 260.8
  arrest 429.16
  rob 482.16
  stint 484.5
  adj substitute 862.8
pinched limited 210.7
  contracted 260.12
  haggard 270.20
  poor 619.7
  straitened 1013.26
pinch-hit
  represent 576.14
  substitute for 862.5
pinch of snuff
  snuff 89.8
  trifle 998.5
pinch pennies 484.5
pin down locate 159.11
  bind 428.10
  stabilize 855.7
  specify 865.11
  fell 913.5

pine
n basketball 747.1
v weaken 16.9
fail 85.48
wish for 100.16
grieve 112.17
languish 393.18
pine away
grieve 112.17
waste 393.19
pine barrens 310.13
pine cone cone 282.5
plant 310.27
pine needle thorn 285.5
leaf 310.19
pine over 112.17
ping 54.3
pinhead top part 198.4
minute 258.7
fool 924.4
pinion
n feather 3.16
member 793.4
v bind 428.10
pink
n pinkness 41.2
radical 611.12
acme of perfection
1002.3
v notch 289.4
perforate 292.15
adj pinkish 41.8
color varieties 41.12
fresh 83.13
radical 611.20
pink elephants 926.10
pinkie 73.5
pink ladies 87.5
pinko 611.12
pink slip 909.5
pinky
pink 41.8
finger 73.5
pin money 728.19
pinnacle summit 198.2
mountain 237.6
tower 272.6
limit 794.5
acme of perfection 1002.3
pin on blame 599.8
attribute to 888.4
pin one's ears back 510.18
pinpoint
n location 159.1
minute 258.7
v locate 159.11
attribute to 888.4
receive 1036.17
adj exact 973.17
pinprick
shallowness 276.1
trifle 998.5
pins 177.15
pins and needles
insensibility 25.1
tingle 74.1
anxiety 126.1
pinstripe
n stripe 47.5
adj striped 47.15
pinstriper 574.3

pinto
n horse 311.11
adj mottled 47.12
pint-size
insignificant 248.6
dwarf 258.13
pinup
photograph 714.3
beauty 1016.8
pinwheel 743.16
pioneer
n traveler 178.1
vanguard 216.2
settler 227.9
engineer 461.14
precursor 816.1
v be in front 216.7
go before 816.3
initiate 818.10
innovate 852.9
adj original 337.5
pioneering
front 216.10
preceding 816.4
pious
pietistic 692.8
sanctimonious 693.5
believing 953.21
pip disease 85.41
seed 310.31
military insignia 647.5
first-rate 999.7
pipe
n screech 58.4
tobacco pipe 89.6
tube 239.6
cylinder 282.4
wind instrument 711.6
v blare 53.10
screech 58.8
bird sound 60.5
transport 176.14
channel 239.15
sigh 318.20
speak 524.25
sing 708.38
blow a horn 708.42
pipe cleaner 89.6
pipe down
v fall silent 51.7
interj silence! 51.14
pipe dream
airy hope 124.4
illusion 976.1
abstractedness 985.2
dream 986.9
pipe-dream muse 985.9
dream 986.17
pipeline
n tube 239.6
inside information 551.2
news channel 552.10
v transport 176.14
piper 710.4
pipes
ship's officer 183.7
bagpipe 711.9
pipette
n drawing off 192.9
tube 239.6
v draw off 192.12

pipe up
vociferate 59.8
blow 318.19
speak up 524.21
strike up 708.37
piping hot 1019.25
pippin 999.7
pips 1036.11
pip-squeak runt 258.4
a nobody 998.7
piquant
appetizing 63.10
pungent 68.6
exciting 105.30
provocative 375.27
alluring 377.8
spirited 544.12
interesting 983.19
pique
n offense 152.2
dudgeon 152.7
v annoy 96.13
stimulate 105.13
provoke 152.24
incite 375.17
rouse 375.19
interest 983.12
piracy
buccaneering 482.7
plagiarism 482.8
pirate
n mariner 183.1
corsair 483.7
plagiarist 483.9
v buccaneer 482.18
plagiarize 482.19
adopt 621.4
pirouette
n whirl 915.2
v rotate 915.9
piss
n humor 2.24
urine 12.5
v urinate 12.14
be discontented 108.6
complain 115.16
make angry 152.23
piss and moan 115.16
piss and vinegar
energy 17.3
gaiety 109.4
liveliness 330.2
piss away 486.5
pissed 153.30
pissed-off 153.30
pissing contest 457.3
pissing match 457.3
piss-poor 1000.8
pistol
n skillful person 413.14
first-rate 999.7
v strike dead 308.18
shoot 904.12
pistol-whip 604.13
piston 904.6
pit
n audience 48.6
deep 275.2
cavity 284.2
well 284.4
indentation 284.6

texture 294.1
tomb 309.16
seed 310.31
arena 463.1
sewer 654.7
auditorium 704.15
stage 704.16
stock exchange 737.7
race 756.3
blemish 1004.1
mine 1058.6
v indent 284.14
the pit 682.1
pit against 456.14
pit bull
sorehead 110.11
boxer 461.2
pitch
n blackness 38.4
tone 50.2
summit 198.2
inclination 204.2
incline 204.4
degree 245.1
plunge 367.1
intonation 524.6
speech 543.2
tuning 709.4
sales talk 734.5
baseball 745.3
field hockey 749.4
soccer 752.1
throw 904.3
flounder 917.8
v establish 159.16
toss 182.55
descend 194.5
tumble 194.8
erect 200.9
incline 204.10
camp 225.11
plunge 367.6
make advances 439.8
play 745.5
shuffle 758.5
throw 904.10
oscillate 916.10
flounder 917.15
adj phonetic 524.30
pitch-black black 38.8
dark 1027.13
pitched battle 457.4
pitcher
baseball team 745.2
thrower 904.7
pitcher's mound 745.1
pitchfork 904.10
pitchforks 316.10
pitch in eat 8.20
set to work 725.15
begin 818.7
pitchiness 38.2
pitchman
publicist 352.9
cheat 357.3
pitch pipe 711.22
piteous
distressing 98.20
pitiful 145.8
pitfall trap 356.12
hidden danger 1006.5

planet 1072.9
planetarium 1072.17
planetary
deviative 164.7
circular 280.11
universal 864.14
celestial 1072.25
plangent
loud 53.11
resonant 54.10
sorrowful 112.26
plaintive 115.19
plank
n strip 271.4
lamina 296.2
platform 609.7
wood 1054.3
v put violently 159.13
face 295.23
plankton 311.29
planned
intentional 380.8
devised 381.12
prepared 405.16
future 839.8
prearranged 965.7
planned obsolescence 390.1
planned parenthood 891.1
plant
n vegetable 310.3
shill 357.5
equipment 385.4
factory 739.3
v establish 159.16
people 225.9
secrete 346.7
tamper with 354.17
fix 855.9
implant 1069.18
adj biological 1068.4
plant and animal life 305.1
plantation
establishment 159.7
peopling 225.2
growth 310.2
farm 1069.8
plant biology 1068.1
plant-eating 8.31
plant growth 14.1
plant oneself 159.17
plaque 549.12
plasma 2.25
plaster
n dressing 86.33
sculpture tool 715.4
adhesive 803.4
pulp 1063.2
v intoxicate 88.23
treat 91.24
smooth 287.5
coat 295.24
cover 295.25
adj on 295.43
plastic
n credit instrument 622.3
thermoplastic 1054.6
resin 1057.1
adj formative 262.9
plasmatic 262.10
docile 433.13
teachable 570.18

changeable 854.6
conformable 867.5
conformist 867.6
influenceable 894.15
ordinary 1005.8
pliant 1047.9
plastic bullet 462.22
plastic surgery surgery 90.2
surgery 91.19
plastic wrap 295.18
plate
n serving 8.10
continent 235.1
plating 295.13
shell 295.15
lamina 296.2
label 517.13
printing surface 548.8
steel plate 713.6
film 714.10
v chromium-plate 295.26
the plate 745.1
plateau
plain 236.1
highlands 237.1
tableland 237.3
degree 245.1
mesa 272.4
interim 826.1
plated
chromium-plated
295.33
layered 296.6
platform
n horizontal 201.3
policy 381.4
arena 463.1
marker 517.10
party platform 609.7
stage 901.13
v make a speech 543.9
platinum 37.7
platinum blond
n hair color 35.9
adj blond 37.9
platitude
generalization 864.8
cliché 974.3
Plato 921.2
Platonic
continent 664.6
Aristotelian 952.12
idealist 1053.8
platoon
military unit 461.22
team 617.7
company 770.3
platter
recording media 549.10
baseball 745.1
plaudit 509.2
plausible
specious 354.27
logical 935.20
sophistical 936.10
believable 953.24
possible 966.6
colorable 968.7
play
n room 158.3
action 328.1

latitude 430.4
joke 489.6
writing 547.10
repute 662.1
stage show 704.4
fun 743.2
frolic 743.5
contest 743.9
sport 744.1
baseball 745.3
football 746.3
basketball game
747.3
tennis 748.2
game 749.3
hockey 749.6
round 751.3
soccer 752.3
bridge 758.3
gambling 759.1
bet 759.3
flicker 1025.8
v jet 238.20
act 328.4
impersonate 349.12
sham 354.21
use 387.10
affect 500.12
stage 704.29
perform 708.39
sport 743.23
compete 744.2
play baseball 745.5
kick 746.5
play basketball 747.4
play tennis 748.3
skate 749.7
play golf 751.4
play soccer 752.4
gamble 759.23
trifle 998.14
flicker 1025.26
playa shore 234.2
plain 236.1
playacting
sham 354.3
acting 704.8
play a joke on 489.14
play along
be willing 324.3
concur 332.9
consent 441.2
play around flirt 562.20
trifle 998.15
play around with
consider 931.12
experiment 942.8
play at cross-purposes
oppose 451.3
go contrary to 779.4
play a waiting game
be patient 134.4
do nothing 329.2
play back 50.14
play ball
cooperate 450.3
play baseball 745.5
play basketball 747.4
playbill 965.3
playbook book 554.1
script 704.21

play both ends against the
middle
play a double game 354.24
exploit 387.16
playboy
sociable person 582.16
dissipater 669.3
player 743.18
play by ear
improvise 365.8
be unprepared 406.6
play 708.39
play-by-play description
account 349.3
circumstances 766.2
play by the rules 644.9
play cat and mouse with 389.7
play date 582.7
play down
minimize 252.9
moderate 670.6
attach little importance to
998.12
play dumb
be silent 51.6
keep secret 345.7
played out
weakened 16.18
tired 21.8
worn-out 393.36
player
competitor 452.2
participator 476.4
motion-picture studio 706.4
actor 707.2
instrumentalist 710.3
frolicker 743.18
athlete 743.19
golfer 751.2
gambler 759.21
component 796.2
influence 894.6
player piano 711.12
play fair 649.6
play fast and loose with
156.4
play favorites 650.8
play for a sucker
deceive 356.19
exploit 387.16
stultify 923.7
play for time 846.11
playful gay 109.14
mischievous 322.6
waggish 489.17
sportive 743.29
play God 640.8
playground 743.11
play hard to get 562.20
play havoc with
spoil 393.10
bungle 414.11
work evil 1000.6
play hide and seek 346.8
play hooky 222.9
playhouse
small space 258.3
theater 704.14
playing card 758.2
playing field arena 463.1
playground 743.11

playmaker
basketball team 747.2
hockey team 749.2
playmate companion 588.3
mistress 665.17
play musical chairs 854.5
playoff baseball 745.1
football 746.1
play off
symmetrize 264.3
offset 338.5
play one's cards close to one's vest 345.7
play one's cards right 321.5
play one's trump card 415.11
play on words
n wordplay 489.8
v joke 489.13
play opposite 704.30
play out 21.5
play politics 468.2
play possum 354.20
playroom
recreation room 197.12
playground 743.11
play Russian roulette 493.6
play safe
take precautions 494.6
keep on the safe side 1007.3
playscape 743.11
playschool 567.2
play second fiddle
efface oneself 139.7
retreat 163.6
retract 168.3
be inferior 250.4
depend on 432.12
play the field 562.20
play the fool
misbehave 322.4
be foolish 923.6
play the game
behave oneself 321.5
conform 579.4
play fair 649.6
follow the rule 867.4
play the lead 704.29
play the market 737.23
play the ponies
gamble 759.23
bet 759.25
play therapy 92.6
play the same old tune 118.8
plaything dupe 358.1
instrument 384.4
toy 743.16
playtime 857.3
play tricks 489.14
play up 997.16
play upon 387.16
play up to
curry favor 138.9
flatter 511.6
cultivate 587.12
play with fire
not know what one is about 414.14
court danger 493.6
take chances 1006.7
playwright 704.22

plaza square 230.8
marketplace 736.2
plea entreaty 440.2
pleadings 598.6
defense 600.2
argument 935.5
plea-bargain sign 437.7
compromise 468.2
plea bargaining 598.12
plead entreat 440.11
enter a plea 598.19
argue 935.16
adduce 957.12
plead guilty
repent 113.7
confess 351.7
plead ignorance 600.11
plead with 375.14
pleasant pleasing 97.6
cheerful 109.11
friendly 587.15
melodious 708.48
good 999.12
rainless 1066.8
pleasantry
pleasantness 97.1
wit 489.1
wittiness 489.2
witticism 489.7
banter 490.1
please
v pleasure 95.6
prefer 371.17
indulge 427.6
interj prithee 440.20
pleasing to the eye 1016.18
pleasure
n enjoyment 95.1
pleasantness 97.1
desire 100.1
will 323.1
option 371.2
command 420.1
amusement 743.1
v please 95.6
pleasure boat 180.3
pleasure principle
psyche 92.28
pleasure-loving 95.4
desire 100.1
sensuality 663.1
pleat
n trench 290.2
pleating 291.2
v furrow 290.3
fold 291.5
pleated furrowed 290.4
folded 291.7
plebe 572.6
plebeian
n common man 606.5
adj common 497.14
populational 606.8
plebiscite vote 371.6
referendum 613.8
pledge
n toast 88.10
oath 334.4
promise 436.1
gage 438.2
member 617.11

debt 623.1
v drink to 88.29
promise 436.4
give security 438.10
contribute 478.14
obligate 641.12
the pledge 668.2
Pleiades nymph 678.9
star 1072.8
plenary great 247.6
unrestricted 430.27
full 794.11
plenary session 423.1
plenipotentiary
omnipotent 18.13
diplomatic 576.17
plenipotentiary power 615.1
plenty
n quantity 247.3
store 386.1
numerousness 884.1
plenitude 991.2
superabundance 993.2
adj sufficient 991.6
plentiful 991.7
adv greatly 247.15
plenum
omnipresence 221.2
council 423.1
assembly 770.2
completeness 794.1
series 812.2
matter 1052.2
universe 1072.1
plethora fullness 794.2
superabundance 993.2
overfullness 993.3
plexus
nervous system 2.14
network 170.3
pliable folded 291.7
weak-willed 362.12
usable 387.23
docile 433.13
teachable 570.18
influenceable 894.15
handy 1014.15
pliant 1047.9
pliers 192.9
plight
n promise 436.1
state 765.1
bewilderment 971.3
danger 1006.1
adversity 1011.1
predicament 1013.4
v promise 436.4
plod
n slow motion 175.2
v plug 175.7
way of walking 177.28
keep doggedly at 360.3
drudge 725.14
plodder
slowpoke 175.5
drudge 726.3
plop
v put violently 159.13
sink 194.6
bubble 320.4
plunge 367.6

adv suddenly 830.9
plot
n plot of ground 231.4
diagram 381.3
intrigue 381.5
stratagem 415.3
real estate 471.6
fable 722.4
field 1069.9
v premeditate 380.7
scheme 381.9
map 381.10
maneuver 415.10
come 839.6
prearrange 965.4
plot a course 182.27
plow maneuver 184.40
furrow 290.3
cultivate 1069.17
plow back into 729.17
plow into
attack 459.15
criticize 510.14
ploy trick 356.6
stratagem 415.3
revel 743.6
pluck
n spunk 359.3
courage 492.1
jerk 905.3
v divest 6.5
flunk 410.17
collect 472.11
strip 480.24
strum 708.40
cheat 759.26
jerk 905.5
harvest 1069.19
plucky
spunky 359.14
enterprising 404.8
courageous 492.16
plug
n hydrant 239.12
stopper 293.4
horse 311.12
publicity 352.4
snare 356.13
commendation 509.3
commercial 1034.20
v plod 175.7
stop 293.7
top 295.21
publicize 352.15
keep doggedly at 360.3
commend 509.11
drudge 725.14
shoot 904.12
plug in 1032.26
plum
desire 100.11
political patronage 609.36
money 728.8
dividend 738.7
good thing 999.5
plumage 3.18
plumb
n vertical 200.2
instrument 200.6
weight 297.6
v plumb-line 200.10

sound 275.9
measure 300.10
perceive 521.9
investigate 938.23
solve 940.2
adj perpendicular 200.12
thorough 794.10
adv perpendicularly
  200.14
absolutely 794.15
exactly 973.21
plumbing 385.4
plumb the depths
lose heart 112.16
sound 275.9
plume
n feather 3.16
v groom 79.20
adorn 498.9
plume of smoke 1067.1
plump
n thud 52.3
v put violently 159.13
sink 194.6
fatten 259.8
plunge 367.6
vote 371.18
soften 1047.6
adj corpulent 257.18
adv suddenly 830.9
plunder
n plundering 482.6
booty 482.11
v pillage 482.17
plunge
n run 174.3
tumble 194.3
decline 252.2
dive 367.1
deterioration 393.3
cheapening 633.4
investment 729.4
trading 737.19
swimming pool 743.12
gamble 759.2
flounder 917.8
v move 172.5
pitch 182.55
descend 194.5
decrease 252.6
gravitate 297.15
dive 367.6
make haste 401.5
rush into 401.7
cheapen 633.6
invest 729.17
trade 737.23
bet 759.25
flounder 917.15
plunger
diver 367.4
speculator 737.11
gambler 759.21
plunk
n thud 52.3
v thud 52.15
put violently 159.13
sink 194.6
plunge 367.6
strike 902.15
adv suddenly 830.9

plural
n number 530.8
adj pluralized 883.7
pluralism
government 612.7
nonuniformity 782.1
mixture 797.1
plurality 883.3
dualism 952.6
plurality
major part 792.6
more than one 883
pluralness 883.1
majority 883.2
pluripresence 221.2
plus
n math terms 253.2
surplus 993.5
v add 253.4
adj additional 253.10
positive 1032.35
adv additionally 253.11
prep with 253.12
plush
n softness 1047.4
adj grandiose 501.21
velvety 1047.15
plus-minus 223.23
plus side 124.1
plus size 257.4
plus-size 257.16
Pluto
nether world deity 682.5
planet 1072.9
plutocracy 618.6
ply
n fold 291.1
lamina 296.2
v touch 73.6
traverse 177.20
navigate 182.13
sail near the wind 182.25
change course 182.30
fold 291.5
use 387.10
urge upon 439.9
importune 440.12
exert 725.8
ply one's trade
work 724.12
trade 731.15
plywood lamina 296.2
wood 1054.3
PM afternoon 315.1
modulation 1034.14
PMS 92.14
pneumatic
bulging 283.15
airy 317.12
comely 1016.18
pneumatological 1039.10
vaporous 1067.9
poach cook 11.5
steal 482.13
poached eggs 10.26
pock
n sore 85.37
swelling 283.4
indentation 284.6
texture 294.1
blemish 1004.1

v indent 284.14
pocket
n atmosphere 184.32
bag 195.2
cavity 284.2
funds 728.14
purse 729.15
game 746.3
string 750.2
v patience 134.8
load 159.15
enclose 212.5
retain 474.5
take 480.13
legislate 613.10
receive 627.3
adj miniature 258.12
pocketbook
record book 549.11
purse 729.15
pocket change 728.19
pocket veto
prohibition 444.2
veto 613.7
pockmarked
spotted 47.13
indented 284.17
pod
n marijuana 87.11
hull 295.16
seed vessel 310.30
group of animals 770.5
v husk 6.9
PO'd 153.30
podcasting
communications 343.5
publication 352.1
podiatrist 90.4
podium 901.13
poem writing 547.10
verse 720.4
thing of beauty 1016.6
poet composer 547.15
author 718.4
poetess 720.11
imaginer 986.12
poetic poetical 720.15
visionary 986.24
poetic justice
justice 649.1
poetics 720.2
poetic license 720.2
poetic prose 721.1
poet laureate 720.11
poetry fluency 544.2
verse 720.1
poesy 720.1
pogrom 308.4
poignant
acrimonious 17.14
sensitive 24.13
painful 26.10
pungent 68.6
deep-felt 93.24
distressing 98.20
vigorous 544.11
spirited 544.12
point
n acrimony 17.5
location 159.1
direction 161.1

leading 165.1
summit 198.2
vanguard 216.2
mountain 237.6
degree 245.1
modicum 248.2
minute 258.7
angle 278.2
point of land 283.9
tip 285.3
intention 380.1
benefit 387.4
joke 489.6
mark 517.5
meaning 518.1
punctuation 530.15
type 548.6
sculpture tool 715.4
tennis 748.2
hockey team 749.2
game 749.3
score 749.6
soccer 752.3
particular 766.3
precursor 816.1
extremity 820.2
period 824.1
grammar 857.4
individual 872.4
topic 937.1
watchman 1008.10
cutlery 1040.2
v direct 161.5
take direction 161.7
sharpen 285.7
gravitate 297.15
mark 517.19
grammaticize 530.16
tend 896.3
point-and-click 714.1
point-and-shoot 714.1
point-blank
plainly 535.4
exactly 973.21
pointer index 517.4
clue 551.3
guide 574.7
point guard 747.2
pointillism 47.3
point in question
topic 937.1
question 938.10
pointless dull 117.6
blunt 286.3
useless 391.9
point man
n vanguard 216.2
employee 577.3
hockey team 749.2
precursor 816.1
v lead 165.2
point of departure 188.5
point of interest 997.5
point of reference 159.2
point of view
viewpoint 27.7
narrator 722.5
opinion 953.6
outlook 978.2
point out
designate 517.18

specify 865.11
call attention to 983.10
point person 577.3
points lending 620.1
interest 623.3
esteem 662.3
point the finger at 599.7
poise
n looks 33.4
equanimity 106.3
behavior 321.1
gesture 517.14
equality 790.1
confidence 970.5
v take off 193.10
equalize 790.6
poison
n poisonousness 82.3
liquor 88.14
killer 308.11
evil 1000.3
venom 1001.3
v empoison 85.52
kill 308.13
corrupt 393.12
work evil 1000.6
radioactivate 1037.10
poisonous nasty 64.7
toxic 82.7
harmful 1000.12
poison pen 512.5
poke
n bag 195.2
signal 517.15
purse 729.15
bundle 770.8
thrust 902.2
hit 902.4
v go slow 175.6
dally 331.14
goad 375.15
signal 517.22
thrust 902.12
hit 902.14
search 938.31
poke at 459.16
poke full of holes 958.4
poke fun at joke 489.13
ridicule 508.8
poke one's nose in
meddle 214.7
pry 981.4
poker
draw poker 759.10
fire iron 1020.12
poker face
unfeeling 94.1
unastonishment 123.1
reticence 344.3
unexpressiveness 522.5
pokey 429.9
poky dull 117.6
slow 175.10
little 258.10
base 661.12
slovenly 810.15
insignificant 998.18
polar
contrapositive 215.5
final 820.11
magnetic 1032.31

polar coordinates 300.5
Polaris
guiding star 574.8
stars 1072.4
Polaroid glasses 29.3
the polar opposite
779.2
pole
n spar 180.13
oar 180.15
summit 198.2
remote region 261.4
tower 272.6
shaft 273.1
beam 273.3
race 756.3
extremity 820.2
base 901.8
axle 915.5
polarity 1032.8
wood 1054.3
v push 904.9
poleax
strike dead 308.18
do for 395.11
polecat
stinker 71.3
wild animal 311.22
beast 660.6
polemic
n quarrel 456.5
contention 457.1
argumentation 935.4
arguer 935.12
adj contentious 110.26
partisan 456.17
argumentative 935.19
pole position
advantage 249.2
race 756.3
precedence 814.1
poles apart
opposite 215.6
different 780.7
pole vault 366.1
police
n policeman 1008.15
police force 1008.17
v tidy 808.12
protect 1008.18
watch 1008.20
police car 179.11
police state 612.4
police station 230.5
policy plan 381.4
polity 609.4
judiciousness 920.7
insurance 1008.4
policyholder 438.7
policy maker 610.7
polio 85.27
polish
n gloss 287.2
smoother 287.4
cultivation 392.3
taste 496.1
good breeding 504.4
elegance 533.1
v shine 287.7
perfect 392.11
buff 1044.8

polish off kill 308.14
accomplish 407.4
end 820.5
polite 504.14
polite society 578.6
political
politic 609.43
governmental 612.16
political action committee
pressure group 609.31
influence 894.6
political activist 330.8
political asylum 1009.1
political convention 609.8
political corruption
political influence 609.29
political corruption 609.34
political detainee 429.11
political election 371.9
political influence
machination 415.4
wire-pulling 609.29
political machine
political party 609.24
association 617.1
political party
party 609.24
association 617.4
political philosopher 610.12
political prisoner 429.11
political science 609.2
politician
expert 413.11
Machiavellian 415.8
statesman 610.2
politico 610.1
politicize
politick 609.38
democratize 611.16
politics
Machiavellianism 415.2
statesmanship 609.3
polity 609.1
political science 609.2
polka dot
spottiness 47.3
mark 517.5
poll
n head 198.6
vote 371.6
balloting place 609.20
returns 609.21
roll 871.6
canvass 938.14
v shorten 268.6
vote 371.18
record 549.15
canvass 938.29
number 1017.17
pollen
n sperm 305.11
v fertilize 78.10
pollinate 78.10
polling booth 609.20
pollute defile 80.17
intoxicate 88.23
misuse 389.4
corrupt 393.12
blaspheme 694.5
adulterate 797.12
work evil 1000.6

pollution
defilement 80.4
unhealthfulness 82.1
misuse 389.1
corruption 393.2
sacrilege 694.2
adulteration 797.3
evil 1000.3
environmental destruction
1073.2
Pollyanna 124.5
Pollyannaish 109.11
poltergeist imp 680.7
psychic phenomena 689.6
specter 988.1
polychrome
n variegation 47.1
v variegate 47.7
adj variegated 47.9
pictorial 712.20
polygenesis 861.3
polygeny 861.3
polygraph 92.8
polyhedral sided 218.7
multilateral 278.11
polymath 413.12
polymer 1054.6
polymers 1054.10
polymorphous 783.3
Polynesian race 312.2
polynomial 883.8
polyp 85.37
polysaccharide 7.5
polysyllabic 545.10
polytropic 364.6
polyunsaturated fat
fat 7.7
oil 1056.1
pomade
n ointment 1056.3
v oil 1056.8
pommel
n saddle parts 901.18
v whip 604.13
pound 902.16
pomp spectacle 33.7
circumstance 501.6
formality 580.1
procession 812.3
pompadour 3.22
pomp and circumstance 501.6
pom-pom 462.12
pompous stuffy 501.22
stiff 534.3
grandiloquent 545.8
ceremonious 580.8
confident 970.21
pond 241.1
ponder hesitate 362.7
consider 931.12
ponderous dull 117.6
bulky 257.19
heavy 297.16
bungling 414.20
stiff 534.3
unwieldy 1013.19
pone 10.29
pontificate
n mastership 417.7
papacy 698.6
v give oneself airs 501.14

talk big 545.6
  criticize 946.14
  dogmatize 970.10
Pontius Pilate 596.5
pontoon 180.11
pony
  n runt 258.4
  horse 311.10
  translation 341.3
  money 728.8
  jockey 757.2
  adj miniature 258.12
  adv on foot 177.43
ponytail 3.5
pooch
  n dog 311.16
  v bulge 283.11
poof
  gone 34.4
  homo 75.15
pooh-pooh
  slight 157.6
  scoff 508.9
  disbelieve 955.5
pool
  landlocked water 241.1
  lake 241.1
  company 617.9
  funds 728.14
  bear pool 737.17
  swimming pool 743.12
  pot 759.5
pool hall 743.11
poop
  n energy 17.3
  power 18.1
  stern 217.7
  v get tired 21.6
pooped weak 16.12
  tired 21.8
  languid 331.20
  worn-out 393.36
poopy 92.39
poor weak 16.15
  humble 137.10
  haggard 270.20
  unskillful 414.15
  disapproving 510.21
  ill off 619.7
  base 661.12
  sparse 885.5
  unsound 936.12
  meager 992.10
  ill-provided 992.12
  paltry 998.21
  inferior 1005.9
poor judgment 948.1
poor man's roulette 759.8
Poor Richard's Almanac
  832.7
poor taste 497.1
poor timing 844.2
pop
  n beverage 10.49
  thud 52.3
  detonation 56.3
  vulgarity 497.1
  father 560.10
  grandfather 560.14
  automobile racing 756.1
  back number 842.8

v thud 52.15
  blast 56.8
  use 87.22
  bulge 283.11
  play 745.5
  adj common 497.14
  adv suddenly 830.9
pope 699.9
pop in enter 189.7
  insert 191.3
pop literature
  writing 547.12
  literature 718.1
pop music 708.7
pop pills 87.22
pop psychology 92.1
poppy 22.10
poppycock
  bull 520.3
  foolishness 923.1
pop quiz 938.2
pop the question
  solicit 440.14
  propose 562.22
populace 227.1
popular
  desired 100.29
  beloved 104.23
  customary 373.13
  communal 476.9
  common 497.14
  approved 509.19
  fashionable 578.11
  populational 606.8
  distinguished 662.16
  lay 700.3
  prevalent 864.12
  usual 869.9
popular belief
  opinion 953.6
  superstition 954.3
populate settle 159.17
  people 225.9
population
  n establishment 159.7
  peopling 225.2
  inhabitants 227.1
  adj populational 606.8
population explosion 251.2
populous
  inhabited 225.12
  crowded 770.22
  teeming 884.9
pop up burst forth 33.9
  be unexpected 131.6
  arrive 186.6
  shoot up 193.9
  play 745.5
  turn up 831.6
  chance 972.11
porcelain
  n ceramic ware 742.2
  adj ceramic 742.7
porch
  propylaeum 189.6
  stoop 197.21
  church 703.9
porcine
  corpulent 257.18
  ungulate 311.45
porcupine 311.22

pore
  n duct 2.23
  outlet 190.9
  opening 292.1
  v scrutinize 27.14
pork food 10.17
  political patronage 609.36
pork barrel
  booty 482.11
  political patronage 609.36
  treasury 729.13
  trading 863.2
pork chop 10.19
porker
  heavyweight 257.12
  swine 311.9
porno film 666.4
pornography
  writing 547.12
  obscenity 666.4
  literature 718.1
porous
  exudative 190.20
  porose 292.20
porpoise
  n marine animal 311.29
  v maneuver 184.40
porridge
  semiliquid 1062.5
  pulp 1063.2
port
  n looks 33.4
  airport 184.22
  destination 186.5
  outlet 190.9
  left side 220.1
  behavior 321.1
  refuge 1009.1
  harbor 1009.6
  circuitry 1042.3
  adj left 220.4
  adv leftward 220.6
portable 176.18
portable classroom 567.10
portage
  transportation 176.3
  fee 630.6
portal entrance 189.5
  porch 189.6
  vestibule 197.19
portal site 1042.18
portcullis 1012.5
portent omen 133.3
  ominousness 133.6
  forewarning 399.2
porter carrier 176.7
  trainman 178.13
  doorkeeper 1008.12
portfolio
  scepter 417.9
  bookholder 554.17
  stock 738.2
portico
  vestibule 197.19
  pillar 273.5
  passageway 383.3
port in a storm 1009.1
portion
  n serving 8.10
  remedy 86.6
  fix 87.20

amount 244.2
  a length 267.2
  share 477.5
  endowment 478.9
  part 793.1
  dose 793.5
  fate 964.2
  v apportion 477.6
  divide 802.18
portion control 7.13
portly 257.18
port of call 1009.6
portrait
  description 349.2
  image 349.5
  portraiture 712.14
  photograph 714.3
  copy 785.1
portrait painter 716.4
portray represent 349.8
  describe 349.9
  enact 704.30
  picture 712.18
pose
  n behavior 321.1
  sham 354.3
  posing 500.3
  gesture 517.14
  v place 159.12
  propose 439.5
  posture 500.13
  postulate 951.12
pose a question 938.19
Poseidon
  mariner 183.1
  spirit of the sea 240.3
  water god 678.10
posh
  grandiose 501.21
  chic 578.13
  upper-class 607.10
  expensive 632.11
posing against
  contraposition 215.1
  symmetrization 264.2
position
  n location 159.1
  navigation 159.3
  rank 245.2
  affirmation 334.1
  remark 524.3
  class 607.1
  policy 609.4
  prestige 662.4
  function 724.3
  job 724.5
  skiing 753.3
  race 756.3
  state 765.1
  classification 809.2
  premise 935.7
  opinion 953.6
  attitude 978.1
  outlook 978.2
  v locate 159.11
position paper
  affirmation 334.1
  announcement 352.2
  policy 381.4
  platform 609.7
  classification 801.3

statement of belief 953.4

positive
  n photocopy 714.5
  print 785.5
  adj downright 247.12
  affirmative 334.8
  unpersuadable 361.13
  helpful 449.21
  real 761.15
  agreeing 788.9
  belief 953.21
  unqualified 960.2
  certain 970.13
  confident 970.21
  dogmatic 970.22
  emphatic 997.21
  numeric 1017.23
  plus 1032.35
positive reinforcement 92.26
posse
  military unit 461.22
  company 770.3
  search 938.15
  police 1008.17
possess
  have 469.4
  take 480.13
  demonize 680.16
  bewitch 691.9
  obsess 926.25
  know 928.12
  haunt 988.6
possessed
  overjoyed 95.17
  frenzied 105.25
  owned 469.8
  bewitched 691.13
  possessed with a demon
    926.29
  obsessed 926.33
  haunted 988.10
possessive
  possessory 469.10
  selfish 651.5
possessive noun 530.5
possible
  latent 519.5
  within the bounds of
    possibility 966.6
  numeric 1017.23
possible action 371.2
possum 311.22
post
  n station 159.2
  standard 273.4
  pillar 273.5
  messenger 353.1
  stronghold 460.6
  mail 553.4
  branch 617.10
  position 724.5
  market 736.1
  basketball game 747.3
  base 901.8
  wood 1054.3
  v place 159.12
  speed 174.8
  send 176.15
  publicize 352.15
  make haste 401.5
  pledge 438.10

record 549.15
wise up 551.9
mail 553.12
commission 615.10
pay 624.16
keep accounts 628.8
list 871.8
adj epistolary 553.14
adv swiftly 174.17
posthaste 401.13
postage 553.5
postage stamp 553.5
postal code 553.9
postal service 553.7
postcard 553.3
postdated 833.3
posted located 159.18
  pledged 438.12
  recorded 549.17
  informed 928.18
poster bill 352.7
  mail carrier 353.6
posterior
  n rear 217.1
  buttocks 217.4
  adj rear 217.9
  succeeding 815.4
  subsequent 835.4
posterity
  kinfolk 559.2
  progeny 561.1
  offspring 561.1
  successor 817.4
  sequel 835.2
postgraduate
  n graduate 572.8
  adj scholastic 568.19
  studentlike 572.12
posthaste
  swiftly 174.17
  in posthaste 401.13
posthumous
  postmortem 307.35
  after death 835.5
post-industrial 835.5
postman
  mailman 353.5
  postal service 553.7
postmark 553.5
postmaster 353.5
postmortem
  n autopsy 307.17
  v examine 938.24
  adj postmortal 307.35
post-natal 1.4
post office
  messenger 353.1
  postal service 553.7
postpartum depression 926.5
postpone
  put away 390.6
  delay 846.9
post position 757.3
postprandial 11.6
postscript
  added to writing 254.2
  sequel 817.1
**post-traumatic stress
  disorder** 92.17
postulate
  n fact 761.3

essence 767.2
curtain-raiser 816.2
premise 935.7
supposition 951.3
axiom 974.2
v propose 439.5
predicate 951.12
posture
  n looks 33.4
  behavior 321.1
  sham 354.3
  gesture 517.14
  opinion 953.6
  attitude 978.1
  v pose 500.13
posy
  n flower 310.24
  bouquet 310.25
  compliment 509.6
  bundle 770.8
  adj affected 500.15
  ostentatious 501.18
  affected 533.9
pot
  n abdomen 2.19
  marijuana 87.11
  container 195.1
  lot 247.4
  wealth 618.3
  trophy 646.3
  ceramic ware 742.2
  jackpot 759.5
  v package 212.9
  put up 397.11
  shape 742.6
  shoot 904.12
  plant 1069.18
potable
  n beverage 10.49
  spirits 88.13
  adj drinkable 8.34
potash 890.4
potato 10.35
potato chip 10.30
potbellied
  corpulent 257.18
  bulging 283.15
potent
  strong 15.15
  powerful 18.12
  sexual 75.25
  virile 76.13
  authoritative
    417.15
  influential 894.13
potentate 575.8
potential
  n talent 413.4
  mood 530.11
  possibility 966.1
  voltage 1032.12
  adj latent 519.5
  possible 966.6
potential energy 17.1
pothead 87.21
pothole 284.3
potion drink 8.4
  dose 86.6
  alcohol 88.7
potluck gamble 759.2
  haphazard 972.4

potpourri perfume 70.6
  performance 708.33
  hodgepodge 797.6
pot roast 10.13
pots and pans 11.4
potshot
  n gamble 759.2
  shot 904.4
  v shoot 904.12
potter
  n ceramist 716.7
  v waste time 331.13
  trifle 998.14
potter's field 309.15
potter's wheel
  wheel 742.4
  instrument of conversion
    858.10
pottery plant 739.3
  ceramics 742.1
  ceramic ware 742.2
POTUS 575.7
pouch 283.11
poultice
  n dressing 86.33
  pulp 1063.2
  v treat 91.24
  relieve 120.5
poultry 311.28
pounce
  n descent 194.1
  leap 366.1
  plunge 367.1
  v descend 194.5
  leap 366.5
  plunge 367.6
pound
  n staccato 55.1
  kennel 228.21
  weight 297.8
  place of confinement 429.7
  money 728.8
  hit 902.4
  v suffer 26.8
  drum 55.4
  pitch 182.55
  injure 393.13
  confine 429.12
  attack 459.14
  beat time 708.44
  din 849.10
  beat 902.16
  pulverize 1051.9
pound-foolish 486.8
pound for pound 943.10
pound out
  do carelessly 340.9
  write 547.21
  play 708.39
  compose 718.6
  produce 892.8
pound the pavement 177.23
pour
  n torrent 238.5
  rainstorm 316.2
  v ladle 176.17
  run out 190.13
  flow 238.16
  rain 316.10
  give 478.12
  disgorge 909.25

abound 991.5

pour it on speed 174.9
  be active 330.14
  work hard 725.13

pour oil on the fire
  excite 105.12
  aggravate 119.2
  incite 375.17

pour one's heart out
  lighten 120.7
  speak up 524.21

pout
  n scowl 110.9
  grimace 265.4
  v look sullen 110.15
  grimace 265.8
  bulge 283.11

poverty poorness 619.1
  scarcity 992.3

POW 429.11

powder
  n medicine 86.4
  makeup 1016.11
  dust 1051.5
  v depart 188.7
  sprinkle 771.6
  pulverize 1051.9
  come to dust 1051.10
  adj powdery 1051.11

powder keg
  threat 514.1
  danger 1006.1

powder puff 1016.11

powder room 12.10

power
  n strength 15.1
  energy 17.1
  effective force 18
  potency 18.1
  country 232.1
  greatness 247.1
  supremacy 249.3
  willpower 359.4
  means 384.2
  talent 413.4
  authority 417.1
  authoritativeness 417.2
  governance 417.5
  vigor 544.3
  control 612.2
  wealth 618.3
  prerogative 642.1
  influence 894.1
  impulse 902.1
  personage 997.8
  v impel 902.11
  adj mechanical 1040.14

power breakfast 8.6

power broker 609.30

power dinner 8.6

power down 1032.26

power dressing 5.10

the power elite 575.15

power failure 1032.20

powerful
  adj strong 15.15
  potent 18.12
  great 247.6
  authoritative 417.15
  vigorous 544.11
  influential 894.13

adv very 247.18

powerhouse
  strong man 15.7
  man of action 330.8
  power station 1032.19

power-hungry 100.28

powerless weak 16.12
  impotent 19.13
  uninfluential 895.3

power lunch 8.6

power of attorney
  commission 615.1
  substitution 862.1

power plant
  propulsion 184.25
  plant 739.3
  powerhouse 1032.19
  machinery 1040.3

powers talent 413.4
  celestial hierarchy 679.3

the powers that be
  the authorities 575.15
  officeholder 610.11
  the government 612.3

power supply 1032.2

power tool 1040.1

power up 1032.26

powwow
  n forum 423.3
  conference 541.5
  political convention
    609.8
  v confer 541.10

PR appearance 33.2
  publicity 352.4
  voting 609.18

practical useful 387.18
  usable 387.23
  occupied 724.15
  operative 889.9
  workable 889.10
  sensible 920.18
  ungullible 956.5
  expedient 966.7
  realistic 987.6
  practicable 995.6
  handy 1014.15

practical joke 489.10

practical wisdom 920.6

practice
  n behavior 321.1
  action 328.1
  custom 373.1
  habit 373.3
  manner 384.1
  experience 413.9
  observance 434.1
  training 568.3
  study 570.3
  bar 597.4
  rite 701.3
  vocation 724.6
  exercise 725.6
  operation 889.1
  tryout 942.3
  notation 1017.2
  v act 328.4
  put into practice 328.8
  use 384.5
  employ 387.10
  perform 434.3

train 568.13
  study 570.12
  rehearse 704.32
  busy oneself with 724.11
  exert 725.8
  play 744.2
  iterate 849.8

practiced
  skilled 413.26
  experienced 413.28

practice law 597.5

practice medicine 90.14

practice what one preaches
  observe 434.2
  keep faith 644.9

practicing
  n iteration 849.2
  adj acting 328.10
  observant 434.4
  pious 692.8

Prado 386.9

pragmatic
  sensible 920.18
  realistic 987.6
  practical 995.6

prairie
  n open space 158.4
  horizontal 201.3
  plain 236.1
  grassland 310.8
  adj rustic 233.6

prairie dog 311.22

praise
  n congratulation 149.1
  thanks 150.2
  approval 509.5
  flattery 511.1
  citation 646.4
  glorification 696.2
  v congratulate 149.2
  give approval 509.12
  flatter 511.5
  honor 646.8
  glorify 696.12

praiseworthy 509.20

Prajnaparamita Sutra 683.9

pram 179.6

prance
  n gait 177.12
  caper 366.2
  v way of walking 177.28
  go on horseback 177.34
  caper 366.6
  strut 501.15
  dance 705.5

prancer horse 311.10
  race horse 311.14

prank
  n trick 489.10
  v dress up 5.42
  ornament 498.8

pratfall tumble 194.3
  collapse 410.3
  goof 975.6

prattle
  n nonsense 520.2
  speech 524.1
  chatter 540.3
  v talk nonsense 520.5
  chatter 540.5
  chat 541.9

pray
  v petition 440.10
  entreat 440.11
  supplicate 696.13
  interj please 440.20

prayer entreaty 440.2
  supplication 696.4
  divine service 696.8
  worshiper 696.9

prayer book 554.1

preach admonish 422.6
  lecture 543.11
  expound 568.16

preacher lecturer 543.5
  informer 551.6
  teacher 571.7
  sermoner 699.3

preamble
  n curtain-raiser 816.2
  v prefix 814.3

prearrange plan 381.8
  prepare 405.6
  contract 437.5
  precontrive 965.4

precarious
  unreliable 971.20
  ticklish 1006.12

precaution
  n precautiousness 494.3
  v forewarn 399.6

precede lead 165.2
  rule 249.11
  antecede 814.2
  go before 816.3
  initiate 818.10
  be prior 834.3

precedent
  n model 786.1
  precursor 816.1
  antecedent 834.2
  verdict 946.5
  adj leading 165.3
  preceding 814.4

precept
  rule 419
  prescript 419.1
  direction 420.3
  a belief 953.2
  maxim 974.1

precinct
  enclosed place 212.3
  nearness 223.1
  sphere 231.2
  region 231.5
  arena 463.1
  election district 609.16

precious
  n endearment term 562.6
  adj beloved 104.23
  downright 247.12
  overnice 500.18
  affected 533.9
  punctilious 580.10
  dear 632.10

precious few 885.4

precious metals
  gold 728.20
  metal 1058.3

precious stone
  jewel 498.6
  gem 1059.7

precip 316.1
precipice cliff 200.3
 slope 237.2
precipitant
 precipitate 401.10
 reckless 493.8
 sudden 830.5
precipitate
 n dregs 256.2
 effect 887.1
 precipitation 1045.5
 v descend 194.5
 gravitate 297.15
 rain 316.10
 hasten 401.4
 fell 913.5
 deposit 1045.11
 adj fast 174.15
 impulsive 365.9
 precipitant 401.10
 unprepared 406.8
 reckless 493.8
 sudden 830.5
 premature 845.8
precipitous
 perpendicular 200.12
 steep 204.18
 precipitate 401.10
 reckless 493.8
 sudden 830.5
précis
 n shortening 268.3
 abridgment 557.1
 iteration 849.2
 v iterate 849.8
precise
 v be accurate 973.11
 adj meticulous 339.12
 fastidious 495.9
 punctilious 580.10
 detailed 766.9
 particular 865.12
 discriminating 944.7
 exact 973.17
precision
 meticulousness 339.3
 fastidiousness 495.1
 elegance 533.1
 accuracy 973.5
preclude
 prohibit 444.3
 exclude 773.4
 prevent 1012.14
precocious 845.8
precognition
 understanding 928.3
 intuition 934.1
 foreknowledge 961.3
presensive 947.2
preconclusion 947.1
precondition
 prime 405.9
 suppose 951.10
preconscious
 n psyche 92.28
 adj subconscious 92.42
preconsider 380.7
precursor
 harbinger 133.4
 leading 165.1
 vanguard 216.2

settler 227.9
 warning sign 399.3
 precedence 814.1
 forerunner 816.1
 antecedent 834.2
 early bird 845.4
 transformer 852.5
 producer 892.7
predate
 date 832.13
 be prior 834.3
predator 480.12
predecessor 816.1
predestine
 predetermine 964.6
 destine 964.7
predetermine
 premeditate 380.7
 prejudge 947.2
 predecide 964.6
predicament
 state 765.1
 urgent need 963.4
 bewilderment 971.3
 danger 1006.1
 adversity 1011.1
 plight 1013.4
predicate
 n affirmation 334.1
 syntax 530.2
 v affirm 334.5
 postulate 951.12
predict
 look forward to 130.6
 foreshow 133.9
 come 839.6
 foresee 961.5
 make a prediction
  962.9
 risk 972.12
predictable
 stable 855.12
 divinable 962.13
 probable 968.6
 reliable 970.17
predilection
 inclination 100.3
 love 104.1
 preference 371.5
 tendency 896.1
 prejudgment 947.1
 disposition 978.3
 prejudice 980.3
predispose 894.7
predominant
 chief 249.14
 governing 612.17
 prevalent 864.12
 influential 894.14
 paramount 997.24
preeminent
 omnipotent 18.13
 top 198.10
 chief 249.14
 authoritative 417.15
 paramount 997.24
preempt 480.19
preemptive strike 459.1
preen groom 79.20
 ornament 498.8
preexist 834.3

prefabricated
 ready-made 405.19
 made 892.18
preface
 n front 216.1
 makeup 554.12
 part of writing 793.2
 curtain-raiser 816.2
 v prefix 814.3
prefect
 teaching fellow 571.4
 executive 574.3
prefecture 417.7
prefer desire 100.14
 have preference 371.17
 offer 439.4
 propose 439.5
 promote 446.2
 favor 650.8
 take the attitude 978.6
preferable 371.25
prefer charges
 arraign 598.15
 accuse 599.7
preferential treatment
 furtherance 449.5
 partiality 650.3
prefix
 n front 216.1
 added to writing 254.2
 morphology 526.3
 curtain-raiser 816.2
 v add 253.4
 preface 814.3
preformed 405.19
pregame 818.15
pregnable
 helpless 19.18
 vulnerable 1006.16
pregnant
 enceinte 78.18
 meaningful 518.10
 beginning 818.15
 critical 843.10
 original 886.14
 productive 890.9
 imaginative 986.18
preheat 1020.17
prehensile
 raptorial 474.9
 knowing 928.15
prehistoric
 prewar 834.5
 former 837.10
 primitive 842.11
preindicate 133.11
prejudge
 be prejudiced 947.2
 forejudge 980.7
prejudice
 n preference 371.5
 tendency 896.1
 prejudgment 947.1
 forejudging 980.3
 disadvantage 996.2
 v prejudice against 980.9
 work evil 1000.6
pre-K 567.2
prekindergarten 567.2
preliminary
 n preparation 405.1

curtain-raiser 816.2
 inauguration 818.5
 adj prior 814.4
 preceding 816.4
 prefatory 818.16
prelude
 n overture 708.26
 precedence 814.1
 curtain-raiser 816.2
 v prefix 814.3
premarital 665.27
premature
 untimely 844.6
 too early 845.8
premeditate
 calculate 380.7
 prearrange 965.4
premier
 n head of state 575.7
 adj first 818.17
 paramount 997.24
premiere
 n theatrical performance
  704.12
 v dramatize 704.28
premise
 n fact 761.3
 curtain-raiser 816.2
 antecedent 834.2
 foundation 901.6
 proposition 935.7
 supposition 951.3
 v prefix 814.3
premises region 231.1
 evidence 957.1
premium
 n extra 254.4
 gratuity 478.5
 interest 623.3
 bonus 624.6
 discount 631.1
 bridge 758.3
 adj expensive 632.11
premonition
 presentiment 133.1
 forewarning 399.2
 extrasensory perception
  689.8
 hunch 934.3
prenatal 818.15
prenuptial agreement 436.3
preoccupy
 appropriate 480.19
 obsess 926.25
 occupy the mind 931.20
 engross 983.13
preordained 964.8
preowned clothing 5.5
prepacked 212.12
prepaid 624.22
preparation
 medicine 86.4
 provision 385.1
 preparing 405.1
 training 568.3
 harmonization 709.2
 earliness 845.1
 foresight 961.1
preparatory school
 preparation 405.1
 secondary school 567.4

prepare cook 11.5
  provide 385.7
  equip 385.8
  make ready 405.6
  take steps 494.6
  write 547.21
  train 568.13
  formulate 718.6
  produce 892.8
prep cook 11.3
prepensely 380.10
preponderance
  superiority 249.1
  dominance 417.6
  majority 883.2
  influence 894.1
preposition
  part of speech 530.3
  prepositions 530.19
prepossessing
  delightful 97.7
  alluring 377.8
preposterous
  overpriced 632.12
  undue 640.9
  absurd 923.11
  unbelievable 955.10
  impossible 967.7
  fanciful 986.20
prepped 405.16
preppie 572.3
prep school
  preparation 405.1
  secondary school 567.4
prerecord 50.14
prerequisite
  n preparation 405.1
  condition 959.2
  requirement 963.2
  adj preparatory 405.20
  requisite 963.13
prerogative
  superiority 249.1
  authority 417.1
  right 642
presage
  n premonition 133.1
  foreknowledge 961.3
  prediction 962.1
  v foreshow 133.9
  predict 962.9
preschool
  n infant school 567.2
  adj scholastic 567.13
prescient 961.7
prescribe
  remedy 86.38
  require 420.9
  advise 422.5
  direct 573.8
  administer 643.6
  legalize 673.9
prescription
  remedy 86.1
  limitation 210.2
  custom 373.1
  precept 419.1
  formula 419.3
  direction 420.3
  possession 469.1
  prerogative 642.1

law 673.3
  rule 869.4
preseason 313.1
presence looks 33.4
  apparition 33.5
  being here 221.1
  behavior 321.1
  existence 761.1
  influence 894.6
  phantom 976.4
  specter 988.1
presence of mind 106.3
present
  n gift 478.4
  tense 530.12
  v manifest 348.5
  put to choice 371.21
  provide 385.7
  offer 439.4
  donate 478.12
  say 524.22
  phrase 532.4
  introduce 587.14
  give 634.4
  dramatize 704.28
  adduce 957.12
  adj attendant 221.12
  existent 761.13
  immediate 838.2
the present time 821.1
  now 838.1
  present tense 838.1
presentable
  giveable 478.23
  tolerable 999.20
  comely 1016.18
presenteeism 221.1
the present hour 838.1
presentiment
  feeling 93.1
  premonition 133.1
  forewarning 399.2
  hunch 934.3
  foreknowledge 961.3
  prediction 962.1
the present minute 838.1
the present moment 838.1
present one's case 598.19
preserve
  n sweets 10.40
  reserve 397.7
  refuge 1009.1
  v reserve 386.12
  conserve 397.8
  cure 397.9
  retain 474.5
  perpetuate 829.5
  be conservative 853.6
  sustain 856.4
  care for 1008.19
preserve one's honor 136.7
preset 437.5
preside
  administer 573.11
  entertain 585.8
  administer justice 594.5
president principal 571.8
  executive 574.3
  head of state 575.7
presidential election
  609.15

press
  n extractor 192.9
  squeezing 260.2
  urge 375.6
  presswork 548.9
  printing office 548.11
  publisher 554.2
  enlistment 615.7
  throng 770.4
  thrust 902.2
  urgency 997.4
  v squeeze 260.8
  hot-press 287.6
  weigh on 297.11
  urge 375.14
  hasten 401.4
  insist 421.8
  bring pressure to bear upon
    424.6
  urge upon 439.9
  importune 440.12
  attach 480.20
  embrace 562.18
  enlist 615.17
  strain 725.10
  thrust 902.12
  densify 1045.9
the press
  informant 551.5
  news 552.1
  journalism 555.3
press charges 599.7
press conference
  conference 541.5
  interview 938.11
press corps 555.4
press into service 387.14
pressman
  printer 548.12
  journalist 555.4
press one's luck
  risk 972.12
  take chances 1006.7
press release
  release 352.3
  message 552.4
pressroom 548.11
press the panic button
  127.11
pressure
  n touching 73.2
  tension 128.3
  squeezing 260.2
  burden 297.7
  urging 375.5
  urge 375.6
  prestige 417.4
  insistence 421.4
  coercion 424.3
  importunity 440.3
  influence 894.1
  thrust 902.2
  urgent need 963.4
  urgency 997.4
  adversity 1011.1
  v urge 375.14
  coerce 424.8
  importune 440.12
pressure group
  interest group 609.31
  party 617.4

influence 894.6
pressure point 208.3
pressure suit
  blackout 184.21
  space suit 1075.11
pressurize 260.8
presswork 548.9
prestidigitation
  juggling 356.5
  illusoriness 976.2
prestige
  respect 155.1
  superiority 249.1
  authority 417.4
  class 607.1
  honor 662.4
  influence 894.1
  notability 997.2
presto
  n music 708.25
  tempo 709.24
  adj music 708.55
  instantaneous 830.4
  presto chango 852.13
  interj attention! 983.22
presume
  hope 124.6
  expect 130.5
  have the audacity 142.7
  imply 519.4
  assume 640.6
  entail 772.4
  judge 946.8
  prejudge 947.2
  suppose 951.10
  think 953.11
  think likely 968.5
presume upon
  exploit 387.16
  impose on 640.7
  inflict on 643.7
presumption
  hope 124.1
  presumptuousness 141.2
  insolence 142.1
  meddling 214.2
  foolhardiness 493.3
  implication 519.2
  assumption 640.2
  entailment 772.2
  prejudgment 947.1
  supposition 951.3
  opinion 953.6
  probability 968.1
presumptuous
  arrogant 141.10
  insolent 142.9
  meddlesome 214.9
  foolhardy 493.9
  presuming 640.11
presuppose
  imply 519.4
  entail 772.4
  prejudge 947.2
  suppose 951.10
preteen 302.8
pre-teen
  n adolescence 301.6
  youngster 302.1
  adj adolescent 301.13
pre-teens 301.2

a belief 953.2
axiom 974.2
print
n indentation 284.6
mark 517.7
imprint 548.3
type 548.6
picture 712.10
numbered print 713.5
photoprint 714.5
offprint 785.5
copy 785.5
impact 887.2
v represent 349.8
mark 517.19
imprint 548.14
engrave 713.9
process 714.15
fix 855.9
printed written 547.22
in print 548.19
engraved 713.11
printer typist 547.18
printworker 548.12
publisher 554.2
output device 1042.9
printing press 548.9
printmaking
printing 548.1
graphic arts 713.1
the print media 555.3
print run 554.5
print shop 548.11
prior
n religious 699.16
adj leading 165.3
preceding 814.4
previous 834.4
former 837.10
priority leading 165.1
front 216.1
superiority 249.1
prestige 417.4
precedence 814.1
sequence 815.1
previousness 834.1
importance 997.1
prism 29.2
prismatic
chromatic 35.16
variegated 47.9
multilateral 278.11
prison 429.8
prisoner captive 429.11
accused 599.6
prisoner of war 429.11
prissy effeminate 77.14
meticulous 339.12
fastidious 495.9
prudish 500.19
stiff 580.9
pristine
unimitated 337.6
unused 390.12
natural 406.13
unadorned 416.6
innocent 657.6
intact 792.10
simple 798.6
new 841.7
primitive 842.11

original 886.14
undamaged 1002.8
privacy
retirement 345.2
seclusion 584.1
aloneness 872.2
retreat 1009.5
private
n enlisted man 461.8
adj interior 207.6
closed 293.9
personal 312.15
privy 345.13
taking 480.25
privatistic 584.9
intrinsic 767.7
particular 865.12
alone 872.8
private detective 576.10
private enterprise 611.8
private practice 90.13
privates 2.13
private sector
capitalism 611.8
economy 731.7
privation loss 473.1
deprivation 480.6
indigence 619.2
privatization 584.1
privatize 611.16
privilege
n superiority 249.1
exemption 430.8
license 642.2
v authorize 443.11
privileged information
secret 345.5
inside information 551.2
privy
n latrine 12.10
hut 228.9
adj covert 345.12
private 345.13
privy council
council 423.1
cabinet 613.3
prix fixe 630.5
prize
n desire 100.11
booty 482.11
monument 549.12
award 646.2
leverage 906.1
lever 906.4
good thing 999.5
the best 999.8
v cherish 104.20
respect 155.4
measure 300.10
price 630.11
get a purchase 906.8
estimate 946.9
value 997.13
adj best 999.16
prized 104.23
prizefight 457.9
prizewinner 413.15
PR man 352.9
pro
n expert 413.11
professional 726.4

gambler 759.21
affirmative 935.14
adj approving 509.17
occupational 724.16
prep in favor of 509.21
proactive
energetic 17.13
enterprising 330.23
pro and con 935.19
probability
expectation 130.1
the future 839.1
tendency 896.1
liability 897.1
prediction 962.1
possibility 966.1
likelihood 968.1
chance 972.1
good chance 972.8
probable error
mathematical probability
968.2
inaccuracy 975.2
probate
n bequest 478.10
v confirm 957.11
probation 942.2
probe
n nurse 90.10
investigation 938.4
search 938.15
feeler 942.4
test rocket 1074.6
artificial satellite 1075.6
v measure 300.10
investigate 938.23
sound out 942.9
philosophize 952.9
probity honesty 644.1
virtue 653.1
problem
annoyance 96.2
enigma 522.8
topic 937.1
question 938.10
bewilderment 971.3
fault 1003.2
trouble 1013.3
problematic
unbelievable 955.10
doubtful 971.17
bewildering 971.27
problem-solve 940.2
proboscis 283.8
procedure
behavior 321.1
rule 373.4
plan 381.1
policy 381.4
manner 384.1
process 889.2
proceed
progress 162.2
behave 321.4
act 328.4
take action 328.5
use 384.5
elapse 821.5
proceed from 887.5
proceedings
activity 330.1

report 549.7
lawsuit 598.1
affairs 831.4
proceeds gain 472.3
yield 472.5
receipts 627.1
production 893.2
process
n manner 384.1
procedure 889.2
v cut or dress the hair
3.22
prepare 405.6
develop 714.15
convert 892.9
gather materials 1054.7
processed
prepared 405.16
made 892.18
processed food 10.1
procession train 812.3
sequence 815.1
processor 1042.2
proclaim
herald 133.13
affirm 334.5
cry 352.13
command 420.8
state 524.23
be prior 834.3
dogmatize 970.10
proclamation
affirmation 334.1
announcement 352.2
decree 420.4
proclivity
inclination 100.3
preference 371.5
tendency 896.1
disposition 978.3
proconsul 575.13
procrastinate
let go 329.5
leave undone 340.7
not face up to 368.13
protract 827.9
be dilatory 846.11
procrastinator
slowpoke 175.5
neglecter 340.5
procreate grow 14.2
generate 78.8
develop 259.7
engender 818.14
originate 892.12
proctor
teaching fellow 571.4
superintendent 574.2
steward 574.4
lawyer 597.1
procumbency 201.2
procure fetch 176.16
elicit 192.14
induce 375.22
acquire 472.8
prostitute oneself 665.21
purchase 733.7
cause 886.11
procurement
provision 385.1
acquisition 472.1

prod
  n goad 375.8
  thrust 902.2
  v touch 73.6
  goad 375.15
  importune 440.12
  thrust 902.12
prodigal
  n wastrel 486.2
  adj exaggerated 355.4
  improvident 406.15
  extravagant 486.8
  diffuse 538.11
  unvirtuous 654.12
  intemperate 669.7
  teeming 884.9
  plentiful 991.7
  superabundant 993.19
prodigal son
  penitent 113.5
  prodigal 486.2
  returnee 859.3
prodigious
  wonderful 122.10
  large 247.7
  huge 257.20
  extraordinary 870.14
  miraculous 870.16
produce
  n vegetables 10.35
  fruit 10.38
  yield 472.5
  receipts 627.1
  groceries 735.7
  production 893.2
  v secrete 13.5
  lengthen 267.6
  do 328.6
  manifest 348.5
  accomplish 407.4
  write 547.21
  dramatize 704.28
  pen 718.6
  cause 886.10
  be productive 890.7
  create 892.8
  bear 892.13
  adduce 957.12
  imagine 986.14
product yield 472.5
  commodity 735.2
  effect 887.1
  end product 893.1
  sum 1017.6
product design 717.5
productivity
  power 18.1
  wordiness 538.2
  productiveness 890.1
  invention 986.3
product liability 641.2
product placement 352.5
profane
  v misuse 389.4
  desecrate 694.4
  adj cursing 513.8
  unsacred 686.3
  impious 694.6
  secularist 695.16
profanity cursing 513.3
  unsanctity 686.1

  sacrilege 694.2
profess affirm 334.5
  sham 354.21
  pretext 376.3
  state 953.12
profession
  acknowledgment 332.3
  affirmation 334.1
  claim 376.2
  occupation 724.4
  vocation 724.6
  confession 953.7
  testimony 957.2
professional
  n expert 413.11
  member of a learned
    profession 726.4
  adj skillful 413.22
  skilled 413.26
  scholastic 568.19
  occupational 724.16
professional development
  college 567.5
  study 568.8
professional ethics 636.1
professional student 570.1
professional wrestling
  457.10
professor expert 413.11
  teacher 571.1
  academic rank 571.3
  gambler 759.21
proffer
  n offer 439.1
  v offer 439.4
  give 478.12
  answer 939.4
  adduce 957.12
proficient
  n expert 413.11
  adj fitted 405.17
  skillful 413.22
  perfected 1002.9
  able 18.14
profile
  n outline 211.2
  side 218.1
  contour 262.2
  description 349.2
  diagram 381.3
  portrait 712.14
  history 719.1
  v outline 211.9
profit
  n incentive 375.7
  benefit 387.4
  gain 472.3
  expedience 995.1
  good 999.4
  v avail 387.17
  make profit 472.12
  expedite one's affair 995.3
  do good 999.10
profitable useful 387.18
  valuable 387.22
  helpful 449.21
  gainful 472.16
  paying 624.21
  expedient 995.5
  good 999.12
profit sharing 476.2

profit-sharing 476.9
profligate
  n reprobate 660.4
  libertine 665.10
  adj prodigal 486.8
  corrupt 654.14
  licentious 665.25
pro forma 580.11
profound
  deep-felt 93.24
  downright 247.12
  huge 257.20
  deep 275.10
  recondite 522.16
  wise 920.17
  learned 928.21
profound thought
  thoughtfulness 931.3
  engrossment 983.3
profuse
  exaggerated 355.4
  liberal 485.4
  prodigal 486.8
  diffuse 538.11
  teeming 884.9
  plentiful 991.7
progenitor 560.8
progeny family 559.5
  offspring 561.1
prognosis
  prognostication 91.13
  verdict 946.5
  prediction 962.1
prognosticate
  hope 124.6
  predict 962.9
  risk 972.12
program
  n exercise 84.2
  announcement 352.2
  plan 381.1
  undertaking 404.1
  government plan 609.6
  platform 609.7
  performance 708.33
  track meet 755.2
  roll 871.6
  schedule 965.3
  software 1042.11
  rocketry 1074.1
  v plan 381.8
  inculcate 568.12
  list 871.8
  schedule 965.6
  automate 1041.20
  computerize 1042.21
programming language
  1042.13
progress
  n progression 162.1
  course 172.2
  travel 177.1
  journey 177.5
  way 182.9
  improvement 392.1
  continuance 856.1
  conversion 858.1
  evolution 861.1
  v advance 162.2
  move 172.5
  travel 177.18

  improve 392.7
  make good 409.10
  evolve 861.5
  prosper 1010.7
progressive
  n left side 220.1
  reformer 392.6
  liberal 611.11
  adj progressing 162.6
  flowing 172.8
  left 220.4
  gradual 245.5
  improving 392.15
  emendatory 392.16
  liberal 611.19
  consecutive 812.9
  modern 841.13
progressive dinner 8.6
progressive lenses 29.3
prohibit
  restrain 428.7
  forbid 444.3
  exclude 773.4
  make impossible 967.6
  prevent 1012.14
prohibition
  restraint 428.1
  ban 444.1
  forbidding 444.1
  prohibitionism 668.3
  exclusion 773.1
  prevention 1012.2
prohibitive
  prohibitory 444.6
  overpriced 632.12
  exclusive 773.9
  preventive 1012.19
project
  n intention 380.1
  projection 381.2
  undertaking 404.1
  task 724.2
  the future 839.1
  v overhang 202.7
  externalize 206.5
  protrude 283.10
  be manifest 348.7
  image 349.11
  intend 380.4
  plan 381.8
  show on screen 714.16
  lie ahead 839.6
  jaculate 904.11
  launch 1074.13
projectile
  n missile 462.18
  ejecta 904.5
  adj trajectile 904.15
projector planner 381.6
  launcher 462.21
  motion-picture projector
    714.12
  rocket launcher 1074.10
prolate
  n sphere 282.2
  adj. oval 280.12
proletarian
  n common man 606.5
  blue-collar worker 607.9
  worker 726.2
  adj working-class 607.10

proliferate
procreate 78.8
grow 251.6
multiply 883.6
produce 890.7
abound 991.5
prolific diffuse 538.11
teeming 884.9
productive 890.9
imaginative 986.18
prolix tedious 118.9
lengthened 267.8
wordy 538.12
talkative 540.9
protracted 827.11
superfluous 993.17
prologue act 704.7
part of writing 793.2
curtain-raiser 816.2
prolong lengthen 267.6
protract 827.9
postpone 846.9
sustain 856.4
prom dance 705.2
performance 708.33
assembly 770.2
PROM 1042.7
prom dress 5.11
promenade
n walk 177.10
path 383.2
dance 705.2
procession 812.3
v go for a walk 177.29
file 812.7
prominence
distinctness 31.2
glory 247.2
height 272.1
protuberance 283.2
conspicuousness 348.4
prestige 417.4
distinction 662.5
notability 997.2
prominent
distinct 31.7
eminent 247.9
high 272.14
protruding 283.14
conspicuous 348.12
authoritative 417.15
outstanding 662.17
notable 997.19
promiscuous
slipshod 340.12
wanton 665.26
mixed 797.14
unordered 810.12
undiscriminating 945.5
purposeless 972.16
promise
n hope 124.1
omen 133.3
commitment 436.2
pledge 436.1
compact 437.1
prediction 962.1
v give hope 124.9
suggest 133.12
observe 434.2
make a promise 436.4

contract 437.5
be probable 968.4
the Promised Land 986.11
promise ring 498.6
promising
of promise 124.12
auspicious 133.17
probable 968.6
promissory note 728.11
promo
promotion 352.5
commendation 509.3
promontory 283.9
promote
advance 162.5
publicize 352.15
motivate 375.12
be instrumental 384.7
improve 392.9
upgrade 446.2
be useful 449.17
commend 509.11
expedite one's affair 995.3
promoter
publicist 352.9
planner 381.6
commender 509.8
supporter 616.9
prompt
n hint 551.4
reminder 989.5
v provoke 375.13
induce 375.22
admonish 422.6
hint 551.10
influence 894.7
remind 989.19
adj eager 101.8
fast 174.15
willing 324.5
quick 330.18
alert 339.14
hasty 401.9
consenting 441.4
punctual 845.9
promulgate
publish 352.10
proclaim 352.13
command 420.8
execute 437.9
pronate 205.5
prone
v lie down 913.11
adj recumbent 201.8
low 274.7
willing 324.5
deferential 433.16
liable 897.5
disposed 978.8
prong fork 171.4
tributary 238.3
pronoun 530.5
pronounce affirm 334.5
announce 352.12
command 420.8
say 524.22
pass judgment 946.13
pronounced
distinct 31.7
downright 247.12
affirmed 334.9

conspicuous 348.12
speech 524.29
pronounce sentence
bring in a verdict 598.20
condemn 602.3
pronto
in short order 174.19
at once 830.8
promptly 845.15
pronunciation 524.5
proof
n manifestation 348.1
proof sheet 548.5
information 551.1
artist's proof 713.7
print 785.5
reasoning 935.1
test 942.2
grounds for belief 957.1
evidence 957.1
demonstration 957.3
confirmation 957.4
v insulate 15.14
print 548.14
adj resistant 15.20
proof positive
manifestation 348.1
proof 957.3
proofread 548.17
proofreader
reader 548.13
examiner 938.17
prop
n theater 704.17
motion-picture studio 706.4
supporter 901.2
propeller 904.6
v strengthen 15.13
aid 449.12
support 901.21
propaganda 569.2
propagate
procreate 78.8
publish 352.10
disperse 771.4
propel
set in motion 172.6
motivate 375.12
impel 902.11
push 904.9
propellant
n propeller 904.6
fuel 1021.1
rocket propulsion 1074.8
adj moving 172.7
propulsive 904.14
propeller 904.6
propensity
inclination 100.3
aptitude 413.5
tendency 896.1
disposition 978.3
proper
downright 247.12
useful 387.18
fastidious 495.9
decorous 496.9
appropriate 533.7
conventional 579.5
right 637.3
rightful 639.8

just 649.7
decent 664.5
orthodox 687.7
characteristic 865.13
accurate 973.16
expedient 995.5
proper fraction 1017.7
proper noun
name 527.3
noun 530.5
property supply 386.2
legal claim 469.1
possessions 471.1
real estate 471.6
sign 517.1
wealth 618.1
theater 704.17
nature 767.4
characteristic 865.4
property rights
possession 469.1
ownership 469.2
prophecy
revelation 683.10
the future 839.1
prediction 962.1
prophesy come 839.6
predict 962.9
prophet
religious founder 684.1
predictor 962.4
visionary 986.13
prophet of doom
pessimist 125.7
warner 399.4
predictor 962.4
prophylactic
n preventive 86.20
contraceptive 86.23
counteractant 900.3
safeguard 1008.3
adj sanitary 79.27
preventive 86.42
precautionary 494.10
protective 1008.23
deterrent 1012.19
propitiate pacify 465.7
atone 658.4
appease the gods 696.15
propitious
promising 124.12
auspicious 133.17
favorable 449.22
timely 843.9
proponent 600.8
proportion
n space 158.1
degree 245.1
size 257.1
symmetry 264.1
portion 477.5
harmony 533.2
equality 790.1
order 807.1
comparison 943.1
comparability 943.3
notation 1017.2
ratio 1017.7
v size 257.15
symmetrize 264.3
proportionate 477.7

make agree 788.7
equalize 790.6
proportional
　spatial 158.10
　proportionate 477.13
　approximate 775.8
proposal
　nomination 371.8
　intention 380.1
　project 381.2
　advice 422.1
　proposition 439.2
　marriage proposal 562.8
　theory 951.2
proposition
　n affirmation 334.1
　project 381.2
　undertaking 404.1
　proposal 439.2
　premise 935.7
　theory 951.2
　supposition 951.3
　axiom 974.2
　v make advances 439.8
proprietary
　n medicine 86.4
　ownership 469.2
　proprietor 470.2
　adj possessive 469.10
　propertied 471.8
proprietary information 210.3
proprietor
　householder 227.7
　proprietary 470.2
propriety
　fastidiousness 495.1
　decorousness 496.2
　elegance 533.1
　social convention 579.1
　decorum 637.2
　justice 649.1
　decency 664.2
　fitness 788.5
　timeliness 843.1
　normality 869.1
　expedience 995.1
propter hoc 888.7
propulsion
　manpower 18.4
　impulse 902.1
　pushing 904.1
pro rata
　proportionate 477.13
　proportionately 477.14
　priced 630.14
prorate
　proportion 477.7
　charge 630.12
prosaic prose 117.8
　simple 499.6
　plain-speaking 535.3
　prosy 721.5
　occupied 724.15
　unimaginative 987.5
proscenium front 216.1
　stage 704.16
proscribe
　restrain 428.7
　prohibit 444.3
　ostracize 586.6
　condemn 602.3

exclude 773.4
banish 909.17
prose
　n prosaicness 117.2
　prose style 721.1
　platitude 974.3
　v platitudinize 117.5
　write prose 721.3
　adj prosaic 117.8
　in prose 721.4
prosecute
　practice 328.8
　pursue 382.8
　execute 437.9
　sue 598.13
prosecuting attorney 597.1
prosecutor 599.5
proselytize 858.16
prosit 88.38
prospect
　n look 27.3
　field of view 31.3
　view 33.6
　hope 124.1
　expectation 130.1
　dueness 639.1
　customer 733.4
　the future 839.1
　foresight 961.1
　possibility 966.1
　probability 968.1
　v mine 1058.14
prospective
　expected 130.13
　future 839.8
prospector 1058.9
prospectus
　intention 380.1
　project 381.2
　prediction 962.1
　schedule 965.3
prosper succeed 409.7
　enjoy prosperity 1010.7
prosperity
　success 409.1
　wealth 618.1
　business cycle 731.10
　prosperousness 1010.1
　good times 1010.4
Prospero 976.2
prosperous
　auspicious 133.17
　successful 409.14
　wealthy 618.14
　in good case 1010.12
prosperous issue 409.1
prostitute
　n harlot 665.16
　v misuse 389.4
　corrupt 393.12
　adj prostituted 665.28
prostrate
　v disable 19.10
　fatigue 21.4
　aggrieve 112.19
　unnerve 128.10
　raze 395.19
　conquer 412.10
　fell 913.5
　lie down 913.11
　adj disabled 19.16

burnt-out 21.10
laid up 85.59
disconsolate 112.28
overcome 112.29
unnerved 128.14
obsequious 138.14
obeisant 155.10
recumbent 201.8
low 274.7
conquered 412.17
deferential 433.16
depressed 913.12
protagonist
　supporter 616.9
　role 704.10
　lead 707.6
protean
　multiform 783.3
　changeable 854.6
protect preserve 397.8
　aid 449.11
　defend 460.8
　play safe 1007.3
　guard 1008.18
protection
　bribe 378.2
　preservation 397.1
　restraint 428.1
　custody 429.5
　pass 443.7
　aid 449.1
　defense 460.1
　precaution 494.3
　policy 609.4
　safety 1007.1
　safeguarding 1008.1
　guard 1008.1
protectionist 428.6
protector
　defender 460.7
　regent 575.12
　keeper 1008.5
protégé 432.6
protein 7.6
pro tem 828.9
proteolytic 806.6
protest
　n complaint 115.4
　demur 325.2
　objection 333.2
　affirmation 334.1
　resistance 453.1
　disapproval 510.1
　nonpayment 625.1
　nonconformity 868.1
　v object 333.5
　affirm 334.5
　oppose 451.3
　offer resistance 453.3
　disapprove 510.10
　not pay 625.6
　not conform 868.4
Protestant
　n non-Catholic 675.20
　adj religious 675.28
protocol
　treatment 91.14
　rule 419.2
　compact 437.1
　etiquette 580.3
　fact 761.3

knowledge 928.1
schedule 965.3
proto-industrial 233.6
proton atom 258.8
　elementary particle 1038.6
protoplasm 305.4
prototype form 262.1
　original 337.2
　model 786.1
　philosophy 932.2
　standard of perfection
　　1002.4
protozoan
　microbic 258.15
　invertebrate 311.50
protract lengthen 267.6
　extend 538.8
　prolong 827.9
　postpone 846.9
　sustain 856.4
protractor 278.4
protrude
　emerge 190.11
　protuberate 283.10
proud prideful 136.8
　vain 140.9
　arrogant 141.9
　grandiose 501.21
　confident 970.21
provable real 761.15
　demonstrable 957.19
　obvious 970.15
prove print 548.14
　result 887.4
　experiment 942.8
　demonstrate 957.10
　confirm 957.11
　verify 970.12
　check 1017.21
proven
　trustworthy 644.19
　proved 957.20
　true 973.13
provender
　n food 10.1
　feed 10.4
　provisions 10.5
　supplies 385.2
　v provision 385.9
provenient 167.4
proverb
　n maxim 974.1
　v aphorize 974.5
provide supply 385.7
　prepare 405.6
　furnish 478.15
provide against
　prepare for 405.11
　take precautions 494.6
provided
　adj supplied 385.13
　prepared 405.16
　adv circumstantially 766.12
　conj in the event that 831.13
　provided that 959.12
provide for
　provide 385.7
　prepare for 405.11
　furnish 478.15
　take precautions 494.6
　finance 729.16

allow for 959.5
care for 1008.19
providence
  precaution 494.3
  thrift 635.1
  divine function 677.13
  sagacity 920.4
  judiciousness 920.7
  foresight 961.1
Providence 964.3
provider 385.6
province sphere 231.2
  region 231.5
  country 232.1
  the country 233.1
  duty 641.1
  diocese 698.8
  function 724.3
  occupation 724.4
  science 928.10
provincial
  n governor 575.13
  peasant 606.6
  adj local 231.9
  rustic 233.6
  idiomatic 523.22
  narrow-minded 980.10
proving ground
  laboratory 942.5
  testing ground 1074.7
provision
  n food 10.1
  groceries 10.5
  providing 385.1
  supplies 385.2
  store 386.1
  preparation 405.1
  stipulation 421.2
  support 449.3
  giving 478.1
  precaution 494.3
  substitution 862.1
  condition 959.2
  foresight 961.1
  expedient 995.2
  v feed 8.18
  provender 385.9
provisional government 612.4
proviso
  stipulation 421.2
  bill 613.9
  condition 959.2
provocateur 375.11
provocative
  appetizing 63.10
  desirable 100.30
  exciting 105.30
  aggravating 119.5
  provoking 375.27
  alluring 377.8
  hostile 589.10
  interesting 983.19
provoke annoy 96.13
  irritate 96.14
  vex 98.15
  stimulate 105.13
  aggravate 119.2
  be insolent 142.8
  incense 152.24
  prompt 375.13
  incite 375.17

sow dissension 456.14
antagonize 589.7
induce 886.11
interest 983.12
provost principal 571.8
  executive 574.3
prow 216.3
prowess skill 413.1
  courage 492.1
prowl
  n stealth 345.4
  v wander 177.23
  creep 177.26
  lurk 346.9
prowler 483.1
proximate
  n person 530.7
  v approach 167.3
  adj approaching 167.4
  near 223.14
  approximate 775.8
  succeeding 815.4
proximity
  nearness 223.1
  relation 775.1
proxy
  n vote 371.6
  deputy 576.1
  ballot 609.19
  voter 609.23
  commission 615.1
  substitute 862.2
  adj substitute 862.8
prude 500.11
prudent
  vigilant 339.13
  cautious 494.8
  economical 635.6
  moderate 670.10
  judicious 920.19
  foreseeing 961.7
prune excise 255.10
  shorten 268.6
  sever 802.11
  cultivate 1069.17
prune-faced
  sour 110.23
  aged 303.16
prurient lustful 75.27
  craving 100.24
  lascivious 665.29
  curious 981.5
pruritus itch 74.3
  symptom 85.9
  twitching 917.5
pry
  n meddler 214.4
  leverage 906.1
  lever 906.4
  inquisitive person 981.2
  v look 27.13
  meddle 214.7
  get a purchase 906.8
  search 938.31
  snoop 981.4
pry loose from 480.22
pry open 292.14
pry out extract 192.10
  elicit 192.14
  get a purchase 906.8
  grill 938.22

search out 938.34
uncover 941.4
PS 817.1
psalm
  n paean 696.3
  sacred music 708.17
  v sing 708.38
the Psalms 701.11
pseudo
  imitation 336.8
  spurious 354.26
pseudonym 527.8
psyche
  psychic apparatus 92.28
  spirit 919.4
psychedelic
  n psychoactive drug 86.13
  drug of abuse 87.3
  adj psychochemical 86.46
  hallucinatory 976.10
psyched up 405.16
psychiatric
  psychological 92.37
  psychotherapeutic 92.38
psychiatric hospital 926.14
psychiatric treatment 92.35
psychiatrist
  psychologist 92.10
  psychiatry 926.19
psychic
  n spiritualist 689.13
  predictor 962.4
  adj occult 689.24
  supernatural 870.15
  mental 919.7
  spectral 988.7
  immaterial 1053.7
psychic energy 92.28
psychic phenomena 689.6
psychic research 1053.1
psycho
  n lunatic 926.16
  psychotic 926.17
  adj crazy 926.27
psychoactive drug
  hallucinogen 86.13
  drug of abuse 87.3
psychoanalysis 92.6
psychoanalyst 92.10
psychoanalyze 92.36
psychobabble
  psychology 92.1
  jargon 523.10
psychochemical
  n drug 87.3
  adj psychoactive 86.46
psychogenic 92.37
psychokinesis 689.6
psychological
  psychiatric 92.37
  mental 919.7
psychological dependence 87.1
psychological warfare 127.6
psychologist 92.10
psychology
  science of the mind 92.1
  anthropology 312.10
  attitude 978.1
psychopathic
  psychological 92.37

psychotic 926.28
psychopathological 92.37
psychophysical 92.37
psychosexual 92.37
psychosis
  mental disorder 92.14
  psychopathy 926.3
psychosocial 92.37
psychosomatic 92.37
psychotherapeutic 92.38
psychotherapy
  therapy 91.1
  science of the mind 92.1
  psychotherapeutics 92.5
psychotic
  n insane 926.17
  adj psychological 92.37
  psychopathic 926.28
psych out
  unnerve 128.10
  solve 940.2
ptomaine poisoning 85.31
pub
  restaurant 8.17
  bar 88.20
puberty
  bodily development 14.1
  adolescence 301.6
pubescence hair 3.2
  bodily development 14.1
  smoothness 294.3
  adolescence 301.6
pubic hair genitals 2.13
  hair 3.2
public
  n bar 88.20
  follower 166.2
  population 227.1
  market 733.3
  adj exterior 206.7
  general 312.16
  published 352.17
  communal 476.9
  common 497.14
  populational 606.8
  well-known 928.27
public acclaim 662.1
public address 543.2
public assistance
  subsidy 478.8
  welfarism 611.7
publication
  informing 343.2
  manifestation 348.1
  dissemination 352.1
  publishing 352.1
  printing 548.1
  information 551.1
  book 554.1
  dispersion 771.1
public baths 79.10
public broadcasting
  radio broadcasting 1034.16
  television 1035.1
public defender 597.1
public domain 469.2
public enemy
  enemy 589.6
  evildoer 593.1
  criminal 660.9
public figure 662.9

publicist
publicizer 352.9
journalist 555.4
commentator 556.4
publicity
publicness 352.4
information 551.1
repute 662.1
public library 558.1
public nuisance
annoyance 96.2
tormentor 96.10
public official
official 575.16
officeholder 610.11
public opinion
political influence 609.29
opinion 953.6
public-opinion poll 938.14
public ownership
communion 476.2
socialism 611.6
public policy 609.4
public radio 1034.16
public records 549.2
public relations 352.4
public relations officer 551.5
public safety 1008.1
public school 567.4
public sector 731.7
public servant
official 575.16
officeholder 610.11
public telephone 347.4
public transportation
transportation 176.3
vehicle 179.1
public vehicles 179.13
public welfare
welfare 143.5
subsidy 478.8
publish divulge 351.5
promulgate 352.10
print 548.14
codify 673.10
disperse 771.4
publisher
informant 551.5
book publisher 554.2
publishing house
press 548.11
publisher 554.2
puce 41.6
pucker
n dither 105.6
anxiety 126.1
wrinkle 291.3
confusion 985.3
v contract 260.7
wrinkle 291.6
pudding food 10.46
softness 1047.4
semiliquid 1062.5
pulp 1063.2
puddle lake 241.1
mud puddle 1062.9
puddle jumper 181.2
pudgy corpulent 257.18
stubby 268.10
puerile childish 301.11
immature 406.11

simple-minded 922.24
puff
n breathing 2.21
pastry 10.41
smoking 89.10
distension 259.2
puff of air 318.3
foam 320.2
publicity 352.4
commendation 509.3
makeup 1016.11
softness 1047.4
v burn out 21.5
use 87.22
smoke 89.14
enlarge 259.4
blow 318.19
publicize 352.15
exaggerate 355.3
boast 502.6
commend 509.11
praise 509.12
let out 909.24
adj exaggerated 355.4
puffed 355.4
puff piece 545.3
puffy corpulent 257.18
distended 259.13
windy 318.21
pug
n foot 199.5
fighter 461.2
print 517.7
boxer 754.2
adj stubby 268.10
pugilist fighter 461.2
boxer 754.2
pugnacious
partisan 456.17
warlike 458.20
puhleez! 440.20
puissant strong 15.15
powerful 18.12
authoritative 417.15
puke
n vomiting 909.8
v feel disgust 99.4
vomit 909.27
pulchritude 1016.1
pule cry 60.2
whine 115.14
Pulitzer Prize 646.2
pull
n drink 8.4
power 18.1
swig 88.7
proof 548.5
strain 725.2
favor 894.2
pulling 905.1
draw 905.2
attraction 907.1
v drink 8.29
smoke 89.14
deflect 164.5
row 182.53
extract 192.10
lengthen 267.6
restrain 428.7
print 548.14
strain 725.10

play 751.4
draw 905.4
attract 907.4
pull a boner
bungle 414.12
make a boner 975.15
pull a fast one 415.11
pull ahead 249.10
pull a stunt
deceive 356.19
trick 489.14
pull away recede 168.2
dodge 368.8
separate 802.8
pull back regress 163.5
withdraw 163.6
retract 168.3
demur 325.4
hesitate 362.7
dodge 368.8
separate 802.8
retreat 903.7
pull down raze 395.19
acquire 472.9
receive 479.6
be paid 624.20
depress 913.4
fell 913.5
pullet fledgling 302.10
poultry 311.28
pull for 403.9
pull in
retract 168.3
arrive 186.6
restrain 428.7
arrest 429.16
stop 857.7
reel in 906.9
pull it together
order 807.4
arrange 808.8
Pullman car 197.10
pull off do 328.6
bring about 407.5
achieve one's purpose
409.8
succeed with 409.11
pull one's leg
fool 356.15
trick 489.14
ridicule 508.8
flatter 511.6
pull one's punches
limit 210.5
allow for 959.5
pull one's weight 476.6
pull out retreat 163.6
retract 168.3
maneuver 184.40
depart 188.6
extract 192.10
abandon 370.5
defect 370.6
separate 802.8
pull out all the stops 430.19
pull rank 424.8
pull strings
maneuver 415.10
exercise influence 894.9
pull the plug on 395.11
pull the trigger 459.22

pull the wool over one's eyes
356.17
pull through
cure 396.15
recover 396.20
pull together
plan 381.8
cooperate 450.3
pull up
maneuver 184.40
extract 192.10
arraign 598.15
stop 857.7
put a stop to 857.11
pull up short 131.7
pull up stakes
disappear 34.2
depart 188.7
decamp 188.14
leave 222.10
flee 368.10
pulmonary 2.32
pulp
n semiliquid 1062.5
paste 1063.2
v soften 1047.6
pulpify 1063.5
pulp fiction 722.1
pulpit rostrum 703.13
platform 901.13
pulpy insipid 65.2
spongy 1047.11
semiliquid 1062.11
pulpous 1063.6
pulsar 1072.8
pulsate drum 55.4
recur 850.5
pulse 916.12
pulse
n plant 310.4
beat 709.26
round 850.3
pulsation 916.3
radio-frequency pulse 1036.10
v resonate 54.6
recur 850.5
pulsate 916.12
flutter 917.12
pulverize
demolish 395.17
come apart 802.9
shatter 802.13
pound 902.16
powder 1051.9
puma 311.21
pumice 287.8
pumice stone 79.17
pummel whip 604.13
pound 902.16
pump
n viscera 2.16
extractor 192.9
poker 759.10
machinery 1040.3
v draw off 192.12
enlarge 259.4
process 892.9
alternate 916.14
interrogate 938.21
pumped up
energetic 17.13

prepared 405.16
overestimated 949.3
pumping iron 84.2
pumpkin 42.2
pun
n wordplay 489.8
ambiguity 539.2
assonance 784.6
v joke 489.13
assonate 784.9
punch
n energy 17.3
power 18.1
zest 68.2
drink 88.9
vigor 544.3
engraving tool 713.8
fight 754.3
mold 786.6
thrust 902.2
hit 902.4
boxing punch 902.6
v indent 284.14
perforate 292.15
mark 517.19
fight 754.4
thrust 902.12
hit 902.14
Punch and Judy 707.10
punch bowl
spirits 88.13
cavity 284.2
punching bag 725.7
punch line 489.6
punch out
check out 188.13
ring in 832.12
beat 902.17
punch the clock 832.12
punctual
meticulous 339.12
observant 434.4
conscientious 644.15
prompt 845.9
punctuate mark 517.19
grammaticize 530.16
emphasize 997.14
punctuation
punctuation marks 530.15
written character 547.9
puncture
n trauma 85.38
hole 292.3
mark 517.5
v collapse 260.10
perforate 292.15
injure 393.13
mark 517.19
disprove 958.4
puncture proof
resistant 15.20
impervious 293.13
pundit expert 413.11
teacher 571.1
clergy 699.13
specialist 866.3
intellectual 929.1
scholar 929.3
pungent intense 15.22
painful 26.10
bitter 64.6

sour 67.5
piquant 68.6
strong 69.10
witty 489.15
spirited 544.12
aphoristic 974.6
punish
torture 96.18
penalize 603.4
chastise 604.10
get even with 506.7
punishment
reprisal 506.2
penalty 603.1
disciplinary measure 604.1
punk
n homosexual 75.14
brat 302.4
a nobody 998.7
tinder 1021.6
adj insignificant 998.18
bad 1000.8
inferior 1005.9
punk rock music 708.1
type of music 708.11
punt
n game 746.3
kick 902.9
v row 182.53
compromise 468.2
play 746.5
bet 759.25
puny frail 16.14
little 258.10
haggard 270.20
meager 992.10
petty 998.20
pupa 302.12
pupil eye 2.9
sight organ 27.9
student 572.1
puppet
sycophant 138.3
miniature 258.6
figure 349.6
instrument 384.4
figurehead 575.5
deputy 576.1
agent 576.3
follower 616.8
toy 743.16
thing of naught 764.2
puppet government
country 232.1
dependent 432.6
puppy member 2.7
impudent person 142.5
boy 302.5
fledgling 302.10
dog 311.16
dandy 500.9
puppy-dog eyes 562.9
puppy love 104.3
purchase
n grasp 474.2
buying 733.1
influence 894.1
footing 901.5
hold 906.2
tackle 906.6
v bribe 378.3

buy 733.7
purchasing agent 733.5
purchasing power
pay 624.4
purchase 733.1
pure clean 79.25
essential 192.18
tasteful 496.7
elegant 533.6
plain-speaking 535.3
honest 644.13
virtuous 653.6
spotless 657.7
chaste 664.4
godly 692.9
thorough 794.10
simple 798.6
genuine 973.15
perfect 1002.6
purebred
upper-class 607.10
wellborn 608.11
purée 1062.5
pure white 37.7
purgatory
torment 96.7
place of confinement 429.7
penance 658.3
hell 682.1
purge
n defecation 12.2
cleansing 79.2
cleanser 79.17
laxative 86.17
release 120.2
homicide 308.2
extinction 395.6
deposal 447.2
elimination 773.2
v clean 79.18
treat 91.24
release 120.6
kill 308.13
murder 308.16
exterminate 395.14
depose 447.4
justify 600.9
acquit 601.4
eliminate 773.5
do away with 909.21
evacuate 909.22
purify clean 79.18
refine 79.22
subtract 255.9
make plain 499.5
sanctify 685.5
simplify 798.4
purist
n obstinate person 361.6
classicist 533.4
pedant 929.5
adj firm 425.7
strict 687.8
puritan
n prude 500.11
ascetic 667.2
adj firm 425.7
Puritan 860.3
purity
color quality 35.6
cleanness 79.1

plainness 499.1
elegance 533.1
probity 644.1
immaculacy 653.2
innocence 657.1
chastity 664.1
godliness 692.2
simplicity 798.1
oneness 872.1
perfection 1002.1
purl ripple 52.11
border 211.10
eddy 238.21
purlieu haunt 228.27
arena 463.1
purloin 482.13
purple
n purpleness 46.1
royal insignia 647.3
v empurple 46.2
adj purpure 46.3
color varieties 46.4
sovereign 417.17
ornate 545.11
purport
n meaning 518.1
v pretext 376.3
intend 380.4
purpose
n resolution 359.1
intention 380.1
function 387.5
intent 518.2
v resolve 359.7
intend 380.4
purr hum 52.13
be pleased 95.12
purse
n funds 728.14
wallet 729.15
v contract 260.7
wrinkle 291.6
purser hand 183.6
attendant 577.5
payer 624.9
treasurer 729.12
purse snatcher 483.2
purse strings 729.15
pursue follow 166.3
practice 328.8
prosecute 382.8
persecute 389.7
court 562.21
elaborate 861.6
specialize 866.4
seek 938.30
pursuer
enthusiast 101.4
lover 104.11
follower 166.2
pursuant 382.4
pursuit
following 166.1
intention 380.1
seeking 382.1
pursuing 382.1
vocation 724.6
specialty 866.1
purulent
puss-filled 2.33
festering 12.21

v extract 192.10
excavate 284.15
mine 1058.14
quart 881.2
quarter
  n pity 145.1
  direction 161.1
  side 218.1
  region 231.1
  heraldry 647.2
  money 728.7
  game 746.3
  basketball game 747.3
  soccer 752.3
  part 793.1
  moment 824.2
  fourth 881.2
  v house 225.10
  divide by four 881.3
  adj fourth 881.5
quarterback
  n football team 746.2
  v direct 573.8
quarter horse 757.2
quarterly
  n periodical 555.1
  adj momentary 850.8
quartermaster
  ship's officer 183.7
  steersman 183.8
  provider 385.6
quarter note 709.14
quarter rest 709.21
quarters 228.4
quartet
  cooperation 450.1
  part music 708.18
  four 879.1
quasar 1072.8
quash cover up 345.8
  extinguish 395.15
  suppress 428.8
quasi
  adj imitation 336.8
  spurious 354.26
  nominal 527.15
  approximating 784.14
  adv imitatively 336.11
  supposedly 951.17
quasilinear 277.6
quaternary
  n four 879.1
  adj four 879.4
quaver
  n trepidation 105.5
  speech defect 525.1
  note 709.14
  trill 709.19
  shake 917.3
  v be weak 16.8
  be excited 105.18
  tremble 127.14
  speak poorly 525.7
  sing 708.38
  shake 917.11
queasy nauseated 85.57
  overfastidious 495.12
queen
  homo 75.15
  mollycoddle 77.9
  ant 311.32

bee 311.33
  sovereign queen 575.11
  princess 608.8
  chessman 743.17
  card 758.2
  chief 997.10
  the best 999.8
queen bee bee 311.34
  chief 575.4
  important person 997.9
Queensbury rules 754.1
queen size
  n large size 257.4
  adj large 257.16
queer
  n homosexual 75.15
  counterfeit 728.10
  v disable 19.9
  spoil 393.11
  hinder 1012.16
  adj homosexual 75.30
  spurious 354.26
  odd 870.11
  insane 926.26
  eccentric 927.5
quell extinguish 395.15
  conquer 412.10
  suppress 428.8
  subdue 432.9
  calm 670.7
quench gratify 95.8
  disincline 379.4
  extinguish 395.15
  suppress 428.8
  fight fire 1022.7
query
  n question 938.10
  v inquire 938.20
  interrogate 938.21
  doubt 955.6
  be curious 981.3
que serà serà 964.11
quest
  n intention 380.1
  pursuit 382.1
  adventure 404.2
  search 938.15
  v pursue 382.8
  seek 938.30
question
  n enigma 522.8
  remark 524.3
  bill 613.9
  topic 937.1
  query 938.10
  doubt 955.2
  gamble 971.8
  v communicate with 343.8
  inquire 938.20
  interrogate 938.21
  doubt 955.6
  be uncertain 971.9
  be curious 981.3
questionable
  deceptive 356.21
  dishonest 645.16
  unbelievable 955.10
  improbable 969.3
  doubtful 971.17
questioning
  n interrogation 938.12

adj communicational
  343.9
  inquiring 938.36
  doubting 955.9
question mark
  enigma 522.8
  question 938.10
questionnaire
  n roll 871.6
  canvass 938.14
  v canvass 938.29
queue
  n braid 3.7
  tail 217.6
  series 812.2
  afterpart 817.2
  v line up 812.6
quibble
  n criticism 510.4
  quiddity 936.4
  v find fault 510.15
  argue 935.16
  cavil 936.9
quiche 10.41
quick
  adj eager 101.8
  hot-tempered 110.25
  fast 174.15
  living 306.12
  willing 324.5
  swift 330.18
  alert 339.14
  impulsive 365.9
  hasty 401.9
  skillful 413.22
  teachable 570.18
  brief 828.8
  sudden 830.5
  prompt 845.9
  smart 920.14
  adv swiftly 174.17
the quick
  sore spot 24.4
  provocation 152.11
  the living 306.3
  inner nature 767.5
quick and dirty
  extemporaneous 365.12
  handy 387.20
  makeshift 995.7
quick-eared 48.15
quicken refresh 9.2
  energize 17.10
  sensitize 24.7
  stimulate 105.13
  accelerate 174.10
  come to life 306.9
  vivify 306.10
  hasten 401.4
  be useful 449.17
  facilitate 1014.7
quick fix 995.2
quick-freeze
  preserve 397.9
  freeze 1024.11
quick on the draw
  sensitive 24.12
  quick 330.18
  alert 339.14
  impulsive 365.9
  reactive 903.9

quicksand marsh 243.1
  danger 1006.1
  predicament 1013.4
quicksilver
  n swiftness 174.6
  changeableness 854.4
  adj active 330.17
  fickle 364.6
  brass 1058.17
quickstep march
  march 177.13
  military march 708.12
quid bite 8.2
  chewing tobacco 89.7
  money 728.8
quiddative 495.13
quid pro quo
  offset 338.2
  tit for tat 506.3
  interaction 777.3
  substitution 862.1
  interchange 863.1
quiescent silent 51.10
  quiet 173.12
  passive 329.6
  inactive 331.17
  permanent 853.7
quiet
  n rest 20.1
  silence 51.1
  composure 106.2
  quiescence 173.1
  peacefulness 464.2
  order 807.1
  v fall silent 51.7
  silence 51.8
  quieten 173.8
  calm 670.7
  order 807.4
  adj vacational 20.10
  soft-colored 35.22
  silent 51.10
  calm 106.12
  reserved 139.11
  quiescent 173.12
  taciturn 344.9
  covert 345.12
  meek 433.15
  pacific 464.9
  tasteful 496.7
  interj silence! 51.14
quiet revolution 392.5
quill
  n feather 3.16
  feather part 3.17
  thorn 285.5
  v fold 291.5
quilt 295.10
quintessential
  essential 192.18
  typical 349.15
  characteristic 865.13
  best 999.16
  perfected 1002.9
quintet
  cooperation 450.1
  part music 708.18
  five 882.1
quintuplets 882.1
quip
  n witticism 489.7

radioactive decay 393.6
radioactive element 1037.5
radioactive isotope 1038.5
radioactive particle 1037.4
radio broadcasting 1034.16
radiocarbon dating 1037.1
radio frequency 1034.12
radio-frequency 1034.28
radioisotope
  radiotherapy 91.8
  radioactive 1037.5
  isotope 1038.5
radiology
  radiography 91.7
  radiation physics 1037.8
  nuclear physics 1038.1
radioluminescence 1025.13
radioman 1034.24
radio signal 1034.10
radio silence
  silence 51.1
  radio signal 1034.10
radio station
  transmitting station 1034.6
  space station 1075.5
radiotelephone 347.5
radio telescope
  radio 1034.3
  observatory 1072.17
radiotherapy
  radiation therapy 91.6
  radiation physics 1037.8
radio transmitter 1034.4
radium
  radiotherapy 91.8
  cauterant 1020.15
radius
  convergence 169.1
  radiation 171.2
  size 257.1
  diameter 269.3
  straight line 277.2
  circle 280.2
raffle 759.14
raft
  n float 180.11
  lot 247.4
  wealth 618.3
  v haul 176.13
rag
  n material 4.1
  garment 5.3
  sail 180.14
  newspaper 555.2
  rabble 606.3
  scenery 704.20
  dance music 708.8
  tempo 709.24
  v berate 510.19
  syncopate 708.43
  play 749.7
ragamuffin 178.3
rag doll 743.16
rage
  n fury 105.8
  fit 152.8
  passion 152.10
  fad 578.5
  violence 671.1
  turbulence 671.2
  frenzy 926.7

mania 926.12
  v be excitable 105.16
  be angry 152.15
  blow 318.19
  bluster 503.3
  storm 671.11
  be insane 926.20
ragged
  raucous 58.15
  tormented 96.24
  rugged 288.7
  shabby 393.32
  nonuniform 782.3
  slovenly 810.15
ragging
  n bantering 490.3
  ridicule 508.1
  game 749.3
  adj ridiculing 508.12
raging
  n violence 671.1
  adj frenzied 105.25
  infuriated 152.32
  stormy 318.22
  blustering 503.4
  turbulent 671.18
  rabid 926.30
rags material 4.1
  clothing 5.1
  tatters 5.5
  remainder 256.1
  refuse 391.4
  poker 759.10
rags-to-riches 1010.12
ragtag 606.3
ragtime
  n dance music 708.8
  tempo 709.24
  adj syncopated 709.29
rah 116.2
raid
  n foray 459.4
  plundering 482.6
  manipulation 737.20
  v foray 459.20
  plunder 482.17
raider assailant 459.12
  plunderer 483.6
rail
  n fence 212.4
  thinness 270.7
  railway 383.7
  horse racing 757.1
  v fence 212.7
rail at scoff 508.9
  berate 510.19
railroad
  n railway 383.7
  game 750.2
  v thrust 902.12
railroad through
  hasten 401.4
  legislate 613.10
raiment
  n clothing 5.1
  v clothe 5.39
rain
  n precipitation 316.1
  rainfall 316.1
  television reception 1035.5
  water 1065.3

v descend 194.5
  precipitate 316.10
  give 478.12
  abound 991.5
  flood 1065.14
rainbow
  n variegation 47.6
  omen 133.5
  halo 1025.14
  iridescence 1025.18
  adj chromatic 35.16
raincoat 5.13
rainfall rain 316.1
  moisture 1065.1
rain on one's parade
  393.11
rain tadpoles 316.10
rainy
  showery 316.11
  stormy 318.22
  moist 1065.15
raise
  n increase 251.1
  height 272.2
  promotion 446.1
  poker 759.10
  v erect 200.9
  increase 251.4
  enlarge 259.4
  emboss 283.12
  leaven 298.7
  communicate with 343.8
  rouse 375.19
  make better 392.9
  promote 446.2
  say 524.22
  train 568.13
  enlist 615.17
  glorify 662.13
  conjure 690.11
  assemble 770.18
  inaugurate 818.11
  produce 892.8
  process 892.9
  elevate 912.5
  farm 1069.16
  breed 1070.6
raise a hand 453.3
raise an alarm 400.3
raise an objection
  dissent 333.4
  disapprove 510.10
raise a question 955.6
raise a ruckus 810.11
raise a stink 115.16
raise Cain
  be noisy 53.9
  be angry 152.15
  create disorder 810.11
raised increased 251.7
  expanded 259.10
  in relief 283.18
  produced 892.17
  made 892.18
  lifted 912.9
raise expectations 124.9
raise eyebrows 661.7
raise money 621.3
raise objections 333.5
raise one's pay 446.2
raise the curtain 351.4

raise the roof
  be noisy 53.9
  be angry 152.15
  create disorder 810.11
raise the spirits 109.7
raise the stakes 759.24
raison d'être
  objective 380.2
  cause 886.9
rake
  n inclination 204.2
  thinness 270.7
  projection 285.4
  libertine 665.10
  v comb 79.21
  incline 204.10
  pull the trigger 459.22
  be promiscuous 665.19
  ransack 938.33
  cultivate 1069.17
rake it in profit 472.12
  grow rich 618.10
rake over the coals 510.18
rakish showy 501.19
  profligate 665.25
rally
  n objection 333.2
  recovery 396.8
  contest 457.3
  call to arms 458.7
  electioneering 609.12
  price 738.9
  tournament 743.10
  game 748.2
  assembly 770.2
  v object 333.5
  incite 375.17
  come about 392.8
  recuperate 396.19
  recover 396.20
  aid 449.11
  call to arms 458.18
  banter 490.5
  scoff 508.9
  come together 770.16
  assemble 770.18
  dispose 808.9
  adduce 957.12
rallying cry
  cry 59.1
  call to arms 458.7
  call 517.16
rally round
  side with 450.4
  form 807.5
ram
  n male animal 76.8
  sheep 311.7
  v sail into 182.41
  thrust 902.12
RAM 1042.7
Ramadan
  fast day 515.3
  holy day 701.14
ramble
  n wandering 177.3
  walk 177.10
  v stray 164.4
  wander 177.23
  be incomprehensible 522.10
  digress 538.9

be insane 926.20
daydream 984.3
muse 985.9
rambunctious 671.20
ramification
  forking 171.3
  fork 171.4
  branch 310.20
  nonuniformity 782.1
  member 793.4
  complexity 799.1
  bisection 875.1
ramjet 181.3
ramp
  n stairs 193.3
  incline 204.4
  deception 356.9
  skiing 753.1
  v be excitable 105.16
  climb 193.11
  rise 200.8
  deceive 356.19
  caper 366.6
  rage 671.11
rampage
  n commotion 810.4
  v rage 671.11
rampant
  ascending 193.14
  vertical 200.11
  lawless 418.5
  unrestrained 430.24
  unruly 671.19
  prevalent 864.12
  raised 912.9
  plentiful 991.7
rampart
  fortification 460.4
  buttress 901.4
  barrier 1012.5
ramrod straight 200.11
ramshackle
  unsteady 16.16
  dilapidated 393.33
ranch
  n farmstead 228.6
  farm 1070.5
  v farm 1069.16
  raise 1070.6
rancher 1070.2
rancid nasty 64.7
  malodorous 71.5
  tainted 393.41
rancor virulence 144.7
  bitterness 152.3
  revengefulness 507.2
  animosity 589.4
R and D 942.1
random
  n haphazard 972.4
  adj unordered 810.12
  vague 971.19
  purposeless 972.16
random testing 938.6
R and R 20.2
range
  n vision 27.1
  field of view 31.3
  earshot 48.4
  scope 158.2
  direction 161.1

habitat 228.18
highlands 237.1
mountain 237.6
degree 245.1
size 257.1
distance 261.1
grassland 310.8
latitude 430.4
arena 463.1
scale 709.6
series 812.2
v extend 158.9
traverse 177.20
wander 177.23
size 257.15
dispose 808.9
classify 809.6
align 812.5
range of motion 158.2
ranger preserver 397.5
  guardian 1008.6
  forester 1069.7
rani
  amphibian 311.26
  sovereign queen 575.11
  princess 608.8
rank
  n standing 245.2
  authority 417.4
  military unit 461.22
  class 607.1
  nobility 608.2
  prestige 662.4
  state 765.1
  continuity 807.2
  category 809.2
  series 812.2
  v rule 249.11
  size 257.15
  order 807.4
  classify 808.11
  categorize 809.6
  align 812.5
  precede 814.2
  estimate 946.9
  rate 946.15
  adj nasty 64.7
  strong 68.8
  malodorous 71.5
  filthy 80.23
  downright 247.12
  rough 288.6
  luxuriant 310.43
  tainted 393.41
  wicked 654.16
  base 661.12
  vulgar 666.8
  terrible 1000.9
rank and file
  army 461.23
  the people 606.1
rankle fester 12.15
  pain 26.7
  provoke 152.24
  decay 393.22
  be remembered 989.13
rank-order 946.9
ransack plunder 482.17
  rummage 938.33
ransom
  n rescue 398.1

recovery 481.3
v redeem 396.12
rescue 398.3
recover 481.6
rant
  n bluster 503.1
  nonsense 520.2
  bombast 545.2
  v be excitable 105.16
  be angry 152.15
  bluster 503.3
  declaim 543.10
  rage 671.11
  overact 704.31
  be insane 926.20
rap
  n thud 52.3
  report 56.1
  criticism 510.4
  discussion 541.6
  condemnation 602.1
  hit 902.4
  tap 902.7
  trifle 998.5
  v thud 52.15
  crack 56.6
  criticize 510.14
  discuss 541.11
  pound 902.16
  tap 902.18
rapacious
  greedy 100.27
  ravenous 480.26
  gluttonous 672.6
rape
  n sexual possession 480.3
  plundering 482.6
  seduction 665.6
  unruliness 671.3
  v possess sexually 480.15
  seduce 665.20
  rage 671.11
rapid
  n rapids 238.10
  adj fast 174.15
  steep 204.18
  constant 847.5
rapid deployment force 461.15
rapid-eye-movement sleep 22.1
rapid fire 847.2
rapid-response 174.15
rapids rapid 238.10
  outburst 671.6
rapist
  sexual pervert 75.16
  seducer 665.12
  violent person 671.9
rap on the knuckles
  n reproof 510.5
  slap 604.3
  v reprove 510.17
rapping
  n speech 524.1
  conversation 541.1
  adj banging 56.11
rapport
  pleasantness 97.1
  accord 455.1
  good terms 587.3
  relation 775.1

rapprochement 587.3
rapt overjoyed 95.17
  persevering 360.8
  absorbed in thought 931.22
  gripped 983.18
  abstracted 985.11
rapture happiness 95.2
  amorousness 104.2
  fury 105.8
  trance 691.3
rara avis 870.4
rare underdone 11.9
  wonderful 122.10
  superior 249.12
  thin 270.16
  rarefied 299.4
  raw 406.10
  other 780.8
  infrequent 848.2
  unusual 870.10
  sparse 885.5
  scarce 992.11
  notable 997.19
rare-earth metals 1058.3
rarefaction 299.2
rarefied diluted 16.19
  dainty 248.7
  thin 270.16
  rare 299.4
  tenuous 764.6
rarin' to go 135.6
rascal
  mischief-maker 322.3
  precious rascal 660.3
rash
  n symptom 85.9
  skin eruption 85.36
  adj impulsive 365.9
  precipitate 401.10
  brash 493.7
rasp
  n scratch 58.3
  v pain 26.7
  grate 58.10
  irritate 96.14
  abrade 1044.7
raspberry 508.3
rassle 457.13
Rastafarian 675.24
rat
  n false hair 3.13
  traitor 357.10
  informer 551.6
  bad person 660.5
  strikebreaker 727.8
  v betray 351.6
  inform on 551.13
  break a strike 727.11
rat-a-tat staccato 55.1
  pulsation 916.3
rat bastard 660.6
ratchet 285.4
rate
  n velocity 172.4
  rank 245.2
  interest 623.3
  price 630.1
  worth 630.2
  ratio 1017.7
  v quantify 244.4
  measure 300.10

reprove 510.17
berate 510.19
price 630.11
deserve 639.5
classify 809.6
precede 814.2
estimate 946.9
rank 946.15
rate of exchange 728.9
rate of interest 623.3
rate of pay 624.4
rather
  v prefer 371.17
  adv to a degree 245.7
  notwithstanding 338.8
  preferably 371.28
  contrarily 779.9
  instead 862.11
  tolerably 999.24
  interj yes 332.18
  right on! 973.25
rathole sty 80.11
  hovel 228.11
rathskeller 88.20
ratify endorse 332.12
  adopt 371.15
  consent 441.2
  authorize 443.11
  secure 855.8
  confirm 957.11
rating rank 245.2
  measurement 300.1
  reproof 510.5
  berating 510.7
  credit 622.1
  valuation 630.3
  motion pictures 706.1
  classification 809.1
  class 809.2
  estimate 946.3
ratings 1035.2
ratio degree 245.1
  intellect 919.1
  comparability 943.3
  rate 1017.7
ratiocinate think about 931.11
  reason 935.15
ration
  n amount 244.2
  portion 477.5
  v budget 477.10
rational mental 919.7
  intelligent 920.12
  sensible 920.18
  sane 925.4
  cognitive 931.21
  reasoning 935.18
  logical 935.20
  open-minded 979.10
  realistic 987.6
  numeric 1017.23
rationale
  explanation 341.4
  announcement 352.2
  reason 886.2
rationalize
  explain 341.10
  plan 381.8
  justify 600.9
  organize 808.10
  classify 809.6

reason 935.15
reason speciously 936.8
rational motive 375.1
rations board 10.6
  store 386.1
rat race
  futility 391.2
  work 725.4
  whirl 915.2
rat's nest
  hodgepodge 797.6
  complex 799.2
  jumble 810.3
rattan rod 605.2
  cane 1054.4
rattle
  n noise 53.3
  noisemaker 53.6
  rattling 55.3
  chatterer 540.4
  throw 759.9
  v weaken 16.10
  ruckle 55.6
  agitate 105.14
  talk nonsense 520.5
  chatter 540.5
  thrust 902.12
  confuse 985.7
rattle off repeat 849.7
  memorize 989.16
ratty rodent 311.44
  shabby 393.32
  infested 910.11
raucous raucid 58.15
  dissonant 61.4
raunchy coarse 497.11
  obscene 666.9
  bad 1000.8
ravage
  n destruction 395.1
  plundering 482.6
  seduction 665.6
  infestation 910.2
  v corrupt 393.12
  destroy 395.10
  plunder 482.17
  seduce 665.20
  infest 910.6
ravages of time
  wear 393.5
  disintegration 806.1
  tract of time 821.3
rave
  n party 582.12
  v be enthusiastic 101.7
  be excitable 105.16
  be angry 152.15
  bluster 503.3
  rage 671.11
  be insane 926.20
raven
  n blackness 38.4
  bird of ill omen 133.5
  v hunger 100.19
  plunder 482.17
  gluttonize 672.4
  adj black 38.8
ravenous
  hungry 100.25
  greedy 100.27
  rapacious 480.26

gluttonous 672.6
ravine valley 237.7
  gulch 284.9
ravioli 10.33
ravish delight 95.10
  corrupt 393.12
  possess sexually 480.15
  plunder 482.17
  seduce 665.20
raw
  n sore spot 24.4
  adj naked 6.14
  sore 26.11
  garish 35.20
  callow 301.10
  windblown 318.23
  crude 406.10
  immature 406.11
  inexperienced 414.17
  coarse 497.11
  cursing 513.8
  vulgar 666.8
  new 841.7
  ignorant 930.11
  cold 1023.14
the raw 6.3
raw data 770.11
raw deal
  injustice 650.4
  bad luck 1011.5
rawhide
  n fur 4.2
  whip 605.1
  v whip 604.13
raw material
  unlicked cub 263.2
  crude 406.5
  materials 1054.1
raw nerve
  sore spot 24.4
  provocation 152.11
ray
  n divergence 171.2
  wave 916.4
  light 1025.5
  radiation 1037.3
  v radiate 171.6
ray of sunshine
  optimist 124.5
  daylight 1025.10
raze level 201.6
  obliterate 395.16
  rase 395.19
  fell 913.5
  abrade 1044.7
razorback 311.9
razor-edged 285.8
razor-sharp 415.12
razz
  n boo 508.3
  v banter 490.6
razzledazzle 501.3
RBI 745.4
re 775.13
reach
  n earshot 48.4
  range 158.2
  inlet 242.1
  degree 245.1
  size 257.1
  distance 261.1

length 267.1
  knowledge 928.1
  v be heard 48.12
  move 145.5
  extend 158.9
  travel 177.19
  sail for 182.35
  arrive 186.6
  arrive at 186.7
  extend to 261.6
  communicate with 343.8
  bribe 378.3
  deliver 478.13
  equal 790.5
  suffice 991.4
reachable 966.8
reach a compromise 468.2
reach an agreement 332.10
reach for the sky 100.20
reach maturity 407.8
reach one's goal 409.8
reach orgasm 75.24
reach out
  extend 158.9
  stretch out 261.5
  be long 267.5
reach the breaking point
  993.13
react
  be affected 93.11
  respond 903.5
  answer 939.4
reaction
  mental disorder 92.14
  feeling 93.1
  regression 163.1
  propulsion 184.25
  resistance 453.1
  conservatism 611.1
  impact 887.2
  counteraction 900.1
  response 903.1
  answer 939.1
  opinion 953.6
reactionary
  n malcontent 108.3
  right side 219.1
  conservative 611.9
  back number 842.8
  reactionist 903.4
  adj regressive 163.11
  right 219.4
  conservative 611.17
  reversionary 859.7
  counteractive 900.8
  reactive 903.9
reactivate
  activate 17.12
  restore 396.11
  militarize 458.19
reactive 903.9
reactor 1038.13
read
  interpret 341.9
  understand 521.8
  declaim 543.10
  copyedit 548.17
  study 570.12
  sound out 942.9
read between the lines
  interpret 341.9

explain 341.10
see through 941.8
reader
 advertisement 352.6
 lecturer 543.5
 elocutionist 543.7
 proofreader 548.13
 textbook 554.10
 journalist 555.4
 academic rank 571.3
 teacher 571.7
 student 572.1
 holy orders 699.4
 input device 1042.4
reading
 measure 300.2
 interpretation 341.1
 rendering 341.2
 speech 543.2
 elementary education
  568.5
 study 570.3
 scholarship 928.5
 signal 1036.11
reading glasses 29.3
read into
 interpret 341.9
 explain 341.10
readjust 858.14
readmit 187.15
read my lips 535.5
read one loud and clear 521.8
read one's mind 689.22
read someone like a book
 perceive 521.9
 see through 941.8
read tea leaves 962.9
read the riot act
 lay down the law 420.10
 reprove 510.17
read up on
 study 570.12
 study up 570.14
 search 938.31
ready
 v repair 396.14
 prepare 405.6
 train 568.13
 adj eager 101.8
 expectant 130.11
 willing 324.5
 quick 330.18
 alert 339.14
 handy 387.20
 prepared 405.16
 skillful 413.22
 cunning 415.12
 consenting 441.4
 teachable 570.18
 prompt 845.9
 foreseeing 961.7
ready-made
 tailored 5.48
 ready-formed 405.19
 made 892.18
ready oneself 570.11
ready-to-wear
 n ready-mades 5.4
 adj tailored 5.48
 ready-made 405.19
 made 892.18

ready wit wit 489.1
 smartness 920.2
reaffirm 849.8
real
 adj land 471.9
 actual 761.15
 substantial 763.6
 obvious 970.15
 true 973.13
 genuine 973.15
 numeric 1017.23
 adv very 247.18
real estate plot 231.4
 land 234.1
 realty 471.6
real estate loan 438.4
realign
 parallelize 203.5
 rearrange 808.13
 change 852.7
realism
 normality 869.1
 genuineness 973.7
 realisticness 987.2
 materialism 1052.6
realistic
 descriptive 349.14
 typical 349.15
 occupied 724.15
 lifelike 784.16
 normal 869.8
 ungullible 956.5
 genuine 973.15
 realist 987.6
 materialistic 1052.12
reality actuality 761.2
 event 831.2
 unquestionability 970.3
 truth 973.1
reality television 1035.2
realize
 externalize 206.5
 do 328.6
 image 349.11
 accomplish 407.4
 profit 472.12
 understand 521.7
 be sold 734.12
 cause 886.10
 establish 892.10
 perform 892.11
 know 928.12
 visualize 986.15
 recognize 989.11
reallocate 808.13
really
 astonishment 122.19
 yes 332.18
realm sphere 231.2
 country 232.1
 occupation 724.4
 hierarchy 809.4
the real McCoy 973.4
real time 1042.18
realtor 730.9
realty 471.6
the real world 973.1
ream
 n paper 1054.5
 v masturbate 75.22
 perforate 292.15

disapprove 510.18
reap shorten 268.6
 acquire 472.8
 harvest 1069.19
Reaper 307.2
reappear
 repeat 849.11
 recur 850.5
reappraise
 reconsider 931.15
 re-examine 938.27
reap the benefit of
 take advantage of 387.15
 get one's deserts 639.6
rear
 n setting 209.2
 hind part 217.1
 rear end 217.1
 rear guard 217.2
 buttocks 217.5
 afterpart 817.2
 v pitch 182.55
 ascend 193.8
 rise 200.8
 erect 200.9
 loom 247.5
 tower 272.10
 foster 449.16
 train 568.13
 produce 892.8
 process 892.9
 elevate 912.5
 farm 1069.16
 raise 1070.6
 adj rearward 217.9
rear admiral 575.20
rear its head 33.8
rearrange
 reorganize 808.13
 re-form 858.12
rear up ascend 193.8
 rise 200.8
 elevate 912.5
reason
 n explanation 341.4
 motive 375.1
 warrant 600.6
 cause 886.2
 intellect 919.1
 sensibleness 920.6
 sanity 925.1
 reasoning 935.1
 argument 935.5
 reasonableness 935.9
 solution 940.1
 v discuss 541.11
 think 931.8
 logicalize 935.15
 conclude 946.10
 philosophize 952.9
reasonable
 justifiable 600.14
 cheap 633.7
 unexcessive 670.12
 intelligent 920.12
 sensible 920.18
 sane 925.4
 logical 935.20
 plausible 968.7
 realistic 987.6
reasoned 935.21

reasoning
 n intellect 919.1
 thought 931.1
 logical thought 935.1
 reason 935.1
 adj mental 919.7
 rational 935.18
reason to believe 957.1
reassemble 396.18
reassert 849.8
reassess 630.11
reassure comfort 121.6
 give hope 124.9
 encourage 492.15
 make sure 970.11
rebate
 n discount 631.1
 v discount 631.2
rebel
 n malcontent 108.3
 revolter 327.5
 anarchist 418.3
 revolutionist 860.3
 v revolt 327.7
 object 333.5
 adj rebellious 327.11
rebellion
 revolt 327.4
 objection 333.2
 anarchy 418.2
rebel yell
 challenge 454.2
 call to arms 458.7
 call 517.16
rebirth
 reproduction 78.1
 revival 396.3
 redemption 685.4
 repetition 849.1
 new start 858.2
reborn
 renascent 396.24
 redeemed 685.9
 regenerate 692.10
 converted 858.19
rebound
 n reverberation 54.2
 recoil 903.2
 elasticity 1048.1
 v reverberate 54.7
 play 747.4
 recoil 903.6
rebuff
 n snub 157.2
 rejection 372.1
 discomfiture 412.2
 refusal 442.2
 resistance 453.1
 recoil 903.2
 repulse 908.2
 v snub 157.5
 reject 372.2
 refuse 442.5
 resist 453.2
 fend off 460.10
 repulse 908.3
rebuild reproduce 78.7
 remake 396.18
 change 852.7
rebuke
 n reproof 510.5

recompose
  restore 396.11
  remake 396.18

reconcile
  bring to terms 465.8
  make agree 788.7
  conform 867.3

reconciliation
  contentment 107.1
  reconcilement 465.3
  adjustment 788.4
  conformity 867.1

recondition
  repair 396.14
  renovate 396.17
  rehabilitate 858.14

reconnaissance
  Air Force mission 184.11
  reconnoitering 938.8

reconnect
  meet 223.11
  communicate with 343.8
  relate to 775.5

reconnoiter
  n reconnaissance 938.8
  v look 27.13
  traverse 177.20
  make a reconnaissance
    938.28

reconsider
  rethink 931.15
  re-examine 938.27

reconstitute
  reproduce 78.7
  restore 396.11
  remake 396.18
  rearrange 808.13

reconstruct
  reproduce 78.7
  remake 396.18
  change 852.7

Reconstruction Era 824.5

record
  n phonograph record 50.12
  supremacy 249.3
  preparedness 405.4
  documentation 549.1
  recording 549.1
  report 549.7
  history 719.1
  chronicle 832.9
  data 1042.15
  v sound 50.14
  write 547.19
  put upon record 549.15
  chronicle 719.5
  teleview 1035.15

record-breaker 249.4

recording
  n tape 50.12
  record 549.1
  registration 549.14
  history 719.1
  transcript 785.4
  adj recordative 549.16

recording system 50.11

record keeping
  registration 549.14
  automation 1041.7

record player 50.11

records 757.4

recount
  n returns 609.21
  summation 1017.11
  v narrate 719.6
  tell a story 722.6
  iterate 849.8
  sum up 1017.19

recoup
  n recovery 481.3
  reimbursement
    624.2
  v redeem 396.12
  recover 481.6
  repay 624.11

recourse
  instrumentality 384.3
  resource 1009.2

recover
  get well 83.7
  recuperate 392.8
  redeem 396.12
  rally 396.20
  rescue 398.3
  regain 481.6
  rehabilitate 858.14

re-cover 295.29

recovery
  improvement 392.1
  reclamation 396.2
  rally 396.8
  rescue 398.1
  regaining 481.3
  business cycle 731.10
  rehabilitation 858.4

recovery room 197.25

re-create
  reproduce 78.7
  remake 396.18
  change 852.7

recreation
  refreshment 9.1
  amusement 743.1

recreational drug 87.3

rec room 197.12

recruit
  n rookie 461.18
  novice 572.9
  newcomer 774.4
  beginner 818.2
  v add to 253.5
  provide 385.7
  avail oneself of 387.14
  restore 396.11
  revive 396.16
  recuperate 396.19
  call to arms 458.18
  employ 615.14
  enlist 615.17

rectangular
  oblong 267.9
  right-angled 278.7
  quadrangular 278.9

rectify refine 79.22
  straighten 277.5
  compensate 338.4
  revise 392.12
  remedy 396.13
  make agree 788.7
  conform 867.3

recto right side 219.1
  makeup 554.12

rector principal 571.8
  director 574.1
  clergyman 699.2

rectory house 228.5
  benefice 698.9
  parsonage 703.7

rectum 2.18

recumbency
  reclining 201.2
  lowness 274.1

recuperate
  get well 83.7
  rally 392.8
  recruit 396.19
  recover 481.6

recur be frequent 847.3
  repeat 849.11
  reoccur 850.5
  recur to the mind 989.14

recursive 849.14

recursively 849.16

recycle 396.12

red
  n redness 41.1
  radical 611.12
  revolutionist 860.3
  adj sore 26.11
  reddish 41.6
  color varieties 41.13
  blushing 139.13
  raw 406.10
  radical 611.20

Red
  n Communist 611.13
  revolutionist 860.3
  adj Communist 611.21

red, white, and blue 647.7

red alert
  warning sign 399.3
  crisis 843.4

red-baiting 389.3

red-blooded
  strong 15.15
  resolute 492.17

redcap carrier 176.7
  trainman 178.13

red carpet 580.1

red cent money 728.7
  trifle 998.5

red corpuscle 2.25

redden make red 41.4
  turn red 41.5
  change color 105.19
  blush 139.8
  show resentment 152.14

reddish 41.6

reddish-brown 40.7

redecorate 498.8

redeem reclaim 396.12
  rescue 398.3
  aid 449.11
  recover 481.6
  pay in full 624.13
  pay for 624.18
  atone 658.4
  regenerate 685.6
  re-form 858.12
  substitute 862.4

redeeming feature 865.4

redemption
  pardon 148.2

reclamation 396.2
  rescue 398.1
  recovery 481.3
  atonement 658.1
  function of Christ 677.14
  redeemedness 685.4
  new start 858.2
  reversion 859.1

redesign
  n reproduction 78.1
  change 852.1
  v reproduce 78.7
  change 852.7

redevelop
  reproduce 78.7
  restore 396.11

red flag
  warning sign 399.3
  signal 517.15

red-handed
  adj guilty 656.3
  adv in the act 656.4

redhead 35.9

red herring fish 10.24
  stratagem 415.3

red-hot fervent 93.18
  zealous 101.9
  heated 105.22
  fiery 671.22
  hot 1019.25

red ink 473.3

rediscover 941.2

redistribute 808.13

red-letter day
  holiday 20.4
  celebration 487.1

red light
  warning sign 399.3
  alarm 400.1
  signal 517.15
  traffic light 1026.4

red-light district
  city district 230.6
  brothel 665.9

redneck
  n hater 103.4
  wilderness settler 227.10
  vulgarian 497.6
  adj not urbane 233.8
  boorish 497.13

redo reproduce 78.7
  ornament 498.8
  repeat 849.7

redolent odorous 69.9
  fragrant 70.9
  recollective 989.21

redouble
  intensify 251.5
  repeat 849.7
  duplicate 874.3

redress
  n compensation 338.1
  reparation 396.6
  restitution 481.2
  recompense 624.3
  atonement 658.1
  v remedy 396.13
  make restitution 481.5
  requite 506.5
  repay 624.11
  atone 658.4

red tape routine 373.5
officialism 612.10
delay 846.2
reduce
n make small 258.9
v weaken 16.10
dilute 16.11
afflict 85.50
relieve 120.5
abase 137.5
quantify 244.4
decrease 252.7
subtract 255.9
contract 260.7
shorten 268.6
slenderize 270.13
conquer 412.10
subdue 432.9
demote 447.3
impoverish 619.6
discount 631.2
cheapen 633.6
moderate 670.6
simplify 798.4
analyze 801.6
depress 913.4
qualify 959.3
chemicalize 1060.8
reduce to 858.11
reduction in forces
deposal 447.2
economizing 635.2
redundancy 993.4
redundant
diffuse 538.11
repetitious 849.14
superfluous 993.17
reduplicate
reproduce 778.6
copy 785.8
repeat 849.7
duplicate 874.3
redux 396.24
red wine 88.17
reebok 311.5
re-echo 55.1
reed tube 239.6
grass 310.5
stem 310.21
arrow 462.6
wind instrument 711.6
woodwind 711.8
reed organs 711.29
reeducate teach 568.10
rehabilitate 858.14
reedy 58.14
reef
n island 235.2
shoal 276.2
point of land 283.9
v slow 175.9
reduce sail 182.50
reefer marijuana
cigarette 87.12
refrigerator truck 1024.4
reek
n stench 71.1
combustion product
1020.16
vapor 1067.1
v have an odor 69.6

stink 71.4
exude 190.15
let out 909.24
smoke 1019.23
vaporize 1067.8
reel
n windlass 906.7
whirl 915.2
swing 916.6
flounder 917.8
v be drunk 88.27
pitch 182.55
eddy 238.21
reel in 906.9
whirl 915.11
oscillate 916.10
flounder 917.15
reel in fish 382.10
wind in 906.9
reeling
n rotation 915.1
adj intoxicated 88.31
rotating 915.14
swinging 916.17
reel off chatter 540.5
repeat 849.7
memorize 989.16
reenactment 396.1
reenlist 825.5
reentry
regression 163.1
return 186.3
repetition 849.1
periodicity 850.2
spacecraft 1075.2
reestablish
reproduce 78.7
restore 396.11
resume 856.6
re-examine
reconsider 931.15
recheck 938.27
refashion
reproduce 78.7
remake 396.18
re-form 858.12
refer 888.3
referee
n arbitrator 466.4
judge 596.1
basketball game 747.3
hockey game 749.3
round 751.3
soccer game 752.3
fight 754.3
umpire 946.6
v mediate 466.6
sit in judgment 946.12
reference
n aspect 33.3
recommendation 509.4
meaning 518.1
punctuation 530.15
relevance 775.4
acknowledgment 888.2
citation 957.5
v refer to 957.14
reference book
book 554.1
work of reference 554.9
directory 574.10

referendum vote 371.6
election 609.15
constitutional referendum
613.8
refer to
avail oneself of 387.14
designate 517.18
mean 518.8
remark 524.24
confer 541.10
relate to 775.5
attribute to 888.4
direct attention to 957.14
call attention to 983.10
refill restore 396.11
complete 794.6
refinance 729.16
refine sensitize 24.7
clarify 79.22
extract 192.16
subtract 255.9
spiritualize 764.4
simplify 798.4
process 892.9
melt 1020.21
refinery refiner 79.13
plant 739.3
refit renovate 396.17
change 852.7
reflect curve 279.6
imitate 336.5
image 349.11
remark 524.24
consider 931.12
remember 989.9
return 1036.16
reflectance 1025.9
reflection bend 279.3
image 349.5
criticism 510.4
aspersion 512.4
remark 524.3
stigma 661.6
reflex 785.7
reaction 903.1
judiciousness 920.7
consideration 931.2
idea 932.1
remembering 989.3
reflected light 1025.9
signal 1036.11
reflector mirror 29.6
observatory 1072.17
reflect upon 510.13
reflex
n conditioning 92.26
impulse 365.1
reflection 785.7
impact 887.2
reaction 903.1
instinct 934.2
v curve 279.6
adj backward 163.12
unpremeditated 365.11
reactive 903.9
involuntary 963.14
reflexive
n voice 530.14
adj unpremeditated 365.11
reactive 903.9
involuntary 963.14

refluence
regression 163.1
course 172.2
eddy 238.12
tide 238.13
reaction 903.1
reflux regression 163.1
course 172.2
eddy 238.12
tide 238.13
reaction 903.1
reforestation
woodland 310.13
forestry 1069.3
planting 1069.14
reform
n reformation 392.5
change 852.1
new start 858.2
v repent 113.7
make better 392.9
restore 396.11
redeem 685.6
change 852.7
re-form 858.12
Reform
n Protestantism 675.10
adj Jewish 675.30
Reformationist
n Protestant 675.20
adj Protestant 675.28
reformatory
n prison 429.8
reform school 567.9
adj emendatory 392.16
refracted 164.8
refractory
n ceramic ware 742.2
adj unwilling 325.5
defiant 327.10
ungovernable 361.12
oppositional 451.8
resistant 453.5
ceramic 742.7
nonconforming 868.5
refrain
n air 708.4
passage 708.24
poetry 720.9
sequel 817.1
repeat 849.5
v not do 329.3
not use 390.5
abstain 668.7
cease 857.6
refreeze 1024.11
refresh freshen 9.2
strengthen 15.13
air 317.11
revive 396.16
renovate 396.17
amuse 743.21
refrigerate 1024.10
refresher course 568.8
refreshment
meal 8.5
invigoration 9.1
refection 9.1
nutriment 10.3
strengthening 15.5
ventilation 317.9

revival 396.3
renovation 396.4
refrigerant
　n coolant 1024.7
　adj refrigerative 1024.12
refrigerate
　preserve 397.9
　freeze 1023.10
　cool 1024.10
refrigerator 1024.4
refrigerator cookie 10.43
refuel 1021.8
refuge reception 187.1
　hiding place 346.4
　pretext 376.1
　preserve 397.7
　protection 1008.1
　sanctuary 1009.1
refugee goer 190.10
　fugitive 368.5
　alien 774.3
refund
　n reparation 481.2
　reimbursement 624.2
　discount 631.1
　v make restitution 481.5
　repay 624.11
　discount 631.2
refurbish
　renovate 396.17
　ornament 498.8
refusal
　unwillingness 325.1
　dissent 333.1
　rejection 372.1
　denial 442.1
　prohibition 444.1
　opposition 451.1
　option 733.2
　repulse 908.2
refuse
　n offal 80.9
　remainder 256.1
　derelict 370.4
　discard 390.3
　waste 391.4
　v be unwilling 325.3
　reject 372.2
　decline 442.3
　prohibit 444.3
　repulse 908.3
refuse comment 344.6
refusenik 327.5
refuse to admit
　deny 335.4
　disbelieve 955.5
refuse to believe 956.3
refuse to pay 625.6
refute deny 335.4
　defend 600.10
　rebut 939.5
　confute 958.5
regain 481.6
regal dignified 136.12
　sovereign 417.17
　noble 608.10
　good 999.12
regale
　n refreshment 9.1
　treat 95.3
　v feed 8.18

feast 8.24
refresh 9.2
gratify 95.8
amuse 743.21
regalia
　formal dress 5.11
　insignia 647.1
　royal insignia 647.3
regard
　n observation 27.2
　look 27.3
　aspect 33.3
　love 104.1
　considerateness 143.3
　respect 155.1
　carefulness 339.1
　good terms 587.3
　esteem 662.3
　particular 766.3
　relevance 775.4
　outlook 978.2
　attention 983.1
　v look 27.13
　cherish 104.20
　be considerate 143.10
　respect 155.4
　care 339.6
　observe 434.2
　relate to 775.5
　think of 931.17
　judge 946.8
　consider 953.11
　heed 983.6
regardless
　adj unconcerned 102.7
　careless 340.11
　incurious 982.3
　inattentive 984.6
　adv anyhow 384.10
　in spite of 338.9
regards
　respects 155.3
　compliments 504.8
　greetings 585.3
regatta
　race 457.12
　tournament 743.10
regency
　mastership 417.7
　government 612.4
　commission 615.1
regenerate
　v reproduce 78.7
　revive 396.16
　redeem 685.6
　re-form 858.12
　adj redeemed 685.9
　converted 692.10
regent 575.12
regift 478.12
regimen diet 7.13
　treatment 91.14
　government 612.1
regiment
　n military unit 461.22
　company 770.3
　v hold a tight hand upon 425.4
　dispose 808.9
regimentation
　strictness 425.1

arrangement 808.1
region
　location 159.1
　area 231.1
　territory 231.5
　land 234.1
　plot 722.4
regional
　locational 159.19
　territorial 231.8
　idiomatic 523.22
register
　n range 158.2
　record 549.1
　memorandum 549.4
　record book 549.11
　registration 549.14
　clerk 550.1
　account book 628.4
　pitch 709.4
　scale 709.6
　organ stop 711.19
　chronicle 832.9
　list 871.1
　v be heard 48.12
　limit 210.5
　represent 349.8
　preserve 397.8
　get across 521.5
　record 549.15
　be taught 570.11
　act 704.29
　agree 788.6
　list 871.8
　protect 1008.18
register a complaint 115.15
registered trademark
　patent 210.3
　label 517.13
registered voter 609.23
registrar
　recorder 549.13
　clerk 550.1
　accountant 628.7
registration
　register 549.14
　index 871.7
registry record 549.1
　registry office 549.3
　memorandum 549.4
　registration 549.14
　account book 628.4
　chronicle 832.9
　list 871.1
　index 871.7
regress
　n regression 163.1
　reversion 859.1
　v go backwards 163.5
　move 172.5
　be behind 217.8
　deteriorate 393.16
　relapse 394.4
　revert 859.4
regret
　n remorse 113.1
　regrets 113.1
　apology 658.2
　v deplore 113.6
regrettable
　distressing 98.20

much to be regretted 113.10
　terrible 1000.9
regroup 858.12
regular
　n partisan 609.27
　customer 733.4
　baseball team 745.2
　adj gradual 245.5
　downright 247.12
　symmetric 264.4
　smooth 287.10
　typical 349.15
　customary 373.13
　habitual 373.14
　uniform 781.5
　thorough 794.10
　orderly 807.6
　constant 847.5
　systematic 850.6
　usual 869.9
　ordinary 1005.8
regularity
　symmetry 264.1
　smoothness 287.1
　constancy 781.2
　order 807.1
　continualness 847.2
　regularness 850.1
　normality 869.1
regular joe 606.5
regulate direct 573.8
　govern 612.11
　legalize 673.9
　make uniform 781.4
　make agree 788.7
　order 807.4
　organize 808.10
　exercise influence 894.8
regulation
　n rule 419.2
　directive 420.3
　direction 573.1
　government 612.1
　law 673.3
　adjustment 788.4
　organization 808.2
　principle 869.4
　adj customary 373.13
　preceptive 419.4
　usual 869.9
regulatory
　directing 573.12
　governing 612.17
regurgitate flow 238.16
　repeat 849.7
　vomit 909.26
　pulp 1063.5
rehabilitate
　restore 396.11
　justify 600.9
　re-form 858.12
　recondition 858.14
rehash
　n iteration 849.2
　summation 1017.11
　v paraphrase 341.13
　iterate 849.8
　sum up 1017.19
rehearse
　report 552.11
　train 568.13

practice 704.32
narrate 719.6
tell a story 722.6
iterate 849.8
sum up 1017.19
reheat 1020.17
reheated 1020.29
reign
  n governance 417.5
  government 612.1
  influence 894.1
  v rule 612.13
  prevail 864.10
reigning
  governing 612.17
  prevalent 864.12
reign of terror
  terrorization 127.7
  despotism 612.9
reimburse
  make restitution
    481.5
  repay 624.11
rein
  n restraint 428.1
  shackle 428.4
  v restrain 428.7
reincarnate
  repeat 849.7
  materialize 1052.9
reindeer
  beast of burden 176.8
  hoofed animal 311.5
reinfect 85.51
reinforce
  n supporter 901.2
  v strengthen 15.13
  intensify 251.5
  add to 253.5
  bolster 449.12
  support 901.21
  confirm 957.11
  stiffen 1046.9
reinforcements 449.8
rein in slow 175.9
  restrain 428.7
reins 573.5
reinstate
  restore 396.11
  justify 600.9
reinstitute
  reproduce 78.7
  restore 396.11
reinvent oneself
  hide oneself 346.8
  act on the spur of the
    moment 365.7
reinvest restore 396.11
  invest 729.17
reissue
  n reproduction 78.1
  print 548.3
  iteration 849.2
  v reproduce 78.7
  print 548.14
  monetize 728.26
  iterate 849.8
reiterate
  v iterate 849.8
  persist 856.5
  adj repeated 849.12

reject
  n derelict 370.4
  discard 390.3
  v repudiate 372.2
  discard 390.7
  refuse 442.3
  prohibit 444.3
  contradict 451.6
  disapprove 510.10
  ostracize 586.6
  exclude 773.4
  eject 909.13
  vomit 909.26
  disbelieve 955.5
  refuse to believe 956.3
rejoice cheer 109.7
  jubilate 116.5
rejoice in 95.13
rejoinder answer 939.1
  rebuttal 939.2
rejuvenate
  make young 301.8
  revive 396.16
rekindle revive 396.16
  ignite 1020.22
relapse
  n regression 163.1
  apostasy 363.2
  lapse 394.1
  conversion 858.1
  reversion 859.1
  v regress 163.5
  invert 205.5
  deteriorate 393.16
  lapse 394.4
  go wrong 654.9
  defect 858.13
  revert 859.4
relate state 524.23
  report 552.11
  narrate 719.6
  tell a story 722.6
  associate 775.6
  compare 943.4
  sum up 1017.19
related kindred 559.6
  connected 775.9
  akin 775.10
related form 784.3
relate to
  communicate with 343.8
  refer to 775.5
relation meaning 518.1
  blood relationship 559.1
  fiction 722.1
  narration 722.2
  story 722.3
  connection 775.1
  relationship 775.1
  involvement 898.1
  comparison 943.1
relations
  copulation 75.7
  kinfolk 559.2
  relationship 775.1
  affairs 831.4
relationship
  blood relationship 559.1
  relation 775.1
relative
  relational 775.7

comparative 943.8
relative humidity 1065.2
relatives 559.2
relativity
  fourth dimension 158.6
  dependence 775.2
  correlation 777.1
  uncertainty 971.1
relativity theory 1018.1
relax
  v unlax 20.7
  compose oneself 106.7
  relieve 120.5
  release 120.6
  be at ease 121.8
  have pity 145.4
  slow 175.9
  not stand on ceremony 581.2
  unbend 670.9
  entertain 743.21
  amuse oneself 743.22
  loosen 804.3
  pause 857.9
  allow for 959.5
  soften 1047.6
  yield 1047.7
  interj cease! 857.13
relay
  n shift 825.3
  v transfer 176.10
relay station 1034.6
release
  n deliverance 120.2
  death 307.1
  press release 352.3
  escape 369.1
  rescue 398.1
  exemption 430.8
  freeing 431.2
  permission 443.1
  relinquishment 475.1
  information 551.1
  message 552.4
  acquittal 601.1
  acknowledgment 627.2
  game 750.2
  disbandment 771.3
  v free 120.6
  rescue 398.3
  exempt 430.14
  unhand 431.5
  extricate 431.7
  permit 443.9
  let go 475.4
  acquit 601.4
  disband 771.8
  detach 802.10
  dismiss 909.19
relegate commit 478.16
  exclude 773.4
  banish 909.17
relent have pity 145.4
  submit 433.6
  be moderate 670.5
  yield 1047.7
relentless pitiless 146.3
  industrious 330.22
  resolute 359.11
  persevering 360.8
  unyielding 361.9
  firm 425.7

constant 847.5
  inevitable 963.15
relevant
  pertinent 775.11
  apt 788.10
reliability
  trustworthiness 644.6
  stability 855.1
  believability 953.8
  dependability 970.4
reliable
  trustworthy 644.19
  stable 855.12
  believable 953.24
  evidential 957.16
  dependable 970.17
  unhazardous 1007.5
relic remainder 256.1
  corpse 307.15
  record 549.1
  antiquity 842.6
  back number 842.8
  memento 989.6
relief remedy 86.1
  relief 120.1
  consolation 121.4
  welfare 143.5
  act of kindness 143.7
  pity 145.1
  outline 211.2
  protuberance 283.2
  lightening 298.3
  aid 449.1
  reinforcements 449.8
  subsidy 478.8
  welfarism 611.7
  visual arts 712.15
  relievo 715.3
  turn 825.2
  interim 826.1
  substitute 862.2
relief pitcher 745.2
relieve give relief 120.5
  comfort 121.6
  lighten 298.6
  aid 449.11
  play 745.5
  take one's turn 825.5
  substitute for 862.5
  disembarrass 1014.9
relieve of 480.21
relieve oneself
  excrete 12.12
  lighten 120.7
  speak up 524.21
relight revive 396.16
  ignite 1020.22
religion
  religious belief 675.1
  theology 676.1
  piety 692.1
  system of belief 953.3
religious
  n clergy 699.16
  adj meticulous 339.12
  conscientious 644.15
  theistic 675.25
  theological 676.4
  sacred 685.7
  pious 692.8
  exact 973.17

religious ceremony 580.4
religious discourse 543.3
religious faith 675.1
religious holiday 850.4
religious order 675.3
religious rites
  celebration 487.1
  ritualism 701.1
relinquish
  give up 370.7
  cease to use 390.4
  surrender 433.8
  resign 448.2
  yield 475.3
  discontinue 857.6
reliquary tomb 309.16
  monument 549.12
  shrine 703.4
  church vessels 703.11
relish
  n taste 62.1
  savor 63.2
  flavoring 63.3
  zest 68.2
  passion 93.2
  pleasure 95.1
  liking 100.2
  appetite 100.7
  v eat 8.20
  savor 63.5
  enjoy 95.13
relocate settle 159.17
  remove 176.11
reluctant slow 175.10
  renitent 325.6
  resistant 453.5
rely on hope 124.6
  rest on 901.22
  depend on 953.16
  trust 953.17
remain be still 173.7
  be present 221.6
  inhabit 225.7
  be left 256.5
  endure 827.6
  persist 853.5
  continue 856.3
remainder
  difference 255.8
  remains 426.1
  part 793.1
  subsequence 835.1
  surplus 993.5
remains
  remainder 256.1
  corpse 307.15
  record 549.1
  antiquity 842.6
remake reproduce 78.7
  reconstruct 396.18
  change 852.7
remand
  n commitment 429.4
  restitution 481.1
  v imprison 429.17
  commit 478.16
  restore 481.4
remark
  n interjection 213.2
  aspersion 512.4
  statement 524.3

commentary 556.2
  attention 983.1
  v comment 524.24
  heed 983.6
remarkable
  wonderful 122.10
  outstanding 247.10
  extraordinary 870.14
  notable 997.19
remarry 563.15
remedial
  curative 86.39
  relieving 120.9
  tonic 396.22
  helpful 449.21
remedy
  n cure 86.1
  relief 120.1
  reparation 396.6
  therapy 396.7
  aid 449.1
  counteractant 900.3
  v cure 86.38
  treat 91.24
  rectify 396.13
  heal 396.15
  aid 449.11
remember
  recall 989.9
  remind 989.19
remembrance
  celebration 487.1
  monument 549.12
  posthumous fame 662.7
  memory 837.4
  recollection 989.1
  remembering 989.3
  reminder 989.5
  memento 989.6
remind 989.19
reminder
  memorandum 549.4
  remembrance 989.5
reminisce 989.10
reminiscence
  memory 837.4
  remembering 989.3
remiss indolent 331.19
  negligent 340.10
  lax 426.4
  dilatory 846.17
remission relief 120.1
  pardon 148.2
  decline 252.2
  reduction 255.2
  restitution 481.1
  acquittal 601.1
  modulation 670.2
  pause 857.3
remit relieve 120.5
  have pity 145.4
  forgive 148.3
  send 176.15
  abate 252.8
  imprison 429.17
  exempt 430.14
  commit 478.16
  restore 481.4
  acquit 601.4
  pay 624.10
  be moderate 670.5

relax 670.9
remittance
  subsidy 478.8
  payment 624.1
remnant
  n remainder 256.1
  adj remaining 256.7
remodel remake 396.18
  re-form 858.12
remonstrate
  object 333.5
  dissuade 379.3
  admonish 422.6
  offer resistance 453.3
remora adhesive 803.4
  curb 1012.7
remorse regret 113.1
  guilt 656.1
remorseless
  unregretful 114.4
  pitiless 146.3
remote aloof 141.12
  distant 261.8
  reticent 344.10
  standoffish 583.6
  secluded 584.8
  selfish 651.5
  farfetched 776.8
remote control 1041.4
remote past 837.3
remote possibility
  possibility 966.1
  small chance 972.9
remove
  n degree 245.1
  v divest 6.5
  take off 6.6
  release 120.6
  move 176.11
  quit 188.9
  extract 192.10
  subtract 255.9
  murder 308.16
  discard 390.7
  exterminate 395.14
  depose 447.4
  eliminate 773.5
  detach 802.10
  eject 909.13
  dismiss 909.19
  evacuate 909.22
removed distant 261.8
  reticent 344.10
  aloof 583.6
  secluded 584.8
  unrelated 776.6
  separated 802.21
  alone 872.8
remove from office 447.4
REM sleep
  sleepiness 22.1
  deep sleep 22.5
remunerate
  remedy 396.13
  make restitution 481.5
  pay 624.10
renaissance 396.3
Renaissance man 413.3
renascent
  reproductive 78.14
  redivivus 396.24

rend pain 26.7
  injure 393.13
  demolish 395.17
  wrest 480.22
  sever 802.11
render
  extraction 192.16
  do 328.6
  translate 341.12
  communicate 343.7
  represent 349.8
  describe 349.9
  execute 437.9
  give 478.12
  deliver 478.13
  pay 624.10
  play 708.39
  convert 858.11
  melt 1020.21
render a service 143.12
render assistance 449.11
rendering extract 192.7
  rendition 341.2
  representation 349.1
  description 349.2
  execution 708.30
rendezvous
  n tryst 582.9
  assembly 770.2
  v come together 770.16
rendition extract 192.7
  rendering 341.2
  representation 349.1
  description 349.2
  restitution 481.1
  execution 708.30
renegade
  n apostate 363.5
  sacrilegist 694.3
  defector 858.8
  adj apostate 363.11
  impious 694.6
  traitorous 858.20
  nonobservant 435.5
renege
  n recant 363.8
  v abandon 370.5
  disregard 435.3
  repeal 445.2
  be unfaithful 645.12
  defect 858.13
renew refresh 9.2
  stimulate 105.13
  revive 396.16
  renovate 396.17
  innovate 841.5
  repeat 849.7
  change 852.7
  resume 856.6
  re-form 858.12
renewable
  remediable 396.25
  convertible 858.18
renewable energy 1021.7
renitent
  reluctant 325.6
  resistant 453.5
  counteractive 900.8
  rigid 1046.11
renounce
  n recant 363.8

v deny 335.4
give up 370.7
reject 372.2
cease to use 390.4
surrender 433.8
relinquish 475.3
swear off 668.8
cease 857.6
renovate
reproduce 78.7
renew 396.17
recover 481.6
innovate 841.5
perfect 392.1
renown glory 247.2
repute 662.1
notability 997.2
rent
n trauma 85.38
crack 224.2
rental 615.6
hire 630.8
break 802.4
v cleave 224.4
inhabit 225.7
open 292.11
lease 615.15
rent out 615.16
adj cleft 224.7
impaired 393.27
severed 802.23
rental car 179.13
rent control 630.5
renter lodger 227.8
tenant 470.4
reoccupy 481.6
reoccur repeat 849.11
recur 850.5
reopen 856.6
reorder 808.13
reorganize
reproduce 78.7
rearrange 808.13
repair
n reparation 396.6
good condition 765.3
v perfect 392.11
mend 396.14
atone 658.4
repairman 396.10
repair shop 739.5
repair to 177.25
reparation
compensation 338.1
repair 396.6
restitution 481.2
recompense 624.3
atonement 658.1
repartee
witticism 489.7
conversation 541.1
answer 939.1
repast 8.5
repatriate restore 481.4
rehabilitate 858.14
repave 295.22
repay
compensate 338.4
be profitable 472.13
make restitution 481.5
requite 506.5

pay back 624.11
repeal
n revocation 445.1
v abolish 395.13
revoke 445.2
repeat
n repetend 849.5
encore 849.6
duplication 874.2
v reproduce 78.7
imitate 336.5
publish 352.10
redo 849.7
recur 849.11
become cyclic 850.5
duplicate 874.3
memorize 989.16
repeatedly 847.6
repeat performance
encore 849.6
repeat 874.2
repeat word for word 849.7
repel disgust 64.4
offend 98.11
cause dislike 99.6
reject 372.2
disincline 379.4
rebuff 442.5
resist 453.2
fend off 460.10
repulse 908.3
prevent 1012.14
repellent
offensive 98.18
resistant 453.5
repulsive 908.4
hideous 1015.11
repent
v think better of 113.7
adj creeping 177.39
reptile 311.47
repentant
penitent 113.9
atoning 658.7
repercussion
concussion 671.8
execution 708.30
impact 887.2
counteraction 900.1
recoil 903.2
repertoire store 386.1
repertory 704.9
repertory company 707.11
repetition
reproduction 78.1
triteness 117.3
tediousness 118.2
imitation 336.1
duplicate 785.3
constancy 847.2
redundancy 849.1
regularity 850.1
continuance 856.1
replication 874.1
repetitive
habitual 373.14
diffuse 538.11
same 781.6
continuous 812.8
repetitious 849.14
ceaseless 856.7

rephrase 341.13
replace
restore 396.11
depose 447.4
come after 835.3
substitute for 862.5
dismiss 909.19
replacement
restoration 396.1
deposal 447.2
successor 817.4
sequel 835.2
exchange 862.1
substitute 862.2
replant 91.24
replay 849.6
replenish provide 385.7
restore 396.11
complete 794.6
replete full 794.11
plentiful 991.7
overfull 993.20
satiated 994.6
replica
reproduction 336.3
the same 778.3
duplicate 785.3
replicate copy 785.8
double 873.5
duplicate 874.3
reply
n communication 343.1
retaliation 506.1
letter 553.2
defense 600.2
reaction 903.1
answer 939.1
v acknowledge 553.11
defend 600.10
react 903.5
answer 939.4
répondez s'il vous plaît 553.15
report
n crash 56.1
account 349.3
announcement 352.2
publicity 352.4
bulletin 549.7
information 551.1
rumor 552.6
commentary 556.2
repute 662.1
explosion 671.7
paean 696.3
note 709.14
criticism 946.2
v present oneself 221.11
communicate 343.7
announce 352.12
inform 551.8
give a report 552.11
accuse 599.7
narrate 719.6
tell a tale 722.6
pass judgment 946.13
reportage 552.1
report card 549.7
reporter
informant 551.5
newsmonger 552.9
journalist 555.4

spokesman 576.5
repose
n rest 20.1
respite 20.2
sleep 22.2
quiescence 173.1
recumbency 201.2
leisure 402.1
moderation 670.1
v rest 20.6
be located 159.10
deposit 159.14
be still 173.7
lie 201.5
trust 953.17
repository
storehouse 386.6
friend 588.1
treasury 729.13
repossess 481.6
reprehensible
blameworthy 510.25
wicked 654.16
guilty 656.3
terrible 1000.9
represent
be in front 216.7
manifest 348.5
delineate 349.8
describe 349.9
mediate 466.6
act for 576.14
enact 704.30
substitute for 862.5
visualize 986.15
representation
spectacle 33.7
reproduction 336.3
display 348.2
portrayal 349.1
delineation 349.1
description 349.2
representative 349.7
sham 354.3
vote 371.6
sign 517.1
bar 597.4
acting 704.8
picture 712.10
copy 785.1
duplicate 785.3
substitution 862.1
idea 932.1
representative
n representation 349.7
sign 517.1
deputy 576.1
legislator 610.3
example 786.2
substitute 862.2
adj representational 349.13
descriptive 349.14
indicative 517.23
deputy 576.16
model 786.8
repress inhibit 106.8
blunt 286.2
cover up 345.8
suppress 428.8
prohibit 444.3
retain 474.5

dominer 612.15
hinder 1012.10
reprieve
  n release 120.2
  pity 145.1
  pardon 148.2
  respite 601.3
  delay 846.2
  v release 120.6
  have pity 145.4
  respite 601.5
reprimand
  n reproof 510.5
  stigma 661.6
  v reprove 510.17
  stigmatize 661.9
reprint
  n print 548.3
  copy 785.5
  iteration 849.2
  v reproduce 78.7
  print 548.14
  iterate 849.8
reprisal requital 506.2
  revenge 507.1
  penalty 603.1
reprise 849.6
repro duplicate 785.3
  print 785.5
  duplication 874.1
reproach
  n reproof 510.5
  accusation 599.1
  disgrace 661.5
  stigma 661.6
  v censure 510.13
  accuse 599.7
  disgrace 661.8
reprobate
  n recreant 660.4
  v censure 510.13
  adj knavish 645.17
  corrupt 654.14
  wicked 654.16
  unsacred 686.3
  unregenerate 695.18
reproduce grow 14.2
  remake 78.7
  grow 259.7
  copy 778.6
  replicate 785.8
  repeat 849.7
  duplicate 874.3
  produce 890.7
reproduction
  bodily development 14.1
  remaking 78.1
  making 78.1
  procreation 78.2
  growth 259.3
  replication 336.3
  picture 712.10
  duplication 785.2
  double 785.3
  repetition 849.1
  imitation 874.1
  proliferation 890.2
reproductive organs 2.13
reprove 510.17
reptile
  n creature 311.3

reptilian 311.24
  beast 660.6
  adj creeping 177.39
  reptilian 311.47
republic country 232.1
  government 612.4
Republican 609.27
republican 612.16
repudiate
  n recant 363.8
  v deny 335.4
  reject 372.2
  refuse 442.3
  not pay 625.6
  exclude 773.4
repugnant
  offensive 98.18
  negative 335.5
  oppositional 451.8
  hostile 589.10
  contrary 779.6
  disagreeing 789.6
  counteractive 900.8
  hideous 1015.11
repulse
  n snub 157.2
  rejection 372.1
  discomfiture 412.2
  refuse 442.2
  resistance 453.1
  recoil 903.2
  rebuff 908.2
  v snub 157.5
  reject 372.2
  rebuff 442.5
  resist 453.2
  fend off 460.10
  repel 908.3
repulsive
  malodorous 71.5
  filthy 80.23
  offensive 98.18
  repellent 908.4
  terrible 1000.9
  hideous 1015.11
repulsive force 908.1
repurpose 387.10
reputable
  honest 644.13
  highly reputed 662.15
  influential 894.13
  notable 997.19
reputation 997.2
reputative
  implied 519.7
  supposed 951.14
repute
  n reputation 662.1
  custom 731.6
  influence 894.1
  notability 997.2
  v suppose 951.10
request
  n proposal 439.2
  expressed desire 440.1
  asking 440.1
  v ask 440.9
requiem dirge 115.6
  last offices 309.4
  sacred music 708.17
requiescat in pace 309.24

require
  prescribe 420.9
  demand 421.5
  oblige 424.5
  charge 630.12
  obligate 641.12
  entail 772.4
  determine 886.12
  need 963.9
  want 992.7
requirement
  demand 421.1
  study 568.8
  requisite 963.2
requisite
  n condition 959.2
  requirement 963.2
  adj needful 963.13
requisition
  n summons 420.5
  demand 421.1
  request 440.1
  appropriation 480.4
  requirement 963.2
  v summon 420.11
  demand 421.5
  request 440.9
  appropriate 480.19
requite remedy 396.13
  make restitution 481.5
  quit 506.5
  repay 624.11
  interchange 863.4
reroute 182.30
rerun 1034.18
rescind delete 255.12
  repeal 445.2
rescue
  n escape 369.1
  saving 398.1
  deliverance 398.1
  liberation 431.1
  aid 449.1
  v redeem 396.12
  come to the rescue 398.3
  liberate 431.4
  aid 449.11
research
  n investigation 938.4
  v search 938.31
  experiment 942.8
research and development
  942.1
researcher
  seeker 938.18
  experimenter 942.6
research paper 556.1
resection 802.2
reseal 734.8
resemble be like 784.7
  be comparable 943.7
resent
  be resentful 152.12
  envy 154.2
reservation
  demur 325.2
  objection 333.2
  preserve 397.7
  stipulation 421.2
  engagement 615.4
  doubt 955.2

qualification 959.1
  prearrangement 965.1
reserve
  n restraint 139.1
  communicativeness 343.3
  reticence 344.3
  reserves 386.3
  preserve 397.7
  conciseness 537.1
  v save 386.12
  not use 390.5
  allot 477.9
  employ 615.14
  postpone 846.9
  prearrange 965.4
  adj unused 390.12
  substitute 862.8
reserve forces 449.8
reservoir
  n lake 241.1
  reserve 386.3
  storehouse 386.6
  v store 386.10
reset sharpen 285.7
  plant 1069.18
reshape reproduce 78.7
  change 852.7
  re-form 858.12
reshuffle arrange 437.8
  rearrange 808.13
reside settle 159.17
  inhabit 225.7
residence
  habitation 225.1
  abode 228.1
resident
  n doctor 90.4
  inhabitant 227.2
  tenant 470.4
  diplomat 576.6
  benefice-holder 699.7
  adj residentiary 225.13
  intrinsic 767.7
residential 228.32
residual 256.8
residue
  remainder 256.1
  extract 893.3
resign give up 370.7
  cease to use 390.4
  submit 433.6
  demit 448.2
  relinquish 475.3
  deliver 478.13
resign oneself to 134.7
resiliency
  lightheartedness 109.3
  pliancy 1047.2
  elasticity 1048.1
resilient
  lighthearted 109.12
  recuperative 396.23
  changeable 854.6
  recoiling 903.10
  pliant 1047.9
  elastic 1048.7
resin
  n gum 1057.1
  v resinize 1057.2
resist oppose 451.3
  contend against 451.4

withstand 453.2
counteract 900.6
hinder 1012.10
resistance
immunity 83.4
defense mechanism 92.23
suppression 92.24
drag 184.27
refusal 325.1
ungovernability 361.4
opposition 451.1
defiance 453.1
withstanding 453.1
defense 460.1
irregular 461.16
counteraction 900.1
hindrance 1012.1
ohm 1032.13
conductance 1033.9
friction 1044.1
hardness 1046.1
toughness 1049.1
resistance movement revolt
327.4
resistance 453.1
resolute
zealous 101.9
resolved 359.11
persevering 360.8
trial 403.16
tough 492.17
resolution
distinctness 31.2
zeal 101.2
will 323.1
determination 359.1
resolve 359.1
perseverance 360.1
intention 380.1
decay 393.6
endeavor 403.1
proposal 439.2
adjustment 465.4
fortitude 492.5
legislation 613.5
passage 708.24
harmonization 709.2
analysis 801.1
itemization 801.2
dissection 802.5
disintegration 806.1
end 820.1
conversion 858.1
solution 940.1
judgment 946.1
verdict 946.5
resolve
n resolution 359.1
intention 380.1
v will 323.2
determine 359.7
intend 380.4
endeavor 403.5
reconcile 465.8
analyze 801.6
itemize 801.7
end 820.5
solve 940.2
decide 946.11
resolvent
n solvent 1064.4

adj disintegrative 806.5
solvent 1064.8
resonance
resoundingness 54.1
reaction 903.1
oscillation 916.1
wave 916.4
resonancy 54.1
resonate vibrate 54.6
oscillate 916.10
resort haunt 228.27
instrumentality 384.3
entertainment 743.13
expedient 995.2
recourse 1009.2
resound
n reverberation 54.2
v sound 50.14
din 53.7
reverberate 54.7
repeat 849.11
resounding triumph 409.3
resource supply 386.2
reserve 386.3
source of supply 386.4
skill 413.1
expedient 995.2
recourse 1009.2
resourceful
skillful 413.22
versatile 413.25
cunning 415.12
respect
n observation 27.2
aspect 33.3
esteem 155.1
regard 155.1
observance 434.1
courtesy 504.1
approval 509.1
good terms 587.3
duty 641.1
honor 662.3
particular 766.3
relevance 775.4
outlook 978.2
attention 983.1
v be considerate 143.10
entertain respect for
155.4
observe 434.2
approve 509.9
relate to 775.5
respectable
honest 644.13
reputable 662.15
tolerable 999.20
mediocre 1005.7
respectful
regardful 155.8
observant 434.4
courteous 504.14
approbatory 509.16
dutiful 641.13
respective
proportionate 477.13
mutual 777.11
particular 865.12
respects regards 155.3
compliments 504.8
respiration 2.21

respirator 91.19
respiratory 2.32
respite
n recess 20.2
release 120.2
reprieve 601.3
interim 826.1
delay 846.2
pause 857.3
v reprieve 601.5
resplendent
illustrious 662.19
gorgeous 1016.20
bright 1025.33
respond sense 24.6
be affected 93.11
defend 600.10
interchange 863.4
react 903.5
answer 939.4
respondent
n accused 599.6
answerer 939.3
adj reactive 903.9
answering 939.6
response sensation 24.1
feeling 93.1
sympathy 93.5
communication 343.1
meaning 518.1
defense 600.2
paean 696.3
responsory report 708.23
passage 708.24
impact 887.2
reaction 903.1
answer 939.1
responsibility
supervision 573.2
commission 615.1
incumbency 641.2
trustworthiness 644.6
attribution 888.1
operation 889.1
liability 897.1
responsible
chargeable 623.9
answerable 641.17
trustworthy 644.19
liable 897.5
responsive
sensitive 24.12
sympathetic 93.20
willing 324.5
communicational 343.9
influenceable 894.15
reactive 903.9
answering 939.6
pliant 1047.9
elastic 1048.7
rest
n respite 20.1
repose 20.1
silence 51.1
quiescence 173.1
step 193.5
remainder 256.1
death 307.1
leisure 402.1
musical pause 709.21
pause 857.3

supporter 901.2
fulcrum 906.3
v repose 20.6
be situated 159.10
deposit 159.14
be still 173.7
ride at anchor 182.16
remain 256.5
do nothing 329.2
plead 598.19
calm 670.7
pause 857.9
depend 959.6
rest assured
hope 124.6
be confident 953.14
be certain 970.9
restate
paraphrase 341.13
iterate 849.8
restaurant
eating place 8.17
dining room 197.11
workplace 739.1
rest easy
be content 107.5
persuade oneself 375.24
restful vacational 20.10
comfortable 121.11
quiescent 173.12
pacific 464.9
tranquilizing 670.15
restimulate 396.16
resting place
tomb 309.16
end 820.1
supporter 901.2
rest in peace 309.24
restitution
compensation 338.1
restoration 396.1
reparation 481.2
reimbursement 624.2
recompense 624.3
atonement 658.1
reversion 859.1
restive restless 105.27
discontented 108.7
impatient 135.6
reluctant 325.6
defiant 327.10
obstinate 361.8
ungovernable 361.12
restless wakeful 23.7
restive 105.27
discontented 108.7
impatient 135.6
bustling 330.20
inconstant 854.7
agitated 917.16
rest one's case 598.19
rest on one's laurels
be content 107.5
take it easy 331.15
restoral 396.1
restore vitaminize 7.20
reproduce 78.7
put back 396.11
return 481.4
justify 600.9
rehabilitate 858.14

adj regressive 163.11
rear 217.9
deteriorating 393.45
reversionary 859.7
retrogress 393.18
retrorocket
rocket 1074.2
spacecraft 1075.2
retrospect
n remembering 989.3
v remember 989.9
retrospective 837.4
retry 874.2
return
n regression 163.1
homecoming 186.3
relapse 394.1
recovery 396.8
gain 472.3
restitution 481.1
retaliation 506.1
reimbursement 624.2
recompense 624.3
dividend 738.7
game 748.2
repetition 849.1
periodicity 850.2
reversion 859.1
production 893.2
reaction 903.1
answer 939.1
signal 1036.11
v reverberate 54.7
regress 163.5
turn back 163.8
restore 396.11
give back 481.4
yield 627.4
play tennis 748.3
repeat 849.11
recur 850.5
revert 859.4
interchange 863.4
answer 939.4
reflect 1036.16
return a verdict 946.13
returnee 859.3
return match 849.6
returns gain 472.3
report 549.7
election returns 609.21
receipts 627.1
roll 871.6
return the favor 863.4
return to the fold
n reversion 859.1
v revert 859.4
reunion
reconciliation 465.3
social gathering 582.10
reunite 465.8
reusable 387.23
reuse 387.10
Reuters 555.3
rev accelerate 174.10
drive 756.4
revamp revise 392.12
renovate 396.17
change 852.7
reveal unclose 292.12
manifest 348.5

disclose 351.4
divulge 351.5
signify 517.17
unfold 861.7
uncover 941.4
revealing
n disclosure 351.1
adj disclosive 351.10
transparent 1029.4
reveille awakening 23.2
morning 314.1
call 517.16
revel
n treat 95.3
celebration 487.1
lark 743.6
v go on a spree 88.28
rejoice 116.5
make merry 743.24
revelation
visibility 31.1
appearance 33.1
surprise 131.2
manifestation 348.1
disclosure 351.1
divine revelation 683.10
unfolding 861.2
intuition 934.1
discovery 941.1
Revelation 683.4
reveler drinker 88.11
player 743.18
revenge
n compensation 338.1
reprisal 506.2
vengeance 507.1
v avenge 507.4
revenue 627.1
reverberate
resound 54.7
repeat 849.11
answer 939.4
reverence
n respect 155.1
obeisance 155.2
piety 692.1
worship 696.1
crouch 913.3
v respect 155.4
worship 696.11
Reverend title 648.5
clergyman 699.2
reverend
venerable 155.12
reputable 662.15
reverie trance 92.19
thoughtfulness 931.3
abstractedness 985.2
dream 986.9
reverse
n reversal 163.3
inverse 205.4
opposite side 215.3
rear 217.1
about-face 363.1
relapse 394.1
discomfiture 412.2
reversion 859.1
reversal of fortune 1011.3
gear 1040.9
v go into reverse 163.7

backwater 182.34
invert 205.5
misinterpret 342.2
repeal 445.2
transpose 779.5
convert 858.11
revert 859.4
adj contrapositive 215.5
contrary 779.6
reversion reverse 163.3
inversion 205.1
relapse 394.1
restoration 396.1
inheritance 479.2
devolution 629.2
change to a former state 859
reverting 859.1
revert regress 163.5
invert 205.5
be behind 217.8
relapse 394.4
repeat 849.11
retrovert 859.4
revetment 295.12
review
n discussion 541.6
periodical 555.1
commentary 556.2
abridgment 557.1
study 570.3
fiction 722.1
narration 722.2
critical notice 723.2
procession 812.3
iteration 849.2
mature thought 931.5
examination 938.3
re-examination 938.7
criticism 946.2
remembering 989.3
v discuss 541.11
write upon 556.5
study 570.12
brush up 570.14
iterate 849.8
reconsider 931.15
examine 938.24
re-examine 938.27
criticize 946.14
remember 989.9
refresh the memory 989.18
reviewer author 547.15
commentator 556.4
analyzer 718.4
critic 723.4
examiner 938.17
judge 946.7
revile scoff 508.9
berate 510.19
vilify 512.10
revise
n revision 392.4
proof 548.5
v reproduce 78.7
redact 392.12
write 547.19
re-examine 938.27
revisionist
n reformer 392.6
Communist 611.13
adj emendatory 392.16

Communist 611.21
revisit 221.9
revitalize 396.16
revival meeting 696.8
revive refresh 9.2
strengthen 15.13
reproduce 78.7
stimulate 105.13
cheer up 109.9
come to life 306.9
perfect 392.11
revivify 396.16
recover 396.20
aid 449.11
restore 481.6
repeat 849.7
be changed 852.6
change 852.7
resume 856.6
remember 989.9
revoke
n repeal 445.1
v deny 335.4
abolish 395.13
repeal 445.2
revolt
n rebellion 327.4
resistance 453.1
strike 727.5
revolution 860.1
counteraction 900.1
v offend 98.11
rebel 327.7
offer resistance 453.3
strike 727.10
revolutionize 860.4
revolting
offensive 98.18
hideous 1015.11
revolution
n overturn 205.2
revolt 327.4
reform 392.5
anarchy 418.2
disruption 802.3
round 850.3
break 852.2
radical change 860.1
circuit 914.2
rotation 915.1
v revolt 327.7
revolutionary
n rebel 327.5
reformer 392.6
radical 611.12
violent person 671.9
revolutionist 860.3
adj rebellious 327.11
original 337.5
emendatory 392.16
radical 611.20
unruly 671.19
changed 852.10
revulsive 860.5
revolutionist 860.6
counteractive 900.8
revolve
invert 205.5
recur 850.5
circle 914.5
rotate 915.9

rightfulness 637.1
due 639.2
prerogative 642.1
justice 649.1
option 737.21
accuracy 973.5
v remedy 396.13
make agree 788.7
arrange 808.8
adj right-hand 219.4
straight 277.6
decorous 496.9
conventional 579.5
rightful 637.3
honest 644.13
just 649.7
orthodox 687.7
apt 788.10
sane 925.4
accurate 973.16
expedient 995.5
adv directly 161.23
rightward 219.7
very 247.18
rightly 637.4
absolutely 794.15
exactly 973.21
right on! 973.24
excellently 999.22
interj yes 332.18
right-about-face
  n reverse 163.3
  change of mind 363.1
  turnabout 859.1
  v do an about-face 163.10
right and left
  extensively 158.12
  all round 209.13
  laterally 218.8
right-angle upright 200.2
  perpendicular 200.12
  right-angled 278.7
right as rain
  adj straight 644.14
  adv right! 973.24
right away at once 830.8
  promptly 845.15
righteous
  right 637.3
  honest 644.13
  virtuous 653.5
  godly 692.9
righteous indignation 152.4
rightful right 637.3
  condign 639.8
  just 649.7
  legal 673.11
  genuine 973.15
right hand 616.7
right-hand
  starboard 219.4
  dexterous 219.5
right-handed 219.5
right-hand man
  subordinate 432.5
  employee 577.3
  right hand 616.7
right of eminent domain 480.5
right off the bat 830.6
right-of-way
  superiority 249.1

road 383.5
right on
  interj congratulations 149.5
  yeah 332.19
  phrs that's it 788.13
  you better believe it! 973.25
the Right Reverend
  n clergyman 699.2
  adj the Noble 648.8
right side 219.1
the right stuff 413.4
the right thing right 637.1
  fairness 649.2
  virtue 653.1
right to vote vote 371.6
  suffrage 609.17
rightward clockwise 161.24
  to the right 219.7
right wing
  right side 219.1
  conservative 611.9
right-wing conspiracy 609.24
right with 788.12
rigid firm 15.18
  meticulous 339.12
  unyielding 361.9
  strict 425.7
  formal 580.9
  permanent 853.7
  immovable 855.15
  exact 973.17
  stiff 1046.11
rigor acrimony 17.5
  meticulousness 339.3
  firmness 425.2
  asceticism 667.1
  violence 671.1
  accuracy 973.5
  adversity 1011.1
  difficulty 1013.1
  cold 1023.1
  rigidity 1046.2
rigor mortis 307.1
rile annoy 96.13
  provoke 152.24
  agitate 917.10
rill 238.1
rim
  n border 211.4
  slope 237.2
  felly 280.4
  v border 211.10
rime 1023.7
rind exterior 206.2
  shallowness 276.1
  skin 295.3
  lamina 296.2
ring
  n ringing 54.3
  circle 280.2
  encircling thing 280.3
  bulge 283.3
  telephone call 347.13
  fighting 457.9
  arena 463.1
  jewel 498.6
  association 617.1
  clique 617.6
  insignia 647.1
  ecclesiastical insignia 647.4
  boxing 754.1

halo 1025.14
  atomic cluster 1038.7
  v din 53.7
  tintinnabulate 54.8
  check out 188.13
  encircle 209.7
  telephone 347.19
ring a bell 903.8
ringer impostor 357.6
  substitute 862.2
ring in arrive 186.6
  inaugurate 818.11
  punch the clock 832.12
  substitute 862.4
ringing in the ear 54.3
ringleader
  instigator 375.11
  leader 574.6
  politics 610.7
ringlet lock 3.5
  circlet 280.5
  coil 281.2
ringmaster
  theater man 704.23
  circus artist 707.3
rings 725.7
ringside seat 27.8
ringtone
  bell 54.4
  staccato 55.1
ring true 973.9
rink playground 743.11
  hockey 749.1
  lawn bowling 750.3
rinse
  n washing 79.5
  cleanser 79.17
  v wash 79.19
  soak 1065.13
riot
  n revolt 327.4
  free-for-all 457.5
  joke 489.6
  unruliness 671.3
  commotion 810.4
  plenty 991.2
  v vegetate 310.34
  revolt 327.7
  contend 457.13
  rage 671.11
  roister 810.10
riot control agent 462.22
riot police 1008.17
rip
  n trauma 85.38
  drinking spree 88.6
  disrespect 156.3
  tide 238.13
  attempt 403.3
  libertine 665.10
  break 802.4
  v torture 96.18
  be disrespectful 156.6
  speed 174.9
  open 292.11
  injure 393.13
  wrest 480.22
RIP 309.24
rip cord 181.13
ripe
  v ripen 407.8

adj mature 303.13
  prepared 405.16
  seasoned 407.13
  experienced 413.28
  marriageable 563.20
  complete 794.9
  timely 843.9
  perfected 1002.9
ripen fester 12.15
  grow 14.2
  enlarge 259.7
  mature 303.9
  develop 392.10
  bloom 407.8
  evolve 861.5
  perfect 1002.5
ripe old age 303.5
rip into
  lift one's hand against 457.14
  attack 459.15
  criticize 510.14
rip off 482.16
rip-off fake 354.13
  hoax 356.7
  theft 482.4
ripped high 87.24
  drunk 88.33
  tortured 96.25
ripping
  n extortion 192.6
  severance 802.2
  adj excellent 999.13
ripple
  n splash 52.5
  rapids 238.10
  wave 238.14
  roughness 288.2
  wrinkle 291.3
  attempt 403.3
  v babble 52.11
  wrinkle 291.6
  agitate 917.10
ripple effect
  divergence 171.1
  transferal 176.1
  permeation 221.3
  expansion 259.1
  dispersion 771.1
  immediate cause 886.3
rip-roaring noisy 53.13
  turbulent 671.18
riptide 238.13
rise
  n appearance 33.1
  ascent 193.1
  rising 200.5
  acclivity 204.6
  slope 237.2
  hill 237.4
  wave 238.14
  increase 251.1
  height 272.2
  improvement 392.1
  promotion 446.1
  evolution 861.1
  source 886.5
  reaction 903.1
  v wake up 23.6
  appear 33.8
  din 53.7
  move 172.5

hard 1046.10
stony 1059.12
rock music 708.10
rock'n'roll 708.10
Rock of Gibraltar 855.6
rock on 322.4
rock pile 604.2
rocks
genitals 2.13
dough 728.2
danger 1006.1
hidden danger 1006.5
rock-steady 129.2
rock the boat 868.4
rock to sleep
put to sleep 22.20
calm 670.7
rocky
unsteady 16.16
tired 21.7
ill 85.56
rugged 288.7
unsafe 1006.11
hard 1046.10
stony 1059.12
rococo
n ornateness 498.2
adj ornate 498.12
freakish 870.13
fanciful 986.20
rod shaft 273.1
scepter 417.9
gun 462.10
stick 605.2
royal insignia 647.3
nuclear reactor 1038.13
rodent
n creature 311.3
adj rodential 311.44
rodeo 770.1
rodlike 1046.11
roe fish 10.24
female animal 77.9
egg 305.15
hoofed animal 311.5
Roger 332.19
Roget's
vocabulary 526.13
reference book 554.9
dictionary 871.4
rogue horse 311.12
mischief-maker 322.3
rascal 660.3
jockey 757.2
rogues' gallery 714.3
roil
n agitation 917.1
opaqueness 1031.1
v annoy 96.13
provoke 152.24
riot 810.10
seethe 915.12
agitate 917.10
role function 387.5
part 704.10
script 706.3
occupation 724.3
mode 765.4
role model
paragon 659.4
ideal 786.4

standard of perfection
1002.4
role-player 357.1
role-playing 704.8
role reversal
reverse 163.3
change 852.1
conversion 858.1
roll
n bun 10.31
staccato 55.1
boom 56.4
gait 177.12
barrel roll 184.14
wave 238.14
a length 267.2
coil 281.2
cylinder 282.4
record 549.1
document 549.5
film 714.10
bankroll 728.17
throw 759.9
bundle 770.8
roster 871.6
rotation 915.1
swing 916.6
flounder 917.8
v reverberate 54.7
drum 55.4
boom 56.9
bird sound 60.5
progress 162.2
travel 177.18
way of walking 177.28
pitch 182.55
maneuver 184.40
level 201.6
billow 238.22
ball 282.7
smooth 287.5
press 287.6
rob 482.16
push 904.9
trundle 915.10
wallow 915.13
oscillate 916.10
flounder 917.15
go easily 1014.10
roll around 850.5
rollback
regression 163.1
curtailment 252.4
discount 631.1
economizing 635.2
roll back reduce 252.7
retrench 635.5
roll bar 756.1
roll call
legislative procedure 613.6
roll 871.6
rolled into one 872.10
roller dressing 86.33
billow 238.14
cylinder 282.4
smoother 287.4
game 745.3
rotator 915.4
wave 916.4
pulverizer 1051.7
rollerblade 177.35

rollercoaster
comparisons 854.4
changeable 854.6
roller coaster 743.15
roller-skate 177.35
roller skates 179.21
rollick
n frolic 743.5
v rejoice 116.5
bluster 503.3
play 743.23
roll in arrive 186.6
indulge 669.4
roll-in 749.6
rolling
n progression 162.1
maneuvers 184.13
throwing 904.2
rotation 915.1
television reception 1035.5
adj resonant 54.10
thundering 56.12
hilly 237.8
knobby 272.18
wavy 281.10
rotating 915.14
swinging 916.17
rolling pin 282.4
rolling stone
wanderer 178.2
changeableness 854.4
rotator 915.4
roll in the aisles 116.8
roll into one
put together 800.5
combine 805.3
roll it 818.7
roll of the dice 759.2
roll on march on 162.3
travel 177.18
elapse 821.5
roll out get up 23.6
manifest 348.5
roll out the red carpet
pay homage to 155.5
receive 187.10
welcome 585.9
honor 646.8
roll over 729.17
roll over and play dead
354.20
Rolls-Royce 249.4
roll up one's sleeves
prepare oneself 405.13
set to work 725.15
roll with the punches
keep cool 106.9
accept 134.7
Rolodex 871.7
roly-poly
n heavyweight 257.12
adj corpulent 257.18
roman 548.6
Roman calendar 832.8
Roman candle 517.15
Roman Catholic
n Catholic 675.19
adj Catholic 675.29
romance
n love affair 104.5
fabrication 354.10

figment of the imagination
986.5
idealism 986.7
v narrate 722.6
idealize 986.16
Roman Christianity 675.7
Romanism 675.8
romanization 546.5
Roman numerals 1017.4
romantic
n visionary 986.13
adj sentimental 93.21
loving 104.26
fictional 722.7
visionary 986.24
Romeo 104.12
Romeo and Juliet 104.17
Rome wasn't built in a day
134.13
romp
n mannish female 76.9
schoolgirl 302.8
victory 411.1
frolic 743.5
horse race 757.3
v exude cheerfulness 109.6
rejoice 116.5
caper 366.6
play 743.23
rompers 5.30
roof
n top 198.1
abode 228.1
home 228.2
house 228.5
roofing 295.6
v top 295.21
rook
n chessman 743.17
cheater 759.22
v deceive 356.19
cheat 759.26
rookery sty 80.11
birdhouse 228.23
birthplace 886.8
rookie recruit 461.18
novice 572.9
newcomer 774.4
beginner 818.2
room
n latitude 158.3
compartment 197
chamber 197.1
interval 224.1
quarters 228.4
capacity 257.2
latitude 430.4
opportunity 843.2
v inhabit 225.7
house 225.10
room and board 385.3
roomer lodger 227.8
tenant 470.4
rooming house 228.15
roommate 588.3
room temperature 1019.3
roomy
comfortable 121.11
spacious 158.11
broad 269.6
airy 317.12

roorback 552.6
roost
  n birdhouse 228.23
  v settle 159.17
  sit 173.10
  inhabit 225.7
rooster
  male animal 76.8
  poultry 311.28
root
  n plant root 310.22
  etymon 526.2
  morphology 526.3
  source 886.5
  foundation 901.6
  v vegetate 310.34
  encourage 492.15
  applaud 509.10
  fix 855.9
  lodge 855.10
  search 938.31
root and tuber 310.68
root around 938.22
rooted
  confirmed 373.18
  innate 767.8
  traditional 842.12
  established 855.13
rooter enthusiast 101.5
  commender 509.8
rooting out 395.6
root of all evil 728.1
root out dislodge 160.6
  excise 255.10
  exterminate 395.14
  eliminate 773.5
  search out 938.34
rope
  n cigar 89.4
  cord 271.2
  latitude 430.4
  hanging 604.7
  execution 605.5
  game 745.3
  v restrain 428.10
  catch 480.17
  bind 800.9
roped off 429.20
rope enough to hang oneself
  430.4
rope in deceive 356.19
  lure 377.5
rope ladder 193.4
rope off
  circumscribe 210.4
  quarantine 429.13
ropes 894.3
rosary 696.4
rose
  n pinkness 41.2
  nozzle 239.9
  insignia 647.1
  heraldry 647.2
  adj pink 41.8
Rose Bowl 746.1
rose-colored glasses
  optimism 124.2
  idealism 986.7
rosé wine 88.17
rosin
  n gum 1057.1

  v resin 1057.2
roster record 549.1
  baseball team 745.2
  football team 746.2
  basketball team 747.2
  roll 871.6
  schedule 965.3
rostrum prow 216.3
  nose 283.8
  pulpit 703.13
  platform 901.13
rosy pink 41.8
  red-complexioned 41.9
  fresh 83.13
  cheerful 109.11
  optimistic 124.11
  thriving 1010.13
rot
  n filth 80.7
  disease 85.41
  rottenness 393.7
  bull 520.3
  blight 1001.2
  v decay 393.22
rota 549.1
rotary flowing 172.8
  periodic 850.7
  circuitous 914.7
  rotational 915.15
rotate move 172.5
  take off 184.38
  invert 205.5
  recur 850.5
  revolve 915.9
rote 989.3
rotgut 88.14
rotor propeller 904.6
  rotator 915.4
rotten unsound 16.15
  nasty 64.7
  malodorous 71.5
  filthy 80.23
  horrid 98.15
  decayed 393.40
  dishonest 645.16
  corrupt 654.14
rotten egg 71.3
rotten luck
  chance 972.1
  ill fortune 1011.5
rotund
  corpulent 257.18
  round 282.8
  convex 283.13
rouge
  n makeup 1016.11
  v make red 41.4
rough
  n roughness 288.2
  diagram 381.3
  combatant 461.1
  vulgarian 497.6
  ruffian 593.3
  golf 751.1
  v roughen 288.4
  mistreat 389.5
  adj acrimonious 17.14
  raucous 58.15
  bitter 64.6
  pungent 68.6
  harsh 144.24

  flowing 238.24
  unsmooth 288.6
  coarse 294.6
  undeveloped 406.12
  vulgar 497.11
  gruff 505.7
  violent 671.16
  boisterous 671.20
  nonuniform 782.3
  irregular 851.3
  jolting 917.20
  difficult 1013.17
  adv roughly 288.11
roughage 7.3
rough-and-ready
  unprepared 406.8
  unrefined 497.12
rough-and-tumble
  n commotion 810.4
  adj boisterous 671.20
rough-hew 288.4
roughhouse
  n misbehavior 322.1
  commotion 810.4
  v misbehave 322.4
  create disorder 810.11
rough idea 784.3
rough it 225.11
roughly speaking
  approximately 223.23
  generally 864.17
roughneck
  n vulgarian 497.6
  ruffian 593.4
  adj boorish 497.13
rough sketch 942.2
rough up
  roughen 288.4
  mistreat 389.5
  injure 393.13
  punish 604.15
  beat 902.17
roulette 759.12
round
  n drink 88.7
  step 193.5
  sphere 231.2
  degree 245.1
  circle 280.2
  music 280.9
  routine 373.5
  route 383.1
  rondo 708.19
  occupation 724.4
  18 holes 751.3
  fight 754.3
  series 812.2
  turn 825.2
  revolution 850.3
  circuit 914.2
  whirl 915.2
  v turn round 163.9
  curve 279.6
  encircle 280.10
  round out 282.6
  circle 914.5
  turn 914.6
  rotate 915.9
  number 1017.17
  adj circular 280.11
  rotund 282.8

  elegant 533.6
  candid 644.17
  full 794.11
  circuitous 914.7
  adv about 209.12
  around 915.16
roundhouse
  garage 197.27
  repair shop 739.5
rounding out 407.2
round of applause 509.2
round off
  complete 407.6
  number 1017.17
round robin 914.2
round table 423.3
round the clock
  adj uninterrupted 812.8
  adv continuously 812.10
round trip
  journey 177.5
  game 745.3
  circuit 914.2
roundup 770.1
rouse energize 17.10
  awake 23.4
  wake someone up 23.5
  excite 105.12
  elicit 192.14
  arouse 375.19
roustabout hand 183.6
  longshoreman 183.9
rout
  n retreat 163.2
  discomfiture 412.2
  rabble 606.3
  attendance 769.6
  throng 770.4
  multitude 884.3
  agitation 917.1
  v overwhelm 412.8
route way 383.1
  path 383.1
routine
  n exercise 84.2
  run 373.5
  manner 384.1
  act 704.7
  order 807.1
  series 812.2
  software 1042.11
  adj medium 246.3
  habitual 373.14
  orderly 807.6
  frequent 847.4
  prevalent 864.12
rove
  n wandering 177.3
  v stray 164.4
  wander 177.23
roving eye 562.12
row
  n series 812.2
  v navigate 182.13
  paddle 182.53
row
  n noise 53.4
  quarrel 456.6
  turbulence 671.2
  commotion 810.4
  agitation 917.1

v be noisy 53.9
quarrel 456.12
push 904.9
cause trouble 1013.14
rowdy
n mischief-maker 322.3
combatant 461.1
vulgarian 497.6
ruffian 593.3
adj noisy 53.13
misbehaving 322.5
boorish 497.13
boisterous 671.20
royal
n volume 554.4
potentate 575.8
adj dignified 136.12
sovereign 417.17
good 999.12
royal blue 45.3
Royal Canadian Mounted
Police 1008.17
royal charter 642.1
Royal Highness 648.2
royalist 611.9
royal pain 96.2
royalty
sovereignty 417.8
potentate 575.8
aristocracy 608.1
nobility 608.2
dividend 624.7
rpm velocity 174.1
revolutions 915.3
RSVP 553.15
rub
n touch 73.1
contact 223.5
disaccord 456.1
bone of contention 456.7
crisis 843.4
crux 1013.8
friction 1044.1
v pain 26.7
stroke 73.8
treat 91.24
contact 223.10
polish 287.7
represent 349.8
banter 490.6
frictionize 1044.6
dry 1066.6
rubber
n contraceptive 86.23
eradicator 395.9
bridge 758.3
softness 1047.4
elastic 1048.3
v be curious 981.3
elasticize 1048.6
adj rubbery 1048.8
rubber band 1048.3
rubber bullet 462.22
rubber check
arrears 623.2
counterfeit 728.10
rubberneck
n traveler 178.1
sightseer 918.3
inquisitive person 981.2
v journey 177.21

be long 267.5
sightsee 918.6
be curious 981.3
adj spectating 918.7
rubber stamp
n ratification 332.4
v ratify 332.12
rubbish
n remainder 256.1
derelict 370.4
rubble 391.5
nonsense 520.2
rabble 606.3
trivia 998.4
v be disrespectful 156.6
censure 510.13
rubble rubbish 391.5
rock 1059.1
rubdown 1044.3
rub down rub 1044.6
tend 1070.7
rube
n bungler 414.9
simple soul 416.3
peasant 606.6
oaf 924.5
adj not urbane 233.8
rub elbows with 582.17
rub it in 96.13
rub off wear 393.20
abrade 1044.7
rub out delete 255.12
kill 308.14
obliterate 395.16
abrade 1044.7
rub salt in the wound
irritate 96.14
aggravate 119.2
impair 393.9
rub the wrong way 288.5
ruby 41.6
ruckus noise 53.4
quarrel 456.6
turbulence 671.2
commotion 810.4
rudder 573.5
ruddy red 41.6
red-complexioned 41.9
fresh 83.13
blushing 139.13
curse 513.10
rude raucous 58.15
hale 83.12
impudent 142.10
undeveloped 406.12
coarse 497.11
discourteous 505.4
inelegant 534.2
populational 606.8
unlearned 930.13
rude awakening
awakening 23.2
disillusionment 977.1
rudiment
embryo 305.14
foundation 901.6
rudimentary
basic 199.8
dwarf 258.13
undeveloped 406.12
beginning 818.15

original 886.14
rue
n pity 145.1
v regret 113.6
ruffian
mischief-maker 322.3
combatant 461.1
vulgarian 497.6
rough 593.3
ruffle
n staccato 55.1
agitation 105.4
edging 211.7
fold 291.1
confusion 985.3
v drum 55.4
annoy 96.13
perturb 105.14
provoke 152.24
wrinkle 288.5
fold 291.5
beat time 708.44
disarrange 811.2
agitate 917.10
confuse 985.7
ruffles and flourishes 708.27
rug wig 3.14
carpet 295.9
blanket 295.10
bedding 901.20
rugged strong 15.15
hale 83.12
harsh 144.24
ragged 288.7
wrinkled 291.8
strict 425.6
sturdy 763.7
difficult 1013.17
ruggedly 15.23
ruin
n wreck 393.8
destruction 395.1
defeat 412.1
loss 473.1
antiquity 842.6
v spoil 393.10
destroy 395.10
defeat 412.6
bankrupt 625.8
seduce 665.20
rage 671.11
thwart 1012.15
ruins remainder 256.1
wreck 393.8
antiquity 842.6
rule
n mean 246.1
supremacy 249.3
straightedge 277.3
measure 300.2
norm 373.4
governance 417.5
law 419.2
direction 420.3
decree 420.4
government 612.1
ordinance 673.3
game 752.3
model 786.1
the book 869.4
influence 894.1

syllogism 935.6
axiom 974.2
v oversee 249.11
wield authority 417.13
command 420.8
sway 612.13
prevail 864.10
exercise influence 894.8
pass judgment 946.13
rule against 444.3
rulebook 869.4
rulebook slowdown 727.5
rule off 300.11
rule of law 612.7
rule of thumb 942.1
rule out
excise 255.10
close 293.6
obliterate 395.16
prohibit 444.3
make impossible 967.6
prevent 1012.14
ruler superior 249.4
straightedge 277.3
governor 575.6
potentate 575.8
rod 605.2
rule the roost 612.14
rule with an iron fist
612.15
ruling
n decree 420.4
law 673.3
verdict 946.5
adj powerful 18.12
chief 249.14
authoritative 417.15
governing 612.17
prevalent 864.12
influential 894.14
ruling class
the best 249.5
mastership 417.7
the authorities 575.15
upper class 607.2
rum
n spirits 88.13
adj odd 870.11
excellent 999.13
rumble
n audio distortion 50.13
noise 53.4
reverberation 54.2
boom 56.4
fight 457.4
report 552.6
v reverberate 54.7
boom 56.9
speak 524.25
rumble seat 217.1
ruminant 931.21
ruminate chew 8.27
consider 931.12
rummage
n search 938.15
v ransack 938.33
rummage sale 734.3
rumor
n report 552.6
v publish 352.10
report 552.11

rump buttocks 217.4
  remainder 256.1
rumple
  n wrinkle 291.3
  v ruffle 288.5
  wrinkle 291.6
  disarrange 811.2
  agitate 917.10
rumpus
  n noise 53.4
  quarrel 456.6
  turbulence 671.2
  commotion 810.4
  v be noisy 53.9
rumpus room 197.12
rumrunner 732.5
run
  n trauma 85.38
  direction 161.1
  course 172.2
  sprint 174.3
  migration 177.4
  journey 177.5
  voyage 182.6
  flight 184.9
  lair 228.26
  stream 238.1
  flow 238.4
  average 246.1
  a length 267.2
  routine 373.5
  route 383.1
  path 383.2
  freedom 430.1
  race 457.12
  engagement 704.11
  impromptu 708.27
  ornament 709.18
  home run 745.3
  round 751.3
  series 812.2
  continuance 856.1
  generality 864.3
  amount made 893.4
  trend 896.2
  v fester 12.15
  exercise 84.4
  extend 158.9
  move 172.5
  speed 174.8
  travel 177.18
  migrate 177.22
  navigate 182.13
  pilot 182.14
  sail before the wind
    182.22
  float 182.54
  meet 223.11
  flow 238.16
  flee 368.10
  nominate 371.19
  hunt 382.9
  injure 393.13
  make haste 401.5
  print 548.14
  direct 573.8
  guide 573.9
  run for office 609.39
  go into politics 610.13
  smuggle 732.8
  play 746.5

  ski 753.4
  race 757.5
  elapse 821.5
  endure 827.6
  operate 889.5
  be operative 889.7
  incur 897.4
  thrust 902.12
  corner 1013.16
  melt 1020.21
  computerize 1042.21
  liquefy 1064.5
  raise 1070.6
runabout 178.2
run across
  meet 223.11
  come across 941.3
run afoul 98.15
run afoul of 457.15
run aground
  shipwreck 182.42
  come to grief 1011.10
run amok
  go berserk 671.15
  riot 810.10
  be insane 926.20
the runaround
  avoidance 368.1
  circumvention 415.5
**run around like a chicken
  with its head cut off**
  be excitable 105.16
  bustle 330.12
run a temperature
  take sick 85.47
  get excited 105.17
run a tight ship 425.4
runaway
  n fugitive 368.5
  adj fugitive 368.16
  escaped 369.11
run away
  run along 188.12
  flee 368.10
run circles around
  outdo 249.9
  defeat 412.9
run counter to
  deny 335.4
  oppose 451.3
  go contrary to 779.4
  counteract 900.6
run down
  burn out 21.5
  fail 85.48
  quiet 173.8
  sail into 182.41
  decline 393.17
  arrest 429.15
  capture 480.18
  disparage 512.8
  run over 910.7
  trace 938.35
  discover 941.2
  underestimate 950.2
run-down tired 21.7
  unhealthy 85.54
  dilapidated 393.33
  worn-out 393.36
run dry 388.4
run for it 368.10

run for one's life
  run off 188.12
  flee 368.10
run for one's money 457.2
run from 182.36
rung step 193.5
  degree 245.1
run in sail into 182.41
  thrust in 191.7
  interpose 213.6
  arrest 429.16
  capture 480.18
  visit 582.19
run-in
  n quarrel 456.6
  adj accustomed 373.15
run in circles
  be impotent 19.7
  be useless 391.8
run in opposition to 779.4
run in pursuit of 382.8
run interference for
  back 449.13
  facilitate 1014.7
run in the family 767.6
run into total 792.8
  sail into 182.41
  meet 223.11
  cost 630.13
  be converted into 858.17
  collide 902.13
  come across 941.3
run into a brick wall 857.7
run into debt
  borrow 621.3
  go in debt 623.6
run into the ground 993.10
run it by again 849.7
run its course
  come to an end 820.6
  elapse 821.5
**run it up the flagpole and see
  who salutes** 942.8
run neck and neck 174.14
runner speeder 174.5
  sled 179.20
  channel 239.4
  branch 310.20
  messenger 353.1
  smuggler 732.5
  jockey 757.2
  member 793.4
runner-up 411.2
running
  n pus 12.6
  exercise 84.2
  motion 172.1
  direction 573.1
  supervision 573.2
  candidacy 609.10
  operation 889.1
  melting 1020.3
  liquefaction 1064.1
  adj flowing 172.8
  fast 174.15
  pouring 238.24
  cursive 547.22
  continuous 812.8
  present 838.2
  prevalent 864.12
  operating 889.11

  adv consecutively 812.11
running away
  absence 222.4
  flight 368.4
running back 746.2
running commentary 556.2
running head
  label 517.13
  caption 937.2
running mate 610.9
running sore 1001.1
running start
  advantage 249.2
  beginning 818.1
  earliness 845.1
running wild 926.30
runny exudative 190.20
  fluid 1061.4
runoff outflow 190.4
  election 609.15
run off
  run along 188.12
  flee 368.10
  print 548.14
  drive out 909.14
run off at the mouth
  talk nonsense 520.5
  chatter 540.5
  persist 856.5
run off with
  steal 482.13
  abduct 482.20
run of luck
  chance 972.1
  stroke of luck 1010.3
run of the mill
  average 864.3
  mediocre 1005.8
run on march on 162.3
  chatter 540.5
  continue 812.4
  elapse 821.5
  endure 827.6
  continue 856.3
run out
  v burn out 21.5
  exit 190.12
  empty 190.13
  find vent 369.10
  be consumed 388.4
  perish 395.23
  protract 538.8
  come to an end 820.6
  elapse 821.5
  eject 909.13
  drive out 909.14
  adj past 837.7
  obsolete 842.15
run out of gas
  weaken 16.9
  stall 410.16
  flop 704.28
  fall short 911.2
run out on 370.5
run over
  overflow 238.17
  browse 570.13
  iterate 849.8
  overrun 910.7
  think over 931.13
  examine 938.24

sad story 115.4
safari 177.5
safari park 743.14
safe
    n treasury 729.13
    adj cautious 494.8
    secure 1007.4
    protected 1008.21
safe bet 966.1
safe-conduct 443.7
safecracker 483.3
safe-deposit box 729.13
safeguard
    n pass 443.7
    precaution 494.3
    safety 1007.1
    palladium 1008.3
    bodyguard 1008.14
    v defend 460.8
    protect 1008.18
safe house
    hiding place 346.4
    retreat 1009.5
safekeeping
    storage 386.5
    preservation 397.1
    custody 429.5
    protection 1008.1
safe room 197.17
safe sex 75.7
safe to eat 8.33
safety
    football team 746.2
    game 746.3
    security 1007.1
    safeness 1007.1
    protection 1008.1
    safeguard 1008.3
safety belt
    life preserver 397.6
    safeguard 1008.3
safety catch 428.5
safety net
    precaution 494.3
    safeguard 1008.3
safety valve
    outlet 190.9
    precaution 494.3
    safeguard 1008.3
saffron 43.4
sag
    n sinkage 194.2
    hang 202.2
    cheapening 633.4
    declining market 737.5
    v drift off course
        182.29
    sink 194.6
    hang 202.6
    decrease 252.6
    curve 279.6
    cheapen 633.6
saga 719.3
sage
    n master 413.13
    wise man 921.1
    adj wise 920.17
Sahara 891.2
sahib man 76.7
    master 575.1
    Sir 648.3

said speech 524.29
    former 814.5
sail
    n sailboat 180.3
    canvas 180.14
    voyage 182.6
    v glide 177.35
    navigate 182.13
    get under way 182.19
    float 182.54
    fly 184.36
    go easily 1014.10
sailboat 760.2
sailing ship 180.3
sailor traveler 178.1
    mariner 183.1
sailplane
    n glider 181.12
    v fly 184.36
sail through 1014.8
saint
    n holy man 659.6
    celestial being 679.1
    angel 679.1
    religious prophet 684.2
    believer 692.4
    v glorify 662.13
    sanctify 685.5
    ordain 698.12
sainthood
    sanctification 685.5
    godliness 692.2
Saint Nicholas 678.13
sake motive 375.1
    intention 380.1
salaam
    n obeisance 155.2
    crouch 913.3
    v make obeisance
        155.6
    bow 913.9
salad food 10.37
    hodgepodge 797.6
salad bar 8.17
salad days 301.1
salamander
    amphibian 311.26
    spirit 678.6
    fire iron 1020.12
salaried worker
    bourgeois 607.6
    worker 726.2
salary
    n pay 624.4
    v pay 624.10
sale transfer 629.1
    selling 734.2
    wholesale 734.1
    closing out sale 734.3
sales 734.13
sales associate 577.5
salesmanship
    promotion 352.5
    inducement 375.3
    selling 734.2
salesperson 730.3
sales pitch 734.5
salient
    n region 231.1
    protuberance 283.2
    adj protruding 283.14

conspicuous 348.12
    notable 997.19
saline 68.9
saliva
    digestive juice 2.17
    humor 2.24
    digestion 7.8
    spittle 13.3
salivary glands
    digestion 2.17
    digestive system 2.18
    ingestion 7.8
salivate 13.6
sallow
    v yellow 43.3
    adj colorless 36.7
    yellow 43.4
    yellow-faced 43.6
sally
    n journey 177.5
    attack 459.1
    witticism 489.7
    v set out 188.8
    emerge 190.11
sally forth set out 188.8
    emerge 190.11
salmon
    n marine animal 311.29
    jumper 366.4
    adj pink 41.8
salon parlor 197.5
    museum 386.9
    society 578.6
    social gathering 582.10
    market 736.1
    company 770.3
saloon bar 88.20
    parlor 197.5
    cabin 197.9
salsa 10.9
salt
    n saltiness 68.4
    mariner 183.1
    preservative 397.4
    veteran 413.16
    wit 489.1
    v flavor 63.7
    tamper with 354.17
    preserve 397.9
    falsify accounts 628.10
    adj flavored 62.9
    salty 68.9
    witty 489.15
salt-and-pepper 39.4
salt away 386.10
salt flat plain 236.1
    wasteland 891.2
salt-free diet 7.13
saltine 10.30
salt in the wound 96.3
salt of the earth
    person of honor 644.8
    good citizen 659.3
    the best 999.8
salt water ocean 240.1
    water 1065.3
¡salud! 88.38
salute
    n obeisance 155.2
    celebration 487.1
    greeting 585.4

    v pay homage to 155.5
    greet another ship 182.52
    praise 509.12
    signal 517.22
    address 524.26
    greet 585.10
    interj toast 88.38
salvage
    n reclamation 396.2
    preservation 397.1
    rescue 398.1
    recovery 481.3
    recompense 624.3
    fee 630.6
    v redeem 396.12
    rescue 398.3
salvageable
    remediable 396.25
    rescuable 398.4
salvager
    mender 396.10
    rescuer 398.2
salvation
    reclamation 396.2
    preservation 397.1
    rescue 398.1
    function of Christ 677.14
    redemption 685.4
salve
    n balm 86.11
    gratuity 478.5
    moderator 670.3
    ointment 1056.3
    v medicate 91.25
    relieve 120.5
    redeem 396.12
    oil 1056.8
salvo detonation 56.3
    volley 459.9
    celebration 487.1
    shot 904.4
    qualification 959.1
Samaritan 592.1
same identical 778.7
    uniform 781.6
    former 814.5
same old story 837.2
same old thing
    tedium 118.1
    regularity 781.2
sample
    n taste 62.4
    specimen 786.3
    part 793.1
    feeler 942.4
    subject 942.7
    v taste 62.7
    canvass 938.29
    experiment 942.8
    adj typical 349.15
sampler 938.16
Samson 15.6
samurai 608.3
sanctify
    glorify 662.13
    hallow 685.5
sanctimonious
    hypocritical 354.33
    prudish 500.19
    zealous 692.11
    self-righteous 693.5

sanction
  n ratification 332.4
  consent 441.1
  authorization 443.3
  approval 509.1
  legalization 673.2
  v ratify 332.12
  consent 441.2
  authorize 443.11
  approve 509.9
  legalize 673.9
sanctioned
  authorized 443.17
  legal 673.11
sanctity sacredness 685.1
  sanctitude 685.1
  godliness 692.2
sanctuary
  hiding place 346.4
  preserve 397.7
  holy of holies 703.5
  refuge 1009.1
sanctum
  sanctum sanctorum 197.8
  retreat 584.6
  sanctuary 703.5
  refuge 1009.5
sand
  n grain 1051.6
  grain of sand 1059.2
  v grind 287.8
  buff 1044.8
sandalwood 70.4
sandbag
  n weight 297.6
  v weight 297.12
  defeat 412.9
  attack 459.15
  bet 759.25
  beat 902.17
  club 902.20
sandbagger 483.5
sandbar island 235.2
  shoal 276.2
  hidden danger 1006.5
  sand 1059.2
sandblast grind 287.8
  buff 1044.8
a sand castle 16.7
sand dune hill 237.4
  sand 1059.2
sandhog 284.10
sanding 1044.2
sandman 22.11
sand painting 712.12
sandpaper
  n roughness 288.2
  v grind 287.8
  buff 1044.8
sands shore 234.2
  hidden danger 1006.5
sands of time 821.3
sandstone 1059.1
sandstorm 318.12
sand trap 751.1
sandwich
  n food 10.32
  v interpose 213.6
sandwich board 352.7
sandwich cookie 10.43
sandy yellow 43.4

granular 1051.12
  stony 1059.12
  dry 1066.7
sane intelligent 920.12
  sensible 920.18
  sane-minded 925.4
  logical 935.20
  realistic 987.6
sanguine
  n personality type 92.12
  adj sanguineous 41.7
  red-complexioned 41.9
  cheerful 109.11
  hopeful 124.10
  expectant 130.11
sanitary hygienic 79.27
  healthful 81.5
sanitary landfill
  receptacle of filth 80.12
  derelict 370.4
  trash pile 391.6
sanitation
  cleansing 79.3
  hygiene 81.2
sanitization 79.3
sanity
  intelligence 920.1
  sensibleness 920.6
  saneness 925.1
sans absent 222.19
  without 992.17
sans serif 548.6
sans souci 107.7
Santa Claus
  giver 478.11
  cheerful giver 485.2
  Santa 678.13
sap
  n essential content
    196.5
  dupe 358.2
  entrenchment 460.5
  essence 767.2
  fool 924.3
  fluid 1061.2
  v weaken 16.10
  excavate 284.15
  undermine 393.15
  overthrow 395.20
  spiritualize 764.4
sapidness 63.1
sapient 920.19
sapling
  youngster 302.1
  sprout 302.11
  tree 310.10
sapphire 45.3
sapphire blue 45.3
sappy
  sentimental 93.21
  immature 301.10
  foolish 923.9
  fluid 1061.4
sarcasm wit 489.1
  irony 508.5
sarcoma 85.39
sarcophagus 309.11
sardonic 508.13
sardonic grin
  smile 116.3
  scornful laugh 508.4

sartorial
  clothing 5.45
  tailored 5.48
sash waistband 5.19
  frame 266.4
sashay travel 177.18
  way of walking 177.28
sass
  n back talk 142.4
  v talk back 142.8
sassy 142.10
Satan demon 680.6
  liar 357.9
  the Devil 680.3
  nether world deity 682.5
satanic cruel 144.26
  diabolic 654.13
  demoniac 680.17
  execrable 1000.10
Satanist 680.15
sate gratify 95.8
  satiate 994.4
sated languid 331.20
  satiated 994.6
satellite
  hanger-on 138.6
  follower 166.2
  country 232.1
  dependent 432.6
  disciple 616.8
  escort 769.5
  moon 1072.11
  artificial satellite 1075.6
satellite communication 347.1
satellite network 1034.8
satellite television 1035.1
satiety 107.1
satin
  n smooth surface 287.3
  fine texture 294.3
  softness 1047.4
  adj smooth 294.8
satire wit 489.1
  sarcasm 508.5
  burlesque 508.6
  lampoon 512.5
satirist
  humorist 489.12
  lampooner 512.7
  poet 720.11
satirize
  burlesque 508.11
  lampoon 512.12
satisfaction
  pleasure 95.1
  contentment 107.1
  compensation 338.1
  reparation 396.6
  observance 434.1
  duel 457.7
  restitution 481.2
  payment 624.1
  recompense 624.3
  atonement 658.1
  sufficiency 991.1
  satiety 994.1
satisfactory
  satisfying 107.11
  convincing 953.26
  sufficient 991.6
  tolerable 999.20

satisfy feed 8.18
  gratify 95.8
  content 107.4
  indulge 427.6
  observe 434.2
  pay 624.10
  pay in full 624.13
  atone 658.4
  convince 953.18
  suffice 991.4
  satiate 994.4
satisfying 97.6
saturate fill 794.7
  imbue 797.11
  overload 993.15
  satiate 994.4
  soak 1065.13
saturated fat 1056.1
saturation
  colorfulness 35.4
  color quality 35.6
  fullness 794.2
  imbuement 797.2
  overfullness 993.3
  satiety 994.1
  soaking 1065.7
saturation point
  fullness 794.2
  satiety 994.1
  radiation 1037.1
saturation raid 459.4
Saturn 1072.9
satyr
  sexual pervert 75.16
  lecher 665.11
  forest god 678.11
sauce
  n cooking 11.1
  liquor 88.14
  back talk 142.4
  hodgepodge 797.6
  admixture 797.7
  pulp 1063.2
  v flavor 63.7
  talk back 142.8
saucer tableware 8.12
  circle 280.2
saucer eyes
  optic part 2.9
  eye 27.9
  defect 28.6
saucer-shaped
  parabolic 279.13
  concave 284.16
saucier 11.3
saucy impudent 142.10
  defiant 454.7
sauna bath 79.8
  bathing place 79.10
saunter
  n slow motion 175.2
  walk 177.10
  gait 177.12
  v go slowly 175.6
  wander 177.23
  way of walking 177.28
sausage 10.21
sausage meat 10.13
sauté brown 40.2
  cook 11.5
savable 398.4

savage
  n barbarian 497.7
  brute 593.5
  violent person 671.9
  v torture 96.18
  mistreat 389.5
  injure 393.13
  rage 671.11
  work evil 1000.6
  adj cruel 144.26
  pitiless 146.3
  infuriated 152.32
  deadly 308.23
  warlike 458.20
  unrefined 497.12
  fierce 671.21
savagery cruelty 144.11
  unrefinement 497.3
  violence 671.1
  unenlightenment 930.3
savanna
  horizontal 201.3
  the country 233.1
  plain 236.1
  grassland 310.8
savant expert 413.11
  specialist 866.3
  wise man 921.1
  scientist 928.11
  scholar 929.3
save
  n soccer action 752.3
  v store up 386.11
  reserve 386.12
  not use 390.5
  preserve 397.8
  rescue 398.3
  aid 449.11
  retain 474.5
  economize 635.4
  redeem 685.6
  stop from scoring 752.4
  be conservative 853.6
  play safe 1007.3
  prevent 1012.14
  prep off 255.14
  excluding 773.10
  conj unless 959.16
save-all
  n niggard 484.4
  adj stingy 484.9
the saved 692.5
saved soul 679.1
save face 136.7
save for a rainy day
  reserve 386.12
  economize 635.4
save one's neck
  rescue 398.3
  benefit 592.3
  be safe 1007.2
save the day 592.3
save your breath! 51.14
saving grace
  extenuation 600.5
  characteristic 865.4
savings reserve 386.3
  funds 728.14
savings account
  account 622.2
  funds 728.14

savings institution
  lending institution 620.4
  bank 729.14
savior preserver 397.5
  rescuer 398.2
  redeemer 592.2
savoir-faire skill 413.1
  mannerliness 504.3
savor
  n taste 62.1
  relish 63.2
  odor 69.1
  passion 93.2
  characteristic 865.4
  v eat 8.20
  taste 62.7
  relish 63.5
  flavor 63.7
  enjoy 95.13
savory
  n food 10.8
  adj edible 8.33
  flavored 62.9
  tasty 63.8
  fragrant 70.9
  delectable 97.10
savvy
  n skill 413.1
  smartness 920.2
  understanding 928.3
  discrimination 944.1
  v understand 521.7
  know 928.12
saw
  n notching 289.2
  maxim 974.1
  platitude 974.3
  cutlery 1040.2
  v fiddle 708.41
  sever 802.11
sawbones doctor 90.4
  surgeon 90.5
sawbuck money 728.7
  trestle 901.16
sawdust
  remainder 256.1
  powder 1051.5
sawed-off 258.13
sawhorse 901.16
sawmill 739.3
sawtooth
  n projection 285.4
  adj angular 278.6
  rugged 288.7
saw wood 22.13
saxophonist 710.4
say
  n supremacy 249.3
  affirmation 334.1
  vote 371.6
  authority 417.1
  free will 430.6
  remark 524.3
  speech 543.2
  turn 825.2
  influence 894.1
  v take leave 188.16
  affirm 334.5
  announce 352.12
  utter 524.22
  state 524.23

  answer 939.4
  suppose 951.10
  adv approximately 223.23
say again 849.7
say a good word for 509.11
say ah! 292.23
say amen to 332.12
say a mouthful 973.10
say a word to the wise 399.5
say aye 441.2
say goodbye to 370.5
say hello 585.10
say in a roundabout way
  prevaricate 344.7
  circumlocute 538.10
  go roundabout 914.4
say in defense 600.10
saying
  affirmation 334.1
  remark 524.3
  maxim 974.1
say in reply 939.4
say it all 1017.19
say loud and clear
  affirm 334.5
  speak up 524.21
say no refuse 442.3
  restrain oneself 668.6
say nothing 51.6
sayonara! 188.22
say one's prayers 696.13
say out loud
  affirm 334.5
  speak up 524.21
say over and over 849.10
say right to one's face 454.3
say-so
  affirmation 334.1
  command 420.1
  free will 430.6
  administration 573.3
  influence 894.1
say the word
  command 420.8
  permit 443.9
say to oneself 542.3
say uncle flinch 127.13
  lose 412.12
  surrender 433.8
say under one's breath 345.9
say what one thinks 644.12
say yes 441.2
scab
  n sore 85.37
  crust 295.14
  strikebreaker 727.8
  blemish 1004.1
  v crust 295.27
  break a strike 727.11
  blemish 1004.4
scabies 85.41
scads lot 247.4
  plenty 991.2
scaffold
  execution 605.5
  scaffolding 901.12
scalawag horse 311.12
  rascal 660.3
scald
  n trauma 85.38
  burn 1020.6

  v injure 393.13
  be hot 1019.22
scalding 1019.25
scale
  n range 158.2
  map 159.5
  ladder 193.4
  step 193.5
  degree 245.1
  size 257.1
  blanket 295.12
  crust 295.14
  flake 296.3
  weighing 297.9
  measure 300.2
  gamut 709.6
  break 802.4
  series 812.2
  v flake 6.11
  climb 193.11
  layer 296.5
  raid 459.20
  break 802.12
scale down
  n make small 258.9
  v reduce 252.7
scales of justice 649.1
scale up 259.4
scaling raid 459.4
  disruption 802.3
scallop
  n notching 289.2
  v cook 11.5
  convolve 281.4
  notch 289.4
scalloped cooked 11.7
  notched 289.5
scalp peel 6.8
  trade 737.23
scalper salesman 730.3
  speculator 737.11
scaly flaky 296.7
  powdery 1051.11
scam
  n deception 356.9
  cheating 759.13
  v deceive 356.14
  swindle 356.19
scamp
  n mischief-maker 322.3
  rascal 660.3
  v slight 340.8
  stint 484.5
scamper
  n run 174.3
  haste 401.1
  v speed 174.8
  hasten off 188.10
  make haste 401.5
scan
  n field of view 31.3
  examination 938.3
  v browse 570.13
  rhyme 720.14
  itemize 801.7
  examine 938.24
  examine cursorily 938.26
  receive 1036.17
scandal slander 512.3
  gossip 552.8
  abomination 638.2

iniquity 654.3
disgrace 661.5
immodesty 666.2
scandalize 661.7
scandalmonger 552.9
scandal sheet 555.2
scanner 1042.4
scanning
  n metrics 720.6
  televising 1035.3
  radar 1036.8
  adj metric 720.16
scant
  v limit 210.5
  stint 484.5
  adj narrow 270.14
  incomplete 795.4
  sparse 885.5
  meager 992.10
scantily clad 6.13
scanty narrow 270.14
  incomplete 795.4
  sparse 885.5
  meager 992.10
  scarce 992.11
scapegoat
  sacrifice 696.7
  whipping boy 862.3
  oddity 870.4
scar
  n precipice 200.3
  slope 237.2
  mark 517.5
  blemish 1004.1
  v mark 517.19
  blemish 1004.4
scarab 691.5
scarce infrequent 848.2
  in short supply 885.5
  sparse 992.11
scarcely any 885.4
scarcely to be expected 969.3
scarcity
  infrequency 848.1
  fewness 885.1
  underproduction 892.5
  scarceness 992.3
scare
  n fear 127.1
  v frighten 127.15
scarecrow figure 349.6
  eyesore 1015.4
scared to death
  afraid 127.22
  terrified 127.26
scaredy-cat
  weakling 16.6
  coward 491.5
scare off 379.3
scare tactics
  terrorization 127.7
  coercion 424.3
  threat 514.1
scare up 472.9
scarf
  n food 10.2
  joint 800.4
  v hook 800.8
scarf down 8.22
scarlet red 41.6
  prostitute 665.28

scarp precipice 200.3
  incline 204.4
  slope 237.2
scary fearful 127.23
  frightening 127.28
scat! 909.31
scathe
  n impairment 393.1
  v criticize 510.20
  work evil 1000.6
scathing
  acrimonious 17.14
  caustic 144.23
scatter
  n deflection 164.2
  rarity 299.1
  dispersion 771.1
  v deflect 164.5
  radiate 171.6
  interspace 224.3
  rarefy 299.3
  overwhelm 412.8
  squander 486.3
  disperse 771.4
  disband 771.8
  shatter 802.13
  part company 802.19
  loosen 804.3
  disarrange 811.2
scatterbrain
  frivolous person 924.7
  flightiness 985.5
scatter to the winds
  squander 486.3
  disperse 771.4
scavenge 79.18
scavenger
  sweeper 79.16
  creature 311.3
scenario project 381.2
  playbook 704.21
  script 706.3
  effect 887.1
  solution 940.1
scene look 27.3
  view 33.6
  outburst 152.9
  setting 209.2
  arena 463.1
  act 704.7
  scenery 704.20
  landscape 712.11
scenery view 33.6
  arena 463.1
  decor 704.20
scenic route
  vacation 20.3
  route 383.1
scent
  n odor 69.1
  sense of smell 69.4
  fragrance 70.1
  perfumery 70.2
  track 517.8
  clue 517.9
  hint 551.4
  v odorize 69.7
  smell 69.8
  perfume 70.8
  catch the scent of
    941.6

scepter rod 417.9
  royal insignia 647.3
schedule
  n plan 381.1
  chronicle 832.9
  list 871.1
  program 965.3
  v plan 381.8
  allot 477.9
  spend 626.5
  list 871.8
  line up 965.6
scheduled
  planned 381.12
  listed 871.9
  slated 965.9
schematic
  diagrammatic 381.14
  analytical 801.9
scheme
  n trick 356.6
  plan 381.1
  project 381.2
  intrigue 381.5
  stratagem 415.3
  plot 722.4
  outline 801.4
  v premeditate 380.7
  plot 381.9
  maneuver 415.10
  plot 839.6
  prearrange 965.4
schism desertion 370.2
  falling-out 456.4
  sect 675.3
schizoid
  n personality type 92.12
  psychotic 926.17
  adj crazy 926.27
  psychotic 926.28
schizophrenia
  mental disorder 92.14
  dissociation 92.20
  dementia praecox 926.4
schizophrenic
  n psychotic 926.17
  adj psychotic 926.28
schlep 175.12
schlock 1005.6
schmaltz 93.8
schnapps 88.13
schnoz 283.8
scholar
  student 572.1
  specialist 866.3
  wise man 921.1
  scientist 928.11
  scholastic 929.3
scholarship
  subsidy 478.8
  studiousness 570.4
  fellowship 646.7
  erudition 928.5
scholastic
  n theologian 676.3
  scholar 929.3
  adj institutional 567.13
  academic 568.19
  studious 570.17
  learned 928.21
  book-learned 928.22

school
  n educational institution
    567.1
  teaching 568.1
  order 617.5
  sect 675.3
  style 712.7
  group of animals 770.5
  system of belief 953.3
  v teach 568.10
  adj scholastic 567.13
schoolbook book 554.1
  textbook 554.10
schoolboy boy 302.5
  schoolchild 572.3
schoolbus 179.13
schooled 928.18
schoolgirl
  schoolmaid 302.8
  schoolchild 572.3
schoolhouse 567.10
schooling
  teaching 568.1
  learning 928.4
school library 558.1
school of thought 952.1
schoolroom 567.11
schoolteacher 571.1
schoolwork 568.1
sciatic 217.10
science art 413.7
  -ology 928.10
science fiction 1075.1
science museum 386.9
science park 739.1
scientific
  technical 928.28
  exact 973.17
  realistic 987.6
scientist 928.11
scintilla hint 248.4
  spark 1019.15
  glitter 1025.7
scintillate joke 489.13
  be brilliant 920.11
  glitter 1025.25
scintillating
  witty 489.15
  smart 920.14
  burning 1019.27
  glittering 1025.36
scion insert 191.2
  sprout 302.11
  branch 310.20
  descendant 561.3
  member 793.4
scissor 802.11
sclerosis symptom 85.9
  hardening 1046.5
scoff
  n food 10.2
  indignity 156.2
  gibe 508.2
  v jeer 508.9
  disbelieve 695.14
scofflaw 660.9
scold
  n bitch 110.12
  faultfinder 510.9
  v bird sound 60.5
  reprove 510.17

unessential 768.4
eventual 831.11
substitute 862.8
unimportant 998.16
secondary disease 85.1
secondary meaning 518.1
secondary product 893.3
secondary school 567.4
secondary smoke 89.1
second banana 704.10
second best 1005.4
second chance 396.3
second childhood
  old age 303.5
  senility 922.10
second-class 1005.9
second-class citizenship 791.1
second cousin 559.3
second-degree burn
  trauma 85.38
  burn 1020.6
second down 746.3
second edition 785.5
second estate 607.2
second fiddle
  inferiority 250.1
  inferior 250.2
  subservience 432.2
secondhand
  used 387.24
  old 842.18
second helping 8.10
second home 228.8
second-honeymoon 563.16
second lieutenant 575.18
second look
  repetition 849.1
  re-examination 938.7
second mate 183.7
second mortgage 438.4
second nature 373.3
second opinion 946.3
second person 530.7
second prize 646.2
second rank 250.6
second-rate 1005.9
seconds tobacco 89.2
  commodity 735.2
second-story thief 483.3
second string
  n inferiority 250.1
  team 617.7
  substitute 862.2
  adj inferior 250.6
second thoughts
  irresolution 362.1
  reverse 363.1
  mature thought 931.5
second to none
  peerless 249.15
  peerlessly 249.18
second wind 396.3
secrecy invisibility 32.1
  concealment 345.1
  secretness 345.1
  hiding 346.1
  seclusion 584.1
secret
  n confidence 345.5
  adj invisible 32.5
  close 345.11

secretive 345.15
concealed 346.11
recondite 522.16
intrinsic 767.7
secret agent
  operative 576.9
  inquirer 938.16
secretariat 594.4
Secretariat
  horse 311.15
  United Nations 614.2
secretary writer 547.13
  recorder 550.1
  executive 574.3
  public official 575.17
  delegate 576.2
  agent 576.3
  table 901.15
Secretary of the Treasury 729.12
secret ballot 371.6
secrete excrete 12.12
  produce 13.5
  keep secret 345.7
  hide away 346.7
  store up 386.11
  be damp 1065.11
secretion
  excretion 12.1
  secreta 13.1
  concealment 346.1
  moisture 1065.1
secret police
  surveillance 938.9
  police 1008.17
Secret Service 576.10
secret service
  intelligence service 576.12
  surveillance 938.9
secret weapon arms 462.1
  salient point 997.6
sect party 617.4
  school 617.5
  system of beliefs 675.1
  sectarism 675.3
sectarian
  n dissenter 333.3
  sectary 675.18
  nonconformist 868.3
  adj dissenting 333.6
  partisan 617.19
  sectary 675.26
sectarianism 617.13
section
  n region 231.1
  plot 231.4
  military unit 461.22
  part of book 554.13
  passage 708.24
  part 793.1
  part of writing 793.2
  severance 802.2
  class 809.2
  classifications 809.5
  v apportion 802.18
sectional
  regional 231.8
  partisan 617.19
  partial 793.7
sector semicircle 280.8
  part 793.1

secular
  n layman 700.2
  adj unsacred 686.3
  secularist 695.16
  lay 700.3
  momentary 850.8
  hundredth 882.29
  realistic 987.6
  material 1052.10
secular humanist 695.13
secure
  v fetch 176.16
  elicit 192.14
  close 293.6
  bind 428.10
  guarantee 438.9
  defend 460.8
  acquire 472.8
  receive 479.6
  fasten 800.7
  make sure 855.8
  stop work 857.8
  protect 1008.18
  adj fast 800.14
  stable 855.12
  belief 953.21
  reliable 970.17
  assured 970.20
  confident 970.21
  safe 1007.4
securities 738
security hope 124.1
  veil of secrecy 345.3
  guaranty 438.1
  surety 438.1
  stability 855.1
  reliability 970.4
  confidence 970.5
  safety 1007.1
  protection 1008.1
  prosperity 1010.1
security blanket 901.1
security camera 714.11
Security Council 614.2
security risk 357.11
sedate
  v put to sleep 22.20
  relieve 120.5
  moderate 670.6
  adj staid 106.14
  solemn 111.3
  dignified 136.12
sedative
  n sleep-inducer 22.10
  anesthetic 25.3
  sedative hypnotic 86.12
  drug 87.3
  moderator 670.3
  adj sleep-inducing 22.23
  calmative 86.45
  palliative 670.16
sedentary inert 173.14
  inactive 331.17
sedge 310.5
sediment
  n deposit 176.9
  dregs 256.2
  v precipitate 1045.11
sedimentary rock 1059.1
sedition
  rebelliousness 327.3

treason 645.7
seduce enamor 104.22
  lure 377.5
  betray 665.20
seductive
  desirable 100.30
  alluring 377.8
see
  n diocese 698.8
  v sense 24.6
  behold 27.12
  attend 221.8
  perceive 521.9
  visit 582.19
  bet 759.25
  spectate 918.5
  know 928.12
  think of 931.17
  detect 941.5
  heed 983.6
  visualize 986.15
  interj attention! 983.22
see about 931.14
see both sides 979.7
seed
  n sperm 305.11
  stone 310.31
  lineage 560.4
  offspring 561.1
  card 758.2
  vital force 886.7
  v plant 1069.18
seedbed 1069.11
seed clouds 316.10
seedling sprout 302.11
  plant 310.3
  tree 310.10
see double
  see badly 28.8
  be drunk 88.27
seed pod 310.30
seedy tired 21.7
  ill 85.56
  shabby 393.32
  slovenly 810.15
  inferior 1005.9
see eye to eye
  concur 332.9
  agree 788.6
see fit 371.17
see how the wind blows 494.6
seeing
  n vision 27.1
  distinctness 31.2
  observatory 1072.17
  adj visual 27.20
Seeing Eye dog
  aid to the blind 30.6
  dog 311.16
see in perspective 925.2
see in retrospect 989.9
see into perceive 521.9
  investigate 938.23
see it through
  prosecute to a conclusion 360.5
  be thorough 794.8
  continue 856.3
  persist 856.5
seek pursue 382.8
  endeavor 403.5

solicit 440.14
　hunt 938.30
　be curious 981.3
seek asylum 1009.7
seek refuge 1009.7
seem 33.10
seeming
　n aspect 33.3
　exteriority 206.1
　sham 354.3
　illusoriness 976.2
　adj apparent 33.11
　exterior 206.7
　specious 354.27
　illusory 976.9
seemly decorous 496.9
　appropriate 533.7
　conventional 579.5
　right 637.3
　decent 664.5
　expedient 995.5
see off 188.16
see one's way clear to 441.3
seep
　n exuding 190.6
　v exude 190.15
　trickle 238.18
　be damp 1065.11
seepage
　sorption 187.6
　entrance 189.1
　exuding 190.6
　trickle 238.7
see red 152.18
seesaw
　n playground equipment
　　743.15
　interaction 777.3
　alternation 916.5
　oscillator 916.9
　v change 854.5
　alternate 916.13
　adj reciprocal 777.10
　alternate 916.19
　adv reciprocally 777.12
　to and fro 916.21
seethe
　n agitation 917.1
　v be excitable 105.16
　be angry 152.15
　bubble 320.4
　fume 671.12
　come together 770.16
　mill 915.12
　flounder 917.15
　be hot 1019.22
　boil 1020.20
　soak 1065.13
see the cloven hoof 941.8
see the difference 944.6
see the future 962.9
see the glass half empty 125.9
**see the handwriting on the
　wall**
　anticipate 845.6
　foreknow 961.6
see the inside of 941.8
see the last of
　not use 390.5
　relinquish 475.3
　eject 909.13

see the light
　appear 33.8
　come to life 306.9
　be published 352.16
　perceive 521.9
　be converted 692.7
**see the light at the end of the
　tunnel** 124.8
see the light of day
　be born 1.2
　appear 33.8
　be published 352.16
　originate 818.13
see to
　prepare for 405.11
　operate 889.5
　seek 938.30
　attend to 983.5
　care for 1008.19
see what one can do
　see what can be done 403.10
　experiment 942.8
see which way the wind blows
　942.9
see ya! 188.22
see you later! 188.22
segment
　n straight line 277.2
　portion 477.5
　sect 675.3
　part 793.1
　part of writing 793.2
　v analyze 801.6
　apportion 802.18
segregate
　quarantine 429.13
　exclude 773.6
　differentiate 780.6
　separate 802.8
　discriminate 944.4
seismic 671.23
seismic wave 916.4
seismograph 916.8
seismology 916.7
seize
　take command 417.14
　arrest 429.15
　hold 474.6
　take hold of 480.14
　understand 521.7
　usurp 640.8
　secure 855.8
　fix 855.10
　stop 857.7
　infest 910.6
　know 928.12
seize on select 371.14
　fasten upon 480.16
　think of 931.16
　pay attention 983.8
seize the day
　make no provision 406.7
　squander 486.3
seize the opportunity
　use the occasion 843.7
　improve the occasion 843.8
seize up be still 173.7
　fix 855.10
　stop 857.7
seizure pang 26.2
　attack 85.6

symptom 85.9
　outburst 105.9
　authority 417.12
　arrest 429.6
　hold 474.2
　seizing 480.2
　take 480.10
　usurpation 640.3
　overrunning 910.1
　spasm 917.6
　frenzy 926.7
seldom
　infrequently 848.4
　unusually 870.17
select
　n the best 999.8
　v make a selection
　　371.14
　designate 517.18
　appoint 615.11
　specify 865.11
　discriminate 944.4
　adj chosen 371.26
　particular 495.13
　exclusive 773.9
　best 999.16
select a jury 598.16
select committee 423.2
selected works 554.7
selection
　choice 371.1
　indication 517.3
　excerpt 557.3
　appointment 615.2
　grouping 808.3
　specification 865.6
selective service
　service 458.8
　enlistment 615.7
selectman 575.17
selectperson 610.3
self psyche 92.28
　ego 865.5
　soul 919.4
self-abasement
　humiliation 137.2
　unselfishness 652.1
　crouch 913.3
self-absorbed
　unfeeling 94.9
　selfish 651.5
self-abuse 75.8
self-accusing 113.8
self-acting
　voluntary 324.7
　automated 1041.22
self-address 542.1
self-adhesive 803.12
self-adjusting 1041.22
self-admiring vain 140.8
　selfish 651.5
self-admission 351.3
self-adulation 502.3
self-advancement 651.1
self-advertisement
　self-approbation 502.3
　selfishness 651.1
self-analysis 113.3
self-appointed
　presumptuous 141.10
　meddlesome 214.9

self-approbation
　complacency 107.2
　vanity 140.1
　self-praise 502.3
self-assertive 359.15
self-assured
　composed 106.13
　confident 970.21
self-avowal 351.3
self-centered
　unfeeling 94.9
　egotistic 140.10
　selfish 651.5
self-complacent
　complacent 107.10
　vain 140.8
self-conceit 140.4
self-confessed
　accepted 332.14
　disclosive 351.10
self-confidence
　equanimity 106.3
　pride 136.1
　confidence 970.5
self-congratulating 140.8
self-conscious 139.12
self-contained
　independent 430.22
　unsociable 583.5
　selfish 651.5
　separate 802.20
**self-contained underwater
　breathing apparatus** 367.5
self-content
　n complacency 107.2
　vanity 140.1
　adj complacent 107.10
　vain 140.8
self-contradiction
　inconsistency 789.2
　impossibility 967.1
　error 975.1
self-control
　n equanimity 106.3
　patience 134.1
　self-command 359.5
　restraint 428.1
　temperance 668.1
　moderation 670.1
　v self-govern 1041.21
self-deception
　deception 356.1
　illusion 976.1
self-defeating 923.10
self-defense
　defense 460.1
　justification 600.2
self-deluding 976.8
self-denial
　self-control 359.5
　unselfishness 652.1
　asceticism 667.1
　temperance 668.1
　moderation 670.1
self-dependent 430.22
self-deprecating
　self-abasing 137.12
　self-effacing 139.10
self-destruct
　blow up 395.18
　be destroyed 395.22

send down 909.17
sender 347.2
send flying 412.7
send for 420.11
send forth send 176.15
  issue 352.14
  start 904.13
  disgorge 909.25
send headlong 913.5
sending 343.2
send in one's papers 448.2
send off send 176.15
  begin 818.7
  start 904.13
  repulse 908.3
  dismiss 909.18
send-off
  leave-taking 188.4
  beginning 818.1
send one's condolences 147.2
send one's regards 504.13
send out
  commission 615.10
  disgorge 909.25
  vaporize 1067.8
send packing
  reject 372.2
  repulse 908.3
  drive out 909.14
  dismiss 909.18
send the wrong message
  pervert 265.6
  misrepresent 350.3
send to Davy Jones's locker
  367.8
send to hell 682.6
send to jail 429.17
send to kingdom come 308.13
send to the gas chamber
  604.17
send up commit 429.17
  lampoon 512.12
send-up 512.5
send up a trial balloon 942.9
send up the river
  imprison 429.14
  commit 429.17
send word
  communicate 343.7
  inform 551.8
senescence 303.6
senile
  n dotard 924.9
  adj stricken in years 303.18
  old-fogyish 842.17
  decrepit 922.23
senior
  n superior 249.4
  elder 304.5
  undergraduate 572.6
  chief 575.3
  bridge 758.3
  adj authoritative 417.15
  previous 834.4
  older 842.19
senior citizen 304.2
senior high school 567.4
seniority
  superiority 249.1
  eldership 303.3
  prestige 417.4

oldness 842.1
senior moment 990.1
señor 76.7
señora 77.8
señorita 77.8
sensate 24.14
sensation
  physical sensibility 24
  sense 24.1
  feeling 93.1
  thrill 105.2
  marvel 122.2
  success 409.4
  brain 919.6
sensational
  emotionalistic 93.19
  lurid 105.32
  wonderful 122.10
  gaudy 501.20
  vigorous 544.11
  grandiloquent 545.8
  superb 999.15
sense
  n sensation 24.1
  feeling 93.1
  milieu 209.3
  meaning 518.1
  consensus 788.3
  intelligence 920.1
  sensibleness 920.6
  cognizance 928.2
  idea 932.1
  hunch 934.3
  logic 935.9
  discrimination 944.1
  suggestion 951.5
  opinion 953.6
  v perceive 24.6
  feel 93.10
  understand 521.7
  intuit 934.4
  detect 941.5
senseless
  unconscious 25.8
  cruel 144.26
  meaningless 520.6
  unordered 810.12
  unintelligent 922.13
  foolish 923.8
  unwise 923.10
  insane 926.26
  illogical 936.11
  inanimate 1055.5
sense of duty 641.2
sense of hearing 48.1
sense of humor 489.11
sense of relief 120.4
sense of rhythm 708.31
sense of right and wrong 636.5
sense of touch 73.1
sense of wonder 122.1
sense organ 24.5
senses five senses 24.5
  wits 919.2
  sanity 925.1
sensible sentient 24.11
  sensitive 93.20
  grateful 150.5
  weighable 297.19
  cheap 633.7
  substantial 763.6

intelligent 920.12
  reasonable 920.18
  sane 925.4
  knowing 928.15
  logical 935.20
  realistic 987.6
sensitive sensory 24.9
  responsive 24.12
  sore 26.11
  sensible 93.20
  excitable 105.28
  touchy 110.21
  confidential 345.14
  fastidious 495.9
  discriminating 944.7
  tolerant 979.11
  pliant 1047.9
sensitize 24.7
sensory
  n brain 919.6
  adj sensorial 24.9
  sensual 663.5
sensual sexual 75.25
  sensualist 663.5
  lascivious 665.29
sensuous sensory 24.9
  delightful 97.7
  sensual 663.5
sentence
  n remark 524.3
  phrase 529.1
  judgment 598.9
  condemnation 602.1
  part of writing 793.2
  verdict 946.5
  maxim 974.1
  v condemn 602.3
  pass judgment 946.13
sentence of death 307.1
sentient 24.11
sentiment feeling 93.1
  sentimentality 93.8
  love 104.1
  idea 932.1
  opinion 953.6
  attitude 978.1
sentimental
  maudlin 93.21
  loving 104.26
  foolish 923.8
sentry warner 399.4
  watchman 1008.10
separable
  different 780.7
  severable 802.26
  discriminable 944.9
separate
  v refine 79.22
  diverge 171.5
  bound 211.8
  partition 213.8
  interspace 224.3
  open 292.11
  quarantine 429.13
  fall out 456.10
  sow dissension 456.14
  divorce 566.5
  disband 771.8
  segregate 773.6
  differentiate 780.6
  apportion 793.6

analyze 801.6
  divide 802.8
  part company 802.19
  classify 808.11
  discriminate 944.4
  adj secluded 584.8
  different 780.7
  distinct 802.20
  alone 872.8
separate oneself
  keep one's distance 261.7
  dissent 333.4
separate returns 630.9
separate the wheat from the
  chaff
  select 371.14
  discriminate 944.4
separatist
  n dissenter 333.3
  apostate 363.5
  adj repudiative 363.12
separator
  extractor 192.9
  sieve 802.7
sepia 40.3
seppuku 308.5
septet
  cooperation 450.1
  part music 708.18
  poetry 720.9
  seven 882.3
septic unhealthful 82.5
  diseased 85.60
  putrefactive 393.39
septicemia 85.31
septic tank 80.12
septuagenarian
  old man 304.2
  seventy 882.7
septum 213.5
sepulcher 309.16
sequaciously 138.15
sequel following 166.1
  continuation 817.1
  consequence 817.1
  follow-up 835.2
  effect 887.1
sequence
  following 166.1
  consistency 803.2
  continuity 807.2
  series 812.2
  progression 815.1
  subsequence 835.1
  effect 887.1
  thoughts 931.4
sequester
  reserve 386.12
  attach 480.20
  separate 802.8
sequester oneself
  seclude oneself 584.7
  stand alone 872.6
  find refuge 1009.8
sequitur 817.1
seraglio 563.10
seraph 679.1
sere worn 393.31
  wasted 393.35
  unproductive 891.4
  dried 1066.9

serenade
 n courtship 562.7
 v court 562.21
 sing 708.38
serendipity
 discovery 941.1
 chance 972.1
serene calm 106.12
 pacific 464.9
 equable 670.13
 light 1025.32
serf sycophant 138.3
 subject 432.7
 retainer 577.1
sergeant
 Army noncommissioned
  officer 575.19
 Navy officer 575.20
 policeman 1008.15
sergeant-at-arms
 ship's officer 183.7
 policeman 1008.15
Sergey Brin and Larry Page
 618.8
serial
 n part 554.13
 periodical 555.1
 radiobroadcast 1034.18
 television broadcast 1035.2
 adj journalistic 555.5
 consistent 803.11
 consecutive 812.9
 periodic 850.7
serial comma
 diagonal 204.7
 grammatical terms 857.4
serial killer 308.11
serial number 517.11
series following 166.1
 edition 554.5
 hockey 749.1
 set 770.12
 classifications 809.5
 succession 812.2
 sequence 815.1
 round 850.3
 mathematical progression
  1017.8
serif 548.6
serious zealous 101.9
 sedate 106.14
 solemn 111.3
 great 247.6
 resolute 359.11
 lofty 544.14
 cognitive 931.21
 weighty 997.20
 dangerous 1006.9
sermon
 reproof 510.5
 lecture 543.3
 lesson 568.7
sermonize
 lecture 543.11
 expound 568.16
serpent snake 311.25
 traitor 357.10
 beast 660.6
serpentine
 n variegation 47.6
 v convolve 281.4

adj deviative 164.7
 flowing 238.24
 curved 279.7
 convolutional 281.6
 coiled 281.7
 reptile 311.47
 cunning 415.12
serrate
 v notch 289.4
 adj angular 278.6
 rugged 288.7
 notched 289.5
serum humor 2.24
 blood 2.25
 antitoxin 86.27
 transfusion 91.18
servant
 hanger-on 138.6
 instrument 384.4
 underling 432.5
 subject 432.7
 employee 577.3
 servitor 577.2
 assistant 616.6
 believer 692.4
 worker 726.2
serve
 n game 748.2
 v copulate 75.21
 be inferior 250.4
 act 328.4
 be instrumental 384.7
 avail 387.17
 summon 420.11
 lend oneself 449.18
 do duty 458.17
 give 478.12
 work for 577.13
 officiate 724.13
 play tennis 748.3
 shuffle 758.5
 suit 788.8
 tend 896.3
 throw 904.10
 suffice 991.4
 expedite one's affair 995.3
 do good 999.10
serve an apprenticeship
 570.11
serve-and-volley 748.2
serve as 349.10
serve notice 551.8
serve one right
 requite 506.5
 punish 604.10
 get one's deserts 639.6
 be just 649.5
serve out 477.8
serve time
 be imprisoned 429.18
 take one's turn 825.5
service
 n serving 8.10
 food service 8.11
 act of kindness 143.7
 rigging 180.12
 obedience 326.1
 instrumentality 384.3
 benefit 387.4
 subservience 432.2
 aid 449.1

military service 458.8
 military branch 461.21
 servanthood 577.12
 ceremony 580.4
 divine service 696.8
 rite 701.3
 task 724.2
 game 748.2
 throw 904.3
 v copulate 75.21
 repair 396.14
serviceable
 modal 384.8
 useful 387.18
 helpful 449.21
serviceable life 827.1
service academy 567.6
serviceman
 mender 396.10
 military man 461.6
service medal 646.6
servile slavish 138.13
 inferior 250.6
 subject 432.13
 downtrodden 432.16
 submissive 433.12
 deferential 433.16
 serving 577.14
serving
 n service 8.10
 rigging 180.12
 adj acting 328.10
 helping 449.20
 servitorial 577.14
serving suggestion 8.10
servitude
 subjection 432.1
 service 577.12
sesquicentennial 850.4
sesquipedality 545.3
session
 ecclesiastical council 423.4
 conference 541.5
 assembly 770.2
 moment 824.2
set
 n navigation 159.3
 direction 161.1
 course 172.2
 flow 238.4
 form 262.1
 sprout 302.11
 edition 554.5
 clique 617.6
 setting 704.19
 motion-picture studio 706.4
 game 745.3
 bridge 758.3
 company 770.3
 collection 770.12
 group 784.5
 all 792.3
 cohesion 803.1
 class 809.2
 trend 896.2
 disposition 978.3
 radio 1034.3
 v be pregnant 78.12
 place 159.12
 establish 159.16
 direct 161.5

take direction 161.7
 sit 173.10
 sink 194.6
 flow 238.16
 form 262.7
 sharpen 285.7
 heal 396.21
 prime 405.9
 prescribe 420.9
 allot 477.9
 typeset 548.16
 impose 643.4
 put to music 708.46
 make agree 788.7
 fasten 800.7
 cohere 803.6
 fix 855.9
 specify 865.11
 tend 896.3
 thicken 1045.10
 solidify 1046.8
 plant 1069.18
 adj trite 117.9
 located 159.18
 circumscribed 210.6
 sharp 285.8
 firm 359.12
 obstinate 361.8
 customary 373.13
 confirmed 373.18
 planned 381.12
 prepared 405.16
 fast 800.14
 cohesive 803.10
 established 855.13
 fixed 855.14
 assured 970.20
 hardened 1046.13
set about
 undertake 404.3
 begin 818.7
set above 371.17
set a course 818.8
set afire 375.18
set afloat cause 886.10
 start 904.13
set against
 v offset 338.5
 sow dissension 456.14
 antagonize 589.7
 compare 943.4
 adj oppositional 451.8
 hostile 589.10
set against one another 215.4
set a limit 944.4
set an example 786.7
set apart
 v partition 213.8
 interspace 224.3
 excise 255.10
 reserve 386.12
 allot 477.9
 dedicate 477.11
 sanctify 685.5
 segregate 773.6
 differentiate 780.6
 separate 802.8
 characterize 865.10
 discriminate 944.4
 adj sanctified 685.8
 segregated 773.8

worthless 391.11
shoddy 393.32
niggardly 484.8
cheap 633.7
base 661.12
slovenly 810.15
paltry 998.21
terrible 1000.9
inferior 1005.9
shack 228.9
shackle
　n restraint 428.4
　curb 1012.7
　v bind 428.10
　confine 429.12
　hamper 1012.11
shack up 75.21
shade
　n color 35.1
　degree 245.1
　hint 248.4
　admixture 797.7
　psyche 919.4
　phantom 976.4
　specter 988.1
　protection 1008.1
　shadow 1027.3
　screen 1028.1
　v color 35.14
　blacken 38.7
　cloud 319.7
　conceal 346.6
　portray 712.18
　darken 1027.9
　screen 1028.5
shade of difference
　margin 780.2
　distinction 944.3
shades spectacles 29.3
　eyeshade 1028.2
shade tree 310.10
shading
　n blackening 38.5
　gradation 245.3
　treatment 712.8
　darkening 1027.6
　televising 1035.3
　television reception 1035.5
　adj screening 1028.6
shadow
　n omen 133.3
　hanger-on 138.6
　follower 166.2
　degree 245.1
　hint 248.4
　remainder 256.1
　thinness 270.7
　slim 270.8
　image 349.5
　treatment 712.8
　spirit 764.3
　reflection 785.7
　psyche 919.4
　phantom 976.4
　specter 988.1
　protection 1008.1
　darkness 1027.3
　shade 1028.1
　v look 27.13
　color 35.14
　blacken 38.7

foreshow 133.9
follow 166.3
cloud 319.7
lurk 346.9
image 349.11
make unintelligible 522.12
trace 938.35
darken 1027.9
shade 1028.5
shadow-box 754.4
shadowing
　n following 166.1
　ambush 346.3
　pursuit 382.1
　surveillance 938.9
　darkening 1027.6
　adj shading 1028.6
shadow of death 307.1
shadow of doubt 955.2
shady dishonest 645.16
　disreputable 661.10
　shadowy 1027.16
　shaded 1028.7
shady character 415.6
shady past 661.6
the shady side 303.5
shaft
　n feather part 3.17
　air passage 239.13
　tower 272.6
　pole 273.1
　hole 275.2
　pit 284.4
　arrow 462.6
　monument 549.12
　base 901.8
　mine 1058.6
　v mistreat 389.6
shag
　n hair 3.2
　head of hair 3.4
　tobacco 89.2
　texture 294.1
　v fetch 176.16
shaggy hairy 3.24
　rough 288.6
　nappy 294.7
　disheveled 810.14
shaggy dog story 488.3
shah 575.9
shake
　n beverage 10.49
　speech defect 525.1
　trill 709.19
　instant 830.3
　quake 917.3
　flutter 917.4
　search 938.15
　wood 1054.3
　v be weak 16.8
　weaken 16.10
　disturb 105.14
　be excited 105.18
　tremble 127.14
　frighten 127.15
　daunt 127.18
　unnerve 128.10
　startle 131.8
　face 295.23
　age 303.10
　evade 368.7

break the habit 374.3
sign 437.7
speak poorly 525.7
greet 585.10
dance 705.5
sing 708.38
thrust 902.12
oscillate 916.10
wave 916.11
alternate 916.14
agitate 917.10
quake 917.11
ransack 938.33
freeze 1023.9
shake a leg
　v be active 330.14
　interj make haste 401.17
shakedown
　extortion 480.8
　search 938.15
　tryout 942.3
shakedown artist 480.12
shakedown cruise
　voyage 182.6
　tryout 942.3
shake hands near 223.7
　sign 437.7
　make up 465.10
　greet 585.10
　strike a bargain 731.19
shaken
　disturbed 105.23
　unnerved 128.14
　startled 131.13
　agitated 917.16
　confused 985.12
shake off evade 368.7
　free oneself from 431.8
　do away with 909.21
shake one's fist at
　defy 454.3
　threaten 514.2
shake on it
　come to an agreement 332.10
　strike a bargain 731.19
shakeout
　elimination 773.2
　classification 801.3
　grouping 808.3
　distinction 944.3
shaker
　gambling wheel 759.16
　agitator 917.9
Shaker
　n abstainer 668.4
　adj abstinent 668.10
the shakes
　shaking 917.2
　delirium tremens 926.10
shake up weaken 16.10
　wake someone up 23.5
　disturb 105.14
　censure 510.13
　rearrange 808.13
　agitate 917.10
　soften 1047.6
shake-up
　rearrangement 808.7
　expedient 995.2
shaky unsteady 16.16
　fearful 127.23

jittery 128.12
stricken in years 303.18
unaccustomed 374.4
inarticulate 525.12
fragile 764.7
loose 804.5
shaking 917.17
unreliable 971.20
unsafe 1006.11
feeling cold 1023.16
shaky ground 1006.2
shallow
　n shoal 276.2
　v become less deep 276.3
　adj insignificant 248.6
　depthless 276.5
　superficial 922.20
　half-learned 930.14
　trivial 998.19
shallowness
　exteriority 206.1
　depthlessness 276.1
　superficiality 922.7
　slight knowledge 930.5
　inattention 984.1
　triviality 998.3
shallows
　shoal 276.2
　hidden danger 1006.5
shalom!
　farewell! 188.22
　peace! 464.11
sham
　n fakery 354.3
　fake 354.13
　hoax 356.7
　impostor 357.6
　pretext 376.1
　affectation 500.1
　display 501.4
　v fake 354.21
　affect 500.12
　adj imitation 336.8
　spurious 354.26
　assumed 500.16
shaman
　n witch doctor 690.7
　adj sorcerous 690.14
shamble
　n slow motion 175.2
　gait 177.12
　v plod 175.7
　way of walking 177.28
shambles
　butchery 308.3
　place of killing 308.12
　destruction 395.1
　battlefield 463.2
shame
　n chagrin 96.4
　regret 113.1
　humiliation 137.2
　abomination 638.2
　iniquity 654.3
　disgrace 661.5
　decency 664.2
　v humiliate 137.4
　disgrace 661.8
　interj God forbid! 510.27
shamed
　humiliated 137.14

pull back 903.7

sheet whiteness 37.2
blanket 295.10
lamina 296.2
newspaper 555.2
part of writing 793.2
paper 1054.5
sheet ice 1023.5
sheet lightning 1025.17
sheet metal 1058.5
sheet music 708.28
sheet of fire 1019.13
sheet of rain 316.1
sheik 104.12
sheikh ruler 575.9
prince 608.7
clergy 699.12
sheikhdom 417.7
shekels 728.2
shelf shoal 276.2
layer 296.1
storehouse 386.6
ledge 901.14
shelf ice 1023.5
shelf life 827.1
shell
n ear 2.10
exterior 206.2
frame 266.4
cavity 284.2
crust 295.14
seashell 295.15
hull 295.16
armor 460.3
cartridge 462.17
shot 462.19
stage 704.16
electron 1033.3
atom 1038.4
v husk 6.9
pull the trigger 459.22
shellac
n liquor 88.14
v color 35.14
defeat 412.9
shellacked drunk 88.33
sleek 287.11
defeated 412.15
shellacking
painting 35.12
victory 411.1
utter defeat 412.3
shellfish 10.25
shell game 356.10
shell out give 478.12
pay out 624.14
spend 626.5
shell shock 92.17
shelter
n quarters 228.4
cover 295.2
protection 1008.1
refuge 1009.3
v house 225.10
protect 1008.18
sheltered
quiescent 173.12
protected 1008.21
shelve incline 204.10
put away 390.6
postpone 846.9

shenanigans
buffoonery 489.5
prank 489.10
shepherd
n guide 574.7
clergyman 699.2
escort 769.5
guardian 1008.6
herder 1070.3
v guide 573.9
escort 769.8
care for 1008.19
drive 1070.8
sherbet 10.47
sheriff 1008.15
Sherlock Holmes 576.10
Shetland pony 311.10
she-wolf bitch 110.12
witch 593.7
violent person 671.9
shibboleth
password 517.12
catchword 526.9
shield
n cover 295.2
shell 295.15
heraldry 647.2
safeguard 1008.3
v cover 295.19
defend 460.8
protect 1008.18
shield-bearer 176.7
shielded
covered 295.31
protected 1008.21
shift
n shirt 5.15
dislocation 160.1
deviation 164.1
moving 176.4
trick 356.6
stratagem 415.3
work shift 825.3
change 852.1
conversion 858.1
expedient 995.2
v deviate 164.3
move 172.5
remove 176.11
change course 182.30
vacillate 362.8
dodge 368.8
live by one's wits 415.9
be dishonest 645.11
be changed 852.6
change 854.5
convert 858.11
quibble 936.9
shift about 645.11
shifting
n deviation 164.1
changing 854.3
quibbling 936.5
adj deviative 164.7
wandering 177.37
inconstant 854.7
unreliable 971.20
shifting sands 854.4
shiftless
indolent 331.19
improvident 406.15

shift the blame
impose on 643.7
be unfaithful 645.12
shifty
covert 345.12
secretive 345.15
deceitful 356.22
evasive 368.15
cunning 415.12
dishonest 645.16
treacherous 645.21
inconstant 854.7
unreliable 971.20
Shiite
n Muslim 675.23
adj Muslim 675.31
shill
n decoy 357.5
by-bidder 733.6
v bid 733.9
shillelagh 273.2
shilling 728.8
shimmer
n glitter 1025.7
v glitter 1025.25
shimmy 705.5
shin
n part the body 2.7
leg 177.14
v climb 193.11
shindig party 582.12
dance 705.2
assembly 770.2
shine
n bootleg liquor 88.18
love 104.1
polish 287.2
glow 1025.2
daylight 1025.10
v polish 287.7
perfect 392.11
cut a dash 501.13
be eloquent 544.7
be somebody 662.10
look good 1016.16
give light 1025.24
buff 1044.8
shiner 85.38
shine through 31.4
shingle
n grain 1051.6
wood 1054.3
gravel 1059.3
v cut the hair 3.22
cover 295.23
overlap 295.30
shin guard
soccer equipment 752.1
safeguard 1008.3
shining
n abrasion 1044.2
adj illustrious 662.19
gorgeous 1016.20
luminous 1025.31
shiny 1025.34
shining example
paragon 659.4
ideal 786.4
shiny clean 79.25
sleek 287.11
luminous 1025.31

shining 1025.34
ship
n boat 180.1
part of fleet 180.10
aircraft 181.1
dirigible 181.11
v haul 176.13
send 176.15
shipmaster 183.7
shipmate 588.3
shipment
transportation 176.3
freight 176.6
ship of war 180.6
shipshape trim 180.20
tidy 807.8
ship's log 549.11
shipwreck
n debacle 395.4
misfortune 1011.2
v wreck 182.42
destroy 395.10
shipyard plant 739.3
harbor 1009.6
shirk
n shirker 368.3
v idle 331.12
leave undone 340.7
slack 368.9
shirt
n clothing 5.15
soccer 752.1
v cloak 5.40
shit
n defecation 12.2
feces 12.4
bullshit 520.3
bad person 660.5
nothing 762.3
v defecate 12.13
shitcan 391.7
shitfaced 88.33
shithead 660.5
shithouse 12.10
shit in one's pants 127.11
shit-kicker 606.6
shitkickers 5.27
shit list 871.1
shitload 884.3
shit or get off the pot 328.5
shitty
excremental 12.20
filthy 80.23
bad 1000.8
shitwork 725.4
shiv 1040.2
shiver
n thrill 105.2
trepidation 105.5
scrap 248.3
piece 793.3
shake 917.3
v be excited 105.18
tremble 127.14
shatter 802.13
shake 917.11
freeze 1023.9
shiver my timbers! 122.19
shoal
n shallow 276.2
group of animals 770.5

multitude 884.3
v become shallow 276.3
adj shallow 276.5
shock
n head of hair 3.4
stupor 22.6
symptom 85.9
trauma 85.26
pain 96.5
start 131.3
concussion 671.8
bunch 770.7
impact 902.3
shake 917.3
misfortune 1011.2
electric discharge 1032.6
v offend 98.11
agitate 105.14
terrify 127.17
startle 131.8
shake 917.11
electrify 1032.26
shock absorber 670.3
shocking horrid 98.19
frightening 127.30
surprising 131.11
downright 247.12
disgraceful 661.11
sudden 830.5
terrible 1000.9
shock-resistant 1049.4
shock tactics 459.1
shock therapy 92.35
shock troops 461.15
shock wave
air speed 184.31
wave 916.4
shod 5.45
shoddy
n fake 354.13
rubbish 391.5
adj spurious 354.26
worthless 391.11
shabby 393.32
cheap 633.7
base 661.12
slovenly 810.15
paltry 998.21
terrible 1000.9
shoe
n footwear 5.27
bowling 750.1
automobile racing 756.1
v cloak 5.40
the shoe is on the other foot
what goes around comes
around 506.10
permanence 852.14
shoemaker 5.38
shogun 575.9
shoo
v do away with 909.21
interj go away! 909.31
begone 909.32
shoo-in
sure success 409.2
victor 411.2
horse race 757.3
sure thing 970.2
shook startled 131.13
confused 985.12

shook up 128.12
shoot
n pang 26.2
journey 177.5
rapids 238.10
gutter 239.3
sprout 302.11
branch 310.20
offshoot 561.4
warp 740.3
deposit 1058.7
rocket launching 1074.9
v suffer 26.8
inject 87.22
immunize 91.28
speed 174.8
row 182.53
float 182.54
strike dead 308.18
vegetate 310.34
hunt 382.9
pull the trigger 459.22
execute 604.17
explode 671.14
film 706.8
photograph 714.14
play basketball 747.4
play hockey 749.7
play golf 751.4
fire off 904.12
shine 1025.24
launch 1074.13
shoot ahead
spurt 174.12
outdistance 249.10
hustle 330.13
shoot back 939.4
shoot craps 759.23
shoot down
strike dead 308.18
do for 395.11
end 820.5
shoot 904.12
shooter 904.8
shoot from the hip
be impatient 135.4
act on the spur of the
moment 365.7
prejudge 947.2
shoot full of holes 958.4
shooting
n pang 26.2
killing 308.1
hunting 382.2
gunfire 459.8
capital punishment 604.7
hockey game 749.3
throwing 904.2
adj painful 26.10
shooting gallery 87.20
shooting script
playbook 704.21
script 706.3
shooting star
omen 133.5
meteor 1072.15
shoot it out with 457.17
shoot off one's mouth
bluster 503.3
talk nonsense 520.5
speak 524.20

chatter 540.5
shootout 752.3
shoot out 283.10
shoot straight with 649.5
shoot the breeze
speak 524.20
converse 541.8
shoot the works
be determined 359.8
persevere 360.7
do one's best 403.14
do to perfection 407.7
court danger 493.6
risk 972.12
shoot up grow 14.2
inject 87.22
spring up 193.9
increase 251.6
expand 259.7
grow higher 272.12
protrude 283.10
vegetate 310.34
shop
n occupation 724.4
market 736.1
workplace 739.1
office 739.7
casino 759.19
v inform on 551.13
market 733.8
shop around
choose 371.13
shop 733.8
be discriminating 944.5
shop at 731.17
shopkeeper 730.2
shoplift 482.13
shoplifter 483.1
shopper 733.5
shopping-bag lady
homeless person 331.10
poor person 619.4
shopping center
metropolis 208.7
city district 230.6
marketplace 736.2
shopping list
purchase 733.1
list 871.1
shopping mall 739.1
shopping spree 733.1
shop steward 727.4
shoptalk 523.10
shopworn 393.31
shore
n border 211.4
side 218.1
coast 234.2
v buttress 449.12
support 901.21
adj aquatic 182.58
coastal 234.7
shore bird 311.27
shore leave 20.3
shoreline
n shore 234.2
adj coastal 234.7
shore patrol 1008.17
shore up
strengthen 15.13
buttress 449.12

support 901.21
stiffen 1046.9
shorn 252.10
shorn of 473.8
short
n car 179.10
motion pictures 706.1
bear account 737.12
v electrify 1032.26
adj insignificant 248.6
little 258.10
brief 268.8
low 274.7
taciturn 344.9
gruff 505.7
concise 537.6
poor 619.7
incomplete 795.4
fleeting 828.8
falling short of 911.5
wanting 992.13
imperfect 1003.4
adv abruptly 268.13
shortage
deficiency 795.2
shortcoming 911.1
want 992.4
imperfection 1003.1
shortchange 356.18
short-circuit 1032.26
shortcoming
inequality 791.1
falling short 911.1
want 992.4
imperfection 1003.1
fault 1003.2
shortcut cut 268.5
straight line 277.2
route 383.1
shorten
n make small 258.9
v reduce 252.7
subtract 255.9
contract 260.7
abbreviate 268.6
be brief 537.5
abridge 557.5
shorten sail
reduce sail 182.50
take precautions 494.6
shorter 252.10
shortfall
deficiency 795.2
shortcoming 911.1
want 992.4
short fuse
irascibility 110.2
hot temper 110.4
shorthand
n phonetic symbol 546.2
stenography 547.8
adj written 547.22
stenographic 547.27
shorthanded 992.12
short list 871.1
short-lived 828.7
short memory 990.1
short odds 759.6
short of breath 21.12
short-order cook 11.3
short range 223.2

short rations 515.2
shorts
  bear account 737.12
  soccer 752.1
short shrift
  pitilessness 146.1
  repulse 442.2
shortsighted
  poor-sighted 28.11
  undiscerning 922.14
  unwise 923.10
  narrow-minded 980.10
shortstop 745.2
short story 722.3
short story writer
  author 547.15
  scribe 718.4
short subject 706.1
short supply 992.1
short temper
  irascibility 110.2
  hot temper 110.4
short-term 828.8
short-term memory 989.1
short time
  shortness 268.1
  little while 828.3
shortwave
  n radio wave 1034.11
  v broadcast 1034.25
  adj radio 1034.28
shorty 258.4
shot
  n detonation 56.3
  dose 86.6
  fix 87.20
  drink 88.7
  inoculation 91.16
  disrespect 156.3
  swiftness 174.6
  attempt 403.3
  ball 462.19
  fee 630.6
  cinematography 706.5
  photograph 714.3
  motion picture segment 714.8
  baseball game 745.3
  basketball game 747.3
  tennis game 748.2
  hockey game 749.3
  golf stroke 751.3
  soccer game 752.3
  bet 759.3
  throw 759.9
  portion 793.5
  discharge 904.4
  shooter 904.8
  guess 951.4
  rocket launching 1074.9
  adj variegated 47.9
  unnerved 128.14
  spoiled 393.29
  ruined 395.29
  ended 820.9
shotgun 308.18
shotgun approach 401.1
shotgun wedding 563.3
shot in the arm 86.8
shot in the dark
  gamble 759.2
  guess 951.4

shot-put 904.3
shot through
  variegated 47.9
  permeated 221.15
  apertured 292.19
should
  ought to 641.3
  be necessary 963.10
shoulder
  n bulge 283.3
  type 548.6
  joint 800.4
  supporter 901.2
  buttress 901.4
  shelf 901.14
  v support 901.21
  thrust 902.12
shoulder patch 647.5
shoulder to shoulder
  adv cooperatively 450.6
  hand in hand 769.10
  concurrently 899.5
  phrs side by side 218.12
shout
  n cry 59.1
  cheer 116.2
  laughter 116.4
  v din 53.7
  cry 59.6
  cheer 116.6
  laugh 116.8
  be manifest 348.7
  proclaim 352.13
shout at the top of one's voice
  59.9
shout down
  drown out 53.8
  run over 910.7
shout hallelujah 116.6
shout out 59.8
shout-out
  cry 59.1
  cheer 116.2
  acknowledgment 332.3
shove
  n thrust 902.2
  pushing 904.1
  v set in motion 172.6
  illicit goods 732.7
  thrust 902.12
  push 904.9
shove aside 164.6
shovel
  n cutlery 1040.2
  v ladle 176.17
  excavate 284.15
shove off
  v get under way 182.19
  sail away from 182.36
  depart 188.7
  leave 222.10
  die 307.19
  interj go away 909.32
shoving match 457.4
show
  n appearance 33.2
  spectacle 33.7
  externalization 206.4
  exhibition 348.2
  sham 354.3
  pretext 376.1

  affectation 500.1
  display 501.4
  indication 517.3
  stage show 704.4
  theatrical performance
    704.12
  marketplace 736.2
  illusoriness 976.2
  v show up 31.4
  appear 33.8
  direct to 161.6
  externalize 206.5
  explain 341.10
  manifest 348.5
  disclose 351.4
  signify 517.17
  teach 568.10
  project 714.16
  finish third 757.5
  evidence 957.8
  prove 957.10
show a deficit 623.6
show a lack of respect for
  156.4
show a percentage 472.13
show aptitude for 413.18
show a tendency
  tend 896.3
  be probable 968.4
showboat
  n show-off 501.11
  theater 704.14
  v exercise skill 413.20
  show off 501.16
show business
  the entertainment industry
    704
  theater 743.13
showcase
  n display 348.2
  theatrical performance
    704.12
  counter 736.6
  transparent substance
    1029.2
  v manifest 348.5
show consideration 670.8
show dog 311.16
showdown poker 759.10
  contrariety 779.1
shower
  n bath 79.8
  showering apparatus 79.12
  rain 316.1
  plenty 991.2
  sprinkle 1065.5
  sprinkler 1065.8
  v wash 79.19
  rain 316.10
  give 478.12
  abound 991.5
shower head
  showering apparatus 79.12
  nozzle 239.9
  sprinkler 1065.8
show girl 707.1
show good faith 644.9
show horse 757.2
show how
  explain 341.10
  teach 568.10

showing
  n appearance 33.1
  externalization 206.4
  display 348.2
  indication 517.3
  adj divested 6.12
  visible 31.6
  manifesting 348.9
  disclosive 351.10
show its colors 351.8
show its face 351.8
show kindness 143.9
showman 704.23
showmanship 704.3
show no mercy 146.2
show off
  manifest 348.5
  grandstand 501.16
show-off 501.11
show of hands 371.6
show one's hand 351.7
show one's true colors
  come out 348.6
  confess 351.7
showpiece model 786.1
  standard of perfection
    1002.4
show pity 670.8
showplace 786.1
show preference 650.8
show promise 133.12
show respect for 155.5
showroom display room
  197.24
  salesroom 736.5
show signs of
  appear to be 33.10
  augur 133.11
  evidence 957.8
showstopper 409.4
show the door 909.18
show the ropes 568.10
show the way
  direct to 161.6
  lead 165.2
  explain 341.10
  go before 816.3
show through
  show 31.4
  be transparent 1029.3
show up show 31.4
  appear 33.8
  arrive 186.6
  attend 221.8
  overshadow 249.8
  disclose 351.4
  turn up 831.6
  be discovered 941.9
  disprove 958.4
  disillusion 977.2
showy
  flaunting 501.19
  grandiloquent 545.8
shrapnel 462.19
shred
  n scrap 248.3
  piece 793.3
  v tear apart 802.14
  pulverize 1051.9
shredded
  severed 802.23

powdery 1051.11
shredder 1051.7
shrew 110.12
shrewd cunning 415.12
  artful 920.15
  knowing 928.15
shrewish
  peevish 110.22
  ungovernable 361.12
  partisan 456.17
shriek
  n blare 53.5
  screech 58.4
  cry 59.1
  laughter 116.4
  v blare 53.10
  screech 58.8
  cry 59.6
  wail 115.13
  laugh 116.8
  sigh 318.20
  speak 524.25
shrift pardon 148.2
  confession 351.3
shrill
  n screech 58.4
  v squawk 58.8
  adj strident 58.14
  dissonant 61.4
shrimp
  n runt 258.4
  a nobody 998.7
  v fish 382.10
shrine
  n tomb 309.16
  monument 549.12
  holy place 703.4
  v enclose 212.5
shrink
  n psychologist 92.10
  v suffer 26.8
  flinch 127.13
  efface oneself 139.7
  recede 168.2
  retract 168.3
  decrease 252.6
  reduce 252.7
  shrivel 260.9
  demur 325.4
  dodge 368.8
  languish 393.18
  waste 473.5
  draw back 903.7
shrink from 99.5
shrinking violet 139.6
shrink-wrap
  package 212.9
  bind 800.9
shrivel shrink 260.9
  age 303.10
  languish 393.18
  dry 1066.6
shroud
  n cover 295.2
  graveclothes 309.14
  supporter 901.2
  v clothe 5.39
  wrap 295.20
  conceal 346.6
  protect 1008.18
shrouded in darkness 1027.13

shrouded in mystery 522.18
shrubbery 310.9
shrug
  n gesture 517.14
  v accept 134.7
  submit 433.6
shrug off
  not care 102.4
  discard 390.7
  submit 433.6
  underestimate 950.2
  dismiss 984.4
shrug the shoulders 517.21
shrunk
  reduced 252.10
  dwarf 258.13
  shrunken 260.13
shtick 704.7
shuck
  n hull 295.16
  v husk 6.9
shudder
  n thrill 105.2
  trepidation 105.5
  shake 917.3
  v be frequent 847.3
  shake 917.11
  freeze 1023.9
shuddering halt 857.2
shuffle
  n slow motion 175.2
  gait 177.12
  prevarication 344.4
  substitution 862.1
  quibble 936.4
  confusion 985.3
  v go slow 175.6
  way of walking 177.28
  slip away 369.9
  dance 705.5
  rearrange playing cards
    758.5
  mix 797.10
  confuse 811.3
  change 854.5
  substitute 862.4
  quibble 936.9
shuffle off 368.12
shun snub 157.7
  avoid 368.6
  abstain 668.7
shunt
  n pushing 904.1
  v avoid 164.6
  remove 176.11
  push 904.9
shush
  n sibilation 57.1
  v silence 51.8
  sibilate 57.2
  cover up 345.8
  interj silence 51.14
shut
  v close 293.6
  turn off 857.12
  adj closed 293.9
shut away 429.12
shutdown closure 293.1
  cessation 857.1
shut down
  close shop 293.8

suppress 428.8
  go bankrupt 625.7
  stop work 857.8
  turn off 857.12
shut down on 51.8
shut-eye 22.2
shut in enclose 212.5
  confine 429.12
shut-in
  n sick person 85.43
  recluse 584.5
  adj unhealthy 85.54
  enclosed 212.10
  restricted 428.15
  confined 429.19
  recluse 584.10
shut off
  v separate 802.8
  turn off 857.12
  obstruct 1012.12
  adj secluded 584.8
  separated 802.21
shut one's mouth 51.5
shutout 412.3
shut out
  v close 293.6
  defeat 412.9
  prohibit 444.3
  exclude 773.4
  obstruct 1012.12
  adj defeated 412.16
shutter 1028.5
shutterbug 716.5
shut the door in one's face
    442.5
shut tight 1012.12
shuttle
  n train 179.14
  aircraft 181.1
  air travel 184.10
  loom 740.5
  oscillator 916.9
  spacecraft 1075.2
  v alternate 916.13
shuttlecock
  n oscillator 916.9
  v alternate 916.13
shuttle diplomacy 609.5
shut up
  v be silent 51.6
  enclose 212.5
  close 293.6
  close shop 293.8
  confine 429.12
  refute 958.5
  adj recluse 584.10
  interj silence 51.14
shy
  n avoidance 368.1
  retreat 903.3
  throw 904.3
  v be frightened 127.12
  flinch 127.13
  be startled 131.5
  turn aside 164.6
  retract 168.3
  demur 325.4
  hesitate 362.7
  avoid 368.8
  pull back 903.7
  throw 904.10

quibble 936.9
  adj fearful 127.23
  timid 139.12
  receding 168.5
  demurring 325.7
  wary 494.9
  incomplete 795.4
  alone 872.8
  doubting 955.9
  wanting 992.13
shy away recede 168.2
  dodge 368.8
  pull back 903.7
shylock 620.3
shyster cheat 357.3
  trickster 415.6
  lawyer 597.3
  rascal 660.3
sí 332.18
siamese connection 239.6
Siamese twins 873.4
Siberia
  remote region 261.4
  cold place 1023.4
Siberian husky 176.8
Siberian tiger 311.21
sibilant 57.3
sibling
  n kinfolk 559.2
  adj related 559.6
sic 973.20
sick ill 85.56
  disconsolate 112.28
  weary 118.11
  insane 926.26
sick and tired of
  weary 118.11
  satiated 994.6
sick as a dog 85.56
sicken
  disagree with 82.4
  take sick 85.47
  afflict 85.50
  offend 98.11
  deteriorate 393.16
sick joke 489.6
sickle 279.5
sick leave 222.4
sickly colorless 36.7
  unhealthy 85.54
sickness disease 85.1
  insanity 926.1
sic on incite 375.17
  sow dissension 456.14
side
  n aspect 33.3
  conceit 140.4
  incline 204.4
  border 211.4
  flank 218.1
  straight line 277.2
  pretensions 501.2
  boasting 502.1
  bluster 503.1
  lineage 560.4
  faction 617.4
  role 704.10
  playbook 704.21
  lawn bowling 750.3
  team 752.2
  interest 935.14

overcome 412.7
suppress 428.8
refute 958.5
interj hush 51.14
silent
n motion pictures 706.1
adj still 51.10
taciturn 344.9
unexpressed 519.9
silent majority
middle class 607.5
party 617.4
mediocrity 1005.5
silent partner 616.2
silent person 49.2
silent treatment 909.4
silhouette
n outline 211.2
contour 262.2
drawing 712.12
portrait 712.14
reflection 785.7
shadow 1027.3
v outline 211.9
silicon chip
electronic circuit 1033.8
circuitry 1042.3
silicone 1056.2
silk material 4.1
smoothness 287.3
fine texture 294.3
softness 1047.4
silk-screen printing
printing 548.1
stencil printing 713.4
silk stocking 607.3
silk-stocking
n nobleman 608.4
adj socially prominent 578.16
silk-stocking district 609.16
silkworm 271.5
silky threadlike 271.7
smooth 287.10
sleek 287.11
fine-textured 294.8
velvety 1047.15
silly
n fool 924.6
adj nonsensical 520.7
foolish 923.8
dazed 985.14
trivial 998.19
silo granary 386.7
rocket launcher 1074.10
silt deposit 176.9
dregs 256.2
silted up 293.11
silver
n tableware 8.12
whiteness 37.1
alabaster 37.2
money 728.1
precious metals 728.20
v whiten 37.5
gray 39.3
adj white 37.7
gray 39.4
eloquent 544.8
brass 1058.17
Silver 311.15

silver dollar 728.7
silver lining 124.2
silver mine 1058.6
the silver screen 706.1
silver-tongued
eloquent 544.8
melodious 708.48
silverware
tableware 8.12
hard goods 735.4
silver wedding anniversary 850.4
s'il vous plaît 440.20
SIM 347.4
SIM card 347.4
simian 311.22
similar
approximate 775.8
like 784.10
comparative 943.8
simile similarity 784.1
comparible 943.1
simmer
n boiling 1020.2
v cook 11.5
be angry 152.15
bubble 320.4
seethe 671.12
be hot 1019.22
boil 1020.20
simmer down 106.7
Simon Legree 575.14
simp 924.8
simpatico 587.15
simper
n smile 116.3
v smile 116.7
mince 500.14
simple
soft-colored 35.22
humble 137.10
homelike 228.33
mere 248.8
artless 416.5
tasteful 496.7
ordinary 499.6
elegant 533.6
plain-speaking 535.3
informal 581.3
real 761.15
essential 767.9
plain 798.6
one 872.7
mentally deficient 922.22
ignorant 930.11
gullible 954.9
genuine 973.15
easy 1014.13
simple existence 761.6
simple fact 761.3
simple machine 1040.5
simple matter 1014.3
simpleminded
artless 416.5
mentally deficient 922.22
simpleton 924.8
simplicity
prosaicness 117.2
rusticity 233.3
decrease 252.1
artlessness 416.1

restraint 496.3
ordinariness 499.1
clearness 521.2
elegance 533.1
plain speech 535.1
informality 581.1
simpleness 798.1
purity 798.1
oneness 872.1
mental deficiency 922.9
ignorance 930.1
gullibility 954.2
facility 1014.1
simulate imitate 336.5
fake 354.21
affect 500.12
adopt 621.4
resemble 784.7
simulation
imitation 336.1
sham 354.3
adoption 621.2
similarity 784.1
simultaneous 836.5
sin
n blackness 38.4
iniquity 654.3
wrongdoing 655.1
misdeed 655.2
error 975.1
v do wrong 654.8
transgress 655.4
since
adv subsequently 835.6
ago 837.15
ever since 837.17
conj because 888.10
sincere zealous 101.9
resolute 359.11
artless 416.5
candid 644.17
genuine 973.15
the sincerest form of flattery 336.1
since time began
for a long time 827.14
since 837.17
sine qua non 196.5
sinew muscularity 15.2
power 18.1
vigor 544.3
sinewy
able-bodied 15.16
vigorous 544.11
tough 1049.4
sinful wrong 638.3
immoral 654.16
wicked 655.5
ungodly 695.17
bad 1000.7
sing
n musical occasion 708.32
v bird sound 60.5
be pleased 95.12
exude cheerfulness 109.6
rejoice 116.5
wind sound 318.20
betray 351.6
speak 524.25
inform on 551.13
vocalize 708.38

poetize 720.13
sing a different tune
n change one's mind 363.6
v be changed 852.6
change 852.7
convert 858.11
singe
n burn 1020.6
v stain 1004.6
burn 1020.24
singer
entertainer 707.1
lead 707.6
vocalist 710.13
Singer 741.3
single
n celibate 565.2
baseball hit 745.3
individual 872.4
v hit a baseball 745.5
adj unmarried 565.7
simple 798.6
characteristic 865.13
one 872.7
single file 812.2
single-handed 872.8
single-minded
resolute 359.11
persevering 360.8
artless 416.5
engrossed 983.17
singleness of purpose 360.1
single out
select 371.14
specify 865.11
call attention to 983.10
singlet 342.1
single vote 371.6
sing out 59.8
singsong
n regularity 781.2
repetitiousness 849.4
adj tedious 118.9
monotonous 849.15
sing the blues
hang one's head 112.15
lament 115.10
sing the praises of
praise 509.12
glorify 696.12
sing 708.38
sing the same old song
harp on 118.8
dwell on 849.9
singular
n number 530.8
adj wonderful 122.10
particular 865.12
characteristic 865.13
odd 870.11
one 872.7
sole 872.9
eccentric 927.5
sinister
adj ominous 133.16
oblique 204.13
left 220.4
dishonest 645.16
bad 1000.7
adverse 1011.13
adv leftward 220.6

sink
  n washbasin 79.12
  receptacle of filth 80.12
  drain 239.5
  cavity 284.2
  den of iniquity 654.7
  v weaken 16.9
  burn out 21.5
  disappear 34.2
  languish 85.48
  lose heart 112.16
  sadden 112.18
  recede 168.2
  move 172.5
  capsize 182.44
  go down 194.6
  decrease 252.6
  deepen 275.8
  be concave 284.12
  excavate 284.15
  gravitate 297.15
  age 303.10
  submerge 367.7
  scuttle 367.8
  spoil 393.11
  decline 393.17
  ruin 395.11
  founder 410.11
  bankrupt 625.8
  invest 729.17
  make a golf shot 751.4
  flit 828.6
  depress 913.4
  come to grief 1011.10
  fall on evil days 1011.11
sinkhole pothole 284.3
  sewer 654.7
  water 1065.3
sink in
  impress 93.15
  mire 243.2
  get across 521.5
  impress 931.19
  be remembered 989.13
sinking fast 307.32
sinking heart 112.3
sink into despair
  lose heart 112.16
  despair 125.10
sink one's teeth into it 330.11
sink or swim
  adv without fail 970.26
  phrs come what may 359.20
sinner evildoer 593.1
  wrongdoer 660.8
sinuous curved 279.7
  convolutional 281.6
sinus 279.2
sip
  n drink 8.4
  taste 62.2
  nip 88.7
  hint 248.4
  v drink 8.29
  taste 62.7
  tipple 88.24
siphon
  n extractor 192.9
  tube 239.6
  v transport 176.14
  channel 239.15

sir 76.7
Sir 648.3
sire
  n senior 304.5
  father 560.9
  Sir 648.3
  jockey 757.2
  author 886.4
  producer 892.7
  v procreate 78.8
  engender 818.14
  cause 886.10
siren
  n noisemaker 53.6
  spirit of the sea 240.3
  tempter 377.4
  warning sign 399.3
  alarm 400.1
  witch 593.7
  water god 678.10
  bewitcher 690.9
  adj alluring 377.8
Sir Galahad 608.5
sirocco
  hot wind 318.6
  dust storm 318.12
sissy
  n weakling 16.6
  effeminate male 77.10
  spoiled child 427.4
  coward 491.5
  sister 559.3
  adj effeminate 77.14
  cowardly 491.10
sister woman 77.6
  nurse 90.10
  female sibling 559.3
  member 617.11
  nun 699.17
  layman 700.2
  likeness 784.3
Sister 648.5
sister-in-law 564.2
sit be pregnant 78.12
  be seated 173.10
  convene 770.17
sit around 331.12
sit at 221.8
sit at the feet of 570.11
sit back 329.2
sitcom 1035.2
sit-down meal 8.5
  conference 541.5
  strike 727.5
  assembly 770.2
site
  n location 159.1
  arena 463.1
  v locate 159.11
  place 159.12
  establish 159.16
sit idly by 329.3
sit-in
  objection 333.2
  assembly 770.2
sit in 333.5
sit in for 862.5
sit in judgment
  administer justice 594.5
  try 598.18
  hold the scales 946.12

sit in on 48.10
sit it out 329.2
sit on cover up 345.8
  suppress 428.8
  participate 476.5
  appropriate 480.19
  disapprove 510.18
  try 598.18
  rest on 901.22
sit on a barrel of gunpowder
  court danger 493.6
  take chances 1006.7
sit on the fence
  n be a timeserver 363.9
  v hesitate 362.7
  dodge 368.8
  remain neutral 467.5
sit on the sidelines
  do nothing 329.2
  remain neutral 467.5
sitter 1008.8
sit through 134.7
sit tight hide 346.8
  stay with it 360.4
  wait 846.12
sitting duck dupe 358.2
  exposure 1006.3
  easy thing 1014.3
sitting pretty
  cheerful 109.11
  successful 409.14
  victorious 411.7
sitting room 197.5
situate
  v locate 159.11
  adj located 159.18
situation location 159.1
  placement 159.6
  environment 209.1
  occupation 724.5
  state 765.1
  mental outlook 978.2
  predicament 1013.4
sit up rise 200.8
  wait 846.12
sit up and take notice 983.8
sitz bath 79.8
six playing card 758.2
  number 882.2
six feet under
  adj dead 307.29
  adv buried 309.23
sixfold
  v multiply by six 882.16
  adj six times as much 882.18
six of one and half a dozen of the other
  n ambiguity 539.1
  the same 790.3
  choicelessness 963.6
  adj coinciding 778.8
  indistinguishable 945.6
sixteen 882.7
sixteenth note 709.14
sixteenth rest 709.21
sixth
  n interval 709.20
  adj ordinal number 882.18
  n fraction 882.14
sixth sense senses 24.5
  extrasensory perception 689.8

  intuition 934.1
sixtieth 882.27
sixty 882.7
sixty-four dollar question 522.8
sixty-fourth note 709.14
sixty-fourth rest 709.21
sizable large 247.7
  considerable 257.16
size
  n dimension 257.1
  largeness 257.1
  extent 300.3
  semiliquid 1062.5
  v adjust 257.15
  measure 300.10
  classify 808.11
  examine 938.24
size up scrutinize 27.14
  measure 300.10
  examine 938.24
  estimate 946.9
sizzle
  n energy 17.3
  hissing 57.1
  v hiss 57.2
  drug use 87.22
  be angry 152.15
  speed 174.9
sizzler
  speeder 174.5
  hot day 1019.8
skate glide 177.35
  play hockey 749.7
skateboard
  n skates 179.21
  v glide 177.35
skateboard park 743.11
skate on thin ice 1006.7
skating rink 743.11
skedaddle
  n flight 368.4
  v be frightened 127.12
  speed 174.9
  depart 188.7
  leave 222.10
  flee 368.11
  lose one's nerve 491.8
  interj go away! 909.32
skedaddling
  absence 222.4
  flight 368.4
  dastardliness 491.3
skeet shooting
  sport 744.1
  trapshooting 904.2
skein cord 271.2
  flock 770.6
skeleton
  n base 199.2
  outline 211.2
  frame 266.4
  thinness 270.7
  thin person 270.8
  corpse 307.15
  diagram 381.3
  wreck 393.8
  abridgment 557.1
  support 901.10
  adj skeletal 2.26
skeleton crew 992.2

skeleton in the closet
skeleton in the closet
secret 345.5
evil 1000.3
skeleton key 292.10
skeptic
n agnostic 695.12
doubter 955.4
adj agnostic 695.20
sketch
n description 349.2
diagram 381.3
treatise 556.1
abridgment 557.1
act 704.7
drawing 712.12
likeness 784.3
v describe 349.9
plot 381.10
outline 381.11
abridge 557.5
act 704.29
portray 712.18
sketchbook
book 554.1
art equipment 712.17
sketchy
incomplete 795.4
imperfect 1003.4
skew
n deviation 164.1
bias 204.3
v squint 28.9
deflect 164.5
diverge 204.9
go sideways 218.5
unbalance 791.3
adj deflective 164.8
askew 204.14
unequal 791.4
skewer
perforate 292.15
stigmatize 661.9
hook 800.8
skew-whiff
askew 204.14
unbalanced 791.5
disorderly 810.13
ski
n skate 179.21
v glide 177.35
sport 753.4
skiboggan 179.20
skid
n slide 194.4
v glide 177.35
maneuver 184.40
slide 194.9
go sideways 218.5
skid row 230.6
skier 753.2
skiing gliding 177.16
sports 753.1
ski jump
n leap 366.1
v leap 366.5
ski lift
cableway 383.8
transport 753.1
skill superiority 249.1
expertise 413.1
skillfulness 413.1

art 413.7
production 892.2
memory 989.1
skilled laborer 726.6
skillful expert 413.22
good 999.12
skim
n gliding 177.16
v touch lightly 73.7
speed 174.8
glide 177.35
float 182.54
slide 194.9
contact 223.10
scratch the surface 276.4
slight 340.8
cheat 356.18
acquire 472.9
take 480.13
browse 570.13
examine cursorily 938.26
skim milk 10.49
skimp
v slight 340.8
stint 484.5
economize 635.4
adj meager 992.10
skimpy sparse 885.5
meager 992.10
skin
n body covering 2.4
fur 4.2
contraceptive 86.23
exterior 206.2
shallowness 276.1
skin 295.3
blanket 295.12
lamina 296.2
money 728.6
cash 728.7
v peel 6.8
best 249.7
injure 393.13
strip 480.24
overprice 632.7
cheat 759.26
tear apart 802.14
abrade 1044.7
skin(s) 4.2
skin alive best 249.7
defeat 412.9
criticize 510.20
skin and bones
n shrinking 260.3
leanness 270.5
adj wasted 393.35
skin color 35.1
skin-deep
cutaneous 2.27
insignificant 248.6
shallow 276.5
epidermal 295.32
skin diver 367.4
skin flick 666.4
skinflint 484.4
skin game 356.10
skinny cutaneous 2.27
lean 270.17
skinlike 295.32
the skinny
information 551.1

the facts 761.4
the truth 973.4
skinny-dip 182.56
skip
n step 177.11
leap 366.1
wastepaper basket 391.7
lawn bowling 750.3
v exude cheerfulness 109.6
rejoice 116.5
way of walking 177.28
depart 188.7
leave undone 340.7
leap 366.5
caper 366.6
flee 368.11
escape 369.6
dance 705.5
play 743.23
skip it 998.25
skip over slight 340.8
examine cursorily 938.26
skipper
n ship's officer 183.7
v direct 573.8
skirl
n screech 58.4
v screech 58.8
skirmish
n fight 457.4
v contend 457.13
skirt
n dress 5.16
woman 77.6
border 211.4
girl 302.7
v border 211.10
flank 218.4
contact 223.10
evade 368.7
circle 914.5
skirting
n edging 211.7
adj bordering 211.11
flanking 218.6
ski slope 753.1
skit 704.7
skittish
sensitive 24.12
excitable 105.28
frisky 109.14
fearful 127.23
jittery 128.12
shy 139.12
fickle 364.6
skoal! 88.38
skulduggery 356.4
skulk
n shirker 368.3
group of animals 770.5
v lurk 346.9
shirk 368.9
cower 491.9
skull cranium 198.7
death 307.2
skull and crossbones
death 307.2
warning sign 399.3
insignia 647.1
skunk
n stinker 71.3

wild animal 311.22
bad person 660.6
v defeat 412.9
sky
n summit 198.2
height 272.2
the heavens 1072.2
v hit golf ball 751.4
elevate 912.5
sky blue 45.3
skycap 176.7
sky dive
parachute 181.13
plunge 367.1
sky-high 272.15
skyjack 482.20
skyjacker 483.7
skylark
n ascent 193.7
v make merry 743.24
skylight roof 295.6
shine 1025.2
skyline 201.4
skyrocket
n ascent 193.7
v shoot up 193.9
improve 392.7
rocket 1074.12
skyscraper
structure 266.2
tower 272.6
skyward up 193.16
on high 272.21
skywriting 184.1
slab lamina 296.2
wood 1054.3
slack
n refuse 391.4
coal dust 1021.2
v relax 20.7
leave undone 340.7
shirk 368.9
ease up 670.9
loosen 804.3
fight fire 1022.7
adj weak 16.12
apathetic 94.13
inert 173.14
slow 175.10
indolent 331.19
negligent 340.10
lax 426.4
wanton 665.26
loose 804.5
slovenly 810.15
dilatory 846.17
slacker neglecter 340.5
shirker 368.3
slack-jawed 292.18
slacks 5.18
slag dregs 256.2
refuse 391.4
combustion product 1020.16
slake gratify 95.8
relieve 120.5
relax 670.9
satiate 994.4
slalom 753.3
slam
n explosive noise 56.1
disrespect 156.3

sparse 885.5
meager 992.10
slim chance 972.9
slime
　n filth 80.7
　slop 80.8
　mud 1062.8
　v dirty 80.15
slim pickings 992.2
slimy filthy 80.23
　flattering 511.8
　viscous 1062.12
　muddy 1062.14
sling
　n medical dressing 86.33
　slingshot 462.9
　throw 904.3
　v suspend 202.8
　throw 904.10
slingbacks espadrilles 5.27
slingshot
　sling 462.9
　toy 743.16
slink
　n gait 177.12
　v creep 177.26
　convolve 281.4
　lurk 346.9
　cower 491.9
slink off 368.12
slinky thin 270.16
　covert 345.12
　cowering 491.13
slip
　n anchor 180.16
　slide 194.4
　runt 258.4
　thinness 270.7
　pillowcase 295.10
　youngster 302.1
　girl 302.6
　sprout 302.11
　branch 310.20
　avoidance 368.1
　miss 410.4
　bungle 414.5
　proof 548.5
　recording media 549.10
　misdeed 655.2
　ceramics 742.3
　error 975.4
　harbor 1009.6
　mud 1062.8
　v glide 177.35
　float 182.54
　slide 194.9
　decline 393.17
　sink 410.11
　miss 410.14
　bungle 414.11
　give 478.12
　go wrong 654.9
　elapse 821.5
　err 975.9
　fall on evil days 1011.11
slip by 837.6
slipcover 554.14
slip in enter 189.7
　insert 191.3
　interpose 213.6
　intrude 214.5

slip off take off 6.6
　absent oneself 222.8
slip of the tongue 975.4
slip on 5.43
slip one's mind 990.7
slip one a Mickey 25.4
slippery slick 287.12
　deceitful 356.22
　evasive 368.15
　cunning 415.12
　dishonest 645.16
　treacherous 645.21
　unreliable 971.20
　precarious 1006.12
　oily 1056.9
slipshod
　careless 340.12
　lax 426.4
　ungrammatic 531.4
　slovenly 810.15
slipstream 184.30
slip through one's fingers
　369.9
slit
　n crack 224.2
　furrow 290.1
　break 802.4
　v cleave 224.4
　furrow 290.3
　open 292.11
　injure 393.13
　sever 802.11
　adj cleft 224.7
　furrowed 290.4
　impaired 393.27
　severed 802.23
slither
　n gait 177.12
　gliding 177.16
　slide 194.4
　v way of walking 177.28
　glide 177.35
　slide 194.9
slit trench 460.5
sliver scrap 248.3
　intruder 774.2
　piece 793.3
slob bungler 414.9
　slattern 810.7
　ice 1023.5
　mud 1062.8
slobber
　n saliva 13.3
　unction 511.2
　v salivate 13.6
　be stupid 922.12
　be insane 926.20
　moisten 1065.12
sloe
　n blackness 38.4
　adj black 38.8
sloe black 38.8
slog
　n walk 177.10
　hit 902.4
　v way of walking 177.28
　keep doggedly at 360.3
　drudge 725.14
　strike 902.15
slogan
　call to arms 458.7

catchword 526.9
　motto 974.4
slog toward 162.4
slop
　n slime 80.8
　offal 80.9
　sentimentality 93.8
　refuse 391.4
　mud 1062.8
　mud puddle 1062.9
　v overflow 238.17
　moisten 1065.12
slope
　n inclination 204.2
　incline 204.4
　declivity 237.2
　skiing 753.1
　v incline 204.10
sloppy filthy 80.23
　sentimental 93.21
　slipshod 340.12
　bungling 414.20
　lax 426.4
　loose 804.5
　slovenly 810.15
　slimy 1062.14
　watery 1065.16
slosh
　n lap 238.8
　snow 1023.8
　mud 1062.8
　sprinkle 1065.5
　v ripple 52.11
　overflow 238.17
　lap 238.19
　moisten 1065.12
sloshed 88.33
slot
　n crack 224.2
　opening 292.1
　syntax 530.2
　gambling wheel 759.16
　v cleave 224.4
sloth
　apathy 94.4
　wretchedness 96.6
　unconcern 102.2
　dejection 112.3
　despair 125.2
　slowness 175.1
　inaction 329.1
　indolence 331.5
　languor 331.6
　group of animals 770.5
slot machine
　vending machine 736.4
　gambling wheel 759.16
slouch
　n slow motion 175.2
　gait 177.12
　idler 331.8
　bungler 414.8
　v way of walking 177.28
　sink 194.6
　idle 331.12
slough
　n shed skin 2.5
　offal 80.9
　gangrene 85.40
　marsh 243.1
　predicament 1013.4

mud puddle 1062.9
　v shed 6.10
　discard 390.7
slovenly dirty 80.22
　slipshod 340.12
　ungrammatic 531.4
　slipshod 810.15
slow
　v slow down 175.9
　adj dull 117.6
　not fast 175.10
　reluctant 325.6
　indolent 331.19
　languid 331.20
　leisurely 402.6
　late 846.16
　dilatory 846.17
　infrequent 848.2
　dull 922.16
　adv slowly 175.13
　late 846.19
　tardily 846.20
slow burn 152.3
slowdown
　slowing 175.4
　decline 252.2
　economizing 635.2
　strike 727.5
　delay 846.2
slow motion 175.2
slow on the draw 846.16
slowpoke 175.5
slow starter 846.6
slow time
　march 177.13
　time 832.3
slow-up 846.2
slow-witted 922.16
sludge slime 80.8
　refuse 391.4
　ice 1023.5
　mud 1062.8
slug
　n drink 8.4
　slowpoke 175.5
　idler 331.8
　shot 462.19
　line of type 548.2
　type spacing 548.7
　token 728.12
　dose 793.5
　blow 902.5
　v fight 754.4
　strike 902.15
slugger
　baseball player 745.2
　boxer 754.2
sluggish apathetic 94.13
　unconcerned 102.7
　inert 173.14
　slow 175.10
　meandering 238.24
　languid 331.20
　dilatory 846.17
　dull 922.16
sluice
　n outlet 190.9
　watercourse 239.2
　drain 239.5
　floodgate 239.11
　v wash 79.19

flood 1065.14
slum sty 80.11
  city district 230.6
slumber
  n sleep 22.2
  quiescence 173.1
  v sleep 22.13
  stagnate 173.9
slumlord 470.3
slump
  n sinkage 194.2
  decline 252.2
  deterioration 393.3
  cheapening 633.4
  business cycle 731.10
  declining market 737.5
  shortcoming 911.1
  hard times 1011.6
  v sink 194.6
  decline 393.17
  cheapen 633.6
  fall short 911.2
slur
  n aspersion 512.4
  stigma 661.6
  musical execution 708.30
  musical notation 709.12
  v slight 340.8
  defame 512.9
  stigmatize 661.9
  examine cursorily 938.26
  stain 1004.6
slurp
  n drink 8.4
  ingestion 187.4
  v lap up 8.30
  draw in 187.12
slurry 797.6
slush slime 80.8
  sentimentality 93.8
  talkativeness 540.1
  snow 1023.8
  mud 1062.8
slush fund 609.35
slut female animal 77.9
  unclean person 80.13
  dog 311.16
  neglecter 340.5
  strumpet 665.14
  slob 810.7
sly covert 345.12
  cunning 415.12
  cautious 494.8
  shrewd 920.15
smack
  n explosive sound 56.1
  taste 62.1
  heroin 87.9
  hint 248.4
  attempt 403.3
  kiss 562.4
  punishment 604.3
  admixture 797.7
  characteristic 865.4
  hit 902.4
  slap 902.8
  v make explosive sound 56.6
  taste 62.7
  kiss 562.19
  punish 604.12
  hit 902.14

slap 902.19
  adv suddenly 830.9
smackdown 132.1
smacker 728.7
smack hint 248.4 62.3
smack in the middle 819.5
smack of savor of 63.6
  resemble 784.7
smack the lips
  savor 63.5
  enjoy 95.13
small
  adj humble 137.10
  insignificant 248.6
  inadequate 250.7
  little 258.10
  thin 270.16
  ungenerous 651.6
  base 661.12
  narrow-minded 980.10
  meager 992.10
  unimportant 998.17
  adv little 258.16
small business 731.1
small change
  petty cash 728.19
  trivia 998.4
small fortune 884.3
small fry runt 258.4
  young people 302.2
  a nobody 998.7
small-minded 980.10
small potatoes
  a nobody 998.7
  mediocrity 1005.5
small print 959.2
small talk
  chitchat 541.4
  gossip 552.7
small-time 250.7
smarmy
  obsequious 138.14
  insincere 354.32
  suave 504.18
  flattering 511.8
  sanctimonious 693.5
smart
  n smarting 26.3
  v suffer 26.8
  affect emotionally 93.14
  resent 152.12
  adj impudent 142.10
  quick 330.18
  alert 339.14
  witty 489.15
  ridiculing 508.12
  fashionable 578.11
  chic 578.13
  tidy 807.8
  brainy 920.14
smart aleck
  egotist 140.5
  impudent person 142.6
smart money 624.3
smart operator 737.11
smarts intellect 919.1
  smartness 920.2
smash
  n debacle 395.4
  success 409.4
  collapse 410.3

defeat 412.1
  concussion 671.8
  declining market 737.5
  impact 902.3
  hit 902.4
  misfortune 1011.2
  pulp 1063.2
  v billow 238.22
  demolish 395.17
  raze 395.19
  conquer 412.10
  suppress 428.8
  play tennis 748.3
  shatter 802.13
  collide 902.13
  soften 1047.6
  pulverize 1051.9
  pulp 1063.5
smashed high 87.24
  drunk 88.33
  impaired 393.27
  conquered 412.17
  suppressed 428.14
smash hit 409.4
smashing defeat 412.3
smattering
  n hint 248.4
  slight knowledge 930.5
  trifling 998.8
  adj half-learned 930.14
smear
  n soil 80.5
  defamation 512.2
  stigma 661.6
  stain 1004.3
  v color 35.14
  soil 80.16
  coat 295.24
  defeat 412.9
  vilify 512.10
  stigmatize 661.9
  stain 1004.6
  oil 1056.8
smell
  n senses 24.5
  odor 69.1
  smelling 69.4
  hint 248.4
  v sense 24.6
  have an odor 69.6
  scent 69.8
  stink 71.4
  detect 941.6
smell a rat 955.6
smell out trace 938.35
  detect 941.6
smelly odorous 69.9
  malodorous 71.5
smelt extract 192.10
  process 892.9
  melt 1020.21
smelter extractor 192.9
  foundry 739.4
smidgen 248.2
smidgen and skosh 248.2
smile
  n grin 116.3
  greeting 585.4
  v be pleased 95.12
  exude cheerfulness 109.6
  grin 116.7

smile at 508.8
smirk
  n smile 116.3
  scornful smile 508.4
  v smile 116.7
  mince 500.14
smitch and scooch 248.2
smithereen scrap 248.3
  piece 793.3
smitten 104.27
smock 5.17
smog
  n fog 319.3
  miasma 1001.4
  v cloud 319.7
smoke
  n blackness 38.4
  marijuana 87.11
  tobacco 89.1
  smoking tobacco 89.3
  puff 89.10
  spirit 764.3
  ephemeron 828.5
  combustion product 1020.16
  vapor 1067.1
  v blacken 38.7
  dirty 80.15
  use marijuana 87.22
  inhale 89.14
  be angry 152.15
  best 249.7
  cloud 319.7
  preserve 397.9
  let out 909.24
  stain 1004.6
  fume 1019.23
  dry 1066.6
  vaporize 1067.8
smoke out 909.14
smoke signal 517.15
smoker addict 87.21
  tobacco user 89.11
  smoking room 89.13
smoke screen
  cover 356.11
  pretext 376.1
Smokey the Bear 397.5
smoking gun clue 517.9
  proof 957.3
smoking room
  smoking car 89.13
  kitchen 197.14
Smoky the Bear 397.5
smolder
  be excitable 105.16
  be angry 152.15
  stagnate 173.9
  be latent 519.3
  be hot 1019.22
smooch
  n kiss 562.4
  stigma 661.6
  v make love 562.15
  kiss 562.19
smooth
  n smoothness 287.3
  note 709.14
  v level 201.6
  straighten 277.5
  flatten 287.5
  change the texture 294.4

pacify 465.7
talkative 540.9
calm 670.7
make uniform 781.4
facilitate 1014.7
buff 1044.8
adj hairless 6.17
quiescent 173.12
horizontal 201.7
straight 277.6
smooth-textured 287.10
fine 294.8
cunning 415.12
suave 504.18
flattering 511.8
harmonious 533.8
eloquent 544.8
fluent 544.9
uniform 781.5
continuous 812.8
easy 1014.13
oily 1056.9
smooth customer 415.6
smoothie cheater 357.4
slyboots 415.6
smooth operator 415.6
smooth over
pacify 465.7
extenuate 600.12
calm 670.7
smooth-running 1014.14
smooth sailing 1014.1
smooth talker 415.6
smooth the way
facilitate 1014.7
oil 1056.8
smoothy 415.6
smorgasbord
restaurant 8.17
appetizer 10.9
smother
control one's feelings 106.8
wrap 295.20
die 307.23
strangle 308.19
cover up 345.8
extinguish 395.15
suppress 428.8
moderate 670.6
be hot 1019.22
fight fire 1022.7
smothering
violent death 307.5
suffocation 308.6
veil of secrecy 345.3
suppression 428.2
extinguishing 1022.2
smudge
n blackening 38.5
soil 80.5
stigma 661.6
stain 1004.3
combustion product 1020.16
vapor 1067.1
v blacken 38.7
soil 80.16
smoke 1019.23
smug
complacent 107.10
vain 140.8
prudish 500.19

suave 504.18
chic 578.13
smuggle 732.8
smuggler 732.5
smut
n blackness 38.4
blackening 38.5
soil 80.5
dirt 80.6
filth 80.7
dregs 256.2
fungus 310.4
obscenity 666.4
blight 1001.2
stain 1004.3
combustion product 1020.16
powder 1051.5
v blacken 38.7
soil 80.16
snack
n light meal 8.7
piece 793.3
v feed 8.18
pick 8.26
snafu
n complex 799.2
mix-up 810.2
goof 975.6
confusion 985.3
v spoil 393.11
complicate 799.3
confuse 811.3
hinder 1012.16
adj confused 810.16
snafued
queered 393.29
goofed-up 414.22
complex 799.4
snag
n teeth 2.8
projection 285.4
proviso 421.3
fault 1003.2
hitch 1013.8
v acquire 472.9
catch 480.17
snaggle-toothed 285.14
snail shellfish 10.25
slowpoke 175.5
marine animal 311.29
snail's pace 175.2
snake
n serpent 311.25
traitor 357.10
bad person 660.6
v stray 164.4
creep 177.26
convolve 281.4
pull 905.4
jerk 905.5
snakebite 1001.5
snake charmer 707.3
snake eyes 873.3
snake in the grass
traitor 357.10
evil 1000.3
hidden danger 1006.5
snake juice 88.13
snake oil 86.2
snap
n bite 8.2

energy 17.3
crack 56.2
zest 68.2
photograph 714.3
football play 746.3
blackjack 759.11
tap 902.7
trifle 998.5
easy 1014.4
cold weather 1023.3
elasticity 1048.1
v crack 56.7
growl 60.4
show resentment 152.14
close 293.6
be damaged 393.23
speak 524.25
photograph 714.14
hook 800.8
break 802.12
hit 902.14
tap 902.18
throw 904.10
adj unpremeditated 365.11
hasty 401.9
unprepared 406.8
snap back react 903.5
recoil 903.6
snap decision 365.4
snap one's fingers at
disdain 157.3
disobey 327.6
flout 454.4
attach little importance to 998.12
snap out of it
cheer up 109.9
recover 396.20
snappy energetic 17.13
zestful 68.7
fast 174.15
active 330.17
quick 330.18
cold 1023.14
snapshot
n photograph 714.3
v photograph 714.14
snap to it! 401.17
snap up energize 17.10
seize 480.14
snare
n springe 356.13
lure 377.3
hidden danger 1006.5
v trap 356.20
catch 480.17
rob 482.16
snarf 8.22
snarl
n rasp 58.3
grimace 265.4
quarrel 456.5
complex 799.2
v sound harshly 58.9
growl 60.4
show resentment 152.14
wind sound 318.20
trap 356.20
speak 524.25
complicate 799.3
confuse 811.3

hamper 1012.11
snatch
n seizure 480.2
piece 793.3
jerk 905.3
v jump at 101.6
seize 480.14
steal 482.13
abduct 482.20
jerk 905.5
sneak
n dastard 491.6
rascal 660.3
v creep 177.26
lurk 346.9
cower 491.9
smuggle 732.8
sneak attack
deceit 356.3
surprise attack 459.2
sneak in intrude 214.5
join 617.14
sneaking suspicion 951.5
sneak out of
shirk 368.9
slip away 369.9
sneak preview 706.1
sneaky covert 345.12
deceitful 356.22
cunning 415.12
cowering 491.13
sneer
n snub 157.2
scornful smile 508.4
v scoff 508.9
sneeze
n breathing 2.21
sibilation 57.1
v sibilate 57.2
sneeze at disdain 157.3
dismiss 984.4
snicker
n laughter 116.4
scornful laugh 508.4
v laugh 116.8
snide spiteful 144.21
disparaging 512.13
hostile 589.10
sniff
n breathing 2.21
sibilation 57.1
snub 157.2
drawing in 187.5
hint 551.4
v sibilate 57.2
smell 69.8
inhale illicit substance 87.22
draw in 187.12
scent 941.6
sniff at 157.3
sniff out trace 938.35
scent 941.6
snifter 88.7
snip
n deckhand 183.6
scrap 248.3
runt 258.4
minute thing 258.7
piece 793.3
v sever 802.11

socialism
communion 476.2
collective ownership 611.6
government 612.7
socialite
n person of fashion 578.7
aristocrat 607.4
adj upper-class 607.10
socialize
make better 392.9
communize 476.7
attach 480.20
politicize 611.16
social justice 607.1
social ladder 607.2
social mobility
class 607.1
change 852.1
social network 607.1
the social order 606.1
social outcast 586.4
social register 578.6
Social Register
directory 549.9
Bluebook 607.2
social sciences 928.33
social security
welfare 143.5
subsidy 478.8
welfarism 611.7
insurance 1008.4
social services 449.3
social studies 312.10
social system 617.2
social worker
philanthropist 143.8
professional 726.4
society
n population 227.1
humankind 312.1
culture 373.2
fashionable people 578.6
association 582.6
the people 606.1
alliance 617.1
community 617.2
fellowship 617.3
sect 675.3
the laity 700.1
company 769.2
adj associational 617.17
sociology 312.10
sociopathy 92.15
sock
n costume 5.9
comedy 704.6
fight 754.3
blow 902.5
punch 902.6
v clothe 5.40
strike 902.15
sock away store 386.10
not use 390.5
socket 284.2
Socrates 921.2
sod land 234.1
turf 310.6
soda beverage 10.49
extinguisher 1022.3
soda fountain 8.17
soda jerk 577.7

soda pop 10.49
sodden
v soak 1065.13
adj underdone 11.9
intoxicated 88.31
soaked 1065.17
sodomy 75.7
sofa furniture 229.1
bed 901.19
so far
thus far 211.16
limited 248.10
until now 838.4
soft weak 16.12
impotent 19.13
soft-colored 35.22
faint 52.16
effeminate 77.14
sensitive 93.20
sentimental 93.21
loving 104.26
comfortable 121.11
pitying 145.7
light 298.12
out of practice 414.18
unstrict 426.5
lenient 427.7
pacific 464.9
cowardly 491.10
unintoxicating 516.4
phonetic 524.30
moderate 670.10
feebleminded 922.21
gullible 954.9
easy 1014.13
nonresistive 1047.8
slimy 1062.14
pulpy 1063.6
soft drink 10.49
soften blur 32.4
muffle 51.9
feminize 77.12
affect 93.14
relieve 120.5
have pity 145.4
move 145.5
extenuate 600.12
moderate 670.6
cushion 670.8
qualify 959.3
soften up 1047.6
softhearted
sensitive 93.20
kind 143.13
pitying 145.7
softie 16.6
soft in the head
feebleminded 922.21
insane 926.26
soft kill 462.22
soft landing 1075.2
soft lenses 29.3
soft-pedal
silence 51.8
muffle 51.9
extenuate 600.12
soft pornography 666.4
soft sculpture 715.1
soft sell
inducement 375.3
selling 734.2

soft-shell crab 311.29
soft-soap
be hypocritical 354.23
urge 375.14
importune 440.12
flatter 511.6
soft-spoken
suave 504.18
speaking 524.31
soft spot
sore spot 24.4
tendency 896.1
vulnerability 1006.4
soft touch 358.2
soft underbelly 16.4
software 1042.11
softwoods 310.50
softy 16.6
soggy 1065.17
soil
n dirtiness 80.5
region 231.1
land 234.1
v besoil 80.16
vilify 512.10
corrupt 654.10
stigmatize 661.9
seduce 665.20
stain 1004.6
soil one's hands
soil 80.16
condescend 137.8
deign 141.8
incur disgrace 661.7
soiree
social gathering 582.10
assembly 770.2
sojourn
n stay 225.5
v stop 225.8
Sol 1072.14
solace
n consolation 121.4
amusement 743.1
v comfort 121.6
amuse 743.21
solar 1072.25
solar battery 1075.4
solar eclipse
eclipse 1027.8
sun 1072.13
solar energy
energy 17.1
fuel 1021.1
solarium 197.5
solar plexus 2.14
solar power 18.4
solar prominence
flash 1025.6
sun 1072.13
solar system 1072.9
solar wind 1072.13
solder
n sculpture material 715.4
v sculpture 715.5
put together 800.5
stick together 803.9
burn 1020.24
soldier
n ant 311.33
shirker 368.3

military man 461.6
the underworld 660.10
v shirk 368.9
serve 458.17
soldier of fortune 461.17
sold on pleased 95.15
belief 953.21
sole
n fish 10.24
base 199.2
foot 199.5
adj unmarried 565.7
one 872.7
unique 872.9
solecism
ungrammaticism 531.2
specious argument 936.3
blunder 975.5
grammatical error 975.7
solemn
sedate 106.14
dignified 111.3
gloomy 112.24
dull 117.6
reverent 155.9
heavy 297.16
celebrative 487.3
pompous 501.22
lofty 544.14
ceremonious 580.8
pious 692.8
worshipful 696.16
weighty 997.20
solemn oath 334.4
solemn observance
celebration 487.1
ritualism 701.1
solemn promise 436.1
solenoid 907.3
solicit
make advances 439.7
canvass 440.14
solicit advice 422.7
solicitor
petitioner 440.7
lawyer 597.1
canvasser 730.6
solicitous
sensitive 24.12
anxious 126.7
considerate 143.16
careful 339.10
courteous 504.14
solicit votes 609.40
solid
n solid body 1045.6
adj firm 15.18
unanimous 332.15
faithful 644.20
solvent 729.18
substantial 763.6
sturdy 763.7
crowded 770.22
complete 794.9
permanent 853.7
stable 855.12
one 872.7
reliable 970.17
valid 973.14
excellent 999.13
dense 1045.12

hard 1046.10
solidarity
  cooperation 450.1
  accord 455.1
  completeness 794.1
  oneness 872.1
solid citizen 607.6
solid fuel 1074.8
solidify contract 260.7
  cohere 803.6
  combine 805.3
  densify 1045.9
  set 1046.8
solid-state device 1033.12
solidus 204.7
solid waste
  derelict 370.4
  refuse 391.4
  extract 893.3
soliloquy
  self-address 542.1
  monology 542.1
solitary
  n recluse 584.5
  oddity 870.4
  adj alone 584.11
  unique 872.7
  isolated 872.8
  eccentric 927.5
solitary confinement 429.8
solo
  n flight 184.9
  soliloquy 542.1
  song 708.4
  aria 708.15
  keyboard 711.17
  v pilot 184.37
  adj alone 872.8
  adv singly 872.13
soloist 710.1
Solomon judge 596.5
  wise person 921.2
so long! 188.22
so long as 959.15
solstice 313.7
soluble solvable 940.3
  liquefiable 1064.9
solution
  explanation 341.4
  harmonization 709.2
  answer to a problem 940
  resolution 940.1
  expedient 995.2
  liquefaction 1064.1
  decoction 1064.3
solve explain 341.10
  resolve 940.2
  liquefy 1064.5
solvent
  n cleanser 79.17
  thinner 270.10
  dissolvent 1064.4
  adj unindebted 624.23
  sound 729.18
  disintegrative 806.5
  dissolvent 1064.8
soma body 2.1
  physical entity 1052.3
somber
  n gloom 1027.4
  v darken 1027.9

adj soft-colored 35.22
  dark 38.9
  gray 39.4
  solemn 111.3
  grim 112.24
  ominous 133.16
  gloomy 1027.14
  lackluster 1027.17
some
  n quantity 244.3
  plurality 883.1
  adj quantitative 244.5
  skillful 413.22
  plural 883.7
  adv approximately 244.6
somebody person 312.5
  celebrity 662.9
  personage 997.8
someday 839.12
somehow
  in some way 384.11
  by chance 972.19
someplace 159.26
somersault
  n overturn 205.2
  v capsize 182.44
something
  n some 244.3
  thing 763.3
  important person 997.9
  object 1052.4
  prep about 223.26
something else
  n marvel 122.2
  a different thing 780.3
  first-rate 999.7
  adj nothing like 787.5
  excellent 999.13
something extra
  advantage 249.2
  extra 254.4
  gratuity 478.5
  surplus 993.5
something like 784.10
something out of nothing 355.3
something special 997.5
something terrible
  distressingly 247.21
  terribly 1000.14
something to fall back on 386.3
something to spare 993.5
something to write home about
  marvel 122.2
  matter of consequence 997.5
sometime
  adj former 837.10
  occasional 848.3
  adv someday 839.12
some time ago 837.16
somewhat
  n some 244.3
  adv to a degree 245.7
  limited 248.10
somewhere 159.26
somewhere else
  adj abstracted 985.11
  adv away 222.18
somnambulic 22.24

somnambulism
  sleep 22.2
  trance 92.19
  nightwalking 177.9
somnolent sleepy 22.21
  languid 331.20
so much for that
  interj that's that! 407.15
  phrs that's all for 820.14
son male child 559.3
  offspring 561.1
  descendant 561.3
sonar 182.2
sone 50.7
song melody 708.4
  vocal music 708.13
  types 708.14
  poetry 720.1
song and dance
  deception 356.9
  act 704.7
songbird bird 311.27
  singer 710.13
  singing bird 710.23
sonic 50.17
sonic boom sonics 50.6
  noise 53.3
  air speed 184.31
son-in-law 564.2
son of a bitch 660.5
sonogram 91.9
sonorous
  sounding 50.15
  loud 53.11
  resonant 54.10
  grandiloquent 545.8
  melodious 708.48
soon in the future 839.9
  presently 845.16
sooner than
  preferably 371.28
  instead of 862.12
soon to be 840.3
soot
  n blackness 38.4
  blacking 38.6
  dirt 80.6
  dregs 256.2
  combustion product 1020.16
  powder 1051.5
  v blacken 38.7
  dirty 80.15
soothe
  relieve 120.5
  quiet 173.8
  pacify 465.7
  calm 670.7
soothing
  n palliative 86.10
  relief 120.1
  pacification 465.1
  modulation 670.2
  adj palliative 86.40
  sedative 86.45
  relieving 120.9
  pacificatory 465.12
  tranquilizing 670.15
  lubricant 1056.10
soothsayer 962.4
sooty dingy 38.11
  dirty 80.22

sop
  n weakling 16.6
  bribe 378.2
  fool 924.1
  v soak 1065.13
sophisticated
  experienced 413.28
  elegant 496.8
  chic 578.13
  ungullible 956.5
  disillusioned 977.5
sophistry
  insincerity 354.5
  cunning 415.1
  misteaching 569.1
  reasoning 935.1
  illogicalness 936.1
  specious argument 936.3
  philosophy 952.1
sophomore
  undergraduate 572.6
  jockey 757.2
soporific
  n sleep-inducer 22.10
  adj sleepy 22.21
  sleep-inducing 22.23
  sedative 86.45
  apathetic 94.13
sopping wet 1065.17
soprano
  n high voice 58.6
  part 708.22
  voice 709.5
  adj high 58.13
  vocal 708.50
sorcerer
  Satanist 680.15
  necromancer 690.5
  illusoriness 976.2
  diviner 689.16
sorceress 690.8
sordid squalid 80.25
  greedy 100.27
  niggardly 484.8
  disreputable 661.10
  slovenly 810.15
  terrible 1000.9
sore
  n soreness 26.4
  symptom 85.9
  lesion 85.37
  pain 96.5
  adj raw 26.11
  distressing 98.20
  resentful 152.26
  angry 152.30
  hostile 589.10
  disastrous 1011.15
  straitened 1013.26
sorehead
  malcontent 108.4
  grouch 110.11
  complainer 115.9
sore point
  sore spot 24.4
  provocation 152.11
  bone of contention 456.7
sore throat 85.9
sorghum 66.2
sorority
  affiliation 450.2

spaceship
rocket plane 181.4
spacecraft 1075.2
space shuttle
aircraft 181.1
spacecraft 1075.2
space station 1075.5
space suit 1075.11
space-time continuum 158.6
space tourism 1075.1
space travel
space flight 1075.1
astronautics 1075.1
spacious roomy 158.11
large 247.7
voluminous 257.17
broad 269.6
spade
n race 312.3
v ladle 176.17
excavate 284.15
cultivate 1069.17
spaghetti 10.33
spaghetti junction 170.2
spam 1042.19
spammer 1042.17
span
n rig 179.5
short distance 223.2
distance 261.1
length 267.1
breadth 269.1
arch 279.4
bridge 383.9
period 824.1
short time 828.3
two 873.2
v extend 158.9
overlie 295.30
measure 300.10
put together 800.5
double 873.5
spandex 1048.3
spangled spotted 47.13
ornamented 498.11
illuminated 1025.40
spaniel 138.3
Spanish fly 75.6
Spanish inquisition 389.3
spank
n slap 902.8
v reprove 510.17
punish 604.13
pound 902.16
slap 902.19
spanking new 841.10
spar
n mast 180.13
beam 273.3
boxing 457.9
lever 906.4
v quarrel 456.11
contend 457.13
fight 754.4
argue 935.16
spare
n bowling 750.2
surplus 993.5
v have pity 145.4
forgive 148.3
refrain 329.3

not use 390.5
preserve 397.8
exempt 430.14
relinquish 475.3
give away 478.21
afford 626.7
abstain 668.7
adj additional 253.10
remaining 256.7
lean 270.17
reserved 386.15
unused 390.12
leisure 402.5
plain-speaking 535.3
economical 635.6
simple 798.6
occasional 848.3
substitute 862.8
meager 992.10
superfluous 993.17
surplus 993.18
spare no expense 485.3
spare part 386.3
spareribs 10.16
spare room 158.3
spare the rod
be easy on 427.5
indulge 427.6
spare time 402.1
spare tire 2.19
spark
n hint 248.4
inspiration 375.9
prompter 375.10
dandy 500.9
immediate cause 886.3
fire 1019.15
glitter 1025.7
v motivate 375.12
kindle 375.18
court 562.21
cause 886.10
be hot 1019.22
glitter 1025.25
sparkle
n bubbling 320.3
spirit 544.4
spark 1019.15
glitter 1025.7
v exude cheerfulness 109.6
bubble 320.4
joke 489.13
be brilliant 920.11
glitter 1025.25
sparkling water 10.49
spark plug
energizer 17.6
prompter 375.10
sparring partner 754.2
sparse dispersed 771.9
infrequent 848.2
scant 885.5
scarce 992.11
Spartan
n stoic 134.3
man of few words 344.5
adj patient 134.9
strict 425.6
inornate 499.9
plain-speaking 535.3
concise 537.6

abstinent 668.10
meager 992.10
spasm pang 26.2
seizure 85.6
symptom 85.9
pain 96.5
outburst 105.9
bustle 330.4
upheaval 671.5
revolution 860.1
convulsion 917.6
frenzy 926.7
spastic
n sick person 85.43
idiot 924.8
adj convulsive 671.23
irregular 851.3
jerky 917.19
unintelligent 922.17
mentally deficient 922.22
foolish 923.8
spat
n quarrel 456.5
offspring 561.2
v quarrel 456.11
spate flow 238.4
torrent 238.5
quantity 247.3
lot 247.4
rainstorm 316.2
outburst 671.6
throng 770.4
plenty 991.2
superabundance 993.2
spatter
n staccato 55.1
stain 1004.3
sprinkle 1065.5
v splatter 80.18
rain 316.10
sprinkle 771.6
spot 1004.5
moisten 1065.12
spatula
art equipment 712.17
sculpture tool 715.4
spawn
n egg 305.15
offspring 561.2
v reproduce 78.9
originate 892.12
spay 255.11
spaying 255.4
speak sound 50.14
hail a ship 182.52
affirm 334.5
communicate 343.6
command 420.8
signal 517.22
use language 523.18
talk 524.19
remark 524.24
address 524.26
make a speech 543.9
speakeasy 88.20
speaker
loudspeaker 50.8
talker 524.17
speechmaker 543.4
chairman 574.5
spokesman 576.5

Speaker of the House 610.3
speak for
be in front 216.7
represent 576.14
defend 600.10
speak in tongues
talk nonsense 520.5
be incomprehensible 522.10
speak too soon 844.4
speak up affirm 334.5
come out 348.6
brave 492.10
speak out 524.21
spear
n leaf 310.19
branch 310.20
stem 310.21
weapon 462.8
v perforate 292.15
stab 459.25
catch 480.17
spearhead
n vanguard 216.2
v lead 165.2
special
n train 179.14
commodity 735.2
feature 866.2
adj student 572.12
detailed 766.9
other 780.8
classificational 809.7
particular 865.12
notable 997.19
special assistant 616.6
special delivery 553.4
special edition 555.2
special education student
572.4
special effects 706.5
Special Forces 461.15
special interest
pressure group 609.31
interest 983.2
specialist
n doctor 90.4
dentist 90.6
stockbroker 737.10
specializer 866.3
adj specialized 866.5
specialize in
practice 328.8
study to be 570.15
go in for 866.4
special ops 461.15
special police 1008.17
special privilege 430.8
specialty study 568.8
occupation 724.4
vocation 724.6
component 796.2
particularity 865.2
characteristic 865.4
object of special attention
866
speciality 866.1
science 928.10
specie money 728.1
hard money 728.4
species
nomenclature 527.1

race 559.4
kind 809.3
classifications 809.5
biology 1068.1
specific
  n remedy 86.1
  adj circumscribed 210.6
  detailed 766.9
  classificational 809.7
  particular 865.12
specification
  circumscription 210.1
  description 349.2
  indication 517.3
  accusation 599.1
  circumstantiation 766.5
  differentiation 780.4
  designation 865.6
  qualification 959.1
  condition 959.2
specific gravity
  weight 297.5
  density 1045.1
specify
  circumscribe 210.4
  designate 517.18
  name 527.11
  itemize 766.6
  differentiate 780.6
  specialize 865.11
  focus on 937.3
  call attention to 983.10
specimen sample 62.4
  representative 349.7
  model 786.3
specious
  meretricious 354.27
  pretexted 376.5
  sophistical 936.10
  illusory 976.9
speck
  n spottiness 47.3
  modicum 248.2
  minute thing 258.7
  mark 517.5
  intruder 774.2
  stain 1004.3
  v variegate 47.7
  mark 517.19
  sprinkle 771.6
  spot 1004.5
speckle
  n spottiness 47.3
  mark 517.5
  stain 1004.3
  v variegate 47.7
  mark 517.19
  sprinkle 771.6
  spot 1004.5
spectacle sight 33.7
  marvel 122.2
  display 501.4
spectacles 29.3
spectacular
  astonishing 122.12
  gaudy 501.20
  theatrical 501.24
  dramatic 704.33
Spectacular Bid 311.15
spectator audience 48.6
  attender 221.5

recipient 479.3
playgoer 704.27
gambler 759.21
observer 918.1
witness 957.6
spectator sport 918.4
specter apparition 33.5
  frightener 127.9
  spirit 678.5
  phantom 976.4
  ghost 988.1
spectrometer 29.1
spectroscope
  optical instrument 29.1
  astronomical instrument
    1072.17
spectrum
  color system 35.7
  variegation 47.6
  range 158.2
  series 812.2
  optical illusion 976.5
  frequency 1034.12
spectrum analysis 35.10
speculate invest 729.17
  trade 737.23
  gamble 759.23
  consider 931.12
  theorize 951.9
  predict 962.9
speculator
  stock investor 737.11
  gambler 759.21
  theorist 951.7
  philosopher 952.8
speech
  n communication 343.1
  language 523.1
  utterance 524
  talk 524.1
  diction 532.1
  conversation 541.2
  public speaking 543.2
  story teller 722.4
  adj communicational
    343.9
  language 524.29
speech impediment 525.1
speechless mute 51.12
  taciturn 344.9
speechmaker 543.4
speech therapist 90.8
speech-writer 543.8
speechwriter 610.12
speed
  n amphetamines 87.4
  velocity 174.1
  hastiness 401.2
  v move 172.5
  go fast 174.8
  hasten 401.4
  be useful 449.17
  facilitate 1014.7
speedboat 180.4
speed bump
  bulge 283.3
  hindrance 1012.1
speed demon 174.5
speeder racer 174.5
  driver 178.10
speed of light 174.2

speed of sound
  sonics 50.6
  sonic speed 174.2
  air speed 184.31
speedometer 174.7
speed skating 760.7
speedster 174.5
speed up
  accelerate 174.10
  hasten 401.4
speedway 756.1
speedwriting 547.8
speedy fast 174.15
  quick 330.18
  hasty 401.9
  brief 828.8
  sudden 830.5
  prompt 845.9
spell
  n sorcery 690.1
  magic spell 691.1
  period 824.1
  term 824.3
  period of duty 825
  turn 825.2
  round 850.3
  superstition 954.3
  bad influence 1000.4
  v augur 133.11
  fascinate 377.7
  mean 518.8
  orthographize 546.7
  cast a spell 691.7
  take one's turn 825.5
  substitute for 862.5
spellbound
  wondering 122.9
  enchanted 691.12
  gripped 983.18
  dreamy 986.25
spell-checker 1042.18
speller 554.10
spelling bee
  contest 457.3
  spelling 546.4
spell out
  explain 341.10
  simplify 499.5
  make clear 521.6
  spell 546.7
  itemize 766.6
  elaborate 861.6
  particularize 865.9
spend
  use up 387.13
  consume 388.3
  waste 486.4
  expend 626.5
  occupy 724.10
  experience 831.8
spend-all 626.4
spending money 728.19
spendthrift
  n prodigal 486.2
  adj prodigal 486.8
spend time 821.6
spent weakened 16.18
  burnt-out 21.10
  used up 388.5
  worn-out 393.36
  wasted 486.9

paid 624.22
sperm body fluid 13.2
  copulation 75.7
  spermatozoa 305.11
spermatozoa 305.11
spermicide 86.23
spew
  n jet 238.9
  outburst 671.6
  vomiting 909.8
  v salivate 13.6
  run out 190.13
  jet 238.20
  erupt 671.13
  disgorge 909.25
  vomit 909.26
sphere
  n space 158.1
  domain 231.2
  rank 245.2
  ball 282.2
  arena 463.1
  occupation 724.4
  science 928.10
  stars 1072.4
  v ball 282.7
spheres of influence 609.5
sphincter 280.2
spice
  n flavoring 63.3
  zest 68.2
  fragrance 70.1
  admixture 797.7
  v flavor 63.7
spick and span 79.26
spicy zestful 68.7
  fragrant 70.9
  risqué 666.7
  interesting 983.19
spider spinner 271.5
  insect 311.32
spider's web 271.1
spiel
  n sales talk 734.5
  v publicize 352.15
  speak 524.20
  declaim 543.10
spiff up 5.42
spiffy chic 578.13
  excellent 999.13
spigot valve 239.10
  stopper 293.4
spike
  n rig 179.5
  thorn 285.5
  stopper 293.4
  plant part 310.27
  ear of corn 310.29
  card 758.2
  v disable 19.9
  perforate 292.15
  stab 459.25
  adulterate 797.12
  thwart 1012.15
spill
  n tumble 194.3
  overturn 205.2
  overflow 238.6
  stopper 293.4
  lighter 1021.4
  v overflow 238.17

sever 802.11
break off 802.12
divide up 802.18
disintegrate 806.3
blemish 1004.4
adj cleft 224.7
impaired 393.27
severed 802.23
halved 875.6
blemished 1004.8
split decision 754.3
split fifty fifty
 v double 873.5
 adj two 873.6
split hairs
 differentiate 780.6
 quibble 936.9
 discriminate 944.4
split-level 228.5
split off
 diverge 171.5
 interspace 224.3
 dissent 333.4
 separate 802.8
split personality 92.20
split second 830.3
split the atom 1038.17
split the difference
 average 246.2
 compromise 468.2
 share 476.6
split ticket 609.19
splotch
 n spottiness 47.3
 mark 517.5
 stain 1004.3
 v variegate 47.7
 spatter 80.18
 mark 517.19
 spot 1004.5
splurge
 n display 501.4
 v cut a dash 501.13
 spend 626.5
spoil
 n gain 472.3
 booty 482.11
 v mar 393.10
 decay 393.22
 bungle 414.11
 indulge 427.6
 plunder 482.17
 thwart 1012.15
 offend 1015.5
spoilage decay 393.6
 rot 393.7
spoiled brat 302.4
spoiler plunderer 483.6
 automobile racing 756.1
spoil for 100.16
spoke radius 171.2
 step 193.5
 curb 1012.7
spoken
 vernacular 523.20
 speech 524.29
spoken for 421.10
spokesperson
 mediator 466.3
 informant 551.5
 deputy 576.5

sponge
 n washing 79.5
 bath 79.8
 drunk 88.12
 parasite 138.5
 absorption 187.6
 porousness 292.8
 lightness 298.2
 marine animal 311.29
 eradicator 395.9
 pulp 1063.2
 v wash 79.19
 feed on 138.12
 absorb 187.13
 obliterate 395.16
 freeload 634.4
 moisten 1065.12
 dry 1066.6
sponge medical 86.33
spongy
 absorbent 187.17
 porous 292.20
 soft 1047.11
 pulpy 1063.6
sponsor
 n guarantor 438.6
 supporter 616.9
 financer 729.10
 v secure 438.9
 patronize 449.15
 accept the responsibility
 641.9
 finance 729.16
spontaneous
 voluntary 324.7
 unpremeditated 365.11
 instinctive 934.6
 automated 1041.22
spontaneous combustion
 1020.5
spontaneous generation 78.6
spoof
 n hoax 356.7
 v fool 356.15
spook
 n specter 988.1
 v frighten 127.15
 discompose 811.4
 haunt 988.6
spoon ladle 176.17
 make love 562.15
spoonerism
 wordplay 489.8
 word form 526.4
 grammatical error 975.7
spoon-feed 449.16
spoor odor 69.1
 track 517.8
 clue 517.9
 hint 551.4
sporadic
 not highly contagious 85.62
 dispersed 771.9
 nonuniform 782.3
 unordered 810.12
 intermittent 851.3
spore germ 85.42
 microspore 305.13
sport
 n hunting 382.2
 loser 412.5

joke 489.6
banter 490.1
dandy 500.9
fun 743.2
toy 743.16
athletics 744.1
gambler 759.21
misfit 789.4
transformation 852.3
v wear 5.44
hunt 382.9
flaunt 501.17
play 743.23
gamble 759.23
sporting
 n hunting 382.2
 gambling 759.1
 adj fair-minded 649.8
 sports 743.30
sporting goods
 dry goods 735.3
 hard goods 735.4
the sport of kings
 racing 457.11
 horse racing 757.1
sports bra 5.24
sportscaster 1034.23
sportsman
 hunter 382.5
 athlete 743.19
 gambler 759.21
sportsmanship
 competition 457.2
 fairness 649.2
sportswear clothing 5.1
 dry goods 735.3
sporty
 casually dressed 5.47
 showy 501.19
spot
 n spottiness 47.3
 soil 80.5
 drink 88.7
 location 159.1
 modicum 248.2
 advertisement 352.6
 mark 517.5
 stigma 661.6
 lights 704.18
 bowling 750.1
 state 765.1
 intruder 774.2
 crisis 843.4
 stain 1004.3
 predicament 1013.5
 commercial 1034.20
 radar signal 1036.11
 v see 27.12
 variegate 47.7
 soil 80.16
 spatter 80.18
 locate 159.11
 mark 517.19
 sprinkle 771.6
 detect 941.5
 recognize 989.11
 bespot 1004.5
 use radar 1036.17
spot check 938.6
spotless clean 79.25
 honest 644.13

virtuous 653.6
innocent 657.7
chaste 664.4
perfect 1002.6
spotlight
 n publicity 352.4
 lights 704.18
 v manifest 348.5
 emphasize 997.14
 illuminate 1025.29
spotter
 secret agent 576.9
 detective 576.11
 watchman 1008.10
spotty spotted 47.13
 discontinuous 813.4
 irregular 851.3
 sparse 885.5
 spotted 1004.9
spousal abuse
 cruelty 144.11
 mistreatment 389.2
spouse 563.6
spout
 n outlet 190.9
 ascent 193.1
 jet 238.9
 channel 239.8
 rainstorm 316.2
 disgorgement 909.7
 v run out 190.13
 jet 238.20
 pledge 438.10
 chatter 540.5
 declaim 543.10
 erupt 671.13
 overact 704.31
 disgorge 909.25
sprain 393.13
sprawl
 n tumble 194.3
 recumbency 201.2
 oversize 257.5
 v rest 20.6
 tumble 194.8
 lie 201.5
 spread 259.6
 be long 267.5
spray
 n perfume 70.6
 jet 238.9
 branch 310.20
 bouquet 310.25
 foam 320.2
 volley 459.9
 member 793.4
 shot 904.4
 sprinkle 1065.5
 sprinkler 1065.8
 vaporizer 1067.6
 v jet 238.20
 moisten 1065.12
 vaporize 1067.8
spray can 1065.8
spread
 n meal 8.5
 food 10.1
 space 158.1
 divergence 171.1
 transferal 176.1
 increase 251.1

size 257.1
expansion 259.1
breadth 269.1
blanket 295.10
publication 352.1
advertisement 352.6
stock option 737.21
dispersion 771.1
caption 937.2
v extend 158.9
diverge 171.5
radiate 171.6
transfer 176.10
grow 251.6
expand 259.6
broaden 269.4
open 292.11
publish 352.10
be published 352.16
report 552.11
disperse 771.4
generalize 864.9
adj recumbent 201.8
increased 251.7
spreading 259.11
published 352.17
dispersed 771.9
spread-eagle
tumble 194.8
fell 913.5
spread far and wide 352.10
spread it on thick
exaggerate 355.3
commend 509.11
spread like wildfire
spread 259.6
be published 352.16
spread oneself too thin
overindulge 669.5
strain 725.10
overdo 993.10
spreadsheet
arranger 808.5
list 871.1
systems program 1042.12
spree
n drinking bout 88.5
revel 743.6
v go on a spree 88.28
make merry 743.24
sprig youngster 302.1
sprout 302.11
branch 310.20
member 793.4
sprightly
cheerful 109.14
active 330.17
agile 413.23
witty 489.15
spring
n progression 162.1
ascent 193.1
haunt 228.27
lake 241.1
springtime 313.2
leap 366.1
motive 375.1
source of supply 386.4
group of teal 770.6
fountainhead 886.6
bedding 901.20

recoil 903.2
resilience 1048.1
elastic object 1048.3
v speed 174.8
distort 265.5
leap 366.5
blow up 395.18
exempt 430.14
release 431.5
recoil 903.6
have resilience 1048.5
adj seasonal 313.9
spring a leak 393.23
spring allergy 85.34
springboard 1048.3
springbok 311.5
spring break 20.3
spring fever 331.5
spring for
subsidize 478.19
pay for 624.18
spring from 887.5
spring up grow 14.2
burst forth 33.9
shoot up 193.9
mature 259.7
originate 818.13
turn up 831.6
springy quick 330.18
recoiling 903.10
pliant 1047.9
elastic 1048.7
sprinkle
n rain 316.1
spray 1065.5
v variegate 47.7
rain 316.10
baptize 701.17
spatter 771.6
moisten 1065.12
sprinkler
extinguisher 1022.3
shower 1065.8
sprint
n run 174.3
v speed 174.8
sprinter 174.5
sprite fairy 678.8
imp 680.7
specter 988.1
spritz
n jet 238.9
v jet 238.20
rain 316.10
moisten 1065.12
sprocket 285.4
sprout
n seedling 302.11
branch 310.20
offshoot 561.4
upstart 606.7
v grow 14.2
enlarge 259.7
vegetate 310.34
spruce
v clean 79.18
perfect 392.11
tidy 808.12
adj dressed up 5.46
cleaned 79.26
shapely 264.5

chic 578.13
tidy 807.8
spry active 330.17
quick 330.18
agile 413.23
spud 10.35
spume
n lightness 298.2
foam 320.2
sprinkle 1065.5
v foam 320.5
spunk vim 17.2
sperm 305.11
enterprise 330.7
pluck 359.3
fearlessness 492.3
tinder 1021.6
spur
n mountain 237.6
point of land 283.9
projection 285.4
sharpen 285.7
goad 375.8
goad 375.15
member 793.4
v sharpen 285.7
goad 375.15
hasten 401.4
drive 1070.8
spurious
ungenuine 354.26
assumed 500.16
illegitimate 674.7
unauthentic 975.19
spurn
n snub 157.2
v scorn 157.4
reject 372.2
be hard to please 495.8
have nothing to do with
586.5
repulse 908.3
banish 909.17
spur-of-the-moment
extemporaneous 365.12
hasty 401.9
spur on
goad 375.15
urge on 375.16
spurt
n run 174.3
ascent 193.1
jet 238.9
bustle 330.4
outburst 671.6
short time 828.3
disgorgement 909.7
v make a dash 174.12
run out 190.13
shoot up 193.9
jet 238.20
make haste 401.5
disgorge 909.25
sputnik 1075.6
sputter
n staccato 55.1
sibilation 57.1
bluster 503.1
flutter 917.4
v drum 55.4
sibilate 57.2

bluster 503.3
mumble 525.9
flutter 917.12
spy
n informer 551.6
secret agent 576.9
v see 27.12
reconnoiter 938.28
detect 941.5
pry 981.4
spy glass 29.4
spy satellite 1075.6
squab 311.27
squabble
n quarrel 456.5
v quarrel 456.11
squad
military unit 461.22
team 617.7
baseball team 745.2
football team 746.2
basketball team 747.2
hockey team 749.2
soccer team 752.2
company 770.3
squad car 179.11
squadron
military unit 461.22
navy 461.27
air force 461.29
squalid sordid 80.25
base 661.12
slovenly 810.15
terrible 1000.9
squall
n cry 59.1
windstorm 318.11
storm 671.4
v cry 59.6
animal sound 60.2
wail 115.13
blow 318.19
speak 524.25
squamous 296.7
squander
consume 388.3
waste 473.5
lavish 486.3
spend 626.5
square
n instrument 200.6
enclosed place 212.3
block 230.7
plaza 230.8
plot 231.4
straightedge 277.3
old-fashioned person 842.8
conformist 867.2
four 879.1
v plumb 200.10
offset 338.5
make restitution 481.5
pay in full 624.13
agree 788.6
equalize 790.6
quadrate 879.3
adj trite 117.9
corpulent 257.18
symmetric 264.4
quadrangular 278.9
straight 644.14

rule 869.4
stand at attention
  pay homage to 155.5
  stand 200.7
  come to attention 983.14
stand behind
  secure 438.9
  back 449.13
standby
  supporter 616.9
  supporting actor 707.7
stand by adjoin 223.9
  stay near 223.12
  be prepared 405.14
  back 449.13
stand down
  abandon 370.5
  resign 448.2
  make peace 465.9
  stop 857.7
  stop work 857.8
stand fast be still 173.7
  confront 216.8
  be resolved 359.9
  hold one's ground 453.4
  stand firm 855.11
stand for tolerate 134.5
  sail for 182.35
  affirm 334.5
  permit 443.10
  signify 517.17
  designate 517.18
  mean 518.8
stand-in deputy 576.1
  supporting actor 707.7
  successor 817.4
  substitute 862.2
standing
  n station 159.2
  rank 245.2
  class 607.1
  candidacy 609.10
  credit 622.1
  prestige 662.4
  state 765.1
  durability 827.1
  permanence 853.1
  footing 901.5
  adj inert 173.14
standing army 461.23
standing at attention 200.4
standing joke 489.6
standing on end 200.4
standing on its base 200.4
standing on its feet 200.4
standing order
  law 673.3
  rule 869.4
standing ovation 509.2
standing room only
  adj full 794.11
  phrs all present and
    accounted for 221.19
standing upright 200.4
stand in the way 1012.12
standoff
  n contrariety 779.1
  the same 790.3
  stop 857.2
  even chance 972.7
  impasse 1013.6

adj aloof 141.12
  reticent 344.10
  unsociable 583.6
stand on ceremony 580.6
stand one's ground
  hold out 359.9
  offer resistance 453.3
  resist 453.4
  stand fast 855.11
stand one in good stead 387.17
stand opposed 215.4
standout
  n superior 249.4
  paragon 659.4
  celebrity 662.9
  adj eminent 247.9
  notable 997.19
stand over
  supervise 573.10
  govern 612.11
  postpone 846.9
stand pat
  balk 361.7
  bet 759.25
  be conservative 853.6
  stand fast 855.11
standpipe 272.6
standpoint
  viewpoint 27.7
  station 159.2
  outlook 978.2
stand ready 405.14
stand shoulder to shoulder
  450.3
standstill
  quiescence 173.3
  stop 857.2
  impasse 1013.6
stand together
  cooperate 450.3
  agree 788.6
  league 805.4
stand to reason 935.17
stand trial 598.19
stand up
  not weaken 15.10
  ascend 193.8
  stand 200.7
  rise 200.8
  stay with it 360.4
  resist 453.2
  stand the test 942.10
  be true 973.8
  suffice 991.4
stand-up comedian
  humorist 489.12
  comedian 707.9
stand up for
  secure 438.9
  defend 600.10
stand up to
  confront 216.8
  offer resistance 453.3
  brave 492.10
  meet an obligation 641.11
Stanley Cup 749.1
stanza
  musical passage 708.24
  poetry 720.9
  fight 754.3
staphylococcus 85.42

staple
  n source of supply 386.4
  commodity 735.2
  marketplace 736.2
  materials 1054.1
  v fasten 800.8
  adj fixed 855.14
star
  n superior 249.4
  successful person 409.6
  skillful person 413.14
  decoration 646.5
  military insignia 647.5
  celebrity 662.9
  movie star 706.4
  lead 707.6
  chief 997.10
  first-rater 999.6
  heavenly body 1072.8
  v rule 249.11
  dramatize 704.28
  act 704.29
  matter 997.12
  emphasize 997.14
  feature 997.15
  adj chief 249.14
starboard
  n right side 219.1
  adj right 219.4
  adv rightward 219.7
starch
  n carbohydrate 7.5
  energy 17.3
  semiliquid 1062.5
  v stiffen 1046.9
  adj prim 580.9
stardom
  great success 409.3
  distinction 662.5
  notability 997.2
stare
  n gaze 27.5
  v gaze 27.15
  wonder 122.5
  be curious 981.3
stare down gaze 27.15
  defy 454.3
  outbrave 492.11
stargaze 985.9
stark
  adj downright 247.12
  mere 248.8
  inornate 499.9
  plain-speaking 535.3
  simple 798.6
  adv absolutely 794.15
stark-naked 6.14
stark-raving mad 926.30
starlet
  movie actress 706.4
  entertainer 707.4
starlight 1025.12
star of David 882.2
starring 704.10
starry-eyed
  happy 95.16
  visionary 986.24
Stars and Stripes 647.7
Star-Spangled Banner 647.7
start
  n shock 131.3

starting 188.2
  point of departure 188.5
  boundary 211.3
  advantage 249.2
  auto race 756.3
  horse race 757.3
  beginning 818.1
  jerk 905.3
  v startle 127.12
  be startled 131.5
  set out 188.8
  leap 366.5
  hunt 382.9
  break 393.23
  propose 439.5
  drive 756.4
  race 757.5
  come apart 802.9
  begin 818.7
  set in motion 904.13
start all over 856.6
starter
  baseball team 745.2
  light source 1026.1
the starting gun 188.2
starting line
  point of departure 188.5
  boundary 211.3
startle
  astonish 122.6
  start 127.12
  frighten 127.15
  be startled 131.5
  shock 131.8
  alarm 400.3
start the ball rolling
  begin 818.7
  inaugurate 818.11
  set in motion 904.13
start up
  burst forth 33.9
  shoot up 193.9
  protrude 283.10
  leap 366.5
  begin 818.7
  make a beginning 818.8
  inaugurate 818.11
  set in motion 904.13
starvation diet 515.2
starvation wages 992.5
starve hunger 100.19
  die 307.23
  kill 308.13
  stint 484.5
  be poor 619.5
Star Wars 460.2
starwatching 1072.19
star worship 697.1
stash
  n hiding place 346.4
  v secrete 346.7
  store 386.10
stasis inertness 173.4
  inaction 329.1
  permanence 853.1
stat
  n print 785.5
  v copy 785.8
state
  n region 231.5
  country 232.1

grandeur 501.5
pomp 501.6
mode 765.1
v affirm 334.5
announce 352.12
declare 524.23
phrase 532.4
specify 865.11
assert 953.12
adj public 312.16
state assembly 613.1
stated
 circumscribed 210.6
 affirmed 334.9
 published 352.17
 fixed 855.14
 conditional 959.8
 assured 970.20
stately
 dignified 136.12
 grandiose 501.21
 lofty 544.14
 ceremonious 580.8
statement
 affirmation 334.1
 account 349.3
 announcement 352.2
 remark 524.3
 report 549.7
 information 551.1
 declaration 598.7
 bill 628.3
 passage 708.24
 list 871.5
 premise 935.7
 testimony 957.2
 summation 1017.11
state of affairs 831.4
state of emergency
 843.4
state of grace 685.3
state of mind 978.4
state-of-the-art 841.14
state of undress 6.3
state one's case 957.9
state park 397.7
state police 1008.17
state prison 429.8
stateroom cabin 197.9
 room on train 197.10
state secret 345.5
state's evidence 351.2
states' rights 609.4
stateside 232.3
statesman
 expert 413.11
 politician 610.2
state-wide 864.14
static
 n audio distortion 50.13
 meaninglessness 520.1
 pandemonium 810.5
 reception 1034.21
 adj motionless 173.13
 inert 173.14
 passive 329.6
 inactive 331.17
 permanent 853.7
 electric 1032.30
 biostatic 1039.8
static electricity 1032.3

station
 n status 159.2
 rank 245.2
 class 607.1
 prestige 662.4
 position 724.5
 state 765.1
 category 809.2
 farm 1070.5
 v place 159.12
stationary
 motionless 173.13
 passive 329.6
 inactive 331.17
 permanent 853.7
 immovable 855.15
stationed 159.18
stationery
 handwriting style 547.4
 paper 1054.5
statistical
 probable 968.6
 numerative 1017.24
statistician
 calculator 1017.15
 mathematician 1017.16
statistics
 baseball 745.4
 football 746.4
 horse racing records
 757.4
 mathematical probability
 968.2
 figures 1017.14
statuary
 n sculptor 716.6
 adj sculptural 715.6
statue figure 349.6
 work of art 712.9
 sculpture 715.2
statuesque
 dignified 136.12
 giant 272.16
 sculptural 715.6
 comely 1016.18
stature height 272.1
 authority 417.4
 prestige 662.4
status station 159.2
 rank 245.2
 class 607.1
 prestige 662.4
 state 765.1
 category 809.2
status quo state 765.1
 circumstances 766.2
statute
 prohibition 444.1
 law 673.3
statutory
 preceptive 419.4
 legal 673.11
staunch solid 15.18
 close 293.12
 firm 359.12
 devoted 587.21
 faithful 644.20
 strict 687.8
 reliable 970.17
stave step 193.5
 staff 273.2

musical staff 708.29
 poetry 720.9
 supporter 901.2
 wood 1054.3
stave in 292.14
stave off
 fend off 460.10
 prevent 1012.14
stay
 n corset 5.23
 respite 20.2
 sojourn 225.5
 exemption 601.2
 delay 846.2
 stop 857.2
 pause 857.3
 supporter 901.2
 prevention 1012.2
 curb 1012.7
 v be still 173.7
 slow 175.9
 inhabit 225.7
 sojourn 225.8
 stop 293.7
 cohere 803.6
 endure 827.6
 delay 846.8
 postpone 846.9
 wait 846.12
 remain 853.5
 continue 856.3
 cease 857.6
 put a stop to 857.11
 support 901.21
 prevent 1012.13
stay-at-home
 n recluse 584.5
 adj untraveled 173.15
 recluse 584.10
staying
 n habitation 225.1
 prevention 1012.2
 adj resident 225.13
 durable 827.10
 permanent 853.7
 continuing 856.7
staying power
 strength 15.1
 perseverance 360.1
 continuance 856.1
stay of execution 846.2
stay on endure 827.6
 continue 856.3
stay over 225.8
stay put be still 173.7
 cohere 803.6
 stand fast 855.11
stay the course
 stay with it 360.4
 endure 827.6
 stand fast 855.11
stay too long 118.7
stay with it
 hold on 360.4
 continue 856.3
stead location 159.1
 place 159.4
steadfast firm 359.12
 persevering 360.8
 devoted 587.21
 faithful 644.20

uniform 781.5
 durable 827.10
 permanent 853.7
 stable 855.12
 reliable 970.17
steady
 n lover 104.11
 v calm 670.7
 stabilize 855.7
 adj inexcitable 106.10
 unnervous 129.2
 firm 359.12
 persevering 360.8
 faithful 644.20
 sturdy 763.7
 uniform 781.5
 orderly 807.6
 continuous 812.8
 perpetual 829.7
 constant 847.5
 periodic 850.7
 stable 855.12
 continuing 856.7
 reliable 970.17
 unhazardous 1007.5
steady state
 continuity 812.1
 stability 855.1
 automation 1041.9
steak 10.18
steakhouse 8.17
steal
 n bargain 633.3
 basketball game 747.3
 v creep 177.26
 lurk 346.9
 thieve 482.13
 adopt 621.4
 play 747.4
 take 480.13
steal away 368.12
steal one's thunder 1012.15
stealth secrecy 345.4
 cunning 415.1
steal the show 704.29
stealthy covert 345.12
 in hiding 346.14
 cunning 415.12
steam
 n energy 17.3
 power 18.1
 hot water 1019.10
 water 1065.3
 vapor 1067.1
 v cook 11.5
 be angry 152.15
 make angry 152.23
 navigate 182.13
 let out 909.24
 be hot 1019.22
 heat 1020.17
 vaporize 1067.8
steamboat
 n steamer 180.2
 v navigate 182.13
steam-clean 79.18
steamed up 105.20
steamer
 steamboat 180.2
 marine animal
 311.29

steamroller
n force 424.2
pulverizer 1051.7
v level 201.6
raze 395.19
defeat 412.9
coerce 424.8
thrust 902.12
adj coercive 424.12
steamy
lustful 75.27
fervent 93.18
heated 105.22
vaporous 1067.9
steed 311.10
steel
n symbol of strength 15.8
sword 462.5
cutlery 1040.2
hardness 1046.6
v strengthen 15.13
make unfeeling 94.6
harden 1046.7
adj firm 425.7
metal 1058.17
steel mill 739.4
steel oneself
harden one's heart 114.3
be determined 359.8
get up nerve 492.12
steely strong 15.15
gray 39.4
callous 94.12
pitiless 146.3
firm 359.12
unyielding 361.9
strict 425.7
sturdy 763.7
hard 1046.10
like steel 1058.17
steep
n precipice 200.3
slope 237.2
v extract 192.16
imbue 797.11
liquefy 1064.5
soak 1065.13
adj perpendicular 200.12
precipitous 204.18
expensive 632.11
excessive 993.16
difficult 1013.17
steeple tower 272.6
projection 285.4
steeplechase
n leap 366.1
leaping 366.3
v leap 366.5
steer
n sexlessness 75.9
male animal 76.8
cattle 311.6
tip 551.3
v direct to 161.6
take direction 161.7
pilot 182.14
guide 573.9
steerage 182.4
steer clear of
snub 157.7
turn aside 164.6

keep one's distance 261.7
avoid 368.6
have nothing to do with 586.5
steering wheel 573.5
stellar chief 249.14
theatrical 704.33
celestial 1072.25
St Elmo's fire
fire 1019.13
luminescence 1025.13
stem
n fork 171.4
prow 216.3
tube 239.6
shaft 273.1
stalk 310.21
morphology 526.3
type 548.6
lineage 560.4
source 886.5
base 901.8
v progress 162.2
fork 171.7
confront 216.8
contend against 451.4
put a stop to 857.11
stemware 1029.2
stench
n odor 69.1
stink 71.1
v stop 293.7
stencil
n printing 548.1
picture 712.10
graphic art 713.4
v portray 712.18
stenographer
shorthand writer 547.17
recorder 550.1
stentorian
loud-voiced 53.12
vociferous 59.10
step
n velocity 172.4
pace 177.11
gait 177.12
stair 193.5
short distance 223.2
degree 245.1
layer 296.1
act 328.3
attempt 403.2
footprint 517.7
interval 709.20
process 889.2
expedient 995.2
v speed 174.9
walk 177.27
measure 300.10
step aside
turn aside 164.6
dodge 368.8
resign 448.2
separate 802.8
stepbrother
extended family 559.3
stepparent's son 564.3
step by step
by degrees 245.6
in order 807.10

consecutively 812.11
step down
reduce 252.7
reduce electric current 1032.26
step forward
progress 162.2
volunteer 439.10
step in enter 189.7
mediate 466.6
step into the breach
be willing 324.3
volunteer 439.10
mediate 466.6
stepladder 193.4
step lively speed 174.9
hustle 330.13
step off
measure off 300.11
die 307.19
step on it! 401.17
step on one's toes
cause resentment 152.21
offend 156.5
step out 743.24
step out of line
disobey 327.6
go wrong 654.9
misbelieve 688.8
steppe open space 158.4
horizontal 201.3
plain 236.1
grassland 310.8
stepped-up
aggravated 119.4
increased 251.7
step up
n promotion 446.1
v aggravate 119.2
approach 167.3
accelerate 174.10
intensify 251.5
make good 409.10
electrify 1032.26
stereophonic system 50.11
stereoscopic
optical 29.10
spatial 158.10
stereotype
n habit 373.3
printing surface 548.8
v autotype 548.15
make uniform 781.4
fix 855.9
generalize 864.9
sterile ineffective 19.15
sanitary 79.27
dull 117.6
fruitless 391.12
unproductive 891.4
sterling
n money 728.1
adj honest 644.13
monetary 728.30
genuine 973.15
superb 999.15
stern
n rear 217.1
buttocks 217.5
heel 217.7
adj harsh 144.24

unyielding 361.9
strict 425.6
steroid 7.7
stet 855.19
stethoscope 48.8
stevedore carrier 176.7
longshoreman 183.9
stew
n food 10.11
drunk 88.12
dither 105.6
anxiety 126.1
impatience 135.1
dudgeon 152.7
flight attendant 185.4
bustle 330.4
hostess 577.5
brothel 665.9
prostitute 665.16
hodgepodge 797.6
bewilderment 971.3
confusion 985.3
predicament 1013.5
v cook 11.5
intoxicate 88.23
feel anxious 126.6
be impatient 135.4
show resentment 152.14
be angry 152.15
seethe 671.12
be hot 1019.22
boil 1020.20
steward
n ship's crew 183.6
flight attendant 185.4
provider 385.6
bailiff 574.4
agent 576.3
attendant 577.5
major-domo 577.10
treasurer 729.12
jockey 757.2
guardian 1008.6
v treat 387.12
stewardess
ship's crew 183.6
flight attendant 185.4
attendant 577.5
stew over 931.9
stick
n marijuana cigarette 87.12
spar 180.13
slim 270.8
pole 273.1
staff 273.2
punishment 605.2
baton 711.22
field hockey 749.4
supporter 901.2
wood 1054.3
dryness 1066.2
v endure 134.6
place 159.12
be still 173.7
come to a point 285.6
perforate 292.15
deceive 356.19
remain firm 359.9
persevere 360.7
injure 393.13
stall 410.16

stringy
  threadlike 271.7
  tough 1049.4
  viscous 1062.12
strip
  n runway 184.23
  a length 267.2
  line 267.3
  strap 271.4
  stripe 517.6
  stock option 737.21
  horse racing 757.1
  v divest 6.5
  undress 6.7
  peel 6.8
  excise 255.10
  strip clean 480.24
  simplify 798.4
  tear apart 802.14
  dismiss 909.19
stripe
  n streak 47.5
  line 267.3
  slash 517.6
  corporal punishment 604.4
  military insignia 647.5
  nature 767.4
  kind 809.3
  slap 902.8
  disposition 978.3
  v variegate 47.7
  mark 517.19
  whip 604.13
striped streaked 47.15
  netlike 170.11
strip mining 1058.8
strip naked 6.5
stripper nudity 6.3
  dancer 705.3
  entertainer 707.1
  separator 802.7
strip-search 6.5
strive endeavor 403.5
  contend 457.13
  struggle 725.11
strobe light 1025.7
stroke
  n touch 73.1
  seizure 85.6
  paralysis 85.27
  pain 96.5
  act 328.3
  attempt 403.2
  stratagem 415.3
  compliment 509.6
  line 517.6
  upheaval 671.5
  work 725.4
  tennis 748.2
  hockey 749.6
  golf swing 751.3
  instant 830.3
  hit 902.4
  spasm 917.6
  expedient 995.2
  v pet 73.8
  delight 95.11
  encourage 375.21
  exploit 387.16
  flatter 511.6
  rub 1044.6

stroke of luck 1010.3
stroll
  n slow motion 175.2
  walk 177.10
  gait 177.12
  v go slowly 175.6
  wander 177.23
  way of walking 177.28
stroller wanderer 178.2
  baby carriage 179.6
  actor 707.2
strong forceful 15.15
  energetic 17.13
  powerful 18.12
  pungent 68.8
  strong-smelling 69.10
  malodorous 71.5
  hale 83.12
  alcoholic 88.37
  great 247.6
  tainted 393.41
  accented 524.30
  eloquent 544.11
  sturdy 763.7
  influential 894.13
  tough 1049.4
strong-arm
  v exert strength 15.12
  coerce 424.8
  adj coercive 424.12
strongbox
  storehouse 386.6
  treasury 729.13
stronghold
  fortification 460.6
  refuge 1009.1
strong language
  cursing 513.3
  vigor 544.3
strong-minded
  strong-willed 359.15
  intelligent 920.12
strong point
  talent 413.4
  stronghold 460.6
  specialty 866.1
  good reasoning 935.10
strop
  n strip 271.4
  v sharpen 285.7
struck down 445.3
structural
  formal 266.6
  semantic 518.12
  linguistic 523.19
  grammatical 530.17
  organizational 808.15
  constructional 892.15
structure
  n house 228.5
  form 262.1
  arrangement 266.1
  construction 266.1
  building 266.2
  texture 294.1
  clearness 521.2
  syntax 530.2
  plot 722.4
  composition 796.1
  order 807.1
  v construct 266.5

  compose 796.3
  order 807.4
structural engineering 1043.1
structureless 263.4
strudel 10.41
struggle
  n endeavor 403.1
  contention 457.1
  fight 457.4
  exertion 725.3
  v endeavor 403.5
  contend 457.13
  strive 725.11
  flounder 917.15
  have difficulty 1013.11
strum 708.40
strut
  n gait 177.12
  swagger 501.8
  v way of walking 177.28
  show defiance 454.5
  swagger 501.15
stub cigarette 89.5
  tail 217.6
  label 517.13
  extremity 820.2
stubble beard 3.8
  remainder 256.1
  bristle 288.3
  refuse 391.4
stubborn
  persevering 360.8
  obstinate 361.8
  strict 425.7
  tenacious 803.12
  inflexible 1046.12
  tough 1049.4
stubborn as a mule 361.8
stubby 268.10
stub one's toe 414.12
stucco 295.25
stuck fastened 800.14
  cohesive 803.10
  caught 855.16
  baffled 971.26
  at an impasse 1013.24
  stranded 1013.27
stuck-up
  conceited 140.11
  arrogant 141.9
  contemptuous 157.8
stuck with 643.8
stud
  n sex object 75.4
  guy 76.5
  male animals 76.8
  leg 273.6
  bulge 283.3
  horse 311.10
  print 517.7
  philanderer 562.12
  jockey 757.2
  poker 759.10
  v variegate 47.7
  roughen 288.4
  sprinkle 771.6
studded spotted 47.13
  knobbed 283.17
  gnarled 288.8
  bristly 288.9
  nappy 294.7

  ornamented 498.11
  sprinkled 771.10
  teeming 884.9
  illuminated 1025.40
student pupil 572.1
  scholar 929.3
stud farm 1070.5
studied
  intentional 380.8
  affected 533.9
  reasoned 935.21
studio library 197.6
  atelier 712.16
  workplace 739.1
  radio station 1034.6
stud muffin 75.4
study
  n diagnosis 91.12
  library 197.6
  intention 380.1
  discussion 541.6
  treatise 556.1
  branch of learning 568.8
  studying 570.3
  work of art 712.9
  drawing 712.12
  office 739.7
  science 928.10
  consideration 931.2
  thoughtfulness 931.3
  examination 938.3
  engrossment 983.3
  abstractedness 985.2
  retreat 1009.5
  v endeavor 403.5
  discuss 541.11
  learn 570.12
  consider 931.12
  examine 938.24
  pay attention 983.8
  memorize 989.16
stuff
  n fabric 4.1
  essential content 196.5
  equipment 385.4
  game 745.3
  substance 763.2
  essence 767.2
  matter 1052.2
  materials 1054.1
  v nourish 8.19
  gorge 8.25
  cram 196.7
  clog 293.7
  embalm 397.10
  gluttonize 672.4
  fill 794.7
  overload 993.15
  satiate 994.4
stuffed clogged 293.11
  full 794.11
  overfull 993.20
  satiated 994.6
stuffed animal 743.16
stuffed shirt 501.9
stuffing
  n food 10.27
  padding 196.3
  extra 254.4
  blockage 293.5
  embalming 397.3

adj gluttonous 672.6
stuffy malodorous 71.5
  dull 117.6
  airless 173.16
  unyielding 361.9
  perverse 361.11
  prudish 500.19
  pompous 501.22
  old-fogyish 842.17
  conformist 867.6
  narrow-minded 980.10
  unimaginative 987.5
  sultry 1019.28
stultify suppress 428.8
  neutralize 900.7
  make a fool of 923.7
stumble
  n tumble 194.3
  collapse 410.3
  bungle 414.5
  flounder 917.8
  slip 975.4
  v tumble 194.8
  not know one's own mind 362.6
  bungle 414.11
  stammer 525.8
  flounder 917.15
  err 975.9
stumblebum 414.9
stumble on
  arrive at 186.7
  come across 941.3
stumbling block 1012.4
stump
  n remainder 256.1
  public speaking 543.1
  art equipment 712.17
  piece 793.3
  extremity 820.2
  platform 901.13
  v plod 175.7
  way of walking 177.28
  make a speech 543.9
  electioneer 609.40
  go into politics 610.13
  boggle 971.14
  thwart 1012.15
stumper enigma 522.8
  campaigner 610.10
stumpy
  deformed 265.12
  stubby 268.10
  low 274.7
stun deaden 25.4
  deafen 49.5
  din 53.7
  numb 94.8
  astonish 122.6
  terrify 127.17
  startle 131.8
stung 96.23
stun gun 462.10
stunning
  deadening 25.9
  astonishing 122.12
  frightening 127.28
  terrifying 127.29
  surprising 131.11
  excellent 999.13
  beautiful 1016.21

stunt
  n act 328.3
  acting 704.8
  v air maneuver 184.40
  shorten 268.6
stunted dwarf 258.13
  undeveloped 406.12
  incomplete 795.4
  meager 992.10
stunt man 185.1
stupefy deaden 25.4
  numb 94.8
  astonish 122.6
  terrify 127.17
stupendous
  wonderful 122.10
  large 247.7
  huge 257.20
  extraordinary 870.14
stupid dumb 922.15
  foolish 923.8
stupidity
  stupidness 922.3
  foolishness 923.1
  folly 923.4
  blunder 975.5
stupor sleep 22.6
  unconsciousness 25.2
  trance 92.19
  apathy 94.4
  languor 331.6
sturdy strong 15.15
  firm 15.18
  hale 83.12
  stable 763.7
stutter
  n stammering 525.3
  v stammer 525.8
sty pigsty 80.11
  eye disease 85.37
  hovel 228.11
  blemish 1004.1
style
  n clothing 5.1
  aspect 33.3
  form 262.1
  flower part 310.28
  behavior 321.1
  preference 371.5
  manner 384.1
  skill 413.1
  motif 498.7
  name 527.3
  way of speaking 532.2
  fashion 578.1
  lines 712.7
  engraving tool 713.8
  race 753.3
  fight 754.3
  mode 765.4
  kind 809.3
  specialty 866.1
  v name 527.11
  phrase 532.4
style guide 530.1
style sheet 530.1
stylish dressed up 5.46
  skillful 413.22
  modish 578.12
stylus 50.11

stymie
  n golf 751.3
  v stop 1012.13
styptic pencil 260.6
Styx
  river of death 307.3
  Hades 682.4
suave smooth 287.10
  glib 504.18
sub
  n submarine 180.9
  baseball 745.2
  football 746.2
  substitute 862.2
  adj inferior 250.6
subatomic particle
  minute particle 258.8
  elementary particle 1038.6
subclass 809.5
subcommittee
  committee 423.2
  delegation 576.13
subconscious
  n psyche 92.28
  inmost mind 919.3
  adj unconscious 92.42
subconscious urge 934.2
subcutaneous
  n injection 91.17
  adj cutaneous 2.27
subdivide
  analyze 801.6
  apportion 802.18
  classify 809.6
  bisect 875.4
  discriminate 944.4
subdue muffle 51.9
  relieve 120.5
  conquer 412.10
  suppress 428.8
  master 432.9
  moderate 670.6
  calm 670.7
  soften 1047.6
subhead
  n caption 937.2
  v focus on 937.3
subhuman
  cruel 144.26
  animal 311.39
subject
  n citizen 227.4
  vassal 432.7
  syntax 530.2
  discipline 568.8
  field of study 570.3
  passage 708.24
  plot 722.4
  doer 726.1
  topic 937.1
  examinee 938.19
  experimental subject 942.7
  v subjugate 432.8
  adj inferior 250.6
  dependent 432.13
subjection
  inferiority 250.1
  subjugation 432.1
  submission 433.1
subjective
  introverted 92.40

  intrinsic 767.7
  mental 919.7
subjectivism 1053.3
subject oneself 652.3
subject to
  v impose 643.4
  adj liable to 897.6
  contingent 959.9
  conj provided 959.12
subjugate
  conquer 412.10
  subject 432.8
  appropriate 480.19
  domineer 612.15
sublet
  v rent 615.15
  rent out 615.16
  adj employed 615.20
sublimate
  n dregs 256.2
  v refine 79.22
  suppress 106.8
  vaporize 1067.8
sublime
  v refine 79.22
  vaporize 1067.8
  adj blissful 97.9
  distinguished 247.9
  lofty 272.14
  eloquent 544.14
  magnanimous 652.6
  eminent 662.18
  raised 912.9
  gorgeous 1016.20
subliminal
  n psyche 92.28
  adj subconscious 92.42
  instinctive 934.6
submarine
  n sub 180.9
  diving equipment 367.5
  adj underwater 275.13
submerge
  submarines 182.47
  sink 194.6
  overflow 238.17
  submerse 367.7
  flood 1065.14
submersible
  n submarine 180.9
  adj submergible 367.9
submission
  resignation 134.2
  obeisance 155.2
  obedience 326.1
  submittal 433.1
  offer 439.1
  consent 441.1
submissive
  resigned 134.10
  servile 138.13
  assenting 332.13
  compliant 433.12
  conformable 867.5
  pliant 1047.9
  obedient 326.3
  humblehearted 137.11
  obeisant 155.10
  downtrodden 432.16
  consenting 441.4

submit affirm 334.5
nominate 371.19
advise 422.5
comply 433.6
offer 439.4
propose 439.5
obey 326.2
acquiesce 441.3
yield 1047.7
subordinate
n inferior 250.2
junior 432.5
retainer 577.1
nonessential 768.2
v subjugate 432.8
arrange 808.11
adj inferior 250.6
subject 432.13
unessential 768.4
suborn bribe 378.3
induce 886.11
subpar 1000.9
subplot 722.4
subpoena
n summons 598.2
v summon 420.11
summons 598.14
sub rosa 345.17
subscribe abet 449.14
contribute 478.14
belong 617.15
subscript 254.2
subscription
ratification 332.4
giving 478.1
donation 478.6
signature 527.10
subsequent
succeeding 815.4
after 835.4
subservient
servile 138.13
inferior 250.6
instrumental 384.8
subject 432.13
submissive 433.12
deferential 433.16
helping 449.20
subset 793.1
subside quiet 173.8
sink 194.6
decrease 252.6
descend 297.15
decline 393.17
subsidiary
n nonessential 768.2
adj helping 449.20
endowed 478.26
unessential 768.4
subsidize provide 385.7
support 449.12
finance 478.19
treat 624.19
sponsor 729.16
maintain 901.21
subsidy provision 385.1
support 449.3
grant 478.8
treat 624.8
financing 729.2
upkeep 901.1

subsist remain 256.5
live 306.8
support oneself 385.12
exist 761.8
endure 827.6
persist 853.5
subsistence
n accommodations 385.3
support 449.3
existence 761.1
adj meager 992.10
subsistence farming 1069.1
subsisting 761.13
subspecies
humankind 312.1
part 793.1
classifications 809.5
substance
content 196.5
quantity 244.1
meaning 518.1
summary 557.2
warrant 600.6
wealth 618.1
funds 728.14
substantiality 763.1
stuff 763.2
essence 767.2
major part 792.6
topic 937.1
salient point 997.6
matter 1052.2
substance abuse 87.1
substandard
vernacular 523.20
below par 1005.10
substantiate
itemize 766.6
test 942.8
confirm 957.11
materialize 1052.9
substantive
n noun 530.5
adj grammatical 530.17
substantial 763.6
essential 767.9
vital 997.23
substitute
n surrogate 92.31
deputy 576.1
supporting actor 707.7
baseball team 745.2
football team 746.2
successor 817.4
replacement 862.2
v exchange 862.4
adj alternate 862.8
substitution
defense mechanism 92.23
compensation 338.1
switch 862.1
substitute 862.2
subterfuge
secrecy 345.1
concealment 346.1
deception 356.1
trick 356.6
pretext 376.1
stratagem 415.3
quibbling 936.5
subterranean 275.12

subtext 519.2
subtile dainty 248.7
tenuous 764.6
shrewd 920.15
discriminating 944.7
subtitle
n book 554.12
caption 937.2
v focus on 937.3
subtle
soft-colored 35.22
dainty 248.7
thin 270.16
rare 299.4
meticulous 339.12
cunning 415.12
nice 495.11
elegant 496.8
tenuous 764.6
complex 799.4
shrewd 920.15
discriminating 944.7
exact 973.17
subtle distinction
margin 780.2
distinction 944.3
subtotal 253.2
subtract deduct 255.9
separate 802.8
calculate 1017.18
subtropics zone 231.3
hot place 1019.11
suburb 230.1
suburban
surrounding 209.8
urban 230.11
upper-class 607.10
ordinary 1005.8
subversion
overturn 205.2
fall 395.3
indoctrination 858.5
revolution 860.1
refutation 958.2
subversionary 395.26
subversive
n rebel 327.5
saboteur 357.11
radical 611.12
revolutionist 860.3
adj rebellious 327.11
destructive 395.26
radical 611.20
changed 852.10
subway train 179.14
underground area 284.5
subzero 1023.14
succeed
accomplish 407.4
prevail 409.7
triumph 411.3
change hands 629.4
be a hit 704.28
be next 815.2
follow 817.5
come after 835.3
substitute for 862.5
prosper 1010.7
succession
authority 417.12
inheritance 479.2

lineage 560.4
offspring 561.1
devolution 629.2
series 812.2
sequence 815.1
subsequence 835.1
constancy 847.2
thoughts 931.4
successive
consecutive 812.9
succeeding 815.4
subsequent 835.4
successor
follower 166.2
survivor 256.3
heir 479.5
replacement 817.4
sequel 835.2
substitute 862.2
succession 862.1
success story 409.3
succinct short 268.8
concise 537.6
aphoristic 974.6
succor
n remedy 86.1
aid 449.1
v aid 449.11
benefit 592.3
succulent
n plant 310.4
adj edible 8.33
tasty 63.8
delectable 97.10
interesting 983.19
fluid 1061.4
pulpy 1063.6
succumb burn out 21.5
faint 25.5
die 307.18
perish 395.23
lose 412.12
submit 433.6
such 784.3
such as 784.12
suck
n sip 8.4
drink 88.7
drawing in 187.5
v sip 8.29
perform oral sex 75.22
draw in 187.12
draw off 192.12
suck dry exploit 387.16
consume 388.3
strip 480.24
sucked into 898.5
sucker
n sprout 302.11
branch 310.20
dupe 358.2
customer 733.4
cheater 759.22
trusting soul 954.4
v exploit 387.16
suck in drink 8.29
draw in 187.12
lure 377.5
suckle
breast-feed 8.19
drink 8.29

draw in 187.12
foster 449.16
suckling 302.9
suck up to
curry favor 138.9
cultivate 587.12
suction
drawing in 187.5
extraction 192.3
favor 894.2
sudatory secretory 13.7
cleanness 79.1
sudden
adj unexpected 131.10
impulsive 365.9
precipitate 401.10
abrupt 830.5
adv suddenly 830.9
sudden death
fatal disease 85.2
early death 307.4
sudden death overtime 749.3
sudden infant death
syndrome 85.2
suddenly
unexpectedly 131.14
abruptly 268.13
Sudoku
enigma 522.8
riddle 522.9
suds
n beer 88.16
foam 320.2
v foam 320.5
sue petition 440.10
solicit 440.14
court 562.21
litigate 598.13
suet 10.14
suffer
feel pain 26.8
ail 85.46
hurt 96.19
endure 134.5
submit 433.6
countenance 443.10
be punished 604.20
experience 831.8
sufferer
sick person 85.43
victim 96.11
suffer the consequences
604.20
sufficient
satisfactory 107.11
valid 973.14
sufficing 991.6
tolerable 999.20
suffix
n addition 254.2
morphology 526.3
sequel 817.1
v add 253.4
place after 815.3
suffocate die 307.23
strangle 308.19
extinguish 395.15
suppress 428.8
obstruct 1012.12
be hot 1019.22
suffragan 616.6

suffrage vote 371.6
participation 476.1
franchise 609.17
suffragette
suffrage 609.17
women's rightist 642.5
suffuse
pervade 221.7
imbue 797.11
suffused with light 1025.40
sugar
n carbohydrate 7.5
sweetening 66.2
LSD 87.10
loved one 104.10
endearment term 562.6
money 728.2
v sweeten 66.3
sugar daddy
beau 104.12
giver 478.11
suggest promise 133.12
advise 422.5
propose 439.5
signify 517.17
mean 518.8
imply 519.4
hint 551.10
resemble 784.7
evidence 957.8
remind 989.19
suggestion hint 248.4
advice 422.1
proposal 439.2
aspersion 512.4
indication 517.3
clue 517.9
implication 519.2
veiled reference 551.4
admixture 797.7
influence 894.1
supposition 951.5
suicidal
wretched 96.26
dejected 112.22
murderous 308.24
destructive 395.26
unwise 923.10
suicide 308.5
suicide-bomb 308.17
suicide bomber 671.9
suicide bombing
suicide 308.5
bombardment 459.7
suit
n clothing 5.6
entreaty 440.2
solicitation 440.5
courtship 562.7
lawsuit 598.1
accusation 599.1
prayer 696.4
soccer 752.1
playing cards 758.2
bridge 758.3
set 770.12
important person 997.9
v outfit 5.41
please 95.6
be satisfactory 107.6
fit 405.8

agree 788.8
be timely 843.6
conform 867.3
suffice 991.4
suitable eligible 371.24
decorous 496.9
right 637.3
apt 788.10
timely 843.9
sufficient 991.6
expedient 995.5
suite apartment 228.13
furniture 229.1
attendance 769.6
set 770.12
suit oneself 430.20
suitor desirer 100.12
lover 104.11
petitioner 440.7
litigant 598.11
accuser 599.5
suit the occasion 995.3
suit up 5.43
sulfa drug 86.29
sulfate 1060.8
sulfuric 1058.15
sulk
n refusal 325.1
v mope 110.14
sulks
sulks 110.10
blues 112.6
refusal 325.1
sulky
discontented 108.7
sullen 110.24
glum 112.25
unwilling 325.5
obstinate 361.8
perverse 361.11
sullen dark 38.9
sulky 110.24
glum 112.25
unwilling 325.5
obstinate 361.8
perverse 361.11
unsociable 583.5
sully soil 80.16
defile 80.17
vilify 512.10
corrupt 654.10
stigmatize 661.9
seduce 665.20
sultan 575.10
sultry
obscene 666.9
stifling 1019.28
sum
n quantity 244.1
amount 244.2
math terms 253.2
meaning 518.1
summary 557.2
amount of money 728.13
total 792.2
summation 1017.6
v compute 253.6
sum up 1017.19
summa cum laude
646.11
summarization 268.3

summarize
shorten 268.6
abridge 557.5
iterate 849.8
sum up 1017.19
summary
n shortening 268.3
résumé 557.2
iteration 849.2
summation 1017.11
adj short 268.8
concise 537.6
prompt 845.9
summary execution 604.7
summation
math terms 253.2
shortening 268.3
résumé 557.2
testimony 598.8
sum 1017.6
summary 1017.11
summer
n summertide 313.3
hot weather 1019.7
v vacation 313.8
spend time 821.6
adj seasonal 313.9
summer solstice 313.7
summery green 44.4
seasonal 313.9
warm 1019.24
summit top 198.2
mountain 237.6
supremacy 249.3
limit 794.5
acme of perfection
1002.3
summit conference 541.5
summon attract 377.6
call 420.11
invite 440.13
enlist 615.17
conjure 690.11
convene 770.17
summons
n bidding 420.5
invitation 440.4
call 517.16
subpoena 598.2
enlistment 615.7
v summon 420.11
issue a summons 598.14
sumo 457.10
sump
receptacle of filth 80.12
drain 239.5
lake 241.1
marsh 243.1
pit 284.4
sumptuosity 632.1
sumptuous
grandiose 501.21
expensive 632.11
sum total 792.2
sum up
shorten 268.6
iterate 849.8
sum 1017.19
sun
n moment 824.2
light source 1026.1

orb of day 1072.13
v sunbathe 1020.19
dry 1066.6
sunbaked 1019.24
the Sunbelt 231.7
sunblind 1028.1
sun-block 1056.3
sunburn
  n burn 1020.6
  v brown 40.2
sundae 10.47
Sunday
  n day of rest 20.5
  holy day 701.12
  v vacation 20.9
Sunday paper 555.2
Sunday school 567.8
sundown 315.2
sundry
  diversified 783.4
  several 884.7
sunglasses
  spectacles 29.3
  eyeshade 1028.2
sunk
  concave 284.16
  spoiled 393.29
  depressed 913.12
sunless 1027.13
Sunni
  n Muslim 675.23
  adj Muslim 675.31
sunny
  bright 97.11
  cheerful 109.11
  optimistic 124.11
  warm 1019.24
  luminous 1025.31
sunny-side up 10.26
sunrise east 161.3
  dawn 314.3
sun roof 1028.4
sunset
  west 161.3
  evening 315.2
sunshine 1072.13
sunshine yellow 43.4
sun shower 316.1
sun worshiper 697.4
sup
  n drink 8.4
  sip 62.2
  nip 88.7
  hint 248.4
  v dine 8.21
  drink 8.29
  taste 62.7
  tipple 88.24
super
  n volume 554.4
  supporting actor or actress
    707.7
  adj superior 249.12
  excellent 999.13
  magnificent 999.15
superb
  eminent 247.9
  grandiose 501.21
  super 999.15
superannuated 837.1
Super Bowl 746.1

supercalifragilistic-
  expialidocious 122.10
supercalifratilistic 122.10
supercharged 993.20
supercomputer 1042.2
superconductor 1032.14
supercooled 1023.14
superdelegate
  selector 371.7
  nonpartisan 609.28
superego psyche 92.28
  conscience 636.5
  self 865.5
supererogatory 253.1
superficial
  apparent 33.11
  dull 117.6
  spatial 158.10
  exterior 206.7
  insignificant 248.6
  shallow 276.5
  hasty 401.9
  formal 580.7
  frivolous 922.20
  half-learned 930.14
  insufficient 992.9
  trivial 998.19
superfluous
  remaining 256.7
  useless 391.9
  unessential 768.4
  redundant 993.17
superheated 1020.29
superhero
  celebrity 662.9
  ideal 786.4
superhuman
  divine 677.16
  supernatural 870.15
superimpose 295.19
superinfect 85.51
superintendent
  n supervisor 574.2
  policeman 1008.15
  adj supervising 573.13
superior
  n boss 249.4
  chief 575.3
  adj arrogant 141.9
  remarkable 247.10
  greater 249.12
  higher 272.19
  authoritative 417.15
  important 997.17
  above par 999.14
superiority power 18.1
  greatness 247.1
  preeminence 249.1
  dominance 417.6
  precedence 814.1
  abnormality 870.1
  overrunning 910.1
  importance 997.1
  goodness 999.1
superiority complex 92.22
superlative
  n exaggeration 355.1
  the best 999.8
  adj downright 247.12
  supreme 249.13
  high 272.14

exaggerated 355.4
superman 249.4
Superman 15.6
supermarket 736.1
supernatural
  divine 677.16
  occult 689.23
  preternatural 870.15
  spectral 988.7
  immaterial 1053.7
supernova 1072.8
superpose add 253.4
  cover 295.19
superpower 232.1
superscript 254.2
supersede 862.5
supersensitive 24.12
supersize
  adj. large 247.7
  v loom 247.5
supersized 247.7
supersonic
  acoustic 50.17
  transsonic 174.16
superstar
  n superior 249.4
  successful person 409.6
  skillful person 413.14
  celebrity 662.9
  lead 707.6
  chief 997.10
  first-rater 999.6
  adj chief 249.14
superstitious 954.8
superstore 736.1
superstructure 266.2
supervise
  wield authority 417.13
  superintend 573.10
  govern 612.11
supervisor
  superintendent 574.2
  public official 575.17
supine apathetic 94.13
  recumbent 201.8
  low 274.7
  languid 331.20
  submissive 433.12
supper 8.6
suppertime 315.2
supplant depose 447.4
  substitute for 862.5
supple
  v soften 1047.6
  adj timeserving 363.10
  versatile 413.25
  cunning 415.12
  changeable 854.6
  pliant 1047.9
supplement
  n adjunct 254.1
  nonessential 768.2
  sequel 817.1
  v add to 253.5
supplementary
  additional 253.10
  unessential 768.4
supplicate
  entreat 440.11
  pray 696.13
supplier 385.6

supplies
  provisions 10.5
  merchandise 385.2
  store 386.1
supply
  n means 384.2
  provision 385.1
  hoard 386.1
  fund 386.2
  materials 1054.1
  v provide 385.7
  furnish 478.15
supply depot 386.6
supply line 385.1
supply side economics 731.11
support
  n nutriment 10.3
  consolation 121.4
  assent 332.1
  means 384.2
  preservation 397.1
  aid 449.1
  maintenance 449.3
  reinforcements 449.8
  subsidy 478.8
  supporter 616.9
  treat 624.8
  supporting actor 707.7
  financing 729.2
  backing 901.1
  bearer 901.2
  confirmation 957.4
  v strengthen 15.13
  comfort 121.6
  give hope 124.9
  endure 134.5
  ratify 332.12
  provide 385.7
  preserve 397.8
  help 449.12
  subsidize 478.19
  encourage 492.15
  commend 509.11
  benefit 592.3
  defend 600.10
  back politically 609.41
  treat 624.19
  afford 626.7
  enact 704.30
  finance 729.16
  bear 901.21
  confirm 957.11
  care for 1008.19
supporter
  follower 166.2
  suspender 202.5
  attender 221.5
  defender 460.7
  giver 478.11
  friend 588.1
  upholder 616.9
  financer 729.10
  support 901.2
support group 449.2
supporting actor
  assistant 616.6
  motion-picture studio 706.4
  support 707.7
supporting evidence 957.4
suppose imply 519.4
  judge 946.8

assume 951.10
think 953.11
presume 968.5
imagine 986.14
supposed implied 519.7
assumed 951.14
suppress repress 106.8
cover up 345.8
extinguish 395.15
conquer 412.10
restrain 428.8
subdue 432.9
prohibit 444.3
retain 474.5
domineer 612.15
moderate 670.6
cushion 670.8
hinder 1012.10
suppurate fester 12.15
decay 393.22
supranational 312.16
supranational government
612.6
supremacy primacy 249.3
dominance 417.6
influence 894.1
importance 997.1
superexcellence 999.2
supremist
superior 249.4
saddle 417.10
supreme
omnipotent 18.13
top 198.10
superlative 249.13
authoritative 417.15
governing 612.17
almighty 677.17
paramount 997.24
best 999.16
surcease
n respite 20.2
release 120.2
cessation 857.1
v release 120.6
surcharge
n burden 297.7
overcharge 632.5
overfullness 993.3
v falsify accounts 628.10
overprice 632.7
overload 993.15
sure
adj expectant 130.11
secured 438.11
trustworthy 644.19
belief 953.21
evidential 957.16
inevitable 963.15
certain 970.13
reliable 970.17
confident 970.21
adv surely 970.24
interj yeah 332.19
sure as death and taxes
inevitable 963.15
dead sure 970.14
sure bet
sure success 409.2
lock 970.2
good chance 972.8

surefire
successful 409.14
reliable 970.17
Sûreté 1008.17
sure thing
n sure success 409.2
bet 759.3
dead certainty 970.2
good chance 972.8
adv surely 970.24
interj yeah 332.19
surety security 438.1
pledge 438.2
guarantor 438.6
belief 953.1
certainty 970.1
confidence 970.5
safety 1007.1
surf
n breaker 238.14
foam 320.2
wave 916.4
v navigate 182.13
surface
n space 158.1
top 198.1
exterior 206.2
shallowness 276.1
texture 294.1
tennis 748.1
v show 31.4
submarines 182.47
arrive 186.6
emerge 190.11
shoot up 193.9
cover 295.22
come out 348.6
be manifest 348.7
be revealed 351.8
adj apparent 33.11
spatial 158.10
exterior 206.7
shallow 276.5
formal 580.7
insufficient 992.9
surfboard 180.11
surfeit
n overfullness
993.3
satiety 994.1
v fill 794.7
overload 993.15
satiate 994.4
surfing 760.2
surge
n loudness 53.1
ascent 193.1
flow 238.4
billow 238.14
increase 251.1
whirl 915.2
wave 916.4
v din 53.7
run out 190.13
ascend 193.8
flow 238.16
jet 238.20
billow 238.22
come together 770.16
whirl 915.11
surgeon 90.5

surgery operation 90.2
surgical treatment 91.19
hospital room 197.25
severance 802.2
surgical strike 459.1
surly sullen 110.24
gruff 505.7
surmise
n supposition 951.3
guess 951.4
v suppose 951.10
think 953.11
surmount climb 193.11
top 198.9
rise above 272.11
defeat 411.5
overcome 412.7
surname 527.5
surpass excel 249.6
outdistance 249.10
exceed 993.9
do better 999.11
surplus
n difference 255.8
remainder 256.4
overrunning 910.1
excess 993.5
v dismiss 909.19
adj additional 253.10
remaining 256.7
excess 993.18
surprise
n wonder 122.1
astonishment 131.2
surprise attack 459.2
v astonish 122.6
take by surprise 131.7
attack 459.14
surreal odd 870.11
illusory 976.9
surrender
n abandonment 370.3
capitulation 433.2
compromise 468.1
relinquishment 475.1
giving 478.1
transfer 629.1
v weaken 16.9
yield 370.7
give up 433.8
compromise 468.2
relinquish 475.3
deliver 478.13
transfer 629.3
surreptitious
covert 345.12
in hiding 346.14
deceitful 356.22
surrogate
psychological substitute
92.31
deputy 576.1
replacement 862.2
surround
n environment 209.1
setting 209.2
nearness 223.1
circumstances 766.2
frame 901.10
v devour 8.22
extend 158.9

internalize 207.5
envelop 209.6
circumscribe 210.4
bound 211.8
enclose 212.5
circle 280.10
wrap 295.20
besiege 459.19
go around 914.5
surveillance
vigilance 339.4
ambush 346.3
supervision 573.2
shadowing 938.9
survey
n scrutiny 27.6
field of view 31.3
measurement 300.1
treatise 556.1
abridgment 557.1
assemblage 770.1
examination 938.3
canvass 938.14
v scrutinize 27.14
measure 300.10
write upon 556.5
examine 938.24
canvass 938.29
surveyor
measurer 300.9
superintendent 574.2
survival of the fittest 861.4
survive remain 256.5
keep alive 306.11
support oneself 385.12
recover 396.20
endure 827.6
outlast 827.8
live on 839.7
sustain 856.4
persist 856.5
survivor 256.3
susceptible
sensible 24.11
sensitive 93.20
teachable 570.18
influenceable 894.15
liable 897.5
exposed 1006.15
pliant 1047.9
sushi 10.24
suspect
n accused 599.6
v be jealous 153.3
suppose 951.10
think 953.11
doubt 955.6
adj unbelievable 955.10
doubted 955.12
questionable 971.17
suspectitiousness 153.2
suspend release 120.6
hang 202.8
repeal 445.2
depose 447.4
postpone 846.9
interrupt 857.10
dismiss 909.19
suspenders 202.5
suspense anxiety 126.1
expectancy 130.3

inertness 173.4
pendency 202.1
uncertainty 971.1
suspension respite 20.2
release 120.2
pendency 202.1
inactivity 331.1
discontinuance 390.2
repeal 445.1
deposal 447.2
harmonization 709.2
elimination 773.2
interruption 813.2
delay 846.2
pause 857.3
dismissal 909.5
solution 1064.3
suspicion
suspiciousness 153.2
hint 248.4
small amount 258.7
wariness 494.2
leeriness 551.4
admixture 797.7
hunch 934.3
suggestion 951.5
doubt 955.2
incredulity 956.1
suspicious
jealous 153.5
wary 494.9
dishonest 645.16
doubting 955.9
unbelievable 955.10
incredulous 956.4
doubtful 971.17
sustain nourish 7.17
feed 8.18
strengthen 15.13
tolerate 134.5
buoy 298.8
preserve 397.8
maintain 449.12
foster 449.16
defend 600.10
endure 827.6
experience 831.8
protract 856.4
support 901.21
confirm 957.11
sustenance food 10.1
nutriment 10.3
maintenance 449.3
continuance 856.1
support 901.1
suttee suicide 308.5
oblation 696.7
burning 1020.5
suture filament 271.1
sewing 741.1
joint 800.4
svelte 270.16
Svengali hypnotist 22.9
influence 894.6
swab wash 79.19
dry 1066.6
swaddle
n children's wear 5.30
v clothe 5.39
wrap 295.20
bind 800.9

swag
n sinkage 194.2
hang 202.2
inclination 204.2
curve 279.2
booty 482.11
swing 916.6
v sink 194.6
hang 202.6
incline 204.10
curve 279.6
oscillate 916.10
adj drooping 202.10
swagger
n gait 177.12
strut 501.8
boasting 502.1
bluster 503.1
v way of walking 177.28
strut 501.15
boast 502.6
bluster 503.3
swagger stick 273.2
swain
n desirer 100.12
beau 104.12
escort 769.5
v court 562.21
swale marsh 243.1
lowland 274.3
grassland 310.8
swallow
n bite 8.2
swiftness 174.6
ingestion 187.4
recant 363.8
v devour 8.22
endure 134.6
disregard 134.8
condone 148.4
ingest 187.11
consume 388.3
believe 953.10
kid oneself 954.6
swallow one's pride 137.7
swamp
n receptacle of filth 80.12
marsh 243.1
predicament 1013.4
v overflow 238.17
overwhelm 395.21
oversupply 993.14
flood 1065.14
swan whiteness 37.2
bird 311.27
swan dive 367.1
swanky
grandiose 501.21
chic 578.13
swan song
leave-taking 188.4
death song 307.9
theatrical performance
704.12
musical performance 708.33
sequel 817.1
end 820.1
swap
n explosive sound 56.1
bargain 731.5
trading 863.2

v make explosive sound 56.6
trade 731.15
interchange 863.4
swarm
n migration 177.4
assemblage 770.6
multitude 884.3
infestation 910.2
v migrate 177.22
come together 770.16
infest 910.6
superabound 993.8
swarthy 38.9
swashbuckler
combatant 461.1
strutter 501.10
blusterer 503.2
swastika cross 170.4
insignia 647.1
charm 691.5
swat
n blow 902.5
v strike 902.15
SWAT 1008.17
swatch 786.3
swath 812.2
sway
n inclination 204.2
supremacy 249.3
authority 417.5
dominance 417.6
government 612.1
influence 894.1
swing 916.6
flounder 917.8
v pitch 182.55
oblique 204.9
incline 204.10
induce 375.22
persuade 375.23
break down 393.24
rule 612.13
change 854.5
influence 894.7
oscillate 916.10
flounder 917.15
prejudice 980.9
sway-backed 265.12
swear affirm 334.6
administer an oath 334.7
promise 436.4
curse 513.6
blaspheme 694.5
state 953.12
testify 957.9
swear by 953.16
swear in
administer an oath 334.7
call to witness 598.17
swear off
break the habit 374.3
relinquish 475.3
renounce 668.8
sweat
n body fluid 2.24
perspiration 12.7
trepidation 127.5
nervousness 128.2
impatience 135.1
bustle 330.4
work 725.4

confusion 985.3
v perspire 12.16
fear 127.10
await 130.8
be impatient 135.4
trickle 238.18
endeavor 403.5
work hard 725.13
overwork 725.16
be hot 1019.22
be damp 1065.11
sweater shirt 5.15
gambler 759.21
sweat it out
be strong 15.11
await 130.8
be impatient 135.4
wait impatiently 846.13
Swedish bath 79.8
sweep
n vision 27.1
view 33.6
sweeper 79.16
range 158.2
deviation 164.1
gliding 177.16
oar 180.15
bend 279.3
lottery 759.14
v touch lightly 73.7
clean 79.23
extend 158.9
speed 174.9
traverse 177.20
glide 177.35
overflow 238.17
curve 279.6
plunder 482.17
push 904.9
go easily 1014.10
receive 1036.17
sweeper 79.16
sweeping change 860.1
sweepings
remainder 256.1
refuse 391.4
sweep off one's feet
enamor 104.22
take one's breath away 122.7
fascinate 377.7
convince 858.16
sweepstakes
award 646.2
lottery 759.14
sweet
n food 10.40
sweetness 66.1
endearment term 562.6
adj soft-colored 35.22
flavored 62.9
sweetish 66.4
fragrant 70.9
clean 79.25
pleasant 97.6
endearing 104.24
good-natured 143.14
harmonious 533.8
melodious 708.48
sweetbread veal 10.15
organ meat 10.20
sweetener 478.5

sweetheart
  n loved one 104.9
  endearment term 562.6
  good person 659.2
  first-rate 999.7
  v court 562.21
sweet nothings
  flattery 511.1
  endearment 562.5
sweets
  confectionery 10.40
  sweetening 66.2
  loved one 104.10
  endearment term 562.6
the sweet science 754.1
sweet sixteen 301.14
sweet tooth 66.1
swell
  n loudness 53.1
  hill 237.4
  wave 238.14
  distension 259.2
  dandy 500.9
  aristocrat 607.4
  nobleman 608.4
  notation 709.12
  keyboard 711.17
  v din 53.7
  be excited 105.18
  be vain 140.7
  billow 238.22
  grow 251.6
  enlarge 259.4
  increase 259.5
  bulge 283.11
  give oneself airs 501.14
  overextend 993.13
  adj grandiose 501.21
  chic 578.13
  excellent 999.13
swelled head 140.4
swelter
  n sweat 12.7
  sultriness 1019.6
  v sweat 12.16
  be hot 1019.22
swept 238.25
swept-back 217.12
swept up 983.17
swerve
  n deviation 164.1
  bias 204.3
  angle 278.2
  v deviate 164.3
  change course 182.30
  oblique 204.9
  angle 278.5
  dodge 368.8
  be changed 852.6
  pull back 903.7
swift
  fast 174.15
  quick 330.18
  hasty 401.9
  brief 828.8
  sudden 830.5
  prompt 845.9
Swiftie 376.1
swig
  n drink 8.4
  snort 88.7

  v drink 8.29
  booze 88.25
swill
  n drink 8.4
  feed 10.4
  offal 80.9
  snort 88.7
  refuse 391.4
  mud 1062.8
  v drink 8.29
  booze 88.25
  ingest 187.11
swim
  n aquatics 182.11
  v bathe 182.56
  conform 867.4
swim against the tide
  dissent 333.4
  not conform 868.4
  counteract 900.6
swimming pool 743.12
swim suit 5.29
swindle
  n fake 354.13
  fraud 356.8
  theft 482.1
  v cheat 356.18
  steal 482.13
  overprice 632.7
swine
  filthy person 80.13
  pig 311.9
  beast 660.6
  sensualist 663.3
  slob 810.7
swing
  n room 158.3
  gait 177.12
  hang 202.2
  latitude 430.4
  thrust 459.3
  supporting actor 707.7
  jazz 708.9
  rhythm 709.22
  meter 720.7
  playground apparatus
    743.15
  golf 751.3
  trend 896.2
  hit 902.4
  swinging 916.6
  oscillator 916.9
  flounder 917.8
  v turn round 163.9
  way of walking 177.28
  toss at sea 182.55
  hang 202.6
  do 328.6
  accomplish 407.4
  manage 409.12
  be hanged 604.19
  afford 626.7
  be promiscuous 665.19
  syncopate 708.43
  change 854.5
  rotate 915.9
  oscillate 916.10
  wave 916.11
  alternate 916.13
  flounder 917.15
  adj music 708.51

swinger
  person of fashion 578.7
  libertine 665.10
swinging in the wind 160.10
swing into action
  behave 321.4
  take action 328.5
  undertake 404.3
  begin 818.7
swing shift 825.3
swing vote 609.28
swipe
  n criticism 510.4
  hit 902.4
  v rob 482.16
  hit 902.14
swirl
  n excitement 105.4
  eddy 238.12
  coil 281.2
  bustle 330.4
  whirl 915.2
  agitation 917.1
  v eddy 238.21
  convolve 281.4
  whirl 915.11
  agitate 917.10
swish
  n sibilation 57.1
  mollycoddle 77.9
  v ripple 52.11
  rustle 52.12
  sibilate 57.2
  play 747.4
Swiss Army knife 462.5
Swiss cheese 284.6
switch
  n false hair 3.13
  surprise 131.2
  branch 310.20
  apostatize 363.7
  whip 605.2
  plot 722.4
  member 793.4
  change 852.1
  conversion 858.1
  substitution 862.1
  trading 863.2
  v avoid 164.6
  transfer 176.10
  whip 604.13
  trade 731.15
  convert 858.11
  substitute 862.4
  interchange 863.4
switchback
  zigzag 204.8
  race 756.3
switchboard
  telephone 347.8
  stage 704.16
switch hitter 745.2
switch over
  n apostatize 363.7
  v convert 858.11
swivel
  n axle 915.5
  v turn round 163.9
  rotate 915.9
swivet dither 105.6
  confusion 985.3

swollen
  diseased 85.60
  puffed up 136.10
  increased 251.7
  corpulent 257.18
  distended 259.13
  bulged 283.16
  pompous 501.22
  boastful 502.12
  bombastic 545.9
  full 794.11
  overfull 993.20
swoon
  n stupor 22.6
  unconsciousness 25.2
  v faint 25.5
swoop
  n descent 194.1
  plunge 367.1
  v descend 194.5
  plunge 367.6
sword
  n combatant 461.1
  blade 462.5
  cutlery 1040.2
  v stab 459.25
sword of Damocles
  threat 514.1
  dangerousness 1006.2
sworn affirmed 334.9
  promised 436.8
sworn enemy 589.6
sworn statement
  deposition 334.3
  certificate 549.6
  statement of principles 953.4
  testimony 957.2
sycophant toady 138.3
  flatterer 511.4
  follower 616.8
syllabic
  n letter 546.1
  adj phonetic 524.30
syllable
  n speech sound 524.12
  word 526.1
  poetry 720.9
  v syllabify 546.7
syllabus 557.1
syllogism reasoning 935.3
  prosyllogism 935.6
sylvan hinterland 233.9
  woodland 310.40
symbiotic
  cooperative 450.5
  agreeing 788.9
  concurrent 899.4
symbol
  n psychological symbol 92.30
  representation 349.1
  emblem 517.2
  sign 518.6
  letter 546.1
  insignia 647.1
  musical notation 709.12
  example 786.2
  substitute 862.2
  number 1017.3
  v designate 517.18
symbolic indicative 517.23
  meaningful 518.10

semantic 518.12
figurative 519.10
symmetrical
balanced 264.4
harmonious 533.8
orderly 807.6
symmetry
balance 264.1
harmony 533.2
correlation 777.1
agreement 788.1
equality 790.1
order 807.1
sympathetic
sensitive 24.12
responsive 93.20
comforting 121.13
kind 143.13
pitying 145.7
condoling 147.3
in accord 455.3
related 775.9
attracting 907.5
tolerant 979.11
sympathy
sensitivity 24.3
fellow feeling 93.5
inclination 100.3
consolation 121.4
kindness 143.1
pity 145.1
condolence 147.1
patronage 449.4
accord 455.1
good terms 587.3
relation 775.1
attraction 907.1
tolerance 979.4
symphony accord 455.1
harmony 708.3
symposium
drinking 8.3
spree 88.5
forum 423.3
discussion 541.6
compilation 554.7
assembly 770.2
symptom
medical sign 91.13
warning sign 399.3
sign 517.1
hint 551.4
evidence 957.1
synagogue 703.2
synapse 2.14
sync
n agreement 788.1
v make agree 788.7
synchronicity 689.6
synchronized
harmonious 708.49
accompanying 769.9
agreeing 788.9
arranged 808.14
simultaneous 836.6
syncopation
dance music 708.8
tempo 709.24
syncope
unconsciousness 25.2
shortening 268.3

abbreviation 537.4
tempo 709.24
syncrasy 805.1
syndicate
n council 423.1
company 617.9
v combine 805.3
the syndicate
the underworld 660.10
illicit business 732.1
syndication 805.1
syndrome 85.1
synergy
cooperation 450.1
concurrence 899.1
synod council 423.1
ecclesiastical council 423.4
diocese 698.8
assembly 770.2
synonomicon 554.9
synonym word 526.1
the same 778.3
synopsis
shortening 268.3
abridgment 557.1
syntax
grammatical structure 530.2
arrangement 808.1
synthesis
identification 778.2
composition 796.1
combination 805.1
reasoning 935.3
synthesize
identify 778.5
compose 796.3
combine 805.3
reason 935.15
synthesizer
musical instrument 711.1
reasoner 935.11
theorist 951.7
synthetic
n plastic 1054.6
adj imitation 336.8
spurious 354.26
similar 784.10
dialectic 935.22
synthetic fuels 1021.1
syringe
n sprinkler 1065.8
v wash 79.19
moisten 1065.12
syrup
sweetening 66.2
medicine 86.4
adhesive 803.4
semiliquid 1062.5
system plan 381.1
manner 384.1
nature 767.4
order 807.1
orderliness 807.3
outlook 978.2
universe 1072.1
systematic
uniform 781.5
orderly 807.6
regular 850.6
systemic 1001.3
system of government 612.1

system of values 373.2
systems analysis 1041.2
syzygy
juxtaposition 223.3
meter 720.7
T 170.4
TA 571.4
tab
n bulge 283.3
statement 628.3
price 630.1
scenery 704.20
afterpart 817.2
v label 517.20
appoint 615.11
tabby
n iridescence 47.2
cat 311.20
newsmonger 552.9
v variegate 47.7
adj striped 47.15
tabernacle 703.2
table
n meal 8.5
food 10.1
horizontal 201.3
furniture 229.1
plain 236.1
plateau 237.3
steppe 272.4
lamina 296.2
diagram 381.3
register 549.1
record book 549.11
outline 801.4
code 808.4
contents 871.2
board 901.15
summation 1017.11
v put away 390.6
legislate 613.10
postpone 846.9
tableau spectacle 33.7
picture 712.10
table manners 580.3
table of contents
book 554.12
outline 801.4
table 871.2
table setting 498.1
tablespoon 8.12
tablet pill 86.7
lamina 296.2
record book 549.11
monument 549.12
tabloid 555.2
tabloidesque 552.14
taboo
n prohibition 444.1
exclusion 773.1
v prohibit 444.3
exclude 773.4
adj prohibited 444.7
jargonish 523.21
tabular
horizontal 201.7
classified 809.8
tabula rasa void 222.3
revolution 860.1
ignorance 930.1
thoughtlessness 933.1

tabulate record 549.15
classify 809.6
list 871.8
tachometer 174.7
tachycardia
symptom 85.9
pulsation 916.3
tacit
wordless 51.11
implicit 519.8
taciturn
untalkative 344.9
concise 537.6
tack
n direction 161.2
deviation 164.1
cordage 271.3
manner 384.1
harness 385.5
horse racing 757.1
inferiority 1005.3
v deviate 164.3
change course 182.30
fasten 800.8
be changed 852.6
tackle
n rigging 180.12
cordage 271.3
equipment 385.4
harness 385.5
impedimenta 471.3
linemen 746.2
football game 746.3
hockey game 749.6
soccer game 752.3
purchase 906.6
lifter 912.3
v practice 328.8
treat 387.12
attempt 403.7
undertake 404.3
set to work 725.15
football 746.5
hockey 749.7
soccer 752.4
reel in 906.9
tack on 253.4
tacky frail 16.14
unpleasant 98.17
shabby 393.32
vulgar 497.10
gaudy 501.20
base 661.12
adhesive 803.12
slovenly 810.15
inferior 1005.9
viscous 1062.12
moist 1065.15
tact sensitivity 24.3
considerateness 143.3
skill 413.1
courtesy 504.1
intuition 934.1
discrimination 944.1
tactic stratagem 415.3
expedient 995.2
tactical planned 381.12
cunning 415.12
tactician planner 381.6
strategist 415.7

tactile tactual 73.10
  touchable 73.11
tactual sensation 73.1
tad 302.3
tadpole
  fledgling 302.10
  amphibian 311.26
tag
  n scrap 248.3
  label 517.13
  name 527.3
  rabble 606.3
  token 728.12
  sequel 817.1
  afterpart 817.2
  extremity 820.2
  v follow 166.3
  add 253.4
  allot 477.9
  label 517.20
  name 527.11
tag along 166.3
tag sale 734.3
taiga 243.1
tail
  n braid 3.7
  follower 166.2
  rear 217.1
  buttocks 217.5
  cauda 217.6
  added to writing 254.2
  book 554.12
  appendage 793.4
  afterpart 817.2
  extremity 820.2
  v look 27.13
  follow 166.3
  trace 938.35
  adj rear 217.9
  caudal 217.11
  final 820.11
tailback 746.2
tail feather 3.16
tailgate 815.2
tail gunner 185.4
tail off weaken 16.9
  recede 168.2
  decrease 252.6
  cease to exist 762.6
tailor
  n garmentmaker 5.35
  sewer 741.2
  v outfit 5.41
  form 262.7
  sew 741.4
  make agree 788.7
tailored
  custom-made 5.48
  formative 262.9
  apt 788.10
tailpiece rear 217.1
  tail 217.6
  adjunct 254.1
  coda 708.24
  afterpart 817.2
tails
  formal dress 5.11
  opposite side 215.3
tailspin
  air maneuver 184.15
  collapse 410.3

tail wind
  atmosphere 184.32
  wind 318.1
  nautical 318.10
taint
  n infection 85.4
  stigma 661.6
  admixture 797.7
  characteristic 865.4
  fault 1003.2
  stain 1004.3
  v defile 80.17
  infect 85.51
  corrupt 393.12
  stigmatize 661.9
  blaspheme 694.5
  work evil 1000.6
  stain 1004.6
take
  n winnings 251.3
  explanation 341.4
  profit 472.3
  catch 480.10
  booty 482.11
  receipts 627.1
  shot 706.5
  motion picture 714.8
  change 852.1
  production 893.2
  answer 939.1
  v eat 8.20
  take sick 85.47
  pocket 134.8
  condone 148.4
  transport 176.12
  interpret 341.9
  succeed 409.7
  submit 433.6
  acquire 472.8
  receive 479.6
  possess 480.13
  possess sexually 480.15
  catch 480.17
  steal 482.13
  understand 521.7
  adopt 621.4
  entail 772.4
  combine 805.3
  suppose 951.10
  think 953.11
take aback
  dismay 127.19
  surprise 131.7
  startle 131.8
take a back seat
  efface oneself 139.7
  retreat 163.6
  retract 168.3
  be inferior 250.4
  depend on 432.12
take a break
  take a rest 20.8
  intervene 826.3
  pause 857.9
  interrupt 857.10
take a breather 857.9
take a chance
  venture 759.24
  risk 972.12
  take chances 1006.7
take action 328.5

take a cut 328.5
take a dim view of
  shudder at 99.5
  disapprove 510.10
take a dive 356.18
take advantage of
  avail oneself of 387.15
  exploit 387.16
  impose on 643.7
  improve the occasion 843.8
take a flier
  trade 737.23
  chance 759.24
take after
  emulate 336.7
  resemble 784.7
take a hard line 425.5
take a header
  tumble 194.8
  plunge 367.6
take a hike! 909.32
take aim at
  intend 380.4
  pull the trigger 459.22
take a liking to 104.21
take a load off 121.8
take a look at 27.13
take a moment 20.8
take a nap
  take a rest 20.8
  sleep 22.13
take an interest in
  love 104.18
  be curious 981.3
  attend to 983.5
take a nose dive
  decrease 252.6
  plunge 367.6
  decline 393.17
take apart
  demolish 395.17
  tear apart 802.14
  disassemble 802.15
take a peek 27.13
take a percentage 631.2
take a picture 714.14
take a powder
  depart 188.7
  flee 368.11
take a raincheck 329.2
take a reading 300.10
take a second look
  repeat 849.7
  re-examine 938.27
take a short cut 268.7
take a stab at 403.7
take a stand 348.6
take at one's word
  believe 953.10
  trust 953.17
take a turn for the better
  rally 392.8
  recuperate 396.19
take a turn for the worse
  worsen 119.3
  decline 393.17
take a walk
  go for a walk 177.29
  not interfere 430.17
take away
  remove 176.11

  subtract 255.9
take a whack at
  attempt 403.7
  enter 818.9
take back deny 335.4
  recant 363.8
  restore 481.4
  recover 481.6
  apologize 658.5
take by surprise 131.7
take by the hand 449.11
take care
  be careful 339.7
  beware 494.7
  pay attention 983.8
take care of
  kill 308.14
  perform 328.9
  look after 339.9
  bribe 378.3
  accomplish 407.4
  supervise 573.10
  serve 577.13
  punish 604.11
  operate 889.5
  care for 1008.19
take care of number one
  651.4
take center stage 501.12
take charge
  be able 18.11
  take command 417.14
take comfort 121.7
take cover hide 346.8
  take refuge 1009.7
take credit 622.7
take down devour 8.22
  abase 137.5
  raze 395.19
  reprove 510.17
  record 549.15
  disassemble 802.15
  depress 913.4
  fell 913.5
take down a rung 137.6
take effect 889.7
take evasive action 368.8
take exception
  dissent 333.4
  find fault 510.15
take for suppose 951.10
  think 953.11
take for a ride
  kill 308.14
  deceive 356.19
take for granted
  accept 123.2
  expect 130.5
  neglect 340.6
  imply 519.4
  suppose 951.10
  believe 953.10
take heart
  cheer up 109.9
  be comforted 121.7
  be hopeful 124.7
  take courage 492.13
take heed
  be careful 339.7
  beware 494.7
  pay attention 983.8

take hold of
seize 480.14
cohere 803.6
attend to 983.5
take-home pay
pay 624.4
receipts 627.1
standard of living 731.8
take in devour 8.22
see 27.12
hear 48.11
extend 158.9
let in 187.10
absorb 187.13
enter 189.7
attend 221.8
shorten 268.6
deceive 356.14
receive 479.6
capture 480.18
understand 521.7
learn 570.7
host 585.7
include 772.3
entail 772.4
put together 800.5
watch 918.5
take in stride
accept 123.2
patience 134.7
take in the sights 918.6
take into consideration
include 772.3
allow for 959.5
take cognizance of
  983.9
take into custody
arrest 429.15
capture 480.18
take issue with
deny 335.4
oppose 451.3
dispute 457.21
take it be strong 15.11
endure 134.6
submit 433.6
suppose 951.10
think 953.11
suffice 991.4
take it easy rest 20.6
compose oneself 106.7
take things as they come
  331.15
be cautious 494.5
pause 857.9
swim with the stream
  1014.12
take it lying down
take 134.8
submit 433.6
take it on the chin
be strong 15.11
endure 134.6
fail 410.10
take it or leave it
be indifferent 102.5
have no choice 963.11
take it out on 152.16
take it slow relax 20.7
go slowly 175.6
be cautious 494.5

take kindly to
assent 332.8
concur 332.9
consent 441.2
approve 509.9
take leave
vacation 20.9
depart 188.6
bid farewell 188.16
absent oneself 222.8
take leave of one's senses
be foolish 923.6
go mad 926.21
take legal action 673.9
take liberties
have the audacity 142.7
presume on 640.7
taken down a notch 137.14
take notice 983.6
taken up with 983.17
taken with
adj pleased 95.15
fond of 104.29
prep compared to 943.11
take odds 759.25
takeoff flight 184.8
start 188.2
embarkation 188.2
point of departure 188.5
ascent 193.1
imitation 336.1
burlesque 508.6
similarity 784.1
take off remove 6.6
become airborne 184.38
depart 188.7
leave the ground 193.10
excise 255.10
kill 308.13
mimic 336.6
impersonate 349.12
improve 392.7
put an end to 395.12
gesture 517.21
discount 631.2
resemble 784.7
detach 802.10
begin 818.7
take offense 152.13
take off for 161.9
take office 615.13
take on
grieve 112.17
complain 115.16
feel anxious 126.6
be angry 152.15
practice 328.8
treat 387.12
attempt 403.7
undertake 404.3
contend against 451.4
engage 457.16
receive 479.6
employ 615.14
adopt 621.4
set to work 725.15
take one's leave
depart 188.6
separate 802.8
take one's life in one's hands
brave 492.10

risk one's neck 1006.7
take one's medicine
submit 433.6
take one's punishment
  604.21
take one's own life 308.22
take one step at a time 494.5
take one's time
dawdle 175.8
idle 331.12
dally 331.14
take one's leisure 402.4
wait 846.12
take one's word for
believe 953.10
rely on 953.16
take one up on
assent 332.8
acquiesce 441.3
take a dare 454.6
suppose 951.10
take orders obey 326.2
be ordained 698.11
takeout 8.6
take out extract 192.10
excise 255.10
kill 308.14
annihilate 762.7
escort 769.8
end 820.5
take out after
follow 166.3
pursue 382.8
censure 510.13
takeover
appropriation 480.4
stock trading 737.19
combination 805.1
take over
take command 417.14
take possession 472.10
receive 479.6
appropriate 480.19
adopt 621.4
usurp 640.8
combine 805.3
succeed 815.2
take pains
be careful 339.7
make a special effort 403.11
take part 476.5
take pity on 145.4
take place 831.5
take pleasure in 95.13
take possession
appropriate 472.10
take 480.13
take precautions
take steps 494.6
play safe 1007.3
take precedence
rule 249.11
precede 814.2
take pride 136.5
take prisoner
arrest 429.15
capture 480.18
take refuge 1009.7
take refuge in 376.4
take revenge
get even with 506.7

avenge 507.4
take risks 492.9
take shape
be formed 262.8
form 807.5
take shelter 1009.7
take sides with
back 449.13
side with 450.4
take steps
take action 328.5
take precautions 494.6
take stock
take account of 628.9
check 1017.21
take the bait
react 903.5
kid oneself 954.6
take the bull by the horns
be determined 359.8
attempt 403.6
undertake 404.3
brave 492.10
seize the opportunity 843.7
take the cake
best 249.7
triumph 411.3
take the edge off
weaken 16.10
blunt 286.2
moderate 670.6
take the first step 818.10
take the floor
speak up 524.21
make a speech 543.9
legislate 613.10
take the grand tour 918.6
take the heat for
be responsible for 641.6
accept the responsibility
  641.9
take the law into one's own
  hands
have one's will 323.3
violate 435.4
break the law 674.5
take the lead
lead 165.2
be in front 216.7
take command 417.14
direct 573.8
dominate 612.14
initiate 818.10
take the next step 817.5
take the offensive 459.14
take the opportunity 843.7
take the place of
follow after 835.3
substitute for 862.5
take the rap 604.21
take the stand
depose 334.6
call to witness 598.17
take the trouble 324.3
take the wind out of one's
  sails
disable 19.10
sadden 112.18
humiliate 137.6
becalm 173.11
disincline 379.4

refute 958.5
thwart 1012.15
take the words out of one's mouth 845.6
take the wraps off 351.4
take the wrong way 342.2
take things as they come
keep cool 106.9
accept 134.7
take it easy 331.15
take time
spend time 821.6
wait 846.12
take to desire 100.14
fall in love 104.21
practice 328.8
become used to 373.11
avail oneself of 387.14
take to heart
respond 93.11
take amiss 152.13
internalize 207.5
believe 953.10
take to mean 341.9
take to task
reprove 510.17
accuse 599.7
punish 604.10
take to the cleaners
best 249.7
lose 473.4
strip 480.24
take turns 825.5
take under consideration 931.14
take under one's wing
back 449.13
benefit 592.3
care for 1008.19
take up
absorb 187.13
practice 328.8
adopt 371.15
undertake 404.3
patronize 449.15
take possession 472.10
collect 472.11
appropriate 480.19
espouse 509.13
discuss 541.11
write upon 556.5
pay in full 624.13
busy oneself with 724.11
assemble 770.18
include 772.3
enter 818.9
pick up 912.8
engross 983.13
take up a collection 770.18
take up arms
contend 457.13
go to war 458.15
take upon oneself
undertake 404.3
presume 640.6
accept the responsibility 641.9
take up residence 159.17
take up the cause of 449.13
take up with
confer 541.10

associate with 582.18
befriend 587.10
take with a grain of salt
doubt 955.6
allow for 959.5
talcum powder 1016.11
tale lie 354.11
gossip 552.7
story 719.3
yarn 722.3
tally 1017.6
talent ability 18.2
flair 413.4
talented person 413.12
artistry 712.6
smartness 920.2
genius 920.8
talented gifted 413.29
smart 920.14
talent scout 704.27
talisman 691.5
talk
n language 523.1
speech 524.1
diction 532.1
conversation 541.2
oration 543.2
report 552.6
gossip 552.7
lesson 568.7
v communicate 343.6
betray 351.6
signify 517.17
speak 523.18
converse 524.19
discuss 541.11
make a speech 543.9
gossip 552.12
talkative
v loquacious 540.9
adj communicative 343.10
disclosive 351.10
speaking 524.31
wordy 538.12
talk back
be insolent 142.8
answer 939.4
talk dirty 513.6
talk down to
condescend 137.8
give oneself airs 141.8
talking-to 510.6
talk into 375.23
talk of the town
report 552.6
repute 662.1
talk on 540.5
talk out of 379.3
talk out of turn
betray 351.6
speak inopportunely 844.4
talk over
persuade 375.23
confer 541.10
discuss 541.11
convince 953.18
talk shop 541.12
talk show 1034.18
talk-show host 1034.23
talk someone's ear off 524.20
talk to oneself 542.3

talk turkey
speak plainly 535.2
discuss 541.12
talk with 541.8
tall large 257.16
long 267.7
giant 272.16
inflated 502.12
grandiloquent 545.8
unbelievable 955.10
tall order 1013.2
tallow whiteness 37.2
oil 1056.1
tall tale 354.11
tally
n label 517.13
report 549.7
account 628.2
likeness 784.3
agreement 788.1
list 871.1
sum 1017.6
v compute 253.6
coincide 778.4
agree 788.6
list 871.8
number 1017.17
calculate 1017.18
tallyho! 382.13
Talmud scripture 683.5
tradition 842.2
talons
governance 417.5
clutches 474.4
control 612.2
tamas 930.1
tamasic 930.11
tame
v accustom 373.9
domesticate 432.11
moderate 670.6
tend 1070.7
adj inert 173.14
domesticated 228.34
meek 433.15
moderate 670.10
tamp indent 284.14
thrust 902.12
tamper with
meddle 214.7
manipulate 354.17
bribe 378.3
adulterate 797.12
tampon
medical dressing 86.33
wadding 293.5
tan
v brown 40.2
embalm 397.10
prepare 405.6
punish 604.15
adj brown 40.3
tandem
n rig 179.5
adv behind 217.13
tang taste 62.1
zest 68.2
characteristic 865.4
sting 1001.5
tangent
n convergence 169.1

neighbor 223.6
straight line 277.2
adj converging 169.3
in contact 223.17
tangerine 42.2
tangible
touchable 73.11
manifest 348.8
substantial 763.6
tangle
n complex 799.2
v trap 356.20
catch 480.17
complicate 799.3
involve 898.2
hamper 1012.11
tangle with 457.17
tangy 68.7
tank
n reservoir 241.1
storehouse 386.6
prison 429.8
jail 429.9
v package 212.9
prearrange 965.5
tanker ship 1075.2
tank top 5.29
tanned brown 40.3
prepared 405.16
tannery 739.3
tantalizing
appetizing 63.10
delightful 97.7
desirable 100.30
exciting 105.30
disappointing 132.6
alluring 377.8
interesting 983.19
tantamount
reciprocal 777.10
equivalent 790.8
tantric sex 75.7
tantrum 152.8
tao 919.5
Taoist 675.32
tap
n thud 52.3
explosive sound 56.1
touch 73.1
outlet 190.9
tube 239.6
valve 239.10
stopper 293.4
root 310.22
rap 902.7
v listen 48.10
thud 52.15
make explosive sound 56.6
touch 73.6
transport 176.14
draw off 192.12
open 292.11
perforate 292.15
take from 480.21
beat time 708.44
rap 902.18
tapas
breakfast 8.6
serving 8.10
sample 62.4

tap-dance
  dance 705.5
  procrastinate 846.11
  quibble 936.9
tape
  n record 50.12
  medical dressing 86.33
  strip 271.4
  recording media 549.10
  boxing 754.1
  end 820.1
  v sound 50.14
  record 549.15
  put together 800.5
  teleview 1035.15
tape cassette 50.12
tape measure 271.4
taper
  n narrowing 270.2
  lighter 1021.4
  light source 1026.1
  candle 1026.2
  wick 1026.7
  v converge 169.2
  narrow 270.11
  sharpen 285.7
  adj tapered 270.15
tape recorder 50.11
tape recording 50.12
tapestry 712.10
tapeworm
  appetite 100.7
  worm 311.38
tap out fail 410.9
  lose 473.4
  go bankrupt 625.7
taps blare 53.5
  funeral 309.5
  night 315.4
  call 517.16
  end 820.1
tap water 10.49
tar
  n blackness 38.4
  opium 87.16
  mariner 183.1
  v cover 295.22
  coat 295.24
tar and feather 604.16
tarantula 311.32
tardy retarded 175.12
  anachronistic 833.3
  late 846.16
tares 391.4
target
  objective 380.2
  laughingstock 508.7
  fission 1038.8
target audience 733.3
target shooting 744.1
target sports 744.11
tariff 773.4
tarlet 10.41
tarmac 383.6
tarnish
  n stigma 661.6
  stain 1004.3
  v decolor 36.5
  defile 80.17
  vilify 512.10
  stigmatize 661.9

  stain 1004.6
tarot reading 962.2
tarry
  v be still 173.7
  dawdle 175.8
  endure 827.6
  linger on 827.7
  wait 846.12
  continue 856.3
  adj black 38.8
tart
  n pastry 10.41
  strumpet 665.14
  adj acrimonious 17.14
  bitter 64.6
  sour 67.5
  caustic 144.23
tartan check 47.4
  insignia 647.1
Tartar 110.11
Tarzan 15.6
Taser 462.22
task
  n undertaking 404.1
  lesson 568.7
  commission 615.1
  charge 643.3
  job 724.2
  work 725.4
  v accuse 599.7
  impose 643.4
  work 725.16
task bar 1042.18
task force
  military unit 461.22
  navy 461.27
taskmaster 574.2
taste
  n bite 8.2
  senses 24.5
  gust 62.1
  sample 62.4
  liking 100.2
  appetite 100.7
  hint 248.4
  preference 371.5
  fastidiousness 495.1
  tastefulness 496.1
  elegance 533.1
  specimen 786.3
  characteristic 865.4
  discrimination 944.1
  v eat 8.20
  sense 24.6
  taste of 62.7
  savor 63.5
  experience 831.8
  experiment 942.8
taste bud 62.5
tasteful
  in good taste 496.7
  elegant 533.6
  artistic 712.19
tasteless
  wishy-washy 16.17
  insipid 65.2
  dull 117.6
  vulgar 497.10
  inelegant 534.2
  base 661.12
taste perception 62.1

taste test 62.4
tasty good 63.8
  delectable 97.10
tata 188.22
tater
  vegetables 10.35
  baseball 745.3
tatter
  n scrap 248.3
  piece 793.3
  v wear 393.20
tattle
  n gossip 552.7
  v betray 351.6
  inform on 551.12
  gossip 552.12
tattletale
  n informer 551.6
  newsmonger 552.9
  adj telltale 551.19
tattoo
  n fanfare 53.5
  staccato 55.1
  mark 517.5
  constancy 847.2
  hit 902.4
  shot 904.4
  v variegate 47.7
  rain 316.10
  mark 517.19
taught 928.18
taunt
  n indignity 156.2
  gibe 508.2
  v be insolent 142.7
  offend 156.5
  scoff 508.9
taupe gray 39.4
  brown 40.3
taut tense 128.13
  in suspense 130.12
  shipshape 180.20
  rigid 1046.11
tautologic 391.10
tautologically 391.15
tautology
  wordiness 538.2
  redundancy 849.3
  superfluity 993.4
tavern
  restaurant 8.17
  bar 88.20
  inn 228.15
  entertainment 743.13
tawdry gaudy 501.20
  paltry 998.21
tawny 40.3
tax
  n demand 421.1
  taxation 630.9
  charge 643.3
  overdoing 993.6
  v burden 297.13
  accuse 599.7
  charge 630.12
  impose 643.4
  strain 725.10
  task 725.16
taxable income
  pay 624.4
  tax 630.9

tax collector
  taxer 630.10
  collector 770.15
tax-deductible 630.16
tax evasion
  shirking 368.2
  tax 630.9
taxi
  n public vehicle 179.13
  v ride 177.33
  take off 184.38
taxidermy 397.3
taxing
  n burden 297.7
  demand 421.1
  accusation 599.1
  imposition 643.1
  strain 725.2
  adj demanding 421.9
taxonomy
  biological classification
    305.3
  nomenclature 527.1
  classification 801.3
  grouping 808.3
  arrangement 809.1
taxpayer payer 624.9
  good or respectable citizen
    659.3
tax preparer
  recorder 550.1
  accountant 628.7
tax return 630.9
tea meal 8.6
  marijuana 87.11
  afternoon tea 582.13
teach 568.10
teacher preparer 405.5
  adviser 422.3
  tutor 568.1
  instructor 571.1
  master 575.1
  clergy 699.10
  professional 726.4
teacher's pet
  weakling 16.6
  favorite 104.15
teaching assistant 571.4
teach one a lesson 604.10
team
  n rig 179.5
  outfit 617.7
  baseball team 745.2
  football team 746.2
  basketball team 747.2
  hockey team 749.2
  attack 749.5
  lawn bowling 750.3
  golfer 751.2
  squad 752.2
  company 770.3
  two 873.2
  v double 873.5
teamed 805.6
team games 744.12
teammate
  companion 588.3
  co-worker 616.5
teamster
  coachman 178.9
  driver 178.10

team up
cooperate 450.3
befriend 587.11
double 873.5
tear
n humor 2.24
weeping 115.2
v secrete 13.5
tear
n trauma 85.38
drinking spree 88.6
break 802.4
v pain 26.7
speed 174.8
hurry 174.9
open 292.11
injure 393.13
make haste 401.5
rage 671.11
sever 802.11
tear apart
demolish 395.17
find fault 510.15
pull apart 802.14
tear down blacken 38.7
raze 395.19
find fault 510.15
defame 512.9
disassemble 802.15
teardrop tear 2.24
weeping 115.2
drop 282.3
tearful
sorrowful 112.26
teary 115.21
tearing
n severance 802.2
adj welling 2.33
tearjerker 93.8
tear limb from limb
torture 604.16
rip apart 802.14
tearoom 8.17
tear open open 292.11
breach 292.14
tears
secretion 13.2
weeping 115.2
tease
n tormentor 96.10
disappointment 132.1
deceiver 357.1
v annoy 96.13
disappoint 132.2
attract 377.6
importune 440.12
banter 490.5
teaspoon 8.12
teatime 8.6
teats 283.6
technical
skilled 413.26
occupational 724.16
specialized 866.5
scientific 928.28
insignificant 998.17
technicality
technical term 526.5
complexity 799.1
specialty 866.1
an insignificancy 998.6

technical knockout 754.3
technical support 449.3
technician
expert 413.11
skilled worker 726.6
engineer 726.7
specialist 866.3
computer whiz 1042.17
technicolored 35.16
technique
manner 384.1
skill 413.1
art 413.7
artistic treatment 712.8
skiing 753.3
knowledge 928.1
technology art 413.7
engineer 726.7
science 928.10
technospeak 523.9
tech support 449.3
tectonic plate 235.1
tectonics 266.1
teddy bear figure 349.6
toy 743.16
tedious dull 117.6
monotonous 118.9
same 781.6
repetitive 849.15
mediocre 1005.7
tee 751.1
teed off 152.30
teed up 405.16
teeming
n proliferation 890.2
infestation 910.2
adj pregnant 78.18
permeated 221.15
diffuse 538.11
crowded 770.22
swarming 884.9
productive 890.9
infested 910.11
imaginative 986.18
plentiful 991.7
superabundant 993.19
teenage 301.14
teenagehood 301.7
teenager 302.1
tee off on
attack 459.15
criticize 510.14
teeter
n alternation 916.5
oscillator 916.9
v be weak 16.8
vacillate 362.8
change 854.5
alternate 916.13
teeth dentition 2.8
acrimony 17.5
clutches 474.4
speech organ 524.18
sail in the teeth of the wind
182.24
teetotaler 668.4
Teflon-coated 1008.23
tel 237.4
telebanking 729.3
telecast
n television broadcast 1035.2

v publish 352.10
televise 1035.14
adj published 352.17
telecommunication
communications 343.5
signaling 347.1
radio 1034.1
telecommute 724.1
teleconference
telephone call 347.13
conference 541.5
telegram
n telegraph 347.14
message 552.4
v telegraph 347.20
telegraph
n telegraph recorder 347.2
telegram 347.14
v send a message 347.20
telekinesis 689.6
telemarket 734.8
telemarketing 347.13
telemetry
measurement 300.1
semiautomatic control
1041.4
rocketry 1074.1
telepathic
communicational 343.9
psychic 689.24
telepathy
communication 343.1
mental telepathy 689.9
telephone
n communication device
347.4
v phone 347.19
telephone book
reference book 554.9
directory 574.10
telephone number 347.12
telephone operator 347.9
telephoto 714.17
teleport 689.20
telescope
n optical instrument 29.4
observatory 1072.17
v shorten 268.6
televise publish 352.10
telecast 1035.14
television
communications medium
347.3
informant 551.5
news 552.1
electronics 1033.1
TV 1035.1
television personality 1035.2
television repairman 1035.13
television studio 1035.6
telex
n telegraph 347.2
telegram 347.14
v telegraph 347.20
tell
impress 93.15
hill 237.4
communicate 343.7
divulge 351.5
say 524.22
inform 551.8

report 552.11
narrate 719.6
spin a yarn 722.6
have influence 894.10
evidence 957.8
recognize 989.11
matter 997.12
number 1017.17
teller
informant 551.5
banker 729.11
telling
n informing 343.2
fiction 722.1
narration 722.2
numeration 1017.9
adj powerful 18.12
exciting 105.30
vigorous 544.11
influential 894.13
evidential 957.16
notable 997.19
tell it like it is 644.12
tell off 510.18
tell on betray 351.6
inform on 551.13
telltale
n divulgence 351.2
clue 517.9
hint 551.4
informer 551.6
newsmonger 552.9
adj tattletale 551.19
tell the truth
confess 351.7
speak true 644.11
disillusion 977.2
temerity 493.1
temp worker 726.2
temperature 1019.3
temper
n firmness 15.3
hot temper 110.4
anger 152.6
nature 767.4
disposition 978.3
mood 978.4
tempering 1046.4
v strengthen 15.13
mature 303.9
moderate 670.6
imbue 797.11
qualify 959.3
harden 1046.7
toughen 1049.3
temperament
pitch 709.4
nature 767.4
disposition 978.3
temperance
sedateness 106.4
sobriety 516.1
cardinal virtues 653.3
temperateness 668.1
restraint 670.1
temperate
sedate 106.14
sober 516.3
moderate 668.9
mild 670.10
warm 1019.24

cool 1023.12
temperature 1019.3
temper tantrum 152.8
tempest outburst 105.9
  windstorm 318.11
  storm 671.4
tempest in a teacup 998.3
tempest in a teapot 355.2
template 786.6
temple side 218.1
  religious building 703.2
tempo time 709.24
  pulsation 916.3
temporal
  unsacred 686.3
  secularist 695.16
  lay 700.3
  chronological 821.7
  transient 828.7
  timekeeping 832.15
  material 1052.10
temporalty 700.1
temporary
  n worker 726.2
  adj interim 826.4
  transient 828.7
  substitute 862.8
  conditional 959.8
  unreliable 971.20
  makeshift 995.7
temporize
  n be a timeserver 363.9
  v not face up to 368.13
  protract 827.9
  procrastinate 846.11
tempt seduce 104.22
  induce 375.22
  attract 377.6
tempt fate endeavor 403.1
  be foolish 923.6
temptress
  tempter 377.4
  seductress 665.15
tempus fugit 821.17
10 1016.2
ten
  n card 758.2
  number 882.6
  beauty 1016.8
  v intervene 826.3
tenable
  acceptable 107.12
  defensible 460.15
  believable 953.24
tenacious
  resolute 359.11
  persevering 360.8
  obstinate 361.8
  retentive 474.8
  courageous 492.17
  adhesive 803.12
  tough 1049.4
  viscous 1062.12
tenant
  n inhabitant 227.2
  lodger 227.8
  occupant 470.4
  v inhabit 225.7
Ten Commandments
  ethics 636.1
  ten 882.6

tend
  take direction 161.7
  gravitate 297.15
  look after 339.9
  serve 577.13
  have a tendency 896.3
  heed 983.6
  care for 1008.19
  groom 1070.7
tendency
  direction 161.1
  preference 371.5
  aptitude 413.5
  nature 767.4
  inclination 896.1
  probability 968.1
  disposition 978.3
tender
  n attendant 577.5
  v offer 439.4
  give 478.12
  pay 624.10
  adj sensitive 24.12
  sore 26.11
  soft-colored 35.22
  sympathetic 93.20
  loving 104.26
  kind 143.13
  pitying 145.7
  seaworthy 180.18
  light 298.12
  immature 301.10
  careful 339.10
  lenient 427.7
  unbalanced 791.5
  soft 1047.8
tenderfoot
  recruit 461.18
  novice 572.9
  jockey 757.2
  newcomer 774.4
  beginner 818.2
  ignoramus 930.7
tenderize 1047.6
tenderloin
  city district 230.6
  brothel 665.9
tender loving care 449.2
tendon 271.2
tendril filament 271.1
  coil 281.2
  branch 310.20
  part 793.4
tenement sty 80.11
  apartment 228.13
  high rise 228.14
tenet rule 419.2
  a belief 953.2
tennis 748.1
tennis ball
  tennis 748.1
  elastic 1048.3
tennis court
  smoothness 287.3
  playing area 743.11
  tennis 748.1
tennis shoes 5.27
tenor
  n high voice 58.6
  direction 161.1
  meaning 518.1

music part 708.22
  voice 709.5
  mode 765.4
  nature 767.4
  transcript 785.4
  trend 896.2
  adj high 58.13
  vocal 708.50
tenpins 750.1
tense
  n grammar 530.12
  time 821.1
  v strain 725.10
  stiffen 1046.9
  adj restless 105.27
  anxious 126.7
  nervous 128.13
  in suspense 130.12
  phonetic 524.30
  unfriendly 589.9
  rigid 1046.11
tension
  n anxiety 126.1
  tenseness 128.3
  disaccord 456.1
  enmity 589.1
  strain 725.2
  overextension 993.7
  urgency 997.4
  voltage 1032.12
  rigidity 1046.2
  stretching 1048.2
  v stiffen 1046.9
tent
  n medical apparatus 86.33
  canvas 295.8
  v camp 225.11
tentacle 3.10
tentacles 474.4
tentaculum 73.4
tentative
  n attempt 403.2
  adj slow 175.10
  hesitant 362.11
  trial 403.16
  cautious 494.8
  interim 826.4
  substitute 862.8
  ignorant 930.11
  examining 938.37
  experimental 942.11
  unreliable 971.20
  makeshift 995.7
tenterhooks 126.1
tenth
  n fraction 882.14
  adj ordinal number 882.22
ten to one 968.8
tenuous dainty 248.7
  infinitesimal 258.14
  thin 270.16
  rare 299.4
  ethereal 764.6
  incoherent 804.4
tenure possession 469.1
  position 724.5
  term 824.3
  period of duty 825.4
tepee 228.10
tepid indifferent 102.6
  warm 1019.24

tergiversate 854.5
term
  n boundary 211.3
  sign 518.6
  word 526.1
  phrase 529.1
  end 820.1
  time 821.1
  moment 824.2
  duration 824.3
  tenure 825.4
  v name 527.11
terminal
  n destination 186.5
  railway 383.7
  speech component 524.9
  end 820.1
  stop 857.2
  output device 1042.9
  adj unhealthy 85.54
  past hope 125.15
  limital 210.10
  bordering 211.11
  dying 307.32
  deadly 308.23
  completing 407.9
  final 820.11
  disastrous 1011.15
terminal degree 648.6
terminal illness 85.2
terminate
  complete 407.6
  end 820.5
  cease 857.6
  result 887.4
terminology
  nomenclature 527.1
  dictionary 871.4
termite 311.33
term paper 556.1
terra land 234.1
  Earth 1072.10
terrace
  balcony 197.22
  horizontal 201.3
  platform 901.13
terra cotta 715.2
terra-cotta 40.4
terra firma
  ground 199.3
  land 234.1
  foundation 901.6
terrain
  open space 158.4
  region 231.1
  land 234.1
  arena 463.1
terrapin 311.24
terrarium 228.24
terrestrial
  terrene 234.4
  secularist 695.16
  celestial 1072.25
terrible
  horrid 98.19
  frightening 127.30
  remarkable 247.11
  wrong 638.3
  dreadful 1000.9
  hideous 1015.11

therein 207.10
thereof 188.20
thermal
    n hot air 1019.9
    adj warm 1019.24
thermal unit 1019.19
thermochemical
    pyrological 1019.32
    chemical 1060.9
thermodynamic 1019.32
thermometer 1019.20
thermonuclear 1038.19
thermonuclear power
    nuclear energy 18.4
    atomic energy 1038.15
thermonuclear reaction
    fission 1038.8
    fusion 1038.9
thermonuclear weapons
    462.1
thermostat 1019.20
thesaurus
    vocabulary 526.13
    reference book 554.9
    dictionary 871.4
these 865.14
thesis treatise 556.1
    accent 709.25
    meter 720.7
    beat 850.3
    premise 935.7
    supposition 951.3
thespian
    n actor 707.2
    adj dramatic 704.33
thew 15.2
they
    the authorities 575.15
    exclusiveness 773.3
    them 865.5
thick
    n middle 819.1
    v thicken 269.5
    density 1045.10
    adj raucous 58.15
    three-dimensional 269.8
    luxuriant 310.43
    inarticulate 525.12
    familiar 587.19
    teeming 884.9
    stupid 922.15
    unbelievable 955.10
    dense 1045.12
    viscous 1062.12
    adv densely 1045.15
thicken increase 251.4
    grow thick 269.5
    densify 1045.10
    solidify 1046.8
    emulsify 1062.10
thicket
    dense plant growth
        310.15
    bunch 770.7
thick skin
    insensibility 25.1
    callousness 94.3
    shell 295.15
    armor 460.3
thief robber 483.1
    evildoer 593.1

criminal 660.9
thigh body part 2.7
    fowl part 10.23
    leg 177.14
thimbleful 248.2
thin
    v dilute 16.11
    subtract 255.9
    shrink 260.9
    thin down 270.12
    rarefy 299.3
    dissipate 771.5
    liquefy 1064.5
    prune 1069.17
    adj shrill 58.14
    insipid 65.2
    dainty 248.7
    infinitesimal 258.14
    shrunk 260.13
    slender 270.16
    shallow 276.5
    rare 299.4
    tenuous 764.6
    sparse 885.5
    unbelievable 955.10
    meager 992.10
    transparent 1029.4
    adv thinly 270.23
thin air 317.1
    spirit 764.3
thing love affair 104.5
    act 328.3
    preference 371.5
    occupation 724.1
    something 763.3
    mode 765.4
    particular 766.3
    affair 831.3
    specialty 866.1
    object 1052.4
things wardrobe 5.2
    equipment 385.4
    belongings 471.2
thingumajig 1052.5
thin ice 1006.1
think expect 130.5
    care 339.6
    intend 380.4
    cogitate 931.8
    suppose 951.10
    opine 953.11
think ahead
    anticipate 839.6
    foresee 961.5
think back 989.9
think better of
    repent 113.7
    reconsider 931.15
thinker wise man 921.1
    intellectual 929.1
    reasoner 935.11
    philosopher 952.8
think highly of
    respect 155.4
    value 997.13
think little of
    disdain 157.3
    not hesitate 359.10
    disapprove 510.10
    underestimate 950.2
    be inattentive 984.2

attach little importance to
    998.12
think nothing of
    disdain 157.3
    not hesitate 359.10
    underestimate 950.2
    be inattentive 984.2
    attach little importance to
        998.12
    take it easy 1014.12
think out loud 542.3
think over 931.13
think tank 942.5
think the world of 104.20
think the worst of 125.9
think twice
    be cautious 494.5
    be unsure 971.10
thinner
    paint 35.8
    solvent 270.10
    diluting agent 1064.4
thinning
    n weakening 16.5
    shrinking 260.3
    rarefaction 299.2
    dispersion 771.1
    cultivation 1069.13
    adj solvent 1064.8
thin-skinned
    sensitive 24.12
    touchy 110.21
third
    n harmonic interval 709.20
    baseball 745.1
    fraction 878.2
    mediocre 1005.6
    v trisect 878.3
    adj tertiary 877.4
the third-degree 938.13
third-degree burn
    trauma 85.38
    burn 1020.6
the third dimension 269.2
the third estate 606.1
third estate 607.5
third person 530.7
third-rate 1005.9
third string
    n inferiority 250.1
    team 617.7
    substitute 862.2
    adj inferior 250.6
third wheel 769.5
third world
    independents 430.12
    neutral 467.4
    the poor 619.3
thirst
    n craving 100.6
    appetite 100.7
    tendency 896.1
    dryness 1066.1
    v hunger 100.19
    drink up 1066.5
thirsty
    craving 100.24
    needing water 100.26
    absorbent 187.17
    dry 1066.7
thirteen 882.7

thirty-second note 709.14
thirty-something 302.1
thirty-two 882.7
this 865.14
this day
    n the present 838.1
    adv now 838.3
this instant 838.1
thistle thorn 285.5
    insignia 647.1
thistledown down 3.19
    lightness 298.2
    softness 1047.4
this way 766.10
thong
    swimwear 5.29
    strip 271.4
    whip 605.1
Thor thunder 56.5
    rain 316.6
    lightning 1025.17
thorax 283.6
thorn
    affliction 96.8
    bramble 285.5
    adhering thing 803.4
    bane 1001.1
thorny
    prickly 285.10
    difficult 1013.17
thorough
    downright 247.12
    painstaking 339.11
    meticulous 339.12
    confirmed 373.18
    complete 407.12
    cautious 494.8
    thoroughgoing 794.10
thoroughbred
    n aristocrat 607.4
    nobleman 608.4
    horse 757.2
    adj upper-class 607.10
    wellborn 608.11
those 865.14
those left 256.3
though 338.8
thought
    n expectation 130.1
    considerateness 143.3
    swift thing 174.6
    hint 248.4
    advice 422.1
    remark 524.3
    admixture 797.7
    intellect 919.1
    act of thought 931
    idea 932.1
    opinion 953.6
    attention 983.1
    adj cognitive 931.21
thoughtful
    solemn 111.3
    considerate 143.16
    careful 339.10
    courteous 504.14
    judicious 920.19
    cognitive 931.21
thoughtless
    inconsiderate 144.18
    careless 340.11

tighten the screws 119.2
tightfisted 484.9
tight grip 474.2
tight-knit joined 800.13
  dense 1045.12
tight-lipped 344.9
tightrope walking
  defiance 454.1
  daring 492.4
  foolhardiness 493.3
  unreliability 971.6
tights 5.9
tight squeeze
  narrowness 270.1
  narrow escape 369.2
  poverty 619.1
  predicament 1013.5
tightwad 484.4
tighty whities 5.22
tigress
  female animal 77.9
  bitch 110.12
  witch 593.7
  violent person 671.9
tile
  n pavement 383.6
  ceramic ware 742.2
  building material 1054.2
  v cover 295.23
till
  n booty 482.11
  treasury 729.13
  v cultivate 1069.17
  prep until 821.15
till death do us part
  829.13
tiller helm 573.5
  agriculturist 1069.5
till hell freezes over
  to the end 820.13
  for a long time 827.14
  forever 829.12
till one is blue in the face
  105.35
till the cows come home
  for a long time 827.14
  forever 829.12
till the end of time 827.14
till then 826.5
till the soil 1069.17
tilt
  n penchant 100.3
  inclination 204.2
  preference 371.5
  contest 457.3
  tendency 896.1
  v tumble 194.8
  incline 204.10
  contend 457.13
  tend 896.3
  throw 904.10
tilt at windmills
  be impotent 19.7
  be useless 391.8
  be foolish 923.6
timber spar 180.13
  beam 273.3
  tree 310.10
  woodland 310.13
  wood 1054.3
timber wolf 311.19

timbre tonality 50.3
  manner of speaking 524.7
Timbuktu 261.4
time
  n leisure 402.1
  tempo 709.24
  duration 821.1
  period 824.1
  term 824.3
  age 824.4
  turn 825.2
  shift 825.3
  tenure 825.4
  time of day 832.2
  date 832.4
  opportunity 843.2
  v fix the time 832.11
  synchronize 836.4
time bomb 1006.1
time book 832.9
time frame
  boundary 211.3
  plan 381.1
  time 821.1
  period 824.1
time-honored
  venerable 155.12
  customary 373.13
  traditional 842.12
time immemorial 827.4
timekeeper
  recorder 550.1
  hockey 749.6
  boxing 754.3
  timepiece 832.6
  chronologist 832.10
timeless
  almighty 677.17
  dateless 822.3
  perpetual 829.7
  old 842.10
time limit 211.3
timely
  well-timed 843.9
  expedient 995.5
time off
  n vacation 20.3
  interim 826.1
  pause 857.3
  v take one's turn 825.5
time out
  n respite 20.2
  v punch the clock 832.12
timepiece 832.6
the times affairs 831.4
  the present 838.1
time scale 832.9
timetable plan 381.1
  chronicle 832.9
time to spare
  leisure 402.1
  earliness 845.1
time travel 821.1
time warp
  fourth dimension 158.6
  time 821.1
timewise 821.7
timeworn trite 117.9
  stricken in years 303.18
  worn 393.31
  stale 842.14

time zone 832.3
timid fearful 127.23
  shy 139.12
  hesitant 362.11
  cowardly 491.10
timing skill 413.1
  tempo 709.24
  agreement 788.1
  chronology 832.1
timorous
  fearful 127.23
  shy 139.12
  cowardly 491.10
tin
  n money 728.2
  v package 212.9
  put up 397.11
  adj spurious 354.26
  metal 1058.17
tincture
  n color 35.1
  pigment 35.8
  hint 248.4
  heraldry 647.2
  admixture 797.7
  v color 35.14
  imbue 797.11
tinder 1021.6
tin foil 295.18
tinge
  n color 35.1
  trace 62.3
  hint 248.4
  implication 519.2
  admixture 797.7
  v color 35.14
  imbue 797.11
  influence 894.7
tingle
  n smart 26.3
  ringing 54.3
  tingling sensation 74.1
  thrill 105.2
  v have energy 17.11
  suffer 26.8
  ring 54.8
  thrill 74.5
  be excited 105.18
tinhorn
  n gambler 759.21
  mediocrity 1005.5
  adj insignificant 998.18
tinker
  n mender 396.10
  v repair 396.14
  rearrange 808.13
  trifle 998.14
tinkle
  n clinking sound 52.3
  ringing 54.3
  v clink 52.15
  ring 54.8
tinny
  lacking resonance 58.15
  inferior 1005.9
  metallic 1058.17
tin pan alley 230.6
Tin Pan Alley 708.7
tinsel
  n appearance 33.2
  fake 354.13

finery 498.3
  glitter 1025.7
  v decorate 498.9
  glitter 1025.25
  adj spurious 354.26
  specious 354.27
tint
  n color 35.1
  hue 35.6
  engraving 713.2
  admixture 797.7
  v color 35.14
  portray 712.18
tintinnabulation 54.3
tiny insignificant
  248.6
  little 258.11
tip
  n summit 198.2
  inclination 204.2
  point 285.3
  piece of advice 422.2
  gratuity 478.5
  part of tongue 524.18
  clue 551.3
  bonus 624.6
  extremity 820.2
  tap 902.7
  surplus 993.5
  v careen 182.43
  crown 198.9
  incline 204.10
  top 295.21
  warn 399.5
  alert 551.11
  tap 902.18
tip-off
  warning 399.1
  sign 517.1
  clue 517.9
  suggest 551.3
  hint 551.4
tip of the iceberg
  modicum 248.2
  hint 248.4
  sign 517.1
tipping point 407.2
tipple drink 8.29
  booze 88.24
tippytoe
  n creeping 177.17
  v creep 177.26
  adj creeping 177.39
tip sheet 757.4
tipster informant 551.5
  dopester 962.5
tipsy intoxicated 88.31
  inclining 204.15
tip the scales 297.10
tiptoe
  n creeping 177.17
  v creep 177.26
  lurk 346.9
  be cautious 494.5
  adj creeping 177.39
  adv on tiptoe 272.21
tip-top
  n summit 198.2
  adj top 198.10
  superlative 249.13
  first-rate 999.18

tirade
- *n* lament 115.3
- berating 510.7
- wordiness 538.2
- speech 543.2
- *v* wail 115.13

tire
- *n* rim 280.4
- *v* clothe 5.39
- fatigue 21.4
- weary 21.5
- oppress 98.16
- be tedious 118.6

tired clothing 5.45
- fatigued 21.7
- weary 118.11
- worn-out 393.36
- aphoristic 974.6

tireless
- industrious 330.22
- persevering 360.8

tires 756.1

tiresome
- fatiguing 21.13
- annoying 98.22
- boring 118.10
- prosaic 721.5

tissue
- *n* material 4.1
- network 170.3
- structure 266.1
- organic matter 305.1
- weaving 740.1
- *v* weave 740.6

titan 257.13

titanic large 247.7
- huge 257.20

tit for tat offset 338.2
- retaliation 506.3
- reciprocity 777.3
- substitution 862.1
- interchange 863.1

tit-for-tat 777.10

tithe
- *n* donation 478.6
- tax 630.9
- tenth part 882.14
- *v* charge 630.12
- *adj* tenth 882.22

Titian
- reddish-brown 40.4
- red 41.6
- redheaded 41.10

titillate tickle 74.6
- delight 95.10
- thrill 105.15
- attract 377.6
- amuse 743.21
- interest 983.12

title
- *n* possession 469.1
- ownership 469.2
- estate 471.4
- name 527.3
- book 554.1
- book part 554.12
- prerogative 642.1
- honorific 648.1
- golf 751.1
- class 809.2
- caption 937.2

- *v* name 527.11
- focus on 937.3

titled named 527.14
- noble 608.10

titleholder 470.2

title of respect or address 527.3

title page label 517.13
- book part 554.12
- caption 937.2

titrate 801.6

tits
- *n* bosom 283.7
- *adj* excellent 999.13

tizzy dither 105.6
- confusion 985.3

TKO 754.3

TLC carefulness 339.1
- support 449.3

to at 159.27
- toward 161.26
- into 189.14
- as far as 261.20
- for the purpose of 380.11
- until 821.15

toad sycophant 138.3
- amphibian 311.26

to a degree
- to some extent 245.7
- limited 248.10
- relatively 775.12

toad-stool 310.4

to advantage
- usefully 387.26
- helpfully 449.24
- profitably 472.17
- expediently 995.8

toady
- *n* sycophant 138.3
- assenter 332.6
- *v* fawn 138.7

to a fault 993.23

to a great extent 247.15

to all appearances
- apparently 33.12
- externally 206.10

to a man 332.17

to and fro
- reciprocally 777.12
- alternately 850.11
- changeably 854.8
- back and forth 916.21

toast
- *n* pledge 88.10
- celebration 487.1
- fine lady 500.10
- *v* drink 8.29
- cook 11.5
- drink to 88.29
- be hot 1019.22
- *adj* brown 40.3
- delightful 97.8

to a T
- to completion 407.14
- exactly 973.21
- to a nicety 973.23
- to perfection 1002.11

to a turn
- carefully 339.15
- to completion 407.14
- to a nicety 973.23

to perfection 1002.11

tobacco
- *n* tabac 89.1
- *adj* tobaccoey 89.15

to beat the band
- swiftly 174.18
- utterly 794.16
- to perfection 1002.11

to be brief 537.8

to be desired
- desirable 100.30
- expedient 995.5

to be exact 973.22

to be expected
- *adj* as expected 130.14
- *adv* imminently 840.4
- normally 869.10

to be fair 649.11

to be reckoned with 894.13

to be seen
- visible 31.6
- manifest 348.8

to be specific 865.15

to be sure
- *adv* surely 970.24
- *interj* yes 332.18

toboggan 177.35

to boot 253.11

to come
- approaching 167.4
- future 839.8
- imminent 840.3
- scheduled 965.9

to completion 407.14

tocsin
- warning sign 399.3
- alarm 400.1

to date 838.4

today
- *n* the present 838.1
- *adv* now 838.3

toddle off 175.6

toddler 302.9

to die for 100.3

to-do
- excitement 105.4
- bustle 330.4
- commotion 810.4
- agitation 917.1

to-do list 871.1

toe base 199.2
- foot 199.5

toehold hold 474.2
- wrestling 474.3
- footing 901.5
- purchase 906.2

toe the mark
- obey 326.2
- follow the rule 867.4

toe-to-toe 779.6

to extremes
- intemperately 669.10
- in or to excess 993.23

tofu 10.48

together
- *v* assemble 770.18
- *adj* composed 106.13
- in accord 455.3
- sane 925.4
- *adv* unanimously 332.17
- cooperatively 450.6

- collectively 769.11
- jointly 800.18
- continuously 812.10
- simultaneously 836.7
- concurrently 899.5

togetherness
- accord 455.1
- accompaniment 769.1

toggle 800.8

to good use 387.26

togs clothing 5.1
- garment 5.3

toil
- *n* work 725.4
- *v* work 724.12
- drudge 725.14
- hamper 1012.11

toilet
- *n* latrine 12.10
- stool 12.11
- bathroom 197.26
- casino 759.19
- *adj* cursing 513.8

toiletries 735.6

to infinity 823.4

token
- *n* omen 133.3
- symbol 517.2
- password 517.12
- label 517.13
- sign 518.6
- record 549.1
- counter 728.12
- substitute 862.2
- characteristic 865.4
- evidence 957.1
- memento 989.6
- *v* augur 133.11
- manifest 348.5
- *adj* cheap 633.7
- substitute 862.8

token gesture 354.6

to leeward
- leeward 182.68
- windward 218.9

tolerable
- bearable 107.13
- satisfactory 999.20
- mediocre 1005.7

tolerance
- resistance 87.1
- patience 134.1
- forgiveness 148.1
- leniency 427.1
- latitude 430.4
- liberalism 430.10
- sufferance 443.2
- inclusion 772.1
- inaccuracy 975.2
- broad-mindedness 979.4

tolerate endure 134.5
- be easy on 427.5
- suffer 443.10
- keep an open mind 979.7

toll
- *n* ringing 54.3
- fee 630.6
- tax 630.9
- *v* ring 54.8

tollbooth 228.9

tomahawk 745.5

adv inversely 205.8
contrarily 779.9
Torah 683.3
torch
n blowtorch 1020.14
lighter 1021.4
light source 1026.1
flame 1026.3
v ignite 1020.22
torched 1020.30
torchiere 1026.6
toreador 461.4
torment
n agony 26.6
torture 96.7
tormentor 96.10
harshness 98.4
worry 126.2
punishment 604.2
bane 1001.1
v pain 26.7
annoy 96.13
torture 96.18
desolate 98.12
aggrieve 112.19
make anxious 126.5
bear malice 144.15
persecute 389.7
work evil 1000.6
trouble 1013.13
torn affected 93.23
impaired 393.27
shabby 393.32
alienated 589.11
severed 802.23
tornado outburst 105.9
whirlwind 318.13
storm 671.4
torpedo
n killer 308.11
missile 462.18
ruffian 593.4
rocket 1074.3
v destroy 395.11
attack 459.22
shoot 904.12
torpor apathy 94.4
inertness 173.4
inaction 329.1
languor 331.6
permanence 853.1
torque circle 280.3
necklace 498.6
Torquemada 144.14
torrential flowing 238.24
rainy 316.11
torrid 1019.25
torsion deflection 164.2
distortion 265.1
convolution 281.1
torso 1052.3
tort misdeed 655.2
offense 674.4
tortellini 10.33
tortilla 10.29
tortoise slowpoke 175.5
reptile 311.24
tortoise shell 47.6
**The Tortoise which Supports
the Earth** 901.3
tortoni 10.47

tortuous
distorted 265.10
curved 279.7
convolutional 281.6
grandiloquent 545.8
torture
n agony 26.6
torment 96.7
harshness 98.4
deflection 164.2
punishment 604.2
v pain 26.7
torment 96.18
agonize 98.12
bear malice 144.15
deflect 164.5
pervert 265.6
deform 265.7
misinterpret 342.2
put to the question 604.16
work evil 1000.6
Tory 611.9
to spare
remaining 256.7
unused 390.12
superfluous 993.17
toss
n gamble 759.2
throw 904.3
flounder 917.8
search 938.33
even chance 972.7
v be excited 105.18
put violently 159.13
pitch 182.55
billow 238.22
gamble 759.23
throw 904.10
oscillate 916.10
flounder 917.15
ransack 938.33
toss and turn
keep awake 23.3
be excited 105.18
flounder 917.15
toss-up election 609.15
uncertainty 759.2
stop 857.2
gamble 971.8
even chance 972.7
total
n amount 244.2
math terms 253.2
whole 792.2
sum 1017.6
v compute 253.6
spoil 393.11
demolish 395.17
amount to 792.8
sum up 1017.19
adj great 247.6
downright 247.12
unmitigated 671.17
cumulative 770.23
comprehensive 772.7
whole 792.9
complete 794.9
thorough 794.10
universal 864.14
unqualified 960.2
sound 1002.7

total assets assets 471.7
funds 728.14
total darkness
darkness 38.2
darkness 1027.1
total eclipse
darkness 1027.8
sun 1072.13
totaled high 87.24
spoiled 393.29
disintegrative 806.5
ended 820.9
totalitarian
authoritative 417.15
governmental 612.16
totality whole 792.1
wholeness 792.5
completeness 794.1
all 864.4
universe 1072.1
total lack 222.1
total loss
wreck 393.8
debacle 395.4
failure 410.2
loss 473.1
total recall 989.2
total victory 411.1
total war
death struggle 457.6
war 458.1
tote board 759.17
to tell the truth
truthfully 644.22
truly 973.18
totem symbol 517.2
race 559.4
familiar spirit 678.12
idol 697.3
totem pole
shaft 273.1
symbol 517.2
tote up compute 253.6
sum up 1017.19
to the contrary
adv contrarily 779.9
interj no 335.8
by no means 335.9
to the death
deathly 307.36
throughout 794.17
to the end to completion
407.14
throughout 794.17
to the bitter end 820.13
to the extreme 993.23
to the four winds
from everywhere 158.14
in every direction 161.25
to the good
helpfully 449.24
profitably 472.17
to one's account 622.9
to the heart of 207.13
to the hilt
completely 794.14
throughout 794.17
to the letter 973.21
to the limit
to completion 407.14
utterly 794.16

to the max
utterly 794.16
in excess 993.23
to the nth degree 794.16
to the point
adj concise 537.6
relevant 775.11
apt 788.10
adv plainly 535.4
to the second 845.14
to the side
adj side 218.6
adv aside 218.10
to the tune of
adv at a price 630.17
prep to the amount of 244.7
toting up 253.3
tots 302.2
totter
n gait 177.12
flounder 917.8
v be weak 16.8
go slow 175.6
ways of walking 177.28
tumble 194.8
age 303.10
vacillate 362.8
break down 393.24
change 854.5
flounder 917.15
touch
n senses 24.5
touch 73.1
unfeeling 94.1
contact 223.5
hint 248.4
lightness 298.1
communication 343.1
skill 413.1
knack 413.6
motif 498.7
signal 517.15
implication 519.2
execution 708.30
admixture 797.7
tap 902.7
v sense 24.6
touch 73.6
affect 93.14
excite pity 145.5
contact 223.10
beg 440.15
signal 517.22
borrow 621.3
relate to 775.5
equal 790.5
tap 902.18
touch and go
gamble 759.2
uncertainty 971.8
even chance 972.7
touch a nerve 24.8
touchdown
landing 184.18
score 409.5
game 746.3
touché
adv right! 973.24
phrs that's it 788.13
touched affected 93.23
penitent 113.9

be revealed 351.8
occur 831.5

transplant
  n insertion 191.1
  plant 739.3
  v treat 91.24
  transfer 176.10
  implant 191.8
  set 1069.18

transport
  n happiness 95.2
  fury 105.8
  transportation 176.3
  trance 691.3
  v delight 95.10
  convey 176.12
  fascinate 377.7
  banish 909.17

transportation
  transplacement 176.1
  conveyance 176.3
  banishment 909.4

transpose
  transfer 176.10
  invert 205.5
  compose 708.46
  reverse 779.5
  interchange 863.4

transsexual 75.17

transverse
  n crosspiece 170.5
  diagonal 204.7
  v cross 170.6
  adj transversal 170.9
  crosswise 204.19
  adv crossways 170.13

transvestite
  n sexual pervert 75.16
  adj homosexual 75.30

trap
  n mouth 292.4
  ambush 346.3
  gin 356.12
  lure 377.3
  basketball game 747.3
  soccer 752.3
  hidden danger 1006.5
  v entrap 356.20
  catch 480.17
  play 752.4

trapeze 725.7
trapezoid 278.9
trapper 382.5

trappings
  wardrobe 5.2
  harness 385.5
  belongings 471.2
  finery 498.3

Trappist
  n religious person 667.2
  adj ascetic 667.4

trap shooting 744.1

trash
  n derelict 370.4
  rubbish 391.5
  nonsense 520.2
  rabble 606.3
  poker 759.10
  trivia 998.4
  v be disrespectful 156.6
  censure 510.13

trashy worthless 391.11
  nonsensical 520.7
  paltry 998.21

trauma shock 85.26
  wound 85.38
  psychological stress
  92.17

traumatic 393.27

travail
  n birth 1.1
  work 725.4
  v give birth 1.3
  drudge 725.14

travel
  n progression 162.1
  course 172.2
  transportation 176.3
  journeying 177.1
  traveling 177.1
  v progress 162.2
  move 172.5
  go 177.18
  journey 177.21

travel agency 177.5
travels 177.2

traverse
  n crosspiece 170.5
  v cross 170.6
  travel 177.20
  navigate 182.13
  oppose 451.3
  contradict 451.6
  ski 753.4
  adj transverse 170.9
  adv crosswise 170.13

travesty
  n reproduction 336.3
  bad likeness 350.2
  exaggeration 355.1
  wit 489.1
  burlesque 508.6
  v misrepresent 350.3
  exaggerate 355.3
  burlesque 508.11

trawler 382.6

treacherous
  falsehearted 354.31
  deceitful 356.22
  perfidious 645.21
  unreliable 971.20
  unsafe 1006.11

treachery
  falseheartedness 354.4
  treacherousness 645.6
  unreliability 971.6

treacle sweetening 66.2
  semiliquid 1062.5

tread
  n velocity 172.4
  travel 177.11
  gait 177.12
  step 193.5
  degree 245.1
  v walk 177.27
  stamp 902.22

treading water 182.11

treadmill
  n routine 373.5
  punishment 605.3
  work 725.4
  adj tedious 118.9

tread underfoot
  conquer 412.10
  subdue 432.9
  domineer 612.15

treason apostasy 363.2
  petty crime 645.7
  conversion 858.3

treasure
  n store 386.1
  wealth 618.1
  funds 728.14
  collection 770.11
  good thing 999.5
  v cherish 104.20
  store up 386.11
  hold 474.7
  keep in memory 989.12
  value 997.13

Treasure Island 986.11

treasurer
  executive 574.3
  payer 624.9
  financial officer 729.12

treasury store 386.1
  bank 386.6
  funds 728.14
  cash 728.18
  treasure-house 729.13
  collection 770.11

treasury bill 728.11

treat
  n meal 8.5
  delicacy 10.8
  regalement 95.3
  payment 624.8
  v remedy 86.38
  practice medicine 90.14
  doctor 91.24
  use 321.6
  handle 387.12
  prepare 405.6
  discuss 541.11
  write upon 556.5
  pay for 624.19
  operate on 889.6

treatise tract 556
  piece 556.1

treatment
  medicine 90.1
  therapy 91.1
  medical attention 91.14
  usage 387.2
  preparation 405.1
  discussion 541.6
  treatise 556.1
  script 706.3
  technique 712.8

treaty 437.2

treble
  n stridency 58.6
  air 708.4
  part 708.22
  voice 709.5
  v triplicate 877.2
  adj high 58.13
  vocal 708.50
  triple 877.3

tree
  n cross 170.4
  spar 180.13
  timber 310.10

  genealogy 560.5
  execution 605.5
  v corner 1013.16

tree line 237.2

trek
  n migration 177.4
  journey 177.5
  v journey 177.21
  migrate 177.22

trellis
  n network 170.3
  v net 170.7

tremble
  n trepidation 105.5
  trill 709.19
  agitate 917.3
  v be weak 16.8
  be excited 105.18
  shake 127.14
  fidget 128.6
  quiver 917.11
  freeze 1023.9

tremendous
  terrible 127.30
  large 247.7
  huge 257.20
  superb 999.15

tremor thrill 105.2
  trepidation 105.5
  speech defect 525.1
  trill 709.19
  shake 917.3

tremulous
  fearful 127.23
  jittery 128.12
  inarticulate 525.12
  shaking 917.17

trench
  n crack 224.2
  channel 239.1
  ocean depths 275.4
  valley 284.9
  trough 290.2
  entrenchment 460.5
  shelter 1009.3
  v intrude 214.5
  cleave 224.4
  channel 239.15
  excavate 284.15
  furrow 290.3

trenchant
  energetic 17.13
  acrimonious 17.14
  pungent 68.6
  caustic 144.23
  vigorous 544.11
  sagacious 920.16

trencherman eater 8.16
  glutton 672.3

trench warfare 458.1

trend
  n direction 161.1
  course 172.2
  flow 238.4
  fashion 578.1
  drift 896.2
  v take direction 161.7
  deviate 164.3
  flow 238.16
  tend 896.3

trendsetter 578.7

trendy
fashionable 578.11
faddish 578.15
knowledgeable 928.17
trepidacious 126.7
trepidation
trepidity 105.5
fear 127.5
nervousness 128.1
agitation 917.1
trés bien 332.18
trés bon 999.12
tres chic 5.46
trespass
n intrusion 214.1
violation 435.2
usurpation 640.3
misdeed 655.2
lawbreaking 674.3
overstepping 910.3
v intrude 214.5
violate 435.4
usurp 640.8
do wrong 655.4
break the law 674.5
overstep 910.9
tresses 3.4
trestle
railway 383.7
horse 901.16
trey card 758.2
three 876.1
trial
n annoyance 96.2
tribulation 96.9
attempt 403.2
preparation 405.1
contest 457.3
number 530.8
legal action 598.5
experiment 942.1
test 942.2
adversity 1011.1
adj tentative 403.16
three 876.3
experimental 942.11
trial and error
attempt 403.2
experiment 942.1
trial balloon
question 938.10
feeler 942.4
trial by jury 598.5
trial lawyer 597.1
trials and tribulations 96.9
triangle bell 54.4
love affair 104.5
straightedge 277.3
punishment 605.3
three 876.1
triangulate
v locate 159.11
measure 300.10
adj tripartite 878.4
triannual 876.3
triathlon sport 744.1
track meet 755.2
tribe race 559.4
company 770.3
kind 809.3
classifications 809.5

tribunal
n council 423.1
court 595.1
forum 595.1
platform 901.13
adj judicial 595.7
tributary
n feeder 238.3
adj subject 432.13
tribute demand 421.1
gift 478.4
celebration 487.1
praise 509.5
fee 624.5
tax 630.9
citation 646.4
acknowledgment 888.2
trick
n act 328.3
artifice 356.6
habit 373.3
pretext 376.1
intrigue 381.5
knack 413.6
stratagem 415.3
prank 489.10
mannerism 500.2
style 532.2
bridge 758.3
shift 825.3
characteristic 865.4
quirk 927.2
goof 975.6
illusion 976.1
expedient 995.2
v deceive 356.14
fool 356.15
live by one's wits 415.9
play a practical joke 489.14
trickle
n leakage 190.5
tricklet 238.7
a few 885.2
v leak 190.14
dribble 238.18
tricks of the trade 356.6
tricky deceptive 356.21
deceitful 356.22
cunning 415.12
waggish 489.17
dishonest 645.15
improper 645.18
treacherous 645.21
difficult 1013.17
tricycle 179.8
trident
n fork 171.4
three 876.1
adj tripartite 878.4
tried and true
experienced 413.28
devoted 587.21
trustworthy 644.19
traditional 842.12
proven 942.12
trifle
n hardly anything 248.5
thing of naught 764.2
particular 766.3
triviality 998.5
v waste time 331.13

leave undone 340.7
make love 562.14
be foolish 923.6
dally 998.14
trifle with
disrespect 156.4
do carelessly 340.9
trifurcation 878.1
trigger
n immediate cause 886.3
v kindle 375.18
explode 671.14
cause 886.10
receive 1036.17
trigger-happy
jittery 128.12
warlike 458.20
trigger man
killer 308.11
ruffian 593.4
triglyceride 7.7
trigonal
triangular 278.8
tripartite 878.4
trigonometry 278.3
trihedral sided 218.7
tripartite 878.4
trilateral sided 218.7
triangular 278.8
tripartite 878.4
trilemma 1013.7
trill
n trillo 709.19
v ripple 52.11
bird sound 60.5
leak 190.14
sing 708.38
trilogy 876.1
trim
n ornamentation 498.1
good condition 765.3
v cut the hair 3.22
trim ship 182.49
border 211.10
shorten 268.6
prepare 405.6
defeat 412.9
remain neutral 467.5
ornament 498.8
disapprove 510.18
punish 604.15
cheapen 633.6
fasten 800.7
sever 802.11
tidy 808.12
reel in 906.9
adj in trim 180.19
shipshape 180.20
shapely 264.5
elegant 533.6
chic 578.13
tidy 807.8
trimester
moment 824.2
three 876.1
trim sail 182.20
trim size volume 554.4
makeup 554.12
trinity three 876.1
threeness 876.2
Godhead 677.9

trinket gewgaw 498.4
toy 743.16
trifle 998.5
Trinkgeld 478.5
trinomial
n three 876.1
adj terminological 527.17
trio cooperation 450.1
part music 708.18
three 876.1
trip
n journey 177.5
flight 184.9
tumble 194.3
bungle 414.5
misdeed 655.2
group of animals 770.5
slip 975.4
illusion 976.1
figment of the imagination 986.5
v use 87.22
speed 174.8
way of walking 177.28
tumble 194.8
trap 356.20
caper 366.6
overcome 412.7
bungle 414.11
go wrong 654.9
explode 671.14
dance 705.5
play 743.23
fell 913.5
err 975.9
dream 986.17
tripartite 878.4
tripe food 10.20
bull 520.3
triple
n game 745.3
v intensify 251.5
play 745.5
triplicate 877.2
adj three 876.3
triplicate 877.3
triple crown
ecclesiastical insignia 647.4
horse racing 757.1
three 876.1
triple play 745.3
triplet note 709.14
tempo 709.24
poetry 720.9
three 876.1
triplicate
n reproduce 785.3
triplication 877.1
v copy 785.8
triple 877.2
adj triple 877.3
tripod three 876.1
fire iron 1020.12
tripping
n hallucination 976.7
adj high 87.24
harmonious 533.8
fluent 544.9
trip up
abase 137.5
trap 356.20

overcome 412.7
discompose 811.4
fell 913.5
make a boner 975.15
distract 985.6
tripwire 1006.5
trisect 878.3
trite corny 117.9
habitual 373.14
commonplace 864.16
well-known 928.27
aphoristic 974.6
trivial 998.19
tritium 1038.5
Triton
spirit of the sea
240.3
water god 678.10
triumph
n rejoicing 116.1
great success 409.3
victory 411.1
celebration 487.1
crowing 502.4
v best 249.7
win through 409.13
prevail 411.3
exult 502.9
triumphant
successful 409.14
victorious 411.7
crowing 502.13
triumvirate
cooperation 450.1
government 612.4
three 876.1
trivet
three 876.1
fire iron 1020.12
trivia 551.1
trivial
insignificant 248.6
inadequate 250.7
shallow 276.5
worthless 391.11
quibbling 936.14
trifling 998.19
triviata 998.4
troglodyte
barbarian 497.7
ancient 842.7
troika
cooperation 450.1
three 876.1
Trojan horse
subversive 357.11
language 1042.13
troll
n round 708.19
v fish 382.10
sing 708.38
push 904.9
pull 905.4
roll 915.10
trolley handcar 179.16
streetcar 179.17
trollop reprobate 660.4
strumpet 665.14
slob 810.7
trombonist 710.4
tromp 177.28

troop
military unit 461.22
company 770.3
group of animals 770.5
trooper
cavalryman 461.12
war-horse 461.30
policeman 1008.15
trophy
desire 100.11
victory 411.1
monument 549.12
laurel 646.3
tennis 748.1
memento 989.6
good thing 999.5
tropical 1019.24
tropical fish 311.30
tropical fruit 10.38
Tropic of Cancer 231.3
Tropic of Capricorn
231.3
tropics zone 231.3
hot place 1019.11
trot
n run 174.3
gait 177.12
old woman 304.3
translation 341.3
repetitiousness 849.4
v speed 174.8
go on horseback 177.34
depart 188.7
trot out 348.5
trotter foot 199.5
race horse 311.14
jockey 757.2
troubadour
wanderer 178.2
minstrel 710.14
poet 720.11
trouble
n annoyance 96.2
affliction 96.8
anxiety 126.1
imposition 643.1
exertion 725.1
commotion 810.4
inconvenience 996.3
adversity 1011.1
impediment 1012.6
the matter 1013.3
v distress 96.16
vex 98.15
excite 105.14
concern 126.4
presume upon 640.7
discompose 811.4
agitate 917.10
inconvenience 996.4
beset 1013.13
trouble-free
perfect 1002.6
unhazardous 1007.5
troublemaker
rebel 327.5
instigator 375.11
mischief-maker 593.2
troubleshooter 396.10
troubleshooting 466.1
trouble spot 458.1

trough
n atmosphere 184.32
wave 238.14
channel 239.1
gutter 239.3
cavity 284.2
valley 284.9
trench 290.2
oscillation 916.4
v excavate 284.15
furrow 290.3
trounce best 249.7
defeat 412.9
criticize 510.20
whip 604.13
troupe
n cast 707.11
company 770.3
v act 704.29
trousers 5.18
trousseau 5.2
trove find 472.6
discovery 941.1
trowel 1040.2
truant
n absentee 222.5
shirker 368.3
wretch 660.2
adj absent without leave
222.13
truce armistice 465.5
pause 857.3
truck
n lorry 179.12
communication 343.1
rubbish 391.5
impedimenta 471.3
commerce 731.1
groceries 735.7
relation 775.1
v haul 176.13
trade 731.15
truculent
cruel 144.26
warlike 458.20
gruff 505.7
trudge
n slow motion 175.2
walk 177.10
v plod 175.7
way of walking 177.28
true
v make agree 788.7
adj straight 277.6
firm 359.12
observant 434.4
devoted 587.21
honest 644.16
trustworthy 644.19
faithful 644.20
orthodox 687.7
real 761.15
certain 970.13
truthful 973.13
true believer
orthodox Christian 687.4
believer 953.9
true blue fidelity 644.7
person of honor 644.8
true course
direction 161.2

course 184.34
true meaning 518.1
true to form
typical 349.15
characteristic 865.13
true to life
descriptive 349.14
lifelike 784.16
genuine 973.15
truism
generalization 864.8
axiom 974.2
truly
adv really 761.16
certainly 970.23
interj yes 332.18
trump
n good person 659.2
bridge 758.3
expedient 995.2
v excel 249.6
trump card
opportunity 843.2
influence 894.1
trumped-up 354.28
trumpet
n blare 53.5
v blare 53.10
proclaim 352.13
flaunt 501.17
praise 509.12
speak 524.25
blow a horn 708.42
truncate excise 255.10
deform 265.7
shorten 268.6
truncheon
n scepter 417.9
v whip 604.13
trundle push 904.9
roll 915.10
trunk
cylinder 282.4
nose 283.8
stem 310.21
line 347.17
base 901.8
body 1052.3
trunk line 347.17
trunks 5.29
truss
n bundle 770.8
v bundle 770.20
bind 800.9
trust
n hope 124.1
estate 471.4
commission 615.1
association 617.9
credit 622.1
investment company 737.16
belief 953.1
confidence 970.5
v hope 124.6
commit 478.16
give credit 622.6
believe 953.10
confide in 953.17
trustee fiduciary 470.5
recipient 479.3
treasurer 729.12

trust fund 737.16
trustworthy
  trusty 644.19
  believable 953.24
  reliable 970.17
  unhazardous 1007.5
trusty
  n prisoner 429.11
  person of honor 644.8
  adj trustworthy 644.19
  dependable 953.22
  believable 953.24
  reliable 970.17
truth
  honesty 644.3
  reality 761.2
  certainty 970.1
  trueness 973.1
  axiom 974.2
the truth, the whole truth,
  and nothing but the truth
  973.3
the truth of the matter
  fact 761.3
  existence 761.4
  the real story 973.3
try
  n attempt 403.3
  test 942.2
  v refine 79.22
  attempt 403.6
  try a case 598.18
  experiment 942.8
  sit in judgment 946.12
trying
  n experiment 942.1
  adj weakening 16.20
  fatiguing 21.13
  oppressive 98.24
  examining 938.37
  experimental 942.11
  adverse 1011.13
  troublesome 1013.18
tryout
  audition 48.2
  preparation 405.1
  theatrical performance 704.12
  workout 942.3
trypsin 7.10
tryst 582.9
T-shirt 5.15
tsk tsk! 98.31
T square
  instrument 200.6
  straightedge 277.3
tsunami wave 238.14
  upheaval 671.5
  wave 916.4
tub
  n bath 79.8
  washbasin 79.12
  car 179.10
  ship 180.1
  heavyweight 257.12
  v wash 79.19
tubby corpulent 257.18
  stubby 268.10
tube
  n train 179.14
  pipe 239.6
  cylinder 282.4

wave 916.4
  electronics 1033.10
  v transport 176.14
tuber 310.22
tuberculosis
  epidemic 85.5
  white plague 85.17
tubing 239.6
tub-thumper 543.4
tubular tubate 239.16
  cylindric 282.11
tuck
  n food 10.2
  fold 291.1
  game 746.3
  race 753.3
  v fold 291.5
tuckered out 21.8
tuff 1059.1
tuft flock 3.6
  beard 3.8
  feather 3.16
  growth 310.2
  bunch 770.7
tug
  n strain 725.2
  pull 905.2
  attraction 907.1
  v strain 725.10
  pull 905.4
  attract 907.4
tug-of-war fight 457.4
  pulling 905.1
tuition 568.1
tumble
  n fall 194.3
  collapse 410.3
  jumble 810.3
  flounder 917.8
  v be excited 105.18
  pitch 182.55
  fall 194.8
  be destroyed 395.22
  lose 412.12
  confuse 811.3
  fell 913.5
  wallow 915.13
  flounder 917.15
  confound 945.3
tummy goozle 2.19
  middle 819.1
tummyache 26.5
tumor symptom 85.9
  growth 85.39
  swelling 283.4
tumult noise 53.3
  excitement 105.4
  bustle 330.4
  turbulence 671.2
  commotion 810.4
  agitation 917.1
tundra plain 236.1
  cold place 1023.4
tune
  n melody 708.2
  harmony 708.3
  air 708.4
  pitch 709.4
  v fit 405.8
  harmonize 708.35
  tune up 708.36

make agree 788.7
  organize 808.10
  rearrange 808.13
tune in
  listen in 1034.27
  receive 1036.17
tune out exclude 773.4
  be inattentive 984.2
  listen in 1034.27
tune up tune 708.36
  organize 808.10
  rearrange 808.13
  listen in 1034.27
tuning fork 711.22
tunnel
  n lair 228.26
  channel 239.1
  cave 284.5
  passageway 383.3
  entrenchment 460.5
  v deepen 275.8
  excavate 284.15
tunnel vision
  faulty eyesight 28.1
  narrow-mindedness 980.1
turbid
  disorderly 810.13
  opaque 1031.3
  fluid 1061.4
  slimy 1062.14
turbinado sugar 66.2
turbine 904.6
turbocharger 756.1
turbojet 181.3
turbulent
  noisy 53.13
  tumultuous 105.24
  stormy 318.22
  rebellious 327.11
  bustling 330.20
  violent 671.18
  disorderly 810.13
  agitated 917.16
turd feces 12.4
  bad person 660.5
turf abode 228.1
  sod 310.6
  arena 463.1
  occupation 724.4
  horse racing 757.1
  sphere of influence 894.4
turf war 456.5
turgid
  distended 259.13
  bulged 283.16
  pompous 501.22
  stiff 534.3
  bombastic 545.9
turkey
  poultry 311.28
  failure 410.2
  loser 410.8
  stage show 704.4
  game 750.2
Turkish bath 79.8
turmoil
  excitement 105.4
  anarchy 418.2
  turbulence 671.2
  jumble 810.3
  commotion 810.4

agitation 917.1
turn
  n looks 33.4
  inclination 100.3
  start 131.3
  act of kindness 143.7
  deviation 164.1
  journey 177.5
  walk 177.10
  bias 204.3
  form 262.1
  distortion 265.1
  bend 279.3
  act 328.3
  aptitude 413.5
  show business 704.7
  ornament 709.18
  transaction 731.4
  trading 737.19
  ski move 753.3
  race 756.3
  bout 825.2
  shift 825.3
  crisis 843.4
  round 850.3
  change 852.1
  reversion 859.1
  tendency 896.1
  circuitousness 914.1
  circuit 914.2
  whirl 915.2
  disposition 978.3
  v direct 161.5
  take direction 161.7
  turn round 163.9
  deviate 164.3
  change course 182.30
  oblique 204.9
  distort 265.5
  curve 279.6
  convolve 281.4
  blunt 286.2
  ski 753.4
  recur 850.5
  be changed 852.6
  change 854.5
  turn back 859.5
  tend 896.3
  go around 914.6
  rotate 915.9
turn a blind eye
  take 134.8
  exclude 773.4
  be inattentive 984.2
turnabout
  n regression 163.3
  reverse 363.1
  apostate 363.5
  change 852.1
  reversion 859.1
  v turn 163.9
turn a deaf ear
  be deaf 49.4
  show no mercy 146.2
  exclude 773.4
turn against
  act the traitor 645.15
  defect 858.13
turnaround
  n regression 163.3
  reverse 363.1

v turn 163.9

turn aside
deviate 164.3
avoid 164.6
disincline 379.4
fend off 460.10
digress 538.9
be changed 852.6
pull back 903.7
prevent 1012.14

turn away avoid 164.6
reject 372.2
disincline 379.4

turn back
put back 163.8
avoid 164.6
change course 182.30
repeat 849.11
convert 858.11
change back 859.5
repulse 908.3

turn back the clock
make young 301.8
be conservative 853.6

turncoat
n traitor 357.10
apostate 363.5
convert 858.8
adj traitorous 645.22

turn down invert 205.5
refuse 442.3

turn down the volume
670.6

turned 393.41

turn in go to bed 22.18
invert 205.5
betray 645.14

turn informer 551.12

turning point
crisis 843.4
crucial moment 843.5
urgency 997.4
salient point 997.6

turn in one's badge 448.2

turn inside out
invert 205.5
ransack 938.33

turn into
translate 341.12
become 761.12
be changed 852.6
convert 858.11
be converted into 858.17

turnip 832.6

turn loose 431.5

turn of events 831.2

turn off offend 98.11
disincline 379.4
shut off 857.12
dismiss 909.18
stop 909.19
electrify 1032.26

turn of phrase 529.1

turn of the screw 251.2

turn on excite 105.12
rouse 375.19
inaugurate 818.11
result from 887.5
depend 959.6
electrify 1032.26

turn on a dime 163.9

turn one's back on
quit 188.9
slight 340.8
defect 370.6
reject 372.2
refuse 442.3

turn one's stomach 64.4

turnout wardrobe 5.2
rig 179.5
attendance 221.4
assembly 770.2

turn out outfit 5.41
get up 23.6
invert 205.5
reject 372.2
equip 385.8
be in a certain state 765.5
happen 831.7
result 887.4
eject 909.13
evict 909.15
dismiss 909.19
come true 973.12

turnover pastry 10.41
overturn 205.2
sale 734.1
game 746.3
error 747.3

turn over
transfer 176.10
capsize 182.44
invert 205.5
overturn 205.6
fold 291.5
relinquish 475.3
deliver 478.13
submit 629.3
sell 734.8
think over 931.13

turn over a new leaf
make better 392.9
change 852.7
re-form 858.12

turn state's evidence
betray 351.6
inform on 551.12

turn swords into plowshares
465.11

turntable 50.11

turn the corner
recuperate 396.19
be changed 852.6

turn the other cheek
take 134.8
condone 148.4

turn the tables
invert 205.5
change 852.7
gain influence 894.12

turn the tide 852.7

turn the trick
accomplish 407.4
succeed with 409.11

turn thumbs down 586.6

turn to
be converted into 858.17
practice 328.8
avail oneself of 387.14
undertake 404.3
set to work 725.15
begin 818.7

attend to 983.5

turn up appear 33.8
be unexpected 131.6
arrive 186.6
upturn 193.13
attend 221.8
show up 831.6
uncover 941.4
discover 941.9
chance 972.11

turn up one's nose at
spurn 157.4
reject 372.2
disapprove 510.10
dismiss 984.4

turn upside down
invert 205.5
overturn 205.6
ransack 938.33

turpentine 35.8

turquoise 45.3

turret 272.6

turtle 311.24

tush teeth 2.8
buttocks 217.5

tusk
n teeth 2.8
v gore 459.26

tussle
n quarrel 456.5
fight 457.4
struggle 725.3
v contend 457.13
struggle 725.11

tutelage
dependence 432.3
patronage 449.4
teaching 568.1
instructorship 571.10
disciple 572.2
protectorship 1008.2

tutor
n academic rank 571.3
teacher 571.5
v coach 568.11

tutti-frutti 10.40

tutu 5.9

tuxedo 5.11

TV sexual pervert 75.16
television 1035.1
receiver 1035.11

twain
n two 873.2
adj two 873.6

twang
n rasp 58.3
accent 524.8
speech defect 525.1
v sound harshly 58.9
speak 524.25
nasalize 525.10
strum 708.40

tweak
n pang 26.2
squeezing 260.2
jerk 905.3
v pain 26.7
squeeze 260.8
jerk 905.5

tweedy studious 570.17
pedagogic 571.11

tweenager
adolescence 301.6
youngster 302.1

tweezers 192.9

twelfth 882.24

twelve 882.7

12-hour clock 832.3

twentieth 882.26

twentieth-century 841.13

twenty 882.7

twenty-five 882.7

twenty-four carat 973.15

24-hour 223.15

twenty-four-hour 812.8

24-hour clock 832.3

24-7 812.10

twenty-something 302.1

twenty-twenty 27.21

twerp
bad person 660.5
fool 924.3

twice 874.5

twiddle one's thumbs
do nothing 329.2
idle 331.12

twig
n sprout 302.11
branch 310.20
member 793.4
v see 27.12

twilight
n foredawn 314.4
dusk 315.3
daylight 1025.10
darkishness 1027.2
adj evening 315.8

twilled 291.7

twin
n image 349.5
the same 778.3
likeness 784.3
equal 790.4
v coincide 778.4
double 873.5
duplicate 874.3
adj accompanying 769.9
identical 778.7
analogous 784.11
two 873.6

twine
n cord 271.2
v convolve 281.4
weave 740.6

twinge
n pang 26.2
v suffer 26.8

twinkle
n instant 830.3
glitter 1025.7
v glitter 1025.25

twinkletoes 705.3

twins set 784.5
pair of twins 873.4

twirl
n eddy 238.12
coil 281.2
whirl 915.2
v convolve 281.4
whirl 915.11

twist
n braid 3.7

unadulterated
clean 79.25
unadorned 499.8
unmixed 798.7
unqualified 960.2
genuine 973.15
perfect 1002.6
unaffected
unmoved 94.11
unyielding 361.9
natural 416.6
tasteful 496.7
plain 499.7
elegant 533.6
plain-speaking 535.3
informal 581.3
undeceptive 644.18
uninfluenced 895.5
genuine 973.15
unaffectionate
unfeeling 94.9
unkind 144.16
unafraid
unfearing 492.19
confident 970.21
unaided
adj alone 872.8
adv singly 872.13
unalterable
unyielding 361.9
unchangeable 855.17
inflexible 1046.12
unamazed 123.3
unambiguous
clear 521.11
certain 970.13
unambitious
undesirous 102.8
modest 139.9
unanimous
solid 332.15
agreeing 788.9
unannounced 131.10
unanswerable
exempt 430.30
obvious 970.15
unanticipated
unexpected 131.10
sudden 830.5
unappealing 98.17
unappeased 100.27
unappetizing
unsavory 64.5
unpleasant 98.17
unappreciated 99.9
unapprehended 930.16
unapproachable
peerless 249.15
out-of-the-way 261.9
reticent 344.10
aloof 583.6
inaccessible 967.9
unarguable 970.15
unarmed unfitted 406.9
unprotected 1006.14
unaroused 173.14
unashamed
unregretful 114.4
immodest 666.6
unaspiring
undesirous 102.8

modest 139.9
unimaginative 987.5
unassailable 15.19
unassisted 872.8
unassuming
modest 139.9
natural 416.6
plain 499.7
informal 581.3
undeceptive 644.18
genuine 973.15
unattached
free 430.21
separate 802.20
unattainable
impracticable 967.8
inaccessible 967.9
unattended
separate 802.20
alone 872.8
unprotected 1006.14
unattracted 102.8
unauthorized
prohibited 444.7
illegal 674.6
unavailable 967.9
unavailing
ineffective 19.15
useless 391.9
unavoidable 963.15
unaware
insensible 94.10
inexpectant 131.9
unconscious 930.12
unawed
unastonished 123.3
undaunted 492.20
unbalanced
eccentric 160.12
unjust 650.9
ill-balanced 791.5
insane 926.26
unbathed 80.20
unbearable
insufferable 98.25
downright 247.12
unbeatable
impregnable 15.19
peerless 249.15
unbeaten
unused 390.12
undefeated 411.8
new 841.7
unbecoming
vulgar 497.10
disgraceful 661.11
indecent 666.5
inappropriate 789.7
unbefitting
inappropriate 789.7
untimely 844.6
inexpedient 996.5
unbelievable
fantastic 870.12
incredible 955.10
unbend relax 20.7
straighten 277.5
moderate 670.9
yield 1047.7
unbiased
impartial 649.9

unprejudiced 979.12
unbidden
unwanted 99.11
voluntary 324.7
unwelcome 586.9
unblemished
clean 79.25
honest 644.13
spotless 657.7
chaste 664.4
perfect 1002.6
unblinking
unnervous 129.2
alert 339.14
undaunted 492.20
unblock unclose 292.12
facilitate 1014.7
unborn 762.10
unbound
unrestricted 430.27
untied 430.28
liberated 431.10
unfastened 802.22
unbowed
unweakened 15.21
straight 277.6
undefeated 411.8
unbreakable firm 15.18
nonbreakable 1049.5
unbreatheable 345.11
unbridled
lawless 418.5
unrestrained 430.24
profligate 665.25
intemperate 669.7
unruly 671.19
excessive 993.16
unbroken
directional 161.12
straight 277.6
smooth 287.10
unsubject 430.29
uniform 781.5
continuous 812.8
constant 847.5
undamaged 1002.8
unbuckle
loose 431.6
detach 802.10
unburden
relieve 120.7
lighten 298.6
unload 909.23
unbutton 802.10
uncage 431.6
uncalled-for
unwanted 99.11
impudent 142.10
voluntary 324.7
needless 391.10
superfluous 993.17
uncanny
awesome 122.11
creepy 127.31
deathly 307.28
weird 988.9
uncap 292.12
uncaring
n carelessness 340.2
incuriosity 982.1
adj apathetic 94.13

careless 340.11
unceasing
continuous 812.8
perpetual 829.7
constant 847.5
continuing 856.7
uncensored 430.28
unceremonious 581.3
uncertain
inconspicuous 32.6
irresolute 362.9
ambiguous 539.4
speculative 759.27
relative 775.7
irregular 851.3
inconstant 854.7
doubting 955.9
unsure 971.16
unsafe 1006.11
uncertified
unproved 958.8
unauthoritative 971.21
unchained
unbound 430.28
unfastened 802.22
unchallenged
unanimous 332.15
undoubted 970.16
unchangeable
unyielding 361.9
uniform 781.5
permanent 853.7
not to be changed 855.17
unchanging
almighty 677.17
uniform 781.5
constant 847.5
permanent 853.7
unchangeable 855.17
unchaperoned 340.14
uncharitable
unbenevolent 144.17
narrow-minded 980.10
uncharted 930.16
unchaste
unvirtuous 654.12
sensual 663.5
lascivious 665.23
obscene 666.9
unchecked
lawless 418.5
unrestrained 430.24
permitted 443.16
candid 644.17
permanent 853.7
unauthoritative 971.21
uncirculated 841.9
uncircumcised 688.10
uncircumspec 340.10
uncivilized
cruel 144.26
unrefined 497.12
savage 671.21
unclad 6.13
unclasp release 475.4
detach 802.10
unclassified
open 348.10
unordered 810.12
unknown 930.16
uncle 559.3

unclean
unwashed 80.20
unvirtuous 654.12
unchaste 665.23
obscene 666.9
demoniac 680.17
terrible 1000.9
unclear
inconspicuous 32.6
faint 52.16
formless 263.4
obscure 522.15
illegible 522.19
vague 971.19
unclench 292.12
Uncle Sam
country 232.5
the government 612.3
unclog unclose 292.12
evacuate 909.22
facilitate 1014.7
unclothe 6.7
unclouded visible 31.6
unhidden 348.11
light 1025.32
transparent 1029.4
uncluttered 798.6
uncoded 521.12
uncoil disinvolve 798.5
unfold 861.7
uncollected accounts 628.1
uncolored
colorless 36.7
genuine 973.15
uncombed
unrefined 497.12
disheveled 810.14
uncomfortable
distressed 96.22
unpleasant 98.20
uncommitted
free 430.21
neutral 467.7
cautious 494.8
uncommon
remarkable 247.10
novel 841.11
infrequent 848.2
unusual 870.10
scarce 992.11
uncommunicative
silent 343.10
indisposed to communicate
  344.8
secretive 345.15
cautious 494.8
inexpressive 522.20
unsociable 583.5
uncomplaining
content 107.7
resigned 134.10
submissive 433.12
uncompleted
unaccomplished 408.3
incomplete 795.4
uncomplexity
unadornment 499.3
facility 1014.1
uncomplicated
unadorned 499.8
uninvolved 798.8

easy 1014.13
uncomplimentary 510.21
uncomprehending
undiscerning 922.14
ignorant 930.11
uncompromising
unyielding 361.9
firm 425.7
unconcealed
visible 31.6
unhidden 348.11
unconcerned
insensible 25.6
apathetic 94.13
uninterested 102.7
nonchalant 106.15
incurious 982.3
uncondemned 148.7
unconditional
unrestricted 430.27
thorough 794.10
unqualified 960.2
unconditional love 104.3
unconducive 391.14
unconfined 430.27
unconfirmed
unproved 958.8
unauthoritative 971.21
unconnected
unintelligible 522.13
unrelated 776.6
separate 802.20
incoherent 804.4
discontinuous 813.4
illogical 936.11
unconquered
undefeated 411.8
unsubject 430.29
unconscionable
downright 247.12
overpriced 632.12
dishonest 645.16
unjustifiable 650.12
violent 671.16
excessive 993.16
unconscious
n psyche 92.28
adj asleep 22.22
senseless 25.8
subconscious 92.42
insensible 94.10
unpremeditated 365.11
unaware 930.12
instinctive 934.6
involuntary 963.14
unintentional 972.17
oblivious 984.7
abstracted 985.11
inanimate 1055.5
unconsidered
neglected 340.14
unheeded 340.15
unexamined 340.16
unpremeditated 365.11
unwise 923.10
unthought-of 933.5
unconstitutional 674.6
unconstrained
communicative 343.10
unrestrained 430.24
informal 581.3

candid 644.17
intemperate 669.7
unconsumed
remaining 256.7
unused 390.12
uncontaminated
natural 416.6
perfect 1002.6
uncontested
unanimous 332.15
believed 953.23
undoubted 970.16
uncontrollable
frenzied 105.25
ungovernable 361.12
rabid 926.30
inevitable 963.15
unconventional
informal 581.3
unorthodox 868.6
eccentric 927.5
unconvinced
unbelieving 955.8
uncertain 971.16
uncooked 406.10
uncooperative
inconsiderate 144.18
insubordinate 327.9
obstinate 361.8
unconsenting 442.6
oppositional 451.8
resistant 453.5
uncoordinated 414.20
uncork 292.12
uncorroborated
unproved 958.8
unauthoritative 971.21
uncounted
innumerable 884.10
undecided 971.18
uncouple 802.8
uncouth
countrified 233.7
bungling 414.20
unrefined 497.12
inelegant 534.2
vulgar 666.8
uncover divest 6.5
disinter 192.11
unclose 292.12
disclose 351.4
greet 585.10
unearth 941.4
uncritical
obedient 326.3
unmeticulous 340.13
uncriticizing 509.18
undiscriminating 945.5
credulous 954.4
unction balm 86.11
flattery 511.2
function of Holy Ghost 677.15
sanctimony 693.1
sacred unction 701.5
ointment 1056.3
lubrication 1056.6
uncultivated
countrified 233.7
undeveloped 406.12
fallow 406.14
unrefined 497.12

unproductive 891.4
unlearned 930.13
uncultured
countrified 233.7
undeveloped 406.12
unrefined 497.12
unlearned 930.13
uncurl 277.5
uncut unformed 263.5
undeveloped 406.12
undivided 792.11
complete 794.9
undamaged
preserved 397.13
intact 792.10
unharmed 1002.8
safe 1007.4
undaunted
persevering 360.8
undismayed 492.20
undecided
irresolute 362.9
undetermined 971.18
undecided issue 971.8
undeclared 519.9
undefeated 411.8
undefended 1006.14
undefined
inconspicuous 32.6
formless 263.4
anonymous 528.3
almighty 677.17
vague 971.19
undeflected 277.6
undeformed 1002.8
undemanding
unstrict 426.5
undiscriminating 945.5
undeniable
downright 247.12
real 761.15
obvious 970.15
undependable
fickle 364.6
untrustworthy 645.19
inconstant 854.7
unreliable 971.20
unsafe 1006.11
under
adj lower 274.8
adv below 274.10
prep below 274.11
beneath 432.17
underachiever 572.4
under a cloud
accused 599.15
in disrepute 661.13
unreliable 955.11
doubted 955.12
under advisement 938.38
underage
n deficiency 795.2
shortcoming 911.1
adj immature 301.10
under arrest 429.22
under a spell 691.12
under attack
adj accused 599.15
adv under fire 459.31
underbelly
digestive system 2.18

undeveloped
immature 301.10
unfinished 406.12
inexperienced 414.17
incomplete 795.4
new 841.7
imperfect 1003.4
undeviating
directional 161.12
straight 277.6
uniform 781.5
unchangeable 855.17
exact 973.17
undifferentiated
identical 778.7
uniform 781.5
simple 798.6
continuous 812.8
general 864.11
indistinguishable 945.6
undigested 406.11
undignified
vulgar 497.10
inelegant 534.2
undiluted 798.7
undiminished
unweakened 15.21
unabated 247.14
undivided 792.11
complete 794.9
undirtied 79.25
undiscernible 32.5
undisciplined
disobedient 327.8
lawless 418.5
intemperate 669.7
inconstant 854.7
undisclosed
invisible 32.5
secret 345.11
unrevealed 346.12
unknown 930.16
undiscovered
unrevealed 346.12
unknown 930.16
undisguised
visible 31.6
unhidden 348.11
undeceptive 644.18
genuine 973.15
undismayed 492.20
undisputed
believed 953.23
undoubted 970.16
undistorted
straight 277.6
genuine 973.15
undisturbed
unexcited 106.11
untroubled 107.8
quiescent 173.12
undivided uncut 792.11
joined 800.13
one 872.7
undo take off 6.6
unnerve 128.10
unclose 292.12
do for 395.11
abolish 395.13
demolish 395.17
defeat 412.6

detach 802.10
neutralize 900.7
solve 940.2
undoing
destruction 395.1
defeat 412.1
disassembly 802.6
neutralization 900.2
undoubted
believed 953.23
not to be doubted
970.16
true 973.13
undress
n dishabille 5.20
unadornment 499.3
v unclothe 6.7
undue
overpriced 632.12
wrong 638.3
unowed 640.9
unjust 650.9
excessive 993.16
undulate
v maneuver 184.40
billow 238.22
recur 850.5
wave 916.11
adj wavy 281.10
unduplicated 337.6
undying
immortal 829.9
indestructible 855.18
continuing 856.7
uneager 102.8
unearned 640.9
unearth extract 192.10
uncover 941.4
unearthly
deathly 307.28
heavenly 681.12
godly 692.9
extraneous 774.5
odd 870.11
supernatural 870.15
unbelievable 955.10
weird 988.9
immaterial 1053.7
unease
unpleasure 96.1
discontent 108.1
anxiety 126.1
agitation 917.1
uneasy
pleasureless 96.20
distressed 96.22
restless 105.27
discontented 108.7
anxious 126.7
nervous 128.11
impatient 135.6
agitated 917.16
uneconomical 406.15
uneducated
vernacular 523.20
unlearned 930.13
unembellished
natural 416.6
unadorned 499.8
prosaic 721.5
unemotional 94.9

unemployed
motionless 173.13
idle 331.18
unused 390.12
unencumbered
lightened 298.11
unhampered 430.26
unending
continuous 812.8
perpetual 829.7
continuing 856.7
unendurable 98.25
unenjoyable
unpleasant 98.17
uninteresting 117.7
unenlightened
blind 30.9
ignorant 930.11
unenvied 156.9
unequaled 249.15
unequipped
unfitted 406.9
incompetent 414.19
unequivocal
downright 247.12
unrestricted 430.27
clear 521.11
candid 644.17
unqualified 960.2
certain 970.13
unerring
uncorrupt 653.7
infallible 970.19
exact 973.17
unescorted 872.8
unessential
n nonessential 768.2
adj needless 391.10
circumstantial 766.7
extrinsic 768.4
irrelevant 776.7
superfluous 993.17
insignificant 998.17
unestablished
unplaced 160.10
unproved 958.8
undecided 971.18
unethical
dishonest 645.16
vice-prone 654.11
uneven
rough 288.6
unjust 650.9
nonuniform 782.3
unequal 791.4
irregular 851.3
imperfect 1003.4
uneventful
uninteresting 117.7
tedious 118.9
unexamined 340.16
unexceptional
normal 869.8
ordinary 1005.8
unexhausted
unwearied 9.5
unweakened 15.21
unexpected
unanticipated 131.10
sudden 830.5
unusual 870.10

fantastic 870.12
improbable 969.3
chance 972.15
unexplained
unrevealed 346.12
unknown 930.16
unexplored
unexamined 340.16
unrevealed 346.12
unknown 930.16
unexposed
unrevealed 346.12
unknown 930.16
unfabricated 973.15
unfaded
unweakened 15.21
undamaged 1002.8
unfailing
persevering 360.8
faithful 644.20
permanent 853.7
reliable 970.17
unfair 650.10
unfaithful
nonobservant 435.5
faithless 645.20
unfamiliar
novel 841.11
unusual 870.10
ignorant 930.11
unknown 930.16
unfashionable
old-fashioned 842.16
unconventional 868.6
unfastened 802.22
unfathomable
abysmal 275.11
unintelligible 522.13
infinite 823.3
unfavorable
ominous 133.16
oppositional 451.8
disapproving 510.21
untimely 844.6
disadvantageous 996.6
bad 1000.7
adverse 1011.13
unfed fasting 515.5
ill-provided 992.12
unfeeling
n insensibility 25.1
unfeelingness 94.1
heartlessness 144.10
adj insensible 25.6
unemotional 94.9
heartless 144.25
pitiless 146.3
inanimate 1055.5
unfelt 25.6
unfertile 891.4
unfettered
unbound 430.28
unfastened 802.22
unfilled hungry 100.25
available 222.15
unfinished
undeveloped 406.12
unaccomplished 408.3
unskilled 414.16
incomplete 795.4
imperfect 1003.4

unfit
v disable 19.9
adj unable 19.14
unserviceable 391.14
unfitted 406.9
incompetent 414.19
wrong 638.3
inappropriate 789.7
untimely 844.6
inexpedient 996.5
unflagging
unweakened 15.21
industrious 330.22
persevering 360.8
unflappable
inexcitable 106.10
firm 359.12
stable 855.12
unflattering
undeceptive 644.18
genuine 973.15
unflavored 65.2
unflinching
unnervous 129.2
unhesitating 359.13
persevering 360.8
undaunted 492.20
stable 855.12
unfold spread 259.6
unclose 292.12
explain 341.10
manifest 348.5
disclose 351.4
amplify 538.7
unroll 861.7
result 887.4
unforced
adj voluntary 324.7
unrestrained 430.24
adv at will 323.5
unforeseen
unexpected 131.10
sudden 830.5
chance 972.15
unforgettable
never to be forgotten 989.25
notable 997.19
unforgivable
unjustifiable 650.12
wicked 654.16
unforgotten 989.22
unfortified
unmixed 798.7
unprotected 1006.14
unfortunate
n unlucky person 1011.7
adj ominous 133.16
unsuccessful 410.18
untimely 844.6
inexpedient 996.5
unlucky 1011.14
unfounded false 354.25
unsubstantial 764.8
baseless 936.13
unproved 958.8
unauthentic 975.19
illusory 976.9
unfreeze 1020.21
unfriendly
unpleasant 98.17
averse 99.8

oppositional 451.8
warlike 458.20
unsociable 583.5
inhospitable 586.7
inimical 589.9
unfrozen 1019.24
unfulfilled
pleasureless 96.20
discontented 108.7
unaccomplished 408.3
unfurl disclose 351.4
unfold 861.7
ungainly
bungling 414.20
ungraceful 1015.9
unglued
unnerved 128.14
unfastened 802.22
ungodly
unvirtuous 654.12
godless 695.17
unbelievable 955.10
execrable 1000.10
ungracious
unkind 144.16
discourteous 505.4
inhospitable 586.7
ungrammatical 531.4
ungrateful 151.4
ungrounded
unsubstantial 764.8
baseless 936.13
unguarded
negligent 340.10
unthinking 365.10
artless 416.5
candid 644.17
unintentional 972.17
unalert 984.8
unprotected 1006.14
unguided
unlearned 930.13
unintentional 972.17
unhampered
communicative 343.10
untrammeled 430.26
unqualified 960.2
unhand liberate 431.5
release 475.4
unhappy
pleasureless 96.20
discontented 108.7
uncheerful 112.21
disapproving 510.21
untimely 844.6
inexpedient 996.5
unfortunate 1011.14
unharmed
undamaged 1002.8
safe 1007.4
unharness 431.6
unhealthy
unhealthful 82.5
healthless 85.54
unwholesome 85.55
bad 1000.7
unsafe 1006.11
unheard-of
wonderful 122.10
unrenowned 661.14
novel 841.11

unusual 870.10
unknown 930.16
unheated 1023.13
unheeded 340.15
unheralded 131.10
unhesitant 359.13
unhidden visible 31.6
open 292.17
unconcealed 348.11
unhinged
dislocated 160.9
insane 926.26
unhitch 802.10
unholy unsacred 686.3
ungodly 695.17
execrable 1000.10
unhook 802.10
unhurried slow 175.10
leisurely 402.6
unhurt
undamaged 1002.8
safe 1007.4
unicellular
cellular 305.19
unipartite 872.11
unicorn rig 179.5
heraldry 647.2
unidentified
anonymous 528.3
unknown 930.16
unidentified flying object
1075.3
unidirectional
directional 161.12
unipartite 872.11
uniform
n livery 5.7
insignia 647.1
soccer 752.1
v outfit 5.41
adj symmetric 264.4
smooth 287.10
equable 781.5
agreeing 788.9
simple 798.6
orderly 807.6
continuous 812.8
regular 850.6
one 872.7
indistinguishable 945.6
unify identify 778.5
put together 800.5
combine 805.3
reduce to unity 872.5
unilateral
sided 218.7
unipartite 872.11
unimaginable
wonderful 122.10
fantastic 870.12
unbelievable 955.10
impossible 967.7
unimaginative
dull 117.8
plain-speaking 535.3
prosaic 721.5
unfanciful 987.5
unimpaired
sound 83.11
intact 792.10
undamaged 1002.8

unimpeachable
honest 644.13
inculpable 657.8
believable 953.24
obvious 970.15
accurate 973.16
unimpeded 430.26
unimportant
insignificant 248.6
of no importance 998.16
humble 137.10
unimpressed
unaffected 94.11
unastonished 123.3
unimpressive 998.17
uninfected 79.27
uninfluenced
voluntary 324.7
impartial 649.9
unmoved 895.5
unprejudiced 979.12
uninformed
inexpectant 131.9
ignorant 930.11
uninhabitable 586.8
uninhibited
unrestrained 430.24
profligate 665.25
intemperate 669.7
uninitiated
unskilled 414.16
ignorant 930.11
uninjured 1002.8
uninspired
unaffected 94.11
unimaginative 987.5
unintelligent
unskillful 414.15
unintellectual 922.13
ignorant 930.11
unintelligible 522.13
unintended
unpremeditated 365.11
unintentional 972.17
uninterrupted
directional 161.12
omnipresent 221.13
straight 277.6
persevering 360.8
consistent 803.11
continuous 812.8
perpetual 829.7
constant 847.5
uninvited
unwanted 99.11
voluntary 324.7
unwelcome 586.9
uninvolved
free 430.21
neutral 467.7
uncomplicated 798.8
incurious 982.3
union
convergence 169.1
juxtaposition 223.3
affiliation 450.2
accord 455.1
marriage 563.1
association 617.1
relation 775.1
identification 778.2

unpack disclose 351.4
  unload 909.23
unpaid due 623.10
  unremunerated 625.12
unpalatable
  unsavory 64.5
  unpleasant 98.17
unparalleled
  peerless 249.15
  extraordinary 870.14
  best 999.16
unpardonable
  unjustifiable 650.12
  wicked 654.16
unpayable
  irredeemable 625.13
  expensive 632.11
unperceptive
  insensible 25.6
  undiscerning 922.14
unperformed 408.3
unperturbed
  unexcited 106.11
  untroubled 107.8
  quiescent 173.12
unplanned
  unprepared 406.8
  unintentional 972.17
unpleasant
  unsavory 64.5
  unpleasing 98.17
  unlikable 99.7
  bad 1000.7
unplug 292.12
unpolished
  countrified 233.7
  rough 288.6
  undeveloped 406.12
  unskilled 414.16
  unrefined 497.12
  inelegant 534.2
unpolluted 79.25
unpopular
  disliked 99.9
  unrenowned 661.14
unpopulated 222.15
unpracticed
  unaccustomed 374.4
  inexperienced 414.17
unprecedented
  wonderful 122.10
  original 337.5
  unimitated 337.6
  extraordinary 870.14
unprecise
  unmeticulous 340.13
  inaccurate 975.17
unpredictable
  unexpected 131.10
  fickle 364.6
  unessential 768.4
  inconstant 854.7
  improbable 969.3
  uncertain 971.16
  chance 972.15
  unsafe 1006.11
unprejudiced 979.12
unpremeditated
  unmeditated 365.11
  unprepared 406.8
  premature 845.8

unintentional 972.17
unprepared
  inexpectant 131.9
  careless 340.11
  unready 406.8
  unskilled 414.16
  premature 845.8
  unalert 984.8
unprepossessing 1015.7
unpretentious
  humble 137.10
  modest 139.9
  natural 416.6
  plain 499.7
  unselfish 652.5
unprincipled 645.16
unprintable 666.9
unprocessed 406.12
unproductive
  fruitless 391.12
  nonproductive 891.4
unprofessional 414.16
unprofitable
  fruitless 391.12
  inexpedient 996.5
  disadvantageous 996.6
unpronounced
  silent 51.10
  unexpressed 519.9
unprotected
  helpless 19.18
  unshielded 1006.14
unprovable
  controvertible 958.9
  uncertain 971.16
unproved
  unsound 936.12
  not proved 958.8
  unauthoritative 971.21
  erroneous 975.16
unprovoked 640.9
unpublished 519.9
unqualified
  unable 19.14
  downright 247.12
  unfitted 406.9
  incompetent 414.19
  unrestricted 430.27
  inappropriate 789.7
  thorough 794.10
  unconditional 960.2
  genuine 973.15
  insufficient 992.9
  sound 1002.7
unquantifiable 884.10
unquenchable
  greedy 100.27
  indestructible 855.18
unquestionable
  downright 247.12
  intrinsic 767.7
  believable 953.24
  obvious 970.15
  true 973.13
unravel extract 192.10
  explain 341.10
  extricate 431.7
  disinvolve 798.5
  come apart 802.9
  loosen 804.3
  solve 940.2

unreachable 967.9
unread 930.13
unreadable 522.19
unready
  inexpectant 131.9
  careless 340.11
  unprepared 406.8
  untimely 844.6
  late 846.16
  unalert 984.8
unreal
  spurious 354.26
  unrealistic 762.9
  thin 764.6
  illusory 976.9
  imaginary 986.19
unrealistic
  unreal 762.9
  imaginary 986.19
  visionary 986.24
unrealized
  invisible 32.5
  unaccomplished 408.3
unreasonable
  capricious 364.5
  overpriced 632.12
  unjustifiable 650.12
  unwise 923.10
  fanatic 926.32
  illogical 936.11
  excessive 993.16
unreceptive
  inhospitable 586.7
  uninfluenceable 895.4
unrecognizable 32.6
unreconstructed
  impenitent 114.5
  ungovernable 361.12
  unsubject 430.29
  conservative 611.17
  permanent 853.8
unrecorded 519.9
unredeemable 654.18
unreduced
  undiminished 247.14
  undivided 792.11
unrefined
  countrified 233.7
  rough 288.6
  coarse 294.6
  undeveloped 406.12
  unpolished 497.12
  ill-bred 505.6
  inelegant 534.2
  unlearned 930.13
unregenerate
  obstinate 361.8
  irreclaimable 654.18
  unsacred 686.3
  unredeemed 695.18
unregretful 114.4
unregulated
  permitted 443.16
  illegal 674.6
unrehearsed 365.12
unrelated 776.6
unrelaxed tense 128.13
  rigid 1046.11
unrelenting
  persevering 360.8
  unyielding 361.9

  firm 425.7
  wordy 538.12
  constant 847.5
unreliable fickle 364.6
  untrustworthy 645.19
  inconstant 854.7
  under a cloud 955.11
  undependable 971.20
  inauthentic 975.19
  unsafe 1006.11
unrelieved
  vacant 222.14
  downright 247.12
  same 781.6
  continuous 812.8
unreligious 695.15
unremarkable 1005.8
unremitting
  industrious 330.22
  persevering 360.8
  continuous 812.8
  perpetual 829.7
  constant 847.5
  unchangeable 855.17
  continuing 856.7
unremorseful
  unregretful 114.4
  pitiless 146.3
unrepentance 114.2
unrepentant 114.5
unrequited
  unthanked 151.5
  unpaid 625.12
unreserved
  communicative 343.10
  artless 416.5
  unrestrained 430.24
  candid 644.17
  thorough 794.10
  unqualified 960.2
unresisting
  resigned 134.10
  submissive 433.12
unresolved
  remaining 256.7
  irresolute 362.9
unresponsive
  unfeeling 94.9
  heartless 144.25
  uninfluenceable 895.4
unrest
  trepidation 105.5
  motion 172.1
  agitation 917.1
unrestored 21.7
unrestrained
  fervent 93.18
  communicative 343.10
  capricious 364.5
  lawless 418.5
  lax 426.4
  unconstrained 430.24
  candid 644.17
  incontinent 665.24
  intemperate 669.7
  inconstant 854.7
  excessive 993.16
unrestricted
  undiminished 247.14
  open 292.17
  communicative 343.10

unconfined 430.27
  thorough 794.10
  unqualified 960.2
unrevealing 346.15
unrewarded
  unthanked 151.5
  unpaid 625.12
unripe sour 67.5
  immature 301.10
  unprepared 406.11
  inexperienced 414.17
  untimely 844.6
  premature 845.8
  ignorant 930.11
unrivaled 249.15
unrobed 6.13
unroll unclose 292.12
  disclose 351.4
  unfold 861.7
unruffled
  unaffected 94.11
  unexcited 106.11
  quiescent 173.12
  smooth 287.10
  uniform 781.5
unruly
  defiant 327.10
  ungovernable 361.12
  anarchic 418.6
  unrestrained 430.24
  disorderly 671.19
unsafe 1006.11
unsaid tacit 51.11
  unexpressed 519.9
unsalvageable 125.15
unsanctioned 444.7
unsanitary 82.5
unsatisfactory
  dissatisfactory 108.9
  disappointing 132.6
  insufficient 992.9
unsaturated fat 1056.1
unsavory
  unpalatable 64.5
  insipid 65.2
  unpleasant 98.17
  dishonest 645.16
  disreputable 661.10
unscathed
  undamaged 1002.8
  safe 1007.4
unscented 72.5
unschooled
  unskilled 414.16
  unlearned 930.13
unscientific 936.11
unscramble
  disinvolve 798.5
  solve 940.2
  disembarrass 1014.9
unscratched 1002.8
unscrew 802.10
unscrubbed 80.20
unscrupulous
  unmeticulous 340.13
  dishonest 645.16
unseal 292.12
unsearched 340.16
unseasonable
  inappropriate 789.7
  anachronous 833.3

untimely 844.6
  inexpedient 996.5
unseat
  dislodge 160.6
  depose 447.4
  disjoint 802.16
unseeing blind 30.9
  unwise 923.10
  unaware 930.12
unseemly
  vulgar 497.10
  inelegant 534.2
  wrong 638.3
  indecent 666.5
  inappropriate 789.7
  inexpedient 996.5
unseen invisible 32.5
  unheeded 340.15
  unrevealed 346.12
unselfish
  liberal 485.4
  impartial 649.9
  selfless 652.5
unserviceable 391.14
unsettle excite 105.14
  disorder 810.9
  discompose 811.4
  agitate 917.10
  confuse 985.7
unshaded 348.11
unshakeable 326.3
unshaken
  unweakened 15.21
  unnervous 129.2
  firm 359.12
unshaven 3.25
unsheathed 6.12
unshielded 1006.14
unsightly
  slovenly 810.15
  ugly 1015.6
unsimulated 973.15
unskilled 414.16
unskilled laborer
  726.2
unsmiling
  solemn 111.3
  unhappy 112.21
unsnap 802.10
unsnarl
  straighten 277.5
  extricate 431.7
  disinvolve 798.5
  arrange 808.8
  disembarrass 1014.9
unsociable
  uncommunicative 344.8
  insociable 583.5
  unfriendly 589.9
  misanthropic 590.3
unsoiled clean 79.25
  spotless 657.7
  chaste 664.4
unsold 734.15
unsolicited
  voluntary 324.7
  neglected 340.14
unsolid unsound 16.15
  unsubstantial 764.5
  unreliable 971.20
unsolved 346.12

unsophisticated
  artless 416.5
  unadorned 499.8
  unmixed 798.7
  gullible 954.9
unsound infirm 16.15
  unhealthy 85.54
  unwholesome 85.55
  unorthodox 688.9
  insolvent 729.19
  fragile 764.7
  unwise 923.10
  insane 926.26
  unsubstantial 936.12
  unreliable 971.20
  imperfect 1003.4
  unsafe 1006.11
unsparing harsh 144.24
  industrious 330.22
  strict 425.6
  liberal 485.4
unspeakable
  horrid 98.19
  indescribable 122.13
  insulting 156.8
  wicked 654.16
  base 661.12
  sacred 685.7
  extraordinary 870.14
unspecified
  anonymous 528.3
  general 864.11
  vague 971.19
unspectacular 1005.8
unspoiled
  downright 247.12
  preserved 397.13
  natural 416.6
  intact 792.10
  unmixed 798.7
  undamaged 1002.8
unspoken tacit 51.11
  secret 345.11
  unexpressed 519.9
unsportsmanlike 650.10
unspotted clean 79.25
  honest 644.13
  spotless 657.7
  chaste 664.4
  perfect 1002.6
unstable
  unsound 16.15
  nonuniform 782.3
  unbalanced 791.5
  transient 828.7
  inconstant 854.7
  unreliable 971.20
  unsafe 1006.11
unstained clean 79.25
  honest 644.13
  chaste 664.4
unsteady shaky 16.16
  nonuniform 782.3
  unbalanced 791.5
  irregular 851.3
  inconstant 854.7
  fluttering 917.18
  unreliable 971.20
  unsafe 1006.11
unstick detach 802.10
  loosen 804.3

unstoppable 963.15
unstrap loose 431.6
  detach 802.10
unstructured
  unformed 263.5
  diffuse 538.11
unstuck 802.22
unsturdy 16.15
unsubstantial
  frail 16.14
  weak 16.15
  rare 299.4
  unreal 762.9
  insubstantial 764.5
  unsound 936.12
  unreliable 971.20
  illusory 976.9
  immaterial 1053.7
unsubstantiated 958.8
unsuccessful 410.18
unsuitable
  unacceptable 108.10
  unserviceable 391.14
  vulgar 497.10
  wrong 638.3
  inappropriate 789.7
  untimely 844.6
  inexpedient 996.5
unsuited
  unfitted 406.9
  inappropriate 789.7
unsullied clean 79.25
  natural 406.13
  honest 644.13
  spotless 657.7
  chaste 664.4
unsung disliked 99.9
  unexpressed 519.9
  unrenowned 661.14
unsung hero 492.6
unsupportable
  baseless 936.13
  unprovable 958.9
unsuppressed
  communicative 343.10
  unrestrained 430.24
unsure
  untrustworthy 645.19
  ignorant 930.11
  uncertain 971.16
  unreliable 971.20
  unconfident 971.23
  unsafe 1006.11
unsurpassed
  peerless 249.15
  best 999.16
unsuspecting
  inexpectant 131.9
  unaware 930.12
  trusting 953.22
  credulous 954.8
  unprotected 1006.14
unsustained
  unsound 936.12
  baseless 936.13
  unproved 958.8
unswayed
  impartial 649.9
  uninfluenced 895.5
  unprejudiced 979.12
unsweetened 67.5

unswept 80.20
unswerving
  directional 161.12
  straight 277.6
  firm 359.12
  persevering 360.8
  faithful 644.20
unsymmetrical
  distorted 265.10
  unordered 810.12
unsympathetic
  insensible 25.6
  unfeeling 94.9
  unkind 144.16
  pitiless 146.3
unsynchronized 456.15
untactful
  careless 340.11
  undiscriminating 945.5
untainted clean 79.25
  preserved 397.13
  natural 416.6
  spotless 657.7
  chaste 664.4
  perfect 1002.6
untalented
  unable 19.14
  unskilled 414.16
  unintelligent 922.13
untamed defiant 327.10
  unsubject 430.29
  unrefined 497.12
  savage 671.21
untangle
  extricate 431.7
  disinvolve 798.5
  solve 940.2
untapped 390.12
untarnished
  clean 79.25
  honest 644.13
  chaste 664.4
untaxed 634.5
unteachable 922.15
untenable
  helpless 19.18
  unacceptable 108.10
  baseless 936.13
untended
  available 222.15
  neglected 340.14
untested 958.8
unthawed 1023.13
unthinkable
  unbelievable 955.10
  impossible 967.7
unthinking
  inconsiderate 144.18
  careless 340.11
  unreasoning 365.10
  unintelligent 922.13
  unwise 923.10
  thoughtless 933.4
  credulous 954.8
  involuntary 963.14
  unintentional 972.17
unthoughtful
  inconsiderate 144.18
  unthinking 365.10
  unwise 923.10

untidy dirty 80.22
  slipshod 340.12
  slovenly 810.15
untied adrift 182.61
  unbound 430.28
  liberated 431.10
  unfastened 802.22
until 821.15
until we meet again!
  188.22
untimely
  inappropriate 789.7
  unseasonable 844.6
  premature 845.8
  late 846.16
  inexpedient 996.5
unto 821.15
untogether 810.12
untold secret 345.11
  unexpressed 519.9
  infinite 823.3
  innumerable 884.10
  undecided 971.18
untouchable
  n outcast 586.4
  adj unfeeling 94.9
  disliked 99.9
  out-of-the-way 261.9
  prohibited 444.7
  sacred 685.7
untouched
  unaffected 94.11
  impenitent 114.5
  unused 390.12
  natural 406.13
  intact 792.10
  unmixed 798.7
  new 841.7
  unknown 930.16
  undamaged 1002.8
  safe 1007.4
untouristed
  available 222.15
  abandoned 370.8
untoward
  ominous 133.16
  untimely 844.6
  bad 1000.7
  adverse 1011.13
untracked 346.12
untrained
  unaccustomed 374.4
  unskilled 414.16
untrammeled
  lawless 418.5
  lax 426.4
  unhampered 430.26
  profligate 665.25
untreated 406.12
untried
  inexperienced 414.17
  new 841.7
  unproved 958.8
untrimmed
  unadorned 499.8
  undeceptive 644.18
untroubled
  unexcited 106.11
  unbothered 107.8
  quiescent 173.12
  pacific 464.9

untrue
  adj false 354.25
  nonobservant 435.5
  unfaithful 645.20
  erroneous 975.16
  adv erroneously 975.20
untrust 153.1
untruthfulness 354.8
untwist
  disinvolve 798.5
  solve 940.2
untying 431.2
unusable 391.14
unused
  remaining 256.7
  unaccustomed 374.4
  unutilized 390.12
  new 841.7
  surplus 993.18
unusual novel 841.11
  infrequent 848.2
  nonconforming 868.5
  unordinary 870.10
unutterable
  indescribable 122.13
  secret 345.11
  sacred 685.7
unvarnished
  natural 416.6
  unadorned 499.8
  plain-speaking 535.3
  undeceptive 644.18
  genuine 973.15
unvarying
  tedious 118.9
  uniform 781.5
  constant 847.5
  permanent 853.7
  unchangeable 855.17
unveil divest 6.5
  unclose 292.12
  disclose 351.4
unventilated
  stuffy 173.16
  closed 293.9
unverified
  unproved 958.8
  unauthoritative 971.21
unwanted
  unwished 99.11
  unwelcome 586.9
unwarranted
  overpriced 632.12
  undue 640.9
  illegal 674.6
  baseless 936.13
  unauthoritative 971.21
unwarrantedness 640.1
unwary
  negligent 340.10
  artless 416.5
  rash 493.7
  unalert 984.8
unwashed 80.20
unwatched
  neglected 340.14
  unprotected 1006.14
unwavering
  unnervous 129.2
  persevering 360.8
  stable 855.12

  confident 970.21
unwed 565.7
unwelcome
  unpleasant 98.17
  unwanted 99.11
  inhospitable 586.9
unwieldy bulky 257.19
  onerous 297.17
  bungling 414.20
  stiff 534.3
  inconvenient 996.7
  unmanageable 1013.19
unwilling
  disinclined 325.5
  unconsenting 442.6
  involuntary 963.14
unwind relax 20.7
  compose oneself 106.7
  disinvolve 798.5
  unfold 861.7
unwise
  unintelligent 922.13
  injudicious 923.10
  inexpedient 996.5
unwitting
  unaware 930.12
  involuntary 963.14
  unintentional 972.17
unwont 374.4
unworkable
  unserviceable 391.14
  impracticable 967.8
  inexpedient 996.5
unworldly
  heavenly 681.12
  godly 692.9
  supernatural 870.15
  immaterial 1053.7
unworn
  unweakened 15.21
  undamaged 1002.8
unworthy
  n bad person 660.1
  adj undue 640.9
  wicked 654.16
  worthless 998.22
unwrap
  take off 6.6
  unclose 292.12
  disclose 351.4
unwritten
  unexpressed 519.9
  speech 524.29
  traditional 842.12
unyielding
  impregnable 15.19
  pitiless 146.3
  resolute 359.12
  unbending 361.9
  firm 425.7
  resistant 453.5
  sturdy 763.7
  immovable 855.15
  uninfluenceable 895.4
  inevitable 963.15
  inflexible 1046.12
unzipped 802.22
up
  n increase 251.1
  v ascend 193.8
  increase 251.4

enlarge 259.4
promote 446.2
elevate 912.5
adj awake 23.8
adv upward 193.16
vertically 200.13
on high 272.21
prep toward 161.26
up against
adj contrapositive 215.5
resistant 453.5
prep near 223.25
up and about 83.10
up and at 'em! 459.32
up and down
perpendicularly 200.14
alternately 850.11
to and fro 916.21
up-and-up 644.14
up a tree
unfortunate 1011.14
in trouble 1013.22
cornered 1013.25
upbeat
n improvement 392.1
beat 709.26
round 850.3
adj optimistic 124.11
upbraid 510.17
upcoming
n ascent 193.1
adj approaching 167.4
ascending 193.14
imminent 840.3
upchuck 99.4
update date 832.13
modernize 841.6
updraft
ascent 193.1
wind 318.1
upended 200.11
up for grabs 971.18
up for sale 734.16
up front 818.18
upgrade
n ascent 193.1
acclivity 204.6
improvement 392.1
v make better 392.9
promote 446.2
adj ascending 193.14
sloping upward 204.17
adv slantingly 204.23
upheaval
outburst 105.9
fall 395.3
convulsion 671.5
revolution 852.2
elevation 912.1
upheld 901.24
uphill
n ascent 193.1
acclivity 204.6
adj ascending 193.14
sloping upward 204.17
laborious 725.18
difficult 1013.17
adv up 193.16
slantingly 204.23
uphold buoy 298.8
preserve 397.8

aid 449.12
approve 509.9
defend 600.10
support 901.21
elevate 912.5
confirm 957.11
upholstered 295.34
UPI 555.3
up in arms
adj prepared 405.16
resistant 453.5
at odds 456.16
adv in opposition 451.9
at war 458.23
up in the air 971.18
upkeep
n preservation 397.1
aid 449.3
support 901.1
v aid 449.12
support 901.21
upland area 237.1
uplift
n ascent 193.1
acclivity 204.6
improvement 392.1
elevation 912.1
v elate 109.8
erect 200.9
buoy 298.8
make better 392.9
glorify 662.13
elevate 912.5
upon
adv after which 835.7
prep toward 161.26
atop 198.16
against 223.25
on 295.37
relation to 775.13
up on skilled in 413.27
informed 928.18
versed in 928.19
up one's sleeve 345.17
upper
n excitement 105.3
adj superior 249.12
higher 272.19
upper case 548.6
upper class
the best 249.5
social status 607.2
aristocracy 608.1
upperclassman 572.6
upper crust
the best 249.5
society 578.6
upper class 607.2
aristocracy 608.1
upper hand
advantage 249.2
dominance 417.6
influence 894.1
upper middle class 607.5
uppermost top 198.10
superlative 249.13
higher 272.19
paramount 997.24
uppers 87.4
uppity arrogant 141.9
insolent 142.9

upraised
vertical 200.11
raised 912.9
upright
n vertical 200.2
post 273.4
base 901.8
v erect 200.9
adj vertical 200.11
straight 277.6
honest 644.13
virtuous 653.5
raised 912.9
adv vertically 200.13
uprising
n ascent 193.1
rising 200.5
acclivity 204.6
revolt 327.4
adj ascending 193.14
sloping upward 204.17
uproar
noise 53.3
outcry 59.4
agitation 105.4
turbulence 671.2
commotion 810.4
uproot
dislodge 160.6
extract 192.10
exterminate 395.14
upscale
upper-class 607.10
wealthy 618.15
expensive 632.11
prosperous 1010.12
upset
n anxiety 126.1
dislodgment 160.2
overturn 205.2
fall 395.3
turbulence 671.2
disorder 810.1
revolution 860.1
agitation 917.1
refutation 958.2
bewilderment 971.3
confusion 985.3
frustration 1012.3
v chagrin 96.15
distress 96.16
excite 105.14
concern 126.4
make anxious 126.5
unnerve 128.10
capsize 182.44
overturn 205.6
overthrow 395.20
overcome 412.7
unbalance 791.3
disorder 810.9
discompose 811.4
revolutionize 860.4
agitate 917.10
refute 958.5
bewilder 971.12
confuse 985.7
thwart 1012.15
adj distressed 96.22
excited 105.23
overwrought 105.26

unnerved 128.14
defeated 412.14
disorderly 810.13
agitated 917.16
disproved 958.7
bewildered 971.24
confused 985.12
upshoot
n ascent 193.1
v grow 14.2
shoot up 193.9
expand 259.7
upside-down
inverted 205.7
confused 810.16
upstage
n stage 704.16
v snub 157.5
act 704.29
adj arrogant 141.9
adv on the stage 704.36
upstairs up 193.16
on high 272.21
upstanding
vertical 200.11
honest 644.13
upstart
n impudent person
142.5
vulgarian 497.6
parvenu 606.7
modern 841.4
v shoot up 193.9
adj populational 606.8
upstream
v ascend 193.8
adv up 193.16
upsurge
n ascent 193.1
increase 251.1
v ascend 193.8
upswing ascent 193.1
increase 251.1
improvement 392.1
uptake 939.1
up the ante 759.24
up the creek
unfortunate 1011.14
in trouble 1013.22
uptight
tense 128.13
conformist 867.6
up to
v be able 18.11
adj able 18.14
prepared for 405.18
competent 413.24
sufficient 991.6
prep until 821.15
up-to-date
fashionable 578.11
present 838.2
modern 841.13
informed 928.18
up to no good
dishonest 645.16
wicked 654.16
up to snuff
competent 413.24
in order 807.7
up to par 999.19

v turn round 163.9
deviate 164.3
change course 182.30
oblique 204.9
go sideways 218.5
angle 278.5
be changed 852.6
vegan vegetarian 8.16
diet 8.31
temperance 668.1
vegetable
n plant 310.3
adj vegetal 310.36
passive 329.6
languid 331.20
permanent 853.7
vegetarian
n eater 8.16
abstainer 668.4
adj eating 8.31
vegetable 310.36
abstinent 668.10
vegetate develop 14.2
stagnate 173.9
grow 259.7
sprout 310.34
do nothing 329.2
merely exist 761.10
vegetation
physical development 14.1
inertness 173.4
growth 259.3
plants 310.1
life 310.32
inaction 329.1
mere existence 761.6
vehement
acrimonious 17.14
zealous 101.9
passionate 105.29
industrious 330.22
emphatic 544.13
violent 671.16
vehicle color 35.8
means of transport 179
conveyance 179.1
instrument 384.4
stage show 704.4
film 714.10
veil
n clothing 5.26
cover 295.2
veil of secrecy 345.3
curtain 346.2
pretext 376.1
shade 1028.1
v cover 295.19
keep secret 345.7
conceal 346.6
shade 1028.5
veiled covered 295.31
latent 519.5
vague 971.19
shaded 1028.7
vein
n duct 2.23
thinness 270.7
source of supply 386.4
style 532.2
mode 765.4
nature 767.4

disposition 978.3
mood 978.4
deposit 1058.7
v variegate 47.7
veld the country 233.1
plain 236.1
grassland 310.8
velocity rate 172.4
speed 174.1
gait 177.12
velvet comfort 121.1
smoothness 287.3
texture 294.3
prosperity 1010.1
easy 1014.4
softness 1047.4
vena cava 2.23
venal greedy 100.27
bribable 378.4
corruptible 645.23
vendetta quarrel 456.5
revenge 507.1
animosity 589.4
vending machine 736.4
vendor peddler 730.5
vending machine 736.4
veneer
n shallowness 276.1
blanket 295.12
lamina 296.2
v face 295.23
venerable
dignified 136.12
reverend 155.12
aged 303.16
reputable 662.15
sacred 685.7
old 842.10
traditional 842.12
venerate
respect 155.4
worship 696.11
venerating 155.9
venereal disease 85.18
vengeance
revenge 507.1
deserts 639.3
venial 600.14
venison 10.13
venom
poisonousness 82.3
rancor 144.7
animosity 589.4
violence 671.1
evil 1000.3
bane 1001.3
vent
n parachute 181.13
emergence 190.1
outlet 190.9
air passage 239.13
escape 369.1
v divulge 351.5
evacuate 909.22
ventilate
deodorize 72.4
air 317.11
disclose 351.4
divulge 351.5
make public 352.11
discuss 541.11

refrigerate 1024.10
ventral 2.31
ventricular 2.31
ventriloquist 524.15
venture
n undertaking 404.1
investment 729.4
trading 737.19
gamble 759.2
v attempt 403.6
dare 492.9
presume 640.6
invest 729.17
trade 737.23
chance 759.24
venture capital
supply 386.2
capital 728.15
trading 737.19
venue 159.2
Venus Love 104.7
beauty 1016.9
stars 1072.4
planet 1072.9
Venus's flytrap 356.12
Venus de Milo 1016.9
veracity honesty 644.3
truth 973.1
veranda 197.21
verb 530.4
verbal
n verb 530.4
adj communicational 343.9
semantic 518.12
speech 524.29
vocabular 526.18
grammatical 530.17
genuine 973.15
verbalize 524.22
verbatim
adj genuine 973.15
adv exactly 973.21
verbiage diction 532.1
wordiness 538.2
verboten 444.7
verdant green 44.4
verdurous 310.42
verdict judgment 598.9
solution 940.1
decision 946.5
verge
n border 211.4
insignia 647.1
v take direction 161.7
border 211.10
tend 896.3
verify
experiment 942.8
collate 943.5
confirm 957.11
certify 970.12
check 1017.21
verisimilitude
probability 968.1
genuineness 973.7
veritable
straight 644.14
real 761.15
thorough 794.10
true 973.13
vérité 706.1

vermeil 41.6
vermicelli 10.33
vermicide
vermifuge 86.24
poison 1001.3
vermiform coiled 281.7
wormlike 311.52
vermilion
n redness 41.1
v make red 41.4
adj red 41.6
vermin
creature 311.3
parasite 311.36
rabble 606.3
beast 660.6
vernacular
n dead language 523.2
mother tongue 523.3
nonformal speech 523.5
substandard language 523.6
jargon 523.9
plain speech 535.1
adj local 231.9
common 497.14
colloquial 523.20
usual 869.9
vernal green 44.4
immature 301.10
seasonal 313.9
new 841.7
vernal equinox
season 313.7
orbit 1072.16
versatile fickle 364.6
handy 387.20
ambidextrous 413.25
multiform 783.3
verse
n part 554.13
passage 708.24
poetry 720.1
poem 720.4
part of writing 793.2
curtain-raiser 816.2
maxim 974.1
v inform 551.8
poetize 720.13
versed in
skilled in 413.27
informed in 928.19
version
reproduction 336.3
rendering 341.2
writing 547.10
sect 675.3
score 708.28
story 722.3
verso left side 220.1
makeup 554.12
versus toward 161.26
against 215.7
opposed to 451.10
vertebrate
n creature 311.3
adj chordate 311.40
vertex summit 198.2
angle 278.2
vertical
n upright 200.2
adj top 198.10

upright 200.11
steep 204.18
straight 277.6
vertigo symptom 85.9
  ear disease 85.15
  dizziness 985.4
verve vim 17.2
  passion 93.2
  eagerness 101.1
  gaiety 109.4
  liveliness 330.2
  spirit 544.4
  lively imagination 986.4
very to a degree 245.7
  exceedingly 247.18
vesicle bulge 283.3
  bubble 320.1
  blemish 1004.1
vespers 696.8
vessel duct 2.23
  ship 180.1
  container 195.1
vest
  n waistcoat 5.14
  v establish 159.16
  endow 478.17
  commission 615.10
vestal virgin 565.4
vested clothing 5.45
  established 855.13
vested interest
  estate 471.4
  pressure group 609.31
  prerogative 642.1
vestibule ear 2.10
  entrance 189.5
  portal 197.19
vestige
  remainder 256.1
  print 517.7
  clue 517.9
  record 549.1
  admixture 797.7
  antiquity 842.6
vestment
  clothing 5.1
  garment 5.3
  cover 295.2
vest-pocket
  insignificant 248.6
  miniature 258.12
  shortened 268.9
  concise 537.6
vestry
  ecclesiastical council 423.4
  church 703.9
veteran
  n old man 304.2
  vet 413.16
  combat participant 461.19
  adj experienced 413.28
veterinarian 90.7
veto
  n negative 444.2
  executive privilege 613.7
  v put one's veto upon 444.5
  oppose 451.3
  disapprove 510.10
  legislate 613.10
vex annoy 96.13
  irk 98.15

make anxious 126.5
  provoke 152.24
  trouble 1013.13
V formation 184.12
VHF 1034.12
via 161.27
viable energizing 17.15
  acceptable 107.12
  living 306.12
  workable 889.10
  practicable 966.7
  of importance 997.18
viaduct crossing 170.2
  bridge 383.9
viaggiatory 177.37
vibrant energetic 17.13
  resonant 54.10
vibrate resonate 54.6
  be frequent 847.3
  oscillate 916.10
  shake 917.11
vibrato
  n screech 58.4
  trill 709.19
  adj shrill 58.14
vicar deputy 576.1
  substitute 862.2
vicarious 862.8
vice
  n misbehavior 322.1
  deputy 576.1
  moral badness 654
  viciousness 654.1
  weakness 654.2
  wrongdoing 655.1
  substitute 862.2
  prep instead of 862.12
vice-president
  executive 574.3
  vice-chairman 576.8
  substitute 862.2
viceroy
  governor 575.13
  vice-president 576.8
vice versa
  inversely 205.8
  reciprocally 777.12
  contrarily 779.9
vicinity
  environment 209.1
  nearness 223.1
  region 231.1
vicious cruel 144.26
  vice-prone 654.11
  wicked 654.16
  savage 671.21
  bad 1000.7
  harmful 1000.12
vicious circle
  circle 280.2
  futility 391.2
  sophistry 936.1
  vicissitudes 972.5
vicious cycle 391.2
vicissitude
  changing 854.3
  adversity 1011.1
victim
  sick person 85.43
  sufferer 96.11
  dupe 358.1

quarry 382.7
  loser 412.5
  laughingstock 508.7
  cheater 759.22
  unfortunate 1011.7
victimize cheat 356.18
  persecute 389.7
  outwit 415.11
  overprice 632.7
victor
  successful person 409.6
  winner 411.2
Victorian
  n prude 500.11
  adj prudish 500.19
  antiquated 842.13
victorious 411.7
victory success 409.1
  triumph 411
  win 411.1
victualler 385.6
victuals food 10.2
  groceries 735.7
video
  n television 1035.1
  adj televisional 1035.16
video arcade 743.15
video camera camera
    714.11
  television 1035.1
video-cassette recorder
  record 50.12
  television receiver 1035.11
video game 743.9
video-on-demand 706.1
videotape
  n recording media 549.10
  v record 549.15
vie compete 457.18
  be comparable 943.7
  excel 999.11
Vietcong
  n irregular 461.16
  revolutionist 860.3
  adj revolutionist 860.6
view
  n look 27.3
  field of view 31.3
  aspect 33.3
  appearance 33.6
  intention 380.1
  scene 712.11
  estimate 946.3
  opinion 953.6
  outlook 978.2
  v see 27.12
  look 27.13
  think of 931.17
  take the attitude 978.6
  heed 983.6
viewer
  optical instrument 29.1
  recipient 479.3
  spectator 918.1
  televiewer 1035.12
viewpoint
  standpoint 27.7
  field of view 31.3
  aspect 33.3
  station 159.2
  outlook 978.2

vigil wakefulness 23.1
  vigilance 339.4
vigilant wakeful 23.7
  wary 339.13
  prepared 405.16
  protective 1008.23
vignette
  description 349.2
  drawing 712.12
  print 713.5
vigor strength 15.1
  energy 17.1
  power 18.1
  haleness 83.3
  gaiety 109.4
  force 544.3
vigorish 793.1
viking mariner 183.1
  pirate 483.7
vile nasty 64.7
  malodorous 71.5
  filthy 80.23
  offensive 98.18
  low 497.15
  cursing 513.8
  knavish 645.17
  wicked 654.16
  base 661.12
  obscene 666.9
  paltry 998.21
  terrible 1000.9
vilify berate 510.19
  revile 512.10
  abuse 513.7
  stigmatize 661.9
  blaspheme 694.5
villa 228.7
village
  n hamlet 230.2
  region 231.5
  adj urban 230.11
villain evildoer 593.1
  rascal 660.3
  role 704.10
  actor 707.2
vim verve 17.2
  power 18.1
  gaiety 109.4
  liveliness 330.2
vinaigrette 70.6
vindicate justify 600.9
  acquit 601.4
vindictive 507.7
vine 310.4
vinegar sour 67.2
  preservative 397.4
vineyard 1069.10
vintage 472.5
violate disobey 327.6
  misuse 389.4
  corrupt 393.12
  break 435.4
  possess sexually 480.15
  seduce 665.20
  rage 671.11
  break the law 674.5
  work evil 1000.6
violence acrimony 17.5
  excitability 105.10
  cruelty 144.11
  rage 152.10

mistreatment 389.2
coercion 424.3
vehement action 671
agitation 671.1
violet
n purpleness 46.1
adj purple 46.3
violinist 710.5
VIP celebrity 662.9
influence 894.6
important person 997.9
viper serpent 311.25
beast 660.6
viral marketing 734.2
virgin
n schoolgirl 302.8
single woman 565.4
adj hinterland 233.9
natural 406.13
unmarried 565.7
continent 664.6
intact 792.10
unmixed 798.7
new 841.7
unproductive 891.4
unknown 930.16
undamaged 1002.8
virgule diagonal 204.7
line 517.6
virile potent 76.13
courageous 492.16
virtual 519.5
virtual classroom 567.5
virtual company 739.1
virtual office
branch 617.10
office 739.7
virtue power 18.1
courage 492.1
morality 636.3
probity 644.1
moral goodness 653
virtuousness 653.1
chastity 664.1
goodness 999.1
virtuoso
n superior 249.4
master 413.13
connoisseur 496.6
musician 710.1
first-rater 999.6
adj skillful 413.22
musical 708.47
virtuous honest 644.13
good 653.5
chaste 664.4
pure 999.12
virulent
acrimonious 17.14
poisonous 82.7
rancorous 144.22
resentful 152.26
deadly 308.23
hostile 589.10
violent 671.16
harmful 1000.12
virus infection 85.4
germ 85.42
organism 305.2
poison 1001.3

visa
n ratification 332.4
pass 443.7
signature 527.10
certificate 549.6
v ratify 332.12
visage looks 33.4
face 216.4
vis à vis 790.4
viscera vitals 2.16
heart 93.3
insides 207.4
viscount 608.4
viscous thick 269.8
dense 1045.12
viscid 1062.12
vise 260.6
visible visual 27.20
clear 31.6
apparent 33.11
manifest 348.8
vision
n sight 27.1
optics 27.1
apparition 33.5
deception 356.1
phantom 976.4
figment of the imagination 986.5
visualization 986.6
dream 986.9
specter 988.1
thing of beauty 1016.6
v visualize 986.15
visioning 27.1
visit
n chat 541.3
social call 582.7
v go to 177.25
enter 189.7
attend 221.8
chat 541.9
pay a visit 582.19
visitor traveler 178.1
incomer 189.4
attender 221.5
superintendent 574.2
guest 585.6
examiner 938.17
visor cover 356.11
eyeshade 1028.2
vista field of view 31.3
view 33.6
visual eye 2.28
ocular 27.20
visible 31.6
visualize
think of 931.17
vision 986.15
visual range 31.3
vital
powerful 18.12
hale 83.12
eager 101.8
gay 109.14
organic 305.17
living 306.12
vigorous 544.11
durable 827.10
requisite 963.13
all-important 997.23

vitality
strength 15.1
energy 17.1
power 18.1
haleness 83.3
eagerness 101.1
gaiety 109.4
life 306.1
vigor 544.3
toughness 1049.1
vital statistics 1017.14
vitamin 7.4
vitamin complex 7.4
vitamin deficiency 992.6
vitamin deficiency disease 85.33
vitamin supplement 7.4
vitiate impair 393.12
corrupt 654.10
neutralize 900.7
vitreous 1029.5
vitriolic
acrimonious 17.14
pungent 68.6
rancorous 144.22
hostile 589.10
vituperate
berate 510.19
vilify 513.7
viva! 509.23
vivacious
energetic 17.13
eager 101.8
gay 109.14
active 330.17
spirited 544.12
vive! 509.23
vivid energetic 17.13
sensitive 24.13
colorful 35.19
eager 101.8
representational 349.13
descriptive 349.14
expressive 544.10
remembered 989.22
bright 1025.33
vivifying 17.15
vivisection 802.5
vixen
female animal 77.9
bitch 110.12
witch 593.7
violent person 671.9
viz
by interpretation 341.18
namely 865.18
vocabulary
n jargon 523.9
lexis 526.13
reference book 554.9
dictionary 871.4
adj verbal 526.18
vocal speech 524.29
singing 708.50
vocal cords 524.18
vocalist 710.13
vocalize say 524.22
sing 708.38
vocation motive 375.1
the ministry 698.1
occupation 724.6

specialty 866.1
vociferous noisy 53.13
vociferant 59.10
vogue
n fashion 578.1
repute 662.1
adj stylish 578.12
voice
n vote 371.6
approval 509.1
utterance 524.2
manner of speaking 524.7
speech sound 524.12
active voice 530.14
spokesman 576.5
part 708.22
voce 709.5
singer 710.13
v publish 352.10
say 524.22
tune 708.36
voiceless mute 51.12
phonetic 524.30
voicemail 347.13
voicemail box 553.6
voice recognition 549.10
void
n space 158.1
vacuum 222.3
crack 224.2
nonexistence 762.1
v defecate 12.13
delete 255.12
abolish 395.13
repeal 445.2
neutralize 900.7
evacuate 909.22
adj vacant 222.14
repealed 445.3
nonexistent 762.8
voilà
so much for that! 407.15
attention! 983.22
volatile
n vapor 1067.1
adj light 298.10
fickle 364.6
transient 828.7
inconstant 854.7
superficial 922.20
flighty 985.17
vaporable 1067.10
volcanic fervent 93.18
excitable 105.28
passionate 105.29
hot-tempered 110.25
explosive 671.24
volcano
mountain 237.6
outburst 671.6
volition will 323.1
choice 371.1
volley
n detonation 56.3
salvo 459.9
arrow 462.6
shot 904.4
v play tennis 748.3
volt 1032.12
voltage 1032.12
voluble 540.9

vocation 724.6
game 745.3
circuit 914.2
v exercise 84.4
go slow 175.6
ambulate 177.27
get off 369.7
win hands down 411.4
be free 430.18
liberate 431.9
strike 727.10
play 745.5
walk all over 612.15
walk a tightrope 1013.11
walk away quit 188.9
outdistance 249.10
abandon 370.5
dismiss 984.4
walker
pedestrian 178.6
baby carriage 179.6
walk-in closet 197.15
walking papers
deposal 447.2
dismissal 909.5
walk of life 765.1
walk-on role 704.10
supporting actor 707.7
walk out exit 190.12
strike 727.10
stop work 857.8
walkover 411.1
walk the walk 641.10
walk-through 704.13
walkup 228.13
walkway 383.2
wall
n precipice 200.3
fence 212.4
partition 213.5
slope 237.2
barrier 1012.5
v fence 212.7
fortify 460.9
Wallace's Trotting Register
757.1
walled-in
enclosed 212.10
covered 295.31
wallet 729.15
wall off partition 213.8
quarantine 429.13
wall of silence 345.3
wallop
n blow 902.5
v punish 604.15
strike 902.15
beat 902.17
flounder 917.15
wallow
n marsh 243.1
flounder 917.8
v pitch 182.55
be promiscuous 665.19
bow 913.9
welter 915.13
flounder 917.15
wallpaper 295.23
Wall Street
stock market 737.1
stock exchange 737.7

financial district 737.8
wall-to-wall
adj comprehensive 772.7
same 781.6
thorough 794.10
continuous 812.8
adv continuously 812.10
wall-to-wall carpet 295.9
walnut 40.3
waltz
n easy 1014.4
v win hands down 411.4
dance 705.5
wampum jewel 498.6
money 728.2
names for 728.3
wan
v lose color 36.6
adj tired-looking 21.9
colorless 36.7
deathly 307.28
languid 331.20
lackluster 1027.17
wand fitness 84.1
scepter 417.9
insignia 647.1
wish-bringer 691.6
dowsing 962.3
wander deviate 164.4
roam 177.23
digress 538.9
misbelieve 688.8
be insane 926.20
err 975.9
stray 984.3
muse 985.9
wanderer rover 178.2
alien 774.3
transient 828.4
planet 1072.9
Wandering Jew
displaced person 160.4
wanderer 178.2
wanderlust 177.3
wane
n standstill 173.3
decline 252.2
deterioration 393.3
v disappear 34.2
recede 168.2
move 172.5
quiet 173.8
decrease 252.6
age 303.10
decline 393.17
wangle elicit 192.14
persuade 375.23
plot 381.9
maneuver 415.10
wangling 381.13
wank 75.8
wankered 87.24
wannabe
desirer 100.12
aspiring 100.28
petitioner 440.7
candidate 610.9
want
n desire 100.1
absence 222.1
indigence 619.2

deficiency 795.2
requirement 963.2
lack 992.4
imperfection 1003.1
v desire 100.14
be inferior 250.4
be poor 619.5
necessitate 795.3
fall short 911.2
require 963.9
lack 992.7
be insufficient 992.8
wanted
desired 100.29
welcome 585.12
requisite 963.13
want for lack 795.3
fall short 911.2
be insufficient 992.8
want list 871.1
wanton
n libertine 665.10
strumpet 665.14
v make love 562.14
be promiscuous 665.19
dissipate 669.6
make merry 743.24
adj capricious 364.5
unrestrained 430.24
reckless 493.8
unvirtuous 654.12
wayward 665.26
inconstant 854.7
wapiti 311.5
war
n disaccord 456.1
contention 457.1
warfare 458.1
campaign 458.3
military science 458.5
v contend 457.13
do battle 458.13
warble bird sound 60.5
speak 524.25
sing 708.38
war cry cry 59.1
challenge 454.2
call to arms 458.7
signal 517.16
ward
hospital room 197.25
region 231.5
custody 429.5
dependent 432.6
defense 460.1
stronghold 460.6
election district 609.16
protectorship 1008.2
warden jailer 429.10
executive 574.3
public official 575.17
guardian 1008.6
doorkeeper 1008.12
ward heeler
follower 166.2
partisan 609.27
henchman 610.8
ward off dodge 368.8
fend off 460.10
repulse 908.3
prevent 1012.14

wardrobe
furnishings 5.2
closet 197.15
warehouse
n storehouse 386.6
market 736.1
v load 159.15
store 386.10
warehouse store 736.1
wares 735.1
warfare
contention 457.1
war 458.1
battle 458.1
warhead charge 462.16
rocket 1074.3
warlock 690.5
warlord 575.13
warm
n man 76.5
v energize 17.10
make red 41.4
excite 105.12
heat 1020.17
adj chromatic 35.16
red 41.6
fervent 93.18
zealous 101.9
heated 105.22
comfortable 121.11
kind 143.13
near 223.14
vehement 544.13
hospitable 585.11
cordial 587.16
wealthy 618.15
on the right scent 941.10
calid 1019.24
warm-and-fuzzy 121.13
warm-blooded 1019.29
warmonger 461.5
warm over 117.5
revive 396.16
heat 1020.17
warn forebode 133.10
dissuade 379.3
caution 399.5
alarm 400.3
demand 421.5
admonish 422.6
threaten 514.2
warning
n forewarning 133.4
dissuasion 379.1
caution 399.1
preparation 405.1
demand 421.1
advice 422.1
threat 514.1
tip-off 551.3
adj premonitory 133.15
cautioning 399.7
advisory 422.8
war of words quarrel 456.5
contention 457.1
argumentation 935.4
warp
n deviation 164.1
bias 204.3
distortion 265.1
woof 740.3

meager 992.10
fluid 1061.4
moist 1065.16
WATS line 347.17
watts 1032.18
wave
  n hairdo 3.15
  billow 238.14
  convolution 281.1
  greeting 585.4
  waving 916.2
  oscillation 916.4
  swing 916.6
  v cut the hair 3.22
  billow 238.22
  manifest 348.5
  flaunt 501.17
  signal 517.22
  oscillate 916.10
  undulate 916.11
  flutter 917.12
wavelength
  oscillation 916.4
  radio wave 1034.11
wavelet 238.14
wave off 773.4
wave pool 743.12
waver
  n swing 916.6
  flutter 917.4
  v demur 325.4
  vacillate 362.8
  diversify 782.2
  change 854.5
  oscillate 916.10
  flutter 917.12
  flicker 1025.26
wave the white flag
  surrender 433.8
  make peace 465.9
wavy curved 279.7
  undulant 281.10
  inconstant 854.7
wax
  n whiteness 37.2
  record 50.12
  fit 152.8
  softness 1047.4
  lubricant 1056.2
  v grow 14.2
  increase 251.6
  expand 259.7
  polish 287.7
  evolve 861.5
  oil 1056.8
wax and wane
  change 854.5
  alternate 916.13
waxen 36.7
waxworks 386.9
way room 158.3
  direction 161.1
  progression 162.1
  progress 182.9
  entrance 189.5
  channel 239.1
  behavior 321.1
  custom 373.1
  habit 373.3
  plan 381.1
  route 383.1

manner 384.1
knack 413.6
latitude 430.4
style 532.2
mode 765.4
nature 767.4
continuance 856.1
specialty 866.1
wayfarer 178.1
waylay 346.10
way of life
  behavior 321.1
  preference 371.5
  custom 373.1
  mode 765.4
  specialty 866.1
the way of the world 765.2
way out
  n outlet 190.9
  loophole 369.4
  excuse 600.4
  adj extreme 247.13
  nothing like 787.5
  modern 841.13
  unconventional 868.6
ways and means 384.2
the way the ball bounces
  972.1
wayward
  disobedient 327.8
  perverse 361.11
  capricious 364.5
  unvirtuous 654.12
  wanton 665.26
  inconstant 854.7
weak weakly 16.12
  impotent 19.13
  tired 21.7
  inconspicuous 32.6
  colorless 36.7
  faint 52.16
  insipid 65.2
  thin 270.16
  stricken in years 303.18
  human 312.13
  weak-willed 362.12
  lax 426.4
  cowardly 491.10
  phonetic 524.30
  unvirtuous 654.12
  fragile 764.7
  influenceable 894.15
  uninfluential 895.3
  feebleminded 922.21
  unsound 936.12
  vulnerable 1006.16
weaken
  grow weak 16.9
  enfeeble 16.10
  disable 19.9
  fatigue 21.4
  fail 85.48
  afflict 85.50
  abate 252.8
  thin 270.12
  blunt 286.2
  impair 393.9
  overthrow 395.20
  moderate 670.6
  spiritualize 764.4
  dissipate 771.5

weak-kneed
  weak-willed 362.12
  cowardly 491.10
weakling
  meek soul 16.6
  impotent 19.6
  vacillator 362.5
  coward 491.5
wealth assets 471.7
  gain 472.3
  riches 618.1
  plenty 991.2
  prosperity 1010.1
wealthy
  rich 618.14
  plentiful 991.7
  prosperous 1010.12
wean
  disaccustom 374.2
  convince 858.16
weapon 285.2
wear
  n clothing 5.1
  use 393.5
  disintegration 806.1
  abrasion 1044.2
  v have on 5.44
  fatigue 21.4
  be tedious 118.6
  change course 182.30
  decrease 252.6
  erode 393.20
  waste 473.5
  affect 500.12
  endure 827.6
  abrade 1044.7
wear and tear
  decrement 252.3
  impairment 393.5
  disintegration 806.1
wear away
  weaken 16.9
  disappear 34.2
  decrease 252.6
  subtract 255.9
  consume 388.3
  wear 393.20
  waste 473.5
  disintegrate 806.3
  come to an end 820.6
  abrade 1044.7
wear down fatigue 21.4
  persuade 375.23
  wear 393.20
  influence 894.7
wear off wear 393.20
  come to an end 820.6
wear out
  fatigue 21.4
  oppress 98.16
  wear 393.20
wear thin
  weaken 16.9
  fall flat 117.4
wear well
  enjoy good health 83.6
  endure 827.6
weary
  v fatigue 21.4
  burn out 21.5
  oppress 98.16

  be tedious 118.6
  adj tired 21.7
  gloomy 112.24
  weariful 118.11
  languid 331.20
weary-worn 21.7
weasel
  n sharp vision 27.11
  sled sleigh 179.20
  wild animal 311.22
  man of few words 344.5
  recant 363.8
  v prevaricate 344.7
  equivocate 539.3
  inform on 551.13
  pull back 903.7
weather
  n atmosphere 184.32
  windward side 218.3
  climate 317.3
  air 317.3
  v sail against the wind
    182.24
  ride out the storm 182.40
  wear 393.20
  stand fast 855.11
  be safe 1007.2
  adj side 218.6
weather balloon 317.8
weather-beaten 393.34
weathered 393.34
weather eye
  sharp eye 27.10
  seamanship 182.3
  vigilance 339.4
weather forecast 317.6
weather the storm
  weather 182.40
  recover 396.20
  win through 409.13
  stand fast 855.11
  be safe 1007.2
weather vane
  instrument 317.8
  weathercock 318.16
  changeableness 854.4
  feeler 942.4
weave
  n material 4.1
  network 170.3
  structure 266.1
  texture 294.1
  weaving 740.1
  v loom 740.6
web
  n material 4.1
  network 170.3
  structure 266.1
  filament 271.1
  presswork 548.9
  weaving 740.1
  v net 170.7
  weave 740.6
web-footed 170.12
weblike 170.12
Weblog
  literature 547.12
  computer communications
    1042.19
web of intrigue 381.5
web press 548.9

website 1042.19
website ad 352.6
Webster's 554.9
webzine 555.1
wed
  v join in marriage 563.14
  unite 563.15
  relate 775.6
  put together 800.5
  combine 805.3
  league 805.4
  adj related 775.9
  leagued 805.6
wedding
  marriage 563.3
  joining 800.1
  combination 805.1
wedding anniversary 850.4
wedding bells 563.3
wedding planner 563.3
wedge
  n phonetic symbol 546.2
  v hook 800.8
  secure 855.8
  get a purchase 906.8
Wedgwood blue 45.3
wedlock 563.1
wee 258.11
wee bit 248.2
weed
  n marijuana 87.11
  plant 310.3
  intruder 774.2
  v subtract 255.9
  cultivate 1069.17
weediness 16.3
weed out use 87.22
  extract 192.10
  eliminate 773.5
  cultivate 1069.17
week moment 824.2
  seven 882.3
weekend
  n vacation 20.3
  v vacation 20.9
  spend time 821.6
weep
  n exuding 190.6
  v excrete 12.12
  fester 12.15
  secrete 13.5
  grieve 112.17
  sob 115.12
  exude 190.15
  hang 202.6
  trickle 238.18
  rain 316.10
  be damp 1065.11
weepy tearful 115.21
  exudative 190.20
wee small voice 636.5
wee thing 258.4
weevil 311.36
weigh
  weight 297.10
  measure 300.10
  classify 801.8
  have influence 894.10
  consider 931.12
  compare 943.4
  estimate 946.9

matter 997.12
weigh anchor
  up-anchor 182.18
  embark 188.15
  detach 802.10
weigh heavy on
  burden 297.13
  domineer 612.15
  go hard with 1011.8
weigh in
  appear 33.8
  enter 189.7
  weigh 297.10
  judge 946.8
weigh in the balance 297.10
weight
  n power 18.1
  fitness 84.1
  affliction 96.8
  heaviness 297.1
  paperweight 297.6
  extent 300.3
  prestige 417.4
  formality 580.1
  charge 643.3
  exerciser 725.7
  boxer 754.2
  influence 894.1
  validity 973.6
  importance 997.1
  impediment 1012.6
  v weigh 297.10
  pull down 297.12
  fill 794.7
weightless 764.5
weight-train 84.4
weight training
  exercise 84.2
  sport 744.1
weight-watching 270.9
weird
  n spell 691.1
  fate 964.2
  adj awesome 122.11
  creepy 127.31
  deathly 307.28
  sorcerous 690.14
  odd 870.11
  absurd 923.11
  eccentric 927.6
  eerie 988.9
weirdo
  oddity 870.4
  lunatic 926.16
  freak 927.4
welcome
  n greetings 186.4
  reception 187.1
  receptivity 187.9
  assent 332.1
  liberality 485.1
  hospitality 585.2
  v receive 187.10
  assent 332.8
  be hospitable 585.9
  incur 897.4
  adj pleasant 97.6
  hospitable 585.12
weld
  n joint 800.4
  v sculpture 715.5

relate 775.6
  put together 800.5
  stick together 803.9
  burn 1020.24
welder
  blowtorch 1020.14
  machinery 1040.3
welfare
  n kindness 143.5
  subsidy 478.8
  welfarism 611.7
  good 999.4
  prosperity 1010.1
  adj benevolent 143.15
welfare state
  welfare 143.5
  relief 611.7
  government 612.4
welfare worker 143.8
well
  n lake 241.1
  depth 275.2
  pit 284.4
  source of supply 386.4
  fountainhead 886.6
  v run out 190.13
  jet 238.20
  adj unailing 83.10
  adv ably 18.16
  kindly 143.18
  successfully 409.15
  skillfully 413.31
  excellently 999.22
well-advised 920.19
well-balanced
  composed 106.13
  symmetric 264.4
  stable 855.12
  sensible 920.18
well-being health 83.1
  pleasure 95.1
  contentment 107.1
  comfort 121.1
  good 999.4
  prosperity 1010.1
well-bred
  highbred 504.17
  upper-class 607.10
  wellborn 608.11
well-built
  able-bodied 15.16
  sturdy 763.7
  made 892.18
  comely 1016.18
well-defined
  distinct 31.7
  clear 521.11
well-deserving 509.20
well-developed
  grown 14.3
  expanded 259.12
  mature 303.13
well-disposed
  well-meaning 143.17
  willing 324.5
  favorable 449.22
  approving 509.17
  friendly 587.15
well-educated 928.20
well-established
  sturdy 763.7

established 855.13
  obvious 970.15
well-fed 257.18
well-known trite 117.9
  distinguished 662.16
  real 761.15
  well-kenned 928.27
well-made
  shapely 264.5
  sturdy 763.7
  made 892.18
  comely 1016.18
well-mannered
  mannerly 504.16
  ceremonious 580.8
well-meaning
  well-meant 143.17
  favorable 449.22
  friendly 587.15
  harmless 999.21
well-nigh 223.22
well-off 618.14
well-oiled 88.33
well-prepared 405.16
well-preserved
  young 301.9
  preserved 397.13
well-proportioned
  shapely 264.5
  comely 1016.18
well-put 533.7
well-rounded 413.25
well-suited
  fitted 405.17
  competent 413.24
well-thought-of
  respected 155.11
  approved 509.19
  reputable 662.15
well-to-do 618.14
well-traveled 177.40
well-versed
  skilled in 413.27
  knowledgeable 928.18
  well-informed 928.20
welsh
  n recant 363.8
  v shirk 368.9
  repeal 445.2
  not pay 625.6
welt
  n sore 85.37
  edging 211.7
  bulge 283.3
  blemish 1004.1
  v punish 604.15
welterweight 297.3
wemless 657.7
wench woman 77.6
  girl 302.6
  maid 577.8
  strumpet 665.14
werewolf
  frightener 127.9
  monster 593.6
  evil spirit 680.12
west
  n points of the compass
   161.3
  adj directional 161.14
  adv W 161.18

Western Hemisphere 231.6
wet
  n drink 88.7
  rain 316.1
  weather 316.4
  liberal 611.11
  moisture 1065.1
  v urinate 12.14
  moisten 1065.12
  adj left 220.4
  liberal 611.19
  foolish 923.8
  fluid 1061.4
  moist 1065.15
wetback migrant 178.5
  derogatory names 232.7
  fugitive 368.5
wet behind the ears
  untried 301.10
  immature 406.11
  inexperienced 414.17
wet blanket
  killjoy 112.14
  bore 118.4
  deterrent 379.2
  spoilsport 1012.9
  extinguisher 1022.3
wetlands shore 234.2
  shoal 276.2
wet noodle 452.3
wet-nurse nourish 8.19
  foster 449.16
whack
  n report 56.1
  attempt 403.3
  slap 604.3
  turn 825.2
  hit 902.4
  v crack 56.6
  slap 604.12
  hit 902.14
whale
  n largeness 257.11
  heavyweight 257.12
  behemoth 257.14
  marine animal 311.29
  v fish 382.10
  whip 604.13
  punish 604.15
wham
  n report 56.1
  v crack 56.6
  strike 902.15
whammy
  n gaze 27.5
  malevolence 144.4
  curse 513.1
  spell 691.1
  charm 691.5
  bad influence 1000.4
  v bring bad luck 1011.12
wharf 1009.6
what 864.6
whatever
  n no matter what 864.6
  adv any kind 809.9
**what goes around comes
  around** 887.9
**what goes up must come
  down** 887.9
what's what 761.4

wheat 10.4
whee 95.21
wheedle urge 375.14
  importune 440.12
  flatter 511.5
wheel
  n cycle 179.8
  circle 280.2
  change one's mind 363.6
  helm 573.5
  torture 605.4
  potter's wheel 742.4
  automobile racing 756.1
  roulette 759.12
  round 850.3
  propeller 904.6
  whirl 915.2
  rotator 915.4
  important person 997.9
  v turn about 163.9
  ride 177.33
  recur 850.5
  circle 914.5
  rotate 915.9
  whirl 915.11
wheelchair 179.7
wheeler-dealer
  man of action 330.8
  politics 610.6
  influence 894.6
wheel of fortune
  gambling wheel 759.16
  changeableness 854.4
  fate 964.2
  Chance 972.2
wheeze
  n breathing 2.21
  sibilation 57.1
  joke 489.6
  v burn out 21.5
  sibilate 57.2
whelp
  n boy 302.5
  fledgling 302.10
  dog 311.16
  beast 660.6
  v give birth 1.3
whenever when 821.8
  time 821.12
when hell freezes over
  822.2
when least expected
  unexpectedly 131.14
  suddenly 830.9
where 159.21
whereabouts
  n location 159.1
  adv where 159.21
whereas
  n condition 959.2
  prep when 821.16
  conj because 888.10
whereby 384.12
wherein 207.10
where it's at fact 761.3
  state of affairs 765.2
  essence 767.3
  novelty 841.2
  what's what 973.4
  salient point 997.6
wherever 159.22

wherewithal
  n means 384.2
  funds 728.14
  adv herewith 384.12
whet
  n appetizer 10.9
  incentive 375.7
  v sensitize 24.7
  stimulate 105.13
  intensify 251.5
  sharpen 285.7
  incite 375.17
whew! 122.20
whey 1061.2
whichever
  n whatever 864.6
  adj every 864.15
while
  n time 821.1
  period 824.1
  meantime 826.2
  v spend 387.13
  prep when 821.16
while away
  spend 387.13
  fritter away 486.5
whim caprice 364.1
  quirk 927.2
  figment of the imagination
    986.5
whimper
  n lament 115.3
  v sigh 52.14
  weep 115.12
  whine 115.14
whimsical
  capricious 364.5
  humorous 488.4
  witty 489.15
  inconstant 854.7
  eccentric 927.5
  uncertain 971.16
  fanciful 986.20
whine
  n screech 58.4
  lament 115.3
  v sigh 52.14
  screech 58.8
  cry 60.2
  whimper 115.14
  speak 524.25
  nasalize 525.10
whinny 60.2
whiny
  discontented 108.7
  plaintive 115.19
whip
  n driver 178.9
  goad 375.8
  lash 605.1
  legislator 610.3
  merry-go-round 743.15
  slap 902.8
  v best 249.7
  foam 320.5
  goad 375.15
  hasten 401.4
  defeat 412.9
  give a beating 604.13
  pound 902.16
  slap 902.19

  agitate 917.10
  emulsify 1062.10
  drive 1070.8
whip into shape
  complete 407.6
  arrange 808.8
  perfect 1002.5
whiplash trauma 85.38
  goad 375.8
  whip 605.1
whipped cream 10.40
whippersnapper
  impudent person 142.5
  brat 302.4
  a nobody 998.7
whipping boy 862.3
whip up excite 105.12
  improvise 365.8
  incite 375.17
  seize 480.14
  agitate 917.10
whir
  n rotation 915.1
  v hum 52.13
whirl
  n agitation 105.4
  ride 177.7
  eddy 238.12
  coil 281.2
  bustle 330.4
  round of pleasure 743.7
  wheel 915.2
  v turn around 163.9
  move 172.5
  eddy 238.21
  convolve 281.4
  whirligig 915.11
Whirlaway 311.15
whirling dervish 915.4
whirlpool
  n eddy 238.12
  whirl 915.2
  v rotation 915.11
whirlwind
  outburst 105.9
  wind 318.13
  whirl 915.2
whirlybird 181.5
whisk
  n tap 902.7
  agitator 917.9
  v sweep 79.23
  speed 174.9
  transport 176.12
  foam 320.5
  tap 902.18
  agitate 917.10
whisker
  n bristle 288.3
  v grow hair 3.20
whiskey 88.13
whisper
  n murmur 52.4
  touch 73.1
  mumbling 525.4
  tip-off 551.3
  hint 551.4
  report 552.6
  v murmur 52.10
  sigh 318.20
  tell confidentially 345.9

publish 352.10
say 524.22
speak 524.25
mumble 525.9
tip 551.11
adj murmuring 52.18
whistle
n blare 53.5
noisemaker 53.6
sibilation 57.1
screech 58.4
alarm 400.1
call 517.16
v blare 53.10
sibilate 57.2
screech 58.8
bird sound 60.5
exude cheerfulness 109.6
rejoice 116.5
sigh 318.20
sing 708.38
blow a horn 708.42
whistle-stop campaign 609.13
whit 248.2
white
n whiteness 37.1
color varieties 37.12
cocaine 87.7
egg 305.15
v whiten 37.5
whitewash 37.6
adj pure 37.7
clean 79.25
vacant 222.14
aged 303.16
spotless 657.7
chaste 664.4
white-bearded 303.16
whitecap
body of water 238.14
wave 916.4
white-collar crime 655.2
white-collar worker
bourgeois 607.6
worker 726.2
white corpuscle 2.25
white elephant 1012.6
white flag
peace offer 465.2
signal 517.15
race 756.3
white-hot zealous 101.9
fiery 671.22
hot 1019.25
the White House
house 228.5
head of state 575.7
white knight 460.7
white lie 354.11
white lightning
liquor 88.14
bootleg 88.18
white meat 10.23
white out 35.14
white supremacist 103.4
white tie
n formal dress 5.11
adj dressed up 5.46
white trash
inferior 250.2
wretch 660.2

whitewash
n appearance 33.2
whitening agent 37.4
cleanser 79.17
pretext 376.1
utter defeat 412.3
extenuation 600.5
v color 35.14
whiten 37.5
hide 37.6
scratch the surface 206.6
conceal 346.6
falsify 354.16
acquit 601.4
white water
rapids 238.10
foam 320.2
whittle
n cutlery 1040.2
v form 262.7
sever 802.11
whiz
n sibilation 57.1
skillful person 413.14
first-rate 999.7
v hum 52.13
sibilate 57.2
speed 174.9
whizbang
superior 249.4
dandy 999.7
whiz kid 413.12
who gives a crap? 102.11
whoa! 857.13
whoever 864.7
who knows? 930.18
whole
n contents 196.1
quantity 244.1
inclusion 772.1
totality 792.1
all 864.4
sum 1017.6
adj healthy 83.11
comprehensive 772.7
total 792.9
complete 794.9
one 872.7
unqualified 960.2
sound 1002.7
wholehearted 359.11
whole kit and caboodle 792.4
the whole nine yards 766.2
whole nine yards 792.4
whole note 709.14
whole rest 709.21
wholesale
n sale 734.1
v deal in 731.16
sell 734.8
adj commercial 731.22
sales 734.13
thorough 794.10
extensive 864.13
undiscriminating 945.5
plentiful 991.7
adv cheaply 633.10
wholesome
healthful 81.5
sound 83.11
sane 925.4

whomever 864.7
whomp
n report 56.1
slap 604.3
impact 902.3
v crack 56.6
defeat 412.9
slap 604.12
collide 902.13
whoop
n cry 59.1
v cry 59.6
whoopee
n rejoicing 116.1
festivity 743.3
int goody! 95.21
whoop it up
be noisy 53.9
have a party 582.21
make merry 743.24
create disorder 810.11
whoops! 975.22
whoosh
n sibilation 57.1
v sibilate 57.2
whopper
largeness 257.11
monstrous lie 354.12
whore
n flirt 562.11
reprobate 660.4
strumpet 665.14
prostitute 665.16
card 758.2
v be promiscuous 665.19
whorehouse
disapproved place 228.28
brothel 665.9
whorl
n coil 281.2
v convolve 281.4
Who's Who 549.9
why
n enigma 522.8
adv whyever 888.8
wick
village 230.2
taper 1026.7
wicked
malicious 144.20
wrong 638.3
evil 654.16
wrongdoing 655.5
ungodly 695.17
bad 1000.7
difficult 1013.17
wicker 170.3
wide
adj spacious 158.11
voluminous 257.17
broad 269.6
phonetic 524.30
extensive 864.13
erroneous 975.16
broad-minded 979.8
adv far and wide 261.16
clear 261.19
wide-angle 269.7
wide-awake
awake 23.8
alert 339.14

clear-witted 920.13
wide berth 430.4
wide-body 269.7
widen grow 251.6
enlarge 259.4
expand 259.5
spread 259.6
broaden 269.4
generalize 864.9
wide of the mark
adj irrelevant 776.7
erroneous 975.16
adv wide 261.19
wide open 174.20
wide-ranging
spacious 158.11
broad 269.6
extensive 864.13
broad-minded 979.8
wide receiver 746.2
widespread
spacious 158.11
spread 259.11
broad 269.6
customary 373.13
dispersed 771.9
extensive 864.13
widget 1052.5
widow
n survivor 256.3
widow woman 566.4
v bereave 307.27
leave behind 566.6
widow's peak 3.6
widower survivor 256.3
widow 566.4
width size 257.1
breadth 269.1
wield touch 73.6
use 387.10
wave 916.11
wieldy 1014.15
wiener roast 8.6
Wiener Schnitzel 10.19
wife woman 77.5
married woman 563.8
wig 3.14
wigger 926.16
wiggle
n wriggle 917.7
v be excited 105.18
way of walking 177.28
wriggle 917.14
wigout 926.10
wig out use 87.22
get excited 105.17
lose self-control 128.8
fly into a rage 152.20
go mad 926.22
wigwam 228.10
wiki 1042.19
wild
n wasteland 891.2
adj overzealous 101.12
frenzied 105.25
passionate 105.29
infuriated 152.32
hinterland 233.9
animal 311.39
defiant 327.10
ungovernable 361.12

unrestrained 430.24
reckless 493.8
foolhardy 493.9
unrefined 497.12
profligate 665.25
turbulent 671.18
unruly 671.19
boisterous 671.20
savage 671.21
absurd 923.11
rabid 926.30
distracted 985.10
fanciful 986.20
wild about 101.11
wild animals 311.1
wildcat strike 727.5
wildebeest 311.5
wilderness
  n open space 158.4
  hinterland 233.2
  complex 799.2
  wasteland 891.2
  adj hinterland 233.9
wild-eyed
  frenzied 105.25
  turbulent 671.18
  fanatic 926.32
wildfire 1019.13
wildflower 310.24
wild-goose chase
  lost cause 125.8
  labor in vain 391.3
  abortion 410.5
wild guess 951.4
wildlife 311.1
wildlife preserve 397.7
wild man
  daredevil 493.4
  savage 593.5
wild West 233.2
wiles 415.1
will
  n desire 100.1
  volition 323.1
  resolution 359.1
  willpower 359.4
  choice 371.1
  intention 380.1
  command 420.1
  bequest 478.10
  v see fit 323.2
  resolve 359.7
  bequeath 478.18
willful
  disobedient 327.8
  obstinate 361.8
  intentional 380.8
  lawless 418.5
willies 128.2
willing volitional 323.4
  willinghearted 324.5
  obedient 326.3
  trial 403.16
  consenting 441.4
  teachable 570.18
will-o'-the-wisp
  deception 356.1
  illusion 976.1
  mirage 976.6
  fire 1019.13
  luminescence 1025.13

willowy thin 270.16
  folded 291.7
  pliant 1047.9
willpower will 323.1
  resolution 359.4
wilt sweat 12.16
  weaken 16.9
  fatigue 21.4
  burn out 21.5
  fail 85.48
  languish 393.18
wily deceitful 356.22
  cunning 415.12
  shrewd 920.15
wimp weakling 16.6
  impotent 19.6
  vacillator 362.5
  coward 491.5
wimpish
  weak 16.12
  impotent 19.13
  henpecked 326.5
  weak-willed 362.12
  cowardly 491.10
  uninfluential 895.3
wimpy weak 16.12
  impotent 19.13
  weak-willed 362.12
  cowardly 491.10
  uninfluential 895.3
win
  n victory 411.1
  fight 754.3
  v best 249.7
  persuade 375.23
  triumph 411.3
  acquire 472.8
  race 757.5
win back 396.12
win by a nose 411.3
wince
  n retreat 903.3
  v suffer 26.8
  flinch 127.13
  retract 168.3
  demur 325.4
  pull back 903.7
winch
  n windlass 906.7
  v reel in 906.9
Winchester drive 1042.5
wind
  stray 164.4
  change course 182.30
  curve 279.6
  convolve 281.4
  trap 356.20
  prime 405.9
  rotate 915.9
wind
  n breathing 2.21
  swiftness 174.6
  current 318.1
  bull 520.3
  wind instrument 711.6
  belch 909.9
  fart 909.10
  v fatigue 21.4
  blare 53.10
  air 317.11
  blow a horn 708.42

windbag
  braggart 502.5
  chatterer 540.4
windblown 318.23
wind chill 318.7
wind down
  decrease 252.6
  cease to exist 762.6
  turn off 857.12
windfall find 472.6
  good thing 999.5
winding
  deviative 164.7
  convolutional 281.6
wind instrument 711.6
windjammer
  sailboat 180.3
  mariner 183.1
  braggart 502.5
  chatterer 540.4
windmill
  rotor plane 181.5
  automobile racing 756.1
window
  casement 292.7
  radar 1036.13
window dressing
  appearance 33.2
  front 216.1
  sham 354.3
  ornamentation 498.1
window frame
  structure 266.4
  opening 292.7
window of opportunity 843.2
windowpane
  window 292.7
  transparent substance
    1029.2
window-shop 733.8
window treatment 295.1
windpipe 2.22
wind power 1021.7
windshield 1008.3
wind sock
  flying and landing guides
    marker 184.19
  weather vane 318.16
windstorm
  high wind 318.11
  storm 671.4
windsurfing 182.11
windtalker 576.9
wind tunnel 239.13
windup
  completion 407.2
  game 745.3
  end 820.1
wind up prime 405.9
  complete 407.6
  end 820.5
  turn off 857.12
  result 887.4
windward
  n windward side 218.3
  adj side 218.6
  adv clockwise 161.24
  leeward 182.68
  side 218.9
windy
  n braggart 502.5

  v talkative 540.9
  adj distended 259.13
  rare 299.4
  blowy 318.21
  inflated 502.12
  wordy 538.12
  bombastic 545.9
  thin 764.6
  trivial 998.19
wine
  n kinds of 88.17
  adj red 41.6
wine cellar
  room 197.17
  storehouse 386.6
wine cooler 1024.3
wine lover 496.5
win friends and influence
    people 894.7
wing
  n fowl part 10.23
  adjunct 254.3
  air force 461.29
  party 617.4
  branch 617.10
  scenery 704.20
  company 770.3
  member 793.4
  protectorship 1008.2
  v disable 19.9
  transport 176.12
  fly 184.36
  cripple 393.14
  make good 409.10
wing it improvise 365.8
  do easily 1014.8
wingspan 257.1
win hands down 1014.11
wink
  n nap 22.3
  glance 27.4
  signal 517.15
  hint 551.4
  instant 830.3
  v blink 28.10
  signal 517.22
the wink of an eye 828.3
wink of sleep 22.3
winner superior 249.4
  man of action 330.8
  sure success 409.2
  successful person 409.6
  victor 411.2
  jockey 757.2
  good thing 999.5
winning
  n victory 411.1
  acquisition 472.1
  adj delightful 97.7
  desirable 100.30
  endearing 104.24
  alluring 377.8
  victorious 411.7
  in the money 757.6
  speculative 759.27
  influential 894.13
winnings
  increase 251.3
  gain 472.3
winnow
  n refinery 79.13

v refine 79.22
air 317.11
select 371.14
segregate 773.6
classify 801.8
discriminate 944.4
wino 88.12
win one's wings
succeed 409.7
triumph 411.3
win over
persuade 375.23
convert 858.16
convince 953.18
seem true 973.9
winsome
delightful 97.7
endearing 104.24
cheerful 109.11
alluring 377.8
Winston Churchill 543.6
winter
n wintertide 313.6
cold weather 1023.3
v summer 313.8
spend time 821.6
adj seasonal 313.9
winter break 20.3
winter solstice 313.7
winter storm advisory 400.1
winter storm watch 400.1
winter weather advisory 400.1
wintry seasonal 313.9
cold 1023.14
wipe
n disappearance 34.1
v clean 79.18
dry 1066.6
wipe off the map 395.16
wipeout 34.1
wipe out clean 79.18
excise 255.10
kill 308.14
exterminate 395.14
obliterate 395.16
bankrupt 625.8
declare a moratorium 625.9
annihilate 762.7
end 820.5
wipe up the floor with 604.11
wire
n cord 271.2
telegram 347.14
automobile racing 756.1
end 820.1
electrical device 1032.21
v telegraph 347.20
bind 800.9
electrify 1032.26
wired high 87.24
assured 970.20
wireless
n communications 347.3
radiophone 347.5
radio 1034.1
radio receiver 1034.3
v broadcast 1034.25
adj communicational 347.21
radio 1034.28
wire-puller
schemer 381.7

strategist 415.7
politician 609.30
politics 610.6
influence 894.6
wire service
telegraph 347.2
news 552.1
the press 555.3
wiretap
n surveillance 938.9
v listen 48.10
wiry able-bodied 15.16
threadlike 271.7
tough 1049.4
wisdom
mental grasp 920.1
ripe wisdom 920.5
understanding 928.3
maxim 974.1
expedience 995.1
wisdom tooth 2.8
wise
n aspect 33.3
manner 384.1
adj sage 920.17
learned 928.21
ungullible 956.5
wisecrack
n witticism 489.7
v joke 489.13
wise guy
impudent person 142.6
wiseacre 921.6
wise man
intelligence 920.9
wise woman 921.1
intellectual 929.1
wise to 928.16
wise up 551.9
wish
n desire 100.1
will 323.1
request 440.1
v desire 100.14
request 440.9
wishbone
fowl part 10.23
fork 171.4
wish-bringer 691.6
wishful 100.23
wishful thinking
defense mechanism
92.23
wistfulness 100.4
deception 356.1
credulity 954.1
idealism 986.7
wishing well 691.6
wish list
list 871.1
schedule 965.3
wishy-washy
tasteless 16.17
insipid 65.2
inconstant 854.7
mediocre 1005.7
wisp runt 258.4
bunch 770.7
luminescence 1025.13
wispy frail 16.14
thin 270.16

wistful
wishful 100.23
melancholy 112.23
regretful 113.8
cognitive 931.21
wit
skill 413.1
cunning 415.1
pleasantry 489.1
humor 489.1
humorist 489.12
intelligence 920.1
witch
n bitch 110.12
frightener 127.9
old woman 304.3
hag 593.7
violent person 671.9
sorceress 690.8
eyesore 1015.4
v fascinate 377.7
bewitch 691.9
adj sorcerous 690.14
witchcraft 690.1
witch-hunt
persecution 389.3
investigation 938.4
the witching hour 315.6
with
adv in spite of 338.9
prep at 159.27
plus 253.12
by means of 384.13
in cooperation with 450.8
in company with 769.12
in agreement with 788.12
among 797.17
with abandon 430.32
with a grain of salt
unbelievingly 955.13
conditionally 959.11
with all haste
swiftly 174.17
hastily 401.12
with a straight face
unfeelingly 94.14
solemnly 111.4
with authority 417.18
with a vengeance
powerfully 18.15
extremely 247.22
violently 671.25
utterly 794.16
with bated breath
adj in suspense 130.12
adv in an undertone
52.22
fearfully 127.32
expectantly 130.15
humbly 137.16
secretly 345.17
with care
carefully 339.15
cautiously 494.12
with child 78.18
with difficulty
disadvantageously 996.9
difficultly 1013.28
with dignity
solemnly 111.4
dignifiedly 136.14

with dispatch
quickly 330.26
hastily 401.12
withdraw
n recant 363.8
v use 87.22
retreat 163.6
recede 168.2
retract 168.3
quit 188.9
extract 192.10
subtract 255.9
dissent 333.4
hesitate 362.7
abandon 370.5
repeal 445.2
separate 802.8
stand alone 872.6
withdrawal
substance abuse 87.1
defense mechanism 92.23
unfeeling 94.1
retreat 163.2
recession 168.1
departure 188.1
extraction 192.1
dissent 333.1
reticence 344.3
recantation 363.3
abandonment 370.1
repeal 445.1
resignation 448.1
seclusion 584.1
elimination 773.2
separation 802.1
aloneness 872.2
incuriosity 982.1
with ease 121.14
wither
fail 85.48
decrease 252.6
shrink 260.9
age 303.10
languish 393.18
dry 1066.6
with eyes rolling 118.12
with feeling 93.25
with finesse
skillfully 413.31
discriminatingly 944.9
with flying colors 501.25
with gusto
eagerly 101.13
gaily 109.18
actively 330.25
with haste 401.12
withhold
keep secret 345.7
reserve 386.12
restrain 428.7
deny 442.4
hold back 484.6
abstain 668.7
withholding 442.1
within
adv in 207.10
prep in 207.13
within easy reach 633.7
within range 223.20
within reach
adj present 221.12

cheap 633.7
accessible 966.8
adv near 223.20
within reason
moderately 670.17
reasonably 935.24
with intent 380.10
with interest 983.21
within the realm of
possibility 966.6
with it
adj knowledgeable 928.17
adv in step 788.11
with love 104.31
with malice aforethought
malevolently 144.30
intentionally 380.10
with might and main
powerfully 18.15
by force 18.17
laboriously 725.19
with no strings attached
extremely 247.22
completely 794.14
with no time to spare 845.12
with one foot in the grave
stricken in years 303.18
dying 307.32
with one hand tied behind
one's back 1014.16
with one voice
adj unanimous 332.15
adv unanimously 332.17
cooperatively 450.6
in step 788.11
simultaneously 836.7
concurrently 899.5
with open arms
eagerly 101.13
willingly 324.8
hospitably 585.13
amicably 587.22
without
adv externally 206.10
prep absent 222.19
off 255.14
excluding 773.10
minus 992.17
conj unless 959.16
without a break 812.10
without a clue 971.24
without a stitch 6.14
without charge
adj costless 634.5
adv gratuitously 634.6
without contradiction
332.17
without delay
at once 830.8
promptly 845.15
without difficulty 1014.16
without distinction
adj identical 778.7
indistinguishable 945.6
adv justly 649.10
equally 790.11
withoutdoors 206.11
without doubt
positively 247.19
believingly 953.28
unquestionably 970.25

without end
adj long 267.7
infinite 823.3
perpetual 829.7
innumerable 884.10
adv infinitely 823.4
perpetually 829.10
without equal 249.15
without exception
adj comprehensive 772.7
unqualified 960.2
adv regularly 781.8
always 829.11
universally 864.18
without fail 970.26
without foundation
unsubstantiated 764.8
baseless 936.13
without further ado
suddenly 830.9
promptly 845.15
without hesitation 324.9
without mercy 146.3
without merit 598.21
without question
willingly 324.8
believingly 953.28
unquestionably 970.25
truly 973.18
without rhyme or reason
adj meaningless 520.6
illogical 936.11
adv capriciously 364.7
without shame 645.16
without warning
adj unexpected 131.10
adv unexpectedly 131.14
suddenly 830.9
with permission 443.19
with pleasure 95.19
with pride 136.13
with purpose 380.10
with regard to 775.13
with relish
eagerly 101.13
willingly 324.8
with respect 443.20
with respect to 775.13
withstand oppose 451.3
resist 453.2
defend 453.3
with taste 496.10
with the exception of
prep off 255.14
excluding 773.10
with the understanding
959.12
with tongue in cheek 489.19
witless
unintelligent 922.13
foolish 923.8
unwise 923.10
insane 926.26
unaware 930.12
scatterbrained 985.16
witness
n certificate 549.6
informant 551.5
litigant 598.11
function of Holy Ghost 677.15
spectator 918.1

examinee 938.19
testimony 957.2
eyewitness 957.6
v see 27.12
attend 221.8
depose 334.6
be pious 692.6
spectate 918.5
testify 957.9
witness stand 595.6
wits 919.2
witticism
pleasantry 489.7
maxim 974.1
witty humorous 488.4
amusing 489.15
wizard
n master 413.13
sorcerer 690.5
adj excellent 999.13
wizened dwarf 258.13
shrunk 260.13
haggard 270.20
stricken in years 303.18
wasted 393.35
dried 1066.9
wobble
n irregularity 851.1
shake 917.3
v way of walking 177.28
vacillate 362.8
change 854.5
oscillate 916.10
shake 917.11
woe wretchedness 96.6
affliction 96.8
distressfulness 98.5
sorrow 112.10
evil 1000.3
bane 1001.1
wolf
n discord 61.1
fox 311.19
philanderer 562.12
libertine 665.10
violent person 671.9
v gobble 8.23
gluttonize 672.4
wolf at the door 619.2
wolverine 311.22
woman
womankind 77.3
Eve 77.5
adult 304.1
person 312.5
wife 563.8
mistress 665.17
womanizer 665.10
woman of means 618.7
woman of substance 618.7
woman of the family 77.7
woman of the world 578.7
womb genitals 2.13
vital force 886.7
women's course 753.1
women's liberation
liberation 431.1
women's rights 642.4
womens' marker 751.1
wonder
n awe 122.1

wonderment 122.1
marvel 122.2
miracle 870.8
first-rater 999.6
v marvel 122.5
not know 930.10
be uncertain 971.9
wonder drug 86.4
wonderful
wondrous 122.10
remarkable 247.10
extraordinary 870.14
superb 999.15
Wonderland
utopia 986.11
fanciful 986.20
wondrous
adj wonderful 122.10
miraculous 870.16
adv intensely 247.20
wonkily 204.22
wont
n custom 373.1
habit 373.3
v accustom 373.9
be used to 373.11
adj accustomed 373.15
wontless 374.4
won ton 10.33
woo lure 377.5
solicit 440.14
court 562.21
wood
woodland 310.13
gambler 759.21
firewood 1021.3
lumber 1054.3
wood carving 349.6
woodchuck 311.22
woodcut
scenery 704.20
print 713.5
wooded 310.40
wooden dumb 117.6
inexpressive 522.20
dull 922.16
woodenheaded 922.17
woodland
n the country 233.1
land 234.1
wood 310.13
adj hinterland 233.9
sylvan 310.40
woods hinterland 233.2
woodland 310.13
woodwind 711.8
woodwind
orchestra 710.12
wood instrument 711.8
woodwork 712.2
wool hair 3.2
whiteness 37.2
softness 1047.4
woolens 5.22
woolly hairy 3.24
fluffy 1047.14
woozy 985.14
word
n affirmation 334.1
oath 334.4
account 349.3

Worship 648.2

worst
 v best 249.7
 defeat 412.6
 adj terrible 1000.9

worst-case
 depressing 112.30
 hopeless 125.12

worth
 n benefit 387.4
 assets 471.7
 value 630.2
 preciousness 632.2
 funds 728.14
 importance 997.1
 goodness 999.1
 adj possessing 469.9
 priced 630.14

worthless
 valueless 391.11
 disadvantageous 996.6
 paltry 998.21
 unworthy 998.22
 terrible 1000.9

worthwhile
 valuable 387.22
 gainful 472.16
 expedient 995.5

worthy
 n good person 659.1
 celebrity 662.9
 personage 997.8
 adj dignified 136.12
 eligible 371.24
 competent 413.24
 praiseworthy 509.20
 precious 632.10
 warranted 639.9
 honest 644.13
 reputable 662.15

would-be
 desirer 100.12
 presumptuous 141.10
 nominal 527.15

wound
 n trauma 85.38
 displease 96.5
 v pain 26.7
 hurt 96.17
 offend 152.21
 injure 393.13
 work evil 1000.6

wound up
 completed 407.11
 ended 820.8
 past 837.7

woven webbed 170.12
 loomed 740.7

wow
 n audio distortion 50.13
 success 409.4
 joke 489.6
 first-rate 999.7
 v delight 95.11
 amuse 743.21

wracked 93.23

wraith phantom 976.4
 specter 988.1
 double 988.3

wrangle
 n quarrel 456.5

 v quarrel 456.11
 argue 935.16
 drive 1070.8

wrangler
 oppositionist 452.3
 combatant 461.1
 student 572.7
 arguer 935.12
 herder 1070.3

wrap
 n dishabille 5.20
 wrapper 295.18
 v clothe 5.39
 surround 209.6
 enclose 212.5
 package 212.9
 fold 291.5
 enwrap 295.20
 bundle 770.20
 bind 800.9
 end 820.5

wrapped up
 completed 407.11
 assembled 770.21

wrapped up in
 fond of 104.29
 involved in 898.5
 engrossed 983.17

wrapper
 dishabille 5.20
 wrapping 295.18
 bookbinding 554.14

wrath anger 152.5
 revenge 507.1

wrath of God
 revenge 507.1
 deserts 639.3

wreak havoc
 destroy 395.10
 rage 671.11

wreath circle 280.2
 bouquet 310.25
 trophy 646.3
 heraldry 647.2
 braid 740.2

wreck
 n nervousness 128.5
 car 179.10
 ruins 393.8
 destruction 395.1
 debacle 395.4
 misfortune 1011.2
 v disable 19.9
 shipwreck 182.42
 spoil 393.10
 destroy 395.10
 demolish 395.17
 rage 671.11

wreckage 395.5

wrench
 n pang 26.2
 trauma 85.38
 pain 96.5
 extortion 192.6
 distortion 265.1
 jerk 905.3
 tool 1040.1
 v pain 26.7
 distort 265.5
 misinterpret 342.2
 misrepresent 350.3

injure 393.13
 wrest 480.22
 jerk 905.5

wrest
 n extortion 192.6
 distortion 265.1
 v extort 192.15
 distort 265.5
 wring 480.22

wrestle
 n struggle 725.3
 v contend 457.13
 struggle 725.11

wrestler 461.3

wrestling match 457.10

wretch sufferer 96.11
 miserable person 660.2

wretched squalid 80.25
 miserable 96.26
 distressing 98.20
 unhappy 112.21
 base 661.12
 paltry 998.21
 terrible 1000.9
 adverse 1011.13

the wretched of the earth
 the underprivileged 606.4
 unfortunate 1011.7

wriggle
 n wiggle 917.7
 v be excited 105.18
 wiggle 917.14

wring
 n extortion 192.6
 distortion 265.1
 v pain 26.7
 torture 96.18
 extraction 192.16
 distort 265.5
 convolve 281.4
 wrest 480.22

wringer 192.9

wring one's hands 115.11

wrinkle
 n extra 254.4
 furrow 290.1
 corrugation 291.3
 fad 578.5
 v contract 260.7
 ruffle 288.5
 furrow 290.3
 corrugate 291.6
 age 303.10
 languish 393.18

wrist member 2.7
 joint 800.4
 arm 906.5

wristband circle 280.3
 jewel 498.6

writ document 549.5
 summons 598.2

write represent 349.8
 describe 349.9
 pen 547.19
 author 547.21
 record 549.15
 correspond 553.10
 compose 708.46
 create 718.6
 produce 892.8

write-in vote 371.6

write off forget 148.5
 excise 255.10
 give up 370.7
 discard 390.7
 repeal 445.2
 declare a moratorium 625.9
 keep accounts 628.8
 discount 631.2

write-off excision 255.3
 repeal 445.1
 moratorium 625.2
 tax 630.9
 discount 631.1

writer penman 547.13
 recorder 547.15
 correspondent 553.8
 discourser 556.3
 scribbler 718.3
 author 718.4
 narrator 722.5

writer's cramp 547.2

writhe
 n wiggle 917.7
 v pain 26.8
 suffer 96.19
 be excited 105.18
 distort 265.5
 wiggle 917.14

writing
 representation 349.1
 letter 546.1
 composition 547.2
 scrivening 547.1
 authorship 547.2
 document 549.5
 book 554.1
 elementary education
  568.5
 literature 718.2

written agreement 332.1

the written word 547.10

wrong
 impropriety 638.1
 injustice 650.1
 crime 650.4
 iniquity 654.3
 misdeed 655.2
 offense 674.4
 error 975.1
 evil 1000.3
 v do one an injustice 650.7
 work evil 1000.6
 adj wrongful 638.3
 unjust 650.9
 wicked 654.16
 wrongdoing 655.5
 untimely 844.6
 erroneous 975.16
 mistaken 975.18
 inexpedient 996.5
 bad 1000.7
 adv wrongly 638.4
 erroneously 975.20
 badly 1000.13

wrongheaded
 perverse 361.11
 stupid 922.15

wrong number 660.4

wrought 407.10

wrung pained 26.9
 tortured 96.25